1979

BRITANNICA
BOOK OF THE YEAR

1979

BRITANNICA
BOOK OF THE YEAR

ENCYCLOPÆDIA BRITANNICA, INC.

CHICAGO, TORONTO, LONDON, GENEVA, SYDNEY, TOKYO, MANILA, SEOUL

THE UNIVERSITY OF CHICAGO

*The Britannica Book of the Year is published with the editorial advice
of the faculties of the University of Chicago.*

CONTENTS

SPECIAL REPORTS

QUESTION MARK OVER AFRICA

by Ali A. Mazrui

A cluster of symbols hangs over the African continent—the crescent with its new power born of petroleum, the cross with the prestige of Western technology, the hammer and sickle with its promise of revolutionary redemption, and the baobab tree with its own indigenous inscrutability. But more ominous than all these is that ultimate symbol of bewilderment and uncertainty: the question mark.

Africa is a continent in transition, and nowhere is this more apparent than in its relations with the rest of the world—with the industrialized West, with the so-called second world of socialist countries, and with the less developed third world. Its ties with the West are of long standing, though they have undergone important changes during the 1970s. Its contacts with the socialist countries are comparatively recent, but they have been expanding. As for Africa's relations with the rest of the third world, dramatic shifts have occurred as a result of two recent developments—the rise of Arab economic power, based on petroleum, and the emergence of Cuba as a factor in African wars.

Africa and the Rise of Arab Power. The October 1973 war in the Middle East had both military and diplomatic significance, but it was the economic war waged by the Arabs that fired the imagination of the third world—the utilization of oil as a political weapon, with all its implications for relations between the affluent industrial world and the primary producers of the Southern Hemisphere. A strange paradox has been apparent on the world scene since that time: economic disparities among third world countries have increased—largely because of the rise in oil prices—but so has political solidarity.

Afro-Arab solidarity was dramatically demonstrated when the African states almost unanimously broke relations with Israel in 1973. Immediately the question arose as to whether this action should be rewarded by special economic concessions from

the Arabs. A more recent question has been whether Africa's break with Israel need continue in the wake of Anwar as-Sadat's peace initiative toward Israel.

To understand Afro-Arab relations, one must distinguish between a political alliance and an economic partnership. When African states broke relations with Israel, they were consolidating their political alliance with the Arab world. At the very minimum, a political alliance involves "sharing enemies," and black Africans, by treating Israel as a common enemy for the time being, were asserting solidarity with the Arabs. But in so doing they were not extending political credit to the Arabs. On the contrary, they were paying back an earlier political debt that had been incurred when most of the Arab states broke relations with the white governments of South Africa and Rhodesia. Some Arab countries, like Algeria, Egypt, and Libya, were supporting black liberation movements in southern Africa years before black Africa recognized the Palestinians as a people with a grievance.

When Africans ask for cheaper oil and development aid from the Arabs, they are trying to move beyond a political alliance to an economic partnership. They are saying: "Let us not merely share enemies; let us also share energy. To some extent, let us merge economies." The case for such a proposal does not rest on Africa's break with Israel. It rests on the proposition that a political alliance can best be consolidated by an economic partnership.

The U.S. and Western Europe have been engaged in a similar debate. The North Atlantic Treaty Organization (NATO) was intended as a military and political alliance, and France, especially, has maintained that

Crossed rifles (NATO on left, Soviet on right) symbolize part of the struggle of Africa.

Ali A. Mazrui is professor of political science and director of the Center for Afroamerican and African Studies at the University of Michigan, Ann Arbor; during 1977–78 he was visiting professor in modern Commonwealth history at the University of Leeds, England. His books include Political Values and the Educated Class in Africa *(1978),* Africa's International Relations *(1977), and* Towards a Pax Africana *(1967).*

9

questions of security should not be mixed with questions of trade and monetary stability. The U.S., on the other hand, has often taken a position on the side of greater economic cooperation. When he was U.S. secretary of state, Henry Kissinger urged the Europeans to bear in mind the health of the U.S. economy when they formulated trade and fiscal policies. An alliance based merely on common enemies, he argued, could be very unstable. Similarly, Africans are asking the Arabs to strengthen the Afro-Arab political alliance by exploring the possibilities of an interregional economic partnership.

Should the Arab world agree under the threat that, if they do not, more Africans will resume ties with Israel? It is to be hoped that both Africans and Arabs will seek alternative grounds for agreement. Patience is called for. Economic disagreements among the NATO partners did not break up the alliance. On the contrary, 20 years of patience are just now beginning to bear economic fruit.

The less developed countries generally have a

Rejecting imperialism from any source, many Africans are acquiring a sense of cohesive identity for their continent. The sign is lettered in Arabic, English, and French.

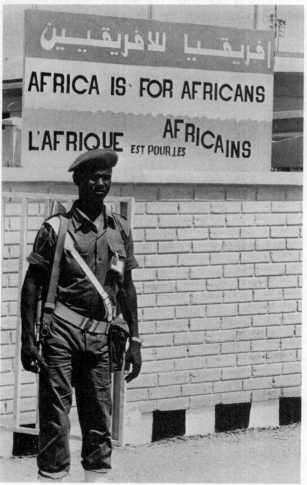

WILLIAM CAMPBELL—SYGMA

good case against the oil producers. A strong argument can be made that the Arabs and the other oil producers should agree on a two-tier pricing system for oil, with one price for the developed world and a lower one for the less developed countries. But in that case, the privileges should be open not just to Africa but to other third world countries, such as India. It is often forgotten that India supported the Arabs in the Middle East for 20 years before most black African states were converted.

In fairness to the oil producers, some effort is being made to share the wealth. The priorities of the Arab members of the Organization of Petroleum Exporting Countries (OPEC) tend to be first, fellow Arabs; second, Muslims; and third, other third world countries provided they show some evidence of sympathy toward the Arab cause. The names of the various aid funds are themselves indicative of cultural solidarity—the Kuwait Fund for Arab Economic Development, the Saudi Development Fund, the Abu Dhabi Fund for Arab Economic Development, the Arab Fund for Economic and Social Development, the Islamic Development Bank. In recent years some of these funds have broadened their base of operations, and in 1975 the Arab Bank for Economic Development in Africa, with lending resources estimated at $1 billion, was established as "the only Arab Fund that concentrates entirely on Africa." The OAPEC Special Account, subscribed by the Arab members of OPEC, operates on the principle of third world solidarity, although special consideration is given to OPEC's need for third world support during periods of possible confrontation with Western oil consumers.

A more recent question for Africans is how to respond to the peace process initiated by Egypt's president in November 1977. If the largest of the Arab countries establishes a rapprochement with Israel, why should Zambia or Guinea abstain? The dilemma is especially acute for those black African countries that sacrificed Israeli technical assistance for the sake of Afro-Arab solidarity. The situation is aggravated by the fact that, of the four front-line Arab states in the confrontation with Israel (Syria, Jordan, Lebanon, and Egypt), only Egypt is within the African continent and a member of the Organization of African Unity (OAU).

In a fundamental sense, Egypt's withdrawal from the anti-Israeli coalition could constitute a substantial deafricanization of the Arab-Israeli conflict as a whole. Yet dilemmas remain. Algeria, probably the most pan-Africanist of the North African states, opposes the Sadat initiative. So does Libya, the most pan-Islamist. Black Africa is thus torn between opposing Arab camps, and the political economy of Afro-Arab relations reflects this painful dialectic.

Cuban Warriors in African Wars. While the rise of Arab power has profoundly influenced African affairs, the most dramatic example of an external force affecting African politics in the 1970s has been Cuba's military intervention in Angola and Ethiopia. This is not the first time Cubans have appeared on the African scene. In November 1964 word began to spread that there were "Spanish-speaking foreigners"—presumably Castro's adversaries in exile—serving as mercenaries for Moise Tshombe's regime in the Congo (now Zaire).

Cuban influences—this time of the left—may also have been present in the Zanzibar revolution of January 1964. The widely publicized report that Cubans were among the Zanzibari revolutionaries probably stemmed from the presence of several trade union leaders, many of whom had adopted the Cuban style of dress. However, Zanzibari militiamen may have been trained in Cuba, and the direction taken by the revolutionary regime could well have been inspired by the Cuban example.

In fact, the effect of Cuba on the whole concept of the third world has probably been crucial. Until the Cuban revolution, Afro-Asian radicals found it hard to identify with Latin America, but this changed with the Cuban assertion of independence from U.S. hegemony. Castro's later drift into military entanglement with the Soviet Union disillusioned some of his nonaligned friends. But his defiance of the U.S. and the social transformation he implemented at home continued to give him an important place among third world leaders. In a vital sense, Castro helped provide the credentials for Latin America's admission into the fellowship of the third world.

Later on, Cubans were hired as a kind of Swiss Guard by African regimes ranging from Sierra Leone to the Congo (Brazzaville). To some extent, this appears to be their current role in Ethiopia. But the first major Cuban intervention came in 1976 during the final stages of the Angolan civil war. There seems little doubt that Cuban support for the Popular Movement for the Liberation of Angola (MPLA) was decisive in tilting the balance against the rival Na-

Angolans waved Cuban flags and carried a large picture of Cuban leader Fidel Castro in a demonstration of support when Castro visited their country.

tional Front for the Liberation of Angola (FNLA) and the National Union for the Total Independence of Angola (UNITA), though other factors were also involved. The UNITA guerrillas are still being kept at bay by Cuban troops.

Some questions about the Cuban intervention remain. It has been suggested in some circles that it is actually a pan-African venture. After all, Cuba's population is at least 40% black in one sense or another. Castro himself has emphasized the African blood flowing in the veins of many Cubans. Certainly there are positive aspects of Castro's claims on the issue of race. Under his revolution, Cuba has witnessed remarkable changes for the better in race relations. But if the U.S. were to send an army consisting entirely of black Americans to participate in a conflict in Zaire, it would not necessarily be a case of pan-Africanism. Before making that judgment, one would have to investigate the race of those who sent the troops, the structure within which the decision was made, and whether or not the motives for the intervention were inspired by solidarity based on shared African ancestry.

It has also been argued that Cuba intervened in Angola in response to a call from the legitimate government of the country, but that surely begs the question. At the time of the intervention, none of the competing factions could be deemed the legitimate government of the country. It may well be that the MPLA was the best qualified of the three movements to rule a newly liberated country in southern Africa, but is this the kind of issue that should have been decided by outside forces? Was the Cuban tail wagging the African dog?

It remains to be seen whether Cuban troops will be used to assist Zimbabwe (Rhodesia) or Namibia (South West Africa) in their struggle for independence from white-dominated regimes. Significantly, no Cubans appeared in Angola while the Portuguese were in occupation, although the MPLA had fought the colonial regime for two decades. Only after the Portuguese had left—and the war had become primarily one among Africans—did Cuban troops and Soviet matériel suddenly become available. The inevitable conclusion is that neither Cuba nor the U.S.S.R. was willing to fight the Portuguese and risk confrontation with NATO.

There is as yet no evidence that Soviet and Cuban liberators are prepared to risk direct confrontation with South Africa by moving into Namibia on the side of the South West Africa People's Organization (SWAPO). There is somewhat more likelihood of Soviet-Cuban support for the Patriotic Front against Ian Smith's regime in Rhodesia, but on balance there seems little doubt that the Soviets and Cubans would prefer to wait until the war becomes a con-

The wares of a bookseller in Addis Ababa illustrate the Communist influence in Ethiopia.

flict among blacks before giving material aid to their favourites. Without denying the difference Cuba has made to prospects in southern Africa, the timing of Cuban intervention raises questions about the extent of Castro's commitment to African liberation.

Spheres of Influence. But is Cuba's involvement in Africa merely an extension of Soviet foreign policy? To say this is a gross oversimplification. Cuba under Castro has aspired to be a major revolutionary force in its own right. In the 1960s it attempted unsuccessfully to export revolution in Latin America, and its African ventures in the 1970s are, in part, a compensation for its earlier failures.

Moscow is also involved in the politics of compensation. Beginning with Sadat's expulsion of Soviet "advisers" from Egypt in 1972, the balance in the Middle East has tilted toward the West. Soviet strategists saw southern Africa as a more promising arena of competition with the West, and the collapse of the Portuguese empire in 1974 and 1975 facilitated Soviet and Cuban penetration in the area.

The Soviets arrived on the African scene with certain advantages. The Soviet Union has usually been at least a decade ahead of the West in identifying major political and social forces in the third world. It recognized the legitimacy of nonalignment as a strategy for newly independent countries when John Foster Dulles was still denouncing it as a kind of diplomatic sin, and the Soviets identified the

Palestinian issue long before the West was shocked out of its relative complacency by the October war and the oil embargo.

Moscow also has been able to deracialize imperialism and thus make its interventions more acceptable in Afro-Asian eyes. It could do this partly because of Russia's role in propagating a new theory of imperialism. It is not always remembered that Marx himself was sympathetic to the British colonization of India. He regarded imperialism as a potentially progressive force that would produce regenerative trends in the Indian social and economic structure. In this respect, he was part of the ethnocentric tradition characteristic of 19th-century Europe, which viewed European culture as a vehicle for the transformation of other societies and imperialism as a civilizing mechanism. Lenin, on the other hand, saw imperialism as a device to prevent revolution in the home country. In *Imperialism: The Highest Stage of Capitalism,* he quotes with relish Cecil Rhodes's argument that empire building was necessary to avoid civil war in England. The theory was persuasive and influential among African intellectuals, and to the extent that Lenin was a Russian, the Soviets benefited.

Similarly, the Soviets deracialized liberation by basing it on class rather than race and by emphasizing shared ideology rather than shared race as the true basis of solidarity. Thus the Soviets could say: "We are coming to help Africa. We may be white, but, in the ultimate analysis, this is a class war, not a race war. Your friends are those who share certain values with you." The Soviets have backed up their claims by providing concrete material support to liberation movements fighting white racism. The use of combat troops from Cuba, itself a racial mosaic, has been part of the pattern.

A major consequence of Soviet penetration has been the appearance of what we will call competitive imperialism, as contrasted with the "monopolistic imperialism" that exists when one imperial system is exclusively in control. Competitive imperialism can be useful to the potential victim. Thus the problems of southern Africa were by and large ignored by the West until the threat of Soviet competition mobilized Washington and other Western capitals into pressuring the white governments toward a solution.

Another illustration is Mozambique. Mozambique is to a large degree under the influence of Moscow because of the support that the Front for the Liberation of Mozambique (Frelimo) and, later, the independent government in Maputo have received from the Soviets. At the same time, Mozambique's

Soviet physician examines a young patient in Mozambique. The Soviet Union is supplying much technical assistance to the country.

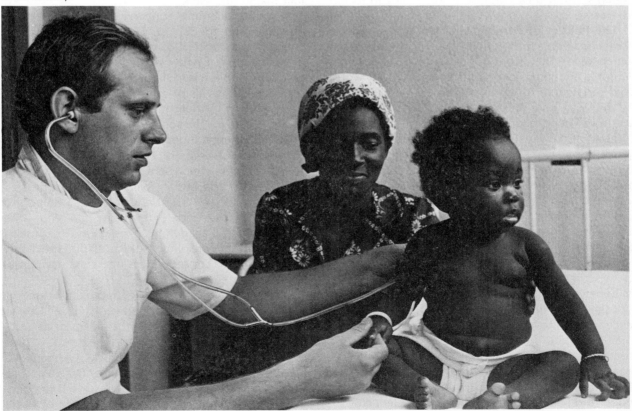

economy is still substantially tied to that of South Africa. Thousands of workers from Mozambique still go to South Africa to work, and South Africa subsidizes the Mozambique economy to the tune of some U.S. $100 million a year. Mozambique derives benefits from both connections.

In another area where competing imperialisms meet, the Horn of Africa, the issue is not liberation but maintaining the territorial integrity of an African country. It is an irony of history that the West drew the African boundaries in all their artificiality and the Soviets are now helping to defend them. The three most populous black countries in Africa, Nigeria, Ethiopia, and Zaire, have all been threatened with secession: Zaire, beginning in 1960 when Katanga Province (now Shaba) first attempted to secede; Nigeria in the Biafran civil war of 1967–70; and, most recently, Ethiopia, where both the Somalis of the Ogaden, aided by Somalia, and the Eritreans have attempted to free themselves from the control of Addis Ababa. In each case, the Soviet Union has been on the side of maintaining the territorial integrity of the country concerned.

Soviet participation in Ethiopia—abetted by the Cuban presence—has been much more extensive than in either the Congo or Nigeria. Cubans and Soviets defended their role in the Ogaden war partly on the grounds that an external power, Somalia, was trying to change the boundary. It is not yet clear how much support they will give Addis Ababa in its bid to keep Eritrea.

The Politics of Foreign Aid. Moscow is readier with armaments than with bread, with military assistance than with economic assistance. The Soviet Union's economic contribution to the third world and certainly to Africa is far more modest than that of the West. Like Western aid, socialist aid includes a strong component of self-interest, but unlike Western aid it involves little straight charity. This is partly because of an ideological distrust of charity as an answer to maldistribution. A related consideration is the socialist fear that charity can result in co-optation and deradicalization. Foreign economic aid must not be allowed to become an obstacle to the emergence of revolutionary consciousness among the workers.

But while socialist aid scores low in terms of charity, it scores high in terms of ideological solidarity. Whenever possible, aid is designed to help promote "progressive change." Of course, there have been exceptions. Moscow poured aid into Egypt in the 1960s, despite the late Pres. Gamal Abdel Nasser's repression of the indigenous Communists. But on balance it is clear that the promotion of "progressive forces" in the third world countries is one of the major motivations behind socialist assistance.

But all aid—whether from the socialist world or from the West—has both costs and benefits. One major dilemma concerns national development as opposed to decolonization. The pursuit of development by third world countries may reduce the pace of decolonization. Aid often brings dependency.

Another dilemma concerns the urban bias in development generally. If the pace of westernization in the countryside is arrested because development is concentrated in the urban centres, the survival of the local culture may be prolonged, for better or for worse. The rural culture may be one of poverty and indigence, but it is also the repository of much that is authentic and distinctive in the society. If development of the countryside can be delayed for a generation or two, the society as a whole may be better able to find a path to "modernization" that is not based almost exclusively on "westernization."

A third dilemma involves capital-intensive versus labour-intensive forms of aid and investment generally. Capital-intensiveness tends to require high levels of skill and thus helps to promote technocracy and elitism. Labour-intensive projects, on the other hand, bring more people into the modern sector of production. To the extent that modernity is conceived as being Western-derived, it is possible to argue that labour-intensive aid projects tend to spread the process of westernization throughout the society, whereas capital-intensive projects affect mainly the elite.

A fourth dilemma concerns stratification more broadly defined. In Africa, Western education changed the concept of class; instead of being defined in terms of who owns what, class came to be based on who *knows* what. Western-educated Africans attained levels of influence and power all out of proportion to their numbers and, in some cases, to their value for the society. The first generation of political leaders at independence—men like Kwame Nkrumah, Julius Nyerere, Nnamdi Azikiwe, Léopold Sédar Senghor—got where they did partly because of the verbal and literary skills acquired from their foreign masters. Western education also helped to produce the secondary levels of the elite—the bureaucrats and academics. Foreign aid that maintains or further consolidates this situation inevitably has significant consequences for class formation and class defense.

On the other hand, in a technologically underdeveloped society, ultimate power is more likely to reside with those who control the means of destruction than with those who possess the means of production. The introduction of modern armaments into otherwise pre-modern societies has given rise to new power structures as soldiers have taken over in one military coup after another. Many of these soldiers were inadequately trained by Western standards, and large parts of Africa have fallen under this "lumpen militariat."

But despite its effects on third world societies, aid represents only a small part of the world's capital flow. Even the richest countries are reluctant to make more than a tiny proportion of their gross domestic product available for purposes of aid. For Africa, as for much of the rest of the third world, the much discussed New International Economic Order has yet to arrive.

Promise and Uncertainty. The centuries of Western imperialism have left enduring cultural and economic legacies in Africa, but the colonial impact did not merely make Africa dependent on the West. It also deepened the West's need for Africa. Africa has 96% of the non-Communist world's diamonds, 60% of its gold, nearly 45% of its cobalt, 35% of its bauxite, nearly 35% of its uranium, and some 80% of its chrome. Approximately half the U.S. supply of manganese comes from Africa. And had Nigeria decided in 1973 to join the Arabs in the oil embargo,

A member of the Popular Movement for the Liberation of Angola (MPLA) practices with a Soviet-made rifle.

the effect on the U.S. economy would have been far more traumatic.

From an African point of view, the most important capitals in the 1970s are Washington and Paris—not London and Paris, as was once the case. British governments in the 1970s have chosen to be moderating influences rather than initiative-takers, except in Rhodesia where Britain retains a legalistic interest. And even there, London is all too eager to share its responsibilities with Washington. Washington's concerns in Africa are mainly strategic and economic, while those of Paris are strategic, economic, and cultural—probably in that order.

African interaction with the second and third worlds has been more limited than with the West. That is why the roles of the Soviet Union and Cuba are so significant. The U.S.S.R. is the most powerful country within the second world, while Cuba represents both the second and the third. The alliance between them and their cooperative ventures in Africa thus serve to expand contacts with both those world groupings.

If the third world is basically tricontinental—encompassing Africa, Asia, and Latin America—Africa is the middle continent. This is true for a number of reasons. Through the Arab-speaking countries of North Africa, it is linked to the Middle East. There are more Arab people in North Africa than there are in Asia, although Asia contains a greater number of Arab states. A second link with Asia is Islam, which is primarily an Afro-Asian religion. And if North Africa provides a bond between the African continent and Asia, it is possible to argue that sub-Saharan Africa is an important link between Africa and Latin America. Millions of people of African ancestry live in Latin America. Portuguese is the language of large areas of black Africa and of Brazil, the largest South American country. The two regions have each had a dependency relationship—Latin America with the U.S., Africa with Western Europe. Both are politically fragmented. Both are rich in mineral resources that might provide an opportunity to influence the world economy through producer cartels. Both are highly dependent on agricultural exports.

Thus Africa stands on the brink of new relationships. With the West, it is groping for new rules to govern an old game. With the socialist countries—especially the U.S.S.R.—what were once tentative contacts are acquiring new implications and new dimensions. Increasing Arab and Cuban influence in Africa—sometimes in competition—is having broad repercussions among the less developed countries generally, especially in relation to the whole doctrine of nonalignment as a guiding principle of third world diplomacy. A new if ambiguous historical era awaits. Whither Africa?

TOWARD A SUN-POWERED WORLD

by Paul Rappaport

Nobody can embargo sunlight; no cartel can control the Sun. Its energy will not run out; it will not pollute the air; it will not poison our waters; it is free from stench and smog. The Sun's power needs only to be collected, stored, and used.

On May 3, 1978, U.S. Pres. Jimmy Carter voiced this strong support of solar energy during a visit to the fledgling Solar Energy Research Institute (SERI) in Golden, Colo. The day of his speech was a special one called Sun Day, the result of a U.S.-based effort headed by environmental advocate Denis Hayes and observed throughout the world with conferences, rallies, demonstrations, and celebrations to promote solar radiation as a clean, renewable, and economically competitive energy source.

On Sun Day President Carter ordered a domestic policy review by all departments in the federal government to investigate how solar energy could become a part of everyday life in the U.S. Finalized in December 1978, the review promised to accelerate appreciably the introduction of several solar energy technologies. The president also earmarked an additional $100 million for solar energy research and development during fiscal year 1979. His presence during Sun Day on the 300-ac site atop South Table Mountain in Colorado marked the future permanent home of SERI.

The interest in solar energy is certainly understandable. The Sun keeps the Earth warm, allows vegetation to grow, and nurtures all life. Significantly it is now also recognized that the Sun's radiation can be harnessed for much—perhaps all—of man's energy needs. Conventional sources of energy—coal, oil, gas, and uranium ore—are becoming seriously limited in supply. Continued burning of fossil fuels also raises the temperature of the atmosphere, causing concern for the future. To date this increase

Paul Rappaport is director of the Solar Energy Research Institute, Golden, Colorado.

has been small, but escalating demands for energy throughout the world could alter climate and perhaps even precipitate such catastrophic effects of atmospheric heating as the melting of the polar caps and consequent flooding of the world's coastal cities. By contrast, solar energy is unlimited in supply, at least for the next 4,000,000,000 years or so. It produces no net increase in the Earth's temperature and can be converted into electricity, mechanical and chemical energy, and other useful forms.

Continuing to use conventional sources of energy causes other problems as well. In the case of oil, the obvious drawback is skyrocketing prices. In 1978 foreign oil cost the U.S. four times what it did five years earlier. Other countries have been affected even more seriously; Japan, for instance, imports 99% of its oil. This dependence on oil is a major factor in world politics and economics and perhaps even future wars. Although coal is abundant in the U.S., the cost of mining it and minimizing the polluting effects of its combustion products continues to rise. Moreover, scientists are concerned about buildup in the atmosphere of one such product, carbon dioxide, and its possible influence on the Earth's surface temperature.

Presently, nuclear power seems an unwise bet as a major energy source for the future. Unanswered questions remain regarding reactor safety and nuclear waste disposal. In addition, many other public concerns have not been properly addressed, creating antagonism toward new reactor power plants. It does not appear likely that nuclear energy will provide more than 5% of the total U.S. energy output for years to come.

In light of such difficulties the case for solar energy appears strong. It is socially acceptable, environmentally benign compared with other sources, and available to all countries of the world. Many foreign countries that lack well-developed utility grids see the opportunity for powering rural villages with local solar energy systems. Utility companies in the U.S. are planning to retrofit conventional plants with solar capabilities, and industries are looking to large solar-powered factories. Cost-conscious people throughout the world have installed solar hot-water heaters as a solution to increasing utility bills.

If solar energy is so good, it is reasonable to ask why it is not being exploited to its full potential. In most cases, the technology of solar energy devices is well understood; what remains is to make them more efficient, reliable, and economical, although in some cases basic research is still a prerequisite. Most importantly, for solar energy to compete with existing energy forms that are already subsidized—to the tune of about $130 billion in the U.S. since World War II—manufacturers and consumers alike need incentives. The transition will not be easy or inexpensive. For example, for solar energy to supply 10–20% of U.S. energy needs by the year 2000 will probably require a public and private expenditure of about $100 billion.

The various solar technologies can be classified in numerous ways. One is to group them by the kind of energy they convert from sunlight: electrical, thermal, mechanical, or chemical (e.g., fuel) energy. Another way is to group them according to levels of technological sophistication and centralization. Perhaps the simplest way, however, is to arrange them into natural collection systems and technological collection systems. In the first category one finds the "collector" to be provided free of charge—be it green plants, the atmosphere, an ocean, or an existing building. The total biosphere participates in natural collection of solar radiation and provides free collector surfaces. On the other hand, technological collection systems are subject to a further economic constraint before collection can even be considered. Man-made collectors must be fabricated, presenting additional construction costs to the energy conversion process. In this second category one finds thermal, photovoltaic, and solar power satellite technologies.

Biomass. For many advocates of solar energy the simplest solution to the energy problem is the use of biomass for energy. Biomass is a catchall term for any form of matter that is living or was once part of a living organism; for example, leaves, wood, corncobs, pea pods, algae, bacteria, kelp, and manure. Although the efficiency of conversion of solar energy by growing plants is only 0.1 to 2%, the U.S. has 900 million ac of land under cultivation for lumber, paper, and food. Through either direct burning or conversion to specialty fuels like ethanol and methanol, the residues associated with forestry and agricultural operations alone could provide as much as 10% of U.S. energy needs.

Creation of "energy plantations" could also produce enormous amounts of biomass. Experiments show that sycamore trees, for example, can be harvested at five-year intervals, yielding 10–16 tons of biomass per acre per year—three times the yield of traditional long-rotation silviculture.

Americans of a century past obtained three-fourths of their energy needs from burning wood, and in much of the world wood is still a primary source of heat. Yet, direct burning of wood is simply one aspect of biomass application. Several U.S. companies have begun production of "densified biomass fuel," or what could be called "instant clean coal." Nature has been making coal for several hundred million years by compressing the biomass of swamps and bogs. So densified, coal has a high energy content but unfortunately often contains sulfur, which becomes a pollutant when the coal is burned. Densified biomass fuels can be made from sawdust, bark, corncobs, pea pods, or coffee grounds by drying these materials to a moisture content of about 10% and compressing them into pellets that resemble dry dog food. In this form the biomass has an energy content higher than many coals, is free of sulfur, and is easy to ship and store.

Although solid fuels are satisfactory for large boilers and heating plants, in recent decades homeowners and other small-scale consumers have become accustomed to more convenient forms of fuel that are automatically dispensed. Such a fuel is wood gas. In 1978 several companies were making gasifiers that convert mill waste and wood chips into a fuel suitable for use in existing oil- and gas-burning equipment. A more sophisticated type of gasifier that uses oxygen instead of air produces a concentrated gas that can be converted to alcohol for automotive fuel or to ammonia for fertilizer.

Whereas these processes are suitable for such dry biomass as wood and straw, about 10% of biomass occurs in wet form; for example, manures and sewage. These materials can be converted by digestion to a gas very similar to natural gas or by fermentation to alcohol. In the late 1970s, thousands of automobiles were running on gasohol, a mixture of biomass ethanol and gasoline.

Wind Power. Uneven heating of the Earth by the Sun gives rise to wind, which is therefore considered a solar energy resource. Even though man has used wind energy for centuries, the maximum energy that can be tapped from the winds is difficult to determine. Careful and exhaustive collection of wind energy data is needed to measure the scope of the wind resource.

Windmills have long been a highly visible sign of man's effort to use air currents for energy, and their presence in Europe and the Middle East since the Middle Ages is well known. During the late 1800s Denmark alone had some 3,000 industrial windmills and another 30,000 household and farm windmills in operation. About six million small windmills have been used in the U.S. since the 1850s, mostly for pumping water and generating electricity. Although the availability of cheap electricity and other relatively inexpensive energy sources ended extensive reliance on windmills, an estimated 150,000 units still spin throughout the country.

Renewed interest today in both large and small windmills for production of electrical and mechanical energy could mark the beginning of another important era of wind power. Private and government-funded research and development is under way for various types of wind turbines. Many of these devices have horizontal propellers, or rotors, with two or more blades. Vertical-axis devices, also called Darrieus or eggbeater turbines, and other innovative machines are also being tested. Large windmills being developed by the U.S. Department of Energy (DOE) are intended for possible integration into the distribution grids of electric utilities. Machines producing as much as 200 kw were tested in New Mexico, Puerto Rico, Rhode Island, and Hawaii in 1978, and plans for building machines ten times as large, with rotors as much as 90 m (300 ft) in diameter, were also going forward. A two-megawatt (two-million-watt) turbine, under construction in 1978 on a mountaintop near Boone, N.C., should meet the needs of about 500 homes.

Despite the revival of interest and centuries of experience using wind energy, the wind is a difficult resource to harness, and reliable wind power is not easily achieved. Fluctuations in wind speed occur as frequently as several times a second. In addition, wind speed and wind characteristics can vary greatly over short distances. Changing weather patterns and shifts in climate also mean changes in the availability and intensity of the winds. And, as is the case with other solar technologies, the storage of energy from wind power is necessary for it to be practical.

Power from the Ocean. Ocean energy resources include tides, waves, currents, salinity gradients, and thermal gradients. The thermal gradients—temperature differences between warm surface waters and cold deeper waters—are caused by the natural storage of solar energy in the surface layers of the ocean.

A number of technologies to tap the energy contained in temperature gradients are being developed under the rubric of ocean thermal energy conversion (OTEC). In general, OTEC systems use heat from warm surface waters to vaporize a fluid like ammonia, which as it expands is passed through a turbine for the production of electricity. Then the vapour is chilled with water taken from the colder regions of the ocean and thereby converted back to a fluid to begin the cycle again.

The largest vertical-axis windmill in the U.S., located at Sandia Laboratories, New Mexico, is capable of generating 60 kilowatts of electric power in a 32-mph wind.

Unlike most other solar technologies, OTEC has the potential of supplying energy around the clock, not just when the Sun is shining. But the temperature differences of 20°–22° C (36°–40° F) that are needed to power these systems efficiently exist mainly in the tropical and subtropical oceans, which are far from many of the densely populated areas of the Earth. Whereas OTEC concepts can be economical, they are centralized and large in scope and require a great deal of capital. Moreover, a wide range of technical, environmental, and political issues must be addressed and resolved before OTEC systems become a viable energy option. The earliest commercial use of OTEC units is projected for the 1990s, with widespread deployment unlikely until the early 21st century.

Solar Heating and Cooling. The best known, simplest, and most practical application of solar technology is the use of heat from the Sun to warm buildings and produce hot water. Numerous "passive" and "active" methods to accomplish these tasks are being used throughout the world.

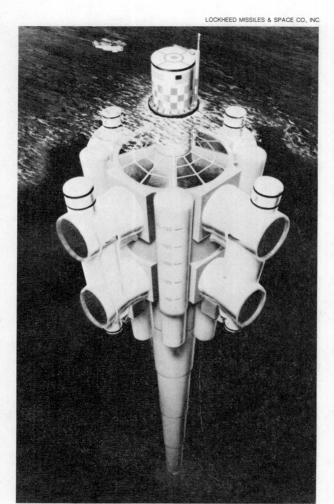

Artist's conception of an ocean thermal energy conversion (OTEC) system. This device would utilize the temperature gradient in the ocean depths to generate 160 megawatts of power.

Passive solar buildings are designed to collect, store, and distribute the Sun's heat. This is accomplished through numerous techniques of building design and proper site orientation. Ideally, the designer begins by positioning the building so that the walls and roof receive maximum solar radiation in winter. Large expanses of window or heat-absorbing wall on the south and few or no window openings on the north serve to maximize solar heat gain in winter, when the Sun is low in the sky. Roof overhangs and movable shutters minimize effects of excess solar radiation in the summer.

Properly designed into a building, passive systems typically provide 40–80% of a building's energy needs for heating and cooling. They often add 5–15% to the cost of conventional construction, mainly because such passive components as movable insulation are not presently mass produced. Many passive buildings, especially owner-built ones, have incurred no added construction costs, and numerous experimental low-cost passive homes have been built in the western and southwestern U.S. as prototypes for low-income housing. In general, passive design represents the most cost-effective method of utilizing solar energy.

In the U.S. both state and federal governments have responded to the recent interest in passive systems. Several states have sponsored residential solar design competitions, built passive test buildings, passed tax credits and property-tax exemption laws that specifically include passive systems, and sponsored workshops and conferences. In addition, the federal government has undertaken a national program to foster passive technology development and utilization and has sponsored a design competition and building demonstration.

With certain exceptions, few passive solar systems lend themselves to economical retrofitting of conventional buildings. Many existing structures, however, can be fitted easily with active systems. The active system consists of six main parts: a collector to capture the solar radiation; a transport system to move the heat from the collector to storage; a storage unit to retain the heat for use at night or on cloudy days; a distribution system to move the heat from storage to living spaces; an auxiliary system, or conventional heating unit, to provide heat that cannot be supplied by the solar system alone; and a system of controls to regulate the total system.

The simplest kind of active collector, called a flat-plate collector, is typically a shallow rectangular box coated inside with a black, heat-absorbing material and faced with glass to retain the heat. It is usually mounted on the roof but can be placed at any location that receives proper southern exposure. Flat-plate collectors use either air or liquid as a circulating medium to absorb and transport the heat. Air and liquid collectors each have their own advantages and disadvantages. Air systems might be simpler in design, be generally easier and cheaper to install, and present fewer freezing and corrosion problems, but they use more electricity and need larger heat storage units than liquid systems. Also, liquid systems are often more practical when solar energy is to be used for domestic hot water.

Most active heating systems are designed to provide 50–90% of a building's heating requirement. Studies conducted by DOE have found that active solar heating makes good economic sense in most parts of the U.S. if it can be financed as part of a new home mortgage, if the alternative is electric resistance heating, and if the solar unit can be installed at a total cost not higher than about $20 per square foot of collector area.

Solar heating systems for residences should always be combined with domestic hot-water systems in order to achieve maximum utilization of the collectors throughout the year. Recent U.S. studies suggest that active hot-water systems currently are a sound financial investment whenever the alternative is electric hot-water heating and can even compete economically with gas hot-water heating in many parts of the country. Most such units are expected to last at least 20 years; typically they will pay for themselves in savings in four to seven years.

Presently solar cooling technology is much less advanced than that for heating equipment. The only cost-effective methods of so cooling private residences are passive methods. Although various types of solar air conditioners are under development, some of which have already found commercial application, they are still too expensive and unreliable for homeowners. Simple techniques can be used to help cool buildings; for example, ceiling vents to expel hot air and draw cool air from a basement or earth-air heat exchanger; porches, eaves, and roof overhangs to ward off the summer Sun; and shutters, transoms, and fans to aid in air flow. Other, more elaborate passive techniques include tall thermal chimneys, which suck the air up and out of the house, and large, roof-mounted bladders of water called roof ponds, which can be used for heating or cooling in nonhumid climates.

Solar Energy for Industry and Agriculture. About 25% of U.S. energy production is consumed in such industrial processes as steam heating, air drying, and heating clean-up water. Solar energy shows potential as an alternate energy source for many of these processes that now require costly natural gas, oil, or electricity. Hit hard by the rising cost of propane and natural gas, farmers are also eyeing solar energy as an option for irrigation pumping, crop drying, water heating, and livestock shelter heating.

Many such industrial and agricultural tasks can be met with low-temperature systems, i.e., below 175° C (350° F), by using flat-plate collectors, shallow solar ponds, and even some passive techniques. Other requirements fall into the intermediate-temperature range, between 175° and 315° C (350°–600° F), which calls for more sophisticated equipment. And fully 60% of industrial-process heat demand is in the high-temperature range, above 315° C, for steelmaking, oil refining, cement and glass manufacture, and chemical production. High-temperature steam can be generated with solar energy using Sun-tracking parabolic collectors and other advanced systems of high cost and still unproven reliability.

In addition to the use of sunlight for heat, conversion of high-temperature heat into electricity is another concept being developed, primarily through design and testing of large-scale, central receiver systems and distributed collector systems. The central receiver system uses a tall "power tower" surrounded by a field of tracking mirrors, called heliostats, that concentrate the Sun onto a boiler located at the tower's top. Steam is generated to drive a turbine for the production of electricity. In 1978 progress was made on a ten-megawatt central receiver pilot plant under construction near Barstow, Calif. A five-megawatt test facility is already operational at Albuquerque, N.M., and is providing valuable experience for the larger plant. Distributed collector systems use a number of comparatively

Rear view (from the west) of a passive solar home located in Pagosa Springs, Colorado. For a front view (from the south-southwest) of same home see page 16.

LAWRENCE C. ATKINSON

small high-temperature heat collectors and channel the energy into central power generating equipment. Some utility companies and the U.S. government are looking into the likelihood of "repowering" existing natural-gas–fired electrical generating plants in the desert southwest with solar thermal power systems. If the economics of such systems appear favourable, use of solar energy in future plants will appear more attractive.

Solar Cells. Photovoltaic cells are very simple semiconductor devices that convert sunlight which strikes them directly into electricity. Used for more than 20 years to power satellites and manned vehicles in space, solar cells promise to help man tap the Sun's unlimited energy and produce pollution-free electric power in large or small quantities.

To date most solar cells have been made with silicon, the Earth's second most abundant material. A typical single-crystal silicon solar cell 7½ cm (3 in) in diameter will generate one-half watt at more than 10% efficiency in bright sunlight. Generally such cells are connected in parallel or series arrangements in flat panels of various sizes that are durable and maintenance-free. Panels of this kind are being used daily for many different applications, from charging

Concentrated sunlight from 1,775 mirror facets strikes a steel target on a 200-foot-high "power tower" at Sandia Laboratories. This mirror array generates enough heat to melt steel.

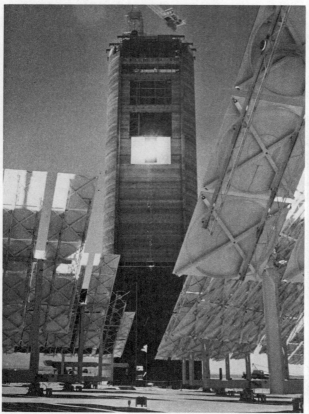

batteries in radios, watches, and pocket calculators to powering remote radio transmitters. In some situations solar arrays are connected to batteries for delivery of electric power at night.

In 1978 DOE funded a solar-cell electric power system for the Papago Indian village of Schuchuli, Ariz. The village formerly relied on kerosene lamps for lighting and muscle power for laundry and had no refrigeration facilities for perishable foods and medicines. More than three million villages throughout the world presently have no electric power, and it is anticipated that solar cells will help improve living conditions for millions of people in less developed countries.

Although solar cells have found useful decentralized applications, their present cost of about $10,-000 per peak kilowatt must be greatly reduced before they can be competitive with other forms of centralized electrical energy. Photovoltaic experts in Europe and the U.S. agree that the U.S. goal of 50 cents per peak watt for flat-panel or concentrator arrays is achievable by 1986, given a major governmental grant program. In 1978 the U.S. government established photovoltaic development as a priority item with the passing of a bill to create a ten-year, $1.5 billion photovoltaic energy research, development, and demonstration program. Its major goal is to double the production of photovoltaic energy systems annually beginning with fiscal year 1979.

Many different approaches are under study to reduce manufacturing costs and improve efficiency. In addition to the single-crystal silicon approach, which is currently the primary technology, work is being pursued on thin films of cadmium sulfide, amorphous (noncrystalline) silicon, and other materials for flat-panel arrays. Another approach is to use concentrating, or focusing, collectors instead of flat panels. In this case cost of the cells is less important than high efficiency, and designs are based on gallium arsenide alloys, silicon, and other photosensitive materials. New approaches and developments occur almost monthly, and some scientists are working to exceed the present cell-efficiency maximum of about 25%.

Large arrays of solar cells are already being used on Earth for a variety of electrical applications. A system of 100,000 cells, for example, provides 25 peak kilowatts of power to a Meade, Neb., farm for pumping irrigation water in the summer; in the fall the system provides electrical energy for fans that dry the crops after harvest. A new ten-unit condominium in Palo Alto, Calif., is the world's first residential application of flat-panel solar cells on a commercial basis, and plans call for construction in 1979 of a 240-kw concentrator photovoltaic array to provide the electrical needs of a community college in Arkansas. Under a

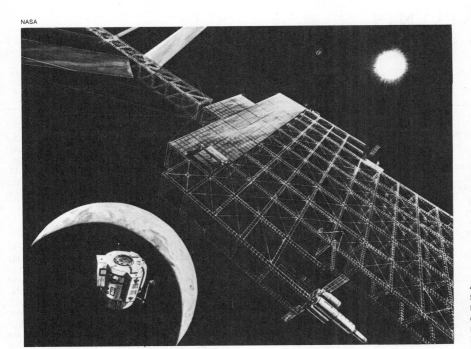

Artist's conception of a solar power satellite which would orbit 22,500 miles above the Earth and beam down electric power in the form of microwaves generated by photovoltaic conversion.

joint agreement between the Saudi Arabian and U.S. governments, a solar village powered by a large photovoltaic array is to be built in Saudi Arabia.

One of the most ambitious photovoltaic conversion processes yet proposed is the solar power satellite (SPS) concept. As envisioned by the U.S. National Aeronautics and Space Administration, such a system would involve constructing and placing generating stations into geostationary orbits around the Earth. Solar energy would be captured on enormous panels of solar cells, converted to microwaves, and beamed to Earth using precisely focused antennas. Beams would be received by large antenna grids on the ground and then converted to high-voltage current. Because the Sun never sets in space, the SPS concept provides nearly continuous power, which can be supplied directly to regions where normal sunlight is low. Considerable work needs to be done in addressing environmental questions, energy storage potential, and the economic effects of the very large investment of tax dollars that would be needed to fund the program.

Legislating Solar. If 1978 marks the dawn of the solar era, much work remains to realize the promise of this ancient energy source. The National Energy Act (NEA), passed by the 95th Congress and signed into law by President Carter in November 1978, should help thousands of homeowners begin efficiently utilizing the solar radiation falling on their homes each day. Provisions in the act allow for a tax credit of 30% of the first $2,000 and 20% of the next $8,000 spent on qualifying solar equipment—and wind power equipment—for a maximum credit of

$2,200. The credit is retroactive to cover systems installed after April 20, 1977, and extends through 1985. In addition, a 15% credit is allowed on expenditures as high as $2,000 for home investments in insulation, weatherstripping, and the like.

Other provisions in the act may hasten the development of solar energy even more than the residential solar and wind tax credits: tax credits for businesses installing solar equipment; provisions encouraging existing utility plants using oil or gas to switch to solar energy; provisions increasing the ceilings on federally insured mortgages when the increase is needed to cover the cost of passive or active solar or wind systems; provisions for secondary financing of solar home-improvement loans; and grants to schools and hospitals for energy-conserving devices.

In addition, a significant amount of solar legislation was passed in the U.S. in 1978 outside the NEA, much of it due to the efforts of a loose-knit group of House and Senate members called the Solar Coalition. Moreover, numerous states passed legislation directed at making solar equipment more economically available to consumers, businesses, and industries.

Probably more important is what can happen in 1979. Members of the 96th Congress should feel strong pressure from groups lobbying in behalf of solar energy issues and consumer protection questions. And the Carter administration is expected to introduce a package of broad-based energy legislation to further strengthen the NEA and extend man's use of power from the Sun.

JANUARY

3 *Cambodia rejects Vietnam peace offer*

Cambodia again refused to negotiate peace with neighbouring Vietnam until all Vietnamese troops had withdrawn from Cambodian territory. The common border, never clearly defined even by the French colonial administrators, became a source of tension soon after the conclusion of the Indochina war in April 1975. Toward the end of 1977 Cambodia attempted to gain control of some 50 villages that Vietnam had designated as new economic areas. About 60,000 Vietnamese troops then attacked an estimated 25,000 Cambodians and drove to within 56 km (35 mi) of Phnom Penh, the capital of Cambodia. The conflict between the two Communist nations had international ramifications because China was backing Cambodia and the Soviet Union was supporting Vietnam.

Gandhi ousted from Congress Party

One day after former prime minister Indira Gandhi was acclaimed president of the Indian National Congress by a power-ful rival faction within the party, she and her followers were formally deprived of membership by party president K. Brahmananda Reddy. The rebel group, which denounced the current leaders as undemocratic and inept, hoped that Gandhi could enforce party unity, regain her former popularity, and eventually avenge the national defeat she and the party suffered at the hands of the Janata Party in March 1977.

4 *Pinochet uses plebiscite to reinforce his control of Chile*

Overriding all objections that he had no power to order a national plebiscite, Chilean Pres. Augusto Pinochet Ugarte called upon voters to approve or reject a single statement that read: "In the face of the international aggression unleashed against the government of the homeland, I support President Pinochet in his defense of the dignity of Chile, and I reaffirm the legitimacy of the republic to conduct in a sovereign way the process of the institutionalization of the country." Because the vote tallies were made by Pinochet's supporters, it was not possible to confirm that 75% of the ballots indicated approval. The president, however, was visibly elated at the outcome and declared that the victory was so overwhelming that no other elections would be needed for at least ten years.

6 *Carter concludes overseas tour*

U.S. Pres. Jimmy Carter returned to Washington, D.C., after a nine-day tour that began on Dec. 29, 1977. After visits to Poland and Iran, he arrived in India and on January 2 addressed the Indian Parliament. Carter then moved on to Saudi Arabia and made a brief side trip to Aswan, Egypt, to discuss Middle East problems with Pres. Anwar as-Sadat. Carter delivered the second major address of his tour in France before government and business leaders and traveled with Pres. Valéry Giscard d'Estaing to Normandy, where they viewed the site of the Allies' D-Day landing during World War II. In Belgium, his last stop, Carter talked with leaders of both the North Atlantic Treaty Organization and the European Com-

U.S. Pres. Jimmy Carter with French Pres. Valéry Giscard d'Estaing at Omaha Beach landing site in Normandy.

U.S. Secretary of State Cyrus Vance (left) turns over St. Stephen's crown to Hungarian officials.

munity. The president later stated that the "constant theme" of his tour was to emphasize "that our modern struggle is not only to establish peace but also to protect the individual from the power of the state."

St. Stephen's crown returned to Hungary

In a solemn ceremony in Budapest, U.S. Secretary of State Cyrus Vance turned over to Hungarian officials the jeweled crown of St. Stephen, a symbol of the nation because it had been used in the coronation of every Hungarian king since Stephen first wore it in the year 1000. Also returned were a sword, scepter, orb, and robe used during the coronations. A captured member of the Hungarian Royal Crown Guard handed over the items to U.S. military personnel in July 1945 to prevent them from falling into Soviet hands. Despite protests from U.S. congressmen and citizens of Hungarian background, the U.S. government went ahead with its plans, explaining that the treasures were being returned to the Hungarian people, not to the Communist government as such. The U.S. gesture was in reality an indication of improved relations between the two countries.

10 *Violence rocks Nicaragua after the assassination of newspaper editor*

Pedro Joaquín Chamorro Cardenal, editor and publisher of the *La Prensa* daily newspaper and a vociferous opponent of the regime of Pres. Anastasio Somoza Debayle, was assassinated by three men who sprayed his car with machine gun and rifle fire. The next night tens of thousands of Nicaraguans in the capital city of Managua set fire to buildings and cars,

looted stores, and hurled stones at soldiers, policemen, and firemen. A bank, a textile company, and other businesses — all reputedly part of Somoza's holdings — also went up in flames. The rioting that continued after Chamorro's burial on January 12 was so fierce that few expected it would subside quickly.

11 *Italian government rejects Communist demands for more active role*

The directorate of Italy's ruling Christian Democratic Party voted unanimously to reject a January 4 demand by the Communist Party for a direct role in the government administration. Though the Communists, Socialists, and three lesser parties had agreed in July 1977 to support the government's economic, social, and antiterrorist programs, the Communists argued that violence across the nation could not be controlled without their active participation in government decisions. On January 12 President Carter, in an unusual move, authorized the State Department to express "U.S. concern" over the prospect of a nondemocratic party participating in the formulation of Italian government policies.

Soviet cosmonauts join two comrades orbiting in space laboratory

Two Soviet cosmonauts linked up their Soyuz 27 spacecraft with the Salyut 6, a manned space laboratory that had been in orbit for a month. The successful docking demonstrated the practicality of multiple linkups in space, the possibility of exchanging crews, and the feasibility of sending rescue missions into space when emergencies arise. The two Soyuz cosmonauts were expected to remain in the

Salyut 6 for five days before returning to Earth.

12 *Firemen end strike in Britain*

More than 40,000 professional and volunteer firemen in Great Britain voted overwhelmingly to end a strike that was called two months earlier after the government refused to grant a 30% increase in pay. The settlement included a 10% annual increase over a two-year period and a six-hour reduction in the weekly work schedule. During the strike, when military personnel using outdated equipment were assigned to fire-fighting duty, there was no appreciable increase in the number of fires or fire-related deaths, but property damage from fires was substantially greater than normal.

13 *U.S. and Japan reach trade accord*

A major agreement designed to reduce Japan's huge surpluses in its trade and balance of payments accounts with the U.S. was reached in Tokyo by negotiators representing the two nations. Among other things, Japan agreed to open up its domestic market to foreign competitors, to remove all quotas on 11 agricultural items, and to increase substantially its importation of manufactured goods, oranges, and citrus juices. Robert S. Strauss, who acted as President Carter's special trade representative, was highly pleased with the results. Nobuhiko Ushiba, Japan's minister for external economic affairs, was less enthusiastic and acknowledged that "Japan has to expect that new economic issues will arise one after another from now on."

15 *Dallas Cowboys win Super Bowl XII*

The Dallas Cowboys won their second National Football League championship by defeating the Denver Broncos 27–10 in Super Bowl XII. The game was played in the Louisiana Superdome in New Orleans before a capacity crowd of 76,000. An estimated 86 million Americans followed the game on television, the largest such audience in the history of televised sports.

16 *Italian government falls*

Premier Giulio Andreotti, the 39th consecutive Christian Democrat to head the Italian government since the fall of Mussolini in 1943, submitted his resignation to Pres. Giovanni Leone. Andreotti stepped down before the lower house of Parliament could call for a no-confidence vote on his rejection of a demand that members of the Communist Party and two lesser groups be given positions in the Cabinet.

18 *Ethiopia denies foreign troops are participating in Ogaden fighting*

A member of Ethiopia's ruling military council denied during a news conference in Addis Ababa, the capital, that Soviet

FEBRUARY

or Cuban military personnel were either fighting or acting as advisers on Ethiopia's behalf. Western intelligence sources, however, estimated that 2,000 Cubans and 1,000 Soviets were in the Ogaden region, actively assisting Ethiopia in its drive against local ethnic Somalis, who reportedly were reinforced by troops from Somalia itself. One week later President Carter told the head of a delegation from the Supreme Soviet that Soviet-U.S. relations would deteriorate if the U.S.S.R. intensified its military involvement in the Horn of Africa.

20 *Suharto silences newspapers and moves against student critics*

In an ostentatious show of strength designed to stifle opposition to his regime, President Suharto of Indonesia banned four of the country's largest newspapers without explanation. Many believed the newspapers were shut down for giving press coverage to students campaigning against official corruption, agitating for social and economic reforms, and demanding that Suharto not run for reelection in the spring. The following day two more newspapers were ordered to suspend publication. The same day two universities were ringed with armoured cars and troops. At the University of Indonesia in Jakarta more than 100 students were arrested and at a private university some 2,000 students fled from a meeting when a low-flying helicopter stirred up dust. The government also banned all student councils and forbade students to participate in political activities. On January 23 a seventh newspaper was banned.

23 *Nicaragua paralyzed by national strike*

Two weeks after the assassination of *La Prensa* editor Pedro Joaquín Chamorro Cardenal, a severe critic of the Somoza government, a general strike gripped the nation. On January 25 the Conservative Party called for the resignation of Pres. Anastasio Somoza Debayle, but he refused to step aside. With about 75% of the country's stores, offices, and factories closed, food, gasoline, and other shortages quickly developed. On January 30 helicopters hovering over the National University in Managua dropped tear gas on demonstrating students. At the height of the disorders Nicaragua's seven Roman Catholic bishops, normally supportive of the government, issued a declaration stating that a solution must be found to the social, political, and economic problems that plagued the nation. Neither Chamorro's brother, who assumed the editorship of *La Prensa*, nor Rafael Cordoba Rivas, who took command of the Union Democratic Liberation party, seemed willing to negotiate with the government.

24 *Fragments of Soviet satellite land in Canada*

Fragments of Cosmos 954, a five-ton Soviet reconnaissance satellite that disintegrated while entering the Earth's atmosphere, fell in a remote area of Canada's Northwest Territories. The first concern of scientists was to determine the fate of the 100 lb of uranium-235 that powered the satellite's reactor. On January 28 debris activated by low-level radiation was

discovered on the ground, but nothing was found to substantiate early fears that humans, fish, or game would be seriously affected. During a news conference on January 30, President Carter said he favoured a total ban on all Earth-orbiting vehicles carrying radioactive materials, unless "fail-safe methods" could be devised to guarantee their safety.

26 *Cyprus gets full-term president*

Spyros Kyprianou, who became caretaker head of the Cyprus government after the death of Archbishop Makarios III in August 1977, officially became president designate when no opposition candidate was named to oppose him in an election scheduled for February 5. His five-year term would commence on March 1.

Tunisian cities erupt in worst civil violence in decades

After months of frustration and smoldering resentment against the government, members of the General Union of Tunisian Workers (UGTT) went on a nationwide general strike. The government responded by declaring a state of emergency. These actions crystallized and intensified opposition to the government of Pres. Habib Bourguiba, who in 1977 ordered a five-year freeze on wages. According to some local sources, nearly 200 persons were killed in Tunisia during confrontations with police and some 400 were arrested. Among those taken into custody on January 28 were Habib Achour, secretary-general of UGTT, and a number of other union officials.

FEBRUARY

2 *Radical Arabs meet in Algeria*

A high-level three-day meeting of leaders from Algeria, Libya, Yemen (Aden), Syria, and the Palestine Liberation Organization met in Algiers to coordinate plans to frustrate Egyptian Pres. Anwar as-Sadat's peace initiative in the Middle East. Iraq refused to attend the meeting because it advocated a more radical position than other Arab leaders were willing to espouse. The results of the meeting were not made public.

3 *Australia reports new uranium find*

A huge deposit of uranium oxide ore, perhaps amounting to one million tons, was reportedly found near Darwin in Australia's Northern Territory. Though the ore was much richer than that at the nearby Ranger Project site, opposition to mining operations was certain to come from the many Australian unions that objected to further development of uranium. In addition, the newly discovered site lay within an area tentatively designated as an extension of the national park system.

China negotiates first trade accord with Common Market

Representatives of China and the European Economic Community (EEC) announced in Brussels that a five-year bilateral trade agreement had been reached. China had earlier established trade links with individual members of the EEC, but formal ties with the organization as a whole required the acceptance of a standard clause giving all parties the right to impose import restrictions on items that threaten to disrupt domestic markets. The Soviet news agency Tass charged that the negotiations had been conducted "in an anti-Soviet spirit with the aim of increasing Chinese access to European technology."

4 *Fragment of satellite recovered in Canada has high radioactivity*

A fragment of Cosmos 954, the Soviet satellite that disintegrated over Canada on January 24, was recovered from the ice covering Great Slave Lake in northern Canada. Scientists reported that the piece

emitted 200 roentgens an hour, a dangerous level of radiation that was many times more intense than that emitted by fragments of the satellite found earlier. In general, most scientists seemed to believe that the satellite's uranium fuel had dissipated on entering the Earth's atmosphere and consequently posed no hazard to human health.

Sri Lanka alters government structure

The structure of the government of Sri Lanka was modified to shift power from the prime minister to a president serving a fixed six-year term. The change, designed to give the nation a stronger and more stable government, was firmly opposed by the Freedom Party, which ruled Sri Lanka under Prime Minister Sirimavo Bandaranaike until July 23, 1977. Junius Richard Jayawardene relinquished his post as prime minister when he was sworn in as president on February 4; on February 6 Ranasingle Premadasa, deputy leader of the ruling United National Party, became prime minister.

PLO leader Yasir Arafat (left) and Syrian Pres. Hafez al-Assad during resistance meeting in Algiers against the Egyptian Middle East peace initiative.

7 Nicaraguan general strike ends

Economic hardships forced an end to a nationwide general strike that began on January 23 with demands that Pres. Anastasio Somoza Debayle resign. Though clashes with the National Guard decreased when the strike ended, opposition to the dictatorial Somoza regime was still widespread. On February 12 the Sandinista National Liberation Front, a guerrilla organization, announced that it was preparing for civil war.

8 Sadat ends visit to U.S.

Pres. Anwar as-Sadat of Egypt ended a six-day visit to the U.S., during which he urged President Carter and other government officials to exert pressure on Israel to be less intransigent in negotiating a peace settlement in the Middle East and to respond positively to Egypt's request for additional arms. Negotiations had bogged down over such fundamental issues as Israeli occupation of and future presence in Arab lands, and the right of the Palestinians to have a land of their own.

9 Canada expels Soviet spies

The Canadian minister of external affairs announced in Parliament that 11 Soviet diplomats were being expelled from Canada for operating a highly sophisticated spy ring, and that two other Soviet nationals would be forbidden reentry for involvement in the same activities. In April 1977 an officer in the counterintelligence division of the Royal Canadian Mounted Police was contacted by a Soviet agent. The man subsequently met his Soviet contact seven times to pass on un-

classified and fabricated data supplied by his superior. In exchange the Canadian received a total of $30,500.

10 Vietnamese ambassador to UN accused of spying, leaves U.S.

Dinh Ba Thi, Vietnam's ambassador to the United Nations, left the U.S. after being notified by the U.S. government on February 3 that his involvement in spy activities abused his "privilege of residence" and made him persona non grata. After proclaiming Thi's innocence, the Vietnamese government ordered him to return home. Cuba and Soviet-bloc delegates supported Vietnam's denunciation of the expulsion order, but a U.S. delegate assured the Assembly that his government had "precise evidence" of Thi's personal involvement. The spy case became public on January 31 when FBI agents arrested an official of the U.S. Information Agency and a Vietnamese residing in the U.S.

Dissolution of EOKA-B reported

The Greek Cypriot terrorist group called EOKA-B sent letters to local newspapers formally announcing its dissolution. The original National Organization of Cypriot Struggle (EOKA) was organized, probably in 1955, by Col. Georgios Grivas. Its purpose was to drive the British from Cyprus and to bring about *enosis*, the union of Cyprus with Greece. After Archbishop Makarios III announced in 1958 that he would accept independence for Cyprus rather than *enosis*, Grivas asked for and received amnesty for his followers and EOKA was disbanded. In 1971 Grivas revived the organization as EOKA-B, but

when he died in January 1974 there was no realistic hope that Cyprus would become part of Greece in the foreseeable future.

12 Immigration policy becomes hot political issue in Britain

Margaret Thatcher, leader of the opposition Conservative Party in Great Britain, told a group of Young Conservatives that "I do not believe we have any hope of promoting the sort of society we want unless we are to follow a policy clearly designed to work toward the end of immigration as we have seen it in these postwar years." Thatcher earlier made headlines when, during a television interview at the end of January, she remarked that many Britons feared they would be "swamped by people of a different culture." The reference was to immigrants from the Caribbean and the Indian subcontinent. A Gallup Poll survey showed that 59% of those interviewed considered immigrants a very serious social problem; 46% said race relations were worsening; and 49% said Britain should offer cash to immigrants who would return home.

13 Sadat visits six countries in Europe

Pres. Anwar as-Sadat of Egypt concluded a five-day visit to Europe during which he sought support for his Middle East peace proposals from the leaders of Great Britain, West Germany, Austria, Romania, France, and Italy.

15 Agreement on black majority rule announced in Rhodesia

Prime Minister Ian Smith of Rhodesia and three of the country's black leaders announced general agreement on a plan that would eventually establish black rule in Rhodesia. Bishop Abel Muzorewa, the Rev. Ndabaningi Sithole, and Sen. Jeremiah Chirau viewed the arrangement as basically acceptable, but the U.S. and Great Britain continued to feel that a successful transition to black rule required the participation of the Patriotic Front. That opinion was reinforced when Joshua Nkomo and Robert Mugabe, co-leaders of the Front, insisted they would continue their guerrilla attacks on Rhodesia from bases outside the country until the Front gained control of the government.

18 Irish Prime Minister Lynch asserts that overseas aid prolongs fighting

Prime Minister John Lynch of Ireland urged "Irish people abroad, especially in the United States," to stop supporting organizations that claim to provide humanitarian aid to residents of strife-torn Northern Ireland. Money given to such groups as the Irish National Caucus and the Irish Northern Aid Committee does not go to widows and orphans, Lynch said, but "to makers of widows and orphans." In an exchange of letters

MARCH

A radioactive fragment from a fallen Soviet nuclear-powered satellite was recovered in northern Canada in early February.

rorists and Cypriot officials seemed to be stalemated. The commandos later claimed that it was the Cypriot National Guard that opened fire on them and that a 12-man unit of the Palestine Liberation Organization quickly joined the Cypriots. The commandos also noted that most of their slain companions died aboard the C-130, which was destroyed by direct fire even though it was stationed more than half a mile from the hijacked plane. After the firing ceased, the terrorists freed the remaining hostages unharmed and surrendered to the Cypriots. On February 22 Sadat cut diplomatic ties with Cyprus.

21 Court halts investigation of RCMP

An official inquiry into alleged illegal activities of the Royal Canadian Mounted Police (RCMP) was stopped by the Quebec Court of Appeals, which concurred with federal officials that the Quebec provincial investigating committee exceeded its powers, and acted unconstitutionally, when it demanded secret RCMP files from a federal officer, a former solicitor general. The court also noted that the investigators violated the Official Secrets Act by making public several documents classified as confidential by the RCMP. The provincial government announced that it would appeal the court decision to the Canadian Supreme Court. Among the alleged illegal activities was a break-in at a Montreal computer firm to search for evidence that the Parti Québécois, which advocates separation from the rest of Canada, had received funds from abroad.

with U.S. Rep. Mario Biaggi (Dem., N.Y.), Lynch implied that the Ad Hoc Committee for Irish Affairs was also fostering violence in Ulster. Biaggi organized the group in the House of Representatives in September 1977.

19 Egyptians launch ill-fated attack against terrorists in Cyprus

In a planned surprise attack on a hijacked plane at Larnaca Airport in Cyprus, 15 of 74 Egyptian commandos were killed during a wildly confusing hour-long gun battle. The affair began in Nicosia on February 18 when two Palestinian terrorists assassinated Yusuf as-Sibai, the edi-

tor of Cairo's daily *al-Ahram* and a close friend of Egyptian Pres. Anwar as-Sadat. In exchange for free passage to the airport, the terrorists released 12 of 30 hostages seized in the Hilton Hotel, the scene of the murder. Seven others were freed when Cypriot officials allowed the terrorists to board a DC-8 aircraft, which took off but was not allowed to land in Kuwait, Somalia, Ethiopia, Greece, or Yemen (Aden). After refueling in Djibouti, it was refused landing rights in Libya and Algeria and had to return to Larnaca. One-half hour later the Egyptian commandos arrived in a C-130 transport, and about two hours later began their surprise attack when negotiations between the ter-

27 Egypt to end special status of resident Palestinians

Prime Minister Mamdouh Salem of Egypt told the People's Assembly that, in the future, Palestinians living in Egypt would no longer enjoy special privileges. Instead of receiving preferential admission to universities and enjoying the same legal rights and business opportunities as Egyptian citizens, they would have the same status as citizens of other sister Arab states. The proposed legislation was a clear expression of Egyptian anger over the alleged role of the Palestinians in the slaying of Egyptian commandos in Cyprus on February 19.

MARCH

2 Iran cuts ties with East Germany

Iran announced that it was recalling its ambassador to East Germany to protest East Germany's support of Iranian students who attacked the Iranian embassy in East Berlin on February 27. The attack was a protest against Iran's suppression of antigovernment riots in Tabriz in mid-February. On March 5 Iran announced that it was also discontinuing all trade and economic ties with East Germany.

China ends National People's Congress

China concluded its fifth National People's Congress, which had convened in Peking on February 26. The main accomplishments of the nation's highest organ of state power were the drafting of a new constitution, the formulation of a ten-year economic plan, and the reappointment of Hua Kuo-feng as premier. Expectations that Vice-Premier Teng

Hsiao-p'ing would replace Hua as premier did not materialize. Several of Teng's closest friends, however, were appointed to positions of importance. In other changes, Yeh Chien-ying relinquished the post of defense minister to become chairman of the Standing Committee of the Congress, a largely ceremonial post equivalent to chief of state. The position of president was not revived, though many had expected that it would be. The new constitution, which replaced that of 1975, revived some articles from China's first Communist constitution, adopted in 1954. The new document placed unprecedented emphasis on economic development and the need to make rapid progress in science and technology, even at the expense of revolutionary ideology.

6 *Prisoner exchange between U.S. and Mexico comes to an end*

The repatriation of U.S. and Mexican prisoners that began in December 1977 ended when 48 Americans and 36 Mexicans returned to their respective countries. Of the 233 Americans who returned earlier, some 70 remained in federal custody. More than 300 Americans were still serving time in Mexican jails, either because they preferred to stay where they were or because they did not qualify for a transfer under the conditions of the exchange treaty. Among those excluded from repatriation were participants in political activities and violators of Mexican immigration laws.

9 *Tito ends visit to the U.S.*

President Tito of Yugoslavia concluded an official four-day visit to the U.S., during which he exchanged views with President Carter on many international problems and expressed a desire to purchase U.S. arms. The 85-year-old Communist leader also manifested annoyance over the freedom given to anti-Communist Yugoslavs in the U.S. to protest his visit and his domestic policies. President Carter spoke

approvingly of Yugoslavia's policy of nonalignment with either superpower and referred to its territorial integrity and independence as "basic foundations of world peace."

Park Tong Sun testifies before House ethics committee

Korean businessman Park Tong Sun concluded his testimony before the U.S. House of Representatives Committee on Standards of Official Conduct. He began his testimony behind closed doors on February 28 under an agreement guaranteeing him immunity from prosecution in exchange for truthful testimony. Park reportedly made no new revelations of importance to further substantiate allegations of South Korean influence-buying on Capitol Hill. Throughout the hearings Park steadfastly denied that he was ever an agent of his government; he explained his friendship with three successive directors of the Korean Central Intelligence Agency as a necessary measure to protect his position as a prospering rice broker to Korea. Some committee members reportedly were not persuaded that Park's government contacts were cultivated solely for business purposes and seemed annoyed with some of his responses, which appeared to be deliberately evasive. Leon Jaworski, special counsel to the committee, stated that the committee wished to question other South Koreans, notably former ambassador Kim Dong Jo, who allegedly was also involved in influence-peddling.

11 *New Italian government formed*

Giulio Andreotti, Italy's caretaker premier since his forced resignation on January 16, formed a new government that consisted mainly of fellow Christian Democrats. Though no Cabinet posts were promised to members of the Communist Party, it and three smaller parties agreed to give parliamentary support to the new government after being assured of a voice in policymaking.

13 *Guatemalan Congress names president*

After determining that none of the presidential candidates had won a majority of the popular votes in the general election of March 5, the Guatemalan National Congress voted 35–0 to name 53-year-old Gen. Fernando Romeo Lucas García president-elect. Twenty-six congressmen chose not to be present when the selection was made. Though the March 5 election had been peaceful, the vote counting was delayed by charges and countercharges of fraud and by sporadic violence. Lucas, who received a plurality of the popular vote, would replace Pres. Kjell Eugenio Laugerud García in July. Both were members of the Partido Institucional Democrático.

14 *UN rejects Rhodesia settlement*

By a vote of 10–0, with five abstentions, the UN Security Council rejected as "illegal and unacceptable" the plan for black

The giant supertanker "Amoco Cadiz" ran aground and split in two off the coast of France on March 17.

KAKU KURITA—GAMMA/LIAISON

Even slingshots were used to fire on airplanes as thousands of demonstrators tried to prevent the opening of Japan's Narita airport in March.

majority rule in Rhodesia that had been signed on March 3 by Prime Minister Ian Smith and three moderate black leaders. Though Great Britain and the U.S. viewed the agreement as a step forward, they withheld their approval (as did Canada, France, and West Germany) because the settlement ignored the Patriotic Front, which swore to continue its guerrilla assaults until its demands for total black rule were met. On March 21 Smith, Bishop Abel Muzorewa, the Rev. Ndabaningi Sithole, and Sen. Jeremiah Chirau were sworn in as members of the Executive Council of the transitional government; the council chairmanship would pass successively from one to the other every four weeks. After the ceremony the four leaders agreed that there would be nine ministries, each jointly administered by one black and one white.

Israel attacks Palestinians in Lebanon

In a coordinated military operation involving land, sea, and air forces, Israel launched major assaults against bases of the Palestine Liberation Organization in southern Lebanon. The action was in response to a Palestinian guerrilla attack on March 11 that took the lives of more than 30 Israeli civilians on a road running between Haifa and Tel Aviv. On March 15 Israel announced that its principal military objectives had been attained and that it had established a "security belt" some 6–10 km (4–6 mi) wide along the border area of southern Lebanon. Prime Minister Menahem Begin then assured all parties that Israel would leave the newly occupied territory as soon as it received assurances that the Palestinians would not be allowed to return to the places from which they had been ejected.

15 *U.S. coal strike nears end*

On the 100th day of a national coal strike involving 160,000 miners, the bargaining council of the United Mine Workers (UMW) voted 22–17 to accept the terms of a new contract negotiated with representatives of the Bituminous Coal Operators' Association (BCOA). Though rank and file members of the UMW rejected a tentative contract in early March, they were expected to approve the latest offer because increased salaries and improved benefits outweighed concessions made to industry. On March 24 the miners ratified the contract with 57% voting approval, and on March 25 a three-year contract was signed by UMW and BCOA representatives. Some 18,000 miners did not return to work immediately because of a brief strike by mine construction workers. A federal court order requiring the miners to return to work on March 13 under provisions of the Taft-Hartley Act was largely ignored, but no action was taken by the government because a settlement seemed imminent.

16 *Aldo Moro kidnapped in Rome*

Former Italian premier Aldo Moro, president of the ruling Christian Democrat Party and one of the country's most respected politicians, was kidnapped in Rome by left-wing terrorists as he was being driven to a special session of Parliament. All five of his bodyguards were slain by the 12 terrorists who fired an estimated 70 rounds of ammunition from Czechoslovak and Soviet automatic weapons. Later in the day Italy's most notorious left-wing terrorist group, the Red Brigades, claimed responsibility for the killings and abduction. One of several anonymous telephone callers said Moro would be killed within 48 hours unless the government released 15 members of the Red Brigades who were being tried with other terrorists in a criminal court in Turin. Thousands of police began an intensive search for Moro and his kidnappers, but immediate success was not expected because the abduction had obviously been carefully planned.

U.S. Senate narrowly approves first Panama Canal treaty

After weeks of prolonged debate and intense lobbying, the U.S. Senate approved the first of two Panama Canal treaties. The 68–32 margin was just one vote more than the required two-thirds majority needed for ratification. The formal agreement, called the Treaty Concerning the Permanent Neutrality and Operation of the Panama Canal, guaranteed the neutrality of the canal after Panama assumed control over it at the end of 1999.

Soviet cosmonauts return to Earth after setting endurance record

Two Soviet cosmonauts returned safely to Earth in their Soyuz 27 capsule after setting a new endurance record of 96 days in space. The previous record was held by three U.S. astronauts who on Feb. 8, 1974, completed 84 days in space aboard Skylab 3. The Soviet spacemen used special exercise equipment to offset the debilitating effects of weightless flight and, according to the Tass news agency, carried out a "wide range of important scientific and technical studies and experiments."

17 *Huge oil spill pollutes Breton coast*

The 230,000-ton "Amoco Cadiz," carrying a capacity load of 1.6 million bbl of crude oil from the Persian Gulf to England, broke in half in heavy seas after striking rocks 5 km (3 mi) off the coast of Brittany. Within a few days strong winds and high-cresting waves drove the oil onto some 115 km (70 mi) of Brittany's beaches, severely damaging the area's tourist and fishing industries. The accident was blamed on a breakdown of the vessel's steering equipment and the inability of a West German rescue tug to control the supertanker in turbulent seas. The American-owned ship was on charter to an affiliate of the Royal Dutch/Shell group when the captain lost control of his vessel. The resultant pollution was the worst such disaster in history.

Bolivia severs ties to Chile

The Bolivian government severed diplomatic relations with Chile when negotiations aimed at giving Bolivia an outlet to the Pacific Ocean "had come to a standstill." All proposals to date had been rejected as unacceptable by either Chile, Bolivia, or Peru. Peru was involved in the dispute because it feared Chile would cede to Bolivia land taken from Peru in the 1879–84 War of the Pacific. Though

Bolivia dispatched troops to its Chilean border, Chile announced its willingness to continue negotiations.

18 *Bhutto sentenced to death*

Former Pakistani prime minister Zulfikar Ali Bhutto, removed from power by a military coup in July 1977, was convicted and sentenced to death by the Lahore High Court on charges of having ordered the unsuccessful murder attempt on Ahmad Raza Kasuri, head of the Pakistan National Alliance. After the five-month trial, the court also imposed death sentences on four ex-members of the Federal Security Force for allegedly hiring gunmen to carry out the assassination. The decision of the court was followed by violent demonstrations in several cities and by appeals from foreign governments to reverse Bhutto's sentence. On March 25 Bhutto filed an appeal with the Supreme Court. His lawyers contended that their client had perforce boycotted the hearings because the five presiding judges were patently biased against him.

19 *France holds critical national elections*

In its most serious attempt in 20 years to win control of the French government, the left-wing coalition of Socialists and Communists narrowly lost the second and final round of the French National Assembly elections. With a record 85% of eligible voters casting ballots, the pro-government parties won 50.49% of the popular vote and 291 of 491 seats in the national legislature. Though the left-wing parties, as expected, had done well in the first round, enough voters apparently had misgivings about left-wing policies and what they would bring the nation to switch their votes to the Gaullists or to others supporting Pres. Valéry Giscard d'Estaing. After the first round of voting, the Communists and Socialists agreed to give their combined votes to each district candidate who had the best chance of winning. The rank and file, however, presumably disregarded this directive. Most opinion polls had predicted a change

in government. On March 31 President Giscard reappointed Raymond Barre premier of the new centre-right coalition government.

22 *Begin and Carter fail to agree on Middle East peace plans*

President Carter and Israeli Prime Minister Menahem Begin ended two days of talks in Washington, D.C., without resolving their differences over policies affecting peace in the Middle East. On March 21 Begin also appeared separately before the U.S. Senate Foreign Relations Committee and the House International Relations Committee. Carter told members of the Senate group on March 23 that Begin had refused to accept any of three proposed compromises as conciliatory steps toward peace. The prime minister, Carter reported, would not allow either Egypt or the UN to assume control over Israeli settlements in the Sinai; would not acknowledge that UN Security Council Resolution 242 required Israel to withdraw from at least portions of the West Bank and Gaza Strip; and would not permit Arabs living in these areas to decide, after five years of experimentation, whether they wanted to remain under international control, join Israel, or become part of Jordan. On March 26 Begin's policies were endorsed unanimously by the Israeli Cabinet and three days later were approved by the Knesset (parliament) by a vote of 64–32.

Suharto reelected in Indonesia

The People's Consultative Assembly (MPR) unanimously reelected General Suharto to an unopposed third consecutive five-year term as president of Indonesia. Suharto's reelection was assured in May 1977 when his Golkar Party won 232 seats in the People's Council of Representatives. Because the Council has 100 seats reserved for presidential appointees, Suharto controlled a minimum of 332 of the 460 Council votes. The 920-member Assembly that elects the president includes all Council members, 207 additional appointees, 130 regional delegates, and

123 members selected on the basis of party strength. The MPR also elected Adam Malik vice-president. He replaced Sultan Hamengku Buwono, who had resigned after pleading poor health. Friends of the sultan, however, reported that his decision was prompted not so much by ill health as by his distress over continuing corruption and recent government suppression of dissent.

24 *Ethiopia gains over Ogaden area*

Ethiopia announced that it had wiped out the last remnants of guerrilla resistance in its southeast Ogaden region and had established full control over the territory. On March 15 the government of neighbouring Somalia reported that it had withdrawn the last of its regular troops from the area, thereby ending its overt support of ethnic Somalis in Ethiopia who sought to separate the Ogaden region from Ethiopia. The outcome of the eight-month-long war became evident after Cuban troops and Soviet personnel joined the conflict on the side of Ethiopia.

26 *Opening of Japan's Narita airport delayed by demonstrators*

The official opening of Japan's new international airport at Narita, some 65 km (40 mi) from Tokyo, was postponed by the government after demonstrators destroyed equipment in the control tower. The opening was scheduled for March 30. Construction of the new facility had been opposed for years by farmers, who were unwilling to accept compensation for their confiscated land, and by environmentalists, who objected to the airport on the grounds of noise and air pollution. The March 26 incident, organized by several radical groups, involved an estimated 20,000 demonstrators who created chaos by hurling firebombs at 13,000 police protecting the area. Emerging from an unguarded sewer tunnel near the control tower, six demonstrators heavily damaged the equipment before police evicted them three hours later. During two days of rioting, scores were injured and 165 were arrested.

APRIL

4 *Angola begins antiguerrilla drive*

The National Union for the Total Independence of Angola (UNITA) announced that it was being heavily attacked by Angolan government troops that were reinforced by Cuban soldiers, Soviet jet fighters, and helicopter gunships carrying napalm bombs. South Africa confirmed that a government offensive was under way and reported that hundreds of Angolan refugees were seeking safety in Namibia (South West Africa). UNITA, which failed to gain control of the country when Portuguese rule came to an

end in 1975, was led by Jonas Savimbi, who had firm support from the Ovimbundu tribe in southeast Angola.

6 *Carter signs legislation raising mandatory retirement age*

President Carter signed into law a bill giving most employees of state and city governments and those in private industry the option of retiring at 70 rather than at the current mandatory age of 65. This provision of the law would take effect on Jan. 1, 1979. The law also stipulated that certain classes of workers in strenuous oc-

cupations, such as police officers and fire fighters, could be made to retire before reaching 70. Corporate executives who received more than $27,000 in annual retirement benefits in addition to Social Security could still be retired at age 65, as could tenured college professors until July 1, 1982. The bill also totally abolished mandatory retirement for federal employees as of Sept. 30, 1978.

7 *Filipinos vote for National Assembly*

In the first national elections permitted by Philippine Pres. Ferdinand E. Marcos

APRIL

since his imposition of martial law on Sept. 23, 1972, Filipinos were allowed to elect 165 members to an interim 200-seat National Assembly. The 1973 constitution, as amended in 1976, not only permitted Marcos to remain as president but also gave him the additional post of prime minister and the power, as leader of the Assembly, to establish laws by decree when, in his own judgment, the Assembly "is unable to act adequately on any matter for any reason." Facing prohibitive odds, the Laban (People's Force) Party nonetheless decided to challenge Marcos's New Society Movement (NSM) in the district of Manila. The Laban, a broad coalition that included the Liberal Party and organizations representing students, labour, and other groups, was led by Benigno S. Aquino, Jr., who ran for office from a prison cell. He and all other Laban candidates in Manila were defeated. After the election Laban demonstrators denounced the government for ballot stuffing and harassment of its poll watchers and accused the Election Committee, who were all Marcos appointees, of falsifying the vote count. On April 9 eight organizers of the antigovernment demonstration, including six Laban leaders, were arrested and faced charges of sedition, incitement to sedition, coercion, and intimidation. Four opposition candidates were among those detained by police. On April 11 two U.S. newspaper correspondents were personally notified that Marcos was unhappy about the election stories they had filed.

Israel admits using cluster bombs during invasion of southern Lebanon

The U.S. government revealed that Israel had violated an agreement with the U.S. by using cluster bombs in its retaliatory raids into southern Lebanon in mid-March. Israel, which had promised the U.S. in 1976 that the antipersonnel weapons would be used only "for internal security and legitimate self-defense," contended that its invasion of Lebanon and its use of the bombs were acts of self-defense because they discouraged further raids into Israel by the Palestine Liberation Organization. On April 12 the Carter administration sought assurances from Israel that in the future field commanders would have no authority to use such weapons without prior approval from responsible political authorities.

Carter defers neutron bomb production

President Carter announced that he was deferring production of the controversial neutron bomb until circumstances warranted an "ultimate decision." The president then explained that U.S. production of these enhanced radiation weapons would depend on the degree of restraint exercised by the Soviet Union "in its conventional and nuclear arms programs and force deployment affecting the security of the United States and Western Europe."

Carter also noted that the Department of Defense would continue its present program of modifying equipment that would be needed to fire the warheads if and when they were produced. There were earlier indications that the U.S. was willing to proceed with production if NATO countries supported the initiative by first promising to deploy the weapons on their territories.

10 Soviet UN official defects

The United Nations announced that its highest ranking Soviet official, 47-year-old Arkady N. Shevchenko, had renounced his Soviet citizenship. The action automatically meant that a replacement would be named to fill his post of undersecretary-general for political and Security Council affairs. Shevchenko went into hiding on April 6. Three days later, in the office of an American lawyer, he met with the Soviet

Demonstrators protesting the Panama Canal treaties picketed the Capitol in April.

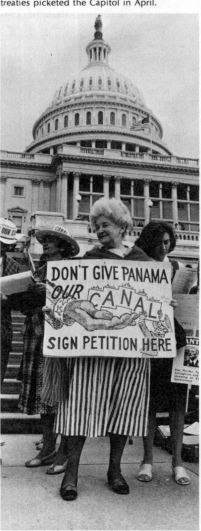

ambassadors to the UN and the U.S. but steadfastly refused to accompany his family on a previously scheduled flight to Moscow that same day. On April 16 Shevchenko met with Soviet officials again but refused to reverse his decision. Ten days later, citing "serious differences of political philosophy and convictions with the present Soviet system," Shevchenko applied for political asylum in the U.S. There were reports that he had been in contact with U.S. intelligence agencies since 1976.

Three former FBI officials indicted

U.S. Attorney General Griffin Bell announced federal grand jury indictments of three former high-ranking officials of the Federal Bureau of Investigation (FBI). Patrick Gray III, former acting director of the FBI, W. Mark Felt, former acting associate director, and Edward S. Miller, former chief of the FBI's counterintelligence section, were all accused of violating the Fourth Amendment, which guarantees that "The right of the people to be secure in their persons, houses, papers and effects, against unreasonable searches and seizures, shall not be violated. . . ." The indictment specifically accused the three of sanctioning illegal break-ins and searches of homes in New York and New Jersey in 1972–73. At that time the FBI was trying to trace the whereabouts of members of the Weatherman group, a radical antiwar faction of Students for a Democratic Society. Bell also announced that the April 7, 1977, indictment of FBI agent John J. Kearney had been dropped because new evidence indicated he was "only carrying out orders" issued by his superiors.

11 Indonesia to free political prisoners

In a joint interview, Admiral Sudomo, chief of the Operational Command for the Restoration of Security, and Gen. Benny Murdani, chief of intelligence, announced that all but a handful of Indonesia's nearly 20,000 remaining political prisoners would be released by the end of 1979. The officials explained that each prisoner would first undergo psychological testing to determine his "Communist ideology" before being granted freedom. An additional 200–300 prisoners, however, would be tried for alleged participation in an attempted army coup in September 1965 that led to the slaughter of hundreds of thousands of Communists and Chinese, mainly in Java. Some months later then president Sukarno was forced to resign.

13 Polisario Front continues to fight for Western Sahara independence

During March, according to news reports, the Polisario Front killed some 400 Moroccan and Mauritanian troops in Western Sahara, a former African province of Spain that had been claimed by Morocco and Mauritania since 1975. The guerrillas had seriously disrupted the economy of the region and undermined morale by repeatedly staging raids and sabotaging freight cars carrying iron ore from Zouerate to the coast. The conflict had also involved France, which sent jet fighters and 1,500 troops to the region in 1977 when eight French nationals were kidnapped by Polisario. Before being turned over to UN Secretary-General Kurt Waldheim in Algiers, the captives were held at military bases in Algeria, which supported Polisario's fight for national independence.

12 *Rhodesian ministers assume office*

The Rhodesian government, in a move toward black majority rule, replaced its Cabinet with an 18-member Council of Ministers. Prime Minister Ian Smith, the only white on the four-man Executive Council, was permitted to nominate nine white ministers, and each of the three black Council members had the right to nominate three black ministers. As previously agreed, one black and one white minister would head each of the nine ministries. On April 28 a crisis developed when the State Council dismissed Byron Hove, a black minister, for violating an executive agreement during discussions with news correspondents. Bishop Abel Muzorewa, who had nominated Hove, threatened to resign, but on May 9 the Executive Council upheld Hove's dismissal. Muzorewa's United African National Council protested the decision but decided it would do more harm than good for Muzorewa to withdraw from the transitional government, at least at that time.

17 *New York Stock Exchange sets record*

The New York Stock Exchange set a new volume record when 63.5 million shares exchanged hands in hectic Monday trading. On the previous business day, a Friday, volume reached 52,280,000 shares, which far surpassed the previous all-time high of 44,510,000 shares traded on Feb. 20, 1976. The Dow Jones Industrial Average opened at 775.21 on Friday and closed at 810.12 on Monday for a gain of 34.91 points. Economists could give no obvious explanation for the phenomenon but noted that large investors had accumulated huge cash reserves that were readily available.

18 *Romanian president ends U.S. visit*

Romanian Pres. Nicolae Ceausescu ended an eight-day visit to the U.S. during which he and President Carter discussed such issues as human rights, expanded trade between their two countries, and the right of every nation to freely choose and develop its own political and economic systems. On the Middle East, Carter would not concede that the Palestine Liberation Organization should represent the Palestinians at a peace conference, though both leaders agreed that any settlement

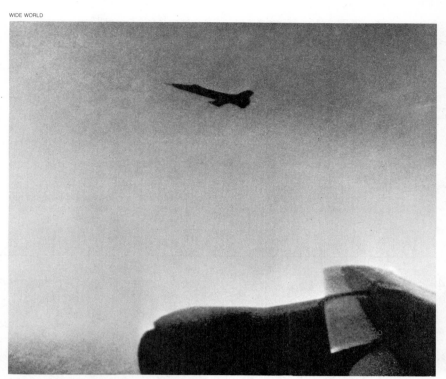

A Soviet fighter plane (upper part of picture) forced down a South Korean airliner on April 20.

had to include Israeli withdrawal from occupied Arab lands, guarantees of security for Israel, and respect for the legitimate rights of the Palestinian people.

Second Panama Canal treaty approved

By a vote of 68–32, the U.S. Senate ratified the Panama Canal treaty, which set down conditions for the operation and defense of the waterway until it was fully turned over to Panama at the end of 1999. The voting was exactly the same as that on March 16 when the Senate approved the first Panama Canal treaty guaranteeing neutrality of the waterway. To preclude future misunderstandings, both treaties included several reservations to the instruments of ratification. Before voting on the second treaty the Senate debated and approved a reservation giving the U.S. the right to use military force, if necessary, to keep the canal open. It further stipulated that such an action shall not be interpreted as interference in the internal affairs of Panama or as a violation of its independence and sovereignty. The reservation was approved on April 17 by Brig. Gen. Omar Torrijos Herrera, Panama's chief of government.

20 *U.S.S.R. downs South Korean jet*

A South Korean Boeing 707 carrying 110 persons on a flight from Paris to Seoul, South Korea, strayed far off course and into Soviet territory on its way to a refueling stop in Anchorage, Alaska. Two persons had been killed and 13 injured by the

time the plane crash-landed on or near a frozen lake about 450 km (280 mi) from Murmansk. Survivors, contradicting an official Soviet version of what happened, said the Korean Air Lines aircraft was fired upon by a Soviet interceptor jet and had to dive sharply before landing. The co-pilot acknowledged that the plane had violated Soviet air space by passing over the Kola Peninsula, a highly sensitive Soviet military area, but he insisted that malfunctioning equipment had caused the navigational error. Soviet authorities detained the passengers at Kem, then moved them to Murmansk on April 22 so they could be picked up the next day by a Pan American rescue plane. On April 29 the pilot and navigator were released in Leningrad and turned over to U.S. officials who acted as intermediaries because South Korea had no diplomatic ties with the U.S.S.R.

25 *Vorster approves Namibia freedom*

South African Prime Minister B. J. Vorster announced that his government was willing to grant independence to Namibia (South West Africa) following a formula worked out in the United Nations Security Council by Canada, France, Great Britain, the U.S., and West Germany. Vorster, however, had first sought assurances that some South African troops could remain in the territory if they were asked to stay by the new Namibian government. The UN group obtained only partial approval for the plan from SWAPO, the South West Africa People's Organization, which had been waging guerrilla

MAY

warfare to win independence for Namibia. Establishment of the new country was expected to occur on Dec. 31, 1978.

27 Afghanistan president killed in coup

Pres. Sardar Mohammad Daud Khan was overthrown and killed in a military coup that caught foreign observers by surprise. Daud died in the capital city of Kabul together with the country's vice-president, the defense and interior ministers, and the commander of the armed forces, all of whom reportedly tried to resist the takeover. The fighting, which continued into the following day, claimed hundreds, perhaps thousands, of lives. On April 30 a Revolutionary Council headed by Nur Mohammad Taraki assumed control of the government. On May 4, in his first public address, Taraki announced that he would follow a policy of active neutrality. The news was greeted with skepticism because Taraki was identified by some sources as the man who had directed a Communist group known as Khalq ("masses").

30 Muslims stream into Bangladesh from neighbouring Burma

Bangladesh officials reported that at least 70,000 Muslims had entered the country from Burma during the previous three weeks and that more were expected to follow. Some reports said many refugees claimed they had been harassed and subjected to indignities before being forced to return to Bangladesh, the land of their ancestors. The World Islamic League in Saudi Arabia urged all Islamic nations to condemn the expulsions. Burma, however, insisted that many of the refugees had entered the country illegally and claimed the trouble started when Burmese immigration officials began checking for illegal Muslim immigrants from Bangladesh. A Burmese news agency reported that the Bengalis tried to impede the inspection by holding mass meetings to organize resistance and by resorting to repeated acts of violence that included the burning and looting of homes and offices belonging to non-Muslims.

MAY

4 South African forces raid Angola

In South Africa's most extensive military action in Angola since its 1975 intervention in the Angolan civil war, South African troops stationed in Namibia (South West Africa) raided guerrilla bases of the South West Africa People's Organization (SWAPO), a nationalistic group determined to undermine South Africa's administrative control over Namibia. South African military sources reported that the raid destroyed SWAPO's main headquarters at Cassinga, about 250 km (160 mi) north of the border, as well as two smaller bases. Disregarding South African claims that the military operation came in response to a recent rise in SWAPO forays into Namibia, the UN Security Council on May 6 condemned the raid, calling it a "flagrant violation" of Angola's sovereignty.

5 Fukuda and Carter confer on trade

Prime Minister Takeo Fukuda of Japan ended five days of talks in the U.S. that concentrated on improving trade relations between the two countries. Fukuda told President Carter that he would make "massive efforts" to cut Japan's current trade surplus of $14 billion, linking the amount of reduction to U.S. efforts to stabilize the dollar against the yen and to control inflation. He promised to hold down Japanese exports to the U.S., particularly steel, automobiles, and colour television sets, and emphasized Japan's commitment to attain a growth rate of 7% by March 1979, a condition that would encourage internal demand for both domestic and foreign goods.

9 Aldo Moro murdered in Italy

The bullet-riddled body of Aldo Moro was found in the luggage compartment of a car parked in the centre of Rome. An anonymous telephone caller told police where the body of the former premier could be found. Despite pleas from Moro's immedi-

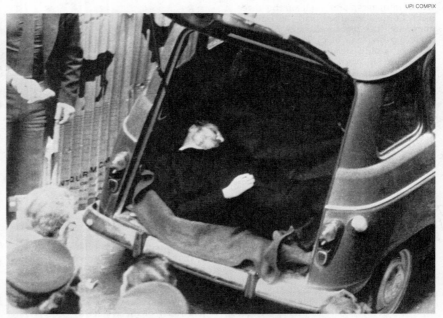

UPI COMPIX

The body of Aldo Moro was found in the trunk of a car in Rome on May 9.

ate family and from Moro himself, who wrote some 20 letters during the 54 days he was held captive, the government steadfastly refused to release 15 imprisoned Red Brigades terrorists, whose comrades kidnapped Moro on March 16. When Moro was buried on May 10, his embittered family excluded official government representatives. On May 13 the government held a "state funeral without the body," thereby ignoring a family request that there be no public mourning. The street where Moro's body was found was covered with flowers and burning candles soon after news of the former premier's death spread throughout Italy.

10 Chinese premier visits North Korea

Chinese Premier Hua Kuo-feng ended a six-day visit to North Korea, his first visit outside China since replacing Mao Tsetung as chairman of the Central Committee of China's Communist Party. During a large rally in the capital city of Pyongyang on May 10, both Hua and Kim Il Sung, the Communist leader of North Korea, demanded that U.S. troops withdraw from South Korea so that the country might be reunited. The omission of a formal joint communiqué was interpreted by some as an indication that the two leaders held different views on such issues as relations with the Soviet Union.

11 Rioting spreads to Iranian capital

After three days of widespread antigovernment riots in Iran, violence erupted in the capital city of Teheran as thousands of demonstrators shouted for the removal of Shah Mohammad Reza Pahlavi Aryamehr. The riots were initiated by religious Muslims who fiercely opposed government reforms that included confiscation of mosque properties as part of a land reform program and permission for women to enter college and appear without veils in public. There were also demands that movie houses and liquor stores be closed down because they made a mockery of Islamic religious precepts. The worst turmoil reportedly occurred in the holy city of Qom on May 9 when shops were burned, barricades erected in the streets, and trains halted. At least a dozen persons were killed.

Guerrillas invade southern Zaire

Secessionist guerrillas of the Congo National Liberation Front (FNLC) invaded Zaire's southeastern Shaba Province and directly attacked Mutshatsha, a railway town, and Kolwezi, an important copper-mining centre. Zairian Pres. Mobutu Sese Seko accused the U.S.S.R., Algeria, and Libya of backing the estimated 4,000 troops that reportedly had active support from Angolan and Cuban forces. On May 19 about 600 French and 700 Belgian paratroopers, using transport planes supplied by the U.S. and U.K., began dropping into Kolwezi to rescue more than 2,500 besieged Europeans and a few Americans. On May 22 the Belgian troops departed after completing the rescue operation. The French Legionnaires, who promised to remain as long as the rebel threat continued, had only a token force left in Kolwezi by May 28. Besides the 44 Europeans found murdered in Kolwezi, initial reports said some 150 other whites and perhaps 300 blacks had lost their lives. Red Cross representatives later announced that more than 850 had died in the Kolwezi fighting. There were also reports that some Europeans had been taken hostage by the retreating rebels.

15 U.S. Senate approves jet sales

After intense lobbying and debate, the U.S. Senate signified by a 54–44 vote that it would not block the sale of U.S. jet fighters to Saudi Arabia and Egypt. President Carter had warned that he viewed arms sales to the Middle East as a package deal and that he would deny Israel's request for arms if sales to the two Arab countries were vetoed by Congress. Though Senate approval was not required by law, the sales could have been blocked if both houses of Congress voted disapproval. The Senate vote guaranteed that Israel would be allowed to buy 15 sophisticated F-15 jets and 75 F-16 fighter-bombers, plus an additional 20 F-15s at a later date; Saudi Arabia would be allowed to buy 60 F-15s, and Egypt would be permitted to purchase 50 F-5 fighters.

Peruvians riot over price increases

The military government of Peru, headed by Pres. Francisco Morales Bermúdez, former commander in chief of the Army,

One of Zaire's air force planes destroyed by rebels in Shaba Province.

announced the implementation of an austerity program demanded by the International Monetary Fund (IMF) as a condition for granting desperately needed foreign credits. When prices for staple foods and other common necessities jumped 50–100%, riots broke out across the country and the universities were closed. Looting, arson, and violence became so widespread that the president on May 19 postponed the June 4 Constituent Assembly elections for two weeks and declared a state of emergency the following day. Campaign speeches were forbidden on radio and television, some publications were banned, and the militia took control of the streets. On May 22 a two-day national protest strike was organized by the Communist-led General Confederation of Peruvian Workers and the nation came to a temporary standstill. Without IMF support, Peru could not avoid defaulting on its foreign debts. It was later reported that talks with the IMF would resume.

16 Dominican Republic holds elections

Ten hours after the polls closed and the vote tallying began in the Dominican Republic, members of the Army and police force ordered a suspension of the vote count. With about one-quarter of the ballots already scrutinized, it seemed highly probable that opposition candidate Antonio Guzmán Fernandez of the Dominican Revolutionary Party (PRD) would unseat Pres. Joaquín Balaguer. Balaguer insisted that he had nothing to do with suspending the count and reiterated public promises made during the campaign that he would respect the will of the voters. After consulting with government leaders in Colombia, Costa Rica, Panama, and Venezuela, and with the secretary-general of the Organization of American States, President Carter issued a public warning on May 19 that U.S. support for

the Dominican Republic would "depend upon the integrity of the election process." On May 26, after a second delay, the election board notified Balaguer that he had lost the election by more than 150,-000 votes.

18 Abortion legalized in Italy

Despite strong opposition from the Vatican, the Italian Senate voted 160–148 in favour of legalized abortion. On April 14 the Chamber of Deputies had signified its approval of state-subsidized abortions by a vote of 308–275. The new law permits abortion on demand for any woman 18 years old or older if she decides that childbirth would endanger her physical or mental health. Women under the age of 18 need the consent of a parent or guardian before undergoing an abortion. Medical certificates are required to terminate pregnancies after the first trimester.

20 Soviet spies arrested in New Jersey

Agents of the U.S. Federal Bureau of Investigation arrested two Soviet citizens, both employees of the UN, on charges of espionage. In a federal grand jury indictment, the two were accused of attempting to recruit a U.S. Navy officer with access to classified information about U.S. Navy antisubmarine capabilities. With the approval of the FBI, the officer communicated with the Soviet agents and received $16,000 in payments for material he transmitted to them. The two Soviet citizens were arrested in Woodbridge, N.J., when they picked up film hidden in an orange juice carton. Bail for each was set at $2 million. The State Department announced that a third Soviet citizen, enjoying diplomatic immunity as a member of the Soviet mission to the UN, would be asked to leave the country because of his involvement in the case.

JUNE

Chiang Ching-kuo is sworn in as president of Nationalist China

Chiang Ching-kuo, the 68-year-old son of the late Chiang Kai-shek and premier since June 1972, was sworn in as president of the Nationalist Chinese government in Taiwan. The new president, who remained chairman of the ruling Nationalist Party (Kuomintang), also became commander in chief of the armed forces. He replaced Yen Chia-kan, who retired from politics. Shieh Tung-min, the Taiwanese-born former governor of Taiwan, was sworn in as vice-president during the same ceremony. Sun Yun-suan, who had served as economics minister, was appointed premier.

21 *Japan's Narita airport opens*

Under heavy security, Tokyo's new international airport at Narita opened with the arrival of 23 flights. Environmentalists and left-wing radicals made a final effort to prevent the opening by polluting the air with heavy black smoke from burning tires and by launching balloons and kites in the path of approaching aircraft.

22 *Brzezinski visits China*

U.S. national security adviser Zbigniew Brzezinski ended a three-day visit to Peking where he spoke with Premier Hua Kuo-feng, First Vice-Premier Teng Hsiao-p'ing, and Foreign Minister Huang Hua. Brzezinski assured the Chinese leaders that President Carter "desires friendly relations with a strong China." On several occasions he publicly noted that both China and the U.S. opposed Soviet involvement in Africa and its efforts to dominate other countries. Brzezinski then flew to Tokyo where he briefed Japanese Prime Minister Takeo Fukuda.

23 *UN disarmament session opens*

The General Assembly of the United Nations began a five-week special session that was described by Secretary-General Kurt Waldheim as the "largest and most representative gathering ever convened to consider the question of disarmament." Though many heads of government were expected to be present, both President Carter and Leonid Brezhnev of the Soviet Union sent representatives. The avowed

purpose of the conference was to seek means to end the weapons race and use the money for economic development.

31 *U.S. congressmen press demands for testimony from Kim Dong Jo*

The U.S. House of Representatives voted 321–46 to request that the government of South Korea make its former ambassador to the U.S. available for testimony before the House Committee on Standards of Official Conduct. Kim Dong Jo had been accused of offering cash to congressmen to influence their voting on matters affecting South Korea. The House vote in effect ratified a resolution passed 31–0 by the House International Relations Committee on May 24. The statement asserted that members of the House would be prepared "to deny or reduce" economic aid to South Korea if Kim did not testify. Such aid, however, would not be denied if U.S. national security or the territorial integrity of South Korea would thereby be placed in jeopardy. The U.S. State Department opposed the resolution, partly because Kim had enjoyed diplomatic immunity while serving as ambassador.

JUNE

1 *Egypt suppresses opposition*

The People's Assembly approved a 13-point legislative measure granting Egyptian Pres. Anwar as-Sadat authority to restrict criticism of his policies. The following day 500 members of the right-wing New Wafd Party met in Cairo and unanimously voted to disband because "all political freedom" had been swept away. On June 5 the left-wing Progressive Union Party announced that it would cease publication of its weekly newspaper but would go to court to challenge the legality of the new law.

5 *China to release 110,000 detainees*

Chinese sources in Hong Kong, quoting broadcasts from China, reported that 110,000 persons recently had been granted freedom. Most had been arrested during the 1957 "antirightist" campaign or during the Cultural Revolution of the late 1960s when Maoist radicals controlled government policy. First Vice-Premier Teng Hsiao-p'ing was reportedly pushing a drive to rehabilitate many of those who had been disgraced or vilified. For the first time the government's Hsinhua news agency openly acknowledged incidents of torture by calling attention to tens of thousands of people in Shanghai, Peking, and elsewhere who had been "cruelly tortured or persecuted."

6 *California mandates tax cuts*

California voters overwhelmingly endorsed a state constitutional amendment

to reduce property taxes 57%. The outcome, closely followed by the rest of the nation, was generally seen as the beginning of a national tax revolt by citizens who claimed that recent tax increases were outrageous and spending at all levels of government was out of control. Howard A. Jarvis, the 74-year-old co-sponsor (with Paul Gann) of Proposition 13, argued that "the only way to cut the cost of government is not to give them money in the first place." The new legislation requires a two-thirds vote (formerly a simple majority) of all California state legislators to increase state taxes and stipulates that two-thirds of all registered voters must approve any new local government taxes. The law meant annual property tax revenues would drop from $12 billion to $5 billion; the $6.6 billion annually allocated to public education would drop to about $2.7 billion. Gov. Edmund "Jerry" Brown announced that the immediate financial crisis facing local and state agencies would be solved by releasing about $5 billion accumulated as a budget surplus.

7 *Chinese leader castigates Vietnam*

Chinese First Vice-Premier Teng Hsiao-p'ing told a group of visiting Thai journalists in Peking that China was cutting its aid to Vietnam because Vietnam had expelled more than 100,000 ethnic Chinese from the country and was "leaning toward the Soviet Union, which is an archenemy of China." Sino-Vietnamese relations had already deteriorated because China was supplying arms to Cambodia

in its border fights with Vietnam. In March the Vietnamese government announced it would nationalize private businesses in the south and grant exit visas to all ethnic Chinese wishing to enter China. By May the Chinese embassy in Hanoi was besieged with requests for entry into China. On May 27 China said it would send ships to evacuate "persecuted" Chinese residents, many of whom had allegedly been ordered to close their businesses and move to undeveloped "new economic zones" in the Vietnamese countryside. By June 20 Chinese ships were riding at anchor near Haiphong and Ho Chi Minh City (formerly Saigon; they were not permitted to dock), the Chinese ambassador to Hanoi had been recalled, Chinese aid had been partially suspended, and three Vietnamese consulates in southern China had been ordered closed. On July 3 China announced that all economic aid to Vietnam was terminated.

12 *Italians reaffirm their support of special police powers*

In a national two-day referendum, Italian voters refused by an impressive majority to repeal the Reale Act which, when it went into effect in 1977, gave police wide options to use guns and tightened restrictions on the release of accused criminals awaiting trial. Reversing its earlier stand, the Communist Party joined the ruling Christian Democrats in supporting strong police powers. The response of the voters was an expected reaction to the terrorism that had plagued Italy in recent years. In the same referendum the voters also

MUNOZ—SIPA PRESS/BLACK STAR

Italian Red Brigades prisoners being led from court in Turin, Italy, in June.

refused by a narrow margin to repeal government subsidies to political parties.

U.S. businessman arrested in Moscow

Francis Jay Crawford, a representative of International Harvester Co. (I.H.), was arrested in Moscow and formally accused on June 17 of having "systematically sold large amounts of foreign currency at speculative prices to Soviet citizens." Brooks McCormick, chairman of the U.S. company, warned the U.S.S.R. that its action could jeopardize future purchases of I.H. farm equipment. It was generally assumed that the U.S.S.R. arrested Crawford in retaliation for the publicized arrest of two Soviet spies in New Jersey on May 20. Usually spies are simply arrested and deported without fanfare. Crawford, who was released from jail on June 26, was given a suspended five-year sentence before leaving the Soviet Union to return to the U.S. on September 8.

15 *Supreme Court rules on snail darter*

The U.S. Supreme Court, by a vote of 6–3, supported a decision of a lower court which ruled that the snail darter, a rare species of perch, was protected by the Endangered Species Act of 1973. As a consequence, the $100 million Tellico Dam, already 80% completed, could not be finished because a dam on the Little Tennessee River could destroy the snail darter's only known habitat. On July 19 the U.S. Senate voted 94–3 to empower an Endangered Species Interagency Committee to grant exceptions to the law when they were clearly justified.

16 *Belgium government crisis resolved*

A complex government crisis was resolved when Belgium's Prime Minister Léo Tindemans withdrew the resignation he submitted to King Baudouin I on June 15. After intense negotiations, the four parties comprising the coalition government reached an agreement on two especially divisive issues. To help reduce the nation's budget deficit, Tindemans was granted powers to cut public spending without parliamentary consent. He then promised to draw up a specific timetable for granting progressive semiautonomy to the three main cultural regions of the country: the bilingual Brussels agglomeration, Flanders, and Wallonia.

23 *Red Brigades trial ends in Italy*

After a 15-week trial in Turin, Italy, and jury deliberations that lasted more than 100 hours, 29 members of the Red Brigades were convicted and sentenced to prison, some in absentia. Two founders of the terrorist organization, Renato Curcio and Pietro Bassi, were each sentenced to 15 years for membership in a terrorist group and for arson, kidnapping, and robbery. They and some others standing trial had been sentenced earlier for similar crimes. Of the 46 accused terrorists being tried, only 15 were in custody because some had never been arrested and others had escaped. Sixteen were acquitted and charges against one were dropped. The trial had twice been postponed, once in 1976 when the chief prosecutor in Genoa and his two bodyguards were murdered, and again in 1977 when the head of the Turin bar association was assassinated and the jurors threatened.

Brazil relaxes some restrictions

The military government of Brazil introduced a number of constitutional reforms that promised greater, but still limited, freedom to the people. Pres. Ernesto Geisel no longer enjoyed the dictatorial powers granted him by Institutional Act number 5, the authority to suspend Congress, or unlimited power to suspend political rights; but he still could declare a state of emergency without consulting Congress. If new political parties met certain standards of representation, they could be registered. Prior censorship of the press was abolished on June 9 as one of the first new reforms, but censorship of radio and television remained in force. In many cases there was no relaxation of restrictive laws.

25 *Argentina wins World Cup*

Argentina defeated The Netherlands 3–1 in overtime to capture its first World Cup football (soccer) championship at River Plate Stadium in Buenos Aires. An es-

Demonstrations against the U.S. Supreme Court's Bakke decision were carried out in Washington, D.C., and other U.S. cities.

MARTIN A. LEVICK—BLACK STAR

JULY

timated 1,000,000,000 people worldwide followed the event on television. Of the 104 national teams that entered the competition, only 16 qualified for the final championship eliminations in Argentina.

26 Palace of Versailles bombed

The south wing of the historic 17th-century Palace of Versailles was severely damaged by a powerful bomb planted by French radicals. Three of the 14 ground-floor rooms, all containing priceless works of art, were virtually destroyed. Though three radical organizations claimed credit for the vandalism, police were initially inclined to place responsibility for the bombing on the Breton Republican Army. As an arm of the Breton Liberation Front, it backs autonomy or independence for the region of France known as Brittany.

28 Supreme Court rules on Bakke case

The U.S. Supreme Court voted 5–4 to uphold a lower court decision requiring the University of California to admit Allan P. Bakke to its medical school at Davis. Bakke, a 38-year-old Caucasian, claimed his civil rights were violated when his application for admission was rejected solely on the basis of race. The school's

minority admission program stipulated that 16 of 100 first-year openings be reserved for minorities, even if their test scores were lower than those of others whose applications were rejected. In announcing the court's decision, Justice Lewis F. Powell, Jr., stated that "preferring members of any one group for no reason other than race or ethnic origin is discrimination for its own sake." The justices clarified their historic decision with an additional 5–4 ruling that gave schools the right to consider race or ethnic background in approving applications. This second ruling, while not endorsing quotas, sanctioned "affirmative action" programs that had been adopted by educational institutions across the country.

Two U.S. reporters accused in Moscow of slandering the U.S.S.R.

Craig R. Whitney of the *New York Times* and Harold D. Piper of the *Baltimore Sun* were summoned to a Moscow court and charged with "publishing slanderous information" about the Soviet Union. The two had filed stories stating that relatives and friends of dissident Zviad Gamsakhurdia believed his televised confession was falsified. The reporters contended that Soviet courts had no jurisdiction over reports published in U.S. newspapers and

noted that the charges of falsification were not made by them but by others. They thus refused to participate in court hearings or to write retractions for their newspapers. On July 18 a Moscow court declared the two, who at the time were vacationing in the U.S., guilty of "slander and defamation" and ordered them to publish retractions and pay court costs and fines. On August 4 Whitney, who had returned to Moscow on July 30, declared that neither newspaper would comply with the court order by printing a retraction and paid costs amounting to about $3,400 "under protest." On August 18 the U.S.S.R. closed the case after withdrawing its demand.

30 UN disarmament session ends

The United Nations General Assembly began winding up its Special Session on Disarmament after adopting a resolution to change the format of the Geneva Conference of the Committee on Disarmament. Membership in the newly formed Committee on Disarmament was increased from 31 to a possible 40 nations, with the chairmanship passing from one country to another each month. Previously the U.S. and the U.S.S.R. had shared the chairmanship. France indicated that it would join the committee.

JULY

1 OAS meeting focuses on human rights

The eighth annual meeting of the General Assembly of the Organization of American States (OAS) ended in Washington, D.C., after several member nations, notably Uruguay and Paraguay, were severely criticized for persistently violating human rights. The criticisms were included in a 70-page report prepared by the Inter-American Commission on Human Rights, which received a mandate to continue its investigations.

7 EEC discusses own monetary system

After a two-day meeting in Bremen, West Germany, the nine member nations of the European Economic Community (EEC) agreed to study a proposal that would stabilize exchange rates by linking together various EEC currencies. The plan, strongly supported by West Germany and France, was viewed less enthusiastically by Great Britain and Italy. The plan included a monetary reserve fund that could reach $50 billion. It was believed that the size would serve as a deterrent to speculation because all the EEC currencies would float as a unit against the U.S. dollar.

Solomon Islands gain independence

The Solomon Islands, which became self-governing in 1960, gained independence

after 85 years of British rule. At a ceremony attended by Prince Richard, duke of Gloucester, Baddeley Devesi was sworn in as governor-general and Peter Kenilorea assumed the office of prime minister.

8 National Front wins Malaysia elections

Malaysia's ruling National Front coalition, under the leadership of Prime Minister Datuk Hussein bin Onn, won an impressive victory in elections for both federal and state offices. The National Front not only secured overwhelming control of the Parliament by eventually winning 131 of the 154 seats but retained its majority in all of the ten contested state assemblies. Three states did not hold elections. Onn later resigned his post as defense minister and assumed charge of Kuala Lumpur, the nation's capital, which had the status of a federal territory.

9 Burmese Muslims to leave Bangladesh

Representatives of Burma and Bangladesh signed an agreement in Dacca that would permit an estimated 200,000 Muslims to begin to return to Burma within the following two months. The exodus from Burma began in April when Muslims claimed they had been harassed and assaulted in the process of being forced to return to their ancestral homes in Ban-

gladesh. Burma, which is predominantly Buddhist, discounted charges of religious persecution by insisting that the trouble began when immigration officials began moving through Muslim communities in search of immigrants who allegedly had entered Burma illegally.

10 Mauritanian president ousted

Pres. Moktar Ould Daddah, who had ruled Mauritania since it gained independence from France in 1960, was overthrown in a bloodless military coup. Radio reports indicated that the country would be run by the Military Committee for National Recovery, with Lieut. Col. Mustafa Ould Salek as its head. The coup came as a surprise to most outsiders, though Mauritania's financial problems were well known. For one thing, its ongoing war against the Polisario guerrillas was proving more costly than had originally been expected.

12 Andrew Young declares that the U.S. also holds political prisoners

Andrew Young, U.S. ambassador to the UN, stirred up a political whirlwind by saying that in U.S. prisons "there are hundreds, perhaps thousands, of people whom I would call political prisoners." His remarks, quoted in the French Socialist newspaper *Le Matin*, brought forth emotional demands in both houses of the

The wife of Soviet dissident Anatoly Shcharansky awaits word of his trial.

U.S. Congress for his immediate resignation or impeachment. The Young interview was published just hours before U.S. Secretary of State Cyrus Vance was to deliver to Soviet Foreign Minister Andrey Gromyko a personal message from President Carter deploring Soviet treatment of dissidents. Though Young had made inflammatory statements on other occasions, President Carter for the first time publicly rebuked the ambassador and said, after telephoning Young, that such remarks were a mistake he did not want repeated. Young later tried to soften his remarks by saying that there were all kinds of political prisoners, but "there is nobody in prison in the U.S. for criticizing the government."

14 *Shcharansky sentenced in U.S.S.R.*

Soviet dissident Anatoly B. Shcharansky, after being convicted in a Moscow court of treason, espionage, and anti-Soviet agitation, was sentenced to three years in prison, to be followed by ten years in a labour camp. Throughout the brief trial, which was closed to Western observers, Shcharansky acted as his own defense lawyer and categorically denied ever working for U.S. intelligence officials. He had been an eloquent spokesman for Jews seeking permission to leave the Soviet Union and had repeatedly contacted Western reporters to publicize their cause.

17 *Economic problems and air hijackings discussed at Bonn meeting*

Leaders of seven major non-Communist industrial nations ended a two-day annual meeting in Bonn, West Germany, during which they discussed inflation, unemployment, balance of trade and payments deficits, currency instability, and other persistent economic problems. Participants included Chancellor Helmut Schmidt of West Germany, Prime Minister Pierre Trudeau of Canada, Pres. Valéry Giscard d'Estaing of France, Prime Minister James Callaghan of Great Britain, Premier Giulio Andreotti of Italy, Prime Minister Takeo Fukuda of Japan, and Pres. Jimmy Carter of the U.S. Roy Jenkins also attended as president of the European Commission. The final communiqué noted that sustained efforts were needed to solve the complex, long-term economic problems currently affecting the industrialized Western countries. In a totally unexpected statement, the seven leaders also took an unprecedented stand against airline hijackings. Should any country refuse to extradite or prosecute hijackers "and/or do not return such aircraft," all flights to and from that country would be canceled. Moreover, all airliners belonging to that country would be refused landing rights.

19 *Egypt and Israel meet in England to discuss peace proposals*

A U.S.-sponsored two-day meeting between the foreign ministers of Egypt and Israel concluded at Leeds Castle, Kent, without any agreement being reached on the future of the West Bank and Gaza Strip. Egypt denied that Leeds signified direct negotiations with Israel, broken off earlier in the year, had resumed. Each nation then bitterly blamed the other for the lack of progress. Egyptian Foreign Minister Muhammad Kamal concluded that negotiations for a lasting peace were "a waste of time." The ten-man Israeli military mission, which had been permitted to remain in Alexandria to carry on technical discussions with its Egyptian counterpart, was thereupon ordered to leave the country. A few days earlier, on July 13, Egyptian Pres. Anwar as-Sadat had held an unexpected meeting with Israeli Defense Minister Ezer Weizman near Salzburg, Austria, at which Sadat submitted new peace proposals, thought to represent a softening of earlier positions.

Quebec modifies French language bill

The Quebec provincial government modified its controversial Bill 101 to permit a wider use of English in the head offices of corporations that, for one reason or another, could not function efficiently using French as their basic language. The change had been urged by businessmen who argued that compliance with the 1977 language bill seriously hampered their ability to operate businesses with headquarters in Quebec. On April 25 policyholders of the Sun Life Assurance Co. of Canada approved by a huge majority the transfer of its head office from Montreal to Toronto. The new language bill was cited as a significant factor in reaching the decision to leave Quebec.

21 *Bolivian presidency seized in coup*

Juan Pereda Asbún declared himself president of Bolivia after deposing Pres. Hugo Banzer Suárez in a military coup. Pereda had been declared winner of the July 9 presidential election, but the national electoral court voided the results on July 19 after declaring that the entire process was riddled with fraud. Independent international observers also condemned the election as totally dishonest. Hernán Siles Zuazo, a former president and Pereda's chief opponent in the July 9 election, went into hiding after the coup along with other defeated candidates. On August 6 Pereda pledged not to be a candidate for president when new elections were held in 1980.

22 *African nations meet in Sudan*

The Organization of African Unity (OAU) ended its annual summit meeting, which began in Khartoum, Sudan, on July 18. The presence of foreign troops in Africa dominated the discussions. Whereas more radical African nations welcomed Cuban and Soviet involvement, moderate African states urged strict nonalignment. The final OAU resolutions opposed the use of force or military intervention to settle African disputes and especially condemned the establishment of foreign military bases in Africa and pacts with non-African powers. The OAU also warned the U.S. not to lift sanctions against Rhodesia. Little progress was reported in settling serious territorial disputes between various African nations.

25 *First "test-tube" baby born in England*

The first documented birth of a human being conceived outside its mother's body occurred in Lancashire, England. The 5-lb 12-oz girl, Louise Joy Brown,

AUGUST

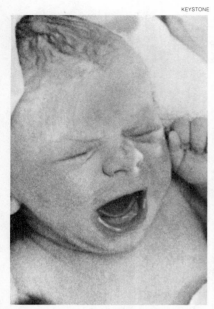
KEYSTONE

Louise Joy Brown, the world's first "test-tube" baby, was born in England on July 25.

was delivered by cesarean section and seemed perfectly normal and healthy. On Nov. 10, 1977, a doctor had surgically removed an egg cell from the mother and fertilized it in vitro with her husband's sperm. After two and a half days the embryo was implanted in her uterus for normal development. Patrick C. Steptoe, the gynecologist responsible for the medical feat, estimated that he had previously performed 200 similar operations without success. His associate was Robert G. Edwards, a specialist in reproductive physiology.

30 *Nonaligned nations meet in Yugoslavia*

Foreign ministers from 87 nonaligned nations concluded a six-day meeting in Belgrade, Yugos. President Tito warned the delegates against "attempts to establish in the vitally important regions of the nonaligned world, primarily in Africa, new forms of colonial presence." In a clear, though implicit, reference to Cuban and Soviet involvement in Africa, Tito pleaded for strict adherence to the principles of nonalignment, which he described as in-

compatible with "power politics, political and economic hegemony, and every kind of external interference and dependence." Though some delegates objected because of Cuba's African policy and its ties to the Soviet Union, the conference voted to hold the 1979 summit meeting in Havana as originally planned.

31 *Arab terrorist attacks Iraqis in Paris*

An Arab terrorist, angered over Iraq's hard-line stand against negotiating peace with Israel, shot his way into the Iraqi embassy in Paris and seized eight hostages. Nine hours later the drama had apparently ended after the man surrendered and police led him to a waiting car. Then suddenly Iraqi guards began firing. In the near total confusion that followed, one French policeman and one embassy guard were slain, and several other persons were wounded. Later three of the Iraqi guards were arrested, but because they enjoyed diplomatic immunity they were merely deported. Iraqi officials were also targets of attack in London on July 28 and in the capitals of Pakistan and Lebanon on August 2.

AUGUST

1 *Indictments issued in Letelier case*

A grand jury in Washington, D.C., indicted three Chileans and four Cuban exiles for complicity in the Sept. 21, 1976, auto-bombing murder of Orlando Letelier. The former Chilean foreign minister, an outspoken critic of Pres. Augusto Pinochet Ugarte, was killed in Washington; Ronni Moffitt also died in the explosion and her husband was wounded. Michael Townley, an American employed by the Chilean secret police (DINA), was subsequently extradited and arrested (April 26, 1978) for involvement in the assassination. On August 11 he admitted in federal court that he both made and planted the bomb. The indictment named Gen. Juan Manuel Contreras Sepúlveda, director of DINA at the time of the murders, as the one who "initiated the action." On September 20 the U.S., Department of State presented a 25-lb box of documentary evidence to the Chilean foreign minister to support its formal request that Contreras and the two other Chileans be extradited to the U.S. to stand trial. The president of Chile's Supreme Court indicated that it would take many months to study the evidence and reach a decision.

U.S. ends Turkish arms embargo

The U.S. House of Representatives, by a vote of 208–205, approved President Carter's request to remove the nearly four-year-old embargo on arms shipments to Turkey. One week earlier the U.S. Senate had signified its approval by voting 57–42 in favour of the change. Both houses of

Congress, however, required the president to report every 60 days on progress toward a settlement of the Greek-Turkish dispute in Cyprus. Carter had wanted a simple repeal of the embargo on the grounds that it was actually impeding a peace settlement and weakening NATO, to which both Greece and Turkey belonged. Restrictions on arms shipments to Turkey had never been absolute. The embargo permitted the transfer of arms to Turkey from other NATO countries and permitted private U.S. firms to sell directly to Turkey; only government-to-government sales were forbidden.

6 *Pope Paul VI dies*

Pope Paul VI, spiritual leader of the Roman Catholic Church, died of a heart attack at the age of 80 at his summer residence at Castel Gandolfo. The Sacred College of Cardinals had elected him the successor of Pope John XXIII on June 21, 1963.

7 *New Colombian president takes office*

Julio César Turbay Ayala of the Liberal Party was sworn in as president of Colombia after narrowly defeating the Con-

"Double Eagle II" after its landing in Miserey, France, in August.

MINGAM—GAMMA/LIAISON

ALAIN KELER—SYGMA

The first papal funeral ever held outdoors was conducted for Pope Paul VI on August 12 in St. Peter's Square, Rome.

servative candidate, Belisario Betancur, in the June 4 national election. In his inaugural address Turbay pledged to strengthen Latin-American economic cooperation and to respect civil liberties while exercising authority that would be "severe within the Constitution and strong within democracy." He also hinted that the long-standing state of siege would be lifted. To ensure political stability Turbay staffed his Cabinet with seven Liberals, five Conservatives, and one member from the armed forces.

President of Honduras ousted

Pres. Juan Alberto Melgar Castro of Honduras was overthrown in a bloodless coup headed by the commanders of the Army, Air Force, and national police. The three-man junta that assumed power recognized Gen. Policarpo Paz García as the new leader of the nation. Melgar seized power in 1975 but promised general elections would be held in April 1980. The junta reiterated that promise and pledged to respect civil liberties and freedom of the press.

Peru receives vital IMF loan

Representatives of the Peruvian government and the International Monetary Fund (IMF) signed a letter of intent entitling Peru to an IMF credit line equal to U.S. $230 million over the next 30 months. The loan not only averted an impending crisis but also implicitly reassured international banking institutions so that they

could reschedule Peru's debts with restored confidence. Before extending the credit, the IMF had first satisfied itself that Peru was now prepared to follow sound economic policies.

10 Canadian premiers reject Trudeau's constitutional proposals

All ten provincial premiers of Canada rejected Prime Minister Pierre Trudeau's proposals for a new constitution that would replace the British North America Act of 1867. Though the premiers found fault with numerous specific proposals, they were especially opposed to Trudeau's plan for a two-stage legislative reform. The first stage would deal only with matters under federal jurisdiction; the second would involve the provinces. The premiers, however, demanded a role in formulating the entire constitution. Before ending the two-day conference the premiers called on Trudeau to discuss the proposed reforms with them again later in the year.

11 State of siege lifted in Bolivia

Bolivian Pres. Juan Pereda Asbún declared an end to the state of siege that he imposed on July 21 after seizing power in a military coup. The new government also relaxed other long-standing restrictions on personal freedom. On August 15 the U.S. government reacted favourably to the changes and to the promise of free elections in 1980 by resuming military aid to the country.

12 China and Japan sign historic treaty

After years of intermittent negotiations, China and Japan signed a ten-year treaty of peace and friendship in Peking. The accord, which pledged mutual respect for each other's sovereignty and territory, also endorsed economic cooperation, cultural exchanges, nonaggression, and noninterference in each other's domestic affairs. The treaty not only ended the state of war that had technically existed between the two countries since the 1930s but substantially enhanced the possibility that Japan would supply China with much of the technology it urgently needed in its drive for rapid modernization. The main obstacle during the negotiations had been China's insistence on an "antihegemony" clause directed at the U.S.S.R. Japan resisted because its relations with the Soviet Union were already deteriorating. By way of compromise, the treaty declared that neither China nor Japan would seek hegemony in the Asia-Pacific region or in any other region and that "each is opposed to efforts by any other country or group of countries to establish such hegemony." The Soviet Union denounced the treaty both before and after it was signed by foreign ministers Sunao Sonoda of Japan and Huang Hua of China. The U.S. welcomed it as a contribution to peace in Asia.

13 Palestinians killed in Beirut blast

A violent explosion that destroyed a nine-story building in Beirut, Lebanon, took

SEPTEMBER

the lives of at least 150 persons belonging to rival Palestinian guerrilla factions. The building served as headquarters for the Palestine Liberation Front (PLF) and contained offices of the rival al-Fatah organization. The pro-Iraqi PLF initially accused the pro-Syrian Popular Front for the Liberation of Palestine (PFLP) of attempting to wipe out its leadership, but a PLF spokesman later denied that any such statement had been made. The Palestine Liberation Organization (PLO) blamed the bombing on "American and Israeli intelligence agents."

14 Smith and Nkomo secretly discuss future of Rhodesia

Rhodesian Prime Minister Ian Smith and guerrilla leader Joshua Nkomo met secretly in Zambia to discuss the possibility of including the coalition guerrilla Patriotic Front in Rhodesia's transitional government. When news of the secret talks became public on August 31, members of both the government and the guerrilla movement expressed conflicting views about the legitimacy and usefulness of the meeting. The two leaders reached no definite conclusions.

16 Canadian government cuts spending

Robert Andras, president of Canada's Treasury Board, announced that the Cabinet had approved budget cuts totaling Can$500 million for fiscal year 1978–79 and additional cuts of Can$1 billion for 1979–80. Substantial savings would be realized through the elimination of 5,000 civil service jobs and special bonuses to bilingual employees. On August 24 Jean Chrétien, the minister of finance, announced that further overall savings would result from a reorganization of certain government programs.

17 U.S. balloonists cross Atlantic

Three Americans completed the first successful transatlantic ballooning when

they landed their helium-filled "Double Eagle II" some 88 km (55 mi) from their intended destination, Le Bourget Airport on the outskirts of Paris. The three, who took off on August 11 from Presque Isle, Maine, established an endurance record of 137 hours 3 minutes and a distance record of 5,023 km (3,120 mi).

19 Theatre fire in Iran kills 430

Arsonists reportedly poured gasoline on the floors of a packed movie theatre in Abadan, Iran, then locked the theatre doors and set the building afire with bombs. The conflagration took the lives of 430 persons. The arrested suspects were described as Muslim extremists who not only considered movie theatres as incompatible with Islamic teachings but also invoked religious ideals as a reason for seeking to reverse many of the shah's policies aimed at liberalizing Iranian society in the name of modernization.

22 Nicaraguan guerrillas seize palace

Twenty-five members of the Sandinista National Liberation Front took control of the National Palace in Managua, Nicaragua, after killing at least six guards and wounding more than a dozen others. Dressed in National Guard uniforms, the guerrillas entered the building when the Chamber of Deputies was in session. Among the estimated 1,000 persons initially held captive were numerous legislators and two relatives of Pres. Anastasio Somoza Debayle. On August 24 a compromise was reached on the guerrillas' demands and they were allowed to fly to Panama with 59 released prisoners and $500,000 in ransom money.

26 Pope John Paul I succeeds Paul VI

Albino Cardinal Luciani, patriarch of Venice, was elected pope of the Roman Catholic Church by the Sacred College of Cardinals. The choice of the 65-year-old Italian prelate surprised most Vatican ob-

servers because it occurred on only the second day of the secret conclave and Luciani had not been considered a leading candidate to succeed Pope Paul VI. He chose the papal name John Paul I.

30 New Danish government formed

Anker Jørgensen, a Social Democrat, remained prime minister of Denmark after persuading the Liberal Democratic Party to become part of a coalition. The new government had the support of 65 Social Democrats, 21 Liberal Democrats, and 2 members of Parliament representing, respectively, Greenland and the Faeroe Islands. The 88 seats held by the coalition were one short of a majority, but right-of-centre groups were expected to support Jørgensen's stringent economic policies. These included a six-month freeze on both prices and profits and a 2% increase (from 18 to 20%) in the value-added tax. There was no direct freeze on wages, but increases were certain to be minimal because of other pressures. Jørgensen's primary goal was to reduce growing deficits both in government spending and in the country's balance of payments. The new government also agreed to continue Denmark's participation in NATO, currently one of the country's most hotly debated political issues.

31 Iceland gets new prime minister

Olafur Johannesson, leader of Iceland's Progressive Party, announced the formation of a coalition government that included the Social Democrats and the People's Alliance. Following the general election of June 25, the leaders of the major parties successively failed to secure the support needed to constitute a viable government. The new coalition, which agreed to maintain Iceland's links to NATO, faced urgent economic problems, including high inflation and troubles in the vital fishing industry. In September Iceland devalued its currency 15% to stimulate exports.

SEPTEMBER

1 Chinese premier visits Romania, Yugoslavia, and Iran

Chinese Premier Hua Kuo-feng ended the first visit ever made to Europe by a Chinese Communist head of state. Hua and his entourage were enthusiastically greeted by Pres. Nicolae Ceausescu and a large crowd in Bucharest, Rom., on August 16. During a state dinner Hua attacked the Soviet Union for attempting to dominate other countries. Another warm welcome was extended to Hua when he arrived in Belgrade, Yugos., on August 21. His talks with President Tito predictably included a discussion of the Soviet Union and events in Africa and Southeast Asia. Though the two leaders did not resolve all

their differences, the meeting was termed mutually satisfactory. Hua's arrival in Teheran, Iran, on August 29 marked the first visit by a Chinese Communist leader to a non-Communist country. No joint communiqué was issued at the end of the visit, apparently a concession to Shah Mohammad Reza Pahlavi, who did not want to antagonize the U.S.S.R.

Estimates of Mexican oil increased

Mexican Pres. José López Portillo announced that the country's proven oil and gas reserves stood at 20,000,000,000 bbl, with probable reserves almost twice that size. The estimate of possible reserves totaling 200,000,000,000 bbl was far greater

than Saudi Arabia's proven reserves of 147,000,000,000 bbl. The president also declared that the nation's added wealth from oil would be used for priorities already established and that a special public budget would account for all oil income and expenditures.

6 Colombia tightens internal security

Colombian Pres. Julio César Turbay Ayala announced tough Cabinet-approved security measures to combat crime and subversion, which had continued to plague the country since he assumed office on August 7. Kidnappers, extortionists, and terrorists would be tried by military courts; arsonists, kidnappers,

Outpourings of vast warmth and congeniality were exhibited by Egyptian Pres. Anwar as-Sadat, U.S. Pres. Jimmy Carter, and Israeli Prime Minister Menahem Begin at a televised session ending the Camp David summit.

and participants in guerrilla organizations would face long imprisonment; illegal strikers would be temporarily suspended from their jobs; and those who printed, distributed, or possessed "subversive propaganda" would be subject to arrest and incarceration. The next day two banks and a store were bombed in Bogotá. The following day guerrillas killed eight peasants for allegedly reporting on their activities. And on September 12 Rafael Pardo Buelvas, a member of the Cabinet in the previous administration, was shot to death. Despite expanded police and military patrols, guerrilla activities continued unabated.

8 *Iran imposes martial law*

Thousands of demonstrators defied a government ban by again taking to the streets shortly after martial law was imposed in Teheran and 11 other cities. Government troops fired on the marchers when they refused to disperse. Officials reported that almost 100 persons were killed in the capital, but unofficial sources estimated the death toll at well over 1,000. The protesters were demanding removal of the shah and establishment of an Islamic state headed by the Ayatullah Ruhollah Khomeini, a religious leader living in exile.

Dominican Republic announces amnesty

Pres. Antonio Guzmán of the Dominican Republic promulgated an amnesty law that three days later resulted in the release of 33 prisoners. Several hundred exiles and prisoners were expected to benefit

from the new law, which was introduced in Congress by Guzmán's Dominican Revolutionary Party (PRD) in fulfillment of a campaign promise. The legislation won quick approval in both the Senate and the Chamber of Deputies.

10 *Martial law declared in Rhodesia*

Rhodesian Prime Minister Ian Smith announced the imposition of selective martial law in various parts of the country as a step toward controlling guerrilla activity. He also warned Zambia and Mozambique to expect reprisals if they continued to provide sanctuary for guerrillas. On September 16 the transitional government announced that blacks would be drafted into the 8,000-man Army, 70% of which already consisted of black volunteers. On September 20 Rhodesia launched a four-day series of raids against 25 suspected guerrilla bases inside Mozambique.

14 *Portugal loses another government*

Portuguese Premier Alfredo Nobre da Costa's nonpartisan government fell after only 17 days in office when the National Assembly, supporting a Socialist motion, voted 141–71 (with 40 abstentions) not to support its program. Pres. António Ramalho Eanes's appointment of Nobre da Costa had angered Socialist Mário Soares, who termed his own dismissal from the premiership unconstitutional.

15 *Trudeau calls for Canada election*

Canadian Prime Minister Pierre Trudeau, whose term was to expire in July 1979,

announced that general elections would be held during the coming spring. The law stipulates that notice of the exact date be given 60 days prior to the election.

16 *Zia becomes Pakistan president*

Mohammad Zia-ul-Haq, who in July 1977 seized power in Pakistan and became chief martial law administrator, assumed the additional post of president after the resignation of Fazal Elahi Chaudhry. The constitution provides that the president be elected by the National Assembly and Senate, but the legislature was dissolved when Zia came to power. As the new chief of state, Zia promised presidential elections in 1979 and said the 1973 constitution would be amended, but not to conform to Islamic law, as some had been demanding.

17 *Camp David meeting ends*

A meeting at Camp David, Md., to resolve the deadlocked Middle Eastern peace negotiations ended on a note of triumph. On September 6 Egyptian Pres. Anwar as-Sadat and Israeli Prime Minister Menahem Begin had begun intensive discussions with President Carter, who assumed the role of both mediator and active participant. Two broad problems lay at the heart of the discussions: Egypt's demand that Israel renounce its claims to sovereignty over occupied Arab lands, and Israel's insistence on secure borders. Despite several dark moments during the course of the talks, Sadat and Begin finally reached agreement on a framework for peace. Many difficult questions still remained, but the two leaders hoped to resolve all major differences within three months and then sign a formal treaty. Among important issues not decided at Camp David were the future status of East Jerusalem and the Golan Heights. Because many Arab nations strongly opposed the conference, U.S. Secretary of State Cyrus Vance departed for the Middle East on September 19 to explain details of the agreement to the Arab leaders of Jordan, Saudi Arabia, and Syria. On September 24 three hard-line Arab nations broke off diplomatic relations with Egypt after a conference in Damascus, Syria, which was also attended by the Palestine Liberation Organization.

19 *Castro ends visit to Ethiopia*

Fidel Castro, president of Cuba's Council of State, ended a week-long visit to Ethiopia, where he conferred with Cuban military personnel. He also attended a celebration commemorating the deposition and imprisonment of Emperor Haile Selassie I on Sept. 12, 1974, which ended imperial rule in Ethiopia. Castro later made brief visits to Algeria and Libya.

20 *Vorster resigns as prime minister*

B. J. Vorster, prime minister of South Africa since 1966, announced his resigna-

SEPTEMBER

tion but said he would seek the largely ceremonial post of president. At the same time he declared that South Africa was no longer willing to accept the UN proposal for independence for Namibia (South West Africa) because conditions agreed to with five Western members of the Security Council in April, and approved in July by the South West Africa People's Organization (SWAPO), had been altered by UN Secretary-General Kurt Waldheim. Vorster further noted that elections for a Constituent Assembly in the territory would be held in November as planned and that independent observers would be welcome. Once constituted, the assembly would be free to determine what role if any the UN would play in Namibia's future. On September 22 SWAPO and several other political parties indicated they would not participate in elections sponsored by South Africa.

Red Brigades leader sentenced

Corrado Alunni, one of the leading figures in the Italian terrorist organization known as the Red Brigades, was sentenced to 12 years in prison for illegal possession of firearms. He was apprehended on September 13 in a Milan apartment that contained machine guns, pistols, explosives, ammunition, and a large sum of money. Alunni was a prime suspect in a dozen murders, including that of former premier Aldo Moro, but murder charges were not brought against him because a long and complicated trial would have resulted.

21 Nigeria lifts ban on political parties

Nigerian head of state Lieut. Gen. Olusegun Obasanjo announced that the state of emergency and the ban against political activity that had been in effect since 1966 were terminated. In a move that brought Nigeria a step closer to civilian rule, military governors in all of the country's 19 states had been replaced by temporary military administrators in July.

22 Government troops regain control of three Nicaraguan cities

After savage fighting, Nicaragua's National Guard established control over Estelí, one of a handful of cities seized on September 9 by left-wing guerrillas and local residents. The city was almost completely destroyed by tanks and rockets before it fell. León was recaptured on September 16 after a three-day battle. Two days later Chinandega fell to government forces. Though there were no accurate reports on fatalities, at least 1,500 persons were believed to have died in the attacks. The rebellion was part of the prolonged and widespread effort to force Pres. Anastasio Somoza Debayle to resign.

26 China terminates talks with Vietnam

China broke off talks with Vietnam after unsatisfactory discussions about the treatment and future of ethnic Chinese living in Vietnam. Before leaving Hanoi, the Chinese vice-foreign minister accused Vietnam of "using the talks to camouflage violence and using violence to undermine the talks." He also charged that Vietnam had abducted, arrested, and even killed Chinese nationals at border passes and in Hanoi. Vietnam denied all the accusations and said China had been totally unreasonable during the negotiations.

27 Indonesia releases political prisoners

The Indonesian government released 1,324 political prisoners who had been detained without trial since an abortive Communist coup in 1965. According to government sources, some 10,000 such prisoners had been released during the year. Of the 16,000 still behind bars, about 400 would stand trial.

28 Botha replaces Vorster in South Africa

Pieter Willem Botha was elected prime minister of South Africa by the ruling National Party. He succeeded B. J. Vorster, who resigned on September 20. Botha announced that he would retain the post of defense minister and would work to improve relations between the races, but he would not even consider abandoning apartheid. On September 29 Vorster replaced the late Nicolaas J. Diederichs as president.

People in Rome grab copy of a newspaper's special edition announcing the death of Pope John Paul I.

Mexican amnesty law enacted

As part of Mexican Pres. José López Portillo's political reform program, scores of political prisoners won freedom when a new amnesty law went into effect. All those convicted or awaiting trial for sedition, incitement to rebellion, conspiracy, and similar crimes benefited from the law provided their actions were nonviolent and committed for political reasons.

29 Pope John Paul I found dead

Pope John Paul I, supreme pontiff of the Roman Catholic Church, was found dead in his Vatican bedroom. After examining the body, three doctors certified that death apparently resulted from cardiac arrest late the previous night. The pope's 34-day reign was the shortest since that of Leo XI, who ruled 18 days in 1605.

18 indicted for massive corruption in U.S. government purchases

A federal grand jury in Baltimore, Md., indicted 18 persons for corrupt practices involving the U.S. General Services Administration (GSA). Twelve present or former GSA managers were accused of taking money or gifts from businessmen in exchange for certifying that the GSA had received office supplies that were never delivered. Three military personnel and one member of the Department of Justice were accused of helping to cover up the operation, of accepting illicit favours, and of signing papers indicating their agencies had received goods that actually had never been delivered. An official and a former official of a Maryland office supply firm were also indicted. On September 20 William Lynch, head of the Narcotics and Dangerous Drugs Division of the Justice Department, was appointed overall coordinator of the criminal investigations concerning the GSA. Preliminary findings indicated that the fraud involved many millions of dollars.

U.S. and Colombia sign drug pact

Representatives of the U.S. and Colombia signed an agreement in Bogotá that coordinated their efforts to combat the illegal production and export of cocaine and marijuana into the U.S. According to a UN specialist, a program of eradication was no longer feasible because the area producing cannabis had reportedly tripled to 300,000 ac since the beginning of 1978. Officials also noted that the estimated $2 billion entering Colombia each year as a result of illegal drug traffic was wreaking havoc on the nation's economy. The antinarcotic program, therefore, concentrated on intense surveillance and control of Colombian and American air corridors traditionally used by smugglers. Among other things, the U.S. promised to train and equip a special Colombian Air Force squad that would patrol the country's Sierra Nevada mountain range and La Guajira Peninsula.

OCTOBER

5 Norway announces austerity program

Norwegian Finance Minister Per Kleppe presented the Labour government's 1979 budget to the Storting (parliament). As expected, it called for strict austerity measures to combat a large foreign debt and generally improve the nation's economic situation. Knowing this could not be done quickly, the government had already announced on September 15 a freeze on wages and prices until 1980. It was hoped that the curbs on wages would both lessen domestic demand for imported items and make Norwegian goods more competitive overseas.

Ecuador sets date for elections

A new electoral court in Ecuador announced that a presidential runoff election and congressional elections would finally be held on April 8, 1979. The previous electoral court had resigned on September 22 after recommending that the results of the July 16 presidential election be annulled as fraudulent. The ruling military junta, however, decided that the runoff election would be held so that Ecuador could return to civilian rule. Jaime Roldos, the candidate of the Concentration of Popular Forces (CFP), was expected to be confirmed, after a vote recount, as the top finisher in the July election, but his runoff opponent was still undetermined. The new president would assume office on Aug. 10, 1979.

6 ERA deadline extended by Senate

The U.S. Senate voted 60–36 to extend the deadline for individual states to ratify the proposed Equal Rights Amendment (ERA). President Carter earlier had indicated his approval of the measure, and the House of Representatives on August 15 had voted 233–189 to extend the original March 22, 1979, deadline to June 30, 1982. Opponents of ERA, however, were certain to take the matter to court. They not only questioned the legality of the extension itself but also the fact that states were allowed to reverse previous votes only if the change was in favour of ratification. Of the 38 states needed for ratification, 35 had approved the amendment, but three later reversed their votes.

10 Rhodesia ends racial segregation

Rhodesia's transitional government announced a program that would end all racial discrimination. In theory the decision would abolish racial segregation and give blacks equal access to such things as housing, educational institutions, and health facilities. In practice, however, few blacks would be in a position to take ad-

Pope John Paul II, the first non-Italian to be elected pope in more than four centuries, blesses crowds after his installation on October 22.

vantage of the changes because they would not be able to afford the costs. Though the abolition of the Land Tenure Act would make it legal for blacks to buy property in formerly all-white areas, owners could still refuse to sell to blacks.

Lévesque clarifies Quebec separation

Quebec Premier René Lévesque, speaking before the provincial National Assembly, clarified some aspects of a planned referendum dealing with Quebec separatism. An affirmative vote, he said, would indicate that Quebecers wanted to establish all their own laws and reserve for themselves the exclusive right to levy taxes. Economic ties with the rest of Canada, however, would continue because there would be unrestricted travel and trade, a common currency, and one central bank. Later, Claude Ryan, a Quebec Liberal, declared it was wishful thinking to suppose that the rest of Canada would accept any such arrangement.

Moi becomes president of Kenya

Daniel Arap Moi, who had been vice-president of Kenya for 11 years before the death of Pres. Jomo Kenyatta on August 22, was elected president. The swearing-in ceremony took place on October 14. Moi, a 54-year-old former teacher, was assured the presidency on October 6

when he was chosen to replace Kenyatta as head of the country's only political party, the Kenya African National Union.

11 Royo named new president of Panama

Aristides Royo was elected president of Panama by the National Assembly of Community Representatives, the nation's congress. Both Royo, who at 38 became the youngest president in Panama's history, and Ricardo de la Espriella, the new vice-president, ran unopposed after being nominated by Brig. Gen. Omar Torrijos Herrera. Many believed that Torrijos, who retained his position as commander of the National Guard, would continue to be the de facto ruler of the country.

12 Uganda and Tanzania report clash

Uganda announced that Tanzanian troops had invaded its territory west of Lake Victoria, but Tanzania characterized the charges as "complete lies." On October 31 Tanzania reported that Ugandan troops, supported by tanks and artillery, had penetrated 32 km (20 mi) into its territory. The following day Uganda announced the annexation of 1,800 sq km (695 sq mi) of Tanzanian territory, a section known as the Kagera salient. On November 4 Ugandan Pres. Idi Amin, apparently pressured by other African and Arab nations, announced that his troops would withdraw from the area. A week later the fighting was still going on, with a reported 10,000 Tanzanians already dead or wounded. On November 27 counterattacking Tanzanian troops were reported to have penetrated 35 km (22 mi) into Ugandan territory.

13 Ullsten becomes Swedish prime minister

Ola Ullsten, whose Liberal Party held only 39 seats in the 349-member Riksdag (parliament), was confirmed as prime minister of Sweden when the Social Democrats and the Centre Party decided to abstain during the voting. Ullsten received only 39 votes, but the 66 votes against him were far short of the constitutional majority required to nullify his plurality. Ullsten replaced Thorbjörn Fälldin, who resigned on October 5 when other parties in the coalition government would not accept the Centre Party's limitations on expanding nuclear power.

15 Figueiredo wins Brazil election

Gen. João Baptista da Figueiredo was elected president of Brazil by an electoral college made up of members of both houses of Congress and of delegates from state assemblies. Figueiredo, who with

South Korean soldiers guard an invasion tunnel that runs under the demilitarized zone from North Korea to South Korea. The discovery of the tunnel was reported by the UN military command in South Korea.

the support of the National Renewal Alliance handily defeated Gen. Euler Bentes Monteiro 355–226, was scheduled to assume office on March 15, 1979. The 60-year-old military officer would be the fifth consecutive general to occupy the presidency since 1964.

16 Karol Wojtyla becomes Pope John Paul II

Karol Cardinal Wojtyla was elected pope of the Roman Catholic Church by the Sacred College of Cardinals. The choice of the 58-year-old archbishop of Krakow, Poland, marked the first time since 1522 that a non-Italian had been elevated to the papacy. Wojtyla succeeded Pope John Paul I, who died suddenly after just 34 days in office.

17 Karpov retains world chess title

World chess champion Anatoly Karpov of the U.S.S.R. successfully defended his title against challenger Viktor Korchnoi, a former Soviet citizen residing in Switzerland. The series, which began on July 18 in the Philippines, was to continue until one player gained six victories. Karpov broke a 5–5 deadlock when he won the 32nd game.

New York Yankees win World Series

The New York Yankees professional baseball team won the sixth and deciding game of the World Series by defeating the Los Angeles Dodgers 7–2. The Yankee victory marked the first time in history that any team won the World Series in four straight games after losing the first two.

19 Argentina agrees to OAS visit

Argentina's ruling military junta agreed to let a delegation from the Organization of American States investigate alleged violations of human rights in the country. No date, however, was set for the visit. Both the U.S. government and local rights groups had repeatedly urged an investigation because of persistent complaints about the Argentine government's infringements of human rights.

20 Rhodesian prime minister visits U.S.

Prime Minister Ian Smith concluded a tour of the U.S. without gaining much new support for his notion as to how black majority rule should be established in Rhodesia. During part of his visit Smith was accompanied by the three black leaders who, with Smith, comprised the Executive Council of Rhodesia's interim government. Though invited by a group of U.S. senators, Smith was initially denied a visa by the State Department because UN sanctions against Rhodesia extended to travel. The U.S. also wished to avoid offending black African nations and feared that such a visit might adversely affect the U.S.-U.K. plans, which called for the inclusion of guerrilla representatives in an all-party conference that would determine Rhodesia's future. Before departing, Smith declared his willingness to meet with guerrilla leaders and negotiate a peaceful transition to black rule provided the talks commenced with no preconditions. Joshua Nkomo, leader of the Zimbabwe African Peoples Union (ZAPU) guerrillas, categorically refused to participate in any such meeting.

21 Cuban prisoners admitted into U.S.

Cuban Pres. Fidel Castro allowed 46 former political prisoners and 33 relatives to fly from Havana to Miami, Fla. The flight, arranged principally by bank executive Bernardo Benes during visits to Cuba, was expected to be followed by others because Castro was reported to be willing to release some 3,000 other prisoners by the end of the year. The new arrivals, who were admitted into the U.S. in accord with the federal Immigration Act, were warmly greeted by the Cuban community in Miami.

23 China and Japan formalize treaty

Japan and China formally implemented the treaty of peace and friendship signed in August when representatives of the two nations exchanged documents of ratification in Tokyo. The convivial affair was attended by Japanese Prime Minister Takeo Fukuda and Chinese Vice-Premier Teng Hsiao-p'ing.

24 Carter urges anti-inflation measures

In a nationally televised speech, President Carter outlined a program that he hoped would lower the U.S. inflation rate to about 6–6.5% in 1979. Because implementation depended largely on voluntary compliance, Carter asked every American "to give this plan a chance to work." Rejecting mandatory wage and price controls as unworkable, the president called for a voluntary 7% limit on pay increases and expressed hope that average price increases would not exceed 5.75%. Carter offered a special inducement in the form of "wage insurance," which Congress would have to authorize. Such legislation would give tax relief to those who adhered to the wage guidelines if the actual inflation rate exceeded 7%. The president also promised that fiscal restraint would characterize government fiscal policy.

25 Israel to expand settlements in occupied Arab lands

Israeli Prime Minister Menahem Begin told the Knesset (parliament) that the government would proceed with a program to expand existing Jewish settlements in territories occupied by Israel during its 1967 war with the Arabs. The announcement, which many saw as a serious obstacle to a peace settlement in the Middle East, was severely criticized by the U.S. as violating the spirit of the Camp David agreements. Israeli Foreign Minister Moshe Dayan, however, denied that Israel had agreed to suspend expansion of existing West Bank settlements.

New premier named in Portugal

Pres. António Ramalho Eanes named 42-year-old independent Carlos Alberto Mota Pinto premier of Portugal. The appointment was an attempt to end a political crisis that began with the collapse of Mário Soares's Socialist-Centre Democrat government in July and continued when Alfredo Nobre da Costa's nonparty government was repudiated by the National Assembly on September 14.

27 *North Korean invasion tunnel found*

The UN military command in South Korea reported the discovery of a large invasion tunnel that began in North Korea, passed under the demilitarized zone, and penetrated 435 m (1,428 ft) into South Korean territory. It was the third such tunnel discovered since 1974. Military authorities estimated that the tunnel, which was constructed 73 m (240 ft) beneath the ground and measured 2 m (6½ ft) in both height and width, was large enough to permit about 30,000 armed troops per hour to enter South Korea during a surprise attack. The general location of the tunnel was first revealed by a defector from North Korea.

29 *Rhodesia delays black rule vote*

Rhodesian Prime Minister Ian Smith announced that "for purely mechanical reasons" it would not be possible to hold parliamentary elections at the end of the year as originally promised. He gave reassurances that blacks would assume control of the country through national elections after unexpected problems encountered in writing the new constitution had been resolved. The delay also meant that Rhodesia would not change its name to Zimbabwe until some time during the first part of 1979.

30 *Soviets sentenced for spying in U.S.*

Two Soviet citizens, convicted on October 13 of espionage, were each sentenced to 50 years in prison by a federal judge in Newark, N.J. While purportedly working for the UN in New York City, the two paid $20,000 to U.S. Navy Lieut. Comdr. Arthur F. Lindberg for documents they believed contained U.S. defense secrets.

PHILIPPE LEDRU—SYGMA

Striking Iranian petroleum workers sit it out in the country's largest refinery in Abadan. The nation's oil production dropped by more than 50%.

With the approval of the Federal Bureau of Investigation (FBI), Lindberg maintained contact with the Soviet agents until the FBI had accumulated sufficient evidence to establish a case against them and make the arrests.

31 *Iranian oil workers strike*

Some 40,000 Iranian petroleum workers went on strike after negotiations with the National Iranian Oil Co. ended without an agreement. The employees were demanding higher wages, an end to martial law, a court trial for the former head of Iran's secret police, and punishment of those responsible for killing hundreds of antigovernment demonstrators during the course of the year. Oil production immediately dropped to less than 50% of normal output, thereby reducing Iran's revenues by about $50 million a day. Most Iranian oil was exported to Europe, Israel, Japan, South Africa, and the U.S.

NOVEMBER

1 *Carter's new monetary policy helps bolster U.S. dollar abroad*

President Carter announced a new monetary policy that almost instantly dramatically strengthened the U.S. dollar on foreign exchange markets. In Tokyo the value of the dollar increased 5%, from a postwar low of 176.08 yen. The Dow Jones industrial average also soared 35.34 points, a record performance for a single day of trading on the New York Stock Exchange. Among other things, Carter's plan included: having the Federal Reserve System raise the discount rate an unusual full percentage point (from 8.5 to 9.5%), thereby making it more costly for banks to borrow money; restricting the expansion of bank credit with the Federal Reserve; vastly increasing the amount of gold to be sold at auction; floating U.S. government securities denominated in foreign currencies so that the money could be used to buy up excess dollars; and doubling the U.S. credit line for certain foreign currencies so that the money could be used to purchase dollars.

2 *Soviet cosmonauts set new record*

Soviet cosmonauts Vladimir Kovalenok and Aleksandr Ivanchenkov descended to Earth in the Soyuz 31 spacecraft after setting a new space endurance record of 139 days and 14 hours. While living aboard the orbiting Salyut 6 space station, they were visited by two pairs of cosmonauts and received supplies from three unmanned vehicles. The flight was evaluated as near perfect by Soviet officials, who expressed optimism that the more than 50 scientific experiments conducted in conditions of weightlessness would yield important data.

3 *Vietnam and the U.S.S.R. sign pact*

Top officials of the Soviet Union and Vietnam signed a 25-year treaty of friendship and cooperation in economic, scientific, and technical endeavours. With China clearly in mind, both of the signatories pledged that in the event of an attack on either nation they would consult immediately and "take appropriate effective measures to ensure the peace and security of their countries."

4 *Sadat rejects Arab offer of aid*

After discussing the matter in Baghdad, Iraq, a coalition of Arab leaders sent Lebanese Prime Minister Selim al-Hoss and three other delegates to Cairo to offer Egypt $50 billion in aid if it would discontinue peace negotiations with Israel. The money would be dispensed over a period of ten years. During an address to Parliament, Pres. Anwar as-Sadat declared that he would neither meet the four-man delegation nor accept the money, for "not all the world's billions can buy Egypt's will."

6 *New York newspaper strike ends*

After an 88-day interval the *New York Times* and the *Daily News* resumed publishing. The strike settlement, which involved ten unions and about 11,000 employees, called for a weekly pay increase of $68 over a three-year period. The agreement also guaranteed the jobs of more than 1,000 pressmen but permitted a reduction in jobs if vacancies occurred through death, retirement, or resignation. A minimum number of workmen, however, had to be maintained at each machine. Publishers estimated that the new contract would result in about one-third fewer pressmen within five years. The *New York Post*, which was silenced by the same strike, resumed publication on October 5 after management promised to accept the same settlement reached by the *Times* and *News*.

14 *Teng visits Southeast Asian nations*

Chinese Vice-Premier Teng Hsiao-p'ing ended a visit to Southeast Asia that included stops in Thailand, Malaysia, Singapore, and Burma. The trip was seen as part of China's new diplomatic offensive and as a significant overture to the four anti-Communist nations. At a banquet in Kuala Lumpur, Malaysian Prime Minister Datuk Hussein bin Onn urged China not to interfere in Malaysia's internal affairs—an allusion to Peking's support of the Malaysian Communist Party. Teng later told Malaysian officials that China's support of the banned party was a matter of principle and could not be withdrawn.

15 *Brazil's ruling party wins election*

Brazil's ruling party, the National Renewal Alliance (ARENA), retained control of both houses of Congress in a national election even though the Brazilian Democratic Movement (MDB), the only other political party, won 60% of the popular vote. ARENA candidates captured 13 of the 23 seats contested in the 67-seat Senate, giving it a majority of 47–20. ARENA also appeared to have secured 227

of the 420 seats in the Chamber of Deputies. Though political speeches were banned on radio and television during the campaign, government officials managed to make many thinly disguised political pleas for ARENA candidates.

18 *Murder of U.S. congressman in Guyana triggers mass suicides and murders*

Leo J. Ryan, a U.S. representative from California, and four other Americans were shot to death by members of the People's Temple as they prepared to leave Guyana by plane. Ryan had gone to Jonestown, a religious commune established by the Temple, to investigate reports that some members of the cult were being held against their will and that some were being subjected to physical and psychological abuses. When Jim Jones, the charismatic but paranoid leader of the San Francisco-based cult, learned that his followers had not killed all those in the Ryan party, he informed his followers that a previously rehearsed suicide ritual would be carried out. Babies were first given a cyanide-poisoned drink, then the others either willingly drank the deadly potion or were murdered. Only a few members of the cult escaped death by fleeing into the jungle. When Guyanese troops arrived at Jonestown after the airport murders they were overwhelmed by the sight of over 900 bodies lying inside and outside the buildings. Jones had died from a bullet fired into his head. Officials later discovered a cache of firearms, hundreds of passports stacked together, and about $500,000 in U.S. currency. Millions more had reportedly been deposited in bank accounts overseas.

19 *Peking wall poster criticizes Mao*

The late Chinese Communist Party chairman Mao Tse-tung was accused in a Peking wall poster of supporting the now disgraced "gang of four." Because the poster was not removed, its message was presumably approved by government officials, notably by Vice-Premier Teng Hsiao-p'ing, who had been vilified as an antirevolutionary by the gang of four and as a consequence lost his important posts. The attack on Mao was seen as part of a gradual but broad campaign to downgrade Mao, thus making it easier for China to abandon many of Mao's most sacrosanct policies in order to establish ties with the West and vigorously push forward its modernization program.

20 *Ethiopia signs pact with U.S.S.R.*

In a Moscow ceremony Ethiopia and the Soviet Union signed a 20-year treaty of friendship and cooperation that called for consultation "in the event of situations which constitute a threat to, or a breach of, international peace." Mutual military assistance was not promised. The pact underscored the Soviet Union's desire to retain a foothold in the Horn of Africa after

substantially supporting Ethiopia in its war against secessionist rebels.

24 *Bolivian president ousted in coup*

Some four months after seizing power, Gen. Juan Pereda Asbún was deposed in a bloodless coup led by Gen. David Padilla Arancibia, commander of the Army. Padilla, who headed the new three-man junta as interim president, promised elections on July 1, 1979, and the transfer of power to a civilian president on Aug. 6, 1979. Pereda had said elections would not be held until May 1980.

25 *Muldoon remains in power as prime minister of New Zealand*

In a general election New Zealand voters gave Prime Minister Robert Muldoon's National Party 49 of the 92 seats in the unicameral legislature, 7 more than were won by Labour Party candidates. The Social Credit Party won the only other seat. In the previous legislature, which had 5 fewer seats, the National Party had 53, the Labour Party 31, one seat was filled by the Social Credit Party, and two were held by independents. The nearly 8%

A vat containing a cyanide-laced drink stands amid scattered corpses in Jonestown, Guyana. More than 900 committed suicide by willingly drinking the potion or were murdered.

WIDE WORLD

drop in National Party representation was attributed in part to Muldoon's often severe criticism of those who found fault with his policies.

27 Japan gets new prime minister

In a complex electoral process established several years earlier, Japanese Prime Minister Takeo Fukuda unexpectedly lost the first round of an election for presidency of the ruling Liberal-Democratic Party to Masayoshi Ohira, the party's secretary-general. Fukuda then withdrew as a candidate in the runoff election, thereby handing Ohira the party presidency and with it the office of prime minister. The election results translated into 748 points for Ohira, 638 for Fukuda, 93 for Yasuhiro Nakasone, and 46 for Toshio Komoto. Before his surprise victory Ohira had campaigned vigorously. He also had the backing of former prime ministers Kakuei Tanaka and Takeo Miki.

29 UNESCO endorses free press

At the end of its 20th General Conference in Paris, UNESCO formally ratified a non-binding compromise declaration endorsing freedom of the press throughout the world. Describing freedom of information as a basic human right and calling attention to the need for greater equality in the flow of news between developed and less developed countries, the UNESCO document urged industrialized nations to assist in improving news organizations in the third world.

UPI COMPIX

Masayoshi Ohira stands to acknowledge cheers after being elected president of the ruling Liberal-Democratic Party of Japan.

30 The Times suspends publication

After management and labour representatives failed to reach a mutually satisfactory settlement of their differences, *The Times* of London suspended publication for the indefinite future. The owner also halted publication of *The Sunday Times* and three weekly supplements. Many predicted that negotiations would be lengthy and some even expressed fears that the 193-year-old newspaper had already published its last issue. Management's demands included an end to wildcat strikes, the utilization of new technology, and a reduction in the labour force. Among other things, workers sought guarantees that the introduction of new technology would not jeopardize their job security.

DECEMBER

3 Vietnam says antigovernment group formed in Cambodia

Radio Hanoi announced that a Kampuchean United Front for National Salvation had been formed in Cambodia to overthrow Premier Pol Pot's regime. The following day the United Front described the Cambodian government as unmatched in history for its ferocity. Meanwhile, Vietnamese troops continued to advance into Cambodia and by December 5 threatened to cut Highway 4, which links the capital of Phnom Penh with Kompong Som, the deepwater port through which Cambodia received its military supplies from China. The Chinese reportedly were advising the Cambodians to resort to guerrilla tactics in order to counter the larger and better equipped Vietnamese forces.

4 Venezuela elects new president

Luis Herrera Campins of the Social Christian Party (COPEI) received 3.7% more votes than Luis Pinerúa Ordaz of the ruling Acción Democrática (AD) in Venezuela's presidential election. Eight other candidates finished far behind. In the congressional elections, COPEI and AD finished even, each winning 21 seats in the 45-seat Senate and 86 seats in the 183-seat Chamber of Deputies. AD, however, would have a one-seat majority in the upper house because two of the three former presidents, all senators for life, were affiliated with AD.

Malaysia admits 600 refugees from Vietnam

Reversing an earlier decision against the admission of additional refugees from Vietnam, the government of Malaysia welcomed 600 people that had arrived in four boats. Less than two weeks earlier 200 refugees had drowned when their boat capsized as it was being towed back to sea by police at Kuala Trengganu. When hundreds of others perished in rough seas off the Malaysian and Thai coasts, the Malaysian government acted. Other countries also offered asylum to limited numbers of refugees. On November 17 the U.S. had said it would add 2,500 "boat people" to the list of 25,000 Vietnamese it had already promised to accept before April 30, 1979. On November 28 the number was again increased by some 22,000. On December 11–12 the UN High Commissioner for Refugees presided over a conference in Geneva that was attended by 38 nations. No immediate solution was found to the problem created by the estimated 200,000 Indochinese refugees, most of whom remained in camps in Thailand and Malaysia.

5 European Monetary System approved

At the end of a two-day meeting, member nations of the European Economic Community (EEC) adopted a new European Monetary System (EMS) that was expected to go into effect on January 2, 1979, the first business day of the new year. Great Britain declined to join, at least temporarily. Ireland and Italy deferred their decisions for a time, then joined. The other participating countries were Belgium, Denmark, France, Luxembourg, The Netherlands, and West Germany. In essence, the new system would link the currency of each nation with those of all the others. If one nation's currency rose or fell more than 2.25% against another's currency, the two countries involved could intervene in the foreign exchange

DECEMBER

markets to bring matters back into a desired balance. To this end a common fund of about $50 billion would support the EMS. On December 29 France effectively delayed inauguration of the EMS by demanding resolution of a dispute with West Germany over agricultural subsidies. France argued that they distort the balance of national economic advantage within the EEC.

Afghanistan signs pact with U.S.S.R.

After two days of talks in Moscow, Afghanistan Prime Minister Nur Mohammad Taraki and Soviet Pres. Leonid Brezhnev committed their countries to a 20-year treaty of friendship and cooperation. Among other things, both nations pledged to continue "to develop cooperation in the military field on the basis of appropriate agreements." Taraki, head of the Revolutionary Council that seized control of the government at the end of April, said Afghanistan would remain officially nonaligned. However, most political observers believed that Taraki's favourable view of Marxism signified much more than a mere continuation of Afghanistan's traditional economic ties with its powerful Soviet neighbour to the north.

6 Spaniards approve new constitution

In a national referendum in Spain, nearly 90% of those who voted gave their approval to a new 169-article constitution that provided for a constitutional monarchy, a parliamentary system of government, and generous individual liberties. Nearly one-third of the eligible voters, however, did not cast ballots. Many of these boycotted the election because the constitution did not meet their expectations. For example, many Basques de-

manded much greater autonomy for their region than the constitution permitted; and others were unhappy that the authority of the central government had been significantly reduced. The new constitution went into effect when it was officially published on December 29. The following day Premier Adolfo Suárez González, who was obliged either to call new elections or to seek a vote of confidence in the legislature, dissolved the Cortes and called for general elections on March 1, 1979.

7 New governor-general named in Canada

Canadian Prime Minister Pierre Trudeau appointed Edward Schreyer governor-general of Canada; he would replace Jules Léger, who was to retire in January. Schreyer, the 42-year-old leader of the New Democratic Party in Manitoba, would be the personal representative of Queen Elizabeth II, Canada's official chief of state.

15 U.S. and China to establish full diplomatic relations

In simultaneous announcements in Washington, D.C., and Peking, President Carter and Chinese Premier Hua Kuo-feng surprised the world by declaring that their two countries had agreed to establish full diplomatic relations as of Jan. 1, 1979. On the same date the U.S. would sever diplomatic relations with the Republic of China in Taiwan. Carter added, however, that even after the U.S. terminated its defense treaty with the Taipei government on Dec. 31, 1979, the U.S. would continue to maintain "cultural, commercial, and unofficial relations with the people of Taiwan." Sen. Barry Goldwater of Arizona immediately claimed

UPI COMPIX

Chinese flock to buy newspapers after U.S. Pres. Jimmy Carter announced normalization of relations between the U.S. and China.

that Carter had no constitutional authority to abrogate the treaty with the Chinese Nationalist government unless the Senate concurred, and he pledged to challenge Carter's unilateral action in the courts. On December 16 China issued an official statement declaring that the future of Taiwan "is entirely China's internal affair." The following day U.S. Secretary of State Cyrus Vance said the U.S. did not expect China to use force to gain control of Taiwan, but he acknowledged that China had made no promise to that effect. In his televised speech, Carter also announced that Chinese Vice-Premier Teng Hsiaop'ing would begin his first visit to the U.S. on January 29. The formal exchange of ambassadors between China and the U.S. and the establishment of embassies were scheduled to take place on March 1, 1979.

Namibian assembly elections held

Results of the December 4–8 election to choose members for the new constituent assembly in Namibia (South West Africa) were announced in Windhoek, the capital. As expected, the conservative multiracial Democratic Turnhalle Alliance scored an easy victory by winning

An old freighter crammed with more than 2,500 Indochinese refugees remained anchored off the coast of Malaysia for weeks until various governments provided aid.

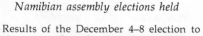
ALAIN DEJEAN—SYGMA

41 of the 50 seats in the new assembly. The Aktur Party, organized by a group of conservative whites, was second with six seats. Three minor parties captured one seat each. The South West Africa People's Organization boycotted the election, as it had promised, because the balloting was not supervised by the UN.

Somoza signs amnesty to promote peace in Nicaragua

Nicaraguan Pres. Anastasio Somoza Debayle, whose rule had been severely challenged most of the year by violent opposition that at times verged on civil war, granted amnesty to all political prisoners. In a radio and television address Somoza said that his action paved the way for a peaceful settlement of the country's problems. Constitutional guarantees had earlier been restored and censorship of radio and television relaxed. The three steps met the basic demands of the Broad Opposition Front but did not satisfy the Sandinista guerrillas who still steadfastly refused to negotiate with the Somoza government. On December 27 Somoza rejected international supervision of a plebiscite that would determine the nation's future leadership.

17 OPEC increases oil prices

On the second day of a meeting held in the capital of the United Arab Emirates, 13 member nations of the Organization of Petroleum Exporting Countries ended an 18-month freeze on the cost of exported crude oil. Beginning on Jan. 1, 1979, the price would be increased every three months until it reached a cumulative total of 14.5% on Oct. 1, 1979. The cost of Arabian light, the norm for other types of crude, would thus rise from $12.70 to $14.54 per barrel after nine months.

Israel and Egypt miss deadline for signing peace treaty

Israel and Egypt failed to sign a peace treaty within the three-month period they had imposed upon themselves at the conclusion of the Camp David summit talks. The two sides had not met since November 16 because neither was willing to compromise on certain issues. Israel, for example, was unwilling to sign an agreement permitting elections that would establish autonomy for Palestinians in the West Bank and Gaza Strip before the end of 1979. Egypt, on its part, would not agree that a peace treaty with Israel would have priority over all other agreements it had already reached with other, notably Arab, countries.

26 Turkey imposes martial law

The Turkish Parliament, by an overwhelming vote, approved a government decree imposing martial law in 13 provinces after a weekend of violence that took some 100 lives. Sections of Maras were destroyed as members of two Muslim sects,

the Sunnis and Alevis (Shi'ites), gave vent to their long-standing political and religious enmity. The politically right-wing Sunnis, who claim to represent nearly 80% of Turkey's population, regard the left-wing, Kurdish-speaking Alevis as Muslim heretics. Turkey's internal problems included external debts in excess of $10 billion, a 70% annual inflation rate, and a 20% unemployment rate.

27 Crisis in Iran reaches acute stage

After two months of political turmoil that disrupted nearly every aspect of Iranian life, Shah Mohammad Reza Pahlavi asked Shahpur Bakhtiar to try to reestablish order by forming a civilian government. Bakhtiar, well-known as an uncompromising critic of the shah and his authoritarian rule, would replace armed forces chief of staff Gen. Gholam Reza Azhari, whose military government was unable to stem Iran's plunge toward economic and social chaos after assuming office on November 6. Bakhtiar faced an awesome task: virtually all transportation had stopped, oil exports had ceased, the central bank and numerous stores had closed, and Iran could no longer meet its own needs for gasoline and kerosene. Hundreds of thousands of demonstrators defied government troops as they shouted "Death to the shah!" and burned cars, buses, and trucks. On December 30 the council of the opposition National Front expelled Bakhtiar from its organization, but he remained steadfast in his determination to gain control of the country. His greatest obstacle was the Ayatullah Ruholla Khomeini, a Shi'ite Muslim, who inspired the antishah and anti-Bakhtiar activities from France by promising to establish an Islamic state in Iran. It was increasingly doubtful whether the shah could retain even a semblance of power as a figurehead monarch.

South Korea frees Kim Dae Jung

Kim Dae Jung, who had opposed South Korean Pres. Park Chung Hee in the 1971 presidential election, was released from prison after serving part of a five-year sentence. He was jailed in March 1976 after denouncing President Park as a dictator and demanding his resignation. Some 5,378 other prisoners were also released or had their sentences reduced. The general amnesty coincided with the inauguration of President Park, who began his fifth consecutive term in office. He became leader of South Korea after a coup in 1961.

31 Investigation of mass murders in Illinois continues

Police authorities in Illinois announced that suspected murderer John Wayne Gacy, a 36-year-old contractor and an admitted homosexual, might also be connected with the sex murders of teenaged boys in neighbouring states. Police using axes, chainsaws, and other equipment had already recovered 26 bodies buried in the crawl space beneath Gacy's one-story, seven-room house in Norwood Park Township in a suburban area of Cook County near Chicago. Another body was found under the garage floor, and two were retrieved from the nearby Des Plaines River. Forensic experts said identification of the remains, most merely skeletons, would be a slow and tedious process. Police planned to continue the search until they were satisfied that all the bodies had been recovered from the house. The case began to break on December 13 when police found in Gacy's house a receipt that came from a pharmacy where a missing 15-year-old boy worked. During a second search eight days later the first three bodies were discovered. Gacy was arrested and held without bond.

The bodies of 27 young men were found buried in the home of John Wayne Gacy in a suburb near Chicago. Two additional bodies were recovered from a nearby river.

UPI COMPIX

Not all the news events of 1978 made prominent headlines. Among items reported less breathlessly in the worldwide press were the following:

Stuart Russell, who likes to frequent Eagles Inn in Oswestry, England, learned that playing snooker can be hazardous to your health. He leaned forward, lined up a shot, coughed, and earned a round of wild applause when he sank two false front teeth in the corner pocket. While trying to recover the teeth, Russell got his hand stuck in the pocket. About 50 patrons tried to free him, but not even liquid detergent would do the job. The expertise of two police officers and six fire fighters was also of no avail until someone suggested removing the table top. Before chalking up his cue, Russell put in his teeth and chalked one up to experience.

Sam Binion, a city bus driver in Chicago, was among several persons asked during a street interview whether they would want a doctor to tell them clearly if death was approaching. Without hesitation, Sam replied that he certainly would. For one thing, he said, it would give him time to get a second medical opinion.

Norman Spatz's troubles began on Sept. 26, 1977, when he was photographed by a hidden camera during a bank robbery in Montreal. Police circulated his picture on a wanted poster that was picked up by six newspapers with more than one million readers. The police failed to locate Spatz, but someone identified his photo as that of a friendly architect living in the neighbourhood. When Spatz was arrested he was incensed that even so-called friends would apparently jump at the chance to turn him in for a mere $500 reward. He was less bothered by the fact that the real bank robber could have shot and killed him as the two stood together in front of the bank teller's window.

A grand jury in Cook County, Ill., indicted a man for theft and fraud because he received $51,000 in Medicaid payments while practicing medicine without a license. After receiving a subpoena, the man fled the country, but not without first writing to the judge to explain that he was suffering from amnesia and could remember nothing whatever about himself. Not even his name, which happens to be Kandaswamy M. Balasubramaniyam.

Dewey Baker, a 26-year-old convicted bank robber, had just been sentenced to a 16-year prison term when he suddenly bolted out of a federal courtroom in San Jose, Calif., and made his escape. As he raced for the door, he heard his three children shouting, "Go, Dewey, go!"

Criminals, detective books assure us, often return to the scene of the crime. Thieves in Chicago did better than that by stealing the scene of the crime. Early one morning seven thieves made off with five bathtubs and a furnace stored in a garage, and that afternoon they returned and stole the garage. They dismantled the 1,400-brick building, then made their getaway with the loot loaded on a truck. Before sundown two of the seven were in police custody, and the owner of a brickyard was wondering how he could have bought a stolen two-car garage without knowing it.

Government agencies of all sorts have often been criticized for selecting names that no printer could possibly squeeze onto a letterhead. One United Nations body solved its problem by adopting the simple acronym CCOP, which every employee doubtless knows stands for: The United Nations Economic and Social Commission for Asia and the Pacific Committee for Coordination of Joint Prospecting for Mineral Resources in Asian Offshore Areas.

Trees grow, even deserts grow, but skyscrapers? If the latest issue of *Facts About Chicago* is to be believed, the city's famed skyscrapers are growing at a phenomenal rate. Comparative statistics in two successive issues of the city's annual brochure indicate that Sears Tower, the world's tallest building, now rises 1,454 ft, four feet higher than it reportedly was a year earlier. An additional story has also been added, apparently just four feet high. The Standard Oil Building grew an astonishing 42 ft in the process of shrinking from 82 stories to 80. But even that was not as startling as what was happening farther north on Michigan Avenue. Water Tower Place grew only one foot while adding 12 new stories. Had he known, Chicago's late Mayor Richard J. Daley might have been tempted to lengthen the city slogan to read, "The city that works . . . miracles."

Large lettering on Louisville, Ky., billboards urged passersby to "Beat Your Wife." Below, in smaller letters, were the words "Go Bowling." Carole Morse, director of the Spouse Abuse Center, doesn't think jokes about such a serious social evil are funny. L. A. Frantz, president of the bowling association, conceded the point and promised that sign painters would change every billboard in town to read "Beat Your Husband."

For reasons as different as human beings themselves, 50.1% of Illinois Bell's Chicago customers are not listed in the telephone directory. Time was when only the famous sought such anonymity, but in recent years truck drivers, office workers, teachers, and other ordinary citizens have joined the list of those unlisted.

International terrorism has been so well publicized—and carried out in such unlikely places—that music lovers in Carnegie Hall have no reason to feel embarrassed. In mid-October, while Seiji Ozawa was conducting the Boston Symphony Orchestra, the sound of gunfire suddenly exploded in the auditorium. Hundreds leaped out of their seats and raced for the exits as members of the orchestra scurried off the stage and ran for cover. The audience gradually

It's pointless to argue about personal tastes. That wise saying from ancient Rome wasn't much comfort to certain California residents when they saw what was happening to their Sunset Boulevard neighbourhood in Beverly Hills. An Arabian sheikh purchased this 58-room mansion for $2.4 million, then began to redecorate it to suit his taste. The outside was painted a garish green, and walls inside the mansion were painted red and orange. Some neighbours and passersby directed their most caustic comments at the Romanesque statues, which were rendered "indecent" by daubs of red paint. Perched along the balustrade, they gaze out across a garden of newly planted plastic flowers.

College president Bill Steed claims he gets excellent results by using hypnosis on his students. All 300 of his pupils major in physical education, but after graduation from Croaker College in California some become cowboys riding on toy horses, others pop entertainers, still others weight lifters or track stars. Most eventually are taken into the homes of celebrities. The student pictured above is starting his workout with a barbell. He's especially good in the bench press event.

regained its composure after being assured that the "gunfire" was merely a malfunctioning speaker system.

After years of wrangling, the U.S. Senate finally approved a revision of the federal criminal code. Among other proposed changes, the senators voted to abolish the current 80 criminal states of mind. Such words as wantonly, maliciously, deliberately, and lasciviously would be replaced by four categories: intentional, knowing, reckless, and negligent. But suppose a motorist intentionally drank too much and then, knowing his car lights were not turned on, sped recklessly down the road and neglected to stop at an intersection. Would he have committed the perfect crime?

NBC news usually doesn't come in over CBS radio stations. But it did, for about two minutes in April, when someone at Western Union crossed the circuits that relay the two networks' broadcasts via satellite to their affiliates across the nation.

It took Bob Speca, Jr., of Philadelphia some 95 hours to set the stage for a new world record on the ballroom floor of the Manhattan Center. Then eight-year-old Michael Murphy, a hemophiliac, was given the honour of tipping over the first of 100,000 dominoes arranged in intricate patterns. Though the benefit event was a clattering success, one television cameraman felt miserable. As he leaned over to get a shot, a press card fell from his pocket and 2,500 dominoes toppled over accidentally.

Five West German teenagers, all apprentices with the Daimler-Benz company in Stuttgart, wrote a new chapter in fuel economy when they built a car that traveled approximately 674 km on one litre of diesel fuel—the equivalent of 1,585 mi per gal. The three-wheel car, which was about 2.7 m (9 ft) long and weighed some 57 kg (125 lb), had an air-cooled, one-cylinder, 200-cc engine with an output of one horsepower. The test run took place at the Hockenheim racetrack. A second car, also designed by apprentices, made a similar test run and proved to be only 7.3% less efficient.

Finnish paratroopers taking part in war games mistook a group of hunters for "the enemy" and began firing blanks in their direction. The startled hunters, not knowing what was happening, returned the fire with live ammunition. Everyone, including perhaps the wildlife, was comforted to learn no one had been hit.

Boston meter maids were reported to have the highest group accident rate among all city employees. Only 10% of the garbage collectors report injuries each year and police average about 40%. But a whopping 85% of the city's 168 meter maids have reported injuries; 19 are collecting workers' compensation. Meter maids have to contend with irate motorists who jam torn parking tickets into their eyes, and they inadvertently strike their hands against the meters with alarming frequency.

Mayors of major cities may have grievous problems, but solutions fortunately don't require international agreements. By contrast, Mayor Maurice Delbove of La Flamengrie, France, merely wanted to put up a stop sign at the main intersection of his village, but he couldn't act without first getting written permission from King Baudouin I of Belgium and Pres. Valéry Giscard d'Estaing of France. The spot in question lies on the border between the two countries, so it belongs to both countries, or to neither country. All things considered, perhaps the mayor ought to authorize an environmental impact study to determine how a stop sign would affect the lives of the village's 208 residents. By the time the study is completed, submitted, studied, rejected, amended, reviewed, revised, discussed, reworded, and approved, someone else will be mayor.

At a cost of $15,865, a sturdy 12-ft-high fence was built on the grounds of the Staton Correction Center in Alabama. The barrier was meant to prevent escapes by inmates working at the prison cannery. Cost projections forced a cancellation of the cannery construction, but not of the fence. It now protects a large area of barren ground.

The Dallas-Fort Worth Regional Airport in Texas will soon lose the distinction of being the largest in the world. The honour will pass to Jidda, a Saudi Arabian city 45 mi west of the sacred city of Mecca. When completed in 1982, the airport complex will occupy about 106 sq km (41 sq mi), almost as large as the city of San Francisco. The most spectacular feature will not be the royal pavilion, or the 200-bed hospital, or the hotel, or the seven mosques, but an immense passenger terminal that will accommodate up to three million Muslims during the annual month of pilgrimage to Mecca. By the time the project is completed, the total cost will approach $7 billion.

When Japanese sports fans first saw "The Great Wall of China," they couldn't believe their eyes. The Tokyo Tower was certainly higher and the Imperial Palace was definitely sturdier, but neither could dribble a basketball. China's "Great Wall" could. When he took the court against the Japanese All-Stars, Mu T'ieh-chu, who stands nearly 8 ft tall and weighs more than 300 lb, made Japan's 6-ft 7-in centre look like a puppet. Though Mu's ball handling would never be the envy of the Harlem Globetrotters, he was remarkably accurate with blind passes to his fast-breaking teammates and was deadly at the foul line. More important, his 21 first-half points helped clinch China's national team's 88–84 victory in the first of seven scheduled games.

Tom Horsley of San Jose, Calif., sued Alyn Chesslet in San Francisco Small Claims Court because she failed to make "a good faith effort" to keep a dinner and theatre date. The judge, dismissing Horsley's $38 claim on the grounds that a date does not qualify as a legal contract, noted wistfully that "vain hopes are often like the dreams of those who wake."

Lawrence V. Skloss wanted to prove that Texans are not just "a bunch of cowboys and Indians." To show that some Texans have class, he took his wife to dinner at La Tour Restaurant in Austin. The eight-course dinner, which began with champagne and caviar, included dinner wines and such exotic items as *bouquetière des légumes, escalopes de veau Escoffier, asperges à la Choron,* and *champignons aux fines herbes.*

53

Divested of its French terminology, the dinner consisted of cauliflower, artichokes, carrots, mushrooms, asparagus, potatoes, and veal scallops. That's language every Texas cowboy can understand. But what they may not understand is why the meal should have cost a classy $2,783, exclusive of tax and tips.

Pacemakers lengthen lives, but they can also endanger them. That was the conclusion reached in an article published in the *British Medical Journal*. Dangerous explosions, radioactivity, and toxic gases were counted among the serious hazards faced by morticians when corpses containing pacemakers are cremated.

City officials in Charleston, S.C., passed an ordinance in 1975 requiring horse owners to diaper their animals. The legislation was greeted with such resounding horse laughs that it was repealed in nine days. But in February 1978 a new law was enacted requiring drivers of horse-drawn carriages to use "adequate devices" to protect the streets. Henry Waagner, an 80-year-old horse and carriage tourist guide, summed up his feelings when he said that the new law "shows what a dumb city we got."

It took August G. Muhrcke just 12 min 32 sec to win a race up 85 flights of stairs in New York City's Empire State Building. But it will certainly take a lot longer than that to explain to the Fire Department Pension Fund Board why he still qualifies for a tax-free disability pension of $11,822 per year. Muhrcke, now 37 years old, was awarded his pension in 1973 after suffering a back injury. It took a while, but he now knows that running for glory can hurt more than the feet.

If washing the dinner dishes is tedious, imagine what it would be like to wash a whole truckload. Such thoughts must have passed through the mind of an unidentified employee of the Gladieux Food Services when he was given such a chore. The company's contract with the Greater Pittsburgh International Airport includes washing the in-flight service tableware as well as preparing the food. Investigators from the Allegheny County district attorney's office finally found the truckload of unwashed dishes and flatware abandoned several miles away in Mount Olivet Cemetery. After firing the employee, the manager of the food service is said to have considered the incident a dead issue.

When U.S. Sen. Jesse Helms of North Carolina suggested a one-minute Senate recess to honour the tribulations of taxpayers, Senate majority leader Robert C. Byrd compromised by ordering one minute of silence "in behalf of nothing."

A weekly shower and a daily 15-minute jog on a treadmill may well increase fertility. The bath seems to induce longer sleep and to produce signs of greater contentment. Those were some of the tentative conclusions reached by scientists who, in an effort to provide Americans with more bacon, ham, and pork chops, were studying the effect of good clean living on pregnant sows in Georgia.

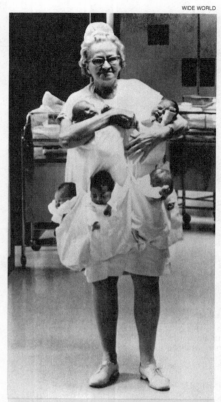

Nurse Vera Leonard, a 30-year veteran at Wesley Long Community Hospital in Greensboro, N.C., was worried about the tiny infants under her care. She wondered how, in an emergency, 30 helpless babies could be carried quickly to safety down five flights of stairs. Her simple but ingenious homemade solution was a smock with six oversized pouches, each large enough to hold a tiny baby wrapped in a blanket. Leonard is satisfied that, if the need ever arises, she and four assistants can evacuate the entire nursery in a matter of minutes.

Insurance salesman Michael Laurin forgot his briefcase during a visit to the Royal Bank of Canada in Guelph, Ont. When he returned to claim it, bank officials reported it was in police custody. In a sense it was. The bomb squad had carried it off to the city dump, then blew off the locks by remote control. Laurin, gazing in disbelief at his disemboweled pocket calculator and mangled briefcase, was only half listening when policemen earnestly explained how logical it was to assume that explosives had been wired to the locks.

Eleanor Grzegorczy of Bay City, Mich., fed apple peelings to her chickens, then realized she had either lost or misplaced her rings. Some time later her daughter-in-law reportedly found the rings inside a chicken egg. Skeptics say such an occurrence is inconceivable.

A special fund set up by the U.S. government handles money sent in by people who want to unburden their consciences. Some letters are signed, others are not. A few warn the office staff not to put the money into their own pockets. A dime found on the street was turned in because the rightful owner was unknown and the coin had

been "minted against the Treasury of the U.S.A." One resident of Tennessee sent a signed check with a note that read: "This $19,000 check is the money I have cheated the government out of over the 23 years I have been in business." Then he added: "The Holy Spirit of God revealed this amount to me."

Titania's Palace, a fully furnished 16-room house built for Sir Neville Wilkinson in 1922, was auctioned off in London for $256,500. That was more than four times the price paid when the palace was last sold in 1967. Everything considered, the price was rather extraordinary because the buyer knew he would never sleep in the bedroom, sit on the living room sofa, or cook a meal in the kitchen. All because Titania's Palace is a dollhouse.

A district court judge in Minneapolis, Minn., refused Michael Herbert Dengler's request to have his name legally changed to the number 1069. Dengler told an interviewer that one potential employer, who refused to hire him as a number, remarked: "You come in here with a name. We'll give you a number."

It cost Minneapolis taxpayers an estimated $3,000 for the first known trial involving raticide. The victim was a white rat that had been shot in an alley by a BB-gun. The boy defendant claimed the rat was a neighbourhood nuisance. The parents of the owner claimed the rat was a pet worth $300 and charged willful destruction of personal property. The police claimed the trial was stupid. Though X-rays introduced as evidence indicated that the rat's spinal cord had been severed, the case was dismissed because the prosecution failed to prove its fundamental premise that the rat was a pet.

Debra Giles filed a complaint with the Colorado Civil Rights Commission after her application for an apartment in Golden, Colo., was rejected. Lawyers for the Golden Ridge Apartments explained that Giles was an insurance risk because she was only 3-ft 7-in tall. A spokesman for the apartment's insurance company quickly demolished that argument by pointing out that little children live in the building and no one considers them insurance risks.

The huge mass of snow that fell on North America and Europe during the winter of 1977–78 produced both expected and unexpected results. Roofs collapsed, trains stopped dead in their tracks, and 300 land mines exploded along the Berlin Wall from the weight of the snow.

Before Muggs arrived, members of Chicago's 12th Fire Battalion lost radios, television sets, clothes, and other items when they were out fighting fires. During his 13 years on duty, the German shepherd bit 72 would-be burglars. When he died in April, Muggs was buried near the firehouse, given a tombstone, and inducted into the station's Hall of Flame.

Bob Peters of Palo Alto, Calif., signed a 70-day "motherhood contract" with his wife without fully realizing what he was getting into. As family chef, economist, psychologist, disciplinarian, recreational director, and a host of other things, Bob stayed home to take care of the house and the four children (ages 4 to 16) while his wife Pat worked as a school secretary. Although he managed to take care of such essentials as shopping for food, cooking, and washing the clothes, he was aware of many failings when he fell exhausted into bed at night. And, it should be noted, he wasted no daylight hours sobbing over soap operas or chatting with neighbours. Bob, by the way, is no 90-lb weakling. He served with the Marine Corps and was an All America defensive end on Stanford University's football team. He might have fared better at home had he been a running back.

The World Cup soccer finals in Buenos Aires, Arg., evoked intense emotions all over the world. When West Germany lost to Austria 2–3, a Berliner leaped from a second-story window because he didn't want to go on living. And in Frankfurt, a distraught nun throttled a man who expressed delight over Austria's victory.

Just as medieval weapons gave way to firearms, and horses gave way to automobiles, so too has the slide rule given way to pocket calculators. Keuffel & Esser Co., which sold some 20,000 precision slide rules each month during the 1950s, finally bowed to changing times and donated its engraving machines to the Smithsonian Institution in Washington, D.C. Still, not everyone was entirely happy with such progress. One man noted that you can see

Christopher Duncan, a 14-year-old from Honolulu, carried along his skateboard when he set out for China with his parents. His "bumpy experience" atop the Great Wall of China did not awaken the dead buried beneath the dirt, bricks, and masonry, but it was probably a historical first for the very historic landmark.

and understand how a slide rule works—but with "electronic gimcrackery" all the "black magic" takes place inside a small plastic box.

Wealthy widow Louise Vanderbilt, who resides in a stately mansion in Providence, R.I., became an overnight advocate of rent controls when told that the cost of her apartment would be increased from $950 to $2,950 per month. The landlord added to her fury by serving notice that after four annual 8% increases, the monthly rent would be $4,013. Vanderbilt thereupon announced that she would petition the city council to enact rent control legislation.

After 21 years as a magistrate, Vera Bray of Bootle, England, resigned in protest after Mark Phillips, husband of Princess Anne, was fined only £15 ($28.50) for his second speeding violation in little more than a year. Bray complained that there is but one law applicable to rich and poor alike, but she would have fined him at least £100.

John and Natalie Weimar always wanted to visit Europe, so once they set out they were determined to make the most of it. During their six-month 1976 journey, they stayed in the best hotels and ate in the finest restaurants. Afterward, in an interview in San Diego, Calif., Natalie estimated the junket cost about $80,000. The total cost was actually a great deal more to them because the Weimars financed the trip with 60 phony credit cards and will spend the next five years in a federal prison.

Finland's Youth Board ordered Donald Duck comics removed from children's libraries. Among other things, the board objected to naked ducks and Donald's common-law marriage.

Lorraine Joswick of Royal Oak, Mich., was beside herself with joy when the lottery ticket she bought turned out to be a $5,000 instant winner. She, her husband, and two grown children then spent the next 40 days trying to discover where the ticket, in the midst of the excitement, had been placed for safekeeping. Moldings and paneling were ripped from the walls and everything movable was turned upside down or inside out until the interior of the house looked as though it had been hit by a tornado. Joswick remembered slipping the ticket under a rug before going to bed, then, in the middle of the night, transferring it to a safer place. She was certain she didn't enter her daughter's bedroom that night, but that is where the ticket was finally found, stuck to the back of a mirror.

Tom Gaskins finally had to admit that business wasn't as good as he anticipated. After trying for nearly ten years to sell snowmobiles in sunny Florida, he had just five sales to his credit. Gaskins was convinced that snowmobiles could be marketed in Florida as an ideal means of transportation across swampy terrain. But there was one drawback. They sink.

All resident foreigners and citizens of Brazil are required by law to deposit the equivalent of about $1,100 with the government before leaving the country. Authori-

ties saw no reason to grant an exemption to Mauro Biscione who was born in Brazil. But Mauro's mother took the matter to the president of the central bank and persuaded him to waive the tax. She explained that she was an Argentine citizen traveling to Toronto to meet her husband and that Mauro was born in Brazil only because the plane made an emergency landing when it became apparent she was about to give birth.

"The objectivities did not specify to the quantifiable of the success of the proposed program." Such sentences as this appeared in a document issued by the U.S. Department of Health, Education, and Welfare. Rep. Robert W. Daniel sarcastically suggested that the unidentified author enroll in the remedial reading program that he was being paid $100 per day to evaluate.

Gaston Ayotte, Jr., president of the city council in Woonsocket, R.I., listened sympathetically to a recommendation from the director of public works, then supported a council vote that transformed "utility men" into "utility persons." With rigorous logic it was also noted that "utility persons" build "personholes" not "manholes." Apparently no council member was man enough to point out that "personholes" was not much of an improvement since it contains the element "son." In any case, utility persons are here to stay, but personholes have been laughed out of existence.

Thirty brand-new cars were test driven in Providence, R.I., by four children ranging in age from 7 to 13. By the time a security guard at the Allens Avenue Shipyard reacted to the sound of crashing metal, the cars had suffered damage estimated at $100,000.

The University of Washington in Seattle used a $25,000 National Science Foundation grant to study human reactions to the unexpected. An experimental group was shown a picture of an octopus in a barnyard. The project director maintained that learning about human reactions to the unusual can help in creating advertisements and aircraft instruments.

San Marino, with an estimated population of 20,700 people, takes pride in being one of the world's smallest republics. But it has equal right to be proud of its voters. During May a group of San Marino citizens flew 4,000 mi from the U.S. to the enclave republic on the east coast of Italy to cast ballots. The Sanmarinese reached their destination in two buses a little after eight o'clock in the evening, only to be informed by officials that the polls had just been officially closed.

Amarillo, Texas, is the home of millionaire Stanley God Bless America Marsh 3—the 3 written, he will tell you, without Roman numerals. To give outward expression to his love of art, he commissioned a monument to the United States. Called "The Great American Dream," it consists of ten Cadillacs half-buried, nose first, in the ground on the outskirts of Amarillo. Stanley's brother apparently loves art too. One Christmas he gave Stanley a red Volkswagen, which he half-buried, nose first, in the front lawn.

DISASTERS OF 1978

The loss of life and property from disasters in 1978 included the following:

AVIATION

January 1, Arabian Sea. An Air India Boeing 747 jumbo jet exploded in midair, cracked in two, and plunged into the Arabian Sea shortly after taking off from Bombay; 213 lives were lost in India's worst air disaster. Three days before the crash the International Proutist Organization, the political arm of a Hindu sect known as Ananda Marga, threatened to blow up Indian airliners.

February 10, Artigas, Uruguay. A DC-3 twin-engine Air Force transport plane, returning to the airport at Artigas because of engine trouble, exploded and burst into flames some 350 yd short of the runway; all 31 persons aboard were killed.

February 11, Cranbrook, B.C. A Pacific Western Airlines Boeing 737 crashed and exploded while dodging a snowblower that blocked its landing path; the 7 survivors of the crash that claimed 41 lives were seated in the tail section, which dropped off the second time the airplane touched down on the runway.

February 24, Guatemala. A twin-engine Piper Comanche airplane carrying 14 Seventh-day Adventist missionaries crashed in a hospital garden when it attempted to make an emergency landing at the airport; six pedestrians and two persons traveling in automobiles near the site of the crash suffered minor burns and all aboard the plane were killed.

March 1, Near Kano, Nigeria. A Nigerian Airways F-28 passenger airplane traveling from Sokoto to Kano collided in midair with a Nigerian Air Force plane conducting a training flight; 18 persons were killed including all 16 civilians on the passenger airplane and 2 crewmen on the military plane.

March 3, Near Caracas, Venezuela. A twin-engine 748 Hawker-Siddeley passenger airplane en route to Cumana crashed into the Caribbean Sea moments after takeoff; 47 persons were killed.

March 16, Near Sofia, Bulg. A Tupelov-134 Bulgarian airliner en route to Warsaw exploded and plunged to the ground 35 mi northeast of the capital shortly after takeoff; all 73 persons aboard were killed.

March 25, Near Rangoon, Burma. A Burmese airliner headed for Mandalay exploded shortly after takeoff; all 48 persons aboard were killed.

April 23, Near Rushville, Ind. A chartered twin-engine Piper Navajo Chieftain, carrying eight officials of the U.S. Auto Club to Indianapolis to begin preparations for the annual Indy 500 race, crashed in a cornfield and exploded during heavy thunderstorms.

A Pacific Southwest Airlines Boeing 727 burst in flames after it collided with a light plane and plunged to the ground in San Diego, California, on September 25. All aboard both planes and several people on the ground were killed.

UPI COMPIX

There was no chance of survival for the nine victims aboard the airplane, which left a crater eight feet deep in the farmland.

June 23, Near St. John's, Newfoundland. A twin-engine chartered Beechcraft 80 crashed shortly after takeoff from St. John's Airport; ten persons were killed including eight members of the Historic Sites and Monuments Board of Canada and two crew members.

June 26, Off the coast of Norway. A Sikorsky helicopter en route to the Stasfjord oil rig in the North Sea crashed 100 mi northwest of Bergen; 13 persons were killed and 5 others of the 18 aboard were missing and believed dead.

August 30, North Las Vegas, Nev. A twin-engine Piper Navajo airplane carrying ten persons crashed moments after takeoff from the North Las Vegas Air Terminal; there were no survivors.

Early September, Near Mexico City, Mexico. A twin-engine chartered airplane carrying 23 passengers crashed and exploded in a mountainous region on the outskirts of Mexico City; three survivors of the crash were badly burned.

September 2, Vancouver, B.C. A twin-engine Otter airplane, making its final approach before landing, crashed into the yacht basin of the Royal Vancouver Yacht Club; a caretaker for the club rescued the 2 survivors among the 13 passengers aboard.

September 3, Near Kariba, Rhodesia. An Air Rhodesia Viscount aircraft was shot down by guerrillas of the Patriotic Front who claimed they thought the airplane carried military personnel; 38 passengers were killed when the plane crashed 35 mi from the Kariba Airport; later, 10 of the 18 survivors were massacred by guerrillas.

September 14, Near Manila, Phil. A Philippine presidential airplane trying to land during a torrential rain smashed through trees and houses and exploded in a fish pond one mile short of the runway; 9 villagers on the ground and 15 of the 24 aboard the plane were killed; no members of the presidential family were aboard the plane.

September 25, San Diego, Calif. A Pacific Southwest Airlines Boeing 727 carrying 135 persons and a private airplane piloted by a student collided in midair and crashed into a San Diego residential area; in addition to the 137 casualties aboard the two aircraft, at least 10 persons were killed on the ground in the worst aviation disaster in the history of the U.S.

October 4, Kuopio, Fin. A DC-3 turboprop Finnish Army airplane carrying 15 persons caught fire, exploded, and crashed into a lake moments after takeoff from Kuopio Airport in central Finland; the disaster claimed the lives of all aboard including three members of Parliament.

October 6, Near Santiago, Chile. A U.S. Navy C-118 airplane crashed into a hill during heavy fog and burst into flames; all 18 persons aboard were killed.

November 15, Colombo, Sri Lanka. A chartered DC-8 Icelandic Airlines jet carrying Indonesian Muslims home from a pilgrimage to Mecca, Saudi Arabia, slammed through rubber and coconut plantations before crashing some four miles short of the airport during a thunderstorm; 79 persons survived the crash but at least 183 others were known dead.

November 19, Leh, India. An Indian Air Force AN-12 transport plane crashed while attempting to land on a mountain airfield in the northern state of Kashmir; 78 persons were killed including all 77 persons aboard the aircraft and one person on the ground.

December 23, Tyrrhenian Sea. A DC-9 Alitalia jet en route from Rome to Palermo, Italy, ditched in the sea and sank a few seconds after it struck the water; 103 of the 129 persons aboard were missing and believed drowned.

December 28, Portland, Ore. A United Airlines DC-8 airplane carrying 185 persons evidently lost power after circling the airport for some 45 minutes because of faulty landing gear and crash-landed in a residential area. Fortunately the two homes the plane plowed through were vacant, but 10 persons on flight 173 from New York City were killed and 18 others were seriously injured.

FIRES AND EXPLOSIONS

January 3, Manila, Phil. A fire that broke out in a Chinese Buddhist temple claimed the lives of 15 persons; it was the city's third major fire in two months.

January 28, Kansas City, Mo. A fire swept through the historic Coates House hotel, where three U.S. presidents had registered as guests after its opening in 1867; 16 persons were killed, some of whom jumped several stories to their death.

February 15, Noyelles-Godault, France. A fire that gutted a house north of Paris was responsible for the deaths of six children and three adults.

February 27, Near Bangkok, Thailand. A boiler explosion at a sawmill and plywood factory claimed the lives of 21 persons and injured at least 40 others.

March 14, Villa Devoto, Arg. A fire started by rioting inmates at Villa Devoto Prison, 10 mi north of Buenos Aires, burned to death or asphyxiated at least 55 persons and injured some 70 others when flames spread rapidly through the cellblock.

May 12, Ankara, Turkey. An engulfing fire that started in a leather worker's shop in a six-story office and shopping complex reduced the centre to a charred shell and killed 42 persons, some of whom jumped to their death.

June 10, Boras, Sweden. A fire that swept through a five-story hotel claimed the lives of 20 teenagers celebrating their graduation from high school and injured 55 others.

June 28, Bolivia, near the Argentine border. Gas from a ruptured pipeline exploded into flames when it came in contact with open fires in private homes; ten persons were killed and six others were seriously injured.

June 28, Damietta, Egypt. A five-year-old mortar shell exploded after it was picked up by a group of military students returning from a training course; at least 20 lost their lives and 20 others were injured.

July 5, Near Taunton, England. A fire that started in the overnight sleeper of a passenger train traveling from Penzance to London killed 11 passengers who were sleeping when the blaze broke out and injured more than 30 others.

July 9, Manila, Phil. A fast-burning fire swept through a crowded downtown theatre; 16 persons were killed and 70 others were injured.

July 11, Near Tarragona, Spain. A tanker truck carrying about 1,500 cu ft of propylene overturned on a bend in the road, rolled over a cement wall, and exploded in a coastal campsite; hundreds of people were engulfed in the flames, about 200 were killed, and over 100 were severely burned.

August 19, Abadan, Iran. A raging fire that engulfed a movie theatre in western Iran claimed the lives of 430 persons who stampeded to bolted exit doors; authorities suspected that Muslim extremists opposed to the shah's modernization plans poured gasoline on the floors, locked the doors, and torched the theatre.

October 10, Caracas, Venezuela. A drunken national guardsman doused a downtown bar with gasoline and set a match to it after quarreling with two of the saloon's patrons; 22 persons lost their lives and 6 others were injured because the emergency exit was blocked by boxes.

October 12, Singapore. A powerful explosion aboard a Greek oil tanker docked for repairs at a Singapore shipyard stunned workers who had climbed aboard after lunch break; at least 57 persons were killed and 86 others were seriously burned.

November 2, Near Villahermosa, Mexico. A fiery explosion resulted when a natural gas pipeline ruptured; the blast, which ripped through several small restaurants and taco stands in the area, killed at least 52 persons.

November 5, Des Moines, Iowa. An early morning explosion followed by a blazing fire gutted a department store in a Des Moines shopping mall; at least ten persons lost their lives in the fiery blast.

November 5, Honesdale, Pa. A fire in the Allen Motor Inn reduced the three-story landmark building to rubble; 11 persons lost their lives in the flames.

November 26, Greece, N.Y. A blazing fire that started in a basement stairwell virtually destroyed a 15-year-old Holiday Inn hotel; at least 25 persons were injured, 6 seriously, and 10 others died after being trapped in rooms or hallways.

December 7, Newark, N.J. An early morning fire swept through a three-story tenement and reduced the building to rubble; 11 persons, including 7 children, were killed in the blaze.

December 9, Ellisville, Miss. An early morning dormitory fire at the Ellisville State School for the mentally retarded claimed the lives of 15 women patients who were overcome by heat and smoke.

MARINE

January 21, Off the southwest coast of Japan. A Singapore-registered freighter sank off the southwest coast of Japan; three Japanese navy vessels rescued 12 crewmen but reported 10 dead and 3 other sailors missing.

February 17, Off the east coast of Korea. A freighter and two fishing boats sank off the east coast of Korea, and seven other fishing boats overturned or went aground when snowstorms created stormy seas; a total of 54 persons were believed drowned.

March 22, Zambezi River, Mozambique. A boat capsized on the flooded Zambezi River; 20 persons were killed.

April 4, Bay of Bengal. A fleet of 100 cargo boats sank in the Bay of Bengal during a violent storm; authorities believed that as many as 1,000 people may have drowned.

April 8, Bay of Bengal. A boat capsized 300 mi northwest of Rangoon, Burma; at least half of the 200 passengers were missing and presumed dead.

April 21, Northeast of Dacca, Bangladesh. An overloaded launch capsized in the Ghorautra River some 200 mi northeast of Dacca; at least 100 of the 600 persons aboard drowned.

May 24, Jamuna River, Bangladesh. A passenger launch capsized during a storm; 30 of the 200 persons aboard drowned.

June 17, Lake Pomona, Kansas. The two-tiered paddlewheel steamboat "Whippoorwill" had just started its dinner/show excursion when a tornado struck, flipped over the showboat, and hurled most of the 46 passengers and 13 crew members overboard; 15 passengers were killed and 14 others were injured, 2 seriously.

June 11, Lake Timiskaming, Ontario. A canoe excursion on Lake Timiskaming was hit by violent thunderstorms accompanied by high winds and four-foot waves; 13 of the 31 persons on the trip, including one teacher and 12 students of St. John's School, Claremont, Ont., drowned when their canoes capsized.

Mid-July, Atlantic Ocean. A boat carrying Haitian refugees from The Bahamas to Florida capsized during a storm; at least ten persons drowned and three others were missing.

July 20, Near Taejon, South Korea. A small motorboat capsized while carrying 17 children to school; 3 boys and the skipper of the vessel swam to safety but 14 others were feared drowned.

October 4, Mediterranean Sea. The "Colo," a 1,598-ton Algerian ship, sank after colliding with the 8,390-ton Italian "Expresso Marilyn"; 26 of the 30 crewmen aboard the "Colo" were missing and believed drowned.

Mid-October, Northern India. A leaky boat capsized in the Hindon River when its passengers panicked after realizing the craft was taking on water; 26 persons were drowned.

October 20, Chesapeake Bay. The 125-ft Coast Guard cutter "Cuyahoga" sank in 70 ft of water minutes after it collided with "Santa Cruz II," a 521-ft Argentine coal freighter. The Coast Guard was unable to rescue 11 of the 29 crew members of the "Cuyahoga."

November 22, Off the coast of Malaysia. A boat packed with Vietnamese refugees sank in the Kuala Trengganu estuary after it was forced back to sea by Malaysian police and villagers; 200 persons were reportedly drowned.

December 2, South China Sea. A boat filled with Vietnamese refugees sank off the coast of Malaysia after having been denied permission to land in that country; at least 143 persons were believed dead.

December 20, Atlantic Ocean. The search for the "München," a 37,000-ton West German freighter, was abandoned after rescue teams found several empty life rafts and barges; the 28 persons aboard the vessel were presumed dead.

December 21, Off Fuerteventura, Canary Islands. A ferry carrying 30 passengers and 2 crewmen sank in heavy seas after it broke apart on rocks; 12 persons were missing and believed dead.

December 24, Philippines. A crowded boat carrying holiday travelers reportedly capsized; 15 persons were killed and one other was missing.

December 28, Off the coast of Portugal. The 315-ft Greek freighter "Tenorga" sank near the entrance to the port of Leixões during a violent storm; 4 persons were known dead and 17 others were missing.

December 31, Off the coast of northwestern Spain. When the Greek supertanker "Andros Patria" cracked in heavy seas and gale force winds, 29 of the 32 persons aboard took to the lifeboats and drowned in rough waters; three men who remained on board were rescued by a helicopter.

On July 11 a tanker truck carrying propylene, a highly flammable industrial liquid gas, exploded in a coastal campsite near Tarragona, Spain. Nearly 200 persons were killed and hundreds were injured.

MINING

February 16, Tatabanya, Hung. A coal mine explosion in Tatabanya, the country's lignite mining centre, killed 26 miners and injured 19 others.

April 3, Near Aleksinac, Yugos. A gas explosion in a coal mine killed 12 persons and injured 26 others.

November 10, Near Changsong, South Korea. Ten coal miners were killed when the pit cage in which they were riding experienced a mechanical failure and crashed down a mine shaft near the eastern town of Changsong.

November 21, Doncaster, England. The last two cars of a four-car train carrying some 70 miners to the surface of a coal pit derailed half a mile underground; 19 men were injured and 7 were killed in the first major British mining disaster since 1973.

MISCELLANEOUS

January–February, U.S. The A-Victoria and A-Texas influenza strains complicated by pneumonia were responsible for over 6,000 deaths in 121 major cities polled across the nation.

January–June, Bombay, India. Water contaminated by sewage accounted for 40,000 cases of jaundice; at least 350 persons succumbed in the first six months of the year.

January 19, Central India. A section of a bridge under construction collapsed and killed at least 70 workers.

March, Simeulue, Indon. An outbreak of cholera claimed the lives of 82 of the 411 persons living on the island of Simeulue.

Late March, Maldives. In the southern islands of the Maldives, 35 persons succumbed to gastroenteritis.

April, Tamil Nadu State, India. Encephalitis affected 98 villages in the southern Indian state of Tamil Nadu; 45 persons died in a five-month period.

April, Maldives. A cholera epidemic spread over 90 islands in the Maldives, affected nearly 5% of the population, and brought fishing and tourism to a standstill; health authorities closed all schools and reported 7,200 cases of cholera and over 200 deaths.

April, Thailand. An outbreak of cholera claimed the lives of 100 persons in Thailand; 2,800 cases of the disease were reported.

April 27, Willow Island, W.Va. When the scaffolding inside a power plant cooling tower collapsed, 51 workers, 11 of them closely related, fell some 170 ft to their death. A team of Occupational Safety and Health Administration investigators found that the concrete poured the previous day was not tested for strength, that necessary bolts to anchor the scaffolding were missing, and that beam sections supporting the concrete-lifting system were not anchored to hold the loads.

A scaffolding inside a power plant cooling tower (foreground) collapsed in Willow Island, West Virginia, in April. Fifty-one workers plunged to their deaths.

UPI COMPIX

April 28, Beirut, Lebanon. A four-story building, housing refugees from Israel's invasion of southern Lebanon, collapsed and killed at least 13 persons; at least 40 were injured, many seriously.

May, India. A scorching heat wave that gripped the plains of India and sent temperatures skyrocketing to an average of 113°F (45°C) claimed the lives of at least 150 people in two weeks.

May, Eastern Samar, Phil. A measles epidemic on Samar, the third largest island of the Philippines, claimed the lives of 17 children.

May 5, Jessore, Bangladesh. A banyan tree, uprooted during a storm, crashed into a marketplace; 30 persons were killed and 100 others were injured.

Mid-May, Nicaragua. Lethal insecticides sprayed during the cotton-growing season killed at least 25 persons and injured some 800 others who failed to take necessary precautions while using the spray.

June, Burundi. An outbreak of cholera claimed the lives of at least 68 persons in Burundi and border villages of Zaire.

June 9–13, Southwestern Iran. A heat wave, the worst in 27 years, claimed the lives of at least ten persons in southwestern Iran.

July, Dallas, Texas. A three-week heat wave with temperatures exceeding 100°F (38°C), compounded by a six-week drought, left at least 21 persons dead from heat stroke; many of the victims were elderly persons who did not have air-conditioned homes.

July 30, Teheran, Iran. The roof and second story of a 60-year-old hospital in need of repair collapsed and buried 28 patients on the first floor; 11 persons were killed and 17 others were injured.

September, Zaire, Rwanda, Burundi. A cholera epidemic affected some 12,000 persons and killed at least 350 others, according to Belgian government officials who sent emergency medical teams into the afflicted African countries.

October, India. A brain-attacking virus, believed to be a type of encephalitis, afflicted between 1,000 and 2,000 persons, mainly in the state of Uttar Pradesh; at least 480 persons succumbed in one month.

October, India. Cholera affected thousands of people and claimed the lives of more than 200 others in flood-ravaged India.

November, Zambia. An outbreak of cholera, reported by the country's health minister, killed 23 persons.

NATURAL

January 12, United Kingdom. A fierce rainstorm accompanied by high tides and 75-mph winds lashed Britain's east coast and damaged hundreds of homes in the worst flooding since 1953; three ships carrying 17 crewmen were lost, 5 persons were killed in traffic accidents, and 2 others were found dead.

January 13, Southeastern Colombia. Floods claimed the lives of 20 persons in southeastern Colombia.

January 13–17, Southeastern Brazil. Floodwaters in the cities of Rio de Janeiro, São Paulo, and Paraíba swept away shantytowns; thousands were left homeless and 26 persons died.

January 14, Japan. A series of earthquakes, centred near the volcanic island of Ō-shima and measuring up to 7 on the Richter scale, damaged homes, cut rail and road links, injured 98 persons, and killed 21 others. After a dam burst, 80,000 cu m of poisonous sludge poured into rivers.

January 25–26, Midwestern U.S. A killer blizzard, accompanied by wind gusts of up to 100 mph and temperatures as low as −50° F (−45° C), ravaged the Midwestern states of Ohio, Michigan, Wisconsin, Indiana, Illinois, and Kentucky, dropped some 31 in of snow, stranded 8,000 motorists, closed airports and factories, and caused more than 100 deaths. Storm damage was estimated in the hundreds of millions of dollars.

January 26–30, Indonesia. Severe flooding in East Java seriously damaged houses and crops; 7,000 people were evacuated and 41 others were killed.

January 28–30, Transvaal Province, South Africa. Three-day floods claimed the lives of 26 persons.

February 2–3, The Alps. In a series of avalanches triggered by strong winds that swept through the Alps, at least 21 persons lost their lives in France, Austria, and Italy.

February 5–7, Northeastern U.S. A paralyzing blizzard, packing winds of up to 110 mph and accompanied by 18-ft tides near the coast, dropped 50 in of snow in Rhode Island and eastern Massachusetts. The severe storm was blamed for at least 60 deaths, some from drowning, others from heart attacks, and still others from carbon monoxide that asphyxiated motorists trapped in cars on impassable highways.

February 10, Southern California. Torrential rains followed by severe flooding destroyed Hidden Springs, a mountain canyon resort in the Angeles National Forest, when a 20-ft wall of water crashed down the canyon; the ports of Los Angeles and Long Beach were closed, zoo animals ran free when the rain battered and smashed cages, and 25 persons were missing and feared dead in the deluge.

March 5, Southern California and northern Mexico. A raging Pacific Coast storm caused massive flooding and a series of mudslides that claimed the lives of 5 persons in southern California and 20 others in northern Mexico; 20,000 people were left homeless.

March 12, Near Aigle, Switz. A thundering avalanche buried 20 skiers under an estimated 15–18 ft of snow; rescue squads found one survivor.

March 17, Delhi, India. A violent tornado roared through the northern outskirts of Delhi uprooting trees, smashing walls, and flipping over crowded buses; 700 persons were injured and 32 others lost their lives in the windstorm that lasted about two minutes.

March 27, Zambezi River, Mozambique. Flooding along the Zambezi River, the worst in a century, caused millions of dollars in property damage, left more than 200,000 people homeless, and killed at least 45 others.

April 16, Orissa State, India. A tornado that swept through Orissa State devastated 500 homes and damaged 1,200 others; over 1,000 persons were injured and nearly 500 were killed. Another tornado in West Bengal State was said to have killed 100 of 800 persons residing in one village.

May 15, Sri Lanka. Floods and landslides left several thousand people homeless and claimed the lives of ten others.

May 16, West Atjeh, North Sumatra, Indon. Massive flooding caused the evacuation of 8,000 persons from their homes; 21 others were killed.

May 18, Myoko Kogen Machi, Japan. A 3-mi river of thick brown mud, 10 ft deep in some places, flowed down a mountain stream, destroyed a dozen buildings in a ski resort, and claimed the lives of victims sleeping inside. When 500 troops and 300 firemen arrived at the scene to implement rescue operations, another avalanche of mud rushed down the mountain and swept 4 officials off their feet; 13 persons were killed including 3 officials.

May 18, Southern Thailand. Violent storms claimed 50 lives in southern Thailand.

June 12, Honshu, Japan. A severe earthquake measuring 7.5 on the Richter scale struck the main island of Honshu; hardest hit was the city of Sendai where power lines and buildings collapsed. In the strongest earthquake to hit Japan in 14 years, 350 persons were injured and 21 were killed.

Mid-June, South Korea. A week of torrential rainfall caused property damage totaling $400,000 and left 2,000 people homeless; 17 persons lost their lives and 10 others were missing.

Summer, India. Widespread flooding as the result of violent summer monsoon rains, the heaviest in memory, channeled a path of destruction throughout the country; an estimated $100 million in damages was assessed; the autumn crop of rice, India's principal grain, was virtually ruined; hundreds of thousands of people were left homeless, and nearly 900 others were believed dead.

June 20, Thessaloniki, Greece. An earthquake measuring 6.5 on the Richter scale claimed the lives of at least 47 persons; 500 apartment buildings and 800 homes were abandoned by residents who feared that the continuing aftershocks indicated another earthquake.

July 10, Afghanistan and Pakistan. Torrential rains followed by severe flooding near the Afghan-Pakistan border resulted in the collapse of hundreds of homes and at least 120 deaths in northwestern Pakistan and in Afghanistan.

July 26, India. Monsoon flooding in six Indian states claimed the lives of nearly 190 persons, 110 of whom drowned in Uttar Pradesh.

July 29–30, The Alps. Snowslides, caused by heat-wave temperatures, claimed the lives of 11 mountain climbers in the Swiss Alps.

August 1, Central Texas. Rain falling at nearly one inch per hour triggered a series of floods that left over 25 persons dead; the city of Albany, where a 20-ft wall of water descended upon the homes of 2,000 residents who spent the night on roofs, in trees, and on top of oil derricks, was hardest hit.

Mid-August, Pakistan. Heavy rains followed by intense flooding from the Hab River, some 30 mi northwest of Karachi, killed over 100 persons.

Mid-August, Northern Philippines. Heavy flooding followed by mudslides throughout northern Philippines left thousands homeless and 45 persons dead; 30 bus passengers were buried under a mudslide when they traveled by foot across mud after the driver refused to chance the mountainside crossing.

September 16, Tabas, Iran. The most powerful earthquake in the world in 1978 completely obliterated the city of Tabas in eastern Iran. The quake, measuring 7.7 on the Richter scale, claimed the lives of at least 25,000 people.

October 26, Philippines. Ferocious Typhoon Rita blasted the Philippines with 130-mph winds, swept some 10,000 homes away, and flooded the country's rice crop; nearly 200 persons lost their lives in the storm, and some 60 others were reported missing.

Early November, Southern India. Heavy monsoon rains triggered widespread flooding and landslides in Kerala State and Tamil Nadu; at least 144 persons were known dead.

November 23, Sri Lanka and southern India. A devastating cyclone that roared through Sri Lanka and the southern coast of India wrecked more than 500,000 buildings, flooded some 45 Indian villages, affected about one million people, and claimed at least 1,500 lives.

RAILROADS

February 24, Waverly, Tenn. A derailed railroad car loaded with liquid propane gas exploded while workers were preparing to transfer the gas to trucks; the blast leveled at least 14 buildings, destroyed two downtown blocks, injured dozens of persons, and claimed the lives of 15 others.

February 25, Saa Pereyra, Arg. A speeding express train carrying over 2,000 passengers to Buenos Aires struck a heavy truck when the driver failed to respond to flashing signals at the crossing; the derailment of all 11 cars resulted in over 120 injuries and nearly 50 deaths.

March 22, Libiri, Zaire. A train crash in eastern Zaire resulted in numerous injuries and 22 deaths.

April 16, Puebla, Mexico. A passenger train crashed into a bus carrying 37 persons from the nearby town of Tlaxcala; 10 passengers on the bus were killed and 16 others were injured.

April 17, Near Bologna, Italy. A southbound Venice to Rome luxury express train collided head on with a northbound Lecce to Milan local during a blinding rainstorm that triggered a mudslide across the tracks and steered the local into the path of the express train. At least 100 persons were injured and 43 were known dead, some of whom were found in the four coaches of the express that rolled 90 ft down an embankment after the impact.

Early May, Vasai, India. The Ahmadabad Express train slammed into a stationary suburban train some 30 mi from Bombay; over 100 persons were injured and 31 were killed.

December 21, Near Munoz, Spain. The locomotive of a train slammed into a school bus carrying over 90 children to a Christmas party and split the vehicle in two; 28 children and one adult were killed and another 63 children were seriously injured.

TRAFFIC

January 3, Sariaya, Phil. A bus traveling to Manila smashed into a parked truck about 50 mi east of the capital; 21 passengers were killed and 38 were injured.

February 15, Aguas Buenos, P.R. A school bus transporting students in rural areas toppled off a narrow road into a 500-ft ravine about 13 mi south of San Juan; of the estimated 60 children aboard the bus, 30 were injured and 11 were killed.

February 16, Tarma Province, Peru. A bus traveling in the Central Province of Tarma plunged over a precipice; 40 persons were killed and 25 others were injured, some seriously.

March 22, Near Birjand, Iran. A collision between a bus and a road tanker in eastern Iran injured 26 persons and claimed the lives of 28 others.

March 27, Near San Luis, Mexico. A head-on collision between two buses some 40 mi south of the border town of San Luis killed at least 30 of the 81 passengers; many of the victims burned to death because of a fire that broke out following the crash.

March 30, Near Teheran, Iran. In the second major Iranian traffic accident in a week, an oil truck, bus, and car collided west of Teheran on the Karaj–Qazvin road; 18 passengers were injured and another 26 were killed.

May 4, Southern Colombia. A tourist bus carrying university students on an excursion to Pasto, a city near the Ecuador border, tumbled over a precipice; 18 were injured and 11 were killed.

May 8, Near Gwalior, India. A bus transporting members of two wedding parties skidded off a bridge in central India and plunged into a river; 35 were injured and 31 others, including the 2 grooms and 9 children, were killed.

June 10, Near Chechaouene, Morocco. A bus plunged into a 500-ft ravine some 30 mi east of the Rif Mountains resort in northern Morocco; at least 23 died and 22 were injured.

July 16, Near Mexico City, Mexico. A truck carrying propane gas flipped over, exploded, and sent fiery gas over one-half mile of a four-lane highway; two trucks, two buses, and a car crashed into the wreckage; 11 persons lost their lives and some 200 others were severely burned.

July 17, Near Cairo, Egypt. An overcrowded bus plunged into the Nile River after colliding with a truck; 11 passengers and the driver escaped injury but 56 others, many of them soldiers, drowned.

July 23, Seoul, South Korea. A swerving city bus crashed through a bridge guardrail and plunged 60 ft into the Han River; 7 persons were seriously injured and 36 others were killed.

July 23, Near Mungling, Nepal. A bus carrying 38 passengers plummeted into the swollen Trusuli River; 25 persons were killed.

August 4, Lac d'Argent, Que. A bus returning from a theatrical performance careened off a roadway and plunged into a lake after its brakes failed; 40 mentally or physically handicapped passengers drowned when the vehicle sank in 60 ft of water.

August 12, Northern Uganda. A bus traveling between Arua and Moyo plunged into a river and killed at least 40 persons; many of the victims were children returning to their villages from school.

Mid-September, Maputo, Mozambique. A truck transporting dozens of farm workers to the town of Xai Xai in Gaza Province overturned and plunged into an irrigation canal; 65 workers were killed and 11 others were injured.

THE ROOTS OF INFLATION

by Paul A. Samuelson

Inflation continued to rage in 1978 throughout every region of the world. Indeed, inflation worsened in the United States to the point that Pres. Jimmy Carter late in the year reactivated guidelines for wage-price controls and gave priority to hard-money and tight-budget programs designed to cool off the economy.

The cost of living, as measured by the consumers' price index, had risen by 11% from 1973 to 1974. The reality of two-digit annual price inflation, interacting with the fivefold increase in the price of oil by the OPEC (Organization of Petroleum Exporting Countries) cartel, brought on the worldwide 1974 recession. At a heavy cost in terms of unemployment, lost output, and depressed profits, U.S. price inflation was brought down in 1975–77 to a base level of about 6%.

But in 1978, the fourth year of vigorous economic expansion, food prices began to accelerate at an ominous rate. And the prices Americans pay for services—the cost of medical care, the premium for car insurance—continued their irreversible rise.

It is no wonder then that polls of public opinion report that people of all classes regard inflation as the number one economic problem. To be sure, the overall rate of U.S. unemployment continued to hover around 6%, a rate that would have been considered fairly high back in the decades of the 1950s and 1960s. Among nonwhite minorities, particularly young urban workers without skills, unemployment rates persist at very much higher levels, 25 and even 50%. Nonetheless, the U.S. had done better than the other leading nations in bringing down overall unemployment; from a peak rate of 9% in 1975 to the autumn 1978 rate of around 6% represented a rapid decline. Moreover, the expansion in total jobs was remarkably great, as more and more women chose to work for pay and as those born in the baby

Paul A. Samuelson, winner of the 1970 Nobel Prize for Economics, is professor of economics at the Massachusetts Institute of Technology. He has served on a number of governmental bodies, among them the Federal Reserve Board and the Council of Economic Advisers. His many writings include the best-selling textbook Economics (1948–76).

SALO—ROTHCO

"Who knows? There may be other economic systems out there many phases ahead of ours."

boom of the 1950s became of an age to seek jobs.

A tight labour market began to put upward pressure on wage rates. Help-wanted advertising rose as a barometer of skilled worker shortages. Corporations yielded to trade union negotiation for collective bargaining contracts, often granting increases in wage rates and pension benefits of 10% per annum over three-year contracts. Nonunion workers, facing increases in the cost of living of 8 to 10%, suffered a drop in their real wage earnings unless they could achieve commensurate hikes in pay. Unit labour costs inevitably rose, rising particularly in that the late 1970s have been years of disappointing productivity improvements. People these days want to enjoy some of the fruits of affluence in a more relaxed pace of labour. As in prosperous Sweden, absenteeism becomes common. Scientists, engineers, and experts in business management continue to improve technology know-how, but not at the extraordinary pace of the epoch just after World War II.

Fortunately, harvests of food and fibre have not been as disastrously bad in the late 1970s as in the earlier years of the decade. Still, Soviet and Chinese shortfalls in crop production continue to put pressure on staple prices. Successful lobbying by U.S. farmers has led to governmental programs that tend to reduce production whenever abundant supplies threaten to keep farm prices down.

Dollar Depreciation. Along with rising wages and raw material prices, recent U.S. inflation has been aggravated by the depreciation of the dollar. Since the autumn of 1977 the exchange rate for the dollar has fallen most relative to the Swiss franc, the Japanese yen, and the West German mark. The dollar has fallen less compared with currencies of other industrial countries, such as the French franc and the British pound sterling. The U.S. dollar has even risen relative to the Italian lira and the Canadian dollar. (*See also* Feature Article: *Another Day, A Different Dollar*.)

When we measure the average drop in the dollar exchange rate, giving weight to each of the countries according to how much we trade with them, the dollar has lost about an eighth of its value in the last five years. During that same period the Swiss franc has almost doubled on a trade-weighted basis, the mark has risen by about 40%, and the yen by about a third. Since there cannot be two different geographic prices for any staple good that can be cheaply shipped from one region to another, the rise in the dollar price of the mark and the yen must mean a greater rate of American inflation for staple goods than for similar staple goods in West Germany and Japan. No wonder then that the inflation rate has not been so high in those countries as in the U.S. And no wonder that the inflation rate has been higher in Italy and Canada than in the United States.

Fortunately, the extra U.S. inflation induced by depreciation of the dollar has been only a small fraction of the dollar's actual percentage depreciation. This shortfall is fortunate because it means that, to potential foreign importers, the costs of American goods have become much more competitive. As the U.S. is able to export more, the deficit in its balance of trade may at long last stop growing and begin to disappear. Reinforcing this favourable tendency for the dollar *eventually* to float upward rather than downward is the fact that West German and Japanese exports to the U.S. are beginning to run into strong competition from now-competitive American products. Detroit car manufacturers face smaller cost increases than do distributors who must import Toyotas and Volkswagens at prices sharply inflated by the appreciation of the yen and mark.

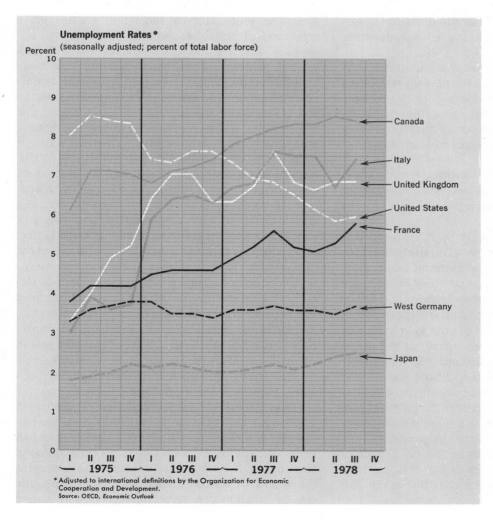

Unemployment Rates (seasonally adjusted; percent of total labor force)

* Adjusted to international definitions by the Organization for Economic Cooperation and Development.
Source: OECD, *Economic Outlook*

By late autumn of 1978, President Carter finally took action to help support the floating dollar. He arranged for a U.S. fund of some $30 billion to be used for dollar stabilization; countenanced higher interest rates in the U.S. and slower economic growth; even showed a willingness to run extra risks of an end-of-the-decade recession, if that was the price of fighting inflation and preventing further dollar depreciation.

Diagnostic Facts. Before choosing a prescription to cure a disease, the expert physician must first attempt to diagnose the nature of the disease. And to formulate a reasoned diagnosis, he must achieve an accurate description of all the symptoms displayed. One can summarize the factual symptoms of modern inflation preparatory to diagnosis and therapy as follows:

1. The worldwide recession of 1973–75 did achieve a general reduction of the two-digit price inflation of the frenzied boom years of the early 1970s. By the late 1970s the U.S. inflation rate compared favourably with most other countries, Japan and West Germany being notable exceptions.

2. As the final years of the decade came into view and as memory of the mid-decade recession began to fade, some new worsening of inflation has become apparent.

3. Virtually every industrialized country is now clearly showing symptoms of the new disease called "stagflation" (*i.e.*, the persistence of uncomfortably rising prices and wages *at the same time* that there seem to exist in the contemporary mixed economy uncomfortably high levels of unemployment and of unused plant capacity).

Popular Fallacies and Half-Truths. People know they hate inflation. Each age needs a scapegoat for real and fancied ills. Inflation is the scapegoat for the modern age.

Suppose your wage goes up by 7%. Suppose at the same time that the OPEC cartel is raising the price of oil, that crops are failing in Eastern Europe, Asia, and the Mississippi Valley, that Iowa farmers are gaining at the expense of urban earners, and finally that productivity growth is languishing in your affluent society. Then most or all of your gain in money earnings will be found to be illusory, as the prices you must pay also rise by around 7%. You blame inflation. But really you should blame the oil and food scarcity and the disappointing productivity trends. For, even if there had been no inflation, you would still have to experience the same disappointing growth in your real income. No wonder, then, that careful, objective economists, like G. L. Bach of the Stanford Graduate School of Business, are hard put to find any broad income class that is the particular victim of inflation.

What then are the primary genuine evils involved in present-day inflation? Here is a brief list.

1. Unexpected and unanticipatable changes in the rate of inflation redistribute incomes in a chaotic and destabilizing fashion. There is rarely anything fair about the process. When the inflation rate is high it is also likely to involve great variability and unpredictability, exacerbating class tensions and decreasing the efficiency of resource use.

2. Modern mixed economies are prone to rates of inflation that accelerate rather than stay constant. Democratic governments feel an imperative need to do something about accelerating inflation before it turns into chronic inflation, like the doubling of prices every decade in so many Latin-American countries, to say nothing of galloping inflations like those of the Confederacy in the American Civil War, the German hyperflation after World War I, and the Hungarian and Chinese destruction of their currencies after World War II. There is little exaggeration in saying that the principal cause of recessions in the Age After Keynes is this felt need of governments to fight inflation by deliberate policies that cool off the economy and slow down its rate of real growth.

3. The brute fact of stagflation creates grave dilemmas of policy. Authorities know how to undertake fiscal and monetary policies that will work against inflation. They know how to undertake those same policies in reverse so as to work against unemployment and stagnating real incomes. But in the presence of modern chronic stagflation, that which helps against inflation hurts unemployment; that which helps against unemployment worsens inflation. Disillusionment over the ability of Washington, Bonn, Stockholm, or Tokyo to "fine tune" the economy comes, not from the inability of analysts to forecast future economic conditions, not from inability to appraise the length and variety of time lags before programs have their intended effect on the future economy. The inability of a jury of the best economic experts to agree upon macroeconomic policies that will ensure reasonable price stability and satisfactory full employment comes from the basic tendency in every modern mixed economy for prices and wages to rise in an inflationary degree *even prior* to conditions of overall demand that will provide what democratic electorates deem to be adequate job opportunity and adequate attainment of the economy's potential for real growth.

Older Theories to Explain Inflation. Beginners in economics are often told: "Inflation results when too much money spending bids against too few economic goods." This touches on both demand and supply. If productivity improvements increase the supply of goods, other things being equal, the rate of inflation can be reduced. If people spend

"Please, folks, use the stairs—they're less crowded."

their money more rapidly or if the central bank prints billions of new dollar bills for release from helicopters, enhanced demand will bid up the prices of goods once all labour and capital resources have become fully employed and further increases in output are severely limited.

Under the relatively pure form of capitalism that obtained a century ago, before the welfare and stabilizing activities of government made ours a "mixed economy," the elementary propositions of the previous paragraph contained much useful truth. As John Maynard Keynes put it in his revolutionary scholarly work of 1936, *The General Theory of Employment, Interest and Money*, the primary task of government used to be to expand total dollar demand by just enough to create enough jobs for all qualified workers seeking employment.

Thus, in 1932, at the bottom of the Great Depression, there was poverty in the midst of potential plenty. Grass grew in the streets. People wanted work. Capitalists wanted to put their idle machines to work. Defying old-fashioned orthodoxy, government could usefully increase its spending and cut down on its taxing. It could aim deliberately for a budgetary deficit and a growing public debt. This way existing dollars would turn over more rapidly, and new dollars could be created to help finance the budget deficit at unchanged low interest rates. Total spending would come into being to produce a new supply of goods commensurate with the additional spending, and no significant price or wage inflation would have to take place.

What would happen, though, once full employment was reached and excess plant capacity was exhausted? Then further new spending, whether brought about by still larger budget deficits or by concomitant Federal Reserve expansion of the money supply, would bid up prices and wages. This economists would call "demand-pull inflation"—as enhanced spending demand pulls or bids up prices and wages of limited goods, labour supplies, and capital capacities. Old-fashioned inflation was simple for political economy to understand.

Stagflation in the Humane Welfare State. Simple demand-pull inflation, prior to the epoch of stagflation and of "cost-push inflation," was easy for governments to control. They needed only to curb the central bank printing of money and the government's overspending by balancing the budget and running a budgetary surplus. And by curbing the total stock of money and its rate of growth, government policy would confront people and business with interest rates that were high enough and with cash balances tight enough to bring the total of demand spending into balance with the full employment supply of goods.

But 1978 was not 1878, nor even 1928. Today everywhere there is the welfare state. Whereas it used to be a case of either work at whatever wage is offered or starve, now there is the humane state.

Unemployment insurance and public welfare payments help to provide a minimum of living standards even if you cannot find employment or will not accept a painfully low wage. Here then is the root cause why unemployed resources no longer put downward pressure on wages and prices: man's humanity to man.

Few would wish to turn the clock back to the inhumane society. In any case, it could not be done politically in any of the modern democracies—the United States, Canada, Japan, Scandinavia, Britain, West Germany, or elsewhere in the developed world. There is thus built into the very nature of the modern mixed economy a problem of *cost-push* inflation intertwined with that of old-fashioned *demand-pull* inflation.

What to do about this modern pathology? John Kenneth Galbraith, the exponent of the new industrial state, believes the only cure is to have an "incomes policy"—permanent governmental controls of prices and wage rates. Milton Friedman, high priest of laissez-faire capitalism, declares that there are no new problems of cost-push inflation. "Adhere strictly to a rule of a constant growth rate in the money supply at an annual rate equal to the slow growth rate of potential high-employment output," Friedman argues in effect, "and in the long run your society will succeed in avoiding price inflation."

Unfortunately a jury of economic experts cannot agree that Galbraith's permanent price-wage controls can be made to work effectively and efficiently in a democratic mixed society. Nor can the jury agree with Friedman's diagnosis that the mixed economies of the last part of the 20th century can be made to behave like the laissez-faire economies of Victorian capitalism.

A core of agreement is discernible among present-day economists. Most of them agree that money matters. Changes in the money supply tend in the longest run to produce changes in the general level of prices in the same direction and (other things being equal) in approximately the same degree. In the shorter run—a year or two ahead—increased money spending can mostly result in expanded production and employment so long as labour markets are slack and industrial equipment is not fully employed.

Those who have studied the several episodes of mandatory wage and price controls, experimented with in the post-World War II period by each of the mixed economies, have usually agreed on the following interpretation: controls work rather effectively in the very short run, for three or six or nine months. But increasingly they become ineffective, inefficient, and inequitable. Bureaucracies to enforce them must proliferate. Courts and tribunals

become jammed with litigation. Supplies of staple goods whose prices have been too rigidly frozen simply dry up. In desperation and impatience, voters, legislators, and Cabinets terminate the controls; and, once the lid on prices and wages is removed, much of what you thought you had gained from putting in such an incomes policy is lost as corporations hasten to raise their prices and workers insist upon achieving higher wage rates.

The Political Business Cycle. U.S. experience in the 1970s, and experience elsewhere, confirms the stagflation dilemma faced by the mixed economy. Nations perforce contrive stop-go policies. When the inflation part of stagflation is hurting the electorate most, governments step on the fiscal and monetary brakes to cool off the rate of price rise. The result is an outright recession or a growth recession (in which, although output does not actually fall, it grows more slowly than the increase in labour supply and productivity tend to make possible). When the costly stagnation cure for inflation is vexing the electorate, the government finds itself releasing the throttle of fiscal and monetary expansion. Thus the old-fashioned business cycle of anarchistic market capitalism has been succeeded by the new-fashioned "political business cycle."

Contemporary history confirms that economies suffer from chronic creeping inflation. Political economy waits upon new innovative research to provide better therapies for the scourge of stagflation, much as medical research seeks for breakthroughs in knowledge to cope better with the scourges of cancer and cardiovascular diseases.

Pessimists believe that a U.S. recession by the end of the decade is inevitable. The new Carter program to defend the dollar may itself contrive such tight-money conditions as to bring on an early 1979 recession. If the president and the Federal Reserve back down from their tough crusade against inflation, the pessimists believe that the recession will merely be delayed. And the longer the delay, the more virulent they expect it to have to be.

Optimists take comfort from the apparent success of the Labour government's "social contract" with the British workers, which seems to have helped reduce the U.K. inflation rate from 25% per year to less than half that rate. This gives hope that the Carter quasi-voluntary price-wage guidelines, reinforced by some monetary and budgetary austerity, can make a contribution to inflation control. Inasmuch as Europe and Japan have scarcely recovered from the 1973–75 worldwide recession, there is less reason to fear that slower U.S. growth will plunge the whole globe into a new recession.

Realists understand that inflation is not a problem that will soon go away.

ANOTHER DAY, A DIFFERENT DOLLAR

by Hamish McRae

In 1978 it was the dollar's turn to be hit on the foreign exchanges; a year or so before it had been the pound, and in another year it might be the French franc or even the Japanese yen. The currency fluctuations that have struck the world economy with apparently ever increasing force since the beginning of the 1970s have been at best a puzzle, at worst a perverse and destructive influence on the creation of wealth by the world economy. By what logic, for example, is the pound worth $2 in February 1976, little more than $1.50 in November of that year, and then $2 again in August 1978?

Faced with these extraordinary variations, it is tempting to seek the existence of some malevolent force, be it the currency speculators or the multinational companies, or perhaps the big international banks. It is also tempting to seek a way back to the relative currency stability of the 1950s and '60s. Then an exchange rate change was a major event, and it appeared to be determined by a government responsible to an electorate rather than by the anonymous forces of the foreign exchange markets.

It is important to resist both temptations, for to yield to the first is to misunderstand fundamentally the nature of the foreign exchange markets, the markets that fix currency values. And to try to return to the fixed rate system of the immediate post-World War II period is on current evidence an impossible goal. There are many ways in which greater currency stability might be achieved, but a return to the system of the 1950s and '60s is hardly one of them.

Essentially, exchange rates—the price of currencies—are now fixed in the same way as the price of goods in any street market; they move in accordance with the supply and demand for a currency on any one day. This has come about because, since 1971, the world's governments have found it impos-

sible to hold their currencies in any fixed relationship with each other. Previously they, through their agents the central banks, had intervened in the foreign exchange markets to try to balance out the supply and demand. Currencies had nominal parities, or par values, fixed in relation to the U.S. dollar. If the supply of the currency exceeded the demand, then the central bank was required to buy the surplus from the market, using its foreign exchange reserves to do so. If the demand exceeded supply, it was required to increase the supply, adding to its reserves the foreign currencies it received in exchange for its own. Thus currencies were held to within 1% (or less) of their par values.

But since the beginning of the 1970s the flows across the exchanges have become too large for governments to match with any confidence. They still intervene to iron out small fluctuations, but they have been unable to maintain even unofficial par values. It follows that the attempts to stabilize exchange rates that are most likely to succeed are those that tackle the reasons *why* supply and demand for currencies are uneven—and therefore attack the problem of currency instability at its source—rather than those that look to intervention as the main method of holding rates together.

How the Foreign Exchange Markets Work. But first a word about the nature of the markets themselves. The superstructure of the floating rate system is exactly the same as that of the fixed rate system; it is the rules that are different. The foreign exchange markets, or "forex" market for short, are simply a series of dealing rooms in banks in all the main financial centres of the world. These are linked by telephone and telex, and dealing moves around the world—from Europe to New York, to the West Coast of the U.S., to Tokyo and Singapore, to the main Middle Eastern foreign exchange market in Bahrain, and back to Europe—following the world time zones. London happens to be the largest such market, with more than 250 banks dealing in foreign exchange, but the market is a truly international one.

Hamish McRae is financial editor of The Guardian, *London. He is co-author, with Frances Cairncross (his wife), of* Capital City: London as a Financial Centre *(1973) and of* The Second Great Crash *(1975), on the effects of the oil monetary crisis on the world economy.*

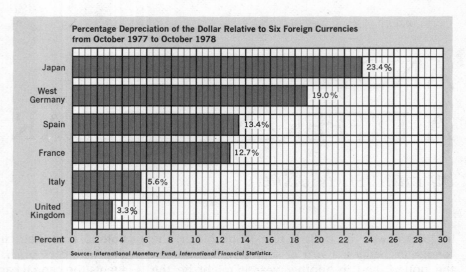

Percentage Depreciation of the Dollar Relative to Six Foreign Currencies from October 1977 to October 1978

Japan	23.4%
West Germany	19.0%
Spain	13.4%
France	12.7%
Italy	5.6%
United Kingdom	3.3%

Percent 0 2 4 6 8 10 12 14 16 18 20 22 24 26 28 30

Source: International Monetary Fund, *International Financial Statistics.*

Most of those 250 are foreign banks that deal in London because it happens to be a convenient place to locate this business.

For the most part, the banks are buying and selling currencies on behalf of clients. There are three types of foreign exchange transactions, though in practice it is difficult to distinguish between them: those corresponding to a trade flow; those corresponding to a capital movement; and those that are purely speculative, where the nature of the deal is to anticipate a profit.

First the trade transaction. All goods traded internationally ought, in theory, to have a corresponding foreign exchange transaction, though in practice banks net out much of the business. If they can match buying and selling orders from among their clients, they do not need to put every tiny transaction through the foreign exchange market.

One might imagine that trading transactions would be one of the market's most stable features. Alas, the reverse is true, for even a small change in the timing of a trading transaction can create a massive swing on the exchanges. If, for example, everyone in Britain thought the pound sterling would fall against other currencies in the near future, they would try to pay early for goods from abroad and delay receipt of foreign currencies earned from exports. But even a change of one day in the pattern of these payments would cause a movement of millions across the exchanges. This phenomenon, known as leading and lagging, vastly increases the pressure on any currency that might be weakening for other reasons.

The second type of foreign exchange transaction relates to a capital movement. Capital movements logically fall into two groups, short-term and long-term, although the difference is more one of intent on the part of whoever controls the funds than of any clear statistical distinction. Thus short-term movements *may* be purely speculative but are not necessarily so; they may, for example, be made in response to international interest-rate differences. And though long-term capital movements are by definition not speculative—they reflect structural payments imbalances in the world, differing investment opportunities, international aid programs, and a host of other factors—there may be little to stop the long-term investor from changing his mind and becoming a short-term one.

Nor can one deduce from where the money is placed whether the movement is of a long- or short-term nature. The oil revenues of Saudi Arabia are placed, to a large extent, in short-term money market instruments in New York, mostly with a three-month maturity. Yet these funds are not likely to be withdrawn suddenly. By contrast, much recent European investment in the U.S. has been in Wall Street. Such an investment would normally be considered long-term; yet there can be little doubt that this money could flow back across the Atlantic if the mood of European fund managers changed.

And the third type of foreign exchange transaction, the purely speculative one? Some element of speculation is inevitable in any market and, with the advantage of hindsight, it is easy to see how speculation made the task of managing the markets in the 1960s an impossible one. But it looks very much as though the massive speculative profits obtainable under the fixed rate regime are no longer possible under a system of floating rates. Under the fixed rate system it was comparatively easy to identify a currency that was ripe for a change in its exchange rate and, more important, relatively cheap to take a speculative position against it.

The sort of profit that might be expected in the event of a change in parity was of the order of 10%. The sterling and French franc devaluations in 1967 and 1969, respectively, were larger than this, the two revaluations of the West German mark, 1961 and 1969, smaller. But the possible penalty for failure was, at most, a movement of 2% in the opposite direction. In practice it was likely to be much less.

These potential profits attracted a great deal of speculation from both financial and international companies. Operators made at least £400 million out of the 1967 devaluation of sterling. But the string of foreign exchange losses by banks in the early 1970s testified to the fact that, under a floating system, profits are very much harder to come by; the risk/reward ratio has changed. So while there remains an element of speculation in the markets, overt speculation is probably less of an unsettling force than leading and lagging of trade flows.

How the Fixed Rate System Worked. How did the fixed rate system manage to survive for 25 years before 1971? The short answer is because it was essentially a dollar-based system, and while the U.S. dominated the world's economy, its currency did the same. The Bretton Woods system—so called after the small New Hampshire town where the 1944 conference that established it took place, although it developed through the '40s and '50s—had three main facets. First, governments were required to peg their currencies to within 1% on either side of a central value. Second, they could use two reserve currencies, the dollar and the pound, as well as gold to intervene on the foreign exchanges. These two reserve currencies could be converted into gold; from the point of view of international settlements they were "as good as gold." Third, countries would be assisted by a new institution, the

International Monetary Fund (IMF), which would help them maintain the par values of their currencies. There were other elements to the system—the Bretton Woods conference also led to the creation of the World Bank group of lending institutions—but this was its core.

In 1949 there was a major devaluation of the pound, together with most European and Commonwealth currencies. But gradually the new rules paved the way for the return to convertibility of all major currencies. By the late 1950s foreign residents could switch in and out of francs, marks, and pounds, as well as dollars. The rules helped avoid the competitive devaluations of the 1930s, and they established a framework of international currency stability that financed the greatest expansion of world trade that has ever occurred. Of course, not all countries shared equally in this prosperity, and the system embraced few countries with centrally planned economies. It was very much a financial system designed for and built to suit the Western industrial world. But with those reservations it was a success.

There were, however, certain flaws in the Bretton Woods system which gradually became apparent. One was the lumpiness of exchange rate changes. If a country could not maintain an exchange rate—if, for example, it did not have sufficient foreign exchange reserves to intervene on the market to keep the currency within its prescribed limits—then it would have to devalue. But devaluation, because of the sudden nature of the change, took on a political significance. Exchange rate decisions came to be taken for political rather than economic reasons and,

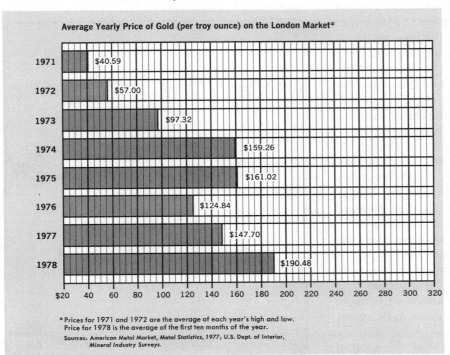

Average Yearly Price of Gold (per troy ounce) on the London Market*

Year	Price
1971	$40.59
1972	$57.00
1973	$97.32
1974	$159.26
1975	$161.02
1976	$124.84
1977	$147.70
1978	$190.48

$20   40   60   80   100   120   140   160   180   200   220   240   260   280   300   320

* Prices for 1971 and 1972 are the average of each year's high and low. Price for 1978 is the average of the first ten months of the year.
Sources: American Metal Market, Metal Statistics, 1977; U.S. Dept. of Interior, Mineral Industry Surveys.

arguably, were resisted too long because it was felt that some stigma attached to this course of action.

It also became apparent that there was a serious asymmetry in exchange adjustment. There was an immediate sanction on countries that found their exchange rates sinking. They were forced to devalue as they ran out of reserves. But there was little corresponding pressure on countries whose exchange rates were being forced up. They could go on adding to their reserves if they so wished and by doing so hold down their currencies on the exchange. This forced most of the onus for adjusting currencies onto the countries that had to devalue.

There was an even more fundamental flaw. The two reserve currencies, the pound and the dollar, ensured that there were sufficient international reserves to support growing world trade. But the only way dollars or pounds could get into the hands of other countries (*i.e.*, into their reserves) was for Britain or the U.S. to run current account deficits and risk reducing confidence in the currency. In the event, weakness, first of the pound, then of the dollar, helped destroy the fixed rate system.

The Floating Revolution. The chronology of the breakdown of the Bretton Woods system is well known. In the early 1950s there seemed to be an eternally insoluble problem of a shortage of dollars. But the U.S. ran substantial current account deficits throughout the 1950s which gradually remedied this. By 1961 it became clear that one major European currency, the West German mark, was undervalued; the markets poured money across the exchanges into it, and it was duly revalued.

Then, throughout the 1960s, the U.S. deficits continued, raising suspicions about the integrity of reserve currencies. Sterling was the first to go. At intervals in the 1950s and '60s sterling was under speculative pressure on the exchanges. Initially it was possible, by a credit squeeze at home and borrowing abroad, to beat off speculators. But on each successive occasion the size of the attack mounted, and the pound was eventually devalued in 1967.

The French franc followed in 1969. Though this was a further demonstration of the mounting pressure of market forces, it was less significant for the system as a whole. For once the concept was accepted that one reserve currency could be devalued, that it was not "as good as gold," it became only a matter of time before the other would become suspect as well. The inevitable happened in August 1971, when Pres. Richard M. Nixon declared the dollar no longer convertible into gold. Since other currencies fixed their rates in relation to the dollar, it was not possible for it to devalue itself against them. The only form devaluation could take was against gold. Nonconvertibility was followed in

December 1971 by a last effort to fix exchange rates, the Smithsonian agreement. It was hailed by President Nixon as "the most significant monetary agreement in the history of the world"—and lasted six months. It established a new set of par values for major currencies, but these were blown apart by flows across the exchanges. First the pound, then the French franc, and subsequently the other European currencies were all forced to float.

Since the Smithsonian agreement, the industrial countries have had no success in fixing international exchange rates. To be sure, some European currencies have been pegged to the mark, the so-called "snake." But this group has been dominated by the mark—the French franc has been only an occasional member—and was effectively simply a mark currency bloc. Even within the "snake" there were repeated revaluations and devaluations.

In the summer of 1978 a new proposal to enlarge the "snake" into a wider form of European Monetary System (EMS) was launched by the European Economic Community's heads of government. But by the end of the year it was still unclear just what form the EMS would take as its inception was delayed by internal dissent among the Community members. More important, there has been no question of the dollar joining in. For the time being the world still had to make do with the floating system.

Why Did It Happen? Why did the fixed rate regime break down? There is no easy answer. The most obvious response, that the scale of financial flows against which governments had to intervene

"The 'floating' dollar."

in the exchanges had risen enormously, is not very helpful. It merely begs the question: why were governments' resources not increased correspondingly?

To some extent, one can link the end of the fixed rate system with the end of the postwar boom—the period of nearly continuous economic growth that ran from the late 1940s to the early 1970s. The boom had a number of features: the growth of international trade, the "economic miracles" of West Germany and Japan, relatively stable prices, the growth of multinational corporations, the growth of the international capital market or "Euromarket," above all the dominance of the U.S. as the foremost economic power in the West. But this is no explanation either; indeed, it is sometimes argued that, to some extent at least, the collapse of fixed exchange rates has been responsible for the economic difficulties of the 1970s.

Perhaps a clue to the most convincing explanation can be gained by viewing the post-1971 arrangement less as a pure float and more as a two-bloc system, with a number of currencies clustering around the dollar (the Canadian, Australian, and New Zealand dollars, for example) and a number around the mark (the "snake" currencies, the Swiss and French francs). The economic policies of countries within these two blocs diverged in the postwar period. In particular, the economic and political priorities of the two most important countries, the world's largest industrial nation—the U.S.—and the world's second largest—West Germany—were rather different. For example, the U.S. was prepared to maintain troops around the world, troops whose salaries and other expenses often had to be paid in foreign currency. West Germany, by contrast, benefited from the payments to foreign troops on its soil. The U.S. sought to build up its overseas investments, permitting its large corporations to invest enormous sums abroad. West Germany, like Japan, sought instead to build up direct exports of goods made in factories at home.

To some extent, as well, the different countries had different priorities with regard to inflation. Though both West Germany and the U.S. maintained low inflation rates throughout the 1950s and '60s, in the U.S. the fight against inflation was never tackled with the same fervour as in Germany. Other countries, such as Britain and Italy, ascribed an altogether lower priority to stable prices than either West Germany or the U.S.

In essence, it is these differences in national priorities that have led to currency fluctuations. Ultimately, the international position of a currency tends to reflect its purchasing power within its "parent" country. This may not be a precise relationship; indeed it hardly ever is. But currencies do tend to adjust themselves to balance out countries' abilities to compete in the international marketplace.

The Path to More Stable Exchange Rates. There are a number of ways in which differing national economic policies might be encouraged to converge. At the string of recent economic summit meetings—at Rambouillet, France, in Puerto Rico, in London, and in Bonn—the major industrial countries, implicitly or explicitly, have been searching for international agreement on economic policies.

There are two broad policy areas in which agreement might lead to greater stability in exchange rates: growth policies and monetary policies. Success in the first is essential if countries are not to have cyclical payments imbalances. When one country—most recently, for example, the U.S.—enjoys a period of faster growth than its main competitors, its trade account tends to deteriorate. Only if the growth performances of industrial nations can be brought into some reasonable relationship can big swings in international trade balances be avoided. Theoretically, it is possible to accommodate these swings—for example, by offsetting capital transfers—and to insulate them from the currency markets. But in practice it is extraordinarily difficult to do so, given the imperfect nature of international cooperation as it exists at present.

International cooperation on monetary policies may be even harder to accomplish. The extent to which the differing rates of growth of the money supply in various countries are responsible for currency fluctuations is the subject of hot debate among economists. There are two ways in which the money supply might affect exchange rates. One is through international capital movements; put at its simplest, if a country prints too much money some of the stuff will try to flow abroad. The other way is through the effect of the growth of money supply on the domestic price level. This affects the trade account, increasing the price of exports and reducing the relative price of imports.

The second of these propositions is not universally accepted, but there is general agreement that relative money supply growth must affect exchange rates *to some extent*. It follows that international agreement on this score would, at the very least, make currency management much easier.

Neither agreement on growth nor coordination of money supply policies will transform a world of unstable currencies into a world of stable ones. Some adjustments would inevitably need to take place, and for all its faults the floating system does allow these to occur. The question in 1978 was not how to get back to fixed rates but, rather, how to inject a greater degree of stability into what will inevitably remain a "second best" currency system.

PEOPLE OF THE YEAR

BIOGRAPHIES

The following is a selected list of men and women who influenced events significantly in 1978.

Abruzzo, Anderson, and Newman

It sounded like a nursery rhyme gone awry: From a field of clover three men flew over the ocean to a barley patch in France. In fact, it was a $125,000 joyride for the U.S. entrepreneurs, whose friends called them "wild men, . . . go-getters, all-or-nothing types . . . looking for the ultimate thrill." In 1978 Ben Abruzzo, Maxie Anderson, and Larry Newman flew a balloon across the North Atlantic to grab the world's imagination and set ballooning records. (*See* AERIAL SPORTS.)

The adventure began several years earlier when Abruzzo and Anderson founded a balloonists' club in Albuquerque, N.M., a mecca for lighter-than-air flight fans. Having floated over Pikes Peak with barely 20 ft to spare, the pair set out in 1977 to commemorate Charles Lindbergh's feat of 50 years earlier by crossing the Atlantic in a novel way. Lindbergh, of course, had flown a small airplane; Abruzzo and Anderson

rode in a balloon that eventually dropped them off Iceland. Dismayed only briefly, they teamed up with Newman, whose skills as a navigator augmented their own abilities as pilots for the August 1978 flight.

In "Double Eagle II" the trio flew 3,000 mi in five days from Merle Sprague's cloverfield in Presque Isle, Maine, to Rachel Coquerel's barley field near Paris. Their craft was equipped in ways that would have made Lindbergh green with envy if not airsickness: a larder of Italian olives (for Abruzzo), sardines (for Anderson), kosher bagels and lox (for Newman); oxygen breathing gear; angora long johns and a portable heater for the subzero cold at 20,-000 ft; 4,000 lb of sand and lead ballast; a mast and sail in case the floatable twinhulled gondola did not reach land; and radios linking them via satellite to land-based meteorologists.

Anderson, at 44 the senior partner aboard, first flew an airplane at 14 before settling down to more terrestrial matters as an engineer and president of a mining company. He viewed the flight of "Double Eagle II" as a historical coda. "What we've ac-

complished is not really to make history, but to complete it," he said after landing amid a mob of ecstatic Frenchmen who tore the balloon fabric to shreds for souvenirs. "Ballooning started here in France in 1783 and since 1873 men have tried to fly the Atlantic. With good luck and good fortune, we've managed to finish that story."

As a boy Abruzzo used to dive from a 60-ft bridge in Rockford, Ill. A busy real estate developer at 41, he confessed to wondering in flight "whether this was worth all the trouble." Afterward he decided, "Unless frontiers are challenged from time to time—whether they be flying a balloon, breaking an altitude record in a plane or writing a fine piece of literature—we don't move forward as a society." Hang glider company president Newman, 31, formerly an industrial jet pilot, drew the short straw to sleep in Lindbergh's bed at the U.S. embassy in Paris.   (PHILIP KOPPER)

Agt, Andreas Antonius Maria van

A nine-month political crisis in The Netherlands ended on Dec. 19, 1977, when Andreas van Agt was sworn in as prime minister at the head of a Christian Democratic-Liberal coalition. Van Agt's success in forming a government followed long negotiations, first with the Socialists and then with the Liberals. These parties had made the biggest gains in the May 25 general election that followed the resignation on March 22 of Joop den Uyl's left-wing coalition. In December 1978, a year after taking office, van Agt stated that his government's highest priority was to reduce unemployment through a redistribution of national income designed to increase the competitiveness of Dutch industry.

Born on Feb. 2, 1931, at Geldrop, Noord-Brabant, van Agt studied law at the Catholic University at Nijmegen, graduating with honours in 1955. He became an academic lawyer, writing widely on legal and ethical issues, and in October 1968 was appointed professor of criminal law at his old university. His political career began in July 1971, when he joined Barend Biesheuvel's incoming right-of-centre Cabinet as minister of justice, a post he retained in the fol-

(Left to right) Maxie Anderson, Larry Newman, and Ben Abruzzo.

LAURENT MAOUS—GAMMA/LIAISON

lowing administration led by Joop den Uyl. As minister of justice van Agt was involved in two major controversies. In 1972 his announcement of the government's intention to pardon the last three Nazi war criminals remaining in Dutch prisons caused such a public outcry that he had to be given police protection, and the decision was revoked; in 1976 he considered resigning after women's action groups prevented police, acting on his authorization, from seizing abortion instruments from a clinic. (A bill to legalize abortion was later approved by the lower house of Parliament but rejected by the Senate.)

In August 1976 van Agt was elected leader of the Christian Democratic Appeal, a grouping of the Catholic People's Party (to which he belonged) with the two other confessional parties (the Antirevolutionary Party and the Christian Historical Union) in anticipation of the 1977 election. In the election campaign his conservative Catholicism, "nonpolitical" image, and his stressing of ethical issues appealed particularly to older people.   (DICK BOONSTRA)

Akuffo, Fred W. K.

When he and other members of the Supreme Military Council overthrew Gen. Ignatius Acheampong in a bloodless coup in July 1978, Lieut. Gen. Fred Akuffo became Ghana's new head of state. The new military leader's previous post had been chief of defense staff of the Army, which had made him second in status to his predecessor. Akuffo promised to clean up corruption and to prepare the country for an early return to parliamentary elections. He made a good start by releasing many political prisoners.

Akuffo was born on March 21, 1937, at Akropong in the British colony of the Gold Coast (which later became Ghana). After graduating from a Presbyterian secondary school, he entered the Army as an officer cadet at age 20. He spent three years in Britain, at the Royal Military Academy, Sandhurst, and then at Abingdon to be trained as a paratrooper. In 1973 he attended the National Defence College in India.

Akuffo moved rapidly up the military ladder after becoming an officer in 1960. He served with the UN peacekeeping force in the Congo; became commanding officer of Ghana's Parachute Battalion; was appointed Army commander at the age of 37; and was chief of defense staff at 39. After an earlier Army coup overthrew the last civilian government in 1972, he became a member (in 1975) of the Supreme Military Council, which ruled the country thereafter.

Though he had a somewhat diffident manner, Akuffo established a reputation for being decisive and, on occasion, tough. It was generally conceded that he would need both these qualities to survive the Herculean task of restoring the country's economy to tolerable levels of growth and stability and to prepare it for a return to civilian rule. He also had the misfortune to come to power at a time when Ghanaian public opinion was showing itself to be tired of any form of continued military rule.   (COLIN LEGUM)

Ali, Muhammad

No man had ever done it before. Perhaps no man would ever do it again. On Sept. 15, 1978, Muhammad Ali became world heavyweight boxing champion for the third time. In 15 rounds, he defeated Leon Spinks, the 25-year-old who had beaten him seven months earlier.

Muhammad Ali was born Cassius Marcellus Clay, Jr., on Jan. 17, 1942, in Louisville, Ky. He first learned to box at the age of 12 in a community recreation centre that was supervised by a local policeman. The peak of his amateur career came during the summer of 1960 when he captured the Olympic light heavyweight championship in Rome. A few months later, Clay turned professional. He won a series of fights, leading to a heavyweight championship match with Sonny Liston in February 1964. When Liston could not answer the bell for the seventh round, Clay became heavyweight champion for the first time.

Ali described his successful boxing style as "float like a butterfly, sting like a bee." He tempted opponents by placing his head within striking range and then backed away at the final moment. The other boxer was pulled off balance, swung at the air, and tired himself out. Ali then moved in for the kill.

Soon after the Liston fight Clay changed his name to Muhammad Ali and announced his membership in the Nation of Islam, commonly called the Black Muslims. In 1966, while the U.S. was at war in Vietnam, he applied for a military draft deferment on the grounds that as a Black Muslim he should be considered a conscientious objector. His request was denied, and when Ali was called up by the U.S. Army in April of 1967 he formally refused induction. Shortly after this, the associations that govern world boxing stripped Ali of his title and suspended his prizefighter's license. He was convicted of violating the Selective Service Act, fined $10,000, and sentenced to five years in jail. Free on appeal, he was vindicated on June 28, 1971, when the U.S. Supreme Court reversed his conviction.

Ali returned to the ring, defeated both Jerry Quarry and Oscar Bonavena, and, in March 1971, unsuccessfully challenged Joe Frazier for the heavyweight title. Following this defeat he spent three years working his way back up the ladder. On Oct. 30, 1974, Ali knocked out George Foreman in the eighth round and became heavyweight champion for the second time. He defended this title against a succession of challengers before losing to Spinks in February 1978.   (VICTOR M. CASSIDY)

Allen, Woody

For comedian/filmmaker Woody Allen, 1978 was a year of triumphant success. His film *Annie Hall* (1977) won most of the major honours in the motion-picture industry, including the U.S. Academy Award, the British Award, the National Society of Film Critics Award, and the New York Film Critics Circle Award. Allen himself won awards for his directing of the movie and his writing (with Marshall Brickman) of the screenplay. Allen's close friend, colleague, and co-star in the film, Diane Keaton, won many awards as best actress of the year.

Critics called *Annie Hall* Allen's first serious comedy. Vincent Canby of the *New York Times* described it as "a comedy about urban love and incompatibility that finally establishes Woody as one of our most audacious film makers, as well as the only Ameri-

MIKE NORCIA—SYGMA

can film maker who is able to work seriously in the comic mode without being the least bit ponderous." The story of *Annie Hall* in many ways parallels the real-life relationship between Allen and Keaton: an on-again, off-again romance between a zany Midwestern singer and a New York comedian suffering from a chronic inability to enjoy life.

But if the comedian Allen was a great success, the serious dramatist Allen did not receive unanimous acclaim. His latest film, *Interiors* (1978), continued to display Allen's concern with failing relationships between men and women, but it departed entirely from the humorous mode that characterized his earlier work.

Born Allen Stewart Konigsberg, on Dec. 1, 1935, in Brooklyn, N.Y., Allen began writing jokes for a public relations firm while still in high school. He became a staff writer for NBC in 1952, writing for television personalities such as Herb Shriner, Art Carney, and Sid Caesar. Encouraged by his agents, Allen worked up his own nightclub act, which he began performing in Greenwich Village clubs.

Allen's first screenplay was *What's New Pussycat?* (1965), followed by *What's Up, Tiger Lily?* (1966). His first Broadway play, *Don't Drink the Water*, opened in 1966. Other films include *Take the Money and Run* (1969), *Bananas* (1970), *Play It Again, Sam* (1972; based on his 1969 Broadway play of the same name), *Everything You Always Wanted to Know About Sex But Were Afraid to Ask* (1972), *Sleeper* (1973), and *Love and Death* (1975). The prolific Allen has also written two books, *Getting Even* (1971) and *Without Feathers* (1975). In 1978 he won an O. Henry Award for his short story "The Kugelmass Episode."   (JOAN NATALIE REIBSTEIN)

Armstrong, Garner Ted

Garner Ted Armstrong made news in 1978 as the unsuccessful principal in a struggle for control of the Worldwide Church of God, a California-based evangelistic sect. In June he lost his positions as operating head of the church and of a church-owned college in Pasadena, Calif. He no longer broadcast "The World Tomorrow," a daily radio program of news and commentary said to reach 30 million people, nor his weekly television newscast.

Armstrong, who was 48 years old in 1978, had been the most articulate spokesman for the Worldwide Church of God and its best fund raiser. His broadcasts helped to build church membership to an estimated 75,000 and its budget to approximately $75 million. In addition to its educational and broadcast activities, the church maintained a large publications department that produced religious books, pamphlets, and periodicals.

Armstrong was expelled from the Worldwide Church of God by his 85-year-old father, Herbert W. Armstrong, who had founded the church in 1934. The elder Armstrong, an advertising executive who became a preacher, was convinced that he had discovered the key to the holy scriptures. He taught that the people of Great Britain and the United States are descended from Ephraim and Manasseh, ancestors of two of the ten lost tribes of Israel. The British and Americans are, thus, God's chosen people. Their natural enemy is Germany, whose inhabitants supposedly are descended from Assyria, Israel's ancient opponent. Armstrong predicted that a final cataclysmic war would soon break out with Britain and the U.S. on one side and the European Common Market nations led by West Germany on the other. This war would go badly for the chosen people, but God would intervene at the final moment, bringing victory and a new order ruled by Christ.

Garner Ted Armstrong quarreled with his father in 1972 and was exiled from the church. Two years later he returned, and Herbert announced that his son was his divinely appointed successor. In the 1978 conflict between the two a third party was involved. Stanley Rader, a lawyer who recently joined the church, had been working closely with Herbert and appeared to have become his second in command. The elder Armstrong stated that his son had disobeyed him, precipitating the crisis. Others claimed, however, that financial problems, theological differences, and Rader's machinations were to blame.

(VICTOR M. CASSIDY)

Bakke, Allan

Allan Bakke hardly seemed to be the stuff of which crusaders are made. A faculty member at the University of California medical school to which Bakke had applied for admission as a student in 1972 described him as "a pleasant, mature person—tall and strong and Teutonic in appearance." But Bakke was also a quiet and intensely private man, not given to public displays of emotion or expressions of opinion. Thus, it was all the more surprising when, in 1978, it was Allan Bakke, a 38-year-old, balding Vietnam war veteran, who helped change the course of social policy in the U.S.

The story began when Bakke could not get into medical school. Despite his good undergraduate and graduate record and excellent scores on the entrance examination

he took for the University of California at Davis and ten other medical schools, Bakke was rejected by Davis. A subsequent application was also rejected. Finally, Bakke sued the university, charging that applicants less qualified than he had been approved for enrollment under a "special admissions" program aimed at increasing the number of minority students. On June 28, after lengthy hearings and appeals through the lower courts, the U.S. Supreme Court ruled that Bakke had been the victim of reverse discrimination and must be admitted to the Davis medical school. As a result, the future of "affirmative action," the federally mandated plan for enhancing minority participation in U.S. economic, political, and social life, was called into serious question. (See LAW.)

Bakke, a descendant of Norwegian forebears, was born in Minneapolis, Minn. His father was a mailman, his mother a teacher. An engineering major at the University of Minnesota, he served with the U.S. Marines and then earned a master's degree in engineering at Stanford University. Later, he obtained a job as an aerospace engineer at the U.S. National Aeronautics and Space Administration's Ames Research Center in Palo Alto, Calif. His work there, plus unpaid volunteer work in a local hospital, led to his interest in medicine—and to his long legal fight to enter medical school. In September 1978, with characteristic quietness, he began his first year of medical-school classes on the Davis campus.

(STANLEY W. CLOUD)

Bee Gees

"Give me eight minutes," the promoter told his pet songwriters. "Eight minutes, three moods. I want frenzy at the beginning. Then I want some passion and then I want some w-i-i-ld frenzy." He got it all. The trio of composers—who, notably, perform their own work—sat down and contrived the music for *Saturday Night Fever*, starring John Travolta (q.v.), the movie that swept the U.S. like an epidemic. The film and its music were largely responsible for "discomania," a social stampede that repopulated the discotheques of the 1960s and inspired a wave of dance contests that raised up memories of 1930s dance marathons. Though the Bee Gees' careers had just begun in the mid–1950s, they had been thoroughly forgotten more than once before; in 1978 they became princes of pop again.

That they could rise like a comet, vanish from musical popularity, and reappear was due to their ability to change styles to suit fickle tastes. This was possible, said one member of the group, "because we were writers . . . when you've got that gift, the ability to create a hook, the catch that makes people hum, you never lose it."

The brothers Gibb (hence the name Bee Gees) are Maurice, Robin, and Barry. Sons of a Liverpool ferryboat bandleader, they first began singing publicly in British movie theatres between the featured films. In 1958 the family moved to Australia, and the young trio rose to the top of the musical heap there. Returning to Britain, they fell in with the people who managed the Beatles. With the help of producer Robert Stigwood, their song "New York Mining Disaster, 1941" became a major hit in 1967, when

Barry, the oldest, was just past his teens. (The younger brothers are twins.)

At times during their career the Bee Gees dominated popular music unlike any group since the Beatles. Once fully half the Top Ten songs were their performances of their own compositions (though none of them reads music). But when, in Robin's words, "we couldn't sell ice cubes in the Sahara," they split up and worked alone.

The family connection brought them back together; they changed styles and rose again "for the second or maybe it was the third time." Their adaptability served them well. As one critic wrote, "Whatever style proved successful; at any given moment, they pursued it . . . . When fashions changed so did they . . . . What mattered first and last was salability." (PHILIP KOPPER)

Begelman, David

An offscreen lion in the very real fiscal jungle that surrounds Hollywood's output of make-believe, David Begelman played the lead in 1978 in a story that dramatized financial hijinks in the $3.2 billion movie business. He faced criminal charges that might have earned him 52 years in prison.

The show began in 1977 when actor Cliff Robertson found documentation of "income" supposedly received by him from Columbia Pictures in a year when he had not worked for the company. It turned out that a check made out to Robertson had been cashed by Begelman, then Columbia's president of film and television operations. This single check snowballed into an avalanche of unsavoury allegations about Hollywood business methods.

Soon there were charges of widespread double-dealing—not just at Columbia but throughout movieland. Actors entitled to shares in films' profits charged that studios regularly played fast and loose with the figures; said actor Tony Curtis, "A studio executive will fly down to Acapulco with 14 of his chicklets and charge the trip against profits."

Begelman, born Aug. 26, 1921, in New York City, was said to have offered qualifications that included a degree from Yale University, but the university denied any record of his graduation. Allies, however, recalled that Begelman had saved Columbia from bankruptcy with such films as *Shampoo*, *The Deep*, and *Close Encounters of the Third Kind*. Others acknowledged "The custom in Hollywood is that you get away with as much as you can until you're caught." Congressional investigations seemed in the offing briefly but never actually materialized.

Begelman pleaded no contest to the theft of $40,000 from Columbia. Forgery charges involving the Robertson check and two others (a director's and a publicist's) were dropped. Begelman was fined $5,000 and placed on probation for three years. He also told the judge that he would produce a documentary for schools and prisons on the dangers of PCP, an illegal drug. He was forced to resign his $400,000-a-year job. But, as an associate pointed out, "David would make more money now as an independent producer even under contract to Columbia than he could make as a studio chief. All he needs to become a millionaire is one big film where he takes a percentage." (PHILIP KOPPER)

Bombeck, Erma

Unlike T. S. Eliot, who "will show you fear in a handful of dust," Erma Bombeck waxes funny about dusting, mid-life dieting, and other domestic drudgeries. Dubbed "the housewives' boffo Boswell," she may reach more readers in a year than that English biographer ever did. At last count, some 800 newspapers carried her thrice-weekly column, "At Wit's End." The year 1978 also brought a television special based on one collection of her light essays, *The Grass Is Always Greener over the Septic Tank*, which sold more than 500,000 hardcover copies. Paperback rights to her latest book, *If Life Is a Bowl of Cherries—What Am I Doing in the Pits?* were auctioned for $1 million.

Her success seemed due to three things.

WARNER BROTHERS, INC.

First, of course, she is funny. Second, she has the rare knack of skirting an issue that polemicists have trampled to death and letting her viewpoint blossom in the sunlight of humour. She'll make a serious point, such as endorsing the notion behind the Equal Rights Amendment, and then disguise it with delicious nonsense that has a far longer shelf life than wearily reasoned rhetoric. For example: "I believe that if things are ever to improve the housewife's lot, change must come through legislation. At the moment I'm mothering a bill that will either raise the driving age of a child to 35 or lower the age of menopause to 12."

Finally, she clearly knows her audience; if she happened to be someone else, she'd be part of it. She writes for family women about the frustrations and foibles of a family woman, herself.

Born in Dayton, Ohio, on Feb. 21, 1927, Bombeck was not always a housewife and writer. Sometimes she was only one or the other. While still in high school, she went to work as a part-time secretary at the local newspaper, then parlayed that job into one as copygirl to work her way through the University of Dayton. She married a sportswriter and left journalism when the first child arrived. Once all three were fledged, she discovered, "I was 37, too old for a paper route, too young for Social Security and too tired for an affair." Her choices clearly limited, she turned to the typewriter, ironed out a few test columns,

and sold them for $3 apiece. Within a year the column was syndicated.

(PHILIP KOPPER)

Bossy, Mike

The day after he signed a professional hockey contract that would make his wallet fatter than a goalie's leg pads, Michael Dean Bossy married his childhood sweetheart. That day, June 24, 1977, was only one of many in Mike Bossy's life that would fit nicely into the works of Hans Christian Andersen.

The fairy tale continued so dramatically throughout the 1977–78 National Hockey League season that when it had finished Bossy had scored more goals and more power-play goals than any rookie in the history of the league. He helped the New York Islanders to the best record in their six-year existence—48 wins, 17 losses, and 15 ties—one that was good enough to give them the Patrick Division championship and the league's third best regular-season mark.

Bossy's 53 goals ranked second to Guy Lafleur, who scored 60 for the NHL champion Montreal Canadiens, but his 25 power-play goals led the league. His 91 points (goals plus assists) were the most by a rookie in 26 years and ranked sixth in the league. The right wing was charged with only six penalty minutes in 73 games, made two fans' all-star second teams, and, almost anticlimactically, won the Calder Memorial Trophy as the league's best rookie.

Born Jan. 22, 1957, in Montreal, Bossy started attracting attention as an uncommon hockey player when he scored 170 goals in one season for his Peewee team. He was only 16 when he started playing for Laval in the Quebec Junior Hockey League. In Bossy's four seasons at Laval he scored 308 goals and 529 points, missing Lafleur's all-time league record by only five goals. The Islanders made the 6-ft 186-lb right-hander the 15th choice in the first round of the 1977 draft of amateur players.

The New York team chose wisely. By the time officials at Laval performed the honorary ceremony of retiring his sweater, Bossy already had established himself as part of the NHL's most productive line with Clark Gillies and centre Bryan Trottier.

(KEVIN M. LAMB)

Botha, Pieter Willem

Piet Botha became South Africa's eighth prime minister on Sept. 28, 1978, following a close contest to succeed B. J. Vorster (*q.v.*), who had unexpectedly announced his resignation a week earlier. Botha had been minister of defense since 1966 and, before that, deputy minister of the interior (1958–61) and minister of community development, public works, and Coloured affairs (1961–66). He made his name in politics as a brilliant organizer of the ruling National Party in Cape Province, becoming its provincial leader in 1966.

Generally known in political circles as "Peevee" (the Afrikaans pronunciation of his initials) or "Piet Wapens" ("Pete Weapons"), Botha was born at Paul Roux in the Orange Free State on Jan. 12, 1916. He was graduated from the University of the Orange Free State and became a professional politician when he was only 20. He was elected to Parliament in 1948.

The new prime minister was known to be

a hard-liner on defense and security affairs and a strong advocate of the government's apartheid policies. He did not, however, support the extremist conservatives in his party on race questions. Although he strongly attacked the policies and attitudes of Western nations toward South Africa, he appeared by no means insensitive to the importance of maintaining reasonable relations with the major Western powers. On the other hand, he tried to make it clear that he would not allow South Africa to submit to coercive pressures, such as economic sanctions.

Botha was mainly responsible for South Africa's decision to intervene militarily in the fighting in Angola in 1975, an enterprise that ended in failure. He was also one of the leaders in the Cabinet who urged rejection of Western proposals for a peaceful settlement in Namibia (South West Africa). His decision to proceed with elections in the territory without UN supervision, despite protests from the UN, started his career as prime minister in open confrontation with the UN, the major Western powers, and the African states.

(COLIN LEGUM)

Brown, Louise Joy

"Some are born great" might well be an unappreciated cliché to Louise Joy Brown when she matures enough to understand it. Not yet six months old at the end of 1978, she had become the centre of international attention in both the popular media and scholarly journals. The baby girl's uniqueness lay in the manner of her conception—on a laboratory bench of Patrick C. Steptoe, a gynecologist practicing in Oldham, England, and Robert G. Edwards, a University of Cambridge physiologist.

Louise, the world's first known test-tube baby, was born to Gilbert and Lesley Brown, a British couple childless for nine years because of a blockage in Lesley's fallopian tubes that prevented eggs from reaching her womb. Steptoe and Edwards used techniques that had been tried on hundreds of similarly afflicted women for more than a decade, but unsuccessfully until Louise; they operated to remove an egg from Lesley, collected sperm from her husband, and combined them in a culture dish. In two and a half days "she was a beautiful eight-cell embryo," said Edwards, noting the last time he saw the mote of life before he and Steptoe implanted it in Lesley's womb. On July 25, 1978, 37 weeks later, the two specialists returned Louise to the outside world by cesarean section, an apparently normal, healthy 5-lb 12-oz infant.

The reasons for Louise's successful birth remained to be published and analyzed in detail, and there was some professional skepticism that the accomplishment could be reliably reproduced. One key factor might have been the early return of the embryo to the womb instead of the four-day wait in culture previously thought optimum. Also of critical importance was the need to coax the womb into a state receptive to implantation, normally a transient condition under the delicate control of brain hormones.

Whereas Steptoe's stated goal had been to

benefit women with reproductive problems, the ramifications of Louise's birth went far beyond the healing arts to stir up many moral and ethical questions. For example, is a newly fertilized egg in culture a human being or only human tissue? Would discarding it constitute an abortion? Could test-tube conception increase the risk of birth defects? If a fertilized egg were implanted into a foster mother because the genetic mother was unable to bear, by legal definition whose child would it be? At year's end Louise slept cozily in her new home, little concerned with such momentous questions and with the future that fate had in store for her. Little, too, did she realize how alarmingly her birth cry still echoed—in the wails of dismay and the shouts of bitter debate from the scientific, legal, religious, and philosophical communities of the world. (*See* Law: *Special Report.*)

(CHARLES M. CEGIELSKI)

Caldwell, Philip

In July 1978 Henry Ford II, chairman of the board of the Ford Motor Co., stunned many in the automotive world by firing Lee Iacocca, president of Ford since 1970. To replace the fiery and hard-driving Iacocca, Ford installed as president his low-keyed vice-chairman of the board, Philip Caldwell.

Many industry observers believed that Ford fired Iacocca because the latter had been gaining so much personal power and acclaim that he had become a threat to the Ford family's control of the company. It was generally believed that Ford planned to have control of the company pass first to his younger brother, William Clay, and then to his son, Edsel. Caldwell appeared to pose no threat to those plans.

Born in Bourneville, Ohio, on Jan. 27, 1920, Caldwell was graduated from Muskingum College, New Concord, Ohio, and then obtained a master's degree in business administration from Harvard University. After serving in the U.S. Navy during World War II, he worked until 1953 in various civilian posts for the Navy. In that year the Navy presented him with a Meritorious Civilian Service award.

Caldwell joined Ford in 1953 and by 1968 had risen to the posts of vice-president and general manager of truck operations. In 1973 he was appointed executive vice-president in charge of international automotive operations—those outside North America. He became vice-chairman of Ford's board of directors in 1977 and also was named a member of the newly formed Office of the Chief Executive, along with Henry Ford and Iacocca. (DAVID R. CALHOUN)

Callaghan, (Leonard) James

The date of a general election in Britain is decided by the prime minister. Few prime ministers like to go the whole term of five years, preferring to choose a favourable moment after about four years rather than risk an unfavourable situation at the end of the term. But James Callaghan, who became prime minister of the United Kingdom in April 1976, chose to have his government continue into the fifth year of the Parliament due to expire in October 1979. He

made the choice even though his government faced the probability of industrial strife and depended on a shaky majority in the House of Commons.

Callaghan's decision not to have an election in October 1978 was the political sensation of the year. It showed cool nerve, self-confidence, and political astuteness that did not stop short of bluff—for he had allowed months of speculation about an autumn election to continue until the latter part of a broadcast on September 7 in which he was confidently expected to announce the election date. Instead, he said a general election then would not help to curb inflation or reduce unemployment. His government would therefore set about consolidating the gains it had made.

In his third year as prime minister, Callaghan's place at the head of the government was unchallenged. Born March 27, 1912, he had come rather late to the leadership, but he had unequaled experience—as an MP since 1945, as foreign secretary (1974–76), home secretary (1967–70), and chancellor of the Exchequer (1964–67). He had established himself in world politics as a considerable figure who could be tough to the point of obstinacy—as in questioning the proposed European Monetary System—but his outgoing personality made him friends among world leaders. To the British electorate he was known as "Sunny Jim." He liked to present himself as a jovial family man with nine grandchildren (and was happy to be photographed kicking a football with some of them on the lawn of the British embassy in Washington, D.C., where his son-in-law, Peter Jay, was British ambassador).

Callaghan was the first person to be named for the newly created Hubert Humphrey Fund International Award in 1978. On that occasion he chose to draw attention to the urgent needs of the third world. To combat world poverty, he said, was both a moral imperative and a matter of self-interest for the developed countries.

(HARFORD THOMAS)

Campbell, Earl

With less than two minutes to play the Houston Oilers wanted to protect their five-point lead by giving the football to their

most dependable running back. If Earl Campbell could just gain nine yards in two plays, the Oilers would have a first down and could keep the ball for the rest of the game. But as Oiler coach O. A. ("Bum") Phillips said with a smile, "He ruined my game plan." He ran 81 yd for a touchdown, the longest carry in the National Football League's 1978 season.

"Campbell is everything they say he is," said Don Shula, who coached the Miami Dolphins team that Campbell outran. "He's all that and more."

What "they" had said about him was plenty. In 1977 Campbell had won college football's most prestigious award, the Heisman Trophy. He led the country with 1,744 yd rushing for the University of Texas and finished his college career with 4,444 yd rushing, the fourth-highest total in college football history. So when the Oilers had a chance to trade for the first choice in the college draft, they gave up a promising player and four other draft choices in order to obtain Campbell.

Despite his impressive college career there was some concern among professional scouts that Campbell's 224 lb might be too much on a 5-ft 11-in frame. He certainly could run through tacklers, they said, but they were not sure whether he could run around them. Those doubts disintegrated under Campbell's quick-stepping feet when he led the NFL in rushing with 1,450 yd and ran for 13 touchdowns. He was not only the NFL's rookie of the year but also, by the vote of the Professional Football Writers of America, its most valuable player.

Campbell was born March 29, 1955, near Tyler, Texas. His father died when he was nine, and his mother was left with 11 children. Before it became apparent that an NFL team would happily pay him a million dollars over several years, Campbell said, "I want to make enough money someday to build my mama a house so that when she goes to bed at night she won't see the big dipper." The biggest star she saw in 1978 was her son Earl. (KEVIN M. LAMB)

Carazo Odio, Rodrigo

In a stunning upset, Rodrigo Carazo Odio defeated the candidate of the dominant Partido de Liberación Nacional (PLN) to capture the presidency of Costa Rica. Carazo's February triumph—in part due to the PLN's ties with fugitive U.S. financier Robert Vesco—marked the seventh peaceful presidential contest in Costa Rica over the past 25 years, an unusual and enviable record in Latin-American politics.

Carazo, a 51-year-old San José economist, campaigned on a reform platform as candidate of a four-party opposition coalition called Partido de Unidad. Speaking from a balcony in downtown San José following announcement of his narrow victory (Carazo captured slightly more than half of the 755,000 votes cast), he pledged, as he had throughout the campaign, to get rid of "waste and corruption."

Indeed, Carazo's campaign had focused not so much on opponent Luis Alberto Monge as on his opponent's party. Appealing to what he sensed was the nation's "enormous desire for change," he lashed out at the government's expanding bureaucracy and budget. But when Carazo talked about getting rid of corruption, he usually meant expelling Vesco, the accused expatriate embezzler. He viewed Vesco's activities in Costa Rica, especially his close association with former president and PLN founder José "Pepe" Figueres Ferrer and with outgoing president Daniel Oduber Quirós, as reprehensible.

In an interview with the Associated Press shortly after the election, Carazo charged that Vesco had been involved in government corruption in Costa Rica, and he vowed that the U.S. financier, wanted by the U.S. Securities and Exchange Commission in connection with the disappearance of $224 million from a mutual fund Vesco controlled, would be asked to leave Costa Rica "as quickly as possible." Vesco's application for Costa Rican citizenship was turned down in August.

Carazo was born in Cartago on Dec. 27, 1926. Through the 1950s and 1960s he was active in the PLN. During this time he served as director of the National Institute of Housing and Urbanization and the Central Bank of Costa Rica. He resigned from the party in 1969 and became a leader of the political opposition.

(JEROLD L. KELLMAN)

Carter, Jimmy

As 1978 began, U.S. Pres. Jimmy Carter's standing in the polls was low—and the trend was down. The public opinion samplings indicated that while many held Carter in fairly high personal regard, they increasingly doubted his competence to be an effective president. In 1977 he had failed to get much of his domestic program, including energy legislation and tax reform, through a Congress that was controlled by his own Democratic Party. Abroad, the president had set equally ambitious goals for himself, seeking a new strategic arms limitation treaty with the Soviet Union and a peace agreement in the Middle East, among other things. But, while there had been no real foreign policy disasters, major accomplishments had eluded him.

Things began to break Carter's way in 1978, however. On two separate, razor-thin votes, the Senate ratified the treaties, negotiated by the Carter administration amid considerable controversy, that would turn the Panama Canal over to Panama by the year 2000. Carter's energy bill, though drastically altered by more than a year of congressional consideration, was finally passed. Moreover, his civil service reform program—the centrepiece of his attempt to reorganize the federal bureaucracy—was passed easily and virtually intact.

Far more significantly, Carter personally played a major role in achieving a breakthrough in the Middle East peace negotiations between Egypt and Israel. Frustrated by months of stalemate, he summoned Egyptian Pres. Anwar as-Sadat and Israeli Prime Minister Menahem Begin to Camp David, Md., in September for 13 days of intense, face-to-face talks. With Carter frequently acting as mediator, agreement was finally reached on the "framework" of a final settlement. In December Carter scored another foreign policy coup. He surprised just about everyone by announcing that, after nearly 30 years, the U.S. and China would have full diplomatic relations beginning in 1979.

As a result, Carter's popularity increased

markedly. Meantime, having wavered between a conservative and a liberal point of view on economic problems, he finally chose the latter and announced a voluntary wage and price control program to deal with inflation. (STANLEY W. CLOUD)

Castro, Fidel

A guerrilla fighter who transformed his country from a corrupt dictatorship into a socialist state, Cuba's Pres. Fidel Castro had by 1978 transferred his revolutionary efforts from Latin America to Africa, notably to Angola and Ethiopia. By the year's end Cuba had diplomatic relations with about 30 African countries.

The basis of Castro's wider success was the economic and military support of the Soviet Union, which in 1978 supplied him with MiG–23 aircraft capable of handling nuclear bombs. In September Castro also conferred with the U.S. and Spain on human rights and in November announced that political prisoners in Cuba would be released.

Born near Birán, Oriente Province, on Aug. 13, 1926, the son of a Spanish immigrant farm worker who became a landowner, Fidel Castro Ruz was educated by the Jesuits before studying law at the Universidad de la Habana. While a student he took part in unsuccessful attempts against dictatorships in the Dominican Republic (1947) and in Colombia (1948). He gained his law degree in 1950 and became a champion of the poor. His uprising against Cuba's dictator Fulgencio Batista in 1953 was crushed, and Castro and his brother Raúl were imprisoned—after he had made his famous "History Will Absolve Me" speech in conducting his own defense. Under a 1955 amnesty both were released.

From exile in Mexico Castro landed in Cuba in December 1956 with a small force. Only 12 escaped to the mountains, but they steadily attracted volunteers. On Jan. 1, 1959, Batista fled before Castro's forces, and on February 16 Castro became Cuba's prime minister. He ruled by decree till 1976. The remnants of the old corrupt regime were swept away, and the major sources of production were nationalized.

Castro's government weathered several crises, including estrangement from the U.S. Economic difficulties were ameliorated by the integration of Cuba's economy with that of the Soviet Union and its Eastern bloc. Under Cuba's constitution of December 1976 Castro became president (of the Council of State), secretary-general of the Communist Party, commander in chief of the Army, and head of the important Agrarian Reform Institute. He continued his long-standing practice of traveling about Cuba by jeep to keep in touch with the people. (MICHAEL WOOLLER)

Collin, Frank

In 1978 Frank Collin made news by threatening to lead a Nazi march in Skokie, Ill., a suburb of Chicago. Collin is the leader of the National Socialist Party of America, a group of about 25 members that had been attempting for several years to spread hatred of Chicago's black population. Failing to gain much notice in this endeavour, Collin shifted his attention to the Jews and decided to carry his message to Skokie.

In 1977 Collin had applied for a permit to

hold a rally in Skokie. Of the town's 70,000 residents, roughly 40,000 were Jewish, many of them survivors of Hitler's concentration camps. All were outraged by Collin's proposal, and many threatened violence.

The Skokie village board tried to prevent a possible riot by acting to block the rally. It passed an ordinance requiring that a $350,000 insurance bond be posted by any group that wanted to hold meetings on public property. Collin then said that he would protest this requirement by leading his followers in a march outside the Skokie village hall. At the same time he turned to the American Civil Liberties Union (ACLU) for legal assistance. (The ACLU is an organization that provides free legal counsel to groups or individuals who believe that their civil liberties are threatened.) Though the ACLU opposes Nazism, it declared that Collin's free speech rights were being violated.

There were legal struggles between the Nazis and the Skokie village board late in 1977 and early in 1978. By June the U.S. courts had ruled in favour of the Nazis on constitutional grounds, and it appeared that Collin would march in Skokie. At the final moment, however, Collin canceled a Skokie rally scheduled for June 25 because, a year after petitioning, he was granted a permit to march in Chicago's Marquette Park, far from Jewish neighbourhoods but near an area of black-white confrontation. This meeting was held on July 9 with 20 to 25 Nazis, more than 2,000 spectators and counterdemonstrators, and several hundred riot-equipped police in attendance.

Frank Collin was born Nov. 3, 1944, the son of a Roman Catholic woman and a Jewish man who was imprisoned in the Dachau concentration camp during World War II. After the war Collin's father emigrated to the U.S., and in 1946 he changed the family name from Cohn to Collin.

(VICTOR M. CASSIDY)

Curcio, Renato

The bearded founder and leader of Italy's Red Brigades terrorists had the best alibi of all when the assassination of former premier Aldo Moro, the most sensational political murder since Fascist times, took place in Rome in May 1978. Renato Curcio was in police custody in Turin, on trial for armed robbery, kidnapping, conspiracy, and armed subversion against the state. He told the court: "The act of revolutionary justice carried out against Aldo Moro is the highest act of humanity possible in this class-ridden society." On June 23 he was sentenced to 15 years in prison for terrorist crimes carried out up to 1974. During the two years and one month that the trial of Curcio and 14 accomplices lasted, no fewer than 17 people, including Moro and his five police bodyguards, were killed by the Red Brigades in their campaign of "total warfare" against the Italian establishment.

At 36, Curcio had every prospect of spending most of the rest of his life in jail. He had already received a seven-year sentence from a Milan court in 1977 for illegally possessing firearms, assaulting a policeman, and resisting arrest. Other charges were pending. He was born at Monterotondo near Rome during World War II. After a strongly Roman Catholic boarding school education he enrolled at the faculty of sociology at the University of Trento. There he joined the Catholic student movement but soon became active in Marxist politics. His teachers found him "bright and diligent," but Curcio refused to take a formal degree on grounds of conscience. He played a prominent part in the 1968 student revolt. In 1969 he married Margherita Cagol, a fellow student, and moved to Milan.

The Red Brigades' acts of terrorism began in 1970. They included a long series of kidnappings, robberies, and murders of lawyers, judges, and police. Curcio was arrested at Pinerolo in September 1974 after being betrayed by a former monk who had infiltrated the Red Brigades organization. In February 1975 he escaped after a raid on the prison at Casale Monferrato led by his wife, who in June that year was shot dead by police during a gun battle. Curcio was recaptured in January 1976 after another gun battle when police discovered him in an apartment in Milan.

(DAVID DOUGLAS WILLEY)

Denard, Robert

The high point in the adventurous career of soldier of fortune Bob Denard, alias Maurin, alias Colonel Bourgeaud, alias Col. Said Moustapha Mahdjou, came on May 13, 1978, with his coup in the Comoros. With a Breton trawler and some 50 mercenaries, Denard, after stopping over in the Canaries and rounding the Cape of Good Hope, organized a night landing on the Itsandra beach. He overthrew Pres. Ali Soilih, the same man he had helped to power three years before (later shot dead "attempting to escape"), and reinstated former president Ahmed Abdallah, who had been deposed in August 1975. Denard was appointed a member of the political and military directorate, then chief of staff of the Comoran Army, and took Comoran nationality under the name of Said Moustapha Mahdjou. But under pressure from African international opinion he had to step down and leave the Comoros in September 1978.

Denard was born in France on Jan. 20, 1929. After enlisting in the French Navy, he served for seven years in Indochina until the Geneva Agreement of 1954. His next field of operations was Morocco, where he appeared to have been employed by the French Special Services in 1955 to fight undercover against Mohammed V in support of Moulay ibn Arafa.

When the former Belgian Congo became independent in 1960, Denard enlisted under the Katangan separatist leader Moise Tshombe and helped to train Tshombe's celebrated "gendarmes." This was followed by an interlude in Yemen, where he was recruited by King Faisal of Saudi Arabia to fight for the royalists. He resurfaced in the Congo where he supported Tshombe against Joseph Mobutu (later Mobutu Sese Seko) and took part in the July "mercenaries' revolt." Leading the sixth commando of "foreign volunteers," entirely made up of French-speaking troops, he fought at

Kisangani. He was wounded there and flown to Salisbury, Rhodesia, for treatment. He went on to Angola and then to France. In 1968, however, Denard returned to Africa and fought with the Biafran separatists under Gen. Odumegwu Ojukwu. In 1977 the leaders of the government in Benin announced his involvement in an attempted coup d'etat in January on behalf of former Benin president Émile Derlin Zinsou and other members of the opposition.

(PHILIPPE DECRAENE)

DeRoburt, Hammer

In 1978 Hammer DeRoburt resumed the presidency of the small Pacific Ocean republic of Nauru, an office he previously had held from independence in 1968 until December 1976. In retrospect, the period when he was out of office (after a dispute over appointments to the Cabinet) appeared as an aberration in Nauru's recent history, for it was DeRoburt who had led the struggle for independence and for control of Nauru's rich phosphate industry. Nearly made president-for-life when the independence constitution was negotiated, he was, in a very real sense, the father of the Nauruan nation. However, to a new generation, secure in the possession of phosphate royalties and political rights, past achievements were no longer sufficient to command unquestioning allegiance. A new, younger administration under Bernard Dowiyogo had taken office in 1976—although DeRoburt was seldom far away from the centre of political life.

Hammer DeRoburt was born in 1922. Educated first on Nauru and then in Australia, he returned to Nauru as a teacher just before World War II. His election to the Local Government Council (LGC) in 1951 was disallowed on a technicality, but he was returned in 1956 and promptly elected head chief of Nauru—a position he still held in 1978. Under DeRoburt the LGC became the vehicle for the pursuit of Nauruan aspirations. He proved to be a hard negotiator with a shrewd appreciation of his opponents' weaknesses and of their capacity to pay. After Nauru had won increased royalties and then, in the mid-1960s, an agreement for control of the phosphate industry, independence and termination of the Aus-

JON BLAU—CAMERA PRESS

tralian-administered UN trust followed as a matter of course in 1968.

In recent times Nauru's position as a leader of the world per capita income table had been challenged by small oil-rich Middle Eastern states, but the Nauruans (numbering some 4,000) were still wealthy. What was more, their long-term future was protected by the investment of community funds in real estate and shipping, although some projects—for example an airline—were expressions of national pride more than of the desire for high financial returns.

(BARRIE MACDONALD)

Engel, Marian

The basic precept of Canadian author Marian Engel is: "Get an original impulse and stick like glue. If you get away from your original impulse, you destroy what you do." Her impulse has led her in all five of her novels to date to deal with women bound by firmly instilled principles who struggle with the problem of breaking away from the past and its precepts. For example, Minn, the heroine of *The Honeyman Festival* (1970), is a woman struggling not to be made over into the image of someone else. *Bear* (1976), which won the 1977 Governor General's Award for Best Fiction, has been called "Canadian literature's strangest and most impossible love story ever." In this novel, Lou, an archivist who goes to northern Ontario to catalog a collection of family papers, has a love affair with the family bear.

Born Marian Passmore in Toronto on May 24, 1933, she spent her childhood in small Ontario towns where her father, a high school teacher, could find work. At the age of 12 she won an award in a temperance essay contest for an article on the evils of liquor. During her years in high school and college she worked as a reporter for the *Sarnia* (Ont.) *Observer*. Although she has the acute eye of a reporter, she later turned to fiction.

After receiving her B.A. degree from McMaster University and her M.A. in Canadian literature from McGill University, Engel taught at Montana State University (1957–58) and at the Study School in Montreal (1958–60). Then she received a Rotary Fellowship for two years of study at the University of Aix-Marseille in France. In 1968, 1973, and 1976 she received Canada Council Senior Arts Fellowships.

In 1962 she married Howard Engel, a producer at the Canadian Broadcasting Corporation. The couple spent a year in Cyprus, which became the setting for her third novel, *Monodromos* (1973). She was made chairman in 1973 of the Writers' Union of Canada, and she became active in promoting an effort to recompense authors for the use of their books in libraries.

Engel also wrote two children's books, *Adventure at Moon Bay Towers* (1974) and *My Name Is Not Odessa Yarker* (1977). In 1978 she was named writer-in-residence at the University of Alberta in Edmonton.

(DIANE L. WAY)

Farber, Myron

When *New York Times* reporter Myron A. Farber began investigating a series of mysterious deaths in a small New Jersey hospital, he had no idea that it eventually would lead to his own jailing on contempt of court charges, heavy fines against his newspaper, and a press freedom case that made him a rallying point for the U.S. journalism profession. In the end the physician who had been accused of murdering hospital patients was acquitted by a jury, and the U.S. Supreme Court refused to hear Farber's case.

The First Amendment constitutional question was never resolved, and journalists throughout the country were left wondering whether state "shield laws" actually enable them to protect the identity of their confidential sources. Because of the Farber case many sources simply stopped talking to reporters on the confidential basis that is essential to investigative reporting.

Farber was a veteran 37-year-old reporter in 1975 when the *Times* received a tip that ten years earlier a dozen postoperative patients had died suddenly at the Riverdell Hospital in Oradell, N.J. Farber's investigation and a series of articles in the newspaper led to the case being reopened by Bergen County authorities. In 1976 Mario E. Jascalevich, the hospital's former chief surgeon, was indicted on three counts of murder and accused of administering the drug curare to the victims in an alleged plot to discredit other physicians.

The murder case came to trial in 1978, and Jascalevich's defense attorney subpoenaed all of Farber's notes and files on the case. Farber, backed by his paper, refused to surrender the documents on grounds that his confidential sources would be revealed. He cited the First Amendment's constitutional guarantee of press freedom and a recent New Jersey shield law that supposedly enabled a reporter to protect the identity of confidential sources.

Judge William J. Arnold, presiding over the murder trial, refused to consider quashing the subpoena until he could inspect Farber's material in private and decide if it was relevant to the trial. Farber and the *Times* refused, contending that the subpoena was too broad and, therefore, invalid. Judge Theodore Trautwein heard the proceedings and held Farber in contempt of court, ordering him to jail until he surrendered the documents, sentencing him to an additional six months, fining him $2,000, and fining the *New York Times* $100,000 outright and $5,000 per day until they complied with the subpoena. Farber served 39 days in jail and the *Times* paid $285,000 in fines.　　　　　(HAL BRUNO)

Figueiredo, João Baptista da

The fifth general to govern Brazil since a military junta took power in 1964, João Baptista da Figueiredo was elected president on Oct. 15, 1978, by a vote of 355–226 in the nation's electoral college. Figueiredo was the candidate of the government party, the National Renewal Alliance (ARENA), and, as such, was virtually assured of the victory, but nonetheless he campaigned vigorously before the election in an effort to become better known. His opponent was Euler Bentes Monteiro of the Brazilian Democratic Movement, the only legal opposition party. In congressional elections later in the year, the MDB cut into ARENA's majority.

After his victory Figueiredo promised a "slow and gradual" return to democracy, stating that "I will promote a political open-

ing" for those who had opposed his candidacy. He pledged to follow his predecessor's domestic and international policies. His major problem was the country's 40% annual rate of inflation, caused primarily by the greatly increased cost to Brazil of its oil imports.

Figueiredo also faced possible opposition from military leaders who were against any further political liberalization. He would be the first president since 1968 to govern without the support of Institutional Act number 5, which had given the nation's chief executive the power to dismiss Congress and to deprive citizens of political rights.

Figueiredo, the son of an army general, was born in 1921 in Rio de Janeiro. He joined the Army in 1935 and served in a number of posts, including instructor with the Brazilian military mission in Paraguay, head of the military police for the state of São Paulo, and head of the president's military household. At the time of his nomination for president, he had become a general and was head of Brazil's National Information Service.　　　(DAVID R. CALHOUN)

Giscard d'Estaing, Valéry

Having won France's parliamentary elections in March 1978 with his "majority parties," Pres. Valéry Giscard d'Estaing stood a good chance of extending his four years as French chief of state to a full presidential term of office expiring in 1981. True, his "majority" was fragile, being composed of such deeply divided groups as Jacques Chirac's Gaullists on the one hand and the "presidential majority" and the centrist parties led by Premier Raymond Barre on the other. But, apparently assured of survival in internal affairs, Giscard left the struggle against unemployment and inflation largely in Barre's hands.

Instead, Giscard concentrated on foreign affairs, in both their political and financial aspects, and in 1978 he was a dominant figure on the international stage. He quickly initiated the repelling of a rebel invasion in May of Zaire's vital Shaba Province by flying in troops from France ahead of those from Belgium and Morocco, and at a meeting of African nations in Paris in May he promoted the organizing of an African security force. In May at the UN General Assembly he called for a European disarmament conference for 1979 to be composed of the 35 countries that met at Helsinki, Fin., in 1975. Having already conferred with West German Chancellor Helmut Schmidt at Hamburg, Giscard launched with him at Bremen, West Germany, in July a Franco–West German plan to form a European Monetary System to stabilize exchange rates. The plan was put to the test at the European Economic Community summit meeting in Brussels in December; although all but Britain eventually agreed to join, France itself delayed inception of the EMS in a dispute over agricultural subsidies. On December 7, he proposed a meeting of Western leaders—U.S. Pres. Jimmy Carter, Schmidt, British Prime Minister James Callaghan, and himself—in the French Caribbean island of Guadeloupe on Jan. 5–6, 1979.

Born at Koblenz, now in West Germany, on Feb. 2, 1926, Giscard d'Estaing came from an aristocratic family. A brilliant academic career led to his becoming an inspec-

tor of finances in 1954 and being elected deputy for Puy-de-Dôme in 1956. Secretary of state for finance from 1959, he served as finance minister in 1962–66 and 1969–74. In May 1974 he succeeded Georges Pompidou as president.　　(PIERRE VIANSSON–PONTE)

Gray, Hannah Holborn

On Oct. 6, 1978, the banner in the quadrangle courtyard at the University of Chicago heralded the inauguration of Hannah Holborn Gray with a verse strangely reminiscent of Shakespeare: "All hail, Hannah, hail to thee, Ph.D. of history . . . Thane of Yale . . . Chicago's president hereafter." Gray, a medieval scholar, became the university's tenth president and first woman to be placed at the helm of a university that has produced some 140 college and university presidents and has claimed 42 faculty and alumni Nobel Prize winners.

Hannah Holborn was born in Heidelberg, Germany, on Oct. 25, 1930. Her fami-

COURTESY, THE UNIVERSITY OF CHICAGO

ly fled to the U.S. in 1934 because her father, a college professor, opposed Hitler's Nazi regime. At the age of 15 she entered Bryn Mawr College and from 1950 to 1952 was a Fulbright scholar at the University of Oxford. She married Charles M. Gray in 1954 and earned (1957) a Ph.D. while teaching at Harvard University (1956–59). She and her husband later joined the history faculty of the University of Chicago. In 1972 the dynamic self-proclaimed feminist was named the first woman dean of arts and sciences at Northwestern University, and in 1973 she was appointed provost of Yale University by its president, Kingman Brewster. It was hardly a surprise when Gray, a respected, witty, yet firm administrator, was formally offered (December 1977) the presidency of the University of Chicago. The first woman to hold such a prestigious academic post, Gray undertook the formidable task of maintaining financial health and academic excellence at the same time. During her brief inaugural remarks she stated that university challenges can be overcome by applying "scrupulous inquiry, precise analysis, and informed judgment." As another banner draped over an entrance to the university administration building so aptly proclaimed, "Vivat Hannah!"

(KAREN JUSTIN)

Guzmán Fernández, Silvestre Antonio

Democracy is a rather uncommon, if desirable, form of government that cannot be willed upon a people but usually seems to evolve from some cruder political arrangement; the process of this evolution is slow, complex, and frustrating. The Dominican Republic is an apparent case in point. On Aug. 16, 1978, Antonio Guzmán was inaugurated president in the first peaceful transfer of power between constitutionally elected governments in 100 years.

From 1930 until his assassination in 1961 Rafael Trujillo, a traditional Latin-American dictator, ruled the Dominican Republic. In 1963 Juan Bosch became president of the country. He was soon overthrown and replaced by a civilian junta under the leadership of Donald J. Reid Cabral. In 1965 this junta was itself overthrown and a civil war began. U.S. troops intervened, ended the war, installed an interim president, and oversaw an election in 1966 that brought Joaquín Balaguer and his Partido Reformista (PR) into power. Balaguer was reelected in 1970 and 1974 but lost to Guzmán in his bid for a fourth term in office.

Silvestre Antonio Guzmán Fernández was born in La Vega, Dominican Republic, on Feb. 12, 1911, to a socially prominent family of modest means. He began working at the age of 15 and rose to an executive position with the Dutch-owned Curaçao Trading Co. In 1948 he and a partner founded a firm that produced rice and exported coffee and tobacco. He eventually became one of the nation's most successful agricultural entrepreneurs.

Guzmán abstained from all political activity until 1963, when he joined the Partido Revolucionario Dominicano (PRD), founded by Bosch, an old friend. In 1963 President Bosch appointed him minister of agriculture. After Balaguer's election in 1966 Bosch, Guzmán, and the PRD went into opposition. After 1966 Bosch moved sharply left toward a wholehearted acceptance of Marxist-style dictatorship, leaving the PRD in 1973. José Francisco Peña Gomez, a prominent attorney, and Guzmán inherited leadership of the PRD.

In the 1974 election the PRD joined in a national front (called the Santiago Agreement) that opposed Balaguer. Guzmán was the front's presidential candidate, but at the last moment the front decided to abstain from voting. They charged the incumbent government with harassment and corruption, and Balaguer became president once more. In 1978 Guzmán was again the candidate of the PRD. The election took place as scheduled on May 16, but one day later the Army suspended the counting of votes. After international protests and charges of vote fraud by both sides in the contest, Guzmán was declared winner of the presidency on July 8.　　(VICTOR M. CASSIDY)

Habré, Hissen

He was pictured in the West as a wild guerrilla leader of the rebel Chad National Liberation Front (Frolinat) in the Tibesti Saharan desert country, whose Toubou tribesmen had held the French ethnologist Françoise Claustre captive for nearly three years. But on Aug. 29, 1978, Hissen Habré won sudden international respectability when he was appointed premier of Chad by Pres. Félix Malloum. The transformation from rebel to premier was brought about by the increasing success of Frolinat in the field and the military and economic insecurity of Malloum's government. Differences about procedure and policy soon soured relations between president and premier, however.

As the French knew, Habré was, in fact, no "wild man." Born in 1942 in northern Chad into the Toubou tribe, he studied at the Institut d'Études Politiques in Paris and gained his diploma in 1971. (He spoke perfect French and was a man of some polish.) Not long after his return to Chad, he was entrusted by then president N'Garta Tombalbaye with a confidential mission to Abba Siddick, at that time leader of the rebellion. Habré went over to Frolinat and became "leader of the Army of the North."

HENRI BUREAU—SYGMA

He did not remain in command of Frolinat, however. In October 1976 he was ousted by another rebel leader, Goukouni Oueddei, with Libyan support. His hostage Françoise Claustre, seized in 1974, was released by Oueddei in January 1977 after the French government paid a ransom of Fr 10 million. Meanwhile, Habré, sometimes reported dead, had escaped with some followers to the Sudan. He emerged in January 1978 as commander of part of Frolinat's forces, and as head of the northern forces signed an accord with Malloum at Khartoum, Sudan, leading to a cease-fire that was supported by Libya. However, this proved as ineffective as a cease-fire arranged in March between Oueddei and the Chad government, also with Libyan backing.

(PHILIPPE DECRAENE)

Hampton, Lionel

Feted at the Newport Jazz Festival, serenaded in New York City, and invited to perform with the Boston Pops Orchestra, Lionel Hampton celebrated his 50th anniversary as a professional musician in 1978. He had become, according to Down Beat magazine, "an institution, one of the living legends of this music we call jazz."

Born in Birmingham, Ala., around 1914, Hampton was sent to his grandparents in Chicago when his father was reported missing with the American Expeditionary Force in World War I. He was educated in Roman Catholic schools, first performing in the Holy Rosary Academy's juvenile fife and drum corps. Hankering to do more drumming, he took a job as a newsboy because the Chicago Defender sponsored a band for its vendors. "I couldn't get to the snare drum first, so I played the bass drum. First I carried it, then I played it."

After high school Hampton's grandmother sent him west with an introduction to a musician in California, where he played percussion for several years. He studied music theory at the University of Southern California and worked with Les Hite's orchestra, which played movie scores. He then joined a series of dance bands and gained such a favourable reputation that when Louis Armstrong appeared in Los Angeles for a recording session he asked Hampton to sit in as his drummer.

By accident Hampton stumbled onto the vibraharp, an instrument then used strictly as a curiosity in large ensembles. He soon introduced the vibes as a major jazz instrument and recalled that it opened "the front door to the electronic age" in popular idioms.

In the 1930s Hampton played vibes with the Benny Goodman Quartet, which besides Goodman on the clarinet included Gene Krupa on drums and Teddy Wilson at the piano. Hampton recalled that this was "the first time black and white ever played together on the stage." After illness sidelined Goodman, Hampton formed his own big band. At the height of the swing era he played to every kind of audience: at debutante parties, at Harlem's famous Apollo Theatre, where Leopold Stokowski came especially to hear him, and at five presidential inaugural balls.

As his own golden anniversary project Hampton produced a record series entitled "Who's Who in Jazz." More than a dozen records were cut the old way—by inviting great jazz artists to a studio and letting them improvise together at will.

(PHILIP KOPPER)

Havlicek, John

For 16 years John "Hondo" Havlicek was so consistent, so reliable, that basketball fans and players did not realize how much he meant to them until they learned he was leaving them. After Havlicek announced Jan. 29, 1978, that he would retire at the end of the National Basketball Association season, his last months as a player became a nationwide celebration. "I don't want it to be emotional or sad," he had said. "I don't want a lot of tears."

He got cheers. Suddenly, people remembered that this was the man who had been a key member of eight Boston Celtics championship teams; so meticulous that he folded his socks on a hanger before leaving the locker room to play; so unselfish that he did not object to being a nonstarter in his first eight seasons, even lending glamour to the "sixth man" role. This was the captain of the best team in basketball history, the man former Celtic coach and general manager Arnold "Red" Auerbach called "the guts of the team."

He was its feet, too. Havlicek was the player who made the Celtics' fast break so fast, hustling so much that nobody called him too short when he was a relatively diminutive 6-ft 5-in forward. He had begun running wherever he went when he was a schoolboy in Martins Ferry, Ohio. During the play-offs in 1976, Havlicek tore a muscle in his foot. The doctor said he could play in the final series only if he soaked his foot in ice water for an agonizing two hours a day. Havlicek soaked his foot four hours a day and finished the play-offs with an average of 25.9 points a game.

Havlicek's career scoring average was 20.8. In his best season, 1970–71, he averaged 28.9 points, 9 rebounds, 7.5 assists, and 45.4 minutes for every 48-minute game. He was the most valuable player of the 1974 play-offs, and he made the league's all-defensive team for five straight years beginning with the 1971–72 season. In his final season he played in his 13th consecutive All-Star Game. No NBA player had played in more than Havlicek's 1,270 regular-season games or shot more than his 23,930 field goal attempts. He ranked second among all-time NBA veterans with 10,513 field goals and 46,471 minutes played. Before playing his last game on April 9, 1978, one day after his 38th birthday, Havlicek received gifts from nearly every NBA team. They were expensive, but not as valuable as his gifts to basketball. (KEVIN M. LAMB)

Haya de la Torre, Víctor Raúl

To a visitor in Lima, Peru, in the spring of 1978, it was like walking through a time warp, for prominent among the names scrawled on walls as the election for a constituent assembly approached was that of Víctor Raúl Haya de la Torre. At the age of 83, 54 years after he had founded the Alianza Popular Révolucionaria Americana (APRA), Latin America's most durable politician was leading his party in what would prove to be a successful electoral effort.

In the election on June 18—Peru's first since 1963—the Apristas won 35.3% of the votes cast and 37 of the 100 assembly seats, 5% and 12 seats more than their nearest competitors. On July 28 Haya was elected president of the assembly, which was to frame a constitution that would return Peru to civilian rule after more than a decade of military dictatorship. He was widely mentioned as a presidential candidate in the election promised for 1980.

This was the first time Haya had actually held office, though he had run for president of Peru three times. Born Feb. 22, 1895, to a wealthy family in Trujillo, he became a student activist, was arrested and deported in 1923. APRA was founded the next year, while he was in exile in Mexico. Its fundamental aims were to end imperialism and to promote Latin-American political unity and the nationalization of land and industry.

The Aprista movement steadily gained adherents, but it was not until 1931 that Haya returned to his country as a presidential candidate. He lost and was jailed again until 1933. For 11 years he worked underground.

In the 1945 election the Apristas backed the successful presidential candidate, José Bustamante. He outlawed the party in 1947 and a year later was himself overthrown by Gen. Manuel Odría. During the disorders Haya took refuge in the Colombian embassy in Lima where he remained for five years, until international pressure secured him a safe conduct out of the country. Haya ran for president twice more. In 1962 he led the field but lacked the necessary one-third plurality, and the military took over before Congress could make the final decision. A year later he was defeated by Fernando Belaúnde Terry, who was ousted by the military in 1968.

"I'm a figure who is almost totally symbolic of the rescue of democracy," Haya told an interviewer. Both antimilitarist and anti-Communist, he had softened his views toward capitalism. As a result, he had added, to his traditional enemies of the right, new enemies on the Communist-Maoist left. Now in the centre—a strange place, perhaps, for an old revolutionary—Haya seemed once more in the ascendant, though his history (and Peru's) stood as a warning against overly facile prediction.

(DAPHNE DAUME)

Hodgkin, Dorothy Mary Crowfoot

Dorothy Hodgkin's presidency (September 1977–September 1978) of the British Association for the Advancement of Science was only the latest in a series of honours and seemed unlikely to be her last. She had won the 1964 Nobel Prize for Chemistry, and in 1965 she received the Order of Merit, an award strictly limited in numbers and in the sovereign's sole gift. She was then already a fellow (1947) and a royal medalist (1956) of the Royal Society and was later to become its first Wolfson research professor (1960–77) and its Copley medalist (1976).

The medium of her achievement was crystallography. In 1933 at Cambridge, she and J. D. Bernal took the first X-ray photographs of a protein, pepsin. Later, at Oxford, following Ernst Chain's experiments with penicillin, she began work on analyzing its crystals. Her current interest in the atomic resolution of insulin had begun in the 1930s; she was also studying the relation of intramolecular peptide chain patterns with the reactions of the molecules themselves.

It was frequently mentioned that she was only the third woman Nobel chemistry laureate (after Marie Curie and her daughter Irène) and the first woman OM since Florence Nightingale. Married in 1937 to Thomas Hodgkin, a specialist in the governments of emergent states, and mother of three children, she appeared to move easily between her family and her work. Her sex, perhaps, predisposed her to maintain a synthesizing element in her career. Interest in archaeology preserved a link with her father's classical scholarship, and crystallography itself brings together chemists and physicists. While remaining involved in laboratory-based research, she readily related scientific development to social problems, urging the British Association to concern itself with such issues as pollution and the development of atomic energy.

Born in Cairo, Egypt, in 1910, Dorothy Hodgkin was educated at the Sir John Leman School in Beccles, England, subsequently reading chemistry at Somerville College, Oxford. After two years at Cambridge, she became Somerville's chemistry tutor (1934), later a university lecturer, and in 1955 a reader. She was chancellor of the University of Bristol from 1970.

(STEPHANIE MULLINS)

Hua Kuo-feng

Always fascinating, Chinese politics had another remarkable year in 1978. It was a period when the People's Republic of China made forays into the backyard of its leading Communist antagonist, the Soviet Union, by seeking ties with Romania and Yugoslavia, two Eastern European Communist countries that have had their own differences with the U.S.S.R. China also discussed oil production with the staunchly anti-Communist shah of Iran, formally ended the technical state of war that had existed between China and Japan since the end of World War II, and opened negotiations with a number of Western corporations in order to speed up China's domestic economic development. Most noteworthy of all, China and the U.S. agreed in December to recognize one another and establish full diplomatic relations.

One man whose position placed him at the centre of all this activity was Hua Kuo-feng, China's 59-year-old premier and Communist Party chairman. Before the death of Premier Chou En-lai in January 1976 and of Chairman Mao Tse-tung the following September, Hua was an obscure party functionary. But in 1978 the successor of China's two great revolutionary leaders was remarkably visible on the international scene. His visits to Eastern Europe and Iran, his first trips outside China, were unprecedented for a top Chinese official. As the year progressed, Hua seemed to swing more and more enthusiastically behind the modernization and liberalization program sponsored by Vice-Premier Teng Hsiao-p'ing. Indeed, it was difficult at times to tell whether Hua or Teng was really in charge.

SVEN SIMON/KATHERINE YOUNG

Although Hua had taken over the top government and party posts before Teng painfully emerged from political disgrace to become vice-premier, it was Teng who seemed to be calling many of the shots, at least where modernization was concerned. In November Hua and even the revered Mao himself were criticized in one of China's periodic outbursts of "politics by wall poster." Many analysts assumed that the man behind the attacks was Teng, who was suspected of trying to wrest the premiership from Hua. But 74-year-old Teng denied any such intention, saying that "a younger man is better for the job." The wall posters then started to come down, and Hua's position in the turbulent world of Chinese politics seemed relatively secure again. The fact remained, however, that Teng spent much of the year personally promoting China's interests through trips abroad, which included visits to non-Communist Southeast Asian countries. And it was Teng who was designated to travel to Washington, D.C., in early 1979 to launch a new era in Sino-U.S. relations. (STANLEY W. CLOUD)

Jabir al-Ahmad al-Jabir as-Sabah, Sheikh

The new emir of Kuwait, Sheikh Jabir al-Ahmad al-Jabir as-Sabah, succeeded his cousin, Sheikh Sabah as-Salim as-Sabah, who died on Dec. 31, 1977. The succession was automatic as Sheikh Jabir had been crown prince since 1966, under the standing arrangement whereby his own Jabir as-Sabah branch of Kuwait's ruling family divides the highest authority in the state with the Salim as-Sabah branch, which had occupied the rulership from 1950 to 1977. No major changes were forecast in Kuwait's foreign or domestic policies as a result of the succession, although Sheikh Jabir's own active political career suggested that he would be more closely involved in running the affairs of Kuwait than was his predecessor.

Sheikh Jabir was born in 1928, the son of Sheikh Ahman al-Jabir as-Sabah, ruler of Kuwait from 1921 to 1950, and was educated privately in Kuwait. From an early age he played a leading role in Kuwait's administration. He entered the Security Department, with special responsibility for the Kuwait Oil Company (KOC) area (1950–56), and was the ruler's special representative with KOC and Aminoil (1956–59) when Kuwait was becoming a leading oil producer. From 1959 to 1962 he was president of the Finance Department and the Housing Department, with budgetary control over all public departments. On Kuwait's acquisition of full independence after the ending of its exclusive treaty relationship with Britain in 1961, he became minister of finance and economy and then minister of finance and industry. As such he presided over the establishment of the Kuwait Fund for Arab Economic Development which, by providing loans on easy terms to other Arab states, pioneered in spreading Arab oil wealth to the needier parts of the Arab world.

In the year following the death of Sheikh Abdullah as-Salim as-Sabah, emir from 1950 to 1965, Sheikh Jabir became prime minister and crown prince by agreement among members of the ruling family. As prime minister he continued to maintain a special portfolio for oil and financial affairs. In August 1976 he resigned, charging that Kuwait's National Assembly, established after independence, had made his government's task impossible by obstructing vital legislation. The emir suspended the parliamentary constitution, and Sheikh Jabir formed a new government.

(PETER MANSFIELD)

Jackson, the Rev. Jesse

In the 1960s black Americans and their white allies won many battles for civil rights and removed the legal obstacles to black advancement. In the late 1970s the black community was turning inward more and more—not toward a philosophy of separatism but toward one of self-help. The Rev. Jesse Jackson typified this change in black activity. During the 1960s he served in the Southern Christian Leadership Conference (SCLC), a national civil rights organization that was led by the late Rev. Martin Luther King, Jr. Jackson participated in numerous marches and sit-ins. In 1966 he was chosen by King to establish a Chicago branch of Operation Breadbasket, the economic arm of the SCLC. Its objective was to improve the economic status of black people in their own community. Operation Breadbasket employed many of the nonviolent direct-action tactics that had proved successful elsewhere in the U.S.

In 1971 Jackson founded Operation PUSH (People United to Save Humanity), a Chicago-headquartered organization that sought to build a strong economic base within the U.S. black community. Instead of leading marches he began to tour the black community, spreading his philosophy with the theme of "PUSH for Excellence." His enemy became not so much the white power structure as the mass media. He denounced popular music, television programs, and black-oriented films that glorified amoral and antisocial conduct. In his view parents and educators must organize to protest and counteract this poison-

WIDE WORLD

ing of young people's minds. Jackson stated that the family is the central unit of society. Black parents must discipline and guide their children, pressing them to succeed in school. An undisciplined adult without work skills will never obtain or keep a good job and will eventually become a drain on the community. Education and a strong family life, Jackson maintained, are the keys to black advancement.

Jesse Louis Jackson was born on Oct. 8, 1941, in Greenville, S.C. He received a B.A. degree from the Agricultural and Technical College of North Carolina, attended the Chicago Theological Seminary, from which he received an honorary doctorate, and was ordained a Baptist minister in 1968. Though he took part in many civil rights activities as a student, it was his work with Operation Breadbasket that made him nationally known. (VICTOR M. CASSIDY)

Jarvis, Howard

On June 6, 1978, the voters of California approved Proposition 13, an initiative on the ballot in a primary election that cut California's property taxes by 57% and reduced the state budget by $7 billion. Proposition 13, which 65% of the California electorate favoured, was the best-publicized and perhaps the most radical of many tax-limitation measures passed throughout the United States in 1978. It started a "taxpayers' revolt," which could lead in time to substantial shrinkage of revenues at all levels of government in the U.S.

Proposition 13 was also called the Jarvis-Gann Amendment after its authors—Howard Jarvis, a retired businessman, and Paul Gann, a real estate salesman. The measure limits the tax on real property to 1% of its full cash value as assessed in 1975–76 and limits increases in assessed values to 2% per year unless the property changes hands. It forbids new property taxes and makes it much more difficult for state or local government in California to increase existing taxes or to impose new ones. In recent years California property taxes had risen rapidly in accordance with the large increases in market values of homes.

When Proposition 13 took effect on July 1, state hiring was frozen, many state and local government workers were laid off, and numerous programs were curtailed or canceled, although the full effect was delayed by distribution of part of the state budgetary surplus to localities. Many Californians, Jarvis included, believed state government had grown too large and were glad that the amendment had this effect.

Jarvis had campaigned for years against high taxes and big government. He was born in Utah on Sept. 22, 1903, to Mormon parents who hoped that he would become a judge. Instead he chose a business career, operating a chain of newspapers, an aluminum foundry, a chemical plant, and an office equipment factory until his retirement in 1962. Jarvis was active in conservative Republican politics, working in the presidential campaigns of Dwight Eisenhower in 1952 and 1956 and Richard Nixon in 1960. He ran unsuccessfully for the U.S. senatorial nomination in 1962 and for state offices in 1970 and 1977. In each of these campaigns he had the same platform: cut taxes.

Even though he lost at the polls, Jarvis

acquired a following, and in 1974 he became director of the Apartment Association. This 8,000-member lobbying group became the base from which he launched his successful campaign for Proposition 13.
(VICTOR M. CASSIDY)

Jawara, Sir Dawda Kairaba

Under the leadership of Sir Dawda Jawara, the tiny West African republic of The Gambia (population about half a million) had become one of Africa's few successful parliamentary democracies. His ruling People's Progressive Party had won three successive elections under completely free conditions since independence in 1965, and Sir Dawda had been president since April 1970 when a republican constitution was adopted to replace the former monarchy under Queen Elizabeth II. In 1978, as current chairman of the Sahel Interstate Committee Against Drought, Sir Dawda toured Western Europe, Canada, and the U.S. to seek aid for the drought-afflicted countries, of which The Gambia was one.

COLIN DAVEY—CAMERA PRESS

President Jawara, who was born on May 16, 1924, completed a science course at Achimota College (Ghana) in 1948 and went on to study at the University of Glasgow, Scotland, where he qualified as a veterinary surgeon in 1953. Although born a Muslim, the son of a Mandinka trader, he received his early education in a Methodist school. It was to the Mandinkas that Alex Haley traced his origins in his best seller *Roots* (1976), which helped to focus world attention on The Gambia and brought a welcome influx of tourists.

Jawara became a Christian when he married in 1955 and changed his first name to David, but ten years later he reverted to the Islamic faith and readopted his original name of Dawda. He first entered politics in 1959, won a seat in the legislature the following year, and became minister of education. When his party won the elections in 1963, he became The Gambia's first prime minister and led his country into independence two years later. He was knighted by Queen Elizabeth in 1966.

Slight of stature and elegant in appearance, with polished manners and a moderate attitude to most aspects of life, Sir Dawda in his politics was essentially pragmatic and careful. He was conciliatory rather than combative in dealing with supporters and opponents alike. A strong believer in the Commonwealth of Nations, he also gave firm support to the Organization of African Unity and to the idea of nonalignment.
(COLIN LEGUM)

John, Patrick Roland

As was the case with many Caribbean politicians, Col. Patrick Roland John—independent Dominica's first prime minister and honorary commander of its 80-strong defense force—eluded political labels. In Caribbean terms he was a socialist but not a revolutionary. After some dalliance with Cuban and Guyanese models of development, he appeared to have rejected them in favour of a mixed economy. Internationally, he made it clear that, in development terms, he saw the island's future bound up with the West. To the surprise of many, one of his first acts after Dominica exchanged its British associated statehood for full independence on Nov. 3, 1978, was to establish diplomatic relations with South Korea.

In terms of domestic politics, John had already proved himself to be tough—some would say ruthless—in his desire for stability. Following the murder of a number of tourists in the mid–1970s and the emergence of a black power movement, he introduced legislation so broadly drawn that it even regulated acceptable modes of dress. Later, he indicated that revolutionary groups would not be tolerated. Personally charming and witty, though with an aggressive streak that some related to his diminutive stature, John was an animated, unpompous, and incisive speaker who obviously enjoyed playing to the gallery.

Born in January 1937, he was educated in Dominica at St. Mary's Academy, a Roman Catholic secondary school where he later taught for five years. In 1956 he left teaching to work as a shipping clerk, then in 1960 became involved in trade unionism. He attended courses on industrial relations and trade unionism in Jamaica and Canada and became general secretary of Dominica's Waterfront and Allied Worker Union, which he had helped to found. In 1965 he was elected to the influential post of mayor of the island's capital, Roseau. Entering the legislature in 1970 as a member of E. O. Le Blanc's ruling Dominica Labour Party, he subsequently held several ministerial posts. When Le Blanc resigned in 1974, John succeeded him as prime minister.
(DAVID A. JESSOP)

John Paul II

Karol Cardinal Wojtyla, archbishop of Krakow, Poland, was elected pope on Oct. 16, 1978. He was the first non-Italian pope in 455 years and the first pope in his 50s for over 100 years. His election overturned most predictions. Commentators had simply not credited the cardinals with the imagination and courage they finally displayed in choosing Cardinal Wojtyla—scholar, theologian, sportsman (skiing and canoeing), and linguist.

Born at Wadowice in southern Poland on May 18, 1920, Karol Wojtyla was the son of a noncommissioned officer in the Polish Army. He lost his mother at an early age. In 1938 he became a student at the Jagiellonian University of Krakow where he studied Polish literature. He wrote poetry and acted in a group known as "Rhapsodic Theatre," which specialized in verse dramas on historical and patriotic themes.

When World War II and German occupation came to Krakow, all cultural life ceased. The university and seminaries were closed down. Wojtyla worked in a chemical factory. But the "Rhapsodic Theatre" continued clandestine performances, and Wojtyla became part of the "cultural underground." In 1942 he disappeared from public view. With no work permit, he could not afford to appear on the streets of Krakow. Already determined to become a priest, he went into hiding in the palace of the archbishop of Krakow, Adam Cardinal Sapieha.

Wojtyla was ordained on Nov. 1, 1946. His abilities had already been recognized, and he was sent to Rome for further studies. His dissertation at the Angelicum was on "The Concept of Faith in St. John of the Cross," and his thesis at the Catholic University of Lublin was on the possibility of basing a moral system on the work of the phenomenologist Max Scheler.

After serving as parish priest and professor, Wojtyla was appointed in 1958 as auxiliary bishop of Krakow—he was the youngest Polish bishop—and in 1964 he became archbishop. The cardinal's hat followed in 1967. This was seen as a "political" gesture; the suppler, more conciliatory Wojtyla was supposed to balance the intransigent primate of Poland, Stefan Cardinal Wyszynski. Though of a different temperament, Wojtyla was always loyal to Wyszynski. He also became known on the wider international scene. He was present at all four sessions of the second Vatican Council (1962–65) and spoke lucidly on religious liberty and atheism. Subsequently, he attended all five Roman synods held between 1967 and 1977 and was elected to the council of the synod in 1971—a good index of popularity.
(PETER HEBBLETHWAITE)

Johnson, Philip

Since its inception more than 40 years ago, the International Style of architecture has thoroughly reordered and come to dominate the skylines of U.S. cities. Conceived in Europe, later characterized by the design dictum that "less is more," this new tradition generated many classic edifices.

First as a writer and museum official, Philip Johnson was the movement's most influential apostle; later, as an architect, he was one of its outstanding activists. His home in New Canaan, Conn., exemplified the style at its best: a transparent "glass house" without interior walls set in a sylvan landscape. In 1956 Johnson collaborated with his mentor, Ludwig Mies van der Rohe, on the Seagram Building in New York City, the apogee of the monumentally unadorned glass box. In 1978 the American Institute of Architects awarded him its gold medal, the profession's highest award, as "one of the most eminent practitioners of the International Style."

Only weeks after the announcement Johnson unveiled his plan for a 660-ft-high New York skyscraper that seemingly repudiated the tradition he had championed. The headquarters for the American Telephone and Telegraph Co. was to be an enormous pink granite tower piled upon eight-story arches with ornamental moldings and topped with a broken pediment. Some shocked observers called it ossified Chippendale, and others compared it to a grandfather clock. At the same time, Johnson's firm was building a low, tile-roofed cultural centre in Dade County, Florida, and finishing a huge, star-shaped church with 10,000 panes of glass rising 120 ft above Garden Grove, Calif. The effect of these projects, the AT&T plan in particular, was to confirm Johnson's role as "at once American architecture's elder statesman and *enfant terrible*."

Johnson denied the labels various critics gave him, including "protopostmodernist." But he maintained that totally unadorned functionalism was a thing of the past; what would follow, he believed, was "art," which had always been his architectural preoccupation. The time had come for styles to diverge. "Let a thousand flowers bloom," he said.

Born in Cleveland, Ohio, on July 8, 1906, Johnson studied philosophy at Harvard University and then joined the newly established Museum of Modern Art in New York City as its first director of architecture. In his 30s he returned to Harvard for an architecture degree and began practicing what he had preached.   (PHILIP KOPPER)

Jørgensen, Anker Henrik

On Aug. 30, 1978, Denmark's prime minister, Anker Jørgensen, succeeded in forming a new government, increasing its support in the Danish Parliament from 66 to 88 of the 179 seats. To achieve this he had broadened his political base—to the consternation of some—by allying the Liberal (Venstre) Party with his own Social Democrats, bitter enemies though they had been. Cynical observers remarked that they would usefully prevent each other from making the disastrous decisions each would make if left on its own. At all events he had a government strong enough to confront a disunited opposition with some confidence. Ever since he first became prime minister in October 1972, Jørgensen had headed minority Social Democrat governments, except for a minority Liberal interregnum from December 1973 to January 1975 during which Poul Hartling was prime minister.

Born into a working-class family in Copenhagen on July 13, 1922, Jørgensen was orphaned while a child. After leaving the Copenhagen orphans' school, he became a working boy, meanwhile continuing his education through a labour union system for promising young workers; as part of this education he was sent to a three-month economic course at Harvard University. He worked in shipyards and warehouses and became a union shop steward in 1947. He was president of the Warehouse Workers' Union, 1956–62, and then rose to become president in 1968 of Den-

mark's largest labour union, that of the unskilled workers. He was elected to Parliament in 1964 from a Copenhagen working-class constituency. When the Danish people in October 1972 "chose Europe," voting in a referendum for Denmark to seek admission into the European Economic Community, Prime Minister Jens Otto Krag resigned in his hour of triumph. Jørgensen succeeded him on October 4, to the surprise of most Danes, for he had held no ministerial post; it continued to be a widespread opinion that he was Krag's "personal invention." But by 1978, after winning elections in 1975 and 1977, there was a general consensus that Jørgensen had grown into his prime ministerial job.   (STENER AARSDAL)

Kain, Karen

A love of music and a desire to express it were the reasons Karen Kain wanted to become a dancer. In 1959 she decided on a career in ballet when she saw Celia Franca's performance of *Giselle* in Hamilton, Ont., the town where Kain was born on March 28, 1951. She began ballet lessons at the age of nine and two years later entered the National Ballet School in Toronto. Graduating at age 18, she joined the corps of the National Ballet of Canada in 1969.

Midway through her second season with the company Kain was plucked from the corps and made a principal dancer, being given only one month to learn the role of the Swan Queen in *Swan Lake*. She danced *Swan Lake* with Rudolf Nureyev in 1972 and subsequently became one of his favourite partners. According to Kain, Nureyev came along when she "needed inspiration" and was helpful to her with his critical advice. The next year she danced the role of Aurora in his New York production of *Sleeping Beauty*. Kain believes that Nureyev's choreography is the hardest in ballet, but she was glad to dance the role because of the challenge it offered her.

With the National Ballet, Kain danced with Frank Augustyn. In 1973 this pair represented Canada at the second International Ballet Competition in Moscow. They won the first prize in the pas de deux category, and Kain herself won the silver medal in

CANADA WIDE

the solo women's division. In Moscow she caught the attention of French choreographer Roland Petit, who created two new roles for her, Albertine in *Les Intermittences du Coeur* (1974) and the title role in *Nana*, a reworking of Émile Zola's novel for the Paris Opéra.

In 1974 Kain's debut in *Giselle* (considered by some to be the most difficult role for a ballerina) was hailed as a triumph. The next year she and Augustyn made a film version for the Canadian Broadcasting Corporation and in January 1977 they danced it at Moscow's Bolshoi Theatre.

It has been said that Kain has the perfect body for ballet, and her dancing has been described as "of such purity and clarity of utterance that the eye is constantly delighted." Clive Barnes, the *New York Times* critic, called her "one of the most talented ballerinas in the Western world." Her versatility allowed her to adapt to any style from the strictly classical to the most contemporary.   (DIANE L. WAY)

Karpov, Anatoly

In a marathon chess match for the world championship at Baguio City, Phil., in which he first appeared to be an easy winner and then the probable loser, 27-year-old Anatoly Karpov of the U.S.S.R. just managed to retain his title, defeating challenger Viktor Korchnoi, formerly of the U.S.S.R. and now stateless, by 6 games to 5, with 21 drawn. (*See* CHESS.) Karpov donated $200,000 of his prize money to the Soviet Sports Committee.

Karpov's progress toward the world championship title was smooth at first. In the 1974 Candidates' tournament he disposed of Lev Polugayevsky and Boris Spassky (both U.S.S.R.) easily enough, but in the Candidates' final (3–2, with 19 draws) Korchnoi gave him a terrific fight. In 1975 Karpov became world chess champion without having to play, when world champion Bobby Fischer (U.S.) declined to play a match except under his own conditions. As world champion Karpov embarked on a course of successful and continuous chess activity unparalleled in the game's history. A string of tournament firsts between 1975 and 1978 included the 1976 Soviet championship.

Born at Zlatoust, Chelyabinsk district, in the southern Urals on May 23, 1951, Karpov moved with his family to Leningrad early in life. There he learned chess at the age of four, becoming a first-category player by the time he was nine. At 15 he won first prize in an international tournament at Trinec, Czech. A year later, at Groningen, Neth., he won first prize in a junior tournament subsequently recognized as the European Junior championship, and in 1969 he became world junior champion at Stockholm without losing a game.

In 1970 he gained the title of international grand master by coming in fourth in an international tournament at Caracas, Venezuela. Continuing successes in 1971–73—including a fourth in the Soviet championship in 1971 and tournament firsts at Moscow; Hastings, England; San Antonio, Texas; and Madrid—showed that he had become a very good world championship prospect as well as one of the world's outstanding tournament players.

(HARRY GOLOMBEK)

Kaunda, Kenneth David

Zambia's Pres. Kenneth Kaunda in 1978 survived the most difficult year of his career since leading his country into independence in 1964. It was highlighted by a suddenly arranged meeting with British Prime Minister James Callaghan (*q.v.*) at Kano, Nigeria, on September 22–23, after Kaunda's indignant outcry at learning of British past connivance in the supplying of oil to Rhodesia despite UN sanctions. At the meeting Kaunda obtained promises of further British aid. His problems were a compound of security troubles due to the Rhodesian conflict spreading into Zambia, economic collapse, disruption of communication routes to the sea, and political rivalries in a year of presidential elections.

That Kaunda survived at all was a measure of his own political standing and astuteness, and also of the loyalty of his friends. Kaunda played a major role as a mediator in the conflicts in southern Africa, working particularly for a peaceful solution in Rhodesia and, later, in Namibia. He had won the presidential election easily in 1968, but things went less smoothly in 1978—he won, unopposed, in December, with about 80% of the votes cast, but others seeking nomination had been disqualified by a somewhat severe interpretation of constitutional regulations.

Kaunda remained committed to his personal philosophy of humanism influenced by a Christian upbringing and the teachings of Mahatma Gandhi. His parents were Church of Scotland mission teachers in Lubwa Mission, Chinsali district, Northern Rhodesia (now Zambia), where he was born in 1924. Subsequently educated in mission schools, Kaunda trained to be a teacher but was deeply offended by the racism he encountered in colonial Northern Rhodesia. In 1943 he joined the anticolonialist African National Congress; his political activities led to his imprisonment for nine months in 1959. He established in 1960 the United National Independence Party, which became the ruling party after Zambia achieved independence in 1964. Kaunda became Zambia's first president and pledged himself to establish "a colour-blind society." But the racial tensions caused by the conflict in Rhodesia inevitably rolled over into Zambia and impeded his efforts to carry out his promise.

(COLIN LEGUM)

Kempes, Mario Alberto

The success of Argentina's long-striding forward in helping his country win Association Football's World Cup in June 1978 capped a rags-to-riches story. Born in Bell Ville, a small town between Rosario and Córdoba in Argentina, on July 15, 1954, Mario Kempes learned the rudiments of his footballing craft kicking a tin can around the streets of his hometown. His talent was quickly spotted, and at age ten Mario was signed by the Talleres club and played in the local youth league.

At 18, Kempes, who was then studying economics in Córdoba, signed for Instituto Córdoba. Goals were his business, and Kempes soon showed his worth by hitting the target 11 times in his first 15 games. Rosario Central swooped in to sign him, and still the goals kept coming. In one of his opening matches for Central, Kempes scored a hat trick against Estudiantes, a former world champion club. In 1974 he finished with 29 goals in 34 games, and in 1975 with 35 in 50 appearances.

The dark-haired, handsome six-footer was selected to play for Argentina in the 1974 World Cup against Bolivia, but he became so exhausted in the thin Andean atmosphere that he had to be removed from the lineup. He later went to West Germany with the squad, playing in three matches but failing to score. Back in his native land he regained his form, averaging nearly a goal a game for the first 22 games in 1976.

Kempes's next move was to Spain, lured by a secret bid from the Valencia club that approached $600,000. He took time to adjust there, but once the season began he was back to normal, finishing with 24 goals in 1977 and 28 goals in 1978. Returning home in May for the World Cup final series, he was top scorer in that competition, with six goals, including two in the final that gave his country the coveted trophy. As to that course in economics, in May 1978 Kempes signed a five-year contract with Valencia worth well over $1 million.

(TREVOR WILLIAMSON)

Kenilorea, Peter

On July 7, 1978, Peter Kenilorea, as the new nation's first prime minister, led the Solomon Islands in the southwestern Pacific, formerly a self-governing British protectorate, to full independence. At the time Kenilorea, a former public servant, had little political experience; he was first elected to the Legislative Assembly in June 1976 and became chief minister soon afterward. In that capacity he led the teams that negotiated both the independence constitution and a financial settlement of $43 million for the Solomons.

As prime minister Kenilorea faced various problems. The Solomons lacked cultural unity, and there was an active secessionist movement in the west; there was not a high level of political awareness among the populace, and there was little enthusiasm for independence in some quarters. There was also a bitter controversy over the granting of citizenship to migrant groups.

Kenilorea was born on Malaita in the eastern Solomons in 1943, the son of a Solomon Islands missionary. He was educated at the local school of the South Seas Evangelical Mission and at the King George VI school at Honiara. In 1963 he was sent to New Zealand for higher secondary education and in 1966–67 attended the teachers' training college at Ardmore, near Auckland.

From 1968 to 1976 Kenilorea worked in the civil service as a teacher at King George VI Secondary School, as a district officer and district commissioner in the eastern Solomons, and for a brief period in 1974–75 as secretary to the chief minister. He tried to enter politics as a candidate from Honiara in 1973 but had to wait until 1976 when he was elected from East 'Are 'Are on Malaita. After the resignation from politics of Solomon Mamaloni, the man who had seemed destined to be the Islands' first prime minister, Kenilorea, backed by other former public servants in Parliament, was chosen as chief minister in his place.

(BARRIE MACDONALD)

Kimball, Spencer W.

It only affected directly about a thousand people, but the announcement nevertheless was regarded as momentous. It came June 9, 1978, from First Presidency (president) Spencer W. Kimball of the Church of Jesus Christ of Latter-day Saints, the Mormons, and two of his counselors. The announcement stated that "all worthy male members of the church may be ordained to the priesthood without regard for race or color."

What the surprise announcement did was to open the door to Mormon priesthood for blacks, who had previously been barred because of tenets in the Mormon scripture that excluded blacks of African descent. Kimball said that he and his counselors had spent many hours in the Upper Room of the Salt Lake City Temple and that God had finally given them a revelation that church policy was to be changed.

The Church of Jesus Christ of Latter-day Saints has about four million members worldwide, and is the largest church to have been founded in the U.S. Few blacks had ever joined the church because of its discriminatory policies. The announcement meant that blacks could now participate fully in temple ceremonies. The church, however, did not abolish its opposition to interracial marriage.

Kimball, a former Arizona banker and insurance executive, acceded to the First Presidency of the Mormon Church on Dec. 30, 1973. He was born in Salt Lake City, Utah, in 1895, and was a grandson of Heber C. Kimball, who had been a counselor to Brigham Young, the man who led the Mormons to Salt Lake City after the death of founder Joseph Smith. Kimball moved to Arizona when his father was sent to head the church in St. Joseph. He was an honour student and athlete in school and was elected president of the student body at the church's Gila Academy, now Eastern Arizona Junior College. While living in Arizona he became interested in Indians and served for 25 years as chairman of his church's Indian Committee.

Klein, Calvin

Business had never been better than in 1978 for U.S. fashion designer Calvin Klein. During that year, a decade after he launched his own company with only $12,000 in capital, Klein was heading a $100 million business empire. Not content with his highly successful lines of womenswear, shoes, scarves, and sheets, in January 1978 Klein showed his first full menswear collection (containing everything from overcoats to neckties), and in March he premiered a complete line of cosmetics (ranging from makeup to soap). Both new ventures were immediate successes, with buyers placing some $10 million in orders in the first month for his menswear and with some $2 million worth of his perfume alone sold in its first six weeks.

Klein's success could be measured not just in dollars but also in the awards he earned from the fashion industry. He was the first designer to win three consecutive Coty Awards for womenswear (1973–75) and the youngest designer of ready-to-wear clothes ever elected to the Coty Hall of Fame (1975). Klein described his design philosophy as the making of "simple, comfortable but stylish clothes—but with nothing overscale or extreme." His clothes are relatively expensive, classic, elegant, and easy to wear, and they have obviously struck a responsive chord among buyers. Moreover, his achievements are said to represent not only the triumph of his particular brand of classical styling but also the maturation of U.S. fashion.

Success, however, has not been an unmixed blessing for Klein. On Feb. 3, 1978, his 11-year-old daughter, Marci, was kidnapped. She was released, unharmed, some ten hours later, after her father paid a ransom of $100,000.

Calvin Richard Klein was born on Nov. 19, 1942, in the Bronx, N.Y. He studied at the Fashion Institute of Technology and after graduating in 1962 went to work as an apprentice designer for a coat-and-suit manufacturer in the garment district. In 1968, when he opened his own company, the fashion industry was in a depressed period, with casual hippie-style clothing and the miniminiskirt defining the range of fashions. The direction Klein took was to provide simple, understated clothing. Noted at first for his suits and coats, he gradually placed more emphasis on sportswear, particularly interchangeable separates.

(JOAN NATALIE REIBSTEIN)

Kucinich, Dennis

Expectations were uncertain but mildly hopeful in November 1977, when 31-year-old Dennis John Kucinich was elected mayor of Cleveland, Ohio. He was the youngest person ever to become mayor of a major American city. Cleveland was beset by economic and social problems on a massive scale, and Kucinich had promised to reverse the decline of what had once been a prosperous industrial city.

Less than a year later Kucinich narrowly avoided being turned out of office in an unprecedented recall election. Government came to a standstill as the mayor battled with Cleveland's political and business establishments. Instead of improving, the city's financial plight grew worse, and by December, Kucinich found himself presiding over the first major U.S. city to default on its obligations since the 1930s.

Born in Cleveland in 1946, Kucinich was raised in the city and graduated from Case Western Reserve University there. His political career began as soon as he was old enough to vote. He served in the city council and was elected clerk of courts before winning the close race for mayor. Kucinich campaigned against the big business "special interests" and won support from Cleveland's mutually hostile black and working-class ethnic communities, despite the opposition of his own Democratic Party.

As mayor, he began to veto city council development programs and insisted that private enterprise be responsible for saving the city's disintegrating central business district. His young Cabinet members were viewed as inexperienced and arrogant, and

most of his major appointments were highly controversial, including that of Police Chief Richard D. Hongisto. When the police staged a "sickout" in a contract dispute, Kucinich ordered Hongisto to patrol the streets personally and later charged that the police force was corrupt. Ironically, it was the firing of Hongisto after he publicly accused Kucinich of trying to force him to commit "unethical acts" that catalyzed the recall movement. Kucinich barely survived the special August election, winning by fewer than 300 votes.

The default came December 15, when the city failed to pay off $15.5 million in short-term notes. Kucinich ostentatiously closed his account at a bank that was demanding repayment from the city, but eventually the financial community agreed to defer drastic action until referenda on two money-raising propositions had been held in February 1979.

(HAL BRUNO)

Kurisu, Hiroomi

As a career military officer, Hiroomi Kurisu has long agonized over what he saw as a dangerous flaw in Japan's military preparedness: in an emergency, the Self-Defense Force (SDF) cannot act without a direct order from the prime minister. Kurisu made sure the nation got this message when in October 1977 he was named chairman of the Joint Staff Council of the SDF, the country's highest military post. In July 1978 he went even further by asserting that he believed the SDF, in the event of a surprise attack, would "without hesitation take prompt supralegal action." Both Prime Minister Takeo Fukuda and Shin Kanemaru, director general of the Cabinet-level Self-Defense Agency, read this as a direct challenge to the principle of civilian control of the military. On July 25 Kurisu was forced to resign. He later denied in a press conference that he was questioning civilian control of the military; he merely wanted the government to rectify a bad situation.

Kurisu was born in Tokyo on Feb. 27, 1920. After graduating in law from the University of Tokyo in 1943, he joined the Ground Defense Force of the SDF and by 1972 had attained the rank of general. Like all policy-minded Japanese, he knew that conservative politicians were unhappy with the U.S.-inspired constitution of 1947, which not only bars war as a weapon of diplomacy but specifically forbids the maintenance of land, sea, and air forces. Conservatives would have liked to amend the constitution to legitimize armed forces, but opposition parties resisted any such change because they viewed the constitution as a bulwark of democracy. The Socialists for their part espoused a policy of unarmed neutrality. But for many Japanese, political realities were the overriding consideration. They approved the U.S.-Japan security treaty (which shelters Japan under the U.S. "nuclear umbrella"), but they doubted the U.S. would aid Japan if it were attacked. They also noted that the Soviet Union had repeatedly violated Japanese air and sea boundaries. In such circumstances, the U.S. would like to see the 260,000-man SDF enlarged and better armed (it started to take shape after the Communist conquest of China in 1949), but for the Japanese this presented great psychological problems. Mindful of World War II and its awful de-

struction, many feared the strengthening of the armed forces might lead to a revival of prewar militarism. And that was unthinkable.

(JOHN RODERICK)

Kyprianou, Spyros

When Archbishop Makarios, first president of Cyprus, died on Aug. 3, 1977, Spyros Kyprianou assumed the functions of acting president. He had been serving as president (speaker) of the House of Representatives and was also leader of the centrist Democratic Party. It was Kyprianou who, on August 8, pronounced the moving funeral oration when the body of the great leader of the Cypriot Greeks was buried on Throni, the highest peak of the Kykkos Mountains. On August 31 the House of Representatives unanimously elected him president of Cyprus, though in practice he had authority only in the Greek portion of the island. In April 1978 Kyprianou rejected Turkish Cypriot proposals for a permanent division of the island as unacceptable, but he was prepared to consider conditionally better negotiating terms offered in July.

Returned unopposed on January 16 for a five-year term, President Kyprianou had already shown strength of mind in refusing the demands of EOKA-B, a clandestine extremist group, after its terrorists had kidnapped (Dec. 14, 1977) and threatened to kill his 21-year-old son. Kyprianou had said that he was prepared to sacrifice his son but never his country, and the son was released. Later he struck bloodlessly at continuing EOKA-B activity by jailing 22 of its ringleaders. In the terrorist attack at Larnaca Airport on Feb. 19, 1978, he dealt firmly with both Egypt's unauthorized commando attempt and the captured Palestinian terrorists, who were not released but convicted and imprisoned.

Kyprianou was born at Limassol, Cyprus, on Oct. 28, 1932. He became a public relations officer for Makarios shortly after the latter's election in 1950 as archbishop of the Church of Cyprus and ethnarch (national leader) of the island's Greek people. When in August 1960 the Republic of Cyprus was established with Makarios as president, Kyprianou became foreign minister, an office he kept until May 1972, when he resigned at the insistence of Greece's military government. On Sept. 5, 1976, when the new House of Representatives was elected in the southern zone of Cyprus, the Democratic Front obtained 21 seats out of a total of 35, and Kyprianou was elected speaker.

(K. M. SMOGORZEWSKI)

Laplante, André

Sharing second prize for piano in the sixth International Tchaikovsky Competition in Moscow in July 1978 made pianist André Laplante a famous and much sought after artist. He endured the tremendous pressure of this competition to become the first Canadian ever to place, much less gain a medal, in the prestigious contest. One of the U.S. judges, Eugene List, identified Laplante's performance of Liszt's Sonata in B Minor as "the finest single piece of piano playing of the entire competition."

Laplante was not a novice in international contests. He had emerged with top prizes in the Marguerite Long-Jacques Thibaud International Competition (Paris, 1973),

the Geneva International Competition (1976), and the First International Piano Competition (Sydney, Australia, 1977). Of his Paris performance, the newspaper *Le Monde* stated that he had an "authentic gift of musical lyricism," and *Le Figaro* called him a "stunning artist."

Born in Rimouski, Quebec, on Nov. 12, 1949, Laplante early began piano lessons but stopped at age seven. Four years later, at the urging of his parents, he resumed and first began to play seriously at the age of 14. He studied at the École de Musique Vincent d'Indy in Montreal, receiving his master's degree in music in 1969. While in Montreal he won a young people's concert competition and made his debut at 15, playing Richard Strauss's *Burleske* with the Montreal Symphony Orchestra. A Canada Council scholarship afforded him seven years of study in Paris with Yvonne Lefébure. In 1975 Laplante began studying with Sascha Gorodnitzki at the Juilliard School in New York City.

Laplante performed as a soloist with all the major Canadian orchestras, playing piano concertos by Brahms, Liszt, Rachmaninoff, Mozart, Tchaikovsky, and others. He also made several concert tours throughout Canada and performed many recitals on the Canadian Broadcasting Corporation network. Abroad, he played in chamber music festivals in France, Hungary, and Portugal. He made his U.S. debut at Carnegie Hall in New York City in October 1978. (DIANE L. WAY)

Lauti, Toalipi

When Tuvalu, comprising nine coral islands in the western Pacific totaling less than 25 sq km (10 sq mi) in area and with a population of about 8,000, was granted independence from the United Kingdom on Oct. 1, 1978, the new microstate's first prime minister was Toalipi Lauti. An unlikely nationalist figure, Lauti had left his industrial relations position in the Nauruan phosphate industry in 1974, when he was elected unopposed from his home island of Funafuti to the legislature of the Gilbert and Ellice Islands Colony. When the Ellice Islands seceded to become Tuvalu in October

1975, Lauti was elected chief minister by a comfortable margin and led his country during the three years that preceded independence, being reelected in September 1977.

Lauti was born in 1932 in the Gulf District of Papua New Guinea, where his father was a pastor for the London Missionary Society. He was educated first at the Ellice Islands School and then, immediately after World War II, was one of a select group sent to Fiji and then to New Zealand for education. After five years spent at St. Andrews School and at the teacher-training college in Christchurch, Lauti returned to a position at the King George V School at Tarawa, headquarters of the Gilbert and Ellice Islands Colony, in 1953. He also acted on occasion as a mediator in industrial disputes in the phosphate industry at Ocean Island and Nauru, where Gilbertese and Ellice Islanders were employed. In 1962 he was appointed labour and training officer at Nauru for the British Phosphate Commissioners (and later for the Nauru Phosphate Corp.).

Antipathy between Gilbertese and Ellice Islanders grew in the 1960s and early 1970s, with the disproportionate representation of Ellice Islanders in education and employment as the most divisive issue. As the Ellice Islanders began to plan a separate future, Lauti, as one who was well educated, had exercised considerable behind-the-scenes political leadership over two decades. At ease in both Tuvalu and Western societies, he was generally perceived as the most suitable leader for the new nation. (BARRIE MACDONALD)

Leakey, Richard

During the past decade Richard Leakey, the son of the famous anthropologists Louis S. B. and Mary Leakey and a man who was at one time reluctant to follow his parents in their field, brought to light in East Africa a series of remarkably important fossils bearing on human evolution. These fossils have forced scholars to reconsider their views on how and when humans first developed. Just as his parents were noted for their work at Olduvai Gorge, Tanzania,

Richard Leakey

Richard Leakey became known for his research at the site of Koobi Fora, along the shores of Lake Turkana (formerly Lake Rudolf) in Kenya. From this site alone in the past ten years workers had uncovered some 400 fossils, representing perhaps 230 individuals, making Koobi Fora the richest and most varied assemblage of early human remains found to date.

Like his father, Leakey proposed controversial interpretations of his fossil finds. In two books written with science writer Roger Lewin, *Origins* (1977) and *People of the Lake* (1978), Leakey presented his view that, some three million years ago, three hominid (humanlike) forms existed: *Homo habilis*, *Australopithecus africanus*, and *Australopithecus boisei*. He argued that the two australopithecine forms eventually died out and that *H. habilis* evolved into *Homo erectus*, the direct ancestor of *Homo sapiens*, modern humans. At Koobi Fora he claimed to have found evidence to support this theory. Of particular importance is an almost complete fossil skull found in 1972, believed by Leakey to represent *H. habilis* and to date from about two million years ago.

Richard Erskine Leakey was born in Nairobi, Kenya, on Dec. 19, 1944. From early childhood he accompanied his parents on their expeditions. At the age of 17 he left school to set up a photographic safari business. When, in 1963, he found an australopithecine jaw while exploring the Lake Natron region, he decided he would, after all, become an anthropologist. In London Leakey completed a two-year secondary education program in six months, but then returned to Kenya before entering college. In 1967 he joined an expedition to the Omo River valley in Ethiopia. It was during this trip that he first noticed the Koobi Fora site, and he led a preliminary search there that uncovered several stone tools and hominid remains. In 1968 Leakey became director of the National Museum of Kenya. (JOAN NATALIE REIBSTEIN)

Lee Kuan Yew

With Communist powers competing vigorously for favours in Southeast Asia in 1978, government leaders in the region found it necessary to coordinate their responses. The collective policy of caution that finally emerged was attributed to some extent to Singapore's behind-the-scenes activity. That and yet another round of lecture tours and official visits to the West drew attention to Prime Minister Lee Kuan Yew as one of the region's more articulate strategists.

The sheer passage of time gave him a special position; having come to power in 1959, he remained the longest-governing leader in Asia. Domestic critics charged that his uninterrupted reign was the result not so much of popularity as of repressive policies that had discouraged support for opposition forces. It was a fact that every seat in Parliament was occupied by Lee's own People's Action Party. But the PAP itself cited the holding of regular general elections as proof of the government's democratic credentials.

In any case, the country's undisputed economic progress (its per capita income was second only to Japan's in Asia) made the nuances of the parliamentary system seem almost irrelevant.

For both Singapore and Lee, it was a hard-earned success story. Born Sept. 16, 1923, into a wealthy family of "Straits Chinese," Lee was educated at the Raffles Institute in Singapore, studied law at Fitzwilliam College, Cambridge, and was called to the bar in 1950 by the Middle Temple in London. Upon returning from England, he became involved in trade union activities. In 1954 he founded the PAP, becoming leader of the opposition in the Legislative Assembly the next year and prime minister in 1959, when Singapore achieved self-governing status. Lee defeated a leftist challenge within the PAP and survived his country's brief merger with the Federation of Malaysia. Declared an independent republic in 1965, Singapore concentrated on economic progress, achieving rapid success in every sector.

In recent years Lee had been concerned about succession. His preferred solution was to give political appointments and electoral opportunities to civil servants, academics, and technocrats in the hope that capable leaders would emerge.

(T. J. S. GEORGE)

Lopez, Nancy

Women had been playing good golf for years, but there was a limit to how much money they could make as long as they were doing it in relative privacy. They needed a drawing card, someone pretty and personable and, above all, very, very good. When they found Nancy Lopez in 1978, Ladies' Professional Golfers' Association Commissioner Ray Volpe said, "We have our Arnold Palmer and Lee Trevino in one package, plus sex appeal. Whether she becomes our Jack Nicklaus remains to be seen."

That day was on the horizon in 1978, when Lopez had what may have been the best rookie season for any athlete in any sport. She set LPGA rookie records by earning $189,813 and winning 9 of 24 tournaments, including the LPGA's featured event. She also set the golf world on its ear in May and June, when she became the first man or woman to win five consecutive tournaments.

"It's kind of neat when everyone looks up to you," Lopez said. "I never dreamed that would happen. I remember when I was an amateur going out to pro tournaments, how much I admired Arnold Palmer and Jack Nicklaus and wanted to get close to them."

She even won when she finally lost. The streak ended at Hershey, Pa., where Lopez failed for the first time in a year to shoot a birdie on the final day of a tournament. But during that week a 29-year-old Harrisburg sportscaster named Tim Melton was among the reporters to interview her, and later in the year she announced her plans to marry Melton early in 1979.

Nancy Marie Lopez, born Jan. 6, 1957, in Torrance, Calif., followed her three-handicap father, Domingo, around the golf course with a sawed-off three wood until he let her start playing when she was eight. She beat her father for the first time when she was 11 and won her first of three New Mexico state women's tournaments when she was 12. In 1975, as an 18-year-old amateur, she finished second in the U.S. Open.

When Lopez decided to turn professional, her father planned to support the venture by selling his automobile body shop. He did not have to. In her first pro event, the 1977 U.S. Open, she finished second and won $7,040.   (KEVIN M. LAMB)

Lucas García, Fernando Romeo

Unable to capture the minimum 50% of the ballots required for electoral victory, Gen. Romeo Lucas García nonetheless succeeded to the presidency of Guatemala when the nation's legislature voted unanimously in his favour. The taciturn former defense minister polled more votes than either of his opponents in the general election, Gen. Ricardo Peralta Méndez and Col. Alfredo Enrique Peralta Azurdia, but the low voter turnout and the intimidation exerted by Azurdia's extreme right-wing National Liberation Movement followers deprived the 53-year old successor to the outgoing president, Gen. Kjell Laugerud García, of a clearcut popular triumph.

All three candidates were military men, and the leftist party in Guatemala was excluded from the March 5 elections. Almost 60% of the country's registered voters failed to cast ballots at all, and another 20% intentionally invalidated their ballots as a gesture of protest. Surprisingly, no disturbances or violence were reported on election day; in light of the widespread vote fraud perpetrated in the 1974 elections and the lack of a civilian or left-leaning candidate on the 1978 ballot, conflict could have erupted easily.

Following repeated delays in the announcement of the final outcome, all three candidates charged fraud. Only Azurdia, though, took action. With 250 armed supporters, he seized the offices of the Electoral Council (overseers of the balloting) but departed on the arrival of armed soldiers and policemen. Finally, three days after the popular voting, the Council declared that no one had won the constitutionally required 50% and that the presidency would be decided by the Congress.

Despite charges of fraud from both Méndez and Azurdia and threats from Azurdia's backers to seize the Electoral Council a second time, the outcome of the election—once the final vote had been announced—was clear. Congress had always endorsed the candidate with the most popular votes, and that candidate in 1978 was Lucas García. Nominee of the Broad Front, he also had the support of the army leadership and the Laugerud administration.

Lucas García was born July 4, 1924, in Chamelco. He attended the Polytechnic Institute and was graduated in 1949. Two years earlier he had entered military service as a cadet, and by 1973 he had risen to the rank of brigadier general. He also became army chief of staff and minister of national defense. From 1958 to 1963 he served as a congressman from Alta Verapaz.

(JEROLD L. KELLMAN)

Mamet, David

During the past three years David Mamet had emerged as one of the leading playwrights in the U.S. In that period he produced nine plays, and the reputation he earned first in his native Chicago grew into a national one. His most recent work, *The Water Engine* (1978), was so successful at the New York Shakespeare Festival's Public Theatre that it was moved to Broadway. His *American Buffalo* (1977) also enjoyed a respectable run on Broadway and was named the best American play of 1976–77 by the New York Drama Critics Circle. According to Richard Eder, writing in the *New York Times Magazine*, Mamet "is not simply an interesting and most individual playwright. He has been showing the kind of creative vitality that does not guarantee greatness but usually goes along with it."

While some reviewers criticized Mamet's work for weaknesses of plot and character development, most granted him a superb ear for dialogue, a way of turning everyday speech into contemporary poetry. He focused particularly on the language of the working class of middle America. His plays are usually short, and most call for just a few actors. There is usually little overt action, the movement taking place within the language of the characters. *The Water Engine*, for example, is a 90-minute fable of the

Great Depression that uses the format of a radio broadcast. The story concerns an inventor who produces an engine that runs on water; the inventor is ultimately murdered, offstage, by a double-dealing patent attorney and his partner.

Mamet was born in Chicago on Nov. 30, 1947. He attended Goddard College in Vermont, where he studied theatre and literature and wrote his first play, *Camel*. After obtaining his degree Mamet held various acting, teaching, and unskilled jobs. He returned to Chicago in 1972, where he succeeded in having his *Duck Variations*, *Mackinac*, *Marranos*, and *Sexual Perversity in Chicago* performed by experimental and community theatre groups. In 1974 *Sexual Perversity* won the Joseph Jefferson Award for the best new Chicago play.

Also in 1974 Mamet and three colleagues formed the St. Nicholas Players theatre company; its first production was Mamet's *Squirrels*, followed later by *The Poet and the Rent*. In 1975 *Sexual Perversity* and *Duck Variations* were produced in New York, where they were warmly received. Other plays include *Lakeboat*, *A Life in the Theatre*, *The Woods*, *Dark Pony*, *The Revenge of the Space Pandas*, and *Reunion*.

(JOAN NATALIE REIBSTEIN)

Marcos, Imelda Romualdez

Even before Imelda Marcos was appointed (1975) governor of metropolitan Manila by her husband, Philippine Pres. Ferdinand Marcos, the vibrant first lady had been the second most powerful figure in the country. In June 1978 her image was further enhanced when she joined the Cabinet to head the newly created Department of Ecology and Human Settlements, with responsibility for planning and developing 1,500 cities and towns.

Then, in August, the interim Parliament overwhelmingly supported a resolution to create a rare husband-and-wife government. If approved by the president, Mrs. Marcos would become the Philippines' first deputy prime minister and the president's officially designated successor. Many believed Marcos himself initiated the move. One clue came shortly thereafter, during the constabulary's anniversary celebrations, when a policemen's chorus sang "Imelda"—with lyrics by Ferdinand Marcos. The first lady displayed the same air of shyness she had shown when named governor of Manila and minister of human settlements. She indicated, however, a willingness to head a ten-man junta after her husband is gone.

Imelda Romualdez, the daughter of a wealthy family from the island of Leyte, was born on July 2, 1931. She made headlines first as Miss Manila of 1953, and again when she married Marcos in 1954. After moving into the presidential palace in 1966, the former beauty queen quickly took advantage of her new position. There was much talk about her growing wealth and the appointments of relatives to both governmental and industrial positions that paid salaries in five- and six-digit figures. When an attempt was made on her life in 1972, she dealt a sharp karate chop to the bolo-wielding assassin. Mrs. Marcos, who also headed numerous charitable and cultural activities, spent $500 million in 1977 for the construction of 14 hotels and only

some $13 million for badly needed public housing. Although 55 model homes were built in Tondo, one of Manila's worst slums, all of the 25,000 poor families remained in shacks because middle-class families occupied the dwellings.

Because Mrs. Marcos had been warmly received during state visits to China, Cuba, and Libya, she was stunned by the welcome accorded her in August 1978, when she traveled to Washington, D.C. Fifteen of the 114 congressmen who signed a letter protesting the alleged rigging of the Philippine elections in April asked pointed and serious questions about her personal wealth and the alleged torture of Trinidad Herrera, a Tondo slum leader, and Colonel Mendes, who was arrested and reportedly subjected to electric shock treatments. Soon after Mrs. Marcos returned home, four prominent Filipinos nominated her for the Nobel Peace Prize, on the basis of a 1976 visit to Libya, where she attempted to persuade Muammar al-Qaddafi to cut off arms shipments to Muslim rebels in the southern Philippines.

(KAREN JUSTIN)

Mickey Mouse

Few performers can boast of half a century of stardom, but in 1978, when Mickey Mouse blew out the 50 blazing candles on his birthday cake, he had accomplished just that.

The beloved Mickey Mouse was born in 1928 on the sketchpad of his creator, Walt Disney. Mickey's origin is shrouded in mystery, but it is widely believed that his features were copied from a little fellow who gleefully scampered across Disney's draw-

UPI COMPIX

ing board while he worked for a farm journal in Kansas City. As a very young mouse, Mickey appeared in his first two adventures, *Plane Crazy* and *Gallopin' Gaucho*, but in October 1928 he became a sensation when *Steamboat Willie*, the first animated cartoon to employ sound, had its New York premiere. The mild-mannered mouse, who spoke with the voice of his creator, became an international favourite, known as Mikki Mausu in Japan, Michael Maus in Germany, and Miguel Ratonocito in Spain and

Latin America. He appeared in hundreds of short cartoons with his friends Minnie Mouse, Pluto, Goofy, and Donald Duck and made a cameo appearance as the sorcerer's apprentice in *Fantasia* (1940).

On Christmas Day 1950 Mickey and company made their television debut. The show was so successful that it was repeated the following year, and the studio scheduled a new series of Mickey Mouse cartoons. During the 1950s he was also host of his own television show, *The Mickey Mouse Club*, which featured boy and girl Mouseketeers sporting black hats with stiff, protruding ears. The demand for Mickey Mouse memorabilia became so great that the famous Mouseketeer hats emblazoned with Mickey's image appeared in retail stores, together with watches, stuffed toys, books, and even clothes.

In 1978 Mickey could be seen strolling down the avenues at Walt Disney World in Orlando, Fla., and at Disneyland in Anaheim, Calif. He was soon to have another home at a $300 million amusement complex planned for Urayasu, Japan. Mickey, a perennial crowd pleaser, declared that his retirement plans were sketchy; this seems easy enough to believe, for Mickey doesn't look any older now than he did the day he was born. (KAREN JUSTIN)

Miller, G(eorge) William

Why would the chairman of a prospering conglomerate leave his position, which pays about $400,000 a year in salary and bonuses, to take a largely thankless job that pays a mere $57,500? No one thought it proper to ask that question of G. William Miller when he left Textron Inc. just before his 53rd birthday to become chairman of the seven-man Board of Governors of the U.S. Federal Reserve System. Broadly speaking, Miller and his colleagues would be responsible for determining the monetary policies of the nation—chiefly because the Fed, which they direct, exercises wide regulatory control over all of the country's 6,000 national banks.

Miller was born in Sapulpa, Okla., on

BRIAN ALPERT—KEYSTONE

March 9, 1925. He graduated in marine engineering from the U.S. Coast Guard Academy in 1945 and in law from the University of California at Berkeley in 1952. After four years with the Cravath, Swaine & Moore law firm in New York City, he joined Textron in 1956 and quickly moved into top executive positions while simultaneously serving on the boards of Allied Chemicals Corp. and other companies. Under Miller's management Textron's profits increased an average of about 10% a year on volume that by 1978 grossed some $2.6 billion annually. Miller became a millionaire and in the process established a reputation for hard work, self-discipline, and managerial know-how. He was also known for his sense of humour and detestation of smoking.

When Miller replaced Arthur F. Burns as head of the Fed, economists were not quite sure what policies the new chairman would follow. They admired his past accomplishments, but many could not discount the fact that Miller had no academic background in banking. He was, moreover, apparently less concerned about theory than about tangible results. Some found this refreshing; others found it disturbing. But all seemed willing to give Miller a chance to try to do for the nation what he had already done for Textron. (ARTHUR LATHAM)

Mohammad Reza Pahlavi Aryamehr

In the early summer of 1978 revolution blazed out in Teheran and other cities in Iran. It was inspired by two strange allies, the "red" Tudeh Party and the Muslim conservatives, united only by their hatred of the reign of the shah of Iran, Mohammad Reza Pahlavi. The head of the Islamic rebellion was the 78-year-old Ayatullah Ruhollah Khomeini, who from exile near Paris was attempting to topple the shah and proclaim an Islamic republic. The Tudeh Party, led by Moscow-based Iraj Eskandare, supported this aim as a step toward a Communist-controlled republic.

The background of the mass uprising was the shah's effort to use income from oil exports—Iran's oil reserves would last only a few decades—to speedily transform his primitive country into a modern industrial and military power able to dominate and stabilize southwestern Asia. Supported by a powerful army and an energetic secret police (Savak), the shah rode roughshod over the Muslim conservatives and sternly repressed any democratic opposition to his centralist planning. In the meantime, members of the royal family, politicians, and others corruptly enriched themselves and scandalized opinion. When he saw that he had gone too far too fast, the shah introduced liberalizing measures and remedied abuses. But at the year's end strikes, riots, and demonstrations continued, and the shah's position became increasingly insecure.

Mohammad Reza was born in Teheran on Oct. 26, 1919, eldest son of Reza Shah Pahlavi, an army officer who in 1925 abolished the Qajar dynasty and proclaimed himself shah-in-shah. On Sept. 16, 1941, during World War II, pro-German Reza abdicated

under Soviet-British pressure in favour of his eldest son. After the war Allied forces withdrew and conditions gradually became normal.

To consolidate the monarchical system the shah needed an heir. Having already divorced two wives unable to produce a son, in December 1959 he married Farah Diba, daughter of an Iranian army officer. A crown prince, Reza, was born in Teheran on Oct. 31, 1960. On Oct. 26, 1967, Mohammad Reza crowned himself and his wife at a lavish ceremony in the Golestan Palace, Teheran. (K. M. SMOGORZEWSKI)

Moi, Daniel Torotich Arap

On the death of Kenya's historic leader, Jomo Kenyatta, on Aug. 22, 1978, his vice-president, Daniel Arap Moi, became acting president. He was then endorsed by the ruling Kenya African National Union (KANU) to stand unopposed in the presidential election. Moi was in many ways the obvious successor to Kenyatta, having served as his deputy since 1966. The fact that he did not belong to the politically dominant Kikuyu tribe (being a Tugen, a small clan of the Kalenjins) was an asset in the tribally divisive politics of Kenya.

Moi was born of peasant stock in the Baringo district of Kenya in September 1924. He received much of his early education at the American Mission School and the Government African School at Kapsabet. He qualified as a teacher in 1945 and soon became headmaster of a small local school. In 1950 he entered politics and was nominated five years later to the Kenya Legislative Council. He campaigned successfully in 1957 in the first elections for African members of the Legislative Council and became successively minister of education and of local government. In 1960 Moi led a breakaway movement from Kenyatta's KANU, which was dominated by the two most influential tribes, the Kikuyu and the Luo. His own Kenya African Democratic Union was essentially an alliance of the smaller tribes that worked closely with a party of local white settlers. After independence (December 1963), his party merged with Kenyatta's in November 1964, and when Kenyatta became president in December

SVEN SIMON/KATHERINE YOUNG

1964, Moi was made minister of home affairs. In 1966 he was chosen to be vice-president. He remained closely loyal to Kenyatta, and as the grand old man of Kenya became less active as a result of age, Moi was given increasing responsibility.

Married, with two children, both studying in the U.S., Moi combined politics with a successful farming and business career. The new president was a tough politician with a strongly independent mind, not renowned for his tolerance of those of his opponents whom he regarded as mischievous or irresponsible. Upon gaining office, he at once initiated drives against corruption and against illiteracy and unemployment.

(COLIN LEGUM)

Mota Pinto, Carlos Alberto de

The choice of Carlos Alberto de Mota Pinto as premier of Portugal on Oct. 25, 1978, came as a surprise to many, but he had emerged as the most acceptable candidate after the defeat of Alfredo Nobre da Costa's government. The Socialists and Centre Democrats approved his selection and seemed likely to give him parliamentary support.

Much more of a known political figure than his predecessor, Mota Pinto was himself a Social Democrat "dissident"; once the party's parliamentary leader, he left in December 1975 after a clash of personalities and a disagreement with the party head, Francisco Sá Carneiro, over the party's organization and its drift to the right. In order to maintain his insecure government, he favoured closer cooperation with Social Democrats and like-minded elements in the Socialist Party.

The new premier was 42 years old, a professor of law and jurist from Portugal's oldest university, in Coimbra. Between 1961 and 1963 his teaching career was interrupted by military service in Portuguese Guinea. After becoming a professor of civil law, he obtained his doctorate in political science in 1970. He rose to be vice-rector of Coimbra University from May 1974 to January 1975, serving on his faculty's Council of Law.

Following the April 1974 revolution, Mota Pinto was elected in April 1975 as a deputy to the Legislative Asssembly for the Social Democrat Party and participated in the drafting of the new constitution. In the first constitutional government, July 1976–December 1977, led by Mário Soares, he served as minister of commerce and tourism.

Mota Pinto's new government, although chosen within a democratic framework, had no formal links with the main political parties and was initiated by Pres. António Eanes. On Dec. 4, 1978, Mota Pinto outlined his program, aimed at restoring the balance of payments and reducing inflation.

(MICHAEL WOOLLER)

Motta, Dick

"The opera isn't over until the fat lady sings," Dick Motta kept telling people. They said his Washington Bullets could never win the National Basketball Association championship, considering that 7 of the league's 22 teams had bettered the Bullets' 44–28 regular season record. But Motta just kept sending his team out on the courts to beat all those better teams until, by June

7, 1978, there were no more teams to beat. The Bullets defeated Seattle 105–99 in the final game of the final series, and nobody could say they weren't the best team in the land.

It was a long opera for Motta, whose 448 NBA victories through the 1977–78 season ranked him ahead of all but two coaches the league had ever had. Motta won those games in only ten seasons, but none of his teams even reached the final round of the play-offs before 1978. People could only wonder how many more games he would have won if he had ever had a team with a dominant centre. But he made do. He persisted. He molded his teams at Chicago and Washington into his own image, aggressive and deliberate, daring the opponent to knock them off. It's us against the world, he told them.

Richard Motta, born Sept. 3, 1931, knew a lot about stretching talent beyond its perceived limits. The youngest son of an Italian truck farmer living near Midvale, Utah, Motta did not even make his high school basketball team. He fought his way to coaching recognition with a six-year record of 122–31 at obscure Weber State in Utah, and in 1968 the Chicago Bulls hired him to coach their third-year expansion team. The first game he coached for them was the first NBA game he saw. The Bulls had won only 29 times the season before he joined them, and only 38 people were interested enough to buy season tickets. Three years later, the fans had their first of four consecutive 50-victory seasons, built around a patient offense and a tenacious defense. Even when the Bulls finished 24–58, worst in the league, in 1975–76, they still had the NBA's best defense, and Motta still was crafty enough to attract the Bullets' job offer after Chicago let him go.

He made them glad in his second season at Washington. In every play-off round after the first one, the Bullets had to play the odd game on their opponent's home court, but they jumped to 3–1 leads in best-of-seven series against both San Antonio and Philadelphia and beat them both, four games to two. They trailed Seattle three games to two before tying the series when substitutes scored 63 points in a 117–82 victory. In the final game they broke Seattle's 22-game home-court winning streak. When Motta repaired to his trout farm in Fish Haven, Idaho, the brooks babbled a little more sweetly than usual. (KEVIN M. LAMB)

Mull, Martin

"Martin Mull is almost famous," *New Times* magazine announced without fear of contradiction early in 1978, a year that ended without disproving the point. Painter, songwriter, satirist, and actor, he stood at the beginning of the year poised on a promising springboard to popularity, a television show that was born as "Fernwood 2-Night" and became "America 2-Night." It was contrived by Norman Lear, creator of "All in the Family" and "Mary Hartman, Mary Hartman," a spoof of soap operas staged in the fictitious town of Fernwood. The "2 Night" series was a spinoff spoof based on the premise that Fernwood might have its own television talk show. With Mull as its loquacious host, Barth Gimble, it gained a devoted but comparatively small following.

Mull's television debut had occurred on "Mary Hartman" as Barth's brother, Garth Gimble, "one of the most odious characters since Cagney smashed a grapefruit in Mae Clarke's face in *Public Enemy*." He was a wife beater but came to an early end impaled on an aluminum Christmas tree. Despite the odium, Mull was seen as a talented performer with the best sense of timing "since Jack Benny turned 39."

Born in Chicago in 1943, Mull "grew up in towns like Fernwood," made a name as a high-school athlete in Connecticut, and then earned honours at the Rhode Island School of Design. His first notably successful appearance as an actor occurred before a select audience in a draft board office. He brought a bag lunch with every carrot stick, the sandwich filling, and both pieces of bread separately wrapped in foil. When an Army interviewer asked what he thought about the draft, he suggested closing the window. Published reports of his military service were unavailable.

In Boston as a struggling artist he posted an unauthorized exhibition called "Flush with the Walls" in the Museum of Fine Arts men's room. Turning to the nightclub stage, according to his wife, "Martin had to take public transportation carrying his guitar, and not get paid, and play to an empty house. But he has a very large ego and that sustained him for a long time."

In California he cut some satiric records, including "I'm Everybody I Ever Loved," before one of Lear's aides recruited him. One of his records, "A Girl Named Johnny Cash," modeled after "A Boy Named Sue," was a near hit, and Martin Mull was on his way to semistardom. (PHILIP KOPPER)

Navon, Yitzhak

Israel's fifth president made his inaugural address to the Knesset on May 29. Speaking in Hebrew and then in fluent Arabic, President Navon appealed to Israel's Arab population and to Egyptian Pres. Anwar as-Sadat to ensure the success of the negotiations for a peace settlement. At 57, he was the youngest of Israel's five presidents. He was also the first not of recent European origin; his family had resided continuously in Jerusalem for more than 300 years.

Navon was born on April 19, 1921, in the Jewish quarter of Jerusalem. He studied Arabic and Islamic culture at the Hebrew University in Jerusalem and worked as a teacher at a night school for working youths. In 1946 he was drafted into the Arabic Department of the Zionist military organization, the Haganah, in Jerusalem and held this position until the conclusion of Israel's war of independence in 1948. He was posted for a short time to the Israeli missions in Uruguay and Argentina, but in 1951 Israel's foreign minister, Moshe Sharett, chose him as his political secretary.

After Navon served two years with Sharett, Prime Minister David Ben-Gurion requested his transfer to the prime minister's office to act as chief of the prime minister's secretariat. Navon remained there until Ben-Gurion's resignation in 1963. In this post Navon served as Ben-Gurion's secretary in his dealings with ministers and foreign dignitaries and as his shield against unwanted interventions.

After leaving the prime minister's office in 1963, Navon joined the Ministry of Edu-

cation and Culture, but by 1965 he was back in politics. He joined Ben-Gurion's Rafi party, a breakaway group from the Labour Party. He was elected to the Knesset and served as deputy speaker for seven years and as chairman of the Defense and Foreign Affairs Committee for four years.

(JON KIMCHE)

Navratilova, Martina

In July 1978 Martina Navratilova finally silenced the doubters who said she had dominated women's tennis early in the year only because Chris Evert chose that time to take a vacation. Not only did Navratilova overcome a 4–2 deficit in the final set to beat Evert 2–6, 6–4, 7–5 but she did it in the championship match of the British Open at Wimbledon, the temple of tennis. In her finest professional hour, though, Martina Navratilova had to say, "I'm very sad that I can't share this with my family."

She had not seen her family since September 1975, when she announced her defection from her native Czechoslovakia on the final day of the U.S. Open. Since then the Communist government of Czechoslovakia had not let her into the country and had not let her family out of it. Navratilova hoped that they at least had been able to reach the Czechoslovak border to see her Wimbledon victory on West German television. She knew that they would have been proud of her. By the end of 1978 she had earned $501,500 by winning 78 of her 86 matches, including two out of four against Evert, and she was ranked first in the world by the Women's Tennis Association.

Navratilova's family could appreciate how difficult it was for her to achieve that goal. Her grandmother once was ranked second in women's tennis in Czechoslovakia, and five years after she was born, on Oct. 18, 1956, in Prague, Martina began playing tennis. She made her first trip outside the country at the age of 13, but she did not see the world's best tennis players until 1973, when the Czechoslovak Tennis Association sent her to the United States to play in a series of tournaments. That was when she began to realize that in order to compete with the best she would have to leave Czechoslovakia.

Navratilova had been popular in the United States even before deciding to become a citizen. She joked with the spectators, and her daring serve-and-volley game was an exciting contrast to Evert's indomitable but conservative baseline strategy.

But Navratilova's style was a hard one to tame. Before 1978 her biggest tournament victories had been on the annual U.S. Virginia Slims tour. From 1974 through 1977 she played in the finals of the national tournaments in France, Italy, Australia, and West Germany, but there was always someone, often Evert, to beat her for the championship. That, however, was not the case in 1978, when she won 10 of 19 tournaments.   (KEVIN M. LAMB)

Noor al-Hussein (Elizabeth Halaby)

The Cinderella story of 1978 culminated on June 15, when Elizabeth (Lisa) Halaby, a 26-year-old U.S. woman, married Hussein ibn Talal, the king of Jordan and a man 16 years her senior. The wedding, a brief Muslim ceremony that took place in Raghdan Palace overlooking Amman, was the fourth for the king but the first for the bride. After the ceremony Hussein proclaimed his new wife, who had taken the Arabic name Noor al-Hussein ("Light of Hussein") and had become a Muslim a few days earlier, the queen of Jordan. This gesture surprised many, for Hussein had not been expected to grant this title to a foreigner.

Observers wondered how a woman from the United States, raised in the liberated atmosphere of the 1960s and '70s and who had had her own career, would adjust to life in the strict and conservative Jordanian society, where many people continued to believe that women are not equal to men. To such questions the new queen replied, "My career is my life with his majesty the king."

Unlike the Cinderella of myth, Lisa Halaby did not exactly move from rags to riches with her marriage. She is the daughter of millionaire lawyer Najeeb E. Halaby, former head of the Federal Aviation Administration, former president of Pan American World Airways, and president of Halaby International Corp. Born on Aug. 23, 1951, in Washington, D.C., Lisa Halaby attended the elite National Cathedral School, transferring to the exclusive Chapin School in Manhattan in 1965 and to the Concord Academy in Massachusetts in 1967. She entered Princeton in 1969 as a member of the university's first coeducational class, graduating with a bachelor's degree in architecture in 1974.

After graduation Halaby worked in urban design in Philadelphia, in Sydney, Australia, and in Teheran, Iran. She first went to Jordan while working for Arab Air Services, a company owned in part by her father that sought to provide Western expertise and technology for Middle Eastern airlines. In 1977 she became director of facilities design and architecture for Alia, the Royal Jordanian Airline, a job that

brought her regularly to Amman. It was about that time that Halaby first met Hussein, whose third wife, Queen Alia, had just died in a helicopter crash.
(JOAN NATALIE REIBSTEIN)

Nyerere, Julius Kambarage

One of the architects of the modern Pan-Africanist movement and of the Organization of African Unity (OAU), Julius Nyerere, president of Tanzania, was in 1978 one of the half dozen or so most influential leaders in the continent. As chairman of the group of "front-line" presidents of Tanzania, Zambia, Mozambique, Angola, and Botswana, he continued throughout 1978 to play a dominant role in the search for peaceful settlements in the conflicts over Rhodesia and Namibia. In July he visited the Ethiopian leader, Lieut. Col. Mengistu Haile Mariam, to confer on developments in East Africa.

During the year Nyerere also faced a military conflict with Uganda in October when Ugandan troops occupied a part of Tanzania. Nyerere's response was to pledge himself to do everything possible to bring about the downfall of Ugandan Pres. Idi Amin. In early December he rebuked the chairman of the OAU, Pres. Gaafar Nimeiry of Sudan, for calling for a cease-fire while Ugandan forces were still occupying Tanzania's Kagera region. Nyerere insisted upon Uganda's renouncing its claim to that area and demanded that the OAU condemn Amin's regime.

When Nyerere first became president of Tanzania (then Tanganyika) in 1962, he chose to be known by the honorific title of Mwalimu, a Swahili word meaning teacher. A moralist of principle, he held that leaders should teach by example. As the founder of his nation he remained committed to the idea of creating an egalitarian socialist society based on the concept of self-reliance.

Born in March 1922, the son of a chief in Butiama, Musoma District, in former Tanganyika, Nyerere became a staunch Roman Catholic. After studying at Makerere College in Uganda, he graduated from the University of Edinburgh, Scotland, and returned home to teach at the St. Francis School, Dar es Salaam, in 1952. From his early school days he was a rebel against the colonial system and a pioneer of the black

nationalist movement. Chief minister of Tanganyika in 1960 and prime minister when the country gained its independence in 1961, Nyerere became its first president in the following year.   (COLIN LEGUM)

Ohira, Masayoshi

Japan's new prime minister in 1978, Masayoshi Ohira, was a farmer's son whose favourite dishes were a bowl of noodles, rice with curry sauce, and a slice or two of raw fish. But behind his country-boy exterior and sleepy-eyed mien existed an accomplished politician and a shrewd negotiator. At 68, Ohira said he sought no new worlds to conquer. "I have no grand plans . . . . I just want the Japanese people to live in happy families in green cities." His main aim was to create middle-sized garden cities as refuges from the noise, pollution, and overcrowding of the Tokyo-Osaka megalopolis. Though he was, like his predecessor, Takeo Fukuda, a product of the conservative bureaucracy, he said he would attempt compromise rather than confrontation in his dealings with the political opposition. One of his first moves after taking office in December was to issue invitations for a Tokyo summit conference of advanced industrial nations in June 1979. Before that, he planned consultations in Washington, D.C., with Pres. Jimmy Carter over the implications of U.S. recognition of China.

Ohira was born on March 12, 1910, on a farm in Shikoku, the smallest of the main Japanese islands, and was an impoverished youth of 16 when his father died. After an older brother helped him through high school, he worked his way through what is now Hitotsubashi University and became an active Christian, joining the YMCA and taking part in Salvation Army activities. When he joined the finance ministry in 1936, he came under the eye of Hayato Ikeda, who, when he became finance minister, made Ohira his private secretary in 1949. The collaboration continued down the years. Ohira became Prime Minister Ikeda's chief Cabinet secretary in 1960 and was credited with suggesting the healing "low posture" policies toward the leftist opposition, which restored the nation to stability after the anti-American confusion of the late 1950s. Later, as Ikeda's foreign minister, he prepared the way for restoration of relations with South Korea. In 1972, as Kakuei Tana-

Masayoshi Ohira

UPI COMPIX

ka's foreign minister, Ohira was the co-architect of normalization of relations with the People's Republic of China.

Ironically, China was an issue when he sought the premiership in December. He had planned to use it in the campaign against Fukuda when the prime minister was struggling to conclude a peace treaty with Peking. Though Fukuda appeared to have a commanding lead after he successfully brought off the treaty negotiations, the ruling Liberal-Democratic Party gave Ohira the nod in its primary balloting. Fukuda then withdrew and Ohira took over. His success was attributed partly to the backing of Tanaka. Though indicted and on trial on charges of accepting bribes in the Lockheed scandal, Tanaka still controlled a large party faction. Ohira acknowledged his friendship for the man who, like himself, had risen from poverty to supreme power. But he said he would maintain the dignity and distance required of the premiership. A few days after assuming his new post, Ohira was attacked by a right-wing youth as he left his official residence. He was not, however, injured by the knife-wielding assailant.   (JOHN RODERICK)

Ould Salek, Mustafa

Leader of the Military Committee for National Recovery that, on July 10, 1978, ousted Pres. Moktar Ould Daddah in a bloodless coup, Lieut. Col. Mustafa Ould Salek succeeded him as head of state in Mauritania. The coup sprang from the mounting dissatisfaction of military leaders with Ould Daddah's conduct of the long-drawn-out war with Polisario guerrillas from the Western Sahara and with the grave economic difficulties arising from it. After the coup Polisario declared a cease-fire, and contacts were made with it. Ould Salek announced that Mauritania's pro-Western policy and understanding with Morocco would continue, and he authorized talks in Paris in November on the Western Sahara. (See MAURITANIA.)

Born in 1936 in Kiffa, Mustafa Ould Salek worked as an assistant primary school teacher from 1954 to 1960, when he joined the Army. He attended a cadet course for reserve officers at the Saumur Cavalry School in France in 1960 and went on to infantry tactics and training at Saint-Maixent during 1963–67. From September 1967 to January 1968 he attended the staff school in Paris, qualifying as a staff officer and, a few months later, as a parachutist. Commissioned as a second lieutenant in Mauritania in February 1961, he rose steadily through the ranks to lieutenant colonel (October 1974), with a colonelcy awaiting him in 1978.

After serving as aide-de-camp to the president of Mauritania from October 1961 to November 1962, Ould Salek was posted to the general secretariat of the African and Malagasy Defense Union at Ouagadougou, Upper Volta, became adjutant to the First Troop of the Mauritanian Guard in 1963, and was local commander in Atar (October 1964 to November 1965). Posted to the headquarters of the Mauritanian armed forces, he was appointed acting chief of staff in December 1965, a position he held until February 1967. Subsequently he was seconded to the Ministry of Defense and became an army inspector (July 1968 to July

1969). From Nov. 1, 1970, to 1975 he was assistant governor and then governor of an administrative region. In July 1977 he took military command of the Third Region (Adras) before being appointed chief of staff after the ministerial reshuffle of Jan. 26, 1978.   (PHILIPPE DECRAENE)

Ozawa, Seiji

Seiji Ozawa, the ebullient music director of the Boston Symphony Orchestra, made history in 1978 when he became the first foreigner to conduct China's Central Philharmonic Orchestra in Peking. Audiences at the June 16–17 concerts gave the 43-year-old China-born Japanese maestro standing ovations after programs of European, Chinese, and Japanese music. The official Chinese news agency, Hsinhua, described the concerts as a smashing success and hoped there would be more of the same. Ozawa later acknowledged it was difficult to evaluate the musicians because they had never heard Brahms and were playing Berlioz for only the second time. But he predicted the Peking group would be on a level with its Japanese counterpart in three to five years. To attain this goal, the Chinese were urged to exchange musicians, even with the Soviet Union, because "music has no boundaries."

Born in Hoten, Manchuria, on Sept. 1, 1935, of a Christian mother and Buddhist father, Ozawa was at home in both the Eastern and Western musical worlds. He studied piano in Tokyo, but gave it up after injuring a hand playing rugby. In 1959, at the age of 24, he was named the outstanding musical talent in Japan. But musicians of Tokyo's prestigious NHK Orchestra wanted an older director, so Ozawa headed for Besançon, France, where he won first prize in an international competition for conductors and attracted the attention of the late Charles Munch, who, as director of the Boston Symphony, was asked to be a judge. Ozawa was then invited to study at Tanglewood in Massachusetts. He received the music centre's coveted Koussevitzky Prize and a scholarship to study with Herbert von Karajan in Berlin. Leonard Bernstein met him there and invited him to tour Japan

AUTHENTICATED NEWS INTERNATIONAL

with the New York Philharmonic. The following year Ozawa directed the Ravinia (Ill.) Festival, and later he led the Toronto and San Francisco orchestras before taking up the baton in Boston in 1973.

Ozawa's first appearance in Europe with the Boston Symphony won critical applause. L'Aurore of Paris commented: "The Orchestra of Boston has found in Ozawa a great sorcerer who has awakened them." Der Abend of Berlin described Ozawa and the orchestra as having "one heart and one soul." But when Ozawa arrived in Japan in 1978 for a tour with the Boston, it was high adventure all the way. True, Ozawa had directed the New Japan Philharmonic for several years, but now he was returning to his native land as director of one of America's greatest orchestras. The homecoming turned into a personal triumph. Everyone, it seemed, wanted Ozawa to know what it meant to have him back. Ozawa shared the excitement and sentimentality of those moments and took advantage of the tour to introduce the musicians to the Japan he knew and loved. One evening was especially memorable. The program, which featured a work composed for the occasion by an American, was dedicated to the late Hideo Saito, Ozawa's former music mentor.

(JOHN RODERICK)

Parker, Sir Roger Jocelyn (Mr. Justice Parker)

It is something of an old English custom: when in doubt, set up a public inquiry and put a leading lawyer in charge of it. This was done in 1977 to advise the British government on whether to go ahead with the construction of a nuclear fuel reprocessing plant at Windscale on the coast of Cumbria. The man named as inspector to head the inquiry was Mr. Justice Parker (knighted on becoming a High Court judge in January 1977). The Windscale inquiry lasted from June 14 until Nov. 4, 1977, and 17 weeks later, on March 6, 1978, Parker's report was published.

Born Feb. 25, 1923, Roger Parker belonged to a distinguished legal family; his grandfather was a law lord and his uncle was lord chief justice from 1958 to 1971. Early in his career he made a name for himself as a commercial lawyer with a reputation for incisive and sometimes ruthless cross-examination. In 1974 he headed the 81-day inquiry into a disastrous explosion at the Flixborough, Humberside, chemical plant and had shown a capacity to cope with a mountain of complex evidence. This ability was needed in the Windscale inquiry, which accumulated a pile of documents said to be 29 ft high.

The Windscale plant would have the capacity to reprocess nuclear waste fuel from foreign countries as well as from U.K. plants. The proposal had created great controversy not only because of the safety hazards involved but because it could be taken to suggest a future commitment to the so-called plutonium economy, dependent for energy supplies on fast breeder reactors using plutonium extracted at plants such as Windscale. In his report, Parker recommended that British Nuclear Fuels Ltd. be allowed to build the reprocessing plant, and the government confirmed the go-ahead decision a few weeks later. This infuriated environmentalists, who had presented a thorough and expertly documented case against the project. Some protested that Parker had ignored key aspects of their case and had oversimplified complex arguments. But there was no provision for appeal against an inquiry voted on in this manner.

(HARFORD THOMAS)

Parton, Dolly

Singer/songwriter Dolly Parton's winning of the Country Music Association's 1978 Entertainer of the Year Award may say as much about the country music field itself as it does about Parton's talents. Distinctions between country and mainstream popular music were no longer cut and dried. The CMA award followed by some two years Parton's crossover into pop/rock music, and since that time several of her records had become simultaneous hits on rock and country stations. In 1978 she was also named best female country artist and best female country album artist by *Billboard*, while her recording "Here You Come Again" was cited as the top country single of the year. At the same time her album "Heartbreaker" was number one on *Billboard*'s chart of country long-playing records. In part, these awards represented the loyalty of Parton's fans but they also indicated increasing acceptance of new artistic ventures.

While Parton's popularity soared and her audience broadened, her crossover did not meet with unanimous critical approval. Although *Billboard*'s Gerry Wood said that Parton "managed her victories without sacrificing her powerful writing and singing talents and . . . showed how Nashville talents can reach the top by stretching beyond the boundaries—once restrictive—of country music," *Rolling Stone*'s Tom Carson disagreed. In a review of "Heartbreaker"

ADAM SCULL—BLACK STAR

he wrote, "Since Dolly Parton's widely publicized crossover from the country genre to the middle of the road mainstream, the quality of her music has gone dramatically downhill while her fame vaults toward the tinsel regions of instant celebrity."

In any event there could be little disagreement that Dolly Parton has come a long way from a childhood of poverty in the mountains of Tennessee. Born on Jan. 19, 1946, near Sevierville, Tenn., she was the fourth of 12 children. She started singing and writing songs as a young child, and was given her first musical instrument, a battered mandolin, when she was six. After graduation from high school in 1964 she moved to Nashville, Tenn., the capital of country music.

In 1967 Parton joined the nationally known band of Porter Wagoner. After seven years she left the group to work independently. In 1976, with her switch to pop, she formed a new group of backup musicians, Gypsy Fever. Among the best-known songs she has written are "Coat of Many Colors," "Tennessee Mountain Home," "Joshua," "Jolene," and "Love Is Like a Butterfly."

(JOAN NATALIE REIBSTEIN)

Pei, I. M.

"An architect . . . has to create an environment for life." I. M. Pei spoke these words not long before his East Building of the National Gallery of Art opened in Washington, D.C., on June 1, 1978. Pei designed this striking structure of triangular forms to house, in effect, three small museums in one, as well as a study centre for the visual arts. Much of the roof is made of glass to provide light and a feeling of openness. Apertures in the marble facade allow additional light and complement the structure's bold geometry.

Pei arrived at his plan for the East Building after inspecting the trapezoid-shaped site in Washington and touring numerous European museums with J. Carter Brown, the director of the National Gallery. Pei and Brown concluded that most museums were too large and monumental, enshrining art while intimidating the viewer. Pei maintained that "the ambience one has to create

I. M. Pei

not only has to be right for the object to be shown in its proper light and proper scale but also right for the individual walking through the museum to look at it." Brown called the East Building "very welcoming— so intimate; you don't expect a building of that size to be so cozy."

Ieoh Ming Pei directed I. M. Pei & Partners, a New York-based firm of architects that has designed many art museums and public buildings throughout the U.S., including the National Center for Atmospheric Research in Boulder, Colo., and the Dallas (Texas) Municipal Center. He was born in Canton, China, on April 26, 1917, and came to the United States to study engineering at the Massachusetts Institute of Technology. There he was influenced by MIT's dean, who urged him to become an architect. By the time that Pei completed college World War II had begun and there was no work for architects. Therefore, he practiced engineering for two years. Later he studied and taught design at Harvard University, coming into contact with the architects Walter Gropius, Marcel Breuer, and Philip Johnson (*q.v.*). In 1948 he began to design urban housing for Webb & Knapp, a large real estate development company. Pei founded his own firm in 1955.

(VICTOR M. CASSIDY)

Pelletier, Monique

Monique Pelletier was appointed minister-delegate for the status of women in the French government on Sept. 12, 1978. Since the beginning of the year, she had been secretary of state in the Ministry of Justice. This was the first time that the government member responsible for women had been given full ministerial rank, the first "minister for women," Françoise Giroud, having had the rank of secretary of state. Pelletier welcomed the opportunity to speak on equal terms with other ministers and declared that she saw herself as "the permanent conscience of the government in questions relating to women."

An energetic 52-year-old mother of seven, Pelletier embarked on the preparation of a reform of laws relating to marriage with the aim of making them more favourable to women. She also began examining the question of pensions for mothers who had had several children, but she rejected as unrealistic proposals for "housewives' salary." The cost of such a "salary," in her estimation, would exceed the total of receipts from income tax.

Monique Pelletier was born at Trouville-sur-Mer, Calvados, on July 25, 1926. A Paris barrister from 1946 to 1958, then a magistrate in juvenile courts, she managed a state-recognized educational institution, L'École des Parents et des Éducateurs, from 1972 to 1977. At the same time she entered local politics, becoming assistant mayor of Neuilly-sur-Seine, the richest suburb of Paris, and a member of the political bureau of the Republican Party, which supported Pres. Valéry Giscard d'Estaing. In 1977 Giscard appointed her to lead a major national investigation into drug addiction and, in particular, the problems of drug abuse among young people. As a minister, she was now concerned with applying the conclusions of her report on drug abuse, especially among teenagers, which had earned her the nickname "Madame Anti-Drogue."

(PIERRE VIANSSON–PONTÉ)

Pertini, Alessandro

Octogenarian Socialist politician Sandro Pertini, best known as a Resistance leader during World War II, was elected seventh president of Italy on July 8, 1978. It was a surprise result to a presidential election that had been moved forward six months because of the sudden resignation of Pres. Giovanni Leone, who had been accused of illegal real estate deals and tax evasion. Pertini, regarded as incorruptible, received a larger majority (83.6%) of the votes of the electoral college than any of his predecessors. But it took ten days and 16 ballots to break the stalemate between Italy's two leading political parties, the Christian Democrats and Communists.

Pertini was born on Sept. 27, 1896, in the village of Stella in Liguria. He served as a machine gunner in World War I, graduating after the war from Genoa University with a degree in law and social sciences. His first steps in politics were as a contributor to the Socialist newspaper *Avanti.* He rapidly identified himself with the anti-Fascist cause and was sentenced to prison six times by different military tribunals, the first time in 1925 when he was arrested for distributing anti-Fascist literature in his native village. He played an important part in helping to smuggle Socialist Party leader Filippo Turati out of the country in 1927 and followed Turati into exile in France, working first as a night taxi driver in Paris and then as a plasterer in Nice. Returning to Italy, he went underground but was betrayed by an informer and sentenced in 1929 to ten years in prison and three years of internal exile. Freed by the Allies in 1943, he was recaptured by the Germans and thrown into jail in Rome. He escaped and thereafter played a prominent part in Resistance activities.

After the war Pertini became secretary of the Italian Socialist Party and had a long and distinguished parliamentary career that culminated in an eight-year period until 1976 as speaker (president) of the Chamber of Deputies.

(DAVID DOUGLAS WILLEY)

Rafshoon, Gerald

In the spring of 1978 the White House belatedly perceived that U.S. Pres. Jimmy Carter was suffering from "an image problem." Many things had gone wrong, those that had gone right went almost unnoticed, and the national polls indicated that the president's popularity was slipping badly. So the call went out for Gerald Rafshoon.

Six months later the word "rafshoon" had taken on a new meaning in political Washington. Used as a verb, to be "rafshooned" meant that a presidential action had been timed and publicized to attract the maximum attention, or it could mean that an action had been downplayed or avoided because it might have a negative impact.

Rafshoon, whose official title was assistant to the president for communications, shrank from his own image as an image-maker. As he saw it, his job was merely to improve communications between the president, the administration, Congress, the Democratic Party, the news media, and the public. But however the job was defined, there was no doubt that Rafshoon soon became one of the most important members of the Carter administration. Whether it was due to Rafshoon's magic touch or because a number of important things finally worked right—such as the Camp David, Md., meeting with Anwar as-Sadat and Menahem Begin on the Middle East—the fact is that the president's ratings in the polls zoomed up after Rafshoon arrived in the White House.

Rafshoon was born in New York City in 1933 and studied journalism at the University of Texas. After working in New York and Atlanta, Ga., he opened an advertising agency in the latter city in 1963. He first came to public attention during the 1976 election when he skillfully handled Jimmy Carter's media campaign. He turned down job offers in the early Carter administration and instead opened a Washington, D.C., office for his advertising and communications firm. Rafshoon was in the midst of

DENNIS BRACK—BLACK STAR

a successful career making television films when the call for help came from the White House.

Although not a policymaker, Rafshoon played a key role in determining how policy was to be presented. It could not be proven, but it was widely believed in Washington that he suggested delaying the announcement of the Camp David accord from early Sunday afternoon—when the news would compete with professional football—to Sunday evening, when there would be a huge television audience. (HAL BRUNO)

Ray, Satyajit

The University of Oxford's award, on June 21, 1978, of an honorary doctorate to the Bengali motion-picture director Satyajit Ray was yet another tribute to one who had long ranked among the very foremost of the world's filmmakers.

Ray was born in Calcutta on May 2, 1922, into a family with strong cultural traditions. His grandfather was an artist; his father a painter and poet and the friend of Nobel laureate Rabindranath Tagore. After studies at the University of Santiniketan, Ray became a commercial artist (the world of advertising was to provide the setting for his film *Company Limited* in 1971). Soon he turned successfully to book illustration. From his youth, however, he had been a passionate devotee of motion pictures, particularly the U.S. films that reached Calcutta, and he was a co-founder of the Calcutta Film Society in 1947.

In 1950 the opportunity to watch and talk to French director Jean Renoir, who was then shooting *The River* in India, inspired Ray to start work on his own first film. This was *Pather Panchali,* adapted from the first of a trilogy of novels which he had illustrated some years earlier. Struggling without money and with collaborators no more experienced than himself (but encouraged at one point by U.S. director John Huston, who happened to be visiting Calcutta), Ray took three years to complete the film. Shown at the Cannes Film Festival of 1956, it was instantly recognized as a classic, the expression of a lyrical and humanist sensibility that was equally to distinguish the concluding parts of the trilogy, *Aparajito* and *The World of Apu,* as well as the best of Ray's films since that time.

Ray's production of more than a score of films was remarkably varied. He ranged from farce (*The Philosopher's Stone*) and children's stories (*The Adventures of Goopy and Bagha*) to Tagore (*Two Daughters*) and dealt with the poor, the old aristocracy (*The Music Room*), and the new bourgeoisie (*Company Limited*). *Distant Thunder* (1973) was an epic treatment of the great Bengali famine of 1943. *The Chess Players,* his most recent film, completed late in 1977 and adapted from a story by Prem Chand about the confrontation of the British colonial rulers and an effete Indian aristocracy, was his first in the Hindi language. (DAVID ROBINSON)

Rorvik, David M.

Orson Welles's 1938 radio play "War of the Worlds," which simulated a newscast of an invasion of New Jersey by beings from

Mars, inadvertently panicked thousands of Americans who trusted in the inviolability of news reportage. Forty years later freelance science writer David Rorvik again put that trust to the test with *In His Image: The Cloning of a Man*, a controversial book published in March by J. B. Lippincott. The profound difference between the efforts of these two men lies in intent: Welles's play merely succeeded too well as good fiction in suspending disbelief; Rorvik's account of an astonishing scientific breakthrough asks to be taken as solid truth, yet without offering one piece of supporting evidence.

In *In His Image*, an aging millionaire spends a vast sum to recruit the medical talent and finance the laboratory research necessary to create an infant boy who is the exact genetic copy, or clone, of his "father" —an heir who is in effect a twin separated some 60 years in time. Formidable questions of common sense and scientific content come up throughout the work, some of which Rorvik fields in ways that many critics found implausible. To explain the total lack of substantiation, Rorvik claims to have disguised or omitted details "to protect the child from harmful publicity and other participants from certain controversy." According to a statement from Lippincott, Rorvik refused "to divulge names or places even to his publisher. David Rorvik assures Lippincott that it [the book] is true. Lippincott does not know."

The great majority of scientists who chose to comment publicly dismissed *In His Image* as a hoax, citing numerous factual errors and pointing out the improbability of making so rapid an advance in cloning techniques while keeping it a secret from other workers in the field. In May a U.S. congressional subcommittee investigating Rorvik's claims listened to more expert criticism but failed to pin down Rorvik himself, who refused to attend despite repeated requests. By year's end Rorvik and Lippincott were facing a severe falloff in sales and a $7 million libel suit filed in July by a British scientist whose work was cited in the book.

A graduate of the University of Montana in 1966 with a master's degree in journalism from Columbia University, New York City, Rorvik worked as a medical reporter for *Time* before turning to free-lance writing. His published works include *Brave New Baby*, *Choose Your Baby's Sex*, and numerous magazine articles on medical topics. A reputable writer on the strength of his past work, Rorvik nevertheless could only rue an interview he gave in 1970 to a Montana newspaper, which printed: "He finds fiction writing more difficult than non-fiction, but is determined to complete his novel, 'The Clone,' and perhaps get it made into a movie."
(CHARLES M. CEGIELSKI)

Rose, Pete

For 16 years Pete Rose had dived headfirst into nearly everything he did on a baseball field. So when he had a chance to become the highest paid player in major league baseball, Rose was not any more bashful about taking the extra dollar than he had been about taking the extra base. As usual, he succeeded.

Soon after the 1978 season ended Rose was courted openly by the richest of baseball's owners until he decided to let the Philadelphia Phillies pay him a reported $3.2 million over the next four seasons. "I think I can put them over the hump," he said of his new team, the National League runners-up from 1976 through 1978. "The team needs leadership."

If that evaluation sounded presumptuous for a newcomer, it should be remembered that Rose has never been the sort of person to call a spade a pitchfork. In the preinflationary 1960s he made it clear that he intended to become the first singles hitter to make $100,000 a year. Ever since he began running out walks as a Cincinnati Reds rookie in 1963, he played with a cocky, aggressive style that prompted him to say the only difference between himself and legendary Ty Cobb was "I don't steal bases and he didn't wear a tie on the road." While shopping for the Philadelphia contract that would assure him $5,400 a game, Rose said, "I feel like I'm the number one player and I just want to get paid like it."

Rose played like it for much of 1978. On May 5 in the fifth inning of a Reds' home game against Montreal, the switch hitter hit a single to left field—the 3,000th hit of his career. He became the 13th player to reach that milestone and, at 37, the youngest.

The pinnacle he sat on July 31 was even less crowded. Rose became the second National Leaguer to hit safely in 44 consecutive games, the first since Willie Keeler did it in 1897 under more liberal hitting rules. His streak would end the next day, 12 games short of Joe DiMaggio's major league record, but in batting .385 for those 44 games Rose had captured the imagination of the country.

A folk hero in Cincinnati, Rose was born there on April 14, 1941. During his years with the Reds he made All-Star teams at four different positions, had 3,164 hits, which left him within 466 of Stan Musial's National League record, and won three National League batting championships. More

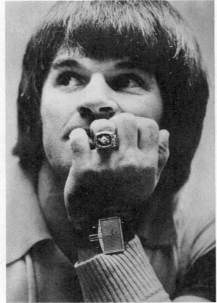

WIDE WORLD

than all that, though, he would be remembered by the message on the T-shirt that he had made to celebrate his 3,000th hit: "Hustle made it happen." (KEVIN M. LAMB)

Rosovsky, Henry

In May 1978, after some four years of planning and discussion, the Harvard College Faculty of Arts and Sciences approved a proposal to restructure undergraduate education at the school, the first such reorganization in more than 30 years. The man who initiated the change and who coordinated the preparation of the detailed proposal was the dean of Harvard's Faculty of Arts and Sciences, Henry Rosovsky.

In 1974 Rosovsky sent a letter to the faculty calling for a major revision of the general education program and for a change to a more structured approach to the curriculum. Rosovsky stated, "At the moment, to be an educated man or woman doesn't mean anything. It may mean that you've designed your own curriculum. It may mean that you know all about urban this and rural that. But there is no common denominator."

Faculty committees were established to examine all aspects of the undergraduate educational system, from the content of the curriculum to the quality of teaching. In May 1977 the faculty as a whole endorsed Rosovsky's key principle of strengthening core requirements. In February 1978 Rosovsky sent to the faculty his synthesis of the recommendations of the faculty committees. It was this basic proposal that received approval (by a vote of 182 to 65) in May.

The new core curriculum, which was to be implemented gradually beginning in 1979, was designed to ensure that students would possess a "basic literacy in major forms of intellectual discourse." Undergraduates would be required to select about one-fourth of their program from a list of core courses in five basic areas: literature and the arts, history, social and philosophical analysis, science and mathematics, and foreign language and culture. In addition, students would have to demonstrate competence in expository writing, mathematics, and foreign languages, either through examinations or through courses.

Rosovsky was born in Gdansk (Danzig), Poland, on Sept. 1, 1927. He moved to the U.S. in 1940 and became a naturalized citizen in 1949. After attending the College of William and Mary and later Harvard (where he received his Ph.D. in 1959), he taught economics at the University of California at Berkeley. He returned to Harvard to teach in 1965 and became dean in 1973. In 1977 he declined an offer of the presidency of Yale University.

(JOAN NATALIE REIBSTEIN)

Rozhdestvensky, Gennady

Music may in theory be a language without frontiers, but it was only after months of delicate negotiations with the Soviet authorities that Soviet conductor Gennady Rozhdestvensky finally took up (in September 1978) his appointment as chief conductor of the London-based British Broadcasting Corporation (BBC) Symphony Orchestra. On the evidence of his first concerts, British music lovers would find his three-year tenure an exhilarating affair.

After performances of such rarities as Sergey Prokofiev's *Ode on the End of the War,* Franz Schrecker's *The Birthday of the Infanta* suite, Benjamin Britten's *Diversions on a Theme,* and Dmitry Shostakovich's *Fourth Symphony,* critics were quick to note the measurably improved form of the orchestra. Both performers and audiences warmed to the personality of a conductor with a markedly expressive style.

Born in Moscow in 1931, Rozhdestvensky showed early prowess as a pianist, graduating from the Moscow State Conservatoire in 1956 and immediately accepting an appointment as an assistant conductor and singing coach at the Bolshoi Theatre. Such was his progress that by the end of the year he had already made his Western European debut, directing several performances during the company's season at the Royal Opera House, Covent Garden. For 13 years (1961–74) he was conductor in chief and artistic director of the U.S.S.R. Radio Orchestra, and after his BBC appointment continued as music director of the Moscow Chamber Opera and professor of conducting at the Moscow State Conservatoire. For five years from 1965 he was in addition principal conductor at the Bolshoi Theatre, and he made numerous appearances throughout the Soviet Union with the Leningrad Philharmonic and U.S.S.R. Symphony orchestras.

Rozhdestvensky traveled widely, appearing in the U.S., Europe, Israel, and Japan, and from 1974 to 1977 was principal conductor of Sweden's Stockholm Philharmonic Orchestra in succession to Antal Dorati. Just before taking up his appointment with the BBC Symphony Orchestra (in succession to the late Rudolf Kempe) he directed, in Leningrad, the premiere of Prokofiev's opera *The Gambler.*

(MOZELLE A. MOSHANSKY)

Sasagawa, Ryoichi

A 79-year-old Japanese rightist, once classified by the American occupation as a war-crimes suspect, made news in 1978 as the chief sponsor of what may have been the biggest space exhibition ever staged outside the U.S. Opened in July on reclaimed land in Tokyo, it attracted two million people in its first four months. Major attractions were Moon rocks, Mercury and Saturn rockets, models of the space shuttle and Viking orbiter, and Eugene A. Cernan, lunar module pilot of the Apollo 10 and 17 moon missions. "I set up the Space Expo to give hope to Japanese children," Ryoichi Sasagawa explained. "The energetic ones run around in fast cars while the others just sit around sniffing glue." For the jovial, white-haired businessman-philanthropist, the $18 million he spent on the four exhibition buildings represented only a part of the money he gave each year to charity and science. Millions had gone to leprosy hospitals in India, to a Philippine cancer clinic, and to other humanitarian projects. Sasagawa, explaining the change in his life after World War II, said: "Before, I was a Japan-firster, but today I realize Japan cannot prosper unless the whole world is at peace too."

Sasagawa, who was born in Osaka, Japan, on May 4, 1899, attracted attention in 1939 when he flew a squadron bomber to Rome and met Benito Mussolini. He next tried to see Hitler, but the Führer was out of town. Having advocated military expansionism as a member of Japan's wartime Parliament, he was imprisoned for four years as a Class A war-crimes suspect, then released. Sasagawa's fortune derived mainly from legalized gambling at the 24 motorboat racing courses that he owned in Japan. He also became one of Japan's most quickly recognized faces through television campaigns that promoted such things as child welfare, traffic safety, respect for parents, and, of course, motorboat racing. In 1970 he sponsored a world anti-Communist convention in Tokyo and in 1977 persuaded the island republic of Tonga to reject a Soviet offer to build an airport because Soviet involvement would threaten peace in that part of the world. Though Sasagawa had been taken to task for his strong ties to the ruling Liberal-Democratic Party and to the Unification Church of the Rev. Sun Myung Moon, he summed up his feelings by saying simply: "All my critics are Red, or jealous, or else spiteful because I don't give them any money." (JOHN RODERICK)

Senghor, Léopold Sédar

President of Senegal from that country's independence in 1960, Léopold Senghor was reelected on Feb. 26, 1978, to another five-year term. He had one opponent and received 82% of the votes cast. In May he reestablished good relations with Guinea after five years of strain, and in the same month visited Paris, to which he returned in November as a mediator in discussions on the Western Sahara conflict. Also in November, an exhibition was held at the Bibliothèque National in Paris honouring him as a writer.

Born Oct. 9, 1906, at Joal, Senegal, Léopold Senghor was educated at the Ngasobil Catholic mission and afterward in Dakar. An outstanding student, he won a scholarship to Paris, where his friends at the Lycée (high school) Louis-le-Grand included Georges Pompidou (later to become president of France) and the West Indian Aimé Césaire. It was a period of Parisian infatuation with Negro jazz, dance, and art. Seeking to rediscover the values of black civilization and culture, Senghor helped found the Association des Étudiants Ouest-Africains and contributed to *L'Étudiant noir.*

Imprisoned for two years during the Nazi occupation in World War II, Senghor became a deputy of the French National Assembly for Senegal in 1946 and served until 1958. Among other important parliamentary and administrative posts in France and Senegal, he was secretary of state to the presidency in Edgar Faure's Cabinet (1955–56) and president of the initial Mali Federation and senator in Senegal (1959–60).

As head of state after the proclamation of Senegal's independence in 1960, Senghor continued his work as a poet. Among Senghor's earlier works, *Chants d'ombre* was published in 1945 and an anthology of contemporary Negro and Malagasy poetry in 1948. In 1956 Césaire and Senghor defined the concept of Negritude ("Black is beautiful"), which gained worldwide significance after the First Congress of Black Writers and Artists in Paris. *Hosties noires* (1948) were followed by *Éthiopiques* (1956) and *Nocturnes* (1961) and *Lettres d'hivernage* (1973). Senghor also did his best to gain recognition for black writers and artists.

(PHILIPPE DECRAENE)

Shcharansky, Anatoly

A leading figure of the Soviet Jewish community, Anatoly Shcharansky was arrested in Moscow on March 15, 1977, and held incommunicado for 16 months in Moscow's Lefortovo prison. Brought to trial for treason, he received a sentence on July 14, 1978, of 13 years, the first three in prison and the rest in a corrective labour camp. His case shocked the West as a striking instance of the Soviet administration's harsh disregard for human rights, despite the fact that, by signing the two United Nations covenants of 1966 and the Final Act of the Conference on Security and Cooperation in Europe at Helsinki, Fin., in 1975, the Soviet Union had undertaken to uphold those rights.

Shcharansky first came to adverse notice by the authorities when he applied in 1973 to emigrate to Israel. Born on Jan. 20, 1948, at Donetsk in the Ukraine, he graduated from the Institute of Physics in Moscow in 1972 as a mathematician and became a computer engineer. His request to emigrate was refused on the grounds that he was a computer scientist in possession of state secrets. He married Natalya (later the Hebrew Avita) Stiglitz in July 1974, and she was permitted to emigrate to Israel shortly afterward.

After the Helsinki conference the pace of Soviet dissidence had quickened, and on May 12, 1976, the Group for the Implementing of the Helsinki Agreement in the U.S.S.R., or Helsinki Group, was formed. Shcharansky joined it as a representative of the Jewish community. Speaking fluent English, he had the task of ensuring liaison between the Helsinki Group and the Western press. "My strength," he said, "is that I do nothing secretly, nothing illegal." But in March 1977 a presumed fellow dissident, Sanya Lipavsky, named Shcharansky as working in a spy ring with U.S. diplomats, the U.S. Central Intelligence Agency, Western journalists, and other dissidents. This was reflected in the charge for which he was eventually condemned, as being "guilty of

WIDE WORLD

espionage and of assisting a foreign country in hostile activity against the U.S.S.R."

(K. M. SMOGORZEWSKI)

Sheehan, George

Counting noses—or fleeting heels and dividing by two—one authority estimated that in 1978 there were 25 million runners in the U.S. The number was rising faster than inflation. *Runner's World*, one of two dozen magazines in the field, doubled its circulation in a year to break 400,000. While some of these subscribers, the joggers, take their exercise casually, many are conscientious, not to say compulsive. One of the most dedicated is George Sheehan, a Red Bank, N.J., cardiologist and father of 12. Sheehan, who runs an average of 30 mi a week, wrote *Running and Being*, one of at least three long-distance best-sellers of the year.

A track star in his youth, Sheehan hung up his spikes for two decades but then began running seriously enough at the age of 44 to enter the famous Boston Marathon. Then it was one of just seven annual 26-mi 385-yd races. By 1978, when he turned 60, there were 260 such recognized events.

The running phenomenon has yet to be satisfactorily explained. At first it seemed to depend on yen for physical fitness, but it continued to gain popularity even after some physicians suggested that running could be hazardous to one's health. Salting his text with practical advice, physiological facts, and quotations from Ralph Waldo Emerson and William James, Sheehan wrote rings around the question: "Why run marathons when nine out of ten of them end in a contest, the human will trying to push the human body beyond endurance? . . . The runner does not run because he is too slight for football or hasn't the ability to put a ball through a hoop or can't hit a curve ball. He runs because he has to. Because in being a runner, in moving through pain and fatigue and suffering, in imposing stress upon stress, in eliminating all but the necessities of life, he is fulfilling himself and becoming the person he is."

Born in Brooklyn, N.Y., on Nov. 5, 1918, Sheehan trained at the Long Island College of Medicine. Head of the department of electrocardiography and stress testing at Riverview Hospital in Red Bank and medical editor of *Runner's World*, he says his best writing is composed while running.

(PHILIP KOPPER)

Shields, Brooke

"Her nude scene is a shocker but Brooke Shields remains a very normal little girl," commented *People* magazine. "She plays a child prostitute with a disconcerting angelic air." Her divorced father, a Helena Rubinstein, Inc. executive and son of a tennis champion, said, "She's still the kid in bluejeans and Top-Siders to me."

Pretty Baby, Shields's starring vehicle, was a popular film in 1978 but set more records for sparking moral outrage than for ticket sales. Its notoriety rested on its subject, the romance and marriage of a very young prostitute in the Storyville district of World War I New Orleans and E. J. Bellocq,

a photographer. Though banned in two provinces of Canada and considered "child pornography" by many, the film was considered by one magazine critic to be "a civilized intelligent work by one of the world's most intelligent and civilized filmmakers" (Louis Malle). Perhaps the most acute observations on the morality of the movie came from the actress herself. "If I were in a Walt Disney movie people would never ask me if the part would affect my life. That's so dumb."

This child actress, one of the most dramatically skilled in living memory, had been in front of cameras for 11 of her 12 years before working for Malle. She worked at her first advertising job as an 11-month-old model. In time her extraordinary face promoted such products as Band-Aids, Ivory soap, and Breck shampoo.

When making *Pretty Baby*, she was chaperoned either by her mother or by an aunt. Daily tutoring kept her from falling behind in her studies at a private Manhattan school. A panel from the *Childrens' Express*, a magazine written and edited by 8- to 17-year-olds, interviewed her for *Rolling Stone* magazine. They found her "relaxed, funny and very friendly." To them, as to many older observers, "Brooke seemed both an adult and a kid."

(PHILIP KOPPER)

Silverman, Fred

When television programming genius Fred Silverman left CBS for ABC in 1975, the price of a share of his new employer's stock rose 2 points. When he moved to NBC in 1978, the stock of its parent company rose 1¼ points. It seemed that Silverman was the Coriolanus of broadcasting, an undisputed leader who could switch sides and win.

The son of a television repairman, Silverman was born in New York City on Sept. 13, 1937. He attended public schools, was graduated from Syracuse University in three years, and went on to Ohio State University, where he analyzed ABC's television programming in a 406-page master's thesis. In it he charged that the network's executives failed to realize that television is "basically a business," not an aesthetic medium.

After earning a reputation as a successful programmer for independent stations, Silverman joined CBS in 1963 to oversee the network's daytime programming. He ordered new soap operas, replaced Saturday morning reruns with original cartoons for children, attracted 40% of the audience, and won a Peabody Award for CBS. Moving up the executive ladder, he fostered the "deruralization" of the network's moribund evening schedules, axing 13 shows and bringing the revolutionary "All in the Family" to the air. Featuring such previously taboo topics as sex and bigotry, it became the most popular show on television.

Typically, Silverman had a hand in every aspect of entertainment programming. He lured talented actors, writers, and producers away from competitors. He supervised promotion spots and planned each night's schedules with an eye on the competition, like a chess player planning a gambit.

He had plenty of detractors, but when CBS claimed nine of the top ten shows it appeared that seven of them were his. Tired of being the network's "custodian of dominance," he moved to ABC in 1975. In two years he took ABC from third place to first in

WIDE WORLD

audience numbers; at one time the network had 15 of the top 20 programs. Detractors said that he depended on sex and violence to attract viewers, but the advertisers did not seem to mind. Early in 1978 NBC hired Silverman as its president and chief executive at a salary said to be between $500,000 and $1 million. Bedeviled by a reputation for sex exploitation and "pandering to low tastes," Silverman said that he would not aim just at high ratings "because we recognize the importance of broadcasting in this country, the reliance that people place on it and the obligation that places on us."

(PHILIP KOPPER)

Smith, Graham

When Graham Smith won an unprecedented six gold medals in swimming at the 1978 British Commonwealth Games, it was not surprising, since he comes from a family renowned in the Canadian swimming world. All of his seven brothers and sisters are competitive swimmers, and in the last three Commonwealth Games they won a total of 18 medals. His father, Don Smith, was a swimming coach for 30 years and the manager of the Canadian swimming team at the 1968 Olympic Games. His mother has been president of Swim Alberta. In August, he won his medals in Edmonton (the town where he was born on June 9, 1958) in a sports arena named for his father, who had designed the pool.

Smith began swimming at the age of six, and by the time he was nine he was already breaking Canadian swimming records. He decided to begin swimming seriously in 1975, and in August of that year he swam in the world championships in South America, where he finished seventh in the 200-m breaststroke. At the 1976 Olympic Games in Montreal both Smith and his sister Becky won medals. Graham won a silver medal in the medley relay, and Becky won a bronze in the freestyle relay and in the individual medley. Graham was Canada's best performing male swimmer at Montreal.

Training for the breaststroke because of his long arms, Smith was ranked fifth in the world in the 200-m breaststroke and sixth in the world in the 100-m breaststroke in 1977. At the Commonwealth Games he won two of his gold medals in those events. The other four were in the 200-m and 400-m individual medleys and the freestyle and medley relays.

In August 1978 Smith was a member of the team representing Canada at the world championships in West Berlin. There he won his first world title, triumphing in the 200-m individual medley and breaking the record he had set in 1977. He also finished second in the 100-m breaststroke.

Aggressive and determined as an athlete, Graham was looking forward to representing Canada at the next Olympic Games, to be held in Moscow in 1980. In the meantime he was attending the University of California at Berkeley on a swimming scholarship. (DIANE L. WAY)

Snepp, Frank W.

On June 20, 1978, Federal District Court Judge Oren R. Lewis ruled in his Alexandria, Va., courtroom that 35-year-old Frank W. Snepp had no right to a jury trial because no questions of fact had to be determined. Snepp freely admitted he used information gained as a CIA employee in Vietnam to write an exposé of the agency and its handling of the final evacuation from Saigon as the war ended. He also said he had not submitted the manuscript of *Decent Interval* to the CIA for approval because he believed the oath of secrecy he signed as a CIA agent was obtained "under duress" and contravened his First Amendment rights of free speech.

The Justice Department, which brought a breach of contract suit on behalf of the CIA, did not contend that Snepp's book revealed classified information. But William Colby, a former director of the CIA, and Stansfield Turner, the current head of the agency, were called to testify. Turner claimed that the publication of the book by Random House in November 1977 clearly had adverse effects on U.S. intelligence operations. The trial lasted less than two days. In a written judgment issued on July 7, 1978, Judge Lewis ruled that Snepp "wilfully, deliberately and surreptitiously breached his position of trust with the CIA" and had irreparably harmed the nation by impairing its ability to collect and protect intelligence. As a consequence, Snepp would lose all direct and indirect profits from the book.

Snepp, who was born in Kinston, N.C., earned a master's degree in international affairs from Columbia University in 1968. His eight years with the CIA included two assignments (1969–71; 1972–75) as a top analyst with the U.S. embassy in Saigon. Because he could not forget the "Vietnamese who had depended on me—people who had made the mistake of trusting us," he was disappointed but not shattered by the court's decision, which he pledged to appeal. If he won, more than just the CIA would be affected. Similar secrecy oaths are required of other U.S. employees, including some in the State Department, the FBI, the National Security Agency, and the Defense Department. (ARTHUR LATHAM)

Somoza Debayle, Anastasio

Nicaragua, the largest country in Central America, has been ruled for more than four decades by a single wealthy family, the Somozas. The president in 1978, Gen. Anastasio ("Tacho") Somoza Debayle, had been in power since 1967, including a two-year period during which he gave up the presidency but continued to rule through a three-man military junta in whose favour he had resigned. Somoza's brother, Luis, had ruled Nicaragua before "Tacho," and before him was their father, the late Anastasio Somoza García. From the dynasty's beginning in 1936 the Somozas had enjoyed considerable support from the U.S. Indeed, the current president, born in León on Dec. 5, 1925, graduated from the U.S. Military Academy, and his son, also named Anastasio, attended Harvard University.

But in 1978 Somoza's hold on his country became shakier than it ever had been before. Trouble had been brewing for some time. In 1977 the U.S. criticized the Somoza government for human rights violations and threatened to cut off U.S. aid if Somoza did not change his ways. In January 1978 one of Somoza's leading domestic critics, Pedro Joaquín Chamorro Cardenal (*see* OBITUARIES), who had been editor and publisher of Nicaragua's largest newspaper, *La Prensa*, was murdered. The crime led to a large demonstration in Managua against Somoza, whom many Nicaraguans suspected of complicity in the murder.

The following August guerrillas led by the Marxist Sandinista National Liberation Front occupied Managua's National Palace, took 1,500 hostages, and forced Somoza to free 59 political prisoners. The fighting escalated a short time later to a full-fledged

JEAN-PIERRE LAFFONT—SYGMA

civil war. Somoza's government troops responded with massive counterattacks, and after 11 days of fighting the rebels had been defeated. Thousands were killed, however, including many civilians who had lived in the towns attacked by the troops.

For the moment the war was ended. But the political fighting continued. The broad coalition that now opposed Somoza demanded his immediate resignation. Somoza adamantly refused. He insisted that he had been constitutionally elected and that he would not step aside until his term ended in 1981. He did, however, offer to conduct a national plebiscite to decide whether the opposition should share power with him. (STANLEY W. CLOUD)

Sonoda, Sunao

On Nov. 28, 1977, Sunao Sonoda became foreign minister of Japan. The appointment was one the 63-year-old politician could hardly have envisioned in 1931 when he finished his formal education as a junior high school graduate on a small island in Kumamoto Prefecture, where he was born on Dec. 11, 1913. He left home in 1938 when he was drafted into the Army, then served in China and in the Pacific area during World War II, gaining distinction as a crack paratrooper and commando leader. But the war, with all its terrible death and destruction, turned Sonoda into a pacifist who never forgot that he would almost certainly have died had the war lasted five more days. He had been scheduled to fly a glider suicide mission against B–29s on Saipan on August 20.

In 1946 Sonoda became head of his village and the following year was elected to the House of Representatives, the lower house of the Diet (parliament). Originally a member of the conservative Democratic Party, he became a Liberal-Democrat when his party merged with the Liberals. Appointed parliamentary vice-foreign minister in 1955, Sonoda actively helped normalize relations with the U.S.S.R., but in 1960 he left his party to protest ratification of the U.S.-Japan mutual security treaty. After rejoining the party he became vice-speaker of the House (1965–67) and minister of health and welfare (1967–68). In 1976 Sonoda energetically supported Takeo Fukuda in his successful bid to become prime minister and was rewarded with the post of chief Cabinet secretary. Since becoming foreign minister in late 1977 he adhered to the belief that Japan should remain only lightly armed. He was also the chief architect of Fukuda's "omnidirectional" international peace diplomacy. For some 30 years Sonoda had sought reconciliation between Japan and China, so it was a great moment in his political life when in August 1978 he represented Japan in Peking at the signing of the long-delayed Sino-Japanese treaty of peace and friendship, the final phases of which he negotiated with Teng Hsiao-p'ing.

Sonoda is a man of fascinating contrasts. Although a sincere pacifist, he holds the highest ranks in such martial arts as karate, judo, kendo, and aikido. Although a political conservative, he married Tenkoko Matsutani, an articulate Socialist member of the House of Representatives. Although a devout Buddhist, he is so well in tune with worldly standards that in 1978 the Japanese tailors' association named him the best-dressed man in Japan.

Steinberg, Saul

Saul Steinberg's one man show at the Whitney Museum in 1978 was an occasion for rethinking notions of popular taste and serious art. His work appeared in magazines, so he must be a cartoonist, but cartoonists aren't honoured in such temples of abstraction. Or are they? In commenting on this event the *New York Times* senior critic observed that Steinberg "is one of the few artists whose work became known to a mass

INGE MORATH—MAGNUM

audience before he was recognized by the critics as an important painter."

Steinberg's patron since the early 1940s was *The New Yorker* magazine. He appealed to its readers through his careful draftsmanship, his hilarious or provocative combinations of unspeakably diverse things, and his elegantly thin ink lines and designs as complicated as the Balkans. He shed new light or perspective on everything he drew: a nose impossibly apart from a face; Mickey Mouse characters toting tommy guns; the map of North America as many New Yorkers insist on seeing it, with everything west of the Hudson River squeezed into uncharted hinterlands.

In Hilton Kramer's words: "He is a master at the delineation of unsuspected affinity; the jukebox is shown to belong to the same species as the Chrysler Building . . . and the kitschiest product of cynical commerce and vulgar sentiment turns out to be the distant disinherited offspring of a once exalted artistic style. Steinberg seems to know the aesthetic genealogy of every object and question and impulse in our culture."

Steinberg was born on June 15, 1914, in Rimnicu-Sarat, Romania, near Bucharest, where his father bound books and made fancy boxes and his mother decorated elaborate cakes. A precocious student, he read Maksim Gorky at 10 and Dostoyevsky's *Crime and Punishment* before he was 13. He went to Milan to study architecture, a profession he eventually deemed impossible, and contributed drawings to a satiric Italian magazine. It paid money and was an outlet for free if veiled expression in the early days of Benito Mussolini's Fascist regime. But, fearing Fascism, Steinberg fled to Portugal and in 1942 moved to the United States. Three years of service in the U.S. Navy, culminating in his commission as lieutenant, provided Steinberg with a wealth of cultural contradictions, violent imagery, and exotica to record and transform in his art. His later subject matter,

often reflecting the profundity of this experience, ranges from urban violence to the Holocaust to the follies of fashion or bureaucracy to Freud. Steinberg has called drawing a way of "reasoning on paper." His doodled universe is a fun-house/horror-house mirror image of our own.

(PHILIP KOPPER)

Steinbrenner, George

More than anyone else George M. Steinbrenner III made it fashionable to hate the New York Yankees again. The chairman of the American Ship Building Co. in Cleveland, Ohio, Steinbrenner became the Yankees' managing general partner after the 1972 season, when they finished fourth in the American League East. In 1976 they won their first American League pennant in 12 years. In 1977 they won the World Series and then did so again in 1978.

Steinbrenner's 1978 Yankees, in winning the team's 32nd pennant and 22nd World Series, had all the makings of the dynasties that preceded them. Those Yankee teams were called the Bronx Bombers with a trace of awe, but Steinbrenner's team was called the Brinks Bombers with a trace of disgust. It was the product of an era that began in 1976 when major-league players first won the right to sell their services to the highest bidder, and it was the product of an owner whose high profile kept his face easily accessible for critics' dart boards.

After the 1976 season Steinbrenner offended catcher Thurman Munson—the American League's most valuable player that year—by giving a multimillion dollar contract to the talented but temperamental outfielder Reggie Jackson. After Billy Martin became the Yankee manager in 1975, Steinbrenner made such frequent threats to fire him that a beer company based a commercial on them in 1978. Soon after that, on July 24, Martin resigned, giving poor health as the reason. Five days later it was announced that Martin would return as manager in 1980, probably the most unbelievable development of all in the Yankees' incredible season.

Under new manager Bob Lemon the Yankees won 48 of their last 69 games, including a one-game play-off with the Boston Red Sox for the American League East Division title. The 1978 Yankees would like to be remembered as the championship team that came back after being 14 games out of first place on July 19, the only American League team ever to win a pennant after changing managers in midseason, and the only major league team ever to win a World Series in six games after losing the first two. More likely, though, they would be remembered as the best team money can buy.

But Steinbrenner was not the only owner to greet players with open wallets, just the most successful. Born July 4, 1930, in Rocky River, Ohio, he received a degree from Williams College. After serving as an assistant football coach for Northwestern and Purdue universities, he went to work for Kinsman Transit Co. in Cleveland in 1957. He became president of Kinsman in 1963 and chairman of American Ship Building Co. in 1967.

(KEVIN M. LAMB)

Stenmark, Ingemar

The most successful ski racer in the alpine disciplines that Sweden has produced and one of the greatest slalomers of all time, Ingemar Stenmark in 1978 was named international alpine skier of the year for a third consecutive season by the authoritative U.S. *Ski Racing* magazine. He also became a specialist to such a degree that he persistently refused to compete in downhill events. It was this that prevented him from perhaps becoming the greatest alpine skier in history.

Stenmark dominated international alpine competition in 1978 to win his third straight World Cup title as well as gold medals for both the slalom and giant slalom in the world championships at Garmisch-Partenkirchen, West Germany. During that season he won seven World Cup races and scored in 13 of the 14 slaloms and giant slaloms. With six consecutive wins gained in the early season, his victory was a foregone conclusion two months before the series

Ingemar Stenmark

WIDE WORLD

ended. In 1976 he had been the first Scandinavian to win the World Cup, after being a close runner-up the year before when Gustav Thöni of Italy won in the last race of the series.

After joining the World Cup circuit in 1974, Stenmark achieved a record number of 28 men's race wins, the last of them on his 22nd birthday in March 1978 (he was born on March 18, 1956, at Tärnaby, Sweden). During the five seasons 1974–78 he placed among the top three in no fewer than 54 of the 72 World Cup races he entered. It was a distinction no man could conceivably have attained without concentrating exclusively on slaloms and giant slaloms, which possibly justified his continued absence from downhill races.

A commanding figure on the snow but unassuming off it, Stenmark was reticent when confronted by newsmen after an event. A perfectionist, he always strove to improve his technique in the two events in which he could outshine any contemporary. There was no particular name to describe his style, merely a consistent ability to negotiate the slalom gates with a minimum of wasted motion.   (HOWARD BASS)

Strauss, Robert

"I'm the best damned appointment Jimmy Carter has made," said Robert Strauss in typical style when he was asked during the summer of 1978 to discuss the work he had done for the Carter administration as its special representative for trade negotiations. While some observers would certainly have disagreed with Strauss's assessment of himself, few would have argued with the proposition that this ebullient Texan was among the most effective of the political operators and troubleshooters in the administration.

Born Oct. 19, 1918, to an immigrant Jewish merchant who settled in Lockhart, Texas, Strauss earned a law degree from the University of Texas. He came by his political skills through association with such legendary Texas wheelers and dealers as former governor John Connally and the late former president of the United States, Lyndon Johnson. Strauss, however, never ran for public office himself, preferring to play the role of political fund raiser and organizer while he founded a highly successful law firm and eventually became a millionaire with investments in banks, a radio station, and real estate.

In 1970 he was elected treasurer of the Democratic National Committee and helped reduce the party's staggering $10 million debt to $2 million. He was elected chairman of the party in late 1972, a year in which the Democrats were bitterly divided in the wake of Sen. George McGovern's massive loss in the presidential election to Richard Nixon. In his efforts to bring the party together again, Strauss begged, cajoled, browbeat, and mediated until, by the 1974 midterm Democratic Party conference in Kansas City, Mo., a fair semblance of order had been restored.

When the eventual nominee, former Georgia governor Jimmy Carter, was elected president in 1976, he rewarded Strauss for his efforts by naming him special trade negotiator, with ambassadorial rank and Cabinet-level status. Strauss's credentials as an expert on international trade were thin,

ARTHUR GRACE—SYGMA

but his reputation as a negotiator and achiever was solid enough for him to win quick confirmation in the Senate. Characteristically, he then launched a series of critical discussions with leading U.S. trading partners, notably Japan, and won some important concessions from them as the U.S. balance of payments deficit continued to grow.   (STANLEY W. CLOUD)

Taraki, Nur Mohammad

After a coup in April 1978, in which Pres. Sardar Mohammad Daud Khan, members of his government, and reportedly several thousand others were killed, a People's Democratic Republic of Afghanistan was established under the leadership of Nur Mohammad Taraki, who assumed the functions of chief of state and prime minister.

A Marxist but also a staunch nationalist, Taraki had the distinction of being a self-made man. He was born in 1917 into a lower middle-class Pushtoon family in Ghazni Province, but there were no records of his actual date of birth or to indicate that he attended the village school. He was taught by his parents and friends in the early stages and passed his matriculation by attending night school while working as a

BALDEV—SYGMA

clerk in the Pushtooni Jetharathi Co. of Bombay, India, in the late 1930s.

After two years in Bombay, where he became an admirer of Mahatma Gandhi, Taraki returned to Kabul. He revisited Bombay in 1946 as a member of an Afghan delegation to buy war surplus goods. In the late 1940s he worked as a junior official in the press department of the Afghan government, and in 1952 he was appointed press attaché at the Afghan embassy in Washington, D.C. On returning to Kabul he worked as a translator for the U.S. embassy there and started his own translation bureau.

Taraki entered politics in 1963 when he founded the Khalq ("masses") Party. The overthrow of the monarchy by Mohammad Daud in 1973 caused a split in the party, with one faction, known as Parcham ("banner"), supporting the Daud regime and the other, led by Taraki, opposing it. In 1977, however, the two factions reunited to form the People's Democratic Party, with Taraki as secretary-general. A noted writer, Taraki held strong pro-Communist views, and the Daud government jailed him for a brief period. The Khalq Party was said to have drawn its inspiration from the Communist Party of India.   (GOVINDAN UNNY)

Thorpe, (John) Jeremy

The most successful leader Britain's Liberal Party had made during the post-World War II period, Jeremy Thorpe in 1978 found himself at the centre of a sensational affair that attracted worldwide attention. On August 4 Thorpe, with three others, was charged with conspiracy to murder a former male model named Norman Scott. Later, Thorpe was charged separately with incitement to murder.

The charges followed more than two years of rumour and speculation which started with a statement by Scott in a court hearing in January 1976 that he had had a homosexual affair with Thorpe in the early 1960s. This Thorpe persistently denied. The charges of attempted murder and incitement to murder were the culmination of police investigations lasting two years and ten months. They arose from a case brought against Andrew Newton, a former airline pilot, after he had shot and killed a Great Dane owned by Scott. Newton claimed that an unidentified Liberal had paid him £5,-000 to silence Scott by murdering him. The subsequent investigation attempted to trace the trail of alleged conspiracy back to Thorpe himself. Preliminary hearings of the case against Thorpe opened at the Minehead, Somerset, magistrates' court on Nov. 20, 1978, and on December 13 he was committed for trial on both charges; his three co-defendants were committed on the charge of conspiracy to murder.

Thorpe had been elected leader of the Liberal Party in 1967 at the age of 37. Born April 29, 1929, the son of a former Conservative MP, he had a successful university career at Oxford and became an MP for North Devon at the age of 30. Under his leadership the Liberal Party reached a peak of postwar success in the general election of February 1974, when Liberal candidates received six million votes (19% of the poll) and 14 Liber-

KEYSTONE

al MP's were elected. His distinctly theatrical style and his wit did not endear him to all his fellow Liberals. His reputation suffered a blow when a report on the collapse of a bank, London and County Securities, raised questions concerning his judgment as a nonexecutive director of the company.

The Scott affair attracted a great deal of publicity in the British press and, later, in the U.S., where television accounts of the affair were shown. Thorpe resigned the leadership of the Liberal Party in May 1976, though a committee of senior Liberals had said they found nothing to support the allegations against him. Thorpe said he would not resign his seat in Parliament and intended to stand again as the Liberal candidate at the next general election. After his first wife died in a car crash in 1970, Thorpe married, in 1973, the countess of Harewood, whose marriage to the earl of Harewood, a second cousin of Queen Elizabeth II, had been dissolved in 1967.

(HARFORD THOMAS)

Touré, Ahmed Sékou

In 1978 Sékou Touré of Guinea, after some preliminary groundwork, swept aside 20 years of hostility toward France as a "misunderstanding" and courted French cooperation. As head of the government since October 1958, when his country became the first former French colony to elect for independence outside Charles de Gaulle's French Community, Sékou Touré (elected president of Guinea in 1961 and reelected in 1968 and 1974) had been pathologically suspicious of France and French plotting. But his country's impoverished economy was inadequately served by Soviet aid. On December 20–22 French Pres. Valéry Giscard d'Estaing paid a formal visit to Guinea and was welcomed by Touré. Earlier, in March, Touré had achieved accord with neighbouring states at a "unity summit" meeting at Monrovia, Liberia.

Ahmed Sékou Touré was born in January 1922 at Faranah, Guinea. After a traditional Muslim education, he entered the Georges Poiret professional school in Conakry. He founded the first Guinean trade union, for postal workers, and eventually became secretary of the Union Générale des Travailleurs d'Afrique Noire, a militant trade union body in the forefront of the struggle for independence. In 1946 he was a founder member of the Rassemblement Démocratique Africain (RDA) and became secretary-general of what was then the leading political party in French Africa, but this brought him into conflict with Félix Houphouët-Boigny, later president of Ivory Coast.

Sékou Touré was elected a deputy to the French National Assembly in 1956 and became secretary of the RDA's parliamentary group. He went on to become vice-president and then president of the Guinean government council. By choosing independence in September 1958 after an overwhelmingly affirmative referendum, he gained immense popularity in Guinea and throughout Africa. His reputation as one of the great progressive leaders of the third world was enhanced by his africanization of the civil service, suppression of traditional chieftaincy, nationalization of insurance and banking, and his militant anticolonial stand. From the late 1960s, however, he was criticized by African nationalists for stifling freedom in Guinea and going back on his ideological and political choices.

(PHILIPPE DECRAENE)

Travolta, John

His mother, a drama coach, once set a long-distance swimming record; his father was a semipro baseball player and an Englewood, N.J., tire dealer. Gene Kelly's brother Fred taught him dancing before he was old enough to leave home. With all that and more behind him, John Travolta in 1978 at the age of 24 won an Academy Award nomination for his first starring movie role and made the cover of *Time* magazine. Despite his youth, however, he had paid his dues.

Determined to become a performer, Travolta got his parents' reluctant blessing to drop out of high school at 16 for a trial year. He went to New York City and persuaded an agent to represent him. After breaking into television via commercials, he had within two years appeared in an off-Broadway play (which lasted five performances) and tackled bit parts in several television shows. Then he landed a minor role in the rock musical *Grease* and doggedly toured the country with a road company.

A short stint on Broadway followed, then a couple of horror films, and finally success in the television series "Welcome Back, Kotter." At the outset of this situation comedy about a high school teacher with a street gang for his troublesome students, the producers could not guess which member of the student "sweathogs" would rise above the others in popular appeal. Travolta soon became the choice. But some critics observed deeper talent and applauded his performance in "The Boy in the Plastic Bubble." This made-for-TV film described the abject lot of a youth raised in a sterile environment because he was born without disease-fighting ability. The young actor and his screen mother, Diana Hyland, 18

years his senior, then had a six-month love affair that ended with her death from cancer.

Though no one said it aloud, the ordeal may have given additional depth to Travolta's film work. During her final illness he was playing the slow-to-mature Tony Manero in *Saturday Night Fever*, a young cock of a Brooklyn roost who discovers that life might have greater challenges than disco dancing, curbside sex, and street fights. Tony's growth provided the film's dramatic gambit, but Travolta's dancing got most of the attention. Travolta, who was born Feb. 18, 1954, in Englewood, N.J., frequented Brooklyn discotheques and danced three hours a day to prepare for his performance in *Saturday Night Fever*. Then in 1978 he played in yet another production of *Grease*, this time as the star of the movie version. Though the film was poorly received by critics it was a major success at the box office.

(PHILIP KOPPER)

Turbay Ayala, Julio César

In a much closer—and, consequently, tenser—election than anticipated, Liberal Party candidate Julio Turbay Ayala defeated his Conservative Party opponent to win a four-year term as president of Colombia. A split in Turbay's Liberal Party and the vigorous campaign waged by Conservative candidate Belisario Betancur combined to make the race so tight that many Colombians feared a renewal of the political violence that had claimed 200,000 lives during the late 1940s and early 1950s.

A professional politician, Turbay represented an anomaly in Latin-American politics, which are generally dominated by the wealthy elite. Born in Bogotá on June 8, 1916, to a middle-class family descended from Lebanese immigrants, he was sometimes called "Turco," a disparaging reference to his Arab forebears. Turbay entered public life at age 22 and over the next 40 years held nearly every high position in the Colombian government: delegate to the House of Representatives, minister of labour, foreign minister, senator, delegate to the UN, ambassador to Great Britain, and ambassador to the U.S.

During those years Turbay built a network of alliances that made him boss of the Liberal Party but also incurred the disapproval of Colombians who disliked machine politics. One of his most vocal detractors was fellow Liberal (and former president) Carlos Lleras Restrepo, who challenged Turbay in an indirect primary for the party's presidential nomination. Turbay turned back the challenge, but he was unable to heal the breach in the party ranks.

Turbay's victory (made official following a recount demanded by Betancur) signaled the emergence of Colombia's middle class into the realm of political power formerly restricted to the very wealthy. While clearly not advocating the drastic social changes some critics claimed must be enacted to save Colombian democracy, Turbay made it clear that he regarded his success as a triumph over the ruling elite.

(JEROLD L. KELLMAN)

Uemura, Naomi

On May 1, 1978, Naomi Uemura accomplished what no one before him had ever done. Traveling alone by dogsled, he reached the North Pole after 57 harrowing days and nights.

Twice during the 800-km (500-mi) trek from Ellesmere Island to the frozen top of the Earth the intrepid explorer feared he would never make it. On the fourth day out a huge polar bear invaded his camp, ate his supplies, and poked his nose against the sleeping bag where Uemura lay tense and motionless. When the bear returned the next day, he was shot dead. On the 35th day the Japanese adventurer settled down on a floe with his malamutes. Suddenly a roaring sound shattered the stillness. The floe had broken up, leaving the explorer and his dogs perilously stranded on a tossing island of ice. After a night of terror, Uemura spotted a metre-wide bridge of ice and raced to safety. Twenty-two days later he planted the Japanese flag atop the globe.

After resting three days, Uemura was airlifted to the northern tip of Greenland to begin an unprecedented solo trek across the largest island in the world. Loneliness and boredom were almost more than he could stand as he fought his way through blinding snowstorms that sometimes lasted for days. When he finally sighted Narsarssuak on August 24 he knew the 2,600-km (1,600-mi) journey was over. The Smithsonian Institution supported the expeditions with supplies and provided communications facilities. In return, Uemura collected specimens and regularly used a NASA Nimbus satellite to relay atmospheric data to waiting scientists.

Naomi Uemura, who stands 5-ft 4-in tall and weighs a slight 130 lb, was born on Feb. 12, 1941, in Hyogo Prefecture, Japan. Shy and diffident by nature, he joined his university alpine club hoping that mountaineering would increase his self-confidence. A few years later he was the first member of a Japanese team of 39 climbers to reach the summit of Mt. Everest, the highest point on Earth. He then made solo ascents to the tops of the highest peaks on four other continents: Mt. Kilimanjaro in Africa, Mt. Aconcagua in South America, Mont Blanc in Europe, and Mt. McKinley in North America. That accomplished, he turned to other exploits. He rafted solo some 6,500 km (4,-000 mi) down the Amazon River and made a 12,000-km (7,500-mi) solo trek across the frozen Arctic wilderness from Greenland to Alaska.

For the present, Uemura was content to write, lecture, and pass the days with his wife, an accomplished calligrapher. But he grew pensive when he realized he had not yet driven a team of dogs to the bottom side of the Earth. (JOHN RODERICK)

Ullsten, Ola

Sweden's first Liberal Party prime minister since the 1930s, Ola Ullsten looked much younger than his 47 years. In his relatively brief but hectic political career he succeeded to the leadership of the small Liberal Party (Folkpartiet) in March 1978, when he was also appointed deputy prime minister in the centre-right government of Thorbjörn Fälldin; from 1976 he had been minister for international development and later minister for immigration. His Liberal minority government succeeded Fälldin's in October 1978 when the coalition collapsed because of disagreements about nuclear policy.

Born at Teg in Umeå, northern Sweden,

June 23, 1931, Ullsten was active as a social worker and in the temperance movement from 1952 to 1957. In 1962 he became chairman of the Liberal Party Youth League, and during 1962–64 he was an editorial writer for the Stockholm *Dagens Nyheter*. He was elected to the Riksdag (parliament) in 1964. Foreign affairs was his principal interest; as far back as 1960 he was attached to John F. Kennedy's presidential election campaign on a foreign affairs study grant.

As development minister Ullsten was prime mover in Sweden's decision in 1977 to write off more than $208 million owed to the country by some of the world's poorest nations. In a recent interview he revealed the tenor of his political thought with noticeable bluntness: "The world is not too poor. But it's deliberately organized by and for those who first achieved economic power, and who are now reluctant to share it with others."

Another of his chief political interests was women's rights. One-third of his Cabinet ministers were women. In his government policy statement after taking office Ullsten told Parliament that "equality of status between men and women is one of the vital premises of this government's policy. . . . All community work must incorporate a bid for greater equality. Men and women must have equal opportunities and equal responsibilities."

(ROGER NYE CHOATE)

Vargas Llosa, Mario

Elected the first Latin-American president of International PEN (Association of Poets, Playwrights, Editors, Essayists, and Novelists) in 1976, Peruvian novelist Mario Vargas Llosa, long known and admired for his fiction and his uncommonly reasonable statements on public affairs, immediately set about reinforcing the club's attempts at helping the victims of repression among writers. A courageous opponent of governmental arbitrariness, he stated: "A writer . . . in any Latin American country is more useful to society if, instead of turning into a mouthpiece of power, . . . he turns into a critic of power." Abhorring censorship, from which he had suffered himself, he wrote recently, "Freedom of information is the first problem a country must solve which wishes truly to solve its other problems."

The works of Vargas Llosa can be divided into two parts: those written before and after his conversion to humour. While not altogether absent from his earlier novels, humour (perhaps comicality and parody would be more precise terms) erupts full-fledged in his fourth novel, *Pantaleón y las visitadoras* (1973), about the military's obsession to organize everything, even sex. The book's protagonist is ordered to create a mobile unit of prostitutes to slacken the thirst of army recruits in Peru's jungle regions. *La tía Julia y el escribidor* (1977), Vargas Llosa's next novel, confessedly autobiographical, concerns his very youthful initiation into literature and marriage. His pre-humour work comprises the short-story collection *Los jefes* (1959) and the novels (all set in Peru) *La ciudad y los perros* (1963), *La casa verde* (1966), and *Conversación en la catedral* (1969), his technically most ambitious and difficult work.

Vargas Llosa was born March 28, 1936, in

SOPHIE BAKER—CAMERA PRESS

Peru's "second city," Arequipa. His first years were spent in the home of his maternal grandparents in Cochabamba, Bolivia, as his parents had separated. Returning to Peru when they were reconciled, he was schooled in Lima and Piura. He studied law and literature in Lima and then went to Spain and Paris with his first wife, Julia Urquidi. His cousin Patricia became his second wife.

The success of his first novel and the later ones have made Vargas Llosa one of the most visible and politically controversial figures in Latin America. He traveled widely and taught in many countries, but since 1974 he has lived in Lima.

(WOLFGANG A. LUCHTING)

Vorster, Balthazar Johannes

South Africa's prime minister since September 1966, John Vorster unexpectedly announced his resignation on Sept. 20, 1978, after his ruling National Party in the previous November had gained the biggest electoral triumph ever achieved in the country's history. The reason for his resignation was ill health. Vorster was elected president of the republic on September 29. In that office he could still be expected to play a major role in South African affairs.

Vorster was a man in the tradition of those leaders who believed both in the political supremacy of Afrikaans-speaking South Africans (Afrikaners) and in rigid segregation between the races through the political system known as apartheid, or separate development. He was nevertheless capable of adopting flexible attitudes when the occasion demanded and was quick to understand the serious consequences of the collapse of Portuguese colonialism in 1974. He offered cooperation with African leaders and with the Western nations in trying to achieve peaceful settlements in Rhodesia and Namibia. He worked closely with the five Western members of the UN Security Council to achieve an internationally acceptable settlement for the problem of Namibia, but in the end he rejected their proposals when they were presented to the

UN Security Council. He resigned at a time when the problems of both Rhodesia and Namibia were reaching their climax.

Vorster was born at Jamestown, Cape Province, on Dec. 13, 1915, and studied law at the University of Stellenbosch, the cradle of Afrikaner nationalism, where he showed early promise as a student leader. His legal career was interrupted by his internment from September 1942 to February 1944 during World War II by Field Marshal J. C. Smuts's government because of his active opposition to the Allies' war effort. He entered Parliament in 1953 and was made a junior minister five weeks later, finally achieving full Cabinet rank in 1961 as minister of justice. When Prime Minister Hendrik Verwoerd was murdered in 1966, the National Party turned to Vorster as its toughest leader to guide South Africa through the difficult years ahead.

(COLIN LEGUM)

Webster, William

When William Hedgcock Webster was named by Pres. Jimmy Carter to be director of the Federal Bureau of Investigation in January 1978, the famed bureau was in a serious state of disarray. Reports of criminal activity by its agents, of bureaucratic power plays, and of investigative blind spots had even tarnished the once shiny reputation of the late J. Edgar Hoover, the FBI's first director. Webster's immediate predecessor in the job, former Kansas City, Mo., police chief Clarence Kelley, had made an effort to get control of the bureau, the closest thing in the U.S. to a national police force, but had been hampered by high-level holdovers from the Hoover days.

Webster was chosen to replace Kelley, who retired, from a list of 17 prospects after Carter's first choice, Alabama federal judge Frank Johnson, declined the job for health reasons. First as a federal judge in the Eastern Missouri district and later as an appellate judge in the 8th Circuit, he had gained a reputation as a moderate of high integrity. If civil rights attorneys were sometimes disturbed by his tendency to side with law-

enforcement officials in procedural matters, they nonetheless regarded him as a fair judge. During the confirmation process in the Senate, both liberals and conservatives found Webster acceptable to run the FBI, with its $500 million annual budget and its 19,000 employees, despite his limited administrative experience.

Probably Webster's most difficult task during his first year in office was handling the cases of more than 60 FBI agents and supervisors accused of using illegal methods—including burglaries and warrantless wiretaps—to investigate the radical "Weatherman" group that was believed to have been responsible for a number of terrorist bombings in the U.S. It took Webster most of the year to make his decision. In December he fired two supervisors, demoted a third, suspended a fourth, and censured two street agents. It was regarded by some as the minimum action he could take, but the director still had to deal with the FBI's cover-up of the illegal activities.

Webster was born March 6, 1924, in Webster Groves, Mo. He was educated at Amherst College and the Washington University law school and served in the U.S. Navy during both World War II and the Korean War. After private law practice and two years as a U.S. attorney, he was appointed to the federal bench in 1971 and to the Court of Appeals in 1973 by former president Richard Nixon.

(STANLEY W. CLOUD)

Weizman, Ezer

A tough talking, uninhibited Israeli Air Force commander, Ezer Weizman underwent a remarkable transformation as minister of defense in the Cabinet of Prime Minister Menahem Begin. He was, in fact, pressing hardest for a peace settlement with Egypt.

Weizman was born in Haifa in 1924, the son of a prominent local manufacturer and nephew of Israel's first president, Chaim Weizmann. During World War II he served as a pilot in Britain's Royal Air Force and afterward became one of the founding officers of the Israel Air Force (IAF). In 1958 he was appointed commander in chief of the IAF and set out to transform and modernize it, particularly its strategy and tactics. It was his meticulous training and detailed preparation that laid the foundation for the success of Israel's air strike against Egypt in June 1967.

In 1966 Weizman was appointed chief of military operations, the second-ranking position in Israel's military hierarchy and the customary stepping-stone to the post of chief of staff. When he learned in 1970 that Prime Minister Golda Meir (see OBITUARIES) had vetoed his appointment as chief of staff, he resigned his commission. He joined the Gahal Party, a forerunner of the Likud, and was nominated as the party's candidate for the Ministry of Transport in the National Unity government.

When the Gahal withdrew from the government later that year, Weizman retired from active political life after sharp differences with Begin over the conduct of the Herut Party. He returned in 1976 when he organized the highly successful Likud Party election campaign.

During 1978 Weizman played a major role in the peace negotiations with Egypt. In

WIDE WORLD

March, while negotiating a new arms agreement in the U.S., he announced that he would abandon his mission and resign his post unless Israel immediately halted work on building new settlements in the Sinai. With Foreign Minister Moshe Dayan he spent considerable time working to persuade the Israeli Cabinet to abandon the policy of retaining Jewish settlements in the Sinai to be administered by Israel.

(JON KIMCHE)

Yeh Chien-ying

Yeh Chien-ying, vice-chairman of the Chinese Communist Party and the grand old man of the Chinese military establishment, became China's nominal chief of state in March 1978 when he was elected chairman of the Standing Committee of the National People's Congress. A long and intense struggle between moderates and radicals preceded the election, but he finally emerged as second only to Chairman Hua Kuo-feng in the Chinese hierarchy. Yeh then saw to it that the Standing Committee was constitutionally strengthened as the highest organ of government. He also used his considerable prestige and his military and political contacts to draw rival factions closer together and gain support for China's new domestic and foreign policies.

Yeh was born into a Hakka merchant family in Mei-hsien, Kwangtung Province, in 1898. Having graduated from the Yunnan Military Academy in 1919, he served as an instructor at the Whampoa Military Academy during 1924–26. He joined the Communist Party in 1927 (or perhaps 1924) and studied in Germany and the U.S.S.R. in the late 1920s. Returning to China, he was named to various Communist army posts, including chief of staff and president of the Red Army School. Yeh's military and organizational talents were much in evidence during the historic Long March (1934–35), when the Communist forces retreated before Chiang Kai-shek's Nationalist army and successfully moved their headquarters in southeast China to Yenan in the northwest. After World War II Yeh accompanied Chou En-lai and other Communists during fruitless negotiations with Chiang. In the civil war that followed, Yeh played a decisive role in driving Nationalist forces from the mainland; in the process he led victorious troops into Peking and became the city's mayor before heading south and assuming control of Kwangtung Province in late 1949. During the following decade he held various military and party posts and traveled widely abroad. When the wild winds of the Cultural Revolution (1966–69) swept across China, Yeh and Chou En-lai worked closely together. In 1971 Yeh replaced Lin Piao as minister of defense when Lin, Mao Tsetung's designated successor, died after an alleged abortive coup. Yeh was thus holding a key position when Mao died in September 1976. In the power struggle that followed, Yeh sided with the moderates and actively participated in the purge of Chiang Ch'ing, Mao's widow and the leader of the radical "gang of four." In his 80s and one of the few surviving veterans of both the Long March and the Communist revolution, Yeh supported China's new policies of economic growth, rapid modernization, political order and stability, and closer ties with the West.

(WINSTON L. Y. YANG)

The 1978 list of Nobel Prize winners contained several mild surprises, but on the whole the new laureates had all been considered likely candidates to win the prestigious international awards. Egyptian Pres. Anwar as-Sadat and Israeli Prime Minister Menahem Begin shared the Peace Prize for taking dramatic steps toward ending decades of intermittent war. Isaac Bashevis Singer was honoured for his contributions to Yiddish literature. Microbiologists Hamilton O. Smith, Daniel Nathans, and Werner Arber were singled out for their basic discoveries about the physiology of genes. Physicist Pyotr Kapitsa was selected for opening the door to low-temperature experimentation, while Arno Penzias and Robert Wilson were awarded the Physics Prize because their discovery provided strong support for the "big bang" theory of the universe's origin. Peter Mitchell gave an explanation of how organisms can convert nutrients into energy, and Herbert A. Simon revealed unseen fundamentals of economic behaviour.

As in past years, critics found something to carp about. Some objected that the Peace Prize was prematurely given to two former terrorists, that the Economics Prize was given to a psychology professor, and that the literature award was bestowed on a man writing in a language of only minor importance. Those who continued to be upset that specific prizes stacked the Nobel deck of cards against such disciplines as astronomy and mathematics were in effect complaining that Alfred Nobel had not written his will differently. From another angle, however, the selections could be viewed as demonstrating the theories with which laureate Simon was honoured. His observation that even the most efficient corporations must often be content with merely satisfactory solutions of complex problems is applicable not only to General Motors but to Nobel committees as well.

Prize for Peace

Since Israel became a state in 1948, its Arab neighbours repeatedly denied its right to exist in the former British protectorate of Palestine. Their pledges to eradicate the new nation, however, were offset by Israel's combative will to survive. The result was decades of war that killed some 40,000 soldiers and civilians. Given this history, Egyptian Pres. Anwar as-Sadat's 1977 meeting with Israeli Prime Minister Menahem Begin in Jerusalem brightened the world's hope that a lasting peace might finally come to the Middle East. When the talks faltered, U.S. Pres. Jimmy Carter offered his good offices for an extraordinary summit conference at Camp David, the presidential hideaway in Maryland. The conference ended with a jubilant White House ceremony at which the two old antagonists signed "A Framework for Peace in the Middle East" and "A Framework for the Conclusion of a Peace Treaty between Egypt and Israel." A little more than a month later Sadat and Begin were chosen from among 50 candidates to share the Nobel Peace Prize and its honorarium of $165,000.

Some observers felt the prize was premature. *The Economist* of London, for example, after noting that Henry Kissinger and Le Duc Tho were honoured for negotiations that failed to end the Vietnam War in 1973, remarked: "Critics correctly called that year's award premature. This year's joint award . . . is vulnerable to similar criticism and, just possibly, to a similarly unwelcome sequel." The notion that the prize was an incentive as well as a reward was confirmed in the official citation, which read in part: ". . . the Nobel Committee wishes not only to honour actions already performed in the service of peace but also to encourage further efforts to work out practical solutions which can give reality to those hopes of a lasting peace as they have been kindled by the framework agreements." But when Begin and Sadat missed their agreed-upon December deadline for concluding a peace treaty, most of the international press blamed Begin's intransigence for the failure. It was somewhat ironic, therefore, that Begin personally appeared to receive his prize in Oslo while Sadat sent a personal representative.

Menahem Begin was born on Aug. 16, 1913, in Brest-Litovsk, then part of Polish Russia and now the Soviet city of Brest. At the age of 16 he joined Betar, an auxiliary of the World Union of Revisionist Zionists, a militant group advocating a Jewish state in Palestine. He earned a law degree at the University of Warsaw and became head of the Polish Betar. During World War II Begin got to Palestine, where he became commander of Irgun Zvai Leumi, an offshoot of the more celebrated Haganah militia. After the war Begin commanded Irgun guerrillas against the British. He was classified as a terrorist and had a $30,000 price on his head. He ordered the bombing of British headquarters in the King David Hotel and directed a notorious raid against an Arab village. Begin later explained that civilians had been warned to abandon the strategic target. When the British protectorate ended, the Irgun became a highly disciplined autonomous group before its integration into the new Israeli Army and later formed the nucleus of Israel's third largest political party, which sent Begin to the Knesset. During the Labour Party's long control of the government, Begin was a leading spokesman for the opposition. When scandals toppled the Labour government in 1977, he became prime minister, leading a coalition that included Orthodox and extremist groups. His hawkish reputation was widely seen as a political trump card when he agreed to negotiate with Sadat. Any statesman with a less militant anti-Arab record probably could not have survived the inevitable domestic criticism.

Anwar as-Sadat, a Muslim, was born in a Nile Delta village on Dec. 25, 1918. A devoutly religious man, he was once an anti-British renegade seeking self-rule for the Egyptian people. In 1936 Sadat and Gamal

Abdel Nasser matriculated in the first class of the Royal Military Academy. After graduation two years later they formed what was to become the Free Officers Committee which was, in Sadat's words, "a secret revolutionary society dedicated to the task of liberation." During World War II he plotted with German spies, hoping thereby to weaken the still considerable British presence in Egypt. But he was betrayed by a female double agent and jailed for two years. He escaped from a detention camp and for a time lived in hiding. Though implicated in terrorist attacks on pro-British officials, he denied participating in a Cabinet minister's assassination. He was, nonetheless, imprisoned for the crime and, as a result, missed the 1948 war against Israel. After his commission was restored in 1950, he served as a captain in the Sinai as liaison between the Free Officers Committee and civilian terrorists. Nasser chose Sadat to announce the overthrow of King Farouk in July 1952. During Nasser's presidency Sadat presided over the National Assembly and became secretary-general of the National Union, which became the Arab Socialist Union, the nation's only political party. His political rise was attributed to Nasser's trust in his apparent lack of political ambition. When Nasser realized death was approaching, he appointed Sadat vice-president. Elected president in his own right in October 1970, he set about reordering Nasser's policies. He abandoned pan-Arab unity as a prime goal, encouraged private enterprise, and guaranteed a constitutional rule of law. And he honoured a campaign promise by waging war against Israel in 1973.

Prize for Literature

"I write about the things I know in the language I know best," explained Isaac Bashevis Singer, whose writings in Yiddish depict "unique characters in unique circumstances, a group of people who are still a riddle to the world and often to themselves." The Nobel citation declared that his "impassioned narrative art . . . brings universal human conditions to life" through the fictional microcosm of Polish Jewry. Like a kosher cook he has concocted an endless array of delights from a few staple ingredients: love, eccentricity, wit, terror, hope, lust, faith, and mystery. Perhaps Singer intended to gently lecture the doubters of his literary alchemy when he said in his acceptance speech: "One can find in the Yiddish tongue and in the Yiddish spirit expressions of pious joy, lust for life, longing for the Messiah, patience and deep appreciation of human individuality. There is a quiet humor in Yiddish and a gratitude for every day of life, every crumb of success, every encounter of love. . . . The ghetto was not only a place of refuge for a persecuted minority but a great experiment in peace, in self-discipline and in humanism. As such it still exists and refuses to give up in spite of all the brutality that surrounds it. . . . My father's house on Krochmalna Street in

Warsaw was a study house, a court of justice, a house of prayer, of storytelling, as well as a place for weddings and Chassidic banquets."

The son and grandson of rabbis, Singer was born in Radzymin, Poland, on July 14, 1904. He grew up in Warsaw, translated *The Magic Mountain* into Yiddish, and became a journalist. Fleeing Nazism, he and his brother went to New York. He worked for the *Jewish Daily Forward*, which serialized his novel *The Family Moskat* after World War II. Saul Bellow made the first translation of one of his stories into English, and after its appearance in a literary magazine Singer began reaching an audience that grew exponentially along with his output. Since his 50th birthday Singer has won two National Book Awards in the course of publishing eight novels, ten children's books, four memoirs, and scores of short stories. His most celebrated works include *In My Father's Court, Gimpel the Fool, A Day of Pleasure, A Crown of Feathers and Other Stories.*

In his Nobel speech Singer said: "I never forget that I am only a storyteller." He then continued: "The storyteller of our time, as in any other time, must be an entertainer of the spirit in the full sense of the word, not just a preacher of social and political ideas. There is no paradise for bored readers and no excuse for tedious literature that does not intrigue the reader, uplift his spirit, give him the joy and the escape that true art always brings."

Jewish Week observed that "many Yiddishists have looked askance at his preoccupation with exotic subjects, his interest in sensuality and the demonic." Singer answered: "Ghosts love Yiddish and as far as I know they all speak it." As for antisensualist criticism: "The Bible and the Talmud are full of sex stories. If these saints are not ashamed of it, why should I be, who am not a saint?" Though Singer "abandoned orthodoxy as a life structure," according to one biographer, the mystical remained a key element in his writing and God a paternal presence in his life. "I always feel that God was very frugal, very stingy in bestowing gifts on us. He didn't give us enough intellect, enough physical strength. But when He came to emotions, to passions, He was very lavish. He gave us so many emotions and such strong ones that every human being, even if he is an idiot, is a millionaire in emotions."

(PHILIP KOPPER)

Prize for Chemistry

The Nobel Prize for Chemistry was awarded to Peter Mitchell, a 58-year-old British biochemist who, since his student days at the University of Cambridge in the 1940s and '50s, has occupied himself with working out a plausible theory of how the cells of living creatures transfer the energy available in oxygen and sunlight into the essential compound adenosine triphosphate (ATP). This compound participates in countless metabolic processes in organisms as small and simple as one-celled bacteria, as complex as human beings, as massive as the giant sequoia.

ATP has been termed the currency of en-

ergy exchange within the cell. Its formation during intracellular chemical reactions is a way in which an organism conserves some of the energy liberated in those reactions instead of setting it free as heat that would be dissipated to its surroundings. The energy saved in the form of ATP can be recovered by the cells when the ATP takes part in reactions that require an external supply of energy in producing substances essential to the organism.

Throughout its life span, every living thing maintains its own precise budget of matter and energy, absorbing both from its environment, rearranging them to meet its requirements, and storing them up or casting them off in different forms. Each of the physical and chemical activities peculiar to each cell plays a part in this ceaseless traffic, changing matter from one location or condition to another, consuming or producing energy as it does so. Foodstuffs are broken down in a series of chemical changes that disrupt the bonds that hold their atoms in molecules, redistributing not only the atoms, to form new molecules, but also the energy associated with those bonds, either retaining it in the bonds of the molecules (including ATP) or letting it go to waste. In other sequences of reactions the complex molecules needed by the cell are assembled from the products of the breakdown of food. The breakdown reactions produce more ATP than they use up, while the building-up reactions use up more than they produce. Other processes such as motion also consume ATP, but the ATP budget is kept in balance by the action of special structures within the cells. In the animal cell, this structure, the mitochondrion—sometimes called the powerhouse of the cell—channels the energy from oxygen molecules into the formation of molecules of ATP; in the plant cell, the chloroplast performs a similar function, obtaining the necessary energy from the photons of light.

The mechanism of storage and utilization of energy outside the mitochondrion or the chloroplast—by the formation and destruction of ATP—has been understood since the middle of the 20th century. In these processes, ATP and its usual companion, adenosine diphosphate (ADP), become directly involved in the chemical reactions, appearing along with the other products or disappearing along with the other starting materials. On the other hand, the transformation of ADP into ATP in the mitochon-

drion or the chloroplast occurs by some mechanism for which no one has yet been able to formulate a chemical reaction that can be experimentally verified in detail.

This mechanism has been the target of Mitchell's efforts. Though other scientists have concentrated on searching for chemical species that convert ADP to ATP, Mitchell has directed attention toward clarifying the involvement of the membranes that partition the interior of the mitochondrion and prevent the substances within the different compartments from mixing. He proposes that enzymes, already known to be fixed within the membranes, are oriented in such a way that as one of them brings about the conversion of ADP to ATP, liberating protons (hydrogen ions), another enzyme simultaneously effects an oxidation-reduction reaction that uses up the protons. The resulting apparent transfer of protons within the mitochondrion links the two interdependent enzymatic actions, permitting the energy available in the proton-consuming reaction—which, in turn, is coupled to the uptake of oxygen—to provide the driving force for the synthesis of ATP. Though a great deal remains to be learned about the workings of this intricate apparatus, Mitchell's ideas have already shown their value by unifying and refocusing the research being conducted on this crucial problem in biochemistry.

Prize for Physics

The Nobel Prize for Physics was divided, one half being awarded to Pyotr Kapitsa of the Soviet Union for research—mostly performed in the 1930s—on the liquefaction of helium and on the unusual properties of the liquid. The other half was shared by Arno A. Penzias and Robert W. Wilson of the U.S. for their discovery—announced in 1965—of a faint electromagnetic radiation that appears to permeate the entire universe. The existence of this radiation lends strong support to the theory that the universe originated in a cosmic explosion several billion years ago.

Kapitsa, who was born in 1894 near St. Petersburg (now Leningrad), was trained at the Polytechnic Institute there and remained on its faculty, but in 1921, while visiting England, he gained admittance to the Cavendish Laboratory at Cambridge for further study with Ernest Rutherford, one of the founding fathers of nuclear physics. At Cambridge Kapitsa took up the investi-

(Above) Pyotr Kapitsa, (right) Robert W. Wilson, and Arno A. Penzias.

gation of the properties of materials subjected to extremely low temperatures or to intense magnetic fields; by 1924 he had built a magnet that produced a field of 500,000 gauss, a record not surpassed until 1956.

For his low-temperature work he needed a reliable method for liquefying helium, which boils at 4.2 K ($-268.94°$ C) and is the most difficult of all gases to condense. The feat had been accomplished by an earlier Nobel laureate, Heike Kamerlingh Onnes of The Netherlands, in 1908, but the procedure required several days to yield only small amounts of impure liquid helium. Kapitsa took advantage of the spontaneous cooling of a gas that expands rapidly enough not to absorb heat from its surroundings, and he overcame the problem that all other substances freeze at the temperatures of his experiments by designing his apparatus so that the helium itself would lubricate the moving parts. The result, demonstrated in 1934, was a machine that produced liquid helium at the unprecedented rate of two litres per hour—the prototype of helium liquefiers now used in cryogenic laboratories throughout the world.

Later in 1934 Kapitsa and his wife, while traveling in the Soviet Union, were trapped there by the confiscation of their passports, and Kapitsa was made director of the new S. I. Vavilov Institute of Physical Problems of the Soviet Academy of Sciences in Moscow. There he built a new low-temperature laboratory and resumed his exploration of the properties of liquid helium, finding that at temperatures below 2.2 K it loses practically all its resistance to flow, seeping through microscopic leaks and creeping mysteriously over the walls of its containers. One of Kapitsa's colleagues at the institute, Lev Landau, won a Nobel Prize in 1962 for developing a quantum mechanical theory that accounts for this unique transition to the "superfluid" state.

During World War II Kapitsa guided the production of large quantities of liquid oxygen for use in the Soviet steel industry. His pacifism, however, led him to decline a chance to engage in the development of nuclear weapons and brought him into conflict with Stalin and Lavrenty Beria. He thereupon forfeited his directorship of the Vavilov Institute and remained under house arrest until after Stalin's death, but in 1955 he was reinstated and reportedly placed in charge of the Sputnik satellite program. Now in his 80s, Kapitsa remains active in research, but he has shifted his attention to the other extreme of the temperature scale, seeking ways to heat plasmas to some temperature (many millions of degrees) at which nuclear fusion would occur at a moderate rate, allowing the energy released to be used for power generation.

At the time that Kapitsa was enlarging the boundaries of modern physics by building his great magnet and liquefying helium, Penzias and Wilson had not yet seen the light of day. Penzias was born in Munich, Germany, in 1933; he went to the U.S. with his parents in 1940, studied at the City College of New York and Columbia University, and joined the Bell Telephone Laboratories in 1961. Wilson was born in Houston, Texas, in 1936; after attending Rice University and the California Institute of Technology, he too joined the Bell Labs,

in 1963. To investigate the intensity of radio waves emitted from the gaseous halo that surrounds our Galaxy, they refined a big horn-shaped antenna that had been built for detecting radio waves reflected from the large, passive Echo satellites orbited by NASA in 1960 and 1964. In May 1964 they tuned this sensitive radio telescope to a frequency of 4,080 MHz and aimed it straight up into the sky, promptly detecting microwave radiation that was more intense than they could attribute to any known source, including the Milky Way, leaky joints in the apparatus, the gases in the Earth's atmosphere, or even the droppings of pigeons that frequented the inside of their antenna. Observations made over a period of months, while the motion of the Earth through space aimed the telescope at different parts of the universe, demonstrated that the excess, or background, radiation did not diverge from any particular place but arrived with equal strength from all directions of the cosmos.

Penzias and Wilson had no explanation for their results, but a colleague suggested that they consult Robert Dicke of Princeton University. Dicke, an astrophysicist, with his associates James Peebles, David Wilkinson, and Peter Roll, had been analyzing the alternative schemes of cosmic genesis by which the known properties of the universe could be accounted for.

One of those theories, first advanced in the 1940s, holds that all the matter and energy of the universe was once compressed in a dense, hot ball that abruptly, at a time between 10 billion and 20 billion years ago —in the so-called big bang—began to expand in all directions. As the dilation proceeded, the constant absorption and reemission of energy by the particles of matter should have caused the whole, growing volume to be uniformly pervaded by an electromagnetic field in which the intensity of the radiation was apportioned in a particular, predictable way among all the wavelengths of the spectrum, from X-rays through visible light all the way out to microwaves and long radio waves. Though the volume of the universe continued to increase, the quantity of radiant energy would, after a time, remain the same but become increasingly diluted, corresponding to a continuous fall in the cosmic temperature. Even now, after billions of years, the wraith of the primeval fireball should still be present. If it could be detected and shown to fit the predicted uniformity and

wavelength distribution, the big bang theory would be rendered more plausible than any theory that implied a different result.

The findings of Penzias and Wilson, which indicate a cosmic background temperature of about 3 K, were found to be in agreement with the inferences drawn by Dicke and his group as to the outcome of the big bang. Since 1965 measurements of the cosmic radiation at several wavelengths—at Bell Labs, Princeton, and other radio observatories—have corroborated the energy-wavelength distribution and confirmed the status of the discovery as one of the principal achievements of 20th-century science.

Prize for Physiology or Medicine

The achievement of successively deeper insights into the nature and function of deoxyribonucleic acids (DNA's) and the rise of a whole new field of science, molecular genetics, have been recognized by several Nobel Prizes during the past two decades. In 1978 the Prize for Physiology or Medicine was divided equally among three microbiologists—Werner Arber of Switzerland and Daniel Nathans and Hamilton O. Smith of the U.S.—for the discovery and application of enzymes that break the giant molecules of DNA into manageable pieces, small enough to be separated for individual study but large enough to retain bits of the genetic information inherent in the sequence of units that make up the original substance. The researches of the three prizewinners, though marked with distinctive creativity, together constitute a notable instance of the evolution of a scientific theme—from its inception in a stage of recognition and rationalization, through its maturation in a phase of refinement and diversification, to its fruition in its generalization and application as an indispensable part of the methodology of research in molecular genetics.

The first of the three stages was the contribution of Arber, who was born in Granichen, Switz., in 1929 and studied at the Swiss Federal Institute of Technology in Zürich, the University of Geneva, and the University of Southern California. He served on the faculty at Geneva from 1960 to 1970 and since then has been professor of microbiology at the University of Basel. The starting point of his work was a phenomenon called host-induced variation when it

(Left) Daniel Nathans and Hamilton O. Smith, (right) Werner Arber

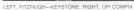

was discovered in the 1940s by an earlier Nobel laureate, Salvador Luria. Luria had observed that bacteriophages (viruses that infect bacteria) not only induce hereditary mutations in their bacterial hosts but at the same time undergo hereditary mutations themselves. During the late 1950s and early '60s Arber and several others extended Luria's work, accumulating experimental evidence supporting a proposal that the effects stemmed from the action of protective enzymes present in the bacterium that modified the DNA of the infecting virus. One of these, the restriction enzyme, is named for its ability to restrict the growth of the bacteriophage by cutting the molecules of its DNA to pieces. By 1968 Arber had developed further knowledge of the action of one of the restriction enzymes, and other scientists had purified another. These, the first members of the class to be studied in detail, belong to a group that attacks DNA's that contain a particular short sequence among the thousands of subunits (like a few consecutive letters in a very long word), but breaks the molecules at random places other than the recognition site.

Smith was born in New York City in 1931 and attended the University of California at Berkeley and Johns Hopkins University in Baltimore, Md. He engaged in research with the U.S. Public Health Service before joining the faculty of the school of medicine at Johns Hopkins in 1973. In 1970 he reported a study of a strain of the bacterium *Haemophilus influenzae*, a common inhabitant of the human respiratory tract that sometimes causes severe complications of the viral disease influenza. In the course of that work Smith and his collaborators isolated a restriction enzyme differing in an important property from those of the type investigated by Arber: it not only recognizes a specific region in a DNA molecule, but it always breaks the DNA at that very site. The reproducible behaviour of this type is the feature that has made it uniquely valuable in molecular genetics. In addition, the procedures introduced by Smith to isolate and purify his enzyme have become a standard method in this field of research; they have been applied to most of the more than 100 known enzymes of this type.

Nathans, born in 1928 in Wilmington, Del., attended the University of Delaware and Washington University in St. Louis, Mo.; he has been a member of the faculty of Johns Hopkins since 1967. When Smith wrote to him about the new restriction enzyme isolated from *H. influenzae*, Nathans was in Israel investigating the structure of the DNA of the simian virus 40 (SV40), which, although it is the simplest virus known to induce cancerous tumours, proved more difficult to decipher than the bacteriophages studied by Arber and Smith. Nathans recognized the potential usefulness of a specific enzyme in cutting up the DNA of SV40 and, after returning to Baltimore, showed in 1971 that Smith's enzyme broke that molecule into 11 well-defined fragments. By employing two more of these enzymes, he broke the viral DNA at other positions and was able to deduce its entire constitution. This achieve-

ment, the construction of a genetic map of a virus, heralded the first application of the new enzymes to the problem of identifying the molecular basis of cancer. Nathans' exposition of the possibilities of applying restriction enzymes to the study of problems in genetics was specifically praised by the Karolinska Institutet.

As fast as the knowledge of the behaviour of the restriction enzymes has been developed, it has been seized by scientists who see these substances as new, powerful tools for seeking the solutions to a multitude of problems related to genetics and heredity. A large group of diseases are definitely hereditary; in humans, the list includes hemophilia, thalassemia, sickle cell anemia, phenylketonuria, and albinism, and possibly diabetes. Studies of the origin of conditions like these are being profoundly influenced by the availability of the new enzymes. Cancer, though not hereditary, is linked to changes induced in the DNA by radiation and chemical compounds, and the restriction enzymes are being used to identify these changes as part of the search for ways to prevent them. The enzymes already have been employed to isolate pieces of DNA that control the formation of the human hormones insulin and somatostatin; by means of the recombinant DNA techniques, the pieces have been incorporated in the DNA of bacteria that can be grown in cultures as a means of manufacturing these hormones, which are very difficult to produce by classical laboratory procedures.

(JOHN V. KILLHEFFER)

Prize for Economics

Herbert A. Simon is not, in the conventional sense, an economist. The Royal Swedish Academy of Sciences, perhaps anticipating criticism of its choice, thus called attention in its citation to Simon's early "publications on structure and decision-making within economic organizations, a relatively new area of economic research." Classical theory holds that business firms function like profit-making automatons endowed with titanic competence and unwavering vision. According to this thesis, corporations seek maximum profits first, last, and always. Traditional analysts would thus assume a single-minded approach by any and all businesses. This approach was convenient but misleading. Simon demonstrated that individual executives work in discrete areas and make decisions on the basis of limited information. Their goals may be either short-term or restricted to a single aspect of corporate activity. Simon concluded that because available information and human comprehension are limited, even chief executive officers could fail to imagine—let alone consider—every possible alternative when determining policies. Consequently executives, and hence corporations, engage in fragmented "satisficing" behaviour, a far cry from undistracted profiteering.

"In his epoch-making book *Administrative Behavior* (1947)," the Academy noted, "and in a number of subsequent works, he described the company as an adaptive system of physical, personal and social components that are held together by a network of intercommunications . . . He rejects the assumption made in the classic theory of the corporate firm of an omniscient, rational, profit-maximizing entrepreneur. He re-

Herbert A. Simon

places this entrepreneur by a number of cooperating decision-makers, whose capacities for rational action are limited both by lack of knowledge about the total consequences of their decisions and by personal and social ties. Since these decision-makers cannot choose a *best* alternative, as can the classic entrepreneur, they have to be content with a *satisfactory* alternative. Individual companies, therefore, strive not to maximize profits but to find acceptable solutions to acute problems. This might mean that a number of partly contradictory goals have to be reached at the same time."

These ideas had wide impact on such diverse things as how companies plan their investments to scholarly analysis of the Kennedy administration's handling of the Cuban missile crisis. The Academy noted that in addition to his influence as an author, Simon was directly involved in "political science, administration, psychology and information sciences." In a colleague's words, Simon "studies reason's limitations in the name of reason." Having explained how quixotic human behaviour affects practical economic reality, he later turned to studying the development of artificial intelligence through computers.

Born in Milwaukee, Wis., on June 15, 1916, Simon earned a doctorate in political science at the University of Chicago. He worked briefly for the International City Managers' Association and the Bureau of Public Administration at the University of California before joining the faculty of the Illinois Institute of Technology. In 1949 he moved to the Carnegie Institute of Technology (now Carnegie-Mellon University) in Pittsburgh where he became Richard King Mellon professor of computer sciences and psychology. The Nobel citation recalled that Simon "has made contributions in . . . science theory, applied mathematics, statistics, operations analysis, economics and business administration." Because the Academy paid attention to these diverse activities, some felt that future Nobel Prizes might be awarded to honour achievements in almost any of the social sciences.

(PHILIP KOPPER)

OBITUARIES

The following is a selected list of prominent men and women who died during 1978.

Abrahams, Harold Maurice, British athlete (b. Dec. 15, 1899, Bedford, Bedfordshire, England—d. Jan. 14, 1978, London, England), represented Great Britain twice in the Olympic Games (1920, 1924) and in 1924 equaled the Olympic record in winning the 100-m dash. He later became an executive in such organizations as the British Amateur Athletic Board and the International Amateur Athletic Federation and covered sports as a radio commentator and as athletics correspondent for *The Sunday Times* (1925–67) in London.

Adoula, Cyrille, Congolese politician (b. Sept. 13, 1921, Léopoldville, Belgian Congo [now Kinshasa, Zaire]—d. May 24, 1978, Lausanne, Switz.), was prime minister of the Congolese Republic (now Zaire) from 1961 to 1964. A founder (1958) of the Mouvement National Congolais, he became a senator in 1960 and minister of the interior after his country's independence from Belgium that year. As prime minister he faced successive crises, including the attempted secession of Katanga (now Shaba) Province under Moise Tshombe. With the help of UN forces, Adoula suppressed the rebellion, but he was replaced by Tshombe in July 1964. Adoula later served as ambassador to Belgium and to the U.S. and as foreign minister before his retirement in 1970.

Ahn, Philip, U.S. actor (b. March 29, 1911, Los Angeles, Calif.—d. Feb. 28, 1978, Los Angeles), was probably best remembered for his role as the Master Kan in the television adventure series "Kung Fu" (1973–75) and as a villanous Japanese warlord in numerous World War II motion pictures. Although he was Korean, Ahn played more than 270 Japanese and Chinese character roles and appeared in such films as *The General Died at Dawn* and *Charlie Chan in Honolulu.* His longtime movie career (1936–67) also included the war films *Halls of Montezuma, China Sky,* and *Battle Zone.*

Alexander, Eben Roy, U.S. journalist (b. Feb. 15, 1899, St. Louis, Mo.—d. Oct. 30, 1978, Roslyn, N.Y.), was managing editor (1949–60) of *Time,* one of the nation's most widely read and prestigious news magazines. Alexander began his career in journalism at the *St. Louis Star* in 1921, then moved (1925) to the *St. Louis Post-Dispatch* before joining *Time* in 1939. He not only knew virtually every editorial job from personal experience but was deeply versed in such diverse fields as politics, religion, music, foreign affairs, and the classics. After a record 11 years in *Time's* highest editorial post, he became executive assistant to Henry R. Luce, a founder of *Time* in 1923. Alexander retired in 1966.

Allen, James Browning, U.S. politician (b. Dec. 28, 1912, Gadsden, Ala.—d. June 1, 1978, Foley, Ala.), Democratic senator (1969–78) from Alabama, whose mastery of parliamentary procedure and ability to wring concessions from opponents placed him at the helm of numerous Senate filibusters. Although he was defeated when he led the opposition to the Panama Canal treaties in 1978, his tactical expertise was generally acknowledged by both Republicans and Democrats. Shortly after graduating in law from the University of Alabama, Allen was elected (1938) to the Alabama House of Representatives and held office until he joined the Navy in 1942. Following World War II he was elected to the Alabama State Senate (1946–50), and later served (1951–55 and 1963–67) as the state's lieutenant governor before filling the U.S. Senate seat vacated by Lister Hill.

Baldwin, Faith, U.S. author (b. Oct. 1, 1893, New Rochelle, N.Y.—d. March 18, 1978, Norwalk, Conn.), gained wide popularity during the Depres-

sion of the 1930s for such romantic novels as *The Office Wife, District Nurse, Honor Bound,* and *Rich Girl, Poor Girl.* Baldwin, whose novels provided an escape for millions of people, earned more than $315,000 in 1936. Her books, depicting rich people with high morals and good breeding, never lost their appeal; she turned out some 85 books in a 50-year career. In the 1960s her monthly column in *Woman's Day* generated scores of letters from satisfied subscribers, and in the late 1970s her final novels, *Thursday's Child* and *Adam's Eden,* continued to delight readers.

Batista i Roca, Josef Maria, Catalan nationalist (b. 1895, Barcelona, Spain—d. Aug. 27, 1978, Barcelona), was a prominent figure in the Catalan nationalist movement for separation from Spain. After studies at the universities of Barcelona, Madrid, Oxford, and Berlin, Batista became professor of ethnography at Barcelona (1921–29), where he was a spokesman for Catalan culture. In 1936 he was appointed diplomatic representative in London of the Catalonian government. When Catalonia lost autonomy after the Spanish Civil War (1936–39), Batista became the exiled spokesman for the cause, as secretary and later president of the Catalan National Council. He also taught Spanish at the University of Cambridge (1948–62), cofounded the Anglo-Catalan Society (1954), and constantly wrote, lectured, and prepared broadcasts on Spanish and Catalan history and affairs. In 1976 he returned to Catalonia as an elder statesman.

Baumgartner, Wilfrid Siegfried, French financial expert (b. May 21, 1902, Paris, France—d. June 1, 1978, Paris), was governor (1949–60) of the Bank of France at the time of the 1958 monetary reform and, as Pres. Charles de Gaulle's minister of finance from 1960 to 1962, played a major role in building up the country's gold and foreign currency reserves. He then became chairman of the Rhône-Poulenc chemical and textiles group, one of the largest manufacturing companies in France. Baumgartner established his reputation as a civil servant in the Ministry of Finance before World War II and gained a reputation as one of Europe's leading monetary experts.

Bedford, D(avis) Evan, British physician (b. 1898, Boston, Lincolnshire, England—d. Jan. 24, 1978, London, England), was internationally recognized

as a leading authority on cardiology. A graduate of the Middlesex Hospital Medical School in 1921, he became associated with the distinguished cardiologist John Parkinson at the Ministry of Pensions Hospital at Orpington, Kent. In 1926 he was in France with Charles Laubry and Louis Gallavardin, world authorities on cardiology, and then returned to London Hospital, where, together with Parkinson, he studied cardiac infarction and published classical papers on electrocardiogram technique. During World War II he treated Prime Minister Winston Churchill's cardiopneumonic illness, and after the war he became a pioneer in the treatment of congenital and valvular heart conditions. He received worldwide honours, including the presidencies of the British Cardiac Society and the European Society of Cardiology, the vice-presidency of the International Society of Cardiology, and the chairmanship of the Council of the British Heart Foundation. He presented his library of rare books on the heart and circulation to the Royal College of Physicians.

Begle, Edward Griffith, U.S. mathematician (b. Nov. 27, 1914, Saginaw, Mich.—d. March 2, 1978, Palo Alto, Calif.), was largely responsible for introducing the "new math" into the U.S. school system. The new math emphasized the theoretical foundations of arithmetic and problem solving rather than rote memorization and computational skills. After earning (1940) his Ph.D. from Princeton University, Begle joined the faculty of Yale University (1942–61) and later of Stanford (1961–78), where he headed the School Mathematics Study Group, an organization funded with $10 million in U.S. government grants. Begle and a staff of nearly 100 formulated curricula for both elementary and secondary schools. In 1972 the group was disbanded because Begle believed they had achieved their goals.

Bennett, Vivienne, British actress (b. July 29, 1905, Poole, England—d. Nov. 11, 1978, South Nutfield, England), became a leading figure on the British stage during the 1930s, known especially for her interpretations of leading women's roles in the plays of Shaw and Shakespeare, the latter at Stratford-upon-Avon and the London Old Vic. During World War II she founded her own company and in the postwar period appeared regularly at the Arts Theatre. In later years she also gave Shakespeare recitals in many countries for the British Council.

Bentley, Nicholas Clerihew, British artist (b. June 14, 1907, London, England—d. Aug. 14, 1978), was a witty illustrator and cartoonist who gained prominence as the author of "pocket cartoons" in the London *Daily Mail.* He also illustrated some 60 books, including several of his own. Following in the footsteps of his father, E. C. Bentley, he was a successful publisher and author of several detective novels. In addition he wrote books on Victorian England and the British monarchy and an autobiography. Many, however, believed that Bentley's greatest talent was manifested in his precise, economical, and immediately recognizable draftsmanship.

Bergen, Edgar, U.S. ventriloquist (b. Feb. 16, 1903, Chicago, Ill.—d. Sept. 30, 1978, Las Vegas, Nev.), who, with his irrepressible wooden sidekick Charlie McCarthy, conveyed laughter into the homes of radio listeners for more than three decades. The pair made their professional radio debut in 1937 on the "Chase and Sanborn Hour" and became famous for their verbal bouts with W. C. Fields. Bergen also introduced such wooden performers as the doltish Mortimer Snerd and the old maid Effie Klinker. After making millions of dollars from his original investment of $35 for the carved head of McCarthy and 25 cents for "Hermann's Wizard's

Edgar Bergen with
Charlie McCarthy

Manual," Bergen announced (Sept. 21, 1978) plans for his retirement on October 11. McCarthy, who was to become the property of the Smithsonian Institution, asked Bergen, "How can you retire, when you haven't worked since you met me?"

Best, Charles Herbert, Canadian physiologist (b. Feb. 27, 1899, West Pembroke, Maine—d. March 31, 1978, Toronto, Canada), was still an undergraduate when he and Frederick Banting, in 1921, using a University of Toronto laboratory made available to them by J. J. R. Macleod, discovered insulin and its use in treating diabetes. In 1923 this discovery merited the Nobel Prize, but Best did not share the honour. Macleod remarked that he was being honoured for discovering Best, and Banting manifested his outrage by giving half his prize money to his colleague. Best also introduced the use of the complex carbohydrate heparin to inhibit blood clotting during heart surgery. He served as head of the University of Toronto's physiology department (1929–65) and director of the Banting and Best department of medical research (1941–67) established at the university in 1923.

Betz, Carl, U.S. actor (b. March 9, 1921, Pittsburgh, Pa.—d. Jan. 18, 1978, Los Angeles, Calif.), spent a major portion of his career in minor roles before gaining wide recognition as Dr. Alex Stone in the television situation comedy "The Donna Reed Show" (1958–63) and later as the tough Texas lawyer in "Judd for the Defense" (1967–69), a role for which he received an Emmy award in 1968. Betz made his Broadway debut in *The Long Watch* (1952), and after playing opposite Veronica Lake in *The Voice of the Turtle* he was signed by 20th Century-Fox. His acting career also included such films as *The President's Lady* (1953), *Inferno* (1953), and his last, *Spinout* (1966).

Bostock, Lyman, U.S. baseball player (b. Nov. 22, 1950, Birmingham, Ala.—d. Sept. 23, 1978, Gary, Ind.), was the congenial star outfielder of the California Angels baseball team and one of the game's highest paid players, with a salary exceeding $400,000 a year. Bostock, who was recruited by the Minnesota Twins in 1975 after spending three years in the minor leagues, compiled batting averages of .282, .323, and .336 in successive seasons. In 1977 he became a free agent and signed with the Angels. Although the 1978 season began slowly for Bostock, who was 2 for 39, he never lost his confidence or sense of humour. He turned over his first month's salary to charity because he hadn't earned it and then returned to his old form. Bostock was accidentally shot to death by the estranged husband of the woman he was escorting.

Boumédienne, Houari (MOHAMMED BEN BRAHIM BOUKHARROUBA), Algerian head of state (b. Aug. 23, 1927, Clauzel, near Guelma, Algeria—d. Dec. 27, 1978, Algiers, Algeria), one of the leaders of his country's struggle for independence from France, was its president from 1965. The son of a small farmer, he had a mainly religious education at the Islamic Institute in Constantine, Algeria, and at al-Azhar University in Cairo. He first went to Egypt to avoid conscription in the French Army. In December 1954, a month after the outbreak of the uprising against France, he switched to military studies in Egypt and then took further training in Morocco. In 1955 he joined a guerrilla unit in western Algeria, adopting his nom de guerre of Bumed-Din (Boumédienne in French transcription), and three years later was in charge of all operations in the western sector. In 1960 he was made chief of staff of the National Liberation Army force with headquarters in Tunisia. In September 1962 Boumédienne led the 30,000 troops armed with Soviet guns and tanks into Algiers in support of Ahmed ben Bella against Yusuf ben Khedda, the head of the first government of the Algerian republic. Ben Bella became premier and Boumédienne minister of defense. But this alliance between the easygoing Ben Bella and the puritanical revolutionary Boumédienne did not last, and in June 1965 Boumédienne used his tanks to depose Ben Bella. He then proclaimed himself president of the Algerian Democratic and Popular Republic, premier, minister of defense, chief of staff, and chairman of the 26-member Revolutionary Council. In 1971 Boumédienne imposed state control on the oil industry at the cost of ending Algeria's special relationship with France. In 1975 he risked war with Morocco by trying to gain territorial access to the Atlantic across the former Spanish Sahara. While negotiating important industrial contracts

with Western countries and at the same time maintaining close ties with the Soviet bloc, he became a leading figure in the nonaligned movement and was host to a summit conference in 1973. The country first learned that Boumédienne was seriously ill on November 18, four days after he returned from Moscow, where he had gone for medical treatment.

Boyer, Charles, French-born actor (b. Aug. 28, 1899, Figeac, France—d. Aug. 26, 1978, Phoenix, Ariz.), whose continental charm and reputation as a great lover assured his success as a box office idol. The top-salaried star for Warner Bros. in 1945, Boyer wooed such glamorous leading ladies as Marlene Dietrich in *The Garden of Allah*, Greta Garbo in *Conquest*, and Ingrid Bergman in *Gaslight*. Probably his most highly acclaimed film was *Algiers* (1938), in which he purportedly invited Hedy Lamarr to "Come with me to the Casbah." He later explained that the lines were invented for publicity. Because of his warm and intriguing voice, Boyer was often typecast in a lover's role although he gave equally superb performances as a rogue, villain, and thief. His later films include *Is Paris Burning?, How to Steal a Million, Casino Royale,* and *Barefoot in the Park.* Reported to have been despondent over the death of his wife of 44 years two days earlier, Boyer consumed an overdose of barbiturates.

Bradshaw, Robert Llewellyn, West Indian politician (b. Sept. 16, 1916, St. Kitts, West Indies—d. May 24, 1978, St. Kitts), became prime minister of St. Kitts-Nevis-Anguilla in 1967, when the three islands became an independent state in association with the U.K. After studying at St. Paul's Anglican School, St. Kitts, he worked as a machinist in the central sugar factory (1922–40). In 1940 Bradshaw founded St. Kitts's trade and labour union and Labour Party. He became a member of the Legislative Council in 1946 and sat in the West Indies Federal Parliament as federal minister of finance (1958–62). When the federation dissolved, he returned to St. Kitts as minister without portfolio until 1966. After briefly serving as chief minister, he became prime minister.

Breech, Ernest Robert, U.S. business executive (b. Feb. 24, 1897, Lebanon, Mo.—d. July 3, 1978, Royal Oak, Mich.), was a corporate troubleshooter who tripled output at Bendix Aviation Corp. and piloted the financially troubled Ford Motor Co. from annual losses of $100 million following World War II to $500 million a year in profits several years later. Breech began his career with the Yellow Cab Co. three years before it merged with General Motors (GM) in 1925. In 1929 he was appointed general assistant treasurer of the company and in 1933 was named president and chairman of the board of North American Aviation Inc., a GM affiliate. After resigning his GM vice-presidency in 1942, he became chief executive officer and chairman of the board of Bendix Aviation Corp. Breech then became executive vice-president and a member of the board of directors of Ford Motor Co. in 1946. He relinquished his chairmanship in 1960 but soon after joined Trans World Airlines and became chairman of the board of that organization.

Brel, Jacques, Belgian-born songwriter (b. April 8, 1929, Brussels, Belgium—d. Oct. 9, 1978, Paris, France), composed nearly 500 compassionate songs and became a French singing idol in the 1950s because of the dramatic intensity with which he sang about loneliness, lost love, war, old age, and death. At the height of his career in 1967, Brel abandoned the concert stage and turned to producing, directing, and acting. He appeared in such French films as *The Risks of the Profession* and *My Uncle Benjamin.* Later, Brel's music gained popularity in the U.S. when his songs were introduced by composer Mort Shuman in the 1968 Broadway musical *Jacques Brel Is Alive and Well and Living in Paris.* When Brel learned in 1974 that he suffered from terminal cancer, he sailed to the Marquesas Islands in the Pacific to live in seclusion. In 1977 he briefly returned to Paris and recorded his last album, *Brel,* the year's biggest hit in France.

Brik, Lili, Russian cultural figure (b. Nov. 11, 1891, Moscow, Russia—d. Aug. 4, 1978, Moscow, U.S.S.R.), became notorious in the 1920s for her ill-fated love affair with Russian poet Vladimir Mayakovsky. Brik, who was married to critic Osip Brik, one of Mayakovsky's closest friends, inspired many of Mayakovsky's poems including *I Love* (1922) and *About This* (1923). Although the poet, a vigorous spokesman for the Communist Party, was hailed in the Soviet Union as the bard of the Bolshevik Revolution, he became increasingly despondent because of the hopelessness of his affair with Brik and in April 1930 took his life. Brik later married Vasily Katanyan, an authority on Mayakovsky's work.

Brugnon, Jacques ("Toto"), French tennis player (b. June 11, 1895, Paris, France—d. March 20, 1978, Paris), was one of the renowned "Four Musketeers" of French tennis who, with Jean Borotra, René Lacoste, and Henri Cochet, captured the Davis Cup for France in 1927 and held it through 1932. Brugnon, regarded as one of the game's greatest doubles players, intimidated opponents with his uncanny reflexes, court tactics, and short backswing, which disguised the direction of his shots. With Marcel Dupont as a partner, he won the French doubles title in 1922 and repeated his victories in 1928, 1930, 1932, and 1934 with Cochet or Borotra. Brugnon's triumphs also included the Wimbledon title in 1926, 1932, and 1933 and the Australian title in 1928. With Suzanne Lenglen he won the French mixed doubles five times (1921–26).

Bryan, Frederick van Pelt, U.S. judge (b. April 27, 1904, Brooklyn, N.Y.—d. April 17, 1978, New York, N.Y.), issued a landmark decision in 1959 by voiding the U.S. government ban on D. H. Lawrence's *Lady Chatterley's Lover,* which had first appeared in Italy in 1928. Bryan ruled that, although some passages might shock readers, the book displayed literary merit and therefore was a legitimate expression of free speech. He held that the book could not be classified as obscene or banned from the mail by the postmaster general, who was not qualified to pass judgment on such matters. In two other far-reaching First Amendment decisions, Bryan ruled (1968) that policemen could not be stationed inside pornography bookshops and (1973) that a police department could not forbid officers from wearing long hair. During his 22 years as a federal District Court judge in New York, Bryan presided over a wide range of complex cases that concerned taxes, antitrust laws, and suits by the Cuban government brought against American banks and businesses that had refused to return holdings because their property in Cuba had been expropriated.

Busia, Kofi Abrefa, Ghanaian politician and academic (b. July 11, 1913, Ashanti, Gold Coast [now Ghana]—d. Aug. 28, 1978, Oxford, England), was prime minister of Ghana from Sept. 30, 1969, to Jan. 13, 1972. He came to power in the first elections after the overthrow (1966) of Pres. Kwame Nkrumah, but his government's economic difficulties led to a military coup while he was visiting England that brought an end to democratic rule. Busia, informed of the coup, chose to remain in England. A scholar and a teacher with degrees from London and Oxford universities, he later became (1943) assistant district commissioner in Ashanti. Busia returned to Oxford in 1946 and obtained a doctorate in philosophy with his thesis—which later became a standard work—*The Position of the Chief in the Modern Political System of Ashanti* (1951). In 1947 he returned to the Gold Coast, where he undertook a government social survey and wrote the authoritative *Social Survey of Sekondi-Takoradi.* He entered the Gold Coast legislature in 1951, led the opposition to Nkrumah in Ashanti, and in 1957 headed the National United Party opposition in Ghana's National Assembly before seeking voluntary exile in The Netherlands and Britain (1959–66), where he held chairs in sociology. He returned to head the interim military government's advisory committees and in 1967 published *Africa in Search of Democracy.*

Carstens, Lina, West German actress (b. Dec. 6, 1892, Wiesbaden, Germany—d. Sept. 22, 1978, Munich, West Germany), created memorable roles in the theatre, in films, and on television during a career of some 60 years. After World War II, she played the title role in Brecht's *Mother Courage and Her Children* in its first performance in Germany and later became a leading member of the Bavarian State Theatre. As a film actress, she won many awards and continued working for both cinema and television when she was over 80.

Carter, Maybelle ("Mother"), U.S. singer (b. May 10, 1909, Nickelsville, Va.—d. Oct. 23, 1978, Nashville, Tenn.), was the grand old dame of the Grand Ole Opry and the matriarch of the Carter Family. Her artistry created a sensation in both folk and country music in the 1930s. Carter, together with her daughters Helen, June, and Anita, brother-in-law A. P., and sister-in-law Sara, formed the original Carter Family in 1927. The Family, whose recordings included such all-time favourites as "Wildwood Flower," "Amazing Grace," "Will the Circle Be Unbroken," and "Wabash Cannonball," became the first group ever named to the Country Music Hall of Fame. After A. P. and Sara left the group, Carter and her daughters were featured (1943–48) on radio station WRVA in Richmond, Va., as Mother Maybelle and the Carter Sisters. Her daughters left the act in the 1950s, but Carter, an accomplished guitarist, autoharpist, and songwriter, continued to be greeted by wild applause when she performed at the Grand Ole Opry.

Catton, Bruce, U.S. writer (b. Oct. 9, 1899, Petoskey, Mich.—d. Aug. 28, 1978, Frankfort, Mich.), received both the Pulitzer Prize and the National Book Award for History in 1954 for *A Stillness at Appomattox,* the third volume of his trilogy about the Army of the Potomac in the U.S. Civil War. He also won wide acclaim for historical novels on the Civil War and for such books as *The War Lords of Washington* (1948), *Mr. Lincoln's Army* (1951), and *Terrible Swift Sword* (1963). Early in his career Catton was a reporter with the *Cleveland News,* the *Boston American,* and the *Cleveland Plain Dealer.* He then accepted (1945) the post of director of information for the U.S. Commerce Department and special assistant to the secretary of commerce (1948). In 1954 he became editor of *American Heritage* magazine and from 1959 was its senior editor.

Chamorro Cardenal, Pedro Joaquín, Nicaraguan editor (b. 1924?, Nicaragua—d. Jan. 10, 1978, Managua, Nicaragua), was editor and publisher of *La Prensa* of Managua, the only newspaper in Nicaragua to oppose the Somoza regime, which came to power in 1933. Chamorro, the leader of the Democratic Union of Liberation, a coalition of outlawed political parties and labour federations, was first arrested and temporarily exiled in 1944 for challenging the dictatorial rule of the Somoza family. Chamorro's newspaper had been subject to strict censorship since December 1974, and Chamorro himself had his civil rights suspended for 20 months. When martial law was lifted in September 1976, *La Prensa* demanded that persons who had disappeared be accounted for and that those jailed without trial be released. In October 1977 Chamorro went to New York to receive Columbia University's Maria Moore Cabot Prize for "distinguished journalistic contributions to the advancement of inter-American understanding." Chamorro was fatally shot in Managua as he was on his way to work. His funeral, attended by some 40,000 people, was followed by widespread rioting, a nationwide strike by labour and business groups, and a demand for Somoza's resignation. Many believed that Chamorro's assassination was instigated by the government.

Chase, Ilka, U.S. actress (b. April 8, 1905, New York, N.Y.—d. Feb. 15, 1978, Mexico City, Mexico), established a reputation as an acid-tongued actress playing Sylvia Fowler in the Broadway play *The Women* (1936) and embellished this image as the hostess of the spicy radio talk show "Luncheon at the Waldorf." Chase, who appeared in such motion pictures as *Now, Voyager, Rich People,* and *The Big Knife,* also launched a successful literary career when she published the autobiographical *Past Imperfect* in 1942. Her world travels earned her fame and fortune and a multitude of material for her books.

Chastenet de Castaing, Jacques, French historian (b. April 20, 1893, Paris, France—d. Feb. 7, 1978, Paris), was the author of a seven-volume history of the Third Republic (1870–1940) and of studies on British and American history. After serving as a liaison officer with U.S. forces in World War I, he spent five years in the diplomatic service, and from 1931 to 1942 he co-edited *Le Temps.* Elected to the Académie Française in 1956, Chastenet was a member of several learned societies and of groups that promoted European and international cooperation.

Chávez, Carlos, Mexican composer (b. June 13, 1899, Mexico City, Mexico—d. Aug. 2, 1978, Mexico City), whose works, marked by distinctively Mexican melodic patterns and rhythmic inflections, were regarded for over half a century as the best in Mexican music. Chávez, who completed his first symphony at age 19, wrote his first significant Mexican ballet, *El fuego nuevo,* in 1921. He later served as conductor of the Orquesta Sinfónica de Mexico (1928) and director of the National Conservatory in Mexico (1928–34). Chávez's compositions not only combined the elements of Mexican-Indian music, utilizing percussion, primitive rhythms, archaisms of harmony and melody, and violence of dramatic change, but also embodied elements of modern European and American music. Some of his most famous works include *Sinfonia de Antigona* (1933), *Concerto No. 1 for Piano and Orchestra* (1940), *Toccata for Percussion Instruments* (1942), and *Concerto for Violin* (1950).

Chávez, Federico, Paraguayan politician (b. 1881?—d. April 24, 1978, Asunción, Paraguay), first gained national prominence as Paraguay's foreign minister, ambassador to France and Spain, and longtime leader of the Colorado Party. The Democratic wing of the Colorado Party secured his election as president of Paraguay in 1949, following a period of great political instability during which his predecessors had held office only briefly. During Chávez's tenure in office he faced growing opposition from the Conservatives, who denounced his policy of nationalization and close association with Argentina. In 1954, when Chávez armed the national police force in an effort to strengthen his regime, Gen. Alfredo Stroessner, commander in chief of the armed forces, led the cavalry in an effective coup that deposed Chávez.

Cheshire, Geoffrey Chevalier, British jurist (b. June 27, 1886, Hartford, England—d. Oct. 27, 1978, Hampshire, England), was Vinerian professor of English law at Oxford University from 1944 to 1949 and the author of several highly authoritative studies on British and international law. Before World War I, he lectured at the University College of Wales, Aberystwyth, and afterward at Oxford, where he gained a reputation as an outstanding academic lawyer and lecturer. His books include *Modern Law of Real Property* (1925; 12th ed., 1976), *Private International Law* (1935; 9th ed., 1974), and *The Law of Contract* (1945; 9th ed., 1976).

Chirico, Giorgio De, Italian artist (b. July 10, 1888, Volos, Greece—d. Nov. 19, 1978, Rome, Italy), founded with the futurist painter Carlo Carrà the Metaphysical School (*scuola metafisica*) of painting. De Chirico, who created works of disquieting intensity and classical stillness, became a top modernist painter. Influenced by the painting of Arnold Böcklin, who juxtaposed the fantastic with the commonplace, and by Nietzsche's descriptions of Turin's squares, De Chirico turned out ominously lighted scenes of deserted piazzas with classical statues, dark arcades, and small, isolated figures overpowered by their own shadows and the

KATHERINE YOUNG

severe, oppressive architecture. While in Paris (1911–15) he created "The Soothsayer's Recompense" (1913) and "The Mystery and Melancholy of a Street" (1914). In 1915 he returned to Italy and modified his earlier style by a denser and more arbitrary arrangement of his unusual forms. Paintings that typify this period include "Grand Metaphysical Interior" (1917) and "The Seer" (1915). By the mid-1920s De Chirico adopted a more realistic and romantic style, which was less widely admired. In 1972 a De Chirico exhibition, the largest retrospective ever seen in New York City, filled four halls and contained some 150 paintings, drawings, and sculptures.

Chorley, Robert Samuel Theodore Chorley, 1st Baron, British jurist (b. May 29, 1895, Kendal, Westmorland [now Cumbria], England—d. Jan. 27, 1978, London, England), was called to the bar by the Inner Temple in 1920 after graduating from Queens College, Oxford. From 1930 to 1946 he was the Sir Ernest Cassel professor of commercial and industrial law at the London School of Economics. In 1945 he was created a peer and became a Labour Party spokesman in the House of Lords. He later served as vice-president of the Howard League for Penal Reform, chairman of the Institute for the Study and Treatment of Delinquency (1950–56), and president of both the Haldane Society (1957–72) and the National Council for the Abolition of the Death Penalty (1945–48).

Christophers, Sir (Samuel) Rickard, British malariologist (b. Nov. 27, 1873, Liverpool, England—d. Feb. 19, 1978, Broadstone, Dorset, England), laid the foundations of a worldwide malaria eradication program through his lifelong pioneering studies. Graduating from the University of Liverpool in 1896, he first studied the disease on an Amazon voyage. In 1898 he joined a malaria commission, and in Central and West Africa associated malaria with blackwater fever and established its endemic character. He entered the Indian Medical Service in 1902 and headed (1910–22) the Central Malaria Bureau. During World War I he directed the Central Laboratory at Basra in Mesopotamia, and when he returned to India, he directed the Central Research Institute in Kasauli (1922–32). As professor of malarial studies at the University of London (1932–38) he directed the Experimental Malaria Unit at the London School of Hygiene and Tropical Medicine. He was made a fellow of the Royal Society in 1926 and was knighted in 1931.

Ciolkosz, Adam, Polish socialist (b. Jan. 5, 1901, Krakow, Poland—d. Oct. 1, 1978, London, England), was chairman of the Socialist Union of Central-Eastern Europe from 1930 to 1957. In 1918 Ciolkosz volunteered for the army of the restored Polish Republic and fought the invading Red Army. After participating in the Silesian Uprising in 1921 he graduated in law from Krakow University. He joined the Polish Socialist Party (pps) in

1921 and was elected to the Sejm (parliament) in 1928. A stalwart democrat, he opposed Marshal Pilsudski's authoritarian regime and was imprisoned in September 1930. After being reelected to the Sejm while in prison, he was set free and became a member of the Central Committee of the pps. But in 1931 a Pilsudskist majority in the Sejm deprived Ciolkosz of his immunity, and he was sentenced to three years in prison. When World War II began, Ciolkosz joined Wladyslaw Sikorski's government-in-exile in Paris, but in June 1940 he fled to London, where he became a member of the Polish Political Council and served as its chairman (1956–59, 1963–67). After the British and U.S. governments formally recognized (July 5, 1945) the new pro-Soviet Polish government, Ciolkosz decided to remain in London. The third volume of his *Historical Outline of Polish Socialism* was completed shortly before his death.

Clay, Lucius DuBignon, U.S. Army general (b. April 23, 1897, Marietta, Ga.—d. April 16, 1978, Cape Cod, Mass.), was the dynamic commander in chief of U.S. forces in Europe and military governor of the U.S. Zone in Germany when the Soviets blockaded Berlin by rail and road for 11 months (1948–49). Clay then engineered the successful Allied airlift of food and supplies into the city. After graduating (1918) from the U.S. Military Academy at West Point, N.Y., Clay held various army engineer assignments before taking charge of the first national civil airport program (1940–41). Soon after the U.S. entered World War II (December 1941), Clay was appointed director of matériel, Army Service Forces, responsible for the production and procurement of troop supplies. In 1945 he became deputy military governor in Germany under Gen. Dwight D. Eisenhower. Following the spectacular Berlin airlift, Clay retired (1949) with the rank of general and entered private business. He also served as adviser (1953–61) to President Eisenhower and then (1961–62) to Pres. John F. Kennedy, who named Clay his special representative to Berlin when a major crisis developed over the building of the Berlin Wall by the East Germans.

Compton, Fay, British actress (b. Sept. 18, 1894, London, England—d. Dec. 12, 1978, England), had a long and varied career on London's West End stage, appearing in review and musical comedy from 1911. Compton established a reputation as author Sir James Barrie's favourite leading lady and starred in such plays as *Peter Pan* (1917) and *Mary Rose* (1920). An actress of considerable versatility, she was Ophelia to the Hamlets of John Barrymore (1925) and John Gielgud (1939) and Ruth in Noel Coward's *Blithe Spirit* (1941). She also played in such films as *The Story of Esther Costello* (1957) and *The Haunting* (1963) and appeared on television as one of the old aunts in the bbc production of "The Forsyte Saga."

Conant, James Bryant, U.S. educator (b. March 26, 1893, Dorchester, Mass.—d. Feb. 11, 1978, Hanover, N.H.), devoted a major portion of his life to the advancement of higher education as both a professor of organic chemistry and the longtime president (1933–53) of Harvard University. Conant's educational philosophy called for a balance between academic and vocational programs in high schools and a diversified general curriculum for colleges. Because of his continued interest in science, he became a central figure in organizing U.S. science policy for World War II, including the testing and development of the first atomic bomb. After the war he served as a senior adviser to the National Science Foundation and to the Atomic Energy Commission. In 1955 he became the first U.S. ambassador to West Germany. Conant returned to the U.S. in 1957 and resumed his public education studies. His writings include *The American High School Today* (1959) and *Slums and Suburbs* (1961). His autobiography, *My Several Lives* (1970), reveals Conant's roles as an innovative public servant, educational reformer, and scientist.

Constanduros, Denis, British writer (b. July 22, 1910, Sutton, Surrey, England—d. Oct. 23, 1978), was an imaginative author of both radio and

television scripts. After studying at the Chelsea School of Art he began writing scripts for broadcasting and produced a highly successful regional series, "The Luscombes." For television he wrote original plays, adapted novels by Jane Austen and H. G. Wells, and created such Henry James dramatizations as "The Spoils of Poynton," "What Maisie Knew," and "The Ambassadors" starring Lee Remick and Paul Scofield.

Cozzens, James Gould, U.S. novelist (b. Aug. 19, 1903, Chicago, Ill.—d. Aug. 9, 1978, Stuart, Fla.), was named recipient of the 1949 Pulitzer Prize for fiction for his World War II novel *Guard of Honor*. He began his writing career while studying (1922–24) at Harvard University and turned out his first

WIDE WORLD

novel, *Confusion*, in 1924. Succeeding novels, including *The Last Adam* (1933), *The Just and the Unjust* (1942), and *By Love Possessed* (1957), quickly rose to the top of the best-seller list. His last opus was a collection entitled *Just Representations*.

Crane, Bob Edward, U.S. actor (b. July 13, 1928, Waterbury, Conn.—d. June 29, 1978, Scottsdale, Ariz.), whose glib radio routines earned him the title role as the ingenious colonel who outwitted the German Army on the television comedy series "Hogan's Heroes" (1965–71). Crane, whose first ambition was to be a drummer, played (1944–46) with the Connecticut Symphony and with several dance bands before turning to radio announcing in the early 1950s. He made his television debut on "The Dick Van Dyke Show," later played the next door neighbour on "The Donna Reed Show," and portrayed an insurance salesman pursuing his medical degree on "The Bob Crane Show." Crane, who was appearing in the play *Beginner's Luck*, was found murdered in his apartment.

Dailey, Dan, U.S. actor (b. 1917, New York, N.Y.—d. Oct. 16, 1978, Los Angeles, Calif.), was a handsome song-and-dance man of the 1940s and 1950s. He appeared in such musicals as *Mother Wore Tights* and *My Blue Heaven*. Dailey, who made his Broadway debut (1934) in *Babes in Arms*, starred in *I Married an Angel* and *Stars in Your Eyes* before signing a motion-picture contract with Metro-Goldwyn-Mayer. After World War II he joined 20th Century-Fox and played opposite the pinup girl with the million-dollar legs, Betty Grable. In later years he appeared on stage in such plays as *The Odd Couple* and *Plaza Suite* and in 1969 and 1970 played Gov. William Drinkwater in the television series "The Governor and J. J."

Daud Khan, Sardar Mohammad, Afghan politician (b. July 18, 1909, Kabul, Afghanistan—d. April 27, 1978, Kabul), became president of Afghanistan on

HUBERT LE CAMPION—SYGMA

July 17, 1973, when he overthrew King Mohammad Zahir Shah, his cousin and brother-in-law. Daud Khan abolished the monarchy and declared Afghanistan a republic. As president he followed a policy of nonalignment, accepting aid from all quarters. Educated in Kabul and in France, he rose to command an army corps in 1939 and held the post of minister of defense from 1946 to 1953. As prime minister (1953–63) he carried out a pro-Soviet policy until he was forced to resign. Daud Khan's overt participation in politics was severely curbed in 1964 when a new constitution debarred members of the royal family from holding political office. He died during a leftist military coup.

Davidson, Jimmy ("TRUMP"), Canadian musician (b. 1909?, Sudbury, Ont.—d. May 2, 1978, Sudbury), was a big-band jazz leader, cornetist, and accomplished baritone who introduced the country to Dixieland music and became one of Canada's most popular entertainers. He formed his first dance-jazz band, Melody Five, in 1925, but reached the height of his career performing (1944–62) at Toronto's Palace Pier with the newly formed big band he modeled after Bob Crosby's Bobcats. In later years, Davidson's Dixieland Sextet, the heart of the big band, delighted millions of listeners with his radio broadcasts "Dixieland Concert," "Jazz Unlimited," and "Dixieland Downbeat."

Davies, Rhys, British writer (b. Nov. 9, 1903, Clydach Vale, Wales—d. Aug. 21, 1978, London, England), depicted the society of Wales in novels and short stories which, though written in English, were deeply rooted in his native land. A careful artist, Davies excelled in the precise medium of the short story, exhibiting poetry and humour in such collections as *The Trip to London* (1946) and *The Chosen One* (1967). His novels, among them *The Black Venus* (1944), were also successful. He was awarded the OBE in 1968.

Davis, Joe, British billiards and snooker player (b. April 15, 1901, Whitewell, Derbyshire, England—d. July 10, 1978, Hampshire, England), was world snooker champion from 1927 until his retirement in 1946. During his career he scored a total of 689 century breaks and held the world record for a maximum break of 147. He also held the world billiard championship from 1928 to 1933 and the British championship thereafter. Davis confirmed

his reputation as the "grand old man" of British snooker when television audiences had an opportunity to admire his finely honed skills and remarkable techniques. He was awarded the OBE in 1963.

Dean, Basil Herbert, British theatrical producer (b. Sept. 27, 1888, Croydon, England—d. April 22, 1978, London, England), was Britain's most prolific theatre producer and director between World Wars I and II. After joining (1907) Annie Horniman's repertory company in Manchester, he became the first director of the Liverpool Repertory Theatre and assisted Herbert Tree at His Majesty's and Alfred Butt at Drury Lane. He directed James Elroy Flecker's *Hassan*, as well as plays by John Galsworthy, W. Somerset Maugham, and Noel Coward. In 1928 he turned to the film industry and founded Ealing Films, Associated Talking Pictures, and British Film Distributors. During World War II he created Entertainments National Service Association (ENSA) which, according to Dean in *The Theatre at War* (1956), performed for over 300 million men and women in the armed forces and in industry. Dean also published several plays and two volumes of autobiography, *Seven Ages* (1970) and *Mind's Eye* (1973).

Debré, Robert, French pediatrician (b. Dec. 7, 1882, Sedan, Ardennes, France—d. April 29, 1978, Paris, France), was renowned for his research on children's infectious diseases and for his role in international child-care agencies. Debré studied literature before attending medical school where he specialized in bacteriology. In 1945 he became chief physician at the Hospital for Sick Children in Paris and gained a preeminent position in French medicine for formulating demographic policies and reorganizing medical studies. His autobiography, *L'Honneur de vivre*, appeared in 1974.

Diederichs, Nicolaas J., South African politician (b. Nov. 17, 1903, Ladybrand, Orange Free State—d. Aug. 21, 1978, Cape Town, South Africa), became president of South Africa on April 19, 1975. Diederichs was also a founder of the Afrikaner nationalist movement which led to the establishment of the Afrikaner National Party. This organization enforced apartheid, a policy of white supremacy based on legalized discrimination against non-Europeans in South Africa. He was appointed minister for economic affairs in 1958 but was especially influential as the country's finance minister (1967–75). Diederichs was nicknamed "Mr. Gold" because he fought to keep gold, South Africa's major export, as the international monetary standard.

Dingle, Herbert, British scientist (b. Aug. 2, 1890, London, England—d. Sept. 4, 1978, Hull, England), spent many years at University College in London as professor (1946–55) of the history and philosophy of science and as professor emeritus. He was, however, more influential as a philosopher who defended and promoted rationalist principles in science. Dingle left school at 14 but in 1915 won a scholarship at the Imperial College of Science and Technology in London. Though he specialized in spectroscopy, his interest in theoretical science became evident when he published *Relativity for All* (1922) just months after Einstein was awarded the Nobel Prize. Forty years later Dingle became involved in a bitter controversy when he challenged some aspects of Einstein's theory. Besides his scientific and philosophical writings, Dingle published books on Wordsworth and Emily Brontë and *Science and Literary Criticism* (1949). He was also president of the Royal Astronomical Society (1951–53).

Docker, Sir Bernard Dudley Frank, British industrialist (b. Aug. 9, 1896—d. May 22, 1978, Bournemouth, England), together with his second wife, Norah, suffered notoriety in the 1950s for a flamboyant style of living during a period of austerity in postwar Britain. Their yacht "Shemara" and Lady Docker's gold-plated Daimler car were frequently featured in newspaper gossip columns. Sir Bernard, knighted in 1939 for services to West-

minster Hospital, was, like his father, a director of the Midland Bank but resigned in 1953. He was chairman and managing director of the Birmingham Small Arms Co. Ltd. (BSA) and its subsidiary, the Daimler Car Co., but he was forced off the BSA board in 1956.

Duke-Elder, Sir (William) Stewart, British ophthalmologist (b. April 22, 1898, near Pitlochry, Perthshire, Scotland—d. March 27, 1978, London, England), was world renowned for his work as a clinician and surgeon, for research on the physiology of the eye, and for his writings. He was graduated from the University of St. Andrews in 1919 and later received doctorates from St. Andrews and the University of London. He was surgeon-oculist to Edward VIII, George VI, and Elizabeth II and consultant to hospitals in both hemispheres. He also directed research at the Institute of Ophthalmology, University of London (1947–65). Duke-Elder's most outstanding publication was his *Text-Book of Ophthalmology* (7 vol., 1932–54), rewritten as *System of Ophthalmology* (15 vol., 1958–76). He was editor in chief of the *British Journal of Ophthalmology* and of *Ophthalmic Literature*. He was knighted in 1933 and became a fellow of the Royal Society in 1960.

Du Vigneaud, Vincent, U.S. biochemist (b. May 18, 1901, Chicago, Ill.—d. Dec. 11, 1978, Scarsdale, N.Y.), was awarded the 1955 Nobel Prize for Chemistry for the isolation and synthesis of the pituitary hormones vasopressin, an antidiuretic, and oxytocin, the principal uterus-contracting agent in labour and milk-releasing agent after childbirth. After receiving (1927) a Ph.D. from the University of Rochester, N.Y., Du Vigneaud studied at Johns Hopkins University, Baltimore, Md., the Kaiser Wilhelm Institute, Dresden, Germany, and the University of Edinburgh, Scotland, before serving (1932–38) as head of the department of biochemistry at George Washington University School of Medicine in Washington, D.C. In 1938 he became professor and head of the biochemistry department at the medical school of Cornell University in New York City. Under his direction, the Cornell laboratories contributed to such major achievements as the synthesis of penicillin and the isolation and development of the structure of the sulfur-bearing vitamin biotin, as well as examining many other sulfur-containing organic compounds. From 1967 to 1975 Du Vigneaud was professor of chemistry at Cornell University in Ithaca, N.Y.

Eames, Charles, U.S. designer (b. June 17, 1907, St. Louis, Mo.—d. Aug. 21, 1978, St. Louis), created (late 1930s) a series of molded plywood formfitting shell chairs that were mass-produced in the 1940s by Herman Miller Furniture Co. after Eames and his wife, Ray, perfected an inexpensive plywood molding process. Eames, a trained architect, headed (1939–41) the experimental design department at Cranbrook Academy of Art, Bloomfield Hills, Mich., and later (1943) became director of research and development for the West Coast operations of the Evans Products Co. in California. He also designed a wide variety of industrial and consumer products and sets for motion pictures, an interest he pursued vigorously after 1955. During the 1960s Eames served as design consultant for a number of major U.S. corporations, and in 1960, together with his wife, was named recipient of the Kauffmann International Design Award, the highest in the field.

Fields, Totie (SOPHIE FELDMAN), U.S. entertainer (b. 1930?, Hartford, Conn.—d. Aug. 2, 1978, Las Vegas, Nev.), was a rotund nightclub and television comedienne who often drew laughs by poking fun at her own obesity. The raucous-voiced Fields performed for three years before Ed Sullivan reviewed (1963) her act at New York City's Copacabana and booked her for his show. Despite continual health problems, including the amputation of a leg, two heart attacks, diabetes, the removal of a breast, and eye surgery, Fields persistently returned to centre stage. When theatrical colleagues named her Entertainer of the Year in January 1978, Fields said, "I don't want anyone feeling sorry for me." Her death was attributed to "apparent heart failure."

Finck, Werner, German cabaret comedian (b. May 2, 1902, Görlitz, Germany—d. July (?), 1978, Munich, West Germany), boldly began (1929) satirizing the Nazis during his comic cabaret sketches in Berlin. Finck was consequently placed in a concentration camp in 1935, and because he was unrepentant, his right to perform was withdrawn in 1939. After World War II he again entertained audiences with his mordant wit.

Flanner, Janet, U.S. writer (b. March 13, 1892, Indianapolis, Ind.—d. Nov. 7, 1978, New York, N.Y.), enchanted millions of readers for nearly 50 years as "Genet," author of the semimonthly "Letter from Paris" which appeared in *The New Yorker* magazine. Her polished prose gave penetrating insights into the political and social conditions in France during the Third, Fourth, and Fifth Republics, and her personal portraits revealed such varied personalities as Queen Mary of England, Pablo Picasso, and Adolf Hitler. As a longtime expatriate in France, Flanner was a striking figure with her bobbed hair, Lanvin suits, and distinctive monocle. She became friends with some of the country's most prominent citizens and produced superb biographies of Charles de Gaulle, Georges Braque, Philippe Pétain, and Henri Matisse. Flanner, who reported only in the third person, characterized her own thoroughness and objectivity: "I act as a sponge. I soak it up and squeeze it out in ink every two weeks."

Foot, Sir Dingle Mackintosh, British lawyer and politician (b. Aug. 24, 1905, Plymouth, England—d. June 18, 1978, Hong Kong), served as solicitor general in the Labour government from 1964 to 1967 and was a prominent defender of civil rights in many notable legal cases in Commonwealth countries. Elected to Parliament as a Liberal in 1931, he served in the World War II coalition government but lost his seat in 1945. He then resumed his legal career, practicing in Britain and in many countries overseas. In 1956, denouncing a "drift to the right" in his old party, he joined the Labour Party, and the following year was elected MP for Ipswich. After failing to be reelected in 1970, he returned to full-time legal practice.

Fosburgh, James Whitney, U.S. painter (b. Aug. 1, 1910, New York, N.Y.—d. April 23, 1978, New York), was an adept landscape artist and gifted still-life painter, who gained international renown when his posthumous portrait of Pres. John F. Kennedy appeared on the cover of *Time* magazine on Nov. 5, 1965. Fosburgh also advised Presidents Kennedy and Lyndon B. Johnson on acquisitions of first-rate American paintings for the White House and served on the committee to ensure its preservation. Other notable portraits included one of Alfred Lunt and Lynn Fontanne and one of Truman Capote. Fosburgh's works were acquired by the Metropolitan Museum of Art in New York City, the Boston Museum of Fine Arts, and the Philadelphia Museum of Art.

François-Poncet, André, French diplomat (b. June 13, 1887, Provins, France—d. Jan. 9, 1978, Paris, France), while French ambassador in Berlin (1931–38) repeatedly and futilely warned his government that Hitler was preparing Germany for war. He studied German literature and philology at the École Normale Supérieure and became professor of modern literature at the École Poly-technique before embarking on a career in journalism in 1911. After distinguished service in World War I and service in government missions, he turned to politics and was twice elected (1924 and 1928) deputy for the Seine département as a moderate

conservative. After holding undersecretaryships in a succession of governments, he was delegated to the League of Nations in 1930 before being named (1931) ambassador to Germany. Following the Munich agreement (Sept. 30, 1938), François-Poncet requested a transfer and for two years served as French ambassador to Italy. When Italy entered World War II (1940), he returned to France and served under Premier Philippe Pétain until he was arrested by German occupation forces and imprisoned in Germany (1943–44). François-Poncet was later consecutively appointed French high commissioner in West Germany (1949) and ambassador (1955) to the newly recognized Federal Republic of Germany. In retirement he remained active as president of the Permanent Commission of the International Red Cross and as a contributor to the newspaper *Le Figaro*. François-Poncet, who was the author of such books as *Souvenirs d'une ambassade à Berlin* (1946), was elected to the Académie Française in 1952.

Frick, Ford Christopher, U.S. sports executive (b. Dec. 19, 1894, Wawaka, Ind.—d. April 8, 1978, Bronxville, N.Y.), was baseball's mild-mannered commissioner (1951–65) but the very vocal president of the National League (1934–51). When Jackie Robinson became baseball's first black major league player, the St. Louis Cardinals threatened a strike. Frick vociferously proclaimed that the league would not sanction this action and warned that any strike would result in the team's expulsion from the National League. Frick was at the helm during some of baseball's most turbulent times, including the Depression, the exodus of players to the armed services during World War II, and the years when franchises changed cities in rapid succession. A former journalist and ghost writer for Babe Ruth, Frick also pioneered baseball broadcasting. In 1934 he became the National League's public relations chief and a natural for the office of league president only nine months later. He helped to establish the Baseball Hall of Fame in 1938, and in 1970 was enshrined in the hall for his many contributions to baseball. His recollections of the game are told in his autobiography, *Memoirs of a Lucky Fan* (1973).

Frings, Joseph Cardinal, West German prelate of the Roman Catholic Church (b. Feb. 6, 1887, Neuss, Germany—d. Dec. 17, 1978, Cologne, West Germany), became a bishop in 1932 and was appointed (1942) archbishop of Cologne during World War II. In numerous pastoral letters he fearlessly condemned Nazi atrocities perpetrated in Germany and in occupied countries. He remained with his flock throughout the Allied bombardments of Cologne, shared their sufferings and privations, and never abandoned his episcopal resi-

dence located in the heart of the city. Made a cardinal by Pope Pius XII in 1946, he retired from his see in 1969 and was succeeded as archbishop by Joseph Cardinal Höffner.

Geer, Will, U.S. actor (b. March 9, 1902, Frankfort, Ind.—d. April 22, 1978, Los Angeles, Calif.), portrayed the feisty grandfather on the television series "The Waltons," the role that earned him an Emmy award in 1975. Geer, who never had an acting lesson, began his six-decade career performing aboard steamboats on the Ohio River. Following his stage debut in *The Merry Wives of Windsor*, he appeared in a number of plays, notably as a free-spirited Georgian in *Tobacco Road*. His special flair for depicting crusty old men also won him many film appearances. Geer was among those blacklisted during the McCarthy era of the 1950s by Hollywood producers, but he returned to the stage in Shakespearean roles and to the screen in such films as *Salt of the Earth* (1954), *In Cold Blood* (1967), and *The Reivers* (1969). Shortly before his death, Geer appeared before a U.S. House select committee to argue against mandatory retirement.

Genn, Leo, British actor (b. Aug. 9, 1905, London, England—d. Jan. 26, 1978, London), was billed as "the man with the black velvet voice" during an acting career that spanned some 40 years. A criminal lawyer by profession, Genn turned from the drama of the courtroom to the limelight of the stage when a friend suggested (1930) the venture as a way to meet prospective clients. Genn, whose legal experience became intertwined with his acting career, wrote legal scenes for films, was given parts as a lawyer, and after World War II joined a British unit investigating war crimes and served as an assistant prosecutor at the Nürnberg trials. Besides acting in both classical and modern dramatic plays, he appeared in such films as *The Way Ahead*, *Caesar and Cleopatra*, *The Snake Pit*, and *The Longest Day*.

Ghashmi, Ahmad al-, North Yemeni politician (b. 1941?—d. June 24, 1978, Sana'a', Yemen Arab Republic), was the short-lived chairman of the Command Council of the Yemen Arab Republic. Ghashmi, who was commander of the armed forces, became chairman of the three-member Command Council that assumed power when Col. Ibrahim al-Hamdi was assassinated on Oct. 11, 1977. Ghashmi was meeting with an envoy dispatched by Pres. Salem Ali Rubayyi of the People's Democratic Republic of Yemen when a briefcase, reportedly containing a top-secret message, exploded, killing both Ghashmi and the envoy. Ghashmi held office only eight months before his assassination.

Gilliam, James William ("Junior"), U.S. baseball player and coach (b. Oct. 17, 1928, Nashville, Tenn.—d. Oct. 8, 1978, Inglewood, Calif.), was a player (1953–66) and coach (1965–78) for the Dodger professional baseball team both in Brooklyn and in Los Angeles. His dexterity and versatility earned him the nickname "Mr. Dependable," and he was named National League rookie of the year in 1953, when he batted .278 and had 63 runs batted in. He began his career at 17 with the Baltimore Elite Giants of the old Negro American League and was dubbed "Junior" by his teammates. As a Dodger, he replaced second base superstar Jackie Robinson, played nearly every position but shortstop, and batted an overall .265. Teammates affectionately renamed Gilliam "the Devil" because his sorcery at the plate made it easier for Maury Wills to steal bases. The Dodgers dedicated their 1978 World Series games to Gilliam, who succumbed 23 days after a massive cerebral hemorrhage.

Gilson, Étienne Henry, French scholar (b. June 13, 1884, Paris, France—d. Sept. 19, 1978, Cravant, Yonne, France), was one of the foremost experts on the history of philosophy and an exponent of Thomism, the scholastic philosophical method devised by Thomas Aquinas. In 1919 Gilson became professor at the University of Strasbourg and then at the Sorbonne (1921–32). From 1932 to 1951 he was professor of medieval philosophy at the Collège de France and was elected to the Académie Française in 1946. His many works included erudite and critical studies of Thomas Aquinas, Duns Scotus, and Dante. Some of his most admired studies include *The Spirit of Mediaeval Philosophy* (1936), *History of Christian Philosophy in the Middle Ages* (1955), and *Modern Philosophy: Descartes to Kant* (with Thomas Langan, 1963.) In 1929 he helped found the Pontifical Institute of Medieval Studies at the University of Toronto, which after 1950 became the centre for his academic activity.

Glass, David, British demographer (b. Jan. 2, 1911—d. Sept. 23, 1978, London, England), was professor of sociology at the London School of Economics and Political Science (LSE) from 1948 (Martin White professor from 1961). As one of the world's foremost authorities on population, he published *Population Policies and Movements in Europe* (1940), *Social Mobility in Britain* (1954), *Population and Social Change* (1972), *Numbering the People* (1973), and studies of fertility patterns in the British population. He was a noted teacher, spending most of his academic career at the LSE, but he traveled widely. During World War II he was engaged in statistical work with the Ministry of Supply, and after 1960 developed a particularly close relationship with the Indian government and academic institutions. He became a fellow of both the British Academy (1964) and the Royal Society (1971) and represented the U.K. at UN and UNESCO conferences.

Gödel, Kurt, Czech-born mathematician (b. April 28, 1906, Brünn [now Brno], Czech.—d. Jan. 14, 1978, Princeton, N.J.), earned a permanent niche in the history of mathematics with the celebrated theorem that bears his name. This philosophical principle states that in any formal system utilizing number theory there exists a proposition that cannot be proved or disproved on the basis of the axioms within that system. A longtime (1953–76) professor at the Institute for Advanced Study in New Jersey, Gödel received the National Medal of Science in 1974. His work *Consistency of the Axiom of Choice and of the Generalized Continuum-Hypothesis with the Axioms of Set Theory* (1940; rev. ed., 1958) is a classic in modern mathematics.

Goodhart, Arthur Lehman, U.S. jurist (b. March 1, 1891, New York, N.Y.—d. Nov. 10, 1978, London, England), was professor at jurisprudence at the University College of Oxford from 1931 to 1951 and the first American ever to become chairman (1937) of the faculty of jurisprudence at Oxford. Goodhart also became the first American head of a college at Oxford when he was elected master of University College in 1951. After graduating from Yale in 1912, he earned a law degree at Cambridge University. He obtained a law fellowship and became a lecturer in jurisprudence there in 1919, a post he held until his appointment as professor at Oxford. An expert on the common law as well as jurisprudence, Goodhart influenced a number of British law reforms.

Grant, Duncan James Corrowr, British painter (b. Jan. 21, 1885, Rothiemurchus, Inverness-shire, Scotland—d. May 8, 1978, Aldermaston, England), emerged as one of the most innovative designers and painters in Britain. He studied at the Westminster and Slade schools of art in London and under Jacques-Émile Blanche in Paris. Grant, whose works are characterized by bold brushwork and bright colours, was included (1912) in the second of the Post-Impressionist exhibitions along with the great French painters of the day. In 1913 he began working with art critic Roger Fry at the Omega Workshops in London, where he showed a flair for designing fabrics and furniture and produced such paintings as "The Lemon Gatherers" and "The Tight-Rope Walkers." Grant was also one of the many talented celebrities associated with the Bloomsbury Group, which met and discussed aesthetic and philosophical questions; in 1919 he became a member of the London Group. In addition to painting, he designed lithographs, stage decor, and collaborated with Vanessa Bell in decorating the interiors of homes.

Gronchi, Giovanni, Italian statesman (b. Sept. 10, 1887, Pontedera, Pisa, Italy—d. Oct. 17, 1978, Rome, Italy), was president of Italy from 1955 to 1962. Beginning in 1902, he participated in political movements that led to the formation of the Chris-

WIDE WORLD

tian Democrat Party. He served for a year in Mussolini's first government, but in June 1924 he joined some 150 other members of the Chamber of Deputies whose opposition to Mussolini led them to set up their own rump parliament. Gronchi left politics in 1926, but during World War II was active in the Italian underground. Between June 1944 and June 1946 he served in four Cabinets and later became (1948) speaker of the Chamber of Deputies. His support of an "opening to the left," which indicated a willingness to include Socialists in a coalition government, made him controversial but did not prevent him from being elected president. In 1960, however, he was accused of favouring a government supported by the neo-Fascists and was criticized for his part in events that brought Italy close to civil war.

Guéhenno, Jean, French writer (b. March 25, 1890, Fougères, Brittany, France—d. Sept. 22, 1978, Paris, France), made his own way from humble origins to bourgeois respectability through the teaching profession and through his writing. He examined the contradictions of his situation in his journals and works such as *Changer la vie* (1961), using it as the basis for a radical critique of contemporary society. From 1928 to 1936 he edited the journal *Europe* in association with the writer Romain Rolland; their correspondence was published in 1975. His biographies of Jean-Jacques Rousseau and Ernest Renan were much admired. He was elected to the Académie Française in 1962.

Halpern, Bernard, French immunologist (b. Nov. 2, 1904, Tarnos Rude, Russia—d. Sept. 22, 1978, Paris, France), was internationally renowned for his work on allergies and on the properties of cancer cells. A Russian by birth, he left that country after the Revolution and became a French citizen while studying medicine in Paris. In 1936 he was appointed director of the Rhône-Poulenc chemical company laboratories but in 1948 joined the Centre National de la Recherche Scientifique. From 1961 he was professor of experimental medicine at the Collège de France and in 1964 became director of the immunoallergic research centre at the Broussais Hospital, Paris. From 1958 to 1961 he was president of the International Association of Allergology.

Hamada, Shoji, Japanese ceramist (b. Dec. 9, 1894, Kanagawa Prefecture, Japan—d. Jan. 5, 1978, Mashiko, Japan), revitalized pottery making in Mashiko, where ceramic arts flourished in ancient times. The town now boasts more than 100 kilns.

Hamada's work is marked by a simple yet elegant economy of design that distinguished him as one of the world's great potters. His works are displayed in various museums, notably in Tokyo's Japan Folk Art Museum, where he held the post of curator for many years. Hamada was designated a "human national treasure" by the Japanese government in 1955, and he received the Culture Medal in 1968.

Hammami, Said, Palestinian Arab nationalist (b. 1941, Jaffa, Palestine [now Israel]—d. Jan. 4, 1978, London, England), was the London representative of the Palestine Liberation Organization. Though a fervent nationalist he was regarded as a "moderate" because of his willingness to consider setting up an independent Palestinian state on the West Bank of the Jordan River, while deferring the question of a single state for all Palestinians to the future. Hammami became a Palestinian refugee in Amman, Jordan, when Israel came into existence in 1948. He joined Yasir Arafat's al-Fatah guerrillas, but after the Palestinians clashed with Jordan in 1970, he moved to Beirut, Lebanon, and into politics, envisaging compromise with Israel. In 1972 he was sent to London, where he publicly espoused antiterrorist policies. Hammami died in his London office at the hands of an assassin, presumably hired by extremists.

Handler, Meyer Srednick, U.S. journalist (b. June 3, 1905, New York, N.Y.—d. Feb. 9, 1978, Santa Barbara, Calif.), was a raconteur noted for recounting his colourful experiences as a foreign correspondent with International News Service (1933–35), United Press (1935–48), and the *New York Times* (1948–73). His dispatches included such spectacular events in history as the fall of France, the German invasion of the Soviet Union, and the Nürnberg trials. In the 1960s Handler returned to the U.S., covered the civil rights movement, and gained the admiration of Martin Luther King, Jr., and Malcolm X; he wrote the introduction to *The Autobiography of Malcolm X*. Handler, who spoke six languages fluently, studied at the University of Chicago, Harvard University, and the Sorbonne in Paris.

Harrah, William Fisk, U.S. gambling executive (b. Sept. 2, 1911, South Pasadena, Calif.,—d. June 30, 1978, Rochester, Minn.), amassed millions of dollars as the enterprising proprietor of Reno and Lake Tahoe gambling establishments that catered to middle-class patrons rather than to high rollers. Without ever venturing into Las Vegas, Harrah built a financial empire in Nevada that earned an estimated $14.6 million during 1977. His first (1937) bingo parlour in Reno was unsuccessful, but after establishing a second several months later on the legendary "Casino Row," he began making plans for a casino that opened in 1946. In 1955 he expanded operations to Lake Tahoe and at the time of his death was considering Australia as a gambling site. Harrah also owned the world's largest vintage automobile museum, which displayed 1,100 cars in Sparks, Nev.

Harrod, Sir Roy Forbes, British economist (b. Feb. 13, 1900, London, England—d. March 8, 1978, Holt, Norfolk, England), developed a theory of economic growth (1939) that became known as the Harrod-Domar model after U.S. economist Evsey Domar formulated it independently some years later. Harrod described the theory in *Towards a Dynamic Economics* (1948) and extended it in *A Supplement on Dynamic Theory* (1952) and *A Second Essay on Dynamic Theory* (1961). After graduating from New College, Oxford, Harrod became senior censor at Christ Church (1930–31), sat on the university Hebdomadal Council (1929–35), and was Nuffield reader in economics (1952–67). He was also joint editor of the *Economic Journal* (1945–61), president of the Royal Economic Society (1962–64), and a member of the British Academy. He was knighted in 1959. His publications include a biography of

John Maynard Keynes, the noted economist, who for a short time had taught Harrod at the University of Cambridge.

Hasselblad, Victor, Swedish inventor (b. March 8, 1906, Göteborg, Sweden—d. Aug. 5, 1978, Göteborg), developed (1941) for the Swedish Air Force a camera that appeared commercially in 1948

KEYSTONE

as the world's first 2¼ in by 2¼ in single-lens reflex camera with interchangeable lenses and magazines. Hasselblad's camera, which earned a reputation as the Rolls-Royce of its field, was widely used by professional photographers and was later adopted by the U.S. National Aeronautics and Space Administration for the first photographs of the Moon. He was also president (1944–66) of his own photography company, Hasselblad Photography, Inc., before he sold the controlling interests to a Swedish industrial group in 1967.

Heger, Robert, German conductor and composer (b. Aug. 19, 1886, Strasbourg, Germany [now France]—d. Jan. 14, 1978, Munich, West Germany), was principal conductor of the operas at Nürnberg (1912–19), Munich (1919–25), Vienna (1925–33), and Berlin (1933–45) and second conductor next to Bruno Walter in London during the German summer seasons. From 1950 to 1954 he served as president of the Munich Academy of Music. His symphonies, piano music, songs, and four operas, including *Der Bettler Namenlos* (1932) and *Der verlorene Sohn* (1936), are marked by the influences of such classical composers as Max Schillings and Richard Strauss.

Hobbs, Carleton Percy, British radio actor (b. June 18, 1898, Farnborough, England—d. July 31, 1978, Maidstone, Kent, England), played over 4,000 roles in radio drama during a 50-year career and possessed one of the most quickly recognized voices in England. He trained at the Royal Academy of Dramatic Art in London and occasionally appeared on the stage, notably at the Lyric Theatre, Hammersmith. He also acted in films and on television, gaining particular success in the role of Sherlock Holmes and as Aristarchus in *I, Claudius*. But it was his voice that, through the productions of the BBC radio Drama Repertory Company, demonstrated his remarkable versatility as a character actor and his expressive range.

Homolka, Oscar, Austrian-born actor (b. Aug. 12, 1898, Vienna, Austria—d. Jan. 27, 1978, Sussex, England), was a leading character actor on stage

and screen whose roles ranged from the humorous to the sinister. After playing in Vienna and Berlin under Max Reinhardt, he performed in London theatre in the mid-1930s. He then traveled to the U.S., where he appeared as the blustering uncle in the Broadway hit *I Remember Mama*. Homolka's film credits include *Sabotage* (1936), *Ebb Tide* (1937), *Ball of Fire* (1942), *Mission to Moscow* (1943), and *Billion Dollar Brain* (1967). He estimated that before he was 30 he had appeared in over 400 plays. He also appeared in some 100 films and on many television shows.

Hornby, Albert Sidney, British lexicographer (b. Aug. 10, 1898, Chester, England—d. Sept. 13, 1978, London, England), compiled the *Oxford Advanced Learner's Dictionary of Current English* (3rd ed., 1974). Based on principles derived from Hornby's experience teaching English in Japan before World War II, it proved phenomenally successful among foreign students. Most of the royalties after 1961 went into a trust for training English teachers from the third world. Hornby's contribution to English studies was publicly recognized by the University of Oxford which awarded him an honorary degree.

Hoytink, Gerrit Jan, Dutch physical chemist (b. Jan. 14, 1925, Alkmaar, Neth.—d. April 11, 1978, Sheffield, England), established an international reputation by applying molecular orbital theory to an explanation of the electronic properties of organic molecules and interpreting electronic spectra of ions with sophisticated measuring techniques. After graduating from the Free University of Amsterdam, where he became (1957) professor of physical chemistry, he joined the faculties of the University of Amsterdam (1960) and of the University of Sheffield (1966). In 1967 he co-founded and became editor of the influential journal *Chemical Physics Letters*.

Hulbert, Jack, British actor (b. April 24, 1892, Ely, England—d. March 25, 1978, London, England), was a light comedian who, together with his wife, Dame Cicely Courtneidge, held the affection of the British public for more than 60 years. They were married after appearing together in *The Pearl Girl* (1913), which launched Hulbert's theatrical career. A long series of comedies and cheerful musicals established the couple as purveyors of refreshing jollity and charm. Their successes include the musical comedies *Follow a Star, Full Swing*, and *The House that Jack Built* and such films as *Jack's the Boy* and *Falling for You*. Hulbert was also a broadcaster and television entertainer. His autobiography, *The Little Woman's Always Right*, appeared in 1975.

Humphrey, Hubert Horatio, U.S. politician (b. May 27, 1911, Wallace, S.D.—d. Jan. 13, 1978, Waverly,

ETHAN HOFFMAN—BLACK STAR

Minn.), a longtime (1949–65 and 1970–77) Democratic senator from Minnesota, was vice-president of the U.S. (1965–69) under Lyndon B. Johnson. Humphrey first pitched his hat into the political arena in 1943 when he unsuccessfully ran for mayor of Minneapolis. But in 1945 he was elected mayor and won wide recognition for creating the first U.S. municipal commission for fair-employment practices. In 1948 he was elected to the Senate where he became a member of the liberal faction, endorsed legislation on civil rights, tax reform, and medical care for the aged and vigorously opposed the Communist Party. Although he lost the Democratic presidential nomination to John F. Kennedy in 1960, Humphrey achieved his most significant legislation victories in the following four years as majority whip in the Senate. He was particularly acclaimed for winning support for the nuclear test ban treaty (1963) and the Civil Rights Act (1964). When Lyndon Johnson announced his political retirement, Humphrey became the 1968 Democratic candidate for president but was narrowly defeated by Republican Richard Nixon. Humphrey then taught political science for two years and served on the board of directors of Encyclopaedia Britannica, Inc., until he was reelected to the Senate in 1970. In 1971 Humphrey's colleagues acknowledged his lifelong devotion to the nation by creating the post of deputy president pro tempore of the Senate for the "Happy Warrior."

Hurry, Leslie, British stage designer (b. Feb. 10, 1909, London, England—d. Nov. 20, 1978, Hundon, Suffolk, England), worked with many of the leading directors in the post-World War II British theatre to design sets for outstanding productions of classical drama, ballet, and opera. Among the most memorable were his sets for Elizabethan and Jacobean plays at Stratford-upon-Avon and in London at the Old Vic and the Aldwych Theatre. Trained as a painter at the Royal Academy Schools, Hurry held one-man shows in London in 1969, 1972, and 1975.

James, Daniel, Jr. ("Chappie"), U.S. Air Force officer (b. Feb. 11, 1920, Pensacola, Fla.—d. Feb. 25, 1978, Colorado Springs, Colo.), was a four-star general in the U.S. Air Force and the highest-ranking black officer in the U.S. armed forces. James, who was decorated for his service as a jet fighter pilot in Korea and Vietnam, was later a spokesman

WIDE WORLD

(1970–75) in the Pentagon for the secretary of defense. In 1975 he became commander in chief of the North American Air Defense Command, responsible for all U.S. and Canadian air space defense forces. James died of a heart attack a few weeks after accepting early retirement.

James, William Owen, British botanist (b. May 21, 1900, London, England—d. Sept. 15, 1978, New Zealand), pioneered research in plant physiology, paleobotany, the extraction of cell organelles, and the medicinal uses of plants. His early work on photosynthesis was followed by a teaching career (1928–58) at the University of Oxford. He became (1959) professor of botany at the Imperial College of Science and Technology in London and emeritus professor after his retirement in 1967. He was elected a fellow of the Royal Society in 1952. His publications include *Plant Respiration* (1953) and *Background to Gardening* (1957).

Jennewein, Carl Paul, German-born sculptor (b. Dec. 2, 1890, Stuttgart, Germany—d. Feb. 22, 1978, Larchmont, N.Y.), was a Neo-Classicist of international renown whose commissions included two panels for the White House, four pylons for the New York World's Fair, a statue and frieze for the Washington Memorial Valley Forge Bell Tower, and a John F. Kennedy medal for the dedication of the Kennedy Center for the Performing Arts in Washington, D.C. Jennewein, whose works are on display at the Philadelphia Museum of Art, the Metropolitan Museum of Art in New York City, and various other museums in the U.S., won numerous awards including the Prix de Rome fellowship for sculpture (1917), the American Numismatic Association art award (1970), and the National Academy of Design award (1972).

John Paul I (ALBINO LUCIANI), pope of the Roman Catholic Church (b. Oct. 17, 1912, Forno di Canale, Veneto, Italy—d. Sept. 28/29, 1978, Rome, Italy), was virtually unknown to the outside world when on Aug. 26, 1978, the Sacred College of Cardinals unexpectedly elected him 263rd pope of the Roman Catholic Church. Because most expected the new pope to come from the ranks of the Vatican curial staff, little was publicly known about the man who emerged from the conclave as the first pope in history to choose a double name: John Paul I. During his 34 days in office—the shortest reign in modern times—John Paul I did nothing to alter church policies but endeared himself to millions of people all over the world with his infectious smile, humble piety, and jovial extemporaneous conversations with his audiences. For his formal installation, John Paul I announced that he would not accept the traditional papal tiara nor be carried by papal throne-bearers to and from the ceremony.

Albino Luciani, the son of a poor Italian family who lived near Belluno, was graduated from the Gregorian University in Rome and was ordained a priest in 1935. He was appointed (1937) deputy director of the seminary in the Belluno diocese where he taught moral theology, canon law, and sacred art. In 1948 he assisted his bishop in the discipline of priests as vicar general of the diocese, and in 1958 he was appointed bishop of Vittorio Veneto. Luciani was made archbishop of Venice in 1969 and cardinal in 1973.

The sudden death of John Paul I, who was discovered the morning after he died of an apparent heart attack while reading in bed, stunned the world.

Jones, Jim (JAMES WARREN JONES), U.S. cult leader (b. May 13, 1931, near Lynn, Ind.—d. Nov. 18, 1978, Jonestown, Guyana), promised his followers a Marxist utopia in the jungles of South America after proclaiming himself messiah of the People's Temple, a San Francisco-based cult. Jones gained a reputation in the 1950s in Indianapolis as a charismatic churchman who championed minorities, the underprivileged, and the sick. But after moving his headquarters to San Francisco, Jones apparently became obsessed by a driving lust for power. Politicians supported his programs and appreciated the fact that Jones could be counted on to appear with 2,000 members at political rallies. There was only minor concern when relatives of some cult members began to charge that Jones was extorting vast sums of money and property. In the face of mounting accusations by reporters and defectors,

from the cult, however, Jones and his followers set up an agricultural commune in Guyana. As dictator of the sect, Jones confiscated passports and millions of dollars and sadistically manipulated his followers with threats of sexual blackmail, brutal beatings with thick paddles, and probable death if they tried to escape. He also staged bizarre rehearsals for a ritual mass suicide. After Rep. Leo Ryan of California arrived in Guyana with a group of newsmen and relatives of cultists to investigate alleged abuses and rescue any disillusioned members, a paranoid Jones ordered the group assassinated. When Jones heard that only Ryan and four others had been killed, he activated his suicide plan. Some cultists obediently responded by squirting cyanide-spiked punch into their children's mouths and freely partaking of it themselves; others were intimidated by armed guards and escorted to the deadly tub of poison; still others escaped into the jungle. In one of the most unthinkable and shocking horrors of recent times, 913 people—including the demented Jones—died. (*See also* GUYANA.)

Josephson, Matthew, U.S. biographer (b. Feb. 15, 1899, Brooklyn, N.Y.—d. March 13, 1978, Santa Cruz, Calif.), was hailed for his sparkling biographies of such French authors as Émile Zola, founder of the Naturalist movement, and Jean-Jacques Rousseau, the great 18th-century philosopher. Josephson, who was in France with a group of expatriates during the 1920s when the Surrealist movement in art and literature flourished throughout Europe, became an adept historian of the period through his associations with Max Ernst, André Breton, and William Carlos Williams. When Josephson returned to the U.S. in the 1930s, he wrote the biographies of such U.S. personalities as Thomas A. Edison and Alfred Smith, but was more widely known as the author of *The Robber Barons* (1934), which chronicled the lives of John D. Rockefeller, Andrew Carnegie, and other 19th-century capitalists.

Kanapa, Jean, French Communist (b. Dec. 2, 1921, Ezanville, Val-d'Oise, France—d. Sept. 5, 1978, Saint-Cloud, France), was a member of the French Communist Party political bureau and its spokesman on foreign affairs. A loyal party member from the era of Stalinism to that of Eurocommunism, he became a vocal critic of Soviet policy after the 1968 invasion of Czechoslovakia. A Communist since 1944, he edited the party journal *La Nouvelle Critique* and was Moscow correspondent of its newspaper *L'Humanité* from 1962 to 1967. When Georges Marchais took over the party leadership in 1970, Kanapa became his closest associate and supporter. His writings include theoretical works and novels.

Kapp, Edmond Xavier, British painter (b. Nov. 5, 1890, London, England—d. Oct. 29, 1978, London), was a versatile and original painter, draftsman, and caricaturist whose works were both highly regarded and eagerly sought by such publications as the *Tatler*, the *Bystander*, and the *Onlooker*. Collections of his drawings appeared in several volumes, with titles such as *Personalities, Pastiche,* and *Minims.* During his almost 70-year career, Kapp received commissions from the British Museum and National Portrait Gallery to execute 25 lithograph portraits of members of the League of Nations at Geneva, from the London Philharmonic Orchestra to produce drawings of the orchestra's activities and personalities, and from UNESCO to draw 20 portraits of its leading delegates in Paris in 1946–47. Kapp, whose work was given a 50-year retrospective exhibition in London in 1961, devoted his later years almost exclusively to abstract painting.

Kappler, Herbert, German SS officer (b. 1907—d. Feb. 9, 1978, Soltau, West Germany), was a Nazi colonel in the SS Elite Guard who was sentenced to life imprisonment for the 1944 massacre of 335 Italians in the Ardeatine Caves south of Rome. Before a five-judge Italian military tribunal in 1948, Kappler admitted giving the execution order and shooting some of the victims himself, but maintained that the executions could be sanctioned

under the rules of war. The Ardeatine massacre (March 24, 1944) was in retaliation for a bombing attack by partisans that killed 32 SS men. Kappler was directed to kill ten times as many Italians. On Aug. 15, 1977, his wife enclosed the 105-lb Kappler in a suitcase and smuggled him out of a military hospital in Rome. The couple escaped to West Germany where under the law he was safe from Italian authorities.

Karsavina, Tamara (MRS. H. J. BRUCE), Russian-born ballerina (b. March 10, 1885, St. Petersburg, Russia—d. May 26, 1978, Beaconsfield, England), electrified audiences as the great interpretive prima ballerina (1909–22) in Sergey Diaghilev's Ballets Russes. The daughter of the famous dancer Platon Karsavin, she was trained at the Imperial Ballet School in St. Petersburg and made her debut at the Maryinsky Theatre on May 1, 1902. She soon was dancing classical roles in *Giselle* and *Swan Lake,* but her interpretive talents shone even brighter when choreographer Michel Fokine created roles for her in such ballets as *The Firebird* and *Petrouchka.* In 1909 she danced with the Diaghilev Ballet in its first Paris season, partnering with Vaslav Nijinsky in *Bluebird.* Karsavina also continued to dance for the Maryinsky but, after marrying British diplomat H. J. Bruce, she left Russia (1918) and in 1922 the Diaghilev company. In England she furthered the development of the English ballet as a founder and vice-president of the Royal Academy of Dancing and as a teacher to Margot Fonteyn. Karsavina published valuable lessons on technique in the journal *Dancing Times,* her autobiography *Theatre Street* (1930), and the text *Classical Ballet: The Flow of Movement* (1962).

Katayama, Tetsu, Japanese politician (b. July 28, 1887, Wakayama Prefecture, Japan—d. May 30, 1978, Fujisawa, Kamagawa Prefecture, Japan), was the head of a coalition government formed by the Japan Socialist Party (JSP), the conservative Democratic Party, and the People's Cooperative Party (Kokkyoto). After eight months (June 1947–February 1948) as the only Socialist prime minister in the history of constitutional Japan, Katayama slipped from power because of confrontations between the leftist and rightist forces within the JSP. After graduating (1912) from Tokyo University in German law, Katayama became a member of the JSP's central executive committee and later a member of the Diet (parliament). Following World War II he became (1946) chief secretary of the JSP and then prime minister. Katayama's continued support for a tenant farming law, a labour union law, and the abolition of the Security Police Law led to much new postwar legislation. During his later years, he served as adviser to the JSP and vigorously fought to protect the Japanese constitution.

Kawasaki, Hideji, Japanese politician (b. Sept. 14, 1911, Mie Prefecture, Japan—d. Feb. 22, 1978, Tokyo, Japan), was elected in 1947 to the first of 11 consecutive terms in the Japanese House of Representatives. As a Liberal-Democratic member of the lower house of the Diet (parliament), he directed his party's youth organization, headed the Japanese section of UNESCO, and traveled to the U.S. and Europe to study social security systems. Kawasaki's abiding interest in sports also made him a logical choice for membership on Japan's Olympic Committee and Field Games Federation.

Keldysh, Mstislav Vsevolodovich, Soviet mathematician (b. Feb. 10 [Jan. 28, old style], 1911, Riga, Latvia—d. June 24, 1978, Moscow, U.S.S.R.), became in effect czar of science when he was unanimously elected (1961) president of the Soviet Academy of Sciences. During the 14 years he held office, the Soviet space program flourished under his direction. After graduating (1931) from the state university in Moscow, Keldysh joined the faculty of its Central Institute of Aerohydrodynamics, where he conducted pioneering research into the theory of vibration analysis of such aircraft structures as wings and landing gear wheels. Keldysh was reportedly named (1943) director of the secret Research Institute No. 1 of the Ministry of Aircraft Industry, where he continued to advance the study of vibrational analysis, and three years later became a member of the Academy of Sciences of the U.S.S.R. In 1947 he served on a special committee of Soviet scientists who evaluated the feasibility of developing a manned space glider proposed by German engineer Eugen Saenger during World War II. He later became (1953) director of the Institute of Applied Mathematics of the Academy of Sciences and, together with such noted colleagues as V. A. Yegorov, was instrumental in developing the trajectories for the first Soviet lunar and space probes. A member of the Central Committee of the Communist Party of the Soviet Union (CPSU), he was buried in the wall of the Kremlin.

Kelly, Stephen Eugene, U.S. publisher (b. May 13, 1919, Brooklyn, N.Y.—d. April 6, 1978, New York, N.Y.), was the publisher of such well-known magazines as *Holiday, Saturday Evening Post,* and *McCall's.* After graduating (1940) from Hamilton College in Clinton, N.Y., he worked for Time Inc. both before and after World War II. Kelly became president (1969) of the Magazine Publishers Association, which represented 161 companies and their 595 magazines, and advanced their advertising revenues to a record $1,970,000,000 in 1977. As president, Kelly confronted two especially challenging problems: the advent of television, which became the number one advertising medium, and rising postal rates in the early 1970s, which threatened to substantially reduce profits.

Kenyatta, Jomo (KAMAU NGENGI), Kenyan statesman (b. *c.* 1894, Ichawevi, Gatundu, Kenya—d. Aug. 22, 1978, Mombasa, Kenya), was president of Kenya from 1964 until his death. His career as a nationalist leader in a former British colony was exemplary: imprisoned before independence and denigrated as a leader of the forces of darkness, he became, as president, the elder statesman of African politics, a stabilizing influence in world affairs, and a sincere friend of the West. In his own country he commanded a respect and affection that overrode tribal divisions and allowed him the luxury of dealing leniently with his opponents. In most of Africa he was admired as a supporter of African unity and a steadfast opponent of all forms of colonialism.

Kenyatta became active in nationalist politics in the 1920s as a member of the Kikuyu Central Association, while working as a legal interpreter. A long stay in Europe during the 1930s allowed him to complete his education, establish links with sympathetic Western intellectuals, and write his classic sociological work, *Facing Mount Kenya.* He helped to organize the fifth Pan-African Congress, held in Manchester, England, in 1945, and in the following year returned to Kenya, where he became principal of a teacher-training college.

His precise role in the Mau Mau uprising of the 1950s remained unclear. Denounced by police informers, he was imprisoned in 1953. His prestige immensely enhanced, he emerged later as president (elected in absentia, 1960) of the Kenya African National Union. After his party won the pre-independence elections in 1963 he became prime minister and in December the following year assumed the presidency of the new republic.

While he restored the confidence of Kenya's white and Asian minorities, Kenyatta was less successful in eliminating intertribal rivalries, which intensified after the assassination of the Luo politician Tom Mboya in 1969. Despite increasing ill-health, Kenyatta weathered later crises but left behind a country whose prosperity, institutions, and unity seemed vulnerable without him.

Kenyon, Dame Kathleen Mary, British archaeologist (b. Jan. 5, 1906, London, England—d. Aug. 24, 1978, Erbistock, Wrexham, Wales), conducted major excavations at Jericho and Jerusalem as director of the British School of Archaeology in Jerusalem (1952–66). Her findings established the sequence of the layers of those cities and provided Palestinian archaeology with a reliable chronological scale. A graduate of Somerville College at Oxford, she joined Gertrude Caton-Thompson's 1929 expedition to what was then Southern Rhodesia. She then worked at Verulamium in England (1930–35), during which period she visited Palestine for the first time. In 1935 she joined the University of London's new Institute of Archaeology, where she later lectured (1948–62) in Palestinian archaeology. She also undertook excavations at Roman Sabratha in North Africa. Kenyon was principal of St. Hugh's College, Oxford (1962–73), and was created a dame of the British Empire in 1973. The last of her many reports and books was *Digging Up Jerusalem* (1974).

Khachaturian, Aram Ilich, Soviet Armenian composer (b. June 6, 1903, Tiflis [now Tbilisi], Georgia, Russia—d. May 1, 1978, Moscow, U.S.S.R.), won widespread popularity in the Soviet Union and the West with his *Piano Concerto* (1936) and such colourful ballets as *Gayane* (1942), with its brassy Sabre Dance, and *Spartak* (1953). Khachaturian, who was trained in Moscow at the Gnesiny Institute and the Moscow Conservatory, was influenced by Maurice Ravel but owed the most to the pulsating rhythms of his Armenian folk heritage. Besides three symphonies (1934, 1943, and 1947) and a violin concerto (1940), he composed film scores, incidental music, and patriotic songs, including the national anthem of the Armenian S.S.R. In 1948 Khachaturian, Prokofiev, and Shostakovich were denounced by the Central Committee of the Communist Party for works that "smelled strongly of the spirit of bourgeois music of Europe and America." Although Khachaturian quickly confessed his guilt and was restored to prominence, after Stalin's death in 1953 he publicly denounced the committee's music policy. He received the Order of Lenin in 1939 and several Stalin prizes; he became a People's Artist of the U.S.S.R. in 1954 and won a Lenin Prize in 1959.

King, Cyril E., U.S. politician (b. April 7, 1921, St. Croix, Virgin Islands—d. Jan. 2, 1978, Charlotte Amalie, Virgin Islands), became the second elected (1974) governor of the U.S. Virgin Islands after serving two years in the Virgin Islands Senate. King was a Washington aide to Minnesota Senator Hubert H. Humphrey (1949–61) and eventually became his senior staff member responsible for research on disarmament for a special Senate subcommittee headed by Humphrey. King returned to the Virgin Islands (1961) when Pres. John F. Kennedy appointed him government secretary (later the elective post of lieutenant governor). In 1969 he became acting governor after Ralph M. Paiewonsky resigned, but when the first popular election was held in 1970, King lost by a narrow margin. His term of office would have expired in January 1979.

Kipnis, Alexander, Russian-born singer (b. Feb. 1, 1891, Zhitomir, Ukraine, Russia,—d. May 14, 1978, Westport, Conn.), whose resonant voice and flair for dramatic interpretation earned him a reputation as one of the most talented basses of the century. Kipnis studied in Warsaw and Berlin, made his singing debut in Hamburg in 1915, and performed with the Chicago Civic Opera for a decade (1923–32) before joining (1940) the Metropolitan Opera Company in New York, where he had engagements through 1945. During his career he sang the title role in *Boris Godunov*, Gurnemanz in *Parsifal*, Baron Ochs in *Der Rosenkavalier*, and Sarastro in *The Magic Flute.* Kipnis began teaching in 1946 and to the end of his life made regular trips from his Connecticut home to New York City in order to work with his students.

Krag, Jens Otto, Danish politician (b. Sept. 15, 1914, Randers, Den.—d. June 22, 1978, Skiveren, Den.), was prime minister of Denmark (1962–68 and 1971–72) and a leading advocate of European cooperation. A Social Democrat, Krag served at the Danish embassy in Washington, then held various ministerial posts before serving as foreign minister from 1958 to 1962. As leader of a series of coalition governments, he brought Denmark into the European Economic Community (EEC) in 1972 and then unexpectedly resigned. After briefly heading the EEC delegation in Washington in 1974, Krag turned to painting and journalism. For his services to the cause of European unity he was awarded the Charlemagne (1966) and Robert Schumann (1973) prizes.

Kuh, Frederick, U.S. journalist (b. Oct. 29, 1895, Chicago, Ill.—d. Feb. 2, 1978, Rockville, Md.), was a *Chicago Sun* foreign correspondent who during World War II earned a reputation for his international news scoops. He was credited with reporting four days in advance the official announcement that Italy would surrender to the Allies and was also 12 hours ahead of other correspondents in relating Bulgaria's peace terms. Kuh, who spent most of his career reporting for Chicago newspapers, also covered (1951–64) the State Department and foreign embassies for the *Chicago Sun-Times* before retiring in 1964.

Kulakov, Fyodor Davydovich, Soviet Communist Party leader (b. Feb. 4, 1918, Fitizh, Kursh region, Russia—d. July 17, 1978, Moscow, U.S.S.R.), was one of the youngest members of the Politburo and a likely candidate to succeed Leonid I. Brezhnev as Soviet party leader. After graduating from an agricultural institute, he worked from 1938 to 1943 as an agronomist and manager of a sugar beet factory and finally as head of the land department of the Zametchino district in the Penza region. In 1934 he joined the Young Communist League and in 1940 became a member of the Communist Party of the Soviet Union (CPSU). From February 1943 he carried out party and local government work as a secretary of the district party committee. He then successively served as head of the agricultural department of the Penza regional committee of the CPSU, chief of the regional agricultural board, and finally chairman of the executive committee of the regional Soviet. He occupied the posts of deputy minister of agriculture from 1955, and in 1958 was appointed minister of grain products of the Russian Federation. From 1960 he served as first secretary of the Stavropol territory party committee. Elected in 1961 to the party Central Committee, he became one of its secretaries and head of its agricultural department three years later. In 1971 he was elected a full member of the Politburo. In February 1978, at a special meeting of the Politburo and Secretariat members, Brezhnev made Kulakov a Hero of Socialist Labour.

Kuo Mo-jo (Kuo K'ai-chen), Chinese author (b. October, 1892, Lo-shan, Szechwan, China—d. June 12, 1978, Peking, China), was one of modern China's most prolific, versatile, and influential writers. After receiving a traditional education, Kuo went to Japan (1913) where, after nine years, he received a medical degree. During those years he also studied foreign languages and literature and co-founded (1921) the Creation Society in Japan for Chinese writers. While translating (1924) a work by Kawakami Hajime, Kuo became a convert to Marxism. In time he gained wide renown as a poet, playwright, novelist, philosopher, historian, autobiographer, and prolific translator of such authors as Goethe, Schiller, Tolstoy, and Upton Sinclair. Kuo's career as a political activist began in 1926 when he returned briefly to China to participate in Chiang Kai-shek's Northern Expedition against the warlords. But when Chiang purged the Communists from his Nationalist Party in 1927, Kuo joined the Communist Nan-ch'ang uprising, then returned to Japan. After the establishment of the People's Republic in 1949, Kuo was given a succession of influential government posts and on many occasions demonstrated his ability to bend with shifting political winds. When Kuo was denounced during the Cultural Revolution (1960s), he readily agreed that his works should be burned. In 1967 he wrote a glowing ode to Chiang Ch'ing, the powerful wife of Chairman Mao Tse-tung. One day after she fell from power, Kuo penned another ode about "the political rogue" which began: "What heartening news!"

Lasswell, Harold Dwight, U.S. political scientist (b. Feb. 13, 1902, Donnellson, Ill.—d. Dec. 18, 1978, New York, N.Y.), revolutionized the field of contemporary behavioural political science through pioneering studies of politics, power, and personality. Lasswell, who earned both his Ph.B. (1922) and Ph.D. (1962) from the University of Chicago, taught political science at his alma mater (1922–38) before serving (1939–45) as director of war communications research at the Library of Congress. While there, he published major works on the "garrison state" and predicted many present-day dictatorships. He then joined (1946) the faculty at Yale University where he was professor of law and political science until 1970. Even though he was turning out such classics as *Psycho-pathology and Politics* (1930) and *World Politics and Personal Insecurity* (1935), regarded as his masterpiece, no political science journal would publish his articles from 1937 to 1950. The importance of his contributions, however, was eventually recognized, and in 1955 Lasswell was elected president of the American Political Science Association. His later writings, which continued to reflect a preoccupation with the mechanisms of the mind, include: *Politics: Who Gets What, When, How* (1936), a study of the elite as primary holders of power; *Politics Faces Economics* (1946); *Power and Society: A Framework for Political Inquiry* (with philosopher Abraham Kaplan, 1950); and *The Policy Sciences: Recent Developments in Scope and Method* (with Daniel Lerner, 1951). In 1976 Lasswell retired from teaching to devote his full attention to the Policy Sciences Center, a research organization partly funded by the U.S. government, and to his writings.

Lear, William Powell, U.S. industrialist (b. June 26, 1902, Hannibal, Mo.—d. May 14, 1978, Reno, Nev.), whose energetic labours produced such diverse inventions as the car radio, the eight-track stereo cartridge, and the automatic pilot for aircraft. Lear, who held some 150 patents in the fields of electronics, aviation technology, and auto engineering, also pioneered the first corporate jet aircraft. In 1939 he founded Lear, Inc., which sold $100 million worth of equipment to the U.S. armed forces during World War II, but he sold (1962) his shares in the company when the board of directors refused to approve plans for a low-priced jet. He then established Lear Jet Corp., which rolled the first "baby jet" off the assembly line in 1963. In 1967 he sold his interest in Lear Jet Corp. for $28 million but his retirement was only temporary; he soon began planning a steam-powered auto and a new turboprop business jet.

Leavis, F(rank) R(aymond), British literary critic (b. July 14, 1895, Cambridge, England—d. April 14, 1978, Cambridge), was an influential and provocative critic of English literature who gave favourable evaluations to authors who complied with his own belief that important literature should be closely related to a criticism of life, and therefore literary critics should base their criticism on the moral position of the author, and devastating reviews to those who deviated. He easily rejected such authors as Gustav Flaubert and James Joyce and lavishly praised Jane Austen, George Eliot, Henry James, and D. H. Lawrence. In 1962 he also bluntly and mercilessly attacked novelist C. P. Snow's fiction and particularly his essay "The Two Cultures and the Scientific Revolution," which criticized devotees of literature and science for ignorance of each other. After graduating from Emmanuel College, Cambridge, Leavis spent the greater part of his career at the University of Cambridge, where his distinction as a teacher of English literature was enhanced by his influence as founder and editor of the literary quarterly *Scrutiny* (1932–53). Cambridge University Press later issued a 20-volume reprint of all the issues. He also became a fellow of Downing College in 1936 and then served as an honorary fellow from 1962 to 1964, when he resigned. Some of his best-known writings include: *Mass Civilisation and Minority Culture* (1930); *Revaluation: Tradition and Development in English Poetry* (1936); *The Great Tradition: George Eliot, Henry James, and Joseph Conrad* (1948); *D. H. Lawrence: Novelist* (1955); and *The Living Principle* (1975). In 1978 he was made a Companion of Honour, one of the highest awards in England.

Leese, Sir Oliver William Hargreaves, 4th Baronet, British army officer (b. Oct. 27, 1894—d. Jan. 22, 1978, near Oswestry, Salop, England), rose to high command in Italy and in Southeast Asia during World War II. He was commissioned in the Coldstream Guards from Eton College and in World War I was awarded the Distinguished Service Order. In 1938 he assumed regimental and staff duties as a colonel in India, where he became an instructor at Quetta. During World War II he was named (1940) deputy chief of staff to the British Expeditionary Force and later formed and trained the Guards Armoured Division. In 1942 he commanded a corps of the 8th Army at the battle of El Alamein. After succeeding Gen. Sir Bernard Montgomery as commander of the 8th Army in December 1943, he moved with his troops to the Italian front. He was promoted to lieutenant general in 1944 and then was given command of the 11th Army Group in the Far East. In 1945 he briefly commanded Allied Land Forces in Southeast Asia before returning to England as general officer commanding, Eastern Command. Leese retired from the armed forces in 1946.

Leibowitz, Samuel Simon, Romanian-born lawyer (b. Aug. 14, 1893, Jassy, Rom.—d. Jan. 11, 1978, New York, N.Y.), became a legend as the dynamic criminal lawyer who, serving without a fee, fought for four years and won a new trial for nine black youths convicted of rape. Although eight of these "Scottsboro Boys" had been sentenced to death and the other to life imprisonment in 1931, the Supreme Court voided the sentence by ruling (1935) that the exclusion of blacks from the jury was unconstitutional; all nine men were eventually released. Leibowitz, who saved all but one of some 140 defendants from the electric chair, also defended gangster Al Capone, but rejected a $250,000 offer to represent seven members of Murder Inc. As a criminal court judge in New York City (1940–69), he advocated the reinstatement of capital punishment and earned the nickname "Sentencing Sam" for dealing out tough sentences to hardened criminals.

Lindner, Richard, German-born artist (b. Nov. 11, 1901, Hamburg, Germany—d. April 16, 1978, New York, N.Y.), earned a niche in the history of modern art first as an illustrator for such magazines as *Vogue* and *Harper's Bazaar* and later for his autobiographical paintings marked by black humour, shock, and a fascinating assortment of women.

"The Meeting" (1953), considered one of Lindner's finest paintings and perhaps his most autobiographical, outlines his past and loss of innocence. His youth is represented by a dreamy young boy in a sailor suit, his flight from Nazi Germany by the figure of mad King Ludwig of Bavaria, his emergence as a painter by portraits of artist friends, and his loss of innocence by a tightly corseted woman with an appetite for power and money.

Lingen, Theo, Austrian actor (b. June 10, 1903, Hanover, Germany—d. Nov. 10, 1978, Vienna, Austria), exploited his stature and angular physique to become a leading comic actor in the German theatre during the 1930s. He first appeared with Bertolt Brecht's company and then with Gustav Gründgens at the State Theatre. In 1943 he took Austrian nationality and until his retirement in 1973 played with the Vienna Burgtheater. Besides his many film credits, including Fritz Lang's *M* and *Das Testament des Dr. Mabuse,* Lingen was also the author of several comedies.

Lipton, Marcus, British politician (b. Oct. 29, 1900, Sunderland, England—d. Feb. 22, 1978, London, England), was a colourful Labour member of Parliament for the Brixton division (1945–74) of Lambeth, London, and for Lambeth Central thereafter. Lipton, who introduced debate on such issues as tax havens, prison conditions, and city slums, had a well-earned reputation for quick wit and facetious remarks. On one occasion he suggested that, to prevent accidents, cows wandering onto public roadways be daubed with luminous paint. A barrister of Gray's Inn, Lipton was a Labour member of the London borough council of Stepney (1934–37) and alderman of Lambeth (1937–56).

Lo Jui-ch'ing, Chinese official (b. 1904, Nan-ch'ung, Szechwan Province, China—d. Aug. 3, 1978, Peking, China), gained political prominence as the minister of public security during the first ten years (1949–59) of the Communist regime. Lo not only helped draft the provisional constitution but also laid the foundation for a national security network. He later served as army chief of staff, with a rank equivalent to that of a four-star general. Lo was serving as vice-premier during the Cultural Revolution when he opposed Mao Tse-tung's contention that people, not weapons, decide wars. Taunted and badgered by the Red Guards, Lo attempted suicide. He was driven from power and disappeared from public view for some ten years but made a stunning reemergence in 1975 when the government again favoured moderation and economic development. In 1977 it became apparent that Lo had regained his power when the government proclaimed him "a leading member of the Military Commission of the Central Committee."

MacArthur, John Donald, U.S. insurance magnate (b. March 6, 1897, Pittston, Pa.—d. Jan. 6, 1978, West Palm Beach, Fla.), was an archconservative who amassed billions of dollars after acquiring (1935) the then bankrupt Chicago-based Bankers Life and Casualty Co. for $2,500. MacArthur peddled dollar-a-month insurance policies door to door, and when other insurance firms collapsed during the Depression, his company swept an open market. In the early 1950s MacArthur, already one of the wealthiest men in the U.S., became Florida's largest property owner by acquiring more than 100,000 ac of land. Other assets included the Citizens Bank & Trust Co., the largest Illinois bank outside of Chicago; Union Bankers Insurance Co. of Dallas, Texas; and various oil wells. MacArthur's death left shipping magnate Daniel K. Ludwig as the last surviving U.S. billionaire.

Macartney, Carlile Aylmer, British historian (b. Jan. 24, 1895, Kent, England,—d. June 18, 1978, Oxford, England), was an authority on Hungarian history and research fellow of All Souls College,

Oxford (1936–65). Although his career was mainly academic, Macartney spent eight years with the League of Nations Union. During World War II he worked in the research department of the British Foreign Office. His many works ranged from studies of *The Medieval Hungarian Historians* (1953) to an analysis of the Hungarian Revolution of 1945, *October Fifteenth* (1957). Other books included *Independent Eastern Europe* (with A.W. Palmer; 1962) and *The Habsburg Empire 1790–1918* (1969). From 1951 to 1957 he held the Montagu Burton chair of international relations at the University of Edinburgh.

McCarthy, Joseph Vincent ("Marse Joe"), U.S. baseball manager (b. April 21, 1887, Philadelphia, Pa.—d. Jan. 13, 1978, Buffalo, N.Y.), shattered baseball records as he led the New York Yankees to eight American League pennants and seven World Series titles between 1931 and 1946. During this period McCarthy became the first manager to pilot a team to four straight World Series championships (1936–39). Many of the superstars of the era considered him the best manager they had ever seen in action. Before joining the Yankees, McCarthy, who had never played major league baseball, led the Chicago Cubs from last place (1926) to a National League pennant in 1929. He retired in 1950 after two years with the Boston Red Sox and was inducted into the Baseball Hall of Fame in 1957.

McCoy, Timothy ("Tim") **John Fitzgerald,** U.S. actor (b. April 10, 1891, Saginaw, Mich.—d. Jan. 29, 1978, Nogales, Ariz.), was one of the big-time cowboys whose acting career included more than 80 films in 45 years. Even as a young man McCoy was fascinated with the Wild West and, after briefly attending college, he traveled to Wyoming where he worked as a cowhand and became an expert on Indian ceremonies and sign language. Sporting a peaked, white ten-gallon hat, the trim six-foot hero appeared in such films as *War Paint, Below the Border, Around the World in Eighty Days,* and the Western extravaganza *The Covered Wagon.* Besides receiving an Emmy award for the "Tim McCoy Show," he was inducted (1974) into the Cowboy Hall of Fame in Oklahoma.

MacDiarmid, Hugh (pseudonym of Christopher Murray Grieve), Scottish poet (b. Aug. 11, 1892, Langholm, Dumfriesshire, Scotland—d. Sept. 9, 1978, Edinburgh, Scotland), sought to inaugurate a Scottish Renaissance by restoring the prestige of the Scots language as a serious medium of poetic expression. MacDiarmid's poetry expressed modern ideas in an eclectic blend of archaic words revived from the 16th century and various Scottish dialects. In 1922 he founded the *Scottish Chapbook,* a periodical that contained his first Scots poetry, which was later published in *Sangschaw* (1925) and *Penny Wheep* (1926). MacDiarmid, who rejected the use of English in Scottish poetry, also employed "synthetic Scots" (an amalgam of elements from various middle Scots dialects, folk ballads, and other literary sources), notably in his masterpiece *A Drunk Man Looks at the Thistle* (1926). After embracing Marxist philosophy, he adopted scotticized English in *To Circumjack Centrastus* (1930), archaic Scots in *Scots Unbound* (1932), and standard English in both *Stony Limits* (1934) and *Second Hymn to Lenin* (1935). His later style was best represented in *A Kist of Whistles* (1947) and *In Memoriam James Joyce* (1955). MacDiarmid became professor of literature to the Royal Scottish Academy in 1974 and president of the Poetry Society in 1976.

McDougald, John Angus ("Bud"), Canadian industrialist (b. March 14, 1908, Toronto, Ont.—d. March 15, 1978, Palm Beach, Fla.), was probably Canada's most powerful financier as chairman and president of Argus Corp. Ltd., the country's most prestigious investment and management company. He was also an executive or director of some 25 other companies with interests in banking, mining, and petroleum. McDougald, a self-made millionaire, was promoted from office boy at Dominion Securities to syndicate manager in two years. In 1975, during one of Canada's most dramatic corporate power struggles, McDougald demonstrated his personal power by squelching an attempt by Power Corp. of Canada Ltd. to take over Argus Corp.

McGinley, Phyllis, U.S. writer (b. March 21, 1905, Ontario, Ore.—d. Feb. 22, 1978, New York, N.Y.), won the Pulitzer Prize for Poetry in 1961 for *Times Three: Selected Verse from Three Decades.* McGinley, whose 18 volumes of poetry and essays were characterized by light verse that commended suburban living, published her last book, *Saint Watching,* in 1969.

McGrath, Paul, U.S. actor (b. April 11, 1904, Chicago, Ill.,—d. April 13, 1978, London, England), was the sinister-voiced host of the radio series "Inner Sanctum Mysteries" (1945–51) and a featured Broadway performer for nearly 45 years with such leading ladies as Helen Hayes and Ruth Gordon. McGrath's most highly regarded performance was opposite Gertrude Lawrence in the comedy *Susan and God* (1937), the first televised Broadway play. He played in more than 30 Broadway productions, including *The Big Knife* and *Command Decision;* seven films, most notably *No Time for Love* and *Advise and Consent;* and such radio melodramas as "The Crime Doctor" (1944–50) and "Big Sister" (1944–54).

Mackintosh, John Pitcairn, British politician (b. Aug. 24, 1929, Midlothian, Scotland—d. July 30, 1978, Edinburgh, Scotland), was admired both as a writer and teacher of politics and as an outspoken back-bench member of Parliament. Elected as member for the Scottish constituency of Berwick and East Lothian in 1966, he represented the right wing of the Labour Party but strongly supported the cause of Scottish devolution. Noted for his intelligence, wit, and independent stance, he served on several parliamentary committees but never held office. He taught politics at universities in Scotland and Nigeria and in 1977 was appointed professor at the University of Edinburgh. Mackintosh, who was widely known as a journalist in the press and on television, wrote the authoritative study *The British Cabinet* (1962).

Mac Liammoir, Micheal, Irish actor (b. Oct. 25, 1899, Cork, Ireland—d. March 6, 1978, Dublin, Ireland), dominated the Irish theatre for 50 years as a leading designer and actor in some 300 productions at Dublin's Gate Theatre, which he founded (1928) with Hilton Edwards. After gaining experience as a child actor in London, he performed with Anew McMaster's Shakespeare Company (1927–28) and later opened the Galway Gaelic Theatre. Besides playing leading Shakespearean roles all over the world, he wrote and appeared in such notable one-man shows as *The Importance of Being Oscar* (1960), a study of Wilde; *I Must Be Talking to My Friends* (1963), a retrospective of ancient and modern Ireland; and *Talking About Yeats* (1970). His many publications in Irish and English included plays, stories, essays, and volumes of autobiography, notably *All for Hecuba* (1946).

Madariaga y Rojo, Salvador de, Spanish writer, diplomat, and historian (b. July 23, 1886, La Coruña, Spain—d. Dec. 14, 1978, Locarno, Switz.), was perhaps Spain's outstanding intellectual and a man of exceptional breadth of interest who wrote prolifically in English, German, and French as well as Spanish. The son of a Spanish army officer, he was trained at his father's insistence as an engineer in Paris but abandoned his career to become a journalist. In 1921 he joined the Secretariat of the League of Nations at Geneva as a press member and the following year was appointed head of its disarmament section. From 1928 to 1931 he was professor of Spanish studies at the University of Oxford. After the Spanish monarchy fell in 1931, he was appointed ambassador to the U.S. and then to France by the Spanish republic, and he was Spain's permanent delegate to the League of Nations from 1931 to 1936. When the Spanish Civil War broke out in July 1936, Madariaga—"equally distant from both sides," as he wrote at the time—resigned and left for England. He became a vocal opponent of the Franco regime and did not return to Spain until April 1976, following Franco's death the previous November.

Among Madariaga's many books are *Englishmen, Frenchmen, Spaniards* (1928; 2nd ed., 1970), *Anarchy or Hierarchy* (1937), *Christopher Columbus* (1939), *Hernán Cortés* (1941), *Spain* (1942), and *The Rise of the Spanish-American Empire* and *The Fall of the Spanish-American Empire* (both 1947). In 1973 he published his memoirs, *Morning Without Noon,* containing anecdotes and vivid pen portraits. Madariaga contributed articles to *Encyclopaedia Britannica* on Columbus and Cortés. He was honorary president of the International Liberal Union and the Congress for Freedom of Culture, founder-president of the College of Europe, and a member of the Spanish and French academies of moral and political sciences.

Mallowan, Sir Max Edgar Lucien, British archaeologist (b. May 6, 1904, London, England—d. Aug. 19, 1978, Devon, England), supervised large-scale excavations in Iraq, notably at Tell Brak (1937–38) and Nimrud (1949–58), and thereby continued a tradition of British archaeological discovery in Mesopotamia that began with Sir Henry Layard in 1842. Mallowan worked with Leonard Woolley at Ur of the Chaldees (1925–30) after graduating from New College, Oxford, and later directed (1931–32) expeditions at the ancient city of Nineveh in Iraq. After World War II, Mallowan served as director (1947–61), chairman (1966–70), and president (from 1970) of the British School of Archaeology, in Iraq. He was professor of Western Asiatic archaeology, University of London (1947–62), and a fellow of All Souls College, Oxford (1962–71). He was also editor (1948–65) of the Near Eastern and West Asiatic series of Penguin Books and editor (1948–71) of the Baghdad School journal *Iraq.* Mallowan, who was knighted in 1968, was the husband of writer Dame Agatha Christie.

Manteuffel, Hasso von, German Army general (b. Jan. 14, 1897, Potsdam, Germany—d. Sept. 24, 1978, Tyrol, Austria), was a superb military strategist whose skillful deployment of tanks repeatedly thwarted Allied offensives in World War II. A major at the outbreak of World War II, he earned rapid promotion and commanded a division at Tunis in North Africa, where his counterattack almost cut communications behind the Allies' front. In the Ukraine his 7th Panzer Division in November 1943 stemmed a victorious Soviet offensive, and in May 1944 his mobile defense checked Marshal I. S. Koniev's drive into Romania. He also commanded the 5th Panzer Army during the crucial Battle of the Bulge that took place in Belgium in December 1944. Manteuffel almost succeeded in breaching the Allied front. After the war, Manteuffel sat in the Bundestag (1953–57) as a Free Democrat, but in 1959 his military past was revived. A court sentenced him to 18 months in prison for ordering a 19-year-old shot for desertion in 1944. After serving four months, Manteuffel was released.

Markov, Georgi, Bulgarian writer (b. 1929, Sofia, Bulg.—d. Sept. 11, 1978, London, England), won national acclaim as a writer and television commentator before he defected from Bulgaria to the West in 1969. In 1961 he published two volumes of short stories and the following year the novel *Men,* a psychological study of a young Bulgarian on the eve of his military service. In 1963 he wrote a successful play entitled *The Cheese Merchant's Good Lady.* His novels *Portrait of My Double* (1966) and *The Women of Warsaw* (1968), as well as his play *The Assassins,* described the problems of contemporary life in Bulgaria and other socialist states. In June 1969, just as his play *The Man Who Was I* was about to be performed, Markov left for Italy. His literary prizes were annulled and he became an "unperson." In 1971 he moved to London, joined the British Broadcasting Corporation's Bulgarian Service, and read broadcasts for Radio Free Europe. On Sept. 7, 1978, while walking past a bus stop in London, Markov became the victim of a bizarre assassination plot. He was jabbed in the thigh with a poison-tipped umbrella and died four days later. Earlier, Markov had reported receiving death threats. When the story broke, Vladimir Kostov, another Bulgarian defector and a friend of Markov, recounted a similar incident that had happened to him in Paris three weeks earlier. Small pellets presumed to have contained poison were found in both men's bodies. Police suspected that Bulgarian agents were responsible for the sophisticated cloak-and-dagger crimes.

Marples, (Alfred) Ernest Marples, BARON, British politician (b. Dec. 9, 1907, Manchester, England—d. July 6, 1978, Monte Carlo, Monaco), was minister of transport in the Conservative government (1959–64) during a period of rapidly expanding car ownership in Britain. His restrictions on traffic in towns, including the introduction of parking meters, made him intensely unpopular with motorists. Earlier Marples served (1957–59) as postmaster general and demonstrated the same exceptional administrative skills that he applied to his comprehensive reorganization of Britain's transport system. He presided over the modernization of the road network and appointed an expert, Thomas Beeching, whose recommendations led to sweeping cuts in the railway system. Marples also founded a major construction company. He was elected to Parliament in 1945 and was made a life peer in 1974.

Martinson, Harry Edmund, Swedish writer (b. May 6, 1904, Jämshög, Blekinge, Sweden—d. Feb. 11, 1978, Stockholm, Sweden), received the 1974 Nobel Prize for Literature for "writings that catch the dewdrop and reflect the cosmos." Martinson, a seaman and a wanderer in his youth, described his childhood in *Nässlorna blomma* (1935; *Flowering Nettle,* 1936) and *Vägen ut* (1936; "The Way Out"). Other significant works include a travel book, *Kap Farväl* (1933; *Cape Farewell,* 1934), and poetry, including the collection *Passad* (1945; "Trade Wind") and the epic cycle of poems *Aniara* (1956; *Aniara, a Review of Man in Time and Space,* 1963), about a spaceship launched from radiation-ravaged Earth. This best-known work was set to music for an opera by Karl Birger Blomdahl in 1959. *Vägen till Klockrike* (1948; *The Road,* 1955), a novel about tramps and other social outcasts, secured his election to the Swedish Academy in 1949.

Mead, Margaret, U.S. anthropologist (b. Dec. 16, 1901, Philadelphia, Pa.—d. Nov. 15, 1978, New York, N.Y.), was internationally known both as an authority on various literate and illiterate cultures and as an irrepressible propagandist for her own ideas. A woman of seemingly limitless energy, she never tired of lecturing the public, formally and informally, on such far-ranging topics as population control, space probes, environmental pollution, world hunger, adolescence, mental health, human sexuality, primitive art, city planning, women's liberation, use of drugs, child rearing, and tribal customs. Though fellow scientists were

Margaret Mead

EDWARD RICE—PHOTO TRENDS

sometimes disturbed that Mead felt the need to air her views on subjects unrelated to anthropology, the attention she attracted also redounded to the benefit of their profession. In 1923 Mead entered the graduate school of Columbia University where, under the guidance of Franz Boas, she obtained a Ph.D. in 1929. During a 1925 field trip in Samoa she gathered material for the first of her 23 books, *Coming of Age in Samoa* (1928), a perennial best-seller and a characteristic example of her reliance on observation rather than statistics for data. Other works include *Growing Up in New Guinea* (1930), *Sex and Temperament in Three Primitive Societies* (1935), *Balinese Character: A Photographic Analysis* (with Gregory Bateson; 1942), *Continuities in Cultural Evolution* (1964), and *A Rap on Race* (with James Baldwin; 1971). During her many years with the American Museum of Natural History in New York City, she successively served as assistant curator (1926–42), associate curator (1942–64), and curator (1964–69) of ethology. Her contributions to science received special recognition when, at the age of 72, she was elected to the presidency of the American Association for the Advancement of Science. In 1979 Margaret Mead was posthumously awarded the Presidential Medal of Freedom, the United States' highest civilian honour.

Meir, Golda, Israeli politician (b. May 3, 1898, Kiev, Russia—d. Dec. 8, 1978, Jerusalem, Israel), infused a new energy into the leadership of Israel as the country's prime minister from 1969 to 1974. In 1906 her family emigrated to Milwaukee, Wis., where Golda trained as a teacher and in 1917 married Morris Myerson. In 1921 the two ardent Zionists settled in Palestine. She became a clerk in the Histadrut (the General Federation of Labour) and later an acting chairman of the Jewish Agency, the highest Jewish authority in British-administered Palestine.

Shortly after proclaiming Israel's independence, David Ben-Gurion, the country's first prime minister, appointed Mrs. Myerson Israel's first ambassador to the U.S.S.R. She spent only nine months in the "cold land of suspicion, hostility and silence"—as she wrote in *My Life* (1975). From April 1949 to 1956 she served as minister of labour and social insurance before becoming foreign minister in June 1956 and changing her name to the Hebrew-sounding Meir. The Suez crisis followed, and Golda Meir represented Israel at the dramatic 1957 UN General Assembly.

In January 1966 she resigned as foreign minister and accepted the post of secretary-general of Mapai (the Israel Labour Party). Following the sudden death of Levi Eshkol, she assumed the office of prime minister on March 17, 1969, at the age of 70. The Arab attack in October 1973 took Israel by surprise and an outcry broke out against those responsible for the "blunder" of unpreparedness. The chief target was Gen. Moshe Dayan, minister of defense, but Golda Meir did not escape criticism. She announced her resignation on April 10, 1974, and stepped down in June. In November

YVONNE PLAUT—CAMERA PRESS

1977 Meir met with her former enemy, Egyptian Pres. Anwar as-Sadat, when he visited Jerusalem. During the moving occasion she told him that the peace negotiations would be difficult, but not as difficult as making the decision to go to war again.

Mellanby, May (LADY MELLANBY), British physiologist (b. 1882, London, England—d. March 5, 1978, London), collaborated with her husband, Sir Edward Mellanby, in research on vitamins and rickets and conducted investigations on biological mineralization. Her special interest was the study of children's teeth and diet. The University of Cambridge made her a doctor of science and the International Association for Dental Research honoured her with a science award in 1975.

Menzies, Sir Robert Gordon, Australian politician (b. Dec. 20, 1894, Jeparit, Victoria, Australia—d. May 15, 1978, Melbourne, Victoria), dominated Australian politics for two decades as the conservative prime minister of the country (1939–41, 1949–66). A lawyer by profession, Menzies served (1929–34) in Victoria's state legislature before entering (1934) the federal Parliament, where he served as attorney general until 1939, when Prime Minister Joseph Lyons died in office. As leader of the United Australia Party, Menzies became prime minister but was forced out of office by the Labor Party in 1941. After founding the Liberal Party (1944), he regained control of the government (1949) and led the country toward rapid industrial growth, sponsored the development of natural resources, and encouraged foreign investments. He also lent controversial support to Britain's intervention in the Suez Canal crisis in 1956 and in the Malaya-Indonesia confrontation in 1960. An outspoken foe of Communism, Menzies unsuccessfully attempted to dissolve the Australian Communist Party in 1951. Because he believed that the security of Australia could best be protected by the U.S., he promoted the Australian, New Zealand, and U.S. (ANZUS) defense pact and Australia's joining (1954) the Southeast Asia Treaty Organization (SEATO). Following the longest continuous tenure as prime minister in the history of Australia, Menzies retired in 1966.

Mercader, Ramón, Spanish Communist (b. unknown—d. Oct. 18, 1978, Havana, Cuba), was the enigmatic assassin of Leon Trotsky, a leader in the Bolshevik Revolution of 1917 and later Joseph Stalin's chief rival for power. Mercader, the son of a Spanish Communist, was probably recruited by Soviet intelligence agents during the Spanish Civil War. After living in the U.S. he went to Mexico, where he took the name Frank Jackson and gradually became a trusted visitor to Trotsky's fortified home in Coyoacán, a suburb of Mexico City. During a visit on Aug. 20, 1940, having asked Trotsky to look over a political article, he pulled out a concealed alpine ax and drove it into Trotsky's skull. Though fatally wounded (he died the next day), Trotsky struggled long enough for help to arrive. Mercader was brutally beaten by the guards and then turned over to the police, but during hundreds of hours of interrogation the assassin kept insisting he was Jacques Mornard, a Belgian, and had acted alone. After nearly 20 years in prison, the maximum sentence under Mexican law, "Jacques Mornard" was quietly released in Mexico City on May 6, 1960. From Czechoslovakia Mercader went to the U.S.S.R., where in 1977 he was declared a Hero of the Soviet Union. Mercader's use of numerous aliases and his conflicting stories to authorities obscured details of his background to the end.

Messel, Oliver Hilary Sambourne, British stage designer (b. Jan. 13, 1904, London, England—d. July 13, 1978, Bridgetown, Barbados), combined elegance and imagination in sets and costumes for plays, operas, and films. He was instrumental in raising stage design to a position of equal importance with acting and directing. After studying at the Slade School of Art in London, Messel began his career in 1926 as a designer for the impresario Charles B. Cochran and by the 1920s was established as Britain's leading designer. He was particularly praised for his costumes and sets for such Cochran revues as Noel Coward's *This Year of Grace* (1928) and *Cochran's 1930 Revue.* After World War II he helped to bring an element of opulence and poetry back to the British stage. He was the author of several books on design and costume, including *Stage Designs and Costumes* (1933).

Messerschmitt, Willy E., German aeronautical engineer (b. June 26, 1898, Frankfurt am Main, Germany—d. Sept. 17, 1978, Munich, West Germany), was the designer of the feared Me 109 fighter, Germany's principal aerial defense against Allied bombers during World War II, the Me 110 two-man fighter-bomber, which was used primarily as an attack aircraft and as a night fighter, and the twin-engined Me 262, the first operational jet fighter, which saw action during the last days of the Third Reich. Educated at the Munich Institute of Technology, Messerschmitt also gained useful knowledge about aircraft construction as a gliding enthusiast. His monoplane prototype of the Me 109 won the world air speed record at 481 mph (775 kph) in April 1939, and some 35,000 Me 109s were produced during the war. Besides the Me 262, he designed the Me 163, a swept-back-wing, rocket-driven plane. After the war Messerschmitt was detained for two years by the U.S. occupation authorities, and during the postwar ban on higher aircraft construction he manufactured prefabricated houses, sewing machines, and enclosed motor-tricycles. In the late 1960s Messerschmitt was named honorary chairman of Messerschmitt-Bölkow-Blohm. In the late 1970s the company employed a force of more than 20,000 workers, who were engaged in the construction of satellites and missiles as well as the Franco-West German airbus and the West German share of the Tornado combat aircraft for the North Atlantic Treaty Organization.

Metcalfe, Ralph H., U.S. politician (b. May 30, 1910, Atlanta, Ga.—d. Oct. 10, 1978, Chicago, Ill.), won a gold medal for the 440-m relay race and two silver medals in the 100-m dash as a member of the 1932 and 1936 U.S. Olympic track teams. After World War II he joined the ranks of Democratic Mayor Richard J. Daley's political organization and became a powerful Chicago alderman and later a U.S. congressman. But in 1972, when blacks reported indignities at the hands of police, he severed ties with Daley, who removed Metcalfe's name from the party slate. Undaunted, Metcalfe ran independently for both his posts as 3rd ward

committeeman and U.S. congressman and won both by a large margin. After Daley's death in 1976, Metcalfe was reconciled with the Democratic Party leaders.

Mikoyan, Anastas, Soviet Communist leader (b. Nov. 25, 1895, Sanain, Armenia—d. Oct. 21, 1978, Moscow, U.S.S.R.), was a shrewd, able, and quick-witted politician who survived Stalin's purges, was never disgraced, and retired into private life with dignity. After graduating from the Armenian ec-

ELLIOTT ERWITT—MAGNUM

clesiastical seminary at Tbilisi, he joined (1915) the Russian Social Democratic Workers' (Communist) Party. In 1917 he began editing an Armenian Communist newspaper in Baku and joined the Communist-controlled Azerbaijani local administration. He remained in Baku during the British occupation that started in July 1918, but on September 15, when Germans and Turks entered the city, he left by sea for Astrakhan with a group of comrades. When a gunboat under British command intercepted them and escorted their ship to Krasnovodsk, 26 commissars were shot, but Mikoyan escaped the death penalty and was held in Ashkhabad prison until February 1919 when he returned to Baku. Having reorganized the local Communist Party, he was instrumental in overthrowing the Azerbaijani Musavat ("Equality") government in April 1920 with the help of the invading Red Army. In 1920 Mikoyan was sent as a party organizer to Nizhny Novgorod (now Gorky). From 1922 to 1926 he worked in Rostov-on-Don as secretary of the regional party organization and supported Stalin against Trotsky. In 1923 Mikoyan was elected to the party's Central Committee and at the 15th party congress (1926) he became a candidate member of the Politburo. He joined the government in 1926 and served successively as people's commissar for foreign trade, for supplies, for the food industry, and again for foreign trade. In 1935 Stalin made him a full member of the Politburo and appointed him a member of the editorial commission for drafting the new constitution. In 1937 Mikoyan became vice-chairman of the Council of People's Commissars, and in 1942 Stalin included him in his five-member Committee of State Defense.

After Stalin's death in 1953, Mikoyan remained a member of the enlarged Politburo and sided with N. S. Khrushchev against G. M. Malenkov. From 1955 to 1964 he was first vice-chairman of the U.S.S.R. Council of Ministers. In 1964 Khrushchev appointed him chairman of the Presidium of the Supreme Soviet to succeed Leonid Brezhnev. Mikoyan's part in removing Khrushchev in October 1964 was obscure but in December 1965 he stepped down from his ceremonial post in favour

of N. V. Podgorny, a Ukrainian. In April 1966 he was not reelected to the Politburo.

Miner, Dwight Carroll, U.S. educator (b. Nov. 4, 1904, New York, N.Y.—d. Aug. 1, 1978, Ridgewood, N.J.), was longtime (1927–73) professor of American history at Columbia University, singled out in a cover story published by *Time* magazine (May 6, 1966) as one of the ten finest college teachers in the U.S. Miner graduated from Columbia in 1926 and, after earning his M.A. the following year, began teaching undergraduates—the joy of his academic life. In 1940 he completed requirements for his Ph.D. Miner's credits include *The Fight for the Panama Route* (1940) and the editing of the 17-volume *Bicentennial History of Columbia* (1954–56). In 1965 undergraduates voted to give him the Mark Van Doren Award for contributing so much to their education.

Montgomery, (Robert) Bruce, British novelist and composer (b. Oct. 2, 1921, Chesham Bois, Buckinghamshire, England—d. Sept. 15, 1978, Devon, England), was the creator of a sparkling series of detective novels that featured the academic sleuth Gervase Fen. Montgomery, who wrote under the pseudonym Edmund Crispin, styled the novels in the "whodunnit" pattern that was executed so well by Dorothy Sayers, a master of the genre. After graduating from St. John's College, Oxford, he turned out *The Case of the Gilded Fly* (1944) and *The Long Divorce* (1951). He was also a talented composer and produced film music, songs, and a well-known chorale, "An Oxford Requiem." In his later years he lived in seclusion in Devon, where he reviewed and anthologized science fiction.

Moon, Keith, British rock drummer (b. Aug. 23, 1947, Wembley, London, England—d. Sept. 7, 1978, London), was a member of The Who rock group whose aggressive drumming helped to make the group one of the internationally best-known British rock bands of the early 1960s. He also played an important part in The Who's successful adaption to the music styles of the 1970s. Moon gained notoriety with outrageous behaviour that included demolishing hotel bedrooms and driving expensive cars into swimming pools. His offstage behaviour was interpreted as a defense mechanism by fellow musicians, who regarded him with affection. Moon's death was ascribed to a drug overdose.

Moreell, Ben, U.S. naval officer (b. Sept. 14, 1892, Salt Lake City, Utah—d. July 30, 1978, Pittsburgh, Pa.), organized and commanded the 250,000-strong naval construction battalion called the Seabees, which erected the shore installations needed to support U.S. ships against the Japanese during World War II. When the government took over the strike-ridden petroleum industry in 1945 and the coal industry in 1946, Moreell was appointed to direct operations and was instrumental in negotiating and drafting settlements. In 1946 he became the first officer of his time to hold the four-star rank of admiral without graduating from Annapolis. After Moreell retired, he became chairman (1947) of Jones and Laughlin Steel Corp. and supervised a half-billion-dollar expansion program.

Morgan, Sir Morien Bedford, British aeronautical engineer (b. Dec. 20, 1912, Bridgend, Glamorgan, Wales—d. April 14, 1978, Cambridge, England), was an expert on guided weapons and on supersonic flight whose studies led to the development of the Concorde. After graduating from St. Catharine's College, Cambridge, Morgan joined (1935) the Royal Aircraft Establishment (RAE) at Farnborough and became chairman (1956) of the Supersonic Transport Aircraft Committee. After serving as controller of aircraft at the Ministry of Aviation (1960–63) and controller of guided weapons and electronics at the Ministry of Technology (1966–69), Morgan returned (1969) to Farnborough as director of the RAE. He was president of the Royal Aeronautical Society (1967–68), was knighted in 1969, and in 1972 was elected a fellow of the Royal Society. In 1972 Morgan retired and became master of Downing College, Cambridge.

Moro, Aldo, Italian politician (b. Sept. 23, 1916, Maglie, Italy—d. May 9, 1978, near or in Rome, Italy), was a lawyer by profession who served as Italy's premier five times during 1963–76 and afterward as the influential president of the Christian Democrat Party (CD). At the age of 24, Moro was a professor of law at Bari University but became interested in politics while president (1939–42) of the Federation of Italian University Catholics and (1945–46) of the Movement of Catholic Graduates. In 1946 he was elected to the Constituent Assembly and in 1948 won election to the first Chamber of Deputies of the new republic. Moro then held Cabinet posts as minister of justice (1955–57) and of education (1957–59) before becoming (1959) secretary of the CD, an appointment he held until 1963. After persuading a party congress to form an alliance with the Socialists, Moro became (1963) premier of the first centre-left coalition to include Christian Democrats, Socialists, Social Democrats, and Republicans. Following two more terms as premier (July 1964–January 1966; February 1966–June 1968), he became Italy's foreign minister, then resumed the post of premier an additional two times (November 1974–January 1976; February 1976–April 1976). In October 1976 he became president of the Christian Democrats and remained a powerful influence in Italian politics even though he held no public office. On March 16, 1978, Moro was kidnapped in Rome by Red Brigades terrorists while on his way to attend a special session of Parliament. After government officials repeatedly refused to release 13 members of the Red Brigades on trial in Turin, Moro was murdered in or near Rome by the terrorist kidnappers.

Mullin, Willard, U.S. cartoonist (b. 1902?, Ohio—d. Dec. 21, 1978, Corpus Christi, Texas), whose comic pen created more than 10,000 original sports cartoons for the *New York World-Telegram* from 1934 to 1966. Although Mullin produced six cartoons a week and preferred prizefighters as subjects, his most enduring caricature was the "Brooklyn Bum," a tramp who, with tattered clothes, flapping soles, cigar butts, and fractured English, epitomized the Brooklyn Dodgers baseball fan. But when the Dodgers moved to Los Angeles in 1958, the beloved Bum sported a beret, a sports shirt, and sunglasses. Mullin also completed hundreds of illustrations for such magazines as *Life, Saturday Evening Post,* and *Newsweek* and did a special cover for *Time* magazine when the New York Mets won the pennant in 1969.

Murphy, Robert Daniel, U.S. diplomat (b. Oct. 28, 1894, Milwaukee, Wis.—d. Jan. 9, 1978, New York, N.Y.), was the talented troubleshooter for a succession of seven presidents. His 40-year diplomatic career involved him in some of the most dramatic international negotiations in history. His expertise was first demonstrated when he developed a liaison with the French underground during World War II and paved the way for the Allies' successful invasion of North Africa. Murphy also presided at the Italian armistice (1943) and helped engineer the Berlin airlift when the Soviets blockaded the city in 1948. He later was appointed ambassador to Belgium (1949–52) and as the first postwar ambassador to Japan (1952–53) helped negotiate an end to the Korean War (1953). He also held the prestigious post of undersecretary of state for political affairs (1959). Although Murphy retired from government service in 1959, he was repeatedly called back to serve in missions abroad. In 1976 he was named by Pres. Gerald Ford to head the Intelligence Oversight Board, which monitors the CIA.

Nabokov, Nicolas, Russian-born composer (b. April 4, 1903, Lubcha, near Minsk, Russia—d. April 6, 1978, New York, N.Y.), received mixed critical reviews for his operas, concertos, and ballet scores but gained international recognition for organizing music festivals in Paris (1952), Rome (1954), and Tokyo (1961) as secretary-general (1951–63) of the now defunct Congress for Cultural Freedom. His most famous compositions include the ballets *Ode* and *Don Quixote* and the operas *Rasputin's Death* and

Love's Labour's Lost. During his youth, Nabokov studied in Russia under Vladimir Rebikov; in Germany, at the Stuttgart Conservatory and the Music Academy of Berlin; and in France, at the Sorbonne. In 1933 he settled in the U.S., becoming a U.S. citizen in 1939, six years earlier than his cousin, the gifted writer Vladimir Nabokov. Nabokov, who delighted the art world with his keen wit, chronicled his international travels and frequent meetings with world-famous musicians in *Old Friends and New Music* (1951) and *Bagazh* (1975).

Nagy, Laszlo, Hungarian poet (b. July 17, 1925, Felsoiszkaz, Hung.—d. Jan. 30, 1978, Budapest, Hung.), exemplified Hungary's literary resurgence after World War II with his rich, brilliant poetic language that drew upon Eastern European folk traditions but was concerned with modern man. Nagy also studied Bulgarian folk poetry and translated the poetry of Federico García Lorca and Dylan Thomas into Hungarian. His collections of poetry include such works as *A nap jegyese* (1954, "Bride of the Sun"), *Deres majalis* (1957, "Fair in Frosty May"), *Himnusz minden idoben* (1965, "Hymn for Anytime"), and *Versben bujdoso* (1973, "Hiding in Poems"). An English translation of his poems was published in 1973 as *Love of the Scorching Wind.*

Nicolson, (Lionel) Benedict, British art historian (b. Aug. 6, 1914, Knole, Sevenoaks, Kent, England—d. May 22, 1978, London, England), was the distinguished editor (1947–78) of *The Burlington Magazine,* a leading British art historical journal. Some of the foremost writers on art history, impressed by Nicolson's own scholarship, were eager to contribute to the magazine and thereby enhanced its reputation. Nicolson was educated at Eton College and Balliol College, Oxford, and studied under the noted U.S. art critic Bernard Berenson in Florence, Italy. He was briefly deputy surveyor of the king's pictures before serving in World War II. His writings include *The Painters of Ferrara* (1950) and *Joseph Wright of Derby* (1968).

Nijinsky, Romola, widow and biographer of Vaslav Nijinsky and one of the last surviving veterans of the Ballets Russes (b. Feb. 19, 1891, Budapest, Hung.—d. June 8, 1978, Paris, France), fell in love with the Russian ballet dancer when she first saw him perform in Budapest with Sergey Diaghilev's Ballets Russes. In 1913 she secured permission to travel to South America as a pupil in Diaghilev's company, pretending affection for another of the leading men in order not to arouse jealousy of the director, who was also in love with Nijinsky. In the same year she married Nijinsky in Buenos Aires, and Diaghilev consequently dismissed him. Romola and Nijinsky had two daughters, and she cared for him from the time (1919) he was diagnosed as a schizophrenic until his death in 1950. During these years she published *Nijinsky* (1933) and *The Diary of Vaslav Nijinsky* (1938), and later *The Last Years of Nijinsky* (1952).

Nikitina, Alice, Russian-born ballet dancer (b. 1909?, St. Petersburg, Russia—d. mid-June, 1978, Monte Carlo, Monaco), joined Sergey Diaghilev's Ballets Russes three years after she fled from the U.S.S.R. in 1920. Nikitina, who appeared in leading roles in Léonide Massine's *Zéphyre et Flore* and *Ode* and in George Balanchine's *La Chatte,* owed her great popular success less to technical excellence than to her beauty and delicate freshness. After Diaghilev died, she appeared in Charles B. Cochran's London revues and danced in concerts. In 1935 she began studying voice and three years later made her operatic debut at Palermo, Italy. She then moved to France, where she opened a ballet school in Paris. Later she opened another ballet school in Nice, France. Her autobiography, *Nikitina by Herself,* appeared in 1959.

Nikodim (BORIS GEORGYEVICH ROTOV), Russian Orthodox metropolitan of Leningrad (b. Oct. 14, 1929, Frolovo, near Ryazan, U.S.S.R.—d. Sept. 5, 1978, Vatican City), became a familiar figure to Christian leaders all over the world as one of the six elected presidents of the World Council of Churches. After graduating from the Pedagogical

Institute of Ryazan, he entered the local Orthodox monastery, where in 1947 he became a heirodeacon and took the name of Nikodim. The archbishop of Ryazan sent him to the Spasso-Preobrazhenski monastery in Yaroslavl, where in 1949 he was ordained priest (hieromonk) and appointed rector of the Nativity Church at Davydov. In 1950 he became rector at Uglich and also started nonresident studies at the Leningrad Seminary and later at the Theological Academy, from which he graduated in 1955. The following year he became a member of the Russian Orthodox Mission in Jerusalem, becoming its head with the rank of archimandrite in 1957. In June 1960 he was consecrated bishop of Podolsk and made responsible for foreign relations of the Russian Church. In 1961 he led the church into the World Council of Churches. Two years later Aleksey, patriarch of all Russia, appointed him metropolitan of Leningrad. He died of a heart attack during an audience with Pope John Paul I.

Nilsson, Gunnar, Swedish racing driver (b. Nov. 20, 1948, Hälsingborg, Sweden—d. Oct. 20, 1978, London, England), won the 1977 Belgian Grand Prix before his promising career was cut short by cancer. A former naval officer, he drove for two seasons with Lotus, becoming their number two driver, before his illness. During his courageous personal fight against the disease, he helped other cancer patients by setting up a fund, the Gunnar Nilsson Cancer Treatment Campaign, which was affiliated with New Charing Cross Hospital in London.

Nobile, Umberto, Italian airship designer and explorer (b. Jan. 21, 1885, Lauro, Italy—d. July 30, 1978, Italy), designed and piloted the airship "Norge," which carried explorer Roald Amundsen and his American companion, Lincoln Ellsworth, from Svalbard (Spitsbergen) over the North Pole to Alaska in 1926 in the first exploration flight to cross the Arctic Ocean. Nobile was rewarded with the rank of general in the Italian Air Service but, when Amundsen criticized his technical skills, a bitter controversy developed. Two years later Nobile set out for the North Pole in the dirigible "Italia." The ship crashed northeast of Svalbard, throwing Nobile and other crew members onto the ice, but then took off again with the rest of the crew, who were never seen again. Amundsen also disappeared in a rescue attempt, and Nobile, severely criticized by a subsequent inquiry, was forced to resign. The controversy continued, and Nobile defended himself in a book about his Arctic adventures, *Gli italiani al Polo Nord* (1959; *My Polar Flights,* 1961). After spending some years designing aircraft for the Soviet Union, he returned to Italy, and in 1945 he was reinstated as a general in the Air Service.

Noble, Ray, British bandleader (b. Dec. 17, 1903, Brighton, England—d. April 2, 1978, London, England), recorded such smash hits of the 1930s as "Goodnight Sweetheart," "Love Is the Sweetest Thing," and "The Very Thought of You." As an arranger he worked for bandleader Jack Payne and for His Master's Voice record company, where he conducted the New Mayfair Orchestra. Noble's English orchestra was in such demand in the U.S. that in 1935 he organized an all-American jazz band, which he conducted until 1937 at the Rainbow Room in New York City. He then moved to Los Angeles and gained even wider popularity as an English stooge on radio with ventriloquist Edgar Bergen and his dummy Charlie McCarthy and on the Burns and Allen radio program. Noble also played for the Jack Benny radio show.

Norrish, Ronald George Wreyford, British physical chemist (b. Nov. 9, 1897, Cambridge, England—d. June 7, 1978, Cambridge), shared the 1967 Nobel Prize for Chemistry with his co-worker (Sir) George Porter and Manfred Eigen for studies of extremely fast chemical reactions. As director of

BOOK OF THE YEAR

the department of physical chemistry at the University of Cambridge (1937–65), Norrish developed research techniques of flash photolysis and flash spectroscopy to measure and study the rapid reactions of free atoms and radicals. His work was detailed in more than 200 scientific papers. A scholar and fellow of Emmanuel College, Cambridge, he was elected to the Royal Society in 1936 and served as president of the Faraday Society (1953–55).

Oakie, Jack (Lewis Delaney Offield), U.S. actor (b. Nov. 12, 1903, Sedalia, Mo.—d. Jan. 23, 1978, Northridge, Calif.), was a happy-go-lucky comic who became a multimillionaire playing mostly secondary roles in such films as *Million Dollar Legs* and *The Affairs of Annabel*. His most memorable performance, and his personal favourite, was his parody of Mussolini in *The Great Dictator* (1940). Oakie entered show business in 1922 and completed more than 100 films in a career that spanned some 40 years. He last appeared in *Daughter of Tugboat Annie* in 1969. He had hundreds of friends, who had standing invitations to attend the parties he held every Sunday at his luxurious mansion.

O Dalaigh, Cearbhall (Carroll O'Daly), Irish jurist (b. Feb. 12, 1911, County Wicklow, Ireland—d. March 21, 1978, County Kerry, Ireland), was president of the Republic of Ireland from December 1974 to October 1976. A linguist, Gaelic scholar, and acknowledged legal expert, he became a judge of the Supreme Court in 1953. He later served as chief justice from 1961 to 1973, then became a judge of the Court of Justice of the European Com-

LESLIE STUART—CAMERA PRESS

munities in Luxembourg. As president of Ireland he attempted to delay legislation that would have lengthened the time during which police could detain suspected terrorists without making formal charges. This action prompted the minister of defense, P. S. Donegan, to describe O Dalaigh as a "thundering disgrace." The Supreme Court upheld the law and O Dalaigh resigned.

Oman, Carola Mary Anima (Lady Lenanton), British writer (b. May 11, 1897, Oxford, England—d. June 11, 1978, Welwyn, Hertfordshire, England), produced carefully researched historical novels and biographies as well as children's books and poetry. The daughter of the historian Sir Charles Oman, she was educated at Wychwood School, Oxford, and served with the Red Cross in World

Wars I and II. Her works include the novels *Princess Amelia* (1924) and *Over the Water* (1935); biographies of *Nelson* (1946), *Sir John Moore* (1953), and *David Garrick* (1958); the children's books *Robin Hood* (1937), *Alfred, King of the English* (1939), and *Baltic Spy* (1940); *The Menin Road and Other Poems* (1919); the historical study *Britain Against Napoleon* (1942); and the autobiographical *An Oxford Childhood* (1976).

Osborn, Sir Frederic James, British town planner (b. May 26, 1885, London, England—d. Nov. 1, 1978, Welwyn Garden City, England), played a major role in the architectural and sociological experiment of Welwyn Garden City, England, one of the main achievements of British town planning between World Wars I and II. In 1912 he was appointed to a post at Letchworth, Britain's first garden city, designed by Sir Ebenezer Howard. With Howard's help and inspired by the ideals of Fabian Socialism, he began to work on a second garden city development in Welwyn after World War I. From 1936, as a leading member of the Town and Country Planning Association, he played a crucial role in the initiation of postwar town planning policies. Osborn was especially concerned with the development of new towns and the need for low-density housing close to open country. He wrote several books, including *Green-Belt Cities: The New Towns* (1946), which called for decentralization as a way of achieving a more human environment.

Page, Sir Denys Lionel, British classical scholar (b. 1908, Reading, England—d. July 6, 1978, Tarset, Northumberland, England), established his reputation with work on the Greek lyric poets, studies of Homer, and editions of Aeschylus and Euripides. As professor of Greek at Cambridge University (1950–73) and master (1959–73) of Jesus College, Cambridge, Page influenced generations of students, while his scholarship in an inevitably controversial field of textual criticism won him wide respect. He was knighted in 1971 and served as president of the British Academy from 1971 to 1974. In later years he was closely involved in excavations on the Greek island of Santorini.

Paul VI (Giovanni Battista Montini), pope of the Roman Catholic Church (b. Sept. 26, 1897, Concesio, near Brescia, Italy—d. Aug. 6, 1978, Castel Gandolfo, Italy), was the spiritual leader of the world's 600 million Roman Catholics for nearly 16 years. Giovanni Battista Montini, who was born into a deeply pious Roman Catholic family, never enjoyed robust health. He was ordained a priest on May 29, 1920, and in 1923 served on the staff of the papal nuncio in Warsaw. After illness brought him back to Rome, he became officially involved in foreign affairs as a member of the Vatican Secretariat of State. Montini, who became the protégé of Eugenio Cardinal Pacelli (Pius XII), was appointed substitute secretary of state in 1937 and in 1944 was named pro secretary of ordinary (nondiplomatic) affairs. In 1954 Montini became archbishop of Milan and in 1958 was named cardinal by Pope John XXIII. On June 21, 1963, Montini, as expected, was elected the 262nd pope and chose the name Paul VI. As pope he carried forward the sweeping reforms instituted by John XXIII during the second Vatican Council, but he held traditionalist views on faith and morals. During Paul's reign both regular abstention from meat on Fridays and the *Index* of condemned books were abolished, the ancient clerical order of the deacon was revived, the procedures for annulment of a marriage were streamlined, and the form of the mass as celebrated since the 16th century was replaced by a new order in which Latin gave way to vernacular tongues and popular music was permitted as a new form of liturgical expression. Paul VI also established an international Synod of Bishops, which first met in 1967 to give guidance to the pope on revisions of canon law, liturgy, and seminaries. Later synods (1971, 1974, and 1977) discussed collegiality, human rights, justice and peace, and celibacy. Paul VI became the first pope since 1809 to travel outside Italy and the first to board an airplane. He used his journeys to the Holy Land, India, New York City,

Portugal, Turkey, Colombia, Switzerland, Uganda, and the Far East to dramatize the need for social justice and to appeal for world peace. Among Paul's most controversial encyclicals were his 1967 *Sacerdotalis Caelibates,* which reaffirmed the tradition of priestly celibacy, and *Humanae Vitae,* which reaffirmed the church's prohibition of any form of artificial birth control. He also declared that women could not become priests, fostered ecumenism, and broadened the international character of the College of Cardinals by selecting members from third world countries. His reforms in church administration included the reorganization of the Congregation of the Holy Office, which he renamed the Sacred Congregation for the Doctrine of Faith, the introduction of non-Italians into the Curia, the establishment of a retirement age of 75 for bishops, and a rule that cardinals could not take part in papal elections after reaching their 80th birthdays. Throughout his reign Paul wrestled with the problems of making needed changes without tearing the whole fabric of the Roman Catholic Church.

Pei, Mario Andrew, Italian-born linguist (b. Feb. 16, 1901, Rome, Italy—d. March 2, 1978, Glen Ridge, N.J.), was fluent in five languages, capable of speaking some 30 others, and commanded a structural knowledge of at least 100 of the world's 2,796 spoken languages. As a graduate student at Columbia University, he learned such early languages as Sanskrit, Old Church Slavic, and Old French. Pei joined the faculty of his alma mater in 1937 and from 1952 until his retirement in 1970 was professor of Romance philology. Besides compiling the companion volumes *The Story of Language* (1945) and *The Story of English* (1952), which provided the general public with a fascinating understanding of linguistics and philology, Pei published *Languages for War and Peace* (1943), a handy guide to 7 key world tongues and 30 minor languages.

Peterson, Ronnie, Swedish racing driver (b. Feb. 14, 1944, Örebro, Sweden—d. Sept. 11, 1978, Milan, Italy), captured ten Grand Prix titles in Formula One racing and was touted, because of his fearlessness, as the man to beat in virtually every race he entered. He started driving go-karts at the

SVENSKT PRESSFOTO/PHOTO TRENDS

age of eight and was Sweden's five-time champion before he entered Formula Three racing in 1968. Peterson, who had raced in more than 100 Grand Prix events and survived some 30 accidents, ranked second behind his team partner, Mario Andretti, in the 1978 world championship driver standings. Peterson was fatally injured in a fiery crash on the first lap of the Italian Grand Prix at Monza in Milan. His death brought demands that the fast and narrow track be closed or remodeled.

Pickles, Wilfred, British entertainer (b. Oct. 13, 1904, Halifax, England—d. March 27, 1978, Brighton, England), was a popular radio and television personality of infectious friendliness whose trademark was his broad Yorkshire accent. A radio broadcaster, Pickles became a national newsreader during World War II and then, in 1946, emceed his own radio quiz program, "Have a Go!," which ran for 21 years. Later television programs in which he appeared included "Ask Pickles," "Dr. Finlay's Casebook," and "For the Love of Ada." He also appeared in various plays and films.

Poulter, Thomas Charles, U.S. explorer (b. March 3, 1897, Salem, Iowa—d. June 14, 1978, Menlo Park, Calif.), was second in command and chief scientist on Richard E. Byrd's second Antarctic expedition (1933–35), aimed at mapping and claiming land in the region of the South Pole. Poulter led the rescue party that revived Byrd, who was near death after spending five months alone in the Bolling Advance Base weather station. In addition to his more than 75 other patents, Poulter designed the 33-ton "Snow Cruiser" used by Byrd to traverse glacier chasms during his third expedition. Early in his career, Poulter headed the departments of chemistry (1925–27) and physics (1927–32) at Iowa Wesleyan College, his alma mater, where he taught James Van Allen, the discoverer of radiation belts around the Earth. After returning from Byrd's Antarctic expeditions, Poulter served as director (1948–54) of the Stanford Research Institute and director of Stanford's Poulter Labs (1954–60). At the time of his death, he was experimenting with implants to aid the deaf.

Prouvost, Jean, French publisher and industrialist (b. April 24, 1885, Roubaix, France—d. Oct. 18, 1978, Ivoy-le-Marron, France), operated his family's wool and textile firm before becoming one of the century's great press barons. During the 1930s his daily *Paris-Soir* reached sales of two million or more, making it the largest newspaper in France, and in the 1950s *Marie-Claire* and *Paris-Match* launched many leading journalists and dominated the market for weekly magazines. From 1950 to 1975 he was also co-owner of the conservative daily *Le Figaro*, and in 1969 he established the top-selling television magazine *Télé 7 Jours*.

Quick, Armand James, U.S. hematologist (b. July 18, 1894, Theresa, Wis.—d. Jan. 26, 1978, Milwaukee, Wis.), developed (1932) a prothrombin time test (Quick test) that assesses the clotting ability of a patient's blood. The test is used to determine the dosage of blood-thinning drugs and to diagnose liver diseases. Quick, who was recognized as one of the top experts of the 20th century on blood diseases, also devised a prothrombin consumption time test that is helpful in diagnosing hemophilia, a hereditary tendency toward excessive bleeding. His research also led to the discovery of warfarin and dicumarol, used as blood-thinning drugs. Quick served as professor of biochemistry and chairman of the department (1944–66) at Marquette University School of Medicine (now Medical College of Wisconsin) after receiving (1928) his M.D. from Cornell University. His numerous books include *Hemorrhagic Diseases* (1957) and *Bleeding Problems in Clinical Medicine* (1970).

Reid, Rose Marie, Canadian-born fashion designer (b. 1912?, Cardston, Alta.—d. Dec. 18, 1978, Provo, Utah), transformed women's swimwear from shapeless, woolen bathing suits into appealing and practical garments more suitable for active swimming. Reid not only incorporated elasticized fibres into her designs but also perfected water-repellent materials to prevent suits from becoming soggy. Between 1946 and 1960, the Rose Marie Reid Co. increased sales by $1 million every year and became the largest U.S. manufacturer of women's bathing suits, with nearly 10% of the total retail sales volume.

Rennert, Günther, German opera producer (b. April 1, 1911, Essen, Germany—d. July 31, 1978, Salzburg, Austria), had worldwide influence as a producer of operas in West Germany and abroad. He regularly worked in New York, Paris, and Glyndebourne, where he served as director from 1959 to 1967. In Salzburg his productions included the established repertory of works by Mozart, Wagner, and Beethoven and such lesser-known operas as Monteverdi's *Poppea*. In his own country he was associated with the State Opera House in Hamburg, which he directed (1946–56), and with the Bavarian State Opera in Munich, where he established his reputation with a moving performance (1945) of Beethoven's *Fidelio*. In 1967 he became director of the Bavarian State Opera.

Riobé, Msgr. Guy, French prelate of the Roman Catholic Church (b. April 24, 1911, Rennes, France—d. July 1978, off Port-Camargue, France), was named bishop of Orléans in 1963 and became noted for his outspoken views on contemporary issues. An admirer of Charles de Foucauld, Riobé was deeply influenced by his experiences as chaplain to the Catholic workers' youth movement and by visits to Africa and Latin America. His stand on such topics as French arms sales, his defense of human rights, and his opposition to conservative traditions in his church made him the centre of frequent controversy. He was also known as a man of deep spirituality who felt that his choice lay between "obeying a certain form of social conformism or following Jesus and his Gospel." Riobé drowned while swimming in the Mediterranean.

Roberts, Brian Birley, British polar specialist (b. Oct. 23, 1912, Woking, England—d. Oct. 9, 1978, Cambridge, England), was head (1946–75) of the polar regions section of the British Foreign and Commonwealth Office. While an undergraduate at Emmanuel College, Cambridge, Roberts led expeditions to Iceland and Greenland, and as a member of the British Graham Land Expedition (1934–37), he completed his doctoral study of Antarctic birds. He later influenced the formulation of both the Antarctic Treaty (1959) and the Convention for the Conservation of Antarctic Seals (1972), which became effective in March 1978. He also served as joint editor of *Polar Record* (1942–75) and was responsible for the impressive development of the library of the Scott Polar Research Institute, Cambridge. His volume *Edward Wilson's Birds of the Antarctic* appeared in 1967.

Roberts, Sir Gilbert, British civil engineer (b. Feb. 18, 1899, London, England—d. Jan. 1, 1978, London), pioneered new design and construction methods in a series of major bridges including the 3,300-ft (1,006-m) Firth of Forth highway bridge in Scotland, the seventh longest in the world. After graduating from the University of London, he became a civil engineer and worked on the Sydney Harbour Bridge and on the Otto Beit suspension bridge across the Zambezi in what was then Southern Rhodesia. A brilliant designer, he adopted new welding methods and the use of high-tensile steel and introduced box columns and girders in the construction of power stations, thereby using less steel. Roberts's designs, which called for lighter construction, better stability, and lower cost, were implemented in such engineering masterpieces as the Severn River Bridge in western England, the Auckland Harbour Bridge in New Zealand, the Volta Bridge in Ghana, and the suspension bridge across the Bosporus in Turkey. Roberts also developed all-welded ships in World War II and designed the Dome of Discovery for the Festival of Britain in 1951, the Babcock 500-ton Goliath crane, and a 210-ft- (64-m-) diameter radio telescope in Australia. In 1965 he was knighted and elected a fellow of the Royal Society.

Robson, Mark, Canadian-born film director (b. Dec. 4, 1913, Montreal, Que.—d. June 20, 1978, London, England), launched his career in the 1940s with a series of low-budget terror films including *The Seventh Victim* (1943) and *Isle of the Dead* (1945) before directing such motion-picture box office hits as *Peyton Place* (1957), *Valley of the Dolls* (1967), and *Earthquake* (1974). With the success of *Champion* (1949) and *Home of the Brave*, Robson accepted a contract offered by Samuel Goldwyn and turned out such films as *Bright Victory* (1951), *The Bridges at Toko-Ri* (1955), *The Harder They Fall* (1956), and *Inn of the Sixth Happiness* (1958), starring Ingrid Berg-

man. In the 1960s his credits included *Nine Hours to Rama* and *Von Ryan's Express*. In 1971 Robson, Robert Wise, and Bernard Donnenfeld formed The Filmakers Group, which was changed from a corporation to a partnership in 1975 and renamed the Tripar Group. Robson died ten days after his collapse on the set of *The Avalanche Express*.

Rochemont, Louis de, U.S. film producer (b. Jan. 13, 1899, Chelsea, Mass.—d. Dec. 23, 1978, near Newington, N.H.), was the originator and producer of the *March of Time* (1935–43), a series of motion-picture documentaries and news reports made in cooperation with *Time* magazine. Notable features in the series included *Inside Nazi Germany* (1938), *The Ramparts We Watch* (1940), and *We Are the Marines* (1942). After becoming an independent producer in 1944, Rochemont turned out the sea saga *Windjammer*, the spy yarn *House on Ninety-Second Street*, the biographical *Martin Luther*, and recently *Animal Farm*, an animated cartoon version of George Orwell's satirical novel.

Rockefeller, John Davison, III, U.S. philanthropist (b. March 21, 1906, New York, N.Y.—d. July 10, 1978, Mount Pleasant, N.Y.), was the grandson of multimillionaire John D. Rockefeller, Sr., founder of the Standard Oil Co. As the eldest of five grandsons, who with their sister became heirs to a family

fortune estimated at $1.5 billion, Rockefeller shunned public life to devote his time and energy to philanthropy. Among the great cultural gifts he left the nation were the Lincoln Center for the Performing Arts in New York City, the India International Centre in New Delhi, the International House of Japan, the Asia Society, and a collection of Asian art that has been bequeathed to the Asia Society. As chairman of the Rockefeller Foundation, he gave substantial support to international agencies, but donated his own funds to found the Population Council, a research centre for family planning. A graduate of Princeton University, Rockefeller served as a trustee or director of some 30 educational and charitable organizations.

Rockwell, Norman, U.S. illustrator (b. Feb. 3, 1894, New York, N.Y.—d. Nov. 9, 1978, Stockbridge, Mass.), was known to virtually every segment of American society as the artist whose name appeared on more than 300 *Saturday Evening Post* covers. The first, which appeared in May 1916 and typified so many others, added a touch of humour to a scene from everyday life. It showed a young boy cheerlessly pushing a baby carriage as two friends, dressed in baseball uniforms, pass by and jeer in boyish delight. Other favourites, and there were many, included a doctor examining a little girl's broken doll, freckle-faced boys carrying

BOOK OF THE YEAR

homemade fishing poles, and a wide-eyed child waiting with bare bottom for an inoculation. For decades Rockwell also produced illustrations for publications of the Boy Scouts of America. On occasion he turned to such serious subjects as racial segregation with a depiction of the murder of three civil rights workers in Mississippi and the image of a small black girl being escorted to school in Little Rock, Ark., by U.S. marshals. But none of Rockwell's pictures, not even those of U.S. presidents, was as popular as the "Four Freedoms," reproduction of which ran into the millions. Rockwell was

CONSTANTINE MANOS—MAGNUM

a careful craftsman with an extraordinary eye for detail (he preferred real people and things as models), but some critics refused to take his artwork seriously. Perhaps mindful of such criticism, Rockwell modestly entitled his autobiography *My Adventures as an Illustrator* (1960). In 1968 and 1972 exhibitions of his works were held in New York City. In 1977 Pres. Gerald Ford presented Rockwell with the Presidential Medal of Freedom.

Rockwell, Willard Frederick, U.S. industrialist (b. March 31, 1888, Boston, Mass.—d. Oct. 16, 1978, Pittsburgh, Pa.), was a financial wizard who became president and chairman of the board of Rockwell International, the giant industrial conglomerate. Rockwell's first important opportunity came when he was named president of Equitable Meter and Manufacturing Co. in 1925. He then set to work expanding the company through mergers and acquisitions, thereby creating Rockwell International. The company name eventually became associated with such diverse industries as power tools, space exploration, textiles, printing, and electronics.

Rodden, Michael ("MIKE") J., Canadian sportsman (b. April 24, 1891, Mattawa, Ont.—d. Jan. 11, 1978, Kingston, Ont.), was an all-around athlete who became the first person to be inducted into both the Hockey Hall of Fame (1962) and the Canadian Football Hall of Fame (1964). As a hockey referee and part-time talent scout, Rodden officiated at some 2,800 games and recommended over a score of hockey players who later skated in the National Hockey League. His football coaching career was equally impressive; his teams held 27 titles including two Grey Cups. While attending Queen's University at Kingston, Rodden earned 15 letters in football and hockey, a school record that still exists. He also served as a sports editor of the *Toronto Globe* and the *Kingston Whig-Standard*.

Ross Williamson, Hugh, British author (b. Jan. 2, 1901, Ramsey, Hertfordshire, England—d. Jan. 13, 1978, London, England), entered journalism on the *Yorkshire Post* a few years after graduation from London University. He then served as editor of *The Bookman* (1930–34) and wrote novels and books on English history, including biographies of parliamentarian John Hampden and Sir Walter Raleigh. He also composed historical plays for small theatres on such figures as Piers Gaveston, Queen Elizabeth I, and W. E. Gladstone and turned J. M. Barrie's *Little Minister* into a musical which was performed at the London Hippodrome. The son of a Congregational minister, he became an Anglo-Catholic and was ordained in the Church of England in 1943, but in 1955 he was received into the Roman Catholic Church. His autobiography, *The Walled Garden*, appeared in 1956.

Rothermere, Esmond Cecil Harmsworth, 2ND VISCOUNT, British newspaper proprietor (b. May 29, 1898, London, England—d. July 12, 1978, London), inherited the publishing empire created by his uncle, Lord Northcliffe, but did not control it with the same autocratic determination. In 1919 Rothermere was elected to Parliament as a Unionist and thus became the youngest member of the House, but he retired ten years later to look after his business interests. He was chairman of the Newspaper Proprietors Association from 1932 to 1961. In 1960 the *News Chronicle* and *Star* were absorbed into his *Daily Mail* and *Evening News*, respectively. In 1971, because of criticism aimed at his economic policies, he resigned as chairman of Associated Newspapers and Harmsworth Publications in favour of his son, Hon. Vere Harmsworth, and became president.

Rubayyi, Salem Ali, South Yemeni politician (b. 1935, al-Mahal, Arabian Peninsula—d. June 26, 1978, Aden, People's Democratic Republic of Yemen), was chairman of the Presidential Council (1969–78) and supreme commander of the armed forces when he was overthrown by Abd-al Fattah Ismail, the politically powerful general secretary of the United Political Organization. When Rubayyi tried to arrest Ismail for presumed complicity in the assassination of Ahmad al-Ghashmi, leader of the neighbouring Yemen Arab Republic, Ismail ordered his Cuban-trained militia to storm the presidential palace. Rubayyi was captured, put on trial, then executed by firing squad.

Rubicam, Raymond, U.S. advertising executive (b. June 16, 1892, Brooklyn, N.Y.—d. May 8, 1978, Scottsdale, Ariz.), was the co-founder (1923), chief executive officer and president (1927–44), and chairman (1944) of Young & Rubicam Inc., one of the largest advertising agencies in the U.S. Rubicam created such ingenious and original slogans that some of them were still in use at the time of his death. In 1932 he hired pollster George Gallup and introduced marketing research, which became a vital tool for advertising agencies around the world. Rubicam was named to the Hall of Fame of the American Advertising Federation in 1974, 30 years after taking early retirement.

Ruck, Berta (AMY ROBERTA OLIVER), British novelist (b. Aug. 2, 1878, India—d. Aug. 11, 1978, Aberdovey, Wales), was a voluminous writer of warm-hearted fiction for young girls. She studied art in Paris and at the Slade School in London and married novelist Oliver Onions (who adopted the name George Oliver). Ruck also wrote magazine fiction for *Home Chat* and other journals, and after the success of *His Official Fiancée*, both as a serial and as a book, she published such charming reminiscences as *A Storyteller Tells the Truth* (1935) and *A Trickle of Welsh Blood* (1967).

Rueff, Jacques Léon, French economist (b. Aug. 23, 1896, Paris, France—d. April 23, 1978, Paris), was the architect of France's 1958 monetary reform program that called for a drastic reduction in borrowing, the removal of nearly all quota restrictions on international trade, and the creation of a new franc valued at 100 old francs. As financial counselor to Charles de Gaulle, Rueff was given the formidable task of finding a cure for chronic inflation

and the decline in value of the franc. His system prepared the road for stability during the 1960s after 50 years of financial difficulties. A graduate of the École Polytechnique, he served from 1930 to 1936 at the French embassy in London. After World War II he was a judge (1952–62) at the Court of Justice of the European Communities and later vice-president of government committees on economic reform and expansion. In 1964 he was elected to the Académie Française; he was the first economist ever to hold this distinction. He also published several books on economic theory, notably *L'Ordre social* (1945).

Sainteny, Jean, French politician (b. May 29, 1907, Le Vésinet, France—d. Feb. 25, 1978, Paris, France), played a central role as intermediary between the U.S. and the North Vietnamese during the Paris peace talks on Vietnam (1968–73). He was able to assume this post because of the exceptional relationship he established with the Vietnamese leaders as French representative in Indochina from 1945 and as delegate to North Vietnam after the French withdrawal in 1954. Returning to France in 1959, Sainteny served as a Gaullist deputy (1962), minister for veterans' affairs (1962–66), and later undertook government missions to China.

Scott, Paul Mark, British novelist (b. March 25, 1920, London, England—d. March 1, 1978, London), established his reputation as a shrewd political and social analyst with four novels that portrayed the turmoil and uncertainty that marked the end of British rule in India. The novels, eventually published in one volume under the title *The Raj Quartet* (1976), bore the titles *The Jewel in the Crown* (1966), *The Day of the Scorpion* (1968), *The Towers of Silence* (1971), and *A Division of the Spoils* (1975). Scott first saw India as an army officer in World War II, returned to England to enter publishing, became director of the literary agents David Higham Associates (1950–60), and then devoted himself to writing. Several of his books were dramatized for television and radio, including his first novel, *Johnnie Sahib* (1952), and *The Alien Sky* (1953). *Staying On*, another story about India, won him the 1977 Booker Prize for fiction.

Secker, Martin, British publisher (b. April 6, 1882, London, England—d. April 6, 1972, Iver, Buckinghamshire, England), whose firm published a select list of distinguished writers including Compton MacKenzie, Arthur Ransome, Hugh Walpole, and D. H. Lawrence. He entered publishing in 1908, founded his own firm in 1910, and in only four years built a reputable list of authors. Following financial difficulties his firm was reconstructed as Secker and Warburg in 1935. Secker left in 1937, became head of the Richards Press, and later founded the Unicorn Press.

Seilern, Count Antoine, Anglo-Austrian art collector (b. Sept. 17, 1901, Frensham Place, Farnham, England—d. July 6, 1978, London, England), amassed a collection of Old Masters that became the envy of many curators of public galleries. The collection was grouped thematically, primarily containing paintings and drawings by Flemish and Italian artists in some way connected with Rubens; at its centre were 33 paintings by Rubens himself. Seilern, the son of Austrian parents, studied art history in Vienna before settling in England in 1938. A very private man, he made generous gifts to the National Gallery and British Museum and would allow students (but never dealers) to visit the collection in his London home.

Selwyn-Lloyd, John Selwyn Brooke Lloyd, BARON, British politician (b. July 28, 1904, Liverpool, England—d. May 17, 1978, Preston Crowmarsh, England), earned opprobrium as foreign secretary for his part in the Suez Canal fiasco of 1956 but was widely admired as speaker of the House of Commons (1971–76). He was Conservative member of Parliament for the Wirral division of Cheshire from 1945 to 1970 before becoming speaker. Educated at Magdalene College, Cambridge, he was called to the bar by Gray's Inn in 1930 and practiced on the Northern Circuit, becoming a king's counsel in 1947. He entered Parliament after World War II and in 1951 became minister of state in the Foreign Office. Selwyn-Lloyd joined the Cabinet as minister of defense in April 1955. He was promoted to foreign secretary in December 1955 and was made chancellor of the Exchequer in July 1960. He introduced austerity measures, including a "pay pause," in July 1961 to resolve a balance of payments crisis and saw the National Economic Development Council launched. After being suddenly dismissed in July 1962, he rejoined the Cabinet in 1963 as lord privy seal and leader of the House of Commons, retaining those positions till the Conservative government's defeat in 1964. He retired as speaker in 1976 and was made a life peer.

Sena, Jorge de, Portuguese writer (b. Nov. 2, 1919, Lisbon, Portugal—d. June 4, 1978, Santa Barbara, Calif.), was generally regarded as Portugal's foremost contemporary poet. His best-known works include *As Evidencias* (1955), *Fidelidade* (1958), *Metamorfoses* (1963), *Arte de Musica* (1968), and *Exorcismos* (1972). Sena was a recognized authority on Luis Vaz de Camões, a 16th-century poet whose literary contributions he explored in such works as *A estrutura de "Os Lusíadas."* He was also noted for such novels as *Andanças do Demónio* and *O Grão-Capitães* and for his plays *Antonio Rei* and *O Indesejado.*

Sena served as an engineer in the Portuguese Ministry of Public Works before leaving the country (1959) to teach Portuguese literature in Brazil at the universities of Assiz and Arquarara. In 1965 he took up residence in the U.S. and taught (1965–70) at the University of Wisconsin and from 1970 at the University of California at Santa Barbara, where he headed the department of Spanish and comparative literature. In 1977 Sena received the Etna-Taormina poetry prize.

Shaw, Robert, British actor (b. Aug. 9, 1927, Lancashire, England—d. Aug. 27, 1978, near Tourmakeady, Ireland), portrayed a cold-blooded assassin in *From Russia with Love* and an Israeli agent in *Black Sunday,* but was probably best remembered as the fearless shark hunter in *Jaws.* Shaw also played leading roles in such films as *The Sting, A Man for All Seasons,* and *The Deep,* but he hoped to be remembered for his writings. Although he penned four books and three plays, his only real success was *The Man in the Glass Booth,* a play that dramatically recounted the trial of Nazi Adolf Eichmann. At the time of his death Shaw was completing another book and recuperating from an ankle sprain he suffered on the set of his last film, *Avalanche Express.*

Siegbahn, Karl Manne Georg, Swedish physicist (b. Dec. 3, 1886, Örebro, Sweden—d. Sept. 26, 1978, Stockholm, Sweden), won (1924) the Nobel Prize for Physics for his discoveries and investigations in X-ray spectroscopy. In 1916 Siegbahn discovered a new group of spectral lines, the M-series. He also developed equipment and techniques that enabled him to determine accurately the wavelengths of X-rays. While he was teaching physics at Uppsala University, he and his associates proved (1924) that X-rays are refracted when they pass through prisms, just as light is. In 1937 he was appointed director of the newly created Nobel Institute of Physics in Stockholm and also became professor of physics at the University of Stockholm. From 1939 to 1962 Siegbahn served as a member of the International Committee on Weights and Measures.

Silone, Ignazio (Secondo Tranquilli), Italian writer (b. May 1, 1900, Pescina dei Marsi, Italy—d. Aug. 21, 1978, Geneva, Switz.), produced powerful antiFascist novels that dramatized the exploitation and forcible suppression of peasants and called for social reform. In 1917 Silone began to work with Socialist groups and in 1921 helped found the Italian Communist Party. He also edited the party's newspaper in Trieste, *Il Lavoratore* ("The Worker") before the Fascists drove him into exile. He settled in Switzerland in 1930, became disillusioned with Communism, left the party, and began a writing career under a pseudonym to protect his family

from reprisals. His first novel, *Fontamara* (1930), created an international sensation and was translated into 14 languages. Other early works that met success were *Pane e Vino* (1937; Eng. trans., *Bread and Wine,* 1937) and *Il seme sotto la neve* (1940; *The Seed Beneath the Snow,* 1942). After World War II Silone returned to Italy. Later works include *Uscita di sicurezza* (1965; *Emergency Exit,* 1968), which describes his shifts from Socialism to Communism to Christianity; and a play, *L'avventura d'un povero cristiano* (1968; *The Story of a Humble Christian,* 1970), which depicts the life of Celestine V, a 13th-century pope.

Silvester, Victor Marlborough, British bandleader (b. Feb. 25, 1900, Middlesex, England—d. Aug. 14, 1978, Le Lavandou, France), sold more than 50 million records and enhanced the standards of formal ballroom dancing for over 40 years with his Strict Tempo Dance Orchestra. After World War I Silvester turned to professional ballroom dancing and won the 1922 world championship with Phyllis Clarke. After opening his first dancing school with his wife, Dorothy, he founded (1935) a dance orchestra, which made its first broadcast in 1937. His reputation and authority grew with the British Broadcasting Corporation's "Dancing Club" in the 1940s and later with "Come Dancing" on television. His books include *Modern Ballroom Dancing* (1932; 57th ed., 1974).

Smith, W. Eugene, U.S. photojournalist (b. Dec. 30, 1918, Wichita, Kan.—d. Oct. 15, 1978, Tucson, Ariz.), created classic pictorial essays that were praised for both intensity and photographic beauty. After covering World War II for *Life* magazine, he returned to the U.S. with large parts of his face shattered by shellfire. During a two-year convalescence, he produced one of his best-known photos, "The Walk to Paradise Garden," which depicts two of his children strolling out of the woods into a sunlit clearing. Photo essays that earned him widespread acclaim include "Spanish Village" (1951), "Nurse Midwife" (1951), and,

H. CARTIER-BRESSON—MAGNUM

more recently, "Minamata: Life Sacred and Profane," a study of grotesquely disfigured Japanese children who lived in a fishing village downstream from a chemical plant. In 1977 Smith joined the journalism and art faculty at the University of Arizona.

Smolenski, Marian Jozef, Polish Army officer (b. c. 1895—d. Jan. 19, 1978, London, England), during World War II served in London in the Free Polish forces under Gen. Wladyslaw Sikorski's Polish government-in-exile. As the head of the special division in charge of liaison with the underground Polish Home Forces, he cooperated with the British

intelligence service by passing on information received from Poland. Earlier he served in Jozef Pilsudski's legions (1919–21), commanded Poland's National Cavalry School, and became head of military intelligence. Following the war, General Smolenski served as head of the Pilsudski Institute in London.

Sobukwe, Robert Mangaliso, South African black nationalist (b. Dec. 5, 1924, Graaff-Reinet, Cape Province, South Africa—d. Feb. 27, 1978, Kimberley, Cape Province), was the nonviolent founder and leader of the Pan-Africanist Congress (PAC), a black-consciousness organization which sought to eliminate apartheid in South Africa. At Fort Hare University he became secretary of the African National Congress (ANC) youth league and later taught at Witwatersrand University and edited *The Africanist.* In 1958 Sobukwe left the ANC and founded the activist PAC. On March 21, 1960, when he and other blacks protested the restrictive pass laws that controlled their lives, police opened fire and killed more than 60 demonstrators in what became known as the Sharpeville massacre. Sobukwe was arrested, charged with incitement to riot, and sentenced to three years in prison. When his prison term ended, authorities enacted a special law that permitted his continued detention on Robben Island for six more years. In 1969 he was sent to Kimberley where he remained under renewed banning orders, and he was denied the right to emigrate to the U.S. where he was offered teaching posts. From 1975 Sobukwe practiced as a qualified attorney.

Spencer, Terence John Bew, British Shakespearean scholar (b. May 21, 1915, Harrow, England—d. March 3, 1978, Birmingham, England), became professor of English language and literature at the University of Birmingham in 1958 and director of the Shakespeare Institute at Stratford-upon-Avon in 1961. In 1964 he became general editor of the New Penguin Shakespeare and the Penguin Shakespeare Library and in 1968 a governor of the Royal Shakespeare Theatre. He was also a member of the board of management of the National Theatre (1968–75). His writings include *Fair Greece, Sad Relic: Literary Philhellenism from Shakespeare to Byron* (1954), *The Tyranny of Shakespeare* (1959), and *Shakespeare: The Roman Plays* (1963).

Steinberg, William (Hans Wilhelm), German-born conductor (b. Aug. 1, 1899, Cologne, Germany—d. May 16, 1978, New York, N.Y.), transformed the languid Pittsburgh Symphony into one of the most reputable ensembles in the U.S., as the disciplined conductor of the orchestra from 1952 to 1972. His receipt in 1968 of an unlimited contract as music director was unprecedented. Earlier, Steinberg served as the music director of the Frankfurt Opera (1929–33) before traveling (1938) to the U.S. where he became the assistant to Arturo Toscanini with the NBC Symphony. In addition to conducting the Pittsburgh Symphony, Steinberg concurrently served as music director of the London Philharmonic (1958–60) and later of the Boston Symphony (1969–72). He retired as music director of the Pittsburgh Symphony in 1976 because of poor health.

Stone, Edward Durell, U.S. architect (b. March 9, 1902, Fayetteville, Ark.—d. Aug. 6, 1978, New York, N.Y.), designed (1937) with Philip Goodwin the Museum of Modern Art in New York City, the first major U.S. public building in the International Style. After studying at Harvard University and the Massachusetts Institute of Technology, Stone toured Europe where he encountered new architectural trends. He won praise for the lavish Art-Deco interiors he designed (1932) for New York City's Radio City Music Hall. Stone had growing doubts about the enduring appeal of the International Style with its stark glass and aluminum structures. After designing (1946) the El Panama Hotel in Panama City, Stone turned to such traditional

HENRI DAUMAN—MAGNUM

materials as concrete, stone, and marble and claimed his first architectural triumph, the U.S. embassy in New Delhi (1954). The temple-like structure was perched on a raised platform fronted by a lavish reflecting pool and enclosed by a lacy concrete grill, one of his trademarks. Although critics described his work as overly romantic, Stone received a steady flow of commissions, including the Nuclear Research Center (1966) near Islamabad, Pakistan, and the Huntington Hartford Gallery of Modern Art (1959; now the New York Cultural Center) in New York City. In Washington, D.C., his works include the National Geographic Society headquarters (1961) and the John F. Kennedy Center for the Performing Arts (1964). After the publication of his autobiography, *The Evolution of an Architect* (1962), Stone completed designs (1964 and 1969) for the 50-story General Motors tower in New York City and the 80-story Standard Oil Building in Chicago.

Strang, William Strang, 1ST BARON, British civil servant (b. Jan. 2, 1893, Rainham, Essex, England—d. May 27, 1978, Newcastle upon Tyne, England), served for 34 years in the British Foreign Office, which he headed as permanent undersecretary of state from 1949 to 1953. After graduating from University College, London, and serving World War I, he joined (1919) the Foreign Office. He accompanied Prime Minister Neville Chamberlain on his fateful 1938 visit to Hitler that brought false hope for "peace in our time." Strang represented (1943) Britain on the European Advisory Commission which charted Germany's terms of surrender and prepared for postwar occupation of the country. After attending the Potsdam Conference in 1945, he was successively appointed political adviser to the British commander in Germany and head of the German section of the Foreign Office. Strang was knighted in 1943 and ennobled in 1954. He published *The Foreign Office* (1955), a workaday account, and memoirs entitled *Home and Abroad* (1956).

Student, Kurt, German Army officer (b. 1890—d. July 1, 1978, Lemgo, West Germany), commanded the paratroop attacks in Norway, the Low Countries, and Crete, which were key elements in Germany's blitzkrieg at the start of World War II. Plans for further paratroop landings were shelved by Hitler after heavy losses in the Cretan operation. Student, who fought in World War I as a pilot, developed his airborne assault tactics as com-

mander of the 7th Flying Division before his appointment as general and commander in chief of airborne forces in World War II. The conduct of his troops in Crete led to his conviction and sentencing to five years' imprisonment by the International Military Tribunal at Nürnberg in 1946, but the sentence was not confirmed.

Sutcliffe, Herbert, English cricketer (b. Nov. 24, 1894, Pudsey, Yorkshire, England—d. Jan. 21, 1978, Crosshills, Yorkshire), was a great England and Yorkshire batsman, especially famous for his first-wicket stands with Jack Hobbs for England and with Percy Holmes of Yorkshire. Sutcliffe first played for his county in 1919 and for England in 1924, when he partnered Hobbs in matches against South Africa. The two scored 26 three-figure partnerships for England, 15 of them against Australia. He and Holmes were an even more powerful combination, turning in 74 three-figure performances (69 of them for Yorkshire), including a record-breaking 555 against Essex in 1932. Sutcliffe headed the batting averages in 1928, 1931, and 1932 with a personal best total of 3,336 runs.

Swanson, Howard, U.S. composer (b. Aug. 18, 1907, Atlanta, Ga.—d. Nov. 12, 1978, New York, N.Y.), attracted national attention when his Short Symphony was performed (1952) by the New York Philharmonic Orchestra under the baton of maestro Dimitri Mitropoulos. Swanson attended (1937) the Cleveland Institute of Music and won a Rosenwald fellowship for studies in Paris, where he remained until 1940. Many of his songs were included in the repertoire of contralto Marian Anderson, and "Night Song," with words by poet Langston Hughes, was sung by Leontyne Price during a 1978 performance at the White House. Swanson's orchestra and piano scores included such favourites as *The Valley, Ghosts in Love,* and *In Time of Silver Rain.*

Trefflich, Henry Herbert Frederick, German-born animal importer (b. Jan. 9, 1908, Hamburg, Germany—d. July 7, 1978, Bound Brook, N.J.), was the prankish proprietor (1928–73) of the largest wild animal dealership in the U.S. He admitted sending 60 monkeys scampering around New York City as advertising agents when business was slow. Trefflich, who was known as the "Monkey King of America," not only provided the chimp Cheetah for Tarzan movies but also supplied the monkeys used for polio research during World War II and for the experiments that led to the discovery of the Rh (rhesus) factor in blood. Profits from his menagerie of elephants, snakes, panthers, and lizards, which were principally sold to zoos and circuses, amounted to as much as $1 million a year.

Tsiranana, Philibert, Malagasy politician (b. Oct. 18, 1910, Anahidrano, Madagascar—d. April 16, 1978, Antananarivo, Madagascar), was president (1959–72) of the Malagasy Republic (renamed Democratic Republic of Madagascar in 1975) who pursued policies of anti-Communism and continued cooperation with the former colonial power, France, and other Western states. Tsiranana, who was trained as a teacher, founded the Madagascar Social Democratic Party in 1956 and headed the provisional government after France granted partial autonomy to Madagascar in 1958. He became the country's first elected president in May 1959, and in 1960 proclaimed the island's full independence from French colonial rule. Tsiranana was overwhelmingly re-elected in 1965 and again in January 1972, but after worker and student riots in May 1972 he handed over power to a military government and finally stepped down in October. In 1975 he was tried and acquitted of responsibility for the assassination of Col. Richard Ratsimandrava, who headed the government briefly in February of that year.

Tunney, Gene (JAMES JOSEPH TUNNEY), U.S. boxer (b. May 25, 1898, New York, N.Y.—d. Nov. 7, 1978, Greenwich, Conn.), became one of the "golden boys" of sports during the 1920s when he captured the world heavyweight boxing title from Jack Dempsey, the "Manassa Mauler," on Sept. 23,

1926. Tunney, who fought as a middleweight before World War I, won the light-heavyweight championship of the American Expeditionary Force in France shortly after the war ended. After winning (1922) the U.S. light-heavyweight championship, he was defeated by Harry Greb—Tunney's only loss in 68 career bouts. The next year he regained the crown from Greb and in 1924 started fighting as a heavyweight. When he challenged Dempsey in 1926, all bets were on the champion, but Tunney dethroned Dempsey. In the inevitable rematch one year later, before a record crowd at Soldier Field in Chicago, Dempsey floored Tunney in the seventh round but failed to move to a neutral corner. The referee had no choice but to delay the count until Dempsey retreated. Tunney staggered to his feet at the count of nine, floored Dempsey in the eighth round, and won a ten-round decision. That night's "long count" became one of the most enduring controversies in sports history. On July 26, 1928, Tunney knocked out Tom Heeney and retired as undefeated champion. He then married and settled into a business career; in the 1960s he was director of several corporations.

Turville-Petre, (Edward Oswald) Gabriel, British Old Norse scholar (b. March 25, 1908, Bosworth Hall, near Rugby, England—d. Feb. 17, 1978, Oxford, England), was Vigfusson reader (1941–53) and professor (1953–75) in ancient Icelandic literature and antiquities at the University of Oxford. Turville-Petre was decorated by the president of Iceland in 1956 and received an honorary doctorate in 1961 from the University of Iceland where he lectured from 1936 to 1938. His publications include *Origins of Icelandic Literature* (1953), *Myth and Religion of the North* (1964), and *Scaldic Poetry* (1976). He also contributed to the *Encyclopaedia Britannica.*

Tweedsmuir of Belhelvie, Priscilla Jean Fortescue Buchan, BARONESS, British politician (b. Jan. 25, 1915, Potterton, Aberdeenshire, Scotland—d. March 11, 1978, Balmedie, Aberdeenshire), was an influential chairman of the European Communities Committee of the House of Lords (1974–77) who helped negotiate a pact that curtailed the dispute between Britain and Iceland over fishing rights. A Conservative member of Parliament for South Aberdeen (1946–66), she was made a life peeress in 1970 and appointed minister of state of the Scottish Office. Tweedsmuir, who strongly advocated closer ties between Britain and Europe, served as a British delegate to the Council of Europe from 1950 to 1953. Her first husband, Sir Arthur Lindsay Grant, was killed (1944) in World War II. In 1948 she married the 2nd Baron Tweedsmuir, son of the author John Buchan.

Unsworth, Geoffrey, British film cameraman (b. 1915, London, England—d. Oct. 29, 1978, France), contributed experience and craftsmanship to such outstanding motion pictures as *Cabaret, Beckett,* and *A Bridge Too Far.* His career began at the Gaumont British Studios. During the 1930s he worked with Alexander Korda at Technicolor Studios and after World War II he joined the Rank Organisation. After the decline of the British film industry, he achieved international recognition for his work on Stanley Kubrick's *2001: A Space Odyssey* and *Murder on the Orient Express.* He was awarded the OBE in 1976.

Volkert, George Rudolph, British aircraft designer (b. July 4, 1891—d. May 16, 1978, Fuengirola, Spain), was chief designer (1912–48) at Handley Page, Ltd., which pioneered the construction of British aircraft. He developed the front-slotted aircraft wing and the multislotted rear flaps, which were later vital for jet-propelled takeoffs. He also designed the Halifax bomber, 6,000 of which were built during World War II. In retirement Volkert won an international reputation as an orchid grower and introduced automatic devices for humidifying, watering, and heating the flowers.

Wallenda, Karl, German-born aerialist (b. 1905, Magdeburg, Germany—d. March 22, 1978, San Juan, P.R.), was a master of the high wire who held crowds in suspense with his breathtaking aerial

WIDE WORLD

acrobatics. Wallenda founded the Great Wallendas, noted throughout Europe for their four-man pyramid and later for the unequaled three-tier seven-man pyramid. The Wallendas performed with Ringling Bros. and Barnum & Bailey Circus from 1928 to 1946. Tragedy was not unknown to the troupe, which performed without the aid of a net. In 1962 Wallenda's son-in-law Richard Faughnan and nephew Dieter Schepp were killed and an adopted son Mario was paralyzed from the waist down when the pyramid collapsed. Wallenda's sister-in-law Rietta fell to her death in 1963, and his son-in-law Richard ("Chico") Guzman was killed in 1972 after touching a live wire in the rigging. Wallenda, who at age 73 attempted a walk between two hotels in Puerto Rico, fell to his death when winds exceeded 30 mph.

Warner, Jack Leonard, U.S. film producer (b. Aug. 2, 1892, London, Ont.—d. Sept. 9, 1978, Los Angeles, Calif.), revolutionized the motion picture industry when he and his brother Harry brought sound to the screen. Warner presented (1927) Al Jolson in *The Jazz Singer,* the first talking feature-length film, four years after founding Warner Brothers Pictures, Inc. The film so delighted movie buffs that the firm was rescued from near bankruptcy and was able to produce (1928) *Lights of New York,* the first full-length all-talking picture, and *On with the Show* (1929), the first all-talking colour film. As one of the top moneymaking studios, Warner Bros. continued to enrapture audiences with gangster movies and musicals in the 1930s and 1940s and later with such box-office hits as *My Fair Lady* (1964) and *The Great Race* (1965). In 1967 Warner Bros. merged with Seven Arts, a distributor of films to television.

Warner, Sylvia Townsend, British writer (b. Dec. 6, 1893, Harrow, England—d. May 1, 1978, Maiden Newton, Dorset, England), established her reputation with her first novel, *Lolly Willowes* (1926), which recounted the fate of a spinster at the mercy of her family. After publishing her second novel, *Mr. Fortune's Maggot* (1927), she wrote short stories for *The New Yorker* magazine and continued to charm readers with *The Corner that Held Them* (1948), set in medieval England, and *Kingdoms of Elfin* (short stories, 1977). *The Espalier* (1925) was her first book of poems, and *Whether a Dove or Seagull* (1934) was a collaborative effort with Valentine Ackland,

her lifelong companion. Warner, who confessed that her first love was music, was one of the editors of a ten-volume study entitled *Tudor Church Music.* She also published a biography of one of her admirers, the English novelist T. H. White, in 1967.

Whitehead, Edward, British executive (b. May 20, 1908, Aldershot, England—d. April 16, 1978, Petersfield, England), became well known as the bearded Commander Whitehead whose urbane yet forceful presence promoted Schweppes tonic water in U.S. advertising campaigns. Before becoming president of Schweppes (U.S.A.) Ltd. in 1953, he served in the Royal Navy Volunteer Reserve in World War II and at the Treasury (1947–50).

Willey, Basil, British scholar (b. July 25, 1897—d. Sept. 3, 1978, Cambridge, England), was a literary historian and critic who cleverly intertwined the literary and philosophical currents of the 17th and 18th centuries in such works as *The Seventeenth Century Background* (1934) and *The Eighteenth Century Background* (1940). A scholar of Peterhouse, University of Cambridge, he lectured in English at Cambridge and in 1935 was elected a fellow of Pembroke College. In 1946 he became King Edward VII professor of English literature at Cambridge. Willey was literary adviser to the committee of translators of The New English Bible and was a contributor and consultant to *Encyclopædia Britannica.* He was also the author of *Nineteenth Century Studies* (1949; second volume, 1956), *Christianity, Past and Present* (1952), *The English Moralists* (1964), and two autobiographies, *Spots of Time, 1897–1920* (1965) and *Cambridge and Other Memories, 1920–1953* (1969).

Williams-Ellis, Sir (Bertram) Clough, British architect and conservationist (b. May 28, 1883—d. April 8, 1978), was the creator of the village of Portmeirion, North Wales, one of the most entertaining architectural "follies" of all time. Although virtually untrained, Williams-Ellis obtained commissions after World War I for a variety of buildings. He excelled in designs that sometimes subordinated or even sacrificed architectural forms to theatrical panorama and ornamentation. Portmeirion, an Italianate tourist village on the Welsh coast, combined charm, whimsy, and frivolity in an idiosyncratic expression of its creator's personality. An ardent conservationist, Williams-Ellis wrote several books and was active on many boards and commissions. He was knighted in 1972.

Wills, Chill (Theodore), U.S. actor (b. July 18, 1902, Seagoville, Texas—d. Dec. 15, 1978, Encino, Calif.), roamed the range, shot up the town, killed villains in black hats, and brought law and order to the West as a gravelly voiced cowboy in hundreds of Westerns and other films. Wills, who became a star as the wry voice of Francis the talking mule in seven motion pictures, became so adept in the role that after the third or fourth film he was able to discard the script in places and improvise. Besides the "Francis" movies, Wills had featured roles in *The Westerner, The Sundowners, From Hell to Texas, Boom Town, Giant,* and the musicals *Meet Me in St. Louis* and *The Harvey Girls.*

Wilson, Michael, U.S. screenwriter (b. July 1, 1914, McAlester, Okla.—d. April 9, 1978, Beverly Hills, Calif.), wrote the scenarios for such motion-picture box-office hits as *Five Fingers* (1952), *The Bridge on the River Kwai* (1957), *The Sandpiper* (1965), and *Planet of the Apes* (1967). In 1952 Wilson shared the Academy Award for the script of *A Place in the Sun,* based on Theodore Dreiser's novel *An American Tragedy.* The following decade was one of great turmoil during which the careers of Wilson and others were disrupted by investigations of the House Committee on Un-American Activities and demands by the Academy of Motion Picture Arts and Sciences that they formally clear themselves of all charges of Communist affiliation. His last screenplay was *Che!* in 1969.

Winston, Harry, U.S. jewel merchant (b. March 1, 1896, New York, N.Y.—d. Dec. 8, 1978, New York), was proprietor of possibly the world's larg-

est independent gem concern and a collector of some of the world's most notable stones. In 1958 he provided the centrepiece of the national jewelry collection when he donated the famed 44.5-carat Hope diamond to the Smithsonian Institution's Hall of Gems and Minerals. Winston nonchalantly sent the sapphire-blue stone by registered mail, explaining, "If you can't trust the U.S. mails, who can you trust?" Winston, characterized as a maverick jeweler, also expertly acquired estate jewelry and at various times owned the Jonker diamond, the Vargas diamond, the Star of the East, and Catherine the Great's sapphire.

Woodhouse, Sir Charles Henry Lawrence, British naval officer (b. July 9, 1893—d. Sept. 23, 1978, Warlingham, Surrey, England), was commander of the light cruiser HMS "Ajax," one of three British cruisers that in December 1939 crippled the German pocket battleship and commerce raider "Graf Spee." The badly damaged ship was forced into port at Montevideo, Uruguay, and four days later was scuttled. During World War I Woodhouse saw action at the battles of the Falklands and Jutland and was promoted to captain in 1934. In 1940 he served in the Admiralty and, after commanding (1943) a battleship at Salerno, Italy, became a rear admiral and director (1944–46) of naval ordnance. He then served with the Pacific Fleet and in 1948 was made commander in chief, East Indies. Woodhouse was knighted in 1949 and retired one year later with the rank of admiral.

Woolley, Frank Edward, English cricketer (b. May 27, 1887, Kent, England—d. Oct. 17, 1978, Chester, Nova Scotia), was one of the greatest all-round cricketers of all time, remembered especially for the fluent grace of his batting. His impressive record in first-class cricket included an aggregate of 58,969 runs, 145 centuries, over 2,000 wickets, and more catches (1,007) than any other cricketer. In each of four successive seasons he scored 2,000 runs and took 100 wickets. During his unusually long career (1906–38), he played for County Kent, and in 67 test matches he scored 3,283 runs for England. In retirement he coached at King's School, Canterbury.

Wrathall, John, Rhodesian politician (b. Aug. 28, 1913, Lancaster, England—d. Aug. 31, 1978, Salisbury, Rhodesia), was appointed president of Rhodesia on Jan. 14, 1976. A chartered accountant who went to Rhodesia in 1936, he worked as a civil servant and accountant before entering politics in 1954 as a member of the United Rhodesia Party. In 1962 he helped found the Rhodesian Front Party and two years later was appointed minister of finance. In this capacity Wrathall was instrumental in protecting the country's economy by devising ways to circumvent UN economic sanctions against Rhodesia. He signed the country's declaration of independence in 1965 and in 1966 became Ian Smith's deputy prime minister.

Wriston, Henry Merritt, U.S. educator (b. July 4, 1889, Laramie, Wyo.—d. March 8, 1978, New York, N.Y.), was the president of Brown University (1937–55) in Providence, R.I., and a firm believer that the essence of education is an "individual search for something significant." To give substance to his vision he hired younger teachers, established new courses, modified old programs, and lessened classroom requirements, hoping thereby to arouse greater student interest in discussing and formulating ideas. He also helped reorganize (1954) the U.S. Foreign Service, and in 1960 was named chairman of the Presidential Commission on National Goals by Pres. Dwight D. Eisenhower. The panel submitted a detailed report suggesting U.S. objectives in economics, government, foreign policy, and the arts and sciences. Before joining Brown University, Wriston taught for 11 years at Wesleyan University, Middletown, Conn., his alma mater, and served as president of Lawrence College in Appleton, Wis.

TERRORISM— WEAPON OF THE WEAK

by Paul Wilkinson

The cliché that "one man's terrorist is another man's freedom fighter" is dangerously misleading; it tends to perpetuate the common fallacy that terrorism is no more than a pejorative for guerrilla warfare.

In fact, terrorism is a very distinctive mode of unconventional warfare. Over the past decade it has been used by a growing number of minorities and factions which either have been too weak to launch a general insurrection or have tried and failed. Terrorism can be briefly defined as the use of threats against life, limb, and property in order to coerce a target government or community into submitting to the terrorists' aims. It has been aptly described as "the weapon of the weak pretending to be strong" and has obvious attractions for desperate and fanatical groups that are unable to win outright political or military victory.

A Distinctive Form of Violence. Characteristic terrorist techniques include bombing, arson, shooting, kidnapping, and hijacking. These methods of intimidation and blackmail are used to gain sensational publicity or to produce a climate of fear and hatred, which the terrorists exploit politically. Thus if terrorism is defined with some precision, it becomes possible to differentiate it from other forms of violence that frequently accompany it. It is a mistake to equate terrorism with guerrilla or partisan warfare in general, although terrorism has played an important auxiliary role in certain major insurgencies since 1945; for example, in Malaya, Indochina, and Rhodesia. Isolated acts of assassination and tyrannicide should also be distinguished from terrorism proper. The former may be motivated merely by vengeance or a desire to remove an individual ruler, or they may be part of an attempted coup. Assassinations become terrorism only when

Paul Wilkinson has been appointed to the new chair of international relations at the University of Aberdeen. His books include Political Terrorism (1974) and Terrorism and the Liberal State (1977).

they are an element in a sustained campaign of coercive intimidation.

All terrorists seek primarily to exploit the psychology of fear. Nevertheless, thousands have been killed or injured in terrorist attacks, and when such attacks occur in societies that are normally peaceable they appear especially heinous. Terrorists often claim to select their victims with the greatest care, but the victim cannot be warned in advance that he is in danger or he would act to save himself. It is obvious, moreover, that the use of such typical terrorist weapons as bombs and submachine guns in modern cities endangers innocent lives. Whatever terrorists say about "warning time" and "selective targets," casualties cannot be predicted with any degree of precision. Nor can one overlook the high probability of error.

In any case, unpredictability is an essential factor in the process of terror. If one knew in advance the identity of the next victim, if there were known measures one could take to avoid harm, then the climate of fear the terrorist wishes to create could not exist. Of course, not all terrorist movements have been equally indiscriminate in their choice of targets. Some have attempted to limit their attacks to specific groups. Others, particularly the more nihilistic and attention-seeking, have deliberately committed mass atrocities in which large numbers of civilians have been killed. Nor is this a new tactic. Such modern nihilistic groups as the Japanese Red Army, which committed the Lod Airport massacre in Israel in May 1972, are actually implementing the doctrines of the anarchist Johannes Most, who was advocating "mass slaughter in public places" over a century ago.

By committing mass atrocities, many terrorists openly defy humanitarian laws of war. The Red Army killers, for example, did not recognize noncombatants or neutrals; women, children, the old, the sick, and foreign nationals lacking the remotest connection with the terrorists' quarrel—all were regarded as expendable for the cause. The degree of cruelty and indiscriminateness evinced varies considerably according to the ideology, personalities, and aims of the terrorist group.

The Debate on Moral Justifiability. Many have condemned specific terrorist outrages, but root-and-branch condemnation of terrorism under any circumstances is rarer. Those who hold to the latter position do so because, in the words of the former British ambassador to Uruguay, Sir Geoffrey Jackson—himself the victim of a terrorist kidnapping—"no injustice, however great, can justify an even greater injustice." Furthermore, whatever terrorists may say, there are always ways of campaigning for change and emancipation that do not involve the murder of the innocent.

However, it is not only the movements themselves and states friendly to their cause that condone terrorism. There is a body of opinion in Western countries that either explicitly or implicitly supports its use under certain circumstances—provided, of course, that the violence is happening to other people and can be hallowed by invoking "national liberation" or "revolutionary struggle." Be-

hind every terrorist campaign are sympathizers, fund raisers, and apologists, innocent or otherwise.

Those who seek to justify terrorism generally use one or more of the following arguments: (1) terrorist morality "transcends" all other norms and values because the realization of the movement's ultimate ends are of such overriding importance that all may be sacrificed for them; (2) terrorism has "worked" in the past and hence it is expedient to use it; (3) the morality of the just vengeance, or "an eye for an eye and a tooth for a tooth"; (4) the morality of the lesser evil, the argument that if one does not use terrorism worse things will happen; and, rather more unusually, (5) some pro-terrorists such as Jean-Paul Sartre and Frantz Fanon have gloried in violence for its own sake as a "cathartic" or "liberative" force. These arguments form one of the major factors complicating efforts toward an effective antiterrorist policy on the part of governments and the international community.

International Terrorist Movements. Terrorism becomes internationalized when it is: (1) directed at foreign countries or targets; (2) concerted by the governments or factions of more than one state; or (3) aimed at influencing foreign publics and poli-

The Lod Airport massacre in Israel, committed by members of the Japanese Red Army in May 1972, involved "mass slaughter in public places" as advocated by 19th-century anarchist Johannes Most.

KEYSTONE

cies. It has recently become fashionable to term all international terrorism "transnational." For purposes of this article, however, this designation will be limited to those terrorists who operate internationally with the express long-term aim of fomenting some kind of global revolution. On this stricter definition, transnational terrorists constitute a small, though exotic, minority of international terrorists.

Even the more fundamental distinction between international and purely internal terrorist movements is easier to draw in theory than to apply in practice. In an era of increasing global interdependence, any severe or protracted campaign of internal terrorism will, at the very least, affect international opinion and the foreign policies and security of neighbouring states. At worst it may bring foreign intervention and an escalation in the conflict.

It is also hard to find a case of exclusively internal terrorism. Even the campaign of the Provisional Irish Republican Army (IRA), though chiefly concentrated within Ulster, has had international repercussions. Terrorists have moved back and forth across the border with the Republic of Ireland. At certain phases of the campaign, terrorists from Ireland have carried out bombings in England. It is true that the Provisionals have generally eschewed the more characteristic methods of international terrorist movements, such as aircraft hijacking and attacks on diplomats, but there have been exceptions. In August 1973 the personal assistant to the senior military attaché at the British embassy in Washington had her left hand blown off by an IRA letter bomb. And in July 1976 the IRA murdered Christopher Ewart-Biggs, British ambassador in Dublin. The Provisionals have also obtained considerable financial aid from sympathizers in North America and have used the European Court of Human Rights as a propaganda platform for attacking Britain.

It is vital to bear in mind the enormous variety of terrorist movements. No single theory can cover them all. Not only are their aims, members, beliefs, and resources extremely diverse, but so are the political contexts of their campaigns. Also, much depends on whether a specific terrorist movement's prime target is a liberal democracy, a colonial regime, a military dictatorship, or a totalitarian state.

A great deal of international terrorism is an overflow from repressive regimes into liberal democracies, whose open frontiers and civic freedoms render them accessible and vulnerable. If the terrorist group remains primarily committed to attacks on representatives of its state of origin, it constitutes no more than a minor hazard or nuisance to the host state, although there is always a danger that some innocent citizens may be harmed. And, of course, the government of the host state will be conscious of its obligations under international law to protect the lives of foreign representatives and citizens who may be at risk. But the crucial point is that the liberal state's involvement in such cases is essentially the result of opportunism and unlucky accident. It is the arena rather than the target.

A far more serious threat to liberal democracies emanates from their own indigenous movements of ethnic separatism or revolutionary dissent, dedicated to the overthrow of the existing order. This threat is amplified by the growing international cooperation among movements and their sponsorship or support by hostile antidemocratic states. Thus a particularly significant and sinister development has been the IRA's cultivation of links with other terrorist movements, facilitating a Europe-wide traffic in terrorist arms, explosives, and attacks. For example, it was no coincidence when, in June 1972, following a meeting between members of the IRA, the Italian Red Brigades, the Popular Front for the Liberation of Palestine (PFLP), and the West German-based Baader-Meinhof gang, there was a bomb attack on the West German embassy in Dublin. The Baader-Meinhof gang claimed responsibility. It would be surprising if these links did not lead to fresh "combined operations." For instance, the Provisional IRA was obviously the prime suspect in the bomb attacks on British army bases in West Germany in August 1978. But those responsible could hardly have managed without the support of German terrorists.

The Current Practitioners. Four major "constituencies" of international terrorism are currently active. First, there are the nationalists and separatists such as the two factions of Euzkadi ta Askatasuna (ETA), which claim to be fighting for Basque autonomy. Other examples are the Front de Liberation du Québec (FLQ), the IRA, and the Puerto Rican Fuerzas Armadas de Liberación Nacional (FALN). Second, and based mainly in liberal democracies, are ideological sects such as the West German Rote Armee Fraktion (RAF; the Baader-Meinhof group), the American Weather Underground, and the Rengo Sekigun, the Japanese United Red Army. A third category comprises exile movements such as the Croatian Ustasha, which has groups in the United States, Australia, West Germany, and many other countries, and the South Moluccans, immigrants in The Netherlands seeking the independence of South Molucca from Indonesia. Finally, there are the transnational gangs which recruit their "mercenaries" from a variety of countries and which have been ready to attack any "imperialist" (i.e., pro-Western) state or adversary group, given the chance. An example was the gang organized by Wadi Haddad and led by the terrorist known as Carlos (Ilich Ramírez Sánchez), which attacked the Organization of Petroleum Exporting

Peace groups in Ulster put up posters condemning IRA terrorism.

Countries conference at Vienna in December 1975 and kidnapped, among others, the Saudi Arabian oil minister.

Some broad political movements are splintered into diverse factions, often with several different ideological tendencies represented in rival terrorist groups. Within the same umbrella movement pro-terror and antiterror factions may coexist uneasily. Often bloody internal conflicts break out between the factions, reflecting power struggles or clashes over strategy and tactics. The histories of the Irish and Balkan movements, for example, are full of internecine struggles. The most important contemporary case is the Palestinian movement. The Palestine Liberation Organization (PLO) was formed in 1964 by an alliance among al-Fatah, the guerrilla fedayeen, and smaller terrorist organizations such as George Habash's neo-Marxist PFLP. The movement has spawned literally scores of terrorist sects, many of them bitterly opposed to the leadership of the PLO chairman, Yasir Arafat. This makes the PLO a particularly unpredictable quantity.

Arafat has managed to garner popular support among the Palestinians in the West Bank and the Gaza Strip. Since the Yom Kippur War of 1973, he has favoured a relatively conventional "government-in-exile" strategy, exerting political and diplomatic pressure by exploiting the official recognition he received from the Arab states at the 1974 Rabat, Morocco, summit and by threatening to use the Arab oil weapon. The official PLO line has been to discourage the use of international terrorism, largely on grounds of expediency. It was beginning to rebound against the PLO's wealthy allies, the Arab oil states; furthermore, by drawing massive Israeli retribution, it was becoming suicidal for the Palestinians themselves. However, in 1976–77 the tenuousness of Arafat's hold over the Palestinian movement became apparent. Groups opposed to any peace that recognized the continuance of Israel, backed by such states as Libya and Iraq (the so-called rejectionist front), openly defied the moderates and carried the terror war into the Arab camp.

The PLO's shift away from reliance on the terrorist weapon did have a marked effect on the pattern of international terrorism. In the period 1970–73 approximately 20% of all international terrorist incidents were directly related to the Palestinian cause. By 1975 the proportion had dropped to 10%. However, Palestinian terrorism is hydra-headed. Arafat has been unable to prevent the activities of terror groups in the Palestinian diaspora, supported by the rejectionist front states. In 1978 a bloody feud between the Abu Nidal group, backed by Iraq, and the official PLO spilled over into attacks on embassies and PLO offices in such diverse locations as London, Paris, Beirut, and Islamabad.

Of the four international terrorist groups that have caused the highest level of indiscriminate casualties in the past decade, three are Palestinian (Black September, the PFLP, and the PFLP-General Command). And in the case of the fourth, the Japanese Red Army, its most brutal attack—the Lod Airport massacre—was made, according to the testimony of the terrorist Okamoto, in order to "inspire Arab fervour" for the Palestinian cause. Thus Palestinian terrorism has played a major role in the escalation of international terrorism. What is more, even if a peace settlement between the Arab states and Israel could be attained, it is highly improbable that international terrorism by the quarreling Palestinian groups would cease. Indeed, it might actually increase in the short term as the "maximalists" tried to wreck any compromise settlement.

Weapon for the Weak. The key point here is that large groups with mass political support are not necessarily the ones that practice international terrorism. Indeed, resort to terrorism is more often than not a symptom of political and military weakness. It is significant that the massive upsurge in international terrorist incidents began in 1967–68 when many Palestinian groups, desperate in the wake of the crushing Arab defeat in the Six-Day War, decided on terrorism as their method of striking back at Israel and its allies.

In many cases, movements which take up international terrorism have been forced to operate abroad by military and police action in their home countries. Conversely, those enjoying mass support and some degree of legitimacy at home generally do not see the need to resort to terror; indeed, because they can hope for power and recognition, they are acutely aware that terrorism might be counterproductive. In other words, a genuine constituency of mass support exerts its own restraints. This is the evolution that many hope will occur in the Palestinian movement, although thus far they have been disappointed. In sum, resort to international terrorism often reflects political weakness, disunity, lack of legitimacy, and uncertainty about its future.

This is still more obvious in the case of tiny ideological sects, such as the Japanese Red Army, which hope to use terrorism as a kind of "propaganda by the deed" to heighten "revolutionary consciousness" and trigger the "people's revolutionary war" of which they dream. Paradoxically, their very use of attacks on the innocent only serves to isolate them further and to alienate potential support.

Despite their minuscule numbers and isolation, however, fanatic revolutionary sects can be a dangerous short-term threat to life and property in liberal states. They are particularly difficult to deal with because their aims and logic are transcendental. For these groups terrorism is a zero-sum conflict: there can be no negotiation, no compromise, over basic aims. When the Italian Red Brigades kidnapped former premier Aldo Moro in March 1978, many well-meaning people harboured the illusion that his captors would respond to appeals to their humanity and reason. But these groups are deadly because they hold life so cheap; many, in the manner of the medieval Assassin sect, are ready to sacrifice themselves.

The ultimate fruitlessness of terrorism by tiny exiled minorities such as the South Moluccans and Croats leads to a similarly intractable situation for the authorities. It is clearly unrealistic for the terrorists to believe that attacks abroad will force Yugoslavia to create a free Croatia or Indonesia a free South Molucca. But this very hopelessness tends to breed a kind of desperate ruthlessness that is comparable psychologically, if not ideologically, to that of the revolutionary sects. These groups are not a significant threat to international order, but they are a bloody hazard to the innocent.

Trends in International Terrorism. International terrorism occurred frequently in Europe, the Middle East, and Latin America in the 19th and early 20th

A hooded member of the Basque terrorist underground movement (ETA) stands guard while journalists are informed of the group's activities.

centuries. In 1958 Raúl Castro adopted the tactic of kidnapping U.S. personnel in Cuba as a weapon of political blackmail. This tactic was copied by the Castroite Venezuelan Armed Forces for National Liberation in the early 1960s. Among its more spectacular ventures, this group kidnapped a Spanish soccer star and hijacked a Venezuelan freighter "to denounce to world opinion the crimes of the Betancourt dictatorship."

However, it was not until 1967–68, when the Palestinian extremist factions adopted a strategy of international terrorism, that the really massive increase in terrorist attacks began. Between 1968 and 1972 they rose by 400%, from roughly 50 incidents per year to over 200. (These figures exclude purely internal attacks and border incursions.) As of 1978, incidents were running at over 250 per year. Almost half were bombings, and more than 50% of these occurred in Europe. During 1975–77 the most frequent forms of terrorism, after bombings, were arson or incendiary attacks, armed assaults, and assassinations; as a group, these had risen at an annual rate of over 40%. Aircraft hijacking, which enjoyed a considerable vogue among terrorists between 1969 and 1972, had declined overall, largely

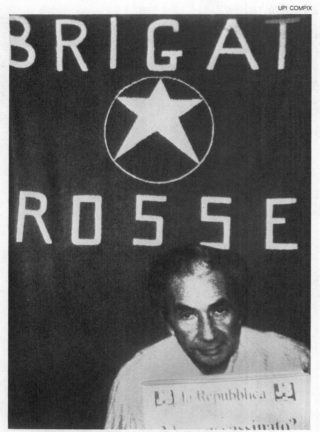

A photo of kidnapped Aldo Moro was produced by his captors, the Italian Red Brigades, in support of their demands.

as a result of stringent security measures. It remained a serious threat, however. The number of hijacks attempted in 1977 (32) was almost double the figure for 1976 (17).

The vulnerability of Western Europe to international terrorist attack—largely because of its accessibility, free media, and the relative openness of its societies—is reflected in the statistics. Over 30% of all international terrorist acts in the past decade have occurred there. Latin America had the next highest share, with over 25%. North America accounted for about 10% of the total. In the late 1970s the Middle East and sub-Saharan Africa were dramatic growth areas for international terrorism, which in both cases was closely interwoven with the wider conflicts in those regions.

The U.S.S.R. and Eastern Europe, by contrast, have an almost zero rating, though it must be remembered that these regimes try to suppress any unwelcome evidence of opposition, and hence there are no really reliable data. Yet it would be wrong to assume that the repressive apparatus of Communist regimes is omnipotent against terrorists, or that the absence of free media necessarily guarantees immunity. The objective of "propaganda by the deed" can still be attained by terrorists if news of their

attacks reaches the foreign media, and the use of terror as a weapon of attrition, leverage, or intercommunal conflict is still feasible, given the volatile relations of many of the national and religious groups within the Soviet empire. News of incidents does occasionally appear in the Soviet press. For instance, it was reported that a Georgian nationalist, Vladimir Shvanya, was sentenced to death in January 1977 after confessing to bomb attacks against government buildings in Tbilisi. Nevertheless, the enormous machinery of surveillance and repressive terror in the U.S.S.R. and the Eastern European states renders any significant antiregime terrorism suicidal if not almost impossible.

Hence the tragic paradox that Western Europe, where basic human rights and political freedom already exist, is the most popular target and arena for terrorists, including both native antidemocratic groups and a substantial overspill from nationalist or revolutionary conflicts elsewhere in the world. Since the early 1970s the situation has been complicated by the emergence of a loose international alliance of terrorists professing aims of "world-revolution" and encompassing both the nihilist gangs of Western Europe (such as the RAF and Red Brigades) and the Palestinian extremists as represented by Wadi Haddad's breakaway PFLP terrorist group. (In fact, it has never been clear whether Haddad was ever really expelled from Habash's PFLP. Some believe the expulsion was simply a move to absolve the PFLP from blame for his terrorist attacks. In April 1978 it was reported that Haddad had died of cancer in an East German hospital. As of late 1978, it was not yet clear what effect the removal of this fanatic leader would have, or who, if anyone, would take over control of his terrorist network. There were also rumours circulating in the Middle East that Haddad was still alive.)

This alliance has given the tiny transnational gangs the considerable practical advantages of support from sponsor states in the forms of cash, firearms, sanctuary, training facilities, forged papers, and the use of the diplomatic pouch to smuggle terrorist weaponry. It has also facilitated another, even more threatening trend: some terrorist movements are now managing to procure various types of advanced weaponry, such as surface-to-air missiles. There is every reason to fear that in due course terrorists will obtain and deploy some kind of nuclear weapon, however primitive, or that they will acquire the necessary firepower to attack a civil nuclear facility and use the threat of sabotaging the plant as a means to blackmail the authorities. It is not generally realized that there have already been numerous bomb attacks by extremists and psychopaths on nuclear facilities in Western Europe and the United States, several of which might easily have triggered a major disaster.

Thus governments and security forces must be prepared to cope with an ever increasing range of terrorist threats to the many prime targets of a vulnerable technological society. Communications systems, computer centres, research laboratories, power stations, oil rigs, pipelines, all are at risk. The danger is that as the authorities make one kind of terrorism, such as aircraft hijacking, more difficult, the terrorists will search out new and potentially more destructive techniques.

Trends in Governmental Response. Worldwide, the response of governments and international organizations to this increasing challenge has been woefully inadequate. Nevertheless, there has been considerable improvement in Western Europe—appropriately enough, since this is the most popular target area—with Britain, The Netherlands, and West Germany in the lead. West Germany adopted a tough "no deals" policy after the massacre of 11 Israeli athletes at the Munich Olympics in September 1972. In dealing with this and with the fanatic terrorism of the Baader-Meinhof gang, which hit Germany in the early 1970s, the West German government acquired a considerable expertise in countermeasures. A major contribution has been the development of a vast computer data bank containing the equivalent of an estimated ten million pages of information on terrorist suspects. Doubts were expressed about its value in light of the failure to rescue the kidnapped industrialist Hanns-Martin Schleyer in the fall of 1977, and further criticisms were voiced when the computer, enlisted to aid the Italians in their search for Moro, could not provide a lead to his whereabouts. In the summer of 1978, however, the computer was instrumental in bringing about the arrest of 15 major West German terrorist suspects, including 4 who were traced to Yugoslavia and 4 to Bulgaria.

There has also been a notable improvement in the machinery of international cooperation in Western Europe. The past few years have seen the emergence of regular meetings among EEC ministers of the interior on the subject, the pooling of intelligence, closer police cooperation, and the drafting of a European Convention on the Suppression of Terrorism, which was signed by 17 of the 19 member states of the Council of Europe in January 1977 (Ireland and Malta were the only nonsignatories). The Convention is especially important because, under its provisions, the ratifying states would treat acts of terrorism within their territories as common crimes. Persons charged with the commission of terrorist acts in any country party to the Convention would be either extradited or brought to trial and would no longer be able to escape punishment by seeking asylum on the grounds that their crimes were politically motivated. As of August 1978 only four countries (Sweden, Austria, West Germany, and Britain) had taken the vital step of ratification. It remained to be seen whether enough states would ratify and implement the Convention to make it effective.

Admittedly, it is not easy to maintain a firm international response. Democratic publics will cheer a success, like the rescue of the passengers of a hijacked West German airliner at Mogadishu, Somalia, in October 1977. Failure in handling a major confrontation with terrorists, on the other hand, can rock a government with a fragile majority. Furthermore, a consistent firm-line policy will almost inevitably increase the number of threats that have to be faced simultaneously.

This was exemplified in August 1978 when Croatian terrorists seized hostages at the West German consulate in Chicago. The Croats, who threatened to kill the hostages unless their demands were met, were trying to force the West German authorities to free Stjepan Bilandzic, founder of a Croatian terrorist group, who was serving a sentence in West Germany for his part in an attempt to assassinate the vice-consul of Yugoslavia stationed in Cologne. The

A woman is overcome with grief after the bodies of the athletes killed in the Munich Olympics massacre of 1972 were returned to Israel.

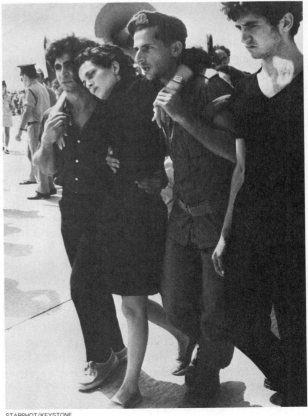

STARPHOT/KEYSTONE

135

A West German Communist Party poster protests the law enacted in 1977 forbidding certain prisoners suspected of terrorist activities any contact with the outside world, including lawyers.

Yugoslavs regarded Bilandzic as one of the most important Croat extremists, and they wanted him extradited. Yugoslavia does not conform to the political and judicial standards of the European Community states, and it is highly questionable whether any Croatian separatist can receive a fair trial there. Moreover, there are many Croatians living abroad in West Germany and elsewhere who could be provoked into retaliation. On the other hand, the Yugoslavs clearly expected full cooperation as the quid pro quo for their assistance in capturing four West German terrorist suspects in Yugoslavia. Indeed, the dilemma did not end with the eventual surrender of the terrorists to local authorities. When West Germany failed to extradite Bilandzic and several other Yugoslav exiles, Yugoslavia released the four West Germans.

The French authorities, on the other hand, had no excuse for their equivocation over several important extradition requests from Italy and West Germany in 1976–77. French uncooperativeness seems to have stemmed from judicial chauvinism and inertia rather than from any rational argument.

International judicial and political cooperation in Western Europe appears to have lagged behind police and military cooperation. In the military field especially, progress has been astonishingly good. British Special Air Service (SAS) teams have assisted the Dutch in handling the South Moluccan sieges, and they provided the "stun" grenades that proved so useful to the West Germans at Mogadishu. Both military and police services in the NATO countries benefit from data exchange on terrorist bombs and techniques, and they have learned much from each other's experiences.

Except for the U.S.-Cuba antihijacking pact of 1973 and Somali-West German cooperation in the Mogadishu rescue operation, the record of international cooperation involving non-NATO countries is abysmal. At Dacca in September 1977, for example, the Bangladesh authorities refused to give the Japanese permission to storm a Japan Air Lines DC-8 hijacked by the Japanese Red Army. And in February 1978 there was a bloody clash between an Egyptian commando force and Cypriot national guards when the Egyptians tried to storm a Cyprus Airways jet commandeered at Larnaca Airport in Cyprus by two Palestinian terrorists who had murdered a well-known Egyptian editor. Fifteen Egyptians were killed in the clash, which seems to have occurred because of a lack of preliminary agreement and coordination between the two governments. As a direct result, Egypt severed diplomatic relations with Cyprus.

This tragic fiasco further underlined the need for proper international machinery to coordinate antiterrorist operations. It has been suggested, for example, that highly trained antiterrorist commando units be organized internationally, possibly under the aegis of the United Nations or the International Civil Aviation Organization, and held ready for use in every major region of the world. If such a squad had been available at Dacca, it is possible that the Bangladesh authorities would have accepted its services, though it is true that, by a tragic coincidence, Bangladesh was experiencing a coup attempt while the hijack was on.

Can International Terrorism Be Curbed? Such are the hazards that may have to be faced by hostages held in unstable and turbulent countries. Given their recent experience of internal violence, the Bangladeshis might well view a single hijack as a relatively trivial incident. The industrialized nations must beware of assuming that their countries' concern about terrorist attacks on their citizens is fully shared or even understood by those who daily struggle to survive in lands that have recently suffered savage repressive terror and where death is a familiar companion.

Nevertheless, in 1977–78 political opinion in the

third world was beginning to harden against terrorism. As terrorism increasingly affects the third world states themselves, striking their own officials, embassies, airlines, and the general public, so their governments are more ready to consider international measures to curb these attacks. One of the most hopeful features of the Mogadishu experience was the clear unwillingness of the Arab states to allow the hijackers to land at their airports. There is also growing interest in a draft UN convention against the taking of hostages.

It cannot be emphasized enough, however, that no international convention, no matter how bold and comprehensive its provisions, is worth the candle unless governments have the will and determination to uphold the rule of law within their own frontiers and to honour their international pledges to extradite terrorists or bring them to trial. As long as terrorist crimes are seen to pay off, bringing such gains as massive publicity, the release of imprisoned comrades, or the capture of cash and weapons, terrorists will continue to violate the human rights of the innocent and exploit every weakness shown by the public authorities.

The international terrorist, whether politically sincere or not, is one who is prepared to commit crimes in the name of revolution. In every sense, he or she is as guilty of crime against humanity as a war criminal. One is forced to ask why those who make a profession of systematically murdering innocent and peaceful citizens should be kept alive at society's expense. The leniency of the jail sentences recently meted out to terrorist murderers in The Netherlands and Italy (14 and 15 years, respectively) is surely an encouragement to further terrorism. And it must be remembered that imprisoned terrorists are a constant incitement to fresh attempts to gain their release.

Throughout the world, politicians are beginning to adopt the position that many observers have long held: society must take drastic measures to reduce the population of terrorist killers and to deter new recruits. Severe punishment should not be regarded as a panacea, however. Until the basic political conflicts that underlie much international terrorism are resolved, high levels of violence are likely to continue. The sting of deterrence must be coupled with the balm of prevention. Nevertheless, there is a greater danger of underreaction than of overreaction on the part of the international community. Ruthless punishment has a vital role in preserving the international rule of law. International terrorism is, after all, a form of war, and one does not normally win wars by loving one's enemies.

West German authorities spread posters of most wanted terrorists throughout the country. The poster campaign, with the aid of a computer data bank, resulted in the arrest of some of the fugitives.

AS SOCIETIES AGE

by Michael S. Teitelbaum

A characteristic common to all industrialized countries, regardless of their political ideologies or economic systems, is that of an aging population. This remarkable uniformity among otherwise diverse societies would warrant comment even if it were of little social or economic significance. But, in fact, the age composition of a population has an impact upon virtually every sector of human society, and the effects of the current aging process in advanced countries will be felt throughout the coming decades with increasing force.

There can be no dispute as to the reality of this aging process. In the United States, for example, the median age of the population in 1850 was 19 years, but by 1950 it was 29.5. The percentage of the population over 65 rose from 4.1% in 1900, to 8.1% in 1950, and to 10.7% in 1975. In England and Wales, the percentage over 65 rose from 7.4% in 1931 to 11% in 1950 and to 14.2% in 1975.

Data on proportions of various countries' population over age 65 and less than age 15 are presented in the accompanying table. It can be seen that in virtually every developed country for which data are available, the proportion of the population over 65 has been rising over the past 25 years. By 1975 the proportions over 65 were 15% or greater in three countries—Austria, East Germany, and Sweden—but were still little more than 8% in Japan, Spain, and Canada. The U.S. figure was intermediate in this range at 10.7%, while England and Wales together and Scotland were both tending toward the more elderly end of the distribution, at 14.2% and 13.3%, respectively.

Also as indicated in the table, the proportions under age 15 in 1975 ranged from 19.4% in Sweden to 31.1% in Ireland. The changes occurring since 1950 were generally moderately negative, with a few small increases.

Michael S. Teitelbaum, university lecturer in demography and fellow of Nuffield College at the University of Oxford, edited Sex Differences: Social and Biological Perspectives *(1976) and is currently working on* The British Fertility Decline.

For purposes of comparing and contrasting the age structures of industrialized countries with that of a typical less developed country, calculations for Mexico are presented at the bottom of the table. Only about 3.5% of the Mexican population in 1950 was over age 65, and this percentage had changed

Nearly one of every two Mexicans in 1975 was under 15 years of age, while the number was fewer than one of every four people in the developed countries.

OWEN FRANKEN—STOCK, BOSTON

very little by 1975. On the other hand, more than 41% were under the age of 15 in 1950, a proportion that had increased to 46.3% by 1975. To put it another way, nearly one of every two Mexicans in 1975 was under 15 years of age. Typically, fewer than one in four people in the developed countries was in this young group.

Causes of Uniform Aging. There is now no mystery as to the relatively uniform pattern of aging among the populations of the developed countries of the world. On the basis of careful demographic work over the past two decades, it is now understood that the age composition of a population is determined primarily by the levels of fertility in the population over the recent past. This is a counterintuitive proposition, for common sense would dictate that populations grow younger or older in response to changes in longevity or mortality—*i.e.*, that the aging of developed countries' populations

ought to be attributable to increased longevity resulting from improved medical and public health practices since World War II. Such interpretations are often made, but they are incorrect because the impact of an improvement in mortality conditions generally affects all age groups and especially the most vulnerable, the young and the old. Thus mortality declines tend to affect both extremes of the age distribution, and their impact upon average age is relatively neutral. In contrast, the impact of a change in fertility affects only one part of the age structure—the very young, or more specifically age 0—and has virtually no impact upon the number of middle-aged or elderly people. Therefore, the effect of a fertility increase is to decrease the average age of the population, while the impact of fertility decline is to increase average age.

An understanding of this basic demographic reality leads immediately to an understanding of the

More and more nursery cribs are standing empty as birthrates fall dramatically in most industrialized countries.

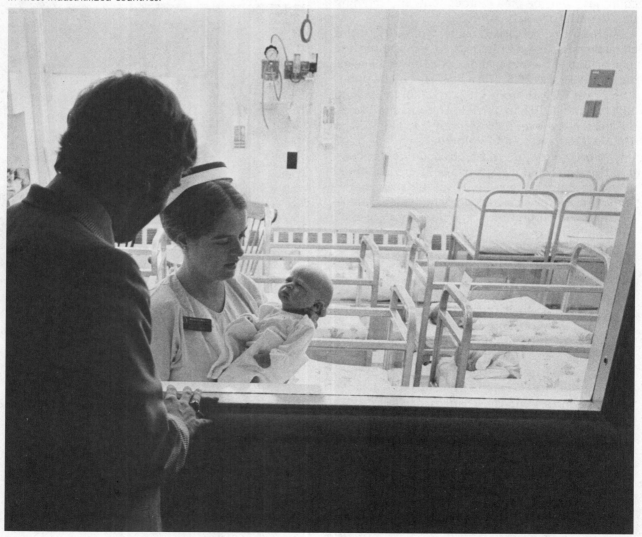

uniformity of increasing age among most populations of developed countries. For a common characteristic of virtually all these populations since the 1960s, and of many from World War II onward, has been a sharp decline in fertility levels. The total fertility rate is the sum of the age-specific fertility rates of women of reproductive age in a given time period. In effect, the rate represents the average number of children that would be born to a group of women if they followed these age-specific fertility rates through their reproductive life spans. In virtually all industrialized countries the trend in total fertility rates from the end of World War II to the latest available data has been one of decline. In many countries there was a short-lived bulge of births during the years immediately following World War II, but in only a few (notably the U.S., Canada, Australia, and New Zealand) did this "baby boom" continue through the 1950s. Since 1965 fertility has turned downward in all but a few of these countries—notably such Eastern European states as Romania and Czechoslovakia which in the 1960s implemented policies to increase birthrates.

This is not the proper place for a discussion of the factors underlying this remarkably uniform experience of fertility decline. The purpose here is to discuss one of its important implications—the aging of the population. Using standard demographic models known as "stable populations," it can be shown that populations with the same mortality levels will have different age structures depending upon their past fertility experiences. Under favourable mortality conditions (life expectancy at birth of 70 years), a population with high fertility over the long term would have over 40% of its population under age 15 and less than 5% over 65 years. With the low fertility levels now characterizing the U.S., U.K., and many other developed countries, only about 20% of the population would be under age 15 and more than 15% would be over age 65. The average age of the high-fertility population would be about 24 years, while that of the low-fertility population would be almost 40 years.

Consequences. Since virtually all industrialized countries have experienced substantial fertility declines in recent years, it follows that the aging of populations is a common phenomenon. The consequences of such shifts in age structure, both real and imagined, are substantial.

REAL CONSEQUENCES. The first social sectors to experience the impacts of declining fertility and an aging population are obvious— the early-age sectors of the medical system (obstetrics and pediatrics) and of the educational system (preprimary and primary schools). The fact that virtually every country in the world has experienced substantial population

Proportions Aged 65 and Over and Less Than 15 years, c. 1950 and c. 1975, and % Change in Proportions Over Period: 30 Developed Countries and Mexico

Country	Proportion 65 and over			Proportion less than 15		
	c. 1950	c. 1975	% change	c. 1950	c. 1975	% change
Australia	.075	.085	+13.3	.299	.280	−6.4
Austria	.106	.150	41.5	.229	.233	+1.7
Belgium	.107	.138	29.0	.206	.226	+9.7
Bulgaria	...	.106	...	...	.222	...
Canada	.077	.084	9.1	.303	.272	−10.2
Czechoslovakia	.077	.118	53.2	.243	.228	−6.2
Denmark	.091	.134	47.3	.263	.226	−14.1
Finland	.067	.103	53.7	.300	.224	−25.3
France	.121	.135	11.6	.233	.237	+1.7
Germany, East	.102	.163	59.8	.245	.211	−13.9
Germany, West	.094	.145	54.3	.213	.215	+0.9
Greece	.075	.122	62.7	.286	.239	−16.4
Hungary	...	.126	...	...	.203	...
Ireland	.107	.112	4.7	.289	.311	+7.6
Italy	...	.120	...	...	.258	...
Japan	.049	.080	63.3	.354	.243	−31.4
Netherlands, The	.071	.108	52.1	.293	.253	−13.7
New Zealand	.092	.087	5.4	.294	.297	+1.0
Norway	.096	.137	42.7	.244	.238	−2.5
Poland	...	.095	...	...	.240	...
Portugal	.070	.102	45.7	.295	.273	−7.5
Romania	.082*	.096	17.1*	.289	.253	−12.5
Spain	.072	.083	15.3	.262	.276	+5.3
Sweden	.102	.151	48.0	.234	.194	−17.1
Switzerland	.096	.127	32.3	.236	.221	−6.4
U.S.S.R.	...	.089†	...	...	.268‡	...
United Kingdom						
England & Wales	.110	.142	29.1	.221	.231	+4.5
Northern Ireland	.098	.111	13.3	.276	.290	+5.1
Scotland	.100	.133	33.3	.246	.246	0.0
United States	.081	.107	32.1	.269	.245	−8.9
Yugoslavia	.056	.085	51.8	.325	.259	−20.3
Mexico	.035	.034	−2.9	.417	.463	+11.0

*1950 data refer to persons aged 60 and over.
†Persons 65–69 roughly approximated as half the known figure for persons 60–69.
‡Persons 10–14 roughly approximated as half the known figure for persons 10–19.
Sources: United Nations *Demographic Yearbook 1948*; additional unpublished data in files of United Nations Statistical Office, New York.

growth over the past century means that most medical and educational planning is keyed to growing numbers of clients over time. The building of new schools and hospitals and the training of teachers and physicians, although partly directed to improvement in services or replacement of natural decay or war damage, has been heavily devoted to the provision of services to the greater numbers of children expected. The baby boom of the 1940s and 1950s caught many planners short, especially in extended-boom countries such as the U.S., Canada, Australia, and New Zealand. In other countries, especially in Europe, much replacement of war losses was necessary. The result was that for a generation medical and educational systems became accustomed to growth.

The fertility declines of the 1960s and 1970s changed all that. Many countries went from severe shortage to awkward glut in only a decade. Suddenly there were too many maternity beds, too many classrooms, too many teachers. Though other factors, such as general economic conditions, increased longevity of female employment, and government attempts to expand medical and educational services also contributed to these surpluses, the fertility declines loomed large. The small age groups born from the late 1960s onward have now reached elementary school age; similar excesses of capacity will likely be experienced on the more advanced educational levels as they progress into secondary school and into higher education.

Aging populations also affect the labour force. In recent years in the U.S., there have been extraordinary numbers of teenagers seeking to enter the labour force. These are the products of the extended baby boom of the 1950s. (The problem has been less severe in the U.K. and in most other European countries, with their smaller and less extended booms.) This is not to say that age structure has been the major factor in the growth of teenage unemployment, which is due primarily to the prevailing depressed economic conditions of the 1970s. It has, however, been a contributing factor.

Beginning in the early 1980s, when the relatively smaller birth groups experienced during the past 10–15 years reach working age, labour supply of teenagers will cease to grow as rapidly. Some commentators even see a labour shortage arising in the 1980s, although so much depends upon economic trends in the interim that little credence can be given to such predictions.

In addition, the spatial mobility of the labour force is thought by some to be affected by its age composition. The argument is that younger workers, relatively free of familial, financial, and housing constraints, are more able and willing to move to areas of new and growing industries, thereby relieving localized shortages of labour and contributing to overall economic growth. The importance of such effects is at least debatable, given the effect on spatial mobility of other important factors such as policies affecting location of industries and the availability and cost of housing in different areas.

Another effect of age structure changes is in crime rates. While criminal statistics often reflect police or judicial attitudes to the prosecution of offenses as well as public attitudes to reporting them, it is still true that crime (and particularly violent crime) shows a characteristic age pattern, with the highest rates being those of young male adult offenders (age groups 15–24 or 15–29). Once again it must be noted that crime rates, like unemployment rates, are heavily affected by overall economic, social, and even cultural conditions; changes in age composition represent only one contributing factor to changes in overall crime rates, but nonetheless a real one. As the children of the baby boom gradually move into their 30s and 40s, one may expect, other things being equal, a resulting decline in crime rates, especially of the violent variety, with the greatest impact in those countries that experienced the most extended and substantial booms.

Meanwhile, the proportion of the population in older age groups increases as that in the younger groups declines. While the need for maternity wards and obstetricians declines in relative terms, that for geriatricians, heart and cancer surgeons, and extended-care nursing facilities increases. The burden of public investment shifts from the needs of the young, such as education and family housing, to those of the old, such as pensions and old-age accommodations.

The implications of age shifts for governmental social security or pension plans has only recently been fully recognized. Most national pension plans are not fully funded; that is, the pensioners are living not off the savings of their own retirement contributions but rather off the contributions and taxes paid by those people currently employed. Thus, if there are changes in the relative proportions of those working and retired, there are consequent financial effects on pension plans. Other things being equal, an increase in the proportion of retired people will cause total benefits to the elderly to decline in real terms (via declines in nominal benefits or, more likely, via inflation), or else will bring about an increase in taxes on the working population. Of course, it is also possible to finance pensions by shifting resources from other sectors such as education or defense, or by raising taxes on industry; each alternative has its own political feasibility and its own social and economic consequences.

The U.S. government recognized only during the past few years that its Social Security system was financially unsound. This was due primarily to the assumptions of age composition built into the actuarial basis of the system, assumptions that implicitly assumed higher fertility levels than had been experienced in recent years. The result of this realization has been the generation of extensive studies by a special commission, submission of numerous legislative alternatives, and a general recognition that the contributions (i.e., earmarked taxes) to the Social Security system must inevitably rise. Indeed, that is precisely the course that the U.S. has chosen to follow. (See SOCIAL AND WELFARE SERVICES: *Special Report*.)

PERCEIVED CONSEQUENCES OF AN AGING POPULATION. Population growth has been a valued phenomenon for millennia ("Be fruitful and multiply" was the biblical form of endorsement) and a near-universal experience in industrialized countries for at least two centuries. It is therefore not surprising that population growth has come to be viewed as "normal" in most developed countries, and as a positive force for increasing national power and welfare. Implied within this perception is the view that slow or zero growth is abnormal; actual negative growth (even of small magnitude) is often perceived as a clear sign of national decline. Such concerns were widely expressed in the 1930s, when fertility was also low although not as low as at present in many developed countries. Perceived negative effects included economic stagnation, military weakness, relative decline of "superior racial stocks," declining opportunity for advancement in a less steeply sloping age structure, and a stodginess and conservatism resulting from the predominance of the middle-aged and elderly. In a memorable, if exaggerated, set of metaphors, the French demographer Alfred Sauvy described such a society as one of "old people ruminating over old ideas in old houses."

Unfortunately, there has been little actual experience with societies characterized by "old" age structures. Before the increase in European population growth in the 18th and 19th centuries, European populations were slow-growing but nonetheless youthful. Fertility was high (though balanced by high mortality), and it will be recalled that it is fertility levels that largely determine age structure. Perhaps the best example of a population that has experienced relatively constant low fertility for several decades is that of Sweden. Swedish total fertility rates were at or below replacement of the current population by 1927 and stayed there until 1941. Even after the end of World War II, Swedish fertility rose to only about 20% above replacement, and for only five or so years. (In contrast, fertility levels in the U.S. rose to nearly 80% above replacement after World War II; in England and Wales the comparable figure was about 35%.)

Yet it is difficult to argue convincingly that Sweden has been characterized by economic stagnation, political conservatism, or lack of opportunity for advancement. In conventional military terms, too, Sweden cannot be said to have weakened substantially, though it is of course a small country that has deliberately rejected the development of nuclear weapons and that can hardly be considered a military superpower.

Future Prospects. Undoubtedly there are real costs resulting from the aging of populations. Disproportionate increases must necessarily occur in expenditures on the needs of the elderly. Certain industries and firms concentrating upon the consumer needs of the young will face a more difficult business climate unless they are able to diversify into other sectors less sensitive to age composition (the recent economic difficulties of one of the leading international suppliers of baby foods provide one notable case in point).

On the other hand, considerable societal savings can be realized in the sectors serving the young, such as the schools. Institutional and political rigidities must be overcome if this is to be done; it is obviously politically expedient to maintain current relative levels of expenditure in sectors such as edu-

"Meanwhile, the proportion of the population in older age groups increases . . ."

cation, with their powerful interest groups and political support. Yet a gradual relative shift of public resources in concert with the gradual transformation of the age structure of society is the only sensible response.

Aging populations are the inevitable mathematical implication of fertility declines to levels compatible with favourable mortality conditions. The alternatives are either logically impossible (continued exponential population growth over the long term) or undesirable (deteriorating mortality conditions). It is fortunate indeed that, given its inevitability, the aging of populations has few clearly negative implications for human welfare.

ARTICLES FROM THE 1979
PRINTING OF THE BRITANNICA

Winston Churchill called the Soviet Union "a riddle wrapped in a mystery inside an enigma." That was in 1939, during the repressive regime of Joseph Stalin.

Much has happened since then. Access to the Soviet Union, especially the freedom to travel about in it, has been greatly expanded since the Stalin era. Nevertheless, the Soviet Union, to many readers of the Britannica, remains one of the major mysteries. This vast country—in fact, the largest on Earth—is obviously very influential and powerful. It is involved in nearly all world affairs and is to be reckoned with at every turn. Yet many remain puzzled. What are the people like? In particular, what kind of government do they really have?

The following lengthy excerpt from Britannica's new article deals primarily with the Soviet constitution, in itself a new development on the political scene. This document was adopted in 1977 after several decades of discussion and, one supposes, of debate. Reading this account of Soviet political realities may help to dispel some of the mystery that surrounds the subject. It also helps to explain why Americans and Soviets do not agree about human rights. In the United States these rights are guaranteed by the Constitution for everyone; in the Soviet Union they are guaranteed for all law-abiding citizens—and that makes a very big difference.

SOVIET UNION

STATE AND SOCIETY

The constitutional framework. In view of the domination exercised over political, economic, social, and cultural life in the Soviet Union by the ruling, monopolistic Communist Party, constitutions and other legal documents are subordinate to the policies of the party and its leadership, centred in the Politburo. The party, however, desires to project an aura of constitutional legitimacy. Hence, it is important that finally, after many years of a somewhat shadowy existence, the Constitutional Commission, appointed in 1962, produced in May 1977 a draft of a new constitution, which, after several months of well-organized discussion in the controlled press, was enacted unanimously into law by the Supreme Soviet in October 1977.

Comparison of the Stalin Constitution—as the "fundamental law" enacted in 1936 was usually called by the Soviet communications media—and the constitution of 1977 reveals no essential changes. The new document is far longer than the old one and in some ways more candid. It much more openly proclaims the ruling and all-penetrating role of the Communist Party of the Soviet Union (CPSU; Kommunisticheskaya Partiya Sovetskogo Soyuza), for example, describing it (Article 6) as "the nucleus of [the] political system." It describes more fully the various legal rights of citizens than did its predecessor. In emphasizing that all rights are accorded by the authorities in return for exemplary performance of duties, however, it in effect limits the rights of citizens more severely than did even the Stalin Constitution.

The fundamental point, however, is that, to a far greater extent than is the case in Western democracies, the Soviet constitution of 1977, like that of 1936, will have meaning only to the extent that the leadership desires and allows it.

The economic foundations. The economic life of the Soviet Union and all other aspects of social activity are dominated by the CPSU. Its Politburo determines economic policy and sees to it that its decisions are enforced by the Soviet government. The CPSU penetrates and guides the government by a system of interlocking membership of party and governmental executive bodies and by many other means. The Soviet economy is held to be "socialist" because its basic principle is state ownership, established by Lenin in 1918 insofar as the main elements (industry, transport, finance, etc.) were concerned and extended by Stalin to agriculture, which Lenin had for pragmatic reasons left largely in the hands of smallholder peasants. Despite state domination of the Soviet economy, not all property is directly administered by state agencies. The state owns and administers land, minerals, water resources, forests, industrial enterprises, banks, large state agricultural enterprises (known as *sovkhozy,* or state farms), means of transport and communication, municipal enterprises, and basic housing funds. In addition to state property, there are two other kinds of property in the Soviet Union, namely cooperative property, predominant in agriculture, and personal property. Most farmers are members of cooperative, or collective, farms, known as *kolkhozy*. Nominally, the land farmed by the collective farmers is assigned to them in perpetuity, but, as is indicated by government-ordered consolidations of collective farms into larger units since the late 1950s, the collective farms in fact exercise whatever control they have over their land within a framework of policies determined by the political authorities.

As for personal property, it includes articles of clothing, household objects, electronic goods, automobiles (in the case of citizens who can afford them, at prices several times higher than in the West, and only after waiting several years), and many other types of goods, including (again for upper-income persons) country cottages, or dachas. Soviet inheritance law with respect to personal property is fairly liberal.

Social and political aspects. According to official doctrine, there are two "friendly" classes in Soviet society, the working class and the collective farm peasantry. There is also a rapidly growing "stratum," the intelligentsia, which, Western observers agree, is by far the most privileged of the three. This does not mean that all members of the intelligentsia are better off than the workers or even, perhaps, than the peasants. Highly skilled workers earn considerably more than the more poorly paid members of the intelligentsia, which roughly corresponds to the professional classes in Great Britain or America. However, the highest ranking writers, scientists, and other professionals are, next to highly placed party and state bureaucrats, the most privileged of Soviet citizens.

As implied by the official slogan, "From each according to his ability, to each according to his work," Soviet society is not egalitarian. However, there is a considerable degree of equality of opportunity. Generally, life is very competitive, and the unofficial guiding principle of distribution of rewards might be described as that of the career open to talents. This is modified by the requirement that to achieve success a person must be not only professionally competent but also politically reliable.

The CPSU, which as of late 1977 had about 16,200,000 members, dominates the political life of the country. The party rules through the formal structures of government, which include the pyramid of soviets ("councils") extending down from the Supreme Soviet of the U.S.S.R. to village soviets, and the system of ministries, headed by the Moscow-centred Council of Ministers and extending down to local representatives of ministries. Nominally, the deputies and presiding officers of the soviets at all levels are elected, but there is only one candidate for any office in those elections, and the selection of candidates is controlled by the CPSU. Party, soviet, and ministerial posts—as well as other positions of influence and power—are allocated in accordance with a "nomenclature" (*nomenklatura*) system, which is operated by the central authorities of the CPSU.

The federal structure. The Soviet Union, in fact a highly centralized state, is nominally a federal republic. Its federal aspect derives from the fact that it consists of 15 theoretically equal republics, each of which has

equal representation in the Soviet of Nationalities, the upper chamber of the bicameral Supreme Soviet, the national legislature. The republics, as well as lower ranking autonomous republics, autonomous regions, and autonomous (formerly national) districts, constitute a means by which symbolic political representation is granted to the numerous ethnic groups of which the Soviet Union is composed. All of the people of the Soviet Union, however, share common federal citizenship. Federal laws have equal force in the territories of the union republics. The federal legislature, under the guidance of the CPSU and the State Planning Committee (Gosplan), determines the federal budget, which includes the budgets of the union republics. Thus the central government in Moscow dominates the economics of the union republics.

This dominance by Moscow is fortified by features of the Soviet system more fundamental than constitutional provisions. Perhaps the most important instrument of central control is the hierarchical, centralized structure of the CPSU. Party headquarters in Moscow, through its centralized control over personnel assignments, can appoint, promote, demote, or transfer even the heads of the party organizations of republics.

The tight control exercised by the Moscow leadership over local economic, political, and cultural life engenders keen resentment among many members of the non-Russian minority nationalities residing in the republics that are named for them. Resistance to Moscow's control has been manifested in a variety of ways; at its mildest it takes the form of anti-Russian jokes and other innocuous verbal behaviour (though even these have at times been punished harshly) or—as after Soviet conquest of the western Ukraine as a consequence of the Nazi–Soviet pact of 1939 and Soviet victory over Germany in 1945—it may be manifested in sanguinary guerrilla warfare. Needless to say, the right of secession from the Soviet Union granted by the constitution (both that of 1936 and that of 1977) has never been exercised. Indeed, any suggestion of dissatisfaction with Moscow's rule on the part of members of non-Russian nationalities is usually regarded as grounds for the imposition of draconian penalties. Of all of the many forms of dissent or opposition to Soviet rule with which the Soviet authorities have had to contend over the years, nationality dissent has aroused the deepest anger and has been punished most severely.

Organs of state power and government. *The Supreme Soviet.* Formally, the Supreme Soviet is the highest organ of state power in the Soviet Union. In keeping with this status, affirmed in the constitution, only the Supreme Soviet can make laws for the entire country. In practice, however, the Supreme Soviet enacts only such legislation as has already been initiated by the CPSU; this is indicated by the fact that the CPSU Central Committee meets before the Supreme Soviet does and lays down the policies that are subsequently endorsed by the latter. It is also clear that the Council of Ministers, nominally appointed by the Supreme Soviet, is in fact a more powerful body than the latter. Despite its limitations, however, the Supreme Soviet is an important body. Its legislative commissions, each of which specializes in a given field of legislation, have been playing an increasingly larger role in bringing to bear on the legislative process the expert knowledge of lawyers, economists, and other kinds of specialists. Thus the competence of the Supreme Soviet to perform its legislative functions has increased. Certainly the Supreme Soviet is not the mere rubber stamp it was in the Stalin era, as is indicated by the increased regularity with which it has met since Stalin's death and by the increased length of its sessions, which, however, are still extremely short by Western standards.

Nonetheless, the Supreme Soviet is far from being a parliament of the Western democratic type. Among the many striking differences, for example, is the fact that in the Supreme Soviet all legislation, including crucially important budgetary legislation, passes unanimously. Quite apart from this, and from the unfailing corre-

Marginalia:

Ownership of property

Soviets

Resistance to Moscow

Role of the CPSU

spondence between CPSU directives and Supreme Soviet legislation, much law is made, despite the apparent lack of constitutionality, by governmental bodies other than the Supreme Soviet, such as the Council of Ministers. There are even many secret laws, not passed by and unknown to the Supreme Soviet.

In form, the Supreme Soviet is bicameral. Members of both chambers are elected (in one-party, one-candidate elections) for four-year terms. One chamber, called the Soviet of the Union, represents, with one deputy for every 300,000 inhabitants, constituents regardless of national origin. The other chamber, the Soviet of Nationalities, is so organized as to take at least symbolic account of the multinational composition of the Soviet population; it has 32 deputies from each of the 15 union republics and for the lower units, designated in descending order as autonomous republics, autonomous regions (*oblasti*), and autonomous districts (*okruga*), respectively 11, five, and one each. The Supreme Soviet normally assembles for regular sessions twice a year. It passes all legislation introduced by its leading members (who are also leading members of the CPSU) unanimously and expeditiously. It sometimes holds special sessions.

The Presidium of the Supreme Soviet. The Presidium of the Supreme Soviet has 37 members, elected by the Supreme Soviet itself and, like the parent body, serving for four years. Between sessions of the Supreme Soviet, which last for only about a week, the Presidium acts for it, performing such functions as convening and dissolving the Supreme Soviet, receiving ambassadors of foreign states, selecting and recalling Soviet diplomats, removing and appointing ministers, instituting and awarding honorary titles, etc. It may also order mobilization of the armed forces and may declare war.

It is obvious that the Presidium is a more powerful body than the Supreme Soviet, although probably somewhat less powerful than the Council of Ministers, which it appoints, and vastly less powerful than the Politburo and Central Committee of the CPSU. Of the 37 members of the Presidium, only its chairman is normally a major party leader and a significant national political figure. Fifteen vice chairmen, one from each of the union republics, serve under the chairman of the Presidium, symbolizing the nominally federal structure of the Soviet state. There are 20 additional members and a secretary.

Both the Supreme Soviet and its Presidium symbolize but do not really exercise power. They legitimize the power of the real ruling force in the Soviet polity, the CPSU. The Presidium also provides an instrument through which the CPSU can deal with foreign states in a manner more understandable and acceptable to the latter than direct transactions with the party would be. With regard to very important business, however—such as negotiations in the area of arms control—the general secretary of the CPSU has dealt with presidents of the United States, dramatically displaying the superordination of party to state in the Soviet Union.

The Council of Ministers. Nominally subordinate to the Supreme Soviet and, between Supreme Soviet sessions, to its Presidium, the Council of Ministers is in fact the most important governmental and administrative agency in the country; in fact, it is designated in the constitution as the "government" of the Soviet Union. According to the constitution, the decrees and ordinances issued by the Council of Ministers must conform to law as promulgated by the Supreme Soviet, but the Supreme Soviet has never overruled any decree of the Council of Ministers. This is not really surprising, since both bodies are dominated by the most powerful leaders of the CPSU.

Working under the direction of the council are ministries of two kinds, the extremely centralized all-union ministries (somewhat equivalent to departments of the U.S. federal government) and slightly less centralized union republican ministries, so-called because in addition to their Moscow headquarters they have local headquarters in the capitals of the union republics. In addition, there are under the council various state committees and special agencies, some of which wield enormous power; one of these is the Committee of State Security (KGB), which controls the Soviet political police and is probably, with the exception of the CPSU itself and perhaps the regular armed forces, the most powerful organization in the country. Both the state committees and the special agencies have ministerial status.

Republican and local state organs. The political structure of republics and autonomous republics is almost identical to that of the country. To a somewhat lesser degree this is also true in the local administrative subdivisions, which are called, respectively, *kraya* (territories, very large in area), *oblasti* (variously translated into English as regions, provinces, etc.), *okruga,* and *rayony;* the last two subdivisions (both translated as districts) may be either rural or urban in character.

The essential element in this system of units is its hierarchical, pyramidal character; the whole constitutes a unified structure. There is no counterpart in the Soviet system to the independent unit of local government such as the American state, county, or city government, each with lawmaking and taxing powers.

The union republics have their own supreme soviets, but they are unicameral rather than bicameral like the Supreme Soviet. Like the federal Supreme Soviet, the supreme soviets of the republics (both union and autonomous) are elected for five-year terms; *oblast* and *rayon* soviets are elected for two and a half years. The soviets elect executive committees, in whose hands most of their power is concentrated. As at all levels of the system, CPSU groups in the local soviets see to it that these bodies carry out party policy.

It is possible that the highly developed "mass participation" in the working of this vast machine affords some satisfaction to some citizens. Official sources, such as speeches by party leaders, and a steady stream of articles on socialist democracy in the controlled press assert that the participation of citizens in local government constitutes a special advantage of the Soviet political system. It is impossible, because of official secrecy, either to confirm or refute such claims by direct investigation, but enough is known about the reality of political life in the Soviet Union to cast doubt on them. It is clear that participation is so hedged about with controls and limits that for most of its alleged beneficiaries it must be more a burden than a privilege.

The electoral system. Little needs to be said about Soviet one-party, one-candidate elections. They are so carefully managed that the official candidates—who are said to represent the bloc of party and nonparty voters—invariably receive virtually 100 percent of all possible votes. All citizens 18 years of age or older may vote, except for the certified insane and criminals confined by court sentence. In fact, voting, though not formally compulsory, is obviously regarded by the authorities as the duty of all citizens; enormous pressure and great fanfare are resorted to in getting people to vote.

THE JUDICIARY, ARMED FORCES, AND PUBLIC ORDER

The judicial system. The Soviet judicial system is highly centralized, hierarchical, and subject to supervision and control by the CPSU. Although far less arbitrary and coercive than it was under Stalin (whose police officials arrested, deported, and did to death millions of persons without anything remotely resembling due process of law), today's system is, by Western and especially by Anglo-American standards, exceedingly defective. There is no equivalent of habeas corpus, no trial by jury, no presumption of innocence, no real independence of the judiciary from ideological and political pressures. Indeed, judges, prosecutors, attorneys, and all others involved in dispensing justice are required to propagate CPSU policy in the judicial field.

Moreover, although the Soviet authorities deny the existence of political crimes in the Soviet Union, they obviously do exist and are dealt with by very special, severe methods. The criminal code of the Russian Soviet

Federated Socialist Republic, largest of the 15 union republics, contains provisions for prosecuting "especially dangerous state crimes" that are clearly political in nature; there are parallel provisions in the codes of the other republics. Loosely drafted, catchall statutes in effect make any publicly expressed criticism of official policy or ideology a crime. Thus, circulating or even having in one's possession written statements that "slander" the state or social system is punishable by long terms in concentration camps, euphemistically described as corrective labour camps. In several important categories of cases, judicial investigation is carried out not by the regular prosecutors but by officials of the security police (KGB). Outside the political sphere there is a system of courts, prosecutors, and attorneys that functions fairly well, subject to the limitations referred to above. In evaluating this system, however, it is necessary to bear in mind that it is subject to CPSU policies, which can change arbitrarily from time to time.

At the apex of the system is the Supreme Court of the U.S.S.R., whose judges are appointed by the Supreme Soviet. Below the Supreme Court (the only national court, apart from military tribunals) stand supreme courts of the union and autonomous republics, provincial, territorial, and city courts, courts of autonomous regions and national areas, and, at the lowest level, the people's courts, the last of which try the overwhelming bulk of all cases. The members of people's courts include a professional judge, who is elected, and two lay "assessors," who theoretically represent the people in the administration of justice at this level. Another so-called popular feature of the people's courts is the openness of their proceedings, though this is restricted in cases involving state security or intimate personal or family matters. Judges at the levels higher than the people's courts are legally trained professionals, appointed rather than elected. There is no institution of judicial review in the Soviet Union, though there is a well-developed system of appealing the verdicts of lower to higher courts.

An important role is played in Soviet justice by the institution of the procuracy. The procurator general of the U.S.S.R. is appointed for a seven-year, renewable term. He in turn appoints lower level procurators for five-year terms. The system of procurators has two main functions. The most unusual of these, in terms of U.S. practice, is supervision of the actions of government officials, with a view to preventing and if necessary prosecuting illegal actions taken by officials. The procurators also conduct criminal investigation and prosecute accused thieves, embezzlers, counterfeiters, and other violators of law. To be sure, prosecution of violators of certain Soviet laws (for example, that of "speculators" for engaging in private trade or other types of prohibited economic activity) is unfamiliar to Westerners.

The armed forces. In the Soviet Union military service is compulsory for all male citizens: two years for the army, three for the navy. There are a very large professional Soviet Army, Soviet Navy, Long Range Air Force, Air Defense Command (established 1955), and Strategic Rocket Force (1960). Most of the armed forces are under the direction of the Ministry of Defense, but the KGB also has several hundred thousand men under arms in such services as the Border Troops, which are equipped with patrol boats, helicopters, aircraft, trained dogs, etc. There is also a vast paramilitary organization known as DOSAAF (Vsesoyuznoye Dobrovolnoye Obshchestvo Sodeystviya Armii, Aviatsii i Flotu S.S.R., or All-Union Voluntary Society for Assistance to the Army, Air Force and Navy of the U.S.S.R.), which, among other functions, provides military training and patriotic indoctrination for schoolchildren. Of great importance also is the GlavPU SA i VMF (Glavnoye Politicheskoye Upravleniye Sovetskoy Armii i Voyenno-Morskogo Flota, or Main Political Directorate of the Soviet Army and Navy), an agency of the CPSU Central Committee, whose task is political supervision and indoctrination of the military forces.

In the late 1970s it was estimated that the Soviet Union

was spending 11–13 percent of its gross national product annually on its military forces, compared with 6 percent in the U.S.; 5.1 in the U.K., and 3.7 in France. Its army strength was estimated at 1,825,000, its navy at 450,000 (including marines), and its air force at 1,025,000.

Public order. As in the administration of justice, two administrative systems maintain public order. The rough Soviet equivalent of Western police systems is the Ministry of Internal Affairs (Ministerstvo Vnutrennikh Del, or MVD), which controls the militia, or ordinary police, as well as prisons, labour camps, fire prevention services, road safety services, registration of births, marriages, and deaths, etc. The more political aspects of order maintenance are administered by the KGB (Komitet Gosudarstvennoy Bezopasnosti, or Committee of State Security), which performs espionage and counterespionage, guards high officials and state frontiers, and also exercises surveillance over foreign diplomats and press correspondents and in general safeguards the power of the regime.

There is an auxiliary police system known as the *druzhina,* whose more than 5,000,000 members, called *druzhinniki,* normally serve a few hours once a month. Wearing red arm bands, they patrol streets and other public places; they may apprehend violators of public order and turn them over to the militia.

THE SYSTEM OF PUBLIC ORGANIZATIONS

The Communist Party of the Soviet Union. The CPSU is the driving and integrating force and the main control mechanism of state and society in the Soviet Union. This fact is registered in article 6 of the constitution (1977), which states that the party is the "leading and guiding force of Soviet society . . . , of all state organizations and public organizations." Article 100 of the constitution also mentions the CPSU first in a list of organizations having the right to nominate candidates for election to the soviets. Of course these articles suggest only feebly the overwhelming initiatory, mobilizing, and penetrating capacities of the CPSU. Although official doctrine characterizes the party as a public organization, it is in fact the collective ruler of the country, containing within its ranks the men and women who make and enforce national policy. It, not the state through which it rules, dominates all Soviet life.

As of late 1977 its membership numbered more than 16,000,000. Perhaps 100,000 of those members enjoyed some measure of executive authority, but only a few hundred had much power. These were the people who headed the republic and main *oblast* party organizations and the party organizations of major economic and other enterprises and institutions, those who edited leading newspapers, and those who held high military or police positions or headed Central Committee departments and on the basis of such status were full members of the Central Committee or full or alternate members of the party's Politburo (Political Bureau).

The dominance of the party's central headquarters over the rank and file is effected by many means and methods. One of the most important is the nomenclature (*nomenklatura*) system of centralized personnel selection, according to which only party members who pass the screening tests imposed from above by appropriate levels of the party leadership can be promoted to a given post. There are lists of positions for which only Moscow headquarters can clear aspirants; lower levels of the party hierarchy screen candidates for positions at their levels, and so on down the line. Another important principle of party organization that enhances centralized control is known as democratic centralism, the most important components of which are strict party discipline and subordination of the minority to the majority (in practice, of lower to higher ranking organizations) and the obligatory nature of the decisions of higher organs for lower. In addition, Moscow headquarters dominates the Soviet mass media of communication. The CPSU Central Committee's newspaper, *Pravda,* and other Central Committee organs such as the magazine *Kommunist,* set the tone of the national press. Central control is also

MVD and KGB

DOSAAF

Nomenclature system

strengthened by the ladderlike system of political schools (in their role as hurdles for promotion somewhat similar to military academies in the United States armed forces), through which party leaders must pass in order to get to the top.

Komsomol and Pioneers. The All-Union Leninist Communist League of Youth (Vsesoyuzny Leninsky Kommunistichesky Soyuz Molodyozhi, or VLKSM), better known as the Komsomol, according to Soviet sources had nearly 35,000,000 members, between the ages of 14 and 28, in 1976. The Komsomol has grown very rapidly, a growth that reflects in large part the continuing urbanization and industrialization of the country, since Komsomol recruitment is far more successful in the cities than in rural areas. The Komsomol's organizational structure is modelled on that of the CPSU, and many former Komsomol leaders have risen to high posts as executives of the party. The Komsomol is regarded by the party as its reserve and helper, terms that convey some sense of the organization's role as an agency of indoctrination in the official ideology and as a channel for dissemination of CPSU propaganda on domestic and international issues. The Komsomol issues a number of publications, the best known of which is the mass circulation newspaper *Komsomolskaya Pravda* ("Komsomol Truth").

There is general agreement among Western experts on the Komsomol that it has by no means achieved its officially imposed objective of creating a "new Soviet man," imbued with Leninist zeal and self-sacrificing devotion to the ruling party's goals. This verdict is based, in part, on frequent Soviet press reports indicating political apathy, cynicism, and even widespread delinquency among Komsomol members. On the other hand, the Komsomol is a useful device for mobilizing Soviet youth for such drives as the Virgin and Idle Lands Campaign of 1954–56, to settle virgin lands especially in Siberia and Central Asia.

Pioneers

The Komsomol also performs other functions for the party, such as assistance in the work of the Pioneers (All-Union Lenin Pioneer Organization, or Vsesoyuznaya Pionerskaya Organizatsiya Imeni V.I. Lenina), an organization the membership of which embraces Soviet schoolchildren between the ages of nine and 14. Vastly larger in membership than the Boy Scouts and Girl Scouts in the U.S., and, unlike them, an organ of the state, the Pioneers assist the schools in ideological and patriotic indoctrination of children. Pioneers wear a three-cornered red scarf, which according to Soviet sources symbolizes the unity of the Communist, Komsomol, and Pioneer generations. Under the guidance of the CPSU and the Komsomol, the Pioneers seek to instill in children disciplined work habits, love of learning, and identification with Soviet ideology and the social and political system. Children's summer camps and educational and recreational centres aid in the pursuit of these goals.

The trade unions. Soviet trade unions are organized according to broad branches of the economy, covering employees of all ranks within a particular branch, such as medicine or engineering. Collective farmers are not covered. Membership is not compulsory but appears highly advisable on both economic and political grounds. By the later 1970s, total union membership exceeded 113,500,000, accounting for all but a small percentage of the total number of eligible employees. Among the largest unions are those for state farm and allied employees and educational institutions.

The basic units are the enterprise and factory unions, most of which are run by small committees. The activities of the enterprise and factory unions are coordinated by town, provincial, or republican union councils, which are elected at the conferences of the basic unit representatives. At the top is the All-Union Trade Union Congress, which is supposed to be convened every four years. The principal task of the congress is to elect the All-Union Central Council of Trade Unions (or VTsSPS; Vsesoyuzny Tsentralny Sovet Professionalnykh Soyuzov), the Presidium of which is responsible for broad policy and activities. Detailed administrative work is handled by the Secretariat. Individual unions, the structure of which follows this pattern, are closely controlled by the central union authorities.

Union function

Unlike the situation in Western countries with market economics, where the function of trade unions is to advance the economic and other interest of workers in relation to employers, labour unions in the Soviet Union are agents of the state. Strikes are forbidden, if not in law certainly in practice. Worker protests and even brief spontaneous labour stoppages occur now and then, but the outside world learns of these only by word of mouth reports that reach foreigners; they are not reported in the controlled Soviet press. From such reports as have reached the West, it appears that military force has been used to put down labour disturbances and that very severe measures were taken against some of their participants.

In 1977 a number of workers founded a trade union independent of the state. The authorities reacted with repressive measures, but this effort to break the official monopoly of organization of labour was thought by many to be a harbinger of highly significant future developments.

The main function of the trade unions is to stimulate workers to increase their productivity. Among the methods used to achieve this, perhaps the best known is "socialist emulation," in which factory is pitted against factory, industry against industry, in nationwide production contests; winning enterprises are awarded banners and receive much praise in the press. Another important function of the unions is the administration of the social insurance system. They also operate an extensive system of rest homes and sanatoriums and generally play an important role in providing services to workers who are in good standing. Like the other Soviet mass organizations, the unions operate an extensive publications network, which of course functions within the framework of overall directives laid down by the CPSU Central Committee but focusses on matters of special interest to employees, including teachers and other professionals as well as industrial workers. The most important trade union publication is the newspaper *Trud* ("Labour").

SOCIAL CONDITIONS AND SERVICES

The basic principle of distribution of goods and services in the Soviet Union is stated in the constitution as "From each according to his ability, to each according to his work." The interpretation and application of this slogan is of course determined by the supreme leadership of the CPSU and is not subject to public discussion. There is abundant evidence, even in Soviet official sources—guarded though they are on such matters as the existence of pronounced inequality and privilege—that this constitutional principle is interpreted so as to permit very wide differences in income, perquisites, opportunities for domestic and foreign travel, access to quality education, and status and power. The existence of such differences is emphasized in statements by dissidents and by many former Soviet citizens now émigrés. In terms especially of power, but also in access to the best vacation and medical facilities, foreign travel, and many other values, high-ranking party and police executives, military officers, and government officials are at the upper end of the scale, while office workers, unskilled labourers, and collective farmers are at the bottom. Also exceptionally well off, in comparison with ordinary citizens, are writers and performing artists in good standing with the political authorities. Favoured novelists and playwrights receive enormous royalties. Scientists who rise to the coveted status of membership in the Academy of Sciences of the U.S.S.R. are perhaps the most honoured citizens of the Soviet Union. Not only do they enjoy, by Soviet standards, very comfortable incomes, superior recreational and medical facilities, and preferential access for their children to the best institutions of higher education, but they also receive substantial additional emoluments by virtue of their academy membership, in addition to their

Privileged persons

salaries as directors of scientific laboratories. Individual party officials who abuse their positions—for example, by building for their personal use excessively luxurious private homes, using materials illegally obtained at bargain prices—are from time to time sharply criticized or even severely punished, but, according to statements by leading Soviet dissidents, the traditional practice of regularly distributing special pay envelopes to party officials persists.

Soviet society is thus far from being egalitarian. The people are also, by the standards of advanced Western industrial nations, rather poor. The average wage of industrial workers, even at the most generous estimate, is about $200 a month U.S. Though rents are low, and housing, though still of very poor quality, is increasingly abundant, the prices of food and clothing are far higher, in proportion to income, than they are in the West. Both husband and wife usually must work in order to make ends meet, though it should also be said that the overwhelming majority of women apparently want to work at paying jobs. In certain respects, women have achieved much in the Soviet economy, as is exemplified by the dominant role of women in the medical profession. Most of the best jobs in all fields, however, and particularly in industry, politics, and public administration, are occupied by men.

Since Stalin's death, the Soviet authorities have made great efforts to raise the standard of living above the very low level of the Stalin era. Perhaps even more important is the program, begun under N.S. Khrushchev, to raise the incomes of the lowest paid categories of workers and in general to improve the economic situation of the workers and collective farmers. This has involved, among other measures, the extension of social security coverage to the collective farm peasantry, who until the mid-1960s remained outside the social security system. Since the mid-1950s there has been a fairly steady rise in Soviet living standards, though this has not necessarily increased the contentment of the mass of the population and has been interrupted by bad harvests, such as those of 1972 and 1975. There has been substantial improvement in a previously dire housing and very poor food situation. There has also been rapid progress in availability of basic consumer goods—excellent in terms of refrigerators, quite good in terms of washing machines and even of television sets, but still very poor in terms of private automobiles. The Soviet population by the later 1970s, however, was still at a standard of life far below that of all of the developed capitalist countries and of several of the eastern European Communist nations.

Health services. Public health and education are perhaps the areas in which Soviet achievements have been greatest, especially in quantitative terms. The official Soviet claim is that medical services are "free and accessible." It is also asserted in Soviet sources that the Soviet Union has about a quarter of all the physicians in the world and that it has more than 3,000,000 hospital beds. Even if these claims are somewhat exaggerated, and in any case say nothing about the quality of medical care, there is no doubt that the Soviet Union's record in this field has been impressive, particularly in view of the backward conditions that prevailed in the tsarist period and the difficulties that had to be overcome along the way. It is also apparent, however, that Soviet medical services—which are administered centrally by the Ministry of Health—suffer from the evils common to overcentralized, bureaucratically administered programs: excessive time is spent by both doctor and patient in record keeping and patients often experience long delays in getting treatment. Nor can it be said that the Soviet Union has a record of innovation in medical research and development even remotely comparable to that of the United States and other advanced Western nations, and the quality of care available to Soviet citizens (so far as it can be judged on the limited information to which foreign students have access) is not equal to the best offered by Western medicine. There is no

doubt, however, that death rates have been substantially reduced (though beginning in the 1970s the infant mortality rate rose substantially and life expectancy fell slightly), and the health of the population compares well with that of citizens of other industrial countries.

Education. An objective Western observer cannot fail to be impressed by the achievements of the Soviet Union in the field of education, especially quantitatively. At the same time, he will also be struck by the peculiarities of the vast Soviet program as it is viewed from the perspective of Western traditions. According to Soviet statistics, 46,468,000 pupils were enrolled in "general educational" schools of all kinds in 1976–77 (a drop from six years previously, when the figure exceeded 49,000,000). At the level of higher education, with a reported 4,950,000 students in 1976–77, the Soviet educational effort was surpassed quantitatively only by that of the United States, which had about 8,000,000 students in four-year colleges and universities (and another 3,000,000 in two-year institutions).

The Soviet educational system is characterized by extreme centralization and uniformity in structure and curriculum and by heavy-handed political control and political indoctrination. Especially (but not only) in the humanities and social sciences, textbooks and classroom instruction are permeated by Marxist–Leninist propaganda. Applicants for higher education must pass examinations in political subjects and must continue to devote several hours a week to the study of political subjects even after admission to medical or other professional schools.

Even in quantitative terms, however, Soviet education has thus far by no means achieved the goals set by the CPSU leadership. Universal secondary education (10 years of schooling) has not been attained, despite many years of predictions in the official press that it was imminent. Certainly the country is far from having made education equally available to all of its youth. Rural, as contrasted to urban, youth are still at a great disadvantage in access to secondary and still more to higher education. As for access to the best universities, such as the state universities of Moscow and Leningrad, or to the best specialized scientific, economic, and other institutes, children of workers and peasants are at an almost hopeless disadvantage in comparison with children of professional people, administrators, and officials. The advantages of the intelligentsia in this respect are apparently so great that many students of the Soviet Union believe that a hereditary class, or caste, system may be forming, if indeed it has not already taken shape. Great efforts are made to provide opportunities to work toward higher education, by evening or correspondence study, etc., for young people who have chosen or have been forced to take jobs in industry upon graduation from primary or secondary school. It is generally agreed, however, that, useful though such efforts may be to the economy, they come nowhere near to equalizing opportunities for higher education.

Education in the Soviet Union is a formidable instrument of national policy. It provides the national economy, the armed forces, science and engineering, and the communications media with an abundance of reasonably well-trained man- and womanpower. These young people have acquired basic skills in a highly organized setting, in which discipline and conformity to authority are stressed. Also, though almost half of the Soviet population belongs to non-Russian national minorities, an apparently successful effort is made to teach all graduates (at least of the secondary schools and of course of higher educational institutions) to read and speak Russian effectively. Indeed, for non-Russians, mastering Russian—in addition to a "sound" political outlook—is a prerequisite for career advancement. Certainly the educational system is one of the sinews of the Soviet state. It is possible, however, that its successes, by providing for some individuals at least a basis for critical thought, may cause trouble for Soviet rulers in the future.

(FREDERICK C. BARGHOORN)

Standard of living

Politics and education

149

One of the more fascinating articles in the Britannica is titled "Food Supply of the World." The article has been in the encyclopaedia for many years, and, of course, from time to time it requires updating. The abridged version of the new revision that appears below reveals some interesting facts about our world economy. It shows, for example, that western Europe and North America produce more beef than all other areas of the world combined. Careful perusal of the text, and of the statistical tables, reveals many significant things about the world's food supply—including the fact that during 1971–85 supplies in less developed countries will have to double to alleviate present shortages and to take care of population increases.

FOOD SUPPLY OF THE WORLD

When, in the mid-19th century, Europe's population suddenly began to multiply and starvation threatened, its emigrants opened up temperate lands in other continents to provide the needed grain, meat, and dairy products. Since World War II, another population explosion has started, this time in the developing countries and much more rapid than anything previously seen, and will, some say, result in widespread famine. The successes of scientists and the many possibilities of applying agricultural technology in the developing countries, however, offer hope that with appropriate effort sufficient food can be produced for all people. The United Nations has projected that world population may stabilize at some 12,-000,000,000 to 15,000,000,000 around the middle of the 21st century. Technically—in terms of the world's resources of soil and water and knowledge of agricultural techniques—it would be possible to feed this many people; whether it will be possible in practice remains to be seen.

THE FOOD SHORTAGE IN DEVELOPING COUNTRIES

Trends in population and food production. In 1975 the population of the world reached 4,000,000,000, sharply divided in terms of social and economic welfare between 3,000,000,000 in the developing countries and 1,000,-000,000 in the developed countries. (As used in this article, "developed countries" include Europe, the Soviet Union, North America, Australia, New Zealand, and, for the postwar years, South Africa, Japan, and Israel; "developing countries" include, unless otherwise indicated, all other countries.) The trends in food production in each group are shown in Table 1, as of August 1977.

Contrary to popular belief, total food output in the developing countries has expanded as rapidly as in the developed. It is in relation to population that the picture becomes quite different. Taking the average of the years 1961–65 as 100, production per person in the developed countries rose from 81 in 1948–52 (that is, just after World War II) to 94 in 1956–60 and 115 in 1971–76. In developing countries production per person rose fairly steadily after the war till about 1958. Thereafter it was almost stagnant. Population increase each year, about 2.3 percent, absorbed most of the increase in production.

The disquieting paradox persists: the already well-fed peoples are able to expand their food production faster than their requirements grow—despite the fact that in some of the rich countries, notably the United States, governments have deliberately restrained production—whereas for poorly fed peoples the reverse is the case. At the very end of the 1960s, as a result of the "green revolution," there were some signs of an upsurge in food production in certain developing countries, notably in Asia. During the 1970s, however, the surge was not maintained.

Since 1972 the world has been close to crisis in its food supply. In that year, poor crops were harvested in most of the major cereal-producing areas, particularly in the Soviet Union, India, and North America. World stocks were almost depleted. Stocks of cereals (outside China and the Soviet Union), which had been 26 percent of total consumption in 1970, had already fallen to 19 percent in 1972. In 1973, as a result of the poor harvests in 1972, they had been drawn down to 14 percent, and in succeeding years they went even lower.

Table 1: Trends in Food Production*
(1961–65 average = 100)

item	1948–52	1956–60	1971–76
Total			
Developed countries†	68	89	130
Developing countries			
Excluding China	66	87	133
Including China	...	...	133
Per person			
Developed countries†	81	94	115
Developing countries			
Excluding China	89	98	102
Including China	...	...	104

*Excluding fish.
†Including eastern Europe and the Soviet Union.
Source: Food and Agriculture Organization, Rome.

Beginning with the 1973 season, the crop situation was complicated by both shortages and very high prices of fertilizers. Partly but not wholly because of the dramatic rise in petroleum prices, prices of fertilizers rose four- to fivefold. The rise in food and fertilizer prices hit particularly those developing countries, such as India, that did not have oil or some other product that benefitted from the price boom.

As a consequence of the earlier trends, the developed countries exported larger and larger quantities of food to the developing countries. Beginning in the mid-1950s, this trade doubled, while the agricultural exports of the developing group recorded only a modest increase. At the same time the imports of food into developing countries increased more rapidly than food imports into developed countries.

The Food and Agriculture Organization (FAO) of the United Nations has calculated that, if these trends in

Margin notes:
World population, 1975

Exports and imports of food

population and food production continue, the net cereal deficit of the developing market economies would have to rise from 16,000,000 tons in 1969–71 to almost 85,-000,000 tons by 1985 in order to meet the projected increase in demand. Since it is entirely unlikely that the poor countries could finance imports of this magnitude or that rich donor countries would give so much away, ways and means will have to be found to enable the developing countries to feed themselves.

The nature of the problem. The food supply problems of the two groups of countries are therefore radically different. In the advanced countries, where food production increases at 2.7 percent per year, population at 1 percent, and per capita food consumption hardly at all, the central problem has been one of supply management. This is dwarfed by the much vaster and more urgent food supply problems of the developing countries, in which large segments of the population are malnourished or actually hungry. By 1985, simply to cover expected increases in population and modest increases in purchasing power, the food supply of the developing countries will have to expand at an average rate of 3.6 percent a year.

Food scarcity in developing countries

To this challenge, no single or simple solution exists. Progress has to be organized in several directions concurrently; for instance, by making better use of existing food supplies, by increasing agricultural inputs, by strengthening research, agricultural services, and rural institutions, by pursuing appropriate national economic and population policies, and by a concerted expansion of international trade and foreign aid. Objectives in most of these fields were proposed by the FAO in its *Provisional Indicative World Plan for Agricultural Development,* published in 1969, and were subsequently updated in the proposals presented to and broadly agreed on by the United Nations World Food Conference, held in Rome in November 1974.

MAJOR PROBLEMS OF FOOD SUPPLIES

Crop production. Since World War II, food production has expanded more rapidly than during any comparable period in history. Had it not been for the equally rapid rise in population in developing countries, the problem of hunger and malnutrition would have been nearly solved. In the developed countries, almost all the increased output came from higher yields per acre, cereal acreages showing little change except in the Soviet Union, where virgin lands in the east and southeast were brought into cultivation. Wheat yields in Europe, for example, rose from 14.7 quintals per hectare (1,310 pounds per acre) in 1948–52 to 30.2 (2,690) in 1975, an annual increment of 3.1 percent. In the U.S. the average yield of corn (maize) was 24.9 quintals (2,220 pounds) in 1948–52 and 54.1 (4,830) in 1975, an annual increase of 3.5 percent. In the developing countries during the 1960s, expansion of area was responsible for about 40 percent of increased production, higher yields for the remainder.

Some of the increased cereal output in developed countries has been exported (especially from North America to developing countries that faced shortages), but the greater part has gone to livestock feeding. In the years ahead, most of the developed countries will require more feed grain but less wheat, whereas the developing countries need more cereals for both food and feed. To meet this need, intensified use of existing farmland appears generally more economic than expansion of area.

Plant breeding for high yield

To increase yields per acre requires a judicious combination of physical techniques and supporting services. Plant breeding, including increasing the supplies of the much-publicized high-yielding varieties of wheat and rice, should play a major role. In the Far East the Mexican wheat and the Philippine rice seed, together with vastly improved varieties from other sources, already account for 54 percent of the wheat area and 20 percent of the rice area. Elsewhere may be found significant "islands" of progress; *e.g.,* hybrid maize in Kenya, wheat in Turkey, improved rice in Madagascar and Brazil, and wheat throughout Mexico.

In order to succeed, the new varieties require ample balanced fertilizer—as much as 120 kilograms of nitrogen per hectare (about 107 pounds per acre) plus appropriate quantities of phosphate and potash, for example. Fertilizer consumption between 1949–51 and 1972–73 rose in developed countries from 22 to 102 kilograms of plant nutrient per arable hectare (from about 20 to 91 pounds per acre) and in developing countries from 1.4 to 1.7 kilograms (from 1.25 to 1.50 pounds). The FAO's *Indicative World Plan* calculated that in these latter countries fertilizer consumption should increase from 2,600,000 tons (1962) to more than 31,000,000 tons (1985).

A second essential element is water. Around 1962 irrigation was used on some 72,000,000 hectares (178,000,-000 acres), or 19 percent of the harvested crop area, in the countries studied by the FAO in the *Indicative World Plan.* The plan proposed to double this area by 1985, with greater emphasis than previously on groundwater, at a cost of some $36,000,000,000 plus another $11,000,000,-000 for drainage, flood control, and related works.

Irrigation

Other necessary elements include crop protection with pesticides to combat loss of potential production, a loss estimated at more than $50,000,000,000 in the developing countries in 1965. Also, mechanization is expected to increase yields and reduce harvesting losses by more timely sowing and reaping; in suitable environments it makes multiple cropping possible. But the economics of applying mechanical power require careful study where, as in the majority of the developing countries, the farm labour supply is already excessive and destined to become more so.

Better cultivation practices can contribute much; *e.g.,* terracing, contour plowing, planting of shelter belts, growing of grass or legumes in rotation with grain or tilled crops, mulching, and growing legumes in rotation. There is no set formula. Measures must vary according to the environment and are very different, for example, in low rainfall areas of more or less level terrain from those in mountainous terrain.

Where annual winter rainfall exceeds 400 millimetres (16 inches) in the Near East, northwest Africa, and the northern Indo-Gangetic plain, it probably would be profitable to replace the cereal–fallow rotation by alternate rain-fed cropping of cereals and fodder legumes, such as clovers and lucerne (alfalfa), with the possibility of more comprehensive rotations—including grain legumes, such as lentils and chick-peas (gram), oilseeds, or other cash crops—in areas of higher rainfall.

One of the best formulas for providing more employment and at the same time increasing incomes undoubtedly is multiple cropping. In Hong Kong, for instance, 80 percent of the vegetable farmers plant more than four crops a year and 45 percent plant seven to nine crops. While these examples cannot be imitated everywhere, there are many regions of dense population, suitable climate, and good water supply in which multiple cropping could be, but is not, practiced.

Multiple cropping

Livestock and fish. To the world's protein supply, livestock products contribute 35 percent and fish 6 percent. Formerly the production of both was concentrated in a few favoured areas. More than half of the world's milk and nearly half of its meat is produced in Europe and North America. Most of the food fish comes from waters adjacent to Europe, North America, and Japan.

Table 2: Meat Production in Developed and Developing Countries				
item	1948–52 (000,000 metric tons)	1976 (000,000 metric tons)	index (1948–52 = 100)	growth rate compound (percent per year)
Developed countries	32.3	81.9	254	4.0
Developing countries	16.5	39.7	241	3.7
World	48.8	121.6	249	3.9
Source: Food and Agriculture Organization, Rome.				

Between the immediate postwar period (1948–52) and 1976, numbers of cattle increased by 34 percent in Europe (excluding the Soviet Union), 60 percent in North America, as much as 68 percent in Africa, and 63 percent in Latin America. As shown in Table 2, world meat production more than doubled during that period, both in developed countries (including the Soviet Union) and in developing countries (including China).

Fish production between 1950 and 1975 increased only modestly in North America and by 100 percent in western Europe; in the Soviet Union, however, it rose 507 percent, in East and Southeast Asia (including Japan) 205 percent, and in Africa 266 percent. Especially noteworthy was the Latin-American expansion from 640,000 tons to 15,000,000 tons (1970), mainly accounted for by the anchoveta (a small anchovy), processed in Peruvian fish-meal plants for export to industrial countries. Thereafter the catch of anchovetas declined—probably temporarily—because of changes in ocean currents.

Consumption of livestock products

It is in consumption of livestock products that the greatest difference between rich and poor peoples is observed. Thus, meat consumption approaches 230 grams (8.1 ounces) per person per day in the United States and is even higher in Argentina, Australia, and New Zealand; by contrast, it reaches only 58 grams (2.03 ounces) in Mexico, 19 grams (0.7 ounce) in Nigeria, and four grams (0.14 ounce) in India. Similarly, the consumption of milk products, which exceeds 700 grams (25 ounces) per person per day (in terms of fresh milk equivalent) in Scandinavia and 670 grams (23.6 ounces) in the United States, reaches only 75 grams (2.6 ounces) in Tanzania and 13 grams (0.46 ounce) in Thailand.

Table 3: Relative Productivity of Cattle by Region, 1976

region	cattle (000,000)	production meat (000,000 tons)	production milk (000,000 tons)	total*	ratio of production to numbers of cattle
Western Europe	101	8.0	125	205	2.03
United States and Canada	142	13.4	62	196	1.38
Soviet Union	111	6.2	89	151	1.36
Australia and New Zealand	43	1.8	13	31	0.72
Latin America	266	7.9	31	110	0.41
Near East	46	0.8	7	15	0.33
Africa	130	1.7	5	22	0.17
Far East	254	0.9	11	20	0.08

*In milk equivalent, one ton of meat being taken as equal in production to 10 tons of milk.
Source: Food and Agriculture Organization, Rome.

Many lines of attack can be pursued simultaneously. Some of the major grassland areas of the developing countries are understocked, and others are hopelessly overgrazed. The introduction of range management would in time greatly augment the carrying capacity of these lands. Fodder crops can be much more widely grown, especially on irrigated land, once the national supply of food crops has become adequate. By-products, often wasted, can be turned into feed concentrates; an example is the successful use of molasses combined with urea for fattening beef cattle. In some regions—*e.g.,* in many parts of Africa—customary forms of land tenure and the hoarding of animals as investment capital impede the introduction of modern cattle raising, as do religious beliefs in parts of southern Asia. Eradication of the tsetse fly from Central Africa would make available 7,000,000 square kilometres (2,700,000 square miles) for cattle raising. The Dairy Development Scheme of the FAO would link the dried milk surpluses of exporting countries to the building of dairy industries in developing countries. These programs will take time. Much more rapid expansion of meat supplies can be achieved by first developing large-scale poultry production and, where acceptable, pig production, though this, as well as beef and dairy expansion, requires the introduction of modern market structures—cold storage, transport, inspection services—and stronger price incentives. A precondition for commercial poultry and pig production is availability of grain supplies beyond human needs.

Expanding fisheries

Fisheries could also expand, since the demand for food fish and fish meal is expected approximately to double between 1965 and 1985. Necessary measures include the introduction of powered vessels and modern gear where these are yet unknown, investment in port facilities, the training of fishermen, and the creation of facilities for cooling the product during storage and distribution. In oceans intensively fished, governments will need to agree upon management and conservation measures, while areas such as the Indian Ocean, the South Pacific, and the Antarctic could be more fully utilized. The culture of fish, especially mollusks, is generally profitable in shallow coastal waters, as is the growing of carp in freshwater ponds.

Better use of existing supplies of food. Another approach to increasing food supplies is to cut down the wastage that occurs at all stages. At the very start of the production process, the land itself in many regions is abused by shifting cultivation, overgrazing, lack of terracing or of tree cover, or poor drainage. The water supply is misused, with wastage of up to 50 percent through faulty design of irrigation systems, overpumping that turns groundwater brackish, or pollution that renders water unusable for either agriculture or fish culture. Animal manures in many countries are used for fuel or simply wasted, and the nutrient value of chemical fertilizers may be partially lost through incorrect application. Investment in extension services to advise farmers about correcting these malpractices would produce important and immediate benefits.

Preventing wastage

In crop husbandry, weeds, pests, and diseases can each cause losses of up to 30 percent. Birds and locusts take a heavy toll, as do primitive harvesting and winnowing methods; even in the United States, with all its modern equipment, studies show grain losses of 5 to 10 percent in the field. In developing countries the percentage is far higher.

In the animal husbandry of the developing countries, high rates of infertility and prenatal mortality are caused by reproductive disorders; poor nutrition results in gastrointestinal parasitism; endemic diseases such as inflammation of the udder reduce milk yields; and other diseases, such as foot-and-mouth disease in Latin America, impede the development of what could be a valuable export business.

Storage losses are notorious. The United States reports 3 to 7 percent grain losses in storage, but in Africa, for example, up to one-third of stored maize may be lost. Yet plastic sheets for drying grain can be had cheaply, and the construction of rat-proof bins and the fumigation of stored grains are not prohibitively expensive.

In the case of perishables, losses are even more serious and the remedies more costly. Thus, in parts of Africa, up to 40 percent of the fruit, vegetables, and eggs sent to urban markets may be lost as a result of faulty packing, infrequent transport, and lack of cold or other suitable storage. In some Near Eastern countries, half the sheep's milk goes bad because of the lack of coolers. In the tropics, fish becomes inedible within 24 hours after removal from the water, which restricts boats without refrigeration to a narrow fishing range. The installation of cold-storage facilities becomes profitable when a sizable urban market has developed and when regular supplies can be counted on.

Agricultural policies. In addition to the technical and scientific progress involved in improving the world's food supply, the social and economic aspects count for as much. In these fields governments have a major responsibility, whether in price and tax policies, in agrarian reform, in creating institutions and services, or in promoting foreign trade.

Prices and taxation. It is not enough for governments to announce a guaranteed price for a product; they must ensure that producers receive that price rather than only half or two-thirds of it. Farmers in developing countries sell their produce at unfavourable moments either because they have insufficient storage, are short of cash, or have been misinformed. In Colombia, for instance, the price of potatoes after harvest falls to one-third of the preharvest level. Remedies include the creation of a sufficient number of local buying points at which official prices are posted and inspectors are present; the construction of more storage space to permit orderly crop disposal; and the provision of credit facilities to relieve farmers from the need to make forced sales.

Taxation policy toward agriculture continues to be of much interest in developing countries. Governments cannot afford to exempt from taxation the farm people who constitute 50 to 80 percent of the population, and yet they must ensure that taxes as well as price policies encourage rather than discourage maximum food production.

Agrarian reform. In many regions, traditional modes of land tenure interfere with expansion of food production either in direct ways or through the perpetuation of a nonprogressive social structure. Where feudal-type estates still exist, for example, the policy of subdividing them must compromise between the need to satisfy land hunger and the desirability of creating farms large enough to be profitable; and, simultaneously with subdivision, new organizations must be established for the marketing, credit, and other services formerly provided, though imperfectly, by the landlords. In several regions of Africa, customary tenures that impede rational land use are being gradually converted to individual or group ownership. In nomadic pastoral economies, where the settlement of nomads may be neither practicable nor desirable, reforms concentrate not on tenure aspects but rather on more rational stocking and range management, on the creation of more water points, and on the provision of veterinary services and supplementary feed supplies. Finally, in districts facing the problem of an excess of very small or badly fragmented farms, costly investments are involved in the consolidation of holdings.

Institutional support. The rapid increases in food output in advanced countries must be attributed in large part to the research and other agricultural services that were built up during previous decades. These services are still embryonic in many developing countries.

Agricultural extension services

Some national governments, sometimes with outside assistance, are building up their agricultural extension services, deliberately linking them to farm credit and marketing facilities, and encouraging the creation of farmers' organizations. To provide recruits for these services and to give farmers some basic agricultural education, training programs at all levels are being established. In some countries, the doubling or even tripling of trained personnel seems to be required.

Agricultural trade. Although less than 10 percent of the world's food crosses national frontiers, and only a few countries, notably in western Europe, import as much as half their supplies, a number of countries, including most of the developing countries, rely on agricultural exports to furnish more than half of their foreign currency earnings. Table 4 illustrates the contrast, with respect to trade in agricultural products.

Table 4: Value of Total Agricultural Trade, 1976*

item	exports	imports
	(000,000,000 $ U.S. at current prices)	
Developed market economies	79.6	95.4
Soviet Union and eastern Europe	6.6	16.8
Total developed countries	86.2	112.2
Developing market economies	40.2	27.0
Asian centrally planned economies	2.5	3.0
Total developing countries	42.7	30.0
World total	128.9	142.2

*The definition of agricultural trade follows that of the FAO *Trade Yearbook.* Agricultural trade excludes forestry and fishery products, with the exception of fish meal and marine oils. Re-exports are normally included.
Source: Food and Agriculture Organization, Rome.

Exports

Paradoxically, the well-fed countries are net importers and the poorly fed net exporters of food. The developed countries' major agricultural exports are composed chiefly of cereals and rice (43 percent); oilseeds, vegetable oils, and sugar (27 percent); and nonfood agricultural products (13 percent). Those of the developing countries include beverages (30 percent); nonfood agricultural products (26 percent); sugar, oilseeds, and vegetable oils (23 percent).

During the decade 1963–73, the volume of the developed countries' agricultural exports rose 73 percent, but that of the developing countries rose only 21 percent (Latin America, 25 percent; Far East, 21; Near East, 35; Africa, 7). Over the 1960s the developed countries benefitted from an increase of some 10 percent in the unit values of their exports, whereas those of developing countries suffered a more than 10 percent decline. Trade in fishery products doubled during the decade, mainly among developed countries, with some export to the developed countries from developing countries (especially fish meal from Latin America). Developing countries themselves do not import much fish.

Many developed countries have maintained tariff and nontariff barriers that shield their farmers from the competition of cheap food imports. Many meetings related to the General Agreement on Tariffs and Trade (GATT) have been devoted to a search for ways of liberalizing trade in farm products, but with little success. Major countries continue to make use of the "waiver" under which they absolve themselves from applying to agriculture the general trading rules of GATT.

Price stabilization

Strong fluctuations in world market prices have always been a particular hazard for countries that are heavily dependent on agricultural exports. Although the most dramatic instances occurred during the Great Depression of the 1930s, price fluctuations persisted during the 1950s and '60s and were particularly marked during the early 1970s. Interested governments have attempted to negotiate international commodity agreements containing price stabilization provisions. Because of economic and political complexities, few such agreements have been concluded, and even in these cases (for example, in wheat) it has often proved to be impossible to hold the price within the prescribed limits. More modest, but often more successful, has been the work of commodity study groups, in which the principal exporters and importers of a product meet regularly to review developments and on occasion to conclude informal trade arrangements.

PROSPECTS

In assessing food-supply prospects, an attempt must be made to determine the expected increase in demand and to see how fully this demand could be met by carrying through the technical and economic programs described above.

Demand for food. What economists call "effective demand for food" is the amount that people want to buy given the money that they have. Future effective demand depends mainly on two factors: growth of population and growth of income.

Population. The biggest challenge facing the world's food supply is the population explosion in the developing countries. During the 1950s, population in these countries (excluding China and other areas of Asia having central planning) grew at 2.4 percent per year (compared with 1.2 percent in developed countries); during the 1960s the rate rose to 2.7 percent in the developing countries (and dropped to 1 percent in developed countries). The rate of growth has been increasing in the developing group but decreasing in the developed.

Income. Estimates based on accepted hypotheses as to the likely rate of growth of national income in the developing countries indicate that between 1969–71 and 1985 per capita demand for food will increase by about 9 percent. Combining this with the expected population growth gives an estimated increase of 66 percent in total food demand. Of the two growth factors, population and income, population will be by far the more influential, accounting for seven-tenths of the estimated increase.

Protein needs

Requirements for food. In the developed countries dietary energy supplies exceed estimated requirements by about 23 percent, while in developing countries they fall short by 5 percent; but 5 percent is an average, and many individuals' diets fall far below the average.

The protein problem is more complex. The advanced countries have an average of 96 grams (3.4 ounces) of protein per person per day, of which more than half is animal protein; this exceeds requirements. The people of the developing countries have an average intake of only 57 grams (2 ounces) of protein per day, much of which is diverted from its true protein functions in an attempt to meet energy deficits. Among developing countries wide differences occur, largely because of ecological and cultural conditions. In moving from the diets of developed countries, which have animal products as the main source of protein, through diets based on wheat, maize, sorghum, or rice, and on to root and tuber diets, the protein intake diminishes, the quality of dietary protein declines because of imbalances in the amino acid content, the protein–energy balance deteriorates, and the gap between intake and recommended allowances widens.

Prospective supply. In the developed countries, apart from a few poorer regions of Europe, no change in dietary energy supplies is anticipated in the near future; but in the developing countries—to eliminate the present shortage, cover the population and income increase, and provide a 10 percent safety margin—energy supplies will have to be almost doubled between 1969–71 and 1985. This lies within the capacity of most, though not all, of the developing countries, provided that they pursue vigorous policies of agricultural investment and modernization.

In developed countries, no overall supply problem exists for protein. What is expected to occur is a rearrangement of the sources of protein; namely, an increase in the proportion represented by animal protein. Public assistance to supplement the incomes of specially disadvantaged groups may remain necessary, since protein foods will still be relatively expensive items in the diet.

In developing countries, it is improvement in the quality of protein and its availability to poorer people that requires attention. Part of the problem is to change traditional dietary habits through nutrition education in order to diversify the diet and obtain a better use of the available food supply. Part lies in asking the plant breeder to develop species of, for example, rice and wheat, with nutritionally more satisfactory amino acid content, as is being attempted with maize. Pulses and high-protein oilseeds can become significant supplements to cereal and starchy root diets. Much can be accomplished and relatively quickly in expanding the production of pigs, poultry, and fish. Further, the fortification of certain staple foods with amino acids, minerals, and vitamins, though costly, might be justified in particular circumstances in which specific nutrient deficiencies have been identified.

New foods

More unconventional sources of protein are already being developed in advanced countries: "artificial meat" from soya meal; fish protein concentrate, an odourless flour for mixing into other foods; food yeast from the by-products of pulp and paper manufacture. Certain seaweeds are eaten in Japan and, to a lesser extent, in other Far Eastern countries. Interest has focussed on *Chlorella,* an alga that multiplies itself at fantastic speed and that, if it could be made acceptable for human consumption, would constitute an almost unlimited source of protein. Not least important is the work on single-cell protein; several factories already transform petroleum waxes into protein intended for animal feeds, and there is potential for human use as well.

INTERNATIONAL AID

The task of feeding the huge populations of the 1980s and feeding them at least somewhat better than today presents a challenge to scientists, educators, economists, administrators, and farmers. The greatest efforts are needed in the countries least equipped to carry out the needed programs. The rich nations already have the necessary knowledge and skills; the poor have first to attain them. Indubitably the main impetus must come from the peoples of the developing countries themselves; they and their governments must mobilize the investments and train the manpower. Yet a role remains for assistance and aid from the rich countries. Those who have plenty in terms of capital, skills, and commodities can do much to help the less fortunate nations win their battle against poverty.

Food aid. In the 1950s the United States began a large program for transferring much of its surplus food on concessional terms to needy countries. Other advanced countries also initiated such transfers on a more modest scale. Finally, in 1962, the FAO World Food Program was established to undertake multilateral food aid. Its activities include emergency feeding after such disasters as earthquakes or floods and economic and social development projects such as maternal and child feeding, animal production and dairy development, land development and improvement, land settlement, and forestry. Care is exercised that food transferred under these programs jeopardizes neither the market for the output of farmers in recipient countries nor the market for normal commercial exporters. Of course food aid, bilateral and multilateral, cannot be contemplated as a permanent element in the food supply of the poorer countries, which ultimately must become economically independent; but it does provide valuable assistance during the transitional period in which they are modernizing their agriculture. The World Food Conference agreed on a minimum target of 10,000,000 tons of food aid a year.

The FAO World Food Program

Technical and financial aid. The net flow of financial resources to developing countries for all purposes, according to calculations by the Organization for Economic Co-operation and Development (OECD), rose from $9,200,000,000 in 1961 to about $40,000,000,000 in 1975. Of this, $16,000,000,000 was official assistance and $22,000,000,000 private capital flow; but official development assistance, in terms of the gross national product of donor countries, fell from 0.52 percent to 0.36 percent. A more positive element has been the increasing attention given to agriculture. Total OECD assistance to the agricultural sector was $2,633,000,000 in 1975. In 1968 the World Bank announced its intention of quadrupling its assistance to agriculture over the following five years; already in fiscal 1971–72 World Bank and International Development Association loans and credits to this sector totalled $436,000,000. By 1975 it was $1,858,000,000, but in fiscal 1976 the total dropped to $1,628,000,000. Technical assistance has expanded more rapidly than financial aid, indeed by more than 10 percent a year. Of expenditure through the UN system, agricultural projects during 1964–74 accounted for about one-third.

The World Food Conference of November 1974 called for the establishment of an International Fund for Agricultural Development, in order to obtain the necessary great increase in external financial assistance for the agriculture of the developing countries. It also agreed on a wide range of other measures, particularly concerning the acceleration of the increase in food production in the developing countries, and a coordinated system of national stock policies embodied in an International Undertaking on World Food Security. If the follow-up to the World Food Conference lives up to professions of intent, a beginning will have been made in the establishment of a world food policy.

International Fund for Agricultural Development

BIBLIOGRAPHY. Current statistical and other information may be found in the following Food and Agriculture Organization (FAO) publications: *Trade Yearbook; Production Yearbook; FAO Yearbook of Fisheries Statistics; The State of Food and Agriculture; Monthly Bulletin of Agricultural Economics and Statistics.* See also *Provisional Indicative World Plan for Agricultural Development* (1969); UNITED NATIONS WORLD FOOD CONFERENCE, *Assessment of the World Food Situation, Present and Future* (1974); *The World Food Problem: Proposals for National and International Action* (1974); *Report of the World Food Conference* (1975).

(ADDEKE HENDRIK BOERMA)

BOOK OF THE YEAR
1978

Aerial Sports

One of the few great aerial challenges remaining for mankind was spectacularly overcome in 1978 with the conquest of the Atlantic Ocean by three U.S. balloonists.

Ballooning. In a six-day flight that recalled Charles Lindbergh's epic solo in 1927—and followed roughly the same route—Ben Abruzzo, Maxie Anderson, and Larry Newman (*see* BIOGRAPHIES) piloted their helium-filled "Double Eagle II" balloon from Presque Isle, Maine, across the Atlantic to Miserey, France, just 88 km (55 mi) short of their hoped-for goal of Paris' Le Bourget Airport. In so doing they established new world records for balloons of 137 hours 3 minutes duration in flight and 5,023 km (3,120 mi) distance.

Their successful August flight was the 18th attempt to cross the Atlantic in a balloon. Only two weeks earlier, two British balloonists had flown to within 240 km (150 mi) of the French coast before ditching. In all, seven balloonists have lost their lives in Atlantic crossing attempts since the first was tried in 1873.

Abruzzo and Anderson had attempted an Atlantic flight in 1977 in a balloon named "Double Eagle I," but they were forced into the sea off Iceland by adverse winds. For their 1978 effort they acquired Newman, a pilot noted for his navigational skills. Their balloon, which featured a catamaran type of gondola equipped with 800 sq ft of sail, was in part designed by Ed Yost, who himself set duration and distance records with an attempted transatlantic flight in 1976.

The Double Eagle team had to brave both a blistering Sun and nighttime temperatures that fell to −13° C (8° F), but their chief problem was that of conserving ballast. Balloons can be steered only by changing altitudes in search of different wind directions, and ballast plays a vital role. The "Double Eagle II" was launched with more than 4,000 lb of ballast, of which 3,275 lb were jettisoned during the flight.

In a historic July 22, 1978, flight, Anderson and U.S. balloonists Chauncey Dunn and Fred Hyde became the first to cross the 14,000-ft-high continental divide of North America in a lighter-than-air ship.

Gliding. At the 16th World Gliding Championships at Châteauroux, France, in July, George Lee of Britain took first place in the Open Class with 10,163 points in an AS-W 17. Bruno Gantenbrink of West Germany finished second with 10,018 points in a Nimbus, and François-Louis Henry of France won third with 9,919 points in a Nimbus.

The 15-m class competition was won by Helmut Reichmann of West Germany with 10,544 points in an SB-11. Karl Striedieck of the U.S. was second with 10,500 points in an As-W 20, and Goran Ax of Sweden finished third with 10,142 points in an As-W 20. In the Standard Class, Baer Selen of The Netherlands was first with 10,681 points in an As-W 19; Leonardo Brigliadori of Italy second with 10,321 points in a Cirrus; and Michel Reculé of France third with 10,185 points in a Cirrus.

Karl Striedieck and Wally Scott of the U.S. took first and second places, respectively, in the 1978 Smirnoff Transcontinental Sailplane Derby May 2 through May 17, with Ingo Renner of Australia placing third. The Los Angeles to Washington, D.C., contest was terminated at St. Louis because of bad weather. Renner won the Australian National Gliding Championships in January.

David Wapier Speight, Dick Georgeson, and Bruce Lindsay Drake of New Zealand set an astonishing world record for distance to a goal of 1,254.26 km (779.36 mi), all of it over New Zealand. On July 5, 1978, Gary Patmor of the U.S. claimed a world hang glider altitude record of 3,266 m (10,715 ft) over Bishop, Calif.

Parachuting. At the 14th World Parachuting Accuracy and Style Championships at Zagreb, Yugos., in September, first place for overall men's team performance went to East Germany, second

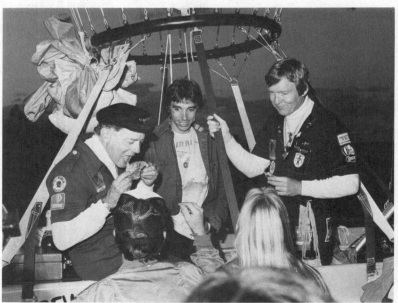

Balloonists Ben Abruzzo, Larry Newman, and Maxie Anderson (left to right) appear confident at the start of their historic crossing of the Atlantic aboard the "Double Eagle II" in August.

One of the competitors in the International Flying Wing contest got a bird's-eye view of Monaco from an altitude of 3,000 feet.

place to the U.S.S.R., and third to West Germany. In the women's team competition, the U.S.S.R. won first place overall; the U.S., second place; and East Germany, third.

Cheryl Stearns, the only female member of the U.S. Army's Golden Knights parachute team, won the women's absolute championship and set a world record for style performance of 6.3 sec. Two East German jumpers and one from the U.S.S.R. tied for first place in accuracy.

On Aug. 6, 1978, Mrs. Ardath Evitt, a 74-year-old Illinois great-grandmother, became the world's oldest woman parachutist with a jump at Kelly Field near Mooresville, Ind. She was trained by her grandson, Clyde Taylor, who made the jump with her. (MICHAEL D. KILIAN)

Afghanistan

A people's republic in central Asia, Afghanistan is bordered by the U.S.S.R., China, Pakistan, and Iran. Area: 653,000 sq km (252,100 sq mi). Pop. (1977 est.): 20,882,000, including (1978 est.) Pashtoon 50%; Tadzhik 25%; Uzbek 9%; Hazara 9%. Cap. and largest city: Kabul (pop., 1976 est., 749,-000). Language: Dari Persian and Pashto. Religion: Muslim. President to April 27, 1978, Sardar Mohammad Daud Khan; afterward prime minister and president of the Revolutionary Council, Nur Mohammad Taraki.

A bloody coup spearheaded by elements of the armed forces on April 27, 1978, led to the overthrow of the five-year-old Sardar Mohammad Daud government and establishment of a pro-Soviet regime headed by Nur Mohammad Taraki (see BIOGRAPHIES). Taraki renamed the country the People's Democratic Republic of Afghanistan. Although he professed a nonaligned policy, there were signs that he was leaning heavily on the Soviet Union for economic aid and advice. A 20-

year treaty of friendship and cooperation with the Soviet Union was signed in December.

The new government faced its first challenge in August. A terse announcement on August 17 said the defense minister, Gen. Abdul Khadir, one of the coup leaders, had been arrested after the discovery of an alleged plot to overthrow the government. Khadir's arrest came on the heels of attempts by Taraki to purge the ruling People's Democratic Party (PDP) of prominent leaders of the Parcham ("banner") wing, which had united with the

AFGHANISTAN

Education. (1975) Primary, pupils 694,240, teachers 19,-158; secondary, pupils 172,263, teachers 7,835; vocational, pupils (1974) 4,516, teachers (1973) 445; teacher training (1974), students 7,173, teachers 392; higher (1974), students 10,956, teaching staff 982.

Finance. Monetary unit: afghani, with (Sept. 18, 1978) a free rate of 38 afghanis to U.S. $1 (75 afghanis = £1 sterling). Gold, SDR's, and foreign exchange (June 1978) U.S. $332,510,000. Budget (1975–76 est.): revenue 12,947,000,000 afghanis; expenditure 12,999,000,000 afghanis. Money supply (March 1978) 20,883,000,000 afghanis.

Foreign Trade. (1976–77) Imports c. U.S. $328 million; exports c. U.S. $297 million. Import sources (1975–76): U.S.S.R. 24%; Japan 19%; West Germany 12%; India 12%; U.S. 7%. Export destinations (1975–76): U.S.S.R. 39%; Pakistan 13%; India 12%; West Germany 10%; U.K. 7%. Main exports: fruits and nuts 30%; cotton 22%; natural gas 13%; carpets 8%; karakul (persian lamb) skins 7%.

Transport and Communications. Roads (1974) 17,973 km. Motor vehicles in use (1976): passenger 20,300; commercial 8,500. Air traffic (1976): 258 million passenger-km; freight 13 million net ton-km. Telephones (Dec. 1975) 25,-000. Radio receivers (Dec. 1975) 113,000.

Agriculture. Production (in 000; metric tons; 1977): corn 817; wheat c. 2,640; rice 461; barley c. 407; grapes c. 430; cotton, lint c. 54; wool, clean c. 14. Livestock (in 000; 1976): cattle c. 3,676; sheep c. 18,000 (including, karakul sheep c. 7,000); horses c. 370; asses c. 1,250; goats c. 2,350; camels c. 290.

Industry. Production (in 000; metric tons; 1975–76): coal 150; natural gas (cu m) 2,959,000; cotton fabrics (m) 60,400; rayon fabrics (m) 35,200; cement 147; electricity (kw-hr) c. 748,000.

Afghanistan

Troops and tanks remained in the streets of Kabul, Afghanistan, for many days after a military coup in April.

Khalq ("masses") wing to form the PDP. Khadir belonged to the Parcham faction. So did Deputy Prime Minister Babrak Karmal, whom Taraki appointed ambassador to Czechoslovakia.

Despite outward expressions of friendliness, neither Iran nor Pakistan had yet shown any indication that it would welcome the continued existence of a pro-Soviet regime on its doorstep.

(GOVINDAN UNNY)

African Affairs

The African continent's major concern during 1978 was over the degree of foreign intervention in its conflicts. The most serious of the conflicts continued to be those in the Horn of Africa, in northwest and Saharan Africa over the former Spanish Sahara and Chad, in west-central Africa between Angola and Zaire, and in southern Africa over Rhodesia (Zimbabwe), Namibia (South West Africa), and South Africa. Although the number of states recognizing the Saharan Arab Democratic Republic increased to 20, it still seemed far from achieving its independence from Morocco and Mauritania. The continent's total number of independent states remained at 50, including South Africa but excluding the two nominally independent homeland states in South Africa.

The Organization of African Unity. This continental movement of all the independent states, excluding only South Africa, held its annual summit conference in July in Khartoum, Sudan. The president of Sudan, Gen. Gaafar Nimeiry, became chairman of the OAU for 1978–79. The two crucial issues that dominated its discussions were foreign intervention in the continent and intra-African conflicts. Attempts to get agreement to condemn Soviet-Cuban as well as Western intervention failed, but a consensus resolution was adopted opposing all forms of external intervention taken against African wishes. Conciliation bodies were established to deal with the conflicts between Algeria and Morocco-Mauritania over the Western Sahara, and between Chad and Libya. A report by a conciliation commission which described the Eritrean conflict as the main reason for bad relations between Sudan and Ethiopia was adopted. The OAU gave broad support to the initiative of the five Western members of the Security Council for a peaceful settlement in Namibia. It also reaffirmed its backing for the Patriotic Front in Rhodesia.

Southern Africa. Simultaneous with their support for the armed struggles of the Patriotic Front and the South West Africa People's Organization (SWAPO), the five "front-line" African states (Tanzania, Zambia, Mozambique, Botswana, and Angola) attempted, in cooperation with the major Western powers, to achieve peaceful settlements of the conflicts over Rhodesia and Namibia. Their failure to produce positive results led to a further dangerous escalation of violence in the subcontinent and to a sharper confrontation with South Africa itself.

In Rhodesia the regime led by Ian Smith succeeded, in March 1978, in getting the agreement of Bishop Abel Muzorewa, Ndabaningi Sithole, and Chief Jeremiah Chirau to an internal settlement that promised majority rule by the end of the year. This was later postponed to April 1979. The settlement was opposed by the Patriotic Front, the OAU, and the Western powers. The level of armed conflict rose sharply after March, and by November Smith announced that it was causing the loss of one life every hour. Almost two-thirds of Rhodesia was placed under martial law. Britain and the U.S. continued to seek support for their proposals for an internationally acceptable settlement. Meanwhile, the fighting spread dangerously into neighbouring Zambia, Mozambique, and Botswana.

In Namibia the Western plan for an internationally acceptable settlement was endorsed by the UN Security Council and received general support from both South Africa and the SWAPO guerrilla movement. The plan became stalled when the South African government decided to press ahead with its own elections in Namibia in December, without international supervision and against the wishes of SWAPO and other Namibian parties. South Africa's main objections to the plan involved the proposal to introduce a large UN peacekeeping force into Namibia and the lack of clarity about the future status of Walvis Bay. The Africa group at the UN pressed for immediate economic sanctions against South Africa, and on November 21 the UN General Assembly approved a proposal for an oil embargo.

Inside South Africa, urban black resistance continued in the black township of Soweto, near Johannesburg, and elsewhere, although on a somewhat reduced scale. There was a rise in the number of security incidents involving the clandestine guerrilla movements, the African National Congress (ANC) and the Pan-African Congress (PAC), resulting in some deaths and several major trials. Of special importance to the Pretoria regime was the decision of Transkei, the first black homeland to be granted a form of independence, to sever its diplomatic relations with South Africa.

The Horn of Africa. The war in the Ogaden Province of Ethiopia reached its climax in March, when Somalia decided to withdraw its regular units after they had been worsted in fighting with the Ethiopian Army, supported by Cuban commando troops and Soviet weapons. Nevertheless, fighting by insurgents continued in Ogaden for the rest of the year. Meanwhile, the thrust of the Ethiopian campaign switched to Eritrea, where three factions of the Eritrean secessionist movement kept up their 15-year-old armed struggle. A major offensive was launched in May, but the Cubans and South Yemenis were reluctant to become involved in Eritrea, preferring that the problem there should be solved by political means. The Ethiopian Army, with continued military support from the Soviets, recaptured most of the major Eritrean settlements, but the countryside remained largely in rebel hands, and the province was far from pacified at year's end. Armed resistance continued in several other Ethiopian provinces—notably Bale, Sidamo, and Tigre. None of the Western powers was engaged in the conflict, but a number of regional powers took sides. The Arab states (chiefly Saudi Arabia, Egypt, Sudan, and Iraq), as well as Iran, continued to back Somalia and the Eritreans. Kenya was the only black African country that openly supported Ethiopia.

Coups and Inter-African Relations. Three successful coups occurred during the year. The idiosyncratic regime of Pres. Ali Soilih in the Indian Ocean island republic of the Comoros was overthrown in May by a small military expedition led by a soldier of fortune, Col. Robert Denard (*see* BIOGRAPHIES), acting on behalf of the leaders previously ousted by Soilih. Two weeks later, Soilih was killed in an attempt to escape house arrest. The military coup in July that overthrew Pres. Moktar Ould Daddah of Mauritania was a direct outcome of the frustrations produced by the fighting in neighbouring Western Sahara. In Ghana the military leader, Gen. I. K. Acheampong, was replaced by his own senior colleagues in July. There were also a number of failed coups, notably against Pres. Idi Amin of Uganda, who escaped two known attempts to overthrow him.

The Intra-African disputes continued to follow the pattern of recent years. The most serious was the invasion of Ethiopia by Somali forces. In May the Shaba Province of Zaire was invaded for the second time across the Angolan border by forces of the National Front for the Liberation of the Congo (FNLC). At the end of October, Ugandan troops invaded Tanzania and laid claim to the Kagera triangle. Amin claimed this was in retaliation for a Tanzanian attack, but he was apparently pursuing Ugandan rebel soldiers who had crossed the border in fairly large numbers after a mutiny in their barracks. Algeria came close to open hostilities with Morocco and Mauritania in their dispute over the Western Sahara.

There were also signs of improved relations between neighbours. Following the OAU's intervention, Angola and Zaire agreed in October to end their disputes and to promote cordial relations. Continued conflict between Guinea's Pres. Sékou Touré and his two neighbours, Pres. Félix Houphouët-Boigny of Ivory Coast and Pres. Léopold Senghor of Senegal, was finally ended as a result of Liberian and Sierra Leonean mediation. The Chad regime made peace with one of the rebel leaders, Hissen Habré (*see* BIOGRAPHIES), who was once supported by Libya; he returned home to become premier at the end of August. The reconciliation effort between Sudan's President Nimeiry

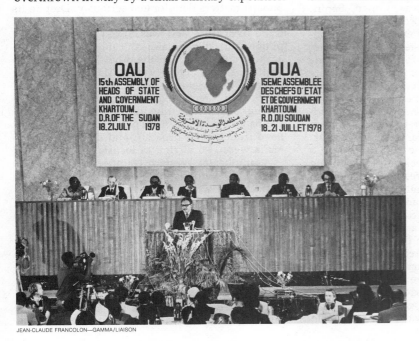

The 15th Assembly of the Organization of African Unity opened in Khartoum, Sudan, on July 18.

A metal sculpture in the shape of the African continent was erected outside the Dar El Beida Airport near Algiers to honour the third African Sports Games, held in the Algerian capital from July 13 to 28.

and one of the leaders of his exile opposition, former prime minister Sadik al-Mahdi, continued to make progress.

Political Systems. The 16-nation Economic Community of West African States (ECOWAS), launched at the end of 1976, showed signs of increasing activity during the year, mainly in developing regional communications projects and removing trade barriers. All hope of resurrecting the East African Community (Kenya, Uganda, and Tanzania), which had collapsed in 1977, was finally abandoned.

Political developments showed movement both toward and away from democratic systems. Sierra Leone was formally converted into a single-party state, while Mozambique followed Angola's example in formally adopting a Marxist-Leninist system. This made ten such regimes in the continent, the others being Guinea-Bissau, Cape Verde, São Tomé and Príncipe, Madagascar, Congo, Benin, Ethiopia, and Somalia (whose disenchantment with the Soviet Union did not extend to abandoning its formal Communist system). On the other hand, a return to parliamentary democracy made progress in Upper Volta, where free elections were held; in Nigeria, where political parties returned in preparation for full parliamentary elections in 1979; and in Ghana, where the new military leadership promised an early return to civilian politics. The experiment with a three-party parliament survived in Senegal, despite some difficulties, but a similar experiment in Egypt looked less promising after Pres. Anwar as-Sadat resorted to political repression against some opposition parties.

External Relations. Soviet and Cuban involvement in the continent increased during the year. More Cuban forces (possibly as many as 25,000) were committed in Angola. In the Horn of Africa late in 1977 the Soviets mounted a massive airlift to support Ethiopia's military regime; several thousand Cuban troops were involved in the fighting in the Ogaden and elsewhere in Ethiopia; and three Soviet generals helped to plan military strategy. After the second invasion of Shaba, an African force from Morocco, Ivory Coast, and Gabon (with French and U.S. logistical support) went to Zaire's assistance. At a summit meeting in Paris in May, the francophone African Community considered the establishment of a permanent Inter-African Army. This idea had the support of Egypt, Morocco, and Sudan, among others, but it was strongly opposed by most African leaders, who insisted that any such force should be free of external links. African cooperation with the Western initiatives in Rhodesia and Namibia continued to be a major feature of the continent's external relations. China's relations with most African countries remained positive, except in the case of Angola and, especially, Ethiopia, which criticized Peking for supporting the Somalis.

Economic Performance. There was little sign of improvement in the overall economic picture. For most countries (notably Zaire, Zambia, and Sudan) matters deteriorated seriously. Despite its oil wealth, Nigeria encountered major balance of trade difficulties and was forced to seek two $1 billion loans. Ghana also continued to experience economic troubles. On the other hand, countries such as Kenya, Ivory Coast, Malawi, and Tanzania were reasonably buoyant. Low agricultural production remained a depressing feature throughout the continent. Some areas—notably the Sahel countries, Ethiopia, and Somalia—suffered from serious drought, and Ethiopia and Somalia were also victims of locusts.

A number of Western countries—led by Sweden, The Netherlands, and Britain—took the initiative in writing off some of the debt owed from previous loans in order to reduce the burden of indebtedness that was proving crippling to many African economies. The African, Caribbean, and Pacific (ACP) countries began their negotiations with the European Economic Community to improve the terms of the Lomé Convention (1975), which was due for renewal.

(COLIN LEGUM)

See also Feature Article: *Question Mark over Africa;* Dependent States; articles on the various political units.

Agriculture and Food Supplies

A record world grain crop reflecting unusually good weather conditions throughout the world in 1978 assured a strong advance in food production in both the developed and less developed countries. Although a few less developed countries faced serious food shortages and the problem of widespread chronic malnutrition continued, as a group these nations regained the ground lost during the early 1970s and advanced beyond it.

Agreement still was not reached on the new international system of nationally held grain reserves recommended by the 1974 World Food Conference, but negotiations were expected to enter a decisive stage in early 1979. At that time a new Food Aid Convention appeared likely to be adopted that would assure a minimum level of food aid of 10 million tons. The flow of foreign official assistance to agriculture appeared to be increasing again after a decline in 1976.

AGRICULTURE AND FOOD PRODUCTION

Production Indexes. World agricultural output (excluding China) increased about 2.5% in 1978 according to preliminary estimates (in December)

contained in indexes prepared by the Economics, Statistics, and Cooperatives Service (ESCS) of the U.S. Department of Agriculture (USDA). Both the developed and less developed countries participated equally in the gains. Among the major developed regions agricultural output grew the most in the U.S.S.R. and Western Europe, largely because of bumper grain crops, while only the United States—where acreage reduction programs were in operation—recorded a decline.

Total world food production increased almost 3%, approximating the average 2.6% rate of annual increase over the preceding two decades. Output in the developed countries increased a little faster than the rate for the world, while that in the less developed countries was closer to 2.5%. The major less developed regions all registered gains, with the largest in West Asia and Africa. Nevertheless, because of rapid population growth, per capita food production in the less developed countries as a group stood at an index of 109 (1961–65 = 100), essentially unchanged from 1977. Small per capita gains in both West and South Asia were offset by a small decline in East Asia, while per capita output remained unchanged in Africa and Latin America.

Relatively few countries—seven in Africa and five in Asia—were reported (in November) by the Food and Agriculture Organization (FAO) of the United Nations to be affected by abnormal food

While soldiers from Somalia and Ethiopia were at battle, another kind of war was going on in their land. Millions of locusts were stripping the land bare and threatening to overrun the rest of Africa.

WIDE WORLD

shortages. Some were the result of internal disorders rather than natural causes. The food situation was particularly serious in Ethiopia, Laos, and Vietnam. In the Sahel region of northern Africa, harvest prospects were poor in Mauritania and parts of Upper Volta. Many countries were reportedly threatened by desert locust infestations in 1979 because of extensive breeding of the insect pest in the Horn of Africa, in the interior of Sudan and around the Red Sea, in eastern Arabia, and near the juncture of Pakistan and southeastern Iran.

Per capita food production in the developed countries increased a little more than 2%, while that for the world (excluding China) rose about 1.5% in 1978. The average annual increase in per capita food production during the past 20 years was: world, 1.1%; developed countries, 1.4%; and less developed countries, 0.5%.

Grains. Weather conditions were unusually favourable for grain production in 1978, and no major region suffered a serious production shortfall. Total grain utilization was increasing more slowly than output, leading to a buildup in stocks to the highest level relative to utilization since the late 1960s.

World grain production (wheat, coarse grains, and milled rice) was forecast—based on December estimates of crops already harvested in the Northern Hemisphere and pre-harvest reports in the Southern Hemisphere—to exceed 1,400,000,000 metric tons in 1978–79, about 6.5% above the previous year's output of 1,322,000,000 tons. Bumper crops in Western Europe and the U.S.S.R. were chiefly responsible for the increase. The area devoted to grains expanded only about 2 million ha, but yields were forecast to rise 6% above 1977–78's two tons per hectare (1 ha=2.5 ac). Total grain utilization was forecast to increase a little less than 3% above the 1,330,000,000 tons of 1977–78, while world trade in grains was likely to rise only about 1% above the 166 million tons of 1977–78.

World grain stocks were expected to increase by the end of 1978–79 to approximately 40 million tons above the 185 million held at the beginning of the season. Such stock levels equaled about 16.5% of total grain utilization, the largest such percentage since the end of the 1960s when they ranged between 18 and 20%. (These percentage estimates are compatible with, but lower than, those published by FAO because of that organization's apparently less comprehensive estimate of stocks and utilization in the U.S.S.R. and China.) The U.S. continued to hold nearly two-fifths of the total.

Wheat crops were forecast to be larger in all major regions except the U.S. and Eastern Europe in 1978–79. Although harvested area of wheat and coarse grains was unchanged at about 576 million ha, average yields increased almost 11% from 1.69 tons per ha in 1977–78. The largest production increases were in the U.S.S.R., Western Europe, and Australia. U.S. output fell because of government acreage reduction measures and low wheat prices that discouraged plantings.

World output of coarse grains was expected to be about 5.6% above the 694 million tons produced in 1977–78. Total yields were also expected to rise 5.6% above the 1.98 tons per ha achieved in 1977–78, while harvested area remained unchanged at about 350 million ha. A strong recovery in Soviet production, substantially larger crops in Western Europe, and a record U.S. corn crop—smaller plantings due to the government acreage reduction program were offset by record yields—all contributed to the increase. Estimates of recovery in both Australian barley and sorghum production and Brazilian corn output and a reduction in Argentine coarse grains were more tentative because of the later harvest and the possibility of some shift from those crops to the more profitable soybeans in those South American countries.

World production of milled rice in 1978–79 (calendar 1979) was projected to increase about 7 mil-

Table I. Indexes of World Agricultural and Food Production (excluding China)
1961–65=100

Region or country	Total agricultural production						Total food production						Per capita food production					
	1973	1974	1975	1976	1977	1978*	1973	1974	1975	1976	1977	1978*	1973	1974	1975	1976	1977	1978*
Developed countries	131	129	128	134	137	141	133	131	130	137	140	144	120	118	116	121	122	125
United States	122	117	126	129	138	134	128	122	134	137	144	142	115	109	118	120	125	123
Canada	123	112	127	138	141	142	124	112	128	143	142	144	106	94	106	116	114	115
Western Europe	123	128	125	123	128	133	123	128	125	123	128	134	115	119	115	113	117	122
EEC	122	125	121	118	126	129	122	125	121	118	125	129	114	116	112	109	115	119
Eastern Europe	135	140	137	144	144	145	135	140	137	144	144	146	126	130	126	132	131	132
U.S.S.R.	155	145	130	153	149	162	155	144	128	153	147	161	139	128	113	133	128	138
Japan	110	110	115	109	117	115	110	111	115	109	117	115	98	97	100	93	99	97
Oceania	117	119	125	124	122	124	127	127	137	138	134	134	107	105	112	111	106	107
South Africa	119	146	134	134	145	147	124	154	141	141	152	153	94	114	102	100	105	103
Less developed countries	130	134	141	145	151	154	132	135	145	149	154	158	103	103	107	108	109	109
East Asia	145	149	154	166	170	174	141	147	154	165	168	171	110	112	115	121	120	119
Indonesia	130	138	140	145	146	156	130	140	141	145	145	155	103	108	107	107	104	109
Philippines	143	146	161	172	173	173	145	147	163	173	175	175	108	107	116	120	118	116
South Korea	139	144	158	175	185	193	135	141	155	172	179	187	107	109	118	129	132	135
Thailand	159	156	162	167	168	173	154	157	167	174	170	176	115	114	118	121	116	117
South Asia	129	124	138	135	147	152	130	124	140	137	150	154	104	97	107	103	110	111
Bangladesh	117	110	124	117	129	130	119	115	130	120	133	133	93	87	96	87	94	91
India	129	122	139	135	147	152	130	122	140	136	149	154	104	96	108	103	111	112
Pakistan	157	162	155	165	181	176	159	164	161	177	191	183	119	119	114	121	127	118
West Asia	129	144	154	169	166	171	127	141	154	168	165	172	96	104	110	117	112	113
Iran	145	160	179	192	190	196	108	116	129	134	128	129	108	116	129	134	128	129
Turkey	125	136	150	163	163	165	95	100	111	116	113	114	95	99	110	115	113	113
Africa	119	126	127	129	126	129	119	126	129	131	127	131	93	95	95	94	89	89
Egypt	120	118	119	122	118	120	124	125	131	135	129	133	97	95	98	99	92	93
Ethiopia	111	114	103	106	100	87	111	112	101	105	98	85	87	86	76	76	70	59
Nigeria	112	119	121	123	125	128	113	119	122	124	126	129	87	90	89	88	87	87
Latin America	130	138	142	145	153	155	138	145	151	158	162	166	105	108	109	111	111	111
Mexico	141	143	151	148	153	162	152	150	169	165	166	179	108	103	112	105	102	106
Argentina	115	122	123	133	135	147	120	126	127	138	138	151	105	109	108	116	114	124
Brazil	137	150	153	157	168	162	153	162	167	184	191	182	116	120	120	129	130	120
World	131	131	132	138	142	145	133	132	135	141	144	148	115	113	113	117	118	120

* Preliminary.
Source: U.S. Department of Agriculture, Economics, Statistics, and Cooperatives Service.

lion tons above the 247 million tons of 1977–78. Harvested area was expected to rise about 1.5% above the 143 million ha of 1977–78, and yields were projected to be about 1% above the 2.55 tons per ha (rough basis) achieved then. The increased output resulted from larger crops in several major producing areas, including Bangladesh, India, Indonesia, Thailand, and China; some uncertainty existed about the size of the late rice crop in China.

Utilization of coarse grains and rice each increased about 3% above the 1977–78 levels of 688 million and 243 million tons, respectively, compared with a 2% rise in wheat consumption from 399 million tons. Growth in wheat consumption usually about matches population growth except when the price spread between wheat and lower priced coarse grains is narrow enough to give livestock feeders an incentive to buy wheat for animal feed. But the spread was wide in 1978–79, particularly in the U.S. because of plentiful supplies of corn.

Demand for coarse grains was also stimulated by a general increase in the feeding of poultry and hogs to compensate for a decline in beef production in many countries, by increased imports in some less developed countries in the Middle East and Asia that were attempting to increase meat production and consumption, by Soviet and Eastern European efforts to expand livestock production, and by a potential reduction of cassava imports from Thailand into Western Europe for feed. The reduced value of the U.S. dollar in some markets for U.S. grains may also have made their purchase for feeding more attractive. Rice stocks in several Asian countries were sufficiently ample to allow some substitution of rice for wheat in human con-

sumption throughout the world. Excessive rice stocks in Japan probably produced this effect along with the greater use of rice in compound feeds.

World trade in wheat in 1978–79 (July–June) was expected, at about 73 million tons, to be almost unchanged from 1977–78. Reduced imports by the U.S.S.R., Eastern Europe, Western Europe, and Japan were largely offset by small increases spread among China and other countries. Among the major exporting regions only Western Europe registered gains, because of strongly subsidized sales of soft wheat to Brazil, Poland, and some Mediterranean countries. U.S. wheat exports were forecast to continue at about 31 million tons, but sales by Canada and Australia were both expected to be lower.

World trade in coarse grains was forecast to rise about 3 million tons above the 83 million in 1977–78, in part spurred by rising poultry and hog production. Increased shipments were expected for all the major exporters except Argentina and Brazil, where drought reduced supplies. Among the major importers only Western Europe, because of bumper grain crops, was expected to import less coarse grains. World rice trade was expected to decline only very little in 1979 from the previous year's 8.7 million tons.

Carry-over world wheat stocks in 1978–79 were forecast to rise about 15 million tons above carry-in stocks of 81 million, to a level equal to about 23% of world wheat consumption. U.S. wheat stocks were expected to decline about 4 million tons from the 32 million-ton carry-in level, and the U.S. share of world wheat stocks to drop from about 40% to less than 30%. Coarse grain stocks were forecast to jump 23 million tons above the 1978–79

The record U.S. grain crop stuffed all available grain elevator space; the surplus had to be stored outside.

carry-in level of 82 million tons. U.S. coarse grain stocks were forecast to grow almost 13 million tons from the 40 million carry-in total and to continue at about 50% of world stocks.

Acreage reduction programs were announced for the 1979 (1979–80 season) wheat and feed grain crops in the U.S. They sought to maintain U.S. wheat stocks at about 7.5% of world wheat use and U.S. feed grain stocks at 6% of world coarse grain use; U.S. wheat stocks were forecast to equal about 7% and coarse grains about 7.5% of world utilization by the end of 1978–79. World rice stocks were forecast to increase about 2.5 million tons (milled) over carry-in stocks of 22 million.

Starchy Roots. The FAO estimated (in July) that recorded production of cassava (excluding China) exceeded 110 million tons (more than 30 million tons cereal-energy equivalent) in 1977, with a 3% increase anticipated for 1978. About two-thirds is consumed as food directly or converted into starchy foods in the less developed countries.

Much of the information on production and consumption of cassava is difficult to obtain—less than an estimated 15% of cassava consumed as food in the producing countries moves through commercial channels. Per capita food use of the product has probably been declining in recent years, partly because of increased grain production and grain storage in most cassava-producing countries that has encouraged a shift in consumer demand toward cereals. Nevertheless, in 1978 it remained the leading supplier of carbohydrates in most rural areas in tropical Africa, Latin America, and the Pacific islands. In many of those areas rough terrain makes it difficult to cultivate cereals.

Protein Meal and Vegetable Oil. World production of protein meals (44% soybean meal equivalent) in 1978, from crops harvested in the Southern Hemisphere in 1978 and in the Northern Hemisphere in 1977, was estimated at 78.8 million (almost 18% above 1977) and 35.2 million tons, respectively. Total production of fats and oils was estimated at 52.7 million tons, about 10% above that in 1977. An 18% reduction in the 1978 Brazilian soybean crop because of drought was more than offset by a one-third increase in both the 1977 U.S. soybean (to 48 million tons) and cottonseed crops, larger 1977 Canadian rapeseed output, and record 1978 Argentine soybean and sunflower production.

Apparent world consumption (world production adjusted by changes in U.S. soybean and soy product stocks) of both protein meals (77.6 million tons) and edible vegetable oils (35.1 million tons) increased an estimated 11% in 1978 over the depressed 1977 level. Strong growth in pork and

poultry production helped boost meal use, but the rate of increased use exceeded that for meat production, particularly in the EEC. Levies there on feed grain imports resulted in greater use of low-protein grain substitutes, such as cassava, that required larger proportions of protein meals in feed rations. The lower value of the U.S. dollar in several markets probably also stimulated the importation and use of protein meals.

For 1979 to be another year of record world output of both protein meals and edible vegetable oils depended upon forecasts of sharp increases in the 1979 Brazilian (36%, to 13.5 million tons) and Argentine (23%, to 3.2 million tons) soybean crops. World production of fats and oils was forecast to reach 55 million tons. The 1978 U.S. soybean crop, at 49.3 million tons, was only 1.3 million larger than in 1977, and a 25% decline in the 1978 U.S. cottonseed crop to 3.8 million tons more than offset a 30% increase in the 1978 U.S. sunflower crop. Other increases in 1979 oil and meal output were expected to come from larger 1978 Senegalese peanut, 1979 Malaysian palm oil (to 1.9 million tons), and 1978 Canadian rapeseed production (to 3.2 million tons). Philippine copra output was expected to decline 10% to 2.4 million tons because of poor weather.

Apparent world consumption of protein meals and vegetable oils was forecast (in December 1978) to increase about 8 and 7%, respectively, in 1979. Higher soybean prices, 25–30% (in dollars) above a year earlier, were a major factor in the forecast slowdown in the growth of consumption, as well as the greater price competition from grains because of the large 1978–79 corn harvest.

U.S. exports of soybeans and products remained strong after the autumn of 1977 and were expected to continue strong at least through the spring of 1979 when new crop Brazilian and Argentine soybeans would become available. U.S. soybean, soybean meal, and soybean oil exports for 1978–79 (October–September) were forecast at 20.4 million (up 7%), 5.7 million (up 4%), and 800,000 (down 13%) tons, respectively.

Meat. Total meat production in the world commercial meat economy (major importers: United States, EEC, Japan, and Canada; major exporters: Argentina, Australia, Mexico, Central America, Uruguay, and New Zealand) was expected (in October) to equal approximately the 55 million-ton output of 1977. Increases in pork and poultry output compensated for a decline in beef and veal.

Overall numbers of cattle in these areas have been declining since their 1975 peak, while beef production leveled off in 1976 and 1977 and fell thereafter. The cutback in beef production and the general reduction in slaughter rates (percentage of herd slaughtered) in 1978, together with some indications of a trend toward a rise in the average weight of cattle slaughtered, were signs that a general rebuilding of herds might soon begin.

If major producers should begin to hold back heifers for breeding in anticipation of future higher slaughter rates from larger herds at favourable prices, beef production could drop sharply as early as 1979. The higher prices that would result from such a production decline could provide incentives

Table II. Annual Rates of Increase of Food Production

	Total production (%)			Per capita production (%)		
	1959–78	1959–68	1969–78	1959–78	1959–68	1969–78
Developed countries	2.4	2.8	2.1	1.4	1.6	1.2
Less developed countries*	3.0	2.7	3.0	0.5	0.3	0.6
World*	2.6	2.8	2.3	1.1	1.2	1.0

*Excludes China.

Source: U.S. Department of Agriculture, Economics, Statistics, and Cooperatives Service.

for a buildup in herds in 1980 and 1981 and result in a further drop in beef output. Higher pork and poultry production could dampen such price increases, but probably not enough to offset fully the rise in beef prices.

Conditions in the U.S. could prove to be representative of the world commercial beef economy. U.S. beef production in 1978 was expected (in December) to decline about 4% from the 1977 level of about 11.2 million tons. Cattle numbers on Jan. 1, 1979, might be down to 111 million head, nearly 5% below January 1978 and 16% under their 1975 peak. But even though a parallel drop in the cow herd suggested a smaller calf crop in 1979, that crop might still exceed the total calf and cattle slaughter for the first time since 1975. The reduced slaughter was expected to result from a 25% drop in nonfed-steer and heifer slaughter and a 20–25% drop in the cow slaughter that would more than offset a slight rise in fed-cattle slaughter.

The U.S. imported beef in 1978 at the rate of a million tons a year, equal to about 9% of domestic production. Except for Central America, the trend in beef production and cattle numbers was also downward in the countries that usually supplement U.S. meat supplies. Thus, beef imports were not likely to be sufficient to maintain current per capita U.S. beef consumption in 1979.

The EEC livestock industry was more insulated from the effect of outside prices because of protectionist features of its common agricultural policy. Cattle numbers there began to rise a little during 1977, although beef and veal production grew about 1.5–2% in 1978 and might continue at that rate well into 1979.

Pasture conditions in Australia and New Zealand at the end of 1978 were excellent, and there were indications that the rate of herd liquidation

there would soon be reduced. Total meat production in those countries in 1978–79 (October–September) was forecast to drop about 8%—beef, 15%—from a year earlier. Beef exports, at 1.3 million tons, were expected to be about 12% lower than in 1977–78. Argentina's cattle slaughter continued to increase in 1978, and beef exports were higher than a year earlier. However, beef production might decline in 1979 if the herd liquidation had run its course.

Dairy. The expansion in world milk production slowed in 1978, but output in 36 major producing countries was expected (as of September) to exceed the 397 million tons in 1977 by about 1%. Major production gains were in prospect for the U.S.S.R. because of favourable pasture conditions and rising numbers of cows and also in the EEC because of good pastures there and the continuing attractiveness of producer incentives. U.S. output was expected to decline slightly because higher slaughter cow prices were bringing about reduction in cow numbers. Output was also falling in Australia and New Zealand.

Income support programs for the dairy industries in most of the developed countries tended to maintain milk production at levels in excess of demand for fluid milk and milk products. The principal method by which governments supported their dairy industries was intervention in the dairy products market—particularly the butter and nonfat dry milk (NFDM) complex—to accumulate or dispose of stocks.

A continuing decline in per capita butter consumption contributed to a buildup of total butter stocks in the 36 major producing countries, although U.S., New Zealand, and Eastern European stocks declined somewhat. Butter sales were hurt by higher retail prices that resulted from higher

In an effort to increase sheep production, U.S. scientists worked at ways to increase the birthrate among sheep. Ewes normally have one offspring at a time, but breeds were developed for greater incidence of twins and triplets.

support prices and also by competition from vege-table-oil substitutes. Total butter stocks were expected to rise about 9% above the 755,000 tons held at the end of 1977 and to represent about 15% of consumption. But these stocks grew more slowly in 1977, partly because rising incomes and high beef prices helped to strengthen the demand for cheese, thus diverting milk supplies away from the production of both butter and NFDM. By far the largest stock increases occurred in the EEC, where they were expected to rise 14%. This was due in part to a 35% increase in U.K. production to more than 500,000 tons, representing almost one-third of EEC consumption and at least 60% of total stocks. EEC intervention stocks, at 392,000 tons in July, were double those on January 1.

EEC stocks of NFDM were also expected to increase despite an overall decline in stocks in the major producing countries of about 11% from the 1,640,000 tons held at the end of 1977. Although EEC stocks had fallen about 20% in 1977 to about 950,000 tons, a 6% rise was expected by the end of 1978. EEC intervention stocks stood at a seasonal peak of about 876,000 tons in July, but were lower than in 1977. Four-fifths of the EEC's output of NFDM in 1977 was aided by subsidies for feed use. Some of the most substantial stock reductions occurred in Canada and the United States because of strong export sales.

Sugar. World production and consumption of sugar were in near balance in 1978–79, and prices strengthened to 9.3 U.S. cents a pound in October after declining steadily during the year to a low of 6 cents per pound (London daily, Caribbean raw basis) in July. Total output was estimated (in November) to be about 2% lower than the record 1977–78 crop of 92.1 million tons (raw value).

Consumption was expected to be a record, almost 4% above the 86 million tons of 1977–78.

World sugar consumption grew at about the same pace as population in the 1970s, with per capita consumption hovering around 20 kg (45 lb) a year. In recent years there was increased per capita use in some less developed countries.

World net import requirements for sugar in calendar 1979, an estimated 21 million tons, were expected to be little changed from 1978. World sugar stocks—29 million tons at the beginning of 1978–79, or one-third of annual world use—were expected to increase much less than during the preceding year.

Brazil reduced its production goal for 1978–79, and output was expected to decline by about 1 million tons. That country, the leading producer of "gasohol," planned to convert about one-fourth of its sugarcane crop, the equivalent of about 2.1 million tons of sugar, into about 2,200,000,000–2,400,000,000 litres of alcohol for automotive use. Brazil planned to build or expand some 150 gasohol projects, and several other countries were also interested in its manufacture from sugarcane or cassava.

Other producers expected to have smaller crops included the EEC, Cuba, Australia, the Philippines, Argentina, and India. The U.S.S.R., Poland, and South Africa were expected to produce about the same amount as in 1977–78.

Sugar faced increased competition from high-fructose corn syrup (HFCS), partly because of relatively low corn prices. Most HFCS production capacity was in the U.S. The FAO estimated that HFCS consumption in the U.S., Canada, the EEC, and Japan would reach 2.5 million tons in 1980 and 3.4 million in 1985.

As of October, 32 of the 55 signatory countries had ratified the International Sugar Agreement (ISA). However, the U.S., the single largest importer, was not among them because the 95th U.S.

A Michigan Department of Agriculture doctor waits for a tranquilizer to take effect on a PBB-infected cow. More than 35,000 cattle who had been fed PBB-contaminated feed had to be destroyed and buried.

A Texas farmer displays a
sack of onions from
Mexico. More than 200
U.S. farmers blockaded
the international bridge
at Hidalgo in March to
protest imports of Mexi-
can beef and produce.

Congress could not agree on a bill that coupled
establishment of a new domestic support program
for sugar with authorization for U.S. ratification.
The U.S. administration announced that it would
pursue authority for both in the next congressional
session. The other signatories were expected to advance the previously extended ratification deadline of Dec. 31, 1978. For the interim the U.S. secretary of agriculture announced on October 25 that
imports of sugar into the U.S. would be monitored
to assure that those from nonsignatory countries
would not exceed the level permitted by the ISA.

Because sugar prices continued below the 11-
cent minimum called for in the agreement, export
quotas for 1979 were reduced in April from 85% of
the basic export tonnage of 15.3 million tons to
82.5% (12.6 million tons), with minor adjustments
for certain small producers considered hardship
cases. Contributions to the stock fund, which were
to be used for withdrawing 2.5 million tons of
stocks from the market, were delayed until Jan. 1,
1979, because of the provisional status of the ISA.

Coffee. World coffee production was expected
to increase an estimated 9% above the previous
year's 68.5 million bags (60 kg each). Brazilian output continued to recover from the 1975 frost, rising
14% above the 17.5 million bags of 1977–78. Brazil's already largely harvested 1978–79 crop was
not seriously affected by an August frost, but the
USDA reduced earlier estimates of a 24 million–26
million-bag harvest to a tentatively estimated 18
million–21 million bags for 1979–80; this delayed
recovery to pre-1975 frost levels until 1980–81. El
Salvador and Ivory Coast output also recovered.

Exportable world production (harvested production less domestic consumption in producing
countries) climbed an estimated 10% above the
51.4 million bags of 1977–78.

The International Coffee Organization (ICO)
monthly average composite price for green coffee
continued to recede with little interruption from
the April 1977 peak of $3.34 per pound to a low of
about $1.43 in July–August 1978. In November af-
ter news of the Brazilian frost it was $1.56. Concern
over falling prices had led the Brazilian and
Colombian governments to hold a meeting in August, attended also by Costa Rica, El Salvador,
Guatemala, Honduras, Mexico, Venezuela, and
the Ivory Coast (observer). The delegates recommended that the ICO establish a unified position for
negotiating with consumers and also create a
mechanism to stabilize prices that would guarantee remunerative prices to producers and guarantee adequate supplies to consumers. The ICO,
meeting in September, failed to agree on the
raising of the trigger price that calls forth export
quotas when export prices fall below that level,
which stood at 77 cents per pound.

Cocoa. The 1978–79 cocoa bean harvest was
forecast (in December) to be nearly 5% below the
1,480,000 tons of 1977–78, largely because of unfavourable growing conditions in the major producing areas of West Africa and Brazil. The
combination in 1977–78 of a moderate recovery in
production, a smaller cocoa grind, and a moderate
growth in season's-end stocks contributed to a fall
in cocoa bean prices from their peak of $2.01 per
pound in July 1977 to a low of $1.29 in February

1978; however, by October, the beginning of the 1978–79 season, they had climbed back to $1.70 per pound. Although prices in 1978 averaged somewhat lower than in 1977 and were expected to ease as the crop came on the market in 1979, they remained high enough to restrain consumption. Thus, the 1979 cocoa grind was expected roughly to equal 1978's 1,360,000 tons, perhaps permitting a small addition to stocks by the end of 1978–79.

The cocoa grind had declined an average 2% yearly without interruption since 1973, roughly corresponding to an overall strong rise in cocoa prices. Competition from more stable-priced substitutes and extenders was becoming increasingly significant and inhibited investment by some producers that might reverse the downward trend in production. Nevertheless, cocoa bean exporters profited greatly from the high prices of recent years; foreign exchange earnings totaled an estimated $4 billion in 1977, compared with an average $2 billion for 1975 and 1976.

The Ivory Coast was steadily increasing production with the introduction of improved hybrid varieties and might soon replace Ghana as the world's leading producer of cocoa beans. Low government prices paid to producers and encouragement of food crops, together with other economic and political factors, contributed to the decline in Ghana's industry. The Nigerian industry faced similar problems. Brazil was driving to increase output and planned, perhaps optimistically, to produce 700,000 tons by 1985.

The International Cocoa Agreement was to expire on Sept. 30, 1979, and negotiations for its renewal under the auspices of UNCTAD (United Nations Conference on Trade and Development) were scheduled to be held in Geneva in January 1979. The economic provisions of the expiring ICA were never invoked because prices had remained high during the agreement's lifetime.

Tea. Producers continued to respond to strong prices for tea brought about by high coffee prices in recent years. World tea production in 1978 (excluding China) was forecast in October to exceed slightly the 1977 record of 1,420,000 tons. Larger tea supplies and an easing of coffee prices led to a decline in the London auction price for all teas from the April 1977 peak of $1.87 per pound, although the July 1978 price of 96 cents remained well above those of the last decade.

Combined Asian-Oceanic output was unchanged from 1977 at 1,190,000 tons. India was expected to approximate its 1977 harvest (562,800 tons, a record), as was Sri Lanka (208,600 tons, about 5,000 below the 1975 record). In the latter country nationalization of the tea industry was followed by reduced fertilizer usage and a slowdown in the expansion of area and in the replacement of unproductive bushes. Indonesia's harvest was expected to exceed slightly the 64,500 tons of 1977.

African output might grow 8% above the 184,-900 tons of 1977 because of a sharp increase in Kenyan production. South American output probably declined about 19% from 44,000 tons in 1977 because of a poor Argentine harvest.

Indian tea exports, which nearly doubled in value to $604 million in 1977 despite a 6% decline in quantity to 223,980 tons, moved slowly in the first half of 1978. The value of Sri Lankan tea exports

A machine developed in Hungary covers vegetables with perforated foil to keep them free from frost and to speed up growth. One and a half acres of land can be blanketed in a day.

Workers in California began picking lettuce again from a new crop after heavy rains destroyed the previous one. The shortage of lettuce drove the price up to $1.49 per head in the East, but prices fell back after the new crop came in.

was expected to be sharply lower than the $382 million earned from 185,542 tons in 1977. World tea exports totaled 774,045 tons in 1977.

The UNCTAD Preparatory Meeting on Tea that met in January in Geneva ratified a recommendation by the Intergovernmental Group on Tea in October 1977 for a joint UNCTAD-FAO study of the feasibility of an international tea stocking arrangement. An Intergovernmental Group of Experts on Tea was to meet in September 1978 in Geneva to consider the study prior to another preparatory meeting later in the year.

Cotton. World cotton production was forecast (in December) to decline about 6.5% in 1978–79 from 63.5 million bales (480 lb per bale) in 1977–78. The decrease resulted from a somewhat greater than 3% decline in planted area, which reflected relatively low prices at planting time in the Northern Hemisphere, and also from adverse weather that helped reduce yields about 2.5% from the 1978 level. Yields fell most in the U.S., where production declined about 24% from the 14.4 million bales of 1977–78. Production outside the U.S. was expected to decline slightly.

Utilization of cotton throughout the world was expected to rise about 2% from the 60.8 million bales of 1977–78 and to exceed production, resulting in a 2.5 million–3 million-bale reduction in stocks (nearly 1 million in the U.S.) from beginning stocks of about 24.2 million bales. Increased mill use in the non-Communist countries outside the United States was largely responsible, particularly in Japan, Taiwan, and South Korea. U.S. cotton use was expected to decline slightly in 1978–79.

Cotton exports were expected to exceed the 1977–78 world total of 18.9 million bales by about 900,000 bales. U.S. cotton exports could exceed those of 5.3 million bales a year earlier by about 300,000 bales. Imports by China could rise 15–20% above the 1.8 million bales of 1977–78.

The tight cotton market resulted in a strengthening of cotton prices during the early part of the 1978–79 season. The Outlook "A" Index (average of five lowest priced of ten selected growths, cost-insurance-freight Northern Europe) averaged nearly 79.4 cents per lb in November 1978, the highest since November 1977.

Tobacco. World production of leaf tobacco in 1978 was estimated (in December) to exceed the 1977 output of about 5,450,000 tons (farm-sales weight) by slightly less than 3%. The major increases in output, from the U.S., India, Canada, Brazil, and Turkey, were attributable to both higher yields resulting from excellent weather and larger planted areas. Flue-cured, burley, and oriental tobacco crops were only slightly higher than 1977's 2.3 million, 590,000, and 909,000 tons, respectively.

World production of cigarettes was believed to have increased about 3% in 1978 above the 4,130,000,000,000 pieces of 1977. Manufacturers continued to adopt new technology that reduced the amount of tobacco used per cigarette. World trade in tobacco rose about 5% above the 1,270,000 tons of 1977. Beginning world stocks in 1979 might increase to 6.4 million tons, compared with 6.3 million at the beginning of 1978, because of larger supplies and a declining demand resulting from antismoking publicity and legislation in 1978.

INTERNATIONAL FOOD SECURITY

Grain Reserves. The long series of tortuous negotiations that had begun in 1975 toward the establishment of an international system of nationally held grain reserves ground to a halt in November 1978, apparently a failure, because the U.S. and the EEC were deadlocked over key provisions of a Wheat Trade Convention (WTC) to replace the 1971 International Wheat Agreement (IWA). But the two sides continued private talks, and an agreement was reached which restored hopes that an overall international agreement could still be

**Agriculture and
Food Supplies**

Nervous Capitol Hill police became
goatherds after farmers protesting
low farm prices turned loose 50 of
the animals on the U.S. Capitol
grounds.

reached in the third session of a 67-country conference sponsored by UNCTAD and scheduled for Jan. 22–Feb. 9, 1979.

A USDA press release on December 28 provided few details on the bargain, stating that the two parties had agreed on international wheat price support levels and the resolution of other unspecified differences between them. Accumulation of reserve stocks under a WTC would begin when the world export price indicator fell to $140 per metric ton ($3.81 per bushel), with a joint program of additional measures to be developed if the price continued to decline to $125 ($3.40). The additional measures presumably might include the further acquisition of stocks and the adoption of production controls. To what degree they might be mandatory or consultative in nature was not indicated. Also left unanswered were the total level and individual national levels of stock acquisition obligations, the trigger points for release of stocks, the measures such as adjustment of consumption or trade policies that might be adopted should a rise in wheat prices continue unchecked, and obligations for financial assistance to less developed countries for stockholding. The paucity of information released on the agreement no doubt reflect-

ed the expected delicacy of the negotiations that would be required to obtain the agreement of the other countries at the UNCTAD meeting.

The U.S. earlier had proposed a total stock of 30 million tons (including 5 million tons of rice) and reportedly called for the accumulation of stocks to begin at $145 per ton ($3.95 per bushel). The EEC, a substantial net exporter of wheat in 1978–79, was said to advocate a stock of 15 million tons with accumulation to begin at $115 ($3.13). Argentina and Canada were reported to be slightly above the U.S. proposal and Japan slightly below that of the EEC. The former are traditional exporters, and the latter is a substantial importer. Many of the less developed countries, which are mostly importers of wheat, presumably favoured maintaining wheat prices at the lower end of the range.

Under the present U.S. domestic grain stabilization and reserve program, stocks may be accumulated in two ways. Under the first a farmer may obtain a government loan, using his grain as collateral. He has the option of keeping the loan money and delivering the grain to the government if prices fall lower than the loan rate ($2.35 per bushel or $86 per metric ton of wheat) or of selling the grain and repaying the government if prices

Table III. World Production and Trade of Principal Grains (in 000 metric tons)

	Wheat Production 1961–65 average	Wheat Production 1977	Wheat Imports− Exports+ 1974–77 average	Barley Production 1961–65 average	Barley Production 1977	Barley Imports− Exports+ 1974–77 average	Oats Production 1961–65 average	Oats Production 1977	Oats Imports− Exports+ 1974–77 average	Rye Production 1961–65 average	Rye Production 1977	Rye Imports− Exports+ 1974–77 average	Corn (Maize) Production 1961–65 average	Corn (Maize) Production 1977	Corn (Maize) Imports− Exports+ 1974–77 average	Rice Production 1961–65 average	Rice Production 1977	Rice Imports− Exports+ 1974–77 average
World total	254576	386596	−64236[1] +62611[1]	98474	173094	−12740[1] +12482[1]	47775	52472	−1344[1] +1377[1]	33849	23767	−762[1] +784[1]	216429	349676	−54364[1] +54158[1]	254711	366505	−8764[1] +8988[1]
Algeria	1254	c1200	−c1430	476	c400	−97	28	c60	—	—	—	—	4	c7[2]	−64	7	c2[2]	−4[1]
Argentina	7541	5300	+3069	679	494	+58	676	570	+107	422	170	+30	4984	8300	+4491	193	320	+99
Australia	8222	9350	+8888	978	2560	+1773	1172	c962	+306	11	c12	+1[1]	176	145	−1[1] +12	136	530	+213
Austria	704	1072	−5 +22	563	1212	−43	322	279	−12	393	351	—	197	1159	−49 +1[1]	—	—	−36
Bangladesh	37	218[2]	−1298	15	17[2]	−1[1]	—	—	−1[1]	—	—	—	4	c2[2]	—	15048	c19300	−290
Belgium	826	c750	−1042[3] +551[3]	485	c700	−1227[3] +328[3]	389	c110	−64[3] +10[3]	120	c50	−13[3] +4[3]	2	c30[2]	−1843[3] +505[3]	—	—	−95[3] +33[3]
Brazil	574	2066	−2670	26	56[2]	−20	20	34	−24	17	14	—	10112	19122	−2 +1262	6123	8941	−15[1] +135
Bulgaria	2213	c3012	−c90 +c167	694	c1750	−120 +c20	141	c60	—	58	c20	−17[1]	1601	c2555	−c340 +c76	37	c70[2]	−6[1]
Burma	38	60[2]	−8[1]	—	—	—	—	—	—	—	—	—	58	c64[2]	+4[1]	7786	9460	+c430
Canada	15364	19651	+11518	3860	11515	+3220	6075	4303	+265	319	392	+187	1073	4303	−853 +113	—	—	−74
Chile	1082	1219	−903	74	143	−6[1] +c14	89	124	+5[1]	7	16	−5[1]	204	355	−112 +2[1]	85	95	−33
China	22200	c40000	−c5000	14200	c15400	−c200	1600	c1900	—	—	—	—	c22500	c33500	−c1000 +c100	c86000	c129000	−c40 +c2500
Colombia	118	c60	−c343	106	81	−c48	—	—	−9[1]	—	—	—	826	753	−13[1] +3[1]	576	1329	+46
Czechoslovakia	1779	c5244	−c596	1556	c3100	−51 +c113	792	c600	+15	897	c870	−1[1] +42	474	c600	−c620	—	—	−c71
Denmark	535	c605	−14 +207	3506	c6084	−170 +486	713	c288	−33 +6	380	c320	−3[1] +41	—	—	−244	—	—	−11 +1
Egypt	1459	1872	−2427	137	c125	−24 +1[1]	—	—	—	—	—	—	1913	c2900	−464	1845	2270	+168
Ethiopia	540	592	−24 +1[1]	628	c830	—	5	c5	—	—	—	—	743	c1150	—	—	—	−1[1]
Finland	448	295	−6 +76	400	1447	−6[1] +16[1]	828	1022	−2[1] +38[1]	141	80	−10	—	—	−97	—	—	−13
France	12495	17450	−263 +6740	6594	10290	−72 +3071	2583	1928	−1[1] +117	367	376	−2[1] +50	2760	8614	−741 +2330	120	18	−194 +19
Germany, East	1357	c3100	−c1410	1291	c3400	−c500	850	c650	−2[1]	1741	c1500	−8[1]	3	c2[2]	−c1820	—	—	−46[1]
Germany, West	4607	7181	−1577 +770	3462	7497	−1566 +338	2185	2723	−329 +43	3031	2538	−78 +87	55	571	−3323 +283	—	—	−161 +38
Greece	1765	c1716	−83[1] +c119	248	c702	−55 +6[1]	143	c81	—	19	c5	—	239	c556	−892	88	c92	−4[1] +8[1]
Hungary	2020	c5312	−28 +c880	970	c750	−c184 +5[1]	108	c64	−25	271	c147	−6[1] +13[1]	3350	c6150	−c27 +c700	36	c51	−13 +1[1]
India	11191	29082	−4435 +2[1]	2590	2296	−1[1]	—	—	—	—	—	—	4593	c6800	−3[1]	52733	c74000	−126 +33[1]
Indonesia	—	—	−851	—	—	—	—	—	−1[1]	—	—	−1[1]	2804	3030	−26 +65	12396	23235	−1279
Iran	2873	c6200	−c1218	792	c1600	−c240	—	—	—	—	—	—	24	c80[2]	−157	851	c1650	−c350 +2[1]
Iraq	849	696	−c630 +5[1]	851	458	−c17	—	—	—	—	—	—	2	c30[2]	−12[1]	142	199	−195
Ireland	343	c239	−201 +20	575	c1359	−94 +46	357	c127	−13 +1	1	c1	—	—	—	−256	—	—	−3[1]
Italy	8857	6329	−2399 +22	276	677	−1070	545	355	−130 +1[1]	87	31	−5	3633	6456	−4323 +4	612	721	−48 +395
Japan	1332	236	−5633	1380	206	−1628	145	18	−157	2	c1	−65	96	11[2]	−8215	16444	17000	−41 +84
Kenya	122	c180	−c45 +5	15	c33	−1[1]	2	c5	—	—	—	—	1110	c1700	+75	14	34[2]	−3[1]
Korea, South	170	c90	−1652	1148	c814	−339	—	—	—	18	c6	—	26	c83[2]	−800	4809	8340	−271
Malaysia	—	—	−360[1]	—	—	—	—	—	−4[1]	—	—	—	8	c25[2]	−262[1]	1140	c2010	−262 +18[1]
Mexico	1672	2451	−380 +26	175	409	−70	76	46	−5	—	—	—	7369	8991	−1628 +1[1]	314	481	−24 +1[1]
Morocco	1516	1288	−c1260	1514	1347	−34[1]	18	8	—	2	c2	—	405	184	−18	20	18[2]	—
Netherlands, The	606	661	−1654 +848	390	287	−336 +208	421	94	−46 +87	312	74	−44 +14	—	c4[2]	−4734 +2052	—	—	−149 +83
New Zealand	248	370	−72 +5[1]	98	316	−1[1] +35	34	71	—	—	c1	—	16	232[2]	+36	—	—	−6[1]
Nigeria	16	c7[2]	−554	—	—	—	—	—	—	—	—	—	997	c1395	−7[1]	207	c600	−c110
Norway	19	65[2]	−288	440	630	−93	126	360	+16	3	8	−60	—	—	−89 +1[1]	—	—	−7
Pakistan	4153	9155	−1050	118	127	+32[1]	—	—	−9[1]	1	c1	−1[1]	514	c864	+c1[1]	1824	4356	+706
Peru	150	c150	−709	185	c170	−26	4	c1	—	—	—	—	490	c700	−250 +c1[1]	324	580	−51 +2[1]
Philippines	—	—	−580	—	—	—	—	—	−3[1]	—	—	—	1305	3037	−c110	3957	7150	−95
Poland	2988	5310	−2030	1368	3404	−c1040 +c50	2641	c2600	−c62 +4[1]	7466	c6200	−c155 +c76	20	c220	−c1400	—	—	−78
Portugal	562	c196	−347	61	c34	−91	87	c55	—	177	90	−10	617	402	−1112 +2[1]	167	112	−71 +1[1]
Romania	4321	c6540	−c523 +c983	415	1626	−78	154	c60	—	95	c50	−28[1]	5853	10103	−c410 +c320	40	c50	−52
South Africa	834	1815	−3[1] +155	40	63[2]	−5[1] +5	107	72	−6[1] +c20	10	4	−1[1]	5248	9714	−c30 +c2380	2	3[2]	−c90 +2[1]
Spain	4365	4045	−81 +28[1]	1959	6707	−33 +74	447	428	—	385	218	—	1101	1885	−3987 +1[1]	386	379	+46
Sweden	909	c1562	−11 +766	1167	c1992	−26[1] +150	1304	c1399	−23 +65	142	c364	−1[1] +117	—	—	−66	—	—	−20
Switzerland	355	338	−352	102	175	−510	40	45	−147	52	32	−22	14	139[2]	−261	—	—	−25
Syria	1093	1217	−160 +1[1]	649	337	−10[1] +22[1]	2	2	—	—	—	—	7	c30[2]	−12[1]	1	c3	−71
Thailand	—	—	−86	—	—	—	—	—	—	—	—	—	816	1677	+2059	11267	13590	+1732
Turkey	8585	16715	−411 +148	3447	c4750	−23 +c115	495	380	—	734	715	—	950	c1200	—	222	c253[2]	−35
U.S.S.R.	64207	92042	−6260 +2447	20318	52653	−c1440 +c686	6052	18379	−c160 +c22	15093	8471	−230[1]	13122	10993	−c6100 +c300	390	2200	−c260 +c46
United Kingdom	3520	5229	−3534 +120	6670	10784	−720 +474	1541	771	−38 +6	21	38	−25[1] +1[1]	—	2[2]	−3540 +42	—	—	−168 +21
United States	33040	55134	−40 +26616	8676	9056	−256 +1123	13848	10856	−13 +219	828	432	−10 +63	95561	161485	−47 +37045	3084	4501	−2[1] +2065
Uruguay	465	c160	+58	28	c44	−5 +7	66	c25	+1[1]	—	—	—	148	c121	+12[1]	67	228	+89
Venezuela	1	c1	−697	—	—	—	—	—	—	—	—	−8	477	c800	−337	136	508	−34 +25
Yugoslavia	3599	5622	−559 +5	557	650	−7 +13	343	309	−3[1] +4	169	87	−3[1]	5618	9856	−28[1] +282	23	28[2]	−20[1]

Note: (—) indicates quantity nil or negligible. (c) indicates provisional or estimated. [1]1974–76 average. [2]1976. [3]Belgium-Luxembourg economic union.
Sources: *FAO Monthly Bulletin of Statistics; FAO Production Yearbook 1976; FAO Trade Yearbook 1976.*

(M. C. MacDONALD)

rise higher than the loan rate. Under the second he may also obtain a loan using his grain as collateral, receive advance payments to finance storage up to three years, and receive a waiver of interest charges after the first year of the three-year loan contract, but he can only sell his grain when prices rise above a designated trigger point (currently set at 140% of the loan rate). In the current program the government would call all loans for wheat if the price rose to 175% of the loan rate. The system was designed to moderate price swings by removing grain from the market when prices are low and supplies are great and releasing it when supplies are scarce and prices high.

As of the end of 1978 the U.S. domestic wheat program did not authorize the government to buy stocks directly for placement in a reserve. If the stock accumulation policies agreed to with the EEC should become part of a new WTC, the issue might be raised as to whether the U.S. government would need such authority to fulfill its international obligations since farmers might conceivably not choose to place their grain in reserve at the international acquisition trigger prices. The case was not clear. Prices in December 1978 were near the proposed trigger point, but the U.S. already held 11.2 million tons in reserve, and much would depend upon the level of stockholding obligations and other measures yet to be determined in a WTC.

In a bill that died in the 95th Congress, the U.S. administration had proposed an International Emergency Wheat Reserve intended to establish a special 6 million-ton U.S. reserve. Its purpose was to deal with foreign emergencies and disasters and to guarantee that the United States would be able to honour its food aid commitments when grain supplies were tight. The administration announced that it intended to reintroduce similar legislation in 1979.

The question of subsidies was one that generated considerable controversy, in both the grain negotiations and the multilateral trade negotiations (MTN) taking place at the same time. One reason that the U.S. adamantly opposed a grain agreement with rigid price provisions that merely set maximum and minimum sales prices without other actions affecting underlying supply-demand factors was that the pre-1971 IWA (the 1971 IWA had only consultative provisions) broke down partly because countries evaded the floor export price of that agreement by subsidization of producers or exporters.

Just as the grain negotiations were approaching a close in December, a group of U.S. wheat producers were seeking to have countervailing duties (those imposed on foreign goods to offset the advantage those goods achieved by subsidization in their country) applied under the U.S. Trade Act of 1974 to EEC products imported into the U.S. This would be in retaliation for heavy EEC subsidies paid on EEC wheat, which, the U.S. producers claimed, unfairly undercut U.S. sales in traditional U.S. markets. Wheat is much more costly to produce in the EEC than in the U.S., and the EEC maintains domestic producer prices and, thus, farm income partly by subsidization of lower quality wheat exports. In effect, the EEC finances most of

these subsidies by proceeds from the import levies its members apply under the CAP to imported higher quality wheat.

Such subsidies and the application of countervailing duties constituted a central issue in the MTN. The U.S. Congress in 1978 had failed to renew the administration's authority to waive countervailing duties—the authority to waive was to expire Jan. 4, 1979—and the EEC was making its acceptance of a code to regulate subsidies contingent upon renewal of the waiver authority. When the MTN appeared on the verge of breaking up, the U.S. administration reiterated its pledge to request renewal authority from the Congress in 1979. Under a provision of the 1974 Trade Act authorizing U.S. participation in the MTN, the Congress would also have in 1979 the opportunity to accept or reject the subsidy code and the other elements in any nontariff trade barrier package agreed to by negotiators in the MTN. There appeared to be a strong linkage between the MTN and WTC negotiations, but the nature of it was not entirely clear.

The UNCTAD grain conference was also expected to adopt a Coarse Grains Trade Convention and a new Food Aid Convention. The former was expected to have only consultative provisions.

Food Aid. Completion of negotiations of a new Food Aid Convention was delayed by the failure to conclude a WTC in 1978. However, there appeared to be basic agreement on its provisions, and the January 1979 UNCTAD grain conference was expected to approve the convention. General acceptance appeared to exist for an overall minimum food-aid goal of 10 million tons of grain. The U.S. offered to provide 4,470,000 tons (more than double its commitment under the old convention) and to join with others in providing increased food assistance to meet extraordinary situations. Provisional contributions pledged by other donors totaled about 3.3 million tons in December 1978.

The FAO's preliminary estimates of food aid allocations of cereals in 1978–79 indicated a total of nearly 10 million tons. U.S. commitments were 66% of the total, the EEC 13%, and Canada 10%. Actual shipments totaled 9.4 million tons in 1977–78, with the U.S. share 63%, the EEC 16%, and Canada 11%. These countries had similar shares in 1976–77. Such shipments had fallen as low as 5.7 million in 1973–74 during the years of scarcity that followed poor grain crops throughout the world in 1972. In the developed countries during the period of grain surpluses preceding 1972, shipments, motivated in part by surplus disposal aims, reached 12.6 million tons in 1971–72, of which the United States provided 9.3 million. Thus, one of the primary goals of a new Food Aid Convention was to assure the more regular availability of food aid in times of both plenty and scarcity.

Food aid shipments of nonfat dry milk were estimated by the FAO to have increased almost 20% in 1977–78 over a year earlier, to 195,000 tons. However, those of vegetable oils declined about 10% to 220,000 tons.

Contributions to the International Emergency Food Reserve totaled (in November) about 315,000 tons of cereals, of which the FAO reported about 277,000 had been utilized. Some of the allocations

Alfalfa test plots at the University of Minnesota contain precise amounts of radioactive materials which enable scientists to measure the nitrogen-fixing characteristics of various strains of alfalfa.

were to Vietnam (to assist refugees and displaced persons from Cambodia in August) and to Afghanistan (to assist flood victims). The FAO's Committee on Food Aid Policies and Programs in October established the reserve on a continuing basis by providing for annual replenishments as recommended by the World Food Council.

The reserve depended upon voluntary pledges. Total pledges between 1976 and 1978 amounted to $105 million, of which $30 million were by Sweden, $27 million by the U.S., $12 million by West Germany, and smaller amounts by the EEC, Norway, the United Kingdom, Canada, Australia, The Netherlands, Japan, and Switzerland. At the end of 1978, $31 million had been pledged for 1979, $27 million by the U.S.

As of October 1979, $716 million of the $750 million target for the UN World Food Program for the 1977–78 biennium had been pledged. For the 1979–80 biennium, 73% of the targeted $950 million had been pledged. The U.S. pledge for 1979–80 was $220 million, compared with $188 million in 1977–78. Most U.S. food aid, however, was granted under bilateral programs. Thus, concessional sales of farm commodities under Public Law 480 Title I were authorized at $800 million in fiscal 1978.

Information Systems. The World Food Conference recommended an expansion of food information activities as an important contribution to world food security. Through its Global Information and Early Warning System, the FAO expanded the collection and dissemination of information to

meet the needs of decision makers, particularly those in less developed countries that did not have the resources to maintain worldwide data collection and analysis systems. In cooperation with the World Meteorological Organization (WMO), the FAO began operation of a weather forecasting system for parts of West Africa.

In late 1979 the USDA planned to start making regular operational use of a remote-sensing system using Earth resources satellites in agricultural forecasts. At first top priority was to be given to providing early warning of major events such as droughts and floods. The high costs involved and the developing state of the technology suggested that such techniques, although growing in importance, would for a long time supplement rather than replace traditional forms of estimation of crop production, land use, and resource inventory assessment.

AGRICULTURAL DEVELOPMENT

Foreign Assistance. The less developed countries received sharply increased commitments of external assistance to their agricultural sectors in 1977, and many donors were providing an increasing proportion of their aid to the poorest countries and to meet the needs of small farmers. Official commitments (excluding the centrally planned countries) of external assistance to agriculture in the less developed countries—broadly defined to include rural infrastructure, agro-industries, fertilizer production, and regional river basin projects

Agriculture and Food Supplies

—totaled an estimated $6.7 billion in 1977, compared with about $4.9 billion in 1976 and $5.5 billion in 1975, according to the Organization for Economic Cooperation and Development (OECD) and the FAO. The 1977 total represented about $6.1 billion in 1975 prices, about 12% above 1976 and 22% above 1975. In terms of the OECD's "narrow" definition of agriculture, roughly equivalent to direct use in food production, total commitments increased from nearly $3.4 billion in current prices in 1976 to almost $4.8 billion in 1977.

Aid commitments by multilateral lending agencies to agriculture were estimated at $3,742,000,-000 in 1977 in current prices, more than $1 billion higher than in 1976 and some $700 million higher than in 1975. About one-third of the total funding of international financial organizations for economic development was going to agriculture, compared with only 19% in 1971–72.

The World Bank complex continued to be the largest foreign lender to agriculture in the less developed countries, accounting for more than two-thirds of all multilateral lending and some two-fifths of total external assistance. In 1977 World Bank loans and interest-free credits from the International Development Association (IDA) were al-

most 50% above the average for 1974–76. These institutions approved $2,770,000,000 in new commitments to agriculture in less developed countries in the first half of 1978, compared with $2,909,000,000 in the first half of 1977.

The World Bank in 1978 was seeking a $30 billion general capital increase for its regular, non-concessionary program for 1982–86, or $40 billion for 1982–87. The U.S. subscribed approximately 25% of the bank's capital and 31% of that for the IDA, which received a $7.6 billion replenishment for fiscal 1978–79.

All the regional development banks also increased their lending to agriculture in 1977. The African, Asian, and Inter-American development banks were also seeking replenishment of either their ordinary capital or their concessional funds to adjust for the effects of inflation and to expand their lending activities.

The International Fund for Agricultural Development (IFAD), which began operation in December 1977 with initial funding of about $1 billion intended for commitment over two to three years, approved its first loans in April to Sri Lanka and Tanzania. IFAD programs were to be executed in cooperation with other development institutions. The IFAD board determined that two-thirds of its funds would be reserved on the softest terms for agricultural projects in countries with per capita incomes under $300.

Bilateral commitments to agriculture by the developed countries were estimated at $2,545,-000,000 in 1977, an increase of more than $800 million over 1976, and constituted about 38% of total external assistance. Bilateral commitments from the Organization of Petroleum Exporting Countries were about $70 million higher than in 1976 but less than three-fifths of 1975 pledges.

UNCTAD meetings in November on the establishment of a proposed Common Fund to finance price stabilization arrangements for primary commodities recessed until February 1979. Negotiators for the industrialized and less developed countries failed to resolve differences over the size and use of the fund, particularly with regard to the proposal by the less developed countries to use some of the proceeds for development aid. Although the industrialized nations offered to contribute to a common fund, the expectations of the less developed countries substantially exceeded what the industrialized countries were prepared to offer.

Research. Funding of the programs and budgets of the nine international agricultural research institutes and two programs sponsored by the Consultative Group on International Agricultural Research was expected to be increased in 1979 about 20% from the $86 million contributed by national governments, foundations, and regional and international organizations. A new activity that the Consultative Group decided to undertake was the establishment of a small group to help provide assistance for strengthening national research programs in the less developed countries.

(RICHARD M. KENNEDY)

See also Environment; Fisheries; Food Processing; Gardening; Industrial Review: *Alcoholic Beverages, Textiles; Tobacco;* United States: *Special Report.*

Rhubarb consumption in the U.S. has declined steadily in recent years because of the high cost of hand harvesting. USDA engineer Dale Marshall has developed a mechanical harvester which reduces harvesting costs by about 50%.

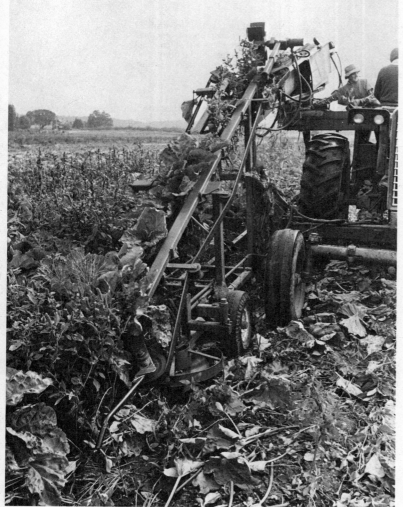

SCIENCE AND EDUCATION ADMINISTRATION—USDA

Albania

A people's republic in the western Balkan Peninsula, Albania is on the Adriatic Sea, bordered by Greece and Yugoslavia. Area: 28,748 sq km (11,100 sq mi). Pop. (1978 est.): 2,687,000. Cap. and largest city: Tirana (pop., 1975 est., 192,000). Language: Albanian. Religion: officially atheist; historically Muslim, Orthodox, and Roman Catholic communities. First secretary of the Albanian (Communist) Party of Labour in 1978, Enver Hoxha; president of the Presidium of the People's Assembly, Haxhi Leshi; chairman of the Council of Ministers (premier), Mehmet Shehu.

Albania's "unbreakable friendship" with China ended abruptly on July 7, 1978, when a note was delivered to the Albanian embassy in Peking announcing that China was severing all economic and military ties with its erstwhile ally. Significantly, the note was sent on the first anniversary of a lengthy statement published in *Zeri i Popullit* ("Voice of the People"), the Albanian party organ, attacking China's "three-world" theory, which justified the Sino-U.S. rapprochement, and accusing the Chinese of betraying revolutionary principles for the sake of power politics. Since 1954 China had supplied Albania with aid amounting to $5 billion as well as some 6,000 technicians, while about 2,000 Albanians had been trained in China. The last 150 Chinese working in Albania left at the end of July.

Denouncing Yugoslavia as well as China ideologically, Albania late in 1978 was seeking aid from India and increased trade with Greece and Turkey and the European Economic Community. In October the Enver Hoxha automobile and tractor complex at Tirana produced its first tractor.

(K.M. SMOGORZEWSKI)

Albania

Algeria

A republic on the north coast of Africa, Algeria is bounded by Morocco, Western (Spanish) Sahara, Mauritania, Mali, Niger, Libya, and Tunisia. Area: 2,322,164 sq km (896,592 sq mi). Pop. (1977 prelim.): 17,272,000. Cap. and largest city: Algiers (pop., 1975 UN est., 1,179,000). Language: Arabic, Berber, French. Religion: Muslim. President to Dec. 27, 1978, Col. Houari Boumédienne; interim president from December 27, Rabah Bitat.

An era in Algeria's history ended on Dec. 27, 1978, when Pres. Houari Boumédienne (*see* OBITUARIES), the country's ruler for 13 years, died after having been in a coma for almost six weeks. In keeping with the 1976 constitution, Rabah Bitat, speaker of the National Assembly, was proclaimed interim president by a special session of the Assembly.

Relations with France dominated Algeria's foreign policy in early 1978. Their lowest point had been reached in December 1977 over the question of the French hostages taken by the Algerian-sup-

Algeria

Moroccan troops captured in the Western Sahara were presented to reporters in July.

ported Popular Front for the Liberation of Saguia el Hamra and Río de Oro (Polisario Front), which sought independence for Western Sahara. (The hostages were later released.) In January and March 1978 eight French companies were nationalized, and French imports were banned wherever possible. On February 9, however, Pres. Valéry Giscard d'Estaing of France called for a new era in Franco-Algerian relations, to which Algeria responded favourably in April.

Relations worsened again in the spring when France's involvement in Zaire prompted Algerian President Boumédienne to denounce French neocolonialism. It was only after the July 10 coup in Mauritania, one of the countries fighting against the Polisario Front, that France and Algeria were able to pursue their reconciliation. President Boumédienne reiterated on July 22 that the main issue in the Western Sahara was simply one of sovereignty, and the Franco-Algerian reconciliation was sealed by a visit by Foreign Minister Abdel-Aziz Bouteflika to Paris on August 1.

Algeria maintained close links with Libya. At a meeting in Algiers, February 15–27, the two countries decided to form joint industrial enterprises. Libyan Pres. Muammar al-Qaddafi made an eight-day visit to Algiers in early June. These contacts also formed part of Algeria's involvement in Middle Eastern affairs directed against Egypt's peace initiative with Israel. After a 13-day tour of ten Arab states, the U.S.S.R., Yugoslavia, and Malta, President Boumédienne was host to a "rejection front" meeting in Algiers on January 31. Algeria also participated in the post-Camp David meeting in Damascus, Syria, in late September, where an effort was made to organize Arab opposition to the peace proposals.

Relations with Spain were complicated by Algeria's support for the independence movement in the Canary Islands. Following the attempted assassination, in Algiers on April 5, of the movement's leader, Antonio Cubillo, the Algerian authorities arrested two Spaniards said to be responsible for the attack; one was later sentenced to death.

At the March 25 congress of the General Union of Algerian Workers, President Boumédienne announced a one-third increase in the national minimum wage and, during the National Union of Algerian Peasants conference on April 24, he announced that the agrarian reform was a success (a view not shared by most observers). It was announced in June that U.S. $1.7 billion was to be spent developing the Tamenrasset region. On June 19 the final part within Algeria of the trans-Sahara highway was opened. (GEORGE JOFFÉ)

Andorra

An independent co-principality of Europe, Andorra is in the Pyrenees Mountains between Spain and France. Area: 464 sq km (179 sq mi). Pop. (1976 est.): 29,000. Cap.: Andorra la Vella (commune pop., 1975 est., 10,900). Language: Catalan (official), French, Spanish. Religion: predominantly Roman Catholic. Co-princes: the president of the French Republic and the bishop of Urgel, Spain, represented by their *veguers* (provosts) and *batlles* (prosecutors). An elected Council General of 24 members elects the first syndic; in 1978, Julià Reig-Ribó.

In the partial elections to Andorra's Council General of the Valleys, held Dec. 14, 1977, the Andorran Democratic Association won 2 of the 12 contested seats from the Conservatives. As a result, the 24-seat Council General was split evenly between the two parties.

Planning a solemn celebration of the 700th anni-

Andorra

GERARD RANCINAN—SYGMA

Tiny Andorra for the first time in 700 years welcomed its two co-princes on a joint visit October 19. Valéry Giscard d'Estaing of France shakes hands with the crowd as Msgr. Joan Martí Alanis, bishop of Urgel, looks on.

versary of Andorra's independence, established on Sept. 8, 1278, the Council General invited the two co-princes—the president of France and the Spanish bishop of Urgel—to honour the ceremony with their presence. There was at first disappointment when the French president, Valéry Giscard d'Estaing, informed the Council General that he would not be able to attend personally, and it was decided to abandon the celebrations. But later the French president found it possible to make the historic visit after all, and on October 19 he joined his co-prince, Msgr. Joan Martí Alanis, bishop of Urgel, in the first meeting ever of co-princes on Andorran soil. There they were welcomed by the first syndic, Julià Reig-Ribó. During the celebrations they unveiled a monument commemorating the principality's 700 years of independence and peace. Giscard spoke of French support in education and technical matters.

Meanwhile, Andorra prospered through the sale of duty-free goods. About four million tourists visited the principality yearly, and their expenditure constituted the major part of Andorra's income. The advantages of Andorra as a tax haven were explained in a brochure published by the Empresa de Planificacio de Finances i de Serveis.

(K. M. SMOGORZEWSKI)

ANDORRA

Education. (1974–75) Primary, pupils 3,779, teachers (including preprimary) 142; secondary, pupils 1,626, teachers 120.

Finance and Trade. Monetary units: French franc and Spanish peseta. Budget (1976 est.): revenue 454 million pesetas; expenditure 357 million pesetas. Foreign trade (1977): imports from France Fr 681,838,000 (U.S. $138.8 million), from Spain 5,354,610,000 pesetas (U.S. $70.5 million); exports to France Fr 18,870,000 (U.S. $3.8 million), to Spain 126,983,000 pesetas (U.S. $1.7 million). Tourism (1976) 6.5 million visitors.

Communications. Telephones (Jan. 1976) 3,860. Radio receivers (Dec. 1975) 6,600. Television receivers (Dec. 1969) 1,700.

Agriculture. Production: cereals, potatoes, tobacco, wool. Livestock (in 000; 1976): sheep c. 25; cattle c. 3; horses c. 1.

Angola

Angola

Located on the west coast of southern Africa, Angola is bounded by Zaire, Zambia, Namibia (South West Africa), and the Atlantic Ocean. The small exclave of Cabinda, a district of Angola, is bounded by the Congo and Zaire. Area: 1,246,700 sq km (481,353 sq mi). Pop. (1978 est.): 6,831,000. Cap. and largest city: Luanda (pop., 1970, 480,600). Language: Bantu languages (predominant), Portuguese (official), and some Khoisan dialects. Religion: traditional beliefs about 45%; Roman Catholicism about 43%; Protestantism 12%. President in 1978, Agostinho Neto; premier to December 9, Lopo do Nascimento.

Throughout 1978 the government's relations with the opposition movements and with South Africa remained hostile. After a difficult start, however, there was some rapprochement with Zaire. The grave concern aroused by the instability of the country's economy and political situation led some Western powers to offer assistance.

Early in the year the Front for the Liberation of the Enclave of Cabinda (FLEC), which had set up a provisional government on May 1, 1977, was forced to seek peace. It had failed to gain support from either of the two main opposition movements, the National Front for the Liberation of Angola (FNLA) and the National Union for the Total Independence of Angola (UNITA), neither of which was anxious to see Angola deprived of Cabinda's oil. U.S. interests also favoured the

American Literature: see Literature

Anglican Communion: see Religion

ANGOLA

Education. (1972–73) Primary, pupils 536,599, teachers 13,230; secondary, pupils 59,209, teachers 3,060; vocational, pupils 15,511, teachers 1,107; teacher training, students 3,388, teachers 330; higher, students 2,942, teaching staff 274.

Finance and Trade. Monetary unit: kwanza, with a free rate (June 30, 1978) of 30 kwanzas to U.S. $1 (56 kwanzas = £1 sterling). Budget (1974 est.) balanced at 19,475,000,000 kwanzas. Foreign trade (1974): imports 15,853,000,000 kwanzas; exports 31,215,000,000 kwanzas. Import sources: Portugal 22%; West Germany 13%; U.S. 10%; South Africa 10%; U.K. 7%; France 7%; Italy 5%; Japan 5%. Export destinations: U.S. 38%; Portugal 27%; Canada 8%; Japan 6%. Main exports: crude oil 48%; coffee 20%; diamonds 8%.

Transport and Communications. Roads (1974) 72,323 km. Motor vehicles in use (1974): passenger 133,512; commercial (including buses) 26,943. Railways: (1975) c. 3,000 km; traffic (1974) 418 million passenger-km, freight 5,461,000,000 net ton-km. Shipping traffic (1974): goods loaded 10,040,000 metric tons, unloaded 3,980,000 metric tons. Telephones (Jan. 1977) 31,200. Radio licenses (Dec. 1975) 116,000.

Agriculture. Production (in 000; metric tons; 1977): corn c. 450; millet c. 85; cassava (1976) c. 1,600; sweet potatoes (1976) c. 165; dry beans c. 70; bananas c. 320; palm kernels c. 13; palm oil c. 42; coffee c. 72; cotton, lint c. 13; sisal c. 25; timber (cu m; 1976) c. 7,836; fish catch (1976) c. 154. Livestock (in 000; 1976): cattle c. 3,000; sheep c. 205; goats c. 910 ; pigs c. 360.

Industry. Production (in 000; metric tons; 1975): cement 699; iron ore (metal content) 3,388; diamonds (metric carats) c. 460; crude oil (1977) c. 8,640; petroleum products c. 800; electricity (kw-hr) c. 1,305,000.

status quo; the U.S.-owned Cabinda Gulf Oil Co. was relying on the Cuban-trained forces of Pres. Agostinho Neto to protect its employees and plant.

During a visit to Nigeria in January, Neto stoutly denied Zaire's charge that Angola was plotting against it. In March Angola accused Zaire of launching a raid against the town of Caianda, in a salient between Zaire and Zambia, and of assisting hostile guerrilla forces. Zaire denied the charges, while the guerrillas claimed Cuban forces were waging a campaign against villages along the Angola-Zaire border. Relations with Zaire were strained further in May by the unsuccessful invasion of Zaire by Katangese rebels, believed to be based in Angola. (See ZAIRE.)

Reports that Neto was visiting Moscow in April to receive treatment for a serious illness were said to be unfounded. Instead, Soviet Pres. Leonid Brezhnev promised all-out support for Neto's government, and in May the visit of a Soviet delegation to Luanda led to a series of agreements covering trade and technical and scientific affairs. Fresh supplies of military equipment from the U.S.S.R. enabled a joint Angolan-Cuban force to launch a fresh attack on the UNITA guerrillas in the south. Both sides claimed successes, but the outcome was uncertain. In June there were reports that a number of senior Soviet officers had arrived in Angola to take over important command and planning posts formerly held by Cubans. This was followed by increased pressure on the guerrillas. Meanwhile, in May, South African troops striking at South West Africa People's Organization (SWAPO) bases inside Angola had attacked Cassinga, about 250 km (160 mi) north of the border.

Talks were held in Brazzaville, Congo, in July and August between Angolan and Zairian delega-

tions and, secretly, between Neto and Pres. Mobutu Sese Seko of Zaire. Shortly thereafter, it was announced that diplomatic relations between the two countries would soon be reestablished, although the promises of détente elicited some skepticism. On October 15 Mobutu paid his first state visit to Luanda. On November 6 it was announced that the Benguela Railway, closed in 1975, had been reopened, permitting Zambian and Zairian copper to reach Western markets by way of the Angolan port of Lobito.

The concern of the Western powers over the continuing troubles in central Africa led to a visit in July from Claude Cheysson, the European Economic Community's commissioner responsible for relations with third world countries, who discussed the possibility of supplying aid. He was preceded by Donald McHenry, U.S. deputy permanent representative at the UN, who visited Angola in June. McHenry returned in July as leader of a delegation, representing five Western nations, that was attempting to make a plan for Namibia's future. He was followed in November by Richard M. Moose, Jr., assistant secretary of state for African affairs and the highest-ranking U.S. official to visit Angola since independence.

In December it was announced that the posts of premier and vice-premier had been abolished; the premier and six government ministers, including three vice-premiers, were dismissed.

(KENNETH INGHAM)

Antarctica

During the 1977–78 summer field season, 11 nations maintained stations in Antarctica and scientists from 14 nations conducted research. Emilio Marcos Palma was the first human born in Antarctica, on Jan. 7, 1978. His father was commander of Argentina's Esperanza Base on the Antarctic Peninsula.

International Research Projects. The five-nation International Antarctic Glaciological Program (IAGP) included two scientific traverses by the Soviet Union, French drilling of a 905-m ice core at Dome C in East Antarctica, Australian drilling of two intermediate ice cores on the Law Dome near Casey Station, and more than 17,000 km of radio echo sounding flights by U.S., British, and Danish scientists using a U.S. Navy Hercules aircraft. A large lake, more than 13 km long, was discovered buried under 3½ km of ice close to the Ellsworth Mountains.

Representatives of the 13 Antarctic Treaty nations met in Canberra, Australia, in February and March in a special consultative meeting to resolve the issue of living marine resources. In July they met again in Buenos Aires, Arg., to develop a convention to regulate fishing in Antarctic waters. It was expected that if an agreement was reached, it would be ratified during the tenth Antarctic Treaty Consultative Meeting, scheduled for Washington, D.C., in 1979. The 1972 Convention for the Conservation of Antarctic Seals was ratified and went into effect on March 11.

The 15th SCAR (Scientific Committee on Antarc-

PHOTOS, PAUL DEARING—U.S. NAVY

(Left) A huge cargo plane bringing supplies for Operation Deep Freeze—the U.S. Navy's support force for Antarctic scientific research— taxis to a test drilling site on the Ross Ice Shelf. Test ice cores (below) are spread out by a scientist for study.

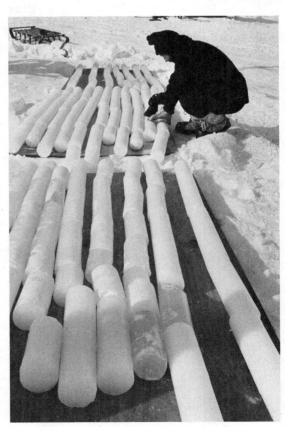

tic Research) met at Chamonix, France, in May. The delegates endorsed international research projects in northern Victoria Land, on Antarctic seabirds, and two dealing with global climate and global pollution levels. Regulation of tourism was discussed, and several international scientific workshops were approved.

Scientific Programs. ARGENTINA. A full scientific program was conducted at Almirante Brown, and meteorologic programs were conducted at the other five Argentine bases, all operated by the armed forces. Besides the birth of a child, a marriage occurred at Esperanza Base, and eight families, including two pregnant women and 19 children, wintered over. Argentina also established a customs house and an immigration office, presumably to reinforce its territorial claims.

AUSTRALIA. Research continued at Casey, Davis, and Mawson stations in Antarctica and at the sub-Antarctic Macquarie Island. Plans were announced to increase the level of Antarctic work by rebuilding all four research stations, increasing the size of the scientific staff by 15 persons, expanding the marine research program, and designing and building a ship for marine research and supply voyages.

CHILE. According to press reports, Chile planned to build a new base at Marguerite Bay to "reinforce its presence in the Antarctic."

FRANCE. In addition to the IAGP science program, research was conducted at Dumont d'Urville Station on the Adélie Coast. The 905-m ice core was thought to contain a climatic record of 25,000 years. Glaciologists also worked at the South Pole to complete a geochemical study.

JAPAN. Showa Base operations continued. Japanese scientists joined with Americans to find more than 300 meteorites preserved in the ice cover at the Allan Hills. Laboratory analysis at the Smithsonian Institution, Washington, D.C., indicated that one meteorite is a unique specimen, the first of a new class of achondrite meteorites, and another is a rare carbonaceous chondrite meteorite containing amino acids.

NEW ZEALAND. Scientific programs were conducted in the Dry Valleys and within helicopter range of Ross Island. The rebuilding of Scott Base and U.S.-New Zealand joint logistics continued, as did the cooperative study of volcanic Mt. Erebus.

NORWAY. Norwegian scientists joined U.S. scientific teams in Marie Byrd Land for geologic investigations and in the Weddell Sea for oceanographic research, but Norway did not send an independent expedition to Antarctica during the 1977–78 season.

POLAND. Construction on Arctowski Base at 62° 10' S, 58°28' W was completed, and a multidisciplinary research program was conducted. Two U.S. scientists worked four months at the base.

SOUTH AFRICA. The 19th South African National Antarctic Expedition resumed the earth sciences research program and continued investigations of the magnetosphere and ionosphere. Sixteen men wintered over at SANAE Base, now buried under ten metres of ice and snow. A new base would be built above the ground surface.

UNITED KINGDOM. British research activities again centred in the Antarctic Peninsula area,

Krill populations in Antarctic waters

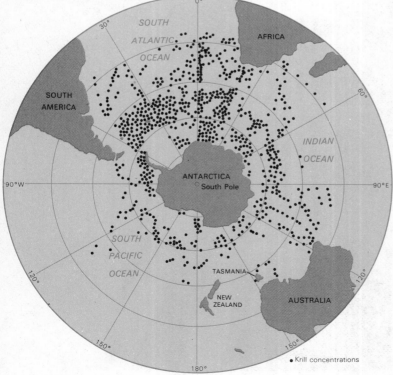

• Krill concentrations

with primary efforts being devoted to geochemical sampling. A marine research program, the Offshore Biological Project, was initiated in the Scotia Sea south of South Georgia. Severe weather and heavy ice hampered resupply of peninsula bases and delayed the completion of Rothera Base. Cooperative geologic projects with U.S. scientists were conducted near the Ronne Ice Shelf, Coats Land, and along the Orville Coast.

U.S.S.R. Some 500 men and women and six ships made up the 23rd Soviet Antarctic Expedition. Research was conducted at the six permanent bases, at Druzhnaya summer station on the Filchner Ice Shelf, and in the seas around Antarctica. Deep drilling continued to about 1,000 m at Vostok Station, where an ice core more than 50,000 years old was recovered. Construction began on an airfield for heavy aircraft at Molodezhnaya in Enderby Land, and modernization of Mirnyy Station was completed. Observations were made in the Scotia and Davis seas in conjunction with Polex-South, part of the international Global Atmospheric Research Program.

UNITED STATES. More than 325 scientists worked on 90 projects during the summer. Research in the new krill laboratory at Palmer Station resulted in important life cycle discoveries with relevance for the international negotiations on living marine resources. The Ross Ice Shelf Project burned two holes through the 420-m ice shelf, enabling deployment of television cameras and fish traps to study the below-ice fauna. More than 200 amphipods and other crustaceans and 109 cm of bottom sediment were collected. A multination geologic survey in Marie Byrd Land discovered 300 million-year-old plant fossils, causing geologists to rethink the origin of that region. At the Cumulus Hills more than 100 vertebrate fossils were discovered, some from animals as large as a small deer.

Geologists visited the Orville Coast to collect data that would complete the geologic mapping of the exposed areas of Antarctica. A special study was begun to determine the environmental impact of the U.S. Antarctic Research Program and to plan base development for the next 30 years. Construction of a new Siple Station began at the base of the Sentinel Mountains in Ellsworth Land. The interdenominational "Chapel of the Snows" at McMurdo Station, built by Navy SeeBees in 1955–56, was destroyed by fire on August 22.

WEST GERMANY. The research ship "Walther Herwig" and a fishing trawler were again sent to the Bellingshausen and Scotia seas to continue investigations of commercial fishing opportunities. Press reports discussed the possibility that West Germany would build a permanent research station and seek consultative status in the Antarctic Treaty.   (PETER J. ANDERSON)

Anthropology

The year 1978 was marked by the announcement of newly discovered fossils, new interpretations of known fossils, and continuing debate on the entire course of human evolution. For the last few decades paleontologists have placed the separation

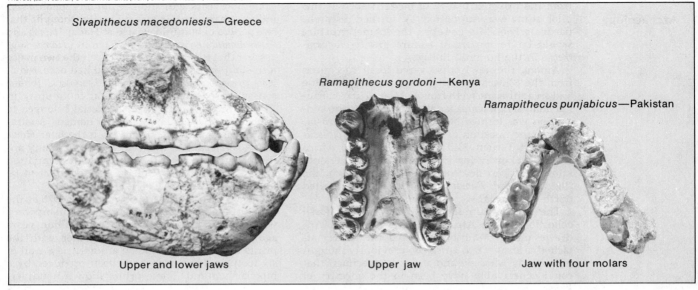

Sivapithecus macedoniesis—Greece

Ramapithecus gordoni—Kenya

Ramapithecus punjabicus—Pakistan

Upper and lower jaws

Upper jaw

Jaw with four molars

between the human, or hominid, line and the line leading to the modern African apes in the Miocene (approximately 16 million years ago), although a much more recent date of divergence is preferred by some anthropologists working with the blood proteins of recent primates. The controversial fossils relevant to the earlier date belong to the genus *Ramapithecus*; they have been found in India and Pakistan spanning a time period between 11 million and 9 million years ago and at Fort Ternan in western Kenya, dated at 14 million years ago. Recent reanalyses of these fossils, as well as the discovery of new material in Pakistan and Turkey, have shaken the confidence of many anthropologists concerning the position of this material as the earliest distinct step in the hominid lineage. *Ramapithecus* was now seen as being much more ape-like than had previously been thought.

It once was believed that *Ramapithecus* closely resembled *Homo sapiens* in its dental characteristics. Among the characteristics that separate it from modern African apes are a general robusticity of the bone supporting the teeth, a more vertical face, thicker enamel on the teeth, more rounded tooth cusps, and an expanded chewing surface. These point toward a diet that was tougher and more difficult to chew and are consistent with the hypothesis that man first became distinct in a relatively open grassland environment where he adapted to a diet of seeds and rhizomes.

However, the ramapithecines are not the only fossils with these characteristics. Most are shared by the Middle Miocene apes belonging to the genus *Sivapithecus,* which either accompanied *Ramapithecus* into Eurasia when a connection was formed between the Eurasian and African land masses at the end of the Early Miocene (16 million years ago) or were part of the radiation that produced *Ramapithecus* after the arrival in Eurasia. The only characteristics that *Ramapithecus* shares with the later hominids but not with *Sivapithecus* are a greater robusticity of the bone supporting the teeth, a less projecting face, a slight reduction in the size of the last lower molar, and a slightly

greater wear gradient on the molar teeth. This is not strong evidence upon which to define the origin of a new phylogenetic lineage.

In addition, David Pilbeam in 1977 announced the discovery of a radius (forearm bone) from the Potwar plateau, Pakistan, which may belong to *Ramapithecus*. If the association is correct it indicates that *Ramapithecus* had a generalized form of locomotion similar to the African Early Miocene apes and, therefore, had not diverged from them in its locomotor pattern. On the other hand, reanalysis of Fort Ternan, the Kenyan *Ramapithecus* site, indicates a woodland-bush environment rather than a forest, suggesting that *Ramapithecus* had made the adaptive transition to a more open habitat before migrating to Eurasia.

One of the most interesting new analyses showed that the enamel prism structure of the teeth of *Ramapithecus* and modern man is distinct

(Below) The footprint from what may have been one of man's early ancestors was left 3.5 million years ago in the soil of Tanzania. The impression is about 6 inches long and 4.4 inches wide.

from the prism structure of modern apes. If this pilot study was supported by further research, particularly on Miocene apes, the enamel structure would be an important feature linking *Ramapithecus* in the hominid lineage.

Among the newly discovered fossil specimens from the Miocene were a series of ramapithecine and sivapithecine teeth from Pasalar, Turkey. Faunal analysis indicates a date shortly after the connection was formed between Africa and Eurasia, raising the question of the origin of *Ramapithecus* from Fort Ternan. Did it migrate back to Africa after initial evolution in Eurasia, or is it the only known African descendant of an unknown line that produced *Ramapithecus* before it migrated north to Eurasia?

The problem stimulated both analysis and fossil collection in the African Early Miocene. P. Andrews and T. Mollison analyzed the matrix attached to *Sivapithecus africanus*, previously thought to be Early Miocene and the only specimen that could conceivably have been in the ancestry of *Ramapithecus* and *Sivapithecus*; their work indicated that there is no clear evidence for its Early Miocene date and that *S. africanus* could be a Middle Miocene contemporary of *Ramapithecus*. Both the search for fossils and reanalysis of existing fossils from the African Early Miocene increased the number of known primate species and illustrated the adaptive diversity at this time period. However, the question of the origin of the line leading to *Ramapithecus* and *Sivapithecus*, as well as the position of *Ramapithecus* in the ancestry of modern *Homo sapiens*, awaited further developments.

An additional uncertainty in the early evolution of the hominids was the absence of fossils in the critical period prior to the Late Pliocene and Early Pleistocene of Africa and the Early Pleistocene of Java, when indisputable hominid material becomes plentiful. It is possible, however, to deduce the general course of evolution during this period from the earliest hominid-bearing Pliocene sites. The two relevant sites are Hadar in Ethiopia

(3 million years ago) and Laetolil in Tanzania (3.5 million years ago). It was originally thought that two genera of hominid existed at Hadar, *Homo* and *Australopithecus*, and one at Laetolil, *Homo*, suggesting that the divergence between the two major forms of Plio-Pleistocene hominid had occurred at least prior to 3 million years ago. Donald C. Johanson surprised the anthropological community in 1978 by suggesting that this material belonged to one species, which he informally named "Australopithecus afarensis," from which the later *Homo* and *Australopithecus* evolved. However, many anthropologists still felt the morphological variation among the Hadar specimens was too great to be incorporated in one evolving lineage.

Laetolil was also in the news during 1978 as the result of the discovery of footprints contemporary with the early hominid levels (3.5 million years ago). Preserved as ash casts, together with the prints of numerous Pliocene animals, is a trail of six footprints that may have been produced by a bipedal hominid. These prints show a nondivergent big toe, lack of a well-developed arch, and a shorter and wider foot than is characteristic of modern man. In addition, the feet cross over each other, with the right foot on the left side of the midline and the left foot on the right side in what could be interpreted as a staggering gait. The possibility exists that they were made by a quadrupedal primate and that the prints of the forefeet had disappeared.

It has long been debated whether *Homo erectus*, in the sense of the fossils found in Africa and Asia, ever occupied Europe, or whether a form closer to anatomically modern *Homo sapiens* was the only inhabitant. A newly discovered fossil from East Germany, first described in English in 1978, is relevant to this controversy. The Bilzingsleben skull fragments from the Thüringen basin (dated to the Holstein or Mindel-Riss Interglacial Stage of the Middle Pleistocene) were interpreted by Emanuel Vlcek as a European form of *Homo erectus* with affinities to the *erectus* fossils from Olduvai Gorge, Tanzania; Sangiran, Java; Chou-k'ou-tien, China; and Vertesszollos, Hung. Chris Stringer from the British Museum (Natural History) also emphasized Bilzingsleben's similarity with the Petrolona skull from Greece. Petrolona traditionally had been interpreted as a rather aberrant Neanderthal, but redating of the cave in which it was found pushed it back in time at least to the Holstein. Vlcek suggested that *Homo erectus*, as represented by Bilzingsleben, Vertesszollos, and possibly Petrolona, was living contemporaneously in Europe with early *Homo sapiens*, but this opinion was far from universal. (LESLIE C. AIELLO)

See also Archaeology.
[411–413; 10/36.B]

The Petrolona skull found in Greece is classified by some anthropologists as *Homo erectus* and may have been contemporary in Europe with early *Homo sapiens*.

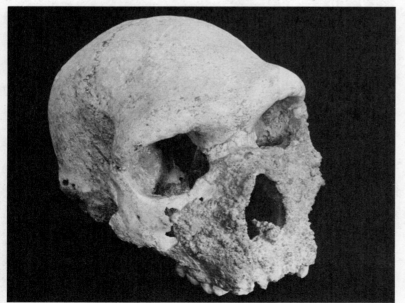

© CHRIS STRINGER

Archaeology

Eastern Hemisphere. Perhaps the most spectacular finds of the year came from an evidently royal tomb at Vergina in northern Greece, claimed to have been the burial place of Philip II of Macedonia, father of Alexander the Great. First encountered in 1977, the site underwent further clearance that yielded golden caskets and a variety of objects in gold, silver, ivory, and copper. There was not complete agreement as to whether the principal personage in the tomb was Philip II.

The archaeological year also was notable for an increase in the number of salvage efforts planned to rescue sites that would be flooded by waters behind new dams. New dams on the Euphrates in southern Turkey and on a tributary of the Tigris in Iraq were cases in point.

As to advances in technical methods for the study of archaeological materials, articles in *Science* reported on both a means for enriching radioactive carbon samples so as to achieve a much longer dating range (to about 75,000 years ago) and a method by which much smaller samples may be dated. *Science* also noted a method that used chemical isotopes to achieve the identification and thus proper assembly of scattered fragments of Greek marble inscriptions.

In a closely reasoned study, Oscar White Muscarella of the Metropolitan Museum of Art in New York City questioned the authenticity of various supposed ancient Near Eastern objets d'art in 27 U.S. and European museums. Muscarella provided evidence to support his belief that forgers and dealers have bilked the museum "experts" of millions of dollars.

Death brought an end to several distinguished archaeological careers during the year: Sir Max Mallowan (*see* OBITUARIES), excavator of the Assyrian capital of Nimrud; Dame Kathleen Kenyon, well known for her work at Jericho and Jerusalem; the director of excavations for the Iraqi government's antiquities service, Fuad Safar; and Vladimir Milojcic, professor of prehistory at Heidelberg University and excavator of various sites in northern Greece.

PLEISTOCENE PREHISTORY. Continuing excavations in caves in France and Spain yielded materials covering the long time range from the Mindel glaciation, which began about 2.5 million years ago, to the beginning of the Holocene Epoch, about 10,000 years ago. At the Arago cave in the French Pyrenees, pre-Neanderthal types of human fossils were recovered along with evidence of a Tayacian flint industry. Henry de Lumley continued his work at the Grotte du Lazaret, where hut foundations within the cave had been found together with tools of the Acheulian industry. A series of radioactive-carbon age determinations were made on Spanish samples from upper Solutrean layers (20,000 to 17,000 years ago) and from a Magdalenian layer (16,500 years ago).

André Leroi-Gourhan of the University of Paris continued his exposure of the great open-air Magdalenian site of Pincevent on the Seine River. Now treated as a national monument, Pincevent provides a much more comprehensive impression of the daily lives of the people of the Magdalenian horizon than do the contemporary caves, for all that the caves do yield the best of the upper Paleolithic art.

Few reports on archaeological finds (artifacts rather than human fossils) in Africa appeared in 1978. A Belgian expedition recovered a sequence of

An Iron Age village (top) was recreated in England's West Country as part of a BBC television experiment concerning daily life *c*. 300 BC. Ten people lived in the village for a year. (Bottom) In an Iron Age hut, participants prepared meals from food they raised themselves.

tools in Zaire, with some radiocarbon age determinations of as much as 45,000 years. In Australia the Western Australian Museum claimed the recovery of stone tools on the Murchison River that were estimated to be 100,000 years old, far older than any archaeological evidence yet noted in Australia.

NEAR EAST. For Egypt the study of the hair of a mummy found in 1898, compared with a lock of hair found in an inscribed locket in Tutankhamen's tomb, established that the body was that of Queen Tiy, the mother of Akhenaton. The private tomb of another pharaoh, Horemheb, Tutankhamen's commander in chief and later pharaoh himself, was cleared at Saqqarah and yielded a spectacular group of reliefs. A new Oriental Institute (University of Chicago) effort was begun by Janet Johnson and Donald Whitcomb at the site of Quseir on the Red Sea coast, a port town of importance in the Roman and Mamluk periods.

Israeli archaeologists reported making a considerable number of new architectural discoveries in clearances about the Jerusalem Temple. In Syria

A royal tomb (far right) found in northern Greece is thought by some to be the burial place of Philip II of Macedonia, father of Alexander the Great. A golden casket (right) found in the tomb might have contained the remains of Philip II.

broad exposures, pertaining particularly to the earlier half of the second millennium BC, were made at Terqa on the Euphrates River, a site with important southern Mesopotamian connections.

McGuire Gibson of the Oriental Institute began a new excavation at Umm al-Hafriyat in southern Iraq, a site with indications of a rich yield in information concerning the time of formation of the earliest literate urban development in southern Mesopotamia, about 3750–2500 BC. The resumption of work by the Iraqi Department of Antiquities at the late 5th-millennium BC village site of Arpachiyeh yielded a new and spectacular variety of motifs of the Halafian painted pottery repertoire. One of the most interesting reports on the salvage effort on a Tigris River tributary in Iraq was that of T. Cuyler Young of the Royal Ontario Museum. Working jointly with Nicholas Postgate, director of the British School of Archaeology in Iraq, on Tell Madhur, he tested a sequence of Ubaid, Early Dynastic I, and Akkadian levels (about 4000 to 2250 BC). The Iraqi government made substantial concessions and provided aid to archaeologists joining in this salvage effort.

In Turkey a large salvage effort was about to begin before dams were built on the Euphrates. A survey that located sites in a plain near Malatya and in another east of Adiyaman was prepared by an Istanbul University team under the direction of Mehmed Ozdogan, and various Turkish and foreign excavations there were to begin in 1979. Elsewhere in Turkey, the early village site of Erbaba yielded a rich collection of early agricultural evidence. At Demirci Huyuk a broad area of the Early Bronze Age town within a fortification wall was exposed by Manfred Korfmann's team. The Italian expedition at Arslantepe-Malatya recovered a remarkably fine cache of early 3rd millennium BC metal tools and weapons.

GRECO-ROMAN REGIONS. In Greece concern for the conservation of the monuments on the Acropolis in Athens increased. The German Institute continued its long-range program on the site of Tiryns and discovered a variety of Mycenaean cult objects. The British also worked on Mycenaean levels at Sparta and on late Bronze Age levels at Assiros in Macedonia. The remarkable royal tomb at Vergina, mentioned above, was sure to take its place as one of the century's archaeological hallmarks.

In Italy a life-size terra-cotta statue of the goddess Minerva was found in a cave at Lavinium, 30 km (18½ mi) south of Rome. A number of broken statues also appeared. Near Metapontum, southwest of Taranto, the University of Texas was excavating a colonial Greek town, recovering proto-Corinthian, Rhodian, and Italic pottery. Underwater investigations at the site of a Roman bridge over the Garigliano River, 150 km (95 mi) south of Rome, yielded a large collection of coins, tools, statues, and jewelry, perhaps votive objects offered from the bridge.

The remains of a Roman mint of the age of Augustus were found in Luxembourg. In North Africa, the large-scale urban salvage effort at Carthage (Tunis) continued, with U.S., British, Bulgarian, Canadian, Danish, Dutch, French, West German, and Italian—as well as Tunisian—involvement.

ASIA AND AFRICA. Chinese archaeologists appeared to have concentrated their attention on early Neolithic sites, and the same seemed to be true in Japan where much work was done on the sites of early Jomon villages (about 4000–2000 BC). A fair portion of the Japanese excavations were actually salvage operations. There was a virtual explosion of archaeological activity in Australia, New Guinea, and Tasmania, where the picture of the area's cultural history over the last 25,000 years was at last coming into focus. Domesticated pigs appear to have been introduced into highland New Guinea by about 8000 BC and horticultural activities began soon afterward.

Perhaps the most interesting of many short reports on post-Pleistocene archaeological activities in Africa was that of an alignment of basalt pillars at Namoratunga in Kenya. The stones were oriented toward certain stars and constellations and suggested the existence of a calendar at about 300 BC. Two sites with stone pillars set in circles were also excavated in The Gambia and dated to about 200 BC to AD 800. The remains of a number of furnaces (of about AD 1 to 500) were uncovered on the western shore of Lake Victoria, Tanzania, and there was evidence to suggest that high-carbon steel was being produced. (ROBERT J. BRAIDWOOD)

Western Hemisphere. Through field studies, continuing research, and cultural resource management programs, a number of archaeological insights were gained during the 1977–78 field season in the Western Hemisphere.

UNITED STATES. In 1978 the U.S. Congress failed to take action on the Cultural Property Implementation Act. This law, in part defeated by lobbyists representing the primitive art market, would have ratified a UNESCO accord making it illegal to export artifacts and primitive art from third world countries. Failure to ratify meant that the U.S. had yet to take a strong stand in opposing the continuing and highly profitable international art market in cultural items. From an archaeological point of view this postponement suggested that massive (and in some cases, total) destruction of archaeological sites would continue unabated.

As a reflection of this continuing loss of nonrenewable archaeological resources, the 1977–78 field season in the U.S. was dominated by a large number of intensive regional surveys in compliance with recently enacted state and federal environmental protection legislation. These surveys yielded new estimates of densities of prehistoric cultural resources throughout the U.S., showing them to be greater than previously believed. In addition, the surveys raised questions regarding the adequacy and accuracy of earlier surveys.

In California, for example, a 1.5% sample of 800,000 ha (1 ha = 2.47 ac) revealed a projected density of more than 10,000 historic and prehistoric sites, all within only a small segment of the Mojave Desert. Similarly, a 20% sample of 65,000 ac of a reservoir revealed no less that 1,400 sites in a partial sampling of the area studied.

The ongoing threat to the archaeological resources remaining in the U.S., in combination with the need for cost effectiveness and accuracy of methods utilized for site detection, stimulated the development of new techniques to identify and define the location of buried remains. At Valley Forge, Pa., a team under the direction of John Cotter and Bruce Beven used both a cesium magnetometer and a ground-penetrating radar unit to identify and then verify subsurface Revolutionary War remains. Under the direction of Joel Grossman, the Rutgers Archaeological Survey Office applied the newest generation of ground-penetrating radar. In exploring the subsurface remains of the Raritan Landing (a Colonial and Revolutionary period port community in New Jersey) the radar was used to develop a polychrome (six-colour) map of remains that were buried beneath four feet of shale. Evaluation of this material through the use of traditional techniques would have been extremely difficult.

Japanese archaeologists directed the building of a mini-pyramid on the sands at Giza in an attempt to recreate the construction methods used for the Cheops pyramid 4,500 years ago.

EARLY MAN. Since the discovery of Folsom and Clovis projectile points (in the first quarter of the 20th century) in association with extinct large animals, archaeologists have debated the antiquity of early man in the Western Hemisphere. During the year several site reports added fuel to the controversy. They presented new examples of remains of extinct large animals found together with manmade tools. For example, work at the Shriver site in Daviess County, Missouri (by Michael J. Regan and others from the University of Missouri, the University of Kansas, and Texas A & M), revealed a deposit containing fluted points overlying a stratum containing only flake and core tools. In the absence of material that could be dated by using the radioactive carbon technique, thermoluminescent dates from the more recent, fluted-point stratum yielded age determinations of between 8690 (±1000) and 12,855 (±1500) BC. While no comparable dates were derived from the deeper flake and core tool-bearing stratum, the authors suggested that this distinctive assemblage was in excess of 15,000 years old. This was older than estimates for the Folsom and Clovis points.

Also during 1978, however, Don Keller and Eileen Camilli of the Museum of Northern Arizona reinvestigated stone-tool-bearing sites situated along the Little Colorado Valley. This material, referred to as the Tolchaco Complex, had been previously regarded as older than the Folsom and Clovis remains. But the investigation suggested that Tolchaco dates to a more recent, Paleo-Indian period (about 10,000–7000 BC) or even to later Pueblo occupations (extending into the Christian era).

Recent research in both North and South America provided evidence for the association of Paleo-Indian projectile points and other artifacts with an expanded inventory of extinct Pleistocene animals. In Texas continued excavations of the Paleo-Indian Lubbock site (by Eileen Johnson and Vance Holiday of the Museum of the University of Texas) produced Clovis period material that was radiocarbon-dated to 12,055 (±95) BC. Also, the first definite direct association of Clovis tools with an extinct variety of short-faced bear (*Arctodus*) was unearthed. This is the first reported occurrence of this animal with early human tools.

MESOAMERICA. A major archaeological find occurred in Mexico City in February when construction workers accidentally discovered a carved Aztec monolith seven feet below a busy city street. Roughly circular and weighing almost ten tons, the andesite stone monolith bears a representation of the Aztec moon goddess Coyolxauhqui and was probably sculpted late in the 15th century.

After the discovery the site was cordoned off, and a full-scale archaeological dig was ordered. As they progressed, archaeologists uncovered the complete foundation of the Great Temple, the most important pyramid in the Aztec capital of Tenochtitlán, and also 19 small stone chambers containing offerings to the gods.

In other parts of Mesoamerica research focused on evidence of long-distance trade and its role in regional growth. In addition, the application of techniques for the gathering of information about

Students and other volunteers working at the site of the ancient Roman Verulamium at St. Albans, England, uncovered a seven-foot-square floor mosaic said to be among the finest ever found in Great Britain.

KEYSTONE

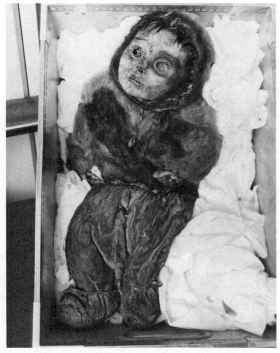

Two bird hunters seeking refuge in a cave in Greenland found several mummified corpses, including that of a seven-month-old child who died about 350 years ago.

food remains was being studied. Research continued into the nature and function of large urban ceremonial centres, with an increased emphasis on the centre and its relation to the hinterland.

Preliminary results were reported from three long-term projects within the Maya lowlands. In Guatemala, work at Quiriguá and surrounding smaller mound complexes (under the direction of Robert Sharer of the University of Pennsylvania) entered its final season. Four construction phases were defined for the period between AD 600 and 950. A number of secondary administrative centres and nonelite residences were identified surrounding the elaborate site core.

In the lowlands of Honduras a Harvard University team (led by Gordon Willey, with the assistance of Richard Leventhal and William Fash) completed the second year of a regional survey program around the Mayan centre of Copán. No fewer than 300 secondary mound centres were identified to the north and to the east of the main centre of Copán. These smaller sites, consisting of from 2 to 3 mounds to as many as 50, were each organized around a court area. The mounds varied in both size and complexity, and appeared to represent differences in the status and wealth of the resident populations.

SOUTH AMERICA. In South America sites were regularly being robbed for the antiquities market and also were being obliterated by urban development. One estimate placed archaeological attrition at no less than 2.4 sites per week in the Quito area of Ecuador.

In an effort to record the dwindling archaeological remains, the Museo del Banco Central of Ecuador, in conjunction with private and federal agen-

cies, supported a program of archaeological survey and excavation. Working under this program, Emile Peterson reported on the early site of Cotocallao prior to its imminent destruction by commercial development. His excavation revealed a number of square-cornered, multiroomed house remains, constructed with outer walls of vertical posts and interior rooms separated by partitions of woven matting. Food remains of corn, beans, deer, rabbit, and waterfowl were also recovered.

Several large-scale, long-term, multidisciplinary studies of the most prominent pre-Inca urban centres in Andean Peru were initiated during the 1977–78 season. At the coastal capital of Chan-Chan, Michael Moseley was working with James Kus, both under the auspices of Chicago's Field Museum of Natural History. With specialists in soils, pollen, and hydrology, they studied the Chimu social and economic organization as it was reflected by the construction and maintenance of regional irrigation systems. In the Andean Highlands of Peru, William Isabell of the State University of New York began a six-year investigation of the pre-Inca capital of Huari, which enjoyed dominance over much of the Peruvian highlands and coast nearly a thousand years before the Inca expansion in the 1400s. (JOEL W. GROSSMAN)

See also Anthropology.
[723.G.8.c; 10/41.B.2.a.ii]

Architecture

In 1978 the twin problems of design and economic pressure were once again the subjects to which much attention was devoted by architectural organizations and periodicals. Balancing the question of what a building should look like from an aesthetic viewpoint with how much it would cost to build and to maintain has always occupied the architectural profession. Because economic factors in 1978 looked generally more hopeful, continuing the trend of the previous year, there was a noticeable leaning during the year toward concern with quality of design.

The design-economic conflict is most easily discernible in commercial and industrial developments, particularly those of a speculative nature, where return to the developer per square foot looms large in the client's priorities. One relatively new factor in reconciling such conflicts was the growing field of architectural research, whereby studies are undertaken to determine the needs and wishes of the client or users of the building proposed and research is carried out in such areas as new technologies applicable to building and new techniques of construction and use of materials. Indeed, the importance of the research field was indicated by the fact that *Progressive Architecture* magazine began including research prizes in its annual series of design awards.

In its opening issue of 1978 the U.S. magazine *Architectural Record* again emphasized the need for architects to concern themselves with quality of design coupled with the appropriate research techniques and business acumen. The editors wrote ". . . by understanding how people feel about their

Archery:
see Target Sports

© JOHN DONAT

John Winter & Associates designed a house in Highgate, London, that consisted of a braced steel cage with a single supporting brick wall.

environment, architects will be able to do a better job of designing it." They also hoped that architects would "work to dispel the commonly held notion that quality in design and profit-making in the marketplace are incompatible goals."

Looking overall at new buildings completed and still in the design stage in 1978, it was possible to identify two main trends. One was a growing tendency toward historical allusion, often taking the form of neomodern references as the younger generation of architects looked back to the buildings heralded as "pioneer" in the 1920s and 1930s and saw that in fact they now appeared to constitute as distinct a "style" as, say, the neo-Gothic of the 19th century. The other trend was toward increasing complexity of form, often using industrial-looking components. Such a mode was exemplified in 1977 by the Centre National d'Art et de Culture Georges Pompidou in Paris, which was described as "tubage." In designs of this type structural elements such as steel braces are actually important features of the design. Spatial variation and complexity are important in contrast to designs of the neomodern type, which tend more toward axial plans and formality of spatial distribution.

Awards. The trends noted above could be seen quite clearly in the series of buildings singled out by *Progressive Architecture* for its awards, reported in January 1978. The top award in the design category went to Edward Mills for "the Pink House" in Friendship, Md., a single-family residence on four floors composed of a multiplicity of pink and peach-coloured jutting and intersecting geometrical elements approached by a long ramp. The lowest level incorporated an indoor swimming pool. The design was commended by the majority of the selection panel, but such was its assertive character that at least one member went on record as violently opposing it on the grounds that it was disorganized and fragmented. Those in favour saw it as an exciting concept in spatial complexity.

It would be difficult to find a clearer example of allusion to historicism than the Pavillon Soixante-Dix, St. Sauveur, Quebec, which also received a *Progressive Architecture* award. The building was a ski lodge reminiscent of Moorish architecture with an arched entrance and minaret-like chimney tops. The dormers and hipped roof were designed to blend with the existing old buildings of the town. Architects were Peter D. Rose with Peter Lanken and James V. Righter.

Westlake Park in Seattle, Wash., also won a *Progressive Architecture* award. This complex was typical of the imaginative multiuse downtown complexes that became popular in the 1970s. Architects Mitchell/Giurgola designed the project incorporating "glazed streets," a public garden, monorail terminal, retail units, a hotel, parking area, and restaurant. There were three interior shopping levels.

In January 1978 the leading English architectural magazine *Architectural Review* singled out a number of projects in progress during 1978 for "preview." In these designs, too, one could detect the dual strands of design concepts outlined above. In the field of housing, notable projects included a private house in Cornwall by architects Colquhoun & Miller. It had certain echoes of the modern International Style, consisting of one-story, rendered, load-bearing concrete walls with a flat roof and large window areas. The windows were designed to gain maximum benefit from the sloping site, which afforded superb views. In contrast, a house in Highgate, north London, by architects John Winter & Associates, consisted of a braced steel cage with a single supporting brick wall. The living areas were raised to upper level to take maximum advantage of the view.

In the field of commercial and industrial architecture, Melvin, Lansley and Mark were architects for a new office complex near Swindon, Wiltshire, for a firm of engineers, Sir William Halcrow & Partners. Set in an 18th-century park, the new project was linked visually with an existing mansion. New structures were of brick with a column and floor structure of concrete and lattice roofs. The complex would ultimately incorporate a variety of social and athletic facilities. Low-level energy consumption was a feature of the project, which was due for completion by mid-1979.

The most distinctive project previewed among educational buildings was the Sainsbury Centre for the Visual Arts at the University of East Anglia, Norwich, by Foster Associates. This building, which received one of the seven Royal Institute of British Architects (RIBA) awards for 1978, fell squarely in the category where industrial components form a major design feature. The steel prismatic structure covered a total area of 6,100 sq m. The walls and roof of the single-story building were clad with silver-coloured aluminum. Cost of the centre, completed in 1978, was about £2 million. It was designed to house the Sainsbury Collection of 500 items, including contemporary painting, sculpture, drawing, and primitive and Oceanic sculpture.

In May the American Institute of Architects awarded its Gold Medal for 1978 to Philip C. Johnson (*see* BIOGRAPHIES), whose important works included his own "glass house" at New Canaan, Conn. (1949); the Seagram Building in New York City (1958, with Ludwig Mies van der Rohe), a building that is among the prototypes of the glass office tower; and the IDS Center, Minneapolis, Minn. (1974). Johnson was also in the news when his design for the new headquarters of the American Telephone and Telegraph Co. in New York City was announced. It attracted such attention that the *New York Times* ran a two-column illustration showing the rendering of the controversial design. The building, which represented an extraordinary departure from Johnson's earlier uncompromisingly modern work, consisted of a distinct base, shaft, and capital as did the pioneer skyscrapers of the 19th century. The whole was capped by a 30-ft broken pediment, which led critics to christen it "Chippendale skyscraper" and "grandfather clock." The architect stated his purpose as the "pursuit of an alternative to modern architecture." The 37-story granite building was to occupy a prominent site on Madison Avenue at 56th Street.

RIBA awarded its Gold Medal for 1978 to the Danish architect Jørn Utzon, best known as the architect of the Sydney (Australia) Opera House.

Museums, Educational, and Cultural Buildings. The opening of the new East Building of the National Gallery of Art in Washington, D.C., in June generated great interest. The building, designed by I. M. Pei (*see* BIOGRAPHIES) and Partners, occupies the last major available site between Pennsylvania Avenue and the Mall. The plan of the building, consisting of two distinct but connected triangular structures, reflects the irregular trapezoidal shape of the site. One "wedge" provides a variety of exhibition spaces, while the other houses administrative facilities and the Center for Advanced Study in the Visual Arts. The atrium connecting the two wedge structures provides a vast, skylighted commons space with access to each level and area of the building. In addition, a multistory underground complex contains service facilities, parking space, and a large cafeteria.

The new building, though strikingly original, recalls the neoclassical National Gallery of 1941 in both scale and materials. The cornice line of the other buildings on the Mall is preserved, and the exterior is faced with pink Tennessee marble from the same quarry as that of the main building. Detailing of the $94 million project is of the highest quality. Exposed concrete was tinted with pink dust to complement the marble veneer; railings, doors, and window frames are of stainless steel; and all the "mechanics" of the building, such as machinery for climate control, ducts, and cables, are hidden from view. This meticulous, finished quality offers sharp contrast to the polychrome, "inside-out" appearance of another major art centre of the '70s—the Centre National d'Art et de Culture Georges Pompidou. Pei's art museum was hailed as a work of art in itself.

The Teheran Museum of Contemporary Art in Iran was opened late in 1977. Set in the Park Farah on the north side of the city, the building covered

The new East Building of the National Gallery of Art in Washington, D.C., was designed by I. M. Pei and Partners.

The Robert Elliott House in Chevy Chase, Maryland, is a Gothic Revival cottage enlarged by a matching addition.

an area of approximately 7,000 sq m. The most distinctive architectural feature was the series of light-admitting towers topped by windows at the front and by curving roof elements at the back. These "light scoops" were reminiscent of the work of José L. Sert at Saint-Paul-de-Vence, France, and at Barcelona, Spain.

The museum was designed by Kamran Diba with Nardir Ardalan, and Diba was also appointed its first director. The interior consisted of an entrance area with a circular ramp leading down to the library, auditorium, and offices and a series of galleries connected by ramps leading off the entrance lobby in a spiral pattern and enclosing a terraced courtyard. The collection housed in the museum included important examples of modern European and American art as well as a major collection of Iranian works of the 20th century.

Also in Iran, the result of the competition for the Pahlavi National Library was announced. There were more than 600 entries, and first prize was awarded to von Gerkan, Marg and Partners, a firm from Hamburg, West Germany. The proposed building incorporated a research library, public library, and the Iran studies centre.

Architect Barton Myers, in association with R. L. Wilkin, won a limited competition for the new Citadel Theatre in Edmonton, Alta. The project included a total of three separate theatres in one: the 700-seat Shocter Theatre, with a proscenium stage; a 300-seat experimental theatre; and a cinema-lecture hall able to accommodate 250. The Shocter Theatre was paneled inside with fireproofed redwood. The exterior of the theatre is of concrete clad with brick and then wrapped in a glass skin supported by an exposed steel frame.

The New Massey Hall, Toronto, Ont., was designed jointly by Arthur Erikson and Mathers & Haldenby of Toronto. The $34 million building was part of the central city cultural complex and was to house the Toronto Symphony Orchestra and the Mendelssohn Choir. The hall was to be surfaced with reflective glass, the effect of which would be to make the exterior skin of the building transparent after dark. Technical innovations included an energy-saving feature whereby the heat generated by the hundreds of electric lights could be distributed throughout the building.

British architect Michael Brawne designed the Scientific and Technological Information Centre for the Pakistan Science Foundation at Islamabad. The building was to house a central coordinating and distribution centre for a network of specialist libraries and would include teaching rooms and offices as well as the library. The plan was L-shaped and the structure was of reinforced concrete. The site was on the edge of Quaid-i-Azam University outside Islamabad, and the master plan for the university was prepared by U.S. architect Edward Durell Stone (*see* OBITUARIES).

The St. Louis, Mo., Art Museum was fully open again in 1978 after two years of restoration and renovation that cost $6.6 million. The building of a $4 million annex to house offices and services was begun and was scheduled to be completed in 1979. The annex design consisted of a stepped four-level structure with alternating horizontal bands of buff brick and solar bronze glass windows; it would contain 45,000 sq ft and be connected to the main building by a sculpture garden and restaurant. The original 19th-century Art Museum building was designed by Cass Gilbert. Architects for the renovation and for the new annex were Hardy Holzman Pfeiffer Associates of New York. The renovation created 10,000 sq ft of new display space from storerooms and offices.

Designs for the Humphrey Institute of Public Affairs to be built at the University of Minnesota were unveiled by U.S. Vice-Pres. Walter Mondale. Conceived as a tribute to the late vice-president and senator Hubert H. Humphrey, the building was designed by Carson, Lundin & Thorson, P.C. to occupy a site overlooking the Mississippi River at the entrance to the campus. The design featured corner towers and a central block defined by four large windows. It was to incorporate an old building and to be faced with Minnesota granite. The projected cost was $4 million.

Public and Commercial Buildings. Plans to expand Dulles International Airport near Washington, D.C., in order to provide improved baggage-loading facilities excited controversy. Built in the early 1960s, the airport, designed by Eero Saarinen, included contingency expansion plans for up to 600 extra feet of space on each side of the terminal. However, the Federal Aviation Administration announced that it intended to push the long wall facing the airfield outward instead of adhering to the Saarinen design. Community groups in the Washington area were concerned that the proposed expansion would spoil the appearance of the building. The estimated cost of expansion was put at $6.7 million, and the architects chosen were Hellmuth, Obata and Kassabaum of St. Louis.

A new headquarters for General American Life Insurance Co. at St. Louis was designed by Johnson/Burgee. The building's central space consisted of a cylindrical rotunda 103 ft in diameter and 90 ft high with a flat ceiling. The main structure was a 208-foot-square volume broken along a diagonal. One of the resultant three-story triangular sections was supported by three-story columns, creating a shaded plaza of roughly one-half of the ground-plan area. Cost per square foot was $66.

A multiuse complex of shopping mall, offices, hotels, housing units, gardens, and parking was announced for a 30-ac site in Jerusalem. The complex, to be known as Mamilla, was expected to cost $150 million, and the architect was the Israeli Moshe Safdie in association with French planner Gilbert Weil.

Two firms of San Francisco architects and planners won a competition to design the master plan for the proposed new capital city of Alaska, which was to be built 70 mi north of Anchorage near Mt. McKinley. The winning design consisted of a linear city plan sited on a ridge between 700 and 800 ft above sea level and featuring covered arcades lining each side of the main street with a complex indoor circulation area. The only vehicles that would be permitted on the main street would be small public buses.

In Washington, D.C., the new Soviet embassy was begun on a 12-ac site to the north of George-

town. The complex, designed by Soviet architect Mikhail Posokhin with local associate John Carl Warnecke, included housing, a school, clubhouse, clinic, and a nine-story office building and ambassador's residence which itself included a concert hall. The whole complex was to cost $70 million.

The building of the new U.S. embassy in Moscow was intended to coincide with that of the Soviet embassy in Washington, but construction was slightly delayed. Work began in the spring on the eight-story chancery, which was to form the central element. Two rows of low-rise terrace houses would border a central park. Architects were Skidmore Owings & Merrill with Gruzen & Partners. Skidmore Owings & Merrill were also architects for an unusual office building to be built in Chicago featuring three atria stacked vertically. Completion was scheduled for 1979.

The AMMJ Sports Club at Amstelveen, Amsterdam, was designed by Jelle Jelles and featured a series of timber-clad pitched roofs with a diamond-shaped window in each gable providing observation areas. Diagonal timber boarding was used throughout, and the building exemplified the enormous popularity of the 45° angle in contemporary architecture. (SANDRA MILLIKIN)

See also Engineering Projects; Historic Preservation; Industrial Review.
[626.A.1–5; 626.C]

Philip C. Johnson, winner of the Gold Medal of the American Institute of Architects, holds a model of the 660-foot-high new AT&T building to be erected in New York City.

STEPHEN SHORE, NEW YORK

THE UNLIKELY TREASURES OF COLUMBUS, INDIANA

by Joseph B. Gill

Columbus, Indiana, is a small town in the southern part of the state, nestled midway between the cities of Indianapolis and Louisville, Kentucky. On a map it looks no more impressive than any other city with a population of 30,000. However, it has something possessed by no other town of its size—one of the world's outstanding collections of architectural treasures.

Though Columbus has become a laboratory for contemporary architecture, the town's first such landmark, the First Christian Church, completed in 1942, was not intended to launch an architectural revolution. It was intended only as a gift from Will G. Irwin and his sister, Linnie I. Sweeney, to the congregation of which they were members. Eventually it would be Irwin's grandnephew, J. Irwin Miller,

Miller's wife, Xenia, and his sister, Clementine Tangeman, who would dedicate themselves to making Columbus the spectacular architectural showplace it is today.

Eliel Saarinen and his son, Eero, both of whom had achieved world renown as architects, were called from Cranbrook Academy near Detroit to design the First Christian Church. Constructed in the downtown area, it was one of the first churches in the United States with a contemporary design. Its 166-ft bell tower, terraced lawns, and sanctuary building with simple, grid-patterned facade comprise a quiet centre around which growth and change in Columbus have evolved.

Twelve years passed before Columbus acquired its next architectural wonder. Miller, who at the time was chairman of the board of Cummins Engine Co., a diesel-engine manufacturing firm headquartered in Columbus, asked Eero Saarinen to return to the town in 1954 to design new quarters for the Irwin Union Bank and Trust Co. Encouraged by the bank's design, a foundation established in part by Miller made an offer to the community that eventually led to the design of more than 40 other architectural masterpieces. The Cummins Engine Foundation, a charitable trust chartered in 1954, agreed to pay the architects' fees on public buildings, when requested to do so and if the public authority agreed to certain terms governing the choice of architects.

Initially, school buildings were the sole recipients

The North Christian Church, designed by Eero Saarinen, was completed in 1964.

BALTHAZAR KORAB

(Left) First Christian Church by Eliel and Eero Saarinen. (Below) Cleo Rogers Memorial Library by I. M. Pei.

of the foundation offer. But eventually the excitement of the architectural revolution caught on, and many other kinds of buildings, unlikely targets of special attention by architects elsewhere, were sponsored and planned.

Harry Weese of Chicago was called on in 1957 to design the first foundation project, the Lillian C. Schmitt Elementary School. A sawtoothed roof dominates the single-story structure which has ten classrooms opening onto a playground area designed by a school patron. Other notable architects who designed schools in Columbus include John Carl Warnecke of San Francisco; Norman Fletcher of Boston; Edward Larrabee Barnes of New York City; Gunnar Birkerts of Birmingham, Mich.; John M. Johansen of New Canaan, Conn.; Eliot Noyes, also of New Canaan; Hardy Holzman Pfeiffer Associates of New York City; Mitchell-Giurgola Associates of Philadelphia; and Paul Kennon and Truitt Garrison of Los Angeles and Houston, Texas, respectively.

Though the town's schools are remarkable, there are many other outstanding architectural projects. For example, Eero Saarinen's North Christian Church, completed in 1964 and the last building he designed before his death in 1961, is probably the town's most notable landmark. Saarinen worked closely with members of the congregation to find out how he could best express the church's concern in his design. A 192-ft spire surmounts the roof

peak of the hexagonal structure, and landscaping of the surrounding grounds gently reflects the slope of the roof. According to the plan, the sanctuary is the centre of the church and the communion table the centre of the sanctuary.

Kevin Roche, John Dinkeloo & Associates designed the Columbus Post Office in 1970. Its mirrored glass exterior reflects neighbouring downtown architectural landmarks. From the inside, however, the glass walls are transparent, allowing a clear view of the Columbus skyline.

The Cummins Engine Co. Technical Center was designed in 1968 by Weese. Two separate concrete buildings, one six stories high and the other two stories, form an attractive, functional facility for the professional engineering staff and for research and engine testing.

The Cleo Rogers Memorial Library was designed in 1969 by I. M. Pei. The asymmetrical entrance and window recessions within a crisp, rectangular profile give this building a monumental character. The structure provides not only the usual library services but also a large meeting space. The plan includes, as well as reference department and technical service areas, a main reading room with high coffered concrete ceilings, a mezzanine, and a small gallery suitable for art displays.

The city's daily newspaper, *The Republic*, moved into a Myron Goldsmith-designed building in 1971.

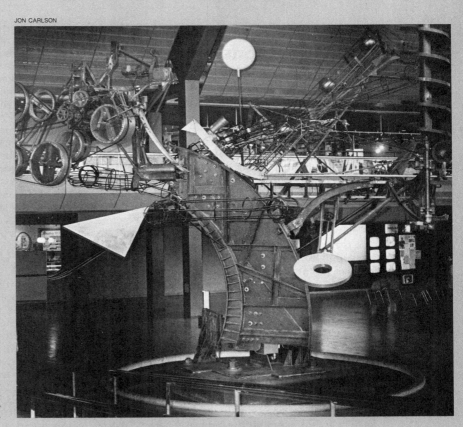

(Opposite page) Interior of Mt. Healthy Elementary School. (Right) "Chaos 1" by Jean Tinguely, located in The Commons.

The glass-walled structure allows the bright-yellow offset press to be seen in full operation from the outside. The design encourages a smooth flow among editorial, advertising, circulation, and accounting services. Visitors are greeted by a large aerial-view map of Columbus as it appeared in 1886.

The Commons-Courthouse Center complex, designed by Cesar Pelli, occupies a two block area near the centre of downtown. "Superblock," as it was named during construction, includes a shopping complex and a large civic mall. Mr. and Mrs. Miller and Mrs. Tangeman donated The Commons to the city as a public meeting space. Many activities— concerts, ballets, flea markets—take place there year-round. The east wall bordering the town's main street is of clear glass. Brown glass surrounds the remainder of the building.

Two of the structures that might eventually dominate Columbus architecture are waiting in the wings. The Cummins Engine Co. has planned a $23 million corporate headquarters downtown, adjacent to Irwin Union Bank and Trust and the Post Office. Construction is scheduled to begin early in 1979, with a projected completion date of sometime in 1981. Kevin Roche designed the six-square-block facility as a complement to the surrounding central city architecture. The second projected structure is a new city hall. Designed by Douglas Merrill and Charles Bassett of San Francisco, the three-story

building is to be triangular in shape, and its grounds will be dramatically landscaped. Plans are being formulated to restore the present city hall, originally built in 1895, for another use.

While the public buildings are most outstanding, many private firms and individuals have either constructed architecturally notable offices or rehabilitated old buildings to serve new purposes. Most new commercial construction is done in the shadow of architectural landmarks. The major structures have provided an atmosphere that encourages quality among the lesser buildings as well. Thus Columbus has avoided the glut of "highway architecture" common to most American towns. The most notable renovation project houses the Visitors' Center. The two-story former dwelling in the centre of town not only serves as an information and tourist office but also boasts the state's only branch of the Indianapolis Museum of Art. The brick exterior and original interior woodwork of the structure have been fully restored.

There are even more architectural wonders in Columbus. Each contributes to an atmosphere that is as unlikely as it is unique. In the middle of the quiet Indiana countryside sits an architectural showplace of the world.

Joseph B. Gill is city editor of the Columbus daily newspaper, The Republic.

Arctic Regions

June 20, 1978, marked one year of operation for the trans-Alaska pipeline. In that year about 278 million bbl of oil had been pumped from Prudhoe Bay to Valdez, providing an estimated 10% of U.S. oil needs. Described as "possibly the largest, most difficult engineering and construction project ever undertaken by mankind," the pipeline was named the outstanding engineering achievement of 1978 by the American Society of Civil Engineers.

Among major measures passed by the tenth Alaska legislature was a bill to provide the mechanism whereby the Northwest Alaskan Pipeline Co. could issue up to $1 billion in tax-free bonds for construction of the Alcan pipeline, a natural gas pipeline from Prudhoe Bay through Canada to the lower 48 states. The state backing was expected to provide a significant boost for the $4 billion Alaskan portion of the project. The Petroleum Industry Research Foundation estimated the cost of the mammoth Alcan gas pipeline at $14 billion, substantially above the $10 billion estimate included in the Canada-U.S. agreement on the project reached late in 1977. Inflation and continued delays in passing appropriate U.S. legislation, plus the availability of large gas reserves in the more accessible parts of western Canada, were among the key factors jeopardizing eventual construction.

The feasibility of piping natural gas from Siberia across the Bering Strait to Alaska was being studied by Lorcan, a company based in Calgary, Alta. The pipeline would probably link up with the proposed Alcan pipeline. The government-owned corporation Petro-Canada issued estimates in June indicating a potential 125 trillion cu ft of natural gas in unexplored offshore areas of Canada's Arctic archipelago. This was much more than the reserves of 20 trillion–25 trillion cu ft required before a pipeline from that region could be built economically.

The Alaska lands bill, called the most important piece of conservation legislation in this century by environmentalists, passed the U.S. House of Representatives by a landslide vote in May. However, the measure was strongly opposed by pro-development Alaskans, including both of the state's senators, and no action had been taken on it in the Senate when Congress adjourned in October. As passed by the House, the bill would provide for about 100 million ac in Alaska to be classified as national parks, wildlife refuges, and wilderness. On December 1 Pres. Jimmy Carter placed 56 million ac of federal lands in Alaska under the National Park System, thereby preventing any oil or mineral development on them unless Congress specifically acted to the contrary. An additional 54 million ac were withdrawn from development for three years by the secretary of the interior. In August some 15,000 sq mi of the northern portion of the Yukon were set aside for the creation of Canada's first national wilderness park. Further development of resources in the area was prohibited, but the action would not prejudice land claims discussions or traditional native hunting, fishing, and trapping activities.

In May the U.S. Fish and Wildlife Service announced plans to rescind the special waterfowl-hunting privileges of Native Americans who had become "part of the cash economy" in order to enforce the terms of a 1916 treaty with Canada and Mexico. Native representatives predicted that, since nearly all native people were at least partly integrated into the cash economy, strict enforcement of the treaty would, in effect, eliminate wildfowl as a food source. In June the International Whaling Commission voted to permit harvesting of 18 bowhead whales in 1979—a 50% increase over the 1978 quotas. However, Eskimos claimed the quotas were substantially less than were required to meet the needs of nine traditional Alaskan villages where whaling satisfies important cultural and nutritional needs.

After more than a year of negotiations, the government of Canada and the Committee for Original Peoples Entitlement (COPE), representing the

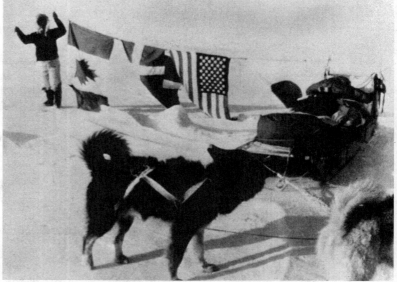

Japanese explorer Naomi Uemura stringing flags at the North Pole in May. Having traveled by dog sled for 57 days, he was the first person to make a solo journey to the pole.

Areas:
see Demography; *see also the individual country articles*

WIDE WORLD

approximately 2,500 Inuit of the western Arctic, made public a joint position paper containing the elements of a land claims agreement. The main points included special wildlife-harvesting rights for the Inuit, ownership of 37,000 sq mi of land, and financial compensation with a 1978 value of $45 million. As of July 1 the Cree Indians and Eskimos of the James Bay communities in Arctic Quebec assumed responsibility for the education of native people within their territory. The creation of native-run schools was a major point of the James Bay and Northern Quebec Agreement, the first native land claims agreement reached in northern Canada. The Naskapi Indians, the only native people in northern Quebec who had not yet made a settlement, agreed to accept $9 million in cash, exclusive hunting and fishing rights, and a land agreement with the provincial and federal governments. Midway through the year the minister of Indian and northern affairs, Hugh Faulkner, threatened to suspend all native land claims activity for six months to a year because of frustration over stalemated negotiations in the Mackenzie Valley. The rival Dene Nation and Métis Association had split over the desire of the Dene to create a self-governing, all-native form of government within the Northwest Territories.

Early in the year the first contract was signed for the 28,000-ton "Arctic," Canada's first icebreaking bulk carrier, to deliver lead-zinc concentrate to Europe from mines in Strathcona Sound in the Canadian Arctic islands. Approval of the design of Canada's first combination nuclear and gas-turbine icebreaker was announced in March by the federal government. The 150,000-shaft horsepower vessel, capable of maintaining continuous forward motion in ice ten feet thick, was scheduled to begin operations in 1985. The Soviets' 75,000-hp, nuclear-powered icebreaker "Sibir" convoyed a cargo ship 3,360 nautical miles through heavy pack ice from Murmansk to the Bering Strait, two months ahead of the regular start of the brief Northeast Passage shipping season. The voyage, which was assisted by navigational and communications satellites, demonstrated a growing Soviet capability in the art of ice navigation.

Radioactive fragments from the Soviet satellite Cosmos 954, which crashed in the Northwest Territories on January 24, were found in June by prospectors on the north shore of Lake Athabasca in northwestern Saskatchewan. Over 220 lb of debris, some of it dangerously radioactive, had been recovered previously after a search over an area of about 80,000 sq km. Canada, which planned to recover the $12 million-plus cost of the search from the Soviet Union, referred the question of safeguards for nuclear power technology in space to the UN.

In April a three-man party of the Nihon Arctic expedition, accompanied by two Canadian Eskimos, reached the North Pole, the first Japanese to accomplish this feat. Shortly thereafter another Japanese, 37-year-old Naomi Uemura (see BIOGRAPHIES), became the first person to attain the North Pole alone by dogsled after struggling 57 days across 500 mi of frozen ocean ice.

(KENNETH DE LA BARRE)

Argentina

Argentina

The federal republic of Argentina occupies the southeastern section of South America and is bounded by Bolivia, Paraguay, Brazil, Uruguay, Chile, and the Atlantic Ocean. It is the second-largest Latin-American country, after Brazil, with an area of 2,776,900 sq km (1,072,200 sq mi). Pop. (1978 est.): 26,393,000. Cap. and largest city: Buenos Aires (pop., 1978 est., 2,982,000). Language: Spanish. Religion: mainly Roman Catholic. President in 1978, Lieut. Gen. Jorge Rafael Videla.

Lieut. Gen. Jorge Rafael Videla was confirmed in office as president for a second three-year term on May 2, 1978, but he was later replaced in the junta by his supporter, Gen. Roberto Viola, who was also given command of the Army. Adm. Eduardo Massera, the second member to retire from the junta, was replaced on September 15 by Adm. Armando Lambruschini. Brig. Gen. Orlando Agosti, the last member of the original junta formed in 1976, was due to retire in January 1979.

A highlight in 1978 for the country was the football World Cup championship held in June, to which Argentina was host at a cost of about $700 million, and which Argentina won (see FOOTBALL: Association Football [Soccer]). But, although this event provided a temporary respite from economic difficulties, the social and political climate continued to be unsettled. Trouble had begun in 1977 with strikes on the railways and on the Buenos Aires subway in October, followed by strikes by petroleum and electrical power workers and then by dock, airline, and bank employees. The end to work stoppages coincided with the granting of a raise in minimum wages late in 1977. In spite of these problems, labour-government relations generally improved in 1978, and a delegation was sent to the International Labour Organization conference in Geneva consisting of members of government-approved labour unions (the group of 25) led by Ramón Baldassini. Strike action took place in

Scoreboard proclaims victory, and the fans go wild as Argentina wins the World Cup football (soccer) championships in June.

OSWALDO ARMAS—SIPA PRESS/BLACK STAR

July when dock workers refused to work overtime, but it came to an end following the introduction of an outside work force and the granting of limited wage increases.

Terrorist activities were less intensive than in previous years, and in December 1977 President Videla stated that subversive groups retained only 15% of their former strength. Activities appeared to be directed mostly against the authorities. In April Miguel Tobías Padilla, undersecretary for economic coordination, was killed; in June a bomb was placed in the house of the secretary of the Army General Staff, Gen. Reynaldo Bignone. A bomb explosion also destroyed most of an apartment building and killed the 15-year-old daughter of Admiral Lambruschini in August.

Concern continued to be voiced by relatives and national and international organizations over the fate of missing persons. From February onward, lists of names of prisoners held by the state were published, with official estimates of persons detained totaling about 4,000. Nevertheless, the Inter-Parliamentary Union leadership, representing some 70 nations, issued a statement in April deploring the treatment of various Argentine politicians since the military coup. In the same month a report of the International Commission of Jurists asserted that in the previous four years 23 judges and lawyers had been killed and 41 who disappeared were still unaccounted for, while 109 had been detained uncharged. In May, Antonio Sofia, the Argentine League for Human Rights leader, was arrested. On the other hand, Alfredo Bravo, the co-chairman of the Permanent Assembly for Human Rights, was released after nine months and put under house arrest, as Jacobo Timerman, the publisher of *La Opinión*, had been two months earlier. Julián Delgado, the publisher of the daily *Cronista Comercial*, was kidnapped in June.

The most prominent prisoner since the coup, María Estela Martínez de Perón, was convicted in 1978 of charges of misuse of funds and abuse of power, and accusations of fraud remained pending against her. The former president, widow of Juan Perón, was transferred from a naval base to her villa in San Vicente, Buenos Aires Province, at the end of August.

There were attempts by various political party leaders to demand a return to democracy, and on April 10 Ricardo Balbín, the head of the Radical Party, chaired a meeting of several leaders including members of the previous Peronist government. A document was published demanding the reestablishment of political freedom; as a consequence, party leaders were detained and reprimanded. President Videla said on August 1 that with the defeat of terrorism he would strive for a "civic-military convergence" that would lead to the restoration of democracy.

During the year relations improved with Bolivia, Peru, Paraguay, and Uruguay, but they deteriorated with Chile over the Beagle Channel issue. In December Argentina and Chile agreed to accept the mediation of a papal representative in the dispute. (*See* CHILE.) The dispute with Britain over the Falkland Islands was exacerbated by the continuing (since 1976) occupation of uninhabited Southern Thule Island in Britain's South Sandwich Islands by Argentine scientists. Trade was expanded with Eastern European, Middle Eastern, and African countries, and an important agreement was signed with China for the sale of three million metric tons of wheat and 75,000 metric tons of cotton over three years.

Relations between Argentina and France deteriorated following the disappearance in December 1977 of two French nuns, who were presumed to have been detained or killed by the authorities. Admiral Massera visited Paris in April and was said to have arranged meetings with various Peronist exiles. General Videla visited various Latin-American countries and later Europe on the death of Pope Paul VI.

The gross national product grew by 4.7% in real terms in 1977 but fell by 5.1% during the first half of 1978 with a decline in the industrial sector of 10%. The excellent performance of the nation's exports resulted in a trade surplus of U.S. $1.3 billion in the first half of 1978 and an overall balance of payments surplus of $2,638,000,000. Foreign reserves totaled $5,770,000,000, permitting the early repayment of a $1 billion commercial loan contracted in 1976 and a return to a credit position with the International Monetary Fund. Inflation continued to rage in 1978 and reached a rate of about 94% during the first eight months of the year, as compared with 160% in 1977 as a whole.

(BARBARA WIJNGAARD)

ARGENTINA

Education. (1976) Primary, pupils 3,601,243, teachers 199,256; secondary, pupils 445,397, teachers 59,765; vocational, pupils 837,659, teachers 109,939; higher, students 601,395, teaching staff 39,007.

Finance. Monetary unit: peso, with (Sept. 18, 1978) a free rate of 847 pesos to U.S. $1 (free rate of 1,659 pesos = £1 sterling). Gold, SDR's, and foreign exchange (April 1978) U.S. $4,565,000,000. Budget (1977 actual): revenue 1,271,570,000,000 pesos; expenditure 2,125,850,000,000 pesos. Gross national product (1975) 1,310,700,000,000 pesos. Money supply (April 1978) 4,018,300,000,000 pesos. Cost of living (Buenos Aires; 1975 = 100; April 1978) 3,348.

Foreign Trade. (1976) Imports 454,030,000,000 pesos; exports 741,953,000,000 pesos. Import sources: U.S. 18%; Brazil 12%; West Germany 11%; Japan 8%; Italy 5%; Chile 5%. Export destinations: Brazil 11%; Italy 10%; The Netherlands 9%; U.S. 7%; U.S.S.R. 6%; Japan 5%; West Germany 5%; Chile 5%. Main exports: meat 13%; corn 9%; wheat 9%.

Transport and Communications. Roads (1976) 207,262 km. Motor vehicles in use (1976): passenger 2,588,000; commercial (including buses) 1,101,000. Railways: (1976) 40,113 km; traffic (1976) 14,481,000,000 passenger-km, freight 11,039,000,000 net ton-km. Air traffic (1977): 4,801,000,000 passenger-km; freight 126.7 million net ton-km. Shipping (1977): merchant vessels 100 gross tons and over 401; gross tonnage 1,677,169. Shipping traffic (1976): goods loaded 15,299,000 metric tons, unloaded 9,154,000 metric tons. Telephones (Jan. 1977) 2,539,500. Radio receivers (Dec. 1973) 21 million. Television receivers (Dec. 1974) 4.5 million.

Agriculture. Production (in 000; metric tons; 1977): wheat 5,300; corn 8,300; sorghum c. 6,730; barley 494; oats 570; rice 320; potatoes 1,777; sugar, raw value c. 1,666; linseed c. 810; soybeans 1,270; sunflower seed 900; tomatoes c. 550; oranges 800; lemons 297; apples 820; wine c. 2,550; tobacco 80; cotton, lint 166; beef and veal 2,909; cheese c. 225; wool c. 90; quebracho extract (1976) 92; fish catch (1976) 282. Livestock (in 000; June 1977): cattle 59,561; sheep c. 34,000; pigs c. 4,200; goats c. 3,500; horses (1976) c. 3,500; chickens c. 36,000.

Industry. Fuel and power (in 000; metric tons; 1977): crude oil 22,483; natural gas (cu m; 1976) 7,710,000; coal 510; electricity (excluding most industrial production; kw-hr) 27,334,000. Production (in 000; metric tons; 1977): cement 6,011; crude steel 2,673; cotton yarn 95; nylon, etc., yarn and fibres 60; passenger cars (including assembly; units) 168; commercial vehicles (including assembly; units) 68. Merchant vessels launched (100 gross tons and over; 1977) 79,000 gross tons.

Art Exhibitions

To mark the opening of the new East Building of the National Gallery of Art in Washington, D.C., designed by I. M. Pei and Partners (*see* ARCHITECTURE; BIOGRAPHIES), the gallery mounted an exhibition entitled "The Splendor of Dresden: Five Centuries of Art Collecting." Hailed as probably the most lavish and expensive exhibition ever held in the U.S., it reportedly cost over $1 million and included more than 700 works of art lent by eight Dresden museums. This was the first time these works had ever left East Germany. That they had been preserved at all was remarkable, considering the terrible destruction suffered by Dresden in World War II.

The show, called "the most comprehensive exhibit ever devoted to the history of collecting," traced the changes in artistic taste from the 16th to the 20th century and included a very wide range of paintings, sculpture, decorative objects, and porcelain. Among the latter were some of the first pieces of Meissen ever produced. Priceless examples of Old Master paintings included works by Titian, Holbein, Rembrandt, Rubens, and Nicolas Poussin. After its Washington showing, the exhibition traveled to the Metropolitan Museum of Art, New York City, and was to go on to San Francisco in 1979. The new East Building was also the venue for a number of smaller exhibitions during the summer, including one entitled "Aspects of Twentieth Century Art" and another devoted to "American Art at Mid-Century: the Subjects of the Artist." The latter show contained, for example, the "Voltri" sculptures of David Smith and several of de Kooning's "Women."

A number of other exhibitions devoted to historical subjects were worthy of note. "The Arts Under Napoleon" was the title of a show at the Metropolitan Museum of Art in the summer. Works illustrating the peculiar and distinctive elements of the French Empire style were drawn primarily from the museum's own vast collections, supplemented by items lent by the Audrey B. Love Foundation. The show focused on the decorative arts, with examples including furniture, clocks, drawings, sculpture, and silver.

The history of connoisseurship and collecting was the underlying theme of "'The Noble Buyer': John Quinn, Patron of the Avant-Garde" at the Hirshhorn Museum and Sculpture Garden, Smithsonian Institution, Washington, D.C. Quinn was a U.S. collector who patronized the lesser-known contemporary artists of his day rather than Old Masters, although many of the artists whose work he collected became the "Old Masters" of the 20th century. He began collecting contemporary art on a large scale in 1909 and continued until his death in 1924. His collection, which was never cataloged or exhibited as a whole during his lifetime, was sold at auction after his death.

The exhibition, which drew from over 40 public and private collections, explored Quinn's evolving taste. Works on show at the Hirshhorn included examples by Van Gogh, Gauguin, Cézanne, Bran-

"Brick Knot" by London artist Wendy Taylor was one of the more unusual pieces in the second Hayward Annual Exhibition of Contemporary Art at the Hayward Gallery in London in August.

cusi, Matisse, and Picasso. There were also canvases by American artists of the early 20th century and by members of the Vorticist School in Britain. When Quinn died his collection consisted of over 2,500 works, but only 500 of them could now be positively identified. Of these, 79 were in the Washington exhibition.

"Karl IV Statesman and Maecenas," held at Nürnberg, West Germany, was a historical exhibition commissioned by the State of Bavaria to mark the 600th anniversary of the death of Holy Roman Emperor Charles IV. Works on display included historical documents, works of art, and religious objects. An exhibition at the Boymans-van Beuningen Museum at Rotterdam, Neth., was devoted to "The History of Tea Drinking in Holland," an activity that became popular in the 17th century but, because it was expensive, was enjoyed only by the very rich until about 1750. The exhibition included books about tea drinking, paintings, and examples of decorative arts, as well as all manner of objects and furniture used in connection with preparing and drinking tea.

"Great Victorian Pictures," a traveling Arts Council of Great Britain exhibition, was as much a commentary on the history of Victorian taste as upon art itself. It comprised 60 examples of popular art which the Victorians thought of as great, though they were by no means the Victorian paintings that would be considered "great" by the standards of modern taste. The paintings, selected for their public impact at the time, ranged from historical and religious subjects to landscape and animal pictures. The exhibition was seen at the Royal Academy in London in the summer, but before its London showing it had traveled to Leeds, Leicester, and Bristol.

Another historical exhibition, at the Château de Sceaux near Paris, was "Voltaire, Voyageur de l'Europe," the first of a series of Voltaire exhibitions commemorating the bicentenary of his death. Included were many portraits of Voltaire's contemporaries. "Van Dyck in Check Trousers" was the droll title of an exhibition at the Scottish National Portrait Gallery, Edinburgh, in the summer. It derived from a remark made by the Victorian artist Sir John Millais about the problem of dress in modern portraiture, the point being that the dignified dress of one period can look ridiculous in a later period, thus robbing the subject of the dignity such garb was intended to give him. In exploring this interplay between art and dress, the exhibition provided an entertaining display of taste in aristocratic costume in the 18th and 19th centuries in Britain. Included were models dressed to resemble historical figures.

Important exhibitions were devoted to primitive and non-Western art subjects. The Bishop Museum in Honolulu held what was possibly the most important exhibition of the art of the South Seas ever shown. It comprised material collected by Capt. James Cook on his three voyages to the South Seas between 1768 and 1779. These native artifacts were referred to at the time of Cook's voyages as "curiosities" and were only now beginning to be appreciated for their intrinsic quality and artistic achievement. An exhibition at the Petit Palais in Paris was made up of sculptures and objects illustrating the art of Java, Indonesia, in the 8th and 9th centuries, taken from the Temple of Borobudur. Objects from other sources nearby were also on display and helped to illustrate the distinction between Buddhist and Hindu art.

"Smoking Pipes of the North American Indian" was the title of an exhibition at the Museum of Mankind in London, which showed an impressive variety of 100 pipes. Pipe smoking was a ceremonial and religious ritual among the Indians, and the examples of the pipes they created showed great skill and craftsmanship. Each tribe had its own distinctive style. The earliest examples, dating from *c.* 100 BC to AD 200, were made by the Hopewell people. A fine example on show was a stone pipe wrought in the form of a bird eating a fish. Some pipes of the 19th century from the northwestern U.S. portrayed white men, illustrative of the increasing influence of white settlers on Indian cultures.

The art of the recent past, especially that of the period from Impressionism to World War II, continued to provide popular subject matter for exhi-

Carl Andre, the controversial American sculptor who likes to pile up bricks and things, stands amid a collection of his works at the Whitechapel Art Gallery, London, during an exhibit held in March.

KEYSTONE

bitions around the world. "Monet's Years at Giverny: Beyond Impressionism" was held at the Metropolitan Museum of Art in the late spring. It concentrated on paintings of flowers, especially the waterlilies, inspired by Monet's two gardens at Giverny, about 40 mi northwest of Paris, where the artist lived and worked from 1883 to 1926. The two gardens—one a flower garden and the other a water garden—had been restored and were opened to the public for the first time in the autumn of 1978. The exhibition was made up of 81 paintings from public and private collections in Europe and North America, including a group of 25 lent by the Musée Marmottan, Paris. After leaving New York the show traveled to St. Louis, Mo., where it was on view from August to October.

"From Manet to Toulouse-Lautrec: French Lithographs 1860–1900," shown at the British Museum, was an exhibition of both black and white and colour lithographs, produced over a 40-year period and drawn from the museum's own collection. It was part of the bequest of Campbell Dodgson, a former keeper of prints and drawings at the museum. The exhibition was a fine introduction to the public of this lesser-known aspect of the museum's collection. Picasso's private collection of 38 paintings and 22 drawings was on show in Paris at the Pavillon de Flore. The collection was formed by the artist somewhat haphazardly, often as a result of gifts or exchanges from fellow artists, and critics found the quality of the collection uneven. There were, however, three fine Cézannes and seven works by Matisse. Eventually the collection would be on permanent display at the Hôtel Salé in the Marais area of Paris, which was destined to become a Picasso museum.

An exhibition at the Grand Palais, Paris, "De Renoir à Matisse," consisted of 11 masterpieces lent by museums in Moscow and Leningrad, together with 11 related works drawn from Paris collections. Viewers could compare, for example, a painting by Gauguin with another by Van Gogh of the same model, or in another instance Cézanne's version of a painting by Delacroix with the Delacroix original, a thought-provoking and educational exercise. "Paintings from Paris," a touring exhibition consisting of 82 items of painting and sculpture of the early 20th century from the Musée d'Art Moderne de la Ville de Paris, was seen in England at Oxford, Norwich, Manchester, and Coventry. It included works by Matisse, Rouault, Braque, Léger, and Picasso.

An exhibition at the Musée d'Art Moderne de la Ville de Paris comprising 81 masterpieces of 20th-century painting was drawn from the Thyssen-Bornemisza collection housed at the Villa Favorita, Lugano, Switz. Examples on display included works by Picasso, Braque, Derain, Gris, Mondrian, Kandinsky, and Dali. "Dada and Surrealism Reviewed," shown at the Hayward Gallery, London, from January to March, was described as "an exhibition about Surrealism, not a Surrealist exhibition." Organized by the Arts Council of Great Britain, the show attempted an art-historical analysis of the literary and artistic movement. Each of the 17 sections into which the exhibition was divided was based on a Dada or Surrealist magazine or group of magazines. Works on display included literature as well as painting, sculpture, photographs, and objects.

The year saw the usual number of large shows devoted to the work of individual artists, often celebrating anniversaries of the birth or death of the honoured subject. A large retrospective devoted to the works of the 19th-century French painter Gustave Courbet was mounted at the Royal Academy, London, in the winter. Again, photographs and literary source material provided an important supplement to the artistic works. The paintings were grouped by subject. Although the painter was best remembered for his large Realist scenes, the show included portraits and still life, landscape, and animal subjects.

The celebrated wood engraver, artist, and naturalist Thomas Bewick had died 150 years previously, and the anniversary was marked by an impressive show devoted to him at the Laing Gallery, Newcastle upon Tyne. A native of Northumberland, Bewick transformed the craft of book illustration in wood engraving into a sophisticated art form. The exhibition revealed his versatility, showing many types of printing and silver engraving as well as some exquisite drawings of birds and other animals prepared for transfer to woodblocks.

The 500th anniversary of the birth of the Italian painter Giorgione was commemorated by an exhibition at Castelfranco Veneto, Italy, organized in conjunction with a number of lectures and concerts devoted to him. Only 20 undisputed pictures by Giorgione still existed, and one of these was the altarpiece in the cathedral at Castelfranco Veneto. The year also marked the 300th anniversary of the death of Jacob Jordaens, a 17th-century Flemish artist and contemporary of Rubens. This anniversary was celebrated by two exhibitions in the artist's native city of Antwerp—one at the Royal Museum of Fine Arts and the other at the Plantin-Moretus Museum. The show at the Royal Museum comprised 42 paintings, while the other exhibition was devoted to drawings, etchings, and prints. In addition, enthusiasts of Jordaens's work could see the house in which the artist lived and worked.

The 50th anniversary of the death of the Scottish architect Charles Rennie Mackintosh was marked by a show of his watercolours. Mackintosh's significance as an architect and furniture designer was widely appreciated, but his work as a watercolourist, an art form to which he devoted himself in his declining years, was less well known. The show included over 60 works, including studies of flowers and views of Italy, Spain, and southern France. The exhibition was shown in Glasgow, Edinburgh, London, Brighton, and Dundee.

A major retrospective of the Abstract Expressionist painter Mark Rothko opened at the Solomon R. Guggenheim Museum in New York City in October. The approximately 150 paintings and works on paper, borrowed from public and private collections in the U.S. and Europe as well as from the Rothko estate, made it possible to trace the artist's development from the early 1920s to shortly before his death in 1970. Following the showing at the Guggenheim, the exhibition was scheduled to

Three expositions of his works marked the 85th birthday of Joan Miró. He stands among some of his works at the Madrid Modern Art Museum.

travel to Houston, Tex., Minneapolis, Minn., and Los Angeles.

The English sculptor Henry Moore celebrated his 80th birthday in July, and to mark the occasion the artist presented 36 sculptures to the Tate Gallery, London. A hugely successful exhibition devoted to Moore's later work was held at the Serpentine Gallery and in Kensington Gardens, London.

A number of exhibitions were devoted to the work of architects. The work of the Finnish architect Alvar Aalto, who died in 1976, was shown by means of models, drawings, paintings, furniture, glass, and photographs at the Royal Academy, London, in the autumn. In evidence were Aalto's celebrated clean "functional" forms, combined with a sensitivity to the human scale. The great architect of High Victorian Gothic, Sir Gilbert Scott, was the subject of an exhibition at the Victoria and Albert Museum, London, consisting of drawings (some of them beautifully coloured and detailed) and photographs. The show enabled visitors to make a reappraisal of Scott, best known to the layman as the architect of the St. Pancras Hotel, London, and for his many church restorations.

The Brighton (England) Museum and Art Gallery organized a definitive and comprehensive exhibition devoted to the Arts and Crafts architect and designer C. F. A. Voysey. Many of Voysey's original architectural drawings were on view, as well as photographs of exteriors and interiors. His talent as a designer was clear from the examples of furniture, as well as from designs for such varied objects as clocks, keys, light fixtures, wallpapers, and tiles. An exhibition devoted to the work of Le Corbusier, the Swiss-born architect who settled in Paris in 1917, was held at the Jahrhunderthalle Höcht of Frankfurt, West Germany. It included canvases done during his early period as a painter, as well as photographs of his buildings situated as far afield as India, Japan, France, and the U.S. The work of G. B. Piranesi, an 18th-century Italian artist and engraver who specialized in architectural subjects, was shown in a large exhibition at the Hayward Gallery in the spring. Large sections were devoted to his prints depicting Roman antiquities and to the fantastic and awesome interiors of the *Carceri d'invenzione* ("Imaginary Prisons") series. Aspects of the Baroque, Rococo, Neoclassical, and Romantic came together in Piranesi's unique and visionary style.

"Some Old Favourites" at the Tate Gallery, London, provided a lesson in the way a museum could mount an exhibition by drawing on its own resources. This show was part of a small-scale series of exhibitions designed to give the public an opportunity to see works of art not normally on display. The 41 pictures included works by John Singer Sargent, Sir Alfred Munnings, and Henry Tuke. Another such show at the Tate was "Artistic Licence," which juxtaposed pairs of pictures bearing the same title or devoted to similar subjects but by different artists. This thought-provoking and illuminating show included 13 pairs of works ranging in date from 1904 to 1971.

Also stimulating was an exhibition devoted to self-portraits from 1490 onward, held at the Kunsthalle in Hamburg, West Germany. The show, which provided an interesting physical and psychological study, included representations by such painters as Luca Signorelli from the earlier period as well as Rembrandt, Velázquez, Goya, and Miró. Finally, on a sweeter note, the Musée des Arts Décoratifs in Paris held an original exhibition entitled "Sucre d'Art," made up of masterpieces of popular confectionery from many different countries. The widely diverse subjects included animals, the leaning tower of Pisa, representations of famous works of painting and sculpture, and even the Concorde.

(SANDRA MILLIKIN)

See also Art Sales; Museums; Photography.
[613.D.1.b]

Art Sales

Market Trends. The 1977–78 art market season culminated in the sale of the Robert von Hirsch collection at Sotheby's in London in June 1978. The sale realized £18.4 million, by far the highest total ever recorded for a public auction. The previous autumn it had been announced that Sotheby's would auction furniture from the New York home of the Wildenstein art-dealing dynasty, and this seemed likely to outstrip the 1977 Mentmore Towers sale total of £6.4 million. In the event, the furnishings were sold privately for Fr 75 million (£8.8 million) to Akram Ojjeh, a Saudi Arabian businessman. Ojjeh said he planned to put the furniture aboard the liner "France," which he had also acquired.

Buyers in the big-time market were few but very important. First among them were the J. Paul Getty Museum of Malibu, Calif., and the British Rail Pension Funds. The museum would have spending power of $50 million a year under the terms of Getty's will. The last purchase approved by Getty before his death provided a foretaste of the future —a $5 million 4th-century Greek bronze statue.

Three copies of the Gutenberg Bible, printed in Mainz, Germany, in the 15th century, were sold in 1978. The "Schuckburgh" Bible was purchased by the city of Mainz for the Gutenberg Museum for $1.8 million.

The sale caused some furor because it was said the figure had been recovered off the Italian coast and exported illegally. The British Rail Pension Funds had already spent over £20 million on works of art by 1978, buying on the advice of Sotheby's. Questions were asked in Parliament as to the ethics of this practice.

Another significant development in the big-time field was the manner in which West German museums swept the board at the Hirsch sale. The museums had decided in advance who should have what from the sale and had raised the money from state and local governments, as well as private sources. The effort had been organized by Hermann Abs, former chairman of the Deutsche Bank.

Works of Art. The German museums' purchases at the Hirsch sale totaled over £5 million. They acquired most of the superlative lots, including a 5¾-in Mosan enamel medallion from a retable of about 1150, at £1.2 million; an enamel armband probably worn by the emperor Frederick Barbarossa at his coronation, at £1.1 million; a Dürer watercolour landscape at £640,000; a Dürer pen-and-ink drawing at £300,000; and a white Meissen bird figure at £105,000. All these prices far exceeded any previously conceivable levels.

The French museums also were busy buying and preempting items at auction. They undermined Sotheby's May auction in Monte Carlo by acquiring a table made by Martin Carlin for Mme du Barry for Fr 580,000 after the French government had denied it an export license. The Greeks paid an auction record price of Fr 3.4 million in Paris for Delacroix's oil "Grec à cheval," inspired by the Greek War of Independence. British museums launched appeal after appeal for funds to retain major British art works in the country. They acquired two Stubbs paintings, "The Haymakers" and "The Reapers," valued at around £1 million, and a portrait of the brewer Ben Truman by Gainsborough, valued at £450,000.

Agitation in Britain concerning the export of works of art centred on the secret dispersal of the treasures from Warwick Castle by Lord Brooke. The only known portrait of Queen Elizabeth I in her coronation robes was sold at Sotheby's in December 1977 to the National Portrait Gallery for £35,000. But this paled into insignificance beside the appeal to keep two of Canaletto's four paintings of the castle in Britain for £550,000 and the mysterious sale of the Warwick vase, a celebrated Roman sculptured stone piece discovered in the 18th century and weighing seven tons. It disappeared from the castle in March and turned up in a London warehouse; the buyer's identity and the price remained a mystery.

There was international agitation about the return of looted art works to their countries of origin and argument over the UNESCO convention on the subject. The U.S. drafted a bill to implement the convention. Interest in primitive tribal art continued to increase. The George Ortiz collection made £1.6 million at Sotheby's in June, with one item, a Hawaiian wood figure believed to have been collected by Capt. James Cook in 1779, going for £250,000; in 1969 it had sold at Sotheby's for £12,000. Two weeks earlier Christie's had sold a Jokwe tribe wood carving from the Angola-Zaire region for £220,000.

Other sensational offerings included the Kingston tureens, chefs d'oeuvre of the French gold- and silversmith Juste-Aurèle Meissonier. They sold for SFr 2,450,000, by far the highest auction price ever paid for silver. The year saw extraordinary prices for works of art connected with U.S. history. In June $980,000 was paid in Los Angeles for a painting entitled "The Jolly Flatboatmen" by George Caleb Bingham, a 19th-century American genre painter. The composition was famous, but there were four versions. No American painting had previously approached this price at auction.

Books. No less than three copies of the Gutenberg Bible, the first significant printed book using movable type, came on the market during the year. In April H. P. Kraus, a New York dealer, sold one to the city of Mainz, West Germany, where it had originally been printed. Shortly thereafter, Christie's auctioned a second copy in New York that went for $2 million to Martin Breslauer, acting on behalf of the State Museum of Baden-Württemberg, West Germany. Bernard Quaritch of London negotiated the sale of the Gutenberg Bible from the Pforzheimer collection to the University of Texas for $2.4 million. The famous Pforzheimer collection, with its remarkably complete assembly of pre-1700 English books, was also on offer by Quaritch. The continental books, peripheral to the main collection, were sold at Sotheby's in June for £179,828.

In March it was revealed that H. P. Kraus had purchased the remainder of the great library formed by Sir Thomas Phillipps (1792–1872) from the Robinson Trust for a reputed £1 million. The books were still packed in 280 crates, and neither buyer nor seller had a clear idea of what they contained. In July Christie's completed its dispersal of the Evelyn family library, begun by the 17th-century diarist John Evelyn. The library had brought a total of £818,836.

Other notable library dispersals included books concerned with the spread of printing in Europe from the Broxbourne Library, which made £701,-445 at Sotheby's in November 1977 and £610,915 in May, and Caxton's *De proprietatibus rerum* of 1472, which made £34,000. Books of French interest from the library of Robert von Hirsch were dispersed in Paris in June for a total of Fr 2,130,-000, while his private press books were sold by Sotheby's, Chancery Lane, for £159,168. They included a Doves Press Bible that made £62,000, an auction record price for a press book.

U.S. buyers were once again avid for relics of their history. A single-sheet expense account submitted in 1774 by Paul Revere sold for $70,000 at Sotheby's in New York in April, and a collection of documents embellished with the signatures of all the signers of the Declaration of Independence sold for $195,000. A manuscript of the Persian poet Firdausi's *Shahnama*, the Book of Kings, dating from 1602 with 62 fine miniature paintings, made £310,000 at Sotheby's in March. In the same sale an Arabic manuscript dated 1315, al-Jazari's *Book of Knowledge of Ingenious Mechanical Devices*, made £160,000.

The Robert von Hirsch collection brought in a record £18.4 million when it went on the block at Sotheby's in London in June. The medallion shown brought £1.2 million.

KEYSTONE

One of the Kingston tureens, fashioned in 1735–38 for the duke of Kingston by the French silversmith Juste-Aurèle Meissonier, was acquired in 1978 by the Cleveland Museum of Art. The two tureens brought a record auction price for silver of SFr 2,450,000. The second tureen went to Baron Thyssen.

Musical scores, some printed, some transcribed by hand, from the collection formed by Louis Alexandre, comte de Toulouse, the illegitimate son of Louis XIV, sold for £120,000 at Sotheby's in June. A richly illuminated *Hours of the Virgin, c.* 1430, made £130,000 in July, while the heavily corrected manuscript of Jane Austen's unfinished novel *The Watsons* sold for £38,000.

(GERALDINE NORMAN)

Astronomy

Solar System. The universe relinquished several of its secrets in 1978, one of the most interesting being the presence of a moon orbiting Pluto, the ninth and outermost known planet of the solar system. On June 22 James W. Christy of the U.S. Naval Observatory examined photographic plates of Pluto taken in April and May and noticed that the images, rather than being circular, were slightly elongated. By comparing them with plates taken in 1965 and 1970, he established the existence of a small satellite in orbit around Pluto. Because of the planet's great distance from Earth—4,500,000,000 km (2,800,000,000 mi)—it has been difficult to determine its properties since its discovery in 1930. By using the orbital period of the newly discovered moon (6.3867 days), the mass of Pluto was calculated to be only 1/380 that of the Earth, much less than currently accepted estimates. Subsequent studies confirmed the existence of the satellite, offering estimates of 2,700 km (1,600 mi) for its diameter and a separation of about 19,000 km (12,000 mi) from Pluto. As a name for the new moon, discoverer Christy suggested Charon, the boatman who ferried souls of the dead into Pluto's underworld, although Persephone, who was Pluto's queen, might be equally appropriate.

To the approximately 2,000 asteroids (or minor planets) currently known to exist, two quite interesting ones were added in 1978. On June 7 the minor planet 532 Herculina passed directly in front of a bright (6th magnitude) star. This event was predicted and observed by at least three independent groups. However, Edward Bowell and

Michael A'Hearn of the Lowell Observatory at Flagstaff, Ariz., also observed another occultation 1½ minutes before the expected one. This event had two likely explanations: it was due either to a second asteroid about 50 km (30 mi) in diameter orbiting Herculina at a distance of about 970 km (600 mi) or to a separate minor planet. In an independent study Eleanor Helin of the California Institute of Technology announced the detection of an extraordinary new asteroid that at the time of discovery was within 27 million km (17 million mi) of Earth. Just 3.2 km (2 mi) in diameter, the tiny asteroid orbits the Sun in only nine months, sooner than any other known asteroid.

On June 30, 1908, a unique event in recorded history occurred in the Tunguska region of Siberia: a huge explosion with a TNT-equivalent yield of at least ten megatons. In the intervening half century, the cause of this great explosion had elicited speculations that included collision of the Earth with a tiny black hole, a piece of antimatter, an errant spaceship, or a large meteorite. Recently a Czechoslovak astronomer, Lubor Kresak of the Slovak Academy of Sciences, appeared to have settled the issue. By comparing eyewitness accounts of the incoming event with deductions from the ground damage still in evidence, he was able to make a fairly precise determination of the arrival direction. This agrees with the direction (radiant) of the daytime β Taurid meteor shower. Because the shower was known to arise from Comet Encke, Kresak concluded that the Tunguska event was caused by the impact of a large cometary fragment with the Earth.

In 1976 J. B. Hartung of the State University of New York at Stony Brook, using 12th-century Canterbury chronicles, suggested that a naked-eye

Elongation of Pluto's image in photographic plates taken at the U.S. Naval Observatory in April and May established the presence of a comparatively large moon in orbit around the planet.

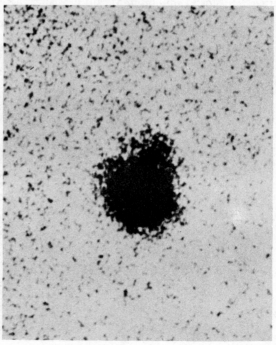

observation of a fiery event emanating from the upper horn of the crescent Moon on June 25, 1178, could have been of a meteorite impact with the Moon, present evidence of which is the lunar crater Giordano Bruno. In 1978 Odile Calame and J. Derral Mulholland of the Centre for Geodynamic and Astronomical Studies and Research in Grasse, France, found evidence for free lunar oscillations in laser-ranging data obtained for studies of the Earth-Moon separation. Combining these results with data from the Soviet Luna 24 landing site, they concluded that the 12th-century chronicles quite possibly do record a lunar meteorite impact that has left the Moon "ringing" to the present time.

Sun. The year brought with it a resurgence of interest in the Sun, especially in the way it affects long-term variations in the weather on Earth. Part of the impetus derived from historical studies suggesting that the present behaviour of the Sun may not be truly representative. For example, during the past few years John A. Eddy of the High Altitude Observatory in Boulder, Colo., presented strong evidence for connections between long-term changes in the level of solar activity (as indicated by the number of sunspots) and such terrestrial phenomena as fossil radiocarbon in tree rings. Most striking is the "Maunder Minimum," a period lasting from about AD 1645–1715 during which there was a nearly complete suppression of the normal sunspot cycle. Eddy also found evidence in historical records of an increase in the rate of solar rotation between 1625 and 1645, which may have given rise to the sunspot disappearance. The period of the Maunder Minimum also corresponds to a very cool time on Earth called the Little Ice Age. Similarly, a period of high solar activity between the 11th and 13th centuries was found to correspond to a warm period on Earth.

Recently scientists at Yunnan Observatory in China, collectively called the Ancient Sunspot Records Research Group, found ancient Chinese sunspot records dating to 43 BC that support the concept of long-term solar variability and indicate that the Sun may be in an anomalously quiet period at present. Also striking was a report by W. C. Livingston of Kitt Peak National Observatory in Arizona that the temperature of the Sun dropped about 6 K (6° C; 10.8° F), which is equivalent to a 0.5% decrease in luminosity, since the minimum of solar activity in the summer of 1975. He concluded that there is an inverse relationship between sunspot activity and the visual luminosity of the Sun, one that might well be linked with cyclical cooling of the temperature of the Earth.

Supernovas. The death of a massive star may be accompanied by a vast explosion that shines for a month or more with the light of 100,000,000,000 Suns. Only six such events were known to have been seen in our Galaxy, the Milky Way, in the past 2,000 years, the most famous one giving rise to the Crab Nebula. The observation of its explosion on July 4, 1054, is well documented in Chinese, Korean, and Japanese records. It has been a puzzle, therefore, ever since the Eastern sightings were brought to light in the West a half century ago, that no such report existed in European or

AUTHENTICATED NEWS INTERNATIONAL

IBM scientists using a computer demonstrated that the spiral shape of some galaxies is caused by localized chain reactions of exploding stars. Superposed are an actual photo of galaxy M81 and a computer-simulated pattern.

Arabic records of the time. In 1978 Kenneth Brecher of the Massachusetts Institute of Technology and Elinor and Alfred Lieber of Jerusalem reported their find of such an eyewitness sighting by an 11th-century Arabic physician named Ibn Butlan, leading to the expectation that other old medical and meteorological records contain valuable astronomical data.

The Crab Nebula contains a pulsar, the rapidly rotating collapsed remnant of the original star. Though the object was known to be spinning more slowly each year, Jerome Kristian of the Hale Observatories in California was able for the first time to detect its decreasing luminosity. The measured rate of decline in optical brightness of about 0.5% per year suggested an origin for its radiation far from the stellar surface. In what appeared to have been a rare successful prediction in theoretical astrophysics, Franco Pacini of the University of Rome had calculated in 1971 that the pulsar should show just this behaviour.

Galaxies. The origin and persistence of the spiral structure evident in some galaxies has been a mystery since their discovery two centuries ago. Though the gravitational theory of spiral density waves could account rather well for some spiral arm features, their origin remained unknown. Recently Humberto Gerola and Philip E. Seiden of IBM proposed a simple and elegant solution. The process involves a chain reaction that condenses stars from gas in the galaxy by supernova explosions. By assuming a certain probability for star formation in the surrounding interstellar gas, they applied their theory to generate computer models with a striking resemblance to actual galaxies. No doubt both dynamical gravitational and supernova-induced statistical phenomena play a role in shaping galaxies.

Whereas the bright stars mark the large-scale features of galaxies, it is questionable whether they represent all the matter present. Using a very

Association Football: see Football

Astronautics: see Space Exploration

Australia

sensitive, newly designed photometer, Dennis Hegyi and Garth Gerber of the University of Michigan reported detection of light from matter (probably stars too dim to be seen individually) around the spiral galaxy NGC 4565 in the constellation Coma Berenices. This previously unseen matter represents the mass of several billion stars, comparable to all the heretofore detected mass in that galaxy.

Our own Galaxy also provided a surprise in 1978. Marvin Leventhal of Bell Laboratories, Murray Hill, N.J., and C. J. MacCullum and P. D. Stang of Sandia Laboratories in New Mexico reported the first definite observation of gamma rays with an energy of 511 keV (thousand electron volts) emanating from the galactic centre. Photons of such energy are a characteristic result of the mutual annihilation of electrons and their antimatter counterparts, positrons. In a seemingly lopsided universe composed almost entirely of ordinary matter, the confirmed presence of at least some antimatter in the galactic centre was significant.

In studies of the nucleus of the relatively nearby galaxy M87 (50 million light years away), a group of optical astronomers led by W. L. W. Sargent of the Hale Observatories presented evidence for a large concentration of nonluminous matter equivalent to about 5,000,000,000 solar masses residing within a radius of about 360 light years. This result was supported by the detection of a "spike" of light, representing a concentration of stars gravitationally bound to some large mass at the centre of M87, by another group at the Hale Observatories. Because M87 is an active galaxy, emitting X-rays, gamma rays, and nonthermal radio-frequency radiation, as well as possessing an extended jet of matter to one side, some extraordinary energy source must power it all. Whereas the investigators concluded that the source might be a central, supermassive black hole, further deductions awaited the improved observing capability from Earth orbit that the planned Space Telescope should provide by 1983.

Quasars and Cosmology. The most fundamental observation of modern cosmology is that light from galaxies and other luminous bodies beyond the Milky Way shifts toward the red end (toward longer wavelengths) of the spectrum with increasing distance from the observer. This red shift, which is a function of the velocity with which the light source appears to be receding from the observer, is most frequently interpreted as arising from the expansion of the universe following an initial "big bang" of creation; it allows measurement of extragalactic distances by means of a proportional relationship, called Hubble's law, between the recessional velocity of a light source and its distance from the Earth. Correlation of distance with red-shift–indicated velocity, however, does not seem to fit quasars at all well. Furthermore, assuming that quasars are at the enormous distances indicated by their red shifts gives them characteristics difficult to explain, including huge luminosities (greater than one trillion suns) and apparent recessional velocities greater than the speed of light. The nature of quasar red shifts has been questioned since their discovery—most dis-

concertingly by Halton C. Arp of the Hale Observatories. Adding to an already impressive list of anomalous examples, in 1978 he presented evidence that near the galaxy M82 lie three quasars, all with roughly equal red shifts much greater than that of M82 yet aligned with an "explosion feature" of the galaxy. A similar result with five quasars unusually close to the galaxy NGC 3384 was also found. Whether these were chance associations or physically connected phenomena remained the key question. On the other hand, Alan Stockton of the University of Hawaii developed convincing evidence that the prototypical quasar 3C 273 and about ten others are in fact at their red-shift–indicated distance by showing that near each quasar studied lie galaxies with the same red shift. Thus, the great debate over the nature of quasar red shifts continued unabated.

The second most important support for the big bang picture of the expanding universe is the existence of microwave radiation left over from the initial fireball. Ever since its discovery in 1965 by Arno Penzias and Robert Wilson of Bell Laboratories (*see* NOBEL PRIZES), scientists have sought evidence of the motion of the Earth with respect to the universe by looking for slight temperature differences in the radiation field reaching Earth from different directions. Recently two groups working independently conducted measurements sufficiently sensitive to detect this anisotropy. Using a balloon-borne radiometer, David Wilkinson and Brian Corey of Princeton University found an anisotropy in the radiation that implied a motion of the Earth (and solar system) toward the constellation Leo at a velocity of about 320 kilometres (200 miles) per second. A group from the University of California at Berkeley, consisting of George F. Smoot, Marc V. Gorenstein, and Richard A. Muller, using a Dicke radiometer flown aboard a U-2 aircraft at an altitude of 21 km (13 mi), found a velocity of about 390 kilometres per second in roughly the same direction. The consistency of these results provided the first believable evidence for the overall (nonperiodic) motion of the Earth through the universe. (KENNETH BRECHER)

See also Earth Sciences; Space Exploration.
[131.A.1–3; 131.F.1–2; 132.A.1–3; 132.D.4 and 7; 133.A.4.a; 133.B.2.b; 133.C.3.e; 224.D.6.e–g]

Australia

A federal parliamentary state and a member of the Commonwealth of Nations, Australia occupies the smallest continent and, with the island state of Tasmania, is the sixth largest country in the world. Area 7,682,300 sq km (2,966,200 sq mi). Pop. (1978 est.): 14,212,900. Cap.: Canberra (metro. pop., 1976, 196,538). Largest city: Sydney (metro. pop., 1977 est., 3,121,750). Language: English. Religion (1971): Church of England 31%, Roman Catholic 27%; Uniting Church 17%. Queen, Elizabeth II; governor-general in 1978, Sir Zelman Cowen; prime minister, Malcolm Fraser.

Domestic Affairs. Prime Minister Malcolm Fraser faced a major crisis in August 1978, when a royal commission report found a senior minister,

Sen. Reginald Withers, guilty of misconduct. The commission was set up to inquire into allegations by D. M. Cameron, Liberal member of the House of Representatives for Fadden, that the finance minister, Eric Robinson, had influenced the redistribution (reapportionment) of federal electoral divisions in Queensland. The report of the royal commissioner exonerated Robinson but, to the chagrin of the Liberal senators in Canberra, found that their leader, Senator Withers, had been guilty of impropriety. The royal commissioner, Mr. Justice D. G. P. McGregor, said that Senator Withers had used his position to further a political purpose by an approach to the distribution commissioners. Withers, said McGregor, influenced the distribution commissioners' report by setting out to try to change the name of a proposed electoral division. Since Withers knew that there was political advantage to be gained from adopting a particular name for an electorate, his behaviour amounted to impropriety.

Faced with the royal commission report, Fraser had no alternative but to dismiss Withers, who had been minister for administrative services. Meanwhile, his Liberal Party colleagues were thrown into turmoil. Victoria's minister for public works, Robert Dunstan, resigned, observing that Fraser was sacking his best mates.

The Fraser ministry had also faced political embarrassment in February, when former governor-general Sir John Kerr was appointed Australian ambassador to UNESCO. The appointment was vigorously opposed by editorial writers and professional career diplomats, who recalled Sir John's controversial role in the dismissal of Gough Whitlam's Labor government in 1975. Sir John resigned the post, hoping thereafter to be free of the imputation that he was a divisive figure in Australian politics.

On July 1, 1978, the uranium-rich Northern Territory achieved self-government, and in November the Aboriginals approved uranium mining on tribal land in the Alligator Rivers area. A British offshoot, the racist National Front, held its first meeting in Melbourne. Wide-ranging changes in the country's immigration policy took effect in June. (*See* Special Report.) In June Australia purchased the Cocos Islands from John Clunies Ross.

Australia's long-time Liberal prime minister, Sir Robert Menzies, died May 15, aged 83 (*see* OBITUARIES).

Foreign Affairs. During the year the main emphasis in Australian foreign policy switched from defense and security to the promotion of multinational trade negotiations and discussions on the need for a new approach to world economic issues. With its large uranium reserves, Australia had a vital interest in the development and use of nuclear energy. Foreign Minister Andrew Peacock was at great pains to explain, in May, that the government's decision to permit the mining and export of uranium was consistent with Australia's international responsibilities regarding nuclear nonproliferation.

Since trade and foreign policy were becoming increasingly linked, the Departments of Trade and Foreign Affairs cooperated more and more closely. The deputy prime minister and trade minister, Douglas Anthony, spent much of the year trying to negotiate sales of Australian uranium with countries willing to accept Australian safeguards. Anthony was unable to achieve his prime objective, the sale of uranium to the U.K. The British and Australian governments did agree on a safeguards contract, negotiated, as the British minister of energy, Anthony Wedgwood Benn, put it, in full conformity with the U.K.'s obligations as a member state of the European Atomic Energy Community (Euratom). However, the agreement was vetoed by the European Economic Community (EEC) because of a clause that would have re-

The Alligator Rivers area of the Northern Territory is the site of large uranium deposits. The Australian government is carefully considering what mining might do to the spectacular landscape.

MICHAEL JENSEN—AUSTRALIAN INFORMATION SERVICE

Athletics:
see articles on the various sports

The sale of 50,000 tons of beef to the U.S. helped to increase farm income in Australia. Beef is shown being loaded aboard a freighter at Sydney.

quired Australian government approval for any transfer of nuclear fuel of Australian origin out of Britain. This conflicted with the Euratom treaty, which insisted on the free transfer of nuclear fuel among member countries. Anthony remained optimistic, however, and safeguards agreements were successfully concluded with Finland and were sought with the Philippines and Iran.

In May U.S. Vice-Pres. Walter F. Mondale visited Australia and was followed a little later, on the 25th anniversary of the battle of the Coral Sea, by U.S. Pres. Jimmy Carter's son Chip. These visits were intended to illustrate the tangible interest the U.S. took in its South Pacific ally, but the emphasis on "close personal relations," as Peacock put it, backfired when President Carter himself proved too busy to see Fraser during the prime minister's trip to the U.S. on June 1–6. Fraser went on to visit London, Paris, and Bonn, conferring on economic issues with heads of government in each capital.

The Australian and Japanese foreign ministers met in Canberra in June, and it soon became clear that the two nations had different perspectives on the way to improve Australian-Japanese relations. The Japanese foreign minister, Sunao Sonoda, thought Australia should drop its discriminatory tariffs against Japanese imports, especially motor vehicles and electrical goods. He pointed out that, while Japan as a world trader had a huge surplus, in bilateral trade with Australia the balance of payments was in Australia's favour. For Australia, Peacock reported the government's hopes that the Japanese would lift their restrictions on beef imports, and he agreed to negotiate over the use of Australian ports for Japanese fishermen when Australia proclaimed its 200-mi fishing limit. Sonoda noted that Japan was not necessarily seeking a balance in bilateral trade with Australia but, in view of the trade imbalance, it hoped Australia would abolish restrictions on manufactured imports. Sonoda also said that Japan was very interested in obtaining stable, long-term uranium supplies from Australia and that he hoped Japan would cooperate in the development of Australian uranium, natural gas, coal, and other energy and mineral resources. Agreement on such cooperation was reached August 2.

The Economy. The Australian economy remained weak during 1978, with unemployment continuing at a high rate of 6%. By June the Commonwealth Employment Service (CES) reported 393,842 unemployed. For every vacancy listed with the CES, there were 23 persons seeking work, as compared with 17 persons in June 1977 and 12 in June 1976.

Although the Fraser government failed to reduce unemployment, it was successful in its attack on inflation. Opponents of the government argued that there was a link between high unemployment and low inflation and that the cost in terms of the numbers of unemployed was too high. Even so, as the Australian Labor Party (ALP) premier of New South Wales admitted, credit had to be given where credit was due. By mid-1978 Australia's inflation rate was down to 7.9% from 13.4% in mid-1977. The *Economic Outlook* published by the Organization for Economic Cooperation and Development (OECD) forecast that Australia's inflation rate would be average among the 24 OECD member countries.

Primary producers were finding it very difficult to penetrate foreign markets. Many believed that their exports of meat and grain were being kept at bay by unfair trading methods employed by the EEC. A sale of 50,000 tons of beef to the U.S. during

---

AUSTRALIA

Education. (1977) Primary, pupils 1,874,631, teachers 83,405; secondary and vocational, pupils 1,-120,161, teachers 76,031; teacher training, students 44,817, teachers 3,760; higher, students 198,488, teaching staff 18,382.

Finance. Monetary unit: Australian dollar, with (Sept. 18, 1978) a free rate of A$0.87 to U.S. $1 (A$1.70 = £1 sterling). Gold, SDR's, and foreign exchange (June 1978) U.S. $2,376,000,000. Budget (1977 actual) revenue A$23,284,000,000; expenditure A$25,804,000,000. Gross national product (1977) A$85.6 billion. Money supply (April 1978) A$11,433,000,000. Cost of living (1975 = 100; Jan.–March 1978) 133.4

Foreign Trade. (1977) Imports A$12,305,000,000; exports A$12,036,000,000. Import sources: U.S. 21%; Japan 19%; U.K. 11%; West Germany 7%. Export destinations: Japan 33%; U.S. 9%; New Zealand 5%. Main exports: coal 11%; wool 10%; wheat 8%; iron ore 8%; beef 6%. Tourism (1976): visitors 532,-000; gross receipts U.S. $306 million.

Transport and Communications. Roads (1974) 837,866 km. Motor vehicles in use (1976): passenger 5,284,000; commercial 1,260,500. Railways: (government; 1976) 40,753 km; freight traffic (1975–76) 30,-820,000,000 net ton-km. Air traffic (1977): 19,240,000,000 passenger-km; freight 413.2 million net ton-km. Shipping (1977): merchant vessels 100 gross tons and over 424; gross tonnage 1,374,197. Shipping traffic (1975–76): goods loaded 158,-621,000 metric tons, unloaded 26,889,000 metric tons. Telephones (June 1976) 5,501,500. Radio licenses (June 1974) 2,851,000. Television licenses (Dec. 1975) c. 3.7 million.

Agriculture. Production (in 000; metric tons; 1977): wheat 9,350; barley 2,560; oats c. 962; corn 145; rice 530; potatoes 765; sugar, raw value c. 3,300; tomatoes c. 175; apples 310; oranges c. 357; wine c. 346; wool, clean 442; milk 5,897; butter 118; beef and veal 1,934; mutton and lamb 551. Livestock (in 000; March 1977): sheep 136,477; cattle 32,060; pigs 2,254; horses (1976) c. 446; chickens 43,356.

Industry. Fuel and power (in 000; metric tons; 1977): coal 78,240; lignite 29,921; crude oil 21,154; natural gas (cu m) 6,700,000; manufactured gas (cu m; 1975–76) c. 7,160,000; electricity (kw-hr) 83,883,-000. Production (in 000; metric tons; 1977): iron ore (64% metal content) 97,460; bauxite 26,070; pig iron 6,753; crude steel 7,313; aluminum 248; copper 152; lead 180; tin 5.4; zinc 247; nickel concentrates (metal content; 1975–76) 81; uranium (1976) 0.4; gold (troy oz; 1976–77) 495; silver (troy oz; 1976–77) 26,960; sulfuric acid 1,750; cement 5,023; newsprint 209; cotton yarn 21; wool yarn 19; passenger cars 338; commercial vehicles 61. Merchant vessels launched (100 gross tons and over; 1977) 87,800 gross tons. Dwelling units completed (1977) 137,000.

June helped to lift some of the gloom on Australian farms. No sooner was the sale made, however, than dock workers in Sydney began a series of selective bans to protest the high domestic prices for beef resulting from the increased demand for cattle to supply the overseas customers. Despite new, large discoveries in the Northern Territory, uranium failed to materialize as the saviour of the economy. Uranium producers blamed the government for not taking a sufficiently dynamic approach.

To counter one cause of the government's predicament, the lack of foreign investment in Australia, the treasurer, John Howard, devised a new scheme called "naturalization." Its purpose was to ease some of the restrictions, imposed when the world economy was stronger, that prevented companies lacking majority Australian ownership from undertaking new mining projects. Under Howard's plan, foreign companies with 25% Australian ownership, but with a majority of Australians on their boards, could consider themselves in the process of becoming "naturalized." Investments of less than A$5 million would not need government approval, and the government would not intervene in foreign takeovers where the assets of the companies involved were less than A$2 million. The government would also waive its insistence on approving real estate purchases of less than A$250,000. According to Howard's guidelines, foreign companies would have to make a public commitment to increase their Australian equity to 51% in due course. Critics of the government pointed out that there were no deadlines for attaining 51% Australian equity and no sanctions to compel companies to keep their word, although it was hoped that the Foreign Investment Review Board would monitor progress.

Although the parliamentary ALP opposition was too small to effect any changes in government emphasis on economic policy, the ALP leader, William Hayden, attempted to provide an alternative solution to Australia's trading and balance of payments problems. While Prime Minister Fraser and his minister for special trade representations, R. V. Garland, concentrated on trying to improve trading terms with the EEC, Hayden suggested that a better solution would be to increase exports to Australia's near neighbours in India, Southeast Asia, and Indonesia.

Hayden's views were largely ignored, however, and despite what Garland described as an atmosphere of "anger and frustration," Australia continued its largely unsuccessful efforts to remedy the growing imbalance of trading opportunities. Garland considered that the EEC's policies were based on unrealistically high domestic support prices underwritten by high variable levies on imports—usually amounting to de facto embargoes—and export subsidies. EEC support prices were generally set well above the prevailing world market prices in order to support and maintain the incomes of the least efficient European producers. In addition, EEC agricultural surpluses were thrown on available world markets at almost any price, putting—in Garland's view—an unreasonable burden on Australia's efficient farmers.

In June, in the face of falling world acceptance of Australian primary products, Anthony offered a tariff cut of 40% to the developed nations participating in the multilateral trade negotiations in Geneva. The 40% reduction was to be made in eight annual steps, beginning in 1980, and was designed to help the global effort to ease trade restrictions. Anthony admitted that the government was making an "offer" and was not committing itself to tariff reduction. This would take place only if better access to foreign markets could be assured for Australian agricultural products.

The treasurer continued the attack on inflation in the 1978–79 budget announced in August. He predicted growth of private investment but admitted there might be an even higher rate of unemployment in 1979 as a result of the government's depressive measures. In order to maintain the falling exchange rate, encourage overseas investment, and keep the deficit below A$3 billion, Howard increased the personal income tax by $1\frac{1}{2}$%. He also made sweeping changes in Australia's health care system (Medibank) by abolishing the element of compulsory health insurance, and introduced a scheme whereby the government paid 40% of the costs of doctors' services and provided free basic hospital treatment. The tax on motor vehicles made in Australia was reduced from 27.5 to 15% in an attempt to boost sales, but this was offset by a huge rise in the cost of gasoline—16 cents a gallon—caused by the decision to impose a state levy on crude oil production.

The budget also included stiff increases in indirect taxes on beer, spirits, and cigarettes, which critics feared would have a further depressive effect on the economy. Hopes for a consumer-led recovery diminished even more as the spectre of rising unemployment inevitably led to an increase in the already high savings ratio.

A strike of telecommunications technicians lasting more than four weeks disrupted communications throughout Australia before it was settled on August 29.   (A. R. G. GRIFFITHS)

See also Dependent States.

The funeral cortege awaits the casket of former prime minister Sir Robert Menzies, who died on May 15 in Melbourne.

WIDE WORLD

NEW AUSTRALIANS— THE NEW STANDARDS

by A. R. G. Griffiths

Far-reaching changes were made in Australia's immigration policies and procedures in June 1978, effectively raising immigration quotas and changing the rules for selecting migrants. The new system was not without opponents, and the debate was exacerbated by the entry into Australia—often illegally—of refugees fleeing the Communist-dominated countries of Southeast Asia.

Under the new immigration procedures, annual immigration targets were replaced by a three-year program designed to help the government provide a more reliable base for private- and public-sector planning. According to the minister for immigration and ethnic affairs, Michael MacKellar, a net gain of 70,000 migrants was sought for each year of the three-year period, 23,000 per year more than under the previous regulations. This would require a gross intake of 90,000 immigrants per year, and the net annual intake of "workers" would be about 27,000.

The new selection process, which was to be introduced in January 1979, was called the "numerical multifactor assessment system" (NUMAS). This grand title was a euphemism for a points system, under which potential migrants were scored for such factors as family ties with Australia, occupational skills and the demand for such skills, literacy in their mother tongue, knowledge of English, and prospects for successful settlement. Under the new policy the government was to relax the criteria for family reunions, make a greater effort to attract people with capital, and expand the terms of reference of the Committee on Overseas Professional Qualifications to cover technical qualifications. On the negative side, it would be more difficult for people with temporary entry permits to change their status to that of permanent residents.

Since the end of World War II all political parties, and most sections of the community, had supported a massive immigration program. Apart from the very large contingent from the U.K., the Australian com-

Author of Contemporary Australia, *A. R. G. Griffiths is a senior lecturer in history, The Flinders University of South Australia.*

munity was enriched by the cultural contributions of the hundreds of thousands of Greeks, Italians, Germans, Yugoslavs, and other ethnic groups who settled in Australia. These migrants went through several stages of assimilation. At first they were stigmatized as "Refos," "DP's," "New Australians," and —less politely—"Wogs," "Dagos," "Ities," and "Pommie bastards." But as Australian society became more cosmopolitan the role of its ethnic groups changed, and the "New Australians" came to be seen by the rest of society as trend setters. Ethnic newspapers had flourished since 1945, but with the new acceptance and enthusiastic imitation, ethnic radio and even some ethnic television programs became more and more common. It was chic to eat at ethnic restaurants, and advertising agencies featured migrants engaged in their most colourful activities—drinking wine, folk dancing, teaching skiing, or eating exotic foods.

The world energy crisis of 1973 diminished the ability of the hard-hit Australian economy to absorb new settlers. Although their diverse behaviour patterns were now heartily welcome, the immigrants faced increasing difficulties in bringing out their relatives. So the sense of isolation from the mainstream of Australian society remained.

Government and Opposition Views. The accepted attitude to immigration in times of high unemployment and a stagnant economy was that a vigorous immigration program merely brought out people who would be a charge to the taxpayer through unemployment and social service welfare payments. But in February 1978 MacKellar tried to pave the way for a change in governmental and public attitudes by initiating a public discussion through a Green Paper on *Immigration Policies and Australia's Population*.

On February 27 he told the Council of Management of the Australian Retailers' Association in Sydney that Australians seemed too little aware, as a nation, of the link between the country's economic future and the decisions that had to be made about population growth. Understandably, said MacKellar, Australians in 1978 were focusing on the economic and employment problems of the moment. But they ought to ensure that preoccupation with present problems did not blind them to long-term solutions. He argued that a properly constituted program of population growth could yield a range of economic benefits. New migrants could fill gaps in the labour supply and thus extend employment in ancillary occupations. Migrants could bring with them capital that could be invested in new technologies.

MacKellar was convinced of the importance to Australia's future of an active and selective approach to immigration, but he knew that, to be fully effec-

Most new settlers to Australia arrive by air. The arrivals are cleared by customs at Kingsford Smith International Airport, Sydney.

tive, government programs had to be in tune with the community and enjoy its support. His greatest hope was that public opinion could be persuaded to accept the view that there was "little doubt that adding a steady stream of new consumers to the Australian market was a strong factor in stimulating the economy in the past."

The Australian Labor Party (ALP) opposition was highly critical of the new program. Moses Cass, the opposition spokesman on immigration, charged that the federal government had increased immigration in order to maintain a docile work force through high unemployment. Cass believed that the role immigration played in aggravating unemployment was not the fault of the individual migrant, yet it was the migrant who suffered most. In August 1978 Cass provided figures which, he said, showed that of the 56,000 migrants who had arrived since January 1977, 18% were unemployed, compared with a national average of 7%.

The Vietnamese Refugees. An element of increasing importance in the public debate on immigration was the influx of refugees in the wake of the Vietnam war. Besides its normal immigration program, Australia was asked by the UN to act as a

resettlement country, along with the U.S., France, and Canada, for the stream of refugees leaving Vietnam, Cambodia, and Laos. The representative of the UN High Commissioner for Refugees (UNHCR) in Jakarta, Indonesia, called for Australia to be prepared to take more than 9,000 such refugees (*see* MIGRATION, INTERNATIONAL). But the orderly acceptance of the official refugees was jeopardized by the increasing number of Vietnamese traveling in small boats who entered Australia illegally but were being allowed to stay and settle there.

Thus, while the government, optimistically and without much success, tried strenuously to attract very wealthy migrants, who would bring large capital sums with them, and migrants who were prepared to work in outback parts of the country where most Australians were reluctant to live, the most colourful and contentious group of immigrants were neither wealthy nor mobile. Thousands of these "boat people" sailed from Vietnam and many, after stopping in Malaysia, Singapore, and Indonesia, found their way to Darwin, capital city and port of Australia's Northern Territory.

When the first refugee immigrants arrived they were treated as brave escapees from the Communist

211

way of life. Australian troops had, after all, died in the jungles of Vietnam trying to preserve the democratic freedoms which the boat people were risking their lives to enjoy. But when the trickle became a flood, and stories of piracy, murder, hijacking, and corruption became so prevalent that the government was forced to investigate them, public opinion changed. Farmers pointed out the dangers to Australia's agriculture resulting from the Vietnamese disregard of plant and animal quarantine laws. Wharf labourers in Darwin and other sections of the labour movement urged the government to stop the boat people. The Vietnamese embassy in Canberra warned Australia not to encourage "fascist terrorists" to plot the overthrow of the government of Vietnam within the safety of Australia's shores.

In response, Australian immigration officers were sent to Malaysia and Singapore to talk to prospective emigrants and to try to dissuade them from making the hazardous crossing. By a greatly accelerated program of processing, it was hoped that Australia could then take 10,000 Vietnamese refugees during 1978–79. But this liberal attitude on the part of the government was in advance of public opinion. Most Australians would have preferred to see the Vietnamese remain at home—a point of view reinforced by newspaper accounts that pictured the Vietnamese as unwilling to learn English, being given preferential employment before out-of-work Australians, and importing Southeast Asian feuds into Australia with them.

Jumping the Queue. The labour movement was particularly opposed to the ad hoc acceptance of Vietnamese refugees. After traveling to Southeast Asia to investigate the refugee problem, the ALP leader, William Hayden, reported that there was no way the Thais, or any other Southeast Asian government, could continue to cope indefinitely with the large number of refugees in camps. Rather than attempting any unilateral solution, Hayden urged the Australian government to seek an international conference on the refugee problem in Southeast Asia, after which the developed nations, preferably under UN auspices, could efficiently provide assistance for the refugees.

Hayden concluded by putting the ALP's point of view very strongly: 1,600 refugees had arrived in Australia by July 1978, and a great many of them had paid something to get in. This group was, in effect, jumping the queue, avoiding the guidelines and selection procedures established to control migration. Hayden said it was obvious that there was some sort of "lucrative racket" for bringing Indochinese refugees to Australia: "People don't conjure boats from nowhere. It seems that those who have the resources can buy a passage easily enough. There is a

great belief, especially in sections of Bangkok, that those refugees who can raise the resources to buy a passage are virtually guaranteed access to and settlement in Australia." If this was true, Australia's resettlement program was no longer in the hands of the government. And that, concluded Hayden, was unacceptable.

The Australian working class, and especially the members of trade unions, had traditionally opposed Asian immigration into Australia. Since the days of the 19th-century gold rushes when Chinese coolies entered Australia, the labour movement had supported the "white Australia policy," as it used to be called without self-consciousness. In the case of the Vietnamese refugees there was an added point to ALP hostility, since the ALP had opposed the Vietnam war and regarded the defeat of the South Vietnamese and the withdrawal of the U.S. from Southeast Asia as victories for reason. Some argued that many so-called refugees were leaving Vietnam for economic rather than political reasons; they had been self-employed business people who, under the new regime, could no longer operate in the entrepreneurial way.

MacKellar faced a difficult and delicate task. At midyear he was forced to spend three weeks in Southeast Asia explaining to government officials that the inland of Australia was barren and that the country could not absorb "millions of refugees." In all the countries he visited—Indonesia, the Philippines, Thailand, Malaysia, and Singapore—he found governments convinced that Australia was a large, wealthy, and underdeveloped country capable of taking in the Indochinese boat people. The Malaysian part of MacKellar's tour was the most crucial, since the Malaysian government was considering closing its doors to the boat people and enforcing its decision with concentrated naval patrols. In that case, the boat people would simply sail on to Darwin via Indonesia.

In Malaysia MacKellar was confronted by the sight of two boats in the final stages of preparation for the voyage to Darwin. Using a camp public address system, MacKellar appealed to the 5,700 refugees there to be patient and to wait until they could be properly processed and flown to Australia with health and immigration clearances. How long the refugees and the Australian community would stay patient remained to be seen. In the meantime, Australia was a major contributor to the UNHCR's 1978 program, giving an immediate cash grant of U.S. $1.5 million in the hope that the maintenance of suitable reception facilities in the countries of Southeast Asia would discourage refugees from making their own way to Australia and allow orderly processing of applications for entry.

Austria

A republic of central Europe, Austria is bounded by West Germany, Czechoslovakia, Hungary, Yugoslavia, Italy, Switzerland, and Liechtenstein. Area: 83,853 sq km (32,376 sq mi). Pop. (1977 est.): 7,518,300. Cap. and largest city: Vienna (pop., 1977 est., 1,590,100). Language: German. Religion (1978): Roman Catholic 90%. President in 1978, Rudolf Kirchschläger; chancellor, Bruno Kreisky.

During 1978 parliamentary and public discussion in Austria focused mainly on two topics: the economy and energy. While the government continued its deficit spending with emphasis on the safeguarding of employment, the opposition called for general economies, reduction of the public debt, and a balanced budget. At the centre of these discussions was the finance minister and vice-chancellor, Hannes Androsch, whose resignation the opposition demanded on the grounds that his interest in a tax consultancy firm was incompatible with his ministerial office.

The campaign against Androsch was touched off

Austria

by the introduction on July 1 of a new "transit" tax on all heavy trucks, whether Austrian or foreign, as a contribution to the costs of maintaining and improving the Austrian road network. Chaos ensued when truck drivers blockaded the frontiers, bringing already congested tourist traffic almost to a standstill. Normal conditions returned when the government, while refusing to repeal the tax, offered haulers some administrative reliefs and compensation for losses incurred.

Verbal "atomic warfare" continued to rage over the planned inauguration of the Zwentendorf nuclear power station — Austria's first — and the related problems of plant security and nuclear-waste disposal. After the contesting parties failed to reach an agreement, it was decided to hold a referendum. This took place on November 5, when 50.5% of the electorate voted against Zwentendorf's being brought into operation. Chancellor Bruno Kreisky had threatened to resign if Zwentendorf was rejected but was persuaded to remain in office by the ruling Socialist Party of Austria (SPÖ) leadership.

At its 24th congress in May the SPÖ adopted a new program "for the realization of social democracy," setting policy guidelines up to the year 2000. Kreisky was reelected party leader.

Vienna was again the scene of a number of international conferences and meetings: the talks between NATO and the Warsaw Pact member countries on mutual and balanced force reductions continued there during October–December 1977; during July–August 1978 UN law experts met to finalize the Vienna Agreement on the Succession of States in Respect of Treaties; and in July, through the intermediary of the Socialist International, Egyptian Pres. Anwar as-Sadat had talks with leading Israeli politicians. In April, in Salzburg-Klessheim, a European Democratic Union comprising right and centre parties was founded.

During the year two members of the Austrian contingent of the UN Disengagement Observer

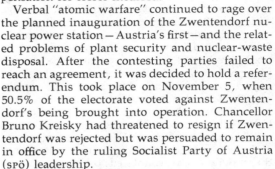

Truck drivers blockaded highways in Austria protesting a law that went into effect in July levying a special tax on trucks passing through Austria.

AUSTRIA

Education. (1976–77) Primary, pupils 974,775, teachers (1975–76) 54,922; secondary, pupils 174,124, teachers 12,650; vocational, pupils 172,756, teachers 3,704; teacher training, students 6,254, teachers (1975–76) 1,544; higher (including 4 main universities), students 89,612, teaching staff 10,624.

Finance. Monetary unit: schilling, with (Sept. 18, 1978) a free rate of 14.27 schillings to U.S. $1 (27.95 schillings = £1 sterling). Gold, SDR's, and foreign exchange (June 1978) U.S. $4,723,000,000. Budget (1976 actual): revenue 138 billion schillings; expenditure 171,670,000,000 schillings. Gross national product (1977) 790.5 billion schillings. Money supply (May 1978) 154,940,000,000 schillings. Cost of living (1975 = 100; May 1978) 116.9.

Foreign Trade. (1977) Imports 234,290,000,000 schillings; exports 161.9 billion schillings. Import sources: EEC 65% (West Germany 42%, Italy 9%); Switzerland 6%; France 5%. Export destinations: EEC 50% (West Germany 27%, Italy 9%, U.K. 5%); Switzerland 7%. Main exports: machinery 23%; iron and steel 10%; chemicals 8%; textile yarns and fabrics 7%; timber 5%; paper and board 5%. Tourism (1976): visitors 11,540,000; gross receipts U.S. $3,146,000,000.

Transport and Communications. Roads (1976) 102,858 km (including 722 km expressways). Motor vehicles in use (1976): passenger 1,828,100; commercial 151,000. Railways (1976): 6,493 km; traffic 6,712,000,000 passenger-km, freight 10,929,000,000 net ton-km. Air traffic (1977): 911 million passenger-km; freight 11,173,000 net ton-km. Navigable inland waterways in regular use (1976) 358 km. Telephones (Jan. 1977) 2,281,300. Radio licenses (Dec. 1976) 2,191,000. Television licenses (Dec. 1976) 1,974,000.

Agriculture. Production (in 000; metric tons; 1977): wheat 1,072; barley 1,212; rye 351; oats 279; corn 1,159; potatoes 1,628; sugar, raw value c. 495; apples 264; wine 248; meat 591; timber (cu m; 1976) 13,175. Livestock (in 000; Dec. 1976): cattle 2,502; sheep 174; pigs 3,878; chickens 13,359.

Industry. Fuel and power (in 000; metric tons; 1977): lignite 3,128; crude oil 1,790; natural gas (cu m) c. 2,340,000; manufactured gas (cu m) c. 790,000; electricity (kw-hr) 37,681,000 (67% hydroelectric in 1975). Production (in 000; metric tons; 1977): iron ore (31% metal content) 3,435; pig iron 2,964; crude steel 4,296; magnesite (1976) 926; aluminum 134; copper 35; zinc 16; cement 5,993; paper (1976) 1,185; petroleum products (1975) c. 7,710; plastics and resins (1976) 404; fertilizers (nutrient content; 1976–77) nitrogenous c. 239, phosphate c. 101; rayon, etc., filaments and fibres (1975) 84.

Force in the Golan Heights were killed and others wounded; in March Kreisky stated that Austria would not supply troops to the UN Interim Force in Lebanon. In June the UN decided to transfer the headquarters of its Relief and Works Agency for Palestinian Refugees from Beirut to Vienna.

The final stages of Austria's new family legislation were completed in Parliament in June. Affected were spouses' inheritance, property, and divorce rights.

Austria's economy fared better than average among the 24 member countries of the Organization for Economic Cooperation and Development. Forecasts for 1978 were: real growth in gross national product, 1.5%; inflation rate, 4%; unemployment, below 2.5%; export growth, 4.5%; import growth, 2–2.5%. To maintain the growth rate Parliament approved an extensive government program whereby over a ten-year period 500 billion schillings would be injected into the economy. The adverse effect on the balance of payments of the long-term capital imports required to finance the program was countered by comparatively drastic import restrictions, including (from January 1) a 30% value-added tax on luxury goods such as private cars. At the same time exports were encouraged, though without devaluation of the schilling. (ELFRIEDE DIRNBACHER)

The Bahamas

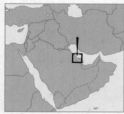

Bahrain

Bahamas, The

A member of the Commonwealth of Nations, The Bahamas comprise an archipelago of about 700 islands in the North Atlantic Ocean just southeast of the United States. Area: 13,864 sq km (5,353 sq mi). Pop. (1978 est.): 226,000. Cap. and largest city: Nassau (urban area pop., 1976 est., 125,400). Language: English (official). Religion (1970): Baptist 28.8%; Anglican 22.7%; Roman Catholic 22.5%; Methodist 7.3%; Saints of God and Church of God 6%; others and no religion 12.7%. Queen, Elizabeth II; governor-general in 1978, Sir Milo B. Butler; prime minister, Lynden O. Pindling.

Following its crushing defeat of the opposition parties in the 1977 election, the ruling Progressive Liberal Party (PLP) continued its middle-of-the-road policies for "generating stability, bahamanization, and the encouragement of overseas investment." Early in 1978, in an effort to promote greater efficiency, Prime Minister Lynden O. Pindling reshuffled his Cabinet, reorganized civil service responsibilities, and set up advisory committees.

The marked improvement in the economy that began in late 1977 was largely attributable to an increase in North American tourist arrivals. With visitor expenditure at U.S. $412.4 million in 1977, hotels hired more workers or rehired those previously laid off. The expulsion of illegal immigrants —principally Haitians working in the tourist industry—also had the effect of creating more jobs. Offshore banking and finance continued to be buoyant. The government actively encouraged the growth of captive insurance companies and hoped that The Bahamas would soon rival Bermuda in this field, especially in view of political uncertainties there. Inflation (3.1% in 1977) was expected to increase to 8 or 9% in 1978. Population growth continued at approximately 3.7% and unemployment at 21%. (DAVID A. JESSOP)

Bahrain

An independent monarchy (emirate), Bahrain consists of a group of islands in the Persian Gulf, lying between the Qatar Peninsula and Saudi Arabia. Total area: 662 sq km (256 sq mi). Pop. (1978 est.): 277,600. Cap.: Manama (pop., 1976 est., 105,400). Language: Arabic (official), Persian. Religion (1971): Muslim 95.7%; Christian 3%; others 1.3%. Emir in 1978, Isa ibn Sulman al-Khalifah; prime minister, Khalifah ibn Sulman al-Khalifah.

In 1978 Bahrain, in common with other Gulf states, experienced a slowdown in economic growth originating principally in the decline in the real estate market, which had boomed after the oil price increases of 1973 and then had become saturated. A two-year budget of $705 million announced in January showed a 12% increase in expenditure for 1978, compared with a 30% increase in 1977.

In April relations with Qatar deteriorated with the revival of a border dispute over virtually uninhabited Hawar Island, involving potential oil

BAHAMAS, THE

Education. (1976–77) Primary, pupils 32,162, teachers (state only) 768; secondary, pupils 29,597, teachers (state only) 649; vocational (1971–72), pupils 427, teachers 60; teacher training (1974–75), students 627, teachers 58; higher (at universities overseas; 1974–75), students c. 400.

Finance and Trade. Monetary unit: Bahamian dollar, with (Sept. 18, 1978) an official rate of B$1 to U.S. $1 (B$1.96 = £1 sterling). Budget (1976 actual): revenue B$134 million; expenditure B$141 million. Cost of living (1975 = 100; April 1978) 112. Foreign trade (1976): imports B$2,892,600,000; exports B$2,601,300,000. Import sources (1975): Saudi Arabia 38%; Nigeria 18%; Libya 14%; Indonesia 7%; U.S. 7%; Iran 5%. Export destinations (1975): U.S. 76%; Liberia 5%. Main exports (1975): crude oil 56%; petroleum products 40%. Tourism: visitors (excludes cruise passengers; 1976) 940,000; gross receipts (1975) U.S. $317 million.

Transport and Communications. Shipping (1977): merchant vessels 100 gross tons and over 109; gross tonnage 106,317. Telephones (Jan. 1977) 58,000. Radio receivers (Dec. 1975) 95,000. Television receivers (Dec. 1964) c. 4,500.

BAHRAIN

Education. (1976–77) Primary, pupils 45,953, teachers 1,939; secondary, pupils 17,444, teachers 749; vocational, pupils 1,042, teachers 82; higher, students 622, teaching staff 78.

Finance and Trade. Monetary unit: Bahrain dinar, with (Sept. 18, 1978) a free rate of 0.385 dinar to U.S. $1 (0.754 dinar = £1 sterling). Gold, SDR's, and foreign exchange (June 1978) U.S. $552 million. Budget (1977 est.): revenue 235 million dinars; expenditure 250 million dinars. Foreign trade (1977): imports 802.8 million dinars; exports 720.7 million dinars. Import sources: Saudi Arabia 45%; U.K. 11%; Japan 9%; U.S. 7%. Export destinations: Saudi Arabia 14%; Japan 14%; United Arab Emirates 9%; U.S. 8%; Australia 7%; Singapore 6%. Main exports: petroleum products 78%; aluminum 6%.

Industry. Production (in 000; metric tons; 1975): aluminum 116; crude oil (1977) 2,804; natural gas (cu m) 2,150,000; petroleum products (1976) c. 10,700; electricity (kw-hr) c. 400,000.

concession rights. In March the government announced plans to take over 100% ownership of the producing and local marketing facilities currently controlled by the Bahrain Petroleum Co. Formal agreements would be retroactive to January 1 and would increase government revenue by an expected $4 million. Refining was not to be affected. A slight increase in crude oil production, after an earlier decline, and a 13% increase in natural gas production as a result of the introduction of new recovery techniques were announced for 1977.

In January 1978 a riot involving rival factions of Bahraini students at Kuwait University left four injured. It was followed by reports of a wave of preventive arrests. (PETER MANSFIELD)

Bangladesh

An independent republic and member of the Commonwealth of Nations, Bangladesh is bordered by India on the west, north, and east, by Burma in the southeast, and by the Bay of Bengal in the south. Area: 143,998 sq km (55,598 sq mi). Pop. (1978 est.): 84,655,000. Cap. and largest city: Dacca (pop., 1974, 1,679,600). Language: Bengali. Religion: Muslim 85%, with Hindu, Christian, and Buddhist minorities. President in 1978, Maj. Gen. Ziaur Rahman.

BANGLADESH

Education. (1974–75) Primary, pupils 8,192,022, teachers 155,023; secondary, vocational, and teacher training, pupils 2,699,421, teachers 106,498; teacher training, students 7,627, teachers (1973–74) 580; higher, students (1973–74) 424,590, teaching staff 14,823.

Finance. Monetary unit: taka, with (Sept. 18, 1978) a free rate of 14.51 taka to U.S. $1 (28.44 taka = £1 sterling). Gold, SDR's, and foreign exchange (June 1978) U.S. $270 million. Budget (1977–78 est.): revenue 11,727,000,000 taka; expenditure 9,063,000,000 taka (excludes development budget 12,540,000,000 taka). Gross domestic product (1976–77): 104,940,000,000 taka. Money supply (March 1978) 12,083,000,000 taka. Cost of living (1975 = 100; May 1978) 109.2

Foreign Trade. (1977) Imports 17,806,000,000 taka; exports 7,314,000,000 taka. Import sources (1976): U.S. 16%; Canada 7%; India 7%; Japan 7%; U.K. 6%; Iran 5%. Export destinations (1976): U.S. 16%; U.K. 9%; Italy 6%; Mozambique 5%. Main exports: jute products 46%; jute 25%; leather c. 9%.

Transport and Communications. Roads (1976) 6,300 km. Motor vehicles in use (1976): passenger 20,000; commercial 9,370. Railways: (1976) 2,874 km; traffic (1973–74) 3,331,000,000 passenger-km, freight 639 million net ton-km. Navigable waterways (1976) c. 8,000 km. Air traffic (1976): 426 million passenger-km; freight 9.7 million net ton-km. Shipping (1977): merchant vessels 100 gross tons and over 133; gross tonnage 244,314. Shipping traffic (1975–76): goods loaded 1,255,000 metric tons, unloaded 3,629,000 metric tons. Telephones (Jan. 1976) 80,100. Radio receivers (March 1969) 531,000. Television receivers (March 1970) 10,000.

Agriculture. Production (in 000; metric tons; 1977): rice c. 19,300; potatoes c. 950; sweet potatoes (1976) 790; sugar, raw value (1976) c. 580; onions c. 151; mangoes c. 290; bananas c. 600; tea c. 34; tobacco 64; jute 1,026; meat c. 232; timber (cu m; 1976) 14,776; fish catch (1976) c. 640. Livestock (in 000; 1977): cattle c. 26,500; buffaloes c. 445; sheep c. 1,200; goats c. 8,000; chickens c. 51,000.

Industry. Production (in 000; metric tons; 1976–77): crude steel 108; cement 313; natural gas (cu m; 1974–75) c. 510,000; petroleum products (1974–75) 773; fertilizers (nutrient content) nitrogenous c. 130, phosphate c. 21; jute fabrics 498; cotton yarn 37; paper 48; electricity (kw-hr; 1976) c. 1,380,000.

Bangladesh

The lifting of the ban on political activities and the subsequent June 3, 1978, presidential election and the December parliamentary elections were considered important steps toward the restoration of democracy in Bangladesh. Maj. Gen. Ziaur Rahman retained the presidency with a massive majority. There were reports that the presidential elections had been rigged, but there was no conclusive proof. In any case, President Zia's victory had been freely predicted since the political groupings supporting his opponent, Maj. Gen. M. A. G. Osmany, had been largely discredited.

After the election President Zia moved steadily ahead with his plans to relax martial law in stages. He had already relaxed press censorship, released a number of political prisoners, and eased restrictions on public meetings in Dacca and other towns. On September 1 he announced the formation of his own political party with himself as chairman. The new party, Bangladesh Jatiotabadi Dal (Bangladesh Nationalist Party, or BJD), was an offshoot of the six-party political front formed just before the presidential election. The BJD included the National Awami Party (Bhashani group), the Muslim League, the United People's Party, a splinter group of the Awami League, and the Jatiyatabadi-Ganatantrik Dal (Jagodal). The last named, also launched before the June election, was to be the major partner. All the groupings were represented in the Cabinet formed at the end of June, though Jagodal held a major portion of the portfolios.

By forming the new party, Zia resolved the conflict that had been developing between Jagodal, headed by his own vice-president, Justice A. Sattar, and the six-party political front. Sattar, who was convener of Jagodal, had been campaigning hard for its recognition as the major political party. By merging Jagodal into the new BJD, Zia gained a free hand to rally his supporters for the parliamentary elections, to be held on Feb. 12, 1979. The elections would, be hoped, usher in democratic civilian rule. Meanwhile, martial-law provisions against political activity would be suspended. Nevertheless, 12 parties decided to boycott the elections.

After the abortive coup by a section of the Air Force in October 1977, Zia sought to pacify the

Major General Ziaur Rahman was elected president of Bangladesh by a landslide in June.

WIDE WORLD

armed forces and the police by improving their wages and working conditions. There was no visible opposition to him from the military during 1978, and increased diligence on the part of the police helped improve the law and order situation.

On the economic front, Zia achieved moderate success, mainly through decentralization of the administrative system in rural areas. A realistic approach was evident in the draft two-year plan for 1978–80, which envisaged real growth of 5.5% and an increase of just under 3% in per capita income. Top priority was allocated to agriculture, as well as to small-scale and cottage industries and family planning. Food production rose from 11 million metric tons in 1976–77 to 13 million tons in 1977–78.

Abroad, there were signs of increasing confidence in the country's stability. The Bangladesh Aid Group and the oil-producing countries of the Persian Gulf together promised a total of $1.1 billion in aid for the fiscal year 1977–78. On June 30, 1978, the day following the formation of his government, Zia announced a surplus budget for 1978–79, with revenue totaling 13,760,000,000 taka and expenditure set at 10,530,000,000 taka.

Relations with Burma were strained by a massive influx of Muslim refugees from Burma into Bangladesh. Agreement on their repatriation was reached in July, although Burma claimed that many of the refugees were originally illegal immigrants from Bangladesh (or former East Pakistan).

(GOVINDAN UNNY)

Barbados

The parliamentary state of Barbados is a member of the Commonwealth of Nations and occupies the most easterly island in the southern Caribbean Sea. Area: 430 sq km (166 sq mi). Pop. (1978 est.): 270,200; 91% Negro, 4% white, 4% mixed. Cap. and largest city: Bridgetown (pop., 1970, 8,900). Language: English. Religion: Anglican 53%; Methodist 9%; Roman Catholic 4%; Moravian 2%; others 32%. Queen, Elizabeth II; governor-general in 1978, Sir Deighton Lisle Ward; prime minister, J. M. G. Adams.

During 1978 most of the government's emphasis

Barbados

BARBADOS

Education. (1976–77) Primary, pupils 38,141, teachers 1,561; secondary, pupils 25,880, teachers 1,245; vocational, pupils 679, teachers 46; teacher training, students 252, teachers 23; higher, students 2,032, teaching staff (1971–72) 111.

Finance and Trade. Monetary unit: Barbados dollar, with (Sept. 18, 1978) an official rate of Bar$2 to U.S. $1 (free rate of Bar$3.92 = £1 sterling). Budget (1976–77 est.): revenue Bar$182,480,000; expenditure Bar$276,275,-000. Cost of living (1975 = 100; May 1978) 121.7. Foreign trade (1977): imports Bar$549,050,000; exports Bar$190.6 million. Import sources: U.K. 26%; U.S. 19%; Trinidad and Tobago 10%; Canada 7%; Venezuela 7%. Export destinations: U.S. 32%; Trinidad and Tobago 11%; Ireland 10%; U.K. 10%; Canada 6%. Main exports (1976): sugar 27%; clothing 18%; petroleum and products 13%; electrical parts 7%; chemicals 6%; molasses 5%. Tourism (1976): visitors 224,000; gross receipts U.S. $83 million.

Agriculture. Production (in 000; metric tons; 1976): sweet potatoes c. 3; corn c. 2; sugar, raw value c. 106.

was on rectifying a worsening balance of payments situation and on widening diplomatic and trade ties so as to increase the possible sources of aid and investment. Prime Minister J. M. G. ("Tom") Adams stressed that ties with China, North and South Korea, the Middle East, and Eastern Europe "would avoid unnecessary ideological commitments irrelevant to the situation."

In November 1977 Foreign Minister Henry Forde had announced that Barbados was considering full membership in the nonaligned movement, but no positive steps were taken in that direction during 1978. Meanwhile, the country was in the forefront of moves to encourage interdependence among the small islands of the eastern Caribbean. Although Barbados continued to enjoy a higher standard of living than the rest of the region, the economy remained an area of serious concern. Inflation was expected to exceed the 8% recorded in 1977, while unemployment seemed likely to remain at 15–16%.

The defeat of the ruling Barbados Labour Party's candidate in a by-election served to reunite factions of the opposition Democratic Labour Party under the leadership of former prime minister Erroll Barrow. (DAVID A. JESSOP)

Baseball

More than 40 million spectators—a record—paid to watch major league baseball in 1978, one of the most memorable years in the sport's history. The Los Angeles Dodgers became the first team to draw three million in one season (3,347,776 for 80 home dates). Champions of the National League, they were defeated in the World Series by the New York Yankees, who culminated a remarkable season by capturing their 22nd World Series title.

World Series. The Yankees, dismissed as noncontenders when they were 14 games out of first place in mid-July, beat the Dodgers 7–2 in Los Angeles on October 17 to clinch their second straight World Series championship 4 games to 2. In doing so, the Yankees became the first team ever to lose the first two games of the Series and then win four straight.

"That's the story of our whole team the whole year . . . we never gave up," said shortstop Bucky Dent, voted most valuable player for the Series. Dent batted .417 for the Series and had seven runs batted in, including three in the final game.

The Dodgers dedicated the Series to the memory of Jim Gilliam (see OBITUARIES), their popular 49-year-old coach who died on the eve of the Series after being felled by a brain hemorrhage.

Second baseman Davey Lopes, one of Gilliam's greatest admirers, hit two home runs and batted in five runs on October 10 as the Dodgers won the opener 11–5 in Los Angeles. In the second game at Dodger Stadium, Ron Cey hit a three-run homer and rookie Bob Welch struck out Reggie Jackson with two out and two runners on in the ninth inning as Los Angeles won again 4–3.

But in the third game at Yankee Stadium on October 13, the Yankees prevailed 5–1 behind pitcher Ron Guidry. The game featured excellent defensive work by third baseman Graig Nettles. The fourth game on October 14 went to the Yankees in ten innings 4–3, evening the Series at two games each. Lou Piniella's single drove in the winning run after the Dodgers argued in vain that Jackson had illegally interfered with a thrown ball, helping the Yankees score a sixth-inning run. Jackson, caught between first and second base, was hit by shortstop Bill Russell's throw, which bounded into foul territory. "He intentionally moved into the ball," said Dodger manager Tom Lasorda. The jittery Dodgers committed three errors while the Yankees collected 18 hits to capture the fifth game the next day in New York 12–2 behind rookie Jim Beattie, who pitched his first complete game ever in the major leagues. The Yankee triumph in the final contest featured excellent pitching by veteran Catfish Hunter and relief ace Rich Gossage plus a home run by Jackson, who batted in eight runs during the Series.

Regular Season. The Yankees, however, were not looking like a championship team in midseason. They trailed first-place Boston by 14 games on July 19. Five days later controversial Billy Martin, the manager who had led them to a World Series victory in 1977, resigned for the "good of the club" after an outburst against Yankee owner George Steinbrenner (*see* BIOGRAPHIES). Bob Lemon, fired less than four weeks earlier by the Chicago White Sox, was hired to take Martin's spot. Martin's departure drew adverse fan reaction in New York,

The Cy Young award was unanimously awarded to the Yankee fireballer Ron Guidry, whose record of 25–3 was the best in the American League since 1934.

where, in a bizarre announcement shortly thereafter, he was introduced before a game as "the rehired Yankee manager for the 1980 season." Yankee fans appeared to be appeased by Martin's reappearance in the organization.

Meanwhile, the club went on a tear, winning 52 of its last 73 regular-season games. By virtue of seven wins in eight meetings with Boston, the Yankees at one time went 3½ games ahead of the Red Sox. But by winning its final regular-season game while the Yankees lost, Boston caught New York and forced a one-game playoff in Boston on October 2, the first for the American League since

Pete Rose tips his cap to the crowd from first base after having hit safely in his 38th consecutive game, a new National League record. He went on to extend the streak to 44 games.

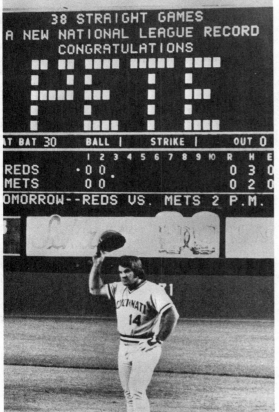

WIDE WORLD

Final Major League Standings, 1978

American League
East Division

Club	W.	L.	Pct.	G.B.	N.Y.	Bos.	Mil.	Balt.	Det.	Clev.	Tor.	Cal.	Chi.	K.C.	Min.	Oak.	Sea.	Tex.
* New York 100	63	.613	...	...	9	5	9	11	9	11	5	9	5	7	8	6	6
* Boston 99	64	.607	1	7	...	10	8	12	7	11	9	7	4	9	5	7	3
Milwaukee ...93	69	.574	6½	10	5	...	8	8	10	12	5	7	4	4	9	5	6
Baltimore 90	71	.559	9	6	7	7	...	7	9	8	4	8	2	5	11	9	7
Detroit 86	76	.531	13½	4	3	7	8	...	10	9	7	9	4	4	6	8	7
Cleveland 69	90	.434	29	6	8	5	6	5	...	10	4	2	5	5	4	8	1
Toronto 59	102	.366	40	4	4	4	4	4	4	...	3	6	5	4	4	2	7

West Division

Club	W.	L.	Pct.	G.B.	K.C.	Cal.	Tex.	Min.	Chi.	Oak.	Sea.	Balt.	Bos.	Clev.	Det.	Mil.	N.Y.	Tor.
Kansas City....92	70	.568	...	...	6	7	7	7	10	12	8	6	6	6	6	6	5
California 87	75	.537	5	9	...	5	12	8	9	9	6	2	6	4	5	5	7
Texas 87	75	.537	5	8	10	...	9	4	9	12	4	7	9	3	4	4	4
Minnesota ...73	89	.451	19	8	3	6	...	7	9	6	5	2	5	6	7	3	6
Chicago........71	90	.441	20½	8	7	11	8	...	7	7	1	3	8	2	4	1	4
Oakland 69	93	.426	23	5	6	6	6	8	...	13	0	5	6	4	1	2	7
Seattle 56	104	.350	35	3	6	3	9	8	2	...	1	3	1	2	5	5	8

*Tied at end of regular season; New York won play-off game.

National League
East Division

Club	W.	L.	Pct.	G.B.	Phil.	Pitt.	Chi.	Mon.	St.L.	N.Y.	Atl.	Cin.	Hou.	L.A.	S.D.	S.F.
Philadelphia...90	72	.556	...	...	11	14	9	10	12	4	5	6	5	8	6
Pittsburgh 88	73	.547	1½	7	...	11	11	9	11	10	7	8	5	5	4
Chicago 78	83	.488	11	4	7	...	7	15	11	7	7	6	4	7	4
Montreal 76	86	.469	14	9	7	11	...	9	8	7	4	6	4	6	5
St. Louis 69	93	.426	21	8	9	3	9	...	11	7	4	5	7	3	3
New York 66	96	.407	24	6	7	7	10	7	...	6	5	5	5	5	3

West Division

Club	W.	L.	Pct.	G.B.	L.A.	Cin.	S.F.	S.D.	Hou.	Atl.	Chi.	Mon.	N.Y.	Phil.	Pitt.	St.L
Los Angeles ...95	67	.586	...	...	9	11	9	11	13	8	8	7	7	7	5
Cincinnati 92	69	.571	2½	9	...	12	9	11	12	5	8	7	7	4	8
San Francisco 89	73	.549	6	7	6	...	10	12	7	8	7	9	6	8	9
San Diego 84	78	.519	11	9	9	8	...	10	10	5	6	7	4	7	9
Houston 74	88	.457	21	7	7	6	8	...	10	6	6	7	6	4	7
Atlanta 69	93	.426	26	5	6	11	8	8	...	5	5	6	8	2	5

One of the standout performers of the 1978 World Series was Graig Nettles, New York Yankee infielder whose diving catches around third base provided some of the most exciting moments of the games.

1948. In a taut contest, the Yankees won 5–4 on Dent's three-run homer, Jackson's solo homer, and clutch relief pitching by Gossage to capture the East Division crown.

For the third straight season, the Yankees' foe in the American League championship series was the Kansas City Royals. They won the West Division crown by five games over California and Texas.

Repeat winners in the National League were the Dodgers, who beat the Cincinnati Reds by 2½ games for the West Division crown, and the Philadelphia Phillies, who withstood a charge by the Pittsburgh Pirates to take the East Division by 1½ games.

With Dodger first baseman Steve Garvey starring, the National League beat the American League 7–3 in the All-Star Game on July 11 at San Diego, Calif. The victory was the 7th straight for the National League and 15th in the last 16 years.

Pete Rose (*see* BIOGRAPHIES), the Cincinnati Reds' veteran, achieved the most outstanding individual performance during the season by hitting safely in 44 straight games. The 37-year-old third baseman thus fell 12 games shy of Joe DiMaggio's major league record established for the 1941 Yankees. However, Rose tied for the second longest streak with Willie Keeler, who hit in 44 straight games for Baltimore of the National League in 1897. At the end of the season, Rose became a free agent and was hired by the Phillies for $3.2 million over four years.

Rod Carew, the Minnesota Twins' perennial batting star, hit .333 to capture another American League crown, his seventh. Guidry, the Yankees' spectacular southpaw, paced league pitchers with a 25–3 record (including the play-off victory at Boston). Other American League pitchers who won 20 or more games were New York's Ed Figueroa, Kansas City's Dennis Leonard, Milwaukee's Mike Caldwell, Boston's Dennis Eckersley, and Baltimore's Jim Palmer. Gossage led relievers with

27 saves. Boston's Jim Rice led the league in home runs with 46 and in runs batted in with 139. Detroit's Ron LeFlore had 68 stolen bases.

Dave Parker of the Pittsburgh Pirates batted .334 to capture his second National League title in a row. George Foster of the Cincinnati Reds hit 40 home runs and drove in 120 runs to lead those departments. Omar Moreno of Pittsburgh had 71 stolen bases. Gaylord Perry of San Diego and Montreal's Ross Grimsley were the only pitchers to win 20 or more games. San Diego's Rollie Fingers led relief pitchers with 37 saves.

Parker won the most valuable player award in the National League, while Rice of the Red Sox gained the honour in the American League. Guidry was the unanimous choice for the American League's Cy Young award, and San Diego's veteran Gaylord Perry won the prize in the National. Rookies of the year were Lou Whitaker of Detroit in the American and Bob Horner of Atlanta in the National League. Bob Lemon of the Yankees was named the American League's manager of the year, while Joe Altobelli of the San Francisco Giants won the National League award.

Play-offs. The New York Yankees won their 32nd pennant by beating the Kansas City Royals 3 games to 1 in the American League play-off. It marked only the third time in modern major league history that a team had changed managers in midseason and won a pennant. Moreover, only Boston's 1914 "Miracle Braves" had rallied from a greater deficit—15 games back on July 4.

The Dodgers beat the Phillies 3 games to 1 for the National League pennant, clinching it on October 7 with a 4–3 victory in ten innings at Los Angeles on a single by Russell.

Latin America. When the major league baseball season ends in North America, many players sign on with teams in Venezuela, Puerto Rico, Mexico, and the Dominican Republic for the "winter ball" season of about 60 games. During the last season,

Caracas won the title in Venezuela, Mayagüez in Puerto Rico, Culiacán in Mexico, and Águilas Cibaeñas in the Dominican Republic. In the Caribbean Series at Mazatlán, Mexico, the winner was Mayagüez.   (ROBERT WILLIAM VERDI)

Japan. Once called a "permanent B-class team," the Yakult Swallows of Tokyo clinched the Central League pennant for the first time since its founding in 1950. Cited as the chief driving force behind the victory was Tatsuro Hirooka's skillful management.

In the Pacific League the Hankyu Braves of Nishinomiya won the pennant for the fourth straight season. It was also the second time that Hankyu had won both halves of the season since the split-season system was introduced. Despite the one-month absence of manager Toshiharu Ueda because of illness and frequent injuries among leading players during the second half of the season, the overall team power, backed by excellent performances of both young and veteran players, brought victory to the Braves.

In the best-of-seven Japan Series the Yakult Swallows beat the Hankyu Braves 4 games to 3 to win the championship for the first time in their 29-year history. In the final game pitching ace Hiromu Matsuoka shut out Hankyu 4–0, scattering seven hits.

For the eighth consecutive year Sadaharu Oh of the Yomiuri Giants of Tokyo captured the runs-batted-in laurel of the Central League, with 118. Though he failed to obtain the home-run title, he hit 39 to raise his world-record total to 805. Jitsuo Mizutani of the Hiroshima Toyo Carp was the Central League's leading hitter with .348, and Koji Yamamoto of Hiroshima won the home-run crown with 44. Tsutomu Wakamatsu of Yakult captured the most valuable player award.

In the Pacific League Kyosuke Sasaki of the Kintetsu Buffaloes of Osaka captured the batting title with .354. Bob Mitchell of the Japan Ham Fighters of Osaka slammed 36 home runs to win that title, and Bobby Marcano of Hankyu batted in the most runs with 94. Pitcher Hisashi Yamada of Hankyu was chosen as the most valuable player in the first half, while pitcher Keiji Suzuki of Kintetsu won in the second half. Yamada was given the MVP award for the entire season for an unprecedented third straight year.   (RYUSAKU HASEGAWA)

Basketball

United States. PROFESSIONAL. When the Washington Bullets won their first National Basketball Association (NBA) championship in 1978, it was only the prelude to a series of stunning off-court developments. The Portland Trail Blazers, heavy favourites to make a successful defense of their NBA crown, were crippled by key injuries, especially to superstar centre Bill Walton. After the season ended Walton claimed that the Trail Blazers had pressured him to take pain-killing medication so that he could play on an injured foot. Walton demanded to be traded and threatened legal action that could have wide implications for the treatment of injured professional athletes.

So, for the ninth straight year, the league failed to produce a repeat champion. Portland was knocked out in the first round of the play-offs by the Seattle SuperSonics, who capped an astonishing turnabout from their previous season by extending the final series to seven games before succumbing to the Bullets.

It was a sweet triumph for Washington and especially for coach Dick Motta (*see* BIOGRAPHIES), who had failed to take the Chicago Bulls all the way in eight stormy seasons there. Motta's Bullets won a siege of psychological warfare from the powerful Philadelphia 76ers in the Eastern Conference finals, and that victory gave them enough momentum to spoil the SuperSonics' Cinderella story in the championship round. A major factor in the series was the domination of Marvin Webster, the 7-ft 1-in Seattle centre, by 6-ft 7-in Wes Unseld of the Bullets.

The champions' feat was remarkable in view of eight consecutive losses during their two previous NBA final play-offs, in 1971 and 1975. This time they triumphed in successive play-off series against San Antonio, Philadelphia, and Seattle, despite yielding the home-court advantage to each of them. In the NBA the home team wins approximately 70% of the time, and so the Bullets had to do it the hard way.

The era of escalating salaries and widening freedom from contract restraints continued in 1978. The Denver Nuggets persuaded their superstar, David Thompson, to keep his kangaroo leaps in the shadow of the Rockies by giving him a five-

Bob Dandridge of the Washington Bullets managed to get a pass by the Seattle SuperSonics in NBA championship play. The Sonics lost the final game 105–99 before a home crowd in June.

UPI COMPIX

year contract. The $800,000 annual salary made Thompson the highest-paid pro athlete, vaulting him above such other millionaires as baseball's Catfish Hunter and football's O. J. Simpson. The gold rush of free agents gained impetus with Seattle's Webster being signed by the New York Knicks for some $3 million over five years.

Another startling event was Rick Barry's shift from the Golden State Warriors to the Houston Rockets. The 34-year-old forward elected to play until 1980 in Houston for $1 million. Also on the move were two entire NBA franchises in a surprising switch that bounced the Braves completely across the country to San Diego after eight years in Buffalo. The most intriguing part of that deal was that Buffalo owner John Y. Brown swapped teams with the Boston Celtics' Irv Levin. Brown's first move in Boston was to retain Arnold ("Red") Auerbach, mastermind of the dynasty that captured 13 NBA titles there, eight of them in succession. With extensive West Coast business interests, Levin was happy to surrender all that tradition for a San Diego base of operations.

One major headache remained for NBA Commissioner Lawrence F. O'Brien, acclaimed for stilling the league's turbulent waters by employing the political expertise he learned as campaign strategist and White House aide for Pres. John F. Kennedy. It was solved by a group's purchase of the New Jersey Nets with a plan to pay off some $20 million in debts, which had brought the franchise to the brink of bankruptcy.

COLLEGE. In a year of renewed interest and rapid growth in collegiate basketball, the University of Kentucky swept to its first National Collegiate Athletic Association (NCAA) crown in 20 years. The Wildcats, ranked first in the country during the season, had been expected to win the tournament, but that did not lessen the joyous mixture of relief and pride that engulfed the state after stubborn Duke was vanquished 94–88 in the championship game.

It had been a long wait for Kentucky, where basketball and bluegrass share top billing. Nobody

felt the pressure more than coach Joe B. Hall, especially with the ghost of Adolph Rupp, longtime architect of Kentucky champions, shadowing him. Rupp had won 880 games and four national titles in 41 seasons at Kentucky, and Hall knew that failure to bring home another one would be blamed on him. However, Jack ("Goose") Givens made sure that would not happen, unleashing a 41-point barrage on Duke in the final game on March 27. The 6-ft 4-in Kentucky forward riddled a zone defense with 23 points in the first half, personally scoring his team's final 16.

Perennial champion UCLA was missing from the final four in 1978. In the semifinals Kentucky beat Arkansas 64–59, and Duke survived a Notre Dame rally 90–86. The ensuing collision between the two Southern powerhouses provided a satisfying finish for an outstanding season, with higher television ratings and gate receipts reflecting nationwide enthusiasm for the college game.

The University of Texas proved that basketball was growing in popularity by winning the National Invitational Tournament (NIT) with a 101–93 decision over North Carolina State. It was the first NIT title for Texas and the first for a Southwest Conference team. The Longhorns' success, coupled with a third-place NCAA finish by Arkansas, indicated that basketball was gaining popularity in places where football had long been unrivaled.

There was an unusual degree of unanimity in the selection of 1978 All-American teams. Both wire services, the National Association of Basketball Coaches, and the United States Basketball Writers Association named the same five men to the first team: guards Phil Ford, North Carolina, and Butch Lee, Marquette; centre Mychal Thompson, Minnesota; and forwards Larry Bird, Indiana State, and David Greenwood, UCLA. Ford also was the near unanimous choice as college player of the year.

One of 1978's most significant sports stories concerned the rapid strides made by women's athletics. College basketball was a leader in that growth, with UCLA defeating Maryland 90–74 to win its first Association for Intercollegiate Athletics for Women championship. Montclair (N.J.) State took third place in the tournament by beating Wayland (Texas) Baptist in overtime, 90–88. The standout for UCLA was Ann Meyers, a four-time All-American who went out in style by scoring 20 points and grabbing 10 rebounds in the championship game.

(ROBERT G. LOGAN)

World Amateur. The eighth World Basketball Championships were contested in October 1978 in Manila. Fourteen teams took part, including defending champion Soviet Union, the Philippines as the host country, and the gold and silver medalists in the 1976 Olympics, the U.S. and Yugoslavia. Other contestants were the winners of the various zones and three invited teams—South Korea, Puerto Rico, and Italy.

The Soviet Union and the Philippines had automatic entry to the final eight, and after the first round of the play-offs the following teams qualified to join them: Yugoslavia, Brazil, U.S., Italy, Canada, and Australia. Yugoslavia, the Soviet Union, Italy, and Brazil earned the right to play

Duke University's Jim Spanarkel had a ball but no place to go as he was surrounded by Kentuckians in the NCAA tournament in March. The University of Kentucky won the championship 94–88.

UPI COMPIX

Carol Blazejowski of Montclair State College, New Jersey, goes up and over to score a basket in the semifinals in the Women's Collegiate Basketball Tournament in Los Angeles on March 23. Despite her effort, UCLA won the game 86–77.

for first through fourth place before a capacity crowd of 25,000 in the Araneta Coliseum. The first game, to decide third and fourth place, was played between the flamboyant and exciting Brazilians and the skillful, experienced Italian team. In the last 0.4 second Brazil scored in a spine-tingling 86–85 triumph. In the championship game Yugoslavia pulled off an 82–81 overtime win over the Soviet Union in a frantic finish. At the end of regulation playing time the score was tied at 73 all. Then, through brilliant shooting by Drazen Dalipagic, Yugoslavia gained a lead of 82–77 with less than a minute to go. Sergey Belov put in two consecutive baskets in a span of 30 seconds for the Soviet Union, but time ran out, leaving the Yugoslavs the world champions. The U.S. finished fifth and Canada sixth.

The first Commonwealth basketball championship took place in Great Britain during August 1978. Seven teams competed, and Canada was the undefeated winner of the championship. New Zealand placed second and England third.

The ninth Asian basketball championship tournament was played during Nov. 28 – Dec. 10, 1977, 14 teams taking part. China was a surprise winner with South Korea and Japan second and third, respectively. The ninth African basketball championship took place in Dakar, Senegal, Dec. 24, 1977–Jan. 1, 1978, with ten teams competing. Senegal beat Ivory Coast in the final, 103–72, and Egypt was third. The 16th European championship for women was played in Poznan, Poland, May 20–30, 1978. Once again the Soviet women won, with Yugoslavia and Czechoslovakia second

and third, respectively. In the men's European Champions' Cup, Real Madrid of Spain defeated Mobilgirgi of Varese, Italy, 75–67. In the European Women's Cup GEAS Sesto of San Giovanni, Italy, triumphed over the Czechoslovak team Spartak CKD of Prague, 74–66. The men's European Cup-Winners' Cup was an all-Italian final; Palacanestro Gambetti of Cantù beat Palacanestro Sinudyne of Bologna. In the Ronchetti Cup for women Leski Spartak beat Slovian Bratislava, 50–49. The Korac Cup was an all-Yugoslav final with KK Partizan of Belgrade triumphing over KK Bosna of Sarajevo, 117–110.   (K. K. MITCHELL)

Belgium

A constitutional monarchy on the North Sea coast of Europe, Belgium is bordered by The Netherlands, West Germany, Luxembourg, and France. Area: 30,521 sq km (11,784 sq mi). Pop. (1978 est.): 9,837,500. Cap. and largest urban area: Brussels (pop., 1978 est., commune 150,000). Language: Dutch, French, and German. Religion: predominantly Roman Catholic. King, Baudouin I; prime ministers in 1978, Léo Tindemans and, from October 20, Paul Vanden Boeynants.

Belgium

Belgium's economic situation, widespread unemployment (6.6% of the work force in August), and the state of public finances were the government's major preoccupations in 1978. With a budget deficit of about BFr 80 billion and a similar one forecast for 1979, stemming the growth of public expenditures had become an absolute necessity. To this end an anticrisis plan was elaborated covering the whole range of public expenditures (social security, unemployment benefits, pensions, etc.) and providing for fiscal measures and greater state intervention in the energy and banking sectors. The Liberal opposition warned that the plan did nothing to reduce government expenditures and only gave powers to the trade unions to the detriment of Parliament.

Prime Minister Léo Tindemans was unable to achieve agreement within the government on additional credits for the Departments of State Insurance and Employment. Faced by this and by a demand from the Front Démocratique des Francophones, one of the partners in the government coalition, that the anticrisis bill and the institutional reforms bill be discussed in Parliament simultaneously and action concluded before the summer recess, he tendered his resignation on June 15. King Baudouin asked him to carry on because of "the seriousness of the economic and budgetary situation," and on June 19 he announced that a compromise had been reached among the coalition parties.

Early in January, new negotiations among the majority parties had been needed to clear up points of the so-called Egmont Pact of June 1977, which was to reshape the country's institutions by granting autonomy to the Flemish, French-speaking, and Brussels regions. Late in July 1978 an ad hoc commission at last started the first reading of the institutional reforms bill. It was faulted on fundamental points by the Council of State and found

U.S. Pres. Jimmy Carter and Belgium's King Baudouin attend an honour guard reception for President Carter during his visit to Belgium in January.

inconsistent with the constitution. The government decided, however, to ignore the objections in order not to upset the delicate balance among the majority parties.

In late September the ad hoc commission approved the bill, but the Flemish Social Christians then had second thoughts about its lack of constitutionality. When Parliament resumed, Prime Minister Tindemans, himself a Flemish Social Christian, was invited by the leaders of the other coalition parties to ask for a vote of confidence on each article of the bill. Tindemans refused and announced his resignation. Paul Vanden Boeynants, minister of defense and a former prime minister (1966–68), formed a new interim government, identical to the previous one except for the outgoing prime minister. After an inconclusive general election on December 17, Vanden Boeynants's government resigned. However, he continued with his Cabinet to serve in a caretaker capacity until a new government could be formed.

A report by a U.S. industrial consulting firm published during the year indicated that the Belgian steel industry would need a complete reorganization in order to survive. Some 25,000 jobs would still be lost by 1985. A new industrial policy submitted to Parliament provided for support to traditional industrial activities and the development of new industries, less dependence on foreign decision-making centres, more foreign investments and encouragement of labour-intensive activities, and stimulation of industrial research. The Liberal opposition's alternative called for lower taxes, workers' financial participation, and lowering of the pension age.

Trade unions claimed new jobs could be created by the introduction of a 36-hour workweek, but without any loss of wages or cuts in social benefits. The idea was rejected by the Federation of Belgium Industries, which favoured an extension of part-time work. During collective bargaining several industries had to yield to the unions' demand, notably the oil industry. In August, the Antwerp RBP

BELGIUM

Education. (1976–77) Primary, pupils 935,804, teachers (1970–71) 51,692; secondary and vocational, pupils 830,-748, teachers (1967–68) 88,030; higher, pupils (1975–76) 159,652, teaching staff (universities only; 1973–74) c. 5,-300.

Finance. Monetary unit: Belgian franc, with (Sept. 18, 1978) a free commercial rate of BFr 31.13 to U.S. $1 (BFr 61 = £1 sterling). Gold, SDR's, and foreign exchange (June 1978) U.S. $5,926,000,000. Budget (1977 actual): revenue BFr 756.5 billion; expenditure BFr 923.9 billion. Gross national product (1977) BFr 2,883,000,000,000. Money supply (March 1978) BFr 751.2 billion. Cost of living (1975 = 100; June 1978) 121.4.

Foreign Trade. (Belgium-Luxembourg economic union; 1977) Imports BFr 1,442,600,000,000; exports BFr 1,343,-600,000,000. Import sources: EEC 67% (West Germany 23%, France 16%, The Netherlands 16%, U.K. 8%); U.S. 6%. Export destinations: EEC 71% (West Germany 22%, France 19%, The Netherlands 17%, U.K. 7%). Main exports: chemicals 12%; machinery 12%; motor vehicles 12%; iron and steel 10%; food 9%; textile yarns and fabrics 6%; petroleum products 5%. Tourism (1976) gross receipts (Belgium-Luxembourg) U.S. $959 million.

Transport and Communications. Roads (1976) 114,814 km (including 1,035 km expressways). Motor vehicles in use (1976): passenger 2,700,500; commercial 237,-300. Railways: (1976) 3,998 km; traffic (1977) 7,660,000,000 passenger-km, freight 6,468,000,000 net ton-km. Air traffic (1977): 4,051,000,000 passenger-km; freight 348.2 million net ton-km. Navigable inland waterways in regular use (1976) 1,539 km. Shipping (1977): merchant vessels 100 gross tons and over 271; gross tonnage 1,595,489. Shipping traffic (1976): goods loaded 33,754,-000 metric tons, unloaded 60,111,000 metric tons. Telephones (Jan. 1977) 2,949,800. Radio licenses (Dec. 1976) 4,272,000. Television licenses (Dec. 1976) 2,856,000.

Agriculture. Production (in 000; metric tons; 1977): wheat c. 750; barley c. 700; oats c. 110; potatoes c. 1,280; tomatoes c. 140; apples c. 120; sugar, raw value c. 770; pork c. 620; beef and veal c. 247; milk c. 3,600; fish catch (1976) 44. Livestock (in 000; Dec. 1976): cattle 2,823; pigs 4,813; sheep 82; horses 49; chickens c. 30,700.

Industry. Fuel and power (in 000; 1977): coal (metric tons) 7,068; manufactured gas (cu m) c. 2,050,000; electricity (kw-hr) 47,094,000. Production (in 000; metric tons; 1977): pig iron 8,913; crude steel 11,262; copper 572; lead 122; tin 5.1; zinc 259; sulfuric acid 2,013; fertilizers (nutrient content; 1976–77) nitrogenous c. 650, phosphate c. 480; cement 7,762; newsprint 83; other paper (1975) 599; cotton yarn 43; cotton fabrics (1976) 63; wool yarn 77; woolen fabrics (1976) 34; rayon and acetate yarn and fibres 26. Merchant vessels launched (100 gross tons and over; 1977) 169,000 gross tons.

refinery, a subsidiary of Occidental Petroleum Corp., was closed down. Workers occupied the premises, and trade unions demanded that the government take over the refinery's activities.

After considerable hesitation, the government acceded to the request of Pres. Mobutu Sese Seko of Zaire and sent paratroops to Kolwezi to help in the rescue of whites threatened by the invasion of Katangese rebels. (*See* ZAIRE.) New tensions with Belgium's former colony, arising from criticism of Foreign Minister Henri Simonet by Mobutu, were settled after mediation by King Hassan of Morocco.

(JAN R. ENGELS)

Benin

A republic of West Africa, Benin is located north of the Gulf of Guinea and is bounded by Togo, Upper Volta, Niger, and Nigeria. Area: 112,600 sq km (43,475 sq mi). Pop. (1978 est.): 3,341,000, mainly Dahomean and allied tribes. Cap.: Porto-Novo (pop., 1973 est., 97,000). Largest city: Cotonou (pop., 1973 est., 175,000). Language: French and local dialects. Religion: mainly animist, with Christian and Muslim minorities. President in 1978, Lieut. Col. Mathieu Kerekou.

Benin's relations with France and with several of the other French-speaking African nations suffered in 1978 from the effects of the raid by some 80–100 mercenaries on the Cotonou airport in January 1977. The government blamed France and Gabon in particular for having "given active support to subversive intrigues against Benin at the time of the mercenary aggression on Jan. 16, 1977." In January 1978 France recalled its ambassador temporarily for consultation following renewed criticism from Benin. Then in July, at the Organization of African Unity summit conference in Khartoum, Sudan, Pres. Mathieu Kerekou publicly attacked Morocco and Gabon, once more accusing them of involvement in the airport affair. As a result of this, Pres. Omar Bongo of Gabon expelled 10,000 nationals of Benin who had settled as immigrant workers in Gabon.

(PHILIPPE DECRAENE)

Bhutan

Benin

Bhutan

A monarchy situated in the eastern Himalayas, Bhutan is bounded by China and India. Area: 46,100 sq km (17,800 sq mi). Pop. (1978 est.): 1,262,000, including Bhutia 60%, Nepalese 25%, and 15% tribal peoples. Official cap.: Thimphu (pop., approximately 10,000). Administrative cap.: Paro (population unavailable). Language: Dzongkha (official). Religion: approximately 75% Buddhist, 25% Hindu. Druk gyalpo (king) in 1978, Jigme Singye Wangchuk.

King Jigme Singye Wangchuk's visit to New Delhi in March 1978 resulted in an agreement with India for the sale of Bhutan's surplus forest products to other countries. Previously, forest products, Bhutan's main exports, were sold entirely to India, and the agreement was seen as a first step toward opening Bhutan's trade relations with other nations.

The king's visit, second since the Janata Party government was formed in India in March 1977, provided an opportunity to review Indian economic assistance during talks held between the king and the Indian ministers of finance and industry. India agreed to implement the Rs 1.5 billion (about U.S. $186 million) hydroelectric project in Chukha. When completed in 1984, the project would have a capacity of 336 Mw. Initially India was to bear the entire cost of the project and would buy its surplus power. A cement plant with a capacity of 100,000 metric tons, constructed by India, was scheduled to begin production at the end of 1978.

Indian Minister for Foreign Affairs Atal Bihari Vajpayee visited Thimphu during the year and assured the king of India's continued respect for Bhutan's separate identity. (GOVINDAN UNNY)

Billiard Games

Billiards. The Billiard Federation of USA played host to the 33rd world amateur Three-Cushion Billiards Championship, which was held in Las Vegas, Nev., during May 1978. Challenging the contingent of eight international billiard stars, led by 14-time champion Ray Ceulemans of Belgium, were four U.S. contestants, Frank Torres, Carlos Hallon, Al Gilbert, and Larry Johnson. The others included Nobuaki Kobayashi, the 1974 world champion from Japan; his countryman Junichi Komori; Muhammad Mustapha Diab of Egypt;

Belize: *see* Dependent States

Bermuda: *see* Dependent States

Bicycling: *see* Cycling

The 33rd world amateur Three-Cushion Billiards Championship was held in Las Vegas, Nev., in May, giving Americans the opportunity of seeing the legendary Ray Ceulemans of Belgium win his 15th title.

Humberto Suguimizu of Peru; Ludo Dielis of Belgium; Peter Thogersen of Denmark; and Galo Legarda of Ecuador.

From the first round Ceulemans set a blazing pace, scoring a 60–10 victory over Johnson in just 26 innings. In the next round he triumphed over Torres 60–14 in 27 innings, setting a new two-game world championship record of 2.264 points per inning. By the next to last round Ceulemans was already the undisputed winner of the crown for the 15th time in his career. Kobayashi, in second place with a loss and a tie, could not overtake the champion, even with a victory. In fact, Ceulemans finished off the final match 60–27 in 25 innings, the shortest match of the tournament. In doing so, he set a new world tournament record of 1.679 average per inning and 22 game points. Finishing in third place was Komori, while fourth place went to Dielis and fifth to Gilbert.

Following the tournament Ceulemans made a tour of several cities, giving those in the U.S. their first opportunity to observe his unequaled talent. The world tournament for 1979 was scheduled to take place in Peru.

Pocket Billiards. One hundred and forty-four finalists, the survivors of some 2,400 original contestants, participated in the second national Eight-Ball Tournament sponsored by the Billiard Congress of America during the first week of November in Louisville, Ky. Representing a 100% increase in contestants over the initial year, the players came from as far as Hong Kong, Newfoundland, and Sweden. The tournament also included a new and separate women's division of 26 finalists.

In the men's division defending champion Tom Kilburn of South Bend, Ind., was hard pressed to retain his title and was eliminated from the tournament at the three-quarter mark. By the last night of the three-day contest the two remaining combatants were fellow Floridians Bob Williams of West Palm Beach and Michael Carella of Tallahassee. The latter had been forced to fight his way through the losers' bracket to gain a chance at the title. In a sharply played contest Williams took the lead by winning the first game of the "race to seven"

championship match. Carella then cleared the table to take the next game. And so the match went, with near-perfect playing until a stymied break by Williams gave Carella an opportunity to forge ahead. He did exactly that, eventually winning the contest by seven games to five after Williams left a three-inch side-pocket shot hanging on the edge.

In the women's division two unheralded contestants from the Pacific coast startled the crowds by relegating the favourite, Gloria Walker, holder of women's world six-ball, eight-ball, and nine-ball titles, to third place. Kitty Stephens of San Francisco and Melodie Horn of Portland, Ore., began the final match. In a "race to five" the contestants traded games in the early stages. At three apiece Stephens cleared the table with a finesse that brought cheers from the stands. In what turned out to be the final game, Horn broke. She made two difficult shots and appeared to be in position to catch up with her opponent. Instead, she missed an open corner-pocket shot. Stephens came to the table and took command, clearing the table for the title.

The third World Open Pocket Billiards Championship took place in August at the Biltmore Hotel in New York City with 51 men and one woman participating. It was accompanied by an 8-woman invitational match led by U.S. Women's Open champion Jean Balukas. Balukas had the distinction of also playing in the Men's Open, having won a qualifying tournament as a "fill in" in Brooklyn. During the seven-day tournament the field of professional players was boiled down to the final foursome of defending champion Allen Hopkins, Ray Martin, Steve Mizerak, and Pete Margo. Playing almost flawless billiards in the semifinal round, Martin ran 99 and 54 to defeat Margo handily. Coming from the losers' bracket, Hopkins had to defeat Mizerak twice, 150–30 and 150–69, to earn a meeting with Martin in the final match. In the 200-point championship match Hopkins was leading 129–51 when a missed side-pocket shot brought Martin to the table. With a run of 50, followed shortly by another of 30, he was soon ahead, finally winning 200–154 for the title.

Balukas, while losing in the third round of the Men's Open, did continue to forge ahead in the Women's Invitational. Narrowly defeating Vicki Frechen, she went on to meet Billie Billing, who had triumphed over Gloria Walker twice in her bracket. Now in complete control, Balukas won 100–28 in the final.

In collegiate billiards the Association of College Unions-International held its annual National Intercollegiate Billiards Championships at Florida State University in Tallahassee in April. Bringing together the men and women winners of regional play-offs, the championship finals found Steven Cusick, a senior from the University of Illinois at Urbana, winning over David Yao of UCLA by a score of 100–44. In the women's division Maridana Heydon, a junior from Oregon State University, defeated Francis Cockrum from Northeastern Oklahoma State University, 50–31.

(ROBERT E. GOODWIN)

[452.B.4.h.v]

Bolivia

A landlocked republic in central South America, Bolivia is bordered by Brazil, Paraguay, Argentina, Chile, and Peru. Area: 1,098,581 sq km (424,165 sq mi). Pop. (1978 est.): 4,886,700, of whom more than 50% are Indian. Language: Spanish 78%, Quechua 15%, Aymara 7%. Religion (1975 est.): Roman Catholic 94.2%. Judicial cap.: Sucre (pop., 1976, 63,347). Administrative cap. and largest city: La Paz (pop., 1976, 654,713). Presidents in 1978, Col. Hugo Banzer Suárez to July 21 and Juan Pereda Asbún to November 24; head of the three-man military junta from November 24, Gen. David Padilla Arancibia.

Following Pres. Hugo Banzer's announcement on Dec. 1, 1977, that he would not run for president in the July 9, 1978, elections, Air Force Gen. Juan Pereda Asbún was nominated as official candidate of the ruling coalition. The period before the July elections was marked by intimidation of the opposition, fears of electoral fraud, and complaints of the government's overt illegal support of the official candidate. The elections themselves were marred by incidents of fraud, which were denounced by international and local observers. The total vote cast exceeded the number of registered voters by 50,000, and General Pereda himself requested annulment of the results: of the votes that had been counted he had gained 50.1%, with former president Hernán Siles Zuazo running second with 21.8%.

On July 19 the National Electoral Court voided the election, and new elections were ordered. President Banzer announced that he would leave his office on August 6 as planned. A military junta would likely exercise the presidency in the meantime. General Pereda then withdrew to Santa Cruz and organized a coup d'etat in cooperation with the Falange Socialista Boliviana, the Army under Gen. Alonso Villapando, and the Air Force. On July 21, after a 24-hour rebellion, Banzer resigned

Bolivia

BOLIVIA

Education. (1975) Primary, pupils 912,998, teachers 39,835; secondary, pupils 124,092, teachers 8,044; vocational, pupils 37,498, teachers 718; teacher training (1973), students 5,896, teachers 314; higher (including 9 universities), students c. 49,850, teaching staff (universities only, 1974) 2,270.

Finance. Monetary unit: peso boliviano, with (Sept. 18, 1978) an official rate of 20 pesos to U.S. $1 (free rate of 39.19 pesos = £1 sterling). Gold, SDR's, and foreign exchange (June 1978) U.S. $181.2 million. Budget (1977 actual): revenue 7,641,000,000 pesos; expenditure 10,954,000,000 pesos. Gross national product (1976) 58,109,000,000 pesos. Money supply (March 1978) 7,337,000,000 pesos. Cost of living (La Paz; 1975 = 100; April 1978) 117.9.

Foreign Trade. Imports (1976) U.S. $555 million; exports (1977) U.S. $600 million. Import sources: U.S. 26%; Argentina 15%; Brazil 14%; Japan 11%; West Germany 8%. Export destinations (1976): U.S. 34%; Argentina 23%; U.K. 9%. Main exports: tin 54%; crude oil 11%; natural gas 11%; tungsten 8%; zinc 7%; silver 5%.

Transport and Communications. Roads (1975) 37,075 km. Motor vehicles in use (1975): passenger 22,500; commercial 30,100. Railways: (1977) 3,787 km; traffic (1975) 310 million passenger-km, freight 465 million net ton-km. Air traffic (1977): 558 million passenger-km; freight 27.7 million net ton-km. Telephones (Jan. 1974) 49,000. Radio receivers (Dec. 1976) c. 426,000. Television receivers (Dec. 1976) c. 45,000.

Agriculture. Production (in 000; metric tons; 1977): barley 60; rice (1976) 113; corn (1976) c. 300; wheat (1976) c. 70; cassava (1976) c. 300; potatoes 679; sugar, raw value (1976) 213; bananas c. 250; coffee c. 17; cotton, lint c. 16; rubber c. 3. Livestock (in 000; 1976): cattle c. 2,926; sheep c. 7,767; goats c. 2,848; pigs c. 1,186; horses c. 360; asses c. 720.

Industry. Production (in 000; metric tons; 1976): cement 232; crude oil (1977) 1,623; electricity (kw-hr; 1975) c. 1,000,000; gold (troy oz; 1975) 53; tin 30; lead 16; antimony 15; tungsten (oxide content) c. 3; zinc 48; copper 4.8; silver (troy oz) c. 6,400.

amid threats that La Paz would be bombed. A state of siege was declared while General Pereda took power in La Paz. Banzer's plans to be a candidate in the next presidential election (splitting support for Pereda and thus making an opposition win likely) and his lack of progress in gaining Bolivian access to the sea probably were major factors in touching off the coup.

In August Pereda stated that new elections

Bolivia's new military junta are (from left to right): Gen. David Padilla Arancibia, Gen. Antonio Sempertegui, and Rear Admiral Moises Vásquez Sempertegui. The gesture they are exhibiting is a Bolivian way of showing approval.

would be held in 1980 and that he would not then be a candidate for the presidency. The repressive laws of compulsory civil service and laws of national security were withdrawn, and Bolivian universities were reopened. International recognition of the new regime was granted, and U.S. military and economic aid resumed, following a 25-day suspension. The delay of elections until 1980 was not acceptable to the military, and on November 24 Pereda was overthrown in a bloodless coup. Power was assumed by a three-man military junta headed by the army chief of staff, Gen. David Padilla Arancibia. Padilla said elections would be held on July 1, 1979, with the elected president assuming office on August 6. In December some disagreement within the junta over the question of the Army's "return to barracks" was reported.

Political uncertainty, export dependence on tin, and declining petroleum revenues undermined the five-year plan. The balance of payments deficit rose from $112 million in 1976 to $214 million in 1977. Mercedes Benz and Renault won contracts to produce light trucks and automobiles locally to fulfill Bolivia's motor-vehicle assignments under the Andean Group industrial program.

(MICHAEL WOOLLER)

Botswana

Botswana

A landlocked republic of southern Africa and a member of the Commonwealth of Nations, Botswana is bounded by South Africa, Namibia (South West Africa), Zambia, and Rhodesia (Zimbabwe). Area: 576,000 sq km (222,000 sq mi). Pop. (1978 est.): 766,000, almost 99% African. Cap. and largest city: Gaborone (pop., 1976 est., 36,900). Language: English (official) and Setswana. Religion: Christian 60%; animist. President in 1978, Sir Seretse Khama.

Border tension between Botswana's newly formed National Defence Force (NDF) and Rhodesian security forces developed during February 1978 as Botswana was increasingly used by guer-

Zimbabwean people huddle in a UN refugee camp in Francistown, Botswana, a temporary refuge from the fighting in southern Rhodesia.

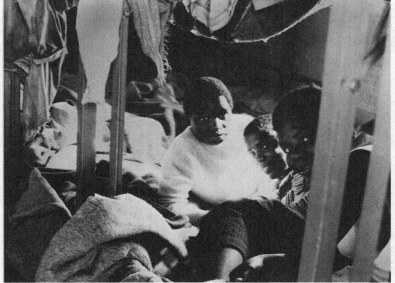

ADN-ZENTRALBILD/EASTFOTO

BOTSWANA

Education. (1977) Primary, pupils 137,290, teachers 4,-495; secondary, pupils 15,496, teachers 649; vocational, pupils 1,754, teachers 233; teacher training, students 646, teachers 46; higher, students 465, teaching staff 62.

Finance and Trade. Monetary unit: pula, with (Sept. 18, 1978) an official rate of 0.83 pula to U.S. $1 (free rate of 1.62 pula = £1 sterling). Budget (1977–78 est.): revenue 94.2 million pula; expenditure 73.3 million pula (excludes development expenditure: 65.8 million pula). Foreign trade (1975): imports 159.3 million pula (80% from South Africa); exports 105 million pula (47% to U.K., 24% to South Africa, 22% to U.S.). Main exports: meat and products 35%; diamonds 31%; nickel 21%.

Agriculture. Production (in 000; metric tons; 1976): sorghum 56; corn 62; millet c. 5; peanuts c. 7; beef and veal c. 46. Livestock (in 000; 1976): cattle c. 2,200; sheep c. 425; goats c. 1,050; chickens c. 560.

Industry. Production (in 000; 1976): diamonds 2,361 metric carats; copper ore (metal content; 1975) 11; nickel ore (metal content; 1975) 13; coal 224 metric tons; electricity (1975) 274,000 kw-hr.

rillas of the Zimbabwe (Rhodesia) People's Revolutionary Army. The conflict culminated in the abduction on March 30 of more than 400 black Rhodesian children (all but 27 later returned). On March 31 the NDF killing of an 18-year-old vacationing Briton, Nicholas Love, and his two South African companions heightened the diplomatic tension. During his visit to London in May the president, Sir Seretse Khama, expressed regret at the incident, and an official inquiry and trial of those responsible was promised.

Gaborone was the site in October of an unprecedented meeting between unionists affiliated with the Organization of African Trade Union Unity and South African black unionists.

Despite the establishment of the first resident Soviet ambassador in January, Botswana remained dependent upon aid from the West and South Africa. With the latter, a joint exploitation of the rich diamond deposit at Jwaneng, newly discovered by the De Beers Botswana Co., was developed to mutual profit. (MOLLY MORTIMER)

Bowling

Tenpin Bowling. WORLD. The Fédération Internationale des Quilleurs (FIQ), the governing body of pin bowling sports, reported at the end of the 1977–78 season 59 member federations and more than ten million individual members. The Bowling World Cup, held in London, was won by Arne Ström (Norway), who beat Philippe Dubois (France) 609 pins to 606. In the women's final Rea Rennox (Canada) defeated Lauren LaCost (U.S.), 570–542.

In the seventh American Zone championships, held in Panama in November 1977, U.S. bowlers swept all eight gold medals. Dale Euwer of Topeka, Kan., was the individual star with four gold medals. The men's eight-player event was won by the U.S. with 12,698, with Mexico runner-up at 12,-542; in the five-man event the U.S. bowled a new record of 6,102 pins, Guatemala finishing second with 5,647; in the men's doubles the U.S. won with a score of 2,585, defeating Venezuela by 14 pins; the all-events individual title was won by Euwer with 5,921, Wade Smith (U.S.) placing second with 5,788. In the women's division the U.S. sextet bowled 6,527, second place being taken by Canada with 6,404; in the five-player event the winning score of the U.S. team was 5,440, with Canada second at 5,371; in doubles the U.S. bowled 2,283 to win, and another U.S. pair finished second with 2,245; in the individual competition Cindy Schuble and Betty Brennan (both U.S.) finished first and second with 4,512 and 4,497.

A new tournament format adopted for FIQ championships was tried at the fifth Asian Zone championships held in August 1978 in Bangkok, Thailand. The number of bowlers on a team was reduced to six men and six women, events being singles, doubles, trios, fives, and masters for the 16 best men and women. In the men's division the Japanese dominated; they won the five-man competition with 5,689, while the Philippines placed second with 5,391; Singapore won the trios with 3,490, with Japan second at 3,399; the Japanese pair bowled 2,331 to win, Singapore finishing second with 2,312; a special singles competition included for the first time was won by Michio Matsubara (Japan) with 1,289, runner-up being Danny Fejeran (Guam) with 1,186. In the women's division Japan won the five-player event with 5,-524, with the Philippines second at 5,192; in the trios the Philippines won with 3,457, while Japan was second with 3,435; the Philippines won the doubles; and Bong Koo of the Philippines was the first singles champion, second place being won by Kumiko Inatsu (Japan). In the men's masters'

Mark Roth finished fourth in the Firestone Tournament of Champions. Roth set a record for earnings in 1978, winning more than $118,000 despite sore-thumb problems.

PROFESSIONAL BOWLERS ASSOCIATION

event Japan won all three medals; first place went to Kiyoshi Taneda with 410, second to Matsubara with 407, and third to Kosaku Tatemoto with 388. In the women's masters' event Ruth Guerster (Australia) won with 402, while Bong Koo finished second with 387.   (YRJÖ SARAHETE)

UNITED STATES. Mark Roth, a 27-year-old New Yorker whose persistent sore-thumb problems had become a part of Professional Bowlers Association (PBA) folklore, coped with his handicap well enough to win eight PBA tournaments in 1978 and set a record for single-season earnings. With several tournaments remaining, the right-hander had already won over $118,000, surpassing the $110,-883 total that Earl Anthony of Tacoma, Wash., had won in 1976. Roth rested his thumb by sitting out 9 of the first 30 PBA events but was virtually certain to be named Bowler of the Year for the second time in succession. Anthony, winner of the $30,000 first prize in the Firestone Tournament of Champions at Akron, Ohio, suffered a heart attack in mid-June. He was able to return to competition in late August, however, finishing in third place in a tournament at Waukegan, Ill.

In the 75th American Bowling Congress tournament, in St. Louis, Mo., Bill Beach of Sharon, Pa., was the only multiple winner, taking the singles title with 701 and the nine-game all-events championship with 1,941 in the Classic Division for professional bowlers. Steve Fehr and Dave Newrath, Cincinnati, Ohio, led the doubles entrants with 1,300, and the Untouchable Lounge, Kirksville, Mo., was the sponsor of the five professionals who won the Classic Division team championship with 2,911. Regular Division winners included: team, Berlin's Pro Shop, Muscatine, Iowa, 3,077; singles, Rich Mersek, Cleveland, Ohio, 739; doubles, Bob Kulaszewicz and Don Gazzana, Milwaukee, Wis., 1,352.

Membership in the Women's International Bowling Congress (WIBC) reached a record 4,209,-220. One of the year's most remarkable events in women's bowling occurred on June 12 in the City Employees' League in Santa Cruz, Calif. There, Diane Ponza, bowling just her ninth game in adult competition and using an eight-pound ball—half the allowable weight—rolled a 300. The perfect score was one of 49 bowled in WIBC-sanctioned play during the 1977–78 season, 15 over the record set in 1976–77. In the WIBC tournament at Miami, Fla., the Open Division winners were: team, Cook County Vending Co., Chicago, 2,956; singles, Mae Bolt, Berwyn, Ill., 709; doubles, Annese Kelly, New York City, and Barbara Shelton, Jamaica, N.Y., 1,211; all-events, Annese Kelly, 1,896. Division One champions included: team, Joyner Garden Center, Alexandria, Minn., 2,706; singles, Norma Walker, Tacoma, Wash., 659; doubles, Jeannie Hand, Fairview, Ill., and Judy Hart, Canton, Ill., 1,201; all-events, Sandy Klingshirn, Boca Raton, Fla., 1,852.

Duckpins. The Troc Pleasure Palace club of Baltimore, Md., bowled 2,271 to win the men's team championship in the 1978 National Duckpin Tournament. The women's team title was won by IBEW (International Brotherhood of Electrical Workers) Local No. 42, Glastonbury, Conn., with 2,129.

Cook County Vending Co. of Chicago won the Women's International Bowling Congress tournament. The winning team (left to right): Sandy Lutz, Kathy Klopp, Sheila Clegg (captain), Dee Sipos, and Joan Karge.

Other champions included: men's singles, Jim Simmons, Baltimore, 599; women's singles, Doris Gravelin, Jewett City, Conn., 493; men's doubles, Nick Tronsky, Kensington, Conn., and Dan Lopardo, Torrington, Conn., 993; women's doubles, Chickey Balesano and Cathy Dyak, Manchester, Conn., 838. The mixed championship team winner was Greenway No. 5, Glen Burnie, Md., with 2,161. (JOHN J. ARCHIBALD)

Lawn Bowls. At the Commonwealth Games at Edmonton, Alta., England's David Bryant won the singles championship for the third time. He also won the International Masters, beating Richard Folkins of the United States in the final at Worthing, England. D. McGill (Scotland) and W. Moseley (South Africa) were third and fourth, respectively. After 16 years Bryant remained the dominant figure in lawn bowls. Another world figure, Harry Reston of Scotland, announced his retirement from international competition and promptly won the Scottish National Singles title for the first time.

In the British Isles women's home internationals finals at Cardiff, Wales, Wales won the singles and the fours. Ireland was champion in the pairs competition. (C. M. JONES)

Brazil

A federal republic in eastern South America, Brazil is bounded by the Atlantic Ocean and all the countries of South America except Ecuador and Chile. Area: 8,512,000 sq km (3,286,500 sq mi). Pop (1977 est.): 113,208,500. Principal cities (pop., 1975 est.): Brasília (cap.; federal district) 763,300; São Paulo 7,198,600; Rio de Janeiro 4,857,700. Language: Portuguese. Religion: Roman Catholic 91%. President, in 1978, Gen. Ernesto Geisel.

Domestic Affairs. Dissatisfaction with the political system established in the country after the revolution of 1964 increased during the year. Students protested against the government's restrictive measures, and there were demands for

Brazil

Boxing:
see Combat Sports

immediate reform. Even members of the government party, the National Renewal Alliance (ARENA), expressed dissatisfaction with conditions and called for reforms. One ARENA leader declared publicly that unless the redemocratization of the nation came soon there would be an "explosion." Pres. Ernesto Geisel had consistently promised a gradual return to a "state of law" with a "perfecting" of the political institutions.

One of the most bitterly criticized measures was the so-called Institutional Act number 5 (AI-5). Adopted on Dec. 13, 1968, it gave the president power to cancel the mandate of any elected or appointed government official and to annul his political rights for a period of ten years. Those persons, known as *cassados* (the "annulled ones"), lost their right to participate in the political life of the nation permanently under article 185 of the constitution.

There were some dissidents who believed that President Geisel was too lenient toward subversive groups. Declaring himself dissatisfied with conditions, the former minister of the Army, Gen.

BRAZIL

Education. (1974) Primary, pupils 19,286,611, teachers 887,424; secondary, pupils 628,178; vocational, pupils 782,827; teacher training, students 270,723; secondary, vocational, and teacher training, teachers 156,174; higher, students 954,674, teaching staff 64,479.

Finance. Monetary unit: cruzeiro, with a free rate (Sept. 18, 1978) of 19.18 cruzeiros to U.S. $1 (37.58 cruzeiros = £1 sterling). Gold, SDR's, and foreign exchange (March 1978) U.S. $7,273,000,000. Budget (1977 actual): revenue 242,893,000,000 cruzeiros; expenditure 241,850,000,000 cruzeiros. Gross national product (1977) 2,286,700,-000,000 cruzeiros. Money supply (April 1978) 352.6 billion cruzeiros. Cost of living (São Paulo; 1975 = 100; May 1978) 268.8.

Foreign Trade. (1977) Imports 181,480,000,000 cruzeiros; exports 167,102,000,000 cruzeiros. Import sources: U.S. 20%; Saudi Arabia 11%; Iraq 9%; West Germany 8%; Japan 7%. Export destinations: U.S. 18%; West Germany 9%; The Netherlands 8%; Japan 6%; Italy 6%. Main exports: coffee 19%; soybeans 18%; iron ore 7%.

Transport and Communications. Roads (1976) 1,489,-064 km. Motor vehicles in use (1976): passenger 6,348,600; commercial 737,400. Railways: (1975) 33,000 km; traffic (1974) 10,649,000,000 passenger-km; freight 55,220,000,-000 net ton-km. Air traffic (1976): 10,366,000,000 passenger-km; freight 488 million net ton-km. Shipping (1976): merchant vessels 100 gross tons and over 538; gross tonnage 3,329,951. Telephones (Jan. 1977) 3,987,000. Radio receivers (Dec. 1975) 16,980,000. Television receivers (Dec. 1975) 10,680,000.

Agriculture. Production (in 000; metric tons; 1977): wheat 2,066; corn 19,122; rice 8,941; cassava (1976) 26,-816; potatoes 1,896; sweet potatoes (1976) c. 1,730; peanuts 395; sugar, raw value c. 8,400; dry beans 2,327; soybeans c. 12,100; coffee 950; cocoa 237; bananas 8,101; oranges 7,058; cotton, lint c. 570; sisal 225; tobacco 357; rubber c. 20; timber (cu m; 1976) c. 164,000; beef and veal 2,286; pork 834; fish catch c. 950. Livestock (in 000; 1976): cattle c. 97,000; pigs c. 36,800; sheep c. 17,300; goats c. 6,800; horses c. 9,600; chickens c. 300,000.

Industry. Fuel and power (in 000; metric tons; 1977): crude oil 8,700; coal c. 3,500; natural gas (cu m; 1976) c. 740,000; manufactured gas (cu m; 1976) c. 516,000; electricity (kw-hr; 1976) 88,380,000 (92% hydroelectric in 1975). Production (in 000; metric tons; 1977): pig iron c. 9,300; crude steel 11,172; iron ore (68% metal content; 1976) 67,100; bauxite (1976) c. 1,000; manganese ore (1976) 2,881; gold (troy oz) c. 180; cement c. 21,000; asbestos (1973) 819; wood pulp (1975) 1,301; paper (1975) 1,643; fertilizers (nutrient content; 1976–77) nitrogenous 195, phosphate c. 822; passenger cars (units) 464; commercial vehicles (units) 455. Merchant vessels launched (100 gross tons and over; 1977) 380,000 gross tons.

Sylvio da Frota, became the recognized leader of a dissenting right-wing group, which apparently included some high officers of the armed forces and a few members of Congress. Earlier, when Frota had publicly acknowledged that he was a candidate for the presidency in 1978, Geisel had promptly dismissed him from office. The president had repeatedly declared that no public discussion of the question of his successor would be tolerated before Jan. 1, 1978.

At a meeting with leaders of ARENA, on Dec. 1, 1977, President Geisel admitted that most emergency laws could now be considered "dispensable." The president also announced that Sen. Petrônio Portella had been entrusted with the mission of gathering suggestions from leaders of all classes regarding the reforms to be adopted.

On Jan. 5, 1978, Geisel declared before a group of leaders of ARENA that he had selected Gen. João Baptista da Figueiredo (*see* BIOGRAPHIES) to be the next president of the republic and Antonio Aureliano Chaves, governor of the state of Minas Gerais, to be the vice-president. At its national convention (April 8–9, 1978) ARENA endorsed the president's choice. General Figueiredo, who took part in the 1964 revolution, had served as the head of the National Intelligence Service since the beginning of Geisel's administration.

Gen. Hugo Abreu, head of the president's military office, resigned in January because, it was said, he disagreed with Geisel's choice. He became the leader of the National Redemocratization Front, which selected Gen. Euler Bentes Monteiro as an alternative candidate. The Front advocated immediate adoption of democratic practices.

The national Congress reopened on March 1, 1978. In June the authorities lifted the prior censorship of the press, which had existed for almost ten years. A package of reforms was presented to President Geisel on June 23 and introduced in Congress three days later. The reforms were to be adopted by Congress within 90 days as constitutional amendments. They included, among other provisions, the creation of a constitutional council and the revoking of all emergency laws.

On October 15 Figueiredo was elected president by a vote of 355–226 in the electoral college, composed of both houses of Congress and representatives of the state assemblies. He would take office March 15, 1979. Brazilians went to the polls on November 15 to elect all 420 members of the Chamber of Deputies, the lower house of Congress; 23 of the 67 senators; and 846 state legislators. At the year's end the final results were not yet available, but it appeared that the opposition Brazilian Democratic Movement had cut into the majority by which ARENA controlled Congress. Late projections of the vote showed the opposition with 191–193 of the deputies in the lower house to ARENA's 227–229. In the Senate ARENA held a strong majority of 47–20, but one-third of these were government appointees.

The Economy. The national economy was still staggering under the impact of the 1973 increase in the price of imported oil. Redoubled efforts were made to control the resulting high rate of inflation, which in mid-1978 was said to be about 35%. It was estimated to have been 38.3% for the 12-month period from July 1977 to June 1978. Exports continued to increase, especially those of manufactured products. Drastic measures were taken to curtail government expenditures, to decrease imports, to reduce traveling abroad, and to decrease the consumption of gasoline.

Despite all efforts to slow down the economy, growth was estimated at 5.6–6% for 1977. The foreign currency reserves were believed to have reached $8.2 billion by the middle of 1978. Exports of coffee, soybeans, and other agricultural products were greatly decreased by a severe drought early in 1978. The cruzeiro continued to be periodically devalued. On Sept. 15, 1977, it was set at 14.92/15.02 to one U.S. dollar. By August 1978 it had become 18.585/18.685.

Manaus, one of Brazil's burgeoning cities, is a seaport on the Amazon River 1,000 miles away from the ocean.

Foreign Relations. In 1978 President Geisel made official visits to Mexico (January 15–18), Uruguay (January 25–28), and West Germany (March 6–10). U.S. Pres. Jimmy Carter visited Brazil on March 29–31. His visit was said to have resulted in a better understanding of the two governments' points of view, some of which had seemed to be divergent.

Relations with Argentina were somewhat strained by conflicting interests regarding proposed plans for the construction of hydroelectric plants on the Paraná River. On July 3–4 an important treaty was signed at Brasília by the representatives of the eight nations with frontiers in the Amazon River valley. This treaty, called the Treaty of Amazonic Cooperation (Amazon Pact), provided for the exclusive occupation and development of the area by the signatory parties (Bolivia, Colombia, Ecuador, Guyana, Peru, Suriname, Venezuela, and Brazil).   (RAUL D'EÇA)

Bulgaria

Burma

Bulgaria

A people's republic of Europe, Bulgaria is situated on the eastern Balkan Peninsula along the Black Sea, bordered by Romania, Yugoslavia, Greece, and Turkey. Area: 110,912 sq km (42,823 sq mi). Pop. (1977 est.): 8,785,700, including 85.3% Bulgarians (but excluding some 210,000 Macedonians classified as Bulgarian according to official statistics), 8.5% Turks, 2.6% Gypsies, and 2.5% Macedonians. Cap. and largest city: Sofia (pop., 1975, 965,700). Language: chiefly Bulgarian. Religion: official sources classify 35.5% of the population as religious, although this figure is suspect since the regime promotes atheism. Of those who practice religion, it is estimated that 85% are Bulgarian Orthodox, 13% Muslim, 0.8% Jewish, 0.7% Roman Catholic, and 0.5% Protestant, Gregorian-Armenian, and others. First secretary of the Bulgarian Communist Party and chairman of the State Council in 1978, Todor Zhivkov; chairman of the Council of Ministers (premier), Stanko Todorov.

The propaganda war between Bulgaria and Yugoslavia heated up in 1978. Speaking on June 15 at Blagoevgrad, Bulgaria's chief of state, Todor Zhivkov, stated that Bulgaria was prepared "immediately and unconditionally" to sign a declaration with Yugoslavia on the inviolability of their frontiers and mutual renunciation of territorial claims. The Yugoslav Federal Secretariat for Foreign Affairs replied on June 29 that Zhivkov had said nothing about the basic problem affecting Bulgarian-Yugoslav relations, namely, that Bulgaria persistently denied the existence of the Macedonian national minority in Bulgaria and was pursuing a policy of assimilation; the Bulgarian offer would be meaningful only if Bulgaria accepted the existence of the Macedonian nation and of the Republic of Macedonia as a member of the Yugoslav federation.

Bulgaria countered on July 24 by declaring, first, that the population of the district of Blagoevgrad (formerly called Pirin Macedonia) always was and continued to be part of the Bulgarian nation; and,

second, that Bulgaria "recognizes the existing realities" in Yugoslavia and considers that "what nationalities exist on the territory of Yugoslavia is a purely internal question."

Bulgaria cooperated with West Germany in June when four suspected terrorists (one of them an escapee from West Berlin's Moabit Prison) were arrested at a Bulgarian Black Sea resort and returned to West Germany.

Georgi Markov (*see* OBITUARIES), a well-known writer who had defected from Bulgaria in 1969, died in London under mysterious circumstances on September 11. (*See* CRIME AND LAW ENFORCEMENT.)   (K. M. SMOGORZEWSKI)

Burma

A republic of Southeast Asia, Burma is bordered by Bangladesh, India, China, Laos, Thailand, the Bay of Bengal, and the Andaman Sea. Area: 676,-577 sq km (261,288 sq mi). Pop. (1978 est.): 33,550,000. Cap. and largest city: Rangoon (pop., 1973, 2.1 million). Language: Burmese. Religion (1977): Buddhist 80%. Chairman of the State

BURMA

Education. (1976–77) Primary, pupils 3,686,773, teachers 79,653; secondary, pupils 1,038,898, teachers 29,361; vocational, pupils 8,141, teachers 714; teacher training (1974–75), students 4,428, teachers 301; higher, students 84,981, teaching staff 3,319.

Finance. Monetary unit: kyat, with (Sept. 18, 1978) a free rate of 6.77 kyats to U.S. $1 (13.27 kyats = £1 sterling). Gold, SDR's, and foreign exchange (June 1978) U.S. $118.4 million. Budget (1976–77 est.): revenue 16,-677,000,000 kyats; expenditure 17,318,000,000 kyats.

Foreign Trade. (1977) Imports 1,320,200,000 kyats; exports 1,586,800,000 kyats. Import sources (1975): Japan 33%; China 9%; U.K. 8%; U.S. 7%; West Germany 7%; South Korea 5%. Export destinations (1975): Indonesia 14%; Singapore 13%; Sri Lanka 11%; Japan 10%; The Netherlands 6%; Mauritius 6%. Main exports: rice 56%; teak 25%; oilcakes 5%.

Transport and Communications. Roads (1975) 21,956 km. Motor vehicles in use (1976): passenger 37,800; commercial (including buses) 40,500. Railways: (1976) 4,347 km; traffic (1976–77) 2,781,000,000 passenger-km, freight 394 million net ton-km. Air traffic (1976): 168 million passenger-km; freight 1.2 million net ton-km. Shipping (1977): merchant vessels 100 gross tons and over 56; gross tonnage 67,502. Telephones (Jan. 1977) 31,500. Radio licenses (Dec. 1974) 659,000.

Agriculture. Production (in 000; metric tons; 1977): rice 9,460; dry beans $c.$ 181; onions $c.$ 104; bananas $c.$ 239; sesame seed 98; peanuts $c.$ 530; cotton, lint $c.$ 16; jute $c.$ 43; tobacco $c.$ 75; rubber $c.$ 16; timber (cu m; 1976) $c.$ 21,655; fish catch (1976) 502. Livestock (in 000; March 1977): cattle $c.$ 7,696; buffalo $c.$ 1,789; pigs $c.$ 1,800; goats $c.$ 587; sheep $c.$ 206; chickens $c.$ 17,000.

Industry. Production (in 000; metric tons; 1977): crude oil 1,301; electricity (excluding most industrial production; kw-hr) $c.$ 920,000; cement 268; lead concentrates (metal content; 1976) 3.2; zinc concentrates (metal content; 1976) 4.1; tin concentrates (metal content) $c.$ 0.3; tungsten concentrates (oxide content; 1976) 0.2; nitrogenous fertilizers (nutrient content; 1976–77) 55.

Council in 1978, U Ne Win; prime minister, U Maung Maung Kha.

In elections to the People's Assembly (parliament) on Jan. 1–15, 1978, all 464 seats were won by candidates of the ruling Burma Socialist Program Party, the only approved political party in the country. There were no rival candidates. The new People's Assembly held its first session on March 2 and reelected U Ne Win chairman and president and Gen. U San Yu general secretary of the State Council. It also chose a 17-member Council of Ministers, headed by U Maung Maung Kha as prime minister, and 19 deputy ministers.

With the economy showing no significant improvement, the government in February appealed to the Burma Aid Group in Paris for assistance of U.S. $250 million to $300 million. The group, sponsored by the World Bank, responded politely, although no concrete commitments were made. In 1976–77 the group had given Burma $200 million.

U Ne Win's two visits to Peking in 1977 were followed by Chinese Vice-Premier Teng Hsiao-p'ing's visit to Rangoon in January 1978. Despite improved relations, there was nothing to indicate that China had stopped aiding guerrillas of the Burmese Communist Party, who continued to menace security. Relations with Bangladesh were strained by a mass exodus of Muslims from Burma across the border into that country. Claiming that many of them had originally entered Burma illegally, Burma in July agreed to the repatriation of all "lawful Burmese nationals." By November some 5,000 had returned.   (GOVINDAN UNNY)

Burundi

Burundi

A republic of eastern Africa, Burundi is bordered by Zaire, Rwanda, and Tanzania. Area: 27,834 sq km (10,747 sq mi). Pop. (1978 est.): 4,068,000, mainly Hutu, Tutsi, and Twa. Cap. and largest city: Bujumbura (pop., 1976 est., 157,100). Language: Kirundi and French. Religion: Roman Catholic 61%; most of the remainder are animist; there is a small Protestant minority. President in 1978, Lieut. Col. Jean-Baptiste Bagaza; prime minister, Lieut. Col. Edouard Nzambimana.

Burundi's payment to Tanzania of TShs 3,750,-000 in compensation for its raids into Tanzanian territory in 1973 began a new era of cooperation between the two countries, intensified by the breakdown of the East African Community and marked by the visit to Burundi in May 1978 of

BURUNDI

Education. (1975–76) Primary, pupils 130,046, teachers (1974–75) 4,159; secondary, pupils 7,143, teachers (1971–72) 343; vocational, pupils 982, teachers (1971–72) 290; teacher training, students 5,381, teachers (1971–72) 243; higher, students 649, teaching staff (1974–75) 133.

Finance. Monetary unit: Burundi franc, with (Sept. 18, 1978) an official rate of BurFr 90 to U.S. $1 (free rate of BurFr 174.77 = £1 sterling). Gold, SDR's, and foreign exchange (June 1978) U.S. $72,750,000. Budget (1977 actual): revenue BurFr 7,216,300,000; expenditure BurFr 7,-003,700,000.

Foreign Trade. (1977) Imports BurFr 6,676,000,000; exports BurFr 8,511,000,000. Import sources (1976): Belgium-Luxembourg 18%; France 13%; West Germany 11%; Iran 8%; The Netherlands 6%; Italy 6%; Kenya 5%; U.S. 5%. Export destinations (1976): U.S. 43%; West Germany 17%; Belgium-Luxembourg 5%; U.K. 5%. Main export coffee 94%.

Agriculture. Production (in 000; metric tons; 1977): corn $c.$ 140; cassava (1976) $c.$ 896; potatoes (1976) $c.$ 149; sweet potatoes (1976) $c.$ 842; sorghum $c.$ 120; dry beans $c.$ 153; bananas $c.$ 932; coffee $c.$ 22; cotton, lint (1976) $c.$ 2. Livestock (in 000; Dec. 1975): cattle 800; sheep 311; goats 653; pigs 46.

The Irish technique of cutting peat is demonstrated to Burundi nationals. Burundi has large deposits of valuable peat that have never been tapped.

CAMERA PRESS/PHOTO TRENDS

Tanzania's president, Julius Nyerere. The old Tanzanian Central Railway, refurbished with Canadian finance, helped transport landlocked Burundi's exports and oil supply. Together with Rwanda and Zaire, Burundi and Tanzania formed the Community of the Great Lakes, with plans to develop the natural gas deposits of Lake Kivu. A treaty signed near Rusomo Falls by Burundi, Rwanda, and Tanzania set up joint management and development of the Kagera River basin.

The 1978–82 five-year plan launched by Prime Minister Edouard Nzambimana in a January speech called for a unified national effort in overcoming food shortages and diversifying exports. The government hoped that major foreign investment would aid urgent agricultural and transport projects. West Germany promised DM 38 million for road transport and rural electrification projects, while the EEC agreed to finance the development of peat from the Akanyaru basin as a main source of future energy. (MOLLY MORTIMER)

Cambodia

Cambodia

A republic of Southeast Asia, Cambodia (officially Democratic Kampuchea) is the southwest part of the Indochinese Peninsula, on the Gulf of Thailand, bordered by Vietnam, Laos, and Thailand. Area: 181,035 sq km (69,898 sq mi). Pop. (1977 est.): 8,580,000 according to official figures, although foreign observers estimated that figure to be overstated by as much as three million persons. It is estimated to comprise: Khmer 93%; Vietnamese 4%; Chinese 3%. Cap.: Phnom Penh (pop., 1976 est., between 40,000 and 100,000). Language: Khmer (official) and French. Religion: Buddhist. Head of state in 1978, Khieu Samphan; premier, Pol Pot.

Striving to break out of its isolationist shell during 1978, Cambodia found its steps dogged by a continuing reputation for excessive cruelty at home and by its protracted border dispute with Vietnam.

Vice-Premier and Foreign Minister Ieng Sary,

Members of a commune south of Phnom Penh are put to work digging an irrigation canal. The photograph was taken by a Yugoslav journalist who was permitted to enter Cambodia early in the year.

UPI COMPIX

CAMBODIA

Education. (1973–74) Primary, pupils 429,110, teachers 18,794; secondary, pupils 98,888, teachers 2,226; vocational, pupils 4,856, teachers 202; teacher training, students 553, teachers 18; higher, students 11,570, teaching staff 276.

Finance. Monetary unit: riel, with (Sept. 18, 1978) a nominal free rate of 1,200 riels to U.S. $1 (2,351 riels = £1 sterling); the general internal use of currency was suspended from 1975, a system of rationing being in use. Budget (1974 est.): revenue 22.8 billion riels; expenditure 71 billion riels.

Foreign Trade. (1973) Imports 14.2 billion riels; exports 2,732,000,000 riels. Import sources: U.S. c. 69%; Thailand c. 11%; Singapore c. 5%; Japan c. 5%. Export destinations: Hong Kong c. 23%; Japan c. 22%; Malaysia c. 18%; France c. 12%; Spain c. 10%. Main export rubber 93%.

Transport and Communications. Roads (1976) c. 11,000 km. Motor vehicles in use: passenger (1972) 27,200; commercial (including buses; 1973) 11,000. Railways: (1977) c. 612 km; traffic (1973) 54,070,000 passenger-km, freight 9,780,000 net ton-km. Air traffic (1975): 42 million passenger-km; freight 400,000 net ton-km. Inland waterways (including Mekong River; 1977) c. 1,400 km. Telephones (Dec. 1975) 71,000. Radio receivers (Dec. 1975) 110,000. Television receivers (Dec. 1974) 26,000.

Agriculture. Production (in 000; metric tons; 1976): rice c. 1,800; corn c. 70; bananas c. 90; oranges c. 34; dry beans c. 17; rubber c. 15; jute c. 3. Livestock (in 000; 1976): cattle c. 1,900; buffalo c. 870; pigs c. 900.

traveling almost constantly, established fresh contacts with Eastern European, nonaligned, and Asian countries. Cambodia's immediate neighbours in the Association of Southeast Asian Nations received special attention. In May agreement was reached to resume economic and trade links with Singapore after a three-year break. This was followed by the appointment of the first Malaysian ambassador to Phnom Penh. Contacts with Thailand led to a significant improvement in relations by July, despite sporadic violence on the Cambodian-Thai border, a steady outflow of refugees into Thailand, and suspicions of collusion between Khmer Rouge elements and Thai Communist insurgents. In August there were reports that Phnom Penh was looking into the possibility of joining the Lower Mekong Development Planning Project, comprising Thailand, Laos, and Vietnam.

There was little improvement in the world's view of Cambodia as a repressive state. In April U.S. Pres. Jimmy Carter described the government as the worst violator of human rights in the world, and Britain asked the UN Human Rights Commission to undertake an investigation. Western sources maintained that one million–two million of Cambodia's claimed population of eight million had died of hunger and disease or in purges since the Communist takeover. In September former president Lon Nol, emerging from his seclusion in the U.S., put the figure at three million.

Impressions of excessive harshness were only strengthened when Premier Pol Pot gave what amounted to the first exposition of Cambodia's state philosophy. In an unprecedented interview in March, he told visiting Yugoslav journalists that his country was developing a new kind of socialism for which there was no model. To achieve its objective, the leadership was abolishing all vestiges of the past such as educational institutions, money, cities, and the family.

In the border war with Vietnam, the advantage swung to the Vietnamese. In December it was reported that a pro-Vietnam Khmer force had been established and that the Vietnamese had penetrated into eastern Cambodia.

The quarrel with Vietnam underlined the preeminence of China in Cambodian affairs. Ieng Sary visited Peking several times. A military team headed by Defense Minister Son Sen went to China in July, and Chinese technical teams were busy throughout the year assisting the government's reconstruction efforts.   (T. J. S. GEORGE)

Cameroon

A republic of west Africa on the Gulf of Guinea, Cameroon borders on Nigeria, Chad, the Central African Empire, the Congo, Gabon, and Equatorial Guinea. Area: 465,054 sq km (179,558 sq mi). Pop. (1978 est.): 7,980,700. Cap.: Yaoundé (pop., 1976, 313,700). Largest city: Douala (pop., 1976, 458,400). Language: English and French (official), Bantu, Sudanic. Religion: mainly animist, with Roman Catholic (24%), Protestant, independent Christian, and Muslim minorities. President in 1978, Ahmadou Ahidjo; prime minister, Paul Biya.

Legislative elections on May 28, 1978, resulted in victory for the 120 deputies nominated by the only legal party, the Union Nationale Camerounaise, whose candidates gained 99.98% of the votes cast.

Although Pres. Ahmadou Ahidjo refused to commit his country to any grouping too closely identified with France, he was anxious to maintain relations with the former colonial power, with francophone African states, and with the European Economic Community. In April he discussed the French intervention in Chad with French Pres. Valéry Giscard d'Estaing.

CAMEROON

Education. (1975–76) Primary, pupils 1,122,900, teachers 22,209; secondary, pupils 106,266, teachers 3,309; vocational, pupils 31,135, teachers 1,145; teacher training, students 1,284, teachers 132; higher, students 7,187, teaching staff 376.

Finance. Monetary unit: CFA franc, with (Sept. 18, 1978) a parity of CFA Fr 50 to the French franc and a free rate of CFA Fr 218.81 to U.S. $1 (CFA Fr 428.75 = £1 sterling). Budget (1976–77 est.) balanced at CFA Fr 128 billion.

Foreign Trade. (1976) Imports CFA Fr 221 billion; exports CFA Fr 160 billion. Import sources (1976): France 45%; U.S. 8%; West Germany 7%; Japan 6%; Italy 5%. Export destinations (1976): France 25%; The Netherlands 23%; West Germany 9%; Italy 6%; U.S.S.R. c. 5%; Gabon 5%. Main exports (1976): coffee 32%; cocoa 20%; timber 10%.

Transport and Communications. Roads (1975) 43,500 km. Motor vehicles in use (1975): passenger 51,949; commercial 28,953. Railways: (1977) 1,173 km; traffic (1976) 270 million passenger-km, freight 442 million net ton-km. Telephones (June 1973) 22,000. Radio receivers (Dec. 1974) 603,000.

Agriculture. Production (in 000; metric tons; 1977): corn c. 360; millet c. 360; sweet potatoes (1976) c. 160; cassava (1976) c. 800; bananas c. 105; peanuts c. 193; coffee c. 90; cocoa c. 90; palm kernels c. 47; palm oil c. 82; rubber c. 16; cotton, lint c. 20; timber (cu m; 1976) c. 8,252. Livestock (in 000; Dec. 1975): cattle c. 2,655; pigs c. 412; sheep c. 2,105; goats c. 1,633; chickens c. 9,382.

Industry. Production: aluminum (1977) 57,000 metric tons; electricity (1976) 1,330,000,000 kw-hr.

An important landmark for the country's economy was its entry into the "club" of African oil producers. In 1978 Cameroon was expected to export 800,000 metric tons of crude oil, and this figure was expected to double in 1979.

(PHILIPPE DECRAENE)

Cameroon

Canada

Canada is a federal parliamentary state and member of the Commonwealth of Nations covering North America north of conterminous United States and east of Alaska. Area: 9,976,139 sq km (3,851,809 sq mi). Pop. (1978 est.): 23.5 million, including (1971) British 44.6%; French 28.7%; other European 23%; Indian and Eskimo 1.4%. Cap.: Ottawa (metro pop., 1977 est., 702,200). Largest cities: Toronto (metro pop., 1977 est., 2,849,000); Montreal (metro pop., 1977 est., 2,809,900). Language (mother tongue; 1976 census): English 61%; French 26%; others 13%. Religion (1971): Roman Catholic 46%; Protestant 42%. Queen, Elizabeth II; governor-general in 1978, Jules Léger; prime minister, Pierre Elliott Trudeau.

Canada

Domestic Affairs. On April 20, 1978, Pierre Elliott Trudeau celebrated his tenth anniversary as prime minister of Canada. Although he was now fourth among Canadian prime ministers in length of service and one of the longest serving world leaders, Trudeau found little comfort in the anniversary. There were many signs that English-speaking Canadians were beginning to turn away from his leadership. The most striking came on October 16, when 15 by-elections to fill vacant seats in Parliament were held across Canada. Trudeau and the governing Liberal Party were decisively rebuffed, with 10 of the 15 seats going to the official opposition, the Progressive Conservatives. During the year a Liberal government was swept from office in Nova Scotia, while that in Prince Edward Island (the only Liberal government left on the provincial level) was almost dislodged. In Saskatchewan the Liberal Party was annihilated, leaving only two Liberal members in legislatures west of the Great Lakes.

Problems of national unity still loomed, with the separatist administration in Quebec preparing a referendum for 1979 on the proposed link of "sovereignty-association" with the rest of Canada. Economic conditions in 1978 were disappointing. Unemployment stood at record levels, the Canadian dollar had sunk to its lowest point since the depression of the 1930s, and the cost of living was beginning to climb again after three years of controls. The Trudeau Cabinet seemed tired and indecisive, unable to formulate new policy initiatives and inept in administration. The prime minister had decided not to call a general election in 1978, but he would have to do so by 1979.

The October by-elections were a rude shock to the Liberals. They suffered a net loss of five seats, although they did take one from the Conservatives in Quebec. The Conservatives won six large urban districts in the vital Toronto-Hamilton area. The Liberals' share of the popular vote fell from 41% in the last general election in 1974 to 30%, while the

ULUSCHAK—EDMONTON JOURNAL, CANADA/ROTHCO

"All very well, but will we have a
COUNTRY for the constitution by
1981?"

Conservatives gained 8% to win 48% of the total. The Liberals still held a majority in Parliament, with 136 seats to 97 for the Tories; 17 New Democratic Party members, 9 Social Credit representatives, and 5 independents made up the remainder of the 264-seat House of Commons.

The four provincial elections in 1978 offered no solace to the Liberals. The first, in Prince Edward Island on April 24, saw Alex Campbell's Liberal administration, after 12 years in office, fall from 24 to 17 seats in the 32-member legislature. The Conservative opposition grew from 8 to 15. On September 11 Campbell announced his resignation from the premiership and from politics. His successor was Finance Minister Bennett Campbell (no relation). The Liberal defeat in Nova Scotia flowed from voter dissatisfaction with a government that had been in power for eight years, but it also reflected anti-Trudeau sentiment. In the September 19 election the Conservatives won 31 of

the 52 seats in the legislature, which had been enlarged by 6 seats. The Liberals fell from 30 to 17 seats, while the New Democratic Party won 4 seats, a gain of one from its previous showing. Conservative leader John Buchanan succeeded Gerald Regan as premier on October 5. Saskatchewan was the third province to go to the polls. On October 18 Premier Allan Blakeney's New Democratic Party administration gained a comfortable victory. The NDP won 44 seats, compared with the 39 it had held previously, while the Conservatives increased their standing from 7 to 17. Both parties gained at the expense of the Liberals, who had formed the government as late as 1971. Going into the election with 11 seats, the Liberals lost them all. Blakeney's campaign had emphasized the need for legislation to assure provincial control over natural resources.

The fourth contest was in New Brunswick on October 23, when Premier Richard Hatfield's Con-

CANADA

Education. (1976–77) Primary, pupils 2,753,553, teachers (including preprimary; 1972–73) 142,900; secondary, vocational, and teacher training, pupils 2,577,190, teachers (1970–71) 101,844; higher (including 45 main universities), students 613,120, teaching staff 50,003.

Finance. Monetary unit: Canadian dollar, with (Sept. 18, 1978) a free rate of Can$1.17 to U.S. $1 (Can$2.29 = £1 sterling). Gold, SDR's, and foreign exchange (June 1978) U.S. $4,743,000,000. Budget (1977–78 actual): revenue Can$40,520,000,000; expenditure Can$46.7 billion. Gross national product (1977) Can$207,710,000,000. Money supply (April 1978) Can$26,950,000,000. Cost of living (1975 = 100; June 1978) 126.4.

Foreign Trade. (1977) Imports Can$42,-070,000,000; exports Can$44,199,000,000. Import sources: U.S. 70%; EEC 8%. Export destinations: U.S. 70%; EEC 10%; Japan 6%. Main exports: motor vehicles 23%; metal ores 6%; machinery 6%; nonferrous metals 6%; timber 5%; newsprint 5%; wood pulp 5%; natural gas 5%. Tourism (1976): visitors 13,002,-000; gross receipts U.S. $1,641,000,000.

Transport and Communications. Roads (main; 1975) 860,719 km. Motor vehicles in use (1975): passenger 8,870,000; commercial 2,112,000. Railways (1976): 70,471 km; traffic 2,942,000,000 passenger-km, freight (1975) 197,089,000,000 net ton-km. Air traffic (1977): 24,910,000,000 passenger-km; freight 620 million net ton-km. Shipping (1977): merchant vessels 100 gross tons and over 1,283; gross tonnage 2,822,948. Shipping traffic (includes Great Lakes and St. Lawrence traffic; 1977): goods loaded 118,296,-000 metric tons, unloaded 58,334,000 metric tons. Telephones (Jan. 1977) 13,785,600. Radio receivers (Dec. 1975) 21.9 million. Television receivers (Dec. 1975) 9,390,000.

Agriculture. Production (in 000; metric tons; 1977): wheat 19,651; barley 11,515; oats 4,303; rye 392; corn 4,303; potatoes 2,488; tomatoes c. 393; apples 402; rapeseed 1,776; linseed 610; soybeans 517; tobacco c. 103; beef and veal 1,139; pork c. 548; timber (cu m; 1976) 132,393; fish catch (1976) 1,136. Livestock (in 000; Dec. 1976): cattle 13,717; sheep 418; pigs 6,170; horses (1975) c. 345; chickens c. 85,779.

Industry. Labour force (Dec. 1977) 10,612,000. Unemployment (Dec. 1977) 8.3%. Index of industrial production (1975 = 100; 1977) 108.5. Fuel and power (in 000; metric tons; 1977): coal 23,201; lignite 5,479; crude oil 64,680; natural gas (cu m) 79,-040,000; electricity (kw-hr) 316,549,000 (74% hydroelectric and 4% nuclear in 1975). Metal and mineral production (in 000; metric tons; 1977): iron ore (shipments; 61% metal content) 54,460; crude steel 13,632; copper ore (metal content) 782; nickel ore (metal content; 1976) 263; zinc ore (metal content) 1,301; lead ore (metal content) 327; aluminum (1975) 878; uranium ore (metal content; 1976) 4.8; asbestos (1976) 1,550; gold (troy oz) 1,750; silver (troy oz) 42,600. Other production (in 000; metric tons; 1977): cement 9,922; wood pulp (1975) 14,707; newsprint 8,155; other paper and paperboard (1975) 3,160; sulfuric acid (1976) 2,840; synthetic rubber 238; passenger cars (units) 1,162; commercial vehicles (units) 613. Dwelling units completed (1977) 251,000. Merchant vessels launched (100 gross tons and over; 1977) 181,000 gross tons.

servative administration, in office since 1970, won a close victory over the Liberal opposition. The Conservatives took 30 seats to the Liberals' 28, giving Hatfield his third term as leader of the government. The major parties tied in the popular vote with 44.5% each, leaving only a small fraction for the New Democratic Party and the Parti Acadien, which had campaigned for a separate province for the French-speaking Acadians.

Although the election results showed that English-speaking Canadians disapproved of the Trudeau administration and only Quebec remained loyal, it was premature to conclude that this represented a break between English- and French-speaking Canada. After ten years, many voters felt the Trudeau government had been in power too long. But whether a protest vote in by-elections could be turned into a government defeat remained to be seen. The Progressive Conservatives, under their 39-year-old leader from Alberta, Joseph Clark, seemed to offer a possible alternative government. The party was handicapped in that it held only two seats in Quebec, and it urgently needed to build up support in that province.

Francis Fox resigned as solicitor general on January 27, after a revelation of personal misconduct before he entered the Cabinet, and Jean-Jacques Blais took on the politically sensitive portfolio, which involved responsibility for the penitentiary service and the Royal Canadian Mounted Police. Blais's job as postmaster general was given to Gilles Lamontagne, a former mayor of Quebec City. On August 2 Ron Basford, minister of justice and a ten-year veteran of the Cabinet, announced he was returning to private life. Otto Lang, serving as minister of transport, assumed the additional responsibility of the justice portfolio. Lang also continued as minister responsible for the Canadian Wheat Board.

The government suffered an embarrassing loss on September 8 when John Munro, minister of labour for almost six years, resigned because he had "transgressed" guidelines set down by Trudeau to govern relations between Cabinet ministers and the judiciary. Munro revealed that he had unthinkingly called a provincial court judge on behalf of a constituent. An acting replacement was named in the person of André Ouellet, minister of

Premiers of Canada's ten provinces met in Ottawa with Prime Minister Pierre Elliott Trudeau in February to seek a cure for Canada's ailing economy.

state for urban affairs. A larger reorganization occurred on November 24 when Trudeau named Robert Andras to the newly created post of president of the Board of Economic Development Ministers. The new superministry would be responsible for coordinating the federal government's industrial strategy. Three new members were appointed to the Cabinet, while six other ministers were given different or additional portfolios.

In the realm of federal-provincial affairs, Prime Minister Trudeau unveiled an ambitious plan to revise Canada's constitution. His proposals, introduced into Parliament on June 20, envisaged a two-stage process of constitutional change. The first phase, to be enacted by July 1, 1979, included a charter of rights and freedoms, among them minority language rights, that would be binding on the federal government. Provinces could agree to accept the provisions of this charter, although there would be no obligation upon them to do so. The federally appointed Senate would be replaced by a new House of the Federation, designed to reflect regional and provincial interests. Members would be named, in equal numbers, by the federal House of Commons and by the provincial legislatures, according to party standings. For the first time the chamber would have authority to approve Supreme Court appointments and nominations to many federal agencies. A system to give the provinces a voice in Supreme Court appointments also formed part of the Trudeau package.

A second phase of reform, targeted for 1981, would see change in the more difficult area of the division of legislative powers between Ottawa and the provinces. This phase would also include agreement on an amending formula for the constitution and adoption of a procedure whereby Canada's constitution would cease to be a statute of the British Parliament.

The scheme represented Trudeau's third attempt to achieve a national consensus on changes in the British North America Act, which currently served as Canada's basic law. The plan got a cool reception from the provincial premiers when they met for their annual conference at Regina, Sask., on August 9–10. Significantly, Premier René Lévesque of Quebec took an active part in the discussion and allied his province with the others in a common front against Ottawa.

A federal-provincial conference held in Ottawa October 30–November 1 failed to achieve agreement on Trudeau's constitutional reforms. It decided to set up a committee of designated Cabinet ministers to consider the proposed charter of human rights as well as the distribution of powers and the reform of Canada's federal institutions. Another meeting would be held in early 1979. In the face of this setback, it appeared unlikely that Prime Minister Trudeau's timetable for constitutional change could be met.

A first ministers' conference on the economy, November 27–29, also ended indecisively. Few concrete steps were taken to boost economic growth. The federal government proposed deferring for six months a $1 a barrel increase in the price of Alberta oil, scheduled to begin Jan. 1, 1979. The provinces were reluctant to accept this arrangement because some of the grants they received from Ottawa were tied to the income of the "have" provinces. Alberta, one of this group, would suffer a lower provincial income because of the deferral, thus reducing equalization grants to some of the other provinces.

The Economy. The sluggish state of the economy reflected adversely on the Trudeau government. There seemed little prospect of attaining the 4.5–5% rate of real economic growth targeted by the Finance Ministry. The actual increase was expected to be around 3%. Foreign trade, especially sales to the U.S., held up well; the merchandise surplus for the first eight months of the year was higher than that for 1977. However, domestic demand was slack, reflecting a slight decline in the real income of consumers. Even temporary measures of tax relief failed to provide stimulation.

Yet the economic picture was not entirely dark. While unemployment reached levels comparable to those of the '30s (the seasonally adjusted rate for September was 8.5%), more jobs were created in the first five months of 1978 than in the whole of 1977. The consumer price index was 8.6% higher in September than it had been a year before, but much of this growth reflected higher food prices — a component that was largely beyond Canada's control since much of the country's fresh fruits and vegetables was purchased abroad. Overall, the economy was more competitive in 1978, with wage and salary settlements moderating significantly. Wage and price controls, imposed in October 1975, were lifted, for the most part, in April.

Much attention was directed to the poor health of the Canadian dollar, which in early October fell below 84 U.S. cents, the lowest in 45 years. The main causes were a current account deficit expected to exceed the 1977 level and loss of investor confidence. The government resorted to heavy foreign borrowing to prop up the dollar, sold off foreign exchange reserves, and raised the Bank of Canada lending rate six times during the year. On November 5 the rate was increased to 10.75%.

Prime Minister Trudeau returned from the Bonn, West Germany, economic summit conference in July determined to support increased economic growth. In a dramatic speech on August 1 he outlined a reordering of government priorities and promised a $2 billion reduction in the current and planned expenditures of his government. No growth in the federal public service would be permitted over the next year, and some functions now undertaken by the government would be returned to the private sector. The Post Office, long a scene of labour unrest leading to interrupted service, would be transformed from a government department into an autonomous crown corporation. On August 24 Jean Chrétien, the finance minister, announced that family allowance payments for seven million children would be cut by $20 a month beginning in 1979. On September 1 it was announced that unemployment insurance regulations would be tightened in order to reduce the number of claimants by 10%. Restraint in government spending was to be a principal weapon of the Trudeau government in the fight against inflation.

Finance Minister Chrétien presented a cautious

Vladimir Souvorov takes a last look at Canada before leaving the country. The second secretary for the Soviet embassy in Ottawa and 12 other Soviets were expelled for espionage.

first budget to Parliament on April 10. Rejecting the large income tax reductions proposed by the opposition, Chrétien decided to give an immediate fillip to the economy by compensating the provinces for a reduction in their consumer sales taxes. They were given the option of reducing the tax by 2% for a nine-month period (chosen by Saskatchewan and British Columbia) or 3% for six months (selected by Ontario, Manitoba, and the Atlantic Provinces). Quebec did not immediately announce its response, and Alberta and the two federal territories did not levy a sales tax. Chrétien agreed to pay about two-thirds of the cost, with the provinces making up the remainder. With revenues of only $36 billion predicted for the fiscal year 1978–79 and expenditures set at $46.9 billion, Chrétien faced a large deficit on government operations. Taking nonbudgetary items into account, the deficit was estimated at about $11.5 billion.

The Chrétien budget, although approved by the House of Commons, led to an acrimonious controversy with Quebec. The provincial finance minister, Jacques Parizeau, cut Quebec's entire 8% sales tax on selected items, mostly manufactured in Quebec, such as textiles, clothing, shoes, and home furniture. The tax was to be removed from these articles until March 31, 1979, and from hotel rooms permanently. Parizeau then demanded the same compensation for his tax changes that had been offered to the other provinces.

After a long controversy, Chrétien decided to pay $186 million directly to Quebec taxpayers who had been on the federal tax rolls in 1977. In addition, Ottawa agreed to pay $40 million directly to Quebec, using the formula that applied to other provinces. After having accepted the plan on June 7, Parizeau rejected it a week later, stating that he would prefer the money to be regarded as a tax credit for 1978 and to have the taxpayers pay it directly to the Quebec government. Chrétien rejected this proposal, and the tax rebates were sent to Quebec taxpayers in due course.

A second federal budget was brought down on November 16 in an effort to provide mild stimula-

tion to the economy. The manufacturers sales tax was lowered from 12 to 9%, providing a tax reduction of about $1 billion, while taxpayers were also helped by a doubling of the maximum employment expense deduction for federal income taxes. There were also changes in federal tax credits for businesses. The budget endeavoured to steer a course between promoting domestic demand too strongly and harming the recently acquired cost competitiveness of the Canadian economy. The tax concessions pushed the cash deficit to $12.1 billion for fiscal 1978–79.

Foreign Affairs. Canada's relations with the Soviet Union were strained during 1978. On January 24 a Soviet satellite powered by about 100 lb of enriched uranium fell through the atmosphere and disintegrated over the sparsely populated Northwest Territories and northern Saskatchewan. Two U.S. airplanes equipped with radiation sensors joined the search, along with low-flying Canadian Hercules aircraft. Radioactive debris from the fallen satellite was later found near Fort Reliance at the northeast corner of Great Slave Lake. About 220 lb of fragments were recovered from the five-ton satellite, but the reactor core was not found. Canada stated it would claim part of the more than $12 million spent in the search from the Soviet Union under a 1972 international convention. (*See* SPACE EXPLORATION.)

On February 9, while the search was going on, Canada expelled 13 Soviet officials for plotting to infiltrate the Royal Canadian Mounted Police security service. Two of the officials had already left Canada, but the remaining 11 were ordered to leave within a short period.

Canada was a member of a five-nation team (with Britain, France, West Germany, and the U.S.) established to work out independence arrangements for Namibia (South West Africa). The plan called for majority African rule based on elections supervised by UN troops. (*See* SOUTH AFRICA.) Canada also took part in the UN peacekeeping mission in southern Lebanon, supplying 80 signal personnel in April.   (D. M. L. FARR)

PETRODOLLARS ON THE PRAIRIE

by Peter Ward

The strongest regional base of Canada's uncertain economy is located in Alberta, the westernmost of the three Prairie Provinces, where vast reserves of crude oil and natural gas have created a strong centre of prosperity. Alberta's metamorphosis from a frontier pastoral land to a burgeoning industrial region began when the first oil flowed from discoveries in the Leduc Field in 1947. The economic boom came of age in 1973, when the price rise forced by the Organization of Petroleum Exporting Countries (OPEC) magnified the value of Alberta's energy reserves sixfold in five years. OPEC's exercise in price fixing also altered the face of Canada by dramatically shifting the centre of economic gravity westward.

Black Gold. Revenues from crude oil and gas have made Alberta's taxes and unemployment rate the lowest in Canada and its growth and optimism the highest. Royalty payments are rolling into the provincial coffers at a rate of nearly $4 billion annually, enough to cover more than half the province's yearly budget and provide capital for a fund designed to ensure its continued prosperity.

In 1978 the provincial budget of Alberta showed a surplus of $780 million, compared with a deficit of more than $12 billion for the federal government. Each year more than $1 billion in energy revenue goes into the Alberta Heritage Savings Trust Fund, which was expected to have a balance of $4.5 billion at the end of fiscal 1978–79. AHSTF money is used to make loans to other provinces, to finance social improvements of long-term benefit to Alberta, and to invest in projects that will help establish a solid economic base for the province. Alberta is the only Canadian province without a sales tax, and its citizens pay the lowest medical insurance premiums in the nation. Its unemployment rate in the summer of 1978 was 4.7%, compared with a national average of 8.4%, and its economy was expected to grow by more than 6% in 1978, at least two percentage points higher than the growth rate of Canada as a

whole. Between 1968 and 1978 Alberta's gross provincial product rose nearly 500% to more than $25 billion, substantially above the increases for all of Canada and for Ontario, the most industrialized province. With 1.9 million people—8% of Canada's population—Alberta was responsible for 11% of the nation's GNP, and the proportion is growing larger each year.

Under these circumstances, it is natural that Canadian population and investment would shift westward, a trend that has been accelerated by the large amounts of capital leaving the old financial centre of Montreal because of nervousness over Quebec separatism. Ontario has been the prime beneficiary of Montreal's decline, but Alberta has been the psychological winner. Ontario and Quebec are interdependent in many ways, whereas Alberta's prosperity is internally generated.

Presiding over this flourishing scene is Premier Peter Lougheed, whose Progressive Conservative government came to power in 1971 and, as of 1978, held 69 of the 75 seats in the provincial legislature. Like the oil sheikhs half a world away, his goal is to strengthen the economy and provide for the future through diversification, and he hopes thereby to increase Alberta's voice within the Canadian confederation partnership and to diminish the traditional dominance of Ontario and Quebec. Lougheed reacts with growing annoyance to federal policies that he feels limit Alberta's scope for development. He wants the rules changed to encourage industrialization of the province by improving the access of Alberta-based companies to U.S. and central Canadian markets, and he has a six-point development plan to accomplish these aims.

The Two-Price Policy. Alberta's petroleum resources were initially developed through a national two-price system for oil and through construction of a network of pipelines from Alberta to the industrial centres of Ontario. All of Canada west of Kingston, Ont., was forced to use Canadian-produced oil although, until 1973, the domestic product cost $1 a barrel more than imported crude. Before the 1973 price spiral began, gasoline and fuel oil cost as much as five cents a gallon less in eastern Canada than in the west because the products sold in the east were refined from cheaper oil imported from the Middle East or Venezuela. Thus provided with a captive market, Alberta's producing companies were encouraged to expand exploration. As a result, Canada, overall, was self-sufficient in energy during the late 1960s and early 1970s, with more domestic oil being exported to the U.S. Midwest than was imported to meet the needs of eastern Canada.

The Canadian constitution places natural resources under provincial jurisdiction. At pre-1973

Peter Ward operates Ward News Service in the Parliamentary Press Gallery, Ottawa, and is a contributing editor for Canadian Business *magazine.*

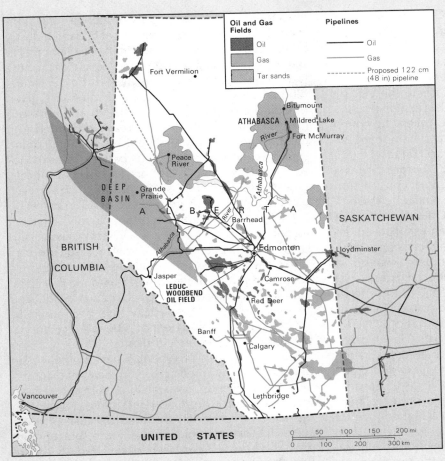

Oil and Gas Fields
- Oil
- Gas
- Tar sands

Pipelines
- Oil
- Gas
- Proposed 122 cm (48 in) pipeline

Fort Vermilion

ATHABASCA
Bitumount
Mildred Lake
Fort McMurray
Athabasca River

Peace River

DEEP BASIN
Grande Prairie

ALBERTA

Barrhead
Athabasca River

SASKATCHEWAN

BRITISH COLUMBIA

Edmonton
Lloydminster

Jasper

LEDUC-WOODBEND OIL FIELD

Camrose

Red Deer

Banff

Calgary

Vancouver

Lethbridge

UNITED STATES

0   50   100   150   200 mi
0   100   200   300 km

prices, oil produced a modest amount of royalty revenue for Alberta. The neighbouring province of Saskatchewan, with smaller deposits of primarily heavy oil, also received some benefit from the federal two-price policy. So did British Columbia, which has considerable reserves of natural gas.

As the price of crude oil on world markets rose after 1973, Canadian crude suddenly became cheaper than foreign oil. Alberta sought to have its oil priced at world levels, but federal policy held it down, giving Canadian industry an international advantage at the expense of Alberta's royalty revenues. Oil exported to the U.S.—by that time a million barrels daily—was subject to an oil export tax that effectively brought the price up to world levels, and revenue from this tax was used to subsidize the more expensive foreign crude oil used in eastern Canada. With Alberta's reluctant agreement, one price level for oil, below the international price, came into force for all of Canada.

Lougheed was displeased with the reduced royalty revenue, and he was also angered by the federal government's demands for a share in the "windfall" increase in Alberta's oil profits. The federal government refused to allow oil companies to deduct royalty payments made to provincial governments from

income when calculating federal corporation tax. In addition, a federal crown corporation, Polysar Ltd., built a huge petrochemical complex at Sarnia, Ont., using Alberta natural gas as a feedstock. Lougheed saw this as taking industrial development and jobs away from Alberta and giving them to Ontario. His answer was to begin building a petrochemical complex in Alberta as a cooperative venture between government and private industry, and he vowed that no more natural gas would be exported to eastern Canada for petrochemical complexes there.

Tug of War with Ottawa. Western Canadians have always complained that unfair federal regulations benefit Ontario and Quebec, but they have been outnumbered. Politically, the majority population of central Canada calls the tune. In the 1974 general election, the Liberal Party retained power while winning only 13 out of 68 parliamentary seats in the four western provinces. In the next election, Ontario and Quebec will be entitled to 75 and 95 seats, respectively, out of a national total of 282.

Energy disputes between Alberta and the federal government during 1978 centred on natural gas. Major new discoveries were made in Alberta during 1977–78, at the same time the U.S. was considering a pipeline through Canada to bring Alaskan natural gas south to the lower 48 states. Construction of the pipeline would provide a further boost to Alberta's economy, although in the long run it would decrease the value of the new natural gas finds.

Lougheed's response was to seek federal permission to sell some surplus natural gas to the U.S. on short-term contracts. He knew that exploration activity in Alberta would decrease unless he found markets for new gas discoveries, and he wanted the high prices available through export contracts to the U.S. He also wanted to offer U.S. border points a short-term gas supply, so that eventual construction of the Alaska natural gas pipeline would be assured. But the National Energy Board in Ottawa, in an effort to preserve resources for Canadian use, had not issued new natural gas export contracts since 1970. Futhermore, the federal government sought to revoke an agreement with Alberta on natural gas pricing that set the price level at 85% of the energy equivalent value of crude oil. The price of oil as of Aug. 1, 1978, in Canadian dollars, was $13.84 per barrel in Toronto and $14.15 per barrel in Chicago.

In short, Ottawa's aim was to create markets for Alberta's new gas discoveries in Ontario and Quebec by lowering the price of natural gas to Canadians. Alberta, not unnaturally, would prefer to earn more royalty revenue by selling at a higher price to the U.S. Ottawa controls exports of energy outside Canada through the National Energy Board; Alberta controls exports of energy outside the province. As of late 1978, industry spokesmen predicted that the standoff disagreement might be settled by winter, with a compromise that would allow some exports to the U.S. but would effectively lower the price of natural gas to Canadians.

Another grievance of western Canadians involves the prevailing system of freight rates. Railroad freight rates increase from west to east according to the degree of "value added" in manufacturing. Thus raw materials can be shipped from west to east at a cheaper rate than manufactured goods, while finished products travel to the west from industrialized Quebec and Ontario more cheaply than if they were being shipped in the other direction. Such policies inhibit the creation of any western manufacturing industry and, combined with tariff rates set by the federal government, force western Canadians to buy domestically produced goods, even though comparable products are available at lower prices in the U.S. Lougheed is a leader in the fight to change the rules—a necessary first step in his six-point plan for development of the province.

Six Steps Toward the Future. Lougheed's first aim is to establish an industry for processing Alberta's diversified agricultural products within the province itself. Freight rates and tariffs must also be changed if the second priority of Alberta's development scheme is to be met: a secondary industry based on crude oil and natural gas. Alberta hopes to sell to central Canada and to the West Coast of the U.S., which Lougheed considers to be "a natural Alberta market." Petroleum production has given Alberta the beginnings of a research and development capability, which has already expanded into the computer-electronics field. As his third point, Lougheed hopes that the R&D base can be expanded especially in such sectors as pharmaceuticals. Export volumes for such products are small, minimizing Alberta's geographic disadvantages.

The fourth development priority involves making Alberta the financial centre for western Canada, and Lougheed has been deeply involved with European bankers who have expressed interest. In addition, a considerable but undetermined amount of capital has flowed to Alberta from Quebec and Ontario, and Japanese investors, especially, are becoming involved in the development of Alberta's recreational possibilities, Lougheed's fifth step.

The sixth prong of Alberta's development plan depends on continued activity in the Canadian Arctic. Alberta intends to maintain its role as the gateway to Canada's north. Oil and gas exploration in the western Arctic has declined because of more accessible energy finds in the south, but enough proven reserves have been discovered to ensure that the slackening of activity is only temporary. One of Lougheed's tactics to ensure Alberta's continued influence in northern development was the purchase in 1977 of Pacific Western Airlines, a major regional airline in western Canada.

Eventually the royalty bonanza from conventional crude oil and natural gas will run dry, but Alberta has additional energy reserves that guarantee the future. More than half the coal reserves in Canada are located in Alberta, and so is the largest single deposit of petroleum-bearing sand. The Athabasca Tar Sands in the northeastern part of the province contain estimated oil reserves of up to 600,000,000,000 bbl—more than in the entire Middle East—some 250,000,000,000 bbl of which can be recovered with existing techniques. Extraction of usable oil from the tar-like sands is expensive and difficult, but it is becoming economically feasible as world oil prices rise. The Great Canadian Oil Sands Co. Ltd., which began production in 1967, turned a profit for the first time in 1974, after the OPEC oil crisis. In 1978 the much larger Syncrude Ltd. plant began producing 129,000 bbl daily, and two more extraction plants are in the planning stage. And when the day comes that oil is too precious to burn as a fuel, Alberta plans to be there, equipped to exploit the possibilities of the future in petrochemicals.

Cape Verde

An independent African republic, Cape Verde is located in the Atlantic Ocean about 620 km (385 mi) off the west coast of Africa. Area: 4,033 sq km (1,557 sq mi). Pop. (1978 est.): 311,000. Cap.: Praia (pop., 1970, 21,500). Largest city: Mindelo (pop., 1970, 28,800). Language: Portuguese. Religion: mainly Roman Catholic. President in 1978, Aristide Pereira; premier, Maj. Pedro Pires.

The November 1977 congress of the African Party for the Independence of Guinea-Bissau and Cape Verde (PAIGC) failed to approve the hoped-for merger with Guinea-Bissau because of differences between the two countries. One of the problems, to which Pres. Aristide Pereira of Cape Verde drew attention after being reelected secretary-general of PAIGC, was the extreme poverty of drought-stricken Cape Verde, even compared with Guinea-Bissau. The congress also appeared uncertain about the ideological line it should adopt, although it rejected with equal firmness Marxism-Leninism and Western-style democracy. It did, however, pledge support to all liberation movements, especially the Polisario guerrillas of Western Sahara.

Cape Verde continued to rely mainly on the Western powers for food supplies, and President Pereira announced that his country's ties with the U.S. were to be strengthened. A similarly pro-Western line was taken by Premier Pedro Pires in mid-1978 when he laid the blame for international clashes in Africa on the Africans themselves. They had sought outside aid in interfering in the internal affairs of their neighbours, he said, and had wasted money on the purchase of arms after accepting conditions from the suppliers that were not to Africa's advantage.   (KENNETH INGHAM)

CAPE VERDE
Education. (1976–77) Primary, pupils 56,000, teachers 1,346; secondary, pupils 6,827, teachers 253; vocational, pupils 677, teachers 80; teacher training, pupils 370, teachers 32.

Finance and Trade. Monetary unit: escudo Caboverdiano, at par with the Portuguese escudo and with a free rate (Sept. 18, 1978) of 45.65 escudos to U.S. $1 (89.45 escudos = £1 sterling). Budget (1974 est.) balanced at 265,120,000 escudos. Foreign trade (1976): imports 911.4 million escudos; exports 48,030,000 escudos (excluding transit trade). Import sources: Portugal 58%; The Netherlands 5%. Export destinations: Portugal 63%; Angola 14%; Zaire 5%; U.K. 5%. Main exports: fish 29% (including shellfish 16%); bananas 19%; salt 9%.

Transport. Ships entered (1972) vessels totaling 5,977,000 net registered tons; goods loaded (1975) 20,000 metric tons, unloaded 145,000 metric tons.

Central African Empire

The landlocked Central African Empire is bounded by Chad, the Sudan, the Congo, Zaire, and Cameroon. Area: 624,977 sq km (241,305 sq mi). Pop. (1978 est.): 1,912,000 according to estimates by external analysts; recent official estimates range up to 1,100,000 persons higher. Cap. and largest

---

CENTRAL AFRICAN EMPIRE
Education. (1974–75) Primary, pupils 215,887, teachers 3,137; secondary, pupils 18,781, teachers 345; vocational (1973–74), pupils 1,729, teachers (1973–74) 141; teacher training, students 539, teachers 47; higher, students 318, teaching staff (1971–72) 6.

Finance. Monetary unit: CFA franc, with (Sept. 18, 1978) a parity of CFA Fr 50 to the French franc and a free rate of CFA Fr 218.81 to U.S. $1 (CFA Fr 428.75 = £1 sterling). Budget (1977 est.) balanced at CFA Fr 17.6 billion.

Foreign Trade. (1976) Imports CFA Fr 13.2 billion; exports CFA Fr 12,504,000,000. Import sources: France 45%; West Germany 11%; The Netherlands 5%; South Africa 5%. Export destinations: France 44%; Italy 14%; Belgium-Luxembourg 9%. Main exports: coffee 33%; timber 17%; diamonds 17%; cotton 17%.

Agriculture. Production (in 000; metric tons; 1977): millet c. 45; cassava (1976) c. 850; corn (1976) 38; sweet potatoes (1976) c. 61; peanuts c. 40; bananas c. 73; coffee c. 10; cotton, lint c. 17. Livestock (in 000; 1976): cattle c. 610; pigs c. 62; sheep c. 76; goats c. 566; chickens c. 1,243.

Industry. Production (in 000; 1975): diamonds (metric carats) c. 338; cotton fabrics (m) 6,000; electricity (kw-hr) 52,000.

Cape Verde

Central African Empire

Chad

city: Bangui (pop., 1968, 298,600). Language: French (official); local dialects. Religion: animist 60%; Christian 35%; Muslim 5%. Emperor, Bokassa I; premiers in 1978, Ange Patassé and, from July 14, Henri Maïdou.

In his first major ministerial reshuffle since his coronation in 1977, Emperor Bokassa I in July 1978 increased his Cabinet from 23 to 29 and appointed Henri Maïdou premier to replace Ange Patassé (said to be receiving medical treatment in Switzerland).

The country's foreign relations were marked by less imperial caprice than previously, although Bokassa did declare the European Economic Community's diplomatic representative in Bangui "undesirable." In June he granted a diamond-mining concession of more than 30,000 sq km to Israeli Gen. Samuel Gonen.   (PHILIPPE DECRAENE)

Chad

A landlocked republic of central Africa, Chad is bounded by Libya, the Sudan, the Central African Empire, Cameroon, Nigeria, and Niger. Area: 1,284,000 sq km (495,755 sq mi). Pop. (1978 est.): 4,285,000, including Saras, other Africans, and Arabs. Cap. and largest city: N'Djamena (pop., 1975 est., 224,000). Language: French (official). Religion: Muslim 52%; animist 43%; Roman Catholic 5%. President in 1978, Brig. Gen. Félix Malloum; premiers, Brigadier General Malloum and, from August 29, Hissen Habré.

The major political event of 1978 was the appointment on August 29 of Hissen Habré (see BIOGRAPHIES), formerly leader of the Toubou rebellion, as premier. A cease-fire agreement had been reached on January 22 at Khartoum, Sudan, although fighting had continued and many French women and children had been evacuated from Chad in April. In naming Habré, Pres. Félix Malloum took the opportunity to reshuffle his Cabinet and reorganize the Army. But disagreement soon arose between the president and Habré, whose entry into the government did not end clashes be-

---

A.F.P./PICTORIAL PARADE

Hissen Habré, former rebel leader in Chad, became premier in August. He stands (centre left) with Pres. Félix Malloum (centre right) and members of the Cabinet.

tween the nationalists of the Chad National Liberation Front (Frolinat) and the Army. Thirty persons were killed in August in hostilities within the Front itself. Urban terrorism also persisted, and a hand grenade exploded in the capital on August 19. A Frolinat faction operating on the Nigerian border near Lake Chad kept two civilians (Christian Masse of France and André Kümmerling, a Swiss) hostage from January 18 to April 14.

In September Malloum paid an official visit to Peking seeking aid, but France continued to be Chad's chief support, maintaining a force of some 1,200 French soldiers as well as a squadron of Jaguar fighter-bombers. In November Malloum was received in Paris by Pres. Valéry Giscard d'Estaing. (PHILIPPE DECRAENE)

CHAD

Education. (1975–76) Primary, pupils 213,283, teachers 2,528; secondary, pupils 12,382, teachers 528; vocational, pupils 675, teachers (1965–66) 30; teacher training (1973–74), students 199, teachers 26; higher, students (1975–76) 2,200, teaching staff (1973–74) 94.

Finance. Monetary unit: CFA franc, with (Sept. 18, 1978) a parity of CFA Fr 50 to the French franc and a free rate of CFA Fr 218.81 to U.S. $1 (CFA Fr 428.75 = £1 sterling). Budget (1977 est.) balanced at CFA Fr 16,182,000,000. Cost of living (1975 = 100; Dec. 1977) 117.2.

Foreign Trade. (1976) Imports CFA Fr 27,593,000,000; exports CFA Fr 14,861,000,000. Import sources (1975): France 37%; Nigeria 10%; The Netherlands 7%; U.S. 6%; U.K. 5%; Cameroon 5%. Export destinations (1975): Nigeria 20%; France 7%; Congo 5%. Main exports (1975): cotton 69%; meat 6%.

Chemistry

Discoveries of "organic metal" compounds, chemical lasers, and a silicate sieve numbered among the noteworthy events in chemistry during the past year. To these were added the archaeological implications of a snip of hair from an Egyptian mummy, exciting finds in interstellar chemistry, and an important chemical anniversary.

Chemical Industry: see Industrial Review

Organic Chemistry. The year 1828 traditionally marks the birth of organic chemistry, when the pioneering German chemist Friedrich Wöhler reported the first laboratory synthesis of a naturally occurring organic compound: the transformation of ammonium cyanate into urea. Interestingly, 150 years later the nature of this reaction was still being debated.

The study of mechanism is fundamental to chemistry; indeed, in October Peter Mitchell of Glynn Research Laboratories in the U.K. was awarded the Nobel Prize for Chemistry for his research into the mechanism of energy supply in living cells. His theory, called chemiosmotic coupling, relates to the way in which chemical energy is stored and used to form the energy-rich compound adenosine triphosphate, or ATP.

Perhaps the most complex chemical synthesis of the year—that of erythronolide B—was announced in July by Elias Corey and co-workers from Harvard University. This compound (1) is the biological precursor for the erythromycins, an important family of broad-spectrum antibiotics. Close runners-up were the syntheses of the potent antibiotics mitomycin A by Yoshito Kishi of Harvard and thienamycin by David Johnston of Merck, Sharp and Dohme Research Laboratories. Another notable synthesis was that of a form of naloxone, a compound structurally related to the opiates that competes with them in the body to counteract their effects. One of the most structurally interesting new compounds was kekulene (2), a 12-ring "superbenzene" prepared by H. A. Staab and his team at the Max Planck Institute in Heidelberg, West Germany.

Many organic molecules are chiral; *i.e.*, they exist in mirror-image forms (isomers) that differ in the manner of left- and right-handed gloves. Chirality in an organic molecule is due usually to the presence of one or more carbon atoms to which are attached four different substituent groups. Incorporating chirality into a compound often results in low yields of optically active products. (Members of chiral pairs are said to be optically active because they can rotate the plane of a beam of polarized light.) Ernest Eliel and his group from the University of North Carolina, however, succeeded in achieving an almost 100% yield of atrolactic acid methyl ester (3) by a series of highly stereospecific reactions—ones dependent on the spatial arrangement of the atoms in the reactants.

Recent improvements in synthesis have come by employing novel reagents and from new concepts in synthesis design, such as the biomimetic approach, in which chemists try to mimic the biosynthesis of natural products. Interest was increasing in the use of enzymes and microorganisms for these syntheses. George Whitesides and co-workers from the Massachusetts Institute of Technology, for example, developed a process by which enzymes can be immobilized on a synthetic gel and used to make relatively large amounts of ATP from adenosine and acetyl phosphate. Several companies were also exploiting immobilized enzymes, including Snamprogretti SpA in Italy, which used them to produce a special milk for people unable to tolerate milk sugar, or lactose.

Another burgeoning field of development was polymer chemistry, some new products being a transparent form of nylon with good mechanical and electrical properties, a polyoxyethylene stearate for preventing glass bottles from breaking, a "barrier" polymer impermeable to gases, and an electrically conducting polymer for use in reprographic processes. Electrical conduction was a feature of recent investigations on "organic metals," polymers that possess some of the electrical and optical properties of metal atoms in bulk. These could be made from doped polyacetylene and formed into thin films to replace wire in simple electrical circuits. Their discoverers, Alan MacDiarmid and his group from the University of Pennsylvania, expected to produce films with electrical properties ranging from insulator to semiconductor to metal.

Physical Chemistry. In the past few years many of the considerable advances made in understanding the physical principles underlying chemical phenomena have relied on the development of lasers, instrumentation, and computer analysis. Working on gas-phase reaction kinetics, H. Hippler and his team from the University of Göttingen, West Germany, studied the decomposition of cycloheptatriene and several derivatives caused by intense bursts of laser light. They finally confirmed a theory advanced years ago that more complex molecules take longer to decompose. In the field of solution kinetics, micelles—aggregates of detergent-like molecules that mimic enzyme sites in biological systems—proved responsible for promoting the fastest transfer of protons (hydrogen ions) so far observed. As part of their work Janos Fendler and Jose Escabi-Perez of Texas A & M University showed that certain micelles form a sphere containing a tiny "pool" of water in which the chemistry differs markedly from that of bulk water.

Theoretical investigations of chemical bonding made steady progress as the computers that carry out lengthy calculations on small molecules became more sophisticated. Spectroscopy, however, was still providing a practical route to the study of bonding. Typically, G. Trudeau and his team at the University of Montreal used infrared spectroscopy to prove that, of a range of fluorocarbon anesthetics, the most potent are those that break the hydrogen bonds of proteins on the surface of cell membranes and then link to the surface by their own hydrogen bonds.

Spectroscopy continued to be used for determining structures and identifying molecules. Interstellar chemistry provides clues about the evolution of stars, the solar system, and the universe, and during the past decade radio astronomers have employed microwave spectroscopy to identify nearly 50 molecules in the space between stars. In the past year methane was detected outside the solar system by scientists at Kitt Peak Observatory in the U.S. More recently cyanotetra-acetylene (HC_9N)— the largest known interstellar molecule—was identified by Harold Kroto and his team at the University of Sussex, England.

Important practical developments emerged from the field of photochemistry in 1978, including an unprecedented reaction observed by Bernhard Kraeutler and Allen Bard of the University of Texas. They found that illumination of acetic acid containing pellets of a semiconductor, n-TiO_2, surprisingly produced methane and carbon dioxide. The semiconductor acted as a "molecular electrolytic cell," the illuminated side being at a

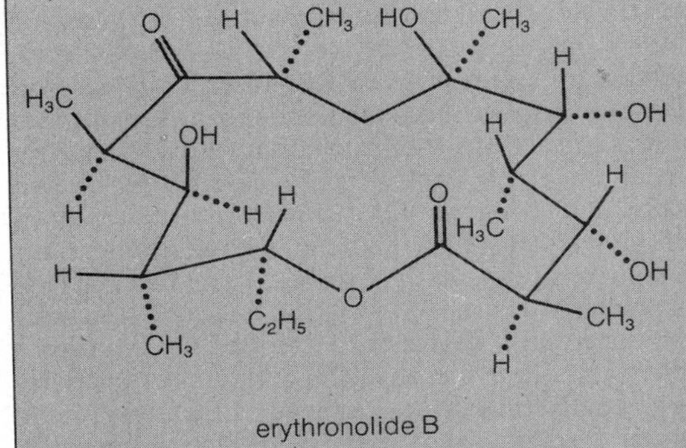

erythronolide B

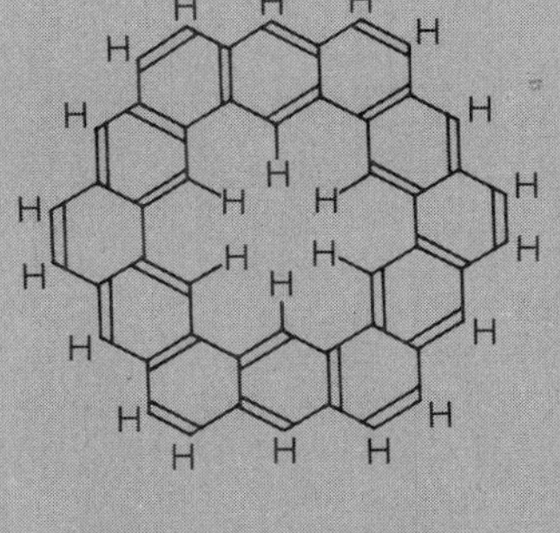

kekulene

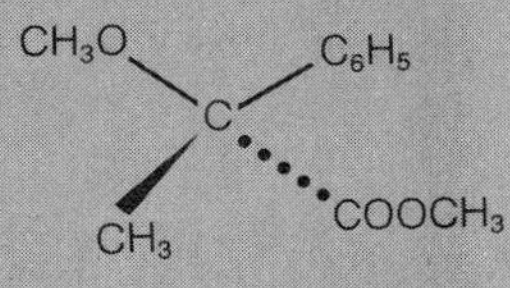

S—(+) atrolactic acid methyl ester

different electrochemical potential relative to the dark side. Several new theories relating to photochemistry were also proposed. Heavy debate concerning the mechanism of human vision prompted fresh ideas from Aaron Lewis of Cornell University, Ithaca, N.Y., and later from Arie Warshel of the University of Southern California. Both investigators concentrated on the first stages of the process, considering that the crucial changes in rhodopsin, a purple pigment found in the rods of the retina, occur before the well-characterized transformation of its pigment-carrying portion, retinal, from one isomer to another.

Solid-state lasers have been increasingly employed in chemistry since the late 1960s because their high light intensities alter thermal equilibriums in solutions and gases such that reactions occur which are otherwise unlikely or impossible. One application of the technique is laser impurity separation. Scientists at Bell Laboratories, Murray Hill, N.J., used lasers to purge trace impurities from silane, a compound of silicon and hydrogen, thereby improving the performance of silicon semiconductors that rely on silane for one stage of their manufacture.

Inorganic Chemistry. In February E. M. Flanagan and his team of chemists at Union Carbide Corporation, Tarrytown, N.Y., announced the preparation of silicalite, a stable form of silica with unusual solid-state properties. This new material has a network of intersecting channels that endow it with the characteristics of a "molecular sieve" such as zeolite. When added to mixtures of benzene and water, for example, silicalite traps the benzene while allowing the water to pass through its micropores. Unlike other molecular sieves, silicalite has potential applications to wastewater treatment; zeolites, by contrast, are commonly employed as drying agents. Recently Joseph Shabtai of the Weizmann Institute in Israel encapsulated hydrogen in zeolites in his attempt to store the gas for use as a multipurpose fuel.

Particularly striking catalytic properties were found for metal cluster compounds, which are molecules made up generally of three or more metal atoms surrounded by other groups or ions, called ligands, to form polyhedral arrays. Such

arrangement of rhodium atoms in carbonyl clusters

$[Rh_{13}(CO)_{24}H_3]^{-2}$

4 $[Rh_{15}(CO)_{27}]^{-3}$

is their importance that in March the American Chemical Society devoted a large symposium to this topic. In key papers at that meeting, Albert Cotton of Texas A & M University described the chemistry of molybdenum and tungsten clusters; Paolo Chini of the University of Milan, Italy, reported the largest known cluster containing 19 platinum atoms, and Geoffrey Ozin of the University of Toronto spoke of "naked" clusters, which contain groups of metal atoms with no ligands. The arrangement of rhodium atoms in two large clusters synthesized by Chini is shown in (4).

Among such compounds with industrial uses was one rhodium cluster, developed by Roy Pruett at Union Carbide Corporation, that efficiently catalyzes the formation of ethylene glycol; another, synthesized by Earl Muetterties at Cornell University, ensures the hydrogenation of 1-hexene within one second at 24° C (75° F)—a rate almost too fast to measure. In related research clusters of platinum atoms were photochemically deposited on the surface of a semiconductor (n-TiO_2) by Kraeutler and Bard. These naked clusters were shown to act as hydrogenation catalysts, and the way in which they were formed could have applications to controlling metal deposition in the manufacture of printed circuits.

Bioinorganic chemistry remained an important field of research because the active sites of many biologically important molecules contain metal atoms. By modeling the environment of the metal atom, scientists can learn something of biological

Unit cell of Union Carbide's silicalite molecular sieve. Each junction represents a silicon atom, and the four large holes represent part of the continuous pore structure of the unique material.

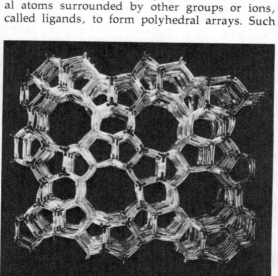

COURTESY, MOLECULAR SIEVE DEPT., LINDE DIV., UNION CARBIDE CORP.

UPI COMPIX

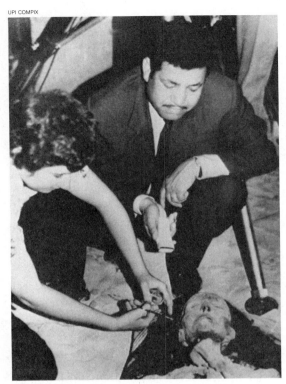

U.S. researcher and Egyptian official sample hair from a mummy. Sophisticated analyses of the lock and of one found in King Tutankhamen's tomb helped to identify the mummy as his grandmother.

processes. Some of the best models developed recently were for the iron-sulfur proteins known as ferrodoxins and rubredoxins, both of which are essential to electron-transport processes in living organisms. Models for nitrogen fixation were also under active study.

Before a biological system is simulated, its structure must be determined. In 1978 one of the most important X-ray studies was of the structure of oxymyoglobin by Simon Phillips at the Medical Research Council laboratory in Cambridge, England. This substance forms in muscle when oxygen binds to the heme protein myoglobin. The work was expected to aid the understanding of how hemoglobin (effectively four molecules of myoglobin) transports oxygen in the blood.

Analytical Chemistry. Whereas many analytical techniques were finding ever-widening application throughout industry, neutron activation analysis (NAA) and scanning electron microprobe analysis recently carved a niche in forensic science and archaeology. In NAA, the sample to be studied is bombarded with a neutron beam, thereby causing its constituent elements to become radioactive; each such "activated" element emits detectable gamma radiation characteristic of its identity, a telltale sign of its presence even in very minute amounts. K. K. S. Pillay at Pennsylvania State University recently demonstrated that it was possible for police forces to "fingerprint" human hair using NAA and to establish a file of gamma ray spectra for each hair sample. Somewhat analogous to NAA, scanning electron microprobe analysis involves bombardment of the sample with a beam of elec-

trons; each element in the sample disperses the collision energy in the form of detectable X-ray emissions, which again are characteristic of the element involved. This method was employed to study an Egyptian mummy that was without identifying marks on its coffin or wrappers. The technique showed that a sample of hair removed from the mummy was virtually identical to an identified sample of hair from a box found in King Tutankhamen's tomb—strongly supporting other evidence that the mummy was Queen Tiye, his grandmother.   (GORDON WILKINSON)

See also Materials Sciences; Nobel Prizes.
[122.A; 122.D–E; 123; 125]

Chess

The world championship chess matches, for both men and women, were held in 1978. Viktor Korchnoi, a former Soviet grand master and now stateless, won his final match in the Candidates at Belgrade, Yugos., over the turn of the year, defeating Boris Spassky (U.S.S.R.) 10½–7½ in January. Negotiations over the site of his match against the defending champion, Anatoly Karpov (*see* BIOGRAPHIES), eventually settled on Baguio in the Philippines. The winner was to be the first to win six games, draws not counting, and Karpov successfully defended his title in the longest world championship match in chess history. The score was 6–5, with 21 games drawn.

The match, which lasted three months, from July 18 until October 17, was full of personal animosity between the contestants. At one stage Karpov was leading by 5–2, but Korchnoi fought back with great fire and resolution and came within an ace of turning the tables. The match for the women's world championship, also held in the autumn of 1978, was not so bitterly or so closely contested. Seventeen-year-old Maya Chiburdanidze (U.S.S.R.) beat Alla Kushnir (formerly U.S.S.R., now Israel) in the final of the Candidates by 7½–6½ and went on to defeat the defending world champion, Nona Gaprindashvili (U.S.S.R.), 8½–6½, thereby becoming the youngest world champion ever.

The 1977 Soviet championship tournament, held in December 1977, resulted in a tie between

Champion Anatoly Karpov ignores his opponent, Viktor Korchnoi, as the two men wait to start at the 13th World Chess Championship in Baguio, Philippines. Karpov ultimately won the match 6 games to 5.

WIDE WORLD

Pirc Defense (32nd and last game of the world championship match at Baguio, Philippines, 1978).

White A. Karpov	Black V. Korchnoi	White A. Karpov	Black V. Korchnoi
1 P–K4	P–Q3 (a)	22 N–N3	R–QR1
2 P–Q4	N–KB3	23 P–B3	R–R5
3 N–QB3	P–KN3	24 B–Q3	Q–R1
4 N–B3	B–N2	25 P–K5	PxP (j)
5 B–K2	0–0	26 QxKP	NxP
6 0–0	P–B4 (b)	27 BxQNP	R–R2
7 P–Q5 (c)	N–R3 (d)	28 N–R4	B–B1
8 B–KB4	N–B2	29 B–K2 (k)	B–K3
9 P–QR4	P–N3	30 P–QB4	N–QN5
10 R–K1	B–N2	31 QxP (l)	Q–N1
11 B–B4 (e)	N–R4 (f)	32 B–B1	R–B1
12 B–KN5	N–B3 (g)	33 Q–KN5	K–R1
13 Q–Q3	P–QR3	34 R–Q2	N–B3
14 QR–Q1	R–N1	35 Q–R6 (m)	R–N1
15 P–R3 (h)	N–Q2	36 N–B3	Q–KB1
16 Q–K3	B–QR1	37 Q–K3	K–N2
17 B–R6	P–QN4	38 N–N5	B–Q2
18 BxB	KxB	39 P–QN4	Q–R1
19 B–B1	N–B3	40 P–N5	N–QR4
20 PxP	PxP	41 P–N6	R–N2
21 N–K2 (i)	B–N2		and Black resigns (n)

(a) A strange choice for Korchnoi to make at this vital stage in the match; one would have thought him well content with his well-tried Open Defense to the Ruy Lopez, or with the French Defense, in both of which he is a great expert. (b) Transposing to a variation resembling the Sicilian Defense. More in the main line of the Pirc here is 6..., P–B3. (c) Exchange of pawns results only in equality; *e.g.*, 7 PxP, PxP; 8 QxQ, RxQ; 9 B–K3, P–N3; 10 KR–Q1, B–Q2; 11 N–K5, N–K1; 12 NxB, NxN; 13 P–B4, BxN and White's two bishops should not do more than compensate for his bad pawn structure. (d) Preferable here seems 7..., B–N5. (e) Threatening P–K5; hence Black's attempt at a diversion on the king-side. (f) But this leaves the knight badly placed; better was 11..., N–Q2. (g) An obvious waste of time; instead 12.., P–KR3 would have posed White an awkward question. (h) Liquidation of material after 15 P–K5, PxP; 16 NxP, P–N4; 17 PxP, PxP; 18 NxQNP, N(B2) xP leaves White nothing. (i) A strong move; the knight is to be brought over to the king-side so as to reinforce the attack there. (j) And not 25.., KNxP; because of 26 N–B5 ch, PxN; 27 Q–N5 ch, K–R1; 28 QxP, when White wins. (k) Threatening to win a piece by B–B3, and P–B4. (l) Once this pawn has gone Black's position is lost beyond repair. (m) Threatening NxP ch. (n) The game was adjourned after White's 41st move and Black sealed his last and 41st move. But he failed to resume the game the next day since White could win a piece by R–R2.

Iosif Dorfman and Boris Gulko; since the play-off also ended in a tie, they shared the title. First prize in the Hastings Premier tournament (December 1977–January 1978) was won by the Israeli grand master Roman Dzhindzhikhashvili. Lajos Portisch (Hung.) was first at Wijk-aan-Zee, Neth., in January, half a point ahead of Korchnoi. The European Junior championship, held at Groningen, Neth., December 1977–January 1978, was won by Shaun Taulbut (England). Walter Browne, who had won the U.S. championship in 1977, walked out before the first round of the 1978 U.S. championship because of a dispute about lighting. The event, which was won by Lubomir Kavalek, was held at Ambassador College, Pasadena, Calif.

There was much computer chess activity throughout the year. A match of ten games was played in February between the English boy prodigy Nigel Short and the Minneapolis-based computer program Chess 4.6, which had won the world computer championship. Both contestants were 12 years old. Victory went to Short by 6½–3½. At Edinburgh, Scotland, in April, a one-game match between "Master," the European computer chess champion, and Michael Clarke was won after 40 moves by the human player. In August and September the Scottish international master David Levy, who had made a £1,250 bet that no computer would beat him in a match by the autumn of 1978, won his bet and the match by 3½–1½ against the 4.7, an improved version of 4.6.

As a final preparation for their world championship match, both Karpov and Korchnoi played in one international tournament. Korchnoi, playing in a comparatively weak tournament at Beersheba, Israel, won first prize 4 points ahead of the rest of the field. In contrast, Karpov, in one of the strongest tournaments of the century at Bugojno, Yugos., came equal first with Spassky and a point ahead of the young Dutch grand master Jan Timman. Later, in July, Timman showed his great strength by coming first in the IBM grand master tournament at Amsterdam. First prize at the Swiss system tournament at Lone Pine, Calif., went to the Danish grand master Bent Larsen, despite his losing in the first round to the English master Jonathan Speelman. Speelman later won the British championship at Ayr, Scotland. At another strong international tournament, at Las Palmas in the Canary Islands, first prize was shared by the Hungarian grand master Gyula Sax and the Soviet grand master V. Tukmakov. Gulko and Timman shared first prize at another very strong Yugoslav international tournament, at Niksic in July.

Initial zonal qualifying tournaments for the world championship were held. In the strongest of these, the U.S.S.R. zonal at Lvov, first place went to Yuri Balashov, who qualified for the interzonal along with Rafael Vaganian. Three major international tournaments were also held in the Soviet Union during the summer of 1978, all won by Soviet grand masters: David Bronstein at Jurmala; former junior world champion Aleksandr Belyavsky at Kiev; and V. Tukmakov at Vilnius. In November the World International Team Championships (or Olympiads as they are usually miscalled) were held by the World Chess Federation (FIDE) at Buenos Aires, Arg. For the first time since they began taking part in such events in 1952, the Soviets failed to win, being beaten by Hungary. The formidable Soviet women's team won the title with ease.   (HARRY GOLOMBEK)

Chile

A republic extending along the southern Pacific coast of South America, Chile has an area of 756,-626 sq km (292,135 sq mi), not including its Antarctic claim. It is bounded by Argentina, Bolivia, and Peru. Pop. (1978 est.): 10,847,600. Cap. and largest city: Santiago (metro. pop., 1978 est., 3,917,000). Language: Spanish. Religion: predominantly Roman Catholic. President in 1978, Gen. Augusto Pinochet Ugarte.

In a referendum held on Jan. 4, 1978, 75% of the votes cast indicated support of the ruling military regime. The referendum was held in response to a resolution critical of the regime passed in the UN General Assembly. Although substantial opposition to the referendum was expressed by various exiled Chilean political groups, Roman Catholic officials, the world press, and even by the Navy and Air Force members of the junta, it was generally accepted that its result led to a strengthening of the regime's self-confidence.

Although political parties were still banned and stringent restrictions on the press and the labour unions remained in force, there was a considerable measure of political liberalization during the year.

CHILE

Education. (1976) Primary, pupils 2,243,274, teachers 57,164; secondary, pupils 307,946, teachers 19,341; vocational, pupils 157,989, teachers 11,509; higher (including 6 main universities), students 147,049, teaching staff (1974) 22,211.

Finance. Monetary unit: peso, with (Sept. 18, 1978) a free rate of 32.91 pesos to U.S. $1 (64.48 pesos = £1 sterling). Gold, SDR's, and foreign exchange (June 1978) U.S. $1,012,000,000. Budget (1978 est.): revenue 81,694,-000,000 pesos; expenditure 82,863,000,000 pesos. Gross domestic product (1977) 321,188,000,000 pesos. Money supply (Dec. 1977) 18,314,000,000 pesos. Cost of living (Santiago; 1975 = 100; June 1978) 825.4.

Foreign Trade. (1977) Imports U.S. $2,367,000,000; exports U.S. $2,190,000,000. Import sources: U.S. 20%; Argentina 12%; Japan 11%; West Germany 8%; Iran 7%; Venezuela 6%; Brazil 5%; Ecuador 5%. Export destinations: Brazil c. 14%; Japan c. 14%; West Germany c. 12%; U.S. c. 12%; U.K. c. 6%. Main exports: copper 54%; metal ores c. 10%.

Transport and Communications. Roads (1976) 75,197 km. Motor vehicles in use (1976): passenger 262,500; commercial 155,700. Railways (1976): c. 10,100 km; traffic 2,-460,000,000 passenger-km, freight (1977) 1,999,000,000 net ton-km. Air traffic (1976): 1,228,000,000 passenger-km; freight 75.7 million net ton-km. Shipping (1977): merchant vessels 100 gross tons and over 143; gross tonnage 405,-971. Telephones (Jan. 1977) 473,400. Radio receivers (Dec. 1976) c. 3.3 million. Television receivers (Dec. 1976) c. 800,000.

Agriculture. Production (in 000; metric tons; 1977): wheat 1,219; barley 143; oats 124; corn 355; potatoes 928; rapeseed 83; dry beans 112; tomatoes 172; sugar, raw value (1976) 319; apples 138; wine c. 600; beef and veal c. 208; wool c. 11; timber (cu m; 1976) 8,816; fish catch (1976) 1,264. Livestock (in 000; 1977): cattle 3,389; sheep (1976) 5,607; goats (1976) c. 800; pigs c. 700; horses (1976) c. 450; poultry (1976) c. 19,800.

Industry. Production (in 000; metric tons; 1977): crude oil 950; natural gas (cu m) c. 1,170,000; petroleum products (1975) c. 3,770; coal 1,236; electricity (kw-hr) 9,850,000; iron ore (61% metal content) 7,963; pig iron 425; crude steel (ingots) 506; copper ore (metal content) c. 1,050; nitrate of soda (1975) 727; manganese ore (metal content; 1975) 7.7; sulfur (1975) c. 21; iodine (1975) 2; molybdenum concentrates (metal content; 1975) 9.1; gold (troy oz; 1975) 129; silver (troy oz; 1975) 6,236; nitrogenous fertilizers (1976–77) 100; woven cotton fabrics (m; 1975) 54,000; fish meal (1975) 169.

On March 9 Pres. Augusto Pinochet Ugarte announced the lifting of the state of siege (which had been in force since Sept. 11, 1973) at the expiration of its current term on March 11, although a state of emergency remained in effect; the pedestrian curfew was also lifted on April 1. The government declared a general amnesty on April 19 for all political prisoners who had been jailed by military tribunals since September 1973. A new Cabinet was formed between April 12 and 21, containing four new civilian ministers (11 out of 16 ministers were now civilians). On July 12 a UN committee was permitted to begin a study on violations of human rights in Chile.

The most serious internal disruption within the junta in its five years in power occurred on July 24, when Gen. Gustavo Leigh Guzmán was dismissed from his post as commander in chief of the Air Force and member of the military junta; he was replaced by Gen. Fernando Matthei Aubel. This was the first change in the composition of the four-man junta since its seizure of power in 1973.

The first draft of a new constitution was submitted to the president for his consideration on August 17. Its principal provisions included the strengthening of presidential powers, the creation of an eight-year nonrenewable term for the president, and the maintenance of a bicameral Congress composed of a Senate and a Chamber of Deputies. In a speech celebrating the fifth anniversary of the coming to power of the junta, President Pinochet announced that the draft constitution would be submitted to a plebiscite for approval at a yet undecided date. Other official announcements indicated that mixed military-civilian rule would prevail from 1985 to 1991. Direct presidential elections were scheduled for 1991.

Chile

The effects of the investigation into the Sept. 21, 1976, assassination in Washington, D.C., of Orlando Letelier, a Cabinet minister in the late Salvador Allende's government, placed a strain on relations with the U.S. and did not improve Chile's world image. A Watergate-type scandal arose, and some commentators believed that responsibility for the assassination might lead directly to high levels of the Chilean government. Michael Townley, a U.S. citizen and former agent of the Chilean police organization, DINA (dissolved on Aug. 6, 1977), pleaded guilty on Aug. 11, 1978, to complicity in the Letelier murder. The U.S. presented the Chileans with evidence for the extradition of three army officers, including Gen. Juan Manuel Contreras Sepúlveda, former head of DINA.

There was a severe deterioration of relations with Argentina in 1978. On January 25, Argentina officially rejected the ruling by an international court of arbitration that awarded three islands in the Beagle Channel (Pictón, Lennox, and Nueva) to Chile. A 180-day negotiation period, ending November 3, was established in February, and, although the sixth round of talks began on September 13 in Santiago, little progress was made. In December the situation reached crisis proportions, with armed forces of both countries put on alert. Late in the month, however, both sides agreed to accept papal mediation, and on December 23 Pope John Paul II designated Antonio Cardinal Samorè, an expert on Latin-American affairs, as his personal envoy to mediate the dispute.

The issue at stake was not really the fate of those small islands but rather the question of the control of the Antarctic and Cape Horn, and also over potential supplies of fish, krill, minerals, and petroleum. Bolivia broke off diplomatic relations with Chile on March 17 over the problem of access to the Pacific Ocean. It was reported that Chile was considering rejoining the Andean Group, from which it had withdrawn in October 1976.

The economic situation evolved favourably for Chile in 1978. In spite of heavy debt-servicing obligations, inflationary pressures, and substantial unemployment, high gross domestic product (GDP) growth rates in 1977–78, balance of payments surpluses, and export diversification programs all contributed to Chile's position of gradually improving economic strength. The GDP grew by 8.6% in 1977. The huge inflation of recent years (340.7% in 1975, 174.3% in 1976, 63.5% in 1977) was checked by stringent government measures, and forecasts indicated a rate of inflation of 25–30% in 1978.

The trade balance showed a deficit of $69.4 million in 1977 (exports, $2,190,300,000; imports, $2,-

259,700,000) and was expected to register a deficit of about $350 million in 1978. However, the government's export-diversification program reduced dependence on copper exports, which accounted for 54% of export revenue in 1977, as against 60% in 1976 and 82% in 1973. The overall balance of payments was expected to result in a surplus of more than $300 million in 1978, and gross internal reserves would probably reach more than $1 billion. Although Chile's large foreign debt was a cause of some concern, recent foreign investments, particularly in mining and oil projects, indicated increasing international confidence in the nation's economic recovery. (MONIQUE MERRIAM)

China

China

The most populous country in the world and the third largest in area, China is bounded by the U.S.S.R., Mongolia, North Korea, Vietnam, Laos, Burma, India, Bhutan, Nepal, Pakistan, and Afghanistan and also by the Sea of Japan, the Yellow Sea, and the East and South China seas. From 1949 the country has been divided into the People's Republic of China (Communist) on the mainland and on Hainan and other islands, and the Republic of China (Nationalist) on Taiwan. (*See* TAIWAN.) Area: 9,561,000 sq km (3,691,521 sq mi), including Tibet and excluding Taiwan. Population of the People's Republic (1978 est.): 960 million, according to official figures; unofficial estimates ranged upward to 1,003,900,000 in 1978. Capital: Peking (metro. pop., 1975 est., 8,487,000). Largest city: Shanghai (metro. pop., 1975 est., 10,888,000). Language: Chinese (varieties of the Peking dialect predominate). Chairman of the Permanent Standing Committee of the National People's Congress (nominal chief of state) from March 5, 1978, Yeh

Chien-ying; chairman of the Communist Party and premier, Hua Kuo-feng.

Probably the most significant internal development in 1978 was the concurrent convocation in February, immediately after the second plenary session of the Communist Party Central Committee, of the fifth National People's Congress (NPC), the nominal legislature, and of the fifth National Committee of the Chinese People's Political Consultative Conference (CPPCC), a front organization with little or no real power. The meetings of these two assemblies launched a new era in post-Mao China. They also marked the reemergence on the political scene of a large number of ex-officials, intellectuals, and social leaders purged during the Cultural Revolution of the late 1960s.

The second plenum of the Central Committee, held February 18–23, reaffirmed the decisions of the 11th Communist Party congress in August 1977. These included elimination of most vestiges of the Cultural Revolution, establishment of the new leadership with Hua Kuo-feng (*see* BIOGRAPHIES), and reinstatement of Teng Hsiao-p'ing to his former high posts. Teng became the third-ranking member in the party hierarchy, after Hua and the octogenarian Gen. Yeh Chien-ying (*see* BIOGRAPHIES), who was then defense minister.

On the recommendation of the party, the fifth NPC, held from February 26 to March 5, appointed Hua and Teng as premier and first vice-premier, respectively, and elected Yeh chairman of its Standing Committee and thus ceremonial chief of state. As holder of the three highest posts, party chairman, head of the Military Affairs Commission, and premier, Hua emerged as the dominant figure in the political structure. However, Teng's proven ability, experience, and popularity enabled him to dominate emerging economic, educational, and foreign policies.

In February the fifth National Committee of the Chinese People's Political Consultative Conference assembled in Peking for its first session. Communist Party Chairman Hua Kuo-feng, pictured next to the late Mao Tse-tung, presided over the meeting.

中国人民政治协商会议第五届全国委员会第一次会议

KEYSTONE

On March 5 the NPC adopted a new constitution stressing the importance of economic, educational, and scientific development. It reflected a shift in the official ideology from revolutionary radicalism to moderate and pragmatic policies. While Mao Tse-tung's successors continued to praise him publicly as a great leader, they no longer took Mao's Thought as dogma.

A number of Mao's favourite internal policies were being reversed. Ideology and political studies were downgraded. In a freer and more open economy, the long-condemned material incentives and bonuses to encourage production were revived. A series of sweeping changes were made in the educational system, including the reinstitution of entrance examinations and of special schools for talented students. On the eve of the 29th anniversary of the People's Republic, October 1, Hua declared that "in order to greatly speed up our socialist construction we must further emancipate our minds, be bolder, devise more measures, and quicken our step." (See Special Report.)

In late November wall posters appeared in Peking that, for the first time, directly criticized Mao and linked him with the discredited hard-line "gang of four." Some posters also called for democracy, praised the U.S., and indirectly criticized Hua. The flurry of wall posters and street rallies coincided with a high-level party meeting, and it was widely rumoured that Teng might replace Hua in at least one of his positions. This did not occur, however. Subsequently, Teng and Hua appeared together in what was apparently meant as a demonstration of unity, and there were indications that official efforts were being made to dampen popular enthusiasm for change.

On December 15 it was announced that the long-delayed normalization of relations with the U.S. would take place on Jan. 1, 1979. As of that date the U.S. would break relations with Taiwan and give one year's notice of termination of the U.S.-Taiwan mutual security treaty. Teng was to visit the U.S. early in the new year.

New Constitution and Leadership. The fifth CPPCC, the official organ for carrying out the party's united-front policy, was opened on February 24 and attended by 1,989 delegates. The convocation of this body, which had not met since 1964, reflected the new leadership's emphasis on harmony after years of political turmoil and was designed to demonstrate and consolidate the unity of the new leadership, as well as to rally support from groups outside the Communist Party structure. The CPPCC "unanimously" elected Teng as its chairman and called on people in all walks of life to carry out the decisions of the fifth NPC.

At a preliminary meeting on February 25, the NPC elected its presidium and endorsed the agenda recommended by the second plenum. The Congress was formally opened on February 26, with 3,456 delegates in attendance. In his unusually lengthy political report, Hua stated that elimination of the gang of four had opened the way for a new era of "socialist construction." He implied that measures aimed toward modernization should be made to seem consistent with Mao's wishes. These measures should include strength-

ening central planning, improvement of education and research, stepping up technological innovation, the use of pay incentives in production, development of foreign trade, and military preparedness to "liberate Taiwan." With little or no debate, the Congress approved Hua's report, the ten-year (1976–85) economic plan, new lyrics for the national anthem that eliminated an embarrassing legacy of the Cultural Revolution, and the new constitution.

The 1978 constitution was the third since the birth of the People's Republic. It declares Marxism-Leninism-Mao Thought to be "the guiding ideology" of China but puts social imperialism before imperialism as a menace to world peace. A significant aspect of the new constitution was the accent on individual freedom and legal protection. The independence of the judiciary and the office of procurator (public prosecutor), contained in the 1954 constitution but abolished in the 1975 version, were partly restored. Chapter three of the new constitution provides that "citizens enjoy" the basic freedoms (art. 45). However, they "must support the leadership of the Chinese Communist Party" (art. 56).

CHINA

Education. (1976–77) Primary, pupils 146,164,200, teachers (1964–65) c. 2.6 million; secondary and vocational, pupils c. 45 million; higher, students c. 1 million.

Finance. Monetary unit: yuan, with (Sept. 18, 1978) a free rate of 1.69 yuan to U.S. $1 (3.30 yuan = £1 sterling). International reserves (1977 est.) U.S. $2 billion. Budget (1960 est.; latest published) balanced at 70,020,000 yuan. Gross national product (1976 est.) U.S. $343 billion.

Foreign Trade. (1976) Imports c. U.S. $6.1 billion; exports c. U.S. $7.2 billion. Import sources: Japan c. 30%; West Germany c. 11%; France c. 6%; Australia c. 5%. Export destinations: Hong Kong c. 20%; Japan c. 17%. Main exports: foodstuffs (meat and products, cereals, fruits and vegetables) c. 30%; textiles and clothing c. 25%; crude oil c. 15%.

Transport and Communications. Roads (1976) c. 808,000 km. Motor vehicles in use (1976): passenger c. 50,000; commercial (including buses) c. 1.5 million. Railways: (1976) c. 48,000 km; traffic (1959) 45,670,000,000 passenger-km, freight (1971) 301,000,000,000 net ton-km. Air traffic (1976): c. 1,410,000,000 passenger-km; freight c. 176 million net ton-km. Inland waterways (including Yangtze River; 1976) c. 160,000 km. Shipping (1977): merchant vessels 100 gross tons and over 622; gross tonnage 4,245,446. Telephones (1976) c. 5 million. Radio receivers (Dec. 1970) c. 12 million. Television receivers (Dec. 1976) c. 350,000.

Agriculture. Production (in 000; metric tons; 1977): rice c. 129,000; corn c. 33,500; wheat c. 40,000; barley c. 15,400; millet c. 20,000; potatoes c. 41,600; dry peas c. 4,900; soybeans c. 13,000; peanuts c. 2,800; rapeseed c. 1,300; sugar, raw value c. 4,200; pears c. 1,000; tobacco c. 1,000; tea c. 310; cotton, lint c. 2,300; jute c. 1,400; cow's milk c. 3,800; beef and buffalo meat c. 2,100; pork c. 10,000; timber (cu m; 1976) c. 194,000; fish catch (1976) c. 6,800. Livestock (in 000; 1976): horses c. 7,000; asses c. 11,700; cattle c. 64,500; buffaloes c. 30,200; sheep c. 75,000; pigs c. 240,000; goats c. 62,000; chickens 1,330,000.

Industry. Fuel and power (in 000; metric tons; 1977): coal (including lignite) c. 460,000; coke (1975) c. 30,000; crude oil c. 92,000; electricity (kw-hr; 1976) c. 125,000,000. Production (in 000; metric tons; 1976): iron ore (metal content) c. 34,000; pig iron c. 30,000; crude steel (1977) c. 25,000; lead c. 100; copper c. 100; zinc c. 100; bauxite c. 1,000; aluminum c. 160; magnesite c. 1,000; manganese ore c. 300; tungsten concentrates (oxide content) c. 12; cement c. 30,000; sulfuric acid (1966) c. 2,500; fertilizers (nutrient content) nitrogenous c. 3,000, phosphates c. 1,200, potash c. 310; cotton yarn (1969) c. 1,450; cotton fabrics (m) c. 8,000,000; man-made fibres c. 160; paper c. 5,500.

During the closing session on March 5, the Congress "unanimously" elected Yeh as chairman of the Standing Committee and "decided on the appointment of Comrade Hua Kuo-feng as premier of the State Council," composed of 13 vice-premiers and some 30 ministers. Five of the vice-premiers, including Defense Minister Hsu Hsiang-ch'ien, who succeeded Yeh, were newly elected. Newly created ministries or ministry-level agencies included the State Economic Commission headed by K'ang Shih-en, former petroleum minister and now a vice-premier, and a state scientific and technological commission headed by Vice-Premier Fang Yi. Of the 37 State Council agencies, 28 were concerned with the economy.

To mobilize the country in the cause of development, a series of national conferences was held during the year on agriculture, industry, science, education, health, army political work, and finance and trade. Teng, the architect of the "four modernizations" policy (in agriculture, industry, national defense, and science and technology), played a prominent role, especially in the National Science Conference in March and the National Conference on Education in late April. To speed up the acquisition of scientific and technological expertise, China was planning to send a large number of students to Western universities.

Teng's increasing importance in the Chinese power structure was underlined in October, when his old enemy, Wu Te, was removed as mayor of Peking. For some months Wu had been the subject of a wall poster campaign, in which he had been called, among other things, "the rat's tail of the gang of four." Although Wu remained on the Politburo, it was reported that he had been sent to a "cadre school" for ideological reform.

The Economy. The ten-year economic plan replaced the fifth five-year plan, which was supposed to have started in 1976. In presenting the plan to the Congress, Hua stated that China intended to complete 120 large industrial complexes in the next eight years. He predicted that by 1985 a solid foundation for the mechanization of agriculture would have been laid, enabling China to produce 400 million metric tons of grain annually. In each of the remaining eight years of the plan, the value of industrial output was to increase by more than 10% and agricultural production by as much as 5%.

Official hard statistics were unavailable, but China's grain production and steel output for 1977 were estimated at 275 million tons and 22 million tons, respectively. At the National Finance and Trade Conference in July, Hua reported that in the first six months of 1978 there had been "a 24% rise in industrial production over the corresponding 1977 period." Most of China's agricultural regions suffered from prolonged drought in the first half of the year, causing China to make additional grain purchases abroad.

In a reversal of Mao's policy of economic self-reliance, China decided to accelerate the modernization process by stepping up the volume of foreign trade, especially the purchase of machinery and technology from Japan and the West. In January, China concluded an agreement with France

on scientific and technological cooperation, its first with a Western power. On February 16 China and Japan signed an eight-year (1978–85), U.S. $20 billion trade agreement involving the exchange of Chinese oil and coal for Japanese industrial plant and technology. On April 3 China and the European Economic Community signed a five-year trade agreement. The Carter administration approved the sale of airborne geologic-exploration equipment to China, and five U.S. oil companies sent high-level delegations to discuss China's oil exploration. Kaiser Engineers, Inc., was awarded a contract to develop Chinese iron mines.

Foreign Relations. Officially, the new leadership reaffirmed Mao's "three world theory," which damned the two superpowers as the potential source of a new world war. Because of its "unbridled acts of aggression and expansion . . . Social Imperialism is the major threat to world peace and security," declared Foreign Minister Huang Hua at the UN General Assembly on September 28. In an effort to counter Soviet expansionism, Peking continued to cultivate friendships with second and third world countries. At the same time, relations with the industrialized nations were strengthened by the new trade accords.

A stream of dignitaries from the third world visited China during the year. Oman and China established diplomatic relations in May, and Libya recognized Peking in August without calling it the sole legal government of China. Peking's ties with India, Sri Lanka, and members of the Association of Southeast Asian Nations were improved. Relations with Vietnam were seriously strained, however, and China's cultivation of relations with the West and Yugoslavia caused a complete break with Albania, once its main European ally.

After years of self-imposed isolation, Chinese leaders launched a diplomatic campaign to re-win old friends and make new ones. Between January and October, Hua, Teng, Vice-Premier Li Hsien-nien, and others led friendly missions to some 40 countries, 9 of them in Europe. On a visit to Zaire in June after attending the UN General Assembly Special Session, Huang attacked the U.S.S.R.'s aggressive policies and labeled the invaders of Zaire's Shaba Province as "Soviet-Cuba mercenaries." Hua's trip to North Korea in May and his 17-day tour of Romania, Yugoslavia, and Iran in Moscow's backyard in August were highly significant and enhanced his image both at home and abroad.

Relations with the Soviet Union showed no signs of improvement. Just two days before the opening of the NPC, Moscow made an overture toward Peking, but it was rebuffed on March 9. China insisted that no improvement could take place until the Soviets withdrew many of the one million soldiers stationed on the Sino-Soviet frontier and in Mongolia. Early in April Soviet Pres. Leonid Brezhnev toured military bases in the border regions and attended maneuvers near Khabarovsk in what was regarded as a clear rebuke to Peking's call for a pullback.

On May 9 a Soviet patrol crossed into China's Yuehyapao district south of Khabarovsk, not far from the site of the hostilities along the Ussuri River in 1969. Peking charged that the incursion—

in which, it claimed, some Chinese had been wounded—constituted an organized military provocation. It demanded an apology, punishment for those responsible, and a guarantee against any recurrence. On May 12 Moscow expressed regret for the incident but denied that its troops had fired on or wounded Chinese citizens. The incident constituted a setback to the Sino-Soviet border negotiations, which had just been resumed following the return of the Soviet negotiator to Peking in April.

Sino-Vietnamese relations deteriorated to the breaking point during the year, exacerbated by increased Soviet influence in Vietnam, Peking's aid to Phnom Pehn in the Cambodia-Vietnam conflict, and Vietnam's harsh treatment of its ethnic Chinese minority. An overwhelming percentage of the more than 1.5 million Chinese in Vietnam had lived in and around Ho Chi Minh City (Saigon). Friction began in March when Hanoi launched a campaign to "eradicate bourgeois trading" and close down private businesses. Chinese entrepreneurs were driven to the so-called new economic zones created out of abandoned land for agricultural purposes. In May the Chinese exodus from Vietnam began, and by June 140,000 had fled. A Chinese party that had arrived in Hanoi with the intention of establishing a consulate general in Ho Chi Minh City was not permitted to go there, and two Chinese ships sent to evacuate Chinese refugees were not allowed to enter Vietnamese waters. On July 3, shortly after Hanoi became a full member of the Moscow-dominated Council for Mutual Economic Assistance (Comecon), Peking announced the cancellation of its entire Vietnamese aid program.

The flood of over 160,000 refugees strained Chinese welfare facilities, and in mid-July Peking closed the frontier except to holders of Chinese entry certificates and Vietnamese visas. It also invited Hanoi to hold high-level talks aimed at an overall settlement of the dispute. The first meeting of the Chinese and Vietnamese deputy foreign ministers, on August 8 in Hanoi, got off to an acrimonious start. The talks were broken off following a violent border clash, with some casualties, on August 25. They were resumed in early September amid new charges and countercharges and broke up again on September 26.

The long-term trade agreement between China and Japan laid a solid foundation for resumption of the negotiations for a treaty of peace and friendship, deadlocked since 1975 because of Peking's insistence on the inclusion of an antihegemony clause aimed at Moscow. Late in March the Japanese prime minister, Takeo Fukuda, decided to resume peace treaty talks with the Chinese leaders, but the appearance of a fleet of Chinese boats in waters off the Tiao Yu T'ai (Senkaku) Islands, occupied by Japan but claimed by both China and Taiwan, caused an abrupt halt in the negotiations. Subsequently, Peking said the incursion was an accident and the dispute was shelved.

Despite Moscow's protest, talks began on July 21. Foreign Minister Sunao Sonoda of Japan arrived in Peking on August 8 to meet his counterpart, and shortly afterward a compromise formula

More than 160,000 ethnic Chinese fled Vietnam during the May–July exodus.

was reached. Both China and Japan declared that they sought no "hegemony in the Asia-Pacific region or in any other region," but they opposed efforts by others to establish dominance. It was also agreed that "The present treaty shall not affect either country's relations with third countries." On August 12 the two foreign ministers put their signatures on the new treaty. The formal ratification, which took place in Tokyo on October 23, was attended by Teng and Fukuda.

The most notable breakthrough in foreign relations came at the end of the year, with the announcement that the U.S. and China would extend formal recognition to each other at the start of 1979. On April 11 Pres. Jimmy Carter had referred to normalization "over a period of months," leading some observers to believe he had set a target date for full diplomatic recognition after the November congressional elections. Similarly, the president's national security adviser, Zbigniew Brzezinski, upon leaving Peking after a visit on May 20–22, had said Sino-U.S. normalization was "vital and beneficial to world peace." Nevertheless, the timing of the announcement was unexpected. The U.S. agreed to China's preconditions for normalization—derecognition of Taiwan (though Carter assured the American public that unofficial cultural and economic ties would be maintained), termination of the mutual security treaty, and withdrawal of remaining U.S. personnel on Taiwan (fewer than 1,000 men). U.S. officials indicated that, in return, China had tacitly agreed not to oppose continued U.S. arms sales to Taiwan and had agreed to termination of the security treaty on one year's notice rather than before relations were restored. Peking also agreed not to raise objections to a U.S. declaration of continued interest in Taiwan. Teng's visit to the U.S.—the first by a high-level Chinese official—was scheduled for late January 1979, and ambassadors were to be exchanged in March.　(HUNG-TI CHU)

CHINA AFTER MAO

by Richard Harris

Mao Tse-tung was a revolutionary who could never leave well enough alone. He always wanted more and better, but ended up with much worse, living ten years too long and leaving China seriously damaged by the conflicts he encouraged. While personally a committed Marxist, he also, rightly, saw himself as the hero of the national revolution and was revered as such by the nation at large.

These are some of the facts that China's present leaders must keep in mind as they plan the country's future. Since Mao's death in 1976, the way has been cleared for economic growth without political interference; old cadres have been rehabilitated, material incentives are being offered rewarding "each according to his work," and order and discipline have been restored. China under Hua Kuo-feng (see BIOGRAPHIES) is glad to be relieved of the political tensions that have lasted since the Cultural Revolution of the late 1960s. For the present, at least, violent winds of political change have abated.

The new leadership was brought about by chance and compromise. Hua holds the nominal title as Mao's successor while Teng Hsiao-p'ing has been restored to the posts he held before his fall from grace in 1975. Teng's appeal at the 11th party congress in 1977 for honesty, attention to the facts, less empty talk, and more hard work seems certain to pervade post-Maoist China.

Rather than a struggle for power between the experienced and forceful Teng and the relatively unknown and more uncertain Hua, the evidence appears to suggest a general acceptance of compromise. This leaves Teng free to press his policies with the help of the strong backing he enjoys, especially from the Army.

But it would be wrong to think that China has achieved a new stability. Contrary to much of the reporting in the Western press, there was never a clear division between the Chou En-lai moderates and the now discredited "gang of four" extremists. The struggles in China that intensified after the tenth party congress in 1973 disrupted labour disci-

---

Richard Harris is deputy foreign editor and Asian specialist, The Times, London. *His works include* Independence and After *and* America and East Asia.

PADRY—LE HERISSON, PARIS/ROTHCO

pline, gave rise to crime and corruption, seriously damaged industrial production, disappointed the younger generation, and generated a loss of confidence among the managers who controlled the country's working life. It has been convenient to blame all these failings on the gang of four; they have been the scapegoat on which China has flung the blame for unwanted Maoist policies. Another way of emphasizing the break with Mao has been through praise of the dead Chou En-lai. However, during the Cultural Revolution and afterward, many, many thousands rose to power in provincial and lower posts. They saw themselves as faithful Maoists, not associated with any power struggle led by the gang of four. They clung to their positions from motives of career as well as ideology, and they have probably not been dislodged. The post-Maoist settlement will take time.

More Rehabilitation, Less Egalitarianism. It is against this unstable background that the steps toward rehabilitation must be viewed. Most of the leading figures who suffered during the Cultural Revolution have been restored to public life. In an even more beneficial move, many thousands of less important people have been freed from the "rightist" label they incurred for their opinions in campaigns as far back as Mao's short-lived "100 flowers" experiment in free speech in 1956–57. They can now hope to enjoy better jobs and social status.

In his writings and speeches Mao veered from one side to another and in the process struck many attitudes. He relished the conflict of opposites. One such was the "contradiction" between "red" and "expert," one with echoes in the Chinese past. It posed a choice between the politically-sound-but-not-necessarily-talented and the talented-irrespective-of-political-fervour. Mao always came down on the side of redness, but his successors have no difficulty in coming down as firmly for expertise in the name of modernization. After all, as one of Mao's thoughts puts it, "The economy is the goal. Politics are only the way that leads to the goal."

Great importance has been given to incentives for the peasant. His labour may not now be used except for his own benefit, and he must be assured that any rise in production will increase his income. At the same time, under the new discipline, mismanagement by commune and district authorities will bring officials to task.

Perhaps the most marked break with Mao's predilections has been the move away from an excessive egalitarianism. The emphasis during the Cultural Revolution and afterward on ideological purity over ability in higher education has badly damaged the Chinese economy. The price paid in terms of China's backwardness in science and technology is openly acknowledged. Gifted pupils who came of "bourgeois" families have suffered—an appalling neglect of talent. The educational reforms have probably affected more people than any other changes since Mao's death. Entry to higher education will again be by examination, scholarship will be valued, and the part-work part-study schemes that interrupted the educational process are lapsing.

In a country where education has always been highly valued, the reversion to earlier ways has brought with it a respect for the past that the Cultural Revolution cruelly tried to destroy. Confucius and other figures from the Chinese past are again honoured; bookshops stock the standard classics; and the traditional theatre has turned its back on the empty revolutionary sloganizing imposed by Mao's wife, Chiang Ch'ing. Under Mao the "new" China was emphasized in contrast to the old. It may be said of China after Mao that it will look back on its revolutionary course with a more critical eye and with less inclination to think of it as a break with history. Tradition will again make itself felt.

Foreign Policy Objectives. The priority given to economic development has led to a new emphasis in foreign policy. To obtain the scientific and technological expertise it now lacks, China needs to forge closer ties with the West and with Japan. On one front, however, the position is unchanged. The Soviet Union is still seen as China's main enemy, and containment of Soviet influence wherever possible, as the first task of diplomacy. Today a less ideological China makes friends with any governments that are suspicious of the Soviets, including Soviet-bloc member Romania and nonaligned Yugoslavia.

Mao's three-world theory has been reaffirmed: By their very nature, the two superpowers, the U.S.S.R. and the U.S., impinge on the national interests of all others, and their power should be curbed. Of the two, the Soviet Union is now much the greater threat. The second world includes the industrialized countries, some of them allied to the U.S. but all of them tending to be manipulated in the interest of the superpowers. China's true friends are those countries in the third world whose national identity is most threatened by superpower intervention.

To some extent this formulation drains China's foreign policy of its revolutionary content. That also helped to transform relations with the U.S. in 1978. Zbigniew Brzezinski's visit in the spring warmed Chinese hearts by its strongly anti-Soviet stance. Then came the spur of the treaty with Japan. Under Teng's active urging, a formula was found whereby China would make no declaration about not using force against Taiwan but allowed the Americans to declare that they would continue to supply Taiwan with defensive weapons. This enabled Washington to fulfill Chinese demands for withdrawal of recognition from the Taiwan government, withdrawal of the remaining U.S. troops on the island, and formal breaking of the security treaty—though the last would not take place until the end of 1979.

Teng's visit to Washington in January, following his visit to Tokyo in the autumn, would thus strengthen—in Chinese eyes—China's international position vis-à-vis the Soviet Union. It now remained for the Peking government to represent its political character and economic advance in such a way as to promote Chinese patriotic feeling among the population of Taiwan. This may be a slow process, but one result of the U.S. exchange of ambassadors with China planned for March would be to limit the anti-Communist arguments on which Taiwan has based its claims to separateness. Teng has already made it clear that Taiwan will enjoy special consideration, including concessions over its higher standard of living, and it is noteworthy that wall posters in Peking stated publicly for the first time that Taiwan's economy was far above China's level.

This desire to achieve the total unity and independence of China—an objective in Chinese minds since the early years of this century—also applies to Hong Kong. But the question of British control there is secondary to the Taiwan issue, since Hong Kong presents no political threat and offers certain economic advantages. Realizing that the lease on the New Territories (which China in theory does not recognize, along with all other 19th-century "unequal" treaties) expires in 1997 and might soon cast its shadow over the Hong Kong economy, the Chinese have, in various oblique ways (such as investing in Hong Kong themselves), made it plain to the business community that they need not worry. There is no question, however, but that Hong Kong will eventually return to Chinese rule.

The treaty of peace and friendship signed with Japan in August 1978 was seen by most observers primarily as a gain for China in its effort to dispel Soviet influence in Japan. A much greater effect in the long run may be the initiation of a new era in Sino-Japanese relations. The two countries have had contacts for over a thousand years, and as a result they have much in common—neither really regards the other as "foreign." In time, Japan, though anxious to be linked politically as well as economically to the Western powers, may find that a peaceful China concentrating on economic growth is a partner not to be spurned.

Southeast Asia is another area that the Chinese have known for hundreds of years and where they now wish to establish a new relationship. Their efforts are complicated by the tensions surrounding the huge colonies of overseas Chinese scattered throughout the region, as well as by their fears of Soviet encroachment. Both themes are present in their relationship with the Vietnamese, whose inclination toward the Soviets led China to give its patronage to Cambodia. The awkward result has been a war between Cambodia and Vietnam, in which China finds itself in the somewhat embarrassing role of Cambodia's supplier.

In considering China's world outlook, one does well to remember that the national aims first defined at the beginning of the century arose from China's reaction to Western power. It became China's objective to win equality with the West in every sense. This goal is shared by the Communist government as much as by any other. In a sense, therefore, the long-term focus of China's foreign relations lies with the West rather than with the Soviet Union or with any other industrially backward power. Just as Japan's association with the West developed as a result of its economic growth, so China may be expected to veer more in that direction and away from a rigidly ideological view of the world.

The Revolution Lives. None of this should be taken to imply that China will become less totalitarian. The restoration of social discipline in China coupled with a more relaxed political attitude has lightened the ideological burden on the Chinese but has not removed it. Dedication to revolutionary ends and the affirmation of political loyalty are still required. As Hua reminded the National People's Congress in February 1978, Marxism–Leninism–Mao Tse-tung Thought (the clumsy label for China's ideology) will continue to maintain its primary position in science and culture. There will be none of the "bourgeois liberalism dreamt of by reactionaries inside the country and outside."

How firm is Hua in this conviction? It is worth putting the question, since China in recent years has experienced real eruptions of political uncertainty. The most considered was a lengthy wall poster put up in Canton in late 1974 and widely copied. It expressed disillusion with the Cultural Revolution and complained that China had no written law, that the masses had no real democratic rights, and that officials were not accountable. Two of its three authors later submitted self-criticisms. One, Li Cheng-tien, refused to do so and received a sentence of "labour reform." The other occasion was the mass demonstration in Peking in April 1976, honouring the recently deceased Chou En-lai and, by implication, most certainly directed against Mao.

So it may be said that a less ideological China is not a settled country ideologically. A cautious leader such as Hua may wish to evade any ideological crisis, whereas Teng might go further in repudiating Maoism. But throughout China there must be considerable skepticism, cynicism, and disillusion on the part of the young who were caught up in the Cultural Revolution and for a brief moment saw themselves as an idealistic advance guard. Millions were later sent to the countryside; thousands more escaped to Hong Kong. All of them felt their future to be insecure and their political ideas confused. Here then are the seeds of change in a future China, although there is no commanding figure in China today capable of reshaping the country's political doctrine. Whatever his talents, Hua shows no sign of being an original political thinker.

The present leadership plays down Mao's fear of counterrevolution. Speaking of Maoism in the past, Teng complains that "They make this a blind faith and do not allow people to use their brains, much less to discern truth from falsehood." In all matters that concern China's economic progress, brains can certainly be used more freely now. But though there is greater freedom for artists and writers, there is no real release from China's traditional totalitarian controls. The writer, like all others, must serve the revolution. It would be a mistake to think that China has moved very far in the short period since Mao's death from those totalitarian political assumptions that have ruled the country for 2,000 years.

Colombia

A republic in northwestern South America, Colombia is bordered by Panama, Venezuela, Brazil, Peru, and Ecuador and has coasts on both the Caribbean Sea and the Pacific Ocean. Area: 1,138,914 sq km (439,737 sq mi). Pop. (1978 est.): 25,867,500. Cap. and largest city: Bogotá (pop., 1978 est., 3,831,100). Language: Spanish. Religion: Roman Catholic (96%). Presidents in 1978, Alfonso López Michelsen and, from August 7, Julio César Turbay Ayala.

In congressional elections on Feb. 26, 1978, the Liberal Party won a clear majority in both chambers. Julio César Turbay Ayala (see BIOGRAPHIES) was chosen as the sole Liberal Party presidential candidate, although he did not have the support of all factions of the party. Belisario Betancur of the Conservative Party was his leading challenger. In the presidential elections, held on June 4, Turbay Ayala was victorious by a narrow margin, receiving 2,506,228 votes to 2,358,644 for Betancur. The abstention rate of about 60% reflected the electorate's dissatisfaction with the political system and the lack of alternatives to the existing two-party system. The elections marked the end of the National Front coalition pact between the Liberal and Conservative parties, but in light of the support

shown for the Conservative Party, Turbay Ayala appointed five Conservatives to his Cabinet when he took office on August 7.

An official report presented to the new president on the illegal drug trade in the three northern provinces of La Guajira, Magdalena, and El Cesar revealed that about 70,000 ha were planted in marijuana, which was expected to yield a crop worth about $1 billion in 1978. Approximately 50 airstrips and 100 coastal landing points to service the trade were located; many of these were destroyed and much of the crop was drenched with incendiary materials.

Violence and organized crime showed no signs of abating in 1978. Kidnappings of prominent people included those of the local head of Texas Petroleum Co. and a former ambassador to France. On September 12 Rafael Pardo Buelvas, a former minister of the interior, was shot dead by the M-19 guerrilla group. This led to a government drive against guerrillas and violence and the passing of a new security law. The two other main guerrilla groups, the Colombian Revolutionary Armed Forces and the National Liberation Army, formed an alliance. In other disturbances during the year, the National University was closed temporarily during the election period, after one student had been killed and several injured; riots followed an increase in bus fares; and there were frequent one-day strikes by bus drivers, public sector employees, teachers, and medical workers.

The economy remained relatively stable, and the rate of inflation was not expected to top 20%. The peso had been devalued by only 2.7% against the U.S. dollar by the end of July. Coffee production for 1977–78 was forecast at a record 9.8 million bags, but exports for the year were not expected to match 1977 levels when prices reached their peak.

(SARAH CAMERON)

Police and soldiers drive off students at the National University of Colombia in Bogotá during riots that erupted prior to the June presidential elections.

Colombia

Colonies:
see Dependent States

COLOMBIA

Education. (1975) Primary, pupils 3,953,242, teachers 131,211; secondary, pupils 977,648, teachers 51,232; vocational, pupils 260,963, teachers 14,894; teacher training, students 67,664, teachers 3,995; higher, students 192,887, teaching staff 21,163.

Finance. Monetary unit: peso, with (Sept. 18, 1978) a free rate of 39.22 pesos to U.S. $1 (free rate of 76.85 pesos = £1 sterling). Gold, SDR's, and foreign exchange (June 1978) U.S. $2,059,000,000. Budget (1977 actual): revenue 63,417,000,000 pesos; expenditure 57,597,000,000 pesos. Gross national product (1975) 411,570,000,000 pesos. Money supply (Sept. 1977) 90,661,000,000 pesos. Cost of living (Bogotá; 1975 = 100; March 1978) 173.

Foreign Trade. Imports (1977) 62,963,000,000 pesos; exports (1976) 54,221,000,000 pesos. Import sources (1976): U.S. 42%; West Germany 10%; Japan 8%. Export destinations: U.S. 29%; West Germany 15%; Venezuela 6%; The Netherlands 6%. Main exports: coffee 53%; textile yarns and fabrics 7%. Tourism (1976): visitors 522,000; gross receipts U.S. $146 million.

Transport and Communications. Roads (1976) 56,667 km. Motor vehicles in use (1976): passenger 355,700; commercial 63,000. Railways (1976): c. 3,420 km; traffic 511 million passenger-km, freight 1,247,000,000 net ton-km. Air traffic (1977): 3,340,000,000 passenger-km; freight 176.1 million net ton-km. Shipping (1977): merchant vessels 100 gross tons and over 52; gross tonnage 247,240. Telephones (Jan. 1977) 1,295,900. Radio receivers (Dec. 1976) 2,808,000. Television receivers (Dec. 1976) c. 1.8 million.

Agriculture. Production (in 000; metric tons; 1977): corn 753; rice 1,329; potatoes 126; cassava (1976) c. 1,900; sorghum 406; soybeans 109; bananas c. 1,300; cane sugar, raw value 823; palm oil 49; coffee c. 558; tobacco 64; sisal c. 42; cotton, lint 174; beef and veal c. 579; timber (cu m; 1976) c. 23,002. Livestock (in 000; Dec. 1976): cattle 24,385; sheep c. 2,158; pigs 1,909; goats c. 651; horses (1975) c. 1,500; chickens c. 54,200.

Industry. Production (in 000; metric tons; 1977): crude oil 7,099; natural gas (cu m; 1975) c. 1,625,000; coal (1975) c. 3,200; electricity (kw-hr; 1976) c. 14,500,000; iron ore (metal content) 460; crude steel 210; gold (troy oz) c. 296; emeralds (carats; 1973) 109; salt (1975) 926; cement 3,297; paper (1975) 240.

Combat Sports

Boxing. During the year Muhammad Ali (*see* BIOGRAPHIES) became the first boxer in history to be crowned heavyweight champion three different times. With relative ease he regained his title from Leon Spinks (U.S.), who seven months earlier defeated Ali in an exciting Las Vegas match. The Ali-Spinks rematch was held in the Superdome in New Orleans, La., on September 15. It drew an all-time record crowd of 70,000 fans, who paid just under $6 million at the gate, another record. Each of the fighters received something around $2 million, a combined purse never before equaled. Promoters got additional revenues from a televised broadcast of the fight. The match was sanctioned by the World Boxing Association (WBA) and acknowledged by most other boxing organizations as a legitimate world heavyweight championship bout. But the World Boxing Council (WBC) continued to insist that Spinks could not give Ali a return match until he first defended his title against Ken Norton (U.S.). When it became clear that the Ali-Spinks rematch would be held, the WBC declared that in its eyes Norton was the reigning world heavyweight champion. Larry Holmes (U.S.) later dethroned Norton on a split decision in Las Vegas and became the WBC world heavyweight champion.

In the light-heavyweight division, Mate Parlov (Yugos.), former European champion, won the WBC title by knocking out Miguel Cuello (Arg.) in nine rounds. Parlov thus became the first boxer from a Communist country to win a professional world boxing title. He then successfully defended his title by outpointing John Conteh (England) but later lost the title to Marvin Johnson (U.S.). WBA champion Víctor Galíndez (Arg.) was dethroned when he was knocked out in the 13th round by Mike Rossman (U.S.). Hugo Corro (Arg.) became the undisputed world middleweight champion when he outpointed Rodrigo Valdés (Colombia). Corro later retained his title in a bout against Ronnie Harris (U.S.). Rocky Mattioli, an Italian-born Australian, retained the WBC junior middleweight title with victories over Elisha Obed (The Bahamas) and José Durán (Spain).

A new WBA junior middleweight champion was crowned when Masashi Kudo (Japan) won a decision over Eddie Gazo (Nicaragua). Carlos Palomino (U.S.) and José Cuevas (Mexico) continued to rule the welterweights. Palomino, the Mexican-born WBC champion, beat Ryu Sorimachi (Japan), Mimoun Mohatar (Morocco), and Armando Muniz (U.S.). WBA champion Cuevas stopped three U.S. challengers, Harold Weston in nine rounds, Billy Backhus in one, and Pete Ranzany in two. In the junior welterweight division Saensak Muangsurin (Thailand) retained his WBC title by stopping Jo Kimpuani (Zaire) and Francisco Moreno (Venezuela); Antonio Cervantes (Colombia) remained WBA champion after bouts with Tongta Kiatarjupak (Thailand) and Norman Sekgapane (South Africa).

Roberto Durán (Panama), a six-year WBA lightweight champion, defeated WBC champion Esteban de Jesús (Puerto Rico) and became the only undisputed world boxing champion besides middleweight Corro. Durán later defeated Monroe Brooks (U.S.). Alexis Argüello (Nicaragua) won the WBC junior lightweight title with a victory over Alfredo Escalera (Puerto Rico). Sam Serrano (Puerto Rico) remained WBA champion after outpointing Mario Martínez (Nicaragua).

Danny López (U.S.) retained the WBC featherweight crown by stopping David Kotei (Ghana), José De Paula (Brazil), and Juan Malvarez (Arg.). López also beat Fel Clemente (Philippines) on a disqualification. Cecilio Lastra (Spain), fighting for the WBA title, outpointed Rafael Ortega (Panama) but was later beaten by Eusebio Pedroza (Panama). Pedroza then defeated Ernesto Herrera (Mexico). WBC junior featherweight champion Wilfredo Gómez (Puerto Rico) retained his title and preserved his unbeaten record by stopping Carlos Zárate (Mexico), the bantam champion. Ricardo Cardona (Colombia) took the WBA title from Soo Hwan Hong (South Korea) and retained it against Rubén Valdéz (Colombia). Bantam champions Zárate and Jorge Luján (Panama) retained their respective titles. Zárate, the WBC champion, beat Alberto Dávila (U.S.) and Andrés Hernández (Puerto Rico); Luján successfully defended his WBA title by beating Roberto ("Kid") Rubalding (Mexico) and Dávila.

Whereas Miguel Canto (Mexico) remained WBC flyweight king, outpointing Shoji Oguma (Japan), the WBA title changed hands when Betulio González (Venezuela) outpointed Guty Espadas (Mexico). Yoko Gushiken (Japan) continued to reign as WBA junior flyweight champion with three successful defenses, but the WBC title changed hands when Freddy Castillo (Mexico), after defeating Luis Lumumba Estaba (Venez.), was beaten by Netrnoi Vorasingh (Thailand), who was in turn knocked out by Kim Sung Jun (South Korea).

Muhammad Ali (right) backs away from a left jab thrown by Leon Spinks in their heavyweight championship bout in September. Ali outpointed Spinks to regain the heavyweight title for the third time.

Table I. Boxing Champions
as of Dec. 31, 1978

Division	World	Europe	Commonwealth	Britain
Heavyweight	Larry Holmes, U.S.* Muhammad Ali, U.S.†	Alfredo Evangelista, Spain & Uruguay	John L. Gardner, England	John L. Gardner, England
Light heavyweight	Marvin Johnson, U.S.* Mike Rossman, U.S.†	Aldo Traversaro, Italy	Gary Summerhays, Canada	Bunny Johnson, England
Middleweight	Hugo Corro, Arg.	Alan Minter, England	Ayub Kalue, Uganda	
Junior middleweight	Rocky Mattioli, Italy and Australia* Masashi Kudo, Japan†	Gilbert Cohen, France	Maurice Hope, England	Jimmy Batten, England
Welterweight	Carlos Palomino, U.S.* José Cuevas, Mexico†	Henry Rhiney, England	Clyde Gray, Canada	Henry Rhiney, England
Junior welterweight	Saensak Muangsurin, Thailand* Antonio Cervantes, Colombia†	Fernando Sánchez, Spain	Jeff Malcolm, Australia	Clinton McKenzie, England
Lightweight	Roberto Durán, Panama	Jim Watt, Scotland	Hogan Jimoh, Nigeria	Charlie Nash, N. Ireland
Junior lightweight	Alexis Argüello, Nicaragua* Sam Serrano, Puerto Rico†	Natale Vezzoli, Italy	Johnny Aba, Papua New Guinea	. . .
Featherweight	Danny López, U.S.* Eusebio Pedroza, Panama†	Roberto Castañón, Spain	Eddie Ndukwu, Nigeria	Dave Needham, England
Junior featherweight	Wilfredo Gómez, Puerto Rico* Ricardo Cardona, Colombia†	. . .	. . .	. . .
Bantamweight	Carlos Zárate, Mexico* Jorge Luján, Panama†	Juan Francisco Rodríguez, Spain	Johnny Owen, Wales	Johnny Owen, Wales
Flyweight	Miguel Canto, Mexico* Betulio González, Venez.†	Franco Udella, Italy	Patrick Mambwe, Zambia	Charlie Magri, England
Junior flyweight	Kim Sung Jun, South Korea* Yoko Gushiken, Japan†	. . .	. . .	. . .

*World Boxing Council champion. †World Boxing Association champion.

In Europe, heavyweight Alfredo Evangelista (Spain), lightweight Jim Watt (Scotland), junior lightweight Natale Vezzoli (Italy), and flyweight Franco Udella (Italy) retained their titles. Aldo Traversaro (Italy) won the vacant light-heavyweight championship. Alan Minter (England) regained the middleweight crown by stopping Angelo Jacopucci (Italy), who died a few days later from brain damage. Minter later defeated Gratien Tonna (France). Alain Marion took the welterweight title by knocking out Jörg Eipel (West Germany), who went into a coma and had to undergo brain surgery. Jorgen Hansen (Denmark) subsequently beat Marion but lost on a disqualification to Josef Pachler (Austria), who in turn lost to Henry Rhiney (England). In the junior welterweight class Colin Powers (England) stopped Jean-Baptiste Piedvache (France) but lost to Fernando Sánchez (Spain). Roberto Castañón (Spain) took the featherweight title from Manuel Masson (Spain). And Juan Francisco Rodríguez (Spain) took the bantamweight title from Franco Zurlo (Italy).   (FRANK BUTLER)

Wrestling. Athletes from the Soviet Union dominated both the freestyle and Greco-Roman wrestling events at the World Games, which were held during August in Mexico City. In the freestyle competition, the U.S.S.R. won six individual titles and amassed a total of 54 points to finish in first place. East Germany won two gold medals but finished a distant second with 21 points. Iran, which scored 19 points, was followed by Japan, whose 18 points included one gold medal. Bulgaria and the U.S. tied for fifth place at 17½ points each. In the Greco-Roman events, the Soviet Union

team once again took six of the ten individual championships and scored a total of 53 points. Romania, which had 36 points for a solid second-place finish, captured three gold medals. Bulgaria won the only other gold medal and finished third (30 points). Other top teams included Poland (23), Yugoslavia (15), and West Germany (11). The 1978 National Collegiate Athletic Association (NCAA) championships were the closest in history. Defending champion Iowa State was narrowly defeated by Iowa 94½–94. Oklahoma State was third with 86¼.   (MARVIN G. HESS)

Fencing. The world fencing championships in July were witnessed by enthusiastic fans who followed the action in the Sporthalle arena in Hamburg, West Germany. The eight events included the women's individual and team foil competitions and the men's individual and team events with the foil, sabre, and épée. The Soviet Union's

John Peterson is successfully thrown by Mark Lieberman of the New York Athletic Club in a match at the national AAU freestyle wrestling championships in Ames, Iowa, in April. Peterson, an Olympic medalist, eventually won the bout.

Table II. World Wrestling Champions

Weight class	Freestyle	Greco-Roman
48 kg (105.5 lb)	Serge Kornilaev, U.S.S.R.	Constantin Alexandru, Romania
52 kg (114.5 lb)	Anatol Beloglazo, U.S.S.R.	Vakhtang Blaguidze, U.S.S.R.
57 kg (125.5 lb)	Hideaki Tomiyama, Japan	Chamil Serikov, U.S.S.R.
62 kg (136.5 lb)	Vladmir Jumine, U.S.S.R.	Boris Kramorenko, U.S.S.R.
68 kg (149.5 lb)	Pavel Pinigin, U.S.S.R.	Stefan Rusu, Romania
74 kg (163 lb)	Lee Kemp, U.S.	Arif Niftoullaev, U.S.S.R.
82 kg (180.5 lb)	Magomedkham Arazilov, U.S.S.R.	Ion Draica, Romania
90 kg (198 lb)	Uwe Neupert, E. Germany	Stoian Nikolov, Bulgaria
100 kg (220 lb)	Harald Buttner, E. Germany	Nikolai Balbochine, U.S.S.R.
100+ kg	Soslan Andyev, U.S.S.R.	Aleandre Kolchinski, U.S.S.R.

WIDE WORLD

During the world junior fencing championships in Madrid, Baianov (centre) won a gold medal in the sabre event. His two Soviet teammates finished third and fourth.

three victories came in the two women's events and in the men's individual sabre competition. Hungary's two gold medals were awarded to its sabre and épée teams. Poland, West Germany, and France each finished with one first place victory. The overall results were expected inasmuch as fencers from Eastern European countries had dominated the sport for more than two decades and traditionally arrived in top form for the annual international contests. In the men's individual foil event, Didier Flament of France finished first ahead of Soviet fencer Aleksandr Romankov. As also happened in all of the other individual events, a fence-off was needed to decide the winner. In men's sabre, Viktor Krovopouskov of the U.S.S.R. was victorious. Olympic gold medalist Alexander Pusch of West Germany avenged his 1977 defeat by recapturing the épée title. In the women's foil, the only weapon used by women fencers, Valentina Sidorova of the U.S.S.R. remained champion. Poland won its only first place medal when its men's foil team outscored France. As the ten-day program came to an end the fans as well as the coaches and athletes were evaluating all performances with an eye to the 1980 Olympics. The Soviets were obviously pleased; Hungary remained a power in the men's sabre and épée; and West Germany had cause to rejoice because Harald Hein and Cornelia Hanisch both finished third in their respective foil events. U.S. fencers continued to lag behind world contenders, but enthusiasm was mounting dramatically, mainly because junior Olympic programs were flourishing under the patronage of the Amateur Fencers League, which governs the sport in the U.S. In the National Collegiate Athletic Association championships, Notre Dame won its third consecutive team title.

(MICHAEL STRAUSS)

Judo. Twenty-year-old Yasuhiro Yamashita firmly established himself as the world's top judoka in 1978 by winning the All-Japan championships for the second consecutive year and capturing both the open and heavyweight classes

in the 26-nation Jigoro Kano Cup international championships at Tokyo's Nippon Budokan in November. The Tokai University student beat Chonosuke Takagi in the finals of the national championships at the Budokan in April; third place was shared by Sumio Endo and Tsukio Kawahara. Some 184 judoka competed for the Jigoro Cup in the largest international tourney since the 1976 Montreal Olympics. Japan dominated the action by winning seven of the eight different weight classes. Yamashita defeated European champion Jean-Luc Rouge of France in the open and then Olympic open champion Haruki Uemura in the finals of the heavyweight class. Dietmar Lorenz of East Germany prevented a complete sweep by the Japanese by pinning Olympic champion Kazuhiro Ninomiya to grab the light-heavyweight title. Olympic champion Isamu Sonoda of Japan took the heavy-middleweight title, and three-time world champion Shozo Fujii won the middleweight class. Kazuro Yoshimura captured the light-middleweight crown, Katsunori Akimoto the welterweight title, and Katsumi Suzuki, with a great last-day effort, the lightweight class. In Japan's first women's national championships, 13-year-old Kaori Yamaguchi won the 50-kg (110-lb) class, while Hiromi Fukuda took the top 65-kg (143-lb) class.

Karate. During 1978 Japanese karateka were involved in competitions that extended from the first Yokohama city championships in March to the Asian championships in Taiwan in December. After the Osaka city tournament in April, the Japanese competed in the World Deaf Games in Italy in May; the Italians won most of the weight-class titles. The outstanding performer of the year was Wado-kai stylist Hisao Murase, who during May captured the individual competition in the All-Japan Industrial Championships at Yokosuka; Nissan Motors took the team title. Murase, the 1976 Wado-kai champion, had to be satisfied with runner-up honours in the All-Japan Wado-kai Championships, as Zenichi Ono, the small (5-ft-6 in;

140-lb) 1975 champion, climaxed his comeback by grabbing first place in July at Tokyo's Nippon Bukodan. But Murase reached the high point of his career in September by capturing the *kumite* (sparring) title in the prestigious All-Japan All-Styles Championships in Nagano Prefecture, defeating Kihei Sakamoto, a Goju-kai specialist. Sakamoto, who had been runner-up in the previous All-Styles Championships two years earlier, was beaten with an upper straight punch (*jodan-zuki*). Hiromasu Miyano, who won the kata (prescribed forms) contest in the fourth All-Styles World Championships in December 1977, took the kata title in the All-Japan All-Styles tournament. Tokyo won first place in the team *kumite* competition; Saitama Prefecture was second and Osaka third. In other key tournaments, Toshiro Mori surprised favourite Mikio Yahara with a sudden footsweep and follow-up face punch to win the Japan Karate Association (JKA) *kumite* competition in June, and Tochigi Prefecture won the team title in the 17th All-Japan Bogu (protective equipment) Championships. Hiroichi Murayama of Chiba Prefecture took first place in the 18th All-Japan Shito-kai Championships at Nara during August. M. Harada won the title in the Tokyo Championships in August, and Joko Ninomiya won the contact karate competition of the Kyokushin-kai All-Japan Open Championships in November. During the All-Japan Goju-kai Championships at Fukuoka in October, Eiji Yoshida won the individual title and Fukuoka the team title.

Sumo. *Yokozuna* (grand champion) Kitanoumi completely dominated traditional Japanese sumo wrestling in 1978 by winning five of the six 15-day annual *basho* (tournaments) and breaking the great *yokozuna* Taiho's all-time record of 81 victories in a single year. Kitanoumi won 82 of the 90 bouts that top *rikishi* (wrestlers) fight each year. The 5-ft 11-in, 375-lb powerhouse also took over second place on the all-time list of most career *yusho* (championships) by registering his 14th tournament title in September, but he still had far to go to equal Taiho's prodigious record of 32 lifetime championships. Although Kitanoumi won five straight *yusho*, he failed to get the sixth, which would have equalled the record jointly held by Futabayama and Taiho, two of sumo's greatest champions, who fought, respectively, in the 1930s and 1960s. Although Kitanoumi lost only four bouts in the first five *basho*, he suffered four more losses in the Kyushu tournament and finished in third place. His overall performance during 1978, however, guaranteed that he would be named *Rikishi* of the year for the fourth time. Sharing the year's honours was Wakamisugi, who after the Natsu (summer) *basho* in May was promoted from the rank of *ozeki* to the top rank of *yokozuna*, from which there is no demotion. *Yokozuna* who perform poorly go into retirement. Wakamisugi celebrated his promotion by adopting the name Wakanohana, which had been made famous by his stable boss, Futagoyama Oyakata, when he was a *yokozuna* in the late 1950s and early 1960s. The new *yokozuna* was runner-up to Kitanoumi in every tournament during the year except one and captured the Kyushu *basho* title with his first perfect 15–0 record and his second career *yusho*. Kitanoumi won the Tokyo Hatsu (New Year's) *basho* in January with a 15–0 record, then defeated *ozeki* Wakamisugi in a play-off for the Osaka Haru (spring) *basho* title after the two finished with identical 13–2 records. Kitanoumi won the Tokyo Natsu *basho* with a 14–1 mark, again overpowering Wakamisugi in a play-off. Kitanoumi fought it out with the third *yokozuna*, 31-year-old Wajima, for the Nagoya *basho* title, muscling Wajima out of the 14-ft 10-in *dohyo* (clay ring) on the 14th day and finishing with his second perfect 15–0 performance of the year. Kitanoumi captured his fifth straight tourney title with another strong 14–1 performance in the Tokyo Aki (autumn) *basho* in September. Takamiyama (Hawaiian-American Jesse Kuhaulua) also came in for his share of the honours in 1978 by setting a new *kinboshi* (gold star) mark of 12. The honour is merited by *maegashira*-ranked wrestlers in the top division whenever they upset a *yokozuna*. Several former *makunouchi rikishi* (wrestlers belonging to the highest six divisions) had their topknots clipped in retirement ceremonies after being demoted to the second-highest *juryo* division. These included former *komusubi* Haguroiwa and former *juryo* wrestler Kiyonohana, the only *rikishi* of Chinese descent. The biggest social event of the sumo year was Kitanoumi's marriage to Tomiko Ishikawa, the 24-year-old daughter of a restaurant proprietor in Kawasaki. The marriage on September 30 was highlighted by a $500,000 wedding banquet that rivaled in its lavishness the wedding banquet of Taiho in the mid-1960s. More than 1,500 select guests were invited to the affair, which was televised live by NHK-TV. The bride appeared in three different $50,000 kimonos.

Kendo. In the top event of 1978, two policemen fought for the national title in the finals of the All-Japan Kendo Championships in December at Tokyo's Nippon Budokan. M. Ishibashi scored two *men* (helmet) strikes to one for Y. Nishikawa to win the championship. The All-Japan Team Championships and the All-Japan Women's Championships were held at the Osaka Central Gymnasium in May. Osaka outpointed Kanagawa Prefecture 4–1 to win the team title. The women's contest was a virtual repeat performance of the 1977 match, as C. Nemoto of Osaka was again victorious over Y. Horibe in a close 2–1 match. Horibe was also runner-up in the All-Japan Women Students Championships in July at the Budokan, losing to R. Ritan of Hokkaido Junior College 0–2 in the finals. K. Kishimoto of Doshisha University beat K. Hayashi of Hosei University 2–1 in the men's university event. Yukio Ono, police kendo champion for three years, had to settle for second place in the All-Japan Police Championships at the Budokan in June. Koji Kasamura of the Kanagawa prefectural police department was victorious 1–0 (*kote*). In April three high-ranking Japanese kendoists gave demonstrations during the European championships, which were held in Chambéry, France. The visiting Japanese also held a special training class. France won both the team and individual European titles.

(ANDREW M. ADAMS)

Commonwealth of Nations

A year of unspectacular but continuing success in cementing economic and social links among Commonwealth countries, 1978 was epitomized by the Commonwealth Games at Edmonton, Alta., in August, where the friendly endeavour of 46 member nations and affiliates contrasted with the cost and strife of the 1976 Montreal Olympics. Commonwealth membership grew to 39, including Nauru and with the Solomon Islands, Tuvalu, and Dominica as new members.

Regional cooperation was emphasized both in exclusively Commonwealth bodies like the South Pacific Forum and in associations with non-Commonwealth members, such as the Association of Southeast Asian Nations (ASEAN). An important regional summit conference, held February 13–16 in Sydney, Australia, joined Australia, New Zealand, Fiji, Papua New Guinea, Tonga, Western Samoa, Nauru, India, Bangladesh, Sri Lanka, Malaysia, and Singapore. It was a success despite terrorist activity, the first such at a Commonwealth meeting. Task forces were set up to deal with trade, terrorism, energy, and drugs.

Now a preeminent Commonwealth power, Australia mourned its former prime minister and great Commonwealth statesman Sir Robert Menzies (*see* OBITUARIES), who died in May. Australia acquired the Cocos Islands from John Clunies Ross, whose family had owned the land since the mid-19th century, and continued to underpin Papua New Guinea economically. Australia's special relationship with Malta was disturbed when Maltese Prime Minister Dom Mintoff demanded more economic aid from Australia. Together with many Southeast Asian and Pacific countries, Australia felt the effects of the great exodus of refugees from Southeast Asia. (*See* AUSTRALIA: *Special Report.*)

Commonwealth Africa also faced a serious refugee problem, and in the death of Kenya's Jomo Kenyatta (*see* OBITUARIES) in August lost a senior statesman. But the Rhodesia problem overshadowed all others. (*See* RHODESIA.)

In the Caribbean, Jamaica and Guyana strengthened ties with Communist Cuba. The Caribbean Group for Cooperation in Economic Development, a consortium under the aegis of the World Bank, held its first meeting in June. With a minimum fund of $125 million, it would direct attention to Jamaica, Guyana, and Barbados, because of their dependence on oil and falling export prices, and to smaller islands facing economic difficulties.

Great Britain directed aid toward the poorest Commonwealth countries, which received 80% of the £514 million in bilateral aid allocated in 1976. This was supplemented by the announcement in August of debt cancellations amounting to £864 million of principal and £64 million of annual interest until the year 2001. The budget of the Commonwealth Fund for Technical Cooperation was increased to £12 million for 1978–79. The Commonwealth Development Corporation's 1978 report showed almost all its 23 new projects (£45 million) in the poorest Commonwealth areas centred on "renewable natural resources." Commitments for 1977 totaled £333.9 million.

The Commonwealth Foundation, which already coordinated over 300 professional bodies, met in London to plan an extension of its work. In April a two-day Commonwealth ministerial meeting, also in London, followed up the work of the UN Conference on Trade and Development by setting up a Common Fund for the stabilization of 18 key commodities traded by Commonwealth members.

(MOLLY MORTIMER)

See also articles on the various political units.
[972.A.1.a]

Comoros

An island state lying in the Indian Ocean off the east coast of Africa between Mozambique and Madagascar, the Comoros in 1978 administratively comprised three main islands, Grande Comore, Moheli, and Anjouan; the fourth island of the archipelago, Mayotte, continued to be a de facto dependency of France. Area: 1,792 sq km (692 sq mi). Pop. (1978 est.): 311,000. Cap. and largest city: Moroni (pop., 1976 est., 18,300), on Grande Comore. Language: French. Religion: mainly Muslim. President to May 13, 1978, Ali Soilih; co-presidents from May 24, Ahmed Abdallah and Mohammed Ahmed; president from October 3, Ahmed Abdallah; premiers, Abdallah Mohammed and, from December 22, Salim Ben Ali.

Marchers carrying a giant Canadian flag participated in the official opening of the XI Commonwealth Games at Edmonton, Alberta, in August.

CANADIAN PRESS

COMOROS

Education. (Including Mayotte; 1976–77) Primary, pupils 34,181, teachers 849; secondary, pupils 2,541, teachers 115; teacher training, students 45, teachers 3.

Finance and Trade. Monetary unit: CFA franc, with (Sept. 18, 1978) a parity of CFA Fr 50 to the French franc and a free rate of CFA Fr 218.81 to U.S. $1 (CFA Fr 428.75 = £1 sterling). Budget (1976 est.) balanced at *c.* CFA Fr 1 billion. Foreign trade (including Mayotte; 1974): imports CFA Fr 6,203,000,000; exports CFA Fr 2,138,000,000. Import sources: France *c.* 50%; Madagascar *c.* 15%; Kenya *c.* 5%. Export destinations: France *c.* 75%; Madagascar *c.* 9%; Italy *c.* 7%. Main exports (1972): vanilla 41%; essential oils 33%; cloves 11%; copra 6%.

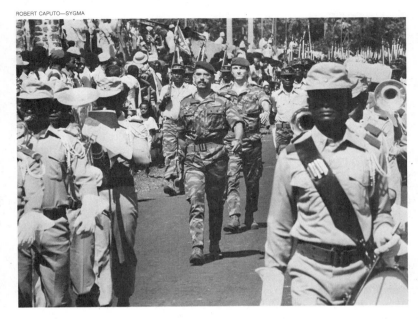

White mercenaries hired by two wealthy Comorans led a military parade after they had seized power in the Comoros. Robert Denard was hailed as "No. 1 President" by the Comorans.

ROBERT CAPUTO—SYGMA

On May 13, 1978, Pres. Ali Soilih was overthrown by a coup organized outside the country and commanded by former French mercenary Robert Denard (*see* BIOGRAPHIES). Soilih was said to have been shot "while attempting to escape"; this brought some discredit on the new regime, although Soilih had been extremely unpopular.

The reinstatement of former president Ahmed Abdallah (overthrown by Soilih in August 1975) took place in stages. First, a political and military directorate promised a new constitution; a few days later it reappointed Abdallah Mohammed as premier; on May 24 a "federal and Islamic republic" was proclaimed under two co-presidents, Ahmed Abdallah and Mohammed Ahmed; on July 22 an exclusively political leadership replaced the joint directorate. In a referendum held on October 1, the new constitution was approved by over 90% of the voters. Two days later Mohammed Ahmed resigned, leaving Ahmed Abdallah sole president.

The French government established diplomatic relations with the new regime in July, following a visit to France by Ahmed Abdallah in June, and cooperation agreements were signed November 10. In July the Comoran delegation to the Khartoum, Sudan, summit of the Organization of African Unity was expelled when the other members denied that it was representative.

(PHILIPPE DECRAENE)

Computers

To no one's surprise, computer technology continued to make great strides during 1978. Many of these advances resulted in smaller, faster, and less expensive data-processing machinery capable of being utilized by people who lack in-depth knowledge of the devices they manipulate.

At least as important as the technological breakthroughs, however, was the vastly increased awareness on the part of people having no direct involvement with computers that their lives were growing inextricably linked with these electronic marvels. Few saw the linkage as an unalloyed blessing. While *Time* magazine waxed ebullient in a February 20 cover story on the labour-saving benefits of computers, stories of computer-related fraud, theft, and invasion of privacy raised a good many doubts.

Mainframes, Minis, and Micros. To an unprecedented extent the minicomputer dominated the attention of the computer world during 1978. Even mainframes—the huge machines costing millions of dollars—increasingly came to be composed of teams of minicomputers, each mini managing a specific slice of the total operation.

But most importantly, the minicomputers not formed into mainframe configurations at last made it feasible for small businesses and (in the least sophisticated versions) for individuals to utilize computer technology. As a consequence, minicomputers became the fastest-growing segment of the computer industry. Their comparatively low cost, in both purchase price and operational overhead, and their ability to function well in less than the optimal environmental (air-conditioned, dust-free) conditions demanded by mainframes made the minis highly appealing; in 1978 they comprised about 20% of the $9 billion volume of the U.S. computer industry.

Recognizing that minis had exhibited an annual growth rate of 35% while mainframes had only expanded at a 15% rate, the dominant mainframe manufacturer, IBM Corp., entered the minicomputer industry by expanding its sales of small business computers. The resulting competition and the continuing technological sophistication of the minis—especially insofar as the capabilities of the microprocessor "miracle" silicon chip were concerned—produced about a 20% annual drop in minicomputer prices.

While the mini makers could be said to have profited in ways that did not directly threaten IBM's total dominance in the computer marketplace, that was not the case with a host of other

Comoros

Communications: *see* Industrial Review; Television and Radio

"Now here's my plan
. . . . ."

Showing that a computer can be trained to do almost anything, officials of a clothing store in Chicago demonstrated a computer programmed to design men's suits.

small computer companies. A major development of 1978 was the coming to prominence of several new computer makers that offered mainframes capable of running on IBM software but selling at lower prices than the IBM equipment. They were able to accomplish this through extensive use of microprocessor chips.

IBM countered by reducing its mainframe prices (and thereby raising price/performance ratios to all-time highs) and by introducing new models. In April IBM chairman Frank T. Cary reported that the company had the largest backlog of orders in its history and expected to add 10,000 people to its manufacturing divisions. Earlier in the year, IBM had announced that its gross income for 1977 was $18.1 billion, up 11% from 1976.

One area of computers in which IBM was no force at all during 1978 was the so-called home computer. Another example of how the microprocessor chip could reduce the size, cost, and operating complexity of data-processing devices, the home computer promised a future of totally automated domiciles. According to David Chung, Umtech's vice-president, "We will use the computer for all our financial work. For printouts of recipes, letters, medical records, self-improvement classes, shipping at home. We'll be able to interrogate it about our stocks and brew coffee with it."

Software and Magnetic Media. As computer hardware grew ever more sophisticated during 1978, the gap between the devices themselves and the software, the body of instructional material conceived to control them and to utilize their extraordinary capabilities, grew ever wider. In fact, the dearth of home computer programs constituted one major drag on sales of the devices. Manufacturers emphasized the rapid creation of libraries of cassette computer programs in order to woo small businessmen who had previously shied away from computers because of the high cost of hiring expensive programming personnel.

Keeping pace with the advances in hardware was the growth in magnetic media used to organize and store information. Cognizant of the limitations of computer tape (primarily the slowness of retrieval), manufacturers developed various forms of disks. In contrast to tape, which stores and processes information in sequence, disks permit random access to data. Although tape can store much more information than a disk for the same expenditure, it frequently consumes much more of the computer's time—a cost factor not to be overlooked. On the other hand, disks are far more sensitive and demanding of a clean, uncontaminated environment. A particle of dust can result in the destruction of much of a disk's stored information. Recently, the floppy disk—offering the best of both tape (low cost) and disk (quick retrieval)—has grown increasingly popular.

In mid-September Rockwell International set the computer world buzzing with its announcement of the first commercial production of bubble-memory devices. These solid-state units can store 256,000 bits of information in a device about the size of a shirt button, making it practical at last to put computers anywhere. And since the bubble-memory devices are relatively unaffected by dirt, they make possible computer installations in gas stations, factories, and other places previously deemed unsuitable for data-processing machinery.

Applications. Increasingly during 1978 the computer's unparalleled capabilities were put to improving the quality of human life. Researchers at the University of Illinois Medical Center, for example, sought to find new ways of regulating fertility—and thus safer forms of contraception—by feeding data relating to fertility-regulating agents in plants into an IBM 370/168. Drawing upon everything from scientific journals to folklore from throughout the world, they analyzed more than 5,000 plants; the computer was programmed to list the plants in ranked order according to their supposed ability to regulate fertility. The plants that emerged at the top of the list were then subjected to further study.

Even the car makers were finding new ways to incorporate computer technology into their products. Microprocessors appeared in only a few 1978 domestic automobiles, but starting in 1980 nearly all of the ten million new cars produced in the U.S. would possess the tiny electronic devices to enhance fuel economy. In West Germany, Volkswagen and Blaupunkt worked on perfecting a computer system designed to route drivers in such a way that traffic congestion would be minimized. The system comprises a small computer in the car which communicates with a network of computers along the side of the road.

Perils of Progress. With greater frequency than ever before individuals both inside the computer community and out discussed the sombre side of life in the electronic era. The basic issue involved security—the ability to make certain that the data stored in huge computer memory banks could not be tapped by unauthorized persons or utilized for unintended purposes.

Always a problem, computer security became more complicated with the growth of distributed data processing (DDP). With DDP, multiple computer systems are placed in a variety of physical locations. In many instances, each of the systems has access to the central processor. Clearly, when a large number of people at remote locations can tap into the stored data, security becomes difficult to maintain.

Interestingly, a number of nations—especially Sweden, France, and West Germany—displayed their concern about computer security by adopting privacy laws that restricted the flow across national borders of computerized information about citizens. The U.S. opposed these laws on the grounds that the U.S. economy and system of government were based upon the free flow of information and because U.S. manufacturers were by far the world's largest exporters of computers and communications equipment.

Concerns about privacy, though, were not restricted to countries in Western Europe; fears were expressed in the U.S. as well. In 1952 the U.S. government had one computer, a Univac I; in 1978 it owned or leased 11,000 computers plus 56,000 terminals. Government computers had data on virtually every citizen, and that data included financial, health, and employment information. The main threat to personal privacy was posed by the access that unauthorized individuals had to these data. Authorities claimed that many government databanks—manufactured before computer crime became epidemic during the 1970s—present few difficulties to the computer technician desiring to manipulate the system for illegal purposes.

(JEROLD L. KELLMAN)

See also Industrial Review: *Special Report.*
[735.D; 10/23.A.6–7]

Congo

A people's republic of equatorial Africa, the Congo is bounded by Gabon, Cameroon, the Central African Empire, Zaire, Angola, and the Atlantic Ocean. Area: 342,000 sq km (132,047 sq mi). Pop. (1978 est.): 1,434,000, mainly Bantu. Cap. and largest city: Brazzaville (pop., 1974 prelim., 299,-000). Language: French (official) and Bantu dialects. Religion: Roman Catholic 38%; most of the remainder are animist. President in 1978, Col. Joachim Yhombi-Opango; premier, Maj. Louis Sylvain Ngoma.

Congo

CONGO
Education. (1974–75) Primary, pupils 307,194, teachers 5,053; secondary, pupils 81,541, teachers 1,703; vocational, pupils 5,526, teachers 390; teacher training, students 901, teachers 50; higher, students 3,007, teaching staff 225.
Finance. Monetary unit: CFA franc, with (Sept 18, 1978) a parity of CFA Fr 50 to the French franc and a free rate of CFA Fr 218.81 to U.S. $1 (CFA Fr 428.75 = £1 sterling). Budget (1977 est.) balanced at CFA Fr 61,404,000,000.
Foreign Trade. (1976) Imports CFA Fr 41,896,000,000; exports CFA Fr 59,870,000,000. Import sources: France 45%; West Germany 8%; Gabon 7%; U.S. 5%. Export destinations: U.S. 30%; Italy 15%; France 12%; Spain 8%. Main exports: crude oil 61%; timber (1974) 19%.
Transport and Communications. Roads (1976) c. 11,-000 km. Motor vehicles in use (1974): passenger 19,000; commercial (including buses) 10,500. Railways (1976): 795 km; traffic 246 million passenger-km, freight 508 million net ton-km. Air traffic (including apportionment of Air Afrique; 1976): 137 million passenger-km; freight 14.2 million net ton-km. Telephones (Dec. 1974) 10,000. Radio receivers (Dec. 1975) 81,000. Television receivers (Dec. 1973) 3,800.
Agriculture. Production (in 000; metric tons; 1976): cassava 761; sweet potatoes c. 96; peanuts 23; sugar, raw value c. 46; bananas 24; coffee c. 1; cocoa c. 2; palm oil c. 5; tobacco c. 2. Livestock (in 000; 1976): cattle 50; sheep 52; goats 101; pigs 44; chickens 843.
Industry. Production (in 000; metric tons): crude oil (1976) 2,002; potash (oxide content; 1975) 462; cement (1975) 55; electricity (kw-hr; 1976) 120,000.

The continued existence of factional struggles within the Congolese leadership was indicated by the increasing calls for "revolutionary vigilance." The trial of the accused assassins of former president Marien Ngouabi opened on Jan. 3, 1978. Ten of the 42 defendants were sentenced to death on February 6, and the sentence was carried out the next day. On August 14, Pres. Joachim Yhombi-Opango announced the discovery of a further plot and the arrest of several officers and civilians.

Despite the unsettled political situation, the economy remained relatively strong, thanks to the production in 1977 of three million metric tons of crude oil. The Congo became the 13th state to officially recognize the Saharan Arab Democratic Republic (Western Sahara).

(PHILIPPE DECRAENE)

Consumerism

Undoubtedly a highlight of 1978 was the ninth Congress of the International Organization of Consumers Unions (IOCU), which was held July 10–14 in London. Approximately 400 delegates representing nearly 40 countries and various international bodies met together for five days to discuss diverse consumer problems under the heading of "A World in Crisis: The Consumer Responses."

The conference split into small groups to discuss specific topics such as the problems of low-income consumers, the mass media, consumer surveys, local consumer groups, promotional activities of consumer groups and their representation at different levels, consumer advice centres and adult consumer education, and the topics of food and energy, perhaps more immediately pertinent to all consumers everywhere. Speakers at the congress urged that consumer organizations continue the battle for nutritional foods obtainable at reasonable prices and that they redouble their efforts to expose foods that lack nutritional value. The congress further resolved that all consumer organizations acting through IOCU should support and urge their respective national governments to assist food-deficient less developed countries to achieve a substantial degree of food self-sufficiency.

Speaking to the congress on the energy crisis, the IOCU president reminded delegates that it was a challenge for consumer organizations to have the opportunity to explain to their members and to the public at large what the basic issues of the problem are, to distinguish the various issues and interests at stake, and to give practical help and advice. In particular, delegates referred to the problems posed by nuclear energy, the need for conservation and greater energy efficiency, and the need to continue to search for alternative methods of supplying energy. Other major topics discussed included the necessity of providing greatly improved information for consumers; for example, the results of tests of the many devices on the market for which fuel saving claims are made.

National Development. In 1978 the consumer movement in the United States placed greater emphasis on state and local political campaigns to gain voting power. This was done by supporting candidates who favoured consumer protection legislation. Ralph Nader and the Consumer Federation of America led a nationwide campaign for candidates in favour of consumer interests.

Increased attention was given to the consumerism movement at the state level as a result of the February 1978 defeat by the U.S. Congress of a bill to create a consumer protection agency. This agency would have represented consumer interests to other government agencies through the process of intervention. It would have been an "umbrella" agency for all consumer activities. The bill was defeated after an eight-year debate before Congress, with the major argument being that there was already too much government regulation.

In response to the defeat, U.S. Pres. Jimmy Carter gave White House Consumer Adviser Esther Peterson permission to lobby before regulatory agencies for consumer causes. To gain momentum in this area, Peterson began to coordinate the efforts of the various consumer offices in federal agencies and departments. President Carter directed the White House Office of Consumer Affairs to participate in domestic policy decisions that affect consumers and to examine current programs offered by the federal government in order to make recommendations for their improvement. The president favoured legislation to establish a consumer cooperative bank agency as well as a procedure for consumers to gain more participation in government decision-making. Consumerists supported a bill that would pay the legal costs of their appearances before congressional committees and federal agencies.

In August, Congress passed a bill creating the consumer cooperative bank. This bank was to provide $1.5 billion in loans over the following five years as well as technical assistance to managers of consumer cooperatives. Such coops sell a wide variety of products and services but are most often found in the food industry. The federal bank would provide funds for a coop that had expanded too rapidly and needed additional capital.

The Consumer Product Safety Commission issued rules in 1978 clarifying the responsibility of industries to report potentially hazardous products to the commission. In the regulation that generated the most debate, the commission required companies to notify it within 24 hours once a corporate official learned that a product did not comply with a safety standard or that the item contained a defect that could create "a substantial risk of injury."

The Federal Trade Commission proposed a trade regulation rule that would make it easier for buyers of consumer products to take advantage of the full warranty provided by manufacturers. Under the proposed rule certain requirements demanded by the warrantor would be considered unreasonable. These included requiring the consumer to fill in and return a registration card shortly after purchase in order to make the warranty effective and to pay the cost of mailing the product to and from the warranty service point.

In Canada a bill was introduced in Parliament that would enable a citizen to sue for damages on behalf of a number of people with the same grievance. Quebec would be a pioneer under this Class Action Act in that the provincial government would give assistance in the form of a grant for the preparation and presentation of the action when the costs were beyond the plaintiffs' means. The Canadian Standards Association in the summer of 1978 began testing household appliances for the amount of energy they use, and Ontario put into law a warranty program for new homes that would guarantee that the building had been constructed in accordance with the Ontario Building Code, was free from major structural defects and defects in material, and was fit for habitation.

Joseph Marshall of Falls Church, Virginia, aired consumer complaints before a House investigations subcommittee concerning the safety problems of some Firestone steel-belted radial tires.

WIDE WORLD

The French Cabinet approved a bill that would impose stricter controls on outdoor advertising with the aim of protecting France's environmental and architectural heritage. The Consumer Protection and Information Act, also known as the Scrivener Act, came into force in January, nearly three years after French consumer organizations had published their draft consumer law; the safety and health of consumers, honest information on products, and equality in conditions of contract for both buyer and seller were among its wide-ranging terms.

In the United Kingdom regulations were prepared to control the production of cosmetics and to eliminate harmful substances from them. The Unfair Contract Terms Act came into force during 1978, as did the Consumer Safety Act and regulations concerning unit pricing for meat. A Consumer Information Act was introduced in Ireland during 1978, some six years after the Consumers' Association of Ireland first advised the government on the need for law reform in that direction. The act made it a criminal offense to describe goods or services falsely.

International Cooperation. A noticeable characteristic of the consumer movement continued to be the ready cooperation between consumer organizations internationally. As an example the results of a comparative test on outboard motors, the first worldwide test organized by IOCU and aimed at serving consumer needs in developed and less developed countries alike, were presented at a press conference in Hong Kong in April.

A planned UNESCO Literacy Project, which aimed to finance and provide training in basic literacy and nutrition for leaders who would then go to live and work in India, was to relate in particular to education in nutrition and include recognition of adulterated foodstuffs. The primary aim of the first gathering of the World Intellectual Property Organization, meeting in Geneva in July, was to explore how trademarks, patents, and the like could be used to improve the protection of consumers, particularly in less developed countries.

The Consumer Information Service of the European Economic Community was involved during the year in helping consumer and environmental protection bodies produce audiovisual materials on European topics. The EEC Commission also presented the Council of Ministers with proposals concerning the quality of water for agricultural use, permissible levels of sound emissions from power lawn mowers and air compressors, and proposals to set up a group of experts to study returning of agricultural wastes to the land. The aim of the latter proposal was to encourage the use of techniques that would ensure the "health protection" of fruit crops.

(ISOLA VAN DEN HOVEN; EDWARD MARK MAZZE)

See also Economy, World; Industrial Review: *Advertising.*
[532.B.3; 534.H.5; 534.K]

The Ford Motor Company was indicted on criminal charges in Indiana after the gas tank in this Ford Pinto exploded when hit from behind on August 10. Three teenage girls riding in the car were killed.

So-called generic products, which list only the name of the contents, were introduced and offered to buyers as food shopping bargains.

Contract Bridge

The year 1978 was notable for the peaceful coexistence that was restored to the tournament bridge world. Top-level international bridge had long been bedeviled by accusations of wrongdoing, and so the president of the World Bridge Federation (WBF), Jaime Ortiz-Patino, ensured that any such charges were dealt with promptly and thoroughly. For example, the Italian Bridge Federation was suspended from the WBF, but when it made the required changes in its constitution it was welcomed back. The Pairs Olympiad in New Orleans, La., was played in an excellent spirit, and though the Italians for once failed to take a title, they were so strong in depth that they later were major challengers for honours in other tournaments.

Perhaps the most romantic story of the 1978 Olympiad related to the women's pairs championship. In 1969 C. C. Wei, a Taiwanese shipbuilder based in New York and a bridge enthusiast whose interest lay in innovation rather than in play, had created the Precision Club system and had persuaded Taiwan to play it, with some success, in world championships. The bridge-playing member of Wei's family was his wife, Katherine. A relative beginner in 1969, she set out to become a champion and in New Orleans in 1978 achieved her ambition when she won the Ladies' Pairs Olympiad with Judi Radin for the U.S.

Brazil, which in 1976 had taken the Teams Olympiad title from Italy, triumphed again in 1978 when Marcelo Branco and Gabino Cintra won the Open Pairs Olympiad title after a titanic struggle with the young Canadian pair, Eric Kokish and Peter Nagy. They thus became the second pair to hold both Olympic titles at the same time (the first was Pierre Jais and Roger Trézel of France, in 1962). The Mixed Pairs championship was won by Barry Crane and Kerry Shuman (U.S.).

The Venice Cup, a world team championship for women, was organized for the first time as a full-scale event. The zonal representatives were the U.S., Italy, Argentina, Australia, and the Philippines. Predictably, Italy and the U.S. were the finalists, and though Italy took a good lead in the first session, the U.S. sextet, Emma Jean Hawes, Dorothy Hayden Truscott, Jacqui Mitchell, Gail Moss, Mary Jane Farrell, and Marilyn Johnson, with Ruth McConnell as nonplaying captain, outplayed their opponents in the remaining three sets to win by a comfortable margin.

A nonchampionship competition, a team event for the Julius Rosenblum Memorial Trophy, almost upstaged the main events. The 64 teams that began the competition were full of champions, with a heavy North American representation that was expected to sweep the board. It was no surprise to find Brazil with its Olympic Team champions as one of the finalists. It was a surprise to find a five-man Polish team (deprived of their top players through illness) there, and it was an even greater surprise to witness the Poles outscoring their opponents by over two points to one to win the competition.   (HAROLD FRANKLIN)

Costa Rica

A Central American republic, Costa Rica lies between Nicaragua and Panama and has coastlines on the Caribbean Sea and the Pacific Ocean. Area: 50,898 sq km (19,652 sq mi). Pop. (1977 est.): 2,-070,600, including white and mestizo 98%. Cap. and largest city: San José (metro. pop., 1977 est., 534,400). Language: Spanish. Religion: predomi-

Costa Rica

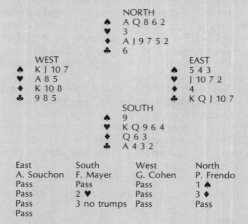

It would appear difficult to select the best played hand of a tournament that involved hundreds of the world's top players and thousands of deals. However, a panel of bridge journalists voted almost unanimously for the following:

```
                          NORTH
                          ♠ A Q 8 6 2
                          ♥ 3
                          ♦ A J 9 7 5 2
                          ♣ 6
        WEST                              EAST
        ♠ K J 10 7                        ♠ 5 4 3
        ♥ A 8 5                           ♥ J 10 7 2
        ♦ K 10 8                          ♦ 4
        ♣ 9 8 5                           ♣ K Q J 10 7
                          SOUTH
                          ♠ 9
                          ♥ K Q 9 6 4
                          ♦ Q 6 3
                          ♣ A 4 3 2
```

East	South	West	North
A. Souchon	F. Mayer	G. Cohen	P. Frendo
Pass	Pass	Pass	1 ♠
Pass	2 ♥	Pass	3 ♦
Pass	3 no trumps	Pass	Pass
Pass			

Dealer, East. Love all.

West was Gilles Cohen, a young professor of mathematics from Paris. South, the declarer, was Federico Mayer of Italy, past European champion and a close runner-up in the 1970 Olympiad.

Cohen led the jack of spades, and dummy won with the queen and led a heart for the king and Cohen's ace. As the cards lay, a club switch would have worked well, but Cohen, unable to visualize his partner's holding in the suit, continued with the king of spades. This left Mayer with a problem of transportation, which he solved by leading a low diamond toward the queen. If Cohen had won with the king, this would have left declarer with nine tricks for a very high score. Cohen, with no marked hesitation, played the ten, and when declarer continued with a second diamond, he followed with the eight. Declarer now had to consider two possibilities: that West had declined to take a trick with K 10 8—impossible to imagine; or that East had played low from K 4—a play that any expert might have conceived, likely to mislead declarer if West had begun with 10 8. Mayer credited East with having made this intelligent play and played the ace only to find that it was West who had made a super-intelligent play.

nantly Roman Catholic. Presidents in 1978, Daniel Oduber Quirós and, from May 8, Rodrigo Carazo Odio.

The presidential election of Feb. 5, 1978, resulted in a victory for Rodrigo Carazo Odio (see BIOGRAPHIES) of the conservative opposition group, Partido de Unidad, over Luis Alberto Monge of the ruling Partido de Liberación Nacional (social democratic). Carazo was inaugurated on May 8.

Relations with Nicaragua worsened during the year as the result of an incident on Oct. 14, 1977, when Nicaraguan aircraft shot at three boats on the Costa Rican side of the Frío River; one of the boats was carrying Mario Charpentier Gamboa, the Costa Rican minister of public security. On Sept. 18, 1978, Nicaragua recalled its ambassador to Costa Rica after accusing Costa Rica of harbouring Nicaraguan guerrillas. In November Costa Rica broke diplomatic relations with Nicaragua.

The economy grew by an estimated 7% in 1978. The trade deficit, which amounted to $217 million in 1977, was expected to narrow, but the cost-of-living index was expected to rise by 8%.

The application of the fugitive U.S. financier Robert Vesco for Costa Rican citizenship was denied. Vesco had left the country in April on a business trip to the Bahamas. (CHRISTINE MELLOR)

Court Games

Handball. Fred Lewis of Miami, Fla., won his fifth U.S. National Open handball title by defeating defending champion Naty Alvarado of Juárez, Mexico, 21–17, 21–6 at Tucson, Ariz. The upset win over Alvarado, who had won six out of eight Spalding professional handball tournaments during the season, made Lewis the second most successful handball player ever, behind Jim Jacobs, who won six National Opens.

In the United States Handball Association (USHA) open doubles competition, Stuffy Singer (Los Angeles) and partner Marty Decatur (New York) defeated defending champions Matt Kelly and Skip McDowell of Long Beach, Calif., 7–21, 21–2, 11–3. In masters play for men over 40, Rene Zamorano of Tucson defeated Jim Faulk of Dallas, Texas, 21–13, 21–12 for the singles title, while Pete Tyson and Dick Roberson of Austin, Texas, defeated Mel Dinner and Tom Kelly of San Francisco 21–7, 19–21, 11–9 for the doubles championship. In golden masters play for men over 50, Jack Briscoe of St. Louis, Mo., successfully defended his singles crown by defeating Chicago's Leo Kilcoyne, 21–17, 21–16, while Ken Schneider and Bud Perelman of Chicago topped Bob Nedd and Stan Clawson of Palo Alto, Calif., 21–12, 21–5. Reg Chapman and Al Klein from Las Vegas, Nev., won the super masters doubles for men over 60, beating Lee Shinn of Salem, Ore., and Dave Weinberg of Chicago, 21–19, 21–13.

Lake Forest (Ill.) College won its fifth USHA intercollegiate handball title by winning the doubles and B-singles competition in the national intercollegiate handball tournament, held on its home courts. Mike Lloyd of Memphis (Tenn.) State University successfully defended his A-singles cham-

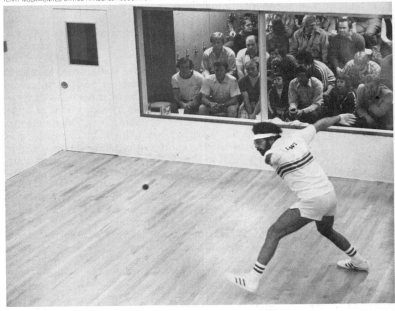

Fred Lewis of Miami, Florida, demonstrates the form that earned him his fifth U.S. National Open handball championship in Tucson, Arizona.

pionship by again stopping Steve Stanisich of Montana Tech 21–4, 21–8.

(TERRY CHARLES MUCK)

Jai Alai. The 1978 world amateur jai alai championships took place at Biarritz, France, in one of Europe's newest frontons from August 28 to September 10. The team of Alex Aperribay and Totorica of Barcelona, Spain, captured first place and the gold medal. The boys, both teenagers, displayed tremendous ability and did not lose a match. It is interesting to note that this same team finished in last place in the 1976 tournament. France, the defending world champions, managed only a third place, while teenage brothers Eduardo and Lallo Elordui took second place for Mexico. The United States, represented by 17-year-old Mike McGee of Boca Raton, Fla., and Mike Faedo, 23, of Tampa, Fla., finished fourth, while Italy trailed the field in fifth place. It was the first time since 1952 that Italy had participated in international jai alai competition. The next world tournament was tentatively scheduled to be played in Mexico in 1980. The U.S. amateur jai alai championships were played in Fort Pierce, Fla., in July. Winning the tournament were Mike McGee, playing the frontcourt and Mike Faedo playing the backcourt. Runners-up were Charles Nickerson of Daytona Beach, Fla., and Gilbert Trujillo, Jr., of Miami.

Professional jai alai continued to grow at a record pace in the U.S. A new fronton opened in Reno, Nev., the second for that state. Florida remained the centre of the sport, and there were also professional frontons in Rhode Island and Connecticut.

(ROBERT H. GROSSBERG)

Volleyball. In a surprise defeat of Japan, Cuba won the women's world volleyball championship in 1978. The United States finished fifth, the highest standing for a U.S. team in many years. In third, behind the second-place Japanese, was the host team from the U.S.S.R.; Korea finished fourth.

The men's world championship was won by the Soviet Union, which defeated Italy in the championship match. Italy, the host team, reached the finals by upsetting Cuba, which finished third. Korea was fourth and Czechoslovakia was fifth. The U.S. was a disappointing 19th. By virtue of their performances in the world championships the Cuban women and the Italian men qualified for the 1980 Olympic Games; the Soviet men and women also qualified as the host teams, as did the Japanese women and Polish men by virtue of being the defending Olympic champions. The remaining teams for the Olympics were to be determined in 1979 during the continental championships and in early 1980 in the final Olympic qualification tournament. The U.S. women were favoured to win the North American continental title in April 1979, while Cuba was the choice for the men's title.

A U.S. volleyball event worthy of special note in 1978 was the tournament connected with the first annual National Sports Festival. Winners were the West men and the South women. From that event the national junior volleyball teams were selected, and the U.S. squads of juniors (age 20 and under) then went on to the Pacific Rim Championships. There the U.S. boys defeated Japan to win first place, and the girls finished second behind Japan.

(ALBERT M. MONACO, JR.)

Cricket

All the major cricketing nations were engaged in one or more series of test matches in 1977–78. England, Australia, and Pakistan refused to select players who had signed for Australian promoter Kerry Packer's World Series. West Indies began a series against Australia with Packer players, but after two tests captain Clive Lloyd resigned be-

cause of disagreements with the selectors. His colleagues left with him, and thereafter West Indies played with a non-Packer eleven.

England's three drawn games in Pakistan demonstrated how difficult it was for a visiting team to win on the slow pitches (fields) prevalent there. G. Boycott, England's outstanding batsman, took over the team captaincy after J. M. Brearly broke his arm before the third test. Slow left-arm P. H. Edmonds had figures of 7 for 66 in the third test, the best by any bowler in a test in Pakistan. Javed Miandad, Haroon Rashid, and Mudassar Nazar dominated the Pakistan batting, the last two making centuries, and spin bowlers Abdul Qadir and Iqbal Qasim took the most wickets.

England then drew a three-match series in New Zealand. At Wellington the New Zealand team beat England for the first time in 48 years, by 72 runs. Boycott sent New Zealand in to bat, and when the field deteriorated England was bowled out for 64. Fast bowlers thrived—R. J. Hadlee and R. O. Collinge took 16 wickets for New Zealand, and R. G. D. Willis and C. M. Old gained 14 for England. At Christchurch, England won chiefly because of the play of I. T. Botham, who made his first test century, followed by 30 not out, took 8 wickets, and held 3 catches, and also of Edmonds, who made 50 batting tenth and took 6 wickets and 5 catches. The feature of the draw at Auckland was a century in each innings by G. P. Howarth for New Zealand and an eight-hour 158 by C. T. Radley. For England Botham took 5 more wickets in an innings, and for New Zealand S. L. Boock, slow left-arm, took 5 for 67, thus setting a new record for number of wickets in a New Zealand season.

When India traveled to Australia, the host team was virtually second-string eleven because of the

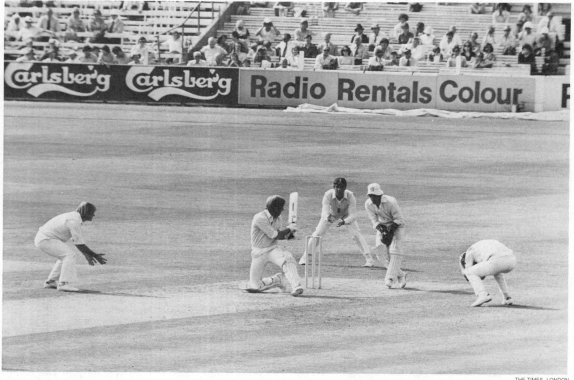

M. G. Burgess, captain of New Zealand's cricket team, defends the wicket with a hook stroke during the first test match against England at the Oval, London.

Test Series Results, November 1977–August 1978

Test	Host country and its scores		Visiting country and its scores		Result
1st	Australia	166 and 327	India	153 and 324	Australia won by 16 runs
2nd	Australia	176 and 342 for 8 wkt	India	402 and 330 for 9 wkt dec	Australia won by 2 wkt
3rd	Australia	213 and 164	India	256 and 343	India won by 222 runs
4th	Australia	131 and 263	India	396 for 8 wkt dec	India won by an innings and 2 runs
5th	Australia	505 and 256	India	269 amd 445	Australia won by 47 runs
1st	Pakistan	407 for 9 dec and 106 for 3 wkt	England	288	Match drawn
2nd	Pakistan	275 and 259 for 4 wkt dec	England	191 and 186 for 1 wkt	Match drawn
3rd	Pakistan	281	England	266 and 222 for 5 wkt	Match drawn
1st	New Zealand	228 and 123	England	215 and 64	New Zealand won by 72 runs
2nd	New Zealand	235 and 105	England	418 and 96 for 4 wkt dec	England won by 174 runs
3rd	New Zealand	315 and 382 for 8 wkt	England	429	Match drawn
1st	West Indies	405	Australia	90 and 209	West Indies won by an innings and 106 runs
2nd	West Indies	288 and 141 for 1 wkt	Australia	250 and 178	West Indies won by 9 wkt
3rd	West Indies	205 and 439	Australia	286 and 362 for 7 wkt	Australia won by 3 wkt
4th	West Indies	292 and 290	Australia	290 and 94	West Indies won by 198 runs
5th	West Indies	280 and 258 for 9 wkt	Australia	343 and 305 for 3 dec	Match drawn
1st	England	452 for 8 wkt dec	Pakistan	164 and 231	England won by an innings and 57 runs
2nd	England	364	Pakistan	105 and 139	England won by an innings and 120 runs
3rd	England	119 for 7 wkt	Pakistan	201	Match drawn
1st	England	279 and 138 for 3 wkt	New Zealand	234 and 182	England won by 7 wkt
2nd	England	429	New Zealand	120 and 190	England won by an innings and 119 runs
3rd	England	289 and 118 for 3 wkt	New Zealand	339 and 67	England won by 7 wkt

Packer disqualifications, and the former captain, R. B. Simpson, aged 41, returned to lead the side after a ten-year absence from test cricket. Australia won an exciting series before a far bigger public than watched the Packer World Series. Australia won the first test at Brisbane and the second at Perth. India won the third at Melbourne and the fourth at Sydney. In a splendid finish Australia won the fifth at Adelaide by 47 runs after India, needing 493 to win, made 445 in the fourth innings. Simpson, with two centuries and other big scores, was Australia's outstanding batsman, and he had strong support from P. M. Toohey and G. J. Cosier. Fast bowler J. R. Thomson was penetrative, and fast-medium W. M. Clark took most of the wickets. Leading Indian batsmen were G. R. Viswanath, S. M. Gavaskar, who made three centuries, and M. Amarnath. For bowling India relied on the spin of captain B. S. Bedi and B. S. Chandrasekhar, who shared 59 out of 94 wickets taken.

In a five-match series at home West Indies won against Australia. West Indies took the first two matches easily, at Port of Spain and at Bridgetown. Before the third at Georgetown, Lloyd and the Packer players withdrew, and the new West Indies team was beaten. This new team recovered to win the fourth at Port of Spain by 198 runs. The fifth at Kingston ended in draw when spectators rioted following a controversial umpires' decision against a home player. The match was abandoned, with 6.2 overs remaining and Australia needing to take one wicket for victory.

During the series A. I. Kallicharran, the new West Indies captain, scored the most runs, and he and other newcomers, L. Gomes and B. Williams, all made centuries. Fast-medium bowlers V. A. Holder and N. Phillip and spinners R. R. Jumadeen and D. R. Parry were the most effective. For Australia new young batsmen Toohey and G. N. Wood made centuries, and B. Yardley was a successful off-spinning all-rounder. Thomson was the bowling spearhead, supported by Clark and spinners Yardley and J. R. Higgs.

England at home played three-match series against Pakistan and New Zealand and won both easily. Pakistan, without its Packer players, was no match for England, losing the first two tests at Edgbaston and Lord's. The weather ruined the third at Headingley, Leeds. Fast bowlers Willis and Old played havoc, Old (7 for 50) taking 4 wickets in 5 balls at Edgbaston. D. I. Gower, a brilliantly promising 21-year-old left-hander, batted beautifully in all three matches, while Radley made one century and Botham two. Botham established a world record by also taking 8 for 34 at Lord's, the first man to make a century and take 8 wickets in an innings in the same match. G. A. Gooch made a successful return to test cricket as an opening batsman, and spinner Edmonds took 4 for 44 at Edgbaston and 4 for 6 at Lord's. Pakistan's best batsman was Sadiq Mohammad, who made scores of 79 and 97, while Mohsin Khan, who averaged 38 in 5 innings with a top score of 46, was consistent. The most successful bowlers were fast-medium Sikander Bakht; medium-paced Nazar, who also was a steady opening batsman; and Sarfraz Nawaz in the one match when he was fit.

New Zealand put up a better fight but lost all three games at the Oval, at Trent Bridge, Nottingham, and at Lord's. At the Oval, Willis, Botham, and Edmonds bowled well after Gower had made his first test century. Boycott was fit for the second test and made 131, and Botham and Edmonds shared 15 wickets. New Zealand led England on the first innings at Lord's, but fast bowling by Willis and Botham had them out for 67. Howarth was New Zealand's outstanding batsman, and B. A. Edgar, 21-year-old wicketkeeper batsman, was also impressive. Hadlee and Boock were the most successful bowlers.

In English county cricket Kent won the championship, with Essex second and Middlesex third. In the one-day competitions Kent won the Benson and Hedges Cup, beating Derbyshire by 6 wickets. Sussex won the Gillette Cup, defeating Somerset by 5 wickets, and Hampshire won the John Player League on a better run-rate than Somerset and Leicestershire, all three tying on points.

(REX ALSTON)

[452.B.4.h.ix]

Crime and Law Enforcement

Violent Crime. TERRORISM. Terrorist violence in 1978 reached new dimensions of savagery and scope, threatening the stability of governments in a number of countries. Nowhere was this threat more apparent than in Italy, which had been plagued in recent years by a growing incidence of terrorist murders, maimings, kidnappings, and bombings. These attacks culminated in March when radical Red Brigades terrorists kidnapped Aldo Moro (*see* OBITUARIES), five times premier of Italy and president of the ruling Christian Democrat Party. Moro's abduction took place in broad daylight in the streets of Rome as he was being driven to attend Parliament. In a lightning ambush, his bodyguards were gunned down and the elderly statesman was taken captive.

The kidnapping came at a time when many of the Red Brigades' leaders were being tried in Turin on charges of armed subversion. As Italian authorities, aided by other European law enforcement agencies, began a massive search for the former premier, his captors demanded the release of their imprisoned colleagues in exchange for Moro's life. Despite anguished pleas from Moro, the government held firm in its decision not to bargain with the Red Brigades. Finally, after 54 days, Moro's bullet-ridden body was found in a Rome street, bundled in the back of a stolen car.

In the furor that followed, many observers speculated whether Italian democracy could long survive such barbarous attacks. But the prosecution of the Red Brigades members continued on schedule. In June, Italy's most celebrated postwar trial come to an end with the sentencing of the Red

Brigades' founder, Renato Curcio (*see* BIOGRAPHIES), to 15 years' imprisonment. The other 28 members were sentenced, in person or absentia, to between 2 and 15 years for crimes associated with the terrorist organization; 16 defendants were acquitted and charges against one were dropped. The jury took over 100 hours to reach a verdict—the longest deliberation in Italian legal history.

In September the much criticized Italian police achieved what seemed to be a breakthrough in their hunt for Moro's killers. In a well-planned and executed raid in Milan, they captured Corrado Alunni, alleged to be the supreme commander of the Red Brigades and mastermind of the Moro kidnapping. Alunni was subsequently charged with illegally possessing weapons. Only seven days after his arrest, he was convicted and sentenced to 12 years' imprisonment—lightning justice in a country widely believed to have the slowest judicial system in Western Europe. Later, however, commentators began to wonder whether Alunni was in fact a significant Red Brigades leader.

Influenced in part by the publicity attending the Moro case, leaders of seven Western democracies signed a joint declaration in July pledging to institute sanctions against any state that harboured airplane hijackers. This represented the first broad international decision to extend the fight against terrorism into the sphere of interstate relations. The signatories included the U.S., the U.K., Canada, France, Italy, West Germany, and Japan.

Further evidence of growing international cooperation in combating the terrorist threat came from Eastern Europe. In May Yugoslav authorities seized four alleged West German terrorists, and in June Bulgarian authorities arrested another group of West German terrorist suspects and deported them to West Germany. Yugoslavia released its prisoners in November, after West Germany refused to extradite several Yugoslavs. Nevertheless, these developments suggested that terrorists could no longer look to Eastern Europe as a completely safe haven. (*See also* Feature Article: *Terrorism—Weapon of the Weak*.)

ASSASSINATION. On November 27 George Moscone, the mayor of San Francisco, and Harvey Milk, a member of the Board of Supervisors, were shot and killed in their offices in the San Francisco city hall. Shortly afterward, Dan White, a former supervisor, surrendered to police. White, an ex-fireman and policeman elected on a law-and-order platform, had resigned as supervisor and then asked to be reinstated, but Moscone had refused to permit him to withdraw his resignation. The assassination came only a week after the shaken city learned that more than 900 members of the San Francisco-based People's Temple had committed mass suicide in Guyana. (*See* GUYANA.)

During the year the U.S. House of Representatives Select Committee on Assassinations held highly publicized hearings on past acts of violence —the assassinations of Pres. John F. Kennedy and the black civil rights leader Martin Luther King, Jr. Most of the testimony appeared to support the 1964 Warren Commission's finding that Lee Harvey Oswald acted alone in killing Kennedy. The most serious challenge came from two acoustics

One of the five bodyguards slain while protecting former Italian premier Aldo Moro lies in the street following an ambush in which Moro was kidnapped. Moro was later murdered.

SVEN SIMON/KATHERINE YOUNG

experts, who claimed that analysis of a recording of sounds transmitted by a policeman's radio indicated there was a fourth shot, which Oswald could not have fired.

The subject of assassination became a matter of concern in England during September. Georgi Markov, a Bulgarian defector and Bulgarian-language broadcaster on the BBC and Radio Free Europe, died mysteriously after claiming to have been jabbed with the point of an umbrella in a London street. (*See* OBITUARIES.) Markov had previously reported receiving death threats. Although a postmortem failed to reveal any cause of death, Scotland Yard began working on the theory that Markov's death might have been ordered by Bulgarian authorities. Support for this theory grew when it became known that an alloy ball, presumed to have been filled with poison, had been found in Markov's leg. It was also reported that another Bulgarian defector had survived a similar attack in Paris in August. Adding to the mystery, a broadcasting colleague of Markov's and fellow Bulgarian defector, Vladimir Simeonov, was found dead in his London home early in October.

PUNISHMENT AND VIOLENT CRIME. After pleading guilty in May to six murders and seven attempted murders, David Berkowitz, the "Son of Sam" killer who terrorized New York City in 1977, was sentenced to 547 years in jail (315 years to be served consecutively), although under New York law the sentence, in reality, amounted to 25 years to life. One of the sentencing judges lamented that he was unable to send Berkowitz to the electric chair since capital punishment had been abolished in New York State. Calls to reintroduce the death penalty for acts of terrorism and other particularly heinous crimes arose in countries as far apart as Northern Ireland and Australia.

South Africa reported hanging 61 persons in 1976 and 90 in 1977. All of those executed were said to be men, and all but three were nonwhites. Spain's Congress of Deputies voted to abolish the death penalty and outlawed the use of the garrotte, an iron collar that strangled or snapped the neck of the person being executed. Capital punishment could still be applied under the Spanish military justice system.

In Saudi Arabia, which observed the draconian Shari'ah law of Islam, a princess who had secretly married or had an affair with a commoner was reported to have been publicly shot; the man was beheaded. Two British citizens working in Saudi Arabia were publicly flogged in May for offenses involving the manufacture of alcoholic beverages.

Nonviolent Crime. WHITE COLLAR AND POLITICAL OFFENSES. U.S. efforts to place legal restraints on corporate bribery moved forward with passage of a law in late 1977 providing for fines of up to $1 million for U.S. companies found to have bribed foreign governments in an effort to obtain business contracts or to influence legislation or regulations. The law also prescribed fines and prison terms for company officials involved in such activities. Investigations, mainly by the Securities and Exchange Commission, had uncovered more than 300 cases of corporate bribery, the most notorious of which involved the Lockheed Corp.

As part of its continuing search for broader international solutions to the problem of corporate bribery, the UN sponsored a working group on corrupt practices. Meanwhile, Switzerland, long a haven for "dirty money"—including U.S. company slush accounts—announced that its banks would no longer accept funds they knew or suspected to be the proceeds of criminal activities. The ban, however, did not extend to funds deposited in Swiss banks in violation of exchange control regulations in the country of origin or in order to evade tax payments.

The U.S. House of Representatives Ethics Committee pursued its investigation of the "Koreagate" scandal involving allegations of widespread influence buying in Washington by South Korean agents. Park Tong Sun, a suspected South Korean government agent, received immunity from prosecution to testify before the committee. In his evidence he claimed that he had paid out about U.S.$750,000 in personal gifts and contributions, mostly to 30 present and former members of Congress, between 1970 and 1975. Following these revelations former U.S. congressman Richard Hanna pleaded guilty to conspiring to commit bribery by using his congressional position to help Park in return for almost $250,000. Hanna was sentenced to six months to two and a half years in prison, a punishment described by the official Soviet news agency Tass as "amazingly soft."

In a display of much harsher justice, Soviet authorities conducted show trials of a number of dissidents. The severe punishments meted out produced a storm of international protest and threatened to undermine détente between the U.S.S.R. and the U.S. Perhaps in response to these protests, Soviet authorities adopted a more lenient approach toward a U.S. businessman, Francis Jay Crawford, tried in September for alleged currency violations. Crawford was convicted but given a five-year suspended sentence and allowed to leave the country.

In Pakistan former prime minister Zulfikar Ali

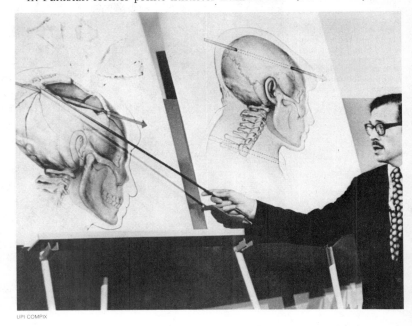

Michael Baden, chief medical examiner for New York City, testifying before the U.S. House Select Committee on Assassinations, demonstrates the path of the bullet that killed Pres. John F. Kennedy.

Bhutto was sentenced to death in March after being found guilty of conspiring to murder a political opponent in 1974. An appeal by Bhutto to the Supreme Court was still pending at year's end. In the U.K. a former leader of the Liberal Party, Jeremy Thorpe (*see* BIOGRAPHIES), and three other defendants were committed for trial on charges of conspiring to murder a man said to have been involved with Thorpe in a homosexual affair.

THEFT AND FRAUD. In perhaps the most bizarre theft of 1978, thieves in March stole the coffin containing the body of the actor Charlie Chaplin from its grave in a Swiss village. The body was subsequently recovered in a cornfield. Two political refugees, a Bulgarian and a Pole, were convicted of the theft and of making ransom demands.

Two crimes involving very large sums of money took place in the U.S. In November, Stanley Mark Rivkin, a 32-year-old computer expert, was arrested and charged with having stolen $10.2 million from the Security Pacific National Bank in Los Angeles. Part of the money was used to buy diamonds from the Soviet Union. The complex crime, which involved manipulation of the wire transfer system for moving funds among banks, was not even known to the bank until it was informed by the FBI. In a more conventional robbery, seven masked men held up the Lufthansa cargo facility at Kennedy International Airport, New York City, on December 11, escaping with a shipment of U.S. currency, estimated at between $3 million and $5 million, and a quantity of jewelry.

In Italy the industry producing fake high-quality brand-name goods was reported to be booming. Almost perfect counterfeits of such items as Gucci leathers and Pucci dresses were widely available, and the trade in the fakes was estimated at some $100 million a year. The forgers were said to be moving into increasingly sophisticated product lines, including electronic heart pacemakers.

European merchants found it necessary to "guarantee mercury-free" oranges after it had been discovered that some fruit exported from Israel had been injected with the poisonous substance. An extremist Arab group claimed credit for the tainted oranges.

KEYSTONE

In the U.S. the illicit cigarette trade was said to be costing local governments some $400 million–$500 million in lost revenue each year. Bootleggers bought large quantities of cigarettes in tobacco-producing states like North Carolina where cigarette taxes were low and smuggled them into high-tax states like New York. Disguised with forged or stolen revenue stamps, the smuggled goods were eventually retailed to the public through organized crime distribution channels.

Law Enforcement. Law enforcement authorities in the U.S. received encouraging news with the release of the latest FBI *Uniform Crime Report* statistics, which showed that reported crime fell 4% during calendar 1977 as compared with 1976. With this trend apparently continuing, the Carter administration unveiled plans to revamp the U.S. Justice Department's principal crime-control agency, the Law Enforcement Assistance Administration. The LEAA would be split into three separate units dealing, respectively, with grant giving, research and development, and judicial statistics.

The FBI continued its search for a fresh identity under the leadership of a new director, William H. Webster (*see* BIOGRAPHIES), a former federal judge. Webster promised that the bureau would operate "strictly within the framework of the Constitution." Meanwhile, former FBI director L. Patrick Gray and other high-ranking members of the bureau faced the possibility of trial on a variety of charges stemming from their alleged authorization of past FBI "bag jobs" (illegal break-ins).

Following more than 22 months of intensive inquiries, the FBI achieved a significant breakthrough in the investigation of the 1976 car bomb assassination of Orlando Letelier, who had been Chile's ambassador to the U.S. under the Salvador Allende regime. In August a federal grand jury indicted seven men allegedly involved in the killing, including two Chilean agents and the country's former secret police chief, Brig. Gen. Juan Manuel Contreras Sepúlveda, a close friend and adviser of the current Chilean president.

In September the Washington, D.C.-based Police Foundation released a survey that showed startling variations in methods and costs among larger U.S. police departments. Thus, of the three surveyed departments serving populations exceeding one million, Houston, Tex., spent about $37 per capita on police, Philadelphia $83, and Detroit $140. The number of sworn officers per 1,000 population varied from 5.69 to 1.37.

The importance of police response time came under attention in another controversial study. Based on analysis of police activities in Kansas City, Mo., the findings suggested that the tens of millions of dollars spent during the past decade to cut police response time had achieved very little. The average citizen waited so long to report a crime that police usually could not make an arrest at the scene no matter how rapidly they responded.

The West German police were increasing their use of highly sophisticated technology to combat terrorism. More than 1,300 video consoles at border crossings, airport terminals, transportation centres, and police outposts were linked with a vast computer data bank in the headquarters of the

Federal Bureau of Criminal Investigation at Wiesbaden. Eventually, officials hoped to equip all police with miniature terminals so that questions could be transmitted to the computer from any beat. There were objections from civil libertarians who feared the information could fall into the hands of unscrupulous police officials.

In Britain a Royal Commission on Criminal Procedure began examining the power of the police. Presenting testimony before the commission, Sir David McNee, commissioner of London's metropolitan police, urged the extension of law enforcement powers to include, among other things, the right to hold arrested persons for up to 72 hours before charging them; wider authority to search people, vehicles, houses, and bank accounts; and wider rights to take fingerprints, blood, and other body specimens. Opposition came from civil libertarians and other groups. Crime in London was reported to have risen more than 12% in 1977, while police were 4,000 under authorized strength.

Reflecting concern over the repressive use of force by some police agencies, the Carter administration placed new restrictions on the export of police weaponry and crowd-control devices. The restrictions forbad U.S. firms to sell firearms and such nonlethal items as tear gas to foreign police. The president of the International Association of Chiefs of Police, with members in 63 nations, called for a "careful, thoughtful reconsideration" of the regulations.   (DUNCAN CHAPPELL)

See also Prisons and Penology.
[522.C.6; 543.A.5; 552.C and F; 737.B; 10/36.C.5.a]

Cuba

The socialist republic of Cuba occupies the largest island in the Greater Antilles of the West Indies. Area: 110,922 sq km (42,827 sq mi), including several thousand small islands and cays. Pop. (1978 est.): 9,648,900, including (1953) white 72.8%; mestizo 14.5%; Negro 12.4%. Cap. and largest city: Havana (pop., 1978 est., 1,981,300). Language: Spanish. Religion: Roman Catholic (49%). President of the Council of State in 1978, Fidel Castro Ruz.

Cuba experienced political stability during 1978, but economic progress was slowed. Institutional changes to bring the administrative system more into line with those of other member countries in the Soviet-dominated Council for Mutual Economic Assistance (CMEA or Comecon) continued. The elected Assembly was designated as "the supreme organ of state power" and the Communist Party as "the superior and leading force in the state and society."

The Cuban involvement in Africa prevented the further development of trade relations with the U.S. and led to the breaking off of an economic cooperation agreement with Canada. However, the Cuban and U.S. interest section offices, established in September 1977, were used for rapid government-to-government communications with reference to Africa. The French newspaper *Le Nouvel Observateur* reported in May that the num-

ber of Cuban troops in Africa was estimated at about 34,000; however, other estimates ranged as high as 50,000. Cuban forces remained heavily engaged in Angola against the National Union for the Total Independence of Angola (UNITA). South African sources stated that Cuban casualties had been heavy and that morale among army conscripts was low.

Zaire accused Angola of having armed and supplied the rebels who invaded its Shaba Province copper region on May 11 and of having assured its own security through the presence of an occupation army of 25,000 Cubans. The U.S. supported these allegations, but they were denied by the U.S.S.R., Cuba, and East Germany. The matter did not reach the UN Security Council, since Zaire believed the invasion to be an African matter. In September Pres. Fidel Castro (*see* BIOGRAPHIES) visited Addis Ababa, returning a visit of the Ethiopian head of state, Col. Mengistu Haile Mariam, to Havana in April. The Cuban leader was reported to have maintained his position that the Ethiopian government should negotiate a settlement with the Eritrean secessionists rather than resort to force. However, the participation of the Cuban Army and Air Force in the Eritrean war was widely reported from mid-July. Soviet and Cuban advisers were said to be strengthening and training the Ethiopian Army, as well as engaging in antiterrorist activities.

At the six-day conference of foreign ministers of the nonaligned nations, opened in Belgrade, Yugos., at the end of July, Cuba was called to account by Egypt and several other nations for its involvement in Angola and Ethiopia on behalf of the U.S.S.R. Cuba, in turn, spoke against U.S. imperialism. The ministers eventually sidestepped a position on Cuba's military actions, however, and an overt split was avoided.

The World Festival of Youth and Students took place in Havana from July 28 to August 5, the first

Havana was the site in July of the annual World Youth Festival. It was the first time that the festival had been held in the Western Hemisphere.

Cuba

Crops:
see Agriculture and Food Supplies

time it had been held in the Western Hemisphere. The 180-strong British delegation (one of the smallest) called for freedom of speech and the observation of human rights, but its speaker was hissed. The U.S.S.R. sent about 1,000 delegates and East Germany, 750. Cuba's Isle of Pines, said to be the scene of Robert Louis Stevenson's book *Treasure Island*, was ceremonially renamed the Isle of Youth by Castro.

In early September the Spanish premier, Adolfo Suárez, visited Havana. Talks were held on technology, trade, and imports of Cuban sugar to Spain, and a four-cornered oil import-export agreement was signed involving Spain, the U.S.S.R., Cuba, and Venezuela. Under its terms, the U.S.S.R. would divert 10,000 bbl of oil a day to Spain, while Venezuela would export a similar amount to Cuba, thus saving large freight costs. No details of currency settlements under the accord were released.

In an effort to improve relations with the U.S., the Cuban government, beginning in September, made three goodwill gestures: the release of 1,000 political prisoners (Amnesty International estimated the total number on the island at about 3,000); agreement to the freeing of 66 U.S. citizens and their family members; and permission for a visit by an exile group, led by the Rev. Manuel Espinosa, to examine conditions on the island.

Economic development was still dominated by the key role of sugar as a hard-currency earner. Under the 1978 plan, economic growth was set at 7.4%, as against 4.1% in 1977; stimulus was to be provided by increased productivity and by cutting private consumption levels, especially of coffee. With a 2.5 million-ton annual quota available to Cuba under the International Sugar Agreement, it was hoped that larger placements of sugar could be made on international markets. The current crop was estimated at about 7.3 million tons, compared with about 6 million in 1973–74. Other areas expected to show growth were construction and its supplying industries and tourism. New electrical capacity of 270 Mw was forecast, and the output of electrical machinery, agricultural equipment, and trucks was to be increased.

Cuba and the U.S.S.R. signed a 1978 trade agreement raising the value of their trade to 4 billion rubles, compared with 3,450,000,000 rubles in 1977 and 2,870,000,000 rubles in 1976. On April 24 the two countries published a joint declaration promising further assistance and support to the liberation movements in southern Africa.

(MICHAEL WOOLLER)

Cycling

A regrettable feature of the 1978 season was the retirement, following illness, of Eddy Merckx of Belgium, who had dominated international road competition for nearly a decade. Merckx's successor might prove to be Bernard Hinault (France), who won the Tour de France convincingly on his

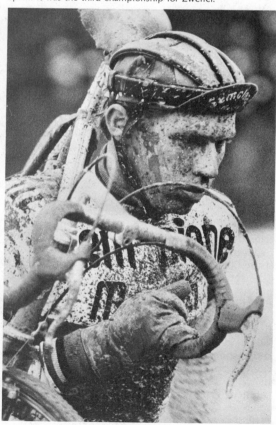

A tired and splattered Albert Zweifel of Switzerland carries his bicycle after winning the professional world cycling title in Spain. It was the third championship for Zweifel.

KEYSTONE

CUBA
Education. (1977) Primary, pupils 1,846,075, teachers 82,520; secondary, pupils 642,624, teachers 49,586; vocational, pupils 187,819, teachers 11,503; teacher training, students 118,000, teachers 4,200; higher (university only), students 122,456, teaching staff 9,934.
Finance. Monetary unit: peso, with (Sept. 18, 1978) a free rate of 0.75 peso to U.S. $1 (1.46 peso = £1 sterling). Budget (1975 est.) balanced at c. 4.5 billion pesos. Gross national product (1976 est.) U.S. $8,120,000,000.
Foreign Trade. (1976) Imports 3,065,000,000 pesos; exports 2,694,000,000 pesos. Import sources (1974): U.S.S.R. 47%; Japan 8%; United Kingdom 5%. Export destinations (1974): U.S.S.R. 36%; Japan 17%; Spain 7%; East Germany 5%. Main exports (1974): sugar 86%; nickel and copper ores 6%.
Transport and Communications. Roads (1975) 27,013 km. Motor vehicles in use (1973): passenger c. 70,000; commercial (including buses) c. 33,000. Railways: (1977) 14,730 km; traffic (1975) 695 million passenger-km, freight 1,825,000,000 net ton-km. Air traffic (1976): 663 million passenger-km; freight 14.2 million net ton-km. Shipping (1977): merchant vessels 100 gross tons and over 315; gross tonnage 667,518. Telephones (Dec. 1974) 289,000. Radio receivers (Dec. 1975) 2.1 million. Television receivers (Dec. 1975) 600,000.
Agriculture. Production (in 000; metric tons; 1977): rice c. 420; corn (1976) c. 125; cassava (1976) c. 254; sweet potatoes (1976) c. 250; tomatoes c. 186; sugar, raw value c. 6,485; bananas c. 92; oranges c. 148; coffee c. 25; tobacco c. 45; jute c. 6; beef and veal c. 204; fish catch (1976) c. 204. Livestock (in 000; 1977): cattle c. 5,644; pigs c. 1,506; sheep c. 346; goats c. 94; horses (1976) c. 833; chickens c. 18,885.
Industry. Production (in 000; metric tons; 1975): crude oil 226; petroleum products c. 5,410; electricity (kw-hr) c. 6,150,000; copper ore (metal content) 2.8; chrome ore (oxide content) 13; nickel ore (metal content) 37; salt 157; paper 120; sulfuric acid 418; cement (1976) 2,501; steel 298.

A.F.P./PICTORIAL PARADE

Cyclists were bunched together in the early going of the Tour de France bicycle race in July. Bernard Hinault (right) was the eventual winner by nearly four minutes after more than 108 hours of racing.

first attempt. But in the world road championship on the notorious Nürburgring in West Germany he was outmaneuvered by Gerrie Knetemann (Neth.), who beat defending champion Francesco Moser (Italy) in a sprint finish.

1978 Cycling Champions

Event	Winner	Country
WORLD AMATEUR CHAMPIONS—TRACK		
Men		
1,000-m time trial	L. Thoms	East Germany
Sprint	A. Tkac	Czechoslovakia
Tandem sprint	V. Vackar and M. Vymazal	Czechoslovakia
Individual pursuit	D. Macha	East Germany
Team pursuit		East Germany
50-km points	N. de Johkheere	Belgium
50-km motor-paced	R. Podlesch	West Germany
Women		
Sprint	G. Tsareva	U.S.S.R.
Individual pursuit	K. van Oosten-Hage	The Netherlands
WORLD PROFESSIONAL CHAMPIONS—TRACK		
Sprint	K. Nakano	Japan
Individual pursuit	G. Braun	West Germany
One-hour motor-paced	W. Peffgen	West Germany
WORLD AMATEUR CHAMPIONS—ROAD		
Men		
100-km team time trial		The Netherlands
Individual road race	G. Glaus	Switzerland
Women		
Individual road race	B. Habetz	West Germany
WORLD PROFESSIONAL CHAMPION—ROAD		
Individual road race	G. Knetemann	The Netherlands
WORLD CHAMPIONS—CYCLO CROSS		
Amateur	R. Libotin	Belgium
Professional	A. Zweifel	Switzerland
MAJOR PROFESSIONAL ROAD-RACE WINNERS		
Het Volk	F. Maertens	Belgium
Milan–San Remo	R. de Vlaeminck	Belgium
Paris–Roubaix	F. Moser	Italy
Amstel Gold Race	J. Raas	The Netherlands
Ghent–Wevelghem	F. Vanden Haute	Belgium
Flèche Wallonne	M. Laurent	France
Liège–Bastogne–Liège	J. Bruyere	Belgium
Tour of Flanders	W. Godefroot	Belgium
Grand Prix of Frankfurt	G. Braun	West Germany
Bordeaux–Paris	H. van Springel	Belgium
Autumn Grand Prix	J. Raas	The Netherlands
Tour of Lombardy	F. Moser	Italy
Grand Prix des Nations time trial	B. Hinault	France
Tour de France	B. Hinault	France
Tour of Italy	J. de Muynck	Belgium
Tour of Spain	B. Hinault	France
Tour of Switzerland	P. Wellens	Belgium
Tour of Luxembourg	L. Peeters	Belgium
Tour of Britain	J. van de Velde	The Netherlands
Four Days of Dunkirk	F. Maertens	Belgium
Dauphiné Libéré	M. Pollentier	Belgium
Paris–Nice	G. Knetemann	The Netherlands

A new event on the international stage-race calendar was the five-day professional Tour of Britain over a Glasgow–London route. It was won by Johan van de Velde (Neth.). In the 14-day amateur Tour of Britain ("Milk Race"), Eastern Europeans took the major prizes, Jan Brzezny (Poland) being best individually and the U.S.S.R. the strongest team. Later in the season Soviet riders outclassed the opposition in the Tour de l'Avenir (the amateur Tour de France), taking not only the team prize but the first four places, led by Sergey Sukhorutchenkov. The U.S. entered a team for the first time in the Tour de l'Avenir, but the high Alpine passes were less to their liking than the shorter, steeper hills of the Milk Race.

Remarkably fast times were recorded in the world track championships in Munich, West Germany, several riders even beating records that had been established at high altitude in Mexico City. East Germans were again prominent in the amateur series, taking the individual and team pursuits and the 1,000-m time trial. Olympic champion Anton Tkac from Czechoslovakia won the amateur sprint title with fine riding, while his compatriots Vladimir Vackar and Miroslav Vymazal were declared winners of an unsatisfactory tandem sprint over the U.S. riders Gerald Ash and Leigh Barczewski. The Czechoslovaks were disqualified in the first final match for causing their opponents to crash, wrecking the tandem and breaking Ash's collarbone. Union Cycliste Internationale officials offered to award the title jointly to the two pairs, but the U.S. riders refused.

(J. B. WADLEY)

Cyprus

An island republic and a member of the Commonwealth of Nations, Cyprus is in the eastern Mediterranean. Area: 9,251 sq km (3,572 sq mi). Pop. (1977 est.): 613,000, including Greeks 82%; Turks 18%. Cap. and largest city: Nicosia (pop., 1977 est., 146,000). All these population figures should be considered unreliable, as they do not take into ac-

Cyprus

Czechoslovakia

count the extensive internal migration or the recent and reportedly extensive Turkish immigration and Greek emigration, for which authoritative data are not available. Language: Greek and Turkish. Religion: Greek Orthodox 77%; Muslim 18%. President in 1978, Spyros Kyprianou.

On April 22, 1978, the Greek Cypriot interlocutor, Tassos Papadopoulos, rejected Turkish Cypriot proposals aimed at resumption of the intercommunal talks, broken off by the Cyprus government the previous May. The Turks had offered to permit the Greeks to reoccupy the Varosha district of Famagusta and to relinquish their rights to territory within the British sovereign base areas and in the zone currently patrolled by the UN peace-keeping force. Their proposals for a future constitution included a weak central government. A more satisfactory proposal was floated on July 21, when the Turkish Cypriot "president," Rauf Denktash, offered to permit the Greeks to begin reoccupying Varosha under UN supervision as soon as intercommunal talks were reactivated. He intimated that new negotiations could take place within the framework agreed upon prior to the last round of talks. On July 24 Pres. Spyros Kyprianou (see BIOGRAPHIES) agreed to resume talks within that framework as soon as the Greeks were allowed back into Varosha. A 12-point U.S. proposal aimed at getting negotiations under way was put forward under UN auspices in November but was rather coolly received.

President Kyprianou was returned unopposed for a five-year term on January 26. On July 16 he dismissed Papadopoulos amid reports of an alleged conspiracy but later declared him uninvolved. On February 10 the underground organization EOKA-B announced its dissolution.

On February 18 Palestinian terrorists killed a prominent Egyptian editor in a Nicosia hotel, seized a number of hostages, and made their way to Larnaca airport, where they took over a Cyprus

Dead Egyptian commandos lie on the ground at Larnaca airport in Cyprus after a bloody shoot-out with Cypriot police and troops.

CYPRUS

Education. 1976–77 (Greek schools) Primary, pupils 54,593, teachers 2,110; secondary, pupils 44,059, teachers 2,136; vocational, pupils 6,574, teachers 442; teacher training, students 97, teachers 15; higher, students 685, teaching staff 63. (Turkish schools) Primary, pupils 18,220, teachers 593; secondary, pupils 10,504, teachers 514; vocational, pupils 811, teachers 134; teacher training, students 68, teachers 4.

Finance. Monetary unit: Cyprus pound, with (Sept. 18, 1978) a free rate of C£0.36 to U.S. $1 (C£0.71 = £1 sterling). The Turkish lira is also in use in North Cyprus (Turkish Federated State). Gold, SDR's, and foreign exchange (June 1978) U.S. $300.2 million. Budget (1977 est.): revenue C£68,735,000; expenditure C£74,320,000. Excludes budget of Turkish Federated State: for 1976 this was balanced at 1,338 million Turkish lira.

Foreign Trade. (South only; 1977) Imports C£254 million; exports C£133 million. Import sources: U.K. 19%; Italy 9%; Greece 8%; West Germany 8%; U.S. 6%; France 5%; U.S.S.R. 5%; Japan 5%; Iraq 5%. Export destinations: U.K. 29%; Saudi Arabia 13%; Lebanon 9%; Libya 5%. Main exports: potatoes 15%; clothing 9%; cement 8%; cigarettes 5%; citrus fruit 5%; wine 5%; footwear 5%. Tourism (1976): visitors 180,000; gross receipts U.S. $50 million.

Transport and Communications. Roads (1976) 9,838 km. Motor vehicles in use (1976): passenger 68,800; commercial 15,300. Air traffic (1977): 393 million passenger-km; freight 16.7 million net ton-km. Shipping (1977): merchant vessels 100 gross tons and over 800; gross tonnage 2,787,908. Telephones (Jan. 1977) 77,200. Radio licenses (Dec. 1975) 206,000. Television licenses (Dec. 1974) 85,000.

Agriculture. Production (in 000; metric tons; 1977): barley 66; wheat (1976) 66; grapes c. 165; potatoes (1976) c. 135; oranges c. 40; grapefruit (1977) c. 57; olives c. 20. Livestock (in 000; Dec. 1975): sheep c. 420; cattle c. 33; pigs c. 115; goats c. 320.

Industry. Production (in 000; metric tons; 1976): asbestos c. 33; iron pyrites (exports) 145; copper ore (exports; metal content) c. 11; chromium ore (oxide content; 1975) 14; petroleum products (1975) 315; cement (1977) 1,074; electricity (kw-hr; 1977) 883,000.

Airways plane. The following day Egyptian commandos landed at the airport, but their attempt to storm the plane was frustrated by the Cyprus National Guard, and 15 Egyptians were killed. Diplomatic relations with Egypt were broken off on February 22. Egypt maintained that the Cyprus government had been informed of its intentions, but Kyprianou denied this and protested against the violation of Cyprus' sovereignty. The Palestinians were sentenced to death in Nicosia on April 4, but Kyprianou commuted their sentences to life imprisonment.

For the first time in four years tensions within the Turkish Cypriot community resulted in public demonstrations and bitter controversy in the press, aroused by the effects of inflation and troubles with immigrants from the Turkish mainland. The prime minister, Necat Konuk, resigned March 24 and was succeeded by Osman Orek. Seven members of Orek's nine-man Cabinet resigned at the end of November over the granting of exploitation rights to a foreign company.

(L. J. D. COLLINS)

See also Turkey.

Czechoslovakia

A federal socialist republic of central Europe, Czechoslovakia lies between Poland, the U.S.S.R., Hungary, Austria, and East and West Germany.

Area: 127,877 sq km (49,374 sq mi). Pop. (1978 est.): 15,138,000, including (1977 est.) Czech 64%; Slovak 30%. Cap. and largest city: Prague (pop., 1978 est., 1,182,900). Language: Czech and Slovak (official). General secretary of the Communist Party of Czechoslovakia and president in 1978, Gustav Husak; federal premier, Lubomir Strougal.

After the political turmoil of the previous year, the Czechoslovak authorities and the opposition Charter 77 group achieved a kind of uneasy coexistence in 1978. Although it would be an exaggeration to suggest that the government had learned to live with the opposition, the kind of large-scale mass denunciations characteristic of 1977 were not repeated. The policy was essentially one of ignoring the charter activists publicly while continuing their harassment through legal and administrative methods.

The charter activists themselves continued their campaign of pressure to constrain the authorities to abide by their own legal norms. One of the official charter spokesmen, Jiri Hajek, stated in an interview in the West German magazine *Der Spiegel* (January 1978) that the charter was not, strictly speaking, a movement but a citizens' initiative deriving its status from the country's legal system. Later in the year Hajek gave up his role as spokesman and was replaced by Jaroslav Sabata. Marta Kubisova, another spokesman, resigned for health reasons and was replaced by the playwright Vaclav Havel. A committee was set up to help those victimized for their support of the charter.

Representatives of the charter held a normal meeting with their counterparts from the Polish opposition committee KSS "KOR" (Committee for Social Self-Defense), and it was after this event that Sabata was arrested by the authorities. By the end of September, 18 charter documents had been issued, and the charter itself counted just under 1,000 signatories. The document issued on the tenth anniversary of the Soviet invasion of Czechoslovakia denounced that act and the occupation of the country by Soviet forces as illegal.

The authorities were also considering taking steps to curb the flourishing *samizdat* (unofficially circulated) literature, known as "Padlock Editions," to which many outstanding figures had contributed. One author, Jiri Grusa, responsible for the novel *The Questionnaire*, was arrested by the authorities, a move that elicited strong protests. (*See* LITERATURE: *Eastern European Literature.*) At the beginning of November the Charter 77 movement appealed in an open letter to UN Secretary-General Kurt Waldheim and the heads of states that had signed the 1975 Helsinki accords to investigate human rights conditions in Czechoslovakia. Also in November, the International Labour Office in Geneva published a dossier of widespread discrimination against the Charter 77 group by the Czechoslovak government.

Within the Communist Party, the conflict between the conservative faction around Gustav Husak and the hard-liners led by Vasil Bilak reached serious proportions during a plenum of the Central Committee in December 1977. Husak was criticized for his handling of both the Charter 77 challenge and the economy. He was evidently able to fight off his challengers. Although he accepted hard-liner Milos Jakes's elevation to the Central Committee Secretariat (the key policy-making body), he was able to balance this by the appointment of two of his own supporters.

It would have been expected that the 30th anniversary of the Prague coup of February 1948 would have been used as an occasion to trumpet forth the achievements of the regime. In fact, the celebrations were held in rather a low key. On the other hand, it was evidently felt that a major campaign had to be mounted to counteract any possible response to the tenth anniversary of the Soviet invasion, and much space in the press was devoted to denouncing the reform movement that preceded it. The third anniversary in 1978 was the 60th year of the founding of the republic. In that context, the authorities attempted to demonstrate that an independent Czechoslovakia could not have come about without the 1917 Russian Revolution, and that the Communist Party had always promoted the best traditions of Czechoslovak statehood.

Husak made one important foreign visit, to West Germany in April, where he was rather coldly received. He in turn welcomed the Soviet leader Leonid Brezhnev at the end of May. Brezhnev once again endorsed Husak, who formally restated the official position of gratitude for the invasion of 1968. Other foreign developments included the continuing series of negotiations with the Vatican, which in January 1978 produced an important partial agreement. It regulated the position of the Roman Catholic Church in Slovakia by creating a separate Slovak ecclesiastical province, with an archbishopric at Trnava. Frantisek Cardinal Tomasek was elevated to the archbishopric of Prague. Official comment on the election of a Pol-

The 30th anniversary of the Communist coup in Czechoslovakia was celebrated in February in Prague.

KEYSTONE

ish pope was confined to the barest factual reports. Throughout the year there were repeated, virulent attacks on Eurocommunism, which was described as "alien and unacceptable."

There was no significant improvement in the uneven performance of the economy, a central political issue given the government's dependence on consumer satisfaction as the trade-off for political inactivity. The Statistical Office reported that plan targets had been fulfilled "in principle" in the first half of 1978, but there were considerable variations from sector to sector and from enterprise to enterprise. In the building construction industry, for example, out of 235 enterprises, 77 failed to meet their targets, although this was an improvement over the 1977 figure of 104.

A substantial increase in growth of foreign trade was recorded, but this was primarily with other socialist countries. The country's deteriorating foreign trade balance of the previous four years showed no change. The standard of living maintained an increase, in terms of cash incomes at least (increases in real terms were not published). Retail trade rose by 6%, mostly derived from a higher volume of consumer durables.

(GEORGE SCHÖPFLIN)

CZECHOSLOVAKIA

Education. (1976–77) Primary, pupils 1,882,371, teachers 93,192; secondary, pupils 137,062, teachers 8,384; vocational and teacher training, pupils 307,303, teachers 16,625; higher (including 9 main universities), students 168,310, teaching staff 17,367.

Finance. Monetary unit: koruna, with (Sept. 18, 1978) a commercial rate of 5.25 koruny to U.S. $1 (10.30 koruny = £1 sterling) and a tourist rate of 8.88 koruny to U.S. $1 (17.40 koruny = £1 sterling). Budget (1976 est.): revenue 292,165,000,000 koruny; expenditure 290,071,000,000 koruny. Gross national product (1976 est.) U.S. $57,250,-000,000.

Foreign Trade. (1977) Imports 63,003,000,000 koruny; exports 61,161,000,000 koruny. Import sources (1976): U.S.S.R. 33%; East Germany 12%; Poland 9%; Hungary 6%; West Germany 6%. Export destinations (1976): U.S.S.R. 34%; East Germany 13%; Poland 9%; Hungary 6%; West Germany 5%. Main exports (1976): machinery 37%; iron and steel 10%; motor vehicles 9%; chemicals 5%.

Transport and Communications. Roads (1974) 145,455 km (including 79 km expressways). Motor vehicles in use (1976): passenger 1,558,700; commercial 275,400. Railways (1976): 13,186 km (including 2,714 km electrified); traffic 17,920,000,000 passenger-km, freight (1977) 71,550,000,000 net ton-km. Air traffic (1977): 1,414,000,-000 passenger-km; freight 17,210,000 net ton-km. Navigable inland waterways (1976) c. 480 km. Shipping (1977): merchant vessels 100 gross tons and over 14; gross tonnage 148,689. Telephones (1977) 2,743,400. Radio licenses (1975) 3,916,000. Television licenses (1976) 3,793,000.

Agriculture. Production (in 000; metric tons; 1977): wheat c. 5,244; barley c. 3,100; oats c. 600; rye c. 870; corn c. 600; potatoes c. 4,100; sugar, raw value c. 939; beef and veal c. 378; pork c. 765. Livestock (in 000; Jan. 1977): cattle 4,654; pigs 6,820; sheep 797; chickens 42,559.

Industry. Index of industrial production (1975 = 100; 1977) 112. Fuel and power (in 000; metric tons; 1977): coal 27,957; brown coal 93,236; crude oil 125; petroleum products (1975) 15,233; natural gas (cu m) 950,000; manufactured gas (cu m) 7,680,000; electricity (kw-hr) 66,296,000. Production (in 000; metric tons; 1977): iron ore (26% metal content) 1,993; magnesite (1975) 2,885; pig iron 9,887; crude steel 15,043; cement 9,750; sulfuric acid 1,277; fertilizers (nutrient content; 1976) nitrogenous c. 562, phosphate 412; cotton yarn 125; cotton fabrics (m) 571,000; woolen fabrics (m) 64,700; man-made fibres 146; paper (1976) 832; passenger cars (units) 159; commercial vehicles (units) 80. Dwelling units completed (1976) 136,000.

Dams: see Engineering Projects

Dance

The crucial funding problems that beset many dance institutions in the United States in 1977 did not totally disappear in 1978, but the financial situation was so much improved that companies were able to announce, for the first time in some seasons, long-range plans. One such company, for example, was the American Ballet Theatre; on the brink of suspending all operations at the end of 1977, it went into fiscal reorganization and received a $1 million matching grant from the National Endowment for the Arts (a federal agency). The New York City Ballet, also in financial straits, received a huge grant from the Endowment, and other companies found essential support from their state and municipal agencies as well as from the national offices.

The New York City Ballet's activities included its regular winter, spring, and fall engagements at New York City's Lincoln Center and a summer month (July) at Saratoga Springs, N.Y., along with various other performances. In matters of personnel the major coup was the obtaining of Mikhail Baryshnikov for its roster of principals. The famed virtuoso, who had been a regular member of the American Ballet Theatre (although he had danced as a guest artist with other troupes) ever since his defection from the U.S.S.R. in 1974, made his final appearance with ABT in *Giselle*, the great romantic classic that had launched his triumphant career with the company. His debut with the New York City Ballet took place in Saratoga Springs in the Alexandra Danilova-George Balanchine staging of the comedy classic *Coppélia*, a ballet he had previously danced in other versions. Subsequently, he performed in such Balanchine ballets as *Stars and Stripes* (the last movement), *Jewels* (the second, or "Rubies," movement), and, on television, *Prodigal Son*. He starred (with Patricia McBride as his partner) in a revival of Balanchine's two-act *Harlequinade*.

In leaving ABT for the New York City troupe, Baryshnikov suggested that his common ancestral ballet heritage with Balanchine at Leningrad's Maryinsky-Kirov Theatre reinforced his desire to learn the Balanchine repertory under the supervision of the ballet master himself. With NYCB, however, he also danced ballets by Jerome Robbins, including *Other Dances*, a piece created for him when he was still with ABT but which was subsequently acquired by the NYCB.

The NYCB's major premieres included Balanchine's *Kammermusik No. 2*, which featured in one section an ensemble of male dancers (unusual in Balanchine ballets); *Ballo della Regina*, with Merrill Ashley and Robert Weiss as principals; and the Balanchine-conceived *Tricolore* in three sections, each choreographed by a different man (Robbins, Peter Martins, Jean-Pierre Bonnefous). *Tricolore* completed a ballet trilogy (the others being *Stars and Stripes* and *Union Jack*) described by Balanchine as "Entente Cordiale." A brief illness kept Balanchine from choreographing *Tricolore* himself, and he assigned the three others to carry out his plans.

Earlier, Martins's first choreography was *Calcium Light Night*, a modern ballet-style pas de deux given its official premiere by NYCB following previews by Martins's own ballet ensemble.

ABT not only lost Baryshnikov through defection to NYCB but also its other premier danseur, Ivan Nagy, through retirement. Nagy, who had been *premier danseur noble* with ABT for ten years, decided to retire at the age of 35. The onetime defector from Hungary was the centre of a celebration in his honour in the fall at the Metropolitan Opera House in New York City and a final gala, his last appearance as a dancer, on December 15 at the John F. Kennedy Center for the Performing Arts in Washington, D.C.

ABT produced a new ballet by Glen Tetley, *Sphinx*, with Martine van Hamel, Clark Tippet, and Kirk Peterson in the principal roles. Two new stars joining ABT were Anthony Dowell from the U.K., leaving Britain's Royal Ballet, and Australia's John Meehan. Rudolf Nureyev appeared as guest artist with ABT during the company's spring season at the Metropolitan Opera House in *Swan Lake*, with Cynthia Gregory, the troupe's American prima ballerina, as Odette-Odile.

Nureyev made many appearances in New York City (and elsewhere in the U.S.) during the spring and summer. He opened on Broadway (Minskoff Theatre) with the Murray Louis Dance Company, a modern dance group, and appeared in the U.S. premieres of *Canarsie Venus* and *Vivace*, both choreographed especially for him by Louis. Next, he continued at the Minskoff as guest artist with the Dutch National Ballet and danced in the local premieres of *Faun* (a new treatment of Claude Debussy's *Afternoon of a Faun* choreographed by Toer van Schayk) and Rudi van Dantzig's *About a Dark House*. Later in the summer he appeared with the London Festival Ballet at the Metropolitan Opera House.

The major debut of a foreign company was that of the Ballet Nacional de Cuba, founded and directed by Alicia Alonso and with Alonso as its star. Alonso, who had risen from chorus dancer in U.S. musicals to ballerina status over a 20-year period, was bringing to the Metropolitan and the Kennedy Center an internationally known major ballet troupe that had begun modestly in 1948 as Ballet Alicia Alonso in her native Havana. The historic U.S. debut occurred 30 years later, May 30, 1978, in Washington, D.C., with Alonso dancing the title part in *Giselle*, the ballet with which she was most closely associated. The Cuban dancers, however, introduced works new to U.S. audiences, most of them choreographed by Cubans. These included *Tarde en la Siesta*, *Ad Libitum*, and *La Péri*, all created by Cuba's leading choreographer, Alberto Mendez; *The House of Bernarda Alba*, choreographed by Ivan Tenorio; *Canto Vital* (Azari Plisetski); *Carmen* (Alberto Alonso); and *Genesis* (Alicia Alonso).

The Dance Theatre of Harlem, the nation's only all-black classical ballet company, offered as its major accomplishment of the year a special creation incorporating speech, song, and dance, *His Love Is Everlasting*, conceived and written by Karel Shook (co-director with Arthur Mitchell of the troupe).

New York City's Cathedral of St. John the Divine housed the art of dancing during the year. Its major visitor was the José Limón Dance Company with Erik Bruhn as guest artist, with Bruhn dancing in *The Moor's Pavane*. The company also danced Limón's *Choreographic Offering* (to music of Bach) and *Missa Brevis* (Kodaly). At the end of the year the Limón dancers opened an engagement at the City Center with works by Limón, a new solo choreographed by Murray Louis, and dances mirroring the origins of modern dance.

Modern dance events on and off Broadway—in Broadway theatres, concert halls, churches, stu-

Mikhail Baryshnikov, who left the American Ballet Theatre in May to join the New York City Ballet, danced the role of Frantz in *Coppélia* at Saratoga Springs, New York, in his first performance with the NYCB.

MARTHA SWOPE

dios, lofts—and across the country from San Francisco to Boston were too numerous to list. In addition to the Limón company the nationally (and even internationally) noted modern dancers active during the year included Merce Cunningham and his dancers in the world premiere of *Inlets* (John Cage), first given on a college campus and then on Broadway; Paul Taylor's company in his new *Aphrodisiamania, Airs, Polaris, Dust*; and the Murray Louis Dance Company performing not only with Nureyev on Broadway but also in another Broadway engagement in a joint season with the Alwin Nikolais Dance Theater. The modern dance-gymnastics group, Pilobolus, continued to be a popular theatre attraction.

The chief highlights of the year in modern dance involved the Martha Graham Dance Company and the Alvin Ailey American Dance Theater. The latter celebrated its 20th birthday with repertory seasons featuring new works but focusing upon a gala that starred former members of the company such as Carmen de Lavallade, James Truitte, George Faison, and Hector Mercado. Ailey himself danced for the first time in more than a decade. As for the veteran Martha Graham, whose companies had been performing for more than half a century, her current troupe played a season at the Metropolitan Opera House, marking the first time in history that Graham had appeared there. Three of the troupe's offerings were new Graham dances, among them *Ecuatorial* (to music of Varèse and with decor by Marisol) and *The Owl and the Pussycat* (to music of Carlos Surinach), with the Broadway and nightclub star Liza Minelli as guest artist. (WALTER TERRY)

Two full-length works—a classical revival and a creation—went into the repertory of the Covent Garden Royal Ballet during the 1977–78 season. Ninette de Valois supervised what amounted to the fifth production of *The Sleeping Beauty* (Tchaikovsky) since 1939. This latest revival, designed by David Walker, restored Petipa's choreography,

as originally reproduced for the company by Nicolas Sergeyev in 1939, but with some additional choreography by Frederick Ashton. Kenneth MacMillan, former artistic director, now resident choreographer, was responsible for *Mayerling* (Liszt, arranged and orchestrated by John Lanchbery). This three-act work, designed by Nicholas Georgiadis, contained many fine roles, especially for Lynn Seymour as Mary Vetsera, Merle Park as Marie Larisch, and David Wall as Crown Prince Rudolf. The season ended with three Royal Ballet principals leaving the company, possibly temporarily: Anthony Dowell to American Ballet Theatre, Lynn Seymour to direct the Ballet of the Bavarian State Opera in Munich, and Ann Jenner to the Australian Ballet.

The Sadler's Wells Royal Ballet, which spends most of its year touring, took advantage of the experience gained from the Gulbenkian International Choreographic Summer School by one of its dancers, David Bintley; he created *The Outsider* (Josef Bohac's *Suita Drammatica*). The other creation was by Jonathan Thorpe, on loan from Northern Ballet Theatre, whose *Game Piano* (Prokofiev) was designed by Ballet Rambert's Zoltan Imre. John Cranko's *Brouillards* (Debussy), originally created for the Stuttgart Ballet, was taken into the repertory, and MacMillan's *Solitaire* (Malcolm Arnold) virtually became a new ballet in designs by Barry Kay.

Britain's other major classical company, London Festival Ballet, made its first excursion into the more contemporary field with Tetley's *Greening* (Arne Nordheim), originally created for Stuttgart. Ronald Hynd created a new version of a work originally given by the Diaghilev Ballet in 1927: *La Chatte* (Henri Sauguet) had designs by Peter Docherty. Festival Ballet's year, at home and abroad, was mainly given over to Nureyev's *Romeo and Juliet* (Prokofiev), which was chiefly responsible for the company's first triumphant New York season. The annual summer season at London's Festival Hall was dedicated to the company's founder, Julian Braunsweg, who died in March.

As in recent years it was the more contemporary companies that were the most stimulating, especially on the musical side. Tetley returned to create a work for the British company he was most associated with, Ballet Rambert. His *Praeludium* (Webern) was his offering to Dame Marie Rambert, celebrating her 90th birthday during the company's Sadler's Wells season. Other works new to the repertory included Jaap Flier's *Episode 1* (Alan Posselt), Sara Sugihara's *Sleeping Birds* (Brahms), and Imre's *Laocoon* (sound collage of Liszt); all the works were designed by Nadine Baylis.

London Contemporary Dance Theatre toured throughout Britain with one overseas tour, to Egypt. New works included Siobhan Davies's *Sphinx* (Barrington Pheloung), Micha Bergese's *Continuum* (Morris Pert), and Richard Alston's *Rainbow Bandit* (sound collage).

Each of the two major regional companies added a full-length classic to its repertory. Scottish Ballet became the first British company to mount the famous Danish classic, Auguste Bournonville's

In 1978, for the first time since its founding in 1948, the Ballet Nacional de Cuba, led by prima ballerina Alicia Alonso, visited the United States. Alonso danced *Giselle* with Jorge Esquivel.

© STEVEN CARAS

Napoli (Paulli/Helsted/Gade/Lumbye); it was produced by Poul Gnatt and designed by Peter Cazalet. Opportunity was given to potential choreographers within the company in a program, Nework '78, in which ten of Scottish Ballet's dancers created ten works. For Northern Ballet Theatre, based in Manchester, there was a successful production of Coppélia, produced by Peter Clegg, which was placed in a Lancashire setting. Other new works for the company included André Prokovsky's Daydreams (John Riley), Terry Gilbert's Into the Sun (Stephen Montague), Geoffrey Cauley's Last of Three (Britten), and Royston Maldoom's Area Without Measure (Anthony Moss).

"New dance" groups continued to proliferate, some on a temporary basis, others more permanent. Among the latter were Extemporary Dance Group, the longest established, and the Rosemary Butcher Dance Company, working mainly at Hammersmith's Riverside Studios in London. Britain's first black dance company, MAAS Movers, was developing into an important addition to the dance scene. There was a new upsurge of mime groups, the most important being The Moving Picture Mime Show.

The Irish Ballet, based in Cork, had become firmly established since it was started by Joan Denise Moriarty in 1974; it toured Ireland extensively besides giving regular seasons in Cork and Dublin. The major creations of the 1977–78 season were by Domy Reiter-Soffer: Chariots of Fire (Christou/Mamangakis/Xenakis) and Shadow Reach (John McCabe).

In France, the Paris Opéra Ballet's principal creation was Romeo and Juliet (Prokofiev), choreographed by Yury Grigorovich from Moscow. There were also programs given over to the works of one choreographer. "Homage to Lifar" consisted of his Les Mirages (Sauguet), Phèdre (Auric), and Suite en blanc (Lalo); "An Evening of Balanchine" had his Four Temperaments (Hindemith), Divertimento No. 15 (Mozart), and dances from Orphée et Eurydice (Gluck).

In West Germany, the Stuttgart Ballet revived a work by Cranko, its artistic director until his death in 1973: Carmen (Wolfgang Fortner/Wilfried Steinbrenner). John Neumeier's Der Fall Hamlet (Copland) was taken into the repertory, and MacMillan created My Brother, My Sisters (Schoenberg). The major additions to the Hamburg State Opera Ballet's repertory were two entirely new versions of Tchaikovsky classics by Neumeier, The Nutcracker and The Sleeping Beauty. There was a more traditional production of The Sleeping Beauty, for the Bavarian State Opera Ballet in Munich, by Rosella Hightower; also a full-evening work by Dieter Gackstetter, Rilke (Walter Haupt).

An all-Stravinsky program was given by the Ballet of the Twentieth Century in Belgium. Maurice Béjart made a new version of Petrushka for Bolshoi guest star Vladimir Vasiliev; Micha van Hoecke's Symphony of Psalms completed the program. Full-evening works by Béjart were Heliogabale (Pierre Henry/Chad/Bach/Nina Rota) and Gaîté Parisienne (Offenbach).

For the Dutch National Ballet, van Dantzig created three new works: Four Last Songs (Strauss),

Merle Park and David Wall danced leading roles in the Covent Garden Royal Ballet production of Mayerling.

Gesang der Junglingen (Stockhausen), and About a Dark House (Haubenstock-Ramati). From Hans van Manen there was 5 Tangos (Piazolla); and from van Schayk, Pyrrhic Dances (17th-century French) and Faun.

In Denmark, Bournonville's The Toreador (Erling D. Bjerno after Helsted), a classic not seen for 48 years, was revived for the Royal Danish Ballet. It was produced by Flemming Flindt, who retired as ballet master at the end of the season to be replaced by Henning Kronstam. In Austria, the Vienna State Opera Ballet had a new work by van Manen, Erstes Grand Trio (Schubert), Erich Walter's Pelléas and Mélisande (Schoenberg), and revivals of Todd Bolender's The Still Point (Debussy) and Souvenirs (Barber). There were Balanchine revivals for Hungary's Budapest State Opera Ballet: Serenade (Tchaikovsky), Symphony in C (Bizet), and Apollo and Agon, both by Stravinsky. The company's own choreographer, Laszlo Seregi, mounted a new version of Sylvia (Delibes) and On the Town (Bernstein).

In Italy the major creation for the La Scala, Milan, ballet was a full-length work, Homage to Picasso (Hindemith/Ligeti/Xenakis/Ragnar Grippes). The ballet company at Venice's Teatro La Fenice staged a new version of Giselle by Polyakov; new works included Ugo dell'Ara's Berhkristal and Vantagio's I Dodici (Tischenko). The Rome Opera Ballet's new artistic director, André Prokovsky, created Seven Deadly Sins (Weill), revived his Soft Blue Shadows (Fauré) and Gounod Divertimento, and mounted a new production of The Sleeping Beauty.

(PETER WILLIAMS)

See also Music; Theatre.

[652]

Danish Literature:
see Literature

Deaths:
see Demography; see also obituaries of prominent persons who died in 1978, listed under People of the Year

Defense

The dominant defense issue in 1978 was the growing willingness of the Soviets to use their global military capabilities to further their political ends, in Africa and elsewhere. This contrasted with the Western powers' failure to match the increase in Soviet and Warsaw Treaty Organization (Warsaw Pact) capabilities, where necessary, and the Western lack of political will to use the capabilities they did have. Thus, given the instability of many governments in the third world, the Soviets were offered an irresistible temptation to seek short-term political gains, although their long-term value was debatable.

The costs to the Soviet Union would remain minimal as long as it used Cuban and/or local troops for any fighting and as long as it did not face any Western military opposition, direct or indirect. It was notable that on the one occasion when a Soviet-backed force was forcefully blocked by the West (the attempted invasion of Shaba Province of Zaire, in May–June, halted by French, Belgian, and Moroccan troops with U.S. logistic and communications support), the probe was withdrawn, at least temporarily. The total forces involved were very small, about 3,000–4,000 on the Western side and, on the other, a somewhat larger, although very uncertain, number of the former Katanga gendarmerie, with some Cuban advisers. This episode underlined the fact that the political will to use force was becoming even more important than the possession of such force in determining the perceptions East and West held of each other's politico-military power and the third world's perception of both.

The U.S. debate on its relations with the Soviet Union (*see* Special Report) emphasized the uncertainty characterizing Pres. Jimmy Carter's foreign and strategic policies. This increased Western Europe's ever present doubts about the credibility of the U.S. nuclear guarantee, on which NATO depended if conventional force should fail to stop a Soviet attack. The major Western European powers, notably West Germany, became increasingly assertive of their views of what constituted Western defense interests. Thus when the U.S. seemed willing to stand by and let the copper-rich Shaba Province fall to a Soviet-backed force, France and Belgium intervened—the first time Western European countries had taken such an action on their own.

European perceptions about U.S. loss of will were shared by America's non-NATO allies, especially Japan and Israel, and by China, which, under its new leadership, argued vehemently for a common front against Soviet expansionism. All feared that the Soviets, sharing these perceptions, would be encouraged to push harder and more often. All held, in varying degrees, the view that

U.S. Pres. Jimmy Carter (at podium) addressed the opening session of the NATO heads of state meeting in Washington, D.C., in May.

a new cold war was emerging and that détente was either dying or dead.

These shifts in perceptions meant that quantitative data on defense spending and forces in being came under increasingly critical examination for evidence of Soviet strength and Western, or non-Soviet, weakness. Defense spending, expressed as a percentage of gross national product (GNP; *see* TABLE), is a major indicator of the importance attached to force in national policies and priorities. High rates of inflation, particularly since 1973, made comparisons of monetary outlays on defense very misleading, since unless spending rose by more than the rate of inflation, defense expenditure would decline in real terms, as in the case of Britain. Increases in real terms, on the other hand, would require very large rises in cash spending.

In the Soviet bloc, especially the Soviet Union, defense spending as a percent of GNP had remained relatively constant, while the West, through cumulative reductions, had experienced a sharp relative decline. Thus for the U.S., revised figures showed that, at the height of the Vietnam war in 1967, defense spending was at a post-1945 peak of 9.8% of GNP ($79,576,000,000), falling to 5.9% of GNP ($88,983,000,000) in 1975. Three years later, in 1978, the defense budget had risen by the apparently enormous figure of $24,017,000,000 — to $113 billion — but this meant a rise in real terms of only 0.1%, to 6% of GNP.

Inflation also compounded the problem of rising manpower costs in Western military forces, where conscripts could no longer be paid a pittance. In the U.S. the change from a conscript to an all-volunteer system of military recruitment, as part of the reaction to the Vietnam war, meant that nearly half the defense budget went to personnel costs, direct and indirect — and even so it was proving difficult to recruit and retain sufficient high-quality personnel. In contrast, the Soviet bloc countries maintained universal conscription with minimal pay for conscripts. Thus the Soviet Union's 1977 defense spending, estimated at 11–15% of GNP ($130 billion–$147 billion), provided 3,638,000 military personnel, as against 2,068,800 for the U.S. In Europe, on the crucial Central Front, NATO had, by 1978, only 626,000 combat personnel (666,000 including French forces in West Germany). Against these, the Warsaw Pact had 943,000 personnel, 638,000 of which were Soviet. Because they minimized manpower costs, the Soviets also enjoyed certain advantages in third world conflicts. In economic terms, they were much better able to afford troop losses, and as a closed society, they could avoid the adverse political effects of any losses that did occur.

UNITED STATES

The Carter administration quite naturally took a more optimistic view of its defense posture, stressing that the long-term economic and political strengths of the West were as much a part of its strategic situation as its military spending. The estimated U.S. defense expenditure for 1978–79 (fiscal year 1979), at $115 billion, provided for total armed forces of 2,068,800 (115,000 women). Secretary of Defense Harold Brown's main concern was

The U.S. Defense Department tested a method of storing intercontinental ballistic missiles underground. In a demonstration of the system, the breakout mechanism punches through five feet of earth and ten inches of concrete in less than one minute.

to improve U.S. and NATO conventional defensive capabilities, and he shared the view, most strongly advocated by former defense secretary Robert S. McNamara, that NATO could fight a prolonged conventional defense against the Warsaw Pact if appropriate steps were taken. Whether NATO had ever had this capability was questionable in the 1960s and very doubtful in 1978.

The U.S. Army of 774,200 had only four armoured, five mechanized, and five infantry divisions (one infantry division was to be mechanized in 1979), plus one airmobile and one airborne division and one armoured, two infantry (one in Berlin), and two special mission brigades. Each U.S. division had 17,000–18,000 men and, if armoured, 324 tanks, with 4,500 men and 108 tanks in a brigade. Armour remained at about 10,500 medium tanks, including 3,300 M-48s and 7,150 M-60s, plus 1,600 M-551 Sheridan light tanks. A new tank, the XM-1, had been accepted for service, with 110 scheduled for delivery in fiscal 1979 and 569 in fiscal 1980. Development of a new mechanized infantry combat vehicle (MICV) had been dropped on cost grounds. As a stopgap, 1,200 additional M-113 armoured personnel carriers (APC's) were to be produced, although the M-113 was inferior to the Soviet BMP MICV. Existing forces included 22,000 M-577, M-114, and M-113 APC's.

The provision of tanks and MICV/APC's was vital for any forces committed to NATO, since only mechanized forces could fight in a sophisticated combat zone such as western Europe. The five infantry divisions were useful only for the Pacific area and would have to be mechanized as the U.S. withdrew from its Pacific commitments. The 30,-000-man U.S. force in South Korea was reduced by one brigade, although this was a significant slowdown from the Carter administration's original plans. The Strategic Reserve in the U.S. was still overoriented to reinforcing the Pacific; the Reserve proper included three infantry and one airborne division, chiefly suited to the Pacific, plus

Approximate Strengths of Regular Armed Forces of the World

Country	Military personnel in 000s			Warships			Total major surface combat vessels	Jet aircraft[3]		Tanks[4]	Defense expenditure as % of GNP
	Army	Navy	Air Force	Aircraft carriers/cruisers[1]	Submarines[2]	Destroyers/frigates		Bombers	Fighters/reconnaissance		
I. NATO											
Belgium	63.4	4.3	19.4	—	—	4	4	90 FB	40, 18 R	386	3.4
Canada	29.3	14.2	36.5	—	—	3	23	—	120	146	1.8
Denmark	21.0	6.1	6.9	—	6 C	2	2	58 FB	40, 16 R	320	2.5
France[5]	324.4	68.2	100.8	2 CV, 1 CA	21, 4 SSBN	42	45	33 SB, 318 FB	140, 45 R	1,060	3.6
Germany, West	336.2	36.5	106.2	—	24 C	17	17	373 FB	60, 111 R	3,779	3.4
Greece	150.0	17.5	22.6	—	7	16	16	133 FB	84, 20 R	1,170	5.0
Italy	251.0	42.0	69.0	3 CA	9	19	22	162 FB	72, 36 R	1,650	2.4
Luxembourg	0.6	—	—	—	—	—	—	—	—	—	1.1
Netherlands, The	75.0	17.0	17.7	—	6	18	18	108 FB	36, 18 R	800	3.6
Norway	20.0	9.0	10.0	—	15 C	5	5	54 FB	29, 13 R	116	3.1
Portugal	40.0	14.0	9.5	—	3	3	3	18 FB	—	113	3.3
Turkey	390.0	45.0	50.0	—	11	13	13	271 FB	33, 35 R	2,800	5.7
United Kingdom	160.8	67.8[6]	84.6	1 CV, 2 LPH, 2 CA	17, 10 SSN, 4 SSBN	66	71	112 B, 134 FB	96, 54 R	900	5.0
United States	965.7[6]	532.3	570.8	3 CVN, 10 CV, 7 CAN, 20 CA	5, 70 SSN, 41 SSBN	132	172	2,164 FB, 432 SB, 282 B	741, 192 R	10,500	6.0
II. WARSAW PACT											
Bulgaria	115.0	10.0	25.0	—	4	—	—	72 FB	137	1,925	2.5
Czechoslovakia	140.0	—	46.0	—	—	—	—	170 FB	247, 72 R	3,400	3.8
Germany, East	105.0	16.0	36.0	—	—	1	1	35 FB	270, 16 R	2,500	5.9
Hungary	91.0	—	23.0	—	—	—	—	—	116	1,000	2.6
Poland	222.0	22.5	62.0	—	4	1	1	6 B, 218 FB	420, 81 R	3,800	3.0
Romania	140.0	10.5	30.0	—	—	—	—	75 FB	237, 15 R	1,700	1.7
U.S.S.R.	1,825.0	433.0[6]	1,380.0[7]	1 CV, 2 CVH, 35 CA	134, 40 SSN, 70 SSBN, 20 SSB, 45 SSGN, 24 SSG	204	242	135 SB, 4,000 FB, 801 B	3,000, 700 R	50,000	11–15
III. OTHER EUROPEAN											
Albania	30.0	3.0	8.0	—	3	—	—	—	101	100	...
Austria	33.0	—	4.0	—	—	—	—	30 FB	—	270	1.1
Finland	34.4	2.5	3.0	—	—	2	2	—	40	—	1.3
Ireland	13.2	0.7	0.7	—	—	—	—	—	—	—	1.6
Spain	240.0	40.0[6]	35.5	1 CVH	8	28	29	45 FB	76, 22 R	680	1.7
Sweden	40.6	11.8	13.3	—	17	10	10	90 FB	306, 54 R	650	3.4
Switzerland[8]	10.5/580.0	—	8.0/45.0	—	—	—	—	287 FB	35, 18 R	640	1.9
Yugoslavia	200.0	27.0	40.0	—	5	1	1	131 FB	120, 40 R	2,150	5.2
IV. MIDDLE EAST AND MEDITERRANEAN; SUB-SAHARAN AFRICA; LATIN AMERICA[9]											
Algeria	70.0	3.8	5.0	—	—	—	—	50 FB, 24 B	90	350	3.9
Egypt	350.0	20.0	25.0	—	12	5	5	326 FB, 28 B	108	1,600	...
Iran	285.0	28.0	100.0	—	—	7	7	361 FB	56, 16 R	1,620	10.9
Iraq	180.0	4.0	28.0	—	—	—	—	190 FB, 22 B	115	1,800	10.2
Israel[8]	138.0/375	5.0/8.0	21.0/25.0	—	3	—	—	525 FB	14 R	3,000	29.9
Jordan	61.0	—	6.6	—	—	—	—	32 FB	44	500	15.5
Lebanon[10]	7.0	—	0.5	—	—	—	—	11 FB	10	—	...
Libya	30.0	3.0	4.0	—	3	1	1	110 FB, 12 B	24	2,000	1.8
Morocco	81.0	2.0	6.0	—	—	—	—	41 FB	—	90	3.6
Saudi Arabia	45.0	1.5	12.0	—	—	—	—	60 FB	18	325	13.6
Sudan	50.0	0.6	1.5	—	—	—	—	12 FB	10	130	5.4
Syria	200.0	2.5	25.0	—	—	2	—	110 FB	282	2,500	16.4
Ethiopia[11]	90.0	1.5	2.0	—	—	—	—	91 FB, 2 B	—	504	...
Nigeria	221.0	4.5	6.0	—	—	1	1	24 FB	—	—	7.8
Rhodesia	9.5	—	1.3	—	—	—	—	28 FB, 7 B	—	—	7.7
Somalia	50.0	0.5	1.0	—	—	—	—	15 FB, 3 B	7	80	...
South Africa	50.0	5.5	10.0	—	3	4	4	32 FB, 18 B	52	170	5.1
Zaire	30.0	—	3.0	—	—	—	—	—	17	—	...
Argentina	80.0	32.9[6]	20.0	1 CVH, 2 CA	4	9	12	153 FB, 9 B	16	100	...
Brazil	182.0	49.0[6]	42.8	1 CVH	10	15	16	39 FB	15	60	1.1
Chile	50.0	24.0	11.0	3 CA	3	8	11	38 FB	17	76	1.1
Colombia	60.0	9.0[6]	6.5	—	2	12	12	—	18	—	...
Cuba	130.0	9.0	20.0	—	—	—	—	30 FB	118	600	0.6
Mexico	332.0	19.0[6]	6.0	—	—	3	3	—	—	—	3.1
Peru	65.0	14.0	10.0	4 CL	8	7	11	34 B, 71 FB	18	310	
V. FAR EAST AND OCEANIA[9]											
Afghanistan	100.0	—	10.0	—	—	—	—	74 FB, 30 B	40	700	...
Australia	32.0	16.3	21.6	1 CVH	6	11	12	56 FB, 22 B	—	87	2.9
Bangladesh	65.0	3.5	5.0	—	—	2	2	—	9	30	...
Burma	153.0	9.0	7.5	—	—	2	2	—	—	—	...
China	3,625.0	300.0[6]	400.0	—	1 SSN, 73	23	23	500 FB, 590 B	4,700	10,000	10.0
India	950.0	46.0	100.0	1 CV, 1 CL	8	25	27	245 FB, 50 B	385, 6 R	1,700	3.1
Indonesia	180.0	39.0[6]	28.0	—	3	11	11	16 FB	—	—	3.5
Japan	155.0	41.0	44.0	—	14	46	46	96 FB	248, 14 R	690	0.9
Korea, North	440.0	27.0	45.0	—	15	3	3	340 FB, 85 B	230	1,950	10.5
Korea, South	580.0[6]	32.0	30.0	—	—	9	9	246 FB	10 R	1,000	6.5
Laos[12]	46.0	—	2.0	—	—	—	—	—	10	—	...
Malaysia	52.5	6.0	6.0	—	—	2	2	16 FB	—	—	4.4
New Zealand	5.7	2.7	4.1	—	—	4	4	13 FB	—	—	1.8
Pakistan	400.0	11.0	18.0	—	4	7	7	175 FB, 11 B	49, 13 R	1,000	4.6
Philippines	63.0	20.0[6]	16.0	—	—	8	8	40 FB	—	—	3.4
Singapore	30.0	3.0	3.0	—	—	—	—	88 FB	—	—	6.3
Taiwan	369.0[6]	35.0	70.0	—	2	33	33	300 FB	8 R	150	8.3
Thailand	141.0	28.0[6]	43.0	—	—	3	3	14 FB	4 R	—	4.1
Vietnam[13]	600.0	3.0	12.0	—	—	—	—	150 FB, 10 B	140	900	...

Note: Data exclude paramilitary, security, and irregular forces. Naval data exclude vessels of less than 100 tons standard displacement. Figures are for July 1978.
[1] Aircraft carriers (CV); helicopter carriers (CVH); helicopter landing platforms (LPH); heavy cruisers (CA); light cruisers (CL); N denotes nuclear.
[2] Nuclear submarines (SSN); ballistic missile submarines (SSB); guided (cruise) missile submarines (SSG); coastal (C); N denotes nuclear.
[3] Bombers (B), fighter-bombers (FB), strategic bombers (SB), reconnaissance fighters (R); data exclude light strike/counter-insurgency (COIN) aircraft.
[4] Medium and heavy tanks (31 tons and over).
[5] French forces were withdrawn from NATO in 1966, but France remains a member of NATO.
[6] Includes marines.
[7] Figure includes the Strategic Rocket Forces (375,000) and the Air Defense Force (550,000), both separate services.
[8] Second figure is fully mobilized strength.
[9] Sections IV and V list only those states with significant military forces.
[10] Figures approximate, given Lebanon's civil war and division.
[11] Ethiopia also has 17,000 Cuban plus other Soviet bloc troops and a 100,000-strong People's Militia.
[12] Lao People's Liberation Army.
[13] Substantial equipment of former South Vietnamese forces not included.
Sources: International Institute for Strategic Studies, 18 Adam Street, London, *The Military Balance 1978–79, Strategic Survey 1977.*

The U.S. Army purchased eight XM-2 tanks for testing purposes. The new vehicle has a top speed of 42 mph and bristles with guns and other weapons.

one armoured, one mechanized, and one airmobile division, usable in Europe. Designated as reinforcements for Europe were one armoured and two mechanized divisions, plus one armoured cavalry regiment. All but one mechanized division had their heavy equipment stockpiled in West Germany.

A significant improvement in U.S. ability to reinforce NATO was planned. Equipment for three more divisions was to be stockpiled in Europe, and air transport would be reorganized to provide the capability for shifting five divisions and 60 tactical air squadrons to Europe in ten days instead of one division and 40 squadrons. U.S. Army personnel in Europe totaled 198,400; of these 189,000 were in West Germany, where the 7th Army included two armoured and two mechanized divisions and one armoured and two mechanized brigades. Total U.S. forces in western Europe amounted to about 300,000 personnel, a major improvement over Vietnam war levels but still far short of the 434,000 stationed there in 1962, when they faced a smaller Soviet force.

This reorganization of U.S. forces toward a largely European role raised questions about the future of the U.S. Marine Corps (USMC) and the Navy. The USMC, with a strength of 191,500 personnel, 575 M-60 medium tanks, and 364 combat aircraft, was nearly one-quarter as large as the Army, while its 64 amphibious warfare ships absorbed a significant portion of the Navy's resources. Because of its amphibious role, the USMC could not carry sufficient heavy equipment to operate in Europe, and it was doubtful whether its amphibious capability was a sufficient asset in Europe to justify its costs. The Carter administration was therefore attempting to upgrade the USMC into a less mobile force with heavier equipment, more suitable for European operations.

Similarly, the U.S. Navy's traditional missions of sea control (securing convoy routes for the movement of U.S. and allied troops and supplies) and force projection (assisting these forces to secure beachheads) were under question. If the Soviets' assumption that they could win a blitzkrieg-type war in Europe in under 30 days was correct,

then NATO would not be able to mobilize its larger reserves or receive U.S. seaborne reinforcements or supplies. This would make redundant the heavy Navy investment in antisubmarine warfare (ASW) capabilities and in the ability to fight a protracted war at sea. The Carter administration, hoping that NATO could hold out longer than 30 days, wished to maintain a sea-control/ASW capability. It had halted the Navy's decline in the last decade from over 300 to 172 major surface combatants, and missile capabilities were being improved with the deployment of the medium-range (70-mi) Harpoon antishipping missile and tactical versions of the Tomahawk sea-launched cruise missile (SLCM).

The president and the Navy remained at loggerheads, however, over the Navy's request for a fifth nuclear-powered aircraft carrier, and in August Carter vetoed a defense appropriations bill because it included funding for the carrier. The cost of a carrier group, including its specialized naval aircraft, was certainly very high, although no other weapons system could offer such an effective mix against a potential Soviet attack by submarines, cruise missiles, and land-based naval aircraft. The Navy was also experiencing cost escalations and building difficulties with the Ohio-class nuclear ballistic missile submarines (SSBN's), each of which would carry 24 Trident submarine-launched ballistic missiles (SLBM's). The first 4 Ohio- (formerly Trident-) class SSBN's were under construction, with 12 more scheduled.

The Air Force was deploying a mix of new fighters to ensure a future level of 2,500 combat aircraft. The less expensive F-18 was being developed to add to the F-15 Hornet and the F-16. Overall force levels were 570,800 personnel and about 3,400 combat aircraft, including 1,100 F-4 Phantom, 216 F-15, and 96 A-7D fighter/ground-attack planes, plus 282 F-111 E/F tactical bombers, 48 A-10A close support (antitank) aircraft, and 192 RF-4C Phantom reconnaissance fighters. Electronics warfare aircraft (known as Wild Weasel) were emerging as a distinct category. The major deployments were: in the U.S., 82,000 personnel in the Tactical Air Command (TAC), with 43 fighter and 5 reconnaissance squadrons, and 64,500 in the

The F-16 fighter-bomber, considered to be the most maneuverable fighter in the sky, is one of the U.S. Air Force's new weapons. The plane is smaller than the F-15 and costs about half as much to build.

Military Airlift Command (MAC); in Europe, 76,-000 personnel in U.S. Air Force, Europe (USAFE), with 25 fighter, 3 reconnaissance, and 2 tactical airlift squadrons; and in the Pacific, 31,100 personnel in Pacific Air Forces (Pacaf), with 9 fighter and 1 reconnaissance squadron.

U.S. air defenses, under the Aerospace Defense Command, remained negligible. The Safeguard antiballistic missile (ABM) system was deactivated, leaving only 141 F-106A interceptors (regular Air Force) and 190 Air National Guard interceptors, all elderly aircraft. The Air Force was, however, involved in a major effort to protect U.S. satellites against Soviet hunter-killer satellites. Offensive space-borne systems under development included antisatellite lasers, which might be usable as an ABM system.

U.S.S.R.

The Soviet Union continued its qualitative upgrading at all levels. Strategically, development and deployment of its fourth-generation intercontinental ballistic missiles (ICBM's; SS-16, 17, 18, and 19) and SLBM's (SS-NX-17 and 18) was well under way, posing a major threat to the U.S. Minuteman ICBM force by 1981. Soviet missile accuracies were now approaching or bettering those of the U.S., while the Soviet advantage in throw weight (payload) was increasing. The SS-20 land-mobile intermediate-range ballistic missile (IRBM) was being deployed to replace 500 SS-4 medium-range ballistic missiles (MRBM's) and 90 SS-5 IRBM's targeted on Western Europe. A fifth generation of strategic missiles was under development.

Contrary to widespread Western expectations, there were no numerical reductions in either strategic or conventional forces as the quality of Soviet equipment, now generally up to Western standards, improved. The Soviets maintained a total of 3,638,000 military personnel, superior both to NATO on their Western frontiers and to China in the East. Nor, despite continuing economic problems, were there any signs that the high level of defense spending would be reduced.

The Army of 1,825,000 comprised 46 tank, 115 motor rifle (mechanized), and 8 airborne divisions, with 11,000 men and 325 tanks in each tank division, 13,000 men and 266 tanks in a mechanized division, and 7,000 men in an airborne division. Tank strength increased to 50,000, compared with 34,000 in 1967, and the T-72 and T-62 were replacing the T-54/55 in front-line service. Armoured fighting vehicles (AFV's) totaled 55,000, including the BMP MICV. Deployment remained relatively unchanged, with 31 divisions (16 tank) in Eastern Europe, 64 divisions (22 tank) in the European U.S.S.R., concentrated against western Europe, and 44 divisions (6 tank) on the Sino-Soviet border, including 3 in Mongolia. The remaining divisions were in southern and central U.S.S.R.

The 455,000-strong Air Force was designed to support the rapid blitzkrieg-type advances called for by Soviet military doctrine. Its 4,650 combat aircraft included increasing numbers of Su-17 Fitter C/D's (530), MiG-23/27 Flogger-B/D's (1,300), and Su-19 Fencer A's (190), whose improved range (about 1,100 mi), payload, and avionics gave the

Soviets a much increased deep interdiction capability. The Soviets had retained and upgraded the Air Defense Force, which remained a separate service. It included 550,000 personnel, 2,720 interceptors, 10,000 surface-to-air missile (SAM) launchers at over 1,000 sites, and four ABM sites around Moscow. The Air Transport Force, with 1,300 aircraft, continued to provide rapid support for Soviet allies in Africa.

The Navy, with 433,000 personnel, also continued to expand. It was now clearly an instrument for projecting Soviet power as well as for denying the sea to the West in a major conflict. The Soviet submarine force remained the world's largest, with 40 nuclear-powered and 134 diesel submarines, plus 45 nuclear- and 24 diesel-powered submarines with long-range cruise missiles (LRCM's). The SS-N-3 Shaddock LRCM, first deployed in 1962 (450-mi range; kiloton-range warhead), was to be replaced by the SS-N-12 (range estimated at 1,000+ mi; kiloton-range warhead). Although designed primarily for antishipping use, Soviet LRCM's could also strike at coastal cities. The widespread deployment of LRCM's and the extended range of the SS-N-12, which could now be verified, meant that Soviet attempts to limit U.S. and allied LRCM range and deployment in the negotiations for a second strategic arms limitation talks agreement (SALT II) constituted another attempt to secure unilateral Western concessions.

The first Soviet carrier, the "Kiev," was closer to the U.S. Invincible-class minicarrier, currently under construction, than to full-size U.S. carriers. The Kiev class (another on trials, one building) carried 20 ASW helicopters and 12 vertical takeoff and landing (VTOL) aircraft similar to the U.K. and USMC Harrier, suitable for point defense or support of landings. The two Moskva-class helicopter carriers were also known as helicopter cruisers, since they combined a cruiser's missile armament with 20 ASW helicopters. The Soviets had 24 modern cruisers and 59 modern ASW destroyers.

Although primarily oriented toward defensive ASW, the Navy was also capable of global operations, including offensive operations in Europe. With the introduction of the Backfire B bomber (30 deployed), whose 5,500-mi range could be considerably extended by in-flight refueling, the Naval Air Force of 770 combat aircraft was acquiring a longer-range capability for antishipping operations. Like the 280 Tu-16 Badger medium bombers, the Backfire carried air-to-surface missiles (ASM's). The cumulative effect of the Soviet naval buildup was to threaten NATO's northern flank in Norway and neutral Sweden. Greece and Turkey were similarly vulnerable, and the eastern end of the Mediterranean, including Israel, was within easy reach of Soviet operations.

NATO

The Western European members of NATO shared the U.S. view that their conventional defense capabilities needed upgrading, and the Long Term Defense Program, designed to achieve this goal, was accepted at the meeting of NATO heads of state in Washington in May 1978. The Europeans, however, doubted that these measures alone were

sufficient. In northern and central Europe the basic balance, even including the two French divisions in West Germany (which would fight with NATO), had swung increasingly in favour of the Warsaw Pact. The peacetime balance, in divisional equivalents, was: armour, 10 NATO versus 32 Pact (including 22 Soviet); mechanized, 13 NATO versus 33 Pact (including 20 Soviet); infantry and airborne, 4 NATO versus 5 Pact (including 3 Soviet). If reinforcements were added, the Pact advantage would increase. In available tactical aircraft, or those which could be quickly redeployed, including U.S. dual-based and French aircraft, NATO had 1,950 fighter/ground-attack planes to the Pact's 1,350 (925 Soviet), 650 interceptors to the Pact's 2,025, and 380 reconnaissance planes to the Pact's 550 (350 Soviet).

Above all, NATO was worried by the Pact's superiority in main battle tanks, since these remained the key to rapid offensive operations. Main battle tanks in operational service (excluding reserves to replace war losses) totaled 7,000 for NATO as against 21,100 for the Pact (13,650 Soviet), while in total conventional artillery NATO had only about 2,700 to the Pact's more than 10,000. To offset this Pact supremacy, NATO still sought to exploit its diminishing technological superiority for defensive purposes. Hence its increased reliance on precision guided munitions and more accurate conventional antitank and antipersonnel weapons, and its interest in tactical versions of the LRCM.

While NATO's European members could understand why the U.S. might want to accede to Soviet demands for limits on LRCM range to secure a SALT II agreement, they strongly opposed any U.S. limits on the transfer of LRCM technology, particularly since SALT II would leave untouched the vast Soviet nuclear strike forces targeted on western Europe. European-U.S. differences came to a head over the neutron bomb, an enhanced-radiation weapon designed to incapacitate enemy troops by

About 20 MiG-23s have been placed in Cuba by the Soviets despite strong U.S. protests.

radiation rather than blast. Because this radiation would be short-lived, the long-term damage would be much less than with existing NATO tactical nuclear weapons. The neutron bomb (actually a miniaturized hydrogen bomb) had been proposed in 1958 but rejected by successive U.S. administrations. President Carter approved its development, and British Prime Minister James Callaghan and West German Chancellor Helmut Schmidt agreed to support a U.S. decision to produce it despite opposition from the left wings of their own parties.

They were therefore appalled when, in April, Carter announced that he would defer production of the neutron bomb, although his national security advisers advocated going ahead. The Western Europeans would have accepted — albeit reluctantly — an early decision not to produce. But, having incurred all the political costs of supporting production, they found themselves in an embarrassing situation. The president's subsequent modification of his decision, approving modernization of U.S. tactical nuclear stockpiles so as to facilitate their rapid conversion to neutron weapons, was a sensible compromise. It came too late to repair the damage, however, and influential Western European leaders were seriously questioning whether the U.S. would honour its nuclear guarantee of Western Europe.

UNITED KINGDOM

Britain's armed forces continued their decline to a total of only 313,253 personnel, although defense spending, at $13,579,000,000, remained at about 5% of GNP. There were reports of low morale re-

sulting from low pay, the hazards of service in Northern Ireland, and frustration over the continued failure to replace obsolete equipment. The Army of 160,837 was geared to defend West Germany, and the British Army of the Rhine (BAOR), at a nominal strength of 55,000 men, was being reorganized. Development of a new tank, the MBTB-80, was authorized.

The Navy, with 67,770 personnel, provided the strategic nuclear deterrent, with four SSBN's, each carrying 16 Polaris A-3 SLBM's; this force required modernization, possibly with U.S. LRCM's. The last Royal Navy aircraft carrier, the "Ark Royal," was retired, leaving one operational ASW/commando carrier, 2 helicopter cruisers, 11 guided weapon destroyers, and 55 frigates. The Air Force of 84,646 personnel included 48 Vulcan B-2 medium bombers and 50 Buccaneer S-2 strike aircraft, aging but still able to deliver nuclear weapons. The biggest single improvement was the planned introduction of 385 Tornado multirole combat aircraft, developed in collaboration with West Germany and Italy.

FRANCE

French forces remained roughly constant, at 502,-800, as did defense spending, at 3.6% of GNP ($17,-518,000,000). France remained a member of NATO, although it did not participate in NATO planning. The nuclear *force de frappe*, still the main defense priority, included 64 SLBM's in four SSBN's; a fifth SSBN was under construction and a sixth had been approved. The 18 S-2 land-based IRBM's were being replaced by the S-3, with a longer range and larger warhead. Besides the 33 Mirage IVA strate-

A new "jump-jet," which takes off from a steel ramp, has been developed by the British Royal Navy. The plane will be used on new British minicarriers.

gic nuclear bombers, the 105 Mirage IIIE fighter-bombers could deliver tactical nuclear weapons, as could the 30 Pluton SSM's. The Gaullist argument that French nuclear weapons were necessary to ensure the U.S. nuclear guarantee seemed increasingly convincing, given European-U.S. differences.

The Army of 324,400 was being reorganized. Tank strength remained at 1,060 AMX-30 main battle tanks. Deployment reflected France's dual concerns of defending West Germany, where two mechanized divisions were stationed, and protecting French and Western interests overseas. Although French troops had been withdrawn from Zaire, they were present in Djibouti (4,000), Senegal (1,000), Chad (1,500), Ivory Coast (400), and Gabon (450) and formed part of the UN Interim Force in Lebanon (UNIFIL). The Navy of 68,200 retained its two aircraft and one helicopter carrier. The 100,800-strong Air Force was divided into the Air Defense Command and the Tactical Air Force.

WEST GERMANY

West Germany's armed forces, at 489,900, remained the largest European contribution to NATO. Defense expenditure, at $21,355,000,000, amounted to 3.4% of GNP. The Army of 336,200 had 1,342 M-48A-2 and 2,437 Leopard 1 main battle tanks, with 1,800 Leopard 2s on order. It was also being reorganized, into 15 armoured brigades, 17 armoured infantry brigades, and 3 airborne brigades. The 106,200-strong Air Force had 60 F-4F Phantom, 144 F-104G Starfighter, and 84 G-91R-3 (to be replaced by 175 Alpha Jet) fighter-bombers; 210 Tornado fighter-bombers were on order. Its SSM squadrons had 72 Pershing 1A SSM's with high-kiloton-range nuclear warheads under dual U.S.-West German control. The Naval Air Arm's 85 F-104G Starfighter fighter-bombers were to be replaced by 110 Tornadoes.

DISARMAMENT AND ARMS CONTROL

The UN had designated the 1970s as the Disarmament Decade, but the tenth UN General Assembly Special Session on Disarmament was largely an exercise in futility. Those heads of government who attended made propaganda speeches, attacking their enemies and suggesting abolition of weapons their countries did not have and could not get. The session's only concrete achievement was to expand the 31-member, Geneva-based Conference of the Committee on Disarmament (CCD) into a 40-member Committee on Disarmament, including China and France, and to abolish the superpower co-chairmanship. France, which had always refused to take part in the CCD, agreed to participate in the new body, but China seemed unlikely to do so. The new committee was probably too large for effective negotiations.

The three major areas for arms control negotiations proper were SALT, the Mutual (and Balanced) Force Reduction (M[B]FR) talks in Vienna, and efforts aimed at implementing the 1968 nonproliferation treaty (NPT). Toward the end of the year there appeared to be progress in SALT, but new problems arose late in December, and a three-day meeting between U.S. Secretary of State Cyrus

Vance and Soviet Foreign Minister Andrey Gromyko failed to resolve them. The Carter administration still hoped that SALT II could be signed at a Carter-Brezhnev summit in the spring of 1979. It seemed questionable whether a SALT II agreement acceptable to the Soviets could receive U.S. Senate ratification. Some conservative senators were threatening to oppose any SALT II as a means of retaliating against the administration for its diplomatic recognition of China.

The M(B)FR negotiations between 19 NATO and Warsaw Pact members, under way since 1973, seemed increasingly futile. The Soviets did accept the Western idea that each side's forces should be reduced to a common ceiling of 700,000 ground troops and 900,000 ground and air personnel. However, the Pact insisted that its ground forces were only 805,000 strong, requiring a cut of 105,-000, whereas Western estimates gave them over 950,000 ground troops, requiring a cut of 250,000. The Soviets also proposed a first-stage reduction of 11–15% by each side, but this was also based on their figures.

The Carter administration made some progress toward limiting the spread of nuclear power plants that could give their owners a weapons-manufacturing capability. The Conference of Atomic Energy Suppliers, set up in 1978 to establish safeguards on such exports, now included 16 countries. Three basic problems remained, however. First, the U.S. needed nuclear energy less than its allies, who could not afford to delay development of nuclear power plants and export markets. Second, the strategic motives for acquiring nuclear weapons were being increased by the Carter administration's apparently uncertain defense and foreign policies. Third, the problems involved even in slowing down nuclear proliferation were so complex that there was no agreement, within the U.S. or the Western alliance, about which mix of policies could achieve the desired goal.

THE MIDDLE EAST

The U.S.-Egyptian-Israeli summit at Camp David, Md., in September made the conclusion of a separate peace between Israel and Egypt a distinct possibility. (See MIDDLE EASTERN AFFAIRS.) Such a treaty would have advantages for both sides. Egypt wanted to regain the territories it had lost to Israel in 1967 but could not recover by force, while Israel could gain more security by trading these territories for a peace treaty with Egypt than by retaining them. Even so, this alone would not remove the chances of war in the Middle East. If Pres. Anwar as-Sadat were deposed, Egypt's military machine could once again be turned against Israel. Israel still had to deter attacks by Syria, which had effectively taken control of Lebanon, and by Jordan. It seemed certain that the Palestinian nationalists would continue to use terror in pressing their claims for a homeland and that the Soviet Union would continue to support anti-Western Arab governments.

Israel spent 29.9% of its GNP on defense ($3,310,-000,000), one of the highest levels in the world. Its 164,000-strong forces could be increased to 400,000 in 24 hours. The Army of 138,000 (375,000 mobilized) comprised 20 armoured, 9 mechanized, 9 infantry, and 5 parachute brigades, each about 3,500 men strong, with 3,000 main battle tanks and 4,000 armoured fighting vehicles. The Air Force of 21,000 (25,000 mobilized) had 25 F/TF-15 Hornet fighter/ground-attack/interceptors (15 more, along with 75 F-16 fighters, on order from the U.S.), 170 F-4E Phantoms, 30 Mirage III-CJ/BJ's, and 50 Israeli-built Kfir C2s, plus 250 Skyhawk fighter-bombers. The small coast defense Navy of 5,000 (8,000 mobilized) was based on 18 fast patrol boats armed with the Gabriel SSM. Qualitatively, these forces were perhaps the best in the world, but their long-term problem was to maintain an edge to deter attacks by the quantitatively superior Arab forces. Hence Israel's development of its nuclear stockpile, estimated at 80–100 Hiroshima-size (15-kiloton) weapons. Officially, Israel refused to confirm or deny its existence.

Egypt's defense spending for 1978–79 totaled $2.8 billion, a substantial decrease from the 1975 level of $6,103,000,000. This still provided armed forces totaling 395,000, but Egypt's main problem was lack of spare parts for its Soviet equipment, making the combat value of its forces uncertain. The Army of 350,000, including the 75,000-man Air Defense Command, had 850 T-54/55 and 750 T-62 tanks, plus 3,000 MICV/APC's. The Air Force had 612 operational aircraft, with more grounded because of lack of spare parts. On order were 50 F-5E/F short-range interceptors and 14 C-130H transports from the U.S. and 14 Mirage interceptors from France.

Perhaps the major threat to stability in the Middle East came from Syria, whose Pres. Hafez al-Assad was a leader in the "Front of Steadfastness" of states opposing an Egyptian-Israeli treaty. Syria continued to obtain Soviet military aid, and this, combined with defense spending of $1,121,-000,000 (16.4% of GNP), provided armed forces totaling 227,500. The Army of 200,000 was equipped with 200 T-34, 1,500 T-54/55, and 800 T-62 tanks, plus about 1,800 APC's and MICV's. Some 30,000 troops were in Lebanon as part of the Arab Deter-

rent Force. The Air Force of 25,000 included 50 MiG-17 and 60 Su-7 fighter-bombers and 220 MiG-21PF/MF, 50 MiG-23, and 12 of the new MiG-27 interceptors.

Iran's massive armed forces of 413,000, costing $9.9 billion (10.9% of GNP), were being used by the shah in an effort to control the increasingly widespread and violent civil disturbances that were threatening his regime. They seemed loyal to him, but this was not an absolute certainty. The doubtful future of the regime called into question their long-term combat value as well as their continued receipt of sophisticated Western equipment. In December the disturbances forced cancellation of a $575 million deal with a U.S. firm for a factory to produce military helicopters. The Army of 285,000 had 760 Chieftain, 400 M-47/48, and 460 M-60A1 medium tanks, 250 Scorpion light tanks, and about 325 M-113 and 500 BTR-40–152 APC's. The Air Force of 100,000 was equipped with 56 of the new U.S. F-14A Tomcat fighters and 32 F-4D, 177 F-4E, 12 F-5A, and 140 F-5E fighter-bombers. The 28,000-strong Navy included three destroyers with Standard SSM/SAM's and four frigates with Seacat SAM's and Seakiller SSM's.

AFRICA SOUTH OF THE SAHARA

With Ethiopia's victory over Somalia in the Ogaden, the focus of interest shifted south, to the guerrilla war in Rhodesia, and to the increasing Cuban-Soviet military presence in Africa. The latter was more important in the long run. Since most African armies were largely paper forces, useful only for maintaining their governments in power, a relatively small number of well-trained and equipped Cuban troops and/or advisers, backed by unlimited Soviet arms supplies, could exert an influence out of all proportion to their numbers. Cuba's armed forces, totaling 159,000 men, cost an estimated $784 million, mostly paid by the Soviets. Overseas deployments included 17,000 in Ethiopia, 25,000 in Angola, substantial numbers in Mozambique and Zambia, and other forces in Algeria, Benin, Congo, Guinea, Libya, Sierra Leone, Tanzania, Uganda, and Yemen (Aden).

In Rhodesia Ian Smith, having finally agreed to black participation in the government, was attempting to form a coalition with three black leaders, Bishop Abel Muzorewa, Ndabaningi Sithole, and Chief Jeremiah Chirau. Opposing them was Robert Mugabe's Patriotic Front, supplied and trained by the Soviets and supported by Angola and Mozambique. Angola's forces totaled 33,000, mostly in the Army; some 25,000 Cubans were serving with these forces, assisted by several hundred Soviet advisers. The Cubans operated heavy equipment and aircraft in actions against Namibia (South West Africa) and against antigovernment guerrilla groups in Angola, where Cuban losses were significant. Mozambique's army of 20,000 was to be expanded to 30,000, with Cuban, East German, and Soviet advisers, as well as some from Romania and China. Zambia, directly involved because the Patriotic Front was based on its territory, had armed forces of only 14,300—less than those of the Front itself. The Front's bases were subject to increasingly heavy Rhodesian raids.

Gas masks and chemical-proof suits developed by the British Army have been purchased for use by NATO combat troops.

LONDON DAILY EXPRESS/PICTORIAL PARADE

Rhodesian defense spending of $242 million (7.7% of GNP) provided an army of 9,500, reinforced by 15,000 Territorial Army and Police Reserves on active duty at any one time and supported by the paramilitary British South African Police. The 1,300-man Air Force had seven Canberra light bombers and ten Hunter FGA9 and 18 FB9 fighter-bombers. Although small, these forces were efficient and relatively superior in local terms. This superiority was being threatened, however, by the sharp increase in Soviet support for the guerrillas.

South Africa was not providing much assistance to Rhodesia, although this might change if the collapse of the Rhodesian government seemed imminent. South Africa's defense expenditure had risen to $2,622,000,000 (5.1% of GNP), providing total armed forces of 65,500. The Army had 50,000 plus 138,000 active reserves (Citizen Force). Some Citizen Force units were deployed on the Angolan border and in Namibia, where South Africa was attempting to satisfy UN and, more importantly, U.S. pressures for Namibian independence while retaining control over this large and valuable territory. The 10,000-man Air Force was the strongest in southern Africa.

SOUTH, SOUTHEAST, AND EAST ASIA

The regional military balance in the Indian subcontinent was significantly altered by the April coup that brought a pro-Soviet government to power in Afghanistan, always regarded by the British as the most likely direction for a Russian thrust at India in the days of the British Empire. Afghanistan's armed forces before the coup were sizable, including a 100,000-man army, with 700 medium tanks, and a 10,000-man air force with 50 MiG-17 and 24 Su-7BM fighter-bombers and 40 MiG-21 interceptors. Pakistan was the most immediately threatened, especially since its forces were tied up in defense against India. Pakistan's defense spending, however, had dropped to 4.6% of GNP ($938 million). It maintained an army of 400,000, equipped with 250 M-47/48 and 700 T-59 medium tanks, and an air force of 18,000. India still maintained the largest forces in Asia after China, at a cost of only 3.1% of GNP ($3,570,000,-000). These included an army of 950,000, equipped with 1,700 medium tanks, and an air force of 100,-000 with 50 Canberra light bombers and 245 fighter-bombers. The Navy of 46,000 had grown steadily to include one aircraft carrier, 25 frigates, and 8 submarines.

Elsewhere, the Asian military balance remained relatively unchanged, despite increased tension between Vietnam and Cambodia and between Vietnam and China. Chinese defense spending remained at about $35 billion (10% of GNP). China maintained total armed forces of 4,325,000, including an army of 3,625,000 with about 10,000 tanks. The new leadership was anxious to modernize these forces, preferably by purchasing the rights to build Western military equipment. China continued to build a nuclear and thermonuclear stockpile, but it still had only a theatre nuclear force, relying on Tu-16 medium bombers and F-9 fighter-bombers for delivery. The strategic missile force lacked operational ICBM's in any quantity and had only 30–40 CSS-2 IRBM's (1,500–1,750-mi range, high kiloton/megaton warhead) and 40 CSS-1 MRBM's (700-mi range).

In Indochina, hostility between Vietnam and Cambodia erupted into sporadic fighting. Because the North Vietnamese had always relied on the Soviet Union for political and military support, they were regarded as hostile by China, and this carried over to the new state created by the North Vietnamese conquest of the South. China also feared a Vietnamese annexation of Cambodia, although that country's brutal regime made it an embarrassing ally. Cambodia's armed forces totaled 70,000 men, with no heavy equipment or aircraft. In contrast, Vietnam's Army of 600,000 (40,000 in Laos) had 900 medium tanks, with supporting artillery, and the 12,000-man Air Force included 120 MiG-17 and 30 Su-7 fighter-bombers, plus 70 MiG-19/F6 and 70 MiG-21F/PF interceptors. Vietnam had also captured large quantities of South Vietnamese equipment.

North and South Korea maintained modern armed forces of 512,000 and 642,000, respectively, costing the North 10.5% of GNP ($1,030,000,000) as against the South's 6.5% ($2.6 billion). Taiwan also maintained large forces, adequate to deter a Chinese attack that was politically unlikely. Its armed forces totaled 474,000 and cost 8.3% of GNP (about $1,670,000,000). Japan continued to spend the least of all developed countries on defense, amounting to only 0.9% of GNP ($8,570,000,000). Japanese forces, totaling 240,000, included a 155,-000-man army with 1 mechanized and 12 infantry divisions. Speculation continued that South Korea and Taiwan had made significant steps toward manufacturing nuclear weapons. Japan's nuclear energy and fuel supply programs were moving it closer toward the ability to exercise a nuclear option, though it still lacked the political will to do so.   (ROBIN RANGER)

See also Space Exploration.
[535.B.5.c.ii; 544.B.5–6; 736]

Members of Japan's first parachute unit formed since World War II check their gear before a jump. The troop is composed of 1,400 men whose average age is 21.

DÉTENTE, ENTENTE, OR COLD WAR?

by Robin Ranger

In 1978 the U.S. and its allies were debating the most important foreign policy question since the Vietnam war: Had a new cold war started between the U.S.S.R. and the West? The term "new cold war" suggested that, as in 1947, the U.S. and its allies faced a Soviet Communist drive for political expansion on a global scale, using both political and military means, but in this cold war—unlike the first one—the Soviets enjoyed the advantage.

Now as then, it was said, the West could only halt this expansion, and so preserve the politico-military balance, by containing and matching Soviet pressures. It was to be hoped that this could be achieved by means short of total war, conventional or nuclear. However, the Soviet strategic buildup and recent technological changes meant that the strategic nuclear balance no longer tilted toward the West. Given that the Soviets now had strategic superiority, the U.S. must strive to change the balance in its favour.

A Change of Mood. These hard-line, hawkish views, once largely confined to the right wing of the Republican Party, enjoyed increasingly wide support in the U.S. as the Nixon-Kissinger policy of superpower détente appeared to be failing. By the 1976 presidential election, Richard Nixon's successor, Gerald Ford, had banned the word "détente" from his campaign vocabulary as a political liability. The Democratic victor, Jimmy Carter, had difficulty sustaining those aspects of détente that he supported, notably the drive to control the strategic arms race, while taking actions the Soviets regarded as contrary to détente, such as his human rights campaign. By 1978 Carter's assistant for national security affairs, Zbigniew Brzezinski, was arguing that the new cold war was on. This view was supported by influential Democratic senators like Henry Jackson of Washington and Sam Nunn of Georgia, as well as by a substantial number of Democratic congressmen and large sections of the American public.

Robin Ranger is an associate professor in the Department of Political Science, St. Francis Xavier University, Antigonish, Nova Scotia, and a Department of National Defence Fellow in Strategic Studies.

This was in sharp contrast to the public mood in 1972, when Nixon and Leonid Brezhnev held their Moscow summit. Advocates of détente in 1978 were a defensive minority, although they included such notable names as former secretary of state Henry A. Kissinger. They maintained that détente, a relaxation of East-West tensions and a move away from confrontation toward cooperation, was dictated by the overriding need of both sides to avoid nuclear war and control the strategic arms race via the strategic arms limitation talks (SALT). Both sides could still gain more from cooperation, however limited, than from the confrontation of a cold war, old or new, although some areas of competition would remain. President Carter seemed to agree with these principles, the most eloquent and persuasive advocate of his version of détente being the president's special adviser on Soviet affairs, Marshall Shulman. Secretary of State Cyrus Vance clearly shared these views, as did Paul Warnke, Carter's chief SALT negotiator until his resignation in October 1978, and, with some reservations, Secretary of Defense Harold Brown.

The Carter administration defended détente by stressing that Nixon and Kissinger had oversold the concept, to the point where they seemed to be talking about entente—a situation of positive cooperation based on complementary, not competitive, interests. This raised expectations that could never be fulfilled and endangered the progress that had been, and could be, made. When—as was inevitable —the Soviets' behaviour fell short of that envisioned for entente, the implication was that both entente and détente had failed, presumably leaving a new cold war as the only alternative. This argument also pinpointed one of the major problems in this new debate on U.S. policy toward the U.S.S.R.: all of the key terms—cold war, détente, new cold war—were extremely vague and so could be used or misused as the protagonists saw fit.

The First Cold War. Détente originally meant a relaxation of the tensions of the cold war. The first cold war is now history, but its main features need recapitulation if the concept of the new cold war is to be understood. The first cold war lasted from Pres. Harry S. Truman's enunciation of the Truman Doctrine in 1947 to the Cuban missile crisis of 1962. By 1947 Truman and his advisers realized that, with Europe devastated by World War II, the Soviet Union had become the dominant power in the continent. Under Stalin's brutal dictatorship, the U.S.S.R. was consolidating its control over the Eastern European states occupied during the war and was threatening a Western Europe that had neither the political will nor the military capability to resist. The Truman Doctrine accordingly stated that the

U.S. would support any free society resisting Soviet expansion. It formed the basis for the North Atlantic Treaty Organization (NATO), established in 1949.

The basic pattern of the cold war in Europe was thus clear. The continent was to be divided into two parts: a Soviet sphere of direct political and military control and a U.S. sphere of influence that would resist the establishment of further Communist governments controlled from Moscow. Each superpower viewed its competition as total, a zero-sum game in which a U.S. gain meant a Soviet loss and vice versa. Historically such rivalry between major powers had always led to war. But, even in 1947, neither Washington nor Moscow could risk full-scale war, because of its unpredictability and the unprecedented losses both sides would suffer.

Although neither superpower had more than a handful of nuclear weapons in 1947, they already provided a strong incentive to avoid direct conflict, and this was reinforced by subsequent technological advances. However, this did not exclude (indeed it facilitated) the use of all other forms of Soviet power to achieve political objectives, necessitating contravening Western action. Hence the introduction of the term cold war to cover a state of conflict by all means short of total war. The Soviet-instigated North Korean invasion of South Korea in 1950 globalized the cold war, and the victory of Mao Tsetung's Communist Party in the Chinese civil war was seen, wrongly, as creating a worldwide Communist monolith controlled from Moscow. The military

containment of Communism thus seemed to be a prerequisite for political and economic reconstruction in Western Europe and elsewhere. Eventually, however, this policy produced an unselective overreaction, especially in military terms, to local political changes in the third world that did not adversely affect fundamental Western interests.

Even after Stalin's death in 1953, the Soviets were seen as an expansionist power, waging the cold war with increased strength and vigour. So while they sought specific accommodations with the U.S.S.R. —often successfully—the Eisenhower (1953–61) and Kennedy (1961–63) administrations continued to base U.S. policy on the cold war principle of politico-military containment. The underlying assumptions were widely shared by the American public and politicians, forming the basis for a bipartisan foreign policy. It was difficult, in the cold war period, to be too anti-Communist, as, by 1972, it was difficult to be too pro-détente, both oversimplifications being equally dangerous.

Through Crisis to Détente. The 1962 Cuban missile crisis arose out of Soviet Premier Nikita Khrushchev's attempt to remedy Soviet strategic inferiority by placing intermediate- and medium-range ballistic missiles in Cuba. Pres. John F. Kennedy forced the Soviets to withdraw by deploying overwhelming conventional forces locally and nuclear forces strategically. But the brush with nuclear war made both sides realize the need to rethink their relationship. The result was President Kennedy's

The SALT negotiations continued. Secretary of State Cyrus Vance (centre, left side of table) led the U.S. delegation, and the Soviets were led by Foreign Minister Andrey A. Gromyko (centre-right).

V. KOSHEVOY—TASS/SOVFOTO

The Soviet Backfire bomber, seen for the first time in the West, was photographed from a Swedish plane in a flight over the Baltic. The plane was part of a controversy holding up agreement between the U.S. and the U.S.S.R. on arms limitations.

June 1963 American University speech, setting out the principles of détente in its proper sense—a relaxation of tensions and the avoidance of unnecessary confrontations. Despite their major differences, Kennedy indicated, the U.S. and Soviet governments must distinguish between their major interests—those they would be prepared to defend by force—and lesser interests, where their differences could be settled by negotiation. Above all, both sides must avoid risking nuclear war. Détente, in its initial form, thus meant the replacement of an undiscriminating cold war policy of military containment by more selective policies. Détente did not mean the end of all containment everywhere and its replacement with global cooperation. It did mean that Americans would have to accept the idea that not all East-West issues were part of a zero-sum game. In many cases, both sides could gain more from cooperation than from confrontation and competition.

President Kennedy died before he could follow through on his initiation of détente. His successor, Lyndon Johnson, followed a cold war policy toward China, necessitating an increasing U.S. military commitment to the defense of South Vietnam that, in the end, destroyed the domestic consensus on foreign policy that had lasted since 1947. President Johnson proved unable to formulate a coherent policy toward Moscow, although he continued a policy of limited détente.

When Richard M. Nixon became president in 1969, he and his chief foreign policy adviser, Henry A. Kissinger, both realized that the Vietnam war had made a broadening of the U.S.-Soviet détente and the initiation of détente between the U.S. and China both electorally popular and politically necessary if the internal U.S. divisions were to be healed. In addition, Kissinger argued that both superpowers shared a common interest in restraining the strategic arms race. Logically, if each side recognized the other's strategic independence and accepted the division of Europe, both could benefit from much wider cooperation, moving, in effect, from détente to entente, although Kissinger never used the term. The Eastern bloc needed Western technology and foodstuffs; the West needed their markets. Eventually, as contacts increased, the East would find itself tied down by a cumulative network of advantages, just as Gulliver was tied down by the Lilliputians. By the 1972 Moscow summit, Kissinger was describing détente as an irreversible entente.

Cracks in Détente. Instead, the superpower relationship deteriorated to a point where it was argued that, at worst, a new cold war had emerged or, at best, the crucial elements of détente could be preserved only with difficulty. What did the Soviets do between 1972 and 1978 to cause this? Equally important, how were their actions perceived by the U.S.? Perception has always been a major problem in interpreting Soviet actions. Since the Soviet Union remains a tightly closed society, Western analysts almost never know what Soviet policies really are or how they are evolved. Hence, there is a natural tendency to select and interpret Soviet actions according to one's prejudices. However, certain Soviet actions are usually cited in the new cold war-détente debate.

In 1973, the Soviets aided and approved the Arab attack on Israel in the so-called Yom Kippur War. From 1974 onward it became clear that the Soviets were circumventing the 1972 SALT I agreements both in letter and in spirit. These agreements comprised two parts, the legally binding treaties and the crucial U.S. interpretations of their provisions,

U.S.–Soviet Strategic Balance, July 1978

Weapons systems	Range (mi)	Payload[1] (000 lb)	Missile warhead yield[2]	CEP[3]	Bomber speed (Mach)	Number deployed
UNITED STATES						
Intercontinental ballistic missiles (ICBM)						
Titan II	6,300	8	9 mt	0.5	—	54
Minuteman II	6,000+	1−	1–2 mt	0.4	—	450
Minuteman III	7,000+	2	3 x 170 kt[4]	0.15	—	550
Total deployed						1,054
Submarine-launched ballistic missiles (SLBM)						
Polaris A-3	2,880	1	3 x 200 kt[5]	0.5	—	160
Poseidon C-3	2,880	2–3	10 x 50 kt[4]	0.3	—	496
Total deployed (in 41 nuclear submarines)						656
Manned bombers						
B-52 D	10,000	60	—	—	0.95	125
B-52 G/H	12,500	70	—	—	0.95	241
F-111A	6,000	37.5	—	—	2.5	66
F-111A/E	2,900	28	—	—	2.5	282
Total deployed						714
SOVIET UNION						
Intercontinental ballistic missiles (ICBM)						
SS-9 Scarp	7,500	12–15	18–25 mt or 3 x 5 mt[5]	0.5	—	190
SS-11 Sego	6,500	1.5–2	1–2 mt or 3 x 100–300 kt[5]	0.3–0.5	—	780
SS-13 Savage	5,000	1	1 mt	0.7	—	60
SS-16	5,000	2	3 x 150 kt[4]	0.3	—	...
SS-17	6,300	6	5 mt or 4 x 900 kt[4]	0.3	—	60
SS-18	6,300	16–20	18–25 mt or 8 x 2 mt[4]	0.2–0.34	—	110
SS-19	6,300–7,000	7	5 mt or 6 x 1–2 mt[4]	0.2–0.34	—	200
Total deployed						1,400+
Submarine-launched ballistic missiles (SLBM)						
SS-N-5 Serb	750	1.5	1–2 mt	1–2	—	21
SS-N-6 Sawfly	1,750–2,000	1.5	1–2 mt or 3 x 2–3 kt[4]	1	—	528
SS-N-8	4,850	2–3	1–2 mt	0.5	—	394
SS-NX-17	3,000+	3+	1 mt	0.2–0.3	—	12
SS-N-18	5,000+	5+	3 x 1–2 mt[4]	...	—	...+
Total deployed (in 70 nuclear submarines)						955+
Manned bombers						
Tu-95 Bear	8,000	40	—	—	0.78	100
Mya-4 Bison	7,000	20	—	—	0.87	35
Tu-16 Badger	4,000	20	—	—	0.8	585
Tu-? Backfire B	5,500	17.5	—	—	2.5	80+
Total deployed						800+

[1] As used here, "payload" refers to a missile's throw weight or a bomber's weapons load.
[2] Yield is given in kilotons (kt) or megatons (mt).
[3] Circular Error Probable: the radius (in nautical miles) of a circle within which at least half of the missile warheads aimed at a specific target will fall.
[4] Multiple independently targeted reentry vehicle (MIRV); the figure to the left of the multiplication sign gives the number of warheads and the figure to the right is the yield per warhead.
[5] Multiple reentry vehicle (MRV); the figure to the left of the multiplication sign gives the number of warheads and the figure to the right is the yield per warhead.
Sources: International Institute for Strategic Studies, *The Military Balance 1978–1979* and Adelphi Papers No. 140 *The Future of the Land-based Forces* by Colin Gray.

which were not legally binding. The Soviet defense that they had not violated the SALT I treaties was technically correct but misleading, since the treaties and the interpretations had been sold to the U.S. Senate and the public as an integral package. Moreover, the Soviets had not restrained either their qualitative strategic force improvements (*see* TABLE) or quantitative and qualitative increases in their conventional forces. SALT II, to remedy the defects of SALT I and stabilize an increasingly unstable strategic balance, was promised for 1975–76; it was still awaited in 1978, and by then there seemed little hope that it could contribute to strategic stability.

Between 1975 and 1978 the Soviets engaged, for the first time, in military intervention in Africa. In 1975 Cuban troops with Soviet supplies were used to secure victory for the pro-Soviet guerrilla forces in the former Portuguese colonies of Angola and Mozambique and then to suppress opposition guer-

rillas. Cuban advisers were sent to any African government that could be persuaded to ask for them, and when the pro-Soviet Ethiopian government faced defeat in its war with Somalia in 1977, the Soviets added, to large Cuban forces, key combat and support personnel from the U.S.S.R. and other members of the Warsaw Pact, commanded by a Soviet major general. Meanwhile, President Carter's attempts to secure improved treatment of Soviet dissidents backfired when the Soviet leadership, viewing this as intolerable interference in their domestic affairs, reacted by even more ruthless suppression. Similarly, Carter's efforts to secure a SALT II that would reduce the strategic forces on both sides was attacked by the Soviets as a departure from the guidelines for SALT II accepted by President Ford.

The West's Reaction. How far the Soviets were reverting to cold war policies—if, indeed, they had ever completely abandoned them—was debatable. But most critics of détente agreed that the Soviets were acting as if the cold war was still on, albeit in a more sophisticated form. If so, they argued, the U.S. and its allies had no alternative but to return to a policy of selective containment. The West should not repeat its earlier mistakes by supporting all governments that claimed to be anti-Communist and trying to topple all governments that were anti-Western or pro-Communist. But the West could not avoid supporting, with force if necessary, governments whose survival was in the West's vital interest. The U.S. should not automatically resort to force in a crisis, but neither should it shrink from using force when necessary.

But were these assessments too pessimistic? American opinion, among the general public as well as among politicians, policy-makers, and analysts, seemed to be tending toward the view that a new cold war was on and that the Soviet Union was responsible for starting it. Superpower entente had ceased to be a possibility and détente had largely evaporated, except perhaps in the original, 1963, sense. The administration's official position was that SALT II was essential for the survival of mankind and that détente, in some form, had to be preserved. Brzezinski took the view that if a new cold war was on the U.S. and its allies must respond accordingly. The president vacillated between the two positions.

The Brzezinski view clearly enjoyed widespread support. Indeed, among conservatives the argument was not so much about whether there was a new cold war as about how rapidly it might get hot, involving perhaps another Korean War-level conflict, and how strongly the U.S. should react to Soviet moves. Unquestionably, détente, or entente, would be a preferable state. But in 1978 new cold war seemed to be the more accurate term.

Demography

The world's population increased to an estimated 4,100,000,000 by mid-1977, reflecting an annual growth rate of about 2%. The various regions differed significantly, however; while the growth rate for northern America, Europe, and the Soviet Union was less than 1%, that for Latin America and Africa exceeded 2.5%. Thus, at its current growth rate of 3.4%, Mexico's 1978 population of about 67 million would double by the year 2000. In contrast, Sweden, at 0.1%, would require 700 years to double. In the U.S. doubling would take 116 years at the current rate of 0.6%.

There was some evidence to suggest that the rate of world population growth was declining, but even if this was so, it would not immediately affect the annual increase in the number of persons in the world (over 70 million in 1977). The birthrate fell in some less developed countries, although this was often counterbalanced by a concurrent decline in the death rate. In some more developed countries the rate of natural increase was negative (death rates exceeded birthrates in Austria, West Germany, East Germany, and Luxembourg), while in others growth was borderline (Denmark, France, Italy, Norway, Sweden, and Switzerland). As of July 1, 1978, the total population of the U.S., including members of the armed services overseas, was 218,502,000.

Birth Statistics. There were an estimated 3,313,000 live births in the U.S. in 1977, about 5% more than in 1976. The birthrate rose to 15.3 births per 1,000 population, approximately 4% over 1976

and the first increase since 1972. The fertility rate (live births per 1,000 women 15–44 years of age) also increased, by more than 2%, from 65.8 in 1976 to 67.4 in 1977. Aside from a small rise in 1969–70, this was the first interruption in a declining trend that began in 1957 when the rate was 122.7. The rise in the number of births and the birthrate resulted from an increase in the number of women in the childbearing ages as well as in the rate of childbearing. This trend could continue since, according to census projections, women of childbearing age would increase 6% by 1980.

According to final statistics for 1976, the birthrate for all racial groups remained substantially the same as in 1975. The rate for whites remained at 13.8, while the "all other" group declined from 21.2 to 21.1 and the black population from 20.9 to 20.8. A significant change occurred in the fertility rate. The white fertility rate dropped 1.3% to 62.2 live births per 1,000 women aged 15–44, the non-white rate fell 1.9% to 87.6, and the black rate fell 2.2% to 87.2. From 1970 to 1976 the fertility rates dropped 26% for whites and 22% for all others.

In terms of mothers' age, birthrates declined for women in all age groups except those 30–34. Decreases were greatest among teenagers and women 40 years and older. Birthrates decreased for all birth orders except the third, and the National Center for Health Statistics attributed the increase in third-order births to previously postponed births rather than a rise in the rate of childbearing. Since the peak year of 1957 the birthrates for mothers aged 35–39 had decreased by 69%. Fifth- and higher-order births had declined 83% since 1961.

An estimated 468,100 illegitimate live births occurred in 1976, 5% more than in 1975; the increase was 6% for whites and 4% for blacks. Nevertheless, this represented a slowing in the rate of increase from previous years. The largest rate increases were found among women in their 20s. Women 15 and younger had fewer illegitimate births. The illegitimacy rate (illegitimate births per 1,000 unmarried women) declined about 0.4% (24.8 to 24.7), reflecting a 3% decline among black women (85.6 to 83.2); the rate for white women increased slightly (12.6 to 12.7). The illegitimacy ratio (illegitimate births per 1,000 total live births) rose almost 4%, from 142.5 to 147.8. In 1976 about 8% of all white births and 50% of black births were to unmarried women.

Natural increase (excess of births over deaths) added an estimated 1,415,000 persons to the U.S. population in 1977, 11% more than in 1976. The rate of natural increase rose 9% to 6.5 per 1,000 population. UN estimates for the period 1965–76 indicated that the world rate was 19; regional rates were Africa 26, North America 10, Latin America 28, Asia 22, Europe 6, Oceania 19, and the U.S.S.R. 10.

Death Statistics. There were 1,898,000 deaths in the U.S. in 1977, according to provisional statistics, and the death rate was 8.8 per 1,000 population, about 1% less than in 1976. Data for the first half of 1978 showed an increase in the number of deaths over the first half of 1977, and for the 12-month period ended June 1978, the death rate was

Table I. Birthrates and Death Rates per 1,000 Population and Infant Mortality per 1,000 Live Births in Selected Countries, 1977 [1]

Country	Birth-rate	Death rate	Infant mortality	Country	Birth-rate	Death rate	Infant mortality
Africa				Norway [2]	13.3	10.0	10.5
Egypt	37.7	11.8	101.3	Poland [2]	19.5	8.8	24.0
Mauritius [2]	26.1	7.8	40.2	Portugal [5]	19.0	10.4	38.9
Nigeria	49.2	20.7	...	Romania [2]	19.5	9.6	31.4
South Africa [3]	43.1	13.9	...	Spain [2]	18.3	8.0	16.4
Tunisia [2]	36.4	6.4	52.1 [4]	Sweden	11.6	10.7	8.0
Asia				Switzerland	11.5	8.7	10.7 [2]
Cyprus [2]	19.6	9.8	26.9	United Kingdom [2]	12.1	12.2	15.7
Hong Kong	17.7	5.3	13.9	Yugoslavia	17.6	8.4	35.2
Israel	26.1	6.9	22.9 [2]	North America			
Japan	15.5	6.1	9.3 [2]	Antigua	19.7	6.8	24.5
Kuwait [2]	43.3	4.8	34.3	Bahamas, The [2]	25.1	4.6	24.8
Philippines [5]	26.7	6.3	58.9 [4]	Barbados [2]	18.6	9.2	28.3
Singapore	16.8	5.2	12.2	Canada [2]	15.8	7.2	14.3 [5]
Syria [5]	47.8	14.8	112.5	Costa Rica [2]	29.3	4.6	33.6
Taiwan	23.8	4.7	12.9 [2]	Cuba [5]	20.7	5.4	27.3
Thailand [2]	24.1	5.5	25.5	El Salvador [2]	40.2	7.5	55.2
Europe				Guatemala [4]	42.8	11.8	75.4
Austria	11.3	12.2	16.9	Jamaica [2]	30.0	7.1	20.4
Belgium	12.4	11.4	11.7	Mexico [2]	34.6	6.5	54.7
Bulgaria [2]	16.5	10.1	23.5	Panama [2]	32.2	5.2	35.6
Czechoslovakia	18.5	11.5	19.9	Puerto Rico [5]	22.4	6.1	20.9
Denmark [2]	12.9	10.6	10.1	United States	14.9	9.1	14.3
Finland	13.9	9.4	12.0	Oceania			
France	14.0	10.1	11.5	American Samoa [2]	36.5	4.4	18.8
Germany, East [2]	11.6	14.0	14.1	Australia	16.1	7.7	14.3 [5]
Germany, West	9.5	11.4	17.4 [2]	Fiji [2]	28.6	4.4	17.2
Greece [2]	16.0	8.9	22.5	Guam [2]	32.7	5.0	18.0
Hungary	16.7	12.4	26.1	New Zealand [4]	17.3	8.3	13.9 [2]
Iceland	17.8	6.6	10.1	Pacific Islands,			
Ireland [2]	21.6	10.5	14.6	Trust Terr. of [2]	32.4	4.4	20.6
Italy [2]	14.0	9.7	19.1	Western Samoa	35.0	7.0	40.1
Netherlands, The	12.5	7.9	9.5	U.S.S.R. [2]	18.4	9.5	27.7 [4]

[1] Registered births and deaths only.
[2] 1976.
[3] 1975–1980 UN estimate.
[4] 1974.
[5] 1975.
Sources: United Nations, *Population and Vital Statistics Report*; various national publications.

continued on page 300

Table II. World Populations and Areas[1]

	AREA AND POPULATION: MIDYEAR 1977			POPULATION AT MOST RECENT CENSUS					Age distribution (%)[2]					
Country	Area in sq km	Total population	Persons per sq km	Date of census	Total population	% Male	% Female	% Urban	0–14	15–29	30–44	45–59	60–74	75+
AFRICA														
Algeria	2,322,164	17,272,000	7.4	1977	17,272,000	49.7	50.3	52.0	47.5	——40.1——			——12.4——	
Angola	1,246,700	6,927,000	5.6	1970	5,646,166	52.1	47.9	14.2	...	...			...	...
Benin	112,600	3,286,000	29.2	1961	2,082,511	49.0	51.0	9.3	46.0	22.7	16.4	9.3	——5.6——	
Botswana	576,000	710,000	1.2	1971	574,094	45.7	54.3	8.4	46.1	21.7	12.8	9.0	5.0	5.4
British Indian Ocean Territory	60			1971	110									
Burundi	27,834	3,966,000	142.5	1970–71	3,350,000	47.6	52.4	3.5	44.1	25.0	17.0	9.8	3.0	1.0
Cameroon	465,054	7,820,000	16.8	1976	7,663,246	49.0	51.0	28.5	43.4	——48.3——			——8.3——	
Cape Verde	4,033	306,000	75.9	1970	272,071	48.2	51.8	19.7	47.0	20.8	14.2	8.7	6.2	3.0
Central African Empire	624,977	1,870,000	3.0	1959–60	1,177,000	47.8	52.2	6.8	40.0	21.9	25.7	10.4	——2.0——	
Chad	1,284,000	4,197,000	3.3	1975	4,030,000	...	...	...	...	...	...	...	...	...
Comoros[3]	1,792	305,000	170.2	1966	244,905	49.2	50.8	13.5	44.1	23.6	15.7	8.7	4.2	3.8
Congo	342,000	1,440,000	4.2	1974	1,300,120	48.7	51.3	39.8	...	...	...	...	...	...
Djibouti	23,000	231,000	10.0	1960–61	81,200	...	...	57.4	...	...	...	...	...	...
Egypt	1,002,000	37,218,000	37.1	1977	40,000,000	51.0	49.0	...	53.1	——48.5——			——16.4——	
Equatorial Guinea	28,051	322,000	11.5	1965	277,240	52.8	47.2	...	...	...	...	...	...	...
Ethiopia	1,225,400	28,556,000	23.3	1970	24,068,800	50.7	49.3	9.7	43.5	27.0	16.3	8.8	3.7	0.7
French Southern and Antarctic Lands	7,366	—	—	—	—									
Gabon	267,667	1,165,000	4.4	1970	950,009	47.9	52.1	26.9	35.4	19.2	22.2	16.3	6.3	0.6
Gambia, The	10,403	553,000	53.2	1973	493,499	51.0	49.0	15.0	41.3	——44.1——			——14.6——	
Ghana	238,533	10,461,000	43.8	1970	8,559,313	49.6	50.4	28.9	46.9	24.4	15.8	7.5	3.8	1.6
Guinea	245,857	4,642,000	18.9	1972	5,143,284	...	...	...	43.1	——56.9——				
Guinea-Bissau	36,125	932,000	25.8	1970	487,448	48.7	51.3	11.1	44.6	——55.4——			...	...
Ivory Coast	322,463	6,881,000	21.3	1975	6,702,866	52.0	48.0	32.4	...	...	...	...	...	...
Kenya	580,367	14,337,000	24.7	1969	10,942,705	50.1	49.9	9.9	48.4	25.1	13.6	7.5	3.9	1.5
Lesotho	30,355	1,242,000	40.9	1976	1,213,960	...	...	...	...	...	...	...	...	...
Liberia	97,790	1,554,000	15.9	1974	1,503,368	51.0	49.0	...	41.0	——59.0——				
Libya	1,749,000	2,596,000	1.5	1973	2,249,222	53.0	47.0	...	48.8	22.2	15.3	8.2	4.0	1.6
Madagascar	587,041	8,520,000	14.5	1966	6,200,000	49.2	50.8	...	46.5	22.3	15.2	10.1	——5.9——	
Malawi	118,484	5,562,000	46.9	1977	5,561,821	48.0	52.0	...	...	...	...	...	...	...
Mali	1,240,142	6,468,000	5.2	1976	6,035,272	49.0	51.0	...	...	...	...	...	...	...
Mauritania	1,030,700	1,420,000	1.4	1977	1,420,000									
Mauritius	2,040	909,000	445.6	1972	851,334	50.0	50.0	42.9	40.3	28.6	14.5	11.0	4.9	0.7
Mayotte	378	47,000	124.3	1966	32,607									
Morocco	458,730	18,359,000	40.0	1971	15,379,259	50.1	49.9	35.4	46.2	22.4	16.0	8.3	5.3	1.8
Mozambique	799,380	9,899,000	12.4	1970	8,168,933	49.4	50.6	...	45.3	22.5	19.1	9.1	3.8	0.3
Namibia (South West Africa)	824,268	905,000	1.1	1970	763,630	50.8	49.2	24.9	...	...	...	...	...	...
Niger	1,186,408	4,859,000	4.1	1959–60	2,611,473	49.7	50.3	...	...	...	...	...	...	...
Nigeria	923,800	78,660,000	85.1	1973	79,760,000	...	...	...	...	...	...	...	...	...
Réunion	2,512	521,000	207.4	1974	476,675	...	...	...	...	...	...	...	...	...
Rhodesia (Zimbabwe)	390,272	6,740,000	17.3	1969	5,099,350	50.3	49.7	16.8	47.2	25.4	15.7	8.4	——3.3——	
Rwanda	26,338	4,368,000	165.8	1978	4,820,000	49.0	51.0	...	...	...	...	...	...	...
St. Helena	412	6,000	14.6	1976	5,147	...	...	29.4	35.3	24.6	15.8	11.7	9.5	3.0
São Tomé & Príncipe	964	82,000	85.0	1970	73,811	50.8	49.2	...	...	...	...	...	...	...
Senegal	196,722	5,239,000	26.6	1976	5,085,388	49.2	50.8	...	...	...	...	...	...	...
Seychelles	443	62,000	139.8	1977	61,950	50.0	50.0	37.1	39.9	26.3	14.0	10.8	6.8	2.1
Sierra Leone	71,740	3,191,000	44.5	1974	2,729,479	39.6	60.4	...	36.7	27.2	19.4	9.0	——7.6——	
Somalia	638,000	3,350,000	5.2	—	—									
South Africa	1,222,375	26,892,000	22.0	1970	21,794,328	49.2	50.8	47.9	40.8	26.1	16.7	10.0	5.0	1.3
Bophuthatswana[4]	40,430	1,039,000	27.5	1970	880,312	46.9	53.1	14.2	44.7	26.4	12.5	——13.5——		1.3
Transkei[4]	41,002	2,061,000	50.3	1970	1,745,992	41.2	58.8	3.2	46.4	22.8	14.1	——15.3——		1.2
Sudan	2,503,890	16,953,000	6.8	1973	14,819,000[5]	...	...	...	...	...	...	...	...	...
Swaziland	17,364	509,000	29.3	1976	499,046	...	...	...	...	...	...	...	...	...
Tanzania	945,087	16,073,000	17.0	1967	12,313,469	48.8	51.2	5.5	43.9	24.7	15.4	8.6	4.1	3.3
Togo	56,785	2,348,000	41.3	1970	1,953,778	48.1	51.9	...	49.8	21.5	15.1	8.0	3.6	2.0
Tunisia	164,150	6,065,000	36.9	1975	5,588,209	50.8	49.2	49.0	43.7	25.6	14.7	10.0	4.9	0.9
Uganda	241,139	12,353,000	51.2	1969	9,548,847	50.5	49.5	7.7	46.2	24.0	15.7	8.3	4.2	1.6
Upper Volta	274,200	6,317,000	23.0	1975	6,144,013	...	...	...	45.3	——43.4——			——11.3——	
Western Sahara	266,769	139,000	.5	1970	76,425	57.5	42.5	45.3	42.9	27.2	16.3	7.4	4.4	1.8
Zaire	2,344,885	26,376,000	11.2	1974	24,327,143	...	...	...	...	...	...	...	...	...
Zambia	752,614	5,302,000	7.0	1969	4,056,995	49.0	51.0	26.9	46.3	24.0	16.6	9.4	3.0	0.7
Total AFRICA	30,232,055	440,383,000	14.6											
ANTARCTICA total	14,244,900	[6]	—		—				—	—			—	
ASIA														
Afghanistan	653,000	20,330,000	31.1											
Bahrain	662	267,000	403.3	1971	216,078	53.8	46.2	78.1	44.3	25.3	16.9	9.0	3.7	0.8
Bangladesh	143,998	80,558,000	559.4	1974	71,479,071	51.9	48.1	8.8	48.1	22.0	15.6	8.7	4.6	1.1
Bhutan	46,100	1,232,000	26.7	1969	1,034,774	...	...	...	...	...	...	...	...	...
Brunei	5,765	190,000	33.0	1971	136,256	53.4	46.4	63.6	43.4	28.0	15.7	8.1	3.9	0.9
Burma	676,577	31,512,000	46.6	1973	28,885,867	49.7	50.3	...	40.5	——53.4——			——6.0——	
Cambodia	181,035	8,580,000	47.4	1962	5,728,771	50.0	50.0	10.3	43.8	24.9	16.8	9.8	4.1	0.6
China	9,561,000	866,376,000	90.6	1953	574,205,940	51.8	48.2	13.3	35.9	25.1	18.8	12.9	6.3	1.0
Cyprus	9,251	613,000	66.3	1976	612,851	...	...	...	...	...	...	...	...	...
Hong Kong	1,050	4,514,000	4,299.0	1976	4,420,390	51.0	49.0	...	30.0	30.2	15.4	14.9	7.3	1.7
India	3,287,782	625,810,000	190.3	1971	547,949,809	51.8	48.2	19.9	41.9	24.1	17.8	10.2	4.9	1.1
Indonesia	1,919,494	138,134,000	72.0	1971	118,367,850	49.3	50.7	17.5	44.0	23.9	18.6	9.1	3.8	0.7
Iran	1,648,000	34,274,000	20.8	1976	33,591,875	51.0	49.0	46.8	46.2	——49.6——			——4.2——	
Iraq	437,522	12,171,000	27.8	1977	12,171,480	51.0	49.0	63.5	...	...	...	...	...	...
Israel	20,700	3,591,000	173.5	1972	3,147,683	50.3	49.7	85.3	32.6	26.9	15.6	13.6	9.2	2.0
Japan	377,619	113,860,000	301.5	1975	111,939,643	49.2	50.8	75.9	24.3	24.9	23.1	15.9	9.2	2.5
Jordan	95,396	2,874,000	30.1	1961	1,706,226	50.9	49.1	43.9	45.4	26.1	13.7	7.5	5.1	1.8
Korea, North	121,200	16,665,000	137.5	—	—									
Korea, South	98,859	36,436,000	368.6	1975	34,678,972	50.0	50.0	48.4	38.0	28.2	17.9	10.2	4.6	1.0

Table II. World Populations and Areas[1] *(Continued)*

Country	AREA AND POPULATION: MIDYEAR 1977 Area in sq km	Total population	Persons per sq km	POPULATION AT MOST RECENT CENSUS Date of census	Total population	% Male	% Female	% Urban	Age distribution (%)[2] 0–14	15–29	30–44	45–59	60–74	75+
Kuwait	16,918	1,129,000	66.7	1975	994,837	54.7	45.3	85.9	31.3	60.0	43.0	16.8	—0.9—	
Laos	236,800	3,462,000	14.6	—	—	—	—	—	—	—	—	—	—	—
Lebanon	10,230	3,053,000	298.4	1970	2,126,325	50.8	49.2	60.1	42.6	23.8	16.7	9.1	—7.7—	
Macau	16	267,000	16,687.5	1970	248,118	51.4	48.6	100.0	37.6	28.9	15.0	11.3	5.9	1.1
Malaysia	329,747	12,600,000	38.2	1970	10,434,034[7]	50.4	49.6	26.1	44.9	25.5	15.2	9.2	—5.2—	
Maldives	298	141,000	473.2	1978	143,046	52.6	47.4	20.7	...	...	...	...	...	...
Mongolia	1,565,000	1,532,000	1.0	1969	1,197,600	49.9	50.1	44.0	...	...	...	...	...	...
Nepal	145,391	13,619,000	93.7	1971	11,555,983	49.7	50.3	13.8	40.5	25.5	18.7	9.7	—5.6—	
Oman	300,000	817,000	2.7	—	—	—	—	—	—	—	—	—	—	—
Pakistan	796,095	75,250,000	94.5	1972	64,892,000	53.0	47.0	25.5	44.0	—56.0—				
Philippines	300,000	45,028,000	150.1	1975	41,831,045	50.0	50.0	...	43.5	28.4	14.9	8.6	3.7	0.8
Qatar	11,400	192,000	16.8	—	—	—	—	—	—	—	—	—	—	—
Saudi Arabia	2,240,000	9,520,000	4.2	1974	7,012,642	...	...	...	...	...	...	...	...	...
Singapore	602	2,308,000	3,833.9	1970	2,074,507	51.2	48.8	100.0	38.8	28.1	16.9	10.5	4.9	0.8
Sri Lanka	65,610	13,940,000	212.5	1971	12,689,897	51.3	48.7	22.4	39.3	27.8	15.9	10.5	5.2	1.3
Syria	185,180	7,845,000	42.4	1970	6,304,685	51.3	48.7	43.5	49.3	22.4	14.3	7.5	4.8	1.7
Taiwan	35,982	16,678,000	463.5	1975	16,206,183	51.8	48.2	...	36.7	29.8	16.4	11.7	4.6	0.8
Thailand	542,373	44,035,000	81.2	1977	44,035,100	50.0	50.0	...	...	...	...	...	...	...
Turkey	779,452	42,134,000	54.0	1975	40,347,719	50.1	49.9	41.8	39.8	26.8	16.1	9.4	5.8	1.3
United Arab Emirates	83,600	698,000	8.3	1975	655,973	...	...	...	...	...	...	...	...	...
Vietnam	338,392	51,152,000	151.2	—	—	—	—	—	—	—	—	—	—	—
Yemen (Aden)	287,680	1,797,000	6.2	1973	1,590,275	49.5	50.5	33.3	47.3	20.8	15.8	8.6	—6.6—	
Yemen (San'a')	200,000	7,075,000	35.4	1975	5,237,893	47.6	52.4	8.2	46.7	—53.3—				
Total ASIA[8,9]	44,586,814	2,419,950,000	54.3											
EUROPE														
Albania	28,748	2,618,000	91.1	1960	1,626,315	51.4	48.6	30.9	42.7	—57.3—				
Andorra	464	31,000	66.8	1975	26,558	...	...	...	...	...	...	...	...	...
Austria	83,853	7,518,000	89.7	1971	7,456,403	47.0	53.0	51.9	24.4	20.5	18.3	16.5	15.5	4.8
Belgium	30,521	9,823,000	321.8	1970	9,650,944	48.9	51.1	...	23.5	21.0	19.4	17.1	14.4	4.6
Bulgaria	110,912	8,786,000	79.2	1975	8,727,771	49.9	50.1	58.0	...	...	...	...	...	...
Channel Islands	194	130,000	670.1	1971	126,363	48.5	51.5	...	21.8	21.4	18.4	18.1	14.9	5.3
Czechoslovakia	127,877	15,031,000	117.5	1970	14,344,987	48.7	51.3	55.5	23.1	24.8	18.4	16.7	13.6	3.4
Denmark	43,075	5,089,000	118.1	1976	5,072,516	...	...	...	...	...	...	...	...	...
Faeroe Islands	1,399	42,000	29.9	1970	38,612	52.2	47.8	...	31.8	23.0	16.5	16.0	9.4	3.3
Finland	337,032	4,742,000	14.1	1975	4,717,724	...	...	...	...	...	...	...	...	...
France	544,000	53,086,000	97.6	1975	52,655,802	48.9	51.1	70.0	22.6	24.4	17.8	16.2	13.3	5.6
Germany, East	108,328	16,765,000	154.8	1971	17,068,318	46.1	53.9	73.8	23.3	19.9	20.1	14.7	16.9	5.1
Germany, West	248,629	61,396,000	246.9	1970	60,650,599	47.6	52.4	...	23.2	21.3	19.7	16.6	15.0	4.2
Gibraltar	6	30,000	5033.3	1970	26,833	48.1	51.9	91.9	22.9	22.7	21.1	18.7	11.2	3.4
Greece	131,990	9,284,000	70.3	1971	8,768,641	49.8	50.2	53.2	24.9	20.4	21.9	16.5	12.5	3.8
Hungary	93,032	10,644,000	114.4	1970	10,322,099	48.5	51.5	45.2	21.1	23.6	20.5	17.7	13.6	3.5
Iceland	103,000	221,000	2.1	1970	204,930	50.6	49.4	...	32.3	25.1	16.4	13.7	9.0	3.5
Ireland	70,283	3,199,000	45.5	1971	2,978,248	50.2	49.8	52.2	31.3	22.0	15.2	15.9	11.6	4.0
Isle of Man	572	63,000	110.1	1976	61,723	47.5	52.5	...	20.5	19.1	15.6	17.3	20.2	7.3
Italy	301,262	56,390,000	187.2	1971	54,136,547	48.9	51.1	...	24.4	21.2	20.7	17.0	12.8	3.9
Jan Mayen	373	—	—	1973	37	...	...	—	...	...	...	...	...	...
Liechtenstein	160	24,000	152.5	1970	21,350	49.7	50.3	...	27.9	27.1	18.6	14.5	9.3	2.6
Luxembourg	2,586	357,000	138.0	1970	339,841	49.0	51.0	68.4	22.1	20.5	21.4	17.5	14.6	3.9
Malta	316	326,000	1,031.6	1967	314,216	47.9	52.1	94.3	29.8	25.9	17.6	13.8	10.2	2.7
Monaco	1.90	25,000	13,157.9	1968	23,035	45.2	54.8	100.0	12.9	17.5	18.4	20.9	21.2	9.1
Netherlands, The	41,160	13,871,000	337.0	1971	13,060,115	49.9	50.1	54.9	27.2	24.6	17.9	15.6	10.9	3.7
Norway	323,886	4,042,000	12.5	1970	3,874,133	49.7	50.3	42.4	24.4	22.5	16.0	18.8	13.5	4.8
Poland	312,677	34,786,000	111.3	1974	33,635,900	48.5	51.5	54.1	24.3	27.5	19.0	15.3	11.1	2.7
Portugal	91,632	9,737,000	106.3	1970	8,663,252	47.4	52.6	...	28.4	21.9	19.0	16.2	11.2	3.3
Romania	237,500	21,678,000	91.3	1977	21,559,416	49.3	50.7	47.5	...	...	...	...	...	...
San Marino	61	21,000	344.3	1947	12,100	49.3	50.7	...	28.4	—71.6—				
Spain	504,750	36,351,000	72.0	1970	33,956,376	48.9	51.1	54.7	27.8	22.0	19.9	16.1	10.8	3.4
Svalbard	62,050	—	—	1974	3,472	...	...	...	...	...	...	...	...	...
Sweden	449,964	8,264,000	18.4	1975	8,208,544	49.7	50.3	82.7	20.7	21.3	18.8	18.1	15.4	5.7
Switzerland	41,293	6,327,000	153.2	1970	6,269,783	49.3	50.7	52.0	23.4	23.7	20.2	16.3	12.5	3.9
United Kingdom	244,035	55,852,000	228.9	1971	55,515,602	48.5	51.5	...	24.1	21.0	17.6	18.3	14.3	4.7
Vatican City	.44	1,000	2,272.7	—	—	—	—	—	—	—	—	—	—	—
Yugoslavia	255,804	21,718,000	84.9	1971	20,522,972	49.1	50.9	38.6	27.2	24.6	22.7	13.5	9.8	2.2
Total EUROPE[9]	10,504,490	669,509,000	63.7											
NORTH AMERICA														
Anguilla	91	7,000	76.9	1960	5,810	44.5	55.5	...	45.7	18.8	11.8	12.9	7.3	3.5
Antigua	440	72,000	163.6	1970	64,794	47.2	52.8	33.7	44.0	24.2	12.0	11.7	—8.0—	
Bahamas, The	13,864	218,000	15.7	1970	168,812	50.0	50.0	71.4	43.6	24.3	16.8	9.8	4.4	1.1
Barbados	430	258,000	601.2	1970	235,229	48.0	52.0	3.7	35.9	27.2	12.9	12.8	8.7	2.5
Belize	22,965	149,000	6.5	1970	119,934	50.6	49.4	54.4	49.3	22.5	13.0	8.7	5.0	1.5
Bermuda	46	58,000	1,260.9	1970	52,330	50.2	49.8	6.9	30.0	25.8	20.5	14.4	7.7	2.0
British Virgin Islands	153	12,000	78.4	1970	10,298	53.0	47.0	21.9	39.2	29.1	14.7	10.0	5.1	1.9
Canada	9,976,139	23,291,000	2.3	1976	22,992,604	49.8	50.2	75.5	...	...	...	...	...	...
Canal Zone	1,432	38,000	26.5	1970	44,198	53.9	46.1	5.8	31.8	31.3	19.8	14.1	2.2	0.8
Cayman Islands	288	14,000	48.6	1970	10,068	46.8	53.2	61.1	37.1	21.7	16.0	11.1	7.4	2.9
Costa Rica	50,898	2,071,000	40.7	1973	1,871,780	50.1	49.9	40.6	43.3	27.0	14.2	8.4	4.4	2.7
Cuba	110,922	9,618,000	86.7	1970	8,569,121	51.3	48.7	60.3	27.0	25.0	16.9	12.1	6.8	2.2
Dominica	772	80,000	103.6	1970	70,302	47.4	52.6	46.2	49.1	21.2	11.2	10.0	6.3	2.2
Dominican Republic	48,442	4,978,000	102.8	1970	4,006,405	50.4	49.6	40.0	47.2	24.8	15.2	7.8	3.8	1.2
El Salvador	21,041	4,253,000	202.1	1971	3,554,648	49.6	50.4	39.4	46.2	25.1	15.2	8.2	4.3	1.0
Greenland	2,175,600	50,000	.02	1970	46,531	52.5	47.5	...	43.4	24.8	18.8	8.5	3.9	0.6
Grenada	344	108,000	312.5	1970	96,542	46.2	53.8	...	47.1	23.0	11.6	9.4	6.6	2.2
Guadeloupe	1,705	365,000	214.1	1974	324,500	...	...	41.9	41.2	22.8	14.3	10.4	5.3	1.7
Guatemala	108,889	6,436,000	59.1	1973	5,211,929	50.0	50.0	33.6	45.1	26.7	15.1	8.3	—4.8—	
Haiti	27,700	4,749,000	171.4	1971	4,329,991	48.2	51.8	20.4	41.5	25.8	16.5	9.5	5.0	1.7

Table II. World Populations and Areas[1] (Continued)

	AREA AND POPULATION: MIDYEAR 1977			POPULATION AT MOST RECENT CENSUS					Age distribution (%)[2]					
Country	Area in sq km	Total population	Persons per sq km	Date of census	Total population	% Male	% Female	% Urban	0–14	15–29	30–44	45–59	60–74	75+
Honduras	112,088	2,926,000	25.9	1974	2,656,948	49.5	50.5	37.5	48.1	25.8	13.9	7.8	3.6	0.9
Jamaica	10,991	2,087,000	189.9	1970	1,797,401	49.8	50.2	41.4	37.5	25.1	15.2	12.4	7.5	2.3
Martinique	1,079	374,000	346.6	1974	324,832	...	...	...	39.5	25.0	14.2	11.8	7.3	2.2
Mexico	1,972,546	64,594,000	32.7	1970	48,225,238	49.9	50.1	58.7	46.2	25.6	14.6	8.0	4.4	1.2
Montserrat	102	12,000	119.2	1970	11,458	46.9	53.1	31.7	37.9	20.6	9.8	12.1	10.7	8.9
Netherlands Antilles	993	245,000	246.7	1972	223,196	48.8	51.2	...	38.0	26.7	...			
Nicaragua	128,875	2,312,000	17.9	1971	1,877,972	48.3	51.7	48.0	48.1	25.6	14.1	7.4	3.6	1.1
Panama	75,650	1,771,000	23.4	1970	1,428,082	50.7	49.3	47.6	43.4	26.1	15.2	9.6	4.3	1.4
Puerto Rico	8,897	3,261,000	366.5	1970	2,712,033	49.0	51.0	58.1	36.5	26.1	15.9	11.9	7.1	2.5
St. Christopher-Nevis (-Anguilla)[10]	269	50,000	477.9	1970	45,327	46.9	53.1	31.7	48.4	18.9	9.5	12.1	8.7	2.4
St. Lucia	623	115,000	184.6	1970	99,806	47.2	52.8	36.9	49.6	21.3	11.6	9.8	5.5	2.2
St. Pierre & Miquelon	242	6,000	24.8	1974	5,840	49.4	50.6	...	33.8	24.7	18.0	12.9	—10.5—	
St. Vincent	389	95,000	244.2	1970	89,129	47.4	52.6	...	51.2	21.7	11.0	8.8	—7.2—	
Trinidad and Tobago	5,128	1,161,000	226.4	1970	931,071	49.4	50.6	...	42.1	26.2	14.2	10.8	—6.8—	
Turks and Caicos Islands	500	7,000	14.2	1970	5,558	47.4	52.6	—	47.1	20.4	12.0	11.1	7.0	2.5
United States	9,363,123	216,817,000	23.2	1970	203,211,926	48.7	51.3	73.5	28.6	24.0	17.0	16.3	10.4	3.7
Virgin Islands (U.S.)	345	96,000	279.4	1970	62,346	49.9	50.1	24.4	35.7	28.3	19.4	10.8	4.4	1.4
Total NORTH AMERICA	24,244,001	352,646,000	13.4											
OCEANIA														
American Samoa	197	32,000	162.4	1974	29,190	50.5	49.5	...	44.9	25.7	15.5	9.5	3.5	0.9
Australia	7,682,300	14,335,000	1.9	1976	13,915,500	50.0	50.0	86.0	27.2	25.5	18.3	15.7	9.8	3.2
Canton and Enderbury Islands	70	—	—	1970	0	—	—	—	—	—	—	—	—	—
Christmas Island	135	3,000	22.2	1971	2,691	64.4	35.6	0	30.8	34.6	22.0	10.8	1.4	0.4
Cocos Islands	14	1,000	71.4	1971	618	49.0	51.0	0	27.3	38.6	21.8	8.9	3.3	0.2
Cook Islands	241	19,000	78.8	1976	18,128	51.3	48.7	...	...	...	...	...	...	...
Fiji	18,272	600,000	32.8	1976	588,068	50.5	49.5	...	41.1	29.8	16.2	8.8	3.3	0.8
French Polynesia	3,265	137,000	42.0	1971	117,664	53.1	46.9	19.0	45.5	23.7	16.6	9.0	3.7	1.5
Gilbert Islands	272	55,000	202.2	1973	51,926	49.3	50.7	...	44.1	24.8	15.3	9.7	5.1	1.1
Guam	549	97,000	176.7	1970	84,996	55.7	44.3	25.5	39.7	29.1	19.3	8.9	2.5	0.5
Johnston Island	3	1,000	333.3	1970	1,007	...	...	0	...	...	...	...	...	...
Midway Islands	5	2,000	400.0	1970	2,220	...	...	0	...	...	...	...	...	...
Nauru	21	8,000	381.0	1977	7,254	52.1	47.9	0	44.2	33.1	11.4	8.5	—2.8—	
New Caledonia	19,079	136,000	7.1	1976	133,233	52.0	48.0	...	38.6	26.3	18.6	10.4	4.9	1.2
New Hebrides	11,870	99,000	8.3	1967	77,988	52.1	47.9	12.0	45.6	26.0	15.5	8.5	—4.4—	
New Zealand	268,704	3,106,000	11.6	1976	3,129,383	49.9	50.1	...	29.1	26.0	17.3	14.5	10.0	3.1
Niue Island	259	4,000	15.4	1976	3,843	50.2	49.8	24.8	46.2	23.8	13.6	7.9	5.8	2.6
Norfolk Island	35	2,000	57.1	1971	1,683	49.0	51.0	0	25.2	20.7	19.7	18.9	12.5	2.9
Pacific Islands, Trust Territory of the	1,880	124,000	66.0	1973	114,973	51.7	48.3	...	46.2	25.8	12.7	9.1	—5.9—	
Papua New Guinea	462,840	2,874,000	6.2	1973	2,489,935	52.0	48.0	11.1	45.2	24.5	17.4	9.9	1.4	1.6
Pitcairn Island	4	65	16.2	1976	74	...	...	0	...	...	...	...	...	...
Solomon Islands	28,529	207,000	7.3	1976	196,823	52.2	47.8	...	47.8	24.1	14.5	8.4	3.6	1.3
Tokelau	10	2,000	200.0	1974	1,574	46.1	53.9	...	48.2	18.3	14.3	9.4	—9.6—	
Tonga	750	91,000	121.3	1976	90,128	51.1	48.9	...	44.4	26.2	14.8	9.5	4.0	1.1
Tuvalu	26	7,000	269.2	1973	5,887	46.3	53.7	...	40.8	23.3	14.5	13.4	6.4	1.6
Wake Island	8	2,000	250.0	1970	1,647	...	...	0	...	...	...	...	...	...
Wallis and Futuna	255	9,000	35.3	1976	9,192	50.0	50.0	...	46.6	23.6	14.0	9.9	5.1	0.8
Western Samoa	2,849	152,000	53.4	1976	151,515	51.7	48.3	21.1	48.2	26.0	12.6	8.7	3.5	1.0
Total OCEANIA	8,502,442	22,105,000	2.6											
SOUTH AMERICA														
Argentina	2,776,900	26,056,000	9.4	1970	23,390,050	49.7	50.3	80.4	29.3	24.6	19.9	15.4	8.6	2.2
Bolivia	1,098,581	4,788,000	4.4	1976	4,647,816	49.1	50.9	...	41.6	26.8	15.6	9.6	4.7	1.7
Brazil	8,512,000	113,208,000	13.3	1970	93,139,037	49.7	50.3	55.9	42.2	26.7	16.3	9.4	—5.1—	
Chile	756,626	10,656,000	14.1	1970	8,884,768	48.8	51.2	75.1	39.0	25.5	16.6	10.4	5.6	2.9
Colombia	1,138,914	24,894,000	21.9	1973	20,575,657	48.6	51.4	63.6	44.1	27.3	14.9	8.5	4.1	1.0
Ecuador	281,334	7,550,000	26.8	1974	6,521,710	50.1	49.9	41.3	44.6	26.5	14.7	8.4	4.6	1.3
Falkland Islands	16,265	2,000	0.1	1972	1,957	55.2	44.8	44.7	26.7	22.4	—51.9—			
French Guiana	90,000	64,000	0.7	1974	55,125	52.1	47.9	76.5	37.9	27.7	16.7	10.7	5.5	1.5
Guyana	215,000	800,000	3.7	1970	699,848	49.9	50.1	33.3	47.1	25.1	13.4	9.0	4.4	1.0
Paraguay	406,752	2,805,000	6.9	1972	2,357,955	49.6	50.4	37.4	44.9	25.4	14.5	9.2	4.5	1.5
Peru	1,285,216	16,358,000	12.7	1972	13,538,208	50.0	50.0	59.6	43.9	25.8	15.6	8.7	—5.9—	
Suriname	181,455	447,000	2.5	1971	384,903	50.0	50.0	...	48.0	—52.0—				
Uruguay	176,215	2,814,000	16.0	1975	2,763,964	49.1	50.9	...	...	...	...	...	...	...
Venezuela	899,180	12,737,000	14.2	1971	10,721,522	50.0	50.0	75.0	35.1	31.7	17.5	10.0	4.4	1.3
Total SOUTH AMERICA	17,834,438	223,179,000	12.5											
U.S.S.R.[9]	22,402,100	258,932,000	11.6	1970	241,720,134	46.0	54.0	56.3	30.9	19.9	23.5	13.8	—11.8—	
in Asia[9]	16,831,038	67,691,000	4.0											
in Europe[9]	5,571,064	191,241,000	34.3											
TOTAL WORLD[11]	150,149,140	4,127,772,000	27.5											

[1]Any presentation of population data must include data of varying reliability. This table provides published and unpublished data about the latest census (or comparable demographic survey) and the most recent or reliable midyear 1977 population estimates for the countries of the world. Census figures are only a body of estimates and samples of varying reliability whose quality depends on the completeness of the enumeration. Some countries tabulate only persons actually present, while others include those legally resident, but actually outside the country, on census day. Population estimates are subject to continual correction and revision; their reliability depends on: number of years elapsed since a census control was established, completeness of birth and death registration, international migration data, etc.

[2]Data for persons of unknown age excluded, so percentages may not add to 100.0.

[3]Excludes Mayotte, shown separately.

[4]Transkei received its independence from South Africa on Oct 26, 1976; Bophuthatswana received its independence from South Africa on Dec. 6, 1977. Both are Bantu homeland states whose independence is not internationally recognized.

[5]Sudan census excludes three southern autonomous provinces.

[6]May reach a total of 2,000 persons of all nationalities during the summer.

[7]West Malaysia only.

[8]Includes 18,130 sq km of Iraq-Saudi Arabia neutral zone.

[9]Asia and Europe continent totals include corresponding portions of U.S.S.R.

[10]Excludes Anguilla, shown separately.

[11]Area of Antarctica excluded in calculating world density.

continued from page 296

8.9, compared with 8.7 in the corresponding period a year earlier. The age-adjusted death rate dropped in 1976 to 6.3 per 1,000 population, the lowest level ever recorded in the U.S. The sex age-adjusted death rate also declined between 1975 and 1976, about 2.4% for the male population and 2.1% for the female. Despite the larger reduction for males, their age-adjusted death rate (8.3) was almost twice as high as that of females (4.6). The age-adjusted death rate for whites declined 1.6% and for nonwhites, 2.4%. As in previous years, however, the age-adjusted rate for persons other than white was 1.4 times that for the white group.

The ten leading causes of death in 1977, accounting for 83% of all deaths, are shown below. In the absence of a major influenza epidemic, the death rate for influenza and pneumonia fell 19.8%. There were also declines in mortality resulting from heart disease (−2%), cerebrovascular diseases (−4.3%), diabetes (−5.5%), and certain diseases

Cause of death	Estimated rate per 100,000 population
Diseases of the heart	331.6
Malignant neoplasms	179.1
Cerebrovascular diseases	84.5
Accident	48.5
Influenza and pneumonia	23.1
Diabetes mellitus	15.5
Cirrhosis of the liver	14.5
Arteriosclerosis	13.4
Suicide	13.1
Certain diseases of early infancy	10.8

of infancy (−6.9%). Increases were reported for malignant neoplasms (2%), automobile accidents (7%), and suicide (8.7%).

Expectation of Life. The expectation of life at birth was a record high 73.2 years for the U.S. population in 1977, up 0.5% from 72.8 years in 1976. Between 1975 and 1976 life expectancy values rose for both men and women, to 69 for males and 76.7 for females. Since 1950, five years had been added to the average lifetime of the population, with the greatest extension being experienced by nonwhites (7.5 years, compared with 4.4 years for whites). Differentials by race had been decreasing slowly, however; the white-nonwhite difference in 1900 was 14.6 years, in 1950 it was 8.3 years, and in 1975 it was 5.3 years.

Life expectancy throughout the world rose in 1976–77; reported values were highest for northern America (73), Europe (71), the U.S.S.R. (69), and Oceania (68) and lowest for Africa (46), Asia (58), and Latin America (62). Sweden recorded record values of 72.07 years for males and 77.65 years for females in the period 1971–75, and life expectancy values of over 70 years were also reported for Denmark, Iceland, Israel, Japan, The Netherlands, Norway, and Switzerland.

Infant and Maternal Mortality. In the mid-1960s health statisticians had doubted that the infant mortality rate for the U.S. would drop below 20 in the following decade. The recent declining trend in infant mortality, therefore, was of considerable significance. There were an estimated 46,500 deaths of infants under one year of age in 1977, approximately 3% less than in 1976, and the infant mortality rate, at 14 per 1,000 live births, was about 8% below 1976 and 36% below the 1968

rate of 21.8. The rate for the 12-month period ended June 1978 was 13.9, compared with 14.5 in the corresponding period a year earlier.

There were 310 maternal deaths associated with childbearing in 1977, a drop of 20% from 1976. The maternal mortality rate was 9.4 deaths per 100,000 live births. In the last quarter century this rate had fallen about 85%. According to final data for 1976, the maternal death rate for whites was 9 and for all others, 26.5. However, between 1975 and 1976 the rate for white mothers declined only 1.1%, while that for nonwhite mothers dropped 8.6%. UN data indicated a decline in maternal deaths around the world. Recent rates in the more advanced countries were as low as 3 (Denmark, Finland, Norway). In contrast, the Philippines reported 138 and Mexico, 108; in some less developed countries the rate was probably higher.

Table III. Life Expectancy at Birth, in Years, for Selected Countries [1]

Country	Period	Male	Female
Africa			
Burundi	1975–80	41.4	44.6
Egypt	1975–80	53.7	56.1
Liberia	1975–80	44.4	47.6
Madagascar	1975–80	44.4	47.6
Nigeria	1975–80	41.9	45.1
Upper Volta	1975–80	37.5	40.6
Asia			
Hong Kong	1976	68.0	75.5
India	1976–81	53.8	52.6
Indonesia	1975–80	48.7	51.3
Israel [2]	1976 [3]	71.6	75.4
Japan	1976 [3]	72.2	77.4
Korea, South	1975	66.0	70.0
Pakistan	1975–80	52.4	52.1
Taiwan	1976 [3]	68.8	73.7
Thailand	1975–80	57.6	63.2
Europe			
Albania	1975–80	68.0	70.7
Austria	1975–80	68.7	75.5
Belgium	1968–72	67.8	74.2
Bulgaria	1969–71	68.6	73.9
Czechoslovakia	1975 [3]	66.9	73.7
Denmark	1975–76 [3]	71.1	76.8
Finland	1975 [3]	67.4	75.9
France	1974 [3]	69.0	76.9
Germany, East	1975	68.5	74.0
Germany, West	1973–75	68.0	74.5
Greece	1970	70.1	73.6
Hungary	1974	66.5	72.4
Iceland	1975–76 [3]	73.0	79.2
Ireland	1974–76 [3]	66.8	70.7
Italy	1970–72	69.0	74.9
Netherlands, The	1975 [3]	71.4	77.6
Norway	1974–75	71.7	78.0
Poland	1975 [3]	67.0	74.3
Portugal	1975–80	66.1	72.7
Romania	1974–76	67.4	72.0
Spain	1970 [3]	69.6	75.1
Sweden	1976 [3]	72.1	77.9
Switzerland	1968–73	70.3	76.2
United Kingdom	1973–75	69.2	75.5
Yugoslavia	1970–72	65.4	70.2
North America			
Barbados	1975–80	68.0	73.0
Canada	1975–80	69.6	75.6
Costa Rica	1975–80	68.5	72.1
Guatemala	1975–80	54.9	56.6
Mexico	1975–80	63.6	67.4
Panama	1975–80	66.3	69.5
Puerto Rico	1975–80	70.6	75.3
United States	1976 [3]	69.0	76.7
Oceania			
Australia	1975–80	69.7	76.0
New Zealand	1975–80	69.4	75.6
South America			
Argentina	1975–80	66.1	72.9
Brazil	1975–80	60.7	66.7
Chile	1975–80	61.3	67.6
Peru	1975–80	56.3	60.0
Suriname	1975–80	64.8	69.8
Uruguay	1975–80	67.3	73.3
Venezuela	1975–80	64.6	68.3
U.S.S.R.	1975–80	67.1	74.7

[1] Projection.
[2] Jewish population only.
[3] Actual.
Sources: United Nations, *Selected World Demographic Indicators by Countries, 1950–2000;* official country sources.

Marriage and Divorce Statistics. There were an estimated 2,176,000 marriages in the U.S. in 1977, about 2% more than in 1976, and provisional data for the first half of 1978 indicated an increase of about 4% over the corresponding period of 1977. The number of marriages had peaked in 1973 at 2,284,108, then subsided through 1974–76. The marriage rate in 1977 was 10.1 per 1,000 population, 2% over the previous year. According to final data for 1976, the median age at first marriage was 21 years for brides and 23.8 for grooms. The median age at remarriage continued to fall to 31.7 years for brides and 35.1 years for grooms. The proportion of marriages that were first marriages dropped somewhat to 68% for grooms and 66.3% for brides.

Special tabulations prepared by the UN indicated that marriage rates varied considerably from country to country, reflecting differing social conditions as well as statistical limitations. Consensual unions may not be recorded as marriages, which probably accounts for the low rates of some African and Latin-American countries. In Europe marriage rates in 1975 ranged from 5.4 in Sweden to 9.7 in Poland; the rate in the U.S.S.R. was 10.7.

Divorces continued to increase in 1977; according to provisional statistics, there were 1,097,000 divorces in the U.S., 1.8% more than in 1976. The number of divorces had doubled in a decade. There was a corresponding increase in the divorce rate, from 5 divorces per 1,000 population in 1976 to 5.1 in 1977. However, the annual rate of increase had been declining, and the 1975–76 increase of 2% was the smallest since 1967. The median duration of marriage ending in divorce was 6.5 years, the same as in the two previous years, with most divorces occurring among persons 25–39 years of age. The number of children under 18 involved in divorce was 1,117,000, representing the first decline in this figure since 1960. In 1976, 44% of divorcing couples had no children, compared with 37% in 1964.

In 1975, when the U.S. rate was 4.8 divorces per 1,000 population, "high" divorce rates in Europe were recorded for Sweden (3.14), East Germany (2.47), and Hungary (2.46) and low rates for Northern Ireland (0.28), Greece (0.41), and Belgium (1.12). Complete correspondence between rates of divorce around the world is not possible because of measurement problems and differences in social customs. (ANDERS S. LUNDE)

[338.F.5.b; 525.A:10/36.C.5.d]

Denmark

A constitutional monarchy of north central Europe lying between the North and Baltic seas, Denmark includes the Jutland Peninsula and 100 inhabited islands in the Kattegat and Skagerrak straits. Area (excluding Faeroe Islands and Greenland): 43,075 sq km (16,631 sq mi). Pop. (1978 est.): 5,099,000. Cap. and largest city: Copenhagen (pop., 1977 est., 689,300). Language: Danish. Religion: predominantly Lutheran. Queen, Margrethe II; prime minister in 1978, Anker Jørgensen.

The major event in Danish politics in 1978 was the establishment of a new government on August 30. Prime Minister Anker Jørgensen (*see* BIOGRAPHIES) increased his government's backing from 66 to 88 of the Folketing's (Parliament's) 179 seats by forming a coalition between his Social Democrat Party and the Liberal Democrat (Venstre) Party, which held 22 seats. Though still a minority government, it was strong enough in the face of a disunited opposition. The leader of the Liberal Democrats, Henning Christophersen, became foreign minister.

Denmark

The main problems facing the country were unemployment (around 200,000 by December 1977), foreign debt, and a rising balance of payments deficit, as well as a budget deficit and some inflation. Nevertheless, the Danish krone, linked to the West German mark in the European currency "snake," remained strong. The new government's program centred on the economy. It at once raised the sales tax from 18 to 20%; later, to permit compensatory measures for low-income groups, the tax was increased to an irritating 20¼%.

The presence of the Liberal Democrats in the government drew considerable hostility from the trade unions, and the chairman of the Landsor-

---

DENMARK

Education. (1975–76) Primary, pupils 555,521; secondary, pupils 228,287; primary and secondary, teachers (1975–76) 58,425; vocational, pupils (1975–76) 62,955, teachers (1973–74) c. 4,200; teacher training (1975–76), students 15,934, teachers 1,216; higher (including 5 main universities), students (1975–76) 106,340, teaching staff (1971–72) 10,467.

Finance. Monetary unit: Danish krone, with (Sept. 18, 1978) a free rate of 5.43 kroner to U.S. $1 (10.63 kroner = £1 sterling). Gold, SDR's, and foreign exchange (June 1978) U.S. $2,748,700,000. Budget (1976–77 est.): revenue 66,996,000,000 kroner; expenditure 79,270,000,000 kroner. Gross national product (1976) 230,920,000,000 kroner. Money supply (April 1978) 59,130,000,000 kroner. Cost of living (1975 = 100; May 1978) 132.3.

Foreign Trade. (1977) Imports 79,637,000,000 kroner; exports 60,436,000,000 kroner. Import sources: EEC 48% (West Germany 20%, U.K. 11%, The Netherlands 6%); Sweden 13%; U.S. 6%; Norway 5%. Export destinations: EEC 45% (West Germany 15%, U.K. 14%, Italy 5%); Sweden 14%; Norway 7%; U.S. 6%. Main exports: machinery 21%; meat 14%; chemicals 7%; dairy produce 5%; fish 5%. Tourism (1976): visitors 16,232,000; gross receipts U.S. $803 million.

Transport and Communications. Roads (1976) 66,515 km (including 397 km expressways). Motor vehicles in use (1976): passenger 1,339,800; commercial 248,600. Railways: (1976) 2,511 km; traffic (1975–76) 3,415,000,000 passenger-km, freight 1,805,000,000 net ton-km. Air traffic (including apportionment of international operations of Scandinavian Airlines System; 1977) 2,567,000,000 passenger-km; freight 124,120,000 net ton-km. Shipping (1977): merchant vessels 100 gross tons and over 1,407; gross tonnage 5,331,165. Shipping traffic (1976): goods loaded 7,-168,000 metric tons, unloaded 30,894,000 metric tons. Telephones (including Faeroe Islands and Greenland; Jan. 1977) 2,528,600. Radio receivers (Dec. 1976) 1,753,000. Television licenses (Oct. 1977) 1,737,000.

Agriculture. Production (in 000; metric tons; 1977): wheat c. 605; barley c. 6,084; oats c. 288; rye c. 320; potatoes c. 800; rutabagas (1976) 1,071; sugar, raw value c. 566; apples c. 128; rapeseed c. 71; butter 131; cheese 177; pork 744; beef and veal 243; fish catch (1976) 1,912. Livestock (in 000; July 1977): cattle c. 3,095; pigs c. 7,811; sheep c. 59; horses c. 56; chickens c. 15,417.

Industry. Production (in 000; metric tons; 1977): crude steel 686; cement 2,307; fertilizers (nutrient content; 1976–77) nitrogenous 109, phosphate 87; crude oil (1975) 167; petroleum products (1975) 7,662; manufactured gas (cu m) 305,000; electricity (kw-hr) 22,482,000. Merchant vessels launched (100 gross tons and over; 1977) 633,000 gross tons.

In May fishermen blocked the harbour at Elsinore, halting all traffic. The protest was over reduced fishing quotas in the Baltic.

ganisationen (LO, the Danish trade union federation), Thomas Nielsen, proclaimed his resistance to the new government. The LO gave notice that it would press for the introduction of "economic democracy"—direct sharing by the workers in industrial profits—a scheme rejected by all the bourgeois parties as an impossibility. In response, the employers spoke of a wage cut of some 6%, to be combined with a lowering of taxes so there would be no cut in the workers' real purchasing power. In its turn, the government promised that workers' "real income" would not be cut, but it insisted that a strict incomes policy was an absolute necessity if the competitive power of Danish industry was to be reestablished.

As a result, prospects for labour negotiations were bleak. The government spoke of "three-part" negotiations between government, unions, and employers. Nielsen expressed willingness to attend any negotiations but saw no possibility of agreement while the Liberal Democrats remained in the government. The Social Democrat rank and file were also dissatisfied with the new coalition government. A pensions reform was, if not canceled, at least postponed "until better times." On December 11, however, the LO dropped its demand for workers' profit-sharing, enabling wage negotiations to go forward.

There was uncertainty about the budget, which was based on the calendar year instead of a year running from April 1 to March 31. The budget had originally been introduced on condition that no changes in economic policy would be made, but the new government was working precisely to make such changes. If the first budget remained valid, there would be a deficit of 16 billion kroner. Including interest charges on foreign and domestic debt and repayments, the state would have a "financing requirement" of some 41 billion kroner.

The balance of payments deficit was calculated at about 10 billion kroner.

Some major projects were canceled, including the bridge over the Great Belt. All parties agreed, however, that natural gas should be introduced, possibly between 1982 and 1983. This would involve Danish findings in the North Sea and imported West German natural gas, to be "repaid" when the Danish system was fully operational.

Denmark was involved in a fisheries dispute with the European Economic Community (EEC) and Britain. The British authorities—under protest from the other EEC members—had widened Britain's North Sea territory at the expense of the Danish fishing industry, and the Danes threatened to take the matter up in the European Court. On September 19 a referendum confirmed an earlier resolution in the Folketing to lower the voting age from 20 to 18. Home rule for Greenland was approved by the Folketing on November 17, and the proposal would be submitted to the Greenlanders in January 1979.　　　(STENER AARSDAL)

See also Dependent States.

Dependent States

In 1978 three dependent states, Dominica in the Caribbean and the Solomon Islands and Tuvalu in the Pacific, achieved independence. (*See* DOMINICA; SOLOMON ISLANDS; TUVALU.) Throughout the year, ethnicity, the nonpejorative word for racial and national awareness, continued to erode the line between colonies and minorities; that is, between dependent territories and dependent peoples. Minorities, though without specific status under the UN, made claims through human rights bodies to be recognized as peoples with rights to self-determination and territory.

Dentistry:
see Health and Disease

Europe and the Atlantic. Argentina continued to press its claim to the British colony of the Falkland Islands and the British Antarctic territories. An Argentine scientific-naval expedition remained on uninhabited Southern Thule Island in the South Sandwich Islands, a Falklands dependency, where it had landed in December 1976 without British permission. In spite of Argentina's claimed sovereignty, talks between British and Argentine representatives continued during the year. There was some separatist violence in the Azores (which had already been granted some autonomy by Portugal), earning verbal support from Col. Muammar al-Qaddafi of Libya. In Saint Pierre and Miquelon a general strike was called on June 13 to protest against economic hardship and neglect by the French government.

Legislation to give Greenland home rule in May 1979 was approved by the Danish Parliament in November. Greenland would remain under the Danish crown, and its foreign relations would be conducted by Denmark. The ruling coalition was returned in general elections in the Faeroe Islands November 7. The coalition supported continuing close ties with Denmark while seeking increased devolution of internal authority. Talks on a new fishery agreement between the Faeroes and the European Economic Community began in Brussels in November.

Discussions between Spain and Great Britain on the future status of Gibraltar took place in a more relaxed atmosphere in 1978. Joint Anglo-Spanish working parties seeking means of cooperation in the Gibraltar dispute were set up in July as the result of a meeting between the British foreign secretary, David Owen, and the Spanish foreign minister, Marcelino Oreja, in Paris in March.

Breton separatists of the Breton Liberation Front exploded a powerful bomb that wrecked three rooms of the Palace of Versailles, near Paris, on June 26; there were over 20 bomb attacks in Brittany itself. Eight men were convicted in July for their parts in various bombings. In Corsica separatists of the Corsican National Liberation Front made over 200 small bomb attacks.

Queen Elizabeth II of England visited Guernsey on her June tour of the Channel Islands.

In Britain the Shetland and Orkney Islands continued their search for a satisfactory formula for home rule outside any scheme for general Scottish devolution.

Caribbean. During 1978 the British Caribbean governments were principally concerned with moves toward independence. They also had to cope with severe balance of payments deficits and the attempt to resolve conflicts of economic interest over the location of industries. Representatives of the St. Lucia government and opposition attended a constitutional conference on independence in London. Prime Minister John Compton announced that the island would become independent on

continued on page 308

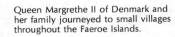

Queen Margrethe II of Denmark and her family journeyed to small villages throughout the Faeroe Islands.

BJARNE LUTHCKE—NORDFOTO/PICTORIAL PARADE

ANTARCTIC

Claims on the continent of Antarctica and all islands south of 60° S remain in status quo according to the Antarctic Treaty, to which 19 nations are signatory. Formal claims within the treaty area include the following: Australian Antarctic Territory, the mainland portion of French Southern and Antarctic Lands (Terre Adélie), Ross Dependency claimed by New Zealand, Queen Maud Land and Peter I Island claimed by Norway, and British Antarctic Territory, some parts of which are claimed by Argentina and Chile. No claims have been recognized as final under international law.

AUSTRALIA

CHRISTMAS ISLAND

Christmas Island, an external territory, is situated in the Indian Ocean 1,410 km NW of Australia. Area: 135 sq km (52 sq mi). Pop. (1977 est.): 3,300. Cap.: The Settlement (pop., 1971, 1,300).

COCOS (KEELING) ISLANDS

Cocos (Keeling) Islands is an external territory located in the Indian Ocean 3,685 km W of Darwin, Australia. Area: 14 sq km (5.5 sq mi). Pop. (1977 est.): 447.

NORFOLK ISLAND

Norfolk Island, an external territory, is located in the Pacific Ocean 1,720 km NE of Sydney, Australia. Area: 35 sq km (13 sq mi). Pop. (1977 est.): 1,600. Cap. (de facto): Kingston.

DENMARK

FAEROE ISLANDS

The Faeroes, an integral part of the Danish realm, are a self-governing group of islands in the North Atlantic about 580 km W of Norway. Area: 1,399 sq km (540 sq mi). Pop. (1977 est.): 41,600. Cap.: Thorshavn (pop., 1977 est., 11,600).

Education. (1977–78) Primary, pupils 6,074; secondary, pupils 2,403; primary and secondary, teachers 466; vocational, pupils (1976–77) 813, teachers (1966–67) 88; teacher training, students 118, teachers (1966–67) 12; higher, students 25.

Finance and Trade. Monetary unit: Faeroese krone, at par with the Danish krone, with (Sept. 18, 1978) a free rate of 5.43 kroner to U.S. $1 (10.63 kroner = £1 sterling). Budget (1976–77 est.): revenue 315,692,000 kroner; expenditure 315,512,000 kroner. Foreign trade (1976): imports 790 million kroner; exports 631 million kroner. Import sources: Denmark 66%; Norway 19%. Export destinations: Denmark 22%; U.S. 16%; U.K. 15%; Italy 10%; Spain 7%; Norway 7%; France 6%; Sweden 6%. Main exports: fish and products 78%; fish meal 10%.

Transport. Shipping (1977): merchant vessels 100 gross tons and over 172; gross tonnage 57,110.

Agriculture and Industry. Fish catch (1976) 342,000 metric tons. Livestock (in 000; 1976): sheep 69; cattle c. 2. Electricity production (1975–76) c. 93 million kw-hr (c. 59% hydroelectric).

GREENLAND

An integral part of the Danish realm, Greenland, the largest island in the world, lies mostly within the Arctic Circle. Area: 2,175,600 sq km (840,000 sq mi), 84% of which is covered by ice cap. Pop. (1977 est.): 49,700. Cap.: Godthaab (pop., 1977 est., 8,545).

Education. (1977–78) Primary, pupils 9,347; secondary and vocational, pupils 2,626; primary, secondary, and vocational, teachers 1,021; higher, students 516.

Finance and Trade. Monetary unit: Danish krone. Budget (1975 est.): revenue 73.6 million kroner; expenditure 77.2 million kroner. Foreign trade (1976): imports 778 million kroner (98% from Denmark); exports 517 million kroner (44% to Denmark, 15% to Finland, 12% to U.S., 8% to West Germany, 7% to France, 5% to Italy). Main exports: fish and products 47%; zinc ores 36%.

Agriculture. Fish catch (1976) 45,000 metric tons. Livestock (in 000; Nov. 1975): sheep 20; reindeer 2.5.

Industry. Production (in 000; metric tons; 1975): lead ore (metal content) 24; zinc ore (metal content) 85; cryolite (1974) 38; electricity (kw-hr) c. 124,000.

FRANCE

FRENCH GUIANA

French Guiana is an overseas département situated between Brazil and Suriname on the northeast coast of South America. Area: 90,000 sq km (34,750 sq mi). Pop. (1978 est.): 60,000. Cap.: Cayenne (pop., 1978 est., 32,900).

Education. (1977–78) Primary, pupils 10,838, teachers 600; secondary, pupils 5,624, teachers (1972–73) 229; vocational, pupils 210, teachers (1972–73) 79; teacher training, students 39.

Finance and Trade. Monetary unit: French (metropolitan) franc, with (Sept. 18, 1978) a free rate of Fr 4.38 to U.S. $1 (Fr 8.57 = £1 sterling). Budget (total; 1976 est.) balanced at Fr 190,578,000. Foreign trade (1977): imports Fr 691,860,000; exports Fr 33,810,000. Import sources (1976): France 62%; Trinidad and Tobago 16%; U.S. 5%. Export destinations (1976): U.S. 61%; France 11%; Martinique 10%; Guadeloupe 5%; Switzerland 5%. Main exports (1976): shrimp 61%; timber 14%.

FRENCH POLYNESIA

An overseas territory, the islands of French Polynesia are scattered over a large area of the south central Pacific Ocean. Area of inhabited islands: 4,182 sq km (1,615 sq mi). Pop. (1977 census): 137,400. Cap.: Papeete, Tahiti (pop., 1977 census, 62,700).

Education. (1975–76) Primary, pupils 28,658, teachers 1,510; secondary, pupils 7,280, teachers 424; vocational, pupils 1,719, teachers 142; higher, students 111, teaching staff 7.

Finance and Trade. Monetary unit: CFP franc, with (Sept. 19, 1977) a parity of CFP Fr 18.18 to the French franc and a free rate of CFP Fr 79.57 to U.S. $1 (CFP Fr 155.91 = £1 sterling). Budget (1977) balanced at CFP Fr 11.2 billion. Foreign trade (1977): imports CFP Fr 29,187,000,000 (53% from France, 19% from U.S. in 1976); exports CFP Fr 1,464,000,000 (82% to France in 1976). Main exports (1974): nuclear material c. 75%; coconut oil 15%. Tourism (1976): visitors 117,000; gross receipts U.S. $49 million.

GUADELOUPE

The overseas département of Guadeloupe, together with its dependencies, is in the eastern Caribbean between Antigua to the north and Dominica to the south. Area: 1,705 sq km (658 sq mi). Pop. (1977 est.): 324,100. Cap.: Basse-Terre (pop., 1977 est., 15,800).

Education. (1974–75) Primary, pupils 75,036, teachers 2,473; secondary, pupils 35,624, teachers 840; vocational, pupils 7,516, teachers 381; teacher training (1973–74), students 304, teachers 22; higher, students 1,614, teaching staff 33.

Finance and Trade. Monetary unit: French (metropolitan) franc. Budget (1972 est.) balanced at Fr 583 million. Cost of living (Basse-Terre; 1975 = 100; April 1978) 126. Foreign trade (1977): imports Fr 1,843,600,000 (74% from France, 5% from U.S. and Puerto Rico in 1976); exports Fr 387,550,000 (84% to France, 11% to Martinique in 1976). Main exports (1976): bananas 42%; sugar 35%; rum 6%; wheat meal and flour 6%.

MARTINIQUE

The Caribbean island of Martinique, an overseas département, lies 39 km N of St. Lucia and about 50 km SE of Dominica. Area: 1,079 sq km (417 sq mi). Pop. (1977 est.): 319,000. Cap.: Fort-de-France (pop., 1974 census, 98,800).

Education. (1976–77) Primary, pupils 80,342, teachers 3,390; secondary, pupils 46,280, teachers 2,592; vocational, pupils (1973–74) 4,819, teachers (1972–73) 245; teacher training (1972–73), students 219, teachers 20.

Finance and Trade. Monetary unit: French (metropolitan) franc. Budget (1974 est.) balanced at Fr 291 million. Cost of living (Fort-de-France; 1975 = 100; March 1978) 130.2 Foreign trade (1977): imports Fr 2,098,590,000; exports Fr 630,350,000. Import sources (1976): France 61%; West Germany 8%; Venezuela 6%; Saudi Arabia 5%. Export destinations (1976): France 68%; Guadeloupe 21%; Italy 7%. Main exports (1976): bananas 57%; petroleum products 17%; rum 11%.

MAYOTTE

An African island dependency of France that was formerly a part of the Comoros, Mayotte is in the Indian Ocean off the east coast of Africa. Mayotte voted to remain a part of France in February 1976. Its current administrative status of "special collectivity" was designated on Sept. 17, 1976. Area: 378 sq km (146 sq mi). Pop. (1978 est.): 48,600. Cap.: Dzaoudzi (pop., about 3,200).

Education. (1976) Primary, pupils c. 3,000.

Finance and Trade. Monetary unit: French (metropolitan) franc. Main exports: vanilla, essential oils, copra.

NEW CALEDONIA

The overseas territory of New Caledonia, together with its dependencies, is in the South Pacific 1,210 km E of Australia. Area: 19,079 sq km (7,366 sq mi). Pop. (1977 est.): 136,000. Cap.: Nouméa (pop., 1976 census, 56,100).

Education. (1977) Primary, pupils 32,766, teachers 1,489; secondary, pupils 7,268, teachers 467; vocational, pupils 2,461, teachers 252; teacher training, students 150, teachers 25; higher, students 411, teaching staff 30.

Finance and Trade. Monetary unit: CFP franc. Budget (1977 est.) balanced at CFP Fr 11,887,000,000. Foreign trade: imports (1977) CFP Fr 26,082,000,000; exports (1976) CFP Fr 26,195,000,000. Import sources (1976): France 39%; Australia 10%; Singapore 9%; Bahrain 8%; Iran 5%. Export destinations: France 51%; Japan 29%; U.S. c. 10%. Main exports: ferronickel 44%; nickel castings 27%; nickel 24%.

RÉUNION

The overseas département of Réunion is located in the Indian Ocean about 720 km E of Madagascar and 180 km SW of Mauritius. Area: 2,512 sq km (970 sq mi). Pop. (1978 est.): 488,000. Cap.: Saint-Denis (pop., 1974 census, 104,600).

Education. (1976–77) Primary, pupils 127,771, teachers 4,397; secondary and vocational, pupils 53,393, teachers 2,627; teacher training (1973–74), students 319, teachers 22; higher, students 1,720.

Finance and Trade. Monetary unit: French (metropolitan) franc. Budget (1975 est.) balanced at Fr 2,471,000,000. Cost of living (Saint-Denis; 1975 = 100; April 1978) 123.8. Foreign trade (1977): imports Fr 2,465,270,000; exports Fr 560,730,000. Import sources (1976): France 61%; South Africa 6%; Madagascar 6%. Export destinations (1976): France 69%; Portugal 15%; U.K. 8%. Main exports (1976): sugar 78%; essential oils 11%.

SAINT PIERRE AND MIQUELON

The self-governing overseas département of Saint Pierre and Miquelon is located about 20 km off the south coast of Newfoundland. Area: 242 sq km (93 sq mi). Pop. (1977 est.): 6,100. Cap.: Saint Pierre, Saint Pierre.

Education. (1977–78) Primary, pupils 1,158, teachers 50; secondary, pupils 505, teachers 55; vocational, pupils 128, teachers 19.

Finance and Trade. Monetary unit: French (metropolitan) franc. Budget (1973 est.) balanced at Fr 3.4 million. Foreign trade (1974): imports Fr 125,553,000; exports Fr 59,352,000. Import sources: Canada 54%; France 38%. Export destinations (excluding ship's stores): Canada 70%; U.S. 25%; France 5%. Main exports: petroleum products (as ship's stores) 53%; cattle 30%; fish 12%.

WALLIS AND FUTUNA

Wallis and Futuna, an overseas territory, lies in the South Pacific west of Western Samoa. Area: 255 sq km (98 sq mi). Pop. (1976 census): 9,200. Cap.: Mata Utu, Uvea (pop., 1976 census, 558).

NAMIBIA (SOUTH WEST AFRICA)

South West Africa has been a UN territory since 1966, when the General Assembly terminated

South Africa's mandate over the country, renamed Namibia by the UN. South Africa considers the UN resolution illegal. Area: 824,268 sq km (318,251 sq mi). Pop. (1977 est.): 905,200. National cap.: Windhoek (pop., 1975 est., 77,400). Summer cap.: Swakopmund (pop., 1975 est., 13,700).

Education. (1973) Primary and secondary: Bantu, pupils 116,320, teachers 2,662; Coloured, pupils 15,941, teachers 797; white, pupils 22,775, teachers 1,232.

Finance and Trade. Monetary unit: South African rand, with (Sept. 18, 1978) an official rate of R 0.87 to U.S. $1 (free rate of R 1.70 = £1 sterling). Budget (1976–77) balanced at R 58 million (excludes capital expenditure of R 62 million). Foreign trade (included in the South African customs union; 1976 est.): imports c. R 500 million (c. 80% from South Africa in 1972); exports c. R 700 million (c. 50% to South Africa in 1972). Main exports: diamonds c. 45%; other minerals c. 20%.

Agriculture. Production (in 000; metric tons; 1976): corn c. 15; millet c. 20; beef and veal c. 142; sheep and goat meat c. 24; fish catch c. 574. Livestock (in 000; 1976): cattle c. 2,850; sheep c. 5,000; goats c. 2,000; horses c. 42; asses c. 63.

Industry. Production (in 000; metric tons; 1976): lead ore (metal content) 40; zinc ore (metal content) 48; copper ore (metal content) 39; tin concentrates (metal content) 0.7; vanadium ore (metal content; 1975) 0.6; diamonds (metric carats) 1,694; salt (1975) 209; electricity (kw-hr; 1963) 188,000.

NETHERLANDS, THE

NETHERLANDS ANTILLES

The Netherlands Antilles, a self-governing integral part of the Netherlands realm, consists of an island group near the Venezuelan coast and another group to the north near St. Kitts-Nevis. Area: 993 sq km (383 sq mi). Pop. (1978 est.): 245,000. Cap.: Willemstad, Curaçao (pop., 1970 est., 50,000).

Education. (1973–74) Primary, pupils 38,170, teachers 1,492; secondary and vocational, pupils 12,104, teachers 631; higher (university only), students c. 150, teaching staff c. 15.

Finance. Monetary unit: Netherlands Antilles guilder or florin, with (Sept. 18, 1978) a par value of 1.80 Netherlands Antilles guilders to U.S. $1 (free rate of 3.51 Netherlands Antilles guilders = £1 sterling). Budget (1972 rev. est.): revenue 122 million Netherlands Antilles guilders; expenditure 121 million Netherlands Antilles guilders. Cost of living (Aruba and Curaçao; 1975 = 100; Dec. 1977) 114.2

Foreign Trade. (1976) Imports 6,602,000,000 Netherlands Antilles guilders; exports 4,535,000,000 Netherlands Antilles guilders. Import sources (1975): Venezuela 57%; Saudi Arabia 17%; U.S. 6%; Nigeria 6%. Export destinations (1975): U.S. 62%; The Netherlands 5%. Main exports (1975): petroleum products 91%; crude oil 5%. Tourism: visitors (1976) 276,000; gross receipts (1974) U.S. $150 million.

Transport and Communications. Roads (1972) 1,150 km. Motor vehicles in use (1975): passenger 50,136; commercial 5,650. Shipping traffic (1974): goods loaded c. 37,323,000 metric tons, unloaded c. 45,930,000 metric tons. Telephones (Jan. 1977) 48,000. Radio receivers (Dec. 1975) 132,000. Television receivers (Dec. 1975) c. 35,000.

Industry. Production (in 000; metric tons; 1975): petroleum products c. 22,110; phosphate rock 82; electricity (kw-hr) c. 1,400,000.

NEW ZEALAND

COOK ISLANDS

The self-governing territory of the Cook Islands consists of several islands in the southern Pacific Ocean scattered over an area of about 2.2 million sq km. Area: 241 sq km (93 sq mi). Pop. (1978 est.): 19,600. Seat of government: Rarotonga Island (pop., 1976 census, 9,800).

Education. (1975) Primary, pupils 5,339; secondary, pupils 1,276; primary and secondary, teachers 360; teacher training (1971), students 75.

Finance and Trade. Monetary unit: Cook Islands dollar, at par with the New Zealand dollar, with (Sept. 18, 1978) a free rate of CI$0.95 to U.S. $1

(CI$1.85 = £1 sterling). Budget (1977–78 est.): revenue CI$12,134,000; expenditure CI$12,514,000. Foreign trade: imports (1973) CI$4,947,000 (83% from New Zealand, 5% from Japan); exports (1975) CI$2,908,000 (98% to New Zealand). Main exports: fruit preserves 70%; clothing 13%; oilseeds 8%.

NIUE

The self-governing territory of Niue is situated in the Pacific Ocean about 2,400 km NE of New Zealand. Area: 259 sq km (100 sq mi). Pop. (1976 census): 3,800. Capital: Alofi (pop., 1976 census, 1,007).

Education. (1976) Primary, pupils 906, teachers 56; secondary, pupils 447, teachers 29; vocational, students 22, teachers 2; teacher training, students 10, teachers 1.

Finance and Trade. Monetary unit: New Zealand dollar. Budget (1975–76): revenue NZ$579,000 (excluding New Zealand subsidy of NZ$2,516,000); expenditure NZ$3.7 million. Foreign trade (1975): imports NZ$2,095,000 (79% from New Zealand); exports NZ$197,000 (73% to New Zealand). Main exports: fruit preserves 43%; copra 37%; plaited ware 11%; honey 6%.

TOKELAU

The territory of Tokelau lies in the South Pacific about 1,130 km N of Niue and 3,380 km NE of New Zealand. Area: 10 sq km (4 sq mi). Pop. (1976 census): 1,575.

NORWAY

JAN MAYEN

The island of Jan Mayen, a Norwegian dependency, lies within the Arctic Circle between Greenland and northern Norway. Area: 373 sq km (144 sq mi). Pop. (1973 est.): 37.

SVALBARD

A group of islands and a Norwegian dependency, Svalbard is located within the Arctic Circle to the north of Norway. Area: 62,050 sq km (23,957 sq mi). Pop. (1977 est.): 3,500.

PORTUGAL

MACAU

The overseas territory of Macau is situated on the mainland coast of China 60 km W of Hong Kong. Area: 16 sq km (6 sq mi). Pop. (1977 est.): 266,500.

Education. (1976–77) Primary, pupils 23,508, teachers 1,125; secondary, pupils 9,701, teachers 527; vocational, pupils 4,360, teachers 201; teacher training, students 42, teachers 31; higher, students (1975–76) 113, teachers 9.

Finance and Trade. Monetary unit: patacá, with (Sept. 18, 1978) a parity of 1.075 patacás to the Hong Kong dollar and a free rate of 5.10 patacás to U.S. $1 (10 patacás = £1 sterling). Budget (1977 est.) balanced at 134.2 million patacás. Foreign trade (1977): imports 1,060,400,000 patacás; exports 1,221,500,000 patacás. Import sources (1976): Hong Kong 68%; China 24%. Export destinations (1976): West Germany 23%; France 17%; U.K. 10%; U.S. 10%; Hong Kong 9%; Portugal 5%; The Netherlands 5%. Main export (1975): clothing 81%.

Transport. Shipping traffic (1976): goods loaded 330,000 metric tons, unloaded 411,000 metric tons.

UNITED KINGDOM

ANGUILLA

Formally a part of the associated state of St. Kitts-Nevis-Anguilla, the island of Anguilla comprises a separate administrative entity, having received a constitution separating its government from that of St. Kitts-Nevis in 1976. Area: 91 sq km (35 sq mi). Pop. (1977 est.): 6,500.

Education. (1976) Primary and secondary, pupils 2,200.

Finance and Trade. Monetary unit: East Caribbean dollar, with (Sept. 18, 1978) an official rate of ECar$2.70 to U.S. $1 (free rate of ECar$5.30 = £1 sterling). Budget (1977 est) balanced at ECar$3,285,000 (including U.K. grant of

ECar$1,262,000). Foreign trade (included with St. Kitts-Nevis; 1976 est) exports c. ECar$1 million Main export destinations: Trinidad and Tobago c. 40%; Puerto Rico c. 30%; Guadeloupe c. 14%; U.S. Virgin Islands c. 10%. Main exports: salt c. 40%; lobster c. 36%; livestock c. 14%.

ANTIGUA

The associated state of Antigua, with its dependencies Barbuda and Redonda, lies in the eastern Caribbean approximately 60 km N of Guadeloupe. Area: 440 sq km (170 sq mi). Pop. (1977 est.): 72,-000. Cap.: Saint John's (pop., 1974 est., 23,500).

Education. (1975–76) Primary, pupils 12,875, teachers 469; secondary, pupils 5,082, teachers 231; vocational, pupils 134, teachers 20; teacher training, students 96, teachers 13.

Finance and Trade. Monetary unit: East Caribbean dollar. Budget (1977 est.): revenue ECar$32 million; expenditure ECar$41 million. Foreign trade (1974): imports ECar$143,750,000; exports ECar$66,468,000. Import sources (1973): Venezuela 31%; U.K. 22%; U.S. 16%; Canada 6%. Export destinations (1973): bunkers 37%; U.S. 21%; Switzerland 11%; Canada 9%; Bermuda 5%. Main exports (1973): petroleum products 84%; aircraft and engines (reexports) 6%.

BELIZE

Belize, a self-governing colony, is situated on the Caribbean coast of Central America, bounded on the north and northwest by Mexico and by Guatemala on the remainder of the west and south. Area: 22,965 sq km (8,867 sq mi). Pop. (1977 est.): 129,800. Cap.: Belmopan (pop., 1977 est., 4,000).

Education. (1976–77) Primary, pupils 33,892, teachers 1,237; secondary, pupils 5,593, teachers 342; vocational, pupils 60, teachers 5; higher, students 460, teaching staff 15.

Finance and Trade. Monetary unit: Belize dollar, with (Sept. 18, 1978) an official rate of Bel$2 = U.S. $1 (free rate of Bel$3.92 = £1 sterling). Budget (total; 1977 est.) balanced at Bel$84 million. Foreign trade (1975): imports Bel$185.5 million; exports Bel$129.6 million. Import sources (1970): U.S. 34%; U.K. 25%; Jamaica 7%; The Netherlands 7%. Export destinations (1970): U.S. 30%; U.K. 24%; Mexico 22%; Canada 13%. Main exports (1975): sugar c. 61%; clothing c. 6%; citrus products 5%.

BERMUDA

The colony of Bermuda lies in the western Atlantic about 920 km E of Cape Hatteras, North Carolina. Area: 46 sq km (18 sq mi). Pop. (1977 est.): 56,900. Cap.: Hamilton, Great Bermuda (pop., 1973 est., 3,-000).

Education. (1974–75) Primary, pupils 6,919, teachers 397; secondary, pupils 4,700, teachers 325; vocational, pupils 510, teachers 49.

Finance and Trade. Monetary unit: Bermuda dollar, at par with the U.S. dollar (free rate, at Sept. 18, 1978, of Ber$1.96 = £1 sterling). Budget (1977–78 est.): revenue Ber$78.3 million; expenditure Ber$78.4 million. Foreign trade (1976): imports Ber$143.2 million; exports Ber$44.7 million. Import sources: U.S. 52%; U.K. 13%; Netherlands Antilles 10%; Canada 8%. Export destinations: bunkers 36%; U.S. 14%; U.K. 6%; New Zealand 5%. Main exports: drugs and medicines 39%; petroleum products 34%; aircraft supplies 7%. Tourism (1976): visitors 559,000; gross receipts U.S. $191 million.

Transport and Communications. Roads (1976) c. 240 km. Motor vehicles in use (1976): passenger 12,100; commercial 1,900. Shipping (1977): merchant vessels 100 gross tons and over 88; gross tonnage 1,751,515.

BRITISH INDIAN OCEAN TERRITORY

Located in the western Indian Ocean, this colony consists of the islands of the Chagos Archipelago. Area: 60 sq km (23 sq mi). No permanent civilian population remains. Administrative headquarters: Victoria, Seychelles.

BRITISH VIRGIN ISLANDS

The colony of the British Virgin Islands is located in the Caribbean to the east of the U.S. Virgin Islands. Area: 153 sq km (59 sq mi). Pop. (1977 est.): 12,-000. Cap.: Road Town, Tortola (pop., 1973 est., 3,-500).

Education. (1975–76) Primary, pupils 1,856; secondary and vocational, pupils 830; primary and secondary, teachers 145.

Finance and Trade. Monetary unit: U.S. dollar (free rate, at Sept. 18, 1978, of U.S. $1.96 = £1 sterling). Budget (1977 est.): revenue U.S. $6,-699,000; expenditure U.S. $7,158,000. Foreign trade (1974): imports U.S. $11,606,000; exports U.S. $425,-000. Import sources: U.S. 26%; Puerto Rico 21%; U.S. Virgin Islands 17%; U.K. 15%; Trinidad and Tobago 11%. Export destinations: U.S. Virgin Islands 53%; Anguilla 22%; St. Martin (Guadeloupe) 9%; U.K. 5%. Main exports (mainly reexports): motor vehicles 16%; timber 14%; beverages 10%; fish 7%; iron and steel 6%; machinery 6%.

BRUNEI

Brunei, a protected sultanate, is located on the north coast of the island of Borneo, surrounded on its landward side by the Malaysian state of Sarawak. Area: 5,765 sq km (2,226 sq mi). Pop. (1977 est.): 190,000. Cap.: Bandar Seri Begawan (pop., 1976 est., 48,000).

Education. (1976) Primary, pupils 30,912, teachers (1975) 1,621; secondary, pupils 14,989, teachers (1975) 876; vocational, pupils 278, teachers (1975) 61; teacher training, students 591, teachers (1975) 48.

Finance and Trade. Monetary unit: Brunei dollar, with (Sept. 18, 1978) a free rate of Br$2.25 to U.S. $1 (Br$4.40 = £1 sterling). Budget (1977 est.): revenue Br$1.4 billion; expenditure Br$813 million. Foreign trade (1977): imports Br$680,410,000; exports Br$3,999,980,000. Import sources (1976): U.S. 25%; Japan 17%; Singapore 15%; U.K. 15%. Export destinations (1976): Japan 70%; U.S. 11%; Malaysia 5%. Main exports: crude oil 74%; natural gas 21%.

Agriculture. Production (in 000; metric tons; 1976): rice c. 4; cassava c. 3; bananas c. 2; pineapples c. 2; rubber c. 1. Livestock (in 000; Dec. 1975): buffalo c. 17; pigs c. 14; chickens c. 894.

Industry. Production (in 000; 1976): crude oil (metric tons) 9,846; natural gas (cu m) 9,700,000; electricity (kw-hr; 1975) 230,000..

CAYMAN ISLANDS

The colony of the Cayman Islands lies in the Caribbean about 270 km NW of Jamaica. Area: 288 sq km (111 sq mi). Pop. (1977 est.): 14,000. Cap.: George Town, Grand Cayman (pop., 1970 census, 3,800).

Education. (1976–77) Primary, pupils 2,208, teachers 85; secondary, pupils 1,356, teachers 95.

Finance and Trade. Monetary unit: Cayman Islands dollar, with (Sept. 18, 1978) an official rate of CayI$0.83 to U.S. $1 (free rate of CayI$1.63 = £1 sterling). Budget (1976 rev. est.): revenue CayI$11,-654,000; expenditure CayI$10,420,000. Foreign trade (1976): imports CayI$29,780,000; exports CayI$505,000. Most trade is with the U.S. (about two-thirds) and Jamaica. Main export (1975): turtle products 95%. Tourism (1976) 105,500 visitors.

Shipping. (1977) Merchant vessels 100 gross tons and over 106; gross tonnage 123,787.

FALKLAND ISLANDS

The colony of the Falkland Islands and dependencies is situated in the South Atlantic about 800 km NE of Cape Horn. Area: 16,265 sq km (6,280 sq mi). Pop. (1978 est.): 1,800. Cap.: Stanley (pop., 1978 est., 1,100).

Education. (1977–78) Primary, pupils 102, teachers 6; secondary, pupils 75, teachers 7.

Finance and Trade. Monetary unit: Falkland Island pound, at par with the pound sterling, with (Sept. 18, 1978) a free rate of U.S.1.96 = £1 sterling. Budget (excluding dependencies; 1977–78 est.): revenue FI£1,405,000; expenditure FI£1,352,000. Foreign trade (1976): imports FI£1,063,000 (83% from U.K. in 1971); exports FI£2,374,000 (93% to U.K. in 1971). Main export (1975): wool 97%.

GIBRALTAR

Gibraltar, a self-governing colony, is a small peninsula that juts into the Mediterranean from southwestern Spain. Area: 5.80 sq km (2.25 sq mi). Pop. (1978 est.): 29,300.

Education. (1977–78) Primary, pupils 2,784, teachers (1976–77) 146; secondary and vocational, pupils 1,851, teachers (1976–77) 139.

Finance and Trade. Monetary unit: Gibraltar pound, at par with the pound sterling. Budget (1975–76 est.): revenue Gib£11,807,000; expenditure Gib£13,014,000. Foreign trade (1976): imports Gib£32,416,000 (67% from U.K. in 1975); reexports Gib£13,728,000 (31% to EEC, 16% to U.K. in 1971). Main reexports: petroleum products 87%; tobacco 11%. Tourism (1976) 125,000 visitors.

Transport. Shipping (1977): merchant vessels 100 gross tons and over 6; gross tonnage 10,549. Ships entered (1974) vessels totaling 13,973,000 net registered tons; goods loaded (1975) 6,000 metric tons, unloaded 345,000 metric tons.

GILBERT ISLANDS

The Gilbert Islands comprise 16 main islands, together with associated islets and reefs, straddling the Equator just west of the International Date Line in the western Pacific Ocean. Area: 272 sq km (105 sq mi). Pop. (1977 est.): 54,900. Seat of government: Bairiki, on Tarawa (pop., 1974 est., 17,100).

Education. (1977) Primary, pupils 13,679, teachers 435; secondary, pupils 1,000, teachers 71; vocational, pupils 183, teachers 28; teacher training, students 73, teachers 12.

Finance and Trade. Monetary unit: Australian dollar, with (Sept. 18, 1978) a free rate of A$0.87 to U.S. $1 (A$1.70 = £1 sterling). Budget (1977 est.): revenue A$11,771,000; expenditure A$9,724,000. Foreign trade (1976): imports A$10,062,000; exports A$18,147,000. Import sources (including Tuvalu; 1974): Australia 60%; U.K. 11%. Export destinations (including Tuvalu; 1974): Australia 44%; New Zealand 42%; U.K. 14%. Main exports: phosphates 95%; copra 5%.

Industry. Production (in 000; 1975): phosphate rock (metric tons) 529; electricity (kw-hr) c. 5,000.

GUERNSEY

Located 50 km W of Normandy, France, Guernsey, together with its small island dependencies, is a crown dependency. Area: 78 sq km (30 sq mi). Pop. (1971): 53,700. Cap.: St. Peter Port (pop., 1971, 16,300).

Education. (1977–78) Primary and secondary, pupils 8,071, teachers 457.

Finance and Trade. Monetary unit: Guernsey pound, at par with the pound sterling. Budget (1976): revenue £22,127,000; expenditure £19,269,000. Foreign trade included with the United Kingdom. Main exports (1975): manufactures c. 49%; tomatoes c. 36%; flowers c. 14%. Tourism (1976) 296,000 visitors.

HONG KONG

The colony of Hong Kong lies on the southeastern coast of China about 60 km E of Macau and 130 km SE of Canton. Area: 1,050 sq km (405 sq mi). Pop. (1978 est.): 4,566,900. Cap.: Victoria (pop., 1976 census, 501,700).

Education. (1977–78) Primary, pupils 574,822, teachers 19,073; secondary, pupils 412,346; vocational, pupils 12,192; secondary and vocational, teachers 14,079; higher, students 23,372, teaching staff 3,216.

Finance. Monetary unit: Hong Kong dollar, with (Sept. 18, 1978) a free rate of HK$4.73 to U.S. $1 (HK$9.26 = £1 sterling). Budget (1977–78 est.): revenue HK$8,274,000,000; expenditure HK$8,-245,000,000.

Foreign Trade. (1977) Imports HK$48,701,-000,000; exports HK$44,833,000,000. Import sources: Japan 24%; China 17%; U.S. 13%; Taiwan 7%; Singapore 6%; U.K. 5%. Export destinations: U.S. 32%; West Germany 9%; U.K. 7%; Japan 6%. Main exports: clothing 32%; textile yarns and fabrics 9%; telecommunications apparatus 6%; watches and clocks 5%; plastic toys and dolls 5%. Tourism (1976): visitors 1,560,000; gross receipts U.S. $740 million.

Transport and Communications. Roads (1976) 1,085 km. Motor vehicles in use (1976): passenger 121,460; commercial 38,600. Railways: (1976) 33 km; traffic (1977) 280 million passenger-km, freight 49.2 million net ton-km. Shipping (1977): merchant vessels 100 gross tons and over 113; gross tonnage 609,679. Shipping traffic (1977): goods loaded 6,526,000 metric tons, unloaded 19,110,000 metric tons. Telephones (Jan. 1977) 1,132,400. Radio receivers (Dec. 1975) 2,505,000. Television receivers (Dec. 1975) 857,000.

ISLE OF MAN

The Isle of Man, a crown dependency, lies in the Irish Sea approximately 55 km from both Northern Ireland and the coast of northwestern England. Area: 572 sq km (221 sq mi). Pop. (1977 est.): 61,-000. Cap.: Douglas (pop., 1976 census, 20,300).

Education. (1977–78) Primary, pupils 5,771; secondary, pupils 3,935; vocational, pupils 3,350.

Finance and Trade. Monetary unit: Isle of Man pound, at par with the pound sterling. Budget (1976–77): revenue £31.8 million; expenditure £30.8 million. Foreign trade included with the United Kingdom. Main exports: beef and lamb, fish, livestock. Tourism (1977) 451,300 visitors.

JERSEY

The island of Jersey, a crown dependency, is located about 30 km W of Normandy, France. Area: 117 sq km (45 sq mi). Pop. (1971): 72,600. Cap.: St. Helier (pop., 1971, 28,100).

Education. (1976–77) Primary and secondary, pupils 12,600, teachers 670.

Finance. Monetary unit: Jersey pound, at par with the pound sterling. Budget (1976): revenue £55,168,000; expenditure £39,882,000.

Foreign Trade. (1976) Imports £122,562,000 (80% from U.K.); exports £49,015,000 (70% to U.K.). Main exports: potatoes 12%; motor vehicles 11%; knitted fabrics 10%; machinery 8%; musical instruments 7%; jewelry 7%; tomatoes 7%; chocolate preparations 6%. Tourism (1977): visitors 1,125,000; gross receipts U.S. $120 million.

MONTSERRAT

The colony of Montserrat is located in the Caribbean between Antigua, 43 km NE, and Guadeloupe, 60 km SE. Area: 102 sq km (40 sq mi). Pop. (1977 est.): 12,200. Cap.: Plymouth (pop., 1974 est., 3,000).

Education. (1976–77) Primary, pupils 2,353, teachers 905; secondary, pupils 701, teachers 49; vocational, pupils 50, teachers 7.

Finance and Trade. Monetary unit: East Caribbean dollar. Budget (1977 est.) balanced at ECar$8,-767,000 (including U.K. aid of ECar$1,860,000). Foreign trade (1976): imports ECar$20,803,000; exports ECar$1,122,000. Import sources: U.K. 31%; U.S. 18%; Trinidad and Tobago 13%; Canada 5%; West Germany 5%. Export destinations: Japan 28%; Trinidad and Tobago 14%; Guadeloupe c. 13%; Dominica 11%; Antigua 9%; St. Kitts-Nevis 6%. Main exports (domestic only): cotton 28%; potatoes 22%; cattle 13%; lime juice 8%; recapped tires 5%; tomatoes 5%.

PITCAIRN ISLAND

The colony of Pitcairn Island is in the central South Pacific, 5,150 km NE of New Zealand and 2,170 km SE of Tahiti. Area: 4.53 sq km (1.75 sq mi). Pop. (1977 census): 70, all of whom live in the de facto capital, Adamstown.

ST. HELENA

The colony of St. Helena, including its dependencies of Ascension Island and the Tristan da Cunha island group, is spread over a wide area of the Atlantic off the southwestern coast of Africa. Area: 412 sq km (159 sq mi). Pop. (1976 census): 5,100. Cap.: Jamestown (pop., 1976 census, 1,500).

Education. (1975–76) Primary, pupils 774; secondary, pupils 509; primary and secondary, teachers 68; teacher training, students 5, teachers 2.

Finance and Trade. Monetary unit: St Helena pound, at par with the pound sterling which is also used. Budget (1975–76 est.): revenue St.H£1,-482,000; expenditure St.H£1,544,000. Foreign trade (1975–76): imports St.H£1,192,000 (61% from U.K., 28% from South Africa in 1968); exports nil.

ST. KITTS-NEVIS

This associated state consists of the islands of St. Kitts and Nevis (Anguilla received a separate constitution in 1976). Area: 269 sq km (104 sq mi). Pop. (1977 est.): 49,700. Cap.: Basseterre, St. Kitts (pop., 1975 est., 16,800).

Education. (1977–78) Primary, pupils 8,900, teachers 339; secondary, pupils 5,305, teachers 316; vocational, pupils 120, teachers 21; higher, students 69, teaching staff 12.

Finance and Trade. Monetary unit: East Caribbean dollar. Budget (1977 rev. est.): revenue ECar$24 million; expenditure ECar$30 million. Foreign trade (1975): imports ECar$51.4 million; exports ECar$46.8 million. Import sources (including Anguilla; 1971): U.K. 35%; Puerto Rico 14%; U.S. 10%; Trinidad and Tobago 9%; Canada 8%. Export destinations (including Anguilla; 1971): U.K. 61%; Puerto Rico 22%. Main exports (including Anguilla; 1971): sugar 65%; electrical equipment 24%.

ST. LUCIA

The Caribbean island of St. Lucia, an associated state, lies 39 km S of Martinique and 34 km NE of St. Vincent. Area: 623 sq km (241 sq mi). Pop. (1977 est.): 115,500. Cap.: Castries (pop., 1970 census, 3,600).

Education. (1977–78) Primary, pupils 31,091, teachers 947; secondary, pupils 4,417, teachers 233; vocational, pupils 151, teachers 23; teacher training, students 149, teachers 14.

Finance and Trade. Monetary unit: East Caribbean dollar. Budget (1976 est.): revenue ECar$34,019,000; expenditure ECar$32,321,000. Foreign trade (1976): imports ECar$125,708,000; exports ECar$49,911,000. Import sources: U.K. 25%; U.S. 20%; Trinidad and Tobago 15%; Canada 12%. Export destinations: U.K. 45%; Leeward and Windward Islands 17%; Trinidad and Tobago 12%; Barbados 8%; Jamaica 5%. Main exports: bananas 42%; cardboard boxes 17%; coconut oil 10%; clothing 7%. Tourism (including cruise passengers; 1976) 125,500 visitors.

ST. VINCENT

St. Vincent, including the northern Grenadines, is an associated state in the eastern Caribbean about 160 km W of Barbados. Area: 389 sq km (150 sq mi). Pop. (1977 est.): 95,000. Cap.: Kingstown (pop., 1973 est., 22,000).

Education. (1974–75) Primary, pupils 26,122, teachers 1,098; secondary, pupils 4,638, teachers 161; vocational, pupils 97; teacher training, students 60, teachers (1971–72) 11.

Finance and Trade. Monetary unit: East Caribbean dollar. Budget (1977–78 est.) balanced at ECar$29 million. Foreign trade (1976): imports ECar$62,290,000; exports ECar$24,546,000. Import sources (1972): U.K. 28%; Trinidad and Tobago 17%; Canada 9%; U.S. 9%. Export destinations (1972): U.K. 61%; Barbados 15%; Trinidad and Tobago 11%; U.S. 6%. Main exports (1974): bananas 54%; arrowroot 6%.

TURKS AND CAICOS ISLANDS

The colony of the Turks and Caicos Islands is situated in the Atlantic southeast of The Bahamas. Area: 500 sq km (193 sq mi). Pop. (1977 est.): 6,000. Seat of government: Grand Turk Island (pop., 1970, 2,300).

Education. (1976–77) Primary, pupils 1,802, teachers 16; secondary, pupils 671, teachers 34.

Finance and Trade. Monetary unit: U.S. dollar. Budget (1977 est.) balanced at $4,364,000. Foreign trade (1976): imports $4,939,000; exports $1,609,000. Main exports (1974): crayfish 73%; conch meat 25%.

UNITED KINGDOM and FRANCE

NEW HEBRIDES

The British-French condominium of the New Hebrides is located in the southwestern Pacific about 800 km W of Fiji and 400 km NE of New Caledonia. Area: 11,870 sq km (4,583 sq mi). Pop. (1978 est.): 100,400. Cap.: Vila (metropolitan area pop., 1976 est., 17,400).

Education. (1978) Primary, pupils 11,540, teachers 540; secondary, pupils 958, teachers 59; vocational, pupils 283, teachers 33; teacher training, students 17, teachers 1.

Finance. Monetary units: Australian dollar and New Hebrides franc, with (Sept. 18, 1978) a parity of NHFr 16.16 to the French franc and a free rate of NHFr 70.73 = U.S. $1 (NHFr 138.59 = £1 sterling).

Condominium budget (1976 est.): revenue NHFr 872 million; expenditure NHFr 878 million. British budget (1974–75 est.): revenue A$4,450,000; expenditure A$4,221,000. French budget (1976 est.): revenue NHFr 1,496,000,000; expenditure NHFr 1,497,000,000.

Foreign Trade. (1977) Imports NHFr 3,146,000,000; exports NHFr 2,525,000,000. Import sources (1975): Australia 30%; France 25%; Japan 8%; New Caledonia 7%; U.K. 5%. Export destinations (1975): France 43%; U.S. 28%; Japan 15%; New Caledonia 8%. Main exports: copra 40%; fish 40%; manganese 6%; cocoa 5%.

Agriculture. Production (in 000; metric tons; 1976): copra c. 37; cocoa c. 1; fish catch c. 8. Livestock (in 000; 1976): cattle c. 110; pigs c. 64; chickens c. 131.

Industry. Production (in 000; 1975): manganese ore (metal content; exports; metric tons) 19; electricity (kw-hr) 15,000.

UNITED STATES

AMERICAN SAMOA

Located to the east of Western Samoa in the South Pacific, the unincorporated territory of American Samoa is approximately 2,600 km NE of the northern tip of New Zealand. Area: 197 sq km (76 sq mi). Pop. (1977 est.): 34,000. Cap.: Pago Pago (pop., 1974, 4,700).

Education. (1977) Primary, pupils 8,000; secondary, pupils 2,000; primary and secondary, teachers 410; higher, students 836, teaching staff (1971–72) 32.

Finance and Trade. Monetary unit: U.S. dollar. Budget (1976 rev. est.) balanced at $43.9 million (including U.S. federal grants of $40 million). Foreign trade (1976): imports (excluding fish for canneries) $51 million (74% from U.S., 10% from Japan in 1974); exports $65 million (95% to U.S. in 1970). Main exports: canned tuna 89%; watches 6%.

CANAL ZONE

The Canal Zone is administered by the U.S. under treaty with Panama and consists of a 16-km-wide strip on the Isthmus of Panama through which the Panama Canal runs. Area: 1,432 sq km (553 sq mi). Pop. (1977 est.): 38,000. Administrative headquarters: Balboa Heights (pop., 1970, 200).

Education. (1977) Primary and secondary, pupils 9,857, teachers 550; higher, students 1,333, teaching staff (1971) c. 120.

Finance. Monetary unit: U.S. dollar (Panamanian balboa is also used). Budgets (1977): Canal Zone government: revenue $80,850,000, expenditure $82,683,000; Panama Canal Company: revenue $289,363,000, expenditure $285,150,000.

Traffic. (1975–76) Total number of oceangoing vessels passing through the canal 12,157; total cargo tonnage 117,212,000; tolls collected U.S. $134 million. Nationality and number of commercial vessels using the canal: Liberian 1,777; British 1,285; U.S. 1,064; Japanese 1,008; Panamanian 930; Greek 885; Norwegian 685; West German 626; Swedish 332; Dutch 300.

GUAM

Guam, an organized unincorporated territory, is located in the Pacific Ocean about 9,700 km SW of San Francisco and 2,400 km E of Manila. Area: 549 sq km (212 sq mi). Pop. (1977 est.): 97,000. Cap.: Agana (pop., 1974 est., 2,500).

Education. (1976) Primary, pupils 24,600; secondary and vocational, pupils 8,500; primary and secondary, teachers 1,402; higher, students (1975) 3,800, teaching staff (1971–72) c. 140.

Finance. Monetary unit: U.S. dollar. Budget (1975 est.): revenue $117.3 million (including U.S. federal grants of $14.8 million); expenditure $126 million.

Foreign Trade. (1974) Imports $259 million; exports $20 million. Main exports: petroleum products, copra, watches, scrap metal. Tourism: visitors (1976) 205,000; gross receipts (1973) U.S. $90 million.

Agriculture and Industry. Production (in 000; metric tons; 1976): copra 1; eggs 1; fish catch 0.1;

petroleum products (1975) c. 1,100; electricity (kw-hr; 1975) c. 1,300,000.

PUERTO RICO

Puerto Rico, a self-governing associated commonwealth, lies about 1,400 km SE of the Florida coast. Area: 8,897 sq km (3,435 sq mi). Pop. (1977 est.): 3,303,000. Cap.: San Juan (pop., 1976 est., 1,125,000).

Education. (1977) Primary, pupils 520,000; secondary, pupils 158,000; primary and secondary, teachers 27,360; higher, students 100,885, teaching staff (1976) c. 1,042.

Finance. Monetary unit: U.S dollar. Budget (1975–76 actual): revenue $2,005,000,000; expenditure $1,901,000,000. Gross domestic product (1976–77) $9,717,000,000. Cost of living (1975 = 100; April 1978) 110.4.

Foreign Trade. (1976–77) Imports $6,108,000,000 (60% from U.S., 10% from Venezuela); exports $4,480,000,000 (86% to U.S.). Main exports (1974–75): chemicals 25%; petroleum products 14%; clothing 11%; machinery 11%; fish 8%. Tourism (1976–77): visitors 1,376,000; gross receipts $424 million.

Transport and Communications. Roads (1974) 16,827 km. Motor vehicles in use (1975): passenger 626,600; commercial 106,400. Railways (1976) 96 km. Telephones (Jan. 1977) 515,500. Radio receivers (Dec. 1975) 1,760,000. Television receivers (Dec. 1975) 630,000.

Agriculture. Production (in 000; metric tons; 1977): sugar, raw value 243; pumpkins (1976) 17; pineapples c. 38; bananas c. 113; oranges 32; coffee c. 12; tobacco (1976) 2; milk 437; fish catch (1976) 81. Livestock (in 000; Jan. 1976): cattle 562; pigs 269; poultry 4,969.

Industry. Production (in 000; metric tons; 1976): cement 1,390; beer (hl) 594; rum (hl) c. 730; petroleum products (1975) 9,143; electricity (kw-hr) c. 17,150,000.

TRUST TERRITORY OF THE PACIFIC ISLANDS

The Trust Territory islands, numbering more than 2,000, are scattered over 7,750,000 sq km in the Pacific Ocean from 720 km E of the Philippines to just west of the International Date Line. Area: 1,880 sq km (726 sq mi). Pop. (1976 est.): 126,000. Seat of government: Saipan Island (pop., 1972 est., 10,700).

Education. (1975–76) Primary, pupils 30,285, teachers 1,526; secondary, pupils 7,951, teachers 525; vocational, pupils 257, teachers (1973–74) 13.

Finance. Monetary unit: U.S. dollar. Budget (1975–76 est.): revenue $72,356,000 (including U.S. grant of $68.6 million); expenditure $61,841,000.

Foreign Trade. (1976) Imports c. $38 million (c. 50% from U.S., c. 27% from Japan in 1972); exports $4.8 million (54% to Japan in 1972). Main exports: fish 62%; copra 33%.

Agriculture. Production (in 000; metric tons; 1976): sweet potatoes c. 3; cassava c. 5; bananas c. 2; copra c. 8; fish catch 6. Livestock (in 000; June 1976): cattle c. 17; pigs c. 18; goats c. 7; chickens c. 170.

VIRGIN ISLANDS

The Virgin Islands of the United States is an organized unincorporated territory located about 60 km E of Puerto Rico. Area: 345 sq km (133 sq mi). Pop. (1976 est.): 95,000. Cap.: Charlotte Amalie, St. Thomas (pop., 1970, 12,200).

Education. (1977–78) Primary, pupils 16,639, teachers 847; secondary and vocational, pupils 15,426, teachers 792; higher, students 2,061, teaching staff 58.

Finance. Monetary unit: U.S. dollar. Budget (1975–76 est.): revenue $121 million; expenditure $113 million.

Foreign Trade. (1976) Imports $2,678,800,000; exports $2,010,200,000. Import sources: Iran 43%; Nigeria 14%; Qatar 10%; United Arab Emirates 9%; U.S. 8%; Libya 8%. Export destinations: U.S. 96%. Main export: petroleum products. Tourism: visitors (excluding cruise passengers; 1976) 539,000; gross receipts (1973) U.S. $100 million.

continued from page 303

December 13, but because of procedural difficulties independence was postponed to 1979. Economically, St. Lucia remained the most buoyant of the associated states, and work was proceeding rapidly on a U.S.-financed, $150 million oil transshipment facility. Elections were due by May 1979. Throughout 1978 the opposition, which opposed independence without elections, was split into moderate and radical factions, thereby playing into the hands of the government.

St. Vincent's prime minister, Milton Cato, broke up the coalition between his St. Vincent Labour Party and the People's Political Party over the question of independence. After a constitutional conference in London, a date of Jan. 21, 1979, was announced for independence, but it seemed unlikely that this could be achieved. The Marxist Youth Liberation Movement appeared to be gaining support among the young.

In an about-face, the Antiguan government announced late in 1978 that it had no intention of being the last associated state to achieve independence, now sought for 1979. The opposition, committed to independence even when Prime Minister Vere Bird's Antigua Labour Party opposed it, called for a general election to take place first. A new agreement was reached with the U.S. government whereby a rental would be paid for the use of military bases. A controversy developed over the possible shipment, through Antigua, of arms and other strategic equipment destined for South Africa, in contravention of the UN embargo.

Britain had suggested that Guatemala's claim to Belize (former British Honduras) might be resolved by the ceding of land, but this line was abandoned when it became clear that the Belize government would not accept such terms. The new Guatemalan regime seemed prepared to take a more conciliatory attitude toward the issue. In

June it was agreed that both the government and the opposition parties should participate in any further meetings. In late September all-party discussions were held in New York in an attempt to resolve the matter, and at the end of November Britain put forward new proposals.

Among the smaller British dependencies, Montserrat experienced labour difficulties with its civil servants over payment of a cost-of-living allowance. The Turks and Caicos government disagreed with the British governor over its desire to establish casinos; it was also involved in negotiations with the U.S. government over future rent for bases on the islands. In the Cayman Islands, construction began on a $138 million oil transshipment facility. The islands' legislature told a delegation from the UN Committee on Decolonization that it was happy to remain a dependency.

The British Virgin Islands also showed no desire for independence, nor did it wish to join the U.S. Virgin Islands (where Cyril Emanuel King, the second popularly elected governor of the territory, died on Jan. 2, 1978 [*see* OBITUARIES]). After the rioting of late 1977 in Bermuda, a royal commission was formed under Lord Pitt. Its recommendations included an end to what was, to all purposes, a system of racial discrimination, as well as a move to full independence. Discussions to that end began in late 1978. Despite continuing local agitation for a stronger regional identity for the French Antilles, Guadeloupe and Cayenne both returned members of France's right-wing majority Rassemblement pour la République (RPR) to Paris in the French elections in March, thereby rejecting autonomy. In Cayenne the abstention rate was 40.3%, suggesting a widespread feeling of electoral impotence. In Martinique, where the elections were marred by pre-election violence, veteran autonomist Aimé Céssaire managed to hold his own. Generally, the French Antilles' economies re-

Demonstrators protested the Panama Canal treaties when U.S. President Carter visited the Canal Zone in June.

Mourners bid farewell to Clemens Kapuuo, leader of the Democratic Turnhalle Alliance, in Namibia (South West Africa) in April. Kapuuo was considered a prime candidate to be the territory's first black president.

mained depressed, with unemployment possibly reaching 35%.

In the Netherlands Antilles, all six islands showed leanings toward independence. Aruba voted by referendum for separate independence, but the Dutch government would agree only to its independence within a federation.

The UN Decolonization Committee's resolution on Puerto Rico called for either full independence or a form of the existing commonwealth association with the U.S. However, the results of an October primary election suggested that many Puerto Ricans would prefer statehood. Controversy over the future of the Panama Canal Zone ended when the U.S. Senate ratified two treaties between the U.S. and Panama providing for the zone's permanent neutrality. The U.S. was to relinquish the canal by the year 2000, and both signatories reserved the right to act against any interference with the canal's operation and to send warships through it. (*See* PANAMA.)

Africa. Negotiations for elections and the framework of a constitution for an independent Namibia (South West Africa) took place during the year between South Africa and five Western member states of the UN, which recognized the insurgent South West Africa People's Organization (SWAPO) and held discussions with it. In October an agreement was reached envisaging free elections under UN supervision in 1979. In the meantime, however, South Africa decided to go ahead with elections for representatives of the Namibian ethnic groups and their parties in December 1978 without UN supervision. These elections were not recognized by the UN and were boycotted by SWAPO, whose external wing, led by Sam Nujoma, continued its guerrilla activities. A major disagreement between South Africa and the UN concerned the former's unwillingness to hand over the Walvis Bay area, with South West Africa's only deepwater port, to Namibia. (*See* SOUTH AFRICA.)

The support of somewhat artificial separatist groups by the Organization of African Unity (OAU), Libya, and the U.S.S.R. was apparent in the Canary Islands. In April Col. Muammar al-Qaddafi of Libya asserted that all islands around Africa (including even Madeira and the Azores, St. Helena, and Ascension) should be forcibly "liberated" from Britain, France, Spain, and Portugal. Spain declared that the Canaries were "not negotiable." A Marxist separatist movement, supported by the OAU, committed several bombings in the islands in January. The separatist leader, Antonio Cubillo, was stabbed and seriously wounded on April 5. In June it was reported that the Spanish government would spend 28.6 billion pesetas on public works in the Canary Islands, including the construction of a naval base on Grand Canary and airport improvement on Tenerife.

Under threat from Morocco and the OAU were the Spanish coastal territories in North Africa, Ceuta and Melilla. The Polisario Front continued its inconclusive guerrilla struggle in what had been Spanish Sahara, ceded by Spain to Morocco and Mauritania early in 1976. To the anger of Morocco, it secured recognition from Spain's Democratic Centre Union Party (the core of the Spanish government) and offered Mauritania's new government a truce in July. (*See* MAURITANIA; MOROCCO.)

Indian Ocean. On May 22 voters on Mayotte Island in the Comoros rejected membership in the Federal and Islamic Republic of the Comoros and confirmed the inhabitants' desire to remain integrally associated with France. The French Navy used Mayotte's deepwater harbour and was linked with the French air base on Réunion. In 1973 France had occupied five small islands off Madagascar, four of them in the Mozambique Channel, and by a decree of Feb. 3, 1978, it declared a 200-mi exclusive economic zone round its Indian Ocean possessions, including these islands. On March 21 Madagascar protested their inclusion in the zone. A conference in the Seychelles on April 27, attended by representatives of the governments of Madagascar, the Comoros, and Seychelles and of left-wing movements in Mauritius and Réunion, called for the dismantling of all military bases in the Indian Ocean.

Pacific. Independence for the British colony of the Gilbert Islands was postponed to 1979 as a result of the dispute over Ocean Island (Banaba) phosphates and the future of the Banabans. Ocean Island phosphate had been the chief support of the Gilbert Islands economy, but the Banabans wished to become an associated state of Fiji. In 1978 newly elected Banaban leaders indicated that they would accept an A$10 million ex gratia payment from the U.K., Australia, and New Zealand—the partners in the British Phosphate Commission—for environmental damage to the island. In March elections in the Gilberts, Naboua Ratieta's government was defeated and a new ministry was formed under the leadership of Jeremiah Tabai, aged 28. Tabai emphasized rural development and abolition of the controversial Defense Force. A fisheries agreement signed with Japan was expected to earn between A$600,000 and A$1 million annually. In February talks were held with the U.S. to resolve disagreements over the sovereignty of some of the Line and Phoenix islands.

In the British-French condominium of the New Hebrides, Walter Lini's majority Vanuaaku Party had boycotted the 1977 general election in protest over the slow progress toward independence and then declared a "people's provisional government." The official government, which clearly lacked public credibility, achieved limited internal self-government in January 1978.

In the French elections in March, New Caledonia and French Polynesia both returned one government and one opposition deputy to Paris. In New Caledonia's elections, held late in 1977, 495 candidates had contested 35 seats in four constituencies. Full independence became an election issue, and about one-third of the successful candidates favoured it. New Caledonia still had not achieved internal self-government; in particular, the nickel industry, the 200-mi exclusive economic zone, and financial policy were French responsibilities. An unprecedented 24-hour general strike was called by the trade unions on June 13 to protest economic conditions. In July Paul Dijoud, the French secretary for overseas territories, indicated that new development policies would be forthcoming and showed more sympathy toward the aspirations of the underprivileged, especially

the Kanaks living on reserves. The Kanak Liberation Party continued to grow. With some self-government given by the 1977 statute, French Polynesia's leaders were trying to reduce economic dependence on France.

In general elections held March 30 in the self-governing New Zealand territory of the Cook Islands, the government of Sir Albert Henry was returned for the fifth time since 1965, and Tom Davis, leader of the opposition, lost his seat. Subsequently, an inquiry found that the prime minister had misused NZ$337,000 in philatelic revenue to provide charter flights from New Zealand for his supporters (there was no provision for absentee votes). Henry and seven other members from constituencies where the fly-in vote had been decisive were dismissed on July 25; a further seat was declared vacant; and Davis was sworn in as prime minister. Davis later announced that absentee votes would be permitted in future elections. Elections in Niue in March saw the return of the longtime prime minister Robert Rex.

Early in 1978 the Norfolk Island Council unilaterally issued a draft constitution for self-government in free association with Australia. In May Australia announced that it would not assume direct control over the island. After integrationist candidates were defeated in council elections, negotiations began with a view to handing budgetary control to a legislative assembly in July 1979. Agreement was reached between John Clunies Ross and the Australian government for the latter to buy the Cocos Islands for A$6,250,000. Australia had had sovereignty over the islands, but the Clunies Ross family had owned the land since the mid-19th century.

In a July 1978 referendum, four Micronesian districts of the Trust Territory of the Pacific Islands—Kosrae, Ponape, Truk, and Yap—supported the proposed constitution for the Federated States of Micronesia, while two—Palau and the Marshalls—already involved in negotiations for a separate future—voted against it. The other district, the Northern Marianas, was scheduled to gain full commonwealth status in association with the U.S. in 1981, when the trusteeship agreement with the

Bikini Atoll, which was abandoned in 1946 after nuclear tests were conducted there, was abandoned again in September 1978 when it was discovered that radiation levels were still too high for human habitation.

UPI COMPIX

UN was terminated. Bikini Atoll, the site of U.S. nuclear tests from 1947 to 1958, was again found to be unsafe for habitation because of radiation levels. The settlers, who had been permitted to return after the island was declared safe in 1969, were removed once again.

The Congress of Micronesia reached a compromise with the U.S. over the use of its 200-mi exclusive economic zone; in particular, highly migratory species of tuna were excluded from zonal control. On Jan. 3, 1978, Peter T. Coleman was sworn in as American Samoa's first elected governor, ushering in internal self-government.

East Asia. An anticorruption drive within Hong Kong's police force resulted in the compulsory retirement of 118 policemen. China was buying land in Hong Kong's New Territories, and economic links between China and Hong Kong continued to expand. In spite of protectionist policies in the colony's export markets, a growth of 9% in its gross national product in 1978 was predicted.

At Britain's behest, negotiations were undertaken in June between the British government and the sultan of Brunei, a British protectorate, looking toward independence in 1983. Malaysia and Indonesia assured the sultan that they would recognize the independence of his wealthy oil state.

(DAVID A. JESSOP; BARRIE MACDONALD; MOLLY MORTIMER)

See also African Affairs; Commonwealth of Nations; United Nations.

Djibouti

An independent republic in northeastern Africa, Djibouti is bordered by Ethiopia, Somalia, and the Gulf of Aden. Area: 23,000 sq km (8,900 sq mi). Pop. (1978 est.): 242,000, most of whom are Cushitic Afars or Somali Issas; there are smaller Arabic and European communities. Capital: Djibouti (pop., 1976 est., 120,000). Language: Arabic and French (official); Saho-Afar and Somali are spoken in their respective communities. Religion: predominantly Muslim. President in 1978, Hassan Gouled Aptidon; primiers, Abdallah Mohamed Kamil from February 5 and Barkat Gourat Hamadou from October 2.

Following the December 1977 resignation of Premier Ahmed Dini Ahmed because of disagreements over the policies of Pres. Hassan Gouled Aptidon, Abdallah Mohamed Kamil became premier on Feb. 5, 1978. In September the president dissolved the Kamil government, and on October 2 the country's third executive since independence was formed under Barkat Gourat Hamadou.

The internal situation remained tense after the terrorist acts that had caused the deaths of six French nationals on Dec. 15, 1977. In January the president spoke out against subversive intrigues aimed at reviving tribal confrontations between Afars and Issas, but the two ethnic groups remained hostile. In May a French technical adviser was taken hostage by an Afar opposition group and held for some days before being released. In July Somali guerrillas attacked the Addis Ababa-

---

DJIBOUTI
Education. (1975–76) Primary, pupils 9,764, teachers 268; secondary, pupils 1,398, teachers 85; vocational, pupils 560, teachers 59; teacher training, students 36, teachers 4.
Finance. Monetary unit: Djibouti franc, with (Sept. 18, 1978) a free rate of DjFr 163 to U.S. $1 (DjFr 320 = £1 sterling). Budget (1978 est.) balanced at DjFr 9,650,000,-000.
Foreign Trade. (1973) Imports DjFr 12,675,060,000; exports DjFr 3,498,540,000. Import sources: France 49%; Ethiopia 12%; Japan 6%; U.K. 6%. Export destinations: France 84%. Main exports: ships and boats 16%; leather and shoes 7%.

Djibouti railway, which had come back into service on June 7, and temporarily halted traffic.

France maintained about 350 technicians and advisers in the country and more than 4,000 military personnel (supported, after September, by Mirage III aircraft). In April and June President Gouled met French Pres. Valéry Giscard d'Estaing in Paris, and in October Djibouti announced its adherence to the Paris-based agency for cultural and technical cooperation among French-speaking states. During November 7–14 a major volcanic eruption 750 mi west of Djibouti was watched by scientists. It was typical of ocean-rift vulcan activity, though it took place on land, in a volcanic rift area. Lava covered a square-mile surface.

(PHILIPPE DECRAENE)

Djibouti

Dominica

Dominica

A republic within the Commonwealth of Nations, Dominica, an island of the Lesser Antilles in the Caribbean Sea, lies between Guadeloupe to the north and Martinique to the south. Area: 772 sq km (300 sq mi). Pop. (1977 est.): 80,000. Cap. Roseau (pop., 1978 est., 16,800). Acting chief of state in 1978, Sir Louis Cools-Lartigue; prime minister, Patrick R. John.

Dominica's ruling party, the Dominica Labour Party, led the island out of associated statehood and into independence on Nov. 3, 1978, under a republican constitution. The island's opposition Freedom Party opposed the move on the grounds that an election or referendum should have been held first. Though Prime Minister Patrick R. John (*see* BIOGRAPHIES) had previously indicated that the government would ensure "that natural resources are locally owned and controlled" under a policy termed "New Socialism," it was clear that by October a drive had begun to attract foreign private investors and aid from Western sources. To

---

DOMINICA
Education. (1977–78) Primary, pupils 18,415, teachers 467; secondary, pupils 5,895, teachers 237; vocational, pupils 351, teachers 15; higher, students 50, teachers 6.
Finance and Trade. Monetary unit: East Caribbean dollar, with (Sept. 18, 1978) an official rate of ECar$2.70 to U.S. $1 (free rate of ECar$5.30 = £1 sterling). Budget (1976–77 est.): revenue ECar$28,517,000; expenditure ECar$30,984,-000. Foreign trade (1976): imports ECar$49.8 million; exports ECar$29.1 million. Import sources (1975): U.K. 30%; U.S. 10%; Canada 10%. Export destinations (1975) U.K. 78%. Main exports (1975): bananas 58%; grapefruit 11%.

Disasters:
see page 56

Disciples of Christ:
see Religion

Diseases:
see Health and Disease

Divorce:
see Demography

The small British colony of Dominica achieved independence in November. The 18th-century Anglican church is in Roseau, capital of the new country.

DOMINICAN REPUBLIC
Education. (1976–77) Primary, pupils 903,521, teachers 17,932; secondary, pupils 136,570, teachers 4,417; vocational, pupils 5,326, teachers 299; teacher training, students 1,353, teachers 49; higher, students 42,395, teaching staff 429.
Finance. Monetary unit: peso, at parity with the U.S. dollar, with a free rate (Sept. 18, 1978) of 1.96 peso to £1 sterling. Gold, SDR's, and foreign exchange (June 1978) U.S. $115.1 million. Budget (1977 actual): revenue 629.3 million pesos; expenditure 625.9 million pesos. Gross national product (1976) 3,791,100,000 pesos. Money supply (May 1978) 458.3 million pesos. Cost of living (Santo Domingo; 1975 = 100; May 1978) 125.9.
Foreign Trade. (1977) Imports 991.7 million pesos; exports 780.4 million pesos. Import sources: U.S. *c.* 50%; Japan *c.* 9%. Export destinations: U.S. 73%; Switzerland 7%; The Netherlands 6%. Main exports: sugar 30%; coffee 24%; cocoa 12%; ferronickel 12%.
Transport and Communications. Roads (1975) 11,844 km. Motor vehicles in use (1976): passenger 77,300; commercial (including buses) 39,400. Railways (including sugar estates; 1976) *c.* 1,700 km. Telephones (Jan. 1977) 127,300. Radio receivers (Dec. 1975) 190,000. Television receivers (Dec. 1975) 158,000.
Agriculture. Production (in 000; metric tons; 1977): rice *c.* 277; corn (1976) *c.* 49; sweet potatoes (1976) *c.* 89; cassava (1976) *c.* 162; sugar, raw value *c.* 1,361; dry beans *c.* 32; tomatoes *c.* 97; peanuts *c.* 62; oranges *c.* 70; avocados (1976) *c.* 131; mangoes *c.* 167; bananas *c.* 310; cocoa *c.* 37; coffee *c.* 60; tobacco *c.* 27. Livestock (in 000; June 1976): cattle *c.* 1,950; sheep *c.* 51; pigs *c.* 821; goats *c.* 355; horses *c.* 174; chickens *c.* 7,400.
Industry. Production (in 000; metric tons; 1976): cement 660; bauxite 621; petroleum products *c.* 1,400; electricity (kw-hr) *c.* 2,690,000.

this end the prime minister, in the face of sharp criticism, visited the U.K., France, the European Economic Community headquarters in Brussels, and Venezuela. The U.K. government agreed in October to provide aid funds on independence amounting to £11 million in the form of grants, interest-free loans, and balance of payments support. The island's government had hoped for approximately £40 million. The government announced its intention to reestablish a sugar industry to satisfy domestic demand.

The island continued to experience balance of payments difficulties and remained almost totally reliant on exports of bananas and grapefruit. Unemployment amounted to at least 20% and illiteracy 70%, making Dominica one of the least developed nations in the Caribbean.

(DAVID A. JESSOP)

Dominican Republic

Covering the eastern two-thirds of the Caribbean island of Hispaniola, the Dominican Republic is separated from Haiti, which occupies the western third, by a rugged mountain range. Area: 48,442 sq km (18,704 sq mi). Pop. (1978 est.): 5,657,000, including (1960) mulatto 73%; white 16%; Negro 11%. Cap. and largest city: Santo Domingo (pop.,

Dominican Republic

1977 est., 1 million). Language: Spanish. Religion: mainly Roman Catholic (94%), with Protestant and Jewish minorities. Presidents in 1978, Joaquín Balaguer and, from August 16, Antonio Guzmán Fernández.

Presidential elections took place on May 16, 1978, after 12 years of uninterrupted rule by Pres. Joaquín Balaguer, leader of the Partido Reformista (PR), but the count was stopped the next day by the military. The count was subsequently resumed

"Of course it's an honest election; the ballot box is locked, isn't it?"

following international protest, and on July 8 Antonio Guzmán Fernández (*see* Biographies) was proclaimed winner with 868,496 votes against 716,358 for Balaguer.

The Electoral Board awarded four disputed Senate seats to the PR, with the effect that the PR continued to control the Senate with a 16–11 majority over Guzmán's party, the Partido Revolucionario Dominicano.

After taking office in August, President Guzmán, in a move to depoliticize the military, dismissed the leading generals who had supported Balaguer. He then promoted a new hierarchy of officers who would be concerned primarily with professional duties. An amnesty law was passed in September under which about 200 political prisoners were released and a number of exiles returned to the country.

African swine fever broke out in the southwest in June, and it was speculated that every pig in the country, including the wild ones, would have to be slaughtered. Sugarcane planted over several thousand acres was affected by a fungal disease, and up to one million metric tons were expected to be lost through drought, pests, and disease. These natural problems, together with low world prices, threatened the nation with reduced earnings from its agricultural exports.   (SARAH CAMERON)

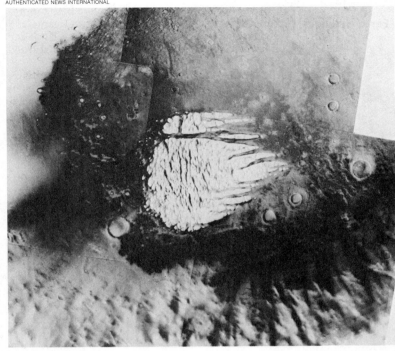

An unusual formation on Mars named "White Rock" was photographed by Viking Orbiter in September. This highly reflective feature in the bottom of a large crater is about 14 × 18 kilometres (8.5 × 11 miles) in size.

Earth Sciences

GEOLOGY AND GEOCHEMISTRY

During the last 20 years international programs have provided the stimulus for many research developments. The International Geophysical Year of 1957–58 established the mechanisms for international cooperation. The Upper Mantle Project of the 1960s was at first organized by disciplines. With the formulation of the global theory of plate tectonics, however, disciplinary and geographic boundaries became unimportant, and the International Geodynamics Project of the 1970s was able to focus on regional problems of earth dynamics. This project, scheduled to end in 1979, leaves a record of remarkable scientific achievement. Because of the success of these programs, national and international committees have been developing plans for a new, international, interdisciplinary project in solid-earth science for implementation during the 1980s.

New Programs. Committee meetings, workshops, and symposia conducted in the United States under the aegis of the U.S. Geodynamics Committee attempted to define a scientific focus for a new program. A subject that presented itself strongly was a detailed examination of crustal processes. Plate tectonics theory (the theory that the Earth's crust consists of rigid plates floating on a viscous underlayer in the mantle) has emphasized the oceanic crust, and there remains much to be learned about the application of the theory to the more complex continental crust. An understanding of crustal evolution has direct bearing on many problems of economic and societal importance, including identification of favourable environments for the concentration of coal, oil, and minerals. This activity led to the production in 1978 of a draft document, "Crustal Dynamics: A Framework for Resource Systems," which was being reviewed and modified by many scientists for presentation to the International Council of Scientific Unions (ICSU).

The International Union of Geological Sciences (IUGS) and the International Union of Geodesy and Geophysics (IUGG) also were preparing plans for consideration by the ICSU. The IUGS proposal, in draft form, was entitled "The Lithosphere: Frontier for the 1980s." The central theme of this proposed program was the current state, dynamics, origin, and evolution of the lithosphere, the upper 70–100 km (43–60 mi) of the Earth. Special attention would be devoted to the continental lithosphere but with due consideration for research on the deeper parts of the Earth that influence the behaviour of the lithosphere. Two special goals were the strengthening of interactions between basic research and applications and the strengthening of the Earth sciences in less developed countries, which contain many of the mineral resources needed by the rest of the world.

Suboceanic Mining. The first attempt to mine the deep ocean floor for manganese nodules was under way in the central Pacific Ocean, about 1,600 km (1,000 mi) SE of Hawaii, under the management of an international consortium of mining companies (U.S., Canada, West Germany, and Japan). The potato-sized rocks were collected from a depth of more than 5 km (3 mi) with a hydraulic pump, then separated from other material that was dropped back to the seafloor, and finally lifted to the drilling ship. The nodules were to be processed at an experimental plant in Ontario for manganese and possibly for nickel, copper, and cobalt.

Drama:
see Motion Pictures; Theatre

Dress:
see Fashion and Dress

Earthquakes:
see Earth Sciences

The effects of the test mining were being monitored by scientists from the National Oceanic and Atmospheric Administration (NOAA). They planned to observe the effect of the discarded materials on the ocean floor.

Lunar and Planetary Science. A surprising discovery was made about isotope abundances in meteorites. Small inclusions in the Allende meteorite contain oxygen with an unusual composition of isotopes. The isotope ratios do not correspond to those expected if the original solar nebula had been chemically homogeneous, as previously supposed. Correlated isotopic anomalies were then discovered in all elements measured to date: magnesium, silicon, calcium, strontium, barium, neodymium, and samarium. The current interpretation of this geochemistry is that the solar system condensed from a mixture of interstellar gas and dust that was disturbed by the shock wave from a supernova explosion. Some of the material ejected by the exploding star was incorporated into the solar nebula and is represented by the meteorite inclusions with anomalous isotopes.

The topic of "Industry in Space" became a feature at the annual lunar science conferences because, at some scale of activity, it must prove more economical to manufacture space structures from materials extracted from the Moon or from asteroids than to manufacture and launch completed satellites from the Earth. Research and analysis of proposed schemes for the extraction and processing of lunar rocks paralleled the consideration of plans for the construction of large power stations in space.

Martian Channels and the Channeled Scablands. The origin of the large channels photographed on Mars by Mariner and Viking spacecraft developed into a topic of considerable debate during the year. Hypotheses included erosion by water, wind, lava, or mudflows. Because there are different classes of channels, scientists believed that there may be different origins. Many of the features, however, most closely resemble

fluvial channels, those produced by water. The reluctance of some investigators to accept a fluvial origin stems from the great size of the channels and the lack of liquid water on Mars today.

In connection with this debate the Channeled Scablands of eastern Washington were reexamined for comparison with the features on Mars. Many features are analogous in form and size in both locations. There is irony in this comparison, because the origin of the Scablands by flooding remained controversial for 50 years after the hypothesis was first proposed in 1923. In 1973, however, paleohydraulic and hydrodynamic studies confirmed the internal consistency between the morphological features of the region and catastrophic flooding. Thus, the Channeled Scablands provide a testing ground for Mars.

High-Pressure Geochemistry. Experimental studies of minerals and rocks at high pressures and temperatures have provided a means for elucidating the processes of origin of many rocks and for calibrating the conditions of depth and temperature that existed during these processes. The range of pressures and temperatures routinely reproduced in the laboratory corresponds to conditions through the crust and down to a depth of about 150 km (95 mi) in the mantle. This range was being extended by scientists in Japan and the U.S.S.R. through the development of massive high-pressure apparatus. An important advance involved the capability for X-ray analysis of samples at high pressures and temperatures while they are within the apparatus.

In the U.S. recent developments centred on the diamond-anvil high-pressure cell. A sample of rock squeezed between two small diamond anvils can be heated by a laser beam to 2,000° C at pressures that are calibrated by observing the spectral shift of a ruby fluorescence line as pressures are increased. It was reported that in a specially designed diamond-anvil cell a steady pressure of 1.7 megabars (25.2×10^6 psi) was achieved, three times higher than any pressure measured before

A Philippine farmer hurriedly harvests his rice as a volcano (background) began erupting.

and greater than that at the core-mantle boundary of the Earth (1.5 megabars). Changes in the physical state of the sample (such as from solid to liquid) can be observed with a microscope through the clear diamond, and a variety of spectroscopic, X-ray, and electrical measurements can be made at the site. The experiments will permit study of the mineralogy, changes of physical state, and properties of material within the Earth to depths of the mantle-core boundary.

Rock-Water Interactions. Many geologic processes involve the interaction between rocks and aqueous solutions. There has been a surge of interest in topics such as interaction between seafloor rocks and seawater, the movement of material by means of heated water in continental and ocean crust as a source of mineral concentrations, solutions of rock and hot water as a source of geothermal energy, and the problems of pollution of groundwater. New programs were beginning to investigate the chemical dynamics of natural rock-water systems where equilibrium is temporary and local.

Soviet geochemists have worked with the theory of metasomatism for many years, and during the year activity began in the U.S. Metasomatism is the change in the chemical composition and physical texture of rocks. Recently geochemists have developed models that provide a basis for calculating the conditions of formation of mineral zones in metasomatic sequence, which influences the origin of many ore deposits.   (PETER JOHN WYLLIE)

[133.A.4.d; 133.C.1.d; 213.A.1–2; 213.D.2; 231.D.1; 232.A.1]

GEOPHYSICS

An exceptionally tragic earthquake in Iran caused the death of an estimated 25,000 persons and left thousands homeless. The shock occurred on Sept. 16, 1978, at latitude 33.3° N, longitude 57.4° E near the town of Tabas and had a magnitude on the Richter scale of 7.7. Other earthquakes that caused fatalities or were of notable size included a magnitude 7.4 shock on Oct. 10, 1977, south of the Fiji Islands and a magnitude 7.5 shock on June 12, 1978, off the coast of Honshu, Japan. The Japanese event caused 22 deaths and produced minor seismic waves.

Several smaller but destructive earthquakes occurred during the year. On Nov. 23, 1977, near Caucete, Arg., a shock of magnitude 7.0 killed nearly 100 and left 20,000 homeless, and on Dec. 19, 1977, a magnitude 5.5 shock in Iran left 589 dead and 4,000 without shelter. On Aug. 3, 1978, a quake of magnitude 7.0 near Copiapo, Chile, caused considerable damage, and on August 13 one beneath the Santa Barbara Channel off California caused $12 million–$15 million in damage in Santa Barbara and Goleta, including a spectacular freight train derailment.

During the year more than 20 volcanoes erupted in various parts of the world, including Tonga, Réunion, Nicaragua, Iceland, Japan, New Zealand, Papua New Guinea, and the Philippines. None was especially severe, although many of the disturbances, such as those at Fuego in Guatemala, Usu in Japan, and White Island in New Zealand, continued for several months.

Research in seismology received a major in-

The devastation of an earthquake was deeply felt in Iran. On September 16, 25,000 persons were killed and thousands more left homeless.

crease in funding with the passage by the U.S. Congress of the Earthquake Hazards Reduction Act in October 1977. Two federal agencies, the National Science Foundation and the Geological Survey, received a total of $55 million in fiscal 1978 to expand research in earthquake hazards reduction. This represented a twofold increase over the previous budgets for those agencies in that field of research. Under the act, funds were scheduled to increase to $70 million in fiscal 1979 and $80 million in fiscal 1980. Research included investigation of the basic causes and mechanisms of earthquakes, development of prediction techniques, inducement of earthquakes by fluid injection, evaluation of methods for controlling or modifying earthquakes, and development of information and guidelines for estimating seismic risk to be used in zoning and disaster preparedness planning. In addition, studies were to be made in the fields of earthquake-resistant structural design and the political and social impact of specific regulations and warning systems.

Another extensive program of research aimed at identifying causative factors of earthquakes in the eastern United States was that of the U.S. Nuclear Regulatory Commission. The design of every nuclear power plant facility must meet stringent criteria to ensure against failure due to environmental accidents such as earthquakes, tornadoes, hurricanes, or floods. To provide more exact information upon which to base seismic criteria for specific sites, the commission established a program of seismic monitoring by means of which more than 200 seismic listening posts were operated on contract throughout the eastern U.S. The information gathered at the posts was correlated with geologic, geomagnetic, and gravitational field data to provide more refined estimates of seismic risk.

During the year a scientist associated with NOAA and the University of Colorado reported that the destructive earthquakes at Long Beach, Calif., in 1933; at Hyuganada, Japan, in 1961 and 1968; and off the coast of Peru in 1970, which was responsible for 66,800 deaths, were all preceded by periods of rapid uplift. The uplifts ranged from 6 to 12 cm and occurred at least three years prior to the shocks. Further research was recommended to determine whether this phenomenon is a true precursor of major earthquakes.

The Consortium for Continental Reflection Profiling (Cocorp) completed a survey of the Rio Grande Rift near Socorro, N.M. This was part of a continent-wide program of subsurface mapping sponsored by the U.S. Geodynamics Project. The survey was accomplished by the application of sophisticated continuous seismic reflection techniques using 37 geophones 134 m apart to measure signals from a system of in-line vibrators. This resulted in a high-resolution subsurface map, which is necessary for a better understanding of tectonic mechanisms in the lower crust and upper mantle.

A scientist at the University of Arizona found a definite inverse relationship between the strength of the geomagnetic field and the amount of carbon-14 in the atmosphere, and in a corroborative finding a scientist from Lamont Geological Obser-

vatory indicated that changes in the magnetic field are inversely related to the temperature. The preliminary conclusion was that global weather changes can be correlated with predicted changes in the Earth's magnetic field.

(RUTLAGE J. BRAZEE)

[213.B and D]

HYDROLOGY

During the past year several major technical symposia concentrated on topics of current hydrologic concern. The National Water Well Association and the U.S. Environmental Protection Agency sponsored the National Ground Water Quality Symposium in Minneapolis, Minn., to discuss groundwater pollution and groundwater protection policies. A two-day symposium at the annual meeting of the American Chemical Society in Miami Beach, Fla., highlighted past and present research in water chemistry and effects of radioactive waste disposal on water resources. At the American Water Resources Association meeting in Florida three symposia dealt with the interrelationship of energy, environment, and economics.

In an environmental message to Congress in June 1978, U.S. Pres. Jimmy Carter announced his intention to reform national water policy by encouraging increased water conservation and improving floodplain management. His policy message had the following objectives: improved planning and management of federal water-resource programs; increased national emphasis on water conservation; enhanced federal-state cooperation in the development of water policy; and increased attention to environmental quality. Nineteen task forces were established to implement the president's water policy.

In 1978 the U.S. experienced above-average streamflow in its five largest rivers—the Mississippi, St. Lawrence, Columbia, Ohio, and Missouri. The flow was striking when compared with that in 1977, when the combined flow of the five rivers averaged about 24% below normal. Also, the record-breaking drought that lasted nearly three years in some areas of the western U.S. came to an end during 1978, and runoff from a near-record snowpack filled most major reservoirs.

During 1978 major flooding that resulted in loss of life and large property damage occurred in California, Nebraska, Arizona, Indiana, Montana, Wisconsin, Texas, Wyoming, and Alabama. Flooding in February caused about $80 million in property damage in southern California and in March about $240 million in property damage in eastern Nebraska. Flash flooding in August in the Hill Country of south-central Texas caused losses of about $63 million.

The upgrading of municipal sewage-treatment plants, improved industrial abatement programs, and other cleanup programs had improved water-quality conditions in Lake Michigan, Lake Ontario, and Lake Erie. The Great Lakes Water Quality Board of the U.S. and Canada International Joint Commission reported reduced phosphorus concentrations in the Great Lakes and declining mercury levels in Lake Erie.

Two important initiatives were undertaken un-

In 1977 the Nicasio reservoir in Marin County, California, resembled a parched desert (far left). Rains during early 1978 filled the reservoir to overflowing and water began flowing down spillways.

der UN sponsorship in 1978, the Anti-desertification Program and the Hydrological Decade for Drinking Water and Sanitation. The former was to deal with the dry areas of the world, particularly on the borders of the major deserts, that have become increasingly incapable of supporting life because of natural or man-made causes. The "Drinking Water Decade" was scheduled to begin in 1980 and had as a goal the development of an adequate potable water supply and sanitary facilities for all the world's people by 1990.

(JOHN E. MOORE)

[222.A.2; 232.A.3; 232.C.1–2]

METEOROLOGY

Research and development in meteorology during 1978 focused largely on new evidence concerning the vagaries of the Earth's climate, the increasing effect on it of man-made factors, and on mechanical and mathematical methods for analyzing meteorological data in hopes that they would lead to an "exact" physical science of weather. Among the methods were the automation of field operations and services, high-capacity, ultrahigh-speed electronic computers for mathematical weather prediction, and space satellites. These tools were also essential for research into the limitations of weather modification and the broader investigations conducted under the Global Weather Experiment (GWE) and its parent program, the Global Atmospheric Research Program (GARP). The latter was by far the most ambitious scientific study ever undertaken of the mechanics of the Earth's atmo-

sphere. Scientists hoped that it eventually would provide worldwide data to permit analysis of global weather patterns and provide a scientific basis for deciding how far in the future it is possible to predict weather.

Every year enormous loss of life and destruction of property adds determination to man's search for solutions to problems of severe storms and other adverse weather. During 1978 this was again dramatized by tragedies resulting from crippling snowstorms in Great Britain and many places in western Europe and by a second consecutive severe winter, this time with especially heavy snowfall, over most of the eastern half of the U.S. In July and August the rivers of northern India, swollen by torrential monsoon rains, inundated thousands of square miles, drowning uncounted numbers of people and livestock. Elsewhere, prolonged droughts desiccated vast regions. Heavy surf from coastal storms swept away miles of valuable beach property in New Jersey, and southern California was devastated by some of the worst winter flash flooding in its history.

The largest national body in numbers of employees and geographic extent of meteorologic coverage during 1978 was that of the Soviet Union. During the year the U.S.S.R. emphasized work on the variations of climate and experiments in weather modification. Although experiments and commercial operations in rainmaking were numerous, neither the techniques nor the practical results showed any great progress. The vital significance of the subject and the optimism of experts in the Soviet Union, the U.S., and several other countries kept it active, however.

Climatology, a relatively passive branch of the atmospheric sciences for many decades, continued the growth that began about 1970. Special advisory boards were organized to investigate the potential hazards to life inherent in fluctuations in climate, whether regional or worldwide in extent and whether natural or man-made in origin. Many research reviews were published by the World Meteorological Organization (WMO), the American Meteorological Society, the U.S. National Academy of Sciences, and other scientific bodies. Findings were incomplete, but evidence of serious future consequences of fluctuations in climate was enough to initiate positive corrective plans.

A study by a team of research specialists from West Germany, Japan, and the U.S. concluded that the cooling trend of the last 30 years seemed likely to continue, at least in the Northern Hemisphere. From 1950 to 1975 the cooling per decade of most climate indexes in the Northern Hemisphere was from 0.1° to 0.2° C (0.2° to 0.4° F). These indexes included sea surface temperatures in the north-central Pacific and the northern Atlantic, air temperatures at the Earth's surface and at various elevations, and the extent of the snow and ice cover at different seasons. Data from the Southern Hemisphere were insufficient for any projections to be made. The scientists also found that in almost all cases the climate varied more markedly from year to year than it did over the long term.

(F. W. REICHELDERFER)

[224.A.3.e; 224.C; 224.D.6]

OCEANOGRAPHY

On Aug. 11, 1978, the Deep Sea Drilling Project (DSDP) completed a decade of ocean-floor exploration from the specially outfitted "Glomar Challenger." By drilling more than 700 holes in the seafloor and dating the sediments recovered, the DSDP provided overall confirmation of the theory of seafloor spreading and of continental drift. According to this theory new molten crustal material rises at mid-ocean ridges, solidifies and spreads laterally as a system of rigid plates that rub against one another at submarine faults, and redescends into the Earth at submarine trenches. The continents were all together in one supercontinent about 180 million years ago; they then drifted apart from one another as the seafloor spread (at the rate of 1–13 cm per year), forming ever widening ocean basins with ridges at their centres.

Besides confirming this overall picture, the DSDP furnished a wealth of detail about how it occurred. At passive margins, where there is no relative motion between seafloor and nearby continent, the drilling found shallow-water sediments and even evidence of former dry-land conditions *below* newer deep-sea sediments. This means that when the original supercontinent broke up, material nearest the lines of breaking sank below the sea. Work in the western Pacific showed that the mid-Pacific seamounts and the Hess Guyot (a large volcanic platform) sank below the ocean's surface during the first 10 million to 20 million years of their existence. This resembles earlier DSDP findings in the central Indian Ocean, where a chain of swamp islands and lagoons sank to form a ridge 1,850 m deep. Coal and peat were recovered from this site. Drilling also continued during the year in the western Pacific near Japan, where there is an active margin (one where the ocean floor is subducted under a continent). It was found that subduction is a smoother process than had been expected, with surprisingly little scraping of material from the Pacific Ocean plate onto the continental area as the ocean plate descends.

The sediment cores recovered by the DSDP were not only useful to geologists but also contained clues about how ocean water and terrestrial climate have changed over the age of the oceans. By measuring carbonate in sediments, project scientists established that the deepest waters of the

Seaside cottages were tumbled together and wrecked after heavy storms hit Massachusetts and the Northeast in February.

UPI COMPIX

A drawing of the Seasat satellite. The satellite, launched from California in June, provided information on the oceans' currents, tides, waves, and storms.

ocean had a temperature of 10° to 15° C (50° to 60° F) about 40 million years ago; the range is now 0° to 4° C (32° to 39° F). Skeletal remains and the silica content of sediments reflected the size of different near-surface populations of marine organisms when the sediment was laid down and thus allowed study of global climate fluctuation during the age of the oceans. Research using these indicators suggested that some fluctuation in climate may be traced back to cyclic variations in the Earth's orbit, but final conclusions had not yet been drawn.

This program of global drilling required impressive technical accomplishments. The drilling vessel was held over the drill site by a computer-controlled system. The system sensed any ship's drift by listening to acoustic beacons placed on the seafloor and then computed motor and steering instructions to counteract the drift. A reentry system allowed removal of the drill string and reemplacement in the same drill hole. For the "Glomar Challenger" this was essential at, for example, mid-Pacific drilling Site 462. There, project scientists had intended to drill down to 140-million- to 160-million-year-old sediments, but the drill encountered a large volcanic complex 500 m thick and about 120 million years old. The drill string had to be removed and replaced 15 times to penetrate this structure.

Drilling became feasible in the deepest parts of the ocean; work during the year in the Mariana Trench was in 7,044 m of water. The deepest holes penetrated more than 1,700 m of sediment. Yet, even this ability was not sufficient for future work. One possibility being discussed by scientists was utilization of the "Glomar Explorer," a much larger vessel with significantly better drilling and lifting capabilities. These capabilities were necessary for future plans, which included deep drilling along the ocean margin just beyond the continental shelf and in the Antarctic Ocean.

On June 26 the first satellite dedicated to oceanographic research was launched from Vandenberg Air Force Base in California. The satellite, Seasat, circled the Earth 14 times per day and scanned 95% of the oceans every 36 hours from an altitude of about 800 km (500 mi). Visual and infrared radiometers mapped sea-surface temperatures to 1°–2° C (34°–39° F) on clear days as well as charting ice fields and cloud patterns. A multichannel microwave radiometer measured atmospheric water content, both to map precipitation on the oceans and to help remove atmospheric effects from the infrared images. A radar scatterometer measured sea-surface wind by sensing the amplitude and direction of tiny surface tension waves. Specially designed radar provided high-resolution pictures of ocean waves, ice fields, and other surface features day and night in all weather by combining many radar returns from each part of the ocean into a detailed image. Finally, a radar altimeter measured the altitude of the satellite to within 10 cm, thus revealing perturbations of the ocean surface due to tides and ocean currents.

(MYRL C. HENDERSHOTT)

See also Disasters; Energy; Life Sciences; Mining and Quarrying; Physics; Space Exploration; Speleology. [213.A; 231.A.3; 231.D and G]

Economy, World

During 1978 the world economy was characterized by slow growth, high unemployment, large trade imbalances, and pronounced monetary instability, as well as a continuing failure to establish the cause of the malaise and then take concerted action. Inflation remained at a high level; there was an increase in protectionist sentiment; and governments continued to pursue domestic policies largely unmindful of their international consequences. Therefore, although some countries managed to achieve improvements in their economies, in terms of the broad objectives accepted by virtually the entire developed world at the end of 1977 the year was an almost total failure. More important, there was nothing to suggest a significantly better performance in 1979.

During 1977 economic growth in the 24 member countries of the Organization for Economic Co-operation and Development (OECD) was approximately 3.5%, a sharp deceleration from the previous year in which the gain had been 5.2%. Given the existence of large-scale unemployment, which was giving rise to social and political pressures, there was general agreement on the need to step up growth in 1978 and beyond. This, however, was not achieved. The reluctant reflationary measures taken in several countries in late 1977 had only a short-term effect, with the result that growth in the first half of 1978 was sluggish. Although the second half appeared to have been marginally better, the latest indications were that during the year as a whole there would be a gain of only some 3.5%. Some countries, particularly Britain and Canada, managed to boost the tempo of economic activity in comparison with 1977, but in the U.S. growth was adversely affected by a severe winter, industrial disputes, renewed inflationary pressure, and a rapid fall in the external value of the dollar. West Germany and Japan, the two principal countries with low inflation and high external payments surpluses, could best afford to stimulate growth, but they failed to take the appropriate measures on time and were expected to register growth largely identical to that in 1977.

Generally speaking, the least sluggish sectors of demand were private consumption and government expenditure. Faced with surplus capacity and weak business confidence, governments found it easier to provide effective stimulus in those areas than in fixed investments. Thus, the latest available figures indicated a rapid expansion in private consumption expenditures in the U.K., Japan, and France. At the same time public spending gained some momentum in the U.S., Japan, West Germany, the U.K., and Belgium, as well as in some small OECD countries. All in all, it seemed that private consumption demand contributed about half of the increase in gross national product (GNP), which was in line with the situation observed in 1977. Public expenditure appeared to have increased its share somewhat, but that of private plant and equipment investment was thought to have declined from the previous year.

The weakness of aggregate demand was mirrored in the trend of output and employment. Although industrial production picked up in the first six months compared with the rather poor performance of the second half of 1977, it seemed that the outcome for the whole of 1978 would not match the gain seen in the previous year. Among the larger economies the U.K., Japan, and France were expected to do better than previously, but—because of a sharp slowdown in the U.S.—the average for this group seemed likely to decline from a growth of 4% to one of 3.5%. Performance in the smaller developed countries was even weaker, bringing industrial growth for the entire OECD area to some 3%, compared with 3.5% in 1977. One result of this was a large measure of surplus capacity in a wide range of industries. Halfway through the year capacity utilization rates in manufacturing were estimated at 80–85%, and the latest estimates provided little evidence of improvement during the second half.

The level of unemployment also remained high throughout the year. It was calculated that in the summer a total of 24 million people were without work, accounting for about 5% of the OECD labour force. This was largely the same as in 1977, with a reduction in the U.S. being offset by increases in Europe. It was clear that unless growth was speeded up the number of jobless was likely to grow. Estimates were that an annual economic growth of 4.5% would be required to absorb the newcomers to the labour market, but there was little evidence that this would be achieved in 1979.

What was particularly discouraging was that slow growth and unemployment coexisted with a high, and possibly accelerating, rate of inflation. In the developed world inflation was of the order of 8% in 1977, though by the end of 1978 there were signs that it had declined somewhat for that year.

Governments remained extremely sensitive to suggestions of an upward movement in prices; this was in fact one of the main reasons for the general reluctance to expand demand sufficiently. As in 1977 West Germany and Japan managed to cut their inflation further and remained at the bottom of the list with 3% and 5%, respectively; in the U.S. the figures pointed to an increase from 5.5% to more than 7%, and in France the government's policy of freeing prices with a view to improving profitability was thought to have increased the rate from about 9% to over 10%. Britain experienced a sharp cutback from some 14% to 8%; Italian inflation was also reduced, but at an estimated 12–13% for the year it was still the highest among the large developed countries. (See Feature Article: The Roots of Inflation.)

As in 1977 the main feature of the international economic scene was monetary instability. Although all indications pointed to a significant reduction in the current account deficits of the OECD area, its distribution remained very uneven, leading to strong pressure on individual currencies. Under the impact of a rapidly rising trade deficit and somewhat lukewarm initial attempts to stem the tide by the government, the U.S. dollar lost heavily up to the end of the year in terms of most

Table I. Real Gross National Products of OECD Countries*
% change, seasonally adjusted at annual rates

Country	Average 1964–65 to 1974–75	From previous year 1977	From previous year 1978†
Canada	5.1	2.6	4.0
France	5.0	3.0	3.75
Germany, West	3.6	2.4	2.50
Italy	4.5	1.7	2.0
Japan	8.6	5.1	5.50
United Kingdom	2.3	0.7	2.75
United States	3.0	4.9	3.75
Total major countries	4.3	5.5	3.25
Australia	4.5	2.6	3.75
Austria	4.7	3.5	0.75
Belgium	4.5	1.8	2.75
Denmark	3.5	1.9	1.0
Finland	4.8	0.8	1.0
Greece	6.3	3.7	4.25
Ireland	3.8	5.0	5.25
Netherlands, The	4.7	2.3	3.0
New Zealand	3.5	0	0.25
Norway	4.6	4.1	3.25
Spain	6.3	2.4	1.25
Sweden	3.3	–2.5	0.25
Switzerland	2.8	4.3	1.25
Total OECD countries	4.3	3.6	3.25

*OECD countries are those listed above and Iceland, Luxembourg, Portugal, and Turkey.
†Estimate.
Source: Adapted from OECD *Economic Outlook*, July 1978.

other currencies. By contrast, the growing external strength of the Japanese economy led to a strong upward pressure on the yen, which—despite a fair amount of resistance by the authorities—rose by some 18% against the dollar between January and late December. The West German mark also gained some strength; the British pound sterling continued its recovery into the first quarter of the year, only to falter and then stabilize in subsequent months. (*See Feature Article: Another Day a Different Dollar.*)

There was little doubt that the international currency fluctuations had a strong adverse effect on business confidence and, therefore, economic growth during 1978. In order to promote exchange-rate stability members of the EEC agreed to establish a new European Monetary System (EMS). This, in effect, was a new and more ambitious attempt to link European currencies together than the original and by now severely truncated currency "snake." Final details were still being hammered out at the end of the year, and Britain was seeking a number of safeguards before agreeing to join.

Other major international economic initiatives during the year included the Bonn summit conference of developed countries and the multilateral trade talks in Geneva. At the Bonn summit, held in July, agreement was reached on a number of measures aimed primarily at boosting growth in the short term. In retrospect, however, they appeared to fall well short of the kind of action required to ensure a substantially faster rate of economic growth. This conclusion was reinforced by the rather disappointing economic indicators for the second half of the year. The aim of the multilateral trade negotiations at Geneva was to reach agreement on a phased reduction on tariffs and a new set of rules governing international trade; at the year's end discussions were still continuing.

On the whole the less developed countries ap-

peared to have grown faster in 1978 than did the developed world. With the exception of the Asian bloc, however, growth in the less developed countries was well below the average for the 1967–72 period. Inflation rates declined but were still at relatively high levels. Current account deficits for these countries, which were reduced in 1977, were believed to have risen to some $30 billion, with the prospects for 1979 looking even worse. However, as a result of an increase in aid disbursements and other capital receipts no special difficulties were envisaged in financing the 1978 deficit. During most of the year major oil-producing countries pursued relatively cautious economic policies. Partly as a result of this but also because of a reduction in oil production, growth rates were comparatively sluggish. In mid-December, however, the Organization of Petroleum Exporting Countries (OPEC) voted to increase the price of its crude oil by 14.5% in 1979. The boost was to take place in four steps, beginning with a 5% rise on January 1. The more developed members of the less developed group (primary producers such as Australia, New Zealand, and southern European countries) pursued generally restrictive fiscal and monetary policies and experienced slower growth rates than industrial countries or other less developed economies.

NATIONAL ECONOMIC POLICIES
Developed Market Economies. UNITED STATES. The U.S. economy started off in the opening quarter of 1978 with a marginal decline of 0.1% in the real GNP. This was mainly attributed to the severe winter and the prolonged coal strikes, but nagging

CHART 1

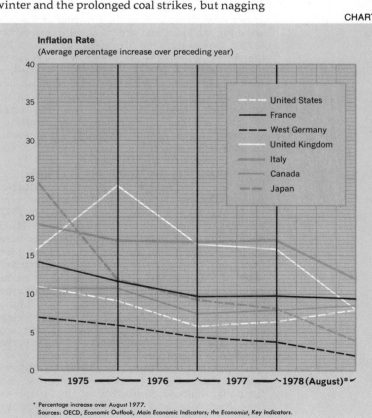

Inflation Rate
(Average percentage increase over preceding year)

United States
France
West Germany
United Kingdom
Italy
Canada
Japan

1975 — 1976 — 1977 — 1978 (August)*

* Percentage increase over August 1977.
Sources: OECD, *Economic Outlook, Main Economic Indicators;* the *Economist, Key Indicators.*

Table II. Percentage Changes in Consumer Prices in Selected OECD Countries

Country	1961–70	Average 1971–75	1976	1977	Latest month* 1977
Canada	2.7	7.3	7.5	8.0	9.4
France	4.0	8.8	9.6	9.8	9.4
Germany, West	2.7	6.1	4.5	3.9	2.4
Italy	3.9	11.3	16.8	17.0	11.9
Japan	5.8	11.5	9.3	8.1	4.2
United Kingdom	4.1	13.0	16.5	15.9	8.4
United States	2.8	6.7	5.8	6.5	7.9
Australia	2.5	10.2	13.5	12.3	7.9
Austria	3.6	7.3	7.3	5.5	3.6
Belgium	3.0	8.4	9.2	7.1	4.1
Denmark	5.9	9.3	9.0	11.1	6.8
Finland	5.0	11.7	14.4	12.6	5.6
Greece	2.1	12.3	13.3	12.1	12.0
Iceland	11.8	24.6	33.0	29.9	51.7
Ireland	4.8	13.3	18.0	13.6	8.2
Luxembourg	2.6	7.2	9.8	6.7	2.9
Netherlands, The	4.0	8.6	8.8	6.4	4.2
Norway	4.5	8.4	9.1	9.1	7.6
Portugal	3.9	15.4	19.3	27.1	17.8
Spain	6.0	12.1	17.6	24.5	16.5
Sweden	4.0	8.0	10.3	11.4	11.2
Total OECD	3.4	8.6	8.6	8.9	

*Percentage increase from corresponding month of previous year.
Sources: OECD, *Economic Outlook*, July 1978; OECD, *Main Economic Indicators*; The Economist, *Key Indicators*.

suspicions remained. By 1978 the recovery from the last recession was in its fourth year and at a highly mature stage. Continuation of the slowdown that was in evidence throughout 1977 was natural, but, owing to the distortions caused by the severe winter, economists had to wait until the second quarter's statistics were published to judge the true underlying trends. The economy then did rebound strongly in the March–June quarter to record a strong growth of 8% in real GNP.

The main factors underlying the moderate growth registered during the first half of the year were higher industrial orders and increased consumer expenditure on durables, especially automobiles. A slowdown in the growth of personal incomes coupled with a slightly higher savings ratio would have held back private consumption, but a rapid rise in installment credit during the spring put considerable bounce into this sector. Private investment, in particular residential investment, slowed down appreciably in response to the ever rising cost of housing and the higher cost of mortgages.

The sharp recovery in the rate of economic activity was mirrored by the industrial production figures. During the opening quarter these were rarely above those of the fourth quarter of 1977, but they expanded by an annual rate of 11.7% during the second quarter. Inventory increases during the first half of the year were slightly lower than sales, leading to a decline in the inventory/sales ratio. Encouragingly, the demand for labour picked up strongly, pushing up the total number of employed to 94.1 million in May, 4.2% higher than in the corresponding month of the previous year. Consequently, the unemployment rate tumbled to about 6%, a lower level than that expected by the administration.

In spite of these sound developments, interest rates in the spring embarked on a relentless rise, the dollar depreciated steadily on the foreign exchange markets, and the stock market fluctuated wildly. The reasons for these lie in the following factors: (1) an upturn in inflation rates and inflationary expectations; (2) a rapid rise in monetary stock; (3) the widening trade deficit; and (4) overcautious measures introduced to check inflation and protect the dollar.

The surge in interest rates was primarily due to market forces—substantial credit demand from both private and public sectors—rather than the result of tighter credit policies of the Federal Reserve Board. Until the beginning of 1978 there was considerable spare capacity in the economy, which kept investment demand down to a level lower than would have been normal in a period of rapid recovery. This limited demand for credit kept interest levels steady until late in 1977. The large federal deficit (estimated at $49 billion for the financial year ended September 1978), which might also have driven up rates, was steadily financed until the summer by foreign central banks striving to limit the appreciation of their own currencies against the dollar. Furthermore, the rapid growth of the labour force delayed the onset of any tightness in the labour market and the inflationary pressures that might produce. By the summer the economy was running close to full employment of productive resources and, after the Bonn summit, foreign intervention slowed down. As a result the inflationary outlook worsened, and the money supply began to run far ahead of the Federal Reserve Bank's target. (In the first eight months it expanded at an annual rate of 8.1%, compared with the Federal Reserve Bank's maximum rate of 6.5%.)

The U.S. government's view throughout the summer and early autumn was that the economy had entered a cyclical deceleration phase (which was certainly true) and that a sharp monetary and fiscal squeeze would result in a steep "V"-shaped recession rather than a "U"-shaped "growth recession." This is not to say, however, that fiscal policy remained expansionary. In May U.S. Pres. Jimmy Carter reduced the scope and postponed the introduction of his proposed tax cuts. Instead of a $24.5 million cut in the fiscal year beginning October 1978, he proposed a $19.4 million reduction effective January 1979. The original tax cuts would have had a largely neutral effect on the economy, tending to offset increased Social Security taxes taking effect Jan. 1, 1979, and higher returns from the income tax caused by inflation pushing more people into higher tax brackets. The revised tax cuts would have produced a budget deficit of about $53 billion. During the summer Congress adopted a more restrictive stance (which sparked a row with the president) and approved still lower tax cuts of $16.3 million. This, together with the pruning of certain programs and the slowing down of others, brought the proposed deficit down to $38.9 billion in October.

While the fiscal policy was being reined back cautiously, monetary policy remained for a while the first line of defense against the rising tide of money supply and inflation. The Federal Reserve Board was fearful of taking tough action, contrary to the will of the Congress and the administration. As a result the too-gradual tightening of the monetary policy was insufficient to wrench the mone-

Table III. Total Employment in Selected Countries

(1975=100)

Country	1974	1975	1976	1977	1978 First quarter	1978 Second quarter
Australia	100	100	103	105	104	105
Canada	98	100	102	104	102	108
France	102	100	99	99	98	97
Germany, West	104	100	99	99	99	98
Italy	99	100	101	106	105	106
Japan	100	100	101	102	100	105
Sweden	98	100	101	101	100	101
United Kingdom	101	100	99	100	99	100
United States	101	100	103	107	108	111

Source: OECD, *Main Economic Indicators.*

tary growth back onto course. Between the end of May and October the federal discount rate (the interest charged by the Federal Reserve Bank for loans) was cautiously raised from 7 to 8.5% in several stages. During the same period the commercial banks' prime rates raced ahead, reaching 10.25% (8% in the spring). Yet there was no sign that the high interest rates were slowing the money supply or inflation sufficiently to restore confidence at home and abroad.

Another phenomenon in evidence from the end of 1977 was the neurotic reaction of exchange markets to movements in the trade account. Despite the fact that exports accounted for less than 6.5% of the GNP and that the balance on invisible trade (including receipts from services such as banking and transportation, and also spending by tourists) wiped out much of the trade deficit, world attention was focused on the U.S. trade deficit. During the first eight months of 1978 the adjusted trade deficit was more than $21 billion, compared with a deficit of $14 billion a year earlier. Oil imports, at an annual rate of $40 billion–45 billion, were undoubtedly one of the main causes. The difficulties encountered by President Carter in obtaining passage of his energy bill also contributed to the weakness of the dollar. Measures announced in the spring and the summer aimed at supporting the currency, such as bilateral currency "swap" agreements and monthly gold sales, seemed to have the opposite effect. The "free fall" of the dollar gained momentum in September. News of congressional approval of a much modified energy program was initially ignored and then dismissed as irrelevant.

The financial world was looking for tough action to control inflation, which in the U.S. was estimated to have shifted to the 7–8% range annually and appeared to be heading toward the 9% range. This required something beyond the fiscal and monetary measures already applied. Therefore, a "national austerity" program was hatched on October 25, calling for voluntary wage and price restraints. A limit of 5.75% for prices and 7% for wages was set. Minor cuts in public spending were also incorporated into this program. After a momentary pause the international markets found the measures to be insufficient, and the plunge of the dollar resumed. The price of gold reached a record $244 an ounce, compared with $165 at the beginning of the year.

On November 1 President Carter unexpectedly rode to the rescue of the dollar by announcing a dramatic but comprehensive package involving a 1% increase in the discount rate, the sharpest rise since 1929, and a credit squeeze in the form of a supplementary reserve requirement on time deposits of $100,000 or more. Monthly gold sales were to be doubled to 1.5 million oz per month. The fourth but equally vital element of the administration's package was $30 billion worth of foreign currency swap facilities lined up within the International Monetary Fund (IMF) and bilaterally with West Germany, Japan, and Switzerland to defend the dollar against speculation. At last the president had taken defensive action and the markets rejoiced. The New York Stock Exchange recorded its largest one-day gain ever in the Dow Jones average, 35 points. The dollar recovered sharply. From its worst levels it rose in just two weeks by 9.5% against the mark, 11% against the Swiss franc, and 6.5% against the Japanese yen. The gold price dropped by 14%.

As calm returned and the year drew to a close, it became clear that the economy was in better shape than had been assumed by the alarmists. Revised data for the third quarter indicated an expansion of 3.4% for the real GNP, reviving hopes that the increase for the year as a whole could be in the region of 3.75%. Personal consumption and business fixed investment outlays were revised upward as well. The continuing low level of inventories was the key factor in preventing the economy from overheating, and it was hoped that in 1979 the restoration of these levels would counteract some of the deflationary pressures unleashed by the tighter fiscal and monetary policies.

Other favourable economic statistics included

CHART 2

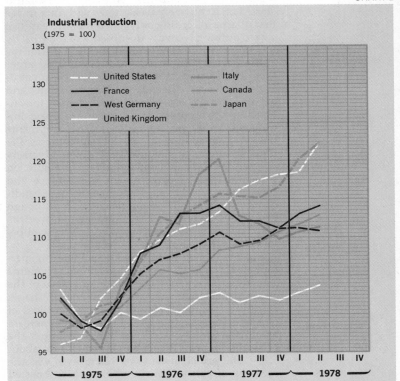

Industrial Production

(1975 = 100)

Source: International Monetary Fund, *International Financial Statistics.*

Table IV. Unemployment Rates in Selected OECD Countries*

% of civilian labour force, seasonally adjusted

Country	Average 1962–73		Peak 1955–73		1975	1976	1977	Latest rates 1977	Number of unemployed latest month 1978 (000)
Australia	1.6	2.6	Aug.	1972	4.4	4.4	5.6	6.1	380
Belgium	2.1	4.0	Feb.	1959	4.5	5.8	6.6	7.1	...
Canada	5.3	7.9	June	1958	6.9	7.2	8.1	8.6	910
Denmark	...	...			6.0	6.1	7.7	8.6	...
Finland	2.4	5.0	Jan.	1968	2.3	4.0	6.1	8.1	...
France	1.8	2.4	Sept.	1972	3.8	4.2	4.8	4.9	910
Germany, West	1.3	4.9	March	1955	4.8	4.7	4.6	4.3	978
Italy	3.6	5.5	April	1959	3.3	3.7	7.1	7.1	1,658
Japan	1.3	1.9	Oct.	1955	1.9	2.0	2.0	2.1	1,305
Netherlands	1.4	2.8	Nov.	1972	4.7	5.1	4.9	5.3	210
Norway	0.9	2.1	Dec.	1958	1.2	1.1	0.9	1.2	...
Spain	...	...			3.8	4.9	5.7	7.0	...
Sweden	2.1	2.9	Nov.	1973	1.6	1.6	1.8	2.1	89
United Kingdom	2.4	3.9	April	1972	3.9	5.4	5.7	5.7	1,339
United States	4.9	7.5	July	1958	8.5	7.7	7.0	6.1	5,870

*Rates not comparable between countries.
Sources: OECD, *Economic Outlook*, July 1978; The Economist, *Key Indicators*.

an improvement in the trend of the trade deficit with exports expanding three times as fast as imports. The oil price increase by OPEC in December, however, seemed likely to add about $4.5 billion to the U.S. oil import bill in 1979. Improved productivity in the second half of the year helped to neutralize the effects of the high inflation rate. The main worry was when the interest rates would peak and at what level. Prime rates rose 1.75% during November to reach 11.5%, and few economists were prepared to say that 12% or higher early in the new year was out of the question. Although the high rates were taking a long time to bite, a sharp slowdown in the economy during the latter part of 1979 was taken for granted.

UNITED KINGDOM. In terms of growth 1978 was a good year for the British economy. Although it started on a relatively weak note (with GNP in the first quarter recording only a nominal increase), it staged a strong recovery in subsequent months. By late 1978 it was estimated that the outcome for the entire year would be a gain of about 3%, larger than at any time since 1973. Rather disappointingly, however, the hoped-for investment- and export-led recovery—considered essential for enhancing productivity and ensuring a basic improvement in the nation's external payments position—failed to materialize. Despite the availability of funds, private investment was adversely affected by lack of confidence and pressure on profits caused by government interference and price controls. All in all, total investment expenditure grew about 2.5% in volume in 1978. Although this represented a marked improvement over the performance of the previous year, it was well below original expectations.

Exports turned in an even less inspiring performance. In 1977 they had recorded a volume growth gain of 6.7%, but, largely because of the rise in the external value of the currency in the six months to March 1978 and the resulting loss of competitiveness in overseas markets, the increase in 1978 was only 3.5%. At the same time the growth of imports accelerated from 4.6% to about 6.5%. The principal cause of this growth was the recovery of private consumption, which boosted demand for imports of finished products as well as a rebuilding of stocks of raw and intermediate materials. Therefore, while in 1977 the effect of foreign trade on economic growth was strongly positive, in 1978 it was neutral if not negative.

Public consumption, which had declined in volume in 1977, recorded a gain in 1978 of more than 2%, but the major stimulus to the economy came from private consumption. As a result of some tax concessions introduced in October 1977, this was already on a marked upward trend at the end of the year. During 1978, however, it was further underpinned by a reflationary spring budget that brought in approximately £2,500 million worth of personal tax concessions. Another favourable force was an inflation rate that was well below the rise in earnings. As a result of these factors, private consumption expenditure gained approximately 5% in 1978, compared with a decline of nearly 1% in 1977.

The strong recovery in private consumption had a positive effect on the level of industrial activity. The index of industrial production in the first half of the year was nearly 3% above the average for 1977 and, although the underlying trend weakened in the fall, the result for the year was expected to be a gain of 2.5–3%. In line with the increase in output, unemployment declined. By October 1978 the number of jobless, expressed as a percentage of the labour force and adjusted for seasonal distortions, was 5.7%, as against 6% a year earlier.

During 1978 the government's major policy objectives were to stimulate growth, keep public expenditure under control, limit the growth of the money supply to 8–12%, and ensure a gradual cutback in inflation to below an annual rate of 10%. Given the failure to achieve a fast enough expansion in exports and investments, the first objective was fulfilled with the aid of a significant fiscal boost to private consumption. This was made possible by the relatively slow growth of public expenditure, which, together with some other factors, caused the borrowing requirement of the public sector to be smaller than expected.

Part of the government's strategy for preventing excessive monetary growth involved a steady and significant increase in interest rates. In January 1978 the Bank of England's minimum lending rate stood at 6.5%. By April (the start of the 1978–79 fiscal year) it rose to 7.5%, and by early December it was up to 12.5%. Furthermore, in an attempt to strengthen their control over interest rates, the authorities abolished the market-related minimum lending rate formula in May and reinstated the administratively controlled bank rate, which had been dropped in favour of the MLR system in 1972.

The main reasons behind the government's relatively strict monetary policy were the need to observe the conditions of the large IMF loan granted to the U.K. at the end of 1976 and to accomplish a further decline in the rate of inflation. Another weapon aimed at the same objective was a continuing effort to restrain the rate of pay increases. Despite strong initial opposition from the trade unions, the third phase of the incomes policy (which expired in August 1978) was unexpectedly well observed, with the great majority of wage settlements conforming to the official guideline of a maximum increase of 10%. Nevertheless, the average rise in earnings during the period of the phase 3 restraint amounted to 15%, due partly to the effect of several allegedly self-financing productivity agreements that provided increases well in excess of 10%. During the second half of the year earnings continued to rise at a rate of approximately 15%, and the result for the whole of 1978 was not expected to be significantly below that figure.

One particularly encouraging feature of the year was the consistent decline in the rate of inflation. In December 1977 the index of retail prices was 12% higher than in the corresponding month of the previous year, but by October 1978 the 12-month gain was down to 7.8%. This was partly the result of the widespread observance of the government's 10% pay guideline and the relatively strict control of the money supply in the previous year. Another major contributor, however, was the appreciation of the pound sterling in late 1977 and early 1978, which had the effect of cutting back the sterling cost of imported products.

As indicated above, sterling did well on the foreign exchange markets in the first quarter of the year, with the result that its effective rate, expressed as a percentage of its value in terms of the world's leading currencies at the end of 1971, rose from 62.2% in 1977 to 65.4% in January–March 1978. The main reasons for this were the improvement in the balance of payments a few months earlier and the weakness of the dollar. However, during the second quarter the dollar gained some strength, which—reinforced by some disappointing trade figures from January onward—led to a sharp reversal of the trend. Although the Bank of England spent large amounts of foreign currency to resist pressure, the effective rate declined to 61.5%, lower than at any time since late 1976. However, renewed pressure on the dollar and the appearance of some favourable economic indications provided a boost in subsequent months, and on the basis of the latest available figures it seemed that the average for the year would be slightly higher than that recorded in 1977.

In regard to external payments, however, performance was generally disappointing. During the year North Sea oil production amounted to approximately 50 million tons, and official calculations indicated that the net benefit to the current account was in the region of £3,500 million, compared with £2,900 million in the previous year. In spite of this and a marked improvement in the terms of trade, the current account recorded an average monthly deficit of £21 million in the first nine months of 1978, compared with a monthly surplus of £24 million in 1977. On this basis, it seemed that the outcome for 1978 would be a deficit of about £200 million.

JAPAN. In the 1977–78 fiscal year (ended March 1978) Japan's real GNP grew by 5.4%. This was a disappointing performance for three reasons: it was nearly 1.5% below the official target; it was marginally below the growth rate achieved in 1976–77 (5.7%); and, as in the previous year, the main stimulus came from exports rather than domestic demand. As a result the country entered 1978–79 under the shadow of much overcapacity in

industry, a relatively high level of unemployment, a very large trade and balance of payments surplus, a strong upward pressure on the yen, and growing international opposition to what were seen as the nation's selfish trade policies.

Nevertheless, the Japanese government failed to take the necessary measures in time. Faced with particularly strong pressure from the U.S., in November 1977 Prime Minister Takeo Fukuda publicly committed himself to a GNP growth of 7% in 1978–79 and a reduction in the current account surplus to $6 billion. However, the authorities took no action to speed growth until the spring of 1978. Even then they could only manage a reduction in the discount rate from 4.25 to 3.50% and a modest increase in public expenditure plans. As a result, in the January–March quarter (the closing quarter of the 1977–78 fiscal year) there was a rapid expansion in exports and a sluggish growth in domestic demand. This, together with the weakness of the dollar, led to a rapid increase in the external value of the yen, and by the end of June 1978 one dollar was worth only 210 yen, compared with 284 yen in November 1977. Not surprisingly, this had a strong adverse effect on the volume of exports as well as the level of domestic business confidence. As a result GNP in the opening quarter of the year grew at an annual rate of only 4.5%.

In spite of the weakness in the volume of exports, their value—expressed in terms of devalued dollars—continued to rise rapidly. This and the continuing unwillingness of the government to

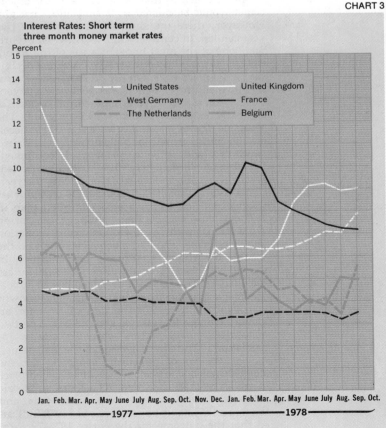

CHART 3

Interest Rates: Short term
three month money market rates
Percent

Source: International Monetary Fund, *International Financial Statistics.*

boost domestic demand led to further speculation in favour of the yen, which rose to 187 against the dollar by the middle of November. Because of its effect on the competitiveness of Japanese exports and business confidence, this had the result of further undermining the real growth prospects for the economy and, at the same time, boosting the dollar-denominated external payments surplus.

Finally, in September the authorities undertook measures to boost domestic demand, partly in order to offset the loss of momentum on the export front. The two main features were the injection of some $7 billion worth of public-works and related expenditures into the economy during the second half of the fiscal year and an increase of approximately $4.5 billion in the amount devoted to residential construction. An additional $1.1 billion was made available for accelerated investment in the electricity and gas industries. The other measures, including schemes to assist small industries and depressed regions, an increase in foreign aid, and $4 billion worth of emergency imports, seemed unlikely to have a significant effect in the short term. According to official claims, the new program was designed to boost GNP growth in 1978–79 by 1.3%, which, the government claimed, would be sufficient to achieve the original growth target of 7%. Nevertheless, although the effect of the extra public expenditure was becoming increasingly pronounced by November, the indications were that GNP growth for the entire fiscal year would not exceed 6%.

Thus, it seemed that, as in 1977–78, the official target would be missed by a substantial margin. However, there the similarity between the two years ended. In contrast to 1977–78, when exports were one of the most buoyant areas of the economy, the signs pointed to an actual volume decline (of 1–2%) in 1978–79. On the other hand, government expenditure, which was generally buoyant in 1977–78, gained further momentum because of a greatly extended public works program. The available figures also indicated a significant acceleration in the growth of both private housing expenditure and private plant and equipment investments, largely in reaction to the unexpectedly sluggish performance recorded during the year. Partial returns for 1978–79 pointed to a somewhat faster expansion in private consumption than in 1977–78. This was because—although the spring wage awards were the lowest on record—inflation fell back further and had a beneficial effect on the volume of private consumption expenditure. In the 1977–78 fiscal year the index of retail prices recorded an average gain of 6.7%, but in subsequent months the trend was consistently downward and in late 1978 the outlook was for an annual average increase of about 4.5%. The two main deflationary factors were the steady appreciation in the external value of the yen, which reduced the cost of the country's imports, and the sluggishness of demand, which discouraged price increases by manufacturers. As a result wholesale prices fell below those of the previous year, and the figures available up to November 1978 indicated that the outcome for the entire 1978–79 fiscal year could be a reduction of some 2%.

Table V. Growth of Real Output in the Developing Countries, 1967–77

% changes in real GNP or GDP

Area	Average 1967–72	1974	1975	1976	1977
Major oil exporters*	9.0	8.0	0.1	12.9	6.3
More developed primary producing countries	6.1	4.4	2.0	3.1	2.7
Europe†	6.5	4.9	2.4	3.7	3.3
Australia, New Zealand, South Africa	5.1	3.4	1.2	2.1	1.4
Less developed countries	6.1	5.3	4.1	4.8	4.9
Africa	5.0	5.6	2.3	4.2	2.2
Asia	4.8	2.7	6.1	5.8	6.4
Latin America and the Caribbean	6.8	7.7	2.6	4.5	4.3
Middle East	8.8	−1.0	8.4	2.1	6.7

*Algeria, Indonesia, Iran, Iraq, Kuwait, Libya, Nigeria, Oman, Qatar, Saudi Arabia, United Arab Emirates, and Venezuela.
†Finland, Greece, Iceland, Ireland, Malta, Portugal, Romania, Spain, Turkey, and Yugoslavia.
Source: Adapted from the International Monetary Fund, *Annual Report 1978.*

Table VI. Consumer Price Changes in the Developing Countries, 1967–77

In %

Area	Average 1967–72	1973	1974	1975	1976	1977
Major oil exporters*	8.0	11.3	17.0	19.0	16.2	15.0
More developed primary producing countries	6.0	11.8	16.7	16.9	15.1	17.8
Europe†	6.8	13.5	18.6	18.2	16.1	20.8
Australia, New Zealand, South Africa	4.6	9.3	13.6	14.6	13.3	12.2
Less developed countries	10.1	22.1	33.0	32.9	32.3	31.5
Africa	4.8	9.3	18.6	16.4	18.8	25.0
Asia	5.4	14.9	27.8	11.5	1.5	8.8
Latin America and the Caribbean	15.9	30.8	40.9	54.6	62.7	51.6
Middle East	4.3	12.7	21.8	20.3	17.4	24.2

*Algeria, Indonesia, Iran, Iraq, Kuwait, Libya, Nigeria, Oman, Qatar, Saudi Arabia, United Arab Emirates, and Venezuela.
†Finland, Greece, Iceland, Ireland, Malta, Portugal, Romania, Spain, Turkey, and Yugoslavia.
Source: Adapted from the International Monetary Fund, *Annual Report 1978.*

Given the relatively sluggish tempo of economic growth, it was not surprising that unemployment continued to rise. In 1977–78 the average unemployment rate (expressed as the percentage of the labour force out of work) was 2%, relatively low by world standards but comparatively high in the Japanese context. By September 1978 the figure reached 2.42%, and the indications were that the average for the fiscal year could reach 2.35%. Industrial production started the year on a relatively strong note but the trend became erratic in the late summer. The injection of extra government spending, however, was expected to have a stabilizing influence, and in late 1978 the outlook was for an average annual gain of about 6%, compared with 3.1% in 1977–78.

On the external payments front the economy was heading for an embarrassingly spectacular improvement, which caused, and subsequently was partly caused by, the appreciation in the external value of the currency. In 1977–78 the current account surplus amounted to $14 billion, and the publicly announced aim of the government was to cut this back to $6 billion. But even though the weakening of competitiveness arising out of the high value of the yen had an adverse influence on the volume of exports, their dollar value continued to rise rapidly. At the same time weak domestic demand restricted the growth of imports, with the result that in the first five months of the 1978–79 fiscal year the trade surplus was $11.3 billion, some 64% higher than in the corresponding period of the previous year. However, as a result of the authorities' determined efforts to step up the outflow of capital in the form of credits, loans, and foreign investment, the overall balance of payments surplus was cut back from $2.7 billion to $1.8 billion during the same period. In late 1978 the indications were that the year as a whole would record a current account surplus of about $18 billion, up by nearly 30% from the preceding year's figure. It was estimated, however, that virtually all this increase was attributable to the appreciation in the dollar; expressed in terms of yen the projected surplus was approximately 3.5 trillion, roughly the same as in the previous year.

WEST GERMANY. The rapid economic growth recorded during the closing quarter of 1977 was not carried into 1978, leading to a swift downgrading of the official growth targets. Despite growing fears about a possible return to stagnation, overcapacity, intractable unemployment, and monetary uncertainty, the government appeared convinced of the adequacy of the measures it had already undertaken and resisted pressure from its European neighbours and the U.S. to embark on any others. By the summer, however, West Germany changed its mind and at the Bonn economic summit conference agreed on the need for more stimulus to the national economy. Yet hardly had the conference ended and the West German Cabinet completed work on its package of tax cuts and reforms than the gloomy clouds lifted, giving way to a much brighter outlook.

Economic statistics for the second quarter of 1978 showed that the GNP rose rapidly after the first three months, enabling the country to overcome the near stagnation of that period. The growth rate of 3% achieved in the first six months appeared to be sustainable for the rest of the year. Furthermore, the strong underlying trends and the tax-cut package described above (to take effect from Jan. 1, 1979) all pointed to an acceleration in the tempo of economic activity.

The main factor promoting growth during 1978 was revival in domestic demand. The boom in the motor industry, which began in 1976, spread to durable goods, textiles, and foreign trade. Demand for housing took off, enabling this sector to contribute positively to economic growth for the first time since 1973. In spite of unused capacity in certain capital goods sectors, industrial investment nudged upward, reflecting the improved business climate. Another success story was inflation, which fluctuated narrowly between 2.5 and 3%, enabling West Germany to maintain the lowest inflation rate among OECD countries except for Switzerland. It was true that the strength of the currency and weak commodity prices played a major role, but the effect of the government's steadfast monetary and fiscal policies during the post-oil crisis years of 1975–76 should not be ignored. The fact that wage increases during 1978 were lower than in 1977 also must have contributed.

In contrast to the above positive economic developments, two major negative factors continued to put a question mark over the quality of the cyclical upswing under way. The first was unemploy-

ment, which remained at 4.1%. As in other OECD countries, this level of unemployment coexisted with severe shortages of skilled labour. The other factor was the high degree of dependence of the economy on exports (which accounted for nearly a third of the GNP). Foreign demand during 1978 was not a particularly bright spot. The rise of the mark, mainly against the dollar, and sluggish international trade kept export growth down.

The West German government viewed the dollar crisis as an urgent international monetary issue but believed that there was little to be done unilaterally to prevent the inexorable rise of the mark. The limited success of the European currency "snake" over the past two years convinced West German policymakers that while Europe could do little to help the dollar it could at least reduce instability among its own major currencies. Therefore, the emphasis of West Germany's international economic policy was on creating a new "zone of stable exchange rates" within Europe.

The mildly expansionary fiscal and monetary policies followed during 1978 could be traced back to 1977, when the government, faced with a prolonged stagnation during the first three quarters (which resulted in a GNP growth rate of 2.5%, compared with a target of 5%), admitted the need

CHART 4

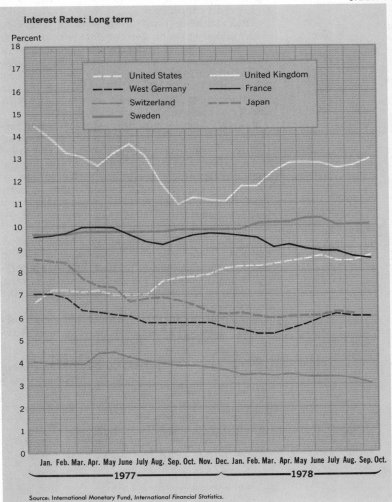

Interest Rates: Long term

Percent

Legend:
- United States
- United Kingdom
- West Germany
- France
- Switzerland
- Japan
- Sweden

Jan. Feb. Mar. Apr. May June July Aug. Sep. Oct. Nov. Dec. Jan. Feb. Mar. Apr. May June July Aug. Sep. Oct.

1977 — 1978

Source: International Monetary Fund, *International Financial Statistics*.

for reflation. The June and September 1977 measures, however, came too late to have any marked influence until the summer of 1978. The budget for 1978, passed by the Bundestag in January, effectively confirmed the changed fiscal stance by providing for a deficit of DM 31 billion, equal to a boost of 1% to the gross domestic product (GDP). As already indicated, the post-Bonn package, which injected a stimulus of an equal magnitude, was intended to prop up the next year's growth rate. So the government completed a U-turn in only two years by admitting the need for continual mini-boosts to spark growth.

The monetary policy of the Bundesbank was in harmony with the federal government's fiscal stance. The target for monetary expansion remained at 8% (the same as in 1978) despite an apparent decline in the inflation rate. Huge speculative movements of foreign exchange in and out of West Germany as one dollar crisis gave way to another throughout 1978 severely complicated the Bundesbank's task of ensuring that there was neither excess liquidity nor shortage of credit. By and large, the authorities were quick to take measures to boost liquidity when faced with outflows and were tolerant of temporary excesses caused by dollar inflows. Clearly, the aim was not to choke off the recovery through creating unnecessarily tight credit conditions.

Thus for the first time in three years West Germany ended a year on a strong note with prospects of even better times in the coming 12 months. The autumn forecast of the country's five leading economic institutes pointed to a GNP growth of at least 4% in 1979 (2.5 to 3% in 1978), coupled with an inflation rate of 3.5%, slightly fewer unemployed, and a mild recovery in export demand.

FRANCE. The encouraging signs of firmer economic activity noticed at the end of 1977 were carried into the opening months of 1978 and proved to be of immense political benefit to the government during the spring election. However, the euphoria did not last long, as indicators in early April began pointing in the wrong direction, and fragility remained the main characteristic of the French economy for the better part of the year.

In September 1977 the Economics Ministry forecast a 4.5% increase in the real GDP for 1978. In April, as the weakness in the economy was becoming apparent, the increase was revised downward. In the summer another correction downgraded the growth target to 3.2%.

Industrial production mirrored economic fluctuations closely. The industrial output index, hav-

ing risen steadily between January and April, fell during the next two months. Some of the decline was due to technical stoppages, but the trend was unmistakable. As a result of the sluggishness of economic activity, the unemployment situation worsened steadily. The numbers out of work (on a seasonally adjusted basis) were just over the million mark in January, but by October their ranks had swollen to 1.1 million and the trend was still pointing upward. Another reason for the sharp rise in unemployment was a change in government policy which, until recently, encouraged employers to keep workers on the payroll.

The progress made in slowing down inflation in 1977 was not maintained during 1978. Even before the government ended the price controls and increased public service tariffs in June, there was considerable evidence of an upward movement in the general level of prices. It gathered strength in the summer, the July increase being the sharpest monthly rise in 15 months. Double-digit inflation was widely expected for the year as whole, representing a serious drift from the original official target of 6.5%. The liberalization of prices was the centrepiece of the government's new economic policy. Despite the heavy price paid initially through increased cost pressures, its ultimate aim was to create new jobs. Whether this would happen remained to be seen.

Like the United Kingdom and Italy, France was trying to bring its balance of trade and balance of payments back into equilibrium. During the first half of 1978 both were in the black, and the trend was expected to continue for the rest of the year. This task was made easier by the decline in the value of the dollar, which reduced the cost of oil imports during 1978.

With the elections safely out of the way, the government introduced several changes in its economic policy. The main one was the gradual dismantling of controls on industrial prices from the beginning of June 1978. This came as a great shock because it was the first time since World War II that a government had attempted to take away such controls. Premier Raymond Barre was convinced that the fundamental economic problems facing France would not be solved unless more resources were devoted to investment. According to this argument the only way investment could be sustained in the long term was to allow prices to rise to a level that improved profitability and in turn attracted more investment. Some controls, however, were retained on the service sector and on distribution margins.

Table VII. Output of Basic Industrial Products in Eastern Europe, 1977

In 000 metric tons except for natural gas and electric power

Country	Hard coal	Brown coal	Natural gas (000,000 cu m)	Crude petroleum	Electric power (000,000 kw-hr)	Steel	Sulfuric acid	Cement
Bulgaria	288	24,864	...	120	29,700	2,592	852	4,668
Czechoslovakia	27,960	93,240	7,608	120	66,300	15,048	1,272	9,756
Germany, East	348	253,704	...	5,412	91,992	6,852	927	12,096
Hungary	2,928	22,524	59,520	2,196	23,388	3,720	631	4,620
Poland	186,108	37,680	59,364	456	109,368	17,444	3,288	21,300
Romania	7,368	19,416	350,004	24,652	...	...	...	...
U.S.S.R.	721,991	...	2,890,488	549,976	1,149,996	147,000	21,108	126,948

Source: UN, *Monthly Bulletin of Statistics.*

CHART 5

Although the declared fiscal policy of the government was to reduce the budget deficit, it did not work out that way in practice. The budget adopted in November 1977 aimed at a deficit of Fr 8.9 billion. A few weeks before the Bonn summit conference the government decided that Fr 20 billion would be more appropriate. The actual figure was expected to be nearly double that, despite an increase in government revenues resulting from indirect tax increases during the summer. Monetary policy was aimed at holding the growth of the money supply at about 12% for the year as a whole. Given the spare resources in the economy and the depressed level of private investment, this policy was not believed to be restrictive during the first half. As inflation gathered force and the budget deficit widened, the liquidity of the banking system increased. However, thanks to firm credit control, the money supply was not expected to exceed 13%.

Developing Countries. In spite of their built-in disadvantages the developing countries continued to cope remarkably well with the aftermath of the mid–1970s recession induced by increased oil prices. Their problems were compounded by harvest failures and declining terms of trade, but they adjusted more rapidly than expected to these potentially damaging economic developments. Indeed, as a group the developing countries experienced faster economic growth during 1977 (the latest year for which statistical data were available) than the richer developed nations. While the latter could not achieve a faster growth rate than 3.5% in 1977, the nonoil-producing developing countries raised their gross national products by an average 4.7%.

It is an accepted fact that the economies of the developing countries are susceptible to the economic fluctuations of the developed world. Rapid economic expansion in the industrialized nations soon stimulates developing economies through higher demand for exports, higher levels of economic assistance, and, in some cases, demand for migrant labour. However, an initial upsurge followed by stagnation tends to create more unsettling influences than a steady but moderate growth. Thus a sharp slowdown in the growth rate of the OECD countries during 1977 (3.5% compared with 5% in 1976) wiped off some of the earlier gains in the developing nations.

MORE DEVELOPED COUNTRIES. These nations, consisting mostly of two groups—primary producers such as Australia, New Zealand, and South Africa, and southern European countries, such as Greece, Yugoslavia, and Turkey—experienced slower growth rates than either the industrial nations or the other nonoil-producing developing countries. Persistent high inflation was probably the main reason for this, although generally restrictive fiscal and monetary policies also contributed to the slowing of economic activity. Not surprisingly, countries that took stabilization measures early in the recession were in a relatively strong position economically in 1978. In contrast, countries that tried to ride it out through greater foreign borrowing only succeeded in postponing the painful measures until late 1976. Consequent-

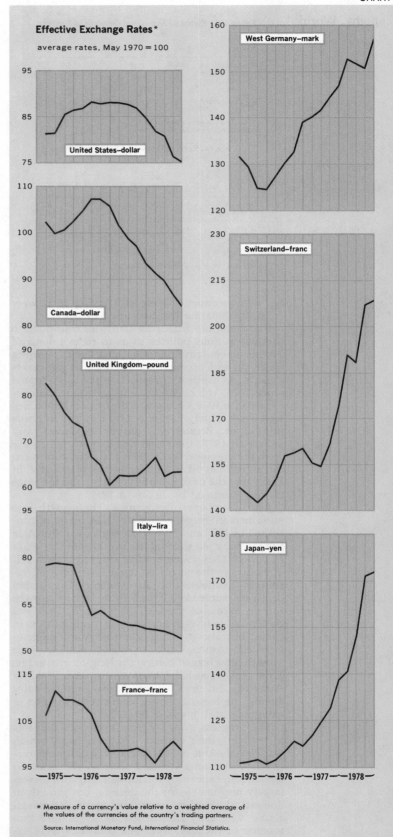

Effective Exchange Rates*

average rates, May 1970 = 100

United States–dollar

Canada–dollar

United Kingdom–pound

Italy–lira

France–franc

West Germany–mark

Switzerland–franc

Japan–yen

—1975——1976——1977——1978—

—1975——1976——1977——1978—

* Measure of a currency's value relative to a weighted average of the values of the currencies of the country's trading partners.

Source: International Monetary Fund, *International Financial Statistics.*

Table VIII. Rates of Industrial Growth in Eastern Europe*

Country	1956–60	1961–65	1971–75	1976	1977
Bulgaria	15.9	11.7	9.0	8.0	5.9
Czechoslovakia	10.5	5.2	6.7	5.5	5.5
Germany, East	9.2	5.9	6.3	5.9	5.2
Hungary	7.5	8.1	6.3	4.1	6.4
Poland	9.9	8.6	10.5	10.7	6.2
Romania	10.9	13.0	13.1	11.5	9.9
U.S.S.R.	10.4	8.6	8.5	4.8	5.2

*Yearly average percentages.
Source: *Ekonomicheskaya Gazeta.*

Table IX. Foreign Trade of Eastern Europe
In $000,000

Country	Exports 1975	Exports 1976	Exports 1977	Imports 1975	Imports 1976	Imports 1977
Bulgaria	4,601	5,382	6,329	5,309	5,626	6,329
Czechoslovakia	7,808	9,035	10,818	8,489	9,706	11,149
Germany, East	10,065	11,361	...	11,265	13,196	...
Hungary	5,355	4,932	5,832	6,223	5,528	6,522
Poland	10,289	11,050	12,336	12,545	13,867	14,674
Romania	5,329	6,100	...	5,330	6,100	...
U.S.S.R.	32,175	37,169	45,161	35,711	38,108	40,817

Source: UN, *Monthly Bulletin of Statistics.*

ly, their economies were still trying to recover from the deflation inflicted upon them.

The major oil-producing countries continued to pursue cautious policies so as to reduce demand pressure, contain inflation, and avoid running large current account and balance of payments deficits. As a result of restrictive policies adopted since 1976, the decline in the inflation rate continued into 1978. Changes in the GDP of these countries were largely influenced by changes in crude oil output. Because oil output expanded only slowly in 1977, their real GDP growth fell to 6% from the previous year's 13%. The trend continued during 1978 as oil output declined significantly. In December the OPEC nations voted to raise the price of their crude oil by 14.5% in 1979.

LESS DEVELOPED COUNTRIES. The growth rate sustained in recent years by these nations continued in 1977 and 1978. However, except in Asia the recovery fell short of the average for the 1967–72 period. This, together with unfavourable developments in the terms of trade, reduced the resources available for investment. The Asian countries succeeded in achieving a GDP growth rate in excess of the 1962–72 average. This was partly due to favourable weather conditions (as in India) but also to the prudent economic policies pursued. Among the countries outside Asia growth rates lagged behind the long-term average. This was especially marked in Africa, Latin America, and the Caribbean area. Inflation rates among the less developed countries remained at extremely high levels of 30–33%.

The progress made by less developed countries in reducing their current account deficits, which was considerable in 1974 and 1976, continued during 1977 but on a reduced scale. A reduction in demand for exports by the industrial countries was largely responsible for the decline, but growth in domestic demand for exportable goods also played a role. The early indications for 1978 were that imports of the less developed countries were expanding more rapidly than exports. A reversal in the terms of trade was also in evidence. These two

factors were expected to push up the trade deficits to a higher level. An IMF forecast placed the 1978 deficit at $30 billion, compared with $22 billion in 1977.

The problem as always was that of finding ways of financing the deficit. Available statistics suggested that this may not have been such a severe headache in 1978. The World Bank estimated in its annual report for 1978 that foreign aid and other capital flows from the industrialized countries would be adequate to finance a $30 billion third world deficit without visible strain. It also suggested that some of the reserves built up by the less developed countries during 1976 and 1977 through borrowings in excess of immediate requirements could be reduced to help finance rapid import expansion.

Over the longer term the only way the less developed countries can finance import growth is by stepping up their exports. The outlook for this, however, was not encouraging. The success of many less developed countries in increasing their exports led to restrictive measures by the industrialized nations in order to protect domestic employment. During 1977 world trade (in dollar terms) increased by about 13% while the value of exports from the less developed countries (excluding oil producers) rose by about 14%. Those countries with low incomes exceeded the average and increased their exports by 22%. The fairly consistent increase in the exports of less developed countries led World Bank observers to the conclusion that the competitiveness of their products was not a transitory phenomenon and that it was likely to continue provided it was not checked by the spread of trade barriers. If such protectionism was held at bay, further rapid economic growth in the less developed countries appeared likely.

However, faster economic growth alone was not sufficient to deal with many of the social and economic problems faced by the less developed countries. Agricultural production, for instance, remained barely ahead of the rise in population. In spite of significant improvements in farming methods, food production was still subject to the vagaries of the weather. Another problem was employment, which had not kept pace with the expansion in the labour force. Rapid urbanization also continued to raise problems.

Centrally Planned Economies. From June 27 to 29, 1978, the 32nd plenary session of the Council for Mutual Economic Assistance (CMEA) was held in Bucharest, Rom. The session approved three programs for long-term cooperation and accepted Vietnam as the tenth full member of the organization. But it was the problem of energy that dominated the discussion. The Bucharest session once again demonstrated that the Soviet Union, by far the strongest member country, was not able to impose its policies concerning some major issues on other member countries.

Before the session it was generally expected that the Soviet Union would try to impose the principle of majority vote in decision making and that the current system requiring unanimity in voting would be abandoned. Shortly before the opening of the session, however, Romania made it clear that "the full realization of national sovereignty is incompatible with any form of supranational management." On June 23 the Polish leader Edward Gierek said at a press conference following his talks with the Hungarian leader Janos Kadar that "none of us is preparing for anything that would require changes in our present system which is functioning efficiently."

These statements made it clear to the Soviet Union that any attempt to introduce the principle of majority rule would be strongly resisted. Other measures aimed at strengthening integration also met with limited success. At the 30th session of the CMEA countries in 1976 it had been decided to embark upon five long-term programs of collaboration between the member countries. Because little progress was achieved, the goal was reduced during the 31st session to three programs covering fuel, energy, and raw materials; machine building; and agriculture and food. During the 32nd session Soviet Deputy Premier Nikolay Baibakow declared that the plans for the implementation of these programs had finally been completed. The extent of the participation by individual nations was, however, still to be decided.

It seemed that the main economic problem faced by CMEA countries was the shortage of energy. The Soviet Union was the main supplier of crude oil and gas and, along with Poland, of coal. In view of the growing demands for energy among the CMEA nations it was deemed necessary to explore for new deposits as well as new sources of energy, and this in turn required large investments. The major emphasis was being put on the construction of nuclear energy plants, and it was envisaged that by 1990 approximately 37 million kw of nuclear power would be produced in Eastern Europe and Cuba and another 4 million kw in the Soviet Union. As far as other sources of energy were concerned, the Soviet Union as the main supplier insisted that its supplies of crude oil and gas to member countries depended on those countries' investments in the exploration of those resources in the Soviet Union. This called for huge capital outlays, and it was estimated that Poland would have to allocate 2.3% of its total investment budget to such projects. The figure for East Germany would be 3 to 3.5%, Hungary 4%, Bulgaria 2.5%, and Romania 2%. The Czechoslovak figures were not disclosed, but it was known that Czechoslovakia was placing more emphasis on reducing consumption of conventional fuels and expanding its own nuclear power base.

The long-term plans covered the period up to the year 1990. Premier Piotr Jaroszewicz of Poland stated during a debate in Bucharest that the problem of energy was of critical importance to the Polish economy, but he stressed the point that nothing was being done to ensure that Poland's short- and medium-term needs for oil and gas would be met.

Not much was revealed in Bucharest of the program for cooperation in machine building. It would appear from Baibakow's speech that all efforts would be concentrated on production of equipment for nuclear power stations and that cooperation in this field would simply serve the program of expanding nuclear energy resources. Nor was much revealed about the third program, dealing with collaboration in agriculture and food industries. Baibakow stressed the need for an increase in the production of grains, fodder, and livestock breeding. Hungarian Premier Gyorgy Lazar declared that agriculture needed as much investment as the energy program. It would seem, therefore, that Lazar drew a parallel between the Soviet demands for investment in energy as a condition for increased deliveries and the similar needs of agricultural exporters (such as Hungary) that lack investment capital. He stated that Hungary had already committed substantial financial resources to agriculture. It is worth noting that the Soviet Union was not only demanding capital equipment and manpower from other countries to enlarge its energy resources but also was raising prices for oil and gas. It seemed possible that Hungary would in turn charge higher prices for its agricultural exports.

In spite of a better harvest in 1978, especially in the Soviet Union, agricultural products were still in high demand, and many CMEA countries had to import large quantities of grain, meat, and other food products. The Soviet Union made it clear that it could not meet food deficiencies within the bloc and that those member countries that are net importers of agricultural products would simply have to rely on their own resources.

CHART 6

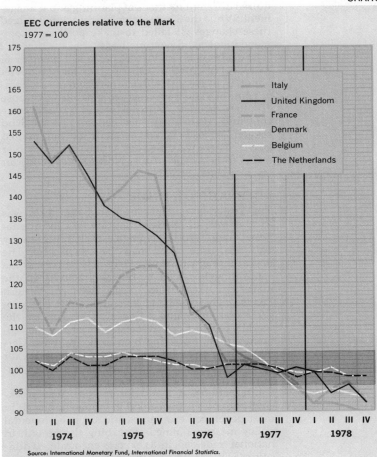

EEC Currencies relative to the Mark
1977 = 100

Italy
United Kingdom
France
Denmark
Belgium
The Netherlands

I II III IV | I II III IV | I II III IV | I II III IV | I II III IV
1974   1975   1976   1977   1978

Source: International Monetary Fund, International Financial Statistics.

Table X. Soviet Trade with Eastern European Countries

In 000,000 rubles, current prices

Country	Exports			Imports		
	1975	1976	1977	1975	1976	1977
Bulgaria	2,059.6	2,276.7	2,658.7	1,931.2	1,663.5	2,494.6
Czechoslovakia	2,019.5	2,320.5	2,680.4	1,891.5	1,648.6	2,436.9
Germany, East	2,980.3	3,217.9	3,661.2	2,643.1	2,275.9	3,066.2
Hungary	1,657.7	1,771.3	2,066.5	1,616.0	1,984.9	...
Poland	2,447.2	2,750.1	3,195.9	2,406.1	2,485.0	2,872.1
Romania	702.1	770.2	1,003.5	828.7	529.8	1,021.9

Source: Ministry for Foreign Trade of the U.S.S.R.

Table XI. Soviet Crude Petroleum and Products Supplied to Eastern Europe

In 000 metric tons

Country	1973	1974	1975	1976
Bulgaria	9,322	10,855	11,553	11,868
Czechoslovakia	14,340	14,836	15,965	17,233
Germany, East	12,985	14,424	14,952	16,766
Hungary	6,294	6,729	7,535	8,435
Poland	12,376	11,855	13,271	14,073

Source: Ministry for Foreign Trade of the U.S.S.R.

In spite of the fact that statistical indicators of many CMEA countries showed general growth, the average increase in national income in 1978 was estimated to be about 5%, which represented a considerable slowing down from previous years. It seemed clear that during the current five-year plans, covering the years 1976–80, a turning point in the region's economic development had been reached. As the possibilities for extensive growth became more limited, new problems arose that required different methods of planning and management. While the 32nd session partly acknowledged these changes, it failed to make positive recommendations as to new methods.

The admission of Vietnam as a full member of CMEA represented a political gain for the Soviet Union in its rivalry with China. From the economic point of view it represented a liability, because all other member countries would have to make contributions to Vietnam's economy. At the 32nd session Yugoslavia was present as an "invited guest." There were also delegations with observer status from Angola, Laos, North Korea, and, for the first time, Ethiopia.

INTERNATIONAL TRADE

The available evidence indicated that 1978 was another year of relatively low growth in international trade. World commerce probably grew by only 5%, little faster than the 4% of 1977. The main cause of this slow rate of expansion was the continuing low level of business activity in the main OECD countries, especially in Western Europe, where demand remained weak. The program of coordinated action agreed upon by the world's seven major industrial nations at the economic summit meeting held in Bonn, West Germany, during July included proposals for stimulating trade but had failed to make any significant impact by the end of 1978.

International demand for imports was weakened both by the poor trend in industrial output in most developed economies and by governmental policy measures aimed at curbing the growth in national trade deficits as exports encountered difficulties. This trend was given further strength by the lack of any rapid growth in the external trade of the less developed countries. A measure of the extent to which import demand weakened in the OECD is provided by the decline in the member countries' combined trade deficit, to $17 billion in 1978 from $32 billion in 1977.

It is likely that the reduction in rates of inflation in many countries produced a lower rate of increase in international trade prices following the 7.5% rise, measured in Special Drawing Rights, in 1977, when inflation rates were on the average much higher. Indeed, for some countries growth in the value of trade at current prices was appreciably less than the increase in real terms. In West Germany, for example, exports in the first half of 1978 were 3% higher in value than in the same period of the previous year but as much as 5% higher in real terms. West Germany's imports over the same period showed only a 4% rise at current prices, though the increase was 9% in volume. In the less developed countries the effect of falling prices for some commodities—such as coffee, cocoa, and tea—made itself felt strongly. Thus, the terms of trade of many nonoil less developed countries deteriorated during 1978, while most industrial countries registered a relative improvement.

Trends in the trade accounts of the developed countries in part mirrored the changes in the strength of domestic demand. Thus the U.S., where economic growth was relatively strong, continued to have a very large trade deficit in 1978, while Japan, West Germany, and Switzerland remained massively in surplus. Surprisingly, fluctuations in exchange rates—mainly, the decline of the dollar and hardening of the mark and the yen—had remarkably little independent effect on the pattern of international trade in 1978. But these swings seemed certain to result in changes in relative costs between the countries concerned and thus were likely to produce their own corrective action on trade imbalances during 1979.

On the basis of provisional data, it seemed probable that the main oil-exporting countries had a combined trade deficit of $18 billion, little more than half the 1977 level of $35 billion. Relatively slow expansion in oil consumption in the industrial countries curbed the increase in export earnings, while imports continued to rise rapidly. In 1978 nonoil less developed countries were obliged to maintain and even increase their imports, but at the same time they suffered a decline in their commodity sales to customers in the industrial states, where demand had weakened. Lower prices for some commodities also added their effect. The net result was a sharp growth in the combined current account deficit of the nonoil less developed countries from $23 billion in 1977 to $33 billion in 1978. The situation was most serious for Caribbean and Latin-American nations, while there was a decline in the aggregate current account deficit of less developed countries in Asia. (EIU)

INTERNATIONAL EXCHANGE AND PAYMENTS

A massive improvement in the current balances of payments of the countries of the OECD relative to the rest of the world took place in 1978. The improvement was shared, on a smaller scale, by the

Table XII. Current Balances of Payments

In $000,000,000

Country	1975	1976	1977	1978*
Canada	−4.7	−3.8	−3.9	−4
France	—	−6.0	−3.2	+2
Germany, West	+4.1	+3.9	+3.8	+7
Italy	−0.6	−2.9	+2.1	+6
Japan	−0.7	+3.7	+11.0	+20
United Kingdom	−4.1	−2.1	+0.5	—
United States	+18.4	+4.3	−15.2	−17
OECD total	+1.2	−18.8	−25.0	+5
Other developed countries	−3.4	−1.6	−0.7	—
Centrally planned economies*	−5.8	−2.6	+2.4	+4
Oil-exporting countries*	+44.3	+44.6	+37.9	+14
Other less developed countries*	−36.3	−21.6	−14.6	−23

*Estimate.
Sources: International Monetary Fund, *International Financial Statistics*; national sources.

other developed countries and the centrally planned economies. Unlike the brief move into balance in 1975, the 1978 change was a result of the recovery of the export prices of the industrial countries relative to those of primary producers rather than a decline in their imports. The recovery strengthened through 1978, reinforced by the rise in value of the European currencies and the yen relative to the dollar (which was still used for most primary commodity prices). This indicated that the improvement in the terms of trade would be sustained. Also, the steady, rather than accelerating, growth in the OECD countries suggested that this improvement would not be offset by a large increase in volume of imports. The improvement relative to the oil-producing countries was assisted by increased output of oil in the U.S., U.K., and Norway, a reminder that the "industrial" countries are also the major producers of primary products.

The year also brought a change in the international policy response to the problems of imbalances and slow recovery from the mid-1970s recession. There were calls by international bodies such as the IMF and the OECD for reflation (use of monetary policies to raise prices) in order to lower the high level of domestic unemployment in the developed countries. Following pressure from the General Agreement on Tariffs and Trade organization, there was recognition that slow growth, rather than aiding international adjustment as had been argued in previous years, was hindering it because slow growth in the expanding sectors offered restricted opportunities to move out of declining industries. The preferred strategy for reflation shifted from a sequence in which the strongest countries lead the rest to emphasis on the responsibility of each country to take the measures that its position permits, more or less without regard for what may be done by the rest. This change resulted both from the unwillingness or inability of the countries designated as "locomotives" under the previous strategy to play that role and from a growing awareness of the relatively limited effect of external stimuli on the internal growth of most individual countries. It also reflected the smaller differences in the international positions of the developed countries that followed from the general improvement in current balances of payments in 1978. Although the new policy, like the old, was promoted by international organizations and conferences, it was not dependent on international coordination.

Current Balances. In contrast to the widespread deficits of 1976 and 1977, in 1978 only two major countries and an unusually low number of smaller OECD countries had deficits. For most countries, therefore, the external balance of payments ceased to be the major immediate problem for policymakers. The increase in the Japanese surplus on current account accounted for nearly one-third of the total improvement by the OECD countries; the rise in the yen exchange rate reinforced the general improvement in the terms of trade of industrial countries. France (which moved back into a small surplus), West Germany, and Italy accounted for another third of the improvement, with the rest divided among the smaller European countries.

Although as a group these probably remained in deficit, most of them improved their balances; Spain and Finland may have moved into surplus, and Norway, Portugal, Denmark, and Sweden reduced their deficits. The only major declines in balances were in The Netherlands, which probably moved into deficit for the first time since 1971 because of the slow growth of its exports, and Ireland, which may have doubled its deficit because of its relatively rapid domestic growth. The United Kingdom remained in balance and there was little change in the Canadian deficit. The U.S. probably had a small deterioration; it did not share in the general improvement in terms of trade because of the decline in the dollar, and the volumes of its exports and imports grew at similar rates.

For most of these countries the change in current balances stemmed almost entirely from changes in merchandise trade, but a few countries also had notable changes in other components. West Germany and the U.K. had substantial increases in their contributions to the EEC budget, reflected in improvements in the balances of France and some of the smaller EEC countries. Higher spending by tourists improved the balances of Italy, Portugal, Spain, and Greece. The U.S. travel deficit may have been reduced as income rose faster than spending. In contrast, the deterioration in the competitive position of the U.K. because of the relatively high value of the pound probably both increased visits abroad and cut income, and West German spending on travel continued to rise.

West Germany, Japan, and the U.S. probably also improved their nontrade balances by increases in their income from interest payments, profits, and other returns on capital. The improvement in the West German figures was exaggerated by the low level in 1977, induced by a change in tax laws, but it also reflected the returns earned on the continued outflow of long-term investment from West Germany. The increase in Japanese earnings reflected a similar process; there was a further large rise in outflows in 1978.

The rise in U.S. earnings, in spite of the large inflows of capital to finance current deficits, can probably be explained by the devaluation of the dollar. Although payments by the U.S. increased rapidly, the rise in other exchange rates increased

Table XIII. Foreign Investment by Major Countries

In $000,000

Country	1973	1974	1975	1976	1977	1978*
	Long-term capital flows					
Germany, West	+4,846	−2,231	−6,840	−126	−5,546	−2,700
Japan	−9,750	−3,881	−272	−984	−3,184	−11,200
United Kingdom	+3,494	+7,405	+2,891	+3,444	+7,439	+1,900
United States	−7,479	−6,416	−19,793	−17,140	−14,414	−14,700
Total	−8,889	−5,123	−24,014	−14,806	−15,705	−26,700
	Net interest, dividends, and profits					
Germany, West	+582	−67	+493	+965	+231	+1,750
Japan	+490	−451	−273	−204	+115	+900
United Kingdom	+2,992	+2,999	+1,695	+2,375	+765	+650
United States	+12,042	+15,457	+12,795	+15,933	+17,507	+19,500
Total	+16,106	+17,938	+14,710	+19,069	+18,618	+22,800

*Estimate.
Source: National sources.

the dollar value of payments to the U.S. (Most investments in the U.S. were denominated in dollars and therefore did not rise in dollar value with a fall in the rate for the dollar. This would be altered, but only for a small part of the total, if the U.S. Department of the Treasury's plan to issue government securities in foreign currencies was carried out.) In addition, most direct investment in the U.S. was fairly recent and probably not yet earning as much as it would when projects were completed, while U.S. investment abroad included a much higher proportion of mature projects.

The fourth traditional provider of long-term investment, the U.K., lost this position; by the end of 1978, its earnings were effectively zero. The most important temporary reasons for this were the large current deficits and consequent government borrowing in the early 1970s, but these loans were being repaid and the interest on them was falling. The more long-lasting reason was the switch to net inward investment by private investors, explained almost entirely by the development of oil production in the North Sea. The rise in payments on these investments reduced the surplus in 1977 and eliminated it during 1978. For the four countries together there was a recovery in net outflows of capital after the low levels of 1976 and 1977, partly because of the higher decline of investment in the U.K. but mainly because of the outflow from Japan.

The centrally planned economies completed the recovery begun in 1977 from their large deficits of the mid-1970s. They achieved the improvement principally by increasing the volume of their exports, rather than on the basis of relative prices, and also by controlling the growth of their imports. The nonindustrial developed countries registered only a small improvement in their balances, resulting from their restraint of imports; they did not share the improvement in the terms of trade of manufactures. Because this rise relied on continued slow domestic growth, it was less secure than that attained by the OECD countries.

The oil-exporting countries' surplus fell in 1978 to its lowest level since 1973, before the rise in oil prices, and was concentrated on Saudi Arabia and a few of the smaller oil producers. All the other major oil exporters were in or approaching deficit, also a return to the pre-1974 situation. The oil producers were hurt both by the deterioration in the

relative prices of all commodities (oil and the others had virtually unchanged prices in dollars relative to 1977) and by the decline in demand for their oil because of the increase in alternative supplies. The other less developed countries suffered a reversal of the entire 1977 rise in their balance. In addition to the fall in their terms of trade, only partially offset by the increase in industrial countries' demand for their exports, their continued need to finance deficits raised their interest payments. The increase in the deficit appears to have affected all areas, and they remained constrained by these deficits.

Reserves and Exchange Rates. The reserves of the nonoil less developed countries and the OECD countries rose during 1978, while those of the oil exporters fell. The rise in those of the less developed countries supported the indication from their borrowing that they more than financed their current deficits and repayments. Unlike the rise in 1977 it appeared to have been widespread. The share of the dollar in other countries' reserves may have fallen because countries chose to place newly acquired funds in a broader range of currencies than in the past, but there was no evidence that they shifted existing holdings out of dollars. This relative decline in the demand for short-term dollar assets, combined with the persistent large current deficit of the U.S., brought pressure on the dollar exchange rate during 1978.

In general, changes in exchange rates reflected current balance positions among industrial countries, although there was a tendency for changes to go too far and be followed by partial reversals. The most important change in exchange-rate policy in 1978 was the move of the U.S. away from a position of only minor intervention to active support of the dollar. This took place in two stages, in January and November. The change reflected both the growing importance of the external sector to the U.S. and the size of the movements in the dollar rate. The effective rate fell over 10% during the year, with most of the decline occurring in the first and third quarters. At the beginning of the year the U.S. attempted to restrain the fall by using "swap" arrangements with other countries. These were supplemented in November by internal policy, including rises in interest rates and a commitment to draw on the IMF. The objective at the end of the year appeared to be to stabilize the dollar rate, at least temporarily. The Canadian dollar fell with the U.S. dollar. The yen rose 25% and the Swiss franc, 20%. There was less change among the EEC currencies, although the mark was revalued within the EEC fixed parity group. The lira fell slightly through the year.

In July the EEC proposed what could be a second major change in the world exchange rate regime: the expansion of its fixed parity group, the "snake," into a European Monetary System to include France, Italy, Ireland, and the U.K. Based on the past performances of the existing members and of the proposed entrants relative to the mark, except for France changes in domestic policies and, probably, extensive temporary support would be required to keep them within the permitted bands of fluctuation. (SHEILA A. B. PAGE)

Ecuador

A republic on the west coast of South America, Ecuador is bounded by Colombia, Peru, and the Pacific Ocean. Area: 281,334 sq km (108,624 sq mi), including the Galápagos Islands (7,976 sq km), which is an insular province. Pop. (1978 est.): 7,814,000. Cap.: Quito (pop., 1978 est., 742,900). Largest city: Guayaquil (pop., 1978, 1,022,000). Language: Spanish, but Indians speak Quechuan and Jivaroan. Religion: predominantly Roman Catholic. In 1978 the country was ruled by a military junta including Vice-Adm. Alfredo Poveda Burbano (Navy), Gen. Guillermo Durán Arcentales (Army), and Gen. Luis Leoro Franco (Air Force).

The military junta held a constitutional referendum on Jan. 15, 1978, and the first round of presidential elections on July 16. The new constitution was approved by 43% of the votes cast (about 25% were spoiled or blank); its principal provisions included granting of the vote to illiterates, extension of the presidential term from four to five years without the option of reelection, and establishment of a single-chamber legislature. A new electoral law announced on February 20 stipulated that presidential candidates must be Ecuadorian-born citizens of Ecuadorian parentage and that former presidents could not run for office, thereby eliminating two candidates. In the first round Jaime Roldos of the Concentration of Popular Forces obtained a plurality of the votes but fell

short of the majority needed for election. An electoral court recommended that the results be annulled because of fraud, but the junta appointed a new court which, in October, set April 8, 1979, as the date for a runoff between Roldos and his closest competitor.

Ecuador's gross domestic product was expected to grow by 7.7% in 1978, as compared with an average 1960–77 growth rate of 7.2%. The 1978 trade balance was expected to be adversely affected by fluctuations in oil revenue (which accounted for over 40% of export receipts) and by escalating imports. Strict measures curbed inflation (the cost-of-living index rose by 12.3% in 1977, as compared with 13.5% in 1976).

Difficulties with the Esmeraldas refinery, pipelines, storage facilities, shrinking export markets, and rising domestic consumption hampered oil production. However, the amended Hydrocarbons Law allowed foreign companies to operate under risk contracts, and substantial investments were made by the state petroleum company, CEPE.

(MONIQUE MERRIAM)

Ecuadorians jammed polling places in January and approved a constitution aimed at ending military rule in the country.

Ecuador

ECUADOR

Education. (1975–76) Primary, pupils 1,254,850, teachers 33,297; secondary, pupils 615,917, teachers 37,230; vocational, pupils 90,535, teachers 5,001; teacher training, pupils 913, teachers 130; higher, students 170,391, teaching staff (1970–71) 2,867.

Finance. Monetary unit: sucre, with (Sept. 18, 1978) an official rate of 25 sucres to U.S. $1 (free rate of 53.68 sucres = £1 sterling). Gold, SDR's, and foreign exchange (June 1978) U.S. $659.7 million. Budget (1977 actual): revenue 16,453,000,000 sucres; expenditure 21,889,000,000 sucres. Gross national product (1977) 148,650,000,000 sucres. Money supply (May 1978) 29,729,000,000 sucres. Cost of living (Quito; 1975 = 100; June 1978) 139.

Foreign Trade. (1977) Imports U.S. $1,508,400,000; exports U.S. $1,228,800,000. Import sources (1976): U.S. 41%; Japan 15%; West Germany 9%; Colombia 5%. Export destinations (1976): U.S. 35%; Panama 13%; Peru 11%; Chile 7%; Colombia 6%. Main exports: crude oil 39%; bananas 14%; coffee 13%; cocoa 5%.

Transport and Communications. Roads (1973) 21,490 km (including 1,392 km of Pan-American Highway). Motor vehicles in use (1974): passenger 43,600; commercial (including buses) 68,400. Railways (1975): 1,200 km; traffic 65 million passenger-km, freight 46 million net ton-km. Air traffic (1976): 318 million passenger-km; freight 7.3 million net ton-km. Telephones (Jan. 1977) 174,000. Radio receivers (Dec. 1971) 1.7 million. Television receivers (Dec. 1975) 252,000.

Agriculture. Production (in 000; metric tons; 1977): rice 316; barley 50; corn (1976) 250; potatoes 347; cassava (1976) c. 590; sugar, raw value c. 372; bananas c. 2,383; pineapples c. 116; oranges c. 325; coffee c. 77; cocoa 70; fish catch c. 223. Livestock (in 000; 1976): cattle c. 2,725; sheep c. 2,150; pigs c. 2,700; horses c. 265; chickens c. 7,500.

Industry. Production (in 000; metric tons; 1976): crude oil 9,490; petroleum products 2,039; electricity (kw-hr) 1,885,000; cement 616; gold (troy oz) 11; silver (troy oz) 47.

Education

Uneven development was perhaps the most marked feature of educational systems throughout the world during 1978. The drive toward universal literacy continued, but—as UNESCO Director General Amadou-Mahtar M'Bow remarked on International Literacy Day in September—achievement remained below expectation. A reduction was forecast in the world illiteracy rate, from 32.4% in 1970 to 25.7% in 1990. If current trends persisted, however, the absolute number of illiterates would rise from 742 million to 814 million in the same period because of the increase in population.

At the fourth Conference of Ministers of Educa-

Elaine Barbour, an elementary school teacher from Colorado, gets a presidential kiss from Jimmy Carter in a White House ceremony in March honouring her as Teacher of the Year. The annual Teacher of the Year awards are sponsored by Encyclopædia Britannica companies, the Council of Chief State School Officers, and the *Ladies' Home Journal*.

Ecumenical Movement:
see Religion

years and three years of higher education), but nothing was done. The system on paper and that in practice remained widely different. Saudi Arabia continued its huge investment in education, with about 12% of the national budget earmarked for that purpose in 1978–79. Particular stress was placed on science and technology in the universities. Support for King Abdulaziz University in Jidda was increased almost 50%.

In the U.S. the educational scene was dominated by the so-called tax revolt, with its implications for retrenchment in the public schools. For some years, voters had shown increasing unwillingness to approve property tax increases for school purposes, but the extent of the "revolt" became apparent in June, when California adopted a referendum proposal known as Proposition 13. The measure cut local property taxes by more than 50% and school budgets by about 10%. Similar proposals were being put forward in other states, and in states with no provision for referenda, legislators were examining spending-restriction formulas. In an action attributed to Proposition 13, Congress cut $1 billion from the appropriation for the Department of Health, Education, and Welfare (HEW), though no actual programs were eliminated.

While other governmental agencies in California could recoup some losses through fees, local school districts had no recourse other than to cut personnel and services. And since California law permits reductions in teaching staff only when enrollments decline, school districts cut positions not covered by the law—in administration, special programs, secretarial, bus, and maintenance services, and, in some cases, athletic programs. The full effect of Proposition 13 was still uncertain because the state had a $5 million surplus to offset the $7 billion tax loss. There was also uncertainty about the effect on federally funded programs that require states to provide matching funds.

Ohio was another state where the schools faced fiscal crisis. Under a 1977 law, Ohio voters must approve tax increases as property values rise, and two-thirds of the votes were negative. Ohio's problems were compounded by a judicial ruling that current differences between the education budgets of rich and poor districts were unconstitutional. Since 1970 some 20 states had reformed education financing to make district-by-district spending more equal, and most other states had study commissions on the problem. The courts had generally held that states must take action to equalize spending among school districts.

Among the developed countries, retrenchment in educational spending seemed to cause the most public anger in Australia, where the allocation for universities and colleges of advanced education was, in effect, cut for 1978–79. An exception was made for technical and adult education, reflecting an emphasis on technical and vocational training evident in many Western countries.

In many advanced countries declining birthrates and falling enrollments made it easier for governments to reduce expenditure. Between 1976 and 1990, school rolls were expected to fall from 12.1 million to 8.1 million in West Germany and

tion and Economic Planning in Asia and Oceania, held in Colombo, Sri Lanka, in July, the minister of education for Sri Lanka, Nissanka Wijeyratne, said the less developed countries had been left none the better for the UN Development Decade. M'Bow conceded that the educational problems of the region were particularly pressing, since 43% of the people were under the age of 15. The conclusions of the conference were predictable: education should be more closely related to work and the skills required to improve economies, and there was a pervading need to train teachers.

China manifested a marked upsurge of enthusiasm and commitment to education. At a national education conference held in Peking, Vice-Premier Teng Hsiao-p'ing went further than any other Chinese leader in rejecting the policies of the previous decade and setting the seal on the new line—a complete overhaul of education as a key to accelerated economic growth. China reportedly had nine million teachers and, as at Colombo, first priority was given to improving their training. China was also anxious to make use of the educational expertise of the West and Japan. A visit by the British secretary of state for education, Shirley Williams, was followed by an announcement expressing the hope that Britain and China would exchange some 2,000 students. The emphasis on science and technology in Chinese schools was becoming almost an obsession. Foreign languages also had high priority, with English being easily the most highly regarded. (*See* CHINA.)

Political changes in another great Asian country, India, did not have the same effect on the educational system. There was much discussion by the Janata government of changing the system inherited from the Congress government (ten years of basic schooling followed by two further from 8.7 million to just over 6 million in England and Wales. It was predicted that by 1984 there would be 50,000 fewer children in Norwegian schools than in 1978. An exception was Ireland, which anticipated an increase of 200,000 between 1974 and 1986.

In the U.S. the 1978–79 school year opened with fewer students in the elementary and secondary schools and more in colleges and universities. Total enrollment, from kindergarten through graduate school, was estimated at 59.8 million, a 1% decrease from the preceding year and the third decline since 1975–76. There were expected to be 600,000 fewer students in kindergarten through eighth grade and 200,000 fewer high school students. Colleges, on the other hand, were told to plan for an additional 300,000. Spending on education was projected to increase from $144 billion to $155 billion, a rise of 8% to keep up with inflation. Of the total, state governments provided $57 billion; local education agencies $43 billion; and the federal government $16 billion. The balance came from miscellaneous sources such as tuition, fees, gifts, and endowments.

Another phenomenon common to most Western countries was the tendency for unemployment to be higher among young people than among adults. In some countries youth unemployment declined slightly in 1978, notably in West Germany and in the U.K., but in France and Sweden it increased. Everywhere attempts were made to alleviate the plight of the young unemployed, chiefly by providing training places in industry (especially medium- and small-sized firms) or through government-supported training workshops. In the U.K. the government pledged that every child leaving school (at 16) would be given employment or a training place within six months. An inquiry by the U.K. Department of Employment found that for every 1% increase in adult unemployment there was a 1.7% rise in employment among boys aged 16 to 18 and a 3% rise among girls. Conversely, when unemployment fell, the young found work faster than adults.

Unemployment was also found within the teaching profession, notably in countries like The Netherlands and the U.K. that had overproduced teachers in the 1960s and now faced declining enrollments. The principal teachers' union in England, the National Union of Teachers, reported that in September 1978 as many as 45,000 qualified teachers—about 10% of the entire teaching force—were unable to get jobs. In the U.S. it was estimated that the number of elementary and secondary teaching positions had fallen by 20,000 in 1978–79, although positions for college instructors rose by 10,000. One result of the end of the teacher shortage was that educational authorities and parents' groups began to intensify demands for higher teaching standards. Even security of tenure, where it existed, began to come under criticism.

As the 1978–79 school year opened, about 15,000 teachers at all levels were on strike in the U.S. Approximately 500,000 students in 21 states were affected, and some of the strikes lasted for weeks. Salary was the principal issue involved. Nevertheless, the 30 strikes that occurred in the opening weeks of school marked a sharp decrease from the peak year of 1975–76, when 203 districts were affected. A Gallup Poll indicated that a majority of Americans believed teachers should not strike, compared with 48% in 1975.

Primary and Secondary Schools. In England and Wales the demand for higher standards led to a major survey of primary school teaching by Her Majesty's Inspectors (an elite corps of government inspectors). Published in September, it revealed that standards in reading had been improving gradually, but the results for mathematics were less reassuring and for science and foreign languages they were distinctly disappointing. The inspectors found that a broad curriculum produced the best results and came out strongly against any "back to basics" campaign. The Labour government held strongly to the view that national testing of students should be carried out by means of light sampling at particular ages, not through mass testing. Many leading figures in the Conservative opposition, however, took the view that there should be much more emphasis on testing and that results should be widely published. Moves in this direction were strongly resisted by the teachers' unions.

In the U.S. it appeared that more students were being "failed" than ever before. Teachers reported that they were now less likely to pass students who failed academically, although the alternatives to the long-held practice of semiautomatic promotion were expensive remedial classes and increased numbers of students in school. A majority of the nation's school board members said they approved of competency testing to assure student mastery of at least minimal learning, and the sentiment was shared by a majority of parents questioned in a Gallup Poll. There was disagreement among legislators and citizens, however, as to just what the students should know before passing on to the next grade or graduating from high school. At a national conference convened by HEW, officials affirmed their belief that the states, not the federal government, should have responsibility for testing.

Japanese elementary school pupils get their lessons from a computer in an experimental program. A classroom teacher is available to give special help.

Teachers Should Be Allowed to Strike, Teens Say

Continuing a conservative trend first noted two years earlier, a majority of junior high school students polled in 1978 named their parents as the single greatest influence in their lives. Television, identified as the biggest single influence by most students in a similar poll conducted in 1975, received only 20% of the vote. One ninth grader said that the greatest influence in his life had been "my mistakes."

The survey of 2,000 junior high school students in all 50 states, conducted by the Encyclopædia Britannica Educational Corp., also asked, "What living person do you admire above all others?" Again, Mom and Dad took the honours; one or the other parent was named by nearly 70%. Among the few celebrities mentioned were John Travolta, Kristy McNichol, Robby Benson, and Steve Martin. Pres. Jimmy Carter got two votes. Several mentioned God.

Inflation was listed as the country's biggest current problem (47%), with crime (24%) and unemployment (10%) next. Most of the youngsters were concerned about the rising prices of "just about everything." One respondent admitted: "Inflation has to be stopped, yet like the experts, I have no solution." More than half believed their parents would be willing to pay higher taxes to improve the quality of their education. Some, however, said their families were opposed to tax increases for whatever purpose. Sixty percent felt that confidence in the U.S. government had not increased during the past year.

One area where conservatism was less apparent involved the right of teachers to strike. Only 18% thought there was no justification for such strikes; 53% felt teachers were justified in striking for higher pay, and 27% believed that teachers should strike to obtain better educational materials. In other areas, however, 75.4% favoured the death penalty for some crimes; 71% believed marijuana should not be legalized, and more than half (equally divided between boys and girls) thought there should be laws restricting the availability of abortions.

A Gallup Poll taken during the year indicated that nearly 65% of teenagers cheat on tests. In the Britannica Poll the percentage of cheaters rose to 83, although 12% of those who admitted cheating said they had done it "only once."

The favourite motion picture of those polled was *Grease*. There was no clear-cut choice of a favourite book. Television had not been abandoned by any means, and "Mork & Mindy" was the favourite program by a wide margin.

Scholastic Aptitude Test (SAT) scores, which had been falling for years, appeared to have stabilized to some degree. In the tests taken in the spring of 1978, average scores for reading and vocabulary remained level, although mathematics scores continued to decline. The SAT, taken by one million students each year, was the most widely used college entrance examination in the U.S. Administrators of the test noted that high school grade averages had declined for the second consecutive year, a phenomenon that was thought to reflect tougher grading standards.

One effect of declining enrollment, particularly in Western Europe, was an acceleration of the closing of small rural schools. There was considerable opposition to this trend, however, on the grounds that schools were vital to the health of rural communities. In the U.K. the movement favouring support of small schools gained strong political backing from the Conservatives.

In Spain, which was taking unsteadily to democracy, it was estimated that children attended primary school for only five months during the 1977–78 academic year, chiefly because of teachers' strikes and a chronic shortage of primary school places. In a controversial move, the government introduced a proposal to give "scholastic checks" (rather like educational vouchers) to parents, enabling them to send their children to private schools.

Religious control of schools was an issue in Ireland. Attempts to create multidenominational schools came to nothing, and the majority of schools remained firmly under the control of the Roman Catholic Church, despite opposition from the principal teachers' union. In Northern Ireland the Free Presbyterian Church of Ulster planned to set up 40 denominational schools on the grounds that proper Christian education was not being provided. In particular, the Free Presbyterians opposed teaching of the theory of evolution.

But it was in some of the African states that primary schools were most disrupted, notably in Rhodesia, where war continued between the Smith regime and the Patriotic Front. Nigeria's efforts to introduce universal primary education by 1980 got off to a ragged start. The most progress was made in the south, already the better educated area, thus accentuating differences between the south and the north. It was reported that some Muslim herdsmen in the north were hostile to any extension of primary schooling. Additional problems were an acute shortage of qualified teachers and resentment over the introduction of school fees by some local authorities. Some educators in South Africa were making efforts toward integrated schooling, and a conference at Grahamstown in September led to a call for a measure of integration. There was little genuine evidence of progress, however.

Paradoxically, the advent of a separatist government in Quebec strengthened the Canadian government's position favouring protection of minority interests in education and led to widespread interest in the subject. In Quebec determined efforts were being made to teach French to English-speaking children in primary schools. The Quebec experience had implications for the teaching of Welsh in Wales, where Welsh was spoken by less than 20% of the population, as well as for

Five students ride in a bus scheduled to carry 80 in a desegregation attempt in Los Angeles. The parents of many white students boycotted the busing of their children long distances into Chicano and black schools.

bilingual programs in the U.S. Results of experiments in Wales published early in 1978 showed that it was possible to teach primary school children from English-speaking homes through the medium of Welsh without any decline in standards. The success of the experiment, however, hinged on the availability of able and well-motivated teachers with a complete command of the Welsh vernacular.

In most U.S. jurisdictions, busing to achieve racial integration was a relatively minor issue in 1978. The major exception was Los Angeles, where some 60,000 students—about 10% of the nation's second largest school district—were bused in a move that climaxed 15 years of litigation. Schools in the Southeast were now the least segregated in the nation. Meanwhile, debate on the educational merits of desegregation continued. David Armor, a researcher for the Rand Corporation, reported that court-ordered integration caused whites to move. "White flight" was also cited by James Coleman, author of the research report that had been used to support desegregation efforts since the mid-1960s. Reversing his original position, Coleman now believed that school desegregation did not further learning by black students, that it was not good for all black students, and that voluntary desegregation programs were preferable to mandatory ones. Critics charged that he had done no original research in 13 years and had misinterpreted the findings of others.

Without controversy, Congress passed a $50 billion, five-year extension of the Elementary and Secondary Education Act (ESEA), designed to improve educational opportunities for disadvantaged and bilingual students. Despite its overwhelming approval by Congress, ESEA received poor marks from the Rand Corporation. Rand researchers called the 12-year ESEA effort a failure, claiming ESEA projects had mistakenly assumed that more money and new technology could bring about massive change. A similar warning that the disadvantaged could not rely solely on outside help was sounded by the Rev. Jesse Jackson (see BIOGRAPHIES). The civil rights leader devoted much of the year to promoting his Project EXCEL, an evangeli-

cal effort to reestablish the values of pride, discipline, and hard work among black students.

In Sweden, the acknowledged leader in secondary school innovation, a new curriculum for the nine-year comprehensive school was announced in 1978. Local education authorities and schools were given greater freedom in the formulation of teaching plans, but it was clear that the central government wished to maintain close supervision over the curriculum. The proposals included making typing and technology compulsory subjects and less streaming (grouping of students according to achievement) and specialization. Teaching hours in the intermediate and senior stages would be reduced to make way for less formal activities, such as class meetings and field trips. In Austria, with a deeply conservative educational system, there were signs that the "experiment" in comprehensive schooling might be extended, notably in Vienna. As in West Germany, the subject of comprehensive schools—similar to general high schools in the U.S.—remained highly political.

The new French minister of education, Christian Beullac, declared his support for the so-called Haby reforms introduced by his predecessor. Basically, these reforms provided for nonselective schools for the 11 to 16 age group. In Italy there was a strong movement in favour of tightening up the school-leaving examination—the *maturita*—taken at 18 for university entry. Following the student strikes and demonstrations of 1968, attempts had been made to create a less selective system for university entrance, and the examination had been made easier.

In the U.K. a government report proposed that the two school-leaving examinations held for 16-year-olds in England and Wales be merged, and that there be a common examination testing across the whole ability range. In an attempt to reduce the competitive pressure on Japanese schoolchildren, the government announced that, beginning in 1979, there would be a uniform entrance examination for all state universities. However, the more prestigious universities indicated that they would continue to hold their own entrance examinations.

If anything, the perennial debate over the secondary school curriculum increased in volume during 1978. There was a tendency to emphasize a "core curriculum" as against allowing students to pursue a multitude of options, and renewed enthusiasm for the teaching of foreign languages. A subject that was relatively new to the curriculum —environmental studies—gained impetus following a UNESCO-sponsored conference in Tbilisi, U.S.S.R., at the end of 1977. Pilot projects were established in places as far apart as Mongolia and Washington, D.C.

Higher Education. In the industrialized countries of the West, the expansion of higher education that had characterized the previous decade and a half appeared not to have brought any marked increase in the proportion of working-class children getting full-time higher education. In Australia a report published by the University of New South Wales Tertiary Education Research Centre showed that abolition of tuition fees by the Labor government in 1974 had had little effect on the accessibility of higher education to the socially disadvantaged. Similarly, educational researchers at the University of Lancaster, England, in evidence presented to an international conference during the summer, indicated that the middle classes had been the chief beneficiaries of the deeper scooping into the "pool of ability" from the early 1960s onward.

Affirmative action to increase the number of disadvantaged students in U.S. colleges and universities remained controversial. The Supreme Court struck down the admissions system used at the University of California Medical School at Davis, which reserved 16 out of 100 openings for minority students, and ordered Allan Bakke (*see* BIOGRAPHIES) admitted. Bakke had sued the university because his application for admission had been rejected while minority students with scores lower than his had been accepted. The court did not rule out consideration of race in determining admissions, however. Harvard University's admissions program, which used race as one factor in admissions decisions but did not have an actual quota, appeared to meet the court's criteria of acceptability. The complicated split decision was not expected to be the last word on affirmative action. At least one pending case, involving voluntary affirmative action programs in industry, could affect educational institutions. (*See* LAW.)

Efforts to contain the cost of higher education were apparent in a number of countries. In The Netherlands the 1979–83 budget for universities reckoned that there would be 30% more students in 1987 than in 1977 but no more resources with which to educate them. The inordinately long courses in Dutch universities—averaging some seven and a half years—were to be reduced to four years, plus two-year postgraduate courses. Similar recommendations were made in West Germany.

A proposal to grant tuition tax credits covering part of the cost of education was introduced in the U.S. Congress but was dropped in the rush toward adjournment. Debate on the measure had centred around the question of whether tax credits should be granted only for college tuition or for elementary and secondary tuition as well. Since the latter proposal would have covered parochial and other religious schools, its constitutionality was in doubt. To help middle-income families faced with skyrocketing college costs, Congress did pass an administration-backed proposal raising the income limit for families eligible for student aid from $15,000 to $25,000.

The job situation for college graduates in the U.S. was brighter than it had been in years. Specialty fields such as petroleum engineering were the most lucrative, but openings in the humanities were up 20%. Doctoral candidates had 20% more job openings than in 1977 and 90% more than in 1976. A study by the American Association of College Professors indicated that the Age Discrimination in Employment Act would not have as much effect on young college staff as had been feared. The act, which prohibited forced retirement before age 70, would go into effect in 1982. A Howard University study projected that, despite affirmative action, it would be 45 years before the percentage of blacks in college teaching positions equaled the proportion of blacks in the population as a whole. Women's advocates, who also continued to cite inadequate representation on college faculties, were heartened when Hannah Gray (*see* BIOGRAPHIES) became president of the University of Chicago.

The trend back to basics, which figured so prominently on the elementary and secondary levels, was also apparent in U.S. higher education. In many institutions, the trendy courses and experimental programs instituted in the '60s had been quietly dropped or absorbed into more traditional departments. A major step in this direction was taken at Harvard, where the faculty voted 182 to 65 to adopt the "core curriculum" proposed by dean Henry Rosovsky (*see* BIOGRAPHIES). In the first major change in the university's curriculum since 1945, students would be required to take about a fourth of their undergraduate program in five basic fields and to demonstrate competency in writing, math, and a foreign language.

Looking toward the future, there was manifest concern over what would happen to higher education systems when the smaller classes born during years of declining birthrates reached college age. In Britain the Labour government favoured taking up the slack by extending higher education to mature adults. A report from Statistics Canada indicated that post-secondary school enrollments would remain stable until 1982 and decline thereafter, partly because of the lower birthrate and partly because there would be less expenditure on higher education.

Special Education. A major report published in England on *Special Education Needs,* called the Warnock Report after its chairman, Mary Warnock, concluded that 17 to 20% of all children needed special education. For the most part, the report held, they should be integrated or mainstreamed—taught in ordinary schools—although it was recognized that the severely handicapped would have to be educated separately. The educational system should extend its embrace to the handicapped before they reached the age of two.

The report also called for massive improvements in in-service teacher training.

Mainstreaming became a fact in the U.S. Beginning with the 1978–79 school year, the public schools became fully responsible for the free and appropriate education of handicapped persons aged 3–18. The Education for All Handicapped Children Act, passed in 1975, had allowed several years in which schools could prepare to meet their biggest challenge since the late 1950s, when the Soviet sputnik called attention to deficiencies in U.S. scientific and technical education. The act requires that, insofar as it is feasible, all handicapped children and youth shall be placed in regular classrooms. An individualized learning program must be designed for each student, endorsed by parents (or appealed if they do not accept the plan), and, to the extent that it is possible, accepted by the student. Congress provided $565 million to implement the act in the 1978–79 school year. Of the 3.7 million students identified as handicapped, more than half had been in regular classes previously. The act mandated that, by 1980, public education services for the handicapped must be provided through age 21.

Largely unnoticed since sputnik, the gifted student—another kind of exceptional student—was receiving more attention in the U.S. Approximately 2.5 million U.S. children and youth were classified as gifted, but according to state data only 4% appeared to be receiving an appropriate education. Since 1972 the U.S. Office of Education had had a unit specializing in the education of the gifted, but funding amounted to only $3,780,000. Recognizing the need, Congress included dramatic funding increases in the Education Amendments of 1978. Funds for this purpose would rise to $50 million by 1983.   (JOEL L. BURDIN; TUDOR DAVID)

See also Libraries; Motion Pictures; Museums.

Egypt

A republic of northeast Africa, Egypt is bounded by Israel, Sudan, Libya, the Mediterranean Sea, and the Red Sea. Area: 1,002,000 sq km (386,900 sq mi). Pop. (1978 est.): 39,636,000. Cap. and largest city: Cairo (pop., 1978 est., 5,247,000). Language: Arabic. Religion: Muslim 93%; Christian 7%. President in 1978, Anwar as-Sadat; prime ministers, Mamdouh Salem and, from October 4, Mustafa Khalil.

For Egypt 1978 was dominated by the continuing efforts of Pres. Anwar as-Sadat (see NOBEL PRIZES) to achieve a general Middle East peace settlement following his own peace initiative toward Israel in November 1977. At home he attempted to curb criticism and to rally support for his policies.

Foreign Affairs. On January 4 President Sadat met both U.S. Pres. Jimmy Carter and West German Chancellor Helmut Schmidt at Aswan. President Sadat said that the Egyptian and U.S. views on the Middle East were "identical," and President Carter said the U.S. would play an active role in the peace process. However, the meeting of the Egyptian-Israeli Political Committee that began in Jerusalem on January 17 ended abruptly the fol-

lowing day with the sudden recall of the Egyptian delegation headed by the foreign minister, despite energetic U.S. attempts to mediate.

In February Sadat toured the U.S. and European countries to promote his own peace initiative. On February 14 Carter agreed to supply 50 F-5E jet fighters to Egypt. The deal, which was approved by the U.S. Senate on May 15, left the Arab-Israeli military balance largely unchanged but was seen as an important shift in U.S. policy.

There was a pause in direct Israeli-Egyptian peace contacts in February after the Israeli Military Committee headed by Defense Minister Ezer Weizman (see BIOGRAPHIES) returned to Israel. Hopes were raised of a resumption of negotiations when Sadat wrote to Israeli Prime Minister Menahem Begin (see NOBEL PRIZES) on March 2, but a visit to Egypt by Weizman, the Israeli Cabinet minister with whom Sadat had the best relations, ended in failure. The stalemate continued for several weeks. Sadat's proposal on May 11 that Israel should return the West Bank area (west of the Jordan River) to Jordanian administration and the Gaza Strip to Egypt as an interim step toward a peace settlement was flatly rejected by Israel. On May 30 Sadat hinted that Egypt would renounce the 1975 Sinai disengagement agreement with Israel in October if there was no progress in negotiations by then. He followed this by strong speeches on June 6 and 7 expressing impatience and threatening war if Israel did not make concessions. Formal proposals by Egypt on July 5 that all Israeli settlements should be removed and the military governments in the West Bank and Gaza be abolished at the beginning of a five-year interim period during which Israel would withdraw from the West Bank, Gaza Strip, and East Jerusalem were rejected by Israel.

Egyptian-Israeli contacts were only resumed during Sadat's visit to Austria, July 7–14, when Sadat held surprise meetings with both Israeli Defense Minister Weizman and opposition leader Shimon Peres. Further talks between the Egyptian

Egypt

A huge crowd led by Egyptian Pres. Anwar as-Sadat gathered at the funeral of 15 commandos killed in the attempted rescue of a hijacked airliner at Larnaca Airport, Cyprus, in February.

KOUSSY—GAMMA/LIAISON

and Israeli foreign ministers at Leeds Castle in the U.K. on July 18–19 ended in stalemate.

Throughout the year President Sadat had to contend with strong and often bitter criticism from Palestinian organizations and such hard-line Arab nations as Iraq, Syria, and Libya without receiving any clear support from moderate regimes such as Jordan and Saudi Arabia. The murder in Nicosia, Cyprus, on February 18 of Yusuf as-Sibai, editor of the newspaper *al-Ahram*, was followed by an unsuccessful attempt by Egyptian commandos at Cyprus's Larnaca Airport to rescue hostages taken by the two Palestinian assassins. Egypt broke off relations with Cyprus.

On August 8 President Sadat accepted an invitation from President Carter to meet him and Israeli Prime Minister Begin at Camp David, Md., on September 5. The meeting lasted 13 days and ended with two agreements entitled "A Framework for Peace in the Middle East" and "A Framework for the Conclusion of a Peace Treaty Between Egypt and Israel." In return for the establishment of normal relations between Israel and Egypt, Israel agreed to return all Sinai to Egypt and remove its settlements from this region. Israel also agreed to freeze the establishment of Jewish settlements in the West Bank during the peace negotiations, but many questions were left open such as future boundaries in the West Bank and Israeli sovereignty in the area. The fact that Palestinians' rights were not mentioned in the agreements, which did not commit Israel to withdraw from all occupied Arab territory, meant that the Palestine Liberation Organization, Syria, and other hard-line Arab states denounced them. Jordan and Saudi Arabia expressed strong dissatisfaction, although Saudi Arabia accepted Egypt's right to recover its own territory as best it could. Undeterred, Sadat declared that this was the only possible way to move toward a general peace. His great satisfaction was that he had achieved his aim of direct U.S. involvement in the Middle East peace process.

Negotiations again broke down in November,

Jubilant throngs greeted Pres. Anwar as-Sadat on his return to Cairo in September from the Camp David meeting.

BOCCON—GIBOD—SIPA PRESS/BLACK STAR

primarily because of Israel's delay in accepting the Camp David agreements. Late in December Egyptian Prime Minister Mustafa Khalil, Israeli Foreign Minister Moshe Dayan, and U.S. Secretary of State Cyrus Vance met in Brussels in an unsuccessful effort to set up future negotiating sessions.

Egypt attempted to strengthen its relations with conservative and pro-Western regimes in Africa. It sent arms to help Somalis fighting the Marxist regime in Ethiopia, and the interception by Kenya on February 15 of an Egyptian aircraft carrying arms to Somalia led to a short-lived crisis with the Kenyan government. On May 30 Egypt warned Ethiopia it would go to war if any power tried to deprive it of the Nile waters or attacked Sudan.

Domestic Affairs. During 1978 President Sadat's earlier moves to liberalize the regime were severely curbed by his own measures to muzzle the opposition. On March 19 five leaders of the extreme Islamic revivalist group al-Takfir Wa al-Hijra were executed for the kidnapping and murder of a former minister of religious endowments in July 1977. The revived New Wafd Party, led by Fuad Serageddin "Pasha," was licensed on February 3. The left brought out the first issue of a successful weekly, *al-Ahali*. But the left suffered continuous harassment by the authorities, and several of its supporters in the provinces were arrested. In his speech on May 2 Sadat showed anger at criticism of the government. There had been strong attacks on ministers over proposals to sell part of the Egyptian motion picture industry to Saudi Arabian interests and to implement a giant tourist project near the Pyramids of Giza (which was later canceled by the president).

On May 7 a new Cabinet was formed under Mamdouh Salem in which the main change was the dropping of veteran Finance and Economic Affairs Minister Abd-al Moneim al-Qaisouni. Sadat then ordered a referendum, which was held on May 21, asking for endorsement of measures to remove from politics and the media those with atheist ideologies and those who had corrupted political life before and after 1952. The government claimed a 98.29% "yes" vote from more than 85% of the electorate. On June 1 the People's Assembly approved the purge law. The New Wafd then announced it was disbanding and the left-wing Progressive Union Party that it was suspending its activities.

On June 19 the Egyptian ambassador to Portugal, Gen. Saad Eddin ash-Shazli, bitterly denounced Sadat as a dictator and, following his dismissal, left Lisbon for Algeria. On June 26 a right-wing and a left-wing member of Parliament were expelled as first victims of the law restricting the president's opponents.

On July 22 Sadat announced his decision to form his own political party, the National Democratic Party (NDP), dissolve the Arab Socialist Union (ASU), and allow more political parties into the country's political system. The ruling centre party, headed by Prime Minister Salem, announced on August 14 that it would merge with the new NDP. On October 2 Sadat asked Mustafa Khalil, former secretary-general of the ASU, to form a new government with a program for over-

Education. (1976–77) Primary, pupils 4,151,956, teachers 125,397; secondary, pupils 1,828,090, teachers 52,700; vocational, pupils 408,540, teachers 25,215; teacher training, students 32,744, teachers 2,830; higher, students 717,053, teaching staff 24,987.

Finance. Monetary unit: Egyptian pound, with (Sept. 18, 1978) an official rate of E£0.39 to U.S. $1 (free rate of E£0.75 = £1 sterling) and a tourist rate of E£0.69 to U.S. $1 (E£1.35 = £1 sterling). Gold, SDR's, and foreign exchange (June 1978) U.S. $472 million. Budget (1977 est.) balanced at E£5,402 million. Gross domestic product (1977) E£7,341 million. Money supply (June 1978) E£3,247.3 million. Cost of living (1975 = 100; March 1978) 135.2.

Foreign Trade. (1977) Imports E£1,881.3 million; exports E£668.5 million. Import sources (1976): U.S. 16%; West Germany 11%; Italy 8%; France 6%; U.K. 6%; U.S.S.R. 5%. Export destinations (1976): U.S.S.R. 24%; Italy 8%; Czechoslovakia 6%; East Germany 5%. Main exports (1976): cotton 27%; crude oil 18%; cotton yarn 10%; fruit and vegetables 10%; petroleum products 7%; rice 5%.

Transport and Communications. Roads (1972) 25,976 km. Motor vehicles in use (1976): passenger 245,600; commercial (including buses) 57,400. Railways: (1976) 4,856 km; traffic (1975) 8,831,000,000 passenger-km; freight 2,260,000,000 net ton-km. Air traffic (1976): 1,739,000,000 passenger-km; freight 21.9 million net ton-km. Shipping (1977): merchant vessels 100 gross tons and over 176; gross tonnage 407,818. Telephones (Jan. 1975) 503,200. Radio licenses (Dec. 1975) 5,120,000. Television licenses (Dec. 1975) 620,000.

Agriculture. Production (in 000; metric tons; 1977): wheat 1,872; barley c. 125; millet c. 830; corn c. 2,900; rice 2,270; potatoes c. 970; sugar, raw value c. 649; tomatoes c. 2,400; onions c. 670; dry broad beans (1976) c. 237; watermelons (1976) c. 1,244; dates c. 417; oranges c. 990; grapes c. 265; cotton, lint 435; cheese c. 229; beef and buffalo meat c. 235. Livestock (in 000; 1977): cattle c. 2,148; buffalo c. 2,294; sheep c. 1,938; goats c. 1,393; asses (1976) c. 1,539; camels (1976) c. 113; chickens c. 26,681.

Industry. Production (in 000; metric tons; 1977): cement 3,167; iron ore (metal content; 1976) 621; crude oil 21,034; petroleum products (1976) 10,380; fertilizers (nutrient content; 1976–77) nitrogenous 200, phosphate 90; salt (1976) 508; sulfuric acid (1976) 31; cotton yarn 206; cotton fabrics (m) 695,000; electricity (kw-hr; 1976) c. 11 million.

hauling the country's political and economic system. The new Cabinet announced on October 4 consisted mainly of technocrats and academics who would tackle Egypt's social and economic problems. Gen. Muhammad Abd-al Ghani al-Gamassi, who as minister of war and commander in chief had been one of the president's mainstays in his peace initiative, was replaced in a surprise move by Gen. Kamal Hassan Ali, whose title was changed to defense minister to symbolize the new orientation toward peace.

Aid totaling some $3.4 billion was pledged to Egypt during the year by the Paris-based International Consultative Group for Egypt under the chairmanship of the World Bank to cover the country's estimated balance of payments deficit. There was a slight improvement in Egypt's economic prospects in 1978 as a result of the rise in Suez Canal and tourist revenues and of new oil discoveries in the Eastern and Western Deserts and the Gulf of Suez. (PETER MANSFIELD)

El Salvador

A republic on the Pacific coast of Central America and the smallest country on the isthmus, El Salvador is bounded on the west by Guatemala and on the north and east by Honduras. Area: 21,041 sq km (8,124 sq mi). Pop. (1978 est.): 4,516,000. Cap. and largest city: San Salvador (pop., 1976 est., 500,000). Language: Spanish. Religion: Roman Catholic. President in 1978, Gen. Carlos Humberto Romero.

El Salvador

The incumbent National Conciliation Party made practically a clean sweep in national elections for congressional deputies and municipal officials, held March 12. The opposition, alleging fraud, boycotted the polls.

The state of general unrest that reigned throughout the year was punctuated by various acts of violence by both government and antigovernment elements. At least 29 persons were killed in March while demonstrating against high unemployment, low wages, and the "law to defend and guarantee public order," which, since its passage in November 1977, had kept the country under a virtual state of siege. The gunfire came from a government-sponsored paramilitary organization known as Orden.

This so-called Holy Week massacre did not prevent further demonstrations by dissident elements, which included a significant sector of the Roman Catholic clergy. Clandestine acts of violence by antigovernment forces included eight kidnappings and murders of several prominent individuals.

In an apparent effort to attack basic social problems, the government launched a five-year rural development program aimed at improving crop production in neglected areas and providing improved rural housing and general welfare.

(HENRY WEBB, JR.)

EL SALVADOR

Education. (1976) Primary, pupils 796,250, teachers (1975) 15,665; secondary, pupils 32,449; vocational, pupils 25,762; secondary and vocational (1975), teachers 1,491; teacher training, students 868, teachers (1975) 55; higher (1975), students 26,692, teaching staff 1,275.

Finance. Monetary unit: colón, with (Sept. 18, 1978) a par value of 2.50 colones to U.S. $1 (free rate of 4.90 colones = £1 sterling). Gold, SDR's, and foreign exchange (June 1978) U.S. $142.3 million. Budget (1977 actual): revenue 1,257,000,000 colones; expenditure 1,077,000,000 colones. Gross national product (1977) 6,498,000,000 colones. Money supply (June 1978) 1,059,400,000 colones. Cost of living (1975 = 100; June 1978) 135.2.

Foreign Trade. (1977) Imports 2,368,200,000 colones; exports 2,419,000,000 colones. Import sources (1976): U.S. 28%; Guatemala 15%; Japan 10%; Venezuela 7%; West Germany 6%; Costa Rica 5%. Export destinations (1976): U.S. 33%; West Germany 14%; Guatemala 14%; The Netherlands 8%; Japan 8%; Costa Rica 6%; Nicaragua 5%. Main exports (1976): coffee 53%; cotton 11%; chemicals 6%; sugar 6%; textile yarns and fabrics 5%.

Transport and Communications. Roads (1974) 10,972 km (including 625 km of Pan-American Highway). Motor vehicles in use (1974): passenger 41,000; commercial (including buses) 19,100. Railways (1976) 602 km. Air traffic (1976): 195 million passenger-km; freight 14 million net ton-km. Telephones (Jan. 1977) 54,200. Radio receivers (Dec. 1975) 1.4 million. Television receivers (Dec. 1975) 135,000.

Agriculture. Production (in 000; metric tons; 1977): corn c. 377; sorghum c. 176; rice (1976) 51; dry beans c. 40; sugar, raw value 286; bananas c. 53; oranges c. 45; coffee c. 180; cotton, lint 71. Livestock (in 000; 1976): cattle 1,109; pigs c. 425; horses c. 82; chickens 3,357.

Industry. Production (in 000; metric tons; 1976): cement 322; petroleum products c. 670; cotton yarn 6; electricity (kw-hr) 1,199,000.

Energy

In November 1978 U.S. Pres. Jimmy Carter signed into law the energy legislation he had requested from Congress in April 1977. During the intervening 18 months there had been a bitter and protracted controversy over the policy embodied in the legislation. As passed, it differed in many respects from the original presidential proposals. The major omission was the crude-oil equalization tax, which would have raised domestic oil prices to world levels but with the difference going to the federal government. Among the provisions of the new legislation were the phased deregulation of the wellhead price of new natural gas production, penalty taxes on new "gas-guzzling" cars, incentives for energy conservation and the use of such new energy resources as solar and geothermal power, and the establishment of national policies governing the regulation of electric utilities by the individual state commissions.

The major event in the coal industry of the United States during the year was the longest industry-wide strike in its history. It began on Dec. 6, 1977, and lasted until March 24 for a total of 109 days. The end of the strike came none too soon, for coal stockpiles at the generating stations of many electric utilities were reaching dangerously low levels. Utilities in more than a dozen states were seriously affected. The situation was not helped by severe cold in the Midwest during January, which sent demand to record heights in some areas at the same time that heavy rains, followed by a sudden temperature drop, froze coal stockpiles into unusable, rocklike masses.

As the duration of the strike lengthened, the governors of several states imposed mandatory cutbacks on electricity consumption by industrial and commercial users, and utilities urged all citizens to reduce their usage as much as possible. Among measures taken by the federal government to alleviate matters were the coordination of large-scale transfers of power to coal-based utilities from those having systems based on nuclear and oil-fired generation, and a cutback of 60% in the power consumption of the nation's three nuclear-enrichment plants. Despite fears of large-scale unemployment as a result of the mandatory cutbacks in industrial consumption, the loss of jobs was minor, as industry instead juggled work schedules and the use of electrical equipment.

Another significant event concerning coal was the defeat of a coal slurry pipeline bill in Congress in July. The bill would have given the right of eminent domain to projects for the construction of pipelines that would carry coal suspended in water. The vote was a victory for the railroads, which feared the loss of much of their coal traffic to this cheaper form of transportation.

The event of greatest significance concerning oil and gas was the official confirmation that discoveries over the preceding several years had made Mexico one of the world's oil giants. In his September state of the nation address to the Mexican Congress, Pres. José López Portillo announced that Mexico's estimated potential resources of oil and gas were the equivalent of 200,000,000,000 bbl. This resource endowment is of the same order of magnitude as that of Saudi Arabia. Although it gave Mexico the potential of producing and exporting oil in quantities that could jeopardize the control of the Organization of Petroleum Exporting Countries (OPEC, of which Mexico was not a member) over world oil prices, President López Portillo stated that Mexico would not use its export capability in a manner that would disrupt world oil markets. The new fields (originally discovered in 1972) are located in the states of Tabasco and Chiapas, on the Isthmus of Tehuantepec, and offshore in the adjacent Gulf of Campeche.

A new device developed in Princeton, New Jersey, is able to create temperatures of 60 million degrees Celsius, another step on the road to being able to obtain energy from nuclear fusion.

UPI COMPIX

The control room of Taiwan's first nuclear power plant. Two other nuclear plants were scheduled to be completed in 1984.

The emergence of Mexico as one of the superstates on the world oil scene carried profound implications for the energy future of the world, especially that of the U.S. It cast doubt on the existing consensus that the world faced an oil supply crisis in the 1980s and called into question the Carter energy policy's underlying assumption of petroleum resource scarcity.

After many months of administrative delays and court battles, the U.S. Supreme Court in February allowed to stand a lower court decision to permit drilling for oil and gas on the continental shelf off the Atlantic Coast. At the end of March drilling began from a ship anchored in 400 ft of water in the Baltimore Canyon area some 85 mi east of Atlantic City, N.J. Six other oil companies or consortia also joined the search. The results were awaited with great interest, for the discovery of oil or gas would indicate the possibility of reducing U.S. dependence on foreign sources of supply, and the location, so near the large consuming centres of the Northeast, would be ideal for supplying those markets.

It was thus a dramatic event when the announcement was made in August that natural gas had been found in the Baltimore Canyon area. The flow of gas from the discovery well (7.5 million cu ft a day) was not in itself commercial but was termed "very encouraging." Further drilling proceeded with the hope that the size of the discovery would prove to be large enough to justify the investment in the pipeline necessary to bring the gas ashore. Further exploration of the Atlantic continental shelf was assured when the Department of the Interior in March leased tracts for drilling in areas off Georgia and Florida.

Among other events concerning oil and gas, OPEC made news in June when it decided at its semiannual meeting not to raise the price of oil, a decision ensuring that world oil prices would not increase during 1978. In the North Sea the "largest object ever moved by man" was installed for production in the Ninian oil field. The "object" was a concrete tower 776 ft high and weighing 600,000 tons. The structure was designed to carry production equipment for the field. A new world record for the water depth of commercial offshore drilling

operations was set with a well drilled in 4,348 ft of water off the mouth of the Congo River in Africa.

Representatives of the 13 members of OPEC met at Abu Dhabi, United Arab Emirates, in December and decided to raise the price of their oil in stages beginning Jan. 1, 1979. By the end of 1979 the total increase would be 14.5%. Many had expected Saudi Arabia to exercise its influence in order to keep the increase below 10%. When questioned, the Saudi representative said that the decision was "a medium solution representing the best we could do under the circumstances."

Debate continued to rage during the year over the future prospects for the world's oil supply as new studies were published. The deep pessimists forecast development of a critical world oil shortage during the 1980s; the moderate pessimists contended that this would not occur until the 1990s; and the optimists foresaw no serious supply problem for the remainder of the century. None of this controversy took into account the new status of Mexico.

Opponents of nuclear power exhibited increased militancy during the year, with occupations or attempted occupations at several operating plants and construction sites. Most notable was the demonstration in June at the site of the Seabrook plant in New Hampshire by 20,000 protesters. Aside from these troubles the prospect for completion of the Seabrook plant was repeatedly cast into doubt and then revived during the year by a series of off-again, on-again court decisions and opinions by environmental and nuclear regulators. By year's end, however, the necessary decisions for completion had been made and upheld.

Two U.S. Supreme Court decisions disposed of other objections raised by nuclear power opponents. In April the court, in a decision that reduced the ability of nuclear opponents to intervene in the process of siting and licensing nuclear power plants, severely limited the power of lower courts to review administrative procedures. In June the court upheld the constitutionality of the Price-Anderson Act, which sets a legal limit of $560 million on the liability of electric utilities resulting from a nuclear accident. If the act had been struck down, it would have cast serious doubt on

Electric bills in Clayton, New Mexico, were expected to go down after this 100-foot-high windmill went into operation in January. The wind blows free in Clayton, and the windmill was expected to generate 200 kw of electricity.

the ability of the utility industry to obtain financing for new nuclear power plants.

In the United Kingdom the House of Commons voted by a large majority to approve construction of a plant at Windscale to reprocess the spent fuel from nuclear power stations in Britain and some other countries. This action was noteworthy because it was directly contrary to the existing U.S. policy to defer nuclear fuel reprocessing until means could be devised to prevent the diversion of plutonium from such plants into weapons manufacture. (*See* ENVIRONMENT.)

Other events relating to nuclear energy included the start-up of Italy's first large-scale nuclear power reactor (840 Mw) at Caorso, near Piacenza; the completion of the first nuclear power reactor (636 Mw) in Taiwan; and the discovery of one of the world's largest deposits of uranium under a lake in northern Saskatchewan.

The testing of geothermal possibilities moved into two new areas in the U.S. during 1978. In June an exploratory well was drilled in New Jersey, the first in a program of 50 wells to be drilled along the Atlantic coastal plain to obtain heat-flow measurements. In July the first test well for geothermal-geopressure energy was drilled in Texas. The purpose of this well was to gather data on the composition and flow behaviour of the fluids contained in deep reservoirs in the Texas-Louisiana Gulf Coast region. The fluids are gas dissolved in hot brine under very high pressure. Thus, such reservoirs constitute potential energy sources in the form of heat, pressure, and gas.

A significant advance in research on nuclear fusion was made at Princeton University. Using a Tokamak machine (a doughnut-shaped magnetic bottle 18 in in diameter), the researchers achieved a temperature of 60 million degrees Celsius, more than twice as high as any temperature previously

achieved. The experiment was important not only because the temperature was achieved but also because it demonstrated, in addition, that the plasma could be held stable at that level. The success of the experiment did not advance the day when fusion power would become feasible, but it did constitute a necessary accomplishment toward that end.

In a field closer to present technology the world's first high-magnetic field magnetohydrodynamics (MHD) generator was successfully operated for ten hours in February at a test facility near Moscow in the Soviet Union. The promise of MHD is the ability to generate electricity directly, without any moving parts, by passing a superheated stream of ionized gas through a magnetic field. The Moscow test was unique in that it used a Soviet MHD installation in combination with a 40-ton superconducting magnet flown from the Argonne National Laboratory in the U.S.; this provided a more powerful magnetic field than had ever been used before in MHD research.

Other events involving unconventional energy sources included: (1) the beginning in May of the first attempt at commercial production of shale oil from the shale deposits of Colorado by burning part of the shale in place, driving off the oil, and pumping it to the surface; (2) the dedication in January of the first federally sponsored wind generator to provide electric power for a U.S. community (Clayton, N.M.), using a 200-kw turbine and twin rotor blades spanning 125 ft; (3) the establishment of the first solar electric system as the sole source of power, for the Papago Indian village of Schuchuli, Ariz., with a capacity of 3 kw; and (4) the approval by voters in Burlington, Vt., of the funding for a wood-fired power plant that would burn 1,200 to 1,500 tons daily of chipped waste wood.   (BRUCE C. NETSCHERT)

COAL

In 1978 many countries continued to increase their coal production capacity in anticipation of future oil shortages, despite the depressed level of economic activity. The recession particularly affected demand from the steel industry, resulting in surplus capacity and a buildup of stockpiles in a number of nations. There was much interest in using coal rather than oil for electricity generation, and research into coal liquefaction and gasification to meet future oil needs continued with a number of projects reaching the pilot-plant stage. Underground gasification of coal deposits not accessible by traditional mining methods also received attention.

World hard coal production reached an estimated 2,464,637,000 metric tons in 1977, 3.2% above 1976. Increases were reported from the U.S., U.S.S.R., China, Poland, South Africa, and Canada. Western European production fell by 2.3%, while Eastern European production, excluding the U.S.S.R., rose by 2.8%. World lignite production gained 1.8% during 1977 to reach 909,792,000 metric tons, with 71.6% mined in Europe.

CHINA. China produced an estimated 490 million metric tons of coal in 1977 (10% from open pits), an increase of 50 million tons over 1976. The southern provinces produced 140 million tons, and with an annual growth rate of 13%, double that of the northern provinces; they hoped soon to become self-sufficient. By the end of 1977 the Kailuan mines were reported to have regained the high levels of output attained before the disastrous earthquake of July 1976. China planned to develop an export trade; Japan took 490,782 tons in 1977, and reports indicated that this could rise to as much as 15 million tons a year in the future. Production might reach 600 million tons a year by 1980 and then was expected to double by 1990. A number of new coalfields were identified, and new productive capacity amounted to some 6 million to 7 million tons during 1977.

UNITED STATES. The 109-day strike called by the United Mine Workers of America (UMW), the longest in the history of the U.S. coal industry, was settled on March 24, 1978. The new three-year contract stipulated that the UMW wage would rise from an average of $7.80 an hour to a new high of $10.20 an hour by the end of 1980. With some changes, U.S. Pres. Jimmy Carter's energy policy, giving priority to coal production and to energy conservation, received congressional approval in October 1978.

Production of bituminous coal and lignite totaled 672 million short tons in 1977 (about 60% from surface operations), a decline of 6.6 million tons from the record level set in 1976. Anthracite production, at 6.6 million tons, remained at about the same level as in 1976. Approximately 481 million short tons of coal were consumed in 1977 by electric utilities, 83 million tons by coke producers, and 68 million by other industrial users. Exports fell by 5.7 million tons to 54.3 million tons. Canada displaced Japan as the principal importer of U.S. coal.

U.S.S.R. A total of 722 million metric tons of raw coal and lignite were produced in the Soviet Union in 1977, an increase of 11 million metric tons over 1976, with about one-third coming from open-pit operations. Main production areas were the Donets and Kuznetsk basins, with, respectively, 31% and 19% of total production. Annual capacity increased by 17.4 million tons, and annual output was expected to reach 805 million tons in 1980. Of the estimated 420,-400,000,000 tons of reserves, more than 70% were in the eastern region; plans were under way to develop these fields and to convey the electrical energy they would generate by high-voltage transmission lines.

EUROPEAN ECONOMIC COMMUNITY. Total hard coal production in 1977, at 233,735,000 metric tons, was 7.2 million tons below the 1976 figure. Belgium, with an output of 7,070,000 tons, registered a drop of 2.3% from 1976. Preparations began in July 1978 for deep-mine gasification trials

sponsored jointly by the Belgian and West German governments. Production in France fell by 726,000 tons to 24.4 million tons of coal and lignite. Hard coal production in West Germany dropped 4.8 million tons to 84.5 million tons; brown coal production, at 122.9 million tons, was 11.6 million tons lower. At the end of 1977 West German stockpiles amounted to a record 32.5 million tons of hard coal.

In the U.K. the introduction of a productivity payment scheme near the end of the National Coal Board (NCB) financial year 1977–78 halted the downward trend in productivity. Deep-mined output, at 104.5 million long tons, was only 2.1 million tons below the amount for the previous year. Open-pit production rose by 20% to 13.3 million tons, some difficulty being experienced in obtaining authorization for future sites. Output from licensed mines increased slightly to 1.2 million tons. The NCB finished a fourth consecutive financial year with a trading profit, £109 million in 1977–78. NCB coal sales to power stations in 1977–78 reached a new record level of 75.7 million tons, although coking sales were the lowest since 1947 because of the depressed steel industry. In 1978 plans were announced to increase overall production to 135 million tons by 1985 and to 170 million by 2000.

POLAND. Hard coal production rose to a new record level of 186 million metric tons, 3.8% over 1976. Lignite production, at 40.7 million tons, remained at about the same level. The increased output in recent years was achieved by the development of new mines and by modernization, both below and above ground. A new hard coal mine at Czeczot was started. Exports rose slightly to 39.3 million tons. By 1985 output was expected to reach 240 million tons a year, dependent on Poland's general economic growth.

JAPAN. Coal production in Japan increased by just over half a million metric tons in 1977, thus halting a steady downward trend. Coal imports increased for the first time in three years, reaching 60,840,-000 tons, an increase of 82,428 tons over 1976. Australia maintained its position as Japan's principal supplier, with 26,450,000 million tons; the U.S. was second with 15,-180,000 million tons, a drop of 13% from 1976.

INDIA. Hard coal production reached 99 million metric tons in 1977, about 2 million tons less than in 1976, partly because of a strike in April 1977. Production targets for future years were being scaled down because of the lack of foreseeable demand. India's coal-based industries were concerned about the quality of the nation's coal and the life of its metallurgical coking coal resources. Plans to import high-grade coking coal to blend with indigenously produced coal were proposed during 1978. Soviet, Polish, and Japanese experts were helping with 71 projects to increase annual productive capacity by 67 million tons in the next six to eight years. Although official estimates placed coal reserves at 84 billion tons (23% coking coal), a program to upgrade existing reserves and establish new ones was under way.

Empty coal cars jammed up in West Virginia during the longest coal strike in U.S. history. Work came to a stop on December 6, 1977, and continued until the new contract was ratified on March 24, 1978.

UPI COMPIX

348

Energy

SOUTH AMERICA. Coal production in 1977 amounted to 8,973,000 metric tons, an increase of about 351,000 tons over 1976. Colombia was the largest producer with 4 million tons, while Brazil produced 3 million and Chile 1,350,000. Venezuela was planning to develop its coal reserves to supply its expanding steel industry.

AFRICA. South Africa produced some 85.4 million metric tons of the estimated total of 90,260,000 tons of hard coal mined in Africa in 1977. South African exports, from the new terminal at Richard's Bay, more than doubled to 12.7 million tons. New mines were being developed for the export trade and also to supply increased demands from thermal power stations. Bosjesspruit Coal Mine, opened in mid-1977, was developed to provide South Africa's second oil-from-coal plant (Sasol II) with 12 million tons of coal a year by 1981.

AUSTRALIA. Despite the worldwide recession in the steel industry, a vigorous expansion policy was being maintained. In New South Wales development began on a steam coal (suitable for use under steam boilers) deposit at Newnes, expected to yield 2 million tons a year by 1981. Subject to government approval, a major steam and coking coal project was planned in the Hunter Valley, along with new loading facilities at Port Kembla and extensions to the Sydney loading facility. In Queensland there was much activity in the development of the coking coal reserves of the Bowen Basin, mainly for the export trade.

Black coal production continued to expand, with 78.3 million tons mined in 1977, some 5% above the figure for 1976. Lignite production in Victoria, where research continued into the extraction of oil from lignite, remained steady at 30.4 million tons. With numerous foreign oil and mining interests buying into the Australian coal industry, its future looked bright. Attention was given to diversification of the export market, and contracts were signed with

One of the world's largest excavators exhumes coal at the Belchatow colliery in Poland.

Pakistan (1977) and Brazil (1978); trial shipments to the U.S. began in March 1978.

CANADA. Total production in 1977, at 31,437,877 short tons, was 12% above that of 1976. Supplies for electricity generating increased, while coking coal demand remained at about the 1976 level. Coal conversion research was keenly pursued. Along with other nations that were developing coal deposits to supply Japan's steel industry, Canada sought to diversify the markets for its output. Though exports increased from 13 million to 13.3 million short tons, with 86% going to Japan, there was little likelihood of growth until the 1980s. Imports from the U.S. rose 800,000 tons to 16.8 million tons in 1977, mainly due to increased demand for electricity generation by Ontario Hydro. (R. J. FOWELL)

ELECTRICITY

World electricity consumption in 1977 rose by 3.7% over the 1976 figure, slightly more than the increase in consumption of primary energy (3.4%) during the same period. The World Energy Conference, which met in Istanbul in September 1977, with 3,000 participants from 70 countries, assessed the current world energy situation and looked at prospects for the year 2020. The resulting picture was fairly gloomy: while primary energy sources were being exhausted, consumption would continue to rise steadily. On the basis of an economic growth at or below the average for the past 50 years, energy consumption in all forms was likely to increase four- or fivefold by 2020 and electricity consumption six- or sevenfold. As a result, the share of primary energy used in electricity production should rise from the current 25% to 40%.

In order to avoid a crisis that would be catastrophic for mankind, there appeared to be only three possible solutions: energy savings, increased use of nuclear power, or the introduction of new energy sources. According to some experts, given the will and a great deal of imagination, savings might reach as much as 50% of consumption in some sectors. But the industrialized countries, and in particular the U.S., would

have to set an example. In this context, although President Carter's program of energy savings, originally halted by Congress, eventually gained approval, the bill passed by Congress was only a pale reflection of the original program. For example, all power stations using fuel oil originally were to have been converted to coal by 1990 at the latest, but the bill eventually allowed many exceptions.

With existing techniques of nuclear fission, a colossal effort of research and of uranium extraction and treatment would be necessary to cope with the development of nuclear power, the share of which in electricity production might rise from the current 7% to almost 65% in 2020. In any case this would give only a respite of a few decades before the uranium supply was exhausted. The use of plutonium, which generates 60 times more heat than uranium does, would extend this period of grace to several centuries. But using plutonium (easily adapted to military purposes) raised once again the question of the risk of proliferation of atomic weapons.

Most new energy sources that appeared feasible were virtually inexhaustible but highly diffuse. This made them difficult and expensive to use so that at present they could compete only with conventional power sources in certain individual cases. Thus, solar energy, which seemed to be one of the most promising of these new sources, could at least partially ensure heating of buildings and sometimes offer economies as compared with traditional methods, but it could not yet produce electricity economically. According to U.S. experts electric current produced by a solar power plant cost 20 times more than that produced by conventional means, and that produced by a voltaic battery 100 times more. Nonetheless, the U.S. and France had already decided to construct small experimental solar power stations. A plant in California would have a capacity of ten megawatts, and the Thémis plant to be built in France's Pyrénées-Orientales would have a capacity of two megawatts. These plants would have, respectively, 2,000 and 350 heliostats—reflectors that, controlled by a central computer, are permanently oriented toward the Sun and project its rays onto a boiler site at the top of a tower. From there the normal operational cycle of conventional thermal power stations takes over. (See Feature Article: Toward a Sun-Powered World.)

On Jan. 1, 1978, the total capacity of the 216 nuclear reactors in service throughout the world amounted to some 108,000 Mw, an increase of 12,700 Mw (13.4%) compared with a year earlier. During 1977, 3 countries joined the 19 already operating nuclear power stations: Finland, with a Soviet pressurized water reactor (PWR) of 420 Mw; South Korea, with a U.S. PWR of 564 Mw; and Taiwan, with a U.S. boiling water reactor (BWR) of 604 Mw. The number of reactors under construction worldwide was put at more than 200, with a total capacity of approximately 200,000 Mw.

In the U.S. orders for reactors had slowed down considerably during the three previous years, and in 1977 they were confined to four installations with a total capacity of 4,976 Mw. President Carter's decision, announced in April 1977, to prohibit the

KEYSTONE

Electrical Power Production of Selected Countries, 1977

By source

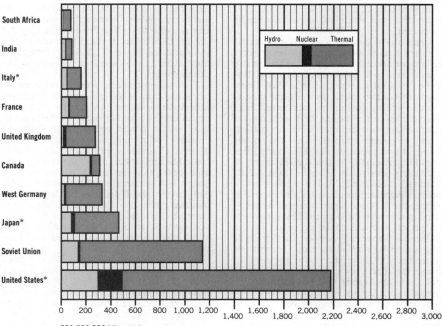

000,000,000 kilowatt-hours

*Includes geothermal.

Sources: United Nations, *Monthly Bulletin of Statistics*; *World Energy Supplies, 1972–76*.

Installed Capacity and Production of Electric Power in Selected Countries, 1976–77

Country	Hydroelectric power		Total electric power	
	Operating plants			
	Installed capacity (000 kw)	Production (000,000 kw-hr)	Installed capacity (000 kw)	Production (000,000 kw-hr)
World	...	...	...	6,916,700
Algeria	300*	500*	1,160	3,960*
Argentina†‡	1,745	5,000	9,856	27,336*
Australia	5,535*	15,595	19,957*	82,464
Austria	6,533	20,511	10,537	37,680
Bangladesh	110	505	915*	1,380*
Barbados	—	—	99	252*
Belgium†‡	502	334	10,942	47,100
Brazil	18,411	81,468	21,796	88,380
Bulgaria†‡	1,887	2,954	7,210	29,700
Burma	181	470	441	912*
Cameroon	199	1,278	227	1,332
Canada†‡	40,052	213,049	65,566	316,548
Central African Empire	11*	51*	17*	53*
Chad	—	—	23*	58*
Chile	1,462	6,234	2,661	9,864
Colombia	2,420	10,000	3,850	13,416*
Congo	17*	65*	34*	120*
Costa Rica	239	1,456	406	1,644
Cyprus	—	—	269	888
Czechoslovakia†‡	1,805	3,465	14,552	66,300
Denmark	9	24	6,570	22,488
Dominican Republic	96*	175*	443	2,690
Egypt	2,550*	7,000*	3,900	11,000
El Salvador	108*	436*	305	1,332
Ethiopia	206	360	320	480*
Finland	2,374	9,379	8,042	31,872
France†‡	18,705	48,200	50,266	210,348
Gabon	—	8*	58*	228*
Germany, East†‡	727	1,174	16,735	91,992
Germany, West†‡	6,175	14,052	81,631	335,316
Ghana	792	4,174	900	4,226
Greece	1,415*	1,870*	4,740	17,400*
Guatemala	103*	305*	333	1,250
Guyana	—	—	95*	396
Hong Kong	—	—	2,919*	8,280*
Hungary	40	163	4,666	23,388
Iceland§#	392	2,349*	523	2,604*
India†‡	9,029	34,827	23,689	90,840*
Iran	804*	3,974	5,130	17,311
Ireland	531*	892*	2,162*	9,312*
Israel	—	—	2,157*	11,112
Italy†‡§#	17,163	40,953	44,831	166,572
Ivory Coast	224*	380*	360*	960*
Jamaica	15*	145*	685	1,404
Japan†‡§#	25,955	88,373	116,871	511,776
Kenya	171	694	284	1,044*
Korea, South	711*	1,789*	5,340	26,556*
Kuwait	—	—	—	5,208*
Lebanon	246	800	608	1,248
Libya	—	—	796*	1,488*
Luxembourg	932*	...	1,157	1,308
Madagascar	40	171*	95	276*
Malawi	59	283	105	276*
Malaysia	...	...	1,361	7,200
Mauritania	—	—	40*	96*
Mauritius	25	55	143	312
Mexico§#	4,616	17,179	12,847	50,052
Morocco	396*	978*	980	3,444*
Mozambique	514*	1,510	793	1,752*
Netherlands, The†‡	—	—	15,009	58,296
New Zealand§#	3,471*	14,922*	5,125*	21,264*
Nigeria	420*	2,525*	960	3,396
Norway	16,959	82,106	17,121	72,492
Panama	15*	110*	363	1,236*
Papua New Guinea	86	260	275	1,039
Philippines	1,138	4,860	3,507	11,412*
Poland	797	2,098	20,131	109,368
Portugal	2,338	4,887	3,588	13,872
Rhodesia (Zimbabwe)	705	4,856	1,192	4,608
Romania	2,705	8,107	12,323	58,272
Senegal	—	—	130*	456*
Singapore	—	—	1,390*	5,112*
South Africa	329*	1,876	15,344	80,196
Spain†‡	11,955	22,508	24,534	93,708
Sri Lanka	195	1,134	281	1,202
Suriname	21	1,176	301	1,335
Sweden†‡	12,497	54,856	26,591	87,576
Switzerland†‡	10,410	26,622	12,016	44,124
Syria	—	—	842	1,788
Thailand	910*	3,637*	2,775	10,296
Togo	2	4	24	76*
Trinidad and Tobago	—	—	454	1,572
Tunisia	29*	53*	426	1,524*
Turkey	1,873	8,360	4,350	20,520
U.S.S.R.†‡	43,131	135,735	228,307	1,149,996
U.K.†‡	2,456	5,121	78,597	283,476
U.S.†‡§#	68,422	286,883	550,369	2,185,404
Yugoslavia	5,143	20,555	10,073	48,636
Zaire	1,159	3,400	1,217	3,502
Zambia	989	6,784	1,261	7,044

*Public sector only. †Includes nuclear (in 000 kw): Argentina 340; Belgium 1,666; Bulgaria 880; Canada 2,666; Czechoslovakia 150; France 2,928; East Germany 950; West Germany 6,328; India 640; Italy 670; Japan 7,441; The Netherlands 524; Spain 1,120; Sweden 3,314; Switzerland 1,006; U.S.S.R. 7,000; U.K. 5,734; U.S. 42,919. ‡Includes nuclear (in 000,000 kw-hr): Argentina 2,527; Belgium 10,037; Bulgaria 4,989; Canada 16,430; Czechoslovakia 442; France 15,100; East Germany 5,271; West Germany 24,262; India 3,253; Italy 3,807; Japan 34,079; The Netherlands 3,872; Spain 7,555; Sweden 15,993; Switzerland 7,561; U.S.S.R. 14,000; U.K. 36,155; U.S. 191,108. §Includes geothermal (in 000 kw): Iceland 3; Italy 421; Japan 55; Mexico 75; New Zealand 192; U.S. 559. #Includes geothermal (in 000,000 kw-hr): Iceland 19; Italy 2,523; Japan 400; Mexico 550; New Zealand 1,233; U.S. 3,616.

Sources: United Nations, *Statistical Yearbook, 1977*; *Monthly Bulletin of Statistics*.

manufacture in the U.S. of fast breeder reactors and to close down the study program on the first U.S. fast breeder on the Clinch River, near Oak Ridge, Tenn., marked the start of a lengthy conflict between the president, who vetoed financing for the project in November 1977, and Congress, which persisted in voting credits for the continuation of research on the prototype. Finally, in August 1978, a compromise was reached whereby $1.5 million would be set aside for basic research on fast breeders, while the Clinch River plant would be brought back into operation only if research proved positive.

In West Germany, despite recent violent antinuclear demonstrations, several bodies expressed support for nuclear power. At the congress of the Social Democratic Party in November 1977 two-thirds of the delegates came out in favour of nuclear power. The following month the government approved a new revision of its energy program, which still aimed to reduce the part played by oil. The building of a limited number of nuclear power stations might be authorized by the states (Länder), provided that reprocessing of irradiated fuels and disposal of wastes could be accomplished; if necessary, this could be done by making use of facilities abroad until the West German centre at Gorleben went into operation. The government called on three institutes to decide the objectives for the nuclear power program up to 1985; their study provided for a capacity of 24,000 Mw, or 22% of the nation's entire estimated electric power capacity at that time.

In the U.K. the Labour Party, at its congress in Brighton in October 1977, voted against a complete halt to the nuclear energy program. After much deliberation, hesitating between the choice of a purely British solution and that of adopting U.S. technology, the government finally, in January 1978, decided on a compromise solution under which it would build two power stations of 1,300 Mw with British advanced gas-cooled reactors (AGR's) and one of a capacity yet to be decided using the U.S.-type PWR.

In Japan 13 nuclear power stations with a total capacity of 11,000 Mw were under construction or on order. Thus by 1985 the total capacity should be in the region of 23,-000 Mw, representing approximately 15% of the nation's electricity generating capacity.

Despite opposition from environmentalists and the inhabitants of some areas, France was proceeding with a particularly ambitious program. By 1985 it aimed to bring into operation 30 reactors of 900-Mw capacity and 6 of 1,300 Mw, giving a total of nearly 35,000 Mw. If this objective was reached, more than half the country's electricity would come from nuclear sources.

In Sweden there was a revival of the conflict over nuclear power. In 1976 it had led to defeat at the polls for the Social Democratic Party, which had governed the country for more than 40 years. The three parties in the subsequent ruling coalition of Centrists, Liberals, and Conservatives were unable to agree on their policy, and the government was forced to resign on Oct. 5, 1978.

In June 1978 the Spanish government approved a general energy plan according to which 35% of total electricity production in 1987 would be provided by nuclear power, 28% by hydroelectric power, 26% by coal, and 11% by fuel oil. In Iran, which in 1978 had no operating nuclear power stations, two West German plants of 1,200 Mw each and two French plants of 900 Mw each were under construction, and two additional plants were provisionally ordered from the West German supplier. Finally, after an agreement between Iran and the U.S. on nonproliferation of nuclear weapons, the way was open for the U.S. to supply between six and eight nuclear power stations to Iran. However, the serious internal upheavals in the country during 1978 jeopardized all projects not already in process of completion.

In Austria there was a national referendum on Nov. 5, 1978, to decide whether the already completed Zwentendorf nuclear power station should be made operational. A majority of 50.5% voted against using the station, thus calling a halt to the government's plans for the development of nuclear energy.   (LUCIEN CHALMEY)

NATURAL GAS

The most important event of the year should have been the passage of President Carter's natural gas bill, but after 18 months of delay Congress approved a much modified and weakened measure in October 1978. In order to encourage exploration and production of natural gas in the United States, the price of newly discovered gas was to be allowed to rise gradually until 1985, when all federal price controls would be lifted. New U.S. gas reserves rose to 11.9

The "Glomar Pacific," a large seagoing rig anchored in the Baltimore Canyon, 85 miles off the New Jersey coast, started drilling in March, beginning Exxon's two years of exploration for oil and natural gas.

Tcf (trillion cubic feet) in 1977, and the administration hoped that its energy policy would lead to further discoveries by 1985 that would be equivalent to 1.4 million bbl a day of oil that would otherwise have to be imported.

Legislative delays and environmental concern also hindered progress on projects to import additional supplies of gas to the U.S. Plans to import more Algerian liquefied natural gas (LNG) to the East Coast were delayed so much that Algeria threatened to sell the gas to other customers. Suggested sites in California for a terminal for Indonesian LNG all met with opposition from environmentalists. On the other hand, it was proposed that U.S. companies should participate in the development of major gas reserves in Siberia. The U.S.S.R. planned to build a 3,000-km pipeline and a coastal liquefaction plant for the export of LNG to the U.S. and Japan. Considerable optimism was generated by the first discovery of gas off the U.S. Atlantic coast, in the Baltimore Canyon. However, further drilling would be needed to prove reserves of more than 1 Tcf, the amount required to make the discovery commercially exploitable. An application for government approval of a plan to import LNG from Iran was under consideration; LNG equivalent to 300 million cu ft a day of gas would be imported through a terminal in Maryland for a 20-year period.

The 400-km Soyuz gas pipeline in the U.S.S.R. was completed, and other links in the system bringing Soviet gas to Western Europe were under way. Construction be-

gan on the 1,422-km pipeline from the Kangan gas field in Iran to the Soviet border. Other major international gas pipeline projects under construction included the 1,178-km Franco-West German link; the Alaska Highway Gas Pipeline Project, running 2,028 mi (3,265 km) through Canada to the U.S.; and the 844-mi (1,359-km) line from the Cactus field in southern Mexico to the Texas border.

Two major projects were announced to bring gas from Algeria across the Mediterranean to customers in Europe. Planning began on the Spanish sector of the Segamo line, which would run through Spain to France. Preliminary agreements between Algeria, Tunisia, and Italy for another trans-Mediterranean pipeline were signed, and contracts were let for its first section, from the Algerian gas fields at Hassi R'Mel 549 km to the Tunisian border. It was planned that the line would then run through Tunisia, under the sea to Sicily, across the Strait of Messina, and into Italy. Work also began on the 286-km undersea pipeline from Sicily to Italy.

Thailand announced that a 725-km pipeline would be built from the newly discovered gas field in the Gulf of Thailand onshore to Bangkok. A pipeline linking southern Iran and Turkey was announced, and Iraq produced plans for a line from the North Rumalia gas fields to the Mediterranean coast. In South America a dual 2,900-km oil and gas pipeline system linking Brazil and Bolivia was proposed, and a pipeline across the Strait of Magellan was completed. This line connected the estimated 1.8-Tcf gas reserves on Tierra del Fuego to the Argentine mainland gas grid system running north to Buenos Aires.

The Frigg gas field, on the median line between the British and Norwegian sectors of the North Sea, was inaugurated in May 1978. Production from this field was scheduled to increase to 1,500,000,000 cu ft a day, a major addition to Britain's gas supplies, currently averaging 4,000,000,000 cu ft a day. The terminal for Frigg gas at St. Fergus in Scotland was also to handle gas from the Brent field, due to arrive in 1980–81. It was announced in July that the first gas field to be discovered in the Irish Sea, the Morecambe field, was of commercial size, with reserves of 2 to 3 Tcf. Appraisal of the field continued simultaneously with surveys to find a site for a shore terminal.

Serious doubt as to the safety of LNG was raised during the year. In Britain the Health and Safety Executive issued a report on potential hazards in the vicinity of Canvey Island, the site of several oil refineries and the LNG terminal where gas arriving from Algeria was stored. The report suggested a number of modifications to plant and procedures at the LNG terminal, but some local residents and the member of Parliament for the area demanded that it be closed.

In the U.S. the General Accounting Office published a report on the hazards of LNG and liquefied petroleum gas in July. This report concluded that catastrophic accidents could occur as a result of natural disasters, sabotage, or various sorts of mishaps. It recommended that LNG be stored only in remote areas and that it should not be transported through densely populated regions. The U.S. gas industry attacked the report as misleading and pointed out the good safety record of LNG and the importance to the U.S. of supplementing its energy resources with the imported product.

The development of facilities to manufacture gas from coal took another step forward with further successful tests on the British slagging gasifier, using U.S. coal. Plans for a pilot plant in Ohio were being prepared, but the U.S. Department of Energy had yet to decide whether such a plant should be built or what process should be used.　　　　　　(RICHARD J. CASSIDY)

PETROLEUM

Generally speaking, oil affairs during 1978 were less acrimonious and dramatic than in the preceding few years. The U.S. Congress finally passed a modified version of President Carter's much debated energy bill in October. For much of the year OPEC appeared to be having second thoughts about raising oil prices or taking action to offset the falling value of the dollar, to which most oil sales were tied, but at their December meeting the OPEC oil ministers agreed to increase the price of oil by 14.5% in stages during 1979. U.S. oil imports in the first nine months of 1978 averaged about 7.9 million bbl per day, 12% less than in the previous year, and for the first time in some years U.S. production marginally increased to 8.7 million bbl per day, or 8.2% more than in 1977; most of the gain was accounted for by Alaskan oil. A new supply problem emerged late in the year when oil exports from Iran were cut off as a result of the political turmoil in that country. Saudi Arabia increased its output to help make up the deficit, but it was feared that there might be severe dislocations unless the Iranian fields resumed production in the near future.

There was an unusual minor reduction in the world's oil production in the first half of 1978 compared with 1977, approximately 1.3%, though this did not include the major Communist producers, which continued to raise their production by some 5%. The OPEC nations registered the largest decline, 8.9%. Of them Nigeria was down 26.2%, followed by Saudi Arabia, Abu Dhabi, and Libya. In May oil production from the British sector of the North Sea reached a monthly average of more than 1 million bbl per day for the first time, production equivalent to that of Alaska.

RESERVES. There was a minor increase in the total world "published proved" reserves at the beginning of 1978, to a total of approximately 653,700,000,000 bbl, compared with 652,000,000,000 in 1977. The Western Hemisphere share rose slightly to 12.8% of the total. The Middle East share was marginally less at 55.9%. The U.S. share remained much the same at 5.4%, while Western Europe totaled 4.2%, the U.S.S.R. 11.5%, Africa 9%, and China 3.1%.

PRODUCTION. World oil production in 1977 increased much less than in 1976, 3.6% compared with 8.5%, and averaged 62,160,000 bbl per day. OPEC production was up only 1.5%. In the Western Hemisphere, in contrast to the decline in 1976, production was up by 1.1% to 16,150,000 bbl a day, with North America up 0.5% and Latin America 1.1%. Production declined in Canada, Brazil, Colombia, Trin-

idad, and Venezuela, but Mexico registered a 16.8% rise to 1,085,000 bbl a day.

Production in the Middle East increased at a much smaller rate than usual, 0.4% to 22,350,000 bbl a day, 32.6% of the world total. Only Abu Dhabi, Dubai, and Saudi Arabia increased their production shares. Saudi Arabia retained its position as the second largest producer of world crude oil with 15% of the total. The Soviet Union was first with 17.8% and the U.S. third at 13.4%, followed by Iran 9.3%, Venezuela 3.9%, Iraq 3.6%, Nigeria 3.4%, and Libya 3.3%. African production rose 7.2% to 6,290,000 bbl a day, 10.2% of the world total. Egypt had a notable increase of 27.8% to 415,000 bbl a day. Southeast Asian production of 2.1 million bbl a day, 3.4% of total world production, was up by 3.4%; Indonesia registered an increase of 11.9% to 1,690,000 bbl a day. Chinese production, at 2.7% of the world total, rose 8% to 1,625,000 bbl a day. The Soviet Union's production rose 4.9% to 11,045,000 bbl a day.

CONSUMPTION. Although the consumption of Western Europe as a whole was lower by 1.9% in 1977 than in 1976, in the world generally there was an increase of 3.1% to 60,980,000 bbl a day, an all-time high. The increase in 1976 had been 6.6%. U.S. consumption rose 5.5% to 17,945,000 bbl a day, 29.2% of the world total. The general Western Hemisphere percentage rise was 4.6% as Canadian consumption dropped slightly below that of 1976. In Europe, West Germany (4.6%), France (3.9%), Italy (3.2%), and the U.K. (3.1%) were the most important oil consumers, but except for a small British increase all registered consumption declines in 1977. The major consuming nations remained the same as in 1976: the U.S.; U.S.S.R., 13% of world total, 8,025,000 bbl a day, increase of 13%; Japan, 8.8%, 5,345,000 bbl a day, increase of 2.6%; and West Germany, 2,855,000 bbl a day, a decrease of 1.3%.

REFINING. In 1977 there was an overall world net decrease in the new additions to refinery capacity for the first time, though

world refining capacity actually increased by 3% over 1977. This was lower than the 4.7% of 1976. In Western Europe refinery capacity decreased by 1.2%, only Italy increasing with 3.9%. In North America the increase was 4.6%, the same figure as that of the U.S. Brazil registered the largest single increase in Latin America with 15.2%. The region as a whole increased by 4.3%.

Elsewhere, Iran had the largest world increase at 35%, but that figure represented only a 1.3% share of world capacity. The Communist countries in general increased by 7.1% to 13,920,000 bbl a day, 18.2% of the total. The U.S. with a total world share of 22.2%, 17,050,000 bbl a day, continued to hold the largest refinery capacity, followed by the Communist group; Japan, 7% and 5,345,000 bbl a day; Italy, 5.9% and 4,510,000 bbl a day; France, 4.5% and 3,465,000 bbl a day; and West Germany, 4% and 3,065,000 bbl a day. The refining capacity of the Middle East, 4.1% of the world total, increased by 10.2% to 3,245,000 bbl per day.

TANKERS. At the end of 1977 the world tanker fleet totaled 332.5 million tons deadweight (dw), an increase of 11.8% over 1976. Ships flying the Liberian flag increased by 7.8%, accounting for 32% of the world total with 107.5 million tons dw, followed by Japan, 8.9%; the U.K., 8.7%; and Norway, 8.6%. Voyages from the Middle East constituted 76% of all tanker movement, and of that total 38% went to Western Europe and 11.5% each to the U.S. and Japan. More than half the tanker fleet consisted of vessels of 205,000 tons dw and over, but of those on order at the end of 1977 more than half ranged from 25,000 to 65,000 tons dw.　　　(R. W. FERRIER)

See also Engineering Projects; Industrial Review; Mining and Quarrying; Transportation.
[214.C.4; 721; 724.B.2; 724.C.1–2; 737.A.5]

Oil workers in Iran went on strike late in the year protesting the shah's rule. Oil production was almost reduced to zero, and the oil-rich nation had to import oil to meet its everyday needs.

PHILIPPE LEDRU—SYGMA

Engineering Projects

Bridges. During 1978 a new set of standards, *BS 5400 Steel and Concrete Bridges*, was issued in Britain, based on the principle of "limit state." Engineers had always appreciated the implications of "limit state" concepts but had not previously written the principle into their standards. By the end of 1978, however, "limit state" was about to be adopted in many countries (in the U.S. under the title of "load and resistance factor design").

Before starting on a new bridge the principal question one had to answer was no longer "Is it technically possible?" Now one had to ask "Is the bridge socially desirable?" and "Can it be built and maintained at a cost that makes best use of limited available resources?" The aim of the "limit state" principle was an acceptable probability that the structure would not become unfit for its expected use during its intended life. In Britain, for example, the "life" of a bridge was 120 years, and this was a measure of what the engineer had to consider when designing such a structure.

Two limit states were stipulated in *BS 5400*. One was serviceability, the condition beyond which a loss of utility might be expected and significant remedial action required. In this connection excessive deformation, corrosion, and vibration are examples of the defects to be avoided. The second limit state was ultimate, the condition beyond which the structure cannot perform its function at all, such as collapse or rupture of a critical component, whatever the cause.

BS 5400 comprised ten parts: (1) General Statement; (2) Loads; (3) Design of Steel Bridges; (4) Design of Concrete Bridges; (5) Design of Composite Bridges; (6) Materials and Workmanship, Steel;

(7, 8) Materials and Workmanship, Concrete, Reinforcement and Prestressing Tendons; (9) Bearings; and (10) Fatigue. All these parts were available to engineers except that dealing with steel bridges. It was delayed in order to take into account the massive research program into the behaviour of steel box girders and plate girders undertaken following the collapse during construction of four such bridges in the past decade.

A particularly significant contribution of the new standards was the part dealing with loading, which provided a comprehensive list of characteristic loads for all types of bridges. The new standards differed from earlier ones in their use of safety factors based on statistically determined materials strength and loading capacity expectations for each element in the plan, rather than using one arbitrarily chosen safety factor for the entire bridge design.

It was also widely recognized, however, that good long-term performance of a bridge would be achieved only if adequate attention was paid during design to durability, detailing, and workmanship. It was more important that sufficient care be given to these aspects of bridge design than that undue regard be paid to apparently precise calculations of stresses made possible by the unthinking use of computers and of data such as loadings and properties of materials that were, at best, imprecise.

Although a massive program of building and replacing small-span bridges continued during 1978, along with renovations of large bridges such as the proposed relaying of the road surface on San Francisco's Golden Gate Bridge, there was relatively little to report about new giant long-span bridges. The Humber Bridge in England, with a main span of 1,410 m (4,620 ft), the longest to be built anywhere, was due to be completed in 1978,

The new Humber Bridge, due to be opened in the north of England in early 1979, will have the longest suspension span in the world. At 1,410 metres (4,626 feet), it will be longer than the Verrazano-Narrows Bridge in New York.

but a combination of unusually bad weather and industrial disputes delayed nearly all aspects of the assembly and erection of the superstructure.

Many proposals continued to be made for the construction of new large bridges to provide crossings of estuaries or connections to offshore islands. Examples included Denmark's Great Belt Bridge and the Messina Bridge between the toe of Italy and the island of Sicily; plans were revived to connect the congested city of Bombay in India with the island of Uran by a combination of tunnel and bridge; and in Japan preliminary work was under way on bridges to connect the islands of Shikoku and Honshu. But while engineers provided preliminary and even complete designs for many such projects, politicians and civil servants in most countries balked at backing their dreams with capital. (DAVID FISHER)

Buildings. Economic and social forces continued to play major and powerful roles in determining the form, context, and use of buildings. The effect of these in combination with architectural aesthetics, new materials, and contemporary structural technology produced some interesting about-faces and paradoxes in building practice.

The growing concern with the quality of life, coupled with the indiscriminate application of the high-rise solution to the problem of mass housing, had led to a marked return in the early 1970s to a "village community" approach to this problem. More recently, however, renewed attempts were made to provide varied and acceptable habitations within a large-structure framework. One such was the "Walden 7" complex in Barcelona, Spain, where 400 dwellings were contained within a single structure, the intricate form of which was far removed from that of the typical slab-sided, regularly structured, prism-like tower of the 1950s and 1960s. However, although one might expect a sophisticated structural solution to such a large and complex building, a basic and simple beam-and-slab reinforced-concrete frame was used.

"Walden 7" could almost be described as a "megastructure," a term that had gained vogue in the last decade to describe single building structures of enormous size envisaged as containing within themselves the essential characteristics and elements of a whole district, town, or even city. Almost all such schemes had remained imaginary, but in Arizona the foremost originator of the concept, Paolo Soleri, had begun the construction of a prototype community for a population of 5,000 within a single structure. Called "Arcosanti," it was described by Soleri as an "arcology" in which architecture and ecology were of equal importance. The main structure was to be a double row of massive concrete trusses, 25 stories high, enclosing a mall one-third of a mile long and more than 300 ft wide. Floors would be constructed across the rows of trusses, with living quarters on the outer surfaces and commercial, educational, and cultural facilities on the interior. The whole structure would be angled to make maximum use of the full potential of solar heating.

In West Berlin a totally different building that could almost equally be termed a megastructure was due to be opened in 1979. The new $400 million International Congress Centre was a 1,050-ft-long, 230-ft-wide structure capable of accommodating up to 13,000 people at any one time in two large halls, eight smaller ones, and many other rooms. Basically the structure consisted of a massive concrete portal frame, surmounted and enclosed by steel roof trusses carried on columns. The centre's stocky, massive shape, like a gigantic upturned ship's hull, formed a curious contrast with the airy, futuristic curved shape of the city's 20-year-old existing congress centre.

It can be argued that the most successful architecture occurs where the structural system chosen makes a natural and positive contribution to the whole building. This was certainly the case at the new computer bureau of the British Steel Corp. at Aldwake, Yorkshire, England, where the understandable desire to give steel the major structural role resulted in a cool and elegant one-story building, the main frame of which consisted entirely of readily available steel components.

Another, and a good deal larger, example of structure contributing positively to the architectural quality of a new building was to be seen in the prestigious new Australian embassy in Paris. The two separate, opposing quadrant-shaped buildings, one housing the chancellery and the other the residential quarters, were built externally of load-bearing precast concrete elements with a white quartz aggregate surface that imparted an immaculately crisp and clear finish. In the chancellery a concrete core contained the services and, between this and the load-bearing facade, specially profiled, precast, prestressed concrete T-beams bridged the 16-m clear span.

A final example involved structural ingenuity on the largest scale. The Renaissance Center in Detroit consisted of a 70-story hotel surrounded by four 39-story office towers. Around the base of the hotel a continuous open atrium space was designed. To accomplish this the support of the hotel was carried by the central elevator shaft core and 12 large columns equally spaced in an outer ring around it. The latter were virtually unsupported laterally for 90 ft so that the atrium was not cluttered with bracing girders from adjacent structures. In the atrium the wind loading and shears from the tower were transmitted to the bell-and-caisson foundation through the elevator shaft cores. (PETER DUNICAN)

Dams. The apparent massive simplicity of most dams is deceptive, few areas of civil engineering presenting a greater challenge or imposing a greater responsibility. As might be expected, by 1978 most of the best sites for large dams had long since been developed. Engineers were thus required to utilize progressively less suitable sites, the development of which was made possible only by advances in analytical techniques and construction methods. Embankment dams, constructed from compacted earthfill or rockfill, were predominant, accounting for more than 80% of large dams and a considerably higher proportion of all dams.

Examples of very large dams completed recently included Kolnbrein (Austria), a concrete double-curvature arch dam 200 m (660 ft) high and containing some 1.6 million cu m (2.1 million cu yd) of concrete, and the Dartmouth (Australia) dam. The latter, a rockfill structure some 180 m (590 ft) high, contained approximately 14 million cu m (19.6 million cu yd) of material. The scale of current projects was well illustrated by Canada's La Grande complex, where some 150 earth and rockfill dams and dikes involved placing approximately 200 million cu m (261 million cu yd) of fill.

New developments in dam engineering included British and U.S. research into the use of rolled lean concretes as an aid to rapid and, therefore, economical construction of concrete dams. Also, bituminous watertight membranes were used increasingly in earthfill and rockfill dams.

Surveillance and safety of dams continued to exercise the minds of dam engineers in the aftermath of the widely publicized Teton Dam failure in the U.S. in 1976 and other lesser known failures elsewhere. Improvements in monitoring the performance of dams and more stringent legislation concerning their construction were expected to play a large part in maintaining an acceptable safety record, particularly with regard to the problem of old dams.

During recent years public interest in the environmental impact of major reservoirs had increased. Engineers had thus been compelled to devote more attention to the consequences of their work. The balance between economic and social benefit on the one hand and possible environmental or ecological harm on the other is a delicate one. In 1978 the confrontation was neatly highlighted by the U.S. Supreme Court decision that the Tellico Dam in Tennessee, completed at a cost of $116 million, could not for the present be filled and commissioned in view of the threat it posed to the habitat of the tiny snail darter fish.

(A. I. B. MOFFAT)

Roads. The year 1978 was marked by an increase in the previously noted trend toward emphasis on maintenance and reconstruction of existing highways rather than new construction, particularly in the developed countries. Construction of new highway facilities on a major scale was more pronounced in the third world nations, although a worldwide trend toward protection of the investment already made in the construction of highways was evident.

In the United States 92% of the 68,260-km (42,-796-mi) interstate system was open to traffic in

Major World Dams Under Construction in 1978[1]

Name of dam	River	Country	Type[2]	Height (m)	Length of crest (m)	Volume content (000 cu m)	Gross capacity of reservoir (000 cu m)
Agua Vermelha	Grande	Brazil	E,G	90	3,990	19,640	11,000,000
Amaluza	Paute	Ecuador	A	170	410	1,157	120,000
Auburn	American (N. Fork)	U.S.	A	213	1,219	4,588	2,914,000
Balimela	Sileru	India	E	70	4,633	22,650	3,823,000
Canales	Genil	Spain	E,R	156	340	4,733	7,070,000
Chicoasen	Grijalva	Mexico	E,R	240	600	12,000	1,660,000
Dartmouth	Mitta-Mitta	Australia	R	180	670	14,100	4,000,000
Emborcacao	Paranaíba	Brazil	E,R	158	1,500	23,500	17,600,000
Fierze	Drin	Albania	E, R	158	400	700	2,620,000
Finstertal	Nederbach	Austria	E, R	158	652	4,500	60,000
Foz do Areia	Iguaçu	Brazil	E, R	153	830	13,700	7,320,000
Grand Maison	Eau d'Olle	France	E	160	550	15,000	140,000
Gura Apelor Retezat	Riul Mare	Romania	E, R	173	480	9,000	210,000
Guri (final stage)	Caroni	Venezuela	E, R, G	162	9,404	77,846	139,000,000
Hasan Ugurlu	Yesil Irmak	Turkey	E, R	175	405	9,100	1,079,000
Inguri	Inguri	U.S.S.R.	A	272	766	3,798	1,100,000
Itaipu	Paraná	Brazil/Paraguay	E, R, G	180	7,900	27,000	29,000,000
Itaparica	São Francisco	Brazil	E, R, G	105	4,700	16,000	12,000,000
Itumbiara	Paranaíba	Brazil	E, G	106	6,262	35,600	17,000,000
Karakaya	Euphrates	Turkey	A, G	173	462	2,000	9,580,000
Kenyir	Trengganu	Malaysia	E, R	150	900	15,900	13,600,000
La Grande No. 2	LaGrande	Canada	E, R	160	23,469	48,200	19,527,000
La Grande No. 3	La Grande	Canada	E, R	98	25,298	33,000	25,470,000
La Grande No. 4	La Grande	Canada	E, R	122	9,113	32,900	7,075,000
Las Portas	Camba	Spain	A	152	484	747	751,000
Miyagase	Nakatsu	Japan	G	155	411	2,010	210,000
Nader Shah	Marun	Iran	E	175	320	7,600	1,620,000
Nurek	Vakhsh	U.S.S.R.	E	300	704	58,901	10,500,000
Oosterschelde	Vense Gat Oosterschelde	Netherlands, The	E	45	9,000	70,000	2,900,000
Oymapinar	Manargat	Turkey	A	185	360	575	310,000
Revelstoke	Illecillewaet	Canada	E, G	153	1,620	13,000	5,180,000
Rogunsky	Vakhsh	U.S.S.R.	E	325	764	62,000	8,600,000
Sayano-Shushenskaya	Yenisei	U.S.S.R.	A	242	1,068	9,117	31,300,000
Sobradinho	São Francisco	Brazil	E, R, G	43	3,900	13,200	34,200,000
Sterkfontein	Nueuejaarspruit	South Africa	E	93	3,060	17,000	2,656,000
Takase	Takase	Japan	E, R	176	362	11,600	76,000
Tedorigawa	Tedori	Japan	E, R	153	420	10,120	231,000
Thomson	Thomson	Australia	E, R	165	1,275	11,000	1,100,000
Tucurui	Tocantins	Brazil	E, G	86	4,200	43,000	34,000,000
Ust-Ilimsk	Angara	U.S.S.R.	E, G	105	3,565	8,702	59,300,000
Warm Springs	Dry Creek	U.S.	E	97	914	23,232	302,000
Yacyreta-Apipe	Paraná	Paraguay/Argentina	E, G	33	69,660	61,200	21,000,000
Zillergrunde	Ziller	Austria	A	180	505	980	90,000
Major World Dams Completed in 1977 and 1978[1]							
Bilandi Tank	Bilandi	India	E, G	32	707	20,571	63,000
Chivor	Batá	Colombia	E, R	237	280	10,800	815,000
Kolnbrein	Malta	Austria	A	200	626	1,580	205,000
Kolyma	Kolyma	U.S.S.R	E, R	130	750	12,550	14,800,000
Mornos	Mornos	Greece	E	126	815	17,000	780,000
Poechos	Chira	Peru	E	49	10,800	18,480	880,00
São-Simão	Paraníba	Brazil	E, R, G	120	3,611	27,387	12,540,000
Toktogul	Naryn	U.S.S.R.	G	215	450	3,200	19,500,000
Ukai	Tapi	India	E, G	69	4,927	25,516	8,511,000

[1]Having a height exceeding 150 m (492 ft); or having a total volume content exceeding 15 million cu m (19.6 million cu yd); or forming a reservoir exceeding 14,800 × 10⁶ cu m capacity (12 million ac-ft).
[2]Type of dam: E = earth; R = rockfill; A = arch; G = gravity.

1978, but the remaining 8% was expected to cost more than 30% of the total bill of $104.3 billion. This increase was attributed to inflation, improved standards of highway construction, safety considerations, and environmental requirements. Much concern was expressed during the year about the deteriorating condition of the first sections of the interstate highways, built as long ago as 1956, and the Federal-Aid Highway Act of 1978 allocated sharply increased funds for interstate maintenance beginning in 1982 and 1983, when the problem was expected to become acute.

Canada's budget for construction and maintenance of highways in 1978–79 was $2,973,000,000, up $101 million over the previous year, but inflation was expected to result in reduced operations. Construction of a 390-km (240-mi) direct highway link between British Columbia and Canada's Northwest Territories was started, with a projected total cost of $63 million.

Progress on the Pan-American Highway System in Central America was impeded in the Darien Gap section when the U.S. Congress failed to allocate construction funds for the 400-km (250-mi) link in Panama and Colombia. The highest toll road in the world, linking Bolivia's capital of La Paz with its principal airport in El Alto, was opened to traffic at altitudes reaching 4,200 m (12,-780 ft) above sea level. In Brazil the 55-km (34-mi) Immigrants Highway linking São Paulo to the port of Santos neared completion despite the necessity for an almost continuous series of viaducts and tunnels.

Costs of highway construction reached new highs throughout the world. A mile-long section of the Ring Road around Brussels, completed by the start of the year, was built at a cost of $70 million, while engineering estimates for the projected four-mile Westway Project along Manhattan Island in New York City totaled $1 billion, including acquisition of the right-of-way.

A ten-year African transportation plan, adopted by the General Assembly of the UN during 1978, was designed to upgrade all modes of transportation, including five major trans-African highway projects in progress. They were the Mombasa-Lagos Trans-African Highway, the Dakar-N'Djamena Highway, the Lagos-Nouakchott Highway, the Cairo-Gaborone Trans-East African Highway, and the Trans-Saharan Highway. Of the existing international road links in Africa in 1978, only 25 were of all-weather standard, while 53 were dry-weather tracks or simply partially improved earth roads. Also in Africa, a 3,200-km (2,000-mi) network of feeder roads was being built by the UN Development Program to serve the famine-troubled Sahel region.

In Saudi Arabia approximately 6,000 km (3,750 mi) of expressways, primary highways, and secondary roads linking major cities and the Saudi-Kuwait border were under design or construction in 1978, at a cost of $2.2 billion. Kuwait started the construction of an ultramodern freeway system to cope with the needs of its population, which had doubled since 1965. In Iraq a $2 billion highway from Ramadi to the port of Basra was under construction, while in Syria a 104-km (64-mi) high-

way between Damascus and the Jordanian border at Dar'a and a 90-km (55-mi) road between Latakia and Tartus were planned at a cost of $200 million.

Overland links between Europe, Africa, and Asia were the subject of much discussion because of the sharp increase in freight traffic by road following the 1973–74 oil crisis and the subsequent business boom in the Middle East. The European Conference of Ministers of Transport called for uniform customs procedures, coordinated traffic and licensing regulations, and better working conditions for drivers. An additional Bosporus Bridge was to be built near Istanbul at a cost of more than $150 million, easing congestion on the present bridge, which carried approximately 102,000 vehicles each day.

In Europe the auto route from Perpignan to Narbonne, linking Paris and the Spanish border, was opened to traffic, making it possible to drive on a continuous expressway from Amsterdam to Valencia, Spain, a distance of some 2,000 km (1,250 mi). East and West Germany agreed on the construction of a $418 million expressway between Hamburg and West Berlin. Construction was under way on the Trans European Motorway, from the Baltic Sea to the Mediterranean and the Black Sea and across Turkey to the borders of Syria, Iraq, and Iran. When completed this project could permit a direct road connection between Europe and Egypt and, by way of the Nile Valley, into central Africa.

A vital link between Pakistan and China was

Workmen in the northern part of the U.S. were kept busy during the summer repairing hundreds of thousands of highway potholes caused by the fierce winter.

opened in July 1978 with the completion of the 800-km (500-mi) Karakoram Highway through the Himalaya, Karakoram, and Hindu Kush mountain ranges. It was built by Pakistani army engineers and Chinese technicians.

In Australia road traffic between the east and west coasts increased 50% following completion of the first connecting paved road. The Japan Highway Planning Corporation announced that it would spend almost $10 billion on seven major highway, bridge, and tunnel projects in 1979 and would build 600 km (375 mi) of expressway costing almost $20 million per kilometre.

A great deal of attention was paid in 1978 to recycling pavements. This involved removing the top layers of worn or damaged pavement by heating or crushing and then mixing fresh material and softeners with the old aggregate to make new asphalt or portland cement mixes.

(HUGH M. GILLESPIE)

Tunnels. The fourth meeting of the International Tunneling Association was held in Tokyo in May 1978. Excluding mining, a record 1,032 km (640 mi) of tunnel were under construction in Japan, providing Japanese engineers with the opportunity to show their visitors some of the most advanced tunneling methods in the world, particularly in the sphere of soft ground tunneling. More than 30 slurry shields were in use in Japan. A unique development was the soil pressure shield, enabling soil to be removed continuously from the face without releasing any pressure. The largest unit of this type was the nine-metre-diameter shield used for the construction of a sewer in Tokyo. Soil excavated by the machine flowed through slits into a bulkhead that acted as a soil-holding chamber; it was removed by screw conveyors at the same rate as it entered so that the soil pressure in the bulkhead was kept constant at the same pressure as at the tunnel face. This eliminated the need for compressed air and was claimed to be cheaper than using a bentonite slurry.

A giant deep-tunnel project, expected to cost about $7.3 billion, is being carried forward underneath Chicago and surrounding communities. Located 200 feet underground, the tunnel is aimed at controlling pollution and flooding.

WIDE WORLD

Progress on the 54-km (33-mi) Seikan undersea tunnel continued, with 70% of the main drive finished and completion scheduled for 1982. Special measures required for driving through areas of very high earth pressure included driving three-metre-diameter side drifts ahead of the drive, which were then filled with concrete to act as the footing for the crown supports in the main tunnel.

A major tunneling development in the U.S. was the Buckskin Mountains Tunnel in Arizona, where for the first time in the U.S. unbolted precast concrete segments were being used for the primary lining. This 11-km (6.8-mi) tunnel was 6.7 m (22 ft) in diameter and was being driven through andesite rock by a machine that averaged 18 m a day. In Chicago one of the world's largest tunneling machines, weighing 700 metric tons, was driving an 8.6-km (5.3-mi) tunnel for a new drainage interceptor. This tunnel was 9 m (28 ft) in diameter, and progress rates of up to 18 m (56 ft) a day were being achieved.

In the U.K. the main tunneling interest was the 19-km (11.8-mi) Kielder water supply tunnel, where a fourth tunneling machine began work to accelerate progress. At Antwerp in Belgium a bentonite slurry shield was being successfully used to drive the first tunnel for the new subway. The soil consisted of fine sand, which would normally have required the use of compressed air for tunneling. The machine was a development of the prototype West German slurry shields first used on the Wilhelmsburg sewer at Hamburg.

French tunneling engineers developed a shield equipped for mechanical precutting of the ground at the tunnel face by using a rock sawing technique. The rock mass to be removed was isolated from the surrounding strata by sawing a groove the depth of the round along the perimeter of the excavation. The method led to considerable savings in the quantities of explosive required and had a particular application for tunnels driven beneath urban areas, where vibrations must be kept to a minimum.

In Sweden construction continued on the 80-km (50-mi) water-supply Bolmen tunnel, which was due for completion in 1984. A feature of interest was the intention to use grouting to limit the ingress of water during construction to only 1.5 litres per second per kilometre of tunnel. The object was to prevent the high-grade Lake Bolmen water from becoming polluted by other waters and to minimize the drop in the groundwater table over the route of the tunnel.   (DAVID A. HARRIES)

Environment

The hazards to life and to the environment involved in the transportation of potentially pollutant, toxic, or otherwise dangerous materials were highlighted in 1978 by some spectacular incidents. (See TRANSPORTATION: *Special Report.*) One of the worst land disasters in this category occurred on July 11 near Tarragona, Spain, when a propylene-filled tank truck exploded in the vicinity of a camping site, causing some 200 deaths. At sea, the most serious oil pollution incident the world had yet

Residents of Brittany struggle to get rid of oil that polluted their beaches after the tanker "Amoco Cadiz" broke apart and unleashed 1.6 million barrels of crude oil into the sea in March.

seen happened when the Liberian-flag tanker "Amoco Cadiz" ran aground on the coast of Brittany, France, on the night of March 16–17, afterward breaking up and releasing its entire cargo of 1.6 million bbl of crude oil.

An emerging issue that promised to dominate environmental debates for the rest of the decade, at least at the governmental level, was the loss of arable land and forests. In February the World Bank published a Sector Policy Paper, *Forestry*, in which it estimated that, at current rates of exploitation, all the world's forests would disappear within 50 years. At the same time, the loss of farmland to erosion, the spread of deserts, and urban development continued largely unabated. Experts calculated that the loss could amount to one-third of the world's arable land by the year 2000.

For environmentalists in the developed countries, however, it was nuclear power and the related problem of nuclear waste disposal that generated the most heated arguments. (*See* Special Report.) In Britain the report by Sir Roger Parker (*see* BIOGRAPHIES) on the application of British Nuclear Fuels Ltd. (BNFL) to build a thermal oxide reprocessing plant at Windscale, Cumbria, was published early in March. Far from resolving differences between those who favoured the nuclear power program and those who opposed it, it served to polarize the debate still further. The European Commission held two public meetings to discuss nuclear power, in November 1977 and again in January 1978, and these, too, concluded with the sides further apart than before. Meanwhile, a new environmental issue that began to gain attention concerned the possible nonthermal effects of exposure to microwave radiation.

Informal groupings of environmentalists continued to gain political stature and expertise. Al-

though they won no seats, their influence was felt in the general election in France and in several Land (state) elections in West Germany.

INTERNATIONAL COOPERATION

United Nations. In his state of the environment report for 1978, presented to the governing council of the UN Environmental Program (UNEP) at its sixth session in Nairobi, Kenya, May 9–25, UNEP Executive Director Mostafa K. Tolba focused on the resurgence of malaria in many parts of the tropics, on the effect of chemicals in the environment, and on the need to use agricultural and agri-industrial residues for the production of food and energy. UNEP's budget for 1978–81 was set at $150 million. In an interview in October, Tolba suggested that UNEP funds used for such specific projects as halting the spread of deserts might be augmented by a "solidarity tax" paid by all governments on profits from the exploitation of global resources.

UNEP collaborated during the year with the International Union for Conservation of Nature and Natural Resources (IUCN) in the compilation of a "World Conservation Strategy," listing major environmental problems, suggesting remedies, and proposing development strategies that would make the most rational use of resources. Agreement on two antipollution treaties and on an action plan for environmentally sound development of sea areas around the world's major oil fields was reached at a conference held in Kuwait, April 15–24, under UNEP auspices.

The seventh session of the UN Conference on the Law of the Sea was held in Geneva, Switz., from March 28 to May 19, and resumed in New York City from August 21 to September 15. The U.S. asserted its belief that all nations have the right to exploit the mineral resources of the seabed, a view that was not shared by the "Group of 77" less developed nations. Progress toward a compromise agreement on seabed mining was made, however, and agreement was reached on procedures for settling disputes over fishing rights within the 200-mi exclusive economic zones established by many countries.

Council of Europe. In December 1977 the Committee of Ministers adopted Resolution (77) 28, recommending that, where administrative and civil procedures failed, the 20 member nations of the Council should resort to criminal prosecution to deal with cases of pollution. To this end it recommended the creation of specialist branches of courts and public prosecutors' offices to deal with environmental cases, the prosecution of groups rather than individuals where appropriate, the creation of special criminal registers, and the exclusion from amnesty of the most serious offenders.

The Parliamentary Assembly, at its meeting in Strasbourg, France, in April 1978, adopted a resolution on conservation of the living resources of the Northeast Atlantic and the Mediterranean that would improve monitoring and the scientific evaluation of conditions in those areas. In June the Rhine Valley Groundwater Working Party decided on a number of measures to improve the monitoring of the Rhine. The second Interparliamentary Conference on the Pollution of the Rhine, held in Paris in September, discussed ways of strengthening cooperation among the states bordering the river.

European Economic Community. The first technical meeting held under the terms of the environmental cooperation agreement signed June 1, 1977, between the EEC and Japan took place in Tokyo on March 30–31, 1978. Representatives from both sides discussed air pollution and the control of hazardous chemicals. The EEC also had an environmental cooperation agreement with Sweden, and on March 9 a technical meeting was held in Brussels to discuss long-range atmospheric pollution and the condition of the Baltic.

The Community environment ministers, meeting on May 30, adopted directives of the European Commission that would control and reduce pollution by oil tankers and lower the lead content of gasoline by 10%. From Jan. 1, 1981, gasoline might contain not more than 0.4 g and not less than 0.15 g of lead per litre. The ministers agreed in principle that the EEC should accede to the Bonn Agreement against North Sea pollution and agree to the protocol of the Barcelona Convention on pollution in the Mediterranean. A directive was adopted setting guide values for contaminants that member governments might use to establish criteria for the quality of fresh water. The ministers instructed the Commission to examine the economic and social implications of regulating the use of chlorofluorocarbon (CFC) propellants in aerosols.

Marine Pollution. The Inter-Governmental Maritime Consultative Organization (IMCO) met for two weeks in London beginning February 6. A U.S. proposal that new oil tankers be required to have segregated ballast tanks was adopted, but the recommendation that old ships be similarly equip-

ped was dropped because of British opposition. The measure, which would have necessitated structural alterations on many ships, was supported in Britain by trade unions representing shipbuilding workers and by the Advisory Committee on Oil Pollution of the Sea. The annual report of the committee, published on May 24, stated that the number of oil pollution incidents around British coasts had increased from 500 in 1975 to 642 in 1977. On June 15 the British government published a White Paper proposing new measures on pollution and safety at sea, including ratification of the IMCO agreement.

Following the "Amoco Cadiz" incident, British and French arrangements for dealing with major pollution incidents came under heavy criticism. In April the Commission reminded the EEC Council of Ministers of proposals it had made almost a year earlier, involving a research program into the ecological impact of oil, techniques for dealing with it, and an information network on antipollution techniques. The Commission also reviewed its earlier recommendations on marine pollution and produced a seven-point program that would coordinate approaches to the problem.

Implementation of the Barcelona Convention ran into technical difficulties at a meeting held in Monaco, January 9–14, organized by UNEP and attended by 17 of the 18 Mediterranean states. No firm agreements were reached, but progress was made on unraveling the complex issues involved. It was recommended that a central data bank be established to correlate relevant information.

NATIONAL DEVELOPMENTS AND POLICIES

Nuclear Energy. The report of the 1977 public inquiry on the proposed reprocessing plant at Windscale was published on March 6, 1978, five weeks after it had been presented to the secretary of state for the environment, Peter Shore. It found in favour of the application, accepting all of BNFL's arguments and rejecting those of its opponents. The government accepted the report and its conclusions, but in order to allow it to be debated in Parliament, it was made the subject of a Special Development Order. On March 22, Parliament approved the report by 186 votes to 56, and on May 15 the Special Development Order was granted by a parliamentary vote of 224 to 80.

The environmental movement angrily rejected the report, and many, who had given evidence at the inquiry claimed their statements had been misunderstood, misrepresented, distorted, or ignored. There were fears that further inquiries—into the first commercial fast breeder reactor, for example—would be boycotted by environmentalists. Friends of the Earth, the principal objector at Windscale, had spent £50,000 in presenting its arguments, and it was doubtful that sufficient funds could be raised to fight another prolonged battle.

On April 29 some 10,000 people from all over Britain demonstrated their opposition to nuclear power in Trafalgar Square, London. Smaller demonstrations took place in other parts of the country. Cases of plutonium contamination were found among workers at the British Atomic Weapons Research Establishment at Aldermaston. As a result, the plant was closed in August for an indefinite period, pending an investigation into health and safety measures and whole-body monitoring of other personnel.

West Germany's plans to expand its nuclear generating capacity were inhibited, partly by difficulties of uranium supply caused by the U.S. Nuclear Non-Proliferation Act of 1978 and partly by opposition from the environmental lobby. Ten new installations were on order, but work was at a virtual standstill throughout the year. The one plant that had been completed, a 1,300-Mw installation at Esenshamm, could not open because of court actions brought by environmental groups.

In Sweden, Prime Minister Thorbjörn Fälldin's coalition government resigned on October 5 because it could not resolve the nuclear issue. It had come to power partly because of its commitment to end nuclear power in Sweden, but once in office it had found this was impossible. Its final attempt, on October 1, consisted of a refusal to permit two new reactors to open until geologic surveys to locate safe sites for waste disposal had been completed. (*See* SWEDEN.)

There were several demonstrations in The Netherlands against the government's plans to supply enriched uranium to Brazil from the Urenco plant at Almelo. On February 1 the Dutch Parliament voted in favour of supplying Brazil, provided it received assurances regarding the use to which the uranium would be put. The assurances were not received, and on June 30 Parliament approved the deal without a vote, in large measure because it feared that a refusal would not be supported by

The Netherlands' British and West German partners in the Urenco consortium. On March 4 the largest antinuclear demonstration ever seen in The Netherlands took place at the Almelo plant; 25,000 to 30,000 people took part, some of them from West Germany. A demonstration of about 4,000 people on June 24 coincided with a much smaller one, by about 500 people, at Capenhurst, Cheshire, England, mounted because of fears that Urenco would simply switch the order from its Dutch to its British plant.

The opening of Austria's first nuclear power station, at Zwentendorf, was made conditional upon the result of a national referendum, held on November 5. In the balloting, 50.5% of the electorate voted against the plant's opening.

U.S. antinuclear groups may have lost, if not the war, at least the battlefield of their own choosing. In April the Supreme Court ruled that federal judges lacked the authority to pronounce on matters relating to nuclear safety and necessity, thus depriving the environmentalists of the recourse to the courts that they had used so successfully in the past. They won a temporary victory when the Nuclear Regulatory Commission ordered work stopped on the proposed plant at Seabrook, N.H., the scene of a number of demonstrations, because of fears that its cooling system might not meet Environmental Protection Agency (EPA) requirements. In August, however, the EPA approved the system, and construction was resumed, though a review of alternative sites was still pending.

Seas and Beaches. The 230,000-ton Liberian-registered tanker "Amoco Cadiz," owned by Amoco International Oil, which ran aground and

Antinuclear adherents held a sit-in in front of the UN to protest construction of the Seabrook (New Hampshire) nuclear generating plant.

Toxic wastes from chemical plants forced the evacuation of hundreds of families from the Love Canal area in Niagara Falls, N.Y.

broke in two off Portsall on the Brittany coast early on March 17, had been carrying 1.6 million bbl of oil, most of it light crude, from the Persian Gulf to Britain. The tanker's steering gear had broken down on the morning of the previous day, but neither its captain nor the captain of the West German tug that went to its assistance called in outside help or gave any warning of impending danger. This failure was severely criticized by a French commission of inquiry that was formed to investigate the disaster.

The entire cargo of the "Amoco Cadiz" spilled into the sea, causing the worst oil pollution incident to date. Almost all the oil drifted onto the Brittany coast, although for a time a slick threatened Guernsey. On March 27 the French authorities announced that they planned to blow up the wreck in the hope of emptying its remaining holds, and on March 30 attempts to do so began. The work of clearing the oil from French beaches started in earnest on April 2. Subsequent claims against the tanker's owners amounted to $1,050,-000,000, compared with $7.5 million paid following the sinking of the "Torrey Canyon" in 1967. Although the sums actually awarded were likely to be much lower than those claimed, it seemed certain that they would far exceed the $50 million limit set by insurers.

Few chemical dispersants were used by the French workers cleaning the beaches and coastal waters. As a result, the ecological damage, though great, was less severe than it might have been, and scientists expected marine life to recover fairly quickly. Immediately after the grounding, the French authorities introduced new navigation rules for ships rounding Ushant. By early June the French Navy had arrested 15 ships for violation of the rules.

On July 24, Greenpeace, a Canadian-based environmental group, showed film and produced eyewitnesses to support its claim that radioactive wastes were being dumped from British nuclear submarines in contravention of the London Con-

vention. The U.K. Atomic Energy Authority replied that the incidents involved barrels of resins used for cleaning purposes and that they contained only insignificant amounts of radioactive materials. On April 25 the last barrels of lead compounds originally intended for use as gasoline additives were removed by Italian divers from the Yugoslav ship "Cavtat," which sank in the Adriatic in 1974.

Seasat, an experimental satellite, was launched from the U.S. on June 26, 1978, and parked in a 500-mi-high orbit to monitor the state of the oceans.

Fresh Water. Denis Howell, minister of state at the U.K. Department of the Environment, announced in Parliament on April 13 that the government would implement Part II of the Control of Pollution Act 1974. This would give water authorities powers to control discharges into most inland and coastal waters and would require details of these discharges to be published. Private individuals would thus be able to bring actions against violators; furthermore, since violation would be a "point in time" offense, two separate charges could be brought if permitted limits were exceeded according to two measurements of the same effluent taken ten minutes apart. Environmentalist jubilation was quickly dampened, however, by news that water authorities were responding by lowering the effluent standards.

The quality of the River Thames appeared to be improving. A routine fish survey in January found a long-spined sea scorpion and a worm pipefish, bringing the total number of species found in the river since 1964 to 95; later a salmon was found. On September 26 the Thames Water Authority approved a £150,000, seven-year pilot scheme to establish a stock of salmon at Runnymede. Fresh water quality also improved in the U.S., although the 1977 report of the president's Council on Environmental Quality pointed out that much more improvement was needed if the 1983 target for water quality was to be attained. Fish were living in the Naugatuck River in Connecticut. Salmon, brown trout, pike, and walleyes were found in the Detroit River and bass in the Mohawk River in New York State.

Toxic Substances. Discussions at government level were held concerning the effect on trade of the U.S. Toxic Substances Control Act of 1976 and of similar Japanese legislation. New West German measures, announced in September 1978, included proposals to bring West German law into line with U.S. law. Through the Chemical Products Groups of the Organization for Economic Cooperation and Development and through UNEP, the EEC sought to bring about modifications that would remove trade restrictions. The matter was discussed at a meeting in Stockholm on April 11–13, organized by the Swedish National Products Control Board and attended by the EEC, the World Health Organization (WHO), the EPA, and UNEP. It was agreed that national controls should be improved and harmonized in order to make the best use of resources.

In 1973 a fire retardant, polybrominated biphenyl (PBB), was accidentally mixed with a batch of animal feed at Mio, Mich., and given to cattle. Many of them died afterward under bizarre circumstances, and others were destroyed. Some time later symptoms began to appear among humans. A small-scale study conducted in 1976 by the Mount Sinai Hospital, New York City, suggested that the effects might be widespread, and in May 1978 Michigan state authorities commissioned a further study, in which 3,000 people were to be examined. It was feared that everyone living in Michigan at the time of the incident could be contaminated and that symptoms reported in hundreds of Michigan children could be those of PBB poisoning. In October, however, a Michigan county judge dismissed the first of many suits brought as a result of the incident. The plaintiff had sought damages for cattle that had been destroyed, but the judge ruled that the levels of PBB in his cattle had not been proved harmful.

On July 27, two years after an explosion in the Icmesa factory at Seveso, Italy, had resulted in the contamination of a large area with dioxin, the parliamentary commission appointed to investigate the affair published its report. Some blame was attached to local authorities, but the 470-page document placed most of the responsibility on the factory management. Early in 1978 several veterans of the Vietnam war made claims against the U.S. government for illnesses they said were caused by exposure, ten years earlier, to a defoliant called Agent Orange, which had been used to deprive the Communist forces of jungle cover. Agent Orange was actually the same substance, dioxin.

On August 7 the Love Canal area of Niagara Falls, N.Y., was declared a disaster area because of chemical contamination. In the 1940s and early 1950s, the site had been used by a chemical company to dispose of waste products, which were buried in metal drums in a manner that was then legal. In time the drums rusted out, and the chemicals percolated to the surface. At least seven of the substances were identified as suspected carcinogens, and the incidence of miscarriages and birth

defects among residents of the area was reported to be far higher than normal. Evacuation of residents was begun, and authorities recommended that pregnant women and children under two leave immediately.

In April the U.S. Department of Health, Education, and Welfare announced that it would issue a health warning to workers who had been exposed to asbestos since the beginning of World War II. It was estimated that between 8.5 and 11.5 million such persons were still living, including 4.5 million who had held wartime jobs in shipyards. Concern had been growing over exposure to asbestos, which was widely used for fireproofing and insulation. There was evidence that asbestos workers and their families ran a high risk of developing a variety of diseases, including several cancers and asbestosis, or "white lung." The effect was delayed, and symptoms might not appear until many years after exposure had ceased.

Atmospheric Pollution. On July 14 heavy rain entering sodium containers caused an explosion at a factory at Trento, Italy, releasing a cloud of sodium hydroxide. No one was injured, but the factory was ordered to close. The Trento factory had been making lead additives for gasoline, and the effects of airborne lead continued to cause concern and argument. On July 5 in Britain suits were filed on behalf of three London children who claimed damages against Shell, British Petroleum, Associated Octel, and the Ford Motor Co. for injuries caused by lead in automobile exhaust. On September 30 the Right Rev. Hugh Montefiore, bishop of Birmingham, used his presidential address to the Birmingham diocesan synod to plead for a reduction in the lead content of gasoline. He said that one-quarter of the children living in Birmingham risked mental injury from this cause. The evidence on which such claims were based continued to be controversial, however, and was opposed by many scientists.

Levels of atmospheric sulfur dioxide in Athens, Greece, fell by more than 50% in the winter of 1977–78, compared with previous years, as the result of a ban on the use of high-sulfur heating oils. The ban had been recommended by the WHO Environmental Pollution Control Project.

For some years, Norway and Sweden had claimed that atmospheric sulfur dioxide originating in Britain was damaging their inherently acid soils by falling as acid rain. Britain argued that it was not possible to track the movement of airborne pollutants over long distances and that under the "polluter pays" principle the degree of British responsibility could not be determined. Discussion of the subject at a NATO conference in May revealed just how little was known about the effect and movement of airborne pollutants. As a first step toward remedying this deficiency, the British Central Electricity Generating Board announced plans for a series of surveys using instruments mounted in aircraft to follow fumes tagged with a radioactive tracer.

The Ozone Layer. The American Manufacturing Chemists Association announced in May that it would soon begin testing for chlorofluorocarbons (CFC's) in the Earth's lower atmosphere from monitoring stations in Ireland, French Guiana, Samoa, and Tasmania. The aim was to locate "sinks" in which CFC's may be absorbed before they can rise into the stratosphere and react with upper atmospheric ozone. Evidence for the existence of such sinks was presented in August, when the Institute for Ecological Chemistry in Munich, West Germany, reported on experiments showing that CFC's can be decomposed by sunlight in the presence of oxygen. Nevertheless, the Swedish Ministry of Agriculture announced in December 1977 that the use of CFC propellants in aerosol cans would be banned as of Jan. 1, 1979. Thus Sweden became the first country to declare an outright ban on aerosols.

In March 1978 the U.S. Food and Drug Administration, the EPA, and the Consumer Product Safety Commission announced that, as of October 15, the bulk manufacture of CFC's for nonessential uses would be forbidden, reducing CFC production about 98% by December. On April 15, 1979, the ban would be extended to bar shipment of CFC's across state lines. Sweden aside, the Europeans generally remained cautious. On September 20, British manufacturers advised the government that evidence of the effect of CFC's on the ozone layer was insufficient to warrant action.

The release of nitrous oxide from nitrogenous fertilizers emerged as a new threat to the ozone layer, but a report by the U.S. National Research Council, *Nitrates: An Environmental Assessment*, published by the National Academy of Sciences, calculated that the effects would be too small to be noticeable until about the year 2000. Indeed, calculations made at the Lawrence Livermore Laboratory in California and published in December 1977 indicated that the effect from fertilizers might be more than offset by the reduction in natural nitrous oxide production resulting from the tilling and draining of more land.

According to a study made in Britain by the Meteorological Office, the depletion of the ozone layer by CFC's, used at the 1973 levels, might be almost exactly counterbalanced by the release of carbon dioxide into the atmosphere from the combustion of fuels. Ozone concentration in the ozone layer had actually increased about 6% since monitoring began in the 1920s.

Microwaves. In January the EPA announced results of a study into the effects of microwave radiation at the currently recommended maximum exposure level, 10 mw per sq cm of body surface. Eight pregnant monkeys were irradiated, and the offspring of six of them died within six months of birth, while no offspring died among the control group. This intensified fears of the nonthermal effects of radiation from radar, VHF radio and television transmissions, broadcasting relay stations, and microwave ovens. For 20 years the Soviet government had set limits for maximum exposure 1,000 times lower than those recommended, but not enforced, in the West.

In January plans to build a military radar station at Cape Cod, Mass., encountered local opposition, and Air Force radiation experts attended a meeting of about 800 residents held to discuss the problem. A U.S. Marine sergeant filed a $1,750,000 lawsuit against the government in June, claiming his sons had been injured by microwaves beamed at the U.S. embassy in Moscow. In October, 163 crew members of the British aircraft carrier HMS "Ark Royal" were given physical examinations following their accidental exposure to microwaves from radar equipment.

Recycling. For some years the use of nonreturnable bottles had incensed environmentalists, but the relative merits of returnable and nonreturnable bottles in terms of cost and the use of materials and energy were far from clear. The British National Waste Management Advisory Council announced research projects costing £50,-000 that would attempt to resolve the issue.

The EEC continued to study ways of conserving materials by reducing waste at the points of production and consumption, increasing the life of goods, modifying designs to facilitate disposal or recycling, and encouraging manufacturers to use recoverable materials where possible. At the same time, the EEC sought to promote selective waste collection systems to facilitate reprocessing. It was estimated in Britain that £150 million a year could be saved by using all the known techniques for recycling. On June 22 the government enlisted the support of voluntary groups in a National Anti-Waste Campaign.

The message was endorsed by the Worldwatch Institute, Washington, D.C., in *Worldwatch Paper 23* by Denis Hayes, published in September. According to the paper, it was technically possible to recover more than 65% of all materials. In practice, however, 70% of all metal was used only once and, of the metal that was recycled, only 0.23% was still in use after five cycles.

In February, Nippon Steel opened a plant in Tokyo that could convert 40 tons of refuse a day into combustible gas, slag for use in construction, and iron. If the experiment was successful, the Tokyo metropolitan government hoped to build more plants of the same type. The process was similar in principle to that used in a blast furnace.

Thousands of seabirds of many species were killed by the oil slick from the "Amoco Cadiz" disaster.

PATRICK ZACHMANN—RUSH/KATHERINE YOUNG

Alternative Technologies. UNEP declared May 3 as "Sun Day," and nowhere was it celebrated more fervently than in the U.S., where the Department of Energy defined it as "a person-to-person effort to spread the word on renewable energy resources." Visiting the Solar Energy Research Institute at Golden, Colo. (in pouring rain), Pres. Jimmy Carter announced that he had asked for an additional $100 million of energy research and development funding to be diverted into solar and other renewable energy projects. In March, 44 congressmen and 26 senators formed a "solar coalition" to lobby for increased spending on solar energy projects.

On February 17 the British government announced plans to accelerate its research and development program into alternative energy sources by investing an additional £6 million over a four-year period; this would bring total funding to about £16 million. In December 1977 the British secretary of state for energy, Anthony Benn, had announced a ten-year, £320 million program to conserve energy.

In an article in the February 1978 issue of *Water Power and Dam Construction*, H. Weyss of the Austrian-based International Institute for Applied Systems Analysis argued that a mixture of solar and hydroelectric energy could make Austria totally independent of fossil fuels and nuclear energy. A report published in the Royal Swedish Academy of Science's journal *Ambio* in April indicated that Sweden could achieve the same independence by using biomass conversion, solar cells, hydroelectricity, wind power, and direct solar heating. The report was by Thomas Johansson and Peter Steen of the Swedish Secretariat for Future Studies.

In September the European Commission recommended that EEC investment in energy saving and alternative sources of energy be increased from about $23 million in 1975–78 to about $75 million for 1979–83. This included the cost of completing the 1-Mw helioelectric power station under construction at Contrasto, Sicily. (*See* Feature Article: *Toward a Sun-Powered World.*)

Urban Problems. There was little substantial improvement in the crisis affecting urban areas. In January it was reported that New York City faced financial difficulties as acute as those that almost bankrupted it in 1975, and in December Cleveland, Ohio, became the first large U.S. city to default on its obligations since the depression of the 1930s. Nevertheless, efforts to understand urban problems intensified. In some cases the resultant studies produced unexpected findings. In Britain, the Centre for Environmental Studies concluded that the development of New Towns, on which Britain had prided itself, was socially and economically deleterious to the older cities.

The UN Habitat and Human Settlements Foundation set up temporary headquarters in Nairobi while it waited for its permanent quarters to be built at Gigiri, Kenya. On April 3–7 the UN Commission on Human Settlements held its first session in New York City. UN Secretary-General Kurt Waldheim appointed Arcot Ramachandran of India as executive director of the UN Centre for Human Settlements. (MICHAEL ALLABY)

World's 25 Most Populous Urban Areas[1]

Rank	City and country	City proper Most recent population	Year	Metropolitan area Most recent population	Year
1	Tokyo, Japan	8,514,100	1978 estimate	27,717,000	1977 estimate
2	New York City, U.S.	7,420,000	1978 estimate	16,590,400	1977 estimate
3	Osaka, Japan	2,707,100	1978 estimate	15,943,000	1977 estimate
4	Mexico City, Mexico	8,988,200	1978 estimate	13,993,900	1978 estimate
5	London, U.K.	6,970,100	1977 estimate	11,517,000	1977 estimate
6	Shanghai, China	5,700,000	1970 estimate	11,396,000 [2]	1975 estimate
7	Los Angeles, U.S.	2,765,000	1978 estimate	10,650,900	1977 estimate
8	São Paulo, Brazil	7,198,600	1975 estimate	10,473,000	1976 estimate
9	Ruhr, West Germany[3]	—	—	10,278,000	1975 estimate
10	Rio de Janeiro, Brazil	4,857,700	1975 estimate	8,601,000	1976 estimate
11	Paris, France	2,299,800	1975 census	8,549,900	1975 census
12	Buenos Aires, Argentina	2,982,000	1978 estimate	8,498,000	1975 estimate
13	Peking, China	...	...	8,487,000 [2]	1975 estimate
14	Calcutta, India	3,148,700	1971 census	8,297,000	1977 estimate
15	Moscow, U.S.S.R.	7,644,000	1977 estimate	7,819,000	1977 estimate
16	Nagoya, Japan	2,085,300	1978 estimate	7,705,000	1977 estimate
17	Bombay, India	...	...	7,605,000 [2]	1977 estimate
18	Chicago, U.S.	2,980,000	1978 estimate	7,564,000	1977 estimate
19	Manila, Philippines	1,454,400	1975 census	7,500,000 [2]	1978 estimate
20	Cairo, Egypt	5,247,000	1978 estimate	7,066,900	1976 estimate
21	Seoul, South Korea	...	...	6,964,900 [2]	1976 estimate
22	Jakarta, Indonesia	...	...	6,178,500 [2]	1977 estimate
23	Philadelphia, U.S.	1,805,000	1978 estimate	5,745,300	1977 estimate
24	San Francisco, U.S.	658,000	1978 estimate	4,723,300	1977 estimate
25	Teheran, Iran	...	...	4,496,200 [2]	1976 census

[1]Ranked by population of metropolitan area.
[2]Municipality or other civil division within which a city proper may not be distinguished.
[3]A so-called industrial conurbation within which a single central city is not distinguished.

WILDLIFE CONSERVATION

In December 1977, in the Volcano National Park in Rwanda, poachers killed the male mountain gorilla Digit, made world famous through Dian Fossey's study of gorillas and a television film that showed him taking and returning her notebook and pencil. One of the poachers, who was caught, explained that the gorilla was killed for the sake of the $20 or so that could be obtained for its head and hands. Later, Uncle Bert, leader of the same gorilla group, and Macho, a female with a three-year-old son, were also shot by poachers.

By then the Fauna Preservation Society (FPS) had set up a Mountain Gorilla Fund, to be devoted wholly to the conservation of the volcano forest area and its gorillas. In August 1978, with the generous backing of Sabena Belgian World Airlines, A. H. Harcourt, a biologist with two years' experience of the Virunga region, and conservationist Kai Curry-Lindahl visited the area. Their report indicated that more than the survival of the gorillas was at stake. The volcano forest acted as a giant sponge, collecting water in the wet season and releasing it in the dry. Its rapid destruction posed a real threat to Rwanda's water supply.

The Magenta petrel, previously known from one specimen collected in 1867 in the central Pacific ocean by scientists in the research vessel "Magenta," was rediscovered by D. Crockett in the Chatham Islands, New Zealand. It proved to be the same species as the Chatham Island tiako, of which only bones had been found. The New Zealand Wildlife Service continued its efforts to preserve the Chatham Island black robin by transferring robins from Little Mangere Island to Mangere Island and planting Olearia cuttings there to provide shelter. Two young had hatched, but the total population remained at seven. The outlook for the takahe, a huge New Zealand rail thought to be extinct but rediscovered in 1948, improved with the hatching of two chicks at the Mount Bruce native bird reserve.

In February the IUCN asked the Canadian government to stop or delay the 1978 killing of baby harp seals (whitecoats) on the ice off Canada's east coast so a reasonable management program could be prepared. Neither action was taken, but permission was given for the killing to be watched by W. J. Jordan, a veterinarian and chief wildlife officer of the Royal Society for the Prevention of Cruelty to Animals, and T. Scott of the International Society for the Protection of Animals. Their report showed that the baby seals were not always killed instantaneously, as was claimed; on the contrary, many of their skulls had not been crushed before skinning began. France, which on May 11 became the 46th country to accede to the Convention on International Trade in Endangered Species of Wild Fauna and Flora, had already (January 26) banned importation of whitecoat skins.

In April a conference convened by Greece and co-sponsored by UNEP, IUCN, and the University of Guelph, Ont., was held in Rhodes to discuss ways of saving the Mediterranean monk seal from extermination. Greece planned to establish a national park in the northern Sporades, an important Aegean centre for the seal. In June the president of Mauritania inaugurated the Banc d'Arguin National Park, off Mauritania's Atlantic coast, which contained the largest known colony of this endangered species. Its numbers there had increased from about 30 in 1973 to about 60 in 1978.

An officially authorized cull of 5,800 gray seal adults and pups in the Orkney Islands was called off in October after Greenpeace's vessel "Rainbow Warrior" impeded the Norwegian sealer "Kvitungen," contracted by the Scottish authorities to carry out the cull. Pending a reexamination of scientific advice, the cull would be limited to 2,000 pups.

Greenpeace was also active during the year in harassing Icelandic, Japanese, and Soviet whalers in the North Atlantic and the Pacific. At the annual meeting of the International Whaling Commission, held in London in June, a Panamanian resolution calling for a ten-year moratorium on commercial whaling was withdrawn, and quotas were set for all important species. The aggregate catch for 1978–79 was put at 16,047, compared with 16,700 for 1977–78.

During the first two weeks following the wreck of the "Amoco Cadiz," 2,700 seabirds of 34 species were brought to the Brest rehabilitation centre. Among the worst affected were 681 puffins, 513 razorbills, 417 shags, and 379 guillemots. Heavy damage to birdlife also followed spillage from the tanker "Christos Bitas" off the Pembrokeshire coast of Wales in October.

On May 15 the U.S. Fish and Wildlife Service designated as protected "critical habitats" five wetland areas used as resting places for the main flock of whooping cranes on their migratory journey from northern Canada to Texas. It also announced that bald eagle nests in the Great Lakes area had increased from 178 in 1965 to 197 in 1977, and the number of young had risen from 187 to 212. Osprey nests had increased from 117 to 159 and young from 120 to 147. Both species were recovering slowly but steadily.

U.S. environmentalists won what might prove to be a Pyrrhic victory when the Supreme Court, ruling in the case of the snail darter versus the Tellico Dam, found in favour of the fish. Under the provisions of the Endangered Species Act of 1973, operation of the dam on the Little Tennessee River had been held up because opening the floodgates would destroy the only known habitat of the three-inch perch. The court ruled that the law, as written, "admits of no exceptions." The door was left open to changes in the act, however, and on November 10 President Carter signed a bill establishing a seven-man, Cabinet-level review board with power to permit construction of federal projects even though extinction of an endangered species would result. Meanwhile, reports from the National Wildlife Federation and the Wildlife Management Institute indicated that some of the larger North American mammals, including elk, antelope, and moose, had made striking comebacks since the early 1900s, to the point where overpopulation was a problem in some areas.

For many years the land iguana of the Galápagos Islands had been endangered by the depredations of feral dogs. In an effort to save the species, the Charles Darwin Foundation of the Galápagos Islands had kept survivors at the Darwin Research Station, where their eggs were placed in incubators, or in semicaptivity on the tiny island of Venecia, where 20 tons of earth had been taken for the iguanas to use for burrowing. A number of eggs had been laid, and in June 1978 the first successful hatching was finally announced.

The cold June in Britain and the consequent scarcity of insect food caused many casualties among bats as mothers abandoned their young and went precipitately into hibernation. Especially affected was the greater horseshoe bat, a cave-roosting species confined to the southwest. To help this bat, protected under the Conservation of Wild Creatures and Wild Plants Act 1973, an anonymous businessman bought Woodchester Park in Gloucestershire where a colony of the bats lived. On July 21 the British government announced that money would be provided to buy 5,500 ac of the Ribble estuary in Lancashire, which was threatened with development. The estuary, a vital resting place for migrating birds and winter residents, was a Grade 1 site of Special Scientific Interest and one of the most important areas of its kind in Europe.

In 1962 the FPS had inaugurated Operation Oryx with the object of reestablishing the Arabian oryx in the countries of its original habitation. This goal came closer in February 1978 when four oryx, all offspring of the FPS-owned female Annie, arrived by air at Amman, Jordan. They were released in good condition into holding pens in the Shaumari wildlife reserve, where the Royal Society for the Conservation of Nature in Jordan had established a captive breeding unit for desert wildlife. Later in the year, four pairs of oryx from the Los Angeles Zoo were introduced into Israel's Hai Bar reserve for biblical animals.   (C. L. BOYLE)

See also Agriculture and Food Supplies; Energy; Fisheries; Historic Preservation; Life Sciences; Transportation.
[355.D; 525.A.3.g and B.4.f.i; 534.C.2.a; 724.A; 737.C.1]

THE INDESTRUCTIBLE GARBAGE

by Jon Tinker

Hannes Alfvén, Swedish Nobel laureate for physics, once commented: "If a problem is too difficult to solve, one cannot claim that it *is* solved by pointing to all the efforts made to solve it." The relevance of Alfvén's thesis to the problems of nuclear waste is becoming increasingly clear. Despite massive research efforts and a plethora of ingenious ideas, the lack of any safe and permanent means of waste disposal appears to be the most intractable roadblock in the way of extended use of atomic power.

Today, the U.S. and half a dozen other countries are hesitating before committing themselves to the breeder reactor, a second generation of nuclear technology that poses waste disposal questions even more ominous than those of ordinary fission reactors. In September 1976 the British Royal Commission on Environmental Pollution warned: "It would be irresponsible . . . to commit future generations to the consequences of fission power on a massive scale unless it has been demonstrated beyond reasonable doubt that at least one method exists for . . . the safe containment of long-lived, highly radioactive waste for the indefinite future."

There are three types of radioactive waste: low-grade, medium-grade, and high-grade, depending on the degree of radioactivity. Low-grade waste consists of mildly radioactive cooling water from nuclear reactors, contaminated laboratory equipment, protective clothing, old containers, and the like. Medium-grade waste is mainly irradiated junk from inside nuclear reactors and reprocessing plants: old pipes, control rods, filters, and ash. High-grade waste comes almost exclusively from the reprocessing plants where the nuclear fuel rods are sent for cleaning and restoring and consists of extremely radioactive decay products.

Storage Techniques. Three separate approaches have been developed for these three types of waste. The first technique, known as dilute-and-disperse, applies to low levels of radioactivity and to short-

lived isotopes. Some reactors, for example, release argon-41, a radioactive isotope of the inert atmospheric gas argon. This argon-41 is allowed to disperse in the air because the amounts involved are small, because argon does not react with anything and thus cannot be incorporated into ecological food chains, and because the half-life of argon-41 is only 1.8 hours. This means that after 1.8 hours its radioactivity will have been reduced to one-half the initial amount, after another 1.8 hours to one-quarter, after another 1.8 hours to one-eighth, and so on. After 20 half-lives—36 hours for argon-41—the radioactivity will have fallen to less than one-millionth of its initial level.

The second technique is known as delay-and-decay and is used for waste contaminated with radioactive isotopes having a medium half-life. Iodine-131, a gas with a half-life of eight days, is produced inside many nuclear reactors. It is liquefied and stored for six months, by which time its radioactivity has declined by ten million times or so, and it can be released safely.

The third technique, called concentrate-and-contain, is the only option currently available for isotopes that are highly radioactive and have half-lives

Scores of drums of radioactive waste await burial in a trench in the Los Alamos Scientific Laboratory in New Mexico.

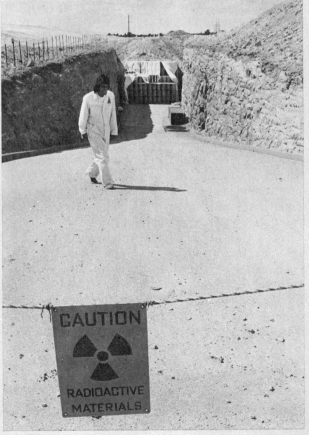

WIDE WORLD

Jon Tinker is director of Earthscan, an agency of the International Institute for Environment and Development.

so long that it is impractical to wait for them to decay. The most dangerous of these wastes is plutonium-239, with a half-life of 24,400 years. For its radioactivity to fall to less than one-millionth of initial levels takes a total of 488,000 years. Nuclear technology at present is unable to guarantee containment on quite this time scale.

How Foolproof? When used fuel rods are removed from a nuclear reactor and taken to a reprocessing plant, they are dissolved in nitric acid and the reusable fuel (uranium and plutonium) is removed in an organic solvent. The liquid that remains is ferociously radioactive. It is first concentrated by evaporation and then carefully transferred into a stainless steel tank. These tanks are fitted with elaborate cooling circuits to prevent the liquors from boiling, rupturing the tanks, and releasing radioactive plutonium and other elements to the soil, the groundwater, and the atmosphere.

But as U.S. nuclear scientist Edward Teller once put it, no foolproof system can be proof against an excessively great fool. Regrettably, the history of nuclear technology suggests that there are fools in this industry as in most others. At the U.S. Atomic Energy Commission (AEC) Hanford plant near Richland, Wash., high-level waste Tank 106T started to leak on April 20, 1973. Not until June 8 did anyone notice, even though fresh wastes were being added to the tank, its level was being recorded every week, and radiation in a borehole in the adjoining ground, which was also being measured, was rising rapidly.

Nor is making a tank foolproof just a matter of protecting it against fools. On Nov. 12, 1972, the hijackers of a DC-9 aircraft threatened to crash it on the AEC's facilities at Oak Ridge, Tenn., unless they were given $10 million and their plane was refueled. Their demands were hurriedly met and they flew to Cuba. The British tanks at Windscale lie little more than 100 mi from the terrorist bombs of Northern Ireland, and no doubt the high-level waste tanks of the French, Indians, Belgians, Chinese, West Germans, Soviets, Canadians, and others are similarly at risk from fools, knaves, and even acts of God such as earthquakes and meteors.

Wanted: A Permanent Solution. To devise procedures capable of keeping this devil's broth safe for hundreds of years has boggled the minds of technologists and politicians alike. Small wonder that both have searched for some permanent means of nuclear waste disposal rather than storage. Many methods have been suggested, ranging from the obviously inane to the barely practicable. In the discussion of these possibilities one can often detect an irrational willingness to consider *any* once-for-all solution that relieves mankind of a custodianship measured in centuries.

The first method that has been suggested is transmutation—bombarding long-lived wastes in an atomic pile so that they are converted into elements with much shorter half-lives. Thus neptunium-237, an isotope with a half-life of over two million years, would be converted to plutonium-238, with a half-life of only 86 years. However, the theory, let alone the technology, is not yet fully developed.

The second method was originally suggested by then AEC chairman James R. Schlesinger: rocketing the waste into the Sun. In theory, of course, this is unexceptionable; the waste would certainly do no harm once it arrived on target. Getting it there is another question, however. The problem of guaranteeing that the waste capsule could survive a crash landing on Earth without releasing its contents seems to be insuperable.

The Hot Mole and Variants. The third proposal is known as the hot mole. The waste would be solidified and placed on the Antarctic icecap. The heat of the waste slug would melt the ice, and the slug would gradually fall downward through the ice sheet, the hole made by its passage freezing above it. Eventually, the wastes would come to rest on the Antarctic rocks a mile and more below the surface. Since the ice sheet is known to have been there for at least one million years, it is thought likely to last that long into the future. However, recent research suggests that there may be a number of lakes beneath the icecap, communicating with each other and with the ocean. This could provide a route for the wastes to reach the biosphere once again.

The fourth suggestion, a variant of the hot mole, was proposed in 1978: embed the waste in a ceramic container, whose melting point, 1,200° C, is higher than that of the most refractory crystalline rocks. Such a waste slug, it is argued, would melt its way down through the rock until it reached the Earth's molten core, or until its wastes decayed sufficiently to reduce the slug's temperature below that of the melting point of the rock. So far, though, even a conventionally heated mole has not been tested.

The fifth method also involves the Earth's interior. The planet's surface is thought to consist of about a dozen tectonic plates floating on a molten core, moving slowly in relation to one another. At a point where two plates are converging, material is forced under one plate and down into the interior. The idea is to place the wastes at the junction of two plates in deep ocean trenches. Unfortunately, calculations suggest it might take 250,000 years for the wastes to be completely engulfed, during which period radioactivity could well escape.

A sixth possibility is to dump the glass blocks on the seabed, preferably in one of the deep trenches six miles or more below the surface. So far, no one is entirely certain that the waste could not irradiate the seawater or the abyssal ooze. A recent theory that tsunamis ("tidal waves") are initiated by masses of methane gas suddenly rising to the surface from the ocean floor has only increased fears that the biosphere might become contaminated. However, if the blocks were dropped down a hole specially drilled to a depth of about half a mile beneath the seabed, and the shaft then sealed, this objection would not apply. No conceivable climatic change could bring the wastes to the surface again, and the seabed area chosen could be one of virtually nil biological activity and of known stability for tens of millions of years in the past. As with most of the other proposals, the requisite technology has yet to be developed.

A seventh possibility, and currently the favourite in most countries, is to deposit the vitrified waste blocks in underground salt mines. Salt is an excellent conductor of heat, and its high solubility in water is powerful evidence that existing salt deposits must have been out of contact with groundwater for long periods of geologic time. West Germany has already established such a waste facility in a salt mine at Asse, and others are in preparation in the U.S. and elsewhere. Since salt is easily mined, it would be a relatively simple matter to monitor the condition of the blocks regularly and to recover them if problems arose. An alternative is to embed the waste in a solid stratum; some rocks underneath Britain, for example, are thought to have remained free of water for at least 60 million years. However, the practical difficulties of placing the wastes deep in solid rock, monitoring them, and if necessary recovering them are considerable.

Despite the powerful psychological pressures to get hot nuclear wastes permanently out of sight and thus out of mind, such materials are still almost entirely stored as liquids in tanks. There, at least, they can be guarded and protected, and any accident or unforeseen circumstance can (it is argued) be remedied quickly.

The Threat to Posterity. Whether these wastes are kept near the surface of the planet or are buried deep beneath it, they will remain furiously radioactive for centuries. How are we to ensure that our descendants a few centuries from now will not dig holes at Hanford or Windscale, will not drill in the deep Pacific, will not explore the lakes beneath the Antarctic icecap? The problem is not that such interference might lead to casualties; every generation leaves a few booby traps for its successors. The risk is that the nuclear wastes might be irrecoverably released into the biosphere.

Is there any way to convey down the centuries to the unimaginable civilizations of the next millennium a taboo against digging in old salt mines, a taboo that must extend as far into the future as King Nebuchadnezzar now lies in the past? Such a responsibility is not a matter of speculation; the wastes already accumulated will indubitably require such cautious treatment for centuries. But if the historical implications of our present technology are worrying enough, the time shadow of the breeder reactor would be substantially greater. Although our present nuclear power plants do indeed produce some wastes with half-lives measured in centuries, the great bulk of present-day high-level wastes consists of isotopes such as strontium-90 and cesium-137, with half-lives of 28 and 30 years, respectively.

If, as the most technologically advanced nations are now considering, the fast breeder reactor is developed commercially, the proportion of plutonium-239 in high-level wastes will increase greatly. Instead of wastes with net half-lives of a few decades, we will be talking of half-lives of tens of thousands of years; instead of centuries of containment, we will have to plan for millions of years.

Although the U.S. is holding back for the moment, France, West Germany, the U.K., and the U.S.S.R. are all actively working on experimental breeders, and India, Italy, and Japan at least are planning to follow. The next year or two will show whether our species can restrain itself from creating a new and awesome problem before it has worked out an answer. We must not, as Alfvén warns, mistake the active search for a solution for a guarantee that a solution is there to be found.

Equatorial Guinea

Equatorial Guinea

The African republic of Equatorial Guinea consists of Río Muni, which is bordered by Cameroon on the north, Gabon on the east and south, and the Atlantic Ocean on the west; and the offshore islands of Macías Nguema Biyogo and Pagalu. Area: 28,051 sq km (10,831 sq mi). Pop. (1978 est.): 327,-000. Cap. and largest city: Malabo, on Macías Nguema Biyogo (pop., 1970 est., 19,300). Language: Spanish. President in 1978, Francisco Macías Nguema.

The flight of Pres. Francisco Macías Nguema's third wife, Monica, in 1978 focused some attention on this impoverished and brutalized West African dictatorship. It was estimated that nearly half the population had fled. Gabon, which took an immigration census after the murder of Gabonese in Equatorial Guinea, was believed to have taken in over 60,000. The few Spanish teachers who remained demanded repatriation when one of their number was detained for "having accommodated a Danish woman, an agent of imperialism," and fined $35,000. In a document published on December 19, the International Commission of Jurists accused Macías of having "completely liquidated his political opponents."

The president's aspirations to divinity brought him into conflict with the Catholic Church. He jailed all priests who refused to begin services "in the name of President Macías and his son"; and on June 30, although over 80% of the population was Catholic, Catholicism was prohibited.

Equatorial Guinea's formerly healthy economy, based on cocoa, timber, coffee, and bananas, was now in total decline, largely because of the flight of peasant farmers and the repatriation of Nigerian workers.   (MOLLY MORTIMER)

EQUATORIAL GUINEA
Education. (1973–74) Primary, pupils 35,977, teachers 630; secondary (1972–73), pupils 4,713; vocational (1972–73), pupils 586; teacher training (1972–73), students 201; secondary, vocational, and teacher training (1970–71), teachers 175.
Finance and Trade. Monetary unit: ekuele, at par with the Spanish peseta, with (Sept. 18, 1978) a free rate of 74.13 ekuele to U.S. $1 (145.25 ekuele = £1 sterling). Budget (1970): revenue 709.4 million ekuele; expenditure 589.3 million ekuele (excludes capital expenditure of 650.7 million ekuele). Foreign trade (1970): imports 1,472,100,-000 ekuele (80% from Spain); exports 1,740,900,000 ekuele (91% to Spain). Main exports: cocoa 66%; coffee 24%; timber 9%. Trade with Spain (1977): imports 176 million ekuele; exports 304 million ekuele.
Agriculture. Production (in 000; metric tons; 1976): sweet potatoes c. 30; bananas c. 15; cocoa c. 7; coffee c. 5; palm kernels c. 2; palm oil c. 5. Livestock (in 000; 1976): sheep c. 31; cattle c. 4; pigs c. 8; goats c. 7; chickens c. 82.

Equestrian Sports

Thoroughbred Racing and Steeplechasing.
UNITED STATES AND CANADA. Louis Wolfson, a Florida owner and breeder, accounted in 1978 for a record five Eclipse Awards in voting conducted by the Thoroughbred Racing Associations, the National Turf Writers Association, and staff members of the *Daily Racing Form*. Wolfson's homebred Affirmed, two-year-old colt champion of 1977, was named best three-year-old colt and horse of the year, and his It's in the Air tied with Mrs. Henry D. Paxson's Candy Eclair for two-year-old filly honours. Wolfson himself was voted best in the owner and breeder categories. It's in the Air, bred by Wolfson's sons, Gary and Stephen, was purchased in midsummer by Wolfson for $300,000 from Jerry Frankel, who had bought her as a weanling for $25,000.

There also was a tie for top honours in the

Coming down the stretch in the Belmont Stakes, Affirmed (right) and Alydar were neck and neck. Affirmed won the race by a nose and took the Triple Crown.

WIDE WORLD

sprinter division between George Pope's J. O. Tobin and Tartan Stable's Dr. Patches. These were the first ties in the history of the Eclipse Awards. Lazaro Barrera, who trained Affirmed, It's in the Air, and J. O. Tobin, was named best trainer for a record third consecutive year.

Seattle Slew, best three-year-old colt and horse of the year in 1977, was the only other Eclipse Award winner besides Affirmed to repeat. He was voted the best older horse and narrowly lost to Affirmed in the balloting for overall best.

Other champions included Hawksworth Farm's Spectacular Bid, two-year-old colt division; Mrs. John Galbreath's Tempest Queen, three-year-old filly; Greentree Stable's Late Bloomer, older mare; Jerome Torsney's Mac Diarmida, turf; Darrel McHargue, jockey; and Ron Franklin, apprentice jockey. On the last day of the year, McHargue surpassed Steve Cauthen's 1977 record for earnings in one year by riding three winners at Santa Anita, bringing his total to $6,188,353.

Affirmed, which defeated Alydar four out of six times during 1977, continued his torrid rivalry with the Calumet Farm colt in 1978. Affirmed, ridden by the 18-year-old Cauthen, won the Triple Crown over Alydar by diminishing margins—1½ lengths in the Kentucky Derby, a neck in the Preakness, and a head in the Belmont Stakes. Alydar, which missed late-season action because of injury, was the first horse ever to finish second in all three Triple Crown events.

Affirmed won an allowance race at Santa Anita early in March to launch his campaign and then scored eight consecutive stakes victories prior to the renewal of the Travers at Saratoga in mid-August. In the Travers Affirmed finished almost two lengths ahead of Alydar but was disqualified for shutting off his rival coming into the stretch turn, and the Calumet colt was awarded first place. Affirmed made two more starts, finishing second to Seattle Slew in the Marlboro and fifth to Exceller in the Jockey Club Gold Cup, during which he was handicapped by a loose saddle. Affirmed's 1978 earnings of $901,541 established a one-year record in U.S. racing.

Seattle Slew won five of seven starts, including three stakes, and retired to stud with earnings of $1,208,726. In brilliant efforts, he won the Marlboro by three lengths and triumphed in the Woodward by four lengths in track record time of 2 min for ten furlongs. Seattle Slew probably ran his best race in defeat. Forced to run extremely fast early by the Wolfson entry of Life's Hope and Affirmed—a half mile in 45.2 sec and six furlongs in 1 min 9.4 sec—he nonetheless battled with the late-charging Exceller in the stretch of the 1½-mi Jockey Club Gold Cup before losing by a nose at the wire.

The most spectacular late-season heroics were accomplished by the gray colt Spectacular Bid. The Maryland-based son of Bold Bidder did not score his first stakes victory until his fifth start, taking the World Playground by 15 lengths in fast time, and then was undefeated in his four remaining starts. Spectacular Bid won the 1 1/16-mi Laurel Futurity in 1 min 41.6 sec to lower the track record by a full second.

Mac Diarmida's first defeat on turf, after ten victories including six stakes, came in the Man o' War when he finished third to Waya. The son of Minnesota Mac clinched the turf championship with victories in the Canadian International and the Washington (D.C.) International.

In 1977 many stud farms in Great Britain were struck by contagious equine metritis, a serious vaginal infection. In the spring of 1978, despite precautionary efforts taken by the U.S. Department of Agriculture, the disease appeared at two major Thoroughbred farms in Kentucky: Gainesway Farm, the hardest hit, and Spendthrift Farm. For a two-week period the Kentucky Department of Agriculture forbade the moving of any stallion or mare from one farm to another. In terms of number of mares getting in foal the Kentucky breeding industry apparently did not suffer appreciably, but there was some disruption of original mating schedules. (*See* VETERINARY SCIENCE.)

In the Queen's Plate, the first event in the Canadian Triple Crown for three-year-olds, Regal Embrace won by a neck from Overskate. The latter gained his revenge, however, by triumphing in the other two, the Prince of Wales Stakes and the Breeders' Stakes, and was subsequently named Canadian horse of the year. In other major races Medaille d'Or won the Coronation Futurity, La Voyageuse took the Canadian Oaks, and Sound Reason triumphed in the Canadian Maturity.

(JOSEPH C. AGRELLA)

EUROPE AND AUSTRALIA. Frost and snow affected the 1977–78 National Hunt season in Britain, and the Cheltenham Gold Cup had to be postponed four weeks. Nevertheless, the race was a fine one as Midnight Court, owned by Mrs. O. Jackson, trained by Fred Winter, and ridden by John Francome, beat the Irish steeplechaser Brown Lad and Master H. The Champion Hurdle was won by the Irish-trained Monksfield from Sea Pigeon and Night Nurse. The Triumph Hurdle for four-year-olds was won by Connaught Ranger from Rodman.

Injury at a late hour foiled Red Rum's bid at the age of 13 to accomplish the near-impossible and win a fourth Grand National Steeplechase, and he retired. In the Grand National nine-year-old Lucius, owned by Mrs. D. Whitaker, trained by G. Richards, and ridden by R. Davies, won in a desperately close finish from Sebastian V and Drumroan. The much-improved Bachelor's Hall won the Mackeson Gold Cup Steeplechase, the Hennessy Gold Cup Steeplechase, and the King George VI Steeplechase. Even Melody won the Massey-Ferguson Gold Cup Steeplechase, and the Whitbread Gold Cup Steeplechase was won by Strombolus. A new £25,000, two-mile, handicap hurdle race, the Royal Doulton Handicap Hurdle, was run at Haydock Park and was won by Royal Gaye. J. J. O'Neill was National Hunt champion jockey with 149 winners, beating the previous record of 125 winners by Ron Barry in 1973. The Grand Steeplechase de Paris at Auteuil was won by Mon Filleul.

On the flat in England in 1978 a feature of the year was the inspired riding of jockey Greville Starkey, who had his best season ever with ten winners. He achieved a unique feat, riding in one season the winners of all four classic races for the

Major Thoroughbred Race Winners, 1978

Race	Won by	Jockey	Owner
United States			
Acorn	Tempest Queen	J. Velasquez	Darby Dan Farm
Alabama	White Star Line	M. Venezia	Newstead Farm
Amory L. Haskell	Life's Hope	C. Perret	Harbor View Farm
Arlington-Washington Futurity	Jose Binn	A. Cordero Jr.	Moreton Binn
Beldame	Late Bloomer	J. Velasquez	Greentree Stable
Belmont	Affirmed	S. Cauthen	Harbor View Farm
Blue Grass	Alydar	J. Velasquez	Calumet Farm
Brooklyn	Nasty and Bold	J. L. Samyn	Meadowhill
Californian	J. O. Tobin	S. Cauthen	El Peco Ranch
Champagne	Spectacular Bid	J. Velasquez	Hawksworth Farm
Coaching Club American Oaks	Lakeville Miss	R. Hernandez	Randolph Weinsier
Delaware	Late Bloomer	J. Velasquez	Greentree Stable
Delaware Oaks	White Star Line	J. Fell	Newstead Farm
Fall Highweight	What A Summer	A. Cordero Jr.	Mrs. B. R. Firestone
Flamingo	Alydar	J. Velasquez	Calumet Farm
Florida Derby	Alydar	J. Velasquez	Calumet Farm
Frizette	Golferette	J. Fell	Randolph Weinsier
Futurity	Crest of the Wave	J. Cruguet	F. W. Hooper
Gulfstream Park	Bowl Game	J. Velasquez	Greentree Stable
Hollywood Derby	Affirmed	S. Cauthen	Harbor View Farm
Hollywood Gold Cup	Exceller	W. Shoemaker	Nelson Bunker Hunt
Hollywood Invitational	Exceller	W. Shoemaker	Nelson Bunker Hunt
Hopeful	General Assembly	D. McHargue	Bertram R. Firestone
Jockey Club Gold Cup	Exceller	W. Shoemaker	Nelson Bunker Hunt
Kentucky Derby	Affirmed	S. Cauthen	Harbor View Farm
Kentucky Oaks	White Star Line	E. Maple	Newstead Farm
Ladies	Ida Delia	A. Santiago	A. U. Jones
Laurel Futurity	Spectacular Bid	R. Franklin	Hawksworth Farm
Man o' War	Waya	A. Cordero Jr.	Daniel Wildenstein
Marlboro	Seattle Slew	A. Cordero Jr.	Tayhill Stable
Matchmaker	Queen Lib	D. MacBeth	Raritan Stable
Matron	Fall Aspen	R. I. Veloz	Joseph M. Roebling
Metropolitan	Cox's Ridge	E. Maple	Loblolly Stable
Monmouth Invitational	Delta Flag	D. Nied	Dogwood Stable
Monmouth Oaks	Sharp Belle	D. B. Thomas	Aisco Stable
Mother Goose	Caesar's Wish	D. R. Wright	Sally M. Benson
Oak Tree Invitational	Exceller	W. Shoemaker	Nelson Bunker Hunt
Preakness	Affirmed	S. Cauthen	Harbor View Farm
Ruffian	Late Bloomer	J. Velasquez	Greentree Stable
Santa Anita Derby	Affirmed	S. Cauthen	Harbor View Farm
Santa Anita Handicap	Vigors	D. McHargue	W. R. Hawn
Sapling	Tim the Tiger	J. Fell	Calumet Farm
Selima	Candy Eclair	A. Black	Mrs. Henry D. Paxson
Sorority	Mongo Queen	G. Roboski	W. W. Rice
Spinaway	Palm Hut	R. Velez	Joseph M. Roebling
Spinster	Tempest Queen	Jorge Velasquez	Mrs. John Galbreath
Suburban	Upper Nile	J. Velasquez	Rokeby Stable
Sunset	Exceller	W. Shoemaker	Nelson Bunker Hunt
Swaps	Radar Ahead	D. McHargue	Sidney H. Vail
Top Flight	Northernette	J. Fell	Peter Brant
Travers	Alydar	J. Velasquez	Calumet Farm
Turf Classic	Waya	Angel Cordero Jr.	Daniel Wildenstein
United Nations	Noble Dancer II	S. Cauthen	Haakon Fretheim
Vanity	Afifa	W. Shoemaker	Swiftsure Stable
Washington (D.C.) International	Mac Diarmida	J. Cruguet	Dr. Jerome Torsney
Widener	Silver Series	A. Cordero Jr.	Dr. Archie R. Donaldson
Wood Memorial	Believe It	E. Maple	Hickory Tree Stable
Woodward	Seattle Slew	A. Cordero Jr.	Tayhill Stable
England			
Two Thousand Guineas	Roland Gardens	F. Durr	J. Hayter
One Thousand Guineas	Enstone Spark	E. Johnson	R. Bonnycastle
Derby	Shirley Heights	G. Starkey	Lord Halifax
Oaks	Fair Salinia	G. Starkey	S. Hanson
St. Leger	Julio Mariner	E. Hide	M. Lemos
Coronation Cup	Crow	P. Eddery	D. Wildenstein
Ascot Gold Cup	Shangamuzo	G. Starkey	Mrs. E. Charles
Eclipse Stakes	Gunner B	J. Mercer	Mrs. P. Barratt
King George VI and Queen Elizabeth Diamond Stakes	Ile de Bourbon	J. Reid	D. McCall
Sussex Stakes	Jaazeiro	L. Piggott	R. Sangster
Benson & Hedges Gold Cup	Hawaiian Sound	L. Piggott	R. Sangster
Champion Stakes	Swiss Maid	G. Starkey	M. Fine
France			
Poule d'Essai des Poulains	Nishapour	H. Samani	Aga Khan
Poule d'Essai des Pouliches	Dancing Maid	F. Head	J. Wertheimer
Prix du Jockey Club	Acamas	Y. Saint-Martin	M. Boussac
Prix de Diane	Reine de Saba	F. Head	J. Wertheimer
Prix Royal Oak	Brave Johnny	H. Samani	Miss M. Darc
Prix Ganay	Trillion	L. Piggott	E. L. Stephenson
Prix Lupin	Acamas	Y. Saint-Martin	M. Boussac
Prix du Cadran	Buckskin	Y. Saint-Martin	D. Wildenstein
Grand Prix de Paris	Galiani	A. Lequeux	A. Ben Lassin
Grand Prix de Saint-Cloud	Guadanini	H. Samani	J. Kaida
Prix Vermeille	Dancing Maid	F. Head	J. Wertheimer
Prix de l'Arc de Triomphe	Alleged	L. Piggott	R. Sangster
Ireland			
Irish One Thousand Guineas	More So	C. Roche	L. M. Gelb
Irish Two Thousand Guineas	Jaazeiro	L. Piggott	R. Sangster
Irish Guinness Oaks	Fair Salinia	G. Starkey	S. Hanson
Irish Sweeps Derby	Shirley Heights	G. Starkey	Lord Halifax
Irish St. Leger	M-Lolshan	B. Taylor	Sheikh Essa Alkhalifa
Italy			
Derby Italiano del Galoppo	Elgay	G. Doleuze	Razza Ascagnano
Gran Premio del Jockey Club	Stone	G. Doleuze	Attilio Palvis
West Germany			
Deutsches Derby	Zauberer	B. Selle	Gestüt Bona
Grosser Preis von Baden Baden	Valour	J. Reid	G. Ward
Grosser Preis von Berlin	First Lord	W. Carson	Stall Weissenhof
Grosser Preis von Düsseldorf	Gimont	R. Prinzinger	Gestüt Rosenau

English and Irish derbies and oaks. His other victories included the Ascot Gold Cup and the Champion Stakes. Shirley Heights was England's best three-year-old colt, winning the English and Irish derbies before injury in August brought his career to an abrupt close. Île de Bourbon won the King Edward VII Stakes at Royal Ascot, and, more importantly, the King George VI and Queen Elizabeth Diamond Stakes from the French Derby winner Acamas.

Acamas and Guadanini were France's leading colts. Fair Salinia from Britain and France's Dancing Maid and Reine de Saba were outstanding three-year-old fillies. They were joined late in the season by Swiss Maid, which took the Champion Stakes from Hawaiian Sound (second in both the English and Irish derbies and the winner of the Benson and Hedges Gold Cup at York) and Gunner B. Of the milers Jaazeiro (Irish Two Thousand Guineas, St. James's Palace Stakes, Sussex Stakes) from Ireland, Homing (Queen Elizabeth II Stakes), and Cistus (second in the French Two Thousand Guineas and winner of Goodwood's Nassau Stakes) stood out. Of the three-year-old sprinters Solinus appeared to be the best in Europe till he was humbled in France by a remarkably fast two-year-old filly, Sigy, which beat him in the Prix de l'Abbaye.

Of older horses Robert Sangster's Alleged, trained by Vincent O'Brien in Ireland and ridden by Lester Piggott, won the Prix de l'Arc de Triomphe, Europe's richest race, for the second time and joined the select band of horses that had done so — Ksar, Corrida, Tantième, and Ribot. Apart from this great win, O'Brien's virus-struck stable had a less successful season than in 1977. Peter Walwyn's stable suffered similarly, and its jockey and 1977 champion, Patrick Eddery, had to yield to Willie Carson (182 winners) in the 1978 unofficial jockeys' championship.

The confused two-year-old picture in England was put straight quite simply by Tromos. After a victory at Ascot he took on some of the best of his age in the Dewhurst Stakes at Newmarket and left them behind. In France Irish River, with victories in the Prix Morny and Grand Critérium, was outstanding. Pitasia, winner of the Prix Robert Papin and the Critérium des Pouliches, was among the best of the fillies. In England Devon Ditty was perhaps the best two-year-old filly.

Mill Reef's success as a sire in 1978 was impressive, his progeny including Shirley Heights and Acamas, among others. In England Henry Cecil was the leading trainer (£383,355).

In Australia the Melbourne Cup, run over 3,200 m at Flemington racecourse and worth A$210,000, was won by Arwon from the New Zealand horses Dandaleith and Karu. He was ridden by Harry White, scoring his third success in the race. The 9 to 2 favourite, So Called, was fifth.

(R. M. GOODWIN)

Harness Racing. In the U.S. the richest harness race ever, the $560,000 Meadowlands Pace, was won by Billy Haughton driving Falcon Almahurst (1 min 55.3 sec), with Flight Director second. Abercrombie won the $128,600 Adios Stake in two straight heats from Flight Director and Pat's Gipsy.

Canadian Elizabeth Ashton astride Sunrise takes a difficult jump in the world three-day event competition in Lexington, Kentucky. It was the first time the meet had been held outside Europe.

In other major pacing events Crakers took the $113,681 Fox Stake, while the Little Brown Jug of $186,760 went to Happy Escort, which later took the $105,381 New York Sires Stake. Scarlet Skipper won the $481,250 Woodrow Wilson two-year-old pace, in 1 min 57.6 sec. In trotting races the Hambletonian was won by Speedy Somolli, which had earlier taken the $233,600 Yonkers three-year-old trot. Winner of the Roosevelt International Trot was Cold Comfort (U.S.) from the New Zealand horse Petite Evander and Hadol du Vivier (France). The Kentucky Futurity went to Doublemint, and Scarlet Skipper took the Kentucky Pacing Derby.

In Australia the trotting find of 1978 was the stallion Maori's Idol (1 min 59.3 sec), which, having run out of trotting competition, later raced against the pacers. In the Uhr "pacing" cup Maori's Idol won two heats and was second to Rip Van Winkle in the final. Pacing sensation of the year was Rip Van Winkle (1 min 57 sec), with earnings of over $200,000. After winning the Perth Cup, the Hunter Cup, and the Miracle Mile, Pure Steel took his earnings past $400,000. Roma Hanover (1 min 57.8 sec) was the fastest mare in Australian pacing history.

In New Zealand Sole Command won the $100,-000 Auckland Cup. The Great Northern Derby went to Main Star. Trotting mare Petite Evander campaigned successfully in the U.S. and Europe, trotting several miles in less than 2 minutes. Trusty Scott won the $75,000 New Zealand Cup from Sapling and Wee Win. New Zealand driver Kevin Holmes won the 1978 world drivers' championship in the U.S.

In France the 1978 Prix d'Amérique for Fr 1 million was won by Grandpré. Istraekc won the $100,000 Prix du Président, and Eléazor took the Prix de France and the marathon Prix de Paris. Top-class filly Ivory Queen won the $80,000 Critérium for three-year-olds at Vincennes, Paris. In Italy Italian entry Doringo won the Gran Premio d'Europa at Milan, and the $100,000 Lotteria Nazionale final went to Last Hurrah. The Tino Trieste for four-year-olds was won by Doringo, and Granite triumphed in the $35,000 Lido di Roma.

A $57,000 mare's championship in Sweden was won by Baroness Hill. The $106,000 Swedish Derby went to Spinoon, and the four-year-old sprinter's championship was taken by Safari Empress. By winning the Aaby Greater Prize, Charme Asserdal became the second Swedish-bred mare to win 1 million kronor. In Finland the Forssa International final was taken by Weiretapper, while Uno Boy won the Finnish championship final. Top three-year-old was Super Mon. In Norway Grand Princess won the Oslo Grand Prix and Stord the Norwegian championship. The three-year-old Grand Prix at Jarlsberg went to Danish-owned Fine Shot, and Finnish-owned Fetard took the four-year-old Grand Prix at Momarken. In Denmark Bjørn Arnhøj won the Danish three-year-old championship, while Tarok gained the overall national championship. Adam Paradiso won the $36,000 Danish Derby in a record 2 min

Ethiopia

7.4 sec over 3,000 m. The $50,000 Grand Prix of The Netherlands was won by Charme Asserdal. The four-year-old Austrian Derby was taken by Derbystan from Clabichon with Grazia third.

(NOEL SIMPSON)

Show Jumping. The 1978 World Show Jumping Championship, held in Aachen, West Germany, in August, was won for West Germany by Gerd Wiltfang, on seven-year-old Roman. Eddie Macken was runner-up for Ireland on Boomerang (beaten only by 0.25 of a time fault), and Michael Matz of the U.S. was third on Jet Run. The team championship went to Great Britain, represented by David Broome on Philco, Caroline Bradley on Tigre, Malcolm Pyrah on Law Court, and Derek Ricketts on Hydrophane Coldstream, with 26.6 penalty points. The Dutch team finished second with 31.3 penalty points, and the U.S. was third with 42.4.

At Lexington, Ky., in September, Bruce Davidson of the U.S. retained his World Three-Day Event Championship, riding Might Tango; John Watson of Ireland was second, on Cambridge Blue, and Helmut Rethemeier of West Germany was third on Ladalco. Their respective scores were 93.4, 120.6, and 122.8 penalty points. The team championship was won by Canada, represented by Juliet Bishop on Sumatra, Mark Ishoy on Law and Order, Cathy Wedge on Abracadabra, and Elizabeth Ashton on Sunrise, with 436.6 penalty points. West Germany was second with 513, and the U.S. was third with 522.2.

(PAMELA MACGREGOR-MORRIS)

Polo. Coronel Suarez, represented by A. Heguy, H. Heguy, J. C. Harriott, and A. Harriott, achieved its 20th Argentine Open success in 1978, beating Santa Ana, represented by G. Dorignac (handicap 9), C. Merlos (9), D. Gonzalez (9), and F. Dorignac (10), in the final by 12 goals to 6. In the U.S. the Abercrombie and Kent team of G. Kent, D. Wigdahl, A. Herrera, and S. MacKenzie became the first team to win both the U.S. Open and the Gold Cup in the same year.

In other contests South Africa, represented by M. Oelrich (5), M. Miller (6), J. Watson (6), and P. Potgieter (6), beat Chile, represented by S. Moreno (4), P. Moreno (5), M. Errazuriz (7), and M. Correa (5); South Africa won 10–5 in the first test and 11–7 in the second. In the Coronation Cup at Windsor, England, South America, with A. Aguerro (6), G. Pierez (8), A. Garrahan (7), and H. Crotto (7), inflicted a defeat on the English team of A. Kent (5), J. Hipwood (8), H. Hipwood (8), and P. Withers (7) — 10–5. In the supporting international match the England II team — R. Watt (4), J. Horswell (5), P. Churchward (5), and R. Ferguson (5) — also lost 6–5 to a Commonwealth team consisting of the prince of Wales (3), A. Devich (6), S. Hill (7), and A. Yakubu (4).

The first Pony Club Polo International between Great Britain and the United States was won by Great Britain 3–0. Stowell Park won the English Gold Cup, defeating Cowdray Park 8–7. In the French Gold Cup, Nigerian Usman Dantata's Anadariya beat Bérengeville. The West German championship and open both went to the BB's.

(COLIN J. CROSS)

Ethiopia

A socialist state in northeastern Africa, Ethiopia is bordered by Somalia, Djibouti, Kenya, the Sudan, and the Red Sea. Area: 1,221,900 sq km (471,800 sq mi). Pop. (1978 est.): 30,037,000. Cap. and largest city: Addis Ababa (pop., 1977 est., 1,327,200). Language: Amharic (official) and other tongues. Religion: Ethiopian Orthodox and Muslim, with various minorities. Head of state and chairman of the Provisional Military Administrative Council in 1978, Lieut. Col. Mengistu Haile Mariam.

In September 1978 Ethiopia celebrated the fourth anniversary of its revolution. Although the leaders of the revolution, with their power centred in the Provisional Military Administrative Council (PMAC), had had many problems to face, the anniversary celebrations demonstrated that the new regime had established firm roots. The major challenges from what were referred to as "internal and external enemies" had been overcome.

Political opposition continued from a number of dissident underground groups — the Ethiopian Democratic Union (EDU), the Ethiopian People's Revolutionary Party (EPRP), the Oromo Liberation Front (OLF) — but it no longer represented a serious threat. In the fighting against the Somali invasion of the Ogaden in the southeast and the Eritrean rebels in the north, the government had largely

ETHIOPIA

Education. Primary (1974–75), pupils 959,272, teachers (1973–74) 18,646; secondary (1973–74), pupils 182,263, teachers 6,181; vocational (1973–74), pupils 5,533, teachers 554; teacher training (1973–74), students 3,126, teachers 194; higher (1973–74), students 6,474, teaching staff 434.

Finance. Monetary unit: birr, with (Sept. 18, 1978) a par value of 2.07 birr to U.S. $1 (free rate of 4.06 birr = £1 sterling). Gold, SDR's, and foreign exchange (June 1978) U.S. $172 million. Budget (1975–76 est.): revenue 1,175,-000,000 birr; expenditure 1,331,000,000 birr. Money supply (April 1978) 1,151,800,000 birr. Cost of living (Addis Ababa; 1975 = 100; May 1978) 164.7.

Foreign Trade. (1977) Imports 727.8 million birr; exports 689 million birr. Import sources (1976): Saudi Arabia 13%; Japan 12%; U.S. 10%; West Germany 9%; Italy 8%; U.K. 6%. Export destinations (1976): U.S. 33%; Djibouti 9%; Saudi Arabia 7%; Japan 7%; Italy 7%; West Germany 6%. Main exports: coffee 75%; hides and skins 7%; pulses 6%.

Transport and Communications. Roads (1976) 23,000 km. Motor vehicles in use (1976): passenger 52,500; commercial (including buses) 13,100. Railways (1976): 988 km; traffic (including Djibouti traffic of Djibouti-Addis Ababa line; excluding Eritrea) 132 million passenger-km, freight 260 million net ton-km. Air traffic (1976): 523 million passenger-km; freight 20.1 million net ton-km. Telephones (Jan. 1977) 73,500. Radio receivers (Dec. 1975) 200,000. Television receivers (Dec. 1975) 20,000.

Agriculture. Production (in 000; metric tons; 1977): barley c. 830; wheat 592; corn c. 1,150; millet c. 230; sorghum 671; potatoes c. 177; sugar, raw value c. 135; linseed c. 50; sesame seed c. 70; chick-peas 114; dry peas c. 110; dry broad beans (1976) c. 200; bananas c. 69; coffee c. 175; cotton c. 24. Livestock (in 000; 1977): cattle c. 26,119; sheep c. 23,149; goats c. 17,064; horses (1976) c. 1,510; mules (1976) c. 1,420; asses (1976) 3,860; camels (1976) 960; poultry c. 52,156.

Industry. Production (in 000; metric tons; 1974–75): cement 117; petroleum products (1976) c. 670; cotton yarn 11.3; cotton fabrics (sq m) 74,000; electricity (kw-hr; 1975–76) c. 674,000.

"Women's Day" in Ethiopia was used as an occasion to celebrate the country's military victories over Somalia.

succeeded in regaining control of the major settlements and wide areas of the countryside. On the domestic front, an All-Ethiopia Peasants' Association had been formed, the *kebeles* (Urban Dwellers' Associations) had been consolidated, and there had been a reorientation of the All-Ethiopia Trade Union.

In these circumstances, the chairman of the PMAC, Lieut. Col. Mengistu Haile Mariam, was able to announce Task Number Four (the previous three tasks were defined as the removal of the emperor, the land reform operation, and the defeat of internal enemies and external aggression). As Colonel Mengistu expressed it, "While continuing our struggle against foreign aggressors, secessionists, and fifth columnists, we have immediately to declare a war against hunger, poverty, disease, and illiteracy." He made it clear that priority would be given to economic development in 1979.

Nevertheless, the government's successes in 1977–78 were not total. It had been generally expected that the new working class party, to be formed through the merger of Ethiopian Marxist-Leninist organizations, would be announced on September 12. As the date approached, however, it was clear that mutual agreement on this merger had not yet been reached. The path toward unity was involving the elimination of some groups, such as Meison (the All-Ethiopia Socialist Movement) and Etch'at (the Revolutionary Organization of Oppressed Ethiopia's United Struggle). There were also signs that other organizations were in trouble because of "right road" opinions. Only Seded (the Revolutionary Flame Organization) was so far beyond criticism.

The military victory was not yet complete, although Keren, the last major town held by the rebels in Eritrea, was recaptured by Ethiopian troops in late November. The Mogadishu-backed West Somalia Liberation Front (WSLF) was still active in the Ogaden. Finally, the PMAC chairman had to announce in his anniversary speech that

"there is a frightening situation in urban areas regarding the shortage of food items" and that "individualism on the part of the peasantry" was a major factor. Subsequent development of this theme in the national press indicated the launching of a crusade against bourgeois farmers and a move toward collectivization.

Natural conditions added to the difficulties. Insufficient rain during the short rains period of February-March meant reduced crops in many areas. Later in the year, heavy and prolonged rain was a factor in promoting the development of the largest swarms of breeding locusts seen in the country for 20 years. It was reported that some 25,000 sq mi in the gorges of the Blue Nile system, inaccessible to surface transport, were infested. An aerial spraying program was undertaken on June 6, but these circumstances, coupled with the displacement of large groups of people in the war areas of the Ogaden, Bale, and Sidamo, resulted in famine or near-famine conditions for an estimated three million people. The southern regions and the highland areas of Welo, Tigre, and Gonder were the worst affected. Fortunately, improving conditions later in the year permitted the more rapid transport of relief supplies and purchased grain from the Ethiopian port of Aseb and from Djibouti.

There were further signs of developing relations with socialist countries and coolness toward the West. Massive military assistance was secured from the U.S.S.R. and Cuba, which supplied equipment and manpower, respectively, and from East Germany, which provided large quantities of trucks. This permitted the opening of an offensive against Somalia in the Ogaden in the spring. Jijiga was recaptured on March 5; by the end of the month the main towns and the road system over the whole of the Ogaden were in Ethiopian hands, although sporadic guerrilla attacks continued. By March 10 the Addis Ababa–Djibouti railway was in operation. The guerrilla activity, which received overt support from Mogadishu, prompted a statement from Mengistu on May 12 that, if Somalia did not desist, "Ethiopia will strike at the very source of destruction." Ethiopia remained firm in its demand for renunciation of all territorial claims by Somalia and payment of reparations as a basis for peace.

After the rapid success in the south, attention turned to the north. Large contingents of militia were trained in the Tatek Camp near Addis Ababa and dispatched to the north, together with supplies of Soviet equipment, much of it manned by Cubans. On June 7 Mengistu reaffirmed the Nine-Point Declaration on Eritrea issued in May 1976 and declared that "those unwilling to seek peace at the dialogue forum will be forced to search for it on the battlefield." This was followed by a four-pronged attack from the south on the Eritrean and Tigrean rebel positions.

On June 17 the Tekeze River was crossed at Om Hajer, opening the way for the fall of Tessenei on July 24. The Mareb River was crossed on July 5. By July 27 the Adwa-Asmera road had been cleared via Adi Ugri. Troops advancing north from Mekele occupied Dekemhare on July 30, and the first convoy of food and gasoline reached Asmera by this route on August 10. The port of Mitsiwa (Massawa) was cleared on July 13, and on November 22 Ethiopian troops entered Asmera after securing the Mitsiwa-Asmera road. The fall of Keren was reported on November 28; Barentu and Agordat had fallen earlier to government troops advancing through the Shire area. However, much of the countryside remained in rebel hands, and an Eritrean spokesman in Rome claimed the Eritreans planned to wage a prolonged "people's war."

The military offensive was accompanied by a political offensive, beginning in Addis Ababa with a large discussion forum on the Eritrean question. This was followed by similar forums in other centres, aimed at consolidating support for the government on the Eritrean issue. In fact, support for the PMAC was at a high level. The "Red Terror," largely directed at elimination of the EPRP, ended in Addis Ababa in February–March, and large numbers of students were released from detention after undergoing political reeducation. The same routine was followed in other major towns. The arming and training of workers' defense squads continued in line with a pledge made by the PMAC. In August the PMAC extended its control by the appointment of several of its members as regional administrators. Some 500 political cadres were trained to replace existing governors at the lowest (*wereda*) level of administration.

Industry was grouped into 14 national corporations covering the major sectors, and measures were taken to increase production, notably of cigarettes, matches, fibre products, and printing. East Germany provided a 10 million birr loan for an oilseed factory in Bahir Dar. The automobile assembly plant in Addis Ababa would shortly reach an output of 500 vehicles annually. Sugar production was 22% above 1974, with 1.5 million quintals produced in the 12 months to September. Ethiopian Airlines expanded its network to Arusha, Tanzania, in October 1977, and the air link with the Sudan was resumed in January. The 10 million birr

extension to Addis Ababa airport was inaugurated in May. East Germany provided a $20 million loan for economic and technical cooperation. Swedish aid of 30 million birr was for water supply and agriculture, while the European Economic Community/European Development Fund covered projects in coffee improvement, low-cost housing, and water development.

Development since the revolution was illustrated in a National Exhibition (Expo '78) opened in September by the Cuban leader, Pres. Fidel Castro, guest of honour at the fourth anniversary celebrations. There were now an estimated 17,000 Cubans in Ethiopia in various capacities. The PMAC chairman paid a state visit to Cuba in April. The anniversary celebrations were followed immediately by the International Conference of Solidarity with the Struggle of the African and Arab Peoples Against Imperialism and Reaction. On November 20, in Moscow, Mengistu and Soviet Pres. Leonid Brezhnev signed a 20-year Soviet-Ethiopian treaty of friendship and cooperation that included a promise of consultation in case of a threat to peace.

European Unity

The European Economic Community (EEC) took three steps during 1978 that appeared to enhance the prospects of greater European unity. It became irreversibly committed to enlarging its membership from 9 states to 12 with the prospective addition of Greece, Portugal, and Spain. At the same time, the Nine took a binding decision at a meeting of the European Council in Copenhagen in April to hold the first Community-wide direct elections to the European Parliament in June 1979. Finally, the Community went further than had been expected in striving for new forms of economic unity by deciding in principle to link members' currency exchange rates to one another.

The international economic crisis again overshadowed most other developments, both within the EEC and in Western Europe as a whole. The Nine found that, once again, they had to grapple with the seemingly intractable problems of low economic growth, high unemployment, recurrent financial upheavals, and the ever present danger of renewed inflation. There were serious disagreements between the European Community (along with members of the European Free Trade Association, or EFTA) and both the U.S. and Japan over questions of international trade. The EEC and the U.S. accused each other of protectionism, while the EEC made clear that it regarded the continuing Japanese trade surplus with Europe as completely unacceptable.

None of the three candidates for EEC, or Common Market, membership actually joined during 1978, but the Community did come to terms with the fact of its prospective enlargement. Early in the year there was concern in Greece that its negotiations with the Community, already nearly three years old, were making no real progress. There was talk in a number of EEC countries, notably France, that the economic, social, and political

An economic conference attended by seven of the leading industrialized non-Communist nations of the world was held in Bonn, West Germany, in July. U.S. Pres. Jimmy Carter (front row, third from right) was urged by the participants to take steps to stabilize the dollar.

costs of the absorption of three relatively poor Mediterranean countries would be too great. There were even suggestions that Greek entry should be held up because Portugal and Spain would seek to take advantage of any precedents established in negotiations with Athens.

In December, however, the prolonged negotiations produced concessions to Greece on the conditions of its transitional period of membership, as a result of which a formal accession agreement was expected to be signed early in 1979. In the meantime, the EEC Council of Ministers agreed that Greece would become progressively involved in the political cooperation meetings of the Community member states. At the same time the EEC took care that the prospect of Greek entry did not further exacerbate its somewhat strained relations with Turkey. Following his tour of the Community in May, the Turkish prime minister, Bulent Ecevit, was promised that, in the context of such political cooperation, the Common Market would consult Turkey on all matters of mutual interest to itself and Greece.

The EEC Commission published its "advice" on Portugal's application for membership, urging acceptance in spite of the formidable economic and political problems facing that country. The member states also contributed to an International Monetary Fund loan for Portugal, the terms of which, however, were criticized in some quarters as being unduly harsh. Formal negotiations on Portugal's membership got under way in the autumn.

Rapid progress was made in the preparation of the Commission's advice on Spain's application. The incorporation of Spain posed serious problems for the Community, partly because France and Italy feared competition from Spanish farmers, and partly because of apprehensions that Spain's relatively modern industries would only add to Europe's crisis of industrial overcapacity and unemployment. However, there was an overriding political commitment to Spain—all of whose major political parties were in favour of EEC mem-

bership—and it seemed likely that the Commission would publish a favourable "recommendation" on the opening of negotiations in 1979.

As 1978 began there were few indications that the time was right for a new initiative to advance economic and monetary union in the Community. The president of the Commission, Roy Jenkins, had urged the establishment of a monetary union but without arousing much support. Then, at the April meeting of the European Council in Copenhagen, Chancellor Helmut Schmidt of West Germany came out strongly in favour of a plan to link the exchange rates of the EEC currencies as a first step toward greater economic and monetary integration. He was supported by Pres. Valéry Giscard d'Estaing of France as well as by the governments of Belgium, The Netherlands, Denmark, and Luxembourg, whose currencies were already linked to the West German mark in the currency "snake," a joint float against the U.S. dollar.

When the European Council next met, in Bremen, West Germany, in July, the heads of government decided in principle to seek agreement on a scheme to link their currencies by the end of the year. Britain appeared to be in a minority when it expressed considerable doubt about the practicability of any plan to link currencies when the underlying economic positions of the participating countries were so different. After strenuous EEC summit negotiations in Brussels in December, Italy and Ireland opted to join the European Monetary System (EMS), while for the time being Britain would remain outside. Inauguration of the EMS, set for Jan. 2, 1979, was delayed, however, by a dispute between France and West Germany over agricultural subsidies.

A major point of discussion in the talks on a new currency system concerned its future relationship with the declining U.S. dollar. The EEC repeatedly urged U.S. Pres. Jimmy Carter to act to stabilize the dollar, and this was emphasized at the economic summit conference of the seven leading non-Communist industrialized nations, held in Bonn, West Germany, July 16–17. At that conference the Euro-

European Economic Community:
see Economy, World; European Unity

peans also insisted that the U.S. administration take effective measures to reduce U.S. dependence on imported energy.

On the other hand, the Nine were frequently divided on questions of economic strategy. The majority of the members supported the view that countries such as West Germany and Japan—which had low rates of inflation and substantial balance of payments surpluses—should do more to reflate their economies and help Europe out of economic stagnation. At the Bonn summit West Germany did finally agree to take additional stimulatory measures. But as the year wore on it became clear that the European economic growth rate as a whole was falling behind the original annual target of 4 to 5% set by the Council of Ministers. The number of unemployed grew to more than six million, with the steel, textile, and shipbuilding industries particularly hard hit.

The problems faced by these and other industries formed the background to the friction that characterized relations between Japan and the EEC during the year. In spite of periodic negotiations between the Japanese government and the Commission, the Japanese trade surplus continued to rise, in terms of volume if not in dollar value. As the year passed, however, there was evidence that the Japanese export offensive in Europe was slackening. Moreover, Japan agreed to limit voluntarily its exports to a number of EEC countries, notably its exports of automobiles to Britain.

Early in the year the Community negotiated an export restraint agreement with the principal suppliers of imported textiles. The crisis in the synthetic textile industry led major European producers to form a cartel to limit output and encourage modernization, but it was declared illegal by the Commission under the Community's antitrust rules. The Commission did agree on a series of similar measures in the steel industry, involving the fixing of output targets and minimum prices. The program was designed to provide breathing space for steel firms to begin modernizing and reducing excess capacity. The slump in the European steel market showed no sign of ending, however, and by midyear there were growing complaints that some EEC producers were ignoring the "anticrisis" plan and breaking the agreed norms for production and pricing.

Fears of chronic political instability and government weakness in a number of countries faded as the year progressed. The victory of the centre-right forces in the French general election in March seemed to assure President Giscard that he would face no serious domestic political challenge for the remainder of the decade. In Italy the strong political challenge of the Communist Party appeared to wane after the kidnapping and murder of the Christian Democrat leader, Aldo Moro. A new right-centre coalition of Christian Democrats and Liberals was formed in The Netherlands, and in Denmark the ruling Social Democrats announced in August that they were forming a coalition with the opposition Liberal Party. The year was marked by closer political cooperation among the Nine on such questions as African policy, human rights, and terrorism. At the Bonn summit the Nine agreed to boycott the airline of any nation that harboured hijackers or refused to release hijacked aircraft. The Nine also closely coordinated policy on the Middle East situation.

Under Danish presidency during the first half of the year, the EEC took steps to increase cooperation between the Community and the countries in

Hundreds of Toyota automobiles and trucks await export from the Japanese port of Nagoya.

EFTA. To the extent that Portugal was both a member of EFTA and a candidate member of the EEC, there was an overlapping interest. Both the EFTA countries and the EEC were desirous of coordinating their policies on questions of mutual interest, such as the international trade negotiations taking place in the so-called Tokyo round of the General Agreement on Tariffs and Trade (GATT). There was speculation that the prospective enlargement of the Community in the south of Europe might bring improved prospects for closer balancing links with the generally prosperous countries of northern Europe gathered in EFTA. However, the policy of neutrality in international relations espoused by Finland, Sweden, Austria, and Switzerland appeared to prohibit those countries from joining the Community. In Norway, which had rejected the EEC in a 1972 referendum, adverse opinion seemed to rule out early membership.

Two other subjects that appeared frequently on the agenda of EEC ministers in 1978 were farm and fishing policy. At the annual EEC farm-price fixing in May, there was general agreement that the EEC common agricultural policy (CAP) should move away from measures that encouraged unwanted surpluses. During the year the Community also agreed that there should be a shift in emphasis from support for northern dairy farmers to assisting southern Mediterranean farmers. In December, however, it appeared that disagreements over farm policy might endanger the EMS. Little progress was made toward a common fisheries policy, leading Britain and other EEC countries to take unilateral measures to conserve fish stocks.

As the year ended the attention of the EEC was focused on the institutional changes that would be necessary in a Community of Twelve. There was no consensus on whether to make the radical move to majority voting in the Council of Ministers, although there was general agreement that the Commission would have to be streamlined. A compromise was also needed on ways of limiting the use of more and more languages, since too many resources were already being employed in translation and interpretation. The year marked the end of the five-year transition period given to Britain, Ireland, and Denmark when they joined the Community.

Other noteworthy events included the first commercial cooperation agreement between the Community and China, but negotiations for a similar agreement with the Eastern-bloc countries of the Council for Mutual Economic Assistance (Comecon) made no progress.   (JOHN PALMER)

See also Defense; Economy, World.
[534.F.3.b.iv; 971.D.7]

Fashion and Dress

"Exercise and keep fit" was the motto for 1978, and jogging became a worldwide mania, providing a bonanza for sportswear manufacturers. T-shirts were dyed in attractive colours or printed with a flower or fruit design centre front. The worldwide best seller was stamped "Fruit of the Loom," the brand name of the U.S. clothing manufacturer that

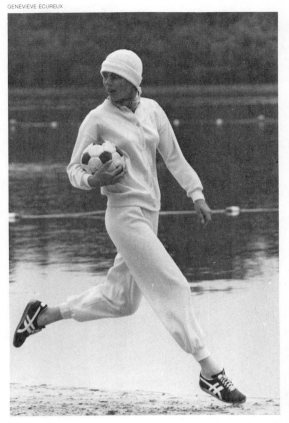

GENEVIEVE ECUREUX

Designers were quick to capitalize on the physical fitness craze, which opened a vast market for warm-up suits, sports shoes, and jogging shorts—not intended exclusively for athletic activities.

originated it, and featured the maker's trademark, a bunch of grapes clustered around an apple, over the left breast. The fad began in Saint-Tropez in the south of France in the summer of 1977, traveled north to Paris in 1978, where it was picked up by tourists, and was brought home to the U.S. by large New York department stores. Late in the summer "Fruit of the Loom" gave way to Mickey Mouse's portrait, in celebration of his 50th anniversary. Mickey's perky ears and nose appeared on every available surface in sportswear, as well as on fancy jewelry and badges.

Jogging outfits included matching vizors and, of course, special sports shoes. Soft bloomers, with their more flattering curve, were preferred to shorts by some enthusiasts. Terry cloth was an alternative to the T-shirt in these "keep fit" outfits, particularly in blousons with gathered waistlines. As skins took on more tan in the course of the summer, shades of terry cloth deepened. Bright yellow, red, or turquoise were top choices.

Blousons were a basic in every 1978 wardrobe. During the winter they appeared in leather with knit collar and cuffs, in tweed with the same rib trimming, or in canvas quilted for extra warmth and stiffness. In the spring wider shoulders and shorter jackets moved in to change the silhouette. Back gussets added bulk and a feeling of ease for sportswear. All aimed to express the desired image of physical fitness.

Skirts were gathered below a flat, hip-level yoke or seam. Some were divided, but they retained their softness so the trouser effect was visible only in movement. Now and then an ironed crease em-

A major silhouette change in 1978 emphasized a broadened shoulder line, narrow pants with a slim fit at the ankle, and higher heels, especially in boots. The hat began to make a comeback for both day and evening.

phasized the trouser effect, or the skirt was neater, with a slight flare. Straight pants were more clinging than ever, with extra-narrow, "cigarette"-shaped legs, but a softer style was also fashionable—rounded and gathered at the hips, cuffed below the calf, inspired by pirates, clowns, or the "sarouel" worn in the Sahara by the camel corps.

In the summer there was a new way with jeans. The mood was definitely changed as jeans were paired off with soft, full-sleeved silk blouses with plunging necklines. Even when ripped off to bermuda or shorts length, jeans were still dressed up with fancy tops, such as bead-embroidered cardigans. Denim was also to the fore in the blouson fad and in the new cropped waistcoat trend. Both were worn with the now classic oversize grandpapa full shirt with a narrow collarband.

Romanticism was apparent in summer dresses featuring a narrow ruffle at the neck and around the shoulder yoke and a deep hem flounce. The preferred floral prints were in the "Liberty" style with mixed colours. Another trend in dresses consisted of a loose chemise worn over "cigarette" pants. For sportswear the same idea was expressed by an above-the-knee sweater dress, with deep armholes, combined with tights. For other occasions tights might be worn under a flimsy, flounced dress in see-through gauze. The newest look consisted of a soft silk tunic, sometimes back-dipping, worn over an equally soft, very slim skirt. This last version prevailed in the fall.

Throughout the year the blazer continued its long career. After passing the winter in plain velvet to accompany soft skirts in light printed wool,

it turned up in fresh white piqué for summer. The all-white cotton outfit, with blazer or bush-jacket and neat, narrow pants at the new above-the-ankle length, was a favourite town look for summer. The desert was the source of inspiration for the competing look in khaki. Both outfits were updated with high-heeled shoes or sandals, eye-catching with the shorter pants length.

At the holiday resorts it was all fullness, flounces, and revealing materials. Transparent cotton voile was preferred for huge skirts with petticoat tiers and lingerie tucks. An alternative was the shapeless nightdress with two straps on either shoulder or—preferably for good shoulders—bare top gathered over the bustline and held up by narrow shoulder straps or a cord.

As clinging and revealing as a second skin were many of the beach clothes in white cheesecloth or cotton muslin. Free-moving, soft, blousy, strapless tops were gathered by a cord at breast level and worn over bathing suits. Some were in terry cloth, others in bright coloured nylon, with some exceptions in metalized cotton. But, on the whole, and particularly on the really sunny beaches, it all boiled down to triangles and strings—when such accoutrements were not dispensed with altogether. The rare one-piece bathing suits maintained the look of bareness with plunging necklines and unexpectedly placed cutouts.

As fall approached, broader shoulders and slimmer hips conferred a trapezoid shape reminiscent of the 1940s, with an added influence from *Star Wars*. Newer than the blazer was the cropped bellboy's spencer, in some cases trimmed with contrasting braid at the front and occasionally belted. In subdued plaids of blended autumn shades, the wraparound skirt that flattens hips became a big winner, while the kilt with flat pleating was every young girl's pick. Cropped waistcoats were matched to skirts in the same fancy materials, and soft plain blouses picked out one of the prevailing colours.

Autumn shades ranged from a deep wine red, named "sangria," to rust, olive drab, and, most notably, black. It was black leather for the stovepipe jeans worn in New York and Italy with full, soft silk blouses; black leather for the flat wrap skirt, seen in Paris with the shortened jacket in speckled tweed and plain velvet collar; black for evening wear with "le smoking" or dinner jacket in satin, silk crepe, or light wool, worn with narrow wrap skirt or shortened trousers; and black again for the "disco dress," bare, sheer, and sexy, designed for modern dances. From the old days of Hollywood came puffed sleeves, feathers and lace, hats and veils, and even gloves.

Jewelry was minute, with a craze for tiny eardrops dangling from a chain hooked into the earlobe and for stickpins and all forms of brooches. Hair fashions ranged from the banana roll in front crowning a shiny mane to a boyish cut called "after punk."

To go with the '40s styles and all the black, lips were vivid and eyes shadowed. After the golden bronze of springtime and terra-cotta foundations with bois-de-rose lipstick, Helena Rubinstein's autumn makeup turned to "Tawny Amber" for

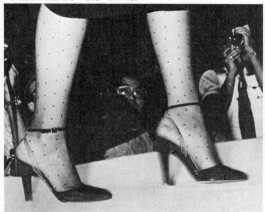
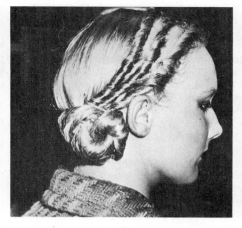

cheeks and "Latin Paradise Pinks," from light to deep, for lips. To put greater emphasis on eyes and lips, Estée Lauder recommended a foundation as close as possible to nature. Her "Great Castle Colours" had all the personality needed to carry off the new autumn clothes. "Antique Walnut" and "Raspberry Wine" outlined lips and "Burnished Burgundy" shadowed eyelids. Elizabeth Arden's "Collection" suggested deep purple and lilac haze for eye shadow and a velvety maroon for lips and nail polish. (THELMA SWEETINBURGH)

Men's Fashions. Men's fashion broke through the barriers of both age and class in 1978. The rules were relaxed to allow a sensible and comfortable style of dress unfettered by conformity to the establishment. British designer Hardy Amies, as famous for his men's ready-to-wear as for his women's haute couture, predicted a further relaxation. "Even business suits are now made in tweeds," he told a London audience of buyers for his latest menswear collections, currently made under license in Britain, the U.S., Canada, Japan, Australia, and New Zealand.

At the menswear trade exhibitions—in London; Paris; Cologne, West Germany; Florence, Italy; and Madrid—there was plenty of evidence to support the new freedom in men's clothes. The two key words at all of these fairs were "soft" and "unstructured." Favoured fabrics included softer woolens, many with open weaves, and soft finished worsteds, while the clothing itself was soft, easy fitting, and comfortable. Jackets were finished with softer interlinings and padding or, in some cases, with none at all. A slightly wider shoulder appeared on some suits. Lapels generally were narrower on jackets, and some narrower cuffs were seen on trousers. Young men began wearing their jackets with the collar turned up, the shirt left unbuttoned at the neck, and the tie knotted at "half mast."

There were more double-breasted styles than previously. Shirts had smaller collar points, and the "penny-round" became popular with younger men. Ties were narrower. Blousons—shown, like jeans, in both denim and cord—were part of the 1978 leisurewear scene. Track suits became fashionable as more men took to jogging.

Two British associations, the Clothing Manufacturers Federation and the Shirt, Collar and Tie Manufacturers Federation, took a critical look at the way some national leaders dress. British Prime Minister James Callaghan was characterized as "a middle-of-the-road dresser"; French Pres. Valéry Giscard d'Estaing "has superb sense of style and knows exactly what suits him"; Canadian Prime Minister Pierre Trudeau "is rather inclined to be a bit too boyishly exuberant at times"; and U.S. Pres. Jimmy Carter's clothes "are surprisingly dull. He should try to make them as cheerful as his smile." (STANLEY H. COSTIN)

See also Industrial Review: *Furs.*
[451.B.2.b and d.1; 629.e.1]

Accessories in 1978 captured the "retro" look—details of earlier eras "quoted" in contemporary ensembles. Designer after designer showed patterned and seamed hose worn with three-inch spiked heels, rolled or pompadoured hairstyles of the 1940s, and everywhere the little hat or veil.

While women's clothing seemed to be stepping backward toward a more formal look, menswear on both sides of the Atlantic showed a more unstructured, relaxed attitude toward the traditional suit and tie.

Fencing:
see Combat Sports

Field Hockey and Lacrosse

Field Hockey. Women's field hockey continued to be dominated by The Netherlands and West Germany, and by the end of 1978 their places among the six women's teams for the 1980 Moscow Olympic Games seemed assured. In the U.K. the Great Britain Hockey Board for men and women, constituted in 1977, formed pools of men and women players from which teams for international matches were chosen. The purpose was to obtain a suitable playing record as a basis of qualification for the Olympic Games.

In men's competition Scotland won the six-nation indoor tournament at Crystal Palace, London, in January 1978, retaining the home countries championship in the process. The visiting nations were France and Italy.

Outdoors the annual four-nation tournament took place in March at Lord's Cricket Ground in London. After beating India, England lost to Australia, which also defeated Scotland. In the remaining match of the two-day program, India defeated Scotland. In the fourth men's World Cup at Buenos Aires, Arg., Pakistan regained world supremacy by beating The Netherlands in the final. Australia finished third and West Germany fourth.

At Hanover, West Germany, in September, West Germany regained the European Cup by beating The Netherlands in the final. England won the bronze medal. It was the first medal won, independently, by an English team in 58 years.

In women's play England tied its match at Wembley, London, in March against the United States, another aspirant for a place at Moscow. A women's team representing Great Britain and Northern Ireland went abroad for the first time in April to play in a four-nation tournament at Amstelveen, Neth. The Netherlands won the tournament and then repeated its triumph by beating West Germany in the final of the World Cup, in Madrid, in September. The U.K. home countries competed in their usual cycle of six matches,

Johns Hopkins' lacrosse team broke Cornell's 42-game winning streak to win the National Collegiate Athletic Association lacrosse championship in May.

Wales emerging with the best record of two wins and a draw.　(SYDNEY E. FRISKIN)

Lacrosse. MEN. In the world championship tournament in July 1978 in England, the host nation received Australia, Canada, and the U.S. at Stockport. In the initial matches the U.S. beat Australia, Canada (by a record international match margin, 28–4), and England; Canada beat Australia and England; and Australia beat England. In the play-off to decide the final standings, Canada beat the U.S. 17–16 in extra time and thus became the world champion. Australia, by beating England 19–9 in the other play-off, finished third with England last. The awards made to the outstanding players throughout the series were: goalkeeper, R. Flintoff (Canada); defense, S. Bevington (England); midfield, J. Butkiewicz (Australia); attack, P. Cann (Australia); fairest and best player, M. French (Canada).

In the U.S., Johns Hopkins University won the National Collegiate Athletic Association championship, with Roanoke College, Salem, Va., winning the title of "the best small college." In the annual North-South encounter, the North won 19–6. Mike O'Neill (Johns Hopkins) was named the best player of the season.

In England, Cheshire again proved itself the champion county by winning the regional championship. Cheadle, a Cheshire club, had an outstanding season by winning the North of England senior flags, the Senior League championship, and the English Club championship (Iroquois Cup). Hampstead defeated Lee to retain the South of England senior flags.　(CHARLES DENNIS COPPOCK)

WOMEN. In the U.S., Philadelphia Colleges unexpectedly defeated Philadelphia I in the 1978 national championship, thus winning the title for the first time in six years. The national squad was selected for the first Great Britain versus U.S. test series, to take place in the following season.

The 1977–78 season in Britain was one of bad weather, shared titles, and epoch-making tours. It began with squad sessions to help select the 17 players for the first official British tour of Australia in the summer of 1978. During the tour the British team played a total of ten matches and returned undefeated after visiting Perth, Adelaide, Hobart, Canberra, and Melbourne. Five were test matches against the Australian national team, which improved considerably with international competition and was defeated by only 6–3 in the final encounter. These were arduous games which Britain won by virtue of superior stickwork and strategy.

In the National Counties Tournament, Cheshire and Middlesex shared the title after an exciting final, as did Bedford and Pendley in the Clubs and Colleges Tournament in April. In the spring an impressive U.S. Colleges team arrived in Britain and won its six matches against universities, defeating the British Universities team 14–3. The players were fast and fit, with a dazzlingly versatile technique. England defeated the English reserves team 11–3 in Nottingham to complete another unbeaten season, which included victories over Scotland 20–1 and Wales 14–1.

(MARGARET-LOUISE FRAWLEY)

Fiji

An independent parliamentary state and member of the Commonwealth of Nations, Fiji is an island group in the South Pacific Ocean, about 3,200 km E of Australia and 5,200 km S of Hawaii. Area: 18,272 sq km (7,055 sq mi), with two major islands, Viti Levu (10,388 sq km) and Vanua Levu (5,535 sq km), and several hundred smaller islands. Pop. (1978 est.): 612,000, including (1976) 49.8% Indian, 44.2% Fijian. Cap. and largest city: Suva (pop., 1976 census, 63,600). Language: English, Fijian, and Hindi. Religion: Christian and Hindu. Queen, Elizabeth II; governor-general in 1978, Ratu Sir George Cakobau; prime minister, Ratu Sir Kamisese Mara.

The return to power of an Alliance Party government in September 1977 had restored political stability, although rivalries within the Indian-dominated National Federation Party continued. The 1976 census showed that, for the first time in 20 years, persons of Indian descent accounted for less than half the population.

Throughout 1978 gradual economic recovery followed the retrenchments of the previous year. Inflation was held to single figures, and there was continued expansion in the sugar industry. The government took over the employment-intensive but uneconomic Vatukoula gold mine. The tourist industry operated below capacity, although capital was injected by Saudi Arabian investors.

Fiji joined other members of the South Pacific Forum in a joint shipping venture and in the cooperative management of their respective 200-mi economic zones. In June, after a visit to China, Prime Minister Ratu Sir Kamisese Mara voiced fears as to the motives and activities of the U.S.S.R. in the Southwest Pacific. (BARRIE MACDONALD)

FIJI

Education. (1976) Primary, pupils 133,529, teachers (1975) 4,274; secondary, pupils 30,712, tea ' s (1975) 1,184; vocational, pupils (1975) 1,938, teachers (1974) 174; teacher training, students (1975) 535, teachers (1974) 50; higher (1975), students 1,810, teaching staff 166.

Finance and Trade. Monetary unit: Fiji dollar, with (Sept. 18, 1978) a free rate of F$0.82 to U.S. $1 (F$1.61 = £1 sterling). Budget (1977 est.): revenue F$134.3 million; expenditure F$150.3 million. Foreign trade (1976): imports F$280,960,000; exports F$162,820,000. Import sources: Australia 28%; Japan 16%; New Zealand 14%; Singapore 12%; U.K. 10%. Export destinations: U.K. 42%; New Zealand 10%; Malaysia 7%; Australia 7%; U.S. 6%; Singapore 5%. Main exports (1975): sugar 72%; petroleum products 12%; gold 6%. Tourism (1976): visitors 169,000; gross receipts U.S. $76 million.

Transport and Communications. Roads (1975) 2,976 km. Motor vehicles in use (1976): passenger cars 18,100; commercial (including buses) 10,200. Railways (1976) 644 km (for sugar estates). Shipping (1977): merchant vessels 100 gross tons and over 33; gross tonnage 10,879. Shipping traffic (1977): goods loaded 536,000 metric tons, unloaded 797,000 metric tons. Telephones (Jan. 1977) 30,800. Radio receivers (Dec. 1975) 300,000.

Agriculture. Production (in 000; metric tons; 1977): sugar, raw value c. 312; rice (1976) c. 24; cassava (1976) c. 91; copra c. 29. Livestock (in 000; Sept. 1976): cattle c. 156; pigs c. 31; goats c. 55; horses c. 35; chickens c. 785.

Industry. Production (in 000; metric tons; 1976): cement (metric tons) 69; gold (troy oz) 66; electricity (kw-hr) 265,000.

Finland

Fiji

Finland

The republic of Finland is bordered on the north by Norway, on the west by Sweden and the Gulf of Bothnia, on the south by the Gulf of Finland, and on the east by the U.S.S.R. Area: 337,032 sq km (130,129 sq mi). Pop. (1978 est.): 4,752,000. Cap. and largest city: Helsinki (pop., 1978 est., 487,500). Language: Finnish, Swedish. Religion (1975): Lutheran 98.2%; Orthodox 1.3%. President in 1978, Urho Kaleva Kekkonen; prime minister, Kalevi Sorsa.

Pres. Urho Kaleva Kekkonen's tenure in the Finnish presidency, uninterrupted since 1956, was predictably extended for a six-year term by 259 of the 300 electors who convened on Feb. 15, 1978. In the January balloting for the electoral college, pro-Kekkonen candidates, representing the six largest parties and ranging from Conservative to Communist, had attracted 82% of the popular vote. Among Kekkonen's four rightist opponents, Raino Westerholm, chairman of the Finnish Christian League, fared best with 25 electoral votes.

Throughout the year Finland was preoccupied with its economy, which faced a fourth successive year of stagnation. On February 17, six days after

FINLAND

Education. (1976–77) Primary, pupils 438,804, teachers 27,414; secondary, pupils 341,421, teachers 21,399; vocational, pupils 88,771, teachers 10,700; teacher training, students 898, teachers 670; higher, students 119,274, teaching staff 5,780.

Finance. Monetary unit: markka, with (Sept. 18, 1978) a free rate of 4.08 markkaa to U.S. $1 (8 markkaa = £1 sterling). Gold, SDR's, and foreign exchange (June 1978) U.S. $1,005,200,000. Budget (1978 est.): revenue 35,721,-000,000 markkaa; expenditure 37,601,000,000 markkaa. Gross national product (1977) 117,890,000,000 markkaa. Money supply (May 1978) 10,679,000,000 markkaa. Cost of living (1975 = 100; June 1978) 138.6.

Foreign Trade. (1977) Imports 30,711,000,000 markkaa; exports 30,938,000,000 markkaa. Import sources: U.S.S.R. 20%; West Germany 14%; Sweden 13%; U.K. 9%; U.S. 5%. Export destinations: U.S.S.R. 19%; Sweden 16%; U.K. 12%; West Germany 10%; Norway 5%. Main exports: paper 23%; machinery 15%; ships 9%; timber 9%; wood pulp 5%; clothing 5%.

Transport and Communications. Roads (1976) 73,763 km (including 186 km expressways). Motor vehicles in use (1976): passenger 1,032,884; commercial 132,679. Railways: (1976) 6,036 km; traffic (1977) 2,974,000,000 passenger-km, freight 6,399,000,000 net ton-km. Air traffic (1977): 1,395,100,000 passenger-km; freight 38,550,000 net ton-km. Navigable inland waterways (1976) 6,675 km. Shipping (1977): merchant vessels 100 gross tons and over 337; gross tonnage 2,262,095. Telephones (Jan. 1977) 1,-936,000. Radio licenses (Dec. 1976) 2,199,600. Television licenses (Dec. 1976) 1,420,900.

Agriculture. Production (in 000; metric tons; 1977): wheat 295; barley 1,447; oats 1,022; rye 80; potatoes 855; sugar, raw value (1976) c. 77; butter 74; cheese 63; eggs 84; timber (cu m; 1976) 32,950; fish catch (1976) 120. Livestock (in 000; June 1977): cattle 1,762; sheep 55; pigs 1,-145; reindeer (1975) 175; horses 29; poultry 11,750.

Industry. Production (in 000; metric tons; 1977): pig iron 1,763; crude steel 2,191; iron ore (metal content; 1976) 770; cement 1,712; sulfuric acid 985; petroleum products (1976) 10,345; plywood (cu m; 1976) 368; cellulose (1976) 3,437; wood pulp (1976) mechanical 1,689, chemical 3,698; newsprint 986; other paper and board (1976) 3,559; electricity (kw-hr) 31,876,000; manufactured gas (cu m) 26,000.

devaluation of the Norwegian krone, the markka was devalued by 8%, bringing to 18% the combined effect of three markdowns in 11 months. A split on this decision precipitated the collapse of Prime Minister Kalevi Sorsa's five-party government. Subsequently, in response to presidential exertions, the coalition withdrew its resignation and was reconstituted minus the small Swedish People's Party. At the 11th hour it averted a near-general 48-hour strike called for March 31 by the Central Organization of Finnish Trade Unions to protest the absence of anti-inflationary measures.

By fall it was evident that Finland was on target for two of its economic goals–8% inflation (the first single-digit reading since 1972) and a substantial surplus on current account. A slight upturn in production was registered, and it was claimed that partially deferred wage settlements and devaluations had increased industrial competitiveness in export markets by one-fifth. Nevertheless, the government shaped its 1979 budget on the assumption that the record 7–8% unemployment rate would continue and that the 4% growth needed to generate new jobs would not materialize. Building on the foundation laid in 1977, it introduced a fourth economic recovery program aimed at stimulating investment through temporary tax relief, tiding local authorities over the worst of the winter, and occupying jobless youth in training programs. Income-tax cuts and increased social benefits were announced, partly to encourage a restrained settlement when centralized pay negotiations got under way in December. Public borrowing was greatly expanded at home and abroad, although foreign debt already amounted to a fourth of the gross national product.

Anticipating the general election due in March 1979, the principal parties held unspectacular conferences. The Communist congress in June did nothing to end the party's 12-year-old divisions; the relative strengths of the "revisionist" majority backing Chairman Aarne Saarinen and the "Stalinist" minority behind Vice-Chairman Taisto Sinisala remained unchanged.

The most concrete manifestation of continuing harmony between neutral Finland and the U.S.S.R. was the laying of a foundation stone on September 14 at Kostamuksha, the largest Finnish construction venture to date in Soviet Karelia, by President Kekkonen and Soviet Premier Aleksey N. Kosygin. On October 5 Defense Minister Taisto Tähkamaa categorically denied that the U.S.S.R. had proposed joint military maneuvers with Finland. UN Commissioner Martti Ahtisaari, appointed special UN representative for Namibia, was the main force behind UN Secretary-General Kurt Waldheim's blueprint for that territory's transition to independence. Finland had 700 troops ready for a UN peacekeeping force in Namibia.

In a major business scandal that rocked the country, Jouko Nordell, former managing director of Salora, a television manufacturer, and four associates were charged with large-scale tax evasion. In connection with the Salora affair, Mikko Laaksonen, director general of the National Taxation Board, and his aide Aake Mesimäki were dismissed on May 26.   (DONALD FIELDS)

Fisheries

Despite a forecast by the Fisheries Division of the UN Food and Agriculture Organization (FAO) that an investment of $30 billion could boost the world fish catch to 120 million–130 million metric tons by the year 2000, the 1978 catch was not expected to exceed the 73.5 million tons of the previous year. A meeting of the FAO Committee on Fisheries in June reported a decline in the catch of less developed nations and a fall in the landings of Peruvian anchoveta, North Sea herring, South African pilchard, and Alaska pollack—warning signs of overfishing that brought reactions in the form of tougher quotas and even total fishing bans.

The almost universal adoption of 200-mi fisheries limits during 1977 had left a high proportion of the world's long-range trawlers with no place to go. For many years nations of the Communist bloc, along with Japan, South Korea, Britain, Spain, Portugal, and France, had invested in ships to fish off the coasts of other nations. Now these traditional fishing "rights" meant little or nothing, and there was intensive negotiation as the deprived nations attempted to set up joint ventures or license arrangements with fish-rich countries.

The Canadian fishery minister, Roméo LeBlanc, adopted an unexpectedly tough line on fisheries policy, to the dismay of the many nations that had traditionally fished off Canada's northeast coast—and had severely overfished cod, haddock, and Alaska pollack. LeBlanc proposed an expansion of the Canadian fishing effort to enable Canada to harvest more of the resource itself and sell fish products to other nations. He estimated that an investment of $90 million would be needed over the next ten years, and he foresaw the need for a new fishing port in Vancouver, B.C., for the use of an anticipated 40–50 trawlers of up to 60-m length. Meanwhile, Japan was already established on the Pacific coast where it had been investing steadily in the herring roe industry—to a point where Japanese buyers almost controlled prices.

Approval for Canada's tough conservation policy was expressed by the Soviet fishery minister, Aleksandr Ishkov, who hoped for steadily increasing collaboration between the two countries, especially in the salmon fishery. Faced with the task of finding employment for a fishing fleet that, in terms of tonnage, represented 53% of the world total, the U.S.S.R. had no choice but to woo the fish-rich countries. It was also stepping up its land-based fish-farming production.

In April a 200-mi fishing zone was declared by Australia, which thus became the possessor of one of the world's largest exclusive fisheries, including the rich prawn grounds within the Gulf of Carpentaria. As a result, Australia became the target of numerous proposals for joint ventures with other nations. One such venture, with British United Trawlers, was already highly successful; three big freezer trawlers were fishing Australian waters to supply a shore-based processing plant. The Australian rock lobster fishery was hoping for another record year; in 1977 it had netted A$200 million.

An Indian confronts federal agents with an oar in a dispute over salmon fishing in the Klamath River in northern California. Federal officials were trying to halt the fishing which the Indians claimed was their right.

During the year a joint Australian-Japanese exploratory squid-fishing program was carried out off Tasmania.

Japan was also negotiating with New Zealand, where its fishing fleet had been very active prior to the establishment of a 200-mi zone. The negotiations were based on the principle of fishing rights for Japan in return for a market for such New Zealand products as meat. Other interested nations were South Korea and the U.S.S.R. Korea was especially anxious for a share in the growing New Zealand squid fishery.

The situation in Europe continued to be dominated by the apparent inability of the European Economic Community (EEC) to act in unison on certain aspects of fisheries. This was hardly surprising, since many of the member countries had too many boats and not enough fish. Furthermore, concerted action required mutual agreement, difficult to achieve when one country's prime food fish was another's raw material for fish meal. It was the Dutch and Danish need for herring that blocked an EEC fishing ban on Britain's northwest coast, forcing the British to take unilateral conservation action by banning all herring fishing outside the Clyde.

Britain continued to assert its need for a preferential 50-mi zone in which it would exercise conservation (and allot fishing rights) in its own way. The mood was encouraged by the EEC's failure to act in conserving west coast herring, although this was a relatively minor issue compared with the possible effect of letting Europe's underemployed trawler fleet loose on the carefully husbanded, but limited, coastal stocks around the British Isles. Alarm was expressed within the EEC over the future membership of Spain, Portugal, and Greece, which between them could muster 2,150 vessels of

over 100 tons. This could present problems even if only a proportion of the ships were unleashed into a "Community Pond," and the prospect seemed to support Britain's proposal for individual rather than collective coastal responsibility.

The fact that Norway was outside the EEC but fished for the same species as the EEC members brought difficulties. For example, the Norwegian and EEC mackerel quota grounds were separated by latitude 60° N. When the fish moved south of this parallel, 96 Norwegian purse seiners "invaded" Bergen harbour demanding to fish farther south—only to be met by a threat of protest action by EEC mackerel boats if this were to happen.

The French west coast was the scene of another major oil spill, when the oil tanker "Amoco Cadiz"

Table I. Whaling: 1976-77 Season (Antarctic); 1976 Season (Outside the Antarctic)
Number of whales caught

Area and country	Fin whale	Sei/ Bryde's whale	Hump- back whale	Minke whale	Sperm whale	Total	Percentage assigned under quota agreement[1]
Antarctic pelagic (open sea)							
Japan	—	1,237	—	3,950	129	5,316	53.2
Norway[2]							
U.S.S.R.	—	621	—	3,950	1,873	6,444	46.8
Total	—	1,858	—	7,900	2,002	11,760[3]	100.0
Outside the Antarctic[4]							
Japan	—	661	—	—	3,540	4,201	
U.S.S.R.	—	679	—	—	3,671	4,513[5]	
South Africa	—	—	—	—	—	—[6]	
Peru	—	—	—	—	—		
Australia	—	—	—	—	995	995	
Iceland	275	3	—	—	111	389	
Others	6	29	5	—	70	110	
Total	281	1,372	5	—	8,387	10,208[5]	

[1] Antarctic only.
[2] Norway had no expeditions in the Antarctic in the 1976–77 season.
[3] Includes others (bottlenose, killer, gray, right, and blue whales).
[4] Excluding small whales.
[5] Includes 163 gray whales.
[6] Whaling ceased after the close of the 1975 season.
Source: The Committee for Whaling Statistics, *International Whaling Statistics.*

Table II. World Fisheries, 1976[1]
In 000 metric tons

Country	Catch Total	Catch Freshwater	Disposition of catch[2] Fresh marketed	Disposition of catch[2] Frozen, cured, canned, etc.
Japan	10,619.9	272.7	3,412.9 [3]	7,217.1
U.S.S.R.	10,133.7	912.4	...	...
China	6,880.0	4,568.0	...	...
Peru	4,343.1	5.3	130.6 [4]	4,207.2 [4]
Norway	3,435.3	1.5	94.6	3,340.8
United States	3,004.0	221.3	965.3	2,030.3
Korea, South	2,406.7	18.5	1,547.8 [5]	857.2 [5]
India	2,400.0	896.8	1,663.2	736.8
Denmark	1,911.6	19.9	153.4	1,759.1
Thailand	1,640.4	169.9	639.2	1,001.3
Spain	1,483.2	21.0	673.4 [6]	707.3 [6]
Indonesia	1,448.0	402.1	...	...
Philippines	1,429.8	200.4	1,143.8	286.0
Chile	1,264.2	...	103.2 [6]	796.3 [6]
Canada	1,135.7	111.1	196.2	905.3
United Kingdom	1,034.2	2.2	491.8 [7]	598.5
Vietnam	1,013.5	176.3	...	...
Iceland	986.1	...	33.7	948.3
Brazil	950.0	109.5	...	...
France	805.9	3.0	...	...
Korea, North	800.0	...	...	...
Poland	750.1	28.4	...	...
Bangladesh	640.0	550.0	...	...
South Africa	638.0	0.1	...	...
Namibia (Southwest Africa)	574.2	0.1	...	...
Mexico	572.3	14.7	137.5	434.8
Burma	501.6	134.4	125.4	376.2
Nigeria	494.8	329.1	...	...
Germany, West	454.4	15.7	77.9 [8]	466.2 [8]
Italy	420.3	23.4	356.0	64.3
Malaysia	412.3	6.1	387.8 [4]	127.8 [4]
Senegal	360.9	10.0	...	...
Faeroe Islands	342.0	...	44.7 [9]	202.5 [9]
Portugal	339.2	0.3	188.9	153.7
Netherlands, The	284.4	2.8	201.0	66.4
Argentina	281.7	9.8	87.5	168.9
Morocco	281.4	0.5	72.2 [6]	162.9 [6]
Germany, East	279.2	19.3	...	...
Ghana	237.7	57.9	...	...
Ecuador	223.4	...	33.7 [4][5][10]	120.2 [4][5][10]
Sweden	208.6	13.5	57.0 [4]	136.0 [4]
Pakistan	205.7	38.6	48.8	135.8
Cuba	204.0	0.5	24.5 [11]	101.6 [11]
Oman	198.0	...	...	...
Tanzania	180.7	150.5	76.2 [6]	16.2 [6]
Panama	171.6	...	2.0	143.0
Other	892.5	...	...	...
World total	73,467.0	9,532.1	19,500	21,400

[1] Excludes whaling.
[2] May include statistical discrepancy.
[3] Includes freezing.
[4] Excludes freshwater fish.
[5] Excludes aquaculture fisheries.
[6] 1975.
[7] Includes cured fish other than herring.
[8] Catch includes imports but excludes exports. Data refer to period between July 1, 1974, and June 30, 1975.
[9] 1974.
[10] 1973.
[11] 1971.

Source: United Nations Food and Agriculture Organization, *Yearbook of Fishery Statistics*, vol. 42 and 43.

grounded off Portsall and broke up, spilling thousands of tons of crude oil. Much of it ended up on the north coast of Brittany, where oyster beds and lobster grounds were affected. Troops and volunteers did their best to scrape and scoop the "black tide" into pits ready to be pumped into tank trucks. Clearance was slowed by the French refusal to use dispersants, despite assurances that they were nontoxic to shellfish, and many of the shellfish were hurriedly transferred to safe beaches in the south.

One of the effects of the 200-mi regime was to present many less developed nations with problems of resource assessment and management that were beyond their capacity to handle. As a result, it was a busy year for the fishery consultants, and the FAO, among others, found a new role as adviser to such nations. The new zones also posed difficult problems of surveillance and protection. At one time, patrols off Namibia (South West Africa) identified 172 foreign fishing vessels.

Polish shipbuilding orders during the year included a series of refrigerated cutters to work in the Gulf of Guinea off West Africa. Five trawlers were ordered from Norway by Vietnam under a Norwegian aid program, and Ghana ordered four big tuna boats from Italy. Demand was good in India, where big business interests were moving into fishing. In Latin America potential production from a large Inter-American Development Bank scheme was estimated by the FAO at 7 million–8 million tons of fish. By the end of 1977 investment in Latin-American fisheries was running at $83 million. Exploratory work by Japan in Argentina was expected to indicate a potential of 100,000 tons a year. In Chile fish meal exports were increasing, and attempts were again being made, with Japanese help, to introduce salmon into the South Pacific.

The Peruvian anchoveta fleet, which had been sold back to private enterprise, was now reduced from 1,500 to 500 vessels, and profits were too low to allow reinvestment in new ones. The only buyer was the state-owned fish meal company, Pescaperu, but this situation was only partly to blame for the depression. The primary cause was lack of fish.

The U.S. west coast tuna industry was also encountering difficulties as a result of the 200-mi regime. The right to cross into adjacent waters in pursuit of tuna was being challenged by Costa Rica, and it might well be joined by other Latin-American states. Costa Rica had demanded $60,000 for a license to seek tuna for 60 days in its waters. In Papua New Guinea, the U.S. tuna giant Star-Kist, a pioneer in establishing joint ventures, was setting up yet another canning enterprise. Meanwhile, the U.S. National Marine Fisheries Service program to reduce the incidental kill of porpoise during tuna purse seining was succeeding beyond the department's wildest hopes.

Antarctic krill continued to make headlines from time to time as a possible future source of fish products, as did the prolific shoals of blue whiting northwest of the British Isles. Hopes ran high that this small herring-like fish could be sold in quantity to Japan for the production of *surimi*, but the project was dogged by high costs. In Norway blue whiting was used to make fish meal, and landings of 100,000 tons were recorded. However, a joint British-Soviet plan to follow suit by transferring catches to a Soviet fish meal factory ship had to be abandoned when the fish failed to appear on schedule outside Faroese limits. Soviet bloc ships had taken much of the 140,000 tons of mackerel caught off Britain's southwest coast, and the question arose as to whether this would be prohibited when a new EEC fisheries policy was eventually hammered out.

Finally, the year saw what could be the "ultimate weapon" against shoal fish. A West German sonar of great power attracted the fish by emitting a special sonic signal and then proceeded to kill them with an acoustic blast, whereupon they floated to the surface to be gathered in.

(H. S. NOEL)

See also Food Processing.
[731.D.2.a]

Floods:
see Earth Sciences; Engineering Projects

Food Processing

The complexity of regulatory controls continued to trouble the U.S. and European food industries. The Carter administration initiated a review of federal food and nutrition policy, involving 14 agencies, and of 12 other agencies conducting food and nutrition research. European Economic Community (EEC) legislation directly affecting foodstuffs now filled 27 volumes and covered raw materials, additives, composition, and labeling, and a number of companies had to engage lawyers to assist in its interpretation. A British food industry representative reported a serious decline in some sectors of the industry because of restrictive legislation. There was a drop in pretax profits as a percentage of sales.

The toxicity and possible carcinogenicity of food additives and contaminants received considerable attention from international organizations, the U.S., and the EEC. A number of toxicologists felt that too much attention was being devoted to carcinogenicity problems to the detriment of research into other aspects of toxicology. Some U.S. and British scientists claimed that an increasing number of people suffered from allergies attributable to certain foods, food additives, and processes. A symposium on the subject was organized in Britain, but the basis of many of the claims was disputed due to lack of corroborative medical evidence.

Government-sponsored investigations in Canada indicated that flour treated with chlorine was toxic to rats. The U.S. Food and Drug Administration (FDA) banned the use of plastic beverage bottles made from acrylonitrile. The EEC announced the withdrawal of three food colours and authorization of one new one. Additional restrictions on the use of saccharin were introduced by U.S. and Canadian authorities. The use of xylitol as a non-caries-producing sweetener was suspended pending receipt of more toxicologic data. Despite further safety testing by international organizations on the use of irradiation for food conservation, irradiated foods still failed to gain public acceptance. Toxicologists in Hong Kong implicated the excessive consumption of salted fish by southern Chinese as a factor in the high incidence of certain forms of cancer. A much debated problem facing legislators was the significance of minute traces of foreign chemicals in foods, now detectable by modern analytical tests.

Processing and Packaging. The need for rapid analytical control of food composition and quality led to numerous innovations. One British invention consisted of a combined optical and acoustic spectrometer that could continuously monitor the composition of liquids and powders. Another British company developed a bottle inspector capable of detecting minute objects such as particles of glass, mold, and other dirt at the rate of 800 bottles per minute. Impending EEC legislation requiring the average weight to be shown on packages stimulated development of a number of advanced checkweighers. A Canadian company developed a laser-operated package-coding system that could handle 30 packs per second.

There were a number of notable innovations in canning technology. Swiss developments included a machine that could produce welded food and beverage cans of superior quality at 450 per minute, a novel sterilizable, peelable can end without sharp edges, said to be competitive with customary scored ends, and a packaging, collating, and cartoning machine with a capacity of 400 tea bags per minute. In anticipation of possible restrictions on the use of hydrogen peroxide as a sterilizing agent for aseptic packaging materials, one Swiss company developed a method of sterilization utilizing high-intensity ultraviolet irradiation, which was successfully applied to the sterilization of plastic containers for individual portions of coffee cream. A British company developed a can capper and seamer with superior hygienic and maintenance characteristics that could operate at the rate of 600 cans per minute.

A French firm commissioned the first fully automatic retort-pouch line in Europe; it could process 100 pouches of high-grade vegetable products per minute. A Swedish company developed a retortable plastic can consisting of a foil/polypropylene laminate with the ends welded to the body and a pull-tab lid. It was said to be lighter than conventional cans, to be free from injurious edges, and to reduce noise levels. A U.S. company announced the development of a novel method of preservation called "hypobaric" storage, which depended on the maintenance of a temperature slightly above freezing with very low air pressure and high humidity. It was said to triple the shelf life of highly perishable products such as strawberries.

Fruit, Vegetable, and Cereal Products. An international specialist criticized the policy, common to many less developed countries, of concentrating on high-yield crops instead of tackling the technical problems of wastage. It was estimated that 50 to 60% of many foods was lost because of infestation and inadequate conservation methods. Among new installations, Sierra Leone

A new device which removes corn kernels intact has been developed by the Science and Education Administration of the U.S. Department of Agriculture. By removing entire kernels, the new device produces up to 20% more edible corn.

SCIENCE AND EDUCATION ADMINISTRATION—USDA

commissioned a fruit-processing factory for the manufacture of jams and juices from local crops of pineapples, mangoes, and oranges; a U.S. company commissioned a $3,450,000 plant for the manufacture of frozen extruded onion ring products for the rapidly expanding fast food industry; and a Swiss company scheduled a $25 million factory in the U.S. to manufacture fructose from starch. A Dutch company developed a machine for dry-peeling onions at 14,000 per hour, while a German company improved the shelf life of jams in sealed jars by exposing them to momentary microwave heating.

Interest in the dietary value of fibre accounted for the introduction of a whole-meal pasta in Britain and the commissioning of a new £20 million factory to meet the demand for breakfast cereals based on bran. A market research report revealed that consumption of whole-meal bread and bran bread had increased at the expense of white bread; 86% of housewives thought whole-meal was very good. An Egyptian research institute successfully fortified Arabic bread and two popular legume foods with soy flour. Swiss scientists established that heated flour had better baking characteristics after long storage than flour treated by heat and irradiation.

Dairy Products. The EEC reported a 14.5% surplus of dairy products over deliveries at the start of 1978, but world stocks of skim-milk powder were 1.6 million tons, compared with 2.3 million tons a year earlier. There was a continuing decline in liquid milk consumption in Europe, coupled with an increase in the consumption of long-life, heat-treated dairy products including low-fat milk. A large modern milk plant in Pakistan was said to be working at only 20% of capacity because of competition from cheap imported skim-milk powder. The U.S. and Sweden reached an agreement whereby the latter would supply certified dried milk products to strict bacteriologic specifications. The use of the enzyme lactase to break down lactose into glucose and galactose was the basis of a new dietetic milk developed in northern Italy and of novel yogurts and ice-cream formulations in the U.S. and Europe.

The production of single packs of safe drinking water for the reconstitution of infant foods was begun in Czechoslovakia. The infant food industry, which had come under considerable attack for its promotional activities in less developed countries, set up a council to establish a code of ethics. It was reported that the decline in breast feeding in the Philippines had resulted in the expenditure of about $33 million for substitute milk formulas in 1978. The packaging of infant formula for the U.S. market was said to consume about 70,000 tons of tinplate annually.

Meat, Unconventional Protein, and Seafood. A Czechoslovak organization developed a continuous smoking tunnel said to be twice as efficient as current plant. A modern combination meat factory and tannery opened in Botswana could produce 20,000 cans of beef and 600 hides daily. A meat-processing factory in the U.S. had a capacity of 5,000 lb of hot dogs per hour and an automatic line processing boneless hams in six hours.

A market research organization reported that sales of textured vegetable protein products in Britain had been disappointing. They were estimated at 15,000–20,000 tons per year, of which the pet-food industry accounted for 8,500 to 13,000 tons and institutional feeding for about 1,500 tons. A world conference on vegetable protein foods was held in The Netherlands. A British pioneer in the development of petroleum-derived protein closed the one remaining European plant.

The restocking of a large number of lakes and rivers with a new strain of crayfish was undertaken in Scandinavia. Proposals were put forward by U.S. scientists for large-scale algal culture as a source of protein; nutrient-rich deep-ocean water would be pumped to the surface by inserting a suitable heat engine between the warm upper layer and the cold depths. South Africa established its first seaweed farm for the production of food-grade emulsifiers. An international workshop was organized in Thailand to promote better utilization of tropical and trash fish for human consumption.

New Foods. Perhaps the most original "new food" developed during the year was a beverage from Japan said to be based on essence of earthworms. A serious proposal was made by two South African scientists for the utilization of locusts; one swarm covering 1,300 sq km would yield 65 million kg of protein. An international organization advocated the more widespread utilization of "bushmeat," including rats, snails, worms, ants, grasshoppers, snakes, and monkeys. It was argued that eating rats would serve the twofold purpose of providing protein and reducing crop damage.

A number of fermented soy protein products, modern versions of Japanese tempeh and Indonesian ontjom, achieved some success in the U.S. A Swiss patent described a process for making protein curd products of animal and vegetable origin by ultrafiltration; they were said to have cheeselike characteristics. A dietetic bread based on edible flax seed was developed in Hungary and successfully introduced in West Germany. In the dessert mix market, many established preparations were being superseded by a new range of milk-based desserts, while yogurt and other fermented milk products showed signs of completely ousting the traditional milk puddings. Yogurt bonbons, salad dressings, pound cakes, pie and bread, and cheese dip and various fermented products containing *Lactobacillus acidophilus* appeared in the U.S. Another U.S. development was a soy-honey product containing 50% protein.

A number of new fish products were developed for the better utilization of the less marketable varieties, including fish-meat dumplings in tomato from the U.S.S.R., tuna sausages, corn-shrimp kropeck, and tenderized bangus (milkfish) from the Philippines, and a new line of processed fish products for the fast food market in Britain. A dehydrated butter for cooking, described as "concentrated butter," was widely introduced in Europe to help reduce the EEC butter surplus.

(H. B. HAWLEY)

See also Agriculture and Food Supplies; Fisheries; Health and Disease; Industrial Review: *Alcoholic Beverages.*
[451.B.1.c.ii; 731.E–H]

Football

Association Football (Soccer). WORLD CUP. Argentina, the host country, became champions of the world when they won the World Cup final on June 25, 1978, in the River Plate Stadium, Buenos Aires, by beating The Netherlands 3–1 in overtime.

The 16-team final tournament's first round, arranged in four groups of four teams each, got off to a dismal start on June 1 when West Germany and Poland ground out a goalless bore before 77,-000 spectators in the River Plate Stadium and millions more watching by satellite television. The goalkeepers were almost as inactive as the fans. But there were some splendid displays of football in other first-round games, as in that between France and Italy. After Bernard Lacombe had scored to give France an early lead, the Italians swung the game around and won it with goals by Paolo Rossi and Renato Zaccarelli. In another contest Hungary took the lead with a goal by Karoly Csapo, but Argentina, managed by Cesar Luis Menotti, showed its potential and particularly the skill and cutting edge of its twin strikers Mario Kempes (*see* BIOGRAPHIES) and Leopoldo Luque; the game was marred when Hungarians Tibor Nyilasi and Andras Töröcsik were ordered off the field in the last five minutes of the game. Argentina next beat France 2–1.

Shocks in the opening round included a 3–1 victory by Tunisia over Mexico; the defeat of Spain by Austria, 2–1; Sweden's 1–1 tie with Brazil, one of the favourites; and Scotland's 3–1 loss to Peru. The Netherlands, managed by Ernst Happel, drew with Peru 0–0 and defeated Iran and Mexico. Scotland was held to a draw by Iran. Argentina suffered its only defeat in the tournament by losing to Italy on a goal by Roberto Bettega. But the two teams remained at the top of their group. The Netherlands, despite losing 3–2 in an all-action tussle with Scotland, qualified for the next round, together with Peru. Poland and West Germany headed their group, and Austria and Brazil theirs.

In the next stage of the competition, the above eight teams played in two groups, or leagues, of four teams each, the winners of each group playing each other in the final, and the runners-up competing in a match for third and fourth places. Argentina, having beaten Poland 2–0 and tied with Brazil, clinched its place in the final with a six-goal spectacular against a dispirited Peru. Kempes and Luque each scored twice, with Alberto Tarantini and René Houseman netting one apiece. The Netherlands, which had already beaten Austria 5–1 and drawn with West Germany 2–2, entered the final by defeating Italy 2–1 in a game with an undercurrent of ill-temper; Erny Brandts of The Netherlands scored accidentally for Italy, injuring his own goalkeeper Piet Schrijvers in collision; but replacement Jan Jongbloed saved superbly for The Netherlands when the Italians, led by Bettega, appeared to be taking control. Brandts tied the score five minutes into the second half, and the Dutch then pounded away at the veteran Dino Zoff's goal until Arie Haan produced a spectacular 30-yd blockbuster to win.

In the play-off for third and fourth places, Italy lost 2–1 to Brazil, which was the only unbeaten team in the tournament but had tied three times. Five minutes before halftime Franco Causio scored to give Italy a 1–0 lead. Eighteen minutes into the second half Nelinho beat Zoff to tie the score, and Brazil then brought on the master architect, Roberto Rivelino. Rivelino set up the attack that led to a blast into the net by Dirceu. The Italians had already lost their grip on the game. Some of the tackling was more agricultural than scientific, and signs of desperation in both teams tarnished the sense of occasion.

The final game, in which host country Argentina was roared along by the huge crowd in the River Plate Stadium on June 25, had all the sense of occasion and more than a touch of drama. There was a delay before the Argentine team appeared, and then they complained about the protective cover on René van der Kerkhof's injured arm, all part of the preliminary psychological battle. The match was far from a classic, yet always maintained the excitement expected.

After 37 minutes Kempes scored Argentina's first goal, set up by Osvaldo Ardiles and Luque. The Dutch, well marshaled by skipper Rudi Krol, pressed, and Haan had a long-range shot stopped by Ubaldo Fillol. Nine minutes before the end of the game Dirk Nanninga, a substitute for Johnny Rep, tied the score, heading in a cross from van der Kerkhof. In the last minute of the game Rob Rensenbrink of the Dutch team cracked the ball against a goal post but did not score. In the first period of overtime the play was even until Kempes scored after his first attempt was blocked by Jongbloed. Five minutes from the end of the game winger Daniel Bertoni scored from Kempes's pass and gave the weary Dutch no chance of bouncing back.

EUROPEAN CHAMPIONS' CUP. Liverpool, the defending champion, retained the club championship of Europe. With a soundly professional performance at Wembley, London, on May 10 the English team defeated FC Bruges, the Belgian representatives, by a single goal, scored by Kenny Dalglish. Until manager Bob Paisley sent onto the field the Irish international competitor Steve Heighway after an hour's play, Liverpool looked as if it was going to have difficulty in scoring. But with almost his first touch the Irishman initiated a series of quick passes for Dalglish to chip the ball over the head of Bruges' goalkeeper, Birger Jensen. Bruges, the first Belgian team to reach the final of the competition, tried to step up the pace and made two substitutions, but their challenge was too late.

EUROPEAN CUP-WINNERS' CUP. Anderlecht of Belgium regained the Cup-Winners' Cup when, in their third final in successive years, they beat FC Austria Wien 4–0. The Austrian team was the first from that country to reach the finals in one of the three major European competitions. The Belgians, however, were far better than their opponents on the night of May 3 in Paris before a crowd just short of 50,000. In Dutch World Cup star Rob Ren-

Argentine players (left) take off in hot pursuit of the ball during World Cup play in Buenos Aires in June. Argentina won the World Cup by defeating The Netherlands 3–1.

senbrink, Anderlecht had a man who could swing the game its way. He opened the scoring in the 13th minute and then put the ball in the goal on a free kick; within two minutes Gilbert van Binst scored off the inside of a post. The second half was played with both sides looking for goals but was marred by some ill-temper. In the closing minutes van Binst surged through for his second, and Anderlecht's fourth, goal.

UEFA CUP. PSV Eindhoven of The Netherlands beat Bastia from Corsica over two legs by an aggregate of 3–0, on April 26 and May 9. PSV had also clinched the Dutch championship earlier in the season and was in splendid form. The first game, at Bastia, was played under a downpour that turned the playing surface into a near morass. Most of the attacking moves broke down, and it was no surprise to find the score sheet blank. At home two weeks later PSV Eindhoven turned on the power, particularly through their midfield men. The brothers van der Kerkhof, Willy and René, were especially outstanding. Willy opened the scoring midway through the first half; a second PSV goal came from Gerry Deykers and then a third from Willy van der Kuylen.

BRITISH ISLES CHAMPIONSHIP. England regained the title by defeating Scotland with a goal by Steve Coppell of Manchester United at Hampden Park, Glasgow, on May 20. The English defense won the major honours for the way they contained a Scotland team that launched persistent raids.

NORTH AMERICAN SOCCER LEAGUE. For the second consecutive year the New York Cosmos won the championship of the North American Soccer League, defeating Tampa Bay 3–1 in the final game of the play-off tournament. Decisive winners of the National Conference's Eastern Division, the Cosmos were led to their play-off triumph by Dennis Tueart, formerly of Manchester City, and by leading defensemen Carlos Alberto and Pino Wilson. (TREVOR WILLIAMSON)

Rugby. RUGBY UNION. Judged on the results achieved in international competition, New Zealand emerged as the strongest country in rugby during 1977–78. The All Blacks' tour of France in October and November 1977 was the first they had ever made of that country separately from a visit to the British Isles. The New Zealand team played

Table I. Association Football Major Tournaments

Event	Winner	Country
World Cup	Argentina	
World Club Cup	Boca Juniors	Argentina
European Super Cup	Anderlecht	Belgium
European Champions' Cup	Liverpool	England
European Cup-Winners' Cup	Anderlecht	Belgium
UEFA Cup	PSV Eindhoven	The Netherlands
Libadores (South American Champions') Cup	Boca Juniors	Argentina

Table II. Association Football National Champions

Nation	League winners	Cup winners
Albania	Dynamo Tirana	Dynamo Tirana
Austria	FC Austria Wien	SW Innsbruck
Belgium	FC Bruges	Beveren
Bulgaria	Lokomotiv Sofia	Merekftanks
Cyprus	Omonia	Apoel
Czechoslovakia	Zbrojovka, Brno	Banik Ostrava
Denmark	BK Odense	Vejle
England	Nottingham Forest	Ipswich
Finland	Valkeakosken Haka	Valkeakosken Haka
France	Monaco	Nancy
Germany, East	Dresden	Magdeburg
Germany, West	FC Cologne	FC Cologne
Hungary	Ujpest Dozsa	Ferencvaros
Iceland	IA Akranes	IA Akranes
Ireland	Bohemians	Shamrock Rovers
Italy	Juventus	Inter-Milan
Luxembourg	Progrès Niedercorn	Progrès Niedercorn
Malta	Valletta	Valletta
Netherlands, The	PSV Eindhoven	AZ '67 Alkmaar
Northern Ireland	Linfield	Linfield
Norway	Lillestrøm	Lillestrøm
Poland	Wisla Krakow	Wisla Krakow
Portugal	FC Porto	Sporting Lisbon
Romania	Steaua Bucharest	Univer. Craiova
Scotland	Rangers	Rangers
Sweden	FC Malmø	FC Malmø
Switzerland	Grasshoppers	Servette
Turkey	Fenerbahce	Trabzonspor
U.S.S.R.	Dynamo Kiev	Dynamo Kiev
U.S.	New York Cosmos	
Wales		Wrexham
Yugoslavia	Partizan Belgrade	Rijeka

eight matches there and achieved a record of won 7, lost 1, points for 199, points against 77. The one match they lost was the first test, the French winning 18–13 at Toulouse. The All Blacks gained revenge in Paris, winning 15–3.

The All Blacks gained an unassailable lead in their three-match test series against the Wallabies of Australia in August and September 1978 by winning the first test 13–12 in Wellington and the second 22–6 at Christchurch. The Wallabies, however, won the third test 30–16 at Auckland.

The Wallabies had previously raised their morale for their tour of New Zealand by winning both tests in their two-match series against Wales in Australia in June. They won the first test 18–8 in Brisbane and the second 19–17 in Sydney. The Welsh record in Australia was won 5, lost 4, points for 227, points against 106.

Wales traveled to Australia as European champions, having earlier in the year triumphed over England, Scotland, Ireland, and France. The Welsh thus achieved their third consecutive triple crown and their second grand slam in three years. They were given a close game at Twickenham in their first match, beating England by only 9–6 (3 penalty goals to 2), but they then proceeded to beat Scotland 22–14 at Cardiff and Ireland 20–16 in Dublin before meeting France, which was also undefeated, in the decisive match at Cardiff. Wales's leading players, Gareth Edwards and Phil Bennett, were in their best form in this match, which Wales won 16–7. France had previously defeated England 15–6 in Paris, Scotland 19–16 at Murrayfield, and Ireland 10–9 in Paris, in a match played on a frozen field. England finished in third place in the championship by beating Scotland 15–0 at Murrayfield and Ireland 15–9 at Twickenham. Ireland opened its campaign by defeating Scotland 12–9 in Dublin, but this proved to be its only victory. Scotland, with four defeats in four games, finished last. After playing his 53rd consecutive game for Wales, Gareth Edwards announced his retirement.

The year was notable for the first extended tour ever made by a U.S. team in Britain. The Eagles played six games in England, winning two and losing four with a points record of 75 for and 124 against. In their most important match they were beaten 37–11 by "an England XV" at Twickenham.

RUGBY LEAGUE. The outstanding event of the European triangular tournament was England's 60–13 defeat of Wales at St. Helens. Since England had previously beaten France 13–11 at Toulouse, they won the tournament convincingly. In the other match Wales beat France 29–7 at Widnes. Australia emphasized its superiority in its part of the world by defeating New Zealand 3–0 in a test series against the Kiwis.   (DAVID FROST)

U.S. Football. Led by the four touchdown passes of quarterback Terry Bradshaw, the Pittsburgh Steelers defeated the Dallas Cowboys 35–31 to become the first team in the National Football League (NFL) to win the Super Bowl three times. Bradshaw, named the game's outstanding player, set a Super Bowl passing record of 318 yd. Dallas, however, did not give up easily. Behind 35–17, with less than seven minutes to play, the Cowboys

rallied behind the passing of Roger Staubach to score two touchdowns. In college football, depending on the poll, Alabama or Southern California was the national champion.

PROFESSIONAL. For years people connected with professional football spoke in reverent tones about the day the National Football League would achieve "parity." It began happening in 1978, when the records of 13 of the 28 NFL teams were within one win or loss of the 8–8 break-even point. The Atlanta Falcons, the Philadelphia Eagles, the Green Bay Packers, the Seattle Seahawks, the San Diego Chargers, and the New Orleans Saints all had their best records of recent years.

But when the regular season ended the only familiar team missing from the play-off tournament was the Oakland Raiders, which failed to qualify for post-season play for the first time in seven years. The Pittsburgh Steelers qualified for the seventh year in a row, and the Dallas Cowboys for the 12th time in 13 years. The Los Angeles Rams and the Minnesota Vikings were there, too, tying a record by winning their respective divisions for the sixth consecutive year.

Minnesota won the Central Division championship in the National Football Conference (NFC) for the tenth time in 11 seasons, despite winning only eight games, losing seven, and tying one. That was one of the problems with parity, which in its purest form would have every NFL team finishing with an 8–8 record.

NFL Commissioner Pete Rozelle clarified his desire for parity by saying he wanted "more close games creating greater interest, not a bunch of mediocre clubs with no one outstanding." The league had the close scores Rozelle hoped for, with almost half of the games being decided by fewer than seven points, but it lacked outstanding teams. Only seven teams, five of them in the American Football Conference (AFC), won more

John Fidler of Gloucester, who is 6 feet 4 inches tall, towered over 5-foot 6-inch Stephen Kenney of Leicester in the John Player Rugby Union Cup final game at Twickenham.

than 60% of their games. That may have been the reason the NFL's television ratings were down from 1977, even though scoring was higher under new rules that encouraged passing by making it harder to rush the passer and cover the receiver.

In order to stress its better balance the NFL changed its scheduling format in 1978, expanding the season from 14 to 16 games and providing for the four best teams in each division to play 12 common opponents. The play-off tournament also grew from eight to ten teams. In each of the two conferences play-off berths went to the three divisional winners and the two best runner-up, or "wild-card," teams.

The divisional winners rested on the first weekend of the play-offs while the wild-card teams from each conference played each other, Atlanta beating Philadelphia 14–13 in the NFC and the Houston Oilers defeating the Miami Dolphins 17–9 in the AFC. Miami was making its first play-off appearance in four years, and none of the others had played a post-season game since the NFL and American Football League merged in 1970. The Oilers were led by rookie halfback Earl Campbell (see BIOGRAPHIES), the league's rookie of the year and, by the vote of the Professional Football Writers of America, its most valuable player.

AFC divisional winners, Denver in the West, Pittsburgh in the Central, and New England in the East, were waiting for Houston. Denver, the defensive power that won the AFC title in 1977, had survived the NFL's only division with four winning teams. New England set an NFL record with 3,165 yd rushing and returned to the play-offs after a one-year absence, and Pittsburgh had the league's best record at 14–2. Besides allowing the fewest yards in the AFC the Steelers scored frequently behind quarterback Bradshaw, whose 28 touchdown passes led the league, and fullback Franco Harris, who became the second NFL runner ever to have six 1,000-yd seasons.

In the American Conference semifinals Pittsburgh, led by Bradshaw and Harris, routed Denver 33–10, while wild-card Houston continued its success with a 31–14 upset win over New England behind the passing of quarterback Dan Pastorini and the running of Campbell. In the AFC finals at Pittsburgh Bradshaw and Harris led the Steelers to a 34–5 triumph over Houston on a wet field.

Minnesota won the NFC Central Division under the tie-breaking formula after Green Bay matched the Vikings' record. The Vikings' rushing total was the lowest in the league, but four Vikings caught more than 50 passes, including league-leader Rickey Young with 88 receptions. Minnesota quarterback Fran Tarkenton set NFL records with 572 passes and 345 completions, but he also threw 32 interceptions.

Los Angeles in the West and Dallas in the East clearly were the class of the NFC. Defending Super Bowl champion Dallas had the best balance. Quarterback Staubach had the best passing rating in the NFL, halfback Tony Dorsett's 1,325 yd rushing ranked third in that category, and no other defense allowed fewer rushing yards. The Rams, who fired newly hired coach George Allen after two exhibition games, went on to have the NFL's best defense

under Ray Malavasi. They allowed an average of 243.3 yd per game and their place kicker, Frank Corrall, led the league with 118 points.

In the National Conference semifinals, Dallas defeated Atlanta 27–20 even though Staubach left the game with an injury in the second quarter. After a halftime tie of 10–10 Los Angeles caught fire and defeated Minnesota 34–10. In the NFC finals Dallas capitalized on Los Angeles mistakes to break a scoreless tie at halftime and win 28–0.

To make room for the new teams in the play-offs, Oakland, the Baltimore Colts, and the Chicago Bears fell out of the play-offs. Oakland's running attack fell from best in the AFC to 11th best, and quarterback Ken Stabler had 30 passes intercepted. Baltimore had risen to prominence in 1975 under young quarterback Bert Jones, and when injuries kept Jones inactive for most of the season the Colts finished with the AFC's worst offense and defense and one of the NFL's worst single-season declines, from 10–4 to 5–11. The Bears had the best rushing tandem in football with Walter Payton running for an NFC-leading 1,395 yd and Roland Harper adding 992 yd, but they lost eight straight games in midseason.

The Bears were one of ten teams to enter the season with a new coach, and nearly all of them suffered transition pains. The St. Louis Cardinals lost eight games before winning six of their last eight under Bud Wilkinson, who had not coached since he finished compiling a 146–29–4 record at the University of Oklahoma in 1963. The Washington Redskins had the opposite problem under Jack Pardee, winning six games and then losing eight of their last ten. The San Francisco 49ers changed coaches before and during the season but finished with the league's worst record, 2–14, partly because halfback O. J. Simpson was injured.

San Diego changed coaches in midseason, hiring Don Coryell after losing three of its first four games. With rookie wide receiver John Jefferson catching a league-leading 13 touchdown passes, the Chargers had the league's best passing offense, winning seven of their last eight games.

COLLEGE. Pennsylvania State University coach Joe Paterno, whose teams had never been elected the national collegiate champions despite three undefeated seasons, often had said the colleges should have a tournament to determine the best team on the field. In 1978 they decided it at the Sugar Bowl in New Orleans, La., where Penn State went into its game against Alabama with the No. 1 ranking and an 11–0 record. After Alabama won the game 14–7, it had an 11–1 record, identical to Penn State's, and it had, at least by some polls, won the national championship.

Penn State's strength was defense, although quarterback Chuck Fusina did win the Maxwell Award, the only player-of-the-year honour that did not go to Oklahoma halfback Billy Sims. With Pete Harris leading the nation with ten interceptions, Penn State was equaled by no one in turnover differential, gaining 21 more than it lost. Its average yield of 54.5 yd rushing per game was 38 yd lower than any other team, and it ranked first in total defense. Also, Matt Bahr led all college field goal kickers by making 22 in 27 tries.

Table III. NFL Final Standings and Play-offs, 1978

AMERICAN CONFERENCE
Eastern Division

	W	L	T
*New England	11	5	0
*Miami	11	5	0
New York Jets	8	8	0
Buffalo	5	11	0
Baltimore	5	11	0

Central Division

	W	L	T
*Pittsburgh	14	2	0
*Houston	10	6	0
Cleveland	8	8	0
Cincinnati	4	12	0

Western Division

	W	L	T
*Denver	10	6	0
Oakland	9	7	0
San Diego	9	7	0
Seattle	9	7	0
Kansas City	4	12	0

NATIONAL CONFERENCE
Eastern Division

	W	L	T
*Dallas	12	4	0
*Philadelphia	9	7	0
Washington	8	8	0
St. Louis	6	10	0
New York Giants	6	10	0

Central Division

	W	L	T
*Minnesota	8	7	1
Green Bay	8	7	1
Detroit	7	9	0
Chicago	7	9	0
Tampa Bay	5	11	0

Western Division

	W	L	T
*Los Angeles	12	4	0
*Atlanta	9	7	0
New Orleans	7	9	0
San Francisco	2	14	0

*Qualified for play-offs.

Play-offs

Wild-card round
Atlanta 14, Philadelphia 13
Houston 17, Miami 9

American semifinals
Pittsburgh 33, Denver 10
Houston 31, New England 14

National semifinals
Dallas 27, Atlanta 20
Los Angeles 34, Minnesota 10

American finals
Pittsburgh 34, Houston 5

National finals
Dallas 28, Los Angeles 0

Super Bowl
Pittsburgh 35, Dallas 31

Pittsburgh Steelers quarterback Terry Bradshaw cocks to throw a touchdown pass to Rocky Bleier (20) in the second quarter of the 13th Super Bowl. Pittsburgh won the game—its third Super Bowl championship—over the Dallas Cowboys 35–31, and Bradshaw, who passed for four touchdowns, was named the game's most valuable player.

Paterno had said that Alabama would be Penn State's most challenging opponent because it had the country's most balanced offense behind quarterback Jeff Rutledge, who threw more touchdown passes in his career than any of Alabama's famous quarterbacks. But although the football writers' poll and the National Football Foundation voted for Alabama as the nation's top team, the football coaches' poll chose Southern California, which also finished 11–1 and had defeated Alabama early in the season. Michigan, which lost to Southern California 17–10 in the Rose Bowl, also lost only once in the regular season and outscored its opponents by a nation-leading 29.4 points per game. And Oklahoma (11–1) and Nebraska (9–3), the Orange Bowl opponents who shared the Big Eight championship, ranked one-two in the country in points scored, rushing offense, and total offense.

Those six teams finished at the top of both major polls before the bowl games. The only surprise among the top ten was Atlantic Coast champion Clemson, which ranked fifth in both points allowed and points scored and then went on to beat Ohio State 17–15 in the Gator Bowl. Near the end of the game Ohio State coach Woody Hayes punched Charlie Baeumann after the Clemson defender had intercepted an Ohio State pass. Afterward Hayes was fired, an unfortunate end to a 33-year coaching career during which he compiled a record of 238 victories, 72 losses, 10 ties, and national championships in 1954 and 1968.

The Orange Bowl, won by Oklahoma 31–24, was an interesting matchup because the contestants had played each other during the regular season. Nebraska won that annual game 17–14 for the first time since 1971, capitalizing on six fumbles against the team that went on to lead the country with 40 points and 427.5 yd rushing per game.

Sims, a junior who won the Heisman Trophy among other awards, had nation-leading rushing figures of 160.2 yd per game, 1,762 yd total, 7.6 yd per carry, and 20 touchdowns. One of his blockers, guard Greg Roberts, won the Outland Trophy, given to the best college lineman.

In the Cotton Bowl, Notre Dame rallied from a 34–12 deficit with less than eight minutes to go to beat Houston, the Southwest champion, 35–34. Quarterback Joe Montana led the Irish charge, passing and running for two of Notre Dame's last three touchdowns.

Canadian Football. Dave Cutler kicked four field goals for the Edmonton Eskimos as they beat the Montreal Alouettes 20–13 at Toronto on November 26 to win the Grey Cup game for the championship of the Canadian Football League (CFL). It was the fourth time in the last five years that Montreal and Edmonton played for the championship and the first time since 1964 that a Western Conference team had won the title on an Eastern Conference field.

Edmonton took a 14–3 halftime lead by scoring a touchdown after a fake field goal kept its drive alive and adding a single and two field goals by Cutler, who led the CFL in scoring with 167 points. The Eskimos finished with the Western Conference's best record, 10–4–2, but Montreal had been second in the East with an 8–7–1 record and had to beat Ottawa in the conference final to reach the Grey Cup game.

Tony Gabriel led CFL pass receivers for Ottawa with 1,070 yd on his 67 receptions, and Tom Clements led the league by completing 63.6% of his passes. Mike Strickland of Saskatchewan was the league-leading rusher with 1,306 yd, and Ralph Brock of Winnipeg led the CFL with 23 touchdown passes and 3,755 yd passing.   (KEVIN M. LAMB)

VIOLENCE IN THE STANDS

by Desmond Morris

Acts of violence associated with sporting events, particularly association football (soccer) matches, have become a cause for increased concern during recent times. To those not closely connected with the world of sports, it appears that such violence must be greater now than ever before. But is this really the case? An alternative explanation could be that it is the concern about violence rather than the violence itself that is increasing.

If one casts an eye back over the long history of sports, it soon becomes clear that violent incidents are by no means a modern phenomenon. Chariot hooligans were as well known to the Romans as soccer hooligans are today. Football itself was repeatedly banned in England, royal proclamations prohibiting it having been issued in 1314 by Edward II, in 1349 by Edward III, in 1401 by Henry IV, and in 1457 by James II of Scotland. Both Henry VIII and Elizabeth I also made similar proclamations, with Henry VIII even making it a penal offense to keep a ground for the purpose of playing football.

In the 17th century, the Puritans attacked the sport of football so savagely, calling it "a bloody and murthering practice" from which "groweth envy, rancour, and malice, and sometimes brawling, murther, homicide, and great effusion of blodd," that it went into a rapid decline, from which it did not recover until the middle of the 19th century. In its new form, with modern rules and regulations, it lost much of its "murderous" quality and went on to become the major spectator sport of the 20th century, involving many millions of onlookers every week throughout the season.

With this change there was far less bloodshed on the field itself, but violence was by no means absent. Vicious tackling and brutal fouling between players often led to emotional explosions and occasional outbreaks of fighting. Among the spectators there were also rowdy scenes, riots, and cases of vandal-

Desmond Morris, a research fellow at Wolfson College, University of Oxford, is the author of The Naked Ape *(1967),* The Human Zoo *(1969), and* Manwatching: A Field Guide to Human Behaviour *(1977).*

ism. Many believed that the behaviour of the onlookers stemmed by example from the behaviour on the field itself. Accordingly, the organizing bodies of association football instigated a reform in refereeing that introduced much stricter penalties for players who broke the rules or "lost control." The result has been improved, cleaner football, with a minimum of incidents between players. But the reform has not had the slightest effect on the behaviour of the spectators, whose acts of violence, both during and after matches, have remained a characteristic feature of the football scene.

Taboos, Rituals, and Thugs. In this respect, at least, it is true to say that football remains today a violent sport. But it is important to recognize that it *remains* so; it has not *become* so. The apparent increase in violence, which so concerns the press, is due to three factors. First, there is, in Western society, a rising tide of objection to acts of violence of any kind, in any context. The popular slogan of the 1960s was "Make love not war," and the legacy of that attitude, today, in the 1970s, is a major tabooshift. Before, social condemnations of misbehaviour were split between the traditional twin taboos of sex and violence. Now, sexual behaviour in all its forms (excepting those, significantly, that are violent) is viewed with greatly increased leniency by society as a whole. This change has left violence as the single major taboo, with the result that it attracts even more attention than before.

A second factor is that the football fans have slowly developed a set of conspicuous rituals with which to express their fierce loyalties and their equally fierce antagonisms. They no longer troop onto the grounds clad in dull, cheap suits and flat caps. Instead, they wear the bright colours of tribal display, and their shouting has become warlike chanting and thunderous, highly rhythmic clapping. They are not only hostile, they are *seen* to be hostile and they are *heard* to be hostile. This, too, increases the public alarm at each sporting event.

Third, there is the association with sporting events of small groups of nonsporting thugs, who do cause damage and who do indulge in real, criminal violence. This small minority, which exists in any society, roaming, as it were, in search of an outlet for its pent-up savagery, has in recent years attached itself more and more to the sporting scene. In the past, the young thug found his outlet in a street gang, a motorcycle gang, or a dance hall gang, but now, almost by chance, he seems to have swung his unwelcome attentions toward the sports grounds, in particular the football grounds.

It is these three factors that seem to explain the apparent increase in violence among the spectators and have led to endless public debate of the problem, especially in the case of football. Emotions have run high, with football fans denounced in the press as "soccer savages" or "mindless morons" who are "worse than animals." The sports authorities have reacted by attempting to penalize supporters in the same way that referees penalized unruly players. When riots or invasions of the playing field have occurred, the authorities have penalized the clubs concerned, either fining them or, in extreme cases, temporarily banning them from playing home games. Individual culprits caught by the police have been fined or imprisoned with increasing strictness by magistrates. But the problem remains.

The "Illusion of Violence." Attempts have also been made to obtain a more objective, scientific assessment of the phenomenon. In the mid–1970s, Peter Marsh, a social psychologist at the University of Oxford, began a long-term study of the behaviour of soccer fans to ascertain, if possible, the nature and causes of their violence. In his published reports, he made it clear that one must be careful to distinguish between "the illusion of violence" and violence itself. Just as the majority of animal species indulge in conspicuous threat displays and counterdisplays, which successfully settle disputes without the drawing of blood, so too do the human football fans indulge in far more display than actual fighting. The very rituals that have been developed—the emblems, the chanting, the clapping, the jeering, and the shouting—which create the *atmosphere* of violent hostility, are, in fact, largely substitutes for violence. They express powerful loyalties and give the impression of impending mayhem, but the blood-shed they promise never comes. Instead, the displays themselves act as symbolic bloodlettings. This degree of ritualization echoes the very nature of sport itself, which is also a symbolic form of hunting or warfare—a form that has replaced the act of killing with the act of scoring a goal.

Marsh has inevitably been criticized for this interpretation. How, for example, could he explain the acts of vandalism and the undeniable acts of true violence that repeatedly do occur? As regards the vandalism, he has pointed out that smashing a window is not smashing a head, and that, although reprehensible, the attack on a store window is already to a certain extent a ritualized form of aggression. This is little comfort to the storekeeper whose premises are vandalized, but it has to be admitted that it is better to have glass fragments on the pavement than blood.

As regards the real violence, Marsh was able to establish that this was typically the work of a tiny minority of hardened thugs who had little to do with the football teams in question. This was clearly proved in one particular case. Marsh himself became instrumental in setting up a young supporters' "travel club" which helped to organize the transportation of fans to away-from-home matches. It is the visiting fans who are accused of causing most of the soccer violence. On the occasion of the first outing of the newly formed fan club, the buses carrying the young fans were met at the outskirts of the "away" town by the police, with whom they cooperated fully.

All should have gone well, but in the press the following day the same stories of vandalism and fighting were reported. Investigations proved that all incidents had been caused by groups of thugs who had nothing to do with the football club in question but who had simply used the occasion as an excuse to cause havoc locally. The worst incidents had occurred before the arrival of the fan club buses, a fact that the police could verify. Had there been no organized fan club, the fans themselves could certainly have been blamed.

The problems of hooliganism that bedevil European and South American soccer at present seem to be largely absent from North American football and soccer. There appear to be two reasons for this. First, the pattern of football attendance is more family-oriented in the U.S. than it is elsewhere, and large, all-male gangs of youths are much less in evidence. Second, the distances between the major playing fields are so much greater that traveling to games away from home becomes virtually impossible on a large scale. Consequently, there are far fewer "territorial invasions," and so clashes between rival bands of supporters are rare.

An injured fan is carried from the stands after being hurt during spectator violence at a soccer game in Manchester, England.

GERARD SCHACHMES—CAMERA PRESS/PHOTO TRENDS

France

France

A republic of Western Europe, France is bounded by the English Channel, Belgium, Luxembourg, West Germany, Switzerland, Italy, the Mediterranean Sea, Monaco, Spain, Andorra, and the Atlantic Ocean. Area: 544,000 sq km (210,040 sq mi), including Corsica. Pop. (1978 est.): 53,196,000. Cap. and largest city: Paris (pop., 1975 census, 2,-299,800). Language: French. Religion: predominantly Roman Catholic. President in 1978, Valéry Giscard d'Estaing; premier, Raymond Barre.

Domestic Affairs. For France 1978 was profoundly marked by the March parliamentary elections, in which, contrary to expectations, the left-wing opposition was defeated by the reigning conservative "majority parties." Pres. Valéry Giscard d'Estaing (see Biographies) was the main architect of the victory, while the left's joint program collapsed.

The first round of the elections on March 12 brought the first surprise. Most opinion polls had given the left a lead over the "majority" parties (Gaullist Rassemblement pour la République or RPR, and the Union pour la Démocratie Française or UDF). However, the latter held its ground, and gains by the left (Socialists, Communists, and Left Radicals), which won 49.7% of the vote, did not seem sufficient to ensure its victory on the second ballot. But the actual results of the second vote on March 19 far exceeded the government's expectations, the majority parties finally winning with 291 seats (a loss of 9) against 200 (a gain of 16) for the left-wing opposition: experts had predicted a final difference of barely 20 seats.

Within the "majority," the RPR, led by Jacques Chirac, remained the largest group with 148 seats, but the balance between "Gaullists" and "non-Gaullists" within the party tipped in favour of the latter. The UDF, which won 137 seats, was formed five weeks before the elections and was an alliance of Jean-Pierre Soisson's Republican Party (formerly Independent Republicans), Jean Lecanuet's Centre National des Indépendants Paysans, and J.-J. Servan-Schreiber's Valois Radicals, all of which supported President Giscard. Six members who campaigned either as candidates for the presidential majority or under various other labels completed the majority coalition.

On the left, the Communist Party, under Georges Marchais, gained more seats (+ 12) than François Mitterrand's Socialist Party (+ 8) for a total of 86 as against the Socialists' 103. The Left Radicals kept ten seats, the Extreme Left only one. (See Political Parties.)

Voter turnout, which already had been very high on the first ballot (83.4%), reached a record 84.7% on the second. The granting of the vote to 1.8 million young people aged between 18 and 21 did not seem to have affected the outcome of the poll, but the electorate of 35.5 million was the youngest in France since 1936. The total of votes gained by the various political parties showed a difference of less than one million votes between the two sides: 14,756,857 for the "majority" against 13,858,839 for the opposition. This was not accurately reflected in the 91-seat gap in the new Assembly because of the skillful transfer of second-round votes between the various "majority" parties.

The left's defeat was probably predetermined on Sept. 23, 1977, when negotiations on its joint program broke down. Unrelenting attacks by the Communist Party against the Socialist Party, and vice versa, destroyed the unifying impulse that had acted so powerfully over the previous three years, halted the country's drift toward the left that had been evident in the 1974 presidential election, and impeded the transfer of votes from one party to the other on the second ballot. The last-minute agreement between Marchais, Robert Fabre, leader of the Left Radicals, and Mitterrand on March 13, allowing candidates of the less successful party to retire in the second round in favour of the better-placed left-wing party, was not enough to wipe out six months of mudslinging. Finally, the prospect of seeing Communists in the government certainly scared a good number of voters.

The left's defeat marked the end of the joint program as drawn up in 1972; it had in any case become an anachronism, and the left-wing parties continued their mutual recriminations long after their electoral failure. Fabre was quick to draw the obvious conclusion from what had happened and announced that he no longer felt bound by the program. He later handed over the presidency of his party to Michel Crépeau and in September accepted an appointment from Giscard to investigate the employment situation and was expelled from his party. However, the encouraging results for

Two children in medieval garb "guarded" a podium when French Pres. Valéry Giscard d'Estaing made an appearance in Burgundy during the election campaign in January.

BOIFFIN-VIVIER—RUSH/KATHERINE YOUNG

Foreign Aid:
see Economy, World

Foreign Exchange:
see Economy, World

Crowds gathered in Paris for the funeral of local Palestine Liberation Organization representative Ezzedine Kalak and an aide, Hammad Adnan, who were killed by terrorists in August.

the left in several by-elections during the summer proved that the opposition, divided as it was, could still capture votes from the majority.

The five parliamentary by-elections produced five successes for the left. It retained the three seats it already held (Seine-Saint-Denis, Gers, and Pas-de-Calais) and gained two, one in Nancy from the UDF and one in Paris from the RPR. The deterioration in the economic and social situation, the unity of the left-wing electorate, and the failure of the majority parties to mobilize their electors and achieve a solid transfer of votes between the two ballots all explained these victories.

In fact, as of the end of 1978 France was divided into four major political groupings: Communists, Socialists, RPR, and UDF. Strengthened by his new parliamentary majority and now finding the means to implement his policies, Giscard tried to defuse the political, economic, and social situation by calling for an end to the "civil war" between the "two nations." On March 28 the first dialogue in 20 years took place between the majority parties and the opposition when Mitterrand spent 90 minutes

with President Giscard at the Élysée Palace. Over the next few days the president held successive talks with union leaders and with Lecanuet, Marchais, Chirac, and Fabre. In October Chirac and Giscard ended their political estrangement. The Élysée visits by Mitterrand and Marchais were described as "historic."

On March 31 President Giscard entrusted Raymond Barre with the task of forming the new government—his third—whose members were named on April 5. As there was no sense in changing a winning team, eight ministers (not counting Barre himself) and a secretary of state remained in the same office as before: Alain Peyrefitte (RPR, justice), Simone Veil (presidential majority, health and family), Christian Bonnet (UDF, interior), Louis de Guiringaud (presidential majority, foreign affairs), Yvon Bourges (RPR, defense), Robert Galley (RPR, cooperation), Alice Saunier-Seité (UDF, universities), Pierre Mehaignerie (UDF, agriculture), and Norbert Segard (UDF, secretary of state for post and telecommunications). Six members of the previous government switched

FRANCE

Education. (1977–78) Primary, pupils 4,618,436, teachers 231,300; secondary and vocational, pupils 4,947,624; teachers 351,825; teacher training (1974–75), students 26,317, teachers 2,691; higher, students 956,262.

Finance. Monetary unit: franc, with (Sept. 18, 1978) a free rate of Fr 4.38 to U.S. $1 (Fr 8.57 = £1 sterling). Gold, SDR's, and foreign exchange (June 1978) U.S. $10,945,000,000. Budget (1978 est.): revenue Fr 389.7 billion; expenditure Fr 398.3 billion. Gross domestic product (1977) Fr 1,870,300,000,000. Money supply (Dec. 1977) Fr 518,050,000,000. Cost of living (1975 = 100; June 1978) 130.2.

Foreign Trade. (1977) Imports Fr 346,360,-000,000; exports Fr 319,220,000,000. Import sources: EEC 49% (West Germany 18%, Italy 10%, Belgium-Luxembourg 9%, The Netherlands 6%, U.K. 5%); U.S. 7%; Saudi Arabia 6%. Export destinations: EEC 49% (West Germany 17%, Italy 10%, Belgium-Luxembourg 10%, U.K. 6%, The Netherlands 5%); U.S. 5%. Main exports: machinery 21%; motor vehicles 12%; food 11%; chemicals 11%; iron and steel 7%.

Tourism (1976): visitors 17,385,000; gross receipts U.S. $3,613,000,000.

Transport and Communications. Roads (1976) 795,777 km (including 3,894 km expressways; excluding c. 690,000 km rural roads). Motor vehicles in use (1976): passenger 16,230,000; commercial 2,145,000. Railways: (1976) 34,299 km; traffic (1977) 51,670,000,000 passenger-km, freight 66,225,-000,000 net ton-km. Air traffic (1977): 27,284,000,-000 passenger-km; freight 1,669,300,000 net ton-km. Navigable inland waterways in regular use (1976) 6,-931 km; freight traffic 12,156,000,000 ton-km. Shipping (1977): merchant vessels 100 gross tons and over 1,327; gross tonnage 11,613,859. Telephones (Jan. 1977) 15,554,000. Radio receivers (Dec. 1975) 18,197,000. Television licenses (Dec. 1975) 14,197,-000.

Agriculture. Production (in 000; metric tons; 1977): wheat 17,450; barley 10,290; oats 1,928; rye 376; corn 8,614; potatoes c. 6,470; sorghum 356; sugar, raw value c. 4,020; rapeseed c. 400; tomatoes c. 670; cauliflowers (1976) c. 480; carrots (1976) c. 518;

green peas (1976) c. 584; apples c. 2,190; peaches (1976) 587; wine c. 5,240; tobacco 53; milk c. 30,100; butter 545; cheese c. 1,004; beef and veal 1,652; pork c. 1,605; fish catch (1976) 806. Livestock (in 000; Dec. 1976): cattle 23,898; sheep 10,915; pigs 11,291; horses (1976) 402; poultry c. 207,543.

Industry. Index of production (1975 = 100; 1977) 113. Fuel and power (in 000; 1977): coal (metric tons) 21,293; electricity (kw-hr) 210,345,000; natural gas (cu m) 7,700,000; manufactured gas (cu m; 1976) 6,100,000. Production (in 000; metric tons; 1977): bauxite 2,027; iron ore (30% metal content) 36,634; pig iron 18.309; crude steel 22,093; aluminum 558; lead 146; zinc 246; cement 28,956; cotton yarn 229; cotton fabrics 176; wool yarn 141: wool fabrics 86; man-made fibres 332; sulfuric acid 4,501; petroleum products (1976) 113,084; fertilizers (nutrient content; 1976–77) nitrogenous 1,462, phosphate 1,490, potash 1,567; passenger cars (units) 3,558; commercial vehicles (units) 454. Merchant shipping launched (100 gross tons and over; 1977) 1,148,000 gross tons.

posts: René Monory (UDF, economy), Michel d'Ornano (UDF, environment), Christian Beullac (presidential majority, education), Robert Boulin (RPR, labour and participation), Jacques Barrot (UDF, trade and crafts), and Jean-François Deniau (UDF, foreign trade). Five new ministers and one secretary of state were appointed: Maurice Papon (RPR, budget), André Giraud (nonparliamentary minister, industry), Joël le Theule (RPR, transport), Jean-Pierre Soisson (UDF, youth, sport, and leisure), Jean-Philippe Lecat (presidential majority, culture and communications), and Maurice Plantier (RPR, secretary of state for veterans). In September Monique Pelletier (see BIOGRAPHIES) was appointed minister for the status of women. At the end of November Jean François-Poncet, secretary-general of the presidency, succeeded Guiringaud as foreign minister.

In the meantime Giscard, not troubled by divisions within the majority parties, strove to emphasize the country's long-term policies. In October, in reply to a question on television about France's place in the world, he recalled that in the year 2000 France would represent only 1% of the world's population, but that it could remain among the vanguard nations in three respects: through its influence in the world, its economic strength, and its standard of living. "France can win through by means of continual adaptation," he declared. Earlier, in a letter to Raymond Barre, he expressed his continued confidence in the premier and made it clear that economic recovery remained the first priority. Giscard stressed that the rate of inflation needed to be brought down significantly and that only international competitiveness could create jobs.

But price rises, at about 10% annually, and rising unemployment, which had reached 1,284,600 by October, did nothing to increase the government's popularity. Barre's tenacious pursuit of policies of economic austerity met with considerable hostility in the country. At the same time, the French economy had entered a new era. Industrial prices were freed after more than 30 years of price controls, and bread prices were also freed after being regulated for two centuries. The government was hoping to restore the taste for industrial competition, but at the same time it had to continue its struggle to combat social inequalities.

During the year serious industrial unrest involved the Renault automotive and Moulinex manufacturing concerns and the naval dockyards (where 60,000 workers went on strike), as well as the railways, electricity, post office, and air traffic control. On October 20 several thousand workers from the shipyards demonstrated in Paris to demand employment protection. In May and June a series of price rises affected railways, electricity, coal, mail delivery and telecommunications, tobacco and cigarettes, stamps, and gasoline and fuel oil. Following this a new wave of increases in the public sector on July 1 affected transport in Paris and rents. To help people cope with the inflation there were rises in pensions, family allowances, minimum allowances to old people, and the minimum industrial wage.

While the Agache-Willot group bought the failing Boussac textile empire for Fr 700 million and the state took financial control of the near-bankrupt steel industry, the automobile industry—one of the strong sectors of the economy—recorded a success. Peugeot-Citroën took over the three European subsidiaries of the U.S. Chrysler group (Chrysler-France, formerly Simca; Chrysler-U.K.; and Chrysler-Spain). This takeover reduced the number of manufacturers in France to two (the other being Renault) and made Peugeot-Citroën easily the leading European producer in the automotive field, with an annual output above 2.3 million vehicles and slightly more than 260,000 employees. The French concern thus rivaled the major U.S. and Japanese manufacturers. Another encouraging sign was the fact that the balance of trade seemed likely to be well in surplus over the year. In December it was reported that China placed a $600 million order for two nuclear power plants with France, as part of a $3.5 billion trade agreement.

During 1978 France had its share of incidents of kidnapping and terrorism. At the end of January the industrialist Baron Édouard-Jean Empain was seized near his Paris home. He was released in March after the police had prevented his family from paying a U.S. $8.6 million ransom. Breton and Corsican separatists were responsible for a number of bomb explosions, the most notorious of which was that which wrecked rooms in a wing of the Palace of Versailles in June. On July 31 a Palestinian shot and wounded an Iraqi diplomat, and in an exchange of fire after the terrorist had surrendered, a French police inspector and an Iraqi security guard were also killed.

A major environmental disaster was the discharge of more than 1.6 million bbl of oil from the tanker "Amoco Cadiz" after it had run aground near Portsall, northwest Brittany, in March and had broken up. (See ENVIRONMENT.)

At the end of October the public realization, through an interview in the magazine L'Express, that the wartime Vichy government's commissioner for Jewish affairs, 80-year-old Louis Darquier de Pellepoix, was living comfortably in Spain as an unrepentant fascist, though now a sick man, produced an outcry and calls that his extradition should be sought. Darquier had deported over 75,000 French Jews to Germany. He had fled to Spain at the Liberation and been condemned to death in absentia.

Foreign Affairs. In dealing with other nations, traditionally the preserve of the president since the regime of Charles de Gaulle, Giscard concentrated mainly on three areas: disarmament, Africa, and Europe. In May he put forward at the United Nations the French plan for disarmament, which aimed to break the U.S.-Soviet dominance; following this, France was to take part in the work of the UN Committee on Disarmament, meeting in Geneva.

In Chad France cooperated with the government against the Chad National Liberation Front (Frolinat). In May, when rebels seized Kolwezi in Zaire's Shaba Province, France and Belgium, at the request of Pres. Mobutu Sese Seko, sent parachutists to defend the 2,500 Europeans there. At a

Franco-African conference in Paris, attended by representatives of 21 African states, France proposed the formation of a Pan-African intervention force. Substantial numbers of French troops were involved in black Africa, an outside force second only to that of Cuba.

Giscard also undertook visits to the Ivory Coast, Brazil, Andorra, and in December to Guinea, where his discussions with Pres. Sékou Touré (*see* BIOGRAPHIES) promised to transform the long-existing coolness between France and Guinea into reconciliation and cooperation. In Paris he received Didier Ratsiraka, Madagascar's head of state, and King Khalid of Saudi Arabia. But the president's efforts were mainly devoted to achieving greater unity for the European Economic Community (EEC). This desire emerged first in the visit to Paris of U.S. Pres. Jimmy Carter, who expressed his enthusiastic support for an economically and politically united Europe. There followed the traditional meetings with British Prime Minister James Callaghan and West German Chancellor Helmut Schmidt. The president's official visits to Madrid and Lisbon, as well as the two visits to Paris of Greek Prime Minister Konstantinos Karamanlis, were directed to the purpose of preparing for the entry of Spain, Portugal, and Greece into the EEC and restoring the geographic balance of the Community by extending it to the whole Mediterranean region.

From the time of the Copenhagen summit in April, at which the EEC member nations decided that the European Parliament would be elected between June 7 and 10, 1979, a common economic and monetary strategy toward the dollar was agreed upon. The European Council at Bremen in July examined the plan to revive monetary cooperation among the members drawn up by Schmidt and Giscard in June at Hamburg. The new European Monetary System was to have been introduced at the turn of the year, but in December its inception was indefinitely deferred because of objections by France on points of detail.

(JEAN KNECHT)

See also Dependent States.

Gabon

A republic of western equatorial Africa, Gabon is bounded by Equatorial Guinea, Cameroon, the Congo, and the Atlantic Ocean. Area: 267,667 sq km (103,347 sq mi). Pop. (1978 est.): 1,300,200. Cap. and largest city: Libreville (pop., 1978 est., 225,200). Language: French and Bantu dialects. Religion: traditional tribal beliefs; Christian minority. President in 1978, Omar Bongo; premier, Léon Mébiame.

In July 1978 Pres. Omar Bongo decided to expel from Gabon the citizens of Benin who were living in the country. This move, affecting more than 10,000 people, was a direct result of the deterioration in relations with Benin after accusations at the Organization of African Unity summit in Khartoum, Sudan, that the Gabon government had taken part in organizing the January 1977 mercenary attack against Benin's Cotonou airport. During

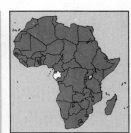

Gabon

GABON
 Education. (1975–76) Primary, pupils 128,552, teachers 2,664; secondary, pupils 19,721, teachers 863; vocational, pupils 2,450, teachers 148; teacher training, students 371, teachers 36; higher, students 1,146.
 Finance. Monetary unit: CFA franc, with (Sept. 18, 1978) a parity of CFA Fr 50 to the French franc (free rate of CFA Fr 218.81 = U.S. $1; CFA Fr 428.75 = £1 sterling). Budget (1977 est.) balanced at CFA Fr 255,792,000,000.
 Foreign Trade. (1977) Imports c. CFA Fr 163 billion; exports CFA Fr 249,620,000,000. Import sources (1976): France 69%; U.S. 6%. Export destinations (1976): France 47%; U.S. 19%; The Bahamas 11%; U.K. 11%; Italy 5%; West Germany 5%. Main export: crude oil 85%.
 Transport and Communications. Roads (1976) 6,878 km. Motor vehicles in use (1974): passenger c. 10,100; commercial (including buses) c. 7,300. Construction of a Trans-Gabon railway was begun in 1974, with planned completion of 670 km by 1980. Air traffic (1976): 190 million passenger-km; freight 14.4 million net ton-km. Telephones (Dec. 1973) 11,000. Radio receivers (Dec. 1975) 92,000. Television receivers (Dec. 1975) 8,000.
 Agriculture. Production (in 000; metric tons; 1976): sweet potatoes c. 3; cassava c. 180; corn c. 2; peanuts c. 2; bananas c. 10; plantains c. 80; palm oil c. 3; coffee c. 1; cocoa c. 4; timber (cu m) c. 2,563. Livestock (in 000; 1976): cattle c. 5; pigs c. 5; sheep c. 59; goats c. 64.
 Industry. Production (in 000; metric tons; 1977): crude oil 11,268; manganese ore (metal content) 1,045; uranium c. 0.6; petroleum products (1976) c. 910; electricity (kw-hr; 1976) c. 230,000.

their removal from Gabon the Beninese were sometimes brutally herded together and often subjected to reprisals by the local population. A considerable number of them were wounded, and official reports admitted that one had been killed.

Despite criticism of his government's attitude in the dispute with Benin, President Bongo played an important role as a mediator in two of the most serious armed conflicts in Africa, the war in Western Sahara and the civil war in Chad. He made several visits to France in this connection to confer with Pres. Valéry Giscard d'Estaing, and in April, when he met the Chad foreign minister there, he denounced Libya's interference in the Chad war.

(PHILIPPE DECRAENE)

Gambia, The

The Gambia

A small republic and member of the Commonwealth of Nations, The Gambia extends from the Atlantic Ocean along the lower Gambia River in West Africa and is surrounded by Senegal. Area: 10,403 sq km (4,016 sq mi). Pop. (1978 est.): 568,-600, including (1973) Malinke 37.7%; Fulani 16.2%; Wolof 14%; Dyola 8.5%; Soninke 7.8%; others 15.8%. Cap. and largest city: Banjul (pop., 1977 est., 51,700). Language: English (official). Religion: predominantly Muslim. President in 1978, Sir Dawda Jawara.

The Gambia's political stability was emphasized in June 1978, when a multiparty by-election, rare in Africa, was held at Bakau. The opposition National Convention Party held the seat against the ruling People's Progressive Party of Sir Dawda Jawara (*see* BIOGRAPHIES).

In his capacity as chairman of the Sahel Interstate Committee Against Drought, Sir Dawda successfully toured Europe and the U.S. in May to raise development funds. The Gambia itself was

GAMBIA
    Education. (1977–78) Primary, pupils 27,523, teachers 948; secondary, pupils 6,980, teachers 354; vocational, pupils 402, teachers 24; teacher training, students 193, teachers 15.
    Finance. Monetary unit: dalasi, with (Sept. 18, 1978) a free rate of 2.04 dalasis to U.S. $1 (par value of 4 dalasis = £1 sterling). Budget (total; 1976-77 actual): revenue 64,-570,000 dalasis; expenditure 84,860,000 dalasis.
    Foreign Trade. (1977) Imports 177,710,000 dalasis; exports 110,170,000 dalasis. Import sources (1976): U.K. 25%; China 13%; The Netherlands 6%; Japan 6%; France 5%; Burma 5%; West Germany 5%. Export destinations (1976): U.K. 30%; The Netherlands 22%; France 10%; Italy 7%; Switzerland 6%; Portugal 5%. Main export: peanut products 89%.

suffering from a two-year drought. Its only export crop, peanuts (groundnuts), fell to the lowest level in 14 years, and a food emergency was declared. The European Economic Community provided immediate aid; the U.S. set up a $2 million soil and water management unit; and Britain provided $3 million as aid to small business and farm units.

Ten years' economic cooperation with Senegal was celebrated in June with an agreement on a $60 million, four-year irrigation development. Earlier, Sir Dawda exchanged visits with Nigeria's head of government, Lieut. Gen. Olusegun Obasanjo, aimed at promoting economic cooperation within the Economic Community of West African States (ECOWAS). Although tourist arrivals had leaped from 300 to 20,000 in a decade, the government remained cautious and aware of tourism's "negative implications" for the Gambian way of life.

(MOLLY MORTIMER)

Gambling

The first legal gambling casino in the United States outside of Nevada opened its doors for business in Atlantic City, N.J., on May 26. During the month of June the casino, in the Resorts International Hotel (formerly the Chalfonte-Haddon Hall), reported that it had taken in $16,038,805 in bets,

about 45% of them on slot machines. Projections for the 12-month period were that the casino would gross more than $200 million in bets, more than double the existing record yearly total for a single casino in the U.S.

Focusing on New York City, federally financed studies indicated that illegal gambling, contrary to widespread belief, did not provide the largest source of revenue for organized crime. These studies revealed that the numbers game and sports bookmaking made relatively small profits and were under the control of competing independent operators. The research included analyses of police records since 1965 and discussions with policemen and informants.

By 1978 some form of wagering was legal in 44 states of the U.S. Twenty-one allowed pari-mutuel betting at racetracks for Thoroughbred and harness horses, 13 had dog races, 14 offered lotteries, 4 had jai alai frontons, 2 provided offtrack betting parlours, and 2 allowed casinos. Offtrack betting, legal only in New York and Connecticut, took in 20% more money in 1977 than in 1976, whereas pari-mutuel betting at tracks increased only 0.5%. Lottery receipts rose 24%, while those for dog racing went up 12.3%, for jai alai 22%, and for casino gambling 20%.

The most significant development during 1978 in the U.K. was the publication in July of the report of the Royal Commission on Gambling under the chairmanship of Lord Rothschild. Examining the whole field of wagering in Great Britain, the report made a total of 304 recommendations. Among the most significant were that a national lottery to benefit good causes should be established, that some casinos should pay more taxes, and that bettors should be given more information about the true odds involved in the various forms of gambling.

Gambling continued during 1978 to be one of the major leisure activities in the U.K. More than £7,000 million was bet, principally on horse and dog racing, football pools, bingo, lotteries, and in casinos. The most popular form of gambling in

Patrons lined up for hours to put their money on the tables when New Jersey's first licensed gambling casino opened in May.

terms of the number of participants was football (soccer) pool betting; approximately 15 million people staked some £230 million on them. Casino gambling, largely attracting the wealthy, continued at about the same level of popularity and accounted for more than half of the total amount of money bet during the year.

The biggest expansion in 1978 in the U.K. was in lotteries. By the end of the year some 350 local authorities were registered to operate them. One new feature was the importation from the U.S. of the instant lottery game, in which the purchaser removes a covering to reveal a winning (or losing) number and thus knows at once whether he has won a prize.　　　　(DAVID R. CALHOUN; GBGB)

See also Equestrian Sports.
[452.C.2]

Games and Toys

Video and other games based on microelectronics made further advances in 1978, supported by a Christmastime trend in toy buying away from the lower-price "stocking fillers" toward more expensive items that could be enjoyed by the whole family. Among the sophisticated electronic games available were chess, embodying a microcomputer that could be programmed for varying degrees of skill; a similar backgammon game; and Master Mind, among the most successful games of the decade, in an electronic form that could be played solo or in competition with other players. Big sellers during the Christmas season included a multicoloured disk named Simon, a robot named 2-XL that could talk, and Merlin, a computer that played ticktacktoe, blackjack, numbers games, and 48 musical notes.

Merchandising of characters associated with popular films and television programs continued to be an expanding sector of the toy trade. *Star Wars* provided a whole range of spin-offs, including the main characters in four-inch articulated-doll form, C3PO playsuits, battery-operated R2-D2s, Force beams, construction kits, and board games. A similar line was based on the new television series "Battlestar Galactica."

With Mickey Mouse celebrating his 50th anniversary during the year (*see* BIOGRAPHIES), he and other Walt Disney characters were much in evidence. However, demand was reported to be disappointing—possibly Mickey had a greater appeal for his contemporaries than for the younger generation. Cuddly rabbits proliferated with the release of an animated film version of Richard Adams's best-seller *Watership Down*.

Among the various articulated "people" toys, Dunbee-Combex-Marx Ltd.'s (DCM's) Playpeople remained popular. Others, besides the *Star Wars* and "Battlestar Galactica" figures, were Micronauts (space-age men, robots, and vehicles) and the Good Eggs (jolly ovoid farmers, policemen, nurses, etc., with various accessories). The larger Action Man and Sindy continued as best-selling dress-up figures for boys and girls, respectively, with new lines of clothes and equipment available; Action Man acquired a girl friend, and

Sindy even ventured into matrimony. A new doll was Baby Wet & Care, which broke out in simulated diaper rash. Mattel's Barbie doll turned 20 in 1978 but continued to register healthy sales.

Additions to DCM's Hornby model railways included a 1/16th scale, butane-fueled replica of George Stephenson's "Rocket." New model car racing circuits included DCM's Aurora Electronic 90 and Ideal's Total Control Racing, both of which enabled cars to change lanes while racing. Also popular were General Mills' slotless Power Passers and Lesney Products' (Matchbox) Speedtrack.

Among construction toys Lego retained a position of leadership, with Meccano and Fischertechnic appealing to the more mechanically minded youngsters. In a class by itself was the aptly named Slime, a modeling material, available with or without a mixture of "worms." Parker Brothers voluntarily recalled almost one million Riviton construction sets after the deaths of two children who swallowed the rubber "rivets."

A newcomer among board games was Skirrid ("The Shapes Game"), which its inventors saw as a potential challenger to the two perennial best-sellers in the field, Monopoly and Scrabble.

In Britain, the previous year's skateboarding boom faded rapidly. Commercial skate parks proved unprofitable, and only a few local authorities provided the facilities needed to maintain interest. Manufacturers who had invested heavily in boards and accessories were faced with a dramatic fall in demand. It seemed likely, however, that skateboarding would continue as a specialist sport among enthusiasts using the more expensive equipment, and it remained popular in the U.S.

A number of toy companies changed hands during the year. Britain's DCM group acquired Aurora, a market leader in the U.S. in the field of slot car racing circuits. Aurora was not a particularly

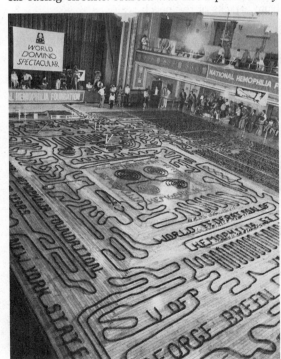

D. GORTON—THE NEW YORK TIMES

Twenty-one-year-old Bob Speca, Jr., of Philadelphia set a new world record when 97,500 dominoes were toppled in 17¾ minutes after he had spent nine days—a total of 95 hours—arranging them on the floor of the ballroom of the Manhattan Center in New York. Speca did not reach his goal of 100,000 dominoes because a press card fell out of a cameraman's pocket and knocked down 2,500 prematurely.

healthy company financially, but DCM had a reputation for buying up companies running at a loss and making them profitable as it had done with Louis Marx Inc. However, after an optimistic forecast in July, it was announced in October that DCM had incurred a £3 million loss in the first half of 1978. This revelation shook the toy industry to its foundations. In order to restore the industry's shaken confidence and DCM's fortunes, the company would have to be successful in the U.S. In another acquisition CBS bought Gabriel Industries, the maker of Tinkertoy.   (JULIA HOBDAY)

Gardening

Most of the trees and shrubs that provide beautiful displays of autumn colour in the northern U.S. have a chill requirement. After becoming dormant in the fall, they cannot resume growth until they have experienced hundreds of hours of temperatures below 7° C (45° F). Using seeds from 42 parent trees on Taiwan, Robert C. Hare of the Southern Forest Experiment Station, Gulfport, Miss., developed varieties of Formosan sweet gum that can produce brilliant fall foliage in the deep South. The colours range from a deep red-purple through bright yellows. The best of the new varieties would be available to the nursery trade in about five years.

Following the loss of so many elms to Dutch elm disease, a National Tree Week was being organized in England to publicize the need for tree planting. Its director, John Yeoman, stated that a massive, 25-year tree-planting program would be required to overcome the losses caused by the 1976 drought, vandalism, neglect, and disease. Meanwhile, there was growing concern over the loss of sycamores from sooty bark disease and of beeches from attacks of the beech scale.

An All-America Rose Selection for 1979 was the Paradise, a hybrid tea rose. The rose is ruby red with tones of pink and lavender.

ALL-AMERICA ROSE SELECTIONS

Three roses were 1979 All-America award winners: Friendship, a clear, bright pink hybrid tea with a strong, sweet fragrance, hybridized by Robert V. Lindquist, Sr., of Hemet, Calif.; Paradise, a ruby red, lavender, and pink hybrid tea, said by the judges to be one of the most distinctive and beautiful roses ever produced, hybridized by Ollie Weeks of Ontario, Calif.; and Sundowner, a large-flowered, gleaming orange, very fragrant grandiflora, hybridized by Sam McGredy IV of New Zealand.

Among English gardeners, hardy herbaceous perennials and ferns were coming back into fashion, possibly because they are easy to grow and not particular as to soil. There was also a growing awareness of bamboos and ornamental grasses, the latter finding favour with flower arrangers and gardeners with difficult sites in dry shade. The New Zealand flax (*Phormium*), introduced into England 200 years ago, was attracting attention because of the introduction of new hybrids. Commercial production of daffodils in England was increasing, and exports had already overtaken those of The Netherlands. Virus-free strains of 30 cultivars had been obtained from the Glasshouse Crops Research Institute and were being built up into commercial quantities. Similar work with tulips was at an early stage. The North of England Tulip Society established a tulip bulb bank based at Chatsworth, the seat of its president, the duke of Devonshire.

Sweet corn has long been among the most preferred garden vegetables, but it loses quality quickly after being picked. A new kind of sweet corn, developed by Douglas Garwood and Roy Creech of Pennsylvania State University, was reported to be capable of staying fresh for several days. In a field evaluation, 90% of the 370 participants rated it superior in sweetness, flavour, tenderness, and texture.

Liberty, a new apple developed by the agricultural experiment station at Cornell University, Ithaca, N.Y., is resistant to apple scab and shows a high degree of resistance or tolerance to cedar apple rust, fire blight, and mildew. Extensive testing indicated that in most years it could be grown without using fungicidal sprays.

Whiteflies have become one of the worst insect pests in greenhouses and a serious problem in many gardens. Robert G. Helgesen and Maurice Tauber of Cornell University found that whitefly numbers could be reduced to an acceptable level in commercial houses by introducing *Encarsis formosa*, a parasitic wasp. The wasp was being used in England, Canada, and The Netherlands with considerable success.

Preliminary reports from the 1978 trapping survey pinpointed a gypsy moth infestation in Seattle, Wash., according to U.S. Department of Agriculture (USDA) officials. Twenty-two male moths were trapped within a three-block area. The gypsy moth also was found for the first time in Muskingum, Stark, and Trumbull counties of eastern Ohio, and large numbers were trapped in Washington, D.C., suburbs. The gypsy moth is a serious pest of forest and fruit trees.

The neem tree, found in India, provided scientists with the first effective natural deterrent to another plant pest, the Japanese beetle. During tests, extracts from neem seeds kept adult beetles from eating sassafras and soybean leaves. T. L. Ladd of the USDA's Beetle Research Laboratory, Wooster, Ohio, said some beetles starved to death rather than consume the treated foliage.

Lovell peach was once widely used as a rootstock for peach in California, but its susceptibility to root-knot nematodes led to its replacement in most areas. A recent survey showed that several old orchards on Lovell rootstock in the San Joaquin Valley had unexpectedly low root-knot nematode populations. An investigation revealed that the nematode eggs had been parasitized by a fungus that often destroyed whole clumps of eggs and occasionally grew into the females, causing egg production to cease prematurely.

(J. G. SCOTT MARSHALL; TOM STEVENSON)

See also Agriculture and Food Supplies; Environment; Life Sciences.

[355.C.2–3; 731.B.1]

German Democratic Republic

A country of central Europe, Germany was partitioned after World War II into the Federal Republic of Germany (Bundesrepublik Deutschland; West Germany) and the German Democratic Republic (Deutsche Demokratische Republik; East Germany), with a special provisional regime for Berlin. East Germany is bordered by the Baltic Sea, Poland, Czechoslovakia, and West Germany. Area: 108,328 sq km (41,826 sq mi). Pop. (1978 est.): 16,757,900. Cap. and largest city: East Berlin (pop., 1978 est., 1,118,100). Language: German. Religion: (1969 est.): Protestant 80%; Roman Catholic 10%. General secretary of the Socialist Unity (Communist) Party and chairman of the Council of State in 1978, Erich Honecker; president of the Council of Ministers (premier), Willi Stoph.

Possibly encouraged by U.S. Pres. Jimmy Carter's stand on human rights and by developments in other Soviet bloc countries, East German dissidents increasingly showed their disaffection toward the regime in 1978. On Dec. 31, 1977, the West German magazine *Der Spiegel* began publishing a manifesto ostensibly written by dissident

officials of the East German Socialist Unity (Communist) Party. The party leadership dismissed the document as a bad joke, gotten up by West German intelligence with the connivance of West German correspondents in East Berlin. Some West German politicians and observers considered, on the other hand, that it represented the tip of an iceberg of dissatisfaction.

The authors of the manifesto introduced themselves as democratic and humanistic socialists and appealed to like-minded comrades in West Germany and West Berlin to join them. Their program was not confined to East Germany alone but rather aimed at bringing about the reunification of Germany, a nation in which Social Democrats, Socialists, and Democratic Communists would outnumber "conservative forces." They would have NATO forces withdrawn from Western Europe. West Germany would leave NATO, East Germany would leave the Warsaw Pact, and a reunified Germany, its neutrality guaranteed by the UN, would be totally disarmed.

Rudolf Bahro, a former Communist Party official turned dissident, was sentenced to eight years' imprisonment in June on charges of spying for the West. He was the author of the book *The Alternative*, which was published in the West in 1977. It strongly criticized the regime and was thought to be the real reason for Bahro's arrest. In a letter sent to West Germany in October, he said that during his secret trial he had made no admission of guilt. He reiterated that he still believed that East Germany should remain noncapitalist, and that he was not hostile to the Soviet Union. What he wanted was a new structure, built on the existing foundations.

There were strong denials in East Berlin of reports by West German intelligence sources that a small number of East German specialists collaborated with Cubans and the Soviets in planning the May invasion of Shaba Province in Zaire. Evidence was building of an increasing East German involvement in this African trouble spot. According to unconfirmed reports, at least 1,000 East German army specialists were serving as instructors or advisers in Africa, and considerable quantities of East German equipment, arms, and ammunition were being supplied to African countries.

Quite apart from evidence gathered by the intelligence services, the cat was let at least partially out of the bag during a well-publicized tour of

German Democratic Republic

GERMAN DEMOCRATIC REPUBLIC

Education. (1976–77) Primary and secondary, pupils 2,599,596, teachers 161,477; vocational, pupils 446,209, teachers 29,975; higher, students 287,614, teaching staff (1974–75) 33,570.

Finance. Monetary unit: Mark of Deutsche Demokratische Republik, with (Sept. 18, 1978) a rate of M 1.98 to U.S. $1 (M 3.87 = £1 sterling). Budget (1976 est.): revenue M 117,588,000,000; expenditure M 117,128,000,000. Net material product (at 1967 prices; 1976) M 147.5 billion.

Foreign Trade. (1976) Imports M 45,921,000,000; exports M 39,536,000,000. Import sources (1974): U.S.S.R. 30%; West Germany 9%; Czechoslovakia 7%; Poland 7%; Hungary 5%. Export destinations (1974): U.S.S.R. 33%; Czechoslovakia 10%; West Germany 10%; Poland 9%; Hungary 6%. Main ex-

ports (1975): machinery 37%; transport equipment 12%; chemicals; textiles.

Transport and Communications. Roads (1976) 118,925 km (including 1,585 km autobahns). Motor vehicles in use (1976): passenger 2,052,200; commercial 248,600. Railways: (1976) 14,306 km (including 1,508 km electrified); traffic (1977) 22,704,000,000 passenger-km, freight 52,142,000,000 net ton-km. Air traffic (1976): 1,448,000,000 passenger-km; freight 50,460,000 net ton-km. Navigable inland waterways in regular use (1976) 2,538 km; freight traffic 1,947,000,000 ton-km. Shipping (1976): merchant vessels 100 gross tons and over 447; gross tonnage 1,486,838. Telephones (Jan. 1977) 2,750,600. Radio licenses (Dec. 1975) c. 6,160,000. Television licenses (Dec. 1975) 5,177,000.

Agriculture. Production (in 000; metric tons; 1977): wheat c. 3,100; barley c. 3,400; rye c. 1,500; oats c. 650; potatoes c. 7,000; sugar, raw value c. 780; cabbages (1976) c. 306; rapeseed c. 315; apples c. 330; pork c. 1,090; beef and veal c. 400; fish catch (1976) 279. Livestock (in 000; 1976): cattle 5,471; sheep 1,870; pigs 11,291; goats 42; poultry 48,445.

Industry. Index of production (1975 = 100; 1977) 111. Production (in 000; metric tons; 1977): lignite 253,699; coal 348; electricity (kw-hr) 91,996,000; iron ore (39% metal content) 72; pig iron 2,626; crude steel 6,849; cement 12,103; sulfuric acid 931; petroleum products c. 18,910; fertilizers (nutrient content; 1976–77) nitrogenous 776, phosphate 383, potash 3,161; synthetic rubber 147; passenger cars (units) 167; commercial vehicles (units) 37.

Africa by the East German defense minister, Gen. Heinz Hoffmann. In Ethiopia, Col. Mengistu Haile Mariam thanked the East Germans for their support. "Progressive comrades from the Soviet Union, Cuba, South Yemen, and East Germany," he said, "are fighting at our side." It was well known that the East Germans had been reorganizing the police in Yemen (Aden) and were helping to improve internal security in Ethiopia. The Rhodesians claimed they had found crates of ammunition stamped with the East German flag.

Although East German politicians constantly emphasized the fraternal relationship between East Germany and the U.S.S.R., it was reliably reported that there were considerable differences between the two countries. The policies on the economy and relations with the West advocated by the East German Communist leader, Erich Honecker, were not completely trusted in Moscow. Honecker wanted the closest possible economic relationship with West Germany in order to expand the East German economy. The Soviet Union felt he was paying too much attention to the West and had not always met delivery dates when supplying Soviet customers with capital goods. Honecker believed the Soviet Union must give the East Germans more latitude in conducting their affairs with West Germany. After all, the Soviets tolerated a fair degree of economic liberalization in Hungary, permitted the Romanians to pursue a largely independent foreign policy, and did not seem unduly upset by the influence of the Roman Catholic Church in Poland.

East Germany was finding it more and more difficult to finance urgently needed Western imports. Normally these were financed by so-called compensation deals—goods for goods. But East Germany had a large trade deficit with its fellows in the Council for Mutual Economic Assistance (Comecon) and was desperately trying to close the gap by increasing its exports to them. This was stretching its productive capacity beyond the limit, and as a result East Germany had to pay cash for many imports from the West.

Honecker's position was not thought to be all that secure in the long term. He was faced not only with economic problems but also with outspoken dissidents and growing unrest among East German citizens who wanted better living conditions. He had opponents in the Communist Party leadership, notably the premier, Willi Stoph. However, Honecker was thought to be reasonably safe as long as Leonid Brezhnev, generally regarded as Honecker's patron, remained in power in Moscow.

(NORMAN CROSSLAND)

Federal Republic
of Germany

Germany, Federal Republic of

A country of central Europe, Germany was partitioned after World War II into the Federal Republic of Germany (Bundesrepublik Deutschland; West Germany) and the German Democratic Republic (Deutsche Demokratische Republik; East Germany), with a special provisional regime for

Berlin. West Germany is bordered by Denmark, The Netherlands, Belgium, Luxembourg, France, Switzerland, Austria, Czechoslovakia, East Germany, and the North Sea. Area: 248,629 sq km (95,996 sq mi). Pop. (1978 est.): 61,352,700. Provisional cap.: Bonn (pop., 1978 est., 284,000). Largest city: Hamburg (pop., 1978 est., 1,680,300). (West Berlin, which is an enclave within East Germany, had a population of 1,926,800 in 1978.) Language: German. Religion (1970): Protestant 49%; Roman Catholic 44.6%; Jewish 0.05%. President in 1978, Walter Scheel; chancellor, Helmut Schmidt.

The government's efforts to expand the economy while maintaining stability met with success in 1978. By autumn West Germany's economic indicators appeared to be switched to green. The popularity of the federal chancellor, Helmut Schmidt, was undiminished, although the coalition parties suffered shocks in two Länder (state) elections.

Domestic Affairs. An economic growth rate of almost 3% was achieved in the first half of the year. Confidence rose with sustained improvement in the business climate for industry—and this despite the drastic fall in the dollar exchange rate and a spate of industrial disputes in the spring. By October inflation had fallen to a mere 2.2%, and unemployment was well below the 900,000 mark.

For nearly three weeks in March and April, IG Metall, the metalworkers' union, called out some 85,000 of its members in southwest Germany in a strike for higher pay, eventually settled with an increase of 5%. The employers retaliated by locking out 145,000 workers in the affected plants. At about the same time the printing workers' union, IG Druck und Papier, called a strike of 2,200 workers after talks had broken down over the introduction of new technology. The employers' answer was to lock out 32,000 workers in 500 printing firms. Subsequently, both unions started litigation in the labour courts to have the lockouts declared illegal.

In the Länder elections in Hamburg and Lower Saxony in June, the Free Democratic Party (FDP) failed to clear the 5% hurdle, the proportion of votes necessary to secure parliamentary seats. It polled 4.8% in Hamburg, where it was in coalition with the Social Democratic Party (SPD), and 4.2% in Lower Saxony, where for the previous 18 months it had been in a government led by the Christian Democratic Union (CDU). Much more than the two larger parties, the Free Democrats suffered from the intervention of groups of environmentalists, standing for the first time in a state election. These groups, supported by many young people, polled 3.9% in Lower Saxony (18% in the constituency where a nuclear fuel reprocessing plant was planned) and 4.5% in Hamburg.

Later, however, the Free Democrats rallied. In the Länder elections in Hesse and Bavaria in October, they managed to comfortably retain their parliamentary representation, polling 6.6 and 5.9%, respectively. This was a tense time for the federal government, formed by a coalition of the SPD and FDP. A change of power in Hesse, ending 33 years of Social Democrat rule, would have increased the opposition's majority in the Bundesrat (the upper house of the federal Parliament, in which the Länder are represented) to two-thirds. Since this would be sufficient to block bills passed by the Bundestag (lower house), it would have placed all government legislation at the mercy of the CDU. The Free Democrats' survival indicated that the federal government was likely to stay the course until the next federal election in 1980.

The Hesse result revived discussion about the long-term strategy of the Christian Democrats. The CDU had emerged once again as the strongest single party in the Hesse state parliament, and once again it was deprived of office by a coalition of Social Democrats and Free Democrats. As in Hesse, so in Bonn. As long as the Free Democrats remained allied to the Social Democrats, there seemed little likelihood of a change of power at the federal level.

The alternative, it was argued, would be to form a fourth party, or rather to extend the operations of the CDU's sister party, the Christian Social Union (CSU) led by Franz-Josef Strauss, beyond the borders of its native Bavaria. The theorists calculated that the CDU, fighting its own battle and therefore less susceptible to conservative CSU influence, would attract Free Democrats and centrist Social Democrats. Strauss's party, fielding candidates federally, would offer a political home for anyone to the right of the CDU. Then, assuming they had an absolute majority, the two parties would form a coalition. Strauss and the CDU chairman, Helmut Kohl, agreed to defer discussion of this and other plans until the spring of 1979. Meanwhile, Strauss was settling down in his new role as premier of Bavaria.

After five and a half years as minister of defense, Social Democrat Georg Leber resigned in February following the disclosure of illegal electronic surveillance by the Military Counterintelligence Service. Under Leber's supervision, the defensive capability of the Bundeswehr and its reputation at home and abroad had continued to grow, but in the months preceding his resignation it had seemed that he no longer had his large and bewilderingly complex department in hand. In December 1977 a Frankfurt newspaper had published a report that three alleged spies in the department had betrayed secret information of "unprecedented value" to East Germany. Shortly afterward the Federal Constitutional Court set aside the decision, for which Leber bore the political responsibility, to stop questioning the sincerity of conscientious objectors, which had made CO status much easier to obtain. Moreover, five young officers who were dismissed from the service by his orders in 1977 after an anti-Semitic incident were subsequently reinstated by a Munich court. Leber was replaced as defense minister by Hans Apel, former minister of finance. In late November the chief of staff, Gen. Harald Wust, resigned, claiming that Apel had not consulted him sufficiently about proposed changes in the organization of the Bundeswehr.

There was also a change at the Interior Ministry. Werner Maihofer resigned as minister in June over a major bungle by the security authorities in the hunt for terrorists. A tip-off about the possible whereabouts of Hanns-Martin Schleyer, the industrialist who was kidnapped (and later murdered) by terrorists in 1977, had been lost by the federal criminal investigation department.

The new minister, Gerhard Baum, formerly Maihofer's deputy, said in September that terrorist groups, far from being subdued by massive police operations and a hunt in which the whole country had been urged to take part, were attracting new recruits. Germany had been spared major terrorist attacks since the Schleyer kidnapping, but in September police came across evidence that something big was being planned. The operation had probably been postponed, if not abandoned, after one of the most wanted terrorists, Willy Peter Stoll, was shot by police in a Düsseldorf restaurant on September 6 and two apartments used as terrorists' headquarters were discovered. Stoll's death reduced to 14 the number of known and most wanted terrorists who were still free. Four others, arrested in Yugoslavia in May, were released in November after Yugoslav authorities turned down Germany's request for extradition. These figures were no guide to the true numerical strength of the terrorist groups, however.

The Bundestag, called from summer recess in August, lifted immunity from one of its members, Uwe Holtz, the Social Democrat chairman of the

Protesters carrying signs saying "Nazis Raus" ("Nazis Go Away") demonstrated in Frankfurt am Main when an NPD (a neo-Nazi party) meeting was scheduled to be held there.

KEYSTONE

German Literature:
see Literature

Bundestag's Development Aid Committee, who was suspected of espionage. He and Joachim Broudré-Gröger, the personal assistant of Egon Bahr, general secretary of the SDP, had been accused of spying by a Romanian defector, Gen. Ion Pacepa. Both were cleared and no charges were brought.

The government came under increasing pressure to get tough with the odd assortment of right-wing extremist splinter groups classified by the authorities as the New Right. In a raid on a NATO camp in north Germany in February, a group of young Nazis overpowered two Dutch guards and stole four automatic weapons. Bank robberies in Hamburg and Cologne were also laid at the door of the New Right. There were estimated to be between 80 and 90 right-wing extremist groups, of which only a dozen or so had a membership of above 250. They were not to be confused with the neo-Nazi National Democratic Party, which after reaching a peak of strength in the late 1960s had shriveled to political insignificance.

After a six-month struggle for political survival, Hans Filbinger, Christian Democrat prime minister of Baden-Württemberg, resigned in August, the victim of disclosures about his past as a naval judge during World War II. His handling of two cases against German sailors in 1945 had prompted the playwright Rolf Hochhuth to comment that "it must be assumed he [Filbinger] is a free man only because those who knew him kept their silence." Filbinger, who fought a libel action against Hochhuth and lost, had passed death sentences on three German naval deserters in 1945 and had condemned another sailor to death in 1943 for looting.

Foreign Affairs. The mid-July meeting in Bonn of the heads of government of the world's seven leading capitalistic nations attracted much publicity and aroused many hopes. In the event, it produced only undertakings and promises. What the world wanted—and indeed expected—from the summit was a correction of two imbalances: between rapid U.S. and slow European growth, and between huge Japanese and West German balance of payments surpluses and other countries' deficits. The U.S. said it would introduce measures to

cut oil consumption and imports by the end of the year. Japan would limit its exports and boost its imports and would double its official aid within three years. France pledged to increase deficit spending to push up its growth rate. Italy promised to create investment. Canada aimed to achieve higher growth and output. Britain made no new commitments beyond saying that it would continue its present policy, which was designed to curb inflation and to reduce unemployment. West Germany promised to reflate by up to 1% of its gross national product, and within a couple of weeks the German government announced tax cuts worth DM 7 billion and increases of about DM 3.5 billion in public spending.

The Bonn summit was preceded by a conference of heads of government of the European Economic Community (EEC) in Bremen. The Nine decided to press ahead with attempts to find a way of bringing about a closer integration of their currency systems. The aim was to coordinate economic policy inside the Community and at the same time form a currency bloc. Further steps toward that end were taken at a meeting held in Brussels in December. (See EUROPEAN UNITY.)

U.S. Pres. Jimmy Carter's talks in Bonn with Chancellor Schmidt in July helped improve their somewhat uneasy personal relationship. There had been differences about the president's stand on human rights, about West Germany's sale of the entire nuclear fuel cycle to Brazil, and about U.S. charges that West Germany had not done enough to stimulate its economy and so assist world recovery. Finally, there was President Carter's deferment in April of a decision to produce the neutron bomb. This prompted Franz-Josef Strauss, a former minister of defense, to comment that for the first time since World War II the U.S. president had "openly knuckled under to a Russian tsar." With 20 Soviet armoured divisions stationed in East Germany, the West Germans were naturally sensitive to the slightest suspicion that the Americans might be weakening in their resolve to defend Western Europe. In July Carter was at pains to allay these suspicions. (See West Berlin, below.)

Soviet leader Leonid I. Brezhnev visited Bonn in

GERMANY, FEDERAL REPUBLIC OF

Education. (1977–78) Primary, pupils 6,014,226, teachers (1976–77) 239,626; secondary, pupils 3,493,023, teachers (1976–77) 166,347; vocational, pupils 2,307,573, teachers 61,912; higher, students 913,308, teaching staff (1973–74) 93,841.

Finance. Monetary unit: Deutsche Mark, with (Sept. 18, 1978) a free rate of DM 1.98 to U.S. $1 (DM 3.87 = £1 sterling). Gold, SDR's, and foreign exchange (June 1978) U.S. $38,224,000,000. Budget (federal; 1977 actual): revenue DM 157,060,000,000; expenditure DM 179,280,000,000. Gross national product (1977) DM 1,193,300,000,000. Money supply (June 1978) DM 206.2 billion. Cost of living (1975 = 100; June 1978) 112.

Foreign Trade. (1977) Imports DM 235,180,000,-000; exports DM 273,610,000,000. Import sources: EEC 49% (The Netherlands 13%, France 12%, Italy 9%, Belgium-Luxembourg 8%, U.K. 5%); U.S. 7%. Export destinations: EEC 45% (France 12%, The Netherlands 10%, Belgium-Luxembourg 8%, Italy 7%, U.K. 6%); U.S. 6%; Austria 5%; Switzerland 5%. Main exports: machinery 31%; motor vehicles 14%; chemicals 12%; iron and steel 6%; textiles and cloth-

ing 5%. Tourism (1976): visitors 7,890,000; gross receipts U.S. $3,211,000,000.

Transport and Communications. Roads (1976) 469,568 km (including 6,435 km autobahns). Motor vehicles in use (1976): passenger 19,180,500; commercial 1,260,000. Railways: (1976) 31,809 km (including 10,680 km electrified); traffic (1977) 38,408,000,000 passenger-km, freight 55,747,-000,000 net ton-km. Air traffic (1977): 15,904,000,-000 passenger-km; freight 1,268,742,000 net ton-km. Navigable inland waterways in regular use (1976) 4,-283 km; freight traffic 45,804,000,000 ton-km. Shipping (1977): merchant vessels 100 gross tons and over 1,975; gross tonnage 9,592,314. Shipping traffic (1977): goods loaded 32,376,000 metric tons, unloaded 104,159,000 metric tons. Telephones (Jan. 1977) 21,161,800. Radio licenses (Dec. 1976) 20,244,000. Television licenses (Dec. 1976) 18,481,-000.

Agriculture. Production (in 000; metric tons; 1977): wheat 7,181; barley 7,497; oats 2,723; rye 2,-538; potatoes 11,347; sugar, raw value c. 2,940; apples 1,175; wine c. 956; cow's milk 22,522; butter c.

536; cheese 692; beef and veal 1,318; pork 2,563; fish catch (1976) 454. Livestock (in 000; Dec. 1976): cattle 14,496; pigs 20,589; sheep 1,091; horses used in agriculture (1975) 342; chickens 88,085.

Industry. Index of production (1975 = 100; 1977) 110.4. Unemployment (1977) 4.5%. Fuel and power (in 000; metric tons; 1977): coal 84,840; lignite 122,-911; crude oil 5,408; coke (1976) 32,780; electricity (kw-hr) 335,400,000; natural gas (cu m) 18,050,000; manufactured gas (cu m) 13,420,000. Production (in 000; metric tons; 1977): iron ore (32% metal content) 2,470; pig iron 29,148; crude steel 38,983; aluminum 1,132; copper 440; lead 310; zinc 488; cement 32,-238; sulfuric acid 4,680; cotton yarn 178; woven cotton fabrics 173; wool yarn 54; man-made fibres 844; petroleum products (1976) 98,468; fertilizers (1976–77) nitrogenous 1,290, phosphate 733, potash 2,217; plastics and resins 6,241; synthetic rubber 433; passenger cars (units) 3,794; commercial vehicles (units) 314. Merchant vessels launched (100 gross tons and over; 1977) 1,373,000 gross tons. New dwelling units completed (1977) 409,000.

Soviet Pres. Leonid I. Brezhnev, accompanied by West German Chancellor Helmut Schmidt, responded to crowds that greeted him at Cologne-Bonn airport May 4, when Brezhnev arrived for talks with the West German government.

May. German sources said the talks went beyond discussion of bilateral problems alone; Brezhnev and Schmidt talked about the wider issues of disarmament, the Middle East, and Africa. Nothing concrete emerged, however. The highest ranking Chinese politician ever to visit West Germany, Fang Yi, a member of China's Politburo, had talks in Bonn in October and made a tour of industrial concerns and research centres. China placed orders for mining equipment worth DM 8 billion with West German firms.

West Germany's reappraisal of its relations with black Africa resulted in a greater sensitivity about its considerable industrial involvement in South Africa. In 1977 the government had narrowed the terms of export credits and reaffirmed its support for the EEC's code of behaviour on employment standards in South African subsidiary companies, but many Germans were not satisfied that the code was being applied. The more positive side of Germany's African policy was the attempt to develop closer relations with the larger pro-Western African states; Schmidt visited Nigeria and Zambia in June. West Germany had many past blunders to make up for, however. There was the long and, to many African minds, still unexplained record of German nuclear cooperation with South Africa. More recently, as Schmidt discovered in June, Africans had become suspicious about the activities of a Frankfurt-based firm that was testing launching systems for commercial satellites in Zaire. In fact, the rocket range had shown little sign of turning into the strategic missile centre described by East German propaganda.

West Berlin. President Carter visited West Berlin in July and renewed the U.S. pledge to defend the city. He said he believed there had been a great improvement in the Berlin situation since the four-power Berlin agreement was signed in 1971, but he did not think anything could hide the deprivation of human rights exemplified by the Berlin Wall.

Brezhnev and Schmidt also briefly discussed Berlin during the Soviet leader's visit to Bonn in May. The Soviet leaders were irritated by the fact that the chancellor accompanied leading statesmen or heads of state who visited Berlin. In Moscow's view this violated the four-power agreement because it implied some degree of federal jurisdiction

over the city. Despite the four-power agreement, the Soviets had not in practice abandoned their claim that West Berlin was a separate entity that should maintain direct relationships with East Germany, the Soviet Union, and other states.

On November 16, East and West Germany signed a major traffic agreement that included the construction of a four-lane highway between West Berlin and Hamburg. The arrangement, which would facilitate travel for residents of West Berlin, was hailed as an important political breakthrough and the most important step for the city since the four-power agreement. Under the pact, West Germany would pay U.S. $3 billion to East Germany over the next ten years to defray the cost of construction.

The mayor of West Berlin, Dietrich Stobbe, was elected chairman of the Bundesrat in October. The office rotated among the premiers of the Länder and was held for a year. The Soviet Union protested the election on the grounds that West Berlin was not a state of the Federal Republic of Germany.

(NORMAN CROSSLAND)

Ghana

A republic of West Africa and member of the Commonwealth of Nations, Ghana is on the Gulf of Guinea and is bordered by Ivory Coast, Upper Volta, and Togo. Area: 238,533 sq km (92,098 sq mi). Pop. (1978 est.): 10,775,000. Cap. and largest city: Accra (pop., 1975 est., 716,600). Language: English (official); local Sudanic dialects. Religion (1960): Christian 43%; Muslim 12%; animist 38%. Chairmen of the National Redemption Council and of the Supreme Military Council in 1978, Gen. Ignatius Kutu Acheampong and, from July 5, Lieut. Gen. Fred W. K. Akuffo.

On July 5, 1978, six and a half years after he had seized power from the elected government of Kofi Busia (see OBITUARIES), Gen. Ignatius Acheampong resigned as head of state. Power passed to Lieut. Gen. Fred W. K. Akuffo (see BIOGRAPHIES), until then chief of defense in the Supreme Military Council (SMC). Acheampong's resignation was probably forced by hostile elements within the ruling elite and reflected disagreements over the eco-

Ghana

GHANA

Education. (1975–76) Primary, pupils 1,157,303, teachers 38,381; secondary, pupils 527,113, teachers 20,892; vocational, pupils 10,964, teachers 661; teacher training, students 10,847, teachers 939; higher, students 9,079, teaching staff 1,103.

Finance. Monetary unit: cedi, with (Sept. 18, 1978) a free rate of 2.70 cedis to U.S. $1 (5.30 cedis = £1 sterling). Gold, SDR's, and foreign exchange (June 1978) U.S. $311.1 million. Budget (1976 actual): revenue 899.4 million cedis; expenditure 1,497,800,000 cedis. Gross domestic product (1975) 6,044,000,000 cedis. Money supply (June 1978) 3,-057,700,000 cedis. Cost of living (Accra; 1975 = 100; Dec. 1977) 282.

Foreign Trade. (1976) Imports c. 972 million cedis; exports 924.3 million cedis. Import sources (1975): U.S. 16%; U.K. 15%; West Germany 11%; Nigeria 7%; Japan 6%; Libya 5%. Export destinations (1975): U.K. 15%; U.S. 11%; The Netherlands 10%; Switzerland 8%; West Germany 8%; Japan 7%; U.S.S.R. 7%; Yugoslavia 5%. Main exports: cocoa 56%; timber 8%.

Transport and Communications. Roads (1974) 35,015 km. Motor vehicles in use (1976): passenger 64,000; commercial (including buses) 46,000. Railways: (1976) 953 km; traffic (1972) 431 million passenger-km, freight 305 million net ton-km. Air traffic (1976): 194 million passenger-km; freight 4.4 million net ton-km. Shipping (1977): merchant vessels 100 gross tons and over 79; gross tonnage 182,696. Telephones (Jan. 1977) 66,300. Radio receivers (Dec. 1975) 1,060,000. Television receivers (Dec. 1975) 33,000.

Agriculture. Production (in 000; metric tons; 1977): corn c. 366; cassava (1976) c. 1,800; taro (1976) c. 1,400; yams (1976) c. 800; millet c. 70; sorghum c. 86; tomatoes c. 100; peanuts c. 100; oranges c. 170; cocoa c. 320; palm oil c. 15; timber (cu m; 1976) 30,025; fish catch (1976) 238. Livestock (in 000; 1976): cattle c. 1,100; sheep c. 1,800; pigs c. 400; goats c. 2,000; chickens c. 11,000.

Industry. Production (in 000; metric tons; 1976): bauxite 267; petroleum products c. 1,095; gold (troy oz) 534; diamonds (metric carats) 2,283; manganese ore (metal content) c. 128; electricity (kw-hr) c. 4,226,000.

nomic crisis and the question of a return to civilian rule. The March referendum on "union government" (a nonparty military-civilian administration), widely believed to have been rigged to give a favourable result, had been followed by extensive civil disobedience. Stringent austerity measures taken by the Akuffo government, including sharp devaluations of the cedi in August and September, led to widespread strikes in November and the declaration of a state of emergency.

After taking over, Akuffo announced the release of detainees held since the referendum and promised that the SMC would yield to a popularly elected government in 1979. In December, following local nonparty elections in which the turnout was disappointingly low, it was announced that political parties would be permitted to function after Jan. 1, 1979.   (MOLLY MORTIMER)

Golf

The 1978 golfing year was particularly memorable for the victories of South African Gary Player in the Masters tournament at Augusta, Ga., and Jack Nicklaus in the British Open at the Royal and Ancient Golf Club at St. Andrews in Scotland. Neither had won a major championship for several years, and it seemed that their long careers as champions might be coming to an end. But at Augusta Player soared to his third Masters success in extraordinary fashion, and after two frustrating years Nicklaus reclaimed his kingdom with mas-

Gibraltar:
see Dependent States

Glass Manufacture:
see Industrial Review

Gliding:
see Aerial Sports

terful golf at St. Andrews. With this victory Nicklaus had won each of the four major titles (Masters, U.S. Open, British Open, and Professional Golfers' Association [PGA]) at least three times since 1962.

As for Player, he set Augusta alight with his last round of 64, which equaled the course record. Going into the final round he was seven shots behind Hubert Green, the leader, but starting at the ninth hole he made seven birdies in ten holes. Especially outstanding was his putting, as he used a smoother stroke than in previous years. Suddenly, Player was in contention, and when he holed a long putt down the wickedly fast slope of the 18th green he took the lead with a score of 277.

First of the challengers was Tom Watson, defending his title, but his tee shot to the 18th finished amid newly planted trees; he could not make the green and finally missed from ten feet in his attempt to tie Player. Needing birdies to tie, Green and Rod Funseth finished in an agony of suspense the like of which even Augusta had rarely known. Green hit a superb eight-iron shot to within four feet of the hole, but after Funseth, who had played with great resource and courage, had narrowly missed his putt, Green also failed. Both joined Watson in a three-way tie for second place, at 278.

Exactly a week later the seven-strokes-behind formula worked again for Player in the Tournament of Champions. This time Severiano Ballesteros of Spain, just 21 and already launched on a prodigious season, was the leader. He had shocked the professional world by winning at Greensboro, N.C., the week before the Masters, and after three rounds he was four strokes ahead of the field. However, his game came apart in the wind on the last day, and Player's closing 67 gained him 12 strokes on the young Spaniard.

As if this were not enough, Player confirmed himself as the comeback golfer of the year by winning the Houston Open, his third victory in as many weeks. Three strokes behind Andy Bean with a round to go, he overtook him with a birdie on the 71st hole and won by a shot. This great stretch of golf established Player as a strong favourite for the U.S. Open at the Cherry Hills Country Club near Denver, Colo. After three rounds he was only a stroke behind Andy North and well ahead of Nicklaus, Watson, Tom Weiskopf, Lee Trevino, and others, but the pressure was mounting. The only major title Player had not won twice or more was the Open, and he desperately wanted to join Nicklaus as the only man to have achieved that distinction. But early in the last round his hopes faded, and the contest finally concerned North, J. C. Snead, and Dave Stockton.

North, one of the tallest players on the tour, was soon five strokes ahead of everyone, but the closing holes were difficult, especially for a man on the threshold of his first great triumph. He began to stumble, his lead vanished, and finally he needed a five on the last hole, one of the toughest par fours imaginable, to beat Snead and Stockton. Twice in the rough and then hitting into a bunker, he faced the prospect of a ghastly collapse. But his nerve held, and after a fine sand shot his putt of five feet was probably the bravest of the year. His winning score of 285 was one over par. Everyone expected a lower total, but the difficulty of the rough restrained everyone, and only a handful broke 70.

For the first time in Open history, in the U.S. or Britain, a player was penalized two strokes for slow play. Robert Impaglia was followed for four holes with his every shot timed by stopwatch, and the penalty was imposed. This had a salutary effect on the subsequent play. Before the event the U.S. Golf Association had declared its intention to penalize without warning.

When Nicklaus won his second British Open at St. Andrews in 1970, it marked his emergence from three lean years. By coincidence the same was true in 1978, when people were starting to wonder whether his ambition and powers of concentration were beginning to wane. Nicklaus swiftly gave the lie to such imaginings by playing some of the most solid golf from tee to green of his life. For three days his putting was unremarkable, but at the beginning of the final round he was only one stroke behind Watson and Peter Oosterhuis of Great Britain, and even with Ben Crenshaw, Simon Owen of New Zealand, and Isao Aoki of Japan. Bob Shearer of Australia and Nick Faldo, by far the most promising young British player, were also in the hunt. The British Open was fulfilling its reputation as the most international of championships, and financially it was the most successful British Open ever. More than 120,000 watched the week's play, beating the previous record by some 30,000; the weather was ideal for golf, and in the minds of thousands for whom Nicklaus had become a hero in the Bobby Jones-Arnold Palmer mold, the right man won.

It was entirely fitting that Nicklaus should win. It was his 17th successive appearance, and his influence on the success of the championship had surpassed even that of Palmer. And the manner of his victory was that of the supreme golfer of the age. Unlike the U.S. Open, where the challengers backed off, at St. Andrews they kept coming. Great finishes by Crenshaw (283) and Ray Floyd (283) and the steadiness of Tom Kite (283) set the pace, and when Owen (283), playing with Nicklaus, chipped in at the 15th for his second straight birdie, he was one ahead. Though Nicklaus must have recalled Watson holing in from off the green at the 15th in his triumph the previous year, his reaction was magnificent. With the wind helping play on the homeward holes for the first time in the championship, his greater experience and control told. A birdie at the 16th to Owen's bogey and a marvelous approach putt at the Road Hole (the 17th), where Owen overshot the green, soon brought triumph to Nicklaus with a score of 281.

The Road Hole, as usual, proved one of the most difficult par fours in existence. Twice in successive rounds Palmer, when going well, bombarded the adjacent hotel with out-of-bounds drives. Ballesteros did likewise when leading late on the second day, and Tsuneyuki Nakajima of Japan took a nine there, with four shots in the bunker by the green.

As if to emphasize that golf is a humbling game, Nicklaus, after winning a tournament in the U.S. the following week, failed to make the cut in the PGA championship at Oakmont, Pa. The winner

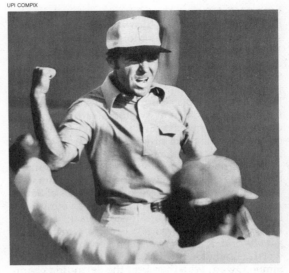

Gary Player of South Africa gave a clenched fist victory salute after winning the Masters competition in Augusta, Georgia, on April 9 with a record final round of 64.

was John Mahaffey, who beat Jerry Pate and Watson on the second hole of a sudden-death play-off. On a course the legendary toughness of which was eased by rains, Watson seemed set for victory when he led Pate by five strokes and Mahaffey by seven with a round to go. But on the final 18 little went right for Watson while Mahaffey was playing the round of his life, putting exceptionally well to score a 66. Pate shot a 68 and Watson a 73. Mahaffey's victory delighted everyone, for he had suffered lean times with injuries, a divorce, and loss of form.

For the second successive year Tom Watson,

Nancy Lopez of Roswell, New Mexico, one of the year's winningest woman golfers, smiles after her fifth straight win on the Ladies Professional Golf Association tour, a record she set by capturing the Bankers Trust Classic at Locust Hill Country Club in Rochester, New York, in June.

UPI COMPIX

with $362,429, was the leading money winner by a huge margin and was also winner of the Vardon stroke-average title. Gil Morgan's victory in the World Series of Golf at Akron, Ohio, after a sudden-death play-off with Hubert Green, was worth $100,000 and gained him second place on the earnings list. Morgan then won the Pacific Masters in Japan and lost a play-off to Bobby Wadkins in the first European Open at Walton Heath, near London. The victory was a first for Wadkins and came on the same day that brother Lanny was winning an Australian tournament 12,000 mi away.

The European professional scene was dominated by Ballesteros, whose winnings of approximately £50,000 were easily a record. Dale Hayes of South Africa was second, followed by three young British players, Nick Faldo, Howard Clark, and Ken Brown. Ballesteros was favoured to win the Colgate World Match Play championship at Wentworth, England, but lost in the second round to Simon Owen, who then beat the defending champion, Graham Marsh of Australia. Floyd, runner-up the previous year, fell to remarkable golf from Aoki, whose short game had few peers in the world. By defeating Owen in the final, Aoki gained the first victory in Europe for a Japanese player.

Bob Clampett of California, age 18, took the U.S. amateur world by storm except for losing to Scott Hoch in a semifinal of the National Amateur. John Cook beat Hoch in the final, and these three, together with Jay Sigel, won the Eisenhower Trophy for the U.S. in the world team championship in Fiji. Canada placed second, and Clampett had the low individual score. The women's event produced a tremendous finish, with Australia beating Canada by one stroke. Cathy Sherk, who had become the second Canadian to win the U.S. women's title, was the lowest individual scorer by four strokes. The U.S. shared fourth place with Britain. In British amateur golf Peter McEvoy became only the fifth player to defend the championship successfully.

Nancy Lopez (*see* BIOGRAPHIES) dominated the women's tournament scene. Her victory in the European Ladies' PGA championship at Sunningdale, Berkshire, England, in August was her eighth of the season. The victory pushed her money winnings to $153,097, breaking the record for a woman in a single season. Her skill, power, and appealing manner made her the greatest attraction to appear in women's golf for many years. Another engaging young player, Hollis Stacy, in only her fourth year on the tour, successfully defended her U.S. Open championship by defeating Joanne Carner and Sally Little of South Africa by one stroke.

The World Cup, played in Hawaii, was won by the U.S. team of Mahaffey and North.

(P. A. WARD-THOMAS)

Greece

A republic of Europe, Greece occupies the southern part of the Balkan Peninsula. Area: 131,990 sq km (50,962 sq mi), of which the mainland accounts for 107,194 sq km. Pop. (1977 est.): 9,284,-000. Cap. and largest city: Athens (pop., 1971, 867,000). Language: Greek. Religion: Orthodox. President in 1978, Konstantinos Tsatsos; prime minister, Konstantinos Karamanlis.

The main preoccupation of the government of Konstantinos Karamanlis in 1978 was to accelerate Greece's entry into the European Economic Community (EEC). While the negotiations were in progress, the prime minister frequently traveled to the EEC capitals. On December 31, following a 17-hour negotiating session in Brussels, agreement was reached on the terms for Greek membership, and it was expected that the membership treaty would be signed early in 1979.

An improved climate between Greece and Turkey followed a meeting between their prime ministers at Montreux, Switz., in March, when it was decided to continue bilateral discussions in the hope of resolving their disputes peacefully. The two prime ministers renewed this resolve when they met again in Washington, D.C., in May during the NATO summit conference.

The détente with Turkey survived two controversial developments: the rejection by Greece of the long-awaited Turkish proposals for a Cyprus settlement in April (*see* CYPRUS) and the decision of the U.S. Congress in August to lift the embargo on arms deliveries imposed on Turkey in 1975 because of the invasion of Cyprus. The lifting of the arms embargo was advocated by the U.S. on the grounds that Turkey was likely to make concessions for a Cyprus solution only after the embargo had been rescinded; the Greek leaders, however, were pessimistic. Although little progress was achieved toward resolving the Greek-Turkish differences on the continental shelf and in the air space of the Aegean Sea, both sides agreed to persevere with their dialogue and to avoid confrontation.

The dispute with Turkey over the Aegean became a major obstacle to the reintegration of Greece into the military structure of NATO, from which it had partly withdrawn after the Turkish invasion of Cyprus in 1974. Reintegration was to be achieved under the face-saving guise of a "special status," which enabled the Greek armed forces to remain under national command except in case of an East-West war. However, Turkey insisted that, before it consented to such an arrangement, NATO's operational jurisdiction in the Aegean, which had been exclusively Greek until 1974, should be redistributed between Greece and Turkey. Greece rejected this as reflecting Turkey's claims for control of the seabed and air space in the eastern half of the Aegean, which would disregard the rights of Greek islands in that area. In September Greece threatened to break off the discussions with NATO and to stay completely out of the organization's military wing if Turkey's objections were not brushed aside.

While trying to patch relations with NATO, Greece also sought to cultivate better links with the Soviet Union and China. Georgios Rallis, the foreign minister, visited Moscow for one week in September, the first Greek foreign minister to do so since the Bolshevik Revolution. China's foreign

Greece

minister, Huang Hua, visited Athens in the same month and signed a cultural agreement.

On the domestic scene, the rapid disintegration of the Democratic Centre Union (DCU) party after its debacle in the November 1977 elections and the resignation of its leader, Georgios Mavros, gave the prime minister's New Democracy Party scope to widen its appeal and recruit some talent from the centre. In May Karamanlis broadened his Cabinet by naming the leader of the New Liberals, Konstantinos Mitsotakis, minister of coordination and appointing a deputy who defected from the DCU as minister of finance. Shortly afterward, several DCU deputies and politicians declared allegiance to Karamanlis, while others decided to remain independent. This left the DCU under its new leader, Ioannis Zidgis, with only 5 of its original 15 deputies.

The question, of course, was whether DCU followers would move to the right, with the defecting deputies, or whether they had not already drifted toward the left and, more particularly, toward Andreas Papandreou's Panhellenic Socialist Movement (Pasok), which had emerged from the elections as the main opposition party, with strong

anti-EEC and anti-NATO platforms. In the nationwide local elections held on October 15 and 22 the leftist opposition managed to retain control of several large municipalities.

On June 20 an earthquake hit Salonika in northern Greece, causing one block of apartments to collapse and at least one-quarter of the buildings in the city to suffer severe damage. Forty-nine persons were killed, all but nine under the ruins of apartment buildings. The city's population of 700,000 fled to the outskirts or the countryside for several months, and the city's economic activity was crippled.

In order to redress the economic damage of the earthquake the government imposed additional tax levies to raise an extra 10 billion drachmas. However, this new burden coincided with increases in the price of gasoline and with stringent regulations against tax evasion, provoking an outcry from the business community. The government argued that illicit, untaxed profits were the cause of excessive consumer expenditure, which was defeating its efforts to contain the rate of inflation below 10% annually and keep the balance of payments on an even keel. Public spending was cut by 20%, but defense expenditure, which absorbed 23.8% of the budget, remained unaffected.

Alleged sex scandals involving prelates, as well as increasing church reactions against government decisions on such questions as abortion and divorce, encouraged a public demand for a complete separation of the Orthodox Church of Greece and the state. At the end of the year discussions were in progress with the church leadership for a takeover by the state of four-fifths of the real property owned by the church and monasteries. In exchange, the state would assume full responsibility for paying the salaries of 9,000 clergy.

(MARIO MODIANO)

Grenada

A parliamentary state within the Commonwealth of Nations, Grenada, with its dependency, the Southern Grenadines, is the southernmost of the Windward Islands of the Caribbean Sea, 161 km N of Trinidad. Area: 344 sq km (133 sq mi). Pop. (1976 est.): 110,000, including Negro 53%, mixed 42%, white 1%, and other 4%. Cap.: Saint George's (pop., 1974 est., 6,600). Language: English. Religion: Christian. Queen, Elizabeth II; governor-general in 1978, Leo de Gale; prime minister, Sir Eric Gairy.

Throughout 1978 Grenada's economy remained in a precarious state, despite improved performance by the island's banana, nutmeg, and tourist industries. On August 12 the government unveiled a five-year plan known as Operation Bootstring after the successful Puerto Rican Operation Bootstrap. The program identified areas for development in which the government was prepared to take shares to the value of 90%.

On January 4 Innocent Belmar, a Cabinet minister, was shot dead. At a subsequent trial the accused were acquitted, with the victim's mother giving evidence for the defense. In September

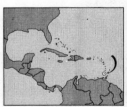

Grenada

Great Britain:
see United Kingdom

Greek Orthodox Church:
see Religion

Greenland:
see Dependent States

GREECE

Education. (1975–76) Primary, pupils 937,123, teachers 31,016; secondary, pupils 546,016, teachers 18,719; vocational, pupils 132,591; higher, students 117,246, teaching staff 6,180.

Finance. Monetary unit: drachma, with (Sept. 18, 1978) a free rate of 37.06 drachmas to U.S. $1 (72.62 drachmas = £1 sterling.) Gold, SDR's, and foreign exchange (June 1978) U.S. $1,020,100,000. Budget (1977 actual): revenue 205,960,000,000 drachmas; expenditure 241,740,000,000 drachmas. Gross national product (1977) 982.2 billion drachmas. Money supply (June 1978) 189,440,000,000 drachmas. Cost of living (1975 = 100; June 1978) 144.7.

Foreign Trade. (1977) Imports 252,150,000,000 drachmas; exports 101,280,000,000 drachmas. Import sources: EEC 42% (West Germany 15%, Italy 9%, France 6%, U.K. 6%); Japan 15%; U.S. 5%; Saudi Arabia 5%. Export destinations: EEC 48% (West Germany 21%, Italy 7%, France 7%, U.K. 5%, The Netherlands 5%); Saudi Arabia 5%; U.S. 5%; Libya 5%. Main exports: fruit and vegetables 21%; textile yarns and fabrics 10%; clothing 8%; chemicals 6%; tobacco 6%; cement 5%; petroleum products 5%; iron and steel 5%; aluminum 5%. Tourism (1976): visitors 3,845,000; gross receipts U.S. $823 million.

Transport and Communications. Roads (1976) 36,574 km (including 91 km expressways). Motor vehicles in use (1976): passenger 495,689; commercial 218,835. Railways (1976): 2,479 km; traffic 1,583,000,000 passenger-km, freight 844 million net ton-km. Air traffic (1977): 4,354,000,000 passenger-km; freight 58,320,000 net ton-km. Shipping (1977): merchant vessels 100 gross tons and over 3,344; gross tonnage 29,517,059. Telephones (Jan. 1977) 2,180,200. Radio receivers (Dec. 1974) 2.5 million. Television receivers (Dec. 1975) 1,140,000.

Agriculture. Production (in 000; metric tons; 1977): wheat c. 1,716; barley c. 702; oats c. 81; corn c. 556; rice c. 92; potatoes c. 936; sugar, raw value (1976) c. 355; tomatoes c. 1,560; watermelons (1976) c. 550; apples c. 260; oranges 582; lemons 202; peaches (1976) c. 330; olives c. 1,370; olive oil 254; wine c. 452; raisins c. 149; tobacco 112; cotton, lint c. 152. Livestock (in 000; Dec. 1976): sheep c. 8,135; cattle (1975) c. 1,300; goats c. 4,524; pigs (1975) c. 750; horses (1975) c. 160; asses (1975) c. 280; chickens c. 29,000.

Industry. Production (in 000; metric tons; 1977): lignite 22,406; electricity (kw-hr) 17,860,000; petroleum products (1976) c. 10,890; bauxite 2,879; magnesite (1976) 1,251; cement 10,557; sulfuric acid 1,098; fertilizers (1976–77) nitrogenous 273; phosphate 169; cotton yarn 87. Merchant vessels launched (100 gross tons and over; 1977) 85,000 gross tons.

GRENADA
   Education. (1971–72) Primary, pupils 29,795, teachers 884; secondary, pupils 4,470, teachers 182; vocational, pupils 497, teachers 10; teacher training, students 101, teachers 6.
   Finance and Trade. Monetary unit: East Caribbean dollar, with (Sept. 18, 1978) a par value of ECar$2.70 to U.S. $1 (free rate of ECar$5.30 = £1 sterling). Budget (1977 est.) balanced at ECar$58 million. Foreign trade (1977): imports ECar$84.8 million; exports ECar$38.4 million. Import sources (1973): U.K. 27%; Trinidad and Tobago 20%; U.S. 9%; Canada 8%. Export destinations (1973): U.K. 33%; West Germany 19%; The Netherlands and possessions 14%; U.S. 8%; Belgium-Luxembourg 5%. Main exports: nutmeg 42%; cocoa 23%; bananas 22%. Tourism (1976): visitors 24,600; gross receipts *c.* U.S. $15 million.

Grenada was openly criticized at the Commonwealth Parliamentary Association meeting in Kingston, Jamaica, because members of the opposition were not included in its delegation.

Prime Minister Sir Eric Gairy maintained the island's links with Chile, sending policemen to be trained at a military academy in Santiago. He also established ties with Taiwan (which he visited) and Yugoslavia. During the year Sir Eric delivered speeches at a number of international forums, including the UN, where he called for further research into unidentified flying objects. Toward the end of the year, Grenada signed the UN Covenant on Human Rights. (DAVID A. JESSOP)

Guatemala

A republic of Central America, Guatemala is bounded by Mexico, Belize, Honduras, El Salvador, the Caribbean Sea, and the Pacific Ocean. Area: 108,889 sq km (42,042 sq mi). Pop. (1978 est.): 6,620,500. Cap. and largest city: Guatemala City (pop., 1973, 700,500). Language: Spanish, with some Indian dialects. Religion: predominantly Roman Catholic. Presidents in 1978, Kjell Eugenio Laugerud García and, from July 1, Fernando Romeo Lucas García.

The general elections of March 5, 1978, resulted in a victory for Gen. Fernando Romeo Lucas García (*see* BIOGRAPHIES), joint presidential candidate of the Partido Institucional Democrático and the Partido Revolucionario, who was inaugurated on July 1. Guatemala maintained its claim to Belize (formerly British Honduras), and no solution to the future of the territory was in sight. However, diplomatic relations with Panama, broken off in May 1977 because of the latter's support for Belizean independence, were resumed on August 17.

From 1975 the economy had shown a satisfactory rate of expansion, despite the 1976 earthquake. The growth in gross domestic product for 1977 was estimated at 11%, and a 7% rate was projected for 1978. The rise was stimulated by good export proceeds from coffee and cotton, foreign currency earned by tourism, and the inflow of earthquake relief funds with a related high level of investment expenditure. The trade and payments balances were favourable, standing respectively at $48 million and $149.2 million in 1977, but lower coffee prices might have an adverse effect in 1978.

Major investment projects included the Agua-

Guatemala

Guinea

Guiana:
see Dependent
   States; Guyana;
   Suriname

GUATEMALA
   Education. (1975) Primary, pupils 706,146, teachers 18,-475; secondary, vocational, and teacher training, pupils 135,801, teachers 7,335; higher (University of San Carlos only), students 22,881, teaching staff 1,411.
   Finance. Monetary unit: quetzal, at par with the U.S. dollar (free rate, at Sept. 18, 1978, of 1.96 quetzales to £1 sterling). Gold, SDR's, and foreign exchange (June 1978) U.S. $790.4 million. Budget (1977 actual): revenue 603 million quetzales; expenditure 644 million quetzales. Gross national product (1976) 4,294,000,000 quetzales. Money supply (May 1978) 694 million quetzales. Cost of living (1975 = 100; June 1978) 135.4.
   Foreign Trade. (1976) Imports 838.9 million quetzales; exports 782.1 million quetzales. Import sources: U.S. 36%; Japan 11%; Venezuela 8%; West Germany 7%; El Salvador 7%. Export destinations: U.S. 35%; El Salvador 11%; West Germany 11%; Japan 8%; Costa Rica 5%; Nicaragua 5%. Main exports: coffee 32%; sugar 14%; cotton 12%; chemicals 8%; textile yarns and fabrics *c.* 5%.
   Transport and Communications. Roads (1975) 13,450 km (including 824 km of Pan-American Highway). Motor vehicles in use (1976): passenger 82,700; commercial (including buses) 50,100. Railways (1976): 904 km; freight traffic 117 million net ton-km. Air traffic (1977): 143 million passenger-km; freight 6.8 million net ton-km. Telephones (Jan. 1974) 53,000. Radio licenses (Dec. 1975) 262,000. Television receivers (Dec. 1975) 110,000.
   Agriculture. Production (in 000; metric tons; 1977): corn 756; sorghum 93; sugar, raw value *c.* 540; tomatoes *c.* 76; dry beans 67; bananas *c.* 550; coffee *c.* 147; cotton, lint 135. Livestock (in 000; March 1977): sheep 612; cattle (1976) *c.* 2,270; pigs (1976) *c.* 840; chickens 11,239.
   Industry. Production (in 000; metric tons; 1976): petroleum products 714; cement 445; electricity (kw-hr) *c.* 1,250,000.

capa and Chixoy hydroelectric schemes and the Eximbal nickel plant with a capacity of 28 million lb a year. The government was also encouraging petroleum exploration, although at mid-1977 production amounted to only 3,200 bbl a day, compared with previous estimates of 6,000 bbl.

(CHRISTINE MELLOR)

Guinea

A republic on the west coast of Africa, Guinea is bounded by Guinea-Bissau, Senegal, Mali, Ivory Coast, Liberia, and Sierra Leone. Area: 245,857 sq km (94,926 sq mi). Pop. (1978 UN est.): 4,762,000; however, a census held on Dec. 30, 1972, reported 5,143,284 persons, of whom 1.5 million were living abroad. Cap. and largest city: Conakry (pop., 1974, 412,000). Language: French (official). Religion: mostly Muslim. President in 1978, Ahmed Sékou Touré; premier, Louis Lansana Beavogui.

The visit of Pres. Valéry Giscard d'Estaing of France to Guinea on Dec. 20-22, 1978, marked the resumption of cooperation between the two countries after 20 years' estrangement. Guinea's reconciliation with its neighbours was formally endorsed on March 18, 1978, in Monrovia, Liberia, when Pres. Ahmed Sékou Touré (*see* BIOGRAPHIES) met the presidents of Togo, The Gambia, Senegal, and Ivory Coast at a "unity summit," with Liberia's president acting as host.

During the year Guinea also tried to attract Western financial investment in exploiting its extensive mineral resources. In May President Touré withdrew permission, granted five years earlier, for the Soviet Union to use an air base near Conakry, and in August he received an important U.S.

delegation led by Richard Moose, assistant secretary of state for African affairs. At the same time, Touré tried to project a more liberal image and encouraged debate within the ruling party. However, the exiled opposition claimed that several thousand political prisoners were still being held; in November it announced that Diallo Telli, former national minister and secretary-general of the Organization of African Unity (1964–72), had died in February 1977 while in detention, after being subjected to torture and deprived of adequate food and water.   (PHILIPPE DECRAENE)

Guinea-Bissau

An independent African republic, Guinea-Bissau has an Atlantic coastline on the west and borders Senegal on the north and Guinea on the east and south. Area: 36,125 sq km (13,948 sq mi). Pop. (1978 est.): 949,400. Cap. and largest city: Bissau (metro. area pop., 1970, 71,200). President in 1978, Luis de Almeida Cabral; premiers, Maj. Francisco Mendès to July 7, Constantino Teixeira, and, from September 28, João Bernardo Vieira.

The changing pattern of rainfall, with ever longer dry periods, continued to have serious effects on Guinea-Bissau's economy in 1978. The hope that self-sufficiency in food production would be achieved by 1977 was frustrated, and attempts to use the rivers for irrigation met with little success. Rice shipments from the U.S. at the beginning of 1978 provided some relief. The U.S. also promised financial assistance for the fishing industry; Norway, Sweden, and The Netherlands promised

help; and there was further financial aid from West Germany. France, too, continued to take an interest and encouraged economic links between Guinea-Bissau and Senegal.

It had been hoped that the ruling African Party for the Independence of Guinea-Bissau and Cape Verde (PAIGC) would approve a merger with Cape Verde at its November 1977 congress, but this did not take place. Differences between the two countries proved insurmountable, and PAIGC was not wholly clear about the political ideology it should adopt. A visit to Portugal by Pres. Luis Cabral in January resulted in agreements on a variety of cultural matters.

On July 7 the premier, Maj. Francisco Mendès, a founding member of PAIGC, was killed in a car accident. He was succeeded by Constantino Teixeira, who on September 28 was replaced by João Bernardo Vieira.   (KENNETH INGHAM)

See also Cape Verde.

Guinea-Bissau

Guyana

A republic and member of the Commonwealth of Nations, Guyana is situated between Venezuela, Brazil, and Suriname on the Atlantic Ocean. Area: 215,000 sq km (83,000 sq mi). Pop. (1978 est.): 845,000, including (1970) East Indian 51.8%; African 31.2%; mixed 10.3%; Amerindian 4.9%. Cap. and largest city: Georgetown (pop., 1970, 63,200). Language: English (official). Religion: Protestant, Hindu, Roman Catholic. President in 1978, Arthur Chung; prime minister, Forbes Burnham.

Guyana

On April 10, 1978, the Guyanese government passed legislation that would permit the constitution to be changed by a two-thirds parliamentary majority instead of by popular referendum. The measure, which was aimed at introducing a socialist constitution, was itself passed by a referendum (97.4% yes vote) in July, after a sporadically violent campaign. The move was attacked by opposition parties, professional associations, and the church as heralding the beginning of a one-party state, and it was alleged that the ballot had been rigged. A constituent assembly was currently examining proposals for the new constitution. Prime Minister Forbes Burnham announced that general elections, due in October 1978, would not be held before October 1979.

The economy remained the chief preoccupation of the People's National Congress government. After 12 months of talks with the International Monetary Fund, the IMF agreed to provide a one-year standby credit of U.S. $19.5 million, plus a loan of $27.3 million. Guyana became an associate member of the Soviet bloc's Council for Mutual Economic Assistance (Comecon). In April Burnham and senior officials visited the Soviet Union, East Germany, North Korea, and Britain to discuss trade assistance and political matters. A Chinese delegation led by Vice-Premier Keng Piao visited Guyana in July. Moves to solve Guyana's border dispute with Suriname and Venezuela began late in the year.

In November Guyana was the scene of one of the most bizarre and horrifying incidents of recent times. In the mid-1970s the Rev. Jim Jones (*see* OBITUARIES), founder and leader of the People's Temple in San Francisco, had taken most of his congregation to Guyana, where they established a commune, Jonestown, near the Venezuelan border. Complaints of abuses within the cult had failed to bring action by either U.S. or Guyanese authorities.

Late in November Rep. Leo Ryan of California, while visiting the commune as a result of such complaints, was approached by several members who asked his help in escaping. As Ryan's party prepared to leave from the nearby Port Kaituma airstrip, they were attacked by Temple members, and Ryan and four others, including three newsmen, were killed. When Guyanese troops reached Jonestown the following day they found that everyone in the commune was dead. The death toll was placed at 913.

As the story was pieced together from the physical evidence and the accounts of the few survivors who escaped into the jungle, Jones, who had become increasingly paranoid, told his followers that since some of Ryan's party were still alive and would bring the authorities, they must now all commit suicide. (Mock suicide rituals had been enacted previously as "tests of loyalty.") Children were poisoned first, and adults were told to consume a soft drink containing cyanide. There were indications that members who resisted were injected with cyanide or shot. Jones himself died of a gunshot wound that, according to the report of the autopsy, was "consistent" with suicide.

The bodies were returned to the U.S. by Air Force transport and taken to Dover Air Force Base, Delaware, for identification. However, survivors accused of crime in connection with the affair were to be tried in Guyana. The FBI, which began an investigation of the case, had jurisdiction only insofar as assassination of a congressman is a federal crime. A large cache of money, jewelry, and arms had been found at Jonestown, and there were reports that as much as $10 million to $15 million in Temple funds had been placed in various bank accounts around the world. It was expected that unraveling the cult's finances would be a lengthy process.   (DAVID A. JESSOP; DAPHNE DAUME)

GUYANA

Education. (1973–74) Primary, pupils 132,023, teachers 4,077; secondary, pupils 64,314, teachers 2,830; vocational, pupils 3,539, teachers 159; higher, students 2,307, teaching staff 231.

Finance. Monetary unit: Guyanan dollar, with (Sept. 18, 1978) a par value of Guy$2.55 to U.S. $1 (free rate of Guy$5 = £1 sterling). Budget (1976 est.): revenue Guy$450 million; expenditure Guy$664 million.

Foreign Trade. (1977) Imports Guy$800.9 million; exports Guy$663 million. Import sources (1976): U.S. 29%; U.K. 23%; Trinidad and Tobago 19%. Export destinations (1976): U.K. 27%; U.S. 20%; Algeria 8%; Trinidad and Tobago 7%; West Germany 6%; Jamaica 6%. Main exports: bauxite 38%; sugar 28%; alumina 11%; rice 10%.

Agriculture. Production (in 000; metric tons; 1977): rice *c.* 300; sugar, raw value *c.* 372; oranges (1976) *c.* 11; copra *c.* 5. Livestock (in 000; 1976): cattle *c.* 280; sheep *c.* 108; goats *c.* 62; pigs *c.* 125; chickens *c.* 10,131.

Industry. Production (in 000; 1976): bauxite (metric tons) 3,203; alumina (metric tons) 247; diamonds (metric carats) *c.* 30; electricity (kw-hr) 396,000.

Gymnastics and Weight Lifting

Gymnastics. In the world gymnastics championships at Strasbourg, France, in October the Soviet Union continued its reign as the leading nation. Its gymnasts won the women's team title and placed second to Japan in the men's events, captured the gold and bronze medals in the men's combined competition, and swept the women's combined medals.

At the tournament the United States won its first gold medals in major international competition since the 1932 Olympic Games and for the first time in 19 world championships. Kurt Thomas won the men's floor exercise, and Marcia Frederick was gold medalist in the uneven parallel bars event. National combined champion Kathy Johnson, eighth in the combined, was a co-winner of a bronze medal in the floor exercise.

Japan had a mixture of veterans and new faces on its winning men's team, which narrowly outscored the U.S.S.R. 579.85 to 578.95. Gold medals were won by Shigeru Kasamatsu on the horizontal bar; Eizo Kenmotsu, parallel bars; and Junichi Shimizu, vault. The other men's gold medals were taken by two 1976 Olympic champions; Nikolai Andrianov of the Soviet Union won the combined title and also earned a gold medal on the rings, while Zoltan Magyar of Hungary continued to dominate the pommeled horse event.

In women's competition the U.S.S.R. featured a powerful team of newcomers to international competition, with only Nelli Kim and Maria Filatova as holdovers from the Olympic championship squad. Elena Mukhina, European runner-up, clearly earned the gold medal in the combined event over teammates Kim and Natalia Shaposhnikova. Mukhina shared the gold medal with Kim in the floor exercise, and Kim won the vault title to repeat her 1976 Olympic triumph. Besides Marcia Frederick, the only other gymnast to crack the Soviet stranglehold was Romania's Nadia Comaneci, star of the 1976 Olympic Games, who won the balance beam event. Although Comaneci was accorded a series of perfect "tens" at Montreal, neither she nor any other gymnast received "tens" in the world championships.

There was little change in the order of finish in the team competitions since the Olympic Games. The first four women's teams, the Soviet Union, Romania, East Germany, and Hungary, had finished in the same order in the Olympics as did the first three men's teams, Japan, the Soviet Union, and East Germany.

A significant change was made in the judging regulations. No judge was permitted to evaluate an athlete from his or her nation. In addition, the gymnasts' routines were, in part, judged on risk, originality, and virtuosity, which tended to reward the flair exhibited by U.S. competitors.

Weight Lifting. Even with a loss in the superheavyweight class, Soviet weight lifters dominated the world championships at Gettysburg, Pa., in

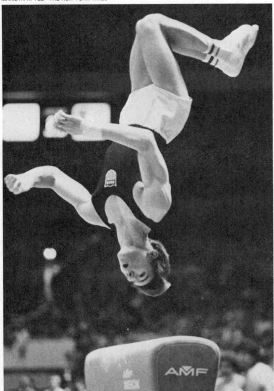

Kurt Thomas of Indiana State appeared destined for a nasty headache during the world gymnastics championships in Strasbourg, France, in October. Thomas, however, won the gold medal in the men's floor exercise, the first gold won by a U.S. athlete in world gymnastics competition in nearly half a century.

October. In the superheavyweight competition Vasily Alekseyev, Soviet six-time world champion, suffered a leg injury and withdrew after the snatch lift. His successor was Jurgen Heuser of East Germany, who lifted a total of 417.8 kg (920.25 lb) in his two efforts. When the awards were tallied, nine Soviet lifters had accounted for five gold and four silver medals to win the team title. Cuba finished second, followed by East Germany and Hungary. The highest finisher for the U.S. was a seventh place by Kurt Setterberg in the 100-kg class.

Only two Olympic Games champions from 1976 won titles. Nikolai Kolesnikov of the Soviet Union repeated in the featherweight division, and David Rigert of the U.S.S.R., considered by many the world's finest lifter pound-for-pound, moved up from middle heavyweight to win the new 100-kg class. Succeeding Rigert in the middle heavyweight division was Rolf Milser of West Germany.

Only three world records were set, all by Yuri Vardanian of the U.S.S.R. in the light heavyweight class. These were individual snatch, the individual clean and jerk, and total lift, 372.5 kg (820.5 lb). Yuri Zaitsev of the U.S.S.R., Olympic runner-up and 1977 runner-up in the heavyweight class, won the title in that event. Poland's Olympic lightweight champion, Zbigniew Kaczmarek, finished second to Yanko Rusev of Bulgaria.

(CHARLES ROBERT PAUL, JR.)

Haiti

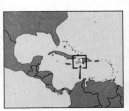

Haiti

The Republic of Haiti occupies the western one-third of the Caribbean island of Hispaniola, which it shares with the Dominican Republic. Area: 27,-700 sq km (10,695 sq mi). Pop. (1978 est.): 4,784,-000, of whom 95% are Negro. Cap. and largest city: Port-au-Prince (pop., 1976 est., 652,900). Language: French (official) and Creole. Religion: Roman Catholic; Voodooism practiced in rural areas. President in 1978, Jean-Claude Duvalier.

Political stability prevailed in Haiti during 1978. In January there was concern over the negation of press freedom following an assault by unknown assailants on the father of the editor of an opposition newspaper, *Jeune Presse*. The owners suspended its publication, and the association of Haitian journalists called for protection for reporters. The U.S. administration indicated in June that it would reduce economic and financial aid to Haiti unless a more determined effort was made to bring about political liberalization and ameliorate the living conditions of lower-income groups.

Official U.S. sources forecast the 1978 economic growth rate at 4–4.5%, compared with just over 1% in 1977, when the island was plagued by drought. The rate of inflation in January–September 1977 was 3.4%, as against 9.4% in 1976. The balance of payments recorded an overall surplus of U.S. $11 million.in 1977; transfers by Haitians living abroad rose to more than $80 million in the year ended September 1977, and foreign assistance disbursements for public-sector investments totaled $59 million during that period.

(ROBIN CHAPMAN)

HAITI

Education. (1976–77) Primary, pupils 266,302, teachers 8,432; secondary, pupils 55,816, teachers 3,324; vocational, pupils (1975–76) 5,356, teachers (1975–76) 474; higher, students 5,195, teaching staff 697.

Finance. Monetary unit: gourde, with (Sept. 18, 1978) a par value of 5 gourdes to U.S. $1 (free rate of 9.80 gourdes = £1 sterling). Gold, SDR's, and foreign exchange (March 1978) U.S. $44.8 million. Budget (total; 1977 actual) revenue 807 million gourdes; expenditure 973 million gourdes. Cost of living (Port-au-Prince; 1975 = 100; Jan. 1978) 110.5.

Foreign Trade. Imports (1976) c. 1,060,000,000 gourdes; exports (1977) 746.5 million gourdes. Import sources: U.S. c. 56%; Netherlands Antilles c. 7%; Canada c. 6%; Japan c. 6%. Export destinations (1976): U.S. 61%; France 10%; Italy 6%; Belgium-Luxembourg 5%. Main exports (1974–75): coffee 23%; toys and sporting goods 14%; sugar 14%; bauxite 13%; textile fibres 9%; essential oils 6%.

Transport and Communications. Roads (1976) c. 4,-000 km. Motor vehicles in use (1974): passenger 15,700; commercial (including buses) 1,500. Railways (1976) c. 240 km. Telephones (Jan. 1977) 17,800. Radio receivers (Dec. 1975) 93,000. Television receivers (Dec. 1975) 13,000.

Agriculture. Production (in 000; metric tons; 1977): rice c. 100; sweet potatoes (1976) c. 92; cassava (1976) c. 147; corn c. 250; sorghum c. 220; sugar, raw value (1976) c. 60; dry beans c. 46; bananas (1976) c. 53; mangoes c. 282; coffee c. 33; sisal c. 13. Livestock (in 000; 1976): pigs c. 1,771; cattle c. 747; goats c. 1,384; sheep c. 81; horses c. 387.

Industry. Production (in 000; metric tons; 1976): cement 232; bauxite (exports) 739; electricity (kw-hr; 1975–76) 137,000.

Handball:
see Court Games

Harness Racing:
see Equestrian Sports

Health and Disease

General Developments. In popular terms perhaps the outstanding medical event of the year was the birth of the first so-called test-tube baby, Louise Joy Brown (*see* BIOGRAPHIES). Delivery by cesarean section took place on July 25 in Oldham General Hospital, Lancashire, England, under the supervision of Patrick Steptoe, a gynecologist who for some years had collaborated with physiologist Robert Edwards from the University of Cambridge. Edwards had spent the better part of his professional lifetime perfecting techniques for fertilizing surgically obtained human eggs with sperm on the laboratory bench. A decade ago he reported success in this effort, believing that his research would allow women rendered infertile by virtue of blocked fallopian tubes to bear children if a way could be found to implant the fertilized egg in the womb. The difficulty lay in preparing the lining of the womb to accept the implantation. Although he and Steptoe appeared to have solved this problem, by the end of the year they had not published full details of the achievement, and some experts wondered whether their success, which followed many failures, might have owed more to chance than to understanding.

That single success, nevertheless, was sufficient to prompt efforts in the U.S. to rescind a 1975 ban on the use of federal funds for research on fertilizing human eggs outside the body. A majority of witnesses argued before a House of Representatives subcommittee that the positive benefits of such techniques now outweighed any possible

hazards. Several days of public hearings were also conducted by the newly created Ethics Advisory Board of the Department of Health, Education, and Welfare (HEW) to stimulate national debate.

In a related development a Florida housewife was awarded $50,000 damages in a lawsuit that charged that her opportunity to become the mother of a test-tube baby had been prevented in 1973 when the chief of obstetrics and gynecology at Columbia-Presbyterian Medical Center, New York City, "maliciously and wantonly" destroyed a laboratory-fertilized culture of her eggs and her husband's sperm. The defendant, Raymond L. Vande Wiele, said that the procedure was untried at the time and that he had acted to prevent an "unauthorized human experiment." (*See* LAW: *Special Report*.)

After two years of intensive investigation the federal Center for Disease Control (CDC), Atlanta, Ga., announced discovery of an environmental source for the organism responsible for Legionnaires' disease, the mysterious lung ailment so named after an outbreak in 1976 in connection with an American Legion state convention in Philadelphia that took the lives of 29 persons and made scores of others ill. The bacterium was found in water in two locations within Bloomington, Ind.—an air-conditioning cooling tower and a nearby creek. The cooling tower was located on the roof of the Indiana Memorial Union, a hotel and social centre where 19 victims of Legionnaires' disease had been housed within two weeks before becoming ill. A large outbreak also occurred in the garment district of New York City in the summer of 1978. The CDC predicted that more cases would be reported in other cities in the years ahead because of the growing ability to identify the organism.

No major developments affected the position of coronary heart disease and cancer as the two major causes of death in the developed nations. Latest figures for the U.K., however, suggested that, as in the U.S., incidence of coronary heart disease might have passed its peak. No firm explanation for the apparent improvement emerged, but experts felt that public awareness of the factors favouring heart attacks had increased and that a tendency, at least among men, to reduce consumption of tobacco, alcohol, and such foods as dairy products, eggs, refined sugar, and fatty meats might be having some effect. The small decline in heart attacks among British men had not been matched by a similar fall among women, whose smoking habits were found not to have altered over the preceding three or four years.

A study of an antigout drug, Anturane, carried out in 26 centres in the U.S. and Canada showed that this preparation appeared to reduce sudden deaths in the months following a heart attack by about 50%. Another Canadian trial suggested that aspirin could produce significant reductions in the risk of a stroke occurring in men who had suffered a transient interference with the supply of blood to the brain. This occurs when brain vessels are affected by the same kind of degenerative process that causes coronary heart disease. Aspirin, which reduces the tendency of the blood to clot, had al-

The World Health Organization, after 20 years of intensive effort, has finally concluded that eradicating malaria everywhere in the world is not an achievable goal for the near future.

ready been shown to reduce the risk of further trouble following a heart attack. In Britain 20,000 doctors aged 50–77 were asked to take either aspirin or a placebo daily for "a few years" without knowledge of which regimen they would be following. The incidence of strokes among those volunteering for the new study would be noted in an attempt to test the theory that a safe daily dose of aspirin could offer significant protection.

The U.S. surgeon general's office reported that smoking was becoming a growing hazard for women. Since 1950 the death rate from lung cancer among men aged 45–64 had doubled, but it had quadrupled among women in the same age group. The first surgeon general's report, issued in 1964, cited the lung cancer hazard of cigarette smoking only for men; for women the data were insufficient to yield similar evidence. Speaking on the 14th anniversary of that report, HEW Secretary Joseph Califano announced a stepped-up drive against smoking. In view of mounting evidence that Pill users who smoked were at increased risk of death from circulatory disease, the label for oral contraceptives was altered to include an appropriate warning.

Catching most health officials by surprise, a prominent U.S. government scientist, Gio Batta Gori of the National Cancer Institute (NCI), announced that some low-tar cigarettes on the market could be smoked in moderation with tolerable risk. Surgeon General Julius Richmond rejected the idea of any safe level of smoking, as did the American Cancer Society and the American Heart Association, and HEW Secretary Califano expressed fear that the report might encourage new smokers.

A letter from the surgeon general to 400,000 U.S. physicians warned about delayed hazards among workers exposed to asbestos since World War II. A sampling showed about 7% of asbestos workers in industry contracted asbestosis, an irreversible lung disease. Another 7% developed a fatal form of cancer affecting the lining of the chest and abdominal cavity. Among exposed workers who smoked, the risk of cancer was 92 times higher than for smokers in other industries. During World War II 4.5 million shipyard workers were exposed to asbestos, and in the past 30 years 3.5 million to 6.5 million others had occupational exposure.

The U.S. government cautioned that very low caloric diets, particularly liquid protein diets, were potentially harmful and should not be used by those seeking to lose weight except under medical supervision. The Food and Drug Administration (FDA) initially reported 16 deaths and a number of severe illnesses among those who had subsisted solely on this diet for weeks or months. The diet came to public attention following publication of a book, *The Last Chance Diet*, in 1976.

Deaths from narcotics overdose dropped 39% in 1977 among 24 U.S. cities surveyed, a phenomenon the Drug Enforcement Administration (DEA) attributed to economics. A decline in the supply of heroin boosted the price of the drug habit to an average of $84 a day, compared with $64 the previous year. The DEA said it could not yet determine if the drop was part of a long-term trend.

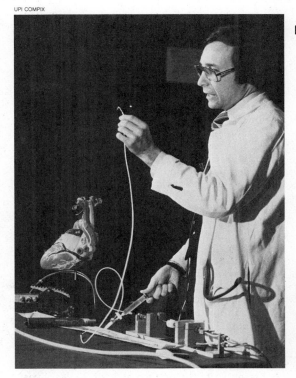

UPI COMPIX

Simon Stertzer, head of the hemodynamics laboratory of Lenox Hill Hospital in New York City, shows a balloon-tipped catheter which helps unclog heart arteries in some patients. In cases where it can be used, it replaces coronary bypass surgery.

International Aspects. Infectious diseases continued to show that their conquest was far from complete. For some years the World Health Organization (WHO) had been announcing the imminent eradication of smallpox from the world. In December 1977 an international commission decided to declare Bangladesh free of smallpox. Four months later WHO experts felt able to suggest that the last case of smallpox had been seen in the Horn of Africa, and the organization offered a reward for a report of a new case anywhere. As it happened, the next confirmed case occurred not in a remote village of a third world country but at the University of Birmingham in England. The victim was a worker at the university Medical School, where smallpox virus was preserved in culture for research purposes. The case closely paralleled an accident in 1973 in which two Londoners died of the disease after a laboratory technician became infected from a culture kept at the London School of Hygiene and Tropical Medicine. Tragically, Henry Bedson, the virologist in charge of the Birmingham laboratory, killed himself within days of the accident and before any cause for the escape of virus particles had been established.

In November 1977 the FDA approved a pneumonia vaccine developed at the University of California, offering promise that effective protection against bacterial pneumonia might eventually be given to all children as a matter of course. An ominous aspect of this development was the support that it gave to findings that certain antibiotics were losing their power to control some of the previously common and dangerous infectious diseases, and that their continued containment would have to depend either upon new techniques or upon refinements of the old.

Controversy in Britain over the practice of vaccinating children against whooping cough continued, with some experts claiming that routine and widespread protection was essential in order to avoid large epidemics and others maintaining that sufficient benefit to the community had not been shown to justify the risk of brain damage to a small proportion of vaccinated infants. Consequently the British government scrapped plans for a publicity campaign scheduled for the autumn of 1977 that urged parents to have their children protected against diphtheria, whooping cough, and poliomyelitis. Six months later and following sustained parliamentary and public pressure, the government announced a compensation plan for children or adults who since July 1948 had been "severely damaged" as a result of a vaccination in the U.K. against diphtheria, tetanus, whooping cough, poliomyelitis, measles, rubella, tuberculosis, and smallpox up to the date that smallpox vaccine had been withdrawn from routine use. Acknowledged victims of vaccine damage would each receive a lump-sum payment of £10,000 without prejudice to any future legal action.

Most authorities regretted the publicity given to the remote, if real, dangers of whooping cough vaccination, because a high level of protection against the disease and other previously common childhood infections was necessary in order to prevent a return to the pattern of 20 or 30 years past. During the summer, for example, an outbreak of poliomyelitis occurred among the inhabitants of the small town of Staphorst in The Netherlands, where the community objected to vaccination on religious grounds. Causing paralysis in more than 20 patients, it was the second serious polio epidemic within the group in eight years.

As widespread resurgence of malaria continued despite 20 years of WHO's eradication campaign, the agency finally admitted that ridding the world of the disease was no longer an achievable goal within the foreseeable future. In India, for example, a highly successful campaign had cut malaria cases from 100 million in 1952 to only 60,000 in 1962, but by the beginning of 1978 this figure had increased a hundredfold. Similar disappointing figures after initial successes were experienced in many other countries, and it was estimated that one-third of the world's population outside China lived in malaria-risk areas.

The return of the disease was due largely to developing resistance to pesticides among malarial mosquitoes. In many countries the organism responsible for malignant malaria, the most dangerous form of the disease, was also becoming increasingly resistant to chloroquine, the standard drug of treatment. As in previous years, doctors in malaria-free countries were warned to be on the lookout for importation of the disease by air travelers. On the positive side successful vaccination of laboratory animals against some malarial forms offered encouragement that an effective treatment for humans would be found in the near future.

Starting in autumn of 1977 a serious outbreak of Rift Valley fever developed among domestic animals in Egypt, making its first appearance in that densely populated country. A viral disease transmitted from animals to man by a mosquito, it led to some tens of thousands of human infections including nearly 100 deaths. The U.S. Department of Agriculture was among the organizations that supported a crash program for the development of a vaccine to protect animals and thus contain the disease.

Medical Economics. In July U.S. Pres. Jimmy Carter unveiled ten general principles for a national health insurance plan for all Americans to be phased in over an extended period in the 1980s. Implementation would depend on the state of the economy and on other demands being made on the federal budget and the taxpayers. Financing for the plan would come from government funding and contributions from employers and employees, and private insurance companies would be given a significant role.

The principles were formulated to ensure freedom of choice for all Americans in selecting physicians, hospitals, and health delivery systems. They would strengthen competitive forces, adopt aggressive cost-containment measures, substantially increase availability of ambulatory and preventive services, attract personnel to underserved regions, assure consumer representation, and seek to eliminate substandard care for the poor. Carter called on HEW to develop legislation from these principles for presentation to Congress in 1979.

The American Medical Association (AMA) reacted favourably to the president's principles, but organized labour and its champion of an alternate proposal, Sen. Edward M. Kennedy (Dem., Mass.), vigorously opposed them as "a piecemeal approach." They objected to the economic reservations placed upon enactment and on the lack of a guarantee that the program would not be stopped

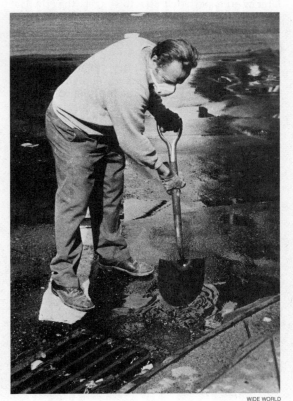

Workmen hosed down and thoroughly cleaned the streets of New York City's garment district after there was an outbreak of Legionnaires' disease in the summer.

WIDE WORLD

in its tracks at any moment. The nation's governors, meeting in Boston, refused to take a stand despite appeals by Kennedy and Carter's aides. Some time before Carter's announcement, Charles Schultze, chairman of the president's Council of Economic Advisers, said it was unrealistic for the administration to propose a new health insurance program at this time.

On a West Coast tour in May, Carter called organized physicians the "major obstacle to progress" in developing a better health care system. "I think doctors care deeply about their patients," he said, "but when they organize into the American Medical Association, their responsibility is to the welfare of doctors and quite often their lobbying groups are the only ones that are heard in state capitals and in the capital of our country."

The U.S. hospital industry voluntarily undertook a 2% reduction in the annual rate of spending increases after the president called for a cost-control bill that would limit hospital revenue increases to 9% a year and place a $2.5 billion ceiling on expenditures, compared with a current $5 billion ceiling. However, the proposal failed to emerge from congressional committees and come before the full Congress. Subsequently HEW asked the industry for a voluntary 9.7% lid on expense increases for 1979.

As a further move toward health cost reduction, a revised version of federal guidelines for health planners called for a maximum of four hospital beds per 1,000 population in any given community. Hospitals that provided care for complicated obstetrical problems needed at least a 75% occupancy to justify continued operation. Moreover, HEW called on Medicare and Medicaid beneficiaries to seek "second opinions" before undergoing recommended hysterectomies, tonsillectomies, and gall bladder surgery. A toll-free hot line was set up to provide local information.

Regulation and Legal Matters. A high proportion of reports relating to cancer published during the year dealt with carcinogens (agents involved in touching off the cancerous process), underscoring current theories that at least 80% of all human cancers are attributable to environmental factors. Studies in the U.S. conducted by the NCI reinforced earlier suspicions that a major component of hair dyes, 2,4-diaminoanisole, caused cancer in experimental animals and aroused interest in a number of other dyes. The FDA proposed that appropriate warnings be printed on the labels of the products involved and that a general warning be displayed in beauty salons.

Although there were an estimated 100,000 chemicals in use, of which some 5% had a known or suspected cancer-causing potential, and although several thousand new names were added to the list of commercial chemicals each year, little agreement emerged concerning the scale or nature of the measures necessary to contain the danger. Nevertheless, during the year the U.S. Environmental Protection Agency, the Health and Safety Executive in the U.K., and the European Economic Commission simultaneously but separately began constructing guidelines for screening new industrial chemicals with a view to introducing legisla-

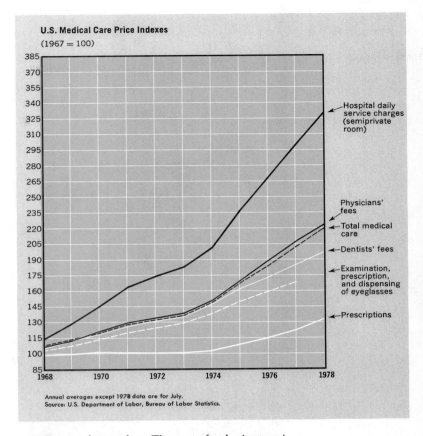

U.S. Medical Care Price Indexes
(1967 = 100)

Hospital daily service charges (semiprivate room)

Physicians' fees

Total medical care

Dentists' fees

Examination, prescription, and dispensing of eyeglasses

Prescriptions

Annual averages except 1978 data are for July.
Source: U.S. Department of Labor, Bureau of Labor Statistics.

tion at some future date. The cost of reducing environmental carcinogens to an "acceptable" level would be enormous, but there seemed no doubt that prevention of avoidable cancers would become a major aim of industrial societies.

The FDA began a nationwide study in March on the possible role of the artificial sweetener saccharin in promoting bladder cancer. The action followed a vote by Congress in 1977 to delay for 18 months a ban on saccharin proposed by the FDA. The ban proposal was made on the basis of a Canadian study that found bladder tumours in the male offspring of rats given a 5% diet of saccharin during gestation. Slated for completion in 1980, the new study was being conducted in the states of New Jersey, Connecticut, Iowa, New Mexico, and Utah and in the Detroit, San Francisco-Oakland, New Orleans, and Atlanta metropolitan areas. Three thousand persons with bladder cancer diagnosed during 1978 and 6,000 randomly chosen healthy individuals living in the same vicinities were to be interviewed and saccharin consumption patterns in the two groups compared. Interestingly, the FDA's National Center for Toxicological Research reported that the cancer risk from saccharin as determined through animal studies was "not persuasive and must be more firmly established by research before the public would accept a ban on saccharin."

Yet another controversial substance, laetrile, which purported to be an effective cancer treatment, was ordered to be made available to terminally ill patients on request of a physician. The U.S. Circuit Court of Appeals in Denver ruled July

Health and Disease

The U.S. Department of Health, Education, and Welfare in April launched a campaign to inform workers who deal with asbestos of the dangers of that substance.

10 that safety and efficacy requirements in the Food, Drug, and Cosmetic Act, under which the FDA had banned laetrile, had no meaning when considered in the context of terminally ill cancer patients. Under such circumstances, the court ruled, laetrile was as effective as anything else. The ruling came in a case appealed from a district court in Oklahoma that had held the FDA ban of laetrile to be in violation of the constitutional rights of the terminally ill. On August 18, however, the FDA recouped when a U.S. appellate court in Chicago upheld a 1977 injunction against a Wisconsin company that had marketed more than $2 million worth of laetrile and apricot pits, from which the substance was extracted. The FDA said it expected the Chicago decision to strengthen chances for a hearing by the U.S. Supreme Court on the agency's power to regulate the drug. In late September, following an NCI Decision Network Committee recommendation, NCI Director Arthur C. Upton called for a clinical trial of laetrile to clear up the vague results obtained from an earlier retrospective study of the medical records of laetrile users.

A drug regulation reform bill introduced in March was pushed for enactment in 1979. Called the "first complete overhaul of federal drug laws since 1938," it included a streamlined system for approving drugs that worked and removing those that did not and a provision for improved patient information on package inserts. Another provision allowed export of drugs awaiting approval for general distribution in the home market.

(DONALD W. GOULD; ARTHUR J. SNIDER)
[424.A.5–6; 424.B.1.a; 425.H; 425.I.2.e.i; 425.J]

MENTAL HEALTH

A British attempt to come to terms with the problem of the mentally ill was made in September 1978 when the government issued a White Paper setting out proposals for a revised Mental Health Act. For many years critics of the law had maintained that patients diagnosed as suffering from mental illness had had their civil rights disregarded in a manner that would not have been tolerated by common criminals. Under existing law, for example, a patient could be detained in a mental hospital or a high-security hospital (which resembled a prison) for life, simply because a psychiatrist had diagnosed mental illness and had decided, with the support of a colleague, that the person concerned was a danger to himself or others.

The White Paper did not propose major reforms concerning compulsory detention but only suggested that patients should have their legal rights clearly explained at the time of detention and that detained patients should have their cases reviewed automatically at regular intervals instead of, as at present, in response to a request for release. It was also suggested that certain kinds of treatment, specifically such measures as psychosurgery and electroconvulsive therapy, should never be administered to voluntarily admitted patients without their consent and should be imposed upon detained patients only in order to save life, prevent violence, or keep a condition from deteriorating—and then only with the support of a second opinion. Some observers felt that the protection given to patients by these recommendations was a sham. An informally admitted patient could be made a detained patient in a matter of minutes, and a "second opinion" could be no more than a signature hastily scribbled on a piece of paper.

Many doctors and scientists believed that such legal and social problems could be eliminated if the biochemical basis of mental disorders could be discovered and if, in turn, drugs could be developed to correct the molecular disturbances that result in disordered thought. As usual, the year produced a crop of papers suggesting various physical explanations for schizophrenia, one of the most serious and commonly diagnosed mental disorders. All manner of chemical abnormalities had been detected in the blood, the urine, or the brains of schizophrenics, but none of the investigations undertaken so far had resulted in the identification of a specific disorder in brain chemistry to which the symptoms and behaviour patterns characteristic of the disease might be imputed.

In one report, for example, which came from Addenbrooke's Hospital in Cambridge and the Institute of Psychiatry at the University of London, investigators measured the concentration of three chemicals—dopamine, glutamic acid decarboxylase, and choline acetyltransferase—in four regions of the brains of diagnosed schizophrenics who had died. Although they found significant differences compared with the brains of mentally "normal" subjects, they could not determine whether such neurochemical abnormalities were related to the illness or were a consequence of prolonged treatment with neuroleptic drugs.

Another recent study at St. Elizabeths Hospital in Washington, D.C., added support to suspicions of a link between abnormally low levels of an enzyme in blood platelets called monoamine oxidase (MAO) and chronic paranoid schizophrenia; MAO was known to be involved in the breakdown of certain chemicals in the body including dopamine and norepinephrine. Other investigators at the University of Florida, who reasoned that if the blood of schizophrenics does contain "schizophrenic factors" then their removal might effect improvement, reported significant remissions in schizophrenics given long-term periodic hemodialysis treatments. The validity of their results, however, remained highly controversial, and the investigators themselves could offer little evidence of exactly what was being filtered out of the blood or how its presence or absence affected human behaviour.

In view of the continuing failure of scientific medicine to meet the problem of mental illness, it was hardly surprising that citizens of the West turned to ancient and traditional methods of treatment for relief. Commenting on the immediate effects of traditional healing methods on the mentally disturbed, T. W. Harding of the World Health Organization's Division of Mental Health said that the results were "almost always striking," and went on to note that "acute psychoses are calmed, family disputes resolved, and hysterical phenomena disappear. More particular emphasis may be placed on their capacity for treating . . . 'acute schizophrenic reactions.' There is a strong impression that the healers' methods are more effective than the techniques of modern psychiatry in this type of illness." (DONALD W. GOULD)
[438.D]

DENTISTRY

As a result of increased productivity and a strong continued emphasis on prevention, during 1978 the U.S. dental profession again succeeded in holding down treatment costs, unlike other sectors of the health care field. The moderate behaviour of dental fees was apparent in the long-term decline in dentistry's portion of the national health bill. In 1955 outlays for dental care were 8.4% of total health expenditures, whereas in 1977 such expenditures amounted to only 6.2%.

Dental scientist Robert Going of Temple University in Philadelphia reported that a well-applied plastic pit and fissure sealant polymerized by ultraviolet light could protect a tooth from further deterioration even if some decay was inadvertently left behind. His study of the teeth of teenaged patients was aimed at determining the viability of bacteria in cavities that had been sealed for five years. Going noted that sealant treatment resulted in an 89% reversal from actively decaying cavities to an inactive state.

At the conclusion of a three-year study conducted in schools of 17 U.S. communities that did not have fluoridated drinking water, scientists at the National Institute of Dental Research (NIDR) in Washington, D.C., reported that a weekly fluoride mouthwash program was an easy, effective, and inexpensive way of reducing cavities. Preliminary results of the study, which involved 75,000 schoolchildren, revealed an average reduction in tooth decay of 35%. James P. Carlos, head of NIDR's National Caries Program, estimated that at least 20 million children in nonfluoridated communities could be helped by the program at an average cost of 50 cents per child per school year.

A chronic, stress-related disorder called bruxism, which involves nocturnal grinding or clenching of teeth, was effectively treated using auditory biofeedback combined with an arousal task. Glenn Clark of the dental school of the University of California at Los Angeles gave each subject in the study a device to use at home during sleep that monitored activity in the masseter muscle, which is responsible for tooth grinding action. When activity in the muscle exceeded the threshold leading to forceful tooth grinding, the device emitted an audible tone to awaken the patient and keep him or her awake for three to five minutes after each occurrence. The study showed that the treatment effectively reduced bruxism in the subjects for at least three weeks. (LOU JOSEPH)
[422.E.1.a; 10/35.C.1]

See also Demography; Life Sciences; Nobel Prizes; Social and Welfare Services.

Historic Preservation

By the end of August 1978, 40 states had ratified or adhered to the International Convention Concerning the Protection of the World Cultural and Natural Heritage. The second session of the World Heritage Committee, established under the terms of the convention, was held in September in Washington, D.C., at the invitation of the U.S. government. The committee approved 12 nominations of outstanding cultural and natural sites to be placed on the World Heritage List. Contributions to the World Heritage Fund amounted to $590,000.

UNESCO, in cooperation with the U.S. government, sent a group of engineers to study the latest U.S. sewage-disposal and conversion plants before finalizing their projects for the Venetian area. However, additional delays occurred in the execution of one of the key projects to protect Venice and its surroundings—control of tidal waters entering the lagoon from the Adriatic. The Italian government rejected all of the proposals submitted because none seemed to meet the criteria for long-term protection against high water while at the same time ensuring that the fragile ecology of the lagoon would not be harmed.

The international campaign to safeguard cultural property in the Kathmandu Valley, Nepal, made considerable progress. During the preparatory period the restoration of Hanuman Dhoka Palace was undertaken under UNESCO/UN Development Program supervision. Experts pre-

STEVE ROSENTHAL—AIA

The renovations of old Faneuil Hall and Quincy Market in Boston attracted many new shops and restaurants and transformed the site into a favourite stopping place for tourists.

A tremendous bomb blast did more than $1 million worth of damage in the Palace of Versailles in June. French Pres. Valéry Giscard d'Estaing had inaugurated the recently restored wing on May 16.

LAURENT MAOUS—GAMMA/LIAISON

pared an inventory of historic buildings, as well as a master plan for the conservation of cultural property. The plight of many monuments and historic buildings in the Kathmandu Valley was exemplified by the case of Swayambhunath Temple (5th century AD). Deforestation of the hill on which it stands had contributed to erosion and the development of slides which now threatened its foundations. Detailed studies were made of the factors leading to slippage following the monsoon rains of 1978, and stabilization and restoration measures were under consideration.

The restoration of older buildings calls for skills that are rapidly disappearing. The Council of Europe began a new project to train artisans in Venice as part of the overall program to revitalize the cultural life of the city. During 1977–78 courses in stone cutting and decorative stucco work were begun under the guidance of skilled artisans. Eventually, courses in other skills required for the restoration of historic buildings would be given.

Another new training project, begun by UNESCO with the help of the International Council of Monuments and Sites, was designed to stimulate the exchange of information on the preservation of historic inner city areas between Western Europeans and Americans and their Eastern European counterparts. Middle-level technical personnel and administrators attended a symposium in June in which the Marais district of Paris and other historic quarters in surrounding cities were used as case studies. Subsequently, those taking part had an opportunity to visit another country (Western Europeans and an American in an Eastern European country and vice versa) to study conservation efforts carried out under a different type of political administration.

In the Marais district of Paris, Greenwich, Fulham, and Kentish Town in Greater London, the historic districts of Kyoto, Japan, and some U.S. cities, an influx of middle-class residents was displacing the inhabitants of former working-class residential areas. In Boston, for example, urban renewal projects had removed most of the low-lying buildings that once surrounded Faneuil Hall and Quincy Market and replaced them with high-rise apartment and office buildings. Renovation of the two historic buildings attracted new stores and restaurants, and Quincy Market, once crowded with pushcarts selling cheap produce to the city's poor, became a major attraction for the middle class and tourists.

Such redevelopments tended to displace the poor or working-class population, which migrated to other marginal districts or to industrial suburbs. Studies showed that such changes often resulted in psychic illnesses and a sense of insecurity among the displaced people. The ideal solution—toward which many renovation projects seemed to be evolving—was to discourage the growth of urban neighbourhoods or small districts composed of a single socioeconomic class (all too frequently the result of zoning regulations, tax structures, or unimaginative development schemes) and to foster a heterogeneous mixture of social classes having complementary and mutually supportive roles.

Growing interest in the conservation of cultural property had its negative aspects. Increasingly, terrorists used attacks on such property to gain public attention. During the spring of 1978, for example, the unoccupied office building of Venice's *Gazzettino* newspaper was bombed and a watchman killed in the first such violent demonstration in Venice. The building, while unimportant architecturally, was near the centre of the historic city. In June a bomb exploded in the Palace of Versailles (France) in the newly restored rooms dedicated to the Napoleonic period. Three of the rooms and their contents (including many paintings of historic importance) were virtually destroyed, and seven others were damaged.

(HIROSHI DAIFUKU)

See also Architecture; Environment; Museums.

Honduras

A republic of Central America, Honduras is bounded by Nicaragua, El Salvador, Guatemala, the Caribbean Sea, and the Pacific Ocean. Area: 112,088 sq km (43,277 sq mi). Pop. (1978 est.): 3,438,388, including 90% mestizo. Cap. and largest city: Tegucigalpa (pop., 1977 est., 316,800). Language: Spanish; some Indian dialects. Religion: Roman Catholic. President in 1978, Col. Juan Alberto Melgar Castro until August 8; thereafter the nation was governed by a three-man military junta headed by Gen. Policarpo Paz García.

A change in the Honduran top command took place on August 8 when the governing Armed Forces Council removed Col. Juan Alberto Melgar Castro as president and transferred power to a three-man junta headed by 46-year-old chief of the armed forces Gen. Policarpo Paz García. The change in command produced no visible shift in the government's basically conservative political orientation. The junta announced that a popular election would be held in 1980, with the intention of returning the country to constitutional government, and began registering voters for that event. Freedom of press and speech continued.

Public accusations of involvement by high government officials in the international drug traffic prompted a government investigation. The first consequence was the suspension of three middle- and low-level Army and police officers.

Several incidents of unrest without bloodshed occurred during the year, including temporary occupation of privately owned rural properties by

Honduras

HONDURAS

Education. (1976) Primary, pupils 483,210, teachers 13,-649; secondary, pupils 78,917; vocational, pupils 2,359; secondary and vocational, teachers 3,910; teacher training, students 2,640, teachers 97; higher (university only), students 12,951, teaching staff 729.

Finance. Monetary unit: lempira, with (Sept. 18, 1978) a par value of 2 lempiras to U.S. $1 (free rate of 3.93 lempiras = £1 sterling). Gold, SDR's, and foreign exchange (June 1978) U.S. $225,450,000. Budget (1977 actual): revenue 457.1 million lempiras; expenditure 454.4 million lempiras. Gross national product (1977) 2,967,000,-000 lempiras. Money supply (March 1978) 478.3 million lempiras. Cost of living (Tegucigalpa; 1975 = 100; June 1978) 120.2.

Foreign Trade. (1977) Imports 1,149,500,000 lempiras; exports 1,008,700,000 lempiras. Import sources (1976): U.S. 44%; Japan 9%; Trinidad and Tobago 7%; Guatemala 6%; West Germany 5%. Export destinations (1976): U.S. 56%; West Germany 12%. Main exports: coffee 33%; bananas 25%; timber 9%.

Transport and Communications. Roads (1976) 9,154 km. Motor vehicles in use (1976): passenger 20,500; commercial (including buses) 30,200. Railways (1976) 1,780 km. Air traffic (1976): 257 million passenger-km; freight 3.6 million net ton-km. Shipping (1977): merchant vessels 100 gross tons and over 63; gross tonnage 104,903. Telephones (Jan. 1977) 19,230. Radio receivers (Dec. 1975) 160,000. Television receivers (Dec. 1975) 47,000.

Agriculture. Production (in 000; metric tons; 1977): corn *c.* 377; sorghum *c.* 62; sugar, raw value (1976) *c.* 88; dry beans *c.* 50; bananas *c.* 1,300; plantains (1976) *c.* 170; oranges *c.* 26; palm oil *c.* 10; coffee *c.* 57; cotton, lint *c.* 5; timber (cu m; 1976) *c.* 3,868. Livestock (in 000; 1976): cattle *c.* 1,800; pigs *c.* 520; horses *c.* 280; chickens *c.* 7,800.

Industry. Production (in 000; metric tons; 1976): petroleum products *c.* 465; silver 0.1; gold (troy oz) 2.3; lead ore (metal content) 20; zinc ore (metal content) 20; electricity (kw-hr) *c.* 590,000.

workers demanding implementation of the government's agricultural reform program and strikes by public health employees for higher wages.

Hurricane Greta swept the nation's Caribbean coast in September, causing extensive damage to coconut and banana crops and destroying many homes. However, there were few human casualties.

(HENRY WEBB, JR.)

Hungary

A people's republic of central Europe, Hungary is bordered by Czechoslovakia, the U.S.S.R., Romania, Yugoslavia, and Austria. Area: 93,032 sq km (35,920 sq mi). Pop. (1978 est.): 10,670,800, including (1970) Hungarian 95.8%; German 2.1%. Cap. and largest city: Budapest (pop., 1978 est., 2,089,500). Language (1970): Magyar 95.8%. Religion (1970): Roman Catholic about 60%, most of the remainder Protestant or atheist. First secretary of the Hungarian Socialist Workers' (Communist) Party in 1978, Janos Kadar; chairman of the Presidential Council (chief of state), Pal Losonczi; president of the Council of Ministers (premier), Gyorgy Lazar.

In an interview given in June 1978 to the *New York Times*, just after the U.S. House of Representatives had granted (May 22) Hungary most-favoured-nation status, Communist Party leader Janos Kadar described U.S.-Hungarian relations as "basically settled." He cited two reasons: pending financial problems had been solved, and the U.S. people had returned to the Hungarian people the

Hungary

Crown of St. Stephen, "a historic symbol of Hungarian thousand-year-old statehood" taken into U.S. custody at the end of World War II. The crown, brought to Budapest by Cyrus Vance, the U.S. secretary of state, and his delegation, was handed over on January 6 to Antal Apro, president of the Hungarian National Assembly.

In June Kadar led a party and government delegation on an official visit to Poland, where they were cordially received. On July 28 Kadar visited the Soviet leader Leonid Brezhnev at Oreanda in the Crimea, and their meeting took place in a reputed "atmosphere of fraternal friendship and complete mutual understanding." In November Kadar paid a three-day state visit to Paris, the first Hungarian Communist leader thus honoured since the 1956 revolution. French Pres. Valéry Giscard d'Estaing greeted him at Orly Airport.

Between the 11th congress of the Hungarian Socialist Workers' Party in March 1975 and January 1978, party membership rose from 754,353 to 816,-593; 20,760 people left the party or were excluded, but some 83,000 joined. In April there were three changes in the party Secretariat: Bela Biszku, aged 57, who had ranked as Kadar's most trusted lieutenant, retired but continued as a Politburo member; Ferenc Havasi, 49, until then a deputy premier, and Mihaly Korom, 51, former minister

of justice, joined the Secretariat. Karoly Nemeth, 56, a secretary since 1974, emerged as a de facto deputy to Kadar. Also in April three new members of the government were appointed: Jozsef Marjai, 55, became deputy premier; Imre Markoja, 47, secretary of state at the Ministry of Justice, became the head of that department; and Istvan Soltesz, 51, became minister of metallurgy and engineering, succeeding the late Tivadar Nemeslaki.

The building of a joint Hungarian-Czechoslovak hydroelectric project on the Danube River between Nagymaros and Gabcikovo, east of Bratislava, Czech., started in the summer; the project included a 750-Mw-capacity power station. At the end of the year an international 750-kv power line linking Vinnitsa in the Ukraine and Albertirsa in Hungary went into operation. Hungary and Yugoslavia agreed to build a system of dams along the Drava River, a Danube tributary that forms a part of the boundary between the two countries; work on the first two dams, at Barcs and Durdevac, was scheduled to start in 1979.

Long-term plans to cope with an increasing flow of traffic across the Danube in Budapest were worked out. They included the building of four more bridges, the widening of the existing six bridges, and the construction of a road tunnel under the river by the end of the century. About 12,800 vehicles an hour crossed the river in each direction. This was expected to double by 1990.

The number of foreigners visiting Hungary rose from 500,000 in 1960 to 12.5 million in 1977. The number of Hungarians traveling abroad reached 4.5 million in the same year.

In July the government took measures against heavy liquor drinking for the second time in the year. Prices for spirits on sale in stores were raised by 25%, and bars were no longer allowed to serve spirits after 9 PM. Alcoholic consumption in Hungary, wine excluded, amounted to more than four litres of pure spirit per capita in 1977 (1 litre = 1.057 quart). (K. M. SMOGORZEWSKI)

HUNGARY

Education. (1977–78) Primary, pupils 1,090,000, teachers 70,007; secondary (1976–77), pupils 95,042, teachers 6,740; vocational (1976–77), pupils 107,439, teachers 7,714; higher, students (1976–77) 64,496, teaching staff 12,579.

Finance. Monetary unit: forint, with (Sept. 18, 1978) a commercial free rate of 37.08 forints to U.S. $1 (72.66 forints = £1 sterling) and a noncommercial (tourist) rate of 18.54 forints to U.S. $1 (36.33 forints = £1 sterling). Budget (1978 est.): revenue 385.9 billion forints; expenditure 389.7 billion forints.

Foreign Trade. (1977) Imports 267,309,000,000 forints; exports 238,590,000,000 forints. Import sources: U.S.S.R. 28%; West Germany 11%; East Germany 8%; Czechoslovakia 6%; Austria 5%. Export destinations: U.S.S.R. 30%; East Germany 9%; West Germany 9%; Czechoslovakia 7%; Poland 5%. Main exports: machinery 22%; motor vehicles 10%; chemicals 9%; meat and meat preparations 7%; fruit and vegetables 5%; iron and steel 5%.

Transport and Communications. Roads (1976) 99,595 km (including 181 km expressways). Motor vehicles in use (1976): passenger 654,794; commercial 125,115. Railways: (1976) 8,187 km; traffic (1977) 13,024,000,000 passenger-km, freight 23,610,000,000 net ton-km. Air traffic (1976): 510 million passenger-km; freight 5.2 million net ton-km. Inland waterways in regular use (1976) 1,302 km. Telephones (Jan. 1977) 1,076,100. Radio licenses (Dec. 1976) 2,559,000. Television licenses (Dec. 1976) 2,477,000.

Agriculture. Production (in 000; metric tons; 1977): corn c. 6,150; wheat c. 5,312; barley c. 750; rye c. 147; potatoes c. 1,400; sugar, raw value c. 410; cabbages (1976) c. 203; tomatoes c. 450; onions c. 230; sunflower seed c. 190; green peas (1976) c. 192; plums (1976) c. 230; apples c. 1,000; wine c. 510; tobacco c. 20; milk c. 2,340; beef and veal c. 130; pork c. 840. Livestock (in 000; March 1977): cattle 1,887; pigs 7,854; sheep 2,350; horses (1976) 156; chickens c. 60,498.

Industry. Index of production (1975 = 100; 1977) 110. Production (in 000; metric tons; 1977): coal 2,926; lignite 22,528; crude oil 2,191; natural gas (cu m) 6.6 million; electricity (kw-hr) 23,324,000; iron ore (24% metal content) 525; pig iron 2,293; crude steel 3,722; bauxite 2,949; aluminum 71; cement 4,621; petroleum products (1976) 9,850; sulfuric acid 632; fertilizers (1976–77) nitrogenous 492, phosphate c. 210; cotton yarn 60; wool yarn 11; commercial vehicles (units) 13.

Ice Hockey

North American. In the competition for the championship of the National Hockey League the Montreal Canadiens were hardly pressed in capturing their third straight Stanley Cup. They beat Boston four games to two in the final series of the playoffs. Individual Montreal honours abounded, with Guy Lafleur winning the Art Ross Trophy for the third consecutive season as the league's leading scorer with 132 points. Ken Dryden and Michel ("Bunny") Larocque earned Montreal's third straight Vezina Trophy for the league's best goaltending, while the team won the Prince of Wales Trophy for finishing tops in the overall-season point standing in the league for a record 19th time. The Canadiens finished 16 points ahead of their nearest rival in the NHL.

In other regular-season accomplishments, the New York Islanders claimed the Patrick Division title, ending a four-year reign by the Philadelphia Flyers. Mike Bossy, the Islanders' rookie right wing with the lightning-fast wrist shot, won the rookie-of-the-year award. He set a new NHL record for rookies with 53 goals, passing Rick Martin's old mark of 44. Denis Potvin was voted the league's top defenseman, and Lafleur was the league's most valuable player for the second year in a row.

The more surprising developments occurred off the ice. Fred ("the Fog") Shero, who had coached the Flyers to two Stanley Cups in seven years, left Philadelphia after the 1977–78 season to become coach and general manager of the New York Rangers. He replaced Ranger general manager John Ferguson and coach Jean-Guy Talbot. The Rangers had finished last in the Patrick Division for the third straight year and were ousted in the playoffs' preliminary round after gaining a wild-card berth.

One of Shero's first moves as Ranger general manager was to complete the signing of Anders Hedberg and Ulf Nilsson, the World Hockey Association superstars who had led the Winnipeg Jets to their second AVCO World Trophy in the 1978 WHA championships with a four-game sweep of the New England Whalers. Ferguson had arranged the deal, in which the two Swedish imports each received a two-year contract worth $1.2 million including signing bonuses. The mammoth expenditure was okayed by Sonny Werblin, the sports businessman who became president of Madison Square Garden Corp. late in the 1977–78 season.

While the Rangers were tossing away bankrolls, their suburban neighbours, the New York Islanders, suffered through a jarring financial setback after it was discovered that principal partner Roy Boe had been transferring funds to his struggling New York Nets in the National Basketball Association. This left the ostensibly prospering Islanders nearly $20 million in debt. After a summer of loan and debt renegotiation, particularly with the NHL itself, the Islanders were refinanced without Boe's participation.

Jack Vickers's one-year effort to relinquish ownership of the financially strapped Colorado Rockies culminated in the transfer of the franchise to Arthur Imperatore, a New Jersey trucking magnate, who hoped eventually to move the team to the New Jersey Meadowlands in 1980. Cleveland solved its continuing financial problems through a creative and speedily executed amalgamation with the Minnesota North Stars. George and Gordon Gund became the principal owners of the new team, which remained in Minnesota.

The NHL experienced its first free-agent arbitration cases over the summer as Minnesota signed Gary Sargent, formerly with Los Angeles, and saw its offer of compensation chosen by Judge Ed Houston over Los Angeles's sealed offer. Thus Rick Hampton, Steve Jensen, and Dave Gardner went to the Kings. When Rogie Vachon, a 33-year-old goalie, signed with Detroit, the Kings were caught in another arbitration situation. This time Judge Houston chose in their favour, and the Kings landed Dale McCourt, a highly promising 21-year-old centre, as compensation.

Although there was a minimum of civil court involvement compared with the previous few seasons of assault cases, the NHL was shocked by the

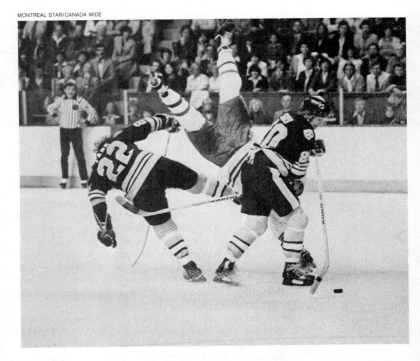

conviction of Don Murdoch, the New York Rangers' 21-year-old right wing, on charges of possession of cocaine. Although Murdoch received a suspended sentence and a $400 fine from a provincial magistrate in Brampton, Ont., NHL Pres. John Ziegler took more punitive action and suspended Murdoch for the 1978–79 season with the option of hearing an appeal at the season's midpoint based on Murdoch's presumed good conduct during his probation. It was the first drug arrest in NHL history, and the NHL Players Association strongly supported Ziegler's disciplinary action.

The WHA conducted merger talks once again with the NHL over the summer, but the rival leagues remained separate. In the fall the WHA began the 1978–79 season reduced to seven teams by the merger of the Houston and Winnipeg franchises in Winnipeg. The Indianapolis Racers went out of business in December.

The WHA fared relatively well in the 1978 amateur draft, signing 20 eligible young players. The individual WHA teams continued their policy of signing underaged players, and by the beginning of the season nine underaged players had signed with the league. The practice led to a dispute with amateur hockey organizations that threatened a series of matches between WHA all-stars and international teams, but a settlement was reached in late November.

Two of hockey's brightest stars left the game. Bobby Hull, seven-time NHL all-star who jumped to the WHL in 1972 for a then-unprecedented $2,750,000, ten-year contract, retired at 39 "for personal reasons." Bobby Orr, a Bruin superstar for ten years before being purchased in 1975 by the Chicago Black Hawks, was forced into retirement at 30 by a knee injury.

In the minor leagues the Maine Mariners won the Calder Cup in their first year in the American Hockey League by beating the New Haven Night-

Steve Shutt of the Montreal Canadiens was sent flying after being checked by Brad Park and Al Sims of the Boston Bruins in the final game of Stanley Cup competition. The Canadiens went on to win the game 4–1, beating the Bruins four games to two in the play-offs.

Hydroelectric Power: *see* Energy; Engineering Projects

Hydrology: *see* Earth Sciences

hawks four games to one. Fort Worth won the Adams Cup in the Central Hockey League, playing a tough seven-game series against Dallas.

(ROBIN CATHY HERMAN)

European and International. The 45th world championships were again contested in three groups by 24 nations, the 8 title contenders competing in Group A from April 26 to May 14 in Prague, Czech. After each had played the other once, the top four played for the title while the others fought to avoid relegation to Group B. The Soviet Union dashed Czechoslovak hopes of a third straight championship by defeating the titleholders 3–1 in the vital final game. The Soviets needed that two-goal margin to recapture the championship; their victory was achieved by having a better record of goals, each country having won nine games. It was the 15th victory for the U.S.S.R.

The host nation was fortunate to be so well placed before the deciding game. In the Czechoslovaks' first-round 6–4 victory over the Soviets, they scored from a doubtful major penalty against a Soviet player, who, it later transpired, was not even on the ice at the time. The ultimate match between the two countries clearly best in the world showed the U.S.S.R. to be the stronger team. Helmut Balderis opened the scoring for the Soviets late in the first period when he outwitted two Czechoslovak defenders and sliced a shot past veteran goalkeeper Jiri Holecek. In the second period, Boris Mikhailov took a bouncing pass from Vladimir Petrov too near the opposing goalie; he then went behind the net and returned the puck for Petrov to score from ideal range. The Soviets went three goals ahead in the final period with a score by Vladimir Golikov before their still-spirited opponents narrowed the margin to two when Ivan Hlinka surprised the Soviet defense. But Czechoslovakia was not given another chance.

Canada, although unable to call upon all its best players because of Stanley Cup play-off commitments, clinched a place in the medals ceremony by a 3–2 triumph over fourth-place Sweden. The six outstanding players in the tournament were generally agreed to be three Soviets, defenseman Vya-

cheslav Fetisov, right wing Aleksandr Maltsev, and left wing Sergey Kapustin, and three Czechoslovaks, goaltender Holecek, defenseman Jiri Bubla, and centre Hlinka. The top scorer was the West German centre, Erich Kuhnackl, with 16 points from 8 goals and 8 assists. Hlinka was next with 14 points, including 10 assists.

The bottom team of the eight countries in Group A was East Germany, which was demoted and replaced by Poland, convincing winner of the Group B matches contested by eight nations on March 17–26 in Belgrade, Yugos. Italy and Yugoslavia, finishing at the foot of this table, were relegated in the next series to Group C and were replaced by The Netherlands and Austria, respectively first and second of the eight teams in Group C. As part of the International Ice Hockey Federation's policy to let as many countries as possible see international matches, Group C was staged on March 10–19 in the incongruously semitropical Canary Islands and included China's first entry since

Boston University's Mark Fidler raises his arms in victory after having shot the puck past Boston College's goaltender, Paul Skidmore. Boston University won the NCAA hockey championship with a 5–3 victory over Boston College.

MANNY MILLAN—"SPORTS ILLUSTRATED" © 1978 TIME INC.

Table I. NHL Final Standings, 1977–78

	Won	Lost	Tied	Goals	Goals against	Pts.
Prince of Wales Conference						
JAMES NORRIS DIVISION						
Montreal	59	10	11	359	183	129
Detroit	32	34	14	252	266	78
Los Angeles	31	34	15	243	245	77
Pittsburgh	25	37	18	254	321	68
Washington	17	49	14	195	321	48
CHARLES F. ADAMS DIVISION						
Boston	51	18	11	333	218	113
Buffalo	44	19	17	288	215	105
Toronto	41	29	10	271	237	92
Cleveland	22	45	13	230	325	57
Clarence Campbell Conference						
LESTER PATRICK DIVISION						
New York Islanders	48	17	15	334	210	111
Philadelphia	45	20	15	296	200	105
Atlanta	34	27	19	274	252	87
New York Rangers	30	37	13	279	280	73
CONN SMYTHE DIVISION						
Chicago	32	29	19	230	220	83
Colorado	19	40	21	257	305	59
Vancouver	20	43	17	239	320	57
St. Louis	20	47	13	195	304	53
Minnesota	18	53	9	218	325	45

Table II. World Ice Hockey Championships, 1978

	Won	Lost	Tied	Goals	Goals against	Pts.
GROUP A Section 1						
U.S.S.R.	9	1	0	61	26	18
Czechoslovakia	9	1	0	54	21	18
Canada	5	5	0	38	36	10
Sweden	4	6	0	39	37	8
GROUP A Section 2						
West Germany	3	4	3	35	43	9
United States	2	6	2	38	58	6
Finland	2	6	2	37	44	6
East Germany	1	6	3	20	57	5
GROUP B						
Poland	6	0	1	51	19	13
Japan	5	1	1	26	17	11
Switzerland	4	2	1	42	32	9
Romania	3	3	1	41	29	7
Hungary	3	4	0	21	36	6
Norway	2	4	1	29	34	5
Italy	1	5	1	32	41	3
Yugoslavia	1	6	0	14	48	2
GROUP C						
Netherlands, The	6	0	1	74	17	13
Austria	5	1	1	65	31	11
Denmark	4	2	1	59	25	9
China	4	3	0	47	30	8
Bulgaria	3	3	1	27	30	7
France	3	4	0	46	39	6
Spain	1	6	0	26	84	2
Belgium	0	7	0	13	101	0

1974. Last-place Belgium was obliged, by the rules, to stand down for a season, and Britain was expected to fill the vacancy.

The season's second most important international tournament was for the Izvestia Cup, in Moscow on Dec. 16–21, 1977. Czechoslovakia thrashed the U.S.S.R. 8–3 on the final day to regain the trophy from the host country, which finished runner-up. Sweden was third, followed by Finland and Canada, the latter represented by a WHA team, the Quebec Nordiques. The world junior (under 21) championship, in Quebec City, from Dec. 22, 1977, to Jan. 3, 1978, was retained by the U.S.S.R. after beating Sweden 5–2 in a play-off. Canada finished third among eight nations.

(HOWARD BASS)

Iceland

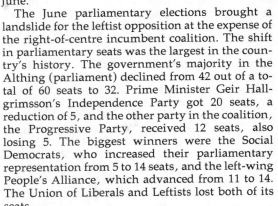

Iceland

Iceland is an island republic in the North Atlantic Ocean, near the Arctic Circle. Area: 103,000 sq km (39,769 sq mi). Pop. (1978 est.): 222,500. Cap. and largest city: Reykjavik (pop., 1978 est., 83,900). Language: Icelandic. Religion: 97% Lutheran. President in 1978, Kristjan Eldjarn; prime ministers, Geir Hallgrimsson and, from August 31, Olafur Johannesson.

Iceland faced serious economic difficulties in 1978. The annual rate of inflation, which reached 50% in 1975, had dropped gradually to 25% by the middle of 1977. It rose again, however, as the result of sharp wage increases, climbing to more than 50% by mid-1978. This created severe operating difficulties for the export industries, and in February the government sought to alleviate them by a 13% devaluation and by legislation that cut

the price increase compensation of wages from 100 to 50%. The move provoked a great deal of unrest in the labour market and a series of sporadic strikes, undoubtedly contributing to the election losses suffered by the government coalition in the municipal and parliamentary elections of May and June.

The June parliamentary elections brought a landslide for the leftist opposition at the expense of the right-of-centre incumbent coalition. The shift in parliamentary seats was the largest in the country's history. The government's majority in the Althing (parliament) declined from 42 out of a total of 60 seats to 32. Prime Minister Geir Hallgrimsson's Independence Party got 20 seats, a reduction of 5, and the other party in the coalition, the Progressive Party, received 12 seats, also losing 5. The biggest winners were the Social Democrats, who increased their parliamentary representation from 5 to 14 seats, and the left-wing People's Alliance, which advanced from 11 to 14. The Union of Liberals and Leftists lost both of its seats.

Immediately after the election the government resigned, although with a majority of two seats it could have continued in power. It remained in office in a caretaker role until the end of August, when Progressive Party leader Olafur Johannesson succeeded in forming a new government in coalition with the Social Democrats and the People's Alliance. The leaders of those two parties, Benedikt Gröndal and Ludvik Josefsson, respectively, had previously failed in their attempts. The new centre-left government's policy platform contained two principal points: Iceland should remain in NATO, and the U.S. Defense Force of about 3,000 personnel should remain at Keflavik air base; and price compensation of wages should be restored for lower- and medium-income wage earners.

To help the export industries, a 15% devaluation took effect on September 5. In addition, to slow down the wage-price spiral, the government instituted heavy subsidies of consumer foodstuffs to hold down the cost-of-living index, financing these partly by tax increases and partly by increased government deficit. Since it was evident that the government would incur serious fiscal deficits in several months if it continued the consumer subsidies, a goal was set to bring government finances into balance before the end of 1979.

Despite these problems, the economy developed relatively favourably during 1978. Real gross national product (GNP) rose by an estimated 3%, and the external terms of trade declined only marginally toward the end of the year. The current account of the balance of payments registered a moderate deficit, estimated at $60 million–$65 million, or some 4% of GNP for 1978 as a whole. There was virtually full employment throughout the year.

In 1977 volcanic activity in the Myvatn region of northeastern Iceland severely damaged the diatomite plant there and prevented the Krafla geothermal steam electricity plant from starting full operations. Volcanic activity was on a much smaller scale in 1978, but it still prevented full operations at the electricity plant from beginning.

(BJÖRN MATTHÍASSON)

Ice Skating:
see Winter Sports

ICELAND

Education. (1975–76) Primary, pupils 30,120; secondary, pupils 16,177; primary and secondary, teachers 2,902; vocational and teacher training, pupils 7,264, teachers 739; higher, students 2,970, teaching staff 575.

Finance. Monetary unit: króna, with (Sept. 18, 1978) a free rate of 305.9 krónur to U.S. $1 (599.5 krónur = £1 sterling). Gold, SDR's, and foreign exchange (June 1978) U.S. $85 million. Budget (1976 est.): revenue 60,342,000,000 krónur; expenditure 58,857,000,000 krónur. Gross national product (1977) 365.9 billion krónur. Money supply (June 1978) 37,071,000,000 krónur. Cost of living (Reykjavik; 1975 = 100; May 1978) 234.9.

Foreign Trade. (1977) Imports 120,969,000,000 krónur; exports 101.9 billion krónur. Import sources: U.K. 11%; West Germany 10%; Denmark 10%; Norway 10%; U.S.S.R. 9%; The Netherlands 8%; Sweden 7%; U.S. 7%. Export destinations: U.S. 30%; U.K. 14%; U.S.S.R. 7%; West Germany 7%; Portugal 6%. Main exports: fish and products 74%; aluminum 15%. Tourism (1976): visitors 70,200; gross receipts U.S. $12 million.

Transport and Communications. Roads (1976) 11,525 km. Motor vehicles in use (1976): passenger 65,700; commercial (including buses) 7,700. There are no railways. Air traffic (1977): 2,004,000,000 passenger-km; freight 28,870,000 net ton-km. Shipping (1977): merchant vessels 100 gross tons and over 375; gross tonnage 166,702. Telephones (Dec. 1976) 95,000. Radio licenses (Dec. 1976) 63,000. Television receivers (Dec. 1976) 55,000.

Agriculture. Production (in 000; metric tons; 1977): potatoes 8; hay c. 390; milk 132; mutton and lamb 15; fish catch 1,374. Livestock (in 000; Dec. 1977): cattle 63; sheep 896; horses 50; poultry 278.

Industry. Production (in 000): electricity (public supply only; kw-hr; 1977) 2.6 million; aluminum (metric tons; 1976) 65.

India

India

A federal republic of southern Asia and a member of the Commonwealth of Nations, India is situated on a peninsula extending into the Indian Ocean with the Arabian Sea to the west and the Bay of Bengal to the east. It is bounded (east to west) by Burma, Bangladesh, China, Bhutan, Nepal, and Pakistan; Sri Lanka lies just off its southern tip in the Indian Ocean. Area: 3,287,782 sq km (1,269,-420 sq mi), including the Pakistani-controlled section of Jammu and Kashmir and the Himalayan state of Sikkim. Pop. (1977 est.): 625,810,000; Indo-Aryans and Dravidians are dominant, with Mongoloid, Negroid, and Australoid admixtures. Cap.: New Delhi (pop., 1971, 301,800). Largest cities: Calcutta (metro pop., 1977 est., 8,297,000) and Greater Bombay (metro pop., 1977 est., 7,605,000). Language: Hindi and English (official). Religion (1971): Hindu 83%; Muslim 11%; Christian 3%; Sikh 2%; Buddhist 0.7%. President in 1978, N. Sanjiva Reddy; prime minister, Morarji Desai.

The year 1978 began eventfully in India. U.S. Pres. Jimmy Carter arrived in the capital on January 1. The same night an Air India Boeing 747 crashed off the Bombay coast, killing 213 people. The next day the Congress Party split for the second time in nine years, and a separate Congress (I)—I for Indira—came into being. Indira Gandhi herself returned to Parliament in November but was later expelled. (*See* below.)

Domestic Affairs. Elections were held in February for assemblies in six states and a union territory. Congress (I) scored impressively in two southern states. In Andhra Pradesh it secured 175 out of 294 seats and formed a government under M. Chenna Reddy. Its tally in Karnataka was 149 out of 224, and Devaraj Urs, whose government had been dismissed by the state governor two months earlier, returned as chief minister. Of 288 Maharashtra seats, 99 went to the Janata Party, 70 to Congress, and 62 to Congress (I), but the two Congress parties formed a coalition government with

Indian police wielded riot clubs against lower caste Hindus who were demonstrating for more jobs in Patna, India. Three people were killed in the demonstrations that took place in late March.

WIDE WORLD

the aid of smaller parties. The government fell in July, when a group under Sharad Pawar joined hands with the Janata Party. Assam and the territory of Arunachal Pradesh got Janata ministries, and in Meghalaya a coalition of regional parties assumed office. On January 2 the Communist Party of India (Marxist) won the elections in Tripura. In Mizoram the People's Conference emerged victorious.

The ruling Janata Party continued to be plagued by dissension. In March the home minister, Charan Singh, demanded that charges of corruption against the prime minister's son be investigated by a commission. A couple of months later he accused the government of being "a bunch of impotents" in dealing with Mrs. Gandhi. Prime Minister Morarji Desai asked for and got Charan Singh's resignation on June 30. Raj Narain, the health minister, also resigned, and so did four junior ministers. Charan Singh and his supporters stayed in the Janata Party, although party elections were postponed in order to prevent further factional trouble.

The government's move to amend the criminal procedure code so as to retain the provision for preventive detention, instituted during Mrs. Gandhi's government's state of emergency, was given up in deference to strong opposition from Socialists within the party. For the same reason, a bill to ban defections was also dropped. The Maintenance of Internal Security Act was repealed. The 45th constitution amendment bill (renumbered 44), introduced to undo the changes effected during the emergency, was adopted by the Lok Sabha (lower house) in August. However, the Rajya Sabha (upper house), in which the two Congress parties together had a majority, refused to accept some important clauses and returned the bill to the Lok Sabha. Among the rejected clauses was a provision for a referendum on changes that might affect the basic features of the constitution. Both houses agreed that the proclamation of an emergency should be made more difficult and should be permissible only in cases of external attack or armed rebellion. The right to property was deleted from the list of fundamental rights. Another constitutional amendment bill was introduced giving statutory status to the Minorities Commission and the Commission for Scheduled Castes and Tribes, both appointed earlier in the year.

The Rajya Sabha adopted a resolution asking the government to appoint commissions of inquiry into charges against relations of the prime minister and former home minister Singh or be guided by a committee of Rajya Sabha members. The government rejected the demand, and the chairman of the house refused to appoint such a committee. The prime minister offered to refer any specific charges against his son to the chief justice.

The commission under Justice J. C. Shah, which had been appointed to go into charges of misuse of power by Mrs. Gandhi, submitted a three-part report. The judge held that Mrs. Gandhi had declared the emergency in order to retain power and "save herself from the legitimate compulsion of a judicial verdict against her." He also held her responsible for the illegal detention of a large number of people and for other excesses. In July six prosecutions were launched in pursuance of the commission's findings, with Mrs. Gandhi figuring in three of them.

A bill to provide special courts for trying those accused of offenses committed in connection with the emergency was referred by the president to the Supreme Court for an opinion on its constitutionality. Other inquiry commissions held former defense minister Bansi Lal culpable of misuse of authority and chief ministers M. Karunanidhi of Tamil Nadu and D. Urs of Karnataka guilty of corruption. A commission under Justice Jaganmohan Reddy, which investigated the withdrawal of Rs 6 million from the State Bank of India by R. S. Nagarwala, a former intelligence agent, was unable to solve the mystery. The inquiry into the Maruti Co. of Mrs. Gandhi's son Sanjay was continuing, but the company itself was ordered dissolved.

The year saw some intergroup clashes. There were attacks on scheduled caste groups (former untouchables) in Belchhi in Bihar and Villupuram in Tamil Nadu and Hindu-Muslim riots in Sambhal, Aligarh, and Hyderabad. Agricultural labourers were fired on in Pantnagar, and Akalis and Nirankaris clashed in Amritsar and Kanpur.

Parliament decided to revive the Press Council. The government appointed a second press commission (the first reported in 1954) to examine press freedom and newspaper economics. The Samachar news agency was dissolved, and its constituent units resumed their separate identities.

Emboldened by the success of her party in some by-elections, Mrs. Gandhi decided to stand for the Lok Sabha from Chikmagalur in Karnataka. In the poll, which was held on November 5, Mrs. Gandhi secured 249,376 votes (55%) and her main opponent, V. Patil of the Janata Party, 172,043 votes (37%). The Kerala chief minister, A. K. Antony, resigned in protest against the decision of the Congress to give tacit support to Mrs. Gandhi and was succeeded by P. K. Vasudevan Nair of the Communist Party of India. Later in November a parliamentary committee found Mrs. Gandhi guilty of breach of privilege and contempt of the House, and on December 19, after a heated debate, a motion calling for her expulsion from Parliament and imprisonment for the remainder of the session was passed. After a week's detention, during which there were widespread violent clashes between her supporters and opponents, Mrs. Gandhi was released on December 26.

The year witnessed the century's worst floods, with the Yamuna and other tributaries of the Ganges registering their highest recorded levels. Several states and the cities of Delhi, Mathura, Agra, Patna, and Calcutta were badly inundated during September and October.

The Economy. In March the National Development Council approved the 1978–83 five-year plan. It envisaged expenditure of Rs 1,162,400,000,000 on development (including a public sector outlay of Rs 693.8 billion). Radical reconstruction of rural life was declared to be its principal objective. The union government's budget for 1978–79, presented on February 28, put revenue receipts at Rs 107,-820,000,000 (including Rs 3,210,000,000 from new

tax proposals) and capital receipts at Rs 65,-850,000,000. Expenditure was set at Rs 108,-990,000,000 and capital disbursements at Rs 75,180,000,000.

In June the Aid-India Consortium announced a credit of $2.3 billion for 1978–79, and Sweden wrote off debts of Rs 1,007,000,000. U.S. aid, suspended since the Bangladesh war of 1971, was resumed with the announcement of a $60 million credit. In January Britain offered credits of £144 million. An agreement was reached with the Soviet Union for the supply of 1.5 million metric tons of crude oil. Protocols were signed with Libya for joint programs involving Rs 12 billion.

The rupee was devalued by small increments in relation to the pound and, in November, in relation to the U.S. dollar. A policy of gold auctions from the Reserve Bank was adopted in an unsuccessful effort to bring down gold prices. Overall, wholesale prices remained steady during the year. The index on October 7 stood at 186.2, only 0.3% higher than in the corresponding week of 1977. In January currency notes of the denominations Rs 1,000, Rs 5,000, and Rs 10,000 were demonetized, and it was later stated that this resulted in Rs 207 million going out of circulation.

The 1977–78 year's grain production was computed at 126 million metric tons. Sugar was decontrolled in August, and 16 sugar mills in Bihar were taken over in October. Accords were reached during the year between various states on the sharing of the waters of the Krishna and Narmada rivers. In February the Caltex Co. was merged into the government-owned Hindustan Petroleum.

People and animals sought whatever high ground was available, in this case the raised railroad tracks, when monsoon rains flooded northern India during September and October.

Indonesia

Foreign Affairs. The Carter visit helped to bring the U.S. and India closer. A private remark by Carter that, following his return, he would send a strong letter to India protesting its refusal to allow inspection of its atomic installations was played down by both sides. Later the U.S. government honoured its obligation to send nuclear fuel for the Tarapur atomic power station. British Prime Minister James Callaghan also visited India in January. Other visitors included the shah of Iran and Premier Pham Van Dong of Vietnam. Desai visited the U.S. in June and addressed the UN Special Session on Disarmament. En route he also visited Brussels and London. While he was in Sydney, Australia, attending the Commonwealth conference, a bomb exploded near his hotel, but he was unhurt. In August he attended Pres. Jomo Kenyatta's funeral in Kenya.

It was announced on October 6 that Anglo-French Jaguar aircraft would be purchased for the Air Force. Three-fourths of the required five squadrons would be manufactured within the country. A contract worth some Rs 13 billion was later signed with the British Aerospace Corp.

(H. Y. SHARADA PRASAD)

INDIA

Education. (1977–78) Primary, pupils 55,772,018, teachers 1,354,460; secondary, pupils 40,702,098, teachers 1,505,565; vocational, pupils 185,251; teacher training, pupils 88,253; higher, students 3,716,350, teaching staff (1970–71) 119,000.

Finance. Monetary unit: rupee, with (Sept. 18, 1978) a free rate of Rs 8 to U.S. $1 (Rs 15.68 = £1 sterling). Gold, SDR's, and foreign exchange (June 1978) U.S. $6,045,000,000. Budget (1977–78 actual): revenue Rs 92,070,000,000; expenditure Rs 114,220,000,000. Gross national product (1976–77) Rs 769,370,000,000. Money supply (April 1978) Rs 182.3 billion. Cost of living (1975 = 100; June 1978) 101.9.

Foreign Trade. (1977) Imports Rs 52,638,000,000; exports Rs 55,621,000,000. Import sources (1976–77): U.S. 21%; Iran 10%; Saudi Arabia 7%; U.K. 6%; U.S.S.R. 6%; West Germany 6%; Japan 6%; Iraq 6%; Australia 5%. Export destinations (1976–77): U.S. 11%; Japan 11%; U.K. 10%; U.S.S.R. 9%. Main exports (1976–77): cotton and jute fabrics 11%; iron and steel 8%; clothing 7%; tea 6%; animal fodder 5%; leather 5%; precious stones 5%; iron ore 5%.

Transport and Communications. Roads (1974) 1,232,300 km. Motor vehicles in use (1976): passenger 799,499; commercial 415,195. Railways: (1975) 60,301 km; traffic (1976–77) 159,940,000,000 passenger-km, freight 154,310,000,000 net ton-km. Air traffic (1976): 7,196,000,000 passenger-km; freight 279.3 million net ton-km. Shipping (1977): merchant vessels 100 gross tons and over 566; gross tonnage 5,482,176. Telephones (Jan. 1977) 2,096,000. Radio licenses (Dec. 1975) 14,075,000. Television licenses (Dec. 1974) 275,000.

Agriculture. Production (in 000; metric tons; 1977): wheat 29,082; rice c. 74,000; barley 2,296; corn c. 6,800; millet c. 10,000; sorghum c. 10,400; potatoes 7,287; cassava (1976) 6,307; sugar, raw value 5,239; sugar, noncentrifugal (1976) c. 7,000; chick-peas 5,366; mangoes c. 8,996; bananas c. 3,553; cottonseed 2,342; rapeseed 1,562; sesame seed c. 450; linseed 431; peanuts c. 5,500; tea c. 560; tobacco 414; cotton, lint c. 1,150; jute (including substitutes) c. 1,262; fish catch (1976) 2,400. Livestock (in 000; 1977): cattle 181,092; sheep c. 40,350; pigs c. 8,732; buffalo c. 60,400; goats c. 70,060; poultry c. 143,000.

Industry. Production (in 000; metric tons; 1977): coal 100,294; lignite 3,628; iron ore (63% metal content) 42,271; pig iron 10,036; crude steel 9,820; aluminum 184; cement 19,183; cotton yarn 846; woven cotton fabrics (m; 1976) 7,940,000; petroleum products (1976) 21,434; sulfuric acid 2,018; caustic soda 517; gold (troy oz; 1976) 101; manganese ore (metal content; 1976) 638; electricity (excluding most industrial production; kw-hr) 90,845,000.

Indonesia

A republic of Southeast Asia, Indonesia consists of the major islands of Sumatra, Java, Kalimantan (Indonesian Borneo), Celebes, and Irian Jaya (West New Guinea) and approximately 3,000 smaller islands and islets. Area: 1,919,494 sq km (741,121 sq mi). Pop. (1977 est.): 138,133,500. Area and population figures include former Portuguese Timor. Cap. and largest city: Jakarta (pop., 1977 est., 6,178,500). Language: Bahasa Indonesia (official); Javanese; Sundanese; Madurese. Religion: mainly Muslim; some Christian, Buddhist, and Hindu. President and prime minister in 1978, Suharto.

In 1978, in the face of rising criticism at home and abroad over burgeoning corruption within his administration, Suharto, a 56-year-old Javanese and former general, was reelected president for a third five-year term. He was the sole candidate nominated by the legislature. Former foreign minister Adam Malik, an outspoken Sumatran, emerged as vice-president. In another political development the first move was made to rehabilitate President Sukarno, who had died in 1970 in disgrace for his purported complicity in the 1965 abortive coup of the Indonesian Communist Party (PKI). In economic affairs the country's "oil bonanza," set in motion by the 1973 oil embargo of the Organization of Petroleum Exporting Countries, of which Indonesia was a member, appeared to peter out, giving rise to concern over a slowdown in Indonesia's economic development.

Suharto's unanimous election by the People's Consultative Assembly (MRP) took place on March 22, against a background of heavy military security, the closing of high schools and universities, and the shutting down of several newspapers. Reporting to the nation, he accepted criticism of his stewardship and invited continued criticism as long as it was "constructive."

For weeks before the election the country was in turmoil as students demonstrated and urged Suharto not to stand for reelection. Restlessness also spread among Muslim groups, intellectuals, and public servants. A major issue was rampant corruption. In an effort to defuse the issue Suharto ordered a cleanup of questionable activities, and at the year's end the first senior army officer, a brigadier general, was indicted for graft. After the election Suharto also loosened the government's tacit control of the press and encouraged newspapers to expose corruption in and out of government.

In foreign affairs Indonesia engaged in dialogues with Vietnam and China, as relations between those two Communist regimes deteriorated. Vietnam's expulsion of overseas Chinese not only exacerbated Sino-Vietnamese relations but served as a pretext for Indonesia, which has a substantial overseas Chinese population, to postpone an earlier decision to extend diplomatic recognition to China. Relations between Indonesia and China had been in suspension for more than a decade, following Indonesia's charge that China was involved in the abortive 1965 Communist coup.

Meanwhile, largely under U.S. pressure, Indonesia continued to release political prisoners allegedly involved in the 1965 putsch. During the year the government announced that all political prisoners except for a hard core of about 400 PKI members would be released during 1979. In Moscow, however, an exiled PKI underground splinter group surfaced for the second time as a rival to a splinter group operating out of Peking. Accordingly, Suharto warned rioting students on election eve that disturbances at home played into Communist hands. The students in turn called on the government to eliminate corruption, narrow the widening gap between rich and poor, and guard against "the reemergence of new-style Communism" if the government failed to meet the students' "moral demands."

Indonesia's economic performance was satisfactory in 1978. The rate of inflation was trimmed from 12 to 10%, and economic growth continued at 7% annually. In May the Inter-Governmental Group of Indonesia, a Western-oriented consortium, extended the government U.S. $2.5 billion in loans as an expression of international confidence in Suharto's stewardship. But in September a leading Indonesian economist warned that Indonesia's oil industry was losing upward of $3.5 million daily because of Japanese and U.S. cutbacks in imported oil. He expressed fear that Indonesia's "oil bonanza" had run its course.

(ARNOLD C. BRACKMAN)

INDONESIA

Education. (1976) Primary, pupils 15,530,124, teachers 514,912; secondary, pupils 2,148,428, teachers 71,079; vocational, pupils 786,916, teachers 33,624; teacher training, students 133,756, teachers 4,475; higher (1975), students 278,200, teaching staff 43,720.

Finance. Monetary unit: rupiah, with (Sept. 18, 1978) an official rate of 415 rupiah to U.S. $1 (free rate of 813 rupiah = £1 sterling). Gold, SDR's, and foreign exchange (June 1978) U.S. $2,086,000,000. Budget (1977–78 est): revenue 3,484,000,000,000 rupiah (excluding foreign aid of 763 billion rupiah); expenditure 4,247,000,000,000 rupiah. Gross national product (1976) 15,035,000,000,000 rupiah. Money supply (March 1978) 2,122,300,000,000 rupiah. Cost of living (Jakarta; 1975 = 100; June 1978) 141.4.

Foreign Trade. (1977) Imports U.S. $6,230,000,000; exports U.S. $10,853,000,000. Import sources: Japan 27%; U.S. 12%; Singapore 9%; West Germany 8%; Thailand 5%; Saudi Arabia 5%; Taiwan 5%. Export destinations: Japan 40%; U.S. 28%; Singapore 9%; Trinidad and Tobago 5%. Main exports: crude oil 63%; timber 9%; rubber 5%.

Transport and Communications. Roads (1974) 95,544 km. Motor vehicles in use (1976): passenger 420,900; commercial (including buses) 263,100. Railways: (1974) 7,610 km; traffic (1976) 3,258,000,000 passenger-km, freight 717 million net ton-km. Air traffic (1976): 3,112,000,000 passenger-km; freight 47.6 million net ton-km. Shipping (1977): merchant vessels 100 gross tons and over 1,032; gross tonnage 1,163,173. Telephones (Jan. 1977) 314,000. Radio licenses (Dec. 1975) 5,010,000. Television receivers (Dec. 1975) 300,000.

Agriculture. Production (in 000; metric tons; 1977): rice 23,235; corn 3,030; cassava (1976) c. 12,500; sweet potatoes (1976) c. 2,478; sugar, raw value c. 1,200; bananas c. 3,152; tea c. 75; copra c. 950; soybeans 527; palm oil c. 495; peanuts c. 556; coffee c. 180; tobacco c. 84; rubber c. 850; fish catch (1976) 1,448. Livestock (in 000; 1977): cattle 6,114; pigs 2,516; sheep 3,286; buffalo 2,458; goats 6,112; horses (1976) c. 704; chickens 102,382.

Industry. Production (in 000; metric tons; 1977): crude oil 83,000; petroleum products (1976) 14,780; coal 230; tin concentrates (metal content; 1976) 22; bauxite (1976) 1,010; electricity (excluding most industrial production; kw-hr; 1976) c. 3,790,000.

Industrial Relations

In 1978, even more than in 1977, it was the economic environment rather than social or technological factors that had the greatest effect on industrial relations. On the positive side most countries achieved modest economic growth, and rates of inflation were declining. For the majority of people standards of living were rising, not falling. But overall recovery from the recession was less marked than had been hoped and was often uncertain. Unemployment remained high, and in some countries continued to rise; considerable efforts by governments to reduce it met with only modest success. It was particularly serious among groups of workers already disadvantaged, and among the young. The possibility of increasing employment by stimulating demand was inhibited by the need to avoid measures that might be inflationary. Against such a background there was limited scope for collective bargainers to secure improvements in wages and working conditions.

The economic stringency might have led to a rise in industrial conflict, with workers and their unions pressing for a return to the regular and sizable improvements that had been customary in the years of high growth. However, abatement of inflationary expectations and a generally realistic appreciation that there was little that could be achieved ensured that most settlements were relatively moderate. Though many negotiations were hard-fought, the year ended without any major industrialized country having suffered a really serious national dispute.

One factor that facilitated bargaining settlements in a number of countries was the shared understanding built up by close and regular consultation between governments, unions, and employers on economic problems. In nearly all democratic countries free collective bargaining was regarded not only as the most effective method so far evolved for determining wages and working conditions but also as a valued basic right, and governments saw their role as a broadly noninterventionary one. For some years, however, it had become increasingly apparent that the results of bargaining were sometimes inconsistent with national economic needs and with the effective operation of a government's economic and related policies. For their part, collective bargainers found it necessary in their negotiations to take more and more account of national needs.

This growing interrelationship between collective bargaining and government policies led to the establishment in a number of countries of bodies in which governments, unions, and employers could meet to exchange views and try to ensure that the courses they pursued were mutually supportive of the national interest. Such consultative institutions did much to facilitate acceptable settlements in 1978.

Given the difficulty of obtaining appreciable direct increases in real wages, in 1978 many unions put increased weight on claims for shorter working hours—mainly in the form of a shorter working week but sometimes also in the forms of longer vacations or earlier retirement. They argued that not only were such changes desirable in the name of social progress but they would create extra jobs, thereby lessening unemployment without causing much loss in efficiency. Employers disagreed; as they saw it the cost of reductions in hours would be substantial, not to mention the lower utilization of plant and loss of production time that would be involved. That lower hours would create appreciably more jobs they considered doubtful. As the year progressed there was no general movement to reduce hours, although in Belgium a number of collective agreements conceded reductions in weekly hours and in several countries minor extensions of vacations were negotiated. A major dispute over a 35-hour-week claim broke out in the steel industry in North Rhine-Westphalia, West Germany, in November. With the prevailing high levels of unemployment, steps to strengthen job security continued to be a noticeable feature of collective bargaining in 1978.

Social and Technological Influences. The social environment influences industrial relations in various ways. Notable in recent years had been the movement to match rising standards of living at home by improved conditions at the workplace. Apart from reduced time spent at work and improved job security, many workers had acquired a greater say in managerial decisions; physical conditions at the workplace had been improved, with increased emphasis on safety; and efforts had been made to improve the intrinsic interest of the work task. Like the rising standards of living, these improvements were, in large measure, made possible by economic growth. Mainly because of the economic climate these "social" improvements had become less marked in recent years than in the early 1970s, but the general movement continued.

Technological advance produces changes in industry that are frequently disturbing to people and

therefore affects industrial relations. In 1978 new technology became more significant than at any time since the introduction of the computer and of automation. A clear-cut example was in printing, where technological innovation threatened the jobs of compositors and led to several disputes and strikes, notably in West Germany, Britain, and the U.S. A second example was telecommunications. However, far wider in its potential effects was the development of microprocessing, though in 1978 this had yet to make any appreciable impact. (*See* INDUSTRIAL REVIEW: *Special Report.*)

Developments in Market Economy Countries. The major industrial relations issue in Britain was the continuation of the "social contract." Phase 3 of the policy held fairly well, although earnings increased by substantially more than the 10% limit that had been set. However, after three years of controls, during which pressure had grown for a return to free collective bargaining, it was clear that further restraint would be difficult to achieve. In July the government published a White Paper calling for a general limit of increases in earnings to 5%. The position taken by the Trades Union Congress in September and by the Labour Party conference in October showed clearly that this was not acceptable, although there was fairly widespread agreement on the need for moderation. The government exhibited considerable firmness, however, and made it clear that it was prepared to use sanctions against firms conceding unduly generous wage increases with which it had contractual relationships, as it had done under Phase 3. Later discussions between the government and unions failed to establish an understanding about moderating wage demands, and in the course of parliamentary debate in December the government dropped sanctions against private firms. By the end of the year no clear pattern of settlement had emerged.

Another British development was the publica-

Mrs. Susan Charlton, mother of two, organized car workers' wives in a campaign urging Ford strikers to return to work in Southampton, England. Her supporters were confronted by many angry strikers.

KEYSTONE

tion in May of a White Paper on *Industrial Democracy*. Its proposals, though far from finding general approval, were much more realistic than those of the 1977 Bullock report. Broadly, the government envisaged the formation of trade union committees that could enter into consultation with company managements, the latter being required to discuss major proposals affecting employees before decisions were made. Although a voluntary approach to greater participation was favoured, there would be statutory backing for workers' rights to representation on the boards of large companies.

In the United States the principal event in industrial relations was the defeat of the administration's labour law reforms, which were lost after a lengthy filibuster in the Senate. The reforms had been intended to remove impediments to labour organization and to strengthen collective bargaining, and their loss angered the unions. Also important was the administration's introduction in October, against a background of rising inflation, of a voluntary code limiting wage and fringe benefit increases to 7% and calling for corresponding moderation in price rises. When Pres. Jimmy Carter announced an administration program of voluntary wage-price controls in October, labour leader George Meany denounced it as too limited in scope. He favoured instead a broad program of mandatory restraints. The major union-employer conflict of the year was the work stoppage in coal mining, which ran for 15 weeks before agreement was reached on wage increases and pensions and sickness payment benefits. Other difficult disputes included a strike for higher wages and seniority rights on the railroads and a strike to prevent job losses that deprived New York City of its major daily newspapers for 12 weeks.

The March general election was the key factor in determining the development of industrial relations in France. The defeat of the left was followed by a series of consultations between government, labour, and management leaders. The wide range of possible measures already under consideration or newly opened up, though restricted by the overall economic austerity, covered such possibilities as improvement in the pay of low-paid workers; strengthening of collective bargaining; revision of industrial tribunals; improvement in physical working conditions; and profit sharing and other forms of worker participation. One initiative, subsequently taken up in an agreement in the metal industries, was for industrial sectors to establish a guaranteed annual minimum income for their workers. On the whole the unions reacted favourably to most of these initiatives.

In West Germany there were some signs of worker discontent. Strikes took place in newspaper publishing concerning technological innovation; in the metalworking industry in north Baden-Württemberg; and on the docks. The employers' use of the lockout in the newspaper and metals disputes strengthened union demands that lockouts should be prohibited by law. However, the West German industrial relations system continued to work well by comparison with most other countries.

Spain continued its efforts to build a new indus-

An unhappy West Virginia coal miner burned a copy of a proposed contract that the United Mine Workers rank and file voted down in March.

trial relations system. Although a bill concerning works councils failed to become law, the overall atmosphere was constructive and the government approached unions and employers to help establish a broad-based agreement on economic policy to succeed the existing Moncloa Pact established by the political parties.

Communist Countries. In the Communist world two events attracted some outside attention. In the Soviet Union a number of dissident workers sought to establish the right to form an independent trade union. Also, the Communist-dominated World Federation of Trade Unions held a congress in Prague, Czech., which was notable for some critical contributions by Western European affiliates. The French Confédération Général du Travail (CGT) declined to put forward a nomination for the post of general secretary, which by custom had always been held by a Frenchman. The CGT did not, however, withdraw from the federation as its Italian equivalent had done earlier.

Less Developed Countries. Among the less developed countries there were many industrial relations problems. A few nations, notably Iran, experienced general strikes, sometimes accompanied by bloodshed. A noteworthy event was the arrest, and in some cases subsequent arraignment before the Court of State Security, of a considerable number of union leaders and workers after a general strike in Tunisia in January. Those convicted included the general secretary of the central trade union, sentenced to ten years' imprisonment.

(R. O. CLARKE)

The views expressed in this article are the author's own and should not be attributed to any organization with which he may be connected.

See also Economy, World; Industrial Review.
[521.B.3; 534.C.1.g; 552.D.3 and F.3.b.ii]

Industrial Review

From the standpoint of industry, 1975, 1976, and 1977 are best characterized as years of recession, recovery, and slow growth. Manufacturing output of the world, excluding the centrally planned economies, fell 7% in 1975, rose 9% in 1976, and then had its rate of growth halved to about 5% in 1977. The signs indicated that this slower growth continued in 1978.

The slowing down of industrial progress in 1977 took place mainly in the developed countries; their output rose by only 4% after a 9% increase in 1976. By contrast, in both the less developed and the centrally planned countries the decline was no more than marginal. There were many reasons for the slow progress: cautious policies influenced by the threat of inflation, budgetary deficits, balance of payments constraints, and depressed business confidence. All resulted in high unemployment and generally weak demand.

One important reason for the hesitancy of the sustained recovery from the deep 1975 recession was the failure of nonresidential investment to swing back from its trough into a growth path, thus generating demand. On previous occasions when productive investment in the major countries fell in absolute terms, a rapid recovery followed. This time, however, productive investment had not quite regained its pre-recession level by 1977. Several factors contributed to this course of events; the most important of them, and the most obvious explanation, is that surplus capacity reached an exceptional level in the recession and remained, on the whole, unusually high; the effects of currency uncertainties and inflation on business confidence may also have played a part.

In the advanced countries belonging to the Organization for Economic Cooperation and Development (OECD) total investment rose appreciably in 1977, but this was largely due to housing and not to industrial investment. Private consumption also rose but less so than in the preceding year; demand from the public sector moved ahead a little, but there was hardly any addition to inventory. This latter point is of considerable importance because in 1976 such stockbuilding accounted for only 1¼% of national output; it provided additional evidence of the bleak view of the economy taken by most businessmen.

Of the three strongest industrial economies, the U.S., Japan, and West Germany, U.S. manufacturing rose by more than 6% in 1977. Japan's advance

Table I. Index Numbers of Production, Employment, and Productivity in Manufacturing Industries
1970 = 100

Area	Relative importance [1] 1970	1977	Production 1976	1977	Employment 1976	1977	Productivity [2] 1976	1977
World [3]	1,000	1,000	124	130	...	...	...	...
Industrial countries	896	869	121	126	...	...	...	...
Less industrialized countries	104	131	153	163	...	...	...	...
North America [4]	409	414	124	131	...	...	...	...
Canada	27	27	127	131	104	103	122	127
United States	381	386	122	130	98	101	124	129
Latin America [5]	59	71	151	154	...	...	...	...
Mexico	13	15	139	145	...	...	...	...
Asia [6]	137	150	132	141	...	...	...	...
India	11	12	129	136	113	...	114	...
Japan	99	98	121	126	99	98	122	128
Pakistan [7]	3	3	117	117	...	...	...	...
Europe [8]	365	339	118	120	...	...	...	...
Austria	6	6	126	130	100	101	126	129
Belgium	11	10	122	121	...	...	...	...
Denmark	5	5	115	117	90	88	128	132
Finland	4	4	123	119	106	104	116	114
France	67	65	126	127	100	99	126	129
Germany, West	104	92	112	115	90	90	124	128
Greece	3	4	166	169	127	132	131	128
Ireland	1	1	128	138	96	99	133	139
Italy	37	35	121	122	108	...	113	...
Netherlands, The	13	12	117	118	86	84	136	140
Norway [9]	4	4	116	116	106	105	102	103
Portugal	3	3	140	143	...	...	...	...
Spain	12	16	153	172	116	...	132	...
Sweden	13	11	114	111	105	101	109	110
Switzerland	12	9	96	100	80	80	120	126
United Kingdom	54	43	103	104	87	88	119	118
Yugoslavia	13	17	154	168	131	137	117	122
Rest of the world [10]	30	26	...	...	...	...	...	...
Australia [7]	14	12	112	108	93	90	121	120
South Africa	6	5	124	117	119	116	104	101
Centrally planned economies [11]	...	...	166	178	...	...	...	...

[1] The 1970 weights are those applied by the UN Statistical Office; those for 1977 were estimated on the basis of the changes in manufacturing output since 1970 in the various countries.
[2] This is 100 times the production index divided by the employment index, giving a rough indication of changes in output per person employed.
[3] Excluding Albania, Bulgaria, China, Czechoslovakia, East Germany, Hungary, Mongolia, North Korea, North Vietnam, Poland, Romania, and the U.S.S.R.
[4] Canada and the United States.
[5] South and Central America (including Mexico) and the Caribbean islands.
[6] Asian Middle East and East and Southeast Asia, including Japan.
[7] Years beginning July 1.
[8] Excluding Albania, Bulgaria, Czechoslovakia, East Germany, Hungary, Poland, Romania, and the U.S.S.R.
[9] Employment and productivity based on 1972=100.
[10] Africa and Oceania.
[11] These are not included in the above world total and consist of Albania, Bulgaria, Czechoslovakia, East Germany, Hungary, Poland, Romania, and the U.S.S.R.

Table II. Industrial Pattern of Recession and Recovery, 1974–77
Percent change from previous year

	World [1] 1974	1975	1976	1977	Developed countries 1974	1975	1976	1977	Less developed countries 1974	1975	1976	1977	Centrally planned economies 1974	1975	1976	1977
All manufacturing	1	−7	9	5	0	−8	9	4	7	3	8	7	9	9	8	7
Heavy industries	2	−10	10	5	1	−10	10	5	10	2	9	7	11	10	9	8
Base metals	2	−15	9	1	0	−16	9	−1	14	4	8	5	6	7	8	3
Metal products	1	−8	9	6	0	−9	8	6	15	3	11	9	12	12	9	10
Building materials, etc.	1	−7	9	6	−1	−9	9	4	8	6	9	9	7	7	6	5
Chemicals	2	−7	12	5	2	−8	13	6	5	0	9	4	11	10	8	6
Light industries	0	−3	8	3	−1	−4	7	3	3	4	7	6	8	6	4	5
Food, drink, tobacco	3	1	6	4	2	1	4	3	3	5	8	8	8	5	3	6
Textiles	−4	−4	8	−1	−5	−7	9	−1	−2	6	6	1	6	6	5	4
Clothing, footwear	0	0	9	1	−2	−3	9	−1	8	11	11	6	7	7	7	6
Wood products	−4	−8	10	4	−5	−8	10	4	1	0	3	5	6	8	4	6
Paper, printing	0	−9	7	4	0	−10	9	3	3	−5	−6	5	6	8	6	5

[1] Excluding centrally planned economies.
Source: UN, *Monthly Bulletin of Statistics*.

Table III. Output per Hour Worked in Manufacturing
1970=100

Country	1970	1972	1973	1974	1975	1976	1977
France	100	114	121	125	121	135	139
Germany, West	100	111	117	121	126	135	139
Italy	100	111	125	130	123	134	142 [1]
Japan	100	114	133	136	131	148	158
U.K.	100	112	118	119	119	123	121
U.S.	100	110	113	116	118	124	127

[1] 1977 not strictly comparable with earlier years.
Source: National Institute, *Economic Review*.

Table IV. Manufacturing Production in the U.S.S.R. and Eastern Europe [1]
1970=100

Country	1975	1976	1977
Bulgaria [2]	154	164	177
Czechoslovakia	140	148	156
East Germany [2]	137	145	152
Hungary	137	143	151
Poland	168	184	209
U.S.S.R.	145	152	160

[1] Romania not available.
[2] All industries.
Source: UN, *Monthly Bulletin of Statistics*.

Industrial unemployment in Italy was high. (Left) Unemployed youth stage protest demonstrations in Milan.

was a mere 4%, however, and West Germany's was 2½%, both low by historical standards. Thus, contrary to the so-called locomotive theory, these economies failed to provide the expected stimulus needed to pull the rest of the world into a path of faster growth. Growth also lagged behind official targets elsewhere, despite the promises and exhortations of politicians.

The Western European manufacturing industry was particularly depressed; its output only grew by about 2% as compared with about 6% in North America and Asia. In 1978 it appeared that the European performance had improved, while that of Japan did not change much. The U.S. growth rate was expected to be reduced, partly because of the severe cold and the coal strike in the winter, causing loss of production that was not compensated for later.

Among the manufacturing industries the most heavily hit by these trends was that of base metals, the output of which actually fell in 1977 in the developed countries. Within this category steel output fell much more. The growth in production of building materials and of some intermediate products such as basic heavy chemicals, wood products, and paper also slowed down appreciably. Generally weak demand affected the consumer goods industries as well, especially textiles and clothing.

In the advanced countries the recovery was best sustained in the U.S., where residential investment was definitely booming and consumer spending was high. Business investment also rose more than elsewhere as a response to improving utilization of industrial capacity, and continued building of inventories also contributed to rising demand. This boom did not spill over to Canada, where private consumption was restrained by the effect on real incomes of inflation and investment remained sluggish.

Industrial growth in Japan in 1977 was 4%, very low for that nation. Sluggish domestic demand resulted in sharp declines in industrial profits and a high level of bankruptcies. Except for exports and public investment, all areas were far weaker than

in 1976. Residential building actually fell, while the growth of consumption and business investment was almost halved.

Industrial activity in France hardly changed. Construction was declining, affecting many supplying industries, and demand in most other areas was poor. The manufacturing industry in West Germany progressed only slightly faster than that of the French. For almost a year there was practically stagnation, though output started to increase toward the end of 1977 as private consumption and housing began to emerge from their depressed conditions. Other investment was weak, and the export industries felt the dual effect of weak markets and the appreciation in value of the mark.

In the United Kingdom the nation's incomes policy kept wages lagging behind inflation, resulting in declining real incomes. Consequently, expenditure in general and all types of investment fell with the sole exception of private manufacturing, and the general stagnation was reflected in the lack of industrial advance. Very similar was the development of the Italian industry, while among the other European countries the results varied from relatively rapid growth in Ireland, Spain, Switzerland, and Yugoslavia to decline in Belgium, Finland, and Sweden. Depressed general conditions caused manufacturing in Australia and South Africa to fall as well.

Productivity in the major industrialized countries rose (with the exception of the United Kingdom) but at a much slower rate than in 1976. Industrial (and other) unemployment remained high and became a major preoccupation for the governments of most industrial nations.

Both the less developed countries and the centrally planned economies achieved a growth rate of 7% in 1977, almost twice as high as in the developed nations. Noteworthy among the first group of countries was the relatively rapid progress of industry in India. The centrally planned economies continued their industrial growth, in the Soviet Union at the same rate as in 1976. This growth was probably a little lower in 1978 because of those nations' somewhat reduced plans.   (G. F. RAY)

Industrial Review

ADVERTISING

The advertising practices of the U.S. broadcasting industry faced tough criticism from private organizations and federal government agencies in 1978. A study initiated by Action for Children's Television found that children saw approximately 25,000 commercials a year on television. An estimated $600 million was spent annually on children's television advertising by consumer goods companies.

The Federal Trade Commission (FTC) continued to study a number of proposals concerning the advertising of children's products, such as toys, and products that affect children's eating habits. Public hearings were held in Washington, D.C., on whether to curtail all advertising aimed at children under eight years of age. A recommendation was considered to balance advertisements for products containing sugar with dental and nutritional messages. Meanwhile, a House of Representatives subcommittee attempted to prohibit the FTC from considering regulations that affect the advertising of foods and other products considered safe by the Food and Drug Administration. The debate on children's advertising seemed certain to continue.

In May the FTC lifted restrictions on price advertising for eyeglasses, contact lenses, and eye examinations in order to encourage competition. In 1978 more than 40 states had restrictions on price advertising of optical products and services. The commission found that the average cost of eyeglasses in states where there were restrictions was 25% higher than in other states. Prices for the same product varied as much as 300% in a single city.

Advertising in the U.S. in 1978 rose 13% over 1977, to $43 billion. This was the third year in which the advertising growth rate had exceeded the growth rate of the economy. Total expenditures by national advertisers in outdoor, newspapers, magazines, and spot and network television had tripled since 1965, making these the five most used media. Advertisers bought more television time than ever before in 1978, and TV accounted for 54% of all national advertising dollar expenditures. Each of the three major television networks, ABC, CBS, and NBC, reached $1 billion in sales. The intense competition for the advertiser's dollar led each network to reshuffle its schedules several times during the year.

For those advertisers who could not afford TV, magazines and newspapers became the major channels for reaching customers. In some areas—notably New York City—this led to problems because of long-running newspaper strikes. There was a major shift in 1978 to the use of celebrities to promote products and services, with actors and athletes being especially prominent. Several consumer groups brought legal actions to require advertisers to show that the celebrities actually used the products and services they endorsed and that the claims they were making were correct. A new industry developed that matched celebrities with advertisers, and during the year one firm billed 400 deals worth $12 million.

One of advertising's most popular spokesmen, 9 Lives Cat Food's Morris, died in Chicago in July at the age of 17.

Statistics published by *Advertising Age* in August indicated that the 100 largest national advertisers in the U.S. increased their advertising and promotion expenditures 14% in 1977, to $8.8 billion. Procter and Gamble maintained its position as the largest national advertiser by spending $460 million. Others in the top five were General Motors, General Foods, Sears Roebuck, and K mart. This was the first time that K mart had appeared on the top five list. Sears Roebuck raised its national advertising expenditures by $45 million, the largest increase among the ten leading national advertisers.

Pharmaceutical firms accounted for three of the top five advertising positions on network radio in 1977. Consumer goods firms such as McDonald's and PepsiCo were among the five largest users of spot television time. The three major network television advertisers were Procter and Gamble, General Foods, and Bristol-Myers. The two leaders among the top five magazine, newspaper, and outdoor advertisers were R. J. Reynolds and Philip Morris. More than half of the money spent in 1977 on advertising on network and spot radio, network and spot television, outdoor, newspapers and magazines, and farm publications came from the 100 leading national advertisers.

With women now comprising 49% of the labour force and holding 41% of professional jobs, a number of firms changed their advertising messages to take this into account. Airline, insurance, oil, and automobile companies were among the leaders in this area. A number of magazines aimed at women showed large increases in advertising revenue in 1978.

In May the U.S. Supreme Court refused to hear a petition from the National Citizens Committee for Broadcasting requesting, in effect, that broadcasters provide free air time for critics of commercial messages. In the late 1960s the Federal Communications Commission (FCC) had mandated free time for such countercommercials, mainly against cigarette ads, but that policy had been reversed as part of a revision of the so-called fairness doctrine in 1974. In refusing the committee's petition that the FCC return to its original policy, the court upheld the FCC ruling that ordinary commercials are not "controversial" messages that require a reply.

Stars and Stripes, the armed forces newspaper, found itself in economic trouble again in 1978 and requested permission from Congress to sell advertising space. In past years this request had been turned down by Congress. However, with the federal government spending more money on advertising each year for military recruiting, it was believed that a favourable response might be forthcoming in 1979.

A once popular advertising medium returned in 1978. A number of large motion picture theatre chains contracted for screen advertising to increase their revenue. This medium, common outside the U.S., had been used with success in the U.S. in the 1950s but declined in importance with the rise of television. With more people attending movie theatres, particularly the young and senior age groups, a number of national advertisers of consumer products put their messages on the screen. Research studies indicated that patrons did not mind an advertising message at the beginning of a film.   (EDWARD MARK MAZZE)

AEROSPACE

Not since the massive tide of technological change in the mid-1950s swept away the piston-engined airliner fleets and replaced them with sleek jets 200 mph faster had aviation seen such significant reequipment activity as in 1978. For a decade the airlines and the aircraft manufacturers had been looking to the time when the present generation of medium- and short-range transports should come up for replacement. The fuel crisis of 1973–74 injected a sense of urgency, the airlines being badly hit, first by the large overnight increase in operating costs and second by the slump in traffic.

The best solution to the problem was determined to be more efficient airframes and engines. For the first time in air transport history new aircraft were to be sold on the basis of economics rather than speed. Estimates showed that to replace the fleets of Boeing 707s, 727s, and 737s, Douglas DC-8s and DC-9s, HS Tridents, BAC One-Elevens, Caravelles, and others, no fewer than 3,000 new airplanes worth $60 billion would have to be built between 1980 and 1992.

In late 1977 Swissair kicked off this mammoth reequipment program by ordering a derivative airliner, a growth version of the DC-9 with a refanned development of the Pratt & Whitney JT8D, the world's most widely used transport engine. This new-wine-in-old-bottles approach only partly exploited the technology that was available

On July 14 United Airlines announced that it had placed a $1.2 billion order for 30 new 767 passenger jets with the Boeing Co. The plane was the first new airliner developed by Boeing since 1968.

for completely new designs, and so the economy characteristics of the plane were not markedly improved. On the other hand there was less risk and fewer introductory problems.

McDonnell Douglas and Boeing also proposed reengined versions of their DC-8s and 707s, but with completely new power plants some 25% more economical than their existing engines and much less noisy. Boeing was fitting the Franco-U.S. CFM56 engines to a 707 for trials and to assess the market, but many experts thought the long-range DC-8s a better bet.

Few people, even five years earlier, could have predicted that the supersonic transport (SST) would make so little impact, and in fact 1978 was as notable for its reverses as for its progress. Load factors on the British and French Concordes continued high, indicating sustained popularity despite premium fares, but the annual utilization remained low owing to the lack of approved routes. In August 1978 British Airways announced that it would have to renegotiate terms for its five Concordes, having lost £17 million during 1977–78. Toward the end of the year crews from the U.S. airline Braniff began training in preparation for an interchange scheme whereby Braniff would take over British Airways and Air France Concordes at New York City and fly them on to Dallas, Texas. Braniff was also planning to extend its service to South America.

The Soviet Union's SST, the Tupolev TU-144, finally began scheduled passenger service in late 1977 on just one route. But persistent rumours about its unsatisfactory performance proved well-founded when service became increasingly sporadic and finally ceased in June 1978. There were no signs that operations would be reinstated. Meanwhile, U.S. engineers, concentrating only on the technical challenge and ignoring the more important political aspects such as overflying and landing rights, concluded that even the decision to launch a second-generation SST could not be made before about 1983–84. On this basis, an actual aircraft could hardly appear before 1990.

In 1978 Europe finally offered a serious challenge to the U.S. in the airliner market. The decision by Eastern Airlines in April to acquire 23 A300 Airbuses, following a successful six-month trial, was a momentous breach of a virtual domestic monopoly held by Boeing, McDonnell Douglas, and Lockheed. Not since the days of the Viscount had there been such a threat to U.S. domination. Almost simultaneously, Pan Am announced an order for a dozen long-range Lockheed L-1011 TriStars, with an option on an additional 14, to replace the last of its once-huge fleet of Boeing 707s. The choice of Lockheed broke Pan Am's traditional liaison with Boeing, and what swung the deal was the British government's guarantee to underwrite the purchase as a means of getting a new version of the TriStar established, using Rolls-Royce RB.211 engines. The U.S. industry and government, which until recently had virtually written off European aviation as a lame duck, complained bitterly about "unfair" competition despite the fact that both aircraft contained substantial contributions from U.S. industry.

Europe also took the next major step. On July 7 Airbus Industrie launched the smaller 200-seat A300B10 on the basis of 60 orders and options from European operators. At that time three other 200-seaters were also being offered: Boeing's 767-200 (once known as the 7X7); the L-1011-400 TriStar from Lockheed; and a McDonnell Douglas contender, the DC-X-200. With so much dangerous competition, particularly from Europe, Boeing acted quickly; only seven days after the A300B10 announcement it launched the 767-200 for its front-line customer, United Airlines. It was the first new Boeing transport in 12 years. Faced with these developments, McDonnell Douglas shortly afterward shelved the DC-X-200, saying that it would in the future concentrate on improving its DC-9s and DC-10s.

Throughout the year the new U.K. nationalized airframe company, British Aerospace Corp. (an amalgam of British Aircraft Corp., Hawker Siddeley Aviation, Hawker Siddeley Dynamics, and Scottish Aviation), sought to collaborate with another

manufacturer on a new airliner. It was wooed by Boeing and McDonnell Douglas but spurned them to reenter Airbus Industrie, from which it had resigned some years earlier owing to lack of confidence in the European wide-body airliner. France held out for tough terms, however, and at the year's end one of the main conditions for a reentry—an order for A300s by British Airways—had not been negotiated.

The British government in July gave its assent for British Aerospace to begin full-scale development of the HS.146, shelved in October 1974 because of a lack of market prospects. Also in July British Airways ordered 19 Boeing 737s to replace its Trident 1s and 2s, and, together with Eastern Airlines, became in September a customer for the second Boeing transport to be launched in 1978—the 174-seat 757.

Laker Airways, which launched its second Skytrain service, from London to Los Angeles, on September 26, announced a massive reequipment program. This included five long-range DC-10s and ten medium-range A300s.

(MICHAEL WILSON)

ALCOHOLIC BEVERAGES

Beer. World beer production in 1977 totaled a record 815 million hectolitres (hl) compared with the previous year's 800 million, itself a record, even though sales were somewhat depressed in both the U.S. and Europe by bad weather during the summer. Production in the U.S., at 200,134,000 hl, remained higher than in any other country and was more than twice that of West Germany (94,336,000 hl), the second largest producer. The U.K. was third with 65,237,-000 hl (1 hl = about 26.5 U.S. gal). West Germany again recorded the highest per capita consumption of beer, with Czechoslovakia, Australia, and Belgium in second, third, and fourth places, respectively. (See Table V.)

For the first time in some years both the U.S. and European countries reported plentiful barley crops in 1978. The generally low nitrogen content of the crop provided an improved yield of beer from a given quantity of barley. Achievement of low-nitrogen barley for malting resulted from close liaison between experimental stations producing new varieties and farmers on the one hand and maltsters and brewers on the other. In Britain the Malting Barley Committee of the Institute of Brewing had for many years been monitoring experiments in barley varieties, arranging for trials and for malting at both the pilot and production stages and finally arranging brewing trials in various breweries around the country. At annual conferences agricultural and brewing interests met to hear the results and to learn which were the recommended varieties for future plantings. The project had already resulted in such excellent new varieties as Ark Royal and had shown how grain might be used economically, allowing high yields of beer from given tonnages.

The bumper harvest did not bring about an undue slump in prices because the grain came onto the market gradually in most

Industrial Review

countries, a circumstance caused by late rains in various parts of Europe. A continuing strong demand for malting-quality grain was expected, in part because of the marked rise in beer consumption in Eastern Europe.

Brewers were watching trends of beer sales in the U.K. with interest. The country was practically the last bastion of ale (as opposed to lager beer) drinking, but lager had increased its market share from 2 to 24.8% in the decade up to 1977. It was estimated, however, that lager's market share would not go much higher before the mid-1980s.   (ARTHUR T. E. BINSTED)

Spirits. The general trend toward "lighter" spirits such as vodka at the expense of "darker," "heavier" varieties like whiskey, continued, especially in the important North American market. White spirits—vodka, gin, rum, tequila—increased their sales in the U.S. in 1977 by 4.2% to 165 million gal at the expense of whiskeys, which fell 1.7% to 219 million gal. White rum was popular as a substitute for vodka and gin, with sales up 20%, and some industry observers considered that it had the best sales prospects of any of the 13 major spirit types sold in the U.S. In Britain vodka's share of the total spirits market moved up two points to 13%, and it was expected to be the number-two spirit by 1981. Smirnoff, the world's largest selling spirits brand, continued to increase its market share in most countries.

Anti-drink lobbies were vocal in several countries, and in the U.S. a "Responsible Drinking" campaign using $2.5 million of free advertising space from the media was sponsored by the Distilled Spirits Council. The plan was for the industry to inform and educate the public rather than be faced by more controls through government legislation.

France's 1978 wine grape harvest was larger than that of the previous year, though still below the 1976 crop.

Releases of Scotch whisky from bond, a fairly reliable guide to retail sales, rose by an encouraging 7.5% in Britain in the 12 months ended Aug. 31, 1978. The world market for Scotch whisky was conservatively estimated to increase at about 5% a year, with growth coming from Europe and Japan rather than the U.S. and U.K. Total exports of Scotch whisky were up 16% in the year ended Sept. 30, 1978, to 99,960,000 proof gal worth £598 million. Exports to EEC countries rose 9.8% to 18,975,000 proof gal despite discriminatory taxation in France and Italy. Shipments to the U.S., the most important export market, were down 7% to 32,331,000 proof gal. Sales to the rest of the world, however, rose nearly 10% to 48,660,000 proof gal.

French grape brandy exports jumped by nearly half (possibly as the result of shipments to the U.S.S.R.) to 260,000 hl of pure alcohol, overtaking cognac exports which, at 236,000 hl, declined 3.7% from the previous year. French liqueur exports showed a rise of 9.2% to 118,000 hl. Armagnac shipments fell 5.3% to 18,000 hl, largely as the result of West Germany switching to grape brandy.   (COLIN PARNELL)

Wine. In 1978, for the second consecutive year, climatic conditions in Europe—which normally supplies 78% of world wine production—were unfavourable for viticulture. Consequently, although world production, estimated at 298.5 million hl, was 3–4% above that of 1977, it was 20 million hl below the 1976 figure and 15 million hl below the 1971–75 average. Although boosted by better harvests in France and

Table V. Estimated Consumption of Beer in Selected Countries
In litres [1] per capita

Country	1975	1976	1977
Germany, West	147.8	150.9	148.7
Czechoslovakia	143.4	139.7	140
Australia [2]	142.1	139.9	136.2
Belgium [3]	130.6	138.0	130.1
New Zealand	133.2	131.0	128.5
Luxembourg	129.0	130.0	127.0
Germany, East	119.7	124.5	126.4
Ireland	128.6	123.0	126.2
United Kingdom	117.6	118.9	119.5
Denmark	117.46	118.83	116.06
Austria	103.8	102.0	103.1
Canada [4]	85.8	86.4	86.0
United States	81.7	82.5	85.6
Netherlands, The	78.96	83.87	83.9
Hungary	72.3	76.4	80.0
Switzerland	71.8	71.1	68.3
Finland	54.7	54.6	55.3
Sweden	60.2	59.1	53.6
Venezuela	50	50	...
Spain	47.0	47.9	46.9
France	44.9	48.66	46.21
Norway	45.44	44.72	45.47
Bulgaria	46	45	...
Yugoslavia	37.8	40.4	...
Colombia	32.8	39.9	40

[1] One litre = 1.0567 U.S. quart = 0.8799 imperial quart.
[2] Years ending June 30.
[3] Excluding so-called "household beer."
[4] Years ending March 31.

Table VI. Estimated Consumption of Potable Distilled Spirits in Selected Countries
In litres [1] of 100% pure spirit per capita

Country	1975	1976	1977
Poland	4.6	5.4	5.8
Luxembourg	3.5	4.1	4.7
Hungary	3.61	4.0	4.4
Germany, East	3.5	3.7	3.7
Canada [2]	3.1	3.16	3.51
U.S.S.R.	3.3	3.3	3.3
United States	3.10	3.12	3.14
Yugoslavia	2.8	3	...
Spain	2.6	3.1	3
Czechoslovakia	2.88	3.00	3
Finland	2.81	3.0	2.99
Sweden	2.97	3.08	2.97
Netherlands, The	3.44	2.48	2.91
Germany, West	3.04	3.33	2.91
France [3]	2.5	2.5	2.5
Iceland	2.40	2.31	2.46
Ireland	2.03	2.03	2.16
Belgium	1.99	1.95	2.10
Italy	2	2	2
New Zealand	1.71	2.00	2
Romania	...	2	...
Norway	1.84	1.87	1.90
Switzerland	1.94	1.80	1.88
Denmark	1.74	1.88	1.80
Cyprus	1.6	1.6	1.7

[1] One litre = 1.0567 U.S. quart = 0.8799 imperial quart.
[2] Years ending March 31.
[3] Including aperitifs.

Table VII. Estimated Consumption of Wine in Selected Countries
In litres [1] per capita

Country	1975	1976	1977
France [2]	103.70	101.27	100.91
Portugal	89.8	97.8	97
Italy	103.9	98.0	93.5
Argentina	83.7	84.8	88.5
Spain	76.0	71.0	65.0
Chile	43.46	47.84	52.30
Luxembourg	41.3	45.3	49.3
Switzerland [3]	43.9	43.5	44.9
Greece	38.0	39.8	39.6
Austria	35.1	36.3	36.1
Hungary	34.2	35.3	35.0
Romania	33.0	30	...
Yugoslavia	28.2	29	...
Uruguay	25.1	25	...
Germany, West	23.3	23.6	23.4
Bulgaria	20	20	...
Belgium	17.2	15.7	17.5
Czechoslovakia	16.3	16.5	16
Australia [4]	11.2	11.2	13.7
U.S.S.R.	13.4	13.4	13.3
Netherlands, The	10.26	11.35	11.73
Denmark	11.48	12.53	11.67
Sweden	8.25	8.47	9.50
Poland	7.5	8.5	9.1
New Zealand	8.8	8.8	9
South Africa	10.41	9.89	9.00

[1] One litre = 1.0567 U.S. quart = 0.8799 imperial quart.
[2] Excluding cider (c. 20 litres per capita annually).
[3] Excluding cider (c. 6 litres per capita 1976–77).
[4] Years ending June 30.

Source: Produktschap voor Gedistilleerde Dranken, *Hoeveel alcoholhoudende dranken worden er in de wereld gedronken?*

Italy, European production at 235 million hl remained below the average for the past decade. European Economic Community (EEC) countries contributed 145 million hl, more than 48% of the world total. Production in South America declined by about 5 million hl to about 35 million hl, Argentina's harvest in particular being reduced by frost and hail. In the U.S. production rose to some 16 million hl.

The French harvest of 58.5 million hl, though higher than that of the previous year, was nevertheless 20% below that of 1976. The most satisfactory levels were reached in the Côtes du Rhône and Beaujolais regions. The quality of the wines was on the whole excellent, with satisfactory alcoholic content and balance of acidity.

Italy produced nearly 67 million hl, close to the average except in Piedmont, Emilia-Romagna, and, especially, Apulia, where production was down. Quality was generally good. Spain, with a production of 28.5 million hl, had an excellent harvest both quantitatively and qualitatively, well above the average for the previous five years. Portuguese production, at 7.5 million hl, was again below average, but the quality of the wines, particularly in the Douro region, was good.

In Algeria production fell to 2.3 million hl, in marked contrast to an annual average of 6 million hl earlier in the 1970s and 12 million hl in the 1960s. Among other important winegrowing countries the U.S.S.R. produced 31 million hl, Romania 10 million hl, and West Germany 8 million hl.

The first World Wine Fair was held in Bristol, England, in July. Although Britain was importing wine from 29 countries and had about 70 commercial vineyards of its own, consumption remained at a low level.

(PAUL MAURON)

AUTOMOBILES

Detroit's executive lineup underwent more changes in 1978 than its automobiles. Ford Motor Co. fired its president, who later gained the same office at Chrysler Corp.; the vice-chairman of General Motors Corp. resigned; American Motors Corp. (AMC) took on a new president and financial officer, and its chairman decided to take early retirement; and, while bringing in a new president, Chrysler moved its former president to vice-chairman. In the meantime its marketing vice-president retired early at the age of 55.

In between all the executive shuffling Detroit managed to bring out perhaps the greatest number of new models in history and to register sales for the 1978 model year second only to the phenomenal totals of 1973. But it was also a year of major recalls. Ford was forced to recall 1.5 million of its subcompact 1971–76 Pintos and 1975–76 Bobcats because of allegations that the fuel tanks could rupture and explode in the event of rear-end collisions. Firestone Tire & Rubber Co. was faced with the largest recall in history, some 10 million of the 500 series steel-belted radial tires.

As if the year was not hectic enough, it was also in 1978 that Volkswagen became the first import manufacturer to build cars in the U.S.; AMC and Renault of France announced plans to affiliate; and Chrysler sold off its European operations to Peugeot-

Citroën of France, making the latter the largest automaker in Europe.

So much was going on in the U.S. that it was almost overlooked when John Z. DeLorean, former GM executive, announced that he would build his long-promoted DMC-12 sports/safety car in Northern Ireland after previously saying that it would be built in Puerto Rico. The two-seat, gullwing sports car was to have been introduced in 1979, but the switch in assembly sites postponed the date to 1980.

In a year filled with surprises the biggest of all probably was the firing of Lee Iacocca as president of Ford Motor Co. and his later hiring as president and chief operating officer of Chrysler Corp. He was replaced by Philip Caldwell (see BIOGRAPHIES). Iacocca was ousted by Henry Ford II, chairman of the firm, reportedly to keep him from gaining control of the company after Ford retired in 1980.

Meanwhile, Richard Terrell, the vice-chairman of GM, decided to take early retirement from General Motors. He cited ill health as one of the chief reasons for his leaving. It was a surprise move because by doing so Terrell took himself out of the running to succeed Thomas Murphy, due to retire as chairman in 1980.

At American Motors Corp., Roy Chapin, Jr., chairman since 1967, announced that he would step down from an active role with the smallest of the domestic automakers. Gerald Meyers, president, took over as chairman. Paul Tippett, Jr., who had been an executive vice-president with Singer Co. and president of its Singer sewing machine operations, was named president to succeed Meyers. At Chrysler, Robert McCurry, vice-president of marketing and recognized as one of those behind Chrysler's offer of cash rebates to sell cars after the Arab oil embargo, made good on his promise to retire at the age of 55.

It was a whirlwind year for executives and for car sales, too. GM, Ford, Chrysler,

and American Motors sold 9,256,808 new cars in the 1978 model year extending from Oct. 1, 1977, to Sept. 30, 1978. It was the second highest model-year total in history, trailing only the 10.1 million sold in 1972–73. GM set an individual sales record of 5,289,313 units, up from 5,131,971 in the 1977 model year and ahead of the previous record of 5,239,695 sold in 1973.

Ford Motor Co. sales also rose, up 8.7%, but they did not reach a record. Ford sold 2,630,837 cars in the 1978 model year and watched as its new compact Fairmont set a new sales record for a car in its first year on the market. The total of more than 420,000 units topped the previous record of 418,000 set by the 1965 Ford Mustang.

Chrysler sales declined to 1.1 million units from 1.2 million in the 1977 model year. One reason cited for the decline was unfavourable publicity generated over the all-new subcompact Dodge Omni and Plymouth Horizon after *Consumer Reports* magazine charged the two with unsafe steering. The charges were refuted by both U.S. and Canadian safety agencies, but for a brief period sales fell. Also contributing to the decline in sales was the fact that Chrysler discontinued the full-size Dodge Royal Monaco and Plymouth Gran Fury in 1978 as a move to boost its overall fuel-economy average. Thus, it was without a market entry in a size segment that proved to be a good seller in 1978.

American Motors scored a sales success with its new compact replacement for the Hornet, the Concord. But the Gremlin, Pacer, and Matador fell flat so that the smallest of the big four sold only 180,099 cars in the 1978 model year. This was down 11.8% from 1977, which itself registered a decline of 21% from 1976. Matador was dropped for 1979.

The first American-made Volkswagens started rolling off the line at the New Stanton, Pennsylvania, plant in April.

WIDE WORLD

All four U.S. automakers unveiled a variety of new model offerings in the fall designed to attract more sales in the 1979 model year. The emphasis was on smaller cars. Ford brought out smaller and lighter versions of the standard-size Ford LTD and Mercury Marquis and restyled models of the subcompact Mustang and Mercury Capri. GM introduced downsized and lighter versions of the Buick Riviera, Oldsmobile Toronado, and Cadillac Eldorado. Chrysler presented smaller and lighter Chrysler New Yorkers and Newports in the standard size segment and a new Dodge St. Regis in the same category, along with two-door versions of the subcompact Dodge Omni and Plymouth Horizon.

Chrysler also brought out new front-wheel-drive models built by Mitsubishi in Japan for distribution in the U.S. They were the Plymouth Champ and Dodge Colt. And for the first time Chrysler brought out subcompact trucks, the Dodge D-50 and the Plymouth Arrow. Both of these were also imports from Mitsubishi. American Motors offered sedan and liftback replacements for the subcompact Gremlin, renamed the Spirit.

GM luxury models sported 114-in wheelbases and overall lengths of about 206 in. All offered front-wheel drive as well, a first for the Riviera. The Riviera also had a 231-cu-in turbocharged V-6 engine as standard in its S model and optional in its luxury version. It became the fourth GM car to offer turbocharging, a method that uses normally wasted exhaust gases to boost engine horsepower so that a normal economy engine can also have the characteristics of a high-performance power plant.

While the new Riviera had the turbo, the new Toronado and Eldorado offered an optional diesel engine, GM's 350-cu-in V-8. The high-mileage diesel was also in the Oldsmobile 88, 98, and Cutlass; the Cadillac Seville; and the Chevrolet and GMC light-duty pickup trucks. Before the end of the 1979 model year all Cadillac models also were to have the diesel as an option. The diesel in the Cutlass was a new, smaller 260-cu-in model, which came with a five-speed manual transmission.

At Ford the new LTD and Marquis were reduced in wheelbases from 121 in, and overall lengths came down to 209–212 in from 224–229 in the previous year. The weight reduction ranged from 600 to 800 lb. Because the cars were smaller and lighter Ford made its 302-cu-in V-8 engine standard in both and its 351-cu-in V-8 an option. It stopped offering the 400- and 460-cu-in V-8s. The 460 was also dropped as an option in the luxury Lincoln in favour of the 400 only.

The new Mustang and Capri (which for the first time was now built in the U.S. rather than in West Germany) were offered in fastback models, and the Mustang also got a notchback version. Four-cylinder engines were standard in both, and sixes and V-8s optional as well as an optional turbocharged 2.3-litre, four-cylinder engine in the Mustang Cobra and Capri Turbo R/S.

The rest of the Ford and Mercury models were little changed for 1979. The automaker

did, however, come out with a special "Collector's Series" edition of the Lincoln and Mark V to commemorate their last year on the market at their large dimensions before they, too, would be downsized in 1980. The Ford Thunderbird, which also would be downsized to become a compact in 1980, offered a Heritage model to signal the end of the line at its present intermediate dimensions.

The changes at Chrysler were extensive. New Yorker and Newport, which had been full-size luxury models, were reduced in size and weight and reclassified as standards. And an ultraluxury version, reminiscent of the former Imperial, was introduced. It was called the New Yorker Fifth Avenue Edition. At Dodge the old Royal Monaco became the St. Regis. Since Chrysler's standard-size cars had become approximately intermediate in size, the mid-size Fury, Monaco, and Charger were dropped in 1979. Two-door sporty versions of the Dodge Omni and Plymouth Horizon were added for '79 to complement the four-door offerings that first appeared in January 1978.

At AMC, while the Spirit name was new, the sedan replacement for the former subcompact Gremlin almost looked like a mirror image save for slight changes in the form of a larger rear quarter window. The liftback Spirit, however, was a new body style.

AMC said that it was counting on Renault to provide it with more models in the future. As soon as the two automakers signed an agreement to affiliate, AMC dealers were to distribute Renault's mini front-wheel-drive Le Car in the U.S. and Renault was to offer AMC's Jeeps in its worldwide markets. Later, perhaps for the 1980 model year, AMC would begin assembling a new Renault called the R-18, a luxury compact, at its Kenosha, Wis., assembly plant.

It was believed that AMC's announced intention to affiliate with a foreign automaker led to the decision by Chrysler to sell its European operations to Peugeot-Citroën of France. Under terms of the deal Peugeot would pay Chrysler $230 million in cash and give it a 15% equity interest in what now would become Europe's largest auto concern with about 18% of the market. Without having to pour money into new products for the European market, Chrysler said it would channel its funds to the U.S. market to develop more fuel-efficient cars in order to meet federal fuel economy standards for the 1980s.

The federal fuel economy laws took effect in the 1978 model year and required each of the four domestic manufacturers to obtain an average of 18 miles per gallon (mpg) from their fleets of cars or face a fine of $5 for every one-tenth mpg they fell below the standard for every car sold during the year. In 1979 the requirement would move up to 19 mpg and in 1980 it would be 20 mpg. The climax to the fuel economy standards and the reason the industry was downsizing its models was that U.S. manufacturers must obtain a 27.5-mpg average from their fleets of cars by 1985.

Meanwhile, the U.S. Environmental Protection Agency, which ranked the fuel economy for both U.S. and imported cars for inclusion on new car window stickers, changed its methods in the fall for the 1979

model year. In the past the EPA listed a city mileage figure, a highway mileage figure, and then one for city and highway combined. Reacting to public outcry that the averages, especially the city/highway combined, were unrealistically high, the EPA for 1979 changed to one "estimated mileage" figure for the cars. It corresponded to the city-only figure for previous years.

Once again the EPA's fuel economy ratings were dominated by imports from carmakers outside the U.S. First on the list was a diesel-powered Volkswagen Rabbit with an estimated rating of 41 mpg. Among the top individual models in the EPA listings, in addition to the Rabbit, were diesel-powered Volkswagen Dasher, Datsun 210, Dodge Colt, Plymouth Champ, Toyota Corolla, Mazda GLC, Chevrolet Chevette, and a three-way tie among the Honda Civic, Plymouth Arrow, and Ford Fiesta.

In addition to dominating the EPA list, the non-U.S. automakers were busy bringing new cars to market. From Japan, Toyota, the top importer in the U.S., unveiled a new Corona and a six-cylinder Celica. Datsun presented a new 280-ZX sports car, a two-door 810 luxury sedan, and a restyled B-210 under the name 210. Honda came out with a four-door model in the Accord line that previously was limited and announced that it would have a sports model in the spring tentatively called the Prelude. Mazda unveiled its sporty two-seat RX-7 rotary-engine sports model and a GLC wagon. From Europe Volkswagen brought out the long-awaited diesel Dasher, and Mercedes introduced its 300TD diesel-powered station wagon. Fiat put the finishing touches on a high-mileage subcompact hatchback tentatively code named the X 1-38.

The year in some respects was one of contrasts. Ford may have fired its president and had to recall several cars, but it also celebrated its 75th year in the business. Chevrolet also commemorated the 25th year on the market for the Corvette, which was chosen as the pace car for the Indianapolis 500-mi race. Only about 6,000 of those special edition cars were built, and speculators quickly drove the $13,000 starting price up to $30,000 and more. After the race prices eased back.

GM also caused a minor stir when it said that it would abandon its traditional once-a-year price increase each fall in favour of a small increase in the fall and others during the year as the need arose. The competition said it would follow suit. Price increases for the 1979 models averaged from 4.1 to 4.6%, or from $235 to $302, depending on the manufacturer.   (JAMES L. MATEJA)

BUILDING
AND CONSTRUCTION

In July 1978 the value of new construction put in place in the U.S. stood at a seasonally adjusted annual rate of $206.9 billion. The level of construction expenditures had exceeded expectations, moving up steadily during the first six months of the year. Despite some of the highest interest rates on record, housing starts during the first nine months remained above a seasonally adjusted annual rate of two million units.

It appeared that the strong housing market was due in large part to the desire of many Americans to invest money in homes to beat inflation. The housing industry was

helped significantly in 1978 by $40 billion in loans made available to savings and loan associations by the Federal Home Loan Bank Board. New six-month lending certificates with flexible interest yields were also a key factor in keeping money available for housing.

The U.S. government reported that new home prices had increased 16% during 1977 and 1978 to an average of approximately $63,000. The median price of a new home had been around $47,900 in 1977 and $27,600 in 1972. It was also reported that in 1977 the six million U.S. families that bought new and used houses stretched their income beyond traditionally safe standards. According to a report by the United States League of Savings Associations, the average home buyer spent $273 each month on the mortgage (exclusive of the down payment), $60 for utility bills, $54 for real estate taxes, and $13 for insurance, for a total of $400.

On a current dollar basis, it was expected that construction expenditures for the year would be in excess of $190 billion, compared with the previous record outlay of $172.5 billion in 1977. In the private sector, construction expenditures moved to successively higher levels of activity in each month of the year, while public sector activity remained strong. When the dollar outlays for the years 1972 through 1978 were adjusted to the 1972 price level, however, the level of activity in 1978 fell considerably below that of 1973.

Investment demand in Canada was weak in 1978, and the value of permits granted for housing construction declined sharply. In Western Europe a rather slow improvement in construction was predicted for 1978 and 1979, despite measures of fiscal stimulation undertaken in several countries. Construction in the U.K., which had risen steadily in 1977, experienced a decline in the first quarter of 1978, attributable mainly to a 23% drop in starts in the public sector. Private housing starts through the first six months of 1978 were 30% above the corresponding period in 1977; private hous-

ing orders remained high, and there was a noticeable increase in the construction of commercial property. Residential building in Japan was down after having risen 7% in 1977, and it appeared that investment in business plant and equipment would remain stagnant.

(CARTER C. OSTERBIND)

CHEMICALS

The U.S. chemical industry scored substantial gains in 1977 and in the first half of 1978. But in other industrialized countries the long-awaited chemical recovery was slow in developing.

In 1977, according to the U.S. Department of Commerce, shipments of chemicals and allied products amounted to $113,891,000,000, 9.4% higher than they were in 1976. In the first half of 1978 they rose to $65,433,000,000, 12.9% above the corresponding period of 1977.

Most of the increase was caused by greater physical volume rather than by higher prices. In 1977 the Federal Reserve Board's index of industrial production for chemicals and allied products averaged 180.7 (1967 = 100), 6.7% higher than the average for 1976. In the same period chemical prices rose only 3%. The U.S. Department of Labor's index of producer prices for chemicals and allied products went from 187.2 (1967 = 100) in 1976 to 192.8 in 1977.

Although the growth in physical output slowed somewhat in the first half of 1978, the same general trend continued. According to preliminary figures the index of chemical production averaged 186.2 for the first six months, 3% higher than that for the full year of 1977. The price index averaged 196.2 for the first half of 1978, 2% above the average for the whole of 1977.

The U.S. Department of Commerce reported that in 1977 chemical exports grew 8.6% to $10,812,000,000, while imports rose only 4.1% to $4,970,400,000. The favourable balance of trade for the U.S. chemical industry, therefore, increased 12.6% in 1977 to $5,841,900,000. During the first three quarters of 1978 the value of

the dollar against other major currencies dropped dramatically. In theory that should have helped the U.S. trade balance for chemicals (and other products) by effectively reducing the price of U.S. exports and increasing the price of imports into the country. No such effect was apparent, however, in the chemical trade figures for the first half of 1978, perhaps because of the time lag between a change in currency value and its effect on trade. In any case U.S. chemical exports did grow in the first six months of 1978 to $5,797,900,000, 7.1% above the figure for the first half of 1977. Imports, however, soared 29.4% in the same period to $3,238,500,000. Net exports of chemicals, as a result, dropped 12% from the first six months of 1977.

Capital investment in the U.S. chemical industry continued at a high level. In the fall 1978 survey taken by the McGraw-Hill Department of Economics, chemical companies estimated that their expenditures for the full year 1978 would amount to $7,480,000,000. They also reported that they intended to boost that by 9% in 1979 to $8,120,000,000. At the same time they said that they expected costs for plant and equipment would be 7% higher than in 1977.

Chemical industries in Western Europe, while continuing to grow in 1977 and the early part of 1978, were experiencing difficulties because of overcapacity in many areas. Commodity chemicals, including plastics, were problem spots. But man-made fibres were probably the most worrisome. Early in 1978 the Commission of the EEC and producers of man-made fibres reached a preliminary agreement under which existing capacities would be cut back by 20%. The plan allowed for special treatment for producers in Italy, where man-made fibre losses had been particularly heavy and where plant utilization was only 50–60%. The overall objective of the plan was to permit fibre producers to break even in 1979.

In West Germany man-made fibre production in 1977 dropped 7% to 707,000 metric tons. The industry was operating at approximately 70% of capacity, lower than it was in 1976. Prices for man-made fibres at the plant were 30% lower than in 1970. Overcapacity in large-volume plastics was also adversely affecting the health of the West German industry. In 1977 chemical sales in the country increased only 1.9%, and in the first quarter of 1978 they declined 2%.

But the outlook was not entirely bleak for West Germany. Experience had showed that chemical business picked up in the fall, and it was expected that the full year of 1978 would register a sales increase of 2–3%. As part of a long-range strategy the industry was turning more and more toward the manufacture of higher value chemical specialties and to more and more investment outside West Germany. The nation's Chemical Industry Association reported that $500 million in capital was transferred out of the country for chemical projects in 1977. It was estimated that another $500 million–$750 million was invested by for-

Industrial Review

eign subsidiaries of West German companies. Though the EEC had the biggest share of West German chemical investment, starting in 1974 the U.S. had become the principal single target. Investments in Brazil and in Japan had been increasing as well.

United Kingdom chemical companies were expecting a sales growth of 2.5–3% in 1978 after a year of no growth in 1977. Their expectations in late 1978 were for a 4–5% growth in 1979. Britain had expected North Sea discoveries of natural gas to revitalize its industry, but projects based on the gas were slow in materializing. In 1976 a government-union-industry working party had established as one goal the construction of four ethylene plants by 1985. In 1978, however, only one plant—in Mossmorran, Scotland—was in the planning stage. A March 1978 study served to dampen hopes further. It concluded that a planned multimillion-dollar gas gathering system was not feasible. The system would have brought ashore liquids associated with North Sea natural gas and would have provided raw material for a large-scale ethylene plant. Study of a more modest system began, but there was no great optimism that even that would be built.

Japanese chemical companies were grappling with problems of overcapacity and sluggish demand. Major chemical companies posted sales and earnings gains during fiscal 1976 (which ended March 31, 1977). They were not able to do so well in 1977, however. Among the 20 largest chemical companies 12 reported lower sales and 6 showed losses. After a two-year study, the Japan Chemical Industry Association recommended consolidation among producers of chlorine and caustic soda, polyvinyl chloride, low-density polyethylene, and polypropylene. A six-month production cartel, which was due to expire at the end of September 1978, improved the situation for makers of nylon, polyester, and acrylic fibres. In the fall of the same year fertilizer makers were planning cutbacks of 20% in ammonia and 40% in urea. Despite these problems Japan's favourable balance of trade in the chemical industry increased 4% in 1977 to $2,006,500,000. The continued strength of the yen, however, made it questionable whether or not the industry could repeat its performance in 1978.

(DONALD P. BURKE)

ELECTRICAL

A relationship, long suspected, between growth in demand for electricity and the market for electrical products was by 1978 believed to be fully established. Recent trends consistently showed annual growth in demand for electricity in the industrialized countries below 7% and electrical machinery markets in the same nations declining, whereas less developed countries had demand growths of up to 30% per annum and also had rapidly growing markets for electrical products. The opportunities in less developed countries attracted manufacturers from the industrialized nations, and although they were beginning to lose ground in some product areas to indigenous industry, there was increasing

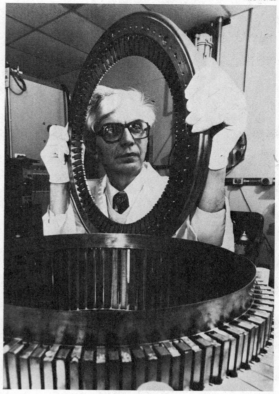

WIDE WORLD

RCA engineer examines component of a 145-kg (320-lb) vacuum switch tube, one of the 12 believed to be the world's most powerful of their kind. A 20-member team designed the water-cooled devices for Princeton University's Plasma Physics Laboratory, where each would be used to control 25 megawatts (million watts) of electric power during nuclear fusion experiments.

scope for them in high-technology products (turbine generators, high-voltage switchgear, etc.) and in mass-produced products (motors, control systems, etc.). One increasingly important complication in assessing overall market strategy was the effect of inflation on trade between the industrialized countries.

The strength of the West German mark and inflated domestic wages were among the factors that persuaded major West German electrical equipment manufacturers to transfer a growing proportion of their budgets into overseas operations. Investment abroad by the industry increased by 10.6% in 1976 and rose by an additional 13.6% in 1977. By 1978 the industry had DM 5.6 billion invested overseas, with the U.S. and Brazil the favourite countries for expansion. Siemens, for example, joined forces with Allis Chalmers in the U.S. to set up a company to manufacture power engineering products.

With the West Germans scanning distant horizons, the flow of investment by foreign electrical companies into West Germany was tailing off. In 1977 the figure rose by DM 332 million to reach a total of DM 4.4 billion. The most interest was shown by U.S. companies, which by 1978 owned 6% of all foreign investment in the West German electrical industry. West German wages overtook those in the U.S., and West German companies were being underbid by up to 25% on many projects.

The same was true of the Swiss electrical industry. Exports increased in 1977 by about 10%, but imports rose by 20%, with switchgear up by 25%. Brown Boveri, the largest Swiss electrical equipment manufacturer, was actively increasing its overseas investment, a recent acquisition

being Turbodyne's Gas Turbine Division in Minnesota.

Although the balance between exports and imports of electrical equipment in West Germany was not as bad as in Switzerland, DED (the West German organization for investment and project coordination in less developed countries) in 1978 had DM 700 million for equity investments and/or loans with equity features available to companies in less developed countries. DED had already initiated production units for cables in Africa and the Far East and for motors, transformers, and batteries in Central and South America.

Toward the end of 1978, following the announcement U.S. Pres. Jimmy Carter's export stimulus package on October 3, there were signs of a trade quarrel brewing between the U.S. and Europe concerning higher U.S. import duties on products subsidized by European governments. In 1977 the U.S. electrical equipment industry increased its sales by 10% to $43 billion and was expected to continue to advance in 1978 but at a somewhat lower rate.

The French electrical industry recorded an increase in exports of 37% in 1977, with imports down by 14%. During the previous four years French exports to the Far East multiplied by nine and to the Middle East by five. In Britain exports of electrical power plant and industrial electrical machinery rose 36% in the first six months of 1978 compared with the same period in 1977, while imports increased by 20%.

Britain was one of the few industrialized countries not accused by the UN Conference on Trade and Development in 1978 of having impeded the local electrical equipment industries in Brazil. AEG (Allgemeine Elektrizitäts-Gesellschaft) and Siemens of

West Germany, Brown Boveri of Switzerland, ASEA (Allmänna Svenska Elektriska Aktiebolaget) of Sweden, ACEC (Ateliers de Constructions Électriques de Charleroi) of Belgium, Hitachi of Japan, and General Electric of the U.S. were alleged to have divided up the Brazilian market to the detriment of the locally owned industry. As a result of the investigation, there was a marked tightening of import laws to encourage increased production in Brazil.

(T. C. J. COGLE)

FURNITURE

The U.S. home furnishings industry continued to profit from the housing boom. Furniture manufacturers' shipments during the first half of 1978 showed a 14% increase in wholesale sales; corrected for inflation, the real growth rate averaged 7%. Wood furniture and upholstery shipments were both 15% above 1977 figures, and tables, principally occasional tables, enjoyed a growth rate of 30%. For the first time in five years, summer and casual furniture sales leveled off, at a 6% annual growth rate. Total retail furniture sales were estimated at $18.8 billion, including bedding, estimated at $176.4 million.

Two significant styling trends gained in importance during the year. "Lifestyle," a merchandising trend featuring casual, easy-to-assemble furniture, spawned hundreds of specialty stores catering to the mobile and young. The second notable trend was "the great room," an all-purpose family room that was actually a throwback to the old family kitchen.

In upholstered furniture, the use of modular units that could be fitted together in many configurations continued to be popular. In the trade, this was referred to as "the pit look." More upholstery manufacturers were offering sleep as well as conventional sofas. Smaller living units

contributed to the popularity of these dual-purpose units, as well as to a significant growth in wall units for books and general storage. Water beds continued to grow in popularity, with sales in 1978 estimated at $275 million. A new type, called a hybrid, combined a water bed with a conventional sleep unit.

U.S. government regulations continued to present problems for the furniture industry. A court decision removed the imminent possibility of a rigid cotton-dust standard in cotton mills, proposed by the Occupational Safety and Health Administration (OSHA). The imposition of wood-dust safety standards, also proposed by OSHA, could cause considerable adjustment in wood furniture-making procedures. An attempt by the Consumer Product Safety Commission to make upholstered furniture cigarette burn-proof still had not been resolved.

Wholesale furniture prices rose 12.5% in 1978, reflecting an estimated 30% increase in the cost of labour and materials, particularly hardwoods. The U.S. Department of Commerce reported a 27% increase in U.S. furniture imports, with 1977 volume reaching $464 million. Imports from Taiwan rose 51% to $75 million. In contrast, U.S. exports totaled only $136 million, 57% of which went to Canada.

(ROBERT A. SPELMAN)

FURS

Additional countries joined the list of those banning the use of such species as spotted cats, populations of which were considered to be endangered. The U.S. now required exporters of otters, lynx cats, and lynx to obtain permits as a means of regulating commerce in those animals. Nations belonging to the Convention on Trade in Endangered Species would meet in March 1979 in Costa Rica for a periodic review.

Prices of furs and fur products in 1978 were about 15% higher than in 1977, reflecting the general inflationary trend. These increases were most noticeable in the U.S. and Canada, because their dollars declined sharply in value relative to other major currencies. Buyers operating with such strong currencies as the Japanese yen, West German mark, and Swiss franc were actually able to buy pelts more cheaply than in the previous year.

Production continued to be a worldwide problem. Despite the recent attractiveness of the industry from the standpoint of profit potential, the attrition of the past decade still had not been offset. This, together with increased demand, resulted in delivery problems for stores. Nevertheless, the current boom prompted the U.S. industry to sponsor its first international fur fair, to be held in New York City in 1979.

The international fur industry again reported excellent business. In many countries 1978 was the fifth or sixth consecutive boom year. Retail fur sales set new records in the U.S., Canada, and Japan. Although final figures were not available at year's end, U.S. projections indicated that volume would reach $750 million, about 15% above the previous year.

Although fashion was considered the main force behind the excellent demand, comfort and economics were not far behind. Severe winters and energy problems were important factors, especially in northern climates. On the economic side, rampant inflation in many areas of the world led consumers to put their rapidly depreciating money into such luxuries as furs, jewelry, and travel. In some countries where widespread affluence was relatively new, the prestige appeal of furs was a major motivation; in Japan, retail fur sales rose more than 30% above the previous year's record of almost $500 million.

(SANDY PARKER)

GEMSTONES

Uncertainty about prices, which continued to trend strongly upward, and frantic activity described the condition of the gemstone industry in 1978. Drastic price changes for diamonds at the source—the Central Selling Organisation in London—were the direct cause of the uncertainty. For the most part these price manipulations were executed in reaction to changing economic and political conditions.

Imposition of a 17% surcharge on rough diamond prices in December 1977 shocked the diamond industry. This surcharge was grossly increased to 40% in March 1978, lowered to 25% by May, to 15% by June, and eventually, in August, dropped completely. Meanwhile, the base price of diamond rough had risen 30% over the December 1977 level. Also, by the end of 1977 a moratorium had been declared on supplying U.S. dealers with rough material weighing over five carats, forcing the dealers to turn to the more expensive secondary market in Europe and elsewhere.

Between September 1977 and September 1978, the steady upward price trend, including surcharges, translated into retail

The president of the environmental group Greenpeace, Patrick Moore (right), was arrested when he tried to protect a seal pup from slaughter during the annual seal hunt off the coast of Labrador.

Industrial Review

price rises of 65 to 121% for finished cut diamonds. Larger sized diamonds of high quality suffered even greater price inflation. Toward the end of 1978 a one-carat, D-Flawless diamond commanded a retail price of $44,000, representing a rise of some 180%. Diamond prices leveled off between June and August, probably because of normally slow gem sales in the summer, but soon began to rise again. There was no evidence of massive consumer resistance, however. Even the prices for older, estate jewelry at the important auctions were much higher than anticipated.

Some of the most severe pressure on diamond prices came from heavy investment buying. With the increase in mining costs and the sharp decline in the relative value of the U.S. dollar, diamonds suddenly seemed an attractive investment. Some retail jewelers, mail-order houses, investment brokers, and other companies jumped into the diamond investment business. Such a surge encouraged fraudulent and illegal enterprise, although industry self-policing, publicity, and court actions helped to weed out some of the more nefarious enterprises. The fluctuating surcharges applied to diamond rough at the source were meant to dampen investment enthusiasm by deliberately creating price uncertainty.

With few exceptions, coloured gemstones participated in the active market. Demand remained strong for medium-priced gems such as tourmaline, aquamarine, and irradiated blue topaz, as well as for higher priced gems such as "imperial" topaz, fancy coloured sapphires, tsavorite, and tanzanite. Tsavorites of over three carats became very scarce. Major producing areas for sapphire and ruby on Thailand's Cambodian border were plagued by guerrilla activity, and prices of Thai rubies and

sapphires rose by 40 to 50%. It was hoped that the good sapphires that entered the market from Yogo Gulch in Montana would help the situation, although these stones tended to be small. Milky-looking Sri Lanka sapphires turned a strong, deep blue by heat and irradiation also came on the market. Because of increased supply, prices of coloured stones in general remained fairly stable.   (PAUL E. DESAUTELS)

GLASS

Worldwide sluggishness in trade continued to affect the glass industry. In Europe the tonnage of glass melted in 1977 was 2.5% below the peak year of 1974. Much of the industry was engaged in modernization and consolidation in preparation for an expected upsurge in demand. The Belgian companies Verlica-Momignies and Bouteilleries Belges Réunies combined their activities under the name Verlipack and now supplied a complete range of glassware for packaging. Pilkington Brothers Ltd. of the U.K. purchased a 50% stake in the Finnish flat glass company Lahden Lasitehdas Oy, thus further consolidating its interests in Scandinavia.

Through its holding company, Scan-Gobain Glas, Saint-Gobain Pont-à-Mousson of France also consolidated its Scandinavian interests by merging Emmaboda Glasverk with Scan Glas Svenska and Söderberg and Cleve. Another French company, La Verrerie Cristallerie d'Arques, joined Sasaki Glass of Japan to set up a company to supply specially designed tableware for the Japanese market. Owens-Corning Fiberglas of the U.S. and Bayer of West Germany jointly planned to build a $47 million glass-fibre insulation plant at Vise in Belgium.

Glass fibre continued to make news, with the bulk of production going to insulation. Owens-Corning Fiberglas planned to set up a plant to produce glass-fibre mats for specialty purposes, such as the replacement of rag felt in roofing. In Japan, Asahi Glass and Mitsubishi Chemical Industries signed

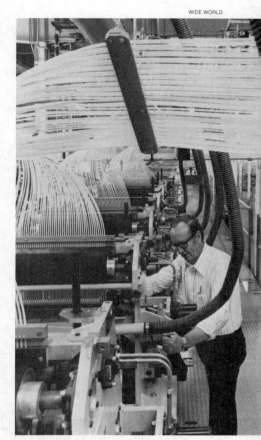

Giant machine fabricates glass-fibre-reinforced foam insulation for liquefied-natural-gas tankers.

an agreement with Allied Chemical of the U.S. to manufacture, under license, a composite glass-fibre thermoplastic resin material for the Japanese automobile industry. It was said to have the same strength as steel at half the weight.

RCA Electro-optics and Devices introduced its first fibre-optics data link for use in communications. This enabled light waves to be transmitted from one point to another through flexible cables consisting of ultrathin strands of glass fibre. The U.S. market in fibre-optics communications, currently around $10 million per year, was expected to grow to $500 million by 1983. It was also predicted that fibre optics would begin to replace telephone cables in the U.S. and Japan by 1979 and in Western Europe two years later. The BBC, in conjunction with Standard Telephones and Cables, was testing colour transmission over optical-fibre cables.

Corning Glass Works developed a range of glasses that reproduced colours in thin layers or in depth. While these had not yet reached the commercial stage, possible applications included the storage of archive material, projection slides, and photographs. The versatility of these new glasses would enable a single glass to take the place of different glasses in such products as stained glass, architectural glass, and tableware. Research laboratories in West Germany developed a fire-resistant glass for building purposes that withstood temperatures of 1,000° C.

The trend in packaging was toward light-

A 353.9 carat diamond was found near Pretoria, South Africa. It was estimated that when cut, the gem would be worth about $11 million.

er weight glass containers, thus reducing the cost of raw materials, energy, and transport. This led to the development of special coatings to protect the strength of the container during filling and use. Pressure to reuse discarded containers continued to grow; the U.K. announced a policy of setting up collection centres, thus following a practice already in use in West Germany, Switzerland, and, to some extent, the U.S. and Australia.

(CYRIL WEEDEN)

INSURANCE

Private insurance sales grew steadily in 1978, approaching $300 billion. Japan and West Germany each accounted for more than 10% of the global market, while the U.S. share was less than 50%. Approximately 90% of total insurance premiums were written by these three countries, Great Britain, France, Canada, The Netherlands, and Australia.

In the U.K. sales growth as of early 1978 was not keeping pace with inflation, despite a rise of 7% in general insurance and 12% in life insurance annual premium volume. Lloyd's membership increased by a record 3,800 individual members to a new high of 14,000. Four existing associations of registered U.K. brokers merged into the new British Insurance Brokers' Association, and brokers were now registered under the Insurance Brokers' Registration Act of 1977. After five years of deliberation, the Royal Commission on Civil Liability recommended changes in the motor vehicle law relating to bodily injuries, including introduction of no-fault compensation with the right to sue for additional damages. Strict liability was proposed in the U.K. and Europe for injuries caused by defective products.

The winter of 1977–78 was bad for domestic insurers in the U.K.; storms caused claims of £15 million in mid-January alone, and a strike by fire-protection personnel led to higher fire losses. Road casualties rose by 3% to 348,000 in 1977. A record liability award of £254,000 to an injured woman was confirmed in the appeals court.

By 1978 U.S. life insurers had more than $3.1 trillion of life insurance in force, and assets exceeded $350 billion. Projected sales growth for the year was close to 10% in life insurance and more than 12% in health insurance. Premium receipts amounted to almost $80 billion: half for life insurance, one-third for health insurance, and one-fifth for annuities. Two out of three persons in the U.S. had life insurance policies, and the average amount of life insurance owned by insured families rose to $37,000. Private insured pension plans, which grew at an annual rate of nearly 15%, now covered 20 million persons.

An increasing number of states were requiring that agents provide prospects with more cost comparison information on life insurance contracts. Several companies introduced new variable and adjustable life insurance policies, which included or permitted added protection to meet inflation. Group dental insurance now covered nearly 50 million persons, up from 13 million eight years earlier, and vision care insurance was very popular. The number of health maintenance organizations (prepaid health plans established under a recent federal law) increased to several hundred, giving insureds a new option in the health insurance market.

U.S. property and liability insurers reported an estimated 12% increase in sales, with premiums amounting to more than $70 billion annually. Statutory underwriting profits, which turned around in 1977 after almost a decade of losses, reached more than $700 million in the first six months of 1978. Including investment profits, policyholders' surplus rose by $2.5 billion to $30 billion at midyear. These results occurred despite 24 catastrophes (involving losses of more than $1 million each) totaling a near-record $482 million in claims.

The trend toward shorter and more readable types of property-liability insurance contracts grew with the introduction of the personal auto policy in most states. Similar personalized wording expanded the use of homeowners' contracts (including new forms for owners of condominiums and older homes) and the business owners' policy. Arson problems plagued the fire insurance business; more than one-fourth of all losses were attributed to that cause.

Automobile rating systems were challenged in many states, with new rating factors advocated to replace the traditional territory, age, sex, and marital status criteria. Tort liability reform continued; more than 20 states had no-fault laws, although there was a slowdown in the adoption of such laws in 1978. Group legal expense insurance was the most rapidly growing type of employee benefit coverage.

Flood risks in the U.S. were now insured under a new federal government program using agents of private insurers for sales and services. Nuclear risks were insured in 1978 with a newly reorganized pool of private insurers called the American Nuclear Insurers.   (DAVID L. BICKELHAUPT)

IRON AND STEEL

The depression in the steel industry that had begun in late 1974 continued in 1978, with no definite upturn in sight. World crude steel output in 1977 was 5 million metric tons less than in 1976, which was itself 30 million tons below the last good year, 1974. There was some upward movement in 1978, and some authorities believed that world output of steel for the year might be slightly above the 1977 figure of 672.2 million tons.

Such improvement as there was in 1978 varied in its extent in different countries. The output of the Communist countries continued to increase, and a number of the less developed countries moved strongly ahead. Among the established Western producers Canada and the U.S. both operated at quite high levels during the year, while many European countries also produced more than in 1977 (though in most cases still only working at about 60% of capacity). The Japanese and British industries were likely to produce less for the second successive year.

The continuance of the depression in the steel industry evoked a reappraisal of policies and the introduction of crisis programs in several of the major producing countries. These last included market protection measures in the U.S., Canada, and the EEC. In practice, however, they were fairly moderate.

In the U.S. 1978 was a year of definite recovery, with demand from the construction and machinery and equipment industries and from steel service centres more

An insurance salesman for 18 years (masked) told a U.S. House committee of how insurance agents pressure old people into buying unnecessary health insurance.

than offsetting some decline in demand from the automotive sector. The steel industry had been operating at about 85% of capacity, and the financial results of many of the major corporations improved significantly over 1977. However, revenue, although improved, was judged inadequate to finance the high cost of the new and replacement equipment that would be required to maintain a competitive U.S. industry over the long term and also to meet the increased cost of equipment for strengthened antipollution standards. In these circumstances attention was focused on the problem of imports, which amounted to 19.3 million metric tons in 1977 (when a number of antidumping suits were introduced against European and Japanese suppliers) and seemed likely to rise to over 20 million tons in 1978.

In the fall of 1977 the U.S. government set up a task force to study and make recommendations on the import issue in relation to the steel industry. The report advised the introduction of a so-called trigger price system. Brought into operation from mid-February 1978 and taking effect in April, this was an arrangement whereby customs officers were furnished with reference, or trigger, prices for each product based on a calculation by the administration of the delivered cost of the most efficient overseas supplier, Japan. Imports at lower prices were liable to receive a punitive tariff imposed by the government. Although U.S. producers were dissatisfied with the results of the system in terms of lowered import tonnage levels, especially from Europe, the administration appeared to anticipate that

One of Republic Steel's new hot metal charging furnaces at its Chicago mill.

the rise in the average price per ton of imports as a result of the system (about 15% by mid-1978) would have a delayed effect and would reduce imports by perhaps some 3.5 million metric tons in 1979.

In the EEC the crisis measures introduced progressively from 1975 were extended and strengthened at the end of 1977 within the framework of the so-called Davignon Plan. The changes then introduced included not only extension to new steel products of the

European Commission-determined mandatory minimum prices and rises in the Commission's recommended minimum prices for products already covered but also, for the first time, the buttressing of the internal market support measures by protection against cheap foreign steel imports. With regard to the latter, the Commission published minimum import reference prices for a wide range of products (in practice some 6% below prevailing EEC internal price lev-

Table VIII. World Production of Crude Steel
In 000 metric tons

Country	1973	1974	1975	1976	1977	1978 Year to date	No. of months	Percent change 1978/77
World	698,100	708,750	645,820	677,070	672,200	—	—	—
U.S.	136,460	131,990	105,940	116,310	113,140	91,450	9	+ 6.7
U.S.S.R.	131,480	136,200	141,330	144,800	146,700	49,900	4	+ 3.3
Japan	119,320	117,130	102,310	107,380	102,400	75,450	9	- 2.6
Germany, West	49,520	53,230	40,410	42,410	38,980	32,080	9	+ 8.5
United Kingdom	26,720	22,400	19,840	22,460	20,490	14,990	9	- 4.6
China*	26,000	26,000	26,500	21,000	23,400	†		
France	25,270	27,020	21,530	23,230	22,100	17,330	9	+ 3.1
Italy	21,000	23,800	21,870	23,460	23,340	18,040	9	+ 3.1
Belgium	15,520	16,230	11,580	12,150	11,260	9,000	9	+ 5.4
Poland	14,060	14,560	15,010	15,640	17,840	6,230	4	+ 6.5
Canada	13,390	13,610	13,030	13,330	13,510	10,990	9	+ 8.9
Czechoslovakia	13,160	13,640	14,320	14,690	15,050	6,300	5	+ 0.3
Spain	10,800	11,500	11,100	10,980	11,170	8,220	9	+ 0.3
Romania	8,160	8,840	9,550	10,970	11,460	†		
Australia	7,700	7,810	7,870	7,790	7,330	5,710	9	+ 3.1
Brazil	7,150	7,520	8,390	9,250	11,250	8,830	9	+ 6.7
India	6,890	7,070	7,990	9,360	10,010	7,070	9	- 5.4
Luxembourg	5,920	6,450	4,620	4,570	4,330	3,620	9	+11.7
Germany, East	5,860	6,170	6,480	6,740	6,850	2,310	4	+ 1.5
South Africa	5,720	5,990	6,830	7,110	7,310	5,920	9	+ 9.0
Sweden	5,660	5,990	5,610	5,140	3,970	3,090	9	+ 9.0
Netherlands, The	5,620	5,840	4,820	5,180	4,920	4,090	9	+ 9.0
Mexico	4,760	5,120	5,280	5,290	5,550	4,410	8	+26.1
Austria	4,240	4,700	4,070	4,480	4,090	3,250	9	+ 3.7
Hungary	3,330	3,470	3,670	3,650	3,720	1,280	4	+ 5.4
North Korea*	2,900	3,200	2,900	3,000	3,150	†		
Yugoslavia	2,680	2,840	2,920	2,750	3,180	2,590	9	+ 9.5
Bulgaria	2,250	2,190	2,270	2,460	2,590	860	4	- 0.2
Argentina	2,210	2,350	2,210	2,410	2,680	1,960	9	+ 1.7
Finland	1,620	1,660	1,620	1,650	2,160	1,690	9	+ 9.0
Turkey	1,350	1,590	1,700	1,970	1,870	1,680	9	+19.4
South Korea	1,160	1,950	1,990	3,520*	4,240	3,500	9	+15.5
Greece	1,090	930	900	1,110	1,000*	†		
Taiwan	540	900	1,010	1,630	1,770	2,530	9	+95.3

*Estimated. †1978 figures not yet available.
Source: International Iron and Steel Institute; British Steel Corporation.

Table IX. World Production of Pig Iron and Blast Furnace Ferroalloys
in 000 metric tons

Country	1973	1974	1975	1976	1977
World	499,900	504,600	468,400	489,500	485,300
U.S.S.R.	95,930	99,870	102,970	105,380	107,370
U.S.	93,520	87,010	72,510	78,810	73,800
Japan	90,010	90,440	86,880	86,580	85,890
Germany, West	37,100	40,220	30,070	31,850	28,960
China	21,000	22,000	22,000	23,000	25,000*
France	20,750	22,520	17,920	19,020	18,250
United Kingdom†	16,880	13,940	11,940	13,910	12,270
Belgium	12,660	13,150	9,070	9,870	8,910
Italy	10,270	11,760	11,410	11,630	11,410
Canada	9,740	9,580	9,310	10,030	9,810
Czechoslovakia	8,660	8,910	9,290	9,480	9,720
Poland	7,900	7,790	7,750	8,040	9,650
India‡	7,340	7,410	8,440	9,780	9,790
Australia‡	7,180	7,520	7,510	7,310	6,700
Spain	6,570	6,910	6,840	6,630	6,710
Romania	5,710	6,080	6,600	7,650*	8,000*
Brazil	5,510	5,980	6,980	7,860	9,380
Luxembourg‡	5,090	5,470	3,890	3,760	3,570
South Africa	4,890	4,660	5,210	5,850	6,070
Netherlands, The	4,710	4,800	3,970	4,270	3,920
Austria	3,010	3,440	3,060	3,320	2,960
Mexico	2,890	3,210	2,050	2,330	2,970*
Sweden‡	2,780	2,980	3,310	2,950	2,310
North Korea	2,700	2,700	2,900	3,200*	3,300*
Germany, East	2,200	2,280	2,460	2,530	2,640
Hungary	2,120	2,290	2,220	2,220	2,290
Yugoslavia	2,110	2,130	2,000	1,920	1,930
Bulgaria‡	1,610	1,530	1,510	1,550	1,610
Finland‡	1,410	1,380	1,370	1,330	1,760
Turkey‡	900	1,320	1,340	1,680	1,740
Argentina‡	800	1,080	1,030	1,280	1,100
Norway	700	660	640	650	550
South Korea‡	460	990	1,190	2,010	2,440

*Estimated. †Estimated adjustment to calendar-year basis. ‡Excluding ferroalloys.
Source: International Iron and Steel Institute

els); imports arriving at lower prices were likely to be punished with extra duties. The arrangement thus resembled in many respects the U.S. trigger-price system. This system, however, was progressively replaced during the year by individual agreements between the Community and the governments of the main foreign supplying countries. Agreements on import levels between the EEC and 15 Western and Eastern countries were reached during 1978, the import reference price arrangements continuing to apply to imports from countries with which no agreement had been made.

The Davignon Plan achieved a measure of success. The pressure of imports was reduced to some extent so far as the Community as a whole was concerned, and prices for EEC products rose internally. However, as a result of renewed price weakness around midyear associated with overproduction in the first half, internal prices increased less than the amount announced as a target at the beginning of the year.

Japanese steel consumption was likely to rise in 1978 for the first time in five years. Demand was reasonably strong from the public works, construction equipment, heavy electrical, and passenger-car industries, but the private building and shipbuilding industries were poorer markets. With regard to exports, higher priority than in the past was given to revenue as against volume. In consequence, export tonnages and total output were expected to be somewhat down over the year, but there was some strengthening of prices on the world market generally, reinforced by the effect of the major appreciation of the yen.

(TREVOR J. MACDONALD)

MACHINERY AND MACHINE TOOLS

The statistics for sales and shipments of machine tools in the U.S. apparently indicated new records in 1978, but because of the recent high rates of inflation the data must be analyzed closely to determine the true picture. The estimated total sales of machine tools for 1978 amounted to $4,225,860,000 and shipments totaled approximately $2,915,640,000. However, in terms of constant dollars (based on 1977 = 100), sales amounted to only $3,604,900,000, a figure exceeded many times in the past. Likewise, the 1978 estimated shipments, based on 1977 dollars, were $2,486,108,000—less than any one year during the period from 1964 to 1970 and also less than in 1974 and 1975. The backlog of unfilled orders increased steadily through 1978 and approached $3.9 billion by the end of the year.

A sharp improvement in sales occurred in October 1978 as a direct result of the International Machine Tool Show held in September at McCormick Place in Chicago. Conventional machines and accessories were on display as well as the newest, most sophisticated equipment, which included many forms of computer-controlled cutting, forming, and measuring machines. Sponsored by the National Machine Tool Builders' Association, the show attracted more than 97,000 visitors, some 6,000 of whom were from outside the U.S. More than 1,000 exhibitors occupied 640,000 sq ft of space, making this the largest industrial exhibition ever held in the U.S. Of the

Part of the crowd of 97,000 visitors who attended the International Machine Tool Show held in Chicago in September.

exhibit area, 37% was occupied by manufacturers of machine tools and accessories from 29 nations outside the U.S.

The increasing importation of machinery from other countries continued to be a serious problem for the U.S. machine tool industry. Revised data showed that about 18% of the U.S. consumption of this equipment came from sources in other nations, compared with less than 10% in 1969. Although the dollar value of U.S. machine exports increased during 1978, for the first time the industry showed an unfavourable balance of trade, amounting to $116.3 million for the first nine months of the year.

Efforts to improve the export sales of the U.S. machine tool industry continued during 1978. At the invitation of the industry, high-level delegations from Romania, Hungary, and China toured the U.S., visiting machine tool builder and user plants. The U.S. industry was represented at shows and trade fairs in South Africa, Mexico, Chile, Argentina, Colombia, Brazil, Japan, and Great Britain.

Conversion to the metric system of measurement proceeded slowly in the U.S. metalworking industry. With the exception of some of the large multinational corporations the industry did not seem to be exerting any great effort to accomplish the conversion. There was little incentive for the machine tool builders to change their machines because they had long supplied the overseas market, which, in most instances, had been metric for a long time. For those exports the measurement-sensitive elements on the machines (lead screws, dials, nameplates) had always been changed to metric units by the builder when an order from outside the U.S. was received, but the basic machine remained unchanged. However, there was a growing tendency for these orders to specify the use

of metric fasteners (nuts, bolts, etc.). This was because they could be obtained locally for replacement purposes whereas, in most cases, machine elements must be obtained from the original equipment manufacturer.

(EDWARD J. LOEFFLER)

NUCLEAR INDUSTRY

A major victory for the opponents of nuclear power took place on Nov. 5, 1978, when the Austrians voted against opening their only nuclear power station. The plant, at Zwentendorf, had been completed for more than a year, but opposition to it forced a referendum on its operation. Austria's chancellor, Bruno Kreisky, made the issue into a political one and thus prevented the vote from being a straight yes-or-no decision about nuclear energy. Most political analysts believed that the result was primarily a modest antigovernment vote as opposed to a true antinuclear vote. But this left the utility with the problem of what to do with a $250 million station.

While Austria's government nearly fell for being pro-nuclear, Sweden's prime minister, Thorbjörn Fälldin, was forced to resign because of his antinuclear stand. Fälldin led his party out of the government coalition because his partners judged the nuclear operators had satisfied the demands of Sweden's stiff nuclear "Stipulation Law" pushed through the legislature a year before by Fälldin in an effort to stop nuclear plants from operating. This law required the operators to demonstrate that nuclear waste could be adequately dealt with to assure virtually absolute safety.

The two issues that dominated the nuclear power controversy were waste disposal and nuclear weapons proliferation. These are connected in that used (or "spent") fuel contains plutonium (which can be used for bombs), unburned uranium, and radioactive waste products. If this spent fuel is not reprocessed, the unburned uranium is lost for further use, the plutonium is not available for fast breeder reactors (an advanced type of reactor that "burns" plutonium and also produces it in two different, but simultaneous, reactions), and there is still the problem of waste.

An international study into these issues was instigated by U.S. Pres. Jimmy Carter at the end of 1977. The International Nuclear Fuel Cycle Evaluation (INFCE), entered into by more than 40 countries, was an attempt to reevaluate the decisions that had been made in the development of nuclear energy technology with the aim of finding ways to lessen the risks of proliferation. In an effort to limit the amount of plutonium, President Carter tried to persuade the advanced countries to stop developing reprocessing and the fast breeder reactor until after the INFCE program, scheduled to end in late 1979. Although these countries would not fully accept this demand, he was able to convince France that it should stop its planned construction of a reprocessing plant for Pakistan.

Another important related event was the issuing of the report of the inquiry into the proposed Windscale facility in Britain, which would be used to reprocess spent fuel from other countries, notably Japan, as well as Britain. The inquiry accepted almost in full the plans of British Nuclear Fuels Ltd. (a government-owned company) to build the plant, and this was later accepted by government and Parliament. Almost immediately a major contract with Japan was signed.

Other major events concerning reprocessing included the start-up of new facilities in France and a small prototype plant in Japan that President Carter tried to stop but finally allowed on a limited basis. (The U.S. has a veto power over the use of all fuel it supplies, which includes most of that used in Japan.)

The fast breeder reactor prototypes in Britain and France (Dounreay and Phénix, respectively) continued to operate well, and France was building a commercial-size breeder, Super Phénix, at Creys-Malville. The major fast breeder effort in the U.S., known as the Clinch River plant, was the centre of a controversy between President Carter and Congress. Carter wanted the project abandoned, but Congress wanted it to be continued. No final decision had been made by the end of the year.

While most countries announced general cutbacks or delays in their nuclear programs (there had not been a domestic order in West Germany since 1975 or an order in the U.S. during 1978), South Korea announced plans to double its nuclear-power capacity through the year 2000 from 20,000 to 40,000 Mw. The only Western country maintaining an expansionist policy was France. The national utility, Électricité de France, was given government approval to order another 10,000 Mw of capacity for 1980–81 in addition to the 10,000 Mw to be ordered in 1978–79. The utility's first four large light-water reactors (the system it adopted after abandoning its own gas-cooled line in the late 1960s) were operating. The extent of French commitment to nuclear power was demonstrated by the appointment of André Giraud, chairman of the Commissariat à l'Énergie Atomique, as minister of industry.

In mid-1978, according to the U.S. Atomic Industrial Forum, there were more than 70 operating reactors in the U.S. (over 50,-000 Mw), representing about 13% of the total electricity supply, and more than 150 reactors outside the U.S. (approximately 56,000 Mw). In 1978 a total of 29 reactor orders were expected, all outside the U.S. By the end of 1978 the Soviet Union was expected to have increased its nuclear capacity by 50% to nearly 12,000 Mw.

The only two countries not to develop light-water reactor systems were Britain and Canada. During 1977 Britain finally rejected the steam generating heavy-water reactor and instead announced that four more advanced gas-cooled reactors (AGRS)

would be built and that the state-run utility would plan a light-water reactor project—something the utility had wanted to do for several years. Coinciding with this announcement, however, was a major accident at one of the two operating AGR stations (the Hunterston B plant in Scotland). It had no radioactive consequences but would take a year to repair.

With the slowdown in reprocessing and fast breeder reactor development, more natural uranium was required. The countries with the largest reserves outside the U.S. were Canada and Australia, both of which supported President Carter's nonproliferation policies and required customer countries to sign safeguards agreements before selling them uranium. The increase in uranium demand meant that previously uneconomic reserves were again interesting. In particular, South Africa discovered that it had become profitable to extract uranium from the ore slimes from its gold fields.

Nuclear fusion experienced some exciting events. After two years of dissension the EEC decided to locate its major fusion project, called JET (Joint European Torus), at Culham in England. In the U.S. the largest working fusion machine of the Tokamak Fusion Test Reactor project, the Princeton Large Torus, achieved results which indicated that plans for fusion to make a contribution to world energy supplies by the year 2025 might be possible.

(RICHARD W. KOVAN)

PAINTS AND VARNISHES

After the recovery of the previous year, the paint industry in most countries experienced little growth during 1978. The U.K., The Netherlands, and Belgium produced some of the best results, with output showing gains of 2–3%. France reported a small decline in volume, while U.S. paintmakers tried to stem a contraction of some 9% experienced early in the year. Production in Japan appeared to be on a plateau, with gains in some sectors roughly balancing losses in others.

The industry's profitability fluctuated as companies grappled with inflation. Determined efforts in the U.S. and U.K. raised the pretax operating profit calculated on net sales to 8–9%, although this was still behind South Africa's 11–13%. At the other end of the scale, the largest paint manufacturers in Norway and Finland were barely breaking even.

The Middle East and Persian Gulf areas continued to provide good export markets for many Western European paint manufacturers. The Netherlands again exported some 40% of production, while U.K. exports continued the upward trend that began in 1974. Many less developed countries would soon have substantial local capacity, however, since paint factories were second only to cement works in these countries' progress toward industrialization. Iran, for example, now had at least 16 large or medium paint factories, unreliably reported to be producing between 250,000 and 2 million gal a year.

The worldwide recession in the shipping industry affected manufacturers of marine coatings. Imperial Chemical Industries Ltd., the U.K.'s largest paintmaker overall, announced its withdrawal from the ma-

A $250 million nuclear power station at Zwentendorf, Austria, stands idle after Austrians voted against putting it into operation.

UPI COMPIX

rine market and the closing of its small specialized factory. In contrast, the world leader, International Paint Co. Ltd., claimed outstanding success for its self-polishing coating for ships' bottoms.

There was considerable interest in powder coatings; two new plants opened in the U.K., adding to that country's existing overcapacity. In Sicily Fiat opened the world's first production line for automatic powder coating of car bodies. Honda and Datsun in Japan were applying powders as priming and top coats on cars and trucks, and Ford in the U.S. was evaluating several thousand experimental vehicles top coated with powders that could be spot refinished with liquid paints. Forecasts indicated, however, that several years would pass before powders gained 10% of the total industrial coatings market.

Pollution and legislation to protect the environment were the themes of the European paint manufacturers' triennial economic congress, held in Italy. A source of worry for many European companies was the effect of the EEC directive on the classification and labeling of paints and varnishes, published in Brussels in November 1977. The annex setting limits above which danger labels would be required was still incomplete, and the industry faced a period of expense and uncertainty.

(LIONEL BILEFIELD)

PHARMACEUTICALS

Legislative and regulatory matters occupied the U.S. pharmaceutical industry during most of 1978. The prime focus was on the Carter administration's drug reform bill, proposed as a solution to the increasingly time-consuming process of securing Food and Drug Administration (FDA) approval of new drug applications. The industry contended that drug safety/efficacy verification had become exorbitantly expensive and that lifesaving drugs were often introduced in Western Europe two to five years before they could be sold in the U.S.

The administration bill aimed at speeding up the process, at least for "significant" therapeutic advances. However, the industry feared that it might encourage poaching by generic drug manufacturers and undermine what so-called research-oriented drug developers regard as proprietary trade secrets. Senate and House subcommittees wrestled with these difficult issues during the summer and into the fall, but no action was taken before Congress adjourned in October.

Also a worry for industry lawyers was what they regarded as encouragement of generic drug manufacturers by the FDA, especially the acceleration of the "maximum allowable cost" system for procurement of drugs in government hospitals and health plans. Even more alarming to the industry was the FDA's role in assisting New York State to compile a price-comparison compendium for physicians and its encouragement of state legislation facilitating substitution by pharmacists of the least expensive drug in filling prescriptions.

In late September the FDA finally issued its Current Good Manufacturing Practices regulations, scheduled to go into effect on March 28, 1979. These would considerably tighten up quality control, expiration dating of most drugs, and apportionment of

clear-cut lines of responsibility within each company. The regulations had been proposed two years earlier, and the first reaction from industry and consumers was largely favourable. Large companies generally would have no trouble complying, although companies might find that the formal controls and detailed staff training mandated by the new procedures were enough of a financial burden to force up prices.

Toward the end of the year the FDA moved to close a gap in the practice whereby high-prestige companies put their name on drugs that were actually made under contract in other manufacturing plants. The new, so-called "man-in-the-plant" regulations specified certain operations and checks that must be supervised directly by personnel of the company claiming to be the manufacturer.

In terms of statistics, 1977 was another good year for U.S. pharmaceutical manufacturers. Census Bureau figures indicated that the total value of all drug shipments at the manufacturers' level was $9,150,000,000, up 4% from $8,770,000,000 in 1976. Over-the-counter drug sales rose 3.5% (to $2,230,000,000 from $2,160,000,000 in 1976). The prognosis for future growth was excellent, based on the trend toward an older population and the growth of third-party health plans.   (DONALD A. DAVIS)

PLASTICS

There were clear signs in 1978 that the plastics materials manufacturing industry—or at any rate the more farsighted part of it—was at last facing up to the longer-term implications of the continuing slowdown in the rate of growth. Firms were no longer prepared to continue profitless operations in the hope of a return to the expansion of the pre-oil-crisis years, when annual growth of at least 15–20% was automatic. In 1978 expansion of plastics production worldwide was, at best, half of that. It was, in fact, an average year, with the U.S. more happily placed than Western Europe and Japan still struggling toward recovery.

The most dramatic expression of the new mood was the decision of two of the largest U.S.-based chemical multinationals, Union Carbide and Monsanto, to sell their entire EEC businesses in, respectively, low polyethylene and polystyrene to British Petroleum. Both the U.S. corporations were closely associated with these product lines (although, of course, these represented only a fraction of their total chemical activities). Each company gave a similar reason for its abandonment of European markets carefully built up over many years: lack of integration in the area into supplies of oil-derived raw materials as feedstocks for its local plants. Each also emphasized its intention to retain its strength in these same products in other markets, especially the U.S. It seemed unlikely that the lesson would be lost on other "commodity" thermoplastics manufacturers whose position in Western Europe seemed manifestly more precarious.

In this situation of gross surplus, prices were naturally depressed. Some manufacturers showed their determination to maintain at least a minimal profitability by making price increases, especially toward the end of the year. A few plastics materials (and petrochemical) plants in Europe

closed down—temporarily, on the face of it, though some of the older and smaller units would probably be scrapped in the not too far distant future. Some expansion plans were also delayed, but not to the extent needed to counterbalance new capacity that was still coming on stream. It appeared that overproduction would become an even more acute problem, at least into the 1980s. The position in Western Europe was exacerbated by low-priced imports from Eastern Europe (including material supplied in lieu of cash in repayment for the provision of technology and plant) and from the U.S., whose shipments became increasingly attractive to hard-currency customers as the dollar weakened.

In contrast to commodity plastics (which constitute by far the greater proportion of total output), the position with regard to higher-priced engineering and specialty polymers continued to be encouraging. The products ranged from those produced in substantial tonnages, such as nylon and ABS, to small volume, ultrahigh-performance materials like polyimides and aramids. Indeed, Monsanto, when withdrawing from the EEC polystyrene market, emphasized its intention to step up its activity in Europe with respect to the related styrene copolymer material ABS. The thermosetting plastics, long regarded as much less glamorous than the thermoplastics, also did well. There was some resurgence of interest in the older thermosets, notably phenolics, with their stable properties, capability of being injection- as well as compression-molded, and, especially, their nonflammable characteristics, which were increasingly in demand.

Another, newer thermosetting class that made progress in 1978, despite environmental problems connected with the isocyanate constituent, was the polyurethanes, which profited from the intense interest in foam insulation for energy saving and the introduction of modified processing techniques such as reaction injection molding. The composites field, using both higher reinforcements such as carbon fibre and improved resin systems, notably epoxies, saw further penetration into important areas of structural use such as aerospace. The scope for general-purpose polyester/glass-reinforced plastics expanded with the improvement of industrialized fabrication techniques, such as those using sheet molding compounds.

The problems with commodity thermoplastics, while severe, differed from those of synthetic rubber and man-made fibres, where substitution of the natural material appeared to have neared the saturation point. The replacement of other substances by plastics, mostly of the large-volume types—PVC, polyolefins, and polystyrene—was generally regarded as still being at an early stage. Sectors such as the building and automotive industries, especially the latter with its constant search for lightness and strength, gave undiminished cause for optimism. Growth potential and scope for innovation remained, although the rate of growth would certainly be less than in previous years.   (ROBIN C. PENFOLD)

PRINTING

The year saw significant changes in production economics and in the economics of the rival printing processes. Dainippon Screen in Japan introduced a desk-top electronic colour scanner unit costing less than $35,000. Other firms offering low-cost scanners included Crosfield Electronics of the U.K. and Dr.-Ing. Rudolf Hell of West Germany. Japan became the world's major scanner market, with Dainippon Screen and Crosfield Electronics sharing the largest market slice.

Electronic previewing and monitoring of colour scanning, pioneered by Toppan Printing in Japan, also became an important feature of units from Hell and from Sci-Tex in Israel. The Toppan and Sci-Tex units were compatible with any make of scanner. Others in this market included Dainippon Screen and Hazeltine in the U.S.

Fully automatic, electronic, computerized "no hands" reproduction, page make-up, and platemaking or cylinder production (for gravure) became a reality. In May 1978, at a meeting of the European Rotogravure Association, Hell demonstrated a linked-up system that covered every process from phototypesetting to colour scanning and integrated these jobs with platemaking or cylinder production. In September Crosfield Electronics demonstrated a computerized combination of makeup and scanning, as well as laser engraving of gravure cylinders coated with an epoxy resin. Meanwhile, the U.S. Optronics system for integrated working was in practical use at Helprint in Finland. One of the world's largest offset plate manufacturers, Kalle of West Germany, a subsidiary of Hoechst, became a sister company to the Eocom laser platemaking system through the acquisition of the U.S. company by Hoechst America.

Gravure increasingly challenged web offset. In Switzerland, Conzett & Huber, in a further development of the Japanese Toppan gravure system, offered simple moiré-free conversion from photolitho reproductions to gravure. Some major European and U.S. catalogs were produced by this system. European printers were being sought by U.S. and Japanese printers as partners in bringing quality medium-run rotogravure to their countries. The initial investment in each case amounted to about $20 million. In Italy, Cerutti experimented with laser cutting or slitting of webs in folders to reduce dust and noise.

The miniwebs—more aptly called eight-page webs—made a considerable impact on the market. Harris of the U.S., Albert of West Germany, Solna of Sweden, and the East German Polygraph group sold dozens of machines within a year of their introduction. Most were used to expand or replace sheet-fed offset capacity. Book printers also turned to web offset. Harris designed an ingenious system by which plating for one section of a book could be carried out on the press while the preceding section was being printed, thus ensuring continuous production. In West Germany Albert announced another system that achieved similar results by "flying plate change."

Taiwan and South Korea became new contenders in the printing export market, shipping primarily to the U.S. but also to West Germany and Australia. Colour separations from a handful of companies in Taiwan were being sent to the U.S. at the rate of several thousand a month.

(W. PINCUS JASPERT)

RUBBER

Production of manufactured rubber goods leveled off after the shortages created by the strike of 1976 had been filled. Profitability for the major manufacturers varied, but in general it lagged behind rates needed to justify investment. The continued high production and sale of automobiles resulted in strong demand for original equipment tires. The replacement tire market also remained strong, even though one tire company executive stated that tire life had increased by a factor of two in the past six years. The adoption of steel-belted radial tires was primarily responsible, although the reduction in the U.S. speed limit to 55 mph may have been an added factor.

The use of solvents in the manufacture of rubber articles, particularly tires, continued to be scrutinized by U.S. government agencies. OSHA proposed strict limits on concentrations of benzene vapour, a known leukemogen, as well as reducing skin contact with solvents containing benzene. The gasoline used to make rubber cements and to freshen rubber surfaces during fabrication contains small amounts of benzene, although benzene as such had not been used for this purpose for many years. The OSHA proposal was rejected by the courts as too restrictive, and a new proposal would probably be drafted.

The Firestone Tire & Rubber Co. voluntarily agreed to recall 10 million steel-belted 500 tires which, according to the National Highway Traffic Safety Administration, were defective. This was the largest tire recall to date. Firestone also agreed to replace the 500s with an improved steel-belted radial. Cost of the recall could exceed $200 million.

Prices of raw materials used in rubber manufacture rose markedly during the

A steel-track rubber tire for use on heavy mining equipment was developed by the Goodyear Tire & Rubber Co.

Table X. Natural Rubber Production

In 000 metric tons

Country	1975	1976	1977
Malaysia	1,478	1,640	1,613
Indonesia	822	848[1]	835[1]
Thailand	349	392	425
India	136	148	152
Sri Lanka	149	152	146
Liberia	83	82	80[1]
Philippines	52	60[1]	65[1]
Nigeria	68	53[1]	59[1]
Zaire	30[1]	30[1]	30[1]
Brazil	19	23	23
Others	129	137	172[1]
Total	3,315	3,565	3,600

[1] Estimate, or includes estimate.
Source: The Secretariat of the International Rubber Study Group, *Rubber Statistical Bulletin.*

Table XI. Synthetic Rubber Production

In 000 metric tons

Country	1975	1976	1977
United States	1,990	2,368	2,418
Japan	789	941	971
France	350	437	479
Germany, West	316	373	424[1]
United Kingdom	261	320	329
Netherlands, The	216	247	240
Italy [1]	200	250	240
Canada	173	210	238
Brazil	129	164	188
Germany, East	144	145	150[1]
Belgium [1]	65	115	125
Romania	99	95	125[1]
Poland	108	117	119
Mexico	60	69	78[1]
Spain	66	79	77
Czechoslovakia	57	56	57[1]
Australia	38	42	44
Argentina [1]	50	45	36
South Africa	32	35	27
Others	1,742	1,875	2,017
Total	6,885	7,983	8,382

[1] Estimate, or includes estimate.
Source: The Secretariat of the International Rubber Study Group, *Rubber Statistical Bulletin.*

year. On Oct. 1, 1977, the New York spot price was 44½ cents per pound for smoked sheets and on Oct. 1, 1978, it was 56½ cents, a 27% increase. The price of nonoil-extended, 1500-type styrene-butadiene rubber (SBR), the most widely used synthetic, increased from 34 cents per pound to 37 cents. Only the price of carbon black did not increase enough to justify production, precluding any plant expansion.

World production of natural rubber in 1977 was estimated at 3.6 million metric tons, an increase of only 35,000 tons over 1976. Production for 1978 was estimated at 3,570,000 tons. The Management Committee of the International Rubber Study Group estimated natural rubber supplies at 3,750,000 tons and synthetic rubber at 8.8 million tons for 1978, while 3.8 million tons of natural rubber and 8.8 million tons of synthetic rubber would be turned into manufactured products. (See TABLES X and XI.) Production of reclaimed rubber in 1977 was equal to that of 1976 (about 200,000 tons). This was the first time for many years that the production of reclaimed rubber had not decreased.

The U.S. continued to be the largest single buyer of natural rubber, purchasing 781,211 tons in 1977. World consumption of natural rubber latex (dry basis) was estimated at 281,000 tons. Statistics on world consumption of synthetic latices were incomplete, but U.S. consumption of the SBR type was 143,000 tons (dry basis). Worldwide consumption of both natural and synthetic rubber was estimated at 12,122,500 tons in 1977.

With fossil fuels, from which synthetic rubber is made, becoming increasingly scarce and expensive, it was predicted that the ratio of natural to synthetic rubber would increase and that natural rubber production would have to double by 1980. Malaysia believed it could accomplish this objective, but the ability of the other rubber-producing countries was questionable. The Soviet bloc countries were increasing their production of SKI-3 and SKI-4 polyisoprene, synthetic counterparts of natural rubber, and were already exporting large quantities to Western Europe and the U.S. at a very competitive price.

Caterpillar, a manufacturer of heavy construction equipment, announced a 100,000-mi passenger tire developed using technology obtained from work on giant tires. It featured a replaceable tread band on a radially wound carcass with high inflation pressure. (JAMES R. BEATTY)

SHIPBUILDING

After a two-year downward slide, the volume of new ship orders worldwide showed signs of steadying at an annual figure of between 10 million and 13 million gross registered tons (grt)—well below the current world shipbuilding capacity of 32 million grt. All the traditional shipbuilding nations faced unemployment and the closure of yards, but only Norway and Sweden took really effective measures to cut capacity. In Japan the reduction was insignificant in relation to the nation's huge shipbuilding capacity. Governments continued to give financial support to their ailing shipbuilding industries. The most practical solution to the problem was a proposal to scrap and build on a large scale; owners would be helped to dispose of vessels and would then place orders for new ships on the basis of one new ship for every two that were scrapped.

In July 1978 the world order book stood at 2,576 vessels totaling nearly 61 million tons deadweight (dw). A year earlier the figure was 85 million tons dw, and in the boom year of 1974 it was 273 million tons dw. The shortage of orders reflected the massive surplus of tonnage in service and the fact that the world's laid-up fleet included 38 million tons dw of tankers and 12.5 million tons dw of dry cargo ships. Japan maintained a massive lead in new orders, with 631 ships totaling 14.9 million tons dw either building or on order. Second came Brazil, where the state yards had orders for 142 vessels totaling 4.9 million tons dw. U.K. yards had 112 ships on order with an aggregate of 2 million tons dw, a figure exceeded by the U.S.S.R. where the 92 ships on order totaled 2.6 million tons dw.

Faced with the prospect of waiting until 1983 for the supply and demand for tankers to come into balance and until 1982 for the bulk carrier market to pick up, shipowners turned their attention to multipurpose cargo liners, roll-on/roll-off vessels, and the smaller categories of containership. Japanese shipbuilders hoped to secure some 40% of all new orders for liquefied natural gas (LNG) carriers, but they would have to compete with South Korea (where confidence in the future was underlined by the building of a new shipyard) as well as with the one Swedish and several European yards specializing in the building of LNG carriers.

Several shipbuilders turned to alternative work, such as the construction of floating process plants. Another source of work was offered by the demand for sophisticated all-purpose vessels for operation in the North Sea in conjunction with drilling rigs. However, after a 12-month spate of orders for reefer ships totaling 77 vessels, this valuable sector of the market was unlikely to provide many more orders. Nearly all the new reefers on order were to replace old tonnage owned by traditional operators of these vessels. Orders for roll-on/roll-off ves-

The world's largest self-propelled seagoing crane vessel was completed in June by a Japanese shipbuilding firm.

sels also dried up as the market showed signs of approaching overcapacity.

The type of ship that offered the greatest hope for many builders was the multipurpose dry cargo liner, for which about 50 standard designs were currently available. This vessel combined the advantages of a self-trimming bulk carrier with the flexibility of a break-bulk cargo ship. The design usually provided for the carriage of 500 to 1,000 containers. Some designs incorporated a large stern ramp that extended the ship's function into the roll-on/roll-off and heavy lift sectors of the market.

In the U.S. the backlog of shipbuilding orders shrank to the vanishing point, and some yards only managed to survive with orders for offshore drilling units. It was estimated that after 1978 the industry would need 45,000 fewer persons, most of them production workers. At mid-1978 U.S. merchant shipbuilding yards had 59 vessels of over 1,000 grt on order, totaling 6 million grt, but the bulk of the order book was provided by 34 tankers totaling 5.4 million tons dw. Failure to encourage the expansion of the U.S.-owned merchant fleet accelerated the approaching storm that threatened the U.S. shipbuilding and allied industries. The absence of a coordinated national shipbuilding policy in the U.S. covering both naval and commercial building could lead to an irretrievable loss of building capability for all vessel types.

With stricter control of world fishing, there was a growing demand for special patrol and protection vessels. Building these provided work for commercial yards without exacerbating the worldwide cargo-carrying overcapacity. The same could not be said for the building of large cargo ships for stock or state ownership.

(W. D. EWART)

TELECOMMUNICATIONS

In 1978 telecommunications technology developed fastest in the area of fibre optics, the technique of transmitting messages in the form of light waves through long glass fibres. Fibre-optic cable appeared in everything from closed-circuit television to telephone networks. At the same time, however, digital communication techniques and semiconductor circuits were being used in new ways. In fact, innovations were appearing so rapidly that the U.S. Congress began reviewing the way in which the U.S. regulates the communications industry.

Fibre and Integrated Optics. No area of electronic technology seemed likely to escape the influence of fibre optics. Military interest was high because fibre-optic communications are hard to tap or jam, and fibre-optic cables and optical circuitry were also beginning to appear in industrial process controls, computers, ships, and planes.

The outstanding advantage of optical fibre, in comparison with electricity flowing through copper wire, is its minimal resistance to energy flow. In dramatic proof of this, Nippon Telegraph and Telephone Public Corp. of Japan succeeded in building a practical communications system in which a fibre-optic cable linked two points some 53 km (33 mi) apart without requiring intermediate amplifiers. Such a distance is far beyond the capabilities of conventional electronics. Other fibre-optic links were used to connect the antenna of a satellite ground station to a colour-television distribution system and to illuminate a car's instrument panel from a single light source.

In perhaps the most significant development of the year in terms of its long-range implications for home and office communications, Bell Telephone Laboratories in the U.S. introduced a telephone that did not need an electricity connection by means of copper wires. Powered by light transmitted on a fibre-optic cable that connects the telephone to a central office, the new phone could handle all the frequencies needed for communications applications in the foreseeable future. This is in contrast to the copper-wire phones which, unless special techniques are employed, can only handle a narrow range of frequencies.

Much research during the year went into integrated optical circuits, which promise to convey signals from place to place much faster and over a wider band of frequencies than do electronic circuits. But not enough was known yet about how to design them, let alone manufacture them as inexpensively as electronic integrated circuits. Nevertheless, both Bell Laboratories and Nippon Electric Co. in Japan produced various components that brought optical transmitters and receivers much closer to reality. Bell deposited layers of various materials on a substrate to build up its filters, switches, and amplifiers. Nippon's filters and other devices used glass rods and lenses.

Telephones. Both the increasing complexity of semiconductor integrated circuits and digital techniques, which code signals as strings of on-and-off pulses instead of as variable waveforms, were improving the telephone. For example, Bell Canada began field testing the "E" phone, with which it hoped to phase out the standard push-button model. The "E" phone is easier to make; 12 integrated circuits do the work that 120 electrical and electromechanical components are required to perform in the standard design. The new phone also uses digital techniques to reproduce a caller's voice accurately and to dial automatically any telephone number stored in its memory circuits.

Telephone central offices were also benefiting from the new technology. In New York City the American Telephone and Telegraph Co. (AT&T) installed the giant new Electronic Switching System No. 4, which was more efficient than its predecessors at switching calls into and out of the international network. In the home, too, digital systems introduced during the year equipped standard television sets to receive special video transmissions such as stock market reports either directly or when hooked up to a telephone.

Electronic Mail. In 1978 Western Union began work on a system for electronically transmitting bills and other computer-generated mass mailings to a central post office in the recipients' areas. Soon afterward the U.S. Postal Service began experiments along the same lines. Essentially, the material is converted into strings of digital pulses for transmission by phone or satellite

Table XII. Countries Having More Than 100,000 Telephones

Telephones in service, 1977

Country	Number of telephones	Percentage increase over 1967	Telephones per 100 population	Country	Number of telephones	Percentage increase over 1967	Telephones per 100 population
Algeria	266,470	79.0	1.5	Lebanon [4]	227,000	74.6	7.4
Argentina	2,539,535	66.3	9.8	Luxembourg	157,829	68.3	44.2
Australia [1]	5,501,508	84.7	39.5	Malaysia	329,644	126.7	2.7
Austria	2,281,251	109.9	29.9	Mexico	3,308,832	255.4	5.2
Belgium	2,949,822	77.1	30.0	Morocco	204,500	41.2	1.1
Brazil	3,987,072	178.5	3.5	Netherlands, The	5,411,619	115.3	39.2
Bulgaria	852,858	178.4	9.7	New Zealand	1,632,478	50.2	52.0
Canada	13,785,647	74.9	60.4	Nigeria [1]	121,032	55.4	0.2
Chile	473,435	63.4	4.5	Norway	1,476,091	56.1	36.6
Colombia	1,295,860	170.5	5.3	Pakistan [1]	239,600	47.3	0.3
Costa Rica	126,879	361.4	6.2	Panama	154,598	167.7	9.0
Cuba [2]	289,000	21.3	3.2	Peru [3]	295,224	119.1	2.0
Czechoslovakia	2,743,387	73.3	18.3	Philippines	541,681	187.9	1.2
Denmark	2,528,585	79.2	48.9	Poland	2,753,204	95.1	8.0
Dominican Republic	127,332	271.9	2.6	Portugal	1,118,970	92.3	12.9
Ecuador	174,046	286.8	2.5	Puerto Rico	515,492	114.1	14.4
Egypt [3]	503,200	42.8	1.4	Rhodesia	190,303	69.8	2.9
Finland	1,935,683	116.9	40.9	Romania [3]	1,076,566	95.1	5.0
France	15,553,798	137.3	29.3	Saudi Arabia	160,000	451.7	2.1
Germany, East	2,750,597	59.6	16.4	Singapore	374,394	252.8	16.3
Germany, West	21,161,787	122.0	34.5	South Africa	2,191,404	73.8	8.3
Greece	2,180,243	276.5	23.8	Spain	8,597,781	179.9	23.9
Hong Kong	1,132,435	275.4	25.3	Sweden	5,673,427	51.0	68.9
Hungary	1,076,064	80.1	10.1	Switzerland	4,016,322	67.7	63.8
India	2,095,962	118.1	0.3	Syria [4]	176,930	93.6	2.3
Indonesia	314,445	85.9	0.2	Taiwan	1,396,022	506.4	8.4
Iran	781,537	266.2	2.3	Thailand [1]	333,761	239.2	0.8
Iraq	319,591	312.4	2.8	Tunisia [1]	126,750	117.3	2.1
Ireland	480,000	89.4	15.1	Turkey	1,130,978	193.3	2.8
Israel	869,042	188.7	24.3	U.S.S.R.	18,000,000	114.3	7.0
Italy	15,240,527	135.6	27.1	United Kingdom	22,012,304	93.5	39.4
Jamaica	108,500	91.3	5.4	United States	155,172,952	57.1	71.8
Japan	48,431,044	202.5	42.6	Uruguay	257,624	32.1	9.2
Kenya	131,843	117.2	1.0	Venezuela	742,050	140.2	5.9
Korea, South	1,681,254	418.8	4.6	Yugoslavia	1,430,575	216.3	6.6
Kuwait	139,880	418.8	12.4				

[1] As of June 30, 1976.   [2] 1974.   [3] 1975.   [4] 1972.
Sources: American Telephone and Telegraph Company, *The World's Telephones, 1977*; Statistical Office of the United Nations, *Statistical Yearbook, 1968*.

and ultimate reconversion to its original format.

An associated and even bigger development was the proposal by AT&T of an Advanced Communications Service that would link the "offices of the future." Special telephone connections would enable all the information-gathering equipment in various offices to "talk" to each other. But doubts as to whether AT&T as a regulated monopoly should be allowed to expand into this new business were immediately raised.

To complicate matters further another entrant in the office communications market was Xerox Corp. The communications network it proposed would not use telephones or just satellites alone. Instead, messages would be relayed from a rooftop microwave antenna and beamed by microwave radio to a multisubscriber collection antenna. Only then would the information be sent to a satellite for distribution.

Satellites. Designers of both commercial and military communications satellites were enthusiastic about the new modulating and coding techniques that emerged during the year. The U.S. National Aeronautics and Space Administration (NASA), for one, began to study "smart" satellites, those capable of deciding how to handle and route messages instead of passively handing them on from one ground station to another.

Satellite Business Systems, the joint venture of IBM Corp., Comsat General Corp., and the Aetna Life & Casualty Co., planned to use satellites to provide large companies with internal communications. Expected to get under way in 1980, this system could compete with both AT&T's and Xerox's in a battle for the office communications market.   (HARVEY J. HINDIN)

TEXTILES

Hopes that renewal of the General Agreement on Tariffs and Trade multifibres agreement for a four-year period from Jan. 1, 1978, would bring greater stability to textile trading were largely unfulfilled during the year. Recession continued to affect the industry, and demand remained weak in most parts of the world. A meeting of the International Federation of Cotton and Allied Textile Industries in London in the fall highlighted the conflicting interests of manufacturers in the developed countries of the West and low-cost suppliers in the less developed countries and southern Europe. The former complained about excessive import penetration and the latter about protectionism.

Many of the industry's problems stemmed from its highly cyclical nature, with fashion trends influencing demand for different types of fabric. For the past few years the knitting industry had been suffering from an oversupply of machine-building capacity and a dwindling market following the collapse of a boom in dress fabrics of textured-filament polyester yarn knitted on double-jersey machines. More recently the trend had been toward 100% cotton denim, creating a demand for mills using shuttleless looms. This, in turn, produced a situation of weaving and dyeing overcapacity at a time when demand for indigo-dyed denim was leveling off in almost all markets.

The current trend was toward pile fabrics that could be man-made fibre velvets or 100% cotton corduroy-type cloths. Because these fabrics, like denims, were woven, overcapacity was not as serious for the loom makers as it had been for the double-jersey machine builders. Meanwhile, there was continued growth in "nonwoven textiles" —neither knitted nor woven—whose high production speed and low conversion cost enabled them to penetrate markets previously held by knitted and woven fabrics.
                                    (PETER LENNOX-KERR)

Wool. For most countries that buy wool, currency fluctuations during 1977–78 had at least as much effect on prices as the levels of supply and demand for the fibre itself. Softening of the U.S. dollar in particular caused wool to be approximately 25% more expensive or cheaper during the course of 12 months, according to the currency used by the buyer.

In market terms crossbred qualities continued to show relatively greater strength than merinos, especially finer Australian merinos. The Australian Wool Corp. bought a large proportion of the offerings under its reserve price scheme at the height of the 1977–78 season, but improved demand and seasonally lower supplies allowed these purchases to be more than balanced by later stockpile sales. There was sufficient confidence at the end of the season in June 1978 to permit raising of the overall floor price by 5%.

The wool-consuming industry established only a very tentative recovery trend during the year. Fashion inclined toward woolens rather than worsteds, but nowhere did confidence in wool itself extend to the point of persuading commercial users to rebuild inventories. However, wool showed no sign of losing ground to man-made alternatives.   (H. M. F. MALLETT)

Cotton. Persistently keen competition from man-made fibres resulted in world usage of raw cotton being reduced to 60.6 million bales in 1977–78, compared with the record level of 62.2 million bales in 1975–76. Most of the curtailment was in Western Europe and the Far East. Global stocks in August 1978 at 23.5 million bales were some 3 million bales more than the abnormally low point reached a year earlier.

Production in 1977–78, at about 64 million bales, was some 6 million bales above the previous season and more than 9 million bales higher than in 1975–76. Major gains were made in the U.S., where the crop totaled 14.5 million bales against 10.7 million bales in 1976–77. The U.S.S.R. was estimated to have produced 12,750,000 million bales and China 9.6 million bales.

Production prospects were severely affected by adverse weather at planting time for the 1978–79 crop. Damage occurred in several countries. Lack of moisture, insect infestation, and intense heat created problems in the U.S., while excessive rains in Pakistan and extensive flooding in the Sudan caused difficulties for farmers in those areas.   (ARTHUR TATTERSALL)

Silk. The dominant feature of the raw silk market was once again the stability of Chinese prices. China expected a worldwide expansion of silk consumption and believed that this could be achieved not only by the provision of funds for promotion in the Western world but also by the mainte-

nance of a stable cost. While 3A 20/22 denier was held at 44.50 yuan per kilo during 1977–78, in October 1977 a considerable discount was offered for the lower grades in an effort to compete with Brazil. This differential was later considerably reduced, and Brazilian prices themselves rose as a result of a partial withdrawal of the government export subsidy.

Japan remained isolated behind its import restrictions and still had its own particular problem to solve—how to ensure a rewarding price for its cocoon farmers and at the same time arrest the decline in domestic consumption. In terms of quantity Japanese consumption of silk had always been much greater than that of the Western countries on account of the traditional silk kimono. Statistics showed that a Japanese used about 15 times as much silk as a European. A grave problem faced not only China but also South Korea when Japan fell away as a foremost customer, and the latter saw no alternative but to reduce production.

In Europe silk enjoyed a good market throughout 1977, but the spring and summer of 1978 brought something of an overall reaction.   (PETER W. GADDUM)

Man-Made Fibres. Continuing overcapacity in the man-made fibres industry led the main European producers to sign a pact in June 1978 with a view to achieving greater balance between supply and demand. Under the pact, capacity within EEC member states would be reduced by about 15% during the next three years. However, the cartel was declared illegal by the EEC Commission under the Community's antitrust rules.

It was increasingly obvious that the polyesters, used as both filament yarns and

A wrinkle-free synthetic fabric that stretches in all directions allows the wearer to create her own style.

WIDE WORLD

staple fibres, were taking the predominant position among conventional textile fibres and could well supersede cotton as the basic world textile raw material. The progress of man-made fibres was largely based on their modification to offer specific properties. Nylon, for example, was being made in a number of versions which could be dyed to different depths or intensity. This enabled a designer to plan fabrics or carpets, which, when dyed, produced a range of effects but with only one fibre. Also important for carpet manufacture was the development of inherently and permanently antistatic nylon fibre. Research work with acrylic fibres was directed toward making them more moisture-absorbent so that when worn in apparel they would behave more "naturally" and absorb perspiration which would then be transmitted away from the body. If this could be achieved, a new all-man-made blend based on polyester and acrylic fibres might emerge to challenge the successful polyester-cotton blend.

(PETER LENNOX-KERR)

TOBACCO

After four disturbed years 1978 was more serene in three major areas of the tobacco business: prices resumed a gentle upward progression after the disruptive leap and collapse of 1974–77; output, at 12,010,000,-000 lb, was broadly in line with world demand; and world consumption of cigarettes (increasingly the most favoured form of tobacco consumption) rose 2%.

World tobacco stocks, equivalent to consumption needs for about 16 months, were moderate but unbalanced. The 13,770,000,-000-lb total included far too much of the oriental type, now deteriorating in Greek, Turkish, and Balkan stockpiles. Excessive 1978 output in those countries, stimulated by political rather than commercial pressures, worsened the problem of unsalable surpluses.

Despite great advances in research on tobacco plant genetics, disease- and pest-control, and knowledge of how to minimize the hazards of tropical agriculture, world average yields per acre had improved only 20% since 1958. Those in major exporting countries of the less developed world, like India, were only about one-third of the 2,-400 lb per ac regularly attained in high-efficiency Japan. The less developed countries, where most of the world's tobacco was produced, could therefore only grow more by planting large acreages, fueling the controversy over the use for tobacco of land with food-crop potential.

Cigarette consumption in 1978 rose almost everywhere except within the EEC, where vigorous antitobacco campaigning coincided with changes in taxation systems to cause a moderate recession. The swing to mild (low tar and nicotine) smoking continued. But in West Germany, which pioneered this trend, sales of mild cigarettes peaked out, suggesting a limit to public acceptance of products low in flavour and aroma. World consumption of cigars and pipe tobaccos continued its long-term decline.

World trade in leaf tobacco continued strong, much aided by the weakness of the currencies of major exporters (the U.S., Brazil, India, Turkey) compared with those of the top importing countries of the EEC and Japan. Increasingly significant was the world trade boom in manufactured tobacco —95% of it in the form of cigarettes—which was rising at more than 10% per annum; earnings per pound were about 2½ times those to be made from selling leaf tobacco. This trade was predominantly in the hands of a few Western countries, although Bulgaria was also a major exporter, shipping some 63 billion cigarettes a year, mainly to the U.S.S.R.

The continued swing to filter types by smokers of the world's annual production of 4.2 trillion cigarettes and the advance of techniques enabling more cigarettes to be made from each pound of tobacco together were allowing gradually increasing cigarette consumption to be satisfied by static or declining production of leaf tobacco. In 1978 additional installations permitted more manufacturers to cut tobacco use (and lower tar and nicotine ratings) by processes that utilized shredded tobacco for cigarettes. This technique and the greater use of factory processes that make robust tobaccos milder while reinforcing the taste elements in the smoke were now preferred to the use of man-made smoking materials in making mild cigarettes. Survivors of the 12 man-made-blend cigarette brands launched amid great excitement in Britain in 1977 now had less than 1% of the market there, and the concept was in eclipse.

(MICHAEL F. BARFORD)

TOURISM

International tourism continued to make headway in 1978. Worldwide receipts approached $62 billion, while arrivals headed for the 260 million mark, both well above the totals for 1977. Despite the continuing decline in the value of the U.S. dollar against other major currencies—particularly in Europe—the number of U.S. tourists bound for Europe increased by 7% in the first half of 1978. Business travel remained buoyant under the influence of steady growth in world trade, though excess capacity in certain industries and the effects of increased protectionism combined to keep growth to single figures. Pleasure travel was stimulated by tax cuts in West Germany, rising real wages in the U.K., and the low personal savings rate in the U.S. Relaxation of exchange controls in Italy, Japan, and the U.K. that began in the autumn of 1977 may also have been a factor.

Great publicity surrounded the attempts of the world's scheduled airlines to agree on new fare structures. In an increasingly "open-rate" situation price-cutting became widespread, and the extensive introduction of promotional fares led scheduled carriers to gain market shares at the expense of charter services. A study by the European Travel Commission concluded that one in five passengers using new promotional air fares (Budget, Super Apex, Standby, or Laker Skytrain) would not have taken the trip without the new fares. The International Air Transport Association (IATA) reported North Atlantic traffic up by 12% in the first half of the year. Intra-European flights were reported growing by 10%, while U.S. carriers expected to fly 222,000,000,000 revenue

passenger-miles in 1978, compared with 193,000,000,000 in 1977.

Greece and Spain welcomed 15% more visitors in 1978. With visitors numbering close to 40 million, Spain's tourist count exceeded the resident population. Austria, Italy, and Yugoslavia reported tourism growing at about 10% per annum, the negative trend experienced in Yugoslav tourism in 1977 being reversed. Japan and Portugal also made good headway, and the Philippines expected that it would reach the one-million tourist mark. Thailand witnessed a growth rate of more than 20% over 1977. Mexico expected 2,250,000 arrivals, while in the Caribbean The Bahamas and Jamaica enjoyed a good winter season with arrivals up by 20 and 40%, respectively. In Africa, Kenya's tourist receipts were expected to exceed $100 million. Tours to China, which began to be sold quietly in 1977, were reported to be gaining rapidly in popularity. China expected 50,000 overseas visitors in 1978. Canada reported a decline in arrivals for the second straight year, while tourism in the U.K., after the success of the Silver Jubilee year, slackened off in the first half of 1978. The problems of the "hard currency" tourist countries in marketing their tourist product were epitomized by Switzerland. That country reported a 20% decline in nights spent there by U.S. travelers but a 12% increase in visitors from West Germany.

Reduced transatlantic air fares resulted in jammed terminals at international airports.

The increasing importance of tourism to certain European countries led to calls to promote and defend the industry. The British Tourist Authority in the U.K. reported that in 1977, for the first time, the number of overseas visitors to Britain (11.5 million) exceeded the number of Britons traveling abroad (11.1 million). Tourism had become the third largest contributor to Britain's invisible exports and contributed no less than 5.8% to total trade. One and a half million people in Britain found their employment in tourism, while visitors to the U.K. were estimated to spend $500 million on shopping for clothes and footwear. In Switzerland, where the dollar reached a historic low of less than SFr 1.5 to $1, the Swiss Tourism Federation and the Swiss Hoteliers' Association urged the federal government to help them "guarantee" tour prices in foreign currency in 1979 so as to give their industry a chance to compete in world markets.

The problems of the peak season were felt acutely in Europe in the summer of 1978, partly because a cool, rainy spell in early June delayed the start of the holiday season. A decision by 2,500 French air traffic controllers to work strictly by the rules, handling only a specified quota of traffic, delayed or stranded thousands at European airports. Their numbers were swelled by many passengers waiting for standby seats at newly introduced discount fares. Meanwhile, news media were expressing concern at the rising level of Mediterranean pollution and its significance for tourism. Ecologists claimed that there were many places on Europe's Mediterranean coast where bathing ought by rights to be prohibited because of coastal pollution. Anger swelled in southwest France as thousands of plastic bottles and other household detritus from neighbouring Spanish cities were washed ashore.

If air travel captured the limelight in 1978, rail travel continued to reinforce its "serious" image in an era of higher-cost energy. The family was the railways' prime marketing target. At least eight European countries offered special discounts to families traveling by train, while several undertook to convey cars by train free provided three or more passengers bought train tick-

ets. In May the U.K. extended its 125-mph High Speed Train network to Anglo-Scottish services.

Work began in 1978 on what was perhaps the world's largest hotel project. The Cosmos Hotel in Moscow, where sports journalists covering the 1980 Olympic Games would be accommodated, was to provide a 1,000-seat convention hall and 3,600 beds. In Nepal the government proposed to turn the picturesque Sherpa villages around Mt. Everest into a Himalayan version of Europe's Alpine resorts.

(CAMILLE SHACKLEFORD)

WOOD PRODUCTS

With regard to worldwide forest resources a significant report was released in the summer of 1978 by the Food and Agriculture Organization (FAO) of the United Nations. It was based on a study of consumption and demand trends for wood products to the year 1994. The report concluded that countries with vast forest resources, such as the United States, Canada, and the Soviet Union, would be called upon to an even greater extent than in the past to supply global industrial wood requirements in future years.

North America and the Soviet Union would continue to produce more wood than they consume, the report forecast. Japan and Western Europe were seen as suffering from wood shortages with increasing frequency, and therefore they would be heavy importers of wood products. The FAO urged large national investments in reforestation to perpetuate the renewable resource and meet the gap between wood-rich and wood-poor countries.

The outlook for the timber supply from public lands was a dominant concern for the U.S. forest products industry in 1978. During the year the Forest Service completed a study to decide the future of 66 million ac of land in national forests.

Throughout 1978 some in the U.S. urged that most of the undeveloped acres in the national forests should be designated as federal wilderness preserves, where no motorized vehicles are allowed, no permanent shelters can be built, and no trees can be harvested or planted. Others argued that most of the lands should be opened up for development to meet the growing needs of the nation for timber, developed recreation, energy, and minerals. About 26 million ac of the roadless lands are potentially productive timber land. The national forests in 1978 were supplying about 16% of the timber growing stock that was cut in the U.S. The Forest Service was to recommend to Congress by January 1979 which areas should be designated as wilderness; which areas for timber harvesting, recreation, and other uses; and which to be studied further.

Strong demand for wood resulting from the continued boom in home building kept production of lumber and plywood at high levels throughout the year. Companies making paper products were plagued by strikes in the second half of 1978. On the bright side the world glut of wood pulp was shrinking to normal inventory levels as 1978 progressed.

The U.S. is both an importer and an exporter of wood. Principal markets for lumber are Canada, Japan, Australia, and

To save wood one company has developed laminated wooden I-beams to replace the traditional 2 × 10 floor joists.

Western Europe. Exports in 1978 were about 4,500,000,000 bd-ft of logs and lumber, about the same level as for 1977. Lumber imports, mainly from Canada, rose in 1978, reaching about 11,500,000,000 bd-ft, 7.5% above 1977, as housing construction continued at near-record-high levels for the second year in a row.

U.S. lumber production in 1978 was expected to total 38,300,000,000 bd-ft, compared with 37,300,000,000 in 1977. Softwood lumber, such as pine and fir, made up about 80% of total production. Between 65 and 70% of all softwood lumber is produced in the western U.S., about 25% in the South, and the balance throughout the rest of the country.

Furniture and flooring demands kept hardwood production at a quick tempo in 1978. The market was also strong for crates and pallets, which use about 30% of hardwood production.

The strength in housing, as well as general inflationary pressures, kept prices of wood products up in 1978. Employment in lumber and wood products industries also increased, particularly for women. The number of women employees rose 30% from 1975 to 1978.

Demand for most paper products was strong in 1978, and production of U.S. paper and paperboard was expected to reach about 64 million tons for 1978, more than 3% above 1977. Production of printing and writing papers was well above that of 1977, reflecting strong demand to supply magazines and copying machines. Consumption of newsprint, most of which comes from Canada, also was high, as was production of containerboard, used for shipping containers. (TAIT TRUSSELL)

See also Agriculture and Food Supplies; Computers; Consumerism; Economy, World; Energy; Food Processing; Games and Toys; Industrial Relations; Materials Sciences; Mining and Quarrying; Photography; Television and Radio; Transportation.

Table XIII. Major Tourism Earners and Spenders in 1977
In $000,000

Major Spenders	Expenditure
Germany, West	$10,805
United States	7,451
France	3,920
Canada	2,829
Netherlands, The	2,454
Japan	2,151
Austria	2,062
United Kingdom	1,921
Belgium/Luxembourg	1,635
Sweden	1,245

Major Earners	Earnings
United States	$6,164
Italy	4,762
France	4,377
Spain	4,003
United Kingdom	3,805
Germany, West	3,804
Austria	3,708
Switzerland	1,943
Canada	1,616
Netherlands, The	1,110

Source: World Tourism Organization.

THE COMPUTER COMES HOME

by Richard Casement

It was becoming increasingly apparent during 1978 that a second industrial revolution was under way. This revolution, so its prophets say, will bring down the cost of many products and enable new goods to be sold on a scale far beyond present-day expectations. But there are also widespread fears that the new technology will lead rapidly to unemployment in numbers that might test the resilience of existing political institutions.

Integrated Circuits. The key to the revolution is a device called an integrated circuit. Until recently it was an obscure piece of technology that few people outside the electronics industry had heard of. It is what makes a computer tick. It made possible the pocket calculator and the digital watch. During 1978 it became clear that few products would be beyond the influence of integrated circuits.

Integrated circuits are a kind of semiconductor. Semiconductors can amplify, switch, store, and control electrical signals. They are made of such materials as silicon and germanium, which, with regard to electrical conductivity, are halfway between metals and insulators. As such, they can be made to conduct electrical current or to block it. On an integrated circuit, thousands of such semiconductor circuits are imprinted on a tiny silicon chip measuring four millimetres square. These circuits can be used to store or process information.

How? Human language uses an alphabet. The English language uses 26 letters, but there is nothing magic about that number. The genetic code employs an alphabet of just four letters, and every instruction for every feature of every living being is coded in those four. A computer uses a two-letter alphabet, 0 and 1, and every number and every word can be represented by a combination of the two. On the computer's integrated circuit, the number one is represented by the presence of an electrical pulse; zero is represented by the absence of such a pulse.

Computers were the first applications of integrated circuits, and their development illustrates how these circuits may affect other products. The Die-

---

Richard Casement is a science correspondent for The Economist, *London, and the author of* Urban Traffic: Policies in Congestion.

bold Group of consultants has compared the modern microcomputer, using integrated circuits, with the first digital computer, the Electronic Numerical Integrator and Calculator (ENIAC) invented by J. Presper Eckert, Jr., and John W. Mauchly. ENIAC cost from $5 million to $10 million; an average microcomputer costs $500. ENIAC required one ten-thousandth of a second to carry out an instruction; a microcomputer needs two-millionths of a second. ENIAC weighed 30 tons; the microcomputer less than 2 lb.

The closer the circuits can be packed together on the silicon chip the cheaper they become, the faster they operate, and the less power they consume. The cost per circuit, $1 in 1960, fell to one cent in 1970 and is expected to be three-tenths of one cent by 1980. During 1978 the standard device packed 16,000 circuits on a 4-mm-square chip. But in September Texas Instruments Inc. unveiled a new standard, with 64,000 circuits on a chip of the same size. In two or three years, 256,000 circuits on a chip are expected, followed by one million circuits in the mid-1980s. Such a chip could store the entire contents of a 50,000-word book.

Microelectronics in the Home. To get an inkling of how such technology might change life-styles, imagine how one might read such a book. One step in this direction was taken during 1978: the first public trials of a British Post Office invention that is attracting worldwide interest from electronics companies. Called Viewdata, it links an ordinary television set with a central computer via a telephone line. Using a keyboard similar to that on a pocket calculator, the user can call up from the computer such data as railroad timetables, cooking recipes, economic information, and legal advice. Take this invention a few years ahead and one can imagine the computerized book. The Library of Congress could be stored on a small central computer in, say, Chicago or Tokyo. A user in London or Paris wants to read *Curtain* by Agatha Christie. He presses the code number for the book; a satellite terminal on the roof of the Chicago library will take about one second of transatlantic telephone time to relay the entire book to the nearest European satellite terminal; more slowly this terminal then relays the book to the user's home, where the information is stored by his personal computer, from which he can call the pages up on his television screen at his leisure.

Farfetched? Not a bit. In the U.S. there are already hundreds of retail computer shops selling personal computers, which by the mid-1980s will be as common as pocket calculators. One 14-year-old schoolboy in California does all his homework on his computer. If it does not have the information he needs, he can ring up the computer of a friend who has it on his.

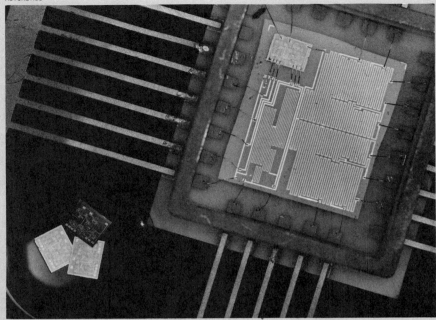

High-technology microminiaturization is evident in photo enlargement of an integrated circuit, or chip (small rectangle near top centre), shown mounted within a larger, mazelike resistor network. Three such packages cover only a fraction of the area of an ordinary contact lens (lower left).

Another invention using integrated circuits that is just about to see the light of day is the portable pocket telephone, developed in the U.S. by Motorola Inc. and Bell Telephone Laboratories, Inc. Public testing is scheduled to start in 1979 in Chicago and Washington, D.C. Meanwhile, the Japanese are working on flat-screen television sets that would eliminate the need for troublesome television tubes; pulse-code modulation for reproducing sound almost perfectly; and facsimile machines to be attached to television sets so that mail can be sent instantly by telephone or radio waves.

Social Implications. A report to the French president on the social implications of new electronic technology was so controversial that its publication was delayed until after the 1978 elections. The report said that microelectronics would play havoc with the employment forecasts in the country's five-year development plan. In Britain, the BBC's "Horizon" program fired the public's alarm with a special report on the same subject; that, too, predicted widespread unemployment. The British prime minister announced a top-level investigation into the social implications.

Advocates of microelectronics responded that new technology has always led to fears of unemployment. They maintained that any employment slack created by such technology in one part of the economy is quickly taken up because resources are freed to expand other sectors; this was what the whole process of rising living standards was about.

Opponents argued that the speed of the integrated circuit revolution is so fast that the slack cannot be taken up rapidly enough; indeed, the productivity gains are so enormous that they wondered whether the slack could be taken up at all. As an example, an electronic telephone exchange would need possibly only one-third the number of workers that are required for an electromechanical one.

One the other hand, it was pointed out that, in a competitive world, no country's industry could abstain from the microelectronic revolution. If it failed to update its products and production technology, its workers would be in danger of losing their jobs anyway. If people want their central heating thermostats computer-controlled in order to save 25% on their fuel bills, they will only buy from the manufacturers who make such thermostats.

Latest Developments. Meanwhile, discoveries and innovations continue, with the two largest electronics companies, AT&T and IBM, spending a total of $6 million a day on research and development. Companies started marketing new, very dense computer memories called magnetic bubbles just as IBM announced that it had discovered the possibility of using bubbles of light for the same purpose. Experiments were also being done on the use of lasers to store information; on computers that could recognize people's voices; and on using subatomic particles to transmit telecommunications signals that could not be jammed.

In California, Stanford University engineers announced a new technique using laser annealing to make the silicon chips themselves. This, they claimed, could enable ten times as many circuits to be packed on the same chip, with the circuits placed only half a micron apart (one-hundredth the thickness of a human hair).

Iran

Iran

A constitutional monarchy of western Asia, Iran is bounded by the U.S.S.R., Afghanistan, Pakistan, Iraq, and Turkey and the Caspian Sea, the Arabian Sea, and the Persian Gulf. Area: 1,648,000 sq km (636,000 sq mi). Pop. (1977 est.): 35,686,000. Cap. and largest city: Teheran (pop., 1976 census, 4,496,000). Language: Farsi Persian. Religion (1976): Muslim 99%; Christian, Jewish, and Zoroastrian minorities. Shah-in-shah, Mohammad Reza Pahlavi Aryamehr; prime ministers in 1978, Jamshid Amouzegar, Jaafar Sharif-Emami from August 27, and Gen. Gholam Reza Azhari from November 6.

In 1978 the regime of Shah Mohammad Reza Pahlavi Aryamehr (*see* BIOGRAPHIES) faced its most dangerous crisis since the shah was restored to the throne after the downfall of Mohammad Mosaddeq in 1953. Long considered a pillar of stability in the Middle East, the regime was rocked by intensifying political turbulence that brought down three governments. Its future was a matter of conjecture at year's end.

The death of a number of religious dissenters when police opened fire on them in the city of Qom in January was followed by a severe clash between the civil authorities and rioters in the northwest city of Tabriz in February, with widespread damage. Rioting took place in many small towns, and Teheran was shaken by major riots in May. Universities there were temporarily closed, and the Teheran bazaar experienced frequent protest strikes and shutdowns. During August, when the Muslim fast of Ramadan was in effect, widespread unrest culminated in further attacks on banks,

IRAN

Education. (1976–77) Primary, pupils 4,775,431, teachers 144,438; secondary, pupils 2,109,381, teachers 84,092; vocational, pupils 201,472, teachers 10,041; teacher training, students 3,356; higher, students 178,389, teaching staff 7,285.

Finance. Monetary unit: rial, with (Sept. 18, 1978) a free rate of 69.92 rials to U.S. $1 (137 rials = £1 sterling). Gold, SDR's, and foreign exchange (June 1978) U.S. $10,-902,000,000. Budget (1977–78 actual): revenue 2,097,000,-000,000 rials; expenditure 2,511,000,000,000 rials. Gross national product (1977–78) 5,347,600,000,000 rials. Money supply (May 1978) 934.5 billion rials. Cost of living (1975 = 100; June 1978) 159.5.

Foreign Trade. (1977) Imports 971 billion rials; exports 1,712,100,000,000 rials. Import sources (1976): West Germany 18%; U.S. 17%; Japan 16%; U.K. 8%; Italy 5%; France 5%. Export destinations (1976): Japan 22%; West Germany 10%; U.K. 9%; The Netherlands 8%; U.S. 8%; France 7%; Italy 6%; U.S. Virgin Islands 6%; Spain 5%. Main exports: crude oil and products 97%. Tourism (1976): visitors 628,000; gross receipts U.S. $142 million.

Transport and Communications. Roads (1975) c. 52,-000 km. Motor vehicles in use (1976): passenger 1,892,000; commercial 105,000. Railways: (state; 1976) 4,525 km; traffic (1974) 2,126,000,000 passenger-km, freight 4,917,000,-000 net ton-km. Air traffic (1976): 3,059,000,000 passenger-km; freight 74.8 million net ton-km. Shipping (1977): merchant vessels 100 gross tons and over 193; gross tonnage 1,002,061. Telephones (Jan. 1977) 782,000. Radio receivers (Dec. 1974) 8 million. Television receivers (Dec. 1975) 1.7 million.

Agriculture. Production (in 000; metric tons; 1977): wheat c. 6,200; barley c. 1,600; rice c. 1,650; potatoes c. 580; sugar, raw value c. 754; onions c. 333; tomatoes c. 256; watermelons (1976) c. 870; melons (1976) c. 420; dates c. 300; grapes c. 917; soybeans c. 103; tea c. 24; tobacco c. 19; cotton, lint c. 180. Livestock (in 000; Oct. 1976): cattle c. 6,650; sheep c. 35,440; goats c. 14,375; horses (1975) c. 350; asses (1975) c. 1,800; chickens c. 63,400.

Industry. Production (in 000; metric tons; 1976–77): cement 6,100; crude oil (1977) 283,230; natural gas (cu m; 1977) 22,850,000; petroleum products (1976) c. 32,500; coal c. 900; lead concentrates (metal content) 48; chromium ore (oxide content) 75; electricity (kw-hr) 17,311,000.

Troops with bayonets and gas masks took to the streets of Teheran to control demonstrators after martial law was proclaimed in Iran by Shah Mohammad Reza Pahlavi in September.

government property, and centres of entertainment. A fire in a movie theatre in Abadan on August 19, believed to have been set by Muslim extremists, caused the deaths of an estimated 430 persons. By the last week in August the tide of rioting and disorder had effectively brought the country to a standstill.

Political dissent took on an increasingly religiously inspired form during 1978 as the Muslim establishment openly criticized the government and called for a return to Islamic principles and the abandonment of such Western reforms as were contrary to their beliefs. The exiled Ayatullah Ruhollah Khomeini, who moved to Paris during the year after being expelled from Iraq, emerged as a symbol of opposition to the shah. Throughout the crisis he urged his followers to avoid any compromise with the regime. Efforts by the prime minister, Jamshid Amouzegar, to negotiate with religious leaders were unsuccessful. Equally, promises by the shah of continuing and far-reaching liberalization, including free elections in 1979, were ineffective. In Parliament control of affairs by the single party, Rastakhiz, was undermined by splits within it and by the emergence of the traditional parties after a hibernation of more than 18 years. Amouzegar resigned in August.

Appointment of Jaafar Sharif-Emami as prime minister on August 27 was made as a concession to the religious classes. The new Cabinet was met with a further surge of rioting, but, after the shooting down of 100 to 200 unarmed demonstrators on September 8, martial law was enforced in Teheran and 11 other major cities with remarkably little bloodshed. Nevertheless, strikes continued. Rioting broke out afresh early in October, with increasingly bloody clashes between soldiers and demonstrators. The shah's gesture in freeing nearly 1,500 political prisoners failed to conciliate the opposition, and various Cabinet changes proved equally futile. By early November strikers had brought the oil industry to a halt. For the first time, the demonstrations took on an overtly anti-American cast, and on November 6, during one of the worst riots in Teheran, an attack on the U.S. embassy was repulsed only with the aid of armed troops.

Sharif-Emami resigned November 5 and was replaced the next day by a military government, headed by the armed forces chief of staff, Gen. Gholam Reza Azhari. A number of prominent persons were placed under arrest, including former prime minister Amir Abbas Hoveida and the former head of Savak, the secret police. A crisis was widely expected on Ashura, the Shi'ite day of mourning (December 11), when thousands threatened to defy a ban on religious processions to march in what amounted to a massive antishah protest. At the last minute the marches were permitted, and the day passed relatively peacefully in Teheran, although there was some violence in other centres, notably Isfahan.

Although a showdown was avoided on Ashura, the situation continued to deteriorate. Oil production, which had picked up somewhat after the military government came to power, was again halted by strikes; exports were cut off, and by the end of December production was insufficient to meet domestic needs. There were also signs that the Army's hitherto unquestioned loyalty to the shah might be weakening, at least among the lower ranks. With the economy in shambles, moves were begun to form a civilian government of prominent members of the opposition, and on December 29 Shahpur Bakhtiar agreed to attempt to form a Cabinet. The position of the shah remained unclear. Palace spokesmen denied persistent rumours that he would abdicate or turn over power to a regency council. Ayatullah Khomeini continued to call for an end to the shah's regime.

On September 16 an earthquake destroyed the city of Tabas in eastern Iran and 40 surrounding villages, killing an estimated 25,000 people.

(KEITH S. MCLACHLAN)

Iraq

A republic of southwestern Asia, Iraq is bounded by Turkey, Iran, Kuwait, Saudi Arabia, Jordan, Syria, and the Persian Gulf. Area: 437,522 sq km (168,928 sq mi). Pop. (1977 census): 12,171,500, including Arabs, Kurds, Turks, Aramaic-speakers, Iranians, and others. Cap. and largest city: Baghdad (pop., 1977, 3,205,600). Language: Arabic. Religion: mainly Muslim, some Christian. President in 1978, Gen. Ahmad Hassan al-Bakr.

In 1978 Iraq maintained its strong opposition to the peace initiative of Egyptian Pres. Anwar as-Sadat and to any kind of political settlement with Israel, but it also remained outside the December 1977 Tripoli alliance of Arab states opposing Egypt and refused to attend the Algiers summit of the Tripoli alliance states on February 2–4, despite strong urging from Algerian Pres. Houari Boumédienne. Iraq predictably condemned the Camp David Egyptian-Israeli agreement as a treacherous conspiracy against the Arabs, but it did not attend the Damascus summit of hard-line Arab states in September. The Arab summit in Baghdad in November failed to take definitive action on the issue.

Because Iraq refused to attend the Algiers summit, Syria on January 29 broke off bilateral talks arranged by Algeria to settle Iraqi-Syrian differences. Because of Syria's continued closure since November 1977 of the Iraq-Turkey rail link through Syrian territory, Iraq was obliged to establish a road bridge bypassing Syria. However, on October 26, following talks held in Baghdad, the presidents of both countries signed a charter of mutual cooperation that appeared to end their long ideological dispute and, in particular, provided for economic and military cooperation through a joint political committee that would meet every three months.

Following the Israeli invasion of Lebanon in March, Iraq sent arms and several hundred volunteers to support the Palestinians and Lebanese leftists; the men were withdrawn after the Israelis left Lebanon. Iraq's relations with the main body of Palestinians, represented in the Palestine Liberation Organization (PLO), worsened considerably during 1978. The PLO blamed the Baghdad-based

Iraq

extremist Abu Nidal group for the assassination of its London (*see* OBITUARIES: *Hammami, Said*) and Kuwait representatives, regarded as moderates. A running warfare then developed with a series of attacks on Iraqi diplomats in London, Paris, and other capitals, widely believed to have been ordered by PLO chairman Yasir Arafat, and reprisals against PLO representatives. The murder in London on July 9 of a former Iraqi premier living in exile, Abdul Razzak an-Naif, also led to a deterioration in relations with Great Britain. On July 26 Britain expelled 11 Iraqi diplomats and officials, charging that they were intelligence agents. Iraq responded by expelling eight British diplomats and two British Airways employees.

The Iraqi Communist Party suffered a severe blow when 21 Communists were executed in May on charges of forming secret groups within the Army. Relations with the U.S.S.R. were also affected. The Iraqi government deplored Soviet support for the Marxist regime in Ethiopia, against which Iraq was aiding Somali and Eritrean nationalists, and—before its rapprochement with Syria—Soviet favouritism toward the rival Baathist regime there. There were some indications of renewed Kurdish nationalist activity during the year but no general recurrence of the revolt. The government announced that it was tripling its investments in the Kurdish Autonomous Region during 1978. The entente with Iran that had defeated the Kurdish revolt was maintained, and the Iraqi regime showed little sympathy for the antishah protests in Iran. In

November the shah's longtime opponent, the Ayatullah Ruhollah Khomeini, was pressured into leaving Iraq, where he had spent many years in exile. Relations with Kuwait continued to improve following the settlement of the border dispute in 1977. In May the two countries agreed to build a railway joining Basra and Kuwait and to link their electric grids.

A record budget for 1978 forecast expenditures of $25.7 billion, a 17% increase over the 1977 figure. It was announced that Iraq had given $2.2 billion in aid in 1977, 80% of which went to non-oil-producing countries. (PETER MANSFIELD)

Ireland

Separated from Great Britain by the North Channel, the Irish Sea, and St. George's Channel, the Republic of Ireland shares its island with Northern Ireland to the northeast. Area: 70,283 sq km (27,136 sq mi), or 84% of the island. Pop. (1977 est.): 3,199,000. Cap. and largest city: Dublin (pop., 1971, 567,900). Language (1971): mostly English; 28% speak English and Irish or Irish only. Religion: 94% Roman Catholic. President in 1978, Patrick J. Hillery; prime minister, John Lynch.

The main issues of 1978 were economic and monetary, with Ireland negotiating from April to join the proposed European Monetary System (EMS). The budget introduced at the beginning of February was designed to relieve taxation and

IRAQ
   Education. (1977–78) Primary, pupils 2,048,566, teachers 78,060; secondary, pupils 664,297, teachers 21,256; vocational, pupils 35,188, teachers 2,333; teacher training, students 27,281, teachers 1,193; higher, students 73,257, teaching staff 3,536.
   Finance. Monetary unit: Iraqi dinar, with (Sept. 18, 1978) a par value of 0.296 dinar to U.S. $1 (free rate of 0.578 dinar = £1 sterling). Gold, SDR's, and foreign exchange (Dec. 1977) U.S. $6,962,000,000. Budget (1976 est.) balanced at 5,045,000,000 dinars. Gross national product (1975) 3,907,400,000 dinars. Money supply (Sept. 1977) 807.8 million dinars. Cost of living (Baghdad; 1975 = 100; Jan. 1978) 119.5.
   Foreign Trade. Imports (1976) 1,024,700,000 dinars; exports (1977) 2,853,800,000 dinars. Import sources (1976): West Germany 21%; Japan 14%; France 8%; U.S. 5%; Italy 5%. Export destinations (1975): France *c.* 16%; Italy *c.* 13%; Brazil *c.* 12%; Turkey *c.* 6%; Japan *c.* 6%; U.S.S.R. *c.* 5%; U.K. *c.* 5%. Main export: crude oil 98%. Tourism: visitors (1976) 630,000; gross receipts (1975) U.S. $78 million.
   Transport and Communications. Roads (1975) 11,859 km. Motor vehicles in use (1975): passenger 98,600; commercial (including buses) 61,800. Railways: (1975) 1,990 km; traffic (1975–76) 704 million passenger-km, freight 2,252,000,000 net ton-km. Air traffic (1977): 1,221,000,000 passenger-km; freight 32.5 million net ton-km. Shipping (1977): merchant vessels 100 gross tons and over 110; gross tonnage 1,135,245. Telephones (Jan. 1977) 319,600. Radio receivers (Dec. 1975) 1,252,000. Television receivers (Dec. 1973) 520,000.
   Agriculture. Production (in 000; metric tons; 1977): wheat 696; barley 458; rice 199; cucumbers (1976) *c.* 102; watermelons (1976) *c.* 393; melons (1976) *c.* 102; tomatoes *c.* 290; dates *c.* 375; tobacco *c.* 10; cotton, lint (1976) *c.* 16. Livestock (in 000; 1977): cattle *c.* 2,550; buffalo *c.* 218; sheep *c.* 11,400; goats *c.* 3,600; camels (1976) *c.* 330; asses (1976) *c.* 607.
   Industry. Production (in 000; metric tons; 1976): cement 2,385; crude oil (1977) 111,220; petroleum products *c.* 5,400; electricity (excluding most industrial production; kw-hr) 4,645,000.

IRELAND
   Education. (1976–77) Primary, pupils 557,548, teachers 18,222; secondary, pupils 276,710, teachers 15,915; vocational, pupils 4,411, teachers 198; higher, students 35,048, teaching staff 3,054.
   Finance. Monetary unit: Irish pound, at par with the pound sterling, with a free rate (Sept. 18, 1978) of U.S. $1.96 = £1. Gold, SDR's, and foreign exchange (June 1978) U.S. $1,908,000,000. Budget (1977 actual): revenue £1,779 million; expenditure £2,335 million. Gross national product (1977) £5,352 million. Money supply (June 1978) £1,120.9 million. Cost of living (1975 = 100; May 1978) 142.2.
   Foreign Trade. (1977) Imports £3,081 million; exports £2,514.2 million. Import sources: EEC 68% (U.K. 48%, West Germany 7%, France 5%); U.S. 9%. Export destinations: EEC 76% (U.K. 47%, West Germany 9%, France 7%, The Netherlands 6%); U.S. 6%. Main exports: machinery 13%; beef and veal 12%; chemicals 10%; dairy products 8%; textile yarns and fabrics 6%; cattle 5%. Tourism (1976): visitors 1,690,000; gross receipts U.S. $253 million.
   Transport and Communications. Roads (1975) 89,006 km. Motor vehicles in use (1976): passenger 551,100; commercial 53,530. Railways: (1976) 2,010 km; traffic (1977) 794 million passenger-km, freight 534 million net ton-km. Air traffic (1976): 1,528,000,000 passenger-km; freight 77.7 million net ton-km. Shipping (1977): merchant vessels 100 gross tons and over 98; gross tonnage 211,872. Telephones (Jan. 1977) 480,000. Radio receivers (Dec. 1974) 886,000. Television licenses (Dec. 1976) 590,000.
   Agriculture. Production (in 000; metric tons; 1977): barley *c.* 1,359; wheat *c.* 239; oats *c.* 127; potatoes *c.* 1,200; sugar, raw value *c.* 185; cabbages (1976) *c.* 138; cow's milk *c.* 4,600; butter 102; cheese *c.* 56; beef and veal *c.* 318; pork *c.* 127; fish catch (1976) 94. Livestock (in 000; June 1977): cattle 7,155; sheep 3,526; pigs 947; horses (1976) *c.* 98; chickens *c.* 10,500.
   Industry. Production (in 000; metric tons; 1976): coal 49; cement 1,569; petroleum products 1,886; electricity (kw-hr; 1977) 9,308,000; manufactured gas (cu m) 270,000; beer (hl; 1973–74) 4,492; wool fabrics (sq m) 3,000; rayon, etc., fabrics (sq m) 16,700.

achieve a wage settlement with the trade unions that would satisfy them but would not feed inflation.

The budget package, delivered by Finance Minister George Colley but to a large extent the brainchild of Martin O'Donoghue, minister for economic planning and development and a new man among the leaders of the Fianna Fail party, seemed to work. Inflation, which had been as high as 20% at the beginning of 1977, came down steadily, reaching 6.2% by mid-June 1978. Agreement was also reached on a nationwide wage package. In June the government published its detailed action program for the economy, a Green Paper which set out proposals on job creation, as well as proposed cuts in public spending. It was controversially thorough and provoked a heated public debate, but the general reaction was positive.

As early as April, the government decided to commit the country to joining the EMS, irrespective of Britain's intent. The proposed system would link all nine members of the European Economic Community. The issue dominated ministerial and summit meetings in Europe, but by year's end, because of objections raised by France in connection with the Community's common agricultural policy, no definite date had been set for the system's inception.

This exercising of Irish political muscle in Europe was backed up by more practical work at the European Parliament. In the late summer Irish delegates took a strong and independent line on specific agricultural issues, including the creation of a European policy for mutton and lamb. Then, at the beginning of October, all three Irish political parties inaugurated their direct election campaigns for the European Parliament, aimed at returning 15 delegates in June 1979 to represent the Republic of Ireland. Most of the political events of the year had a European flavour.

Security remained a serious Irish problem, however. In January the government dismissed the head of the police force, Edmund Garvey, without giving reasons. The reasons, in fact, were numerous and complex, involving a loss of confidence in the force, too much priority given to the arrest and detention of subversives, and too little emphasis on crime prevention and detection, particularly in urban areas. But if urban crime was identified by the government as the main security problem, a very different view was adopted by the British secretary of state for Northern Ireland, Roy Mason. Visiting Dublin in May, he called for more pressure against subversives, while treating other matters of North-South cooperation in a fairly dismissive manner. Previously, in March, Mason had alleged that Provisional Irish Republican Army (IRA) terrorists were operating from bases inside the republic.

In June Seamus Twomey, a former chief of staff of the Provisional IRA, was sentenced. Twomey had escaped from Mountjoy Prison, Dublin, in a hijacked helicopter in October 1973 and had been recaptured in December 1977. He received a five-year jail sentence for his exploit, with a three-year concurrent sentence for IRA membership.

In January the government issued a statement

Ireland

welcoming the European Court of Human Rights ruling on interrogation techniques used by British security forces in Northern Ireland. The court held that, while they did not constitute torture, they amounted to "inhuman and degrading treatment" that contravened the European Convention on Human Rights.

An important archaeological discovery in Dublin aroused much controversy during the second half of 1978. Substantial remains of the old Viking city were unearthed during the course of sinking foundations for civic offices on the banks of the River Liffey. They included the foundations of houses, roadways, docking facilities beside the river, much human detritus of one sort or another, and even the remains of a Viking skeleton. The courts declared the site "a national monument," thus halting construction. Marches of protest were organized, one of which attracted an estimated 20,000 people. Among the protesters were Dubliners dressed in Viking costume who declared they would fight once again for the dear old city. In the event, the government compromised by granting a period of six weeks for further excavations and later making this an unlimited period, until such time as the archaeologists responsible were satisfied. Strong pressure continued on the government to abandon the civic offices altogether and turn the Wood Quay site into a Viking park. In mid-November Prime Minister John Lynch indicated, in connection with the controversy, the need for governments to take note of public opinion, and defenders of Wood Quay anticipated an eventual decision in their favour.

A serious restraint was placed on conversation throughout the country by a prolonged strike of telephone engineers and operators. It ran from February to early May. However, it never quite brought the system to a stop, and partial communication, of an intermittent kind, remained available. As a compensation of sorts, the state radio and television network inaugurated a new television channel in June, following this with a second radio channel in the autumn. It had the look of a plan to stop people from talking and have them look and listen instead. There was plenty of opportunity; from May to October the weather was cold and miserably wet.

On March 21 the former president of Ireland, Cearbhall O Dalaigh (see OBITUARIES), died following a heart attack. He was the only president of Ireland to resign, and did so in circumstances that provoked considerable controversy.

(BRUCE ARNOLD)

See also United Kingdom.

Israel

Israel

A republic of the Middle East, Israel is bounded by Lebanon, Syria, Jordan, Egypt, and the Mediterranean Sea. Area (not including territory occupied in the June 1967 war): 20,700 sq km (7,992 sq mi). Pop. (1978 est.): 3,695,600. Cap. and largest city: Jerusalem (pop., 1978 est., 376,000). Language: Hebrew and Arabic. Religion: predominantly Jewish (1977 est., 84.5%) with Muslim, Christian, and other minorities. Presidents in 1978, Ephraim Katzir and, from May 29, Yitzhak Navon; prime minister, Menahem Begin.

For Israel the year 1978 was essentially one of testing the nation's leaders, Prime Minister Menahem Begin (*see* NOBEL PRIZES) and his ministerial colleagues of the Likud Party. They had come to power in the wake of their surprising electoral victory in May 1977 when the Labour Party was displaced for the first time after 30 years in office. It was also a test for the new and younger leaders of the Labour Party. They had to reconstruct their party, regain public confidence, and demonstrate their authority in opposition to the government.

Alone, almost apart, without a party label or a party following, stood the foreign minister, Moshe Dayan. His influence in the country and abroad was greatly enhanced by year's end but was still challenged by the majority in the Cabinet that was taking a hard line with regard to concessions to Egypt and the Palestinians. Twice he had approved the text of a peace treaty with Egypt, only to be overruled by the Cabinet. Both times he had withheld his resignation, presumably because he could not see how Israel's best interests would be served if he and Defense Minister Ezer Weizman (*see* BIOGRAPHIES) were to abandon the negotiating field to the hard-line "hawks."

As 1978 began, six weeks after the euphoria of the "peace initiative" visit of Egyptian Pres. Anwar as-Sadat (*see* NOBEL PRIZES) to Jerusalem, the mood in Israel had become more sober. The Sadat-Begin meeting at Ismailia in Egypt late in 1977 had concluded without the expected "joint declaration" of peace. The Knesset (parliament) had voted on December 28 for Begin's peace plan, which Sadat had categorically rejected. Within weeks Begin abandoned the plan's more untenable positions: the retention of Jewish settlements in Sinai to be administered by Israel and protected by Israeli troops and the retention of Israeli troops in central Sinai to monitor the free passage of ships through the Strait of Tiran.

As it turned out both Sadat and Begin had lost the initiative at Ismailia. On January 4 Sadat met briefly with U.S. Pres. Jimmy Carter at Aswan, Egypt. With this encounter the initiative passed to the United States. It became a partner in the peace process, as Sadat had desired and as Begin had sought to prevent. However, the formula on the Palestinian question agreed upon at Aswan was accepted by the Israeli government. It stipulated that "the resolution of the Palestine problem must recognize the legitimate rights of the Palestinian people and enable the Palestinians to participate in the determination of their own future." But the Israelis took comfort from President Carter's statement of Dec. 15, 1977, in which he said that because of its intransigence the Palestine Liberation Organization (PLO) had removed itself "from any immediate prospect of participation in a peace discussion."

Negotiations continued when Egyptian Foreign Minister Muhammad Ibrahim Kamal went to Jerusalem to meet with Foreign Minister Dayan and U.S. Secretary of State Cyrus Vance. An early cloud was cast over the proceedings by an uncompromisingly hard-line statement that Kamal made on his arrival January 17. The cloud turned into a storm warning when that same evening Begin responded with somewhat heavy-handed humour that greatly offended the Egyptians. On the next day, after the Israelis and the Egyptians had made their formal opening statements, Egyptian radio announced that Sadat had ordered Kamal and his negotiating team to return to Cairo. The political talks were at an end.

Meanwhile, Sadat flew to Washington and stayed with President Carter at Camp David, Md. A week after Sadat's arrival, Secretary Vance informed the Israeli government that it was the U.S. position that the Jewish settlements in the Sinai were there "contrary to international law." U.S. Assistant Secretary of State Alfred Atherton continued to negotiate in Jerusalem and Cairo between February 21 and March 6, but to no avail.

Begin was to follow Sadat to Washington in an attempt to restore the traditional U.S. support for Israel and to counter the Egyptian leader's undoubted public relations success in the U.S. On the eve of his departure on March 12, 11 terrorists attacked a bus and several other vehicles on the Haifa–Tel Aviv highway. About 30 Israeli passengers and one U.S. citizen died, and many were injured. Nine of the terrorists were killed in the ensuing gunfight. The PLO claimed responsibility.

Begin postponed his journey to Washington. On March 14 Israeli troops crossed into southern Lebanon to occupy "a security belt" that Israel hoped would prevent further terrorist raids across the border. Although the Israeli force was much smaller than was generally claimed, numbering only 6,500 men rather than 25,000, it appeared to have gone into action without any clear objective, causing much damage and many casualties among the normally friendly southern Lebanese. The PLO forces escaped to the north.

Weizman ordered a unilateral cease-fire in southern Lebanon on March 21. On that day Prime Minister Begin arrived in the U.S. for the post-

Israeli troops physically removed squatters from an illegal settlement in occupied Jordan. The squatters were protesting the Camp David peace agreements.

UPI COMPIX

ISRAEL

Education. (1976–77) Primary, pupils 578,658, teachers 31,835; secondary, pupils 77,943, teachers 5,732; vocational, pupils 74,441, teachers 7,652; higher, students 74,-371, teaching staff (1973–74) 13,981.

Finance. Monetary unit: Israeli pound, with (Sept. 18, 1978) a free rate of I£18.45 to U.S. $1 (I£36.15 = £1 sterling). Gold, SDR's, and foreign exchange (June 1978) U.S. $1,749,600,000. Budget (1977–78 est.) balanced at I£122,500 million. Gross national product (1977) I£138,-921 million. Money supply (Sept. 1977) I£17,633 million. Cost of living (1975 = 100; June 1978) 258.5.

Foreign Trade. (1977) Imports I£60,535 million (including I£9,852 million military goods); exports I£32,249 million. Import sources: U.S. 20%; U.K. 10%; West Germany 9%; Switzerland 9%; The Netherlands 9%. Export destinations: U.S. 19%; West Germany 9%; U.K. 7%; Hong Kong 6%; The Netherlands 6%; France 5%; Belgium-Luxembourg 5%. Main exports: diamonds 36%; chemicals 11%; metal manufactures 8%; citrus fruit 6%; machinery 6%. Tourism (1976): visitors 733,000; gross receipts U.S. $292 million.

Transport and Communications. Roads (1974) 10,657 km. Motor vehicles in use (1976): passenger 297,300; commercial 98,100. Railways: (1977) 902 km; traffic (1976) 280 million passenger-km, freight 449 million net ton-km. Air traffic (1977): 4,697,000,000 passenger-km; freight 179,008,000 net ton-km. Shipping (1976): merchant vessels 100 gross tons and over 58; gross tonnage 404,651. Telephones (Jan. 1977) 869,000. Radio receivers (Dec. 1972) 680,000. Television receivers (Dec. 1974) 652,000.

Agriculture. Production (in 000; metric tons; 1977): wheat 230; barley (1976) 20; potatoes 212; peanuts 25; watermelons (1976) c. 110; tomatoes c. 250; onions c. 60; oranges 897; grapefruit 499; grapes 73; apples 100; olives 9; bananas 54; cotton, lint 63; cheese c. 50; fish catch (1976) 26. Livestock (in 000; 1976): cattle 323; sheep 202; goats 140; pigs c. 86; camels 11; chickens c. 11,500.

Industry. Production (in 000; metric tons; 1977): cement 1,852; petroleum products (1976) c. 6,800; sulfuric acid 198; salt 87; fertilizers (nutrient content; 1976–77) nitrogenous 48, potash 645; electricity (kw-hr) 11,164,000. New dwelling units completed (1977) 43,010.

The charred wreckage of a bus stands along a highway leading into Tel Aviv. The bus had been full of tourists returning home after sight-seeing in March when it was attacked by PLO terrorists. After a gun battle, 37 Israelis and 9 Palestinians were killed; 82 Israelis were wounded.

poned meeting with President Carter. This was said to be "serious and candid." Carter left Begin in little doubt that the U.S. found certain positions adopted by the Cabinet majority, be they with Begin's blessing or not, unacceptable. The U.S. stressed Lebanon's territorial integrity and also urged Israel to accept UN Resolution 242 as the basis for negotiations with Egypt. (This resolution called for Israeli withdrawal from territory occupied in the 1967 war.) The Israeli Cabinet rejected this in February. However on April 16, a month after the Washington talks, the Cabinet affirmed its support for the UN resolution.

At this time and especially during the first weeks of May, Israel again became entangled with U.S. policy. This time the issue was the proposed sale by the U.S. of 60 F-15 fighter planes to Saudi Arabia over a four- or five-year period. Begin ordered an all-out campaign against this proposed sale on the grounds that it would change the balance of power on Israel's eastern front. Carter countered by stipulating a package deal that made the sale of 90 F-16 and F-15 aircraft to Israel contingent on Senate approval of the Saudi sale.

Israel urged its friends in the U.S. to oppose this and to urge the U.S. Senate not to vote for the package deal. On May 5 Begin took the unprecedented step for an Israeli leader of urging U.S. Jews to mute their public expressions of dissent from his policies because in so doing they "weaken those who negotiate for Israel." On May 15, despite Be-

gin's appeal and the urgings of Israel's friends, the Senate approved Carter's proposed package arms deal with Israel, Saudi Arabia, and Egypt.

On April 19 Yitzhak Navon (*see* BIOGRAPHIES) was elected president of Israel without opposition. It was a popular choice. Navon, a tenth-generation Israeli, charmed his audience with an inaugural speech delivered with impressive articulation in Hebrew and Arabic. He appealed to Begin and Sadat not to abandon their effort for peace.

At the end of June the Israeli Cabinet began to confront its other major problem, the future sovereignty of the West Bank and Gaza. This issue was of great political importance for Begin and his colleagues. Carter and, especially, the U.S. Department of State did not make matters any easier for Dayan and Weizman. Their objective was to compel Begin to climb down from positions that had been a mainstay for him and his party.

Dayan was left with the seemingly impossible task of bridging the gap between an angry Begin, who resented U.S. pressure, and an angry Carter, who was annoyed by Israeli "legalisms and double-talk." What Dayan wanted was to keep the negotiations going on Carter's terms. But at the same time he wanted to push ahead with Israel's plans for the West Bank so that in five years, when a decision on its autonomy was due, there would be a new relationship established between it and Israel that would be acceptable to all parties.

The year's most significant achievement consisted of two agreements signed by Begin and Sadat at the end of a conference with Carter at Camp David in September. In return for the establishment of normal relations between Israel and Egypt, Israel agreed to return all of Sinai to Egypt and remove its settlements from that region. Israel also agreed to a freeze on new settlements in the West Bank. The rights of Palestinians were to be recognized. Loose ends in the agreements were dealt with by

Dayan and Weizman along with representatives from Egypt and the U.S., and by the end of October a formula had been negotiated that satisfied all three parties.

The formula was rejected by the Israeli Cabinet in early November. Meanwhile, in Baghdad, Iraq, a conference of the opponents of the Camp David agreements had met and denounced them with the support of the Saudi Arabian delegation. Sadat's position in the Arab world was thus becoming more difficult, and he stepped up his demands on Israel. Therefore, the formula agreed on by the negotiators was no longer practical on November 21 when the Israeli Cabinet, at Dayan's urging, belatedly endorsed the Dayan-Weizman formula but without a crucial addition to which the two negotiators had agreed. This had set a target date, with adequate qualifications, for elections to be held in the West Bank.

Again it seemed as if all was lost. But again Dayan and the Egyptians, assisted by Cyrus Vance, found yet another opening. A meeting between Dayan, Vance, and Egyptian Prime Minister Mustafa Khalil was arranged for December 24 in Brussels. Before Dayan left for Brussels, Begin announced that Dayan had been authorized to discuss only procedural questions.

On his return to Jerusalem, before a special Cabinet meeting to hear his report and after he had briefed Begin, Dayan said that he had discussed the outstanding issues "in great depth" with Khalil and Vance. Accordingly, he recommended that the talks be resumed, with both Israel and Egypt making concessions. This was not what Begin had intended, but evidently Dayan believed that the day of decision had come. The Cabinet talked for four hours but made no decision.

Thus, the euphoria of December 1977 had all but evaporated a year later. Begin's command over his party and his colleagues in the Cabinet had weakened. His economic policy of liberating the country from controls and restrictions was in a shambles. There had been crippling strikes among dockworkers, postal employees, and teachers. Inflation was out of control, running at 40% for most of the year and climbing in the last quarter to an annual rate of 80%.

On December 8, Golda Meir, a former Labour prime minister and one of the last of Israel's founding giants, died at the age of 80 (*see* OBITUARIES). Begin and Sadat on December 10 received the Nobel Peace Prize at a ceremony in Oslo, Norway. Begin attended in person, while Sadat sent a proxy.

(JON KIMCHE)

Italy

Italy

A republic of southern Europe, Italy occupies the Apennine Peninsula, Sicily, Sardinia, and a number of smaller islands. On the north it borders France, Switzerland, Austria, and Yugoslavia. Area: 301,262 sq km (116,318 sq mi). Pop. (1978 est.): 56,600,400. Cap. and largest city: Rome (pop., 1978 est., 2,897,500). Language: Italian. Religion: predominantly Roman Catholic. Presidents in 1978, Giovanni Leone until June 15 and,

Alessandro Pertini was greeted by a well-wisher on his way to a meeting of Rome's Chamber of Deputies on July 8. Pertini was elected president of Italy at that session.

from July 9, Alessandro Pertini; premier, Giulio Andreotti.

The kidnapping and murder by Red Brigades terrorists of Aldo Moro (*see* OBITUARIES), former premier and one of the nation's most influential political leaders, was the most dramatic event of a year during which political developments were overshadowed by a serious increase in terrorist violence. The biggest manhunt ever organized in peacetime in Italy failed to track down Moro's killers. Although a small group of alleged Red Brigades members were arrested and sentenced to long prison terms on charges of illegal possession of arms, the crime remained unsolved and continued to weigh heavily on an unstable political situation in which Roman Catholics and Communists formally shared power for the first time in over 30 years.

Domestic Affairs. The year began with a sudden spate of extremist political violence in Rome and the major cities of northern Italy, leaving four dead. Disagreements on economic and social policies among the members of the six-party political alliance that had supported Premier Giulio Andreotti's minority Christian Democrat government for 17 months culminated in the withdrawal of the Communists from the pact. Lacking this support, Andreotti resigned on January 16. The Communists, supported by the Socialists, demanded direct Cabinet participation in an all-party emergency government. Four days before Andreotti resigned and after a hastily arranged visit to Washington, D.C., by the U.S. ambassador to Italy, Richard Gardner, the U.S. Department of State spelled out its strong opposition to participation in the government by the Italian Communist Party. There followed the longest government crisis in Italian postwar history. Almost eight weeks elapsed before Andreotti was able to succeed himself with a new minority administration. Communist demands for greater power sharing were satisfied by a new compromise arrangement, a parliamentary majority in which the Italian Communist Party was formally associated with government for the first time in over 30 years.

The new Cabinet, without Communist members and virtually unchanged from that of the previous administration, met for the first time on March 15. At the meeting Andreotti outlined his program to be presented to Parliament the following day. But shortly after nine o'clock on the morning of March 16 a group of terrorists ambushed the car carrying Aldo Moro, president of the ruling Christian Democrat Party and architect of the new political agreement between Catholics and Communists, on his way to Parliament. Moro's driver and his four police bodyguards were murdered, and the terrorists escaped with their hostage.

The government organized a massive search for the kidnapped leader, mobilizing all the nation's police forces and bringing in the Army to help as well. The Red Brigades terrorists announced in a series of "communiqués" that they were subjecting the former premier to a "people's trial." Two photographs of Moro in captivity were published, and during March and April the terrorists released a series of more than 20 personal letters written by Moro to his family, friends, and political leaders pleading that the government agree to exchange him for imprisoned Red Brigades members. Finally the Red Brigades announced that they had sentenced their hostage to death and that he would be executed. Hundreds of police were dispatched to a frozen lake high up in the Abruzzi Mountains of central Italy after a fictitious report was circulated that the statesman's body had been dumped there.

Pope Paul VI made a vain personal appeal for the life of his friend, while the Italian government stood firm and refused any deal with the terrorists.

However, there were indications that a one-for-one prisoner exchange was being considered at a high level when confirmation came that Moro had been murdered. His body was found on May 9 in the back of a stolen car abandoned symbolically in a narrow street in central Rome halfway between the headquarters of the Communist and Christian Democrat parties. He had been shot.

The Moro affair dominated the political scene in Rome for most of the year. Police arrested various minor accomplices in June in Rome, and in September in Milan they arrested Corrado Alunni, a known Red Brigades leader wanted on previous terrorism charges. Alunni was sentenced to 12 years of imprisonment on two counts relating to past terrorist acts and illegal possession of arms and ammunition. Judicial inquiries into the Moro murder continued without significant result.

In spite of attempts to intimidate judges, lawyers, and jurymen, the much-delayed trial of Renato Curcio (*see* BIOGRAPHIES), founder of the Red Brigades, and a group of 28 of his accomplices (in person or absentia) was successfully concluded. The accused were found guilty and sentenced to up to 15 years in prison on charges relating to political violence in the early 1970s.

On May 18 a controversial bill allowing free abortion on demand for women over the age of 18 was passed by a narrow majority in the upper house of Parliament, the Senate, and became law in June. The implementation of the law caused serious difficulties in Italy's overcrowded hospitals and clinics. Many Roman Catholic physicians took advantage of a clause in the new law allowing them to withdraw from the state abortion scheme on grounds of conscience.

Partial local elections were held in May involving 10% of the total electorate. The results showed a significant swing toward the ruling Christian Democrats and away from the Communists, reversing the trend set in the 1976 general election.

Giovanni Leone, president of Italy, and his family were accused by the press during the early part of the year of tax evasion, questionable real-

Surrounded by iron bars and armed guards, members of the Red Brigades went on trial in Turin in March. Twenty-nine Brigades members were given long prison sentences, some in absentia, and 16 were acquitted.

SYGMA

Italian Literature:
see Literature

estate deals, and improper use of his high office. The president, a former Christian Democrat premier, resigned on June 15 after the Communist Party gave its support to calls for his removal.

Alessandro Pertini (*see* BIOGRAPHIES), an 82-year-old wartime resistance leader and former Socialist speaker of the lower house of Parliament, was elected seventh president of Italy after a difficult ten-day series of ballots by the electoral college, a joint session of both houses of Parliament.

In December the Senate approved the draft of a revision of the concordat on church-state relations signed by Benito Mussolini in 1929, and early acceptance seemed likely. Under the proposal, worked out over ten years of intermittent negotiations, Roman Catholicism would cease to be the state religion of Italy. The future of church-run educational and welfare institutions would be decided at a later date. The influence of the Vatican on Italian domestic politics was considered likely to dwindle under the new Polish pope, John Paul II (*see* BIOGRAPHIES).

On November 8 Fedele Calvosa, public prosecutor of Frosinone, a town between Rome and Naples, was shot dead by terrorists together with his driver and bodyguard. This new triple assassination raised speculation that the centre of extremist political violence might be shifting from the industrial north to central Italy and that the campaign of terror would become more indiscriminate.

Foreign Affairs. The succession of domestic crises prevented Italy from engaging in much activity in international affairs, but Andreotti managed to fit in a visit to the United States from May 28 to June 2 during which he met U.S. Pres. Jimmy Carter and made a speech at the United Nations Special Session on Disarmament. During his visit Andreotti briefed U.S. officials on the new political arrangement with the Communists.

The most significant official foreign visitor to Italy was the Chinese foreign minister, Huang Hua, who spent five days from October 5 to 10 talking to government leaders and touring industrial areas in both the north and south. In Turin the Chinese minister met Giovanni Agnelli, the chairman of Fiat and Italy's leading industrialist.

Negotiations were at an advanced stage between the Fiat organization and the Chinese government for the sale of a tractor plant worth $600 million. During a visit to Peking Italy's Foreign Trade Minister Rinaldo Ossola offered the Chinese a line of credit worth $1 billion for the purchase of Italian products. A formal trade agreement was due to be signed early in 1979.

The Economy. At the end of August Treasury Minister Filippo Maria Pandolfi produced a long-awaited three-year economic stabilization plan for 1979–81. This was an attempt to define a strategy to halt Italy's slide away from its European Community partners. "Popular feeling and political orientation carry us toward Europe, but economic reality tends to push us toward the sidelines," the document said. The aims were radical surgery in public spending (budget deficits in the 1970s reached heights rarely exceeded in other industrialized countries) and a cut in labour and social costs. In December, after initial hesitation, Italy opted to join the proposed new European Monetary System, to be inaugurated in 1979.

On paper Italy had a healthy balance sheet with record currency reserves of $10.7 billion and a balance of payments surplus for practically every month in the year, thanks to buoyant exports and generous spending by millions of foreign tourists. The result was that large Italian companies were again in the market for international loans.

But Andreotti's plan to dampen inflation and to cut the public-sector deficit was not achieved. The series of political crises—the change in government, the Moro murder, and the change of presidents—all combined to leave the country rudderless at times when vital economic decisions had to be made.

Inflation remained at about 11%, an improvement over the 1977 figure of more than 14% but still high enough to cause continuing pressure by the labour unions for higher wages. Imbalances in wages and salaries between workers in the public sector and those in private industry caused a series of damaging strikes by hospital workers and other government employees.

(DAVID DOUGLAS WILLEY)

ITALY

Education. (1977–78) Primary, pupils 4,665,526, teachers 255,267; secondary, pupils 2,945,930, teachers 249,777; vocational, pupils 1,421,515, teachers 126,851; teacher training, students 205,695, teachers 18,899; higher, students 748,425, teaching staff (1975–76) 43,129.

Finance. Monetary unit: lira, with (Sept. 18, 1978) a free rate of 832 lire to U.S. $1 (1,631 lire = £1 sterling). Gold, SDR's, and foreign exchange (June 1978) U.S. $12,961,000,000. Budget (1977 actual): revenue 43,022,000,000,000 lire; expenditure 54,899,000,000,000 lire. Gross national product (1977) 172,397,000,000,000 lire. Money supply (Feb. 1978) 96,236,000,000,000 lire. Cost of living (1975 = 100; June 1978) 152.6.

Foreign Trade. (1977) Imports 41,960,000,-000,000 lire; exports 39,736,000,000,000 lire. Import sources: EEC 43% (West Germany 17%, France 14%); U.S. 7%; Saudi Arabia 6%. Export destinations: EEC 47% (West Germany 19%, France 14%, U.K. 5%); U.S. 7%. Main exports: machinery 23%; motor vehicles 9%; chemicals 7%; food 5%; cloth-ing 6%; textile yarns and fabrics 5%; petroleum products 5%; iron and steel 5%. Tourism (1976): visitors 13,930,000; gross receipts U.S. $2,526,000,-000.

Transport and Communications. Roads (1975) 291,081 km (including 5,431 km expressways). Motor vehicles in use (1976): passenger 16,221,300; commercial 1,059,980. Railways (1976) 19,923 km; traffic (1977) 38,780,000,000 passenger-km, freight 16,080,000,000 net ton-km. Air traffic (1976): 10,780,000,000 passenger-km; freight 468,240,000 net ton-km. Shipping (1977): merchant vessels 100 gross tons and over 1,690: gross tonnage 11,111,182. Telephones (Jan. 1977) 15,241,000. Radio licenses (Dec. 1976) 13,024,000. Television licenses (Dec. 1976) 12,377,000.

Agriculture. Production (in 000; metric tons; 1977): wheat 6,329; corn 6,456; barley 677; oats 355; rice 721; potatoes 3,310; sugar, raw value 1,230; cabbages (1976) 628; cauliflowers (1976) 570; onions 490; tomatoes 3,120; grapes 10,900; wine 6,363; olives 2,550; oranges 1,650; mandarin oranges and tangerines 375; lemons 871; apples 1,810; pears (1976) 1,480; peaches (1976) 1,419; tobacco c. 110; cheese c. 525; beef and veal c. 1,047; pork 902. Livestock (in 000; Dec. 1976): cattle 8,737; sheep 8,445; pigs 9,097; goats 948; poultry c. 117,550.

Industry. Index of production (1975 = 100; 1977) 113.6. Unemployment (1977) 7.1%. Fuel and power (in 000; metric tons; 1977): lignite 1,112; crude oil 1,083; natural gas (cu m) 13,700,000; manufactured gas (cu m) 3,380,000; electricity (kw-hr; 1976) 163,-550,000. Production (in 000; metric tons; 1977): iron ore (44% metal content) 480; pig iron 11,666; crude steel 23,299; aluminum 262; lead 46; zinc 180; cement 38,206; cotton yarn 149; man-made fibres 432; fertilizers (nutrient content; 1976–77) nitrogenous 985, phosphate 383, potash 141; sulfuric acid 2,952; petroleum products (1976) 101,958; passenger cars (units) 1,440; commercial vehicles (units) 144. Merchant vessels launched (100 gross tons and over; 1977) 688,000 gross tons. New dwelling units completed (1977) 149,200.

Ivory Coast

A republic on the Gulf of Guinea, the Ivory Coast is bounded by Liberia, Guinea, Mali, Upper Volta, and Ghana. Area: 322,463 sq km (124,504 sq mi). Pop. (1978 est.): 7,205,000. Cap. and largest city: Abidjan (pop., 1975, 685,800). Language: French (official) and local dialects (Akan 41%, Kru 17%, Voltaic 16%, Malinke 15%, Southern Mande 10%). Religion: animist 65%; Muslim 23%; Christian 12%. President and premier in 1978, Félix Houphouët-Boigny.

In internal politics 1978 was a relatively uneventful year for the Ivory Coast. A minor government reshuffle in February, with the appointment of Amadou Thiam to the post of information minister, was essentially a technical adjustment. In foreign affairs, however, important developments included a rapprochement with Guinea and the strengthening of links with France.

Pres. Félix Houphouët-Boigny visited Cameroon on February 23, and on March 17 a summit meeting at Monrovia, Liberia, brought together the presidents of Guinea, Ivory Coast, Liberia, Togo, and The Gambia and officially confirmed the reconciliation between Guinea and the Ivory Coast. This was translated into concrete terms on April 14, with the establishment of normal diplomatic relations and the signing of a treaty of friendship between the two countries.

Pres. Valéry Giscard d'Estaing of France visited the Ivory Coast on January 11–16, taking the opportunity to revive proposals for an Afro-European solidarity pact. This concept, brought up again at the Franco-African conference in Paris together with that of a joint African intervention force, was supported by President Houphouët-Boigny. On the whole, Giscard's visit was seen as marking a renewed attempt by France to extend its influence in Africa and was attacked on those grounds by Algeria, Libya, and the Soviet Union.

(PHILIPPE DECRAENE)

Ivory Coast

Jamaica

A parliamentary state within the Commonwealth of Nations, Jamaica is an island in the Caribbean Sea about 90 mi S of Cuba. Area: 10,991 sq km (4,244 sq mi). Pop. (1978 est.): 2,115,000, predominantly African and Afro-European, but including European, Chinese, Afro-Chinese, East Indian, Afro-East Indian, and others. Cap. and largest city: Kingston (pop., 1974 est., 169,800). Language: English. Religion: Christian, with Anglicans and Baptists in the majority. Queen, Elizabeth II; governor-general in 1978, Florizel Glasspole; prime minister, Michael Manley.

Throughout 1978 Michael Manley's People's National Party (PNP) government tried to maintain political stability against a background of massive economic problems. At the end of 1977 the island's visible trade deficit stood at Jam$106.3 million and its reserves at minus Jam$201 million. Early in 1978 the island defaulted on one of the terms of a U.S. $74.6 million International Monetary Fund assistance package agreed upon in July 1977. A tough agreement was reached in May 1978 whereby, in return for U.S. $240 million in balance of payments support over three years, the Jamaican government would raise additional revenues of Jam$180.3 million; restrict wage increases to 15%; and devalue the Jamaican dollar progressively to achieve a fall of 43.6% by May 1979. The terms resulted in domestic unrest and left the government little room for maneuver.

Cabinet changes included the resignation of the minister of finance, David Coore; P. J. Patterson became deputy prime minister, reconfirming the PNP's move away from radical socialism. Edward Seaga was returned unopposed as head of the opposition Jamaica Labour Party. Relations with Cuba remained warm while relations with the U.S. improved. (DAVID A. JESSOP)

Jamaica

Jai Alai:
see Court Games

Japan

Japan

A constitutional monarchy in the northwestern Pacific Ocean, Japan is an archipelago composed of four major islands (Hokkaido, Honshu, Kyushu, and Shikoku), the Ryukyus (including Okinawa), and minor adjacent islands. Area: 377,619 sq km (145,799 sq mi). Pop. (1978 est.): 114,689,500. Cap. and largest city: Tokyo (pop., 1978 est., 8,514,100). Language: Japanese. Religion: primarily Shinto and Buddhist; Christian 0.8%. Emperor, Hirohito; prime ministers in 1978, Takeo Fukuda and, from December 7, Masayoshi Ohira.

Domestic Affairs. As a result of a general election held on Dec. 5, 1976, the Liberal-Democratic Party (LDP) had won a paper-thin majority in the (lower) House of Representatives (249 of 511 seats plus the support of independents). The election of July 1977 had given the party an equally narrow margin in the (upper) House of Councillors (124 of 252 seats plus independent support).

Although there were no national elections held during 1978, the LDP's status was affected by significant judicial action and reform within the party. On September 11 the Tokyo High Court declared the Dec. 5, 1976, election unconstitutional on the grounds that Diet seats had not been evenly allotted according to the populations of the electoral districts. For years the LDP had relied on its support in overrepresented rural districts. The court refused to set aside the outcome of the election, however. Within the LDP, members and associates participated for the first time on November 27 in the selection of the two top candidates for the presidency. When Masayoshi Ohira (see BIOGRAPHIES), LDP secretary-general, defeated Prime Minister Takeo Fukuda in this primary election, the latter withdrew from the final election scheduled for December 1. As the new president, Ohira was elected prime minister by the Diet on December 7.

Meanwhile, the LDP could take heart in the results of two local elections. On April 9 Yukio Hayashida, supported by the LDP, won the gubernatorial election in Kyoto and thus brought to an end 28 years of leftist administration. One week later in Yokohama, Michikazu Saigo, formerly a home affairs vice-minister, was elected mayor to succeed Ichio Asukata, who had resigned to become chairman of the Japan Socialist Party (JSP).

As usual, Prime Minister Fukuda's government was absorbed during 1978 in complex economic problems. Among these were a domestic recession alongside a towering balance of payments surplus, with a concomitant rise in the value of the yen. The recession made maintenance of Japan's imports difficult, while the yen value made exports expensive. A slight gain in the economy's output during the last quarter of 1977 brought Japan's gross national product (GNP) to an inflation-adjusted growth rate for the year of 5.1%, compared with a 6% gain in 1976. During the first quarter of 1978 the GNP scored its best gain in five years, running at an adjusted annual rate of 106,490,000,000,000 yen (U.S. $448 billion). The rate of growth in fiscal 1977–78 (ended March 31) thus reached 5.4%. During the second quarter of 1978, however, the rate of growth fell off again, to 4.5% annually.

By the end of April, despite some signs of recovery, Japan's unemployment rate had climbed to the highest level in 19 years. The jobless totaled 1,230,000, or 2.2% of the labour force. On the other hand, the consumer price index in Tokyo continued to show a steadying trend. In March the index in the city areas was up only 0.8% over the previous month, with the annual increase at only 4.8%.

Late in December 1977 the government completed its fiscal 1978 budget. Calling for a total expenditure of 34,295,000,000,000 yen ($145 billion), it was designed to revitalize the national economy. The budget passed the Diet in mid-March. On September 2 the government announced a six-point stimulus plan that included the expenditure of an additional 2.5 trillion yen on public works. Prime Minister Fukuda stated to the Diet on September 30 that he would stake his prestige on fulfilling Japan's commitment (made by him at the economic summit meeting in Bonn,

In an attempt to prevent the opening of the New Tokyo International Airport at Narita, thousands of demonstrators invaded the airfield. Some managed to get into the control tower which they thoroughly wrecked, delaying opening of the airport by several weeks.

KAKU KURITA—GAMMA/LIAISON

West Germany, in July) to achieve a growth target of 7% in fiscal 1978.

Throughout August the government found itself caught up in debates over alleged defects in Japan's Self-Defense Forces (SDF) Law. Even with the famous article 9 of the constitution (which severely restricted armed components of the military), Japan's defense agency proposed a defense expenditure of more than two trillion yen for fiscal 1979. Such an outlay would make Japan the seventh largest defense spender in the world. Nonetheless, the government found it necessary on July 25 to relieve Gen. Hiroomi Kurisu (*see* BIOGRAPHIES) from duty as chairman of the SDF Joint Staff Council. He had stated that in the face of an external threat the SDF might well have to act without prior authorization from the civilian Cabinet. On September 25 the defense agency made public a document stating clearly that the SDF would not resort to arms unless the prime minister had issued an order to mobilize forces under present law and within the framework of the constitution.

Japan's government did face an emergency of another sort, the interruption of the formal opening of the New Tokyo International Airport at Narita, 65 km (40 mi) from downtown Tokyo. After seven years of delay, officials on March 23 finally held ceremonies marking completion of the first phase of the airport complex. Operations were scheduled to begin on April 2, but on March 26 some 20,000 demonstrators—a coalition of farmers whose property had been seized and their mostly student supporters—confronted 13,000 riot policemen mobilized to protect the airport. Early in the afternoon, following a diversionary assault on one of the gates, a handful of red-helmeted protesters were able to gain access to the control tower, where they proceeded to destroy equipment and instruments. In some embarrassment the Cabinet announced on April 6 that a ceremonial opening would be postponed to May 20. On May 12 the Diet passed a law empowering the Transport Ministry to apply stringent measures for security in the airport vicinity. Following a heavily guarded ceremony on May 20 and some arrivals of airplanes on May 21, the airport began full-scale operation on

WIDE WORLD

A major earthquake opened great fissures in a highway near Higashi-Izu in January. Eleven persons were reported killed in the quake, 14 were injured, and 15 were missing.

May 22. Sporadic demonstrations continued, including the destruction on June 23 of radio relay equipment (for international flights) atop Mt. Tsukuba in Ibaraki Prefecture. After three months of operations it was announced on September 1 that even amid insecurity and inconvenience Narita was handling an average of 160 international flights per day involving some 22,000 passengers. The older and more familiar Haneda airport,

---

JAPAN

Education. (1977) Primary, pupils 10,819,656, teachers 473,814; secondary and vocational, pupils 9,156,883, teachers 473,814; higher (including 42 main national universities), students 2,093,935, teaching staff 115,146.

Finance. Monetary unit: yen, with (Sept. 18, 1978) a free rate of 191 yen to U.S. $1 (374 yen = £1 sterling). Gold, SDR's, and foreign exchange (June 1978) U.S. $26.4 billion. Budget (1978–79 est.) balanced at 34,295,000,000,000 yen. Gross national product (1977) 183,600,000,000,000 yen. Money supply (June 1978) 61,462,000,000,000 yen. Cost of living (1975 = 100; June 1978) 122.5.

Foreign Trade. (1977) Imports 19,128,000,-000,000 yen; exports 21,660,000,000,000 yen. Import sources: U.S. 18%; Saudi Arabia 12%; Australia 8%; Indonesia 7%; Iran 6%; Bahrain 5%. Export destinations: U.S. 25%; South Korea 5%. Main exports: machinery 25% (telecommunications apparatus 6%); motor vehicles 19%; iron and steel 15%; ships 10%; instruments 7%; chemicals 6%; textile yarns and fabrics 6%.

Transport and Communications. Roads (1976) 1,078,357 km (including 1,915 km expressways). Motor vehicles in use (1976): passenger 18,475,600; commercial 11,387,200. Railways (1977): 26,849 km; traffic 311,860,000,000 passenger-km, freight 41,585,000,000 net ton-km. Air traffic (1977): 22,813,000,000 passenger-km; freight 1,126,600,000 net ton-km. Shipping (1977): merchant vessels 100 gross tons and over 9,642; gross tonnage 40,035,853. Telephones (March 1977) 48,431,000. Radio receivers (Dec. 1975) 51,630,000. Television licenses (Dec. 1975) 26,030,000.

Agriculture. Production (in 000; metric tons; 1977): rice 17,000; wheat 236; barley 206; potatoes c. 3,200; sweet potatoes (1976) 1,279; sugar, raw value (1976) c. 540; onions c. 1,100; shallots (1975) c. 610; tomatoes c. 1,243; cabbages (1976) c. 3,885; cucumbers (1976) c. 1,055; aubergines (1976) c. 675; watermelons (1976) c. 1,255; apples c. 904; pears (1976) 507; oranges c. 406; mandarin oranges and tangerines c. 4,080; grapes c. 314; tea c. 105; tobacco c. 169; milk 5,713; eggs c. 1,878; pork 1,165; timber

(cu m; 1976) c. 38,134; fish catch (1976) 10,620; whales (number; 1974–75) 9.4. Livestock (in 000; Feb. 1977): cattle 3,875; sheep c. 10; pigs c. 7,900; goats c. 94; chickens c. 255,261.

Industry. Index of production (1975 = 100; 1977) 115.6. Fuel and power (in 000; metric tons; 1977): coal 18,248; crude oil 592; natural gas (cu m) 2,804,-000; manufactured gas (cu m) 6,600,000; electricity (kw-hr; 1976–77) 511,780,000. Production (in 000; metric tons; 1977): iron ore (54% metal content) 660; pig iron 87,693; crude steel 102,405; petroleum products (1976) 210,014; cement 73,136; cotton yarn 442; woven cotton fabrics (sq m) 2,266,000; man-made fibres 1,735; sulfuric acid 6,337; fertilizers (nutrient content; 1976–77) nitrogenous 1,149, phosphate 625; cameras (35 mm; units) 6,827; wristwatches (units) 44,738; radio receivers (units) 17,310; television receivers (units) 14,342; passenger cars (units) 5,429; commercial vehicles (units) 3,077; motorcycles (units) 5,577. Merchant vessels launched (100 gross tons and over; 1977) 9,838,000 gross tons. New dwelling units started (1977) 1,702,400.

closer to the city, handled only domestic flights after the opening of Narita.

The Japanese had their share of natural disasters during the year. A powerful earthquake rocked the northern regions of Honshu on June 12, killing 22 and injuring 340 others. Centred in the Pacific Ocean off Miyagi Prefecture, the quake registered an intensity of 7.5 on the Richter scale in the city of Sendai.

The so-called Lockheed scandal continued to plague the country. On April 3 Hiroshi Itoh, former executive of the Marubeni Co. (which had represented Lockheed in Japan), admitted in court that he had passed yen payments to former prime minister Kakuei Tanaka. Again, on July 5, Kenji Osano, a wealthy businessman, testified on influence brought to bear in order to sell Lockheed Tristar aircraft in Japan.

Foreign Affairs. In a policy speech before the 85th extraordinary Diet session on September 25, Prime Minister Fukuda reviewed his government's efforts to meet the world's expectations of Japan. Contributions to the peace and stability of Asia included the signing of a Sino-Japanese peace treaty in August and Fukuda's visit to the Association of Southeast Asian Nations (ASEAN) meeting in 1977. Fukuda referred to his visit to the Middle East in September, the first ever made by a Japanese prime minister to that area. He called for the fulfillment of Japan's economic pledges made at the July summit meeting of industrial nations and looked forward to the next such meeting, to be held in Tokyo in 1979.

On October 23, some six years after Japan and China had normalized relations, Fukuda and Vice-Premier Teng Hsiao-p'ing of China attended ceremonies in Tokyo to exchange ratifications of the peace treaty. This significant step brought to a climax a long and difficult negotiation, which had virtually been halted in 1975. At issue was Chinese insistence on an "antihegemony" clause, a thinly veiled denunciation of Soviet activities in Asia.

On February 16 in Peking, China and Japan had signed an eight-year private agreement under

China's Vice-Premier Teng Hsiao-p'ing and Prime Minister Takeo Fukuda pledged friendly relations between the two countries when Teng visited Japan in October.

UPI COMPIX

which two-way trade would grow to about $20 billion over three–four years. But on April 15 the chief Cabinet secretary, Shintaro Abe, announced Japan's decision to shelve negotiations for the peace treaty until Tokyo received a formal explanation of a Chinese fishing fleet encroachment into Japanese waters off the Senkaku Islands. The next day China responded indirectly to a visiting Japanese delegation to the effect that the fleet's action had not been planned but was an "accident," and on June 30 Foreign Minister Sunao Sonoda announced that Japan would resume talks.

Sonoda and Chinese Foreign Minister Huang Hua signed the five-article treaty of peace and friendship on August 12 in Peking. Japan publicly announced that the antihegemony clause was not aimed at any specific third party. China in turn indicated in oblique fashion that the 1950 Sino-Soviet treaty of alliance, which defined Japan as a common potential enemy, would be nullified. Sonoda disclosed on August 13 that Premier Hua Kuo-feng of China planned to visit Tokyo in 1979 to further promote Sino-Japanese ties. During his visit to Tokyo in October Teng declared that he understood Japan's close ties with the U.S., but he criticized U.S. efforts toward détente with the U.S.S.R.

Earlier, on February 24, Japan had spurned a Soviet proposal for a Soviet-Japanese treaty of cooperation. Japan's unchanged basic policy was that despite normalization of relations with the U.S.S.R. in 1956, a peace treaty would have to await settlement of the "northern territories" dispute. The latter involved Soviet occupation of the Kuril Islands, off Hokkaido. On June 10 Japan revealed that Etorofu, northernmost of the islets, was being used by the U.S.S.R. as a site for seaborne and air-supported landing maneuvers. It was widely reported in Tokyo that these were Soviet tactics to interrupt Sino-Japanese negotiations. On June 19 in Tokyo, Soviet ambassador Dmitri S. Polyansky delivered his nation's formal protest against Japan's plan to conclude a treaty with China.

After his visit to Peking, U.S. security adviser Zbigniew Brzezinski stopped off in Tokyo on May 23–24 to brief Prime Minister Fukuda and Foreign Ministry officials. The actual timing of the December 15 announcement that the U.S. and China would resume diplomatic relations at the beginning of 1979 apparently came as a surprise to Japanese officials. According to Foreign Minister Sonoda, Prime Minister Ohira was notified via the "hot line" between Washington and Tokyo only a few hours before U.S. Pres. Jimmy Carter announced the move on U.S. television. However, the Japanese government appeared generally pleased with the development, and Sonoda told newsmen that Japanese consultations with both countries had contributed to Sino-U.S. normalization.

Otherwise, relations with the U.S. were dominated throughout the year by Japan's huge trade surplus, an increasing current account surplus, and the concomitant fall in dollar values against the yen. On January 13 in Tokyo, Robert Strauss, U.S. special trade representative, and Nobuhiko Ushiba, external economic affairs minister, concluded a truce in the trade dispute. Strauss warned, however, that the agreement would probably not stem the drive in the U.S. toward protectionism. Ushiba in turn promised that Japan would try to cut its current account surplus for fiscal 1978. Nevertheless, in February it was announced that Japan's current account surplus in 1977 was nearly three times that of 1976 and that foreign currency reserves had reached a record $22.8 billion. On March 1 reserves were pegged at an all-time high of almost $24.2 billion. Much of February's gain was attributed to the Bank of Japan, which was purchasing U.S. dollars to guard against a further decline in the U.S. currency against the yen.

At a bilateral summit meeting in Washington, D.C., on May 3, President Carter assured Fukuda that the U.S. would maintain its presence, in alliance with Japan, in the Asian region. Fukuda promised Carter in return that Japan would do its best in fiscal 1978 to achieve a 7% growth rate and to reestablish trade equilibrium. At the seven-nation summit meeting of industrial democracies in Bonn, Fukuda was again under pressure because of the trade surplus. He set as a target the cutting of Japan's current account surplus to a level of $6 billion (from $14 billion in fiscal 1977) and promised to take strong action to guarantee a 7% growth rate.

Meanwhile, steadily rising export prices due to the rise in value of the yen were beginning to reestablish equilibrium; on September 23 the Finance Ministry announced that in August Japan's balance of payments surplus had declined for the third straight month. In early December the U.S. and Japan reached agreement on measures to increase Japanese imports of U.S. citrus fruits and beef products.

Prime Minister Fukuda returned to Tokyo on September 14 from a ten-day official tour to Iran, Qatar, the United Arab Emirates, and Saudi Arabia. The unprecedented attention to the Middle East dramatized Japan's almost total dependence on external sources of energy, particularly oil. Fukuda reported that he sought understanding among the leaders of those nations of the need to prevent the vicious cycle of a fall in the dollar's value and a rise in oil prices.

Japan's newfound status as an economic power broker was illustrated by several official visits to Tokyo. Pres. Walter Scheel of West Germany was a state guest April 16–22, accompanied by Foreign Minister Hans-Dietrich Genscher. Genscher urged Japan to expand its imports from Western Europe rather than curb exports. Fukuda and visiting Australian Prime Minister Malcolm Fraser agreed that their two nations should cooperate in multilateral trade and in assistance to less developed countries. Fraser arrived in Tokyo on April 19, reportedly to ask Fukuda to explain Australia's position to the U.S. when the latter met with Carter on May 3. In mid-August Foreign Minister Sonoda met with his Indian counterpart, Minister of External Affairs Atal Bihari Vajpayee, in Tokyo. They agreed that Japan and India should strengthen mutual cooperation. A second ministerial meeting was scheduled to be held in New Delhi in 1979.

(ARDATH W. BURKS)

Jordan

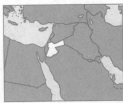

Jordan

A constitutional monarchy in southwest Asia, Jordan is bounded by Syria, Iraq, Saudi Arabia, and Israel. Area (including territory occupied by Israel in the June 1967 war): 95,396 sq km (36,833 sq mi). Pop. (1978 est.): 2,971,000. Cap. and largest city: Amman (pop., 1976 est., 691,100). Language: Arabic. Religion (1961): Muslim 94%; Christian 6%. King, Hussein I; prime minister in 1978, Mudar Badran.

In 1978 Jordan pursued a careful balancing act between Egypt's Pres. Anwar as-Sadat and the Arab states opposed to him. King Hussein expressed only cautious and qualified approval of the Sadat peace initiative. He refused to attend the Camp David, Md., summit in September, despite U.S. urging, although he was gratified by Egyptian proposals that the West Bank be returned to Jordanian administration as a step toward a peace settlement. Throughout the year Hussein called for the restoration of Arab unity, and he deplored Arab failure to react against the Israeli invasion of Lebanon in March. He proposed a reconciliation Arab summit and remained in constant touch with Arab capitals.

Hussein's refusal to denounce President Sadat's policies caused some coolness in relations with Syria. Although there was no rupture, enthusiasm for moves toward Syrian-Jordanian federation diminished. An improvement in relations with the Palestine Liberation Organization (PLO) was encouraged by Algeria and Syria as a means of keep-

JORDAN

Education. (1977–78) Primary, pupils 414,490, teachers 12,757; secondary, pupils 200,916, teachers 9,188; vocational, pupils 8,826, teachers 540; higher, students 17,219, teaching staff 960.

Finance. Monetary unit: Jordanian dinar, with (Sept. 18, 1978) a free rate of 0.30 dinar to U.S. $1 (0.58 dinar = £1 sterling). Gold, SDR's, and foreign exchange (June 1978) U.S. $805 million. Budget (1977 actual): revenue 273 million dinars (including foreign aid and loans of 128 million dinars); expenditure 306 million dinars. Gross national product (1977) 613.9 million dinars. Money supply (June 1978) 348.9 million dinars. Cost of living (Amman; 1975 = 100; Dec. 1977) 153.7.

Foreign Trade. (1977) Imports 454,430,000 dinars; exports 82,060,000 dinars. Import sources (1976): West Germany 17%; U.S. 9%; U.K. 8%; Japan 7%; Italy 6%. Export destinations (1976): Saudi Arabia 11%; Syria 9%; Iran 9%; Kuwait 5%. Main exports (1976): phosphates 28%; oranges 11%; vegetables 7%; machinery (reexports) 7%; chemicals 6%. Tourism (1975): visitors 707,600; gross receipts U.S. $101 million.

Transport and Communications. Roads (excludes West Bank; 1976) 4,152 km. Motor vehicles in use (1976): passenger 39,500; commercial 14,100. Railways (1975) 371 km. Air traffic (1977): 1,131,800,000 passenger-km; freight 40.6 million net ton-km. Telephones (Jan. 1977) 43,700. Radio receivers (Dec. 1975) 529,000. Television licenses (Dec. 1974) 85,000.

Agriculture. Production (in 000; metric tons; 1977): wheat c. 53; barley (1976) 13; tomatoes c. 88; aubergines (1976) c. 40; watermelons (1976) c. 44; olives c. 23; oranges c. 5; lemons c. 9; grapes c. 14; tobacco c. 2. Livestock (in 000; 1976): cattle c. 35; goats c. 474; sheep c. 818; camels c. 18; asses c. 38; chickens c. 2,960.

Industry. Production (in 000; metric tons; 1976): phosphate rock 1,768; petroleum products 1,040; cement 533; electricity (kw-hr) 501,000.

Japanese Literature:
see Literature

Jazz:
see Music

Jehovah's Witnesses:
see Religion

Jewish Literature:
see Literature

Kenya

Elizabeth Halaby, daughter of former Pan American World Airways president Najeeb Halaby, was married in June to King Hussein of Jordan. After the wedding, Halaby took the Arabic name of Noor al-Hussein ("Light of Hussein").

Kenya

ing Jordan out of the Egyptian camp. In March several dozen Palestinian prisoners were released. At the same time the Jordan government remained in constant touch with West Bank mayors, several of whom visited Amman, and continued to subsidize West Bank religious and educational institutions. A visit by the prime minister to Libya in April led to an improvement in relations and a Libyan loan for Jordanian fertilizer projects.

Hussein clearly expressed his disappointment over the Camp David agreements in September because they did not provide for Israeli withdrawal from all occupied territories or the restoration of Arab sovereignty over the West Bank and Gaza. He said Jordan was not committed to an agreement in which it took no part and expressed concern that it would lead to a separate Israeli-Egyptian agreement. Nevertheless, the king refused to join the hard-line states in outright rejection and indicated that he would modify his attitude if changes were made in the terms of the agreements.

In April the king called upon the prime minister to form a National Consultative Council to perform a function similar to that of Parliament, which had been suspended in 1974 and briefly reconvened in 1976. The 60-member council, which was to serve for two years, represented all regions of Jordan but not the occupants of the West Bank. The proportion of PLO representatives was significantly lower than in the suspended Parliament.

Amman continued to enlarge its role as an Arab commercial centre, partially replacing Beirut. In January a stock exchange was opened, and in April the first merchant bank in the country was established. The government claimed that the rate of inflation had been cut by half from the 1977 level of 14.7%. The 1978 budget, introduced in February, showed expenditure equivalent to U.S. $1,192,000,000—a 9.6% increase over 1977—and a deficit of $48 million. Defense expenditure ac-

counted for about one-quarter of the total. Foreign aid in 1978 was estimated at $330 million.

In August, following meetings in Amman of the joint higher committee chaired by the Syrian and Jordanian prime ministers, Jordan and Syria set aside their differences enough to agree on effective and rapid steps toward economic integration. Plans were drawn up for cooperation in agriculture and guaranteed provision of foodstuffs.

On June 15 King Hussein concluded his fourth marriage, to U.S.-born Elizabeth Halaby, daughter of a former Pan American World Airways president of Arab origin. She became a Muslim with the name of Noor al-Hussein (see BIOGRAPHIES) and was proclaimed queen. The king also announced that his third son, two-year-old Prince Ali, would become crown prince when the king's brother, Crown Prince Hassan, succeeded to the throne.   (PETER MANSFIELD)

See also Middle Eastern Affairs.

Kenya

An African republic and a member of the Commonwealth of Nations, Kenya is bordered on the north by Sudan and Ethiopia, east by Somalia, south by Tanzania, and west by Uganda. Area: 580,367 sq km (224,081 sq mi), including 11,230 sq km of inland water. Pop. (1977 est.): 14,337,000, including (1969) African 98.1%; Asian 1.5%. Cap. and largest city: Nairobi (pop., 1978 est., 820,000). Language: Swahili (official) and English. Religion: Protestant 36%; Roman Catholic 22%; Muslim 6%; others, mostly indigenous, 36%. Presidents in 1978, Jomo Kenyatta and, from August 22, Daniel Arap Moi.

The death of Pres. Jomo Kenyatta (see OBITUARIES) on Aug. 22, 1978, left the country facing a constitutional problem. The vice-president, Daniel

KENYA

Education. (1976) Primary, pupils 2,894,617, teachers 89,074; secondary and vocational, pupils 280,388, teachers 11,438; teacher training, students 8,668, teachers 639; higher, students 5,753.

Finance. Monetary unit: Kenyan shilling, with (Sept. 18, 1978) a free rate of KShs 7.58 to U.S. $1 (KShs 14.86 = £1 sterling). Gold, SDR's, and foreign exchange (June 1978) U.S. $446.9 million. Budget (1976–77 actual): revenue KShs 5,863,000,000; expenditure KShs 6,883,000,000. Gross national product (1977) KShs 35,240,000,000. Cost of living (Nairobi; 1975 = 100; March 1978) 134.7.

Foreign Trade. (1977) Imports KShs 10,673,000,000; exports KShs 11,273,000,000. Import sources: U.K. 18%; Japan 12%; West Germany 11%; Iran 9%; Saudi Arabia 7%; U.S. 6%; France 5%. Export destinations: West Germany 17%; U.K. 13%; Tanzania 10%; Uganda 10%; The Netherlands 10%; U.S. 5%. Main exports: coffee 41%; petroleum products 17%; tea 14%; fruit and vegetables 5%. Tourism (1975): visitors 407,400; gross receipts U.S. $98 million.

Transport and Communications. Roads (1976) 50,091 km. Motor vehicles in use (1975): passenger 83,700; commercial 79,200. Railways: (1975) 2,729 km; freight traffic (1976) 3,650,000,000 net ton-km. Air traffic (1975): 879 million passenger-km; freight 19.7 million ton-km. Telephones (Jan. 1977) 131,800. Radio receivers (Dec. 1975) 511,000. Television receivers (Dec. 1975) 38,000.

Agriculture. Production (in 000; metric tons; 1977): corn c. 1,700; wheat c. 180; millet c. 140; potatoes c. 252; sweet potatoes (1976) c. 555; cassava (1976) c. 677; sugar, raw value (1976) c. 173; bananas c. 190; coffee c. 87; tea c. 90; sisal c. 34; cotton, lint c. 7; fish catch (1976) 41. Livestock (in 000; May 1977): cattle c. 7,350; sheep (1975) c. 3,611; pigs c. 70; goats (1976) c. 4,100; camels (1976) c. 564; chickens (1976) c. 15,428.

Industry. Production (in 000; metric tons; 1976): cement 983; soda ash 102; petroleum products c. 2,490; electricity (kw-hr) c. 1,119,000.

Arap Moi (see BIOGRAPHIES), at once became acting president, but the constitution required that an official successor to Kenyatta be elected within 90 days. On October 10 Moi, as sole candidate, was formally elected president. He was to hold office until November 1979, when the term would expire and a new election would take place. Moi appointed Mwai Kibaki, minister of finance, as vice-president. He also abolished the powerful position of minister of state and named its former incumbent, Mbiyu Koinange, to the post of minister of natural resources.

The year had begun with the news that James Ngugi wa Thiong'o, the country's leading novelist and a prominent critic of the government's failure to realize the promises it had made at the time of independence, had been arrested. There was also concern over the possible repercussions of the Somali-Ethiopian war, emphasized by the forcing down by Kenya of an Egyptian plane carrying arms to Somalia. The Egyptians responded by impounding two Kenyan planes, and for a time relations were strained.

Normal diplomatic relations with Uganda were resumed after discussions early in the year. This was followed by a request from Pres. Idi Amin that a large number of refugees who had found sanctuary in Kenya and whom he thought to be a danger to his own country should be returned to Uganda. Hopes of improving economic relations between the two countries received a setback when oil companies in Kenya refused to supply oil to Uganda because of a debt owed to them for oil supplied earlier in the year. There were hopes that the frontier with Tanzania, closed since February 1977,

might be reopened, and Kenya, anxious to restore the lost export trade with its neighbour, made every effort at reconciliation.

The collapse of the East African Community in 1977 meant that the Kenyan corporations that replaced it had had to invest large sums of money, and as a result there had been government overspending. In an attempt to control the resulting inflation a credit squeeze was imposed in July. The situation was not improved by the government's failure to take advantage of the benefits it received from coffee sales in 1977, proceeds of which had been used for consumption and not for investment. It was necessary, too, to protect Kenya's major textile industry by banning the importation of all textiles that might compete with locally produced articles.

Work began on the first phase of a project to develop a semidesert area in the northeast of the country into irrigated farmland capable of supporting 30,000 people. The government received financial assistance from Britain, The Netherlands, the World Bank, and the development fund of the European Economic Community. The Bank of America and the U.S. Export-Import Bank also promised a loan of $16 million to help the government in financing a polyester-fibre manufacturing project in Nanyuki.

In January Kenya Airways inaugurated its jumbo jet service from Nairobi to London, and on March 14 Nairobi's $65 million airport, capable of handling six million passengers a year, was opened. In April a new dry dock, able to deal with almost all the country's naval and merchant shipping, was opened in Mombasa.

The reserves of corn in the country were good, and an excellent harvest was expected in 1978. The government decided to ban the export of corn in

The body of Kenya's president, Jomo Kenyatta, lies in state in Nairobi in August.

Korea

the hope of ensuring that everyone in the country would have enough to eat. One less satisfactory feature of the year was the continuing increase in crime, particularly robbery, forgery, and fraud.

(KENNETH INGHAM)

Korea

A country of eastern Asia, Korea is bounded by China, the Sea of Japan, the Korea Strait, and the Yellow Sea. It is divided into two parts roughly at the 38th parallel.

Relations between the two Koreas followed the familiar pattern of propaganda, denunciation, and occasional violence in 1978. South Korea tried a new approach in June when it proposed to the North the creation of a "consultative body for the promotion of south-north economic cooperation" with a view to promoting mutual trade and technical cooperation. South Korean Pres. Park Chung Hee said "we are ready to hold a pertinent ministerial conference with the North if necessary." He repeated the suggestion in August in an address commemorating the 33rd anniversary of national liberation. At the same time, he made it clear that he was making the proposal from a position of strength as South Korea had "overcome all hardships [and] South Koreans were no longer the people who depended on other countries for their national defense."

North Korea, however, saw it all differently. The ruling Workers' Party's official organ, *Rodong Shinmun*, said in July that the North would not discuss reunification with the South as long as Park Chung Hee remained in power. Park's reelection in July was described as a "shameless and intolerable insult to the Korean people."

An unexpected development of the year was direct diplomatic contact between the United States and North Korea. U.S. Assistant Secretary of State for East Asia Richard Holbrooke was quoted as saying that officials from the two countries had met secretly five times. Furthermore, the presidents of Yugoslavia and Romania were said to have acted as peacemakers. North Korea had

previously insisted on direct talks with the U.S., and in an anniversary report in September Pres. Kim Il Sung reiterated his readiness to "start talks and settle all necessary problems."

South Korea for its part was not amused. After receiving reports that President Tito of Yugoslavia had discussed the Korean problem with the U.S., it expressed displeasure at "meddling" by third parties; Foreign Minister Park Tong Jin said the Korean problem was not a political football that anyone could kick around at will. Whether on account of the South Korean protest or not, nothing tangible seemed to emerge from the U.S.-North Korea contacts.

Republic of Korea (South Korea). Area: 98,859 sq km (38,169 sq mi). Pop. (1978 est.): 37,018,900. Cap. and largest city: Seoul (pop., 1975 census, 6,879,500). Language: Korean. Religion: Buddhist; Christian; Confucian; Tonghak (Chondokyo). President in 1978, Gen. Park Chung Hee; prime minister, Choi Kyu Hah.

With a presidential election due at least 30 days before the expiration of Pres. Park Chung Hee's current term on Dec. 26, 1978, some political heat was expected during the year. But on July 6 Park consummated his reelection in a move barely noticed by the nation. He was the only candidate in an election in which voting rights were confined to a 2,583-member National Conference for Unification set up under the 1972 constitution. In less than two hours the proceedings were over, and Park was in for a sixth consecutive term (counting the 1975 referendum), to begin on December 27. This time it was for six years.

Earlier in the year continuing political problems with the U.S. had vexed the Park administration. Embarrassment was created by reports that in the 1960s and 1970s U.S. intelligence agents had bugged the Blue House, the official presidential residence in Seoul. The U.S. embassy expressed regret, and the Korean government said that it would consider the matter closed. The so-called Koreagate influence-buying scandal also stayed in the headlines as businessman Park Tong Sun testified before congressional investigators in Washington, D.C. Emotions were aroused in Seoul when the chairman of the U.S. House Subcommittee on International Organizations charged that President Park had personally presided over secret strategy sessions in 1970 to plan covert lobbying operations in Washington. The government denied the allegation.

However, in what South Korea considered substantive matters the news was good. In April U.S. Pres. Jimmy Carter announced that he planned to withdraw only 800 U.S. soldiers from the nation by the end of the year instead of the 2,400 originally planned. In July the U.S. Senate approved an amended military aid law which said that further withdrawal of ground troops "may seriously risk upsetting the military balance" in the Korean region and stipulated that any new administration initiative must have "full advance consultation with Congress." The Park government felt so confident that Defense Minister Ro Jae Hyun said he saw no "major difficulties" on account of the troop withdrawal question.

Korean businessman and party giver Park Tong Sun, accompanied by attorney William Hundley, testified before a U.S. House Ethics Committee hearing about gifts to congressmen and others.

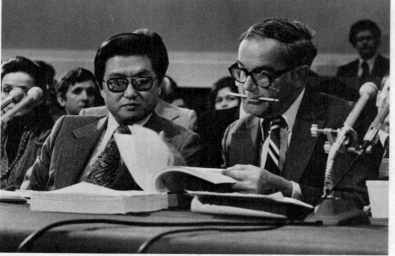

BRIAN ALPERT—KEYSTONE

But South Korea was also clearly intent on strengthening its independent military muscle. According to Park, the North could start a reckless war in order to divert attention from its worsening economic situation and a power struggle over Kim Il Sung's successor. The only way to avoid another fratricidal war, he said in January, was "to build up military power enough to overpower North Korea, and the time will come early in the 1980s." Park added that, while the South was already 10 to 15 years ahead of the North economically, the two sides were just about equal in military strength. Therefore, South Korea would launch a crash program to boost defense industries.

These words were backed by action. In September the first Korean-made ground-to-ground missile was successfully test-fired. The tactical missile, with a range of 150 km (90 mi), was to be mass-produced, marking what officials called a new milestone in the country's defense production. On October 1, Armed Forces Day, the missile was put on public parade along with other new weapons, including a medium-range surface missile; a truck-mounted, multiple-tube rocket launcher; battle tanks; artillery; and electronic cannons.

While Park talked convincingly about stability and power, critics continued to agitate for civil liberties. The opportunities to do so were limited because of tight surveillance and preemptive arrests. On August 8 leading dissident Kim Dae Jung staged a one-day hunger strike to mark the fifth anniversary of his kidnapping from Tokyo. Earlier, in June, some 1,000 students of Seoul National University had organized a daring street demonstration in an apparent bid to attract attention to the dissident movement. Park's Democratic Republican Party (DRP) suffered a setback in the December 12 elections to the National Assembly, receiving only 31.7% of the votes against the opposition New Democratic Party's 32.8%. However, the DRP's ascendancy remained basically unaffected, since Park nominated one-third of the 231-member Assembly. On December 27 some 4,000

prisoners, including Kim Dae Jung, were freed under an amnesty coinciding with Park's inauguration to his new term.

A bizarre incident occurred on April 20 when a Korean Air Lines passenger jet on a scheduled flight from Paris to Seoul strayed into Karelia in the Soviet Union. A Soviet supersonic fighter fired at the airliner and killed two passengers before the Korean pilot landed. The remaining passengers were released three days later.

Rising inflation and consumer prices caused some worries on the economic front, but the real growth for the year was expected to be between 13 and 15% as against the government forecast of 10 to 11%. Growth in 1977 had been 10.3%.

Democratic People's Republic of Korea (North Korea). Area: 121,200 sq km (46,800 sq mi). Pop. (1978 est.): 17,078,000. Cap.: Pyongyang (metro. pop., 1976 est., 1.5 million). Language: Korean. Religion: Buddhist; Confucian; Tonghak (Chondokyo). General secretary of the Central

Passengers depart from a relief plane in Seoul after the plane in which they were previously riding strayed into Soviet airspace and was shot down by Soviet fighter planes. The incident, which resulted in two passengers being killed, occurred in April.

Khmer Republic:
see Cambodia

KOREA: Republic

Education. (1977) Primary, pupils 5,514,417, teachers 112,997; secondary, pupils 3,546,370, teachers 91,113; vocational (1976), students 533,695, teachers 17,624; higher, students 362,686, teaching staff 15,313.

Finance. Monetary unit: won, with (Sept. 18, 1978) an official rate of 485 won to U.S. $1 (free rate of 949 won = £1 sterling). Gold, SDR's, and foreign exchange (June 1978) U.S. $4,185,000,000. Budget (1977 actual): revenue 3,360,800,000,000 won; expenditure 3,298,300,000,000 won. Gross national product (1977) 15,240,400,000,000 won. Money supply (June 1978) 2,282,100,000,000 won. Cost of living (1970 = 100; June 1978) 145.5.

Foreign Trade. (1977) Imports 5,232,500,000,000 won; exports 4,862,700,000,000 won. Import sources: Japan 36%; U.S. 23%; Saudi Arabia 10%; Kuwait 5%. Export destinations: U.S. 31%; Japan 21%; Saudi Arabia 7%; West Germany 5%. Main exports (1976): clothing 24%; textile yarns and fabrics 12%; electrical machinery and equipment 10%; footwear 5%; iron and steel 5%. Tourism (1976): visitors 834,000; gross receipts U.S. $275 million.

Transport and Communications. Roads (1976) 45,514 km (including 1,142 km expressways). Motor vehicles in use (1976): passenger 96,099; commercial 87,528. Railways: (1976) 5,653 km; traffic (1977) c.

16,900,000,000 passenger-km, freight 10,276,-000,000 net ton-km. Air traffic (1976): 4,519,000,000 passenger-km; freight 355.1 million net ton-km. Shipping (1977): merchant vessels 100 gross tons and over 1,042; gross tonnage 2,494,724. Telephones (Jan. 1977) 1,681,000. Radio receivers (Dec. 1976) c. 11 million. Television receivers (Sept. 1977) 3,522,000.

Agriculture. Production (in 000; metric tons; 1977): rice 8,340; barley c. 814; potatoes c. 650; sweet potatoes (1976) c. 1,950; soybeans c. 340; cabbages (1976) c. 900; watermelons (1976) c. 170; onions c. 140; apples c. 327; tobacco c. 138; fish catch (1976) 2,407. Livestock (in 000; 1976): cattle 1,641; pigs 1,247; goats 250; chickens 20,939.

Industry. Production (in 000; metric tons; 1977): coal 17,320; iron ore (56% metal content) 657; crude steel 2,738; cement 14,202; tungsten concentrates (oxide content; 1976) 3.5; zinc ore (1976) 112; gold (troy oz; 1976) 17; silver (troy oz; 1976) 1,838; sulfuric acid 988; petroleum products (1976) 18,204; man-made fibres 379; electricity (excluding most industrial production; kw-hr) 26,586,000; radio receivers (units; 1976) 6,578; television receivers (units; 1976) 2,291. Merchant vessels launched (100 gross tons and over; 1977) 463,000.

KOREA: People's Democratic Republic

Education. (1973–74 est.) Primary, pupils c. 1.5 million; secondary and vocational, pupils c. 1.2 million; primary, secondary, and vocational, teachers c. 100,000; higher, students c. 300,000.

Finance and Trade. Monetary unit: won, with (Sept. 18, 1978) a nominal exchange rate of 0.88 won to U.S. $1 (1.72 won = £1 sterling). Budget (1976 est.) balanced at 12,513,000,000 won. Foreign trade (approximate; 1976): imports c. 750 million won (c. 32% from U.S.S.R., c. 27% from China, c. 13% from Japan); exports c. 800 million won (c. 40% to China, c. 20% to U.S.S.R., c. 9% to Japan). Main exports (1972): zinc and ore c. 30%; lead and ore c. 15%; magnesite c. 15%; iron and steel c. 15%; iron ore c. 12%; cement c. 8%.

Agriculture. Production (in 000; metric tons; 1977): rice c. 4,610; corn c. 1,820; barley c. 340; millet c. 418; potatoes c. 1,300; sweet potatoes (1976) c. 330; soybeans c. 310; apples c. 165; tobacco c. 41; fish catch (1976) c. 800. Livestock (in 000; 1976): cattle c. 816; pigs c. 1,573; sheep c. 268; goats c. 199; chickens c. 17,316.

Industry. Production (in 000; metric tons; 1976): coal c. 40,000; iron ore (metal content) c. 3,800; pig iron c. 3,000; steel c. 3,000; lead c. 78; zinc c. 138; magnesite c. 1,700; silver (troy oz) c. 1,600; electricity (kw-hr; 1965) 13,300,000.

Chinese Vice-Premier Teng Hsiao-p'ing (left) waved to friendly crowds on his arrival in North Korea in September. With him was North Korean President Kim Il Sung.

Committee of the Workers' (Communist) Party of Korea and president in 1978, Marshal Kim Il Sung; chairman of the Council of Ministers (premier), Li Jong Ok.

Infighting over the succession to Pres. Kim Il Sung (said to be suffering from some form of neck cancer) appeared to have cooled down during 1978, but only because his son and presumed heir, Kim Chong Il, was reported grievously ill. Sources close to North Korea said that Kim Chong Il had been pronounced unable to recover from a coma following an assassination attempt during the previous September. Consequently, the succession question was put off for five years, until Kim Pyong Il, the president's son by his second wife, Kim Song Ae, would turn 30. There was no independent corroboration of these reports.

In April President Kim opened the second session of the national legislature, the sixth Supreme People's Assembly. The first session, held in December 1977, had adopted the second seven-year economic development program (1978–84), which called for a 12.1% annual growth in industrial production. The second session discussed the budget for fiscal 1978 and adopted a new labour law aimed at improving production. This followed official claims that 75% of the targeted increase in industrial production during the second development program had been achieved.

The biggest event of the year was the 30th anniversary of the founding of North Korea, on September 9. Delegations from 46 countries were reported to have arrived in Pyongyang to participate in the celebrations. By far the most important of these was the Chinese delegation headed by First Vice-Premier Teng Hsiao-p'ing. His high-profile presence when the Soviet Union was represented by a much lower-ranking personage who was allotted a position 77 places down the line signaled what diplomats considered Pyongyang's swing toward China in the Sino-Soviet dispute.

The effects such a shift could have on the nation's economy, heavily dependent on Soviet supplies, were unclear. Debt repayment problems arising from $370 million owed to Japan had not eased, but the food supply had moved into surplus. The gross national product for 1977 was believed to be about $9 billion (as against the South's $31.5 billion). (T. J. S. GEORGE)

Kuwait

An independent constitutional monarchy (emirate), Kuwait is on the northwestern coast of the Persian Gulf between Iraq and Saudi Arabia. Area: 16,918 sq km (6,532 sq mi). Pop. (1978 est.):

King Khalid of Saudi Arabia (left) greets Sheikh Jabir al-Ahmad al-Jabir as-Sabah of Kuwait upon arriving there in early January to offer his condolences. Sheikh Jabir succeeded Sheikh Sabah as-Salim as-Sabah who died Dec. 31, 1977.

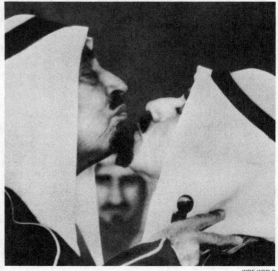

WIDE WORLD

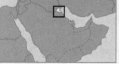

Kuwait

1,198,500. Cap.: Kuwait (pop., 1975 census, 78,100). Largest city: Hawalli (pop., 1975 prelim., 130,300). Language: Arabic. Religion (1975): Muslim 94.9%; Christian 4.5%. Emir, Sheikh Jabir al-Ahmad al-Jabir as-Sabah; prime minister from Feb. 8, 1978, Crown Prince Sheikh Saad al-Abdullah as-Salim as-Sabah.

In January 1978 former interior and defense minister Sheikh Saad al-Abdullah as-Salim as-Sabah was appointed crown prince by the emir, Sheikh Jabir al-Ahmad al-Jabir as-Sabah (*see* BIOGRAPHIES), and on February 16 Sheikh Saad formed a new 19-member Cabinet. In March Sheikh Nawaf as-Sabah became the eighth member of the ruling family in the Cabinet when he joined as information minister.

Kuwait's Arab policy was cautious and mediatory. It tried to help heal the rift caused by Egyptian Pres. Anwar as-Sadat's peace initiative with Israel and to mediate in the Oman-United Arab Emirates border dispute. In July Kuwait refused to break all relations with South Yemen as recommended by an Arab League meeting. Relations with Iraq improved, and in May the two countries agreed to build a railway connecting Basra and Kuwait and to link their electric power grids.

Internally there was some unrest among students, and several newspapers were suspended during the year for violating the publications law. In May a special committee was set up to revise the constitution, and the prime minister promised that the National Assembly would be revived.

In January Kuwait announced the reduction of its oil prices by 10 U.S. cents a barrel, reflecting concern at overpricing of its heavy crude oils and the slackening of world demand. Throughout the year, however, Kuwait expressed concern over its loss of revenues due to the decline of the U.S. dollar, and it agreed to the 14.5% price rise mandated by the Organization of Petroleum Exporting Countries in December. (PETER MANSFIELD)

Laos

Laos

A landlocked people's republic of Southeast Asia, Laos is bounded by China, Vietnam, Cambodia, Thailand, and Burma. Area: 236,800 sq km (91,400 sq mi). Pop. (1978 est.): 3,546,000. Cap. and largest city: Vientiane (pop., 1973, 176,600). Language: Lao (official); French and English. Religion: Buddhist; tribal. President in 1978, Prince Souphanouvong; premier, Kaysone Phomvihan.

In 1978 Laos identified itself clearly with Vietnam against China. In May, in a "back to the land" campaign identical with one started in Vietnam, the several thousand resident Chinese left in the country were asked to give up shopkeeping and "devote themselves to collective productions," such as farming. In a typical case, merchants in the southern town of Paksé were given 25 ha of virgin land to reclaim. Western sources reported that China was assisting ethnic minorities in northern Laos to oppose the Vientiane government, and Laotian Radio reported in July that enemies had been trying to "exploit racial antagonisms in order to destroy the socialist revolution in Laos." French reports suggested that the government faced a measure of resistance from the H'mong minority in the north, as well as from elements of the Pathet Lao garrison at Phong Saly, close to China's Yunnan Province.

The southeast Asian tour of Hanoi's vice-foreign minister, Phan Hien, in July provided an occasion for Vientiane to reaffirm its ties with Vietnam. In the same month reports circulated in Bangkok, Thailand, that the largest airport in Southeast Asia was being built in the Plaine des Jarres in central Laos by Vietnamese troops and Soviet technicians. At least one high-ranking Soviet military leader visited Laos during the year, and a delegation of

Labour Unions: *see* Industrial Relations

Lacrosse: *see* Field Hockey and Lacrosse

the Lao Supreme People's Assembly went to the Soviet Union in August.

Association with France was ended in August, when Laos officially announced the closure of its embassy in Paris. Earlier, it had accused France of hostile activities and expelled two French diplomats from Vientiane. Relations with Laos' Southeast Asian neighbours improved, however. A trade agreement was signed with Thailand in June to sell coffee beans and timber products in return for Thai sugar, textiles, machinery, tobacco, soft drinks, and liquid oxygen. There was also a toning down of Laos' earlier harsh line against the Association of Southeast Asian Nations.

An unexpected development was the decision of the U.S. State Department, reported in June, to give Laos 10,000 tons of rice valued at about $5 million. The program was classified as humanitarian, but officials indicated that they expected it to help improve political relations. While that might depend on a simultaneous improvement of U.S.-Vietnam relations, there was little doubt that Laos needed all the food aid it could get. The UN had estimated the year's grain shortage at about 113,-000 tons, or approximately one-third of national consumption. Other countries had pledged only about 80,000 tons, and the addition of the U.S. quota still left a gap to fill. By October it appeared that, even with substantial new aid, Laos would find it hard to avoid famine conditions. The flooding of the Mekong, officially described as a national disaster, devastated 90% of the agricultural fields in the north and half the arable land in the central region. Loss of life in the southern region was termed "serious." (T. J. S. GEORGE)

Latin-American Affairs

External Relations. Latin America's relations with the outside world improved in 1978, as South American military dictatorships responded to U.S. and Western European diplomatic pressure by lifting states of siege, agreeing to invite the UN Commission on Human Rights, and generally confirming a return to free elections in the 1980s. However, in regard to economic affairs disagreement sharpened, with the Latin Americans uniting to apply pressure for opening U.S. and European markets to their exports, making the International Monetary Fund (IMF) more flexible in respect to trade deficit financing, and discouraging malpractices of multinational companies.

U.S. Pres. Jimmy Carter visited Brazil and Venezuela in March; and Patricia Derian, U.S. State Department coordinator on human rights, then went to Argentina, mainly to raise the question of human rights and persuade Brazil and Argentina to ratify the Non-proliferation of Nuclear Weapons Treaty of 1968. Argentina announced that it would ratify the treaty but failed to respond convincingly on the human rights issue, leading the U.S. government in July to place a ban on a $270 million Export-Import Bank loan sought by Argentina to help finance the purchase of U.S. hydroelectric equipment; the ban was later lifted. Brazil refused to ratify the weapons treaty and Pres. Ernesto Geisel visited West Germany in March to help secure a controversial nuclear deal made with West Germany in 1975. Chile's reaction

A mighty explosion of nearly 60 tons of dynamite signaled the start of construction of the world's largest hydroelectric dam, to be built on the Paraná River on the frontier between Brazil and Paraguay. Construction of the Itaipú Dam started in October and was expected to cost $8.7 billion.

to outside pressure on alleged violations of human rights was to hold a vaguely worded referendum subject to strict controls; on Jan. 5, 1978, the government announced it had won with 75% support.

At the "Tokyo Round" of talks under the General Agreement on Tariffs and Trade (GATT) during 1978, the Latin Americans sought a common position on the opening of U.S. and European Economic Community markets; this was reiterated at the UN Conference on Trade and Development ministerial meeting in March. At the annual meeting of the IMF-World Bank in September, the Latin American representatives attempted to gain help in financing their balance of payments deficits.

Economics. The Latin-American nations (excluding oil-exporting Venezuela and Ecuador) were faced with severe balance of payments problems in 1978. Consequently, the debt-servicing burden on these countries rose sharply, and unless they could increase their foreign earnings by boosting exports, they might be forced to default on their foreign borrowings.

These problems did not affect Venezuela, Ecuador, and Bolivia; the first two, the region's main petroleum-exporting countries, enjoyed economic growth rates well above the Latin-American average of 4.5% during 1977. On Sept. 1, 1978, Pres. José López Portillo of Mexico said in his annual address to the nation that his country's petroleum reserves had been upgraded significantly. As a result, the improvements registered in the Mexican economy in 1978, based on increasing oil exports, were expected to continue.

Regional Integration. The ninth conference of foreign ministers of the member countries of the River Plate Basin Group (Argentina, Bolivia, Brazil, Paraguay, and Uruguay), held in Asunción, Paraguay, between Dec. 5 and 8, 1977, was perhaps the most important in the short history of this regional group. The members reached agreement on backing three major projects: the 201-km (125-mi) Trans-Chaco Highway connecting the northern part of Argentina's road network with that of Paraguay; a railroad program for Bolivia to provide a connection with Brazil that would help to give the Brazilians an outlet to the Pacific (at the Chilean port of Arica); and a natural-gas pipeline linking Uruguay to Bolivia's supplies by way of Argentina's pipeline network.

During the second half of 1977 problems raised by the construction of three joint hydroelectric dams on the Paraná River (the Brazilian-Paraguayan 12,600-Mw Itaipú Dam due in 1983–85, the Argentine-Paraguayan 3,200-Mw Yacyretá-Apipé Dam due in 1985, and the Argentine-Paraguayan 3,500–5,500-Mw Corpus Dam, completion unscheduled) threatened to sour relations between the three participating countries, particularly Brazil and Argentina. Brazil announced that Paraguay had decided not to change the frequency of its electricity system to suit Brazil's 60 cycles a minute (Paraguay, Argentina, and Uruguay all used 50 cycles a minute).

In 1978 attention focused on the ensuing trilateral talks. The shelving of the Corpus project was threatened because the Brazilians were not prepared to allow any of their territory to be flooded

Under a huge portrait of Venezuelan liberator Simón Bolívar, U.S. Pres. Jimmy Carter and Venezuelan Pres. Carlos Pérez talked when Carter visited Caracas in March.

(they had developed the region for rice growing); such flooding was inevitable if full capacity for Corpus at its planned height of 120 m was to be realized. In place of Corpus, Argentina told the Paraguayans that it would develop a project in the middle Paraná region on its own. Then on May 30 Brazil announced it had called off the talks with Argentina and Paraguay that were scheduled for June 7, indicating that a deadlock had been reached. In October, however, news came of a compromise between Argentina and Brazil on the scale of the Corpus project. The agreed-upon height of the dam was reported to be between 103 and 108 m.

Another similar regional group, the as yet limited Amazon Pact, was inaugurated on July 3. Members included Bolivia, Brazil, Colombia, Ecuador, Guyana, Peru, Suriname, and Venezuela.

The Latin American Free Trade Association (LAFTA) reduced tariff barriers within the area; in late 1977 Mexico and Argentina signed three new complementary agreements, to which another was added on May 22, 1978, relating to tariffs governing particular goods. These bilateral accords were designed to prepare the way for more trade among Argentina, Brazil, and Mexico, as well as, though to a lesser extent, Chile and Uruguay.

The Andean Group members (Bolivia, Colombia, Ecuador, Peru, and Venezuela) took a step toward integration when the Sectorial Program for the Motor Vehicle Industry was approved in September 1977, after considerable negotiation. The program consisted of special advantages in this industry conceded to Bolivia by the other members. Success spurred on negotiations for expanding the machine-tools sectorial program.

Border Disputes. During 1978 relations between Chile and Argentina deteriorated rapidly.

On January 25 the Argentine government announced that it considered null and void the judgment made in May 1977 by a special tribunal appointed from the International Court of Justice to settle the territorial dispute on the southern tip of the continent, the so-called Beagle Channel dispute. The tribunal awarded to Chile three small islands across the Beagle Channel from Tierra del Fuego. The issue gained importance during the second half of 1977 with the discovery of a major petroleum deposit by the Chileans nearby in the Magellan Straits and the awarding of exceptionally favourable offshore prospecting contracts to U.S.-based multinational companies.

The Argentine announcement was immediately followed by declarations from Chilean military leaders that "the territorial integrity of the Fatherland" had to be protected at all costs and that the decision made by the tribunal was final. The response in military circles in Argentina was a patriotic outcry; Adm. Eduardo Massera, commander of the Argentine Navy and a member of the ruling three-man junta, instructed the Argentine fleet to sail south to the area in question. Troop maneuvers on either side of the border followed.

Despite two meetings held on January 19 and February 20 between the two military heads of state, Pres. Jorge Videla of Argentina and Pres. Augusto Pinochet of Chile, and an agreement to commence bilateral negotiations to resolve the differences, the tense atmosphere worsened as the year progressed and the negotiations came to an impasse. In April Argentina placed a ban on the export to Chile of "strategic items," loosely defined so as to include trucks, buses, motor-vehicle parts, and other such products. Trade between Chile and Brazil was affected as truck drivers crossing Argentina were purposefully harassed with petty regulations and capricious border and tunnel closings. By midyear air-raid drills and blackouts were ordered in Argentine cities on the Andean foothills, and army reserves were put on alert in both countries.

Meanwhile, Bolivia on March 17 broke off diplomatic relations with Chile over the question of Bolivia's access to the Pacific Ocean. The Bolivian government organized a symbolic march with army units to the Chilean border.

During much of the second half of 1978, negotiations between Chile and Argentina remained deadlocked, prompting the chief Argentine negotiator, Gen. Osiris Villegas, to issue a statement saying that war "may be the only alternative left." Admiral Massera set out on a Latin-American tour, stopping over in Bolivia and Peru, to seek support for the Argentine position. Rumours of a military alliance spread when, in October, the commander of the Argentine Air Force met his Peruvian and Bolivian counterparts in Santa Cruz, Bolivia, ostensibly to celebrate Bolivia's Air Force Day.

Opposition to war, however, was taking shape. In September bishops of Argentina and Chile called for peace; in October, 16 intellectuals from the two countries published a manifesto calling for understanding. But the pacifists were voicing their discontent at a time when their governments were in the hands of the military, making it difficult to negotiate a compromise. The situation became increasingly tense in November, with armed forces of both sides placed on alert. In December, however, after some initial disagreement, both sides indicated their willingness to accept papal mediation.   (PAUL DOWBOR)

See also articles on the various political units.

Law

Court Decisions. This article reviews the important judicial decisions handed down by the various courts throughout the world. During 1978 the most significant decisions involved human relations, business enterprises, freedom of speech, and family matters.

HUMAN RELATIONS. In the most publicized case of the year, *Regents of the University of California* v. *Bakke*, the United States Supreme Court ordered the University of California at Davis to end its practice of "reverse racial discrimination." The university had been reserving 16% of the places in its entering medical school class for minority applicants. To qualify for admission within this special group, one had to be "black, Chicano, Asian or American Indian." Allan Bakke (*see* BIOGRAPHIES) was not a member of any of these minority groups, and his application for admission to medical school was denied even though his overall grade-point average, science grade-point average, and Medical College Admissions Test score were superior to those of some individuals who were admitted because of their minority status.

Bakke sued to compel the university to admit him. The university responded by defending its special admissions program on the grounds of four aims: (1) to partially redress the historic deficit of traditionally disfavoured minorities in medical schools and the medical profession; (2) to counter the effects of societal discrimination; (3) to increase the number of physicians who will practice in communities currently underserved; and (4) to obtain the educational benefits that flow from an ethnically diverse student body. The Supreme Court of California found that the special admissions program discriminated on the basis of race and therefore violated the Fourteenth Amendment to the U.S. Constitution. The U.S. Supreme Court affirmed this judgment and ordered the university to admit Bakke.

In a narrow sense the court based its decision on the fact that the university had discriminated unfairly against Bakke because it could not demonstrate that he would not have been admitted had he been able to compete for the "minority" as well as the "regular" places in the class. Because a majority of the court could not agree upon the precise reason for its order, however, the case impressed most legal scholars as being of doubtful value as a precedent.

It was even difficult for most scholars to make any generalized statement as to the inclination of the Supreme Court on the important matter of "reverse discrimination" because the opinions of the justices tended to overlap one another and not fall into discrete categories. Most, however, tended to attach principal significance to the opinion of Justice Lewis Powell. In two 5–4 decisions, the court outlawed the special admissions program of the university, but also maintained that race could be used as a factor in admission to institutions of higher education; only Justice Powell voted for both of these positions.

In Powell's opinion the case had to be decided under the equal protection clause of the Fourteenth Amendment. Although this clause was first introduced into the Constitution to ensure the emancipation of blacks from their former condition of slavery, it does more than ensure equality between blacks and whites. It is meant to guarantee equality of all persons and to protect all groups from racial discrimination. It prevents the ranking of groups according to the amount of injury they have suffered at the hands of society. There is, according to Powell, no basis in principle for deciding which group at any moment should merit heightened judicial solicitude, and to hitch the meaning of the equal protection clause to these transitory considerations would mean that classifications touching on racial and ethnic considerations might vary with the ebb and flow of political forces.

Justice Powell then turned his attention to the four purposes alleged by the university to justify its special admissions program. The first two purposes, redressing the historic deficit of traditionally disfavoured minorities in medical schools and countering the effects of societal discrimination, were dismissed as invalid for the reasons stated earlier in his opinion and outlined above. The third purpose, increasing the number of physicians who will practice in communities currently underserviced, was not, in Powell's view, served by the special admissions program, because that program was based on the race of the applicant and not on his or her interest in providing health care to the poor or minority population. The fourth purpose, obtaining the educational benefits that flow from an ethnically diverse student body, was considered by Justice Powell to be a valid one, but one reached by the special admissions program of the university through improper means. He maintained that rigid quotas based solely on race are not a constitutionally permissible means for achieving diversity in a student body.

In what was perhaps the most important part of the opinion, Justice Powell then outlined the special considerations that may be taken into account in setting up an educational program aimed at obtaining an ethnically diverse student body. In doing so, he quoted from an amicus curiae brief filed by Harvard University. Under the Harvard College plan, explicitly approved by Justice Powell, race may be taken into account as a factor in admissions, just as a life spent on a farm, residence in a Western state, or a special talent for mathematics, music, or athletics may be taken into account. "A farm boy from Idaho can bring something to Harvard College that a Bostonian cannot offer. Similarly a black student can usually bring something that a white person cannot offer. The quality of the educational experience of all the students in Har-

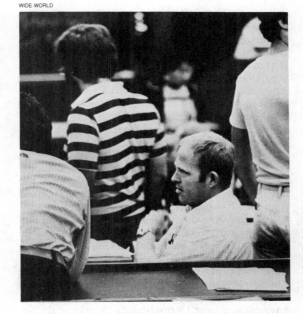

Allan Bakke, whose complaint of reverse discrimination was carried to the U.S. Supreme Court, attended his first class at the University of California medical school in September after the court ruled that he must be admitted.

vard College depends in part on these differences in the background and outlook that students bring with them." Moreover, in order to provide a truly heterogeneous environment, some attention must be paid to numbers. In the words of the Harvard brief, "It would not make sense, for example, to have 10 or 20 students out of 1,100 whose homes are west of the Mississippi. Comparably, 10 or 20 black students could not begin to bring to their classmates and to each other the variety of points of view, backgrounds and experiences of blacks in the United States."

In conclusion Justice Powell held that race, geographic origin, and special interests and talents may all be considered as factors in order to obtain a diverse student body. Some factors, even race, may be weighed more heavily than others. As long as race is not the factor that precludes a candidate from consideration for all admission places, it is a factor that may be weighed. Under this test the special admissions program of the University of California was deficient because it denied Bakke his right to individual consideration without regard to race.

The European Court of Human Rights also decided two important civil rights matters in 1978, both involving Article 3 of the European Convention on Human Rights, which prohibits member states from inflicting "inhuman and degrading" treatment. In *Ireland* v. *U.K.*, the first interstate case to be brought before the court, it ruled that the treatment of detainees by the U.K. security forces in Northern Ireland amounted to inhuman and degrading treatment but not "torture" under Article 3 of the Convention. The court refused to order the U.K. to initiate prosecutions against members of its security forces for their actions. Presumably it would have done so had it found that the actions amounted to "torture."

In *Tyrer* v. *U.K.* the court reviewed the practice of inflicting corporal punishment on young, violent offenders under the law of the Isle of Man. Specifically, it considered the practice of "birching" (beating with a birch rod) such offenders. The U.K. defended the action by contending that birching is merely a form of punishment but not inherently degrading in nature. The court agreed that to be "degrading" the punishment must attain a particular level of debasement higher than the usual element of humiliation involved in punishment in general. It found, however, that such a level had been reached and that the birching law of the Isle of Man infringed Article 3 of the Convention. Authorities in the Isle of Man indicated that they would not honour the decision. This raised constitutional difficulties for the U.K. because it conventionally does not legislate for the Isle of Man (though it has the right to do so) and the latter has complete judicial autonomy.

BUSINESS AFFAIRS. During the year several significant cases were handed down in the area of business. In *Flagg Brothers, Inc.* v. *Brooks,* the U.S. Supreme Court held that section 7–210 of the New York Uniform Commercial Code does not violate the due process clause of the Fourteenth Amendment to the U.S. Constitution. Section 7–210 allows a warehouse to sell stored goods to enforce its lien for unpaid storage charges.

The Federal Supreme Court of Germany reversed its former rule that a shipowner is strictly liable for mishaps that occur during the loading and unloading of cargo. The court held that such a rule does not make sense under modern circumstances, in which it is common for the charterer or consignee to commission special enterprises to do the work of handling cargo. Under the new rule announced by the court it must be decided in each case who was actually responsible for the accident.

The European Court of Justice handed down a new and stricter definition of "market dominance" under Article 86 of the Convention. Under that article an enterprise having market dominance cannot charge prices as high as the market will bear but is limited to prices having a reasonable relationship to the economic value of the product, usually measured by the cost of producing it. The court held that a company is market-dominant for purposes of this rule when it is able to keep a large share of the market, though selling at higher prices than those of its competitors, if it has obtained this station by means of a "flexible overall strategy against new competition." The case involved the pricing practices of United Brands Co. with respect to bananas. Although the court held that United Brands was market-dominant, it also found that it had not been established that its prices were unreasonable (unrelated to cost) under Article 86.

FAMILY RIGHTS. In *Zablocki* v. *Redhail,* the U.S. Supreme Court struck down a Wisconsin statute that required a noncustodial parent to obtain court permission before marrying if that parent was under a court order to support his child. The statute had specified that court permission to remarry cannot be granted unless the marriage license applicant submits proof of compliance with the child support obligation and, additionally, demonstrates that the children covered by the support order are not then, and are not likely to become, public charges. A marriage entered into in violation of the statute was made void thereunder, and the violator was made subject to criminal penalties.

Demonstrators from many U.S. cities paraded in Washington, D.C., on March 18 demanding freedom for the "Wilmington Ten," a group of civil rights workers who had been imprisoned in North Carolina.

Redhail, a Wisconsin resident, admitted paternity of an illegitimate child in a 1972 lawsuit and was ordered to pay $109 per month for support of the child. He was unemployed and indigent and did not make any support payments. In 1974 he applied for a license to marry a woman who was bearing his child. The license was denied because he had not obtained court permission to marry as required by the statute.

By an 8–1 margin, the Supreme Court struck down the Wisconsin statute as unconstitutional. It held that the classification of people according to whether or not they are under a child-support order, subjecting only those under such an order to court review of their marriage license application, denies to such persons the equal protection of the laws, in violation of the Fourteenth Amendment to the U.S. Constitution. The court held that the freedom to marry is a fundamental liberty protected by the Fourteenth Amendment.

The West German Federal Constitutional Court held that the Basic Law was violated by a decision which did not adequately protect the rights of an unborn child. The case involved a situation in which the unborn child was injured when its mother was accidentally hurt at work. Under the statutory social insurance the mother was entitled to protection for her injuries, but the unborn child was not similarly protected. The court held that this discrimination against the unborn child was unconstitutional and that it was entitled to the same protection as its mother.

(WILLIAM D. HAWKLAND)

International Law. The year 1978 did not produce any major developments in the field of international law, although there were indications of more dramatic events in coming years. In one sense the theme for the year could be stated as international lawlessness, exemplified by a report of the Swedish Committee on South Africa that brushed aside international law rules that stood in the way of its proposals for Swedish interference in South Africa's domestic business affairs. The action of Lebanon giving house room to guerrilla forces that were fighting on neighbouring territory also illustrated a loosening of the proper rules of conduct between states at peace with each other. Law broke down completely in the Eritrea-Ethiopia conflict and the war between the Polisario guerrillas and Morocco-Mauritania in the former Spanish Sahara. On the other hand, the earlier wave of aircraft hijacking for political purposes seemed to have died down.

The other theme for the year could be the third world, with its main manifestation a further stage in the organizing of political consciousness on the part of the less developed countries. The North-South dialogue continued without producing anything important, but more significant was the UN Conference on Trade and Development (UNCTAD) meeting on transfer of technology. Although the conference failed to attain its goal of agreement on the text of a code governing such transfers, the occasion marked the culmination of many years of work on the subject and the start of a period of more open political debate that was likely to result in a new settlement of the economic relations between the industrialized and the less developed nations.

Related to this theme was the continuing saga of commercial bribery and the not unrelated one of the place of multinational corporations. The great business bribery scandals of recent years led to a certain amount of new law, particularly the U.S. Foreign Corrupt Practices Act of December 1977 and a report of the International Chamber of Commerce on bribery in the preceding month.

Finally, to complete this survey of general economic law, there was significant organizational activity. The International Law Commission completed its draft articles on the most-favoured-nation clause and submitted them to the UN for consideration at a full diplomatic conference still to be arranged. A coordinating council for associations producing raw materials was agreed upon by 40 less developed countries in Geneva in April, and in the same month 17 African nations agreed to establish a preferential trade area for eastern and southern Africa. The Economic Community of West African States set up the Trade, Customs, Immigration, Monetary and Payment Commission in Lagos to identify policy options and possible trade liberalization under the Treaty of Lagos.

TERRITORY AND SOVEREIGNTY. The most discussed territorial event of the year was undoubtedly the final approval of the Panama Canal treaties by the U.S. Senate and their subsequent ratification in June after much political uncertainty in both the U.S. and Panama. New nations that came into being included the Solomon Islands, previously an Anglo-French condominium; Dominica, a former British Caribbean colony; and Tuvalu (in the Pacific north of Fiji, with only 8,000 inhabitants and 26 sq km of land area). In the China Sea, on the other hand, the status of various island groups continued to be the subject of dispute, with Chinese fishing vessels behaving as if the Japanese-claimed Senkaku Islands were Chinese; farther to the south, the Spratly Islands were still being claimed by the Philippines, Vietnam, China, and Taiwan. In both cases the sharpened interest was believed to be related to the possibility of oil deposits in the surrounding waters.

On the other hand agreement was reached between India and Bangladesh on the sharing of the waters of the Ganges River after 25 years of dispute; it provided for the sharing of the available waters but did not tackle the problem of regulating the flow of the river to take account of monsoon floods and winter droughts. The Amazon Basin agreement went much further. That treaty, signed in July by Bolivia, Brazil, Colombia, Ecuador, Guyana, Peru, Suriname, and Venezuela, provided for the joint development and preservation of the entire Amazon basin and forest and aimed to promote the global integration of the area.

INTERNATIONAL ADJUDICATION. The International Court of Justice was no nearer winning general acceptance of its function, its latest snub being the refusal of Turkey to accept its jurisdiction in the dispute with Greece over the continental shelf in the Aegean Sea. As with the earlier French boycott of the court's hearing of complaints about French nuclear tests by Australia and New Zea-

Mario Jascalevich, whose demand for reporter Myron Farber's notes led to the celebrated "Farber case," flashes a victory sign after a jury in Hackensack, N.J., acquitted him on three counts of murder.

land, the court nevertheless heard arguments as to its jurisdiction in the absence of Turkey. The court also adopted a new set of rules of court aimed at simplifying the procedure, reducing the expense for litigants, and facilitating recourse to chambers of the court and the use of advisory procedures.

Other forms of judicial settlement were more popular. The International Centre for Settlement of Investment Disputes (part of the World Bank group) delivered in August 1977 its first award under the Convention for the Settlement of Investment Disputes. It later settled two more cases, received three new requests for arbitration, and resumed proceedings in a fourth. The number of states that had ratified the convention rose to 71.

Arbitration rules were also adopted by the UN Economic Commission for Europe to apply to disputes relating to certain categories of perishable agricultural products. In August the member states of the Andean Pact agreed to establish a Supreme Court of the Andes states to oversee the process of economic integration.

Two 1977 arbitrations, however, were disputed. The Beagle Channel award to Chile was first rejected by Argentina, and there were suggestions of referring it to the International Court of Justice. Later in the year, however, Argentina agreed to papal mediation. The award in the Franco-British dispute over continental shelf demarcation in the English Channel and Western Approaches was disputed by the U.K. on the basis of faulty line drawing by the surveyor chosen to implement the award geographically. The arbitral tribunal did not, however, upset the award or, for the most part, alter the lines drawn.

MARITIME AFFAIRS. As with international law generally the law of the sea marked time after the spate of bilateral fishing agreements in 1977 (which did, however, continue fairly strongly

during 1978). In particular, the UN Conference on the Law of the Sea held spring and summer sessions in Geneva and New York without reaching any conclusion. New meetings were fixed for 1979, and it was hoped that a final text would be ready for signature in 1980.

Many maritime boundary treaties were signed during the year (U.S.-Cuba; Mexico-Venezuela; The Netherlands-Venezuela; Colombia-Venezuela; Costa Rica-Dominican Republic; Ecuador-Haiti-Panama; India-Indonesia-Thailand; Papua New Guinea-Australia; Finland-Sweden). The dispute in the Barents Sea between Norway and the U.S.S.R., on the other hand, sharpened quite considerably. A sea boundary disagreement of an unusual nature arose between the U.K. and Norway with regard to the Statfjord oil field, which extends under the boundary between the continental shelves of the two nations. The U.K. claimed that it should have more than the 11.12% of the total extraction that it was currently taking, and negotiations were initiated under the bilateral continental shelf treaty.

Marine pollution was a particularly prominent matter during the year, especially because of three major oil tanker disasters near the British Isles. The first, the "Amoco Cadiz," which broke up close to the French coast of Brittany, led not only to recriminations and an extremely thorough French report but also to immediate changes in the traffic separation schemes in those waters and to renewed European pressure against flags of convenience. This disaster was followed by the wrecking of the "Eleni V" and the "Christos Bitas," which caused less damage but emphasized the need for strong continuing control measures. In February, before "Amoco Cadiz," the Conference on Tanker Safety and Pollution Prevention adopted protocols to 1973 and 1974 conventions, which required large tankers to have duplicated steering gear, two radars, and special ballast tanks. In October the coastal states on the Baltic Sea signed an agreement relating to the detection of vessels leaking oil at sea, and the eight Persian Gulf states adopted a framework convention on oil pollution and on an action plan for protection of the marine environment.

EUROPE. The European Court of Justice delivered a major constitutional judgment that emphasized the precedence of European Economic Community law over national law and its direct enforceability by lower courts. Of equal significance was its judgment that the tax imposed by an EEC regulation on isoglucose production (aimed at protecting sugar producers) was discriminatory and so void; this confirmed the newly robust attitude noted in an earlier case relating to a virtual tax on animal feed compounders who did not use skimmed milk powder. The court also held that the no-trawl areas set up within 50 mi of the Irish coast were discriminatory against other EEC fishermen and so unlawful. But in that, as in the two trademark cases of *Hoffmann-La Roche* v. *Centrafarm* and *American Home Products* v. *Centrafarm*, the court left most of its, and the parties', options open.　　　　　　　(NEVILLE MARCH HUNNINGS)

See also Crime and Law Enforcement; Prisons and Penology; United Nations.

TEST–TUBE BABIES— THE LEGAL IMPLICATIONS

by Michael Zander

On July 25, 1978, the world's first "test-tube baby" was born in Oldham, England, to Mrs. Lesley Brown. Mrs. Brown and her husband had been trying to have a child for some nine years. The baby Mrs. Brown eventually had was conceived in a laboratory culture dish under the supervision of gynecologist Patrick Steptoe and research physiologist Robert Edwards. Steptoe and Edwards had been working for over a decade to perfect a technique for fertilizing human eggs outside the human body.

The method used was to take a ripe egg from the wife's ovary and place it in a culture dish together with sperm taken from the husband. The embryo was allowed to develop for two and a half days before being placed in the uterus, where it became implanted and grew like any other fetus. The birth, by cesarian section, took place 38 weeks and 5 days after Mrs. Brown's last menstrual period. The baby was reported by the doctors to be absolutely normal. (*See* BIOGRAPHIES: *Brown, Louise Joy*.)

This development has important medical and social implications, but attention is given here only to the legal issues involved. In most ways these are the same or very similar to those that arise from artificial insemination, where fertilization takes place through placing sperm in the vagina rather than through ordinary sexual intercourse. In artificial insemination the sperm may be taken from the husband (AIH) or from a donor (AID). This is also the case with fertilization in vitro—but this method also permits the ovum to be provided by a donor.

Is the Child Legitimate? Where the sperm and ovum are from a man and woman who are married to each other, the resulting child is unquestionably legitimate. But where either sperm or ovum is taken from a donor not part of the marriage, in most jurisdictions the child is illegitimate—even when the other partner to marriage consents. Some of the

---

Michael Zander is professor of law at the London School of Economics and Political Science and author of several works on law and society.

decisions have gone so far as to hold that artificial insemination by donor is adultery, but this no longer represents the typical approach of courts in common-law countries. There are some places that have statutes legitimizing children born by AID with the husband's consent (they include Arkansas, California, Kansas, and New York), and in other areas the courts have achieved the same result without legislation. But it is still uncertain whether these statutory provisions and judicial decisions will cover the new situation of in vitro fertilization. In practice the illegitimacy may never come to light. There is a strong legal presumption that a child born to a married couple is legitimate. The presumption is rebuttable, but normally only the couple and the doctors would know the true position, and their interest would be to hide the facts. Both AID and in vitro fertilization would normally be undertaken only for married couples, and the child would usually be registered as their child. In the case of AID this usually constitutes a criminal offense, since the register then shows a false entry. But if the marriage survives, the true position will probably never emerge.

It could emerge, however, in a variety of ways. For example, during divorce proceedings, the husband might deny that the child is his and thereby seek to avoid financial responsibility for it. In 1963, in *Gursky* v. *Gursky,* a New York court held that a child conceived through AID was illegitimate but that the husband, because he consented to the AID, was responsible for its financial support. (In 1973 another New York court ruled that *Gursky* v. *Gursky* should not be followed, and that an AID child born to consenting parents was legitimate. Thus the husband was the father for the purpose of an adoption law that required a father's consent for the adoption of his child by the mother's second husband.)

In *People* v. *Sorensen* in 1968, a California court ruled that the mother's husband, having consented to AID, was "the lawful father" and as such liable to support the child. In that case the child was also said to be legitimate, but the trend of the decisions suggests that a husband who consented to the method of conception would be held to support the child even if it was deemed illegitimate.

The fact of illegitimacy might also be revealed in the context of some dispute over inheritance. The child might seek to inherit from the husband-non-father. The law in some jurisdictions permits an illegitimate child to inherit only where there is a provision in a will. On death intestate, other relatives might try to establish that the apparent father of the child could not have conceived him. The child might then find itself disinherited. In some countries, including Britain, it is legally possible for an illegitimate child to inherit from its actual father.

Mrs. Doris Del Zio of New York City, accompanied by her attorney, sued a New York hospital and a doctor for over $1.5 million, charging that her laboratory-fertilized embryo was deliberately destroyed in 1973 just before it was to have been implanted in her womb. The jury granted her $49,000.

For an AID child or one born through in vitro fertilization, however, the attempt to do so would most likely be frustrated through ignorance of the circumstances of the birth and inability to find out the identity of the biological father.

Liability of the Physician. There are various ways in which a doctor might become legally liable for his actions arising out of in vitro fertilization. The child might be born with genetic defects, or there might be complaints that it was defective in some way— perhaps of a distinctly lower intelligence quotient than the couple themselves. A doctor would not be liable to pay damages if he could show that he had taken reasonable care in all the circumstances, but negligence, for instance in muddling batches of semen, could be the basis of a claim. In practice, most doctors would probably try to exclude liability by getting the couple to sign waivers.

If a potentially defective fetus is destroyed in the womb by the doctor, he risks criminal penalties for carrying out an illegal abortion unless local law permits an abortion on such grounds. Conversely, the unjustified destruction of the fetus might be the basis of an action by would-be parents. In the first action of this kind, damages were awarded against the doctor and the hospital. In 1973 gynecologist Raymond Vande Wiele of the Columbia Presbyterian Medical Center in New York City destroyed the specimen culture the day after fertilization. An action was brought for $1,550,000 damages for emotional stress by the would-be parents, Doris and John Del Zio. On Aug. 18, 1978, a New York jury awarded Mrs. Del Zio $24,000 against the hospital and $25,000 against Vande Wiele. The doctor testified that he had intervened because he thought the procedure might prove fatal to Mrs. Del Zio.

Incest. If, in a particular neighbourhood, one donor is used to father numerous children, there is the possibility that his offspring might unwittingly come to marry. Such a marriage would be within the prohibited degrees of relationship, but no criminal offense would be committed since the parties to the marriage would lack the requisite knowledge.

New Legislation Needed. The number of births through artificial insemination is considerable. It has been estimated that 7,000 to 10,000 babies are born each year in the U.S. alone through this means. Fertilization in vitro is a technique for solving certain problems of infertility, and it may come to be as familiar as AIH and AID. Existing laws deal only partially and not always aptly with the problems involved, and there is an urgent need for regulation.

In particular, laws are needed to prescribe medical qualifications for those who handle these procedures and to deal with the nature of the consents that must be obtained, the screening of donors, and whether unmarried persons may benefit. There must also be rules on what records are to be kept and in what circumstances any of the relevant parties may have access to confidential records. The information to be stated on birth certificates should be specified, and there should be rules on the legitimacy and inheritance rights of children born through the assistance of donor sperm or ova.

A further range of even more complex problems is raised by the possibility that an embryo fertilized in the laboratory may be planted in the uterus of a third party, who agrees to hand over the child on birth to the couple for whom the arrangement is made and who may have supplied the sperm or the ovum or both. Does the child belong to the couple or to the woman who bore the child? Who are the parents for the purpose of the birth certificate? What happens if the "hostess" changes her mind and decides to keep the child? How can the anonymity of those concerned be preserved? Must a proposed abortion on health grounds have the consent of the couple whose child is being gestated in the "hostess" womb? The new technology poses problems that must now be faced by legislatures in any country where it is used.

Lebanon

A republic of the Middle East, Lebanon is bounded by Syria, Israel, and the Mediterranean Sea. Area: 10,230 sq km (3,950 sq mi). Pop. (1978 est.): 3,152,-000. Cap. and largest city: Beirut (metro. pop., 1975 est., 1,172,000). Language: Arabic. Religion: recently released 1965 census figures, of questionable reliability, show Christians: 54.5%; Muslims 45.5%. President in 1978, Elias Sarkis; prime minister, Selim al-Hoss.

Lebanon's slow recovery from the civil war of 1975–76 was jeopardized in 1978 by an Israeli invasion of the south of the country in March and heavy fighting between the Syrian-dominated Arab Deterrent Force (ADF) and Lebanese rightists in September-October. In January there were signs that a political entente might be developing among the various Lebanese factions, although security remained disturbed and there were frequent bomb attacks against individual political figures and newspapers. The relative quiet in southern Lebanon was broken by clashes among Palestinians, leading to a general strike in Sidon.

The situation deteriorated sharply in February with a serious clash between Syrian forces of the ADF and right-wing Lebanese militia, mainly of ex-president Camille Chamoun's National Liberal Party. Chamoun emerged as the chief opponent of the Syrian presence in Lebanon, while the Falangists and supporters of ex-president Suleiman Franjieh were more moderate toward the Syrians. There were also renewed clashes in the south, with Israeli forces providing backing for Lebanese rightists fighting Palestinians and leftists.

On the night of March 14, Israel launched a full-scale invasion of southern Lebanon, using tanks and air cover. Although the immediate reason for the invasion was retaliation for a Palestinian guerrilla attack near Tel Aviv on March 11, the Israeli objective was to destroy the Palestinian guerrilla bases in southern Lebanon. Israeli troops immediately occupied a 12-km-deep strip of territory from the coast to the Mt. Hermon foothills, and from March 19 they advanced to occupy all southern Lebanon up to the Litani River except for an enclave around Tyre.

Lebanon

By then troops of the UN Interim Force in Lebanon (UNIFIL) had begun to arrive in accordance with UN Security Council Resolution 425 of March 19. Red Cross estimates said about 1,000 had been killed in the fighting and 80% of the villages in the south had been damaged. Some 200,000 Lebanese and 65,000 Palestinians fled northward, creating a serious refugee problem in Sidon and Beirut. As the UNIFIL forces were deployed, the Israeli troops withdrew by stages until they finally left Lebanese territory by mid-June. However, they remained in close support of the Christian enclaves along the Lebanon-Israel border, where right-wing Christian militia continued to defy both the UNIFIL forces and those of the reconstituted Lebanese Army, which took up positions in the south at the end of July.

On April 19 Prime Minister Selim al-Hoss resigned to enable his Cabinet of technocrats to make way for one of parliamentarians and other political leaders. Failure of the various political factions to agree led to his reappointment on April 28, and on May 15 the same government resumed office. However, Lebanese politicians agreed sufficiently to issue a joint declaration calling for "an end to all Palestinian and non-Palestinian armed action inside Lebanon." The declaration was attacked by

ZOUHAIR SAADEH—GAMMA/LIAISON

Heavy Syrian bombardment turned downtown Beirut, Lebanon, into smoking, charred rubble during fighting in October.

Law Enforcement:
see Crime and Law Enforcement

Lawn Bowls:
see Bowling

Lawn Tennis:
see Tennis

the Lebanese left and by the Syrians but was only moderately criticized by the Palestine Liberation Organization, which insisted on its noninterference in Lebanese affairs.

In May and June the Lebanese Christians were weakened by a deep split between Falangists, concentrated mainly around Mt. Lebanon, and supporters of ex-president Franjieh in the north. Following a reconciliation between Franjieh and the Tripoli Muslim leader, Rashid Karami, there were increasingly frequent incidents between Falangists and Franjieh supporters, culminating in the deaths on June 13 of Franjieh's son Tony and his family under Falangist shellfire. Although Falangist leaders denied they had ordered the attack, Franjieh vowed revenge and more murders took place, including the massacre of 22 Falangist supporters in Bekaa villages on June 28. The Syrians were close to Franjieh, and these events contributed to a further deterioration in relations between the ADF and the Lebanese rightists.

In the first week of July, Syrian forces bombarded Christian East Beirut. Pres. Elias Sarkis threatened to resign on July 6 but withdrew his threat on July 15 under strong pressure both at home and abroad. On August 5 the Syrian forces resumed the shelling in the heaviest bombardment since the civil war. A cease-fire ordered by Syria's Pres. Hafez al-Assad on August 9 restored relative calm for three weeks, although firing by Christian militia prevented the reopening of Beirut port.

Tension increased as the U.S.-Israeli-Egyptian summit at Camp David, Md., approached. A showdown was widely expected in view of Syria's

determination to sabotage any Egyptian-Israeli agreement. The Lebanese Christian leaders' open claims of active Israeli support and the regular overflying of Beirut by Israeli warplanes as a warning to Syria further antagonized the Syrians. The shelling was resumed with increased intensity at the end of September. East Beirut was surrounded by Syrian forces, and on October 6 and 7 Syria committed more troops. President Sarkis visited Saudi Arabia to appeal for other Arab troops to replace the Syrian forces. On October 13 some 500 Lebanese troops moved into the perimeter of the fighting but could not restore calm.

As the situation worsened, Arab foreign ministers met urgently at Beit Eddine, south of Beirut. On October 17 they announced a peace plan involving the withdrawal of Syrian troops a few hundred yards from the perimeter of East Beirut and their replacement by non-Syrian Arab forces. This was carried out, enabling Lebanese Christian civilians in Beirut to leave for the countryside. The Arab plan also provided for unauthorized armed persons to leave the streets or suffer arrest; by the end of October this had been fairly effective, although sporadic outbreaks of fighting continued to occur. Chamoun continued to insist that the Syrians should leave, while the Syrians were determined to enforce internal security in Lebanon.

(PETER MANSFIELD)

Lesotho

A constitutional monarchy of southern Africa and a member of the Commonwealth of Nations, Lesotho forms an enclave within the republic of South Africa. Area: 30,355 sq km (11,720 sq mi). Pop. (1976 prelim.): 1,230,000. Cap. and largest city: Maseru (pop., 1976 prelim., 14,700). Language: English and Sesotho (official). Religion: Roman Catholic 38.7%; Lesotho Evangelical Church 24.3%; Anglican 10.4%; other Christian 8.4%; non-Christian 18.2%. Chief of state in 1978, King Moshoeshoe II; prime minister, Chief Leabua Jonathan.

In February 1978 Transkei introduced restrictions on border crossings from Lesotho, thus cutting off many Basuto migrant workers from South Africa and preventing Basuto traders from bringing food in from South Africa. Reportedly, Transkei hoped to force Lesotho to recognize its independent status. Lesotho reported the dis-

LEBANON

Education. (1972–73) Primary, pupils 497,723; secondary, pupils 167,578; primary and secondary, teachers 32,901; vocational, pupils 3,898, teachers (1970–71) 508; teacher training, students 3,235, teachers (1971–72) 551; higher, students 50,803, teaching staff 2,313.

Finance. Monetary unit: Lebanese pound, with (Sept. 18, 1978) a free rate of L£2.96 to U.S. $1 (L£5.81 = £1 sterling). Gold and foreign exchange (June 1978) U.S. $2,207,300,000. Budget (1978 est.) revenue L£1,403 million; expenditure L£2,083 million.

Foreign Trade. (1977) Imports c. L£4,634 million; exports c. L£1,939 million. Import sources (1976): Romania c. 10%; Turkey c. 7%; Saudi Arabia c. 7%; Iraq c. 7%; France c. 7%; U.S. c. 7%. Export destinations (1976): Saudi Arabia c. 25%; Libya c. 19%; Egypt c. 9%; Syria 5%; Iraq 5%; Kuwait 5%. Main exports (1973): machinery 14%; fruit and vegetables 12%; chemicals 8%; aircraft 6%; clothing 6%; textile yarns and fabrics 5%; motor vehicles 5%. Tourism: visitors (1975) 1,555,000; gross receipts (1974) U.S. $415 million.

Transport and Communications. Roads (1976) c. 7,100 km. Motor vehicles in use (1974): passenger 214,000; commercial (including buses) 24,100. Railways: (1976) c. 425 km; traffic (1974) 2 million passenger-km, freight 42 million net ton-km. Air traffic (1976): 1,800,000,000 passenger-km; freight 525.2 million net ton-km. Shipping (1977): vessels 100 gross tons and over 163; gross tonnage 227,009. Telephones (Jan. 1973) 227,000. Radio receivers (Dec. 1975) 1,321,000. Television receivers (Dec. 1975) 410,000.

Agriculture. Production (in 000; metric tons; 1977): potatoes c. 90; wheat (1976) c. 30; tomatoes (1976) c. 65; grapes c. 100; olives c. 25; bananas (1976) c. 42; oranges c. 188; lemons c. 81; apples c. 177; tobacco c. 4. Livestock (in 000; 1976): cattle c. 84; goats c. 330; sheep c. 234; chickens c. 7,398.

Industry. Production (in 000; metric tons; 1976): petroleum products c. 820; cement c. 1,700; electricity (kw-hr) c. 1,250,000.

LESOTHO

Education. (1976) Primary, pupils 222,017, teachers 4,235; secondary, pupils 16,726, teachers 621; vocational, pupils 836, teachers 109; teacher training, students 393, teachers 401; higher, students 601, teaching staff 95.

Finance and Trade. Monetary unit: maloti, at par with the South African rand, with (Sept. 18, 1978) an official rate of .87 malotis to U.S. $1 (free rate of 1.70 malotis = £1 sterling). Budget (1976–77 est.) balanced at R 29.3 million. Foreign trade (1975): imports R 117.8 million; exports R 11.4 million. Main exports (1974): wool 35%; mohair 16%; livestock 16%; diamonds 9%. Most trade is with South Africa.

Agriculture. Production (in 000; metric tons; 1976): corn c. 130; wheat c. 50; sorghum c. 70; dry peas c. 8; wool c. 2. Livestock (in 000; 1976): cattle c. 580; goats c. 915; sheep c. 1,640.

Lesotho

criminatory measures to the European Economic
Community and the UN.

Great Britain increased its three-year capital aid
of £11.5 million by £2 million, and Abu Dhabi
lent R 637,000 for an airport feasibility study. Nevertheless, Lesotho remained to all intents an economic dependency of South Africa. The 1978–79
budget showed an increase of 53% in expenditure
(total expenditure, R 123,140,000). A new currency, the maloti, equivalent to the rand, was introduced and would circulate alongside the rand.
Lesotho's latter-day hostility toward South Africa,
tempered by awareness of economic realities, was
epitomized by the reception of a five-man Cuban
delegation in June. After South Africa protested,
the Lesotho government agreed that, though diplomatic relations with Cuba would be established,
there would be no Cuban military mission on its
soil.   (MOLLY MORTIMER)

Liberia

A republic on the west coast of Africa, Liberia is
bordered by Sierra Leone, Guinea, and Ivory
Coast. Area: 97,790 sq km (37,757 sq mi). Pop.
(1978 est.): 1,716,900. Cap. and largest city: Monrovia (pop., 1978 est., 229,300). Language: English
(official) and tribal dialects. Religion: mainly animist. President in 1978, William R. Tolbert, Jr.

In his annual address to the nation Pres. William Tolbert called for 1978 to be the year of

Liberia

LIBERIA

Education. (1975) Primary, pupils 157,821, teachers 3,-832; secondary, pupils 32,978, teachers (1974) 1,331; vocational, pupils 851, teachers (1970) 66; teacher training, students 322, teachers 53; higher, students 2,404, teaching staff c. 190.

Finance. Monetary unit: Liberian dollar, at par with the U.S. dollar, with a free rate (Sept. 18, 1978) of L$1.96 to £1 sterling. Budget (1977–78 est.) balanced at L$148 million.

Foreign Trade. (1977) Imports L$463.5 million; exports L$447,420,000. Import sources (1976): U.S. 30%; Saudi Arabia 13%; West Germany 12%; U.K. 8%; Japan 7%; The Netherlands 6%. Export destinations (1976): West Germany 28%; U.S. 19%; Italy 14%; France 8%; Belgium-Luxembourg 8%; The Netherlands 6%; Spain 5%. Main exports: iron ore 61%; rubber 13%; timber c. 8%; diamonds 5%.

Transport and Communications. Roads (state; 1975) 7,282 km. Motor vehicles in use (1974): passenger 12,100; commercial (including buses) 10,000. Railways (1975) 493 km. Shipping (1977): merchant vessels 100 gross tons and over 2,617 (mostly owned by U.S. and other foreign interests); gross tonnage 79,982,968. Telephones (Dec. 1974) 7,000. Radio receivers (Dec. 1975) 264,000. Television receivers (Dec. 1975) 8,800.

Agriculture. Production (in 000; metric tons; 1977): rice c. 230; cassava (1976) c. 310; bananas (1976) c. 64; palm kernels c. 13; palm oil c. 27; rubber c. 80; cocoa c. 3; coffee c. 5. Livestock (in 000; 1976): cattle c. 35; sheep c. 176; goats c. 175; pigs c. 93.

Industry. Production (in 000; metric tons; 1976): iron ore (metal content) 14,010; petroleum products c. 520; diamonds (exports; metric carats) c. 400; electricity (kw-hr) c. 887,000.

"economy, accountability, and self-sufficiency."
The 1976–80 development plan was well under
way, despite a 50% increase in expenditure
through inflation. The 1977 growth rate was good

During a stopover in Liberia on his way home from talks in Nigeria, U.S. Pres. Jimmy Carter was greeted by Liberian Pres. William Tolbert. It was the first official visit of a U.S. president to Liberia, which was founded largely by former slaves from the U.S.

despite increasing labour disputes, with a balance of payments surplus and 49% of the L$412.8 million external debt repaid. During 1976–77 foreign investment rose 52% to L$75.8 million. Firestone extended its rubber cultivation by 22,500 ac; West Germany increased its timber interests; and Britain invested £3,850,000 in small landholding projects. The government continued to set up an industrial free zone in Monrovia.

A joint Liberian-Nigerian economic commission was established following the visit to Monrovia in February of Nigeria's chief of state, Lieut. Gen. Olusegun Obasanjo. Tolbert in March was host to a "unity summit" in Monrovia attended by the presidents of The Gambia, Guinea, Ivory Coast, Senegal, and Togo, for the purpose of patching up past quarrels. In June Tolbert visited Guinea to consolidate relationships. Also in June he went to China, where he asked for economic help, "not misleading ideologies." In April U.S. Pres. Jimmy Carter visited Monrovia during his African tour and had talks with Tolbert.   (MOLLY MORTIMER)

Libraries

The universal availability of publications (UAP) was the theme of the 1978 annual general council of the International Federation of Library Associations and Institutions (IFLA), held at Strbske Pleso, Czech. The meteoric rise of the British Library Lending Division as a major international source of loans and photocopies provided a model

for UAP, and the UAP program called upon every country to collect all its own publications and to make them universally available.

In September 1977 an international congress on national bibliographies had been held at the headquarters of UNESCO in Paris. Its first recommendation had been to draft a model for the legal deposit of publications in national libraries in order to facilitate national bibliographies. This was part of UNESCO's National Technical Information Systems program. The advisory committee and the first plenary session of UNESCO's General Information Program met in Paris in October and November 1977, respectively, and recommended greater international coordination of information resources, as well as the training of professional librarians, to satisfy the information needs of all countries. Simultaneously, the UNESCO Committee on Data for Science and Technology established a World Data Referral Centre in Paris to facilitate the finding of sources of scientific information; it was to collaborate with other international information organizations such as the International Nuclear Information System and the Agricultural Information System. A regional branch of the latter reported good progress in spreading agricultural information in nine Asian countries.

Such international developments necessitated the growth of national networks of libraries in each country, exemplified by the networking activities of the U.S. Library of Congress in Washington, D.C. There in 1977 the Network Advisory Committee formed a task force of technical staff

Interior view of the Illinois Regional Library for the Blind and Physically Handicapped, which opened in June. Consulting architect was Stanley Tigerman & Associates in association with the Bureau of Architecture, City of Chicago. Stanley Tigerman was architect in charge of design; Jerome R. Butler, city architect; and Robert E. Fugman, associate in charge.

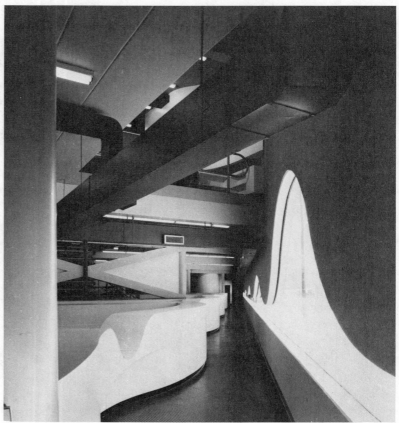

GARY SETTLE—THE NEW YORK TIMES

A portion of the private library of Sigmund Freud was opened in May to scholars at the Columbia Health Sciences Library in New York City. It had previously been housed at the nearby New York State Psychiatric Institute library.

known as the Network Technical Architecture Group, which linked computerized bibliographical organizations to the Library of Congress to form a national network for identifying and locating publications of all kinds, in print, microfilm, and machine-readable forms.

A feature of 1978 was the development of public library service to minority populations and to the disadvantaged. In the U.S. this was exemplified by the publication of guidelines for service to the 11 million Spanish-speaking population, the activities of El Centro Hispanico de Información with a bilingual staff at the Brooklyn, N.Y., Public Library, and the exchanges of staff between Tucson (Ariz.) Public Library and libraries across the border in Mexico. In the U.K. there was the publication of *The Libraries Choice* (Her Majesty's Stationary Office) and *A Public Library Service for Ethnic Minorities in Great Britain* (the Library Association). The National Library of Canada developed a multilingual biblioservice, and Denmark provided library service for immigrant workers.

The domination of the printed word was once more threatened by trials of an information system for the general public using an adapted television set in combination with the telephone. An example was Viewdata, a service offered by the British Post Office. International computer links continued to develop; in France nine medical libraries were equipped with terminals linked to the MED-LARS network in the U.S., and a dozen French

academic libraries were joined to European and U.S. networks and to the French PASCAL network of the Centre National de la Recherche Scientifique.

The training of librarians continued to be an urgent need for less developed countries. The School of Librarianship in Kampala, Uganda, celebrated ten years of intense activity in training East African librarians, and similar efforts were reported in training French-speaking West African librarians, notably at the school in Dakar, Senegal, and at the École Nationale Supérieure des Bibliothécaires near Lyon, France. In India a library science education seminar at Chandigarh stressed the need for research and for the improvement of library training; only five Indian universities were offering training in library science.

The completion of several large library buildings in the U.S.S.R. was reported. These included the National Library of the Turkmen S.S.R. at Ashkhabad, with space for three million volumes and quiet central patios for readers; the new building of the Fundamental Library of the Social Sciences in Moscow, with room for seven million volumes and a large, light, and spacious upper floor for readers; and the new State Public Scientific and Technical Library in Moscow, with ten million volumes and 1,200 seats for readers.

A highlight of public library development was the first year of operation of the library in the Centre National d'Art et de Culture Georges Pompidou in Paris, better known as the Centre Beaubourg. This three-story library, with its entrance on the middle floor, held about 300,000 books, the same number of slides, and large collections of films, microfilms, microfiches, phonograph records, and maps, all with free and open access. Of the 1,300 seats for readers, 250 were equipped with audiovisual apparatus. By February 1978, the end of the first year, the library was able to report an average daily attendance of more than 12,000 persons.

(ANTHONY THOMPSON)

[441.C.2.d; 613.D.1.a; 735.H]

Libya

A socialist republic on the north coast of Africa, Libya is bounded by the Mediterranean Sea, Egypt, the Sudan, Tunisia, Algeria, Niger, and Chad. Area: 1,749,000 sq km (675,000 sq mi). Pop. (1977 est.): 3,014,100. Cap. and largest city: Tripoli (pop., 1973 census, municipality, 551,000). Language: Arabic. Religion: predominantly Muslim. Secretary-general of the General People's Congress in 1978, Col. Muammar al-Qaddafi.

The moves of Egypt's Pres. Anwar as-Sadat toward reconciliation with Israel in 1978 were vehemently opposed by Libyan leader Col. Muammar al-Qaddafi. To express his disfavour Qaddafi joined the meeting of high-level Arab "rejection front" leaders in Damascus, Syria, in September, where he urged action on the part of Arab countries on behalf of the Palestinians.

In June and July Qaddafi enjoyed a successful tour of the Soviet Union and the Eastern bloc countries. The Libyan leader was greeted by huge

Libya

Libyan leader Muammar al-Qaddafi, King Hussein of Jordan, and PLO leader Yasir Arafat (left to right) met in Damascus, Syria, in September to discuss the Egyptian-Israeli peace negotiations.

crowds in all the countries he visited, and opportunities to speak were extended to him. On his way home Qaddafi stopped in Malta to confirm his support for that nation's precarious economy.

Far-reaching changes were set in motion at home by the measures that implemented the egalitarian message in volume two of Qaddafi's *Green Book*, published in early 1978. The first volume had discussed government and political representation. The second, *The Solution of the Economic Problem*, was concerned with the organization of production and the distribution of its benefits; it was preoccupied with the idea that "whoever possesses your needs controls or exploits you" and concluded that in the "final stage profit will automatically disappear and there will be no need for money." The most severe restrictions that resulted from the book were applied to housing. Since only one house per family was to be allowed, all privately owned rental properties were taken over by the government. A limit of 10,000 dinars was placed on personal bank deposits; meanwhile, the movement overseas of funds that would naturally follow such moves was restricted. Gold disappeared from the market, and there were signs of conspicuous consumption of such items as automobiles. Almost all the country's production and commerce were handled by government agencies.

Because traditional Islamic law unambiguously upholds the right of an individual to own property, Qaddafi found himself in conflict with the religious leadership at home and throughout the Islamic world. He responded by imprisoning some local religious leaders opposed to the guidance of the *Green Book*. The people, meanwhile, received constant reminders of the *Green Book*'s message, recited in Koranic style on radio and TV.

Libya had a good year for winter crops with a record level of grain production. Summer crops continued to be severely affected by the shortage of groundwater, and summer crop acreages were declining. Oil remained the main source of revenue, and Libya maintained its share of world production while complaining loudly of the decline in the value of its oil exports because of inflation and the depreciation of the U.S. dollar. The economy

LIBYA

Education. (1976–77) Primary, pupils 568,781, teachers 26,385; secondary, pupils 172,250, teachers 12,025; vocational, pupils 4,990, teachers 403; teacher training, students 21,719, teachers 2,006; higher, students 12,459, teaching staff 350.

Finance. Monetary unit: Libyan dinar, with (Sept. 18, 1978) a par value of 0.296 dinar to U.S. $1 (free rate of 0.580 dinar = £1 sterling). Gold, SDR's, and foreign exchange (June 1978) U.S. $4,478,000,000. Budget (1975 actual): revenue 1,997,575,000 dinars (including petroleum revenue of 1,283,995,000 dinars); expenditure 2,323,530,-000 dinars. Gross national product (1977) 5,182,000,000 dinars. Money supply (Dec. 1977) 1,276,000,000 dinars. Cost of living (Tripoli; 1975 = 100; March 1978) 140.8.

Foreign Trade. (1977) Imports (fob) c. 1,415,000,000 dinars; exports 2,955,500,000 dinars. Import sources: Italy c. 26%; West Germany c. 14%; France c. 9%; U.S. c. 7%; U.K. 6%; Japan c. 6%; Belgium-Luxembourg c. 5%. Export destinations: U.S. c. 36%; West Germany c. 19%; Italy c. 14%; Spain c. 5%. Main export: crude oil 100%.

Transport and Communications. Roads (including tracks; 1976) c. 20,000 km (including 8,700 km surfaced). Motor vehicles in use (1975): passenger 263,100; commercial (including buses) 131,300. Air traffic (1976): 700 million passenger-km; freight 6.9 million net ton-km. Shipping (1977): vessels 100 gross tons and over 53; gross tonnage 673,969. Shipping traffic: goods loaded (1977) 92,720,000 metric tons, unloaded (1975) 9,619,000 metric tons. Telephones (Dec. 1974) 102,000. Radio licenses (Dec. 1975) 106,000. Television licenses (Dec. 1975) 10,-000.

Agriculture. Production (in 000; metric tons; 1977): barley c. 200; wheat c. 70; potatoes (1976) c. 66; watermelons c. 100; tomatoes c. 204; onions c. 44; oranges c. 24; olives c. 100; dates c. 70. Livestock (in 000; 1976): sheep c. 3,360; goats c. 1,125; cattle c. 123; camels c. 120; asses c. 73.

Industry. Production (in 000; metric tons; 1976): petroleum products c. 2,540; crude oil (1977) 100,144; electricity (Tripolitania; excluding most industrial production; kw-hr) 1,490,000.

and its further development were sorely affected by labour shortages, an aftermath of the return of many Egyptian labourers to Egypt in 1977. By June the employment of labour was being controlled at the Cabinet level. (J. A. ALLAN)

Liechtenstein

Liechtenstein

A constitutional monarchy between Switzerland and Austria, Liechtenstein is united with Switzerland by a customs and monetary union. Area: 160 sq km (62 sq mi). Pop. (1977 est.): 24,730. Cap. and largest city: Vaduz (pop., 1976 est., 4,620). Language: German. Religion (1976): Roman Catholic 84%. Sovereign prince, Francis Joseph II; chiefs of government in 1978, Walter Kieber and, from April 26, Hans Brunhart.

In the elections of Feb. 2, 1978, the Patriotic Union Party (PUP) defeated the Progressive Citizens' Party (PCP). A crisis of more than two months followed when the vice-president and former chief of government, Walter Kieber (PCP), refused to relinquish the foreign affairs portfolio. After intervention by Prince Francis Joseph II, the post was abolished; its diplomatic functions were taken over by the new chief of government, Hans Brunhart (PUP), and its juridical and economic functions by Kieber.

The profusion of "letter box" companies registered in Liechtenstein was of concern to fiscal and monetary authorities in Switzerland. The Swiss National Bank endeavoured to reach an understanding that would regularize the principality's adherence to Swiss exchange controls. Fritz Leutwiler, president of the Liechtenstein Central Bank, desired a formal agreement to ensure that Swiss currency measures applied equally in both countries.

In September, Liechtenstein became the 22nd member of the Council of Europe, gaining recognition of full statehood. (K.M. SMOGORZEWSKI)

LIECHTENSTEIN
   Education. (1977–78) Primary and secondary, pupils 3,-807, teachers 176.
   Finance and Trade. Monetary unit: Swiss franc, with (Sept. 18, 1978) a free rate of SFr 1.58 to U.S. $1 (SFr 3.09 = £1 sterling). Budget (1977 rev. est.): revenue SFr 189,670,000; expenditure SFr 189,320,000. Exports (1976) SFr 597.8 million. Export destinations: Switzerland 40%; EEC 30%; EFTA (other than Switzerland) 8%. Main exports: metal manufactures, furniture, chemicals, pottery. Tourism (1976) 74,462 visitors.

Life Sciences

In a year when confirmation of the existence of "genes in pieces" rocked the life sciences by overturning long-standing assumptions about the structure and function of genes in higher organisms (see *Molecular Biology*, below), it seemed easy to overlook progress along other important lines of genetic research. Refinement of recombinant DNA technology and gene-synthesis techniques in recent years had made it possible to provide one kind of organism with functional genes that had been either chemically synthesized or derived from another, sometimes very different species, and thereby to endow the recipient organism with the ability to make, or express, protein products foreign to its nature. These methods had been foreseen early by geneticists as powerful tools to create biological factories for manufacturing important human hormones and enzymes from cultures of rapidly multiplying bacteria.

A significant milestone came late in 1977 when Herbert Boyer of the University of California, San Francisco, and co-workers succeeded in introducing a working synthetic gene for a form of mammalian somatostatin into the bacterium *Escherichia coli* and then extracting the hormone from bacterial cultures. Then in June 1978 a team led by Walter Gilbert of Harvard University announced that a gene for a form of rat insulin, derived from messenger RNA, had been successfully introduced and made to function in *E. coli*. Finally, in September a ten-member team from the City of Hope National Medical Center and Genentech, Inc., both in California, reported that chemically synthesized genes for the two amino-acid chains which together compose the human insulin molecule had been separately inserted and made to function in *E. coli*. To make an intact insulin molecule the two chains subsequently were extracted and purified from separate bacterial cultures and then joined chemically. Whereas complications of the process presented difficulties in adapting it for efficient large-scale production, its existence demonstrated that human insulin indeed could be derived from bacterial sources.

In closely related research Paul Berg and co-workers of Stanford University announced in October the first successful transplant, using DNA recombinant techniques, of a functional gene between mammalian species—specifically, a gene that codes for a part of the rabbit hemoglobin molecule into cells of the African green monkey. Their achievement represented perhaps one of the initial steps toward a future science of genetic therapeutics, whereby defective or absent genes in humans would be routinely replaced by correctly functioning counterparts. (CHARLES M. CEGIELSKI) [339.C]

ZOOLOGY

Several interesting cases of mimicry came to light during 1978. Theodore W. Pietsch and David B. Grobecker of California State University reported on a Philippine anglerfish that utilizes a lure resembling a small fish. Anglers are sedentary marine fish that attract prey by means of a fleshy lure attached to a modified spine on the head. The device conserves energy and is thus of high adaptive value to the fish. In the case of a species of *Antennarius*, the lure was found to be a nearly exact replica of a small fish found in the same region. The lure has stripes and "eyespots," is laterally compressed, and even has "fins." It is whipped about to fool prey into mistaking it for a real fish. This discovery appeared to be the first such of an angler lure resembling a living fish and was considered an example of highly aggressive mimicry.

Life Insurance:
see Industrial Review

COURTESY, WILLIAM EBERHARD, UNIVERSIDAD DEL VALLE, CALI, COLOMBIA AND SMITHSONIAN TROPICAL RESEARCH INSTITUTE, CANAL ZONE

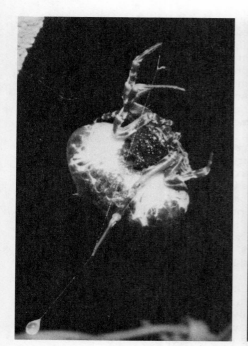 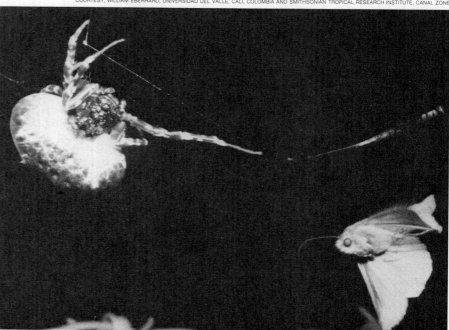

Awaiting prey, the bolas spider holds a sticky ball suspended from its legs by a thread (left). The spider apparently exudes a chemical sex attractant to lure male moths within range of its weapon, which it whips through the air to snare them (right).

Another interesting example involved a "wolf-in-sheep's-clothing" type of behaviour. Thomas Eisner and co-workers at Cornell University, Ithaca, N.Y., reported that an insect larva (*Chrysopa slossonae*) disguises itself as its aphid prey by plucking a waxy wool-like secretion from the aphids and carrying the material around on its own back. This disguise was found to protect it from assault by ants that ordinarily guard the aphids. When the investigators stripped larvae of their woolly disguise, the guardian ants promptly removed the exposed impostors from the aphid colonies. Although other insects were known to carry "trash" as a defense against predators, the present situation was the first known wherein such behaviour results in mimicry of the prey by the predator.

A third case involved chemical mimicry. William G. Eberhard of the Universidad del Valle in Colombia obtained evidence that mature female bolas spiders (*Mastophora* species) apparently mimic the female sex-attractant pheromone of their moth prey (*Spodoptera frugiperda*). A sex pheromone is a specific chemical emitted by a female to attract males of its own species. The bolas spider has an inefficient trapping method that involves the use of a sticky ball of thread instead of the usual web. Its production of sex attractant mimic, however, presumably improves the chances for successful capture of its prey, which were seen at times to make repeated "passes" at the spider! It was concluded that the spider produces the pheromone only when hunting, because prey approach the spider only during this time. Definitive proof would have to await chemical determination of the pheromone.

Many reports during the year touched on aspects of animal reproduction. One finding involved the hormonal control of mating behaviour in the leopard frog, *Rana pipiens*. Carol Diakow of Adelphi University, Garden City, N.Y., found that a pituitary hormone, arginine-8-vasotocin, inhibits the production of the release call in sexually receptive females. These frogs mate by a process known as amplexus (clasping), wherein the male clasps the female from behind and sheds sperm into the water at the same time that she sheds eggs. Unreceptive females emit a release call, which signals the male to cease clasping, but receptive females lack this call. Injection of the hormone brought about a reduction in the number of unreceptive females emitting the release call; injections of an inactive control substance had no effect. The hormone acts by bringing about an accumulation of salt and water in the frog's body, the increased pressure acting through some physiological mechanism to inhibit production of the call. This was shown by placing unreceptive females in a salt solution (Ringer solution), which by itself produced a decrease in the frequency of release calls. Unreceptive control frogs in tap or de-ionized water were unaffected.

Another interesting reproductive study concerned the egg pigments of ground-nesting birds. G. S. Bakken of Indiana State University and co-workers found that the usual vertebrate protective pigment, melanin, is replaced in these eggshells by other pigments that are much less absorptive in near-infrared (near-IR) light. An eggshell must be protectively coloured yet prevented from absorbing too much heat, which would kill the embryo. Although melanin is excellent for protective coloration, it has a high capacity to absorb near-IR. The pigments that replace melanin are protoporphyrins (heme pigments) and bilins (bile pigments). Unpigmented eggshell has a near-IR reflectance greater than 90%. The addition of these nonmelanin pigments did not significantly decrease this reflectance but presumably conferred protective coloration. Melanins were found to be replaced by the other pigments in 25 species of birds from nine families, indicating the widespread nature of the phenomenon and providing a striking example of the use of a specific substance to solve one problem without creating another.

One recent study concerned biochemical differences between skeletal muscle enzymes of two closely related species of North Pacific fish found at different depths. Joseph Siebenaller and George N. Somero of the Scripps Institution of Oceanography, La Jolla, Calif., studied the lactate dehydrogenases (LDH) of Sebastolobus alascanus and S. altivelus—which live at depths of 180–440 m (590–1,440 ft) and 550–1,300 m (1,800–4,260 ft), respectively—to learn if biochemical differences might be related to the different depth distributions. The enzyme LDH catalyzes the important reaction that reduces pyruvic acid to lactic acid. The investigators found that there are indeed pressure sensitivity differences in the LDH's of the two species. When LDH from the shallower species was placed at the pressure normally encountered only by the deeper species, its ability to bind its substrate, pyruvic acid, decreased. Thus, its ability to catalyze its reaction decreased, because substrate binding is the essential first step in the reaction. In addition, the ability of LDH from the shallower species to bind its cofactor (NADH) also decreased when it was placed at the higher pressure. This would also decrease its ability to catalyze its reaction, because the cofactor must be intimately bound to the enzyme for the reaction to take place.

Both results show that if the shallower species were suddenly moved to deeper water, its LDH would function less efficiently. Presumably these biochemical differences were important in establishing the existing differences in depth distribution between the two species. Previous studies had shown that pressure effects indeed were useful in explaining such differences. However, this study also involved closely related species with similar life histories found at nearly identical temperatures, thereby minimizing the possible influence of factors other than water pressure on the results obtained.

Recently, the pineal gland, which functions as a light receptor or "third eye" in some lower vertebrates, was implicated in the control of swimming behaviour in frog tadpoles by A. Roberts of the University of Bristol in the U.K. He found that if tadpoles of the South African clawed frog (Xenopus laevis) were shadowed some of them started to swim. This shadow response depends upon the presence of the pineal eye on the top of the head, although the lateral eyes are not required. At this stage of frog development the pineal eye has photoreceptors, which are connected to the brain by nerves. This connection via the pineal stalk was found to be necessary for the observed response. The pineal had been implicated previously in the regulation of a variety of functions in amphibians, including control of pigmentation, circadian (24-hour) activity patterns, phototaxis (movement in response to light), compass orientation, and the perception of linearly polarized light. These results indicate that the pineal eye could have mediated similar shadow responses in primitive vertebrates before paired, image-forming, lateral eyes evolved.

Finally, a team of British researchers described the case of a dominance hierarchy (pecking order) in sea anemones. R. C. Brace and J. Pavey of the University of Nottingham observed that when two anemones of the same species (Actinia equina) were brought together, aggressive behaviour developed between them such that one "won" and the other "lost." The winner remained open and active, whereas the loser tended to retract its tentacles and sometimes detached from the substrate. Using many such encounters they constructed two hierarchies, based on "aggress first" (initial aggressor) and "win." The initial aggressor almost always won the encounter, and larger anemones tended to be winners. This was regarded as being the first description of a dominance hierarchy in a lower invertebrate. (RONALD R. NOVALES)
[312.C.3.b; 313.J.3.e.vii; 342.A.6.e; 342.C]

Entomology. By 1978 a serious upsurge of malaria became evident in various parts of the world. During the 1960s massive use of DDT against malarial mosquitos had all but wiped out the disease in many countries. Fearing pollution, governments then discontinued use of the insecticide, and populations of mosquitos had been building up since. Even where DDT spraying resumed, the years of insecticidal treatment had often selected resistant strains of mosquitos, some having a new pattern of behaviour; e.g., females that fly into a dwelling for a meal and then fly straight out to rest on exterior walls not treated with insecticide.

V. T. H. Gunaratne, director of the World Health Organization's New Delhi office in India, warned of an additional danger: kala-azar, which is spread by phlebotomid sand flies and had been rare in the DDT era, was increasing alarmingly. Like malaria the disease is caused by protozoal parasites, affects liver and spleen, and causes fever; untreated it is usually fatal within three years. Gunaratne urged health authorities to use DDT again but pointed out that the flies, which formerly hovered within a few feet of the ground, were flying up to ceilings, requiring more spraying.

William S. Bowers of the State Agricultural Experiment Station, Geneva, N.Y., and Rafael Martinez-Pardo of the Instituto de Agroquímica y Tecnología de Alimentos, Valencia, Spain, investigated further the natural insecticides called precocenes that Bowers's group had previously discovered in plants. Precocene II prevented development or caused regression of the corpora allata of insects, the endocrine glands that produce juvenile hormone. Immature stages became premature adults, and lack of the hormone in adult females prevented or reversed development of the ovaries.

Another new kind of insecticide, Dimilin (diflubenzuron), discovered by the Dutch firm of Philips-Duphar B.V. and tested in the U.S. by Thompson-Hayward Chemical Co., was found to inhibit synthesis of chitin, a principal constituent of the exoskeleton that invests insects and related invertebrates. Concentrations of 15–60 ml (0.5–2 oz) per acre were toxic to larvae, which died when attempting to molt, but not to other animals. Neither were fungi affected despite their chitin content. Insects were not all equally susceptible, and Dimilin promised to be the first effective insecticide more toxic to the boll weevil than to natural enemies of cotton pests. The chemical was very stable, however, giving rise to fears that its persistence in the environment might have deleterious effects; but its discovery could well lead to other, safer inhibitors of chitin synthesis.

One reason for the high cost of silk is the need for mulberry leaves in the diet of the silkworm, and much attention has been given to finding substitutes, especially at Kyoto University, Japan. Within the past year Yasuyuki Yamada and Asao Okamoto reported that the 10–40% leaves needed to make "artificial" diets palatable could be replaced by tissue cultures of mulberry cells, but only if grown in light to develop their chlorophyll content. Keizo Hayashiya, noting that caterpillars reared on diets with extracts of leaves were more susceptible to viral disease than those fed fresh leaves, found that a red-fluorescent protein, derived partly from chlorophyll and partly from a protein produced in the silkworm's gut, had antiviral properties. Fortunately, chloroplasts from any source, *e.g.*, spinach, could provide the necessary chlorophyll. Meanwhile, Masaru Kato iden-

tified as labile phenolic compounds the mulberry flavour essential to make the larvae eat, and the way at last seemed clear to produce artificial diets entirely without mulberry.

Molting is a critical process for an insect, when all cuticular structures, including delicate linings of internal breathing tubes and parts of mouthparts and external sense organs, must be detached and replaced. In West Germany Werner Gnatzy of the Johann Wolfgang Goethe-Universität, Frankfurt am Main, and Jürgen Tautz of the Universität Konstanz investigated how mechanoreceptive hairs of a species of caterpillar fared during the changeover. Loosening of the old cuticle from the developing new one occurred some 40 hours before the fourth stage finally shed its skin to reveal the fifth, yet sensitivity of the hairs persisted even up to 30 minutes before the molt. They found that as the old cuticle separated, the dendrite innervating each hair elongated to span the gap. A new hair was laid down under the old cuticle with the elongated dendrite emerging from the new hair's base, and at this point the dendritic extension was pinched off at the moment of shedding the old, the remainder serving the new hair.

(PETER W. MILES)

[313.H.5.o; 321.B.9.c.i; 321.E.2.a; 724.C.8.f]

Ornithology. Birds in urban areas formed the topic of an entire symposium at the 17th International Ornithological Congress in Berlin. Anthony

Large larva of *Toxorhynchites rutilus rutilus,* a nonbiting mosquito, preys on smaller larvae of *Aedes aegypti,* the carrier of yellow fever virus. The predatory mosquito was under study as a biological control agent against several disease-carrying mosquitoes.

J. Erskine of the Canadian Wildlife Service considered urban birds in the context of the Canadian climate and of human settlement in Canada. The harsh winter climate in most of Canada greatly reduces the possibilities of year-round residence by birds and also shortens the growing season, slowing revegetation of disturbed areas. Most Canadian cities and towns are less than 100 years old, and nearly all expanded their boundaries in recent decades with use of private cars for transport. Areas of new construction are populated largely by birds of introduced species previously adapted to urban habitats in Eurasia. Native birds appear gradually as height and density of vegetation increases, but they seldom if ever approach the densities attained by the introduced species.

In summer, except in largely unvegetated areas, urban bird densities are often as high as in the better natural communities nearby, although usually with fewer species than in natural habitats. In winter, however, far more birds inhabit urban centres than the surrounding country. Correlations of urban birds and their habitats must consider such man-influenced factors as age and density of buildings, age and density of vegetation, and income level of owners, as well as the climatic regime; *e.g.*, length of growing season and depth and duration of snow cover.

Veteran British city ornithologist Stanley Cramp spoke on changes in the breeding birds of inner London since 1900. A mainly built-up area of 16 sq km (6.2 sq mi), with large parks, squares, private gardens, several ornamental waters, and a stretch of river had been delimited for the purpose of this long-term study. Cramp reported a steady increase in the diversity of breeding species, with 24 breeding regularly in 1900, 30 in 1950, and 40 in 1957, with any lost species more than offset by new colonizers. A further 17 species nested irregularly, a few quite frequently. In recent years regular censuses, mainly in the large parks, showed increases in the numbers of many breeding species, including several which are entirely or largely insectivorous. The main reasons appeared to be a much more favourable attitude to birds among the general public, better legal protection, active conservation (including the provision of sanctuaries and habitat improvements), and probably the effects of cleaner air.

Brian Bertram of the University of Cambridge discussed cooperative breeding in ostriches. In East Africa ostriches nest communally. A male establishes a territory, and several females lay eggs in a nest within it. Only one of the females, the "major" hen, takes turns with the male in all the work of guarding the nest and subsequently in incubating the eggs. In many nests more eggs are laid than can be covered by an incubating bird. Therefore, before incubation starts a number of eggs are pushed to an outer ring that is not incubated. There are some indications that the major hen's own eggs are unlikely to be among these doomed outer eggs. A pair of ostriches that has hatched chicks apparently competes with other similarly successful pairs for guardianship of all the young; thus, very large mixed broods may be formed.

Neal Griffith Smith of the Canal Zone Biological Area studied aspects of the nesting association of certain tropical birds and tyrant flycatchers in Central and South America with colonies of aggressive social insects. Although it is the birds that choose to nest close to the wasps or bees, and not vice versa, advantages accrue to both partners. For the birds the association provides varying degrees of protection against predators; for the hymenoptera the proximity of the birds provides protection against certain birds and mammals that specialize in eating their larvae. At least in South America, those species of bird that habitually associate with bees and wasps have a peculiar odour, whereas their close relatives, which are not vespiphiles, lack this smell.

A great rarity during the year was the publication of a book on birds from China. Cheng Tsohsin, the distinguished Chinese ornithologist, listed 1,166 species in a book of 571 pages, with 828 distribution maps, giving names in Latin, English, and Russian as well as Chinese.

(JEFFERY BOSWALL)

[313.J.6; 342.A.6.e.iii; 352.B.2.c]

MARINE BIOLOGY

Although ecologists tend to define food webs in terms of biomass, organic matter, or energy, recent work in the U.K. at the Department of Agriculture and Fisheries for Scotland emphasized the importance of species composition and age structure. Relative size structure of herbivorous copepods, which make up a subclass of generally minute crustaceans, and their phytoplankton food was found to be more important than biomass of each trophic level (all the organisms in a step of a food chain) in determining energy transfer along the food chain. Surveys from 1970–74 in the southern North Sea showed several phytoplankton species of *Ceratium* appearing earlier and for longer in the year than in the 1960s. The changes relate to increased salinity from increased flow of English Channel water into the North Sea, induced by increased westerly winds associated with changed atmospheric pressure distribution over the Atlantic.

Studies of meiofauna, very small animals living between sand grains, had been hampered by problems of handling large numbers of samples. These were overcome by embedding samples in resin, using a technique developed for transmission electron microscopy, to provide man-made "fossil" samples of both soft- and hard-bodied forms and of the small protozoans, algae, and fungi attached to the sand grains.

Ghost crabs (species of *Ocypode*) occur commonly on tropical and subtropical beaches, yet knowledge of their ecology is largely anecdotal. In North Carolina *O. quadrata* was found not to be mainly a scavenger as was commonly thought but the top carnivore feeding on filter-feeding mole crabs (*Emerita*) and clams (*Donax*). It appeared to have no competitor or predator in what is a simple food chain.

A new mechanism of buoyancy in deep-water fish was demonstrated in *Acanthonus armatus*. The fish has a relatively massive head which, except

Kryptophanaron alfredi, a species of flashlight fish not seen since its discovery in 1907, made its reappearance in January with six captured specimens. The fish's common name derives from the presence beneath each eye of a light organ filled with luminescent bacteria.

for a small brain, is filled with dilute, low-density fluid, permitting an approach to neutral buoyancy. An intriguing example of "adoption" behaviour was described in mysid crustaceans. Commonly called opossum shrimp, these small animals normally incubate their young in an external brood pouch into which populations in the Adriatic Sea were shown to introduce larvae from other females. The ability to identify and adopt other young of the same species serves to protect accidentally released young from predation by the adults.

Studies on migration of eels showed that elvers (juveniles) of the American eel are able to orient to weak direct-current electric fields. Elver migration could conceivably be influenced by electric fields generated in the major ocean current systems. Crabs in tropical waters are generally more agile and powerful than their temperate-water counterparts. Work on tropical Pacific crabs showed that some families are able to crush mollusks by intense, sustained pressure and that an increase in shell thickness of gastropod mollusks in these regions parallels the increased crushing power of the crabs.

British Antarctic Survey work showed interesting differences in chick development in black-browed and grey-headed albatrosses. The former raises chicks on krill and fish 30 days quicker than the latter, which feed on squid and fish. Interchanging chicks between parents showed that this difference is due to a dietary effect, probably related to the low calorific value and calcium content of squid.

New techniques to produce all-female stocks of salmonid fish for aquaculture included administering the sex hormone 17β-estradiol, which induces male-to-female sex reversal. Unlike males, females reach marketable size before undergoing sexual maturation, so the technique avoids loss of food conversion efficiency, deterioration of flesh quality, and increased susceptibility to infection, all of which occur at maturation. The farming of single-sex stocks of fish also safeguards against accidental establishment of nonindigenous species imported for aquaculture.

(ERNEST NAYLOR)

[354.B.2 and 4]

BOTANY

Attempts to explain how members of a class of hormones called auxins interact with plant cells to promote lengthwise growth of the plant continued to be reported in 1978. In order to identify the possible receptor sites in the cell where auxins might exercise their primary effect, the binding of radioactively labeled auxins to different particulate components of coleoptile cells was followed. (The coleoptile is the first leaf of an emerging seedling of grass or other monocotyledon.) Most binding was to the internal system of membranes called the endoplasmic reticulum (ER), as measured by the correspondence between the distribution of radioactivity and that of one of the ER-localized enzymes. A second binding site was recognized and was suggested to be the tonoplast; *i.e.*, the membrane enclosing the cell's central vacuole.

Because the cell-wall extension that results from auxin treatment was believed to be a consequence of H^+ (hydrogen ion) secretion, it was suggested that auxins bound to the ER might stimulate H^+ transport into the lumen (internal space) of the ER, from which the ions could be carried to the outside of the cell via the Golgi apparatus, a structure that is known to be involved with the transport of materials across the cell membrane. It was also shown, however, that activity of the enzyme ATP-ase, thought to be necessary for H^+ transport, is not associated with the receptor sites. Support for the contention that these most recently reported binding sites are physiologically significant was that the degree of binding of many different auxins and auxin analogs paralleled their effect on coleoptile elongation.

The three major pathways utilized by plants to fix, or incorporate, carbon from atmospheric CO_2 had been recognized for several years, but the functional significance of the C_3, C_4, and CAM (crassulacean acid metabolism) pathways was not always clear. In an investigation of the geographical distribution of species of dicotyledons in North America using the C_4 pathway in relation to many different climatic parameters, strong correlations were found between the frequency of C_4 species and two parameters that strongly affect plant water balance. These correlations indicated that in dicotyledonous plants the C_4 pathway might have evolved as a genetic adaptation to arid conditions, better enabling the plants to cope with water stress. An interesting observation was that the C_3 species within C_4 families also correlated with limited water supply, suggesting that for these families, C_4 photosynthesis is one of several adaptive properties that favour their presence in arid regions. This distribution of C_4 dicotyledons was different from that of the C_4 grasses, however, which had earlier been shown to correlate with temperature; thus the C_4 pathway was thought to confer different ecological attributes to different plant taxa. Other work showed that succulents grown under water stress could switch from the C_3 pathway to the CAM pathway, indicating that changes in CO_2-fixation routes could result as physiological adaptation to dry conditions as well as genetic adaptations.

The marine alga *Prochloron*, a procaryote (a non-nucleated primitive cell) and a possible "missing link" in the evolution of eucaryotic plants (higher plants, formed of cells with well-defined nuclei), was further investigated in 1978. In an analysis of the pigments and pigment/protein complexes of this recently discovered organism it was confirmed that the phycobilin pigments characteristic of the procaryotic blue-green algae (cyanobacteria) is absent, whereas chlorophyll b, hitherto found only in photosynthetic eucaryotes, is present. The P-700/chlorophyll-a/protein complex common to both the procaryotic and eucaryotic photosynthesizers was identified, the proportion of total chlorophyll contributing to this complex being intermediate between the corresponding values for procaryotes and eucaryotes. Also intermediate in value between the two types are the chlorophyll/P-700 ratio and the chlorophyll-a/b ratio. Furthermore, a chlorophyll-a/b–protein complex, identical to that characteristic of eucaryotic plants, was shown to be present, and it was thought likely that this second complex had replaced the phy-

cobilin proteins as light-harvesting components of the photosynthetic unit. The characteristics of the overall pigment complement, along with the previously noted stacking of the photosynthetic membranes, lent strong support to the suggestion that *Prochloron* might represent a transition form between the cyanobacteria and the chlorophyta, and might even be a descendant of the postulated progenitor of the chloroplast.

(PETER L. WEBSTER)

[311.B.4.a; 312.A.3; 321.B.9.d.i; 322.A.7]

MOLECULAR BIOLOGY

Brain Opiates. Specific naturally occurring compounds have long been known to affect mood and perception dramatically. Opium from the poppy and cocaine from coca leaves, for example, give surcease from pain and anxiety, whereas psilocin from a kind of mushroom and mescaline from a desert succulent (peyote) induce hallucinations. Psychoactive compounds have been synthesized and studied, and the successes of psychiatry now depend largely upon their judicious use.

Consider morphine, the major active component of raw opium. Why should it decrease perception of pain, and why upon prolonged ingestion should it induce both tolerance and addiction? The hope of synthesizing nonaddictive analgesics has led to a thorough examination of the chemistry and pharmacology of the opiates. Experiments have made it clear that physiological action is a sensitive function of chemical structure. Minor changes in the structure of the morphine molecule give compounds, called agonists, that mimic the effects of natural morphine and others, called antagonists, that inhibit its effects if administered at the same time. The only way to explain this acute dependence upon chemical structure is to suppose the existence of specific binding sites on neurons (nerve cells) in the brain. Occupancy of such sites by morphine agonists modifies responsiveness of the neuron, whereas occupancy by antagonists

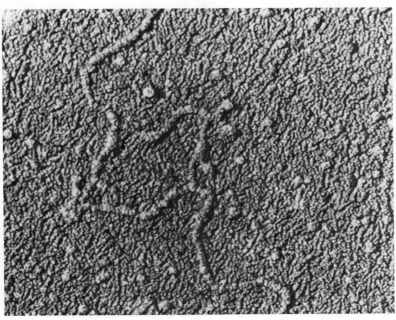

Scientists at the University of Michigan announced success in isolating and photographing single human genes. Runs of DNA that normally pair up to form a double-stranded thread were deliberately mismatched at the site of the gene under study, creating a telltale loop easily located under the electron microscope.

UPI COMPIX

blocks access by morphine or its agonists without modifying responsiveness of the neuron.

Receptor sites, specific for binding opiates, have been shown to exist through techniques making use of radioactively labeled agonists. Such methods also have shown that opiate receptors are plentiful in vertebrate nervous tissue, but not in such other tissues as liver or muscle. Invertebrates, which are not affected by opiates, do not possess these receptors. The abilities of a variety of compounds to bind to opiate receptors match their abilities to act as opiate agonists or antagonists. The anatomic distribution of opiate receptors within the brain is in accord with the known susceptibilities of the different regions of the brain to the physiological actions of opiates.

But why should the vertebrate brain possess receptors for responding to alkaloids derived from plants? To scientists it seemed most likely that these receptors were actually evolved to respond to compounds normally present in the brain. A search was launched for such substances within the brain and recently two were found and isolated. Called enkephalins, they are pentapeptides (a chain of five amino acids) that when injected into the brains of rats exhibit all of the effects of opiates. The amino-acid sequence of one of these enkephalins was found to be identical to that of a portion of β-lipotropin, a chemical known to function as a pituitary hormone. Another segment of β-lipotropin is homologous to the melanocyte-stimulating hormone. It may be that β-lipotropin serves, by fragmentation, as a precursor of other active hormones and neuroregulators.

The enkephalins are the first known representatives of a new class of neurotransmitters. Acetylcholine has long been recognized as a neurotransmitter, which is released by nerve terminals and which excites adjacent nerves. In the past few years scientists have begun to appreciate the fact that many different kinds of neurotransmitters are required to mediate and regulate the flow of signals in the central nervous system. It is, of course, essential to perceive pain, but it is also essential to be able to modify the perception of pain so that under stressful circumstances the pain does not incapacitate the organism and prevent necessary action. The enkephalins are neurotransmitters that allow modification and control of the perception of pain. Other compounds in the brain that modify and control other aspects of brain function were expected to be found.

As of late 1978 the known properties of the opiate receptors and of the enkephalins had not yet provided the key to overcoming tolerance and addiction. Induction of tolerance and addiction by prolonged administration of opiates does not change the quantity or the binding properties of the opiate receptors. Indeed, the enkephalins themselves were shown to be addictive if administered repeatedly in large doses. The explanation for tolerance and addiction seemed to involve the enzyme adenyl cyclase, which is bound to the inner surface of cell membranes and which mediates the actions of many hormones and transmitters. In general terms, a substance that binds to a specific receptor on the cell membrane can activate or inhibit adenyl cyclase. This raises or lowers the intracellular level of cyclic adenylic acid, which, in turn, modifies the action of still other enzymes. The net effect of this cascade of events is a great amplification of the initial signal, such that the binding of a few molecules of the hormone to the cell surface can modify the metabolism of the entire cell.

In the case of brain cells, binding of opiates results in an inhibition of adenyl cyclase. This inhibition is reversible if the opiate is promptly removed. If the opiate is present for many hours, however, there is a compensatory increase in the amount of adenyl cyclase. This counters the inhibitory effect of the bound opiate and thus gives rise to tolerance. When the inhibitory opiate is then removed, as during narcotic withdrawal, the increased amount of adenyl cyclase gives rise to an abnormally high level of cyclic adenylic acid in the neuron. This generates the distressful symptoms and the craving that is seen as addiction.

Genes in Pieces. Present understanding of the molecular details of gene structure and function has been derived almost exclusively from study of the intestinal bacterium *Escherichia coli* and of the viruses that infect this organism. This bacterium is a typical representative of the simple cell class referred to as procaryotes, which lack a true nucleus. Recent technological advances, notably the development of recombinant DNA methodology, has made possible the chemical analysis of gene structure in the far more complex, nucleated eucaryotic cell, which is present in all higher organisms including man. During the past two years analysis of a number of eucaryotic genes led to the surprising conclusion that a fundamental difference may exist between gene structure in procaryotic and eucaryotic cell types.

Consider first the nature of gene structure and function in procaryotic cells. In structural terms a gene is a segment of double-stranded DNA. Each strand of the DNA molecule is comprised of a linear array of four basic constituents called deoxyribonucleotides, which can be abbreviated dA, dG, dC, and dT. The two strands of DNA are said to be complementary because dA on one strand is always opposite dT on the other, whereas dG is always opposite dC. Thus, the sequence of deoxyribonucleotides on one strand is sufficient to specify the nucleotide sequence of the other. It is within the nucleotide sequence of DNA that genetic information is spelled out using this four-component alphabet. (*See* Figure 1.)

The information encoded within the DNA sequence is used to direct the synthesis of proteins, which form cellular structural elements or which act as enzymes. However, DNA does not participate directly in the process of protein synthesis. Rather, genetic information is made available for use within the cell via the synthesis of a working RNA copy of one strand of the gene. This so-called messenger RNA (mRNA) copy is single stranded and complementary and is composed of the four ribonucleotides rA, rG, rC, and rU. Three of the ribonucleotides of RNA are chemically very similar to the deoxyribonucleotides of DNA, and just as dA, dG, or dC occurs in the appropriate strand of

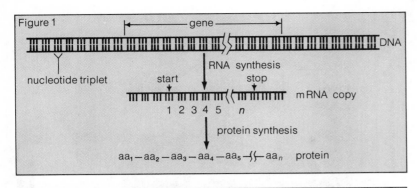

Figure 1

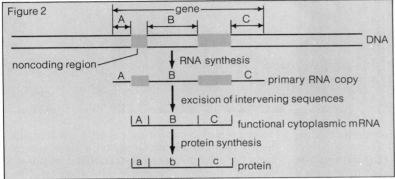

Figure 2

the gene, rA, rG, or rC appears in the mRNA copy. Whereas dT occurs in the gene, rT does not appear in the copy; instead, the ribonucleotide rU replaces it.

Messenger RNA serves to carry the genetic information from the gene to the protein-synthesis machinery where the nucleotide sequence information is used to direct the assembly of a protein from a set of basic components. These are the 20 amino acids that in a protein are linked together in various combinations in a linear fashion. The translation of mRNA information to yield the amino-acid sequence of a protein works in the following way. Each amino acid is specified by a triplet of nucleotides (called a codon) in the message. Because there are 64 triplets of unique sequence and only 20 different amino acids, almost all the amino acids are specified by more than one codon. Moreover, five of the codons can function in a specialized way. The beginning of the protein chain is signaled by one of two codons (AUG or GUG). Subsequent triplets in the mRNA are then read in a nonoverlapping fashion to direct the addition of amino acids to the growing protein chain. However, three of the 64 codons (UAG, UGA, UAA) do not specify an amino acid. When such a triplet is encountered in the mRNA, synthesis of the protein chain terminates. Hence, these three "stop" codons act as would a period in a prose sentence.

This picture of gene expression has been derived primarily from studies of the procaryote *E. coli.* Fundamental to this view has been the idea of colinearity of nucleotide sequence of the gene with the amino-acid sequence of the protein for which it codes; *e.g.,* if the third triplet in the gene specifies the third amino acid in the protein, then triplet 57 will code for amino acid 57. It has become clear, however, that this concept of strict colinearity is

not generally true in eucaryotic cells. Such evidence was first reported in 1977 by Louise Chow, Richard Gelinas, Thomas Broker, and Richard Roberts of Cold Spring Harbor Laboratory, New York, and by Phillip Sharp and his colleagues at the Massachusetts Institute of Technology. They found that runs of a human viral nucleotide sequence which were contiguous on certain cytoplasmic mRNA's were not contiguous on the DNA from which the RNA was presumably copied. This implied the existence of intervening sequences at the DNA level.

Subsequently the interruption of coding regions in a gene at the DNA level by noncoding sequences was rigorously established for several eucaryotic genes. These include antibody and β-globin genes of mouse (β-globin forms part of hemoglobin) and the gene for chicken ovalbumin (a major protein of egg white). Genes containing intervening sequences have been referred to as "genes in pieces" because they clearly violate the principle of colinearity.

The discovery of intervening sequences raised several questions concerning gene expression in eucaryotic cells. First, how is a functional message derived from a DNA segment containing noncoding regions? This point was answered by Philip Leder's laboratory at the National Institutes of Health in Bethesda, Md. Analysis of the mRNA for β-globin showed it to be derived from a larger RNA molecule. Moreover, they demonstrated that the RNA precursor contained not only the coding regions but the intervening sequences as well. Thus, functional mRNA is generated from a direct transcript of the DNA by excision of the intervening sequences and splicing together of the appropriate coding regions. This process has been termed RNA splicing. (*See* Figure 2.)

"Glove-box" sealed environment comprises part of the precautions taken at the National Institutes of Health's so-called P-4 laboratory at Fort Detrick, Maryland, the first U.S. facility certified for maximum-risk genetic research. In March government scientists detailed some of the facility's initial experiments, which would assess the risks connected with recombinant DNA research.

Second, are intervening sequences present in all eucaryotic genes? As of late 1978 the answer to this question appeared to be no. M. L. Birnstiel and his colleagues at the University of Zürich in Switzerland directly sequenced DNA segments corresponding to the genes for the sea urchin histone proteins. Comparison of these sequences with the known amino-acid sequences of this set of proteins demonstrated that the histone genes of this organism do not contain intervening sequences.

The last and most important question concerns the function of intervening sequences within the eucaryotic organism. Although there was considerable speculation, by late 1978 this point had not yet been resolved. It had been well established that gene expression is governed by a variety of regulatory mechanisms, and it is possible that the phenomenon of RNA splicing represents one such mechanism. An alternative, but perhaps related, possibility suggested by Sharp is that splicing provides a mechanism for generating a set of related proteins.

Consider, for example, the primary RNA copy in Figure 2. Suppose the intervening sequence between segments B and C contains a "stop" codon. Further, suppose this particular intervening sequence is not always spliced out. Reading of such an RNA by the protein-synthesis apparatus will occur normally through regions A and B, but the "stop" condon will prevent reading of segment C. Hence, the protein product will be of the form a-b. However, when the intervening sequence between B and C is spliced out, the terminator will be removed, and the protein product will be of the form a-b-c. Sharp's laboratory in fact obtained evidence suggesting that splicing may be responsible for such a phenomenon in certain virally infected cells.

A more general statement of the possible significance of intervening sequences was made by Walter Gilbert of Harvard University, who pointed out that existence of intervening segments affords an organism the opportunity to combine various coding sequences at the DNA level. Such an opportunity could be advantageous for a variety of reasons. For example, it was known that evolutionary development of a species occurs by selection of hardier individuals that arise as a consequence of mutational events at the DNA level. The simplest and by far most frequent type of mutational event results from a single deoxyribonucleotide change in DNA. When such an event occurs in a coding region, it usually causes a change of only a single amino acid in the corresponding protein. Nevertheless, even such a minor change usually destroys the biological activity of the protein. This renders most mutational events unfavourable, and individuals carrying such lesions will be eliminated from the population. Because significant steps in evolutionary development are presumed to reflect the appearance of new proteins which differ in their amino-acid sequence in major ways from existing molecules, evolution by such a mechanism would be an extremely slow and unfavourable process. The existence of intervening sequences, however, suggests that rapid evolution of eucaryotic organisms could occur by a mechanism involving single nucleotide changes. A simple mutational event occurring within an intervening noncoding sequence would leave adjacent coding sequences unaltered. Nevertheless, such an event could reduce the efficiency of splicing at the RNA level such that the intervening sequence is excised only part of the time. When the new mRNA containing the intervening sequence is translated by the protein-synthesis machinery, a radically new protein would result. Because normal splicing of the altered RNA would occur some of the time, however, the original mRNA would also be available to the cell, as would its protein product. As Gilbert stated, such a mechanism would permit evolution to "seek new solutions without destroying the old."

(IRWIN FRIDOVICH; PAUL LAWRENCE MODRICH)
[321.B.5; 321.C.4.c.v; 323.C.4; 339.C]

See also Earth Sciences; Environment.

Liquors, Alcoholic:
see Industrial Review

Literature

The 1978 Nobel laureate for literature, Isaac Bashevis Singer, was surely one of the more popular choices of the decade. An emigrant from Warsaw to New York who kept faith with the Polish-Yiddish culture into which he was born, he seemed, in his life and career, peculiarly representative of all the generations and millions who made the traumatic journey to the New World. In the comparatively short time during which his work had been widely translated, readers everywhere had found themselves involved in a curiously intimate way with Singer's art and the world of his novels and stories, a world in which, as the Nobel citation said, "The Middle Ages rise up . . . and permeate the present, everyday life is interwoven with wonders, reality is spun from dreams." (*See* NOBEL PRIZES; *see* also *Yiddish*, below.)

The appointment in 1976 as president of International PEN of the Peruvian novelist Mario Vargas Llosa (*see* BIOGRAPHIES) had proved to be more controversial, not least because of his sympathy for the idea of allowing the creation of a PEN centre in the Soviet Union. There was something symbolic, too, about a Peruvian at the head of the international writers' organization, at a time when readers and writers elsewhere were turning to the fresh energy and fantasy of novelists like Gabriel García Márquez, Carlos Fuentes, and other Latin-American writers rather as, 30 years earlier, war-

Isaac Bashevis Singer, winner of the 1978 Nobel Prize for Literature.

John Irving, author of *The World According to Garp*.

weary Europeans had looked hopefully to the literature of the United States. Some of this energy was born of freedom from the weight of a cultural heritage so rich it could make a writer feel there was nothing left to say. Moreover, these Latin Americans had the stimulus of a peculiarly expectant and responsive native audience for whom, as the Argentine novelist Julio Cortázar told the PEN congress, "literature is a part of life and not of leisure, part of politics and history."

In Britain an intense debate went on for half the year in the correspondence columns of the *Times Literary Supplement* about whether or how writers should organize at a time when publishing was becoming increasingly concentrated and industrialized. There were some genteel cries of horror at the thought that the Royal Society of Literature might turn into anything like a trade union. Nevertheless, and perhaps noting the effectiveness of the West German and Swedish writers' unions, 44% of voting members opted for unionization when the society took their opinion; 20% were opposed and 35% were "don't knows."

The growing influence of the women's movement showed in the spread of feminist publishing houses in Europe and the U.S. and in a number of novels preoccupied with the changes in consciousness that the movement had brought about—some of them, following the example of Günter Grass in *Der Butt* (*The Flounder*), by men. John Irving's *The World According to Garp* was an interesting case in point.

The workings and aspirations of another international cultural organization which had an embattled year were described with rare candour but no malice by Richard Hoggart, a former assistant director general of UNESCO, in his book *An Idea and Its Servants*. Finally, a more universally admired, and envied, servant of literature and scholarship, the Oxford University Press, celebrated its 500th anniversary with 19,000 titles in stock and printing at the rate of ten million books a year.

ENGLISH

United Kingdom. Cultural pessimists, observing the continuing decline in literacy and the growing vacuity and moral equivocation in the print media, might have considered as the emblematic event of the year the death of F. R. Leavis (*see* OBITUARIES), the most influential English critic and teacher of literature since Matthew Arnold and an even more pugnacious upholder of standards of high seriousness. Pessimists who think, on the other hand, that the English disease is overvaluing the past at the expense of the future might have been dismayed at the attention given to a positive plethora of institutional anniversaries. These ranged, in publishing, from the quincentenary of the mighty Oxford University Press to the 50th anniversary of the once radical, now respectable, firm founded by Victor Gollancz, and, among magazines, from the 150th anniversary of the weekly *The Spectator* to the 25th of the monthly *Encounter* — "One of the few good investments the CIA ever made," a *Spectator* columnist observed, benignly recalling the not quite killing scandal of *Encounter*'s subsidy by the Central Intelligence Agency, revealed in the mid-1960s.

Signs of present liveliness were to be found in another subsidized (by the Arts Council of Great Britain) magazine, *The New Review*, which in its summer issue polled 50 novelists and a handful of critics for their views on the recent performance and likely future of the novel. Not surprisingly, no simple consensus emerged.

FICTION. The fiction that actually appeared during the year confirmed several drifts or trends noted in *The New Review*'s symposium and in a book by J. A. Sutherland, *Fiction and the Fiction Industry*, which usefully analyzed in more detail the history and economy of the form. There was plenty of evidence of the diversification of the "serious" novel — partly as a response to commercial pressures, partly for more complicated cultural reasons — into what are called the genres: science fiction, the moral-political thriller, and the ill-defined but increasingly fashionable category of fantasy.

Another observation amply borne out by current production was made by Raymond Williams, who noted that the "commercial" length of the English novel had shrunk to barely one-sixth of the average 19th-century novel. He suggested that this was largely responsible for what he called "a fiction of diminishing personal relationships," presenting characteristically only "the relationships of two or three who live, in effect, as if they were human beings alone in the world, though there are noises off from the rest of humanity."

In fact this austere critical realist demonstrated part of his case himself, producing an awkwardly short moral thriller, *The Volunteers*, dealing with the breaking point between radical politics and terrorism. But one could note, too, that practically a whole new fiction list (from the rejuvenated firm of Duckworth) had been constructed successfully out of short, elegantly pessimistic novels, barely more than novellas, of a kind most vividly written, in the late 1960s and 1970s, by that list's bright star, Beryl Bainbridge. Something of Williams's generalization did hold with many current novels of this kind, but hardly with those of Bainbridge, whose gifts included the ability to establish character, presence, and place with an almost Dickensian prodigality and energy of registration but with an extraordinary economy of length. Certainly the rich glooms of her Liverpool streets and interiors and her constellation of warty exiles provided a dense enough context for the central figures of her latest novel, *Young Adolf*, though even her formidable imaginative juices were not quite able to digest so historically and lately monstrous a figure as Hitler — not even this young Adolf, dodging the draft on a sorrowful visit to his half-brother, the Liverpool waiter, in 1912.

What was hard to find was the novel that dealt directly with contemporary reality with any distinction, if one excepts a few such things as Graham Greene's rather tired though no doubt well-grounded account of the world of spies and treason in *The Human Factor*. This indicated a difficulty that more and more authors attempted to resolve by joining the flight into historical fiction. At the middle-brow level this produced, for example, a whole swashbuckling shelf of novels about the Victorian Navy. The detective novel, too, seemed to be going backward (Julian Symons's *The Blackheath Poisonings*, with its elaborate late-Victorian furnishings, was one of the happiest flights). And there were more substantial narratives, like M. M. Kaye's huge romantic novel of the British Raj in India, *The Far Pavilions*, or J. G. Farrell's more sophisticated handling of an imperial theme, *The Singapore Grip*, about the last years before the Japanese invasion.

History of a kind was a favourite field for the fantasists, too. In *Gloriana, or, the Unfulfill'd Queen*, Michael Moorcock created a rich parallel universe to Elizabethan myths of Albion and its mistress, setting a great Gormenghastly palace in a midden of a city as gaudy as Shakespeare's London. Robert Nye's *Merlin* — Malory annotated and updated by a very clever (and very dirty-minded) schoolboy — was a less successful sequel to his uproarious *Falstaff*. A richly romantic Elizabethan Devon was the matter of *Moon's Ottery* by that good Devonian poet Patricia Beer. Brigid Brophy's *Palace Without Chairs* was historical in the sense that it was truly "a baroque novel," raising up with hallucinatory clarity the parks and vistas and all the frozen extravagance of some Bohemian capital surviving archaically in the divided middle of *Mitteleuropa*.

Margaret Forster's affectionate imaginary autobiography of *William Makepeace Thackeray* was more modest historical invention, and Len Deighton's *SS-GB* a more recent one, ingeniously using period detail from the 1940s to suggest how it might have happened in Britain if the Nazis had come after all, but selling out an imaginative start to the exigencies of a thriller plot. Anthony Burgess, sui generis as usual, explained how it *would* happen in the fictional second half of *1985*, showing how Orwell got the future wrong in *Nineteen Eighty-four*.

Novelists who did treat with contemporary reality mostly used the comic or ironic standoff, like Allan Massie in his elaborate picaresque comedy *Change and Decay in All Around I See*, or the Amises, father and son. Kingsley Amis dealt roughly with current follies of grandeur about sex in *Jake's Thing*, putting his jaded eponymous don through all the bent hoops of sexology and presenting his jaundiced view of affairs in general and affairs with women in particular. One of the pair of contrasted apartment-mates in Martin Amis's novel ("a man of parts, predominantly private," wrote Norman Shrapnel) seemed to end up with Jake's thing too, but the reality was otherwise, and *Success* turned out to be a clever fugue of modern fantasies.

There was not too much realism or reality, of course, in Iris Murdoch's seaside entertainment, *The Sea, The Sea*, which won her the 1978 Booker Prize. It retired a famous stage director with an infamous diary style to a coastal retreat and entertained him and us with a sea monster and some remarkable coincidences, not excluding the usual lobster quadrille of relationships. Francis King managed conventional naturalism with admired skill and freshness in *The Action*, a psychological novel focused on the relationship of a neurotic brother and sister, and so did Jane Gardam with her child's-eye view of the emotional shock waves loosed in a family by a new birth in *God on the Rocks*.

It was notably a good year for short stories, with collections from William Trevor (*Lovers of Their Time*) and his Irish compatriots John McGahern (*Getting Through*) and Benedict Kiely (*A Cow in the House*); also from Frank Tuohy (*Live Bait*), Leslie Norris (*Sliding*), and Jennifer Dawson (*Hospital Wedding*).

LETTERS, LIVES, HISTORY. It continued to be a good time for the writing of history and a thin time for literary criticism, rare exceptions to the latter case being John Bayley's subtle *An Essay on Hardy* and Peter Conrad's *Shandyism*, which with considerable learning and brilliance proposed Sterne's novel as a central masterpiece linking Shakespeare's minglings of tragedy and comedy with the consciousness of Romanticism. E. H. Carr completed his massive *History of Soviet Russia*, and one of the masterful new generation of historians, Simon Schama, added to his reputation with *Two Rothschilds and the Land of Israel*, which clarified much about the origins of the Jewish settlements in Palestine. In *Protest and Punishment* George Rudé told the grim stories of the social and political dissidents who were transported to Australia between 1788 and 1868, while Gwyn Williams produced a vivid and reliable account of *The Merthyr Rising* of 1831, a bloodier event than Peterloo, which did much to establish the traditionally hard militancy of the Welsh working class.

The cottage industry devoted to Virginia Woolf and her circle continued to pay dividends. Another volume each of the *Letters* and *Diaries* appeared, interspersed with commentaries and new biographical studies, as well as a second volume, *Po-*

Iris Murdoch's *The Sea, The Sea* won for this novelist the 1978 Booker Prize.

lycrates' Ring, of P. N. Furbank's life of E. M. Forster. The second volume of Anthony Powell's memoirs, *Messengers of Day*, recalled the fashionable literary world of the 1920s. Edward Blishen's *Sorry, Dad* marvelously recovered the pain and particularity of growing up clever and absurd amid the dour gentility of a lower middle-class family in a South London suburb between World Wars I and II.

POETRY. The most substantial British political poet of the age, Hugh MacDiarmid (*see* OBITUARIES), died at the age of 86, passionately committed to the end to his own version of Communism and Scottish nationalism and just missing publication of the definitive two-volume edition of his *Collected Poems*. Jeffrey Wainwright was the find of the year, a young poet with a fine moral intelligence and sense of history. Martin Dodsworth thought his *Heart's Desire* "the best first collection to have been published in the last ten years," with one long poem on Thomas Müntzer, the Protestant reformer and leader of the people's army in the Peasants' Revolt of 1525, already "a masterpiece." *The Great Cloak* by the Ulster poet John Montague was a set of strong, unsentimental poems on the breakdown of a marriage and the discovery of new love, and there were fine late love poems in Geoffrey Grigson's *The Fiesta and Other Poems*. Two sonnet sequences, "Lachrimae" and "An Apology for the Revival of Christian Architecture in England," in Geoffrey Hill's *Tenebrae* confirmed him as one of the best half-dozen living English poets.

(W. L. WEBB)

United States. FICTION. The Jewish novel showed no signs of decline in 1978 but rather of development. This was highlighted by the awarding to Isaac Bashevis Singer of the Nobel Prize for Literature. No claim can be made that Jewish novelists in the U.S. historically make up a cohesive school or have achieved an artistic or moral syn-

John Updike, in *The Coup,* wrote a fictional account of an African dictator.

thesis of the human dichotomies. Yet they have shared a willingness to accept the world on its own terms—disorderly, incoherent, absurd.

Singer's work (translated from the Yiddish), which began in the 1930s and continues to the present, has revealed through its ambivalence a perfect balance of faith and skepticism, uniting (through ironic detachment) the sexual and the sacred, the naturalistic and the fantastic, the psychological insight and the parapsychological mystification. As in the novels of Nathaniel Hawthorne the irrational expresses itself typically in the context of "normalcy," where soup and sympathy come to acquire magical properties. "No doubt," asserts Gimpel (one of Singer's Holy Fools), "the world is entirely an imaginary world."

In 1978 Singer produced *Shosha,* a novel about Jewish Warsaw in the 1930s, where the threat of Nazi occupation throws a fence around everyone, locking them into patterns of ultimately fatal foolishness: "so long as Hitler didn't attack, so long as no revolution or pogrom erupted, each day was a gift from God." (See *Yiddish Literature,* below; NO-BEL PRIZES.)

U.S. novelists continued to search for shock-resistant lives and a model of how life can cohere, homing in on twin modes of the art: the integrated, wide-angled, obsessively managed novel and the anarchic novel where mindlessness is virtue. *Picture Palace* by Paul Theroux unpeeled the autobiography of pioneer photographer Maude Pratt —famous for her uncompromising portraits of blacks, louts, and celebrities. The unearthing of old prints triggers memories ("the picture palace of my mind"): public triumphs and private torments —"It's the wounded who take to art."

Son of the Morning provided the focus for another of Joyce Carol Oates's glutinous and hysterical explorations of the fevered mind: "seeing visions and getting whispered personal endorsements from Jesus." Religious irreverence was also the nexus of Max Apple's *Zip,* whose goal is to turn Jesus, renamed "Crab Goldstein," into a middleweight boxing champion.

John Updike's long interest in African literature eventually was bound to produce something like *The Coup,* a tale about Ellellou, dictator of Kush, a sub-Saharan dust bowl ruled by dint of government-by-mythology. Wandering not quite so far was *The World According to Garp* by John Irving, a superb and affecting novel about Vienna, wrestling, boys' schools, and feminism. Richard Stern's brilliant *Natural Shocks* exhibited voyeur Fred Wursup, one of the most appealing fictional men of letters since Saul Bellow's Charlie Citrine.

Important family chronicles were David Plante's

Julia Markus's *Uncle* was winner of the Houghton Mifflin Literary Fellowship Award.

The Family, a dark, commandingly superb depiction of the life of a French-Canadian family in Providence, R.I., during the 1950s, and *Time in Its Flight* by Susan Fromberg Schaeffer, in which the grit of 19th-century doctors' families shakes from the book like iridescent powder. In addition, one remarkable first novel appeared, Julia Markus's *Uncle* (winner of the Houghton Mifflin Literary Fellowship Award), offering totems of young womanhood and completely fouled men.

Feminist fiction continued to explore the taboos and strictures that cast women aside from male society. Coming from diverse backgrounds, the heroines had all been wounded by either gross insults or little cruelties connected to their femaleness. They came from stultifying domestic prisons, disapproved of, humiliated, but ready for battle. The credo of Zane, the heroine of Alix Kates Shulman's *Burning Questions*, is lesbianism, dialectics, and political activism. For the group of women in E. M. Broner's *A Weave of Women*, the answer, after windy consciousness-raising sessions, is a religious "government-in-exile." Careerism is the mode in *Violet Clay* by Gail Godwin: thirtyish Violet broods over Life and Art as she sketches gothic book jackets—"over two hundred women running away from houses."

Finally, popular successes were scored by *Fools Die* by Mario Puzo, a big, messy novel about money, sex, and writing by the author of *The Godfather*, who probably writes about money more than anyone since Balzac; Howard Fast's *Second Generation* (a sequel to *The Immigrants*), about a San Francisco family (an ethnic minestrone) in which good men rise from humble toil, bad men are bankers, and women are lovely and loaded; *Chesapeake* by James Michener, another massive but arbitrarily fragmented community history—a Maryland island, 1583–1978; *War and Remembrance* by Herman Wouk, undigested military history from Pearl Harbor to Hiroshima with Wouk; and *Whistle* by James Jones, conceived as the capstone of his World War II trilogy about manhood tested in combat begun with *From Here to Eternity* (1951) —published posthumously.

In the genre of short story *The Stories of John Cheever* appeared, a mammoth grouping of polished pleasures with those legendary seductive opening lines—*e.g.*, "The first time I robbed Tiffany's it was raining." Barry Hannah offered a remarkable collection, *Airships*, with Faulknerian gothic motifs. Also notable: Susan Sontag's *I, Etcetera*, eight wiry stories, too smart for their own good; and Penelope Gilliatt's *Splendid Lives*, ambivalent observations of life, splendid and otherwise.

HISTORY, BIOGRAPHY, AND BELLES LETTRES. The prizewinning academic histories in 1978 were David McCullough's objective *The Path Between the Seas: The Creation of the Panama Canal, 1870–1914* and Page Smith's *The Constitution*, gathering the intellectual strands lying behind the Founding Fathers' belief that a voluntary compact could restrain man's sinful tendency to abuse power. More contemporary, *The Illusion of Peace* by Tad Szulc described how Nixonian foreign policy operated on two levels: public pronouncements and private deals. In *America in Vietnam* Guenter Lewy was highly critical of the "big war" strategy, arguing that the U.S. never really understood the nature of insurgent warfare. Another Vietnam study was the blockbuster *Decent Interval* by Frank Snepp (*see* BIOGRAPHIES), a former CIA analyst; this was an immense sketch of duplicity and delusion offering not only the local colour of terror, assassination, and shoddy leadership but also broad views of policy and policymakers.

Deception was the subject of three other major works. *Watergate and the Constitution* by legal scholar Philip Kurland argued that a sitting president is immune from legal action—a reminder that, although Watergate is past, the problems it epitomized remain; Allen Weinstein's *Perjury: The Hiss-Chambers Case* obliterated Alger Hiss's "defense by reputation" and minimized Whittaker Chambers's unstable personality, which had been used as prima facie "evidence" of a frame-up; and an extraordinary work by Harvard University professor of ethics Sissela Bok, called *Lying: Moral Choice in Public and Private Life*, examined situations in which last-resort or habitual lying is often justified.

Three important but partisan primers on the "dismal science" of economics also appeared: *Two Cheers for Capitalism*, by neoconservative theoretician Irving Kristol, constituting a paean to God and to Horatio Alger; William Simon's *A Time for Truth*, a powerful case against government encroachment upon business; and Pulitzer Prize-winning Alfred Chandler's *The Visible Hand*, a monumental research effort summarizing much of what is known about the rise of the managerial class in the U.S.

Underscoring the trenchancy of ideology in U.S. society, several important documents were offered. Most controversial was *On Human Nature*, by Harvard University zoologist Edward O. Wilson, guaranteed to inflame feminists, science-for-the-people groups, and others opposed to genetic determinism. He argued that human societies are naturally (*i.e.*, biologically) characterized by male dominance, male aggression, incest taboo, pair bonding, division of labour, etc., and that sociobiology, the discipline he called into being to describe these phenomena, will absorb the social sciences and put them on a firm scientific basis.

Vivian Gornick's *Essays in Feminism* illustrated an insistent abhorrence of all dogmas (like sociobiology) that circumscribe the revolutionary expansion of feminist consciousness; and *The Remembered Gate: Origins of American Feminism* by historian Barbara Berg challenged the usual view that feminism in the U.S. was an outgrowth of the abolition crusade. Crime was "as American as Jesse James" in Charles Silberman's important new book *Criminal Violence, Criminal Justice*, in which he made an uncomfortable assertion: until nonwhites and the poor enter society's mainstream, there is not much courts and cops can do to reduce crime.

Noteworthy efforts in the "New Journalism" were: Steven Brill's *The Teamsters*, lamenting what might have been: why couldn't the Teamsters have become a force for good?; Tom Wicker's *On Press*, a study of U.S. journalism since the era of cold

Walter Jackson Bate won the Pulitzer Prize and the National Book Award for his biography *Samuel Johnson.*

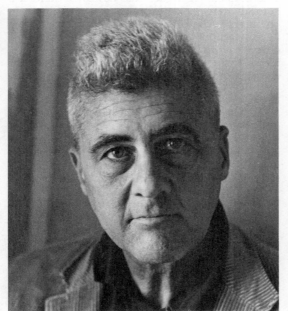

Poet Howard Nemerov won a Pulitzer Prize and National Book Award for his *Collected Poems*, a work spanning three decades.

war certainties, addressing the qualms of those who feel the media have "gone too far" as kingmakers and whistle-blowers; and Susan Sontag's *Illness As Metaphor*, a liberating book that could become the cancer patients' *Common Sense*, studying how cancer has been viewed increasingly as a "form of self-expression" or as "self-caused."

Briefly noted entries in popular nonfiction include *If Life Is a Bowl of Cherries—What Am I Doing in the Pits?* by Erma Bombeck (*see* BIOGRAPHIES), a return to the heartland of Fotomats and carryout chicken from the woman who claims that gym clothes are the No. 1 cause of pollution; and *Metropolitan Life* by urbane literary grump Fran Lebowitz, drolly expanding on city living in general and on phenomena specific to New York such as SoHo conceptual artists and the First Women's Bank.

In the elegiac spirit of *A Thousand Days*, Arthur M. Schlesinger, Jr.'s *Robert Kennedy and His Times*

mounted a massive attack on the RFK conundrum (shy/aggressive, compassionate/ruthless)—the major biography of the year. There is sufficient material in the book to occupy a battery of historians, some of it revisionist (such as a broad defense of John Kennedy's handling of the Cuban missile crisis), some of it startling (Robert Kennedy broke with Lyndon Johnson after the latter spoke of John Kennedy's death as "divine retribution" for the assassination of Rafael Trujillo and Ngo Dinh Diem). And in *American Caesar: Douglas MacArthur 1880–1964*, William Manchester proffered a life so grandiose as to satisfy even the giant ego of its subject: "the best of men and the worst of men."

In the domain of literary biography W. J. Bate won both the Pulitzer Prize and the National Book Award for his study *Samuel Johnson*, disclosing how his subject rose above poverty and erratic personality to achieve literary triumphs. A. Scott Berg's *Max Perkins* detailed the glory days of Scribner's powerful editor who loomed, prospectively, nearest to God, functioning as censor, confessor, and moneybags to his "literary sons."

The most belligerent memoir of the year was *RN: The Memoirs of Richard Nixon*: "I intended to play the role of the President right down to the hilt and right to the end." Thus Nixon, whose words read less like memos here than they did in the newspaper excerpts and more like the last will and testament of a fighter who never willingly rebelled, offers a journal of how the mightiest fell. It may not be worth 1,000 pages, but it does carry weight.

In Search of History by Theodore H. White identified White's own dissatisfactions with the fate of his country; Charles A. Lindbergh's *Autobiography of Values* was a final communion with the cosmos; and Isaac Bashevis Singer's *A Young Man in Search of Love* revealed Singer as a young man in 1930s Warsaw, tormented by philosophical doubts, involved with a much older mistress, and deciding that human culture seems "one huge and complex fig leaf."

POETRY. Cited for a body of work spanning three decades, capsulated in his *Collected Poems*, Howard Nemerov was awarded both a Pulitzer Prize and a National Book Award. Other impressive volumes: *The Dream of a Common Language*, Adrienne Rich's eighth volume, aspired to "a whole new poetry beginning here"; *Stories That Could Be True* by William Stafford, a work of quiet simplicity and Aristotelian golden meanness; James Wright's *To a Blossoming Pear Tree*, with sentimental Wright in Italy, mostly; Robert Creeley's *Hello*, another collection of masterfully reductionist and stenographic poems in the manner of Louis Zukofsky; and two angry, audacious dithyrambs by feminist black poets Nikki Giovanni (*Cotton Candy on a Rainy Day*) and Maya Angelou (*And Still I Rise*).

(FREDERICK S. PLOTKIN)

Canada. Works by major Canadian writers and poets highlighted the 1978 publishing scene. Marian Engel (*see* BIOGRAPHIES), honoured with a Governor General's Award for her last novel, the unusual *Bear*, demonstrated the continuing development of her versatile talents in her new novel, *The Glassy Sea*. In it she tells the story of a woman in retreat from the world (she belongs to an obscure order of Anglican nuns) who, on being forced to enter the world, finally learns to deal with it to the extent of being able to open a (temporary) retreat for other women. Thirty years after the publication of her underground classic *By Grand Central Station I Sat Down and Wept*, Elizabeth Smart returned with her second novel, *The Assumption of the Rogues and Rascals,* a chronicle of survival.

R. Murray Schafer, best known as a musician, was also an accomplished writer, as his novel *Ariadne* proved in language that was both labyrinth and clue. In *No Man's Meat and the Enchanted Pimp*, Morley Callaghan explored what happens to ordinary people in exceptional circumstances. *Who Do You Think You Are?*, the stories of two women whose lives echo and reflect each other, marked a darker tone and a deeper level in Alice Munro's development as a writer. Other important novels were the first English translation of Marie-Claire Blais's *The Fugitive*; the third in Jean-Guy Carrier's series of novels depicting life in rural Quebec, *A Cage of Bones*; André Bruneau's *Moving Out*, which microcosms the French-English conflict within one family; and two books reflecting the experiences of immigrants to Canada, *The Italians* by Frank Paci and *Immigrant* by Stephen Gill.

Among the many collections of short stories were the *Selected Stories of Ernest Thompson Seton*, introducing a new generation to Seton's meticulously detailed world of the wild animals of the western plains and mountains; Margaret Gibson's *Considering Her Condition*, in which the world of madness, of shifting edges and obscure extremes, is once more opened; *Red Dust* by W. D. Valgardson, in which another, but quite different, world of extremes is depicted in stories of survival in the stark environment of the Canadian north; and *Dark Must Yield* by Dave Godfrey, which includes three experimental works among more conventionally styled stories of rural Ontario.

In poetry, Leonard Cohen's long-awaited *Death of a Lady's Man* proved to be a many-layered collection of poems, annotations, second thoughts, and critical comments spiraling into the poet's self-centre, his preoccupation with the possibility that he has failed as a poet—some critics agreed, at least as far as this book was concerned. Miriam Waddington's *Mister Never* explored the concept of absence, especially that vacancy found in unrequited love, hauntingly evoking the search for the "other," the perfect mate. *The Works: Collected Poems* brought together four poems for voices written by Phyllis Gotlieb for the Canadian Broadcasting Corporation (CBC), along with other, earlier work, including haiku. Irving Layton's annual contribution, *The Tightrope Dancer*, uses language as a wire upon which to balance the forces, for both good and evil, that govern his life. In Earle Birney's new book, *Fall by Fury*, the title poem describes, with both horror and humour, the accident that left the poet lame and that vividly brings home to him the passage of time and the increasing physical frailty of old age.

In *Being Alive*, a collection of Al Purdy's work over the last 20 years, the past, its presence in the present, serves as a focus for Purdy's reflections on the wish to be remembered after one has died. Craig Powell, in *Rehearsal for Dancers*, discovers and rediscovers himself and others in images of snow, light, water, and trees. Other books of poetry were Peter Trower's *Bush Poems*, revealing the life of the poet-logger; *Deathwatch on Skidegate Narrows*, an epic poem by Sean Virgo; *The Inks and the Pencils and the Looking Back*, Sean O'Huigin's first major Canadian publication; and *The Pat Lowther Poem*, in which Pat MacKay confronts the violent death of her friend and teacher.

(ELIZABETH WOODS)

FRENCH

France. It was a year for anniversaries. Voltaire and Rousseau, rival geniuses of an age struggling with dilemmas of public conscience and individual identity, died in 1778 and were commemorated, the first by two volumes in a definitive edition of his correspondence, the second by a number of reappraisals, notably G. A. Goldschmidt's *Jean-Jacques Rousseau*. There was also the tenth anniversary of the May 1968 student uprising; the corpse of what had euphemistically been called "the events" was exhumed and found to have enough meat on it for a dozen new books.

The revolution, politically abortive, had been culturally liberating and its spirit lived on, most visibly in the antiestablishment press, the political and erotic comic strip, and science fiction, where there were signs of a distinctive French contribution in a market dominated by translations from the American. Bernard Blanc's investigation *Pourquoi j'ai tué Jules Verne* explicitly rejected the form created by France's pioneer in the field (born 150 years earlier and enjoying a critical revival). In place of Verne's projection of technological achievement, writers were suspicious of material progress and more concerned with exploring "inner space" or elaborating political myths with implications for the present. Jacques Sternberg (*Mai 86*) and Anne Cauquelin (*Potamor*) warned us to avoid the future at all costs.

Heeding them, many novelists looked to the past, and childhood remained a favourite theme. Robert Sabatier dished up a sickly confection called *Les Enfants de l'été*, about two orphans in Provence. It proved very popular. In *Lorelei*, Maurice Genevoix looked nostalgically at a young man's discovery of love in Germany in the innocent days before World War I, and Jean Cayrol, relaxing from the textual density of his recent work, wrote an account of children growing up in 1918, *Les Enfants pillards*. There was a similar mixture of autobiography and fiction in the year's Prix Renaudot winner, *L'Herbe à brûler* by the Belgian novelist Conrad Détrez, and in Bruno Gay-Lussac's *La Chambre d'instance*, but the most grimly compulsive work of this type was Alain Bosquet's merciless dissection of his relationship with his mother, *Une Mère russe*.

The ambiguity of our feelings for others was the theme of Jean-Didier Wolfromm's highly praised novel about a crippled adolescent, *Diane Lanster*, awarded the Prix Interallié. Daniel Boulanger's icy depiction of the moral cripples in the stories of

L'Enfant de Bohème was justly acclaimed, as were Hélène Parmelin's *Le Monde indigo*, Patrick Grainville's *La Diane rousse*, and Raymond Jean's *La Rivière nue*. Hervé Bazin had a mixed reception for *Un Feu dévore un autre feu*.

The search for identity, which inspired so many novelists to retrace the experience of childhood, continued to haunt Patrick Modiano, the year's Goncourt winner with *Rue des boutiques obscures*. Returning to Modiano's favourite background, the German occupation, it described a private detective's efforts to rediscover his past while suffering from amnesia. At least one critic felt that its author's treatment of his theme was becoming repetitive and dangerously facile. Identity was also a keynote in André Wurmser's *Une Fille trouvée*, an honest and moving novel about a writer who is forced to question his beliefs and attitudes when he rediscovers his illegitimate daughter.

The outstanding novel among many examining the condition of women in French society was Claire Etcherelli's *Un Arbre voyageur*, in which the working-class heroine provides shelter for an assortment of children, friends, and lovers during her gradual achievement of political awareness. Marie Cardinal's *Une Vie pour deux* dealt with a comparable situation, and family life was also the subject of Yves Navarre's *Je vis où je m'attache*. Significantly, women writers headed one paperback best-seller list, and the vitality of the women's movement was also recorded in a number of essays, notably Evelyne Sullerot's *Le Fait féminin*.

On the whole, Modiano's work, predictable and confirming a reputation without breaking new ground, was typical of the year's fiction. But there were exceptions. Georges Pérec's *La Vie mode d'emploi* (Prix Médicis), a massive novel, or series of novels, constructed on the analogy of a house in which each room leads to another, was a work of

French novelist André Wurmser, Une Fille trouvée.

LUTFI ÖZKÖK

great poetic power, gaining strength from the constraints imposed on it by its creator. There was delight too for the readers of Jacques Roubaud's *Graal Fiction* and *Graal Théâtre* (the latter written with Florence Delay), two splendid rejuvenations of Arthurian myth in which the discontinuity between past and present, fiction and reality was explored with wonder, irony, humour, and a passion for language. Pérec and Roubaud owed much to Raymond Queneau (d. 1976), who was commemorated by an exhibition at the Bibliothèque Nationale.

Roubaud published a study of the alexandrin, the standard French verse line, in which he looked at the state of prosody in an age when some had questioned whether poetry is still compatible with verse. One sign of a possible return to more structured poetry was the renewed interest in the 16th-century Rhétoriqueurs; Paul Zumthor studied them in *Le Masque et la lumière* and edited a paperback anthology. In fact, poetry appeared healthy. Guillevic published *Du Domaine*, characteristically spare and aphoristic; Joyce Mansour, *Faire Signe au machiniste*; and Jean-Pierre Faye, *Verres*. Yves Martin explored the quality of everyday experience in *Je fais bouillir mon vin*, and Jean-Claude Renard won the Guillaume Apollinaire prize for *La Lumière du silence*.   (ROBIN BUSS)

Canada. Three novels stood out in 1978. In Louis Caron's *Le Bonhomme Sept-heures*, chilling fear assumes a new face and becomes almost "tender" when expressed in words that are, in effect, exorcistic incantations. André Mathieu's *Demain tu verras* attracted considerable attention, but it was questionable whether the book's commercial success was due to its real quality or to the fact that it is set in Quebec and traces the amorous adventures of the protagonist. Finally, *La Grosse Femme d'à côté est enceinte* was the first novel by the playwright Michel Tremblay, author of *Les Belles sœurs*. The novel, taking place in a single day in 1942, was quite different from his other works.

The poems of Marcel Bélanger were published in two new collections, *Fragments paniques* and *Infranoir*. Written some time earlier, they were beautifully structured and full of depth. In *La Belle Conduite*, Normand de Bellefeuille pursues his search for the poetic voice that commingles the themes of day-to-day life, politics, and poetry.

In theatre, the year was highlighted by three plays, each treating different aspects of the same subject, the Quebecois woman. In her first play, *Les Fées ont soif*, Denise Boucher looks at the virginal and promiscuous sides of women; Michel Garneau treats female passion, sadness, and tenderness in his excellent *Quatre à quatre*; and the indefatigable Jean-Claude Germain focuses on the reality of conjugal life in *M'Amour et Conjuga— Scènes de la vie amoureuse québécoise*.

The second volume of René Dionne's *La Patrie littéraire* appeared; the work provides a broad, valuable reference on 19th-century French-Canadian literature. Robert Marteau's *L'Oeil ouvert*, gathering together articles on art criticism that appeared in *Le Jour* in 1974, offers a clear, insightful, and readable commentary.

(ROBERT SAINT-AMOUR)

GERMAN

The political alarms of the previous months continued to be reflected in literature in 1978. It was a time for stocktaking, looking for reasons, abandoning causes, retreating into a private world, warning against "extremism."

Alexander Kluge's *Unheimlichkeit der Zeit*, a collection of clinically told short pieces, fiction-cum-documentary, saw the terrorism of the present as a symptom of the triumph of technology foreshadowed both in the Nazis' treatment of their victims and in the Allied bombing of civilian targets. Bernward Vesper's posthumous autobiography, *Die Reise*, gave direct support to the "Hitler's children" thesis; here was the son of an authoritarian Nazi writer who drifted onto the left-wing student scene in the 1960s and ended as an acccomplice of the terrorists Baader and Meinhof. The hero of Peter Härtling's novel *Hubert* might have been a rather older Vesper. His domineering Nazi father gives him no opportunity to develop a personality, he finds identity only in film heroes, and although relatively successful in the postwar years, he lacks any qualities likely to inspire the respect of the younger generation. This political helplessness of the fathers when confronted with their children was the theme of Paul Kersten's moving *Der alltägliche Tod meines Vaters*.

The outstanding book of the year, acclaimed almost unanimously, was Martin Walser's novella *Ein fliehendes Pferd*. In it the failed liberal intellectual Helmut, the introvert on the run from his revolutionary past and from his own identity, is confronted with the extrovert, vital, successful journalist Klaus. Not even the central scene, in which Helmut disposes of his rival overboard during a brilliantly evoked storm on Lake Constance, resolves the many rich ambivalences of this highly relevant work.

Helmut wished to withdraw into himself, but outside reality constantly intruded. The trend to a new German "inwardness" continued in other critical successes. In Botho Strauss's *Die Widmung*, Richard, abandoned by his wife, spends his time locked up in his apartment writing a self-analysis which he hopes will justify himself to her but which she is unlikely to read. Gerhard Roth's *Winterreise* describes a journey in search of the self. Ingomar von Kieseritzky's *Trägheit* was both an example and a parody of this genre. Its hero represents an extreme case of narcissism; it is also a witty satire on the doctors and psychiatrists we like to believe in.

More conventional novels of social criticism included *Die Vernichtung der Sorgen*, the second volume of Wilhelm Genazino's trilogy on office workers' lives, and Wolfgang Hädecke's *Die Leute von Gomorrha*, a satirical portrait of life after pollution has destroyed our environment. The outstanding novel in this field was *Die Rückfahrt* by the Swiss writer E. Y. Meyer. As technology increasingly threatened the Swiss heritage, Meyer was looking for a "conservative" philosophy that would be neither antisocialist nor antirationalist.

Historical novels were popular. Walter Kempowski's *Aus grosser Zeit* traced the fortunes of the Kempowski family between 1900 and 1918. Arno Surminski's *Kudenow* reminded its readers somewhat nostalgically how awful life had been in the immediate postwar years. These novels were superficially similar in their mixture of documentation and snapshot narrative, but unlike Kempowski, Surminski could not resist sentimental commentary. Siegfried Lenz's richly textured *Heimatmuseum* was probably more important than either. Devoted to the landscape, history, and customs of the Masuren region, it both celebrated "Homeland" and warned against the ideological dangers of such a celebration.

A quite different work, but one equally concerned with the times, was the remarkable *Eumeswil* by the octogenarian Ernst Jünger, an essayistic utopian novel defending "conservative anarchism," the ironic aloofness of one who has seen many movements, ideals, and tyrannies fail.

In the area of lyric poetry, Nicolas Born's *Gedichte 1967–1978* was very favourably received. Other important collections included Johannes Schenk's *Zittern*, two cycles of which described the U.S. and Portugal, respectively, with the eye of the critical left; Erich Fried's *Die bunten Getüme*; and Alfred Andersch's *Empört euch der Himmel ist blau*. Other significant literary enterprises of the year included publication of Thomas Mann's *Tagebücher 1933–1934*, Kurt Tucholsky's *Die Q-Tagebücher 1934–1935*, a four-volume edition of the works of Ingeborg Bachmann, and the *Gesamtwerk* of Konrad Beyer.

As East Germany approached its 30th birthday, the "midlife crisis" seemed to be felt particularly acutely. Werner Heiduczek's *Tod am Meer* was heavily censured for its negative presentation of an orthodox party writer's reckoning with his past.

German novelist Martin Walser's novella *Ein fliehendes Pferd* was highly acclaimed.

LUTFI ÖZKÖK

Jurek Becker's *Schlaflose Tage* and Klaus Poche's *Atemnot* were not even allowed by the authorities to appear in the East. The former described a middle-aged schoolmaster, the latter a middle-aged writer, both of whom realize they are unable to continue without questioning some of the assumptions of their society.

In lyric poetry, too, the most important works could appear only in the West: Bernd Jentzsch's *Quartiermachen*, Günter Kenert's *Unterwegs nach Utopia*, and Rainer Kirsch's *Auszog das Fürchten zu lernen*.　　　　　　　　　　　(J. H. REID)

SCANDINAVIAN

Danish. Denmark was currently preoccupied with Greenland, whose independence seemed imminent. Niels Fenger's *Hvid anorake* was a good, straightforward novel from 1977, but a major artistic work was, without doubt, Thorkild Hansen's *Sidste sommer i Angmagssalik*, much in the tradition of his earlier books, a mixture of narration, description, and commentary. An intense, penetrating, and personal glimpse of Greenland today was given in *Balladen om identiteten*, poems by aaju (Kristian Olsen).

Another Danish preoccupation, problems personal and social, showed in Jytte Borberg's *Det bedste og det værst* (1977), a continuation of the previous year's *Eline Bessers læretid*. Different, but with social overtones, were the poems *Skuffebarn* by a newcomer, Iris Garnov. Two other women made their mark. Elsa Gress's novel *Salamander* (1977), though it had certain affinities with a roman à clef, was ultimately an analysis of the artistic temperament. A very different study of personality and personal relationships was Herdis Møllehave's *Le* (1977), one of the most discussed Danish novels of recent years, rivaled only, perhaps, by Dea Trier Mørch's *Vinterbørn* (1977) with its revealing and moving stories of patients in a maternity ward.

However different, the unemployment problem of the 1970s turned people's thoughts back to the 1930s. Ole Sarvig's highly acclaimed novel *De rejsende* had those years as its setting, while the opportunity was taken to publish a hitherto unknown novel by Harald Herdal, *Arbejdsløs*. Henrik Stangerup published a collection of his own articles in *Mens tid var*, tracing his development as a thinker and writer.

The Danish Academy's 1978 literature prize went to Tage Skou-Hansen, largely for his novel *Den hårde frugt* (1977). His new play, *Nedtællingen*, appeared in 1978. The 1977 prizewinner, Peter Seeberg, produced a controversial and experimental new novel, *Ved havet*, basically a collage of the actions and thoughts of some 40 characters during one day by the sea, and a play, *På selve dagen*, set in an old people's home. Another established writer, Willy-August Linnemann, continued writing of the Flensburg region in *Bølgerne på fjorden* (1977).　　　　　　　　(W. GLYN JONES)

Norwegian. A wide range of psychological, social, and philosophical problems were convincingly discussed in Carl Fredrik Engelstad's novel *Den største blant dem alle*. Also outstanding was a documentary by Per Hansson, *Den siste veien*, dealing with the last months in the life of a 22-year-old student dying of cancer. Novelists continued to show a keen interest in the life of the proletariat. Edvard Hoem's *Gi meg de brennende hjerter* was set in a small industrial town in western Norway at the end of World War I, while the backdrop of Dag Solstad's *Svik. Førkrigsår* was Oslo in the period leading up to World War II. Both were announced as first volumes of trilogies. The repercussions of North Sea oil on people and society in contemporary Norway were convincingly dealt with in Erling Pedersen's novel *Ventetid*.

Conventional male and female roles, respectively, were portrayed in Knut Faldbakken's *Adam's dagbok* and Ebba Haslund's amusing *Behag og bedrag*. In *Musica*, Finn Alnæs combined a number of topical problems with an intense erotic element. Kåre Holt contributed a historical novel, *Sønn av jord og himmel*, centred on the 18th-century apostle of Greenland, Hans Egede. Erling T. Gjeldsvik's *Dødt løp*, set in Spain, was an outstanding debut. Science fiction was well represented by Øyvind Myhre's *Sabøtorene*, with the fight for power moved from earth into space. The problem of identity was central in Sigbjørn Holmebakk's novel *Sønnen*, with illegitimacy and incest as the leading themes. Refreshing humour was a welcome aspect of Terje Stigen's small-town novel *Huset og byen*. Knut Hauge's *Juvet* was set in rural Norway during and after World War II.

Sverre Undæs's *I dette hvite lyset og to andre spill* contained his outstanding play *Vinger*. Major collections of poetry were Hans Børli's *Dag og drøm: Dikt i utvalg*, Paal Brekke's *Dikt 1949–1972*, and Halldis Moren Vesaas's *Dikt i samling*.

The 150th anniversary of Henrik Ibsen's birth was marked by the publication of three valuable works of scholarship: Arild Haaland's *Ibsens verd-*

Halldis Moren Vesaas's collected poems appeared in *Dikt i samling*.

en, Bjørn Hemmer's *Ibsen og Bjørnson*, and Edvard Beyer's *Henrik Ibsen*. (*See* THEATRE: *Special Report*.)

(TORBJØRN STØVERUD)

Swedish. In *Författarnas litteraturhistoria*, a three-volume Swedish literary history, some 90 writers cooperated to present their own favourite authors or genres with a variety of methods and approaches, producing a work at once instructive and entertaining. Many novelists continued to chart the emergence of modern Swedish society, often from the perspective of class struggle. With *Tid och otid*, Lars Ardelius reached the second volume of a trilogy presenting the past 150 years of Swedish history, while Per Agne Erkelius' *Drömmen om Johannes*, based on his father's diaries—also the middle volume of a trilogy—and Per Olov Enqvist's *Musikanternas uttåg* both dealt with life in northern Sweden in the early 20th century.

The humorous mode of social criticism was adopted by author and physician P. C. Jersild in *Babels hus*, a splendid satire on a huge modern hospital which functions as a microcosm of the welfare state. Humorous irony designed to expose the shams of a liberal, bourgeois society formed the basis of Gunder Andersson's *Alla chanser!*, a picaresque account of a provincial lad's attempts to make good in the Stockholm of trendies and exploiters. In *Slöddret skall bort* K. Sivert Lindberg gave a bitter inside view of the burgeoning social services sector and its clients. Quite a different, individualistic view of Stockholm in the recent past was provided by young Klas Östergren, whose novel *Fantomerna* was an attempt to exorcise the phantoms of his early days. Social comment of another kind was found in Margareta Sarri's feminist burlesque, *Mor ror, åran är trasig*, which followed the domestic struggles of a young wife and mother.

In a politically oriented year, two established writers produced novels of a more imaginative-metaphysical kind: Lars Gyllensten's *Baklängesminnen* starts with a man attending his own funeral and ends with him anticipating his own birth, and Sven Delblanc's *Gunnar Emmanuel*, clearly inspired by Swedenborg's *Dreambook*, sees the hero sent off on journeys to past historical epochs in search of his vanished girl friend Vera, who allegorically represents Truth. On the poetic front, Tomas Tranströmer published *Sanningsbarriären*, Tobias Berggren *Bergsmusik*, and newcomer Eva Runefelt *Aldriga och barnsliga trakter*.

(KARIN PETHERICK)

ITALIAN

While the number of Italian readers did not seem to increase, the market was inundated with new books—a sign of both the country's cultural ebullience and the publishing industry's inflationary and ultimately self-defeating policies. There were too many books on the same topical themes, such as the Moro case, the events of 1968, parapsychology, and the Holy Shroud of Turin. Most remarkable and effective was *Giovanni Leone. La carriera di un presidente*, by Camilla Cederna, which included some serious charges against Leone and significantly contributed to his resignation as president of the republic.

P. C. Jersild's *Babels hus* was a satire on modern hospitals.

The country's self-examining mood was well caught by Luca Goldoni who, with *Non ho parole*, achieved an even more devastating satire on contemporary Italian language and life than in his previous success, *Cioè*. In a category of its own was *Questioni di frontiera*, a coherent collection of essays in which Franco Fortini rigorously analyzed some of the major political and literary issues of the day.

While the trend in fiction was away from formal experimentation, the emphasis was still on the country's social and political problems. *Candido ovvero Un sogno fatto in Sicilia* by Leonardo Sciascia was a novel of Voltairean inspiration in which reason and spontaneity are shown to be impotent against the ambiguities of what the narrator describes as the two churches of our time, the Catholic and the Communist. In a mood of deep political skepticism, Sciascia seems to propose literature as the only consolation left to the individual. Alberto Moravia published *La vita interiore*, which, despite being cast in the form of an interview between narrator and protagonist, was distinctly reminiscent of his first novel of almost 50 years earlier, *Gli indifferenti*. The theme was the familiar death wish of the bourgeoisie, represented by a young woman who gradually destroys all the traditional values of her social class and finally her own physical self.

The same conclusion was reached, although by different means, in *Ammazzare il tempo* by the young novelist Lidia Ravera (co-author of the 1977 best-seller *Porci con le ali*). Here the narrator, having been on the barricades in 1968, discovers the gap that already divides and alienates her from the new generation of 1977 and decides to opt out. Among more generally apocalyptic novels, the most significant was *Il pianeta irritabile* by Paolo Volponi, set in a characteristically surreal world where a nuclear explosion has suddenly eliminated all people. An immense catastrophe has also occurred in Antonio Porta's *Il re del magazzino*, where the protagonist is found under the debris of a farm together with 29 letters recording his last days. Some critics detected a turning point in the career of Carlo Cassola, who with *L'uomo e il cane* gave a chilling view of a pitiless society doomed to self-destruction. However, Cassola, who lately had taken a firm stand—particularly with his essay *La lezione della storia*—in favour of a demilitarized utopia, seemed to revert to his usual banalization of human events with *Un uomo solo*, yet another novel about frustrated marriage plans.

A group of novels focused on family life. Ferdinando Camon's *Un altare per la madre* was a touching elegy for the figure of the mother as symbol of a waning peasant culture. *Famiglia* by Natalia Ginzburg included two parallel stories, centred around two characters who, unaware of their own impending death, progressively lose contact with the families (of animals and objects as well as people) that surround them. *Fratelli* by Carmelo Samona, one of the best and most intense books of the year, was about two brothers, sharing a huge old apartment in the middle of a city and unsuccessfully striving, between sanity and madness, to communicate with each other. However, the year's best-sellers were undoubtedly two very straightforward novels, *La sposa americana* by Mario Soldati and *Il cappotto di astrakan* by Piero Chiara. The former is the story of a man who discovers how much he loved his wife only after she has died; the latter has a provincial hero who longs for change and finds it only to discover that he prefers his own fantasies. Finally, Giuseppe Pontiggia's excellent *Il giocatore invisibile* was a new kind of thriller in which a university professor desperately tries to identify the anonymous author of a harsh review directed against him, thus laying bare the misery of a certain type of academic culture.

Some excellent new poetic works appeared, notably *Al Fuoco della controversia* by Mario Luzi, *Dimenticatoio* by Leonardo Sinisgalli, and *Poesie per un passante* by Daria Menicanti. Also very successful were the much awaited collected poems of Eugenio Montale, *Tutte le poesie*, and of Franco Fortini, *Una volta per sempre, poesie 1938–1973*.

(LINO PERTILE)

SPANISH

Spain. The year's Premio de la Crítica for poetry was awarded to J. M. Caballero Bonald for *Descrédito del héroe* and for fiction to Gonzalo Torrente Ballester for *Fragmentos de apocalipsis*. First winner of the new *El Bardo* poetry award was Alvaro Pombo, for *Variaciones*; the same writer also published *Relato sobre la falta de sustancia*, a book of stories widely acclaimed by the critics.

Among new young writers, Eduardo Haro Ibars attracted attention with his collection of "neosurrealist" poems entitled *Perdidas blancas*. Féliz de Asúa published both a book of verse, *Pasar y siete canciones*, and a novel, *Las lecciones suspendidas*, while Luis Antonio de Villena brought out his highly polished *Viaje a Bizancio*. The last poems of Pere Gimferrer, a collection of his verse translated from Catalan to Castilian by the author, was an important work. García Hortelano edited an anthology of verse by the so-called Generation of the '50s: Caballero Bonald, Angel González, Jaime Gil de Biedma, Carlos Barral, and others. Barral issued

J. M. Caballero Bonald won Spain's Premio de la Crítica for his book *Descrédito del héroe*.

the second volume of his memoirs, *Los años sin excusa*.

The politico-polemical novel *Autobiografía de Federico Sánchez*, by the ex-Communist leader in exile Jorge Semprún, raised a storm of extraliterary argument. The same author's novel *La segunda muerte de Ramón Mercader*, previously unpublished in Spain, was much less noticed though superior in quality. Juan Benet, of the same generation but belonging to a different literary world, published an experimental novel, *En el estado*. In the same genre, only better, was *Entre espacios intermedios: Wham!*, by M. Antolín Rato, a mixture of medievalism and science fiction. Other outstanding young authors, occupying a terrain between philosophy and the strictly literary, included Antonio Escohotado, with his *Historias de familia*; Fernando Savater, the prolific author of *Panfleto contra el todo*, a libertarian polemic; and the Catalan Jordi Llovet, winner of the sixth *Anagrama* award for essays, with his *Por una estétic egoísta*.

(ANTHONY KERRIGAN)

Latin America. Cuba's Casa de las Américas prizes went to Claribel Alegría of El Salvador for *Sobrevivo* (poetry), to Costa Rican Joaquín Gutiérrez for *Te acordarás, hermano* (novel), to Mexican David Ojeda for *Las condiciones de la guerra* (stories), to Angus Richmond, Guyana, in the category of Anglo-Antillan literature for *A Kind of Living*, and to Uruguayan Eduardo Galeano's *Días y noches de amor y de guerra* (memoirs). Goodyear's biannual J. M. Arguedas Prize honoured Gregorio Martínez for *Canto de sirena*, a series of monologues in folksy language by an ancient black in southern Peru. Another Peruvian, J. M. Gutiérrez Souza, received Spain's Blasco Ibáñez Prize for his first novel, *Así me dijo Arturo*, about the supernatural and the commonplace. Later, Gutiérrez published in Lima *Sole mía Nada Más*: life as seen by the dead.

Cuba honoured J. Lezama Lima with a posthumous edition of his unfinished novel *Oppiano Licario*, which continued his famous *Paradiso*, and of his last poems, *Fragmentos a su imán*. In the Casa's series "Valoración Múltiple," two volumes were noteworthy: *El teatro latinoamericano de creación colectiva* and *La novela romántica latinoamericana*, both important essay collections. As a complement to the latter, S. Menton published in Colombia, home of the romantic Hispanoamerican novel, *La novela colombiana: planetas y satélites*, a valuable study of Colombian classics and iconoclasts.

Elsewhere, fiction was abundant and good, in some cases appearing to move away from the author's usual concerns. In Mexico, Carlos Fuentes presented an "adventure novel," *La cabeza de la hidra*. Vicente Leñero offered *Los periodistas* and Elena Poniatowska *Querido Diego, te abraza Quela*, both novels. Other interesting fiction was by younger writers: Jorge Aguilera Mora's *U.S. Postage Air Mail Special Delivery* and Esther Seligson's *Tránsito del cuerpo*. Essayist Carlos Monsiváis captivated readers with *Amor perdido*. In Colombia a new publishing house, La oveja negra, announced the first volume of García Márquez's collected works, an initial attempt to publish this important writer in his homeland. Gustavo Alvarez Gardeazábal, second among Colombian novelists in a recent survey, forsook Tuluá, the hometown terrain of his previous fiction, and stunned his public with *El titiritero*, a merciless novel about Colombia's university system. Oscar Collazos brought out a formalistically indulgent novel, *Crónica de tiempo muerto*, mostly about himself.

Neighbouring Venezuela provided an impressive number of narrations: Saúl Ibáñez's stories, *A través de una mirada*, and José Balza's keen look at Caracas via the mass media, *D.*, were considered the most important. Excellent poetry was presented by Rafael Cadenas in *Memorial*. Peru maintained its narrative fertility and quality. Mario Vargas Llosa (*see* BIOGRAPHIES) returned to his origins (*La huída del Inca*, 1952) and wrote a play, *La señorita de Tacna*. Playwright Alonso Alegría finished his new verse drama, *El tierno blanco*. Julio Ramón Ribeyro, called by Vargas Llosa Latin America's "most unjustly neglected narrator," published the third volume of his short stories, *La palabra del mudo III*, containing an absolute masterpiece, "Silvio en el rosedal." His *pensées* were continued with *Prosas apátridas aumentadas*.

Alfredo Bryce Echenique's saga of the suffering rich continued with a hilarious celebration of egotism, *Tantas veces Pedro*, a chronicle of a Latin-American cultural émigré in Paris. A young diplomat, Harry Belevan, attracted attention with *La piedra en el agua*, an experimental novel about fiction and life, and *Antología del cuento fantástico peruano*, containing a dense study of the genre. Another experimenter, José Antonio Bravo, published two novels, *Un hotel para el otoño*, about a writer's return to his youth, and *A la hora del tiempo*, concerning the coexistence of the New and the Old World in a Madrid pension.

Chilean Jorge Edwards published, in Spain, his novel *Los convidados de piedra*, which illuminates the historical conflicts that produced Salvador Allende and the military regime that followed his presidency. Poet Oscar Hahn's significant *Arte de morir*, continuing his "popular poetry," vigorously denounced current Chilean reality. Matilde de Neruda, with Venezuelan Miguel Otero Silva, put out her late husband Pablo Neruda's unpublished diary entries, memoirs, and other writings under the title of *Para nacer he nacido*. In Argentina and the world, curiosity about J. L. Borges was stimulated by Peruvian Carlos Meneses' publication, in Barcelona, of *Poesía juvenil de J. L. Borges*, which collected and studied largely unknown poems written from 1919 to 1922.

Critical literature was dominated by the need for stocktaking: José Juan Arrom's *Esquema generacional de las letras hispanoamericanas*, Argentine Saúl Yurkiévich's *La confabulación de la palabra*, and *Ver/Ser visto* by Alicia Borinsky. Limited to individual writers were Peruvian José Miguel Oviedo's up-to-date and thorough *Mario Vargas Llosa: La invención de una realidad* and Wolfgang A. Luchting's *Mario Vargas Llosa: Desarticulador de realidades*. In Spain an important effort was begun to gather the works of Uruguayan Juan Carlos Onetti and of Peru's great poet César Vallejo.

(WOLFGANG A. LUCHTING)

PORTUGUESE

Portugal. Political censorship under the pre-1974 regime had prevented publication of many works, some of which now saw the light of day. Among those to appear in 1978 was Alexandre Pinheiro Torres's *A Nau de Quixibá*. Written in 1957 and set in the early 1940s, it centres on a conflict between father and son during the latter's visit to São Tomé, then a lonely outpost of the Portuguese empire. A debate on the idea of democracy, defended by the ailing father and opposed by the son, who holds the authoritarian convictions instilled in him by forced political indoctrination, turns gradually into an unsuspected ritual of initiation into manhood for the young visitor.

A clear break with tradition was made by Carlos de Oliveira, one of the most distinguished novelists of the 1940s and the leading figure of the neorealist movement. His *Finisterra* was an admirable novella that appeared to be a remake of the psychological moods and tones that pervaded his highly successful *Casa na Duna*. Another new venture in fiction was *A Personagem* by Maria Ondina Braga. Acutely aware of the status of women in Portuguese society, she drew skillfully the portrait of a narrator who tries to create a fictional character in the pages of her diary. From this dual conflict with herself and her own creation, the new personality of the narrator emerges, breaking out of the old cocoon of domestic docility.

In this scene of lively experimentation, *O Escriba Acocorado* by Rui Knopfli stood out as probably the most remarkable poem published during the year. By reverting to the regular form and metre of the long poem, currently out of fashion, and by adopting a terse poetic diction deeply rooted in Western tradition, Knopfli produced an epic of the individual tragedy of modern man.

Portuguese and world literature suffered a serious loss with the death of Jorge de Sena (*see* OBITUARIES). (L. S. REBELO)

Brazil. Nélida Piñon's latest novel was an unusual departure from the highly personal nature of her previous fiction. *A força do destino* is a parody of the Verdi opera in which Nélida is both a character and the commentator on the events. An exposé of the violence and drug culture of Rio life was presented by José Carlos de Oliveira in *Terror e extrase*, with a plot vaguely resembling the story of Patty Hearst. Other important works of fiction were published by Ignácio de Loyola Brandão, Jorge Andrade, a distinguished playwright turned novelist, and the comic short-fiction writer Chico Anísio. Three highly respected novelists died during the year: Clarice Lispector, Osman Lins, and Juarez Barroso. Barroso's posthumous novel, *Doutora Isa*, evokes his native state of Ceará. Lins's posthumous work deals with the relationship between literature and the media.

Anna Maria Martins published another collection of stories, *Sala de espera*, in which she once again portrays characters lost at the crossroads of their lives. Bernardo Elis's *André Louco* brings together both previously published and new stories about his native Goiás. Murilo Rubião appears to search for the lyrical note of daily existence in the somewhat fantastic stories of *A casa do girassol vermelho*. Rubem Fonseca and Wander Piroli also produced new volumes of short fiction. In the unique Brazilian *crônica* genre, Carlos Eduardo Novaes published a delightful new collection.

Facsimile editions of significant poetic reviews of the Brazilian modernist movement (*Klaxon*, *Revista de antropofagia*, etc.) were published. Waldimir Diniz's volume of poetry *Até o 8° round*, which received a literary prize, is made up of 22 poems about daily life. The initial poem, which gives the volume its title, has eight verses, each presenting one of life's "battles." The poems of Cassiano Nunes's *Madrugada* merited attention not only for their unusual content but also for their graphic appearance. The novelist Accioly Lopes wrote his first volume of verse. The Brazilian theatre remained at a virtual standstill, the most notable publication being an edition of the complete plays of Gianfrancesco Guarnieri.

Brazilian novelist Nélida Piñon's novel *A força do destino* was a parody of Verdi's opera.

LUTFI ÖZKÖK

Three additional volumes of Wilson Martins's *História da inteligência brasileira* appeared, bringing the study into the 20th century; the work remained on the best-seller list. There were several new studies of the works and influence of Guimarães Rosa. Joan Dassin studied the political aspect of the modernist Mário de Andrade's poetry, and João Alexandre Barbosa "rediscovered" the works of the late Érico Veríssimo.

Censorship of newspapers and magazines (with the exception of the literary review *Inéditos*) was lifted, but radio, television, and books remained subject to the censor's whim.

(IRWIN STERN)

RUSSIAN

Soviet Literature. The 150th anniversary of the birth of Leo Tolstoy was marked by the publication of all the great writer's major works. A 22-volume edition of his collected works was launched in an unprecedented print of one million. All central, republican, and regional publishers contributed to the publication of anniversary editions, including reminiscences by Tolstoy's relatives and intimate associates Sonya Tolstaya, Tatiana Tolstaya-Sukhotina, D. Makovitsky, and P. A. Sergeyenko, monographs by M. Khrapchenko, K. Lomunov, and others, and the symposia *Tolstoy and the Artist, Tolstoy and Music,* and *Tolstoy and the Theatre.*

The Soviet Union's major literary award, the biennial Lenin Prize, went to Aleksandr Chakovsky for his novel *Blockade* and to the Belorussian poet Maksim Tank for his poem *Narochanskye Pines.* The annual State prizes went to Viktor Astafiev for his book *Tsar-Ryba,* to Andrey Voznesensky (who lectured in the U.S. during the year) for his volume of verse *A Master of Stained Glass,* to Daniil Granin for his story *Klavdia Vilor,* and to the Kazakh poet Djuban Muldagaliev for his poems *Eagle Steppe* and *Mudflow.* The prize for children's literature was awarded to Anatoly Aleksin for four stories. The 200-volume edition of the Library of World Literature series, published over a period of ten years, was completed by the beginning of the year, and those engaged on the publication were presented with special prizes for their work. Among the winners of the 1978 Komsomol prizes were the young Siberian poet Viktor Potanin and the Tajik poet Gulrukhsor Safieva.

The year saw the publication of an impressive autobiographical trilogy—*Small Land, Rebirth,* and *Virgin Land*—by Soviet Pres. Leonid I. Brezhnev. The work provided a lively documentary record of the period from World War II to the great peacetime movement to develop the virgin lands. The war theme continued to hold an important place in Soviet publications, noteworthy among which were Vasily Bykov's *To Go and Not Return,* Konstantin Simonov's novels *We Shall Not Meet* and *From Lopatin's Notes,* Aleksandr Chakovsky's *Victory,* and Anatoly Rybakov's *The Heavy Sand.*

Major social and moral questions of Soviet life were also popular themes. Among best-sellers showing the tremendous transformations taking place in the villages were Fyodor Abramov's novels *The Don* and *The Last Bow.* Friendship among the

Aleksandr Chakovsky won the Soviet Union's Lenin Prize for his novel *Blockade*.

Soviet peoples was the theme of the novel *Law of Eternity* by the Georgian writer Nodar Dumbadze, and problems of the scientific and technical revolution were well developed in Valentin Kaverin's *A Two-Hour Outing*.

The biggest editions of fiction were put out in the popular Roman-Gazeta pocket series (over 1.5 million copies). Apart from works by such well-known authors as Anatoly Ivanov, Valentin Rasputin, and the Estonian Paul Kuusberg, Roman-Gazeta published poetry and in 1978 devoted a whole issue to young authors.

(ALEKSEY OVSYANNIKOV)

Expatriate Russian Literature. Publication of the third volume of Aleksandr Solzhenitsyn's *The Gulag Archipelago* was doubly a landmark. With the conclusion of this arduous "experiment in literary investigation," the heroic age of "dissident" Russian literature in the post-Stalin age seemed also to be drawing to an end. No single-handed record of the misery of the Soviet prison camp system could be definitive as history, but no subsequent work, surely, would be able to embrace so closely so much of that bitter experience. In this sense, *The Gulag Archipelago* completed the perspective of one age on the history of Stalinism. Now it seemed as if the major part of the most important emigration of creative talent from Russia since the Revolution was completed as well.

This last volume was perhaps the most contentious, defending very deliberately, for example, the cause of the Vlasovites and others who collaborated with the Germans during World War II. It also contained much of Solzhenitsyn's most personal writing; the author appeared as a participant in some of the struggles of the early 1950s as a foreman in the camp at Ekibastuz, taking part in a hunger strike in spite of a rapidly growing tumour. In its final pages a harsh and prescient pessimism seems to anticipate the time when he would be protesting not on his own soil but with the distant voice of exile, speaking from an alien and little-comprehending culture. (In a speech at the Harvard commencement in June, Solzhenitsyn addressed that culture in no less uncompromising terms, berating it for its lack of courage, its corrupted humanism and "spiritual exhaustion."

Of the work of other recent exiles published during the year, Vladimir Maksimov's novel *Farewell from Nowhere* was worth noting for the light it shed on criminal life in the Soviet Union and for the great sweep of country its young hero covers. In *To Build a Castle*, Vladimir Bukovsky describes his life as a dissident, in and out of prisons and psychiatric institutions. Some critics thought he showed an overly naive impatience with compatriots leading decent and difficult lives who had not embraced public dissidence.

Poets suffer most sharply from the separation from their linguistic environment in exile, and the pain and difficulty of the whole process could be seen in two collections (*Konets prekrasnoy epokhi: Stikhotvoreniya 1964–71* and *Chast' rechi: Stikhotvoreniya 1972–76*) published by the most gifted of living Russian poets, Mandelstam's heir Josif Brodsky. In one of the last poems in the second volume, the poet imagines the evening crowd pushing onto a Leningrad tram, all shouting "in the language of the man who has gone away." However, wrote Henry Gifford in a review in the *Times Literary Supplement*, "whatever Brodsky may fear, he is still marvellously at home in the language." (W. L. WEBB)

EASTERN EUROPEAN LITERATURE

Anniversaries are not always useful ways of focusing on history, but the tenth anniversary of the "Prague Spring" and of the Soviet invasion that crushed it helped to remind the world of the spirit that was kindled then and of its tenacious survival in the minds of many.

The good news from Prague was of the extent and quality of the local version of *samizdat* called the "Padlock Editions." Ten years after the "restoration" in Czechoslovakia, there had been little of the kind of reconciliation or accommodation between the regime and the intellectuals that occurred quite quickly in Hungary after the uprising of 1956. Playwrights with international reputations, like Vaclav Havel, Pavel Kohout, and Ivan Klima, and novelists and poets like Ludvik Vaculik and Jiri Grusa were still unpublishable. But by the summer of 1978 more than 100 books by these and other authors had been put into circulation "under padlock." The list was a roll call of most of the country's really gifted writers, showing up sharply the thinness of the official lists. Two issues of a duplicated magazine called *Spektrum* that reached London during the year included philosophical and historical essays, stories, and poems of a similarly high quality.

The bad news was of the penalties such work could involve. Sometimes there was an element of dark comedy in such cases; accounts of how Havel, Kohout, and two of their friends were evicted by police from the annual railwaymen's ball in Prague for fear they would contaminate the proletariat sounded like an episode from one of the more hilarious Czechoslovak films of the 1960s. A more serious matter was the imprisonment of Jiri Grusa, whose novel *The Questionnaire* was described by Eduard Goldstücker as "undoubtedly one of the most important literary works to come out of occupied Czechoslovakia." Grusa appeared to be charged actually for the literary works he had written (construed as "incitement"). It was feared that the authorities were hoping to attack the padlock press through a writer too young to have published much before 1968 and therefore little known in the West and less likely to become the subject of protest. (*The Questionnaire* was shortly to be published in France and West Germany, however.)

Pavel Kohout published abroad, in London and elsewhere, a lively parody of neo-Stalinist angst, *White Book*, in which a schoolmaster succeeds, after years of concentration, in levitating to the ceiling and walking upside down, a defiance of the laws of nature with the gravest ideological consequences. *Laughable Loves* by Milan Kundera (currently being allowed by the Czechoslovak authorities to live and teach in France) was a set of stories mostly about seduction, elaborate stratagems unfolded with a neat but bleak irony which seemed to suggest that sexual love in the author's land had become a sort of faute de mieux activity. The most memorable Czech novel made available in translation, however, was Josef Skvorecky's *The Bass Saxophone*, two novellas prefaced by a short history of jazz in Czechoslovakia in Nazi and Stalinist times. The title story was also about jazz and freedom and loyalty, a tender returning to the small Moravian town that was the setting for *The Cowards*, Skvorecky's earlier novel about growing up in the last days of the Reich protectorate.

Hungary, which had a pleiade of poets larger and more gifted, probably, than those of any other small country since Ireland in the days of the Yeatsian renascence, completed for the time being a long and admirably intelligent program of translation. Done in collaboration with a number of British and American poets, it should release into the broader stream of European and world literature such cherishable talents as those of the magical master Sandar Weöres, Ferenc Juhasz (whose "The Boy Changed into a Stag" was described by W. H. Auden as "one of the greatest poems written in my time"), Laszlo Nagy, and the austere Catholic poet Janos Pilinszky. Several of the poets who appeared in the large anthology *Modern Hungarian Poetry* (edited by Miklos Vajda and published by the Columbia University Press) toured the U.S., where they gave warmly received readings.

Samizdat publishing, now flourishing in Poland (notably in the magazine *Zapis*), started in Hungary as well. *Profile*, edited by Janos Kenedi, was an 850-page literary *journal des refusés*, while *Marx in the Fourth Decade*, edited by Andras Kovacs, contained the replies of 21 young writers and scholars to a questionnaire on Marxism. Writing in *Index*, Romanian novelist Paul Goma reported that Pres. Nicolae Ceausescu's "abolition" of censorship in Romania, announced with fanfares in the summer of 1977, had been replaced with a system of pre-censorship by committees of writers that seemed to be even more vexatious.

(W. L. WEBB)

JEWISH

Hebrew. S. Yizhar figured prominently in the literary headlines of 1978; his novel *Yemei Ziklag* headed a poll on the greatest accomplishments of Israeli literature since 1948. A television movie of "Hirbet Hiz'e," with its perspective of concern for civilian Arab war victims, caused a heated controversy. Two early works, "Ephraim hozer la'aspesset" and "Befa'atei negev," were reissued.

Renowned but out-of-print works by U. Z. Greenberg, S. Y. Agnon, D. Vogel, and N. Bistritsky were also reissued. Retrospective anthologies presented surveys of Israel's first generation of writers. Current novels included three with a socio-historical perspective: A. Megged's *Asa'el*, B. Tammuz's *Requiem leNa'aman*, and D. Tselka's *Philip Arbes*. Tselka's novel and Y. Shabtai's *Zikhron Devarim* were the year's artistic highlights. D. Avidan, P. Sadeh, E. Megged, M. Ben-Shaul, and Zelda issued new poetry collections, and the playwrights A. Wolfson, A. Kenan, and H. Levin saw plays published.

Critical studies by M. Perry, D. Miron, S. Zemach, and K. A. Bertini focused on Hayyim Bialik. G. Shaked brought out the first volume of his history of Hebrew literature from 1880 to 1970 and, with R. Weizer, edited a volume of documents and articles on Agnon. A. Sha'anan issued vol. v of his interpretive literary history, and B. Hrushovski published an outstanding study of Greenberg's poetry. Collected essays appeared on G. Shofman, H. Hazaz, and U. Gnessin.

Among the promising new writers were several poets, including Y. Sharon, M. Galili, and E. Eli, as well as novelists D. Shavit and S. Galender. Anniversaries included the 80th birthdays of S. Halkin and Y. Zemora, the 75th of E. Amir, and the 60th of poets A. Gilboa and A. Kovner. E. Kishon published his 25th book. Several works appeared by Oriental Jews, notably D. Sitan, D. Rabi, and H. and B. Hakak. (WARREN BARGAD)

Yiddish. The 1978 Nobel Prize for Literature was given to Isaac Bashevis Singer (*see* NOBEL PRIZES), the first Yiddish writer to receive this prestigious award. The Swedish Academy noted that Singer's art has its "roots in the Polish Jewish cultural tradition" and that he portrays the life of Eastern European Jewry "as it was lived in the towns and villages, amid poverty and persecution. . . . The language was Yiddish, the language of ordinary people . . . the language of the mothers in which was safeguarded the stories, legends, and reminiscences of hundreds of years."

Singer writes in the tradition of the 19th-century prose masters and in the tradition of the Yiddish classics. He also was influenced by his older brother I. J. Singer and by Sholem Asch, Aaron Zeitlin, and Ephraim Kaganovsky. He created a body of work consisting of stories, novels, and memoirs portraying Jewish life in Poland in the last centuries. He also wrote about the survivors of the Nazi Holocaust and their struggle to adjust themselves to their new life. Some Yiddish critics criticized Singer for stressing negative elements in past Jewish life, but they all seemed to agree that he is a master storyteller.

As of 1978 nearly 150 Yiddish writers lived in Israel, where they continued to write in Yiddish. The Israeli quarterly *Di Goldene Keyt*, edited by Abraham Sutzkever, recently celebrated its 30th anniversary by publishing a special issue with contributions by Israeli, European, and U.S. Yiddish writers. *Bay-Zikh*, a literary journal edited by the poet and critic Itzhak Janosowicz, marked the 30th anniversary of Israel by publishing a thick issue with contributions by Yiddish writers from various countries. The *Jerusalem Almanac* devoted its recent issue to the memory of the Soviet Yiddish writers who perished during the purges.

Collections of poetry by Israeli-Yiddish poets included books by Shloyme Roitman, Rachel Boymvol, and Jacob Shargel. Collections of essays and criticism included works by Abraham Lis, Gabriel Weissman, Yehuda Kersh, and Itzhak Korn. *Der Mabul*, a collection of extraordinary stories by Leil Rokhman, was published a few weeks before he died. The Yiddish work of S. Y. Agnon was published with an introduction by Dov Sadan. A collection of stories by Julien Hirshaut from the U.S. and a volume of poetry by Hayyim Plotkin were published in Israel. In Moscow Aleksandr Lizen published a novel, *Nahumke Esrog*, his first in Yiddish. (ELIAS SCHULMAŃ)

CHINESE

Official discouragement of "indigenous" literature in the past two years appeared to have impaired the quality of literary efforts in Taiwan. Much popular literature was produced in 1978. At best, such efforts as Chiang Hsiao-yun's *Drift with the Tide* entertained with humorous, at times witty, but never unduly disturbing tales. At worst, as in Ma Shen's *Lives in a Bottle*, they irritated with sentimental, pretentious accounts of innocuous love affairs. The more serious writings focused on various moods of personal loss. Szu-ma Chung-yuan's *Wishing Well* is a poetic evocation, in lyrical prose, of a lost Eden, summoned by the power of childhood reminiscences. Yu Li-hua's *The Family Fu* deals with the actualities of disillusionment, failure, and moral and spiritual confusion among members of a family that has emigrated to America. Hsin Tai lacks Yu Li-hua's disciplined grasp of events and situations, but in *Pictures of Four Seasons* she shows some promise in her exploration of her characters' shifting states of mind.

On the mainland the most significant events were the publication of Chinese and Western classics after a long absence and the reappearance of works by writers persecuted during the Cultural Revolution. The government's more flexible and pragmatic political attitudes and policies were not yet reflected in current literature, however. Works like Liang Pin's *Record of a New Life*, Kuan Hua's *Chiang Chun River*, Hsi Ch'ing's *Chu Lui*, Ch'en K'ai's *Spring Time over Ku Ma River*, and *Fired Steel* —the last a collection of short stories by members of the Communist First Heavy Machinery Factory —are didactic exercises designed to inculcate the virtues of patriotism, selflessness, and dedication and to warn against Soviet revisionism, exploitive capitalism, and the "gang of four."

In this context of literary stereotypes—a situation lamented by such official publications as the *People's Daily* and the *Peking Review*—Yu Min's *The First Round* stood out, by virtue of the extensive social panorama it covers and the writer's grasp of the psychology of human motives and behaviour. The ideological principles that give meaning to the characters' lives are never in question, but the human relationships portrayed by the author are seen to be governed by tangibles and intangibles that have to do not with ideology but with the way people are. (JOHN KWAN-TERRY)

JAPANESE

The literary scene appeared quite tame in 1978. Some literary critics even complained of the difficulty in finding good fiction to recommend to the juries awarding literary prizes. Nevertheless, there were several important contributions. One of the most remarkable was by senior novelist Yasushi Inoue, whose *Wadatsumi* ("The Ocean") was impressive for both its scale and subject, though it remained a work in progress (only the first three volumes). Its central character was a young Japanese who went across the Pacific at the beginning of the 20th century to settle in San Francisco, and the book discusses his "americanization" during the period when anti-Japanese regulations were instituted in California. Inoue planned to cover the whole turbulent period through the Pacific War (World War II).

Shinichiro Nakamura's *Natsu* ("Summer"), the second part of a tetralogy, traced the spiritual pilgrimage of a middle-aged author. Nakamura had been regarded as a westernized experimental novelist whose work was too technical to be really sympathetic, but *Natsu*, mainly concerned with the amorous adventures of the protagonist, proved to be an entertaining story. It was also remarkable for its acute psychological analysis and skillful use of erotic motifs derived from classical Japanese literature. Junnosuke Yoshiyuki's *Yugure-made* ("Till the Evening") was another love story, and the description of the young girl, obsessed with virginity despite her liberated sexual behaviour, was curiously appealing. This novel made an interesting pair with Hideo Takubo's *Shokubai* ("A Catalyst"), whose central theme was an involved relationship with a neurotic woman. Yoshiyuki's style was remarkable for its cool delicacy and almost abstract lyricism; Takubo's novel, for its elaborate structure and romantic evocation of prewar Tokyo. Hiroko Takenishi's *Kangengaku* ("Shinto Music") and Yuko Tsushima's *Choji'* ("Favourite") were favourably received contributions by two women novelists.

It was a fruitful year for biography and literary criticism. Takeshi Muramatsu's *Emperor Godaigo* and Shusaku Endo's *Birth of Christ* were entertaining and informative. Also worthy of note were Kozo Kawamori's *Life and Times of Baudelaire* and Shoichi Saeki's *Yukio Mishima*. One of the most active poets, Koichi Iijima, published his lively collected poems and a book on Hakushu Kitahara. (SHOICHI SAEKI)

See also Art Sales; Libraries; Nobel Prizes; Publishing; Theatre.
[621]

Luxembourg

Madagascar

Luxembourg

A constitutional monarchy, the Benelux country of Luxembourg is bounded on the east by West Germany, on the south by France, and on the west and north by Belgium. Area: 2,586 sq km (999 sq mi). Pop. (1977 est.): 356,800. Cap. and largest city: Luxembourg (pop., 1977 est., 76,500). Language: French, German, Luxembourgian. Religion: Roman Catholic 93%. Grand duke, Jean; prime minister in 1978, Gaston Thorn.

In January 1978 Jacques Poos, the minister of finance, declared at a press conference that the Luxembourg government was planning additional exchange controls. Banks in Luxembourg would have to supply more information on foreign exchange operations in addition to the monthly returns they already submitted to the Luxembourg Banking Commission. They would also have to observe criteria set by the Institut Belgo-Luxembourgeois du Change. The proposals were designed to curb speculative currency flights and in particular to defend attacks on the Belgian franc, at par with the Luxembourg franc.

By the end of 1977 Luxembourg banks had accumulated balance sheets totaling LFr 2,115,000,-000,000, or about $58.5 billion. The 20 or so West German banks—the grand duchy's largest single tax source—accounted for two-thirds of this, amounting to some 14% of the balances in their parent banks in the Federal Republic.

Luxembourg, alone among the nine countries of the European Economic Community, issued a stamp in 1978 to celebrate the 20th anniversary of the signing of the Treaty of Rome.

In June the European Commission approved plans to restructure the Saar and Luxembourg steel industries under Arbed of Luxembourg. Arbed would acquire 25% and management control of the Luxembourg-based Métallurgique Minière de Rodange-Athus.   (K. M. SMOGORZEWSKI)

LUXEMBOURG
Education. (1975–76) Primary, pupils 34,980, teachers 1,757; secondary, pupils 8,345, teachers 860; vocational, pupils 13,955, teachers 941; higher, students 427, teaching staff 135.
Finance. Monetary unit: Luxembourg franc, at par with the Belgian franc, with (Sept. 18, 1978) a free commercial rate of LFr 31.13 to U.S. $1 (LFr 61 = £1 sterling). Budget (1978 est.): revenue LFr 39,111,000,000; expenditure LFr 39,363,000,000. Gross domestic product (1976) LFr 86,500,000,000. Cost of living (1975 = 100; June 1978) 120.8
Foreign Trade: see BELGIUM.
Transport and Communications. Roads (1976) 4,970 km (of which 27 km expressways). Motor vehicles in use (1976): passenger 130,719; commercial 9,687. Railways: (1976) 274 km; traffic (1977) 297.5 million passenger-km; freight 567 million net ton-km. Air traffic (1976): 165 million passenger-km; freight 300,000 net ton-km. Telephones (Jan. 1977) 157,800. Radio licenses (Dec. 1975) 176,000. Television licenses (Dec. 1974) 88,000.
Agriculture. Production (in 000; metric tons; 1976): barley 33; wheat 16; oats 12; potatoes 20; apples c. 9; grapes c. 20; wine c. 13. Livestock (in 000; May 1976): cattle 214; sheep 4; pigs 83; chickens 188.
Industry. Production (in 000; metric tons; 1977): iron ore (29% metal content) 1,547; pig iron 3,571; crude steel 4,329; electricity (kw-hr) 1,302,000.

Madagascar

Madagascar occupies the island of the same name and minor adjacent islands in the Indian Ocean off the southeast coast of Africa. Area: 587,041 sq km (226,658 sq mi). Pop. (1978 est.): 8,776,000. Cap. and largest city: Antananarivo (pop., 1975 est., 438,800). Language: French and Malagasy. Religion: Christian (about 50%) and traditional tribal beliefs. President in 1978, Didier Ratsiraka; prime minister, Lieut. Col. Désiré Rakotoarijaona.

Pres. Didier Ratsiraka faced serious economic difficulties and mounting political pressures in 1978. The Merina bourgeoisie of the High Plateaus remained hostile to the government but confined their opposition to passive resistance. Some left-wing elements resorted to direct action, however. In May student protests in Antananarivo degenerated into riots in which three people were killed and more than 150 demonstrators arrested. The disturbances, which originated in a dispute over examinations, spread outside the schools to involve mainly unemployed youths.

On February 4 a special military tribunal sentenced 54 persons to long prison terms for looting during the incidents at Majunga in December 1976. The circumstances surrounding these events remained obscure; they led to the death of about 100 people in pogroms mainly directed against the Comoran minority living in the town.

The Malagasy leadership continued to maintain close cooperation with the countries of the Eastern bloc. President Ratsiraka paid official visits to Moscow in July and to Pyongyang, North Korea, in September. The country also retained close links

MADAGASCAR
Education. (1976) Primary, pupils 1.1 million, teachers (1973) 16,351; secondary, pupils 114,468, teachers (1975) 5,088; vocational, pupils 8,193, teachers 879; teacher training (1973), students 993, teachers 63; higher, students (1975) 8,385, teaching staff (1972) 411.
Finance. Monetary unit: Malagasy franc, at par with the CFA franc, with (Sept. 18, 1978) a parity of MalFr 50 to the French franc (free rates of MalFr 218.81 = U.S. $1 and MalFr 428.75 = £1 sterling). Gold, SDR's, and foreign exchange (June 1978) U.S. $94.3 million. Budget (1977 est.): balanced at MalFr 137 billion.
Foreign Trade. (1976) Imports MalFr 68,430,000,000; exports MalFr 66,040,000,000. Import sources: France c. 41%; West Germany c. 8%; Japan c. 5%. Export destinations: France c. 30%; U.S. c. 21%; Japan c. 11%; West Germany c. 8%; Italy c. 6%. Main exports (1974): coffee 27%; petroleum products 9%; vanilla 8%; meat 7%; cloves 7%; fish 6%.
Transport and Communications. Roads (1976) 27,507 km. Motor vehicles in use (1974): passenger 56,700; commercial (including buses) 43,700. Railways: (1975) 884 km; traffic (1976) 289 million passenger-km; freight 200 million net ton-km. Air traffic (1976): 276.4 million passenger-km; freight 7,830,000 net ton-km. Shipping (1977): merchant vessels 100 gross tons and over 44; gross tonnage 39,850. Telephones (Jan. 1977) 27,700. Radio receivers (Dec. 1974) 855,000. Television receivers (Dec. 1975) 7,500.
Agriculture. Production (in 000; metric tons; 1977): rice 2,200; corn (1976) 123; cassava (1976) 1,348; sweet potatoes (1976) c. 280; potatoes (1976) c. 123; dry beans 76; bananas 440; oranges c. 88; pineapples c. 51; peanuts 40; sugar, raw value (1976) c. 117; coffee 95; cotton 14; tobacco 4; sisal 21; beef and veal c. 113; fish catch (1976) c. 55. Livestock (in 000; Dec. 1976): cattle c. 9,800; sheep c. 720; pigs c. 700; goats c. 1,350; chickens c. 13,250.

with France (to which Ratsiraka paid a state visit in September), although its relations with the former colonial power were somewhat soured by Malagasy territorial demands. In March and April Madagascar asserted its claim to four islands in the Indian Ocean administered by the French overseas département of Réunion: Îles Glorieuses, Europa, Bassas da India, and Juan de Nova. The group covers less than 50 sq km, but Madagascar considered its demand a matter of principle.

Former president Philibert Tsiranana, deposed in May 1972, died on April 16 (*see* OBITUARIES).

(PHILIPPE DECRAENE)

Malawi

A republic and member of the Commonwealth of Nations in east central Africa, Malawi is bounded by Tanzania, Mozambique, and Zambia. Area: 118,577 sq km (45,781 sq mi). Pop. (1977 prelim. census): 5,571,576. Cap.: Lilongwe (pop., 1976 est., 75,000). Largest city: Blantyre (pop., 1976 est., 219,000). Language: English (official) and Nyanja (Chichewa). Religion: Christian 33%; remainder, predominantly traditional beliefs. President in 1978, Hastings Kamuzu Banda.

Malawi's first parliamentary elections since independence were held on June 29, 1978. Forty-seven of the 87 seats were contested, 33 candidates being returned unopposed while seven seats were declared vacant because the candidates could not pass the English language test. All candidates were members of the country's single political party, the Malawi Congress Party, but nearly two-thirds of the sitting members in the constituencies where voting took place were defeated. Among those who lost their seats were two former government ministers.

After having been banned for several years, representatives of the foreign press were allowed into

---

MALAWI

Education. (1976–77) Primary, pupils 663,940, teachers 10,735; secondary, pupils 14,826, teachers 725; vocational, pupils 685, teachers 88; teacher training, students 1,355, teachers 86; higher, students 1,285, teaching staff 122.

Finance. Monetary unit: kwacha, with (Sept. 18, 1978) a free rate of 0.83 kwacha to U.S. $1 (1.62 kwacha = £1 sterling). Gold, SDR's, and foreign exchange (June 1978) U.S. $87,390,000. Budget (1977 actual): revenue 100,870,-000 kwacha (excludes 6,740,000 kwacha of foreign grants); expenditure 131,370,000 kwacha.

Foreign Trade. (1977) Imports 211.8 million kwacha; exports 184,570,000 kwacha. Import sources: South Africa 37%; U.K. 19%; Japan 9%; U.S. 5%. Export destinations: U.K. 42%; U.S. 10%; The Netherlands 7%; South Africa 7%. Main exports: tobacco 47%; tea 23%; sugar 8%; peanuts 5%.

Transport and Communications. Roads (1975) 11,025 km. Motor vehicles in use (1976): passenger 10,200; commercial (including buses) 10,600. Railways: (1975) 566 km; traffic (1976) 62 million passenger-km, freight 204 million net ton-km. Air traffic (1976): 122.4 million passenger-km; freight 4,680,000 net ton-km. Telephones (Jan. 1976) 20,-000. Radio receivers (Dec. 1975) 127,000.

Agriculture. Production (in 000; metric tons; 1977): corn *c.* 1,250; cassava (1976) *c.* 80; sorghum *c.* 105; sugar, raw value (1976) *c.* 90; peanuts *c.* 174; tea *c.* 30; tobacco *c.* 53; cotton, lint (1976) *c.* 6. Livestock (in 000; 1976): cattle *c.* 700; sheep 88; goats 739; pigs 189; poultry *c.* 8,092.

---

the country to cover the elections. Pres. Hastings Kamuzu Banda took the opportunity during a press conference to say that he had no intention of driving the Asians out of Malawi, although they had been entirely removed from the rural areas. He also stressed that there were no longer any political prisoners in jail. The relaxation of the order against the press did not last long, however, and foreign newspapermen were again excluded after the president accused them of misreporting events in the country.

Economically, Malawi continued to prosper. The agricultural sector in particular flourished, and the country, having become self-supporting as far as staple foods were concerned, could afford to export to its neighbours. (KENNETH INGHAM)

Malaysia

A federation within the Commonwealth of Nations comprising the 11 states of the former Federation of Malaya, Sabah, Sarawak, and the federal territory of Kuala Lumpur, Malaysia is a federal constitutional monarchy situated in Southeast Asia at the southern end of the Malay Peninsula (excluding Singapore) and on the northern part of the island of Borneo. Area: 329,747 sq km (127,316 sq mi). Pop. (1977 est.) 12,600,000. Cap. and largest city: Kuala Lumpur (pop., 1975 UN est., 557,000). Official language: Malay. Religion: Malays are Muslim; Indians mainly Hindu; Chinese mainly Buddhist, Confucian, and Taoist. Supreme head of state in 1978, with the title of *yang di-pertuan agong*, Tuanku Yahya Putra ibni al-Marhum Sultan Ibrahim; prime minister, Datuk Hussein bin Onn.

General elections for the federal Parliament and ten state assemblies began on July 8, 1978. The results confirmed the national leadership of Datuk Hussein bin Onn, who was seeking a popular mandate for the first time since he succeeded the late Tun Abdul Razak as prime minister in January 1976. Out of 154 seats in the federal Parliament, the ruling coalition, Barisan Nasional (National Front), won 131, the Democratic Action Party (DAP) gained 16 (including one in Sabah), while Party Islam secured 5. Two independent candidates were elected in Sarawak and Sabah. The National Front was victorious in all the state assembly elections.

One notable feature of the results was the poor performance of Party Islam, which, with 14 seats in the last federal Parliament, had been a member of the ruling coalition until it was expelled in December 1977. Conflict had arisen between it and the country's principal Malay party, the United Malays National Organization (UMNO), over the exercise of political power in the peninsular Malaysian state of Kelantan. After a state of emergency imposed in November 1977 was lifted in February 1978, elections for the Kelantan state assembly were held in March. The outcome was a decisive victory for UMNO, which was a major consideration in the holding of general elections in July.

A second feature of the general elections was the

Malawi

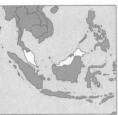

Malaysia

Magazines:
see Publishing

Malagasy Republic:
see Madagascar

relatively strong showing of the DAP, which drew its support primarily from the Chinese community. This performance contrasted with the relatively weak showing of the Malayan Chinese Association, the senior Chinese component within the National Front.

In September, as a result of triennial elections held during the UMNO annual assembly, Datuk Hussein bin Onn was confirmed as president of the country's principal Malay party, although he faced a challenge from former publicity officer Suleiman Palestin, who secured approximately one-quarter of the votes cast. Dato Seri Mahathir Mohamed, the deputy prime minister, was returned unopposed as deputy president of the party. In the contested elections for the three posts of vice-president, the successful candidates were Tengku Razaleigh Hamzah (the minister of finance), Datuk Musa Hitam (the minister of education), and Abdul Ghafar Baba.

In March the head of state, Tuanku Yahya Putra ibni al-Marhum Sultan Ibrahim, rejected an appeal for a pardon by the former chief minister of Selangor, Datuk Harun Idris, who had been convicted on corruption and forgery charges. In August communal tension increased when four Muslim Malays were killed by guards while attempting to desecrate a Hindu temple in Kerling, 35 mi north of Kuala Lumpur. The Malays were members of an extreme fundamentalist group, itself a part of the wider Dakwah (missionary) movement that had gained many adherents among young educated Muslims. The killings marked a bloody end to the almost nightly desecration of Hindu temples during August. Government concern about Islamic fundamentalism was expressed publicly by Deputy Prime Minister Mahathir at the outset of the UMNO annual assembly when he denounced religious extremism.

In March talks between Malaysian and British officials were suspended indefinitely after their failure to reach agreement on terms for the resumption of the joint British Airways-Singapore Airlines Concorde service between London and Singapore via Bahrain. At issue was whether to allow the supersonic airliner to fly through Malaysian air space over the Strait of Malacca. In April

MALAYSIA

Education. *Peninsular Malaysia.* (1976) Primary, pupils 1,608,157, teachers 49,941; secondary, pupils 838,968, teachers 29,915; vocational (1975), pupils 21,134, teachers 930; higher (1974), students 34,524, teaching staff 2,624 *Sabah.* (1976) Primary, pupils 127,271, teachers 5,000; secondary, pupils 52,149, teachers 1,978; vocational, pupils 300, teachers (1974) 30 *Sarawak.* (1976) Primary, pupils 189,347, teachers 5,307; secondary, pupils 71,167, teachers 2,413; higher (1974), students 722, teaching staff 62.

Finance. Monetary unit: ringgit, with (Sept. 18, 1978) a free rate of 2.30 ringgits to U.S. $1 (4.50 ringgits = £1 sterling). Gold, SDR's, and foreign exchange (June 1978) U.S. $2,818,000,000. Budget (total: 1976 actual): revenue 6,166,000,000 ringgits; expenditure 7,414,000,000 ringgits. Gross national product (1977) 30,934,000,000 ringgits. Money supply (June 1978) 6,572,000,000 ringgits. Cost of living (Peninsular Malaysia; 1975 = 100; June 1978) 113.1.

Foreign Trade. (1977) Imports 11,178,000,000 ringgits; exports 14,962,000,000 ringgits. Import sources: Japan 24%; U.S. 13%; Singapore 9%; U.K. 8%; Australia 6%; West Germany 6%; Thailand 5%. Export destinations: Japan 20%; U.S. 18%; Singapore 16%; The Netherlands 7%; U.K. 5%. Main exports: rubber 23%; timber 16%; crude oil 13%; palm oil 12%; tin 11%.

Transport and Communications. Roads (1976) 21,324 km. Motor vehicles in use (1974): passenger 430,400; commercial (including buses) 140,300. Railways: (1976) 1,814 km; traffic (including Singapore; 1977) 1,273,000,000 passenger-km, freight 1,212,500,000 net ton-km. Air traffic (1977): 2,100,000,000 passenger-km; freight 48,395,000 net ton-km. Shipping (1977): merchant vessels 100 gross tons and over 179; gross tonnage 563,666. Telephones (Jan. 1977) 329,600. Radio licenses (Dec. 1975) 450,000. Television licenses (Dec. 1974) 390,000.

Agriculture. Production (in 000; metric tons; 1977): rice c. 2,010; rubber c. 1,595; copra c. 150; palm oil c. 1,643; tea c. 3; bananas c. 455; pineapples c. 284; pepper (Sarawak only; 1976) 35; tobacco c. 10; timber (cu m; 1976) 36,361; fish catch (1976) 517. Livestock (in 000; Dec. 1975): cattle c. 423; buffalo c. 298; pigs c. 1,444; goats c. 369; sheep (Peninsular Malaysia only) c. 46; chickens c. 44,930.

Industry. Production (in 000; metric tons; 1977): tin concentrates (metal content) 65; bauxite 615; cement 1,740; iron ore (56% metal content) 326; crude oil 8,790; petroleum products (Sarawak only; 1976) c. 950; gold (troy oz; 1976) 3.6; electricity (kw-hr) 7,206,000.

Malaysian and Thai security forces resumed joint operations against the insurgent Malayan Communist Party in the Betong area north of their common border. The Vietnamese prime minister, Pham Van Dong, paid a visit to Malaysia on October 12–16 during his tour of capitals of states belonging to the Association of Southeast Asian Nations.   (MICHAEL LEIFER)

About 2,500 Vietnamese refugees were stranded aboard a crowded freighter off the coast of Malaysia when that government refused to allow them to land in November. Canada, France, and the U.S. later agreed to accept the refugees, many of whom had become sick.

Maldives

Maldives, a republic in the Indian Ocean consisting of about two thousand small islands, lies southwest of the southern tip of India. Area: 298 sq km (115 sq mi). Pop. (1978 census): 143,000. Cap.: Male (pop., 1978, 29,600). Language: Divehi. Religion: Muslim. Presidents in 1978, Ibrahim Nasir and, from November 11, Maumoon Abdul Gayoom. Pres. Ibrahim Nasir, in office since 1968, declined to serve a third term. Maumoon Abdul Gayoom, nominated president-elect by the Majlis (Parliament), was sworn in as president on Nov. 11, 1978.

In January Maldives joined the International Monetary Fund and the World Bank, and in February it was admitted as the 43rd member of the Asian Development Bank. The Indian and Kuwaiti governments provided aid for the development of Hulele airport. India operated Maldive International Air's first jumbo jet service, which helped the fast-growing tourist trade.

Tourism was encouraged by free port and no-passport facilities, but suffered a setback as the result of a severe cholera epidemic and President Nasir's January statement that no "hippies" would be admitted. Foreign currency only was accepted at tourist resorts in an effort to fill the $500,000 a year gap left when the British abandoned the air base on Gan Island. As a nonaligned state, Maldives had refused the 1977 Soviet offer of $1 million to lease the island as a fishing base. The many local unemployed, bereft of prosperity, educational facilities, and hospital treatment, claimed the Male government was deliberately neglecting them in revenge for an attempted secession in the 1950s. The government changed Independence Day to March 29, the date when Britain handed over Gan in 1976. (MOLLY MORTIMER)

> **MALDIVES**
> **Education.** (1977) Primary, pupils 4,411, teachers 30; secondary, pupils 641, teachers 55; teacher training, students 30, teachers 11.
> **Finance and Trade.** Monetary unit: Maldivian rupee, with (Sept. 18, 1978) a par value of MRs 3.93 to U.S. $1 (MRs 7.70 = £1 sterling). Budget (1976) revenue MRs 17.2 million; expenditure MRs 35.7 million. Foreign trade (1976): imports MRs 21,498,000; exports MRs 11,755,000. Main destinations: Sri Lanka, Japan, and Thailand. Main exports: Maldive (dried) fish 46%; raw fish 44%; shells 5%.

Mali

A republic of West Africa, Mali is bordered by Algeria, Niger, Upper Volta, Ivory Coast, Guinea, Senegal, and Mauritania. Area: 1,240,142 sq km (478,832 sq mi). Pop. (1977 est.): 6,468,200. Cap. and largest city: Bamako (pop., 1976, 404,022). Language: French (official); Hamito-Semitic and various tribal dialects. Religion: Muslim 65%; animist 30%. Head of the military government in 1978, Col. Moussa Traoré.

There was no relaxation in Mali's internal power struggle or resolution of the country's economic difficulties during 1978. Col. Moussa Traoré strengthened his personal power and that of his government. In February an attempted coup led to the arrest of 43 officers, including the ministers of foreign affairs, transport, and the interior and the head of the security services. Kissima Doukara, former minister of the interior, and Tiecoro Bagayoko, security chief, were sentenced to death.

Mali strengthened its links with both the U.S.S.R. and France. The Soviet deputy-minister of defense visited Bamako in June, and Mali was thought to be the West African country receiving the most Soviet military aid. The French cooperation minister paid two visits, in January and November. France was giving considerable technical and financial aid to Mali, which suffered from inherited economic problems, corruption, and bad management in the public sector.

(PHILIPPE DECRAENE)

Maldives

Mali

Malta

> **MALI**
> **Education.** (1975–76) Primary, pupils 253,351, teachers 9,413; secondary, pupils 48,168, teachers (1974–75) 511; vocational, pupils 2,605, teachers (1970–71) 332; teacher training (1974–75), students 1,839, teachers 126; higher (1974–75), students 2,445, teaching staff 327.
> **Finance.** Monetary unit: Mali franc, with (Sept. 18, 1978) a par value of MFr 100 to the French franc and a free rate of MFr 438 to U.S. $1 (MFr 857 = £1 sterling). Budget (1978 est.) balanced at MFr 61 billion.
> **Foreign Trade.** (1977) Imports MFr 71.4 billion; exports MFr 32.9 billion. Import sources (1976): France c. 35%; Ivory Coast c. 27%; China 7%; U.S.S.R. c. 6%; West Germany c. 5%. Export destinations (1976): France c. 24%; China c. 11%; West Germany c. 10%. Main exports: cotton 43%; peanuts 12%; livestock c. 10%; textile yarns and fabrics c. 5%.
> **Agriculture.** Production (in 000; metric tons; 1977): millet and sorghum c. 850; rice (1976) 237; corn (1976) 81; peanuts c. 230; sweet potatoes (1976) c. 36; cassava (1976) c. 401; cottonseed c. 78; cotton, lint c. 43; beef and veal (1976) c. 38; mutton and lamb (1976) c. 30; fish catch c. 100. Livestock (in 000; 1976): cattle c. 4,080; sheep c. 4,219; goats c. 3,930; camels c. 178; horses c. 150; asses c. 400.

Malta

The Republic of Malta, a member of the Commonwealth of Nations, comprises the islands of Malta, Gozo, and Comino in the Mediterranean Sea between Sicily and Tunisia. Area: 316 sq km (122 sq mi), including Malta, Gozo, and Comino. Pop. (1978 est.): 326,000. Cap.: Valletta (pop., 1977 est., 14,100). Largest city: Sliema (pop., 1977 est., 20,100). Language: Maltese and English. Religion: mainly Roman Catholic. President in 1978, Anton Buttigieg; prime minister, Dom Mintoff.

Foreign policy dominated the Maltese political scene throughout 1978. Prime Minister Dom Mintoff was assured by U.S. Pres. Jimmy Carter that the U.S. was encouraging other countries to help Malta, but in September Mintoff revealed that discussions with Italy and France regarding guarantees for Malta's neutrality had ended fruitlessly; as a result, agreements with Libya and Algeria were being worked out. In July British journalists were barred from Malta and the British Forces Broadcasting Service was closed.

In November Malta appealed to Libya to solve, on a brotherly basis, the median line question involving the continental shelf boundary between the two countries. Exploration for oil had been impeded because of the dispute. Libya, which had been supplying low-cost oil to Malta since 1974, was refusing to refer the question to the International Court of Justice. The matter was especially pressing for Malta, which would need to make up the loss of M£28 million annually after the military bases agreement with Britain and NATO expires in March 1979.

Later, the Maltese government prohibited importation of British textiles and closed down the British Council in retaliation for Britain's request to the European Commission to restrict Maltese textile imports.

The government budgeted for a record expenditure of M£109.2 million in 1978–79. Two highly controversial laws were passed in July, to restructure tertiary education and to prohibit the use (without government authorization) of "Malta" or "nation" in the name of any publication or association. The labour dispute with doctors, which started in June 1977, continued.   (ALBERT GANADO)

MALTA

Education. (1976–77) Primary, pupils 29,063, teachers 1,428; secondary, pupils 25,953, teachers 1,773; vocational, pupils 4,332, teachers 375; higher, students 1,285, teaching staff 125.

Finance. Monetary unit: Maltese pound, with (Sept. 18, 1978) a free rate of M£0.38 = U.S. $1 (M£0.74 = £1 sterling). Gold, SDR's, and foreign exchange (June 1978) U.S. $788.6 million. Budget (1976–77 actual): revenue M£102.8 million; expenditure M£90.2 million.

Foreign Trade. (1977) Imports M£217,680,000; exports M£121,790,000. Import sources: U.K. 26%; Italy 18%; West Germany 11%; U.S. 9%; France 5%. Export destinations: West Germany 31%; U.K. 19%; Libya 11%; ship and aircraft stores 6%; The Netherlands 5%; Italy 5%; Belgium-Luxembourg 5%. Main exports: clothing 42%; machinery 7%; food 7%; petroleum products 6%; printed matter 5%. Tourism (1976): visitors 340,000; gross receipts U.S. $67 million.

Transport and Communications. Roads (1976) 1,271 km. Motor vehicles in use (1976): passenger 56,400; commercial 12,600. There are no railways. Air traffic (1976): 340.3 million passenger-km; freight 3,780,000 net ton-km. Shipping (1977): merchant vessels 100 gross tons and over 44; gross tonnage 100,420. Shipping traffic (1977): goods loaded 161,900 metric tons, unloaded 1,162,000 metric tons. Telephones (March 1977) 62,300. Radio licenses (Dec. 1976) 66,500. Television licenses (Dec. 1976) 63,000.

Materials Sciences

Ceramics. Cost reductions and energy savings continued as central themes within the ceramics industry in 1978. The ceramic dinnerware industry in the U.S. verged on a breakthrough in its application of dry pressing and fast-firing processes, one that was thought to assure continued competitiveness with plastics and other alternatives to ceramics in domestic and world markets. In conventional wet forming processes at least 25% water is added to the clay body to achieve plasticity. By switching to dry pressing, capital equipment and labour required to introduce the water uniformly are avoided and the time and energy required to remove the water prior to firing are

Manufacturing:
see Economy, World; Industrial Review

Marine Biology:
see Life Sciences

saved. In the new process spray-dried powders containing only about 5–7% water are pressed to shape in carefully designed dies on automated hydraulic or mechanical presses. Automatic presses under construction were expected to be capable of producing 10–24 pieces per minute and to be better suited to automatic handling of the dinnerware through the glazing and decorating stages of production prior to delivery to roller-hearth kilns for fast firing.

Because heating ceramics to produce strength and hardness is highly energy intensive, fast firing has received much attention in recent years. For example, by the late 1970s wall tile could be fired to 1,260° C (2,300° F) in as little as ten minutes, for a fuel saving of 50% compared with older methods. Whereas dinnerware firing was much more complex, even high-temperature porcelain could be fired to good quality in 45 minutes with proper compositional modifications. A major problem remaining was the cost and durability of the kiln furniture, which had to withstand rapid, repeated firing cycles.

Energy saving was also essential in the cement-making industry, one of the top ten energy consumers in the U.S. and user of 1.6% of all the world's energy as recently as 1971. Conversion to dry processing had already reduced the energy used in removing water that once had been required for ease in mixing raw materials. Recently a composition change introduced by P. Kumar Mehta of the University of California, Berkeley, was expected to save 25% of the energy consumed in portland cement production. The high iron oxide content in the new formula reduces the amount of lime that must be formed by dissociation of limestone during firing and lowers the firing temperature by 170°–220° C (300°–400° F).

Corning Glass Works, Corning, N.Y., announced a new type of product, called polychromatic glass, that may represent the first photographic medium with true colour permanence. When activated by controlled ultraviolet-light exposures and heat treatments, the glass yields a full range of opaque or transparent colours in two- or three-dimensional patterns. The colours were thought to derive from the formation of subcolloidal metallic particles of silver in a range of shapes and sizes.

Magnetic-bubble memory devices, which can store vast amounts of information on a tiny integrated circuit, achieved their first Bell System application as part of an announcement system to replace current drum recorders that store and deliver standard "call assist" messages. Invented at Bell Laboratories, Murray Hill, N.J., bubble devices employ the formation and movement of magnetic microdomains (which are minute regions of magnetization) in thin-film garnet crystals for the storage and retrieval of bits of information.

Use of glass and graphite fibre grew dramatically as applications expanded for fibre-reinforced plastic. Nearly 2,000,000,000 pounds were used in 1978, about one-quarter in the automotive industry for weight, cost, and fuel savings. New compounding and moulding techniques allowed faster production rates and increased fibre content for improved strength. Although glass fibres were still by far the most common reinforcement, use for graphite in high-performance composites increased as well, and in some cases the cost of graphite fibre was reduced 10–20%. Some initial applications of graphite fibres could be slowed, however, by recent indications that accidental release into the atmosphere of this light, electrically conductive material could cause interference with electronic equipment. (NORMAN M. TALLAN) [721.D.2; 724.C.5]

Metallurgy. The year 1978 was marked by poor markets for most metals, a factor that joined with constantly rising costs to keep expansion and modernization slow. Many of the new plants were in less developed countries trying to increase production for both export and domestic use. Research and development efforts directly concerned with metals also were reduced by diversion of manpower to environmental, safety, and product liability problems as well as by high cost. Modernization, especially to increase efficiency, included several new blast furnaces. Plants for the direct reduction of iron ore without melting, although still a small contributor to world production, continued to multiply. The Soviet Union purchased such a plant, the world's largest, with a capacity of 1.7 million tons a year or about that of a large blast furnace. A direct-reduction steel plant in Qatar with a capacity of 400,000 tons a year started production using the nation's abundant natural gas resources.

The oxygen-argon decarburizing process, which improves the corrosion resistance and weldability of stainless steel, was being used in more than half of U.S. production. Nitrogen and other gases including steam were under study as replacements for the expensive argon.

Continuous casting was in use in an estimated 20% of the world's steel production. Ever larger and faster machines were coming on line; one very large caster was producing 100 × 10-inch slab at 45 inches per minute. Induction stirring of the molten metal during continuous casting, using equipment similar to that for heating, was shown to improve the surface finish and internal quality of slab as well as to allow increased casting speed. A third-generation caster for aluminum was expected to reduce energy consumption for production of sheet by 35% compared with conventional hot rolling of ingots. The French-developed machine was in a U.S. plant.

Numerous developments, particularly in high-formability alloys and high-temperature die material, were making possible "net-shape" isothermal forging of parts to within a few thousandths of an inch of final shape. For some titanium parts a powder preform is made by cold compacting a mixture of pure titanium and master alloy powders. Diffusion of the metals during net-shape forging produces a homogeneous alloy part less expensive than one made with prealloyed powder.

For some years it had been known that rapid quenching of molten metal alloys could cause them to solidify into an amorphous, or glassy, state characterized by an absence of crystalline struc-

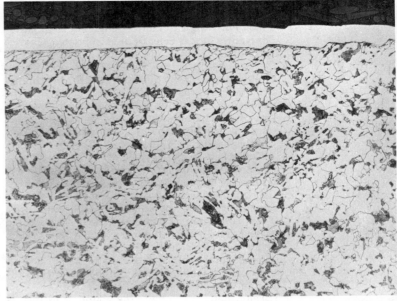

Highly magnified cross section of a steel plate reveals the suitability of chemical explosives in welding a razor-thin ribbon of metallic glass alloy (narrow white strip) to a thicker sheet of ordinary steel (speckled region). The featureless appearance of metallic glass, which possesses no regular atomic structure, contrasts markedly with the graininess of the steel, which is made up of discrete crystal regions.

ture. Such metallic glasses were found to be highly resistant to wear, corrosion, and radiation damage but were previously available only as powders, wires, and thin ribbons because of fabrication limitations imposed by the need to avoid the high temperatures of ordinary welding and casting operations, which would recrystallize, or devitrify, the materials. One method employed for ribbon production involves spraying a jet of molten metal onto a cold rotating drum, which acts to chill the metal at a rate of millions of degrees per second. Recently it was demonstrated that controlled chemical explosions could compress metallic glass powders into strong bulk shapes and weld thin ribbons to conventional metal plates to form protective coatings. A precisely arranged explosion squeezes the glassy material into shape so rapidly that devitrifying levels of heat do not build up.

Few materials except those for photovoltaic cells have been developed especially for solar energy utilization. One recent exception was a black coating electrodeposited on foil in a continuous plating line. The material has as much as 25% greater heat absorption than black paint and was being supplied with pressure-sensitive adhesive backing for application to nearly any surface.

(DONALD F. CLIFTON)

[725.B]

See also Industrial Review: *Glass; Iron and Steel; Machinery and Machine Tools;* Mining and Quarrying.

Mathematics

The major news in mathematics in 1978, as it is every fourth year, was the awarding of the prestigious Fields medals. Regarded as the equivalent for mathematics of the Nobel prizes, these medals are presented at the quadrennial meetings of the International Congress of Mathematicians to persons under the age of 40 who have achieved great distinction in research and show considerable promise for further achievement.

The 1978 Fields medals, awarded in August at the meeting of the International Congress in Helsinki, Fin., went to Pierre Deligne of the Institut des Hautes Études Scientifiques in France, Charles Fefferman of Princeton University in New Jersey, G. A. Margulis of the Soviet Union, and Daniel Quillen of the Massachusetts Institute of Technology. These awards bring to a total of only 24 the number of Fields medals that have been awarded since the prize was established in 1932 by a bequest from the Canadian mathematician John Charles Fields.

Deligne, a Belgian, was cited for his recent introduction of a new strategy called weights theory, which has had important applications in differential equations, and for his solution in 1974 of three famous problems known as the Weil conjectures. These conjectures, formulated about 30 years ago by the French mathematician André Weil, relate on a very abstract level certain properties of prime numbers to the solutions of equations in finite systems of arithmetic. (Prime numbers are those divisible only by themselves and by one.)

Fefferman, at 29 one of the youngest recipients of a Fields medal, was cited for several innovations in classical analysis that have opened new areas of study in the interface of harmonic analysis, complex analysis, and differential equations. His work is dominated by an uncanny insight into the correct generalizations to high dimensions of lower-dimensional theorems; this led Fefferman to the solutions of many problems long thought to be unsolvable. In 1976 Fefferman was the first recipi-

ent of the National Science Foundation's Alan T. Waterman award for individuals who are considered by their colleagues to be in the forefront of science. He was also at age 22 appointed to a full professorship at the University of Chicago, making him the youngest person ever to achieve that rank in the history of U.S. higher education.

Margulis received his Fields medal for his penetrating analysis of the internal structure of objects called Lie groups, which combine algebraic, geometric, and analytical structures into a single object. Because of this special unity, Lie groups permit mathematicians to employ powerful tools of algebra and topology developed in recent decades to unravel centuries-old mysteries posed by differential equations. These accomplishments have led, in turn, to widespread applications in chemistry, physics, and cosmology, making Lie groups one of the most important tools of the applied mathematician.

Quillen was cited as being the prime architect of a new field known as algebraic K-theory that has successfully employed geometric and topological tools to solve major problems from algebra. In 1976 Quillen solved an important problem posed 20 years earlier by a 1954 Fields medalist, Jean-Pierre Serre, concerning the structure of certain abstract spaces. The importance of Quillen's solution is that it showed that many of the generalized spaces that have been the hallmark of 20th-century mathematics can be constructed from elementary components, one dimension at a time, just like the ordinary two- and three-dimensional space of Eu-

Adding extensions to an equilateral triangle in a strict repeating pattern produces shapes that progress from a star to complex "snowflakes" and ultimately to a shape whose perimeter has infinite length yet contains a finite area. Although this construction has been known for 75 years, its properties form part of the recently developed topologic concept of fractals, which seeks to define and describe extremely irregular curves and surfaces.

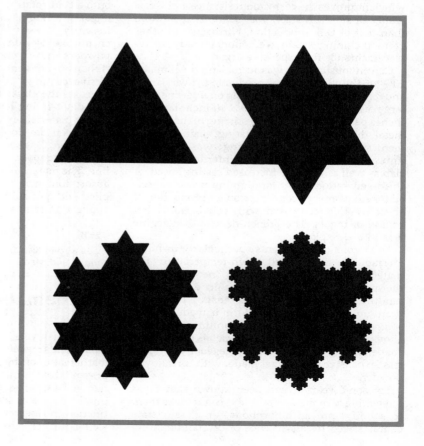

clidean geometry. Mathematics progresses most with theorems that say "this structure is just like that one"; Quillen's work has done just that for many parts of algebra and topology.

Finally, it should be noted that Kurt Gödel died on January 14. Gödel was a premier logician, a man whose name became a legend in such diverse fields as philosophy, computer science, and mathematics. His towering achievement was his proof in 1931 that no axiomatic structure of mathematics can ever be complete nor can it ever be proved internally consistent (*see* OBITUARIES).

(LYNN ARTHUR STEEN)

Mauritania

The Islamic Republic of Mauritania is on the Atlantic coast of West Africa, adjoining Western (Spanish) Sahara, Algeria, Mali, and Senegal. Area: 1,030,700 sq km (398,000 sq mi). Pop. (1977): 1,420,000. Cap.: Nouakchott (pop., 1977, 135,000). (Data above refer to Mauritania as constituted prior to the purported division of Spanish Sahara between Mauritania and Morocco.) Language: Arabic, French. Religion: Muslim. President in 1978, Moktar Ould Daddah until July 10; head of the Military Committee for National Recovery after July 10, Lieut Col. Mustafa Ould Salek.

Against a background of economic and financial crisis due to the continuing war in the Western Sahara and dissatisfaction in the Army following various purges, a coup d'état ousted Pres. Moktar Ould Daddah during the night of July 9–10, 1978. The Military Committee for National Recovery, led by Lieut. Col. Mustafa Ould Salek (*see* BIOGRAPHIES), seized power. At the same time, the Polisario Front, which was fighting for independence for the Western Sahara, decided to call a unilateral cease-fire in Mauritania.

In November Lieut. Col. Ould Salek visited Paris, where talks began with the various parties involved in the Saharan problem. Presidents Félix Houphouët-Boigny of Ivory Coast and Léopold Sédar Senghor (*see* BIOGRAPHIES) of Senegal served as intermediaries.

In September Mauritania's new head of state visited Rabat in search of Moroccan diplomatic support for his peace initiative with the Polisario Front, and he later undertook secret contacts with the Polisario. The latter, meeting at its fourth general congress in Tindouf in September, extended the cease-fire in Mauritania, while continuing its attacks in Morocco.

Accusing the old regime of mismanagement, the new government promised to revive the country's economy. Emphasis was to be put on agriculture, fisheries, and small industry, and the country's massive external debt was to be rescheduled.

(PHILIPPE DECRAENE)

See also Morocco.

Mauritania

Mauritius

The parliamentary state of Mauritius, a member of the Commonwealth of Nations, lies about 800 km E of Madagascar in the Indian Ocean; it includes the island dependencies of Rodrigues, Agalega, and Cargados Carajos. Area: 2,040 sq km (787.5 sq mi). Pop. (1978 est.): 920,000, including (1972) Indian 66%; Creole (mixed French and African) 31%; others 3%. Cap. and largest city: Port Louis (pop., 1977 est., 143,000). Language: English (official); French has official standing for certain legislative and judicial purposes; and Creole is the lingua franca. Religion (1974 est.): Hindu 51%; Christian 30%; Muslim 16%; Buddhist 3%. Queen, Elizabeth II; governor-general in 1978, Sir Abdul Rahman Muhammad Osman; prime minister, Sir Seewoosagur Ramgoolam.

Mauritius

On March 12, 1978, Mauritius celebrated a decade of independence under the same prime minister, though he had governed with a minority coalition since the 1976 elections and was pressed by the opposition left-wing Mauritius Militant Movement. The immediate political problem remained the form of republic within the Commonwealth of Nations that Mauritius should become.

With an unprecedented trade deficit and a budgetary deficit of MauRs 300 million, the year opened gloomily. Despite some diversification of products, Mauritius remained dependent upon sugar, which supplied more than 80% of its export revenue. Although long-term sugar contracts under the Lomé Convention were guaranteed until 1980, escalating costs, low productivity, disease,

MAURITANIA

Education. (1974–75) Primary, pupils 47,000, teachers 1,768; secondary, pupils 5,493, teachers (1973–74) 200; vocational, pupils 1,591, teachers (1973–74) 117; teacher training (1971–72), students 145.

Finance. Monetary unit: ouguiya, with (Sept. 18, 1978) a free rate of 43.61 ouguiya = U.S. $1 (85.46 ouguiya = £1 sterling). Gold, SDR's, and foreign exchange (June 1978) U.S. $26.6 million. Budget (1977 est.) balanced at 7,750,-000,000 ouguiya.

Foreign Trade. (1977) Imports 9,458,000,000 ouguiya; exports 7,156,000,000 ouguiya. Import sources: France *c.* 55%; West Germany *c.* 11%; U.S. *c.* 10%; Spain *c.* 8%. Export destinations: France *c.* 24%; West Germany *c.* 11%; Japan *c.* 15%; Italy *c.* 12%; Spain *c.* 11%; Belgium-Luxembourg *c.* 10%; U.K. *c.* 9%. Main exports iron ore 80%; copper; fish.

MAURITIUS

Education. (1977) Primary, pupils 140,844, teachers 6,-269; secondary, pupils 78,429, teachers 2,452; vocational, pupils 1,141, teachers 93; teacher training (1976), students 700, teachers (1975) 19; higher (1977), students 854, teaching staff 100.

Finance and Trade. Monetary unit: Mauritian rupee, with (Sept. 18, 1978) a free rate of MauRs 6.07 to U.S. $1 (MauRs 11.90 = £1 sterling). Gold, SDR's, and foreign exchange (June 1978) U.S. $75.9 million. Budget (1977–78 est.): revenue MauRs 1,165,000,000; expenditure MauRs 1,201,000,000. Foreign trade (1977): imports MauRs 2,918,000,000; exports MauRs 2,058,400,000. Import sources (1976): U.K. 16%; France 10%; South Africa 10%; Japan 8%; Iran 7%; West Germany 6%; Australia 5%. Export destinations (1976): U.K. 69%; France 9%; U.S. 6%. Main exports (1976): sugar 75%; clothing 12%. Tourism: visitors (1974) 73,000; gross receipts (1975) U.S. $22 million.

Agriculture. Production (in 000; metric tons; 1977): sugar, raw value *c.* 715; bananas (1976) *c.* 5; tea *c.* 4; tobacco *c.* 1; milk *c.* 22. Livestock (in 000; April 1976): cattle *c.* 53; pigs *c.* 5; sheep *c.* 3; goats *c.* 67; chickens *c.* 1,100.

and the risk of cyclones caused observers to be pessimistic about future crops. The two successive five-year plans were on target in their effort to provide more than 100,000 jobs by 1980, largely through the development of an industrial free zone (Export Processing Zone) that offered fiscal incentives to foreign investment in export-oriented industries. One of the most promising developments was the reduction over the decade of the birthrate from 3 to 1.7%, in one of the most densely populated areas of the world. (MOLLY MORTIMER)

Mexico

Mexico

A federal republic of Middle America, Mexico is bounded by the Pacific Ocean, the Gulf of Mexico, the U.S., Belize, and Guatemala. Area: 1,972,546 sq km (761,604 sq mi). Pop. (1978 est.): 66,944,000, including about 55% mestizo and 29% Indian. Cap. and largest city: Mexico City (pop., 1978 est., federal district 8,988,200, metro. area 13,993,900). Language: Spanish. Religion: predominantly Roman Catholic. President in 1978, José López Portillo.

Some of the political reforms promised by Pres. José López Portillo in 1977 began to be carried out in 1978, including the legalization in May of three minority parties, the Mexican Communist Party, the Revolutionary Socialist Party, and the Mexican Popular Party. The Chamber of Deputies was also restructured to allow greater representation for minority groups. Four members of the previous administration were arrested on corruption charges.

In October members of the 20,000-strong Association of Self-Defense for Peasants, formed early in 1977, invaded lands in the Tuxtepec area in the state of Oaxaca. They demanded that 150,000 ha of communal land, which they claimed private farmers had taken from them, be returned to them. The week-long invasion was disbanded by about 200 armed police. The peasants agreed to withdraw, pending a government promise to look into the matter. Agricultural production was affected by drought in the first half of the year and by heavy rains in October in the wheat- and soybean-pro-

ducing area of the state of Sonora, with storm damage estimated at $4.4 million.

Strikes in 1978, including those in steel, textiles, a brewery, copper mining, and telephones, were mainly for wage increases (on an average kept to 12%). A 23-day strike by air traffic controllers was caused by the granting of control of the private company they were working for to the state.

In his annual message to the nation in September President López Portillo stated that proven petroleum reserves were now 20 billion bbl, probable reserves 37 billion bbl, and potential resources 200 billion bbl (including the two former amounts). At the year's end the nation's production of hydrocarbons stood at approximately 1.4 billion bbl a day, 50% over November 1976.

The president also said that government employees would be granted a 12% wage increase if they earned up to 15,000 pesos a month and a 1,800-peso increase if pay was over that amount, and that the annual bonus would be increased from 20 to 40 days' pay. The nation needed to have about three million new houses built by 1982, but only half of that requirement could be fulfilled. Redistribution of land was to proceed, but large plots would only be granted to cooperatives.

On the government front, bills being presented to Congress related to the appointment of temporary governors in states where constitutional powers had been suspended, to the right to work, and to the right to information. An amnesty law for political prisoners was also presented, but it was marred by the kidnapping and killing of the 35-year-old son of Mexico's ambassador to the U.S., Hugo Margain, on August 29. Plans to release prisoners nevertheless proceeded.

President López Portillo also forecast a real growth in the economy of about 5% in 1978 as compared with approximately 2% in 1977. The consumer price index, he said, had increased by 8% during the first half of the year (13% in January–June 1977).

Relations were improved with the U.S.S.R. and Bulgaria as a result of López Portillo's visit to both in May to discuss matters related to oil, technology, and especially agricultural systems. The latter was also a central theme in discussions with

---

MEXICO

Education. (1976–77) Primary, pupils 12,600,620, teachers (1975–76) 253,990; secondary and vocational, pupils 2,999,456, teachers (1975–76) 142,274; teacher training (1975–76), students 111,502, teachers 8,396; higher, students 599,920, teaching staff 30,865.

Finance. Monetary unit: peso, with (Sept. 18, 1978) a free rate of 22.84 pesos to U.S. $1 (free rate of 44.75 pesos = £1 sterling). Gold, SDR's, and foreign exchange (May 1978) U.S. $1,756,000,000. Budget (central; 1977 actual) revenue 194 billion pesos; expenditure 249 billion pesos. Gross domestic product (1976) 1,220,800,000,000 pesos. Money supply (Dec. 1977) 199,040,000,000 pesos. Cost of living (1975 = 100; June 1978) 169.7.

Foreign Trade. (1977) Imports 124,094,000,000 pesos; exports 94,140,000,000 pesos. Import sources: U.S. 64%; West Germany 6%; Japan 5%. Export destinations: U.S. 58%; Brazil 4%. Main exports (1976): crude oil 16%; coffee 10%; cotton 8%; metals and ores 8%; machinery 6%; chemicals 5%;

shrimps 5%; textile yarns and fabrics 5%. Tourism (1975): visitors 3,217,900; gross receipts U.S. $2,142,000,000.

Transport and Communications. Roads (1976) 193,390 km (of which 1,062 km expressways). Motor vehicles in use (1976): passenger 2,641,000; commercial 976,700. Railways: (1974) 24,700 km; traffic (1976) 4,058,000,000 passenger-km, freight 34,821,-000,000 net ton-km. Air traffic (1976): 7,833,000,000 passenger-km; freight 83,400,000 net ton-km. Shipping (1977): merchant vessels 100 gross tons and over 311; gross tonnage 673,964. Telephones (Jan. 1977) 3,309,000. Radio receivers (Dec. 1974) 17,514,000. Television receivers (Dec. 1974) 4,885,-000.

Agriculture. Production (000; metric tons; 1977): corn 8,991; wheat 2,451; barley 409; sorghum c. 3,-350; rice 481; potatoes c. 708; sugar, raw value 2,545; dry beans 745; soybeans 565; tomatoes c. 964; bananas c. 1,351; oranges c. 1,142; lemons c. 611; cottonseed c. 540; coffee c. 270; tobacco c. 57; cotton,

lint c. 327; beef and veal 542; pork 451; fish catch (1976) 572. Livestock (in 000; Dec. 1976): cattle 28,-935; sheep 7,861; pigs 11,986; goats 8,343; horses (1975) c. 5,818; mules (1975) c. 2,648; asses (1975) c. 2,978; chickens 147,705.

Industry. Production (in 000; metric tons; 1977): cement 13,097; crude oil 49,550; coal (1976) 5,650; natural gas (cu m) 23,280; electricity (kw-hr) 50,052,-000; iron ore (metal content) 3,594; pig iron 4,428; crude steel 5,397; sulfur (1976) 2,148; petroleum products (1976) c. 32,740; sulfuric acid 2,032; fertilizers (nutrient content; 1976–77) nitrogenous c. 650, phosphate c. 237; aluminum 43; copper 73; lead 160; zinc 171; antimony ore (metal content; 1976) 2.5; manganese ore (metal content; 1976) 184; gold (troy oz; 1976) 159; silver (troy oz) c. 48,000; cotton yarn (1975) 158; woven cotton fabrics 65; wool yarn (1975) 37; man-made fibres (1976) 166; radio receivers (units; 1976) 1,135; television receivers (units; 1976) 729; passenger cars (units) 200; commercial vehicles (units) 76.

WIDE WORLD

In an attempt to expand trade, Mexican Pres. José López Portillo visited China and Japan. During his visit he toured a petrochemical plant in Peking.

China, which the president visited in late October, when he also went to Japan. Former president Luis Echeverría Álvarez was appointed ambassador to Australia in that month. The resumption of good relations with Spain after some 40 years was marked by a six-day state visit to Mexico in November by King Juan Carlos and Queen Sophia, during which various cooperation agreements were signed. Relations with the U.S. were briefly marred by press reports that U.S. authorities planned to build a fence along the U.S.-Mexican border to stop illegal immigration into the U.S. (*See* MIGRATION, INTERNATIONAL: *Special Report.*)

Four major earthquakes on November 29 caused eight deaths in Mexico City and one in Oaxaca.

(BARBARA WIJNGAARD)

Middle Eastern Affairs

The state of the Middle East was radically altered in 1978 by the first real moves in 30 years toward the conclusion of peace between Israel and its largest Arab neighbour, Egypt. Most other Arab states were opposed in varying degrees to these moves, as a result of which the Arab world was deeply divided.

Egypt-Israel Negotiations and the Front of Steadfastness. At the beginning of 1978 the Arab states were still reacting to the visit of Egypt's Pres. Anwar as-Sadat (*see* NOBEL PRIZES) to Jerusalem in November 1977 and the Israeli-Egyptian political and military negotiations which it initiated. U.S. Pres. Jimmy Carter toured the Middle East in the first week of January but elicited no positive response from other Arab states to Sadat's initiative. In Egypt he assured Sadat that the U.S. would play a positive role in the peace

process, as Egypt wanted, while Sadat declared that U.S. and Egyptian views on the Middle East were identical.

Palestine Liberation Organization (PLO) leaders and the Syrian government declared their strong opposition to Sadat's policies. However, strenuous efforts by Algeria's Pres. Houari Boumédienne (*see* OBITUARIES) to reconcile the rival Baathist regimes in Syria and Iraq were a failure. Boumédienne had hoped to persuade Iraq to join the "Front of Steadfastness" of Arab states opposed to Sadat. Iraq, which had walked out of the front's summit meeting in Tripoli in December attended by Syria, Libya, Algeria, Yemen (Aden; South Yemen), and the PLO, continued to insist that Syria should first reject UN resolutions on the Middle East. It opposed efforts to boycott Egypt entirely and considered Syria almost as guilty as Egypt. On these grounds it refused to attend bilateral talks with Syria or the front's second summit, held in Algiers, February 2–4.

Meanwhile, the Israeli-Egyptian Military Committee, meeting in Cairo, was making some progress over the Sinai question but was encountering difficulties over the issue of Israeli settlements in the occupied territories. The Israeli settlers in the Sinai, who opposed returning the land on which their settlements stood to Egypt, were beginning to put effective pressure on the government of Israeli Prime Minister Menahem Begin (*see* NOBEL PRIZES). The talks broke down after the Israeli-Egyptian Political Committee met in Jerusalem on January 17, despite U.S. attempts to mediate.

In February Sadat made a tour of eight countries, including the U.S., to promote his peace initiative. The announcement on February 14 that the U.S. would sell modern F-15 fighter planes to both Saudi Arabia and Israel, F-16s to Israel, and less advanced F-5s to Egypt—a decision approved by the U.S. Senate on May 15—was seen as a move to encourage Egypt. It was also a measure of U.S. concern about relations with Saudi Arabia, which the U.S. hoped would maintain its moderate oil-price policy. Military experts generally agreed that the sale would not alter the military balance in the Middle East significantly. Israeli opposition was based largely on the political implications.

On February 20 U.S. envoy Alfred Atherton resumed shuttle diplomacy between Israel and the Arab states, but with little result. His visit to Cairo was overshadowed by the assassination in Cyprus of Sadat's friend Youssef as-Sebai by Palestinian guerrillas and the abortive Egyptian attempt to recapture the plane they had hijacked, an incident that led to a worsening of Egypt's relations with the Palestinians. (*See* CYPRUS.) Atherton returned to Jerusalem with a note from Sadat to Begin on Egyptian reactions to Israeli proposals, but no plans for new meetings were announced.

On March 11 attention was diverted to a Palestinian guerrilla raid in Israel, which left 37 dead and 82 wounded, and the subsequent invasion of southern Lebanon by Israel on March 14. The Arabs unanimously deplored the invasion, but they were unable to react because the Syrian-dominated Arab Deterrent Force (ADF) in Lebanon was not deployed south of the Litani River. Only

Israeli Prime Minister Menahem Begin, U.S. Pres. Jimmy Carter, and Egyptian Pres. Anwar as-Sadat held many lengthy and informal discussions during peace talks at Camp David, Maryland.

the Iraqis sent volunteers to support the Palestinians and Lebanese leftists in their rearguard action against the advancing Israelis. Sadat further distanced himself from the other Arab states by publicly deploring the Palestinian raid.

On March 19 the UN Security Council passed Resolution 425, calling for an Israeli withdrawal and establishment of the UN Interim Force in Lebanon (UNIFIL). UNIFIL reached a strength of 1,800 by April 11, including contingents from Iran, France, Sweden, and Norway. The Israelis withdrew in stages and had completely evacuated Lebanese territory by mid-June. They had been only partly successful in their aim of destroying Palestinian guerrillas and their bases south of the Litani. Several hundred Palestinians were killed, but the bulk of them escaped northward or remained in the Tyre enclave.

On May 10 Sadat said Israel should return the West Bank to Jordan and Gaza to Egypt as interim steps toward a peace settlement, but Israel rejected any return to the pre–1967 borders. Begin visited the U.S. in early May for the 30th anniversary of the state of Israel and made strong but unsuccessful appeals for rejection of the sale of arms to Saudi Arabia and Egypt. On May 30 Sadat threatened to end the 1974 Sinai pact with Israel unless progress was made toward peace, and in speeches on June 6 and 7 he threatened war if Israel did not make concessions. Formal Egyptian proposals that all Israeli settlements be removed and the military governments in the West Bank and Gaza abolished were sharply rejected by Israel. A vaguely worded Israeli response to U.S. questions on the future of the West Bank and Gaza and on Palestinian issues failed to satisfy the U.S. and caused a split in the Israeli Cabinet.

Egyptian-Israeli contacts were not resumed until Sadat's visit to Austria, July 7–14, when he held surprise meetings with the Israeli defense minister, Ezer Weizman (*see* BIOGRAPHIES), and opposition leader Shimon Peres. However, no immediate results followed from these meetings or from those held, at U.S. suggestion, in July at Leeds Castle in the U.K. among the Israeli, Egyptian, and U.S. foreign ministers.

On August 8 it was announced that both Sadat and Begin had accepted President Carter's invita-

tion to a U.S.-Israeli-Egyptian summit meeting at Camp David, Md., on September 5. This widened the rift between Sadat and other Arabs, who denounced what they saw as a certain trend toward a separate Israeli-Egyptian peace. After 12 days of negotiations, the Camp David meeting ended with two agreements, "a framework for peace in the Middle East" and "a framework for the conclusion of a peace treaty between Israel and Egypt." These agreements, which surprised the many observers who had expected failure, left many questions open, especially with regard to the future of the Israeli settlements in the West Bank, the length of the period during which Israel had agreed to freeze their development, and the linkage, if any, between Israeli-Egyptian peace and an Israeli withdrawal from the West Bank and Gaza.

As expected, the reaction from the Front of Steadfastness states was bitter denunciation. Among the more moderate Arab states, Saudi Arabia expressed displeasure that the agreements said nothing about Israeli withdrawal from all occupied Arab lands, especially Arab Jerusalem, or about the future of the Palestinian people; however, Saudi Arabia denied itself the right to criticize Egypt for recovering its lost territory by any means possible. Jordan was placed in a dilemma. King Hussein had rejected strong U.S. urging to join the peace talks and emphasized his own view that the agreements were unsatisfactory and inadequate for the Arabs. On the other hand, he was equally reluctant to join the Front of Steadfastness, although he held a surprise meeting with Libya's Pres. Muammar al-Qaddafi and PLO Chairman Yasir Arafat on the Jordanian-Syrian border September 22. The Front of Steadfastness states, meeting in Damascus, announced their intention to boycott Egypt politically and economically and to set up a joint military and political command.

The great weakness of the anti-Sadat front, the split between Syria and Iraq, was apparently ended during a visit by Syria's Pres. Hafez al-Assad to Baghdad on October 24–26. The two countries agreed to bury their differences and form a common front against the Camp David agreements. This paved the way for an anti-Camp David summit meeting which Iraq finally succeeded in holding in Baghdad on November 2. Saudi Arabia and

Jordan attended, along with the Arab Gulf states, but they opposed any attempt to take immediate action against Egypt. The Baghdad meeting agreed to establish a fund to fight the Camp David agreements and to take various sanctions against Egypt if and when it signed a peace agreement with Israel. The meeting also agreed to move the Arab League headquarters from Cairo to Tunis.

Meanwhile Egyptian-Israeli negotiations on their draft treaty began October 12. On October 16 the Israeli Cabinet voted to accept the draft treaty in outline, but both sides continued to press for further amendments. Israel's declared decision to expand its West Bank settlements was openly criticized by the U.S. The October 27 announcement that the Nobel Peace Prize would go jointly to Sadat and Begin was welcomed in Israel but caused some embarrassment in Egypt and provoked bitter comment in the anti-Sadat Arab states. (*See* NOBEL PRIZES.)

Negotiations reached an impasse in mid-November when Israel rejected Egypt's demands that the peace treaty between the two should be linked to a timetable for the establishment of Palestinian self-rule in the Israeli-occupied West Bank and Gaza territories. Israel held that such linkage was in contravention of the Camp David agreements. Egypt in turn objected to the inclusion in the draft treaty of a clause (article 6) that would in effect give priority to its obligation to peace with Israel over its inter-Arab obligations in any future war. Subsequent efforts by the U.S. to achieve a compromise were unsuccessful and at year's end the treaty remained unsigned.

Other Arab Affairs. The deteriorating situation in Lebanon and the possibility that the fighting between Syrian forces and the Lebanese Christian militia during September-October might lead to a renewal of the civil war caused deep concern in Arab states. Saudi Arabia, as the chief paymaster of the Syrian-dominated ADF, was especially involved. After an urgent meeting in Lebanon on October 15–17, the Arab foreign ministers announced a plan to restore order, which included the replacement of Syrian troops on the perimeter of Christian East Beirut by non-Syrian forces. The Saudis later agreed to increase their contingent of 1,000 in the ADF.

During the year there was a violent split within the PLO, marked by assassinations in London, Kuwait, and Paris. A radical wing moved to Baghdad, but the breach seemed to have been smoothed over by the end of August.

Arab states on the perimeter of the Red Sea were closely concerned by the events in the Horn of Africa. With the exception of South Yemen, they supported the Somalis and Eritrean nationalists in their struggle with the Marxist regime in Ethiopia and expressed their anxiety over Soviet and Cuban intervention in the area, especially the Communist forces' use of Aden as a staging area. Saudi Arabia's efforts to wean South Yemen away from the pro-Communist camp having failed, the Saudi government concentrated on attempting to isolate it. However, South Yemen's membership in the Front of Steadfastness was sufficient to prevent these moves from being effective.

Saudi Arabia and the Gulf states were all affected by the massive anti-shah demonstrations in Iran during the year. Saudi Arabia and Iraq both indicated their hope that the shah's regime would survive. Iraq even expelled the Ayatullah Ruhollah Khomeini, a Shi'a religious leader exiled from Iran and the shah's chief opponent.

(PETER MANSFIELD)

See also Energy; articles on the various political units.
[978.B]

Migration, International

Large numbers of ethnic Chinese from Vietnam, estimated by early September 1978 at 160,000, were reported to have crossed the border into China after expulsion by the Vietnamese authorities. (*See* VIETNAM.) In May reports that 200,000 Arakan Muslims had fled from Burma to Bangladesh to escape persecution by the Burmese authorities were discounted by the Burmese, who claimed that many of the Muslims were without national registration papers and had reacted in panic to the announcement of a citizenship check.

People also continued to leave Vietnam for non-Communist countries throughout 1977, and the pace increased during 1978. Largely middle class, the refugees had valuable occupational skills and

			Nonquota immigrants		
Immigration and Naturalization in the United States					
Year ended June 30, 1976					
Country or region	Total immigrants admitted	Quota immigrants	Total	Family— U.S. citizens	Aliens[1] naturalized
Africa	7,723	5,735	1,988	1,797	2,894
Asia[2]	149,881	102,258	47,623	44,239	56,465
China[3]	18,823	14,404	4,419	4,036	11,145
Hong Kong	5,766	5,002	764	674	...
India	17,487	16,462	1,025	839	5,574
Iran	2,700	1,825	875	857	836
Iraq	3,432	3,264	168	164	483
Israel	2,982	2,134	848	731	1,548
Japan	4,258	2,062	2,196	1,862	1,549
Jordan	2,566	2,074	492	471	1,381
Korea, South	30,803	20,011	10,792	10,045	10,446
Lebanon	2,840	2,346	494	466	1,154
Philippines	37,281	20,978	16,303	15,601	16,145
Thailand	6,925	1,782	5,141	4,805	985
Vietnam	3,048	1,027	2,021	1,787	1,412
Europe[4]	72,411	51,374	21,037	18,798	47,480
Germany, West	5,836	1,613	4,223	3,796	4,856
Greece	8,417	6,338	2,079	1,938	6,151
Italy	8,380	6,202	2,178	1,956	7,891
Poland	3,805	2,742	1,063	973	2,768
Portugal	10,511	9,309	1,202	1,065	3,739
Spain	2,254	1,341	913	788	886
U.S.S.R.	8,220	7,998	222	188	535
United Kingdom	11,392	6,649	4,743	4,186	9,345
Yugoslavia	2,820	2,253	567	527	2,447
North America	142,307	107,110	35,197	29,879	43,085
Canada	7,638	3,475	4,163	3,463	3,759
Cuba	29,233	27,999	1,234	476	20,506
Dominican Republic	12,526	10,464	2,062	1,799	1,904
El Salvador	2,363	1,667	696	642	470
Haiti	5,410	4,805	605	553	1,870
Jamaica	9,026	7,398	1,628	1,490	3,849
Mexico	57,863	39,459	18,404	15,392	6,301
Trinidad and Tobago	4,839	4,040	799	724	1,179
Oceania	3,591	2,381	1,210	1,066	760
South America	22,699	15,914	6,785	6,240	8,302
Argentina	2,267	1,663	604	513	1,574
Colombia	5,742	3,542	2,200	2,024	2,029
Ecuador	4,504	3,633	871	824	880
Guyana	3,326	2,895	431	407	980
Peru	2,640	1,624	1,016	977	850
Total, including others	398,613	284,773	113,840	102,019	159,873

Note: Immigrants listed by country of birth; aliens naturalized by country of former allegiance.
[1] Year ended Sept. 30, 1977. [2] Includes Turkey. [3] Taiwan and People's Republic.
[4] Includes U.S.S.R.
Source: U.S. Department of Justice, Immigration and Naturalization Service, 1976 Annual Report and unpublished data from 1977 Annual Report.

Vietnamese "boat people" living off the coast of Thailand. Many of the refugees destroyed their boats after they reached that country so that they could not be forced back out to sea.

left in family units to escape deteriorating living standards and food shortages. The rate of emigration by sea—by the so-called boat people—had risen to about 20,000 a month by November 1978. Many found their way to the U.S., and in November the administration sought to double the previously set intake through April 1979 to 30,000.

The Vietnamese were not welcomed everywhere, however. Thailand and Malaysia imposed restrictions on their entry, and Singapore declined to accept Vietnamese who could not guarantee their eventual resettlement elsewhere. On Dec. 5, 1977, Australian immigration officials flew to Malaysia to select Indochinese for settlement; 2,000 were admitted, bringing the total from 1975 to the end of June 1978 to approximately 9,000. On May 17, 1978, it was announced that Australia would accept a further 9,000 Indochinese in the 12-month period to June 31, 1979. Canada, France, and Britain admitted limited numbers of Vietnamese.

Nonwhites avoiding conscription or seeking higher education accounted for the bulk of 2,800 Rhodesian immigrants to Britain known to the Commonwealth Secretariat in July 1977. They had registered their presence as a result of a decision taken at the UN conference on racial discrimination in 1976. Emigration by whites from Rhodesia quickened during 1978, and in July officials conceded that the white population had fallen by 47,000 during the previous two years. (See RHODESIA.) Most of the emigrants moved to South Africa. Earlier reports of a visit by South African businessmen to certain South American countries in October 1976 spoke of 10,000 Rhodesians expressing a desire to migrate to Uruguay. In April 1977 a spokesman for the Bolivian Interior Ministry announced his government's intention to "encourage the entry of white immigrants of German and Dutch origin especially from Namibia, Rhodesia, and South Africa." Bolivia had approached the World Bank, the Inter-American Development Bank, and private sponsors for funds. On Jan. 7, 1977, Romania had announced that, over the following five years, 11,000 ethnic Ger-

mans would be allowed to leave the country annually. Some 60,000 of Romania's estimated 340,000 ethnic Germans had left since 1945, principally for West Germany. Jews leaving Romania were said to have numbered approximately 2,000 in 1976, a slight drop from the 1975 total. At a conference in Brussels on Soviet Jewry in February 1976 the chairman of the American Conference on Jewry had estimated that 750,000 Jews wished to leave the U.S.S.R.

The oil-producing countries of the Persian Gulf continued to attract workers, not only from the surrounding states of the Middle East but from as far afield as the Philippines, India, and South Korea. Three out of four jobs in the United Arab Emirates were held by foreigners. The number of South Koreans in Kuwait, 10,000 in October 1978, was expected to reach 80,000 by December.

Canada's revised Immigration Act and Regulations, which went into effect on April 10, 1978, sought to link the number of immigrants to the needs of the labour market and long-term demographic trends. In the first six months of 1978, 25,807 immigrants entered Canada; the five main source countries were Britain (14.5%), the U.S. (10.8%), India (6.2%), the Philippines (5.8%), and Hong Kong (5.2%). In Australia new immigration categories and procedures, announced on June 7, 1978, would come into force on Jan. 1, 1979. (See AUSTRALIA: Special Report.)

The U.S. remained a major attraction for migrants, legal or otherwise. (See Special Report.) A new wave of "boat people" consisted of refugees from Haiti; 1,400 Haitian would-be immigrants had arrived between November 1977 and June 1978, when a record 600 landed. The outstanding feature of U.S. immigration, however, was the change in origin of the newcomers, with increasing numbers coming from Asia, Latin America, and the Caribbean rather than from Europe. Notably, immigrants now accounted for well over one-third of the country's annual population growth.

(STUART BENTLEY)

See also Refugees.
[525.A.1.c]

THE INVISIBLE MIGRANTS

by Roberto Suro

The Statue of Liberty and the Berlin Wall are both potent symbols of different philosophies of government. The manner in which a nation rules its borders serves as an important image because it quickly indicates a government's attitude toward the people who live within those borders as well as toward those in the world outside. The most apt symbol of U.S. immigration policy in recent years might be a traffic cop unable to control a busy intersection. He blows his whistle and waves his arms like a windmill, but no one pays attention. The drivers all come and go as they please.

The United States has essentially lost control of its borders. Even though sneaking into the country can be a risky, even physically dangerous business, many enter and leave it as they wish. The U.S. Immigration and Naturalization Service (INS) concedes that about one million people succeed in entering the country illegally each year. They contribute to a permanent population of some eight million to ten million illegal aliens, by the best estimates.

A mere 94 years ago a hungry and growing United States could erect a statue welcoming the globe's "huddled masses." Today the nation remains the most attractive goal to those who leave their homelands in search of a better life. This appeal will grow as long as there is a widening gap between U.S. affluence and the poverty of less developed nations. Determining how many of these eager people the U.S. can handle is controversial. Regardless of where the limits are set, however, there is one aspect to the issue that should not be controversial: the federal government cannot simply default on its responsibility to regulate the number of new immigrants. The growth of the population through immigration cannot simply be a question of how many can get in without getting caught.

Administration Proposals. At the beginning of his administration U.S. Pres. Jimmy Carter showed considerable interest in making sense of immigration policy, and in August 1977 he sent Congress a com-

Roberto Suro is a correspondent in the Midwest Bureau of Time *magazine.*

plex package of measures. His most important proposal to staunch the flood of illegal migrants would attempt to remove their motive for coming—jobs. Carter recommended imposing civil sanctions—a $1,000 fine for each violation—on employers who hire such migrants. But enforcing this rule poses a perplexing web of difficulties. Millions of illegal aliens are already equipped with false documents showing that they are legal residents, and the employers would be stuck with the task of judging whether or not job seekers have obeyed U.S. immigration laws. Hispanic organizations all across the country have been uncommonly united in protesting the proposal. Some 90% of all illegal aliens are from Latin America, and so they believe that employers would avoid hiring any Latinos rather than risk violating the law.

Carter also addressed the tricky question of what to do with the existing population of illegal migrants. Identifying and deporting several million people would require a massive law-enforcement effort that would be difficult to execute without in-

Shoes in hand, an illegal alien walks across the Rio Grande into the United States near El Paso, Texas.

fringing on the rights of native-born Latinos. A mass deportation with roundups and detention camps would produce an altogether ugly spectacle.

Simply allowing the illegal aliens to stay might be just as unpopular, and so Carter chose a middle course. Anyone who could prove that he or she had lived in the U.S. since Jan. 1, 1970, would be given legitimate resident alien status. Anyone who arrived between 1970 and Jan. 1, 1977, would be given a five-year temporary resident alien status. No exact plan was spelled out for these migrants after the five years had passed. Only those arriving in 1977 or later would be subject to deportation.

Carter's immigration proposals were put on the back burner soon after they were announced. The 95th Congress never got around to debating the measures before it adjourned in the fall of 1978. Illegal immigration did not appear to present the kind of crisis that demands immediate attention from the lawmakers.

INS Measures. Carter carried Texas in the presidential election of 1976 only because he had a great deal of support in Mexican-American communities. His initial interest in immigration was at least partially prompted by demands from those supporters. His appointment of Leonel Castillo as commissioner of the INS was also apparently a response to those votes. Castillo, formerly controller of Houston, is a descendant of an illegal alien. He took the important step of shifting the focus of enforcement efforts from the nation's interior, where INS raids were a constant irritant to Latino communities in industrial cities, to the border region where the INS beefed up efforts to stop illegal migrants at the point of entry. Several federal court decisions also limited INS activities in the cities by placing more stringent restrictions on the ability of its agents to raid factories and question people.

In an effort to find humane approaches to the problem, Castillo spent money to make detention centres more comfortable, and he launched what he called an "outreach" program. This involved helping social service agencies set up counseling centres where illegal aliens could safely inquire whether they had any legal claims to residency by way of a relative who was a citizen. Castillo even taped radio commercials in Spanish to encourage illegal aliens to visit the centres. These measures contributed to a morale problem among INS agents. Unnamed INS agents were frequently quoted in the press charging that Castillo was "soft" on illegal aliens and that he was making their jobs more difficult.

But in 1978 the INS also announced plans to build new fences on the two most heavily crossed sections of the border, in Texas and California. Replacing old and worn-out barriers, the 12.5 mi of new

fence were to be 12 ft high and made of tough steel mesh designed to frustrate wire cutters and make climbing a painful experience. The fence, quickly dubbed the "Tortilla Curtain," provoked a remarkably rancorous reaction and demonstrated that illegal immigration is more than a domestic matter.

Mexican Pres. José López Portillo criticized the fence as "a discourteous, inconsiderate act." On the other side of the border, William Clements, governor-elect of Texas, said, "I don't believe that we and Mexico should have any sort of Berlin Wall on our borders." These responses show that the two major factors in devising a workable immigration policy are the unique relationship between the U.S. and Mexico and the U.S. self-image as a nation with a special respect for human dignity.

The Border Problem. About 60% of all illegal aliens are Mexicans, and the heart of the problem lies in the 3,140-km (1,950-mi) border shared by the United States and Mexico. Arturo Vazquez, a sociologist at the University of Illinois, has said, "Northern Mexico and the U.S. border states are not really separated by any overwhelming topographical or linguistic boundaries." There are, of course, enormous cultural differences between the two countries when they are viewed as wholes, but looking at the border region alone, Vazquez says, "The major difference is in the degree of economic opportunity: there is a great deal on one side; little or none on the other."

Mexicans began moving north in search of these opportunities almost as soon as the border was drawn. The seasonal surges in agricultural employment traditionally provided a reliable source of income for Mexicans in the U.S. croplands. In 1942 this migration was legalized in the form of the "Bracero Program," which involved temporary visas for Mexicans working on farms. The program was begun to relieve wartime manpower shortages, but, under pressure from agricultural interests enamoured of the cheap labour it provided, it was extended until 1964. During 22 years some 4.8 million Mexicans were legally recruited and encouraged to make the trip north.

Having taken advantage of such immigration as a profitable source of labour, the U.S. bears some responsibility for causing the influx.

While Carter's proposals languished in Congress, a single development emerged to offer hope. Mexico discovered oil fields with at least 200 billion barrels in potential reserves, equal to about one-third of the world's known oil reserves. Perhaps the best immigration policy for the U.S., therefore, would involve providing the technical assistance that Mexico will need to translate this resource into millions of jobs.

Mining and Quarrying

Mining and quarrying in the United States in 1978 was essentially a replay of 1977. There were no new major projects or trend developments. The absence of aggressive development plans was attributed to low prices for major metals, inflation, and delays because of regulations. The trend toward acquisitions and mergers continued. No national minerals policy was being formulated. The importance of technological development was becoming secondary to legal issues.

On the world scene economic pressures and the absence of U.S. company initiatives created a situation similar to that in the U.S. Political unrest in central and southern Africa was of concern to the world mining community because of the important mines and potential mineral deposits in those areas. A major change occurred when China began to seek assistance overseas in developing its natural resources.

No legislation in the U.S. in 1978 approached in importance the 1977 Surface Mining Control and Reclamation Act. It culminated five years of effort and had twice been vetoed by U.S. Pres. Gerald Ford. After its passage coal operators, who were the principal targets of this environmental legislation, joined with other surface-mining operators to seek through the federal courts to modify some of the more onerous and complex portions of the law. It was expected to be some time before it would be known whether this law has aided the public. It provided environmental protection while delaying the development of new energy sources. For example, the Wyoming Coal Information Committee stated that, largely because of procedures set up by the law, it required up to ten years from the time a mining claim is purchased until the first carload of coal is shipped.

One of the most critical decisions by the U.S. Congress that was awaited by the mining community concerned legislation which would prevent large sections of land in Alaska from being mined. An area of 103 million ac, or 40% of the Alaskan landmass, was declared reserved for national parks, wildlife refuges, wilderness reserves, etc., by the House of Representatives in May. Efforts were being made to modify these strict provisions, and as a result the House passed an amendment that called for a mineral appraisal of the lands to be reported to the president in October 1981. However, the bill was not moving rapidly in the Senate even with U.S. Pres. Jimmy Carter's support.

In July the House of Representatives passed a bill which would license U.S. mining firms to mine deep-sea nodules from the ocean floor provided the work was executed according to environmental regulations. Several international consortiums were formed to exploit the nodules, from which manganese, nickel, cobalt, and copper can be extracted. At the year's end the companies were not operating on a commercial scale but were experimenting on technical aspects of the mining and processing methods while waiting for resolution of the international laws that may regulate exploitation of these resources.

Industry Developments. The trend toward acquisitions and mergers continued in 1978. Anglo American Corp., through affiliated companies, increased its ownership of Inspiration Consolidated Copper Co. to about 75%. Of the remaining shares 20% were owned by the Anaconda Co., which had been acquired by the Atlantic Richfield Co. in recent years. Inspiration stock was removed from the New York Stock Exchange listing.

The pattern of conglomerate mergers attracted Senate antitrust and monopoly committee hearings and stepped up Federal Trade Commission inquiries. U.S. oil companies already owned approximately 37–40% of U.S. copper production.

The oil companies were not finding a bonanza in minerals. Instead, they were learning about a new set of market conditions—mostly depressed and difficult development problems such as water flooding in deep mines.

By the end of 1978 only 3 of 20 oil firms that have dabbled in mining were making a profit from min-

Bulldozers were sent in to knock down vacant buildings in the mining town of Lark, Utah. Kennecott Copper, which owned the land the town sat on, said it needed to expand open-pit mining operations.

A giant bucket excavator is used to dig lignite out of the ground for fueling power stations in Hungary.

erals: Continental Oil Co. from Consolidation Coal Co.; Kerr McGee Oil Co. from uranium; and Occidental Petroleum Corp. from Island Creek Coal Co.

United Nuclear Corp. failed to deliver 27 million lb of uranium, under 1973 and 1974 supply contracts, to General Atomic, a partnership of Gulf Oil Corp. and Royal Dutch/Shell. The state supreme court in Santa Fe, N.M., upheld United Nuclear in a lawsuit against General Atomic in which United Nuclear claimed that it had been victimized by a price-fixing scheme of which General Atomic was a part. The U.S. Supreme Court later declined to review the ruling of the New Mexico court.

In the more celebrated Westinghouse Electric Corp. case, Westinghouse was still faced with 14 lawsuits filed by 20 utilities after it canceled uranium fuel supply contracts in 1975 because of rapidly rising uranium prices. The suits sought delivery of 69 million to 85 million lb of uranium at contract prices over the next 20 years. Westinghouse in turn filed antitrust suits against 29 foreign and domestic uranium producers, alleging price fixing and restraint of free trade.

On the exploration front Phelps Dodge Corp. discovered an important molybdenum deposit near Pine Grove in southern Utah. It is a deep porphyry deposit with 0.29 to 0.38% molybdenum and minor tungsten values. Getty Oil Co. then teamed up with Phelps Dodge for more extensive drilling. Westinghouse formed a joint venture with Cyprus Mines Corp. to develop the Hansen uranium deposit in Fremont and Teller counties in Colorado. The deposit, discovered by Cyprus, was believed to contain 30 million lb of uranium.

Louisiana Land and Exploration Co. and Superior Oil Co. made a rich discovery in 1977 near Aroostook in northern Maine. Additional drilling proved 30 million tons of ore. The ore was of two types: one high in zinc, 3.38%, and one high in copper, 1.68%. The discovery attracted other exploration activity to Maine.

A new underground copper mine was being de-

veloped in Arizona by Oracle Ridge Mining Partners. With engineering completed, construction started at the end of the year; the new mine was expected to be producing early in 1980 at the rate of 2,000 tons per day of ore.

In mining developments outside of the U.S., an Exxon Inc. subsidiary, Esso Minerals Canada Ltd., announced a uranium discovery in northwestern Saskatchewan, Canada, which is probably the largest deposit in that uranium-rich country. The deposit was estimated to contain 100 million lb of uranium oxide. The top of the ore is about 600 ft below the surface of Midwest Lake, necessitating a costly development process. Plans were underway to invest Can$200 million to bring the deposit into production between 1982 and 1984.

Jamaica extended its control over bauxite mining operations in its territory by acquiring a 7% interest in Alcan Jamaica for $4.4 million. In this transaction the government acquired all mineral lands owned by Alcan Aluminum Corp. Alcan was to pay a royalty of 31 cents per long ton of bauxite mined for eight years retroactive to Jan. 1, 1976. In addition, Alcan would pay a production levy based on the price of aluminum ingot for a specified number of years.

The U.S. Export Import Bank agreed to finance purchase of $30,220,000 in U.S. equipment and services for a nickel mine and processing plant in Colombia. Cerro Matoso was a new Colombian firm owned by the government with foreign participation by Hanna Mining Co., Standard Oil Co. of California, and Billiton Overseas Ltd. The total cost of the project was estimated to be about $300 million, with additional financing being provided by the World Bank and a private banking syndicate.

Political unrest in central Africa continued to have grave consequences for the copper-producing nations of Zaire and Zambia. The invasion of Shaba Province in Zaire by Angola-based rebels in May caused a one-month shutdown in the mines. Probably even more serious was the exodus of foreign engineers and technicians, which was expected to be detrimental to the productivity of the mines. Until late in 1978 the Benguela Railway continued to be shut down, a situation that began in 1975 when the Angolan civil war disrupted traffic. The closing of this route, which connects the Shaba mines with the port city of Benguela, Angola, 2,000 mi away, disrupted the exporting of copper. Besides being a major world copper producer, Shaba provides half of the world's cobalt.

Landlocked Zambia, with its connection to the Benguela Railway useless and traffic through Rhodesia restricted for most of 1978, was dependent on the services of the inadequate, Chinese-built Tazara Railway which connects Ndola with Dar-es-Salaam, Tanzania. Because of these transport difficulties, Zambia cut back copper production 15% during the year.

Technological Developments. In China, where technological development of mining had virtually halted during the last decade of Mao Tse-tung's life (1966–76), a giant thrust to modernize began. An eight-year program of capital investment was launched. Large-scale projects, some 120 in number, were scheduled. China was interested particularly in foreign participation in mineral extraction. Several technical missions were sent by the government to the U.S. during the year, one with interest in phosphate and another in coal.

In South Africa a new record-breaking endeavour began during the year. At Vaal Reefs gold mine, in the Klerksdorp area, sinking of the world's largest single-lift mine shaft was begun. The new shaft had a diameter of 34.78 ft and was scheduled to be completed in 1983 to a depth of 1.43 mi. Its cost was estimated at $82 million.

Solution mining was becoming a promising new technique for the mining of uranium. Several pilot-size experiments had been conducted in past years, and in 1978 the first commercial-sized leach facility became operational and four others were in various stages of development. Most of this work was near Corpus Christi, Texas, in a 125-mi belt of poorly consolidated sediments that could not be economically mined by underground methods. Pilot or test work was also being conducted in Wyoming and New Mexico. The in-situ leaching technique held promise of making economically feasible small deposits that do not warrant the expense of shafts and underground mining. Careful determination of the chemical properties of reservoir fluids before mining and continuous monitoring of the local chemical variations during mining proved effective in preventing migration of leach fluids from the mining area.

For more than 25 years scientists and engineers had tried to determine how to recover the uranium present in Florida phosphate deposits. These efforts intensified in recent years because of the increase in the price of uranium. In the fall of 1978 two multimillion dollar purchase contracts were announced by International Minerals and Chemical Corp. (IMC), one with Florida Power & Light Co. for one million pounds of uranium oxide over a period of 12 years valued at $500 million and the other with the Tennessee Valley Authority for 850,000 lb through 1992 for $400 million. IMC successfully extracted the uranium from phosphoric acid, one of the main uses of Florida phosphate rock. The firm's extraction facility, which was expected to cost about $50 million, was scheduled to start operation in 1979. Wyoming Minerals Division of Westinghouse, Gardinier Inc., and Freeport Chemical Corp. also had plants to recover uranium from phosphoric acid in various stages of completion. (JOHN V. BEALL)

Production. The lack of aggressiveness noted above in the mining sector in the U.S. also characterized many of the other developed economies, both domestically and in their investments in the less developed countries. As the table indicates, production during 1977 and 1978, as measured by UN indexes of production, lagged well behind the manufacturing sector. The only exceptions were the centrally planned economies, which are better able to structure the relative growth of one sector with respect to another. These states, for example, showed 49% growth from 1970, while the developed market economies and less developed countries remained at production levels attained as long ago as 1973.

The inelasticity of hydrocarbon energy supplies needed for the maintenance of most countries' general economies resulted from the failure of these countries to develop alternate energy sources and consumption strategies (the U.S. being the most notable offender). This inelasticity was the cause of the somewhat better showing in the petroleum sector (36% growth between 1970 and the first quarter of 1978, compared with 24% for the mining sector as a whole). On the other hand, the metal sector, where many alternatives exist, grew by only 8% between 1970 and the first quarter of 1978. Perhaps most disappointing to planners was the decline in coal production during the 1970s. Despite general recognition of the desirability of converting certain energy-intensive uses of petroleum and natural gas to coal, mid-1978 production indexes for coal were 14% below those of 1970 in the developed countries.

Indexes of Production, Mining, and Mineral Commodities

(1970=100)

	1973	1974	1975	1976	1977	1978 I	1978 II
Mining (total)							
World [1]	114	116	114	120	124	124	...
Centrally planned economies [2]	118	124	132	138	143	149	149
Developed market economies [3]	105	105	101	103	106	105	109
Less developed market economies [4]	123	125	114	126	130	126	...
Coal							
World [1]	96	96	98	100	100	96	...
Centrally planned economies [2]	108	110	114	116	118	118	120
Developed market economies [3]	86	82	84	84	83	76	86
Less developed market economies [4]	104	112	122	124	125	136	...
Petroleum							
World [1]	122	125	120	129	135	136	...
Centrally planned economies [2]	122	130	140	149	157	167	167
Developed market economies [3]	114	115	113	113	120	126	124
Less developed market economies [4]	129	130	116	131	136	128	...
Metals							
World [1]	106	107	103	106	106	108	...
Centrally planned economies [2]	118	119	122	123	124	126	127
Developed market economies [3]	100	98	92	95	93	92	93
Less developed market economies [4]	105	111	104	110	112	119	...
Manufacturing (total)	124	128	126	136	143	147	...

[1]Excluding Albania, China, Mongolia, North Korea, Vietnam.
[2]Bulgaria, Czechoslovakia, East Germany, Hungary, Poland, Romania, U.S.S.R.
[3]North America, Europe (except centrally planned), Australia, Israel, Japan, New Zealand, South Africa.
[4]Caribbean, Central and South America, Africa (except South Africa), Asian Middle East, East and South East Asia (except Israel and Japan).
Source: UN, *Monthly Bulletin of Statistics* (November 1978).

Recognizing the need for an international overview on which mutual planning could be based, the member countries of the Organization for Economic Cooperation and Development in 1976 established Interfutures, a research program designed to provide a theoretical basis for both short- and long-term planning not only for mineral commodities but for a score of other economic and social complexes as well. Preliminary data released by Interfutures in mid-1978 indicated that, at current mineral production levels, demand was unlikely to outstrip reserves by the year 2000 except for a few minerals such as bismuth, silver, mercury, and asbestos (for most of which alternatives or substitutes exist). The most likely cause of imbalances in the world market was seen to be regional or politically conditioned inequities of distribution.

Aluminum. World production of bauxite, the primary ore of aluminum, was estimated to have grown approximately 5.7% in 1977, rising from 79,989,000 metric tons to 84,568,000. Australia, the largest producer with some 26,070,000 tons in 1977, widened its lead over Jamaica (11,433,000 tons) and Guinea (11,320,000). These three countries accounted for nearly 60% of the world total. Production of alumina (aluminum oxide, the chief raw material for the production of aluminum metal) rose some 10.1% to 29,486,000 tons; major producers were Australia (6,659,000 tons) and the U.S. (6,032,000). Output of aluminum metal also increased substantially, from 12,496,000 tons to 13,660,000. The U.S. accounted for approximately 30% of the total.

Antimony. In terms of contained metal, world production of antimony was estimated to have declined slightly during 1977, falling from approximately 69,614 metric tons to about 69,535. Despite a 20.6% drop, Bolivia remained the leading producer with 13,822 tons, ahead of South Africa and China, both estimated to have produced about 12,000 tons. Production of primary antimony fell in the U.S., the world's leading producer at 11,636 tons.

Arsenic. The approximately 14% decline experienced by the arsenic industry in 1976 continued in less extreme form during 1977. Based on preliminary figures, production fell from 34,910 metric tons to 34,315. Few statistics were available for the major producing countries, but they were thought to be, in order, the Soviet Union (7,500 tons), Namibia (South West Africa; 7,300), France (6,900), Sweden (6,724), and Mexico (4,000).

A giant steel cable belt at the Duval Sierrita copper mine near Tucson, Arizona, moves up to 6,400 tons of ore an hour, replacing the work of a dozen trucks.

WIDE WORLD

Cadmium. Preliminary data from the U.S. Bureau of Mines indicated growth of about 4% during 1977; smelter production rose from 16,483 metric tons in 1976 to 17,125. Major producers were Japan (2,765 tons) and the Soviet Union (2,750).

Cement. World production of cement was estimated to have risen about 4.7% in 1977, from 695 million metric tons in 1976 to 728 million. The leading producer continued to be the Soviet Union with 127 million tons, followed by the U.S. with some 74 million and Japan with 63.5 million. Other important producers included West Germany (32.2 million tons), France (29 million), Spain (28 million), Poland (21.3 million), and Brazil (21.1 million). Shipments of prepared cement in the U.S. in 1978 were running about 7% ahead of 1977 through the end of September.

Chromium. World mine production of chromite, the principal ore of chromium, increased by 13.5% in 1977, rising from 8,629,670 metric tons in 1976 to 9,799,571, according to preliminary data from the U.S. Bureau of Mines. More than a third of the total originated in South Africa, which increased production by 38% (2,409,000 to 3,317,000 tons) and thus widened the gap between it and the Soviet Union (2,180,000). No other producer exceeded one million tons. Reinstatement of the U.S. trade embargo against Rhodesia in March 1977 led to increased imports from other producing countries, notably South Africa, the Philippines, and the Soviet Union.

Cobalt. Largely because of continued low production levels in Zaire, world production of cobalt continued a decline begun during 1976. From 17,400 metric tons, or 53% of the world total, in 1975, Zaire's output in 1977 had fallen to about 9,900 tons, an estimated 38.8% of total world production of about 25,500 tons. The remainder was divided among a few countries, most of which limited distribution of data for strategic reasons; they included Zambia, New Caledonia, Cuba, the Soviet Union, and Canada, all of which were estimated to have produced between 1,500 and 2,500 tons. Substantial price rises were announced by Zaire, Zambia, and Finland in September 1978.

Copper. According to preliminary data from the U.S. Bureau of Mines, world mine production of copper rose an estimated 1.3% in 1977, to approximately 7,550,000 metric tons. The U.S. was the major producer with some 1,350,000 tons, followed by Chile (1,050,000), Zambia (819,000), Canada (781,000), and the Soviet Union (744,000). Other major producers included Zaire (427,000), Peru (331,000), and Australia (211,000). Most major producers of refined copper showed modest increases or declines in production levels during 1977, the only important exception being the U.S. where smelter production fell from about 1.4 million tons to under 1.2 million. Total consumption of copper was estimated to have risen 10% during 1977. The May 1978 invasion of Shaba Province in Zaire created fears of a shortage and led to a rise in London prices, but production levels were restored very rapidly.

Gold. World mine production of gold was estimated to have fallen off slightly from the already depressed levels of the mid-1970s, to some 38,490,000 troy ounces. The leading producers continued to be South Africa, whose production fell 2.3% to 22,408,037 oz, the lowest in 16 years. Because of the rise in gold prices during 1977 and 1978, however, South Africa's foreign exchange earnings were characterized in some places as a "mini-boom." Other major producers were believed to have increased production: the Soviet Union to 7.9 million oz, Canada to 1,707,000, and the U.S. to 1.1 million, the first gain in three years. Gold prices exceeding $230 per ounce in 1978 made new operations feasible in a number of countries.

Iron. Preliminary data indicated that 1977 iron ore production fell about 3.6% to 836.9 million metric tons. The major producer was the Soviet Union, with some 237.7 million tons, followed distantly by Australia (97,465,000), Brazil (67 million), the U.S. (55,824,000; down 34.7%, accounting for almost all of the decline in the world total), Canada (54,431,000), China (an estimated 50 million), France (42,271,000), and India (37 million). Most of the decline in the U.S. was attributable to the effects of strikes. It appeared, however, that U.S. domestic consumption fell by only 6%, the difference being made up by imports. World pig iron production declined from 487,700 tons in 1976 to an estimated 482,500 in 1977. Major producers were the Soviet Union (106,350,000 tons; about 22% of the world total), Japan (85,886,000), and the U.S. (73,779,000).

Lead. World production of refined lead fell an estimated 8.1% in 1977, to about 3,715,400 metric tons. At 613,300 tons, the U.S., the major producer, was off 19.8% from the preceding year. Next were the Soviet Union with an estimated 450,000 tons, followed by West Germany (309,400), the U.K. (264,000), and Japan (218,400). Canada, France, Belgium, Yugoslavia, and China produced between 100,000 and 200,000 tons each. U.S. domestic mine production of lead declined from 553,000 tons to 535,000 tons. Environmental constraints on exposure to lead appeared to have had little effect on the U.S. market, which remained buoyant as a result of strong demand from the automobile industry. Batteries and fuel additives accounted for 72.9% of U.S. consumption in 1977.

Manganese. World production of manganese fell by some 2.4% in 1977, according to preliminary figures. Major producers were the Soviet Union and South Africa, with 8.3 million and 5,440,000 metric tons, respectively; together they accounted for approximately 58% of world production of about 23,950,000 tons. Other important producers included Gabon (2.1 million tons), Australia (2 million), Brazil (1.7 million), India (1.6 million), and China (1 million). Ocean Management, Inc., recovered some 700 tons of manganese nodules from depths of up to 5,200 m (17,000 ft) in the Pacific Ocean during the summer and fall of 1978.

Mercury. World production of mercury in terms of 34.5-kg (76-lb) flasks fell approximately 17% during 1977, to about 200,-000 flasks. The major producers, estimated on the basis of previous production levels, were thought to be the Soviet Union (about 58,000 flasks), Spain (38,000), the U.S. (32,000), Algeria (25,950), China (20,000), and Mexico (15,200). Most of the drop was accounted for by the closing of mines in Italy and Yugoslavia and by declines of 22% in China and 16% in Algeria.

Molybdenum. Production of molybdenum rose about 7% in 1977, according to preliminary data from the U.S. Bureau of Mines. Of the world total of some 95,047,000 metric tons, about three-fifths was from the U.S. (55,523,000 tons;). There were only three other major producers, all of whom registered modest gains: Canada (16,431,000 tons), Chile (11 million), and the Soviet Union (an estimated 9.7 million).

Nickel. World mine production of nickel was estimated at some 796,298 metric tons in 1977, a decline of about 3% from 1976. Major producers were Canada (235,362 tons), the Soviet Union (an estimated 168,000), New Caledonia (109,060), and Australia (85,800). New Caledonia retained fourth place despite an 8% decline. Production of refined metal fell by a comparable amount in 1977, to about 745,000 tons; the Soviet Union led with 188,000 tons, followed by Canada, Japan, and New Caledonia. The decline in New Caledonian production would evidently continue; further cutbacks were announced, attributable to slack world demand and deterioration of the franc/dollar parity.

Phosphate Rock. World production of phosphate rock and guano was estimated to have risen by a healthy 7.7% in 1977; the world total amounted to some 115,948,000 metric tons. Major phosphate rock producers were the U.S. at 47,256,000 tons, followed by the Soviet Union with an estimated 24.2 million and Morocco with 17,027,000. Guano production at 24,000 tons, mostly from Chile, was virtually the same as in 1976.

Platinum-Group Metals. Production of the platinum-group metals (platinum, palladium, iridium, osmium, rhodium, and ruthenium) was estimated to have risen by 6.7% during 1977 to an estimated total of 6.4 million troy ounces. Most of it originated in the Soviet Union and South Africa, each with about 3 million oz. Canada, a distant third with 469,000 oz, registered a strong 9.1% gain.

Potash. The 1977 recovery of the world fertilizer market was reflected in potash production. Marketable potash rose 6.2% to a total of 25,772,000 metric tons. The chief producing country was the Soviet Union with an estimated 8.5 million tons, followed by Canada (6,089,000 tons), East Germany (3,244,000), West Germany (2,341,000), and the U.S. (2,229,000). Production levels in the centrally planned economies were generally at or near capacity, while market economies were often substantially below capacity.

Silver. According to preliminary U.S. Bureau of Mines estimates, world mine production of silver rose by some 4.4% during 1977 to approximately 318.4 million troy ounces, reflecting the continued attractiveness of precious metals during periods of inflation. The Soviet Union and Mexico were the world leaders with about 45 million oz each. For Mexico, this represented a 10.3% rise over 1976. Other major producers included Canada (42,758,000 oz), the U.S. (37,733,000), and Peru (37 million). Prices were high (averaging 462.3 cents in New York) and stable throughout 1977.

Tin. World mine production of tin was almost unchanged in 1977, totaling about 230,333 metric tons as against 228,005 tons in 1976. The major producer was Malaysia (58,703 tons), followed by the Soviet Union (an estimated 33,000), Bolivia (32,616), Indonesia (24,021), Thailand (23,100), and China (about 20,000). Smelter production of tin metal totaled about 230,243 tons, compared with 229,861 in 1976. The most important producer was Malaysia (66,-305 tons), followed distantly by the Soviet Union (33,000). Tin prices in New York briefly reached record highs in September 1978 but later fell back sharply.

Titanium. World production fell an estimated 16.1% for rutile (358,601 tons, compared with 427,510 in 1976) and 13.8% for titaniferous slag (712,228 in 1977, down from 826,486) but rose 5.8% for ilmenite, (from 3,197,233 to 3,382,030). Australia continued to be the major producer of ilmenite and rutile, with 1,080,-695 and 324,371 tons, respectively. It was followed among ilmenite producers by Norway (828,359 tons), the U.S. (579,240), and the Soviet Union (400,000). Canada produced most of the titaniferous slags.

Tungsten. Estimated world mine production of tungsten rose about 5.3% during 1977, to 42,927 metric tons. Major producers were thought to be China (about 9,400 tons), followed by the Soviet Union (7,800); the U.S. was third with about 3,175 tons.

Continuing price increases gave rise to fears among U.S. producers and consumers that imports might have to be increased and that alternative materials, such as titanium, tantalum, and columbium carbides, might begin to be substituted. Nevertheless, domestic U.S. production seemed likely to gain some ground with the opening of a major new mine in southern Nevada.

Uranium. The implications of hydrocarbon prices continued to make nuclear power an attractive option, and 1977 production showed a strong increase of 13.8%. Production totaled 30,660 metric tons in the market economy countries for which production figures were available. The U.S., the leading producer among these countries, registered an increase of approximately 10% to about 12,700 tons.

Zinc. World smelter production of zinc was estimated to have fallen sharply during 1977, from 5,806,100 metric tons to only about 5,317,400, according to preliminary estimates. The major producer was thought to be the Soviet Union at 750,000 tons, followed by Canada (494,800), the U.S. (384,200), West Germany (341,700), and Finland (248,600). The U.S. production figures represented a decline of nearly 21% caused by major strikes, consumption cutbacks, and deferral of development. During 1978 trading in zinc futures began for the first time on the Commodity Exchange in New York. (WILLIAM A. CLEVELAND)

See also Earth Sciences; Energy; Industrial Review: *Gemstones; Iron and Steel*; Materials Sciences.

_____

Monaco

Monaco

Monaco

A sovereign principality on the northern Mediterranean coast, Monaco is bounded on land by the French département of Alpes-Maritimes. Area: 1.90 sq km (0.74 sq mi). Pop. (1978 est.): 25,000. Language: French. Religion: predominantly Roman Catholic. Prince, Rainier III; minister of state in 1978, André Saint-Mleux.

The event of the year was the wedding of Princess Caroline of Monaco, aged 21, to Philippe Junot, a 38-year-old Paris businessman. The civil marriage took place on June 28 in the palace throne room. After the nuptial mass, celebrated the fol-

ANDANSON—SYGMA

Princess Caroline of Monaco and her groom, Philippe Junot, meet well-wishers in the streets of old Monte Carlo after their nuptial mass on June 29.

Missiles:
see Defense

Molecular Biology:
see Life Sciences

lowing day, the couple walked through the narrow streets of old Monte Carlo. A pre-wedding ball was attended by about 600 guests, including two former kings — Umberto II of Italy and Michael I of Romania — and Grand Duke Vladimir Kyrillovich, the Russian pretender. Before leaving for their honeymoon at Papeete, on Tahiti, the couple attended a luncheon for friends of the family, including many show business personalities.

In elections to the National Council on January 16, the majority candidates of the National Democratic Union, led by Jean-Claude Rey, took all 18 seats, the Communists losing their only seat.

(K. M. SMOGORZEWSKI)

> **MONACO**
> **Education.** (1976–77) Primary, secondary, and vocational, pupils 4,966, teachers 357.
> **Finance and Trade.** Monetary unit: French franc, with (Sept. 18, 1978) a free rate of Fr 4.38 to U.S. $1 (Fr 8.57 = £1 sterling). Budget (1976 est.): revenue Fr 528 million; expenditure Fr 464 million. Foreign trade included with France. Tourism (1976) 181,000 visitors.

Mongolia

A people's republic of Asia lying between the U.S.S.R. and China, Mongolia occupies the geographic area known as Outer Mongolia. Area: 1,565,000 sq km (604,000 sq mi). Pop. (1978 est.): 1,577,000. Cap. and largest city: Ulan Bator (pop., 1976 est., 334,000). Language: Khalkha Mongolian. Religion: Lamaistic Buddhism. First secretary of the Mongolian People's Revolutionary (Communist) Party in 1978 and chairman of the Presidium of the Great People's Hural, Yumzhagiyen Tsedenbal; chairman of the Council of Ministers (premier), Zhambyn Batmunkh.

On Aug. 23, 1978, at Oreanda, Crimea, Soviet Communist Party leader Leonid Brezhnev received Yumzhagiyen Tsedenbal, first secretary of

Mongolia

Morocco

> **MONGOLIA**
> **Education.** (1975–76) Primary, pupils 129,802, teachers (1974–75) 4,144; secondary, pupils 172,134, teachers (1974–75) 6,511; vocational, pupils 10,936, teachers (1974–75) 755; teacher training, students 1,618, teachers 137; higher, students 9,861, teaching staff 807.
> **Finance.** Monetary unit: tugrik, with (Sept. 18, 1978) a nominal exchange rate of 2.93 tugriks to U.S. $1 (5.73 tugriks = £1 sterling). Budget (1978 est.): revenue 3,660,000,000 tugriks; expenditure 3,650,000,000 tugriks.
> **Foreign Trade.** (1976) Imports c. U.S. $680 million; exports c. U.S. $230 million. Import sources: U.S.S.R. c. 93%. Export destinations: U.S.S.R. c. 81%; Czechoslovakia c. 6%. Main exports (1975): livestock 27%; meat 19%; wool 16%.
> **Transport and Communications.** Roads (1970) c. 75,000 km (including c. 9,000 km main roads). Railways (1977) 1,589 km; traffic (1976) 219 million passenger-km, freight 2,718 million net ton-km. Telephones (Jan. 1977) 37,800. Radio receivers (including loudspeakers; Dec. 1976) c. 220,000. Television receivers (Dec. 1976) c. 34,000.
> **Agriculture.** Production (in 000; metric tons; 1976): wheat 280; oats c. 65; barley c. 35; potatoes c. 27; milk c. 230; beef and veal c. 67; mutton and goat meat c. 128. Livestock (in 000; Dec. 1975): sheep 14,458; goats 4,595; cattle 2,427; horses 2,255; camels c. 650.
> **Industry.** Production (in 000; metric tons; 1977): coal and lignite 3,324; fluorspar 345; cement (1975) 159; electricity (kw-hr) 1,090,000.

the Mongolian People's Revolutionary Party. In a joint communiqué the two leaders branded the Chinese leadership as "obsessed by its pursuit of hegemony" and "gambling on stirring up international tension." According to *The Military Balance 1978–1979*, published by the International Institute for Strategic Studies in London, 3 of the 44 Soviet divisions deployed on the Sino-Soviet border were stationed in Mongolia. During the year China reported incidents involving reconnaissance patrols along the Mongolian border.

Since 1962, when Mongolia became a member of the Council for Mutual Economic Assistance (Comecon), industrialization of the country had progressed. Between 1960 and 1978 the proportion of the labour force engaged in agriculture and animal breeding had fallen from 60 to 45%. During the 1976–80 five-year plan some 40 new industrial enterprises were to be completed with the help of Comecon countries, mainly the U.S.S.R., Poland, East Germany, and Czechoslovakia.

(K. M. SMOGORZEWSKI)

Morocco

A constitutional monarchy of northwestern Africa, on the Atlantic Ocean and the Mediterranean Sea, Morocco is bordered by Algeria and Western (Spanish) Sahara. Area: 458,730 sq km (177,117 sq mi). Pop. (1977 est.): 18,359,000. Cap.: Rabat (pop., 1977 est., 704,100). Largest city: Casablanca (pop., 1977 est., 2,048,100). Data above refer to Morocco as constituted prior to the purported division of Western (Spanish) Sahara between Morocco and Mauritania. Language: Arabic (official); with Berber, French, and Spanish minorities. Religion: Muslim. King, Hassan II; prime minister in 1978, Ahmed Osman.

During 1978 Morocco continued to represent moderate and conservative interests in Africa and the Middle East. King Hassan supported Egyptian Pres. Anwar as-Sadat's Middle Eastern peace initiative throughout the year. Sadat visited Rabat on several occasions and conferred with King Hassan on September 21 immediately after the Camp David summit on peace in the Middle East.

In Africa the king reluctantly repeated his 1977 military aid to Zaire by sending 1,500 Moroccan troops to Shaba Province on June 2, replacing the French and Belgian paratroopers involved in the initial European evacuations from Kolwezi. The Moroccan contingent was airlifted to Shaba by the U.S. Air Force, but despite the generally close relationship between the U.S. and Moroccan governments initial U.S. willingness to sell Cobra gunships to Morocco and to remove restrictions on the use of U.S. arms already delivered was replaced by congressional reluctance to support Moroccan troops in the Western Sahara.

The Sahara exerted an indirect influence on Moroccan foreign policy throughout the year. A Moroccan-Soviet fishing agreement was signed on April 27 only after being reworded so as not to imply Soviet recognition of Moroccan sovereignty over Saharan waters. The Popular Front for the Liberation of Saguia el Hamra and Río de Oro

(Polisario Front) warned that Spanish boats fishing in Saharan waters under a similar agreement would be in danger of armed attack.

In the Sahara itself, the guerrilla war continued, Polisario Front forces controlling the desert while Moroccan troops defended the strategic towns of Layyoun and Samara and the phosphate mines at Bu Craa. To the south, Polisario was hampered by French air strikes from Mauritania and by the more than 7,000 Moroccan troops stationed around the Zouerate iron mine. When Mauritanian Pres. Moktar Ould Daddah was overthrown in a bloodless coup on July 10, his successors, benefiting from a unilateral Polisario cease-fire, renewed peace feelers with the guerrillas. King Hassan declared his support for the new Mauritanian government on July 13, and again in August, when he emphasized that new peace moves in the guerrilla war supported by France and Algeria would be unacceptable if they threatened Moroccan sovereignty over the Western Sahara. Nevertheless, readiness to consider a negotiated settlement was implied by secret negotiations between Morocco and Algeria in April, which were officially confirmed in July.

Moroccan flexibility over the Sahara was undoubtedly linked to the country's poor economic performance. Although a major Soviet-Moroccan

---

MOROCCO

Education. (1976–77) Primary, pupils 1,603,872, teachers (state only) 40,197; secondary and vocational, pupils 484,694, teachers (state only) 22,273; teacher training (1975–76), students 3,953, teachers 486; higher (1976–77), students 45,085, teaching staff (1975–76) 1,642.

Finance. Monetary unit: dirham, with (Sept. 18, 1978) a free rate of 3.98 dirhams to U.S. $1 (7.80 dirhams = £1 sterling). Gold, SDR's, and foreign exchange (June 1978) U.S. $322 million. Budget (1977 est.): revenue 17.4 billion dirhams; expenditure 21,670,000,000 dirhams. Gross national product (1976) 37,710,000,000 dirhams. Money supply (May 1978) 18,366,000,000 dirhams. Cost of living (1975 = 100; April 1978) 133.1.

Foreign Trade. (1977) Imports 14.4 billion dirhams; exports 5,858,000,000 dirhams. Main import sources: France 27%; Spain 9%; Italy 7%; West Germany 7%; U.S. 6%; Iran 5%. Main export destinations: France 25%; West Germany 10%; Spain 7%; Italy 6%; Belgium-Luxembourg 5%. Main exports: phosphates 36%; citrus fruit 10%; vegetables 9%; textile yarns and fabrics 6%. Tourism (1976): visitors 1,108,000; gross receipts U.S. $386 million.

Transport and Communications. Roads (1975) 26,382 km. Motor vehicles in use (1976): passenger 347,400; commercial (including buses) 145,700. Railways: (1976) 1,756 km; traffic (1977) 830 million passenger-km, freight 3,476,-000,000 net ton-km. Air traffic (1976): 1,264,000,000 passenger-km; freight 18.2 million net ton-km. Shipping (1977): merchant vessels 100 gross tons and over 91; gross tonnage 270,295. Telephones (Jan. 1977) 204,000. Radio receivers (Dec. 1975) 1.6 million. Television licenses (Dec. 1975) 460,000.

Agriculture. Production (in 000; metric tons; 1977): wheat 1,288; barley 1,347; corn 184; potatoes c. 280; sugar, raw value c. 340; dry broad beans (1976) 230; tomatoes c. 320; grapes c. 230; oranges c. 570; mandarin oranges and tangerines c. 125; olives c. 260; dates c. 70; fish catch (1976) 281. Livestock (in 000; 1977): sheep c. 14,300; goats c. 4,940; cattle (1976) c. 3,400; horses c. 300; mules c. 400; asses c. 1,200; camels c. 200; poultry c. 21,000.

Industry. Production (in 000; metric tons; 1977): coal 707; crude oil 22; cement 2,596; iron ore (55–60% metal content) 407; phosphate rock (1976) 15,656; manganese ore (metal content; 1976) 117; lead concentrates (metal content; 1976) 83; zinc concentrates (metal content; 1976) 15; petroleum products (1976) c. 2,570; electricity (excluding most industrial production; kw-hr) 3,444,000.

---

phosphate deal was finally signed on March 10, in its April budget the government reduced all public expenditure, except for the military and for limited imports of luxury goods. The economic situation was worsened by a poor harvest and industrial depression during 1976 and 1977.

(GEORGE JOFFÉ)

Motion Pictures

English-Speaking Cinema. UNITED STATES. Hollywood needs its annual miracle and in 1978 it was John Travolta (see BIOGRAPHIES), who, with John Badham's *Saturday Night Fever*, became a teenagers' idol and a major box-office draw. The success of this amiable film released late in 1977, in which Travolta played a clerk in a New York City hardware store who achieved full realization only on the dance floor of a crowded discotheque, was later exceeded by Randal Kleiser's *Grease*, again with Travolta, adapted from a stage musical set in a high school in the late 1950s.

The long-heralded *Superman*, directed by Richard Donner and with Christopher Reeve as the aerobatic hero, had its Washington, D.C., and London premieres in December and seemed likely to rival the success of *Star Wars*.

Grease characterized a pronounced tendency in U.S. films toward nostalgic evocation of the early rock-and-roll era. Others in this category included Martin Scorsese's *The Last Waltz*, a reflective record of the last appearance of The Band, an influential group of the 1960s and early 1970s; and Bob Dylan's idiosyncratic and visually inventive impression of his own music and his own times, *Renaldo and Clara*. Less distinguished examples of the nostalgia mood were Steve Rash's *The Buddy Holly Story*; James Bridges's *September 30, 1955*, which told of the effect upon a group of teenagers of James Dean's death on that date; and Robert Zemeckis's *I Wanna Hold Your Hand*, recalling the excitement of the Beatles' first appearance in New York.

A healthy antidote to slushy nostalgia for college days was provided by *National Lampoon's Animal House*, directed by John Landis and one of the best comedies of the year. Produced by the successful publishing company of the *National Lampoon* magazine, this was an unsentimental and disabused — not to say brutal — view of college life in 1962. Other films evoking the past included Terrence Malick's lushly photographed *Days of Heaven*, set on a large farm in the Texas Panhandle just before World War I, and French director Louis Malle's *Pretty Baby*. The latter, about a child prostitute in the Storyville district of New Orleans during World War I, was noteworthy chiefly for the skilled performance in the title role of 12-year-old Brooke Shields. (See BIOGRAPHIES.)

The nostalgic spirit extended, predictably, to Hollywood's continuing fascination with its own traditions. Hal Needham's *Hooper* was a Burt Reynolds comedy vehicle about the world of Hollywood stuntmen. Three farces satirized Hollywood history and genres. Mel Brooks's *High Anxiety* parodied the Hitchcock-style thriller; *The World's Greatest Lover*, directed by and starring a Brooks

---

Annual Cinema Attendance [1]

Country	Total in 000	Per capita
Afghanistan	19,200	1.1
Albania	9,000	4.1
Algeria	45,000	2.7
Angola	3,700	0.6
Argentina	82,200	3.2
Australia	32,000	3.0
Austria	17,500	2.3
Bahrain	2,000	8.2
Barbados	1,800	7.4
Belgium	25,400	2.6
Benin	1,200	0.4
Bolivia	3,200	0.7
Brazil	275,400	2.6
Brunei	2,500	17.0
Bulgaria	114,600	13.0
Burma	222,500	8.1
Cambodia	20,000	3.0
Cameroon	6,500	1.0
Canada	97,500	4.3
Chile	44,600	5.0
Colombia	163,600	6.8
Cuba	124,300	14.2
Cyprus	6,100	9.5
Czechoslovakia	85,300	5.7
Denmark	19,000	3.7
Dominican Republic	5,200	1.2
Ecuador	38,700	5.6
Egypt	65,000	1.9
El Salvador	14,100	3.5
Finland	9,600	2.0
France	178,500	3.4
Germany, East	79,700	4.8
Germany, West	128,100	2.1
Ghana	1,100	0.1
Grenada	1,100	11.5
Guam	1,000	10.3
Guatemala	15,400	2.8
Guyana	8,700	11.2
Haiti	1,500	0.3
Hong Kong	54,100	12.4
Hungary	74,400	7.0
Iceland	2,300	10.8
India	2,260,000	3.8
Indonesia	112,500	0.9
Iran	123,100	3.7
Iraq	8,300	1.3
Ireland	38,000	13.0
Israel	27,000	7.8
Italy	515,000	9.2
Ivory Coast	10,000	1.5
Japan	171,000	1.5
Jordan	4,300	1.9
Kenya	5,700	0.4
Korea, South	75,600	2.2
Kuwait	4,700	4.7
Lebanon	49,700	18.0
Liberia	1,000	0.6
Libya	23,000	9.4
Luxembourg	1,100	3.2
Macau	2,200	8.0
Madagascar	2,900	0.4
Malawi	2,000	0.4
Malaysia	108,800	9.1
Mali	2,500	0.5
Malta	3,100	9.9
Martinique	2,100	6.0
Mauritius	17,000	18.9
Mexico	251,000	4.2
Morocco	36,300	2.0
Mozambique	4,600	0.5
Netherlands, The	28,300	2.1
New Zealand	11,900	3.8
Nicaragua	7,700	7.7
Norway	18,500	4.6
Pakistan	194,800	3.0
Panama	7,100	4.8
Philippines	318,000	7.6
Poland	144,200	4.2
Portugal	35,700	4.1
Puerto Rico	6,800	2.2
Romania	191,200	8.9
Senegal	5,200	1.2
Singapore	42,000	18.7
Somalia	4,700	1.7
Spain	251,800	6.9
Sri Lanka	55,000	4.0
Sudan	24,000	1.4
Surinam	1,700	5.0
Sweden	22,300	2.7
Switzerland	23,000	3.6
Syria	42,000	5.5
Thailand	71,000	1.7
Trinidad and Tobago	8,400	8.0
Tunisia	12,500	2.3
Turkey	246,700	6.7
U.S.S.R.	4,211,000	16.5
United Kingdom	104,000	1.9
United States	1,032,800	4.9
Upper Volta	1,000	0.2
Venezuela	36,100	3.1
Yemen (Aden)	3,500	2.4
Yugoslavia	80,000	3.7
Zaire	1,700	0.1

[1] Countries having over one million annual attendance.

Olivia Newton-John and John Travolta (centre two) cavort with friends in the movie *Grease*.

alumnus, Gene Wilder, told of the fortunes of a would-be Valentino in the 1920s (and in its oblique way seemed closer to the reality of the period than Ken Russell's ambitious *Valentino*); Robert Moore's *The Cheap Detective*, scripted by Neil Simon, was a complex mass of references to the Humphrey Bogart thrillers of the 1940s, with Peter Falk as a shabby Bogart-type private eye.

Hollywood's own old staple genres seemed to be at a somewhat low ebb. Of musicals, *A Little Night Music*—Stephen Sondheim's stage show adapted from an Ingmar Bergman film—made an uncomfortable transfer to the screen in Harold Prince's version. From the start the idea of an all-black remake of *The Wizard of Oz* looked like a mistake, and Sidney Lumet's *The Wiz*, in the outcome, confirmed that impression. The Western also seemed practically to have disappeared except for Jack Nicholson's reworking of the old formulas in *Goin' South* and Alan Pakula's *Comes a Horseman*, set in Montana just after World War II.

Even the more recent film cycles seemed only halfheartedly pursued, though there were a *Jaws 2* and *Damien—Omen II*. Fascination with the occult was still evident in Irvin Kershner's *Eyes of Laura Mars* and Brian De Palma's *The Fury*, both of which dealt with human beings with supernormal perceptions. The "disaster" film lingered in *Gray Lady Down*, a submarine rescue drama that remained fairly traditional despite new technologies; and *Rollercoaster*, about a pathological subject who plants bombs on attractions in crowded amusement parks.

There were reflections of more specific U.S. anxieties. Guilt and remorse for the Vietnam war were the underlying motives of Hal Ashby's *Coming Home*, about the love of a soldier's wife for a paralyzed victim of the war; in Ted Post's intelligent war story, *Go Tell the Spartans*, with Burt Lancaster as a veteran officer disillusioned in his mission; and again in Karel Reisz's well-structured *Who'll Stop the Rain?* The intention of this interesting film was to transform into terms of action the reflective approach of Robert Stone's novel *Dog Soldiers*, about the widespread moral influence of war.

Other filmmakers attempted to analyze the nature and the ills of present-day society. In *A Wedding* Robert Altman used a comically disastrous marriage ceremony between new rich and old aristocracy as a microcosm of a way of life. Woody Allen's *Interiors* looked like a tribute to Ingmar Bergman in its analysis of the interior crises of a group of gifted and moneyed people. Paul Mazursky's *An Unmarried Woman* dealt, with feeling and perception, with the traumas of divorce. Jeremy Paul Kagan's *The Big Fix* looked awry at a corrupt society, from the point of view of a 1960s dropout reclaimed by the establishment as a private detective.

Union corruption provided the theme of Norman Jewison's *F.I.S.T.*, a novelettish approach to the life and times of a truck drivers' union organizer; and also *Blue Collar*, the first film to be directed by the writer Paul Schrader and an effective, if not entirely convincing, story of the various fates of three men who try to defy an automobile industry union. Less successful were *The Betsy*, a Harold Robbins saga of a Detroit automobile dynasty headed by Laurence Olivier, and J. Lee Thompson's *The Greek Tycoon*, a ludicrous dramatization of 1960s gossip columns about Aristotle Onassis and his circle, with names transparently disguised. An ambitious film that displayed the talents of animator Ralph Bakshi was *The Lord of the Rings*, adapted by Bakshi from J.R.R. Tolkien's epic three-volume fantasy.

Paul Schrader's was one of several promising directorial debuts, which included those of two popular actors: both Burt Reynolds and Warren Beatty chose comedies for their first films, respectively *The End* and the other-worldly *Heaven Can Wait*. Small-scale and independent U.S. productions of note included Claudia Weill's *Girl Friends*, about the tragicomic adventures of a plain but bright Jewish girl in New York, and Mark Rappaport's experimental *The Scenic Route*, which explored effortlessly the gulfs between what was thought and what was said in the course of a complex three-cornered relationship. Robert M. Young's *Alambrista!* used a largely nonprofessional

John Belushi (centre) was the leading home-wrecker in *National Lampoon's Animal House*.

cast in a study of the exploitation of illegal immigrant workers on the fruit farms of the southwestern states.

A number of significant Hollywood veterans died in 1978: Jack L. Warner, last of the first generation of tycoons and of the formidable Warner Brothers; Tim McCoy, a popular Western star of the 1920s; Charles Boyer, the ideal of the sophisticated continental charmer; Edgar Bergen, the ventriloquist made famous by his dummy, Charlie McCarthy; the comic actor Jack Oakie; and Gig Young, a durable light-comedy leading man. (*See* OBITUARIES.)

At the annual award ceremony of the U.S. Academy of Motion Picture Arts and Sciences, the Oscars for best film, best director, and best actress went to Woody Allen's *Annie Hall* and its co-star (with Allen) Diane Keaton. *Star Wars* took seven technical awards—including those for best art direction, best costumes, best film editing, best visual effects, and best original music score (John Williams). The best actor was Richard Dreyfuss, for *The Goodbye Girl*; the best supporting actor and actress were Jason Robards and Vanessa Redgrave, in Fred Zinnemann's *Julia*. (Robards had also won the same award the previous year for his part in *All the President's Men*.) The best foreign-language film was the French *Madame Rosa*, directed by Moshe Mizrahi.

BRITAIN. Although British studios and technicians were kept occupied by U.S. productions, British production proper continued low and underfinanced. One or two big and costly productions—John Guillermin's all-star adaptation of Agatha Christie's *Death on the Nile* and Blake Edwards's addition to a popular comedy series, *Revenge of the Pink Panther*—aimed firmly at an international market. *Watership Down* was a brave attempt by Martin Rosen to bring Richard Adams's best-selling novel to the screen in the form of an animated film.

Some of the most attractive films of the year were made on small budgets. Robert Enders, long a producer in the U.S. and Britain, made his debut as a director with *Stevie*, an effective adaptation of the impressionist stage biography of the poet Stevie Smith, starring Glenda Jackson in her original title role. The Polish director Jerzy Skolimowski made a striking mystery, *The Shout*, which he adapted from a Robert Graves short story. Jack Gold, following an indifferent supernatural thriller, *The Medusa Touch*, made a touching period piece, *The Sailor's Return*, from a David Garnett story about a 19th-century sailor who brings a black bride home to his remote English village.

For the liveliest activity in Britain it was again necessary to look to artists working on small budgets outside the commercial system. Bill Douglas completed his autobiography of a grim Scottish childhood with *My Way Home*, which carried its hero to young manhood, military service, and the first discoveries of a world of culture. This, like Phil Mulloy's *In the Forest*, a Brechtian journey of three grotesque peasants through the history of Britain's working class, was financed by the British Film Institute Production Fund.

Maurice Hatton's *Long Shot* was a loose-limbed satirical farce about the film business. *Jubilee*, by Derek Jarman, a co-director of *Sebastiane*, was a futurist vision drawn from punk culture. *Nighthawks*, directed by Ron Peck, was a notable portrayal of the life and difficulties of a young homosexual school teacher, which avoided both easy stereotypes and patent propagandism.

IRELAND. A small crop of short fiction films indicated the emergence of a distinctive Irish cinema, helped by the existence of the National Film Studios of Ireland and an enterprising system of competitive awards by the Irish Arts Council. The most notable were Bob Quinn's *Poitín* (in Gaelic), a realistic horror comic about illicit whiskey trade in western Ireland; and two short stories by Kieran Hickey, *Children's Voices*, a ghost story set in the early days of sound broadcasting, and *Exposure*, a subtle description of the shifting relationships of three men who find themselves in unconscious rivalry for the attention of a lone woman, stranded, like themselves, in a deserted hotel.

AUSTRALIA. The recently acquired confidence of Australian filmmakers showed in both quantity

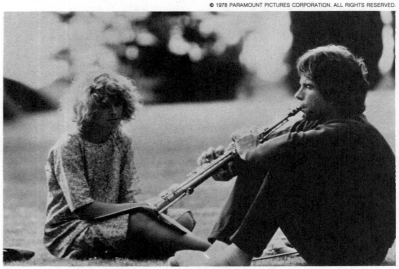

Julie Christie and Warren Beatty in
Heaven Can Wait.

(some 19 feature productions were scheduled for the year) and quality. The first Australian film to compete in the Cannes Film Festival was Fred Schepisi's *The Chant of Jimmy Blacksmith,* a vigorous account of an intelligent 19th-century aborigine who declares a private war on the repressive white settlers. Phillip Noyce's *Newsfront* also made its mark at various international festivals. Through an ingenious combination of documentary film and the fictional story of the rivalry of two newsreel firms, it explored Australian history after World War II.

NEW ZEALAND. In the wake of the Australian miracle there was evidence of an emergent New Zealand cinema. Roger Donaldson's *Sleeping Dogs* was a story—better told than conceived—of a near-future totalitarian terrorist state. Vincent Ward's *State of Siege* achieved the quality of parable in its story of a middle-aged woman in retreat in her lonely cottage and besieged by a night prowler.

CANADA. Canada in 1978 clearly lacked either the confidence or the sense of direction that inspired the Australian film industry. The lack of confidence was intimated by the extensive importation of acting and directorial talent (for instance, Peter O'Toole and David Hemmings for Martyn Burke's *Power Play;* Claude Chabrol to direct one of his least successful thrillers, *Blood Relatives*). More successful, because more authentically indigenous, were two films modestly made for television: Ralph Thomas's *Tyler,* about a young farmer's battle for survival in the face of bureaucracy; and Robin Spry's *Drying Up the Streets,* a disillusioned view of the legacy of the liberated 1960s.

Western Europe. FRANCE. While lightweight bourgeois comedy (Michel Lang's *L'Hôtel de la Plage;* Pierre Richard's *Je suis timide, mais je me soigne*) remained the commercial staple, a number of distinctive trends were discernible in French production. The "affaire" film—recreating in neodocumentary style political situations or incidents closely or remotely based on facts—remained remarkably popular. Thus the veteran André Cayatte's *La Raison d'état* dealt with the elimination of a man who discovers corruption and illicit arms dealing in high official places. Michel Deville's

Dossier 51 considered the threat to individual liberty and privacy implicit in the existence of a secret service. Christian de Chalonge's *L'Argent des autres* was about the efforts of the top executives of a great bank to find a whipping boy for their own deficiencies. Vera Belmont's *Prisonnier de Mao* recreated the processes of guilt and exculpation in Communist China. Joseph Losey's *Les Routes du sud* stood perhaps on the edge of the tradition; scripted by Jorge Semprun, it was almost a parody of the Spanish writer's recurrent theme of exiles still fighting their nation's civil war 40 years later.

A new and very different direction in French production was the historical epic, typified by Ariane Mnouchkine's marathon *Molière;* by the former television director Frank Cassenti's *La Chanson de Roland;* and by Eric Rohmer's disappointing account of *Perceval le Gallois.* Several directors offered individual psychological studies of depth and high quality. In *Le Jument vapeur* Joyce Buñuel depicted humorously and poignantly the nervous breakdown of a housewife. Gérard Blain's *Un Second Souffle* succeeded in never ridiculing its hero, a middle-aged man desperately grasping after lost youth in an affair with a young girl.

Claude Chabrol and François Truffaut continued on their independent ways. Chabrol's *Violette Nozière* recreated—stylishly but at excessive length—a controversial murder case of 1934. Truffaut's *La Chambre verte,* adapted from Henry James, portrayed a man (played by the director) obsessed with his loved dead. In *L'Amour en fruite* Truffaut continued the adventures of Antoine Doinel (Jean-Pierre Léaud), which began some 20 years ago in *Les Quatre Cents Coups (The 400 Blows).*

ITALY. Despite the inroads of television (the Italian cinema was particularly hard hit by the proliferation of independent television stations and film piracy) Italy continued to produce high-quality films. For the second year in succession an Italian movie won the Grand Prix at the Cannes Film Festival, with Ermanno Olmi's *L'albero degli zoccoli (The Tree of Clogs),* a majestic panorama of life on a Lombardy farm at the end of the last century.

Marco Ferreri's *Ciao, Maschio* was a bizarre apocalyptic extravaganza about a group of eccentrics inhabiting a deserted New York City, where a giant gorilla has been washed up on the Hudson River mud flats. Other directors seemed attracted to history, whether recent (Tonino Cervi's dissection of Fascist-era bourgeoisie, *Nest of Vipers*) or more remote, as in Luigi Magni's satirical tragedy about the last days of the Church's temporal power, *In nome del Papa Re*. The 22-year-old Nanni Moretti made his debut in 16-mm filmmaking with an entirely contemporary subject: in *Ecce bombo* he played the hero of his own plotless impression of relationships of the young in present-day Italy.

WEST GERMANY. Eight major young directors, including Rainer Werner Fassbinder and Volker Schlöndorff, collaborated on *Deutschland im Herbst*, an ill-digested collective reflection on events in West Germany in late 1977 — the Schleyer murder, the Kappler incident, the Mogadishu hijacking, and the terrorist deaths in Stammheim prison. Other directors enjoyed more success. A comparative newcomer, Wolfgang Petersen, made *Die Konsequenz*, a touching study of the social tribulations of two young homosexuals, and *Schwarz und Weiss wie Tage und Nächte*, a concentrated study of a man obsessed with the game of chess. Reinhard Hauff directed *Der Hauptdarsteller*, about the effects on a country boy of being chosen for a role in a film, and *Messer im Kopf*, a prizewinner at the Paris Festival, describing a cat-and-mouse game between the police and a politically suspect intellectual whose brain they have injured in the course of a demonstration. After years as a confirmed "underground" filmmaker, Werner Schroeter achieved a considerable critical success with his operatic historical panorama *Il regno di Napoli*.

Women filmmakers were prominent. Ula Stöckl's *A Woman and Her Responsibilities* and Helga Sanders's *The All-Round Reduced Personality* dealt with specifically feminist issues. Margarethe von Trotta made her debut as director with a reflective story of crime and flight, *Das zweite Erwachen der Christa Klages*.

SWITZERLAND. The most interesting Swiss films of the year coincidentally both found their subjects in Jean-Jacques Rousseau. Claude Goretta's *Les Chemins de l'exil* explored the events of 1762, when *Émile* was banned and its author forced into exile in Switzerland and then England. Thomas Koerfer's *Alzire oder der neue Kontinent* described the unsettling effects upon a troupe of actors attempting a production of Voltaire's *Alzire* when the author and Rousseau turn up alive and well to discuss the ethics and philosophy of theatrical representation.

SCANDINAVIA. Sweden's greatest director, Ingmar Bergman, remained in exile. After a U.S.-West German co-production, *The Serpent's Egg*, a disappointing period piece about portents of Nazism in inflation-ridden Berlin, he made one of his most accomplished works, *Autumn Sonata*, as a West German-Norwegian co-production. The film explored the relationship, a web of ancient resentments, between a mother and daughter, played by Ingrid Bergman and Liv Ullmann. Within the Swedish film industry Jörn Donner's *Men Cannot Be Raped* dealt with rape as a personal crisis rather than a legal issue, in a story of a victim's attempt

to exact revenge in kind. Actors Ingrid Thulin and Erland Josephson with the cinematographer Sven Nykvist directed themselves in *One and One*, a meticulous observation of the odd relationship of two middle-aged people. From Denmark the ingenious and accomplished *92 Minutes of Yesterday*, a brief encounter between a Frenchman and a Danish girl who do not speak each other's language, was a notable debut for its director, Carsten Brandt.

SPAIN. In 1978 Spain was claiming persuasively that its filmmakers had as great a freedom of expression as any in the world. Freedom and extensive government financial support seemed to have brought rapid results, and Spanish production showed great vitality. In *La ciutat cremada*, Antoni Ribas instituted a new Catalan cinema with a kind of Catalan *1900*. Luis Berlanga's *La escopeta nacional* lampooned francoist politics with ribald comedy. A special Spanish taste for the bizarre (notable in the greatest Spanish film artist, Luis Buñuel) was evinced in Jaime de Armiñán's *Nunca es tarde* about an aged lady determined on a virgin conception; and again in José Luis García Sánchez's *Las truchas*, about a grand dinner where the guests politely ignore the fact that the fish is rotten and some of their number are noisily expiring in consequence.

Eastern Europe. Apart from Hungary, Eastern European filmmaking seemed to be in the doldrums. The Soviet cinema's major productions were stolid classical adaptations (Sergey Bondarchuk's *The Steppe*, from Chekhov; Igor Talankin's *Father Sergius*, from Tolstoy; Iosif Kheyfits's *Asya*, from Turgenev). Among these, Roman Balaian's *Birjuk*, from Turgenev, revealed more style than the rest, and was a promising debut. Once again

Peter Sellers as Inspector Clouseau impersonating Toulouse-Lautrec in the movie *Revenge of the Pink Panther*.

Yves Montand starred in the French film *Les Routes du sud,* directed by Joseph Losey.

the filmmakers from the republic of Georgia produced what vitality there was; Tengiz Abuladze's *The Wishing Tree* was a likable eccentric comedy of rural tradition and belief. Czechoslovakia turned to historical action stories and escapist comedy in evasion of real contemporary themes. East German and Yugoslav production seemed negligible, but Bulgaria had at least one bright spot with Ivan Nichev's *Stars in the Hair, Tears in the Eyes,* a bittersweet comedy about a touring theatrical troupe and its short-lived triumph.

In Hungary there was a reaction against the literary and theatrical character that had always been strong in Hungarian cinema. Thus, two feature directors, Janos Rozsa and Ferenc Kosa, made socially critical documentaries, respectively *The Battlefield* and *Portrait of a Champion.* Pal Schiffer's *Gyuri* was part reportage, part recreation of the problems of a young gypsy endeavouring to integrate himself into ordinary society. Istvan Darday's four-hour *Three Sisters* used nonprofessional actors and improvisation to explore family relationships. Other established directors pursued more conventional methods with distinguished results. Karoly Makk's *A Very Moral Night* was a comedy about a *fin-de-siècle* brothel that posed as a ladies' pension for an evening. Zoltan Fabri's *The Hungarians* and Sandor Sara's *80 Hussars* both dealt with expatriation. Sandor Simo's *My Father's Happy Years* dealt with a subject rarely discussed in Hungarian films, the situation of a small capitalist in the first days of socialism. In *Just Like at Home* Marta Meszaros made another of her popular investigations of the emotional-social problems of women in Hungary.

Asia. JAPAN. With production levels apparently stabilized, Japanese producers concentrated upon commercially reliable subjects. Nagisa Oshima's *The Empire of Passion* disappointed those who anticipated some kind of sequel to his celebrated erotic study *In the Realm of the Senses.* Instead, it proved to be a somewhat conventional and conventionally made ghost story.

INDIA. The first film festival to be held in South India, in Madras, revealed to an international audience the existence of a rich and independent school of cinema, ranging from John Abraham's parable *Donkey in a Brahmin Village* to Bapu's elevation of the "mystical" genre in *Sita's Wedding. The Boon,* made by Bombay director Shyam Benegal, examined critically the mystical elements of traditional Buddhism.

Africa and the Middle East. ISRAEL. One of the year's most controversial films was Yehuda (Judd) Ne'eman's *Paratroopers,* which critically examined the relationships of a group of Army recruits and, through them, the whole nation's inevitable obsession with militarism. The most popular film, *Lemon Popsicle,* was a ribald comedy about the adventures of a group of adolescents.

MOROCCO. Among 1978's most promising debuts was that of a young Moroccan director, Ahmed el Maanouni, whose *Alyam, Alyam (Oh the Days)* explored perceptively the tensions between the conservative old and the young, yearning for Europe, in a small village. (DAVID ROBINSON)

Nontheatrical Motion Pictures. The output of nontheatrical films in the U.S. in 1978 rose for the second straight year after a three-year decline. Production was 15,400 in 1977 and more than 16,000 in 1978.

Two amateur films, one by a group of University of Southern California cinema students and the other a black-and-white production by two other California students, each took multiple honours in overseas film festivals. One was *El Dorado,* the adventures of a Mexican farmer in Los Angeles. Student director Allan Marcel headed a team of six. The second, *Gravity,* was a spoof of educational films. It was the work of two students from Encino, Calif., David Wechter and Michael Nankin.

In other competition Robin Lehman of New York City for the third year took a grand prize, this one for *Manimals,* at the Melbourne, Australia, Film Festival. *Water* by Dick Young, also of New York, won the Golden Ear of Corn at Berlin's Agriculture Film Competition in the environmental group. At the American Film Festival in New York City the major prizewinner was an Austrian entry, *Young Dr. Freud.* (THOMAS W. HOPE)

See also Photography; Television and Radio.
[623; 735.G.2]

OSCAR TURNS 50

by Daniel Taradash

A time capsule containing the major entertainment artifacts of the 20th century undoubtedly would contain a 13½-in statuette and a conventional large envelope. Made of britannia metal (an alloy), gold-plated, and weighing 8½ lb, the statuette appears to be a figure out of science fiction holding what has been interpreted as a crusader's sword. It stands on a round pedestal that depicts a semiabstract reel of motion-picture film. The envelope, of high-quality bond, has a phrase such as "Best Achievement in Costume Design" in large type on the front; it is sealed and adorned with a red ribbon. These two objects are the Oscar and the envelope holding the name of its winner. They are the featured attractions at the annual awards ceremony of the Academy of Motion Picture Arts and Sciences.

The Academy was founded in 1927 by 36 leaders of the film industry, among them Louis B. Mayer, Darryl Zanuck, Mary Pickford, Cedric Gibbons (who designed the Oscar), Norma Shearer, Jack L. Warner, and the organization's first president, Douglas Fairbanks. Suspected of being an antilabour stratagem, the Academy did not follow that course. Instead, it became an esteemed society of professionals, its primary purposes "to advance the arts and sciences of motion pictures, foster cooperation . . . for cultural, educational and technological progress . . . cooperate on technical research and improvement of methods and equipment." The Academy has lived up to its aims and, particularly in the last decade, has conducted many educational activities. But the statuette and envelope have inevitably been its most famous symbols.

The Awards Ceremonies. Some 250 people attended the first bestowal of the awards. (*Wings* was voted best picture.) The 50th annual presentation, in 1978, was seen by more than 300 million; in addition to 70 million television viewers in the U.S., 50 foreign countries received it, a few directly, some by satellite, and the rest by delayed telecasts. The net-

work fee for the award show is, incidentally, the Academy's primary source of income. Originally held as banquets in hotels, the presentations were moved to theatres in 1944 and since 1969 have been held at the Chandler Pavilion of the Los Angeles Music Center. Network radio broadcasts began in 1945 and television coverage in 1953. The ceremonies are generally held early in April to honour the achievements of the previous year.

The integrity of the awards is undeniable; votes are tabulated in secrecy by the accounting firm of Price Waterhouse. The results are unknown until the envelopes are opened. In addition, nobody, a president of the Academy no more than a trade-journal reporter, could ever pry from Price Waterhouse such information as the number of votes by which somebody won, who finished second, or even how many votes were cast.

Though faultfinders call it "establishment," the Academy has shown an amazing catholicity in its citations in almost all of its 22 categories. Oscars for best picture have gone not only to large-budget blockbusters (*The Greatest Show on Earth, The Godfather*) but also to inexpensive, offbeat movies such as *Marty, One Flew over the Cuckoo's Nest,* and *Annie Hall*. In the Documentary and Short Subjects category it has often paid homage to the unusual and controversial, such as *Interviews with My Lai Veterans, Woodstock,* and *Harlan County, U.S.A.* While Irving Berlin's traditional "White Christmas" was acclaimed best song in 1942, Isaac Hayes's hip "Theme from *Shaft*" won in 1971.

Critics call the awards highly commercialized. Indeed, the trade papers abound with advertisements just before Oscar time. But no one has yet proven any correlation between the ads and the winners. And in some cases offensively large "campaigns" have seemed counterproductive. The commercial gain for an Oscar, of course, can be spectacular. For example, though the award for best picture gave only a little more impetus to the already high-flying *The Godfather,* it meant additional millions to the more chancy *One Flew over the Cuckoo's Nest*.

Many notable moments have occurred at the awards ceremonies. In 1940 Nobel Prize-winning author Sinclair Lewis, accepting a posthumous Oscar for Sidney Howard for the screenplay of *Gone with the Wind* (Lewis had played a small role in the film), remarked: "I know the value of writers. Without their imagination and eloquence, which produce the words we speak, we actors would be nothing." In 1943 Greer Garson, accepting for her performance in *Mrs. Miniver,* was so overwhelmed that she took the better part of an hour for her "thank you" speech. In 1973 Marlon Brando sent a young American Indian actress to the podium to refuse his

Daniel Taradash, president of the Writers Guild of America, West, and president of the Academy of Motion Picture Arts and Sciences, 1970–73, won an Academy Award for his screenplay of From Here to Eternity. *He also wrote the screenplay for* Picnic.

best actor award for *The Godfather* and also to tell the world the plight of her people. (The Academy treated Brando's nonacceptance with serene objectivity: It nominated him again the next year for his performance in *Last Tango in Paris,* though he did not win.) In 1978 Vanessa Redgrave also politicized her acceptance (for her best supporting actress role in *Julia*), referring to her disapproval of Zionism. Toward these irregularities, the Academy has maintained a "freedom of expression" stance. But the audience responded with bravos in 1972 when Jane Fonda, at that time perhaps better known for her anti-Vietnam war protests than for her acting, fondled her Oscar (for best actress in *Klute*) like a newborn babe and spoke up: "There's a great deal to say, but I'm not going to say it tonight. I thank you all very much."

The most moving and cherished of all appearances took place on the same program. The Academy had persuaded Charlie Chaplin to come to Hollywood after 20 years of self-imposed exile abroad to receive a special honorary award. (He was then six days short of his 83rd birthday.) The presentation to him was the last of the evening, and Chaplin was nervous, fearing the possibility of catcalls. But when the inscription on his Oscar was read ("For the incalculable effect he has had in making motion pictures the art form of this century"), the auditorium exploded with a standing, roaring ovation, among the greatest in Academy history. Chaplin's eyes teared, and he expressed gratitude to "you sweet people" in emotion-filled, quavering tones.

For a few statistics, *Ben Hur* received more awards than any other picture (11). *All About Eve* received the most nominations (14). Only three performers have won three times—Walter Brennan, Ingrid Bergman, and Katharine Hepburn. Walt Disney collected far more statuettes than anyone else, most for his short films starring Mickey Mouse; including honorary awards, Disney won 30 prizes. Performers, creative artists, and craftsmen from many countries have won awards in various categories.

Organization and Membership. Nominations and voting for the awards are best explained in terms of the Academy's membership structure. The Academy consists of 12 branches, each of which represents an aspect of filmmaking such as acting or directing. The Board of Governors consists of three members elected by each branch, and the board elects the Academy officers from its own group. Additionally, there are members-at-large, those whose activities do not encompass numbers large enough for separate branches, and associate members, who do not vote.

Balloting for nominations (in almost all cases five in each category) for awards is restricted to members of the branch concerned; writers nominate only writers, directors nominate directors, etc. (Exceptions are Foreign Language Films and Documentaries. In these cases, large committees drawn from all branches make the nominations.) Every voting member is entitled to nomination balloting for best picture, including members-at-large, whose nominations are limited to this category. Price Waterhouse tabulates all nominations. After nominations are announced, all voting members are eligible to vote for all categories.

To become a member of the Academy, a candidate must be sponsored by two members of his particular branch. A committee of each branch determines if the applicant meets the Academy's criteria. These include several meritorious cinema credits—television credits are not considered—or a particularly outstanding contribution to motion pictures. The Board of Governors reserves the final right of acceptance.

It is fair to state that today the Academy leadership prides itself mostly on the Margaret Herrick Library and the Samuel Goldwyn Theater, each in the new Academy building, which opened in Beverly Hills, Calif., in December 1975. The library, which occupies 10,000 sq ft and is open to the public, houses the world's most extensive collection of film-related books, periodicals, and pamphlets and contains one million still photographs. The theatre, reserved for the members, with occasional exceptions, seats more than 1,000.

When actor Gregory Peck became the Academy's 17th president in 1967, he was determined to increase its educational and cultural activities. He and the three presidents who followed him have made the "Academy" in the title a word of meaning. Scholarships and grants are given to students in both the artistic and the scientific sectors. These have ranged from a grant to a young Gambian filmmaker to one to a graduate student at Ithaca (N.Y.) College working on optical techniques.

The Student Film Awards (co-sponsored by AT&T) grow in popularity each year. More than 300 films from college filmmakers throughout the U.S. were entered in the latest contest. The seven finalists were honoured at the Goldwyn Theater before an overflow audience.

The Academy has ended its first 50 years as a distinctive institution, a blend of popular prizes and educational and technological undertakings. The latter, however, will probably always be (as they are now) obscured in the giant shadow cast by the small statuette. And for those who wonder how the prize got its name, former executive director Margaret Herrick, on seeing it for the first time in 1931, exclaimed, "Why, he looks just like my Uncle Oscar!"

Motor Sports

Grand Prix Racing. The 1978 season of Formula One grand prix racing featured effective new cars, with the Lotus 79 quite outstanding, and Michelin tires furnishing strong competition to Goodyear. Renault continued to operate its technically intriguing turbocharged car but without the success hoped for. A number of starting-line accidents during the year culminated in the death of Sweden's Ronnie Peterson (*see* OBITUARIES). The world championship was won at the Italian race by Mario Andretti of the U.S., driving one of Colin Chapman's invincible Lotus 79s, and so the two remaining races were somewhat of an anticlimax.

An unsavoury aspect of the season was the court case brought by Shadow against the Arrows team, which was accused of copying the Shadow design. Another unhappy event was the death from cancer of Swedish driver Gunnar Nilsson (*see* OBITUARIES). An attempt to race the U.S. Indianapolis cars at Silverstone and Brands Hatch was not entirely successful because they could not race in rain and were unsuited to road circuits; however, they did set new lap records at both places.

In the opening grand prix race in January at Buenos Aires, Arg., it was Andretti and Lotus all the way, the Type 78 car winning from Austrian Niki Lauda's Brabham Bt46 and the Tyrrell of France's Patrick Depailler. A Ferrari made the fastest lap. In the Brazilian Grand Prix at Rio de Janeiro the Ferrari of Argentina's Carlos Reutemann beat the Copersucar F5A of Brazil's Emerson Fittipaldi, with Lauda's Brabham third. The Brabham had a 12-cylinder Alfa Romeo engine and the Ferrari used its own 12-cylinder power plant. All the rest used Cosworth-Ford V8 engines except for

Renault. In South Africa at Kyalami, with Andretti's Lotus in trouble, Peterson chased an ailing Tyrrell to snatch victory from Depailler; third place went to John Watson's Brabham. In the U.S. Grand Prix West at Long Beach, Calif.—a real street race with a limit on entrants—Reutemann won easily from Andretti and Depailler.

The European season opened with the Monaco Grand Prix, in which Depailler got away well and won his first grand prix for the Tyrrell-Ford team. Lauda finished second in his Brabham in front of the Ford-powered Wolf of Jody Scheckter of South Africa. Lauda set a new lap record of 134.649 kph. In the Belgian Grand Prix at Zolder, Andretti brought the Lotus's new, skirted Type 79 home first, followed 49.9 sec later by his teammate Peterson in a Lotus 78; Peterson made the fastest lap, at 184.635 kph. Then, in Spain, over the Jarama circuit, Lotus annihilated the opposition, its two drivers, both in Type 79 cars, finishing first and second. Peterson was 59.56 sec behind Andretti, who had the fastest lap at 150.523 kph. The French Grand Prix at Paul Ricard was won by Andretti, with Peterson again second; James Hunt of Britain was third in a McLaren-Ford, and Reutemann set a new lap record at 192.597 kph.

The British Grand Prix at Brands Hatch was a race of changing leaders until Reutemann's Ferrari took the prize. Lauda and Watson were second and third in Brabhams. Although skirts, which aid a racing car's wheel grip in something of a Hovercraft manner, had not been questioned, after the Swedish race, the suction fan—which Bernard Ecclestone's Brabham-Alfa Romeo team claimed was necessary to keep the engine cool—was disallowed because it was said to aid wheel grip unduly; the ruling caused great acrimony. Lauda had won the event in his Brabham.

The German Grand Prix was held at Hocken-

Al Unser (No. 2, centre) drove his turbocharged Lola-Cosworth at an average speed of 161.363 mph to win the 1978 Indianapolis 500, his third victory in the classic race.

Motorboating:
see Water Sports

Motor Industry:
see Industrial Review

heim in hot weather. Of the 24 entrants, 13 did not finish. Andretti won the race, with Scheckter's Wolf WR5 second and Jacques Laffite's Ligier JS9 third. Peterson had the fastest lap, at 211.354 kph. The Austrian Grand Prix, marred by rain, was won by Peterson from Depailler, with Gilles Villeneuve of Canada third in a Ferrari. The Dutch Grand Prix at Zandvoort endorsed Lotus supremacy, with Andretti and Peterson first and second, respectively, ahead of Lauda, who set the fastest lap, at 191.2 kph. The Italian Grand Prix at Monza was marred by an accident at the starting line involving Peterson, who died from his injuries; Lauda won from Watson and Reutemann, and Andretti endorsed his top position with a lap record of 212.562 kph. With no Japanese Grand Prix in 1978, there remained only the U.S. Grand Prix East at Watkins Glen, N.Y., and the Canadian Grand Prix at Mosport. The winner of the former was Reutemann, and the Canadian event was won by Villeneuve's Ferrari.

In sports car racing the 24-hour marathon at Le Mans, France, was won by a two-litre turbocharged Renault-Alphine A442B, on Michelin tires, at 210.19 kph. The Monte Carlo Rally was won by Porsche, the Swedish by Ford, the Circuit of Ireland by Ford, the Swedish Rally by Vauxhall, the Mintex by Vauxhall, the Portuguese by Fiat, the Acropolis by Fiat, the Scottish by Ford, and the 1,000 Lakes by Fiat. Fiat then won in Quebec, but Lancia won at San Remo. By winning in Corsica, Fiat clinched the world championship. The RAC Rally was won by Ford.

(WILLIAM C. BODDY)

U.S. Racing. For Al Unser, a veteran driver from Albuquerque, N.M., and Cale Yarborough of Timmonsville, S.C., three was a significant number in 1978. Unser scored an unprecedented sweep of the three most lucrative and prestigious United States Auto Club (USAC) single-seater oval-track races. He won the Indianapolis 500-mi classic for the third time in his career and then added the Schaefer 500 at Mt. Pocono, Pa., and the California 500 at Ontario. He also became the first USAC driver to win more than $500,000 in a single season.

Christian Léon of France leans into a turn in the 1978 European Endurance Championship at Le Mans, France, in April. Léon and his partner, Jean-Claude Chermarin, were victors in the grueling 24-hour event.

A.F.P./PICTORIAL PARADE

A bullnecked ex-football player, Yarborough won ten Winston Cup stock car races, including the Winston 500 at Talladega, Ala., and the granddaddy of the 500-milers, the Southern 500 at Darlington, S.C., en route to his third National Association for Stock Car Auto Racing (NASCAR) crown. Driving the First National City Travelers Checks Oldsmobile, Yarborough captured five of the new pole position awards, enabling him to surpass $400,000 in winnings.

In each case the veteran had a single "young lion" as a main challenger. For Unser it was Tom Sneva who, through his exploits in two USAC races in Great Britain, edged Unser for the Citicorp Cup, emblematic of the season championship. Second to Unser at Indianapolis after winning the pole position, Sneva garnered a third at Silverstone and a second at Brands Hatch while Unser failed to finish either race. (The respective winners were A. J. Foyt and Rick Mears.) The final point standings for the season were Sneva 4,153 and Unser 4,031.

In the Indianapolis race, Sneva, in a Penske-Cosworth, won the pole position at a record 202.156 mph. But Unser, eight miles per hour slower in qualifying, won the race in a Lola-Cosworth owned by ex-racer Texas Jim Hall. He averaged 161.363 mph, earning $290,363 of the $1,145,225 purse.

Veteran A. J. Foyt won USAC's stock car crown in his Camaro, a title he last held a decade earlier. The dirt car champion was Pancho Carter, the sprint champion was Tom Bigelow, and Rich Vogeler won the midget title.

Meanwhile, in NASCAR's Winston Cup series, which topped $5 million in prizes, Yarborough had to fend off young Tennessean Darrell Waltrip. The two were even after the first half of the season with four victories apiece. But then Yarborough pulled away in his Buddy Baker Oldsmobile to clinch the title. NASCAR's richest race, the Daytona 500, eluded both men. Yarborough had gained the pole position but Bobby Allison in a Ford Thunderbird won the race with an average speed of 159.730 mph after Yarborough's car broke down two laps from the end. Allison also figured in the season's most unusual finish, which occurred in Atlanta's Dixie 500. It took 24 hours to determine that he, not Richard Petty, had won. Chevrolet won the manufacturer's title.

U.S. road racing also crowned its champions. The Sports Car Club of America's (SCCA's) Can-Am title went to Alan Jones of Australia driving a Lola-Chevrolet. In the other SCCA professional series, the Trans-American, Greg Pickett in a Corvette GT won category I and Bob Tullius in a Jaguar XJS took category II.

The International Motor Sports Association, which sanctions the 24 Hours of Daytona and the Sebring 12-Hour races, crowned Peter Gregg (Porsche Turbo) as its Camel GT champion and Walt Bohren (Mazda) as its (Champion Spark Plug) Racing Stock titlist. Dave White in a Porsche won the GT Under 2.5 Litre crown. The Daytona 24 also was a runaway for Porsche: Rolf Stommelin of West Germany, Toine Hezemans of The Netherlands, and Gregg formed the winning team. At

Formula One Grand Prix Champions, 1978

Race	Driver	Car	Average speed
Argentine	M. Andretti	Lotus 78	191.820 kph
Brazilian	C. Reutemann	Ferrari 312T	172.887 kph
South African	R. Peterson	Lotus 78	187.808 kph
U.S. Western	C. Reutemann	Ferrari 312T	140.167 kph
Monaco	P. Depailler	Tyrrell 008	129.325 kph
Belgian	M. Andretti	Lotus 79	179.240 kph
Spanish	M. Andretti	Lotus 79	150.523 kph
Swedish	N. Lauda	Brabham BT46	167.6 kph
French	M. Andretti	Lotus 79	190.405 kph
British	C. Reutemann	Ferrari 312T	187.66 kph
German	M. Andretti	Lotus 79	208.233 kph
Austrian	R. Peterson	Lotus 79	189.950 kph
Dutch	M. Andretti	Lotus 79	188.170 kph
Italian	N. Lauda	Brabham BT46	207.526 kph
U.S. Eastern	C. Reutemann	Ferrari 312T	190.820 kph
Canadian	G. Villeneuve	Ferrari 312T	160.41 kph

WORLD DRIVERS' CHAMPIONSHIP: Andretti 64 pt, Peterson 51 pt, Reutemann 48 pt

CHAMPIONSHIP OF MAKES: Lotus 1st, Ferrari 2nd

Sebring promoter Dave Mendez won his own race in a Porsche, teamed with Bob Garretson and Brian Redman of the U.K.

A future challenge to USAC seemed likely when a rival organization, Championship Auto Racing Teams, Inc., was formed during the year. It announced a 1979 schedule of races in competition with those of USAC. (ROBERT J. FENDELL)

Motorcycles. Kenny Roberts of the U.S., riding a Yamaha, wrested the 500-cc world road race championship of 1978 away from Britain's Barry Sheene (Suzuki) and was barely beaten by Johnny Cecotto (Venezuela) for the 750-cc championship; the 350-cc and 250-cc classes went to Kork Ballington of South Africa (Kawasaki); winners of the 125-cc and 50-cc classes were E. Lazzarini of Italy (Kreidler) and R. Tormo of Spain (Bultaco), respectively; world sidecar champion was Swiss Rolf Biland. The European Endurance Championship, dominated by Hondas, was won by J. C. Chermarin and C. Leon, both of France.

At the Tourist Trophy (TT) races, chief winners were Northern Ireland's Tom Herron (senior, Suzuki), Britain's Mick Grant (classic, Kawasaki), Britain's Charles Mortimer (junior 250-cc, Yamaha), and Rolf Steinhausen of West Germany (sidecar, Yamaha). The Formula One race was won by Britain's Mike Hailwood (Ducati). In the International Six Days' Trial, Czechoslovakia (Jawa) won the World Trophy.

Motocross world champions were Heikki Mikkola of Finland (Yamaha) in the 500-cc class and Gennady Moisseev of the U.S.S.R. (KTM) in the 250-cc class. At the Golden Jubilee speedway world championship at Wembley, London, Ole Olsen of Denmark beat Gordon Kennet of England. Denmark beat Britain in the World Team Cup Event, held at Landshut, West Germany. The "world's fastest" title went to Don Vesco of the U.S., with a speed of 318.59 mph on a turbocharged Kawasaki-powered streamliner. (CYRIL J. AYTON)

See also Water Sports.
[452.B.4.c]

Mountaineering

In the 1977 post-monsoon season a South Korean expedition put one Korean climber and one Sherpa porter on the summit of Mt. Everest via the origi-

nal South Col route. In the 1978 pre-monsoon season one West German and eight Austrian climbers and one Sherpa porter, members of an Austrian expedition, reached the summit by the same route. Reinhold Messner (Italy), Peter Habeler (Austria), and Eric Jones and Leo Dickinson (Great Britain) accompanied the Austrian expedition; Messner and Habeler reached the summit, also by the original route, without the use of oxygen on May 8.

The first ascent without oxygen was probably that of the Chinese-Tibetan expedition in 1975. Nevertheless, the Messner-Habeler ascent became the subject of controversy when some Sherpas who had reached the summit in the past wrote to the Nepalese government doubting it could have been accomplished without oxygen. It was, however, accepted by the climbing world as confirming the place of Messner and Habeler as the finest current climbing partnership. Later, Messner, in the western Himalayas, reached the summit of Nanga Parbat (8,126 m; 26,660 ft) alone after climbing a new route on the Diamir Face without oxygen or support climbers.

In July 1977 a Yugoslav expedition made the first ascent of the southwest face of Gasherbrum I (8,073 m; 26,470 ft) in the Karakoram Range. Also in the Karakorams, the second ascent of K2 (8,611 m; 28,250 ft) was made in August 1977 by a joint Japanese-Pakistani expedition; in June 1978 a new-route attempt on the west ridge of this mountain by a British expedition was abandoned after the death of a member. A Dutch expedition climbed Annapurna I (8,078 m; 26,504 ft) in the Himalayas by a new route in October 1977. Pre-monsoon successes in the Himalayas in 1978 included the south face of Dhaulagiri by the South Pillar—a long-standing problem—by Japanese climbers, and Kangchenjunga South (8,504 m; 27,885 ft), the second highest unclimbed peak in the world, by a Polish expedition.

The Nepalese government announced a list of 47 further peaks made available for climbing, in four categories: for Nepalese expeditions only; for joint Nepalese-foreign expeditions, or for foreign expeditions after Nepalese attempts; for general availability; and for tourist trekking and climbing. Permits were to be given for two-week periods from base camp. The Nepalese government also banned leaders of four expeditions—two Japanese, one Polish, and one Spanish—for transgressing its rules. Entry to Nepal was banned for three years and climbing for five. (JOHN NEILL)

Mozambique

An independent African state, the People's Republic of Mozambique is located on the southeast coast of Africa, bounded by the Indian Ocean, Tanzania, Malawi, Zambia, Rhodesia, South Africa, and Swaziland. Area: 799,380 sq km (308,642 sq mi). Pop. (1977 est.): 9,899,000. Cap. and largest city: Maputo (pop., 1970, 354,700). Language: Portuguese (official); Bantu languages predominate. Religion: traditional beliefs 70%, Christian about 15%, Muslim 13%, with Hindu,

Mozambique

Buddhist, and Jewish minorities. President in 1978, Samora Machel.

Despite continuing guerrilla activity by the opposition Mozambique National Resistance in 1978, the Mozambique Liberation Front (Frelimo) government's authority was felt over the whole country. The protracted electoral process, culminating in the election of the People's Assembly in December 1977, was followed early in January by the appointment of a central national commission of instruction, headed by Pres. Samora Machel and directed at the political education of the people.

Also in January, the Moatize coal mines and the Cabora Bassa hydroelectric scheme were placed under the Council of Ministers. Foreign and local banks were nationalized, and a second state-owned bank was established. Shortly afterward the Portuguese-owned Metalo-Mecanica engineering works was nationalized to avoid economic sabotage. In light of the country's economic difficulties, however, Machel continued to allow foreign-owned private businesses to operate. The scheme to expand Mozambique's fishing industry continued with the assistance of the Norwegian Agency for Development. Much-needed foreign currency also flowed in from the sale of electric power from the Cabora Bassa Dam to South Africa. In March 1978 a new fiscal system was introduced, including a 3% circulation tax on goods and services, a capital revenue tax, a consumer tax, and a national reconstruction tax levied, on a sliding scale, on earnings.

Machel's socializing program encountered numerous obstacles, including frequent disruptions by guerrilla activity, particularly in the north, and lack of enthusiasm on the part of some of his followers. At a meeting of the Frelimo provincial committee in Maputo, he claimed the capital was infested by crime. He also admitted, at a mass meeting of students and teachers on February 16, that the education program in 1976 and 1977 had been a disaster, due to absenteeism and lack of commitment by students. In August charges of incompetence and negligence were leveled by the government against the European managers of the formerly prosperous British-owned Sena Sugar Estates, though it was reported that the breakdown was at least partly attributable to the unwillingness of plantation workers to do their job. Heavy rains in March caused serious flooding in Tete district; the Zambezi burst its banks, killing more than 40 people and rendering 200,000 homeless.

The government's difficulties were aggravated by its support for Robert Mugabe's Patriotic Front guerrilla movement. In reprisal for the Front's attacks on Rhodesia, the Rhodesian government raided guerrilla camps in Mozambique. Although Mozambique military forces were not directly involved, the Army had to be kept on the alert and up to strength to deal with possible border infringements, as well as to counter the activities of Mozambique's own guerrilla movement. The country had 20,000 soldiers under arms, largely supplied with Soviet weapons. Friendship with the U.S.S.R. seemed to cool a little in May, when President Machel visited China and thanked that country for its help. In August, however, there were reports of the arrival of large numbers of Soviet and Cuban technical and military advisers.

In economic terms it was South Africa, rather than the Communist countries, that provided the country's main support, a support that was particularly necessary in view of the shortages of machinery, spare parts, and raw materials to develop Mozambique's own industrial potential. Importation of these necessities had to be strictly controlled by the government because of the lack of foreign exchange. Mozambique still suffered materially from the loss of its transit trade due to the closing of the Rhodesian border, but, unlike Zambia, it did not reopen communications with South Africa through Rhodesia.

(KENNETH INGHAM)

MOZAMBIQUE

Education. (1972–73) Primary, pupils 577,997, teachers 8,345; secondary, pupils 36,155, teachers 1,682; vocational, pupils 17,216, teachers 984; teacher training, students 1,279, teachers 122; higher, students 2,621, teaching staff 326.

Finance and Trade. Monetary unit: Mozambique escudo, with (Sept. 18, 1978) a free rate of 33.22 escudos to U.S. $1 (65.10 escudos = £1 sterling). Budget (1976 est.): revenue 7.1 billion escudos; expenditure 9.3 billion escudos. Foreign trade: imports (1975) 10,472,000,000 escudos; exports (1976) 4,524,000,000 escudos. Import sources: South Africa 18%; Portugal 15%; West Germany 11%; U.K. 8%; Iraq 6%; U.S. 5%; Japan 5%; France 5%. Export destinations: Portugal 25%; U.S. 24%; South Africa 8%; Japan 5%; U.S. 5%. Main exports: cashew nuts 23%; textiles 14%; cotton 12%; sugar 12%.

Transport and Communications. Roads (1974) 39,173 km. Motor vehicles in use (1972): passenger 89,300; commercial (including buses) 21,500. Railways (1975): 4,161 km; traffic 210 million passenger-km, freight (1974) 2,180,-000,000 net ton-km. Air traffic (1976): 312 million passenger-km; freight 5.8 million net ton-km. Telephones (Jan. 1977) 52,300. Radio licenses (Dec. 1975) 200,000.

Agriculture. Production (in 000; metric tons; 1977): corn c. 350; sorghum c. 250; cassava (1976) c. 2,400; peanuts c. 100; sugar, raw value c. 250; copra c. 85; bananas c. 68; cashew nuts (1976) c. 200; tea c. 14; cotton, lint c. 30; sisal c. 23. Livestock (in 000; 1976): cattle c. 1,420; sheep c. 132; goats c. 570; pigs c. 183; chickens c. 16,000.

Industry. Production (in 000; metric tons; 1976): petroleum products c. 440; cement (1975) 258; beer (hl) 655; bauxite c. 2; electricity (kw-hr) c. 1,915,000.

Museums

The premier event of the year was the opening in Washington, D.C., of the $94 million East Building of the National Gallery of Art. A gift of Paul Mellon and Ailsa Mellon Bruce and the Mellon Foundation and designed by I. M. Pei (see BIOGRAPHIES), the structure consists of exhibition areas and the Center for Advanced Study in the Visual Arts. (See ARCHITECTURE.)

In September, the Metropolitan Museum of Art in New York City opened its permanent display of the reassembled Temple of Dendur. Rebuilt and housed in New York at a cost of $9.5 million, the small, well-preserved building was offered to the U.S. people in 1965 by the Egyptian government in gratitude for U.S. help in saving the temples of Abu Simbel during the Aswan High Dam project. The 1st century BC temple stands in the largest enclosed museum space in the world, and its opening coincided with the second phase of the reinstallation of the Metropolitan's vast Egyptian collections.

In Corning, N.Y., the Corning Museum of Glass began construction on a $6 million structure that would triple its exhibition space. The Museums of Contemporary Art in La Jolla, Calif., and in Chicago both began major expansion programs. In Washington, D.C., the old Pension Building was renovated to house the newly organized National Museum of the Building Arts; the museum was to illustrate the arts and industries of engineering, design, landscape and urban planning, and the building trades.

An unusual new museum was the National Museum of Qatar at Doha—unusual because it was uncommon to discover a museum in an Arab country showing interdisciplinary concern as against an interest in the country's art and artifacts alone. Algeria's National Museum of the Moudjahid in Algiers took as its theme the struggle for liberation by Algeria and the overthrow of colonialism. By showing the history of the country's struggle for independence culminating in the Algerian Revolution, it attempted to provide a permanent reminder of the country's recent history.

The West African Historical Museum in Ghana, situated in the castle at Cape Coast, was intended as a chronicle of the history of contact between Europe and West Africa from the 15th century to the present. In Tel Aviv, Israel, the new $10 million Museum of the Jewish Diaspora was opened in May on the campus of Tel Aviv University. It commemorated the customs and achievements throughout history of Jews outside the Holy Land.

In France the Château d'Ecouen, about 15 km (9½ mi) north of Paris, was transformed into a national museum devoted to the Renaissance. The museum opened late in 1977, though it would be several years before the conversion was complete and the building fully furnished.

Other new museums included the Stamford Brewery Museum, at Stamford, England, which opened in July. It featured a complete Victorian brewery restored to its heyday condition, with gleaming brass and copper equipment, a steam engine, and a horse and dray. Local ale was available in the refreshment room. The Ironbridge Gorge Museum, Telford, England, was named as "European museum of the year" at Strasbourg, France, in February. It was a museum of industrial archaeology centred on remaining factory buildings and kilns of the complex initiated by the early civil engineer Thomas Telford (1757–1834).

Acquisitions and Losses. Important museum acquisitions included the Heineman Foundation gift to the Pierpont Morgan Library in New York City; comprising 950 rare books and 1,200 letters and manuscripts, it was valued at $10 million. The Cleveland (Ohio) Museum of Art purchased both a major Picasso painting from 1924, "Still Life with Biscuits," and, together with the Stichting Collectie Thyssen-Bornemisza, Amsterdam, a pair of rococo-style silver tureens described as the "most important works in silver made in Europe since the Renaissance." The J. Paul Getty Museum, in Malibu, Calif., purchased an ancient Greek bronze sculpture of a youth. Attributed to Lysippus and in

EZRA STOLLER © 1978 ESTO

almost perfect condition, the work cost nearly $5 million.

Important archaeological exhibitions continued, as in recent years, in U.S. museums. "Pompeii A.D. 79" began its four-museum U.S. tour in Boston at the Museum of Fine Arts, which helped organize some 300 objects from Italian museums; it drew large crowds throughout its tour.

Major museum losses included a devastating fire which destroyed 1,000 art works, including paintings by Picasso, Dali, and Van Gogh, at the Museum of Modern Art in Rio de Janeiro, Brazil. A fire at Eastman House, the International Museum of Photography in Rochester, N.Y., was attributed to spontaneous combustion. The loss of the original prints of many M-G-M movies strengthened the drive for copying these flammable nitrate-based films onto acetate-based safety stock.

Administration. In a time of financial stringency, museums and their directors were faced with a decline in private and public patronage that made the acquisition and exhibition of works more difficult, and in 1978 tax exemption for gifts to museums, as enjoyed in the U.S., was sought in Britain. Also in Britain, there was a cry for the establishment of a national museums council, with the double object of coordinating museum policy and freeing museums from administration under the Department of Education and Science.

In the United States federal support for museums, which was $5.7 million in 1973, was expected to rise to $30 million in fiscal 1979. And, as evidenced in the continuing rise of new agencies, attention to museum needs continued. One of the four major groups in the newly established Federal Council on the Arts and the Humanities was devoted to federal museums policy. Its purpose was to establish an interagency awareness of museum needs and avoid duplications in funding and other services. The Museum Services Institute, an agency of the U.S. Department of Health, Education and Welfare established in late 1977, was designed

An exhibit of the open form steel sculptures by David Smith was one of the featured attractions when the new East Building of the National Gallery of Art was opened in Washington, D.C., in June.

The Temple of Dendur, housed in the largest enclosed museum space in the world, was opened for viewing in the Sackler wing of the Metropolitan Museum of Art in New York City in September.

to help finance the administrative costs of museums. Of its $4 million initial budget, $3.7 million was distributed among 256 museums. Officials were confident that the program would grow.

Evidence of museums' public awareness and newly organized educational campaigns was seen in Canada; there, the National Museums of Canada granted $600,000 to the magazine *Saturday Night* to develop a periodical in which Canadian museums could utilize their resources more fully by reaching a larger audience.

Although there was no pervasive evidence of museum program cutbacks because of the current economic situation, several museums in California and elsewhere raised their admission prices, and the Isabella Stewart Gardner Museum in Boston

This mosaic portrait of a woman was one of the featured works in the American tour of "Pompeii A.D. 79," which began its tour in Boston.

finally abandoned its free admission policy. For the first time in its 93-year history the Detroit Institute of Arts purchased a work with funds raised by public subscription. The 1953 paper cutout "The Wild Poppies," by Henri Matisse, and a stained-glass window from the design were purchased with the $350,000 raised by the fund drive.

(JOSHUA B. KIND; SANDRA MILLIKIN)

See also Art Exhibitions; Art Sales.
[613.D.1.b]

Music

Classical. Among a number of interesting developments on the international music scene in 1978 was MusicArmenia '78, an international celebration of Armenian music held in London, August 6–13, under the auspices of the newly inaugurated Institute of Armenian Music. Patronized by His Holiness Vasken I, supreme catholicos of all Armenians, Alain Danielou, Yehudi Menuhin, and (until his death in May) the Soviet-Armenian composer Aram Khachaturian (*see* OBITUARIES) and supervised by a nine-man team of trustees and committee members headed by composer-conductor Loris Tjeknavorian, the institute had been established in the fall of 1976 with the aim of encouraging and actively promoting on a worldwide basis the appreciation of Armenian music, both sacred and secular, and the artistry of Armenian musicians.

MusicArmenia '78 presented daily (at London's City University) a series of authoritative lectures by leading academics. These were supplemented by 16 lunchtime and evening concerts held at the university, St. John's Church, Smith Square, and St. Peter's Armenian Church. Music featured included settings of the Armenian liturgy by the "father of Armenian music," Komitas Vardaplat; Tjeknavorian's *The Life of Christ*; and various works by Ludwig Bazil, Grant Beglarian, Rouben Gregorian, Alan Hovhaness, Khachaturian, Ti-gran Mansurian, Ernest Mirzoyan, and Richard Yardumian.

In Paris the Institut de Recherche et de Coordination Acoustique/Musique (IRCAM) marked further progress. Although its director, Pierre Boulez, had devised a multidisciplinary program of research, education, information, and dissemination, he was initially prompted by a desire to cut a way through what he defined as the current crisis of musical creativity. Boulez believed that contemporary composers were faced with special and particular problems, primarily of inadequate tools and of a stagnation in the development of new acoustic and electroacoustic instruments. He believed further that this impasse could no longer be overcome on a strictly individual level and had in consequence drawn together at IRCAM a four-man "think tank" to tackle the problem. This team comprised Yugoslav composer and trombonist Vinko Globokar, Italian composer Luciano Berio, Jean-Claude Risset (director of the University of Aix-en-Provence Music Laboratory), and U.S. composer Gerald Bennett, formerly director of the Basel Music Academy. Each of them was to head a specialist department where European and non-European instruments and voice practices would come under investigation.

In 1978 Vladimir Horowitz celebrated the golden jubilee of his U.S. debut. On January 8 Carnegie Hall in New York was consequently packed to overflowing for what was, simultaneously, Horowitz's first public performance in many years of Sergey Rachmaninoff's taxing third Piano Concer-

Beverly Sills and Sherrill Milnes sang lead roles in Massenet's "Thaïs," which opened at the Metropolitan Opera in New York City in January. It was the first performance of "Thaïs" at the Met since 1939.

to and his first appearance with an orchestra in a quarter of a century. Eugene Ormandy conducted the New York Philharmonic.

The 150th anniversary of the death of Schubert and the 50th of Czechoslovak composer Leos Janacek were observed with numerous worldwide tributes to those masters. They included two especially impressive cycles at London's South Bank complex.

OPERA. In the U.S. the Metropolitan Opera's 1978–79 season got off to a promising start on Sept. 23, 1978, with the much-awaited New York premiere of Benjamin Britten's *Billy Budd*. Despite critical misgivings over certain aspects of the music, acclaim ran high for a cast that included Sir Peter Pears (Vere), Richard Stilwell (Budd), and James Morris (Claggart). Raymond Leppard drew some especially impressive sounds from the pit, while house producer John Dexter and designer William Dudley had between them a field day with an enormous cutaway set of HMS "Indomitable" that seemed magically to expand and contract as the action demanded.

Notable revivals included Wagner's *Tannhäuser*, produced in opulent style by Günther Schneider-Siemssen and brilliantly conducted by music director James Levine; Britten's *Peter Grimes*, with Jon Vickers featured in the title role; and Richard Strauss's *The Woman Without a Shadow*, in which veteran Karl Böhm conducted and Ursula Schröder-Feinen replaced Christa Ludwig as the Dyer's wife.

Houston Opera caught the public eye during October 1978 with a major revival of Rossini's early opera seria, *Tancredi*, in a version that restored a long-lost 80-bar "tragic finale" specially written for the opera's second performance in 1813. Marilyn Horne, singing the title role, scored a brilliant triumph. In this she was joined by Joan Carden, a promising young Australian soprano who made her U.S. debut as Amenaide. Stage design was by John Stoddart, with Nicola Rescigno conducting.

Following a slightly disappointing November 1977 run of Richard Strauss's *Arabella* (starring Kiri Te Kanawa and conducted by Charles Mackerras), Houston achieved another success with an English-language production of Verdi's *Falstaff*. Subtle and totally assured, Donald Gramm's portrayal of the complex title role was the centre-point of a compelling realization. Sir Alexander Gibson conducted.

In November the Lyric Opera of Chicago staged the world premiere of Polish composer Krzysztof Penderecki's *Paradise Lost*, the first premiere of a major opera in the U.S. since 1921. Based on the poem by John Milton and with a libretto by British dramatist Christopher Fry, the opera opened to mixed reviews. Penderecki's score was criticized as being heavy and portentous and the production as static, while a number of the singers and dancers received praise.

Internationally, 1978 was marked by its fair share of controversy, nowhere more so than at Bayreuth, West Germany, where Harry Kupfer brought to Wagner's *The Flying Dutchman* some highly individual notions and a truly remarkable use of production techniques. Not surprisingly,

Music

Vladimir Horowitz performs on the piano while Zubin Mehta directs the New York Philharmonic Orchestra during a rehearsal in September. Mehta had just been named director of the Philharmonic.

Royal Hunt of the Sun to Offenbach's *Orpheus in the Underworld*. Most notable of all was Jean-Claude Auvray's exquisite production of Puccini's *La Bohème*, an unforgettable experience.

A mixed season at Covent Garden was notable for Lorin Maazel's Royal Opera debut in a well-received staging of Verdi's *Luisa Miller* in which Katia Ricciarelli (Luisa) regained her form and Leo Nucci as the Miller impressed with the beauty and strength of his baritone voice. Greater controversy surrounded Götz Friedrich's January production of Mozart's *Idomeneo*. Given that it is an opera that virtually defies successful staging, Friedrich's option of filling the arena with action nonetheless seemed questionable, while Colin Davis (having proclaimed his regard for the score) largely undid his own best intentions by racing through the music with an almost unseemly haste. Vocally, matters were more satisfying, Janet Baker shining as Idamante while Stuart Burrows brought to the part of Idomeneo a beautiful flexibility.

The Covent Garden December 1977 premiere of Donizetti's *Mary Stuart* marked the 25th anniversary of Joan Sutherland's debut in the house but was generally disappointing. By contrast, the New Year *Die Fledermaus* was pure enchantment, with conductor Zubin Mehta leading a cast that included Kiri Te Kanawa (Rosalinde), Hermann Prey (Eisenstein), Hildegarde Heichele (Adele), and Benjamin Luxon (Falke) through an evening in which champagne literally flowed on the stage. A further highlight of the season was Puccini's *The Girl of the Golden West* in a production by Piero Fagioni, again conducted by Mehta and starring Carol Neblett and Placido Domingo.

High point of the 1978 Glyndebourne season was John Cox's production of Mozart's *The Magic Flute*, the stage being dominated by sets of striking originality from David Hockney that caused audiences to break into spontaneous applause. Andrew Davis conducted, and the cast was led by Benjamin Luxon (Papageno) and Isolel Buchanan (Pamina).

SYMPHONIC MUSIC. With the departure of music director Pierre Boulez, the New York Philharmonic seemed set for a less exploratory regime under incoming maestro Zubin Mehta. The Chicago Symphony lost its principal guest conductor Carlo Maria Giulini to Los Angeles, where he became music director of the Philharmonic in the fall of 1978. The Chicago Symphony split most of its summer between the Ravinia Festival under James Levine and a wildly acclaimed European tour under Sir Georg Solti that included, as part of the 1978 Henry Wood Promenade concerts in London's Royal Albert Hall, the British premiere of Sir Michael Tippett's Fourth Symphony.

In Great Britain particular interest was attached to Moscow-born conductor Gennady Rozhdestvensky's (*see* BIOGRAPHIES) appointment as chief conductor from September 1978 of the BBC Symphony Orchestra. On February 2 the Royal Festival Hall was the setting for the premiere of Peter Maxwell Davies' eagerly awaited and, as it turned out, vibrantly impressive symphony from the Philharmonic Orchestra under Simon Rattle. At the Queen Elizabeth Hall the previous November

opinions were divided, but Kupfer's was generally believed to be among the most original Wagner productions of recent years. Danish soprano Lisbeth Balslev was especially impressive as Senta. Simon Estes of the U.S. proved a powerfully convincing Dutchman, while Matti Salminen of Finland was in outstanding form as Daland.

Opera in London continued to be dominated by the Royal Opera at Covent Garden and English National Opera (ENO), the latter not infrequently outstripping the former in both enterprise and musical excellence. The ENO's home, the London Coliseum, was the scene of some particularly notable productions. Foremost among these was a double bill on August 22 that paired, in a strange but effective coupling, Kurt Weill's *Seven Deadly Sins* and Puccini's *Gianni Schicchi*. In the first Julie Covington joined with dancer Siobhan Davies in an adroitly effective production from Michael Geliot that was let down only by some limp choreography. Lionel Friend conducted. There followed a revival of Colin Graham's *Gianni Schicchi* in which David Collis's sets and some marvellous lighting nearly stole the show from a strong cast headed by Eric Shilling.

On April 5 ENO surpassed expectations with a production as enterprising as it was convincing of Bohuslav Martinu's surrealistic *Julietta*. John Stoddart's designs caught to perfection the mood of a thoroughly enjoyable period piece, and a strong cast was led by Joy Roberts (Julietta) and Stuart Kale (Michel). The conductor, Charles Mackerras, had also been in charge of one of the season's outstanding revivals, Janacek's *From the House of the Dead*, while the company's roster elsewhere ranged from a short-notice production of Menotti's *The Consul* and a revival of Iain Hamilton's *The*

the London Sinfonietta, which in 1978 celebrated its tenth anniversary, gave the first performance of Brian Ferneyhough's difficult *Transit*.

Of particular interest during the summer of 1978 was a wide-ranging festival of 20th-century music, held at St. Bartholomew's Church, Spitalfields, that culminated on July 14 with Penderecki conducting the Royal Academy of Music's Symphony Orchestra in a program of his own works. Guests to London included the Vienna Philharmonic, which, conducted by Leonard Bernstein, performed Beethoven's Second and Third Symphonies at the Festival Hall on February 18; the Leningrad Philharmonic under Mariss Jansens; the Pittsburgh Symphony and André Previn; and three concerts in which the London Symphony Orchestra was directed by (and became greatly, it seems, attached to) the elusive Romanian conductor Sergiu Celibidache.

(MOZELLE A. MOSHANSKY)

Jazz. One of the riddles confronting the student of jazz throughout the decade was how to decide exactly where jazz music starts and other music ends. Ever since the late 1950s both classical and popular music had been making inroads into jazz territory, or perhaps it would be at least as truthful to say that jazz had been embarking on policies of imperial aggrandizement with regard to its rivals. Miles Davis's "Sketches of Spain" was an early, brilliant example of the jazz performance that was not a jazz performance, while the Dave Brubeck Quartet's recording of "Take Five" became so popular as to distract people from the jazz content of some of the playing. While such successes brought enormous financial gain to a handful of jazz artists, there was no question but that their eventual effect was to smudge demarcation lines.

In fact, it would be true to say that the most notable change currently being undergone by jazz was its comparative loss of identity; no longer was it possible to know where to look for it or by what canons to judge it when located. The puritan conscience might find a grim satisfaction in the fact that neither Davis nor Brubeck had survived as a significant jazz practitioner of the 1970s, but even more remarkable than their rise and fall was the latest manifestation of this collapse of the old isolationist policies. During 1978, one of the most adamant of all the avant-garde jazz instrumentalists, the pianist Herbie Hancock, arrived in the unaccustomed environment of the "Top Twenty" popular hits, where his temporary eminence was celebrated by audiences who could have had no conception of the cultural roots that had nurtured Hancock's brilliant development.

A contributory reason for the progressive blurring of the outlines of jazz was a lack of new players. The 1970s were depressing, and even alarming, for their failure to produce those enfants terribles without whom no muse can reasonably expect to continue evolving. No more vivid proof of this defection of the young musician could be found than the fact that veterans like Dizzy Gillespie (born 1917), Oscar Peterson (born 1925), and Stan Getz (born 1927) all maintained, and justifiably so, their places as leaders of jazz mastery. A compensating factor was the sustained interest in and contribution to jazz by other countries, whose players more and more tended to overcome the once crippling handicap of having learned their music in outposts of the old jazz empire.

An especially gallant attempt to encompass the whole of jazz history, and to relate its beginnings to the almost unrecognizable offshoots of the

The stage set of the Electric Light Orchestra, built at a cost of £250,000 (about U.S. $500,000), was a smash sensation when the group opened at Wembley, London, in June. The massive set rose 7.6 m (25 ft) and floated above the stage.

KEYSTONE

1970s, was made during the year by a U.S. critic, James Lincoln Collier, whose *The Making of Jazz: A Comprehensive History* was certainly one of the most thorough studies of jazz history ever published. If Collier tended to be a shade brusque in his qualified appraisals of some of the pioneers and disproportionately reverent toward some later lions, his general demeanour was one of welcome sanity in a field not generally distinguished for the level heads of its analysts. Collier was not the first critic, nor would he be the last, to suggest, as he did in the closing chapters of his enormous book, that jazz would benefit from a respite from experiments and a turning inward on its own past.

During 1978 there were at least three deaths that removed famous stylists, none of whom could conceivably be replaced. The modernist trombonist Frank Rosolino won his jazz reputation in the early 1950s with the Stan Kenton Orchestra, but although his technical command was phenomenal his creative ability was so derivative that the glibness without the imagination lent even his best work a faint tinge of freakishness. Lenny Tristano, the blind Chicago-born pianist, would be remembered as one of the most defiantly esoteric musicians of his day, which had long since passed at the time of his death. Tristano enjoyed a brief but intense eminence, especially among some fellow musicians, for his recordings with the saxophonist Lee Konitz in the late 1940s. At the time of his death Tristano had for many years been immersed in teaching, and neither he nor Konitz could be said to have fulfilled the promise of those critics who had once attempted to deify them.

A Swedish group, ABBA, was the most successful pop group to hit Europe since the Beatles.

KEYSTONE

Namibia:
see Dependent
  States; South Africa

NATO:
see Defense

Navies:
see Defense

In terms of both originality and fame the biggest loss of the year was that of Giuseppe "Joe" Venuti, who stands with Eddie South, Stuff Smith, and Ray Nance as the establisher of a school of jazz violin-playing. Venuti's days of jazz fame lasted from the mid–1920s, during his association with such other jazz-inclined members of the Paul Whiteman Orchestra as Bix Beiderbecke and Frank Trumbauer, to the death of his friend and partner, the guitarist Eddie Lang, in 1933. Venuti, however, continued working till the end of his life and enjoyed two successful tours of Europe in the last five years.   (BENNY GREEN)

Popular. Highlighting 1978 was a disco boom and, associated with it, the rare phenomenon of renaissance: ten years after their initial heyday, the Bee Gees (*see* BIOGRAPHIES)—Barry, Robin, and Maurice Gibb—returned to international fame, largely through their songs for the disco film *Saturday Night Fever*. Fraternal differences had split the group in 1969, but the brothers reunited and in 1971 reached No. 1 in the U.S. with "Lonely Days." They had always been famous for slow ballads such as "Massachusetts," but a beat crept in and their big 1976 hit was "You Should Be Dancing." For *Saturday Night Fever* they wrote five songs, all of which became international hits; by January 1978, with the film newly released, Gibb songs were flooding the U.S. airwaves—many as hits for other artists, notably the youngest Gibb brother, Andy, who had three top-selling songs in the U.S. in 1978.

Saturday Night Fever, which made its star John Travolta (*see* BIOGRAPHIES) an international idol, was produced by the Bee Gees' manager Robert Stigwood. A skillful publicist, he produced a second hit film in 1978, *Grease*—again starring Travolta and featuring a Gibb title number—but his reworking of the Beatles' *Sergeant Pepper's Lonely Hearts Club Band*, starring the Bee Gees and Peter Frampton and with a host of celebrities in cameo roles, met with less enthusiasm. Other notable films dealing with popular music were *American Hot Wax*, based on the career of Alan Freed, "founder" of rock 'n' roll, and *The Last Waltz*, Martin Scorsese's movie of The Band's farewell concert.

The insistent disco dance beat dominated the charts. Many of these records came from continental Europe, notably West Germany where Donna Summer was based, as was the group Boney M, whose many hits included the chart-topping "Rivers of Babylon," a setting of the familiar biblical text. Faced with the disco onslaught the "new wave," or punk rock, lost impetus; several groups disbanded, including the notorious Sex Pistols (immediately after their U.S. tour). The survivors, including Talking Heads and the Boomtown Rats, were maturing. Some took a social-political stand, notably the Tom Robinson Band, whose well-crafted songs dealt with such subjects as homosexuality ("Glad to be Gay"). In contrast, Darts were pure entertainment with their slick "doo-wop" recreations such as "Come Back My Love." Several groups featured girl singers, usually somewhat aggressive in style, like Siouxsie of the Banshees; Blondie's Debbie Harry had a more sexual appeal, albeit with sinister undertones.

French punk Plastic Bertrand's "Ça plane pour moi" was a hit in both Europe and America, the first French-language record to enter the U.S. charts since the Singing Nun's "Dominique" in 1963. A distinctive new soloist was Kate Bush, whose "Wuthering Heights" (based on the Emily Brontë classic) topped the British charts in March. Traditional rock 'n' roll came from Bob Seger, whose "Night Moves" brought him stardom after ten years; Seger appeared successfully in Britain in 1978, as did Billy Joel, the sophisticated New York singer-songwriter whose third album, "The Stranger," became a best-seller and yielded four hit singles. Bruce Springsteen, legal problems solved, returned with a fine album, "Darkness on the Edge of Town," and co-authored Patti Smith's hit "Because the Night."

Bob Dylan's 1978 concert tour, made (reportedly) to recoup financial losses on his film *Renaldo and Clara*, became a personal triumph, with Dylan emerging as a master performer as well as a songwriter. Also acclaimed "live" were David Bowie; the Tubes with their satirical theatrics; the Electric Light Orchestra, whose "spaceship" stage set at Wembley, London, caused a sensation; and Bette Midler, who made her U.K. debut in September. In December 1977 the British label Stiff toured its artists with great success. In September Gracie Fields, at 80, sang in her hometown of Rochdale, England.

The single record proved the ideal medium for new bands, and competition was fierce; promotional devices such as picture sleeves and coloured vinyl abounded. Early in 1978 Wings' "Mull of Kintyre" became Britain's fastest selling single ever, surpassing the Beatles' "She Loves You." The Dutch television commercial "Smurf Song" was a favourite novelty, while Nick Lowe's "I Love the Sound of Breaking Glass" caused some controversy as a possible incitement to vandalism. Virtuoso flutist James Galway reached the U.K. top three with "Annie's Song." On August 26 disc jockey Alan Freeman left the BBC after 20 years of service.

Reggae by 1978 had become a cultural focus for blacks, especially in Britain; its lyrics generally dealt with racial subjects. Bob Marley was still its leading exponent; in April he topped an all-star bill at the One Love Peace Concert in Kingston, Jamaica, celebrating political reconciliation. In a lighter vein Althea and Donna's slang song "Uptown Top Ranking" topped the British charts in February. Some strong new talents arose in U.S. country music; Joe Ely, Crystal Gayle, and the blind Ronnie Milsap, voted the Country Music Association's "Entertainer of the Year" for 1977.

In August 1978 The Who celebrated 15 years in music with a new album, "Who Are You," but their performing future was jeopardized by the death of drummer Keith Moon (see OBITUARIES) a month later. In March 1978 top French singer and composer Claude Françoise was killed in an accident. One year after the death of Elvis Presley his records and memorabilia were still an industry, and a musical based on his life story opened in London. (HAZEL MORGAN)

See also Dance; Motion Pictures; Television and Radio; Theatre.

Nauru

Nauru

An island republic in the Pacific Ocean, Nauru lies about 1,900 km (1,200 mi) E of New Guinea. Area: 21 sq km (8 sq mi). Pop. (1977 census): 7,254, including Nauruan 57%; Pacific Islanders 26%; Chinese 9%; European 8%. Capital: Yaren. Language: Nauruan and English. Religion (Nauruans only): Protestant 60%; Roman Catholic 33%. Presidents in 1978, Bernard Dowiyogo until April 19, Lagumot Harris until May 11, and Hammer DeRoburt from May 15.

Pres. Bernard Dowiyogo visited New Zealand in February 1978 in an effort to boost New Zealand's sagging imports of Nauruan phosphate and to request landing rights in New Zealand for Air Nauru. On his return, Dowiyogo faced a political crisis that came to a head in May, when Chief Hammer DeRoburt (see BIOGRAPHIES), who had been deposed 16 months earlier, was reinstated as president. DeRoburt's supporters forced the resignation of President Dowiyogo by defeating a bill dealing with phosphate royalties. Lagumot Harris succeeded Dowiyogo during a brief interregnum but resigned when Parliament rejected an appropriations bill designed to finance the republic, and DeRoburt was elected in the ballot that followed.

The crisis was precipitated because of the islanders' concern for their future. With only 15 years left before the phosphate deposits were due to run out, the Nauru Finance Corp. was investing in other enterprises throughout the Pacific. Some of the investments (for example, those in the Marshall Islands) were seen as giving Nauru undue political influence in the area. In February Nauru celebrated its tenth anniversary as a republic with the issuance of two new postage stamps, sales of which were expected to earn A$60,000.

(A. R. G. GRIFFITHS)

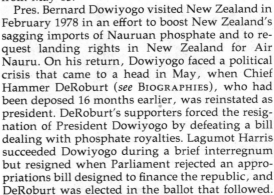

NAURU
Education. (1977) Primary, pupils 1,620, teachers 80; secondary, pupils 505, teachers 39; vocational, pupils 60, teachers 3; teacher training, students 6, teacher 1.
Finance and Trade. Monetary unit: Australian dollar, with (Sept. 18, 1978) a free rate of A$0.87 to U.S. $1 (A$1.70 = £1 sterling). Budget (1975–76 est.): revenue A$45,510,000; expenditure A$26,670,000. Foreign trade (1974): imports c. A$20 million (c. 58% from Australia, c. 30% from The Netherlands); exports c. A$64 million (c. 57% to Australia, c. 23% to Japan, c. 18% to New Zealand). Main export: phosphate c. 100%.
Industry. Production (in 000): phosphate rock (exports; metric tons; 1975–76) 758; electricity (kw-hr; 1976) c. 26,-000.

Nepal

Nepal

A constitutional monarchy of Asia, Nepal is in the Himalayas between India and the Tibetan Autonomous Region of China. Area: 145,391 sq km (56,136 sq mi). Pop. (1977 est.): 13,136,000. Cap. and largest city: Kathmandu (pop., 1976 est., 171,-400). Language: Nepali (official) 52.5%, also Bihari (including Maithili and Bhojpuri) 18.5%, Tamang 4.8%, Tharu 4.3%, and Newari 3.9%. Religion

NEPAL

Education. (1976) Primary, pupils 643,835, teachers 20,-775; secondary, pupils 243,231; teachers 10,609; vocational, pupils 16,815, teachers (1974) 1,278; teacher training, students 2,702, teachers 173; higher (1975), students 23,-504; teaching staff 1,516.

Finance. Monetary unit: Nepalese rupee, with (Sept. 18, 1978) a par value of NRs 12 to U.S. $1 (free rate of NRs 23.51 = £1 sterling). Gold, SDR's, and foreign exchange (June 1978) U.S. $136.4 million. Budget (1977–78): revenue NRs 1,725,000,000 (excluding foreign aid of NRs 1,-121,000,000); expenditure NRs 3,087,000,000 (including development expenditure of NRs 2,148,000,000).

Foreign Trade. (1977) Imports NRs 2,104,100,000; exports NRs 1,018,300,000. Import sources (1976–77): India 72%; Japan *c.* 9%. Export destinations (1976–77): India 69%; Japan *c.* 5%; U.S. *c.* 5%. Main exports (1974–75): jute goods *c.* 33%; raw jute *c.* 13%; curio goods *c.* 11%; jute cuttings *c.* 7%. Tourism (1974): visitors 89,800; gross receipts U.S. $9 million.

Agriculture. Production (in 000; metric tons; 1977): rice 2,285; corn 651; wheat 362; potatoes *c.* 314; millet *c.* 140; jute 56; tobacco 5; buffalo milk *c.* 460; cow's milk *c.* 210. Livestock (in 000; 1976): cattle *c.* 6,653; buffalo *c.* 3,930; pigs *c.* 338; sheep *c.* 2,310; goats *c.* 2,373; poultry *c.* 20,-530.

(1971): Hindu 89.4%; Buddhist 7.5%. King, Birendra Bir Bikram Shah Deva; prime minister in 1978, Kirti Nidhi Bista.

The signing of trade and transit treaties with India in March 1978 followed long and difficult negotiations that had begun in 1971 when the previous treaty expired. It removed a major irritant in Indo-Nepalese relations, as India finally agreed to the Nepalese demand for a separate transit agreement formalizing its transit rights through India.

Indian Prime Minister Morarji Desai's visit to Nepal in December 1977 was followed a few months later by Prime Minister Kirti Nidhi Bista's trip to New Delhi. The visits helped to strengthen friendly relations, which had been disturbed by Indian leaders' demands for the release from prison of the opposition Nepalese Congress Party leader, B. P. Koirala. Koirala was later allowed to return to the U.S. for medical treatment.

Chinese Vice-Premier Teng Hsiao-p'ing was warmly received on his official visit to Nepal, February 3–5. Teng reiterated Peking's full support for King Birendra's proposal to declare Nepal a zone of peace—a proposal to which India had indicated it would not subscribe.   (GOVINDAN UNNY)

See also Historic Preservation.

Netherlands, The

The Netherlands

A kingdom of northwest Europe on the North Sea, The Netherlands, a Benelux country, is bounded by Belgium on the south and West Germany on the east. Area: 41,160 sq km (15,892 sq mi). Pop. (1978 est.): 13,897,900. Cap. and largest city: Amsterdam (pop., 1978 est., 728,700). Seat of government: The Hague (pop., 1978 est., 464,900). Language: Dutch. Religion (1971): Roman Catholic 40.4%; Dutch Reformed 23.5%; no religion 23.6%; Reformed Churches 9.4%. Queen, Juliana; prime minister in 1978, Andreas van Agt.

Andreas van Agt (*see* BIOGRAPHIES), having assumed the prime ministership on Dec. 19, 1977,

presented the new government's first statement of policy in the lower house of Parliament on Jan. 16, 1978. Attention was to be given to limiting salary increases and to reducing public expenditure. The former prime minister, Joop den Uyl, chairman of the Socialist Party (PvdA) in the lower house, criticized the proposals and stated that the distribution of Cabinet posts did not reflect the results of the May 1977 election.

In January, Parliament debated the expansion of the nuclear power station at Almelo (owned by Urenco, a joint West German-British-Dutch company). The purpose of the debate was to examine the proposal of the Dutch government, in agreement with West Germany and Great Britain, to export enriched uranium to Brazil, a state that had not yet signed the nuclear nonproliferation treaty. The proposal gave rise to widespread protest by action groups. (*See* ENVIRONMENT.) In the event, however, the government was empowered to export the enriched uranium, subject to the provision of satisfactory safeguards.

The debate divided the two coalition parties, and the rift was intensified by discussion of the neutron bomb. The Liberal Party (VVD) did not want the government to declare itself opposed to the bomb, but the majority of the Christian Democratic Appeal considered it a serious threat to disarmament and that its introduction should be avoided. On March 8 Parliament passed a resolution opposing production of the bomb. Opinions also differed within the government, and on March 4 the minister of defense, Roelof Kruisinga, resigned. He was succeeded by Willem Scholten.

In October three terrorists of the West German Red Army Faction, Knut Folkerts, Gert R. Schneider, and Christof M. Wackernagel, were extradited to the West German authorities before the judicial department of the Council of State pronounced sentence. Earlier, the High Court of Justice had declared the extradition of the three admissible, and they had appealed to the Council of State. The Dutch government decided to extradite them when they began a hunger strike to protest against their isolation during imprisonment.

The Cabinet's main economic objective was to reduce unemployment to 150,000, and to achieve this the government sought to increase investment by creating and plowing back company profits. This meant restraint in expenditure, including a wage freeze for civil servants. Civil servants struck on June 23 and demonstrated in The Hague on June 26. The Federation of National Trade Unions attacked the government's policy, arguing that there was no guarantee that new jobs would be created and that the burden would fall on the lower-paid workers. Under pressure, the government agreed to discuss some of its measures.

On November 6 the director of the Institute of War Documentation accused the Christian Democratic political leader Willem Aantjes of having been a member of the German SS for some months during World War II. Aantjes announced his resignation from all political posts in order to prepare a refutation of the charge. There were protests over the release on December 4 of Pieter N. Menten, sentenced to 15 years' imprisonment in 1977

NETHERLANDS, THE

Education. (1976–77) Primary, pupils 1,533,012, teachers 60,247; secondary, pupils 794,745, teachers 50,000; vocational, pupils 525,536, teachers 43,100; teacher training, students 10,700, teachers 900; higher (including 11 main universities), students 247,577, teaching staff (university only) 28,800.

Finance. Monetary unit: guilder, with (Sept. 18, 1978) a free rate of 2.15 guilders to U.S. $1 (4.21 guilders = £1 sterling). Gold, SDR's, and foreign exchange (June 1978) U.S. $6,958,000,000. Budget (1977 actual): revenue 87.2 billion guilders; expenditure 94,929,000,000 guilders. Gross national product (1977) 261,790,000,000 guilders. Money supply (June 1978) 64,360,000,000 guilders. Cost of living (1975 = 100; June 1978) 119.9.

Foreign Trade. (1977) Imports 114,271,000,000 guilders; exports 107,208,000,000 guilders. Import sources: EEC 55% (West Germany 24%, Belgium-Luxembourg 14%, France 7%, U.K. 7%); U.S. 8%. Export destinations: EEC 70% (West Germany 31%, Belgium-Luxembourg 15%, France 10%, U.K. 7%,

Italy 5%). Main exports: food 19%; chemicals 14%; machinery 14%; petroleum products 12%; natural gas 6%. Tourism (1976): visitors 2,910,000; gross receipts U.S. $1,061,000,000.

Transport and Communications. Roads (1976) 86,354 km (including 1,839 km expressways). Motor vehicles in use (1976): passenger 3,760,000; commercial 316,000. Railways: (1976) 2,832 km (including 1,712 km electrified); traffic (1977) 8,018,000,000 passenger-km, freight 2,805,000,000 net ton-km. Air traffic (1977): 11,497,000,000 passenger-km; freight 753,040,000 net ton-km. Navigable inland waterways (1976) 4,343 km; freight traffic 30,952,000,000 ton-km. Shipping (1977): merchant vessels 100 gross tons and over 1,254; gross tonnage 5,290,360. Shipping traffic (1977): goods loaded 77,009,000 metric tons, unloaded 248,133,000 metric tons. Telephones (Jan. 1977) 5,412,000. Radio licenses (Dec. 1976) 3,-996,000. Television licenses (Dec. 1976) 3,774,000.

Agriculture. Production (in 000; metric tons; 1977): wheat 661; barley 287; oats 94; rye 74;

potatoes 5,752; tomatoes c. 378; onions c. 500; sugar, raw value c. 904; cabbages (1976) 241; cucumbers (1976) 323; carrots (1976) 162; apples c. 340; rapeseed 30; milk 10,682; butter 182; cheese c. 405; eggs c. 340; beef and veal 382; pork 992; fish catch (1976) 284. Livestock (in 000; May 1977): cattle 4,877; pigs 8,288; sheep 800; chickens 69,875.

Industry. Index of production (1975 = 100; 1977) 107. Production (in 000; metric tons; 1977): crude oil 1,382; natural gas (cu m) 86,500,000; manufactured gas (cu m) 930,000; electricity (kw-hr) 58,291,000; pig iron 3,921; crude steel 4,928; cement 3,891; petroleum products (1976) 58,879; sulfuric acid 1,572; fertilizers (nutrient content; 1976–77) nitrogenous c. 1,253, phosphate c. 307; cotton yarn 28; wool yarn 10; rayon, etc., filament yarn and fibres 34; nylon, etc., filament yarn and fibres (1972) 113. Merchant vessels launched (100 gross tons and over; 1977) 380,000 gross tons. New dwelling units completed (1977) 112,000.

---

for war crimes allegedly committed in Poland in 1941. A special court accepted the 79-year-old Menten's claim that in 1952 the then minister of justice had granted him immunity from further prosecution.

On March 13 South Moluccans seized the provincial administrative building at Assen for 24 hours before being dislodged by Dutch Marines.

(DICK BOONSTRA)

See also Dependent States.

New Zealand

New Zealand, a parliamentary state and member of the Commonwealth of Nations, is in the South Pacific Ocean, separated from southeastern Australia by the Tasman Sea. The country consists of North and South islands and Stewart, Chatham, and other minor islands. Area: 268,704 sq km (103,747 sq mi). Pop. (1978 est.): 3,145,800. Cap.: Wellington (pop., 1977 est., 139,700). Largest city: Christchurch (pop., 1977 est., 172,400). Largest urban area: Auckland (pop., 1977 est., 801,200). Language: English (official), Maori. Religion (1976): Church of England 35%; Presbyterian 22%; Roman Catholic 16%. Queen, Elizabeth II; governor-general in 1978, Sir Keith Holyoake; prime minister, Robert David Muldoon.

After battling with some success to arrest inflation and a balance of payments deficit, the National Party government barely scraped back into office in the November general elections. Its parliamentary representation (with one seat still in dispute) slipped from 53 to 50 in a larger House (increased from 87 to 92), but it continued to have a working majority over the 41-seat Labour opposition and the one Social Credit representative. The government lost two ministers and received only about 40% of the vote. Prime Minister Robert Muldoon responded to charges that his own highly personalized, abrasive leadership was an adverse factor by surrendering the House leadership to a minister of state, David Thomson, and naming six new ministers.

The main election issue was management of the economy. Muldoon had ended a short Labour in-

tervention in a long era of National Party administration by attacking spendthrift policies; in 1978 he had to convince the electorate that factors beyond the reasonable control of the government, such as increased oil and international transportation costs, had made it necessary to curb imports to the extent of raising unemployment to levels unknown since the slump of the 1930s. Unemployment seemed to be easing by September, however,

NEW ZEALAND

Education. (1977) Primary, pupils 522,930, teachers 20,-844; secondary, pupils 232,015, teachers 12,688; vocational, pupils 4,946, teachers 1,706; higher (universities and teacher training only), students 35,967, teaching staff 3,-491.

Finance. Monetary unit: New Zealand dollar, with (Sept. 18, 1978) a free rate of NZ$0.95 to U.S. $1 (NZ$1.85 = £1 sterling). Gold, SDR's, and foreign exchange (June 1978) U.S. $790 million. Budget (1976–77 actual): revenue NZ$4,255,000,000; expenditure NZ$4,491,000,000. Gross national product (1976–77) NZ$12,786,000,000. Cost of living (1975 = 100; 2nd quarter 1978) 147.9.

Foreign Trade. (1977) Imports NZ$3,464,000,000; exports NZ$3,294,900,000. Import sources: Australia 21%; U.K. 17%; Japan 14%; U.S. 14%. Export destinations: U.K. 20%; Australia 13%; Japan 13%; U.S. 11%. Main exports (1976–77): wool 21%; lamb and mutton 12%; beef and veal 10%; butter 8%; wood pulp and paper 5%. Tourism (1976): visitors 384,000; gross receipts U.S. $161 million.

Transport and Communications. Roads (1975) 95,026 km. Motor vehicles in use (1977): passenger 1,210,200; commercial 230,800. Railways: (1976) 4,797 km; traffic (1976–77) 497 million passenger-km, freight 3,600,000,000 net ton-km. Air traffic (1977): 3,608,000,000 passenger-km; freight 121.9 million net ton-km. Shipping (1977): merchant vessels 100 gross tons and over 102; gross tonnage 199,462. Telephones (March 1977) 1,632,000. Radio receivers (Dec. 1975) 2,704,000. Television licenses (Dec. 1977) 849,400.

Agriculture. Production (in 000; metric tons; 1977): wheat 370; barley 316; oats 71; corn (1976) 232; potatoes (1976) c. 250; dry peas c. 62; tomatoes c. 70; apples c. 137; milk 6,635; butter 277; cheese 81; mutton and lamb 511; beef and veal c. 515; wool 221; sheepskins (1976) c. 108; timber (cu m; 1976) 10,019; fish catch (1976) 70. Livestock (in 000; Jan. 1977): cattle 9,472; sheep (June 1976) 56,400; pigs 536; chickens (1976) c. 6,080.

Industry. Fuel and power (in 000; metric tons; 1977): coal 2,090; lignite 167; crude oil (1976) 477; natural gas (cu m) 1,400,000; manufactured gas (cu m) 79,000; electricity (excluding most industrial production; kw-hr) 21,307,000. Production (in 000; metric tons; 1977): cement 910; petroleum products (1976) c. 3,470; phosphate fertilizers (1976–77) c. 375; wood pulp 1,108; newsprint (1976–77) 275; other paper (1976–77) 359.

New Zealand

Netherlands Overseas Territories: *see* Dependent States

New Guinea: *see* Indonesia; Papua New Guinea

New Hebrides: *see* Dependent States

Newspapers: *see* Publishing

when the total approached 50,000. Particularly damaging to morale was the extent of the departure of skilled workers and others for such countries as Australia.

In the year to August a current overseas trading account deficit of NZ$514 million was recorded, a rise of NZ$28 million over 1977. Export receipts were about the same and import payments declined by 5%, but nonmerchandise items such as export freight costs and interest payments rose 16%, or NZ$205 million. Inflation, which had been receding from a mid-1976 high of 17.7%, seemed likely to settle at 11.1% for the year, the lowest since 1974. The budget in June lowered income tax rates, raised gasoline prices, and gave some relief to farmers. The effort to diversify farm product markets continued; protracted negotiations aimed at making Japanese fishing rights and catch limits within New Zealand's coastal zone reciprocal to the extent to which Japan showed interest in buying New Zealand agricultural products and granting trade opportunities.

In foreign affairs the government welcomed the passing of power on July 25 in the Cook Islands from Sir Albert Henry and his family administration to Tom Davis after an inquiry into the funding of flights of New Zealand-domiciled electors to the islands for general elections won by Sir Albert. Firmer ties with Australia seemed to result from a tour by Foreign Minister Brian Talboys.

A rail tunnel was opened through the Kaimai range between the central North Island and Tauranga. Environmentalists persuaded the government to reduce the cut of native timbers in the King Country. The timber-into-paper industry provided one of the biggest industrial upheavals because of strikes at the Tasman Pulp and Paper Co. followed by management changes. The national shipping line launched its first container vessel, and the international and domestic airlines merged under the title Air New Zealand. The social issue of the year again was abortion. New laws effective on April 1 were later modified to enable operating surgeons to take part in the decision process and to permit abortions of pregnancies involving likely mental handicap to the baby.

(JOHN A. KELLEHER)

See also Dependent States.

Nicaragua

Nicaragua

The largest country of Central America, Nicaragua is a republic bounded by Honduras, Costa Rica, the Caribbean Sea, and the Pacific Ocean. Area: 128,875 sq km (49,759 sq mi). Pop. (1977 est.): 2,-312,000. Cap. and largest city: Managua (pop., 1974 est., 313,400). Language: Spanish. Religion: Roman Catholic. President in 1978, Anastasio Somoza Debayle.

Unrest in Nicaragua accelerated to a state of near-civil war in 1978, when the 42-year control of the country by the Somoza family was threatened seriously for the first time. The year's violence began with the assassination on January 10 of Pedro Joaquín Chamorro Cardenal, the nation's most prominent critic of Pres. Anastasio Somoza De-

Sandinista leader Edén Pastora Gómez, who calls himself "Zero," headed the guerrillas who seized the National Palace in Managua, killing at least six guards and holding more than 1,000 people hostage for two days.

bayle. The government, disclaiming responsibility and expressing regrets, conducted an investigation that produced nothing conclusive. Chamorro's supporters responded by leading a general strike that lasted two weeks and also by instigating antigovernment demonstrations that frequently ended in armed clashes between demonstrators and government forces.

On August 22, 24 heavily armed members of the clandestine Sandinista National Liberation Front, disguised as members of the National Guard, raided the National Palace. They held more than 1,000 hostages, including government officials, members of the Chamber of Deputies, and government workers, until the government met their demands to release 59 political prisoners, to provide safe conduct out of the country for them and for the insurgents, and to pay a large cash ransom. At least six members of the National Guard were killed by the invaders.

This dramatic Sandinista success brought antigovernment sentiments to a head. Popular uprisings in the cities of Matagalpa, Masaya, León, Chinandega, Diriamba, and Estelí were subdued, one by one, by government forces. Estimates of civilian deaths ranged from 1,500 to double that number. So concentrated was the slaughter at times that Red Cross workers were forced to cremate bodies in the streets to prevent the spread of disease. Another general strike, which despite the arrest of many participants continued for a month following the August raid, virtually paralyzed the economy.

The Organization of American States, at a meeting of foreign ministers called by Venezuela in September, rejected a motion by the United States that the OAS mediate the conflict. Such action, it was decided, would violate the principle of nonintervention. Nicaragua, however, agreed to accept the friendly cooperation of outside countries, and the OAS accordingly sponsored a visit to the country by a team composed of representatives of the U.S., Guatemala, and the Dominican Republic. The U.S. recommended that a national plebiscite be held to determine the desires of the Nicaraguan people relative to the immediate resignation of Somoza, but the president would agree only to a referendum that would determine whether or not members of the opposition might be included in his Cabinet. The opposition rejected any consideration of a plebiscite. Sporadic bombings and armed clashes continued to break out in Managua and elsewhere, and the Sandinistas issued repeated warnings that an all-out attack to oust Somoza could occur at any time.

The U.S., adhering to the administration's policy of conditioning economic aid upon acceptable performance in the field of human rights, reduced Nicaragua's share of its foreign aid budget severely to a small amount earmarked for nonmilitary purposes. Meanwhile, on November 17, the Human Rights Commission of the OAS reported that the National Guard had committed widespread atrocities in the August–September fighting. Somoza denied the accusations.

The failure of the opposition to have a well-coordinated plan for the nation's future gave rise to considerable speculation concerning its capacity to organize and conduct an effective government in the event Somoza should resign. There was also apprehension about the long-range intentions of the well-organized Sandinistas. While they stated that their desire was to participate in a broadly based democratic post-Somoza Nicaragua, the possibility that their ultimate purpose might be to create a second Cuba caused much concern.

Meanwhile, the year's events had left a tragic toll of death, devastation, and economic catastrophe. Thousands of Nicaraguans left the country, and the flight of capital to other countries was estimated to have amounted to more than $100 million.

(HENRY WEBB, JR.)

Niger

Niger

A republic of north central Africa, Niger is bounded by Algeria, Libya, Chad, Nigeria, Benin, Upper Volta, and Mali. Area: 1,186,408 sq km (458,075 sq mi). Pop. (1978 est.): 4,986,000, including (1972 est.) Hausa 53.7%; Zerma and Songhai 23.6%; Fulani 10.6%; Beriberi-Manga 9.1%. Cap. and largest city: Niamey (pop., 1975 est., 130,000). Language: French (official) and Sudanic dialects. Religion: Muslim, animist, Christian. President in 1978, Lieut. Col. Seyni Kountché.

On Sept. 5, 1978, a ministerial reshuffle left the government with 11 civilian and 6 military members. In the process, Maj. Idriss Arouna, until then considered number two in the regime, was unexpectedly removed. In April, Pres. Seyni Kountché had released most members of the former regime arrested during the 1974 coup. Only former president Hamani Diori and Djibo Bakary (arrested in August 1975) remained in custody.

Niger was able to play an important role as mediator in the Chad conflict. (See CHAD.) In May, President Kountché attended the fifth Franco-African conference in Paris, where he expressed opposition to French proposals for an African intervention force. During the year, Niger became the world's fifth largest producer of uranium. Three-quarters of its production went to France.

(PHILIPPE DECRAENE)

Nigeria

Nigeria

A republic and a member of the Commonwealth of Nations, Nigeria is located in Africa north of the Gulf of Guinea, bounded by Benin, Niger, Chad, and Cameroon. Area: 923,800 sq km (356,700 sq mi). Pop. (1977 est.): 78,660,000, including Hausa 21%; Yoruba 20%; Ibo 17%; Fulani 9%. Cap. and largest city: Lagos (metro. pop., 1977 est., 3.5 million). Language: English (official). Religion (1963): Muslim 47%; Christian 34%. Head of the provisional military government in 1978, Lieut. Gen. Olusegun Obasanjo.

In a television broadcast to the nation on Sept. 21, 1978, Lieut. Gen. Olusegun Obasanjo lifted the 12-year-old ban on political activity. The new constitution was completed, with amendments, and presented to Obasanjo on August 29. It would be formally promulgated in the autumn of 1979, when elections would be held and civilian rule established. The document, which provided for a presidential system based on the U.S. model, had been worked out and completed ahead of schedule by the constituent assembly after 11 months of sometimes hectic debates. The most noteworthy, over a proposal from the northern states for a separate Federal Shari'a Court of Appeal to hear Islamic cases, was settled by a compromise whereby the Federal Supreme Court of Appeal would include three Muslim judges. The military government accepted the new constitution with little change.

The Federal Electoral Commission completed a

U.S. Pres. Jimmy Carter had to reach up to shake hands with a dancer on stilts after a performance during Carter's visit to Nigeria in April.

UPI COMPIX

voters' register in February. The enrollment totaled 47,710,680 over the age of 18 (51% female after women in the northern states were registered in 1977). The official estimate of Nigeria's population, based on the 1963 census and assuming an annual growth rate of 2.5%, was unreliable. The population was believed to total more than 80 million, rather than the official figure of about 78.7 million.

Three political parties emerged after the lifting of the ban: Chief Obafemi Awolowo's Unity Party of Nigeria, the Nigerian People's Party, and the National Party of Nigeria. All of them revived old groupings. Eight of Nigeria's 13 universities experienced student unrest in April after fees for room and board were raised, and there were eight deaths at Zaria and Lagos. Another source of disruption lay in the traditional rulers' objection to federal land decrees, which vested ownership of undeveloped lands in the state.

The economic picture was sombre, despite a gross national product (GNP) of U.S. $25 billion and a rise to fourth place in production of oil within the Organization of Petroleum Exporting Countries. Oil provided 30% of Nigeria's GNP and nearly 90% of the value of exports, revenue, and foreign exchange, but it also produced an internal imbalance. Only 20,000 Nigerians were employed in the oil industry. On the other hand, 75% of the population was engaged in agriculture, which provided only 4.6% of export earnings. Productivi-

NIGERIA

Education. (1973–74) Primary, pupils 4,889,857, teachers 144,351; secondary, pupils 498,744, teachers 19,409; vocational, pupils 22,117, teachers 1,120; teacher training, students 49,216, teachers 2,360; higher (1975–76), students 32,971, teaching staff 5,019.

Finance. Monetary unit: naira, with (Sept, 18, 1978) a free rate of 0.63 naira to U.S. $1 (1.24 naira = £1 sterling). Gold, SDR's, and foreign exchange (June 1978) U.S. $1,-901,000,000. Federal budget (1977–78): revenue 7,-650,000,000 naira; expenditure 8.6 billion naira (including 5,503,000,000 naira development expenditure). Gross domestic product (1975–76) 15,449,000,000 naira. Money supply (March 1978) c. 5,535,000,000 naira. Cost of living (Lagos; 1975 = 100; Jan. 1978) 180.1.

Foreign Trade. (1977) Imports 7,296,800,000 naira; exports 7,620,400,000 naira. Import sources (1976): U.K. 23%; West Germany 16%; U.S. 11%; Japan 9%; France 7%; Italy 6%; The Netherlands 5%. Export destinations (1976): U.S. 35%; U.K. 10%; Netherlands Antilles 15%; The Netherlands 10%; France 9%; West Germany 7%. Main export: crude oil 90%.

Transport and Communications. Roads (1974) 97,000 km. Motor vehicles in use (1973): passenger c. 150,000; commercial (including buses) c. 82,000. Railways: (1975) 3,524 km; traffic (1974–75) 785 million passenger-km, freight 972 million net ton-km. Air traffic (1976): 470 million passenger-km; freight 8.4 million net ton-km. Shipping (1977): merchant vessels 100 gross tons and over 94; gross tonnage 335,540. Telephones (Jan. 1977) 121,000. Radio receivers (Dec. 1975) 5 million. Television receivers (Dec. 1977) 450,000.

Agriculture. Production (in 000; metric tons; 1977): millet c. 2,600; sorghum c. 3,750; corn c. 1,395; rice c. 600; sweet potatoes (1976) c. 200; yams (1976) c. 15,000; taro (1976) c. 1,800; cassava (1976) c. 10,800; tomatoes c. 250; peanuts c. 850; palm oil c. 660; cocoa c. 250; cotton, lint 73; rubber c. 90; fish catch (1976) 495. Livestock (in 000; 1977): cattle c. 11,500; sheep c. 8,100; goats c. 23,600; pigs c. 950; poultry c. 95,000.

Industry. Production (in 000; metric tons; 1977): crude oil 104,299; natural gas (cu m) c. 408,000; cement (1976) 1,270; tin concentrates (metal content) 3.3; petroleum products c. 2,780; electricity (kw-hr:1976) c. 3,400,000.

ty in the agricultural sector was below that of the 1960s. Production of cocoa (the only significant cash crop), cotton, rubber, palm products, and peanuts had fallen, and Nigeria was no longer able to feed itself. Food imports in 1977 cost over 1 billion naira, and total economic growth stood at about 2%. Government incentives were largely restricted to large-scale projects. Even U.S. moves into commercial agriculture (where only 40% Nigerian ownership was necessary) were of little help to the peasant farmers.

The April budget aimed to halt deterioration on the external account. It reflected shortages of essential goods, a fall in revenue because of the decreased demand for oil, and a rise in government expenditure, particularly in connection with the five-year plan and huge defense estimates. Revenue was estimated at 6,820,000,000 naira and expenditure at 10,110,000,000 naira, with the deficit to be made good by external financing.

Nigeria's oil economics remained closely linked to political attitudes in the U.S. The U.S. bought 55% of Nigeria's oil output, and Nigeria was its second-largest supplier. Obasanjo's visit to Washington and U.S. Pres. Jimmy Carter's trip to Nigeria in April brought some accord on attitudes toward Namibia and Rhodesia, but Obasanjo was not to be drawn into a condemnation of Soviet and Cuban roles in southern Africa and in the Horn. In June West German Chancellor Helmut Schmidt also visited Nigeria.   (MOLLY MORTIMER)

Norway

A constitutional monarchy of northern Europe, Norway is bordered by Sweden, Finland, and the U.S.S.R.; its coastlines are on the Skagerrak, the North Sea, the Norwegian Sea, and the Arctic Ocean. Area: 323,886 sq km (125,053 sq mi), excluding the Svalbard Archipelago, 62,048 sq km, and Jan Mayen Island, 373 sq km. Pop. (1978 est.): 4,077,000. Cap. and largest city: Oslo (pop., 1978 est., 460,400). Language: Norwegian. Religion: Lutheran (94%). King, Olav V; prime minister in 1978, Odvar Nordli.

Continuing recession forced Norway's minority Labour government to adopt far more restrictive economic policies during 1978. Earlier hopes that the country could ride out the slump by borrowing against future earnings from offshore oil and gas were finally abandoned. During 1977 Norway's foreign debt had climbed by 30.5 billion kroner to a record 84,950,000,000 kroner. Though investment in offshore oil installations and new ships accounted for more than half of this, much was caused by high imports as a result of consumer spending.

In January consumer credit regulations were tightened, particularly for car buyers, and lower loan ceilings on both state and private banks were imposed. A month earlier interest rates had been allowed to rise to encourage saving, marking a departure from Labour's traditional low-interest policy. In February the Norwegian krone was devalued by 8% against the other currencies of the European joint currency float, or "snake," and a temporary price freeze was announced. The effect was undermined by Finland's subsequent devaluation of the markka and the continuing weakness of the U.S. dollar. In the spring round of wage bargaining between the employers' association and the Norwegian labour union federation, the employers called for a pay standstill to match the temporary price freeze. The unions would not accept this, and the government settled the dispute through an impartial wages board, which awarded moderate increases.

The austerity measures, together with industrial cutbacks and a rise in unemployment, led to a slowdown in consumer spending. The trade gap shrank, and by October earlier estimates of a 20.8 billion kroner payments deficit in 1978 had been revised downward to 12.6 billion kroner. But the

Norway

An oil rig under construction in Oslo is part of Norway's North Sea oil and gas industry.

PHILIPPE HERITIER—CAMERA PRESS/PHOTO TRENDS

Nobel Prizes:
see People of the Year

country was still living beyond its means, and its debt burden was growing. Projections of future oil and gas income were becoming less optimistic, partly because of development delays and partly because oil prices did not rise as fast as expected.

In September a new, rigid freeze on wages and prices was introduced, to last throughout 1979. The unions acquiesced reluctantly, accepting the argument that jobs would be lost if Norwegian industry did not become more competitive. Nevertheless, there were some wildcat protest strikes. The freeze was followed by the most restrictive budget Norway had seen since World War II. It allowed for a very modest rise in government spending in 1979 and aimed at holding private consumption at 1977 levels.

The merchant fleet continued to suffer from the world slump, with about one-quarter of its tonnage laid up. Many Norwegian shipowners had to sell their vessels to foreign owners. The shipbuilding industry saw its order books exhausted, and demand for oil platforms and other offshore equip-

ment was insufficient to provide alternative employment. One major industry that did relatively well was aluminum refining as world demand for the metal improved and prices rose.

A government proposal that Norway should take a 40% holding in Volvo, the Swedish automobile manufacturer, was met by skepticism among industrialists and opposition politicians. Critics said the necessary investment could be better spent in making existing Norwegian industry more competitive. An agreement signed in December was to be approved by shareholders and Parliament early in 1979, and the cost to Norway would be 950 million Swedish kronor.

In January Norway and the U.S.S.R. signed a temporary agreement to regulate fisheries in a disputed area of the Barents Sea, but the Soviets would not accept Norwegian policing of the fisheries protection zone that Norway had unilaterally established in 1977 around the Svalbard Archipelago. Norway's assertion of sovereignty over the archipelago led to a clash with the U.S.S.R. in the autumn. A Soviet plane crashed in the area—on Hopen Island—and Norway took charge of the plane's flight recorder and insisted on its right to open the device and interpret its information. The Soviet ambassador to Norway made a formal protest.   (FAY GJESTER)

Oman

An independent sultanate, Oman occupies the southeastern part of the Arabian Peninsula and is bounded by the United Arab Emirates, Saudi Arabia, Yemen (Aden), the Gulf of Oman, and the Arabian Sea. A small part of the country lies to the north and is separated from the rest of Oman by the United Arab Emirates. Area: 300,000 sq km (120,000 sq mi). Pop. (1978 est.): 843,000; for planning purposes the government of Oman uses an estimate of 1.5 million. No census has ever been taken. Cap.: Muscat (pop., 1973 est., 15,000). Largest city: Matrah (pop., 1973 est., 18,000). Language: Arabic. Religion: Muslim. Sultan in 1978, Qabus ibn Sa'id.

Oman's prospects as an oil producer improved in 1978 with new discoveries in Dhofar, which were expected to compensate for declining output in the country's northern fields. In January an

---

NORWAY

Education. (1976–77) Primary, pupils 396,987, teachers (1975–76) 19,613; secondary, pupils 270,172, teachers (1975–76) 14,240; vocational, pupils 70,082, teachers (1975–76) 6,214; higher, students 73,353, teaching staff (1975–76) 5,651.

Finance. Monetary unit: Norwegian krone, with (Sept. 18, 1978) a free rate of 5.22 kroner to U.S. $1 (10.24 kroner = £1 sterling). Gold, SDR's, and foreign exchange (June 1978) U.S. $2,839,200,000. Budget (1978 est.): revenue 55,062,000,000 kroner; expenditure 70,845,000,000 kroner. Gross domestic product (1977) 190,660,000,000 kroner. Money supply (May 1978) 36,030,000,000 kroner. Cost of living (1975 = 100; June 1978) 128.1.

Foreign Trade. (1977) Imports 68,579,000,000 kroner; exports 46,439,000,000 kroner. Import sources: Sweden 18%; West Germany 15%; U.K. 12%; Japan 7%; U.S. 6%; Denmark 6%; France 5%. Export destinations: U.K. 29%; Sweden 13%; West Germany 9%; Denmark 6%. Main exports: ships 19%; crude oil 16%; machinery 9%; aluminum 7%; chemicals 6%; fish 6%; iron and steel 5%.

Transport and Communications. Roads (1976) 78,116 km (including 172 km expressways). Motor vehicles in use (1976): passenger 1,022,900; commercial 138,700. Railways: (1976) 4,241 km (including 2,440 km electrified); traffic (1977) 2,010,000,000 passenger-km, freight 2,632,-000,000 net ton-km. Air traffic (including Norwegian apportionment of international operations of Scandinavian Airlines System; 1977): 3,470,000,000 passenger-km.; freight 132,003,000 net ton-km. Shipping (1977): merchant vessels 100 gross tons and over 2,738; gross tonnage 27,801,471. Shipping traffic (1976): goods loaded 34,218,-000 metric tons, unloaded 21,966,000 metric tons. Telephones (Jan. 1977) 1,476,000. Radio licenses (Dec. 1976) 1,318,000. Television licenses (Dec. 1976) 1,087,000.

Agriculture. Production (in 000; metric tons; 1977): barley 630; oats 360; potatoes *c.* 484; apples 42; milk (1976) *c.* 1,864; cheese 59; beef and veal (1976) *c.* 62; pork (1976) *c.* 75; timber (cu m; 1976) 8,968; fish catch (1976) 3,435. Livestock (in 000; June 1976): cattle 921; sheep 1,667; pigs 698; goats 68; chickens *c.* 6,594.

Industry. Fuel and power (in 000; metric tons; 1977): crude oil 13,687; coal (Svalbard mines; Norwegian operated only) 455; natural gas (cu m; 1976) 319,000; manufactured gas (cu m) 21,000; electricity (kw-hr) 72,520,000. Production (in 000; metric tons; 1977): iron ore (65% metal content) 3,722; pig iron 1,206; crude steel 734; aluminum 625; copper 20; zinc 69; cement 2,333; petroleum products (1976) 8,143; sulfuric acid 388; fertilizers (nutrient content; 1976–77) nitrogenous 337, phosphate 125; fish meal (1976) 464; wood pulp (1976) mechanical 836, chemical 872; newsprint 437; other paper (1976) 791. Merchant vessels launched (100 gross tons and over; 1977) 530,000 gross tons. New dwelling units completed (1977) 38,600.

OMAN

Education. (1976–77) Primary, pupils 62,800, teachers 2,534; secondary, pupils 2,345, teachers 355; vocational, pupils 209, teachers 48; teacher training, students 25, teachers 4.

Finance and Trade. Monetary unit: rial Omani, with (Sept. 18, 1978) a par value of 0.345 rial to U.S. $1 (free rate of 0.674 rial = £1 sterling). Gold, SDR's, and foreign exchange (June 1978) U.S. $390 million. Budget (1977 est.): revenue 714 million rials; expenditure 770 million rials.

Foreign Trade. (1977) Imports 278.4 million rials; exports 543.7 million rials. Import sources (1976): U.K. 19%; United Arab Emirates 17%; Japan 12%; West Germany 6%; U.S. 6%; India 5%. Export destinations: Japan *c.* 51%; U.S. 15%; The Netherlands 9%; Trinidad and Tobago 9%. Main export: crude oil 100%.

Industry. Production (in 000): crude oil (metric tons; 1977) 17,060; electricity (kw-hr; 1976) 413,000.

Oman

Oman Mining Co., partially financed by Saudi Arabia, was formed with two U.S. companies to extract copper ore in the Sohar area.

A border dispute with the United Arab Emirates over an area claimed by Oman and Ras al-Khaimah was exacerbated by a Kuwait-Ras al-Khaimah agreement in January to establish an oil refinery in the disputed area. Although the rebellion in Dhofar of the Popular Front for the Liberation of Oman (PFLO) had been declared ended by the Oman government, the Algiers summit of Arab hard-line states in February affirmed its support for the PFLO and expressed concern over the continuing foreign military presence in Oman. The Oman government protested strongly. The murder on June 1 of five British ex-servicemen working for Airwork Services in Dhofar was generally attributed to rebels trained in Aden by Cuban advisers.

In May Oman became the second Arab Gulf state (after Kuwait) to establish diplomatic relations with China. (PETER MANSFIELD)

Pakistan

A federal republic, Pakistan is bordered on the south by the Arabian Sea, on the west by Afghanistan and Iran, on the north by China, and on the east by India. Area: 796,095 sq km (307,374 sq mi), excluding the Pakistani-controlled section of Jammu and Kashmir. Pop. (1978 est.): 74,540,000. Cap.: Islamabad (pop., 1972, 77,300). Largest city: Karachi (metro. area pop., 1975 est., 4,465,000). Language: Urdu and English. Religion: Muslim 90%, Hindu and Christian minorities. President to Aug. 14, 1978, Fazal Elahi Chaudhry; chief martial law administrator and president from September 16, Gen. Mohammad Zia-ul-Haq.

The uncertainty that marked the political scene in Pakistan after Gen. Mohammad Zia-ul-Haq's coup in July 1977 continued in 1978. The promised general elections remained postponed. Hopes of return to parliamentary rule receded with the resignation of Pres. Fazal Elahi Chaudhry upon the expiration of his constitutional five-year term in August 1978. General Zia took over the duties of president on September 16, in addition to being chief martial law administrator and chief of the Army staff. Chaudhry had been the first elected president of Pakistan under the 1973 constitution. The constitution, which was not fully suspended when General Zia took over, stipulated that the president should continue in office until a new president was elected jointly by the National Assembly and Senate, but Chaudhry refused to carry on.

Under martial law since July 1977, the regime carried on its work initially without the support of politicians, but General Zia changed this approach because of the growing opposition of his main adversary, the Pakistan People's Party, led by the prime minister he had deposed, Zulfikar Ali Bhutto. The general opened a dialogue in April 1978 with the leaders of the anti-Bhutto Pakistan National Alliance (PNA), a loosely knit grouping of parties that had offered him cooperation. But his efforts to persuade them to identify totally with his regime in a national government did not succeed. On July 5, the first anniversary of his coming to office, Zia announced a 22-member Cabinet with no fixed term and responsible only to him. The Muslim League sent its representatives to the government and later, on August 23, most PNA constituents agreed to join a new, civilian Cabinet.

But martial law continued, and the Military Council remained supreme. Bhutto, now in jail, dominated the restricted opposition politics. Apart from other charges brought against him, he was sentenced to death on March 18 by the Lahore High Court for political murder. Four police officials were convicted with him for the murder of Nawab Mohammad Ahmad Khan, father of a former National Assembly member, Ahmad Raza Kasuri. Bhutto's conviction touched off a worldwide demand for clemency. The Supreme Court of Pakistan was considering his appeal against the sentence. Many of his party colleagues were jailed, and family members were placed under restrictive orders (or arrest in the case of Bhutto's daughter Benazir, on October 3). The government also published lengthy White Papers on Bhutto's electoral misdeeds and his misuse of power and of the mass media.

Pakistan

PAKISTAN

Education. (1975–76) Primary, pupils 5,241,161, teachers 131,663; secondary, pupils 1,749,287, teachers 103,000; vocational, pupils 27,327, teachers 2,137; teacher training, students 17,371, teachers 751; higher, students 280,600, teaching staff 15,437.

Finance. Monetary unit: Pakistan rupee, with (Sept. 18, 1978) a par value of PakRs 9.90 to U.S. $1 (free rate of PakRs 19.40 = £1 sterling). Gold, SDR's, and foreign exchange (June 1978) U.S. $768 million. Budget (1977–78 est.): revenue PakRs 22,929,000,000; expenditure PakRs 23,527,-000,000. Gross national product (1975–76) PakRs 133,180,000,000. Money supply (June 1978) PakRs 42,433,000,000. Cost of living (1975 = 100; June 1978) 123.

Foreign Trade. (1977) Imports PakRs 24,299,000,000; exports PakRs 11,627,000,000. Import sources (1976): U.S. 18%; Japan 12%; U.K. 8%; Saudi Arabia 7%; West Germany 7%; Kuwait 5%. Export destinations (1976): Hong Kong 8%; Japan 8%; U.K. 6%; U.S. 6%; West Germany 6%; Saudi Arabia 6%; Iraq 5%. Main exports (1976–77): rice 22%; cotton fabrics 14%; cotton yarn 10%; carpets 8%; leather 6%.

Transport and Communications. Roads (1976) 49,926 km. Motor vehicles in use (1975): passenger 196,100; commercial (including buses) 91,700. Railways: (1977) 8,815 km; traffic (1976–77) 12,957,000,000 passenger-km, freight 8,677,000,000 net ton-km. Air traffic (1976): 3,410,000,000 passenger-km; freight 148.3 million net ton-km. Shipping (1977): merchant vessels 100 gross tons and over 84; gross tonnage 475,600. Telephones (Jan. 1976) 240,000. Radio licenses (Dec. 1975) 1.1 million. Television receivers (Dec. 1976) c. 415,000.

Agriculture. Production (in 000; metric tons; 1977): wheat 9,155; corn c. 864; rice 4,356; millet c. 305; sorghum c. 400; potatoes c. 331; sugar, raw value c. 783; sugar, noncentrifugal (1976) c. 1,445; chick-peas 649; onions c. 338; rapeseed 289; cottonseed 1,041; mangoes c. 600; tobacco c. 61; cotton, lint c. 500; beef and buffalo meat 324; mutton and goat meat 235; fish catch (1976) 206. Livestock (in 000; 1977): cattle 14,361; buffalo 10,593; sheep 19,749; goats 22,722; camels (1976) c. 900; chickens 35,306.

Industry. Production (in 000; metric tons; 1977): cement 3,175; crude oil 496; coal and lignite (1976–77) 1,-340; natural gas (cu m) c. 5,050,000; petroleum products (1976) c. 3,390; electricity (kw-hr; 1976) c. 10,876,000; sulfuric acid 49; caustic soda 27; soda ash (1976–77) 56; nitrogenous fertilizers (nutrient content; 1976–77) 309; cotton yarn 283; woven cotton fabrics (sq m; 1976–77) 417,000.

On the economic front, the situation remained uneasy, though the picture was not one of unrelieved gloom. There were favourable developments concerning the nation's external account, and crop production was good. Remittances from Pakistani workers, mostly in Persian Gulf countries, were also helpful.

In foreign relations ties with India were improved. Indian External Affairs Minister Atal Bihari Vajpayee visited Islamabad in February, the first Indian senior minister to visit Pakistan in 12 years. While Kashmir remained an outstanding issue as far as Pakistan was concerned, the leaders of the two countries otherwise acknowledged the need for normalization of relations. Subsequently, a treaty concerning the hydroelectric project on the Chenab River in the Indian part of Kashmir was signed. An agreement had been eluding the two sides for the previous eight years. The project was a follow-up to the 1960 Indus Waters Treaty, under which Pakistan had the use of the waters of the Chenab for all purposes and India only for nondrinking purposes. Indian Prime Minister Morarji Desai and General Zia met in Nairobi when attending the funeral of Pres. Jomo Kenyatta of Kenya at the end of August.

Friendly relations with China formed a thread of continuity in Pakistan's foreign policy. The Karakoram highway linking China with Pakistan was opened in June. The new road, 500 mi long, stretched from the border of China's Sinkiang Province to a few miles north of Pakistan's capital of Islamabad. Anxious to establish good relations with Afghanistan's new Communist-oriented regime, Pakistan sent a trade delegation to Kabul in December. (GOVINDAN UNNY)

Panama

Panama

A republic of Central America, bisected by the Canal Zone, Panama is bounded by the Caribbean Sea, Colombia, the Pacific Ocean, and Costa Rica. Area: 75,650 sq km (29,209 sq mi). Pop. (1978 est.): 1,825,500. Cap. and largest city: Panama City (pop., 1978 est., 439,900). Language: Spanish. Religion (1977 est.): Roman Catholic 89%. Presidents in 1978, Demetrio Lakas Bahas and, from October 11, Aristides Royo.

In the fall of 1977 Panama City presented a facade of prosperity: crowded streets, stores displaying foreign goods, numerous automobiles, and the bustle of shoppers. But those people were struggling with a 12 to 15% unemployment level and an inflation rate of about 10%. Many were contending with a wage scale that had been frozen for many months. The economic slowdown had approached the point of stagnation. Much of the reason for the decline lay in unfavourable world conditions and excessive borrowing by the government, to the point of increasing the nation's foreign debt to more than $1 billion. A third major reason was uncertainty about the Panama Canal.

Ambiguities in the treaty agreements of Sept. 7, 1977, and the supplementary statement of Oct. 14, 1977, by U.S. Pres. Jimmy Carter and Panamanian leader Omar Torrijos Herrera precipitated visits to Panama of nearly half the members of the U.S. Senate. Torrijos was the perfect host, providing sight-seeing trips and conferences in which he offered explanations and assurances about the treaties. Early in November 1977, as further inducement to ratify them, he offered to resign from the leadership of his country, abolish martial law, ease press censorship, permit the return of political exiles, and open the way for free elections. Late in January 1978, influenced perhaps by the indication of public opinion polls in the U.S. that no more than one in three persons favoured the treaties, he renewed his offer to resign.

The U.S. Senate was not satisfied with Torrijos's assurances that Panama could operate the canal, nor was it persuaded to approve the pacts by Carter's warning that their defeat would stimulate Communist countries to create dissension in Panama. When the Senate Foreign Relations Committee recommended changes on January 27, Torrijos and his treaty negotiators warned that these might re-

U.S. Pres. Jimmy Carter (second from left) shakes hands with Panamanian leader Gen. Omar Torrijos after the signing of the Panama Canal treaties in Panama in June.

DON GOODE—SYGMA

quire a second plebiscite in Panama, which could reverse the approval given on Oct. 23, 1977.

About seven weeks after the committee recommendation, the Senate approved the first of the agreements, the Neutrality Treaty, with several modifications. Two of these cast in more definite form the unsigned Carter-Torrijos statement of Oct. 14, 1977. They provided that each country, after the year 1999, would be responsible for defending the canal against a threat to its neutrality and that U.S. (and Panamanian) warships would have a right to "go to the head of the line" in case of emergency. To these Panama had no serious objection. A third change was proposed by Sen. Dennis DeConcini (Dem., Ariz.), who was troubled by the spectre of a canal closed by domestic riots and turmoil. His reservation gave the U.S. the right to reopen the canal in such an eventuality, using troops if necessary. Torrijos denounced this change and dispatched copies of the reservation and his complaint to 115 heads of state. Belatedly, the Senate learned that Torrijos rejected the DeConcini reservation and demanded that it be neutralized.

The second treaty, transferring the canal to Panama by stages up to the year 2000 (at noon, Panama time, Dec. 31, 1999), was ratified on April 18. Once again DeConcini proposed a reservation to allow the U.S. an immediate right to safeguard the canal from a threat from whatever source. Since a change of mind by two senators would defeat the agreement, the pro-treaty forces accepted the reservation but added language whereby the U.S. specifically renounced any right to intervene in the internal affairs of Panama. The conclusion of the ratification process inspired jubilation in Panama.

Economic improvement for Panama seemed to be in sight with the completion of Tocumen International Airport and a Canadian guarantee of a large loan to develop the Cerro Colorado copper project. On August 6 Panamanians elected a National Assembly to choose a new president. Torrijos withdrew as a candidate and as chief of state and returned to his old position as head of the National Guard after Aristides Royo was chosen president and sworn in on October 11. Along with the presidency Royo assumed the powers that Torrijos had held as chief of state.

(ALMON R. WRIGHT)

Papua New Guinea

Papua New Guinea

Papua New Guinea is an independent parliamentary state and a member of the Commonwealth of Nations. It is situated in the southwest Pacific and comprises the eastern part of the island of New Guinea, the islands of the Bismarck, Trobriand, Woodlark, Louisiade, and D'Entrecasteaux groups, and parts of the Solomon Islands, including Bougainville. It is separated from Australia by the Torres Strait. Area: 462,840 sq km (178,704 sq mi). Pop. (1977 est.): 2,908,000. Cap. and largest city: Port Moresby (pop., 1976 est., 113,400). Language: English, Police Motu (a Melanesian pidgin), and Pidgin English (or Neo-Melanesian) are official, although the latter is the most widely spoken. Religion (1966): Roman Catholic 31.2%; Lutheran 27.3%; indigenous 7%. Queen, Elizabeth II; governor-general in 1978, Sir Tore Lokoloko; prime minister, Michael T. Somare.

On February 21, Finance Minister Barry Holloway presented Papua New Guinea's 1978 budget, the first to cover an aligned calendar and financial year. The budget forecast an expenditure of 485.8 million kinas and revenue of 476.2 million kinas.

567

Papua
New Guinea

PANAMA

Education. (1977) Primary, pupils 357,753, teachers 12,509; secondary, pupils 92,363, teachers 3,563; vocational, pupils 43,378, teachers 2,182; teacher training, students 1,317, teachers 113; higher, students 34,477, teaching staff 2,171.

Finance. Monetary unit: balboa, at par with the U.S. dollar, with a free rate (Sept. 18, 1978) of 1.96 balboas to £1 sterling. Gold, SDR's, and foreign exchange (June 1978) U.S. $125 million. Budget (1977 actual): revenue 343 million balboas; expenditure 433 million balboas. Gross national product (1977) 2,215,400,000 balboas. Cost of living (Panama City; 1975 = 100; June 1978) 113.6.

Foreign Trade. (1977) Imports 861.2 million balboas; exports 253,050,000 balboas. Import sources (1976): U.S. 32%; Ecuador 18%; Venezuela 8%; Japan 6%. Export destinations (1976): U.S. 49%; Canal Zone 12%; West Germany 9%; Italy 7%. Main exports: petroleum products 27%; bananas 26%; shrimps 12%; sugar 9%.

Transport and Communications. Roads (1976) 7,686 km. Motor vehicles in use (1975): passenger 66,200; commercial (including buses) 19,600. Railways (1976) c. 490 km. Air traffic (1976): 437 million passenger-km, freight 5 million net ton-km. Shipping (1977): merchant vessels 100 gross tons and over 3,267 (mostly owned by U.S. and other foreign interests); gross tonnage 19,458,419. Telephones (Dec. 1976) c. 140,000. Radio receivers (Dec. 1975) 265,000. Television receivers (Dec. 1975) 185,000.

Agriculture. Production (in 000; metric tons; 1977): rice c. 190; corn (1976) c. 55; sugar, raw value (1976) 129; mangoes c. 26; bananas c. 1,000; oranges 62; coffee c. 5; fish catch (1976) 172. Livestock (in 000; 1976): cattle c. 1,361; pigs c. 172; horses c. 164; chickens c. 3,776.

Industry. Production (in 000; metric tons; 1976): petroleum products c. 2,620; cement 311; manufactured gas (cu m; 1977) 1,800; electricity (kw-hr) c. 1,508,000.

PAPUA NEW GUINEA

Education. (1976) Primary, pupils 255,538, teachers 8,067; secondary, pupils 32,050, teachers 1,242; vocational, pupils 9,575, teachers 495; teacher training, students 2,404, teachers 143; higher, students 2,621, teaching staff 333.

Finance. Monetary unit: kina, with (Sept. 18, 1978) a free rate of 0.69 kina to U.S. $1 (1.35 kina = £1 sterling). Gold, SDR's, and foreign exchange (June 1978) U.S. $420 million. Budget (1976–77 est): revenue 432 million kinas (including Australian grants of 175 million kinas); expenditure 436 million kinas.

Foreign Trade. (1977) Imports 533.4 million kinas; exports 571.5 million kinas. Import sources (1975–76): Australia 47%; Japan 14%; Singapore 12%; U.S. 7%; U.K. 5%. Export destinations (1975–76): Japan 29%; West Germany 25%; Australia 15%; U.S. 8%; Spain 6%; U.K. 6%. Main exports (1976–77): copper ores 37%; coffee 26%; cocoa 11%.

Transport. Roads (1975) 18,188 km. Motor vehicles in use (1976): passenger 17,700; commercial (including buses) 19,200. There are no railways. Shipping (1977): merchant vessels 100 gross tons and over 64; gross tonnage 16,217.

Agriculture. Production (in 000; metric tons; 1977): cocoa c. 35; coffee c. 43; copra c. 132; cassava (1976) c. 86; taro (1976) c. 220; yams (1976) c. 170; bananas c. 870; palm oil c. 32; tea c. 6; rubber c. 6; timber (cu m; 1976) 5,892. Livestock (in 000; March 1976): cattle c. 155; pigs c. 1,173; goats c. 15; chickens c. 1,085.

Industry. Production (in 000; 1975–76): electricity (kw-hr) 1,048,000; gold (troy oz; 1977) c. 730; silver (troy oz) 1,450; copper ore (metal content; metric tons) 176.

Palestine:
see Israel; Jordan

Panama Canal Zone:
see Dependent States; Panama

Paper and Pulp:
see Industrial Review

Australian aid accounted for 37.8% of the revenue, international loans for 6.8%, and internal taxation for the remainder. Holloway also announced a National Public Expenditure Plan, under which the government planned particular initiatives to stimulate the food industry and improve nutritional standards by the production of rice, vegetables, sugar, fish, and beef.

While the Papua New Guinea economy made good progress, the nation's relations with Indonesia were under strain as the latter continued "hot pursuit" of rebels who crossed the common frontier. Despite Papua New Guinea's complaints, Indonesian military patrols penetrated 50 km (31 mi) inside the northern sector of the border to destroy a camp where anti-Indonesian separatists were living. Although Papua New Guinea recognized Indonesian sovereignty in West Irian and did not condone rebel activity, Prime Minister Michael Somare refused Indonesian requests for joint military or civilian patrols along the boundary.

(A. R. G. GRIFFITHS)

Paraguay

A landlocked republic of South America, Paraguay is bounded by Brazil, Argentina, and Bolivia. Area: 406,752 sq km (157,048 sq mi). Pop. (1978 est.): 2,888,000. Cap. and largest city: Asunción (pop., 1977 est., 460,800). Language: Spanish (official), though Guaraní is understood by more than 90% of the population. Religion: Roman

Paraguay

Peru

PARAGUAY

Education. (1975) Primary, pupils 452,249, teachers 15,398; secondary, pupils 75,424, teachers 10,406; vocational, pupils 1,361, teachers 67; higher, students 17,135, teaching staff 1,741.

Finance. Monetary unit: guaraní, with (Sept. 18, 1978) a par value of 126 guaranis to U.S. $1 (free rate of 244 guaranis = £1 sterling). Gold, SDR's, and foreign exchange (June 1978) U.S. $399.8 million. Budget (1977 actual): revenue 26,292,000,000 guaranis; expenditure 22,964,000,000 guaranis. Gross national product (1977) 259 billion guaranis. Money supply (June 1978) 36,690,000,000 guaranis. Cost of living (Asunción; 1975 = 100; June 1978) 124.4.

Foreign Trade. (1977) Imports 38,007,000,000 guaranis; exports 34,564,000,000 guaranis. Import sources: Brazil 22%; Argentina 17%; U.S. 12%; Algeria 9%; Japan 9%; West Germany 9%; U.K. 6%. Export destinations: The Netherlands 15%; U.S. 14%; Argentina 13%; West Germany 10%; Switzerland 9%; Brazil 6%; U.K. 5%; France 5%. Main exports: cotton 29%; soybeans 20%; vegetable oils 11%; meat 8%; timber 7%; tobacco 5%.

Transport and Communications. Roads (1973) 15,956 km. Motor vehicles in use (1976): passenger *c.* 25,900; commercial (including buses) *c.* 14,800. Railways: (1976) 498 km; traffic (1973) 26 million passenger-km, freight 30 million net ton-km. Navigable inland waterways (including Paraguay-Paraná River system; 1975) *c.* 3,000 km. Telephones (Jan. 1977) 41,600. Radio receivers (Dec. 1975) 180,000. Television receivers (Dec. 1975) 54,000.

Agriculture. Production (in 000; metric tons; 1977): corn *c.* 372; cassava (1976) *c.* 1,450; sweet potatoes (1976) *c.* 97; soybeans *c.* 375; sugar, raw value (1976) *c.* 58; tomatoes *c.* 54; oranges *c.* 134; bananas *c.* 268; palm kernels *c.* 13; tobacco *c.* 46; cottonseed *c.* 143; cotton lint *c.* 75; beef and veal (1976) *c.* 102. Livestock (in 000; 1976): cattle *c.* 5,049; sheep *c.* 355; pigs *c.* 800; horses *c.* 315; chickens *c.* 8,520.

Industry. Production (in 000; metric tons; 1976): petroleum products *c.* 220; cement 155; cotton yarn 34; electricity (kw-hr) *c.* 700,000.

Catholic (official). President in 1978, Gen. Alfredo Stroessner.

The ruling Partido Colorado captured 89.6% of the votes cast in the Feb. 12, 1978, presidential election. Gen. Alfredo Stroessner was subsequently sworn in for a sixth consecutive five-year term of office on August 15, making his the longest period of unbroken rule by one man in Latin America in the 20th century.

A resolution was passed by the Inter-American Commission on Human Rights on July 1 calling on Paraguay to answer allegations regarding violations of human rights. Although considerable numbers of political prisoners were released during the year, the arrest on July 7 of Domingo Laíno, leader of the opposition Partido Liberal Radical Auténtico, placed a strain on relations with the U.S. and Western Europe; he was freed on August 9.

The 1977 economic growth rate of 11.8% was the highest in Latin America; a growth rate of about 8% was estimated for 1978. The foreign trade balance deteriorated, registering a deficit of $57.4 million in January–June 1978, compared with a surplus of $29.7 million during the first half of 1977. A balance of payments surplus of more than $100 million was forecast for 1978.

(MONIQUE MERRIAM)

Peru

A republic on the west coast of South America, Peru is bounded by Ecuador, Colombia, Brazil, Bolivia, Chile, and the Pacific Ocean. Area: 1,285,215 sq km (496,224 sq mi). Pop. (1978 est.): 16,819,200, including approximately 52% whites and mestizos and 46% Indians. Cap. and largest city: Lima (metro. area pop., 1978 est., 4,376,100). Language: Spanish and Quechua are official; Indians also speak Aymara. Religion: Roman Catholic. President of the military government in 1978, Francisco Morales Bermúdez.

Amid increasing economic hardship, the Peruvian people in 1978 experienced constant alterations in economic policies, the result of repeated changes in Cabinet ministers. This began on January 30 when Gen. Guillermo Arbulu Galliani was succeeded as prime minister, war minister, and Army commander by Gen. Oscar Molina Pallochia. Gen. Francisco Morales Bermúdez retired from the Army but remained president.

Also during the year the military government committed itself to reestablishing constitutional rule. Under the Tupac-Amarú plan, published in October 1977, the government announced that general elections would be held by 1980 to reintroduce a civilian constitutional government. In spite of political unrest, elections were held on June 18 for a 100-member Constituent Assembly to draw up a new constitution within 12 months.

A principal reason for a new constitution was to include in it the reforms undertaken by the armed forces since 1968. However, the late Gen. Juan Velasco's left-nationalist approach was being changed to a large extent under the government of General Morales. The National Agrarian Confederation was dissolved in early June; the industrial community law was modified to allow workers to sell company shares freely; Pescaperu, the state fishing enterprise, was being returned to private hands; many mining projects were opened to private investors, and more encouragement was being given to foreign investment.

In the elections for the Constituent Assembly the moderate leftist Alianza Popular Revolucionaria Americana (APRA), headed by Víctor Raúl Haya de la Torre (see BIOGRAPHIES), won 35.3% of the total votes cast, while the Partido Popular Cristiano captured about 27%; various left-wing parties obtained 30.3%, and although not united they represented a group of opinion opposed to the current trend in economic strategy. The labour front became the major opposition to the government's austerity measures designed to satisfy the International Monetary Fund.

The country had faced high overall deficits in the balance of payments in the previous three years, and in consequence the external debt increased sharply in 1977 to $8,274,000,000. In 1977 the foreign banks established as a condition for the rescheduling of the foreign debt the IMF's approval of the government's future economic policy. After long negotiations at the end of 1977 Peru signed an agreement with the IMF by which it was granted a two-year standby credit of 90 million Special Drawing Rights (U.S. $106 million) subject to a

stabilization program. However, in February 1978 the IMF refused to authorize Peru to draw from the loan a second time, demanding a stricter adherence to the stabilization program. In the middle of May, just before the elections for the Constituent Assembly, the political climate was transformed by the announcement of new austerity measures that included sharp price increases for gasoline, wheat products, milk, and cooking oil. These increases were followed by unrest in several cities, culminating in a two-day general strike on May 22 and 23 during which at least 30 civilians were killed in clashes with police. A state of emergency was declared and then lifted one week before the elections.

Early in August Peru signed a letter of intent with the IMF under which a new standby credit of 184 million Special Drawing Rights ($230 million) over 30 months was granted and an additional austerity program was announced. The government also produced new legislation in July to guarantee the freedom of the press.

(MARTA BEKERMANN DE FAINBOIM)

Philately and Numismatics

Stamps. Throughout 1978 the international stamp market remained active, especially in the auction field. Many small firms, particularly in the U.K. and the U.S., established themselves as philatelic auctioneers, and one of the major auctioneers of fine art, Sotheby Parke Bernet, began regular philatelic sales in the U.S. and the U.K. The London-based firm of Stanley Gibbons International opened a new business in Monaco. Stanley Gibbons Merkur (Frankfurt am Main, West Germany) created a world record for a single-country sale when, in May, the "Rio" collection of classic Brazilian stamps realized DM 1,140,000 (£285,000) in one day; the unique sheet of the 1843 60-reis "Bull's-Eye" issue made DM 151,000 (£38,750).

At the British Philatelic Federation congress held at Worthing in June, new signatories to the Roll of Distinguished Philatelists were Karl K. Wolter (West Germany; elected 1976), Kenneth McNaught (New Zealand), Tomas Barringer

The "A" stamp, which carried no monetary denomination, was issued by the U.S. Postal Service in May after first-class postage rates were raised to 15 cents per ounce. The stamp was printed before the amount of the raise had been decided.

PERU

Education. (1976) Primary, pupils 2,964,500, teachers 74,853; secondary, pupils 687,100, teachers 30,848; vocational, pupils 204,200, teachers 8,318; higher, students 190,635, teaching staff 12,113.

Finance. Monetary unit: sol, with (Sept. 18, 1978) a free rate of 172.3 soles to U.S. $1 (337.7 soles = £1 sterling). Gold, SDR's, and foreign exchange (June 1978) U.S. $312.7 million. Budget (1977 actual): revenue 154,118,000,000 soles; expenditure 172,837,000,000 soles. Gross national product (1977) 1,030,000,000,000 soles. Money supply (April 1978) 194,820,000,000 soles. Cost of living (Lima; 1975 = 100; March 1978) 237.9.

Foreign Trade. (1977) Imports 157,542,000,000 soles; exports 132,662,000,000 soles. Import sources (1976): U.S. c. 32%; Japan c. 8%; West Germany c. 7%; Venezuela c. 5%. Export destinations (1976): U.S. c. 25%; Japan c. 14%; U.S.S.R. c. 8%; Chile c. 6%. Main exports: copper 23%; coffee 12%; fish meal 10%; silver 9%; zinc 7%; iron ore 5%.

Transport and Communications. Roads (1976) 56,940 km. Motor vehicles in use (1976): passenger 299,500; commercial (including buses) 156,100. Railways: (1974) c. 3,-400 km; traffic (1975) 455 million passenger-km, freight 707 million net ton-km. Air traffic (1976): 1,367,000,000 passenger-km; freight 25.9 million net ton-km. Shipping (1977): merchant vessels 100 gross tons and over 681; gross tonnage 555,419. Telephones (Jan. 1977) 295,200. Radio receivers (Dec. 1975) 2,050,000. Television receivers (Dec. 1975) 500,000.

Agriculture. Production (in 000; metric tons; 1977): rice 580; corn c. 700; wheat c. 150; barley c. 170; potatoes c. 1,975; sweet potatoes (1976) c. 190; cassava (1976) c. 475; sugar, raw value 928; onions c. 174; oranges c. 210; lemons c. 78; coffee c. 60; cotton, lint c. 65; fish catch (1976) 4,343. Livestock (in 000; 1977): cattle 4,116; sheep c. 14,500; pigs 1,994; goats c. 2,060; horses (1976) c. 713; poultry c. 30,-000.

Industry. Production (in 000; metric tons; 1976): crude oil (1977) 3,698; natural gas (cu m) c. 480,000; cement 1,966; iron ore (metal content) c. 3,089; pig iron 223; crude steel 349; copper 132; lead 81; zinc 67; tungsten concentrates (oxide content) 1.1; gold (troy oz) 81; silver (troy oz) 35,700; fish meal 857; petroleum products c. 5,520; electricity (kw-hr) c. 8,650,000.

CZECHOSLOVAK NEWS AGENCY/KEYSTONE

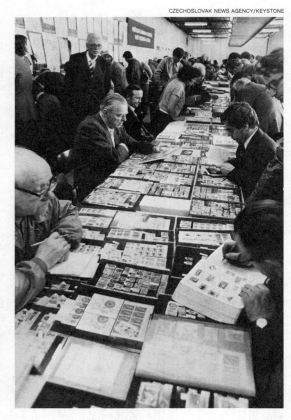

The largest exhibition of postage stamps ever held in the history of philately went on view in Prague, Czechoslovakia, in September. Almost 1.5 million stamps from 140 countries were on display.

(Sweden; at 31 the youngest-ever signatory), George T. Turner (U.S.), Philip Silver (U.S.), and Albert L. Michael (U.K.). The Philatelic Congress Medal was awarded to Robert C. Emery of Worthing.

The British Post Office issued its first postal miniature sheet. Containing four stamps, with a face value of 43½ pence, it was sold at 53½ pence to help finance the forthcoming London 1980 international exhibition. The estimated printing of two million was sold out within a few days. An American precedent was a souvenir sheet of U.S. stamps sold in Toronto at the Capex 78 exhibition in June but not placed on general sale in the U.S. until August.

At Capex 78, the major international exhibition

The likeness of Susan B. Anthony, a leading suffragist, would be on the new U.S. dollar coin scheduled to be issued in mid-1979.

of the year, the four main awards were: International Philatelic Federation's Grand Prix d'Honneur, Hiroyuki Kanai (Japan) for classic Mauritius; Grand Prix National, J. Foxbridge (U.S.) for early Canadian classics; Grand Prix International, John J. Engellau (Sweden) for early Denmark; and the Grand Prix Postal History (a new award at international exhibitions), Paolo Bianchi (Italy) for Italian occupation of East Africa. The 1978 "omnibus" issue commemorated the Silver Jubilee of the coronation of Queen Elizabeth II.

In an effort to cut production costs, the U.S. Postal Service announced that, for the first time, private firms would be invited to bid for printing four forthcoming U.S. commemorative stamps. The experimental production of a 13-cent "mini" stamp designed to save paper costs was successful. Estimates suggested an annual saving of $500,000 would be achieved in the production of the basic letter-rate stamp alone.   (KENNETH F. CHAPMAN)

Coins. After nearly three years of study and debate, the U.S. Congress approved a small-size dollar coin that was expected to be in circulation by mid-1979. Slightly over one inch in diameter, the coin was estimated to cost three cents to produce and to have a life of 15 years, compared with paper dollars costing two cents each but having a life of only about 18 months. After considerable controversy, it was decided that the coin would feature a likeness of the 19th-century women's rights leader Susan B. Anthony.

The long-awaited and much-needed book on grading of U.S. coins went on sale in book and hobby shops in January 1978. It was compiled under the direction of and endorsed by the American Numismatic Association.

Prices of collectors' coins and paper money, especially the rarities, continued to increase. During 1978 one of the five 1913 U.S. liberty head nickels minted was reportedly sold privately for $200,000; another was presented to the Smithsonian Institution. Prices of common gold coins rose in proportion to the market quotations of the metal, placing U.S. $20 gold coins in the $250–$300 range. Among other common coins sought by dealers and collectors alike were U.S. silver dollars and equivalent coins of other countries.

Israeli coin and medal exports had fallen drastically in 1977, to about $2 million, compared with over $9 million a year or so earlier. No definite reason for the change was known, but interest in Israeli numismatic items improved in 1978. Two new higher value coins, a 50 lirot, .500 fine silver, and a 1,000 lirot, .900 fine gold, were dated 1978 and observed the 30th anniversary of Israel's independence.

Large numbers of expertly made counterfeit British gold sovereigns appeared, mostly dated 1963 or 1967. The gold content was practically the same as that of genuine coins, and the fakes were extremely difficult to detect. Proving that the improbable can happen, a handyman of Bristol, England, found a coin on a mudbank that proved to be an excellent silver penny of King Henry I, struck about 1130. It was sold to a London coin dealer for £600.

UPI COMPIX

Representative new coins included: Austria, 1978, 100 schillings, .640 fine silver; British Virgin Islands, 1978, $100, .900 fine gold, 25-sided in recognition of the 25th anniversary of the coronation of Elizabeth II; Cook Islands, 1978, $200, .900 fine gold; Finland, 1978, 25 markkaa, .500 fine silver, in observance of the world skiing championships held in that country in February; Hong Kong, 1978, HK$1,000, .917 fine gold; Isle of Man, 1978, £1, special nonprecious alloy with the edge having alternately reeded and smooth segments for identification by the blind; Norway, 1978, 50 kroner, .925 fine silver, celebrating King Olav's 75th birthday; Panama, 1978, 500 balboas, .900 fine gold; Papua New Guinea, 1978, 100 kina, .900 fine gold; Poland, 1978, 100 zlotys, .625 fine silver; Soviet Union, six silver and one gold coin, dated 1977, in observance of the 1980 Summer Olympics to be held in Moscow, and a one-ruble cupronickel coin in observance of the 60th anniversary of the October Revolution; San Marino, 1977, 1,000 lire, .835 fine silver, commemorating the 600th anniversary of the birth of the Florentine architect Filippo Brunelleschi; Singapore, 1978, Sing$10, silver; Switzerland, 1978, 5 francs, cupronickel, marking the sesquicentennial of the birth of Jean-Henri Dunant, founder of the Red Cross; and Western Samoa, 1978, $100, .917 fine gold, and two other coins marking the 50th anniversary of the first transatlantic flight.

Among the many medals issued was one by the Judaic Heritage Society, in gold, silver, and bronze, honouring Egyptian Pres. Anwar as-Sadat and Israeli Prime Minister Menahem Begin for their peace initiative in November 1977. Sweden commemorated the 500th anniversary of its first dated coin with a medal issued in gold, silver, and bronze.   (GLENN B. SMEDLEY)

[452.D.2.b; 725.B.4.g]

Philippines

Situated in the western Pacific Ocean off the southeast coast of Asia, the Republic of the Philippines consists of an archipelago of about 7,100 islands. Area: 300,000 sq km (115,800 sq mi). Pop. (1977 est.): 45,028,000. Cap. and largest city: Manila (pop., metro. area, 1977 est., 7.5 million). Language: Pilipino (based on Tagalog), English, Spanish, and many dialects. Religion (1970): Roman Catholic 85%; Muslim 4.3%; Aglipayan 3.9%; Protestant 3.1%; others 2.4%. President and (from June 12) premier in 1978, Ferdinand E. Marcos.

An interim National Assembly was elected April 7, 1978, the first legislative body to take office since Pres. Ferdinand E. Marcos declared martial law in 1972. When it was inaugurated on June 12, Marcos took the additional title of premier. As president, he continued to have the power to rule by decree, but his veto of assembly decisions could be overridden by a two-thirds vote.

The assembly had 165 elected members in a total of 200. It was created as a step toward a still-undefined blending of the presidential and parliamentary systems. A 27-member Cabinet was sworn in June 11 with Imelda R. Marcos (see Bi-

UPI COMPIX

Former senator Lorenzo Tanada gestured and shouted defiance after he and others were arrested in antigovernment demonstrations in Manila in April.

OGRAPHIES), the president's wife, as one of the members.

Marcos told the assembly that he would "enlarge the democratic dialogue among all sectors of society," but that martial law would continue during a long transition from authoritarian government. He granted amnesty to 631 military detainees on June 10 and to 444 more on September 11, his 61st birthday.

The assembly elections were controversial. Almost all the seats were won by the New Society Movement headed by Marcos. A hasty coalition of opponents to martial law, the Laban (People's Front) Party, charged fraud, police intimidation, and other irregularities. The largest demonstration against the government since martial law began was held in Manila on the eve of voting, and public protests continued after votes were counted.

The main contest was in Manila. Laban contested the city's 21 assembly seats but lost to a ticket headed by Mrs. Marcos. The opposition list was led by former senator Benigno S. Aquino, Jr., who was in jail. He had been sentenced to death by a military court on Nov. 25, 1977, on charges of subversion, illegal possession of firearms, and murder. However, Marcos then ordered the trial of his main political opponent to be reopened, and proceedings were later suspended. During 1978 a movement began to have Aquino released. Despite support from the head of the Roman Catholic Church in the Philippines and others, he remained imprisoned.

The assembly elections provoked such protest that on May 26 the government announced the postponement of municipal and provincial elections. It said that the disruption in April made it doubtful that the nation could "endure another election."

Two guerrilla wars continued unabated. The main one, centred in the southern islands, was between an estimated 20,000 Muslim rebels seeking autonomy and some 50,000 government troops and local forces. After the breakdown of negotiations in 1977, sporadic ambushes kept much of the southern Philippines unsettled. The leadership of

Philippines

PHILIPPINES

Education. (1975–76) Primary, pupils 8,365,470, teachers 261,817; secondary, pupils 1,591,594; vocational, pupils 662,949; secondary and vocational, teachers 72,778; higher, students 764,725, teaching staff 31,783.

Finance. Monetary unit: peso, with (Sept. 18, 1978) a free rate of 7.36 pesos to U.S. $1 (14.43 pesos = £1 sterling). Gold, SDR's, and foreign exchange (June 1978) U.S. $1,902,000,000. Budget (1977 actual): revenue 24,-803,000,000 pesos; expenditure 27,526,000,000 pesos. Gross national product (1977) 151,980,000,000 pesos. Money supply (June 1978) 14,492,000,000 pesos. Cost of living (1975 = 100; June 1978) 121.1.

Foreign Trade. (1977) Imports 31,609,000,000 pesos; exports 22,951,000,000 pesos. Import sources: Japan 25%; U.S. 20%; Saudi Arabia 8%. Export destinations: U.S. 35%; Japan 23%; The Netherlands 9%. Main exports: sugar 16%; coconut oil 13%; copper ores 8%; fruit and vegetables 8%; timber 6%; copra 6%.

Transport and Communications. Roads (1975) 112,870 km. Motor vehicles in use (1976): passenger 386,-200; commercial (including buses) 281,000. Railways: (1973) 1,150 km; traffic (1976) 780 million passenger-km, freight 40 million net ton-km. Air traffic (1976): 3,050,000,-000 passenger-km; freight 111.9 million net ton-km. Shipping (1977): merchant vessels 100 gross tons and over 504; gross tonnage 1,146,529. Telephones (Jan. 1977) 542,000. Radio receivers (Dec. 1975) 1,850,000. Television receivers (Dec. 1974) 711,000.

Agriculture. Production (in 000; metric tons; 1977): rice 7,150; corn 3,037; sweet potatoes (1976) c. 986; cassava (1976) c. 679; sugar, raw value 2,685; bananas c. 1,210; pineapples c. 440; copra c. 2,400; coffee c. 80; tobacco c. 60; rubber c. 58; pork c. 374; timber (cu m; 1976) 33,527; fish catch (1976) 1,430. Livestock (in 000; March 1977): cattle c. 2,373; buffalo c. 5,150; pigs c. 9,700; goats c. 1,400; horses c. 320; chickens c. 48,230.

Industry. Production (in 000; metric tons; 1976): iron ore (metal content) 354; chrome ore (oxide content) 158; copper ore (metal content) 238; gold (troy oz) 500; silver (troy oz) 1,500; cement (1977) 4,047; petroleum products 8,595; sulfuric acid (1977) 257; coal (1977) 280; electricity (kw-hr) 14,740,000.

the rebel organization, the Moro National Liberation Front, was challenged in an apparent government attempt to split it, but the 42-nation Conference of Islamic States continued to recognize Nur Misuari as the Front's leader.

The other guerrilla action, by the Communist Party's New People's Army, continued on a smaller, more widely scattered scale. The party's chairman, José Maria Sison, was captured and on June 23 was charged with leading a rebellion. This did not seem to hinder the Communist effort to strengthen their rural base areas throughout the islands.

Negotiations with the United States concerning U.S. military bases in the islands were concluded December 31. Under the new agreement the Philippines would receive up to $500 million in aid over five years in return for continued "unhampered" use of the bases by the U.S. Overall security at the installations would be a Philippine responsibility.   (HENRY S. BRADSHER)

Photography

In its technological evolution during 1978 still photography was strikingly marked by its use of sophisticated microelectronic circuitry to perform functions that in the past had been mechanical and directly under the photographer's manual control. As an international industry photography was troubled by the drop of the U.S. dollar in relation to other national currencies and by associated trade imbalances. In general the worldwide market for photographic products and services continued to grow, but, as during the preceding year, profits declined and competitive pressures remained high. Photography maintained and even enlarged its status as a form of visual creativity of interest to museums, galleries, art historians, the academic establishment, and an increasing share of the art-oriented public. The revival or expected return of such quality picture magazines as *Life* and *Look* and the birth of new outlets for photographic reportage breathed fresh life into photojournalism.

Cameras and Lenses. Canon vigorously maintained its position of innovative leadership among manufacturers of sophisticated single-lens-reflex (SLR) 35-mm cameras. Production of its revolutionary AE-1 passed the million mark in 1978, making it one of the most successful high-quality cameras ever marketed. In March Canon introduced another impressive camera, the A-1, which offered the user an unprecedented array of five exposure-automation options plus manual: shutter priority, aperture priority, programmed, automatic flash, and automatic stop-down metering with most Canon non-FD lenses. Other features included an electronically governed cloth focal-plane shutter with a continuous range of speeds from 30 to 1/1,000 sec and an accessory autowinder with a maximum rate of five frames per second.

Another interesting and highly automatic camera was the Konica FS-1, introduced in late 1978. A relatively compact shutter-priority auto-exposure model, it featured a built-in, battery-powered motor-wind system and a semiautomatic method for loading 35-mm film. The user simply dropped a 35-mm cassette into a chamber, placed the film leader in contact with a nonslotted take-up spool, and closed the camera back. The FS-1 did the rest, automatically advancing the film to position the first frame for exposure. The camera had an electronically controlled shutter with speeds from 2 to 1/1,000 sec plus B and accepted any Konica bayonet-mount lens. Nippon Kogaku unveiled the Nikon FE, a fully automatic, aperture-priority sibling of the previously introduced compact Nikon FM. With a newly formulated 50-mm Nikkor f/1.8 standard lens, the FE accepted easily interchangeable viewing screens and could be used with the Nikon MD-11 motor drive and Nikon SB-10 electronic flash unit.

Among compact, non-SLR 35-mm cameras, many new models appeared with built-in miniature electronic flash units, and several makers, including Fuji, Chinon, and Cosina, introduced autofocusing models using the Honeywell Visitronic module. Olympus brought out the smallest rangefinder 35 to date, tentatively designated the XA, with a 25-mm Zuiko f/2.8 lens, aperture-priority exposure automation, shutter speeds from 10 to 1/500 sec, and an unusual "clam shell" dust cover to protect the lens when the camera was not in use. The most unusual 110 pocket camera of the year was the Pentax Auto 110, the first automatic-exposure 110 SLR "system" camera with interchangeable lenses and motor-wind and automatic flash accessories. With a 35-mm SLR configuration but considerably smaller in scale, the new Pentax had a top shutter speed of 1/750 sec and offered a choice of three bayonet-mount lenses.

Polaroid demonstrated its Sonar autofocusing system, which used ultrasonic "chirps" to determine camera-to-subject distance. The heart of the system was an electrostatic transducer that both generated the ranging signals and received their echoes. A high-frequency crystal oscillator measured the elapsed time, microcircuitry calculated subject distance, and a miniature motor moved the outer lens element to the position of sharp focus from ten inches to infinity. The system appeared on modified versions of Polaroid's SX-70 and Pronto!

Numerous technical advances continued to allow the design of increasingly lighter and more compact lenses of improved performance. This effect was particularly striking in the case of zoom and telephoto optics. The new zooms often combined a macro (extreme closeup) focusing capability with the normal zoom range in one continuous adjustment, without the need to switch into a special macro mode. Zoom ranges were widened, too, with such lenses as Tokina's 28–85-mm *f*/4 and Makina's Auto Makinon MC 28–80-mm *f*/3.5 providing the user with a choice of true wide-angle to medium telephoto photography.

Films and Papers. The trend toward establishing a film speed index of ASA 400 as the norm for colour as well as black-and-white continued apace during the year. Kodak introduced Ektachrome 400, an E-6–processed transparency film available in 20- and 36-exposure 35-mm and 120-roll sizes. Although balanced for daylight, it was unusually tolerant of tungsten-, mixed-, and even some fluorescent-light situations, and could be push-processed with good results to exposure indexes of 800 and even 1600. Fuji brought forth a new high-speed black-and-white film, Neopan 400, in 35-mm and 120 sizes. Competitively fine-grained and sharp for such a fast emulsion, it could be push-processed to an exposure index of 1600 with acceptable results. Agfa introduced in Europe its ASA 400 colour print film, Agfacolor CNS 400. It was compatible with Kodak C-41 processing and came supplied in 35-mm and 110 cartridge loads. Another new film was Kodachrome 40, an extraordinarily sharp slide film balanced for 3,400 K that replaced Kodachrome II Professional, Type A. In instant materials Polaroid introduced a colour-improved version of its SX-70 film that also developed to completion in about four minutes, or approximately twice as fast as its predecessor.

For professional use Cibachrome introduced an improved, soft-contrast version of its Cibachrome (positive-to-positive) colour printing paper and supplied two new surfaces, a semi-matte RC-Pearl and an ultra-glossy PS-Brilliant. Reversing a trend by leading manufacturers away from fibre-based papers to RC (resin-coated) materials, Ilford unveiled its Gallerie, a quality chlorobromide black-and-white printing paper available in three contrast grades in most standard sizes.

Cultural Trends. Along with photography's growing status as an art form and the recognition of its role in social-historical documentation, much attention was being turned to its past. As a result collections of important work were being discovered or rediscovered in dusty attics and neglected archives.

Collector Sam Wagstaff's personal and discern-

A new autoradiographic process, developed at the Marshall Space Flight Center, Huntsville, Alabama, is able to bring out details in faded or underexposed photographs. (Top) a faded 1908 photograph; (below) image of the same photo after enhancement.

NASA

Dilemma of fallen cyclist, captured on film by French Press Agency staffer Daniel Janin, took first prize for sports photography in the 17th annual Grand Prix Martini competition.

Year. Top winner in the international World Press Photo Awards for spot news was Leslie Hammond of *The Argus*, Cape Town, South Africa. The Pulitzer Prizes for photography suffered a double embarrassment. It developed that the Pulitzer for spot news photography, eventually awarded to freelancer John W. Blair, had erroneously been given to another photographer because of a United Press International credit blunder. Then, three photographs of Associated Press stringer J. Ross Baughman that won the feature photography Pulitzer were found to have been previously disqualified by an Overseas Press Club jury from its own competition because of questions over the authenticity of the photos and the manner in which they were obtained. Baughman had joined a Rhodesian cavalry unit as an armed soldier to get his eyewitness reportage of Army atrocities.

(ARTHUR GOLDSMITH)

See also Motion Pictures.
[628.D; 735.G.1]

Physics

The Josephson Effect. For many years a major goal of computer technology has been to decrease the machine cycle time, or the time required to carry out the simplest operation. Because the speed of an electronic computer is limited to the speed of electrical conduction, *i.e.*, the speed of light, efforts to decrease machine cycle time have concentrated on spacing logic and memory circuits as closely as possible. The introduction of tiny magnetizable ferrite cores produced a machine cycle time of the order of one microsecond (10^{-6} second), and their replacement by semiconductor switches reduced the cycle time to about 60 nanoseconds (60×10^{-9} seconds). It was possible to increase the speed of semiconductor switches still further but at the expense of high power consumption.

Despite continued advances in the microminiaturization of electronic circuitry, close packing of components has been restricted by the problem of electrical resistance within the circuits and of consequent heat generation, which becomes increasingly troublesome as components are crowded together. One technique with the potential to minimize this difficulty is based on the superconducting Josephson effect. Recent results of small-scale tests in the U.S. at IBM and Bell Laboratories showed that a machine cycle time of a few nanoseconds seemed highly likely. The Josephson effect occurs within a configuration called a Josephson junction, which consists of an extremely thin insulating layer, usually of oxide, between two metals that become superconducting (offer no electrical resistance) when cooled to temperatures near absolute zero. For low electrical currents and low external magnetic fields the junction is superconducting, but it can readily be switched to a resistive state by the application of currents or fields above certain thresholds. The energy consumed or transformed into heat during this operation is extremely small, and switching time between superconducting and resistive states can be quite rapid, on the order of ten picoseconds

ing taste was displayed in a traveling exhibition and accompanying catalog, *A Book of Photographs*, which opened at the Corcoran Gallery in Washington, D.C., early in the year. Late pioneer photojournalist and fashion photographer Martin Munkacsi was given an impressive retrospective at New York City's International Center of Photography, which also held an exhibition and gathering by members of the Photo League, a seminal photographic organization active in the years immediately following World War II. Another backward look was the major Richard Avedon retrospective at New York City's Metropolitan Museum of Art and an accompanying book, which at $50 per autographed copy was probably the most expensive all black-and-white photography book yet published in the U.S. Images of an imperial past were resurrected in Lala Deen Dayal's photographs of India during the height of British rule and in two splendid shows and accompanying books, *Imperial China: Photographs 1850–1912* and *The Face of China as Seen by Photographers & Travelers 1860–1912*, the former from Asia House Gallery in New York City and the latter from the Philadelphia Museum of Art.

Even the most controversial contemporary exhibition of the year, "Mirrors and Windows," at the Museum of Modern Art in Manhattan, was a retrospective, an attempt to summarize the significant achievements in photography as "art" since 1960. It succeeded as a representative, if somewhat familiar, collection of recent formalist, introspective, conceptual, and minimalist trends in photography but was severely criticized for its lack of humanistic, documentary, and photojournalistic work.

At the Pictures of the Year competition co-sponsored by the National Press Photographers Association and the University of Missouri School of Journalism, Michael Wirtz of the *Suburban Trib*, Hinsdale, Ill., was honoured as Newspaper Photographer of the Year and *National Geographic* staffer David Harvey as Magazine Photographer of the

$(10 \times 10^{-12}$ seconds) for individual devices a few microns in length and width.

For practical purposes, using a single Josephson junction as a switch activated by small changes in currents requires a large junction area, which increases capacitance and slows switching time. Using two or more junctions in parallel reduces the required junction area and hence increases the switching speed. Another advantage can be gained by using superconducting lines to connect circuit components. One disadvantage of the technique is that computer designers must cope with the technology of liquid helium, which is needed to bring the circuitry to superconducting temperatures.

Particle Physics. The report in 1977 by Stanford University physicist William Fairbank and co-workers that they had observed niobium spheres with charges which were a fraction of the charge on the electron accelerated speculation on the possibility of "free" quarks. Theoreticians were hardening toward the view that quarks, although apparently the basic building blocks of much of matter, could not exist in isolation but only in combination as protons, neutrons, and certain other subatomic particles.

The niobium spheres that produced the Stanford results had been heated on a tungsten substrate. To test whether tungsten could be the carrier of free quarks a similar experiment was carried out at San Francisco State University by Roger Bland and colleagues using small tungsten particles. Their results showed no evidence for fractional charges. Many centres throughout the world were also ac-

tive in this field and further developments were expected in the near future.

The four known fundamental forces of the physical world are gravity, the strong interaction (which binds atomic nuclei), the weak interaction (involved in radioactive decay), and electromagnetism. Suspecting underlying relationships among them, physicists have long sought a workable theory that explains them as different manifestations of the same basic phenomenon. A partial attempt, the unified field theory of Steven Weinberg and Abdus Salam, devoted itself to a combined picture of the electromagnetic force and the weak interaction. One prediction of this model is that a type of symmetry found in particle interactions, called parity, should be violated in proton-electron collisions; *i.e.*, protons should show a preference for interacting with left-handed, rather than right-handed, electrons. The handedness of an electron depends upon the direction of its spin relative to its direction of motion: an electron with its spin oriented in the direction of motion is right-handed (just as an ordinary screw moves forward when turned to the right, or clockwise), whereas an electron with its spin against the direction of motion is left-handed. Particle interactions that show no preference for handedness are said to conserve parity; preferential interactions, such as that predicted by the Weinberg-Salam theory, violate parity.

Some previous attempts to find such parity violations, *e.g.*, in low-energy laser experiments on atomic bismuth at the universities of Oxford and

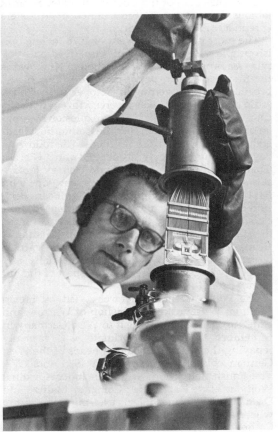 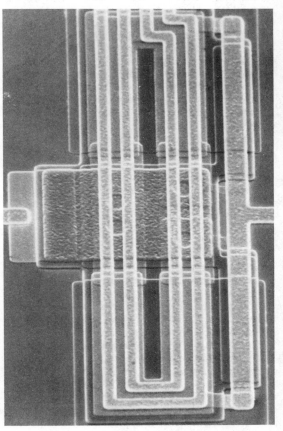

IBM scientist (far left) lowers an experimental memory chip, or integrated circuit, of Josephson junctions into a vat of liquid helium for testing. Scanning electron micrograph of a single Josephson logic circuit (left) reveals four Josephson junctions—the small circular depressions near the centre of the image—and several vertical control lines. The width of each line is about five microns, or 1/5,000 inch.

Washington, detected none within measurable range, although a later experiment at the Institute of Nuclear Physics at Novosibirsk in the Soviet Union, also using bismuth vapour, contradicted these results. In 1978 strong support for the theory came from experiments at the Stanford Linear Accelerator Laboratory (SLAC), in which proton targets in deuterium (hydrogen-2) nuclei were bombarded with polarized electron beams; *i.e.*, beams made up predominantly of either left- or right-handed particles. Left-handed electrons were observed to scatter more strongly during the collisions than right-handed ones by a difference (about one part in 5×10^3) that fit perfectly with the model. Coupled with promising results in earlier experiments involving neutrino-nuclei interactions, the evidence pointed toward the existence of only three fundamental forces—the strong interaction, gravity, and a new, unified force to which physicists, somewhat uncharacteristically, had yet to attach a fitting name.

In midyear scientists at the European Organization for Nuclear Research (CERN) in Geneva announced success in storing the first beam of antiprotons. As part of a project to create colliding beams of protons and their antimatter counterparts, about 240 antiprotons were injected into a magnetic ring 24 m (79 ft) in diameter and kept circulating 85 hours. Of the initial number 80 survived, the disappearance of the remainder being ascribed to collisions with molecules of gas in the ring. The total annihilation that comes from contact between antimatter and the ordinary world of matter and the tendency of a beam of antiprotons to swell from electrostatic repulsion make the storage of these particles extremely difficult. Success at CERN was due to a technique that used a rapid electronic feedback system to keep the particles focused magnetically into a tight beam.

Aside from being a stepping-stone to a greater goal, survival of the beam was in itself significant, because it provided a new experimental lower limit on the lifetime of the antiproton that was several orders of magnitude greater than previous studies, which had only measured the survival time of the antiproton between its creation and its annihilation mere nanoseconds later. Theoretically the antiproton, which was believed to be identical to the extremely stable proton except for its opposite, negative charge, should have a similar lifetime—at least 10^{28} years, which is much longer than the estimated age of the universe itself.

Ultrahigh Pressure Research. In June Peter M. Bell and Ho-Kwang Mao of the Carnegie Institution of Washington (D.C.) reported achievement of the highest sustained pressure ever generated—1.7 megabars or 25×10^6 psi—using a cell made of two clear natural diamond anvils precisely cut and aligned to withstand the load. To measure the pressure, ruby crystals were sandwiched between the two opposing diamond faces and made to fluoresce using laser light. Because the wavelength of ruby fluorescence shifts in a known way with pressure changes, pressure in the diamond cell could be calculated indirectly from measurement of the emitted light.

The experimenters' high-pressure technique du-

plicated pressures within the Earth's core near the core-mantle boundary and was expected to spur geophysical studies of the behaviour of rocks lying deep within the Earth. The record pressure also fell just within the pressure range of one-to-ten megabars within which hydrogen was believed to transform into a liquid metallic state. Once created, metallic hydrogen might be both stable and superconducting at room temperature.

In November a team from Cornell University, Ithaca, N.Y., headed by Arthur L. Ruoff, reported the transformation of the normally gaseous element xenon into a transient metallic state within a diamond-anvil cell at a pressure of 320 kilobars and a temperature of 32 K ($-241°$ C). The change to the metallic form was signaled by a sharp increase in conductivity across xenon-coated microelectrodes mounted between the anvil faces.

(S. B. PALMER)

See also Nobel Prizes.
[111.H; 112.E; 124.G.3; 125.D.8; 735.D; 735.K.1]

Poland

A people's republic of eastern Europe, Poland is bordered by the Baltic Sea, the U.S.S.R., Czechoslovakia, and East Germany. Area: 312,677 sq km (120,725 sq mi). Pop. (1978 est.): 35 million. Cap. and largest city: Warsaw (pop., 1978 est., 1,532,-100). Language: Polish. Religion: predominantly Roman Catholic. First secretary of the Polish United Workers' (Communist) Party in 1978, Edward Gierek; chairman of the Council of State, Henryk Jablonski; chairman of the Council of Ministers (premier), Piotr Jaroszewicz.

The most momentous event of 1978 for the Polish people was the election of Karol Cardinal Wojtyla (*see* BIOGRAPHIES), archbishop of Krakow, as the first non-Italian pope since 1523. This news, broadcast on the evening of October 16 by Polish radio and television, was received throughout the country with joy and pride. The explosion of popular enthusiasm was such that the Communist leadership had to join in the rejoicing. The following day Communist Party leader Edward Gierek, Chairman of the Council of State Henryk Jablonski, and Premier Piotr Jaroszewicz sent Pope John Paul II a message saying that "the significant decision by the conclave of cardinals has caused great satisfaction in Poland. On the papal throne, for the first time in history, a son of the Polish nation is sitting." The pope replied that it was his "earnest desire to see Poland developing spiritually and materially in peace, justice, and respect of the human person."

The Polish Catholic hierarchy, led by Stefan Cardinal Wyszynski, archbishop of Warsaw and Gniezno, paid a six-day visit to West Germany in September. The Polish primate was formally repaying the visits to Poland of heads of the West German episcopal conference in 1975 and 1977. The Polish delegation, which included Cardinal Wojtyla, stayed at Fulda, Cologne, Mainz, and Dachau, the former Nazi extermination camp where about 10,000 Poles, including 858 Roman Catholic priests, perished. Preaching at the Mu-

Poland

Pipelines:
see Energy; Transportation

Plastics Industry:
see Industrial Review

Poetry:
see Literature

Education. (1977-78) Primary, pupils 4,144,544, teachers 187,885; secondary, pupils 420,973, teachers 25,375; vocational, pupils 1,392,972; teacher training, students 27,046; vocational and teacher training, teachers 73,102; higher, students 306,082, teaching staff 51,398.

Finance. Monetary unit: zloty, with (Sept. 18, 1978) a basic rate of 3.32 exchange zlotys to U.S. $1 (6.50 exchange zlotys = £1 sterling) and a commercial and tourist rate of 32 zlotys to U.S. $1 (62 zlotys = £1 sterling). Budget (1978 est.): revenue 1,059,-900,000,000 zlotys; expenditure 1,057,100,000,000 zlotys. Net material product (1976) 1,596,000,-000,000 zlotys.

Foreign Trade. (1977) Imports 48,752,000,000 exchange zlotys; exports 40,982,000,000 exchange zlotys. Import sources: U.S.S.R. 29%; West Germany 7%; East Germany 8%; Czechoslovakia 6%; U.K. 6%. Export destinations: U.S.S.R. 32%; East Germany 9%; Czechoslovakia 8%; West Germany 6%. Main exports (1975): machinery 20%; coal 16%; transport equipment 12%; textiles and clothing 7%; chemicals 6%; food 6%.

Transport and Communications. Roads (1976) 300,822 km (including 139 km expressways). Motor vehicles in use (1976): passenger 1,290,100; commercial 467,100. Railways: (1976) 23,855 km (including 5,988 km electrified); traffic (1977) 44,311,000,000 passenger-km, freight 135,407,-000,000 net ton-km. Air traffic (1977): 1,666,000,000 passenger-km; freight 15,710,000 net ton-km. Shipping (1977): merchant vessels 100 gross tons and over 773; gross tonnage 3,447,517. Telephones (Jan. 1977) 2,753,000. Radio licenses (Dec. 1976) 8,228,-000. Television licenses (Dec. 1976) 6,820,000.

Agriculture. Production (in 000; metric tons; 1977): wheat 5,310; rye c. 6,200; barley 3,404; oats c. 2,600; potatoes c. 49,000; sugar, raw value c. 1,900; rapeseed 700; cabbages (1976) c. 1,563; onions c. 340; tomatoes c. 350; carrots (1976) c. 444; cucumbers (1976) c. 508; apples c. 1,000; tobacco c. 100; butter c. 270; cheese c. 346; hen's eggs c. 526; beef and veal c. 790; pork c. 1,530; timber (cu m; 1976) 21,596; fish catch (1976) 750. Livestock (in 000; June 1977): cattle 13,019; pigs 20,051; sheep 3,934; horses (1976) 2,151; chickens c. 200,000.

Industry. Index of industrial production (1975 = 100; 1977) 124. Fuel and power (in 000; metric tons; 1977): coal 186,112; brown coal 40,680; coke (1976) 17,915; crude oil 460; natural gas (cu m) 7,170,000; manufactured gas (cu m; 1976) 8,010,000; electricity (kw-hr) 109,364,000. Production (in 000; metric tons; 1977): cement 21,298; iron ore (30% metal content) 720; pig iron 81,080; crude steel 17,841; aluminum (1976) 103; copper (1976) 270; lead (1976) 81; zinc (1976) 238; petroleum products (1976) 14,162; sulfuric acid 3,293; fertilizers (nutrient content; 1976) nitrogenous 1,548, phosphate 928; cotton yarn 219; wool yarn 107; man-made fibres 238; cotton fabrics (m) 948,000; woolen fabrics (m) 126,000; passenger cars (units) 279; commercial vehicles (units) 71. Merchant vessels launched (100 gross tons and over; 1977) 492,000 gross tons.

---

nich cathedral, Cardinal Wyszynski emphasized the need for both nations to work for peace and a Christian future.

In June 1978 the plenary Polish bishops' conference adopted a resolution demanding recognition of the Roman Catholic Church as a separate juridical entity; the conference proclaimed once more the church's right and duty to teach religion to the country's youth; it also protested against the press and book publishing censorship and the biased teaching of Polish history.

In March 1977 Poland had ratified the two UN covenants on civil, political, and cultural rights, which had been approved unanimously by the 21st UN General Assembly in 1966. But the government's recognition of these rights left much to be desired, and in 1978 a few citizens' committees, notably the Social Self-Defense Committee, presented to the state authorities petitions demanding observance of the covenants' stipulations. Considering such petitions as "antistate activity," the government ordered a campaign of individual harassment against those who had signed them.

Poland's general economic position improved in 1978. During the first half of the year industrial production rose by 6.2%. It was expected that in 1978 the country would extract about 200 million tons of hard coal, generate 120 billion kw-hr of electric power, and produce 20 million tons of steel. In November Premier Jaroszewicz and three ministers visited Tokyo to discuss Polish-Japanese economic cooperation.

The Communist rulers of Poland had ignored the date of November 11, which commemorated not only the victory of the Allies over Germany in 1918 but also the proclamation in Warsaw of the independence of the restored Polish state at that time. In 1978, the 60th anniversary of these events, these tactics were partly abandoned. On November 6, on the eve of the 61st anniversary of the Russian Revolution, at a solemn meeting of the Sejm (parliament), Gierek paid homage to the will of the Polish nation to recover its lost independence but added that the Russian Revolution and the "great mind of Lenin" had opened the road to Poland's rebirth. On November 11 some 5,000 Poles marched through Warsaw to the tomb of the Unknown Soldier singing patriotic songs of 1793 and 1831—a demonstration not officially planned.

During the year Gierek visited Soviet leader Leonid I. Brezhnev twice: on April 18 in Moscow he was decorated by Brezhnev with the Order of the October Revolution; and on August 3 at Oreanda, in the Crimea, the two leaders "reaffirmed the adherence of their countries to the policy of détente." The most prominent Western visitor to Poland was Pres. Valéry Giscard d'Estaing of France, who in September at the Carpathian mountain resort of Bieszczady discussed with Gierek bilateral affairs and also called for the continuation of détente and for "an end to the quantitative and qualitative arms race."   (K. M. SMOGORZEWSKI)

Political Parties

The following table is a general world guide to political parties. All countries that were independent on Dec. 31, 1978, are included; there are a number for which no analysis of political activities can be given. Parties are included in most instances only if represented in parliaments (in the lower house in bicameral legislatures); the figures in the last column indicate the number of seats obtained in the last general election (figures in parentheses are those of the penultimate one). The date of the most recent election follows the name of the country.

The code letters in the affiliation column show the relative political position of the parties within each country; there is, therefore, no entry in this column for single-party states. There are obvious difficulties involved in labeling parties within the political spectrum of a given country. The key chosen is as follows: F–fascist; ER–extreme right; R–right; CR–centre right; C–centre; L–non-Marxist left; SD–social democratic; S–socialist; EL–extreme left; and K–Communist.

The percentages in the column "Voting strength" indicate proportions of the valid votes cast for the respective parties, or the number of registered voters who went to the polls in single-party states.
[541.D.2]

Police:
see Crime and Law
Enforcement

COUNTRY AND NAME OF PARTY	Affiliation	Voting strength (%)	Parliamentary representation
Afghanistan			
Pro-Soviet government since April 27, 1978	—	—	—
Albania (November 1978)			
Albanian Labour (Communist)	—	99.9	250 (250)
Algeria (February 1977)			
National Liberation Front	—	99.95	261
Angola, People's Republic of			
Movimento Popular de Libertaçao de Angola (MPLA)	—	—	—
Argentina			
Military junta since March 24, 1976	—	—	—
Australia (December 1977)			
National Country	R	...	19 (23)
Liberal	C	...	67 (65)
Australian Labor	L	...	38 (36)
Other		...	0 (3)
Austria (October 1975)			
Freiheitliche Partei Österreichs	R	5.4	10 (10)
Österreichische Volkspartei	C	42.9	80 (80)
Sozialistische Partei Österreichs	SD	50.4	93 (93)
Kommunistische Partei Österreichs	K	1.2	0 (0)
Bahamas, The (July 1977)			
Progressive Liberal Party	CR	55.0	30 (30)
Bahamian Democratic Party	L	...	5 (8)
Free National Movement	L	...	2
Vanguard Party	SD	...	0 —
Bahrain			
Emirate, no parties	—	—	—
Bangladesh			
Military government since Nov. 6, 1975	—	—	—
Barbados (September 1976)			
Democratic Labour	C	...	7 (18)
Barbados Labour	L	...	17 (6)
Belgium (December 1978)			
Vlaams Blok	ER	...	1 (0)
Volksunie	R	...	14 (20)
Front Démocratique Francophone	R	...	10 (11)
Rassemblement Wallon	R	...	5 (4)
Parti Libéral {Flemish	CR	...	22 (17)
{Wallon	CR	...	15 (16)
Parti Social-Chrétien {Flemish	C	...	57 (56)
{Wallon	C	...	25 (24)
Parti Socialiste Belge {Flemish	SD	...	26 (27)
{Wallon	SD	...	32 (35)
Parti Communiste	K	...	4 (2)
UDRT (Brussels anti-tax)	—	...	1 (0)
Benin (Dahomey)			
Marxist-Leninist military government since Oct. 26, 1972	—	—	—
Bhutan			
A monarchy without parties	—	—	—
Bolivia			
Military junta since Nov. 9, 1974	—	—	—
Botswana (October 1974)			
Botswana Democratic Party	C	...	27 (24)
Botswana People's Party	L	...	2 (3)
Botswana National Front	EL	...	2 (3)
Brazil (November 1978)			
Aliança Renovadora Nacional (ARENA)	CR	...	... (199)
Movimento Democrático Brasileiro (MDB)	L	...	... (165)
Bulgaria (May 1976)			
Bulgarian Communist Party {Fatherland			272 (266)
People's Agrarian Union {Front		99.9	100 (100)
Nonparty			28 (34)
Burma (January 1978)			
Burma Socialist Program Party	—	99.0	464 (451)
Burundi (October 1974)			
Tutsi ethnic minority government	—	—	—
Cambodia (March 1976)			
People's Kampuchea Revolutionary Party	—		
Cameroon (May 1978)			
Cameroonian National Union	—	99.98	120 (120)
Canada (July 1974)			
Social Credit	R	5.0	11 (15)
Progressive Conservative	CR	35.6	95 (107)
Liberal	C	42.9	141 (109)
New Democratic	L	15.6	16 (31)
Independents	—	...	1 (2)
Cape Verde Islands (June 1975)			
African Party for the Independence of Guinea-Bissau and Cape Verde (PAIGC)		84.0	56
Central African Empire			
Military government since Jan. 1, 1966	—	—	—
Chad			
Military government since April 13, 1975	—	—	—
Chile			
Military junta since Sept. 11, 1973	—	—	—
China, People's Republic of (February 1978)			
Communist (Kungchantang) National People's Congress	—	...	3,500
Colombia (February 1978)			
Partido Conservador	R	...	86 (66)
Partido Liberal	C	...	109 (113)
Unión Nacional de Oposisión	L	...	4 (20)
Comoros (December 1974)			
Single party rule from Aug. 3, 1975	—	—	—
Congo			
Military government since Sept. 1968	—	—	—
Costa Rica (February 1978)			
Partido de Liberación Nacional	R	...	25 (27)
Partido de Unidad	C	...	27 (16)
Three left-wing parties	L	...	5 (8)
Cuba (November 1976)			
Partido Comunista Cubano	—	...	481
Cyprus (September 1976)			
De facto partition in two parts	—	—	—
Czechoslovakia (October 1976)			
National Front (Communist Party of Czechoslovakia and others)	—	...	...
Denmark (February 1977)			
Conservative	R	8.5	15 (10)
Liberal Democratic (Venstre)	CR	12.0	21 (42)
Christian People's	CR	3.4	6 (9)
Progress (M. Glistrup)	C	14.6	26 (24)
Radical Liberal (Radikale Venstre)	C	3.6	6 (13)
Justice (Retsforbund)	C	3.3	6 (0)
Centre Democrats (E. Jakobsen)	L	6.4	11 (4)
Social Democrats	SD	37.0	65 (53)
Socialist People's	EL	3.9	7 (9)
Left Socialists	EL	2.7	5 (4)
Communists	K	3.7	7 (7)
Djibouti (May 1977)			
Ligue Populaire Africaine pour l'Indépendance (mainly Somali)	C	...	33
Front de Libération de la Côte des Somalis	L	...	30
Dominica (November 1978)			
Dominica Freedom Party	C	...	...
Dominica Labour Party	L	...	...
Dominican Republic (May 1978)			
Partido Reformista	C	...	92 (86)
Partido Revolucionario	SD	...	49 ...
Others	—	...	... (5)
Ecuador (July 1978)			
Partido Conservador	R	...	...
Partido Liberal	C	...	...
Concentración de Fuerzas Populares	L	...	...
Egypt (November 1976)			
Arab {Social Democrats		...	12
Socialist {Egyptian Arab Socialists	—	...	336
Union {National Progressives		...	2
El Salvador (March 1978)			
Partido de Conciliación Nacional	R	...	50 (52)
Partido Popular Salvadoreño	L	...	4 (0)
Equatorial Guinea			
Partido Único Nacional de los Trabajadores			
Ethiopia			
Military government since 1974	—	—	—
Fiji (September 1977)			
Alliance Party (mainly Fijian)	—	...	36 (24)
National Federation (mainly Indian)	—	...	15 (26)
Others	—	...	1 (2)
Finland (September 1975)			
Conservative Party	R	18.4	34 (33)
Swedish People's Party	R	4.7	10 (11)
Centre Party (ex-Agrarian)	C	17.7	39 (35)
Liberal Party	C	4.4	9 (6)
Christian League	C	3.3	9 (4)
Rural Party	L	3.6	2 (5)
Social Democratic Party	SD	25.0	54 (55)
People's Democratic League	K	19.0	41 (37)
Others	—	4.0	2 (14)
France (March 1978)			
Centre-Right:			
Gaullists (Rassemblement pour la République)	R	25.84	148 (185)
Giscardians (Union pour la Démocratie Française)	CR	23.18	137 (54)
Other	—	1.64	6 (36)
Union of Left:			
Parti Radical	L	2.02	10 (12)
Parti Socialiste	SD	28.46	103 (89)
Parti Communiste	K	18.83	86 (73)
Others		...	1 (9)
Gabon (February 1973)			
Parti Démocratique Gabonais	—	...	70
Gambia, The (April 1977)			
People's Progressive Party	C	...	29 (28)
United Party	L	...	2 (3)
German Democratic Republic (October 1976)			
National Front (Sozialistische Einheitspartei and others)	—	99.9	500 (434)
Germany, Federal Republic of (October 1976)			
Christlich-Demokratische Union	R	38.0	190 (177)
Christlich-Soziale Union	R	10.6	53 (48)
Freie Demokratische Partei	C	7.9	39 (41)
Sozialdemokratische Partei Deutschlands	SD	42.6	214 (230)
Deutsche Kommunistische Partei	K	0.3	0 (0)
Ghana			
Military government since 1972	—	—	—
Greece (November 1977)			
National Rally	R	6.82	5 (0)
New Democracy Party	CR	41.85	172 (215)
Democratic Centre Union	C	11.95	15 (57)
New Liberals (mainly in Crete)	C	1.08	2 (0)
Panhellenic Socialist Movement	SD	25.33	93 (15)
Left Alliance (Eurocommunist)	EL	2.72	2 (6)
Greek Communist Party (pro-Moscow)	K	9.36	11 (5)
Others		0.89	— (14)
Grenada (December 1976)			
United Labour Party	L	...	9 (13)
People's Alliance (coalition parties)	—	...	6 (2)

COUNTRY AND NAME OF PARTY	Affiliation	Voting strength (%)	Parliamentary representation
Guatemala (March 1978)			
Movimiento de Liberación Nacional	CR	...	20
Partido Institucional Democrático	CR	...	17
Partido Demócrata Cristiano	C	...	7
Partido Revolucionario	L	...	14
Others	—	...	3
Guinea (December 1974)			
Parti Démocratique de Guinéa	—	100.0	150
Guinea-Bissau (1975)			
African Party for the Independence of Guinea-Bissau and Cape Verde (PAIGC)	—	...	92
Guyana (July 1973)			
People's National Congress	C	...	37 (30)
People's Progressive Party	EL	...	14 (19)
Others	—	...	2 (4)
Haiti			
Presidential dictatorship since 1957	—	—	—
Honduras			
Military junta since Dec. 4, 1972	—	—	—
Hungary (June 1975)			
Hungarian Socialist Workers' Party	} Patriotic People's Front		
Young Communist League			
National Council of Women		97.6	352
Hungarian Federation of Partisans			
Federation of National Minorities			
Iceland (June 1978)			
Independence (Conservative)	R	32.7	20 (25)
Progressive (Farmers' Party)	C	16.9	12 (17)
Union of Liberals and Leftists	L	3.5	0 (2)
Social Democratic	SD	22.0	14 (5)
People's Alliance	K	22.9	14 (11)
India (March 1977)			
Janata (People's) Party and allies:			
Janata (including Jan Sangh, Opposition Congress, Swatantra, Samyukta, and Praja Socialist parties)	—	...	295 (53)
Akali Dal (Sikh Party)	C	...	9 (1)
Dravida Munnetra Kazhagam	R	...	1 (23)
Communist-Marxist (pro-Chinese)	K	...	22 (25)
Five other parties	—	...	14 (3)
Congress Party and allies:			
Congress	C	...	150 (350)
Anna Dravida Munnetra Kazhagam	R	...	19
Communist (pro-Soviet)	K	...	7 (23)
Four smaller parties	—	...	7 (9)
Four independent parties	—	...	14 (28)
Indonesia (May 1977)			
Sekber Golkar (Functional Groups)	—	62.1	232 (236)
United Development Party (merger of four Islamic parties)	—	29.3	99 (94)
Partai Demokrasi Indonesia (merger of five nationalist and Christian parties)	—	8.6	29 (30)
Iran (June 1975)			
Rastakhiz (National Resurgence) Party	—	52.0	268
Iraq			
Military and Baath Party governments since 1958	—	...	...
Ireland (June 1977)			
Fianna Fail (Sons of Destiny)	C	...	84 (69)
Fine Gael (United Ireland)	C	...	43 (54)
Irish Labour Party	L	...	17 (19)
Sinn Fein (We Ourselves)	—	...	0 (0)
Others	—	...	4 (2)
Israel (May 1977)			
Likud (Herut, Liberal Alignment, La'am, and Free Centre)	R	33.4	43 (39)
Torah Front (Agudat Israel and Poalei Agudat Israel)	CR	4.8	5 (5)
National Religious	C	9.2	12 (10)
Democratic Movement for Change	C	11.6	15
Independent Liberal	C	1.2	1 (4)
Civil Rights Movement	L	1.2	1 (3)
Labour Alignment (Mapam, Mapai, Rafi, and Achdut Ha'avoda)	SD	24.6	32 (51)
Democratic Front for Peace and Equality (pro-Soviet)	K	4.6	5 (4)
United Arab List	—	1.2	1 (3)
Others	—	8.0	5 (1)
Italy (June 1976)			
Movimento Sociale Italiano	F }	6.1	35 (56)
Partito di Unità Monarchica	R }		
Partito Liberale Italiano	CR	1.3	5 (20)
Democrazia Cristiana	C	38.7	262 (267)
Partito Repubblicano Italiano	C	3.1	14 (15)
Partito Social-Democratico Italiano	L	3.4	15 (29)
Partito Socialista Italiano	SD	9.6	57 (61)
Democrazia Proletaria	EL	1.5	6 (0)
Partito Comunista Italiano	K	34.4	228 (179)
Südtiroler Volkspartei	—	0.5	3 (3)
Others	—	1.4	5 —
Ivory Coast (November 1970)			
Parti Démocratique de la Côte d'Ivoire	—	99.9	100
Jamaica (December 1976)			
People's National Party	L	...	48 (35)
Jamaica Labour Party	S	...	12 (18)
Japan (December 1976)			
Liberal-Democratic	R	41.8	249 (271)
Komeito (Clean Government)	CR	10.9	55 (29)
New Liberals	CR	4.2	17
Democratic Socialist	SD	6.3	29 (19)
Socialist	S	20.7	123 (118)
Communist	K	10.4	17 (38)
Independents and others	—	5.7	21 (16)
Jordan			
Royal government, no parties	—	—	60
Kenya (October 1974)			
Kenya African National Union	—	...	158 (171)
Korea, North (November 1977)			
Korean Workers' (Communist) Party	—	100.0	579
Korea, South (February 1973)			
Democratic Republican	CR	38.7	73
New Democratic	L	32.6	52
Democratic Unification	S	10.1	2
Independents	—	18.6	19
Kuwait			
Princely government, no parties	—	—	30
Laos, People's Democratic Republic of			
Lao People's Revolutionary Party	—	...	...
Lebanon (April 1972)			
Maronites (Roman Catholics)	—	...	30
Sunni Muslims	—	...	20
Shi'ite Muslims	—	...	19
Greek Orthodox	—	...	11
Druzes (Muslim sect)	—	...	6
Melchites (Greek Catholics)	—	...	6
Armenian Orthodox	—	...	4
Other Christian	—	...	2
Armenian Catholics	—	...	1
Lesotho			
Constitution suspended Jan. 30, 1970	—	—	—
Liberia (October 1975)			
True Whig Party	—	...	41
Libya			
Military government since Sept. 1, 1969	—	—	—
Liechtenstein (February 1978)			
Vaterländische Union	CR	...	8 (7)
Fortschrittliche Bürgerpartei	C	...	7 (8)
Luxembourg (May 1974)			
Parti Chrétien Social	CR	28.0	18 (21)
Parti Libéral	C	22.1	14 (11)
Parti Ouvrier Socialiste	SD	29.0	17 (15)
Parti Social Démocratique	S	9.1	5 (6)
Parti Communiste	K	10.4	5 (6)
Madagascar (June 1977)			
Avant-garde de la Révolution Malgache	C	...	112
Parti du Congrès de l'Indépendance	L	...	16
Others	—	...	9
Malawi (June 1978)			
Malawi Congress Party	—	...	87
Malaysia (July 1978)			
Barisan Nasional (National Front, 12 mainly Malay parties)	—	...	131 (120)
Democratic Action Party (mainly Chinese)	L	...	16 (9)
Party Islam	—	...	5 (14)
Maldives			
Government by the Didi family			
Mali			
Military government since Nov. 19, 1968	—	—	—
Malta (September 1976)			
Nationalist Party	R	48.7	31 (27)
Labour Party	SD	51.3	34 (28)
Mauritania			
Military government since July 10, 1978	—	—	—
Mauritius (December 1976)			
Independence Party (Indian-dominated)	C	...	28 (39)
Parti Mauricien Social-Démocrate	L	...	8 (23)
Mauritius Militant Movement	K	...	34
Mexico (July 1976)			
Partido Revolucionario Institucional	CR	94.4	...
Partido Acción Nacional	C	...	...
Partido Auténtico de la Revolución Mexicana	L	...	...
Partido Popular Socialista	S	...	...
Partido Comunista Mexicano	K	...	...
Monaco (January 1978)			
Union Nationale et Démocratique	—	...	18 (17)
Mongolia (June 1977)			
Mongolian People's Revolutionary Party	—	99.99	336 (295)
Morocco (June 1977)			
Independents (pro-government)	CR	44.7	141 (159)
Popular Movement (rural)	CR	12.4	44 (60)
Istiqlal (Independence)	C	21.6	49 (8)
National Union of Popular Forces	L	14.6	16 (1)
Others	—	...	14 (12)
Mozambique (December 1977)			
Frente da Libertação do Moçambique (Frelimo)	—	...	210
Nauru (November 1977)			
Nauru Party (Dowiyogo)	—	...	9
Opposition Party (DeRoburt)	—	...	8
Independent	—	...	1
Nepal			
Royal government since December 1960	—	—	—
Netherlands, The (May 1977)			
Christian Democratic Appeal (Anti-Revolutionaire Partij, Christelijk-Historische Unie, and Katholieke Volkspartij)	CR	31.9	49 (48)
Boerenpartij (Farmers' Party)	CR	0.8	1 (3)
Volkspartij voor Vrijheid en Democratie	C	18.0	28 (22)
Democrats 1966	C	5.4	8 (6)
Democratische-Socialisten '70	L	0.7	1 (6)
Partij van de Arbeid	SD	33.8	53 (43)
Communistische Partij van Nederland	K	1.7	2 (7)
Seventeen other parties	—	...	8 (15)
New Zealand (November 1978)			
National (Conservative)	CR	39.5	49 (54)
Labour Party	L	40.5	42 (32)
Social Credit	C	16.4	1 (1)
Nicaragua (September 1974)			
Partido Liberal Nacionalista (A. Somoza)	R	60.0	42 (35)
Partido Conservador de Nicaragua	R	...	11 (17)
Others	—	...	0 (1)

COUNTRY AND NAME OF PARTY	Affiliation	Voting strength (%)	Parliamentary representation
Niger			
Military government since April 17, 1974	—	—	—
Nigeria			
Military government since Jan. 15, 1966	—	—	—
Norway (September 1977)			
Høyre (Conservative)	R	24.7	41 (29)
Kristelig Folkeparti	CR	12.1	22 (20)
Senterpartiet (Agrarian)	C	8.6	12 (21)
Venstre (Liberal)	C	3.2	2 (1)
New People's Party	C	1.7	0
Party of Progress	C	1.9	0 } (2)
Arbeiderpartiet (Labour)	SD	42.5	76 (62)
Sosialistisk Venstreparti (Socialist Left)	S	4.1	2
Kommunistiske Parti	K	0.4	0 } (16)
Oman			
Independent sultanate, no parties	—	—	—
Pakistan			
Military government since July 5, 1977	—	—	—
Panama (August 1978)			
National Union Assembly	—	...	505
Papua New Guinea (June–July 1977)			
Pangu Party	—	...	39 (22)
United Party (chief opposition)	—	...	38 (34)
People's Progress Party	—	...	18 (12)
National Party	—	...	3 (10)
Country Party	—	...	1
Papua Besena	—	...	5 (2)
Other	—	...	5
Paraguay (February 1977)			
Partido Colorado (A. Stroessner)	R	69.0	...
Opposition parties	—	31.0	...
Peru (June 1978)			
Partido Popular Cristiano	CR	27	25
APRA (Alianza Popular Revolucionaria Americana)	CR	35.3	37
FOCEP (Frente Obrero, Campesino y Estudiantino Popular)	L	...	12
Socialists	S	...	6
Communists	K	...	6
Others	—	...	14
Philippines			
Martial law since Sept. 23, 1972	—	—	—
Poland (March 1976)			
Front of National Unity	—	99.4	460 (460)
Portugal (April 1976)			
Centro Democrático-Social	CR	15.9	41 (16)
Partido Popular-Democrático	C	20.0	71 (80)
Partido Socialista	SD	35.0	106 (116)
União Democrática Popular	EL	1.7	1 (5)
Partido Comunista Português	K	14.6	40 (30)
Qatar			
Independent emirate, no parties	—	—	—
Rhodesia (August 1977)			
Rhodesian Front (European)	R	85.0	50 (50)
Rhodesian Action Party	—	9.0	— —
National Unifying Force	—	6.0	— —
Romania (March 1975)			
Communist-controlled Socialist Unity Front	—	99.9	349
Rwanda (July 1975)			
National Revolutionary Movement	—	—	—
San Marino (May 1978)			
Partito Democratico-Cristiano	CR	42.2	26 (25)
Partito Social-Democratico	SD	...	9 (9)
Partito Socialista Unitario	S	...	8 (8)
Partito Comunista	K	25.1	16 (15)
Others	—	...	3 (3)
São Tomé and Príncipe (1975)			
Movimento Libertação	—	—	—
Saudi Arabia			
Royal government, no parties	—	—	—
Senegal (February 1978)			
Parti Socialiste	CR	82.5	83
Parti Démocratique Sénégalais	L	17.1	17
Seychelles			
People's Progressive Front (alone in power after the June 5, 1977, coup)	—	—	—
Sierra Leone (May 1977)			
All People's Congress	CR	...	70 (84)
Sierra Leone People's Party	L	...	15 ...
Singapore (December 1976)			
People's Action Party	CR	...	69 (65)
Solomon Islands			
Independent Group	C	...	...
National Democratic Party	L	...	...
Somalia			
Somalian Revolutionary Socialist Party	—	—	—
South Africa (November 1977)			
Herstigte Nasionale Partij	ER	3.2	0 —
National Party	R	64.8	134 122
South African Party	CR	1.7	3 —
New Republic Party	C	11.8	10 —
United Party	C	—	— 41
Progressive Federal Party	L	16.7	17 —
Progressive Reform Party	L	—	— 7
Others	—	...	— 1
Vacant	—	...	1
Spain (June 1977)			
Alianza Popular	R	8.1	16
Union Centro Democratico	CR	34.3	165
Partido Socialista del Pueblo	L	4.3	6
Partido Socialista Obrero Español	SD	28.5	118
Partido Comunista Español	K	9.0	20
Catalans (two parties)	—	...	13
Basques (two parties)	—	...	9
Independents	—	...	3
Sri Lanka (July 1977)			
United National Party	R	...	139 (19)
Freedom Party	C	...	8 (91)
Tamil United Liberation Front	C	...	17 (12)
Communists and others	—	...	2 (44)
Sudan (February 1978)			
Sudan Socialist Union	—	...	304
Suriname (November 1977)			
National Party Alliance (H. Arron)	—	...	24 (22)
United Democratic Party (J. Lachmon)	...	...	15 (17)
Swaziland			
Royal government, no parties	—	—	—
Sweden (September 1976)			
Moderata Samlingspartiet (ex-Höger)	R	15.6	55 (51)
Centerpartiet (ex-Agrarian)	CR	24.1	86 (90)
Folkpartiet (Liberal)	C	11.0	39 (34)
Socialdemokratiska Arbetarepartiet	SD	42.9	152 (156)
Vänsterpartiet Kommunisterna	K	4.7	17 (19)
Switzerland (October 1975)			
Christian Democrats (Conservative)	R	20.6	46 (44)
Republican Movement	R	3.0	4 (7)
Evangelical People's	R	2.0	3 (3)
National Action (V. Oehen)	R	2.5	2 (4)
Swiss People's (ex-Middle Class)	CR	10.1	21 (23)
Radical Democrats (Freisinnig)	C	22.2	47 (49)
League of Independents	C	6.2	11 (13)
Liberal Democrats	L	2.3	6 (6)
Social Democrats	SD	25.4	55 (46)
Socialist Autonomous	EL	1.3	1 (0)
Communist (Partei der Arbeit)	K	2.2	4 (5)
Others	—	2.2	0 —
Syria (August 1977)			
National Progressive Front (dominated by Baath Party)	—	...	159
Others	—	...	36
Taiwan (Republic of China)			
Nationalist (Kuomintang)	—	...	773
Tanzania (October 1975)			
Tanganyika African National Union	C	93.2	218
Zanzibar Afro-Shirazi (nominated)	L	...	52
Thailand			
Revolutionary Council in power since Oct. 20, 1977			
Togo			
Military government since 1967	—	—	—
Tonga (June 1972)			
Legislative Assembly (partially elected)	—	—	21
Trinidad and Tobago (September 1976)			
People's National Movement	C	...	24 (36)
Democratic Action Congress	—	...	2
United Labour Front	L	...	10
Tunisia (November 1974)			
Parti Socialist Destourien	—	99.0	112 (101)
Turkey (June 1977)			
National Action (A. Turkes)	ER	6.4	16 (3)
National Salvation (N. Erbakan)	R	8.6	24 (48)
Turkish Justice (S. Demirel)	CR	36.9	189 (149)
Democratic	C	1.8	1 (45)
Republican Reliance (T. Feyzioglu)	C	1.9	3 (13)
Republican People's (B. Ecevit)	L	41.4	213 (185)
Others	—	...	4 (7)
Tuvalu			
No political parties	—	—	—
Uganda			
Military dictatorship since Jan. 25, 1971	—	—	—
Union of Soviet Socialist Republics (1974)			
Communist Party of the Soviet Union	—	99.8	767
United Arab Emirates			
Federal government of seven emirates			
United Kingdom (October 1974)			
Conservative	R	35.8	276 (296)
Liberal	C	18.3	13 (14)
Labour	L	39.3	319 (301)
Communist	K	...	0 (0)
Scottish National Party	—	...	11 (7)
United Ulster Unionists	—	...	10 (11)
Plaid Cymru (Welsh Nationalists)	—	...	3 (2)
Others	—	...	3 (4)
United States (November 1978)			
Republican	CR	...	159 (143)
Democratic	C	...	276 (292)
Upper Volta (April 1978)			
Union Nationale pour la Défense de la Démocratie	CR	...	13
Union Démocratique Voltaïque	C	...	28
Parti de Rassemblement Africain	L	...	6
Union Progressiste Voltaïque	S	...	9
Independent	—	...	1
Uruguay			
Rule by Council of State from 1973	—	—	—
Venezuela (December 1978)			
COPEI (Social Christians)	CR	...	... (64)
Acción Democrática	L	...	... (102)
Movimiento al Socialismo	SD	...	... (9)
Movimiento Electoral del Pueblo	S	...	... (8)
Movimiento Institucional Revolucionario	EL	...	... (2)
Partido Comunista Venezolano	K	...	... (2)
Vietnam, Socialist Republic of (April 1976)			
Communist Party	K	...	...
Western Samoa			
No political parties	—	—	—
Yemen, People's Democratic Republic of			
National Liberation Front	—	—	—
Yemen Arab Republic			
Military government since 1974			
Yugoslavia (May 1978)			
Communist-controlled Federal Chamber	—	...	220
Zaire (October 1977)			
Legislative Council of the Mouvement Populaire de la Révolution	—	...	268
Zambia (December 1973)			
United National Independence Party	—	80.0	125

(K. M. SMOGORZEWSKI)

Portugal

A republic of southwestern Europe, Portugal shares the Iberian Peninsula with Spain. Area: 91,-632 sq km (35,379 sq mi), including the Azores (2,335 sq km) and Madeira (796 sq km). Pop. (1978 est.): 9,832,800, excluding about 550,000 refugees (mostly from Africa). Cap. and largest city: Lisbon (pop., 1976 est., 847,300). Language: Portuguese. Religion: Roman Catholic. President in 1978, Gen. António dos Santos Ramalho Eanes; premiers, Mário Soares, Alfredo Nobre da Costa from August 28, and, from November 22, Carlos Mota Pinto.

On Dec. 8, 1977, the Socialist government led by Mário Soares had been defeated on a motion of confidence in the Assembly by 159 votes to 100 and had resigned. The government needed a mandate to complete negotiations with the International Monetary Fund (IMF) for the second portion of an export-equalization loan of $50 million that would open the way to a consortium loan of $750 million provided by 14 Western countries. The IMF terms

for the loan required the imposition of austerity policies. Pres. António Eanes began consultations for the formation of a new government immediately, and on December 28 nominated Soares to form a new administration. The Cabinet appointed on Jan. 26, 1978, was a coalition. The offer of three ministries to the Democratic Social Centre (CDS) enabled Soares to form a government with a combined majority of 143 seats in the 263-seat Assembly.

On February 12 Premier Soares gained support in the Assembly for a two-stage economic recovery program that included credit and import austerity measures. On April 5 the premier announced that the minimum wage for 1978 had been raised by 26% for agricultural workers and 31% for industrial workers; unemployment benefits were increased by 18.5–24.4%. Wage agreements were to apply for one year instead of 18 months to permit an annual reappraisal of salaries. The Assembly on April 13 approved the 1978 budget, which projected a deficit of 60,480,000,000 escudos, compared with 48,-540,000,000 escudos in 1977 and 47,170,000,000 escudos in 1976. Most of the projected 1978 deficit was to be funded internally, with only 6% to be raised abroad. Revenue from taxation was raised by 40%, and public service fees were increased by 20 to 50%.

On May 4 the government's negotiations with the IMF were concluded, opening the way for release of the $750 million medium-term loan; the U.S. made $200 million of its $300 million contribution available in mid-May 1978 and the remaining $100 million in October 1978. The main aim of the program agreed on with the IMF was to reduce the balance of payments deficit on current account from $1.5 billion in the year ended in March 1978

Portugal

PORTUGAL

Education. (1976–77) Primary, pupils 1,207,902, teachers 63,647; secondary (1975–76), pupils 334,944, teachers 15,715; vocational (1975–76), pupils 127,885, teachers 14,-166; teacher training (1975–76), students 9,584, teachers 879; higher, students 86,189, teaching staff 7,181.

Finance. Monetary unit: escudo, with (Sept. 18, 1978) a free rate of 45.65 escudos to U.S. $1 (89.45 escudos = £1 sterling). Gold, SDR's, and foreign exchange (June 1978) U.S. $1,231,000,000. Budget (1977 est.) balanced at 159,-173,000,000 escudos. Gross national product (1975) 376.3 billion escudos. Money supply (Dec. 1976) 249,560,000,-000 escudos. Cost of living (Lisbon; 1975 = 100; June 1978) 165.5.

Foreign Trade. (1977) Imports 189,640,000,000 escudos; exports 77,410,000,000 escudos. Import sources: West Germany 12%; U.K. 10%; U.S. 10%; France 8%; Italy 5%; Spain 5%. Export destinations: U.K. 18%; West Germany 12%; France 8%; U.S. 7%; Sweden 6%; Angola 5%. Main exports: textile yarns and fabrics 15%; machinery 11%; clothing 11%; food 8%; wine 7%; cork manufactures 6%; chemicals 5%; wood pulp 5%. Tourism (1976): visitors 2,175,000; gross receipts U.S. $321 million.

Transport and Communications. Roads (1975) 46,241 km (including 66 km expressways). Motor vehicles in use (1976): passenger 1,034,000; commercial (including buses) 288,000. Railways: (1976) 3,591 km; traffic (1977) 5,242,-000,000 passenger-km, freight 884.5 million net ton-km. Air traffic (1977): 3,010,000,000 passenger-km; freight 91.5 million net ton-km. Shipping (1977): merchant vessels 100 gross tons and over 350; gross tonnage 1,281,439. Telephones (Jan. 1977) 1,119,000. Radio licenses (Dec. 1975) 1,519,000. Television licenses (Dec. 1976) 909,000.

Agriculture. Production (in 000; metric tons; 1977): wheat c. 196; oats c. 55; rye 90; corn 402; rice 112; potatoes 1,144; tomatoes c. 790; figs (1976) c. 200; apples c. 89; oranges c. 100; wine 523; olives 265; olive oil 40; cow's milk c. 710; meat 382; timber (cu m; 1976) 7,887; fish catch (1976) 339. Livestock (in 000; 1977): sheep c. 3,657; cattle (1976) c. 1,000; goats c. 700; pigs (1976) c. 1,683; chickens c. 16,800.

Industry. Fuel and power (in 000; 1977): coal (metric tons) 195; petroleum products (1976) 5,370; manufactured gas (Lisbon; cu m) 137,000; electricity (kw-hr) 13,875,000. Production (in 000; metric tons; 1977): iron ore (50% metal content) 52; crude steel 380; sulfuric acid 344; fertilizers (nutrient content; 1976–77) nitrogenous c. 176, phosphate c. 97; cement 4,337; tin 0.2; tungsten concentrates (oxide content; 1976) 1.6; kaolin (1976) 64; preserved sardines (1976) 19; wood pulp (1976) 587; cork products (1976) 264; cotton yarn 85; woven cotton fabrics 57.

WIDE WORLD

Premier Mário Soares (left), shown touring a cement plant with Alfredo Nobre da Costa in 1977, was succeeded by Nobre da Costa in August 1978.

Polo:
see Equestrian Sports; Water Sports

Populations:
see Demography; see also the individual country articles

to about $1 billion in the following year. The program maintained restrictions on wages and money supply and increased levels of taxation, all moves designed to reduce demand and inflation. Higher rates of interest were maintained to help attract foreign capital, increase emigrant remittances, and curb speculative building of inventories. On May 5 the Banco de Portugal announced a 6.5% devaluation of the escudo against a basket of 14 currencies of major trading partners; also, the escudo would be allowed to continue to depreciate at a rate of up to 1½% a month.

The political scene again became turbulent in June, when the CDS publicly criticized the Socialist plan to introduce a comprehensive national health service on British lines. The land reform issue was the breaking point for the coalition government. The CDS, restive over the slowness with which illegally expropriated land was being returned to its owners, called for the resignation of the Socialist agriculture minister, Gonçalves Saias. The Socialists rejected the demand for the minister's resignation, whereupon the CDS withdrew its three Cabinet ministers from the government and its support in the Assembly.

Soares was removed from office by President Eanes on July 27. On August 1 the president addressed the nation and outlined two possible solutions: a restructured alliance of political parties or a presidentially appointed premier whose Cabinet would be composed of persons of recognized competence. If neither solution was possible, general elections would be called under the rules of the constitution. On August 9, after the failure of the president's first alternative, Eanes appointed as premier Alfredo Nobre da Costa, previously head of the state petroleum corporation, Sacor, and later minister of technology in the first provisional government in 1976. His government of political independents (set up on August 28) fell on September 14 after the defeat of its program in the Assembly by 141 votes to 71. The core of the program was very similar to that of the previous government.

Nobre da Costa continued in office in a caretaker capacity while negotiations between President Eanes, the political parties, and the unions continued around a list of 11 candidates for premier, including Nobre da Costa. On October 25 Carlos Mota Pinto (*see* BIOGRAPHIES), an independent left-of-centre deputy and professor of law from Coimbra University, was appointed premier-designate by Eanes with the agreement of both Socialist and Centre parties. His nonpartisan Cabinet, which included seven lawyers and four engineers, was sworn in November 22.

In mid-October the leader of the Communist Party, Alvaro Cunhal, accused Nobre da Costa's caretaker government of creating a civil war atmosphere in the Alentejo region—where security forces had clashed with farm workers—by handing back illegally expropriated land to its legal owners. On October 16, in an attempt to relax tension, the government temporarily suspended the program.

After a year of relative calm, during which the 22% limit on wage increases appeared to have been respected, sporadic labour action and strikes

affected key sectors of the economy. A strike by hotel workers in August seriously affected tourism. Other disputes involved the chemical, building, and farming sectors, as well as the domestic (SATA) and international (TAP) airlines. The most serious, in terms of both length and cost, involved the largely state-run merchant marine; at its height it affected incoming goods to Lisbon and vital supplies to the Algarve, the Azores, and Madeira. Between the first quarters of 1977 and 1978, the real earnings of Lisbon industrial workers (the country's highest-paid) fell by 5%.

On October 17 the Council of Ministers of the European Economic Community (EEC) formally accepted Portugal's application to join the Community and agreed that formal negotiations should begin in 1979. On joining the EEC, Portugal would be allowed a maximum ten years to comply with Community rules and policies.

(MICHAEL WOOLLER)

See also Dependent States.

Prisons and Penology

With more urgency than ever before, the question was asked in many countries in 1978: what can be done to stem the rising tide of crime? The somewhat disparate responses fell into five categories: greater severity of punishment; shorter penalties more swiftly administered; greater certainty of detection; support within the community for relatively minor offenders who have difficulty coping with society; and more effective measures of prevention.

The severest penalty, capital punishment, was also the most debated, and once again opposite actions were taken in different countries. In the U.S., for example, Gov. Hugh L. Carey of New York vetoed a bill in April that would have restored the death penalty, previously abolished by the state Court of Appeals. In France, on the other hand, a movement in favour of abolition, initiated by the French bishops and leading to a prolonged controversy, failed to change the existing law. There were, however, no executions.

A meeting of European ministers of justice in June could not agree on ending capital punishment in all member countries of the Council of Europe. In the U.S. no one had been executed since Gary Gilmore in early 1977, but a number had been sentenced to death. Cuba introduced a new penal code in February 1978 which permitted death by shooting for crimes ranging from some types of murder and robbery to hijacking and rape.

Next in severity were very long prison sentences. Although it was accepted in most countries that some prisoners are so dangerous that they must be detained for prolonged periods, there was less agreement on what constituted a sufficient degree of dangerousness and how lengthy the period of detention should be. There were also practical problems; long-term prisoners had the greatest incentive to escape, for example, and the longest time to plan such a venture.

That was what bank robber Jacques Mesrine did; the most wanted man in France escaped from

This mass of rubble used to be the laundry at the Pontiac (Illinois) Correctional Center before it was set ablaze by rioting prisoners in July. Three guards were killed and vast property damage occurred.

the security wing of Santé prison in Paris in May and was still at large at year's end. Also in the spring, Till Meyer, accused of terrorism, was freed from Moabit prison in West Berlin by two women accomplices. But the further tightening of security as a result of such incidents led to new tensions. In Sydney, Australia, in August, 400 prisoners rioted and damaged parts of the maximum security prison in protest against tight security. Earlier, in France, 600 prisoners went on a hunger strike in a demonstration against special security cells.

Conditions in top-security jails were difficult not only for prisoners but also for staff. All kinds of attempts were made to lessen tensions—for example, by improved grievance procedures for inmates—but considerable problems remained. Prisoners still found it possible to take hostages. Riots broke out, for example, in Málaga prison in Spain, which was almost totally destroyed; at the Villa Devoto prison in Buenos Aires, Arg.; and at the Pontiac (Ill.) Correctional Center, where three guards were killed. Prison officials were also killed outside prisons—as in Turkey, Italy, and Spain— though such acts were probably politically inspired. Nevertheless, it was not surprising that prison staff, feeling the general pressure, sometimes took industrial action.

A Council of Europe publication on the treatment of long-term prisoners spotlighted three factors as being critical to the response of inmates: the interplay between the prisoner's age and the length of his sentence; his personality; and the regime in the institution concerned. Only the last could be affected by prison administrators and then only marginally, in view of the prevalent overcrowding and shortage of resources. A serious problem in the management of long-term prisons was the presence of difficult, mentally abnormal inmates. Many reports had suggested that such individuals should be held in secure psychiatric hospitals. However, health departments were reluctant to open such facilities when their broad strategy was to maintain open-door policies, and correctional departments were sometimes loath to

employ psychiatric nurses in case this was taken as an admission that disturbed prisoners were their permanent responsibility.

The movement against overlong sentences, especially of an indeterminate kind, gathered momentum during the year. Many Western European countries had fixed maximum sentences, with relatively little indeterminacy. Lowering of fixed maximum penalties themselves was recommended in the U.K. in a report by the Advisory Council on the Penal System. The council suggested a two-tier system, with a lowering of the top penalties for the vast majority of cases (in line with what the courts already did) but with higher maximum sentences for the small minority of exceptionally serious offenders.

There was also a tendency to split relatively minor offenders into two types for sentencing purposes. For certain youthful criminals a short period of detention, with a Spartan but active routine, was being envisaged in some countries. For the inadequate and socially deprived of all ages, many penal systems provided various forms of treatment in the community, usually involving support and the learning of new skills and sometimes including an element of reparation. Ordinary representatives of the community and ex-offenders, not just professional correctional or social workers, were increasingly used in such programs.

Certainty of detection had always been more important in restraining crime than the nature of punishment. Some countries, for example the U.K., sharply increased police pay to attract recruits. Efforts to improve police efficiency ranged from the use of sophisticated computers to detailed analyses of local crime and the alerting of neighbourhoods to specific ways of preventing offenses. It was also realized that efforts should be made to speed up the administration of justice, so that the penalty could follow more swiftly upon the commission of the crime. But this proved difficult; often increases in the number of courts and judicial personnel merely kept pace with the increase in crime.

Visitors to a prison in Tijuana, Mexico, were detained in the courtyard until they could be identified and escorted out by the police following rioting which broke out at the prison in June.

Together with rising public irritation over the continuing increase in crime, there also seemed to be a growing realization that the police and the penal system were no substitute for care and control within the community. Under attack for years, the family was still regarded by many as the most important social unit where children learned basic behaviour. An example of parents taking action to protect their children was documented in Harriet Wilson and G. W. Herbert's *Parents and Children in the Inner City* (1978). Some parents, as poor as their neighbours and living in the same deprived, high-delinquency area, decided to protect their children from attack and bad influence. At home they insisted on certain standards of behaviour. Outside, they did some strict chaperoning. Three-quarters of the parents using such old-fashioned methods succeeded in preventing their children from becoming delinquent. Almost none of the other families in the area kept their children from getting into trouble.

(HUGH J. KLARE)

See also Crime and Law Enforcement; Law.
[521.C.3.a; 543.A.5.a; 10/36.C.5.b]

Publishing

With some of the world's leading newspapers failing to appear for prolonged periods in 1978 and their very survival often in doubt, freedom of the press at times seemed a somewhat academic concept. It was nonetheless an issue that attracted much attention, worldwide, during the year. In the West, where the advent of new printing technology was the root cause of much of the disruption, freedom of expression was felt by many journalists to be seriously threatened by the increasing concentration of ownership of newspapers. (See Special Report.) Elsewhere, in many countries, governmental censorship, manipulation of information, and repression of journalists continued unabated.

At the international level on October 16 the UNESCO commission headed by Sean MacBride published its *Interim Report on Communications Problems in Modern Society.* This was followed on November 22 by UNESCO's adoption of a declaration on press rights. First considered in 1970 and the cause of much disagreement, particularly between East and West, the draft declaration was discussed at length by the UNESCO general conference in Paris. The final version was agreed upon by all members. For the Soviet Union it was seen as assigning specific objectives and responsibilities to journalists for the first time in an international agreement; as the West saw it, it nevertheless did not further restrict the free flow of information, as many third world countries had increasingly been wishing to do, calling rather for a "balanced" flow.

Newspapers. On Dec. 1, 1978, *The Times* of London did not appear. This was in itself nothing new; the newspaper had lost several days of publication because of a strike at the beginning of the year. The difference, on December 1, was that the failure to publish came not through disruption by members of the paper's work force but by decision of the management of Times Newspapers Ltd.

Six months earlier management's chief executive had issued an ultimatum: if, by November 30, the company had not secured new agreements with every one of the groups in its work force, covering new working practices, guarantees of uninterrupted production, and a move to new technological processes, it would suspend publication of all its titles (*The Times, The Sunday Times,* and three weekly literary and education supplements). By

The state of press freedom in Nicaragua is evidenced by the front page of Managua's *La Prensa* newspaper after it had been subjected to government censorship. The government said the paper had to fill the censored space with "important" news.

November 30, just 2 of the 54 separate bargaining groups involved had signed such agreements.

Although the issues involved affected virtually all London newspapers, there was considerable misgiving among some other managements, as well as in the unions, about the tactic of setting a challenging deadline. It became clear, too, that management's detailed proposals had been issued only a few weeks in advance. Suspension, therefore, came in an atmosphere of suspicion and recrimination. Although talks went on, most predictions were of a work stoppage lasting months rather than weeks.

The year's one significant effort at expansion in the U.K. got off to an uncertain start. Express Newspapers Ltd., owned since 1977 by the Trafalgar House conglomerate, had several plans for development under its new chairman, Victor Matthews, including a third London evening newspaper and a new "popular" Sunday paper. His first move, however, was a surprise entry into the daily market. On November 2 he launched the tabloid *Daily Star*. The first print order was about 1.5 million, with a target sale of 1 million. Within two weeks fierce publicity battles were being fought with the rival *Daily Mirror* and *The Sun* over the new paper's actual performance, but it seemed clear that it was well below the target and would have to work hard to assure the future of the new jobs and revenue it hoped to create.

In France Robert Hersant was at the centre of a new controversy, over a newspaper he did not actually own. The conservative Paris daily *L'Aurore* was sold in July by industrialist Marcel Boussac to a major supermarket group. The new owners, in an effort to cut losses, quickly proposed a joint printing deal, including some pooled advertising, with Hersant's *Le Figaro* and *France-Soir*. Hersant executives were appointed to senior posts in the *L'Aurore* management. A sharp confrontation rapidly arose, as printers demanded assurances that jobs would not be lost by the joint printing, a dozen journalists left *L'Aurore* because of the extension of Hersant control, and others took the issue to the president of the republic. Hersant abruptly pulled out of the deal, but his appointee then announced reductions in both paging and circulation of *L'Aurore*. Suspicion grew that the paper was being deliberately run down. The independent *Le Quotidien de Paris*, founded in 1974, ceased publication on June 28, 1978.

Control of a newspaper was at the centre of a major governmental scandal that rocked South African politics. Throughout the year the South African press probed secret workings of the Department of Information and, in particular, the use of a secret $75 million fund under the control of its minister, C. P. Mulder, and his close associates. As the so-called "Muldergate" scandal exploded, it was revealed that half the fund had been behind the launching, in September 1976, of a new English-language newspaper, *The Citizen*, ostensibly independent but in fact a government mouthpiece. Percy Qoboza, editor of the black newspaper *The World* and detained since its October 1977 banning, was released in March 1978.

(PETER FIDDICK)

World Daily Newspapers and Circulations, 1976–77[1]

Location	Daily news-papers	Circulation per 1,000 population	Location	Daily news-papers	Circulation per 1,000 population
AFRICA			**ASIA**		
Algeria	4	22	Afghanistan	17	...
Angola	5	21	Bangladesh	21	4
Benin	1	0.3	Burma	7	10
Botswana	1	24	Cambodia	17	10
Cameroon	3	4	China	392	...
Central African Empire	1	0.3	Cyprus	12	123
Chad	4	0.4	Hong Kong	111	350
Congo	3	...	India	835	16
Egypt	16	...	Indonesia	172	...
Equatorial Guinea	1	4	Iran	28	25
Ethiopia	5	2	Iraq	7	17
Gabon	1	...	Israel	25	180
Ghana	4	42	Japan	180	374
Guinea	1	2	Jordan	4	22
Guinea-Bissau	1	11	Korea, North	11	...
Ivory Coast	3	12	Korea, South	30	173
Kenya	3	11	Kuwait	6	86
Lesotho	1	1	Laos	8	...
Liberia	2	9	Lebanon	33	...
Libya	2	...	Macau	7	...
Madagascar	12	...	Malaysia	31	87
Malawi	2	6	Mongolia	1	78
Mali	2	...	Nepal	29	...
Mauritius	11	90	Pakistan	102	...
Morocco	9	21	Philippines	15	...
Mozambique	2	4	Saudi Arabia	11	11
Niger	2	0.5	Singapore	12	239
Nigeria	19	...	Sri Lanka	18	...
Réunion	1	47	Syria	6	...
Rhodesia	3	16	Taiwan	31	...
Senegal	1	5	Thailand	56	...
Seychelles	2	58	Turkey	450	...
Sierra Leone	2	10	Vietnam	29	8
Somalia	1	...	Yemen (Aden)	2	7
South Africa	24	57	Yemen (San'a')	6	10
Sudan	4	...	Total	2,722	
Tanzania	3	14			
Togo	1	3			
Tunisia	5	...			
Uganda	2	3	**EUROPE**		
Upper Volta	1	0.2	Albania	2	48
Zaire	6	...	Austria	30	308
Zambia	2	19	Belgium	30	239
Total	179		Bulgaria	14	238
			Czechoslovakia	30	288
			Denmark	50	341
			Finland	60	450
			France	98	214
NORTH AMERICA			Germany, East	40	452
Antigua	2	136	Germany, West	411	404
Bahamas, The	3	113	Gibraltar	2	173
Barbados	1	109	Greece	106	107
Belize	1	29	Hungary	29	266
Bermuda	1	200	Iceland	5	429
Canada	117	227	Ireland	10	246
Costa Rica	6	100	Italy	78	113
Cuba	16	...	Liechtenstein	1	325
Dominican Republic	10	42	Luxembourg	6	364
El Salvador	12	...	Malta	6	...
Guadeloupe	2	61	Netherlands, The	95	315
Guatemala	11	...	Norway	80	412
Haiti	7	20	Poland	44	248
Honduras	8	...	Portugal	30	70
Jamaica	3	58	Romania	32	170
Martinique	1	71	Spain	115	98
Mexico	256	...	Sweden	144	571
Netherlands Antilles	5	216	Switzerland	97	385
Nicaragua	6	48	U.S.S.R.	691	397
Panama	6	77	United Kingdom	130	...
Puerto Rico	4	132	Vatican City	1	...
Trinidad and Tobago	3	131	Yugoslavia	26	89
United States	1,753	284	Total	2,493	
Virgin Islands (U.S.)	2	152			
Total	2,236				
			OCEANIA		
			American Somoa	2	320
SOUTH AMERICA			Australia	70	394
Argentina	164	...	Cook Islands	1	32
Bolivia	14	35	Fiji	3	...
Brazil	280	39	French Polynesia	4	86
Chile	47	...	Guam	1	177
Colombia	40	...	New Caledonia	1	57
Ecuador	29	49	New Zealand	35	322
French Guiana	1	25	Niue	1	60
Guyana	3	155	Papua New Guinea	1	8
Paraguay	5	52	Total	119	
Peru	35	...			
Suriname	7	...			
Uruguay	30	...			
Venezuela	47	...			
Total	702		Grand total	8,451	

[1]Only newspapers issued four or more times weekly are included.
Sources: UN, *Statistical Yearbook, 1977* (1978); *Editor & Publisher International Year Book* (1978); *Europa Year Book 1978, A World Survey*; various country publications.

For U.S. newspapers 1978 was a year of high controversy and continuing prosperity. Total daily circulation rose about 1% to 61,495,140, the highest level since 1974, according to the 1978 *Editor & Publisher International Yearbook*. Morning circulation hit an all-time high of 26,742,318, up 3% from a year earlier, but evening circulation dropped 1% to 34,752,822. The total number of newspapers fell by 9 to 1,753. The Newspaper Advertising Bureau estimated that advertising revenues amounted to $12.5 billion, up 12% from 1977.

The year's most important casualty, and one that accounted for most of the drop in total evening circulation, was the *Chicago Daily News* (final circulation, 329,000). Founded in 1876 by editor Melville Stone, the paper had a tradition of fostering such literary talents as poet Carl Sandburg, humorist Finley Peter Dunne, and dramatist Ben Hecht; in its heyday it had been noted for its excellent foreign coverage. The paper had lost $21.7 million since 1974 for its owners, Field Enterprises, which continued to publish the morning *Chicago Sun-Times* in competition with the Tribune Co.'s *Chicago Tribune*. The *Daily News*'s demise left Chicago without a major evening newspaper.

Big-city evening newspapers had been losing readers for years, mostly because of population shifts to distant suburbs and because of increased competition from television. But during the same week that the death of the *Daily News* was announced, the nation's second most troubled evening newspaper found a buyer. The *Washington Star* (circulation, 349,000), which lost more readers in the year ended in the spring of 1978 than any other U.S. daily, was bought by Time Inc. for $28 million from Joe Allbritton, a Texas financier who had owned the paper since 1974. Time, which published a stable of magazines including the

weekly news magazine of that name, quickly launched five new local editions of the paper and invested $2 million in automated production equipment.

The other notable newspaper failure of the year was *The Trib* (final circulation, 50,000, down from an initial 200,000), New York City's first major new daily in seven years. A tabloid financed by a number of prominent politically conservative investors, *The Trib* was unable to win enough readers or advertisers with its bland mix of wire-service reports and syndicated features.

The year's boldest new venture was not the launching of a new daily but imperialism by an old one. Hit by declining readership in its hometown, the *Los Angeles Times* (circulation, 1,020,000) opened a 22-member editorial office and launched a new local edition in San Diego, 125 mi away. To meet that invasion San Diego's two dailies each expanded the space and staff they devoted to local news.

The largest new daily of the year was New York City's *Daily Sun* (initial circulation, 600,000), a morning tabloid launched by Australian publisher K. Rupert Murdoch and printed at his *New York Post*. The *Post* (circulation, 622,000) was for a time New York's only major newspaper, when a strike of pressmen shut the city's dailies for nearly three months. The *Post* was also struck, but, after reaching a separate agreement with the unions, returned to the newsstands several weeks before the rival *Daily News* and *Times*. Losses at the latter two papers approached $2 million a day in circulation and advertising revenues during the strike.

The press suffered a number of setbacks in the courts during 1978. In *Zurcher* v. *Stanford Daily*, the U.S. Supreme Court ruled that police could search newsrooms for evidence of crime as long as they obtained a search warrant. Previously, it had been assumed that police first had to seek a subpoena, which, unlike a search warrant, can be challenged in court before any evidence is surrendered. Journalists feared that the court's decision would discourage confidential sources from coming forward with sensitive information, for fear that their names would be turned up during a newsroom search.

In another case that troubled journalists *New York Times* reporter Myron Farber was jailed and fined for refusing to turn over his notes on a New Jersey murder case for inspection by the trial judge. The subpoenaing of Farber's notes was part of a nationwide trend involving judicial demands that reporters testify or surrender their notes in criminal trials. Like Farber a number of subpoenaed reporters declared that they would go to jail rather than comply.

Two U.S. newspapermen ran afoul of courts in the Soviet Union. The *Baltimore Sun*'s Hal Piper and the *New York Times*'s Craig Whitney, who reported for their respective newspapers from Moscow, were convicted of slandering the Soviet television industry after the reporters quoted relatives of an imprisoned dissident as insisting that his televised confession was not genuine. Piper and Whitney were fined a token sum, but their newspapers did not print the retractions demanded by the court;

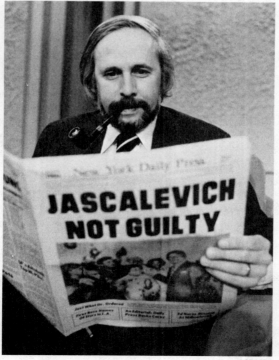

New York Times reporter Myron Farber holds a newspaper headlining the acquittal of Mario Jascalevich on three counts of murder. Farber went to jail for refusing to turn over his notes and files concerning the case.

WIDE WORLD

both journalists were allowed to continue reporting from Moscow.

In one of the largest mergers in recent newspaper history Gannett Co. absorbed Combined Communications Corp., owner of broadcast, newspaper, and related properties worth $370 million. The deal made Gannett the nation's most numerous newspaper chain, with 77 dailies.

As in previous years, the Pulitzer Prizes were not without controversy. The award for spot news photography, which was initially given to Jim Schweiker of United Press International, was later presented to free-lancer John Blair after it was discovered that UPI had mislabeled the winning entry, a photo of a gunman and a hostage. Another photo award went to free-lancer J. Ross Baughman for his pictures of Rhodesian guerrillas, despite doubts about their authenticity.

One Pulitzer not in dispute was the Gold Medal for Public Service, which went to the *Philadelphia Inquirer* for a series on local police brutality by reporters William Marimow and Jonathan Neumann. For the first time in the 60-year history of the awards, three were given to journalists from the same paper, the *New York Times*. Correspondent Henry Kamm won the international reporting prize for his articles on the plight of Vietnamese refugees. Columnist William Safire received the commentary award for his articles on the personal financial dealings of U.S. Office of Management and Budget Director Bert Lance, who later resigned in disgrace. Walter Kerr was given the criticism prize for his theatre reviews.

(DONALD MORRISON)

Magazines. A generally buoyant year for the British magazine market ended with some of the biggest-circulation magazines failing to appear. The major publishing group, International Publishing Corp. Magazines Ltd., found itself in dispute with the National Union of Journalists and from late November was forced to suspend some of its market leaders in the women's field, including *Woman, Woman's Own, Woman's Realm,* and the monthly *Woman's Journal.* After settlement of the dispute publication was resumed, but the time required to start up production meant that some titles would not appear until January. This meant substantial loss of revenue in the lucrative period around Christmas, at a time when most publications were doing better than ever before. November issues of *Ideal Home* and *Homes and Gardens* were running up to 100 pages more than in the same month of 1977.

Faces, a new magazine with a U.S. angle (in its aim of building a publication around pictures and gossip about the famous), was launched in February. It immediately hit production problems over a union-recognition dispute, but it was as much the format's lack of appeal that led to its demise in April. A U.S. connection with better chance of success was formed in April, when the new owners of *The Tatler,* one of the oldest and most old-fashioned "society" magazines, hired a young American woman, Leslie Field, as editor. She announced her intention of raising the magazine's circulation from around 30,000 to a target 50,000 by attracting an international readership.

One of Britain's own oldest titles showed more staying power. *The Spectator,* the conservative political weekly, celebrated its 150th birthday. Another anniversary was *Encounter's* 25th. *The New Review,* the literary monthly started in 1974, changed to quarterly publication with its June issue. *New Statesman,* from April under a new editor, Bruce Page, underwent extensive changes.

In West Germany ten leading feminists attempted legal action to force the magazine *Stern* to keep female nudity off its covers, but the court ruled that nothing could be done under the law. In France *F. Magazine,* a monthly news magazine aimed at French women "who want to understand the world and participate in it intensely rather than follow its fashions," made its first appearance on January 9. Its editor was Claude Servan-Schreiber, formerly of *L'Express, Elle,* and *Marie-Claire.*

(PETER FIDDICK)

In the U.S. in 1978 people were reading more magazines. This was the good news, reflected in advertising and subscription and newsstand sales. Revenue was up an average of 17% over 1977. A good part of the boost was due to both readers and advertisers turning away from electronic media (particularly network television) and back to magazines.

On the dark side the rising postage rates increased second-class mailing costs. In 1979 it would cost 11.6 cents to post a magazine that could be mailed in 1971 for 2.3 cents. Postal increases are passed on to subscribers, and to no one's surprise the cost of an average subscription rose 12.2% in 1978. These continual increases started a trend toward single-copy sales rather than subscriptions. The market share of newsstand sales rose from 48.4% in 1975 to slightly over 53% in 1978.

Publishers continued to seek ways to meet higher costs. A favourite, now almost exhausted, was to reduce the format size of the magazine. In 1978 the most notable example of this was *Fortune.* After 50 years the monthly business magazine became a biweekly and trimmed its format.

The number of new commercial and business and trade magazines published in 1977 dropped to about 300 from some 360 issued in 1976. (Figures for 1978 were not yet available, but seemed to follow the 1977 trend.) No reason was given for the decrease, although traditionally the number of new magazines is in line with the ups and downs in the U.S. economy. The profile for the average new magazine: a monthly directed to a specialized audience with a circulation of 5,000–10,000.

Continuing the trend toward special-interest magazines, the leading new titles published in 1978 included *American Photographer,* a monthly for advanced amateurs to challenge the two leaders, *Popular Photography* and *Modern Photography*; *Your Place,* a "magazine for the new generation of men and women"; and *The Marathoner,* a slick quarterly with a $2.50 cover price for the joggers. The best publicized new magazine in 1978 was *Omni,* a slick $2 monthly from the publishers of *Penthouse.* About $3 million were budgeted to promote this "first magazine of the space age."

Old weekly magazines never die but simply come back as monthlies. First it was the *Saturday*

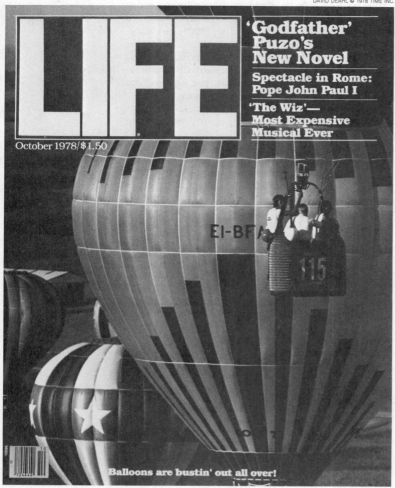

LIFE

'Godfather' Puzo's New Novel

Spectacle in Rome: Pope John Paul I

'The Wiz'— Most Expensive Musical Ever

October 1978/$1.50

EI-BFA

115

O 7

Balloons are bustin' out all over!

After an absence of almost six years, *Life* magazine reappeared on the newsstands in October, this time as a monthly magazine. The new version is slightly smaller than the previous one but still features what original founder Henry Luce called "picture magic."

Evening Post, and in 1978 it was *Life*. The weekly picture magazine, which suspended publication in 1972, was revived by Time Inc. as a showcase for photojournalism about what the "folks are doing" rather than headline news. Another casualty of the 1970s, *Look*, was scheduled to be revived as a pictorial newsmagazine.

A few years earlier there had been a rumour that the new women's movement would kill the traditional women's magazines. Liberated women, it was believed, would not support the kitchen-fashion oriented older titles. This, however, did not happen. In 1978 *McCall's* led the "big five" with a circulation of 6.5 million. Close behind were *Ladies' Home Journal*, 6 million; *Good Housekeeping*, 5 million; *Redbook Magazine*, 4.7 million; and *Cosmopolitan*, 2.5 million. Taking a hint from these new highs in sales (both from subscriptions and at the supermarket checkout stands), publishers in 1978 brought out *Ambiance*, a service magazine "for the very busy woman," and *The Homemaker*, and the Hearst Corp. tested out a new magazine called *Romance Weekly*. But at the same time, publishers acknowledged that the success of *Ms.* meant that the women's market had been segmented and that titles for working women could do as well as the old fashioned magazines; new magazines along these lines were *Self* and *New Dawn*.

In the "death" column, the leading casualty of the year was the magazine/underground newspaper the *Los Angeles Free Press*. Founded in the 1960s, it had been a leading voice of the "flower children" of that era. Except for a few outstanding efforts the ubiquitous underground publications of the 1960s and early 1970s had by 1978 become only history.

Columbia University and the Magazine Publishers Association honoured several magazines in 1978. Winners of the National Magazine Awards were *Architectural Digest*, visual excellence; *Esquire*, essays and criticism; *Mother Jones*, public service; *Newsweek*, service to the individual; *The New Yorker*, fiction and reporting excellence; and *Scientific American*, specialized journalism.

(WILLIAM A. KATZ)

Books. A notable feature of 1978 was the interest shown by China in cooperating with Western countries over publishing matters. Two delegations of publishers from the U.K. visited China, and a reciprocal visit was made to Britain by members of the Chinese National Publications Import Corp. These visits seemed likely to culminate in a greater availability of British books within China. Booksellers and publishers from West Germany, France, and the U.S. were also in contact with China, and the Chinese were represented at the Frankfurt (West Germany) Book Fair.

Western publishers were particularly concerned about the copyright situation in China. No further signatures had been added to the Berne Convention since that of Egypt in 1977, and the widespread piracy of English texts in areas such as Southeast Asia and the Middle East was proving acutely damaging to sales in traditional markets. Spanish publishers faced similar problems in Latin America.

International book fairs mushroomed to the point where it became almost impossible for publishers to attend all of them. In 1978, apart from Frankfurt, major fairs were held in Cairo, Brussels, Warsaw, and Atlanta, Ga. The International Children's Book Fair was held in Bologna, Italy, and the Didacta educational book and equipment exhibition took place in Brussels. All these fairs would be repeated in 1979, with the addition of major fairs in Jerusalem and Moscow.

The 1978 Frankfurt Book Fair (the 30th since the fair's inception), held October 18–23, was attended by 4,731 exhibitors from 78 countries, showing a total of some 282,000 titles. Major participants were the U.K., with 537 exhibitors listed, the U.S. (459), France (188), Switzerland (162), The Netherlands (160), and Italy (151). In anticipation of International Year of the Child, scheduled for 1979, the fair's theme was "Children and Books."

Despite pressure from Australian publishers the Australian attorney general announced that there was no need to change the recent Franki report on reprographic reproduction to afford more remuneration to copyright owners. However, 1978 witnessed the foundation of the U.S. Copyright Clearance Center to control the copying of journals in the U.S. and the establishment, through the Stichting Reprorecht, of a scheme to legalize copying of copyright works in The Netherlands. Discussions between copyright owners and users continued in West Germany, France, and the U.K.

The total turnover in sales of British books rose from £408 million in 1976 to £470 million in 1977. Home sales rose from £232 million to £265 million, and exports rose from £175 million to £205 million. Titles published, including reprints and new editions, reached a record 36,322.

The U.S.S.R. published more than 5,200 book titles in 1978 in addition to some 3,200 titles of children's books. These included classics and modern literature of all the Soviet nationalities.

(JOHN DAVIES)

Book sales in the U.S. in 1978 increased in almost all categories. First novels, works of history, and novels by well-known authors with proven track records (James Michener's *Chesapeake* and Herman Wouk's *War and Remembrance*) boasted unusually strong sales. Cumulative U.S. sales figures in 1978 for January through September, according to the Association of American Publishers, showed a continuation of 1977's upturn in net dollars received in most categories. Unit sales trends were not available, but it seemed likely that, in view of the steady rise in prices, increases in the number of copies sold were modest.

Both adult trade hardback and mass market paperback sales rose 11% from 1977 through September. Among the major book categories mailorder publications had the biggest percentage gain through September, up 16.4% on sales of $160.1 million.

Sales of technical, scientific, business, and medical books rose 8.3% through September on sales of $114.4 million. In the two textbook categories, elementary-high school and college, the former rose 10.1% on sales of $534.5 million and college increased 8.7% on sales of $343.1 million.

U.S. consumer expenditures on books for 1977 were encouraging for the book industry. Estimated expenditures, individual as well as institutional, increased by 11%, compared with 9.6% the year before. Even more significant, unit sales to consumers rose by 4.2% after having dropped consistently for several years.

It was a particularly good year for paperbacks. Mass market paperbacks led the way with a 25.5% dollar gain and a 7.9% unit gain. Adult trade paperbacks posted a 14.5% dollar and a 3.4% unit increase. Children's trade paperbacks and religious, professional, university press, and text paperbacks all outperformed their hardback counterparts, showing dollar increases in excess of 10% and some unit growth.

The year 1977 was reassuring for some hardbound books as well, with adult trade books displaying an impressive 11.8% dollar increase and a 4.4% unit increase and with a good performance posted by professional books and school textbooks. Disappointing records were established by other hardbacks, however, notably by religious books, which showed an 0.8% dollar and 3.7% unit decrease, and by college textbooks, which recorded a 1.4% dollar increase but suffered an 8.6% unit decline.

U.S. book title output in 1977 increased moderately over 1976, while average prices rose significantly in many sectors. The book title count, according to the R. R. Bowker Co., totaled 42,780, including 33,292 new books and 9,488 new editions, for an overall rise of about 2.6% from the 1976 figures. Price averages on a per-volume (not a per-title) basis indicated a 10.5% hike in overall average list prices for hardcover books.

The now familiar theme that mergers and acquisitions by conglomerates were destroying the independence of the major publishing houses they acquired was repeated in 1978. The Authors Guild, a 5,000-member professional authors' association, even urged the Federal Trade Commission to halt "the sinister process" of conglomerate takeover. To refute these and other statements on this issue, the Association of American Publishers (AAP) issued a statement of basic facts regarding the allegations of concentration in the book publishing industry. Quoting U.S. Department of Commerce figures, the AAP declared that the total number of U.S. book publishers had increased from 903 to 1,128 between 1958 and 1976 and published titles rose from 18,000 in 1960 to almost 40,000 in 1976.

Despite this report the merger issue intensified. In June the U.S. Department of Justice brought suit to force CBS to divest itself of Fawcett Publications, Inc., because of alleged anticompetitive effects of that acquisition on the mass-market paperback book business. This was the first such antimerger action in mass-paperback book publishing.

The controversy notwithstanding, mergers and acquisitions continued during the year. The Hearst Corp. acquired Arbor House Publishing Co., Inc., from its founder and sole owner, Donald Fine, who would continue as president and publisher. The acquisition added a general trade publishing house to the Hearst properties, which included Avon Books.

Arco Publishing Co., Inc., a 41-year-old firm that was the largest publisher of test preparation books in the U.S., and Prentice-Hall, Inc., publishers of trade and text books, jointly announced the proposed sale of the assets of Arco to a subsidiary of Prentice-Hall. In a different kind of merger two distinguished independent publishing firms, Charles Scribner's Sons and Atheneum Publishers, announced plans to merge in order to continue operating independently and avoid any possible takeovers by a conglomerate.

Breaking the record for nonfiction and equaling the record for fiction set earlier in the year, paperback rights to *Linda Goodman's Love Signs*, an astrological guide, were auctioned by Harper & Row, Publishers, Inc., to Fawcett Books Group for $2,-250,000 in early December. Part of the deal was that Fawcett would not exercise the reprint license for two years (the usual wait is one year) but had the right to issue the work in mass-market paperback, trade paperback, and in a format of up to 12 volumes, one for each sign of the zodiac. Earlier in the year New American Library established the new fiction record for paperback rights with its purchase of Mario Puzo's novel *Fools Die* for $2,-250,000 from the hardcover publisher, G. P. Putnam's Sons.

(DAISY G. MARYLES)

See also Literature.

[441.D; 543.A.4.e]

THE VANISHING DAILY

by Rex Winsbury

It was no coincidence that two of the world's most prestigious newspapers, *The Times* of London and the *New York Times,* were both shut down for prolonged periods in 1978 by disputes between management and labour unions about technology and jobs. For, faced with the "future shock" of modern electronic technology, newspapers, which exist to report and comment on the world around them, have themselves become an illuminating example of technical, industrial, and social change.

On the one hand, the advent of computerized editing, typesetting, page design, and transmission has raised a host of problems common to many industries but acute in newspapers. These include questions of employment levels and policies, union organization and power, management prerogatives and employee participation, the socially acceptable pace of technological change, and the harnessing of technological change to marketing objectives.

On the other hand, in large part due to the computer, we now live in an "information society" in which the creation, storage, distribution, or selling of information of all kinds is now *the* prime activity in all the major industrialized countries. Newspapers are at the heart of the information business, but information is no longer, as it might have been when *The Times* of London and the *New York Times* were founded, the birthright of newspapers. Having survived, if with depleted ranks, the first fierce onset of television, newspapers must adapt to a world in which information is a commodity dealt with by many different agencies, from Xerox Corp. and the American Telephone and Telegraph Co. to the *Wall Street Journal,* from the British Broadcasting Corporation and the Post Office to Reuters and the *Frankfurter Allgemeine Zeitung.*

Newspapers' Changing Role. This means that newspapers are having to take a fresh look at themselves as "information companies," which may distribute their news and views to the "reader" on paper in the traditional way but may also do it by

Rex Winsbury is the author of New Technology and the Press, *a research paper prepared for Britain's Royal Commission on the Press, and of* New Technology and the Journalist. *He is a member of the editorial staff of the London* Financial Times.

new means, such as teletext display on a television screen, computer retrieval, microfiche and microfilm. This information perhaps may be disseminated at times of the day specified by the reader rather than those fixed by newspaper delivery schedules and perhaps according to a selection made by that same reader for himself rather than one made for him by an editor at the newspaper office.

In short, newspapers, both in their internal production and editorial processes and in their external competitive environment are now entering fully into the electronic era, with challenging implications for their future—and for ours. As citizens, we may have to make choices about what sorts of newspapers and information media we want in the future and about who should own and control them. For throughout the Western world both the stress and the promise of the electronic era are driving publishing (and broadcasting as well) into fewer and fewer hands, into conglomerates and international multimedia organizations with the financial resources and know-how to cope with the changes.

Throughout most of the U.S. and Great Britain, as in many parts of Europe, the effect of competition from television has been to establish a pattern of only one newspaper to each city—and these newspapers are increasingly owned by chains. In the U.S., at a recent count, only 691 of the 1,759 daily newspapers were still independently owned; chains had been gobbling them up at the rate of 55 a year. At the same time the chains themselves have become diversified; an example in 1978 was the acquisition by Gannett Co., the largest chain in the U.S. with 77 newspapers, of Combined Communications of Arizona, owner of television and radio stations, two newspapers, and a large outdoor billboard business. In Great Britain the ultimate fate of *The Times* lay in the hands of a company, the International Thomson Organization, whose headquarters shifted from England to Canada during 1978 and whose main wealth was derived from oil.

But news is one of the commodities about which anxieties over monopoly and concentration are most acutely felt. The free flow of news and views, from a variety of sources, is considered to be one of the basic ingredients of democracy. Thus a rich vein of argument is opened up between those who see these structural technology-driven trends in the newspaper industry as a sinister development, to be reversed by law and law enforcement, and those who see the trends as the inevitable, indeed desirable, response to the rise of television and the risks and rewards of innovation.

New Technology and Old Crafts. Thus the disputes that shut down the *New York Times* (along with other New York newspapers) and *The Times* of

London and also the settlements over new technology that were reached in 1978 in West Germany and Australia, were symptomatic of widespread industrial upheaval. In West Germany, although there were strikes on the issue, the ultimate agreement was made much easier by the fact that all workers in the printing industry belong (in marked contrast to Great Britain and the U.S.) to one union; while in Australia the system of labour law meant that (much as in the U.S. but in sharp contrast to the U.K.) a judge eventually ruled on whether, and how, the new equipment should be used.

In one major respect there was really little in common between the London and New York disputes. In New York it was probably one of the final battles in a war that is practically over. For after a series of union-management clashes in the early and middle 1970s, the U.S. newspaper industry is in the throes of a massive switchover to full electronic technology. But London's Fleet Street is still (with a few exceptions) the last great bastion of the "old technology" of hot metal printing, and *The Times* was the first British paper to attempt a head-on showdown with the unions over the introduction of computerized technology, and the effect this would have on jobs among the skilled craft unions.

What the computer does, or can do, inside a newspaper is to cut out almost all human activity between the first creation of a story or feature article (whether it be edited from a wire service or written by a reporter) and its appearance on the printing plate. Traditionally, this has been the area where the compositors have worked, setting type and making up pages; other skilled men have then made the printing plates, or manned the telex machines that sent the stories from one office to another. The computer, allied to the camera lens and the laser, wholly or substantially replaces all these men. Managements, spotting the implications for profits of drastically cutting down their expensive skilled labour force, were not slow to act. The struggle has been and is often prolonged and bitter.

The compositors are among the oldest craft unions in the world, dating back in Europe to at least the 17th century; they are tightly organized into closed shops (one must be a union member to get a job), and are usually highly paid—in the case of Fleet Street, higher paid than many managers. Theirs is a proud and ancient craft tradition, and, despite controversy about overmanning, the production of newspapers night after night has depended a great deal on their skill and dedication. To displace such men by computers is neither easy nor pleasant.

The Pushbutton Daily. The positive side of the issue is that with profits generated by more efficient technology newspaper companies are and will be both improving their products and creating new jobs in areas of "electronic publishing" that in some cases do away with paper altogether. Many newspaper owners believe that newsprint will be limited in supply by ecological considerations and will get increasingly expensive not only in itself but also to distribute in bulky parcels of printed newspapers. Electronic transmission seems to be the answer. This might mean simply printing the paper in several different places at once and therefore closer to the reader. The great example of this is the *Wall Street Journal*, printed in a dozen U.S. centres from editorial material sent from New York, often by satellite; the *Los Angeles Times* and *New York Times* are using the same techniques for page facsimile transmission, as are the *International Herald Tribune* in Europe and *The Guardian* and *Financial Times* in London. Alternatively, it might mean pure electronic transmission, with the information displayed on a TV-style screen in the office or home.

For newspapers the question is, who controls these developments, and who provides the information they supply? Is it to be the TV networks, or the newspaper companies, or the telecommunications companies? In West Germany there has been a running battle between the (state-owned) television stations and the (privately owned) newspaper groups on this question. In the U.K. there has been a typical British compromise, with the TV networks running their own teletext service under the names Ceefax and Oracle, and the Post Office running another service, Prestel, which links the TV set to the telephone and thence to Post Office computers. The important difference is that newspaper and other publishers, as well as many other organizations, provide the information for Prestel. In the U.S., antitrust rules governing AT&T have complicated the issue. But other computer data base distributors have flourished, while alongside them the *New York Times* has developed its massive computer-based Information Bank, and the *Wall Street Journal* is marketing its computerized News Retrieval Service to the financial community.

Satellites, lasers, facsimile, computer storage and retrieval—a far cry from the chase and the forme and the printer's devil of older times. But there is still the need to communicate, to say something meaningful to someone. When does wisdom degenerate into knowledge? Knowledge into information? Information into data? Data into computer bit rates? Modern technology may swamp us with the trivial or select for us the significant. Therein may lie the long-run survival of newspaper companies—their long tradition of editing out the chaff, on behalf of the public, and adding up the grains of truth. The man in the green eyeshade may be with us for a while yet.

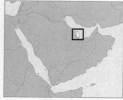

Qatar

Qatar

An independent monarchy (emirate) on the west coast of the Persian Gulf, Qatar occupies a desert peninsula east of Bahrain, with Saudi Arabia and the United Arab Emirates bordering it on the south. Area: 11,400 sq km (4,400 sq mi). Pop. (1978 est.): 200,000. Capital: Doha (pop., 1978 est., 160,-000). Language: Arabic. Religion: Muslim. Emir in 1978, Sheikh Khalifah ibn Hamad ath-Thani.

In April the border dispute with Bahrain involving the nearly uninhabited Hawar Island and potential oil concession rights was revived; Saudi Arabia and the United Arab Emirates (U.A.E.) attempted to mediate. Qatar continued to provide aid to Arab and Islamic countries and to take an interest in their affairs. Special concern was shown toward the Horn of Africa, and in June Somali Pres. Muhammad Siyad Barrah visited Qatar for talks with the emir, Sheikh Khalifah ibn Hamad ath-Thani. In April the emir decreed that the term of office of the 30-member Consultative Council would be extended for four years after its expiration on April 30.

On Jan. 28, 1978, the Qatar riyal was revalued by 1.8% against the U.S. dollar and the former relationship with the Bahrain and U.A.E. currencies thereby restored. Qatar reduced capital expenditure in its 1978 development budget by about 20% from 1977 to about $1.3 billion. The allocation for heavy industry was reduced by about 40% as a result of the completion of several major projects. In April the country's new $284 million iron and steel plant was inaugurated. A $35 million contract to build a liquid gas plant to replace one destroyed by fire in 1977 was awarded in August to a Japanese company. Crude oil output, which fell by 10.7% in 1977 from 1976 levels, increased sharply from March 1978 onward.   (PETER MANSFIELD)

Race Relations

In 1978 the issue of human rights stole some of the limelight from that of race relations. Deterioration rather than progress marked relations between majority and minority races in many parts of the world, with collision courses seemingly set in southern Africa. And there was less optimism about Israeli-Arab relations than there had been at the end of 1977 after the peace initiative of Egyptian Pres. Anwar as-Sadat.

Africa. Southern Africa in 1978 was the area of the world in which uneasy race relations were most widespread, between the black and white races above all. In Rhodesia—Zimbabwe to be—the ruling white minority controlled a country close to full-scale war and was constantly engaged in actions against African guerrilla forces. Yet the rigidity of previous segregation had been considerably modified. The now biracial government of transition included black department heads; access to land ownership, housing, schools, and hospitals by blacks was scheduled; and personal relations between whites and blacks were better than

they had been in the past. But the black African nationalist leaders of the Patriotic Front of guerrilla forces, claiming to be the authentic representatives of black Zimbabwe, would not compromise with the white-led administration. (*See* RHODESIA.)

In South Africa race relations were unsettled with outbursts of violence in African townships, notably Soweto near Johannesburg. They were framed primarily in a social context, with strong political overtones. Some petty restrictions on the black population (no longer to be called "Bantu" from 1978), including some on theatre seating, were lifted, but they were replaced by an even more oppressive insecurity. Blacks who had been born in South Africa and had lived there all their lives were now assigned to one or another of the recently created homelands. Thus, they became foreigners without rights in South Africa proper, nominally forbidden to remain there if unemployed. The citizens of South Africa were now entirely white, the majority black population having the status of temporary, imported labour. In the courts there were trials of blacks charged with violence and subversion, notably of 11 Soweto student leaders, and there were also exonerations of police brutality against blacks. When the banned Pan-African Congress launched an insurgency campaign in November, 23 arrests were made. Some show was made of including the white, Coloured, and Indian populations under a parliamentary umbrella, but few nonwhites set much store by it. In Namibia (South West Africa) there was another confrontation between militant blacks and a proposed administration in which white influence would predominate. (*See* SOUTH AFRICA.)

On September 19 the revelation that British oil companies had over a long period broken sanctions against Rhodesia imposed by Britain and the UN, at first covertly through an arrangement with a French company and later directly, aroused indignation throughout black southern Africa. This was particularly true in Zambia, which had contributed to its own impoverishment through its observance of sanctions. Consternation, accompanied by recriminations, was felt in Britain, where the good name of the government and of the British people it represented seemed badly compromised in one

Puerto Rico:
see Dependent States

Quakers:
see Religion

Quarrying:
see Mining and Quarrying

Faculty members at Vanderbilt University in Nashville, Tennessee, marched in protest against the apartheid policies of South Africa when the South African tennis team appeared in Nashville to take part in the Davis Cup competition in March.

of the world's most acute race relations issues. The work of those in the British government—and in the U.S. administration as well—who had striven to reach a settlement in Rhodesia seemed to be jeopardized by what was interpreted in Africa as an underhanded attempt to shore up white power.

Ethiopia, by the end of the year, had not only defeated Somalia preparatory to restoring full control over the Somali nomads in the Ogaden but was pressing back the separatist forces in Eritrea. A report of genocide was made against the regime of Pres. Idi Amin of Uganda, with regard to alleged mass killings among the Lango and Acholi tribes in February.

A UN conference held in Geneva in August and attended by 123 nations, as part of the UN Decade for Action Against Racism and Racial Discrimination declared in 1973, accused Israel of giving South Africa military assistance. The conferees made a 26-point declaration, which among other things called for mandatory economic sanctions, including an oil embargo, against South Africa and urged governments not to recognize the black homelands set up by South Africa. The nine European Economic Community nations, as well as Australia, Canada, and New Zealand, left the conference session in protest. The U.S. and Israel had already boycotted the conference because of a 1975 UN resolution that equated Zionism with racism.

Australia. On Dec. 21, 1977, Prime Minister Malcolm Fraser dismissed Glenister Sheil from his post as minister of veterans' affairs because of his public support for the introduction of racial segregation in Australia if the Aboriginal population wanted it. In November Aboriginal representatives lobbying in Britain against bauxite mining in Queensland reported that the Anti-Slavery Society hoped to take their case to the UN Human Rights Commission in Geneva. Mick Miller, chairman of the Queensland Land Council, reportedly said, "The Aboriginals have no title to their tribal lands. They must have a permit to be on a reserve, and

a permit to leave. Anyone caught without a permit on a reserve can be fined $200." In November it was announced that Fraser's federal government had signed an agreement with Aboriginals in the Northern Territory for uranium mining to begin at Ranger, 130 mi east of Darwin.

The Americas. The Akawaio tribe in the Upper Mazarui Basin in Guyana occupied 2,590 sq km of land scheduled to be submerged in 1982 beneath the waters of a dammed-up lake. In April 1978 the Amazonia Symposium held in Wisconsin unanimously condemned the scheme as "an act of ethnocide and ecocide against the Akawaio Nation." By contrast, in the United States indigenous peoples had begun to try to exercise some muscle. According to the 1970 census, 792,730 people in the U.S. identified themselves as American Indians. In the spring of 1977 tribes that occupied land rich in coal and uranium, such as the Navajo, joined together in a new group called the Council of Energy Resources Tribes, which finally received financial backing from federal sources. To protest against 11 bills before Congress more than 1,000 tribal people

Members of the National Front, a neofascist group in Britain, staged a rally in London. The three-finger salute signifies white power.

in 1978 participated in a 3,000-mi "Longest Walk" to Washington, D.C.

On June 28 the U.S. Supreme Court in complex opinions on the Allan Bakke (see BIOGRAPHIES) case appeared to give comfort simultaneously to civil rights activists and those opposed to affirmative action. (Bakke had claimed to be a victim of "reverse discrimination" because the University of California medical school's minority admissions plan—reserving 16 places out of 100 for students of minority races—had deprived him, as a white applicant, of a possible place in the school while admitting less qualified blacks.) The court's decision, by a 5 to 4 vote, condemned numerically fixed admissions programs as a form of discrimination but allowed that such factors as minority status or ethnic background could be taken into account. How the Bakke case affected implementation of affirmative action programs with numerical goals was not clear, but in August the U.S. Commission on Civil Rights claimed to be "heartened" by the decision and recommended an "all-out effort on behalf of affirmative action programs." In June the Mormon Church in Salt Lake City, Utah, removed the exclusion of blacks from the priesthood and so from their inner temples.

Europe. In Britain unprovoked assaults and murders of black and coloured people reached an unprecedented level. Attacks were made in particular upon Bengali communities in the East End of London. Racism became "part of the mainstream of politics" according to the Institute of Race Relations. The Conservative Party leader, Margaret Thatcher, expressed an underlying apprehension of many of Britain's white population when she said on television on January 30 that "people are really rather afraid that this country might be rather swamped by people with a different culture." She did not seek repatriation of West Indians and Pakistanis as advocated by conservative politician Enoch Powell, but called for an end to immigration other than on compassionate grounds.

A broad-based movement called the Anti-Nazi League (ANL) was formed to combat racist ideas. At two ANL carnivals in May and September more than 200,000 demonstrators marched in London. The ANL claimed 280 branches since its foundation in November 1977. The Board of Deputies of British Jews, however, suspected the political motives of some member organizations and did not join.

Asia. In India outbreaks of inter-communal rioting and murder between Muslims and Hindus early in October spread throughout the state of Uttar Pradesh. Rioting had already occurred during the year in several Indian states, particularly against the scheduled castes, the former untouchables. Approximately 200,000 Muslims began leaving Burma for Bangladesh in March, but some of them later returned. (Burma had been investigating illegal immigration of Muslims.) After the uneasy quiet of 1977, fighting was again resumed in Lebanon, involving clashes between Christians (of two rival factions), Palestinian and Syrian Arabs, and Israelis. (See LEBANON.)

A second World Romany Congress in Geneva in April consisted of 100 delegates from 25 countries. They included film actor Yul Brynner, who claimed gypsy descent. The congress asked the UN for consultative status as a national minority and to discuss with UNESCO a program to preserve Romany culture; the West German government was asked to provide reparation for the half million gypsies killed in World War II, the sum to be spent on gypsy education. The National Gypsy Council, representing 8,500 gypsy families in England and Wales and their 17,000 children, stated in June that gypsies wished their children to attend ordinary schools. (STUART BENTLEY)

[522.B]

Racket Games

Badminton. In the All-England tournament held in London, March 15–18, 1978, Liem Swie King of Indonesia won the men's singles by defeating fellow countryman Rudy Hartono 15–10, 15–3. The women's championship was won by Gillian Gilks of England, who triumphed in the finals over Saori Kondo of Japan 11–1, 11–9. Men's doubles were taken by Tjun Tjun and Johan Wahjudi of Indonesia 15–12, 15–8 over Christian and Ade Chandra, also of Indonesia. Atsuko Tokuda and Mikiko Takada of Japan defeated Emiko Ueno and Yoshiko Yonekura, also of Japan, 18–16, 15–6, to win the women's doubles, and the mixed doubles were taken by Michael Tredgett and Nora Perry of England 15–7, 15–4 over Steen Skovgaard and Lene Koppen of Denmark.

In the U.S. championships, which took place at Austin, Texas, March 22–25, 1978, Mike Walker of Manhattan Beach, Calif., won the men's singles by defeating Gary Higgins of Alhambra, Calif., 15–9, 4–15, 15–11. Cheryl Carton of San Diego, Calif., triumphed over Pam Bristol of Flint, Mich., 8–11, 11–5, 11–2 for the women's singles title. The men's doubles went to John Britton of Manhattan Beach and Charles Coakley of Newport Beach, Calif., 15–12, 14–17, 15–8 over Higgins and Bob Dickie of Manhattan Beach. Diana Osterhues of Torrance, Calif., and Janet Wilts of Pasadena, Calif., won the women's doubles 17–14, 17–15 over Bristol and Judianne Kelly of Costa Mesa, Calif. In the mixed doubles Bristol and Bruce Pontow of Blue Island, Ill., defeated Coakley and Wilts 15–11, 15–11.

(JACK H. VAN PRAAG)

Squash Rackets. The increasing cost of staging international championships was making it difficult to find sponsors for some of the major championships. Thus, the second World Open championship, which was to have been held in England in September 1978, had to be canceled owing to lack of a sponsor.

The first World Open championship was played at Adelaide, Australia, in October 1977 and was won by Geoffrey Hunt (Australia), who in the final beat Qamar Zaman (Pak.). Hunt went on to win the British Open championship in April 1978 for the fifth time, again beating Zaman in the final. This championship was made memorable by the appearance in the Open Vintage championship (over-55-year-old competitors) of the legendary Hashim Khan, making his first appearance in England since he last won the British Open cham-

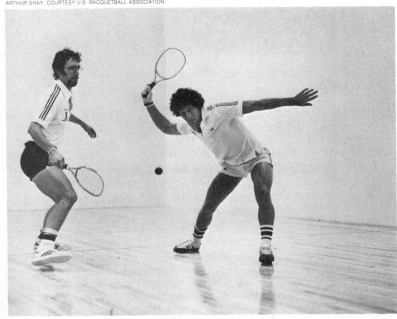

ARTHUR SHAY, COURTESY U.S. RACQUETBALL ASSOCIATION

Charlie Brumfield (left) and Marty Hogan, two of racquetball's top stars, went head to head in National Championship competition in June. Hogan won by the narrow margin of 21–20.

pionship 20 years previously. Now in his early 60s, he had no difficulty in winning the title. The North American Open championship was won by Sharif Khan for the ninth time, while the U.S. Amateur title was won by M. Desaulniers (Canada) when illness compelled co-finalist M. Sánchez (Mexico) to default. The European championships, played near Amsterdam, included for the first time a Ladies' championship, which was convincingly won by England. England also won (for the sixth successive year) the men's championship.

(JOHN H. HORRY)

Rackets. William Boone regained the British amateur singles championship at Queen's Club, London, in February 1978, beating John Prenn by three games to two in the final. In the semifinal Boone had his revenge against Charles Hue-Williams, who had beaten him in the previous year's final. In March Howard Angus regained the Louis Roederer British Open championship, beating Boone and former champion Prenn by 4–1 scores in the final and semifinals, respectively.

This change of titles meant that both Angus and Boone were in line to challenge William Surtees for the world championship, as was Prenn, who had put in his challenge in 1977. It was decided that Angus should play Boone, and the winner would meet Prenn for the right to challenge Surtees. Boone beat Angus 8–5 and Prenn 6–4 and awaited Surtees's acceptance of his challenge.

Angus and Andrew Milne, runners-up in 1977, won the amateur doubles championship for the first time. In the final at Queen's Club in April 1978, they beat Geoffrey Atkins and David Jenkins 4–3, having saved a match point in the sixth game.

Real Tennis. Howard Angus remained the world's outstanding real tennis player. He won the British amateur singles title for the 13th straight year in April 1978, defeating John Ward in straight sets in the final. Angus and Ward together retained the International Bathurst Cup for Great Britain in Paris in May, beating the U.S. 3–2 as Angus won both his singles.

(CHRISTINA WOOD)

Racquetball. In 1970, the first year that statistics were kept, there were only 50,000 racquetball players in the world, all of them playing on handball courts. "Today," reported U.S. Racquetball Association president Bob Kendler, "there are over eight million racquetballers and we can't seem to stop growing by less than 70–90% annually."

A deeper look into the racquetball phenomenon made the growth explosion easier to understand. Racquetball is a combination of virtually every racquet game in existence. It is a cousin of tennis, paddleball, squash, badminton, and even table tennis. Many racquetball enthusiasts also had played one or more of these sports.

Racquetball's growth was mirrored by equipment sales. In 1970 some 228,000 racquetballs were sold in North America. In 1978 the figure exceeded 16 million. One of the biggest strides forward came in 1978 when the Colgate-Palmolive Co. began to sponsor the professional tour of the National Racquetball Club, along with the Seamco Sporting Goods Co. and Leach Industries. Colgate's lead was followed by other corporations, whose overall sponsorship made the professional tour an annual series worth more than $300,000 in prize money and royalties.

(CHARLES S. LEVE)

Refugees

New crises emerged in 1978, in the Horn of Africa and in Bangladesh, while existing refugee situations, notably in southern Africa and Southeast Asia, were exacerbated. The 1978 financial requirements of the United Nations High Commissioner for Refugees (UNHCR), originally estimated at some $72 million, increased sharply and were expected to total $112 million. By November gov-

KELER—SYGMA

Jammed in the trunk of a car for protection, a family fled from Beirut, Lebanon, following bombardment by the Israeli Air Force in March.

ernments had pledged contributions amounting to $66 million. At the 29th session of the Executive Committee of the High Commissioner's Program, held Oct. 9–17, 1978, under the new high commissioner, Poul Hartling, former prime minister of Denmark, Somalia acceded to the 1951 Convention Relating to the Status of Refugees and the 1967 Protocol. Somalia was the sixth state to have acceded since the committee's previous session in October 1977, the others being Costa Rica, the Dominican Republic, São Tomé and Príncipe, Panama, and Spain. This brought the total number of states that were parties to these instruments to 77 and 68, respectively. Some 5,820 separated family members were reunited with the assistance of UNHCR between January 1976 and September 1978.

In Africa refugees and displaced persons at the end of 1977 were estimated at some 3.7 million—an increase of 700,000 over 1976. UNHCR expenditure under general and special programs in 1977 amounted to some $35.6 million, over $13 million of which was allocated from the general programs. In June 1977 the high commissioner had launched an appeal for $16 million, and in April 1978 an appeal was made for over $12 million to assist refugees and displaced persons in the Horn of Africa. UNHCR coordinated its assistance with representatives of national liberation movements recognized by the Organization of African Unity, as well as with the governments of states sheltering refugees. Assistance ranged from relief, accommodation in reception transit centres, and agricultural integration to educational placement. UNHCR appealed to governments for funds to finance a program to assist in repatriating and rehabilitating Zairian nationals in Angola, Sudan, Uganda, Zambia, and other neighbouring countries. This $11,375,000 program would assist an estimated 110,000 persons considered to be in greatest need.

At the end of 1977 there were an estimated 3.9 million refugees and displaced persons in Asia benefiting from UNHCR-financed aid. Total UNHCR expenditure in 1977 was $19.8 million under the special programs and $1.1 million under the general programs. Funds made available in 1978 totaled approximately $29.7 million. In May 1978 UNHCR appealed for $15,565,000 for humanitarian assis-

tance to refugees from Burma who had crossed into Bangladesh. Their number had increased to over 200,000, and 13 camps had been set up in Bangladesh to accommodate them. Later some were repatriated to Burma. In response to a request from the government of Vietnam in April 1978, a three-month emergency relief program was established for assistance to 150,000 refugees and displaced persons from Cambodia. A long-term program was being elaborated by UNHCR in cooperation with the authorities.

Refugees and displaced persons from the Indochinese Peninsula consisted mainly of those who arrived by land in Thailand and the so-called boat people, originating from Vietnam. In October 1978 refugees and displaced persons in Thailand, located in 13 centres and 2 camps, included some 96,000 persons from Laos, 14,000 from Cambodia, and

Burmese Musilms fleeing from religious persecution streamed into Bangladesh in 1978, taxing that country's already strained resources.

BENOIT GYSEMBERGH/CAMERA PRESS

3,200 from Vietnam. The boat people generally arrived in small, fragile craft in the countries bordering the South China Sea or were rescued on the high seas and taken to the first port of call. A two-day conference convened by UNHCR in Geneva in December to consider the Indochinese refugee problem was attended by 38 nations, including Vietnam.

European countries admitted many refugees and displaced persons from the Indochinese Peninsula and Latin America. In Europe, in addition to government expenditure, finance by UNHCR general programs amounting to over $2.2 million was proposed for 1978. Some $2.8 million would be needed in 1979, largely because of programs in Portugal and Spain for the benefit of persons from Africa and the inclusion, in the programs for France, of aid to refugees and displaced persons from the Indochinese Peninsula.

UNHCR signed an agreement with the Honduran government to assist about 10,000 Nicaraguans who took refuge in the south of Honduras following the September disorders in Nicaragua. The program was principally for the construction of temporary housing. (UNHCR)

See also Migration, International.

Religion

Although he wrote most of his last will and testament in 1965, Pope Paul VI expressed in this personal document points of view that anticipated the religious mood in 1978. The pontiff's will was made public shortly after his death in August. In it he advised his spiritual heirs on how they could best manage the relationship between the Roman Catholic Church and other Christian denominations and how they should guide the church in its relationship with the secular world.

Ecumenically speaking, Pope Paul said: "May the work of drawing closer to the separate brothers be continued with great understanding, with great patience, with great love, but without deflecting from the true Catholic doctrine." Addressing himself to the church-world relationship, the pope counseled: "One should not believe that he is benefiting the world by assuming its customs, its tastes, but by studying it, loving it, and serving it."

His words stood in sharp contrast to the popular religious slogan of the 1960s when many church leaders were proclaiming that "the world must set the agenda for the church." Early in the 1970s, the mood shifted. As subscribers to various religious creeds became more and more disillusioned with the secular-scientific world's claims to wisdom, they became increasingly intent on rediscovering the distinctive values of their own religious traditions. Alert to the conservative mood of the times, trendy speakers in 1978 scored easy points with their audiences by deploring trendiness.

Neotraditionalism expressed itself in a variety of religious (and secular) experiences in 1978. Just as several large universities abandoned the faddish experimental courses launched in the 1960s, religious leaders, in a parallel development, attempted to return to the "basics" of their respective faiths. At the mass preceding the conclave that met in August to elect a new pope, leaders of the Roman Catholic Church gave some indication of the kind of man they were looking for by their choice of Scripture lessons. The first, from the book of Isaiah, spoke of the responsibility of the People of God to "bring good news to the poor and to bind up hearts that are broken." The second, from the Letter to the Ephesians, warned of the perils of being "tossed one way and another by every changing wind of doctrine." And the third, from the Gospel of John, urged Christians to "love one another."

On August 26 the College of Cardinals selected as the church's 263rd pope Albino Cardinal Luciani, the 65-year-old patriarch of Venice, who took as his papal name John Paul I. When the smiling Venetian pope died 34 days after assuming office, the cardinals broke a 455-year-old tradition by electing a non-Italian, Karol Cardinal Wojtyla, the 58-year-old archbishop of Krakow, Poland.

In some ways this was a radical step that dramatized the catholicity of Catholicism. In other ways, however, the election of history's first Polish pope was a conservative action. By choosing the name John Paul II, the new pope signaled his intention of following the pattern laid down by his immediate predecessors. And he, like the church of his homeland, had a reputation for theological conservatism. Indeed, it was obvious that the cardinals would not have elected a man who was less than thoroughly orthodox in his doctrinal stance. The election symbolized the cardinal electors' desire for continuity combined with cautious change consistent with the initiatives taken by the Second Vatican Council. (See *Roman Catholic Church*, below.)

At a July convention in Chicago, the Lutheran Church in America, largest and most progressive of the nation's three major Lutheran bodies, engaged in a noteworthy symbolic act when delegates took the first step toward changing the title of its top national and regional leaders from "president" to "bishop." Advocates of the change argued that "president" was borrowed from the worlds of commerce and politics, while "bishop" was rooted in biblical tradition.

As they were accustomed to do every ten years or so, the bishops of the Anglican Communion gathered in July for a Lambeth Conference in Canterbury, England, to seek consensus on major issues facing the church. Although they voted decisively against a moratorium on the ordination of additional women priests, the bishops, on the whole, were more eager to consolidate changes already made than to initiate drastic new ones. A veteran correspondent for *Christian Century* magazine said he had observed at Canterbury "a recovery of Anglican identity and self-confidence." (See *Anglican Communion*, below.)

The ecumenical movement made a few cautious steps toward Christian unity in 1978, but clearly none of the constituent bodies was prepared to take long strides. To no small extent, this was due to the desire of the participating churches to clarify their own identities before entering more fully into deeper relationships with other church bodies.

The general antipathy toward change dashed the hopes of those seeking modifications in traditional church policies and attitudes regarding homosexuality. In a year when such cities as St. Paul, Minn., and Wichita, Kan., repealed ordinances underwriting civil rights for homosexuals, the General Assembly of the United Presbyterian Church was asked to consider a proposal giving the church's general approval to the ordination of homosexuals to the ministry. In the end a compromise was worked out that left responsibility for deciding the issue in the hands of local church governing bodies (presbyteries). At the same time, the assembly went on record as saying that "unrepentant homosexual practice does not accord with the requirements for ordination."

In the realm of ideas, 1978 was not remarkable for any major theological breakthroughs. Theological books tended to reflect the work of competent craftsmen more than the labours of adventuresome spirits. The intellectual climate being what it was, some publishers found it more profitable to recycle the old books of C. S. Lewis, Dorothy L. Sayers, Thomas Merton, and the authors of "devotional classics" than to come forth with freshly minted volumes.

Despite the efforts of main-line churches to move closer to their own traditional centres of belief and practice, they did not go far enough for those still disgruntled over changes introduced in the last 15 years. Thus Archbishop Marcel Lefebvre, ignoring warnings from the Vatican, continued to ordain priests who would serve traditionalist Catholics opposed to the reforms of the Second Vatican Council. Disaffected members of the Episcopal Church in the U.S., angry over the denomination's revised prayer book and its decision to ordain women as priests and bishops, gave birth to the Anglican Catholic Church, a new denomination dedicated to preserving the old ways.

In the meantime, as main-line churches edged rightward, some of the more conservative religious groups experienced internal and external pressures that moved them slightly to the left. In June the president of the Church of Jesus Christ of Latter-day Saints made a dramatic announcement resulting in a fundamental change in his denomination's policy and practice. Saying that he was acting on the basis of a revelation from God, he declared that the denomination's traditional ban on the ordination of black men as priests no longer was in effect. Two days later, Joseph Freeman, Jr., became Mormonism's first black priest. (See *Church of Jesus Christ of Latter-day Saints*, below.)

As Protestant evangelicals continued to enjoy the boom in "born again" religion, they became more susceptible to cosmopolitanizing influences. *Christianity Today*, a leading evangelical journal, hired a new editor, Kenneth Kantzer, who was less a doctrinal hard-liner than his predecessor, Harold Lindsell. Fuller Theological Seminary in Pasadena, Calif., a leading evangelical school, continued to build a faculty that represented a somewhat sophisticated form of evangelical faith.

And the 13 million-member Southern Baptist Convention, much in the spotlight since the election of Jimmy Carter, the country's first Southern Baptist president, reflected its new mainstream status at its annual convention in Atlanta, Ga., by adopting resolutions calling upon the nations of the world to support multilateral arms control agreements and policies guaranteeing human rights. In the past, the Convention had confined itself largely to pronouncements on more traditional "religious" issues.

The forces and counterforces influencing Christianity were also affecting the Jewish religious community. Neotraditionalism was much in favour among Reform and Conservative Jews, the branches of Judaism that had been the most responsive to the dynamics of the secular world. The appeal of tradition was reinforced by the strong emotional impact of "Holocaust," a 9½-hour television special dramatizing the horrors of the Nazi persecution of Jews. In the meantime, Orthodox Jews, who had been strictly traditional all along, showed signs of making some hesitant moves out of their isolated world while at the same time striving to keep their traditions intact. Muslims, too, were struggling to adapt to changes imposed by the cosmopolitan secular world without permitting their faith and its institutions to be transformed beyond recognition. In Saudi Arabia, Iran, and Egypt, Muslim fundamentalists fought, sometimes violently, for the preservation of religious traditions.

In short, as the 1980s drew nearer, it was clear that religious institutions and their members, still not completely recovered from the shocks of the 1960s, continued to long for a period when their emotional and intellectual equilibrium would not be seriously threatened. For most people, it seemed, faith was an instrumental means of coping with change, not a summons to effect change.

Universal as was the desire for homeostasis, however, forces were at work that served to remind the faithful they were living in a fast-changing world. Feminists were not satisfied with the status quo. In June the influential Catholic Theological Society published a research report, "Women in Church and Society," that called into question all traditional teachings used by the church to prevent women from being ordained as priests. And in November several hundred Catholic women meeting in Baltimore, Md., "witnessed" to their belief that they were "called" by God to be priests. Similarly, residents of the third world reminded their co-religionists in North America and Europe that their longing for peace and quiet would not be satisfied until the third world's demands for justice were met.

And all over the world unprecedented events were taking place that could not be met with ready-made formulas. When, for example, Louise Brown (*see* BIOGRAPHIES), the world's first "test-tube baby," was born in July in Lancashire, England, she by her presence served notice to religious leaders that new questions of faith and morals were emerging that required nothing less than the most creative uses of traditionalism.

(ROY LARSON)

PROTESTANT CHURCHES

Anglican Communion. Anglicanism in 1978 was dominated by the 11th Lambeth Conference and by further rumblings over the ordination of women. The Lambeth Conference, which normally meets every ten years, is a gathering of bishops from all over the world. In 1978 it brought together 440 of them, more than ever before. There were also more representatives of the third world. For the first time the bishops did not meet at Lambeth Palace, official London residence of the archbishop of Canterbury, but at Canterbury.

The archbishop of Canterbury, Donald Coggan, had set out the aim and context of the conference as "prayer and waiting upon God," but the bishops could not, and did not wish to, avoid wider considerations. Accordingly, they found themselves debating such diverse issues as political and economic injustice, poverty, racial discrimination, technology, ecology, and war and violence.

The Lambeth Conference has no legislative powers and the bishops represent only themselves. This shocked Archbishop Athenagoras, an official Orthodox observer, who urged the conference to acquire an authoritative status. There was some pressure for this from within the conference itself, but generally the bishops felt it would be alien to the ethos of Anglicanism. They settled instead for Archbishop Coggan's suggestion that there be a "Primates Committee," consisting of senior bishops and meeting at fairly regular intervals.

The bishops turned to the ordination of women, pressured to do so both from Anglicans opposed to women priests and from the Roman Catholic and Orthodox churches, which had repeatedly warned that further extensions of women's ordination would seriously jeopardize prospects for unity. The conference declared its acceptance of both those churches that do ordain women and those that do not and urged churches to respect each other's policies. However, when the General Synod of the Church of England met in November, a motion to allow women's ordination was defeated by opposition among the clergy; both bishops and laity voted in favour.

At the beginning of the year, opposition to women priests (among other things) led to the formal establishment of a breakaway church in North America, composed chiefly of dissidents from the Episcopal Church of the U.S. but also including some Canadians. They consecrated their first bishops in circumstances that caused disputes among the dissidents themselves. In a case involving four breakaway parishes in California, the court ruled that the church buildings were the property of the diocese.
(SUSAN YOUNG)

Baptist Churches. The condition of Baptists within the Soviet bloc remained stable, with slight indications of numerical growth. In England, by contrast, Baptists had declined 30% over the last 25 years. In the U.S. the picture was one of growth, at least for the Southern Baptist Convention, the largest Protestant denomination in the country (over 13 million).

At its annual meeting, the Southern Baptist Convention announced the Bold Mission Thrust, a program of evangelism aimed at bringing the gospel to every person in the world by the year 2000. The program was to be initiated in 1979–82.

An offshoot was the Mission Service Corps, designed to place 5,000 volunteers in mission fields for one- or two-year terms by 1982. A record 279 foreign missionaries were added to the regular overseas corps in 1978. On the negative side, it was noted with concern that baptisms among Southern Baptists were the lowest since 1949, and Sunday school enrollments were down.

Among American black Baptist denominations, the largest, the National Baptist Convention, U.S.A., elected Joseph H. Jackson to a 25th term as president. Education was the theme of the annual meeting in New Orleans, La., in September. A $40,000 grant was given to Meharry Medical College in Nashville, Tenn., affiliated with the United Methodist Church. Meharry had produced 43% of all black doctors and dentists in the U.S. The other major largely black Baptist denomination, the Progressive National Baptist Convention, meeting in Los Angeles, presented Rosa Parks with a special award for her refusal to give up her seat on a bus to a white man in Montgomery, Ala., in 1955. It was this incident that sparked the civil rights movement of the '50s and '60s.

The predominantly white American Baptist Churches, U.S.A., which had entered into a fund-raising program—the Fund of Renewal—with the Progressive National Baptists for the support of minority causes, reported revenue of $6 million, only half of what had been expected. While some saw this as a moral success, others judged the fund a serious failure. The fund's counsel noted: "[Racism] probably had the most seriously negative effect on the campaign of all the problems we encountered."

The Baptist World Alliance, a loosely affiliated organization of world Baptists, met in Manila for six days. A strong stand was taken on human rights, and over $1 million was pledged for world relief.
(NORMAN R. DE PUY)

Christian Church (Disciples of Christ). The church held its 1978 General Board meeting in Chicago, despite some opposi-

The new Anglican cathedral in Liverpool, England, was formally dedicated in 1978 after decades of construction.

tion because of Illinois' failure to ratify the Equal Rights Amendment to the U.S. Constitution. Leaders vowed to hold the 1979 General Assembly in St. Louis while maintaining pressure on Missouri, another state that had not yet ratified ERA.

Women's rights were a major concern of the quadrennial international gathering of Disciples women in June, a meeting that drew a record 5,000 to Purdue University, West Lafayette, Ind. Blacks of the church also held a record-size national meeting, attracting more than 800 to their August convocation in Little Rock, Ark. The Disciples' Reconciliation program celebrated its tenth birthday, having provided some $4 million for race and poverty projects throughout the U.S.

The issue of homosexuality continued to trouble Disciples, particularly early in 1978 following the action of the 1977 General Assembly affirming civil liberties for homosexuals. A task force worked throughout the year on what attitude the church might take on ordination of homosexuals.

Leaders of the church expressed distress over the mass suicide of members of the People's Temple, led by the Rev. Jim Jones, an ordained Disciples minister. (*See* GUYANA.)

(ROBERT LOUIS FRIEDLY)

Churches of Christ. Total membership reached an estimated four million in 1978. Two Florida churches led in growth—Jacksonville with 279 baptisms and the Crossroads Church in Gainesville with 270.

Twenty thousand persons attended the International Soul-Winning Workshop in Tulsa, Okla., in March, and similar workshops were held in St. Louis, Mo., Wichita, Kan., and Sacramento, Calif. A five-night "Unite in Christ" campaign held by 30 congregations in Nashville, Tenn., had a total attendance of 42,000. Stations WPIX in New York City and WJAL in Washington, D.C., were added to the Herald of Truth TV and radio ministry.

In the foreign mission field, approximately 1,400 full-time workers were active in more than 125 countries. The Bammel Road Church in Houston, Texas, instituted its Iron Curtain Printing Ministry, based in Vienna, to place Bibles in Eastern Europe.

Enrollment at 15 accredited Christian colleges totaled 18,481, an increase of 4.5%. Northeastern Christian Junior College in Villanova, Pa., York College in York, Neb., and Ohio Valley College in Parkersburg, W.Va., received full accreditation.

(M. NORVEL YOUNG)

Church of Christ, Scientist. During 1978 an endowment fund was established for the denomination's newspaper, the *Christian Science Monitor.* In opening the fund in June, the Christian Science Board of Directors indicated the church's strengthened commitment to the paper's founding purpose, "to injure no man, but to bless all mankind" (Mary Baker Eddy, 1908), despite spiraling publishing costs.

About 12,000 Christian Scientists from many of the denomination's approximately 3,000 congregations in 57 countries attended the annual meeting of the First Church of Christ, Scientist, in Boston. In a keynote message, DeWitt John, chairman of the

Board of Directors, urged members to put aside "busywork [and] organizational mechanics, . . . The need today is for more healing, more spirituality, meekness, humility." Church officers reported a modest increase in new branch churches and an overall slight decline in membership.

John R. Peterson, the church's general counsel, was named president for a one-year term that would take the denomination into its hundredth year.

(ALLISON W. PHINNEY)

Church of Jesus Christ of Latter-day Saints. The most dramatic change in Latter-day Saint policy since the 1890s came with the announcement on June 9, 1978, that church leaders had received a revelation inviting participation in the Mormon lay priesthood for all worthy male members regardless of race. Heretofore blacks of African descent had been excluded from priesthood functions. Citing the church's vigorous growth in many nations, 83-year-old president Spencer W. Kimball (*see* BIOGRAPHIES) and his two counselors explained that they had actively sought such a revelation in order to extend priesthood blessings to the church's entire male membership. This also meant full participation for worthy church members of all races in temple ceremonies. Kimball announced plans to proselyte more vigorously among blacks, both in the U.S. and overseas.

The dedication in June of a memorial park in Nauvoo, Ill., featured the unveiling of the Monument to Women. Meanwhile, the church's First Presidency counseled against extension of the seven-year deadline for ratification of the Equal Rights Amendment, arguing that it was not in the best interest of women and would polarize the nation.

Church membership exceeded four million by early 1978, maintaining an annual growth rate of approximately 5%. The increasingly international character of the church was evident in the addition of a Briton, a German, and a Japanese Mormon to the First Quorum of Seventy, part of the hierarchy of General Authorities.

(LEONARD J. ARRINGTON)

Joseph Freeman, Jr. was the first black to be ordained into the Mormon priesthood.

WIDE WORLD

Jehovah's Witnesses. A society of Christians whose activities include promotion of home Bible study, Jehovah's Witnesses in 1978 numbered 2,182,341 individuals associated with 42,255 congregations in 205 lands. The Witnesses conducted an average of 1,257,084 free home Bible studies with individuals or families, in which they emphasized the beliefs that the Bible is the inspired word of God, that Jehovah is the only true God, that salvation comes through faith in God's Son Jesus Christ, and that the kingdom of God through Christ will soon be the only government for all mankind. During the year, 95,052 new evangelizers were baptized. Altogether, Witnesses devoted 307,272,262 hours to the spreading of their beliefs.

A series of 112 five-day "Victorious Faith" international conventions were held in 62 countries, with a combined attendance of over one million. The principal discourse was "Jesus Christ—Victorious King with Whom Nations Must Reckon." In keeping with their attention to use of the Bible to improve the quality of family life, the Witnesses released a new handbook entitled *Making Your Family Life Happy.*

(FREDERICK W. FRANZ)

Lutheran Churches. Lutheran cooperative efforts continued in 1978, though the goal of one united denomination still seemed a distant reality. One notable development on the U.S. scene was a proposal by the new Association of Evangelical Lutheran Churches (AELC) that all branches of the church in North America commit themselves to union in principle, then sit down and work out a merger process.

At year's end, the "Call to Union" had the enthusiastic approval of the AELC—formed in a breakaway from the Lutheran Church-Missouri Synod (LCMS)—and the liberal Lutheran Church in America (LCA). But there was hesitance in the more middle-of-the-road American Lutheran Church (ALC), and no sign that either the conservative Missouri Synod or the even more conservative Wisconsin Evangelical Lutheran Synod would go along. Still, discussions continued through a new Committee on Lutheran Unity (ALC, LCA, AELC) and these churches, together with the LCMS, were engaged in a variety of cooperative endeavours through the Lutheran Council in the U.S.A.

Worldwide membership in Lutheran churches remained about the same as in recent years. The latest world count showed some 70.4 million members, with nearly 55 million in the 99 member bodies of the Lutheran World Federation (LWF). In North America the total was 8.9 million members in 15 Lutheran groupings.

Through both the LWF and a counterpart organization in the U.S., notable progress was made in the theological dialogue with Roman Catholics. The international joint commission, completing work on a study of the Eucharist, issued a statement that, though differences remain, there is considerable common understanding of the sacrament. Similarly, theologians of the two churches in the U.S. issued a document on papal infallibility declaring that the often-divisive issue is secondary to common trust in Christ and the gospel. The U.S. dialogue was also marked by issuance of a Lutheran-Episcopal statement citing new areas of understanding of the doctrine of justification by grace.

Churches in many countries expressed their solidarity with black Lutherans in Namibia (South West Africa), who comprised nearly half the population of the territory.

A new *Lutheran Book of Worship*, the product of more than a decade of inter-Lutheran effort, went into distribution in September with an advance sale of 800,000. Lutheran Immigration and Refugee Service, a cooperative agency, continued efforts to find congregational sponsors for Indochinese refugees in the U.S. In recent years it had assisted some 20,000 of these homeless persons.   (NEIL B. MELLBLOM)

Methodist Churches. Wesley's Chapel in City Road, London, the "Mother Church of Methodism," opened by John Wesley on Nov. 1, 1778, was reopened exactly 200 years later. The special service was conducted by the president of the British Conference and attended by Queen Elizabeth II, the Executive Committee of the World Methodist Council (WMC), and other dignitaries. The chapel had been restored at a cost of approximately £1 million, nearly half of which came from the Methodist churches in North America.

In an important legal decision, a California state court ruled that the United Methodist Church (UMC) was a "spiritual confederation" not subject to suit under California law. Dismissing a $266 million lawsuit brought against the UMC on behalf of 160 residents of the bankrupt Pacific Homes for the elderly, the judge said that a contrary ruling would effectively destroy Methodism in the U.S. and would have a chilling effect on all religious movements.

The Oxford Institute of Theological Studies held its sixth meeting at Lincoln College, Oxford, bringing together 100 leading theologians to examine the relationship between "Sanctification and Liberation." The dominant concept was "oppression," and it was estimated that two-thirds of the world's population were oppressed.

In May the government of Transkei declared the Methodist Church of South Africa to be an "undesirable organization" and ordered it to cease all activities. This followed a press conference at which Transkei's prime minister implied that the decision of the church not to send greetings to heads of state was taken in order to avoid recognition of Transkei's independence. A "Methodist Church of Transkei" was set up, although the president of the Methodist Church of South Africa declared this to be "an ecclesiastical disaster."

The Rev. Colin Morris, in his last report to the British Conference as secretary of the Overseas Division, strongly defended a controversial statement about black churches in Britain. It read, "Because the black churches came into being in reaction against white rejection, we have no right to be self-righteous; but we may conclude, more in sadness than in anger, that at the very least such ghetto congregations are guilty of hoarding talents which ought to be diffused throughout the wider Christian community; at worst they are defying the catholicity of the Church." After a lengthy debate, the word "ghetto" was removed, and a further motion urged local churches to enter into and develop creative encounters with black churches.

(PETER H. BOLT)

Pentecostal Churches. Several major denominational conferences highlighted the year. The Church of God (Cleveland, Tenn.) saw 15,000 gather in Kansas City, Mo., in August. Also in Kansas City in August, the Assemblies of God sponsored a Church Growth Convention with more than 3,000 registered participants. The *Yearbook of American and Canadian Churches*

This young woman was one of 400 who were baptized in a portable pool at Shea Stadium in New York City when 55,000 Jehovah's Witnesses from around the world convened there in July.

1978 recognized the Assemblies of God as the fastest growing of the Pentecostal groups in the U.S., with over 2,000 new congregations formed since 1967. The annual convocation of the predominantly black Church of God in Christ drew over 50,000 to Memphis, Tenn., in November—the largest annual denominational conference in the U.S.

In July Anglican charismatics from 25 nations gathered in Canterbury, England, for the first pentecostal service in the cathedral there. The Lambeth Conference of Anglican bishops estimated the total number of Anglican charismatics at 811,000. A new movement developed among charismatics and Pentecostals to sponsor ecumenical Pentecost-eve celebrations. In May 60,000 gathered in Giants Stadium in New Jersey for a rally sponsored by Catholic charismatic and Pentecostal groups, and celebrations were also held in Dallas, Texas, and Oklahoma City. Plans were being laid for 20 Pentecost-eve celebrations in major U.S. cities in 1979.   (VINSON SYNAN)

Presbyterian, Reformed, and Congregational Churches. Human rights figured prominently on the 1978 agenda of the World Alliance of Reformed Churches (WARC). The WARC executive committee, which met July 31–August 5, issued a statement associating itself with the 30th anniversary of the Universal Declaration of Human Rights. The North American and Caribbean Area Council of the WARC adopted a resolution on human rights, and the Presbyterian Church in Taiwan also published a declaration on the subject. On various occasions the president of the WARC, James I. McCord, and its general secretary, Edmond Perret, expressed their concern over human rights violations. Another important issue before the executive committee was the next General Council of the WARC, which was scheduled for 1982.

Studies on the theological basis of human rights were to be pursued by the Alliance on a broader platform involving churches from outside the Reformed family. A new theme for theological studies, the biblical concept of God's "covenant," was launched.

The Alliance continued to be widely involved in the search for unity among the Christian churches. During the year member churches sent in their comments and reactions to reports on dialogues with the Baptist World Alliance and the Secretariat for Promoting Christian Unity of the Roman Catholic Church. An Anglican-Reformed consultation was held in December 1978, and the ecumenical patriarch of Constantinople invited a Reformed delegation to visit Istanbul for preliminary conversations with the Orthodox.

Church union negotiations in Belgium led to formation of the United Protestant Church of Belgium on Sept. 30, 1978. Involved in this merger were the Protestant Church of Belgium, the Reformed Church of Belgium, and the Belgian District of the Reformed (Gereformeerde) Churches in The Netherlands. More than one-quarter of all WARC member churches were currently involved in union talks.

The first meeting of Alliance representatives in Spain took place in March, when the European Area Committee met in Madrid. Karoly Toth, a WARC vice-president, was inducted as bishop of the Danubian district of the Reformed Church in Hungary and later elected president of the Christian Peace Conference.

(INGRID T. TRINDADE)

Religious Society of Friends. Naturally enough, since the search for world peace is a basic element in the Quaker religious view, Friends concentrated their work and prayers on the UN Special Session on Disarmament, held in May and June 1978. As the result of a proposal by Friends, one day during the session was devoted to statements by 25 nongovernmental organizations, including the Friends World Committee for Consultation.

A further expression of Quaker concern for peace was a series of gatherings in the U.S. with the theme "A New Call to Peacemaking." These culminated in a conference in October at Green Lake, Wis., at which 100 Friends met with equal numbers of Brethren and Mennonites, a drawing together of the historic "peace churches."

Another traditional Quaker concern—for equality, particularly between the sexes—led the American Friends Service Committee to announce a policy of "affirmative action" in the hiring of its own employees. Over the next five years this relief and social program agency intended to ensure that its staff in all regions consisted of at least 40% women and 20% Americans of "third world" extraction, as well as a proportion of declared homosexuals.

British Friends held a week-long Yearly Meeting in August at Lancaster, scene of much persecution in early Quaker history. The event was attended by some 1,500 British Friends, out of a total membership of 19,559. (DAVID FIRTH)

Salvation Army. With the appointment of Commissioner Harry W. Williams as international secretary for planning and development in June 1978, the needs of third world countries began receiving even more concentrated attention from the Salvation Army. A number of new programs were being initiated, and humanitarian undertakings operated by specially trained indigenous Salvationists were expected to receive the backing of various governmental and international agencies. In this connection, Salvation Army World Service offices were set up in Washington, D.C., and London.

Salvationists were reminded that their Christian commitment is a costly one when, in June, two young British Salvationist missionary teachers were killed in the guerrilla war in Rhodesia. In August the Army decided to suspend its membership in the World Council of Churches, pending inquiries into that body's granting of funds to the black nationalist Rhodesian Patriotic Front.

Thirty thousand Salvationists from around the world joined with thousands of British Salvationists in staging an International Congress in London from June 29 to July 9. The event marked the passing of a century since Gen. William Booth's Christian Mission changed its name to The Salvation Army. (JENTY FAIRBANK)

Seventh-day Adventist Church. World church president Robert H. Pierson spent three weeks during August–September 1978 visiting congregations in the U.S.S.R. He was the first head of the world church to visit the Soviet Union in an official capacity since the 1917 Revolution.

Despite continuing violence in the area, the church's Middle East College, in Beirut, Lebanon, held its first graduation in three years in June. Adventist work in the Congo was closed by the government (along with that of 12 other denominations), and the oldest SDA mission college in Africa—Solusi in Rhodesia—was moved to a new site because of mounting guerrilla activity.

The 1977 Annual Council voted to include homosexuality with adultery as a valid ground for divorce. It also voted to set up local conciliation panels to mediate disputes that might otherwise go to the secular courts.

World membership reached three million in April 1978, with 243,735 members added in 1977. During 1977 the church sent a total of 1,158 workers overseas, and Seventh-day Adventist World Service distributed more than $6 million worth of relief supplies. (KENNETH H. WOOD)

Unitarian (Universalist) Churches. In 1978 this liberal church movement appeared to be undergoing a slow transformation in two directions. District organizations were gaining authority, producing a decentralization of programming. At the same time, the churches' traditional major concern for social responsibility was receding before a growing interest in self-development and personal growth. Many seminary students were opting for courses in heightened self-awareness, while pulpit emphases and General Assembly resolutions reflected a lessening concern with traditional social issues.

The 17th annual General Assembly of the Unitarian Universalist Church attracted 1,211 official delegates to the campus of Boston University, June 19–24, 1978. Resolutions were passed on the legality of living wills, world hunger, development of hospices, community correctional programs, abortion, and ending the government's tobacco price-support program. Rejected for consideration, by an earlier national poll of parishes, were such subjects as unemployment among blacks, sanctions against South Africa, peace in the Middle East, and organized crime.

Inflation and the resultant high cost of book production led to considerable debate over the future of the denomination's Beacon Press. An average of 70 books were being issued by the press annually at a substantial loss. It was decided to retain the Press but to concentrate its focus on more relevant denominational concerns and to reduce staff and the list of titles.

The jubilee anniversary meetings celebrating the founding of the General Assembly of Unitarian and Free Christian Churches in Britain were held in the spring in Cambridge. The Welsh Department reported that, for the first time, Unitarians in Wales had been invited to be represented on the Welsh Council of Churches and other ecumenical bodies. Resolutions were passed on racism, alcohol advertising, blasphemous libel, disarmament, atrocities in Ethiopia, and One World Week.

The Canadian Unitarian Council elected Brian Reis of Dundas, Ont., as president at the annual meeting in Fredericton, N.B., May 22. (JOHN NICHOLLS BOOTH)

The United Church of Canada. The effort to be relevant as the church in the world, in tension between programs and piety, was a major concern for the United Church in 1978. Four major reports approved by the 27th General Council in 1977 and sent to the 2,369 congregations for study illustrated this tension: "The Lordship of Jesus," "The Environment," "Project Ministry," and "Genetics and Ethics."

The possibility that the province of Quebec might secede from Canada continued to be a vital concern to the church, which had a French-speaking membership of 2,215 in 17 bilingual congregations in Quebec and eastern Ontario. The church was on record as recognizing the "right of peoples to self-determination." The 1980 General Council was to be held in Quebec, if possible in a Francophone setting.

With other religious denominations and secular agencies, the United Church monitored the UN Special Session on Disarmament in May and June. In a letter to ministers and members in April, the moderator, the Rt. Rev. George M. Tuttle, pointed out the opportunity afforded by the special session "for increased awareness of the awesome threat to peace implicit in the widespread stock-piling of arms."

As of 1978, the church had 107 missionaries in 17 countries overseas. The number had been declining in recent years as the Asian, African, and Latin-American churches became more self-sufficient. Conversations with the Presbyterian Church in Canada resulted in a report recommending continued cooperation in related local endeavours and mutual reception of ministers. (The majority of Presbyterians in Canada joined with the United Church in 1925, along with Methodists and Congregationalists.) (NORMAN K. VALE)

United Church of Christ. Under the leadership of its fourth president, Avery D. Post, the United Church of Christ in a non-General Synod year was engaged at all levels in implementation of the ten priorities adopted at the 11th General Synod in 1977.

The priorities included: "Aging," involving development of ministry to the elderly and programs to end discrimination against the elderly in the media; "World Hunger," including support of relevant changes in government policy, work with citizen groups on energy development issues, and support of groups working on hunger issues; "Criminal Justice and Penal Reform," urging changes that will make the U.S. criminal justice and penal systems more equitable, humane, and nondiscriminatory; "The Church and Persons with Handicaps," with a major emphasis on empowering and fully integrating persons with physical, mental, and emotional handicaps into the life of the church; "Evangelism and the Search for Faith"; "Exploitative Broadcasting," advocating a responsible broadcasting industry that will minimize such practices as the use of gratuitous violence and exploitation of sex; "Family Life," involving consideration of the biblical per-

(Above) The body of Pope Paul VI lay in state in August. (Top right) Pope John Paul I greeting crowds after his election on August 27. (Bottom right) Pope John Paul II during installation in October.

spectives, the traditional meanings of family, and the diverse relationships existing in American family life today; "Human Rights," including racial and economic justice, to be addressed in the context of the Christian faith and witness in programs throughout the church; "Local Church Vitality"; and "Women in Church and Society Including Sexism and Racism," involving a systematic approach to the elimination of institutional and cultural sexism.

In addition to these ten priorities, the church continued its support of the "Wilmington Ten," civil rights activists jailed in connection with 1971 racial disorders in Wilmington, N.C. Serious "conversations" were being held with the Christian Church (Disciples of Christ) regarding union. A report on *Human Sexuality, A Preliminary Study*, received by the 11th General Synod, continued to elicit response.

(JOSEPH H. EVANS)

[827.D; 827.G.3; 827.H; 827.J.3]

ROMAN CATHOLIC CHURCH

The year was overshadowed by the death of Pope Paul VI on Sunday, August 6, and by the death of his successor, Pope John Paul I, on Thursday, September 28, after a pontificate of 34 days (*see* OBITUARIES). The 111 cardinals who had gone into conclave on August 25 had to start all over again on October 14. It took them two days and—presumably—eight ballots to elect Karol Cardinal Wojtyla, archbishop of Krakow, Poland, who took the name John Paul II (*see* BIOGRAPHIES).

The pontificate of Pope John Paul I, though brief, was not without significance. The election of the virtually unknown Albino Cardinal Luciani, patriarch of Venice, had been surprising in its swiftness and unanimity, but he rapidly brought a new style to the papacy. He spoke simply and directly to the crowds in St. Peter's Square and at audiences. It was discovered that he had written a book, *Illustrissimi*, in which he addressed imaginary letters to such authors as Dickens and Mark Twain and to fictional characters like Pinocchio and Mr. Pickwick. He avoided the pontifical plural, and instead of the traditional coronation with the tiara, he simply "inaugurated his ministry as Supreme Pastor" (the Mass was televised). His smile made him a well-known and popular figure.

His death, alone in his bedroom, was felt as a shock. In a few brief weeks he had enabled Catholics and the world to glimpse a vision of a church at last reconciled and at peace. But he was never tested by conflict, and it was impossible to predict how his pontificate might have continued. Many cardinals remarked that he "had done what he had to do, and then departed."

The election of his successor was an even bigger surprise. Not only was Cardinal Wojtyla the first non-Italian pope in 455 years but he came from a Communist country, making his appointment politically controversial. Moreover, as popes go, he was young—a mere 58. Unlike his predecessor, he gave an impression of solidity and durability.

In his first few weeks as pope, John Paul II won the affection of the Roman crowds. He made it clear that he would not remain a "prisoner of the Vatican" and distressed some of his aides by driving around Rome in an open car and taking off on weekends by helicopter to visit shrines such as Assisi. In his administration he moved cautiously, confirming top cardinals in their posts but only on a temporary basis.

As he turned to the many dossiers on his desk, he would discover that church-state conflicts were not confined to Communist countries. The Justice and Peace Commission was banned in Bolivia. In South Africa the bishops, shaken by the death of the black nationalist Steven Biko in 1977, warned the government that "politics should be inspired by the spiritual values of the Gospel." Convinced that the Somoza government in Nicaragua offended against these spiritual values, the priest-poet Ernesto Cardenal joined the Sandinista guerrillas, whose protest later turned into full-scale rebellion. (*See* NICARAGUA.)

There was intense interest in Latin America in the preparations for the third meeting of the Latin American Bishops'

Religion

604

Conference, originally scheduled to be held at Puebla, Mexico, in October and postponed until January 1979 because of the death of Pope John Paul I. At their 1968 meeting, the bishops had committed the church to "the struggle for human liberation," but more conservative tendencies could be seen in the preparations for the Puebla meeting. Critics said the documents were too tame and inward-looking. At the last moment, the texts were revised and given more bite.

Many speculated that a Polish pope would make a difference to the Vatican's *Ostpolitik*, but there was little evidence for this in 1978. In February, in a lecture given at the Georgetown Center for Strategic and International Studies, Washington, D.C., Msgr. Agostino Casaroli, the Vatican's "foreign minister," defended the *Ostpolitik*, claiming that it had served to improve the fate of Catholics living in Eastern Europe.

The internal life of the church was no less agitated. The church of Saint-Nicolas-du-Chardonnet in Paris continued to be occupied by supporters of the traditionalist Archbishop Marcel Lefebvre. In July, he ordained more priests at his seminary at Ecône, Switz., against the express orders of the Vatican. Lefebvre thought the new pope's choice of the name John Paul boded no good, but on November 19 he had a surprise meeting with John Paul II about which nothing was reported.

Ecumenism appeared to be in a state of suspended animation. Donald Coggan, the archbishop of Canterbury, made a further plea for intercommunion now when he preached in January in the Catholic Westminster Cathedral. A few weeks later Basil Cardinal Hume, the archbishop of Westminster, addressing the Anglican General Synod, conceded that the desire for intercommunion was widespread but added that there are "other questions to be resolved before we can, as churches, approach the altar of the Lord together." Some commentators concluded that there was a distinction between what could be done "as churches" and what might be done "as individuals."

In the U.S. a group of Episcopalians made approaches to the National Conference of Catholic Bishops and to the Vatican, seeking reunion and expressing their distress at the ordination of women priests and other "liberal" tendencies in the Episcopal Church. In November the Church of England Synod (or rather the clerical part of it) voted against the ordination of women, the main motive being a desire not to upset the Catholic Church and not to create a further obstacle to union. Critics maintained that a church should do what it had to do, come what may, and that in any case the opposition to women priests in the Roman Catholic Church was less solid than it looked.

Pope John Paul's direct experience of ecumenism was limited, but he firmly committed himself to it in his first programmatic speech. He also made it clear that he intended to govern the church "collegially," that is, with the aid of the world's bishops and through the instrument of the

Synod. There was a new mood of hope in the church, if not of optimism. The last years of Pope Paul's pontificate had been oppressive and gloomy. Pope John Paul II's attractive new style lifted the burden.

(PETER HEBBLETHWAITE)
[827.c; 827.G.2; 827.J.2]

THE ORTHODOX CHURCH

The instability of political relationships between Turkey and Greece continued to affect the ecumenical patriarchate of Constantinople (Istanbul), impairing its activities as an international centre and further depleting its flock in Turkey. However, the new Turkish government of Bulent Ecevit seemed to have afforded some relief. The Soviet authorities, while staging spectacular trials of dissidents—some on religious grounds—reduced somewhat the most drastic restrictions on registered church bodies. The quotas of new theological students at the Orthodox seminaries in Zagorsk, Leningrad, and Odessa were expanded slightly, and new buildings were provided to house them.

Representatives of all Orthodox churches met on two festive occasions, both in May 1978: the 25th anniversary of the restoration of the Bulgarian patriarchate in Sofia and the 60th jubilee of the reestablishment of the Russian patriarchate in Moscow. The latter meeting, particularly, provided an opportunity for significant public statements. The archbishop of Finland, Paul, pleaded for "an awakening from the long sleep of history" and for the establishment of new autocephalous (independent) churches in America, Asia, Africa, and Australia. Bishop Dmitri, representing the Orthodox Church in America, emphasized that the autocephaly of his church aimed at serving Orthodox unity both locally and on a world scale.

These comments dramatized the main issue confronting the Orthodox Church in its attempts to organize a Pan-Orthodox council of all the autocephalous churches. In many countries where Orthodoxy was developing but did not possess traditional cultural roots, Orthodox jurisdictions were organized along ethnic lines and were dependent on mother churches abroad. This situation was acknowledged as a hindrance to Orthodox witness and as contrary to Orthodox canon law. It stood on the agenda of the various preparatory meetings organized by the ecumenical patriarchate and was discussed at an international conference of Orthodox theologians in Brookline, Mass., August 28–31.

It also formed the background of the conversations between Patriarch Dimitrios of Constantinople and Patriarch Pimen of Moscow during the latter's visit to Istanbul in October 1977. Disagreement between these two centres would have to be solved, at least in principle, before a council could meet. Moscow favoured the establishment of new independent churches, while Constantinople bitterly opposed the trend. This was demonstrated by its approval of a new "charter" of the Greek Archdiocese in America, whose primate and bishops would continue to be appointed from Istanbul.

The future policies of the patriarchate of Moscow—particularly in the ecumenical field—were put in question by the dramatic

death of the influential metropolitan of Leningrad, Nikodim (see OBITUARIES), which occurred in the Vatican's papal library during an audience with Pope John Paul I on September 5.

(JOHN MEYENDORFF)

EASTERN NON-CHALCEDONIAN CHURCHES

The difficult situation of Christian communities in the Middle East was dramatized by several declarations favouring the Arab political cause by Patriarch Shenouda III of the Coptic Church. Whereas the Maronite Church in Lebanon (an Eastern group accepting papal supremacy) was moving toward the creation of a separate community, the Non-Chalcedonian (and Orthodox) Arab-speaking churches generally identified with Arab nationalism.

In Ethiopia the Marxist regime secularized the cathedral of Addis Ababa and deprived the church of many of its facilities. These measures were taken even though the government had previously established its own puppet patriarch.

Conversations took place aimed at restoring relations between the Armenian "supreme" catholicos of Echmiadzin (Soviet Armenia) and the traditionally anti-Communist catholicos of Cilicia (residing in Antelias, Lebanon).   (JOHN MEYENDORFF)
[827.B; 827.G.1; 827.J.1]

JUDAISM

The most important event in Judaism in 1977 was a public and political one: the visit of Pres. Anwar as-Sadat of Egypt to Jerusalem. Whatever the political consequences, the religious meaning was not lost on leaders of both Judaism and Islam. Delegations of rabbis, principally from the U.S., visited Egypt, and the Synagogue Council of America, which joins Orthodox, Reform, and Conservative Judaism, sent an important group to consult with Muslim counterparts at Cairo University. The beginnings of religious dialogue between Judaism and Islam, which had proved so fruitful in medieval times, appeared to be under way.

A second important public event, the NBC television special "Holocaust," likewise led to important religious interchange, this time between American Christians and American Jews. The program described, through very human characters, what it meant to be a Jew in Hitler's Europe, moving some Christians to wear the Star of David or in other ways express their solidarity with the Jewish people. The timing of these expressions, on the eve of Passover 5738/1978, presented a curious and heartening contrast, in the minds of many Jews, to the riots and pogroms carried out at Passover and Easter in times not long past.

The inner life of Judaism should not be obscured by these public spectacles. One trend likely to have long-term consequences was the continuing nurture of the study of the ethics of Judaism. What was important was that current conceptions of how ethical inquiry is to take place have entered into the framework of Judaic discourse. One of the keenest minds in the field, Rabbi Seymour Siegel, professor of theology and ethics at the Jewish Theological Seminary of America, presented a paper in *Linacre Quarterly* (August 1977) "on telling the truth." In it, he assembles relevant sayings on truth telling found in the rabbinic literature in order to inquire into issues of patient-physician relationships. In so doing, he adduces principles from the ancient sources of Judaic wisdom for examination and analysis in the contemporary context. "Truth is indispensable, but is not the supreme value," he concludes. "Human life is made tolerable because on some occasions it is cast to the ground."

One of the most profound and significant social philosophers of Judaism, Charles S. Liebman of Bar Ilan University, Israel, presented a major statement on "the present state of Jewish identity in the State of Israel and the United States." Liebman comes right to the heart of the matter, which links the social character of the Jewish people with the religious structure of Judaism: "There are two questions which I take to be central to the subject of Jewish identity. First, how does one define Judaism. . . . Second, how intense is the individual's sense of Jewish identity? How important is Judaism to him?" Since social scientists generally ignore Judaism when dealing with the Jews, Liebman's phrasing of the question itself constituted a breakthrough. He further raises the question of Jewish identity in the state of Israel, an unusual initiative, since it has been taken for granted that Israeli nationality and the Jewish identity of Israelis are more or less the same thing.

Liebman points out that "the Israeli's perception of the holocaust strengthens his sense of continuity with historical Judaism and reinforces the feeling that Israelis, like the victims of the holocaust, are isolated and beleaguered because they are Jewish." In consequence, there has been "an increasing overlap in their Israeli and Jewish identity." At the same time, "Judaism has no great meaning in the private life of the individual." American Jews, by contrast, conceive of Judaism primarily in religious terms, but "it is . . . difficult to specify what precisely the American Jew means when he calls himself . . . a religious Jew." American Jewish assistance to Israel "increasingly represents the content of the Jewish religion. And . . . it is religion which still provides the nominal facade and legitimation for the Jewish sense of peoplehood." The two principal communities of Jews in the world thus concur that "religion is an important component of Judaism." But "religion" bears different meanings in different contexts.

The importance of Liebman's reflections becomes clear when one returns to the prospect that peace may yet come to the Middle East. Without crisis in the state of Israel, American Judaism might find itself lacking all content. Debates in American Jewry on whether Judaism would survive the demise of the state of Israel, commonplace (if not public) in the aftermath of the 1973 war, now were joined by quiet reflections on whether Judaism can survive peace.

(JACOB NEUSNER)
[826]

BUDDHISM

The chance discovery in India of four Minor Rock Edicts of the Buddhist king Asoka (reigned c. 273–232 BC)—two in August 1977 and two in March 1978—caused considerable excitement both inside and outside the world of Buddhism. The edicts found in 1977, which mention Asoka's name specifically, state that he had spent 236 days on tour during the previous one and a half years promoting Buddha's teaching (dharma).

Asoka's vision of a worldwide Buddhist community, which had inspired Buddhist leaders during the 1940s, '50s, and '60s, had greatly eroded in recent years. Ironically, it was in the West, especially in North America, that Buddhism's prospects seemed brightest. Zen and Tibetan Buddhism were popular in the West, and Nichiren Shoshu, one of the new Japanese religions of Buddhist origin, was also attracting sizable numbers of Western adherents. Pure Land Buddhism was influential among Asian-Americans and Asian-Canadians. For the most part, Western Buddhists, preoccupied with the personal aspect of their beliefs and practices, showed little inclination to relate Buddhism to social, economic, and political issues.

Buddhism in Asia, however, did not fare as well. In India the Dalai Lama and the Tibetan Buddhist refugees continued to hope against hope for a return to their homeland. In Sri Lanka the special status accorded to Buddhism by the 1972 constitution was threatened by the vocal opposition of the Tamil minority. The Laotian regime had imposed a stern Communist work ethic on the traditionally easygoing Buddhist peasants, who were compelled to work even on Buddhist holidays. Buddhists in Vietnam managed to smuggle their leader Tich Man Giac out of the country to launch a worldwide campaign against religious persecution in his nation; while he received some support in Europe, he was disappointed by the general indifference of Americans.

In China the Panchen Lama, once the second ranking religious leader of Tibet, emerged from 12 years of obscurity early in 1978 as a delegate at the Chinese People's Political Consultative Conference. Meanwhile, Buddhists in Hong Kong and Taiwan were carrying on heated debates regarding the marriage of monks and nuns.

(JOSEPH MITSUO KITAGAWA)
[824]

HINDUISM

On Jan. 30, 1948, Mohandas Karamchand Gandhi was assassinated by a Hindu fanatic. Although he was a skillful politician, Gandhi is remembered and revered by Indians as a holy man, an esteem which during his lifetime won him the title Mahatma, or "Great Soul." The 30th anniversary of his death was marked by special observances throughout India, especially in New Delhi where Prime Minister Morarji Desai used the occasion to stress his government's commitment to Gandhi's spiritual principles.

The powerful relationship between religion and politics in India expressed by Gandhi's life was underscored in 1978 by the growth and activities of the Rashtriya Swayamsevak Sangh (RSS), an organization regarded by many as the paramilitary wing of the Jan Sangh, one of the groups making up the ruling Janata Party. Dedicated to the ideal of a Hindu state, the RSS had been identified throughout its 53-year existence with an aggressive and sometimes violent assertion of Hindu communalism. Although its critics saw it as a serious threat to democracy in India, the organization itself claimed to be simply a cultural group.

The politicizing of Hinduism was further dramatized by a religious ceremony held in

The Dalai Lama (second from left), exiled religious leader of Tibet, attended the 12th World Buddhist Conference in Tokyo in October.

WIDE WORLD

Religion

Ahmedabad during March. A nine-day-long sacrifice, costing about $1,250,000, was conducted by Baba Jai Gurudev, a religious leader who had been jailed for 21 months by former prime minister Indira Gandhi during her "emergency" rule. The sacrifice, supported by the RSS and the Jan Sangh, entailed the offering into sacred fires of some 50,000 qt of milk, 70,000 lb of clarified butter, and 44,000 lb of rice. It was held to usher in the Age of Truth, which the Baba said would begin on March 31, 1982, and would mark the end of deceit, suffering, and want. His critics viewed the sacrifice as an immoral waste of food.

The year saw two archaeological events of religious significance. The first was the discovery of a unique stone image of the Hindu god Siva in the hitherto unknown form of a dwarf (*vamana*). Dating from the Gupta period (*c.* 4th–6th centuries AD), the image added an important piece to the still incomplete picture of the development of Hindu iconography. The other event was the excavation at Apsad in Bihar state of a temple dedicated to the god Vishnu, also of the Gupta period, marking the site of an ancient centre of Hindu thought.

(H. PATRICK SULLIVAN)

[823]

ISLAM

Serious peace negotiations between Egypt and Israel, begun by the trip to Israel by President Sadat in November 1977, were of great interest to Muslims throughout 1978. The Arab-Israeli situation had been the Arab countries' principal concern for more than three decades. (*See* MIDDLE EAST.) Unfortunately, the Lebanese civil war continued, further deepening the religious divisions in that country. (*See* LEBANON.)

The year also saw serious disturbances in Iran, beginning in January with a riot in Qom. The death toll from the disturbances was estimated in the thousands. The protesters represented a wide spectrum of political and religious beliefs, from radical left to conservative Islamic religious positions. The exiled Shi'ah dignitary Ayatullah Ruhollah Khomeini, who during the year moved from Iraq to Paris, became the focus of Islamic opposition to the shah's regime.

The aged Ayatullah Sharietmadari, a theologian living in Qom, generally recognized as one of the most important Shi'ah leaders resident in Iran, was quoted as accepting many of the government's policies but objecting that Islamic values were being overthrown by Western permissiveness. Examples were Western films found to be offensive because of their sex and violence, immodest dress of westernized women, and the use of liquor and drugs. In August at least 377 persons were killed in an arson attack on a movie theatre in Abadan. The government blamed "Islamic Marxists," though religious leaders denied the accusation. It seemed clear that the uprisings were not simply the result of religious reaction. Rather they had developed out of many years of rapid social and cultural change, unaccompanied by the opportunity for political expression. (*See* IRAN.)

In February, 15 U.S. rabbis and Jewish laymen visited Egypt to further interfaith relations. Egypt's ambassador to the U.S., Ashraf Ghorbal, had issued the invitation to the Synagogue Council of America. In June King Khalid of Saudi Arabia inaugurated the mosque his nation had built in Geneva.

In the U.S. the World Community of Islam in the West (formerly the Black Muslims), under the leadership of Wallace Muhammad, was becoming more clearly identified with mainstream Islamic beliefs and practices. While not all former Black Muslims had followed Wallace Muhammad's lead, he continued actively to express his positions. In May he specifically attacked any black separatist philosophy.

(R. W. SMITH)

WORLD CHURCH MEMBERSHIP

Reckoning religious membership throughout the world remains a precarious exercise. Different religions and even different Christian churches vary widely in their theories and methods of counting and reporting. Some simply depend on governments' population figures; for others, "numbering the people" is forbidden by religious law. Some faiths' communities count only adults or heads of families; others include children, retainers, and servants. Where religious liberty obtains, some count contributors; others estimate communicants or constituents.

Procedures vary from country to country within the same religion. On the mission fields quite reliable figures are available, for Buddhism, Islam, and Hinduism, as well as for Christianity. In areas where a religion has prevailed for many centuries (Christianity in Europe, Hinduism in India), official figures usually report whole populations as adherents, although the rise of antireligious ideologies rebukes the casual assumption implicit in that procedure.

Although Albania is the only officially atheist state, the 20th century has produced a number of governments hostile to religion in theory and/or practice. It is difficult if not impossible to get religious statistics from the peoples they control.

The traditional listing of religions, used by scholars since the study of world religions became an academic discipline, makes no provision for several religions that have gained ground subsequently — Baha'i, Cao Dai, Chondokyo, Jainism, the Spiritualist Church of Brazil. Finally, each year brings reports of new genocides or substantial movements of refugees, casting further uncertainty upon statistics on religious adherence.

The reader is therefore advised to reflect carefully upon the statistics and to refer to the articles discussing the different countries and religions when pursuing the subject in depth.

(FRANKLIN H. LITTELL)

Estimated Membership of the Principal Religions of the World

Religions	North America[1]	South America	Europe[2]	Asia[3]	Africa	Oceania[4]	World
Total Christian	230,458,700	165,811,000	338,681,900	88,966,000	126,362,500	17,904,000	968,184,100
Roman Catholic	131,961,500	154,270,000	173,879,300	50,853,000	47,107,000	4,466,500	562,537,300
Eastern Orthodox	4,290,000	537,000	63,498,600	2,040,000	14,215,000 [5]	404,000	84,984,600
Protestant[6]	94,207,200	11,004,000	101,304,000	36,073,000	65,040,500 [7]	13,033,500	320,662,200
Jewish	6,150,170	564,200	3,996,620	3,432,660	164,450	75,000	14,383,100
Muslim[8]	291,200	324,500	8,041,000	402,404,000	134,877,300	87,000	546,025,000
Zoroastrian	250	2,100	7,000	244,000	650	—	254,000
Shinto[9]	58,000	91,000	—	56,003,000	—	—	56,152,000
Taoist	16,000	11,000	—	31,206,000	650	—	31,233,650
Confucian	97,100	83,150	24,000	167,913,000	1,250	40,200	168,158,700
Buddhist[10]	170,250	190,300	272,000	255,366,500	9,000	21,000	256,029,050
Hindu[11]	82,000	836,800	310,000	468,344,400	929,950	495,000	470,998,150
Totals	237,323,670	167,914,050	351,332,520	1,473,879,560	262,345,750	18,622,200	2,511,417,750
Population[12]	359,338,000	236,276,000	744,049,000	2,407,597,000	435,562,000	22,593,000	4,205,415,000

[1] Includes Central America and the West Indies.
[2] Includes the U.S.S.R. and other countries with established Marxist ideology where religious adherence is difficult to estimate.
[3] Includes areas in which persons have traditionally enrolled in several religions, as well as China with an official Marxist establishment.
[4] Includes Australia and New Zealand as well as islands of the South Pacific.
[5] Includes Coptic Christians.
[6] Protestant statistics usually include "full members" (adults) rather than all family members or baptized infants and are therefore not comparable to the statistics of ethnic religions or churches counting all constituents.
[7] Including many new sects and cults among African Christians.
[8] The chief base of Islam is still ethnic, although some missionary work is now carried on in Europe and America (viz. "Black Muslims"). In countries where Islam is established, minority religions are frequently persecuted and their statistics are hard to come by.
[9] A Japanese ethnic religion, Shinto has declined markedly since the Japanese emperor gave up his claim to divinity (1947). Neither does it survive well outside the homeland.
[10] Buddhism has several modern renewal movements which have gained adherents in Europe and America and other areas not formerly ethnic-Buddhist. In Asia it has made rapid gains in recent years and has shown greater staying power under persecution than Taoism or Confucianism. It also transplants better.
[11] Hinduism's strength in India has been enhanced by nationalism. Modern Hinduism has also developed renewal movements that have won converts in Europe and America.
[12] United Nations, Department of Economic and Social Affairs; data refer to midyear 1978.

(FRANKLIN H. LITTELL)

THE BUSINESS OF RELIGION

by Martin E. Marty

Organized religion in America is big business, and it is rapidly getting bigger. While the idea of such wealth may be disturbing to a small antireligious minority, most expressions of concern in 1978 came from within the churches and synagogues themselves. The critics warned lest Mammon, which in the Bible personifies wealth as a false god, might take over where pure and simple faith should rule. As far as the general public was concerned, however, few signs of mistrust had developed. In a Gallup Poll, the sampled citizens ranked clergyman the most trusted among 20 major occupations.

The American Association of Fund-Raising Counsel, Inc., in its publication *Giving-USA,* was able to announce a remarkable $6 billion spurt in charitable giving by Americans during 1977. And while hospitals received a total of $4,750,000,000 and education $4,660,000,000, gifts to religion amounted to $16.5 billion. In the major churches, the average member donated $149.75 in the course of the year. Even among mainline church bodies experiencing membership declines, voluntary gifts increased.

Rendering unto Caesar. Nevertheless, many church leaders were concerned lest public confidence in their financial management erode. Financial officers of large Protestant evangelistic networks met to map strategies against congressional forces working for compulsory "full disclosure" bills. The evangelists argued that they could set or keep their own houses in order, but they did acknowledge that both fund raising and the uses of wealth had become controversial.

Among the fully legal but highly controversial practices were efforts by religious organizations to influence secular economic enterprises. Thus members of the National Council of Churches, among others, were criticized for urging churches to divest their portfolios of investments in firms doing substantial business in South Africa. Others joined many Roman Catholic bishops in the South in siding with

Martin E. Marty is Fairfax M. Cone distinguished service professor at the University of Chicago and associate editor of The Christian Century.

WIDE WORLD

Father Guido Carcich talked with reporters in Washington the day he was indicted by a grand jury. He was charged with misappropriating more than $1 million in charity donations.

organized labour against the industrial giant J. P. Stevens in a union dispute, and suffered rebuke for their activities.

As religious organizations moved beyond their sanctuaries into the marketplace, competitors questioned their tax-exempt status. Thus the heads of small fishing industries accused the Rev. Sun Myung Moon's Unification Church of unfair competition when front groups for the church bought fishing fleets and processing plants. Some years ago it was learned that an evangelist was not required to pay taxes on his church-owned bra and girdle factory. The Roman Catholic Christian Brothers, criticized for nonpayment of taxes on their wine-making business, made amends with remuneration for several previous years. The Church of Jesus Christ of Latter-day Saints was known to hold substantial investments in secular business, portfolios made possible by the tithing of the members.

Most Americans still favoured tax exemption in principle. Nevertheless, the issue had become so debatable that in 1977, Dean Kelley, a staff member of the National Council of Churches, felt called upon to write *Why Churches Should Not Pay Taxes*—a book with a defensive title that would have been unnecessary a few years earlier. Adding to the controversy was the Universal Life Church, a mail-order operation run by Kirby J. Hensley, an illiterate former hobo. Hensley ordained people for a small fee and then helped them remove their homes (reclassified as churches or monasteries or retreat centres) from the tax rolls. In 1976, 211 of the 236 adult residents of Hardenburgh, N.Y., became ministers of the Universal Life Church, leaving other New Yorkers to pay for their children's schooling and setting off complex legal action.

Unwise and Unjust Stewards. Religious fund raisers were also concerned over a series of embarrassments and scandals caused by incompetent or unscrupulous individuals. Miscalculations about population trends and inflation plunged the Pacific Homes in southern California into bankruptcy. Since these homes for the aged were connected with a jurisdiction of the United Methodist Church, the church was sued (unsuccessfully, as it turned out) for $50 million in punitive damages and $216 million in class-action suits.

Roman Catholic agencies, embarrassed by press exposure of questionable fund-raising practices at Boys Town, Neb., several years earlier, now confronted the backlash from the criminal activity of Father Guido Carcich of the Baltimore-based Pallottine Fathers. A genius at raising money, he permitted only 2.5 cents of every dollar to reach the starving children for whom the donations were intended; much of the rest was embezzled or funneled into questionable investments. Let off lightly after plea bargaining, the priest set out on a new course. His archbishop asked people to be forgiving. Least likely to find forgiveness easy were the ethical majority among church fund raisers.

Even the widely respected name of Billy Graham was drawn into controversy when the *Charlotte* (N.C.) *Observer* reported that the Billy Graham Evangelistic Association had not publicized a subsidiary foundation, the WECEF or World Evangelism and Christian Education Fund, despite its assets of over $20 million. Evangelist Graham, who took the exceptional step of defending himself against press attack, explained that too many applicants would approach the WECEF for funds if they knew of its existence. He evidently escaped without much personal taint, although friendly critics questioned whether it was fair to give donors the impression that their offerings were going to soul winning, rather than to the less glamorous task of educating.

Viewing the scene, Father Edwin Dill told 160 fund raisers at a National Catholic Development Conference: "Gone are the days of unquestioned acceptance." Edward Hales, director of field services for the National Association of Evangelicals, observed: "Just as consumerism has come to the fore so has donorism."

Rich and Poor. In this sense, the least plagued houses were the local churches and denominations, whose accounting procedures were ordinarily the most open. Journalist Nino Lo Bello accurately noted that the prosperity of the Roman Catholic Church in the U.S. was partly an illusion; the church

was "land rich but money poor," and many dioceses ran large deficits. Most Protestant churches had fewer than 300 members, all of whom had access to the books. Faced with inflation and far removed from the world of religious high finance, members were tending to keep more of their dollars at home, thus forcing national headquarters to cut back on staff and on agencies of mission and charity.

A few local churches, if they were well located and headed by charismatic pastors, did prosper. Some generated contests to see who could gather the most money on a single Sunday. For one week in June the Garden Grove Community Church in California held the record, with $1,421,000. A week later a church in Kirkland, Wash., topped this, with $1,650,000. Garden Grove reported that the one-Sunday drive did not hurt the weekly average; $60,-000 was still collected on each Lord's Day. That would support most Protestant churches for a year.

Relative newcomers to the world of high finance were Protestant television empires, each of which took in more funds than most large denominational headquarters. Despite a schism between father Herbert W. Armstrong and son Garner Ted (*see* BIOGRAPHIES), their Worldwide Church of God received $75 million in 1977. Oral Roberts of Tulsa, Okla., received over $60 million, recorded a growth rate of 25% annually, and produced half a million letters in support of a hospital venture that Tulsa officials had not wanted. The PTL (Praise the Lord) television network raised $25 million, while the Rev. "Pat" Robertson, head of the rival Christian Broadcasting Network, observed that "We can't really be taken seriously unless we're a $1 billion a year operation."

Much of the money channeled through these empires did go into charity, more of it into spreading the Word. The nonchurched public ignored the activity or tolerated its excesses. Effective criticism came from within the religious community—from Jews who contrasted the prophets' message about the poor with the lavish wealth of some religious enterprises; from Protestants like Adam Daniel Finnerty who, in *No More Plastic Jesus,* tabbed church wealth at $135 billion and asked how much of it reaches Jesus' poor; from Catholics who quoted the 1971 synod of bishops: "The church is obliged to live and administer its own goods in such a way that the Gospel is proclaimed to the poor. If instead the Church appears to be among the rich and powerful of this world, its credibility is diminished."

Religious organizations continued to hold the goodwill of their members, but where there were excesses in their enterprises, they knew they were living on borrowed time. That was why so many of them spent 1978 setting their houses in order, before anyone called down plagues upon them.

Rhodesia

Though Rhodesia declared itself a republic on March 2, 1970, it remained a British colony in the eyes of many other nations. It is bounded by Zambia, Mozambique, South Africa, and Botswana. Area: 390,272 sq km (150,685 sq mi). Pop. (1978 est.): 6,930,000, of whom 96% are African and 4% white. Cap. and largest city: Salisbury (urban area pop., 1978 est., 610,000). Language: English (official) and various Bantu languages (1969 census, Shona 71%, Ndebele 15%). Religion: predominantly traditional tribal beliefs; Christian minority. President in 1978, John Wrathall; prime minister, Ian D. Smith. From March 21 the country was governed by an Executive Council comprised of Smith, Bishop Abel Muzorewa, Ndabaningi Sithole, and Jeremiah Chirau.

On March 3, 1978, after long, grueling talks in Salisbury, Prime Minister Ian Smith, Bishop Abel Muzorewa of the United African National Council (UANC), Ndabaningi Sithole of the African National Council, and Sen. Jeremiah Chirau of the Zimbabwe United People's Organization signed an agreement for Rhodesia, under the new name of Zimbabwe, to be governed by its black majority by December 31. All citizens of 18 or over would be enfranchised and would elect a Parliament with 100 members; 72 seats would be reserved for blacks and 28 for whites, 20 members of the latter to be elected on a preferential voting system by white voters and the remaining 8 by all voters from at least 16 candidates nominated by an electoral college of whites. This reservation system would be reviewed after ten years. There would be a declaration of rights and freedoms, and no one would be deprived of property without adequate compensation. The independence of the judiciary would be guaranteed, while the public services would be filled by persons chosen by a public service board independent of politics. These proposals would be embodied in the future constitution of Zimbabwe.

In the meantime, there would be a transitional

Rhodesia

government comprising an Executive Council consisting of the four signatories, each in turn acting as chairman, and a Ministerial Council consisting of equal numbers of black and white ministers. The black ministers would be nominated in equal proportions by the three black signatories, and the white ministers by Prime Minister Smith. Chairmanship of the Ministerial Council would alternate between black and white ministers. Parliament would continue to convene under the transitional government with the responsibility of enacting the new constitution and legislating for the registration of voters.

At the end of January the leaders of the opposition Patriotic Front, Joshua Nkomo and Robert Mugabe, had had talks with representatives of the

(Left to right) Bishop Abel Muzorewa, Prime Minister Ian Smith of Rhodesia, Sen. Jeremiah Chirau, and the Rev. Ndabaningi Sithole signed agreements in Salisbury in March as an important step toward a transitional government. The election to establish black rule had not yet taken place at year's end.

British and U.S. governments in Malta. The talks did not produce agreement but did enable the Patriotic Front leaders to declare their support for independently observed and supervised elections provided they themselves could play a substantial role during the transitional period of preparation for the elections. When the internal agreement was signed March 3, Nkomo and Mugabe immediately denounced it and said that the guerrilla war would be intensified; however, a meeting between them in Maputo, Mozambique, to unify their forces for an offensive came to nothing.

Britain still hoped to bring the various Rhodesian leaders together for discussions. This hope received a serious setback when the presidents of Tanzania, Zambia, Botswana, and Mozambique and a representative of Angola, meeting in Dar es Salaam, Tanzania, condemned the Salisbury agreement on March 26.

After argument between the black leaders concerning the allocation of offices, the Ministerial Council was chosen in April. Meanwhile, the Executive Council set to work to draft an amnesty for guerrillas who were prepared to lay down arms. In May the amnesty was made public, while the ban on political parties, including Mugabe's Zimbabwe African National Union (ZANU) and Nkomo's Zimbabwe African People's Union (ZAPU), was lifted. On April 6 the council also announced arrangements for the phased release of several hundred political detainees and the withdrawal of restrictions on others. The African internal leaders failed, however, to achieve a cease-fire.

Tensions within the Executive Council and the interim government's inability to secure peace made observers skeptical of supporting the internal settlement. While retaliatory raids by Rhodesian security forces on what were claimed to be guerrilla bases in Mozambique were condemned by those who believed the targets were refugee camps, heavy raids on ZAPU guerrilla bases near Lusaka in Zambia by Rhodesian ground and air forces diminished Nkomo's hopes of launching a rainy-season offensive. The massacre of British missionaries at Umtali by guerrillas in June shocked Britain. Mugabe lost some external support when, in August, ZANU vowed to kill the three black members of the Executive Council and when a ZANU death list containing more than 40 names of African leaders was made public in November. Nor did Nkomo's denial that ZAPU guerrillas had killed some of the survivors after shooting down a civilian aircraft in September allay criticism. The bans against ZANU and ZAPU were reimposed in September.

Secret talks between Nkomo and Smith in Zambia in August led to speculation and brought recriminations both from Smith's black associates in the interim government and from Nkomo's ally, Mugabe. That meeting also split the presidents of the "front line" states; Julius Nyerere of Tanzania and Samora Machel of Mozambique sided with Mugabe and Kenneth Kaunda of Zambia and Agostinho Neto of Angola with Nkomo, while Botswana's Sir Seretse Khama pursued a neutral line. In September the government's decision to conscript blacks into the security forces was criti-cized by whites, already concerned about Smith's concessions to black opinion, and by the blacks themselves, while the declaration of martial law over a large proportion of the country met with widespread hostility.

Britain, supported by the U.S., still considered that a solution could only be found through a conference of all parties concerned. Smith claimed that the internal settlement presented a new situation and requested the withdrawal of sanctions, a request refused by Britain and the U.S. The Patriotic Front continued to insist that it represented the only authentic voice of the black people of Rhodesia. Smith and his supporters, although prepared to take part in it, indicated their skepticism about the outcome of an all-party conference.

Elections to bring into effect full majority rule by December 31 had to be postponed because there was not time to make arrangements. Muzorewa protested against this decision but was overruled by his colleagues. (KENNETH INGHAM)

Rodeo

Tom Ferguson of Miami, Okla., won his fifth consecutive world all-around championship in competitions sponsored by the Professional Rodeo Cowboys Association (PRCA). The 27-year-old athlete also set a new winning mark for a single year. During the regular rodeo season, Ferguson won $79,269 competing in timed events—calf roping, steer wrestling, steer roping, and team roping. At the National Finals Rodeo in Oklahoma City in December, he won the steer wrestling world title in addition to the all-around crown, and his arena earnings climbed to $103,734. Added to that amount were various bonus awards, which brought his year-end total to $128,434. It was more money than any other rodeo cowboy had ever earned in a single season.

Other PRCA champions for 1978 included Jack Ward of Springdale, Ark., in bareback riding; Joe Marvel of Battle Mountain, Nev., in saddle bronc riding; Butch Kirby of Alba, Texas, in bull riding; Dave Brock of Pueblo, Colo., in calf roping; and Arizonans Brad Smith of Prescott and George Richards of Humbolt in team roping. Each champion won $15,000 at the finals, plus a $5,000 bonus; the money was divided between the two team-roping winners. The finals also saw Lynn McKenzie of Shreveport, La., win her first championship in barrel racing; Kenny Call of Newhall, Calif., won the PRCA steer roping world title at the finals of that event held in Laramie, Wyo., in September.

For each of the preceding three years, the PRCA had named world champions solely on the basis of national finals competition, but the association announced that, beginning in 1979, world champions would once again be determined on the basis of total earnings for the entire year, including the finals.

During the year a new organization, Major League Rodeo, Inc., held its first season of team rodeo competition. After six franchise teams battled each other throughout the season, the Denver

Tom Eirikson of Innisfail, Alberta, showed great form in the calf roping event at the Calgary Stampede in July.

Stars and Tulsa Twisters made it to the finals. The Denver team won.

In competitions promoted by the International Rodeo Association, which holds its International Finals Rodeo each January, reigning all-around champion Mike Waters of Linden, Texas, was holding down second place with more than $25,-000 in winnings. However, Dan Dailey of Fort Worth, Texas, was expected to win his first all-around title. He would enter the finals with nearly $30,000 in earnings.

The Girls Rodeo Association, which sanctions barrel racing for women at PRCA rodeos, had held its own "all-girl" rodeos in recent years. During the fall, it sponsored its first National Finals in San Antonio, Texas. Judy Robinson of Alfalfa, Ore., won the all-around championship, competing in seven events. (RANDALL E. WITTE)

Romania

A socialist republic on the Balkan Peninsula in southeastern Europe, Romania is bordered by the U.S.S.R., the Black Sea, Bulgaria, Yugoslavia, and Hungary. Area: 237,500 sq km (91,700 sq mi). Pop. (1977): 21,559,400, including (1966) Romanian 88.1%; Hungarian 7.9%; German 1.6%. Cap. and largest city: Bucharest (pop., 1977, 1,807,000). Religion: Romanian Orthodox 70%; Greek Orthodox 10%. General secretary of the Romanian Communist Party, president of the republic, and

president of the State Council in 1978, Nicolae Ceausescu; chairman of the Council of Ministers (premier), Manea Manescu.

In April Pres. Nicolae Ceausescu and his wife, Elena, paid their fourth official visit to the United States in eight years, demonstrating continuing U.S. interest in Romania's international standing. On April 13 President Ceausescu and U.S. Pres. Jimmy Carter declared their mutual determination to strengthen the process of détente. In May Ceausescu and his wife paid their second official visit to China (the first took place in 1971). A long-term economic and technical cooperation agreement was signed on May 19 in Peking by Ceausescu and Hua Kuo-feng, the head of the Chinese government. President Ceausescu and his wife paid a three-day visit to Great Britain in June. Though this was Ceausescu's second visit to London since he became Romania's leader in 1965, he was the first head of a Warsaw Treaty member country to be accorded the full panoply of a state visit to the British capital.

On August 7 Ceausescu and his foreign minister, Stefan Andrei, met Soviet Pres. Leonid I. Brezhnev, Soviet Foreign Minister Andrey Gromyko, and Konstantin Chernenko, then candidate member of the Politburo and a secretary of the Central Committee, for talks described as "frank and friendly." They doubtless included a warning to Romania on dealing with China. When Ceausescu returned home, the Bucharest weekly *Lumea* commented that "the development of

Romania

Roman Catholic Church:
see Religion

friendship and solidarity with the U.S.S.R. is a top priority in Romanian foreign policy."

A week later, on August 16, Hua Kuo-feng arrived in Bucharest, where he received an enthusiastic welcome. Romania was the first European country to be visited by a Chinese head of state since Mao Tse-tung went to Moscow in 1957. At a dinner in his Chinese guest's honour, Ceausescu proclaimed the determination of both parties to ensure the development of their relations.

On October 13 Brezhnev sent a three-man Communist Party delegation, headed by Gromyko, to Bucharest. According to a Soviet communiqué, the delegates of the two Communist parties during their three-day talks emphasized the determination of their countries to act jointly with other Warsaw Treaty members in promoting the cause of détente.

In mid-November in Belgrade, Yugos., Ceausescu met President Tito for the 18th time. After discussion of Romanian-Yugoslav cooperation and topical multilateral problems, Tito awarded Ceausescu the high order of Hero of Socialist Labour.

The Political Consultative Committee of the seven Warsaw Treaty countries met in Moscow on November 22–23. In a formal declaration they proclaimed their resolve "to set out on the road of firm allegiance to the policy of peace and détente." Ceausescu was able to sign this lengthy document because, at his insistence, it omitted vilification of China and criticism of efforts for peace in the Middle East.

In five speeches of extraordinary boldness made between November 25 and December 1, shortly after his return to Bucharest, the Romanian leader revealed that he had told his comrades in Moscow there was no danger of aggression against any Warsaw Treaty power and therefore no need for any increase in defense expenditures. He proposed the creation of a buffer zone between the military areas of the Warsaw Treaty and NATO "where no armaments would be located and no maneuvers would take place." He added that each national army must act only under the orders of its own high command.

On December 5 Brezhnev delivered his first public rebuke to Ceausescu, although without naming him. Speaking in the Kremlin at a banquet celebrating the signing of the Soviet-Afghan friendship treaty, the Soviet leader denounced "demagogic" advocacy of unilateral disarmament, which could have "irreparable consequences for socialism, freedom and independence."

(K. M. SMOGORZEWSKI)

Rowing

Ten nations shared the 32 titles in world rowing in 1978. East Germany dominated the men's championships in New Zealand with five titles. They also won five out of the six new titles offered for the first time in the women's junior championships in Belgrade, Yugos., and three first places in the women's events in New Zealand. The Soviet Union earned distinction by winning three of the men's junior championships at Belgrade. The eight other nations winning first places were Bulgaria, Czechoslovakia, Great Britain, Italy, Norway, Spain, Switzerland, and West Germany.

The men's and women's world rowing championships, held on Lake Karapiro in New Zealand, were the first to be held in that part of the world. Contesting for the championships in the eight men's events were 89 boats from 26 nations. Since the number of entries in Amsterdam in 1977 was only slightly higher, this disproved forecasts that European countries might not undertake the long journey because of the high cost.

In the men's finals a crowd of 34,000 saw East Germany win the eights by only 0.92 sec after New Zealand had led most of the way. Approaching 1,750 m, the East Germans mounted their finishing burst. West Germany went with them, and so did New Zealand; at the finish line less than a boat's length separated the three crews, with New Zealand third. East and West Germany also won the first two places in coxed fours, separated by 1.31 sec, but it was the Soviet Union's sole victory, in coxless fours, that produced the closest finish. The Soviets led from the start, but in the last 250 m East Germany began to close the gap. The drama mounted until the Soviet boat reached the finish

ROMANIA

Education. (1976–77) Primary, pupils 3,125,584, teachers 147,582; secondary, pupils 996,044, teachers 45,086; vocational, pupils 155,580, teachers 5,388; teacher training, students 19,842, teachers 1,361; higher (including 12 universities), students 174,888, teaching staff 13,662.

Finance. Monetary unit: leu, with (Sept. 18, 1978) a commercial rate of 4.47 lei to U.S. $1 (8.49 lei = £1 sterling) and a tourist rate of 12 lei = U.S. $1 (22.80 lei = £1 sterling). Budget (1978 est.) balanced at 318.5 billion lei.

Foreign Trade. (1976) Imports 30,294,000,000 lei; exports 30,504,000,000 lei. Import sources: U.S.S.R. 18%; East Germany 7%; West Germany 7%; Poland 5%; Iran 5%; U.S. 5%. Export destinations: U.S.S.R. 18%; West Germany 9%; East Germany 7%. Main exports (1973): machinery 9%; transport equipment 8%; petroleum products 7%; meat 7%; chemicals 7%; clothing 6%; timber 5%.

Transport and Communications. Roads (1975) c. 95,000 km (including 96 km expressways). Motor vehicles in use (1976): passenger c. 200,000; commercial c. 100,000. Railways (1975): 11,039 km; traffic 22,380,000,000 passenger-km, freight (1976) 67,560,000,000 net ton-km. Air traffic (1977): 919 million passenger-km; freight 13,749,000 net ton-km. Inland waterways in regular use (1976) 1,628 km. Shipping (1977): merchant vessels 100 gross tons and over 207; gross tonnage 1,218,171. Telephones (Dec. 1976) 984,000. Radio licenses (Dec. 1976) 3,104,000. Television licenses (Dec. 1976) 2,963,000.

Agriculture. Production (in 000; metric tons; 1977): wheat c. 6,540; barley 1,626; corn 10,103; potatoes c. 4,000; cabbages (1976) c. 633; onions c. 290; tomatoes c. 1,150; sugar, raw value c. 755; sunflower seed 807; soybeans c. 193; plums (1976) c. 550; apples c. 455; grapes c. 1,500; linseed c. 48; tobacco c. 47; cheese 138; beef and veal 284; pork c. 770; timber (cu m) 20,587. Livestock (in 000; Jan. 1977): cattle c. 6,129; sheep 14,331; pigs 10,193; horses (1976) 562; poultry 91,503.

Industry. Fuel and power (in 000; metric tons; 1977): coal 7,370; lignite 19,420; coke (1976) 2,472; crude oil 14,650; natural gas (cu m) c. 34,080,000; manufactured gas (cu m) c. 1,300,000; electricity (kw-hr; 1976) 58,266,000. Production (in 000; metric tons; 1976): cement 13,088; iron ore (metal content) 740; pig iron 7,415; crude steel 10,733; petroleum products c. 20,770; sulfuric acid 1,555; fertilizers (nutrient content) nitrogenous 1,331, phosphate 493; cotton yarn (1975) 145; cotton fabrics (sq m) 677,000; wool yarn (1975) 51; woolen fabrics (sq m) 105,000; man-made fibres (1975) 148; newsprint 44; other paper c. 605. New dwelling units completed (1976) 139,000.

line first by 0.27 sec. East Germany won the coxed and coxless pairs as well as the quadruple sculls. The two other gold medals were won by West Germany in single sculls and Norway in double sculls.

In the women's events East Germany had to be content with three golds and a silver after winning all six events in 1977. Bulgaria won two of the remaining gold medals, and the Soviet Union took one by defeating East Germany in the eights. In single sculls Christine Hahn of East Germany achieved the unique distinction of winning the world title for the fifth successive year. U.S. and Canadian women each won one silver and one bronze medal.

At Belgrade the Soviet Union displaced East Germany as the world leader in junior rowing with three gold and two silver medals and a bronze. East Germany won two gold and two silver medals, and the three other gold medalists were Czechoslovakia, Italy, and West Germany. These championships were shared for the first time with the women's junior events, which were dominated by East Germany. The only other country to win a gold medal in the tournament was the U.S.S.R.

At the Henley Royal Regatta in England the Trakia Club from Bulgaria won three events in its first visit and foiled a clean sweep by home crews. The Bulgarians won the Grand Challenge Cup (eights) by three-quarters of a length from the University of Washington, the Stewards' Cup (coxless fours), and the Prince Philip Cup (coxed fours). Oxford completed the 4¼-mi course unchallenged in the 124th University Boat Race after Cambridge sank in rough water two-thirds of a mile from the finish. It was the third sinking in the 149-year-old series, in which Cambridge now led with 68 wins to Oxford's 55.   (KEITH OSBORNE)

Rwanda

A republic in eastern Africa and former traditional kingdom whose origins may be traced back to the 15th century, Rwanda is bordered by Zaire, Uganda, Tanzania, and Burundi. Area: 26,338 sq km (10,169 sq mi). Pop. (1978 census): 4,820,000, including (1970) Hutu 90%; Tutsi 9%; and Twa 1%. Cap. and largest city: Kigali (pop., 1978 census, 118,000). Language (official): French and Kinyarwanda. Religion: Roman Catholic 41%; most of the remainder are animist; there are small Protestant and Muslim minorities. President in 1978, Gen. Juvénal Habyarimana.

Pres. Juvénal Habyarimana received a top-level welcome during his June 1978 visit to Peking, although the Soviet representatives walked out of a

Rwanda

RWANDA

Education. (1976–77) Primary, pupils 434,150, teachers 8,161; secondary, vocational, and teacher training, pupils 12,520, teachers 820; higher, students 1,069, teaching staff 184.

Finance. Monetary unit: Rwanda franc, with (Sept. 18, 1978) a par value of RwFr 92.84 to U.S. $1 (free rate of RwFr 178.08 = £1 sterling). Gold, SDR's, and foreign exchange (June 1978) U.S. $93.6 million. Budget (1976 actual): revenue RwFr 7,318,000,000; expenditure RwFr 5,898,000,000.

Foreign Trade. (1977) Imports RwFr 10,589,800,000; exports RwFr 8,539,800,000. Import sources: Belgium-Luxembourg 21%; Japan 12%; Kenya 11%; West Germany 8%; Iran 8%; France 7%; U.S. 5%. Export destinations: Kenya 81%; Belgium-Luxembourg 6%. Main exports: coffee 72%; tea 9%; tin 6%.

Agriculture. Production (in 000; metric tons; 1977): sorghum c. 155; corn (1976) c. 60; potatoes c. 170; sweet potatoes (1976) c. 675; cassava (1976) c. 416; dry beans c. 164; dry peas c. 58; pumpkins (1976) c. 60; plantains (1976) c. 1,784; coffee c. 20; tea c. 5. Livestock (in 000; July 1976): cattle c. 717; sheep c. 252; goats c. 570; pigs c. 75.

banquet in his honour to protest Chinese accusations of Soviet imperialism in Africa. The president also widened contacts within Africa. During a four-day visit to Uganda a joint committee was established to deal with common interests, especially the transport of landlocked Rwanda's exports to Kenyan ports. As chairman of both the Common African and Mauritian Organization and the Economic Commission of the Great Lakes, Habyarimana was particularly concerned with the economic future.

In July, on the fifth anniversary of the military takeover, Habyarimana announced that presidential and legislative elections and a referendum on a proposed constitution would be held. The constitution was approved in October at a joint meeting of the government and the ruling Revolutionary Movement for National Development, the country's sole political party.   (MOLLY MORTIMER)

Sailing

During 1978 there was continuing discussion of proposed International Ocean Racing (IOR) rules. In the course of this long-unresolved controversy many small clubs and associations abandoned IOR

Spinnaker billowing, the sloop "Circus Maximus" was the first across the finish line in the New-port-to-Bermuda yacht race in June. The boat was co-skippered by John Raby of New York City and Don Ritter of Short Hills, New Jersey.

WIDE WORLD

rules; the new offshore one-design concept was thus given an unexpected boost.

Many yachtsmen began 1978 under the impression that centreboard yachts would soon dominate competition. However, while some centreboarders did well, others performed extremely badly, and a likely rule in 1979 that centreboards must be locked down while racing would make their importance short-lived.

The first major result of 1978 was in the Sydney to Hobart race, notable for the violence of the storm early in the competition, which inflicted structural damage to some yachts and caused several to quit. The winner was the big U.S. Sparkman and Stephens 79-ft ketch "Kialoa" owned by John Kilroy. It reveled in the rough conditions, beating by two hours the Frers 47-ft "Ragamuffin" owned by Sid Fischer of Australia. Another huge U.S. yacht, "Windward Passage," owned by Fritz Johnson, finished third. Perhaps the most remarkable performance was that of fourth-place "Lollipop," a three-year-old half-tonner, owned by Miller and Kline of New South Wales, Australia.

The Sydney–Hobart was also the final event in the Southern Cross team racing series. The earlier races had been dominated by the New Zealand team of one-tonners, and their lead was such that, although only "Jenny H" managed to finish in the Sydney–Hobart, they won the series easily from New South Wales, with Great Britain third.

A single-handed ocean race from the Canary Islands to Antigua took place during the year. The maximum boat length allowed was 6.5 m overall, about the size of a mini-tonner. The winner from a large entry was Daniel Gilard of France in "Petit Dauphine." Kazimierz Jaworski of Poland, sailing "Spanielek," was second.

The Ton Cup events were once more keenly contested. From the designer's point of view this was the year of New Zealand's Laurie Davidson, with his designs winning both the half- and three-quarter-ton world cups.

The Round Britain race attracted a good fleet of multihulled and single-hulled yachts. Chay Blyth and Robert James and their big new trimaran "Great Britain IV" led the fleet home in impressive style, but the surprise winner on handicap was one of the smallest yachts in the fleet, "Ocean Beetle," a half-tonner owned by John Dungey.

Late in the season the International Ocean Racing circuit held a new team racing series, for the Sardinia Cup in the Mediterranean. Strong teams challenged from the U.S., West Germany, and the U.K., but the Italians triumphed with the help of two new Peterson-designed two-tonners, "Dida" and "Yena," crewed by a multinational team.

In the dinghy competition Laurie Smith from England, David Ullman from the U.S., John Albrechtson from Sweden, and Peter Colclough from England dominated their classes. Albert Batzill and his brother Rudolf of West Germany overcame their more famous cousins, the Diesch brothers, for the first time in a world event to win the world Flying Dutchman championship from the Olympic gold-medal pair.

In women's racing, world championships were held in 420s for helmswoman and crew and in

Lasers for single-handed sailors. The British pair of Cathy Foster and Wendy Hilder won the 420 class, and Lyndall Coxon of Australia won the Lasers.

Naomi James of New Zealand sailed into Dartmouth, Devon, England, on June 8 to become the first woman to sail single-handedly round the world by way of Cape Horn. She had left Dartmouth outward on Sept. 9, 1977, in her 19-ton, 53-ft "Express Crusader."   (ADRIAN JARDINE)

San Marino

A small republic, San Marino is an enclave in northeastern Italy, 5 mi SW of Rimini. Area: 61 sq km (24 sq mi). Pop. (1978 est.): 20,700. Cap. and largest city: San Marino (metro. pop., 1978 est., 8,300). Language: Italian. Religion: Roman Catholic. The country is governed by two *capitani reggenti,* or co-regents, appointed every six months by a Grand and General Council. Executive power rests with three secretaries of state: foreign and political affairs, internal affairs, and economic affairs. In 1978 the positions were filled, respectively, by Giordano Bruno Reffi, Alvaro Selva, and Emilio della Balda.

In the general election of May 28, 1978, the Christian Democrats gained one additional seat, bringing their total to 26 in the 60-seat Grand and General Council (parliament). Because the Communists retained their 16 seats (15 at the 1974 election but subsequently increased by the single Statutory Freedoms Movement member) and the Social Democrats and Socialists their 9 and 8 seats, respectively, the overall majority was still with the left.

The previous impasse was thus unresolved. The two co-regents, Francesco Valli and Enrico Andreoli, asked Gian Luigi Berti, the Christian Democrats' leader, to form a new government, but he was unable to do so. Then, on July 17, a left-wing coalition of Communists and the two Socialist parties, led by Communist Party secretary Umberto Barulli, formed a new government with a majority of one. One of the new Council's first acts was to approve a resolution criticizing the trials of dissidents in the U.S.S.R.

In July Antonietta Bonelli, a Communist and a member of the San Marino Foreign Ministry, participated as a "guest" in the conference of nonaligned nations in Belgrade, Yugos., with a view to San Marino's acceptance as a member of the nonaligned movement.   (K. M. SMOGORZEWSKI)

San Marino

São Tomé and Príncipe

An independent African state, the Democratic Republic of São Tomé and Príncipe comprises two main islands and several smaller islets that straddle the Equator in the Gulf of Guinea, off the west coast of Africa. Area: 964 sq km (372 sq mi), of which São Tomé, the larger island, comprises 854 sq km. Pop. (1978 est.): 83,000. Cap. and largest city: São Tomé (pop., 1977 est., 20,000). Language: Portuguese. Religion: mainly Roman Catholic. President in 1978, Manuel Pinto da Costa; premier, Miguel Trovoada.

Early in 1978 Pres. Manuel Pinto da Costa appealed to a number of countries for help against a possible external threat, although he did not specify from which direction he expected the threat to come. Failing to obtain any response from the UN, Costa flew to Angola where Pres. Agostinho Neto offered assistance. This was followed by a visit to São Tomé by the premier of Angola, Lopo do Nascimento, with a view to creating a closer association between the two nations. There was an additional offer of help against would-be attackers from Pres. Omar Bongo of Gabon, who was also chairman of the Organization of African Unity and who for some time had hoped to federate São Tomé with his own country. Costa, however, was wary of Gabon's intervention and went so far as to put Gabonese sympathizers in jail. These latter included some of his own closest associates. Early in May the president paid a brief working visit to Algeria, but while looking for new friends São Tomé continued to retain close links with the old colonial power, Portugal.

São Tomé and Príncipe

SÃO TOMÉ AND PRÍNCIPE

Education. (1972–73) Primary, pupils 12,518, teachers c. 303; secondary (1971–72), pupils 1,621, teachers 126; vocational (1971–72), pupils 280, teachers 36.

Finance and Trade. Monetary unit: dobra (which replaced the São Tomé and Príncipe escudo at par from September 1977), with (Sept. 18, 1978) a free rate of 35.67 dobras to U.S. $1 (69.60 dobras = £1 sterling). Budget (1974 est.) balanced at 150 million dobras. Foreign trade (1975): imports 288,469,000 dobras; exports 180,432,000 dobras. Import sources: Portugal 61%; Angola 13%. Export destinations: The Netherlands 52%; Portugal 33%; West Germany 8%. Main exports (1973): cocoa 87%; copra 8%.

Agriculture. Production (in 000; metric tons; 1977): cocoa c. 9; copra c. 5; bananas c. 1; palm kernels c. 2; palm oil c. 1. Livestock (in 000; 1976): cattle c. 2; pigs c. 3; sheep c. 1; goats c. 1.

SAN MARINO

Education. (1977–78) Primary, pupils 1,623, teachers 132; secondary, pupils 1,209, teachers (1976–77) 108.

Finance. Monetary unit: Italian lira, with (Sept. 18, 1978) a free rate of 832 lire to U.S. $1 (1,631 lire = £1 sterling); local coins are issued. Budget (1977 est.) balanced at 34,-039,000,000 lire. Tourism (1976) 2,435,000 visitors.

Saudi Arabia

A $21 million aid program for São Tomé and Príncipe, for the development of transport services, industry, agriculture, housing, and urban development, was recommended by a visiting UN mission.   (KENNETH INGHAM)

Saudi Arabia

A monarchy occupying four-fifths of the Arabian Peninsula, Saudi Arabia has an area of 2,240,000 sq km (865,000 sq mi). Pop. (1974 census): 7,012,-600. Cap. and largest city: Riyadh (pop., 1976 est., 667,000). Language: Arabic. Religion: Muslim. King and prime minister in 1978, Khalid.

In 1978 Saudi Arabia used its influence in the Middle East and the world to promote a peace satisfactory to the Arabs and to block the expansion of Soviet and Communist power, but it could not heal the rifts in the Arab world that followed Egypt's peace initiative toward Israel. It continued to back moderate policies on oil prices.

Saudi Arabia clearly expressed its reservations about Egyptian Pres. Anwar as-Sadat's initiative but did not condemn it outright. Following a visit to Riyadh by U.S. Pres. Jimmy Carter on January 3–4, Saudi Arabia reiterated its insistence on Israel's complete withdrawal from Arab lands occupied in 1967, including East Jerusalem, as a condition for peace. On February 14 President Carter agreed to the sale of 60 F-15 fighter planes to Saudi Arabia as part of a package deal that included sending similar planes to Israel and less advanced ones to Egypt. The sale was approved by the U.S. Senate on May 15, but only after surmounting considerable opposition in the U.S. Saudi spokesmen denied any connection between the deal and continuing Saudi moderation on oil prices, but they made it clear that Saudi-U.S. relations would be seriously affected if the deal fell through. The sale of the planes was hedged with restrictions to prevent Saudi Arabia from supplying them to another country or training non-Saudis to handle them.

In February the U.S. agreed to provide Saudi Arabia with a $670 million military training program. It was also announced that Saudi Arabia would launch a new $10 billion project to make military electronic equipment under the auspices of the Arab Military Industries Organization. The industry would be located in al-Kharj, a new town to be built 60 mi southeast of Riyadh.

Crown Prince Fahd, the deputy prime minister, denied that Saudi Arabia was using oil as a direct means of pressuring the U.S., but he said in a newspaper interview published March 9 that "the oil lever cannot be dismissed." There were strong hints that Saudi Arabia might have recourse to other sources of arms if it could not get all it wanted from the U.S. Contrary to expectations, a state visit to Paris in May did not result in a deal to buy Mirage fighters, although France continued to supply Saudi Arabia with Crotale ground-to-air missiles.

Saudi Arabia pursued its efforts to heal divisions among the Arabs caused by the Sadat initiative. These efforts were not confined to conservative,

pro-Western Arab states. In April the defense minister visited Baghdad, and in July Crown Prince Fahd and the foreign minister, Prince Saud al-Faisal, toured Egypt, Syria, Jordan, and Iraq.

The Saudis welcomed the announcement that an Israeli-Egyptian-U.S. summit would be held at Camp David, Md., but they were less enthusiastic when the Camp David agreements were announced on September 18. A Saudi government statement said the accords could not be considered a finally acceptable formula for peace because they did not make clear Israel's intention to withdraw from all occupied territories, including Jerusalem, and because they failed to stipulate the right of the Palestinians to self-determination or to mention the Palestine Liberation Organization. The statement added, however, that Saudi Arabia did not accord itself the right to intervene in the affairs of another Arab country. Neither did it question that country's right to recover occupied territory by armed struggle or peaceful means. Saudi Arabia refused the hard-line Arab states' requests that it break with Sadat. It attended the Arab summit in Baghdad in October, which condemned the Camp David accords but failed to produce agreement on sanctions against Egypt.

Saudi Arabia also showed concern over events in southern Arabia and the Horn of Africa. It expressed alarm at increasing Soviet-Cuban support for Ethiopia in its fight against Somali and Eritrean nationalists, and it was especially disturbed by the use of the People's Democratic Republic of Yemen (Aden; South Yemen) as a staging-post for Communist arms and troops. The rapprochement with South Yemen, which had begun in 1976, was not sustained. In January and February there were severe border clashes, and matters worsened in June after the assassination of Pres. Ahmad al-Ghashmi of the Yemen Arab Republic (San'a'; North Yemen), which Saudi Arabia blamed on South Yemen. Subsequently, Pres. Salem Ali Rubayyi of South Yemen, the member of the Aden regime who had most favoured rapprochement with Saudi Arabia, was overthrown and executed. Saudi Arabia led moves to isolate South Yemen within the Arab League, but it strongly denied plans to invade it. Relations with North Yemen remained close.

Saudi Arabia maintained its leading role in international oil and economic diplomacy. The Saudi oil minister, Sheikh Ahmad Zaki Yamani, and other spokesmen regularly expressed concern over the decline of the U.S. dollar and its effect on Organization of Petroleum Exporting Countries (OPEC) revenues. At the same time, they voiced confidence that the dollar would ultimately recover because of the underlying strength of the U.S. economy. Accordingly, Saudi Arabia steadfastly opposed proposals from other OPEC members that payments for oil be made in some alternative to the dollar, such as a basket of currencies. Saudi Arabia also opposed any increase in oil prices while the international oil glut continued. In September, however, the oil minister argued that the glut would end in 1979; since oil price increases would then be inevitable, they should be made gradually to avoid any sudden upward jolt. After the December OPEC meeting, at which it was agreed that oil prices would be raised, in stages, to a total of 14.5% as of Oct. 1, 1979, Sheikh Yamani told a news conference that 14.5% was "a medium solution representing the best we could do under the circumstances."

Looking toward the future, the oil minister warned that the Soviet Union would shortly become a net oil importer and would then seek control over some Middle East oil fields and oil routes. He attacked the lack of Western response to Soviet intervention in Africa and Asia, reflecting Saudi apprehension over events in the Horn of Africa, the Communist takeover in Afghanistan, and instability in Pakistan. In a rare economic policy statement, Crown Prince Fahd, addressing the governors of the Arab Bank for Economic Development in Africa on April 19, expressed deep concern over the crisis in the world economy. He called for a much greater effort to narrow the gap between rich and poor nations, for greater energy saving by the major consumer nations, and for an end to instability in international exchange rates. Saudi Arabia continued to provide large amounts of aid to Arab states and other Asian, African, and Islamic countries through the Saudi Development Fund ($700 million in 1977) and other agencies.

Saudi Arabia's domestic oil output fell sharply during most of 1978. In the first half of the year it averaged 7.1 million bbl a day, as compared with 8,850,000 bbl a day in 1977. In February the government issued a directive to Aramco limiting production of Saudi light crudes to 65% of the total

Saudi Arabia, like most oil-rich nations, is experiencing a fantastic building boom. Apartment buildings under construction are common in Jidda.

(previously, light crudes had accounted for more than 70%). The move was designed to adjust output to reserves, but since the light crudes were subject to stronger international demand, it had an important effect on marketing patterns. Late in the year production was increased to compensate for the precipitous drop in Iranian output caused by the disturbances in that country.

Despite the lowered oil output, the budget for 1978–79, announced on June 1, showed the first increase in three years. Revenues amounted to U.S. $37.6 billion (including $33.3 billion, or 88.5%, from oil), compared with $32 billion in 1977–78. The government went ahead with its large-scale plans for two major industrial areas—at Jubail on the Gulf and at Yanbu on the Red Sea. It was also announced that $6.6 billion would be spent over the next four years to expand the ports of Jidda, Dammam, Yanbu, and Jubail. Chronic port congestion had already been eased considerably, and the amount of cargo handled had increased by 65% in 1977. Work continued on the new airport outside Jidda, which was expected to be one of the largest in the world. It would have the capacity to handle 16,000 passengers a day.

The government claimed that the rate of inflation, which had been running above 30% in 1976, had been halted through importation of cheaper food supplies and an attack on monopoly practices. A determined effort was made to tighten controls over the entry, work, and length of stay of the hundreds of thousands of immigrant workers in the country. The Interior Ministry announced on July 25 that 760 illegal immigrants were being deported.　　(PETER MANSFIELD)

SAUDI ARABIA

Education. (1975–76) Primary, pupils 686,108, teachers 35,139; secondary, pupils 203,314, teachers 13,875; vocational, pupils 4,832, teachers 697; teacher training, students 14,651, teachers 1,156; higher, students 26,437, teaching staff 2,133.

Finance. Monetary unit: riyal, with (Sept. 18, 1978) a free rate of 3.32 riyals to U.S. $1 (6.51 riyals = £1 sterling). Gold, SDR's, and foreign exchange (March 1978) U.S. $26,-020,000,000. Budget (1977–78 est.): revenue 146,493,000,-000 riyals; expenditure 111.4 billion riyals. Gross domestic product (1976–77) 193.1 billion riyals. Money supply (Sept. 1977) 33.3 billion riyals. Cost of living (1975 = 100; 1st quarter 1978) 145.2.

Foreign Trade. (1977) Imports (fob) c. 52,910,000,000 riyals; exports 145.1 billion riyals. Import sources: U.S. c. 23%; Japan c. 15%; West Germany c. 11%; Italy c. 7%; U.K. c. 6%. Export destinations: Japan c. 19%; U.S. c. 16%; France c. 10%; Italy c. 6%. Main exports: crude oil 94%; petroleum products 6%. Tourism (1975) gross receipts U.S. $509 million.

Transport and Communications. Roads (1976) 26,267 km. Motor vehicles in use (1976): passenger 226,200; commercial 178,300. Railways: (1976) 612 km; traffic (1974) 72 million passenger-km, freight 66 million net ton-km. Air traffic (1976): 3,122,000,000 passenger-km; freight 85.2 million net ton-km. Shipping (1977): merchant vessels 100 gross tons and over 119; gross tonnage 1,018,713. Telephones (Jan. 1977) 160,000. Radio receivers (Dec. 1975) 255,000. Television receivers (Dec. 1975) 124,000.

Agriculture. Production (in 000; metric tons; 1977): sorghum 86; wheat (1976) c. 205; barley (1976) c. 22; tomatoes c. 126; onions (1976) c. 37; grapes c. 70; dates c. 265. Livestock (in 000; 1976): cattle c. 180; sheep c. 1,379; goats c. 779; camels c. 614; asses c. 102; poultry c. 9,650.

Industry. Production (in 000; metric tons; 1977): crude oil 457,089; petroleum products (1976) c. 28,600; natural gas (cu m) c. 6,400,000; electricity (excluding most industrial production; kw-hr; 1976) c. 2,250,000; cement (1976) 1,104.

Senegal

A republic of northwestern Africa, Senegal is bounded by Mauritania, Mali, Guinea, and Guinea-Bissau and by the Atlantic Ocean. The independent nation of The Gambia forms an enclave within the country. Area: 196,722 sq km (75,955 sq

Senegal

SENEGAL
   Education. (1977–78) Primary, pupils 313,455, teachers (1975–76) 8,468; secondary, pupils 20,390, teachers (1974–75) 2,705; vocational and teacher training (1975–76), pupils 12,036, teachers (1974–75) 484; higher (1975–76), students 8,213, teaching staff 412.
   Finance and Trade. Monetary unit: CFA franc, with (Sept. 18, 1978) a par value of CFA Fr 50 to the French franc (free rate of CFA Fr 218.81 = U.S. $1; CFA Fr 428.75 = £1 sterling). Budget (1978 est.) balanced at CFA Fr 154 billion. Foreign trade (1975): imports CFA Fr 123,540,000,000; exports CFA Fr 98.7 billion. Import sources: France 31%; U.S. 6%. Export destinations: France 32%; Mauritania 8%; Mali 5%; The Netherlands 5%; U.K. 5%. Main exports: petroleum products 20%; peanut oil 19%; phosphates 18%; fish and products 6%; peanut oil cake 5%.

SEYCHELLES
   Education. (1977) Primary, pupils 10,005, teachers 424; secondary, pupils 4,250, teachers 193; vocational, pupils 159, teachers 20; teacher training, students 150, teachers 22; higher (1976), students 142, teaching staff 13.
   Finance and Trade. Monetary unit: Seychelles rupee, with (Sept. 18, 1978) a free rate of SRs 6.80 to U.S. $1 (par value of SRs 13.33 = £1 sterling). Budget (1977–78 est.): revenue SRs 134.4 million; expenditure SRs 148.5 million. Foreign trade (1976): imports SRs 290,620,000; exports SRs 57.6 million. Import sources: U.K. 30%; Kenya 16%; South Africa 7%; Yemen (Aden) 7%; Japan 5%; Singapore 5%; Australia 5%. Export destinations: ship and aircraft bunkers 66%; Pakistan 15%; Mauritius 5%. Main exports: petroleum products 58%; copra 15%; cinnamon bark 6%; frozen fish 6%; aircraft engine parts 5%. Tourism (1976) 49,498 visitors.

mi). Pop. (1976 prelim.): 5,085,400. Cap. and largest city: Dakar (pop., 1976 prelim., 798,800). Language: French (official); Wolof; Serer; other tribal dialects. Religion: Muslim 80%; Christian 10%. President in 1978, Léopold Sédar Senghor; premier, Abdou Diouf.

Presidential, parliamentary, and local elections were held in Senegal on Feb. 26, 1978. Léopold Sédar Senghor (*see* BIOGRAPHIES) was reelected president with 82.02% of the vote, against 17.38% for his opponent, Abdoulaye Wade, and the governing Socialist Party took 83 of the 100 seats in the National Assembly. On March 13 the Supreme Court dismissed Wade's appeal for the annulment of the presidential election.

Also on March 13 Abdou Diouf was endorsed as premier. The new Cabinet, with Senghor's approval, was constituted so as to strengthen Diouf's authority, and a further move in this direction was the dismissal in a reshuffle on September 19 of Foreign Minister Babacar Ba. Babacar Ba was replaced by Mustafa Niasse. On October 23, to end rumours that he was preparing to retire, Senghor announced that he would continue to exercise his presidential mandate until its expiration in March 1983.

In external affairs the two most important events of the year were the normalization of relations with Guinea when diplomatic relations, broken off on Sept. 18, 1973, were reestablished on May 8, 1978, and President Senghor's official visit to France from May 17 to 20.

The economy continued to be seriously affected by drought. The worst effects of earlier famines were avoided by food imports and aid, but the country's peanut industry, providing the largest source of export revenue, was hard hit, and Senegal was expected to have a much larger trade deficit in 1978 than the high one recorded in 1977.

(PHILIPPE DECRAENE)

Seychelles

A republic in the Indian Ocean consisting of 89 islands, Seychelles lies 1,450 km from the coast of East Africa. Area: 443 sq km (171 sq mi), 166 sq km of which includes the islands of Farquhar, Desroches, and Aldabra. Pop. (1977 census): 61,950, including Creole 94%, French 5%, English 1%. Cap.: Victoria, on Mahé (pop., 1977, 23,000). Language: English and French are official, creole

patois is also spoken. Religion: Roman Catholic 91%, Anglican 8%. President in 1978, France-Albert René.

In April 1978, 21 people were arrested and charged with plotting to overthrow Pres. France-Albert René's government. Accusations that former president James Mancham and some Kenyan ministers were involved were denied, and those arrested were subsequently released. René, backed by the newly formed Tanzanian-trained militia, stated that he would never allow the country to be destroyed by reactionary forces, and on June 9 he declared a one-party state (his Seychelles People's United Party being renamed the Seychelles People's Progressive Front). He also announced (June 5) a five-year plan abolishing private medicine, redistributing land, and expanding public housing.

In the field of foreign affairs, René claimed Tromelin Island (which France had occupied since 1954 with British agreement) under the Treaty of Paris of 1814. Following René's visit to France in September, the French minister for cooperation visited Seychelles in November. René also acted as host in April to a left-wing conference of Indian Ocean states, attended by Madagascar and the Comoros along with the opposition parties of Mauritius and the Communist Party of Réunion. Though Chinese aid followed René's April trip to Peking and a 30-man Soviet embassy was set up, Britain remained the chief economic provider for the Seychelles and the U.S. maintained its satellite tracker there.   (MOLLY MORTIMER)

Sierra Leone

A republic within the Commonwealth of Nations, Sierra Leone is a West African state on the Atlantic coast between Guinea and Liberia. Area: 71,740 sq km (27,699 sq mi). Pop. (1978 est.): 3,220,000, including (1963) Mende and Temne tribes 60.7%; other tribes 38.9%; non-African 0.4%. Cap. and largest city: Freetown (pop., 1974, 314,340). Language: English (official); tribal dialects. Religion: animist 66%, Muslim 28%, Christian 6%, according to outdated statistics; it appears that Islam is rapidly gaining converts from animism, however. President in 1978, Siaka Stevens; prime minister to June 15, Christian A. Kamara-Taylor.

In May 1978 a bill was passed, by the requisite

Seychelles

Sierra Leone

Singapore

SIERRA LEONE

Education. (1976–77) Primary, pupils 218,379, teachers 6,700; secondary, pupils 50,455, teachers 2,297; vocational, pupils 1,690, teachers 154; teacher training, students 1,269, teachers 121; higher, students 2,077, teaching staff 327.

Finance and Trade. Monetary unit: leone, with (Sept. 18, 1978) a free value of 1.02 leones to U.S. $1 (par value of 2 leones = £1 sterling). Budget (1977–78 est.): revenue 144.7 million leones; expenditure 156.7 million leones. Foreign trade (1977): imports 216,460,000 leones; exports 147,440,000 leones. Import sources: U.K. c. 20%; Nigeria c. 13%; Japan c. 8%; China c. 7%; U.S. c. 6%; France c. 6%; West Germany c. 6%. Export destinations: U.K. c. 44%; U.S. c. 35%; West Germany c. 8%; The Netherlands c. 7%. Main exports: diamonds 42%; coffee 27%; cocoa 15%.

Agriculture. Production (in 000; metric tons; 1977): rice c. 600; cassava (1976) c. 87; mangoes c. 55; palm kernels c. 51; palm oil c. 56; coffee c. 5; cocoa c. 5; fish catch (1976) c. 68. Livestock (in 000; 1976): cattle c. 305; sheep c. 68; goats c. 179; pigs c. 36; chickens c. 3,300.

Industry. Production (in 000; metric tons; 1976): bauxite 660; petroleum products c. 295; diamonds (metric carats) c. 1,500; electricity (kw-hr) c. 200,000.

two-thirds majority, authorizing the establishment of a one-party state under the ruling All People's Congress Party (APC). A referendum on the change, necessary according to a 1971 amendment to the Constitution Act, was rushed through in June, with some areas giving virtually 100% approval. According to the bill, all MP's were to declare their adherence to the ruling party within 24 days or vacate their seats. Nine of the 11 opposition Sierra Leone People's Party MP's declared their adherence to the APC and were later followed by the party's leaders, Salia Jusu-Sheriff and George Saffa. Presidential powers were increased, and the president was to be elected for a seven-year term (with a 14-year limit); Siaka Stevens agreed to take office "as if elected." The prime minister was replaced by two vice-presidents (Sorie I. Koroma and C. A. Kamara Taylor), and MP's were to be elected from among "approved party candidates."

The economy suffered from slow growth rates, a balance of payments deficit, and a steep decline in diamond production. Western creditors granted debt relief, and the Mano River (tariff) Union of Sierra Leone and neighbouring Liberia concluded plans for joint highway and hydroelectric power projects to be built by the two countries in the near future. (MOLLY MORTIMER)

Singapore

Singapore, a republic within the Commonwealth of Nations, occupies a group of islands, the largest of which is Singapore, at the southern extremity of the Malay Peninsula. Area: 616 sq km (238 sq mi). Pop. (1978 est.): 2,334,400, including 76% Chinese, 15% Malays, and 7% Indians. Language: official languages are English, Malay, Mandarin Chinese, and Tamil. Religion: Malays are Muslim; Chinese, mainly Buddhist; Indians, mainly Hindu. President in 1978, Benjamin Henry Sheares; prime minister, Lee Kuan Yew.

From the beginning of the year Prime Minister Lee Kuan Yew (see BIOGRAPHIES) placed emphasis on what he regarded as a major priority for the nation. This was the policy of bilingualism, the object of which was to ensure that English became the working language of the country while at the same time encouraging members of the various racial communities to become fluent in their own tongues. One practical outcome of this policy was a radical reform of Nanyang University. From the beginning of the academic year in July, English replaced Chinese as its medium of instruction. Its first-year students began joint courses with those of the English-language University of Singapore. The declared goal was to complete the transfer of instruction from Chinese to English by 1981.

Effective at the beginning of the 1978–79 academic year, the government suspended the requirement for university entrants to possess a suitability certificate. This certificate had been introduced in 1964 in an attempt to prevent Communists from infiltrating institutions of higher education. In August a dispute arose between the government and medical and dental students when it was announced that students who refused to sign a bond committing them to work in a state hospital for up to five years would not be awarded their degrees.

In April a Malaysian Chinese labourer became the first person to be executed for trafficking in drugs under legislation introduced in 1975. In August the first woman was sentenced to death for the same offense. President Lee in an interview in September indicated that he might retire in ten years when a second-generation leadership would be ready to assume responsibility for high office.

The Singapore branch of the Soviet Union's Moscow-Narodny Bank incurred huge losses on loans when a number of large companies to which it had extended credit defaulted on repayments. As a consequence it acquired extensive property and landholdings on the island. (MICHAEL LEIFER)

SINGAPORE

Education. (1977) Primary, pupils 306,349, teachers 11,041; secondary, pupils 153,055, teachers 6,731; vocational, pupils 35,991, teachers 1,662; teacher training, students 1,190, teachers 109; higher, students 20,734, teaching staff 1,116.

Finance. Monetary unit: Singapore dollar, with (Sept. 18, 1978) a free rate of Sing$2.25 to U.S. $1 (Sing$4.40 = £1 sterling). Gold, SDR's, and foreign exchange (May 1978) U.S. $4,334,800,000. Budget (1977–78 est.) balanced at Sing$3,362,000,000 (including transfer to development fund of Sing$611 million). Gross national product (1977) Sing$15,669,000,000. Money supply (May 1978) Sing$4,550,000,000. Cost of living (1975 = 100; June 1978) 105.6.

Foreign Trade. (1977) Imports Sing$25,522,000,000; exports Sing$20,091,000,000. Import sources: Japan 18%; Saudi Arabia 15%; Malaysia 14%; U.S. 13%. Export destinations: U.S. 16%; Malaysia 14%; Japan 10%; Hong Kong 7%; Australia 5%. Main exports: petroleum products 24%; machinery 20%; rubber 11%; food 7%; ship and aircraft stores 6%. Tourism (1976): visitors 1,321,000; gross receipts U.S. $283 million.

Transport and Communications. Roads (1977) 2,237 km. Motor vehicles in use (1977): passenger 142,100; commercial 49,500. Railways (1976) 26 km (for traffic see Malaysia). Air traffic (1977): 7,864,000,000 passenger-km; freight 259,330,000 net ton-km. Shipping (1977): merchant vessels 100 gross tons and over 872; gross tonnage 6,791,398. Shipping traffic (1977): goods loaded 24,675,000 metric tons, unloaded 40,474,000 metric tons. Telephones (Dec. 1977) 455,000. Radio licenses (Dec. 1977) 387,000. Television licenses (Dec. 1977) 329,000.

Seventh-day Adventist Church:
see Religion

Ships and Shipping:
see Industrial Review; Transportation

Skating:
see Ice Hockey; Winter Sports

Skeet Shooting:
see Target Sports

Skiing:
see Water Sports; Winter Sports

Soccer:
see Football

Social and Welfare Services

Social security continued to be dominated during 1978 by the state of the economy. The persistence of unemployment was influencing policy in a number of different areas: unemployment insurance, pensions and retirement, efforts at job creation, and the financing of social security and social assistance. Relatively few general improvements were made in the scope and coverage of social security, reflecting the economic situation and the desire of many governments to hold down or, in some cases, to reduce public expenditure. Nevertheless, there were some advances in family benefits and in the field of pensions.

International Developments in Social Security. There was widespread recognition that adequate compensation for the unemployed is a necessary but only partial response to the unemployment problem. An interesting development in this field was the idea of work sharing. This had come at a time when there had been a certain upturn in economic growth, resulting largely from increased productivity, but no significant fall in unemployment. Official targets for future growth in many countries were not substantially higher than the forecast rise in productivity, so there was reason to think that, even if economic growth continued, unemployment would persist at its current high level or perhaps get worse as more young people and women came onto the labour market. To deal with this long-run problem, the trade unions, especially in Belgium, West Germany, and the U.K., launched a strong campaign in favour of shorter working hours, designed to share existing work.

Work sharing was relevant to social security not only because its success could relieve the pressure on unemployment insurance schemes but also because social security systems could contribute to that success by reviewing the ways they levy contributions on employers and employees. Because of the existence of income ceilings above which little or no contribution may be payable (and, in rare cases, because contributions were on a flat-rate rather than an earnings-related basis), the cost of contributions under most social security systems was higher if a given number of working hours were shared among more employees. To remove the disincentives to work sharing implicit in the methods of financing social security was seen by some as a logical step that could probably be achieved at little or no cost.

While unemployment levels tended to stabilize in 1978, the number of long-term unemployed continued to rise. The vast majority of unemployment insurance schemes paid full benefits for a limited period only, typically six months or a year. After this time, the unemployed received a cut in benefit income and were often transferred from unemployment insurance to social assistance, where benefits were means-tested and procedures in general were more rigorous. There seemed little doubt that the long-term unemployed needed higher, not lower, benefits. Some recognition was given to the problem by the U.K. Supplementary Benefits Commission, which recommended the extension of the "long-term" benefit rate to people who had been unemployed for two years or more.

Early retirement provisions continued to be used as a way of combating the effects of recession. Trade unions and governments saw early retirement as a way of making more jobs available to younger members of the work force, and it was a convenient way for employers to shed excess labour. Furthermore, it directly cut the number of people registered as unemployed, thereby reinforcing its attraction to governments. Government and employers were reluctant to concede permanent reductions in the retirement age, however, and several of the schemes for early retirement had been introduced on a temporary basis. In Belgium the eligibility conditions for a "pre-pension" were relaxed at the beginning of the year. In the U.K. the Job Release Scheme was extended to cover the whole country (rather than being confined to assisted areas) and higher benefits were introduced for married people. To qualify under the Job Release Scheme, a worker had to be age 64 (59 if a woman) and his employer had to agree to recruit a replacement from the unemployment register, though not necessarily for the same job.

The problem of excess labour supply was not universal; indeed, some socialist countries were experiencing the opposite problem. In Hungary a decree was passed at the beginning of 1978 to encourage people who had reached retirement age to continue working. Extra pension rights earned after the normal pension age (60 for men, 55 for women) could now bring the pension up to a maximum of 100% of the worker's wage, and extra paid leave was granted to those who continued working. In the U.S.S.R., with its relatively low retirement ages, efforts were also being made to keep older workers in the labour force.

Renewed emphasis was being placed on family allowances, partly because they had not risen in line with other benefits or with incomes, partly because of new concern about the persistence of poverty in industrialized countries, especially among families, and fears about the falling birthrate. There was a tendency to eliminate help in the form of tax allowances, since it was of greater value to the rich, who paid higher rates of taxation. At the same time, cash allowances or family benefits were being raised.

In The Netherlands, as of October 1978, tax allowances for children were replaced by an increase in family allowances equal to the tax relief an employee earning 40,000 guilders per year would have gotten under the old system. The fact that some families were worse off as a result of the reform was closely related to the fact that it formed part of a plan to make savings in public expenditure. In some other countries the reform was being or had been implemented in such a way as to make almost all families better off. This was the case in West Germany and appeared to be the case in the U.K. All child tax allowances in the U.K. were to be abolished by April 1979, when child benefits would be raised to £4 per child per week (£6 for the first child of a single parent). In early 1978 the benefit was £1 for the first child and £1.50 for subsequent children and for the first child of a single parent.

A change in the system of family support in Canada, announced in August, appeared to diverge somewhat from this trend. The basic rate of allowances was being cut from $25.68 to $20 per child per month, reducing expenditure by $690 million. At the same time, families earning $18,-000 per year or less would receive a tax credit of $200 per year for each child under 18; the credit would be reduced by 5% for families with income over $18,000. Tax credits, unlike tax allowances, do not favour the rich, since their value is unrelated to a person's marginal tax rate.

Another important reform in family benefits was implemented in 1978 with the introduction of the family supplement in France. The supplement, which replaced five other benefits, was worth Fr 340 per month at the beginning of 1978. It was payable to families with a child under three or with at least three children when the family income was below a certain limit, defined in such a way that about 80% of families in the relevant categories could qualify for the benefit. The reform had three main aims: to help young families, to favour families with three or more children (for demographic reasons), and to ensure similar treatment whether or not the mother worked.

Various improvements were made in pensions. In France women receiving the family supplement, and also women caring for a handicapped person, would have pension contributions paid on their behalf by the Family Allowances Fund. A more fundamental reform was implemented in the U.K. with the extension to all employees of earnings-related pension insurance. Many employees, particularly in the public sector and in the better jobs in the private sector, would continue to belong to occupational schemes and would thus be able to contract out of the new earnings-related plan. Everyone, however, would continue to be covered by the basic pension scheme, which paid flat-rate pensions.

The ways in which pensions are adjusted continued to be a topical issue. Switzerland was to make automatic adjustments every two years, equal to the mean of the consumer price index and the national wage index. Adjustments might be more frequent if prices rose by more than 8% in a single year or less frequent if prices rose by less than 5% over two years.

Social assistance or welfare, intended as a purely residual form of social protection, had been taking on vast dimensions, a development not unrelated to the rise in unemployment. In the U.K., where 10% of the population relied on supplementary benefits (the national system of social assistance) to bring their incomes up to the poverty line, a committee set up in 1976 to review the system made its report in July 1978. Among its proposals were replacement of discretionary lump-sum payments by an automatic payment at six-month intervals to all beneficiaries, the incorporation of a small heating allowance into the basic rates of sup-

UPI COMPIX

U.S. abortion foes marched on the Capitol in January to demand a constitutional amendment banning abortions.

plementary benefit, and transfer of the responsibility for meeting housing costs to the local authorities. Some disappointment was expressed over the lack of proposals for more fundamental reform, but the committee had been instructed not to discuss proposals designed to reduce the numbers dependent on supplementary benefits by expanding the national insurance scheme.

(ROGER A. BEATTIE)

U.S. Developments. Social welfare programs were one of the major casualties of the conservative, budget-cutting mood that prevailed in the United States in 1978. Some of the most ambitious social legislation—welfare reform, national health insurance, urban revitalization—languished in Congress, while other programs were trimmed down.

One of those cut back was the Comprehensive Employment and Job Training Act (CETA). Under a four-year extension of the program, public service jobs would be created for about 660,000 people in fiscal 1979, a reduction from the 725,000 jobs that existed before and which Pres. Jimmy Carter had requested. A limit of $13,200 a year was set on wages for these jobs.

CETA suffered not only from the general anti-spending mood in Congress but also from charges of widespread waste and corruption in the program itself. Created to help disadvantaged persons who were victims of discrimination and poor educational opportunities, CETA was found to be providing jobs mostly to educated white males. In many communities CETA workers were used to substitute for regular city or county employees, thus cutting the local payroll.

Another measure scaled down from original plans was the Humphrey-Hawkins full-employment bill. It was stripped of a key provision requiring the government to be the employer of last resort for the hard-core unemployed. A national goal of 3% inflation by 1983 was added to the original goal of 4% unemployment.

An exception to the trend came in the area of assistance for the nation's 20 million to 35 million handicapped persons, as Congress authorized $5.2 billion to be spent for this purpose over the next four years. Existing efforts to provide equal opportunities and legal protection for the handicapped were to be expanded and new ones started, including creation of a National Institute for Handicapped Research and a jobs program patterned after the community employment program for the elderly.

The Equal Opportunity Act, which embraced many of the original "poverty" programs, was extended for three years with one major change. The formula for funding the Head Start program for low-income preschoolers was altered so that the money would eventually be distributed more equally among all the states. In the past emphasis had been placed on 25 states, most of them in the South.

New Food Stamp regulations ordered in 1977 by Congress were spelled out by the Department of Agriculture and slated to take effect Jan. 1, 1979. Eligibility standards were tightened, the requirement that recipients pay cash for stamps was eliminated, and twice-a-year cost-of-living increases were added. The new regulations were expected to trim about 400,000 families from the Food Stamp rolls, but benefits would rise for the remaining 4,380,000 households and additional poor who joined the revised program.

In other areas of social welfare, Congress extended the Older Americans Act for three years and authorized $4 billion for social and legal services, nutrition, health, and other programs for the nation's 35 million elderly; increased the federal government's role in treating and preventing child abuse and neglect; broadened benefits for coal miners suffering from black lung disease; and reauthorized federal assistance for comprehensive health centres for migrant workers and persons living in medically underserved areas and for family planning programs (expanded to include the administration's efforts to curb teenage pregnancy).

Social Security and federal funding of abortions were in the spotlight again in 1978. Concerned about large increases scheduled in payroll taxes, several lawmakers urged reconsideration of the Social Security plan that had been passed in 1977, but action on reducing the taxes was deferred. As a result, the Social Security tax rate (paid by both employer and employee) was scheduled to rise from 6.05% to 6.13% in 1979 and the maximum annual salary taxed from $17,700 to $22,900. This meant that the maximum tax for a worker would increase from $1,070.85 to $1,403.77. For self-employed workers the maximum tax in 1979 was slated to be $1,854.90, compared with $1,433.70 in 1978. (*See* SPECIAL REPORT.)

Congress remained sharply divided over abortion funding, with the House of Representatives favouring tighter restrictions than the Senate. Opponents of abortion succeeded in limiting payments for military personnel and dependents to three types of cases: (1) pregnancies in which the life of the woman is in danger; (2) those involving incest or rape promptly reported to authorities; and (3) those in which two doctors agree that the woman's physical health would be seriously impaired if she had the child. The same three limitations, originally worked out as a compromise in 1977 after a five-month House-Senate battle, were once again imposed on the funding of abortions for low-income women under Medicaid.

In the wake of past reports of abuses and waste, efforts to tighten welfare programs continued. The Department of Health, Education, and Welfare (HEW) announced that the number of persons on the rolls of the largest program—Aid to Families with Dependent Children (AFDC)—had decreased in 1977 for the second straight year. The monthly case load of AFDC recipients was 11,018,158 in 1977, down 2.3% from 11,279,861 per month in 1976. HEW also stepped up its campaign to force absentee fathers of children on welfare to contribute to the support of the children.

Perhaps as noteworthy as what did happen in the social welfare field was what did not. Several welfare reform plans were introduced during the year, including a $20 billion "comprehensive" Carter administration proposal, a $5 billion "no-frills" plan by senators Daniel Patrick Moynihan (Dem., N.Y.) and Alan Cranston (Dem., Calif.), and a broader measure proposed by Sen. Edward M. Kennedy (Dem., Mass.), which had an estimated cost of $7.1 billion for the first year. Welfare reform would be a major issue again in 1979, when the administration was expected to back a low-budget plan.

National health insurance fell victim to the same money-saving mood. The Carter administration announced a set of general national health insurance principles, including universal coverage and comprehensive benefits to be phased in as economic factors allowed. That plan was attacked by Senator Kennedy, who outlined a more comprehensive and expensive labour-backed proposal.

The key elements of President Carter's extensive urban plan—a National Development Bank, public works programs aimed at the hard-core unemployed, and countercyclical revenue sharing—all were sidetracked in Congress. Funds for some smaller items such as inner-city parks and health clinics, social service projects, and urban mass transit were included in other authorization bills.

(DAVID M. MAZIE)

See also Education; Health and Disease; Industrial Review: *Insurance.*
[522.D; 535.B.3.e; 552.D.1]

HOW SECURE IS SOCIAL SECURITY?

by J. W. Van Gorkom

"Plasma coming up."

In recent years the U.S. has witnessed a spate of articles, books, and speeches, all with a common theme: the Social Security system is "bankrupt" and will not be able to pay benefits to today's workers when they reach retirement. While the system does face some long-term financial problems, a closer examination indicates that these dire predictions are based on a superficial understanding of the subject.

This refers, of course, to the retirement and disability aspects of Social Security, collectively known as OASDI, for old age, survivors, and disability insurance. Medicare is also a part of the Social Security system, but its economics are quite distinct.

A Faulty Analogy. When a private insurer sells a retirement policy to an individual, the insurer undertakes to pay him retirement benefits from a certain age until his death. To pay these benefits, the insurer collects premiums from the insured during his working life and invests them. The premiums are based on an actuarial estimate of the obligation assumed. The accumulated premiums and the interest earned thereon constitute an actuarial fund from which the benefits will be paid.

Social Security is financed on a totally different basis, known as "current cost financing." The premiums, in the form of payroll taxes, are not accumulated and invested; they are generally paid out immediately as benefits to those persons who have already retired. No funds are accumulated except for a relatively small contingency reserve. When today's workers reach retirement, their benefits will be paid from taxes collected from the persons who are then working. In essence, the system is based on inter-generational transfers.

It is this absence of an actuarial fund that has caused critics to declare the Social Security system "bankrupt." A private system in such a situation would indeed be bankrupt, but the government has

Jerome W. Van Gorkom is chairman of the board and chief executive officer, Trans Union Corp., Lincolnshire, Ill. He recently received his second appointment to the U.S. Department of Health, Education, and Welfare's Advisory Council on Social Security.

the power to tax future generations of workers and thereby extract from them the money needed to pay future benefits. It does not need an actuarial fund, and use of the word bankrupt is thus misleading.

Critics who understand this difference still claim that the benefits are too uncertain because they depend on the ability of the government to levy taxes in the future. But suppose that fully funded reserves for the system had actually been accumulated. Because the system covers roughly 100 million workers plus their dependents, the reserve would have to aggregate some three to five trillion dollars, or roughly double the entire gross national product.

Where could such an amount be invested? All the listed stocks in the U.S. and all the outstanding federal bonds aggregate less then two trillion dollars. If the Social Security system were to buy up all these assets the form of the economy would be completely changed. The only apparent alternative would be to create a special type of government bond into which the fund could be invested. But payment on any government bond is also dependent on the government's ability to levy taxes in the future!

Planning for the Future. This does not mean that there are no problems with regard to the system's future. In recent years the benefits paid out exceeded the taxes collected, and the tiny contingency fund was on its way to exhaustion. In 1977, however, Congress largely corrected the problem.

First, it eliminated a basic computational error inadvertently built into the system in the legislation of 1972, and this wiped out about one-half of the estimated long-range deficit. Second, it provided for future increases in the tax rate and also that maximum earnings subject to the tax would rise by arbitrary amounts for three years, so that over 90% of all earnings would be covered in 1981. Thereafter the maximum would rise in proportion to the average national increase in all wages. (*See* Table I.)

Table I. OASDI Tax Increases to 1990

Year	OASDI tax rate for employer and employee (percent)	Maximum earnings subject to tax
1977	4.95	$16,500
1978	5.05	17,700
1979	5.08	22,900
1980	5.08	25,900
1981	5.35	29,700
1982–84	5.40	Subject to auto-
1985–89	5.70	matic raises as
1990	6.20	all earnings rise

Table II. OASDI Surplus or Deficit to 2052

Period	Surplus or (deficit)*
1978–2002	1.02% of total covered earnings
2003–27	(1.11) of total covered earnings
2028–52	(4.10) of total covered earnings

*Note: The surplus or deficit is stated as a percentage of "total covered earnings." This measure is used because it is more meaningful than any absolute amount in that it clearly delineates the burden or benefit to the taxpayer.

Without passing judgment on the merits of these changes, it is clear that the financial structure of the system has been substantially strengthened. A more detailed picture can be obtained by examining the report issued in May 1978 by the trustees of the system, covering the period from 1978 to 2052.

The future income and outgo of the system are dependent upon several factors, three of which are critical: (1) the rate of future *wage increases*, which affects both the amount of taxes collected and initial retirement benefits, (2) the rate of future *price increases*, since annual increases in benefits are tied to the Consumer Price Index, and (3) the *fertility rate*, the number of children born to the average woman in her lifetime. From its peak of 3.7 in 1957, it had fallen to 1.8 by 1977. It is significant because it affects the ratio of workers to beneficiaries.

It is impossible to forecast these factors for 75 years with any assurance of accuracy. Nevertheless the forecast is a valuable tool and the assumptions, however difficult or open to argument, must be made. As to the three items described above, here are the trustees' assumptions: (1) Wage rates will rise by gradually decreasing percentages, falling from 7.7% in 1977 to 5.75% in the year 2000 and remaining there through 2052. (2) The Consumer Price Index will rise by various amounts for the next few years, but from 1985 to 2052 it will rise 4% per year. (3) The fertility rate will increase slowly to 2.1 around the year 2000 and remain there until 2052.

Based on these assumptions, the trustees report that over the next 75 years outgo will exceed income by an average of 1.4% of total covered earnings. This deficit, however, does not occur uniformly.

As can be seen in Table II, the system will actually run at a small surplus for 25 years, to the year 2002. This will be followed by a small deficit in the second 25-year period. Not until the third 25 years does a significant problem appear.

A Question of Demographics. This peculiar pattern springs from the fact that the basic financial problem facing the system is a demographic one, which will not manifest itself until well into the future. Today there are roughly three workers for every person receiving OASDI benefits. By 2030 there will be only two workers for every beneficiary. This factor alone will automatically increase the tax burden on the individual worker.

This reduction in the ratio of workers to retirees is the result of the huge surge in births after World War II and the sharp drop in the fertility rate after 1957. Today, the people born at the peak of the baby boom are entering the work force and helping to pay the benefits of the comparatively small number of workers who are already retired. However, shortly after the year 2010, these people will begin to retire and they will be adding very heavily to the benefit rolls for some two decades thereafter. On the other hand, a relatively small number of persons are expected to be moving into the work force.

There is always the possibility that the fertility rate may be higher than projected, but even if it remains low, the situation is by no means hopeless. Much of the burden can be alleviated by gradually raising the retirement age to 68 or higher, starting after the turn of the century. Furthermore, the society envisioned would have a much lower percentage of children, so that funds now spent on child care could be shifted to the care of the elderly. With fewer children, more wives would be encouraged to work, although the forecast assumes some increase from this factor. As a last resort, immigration quotas could be raised.

Without attempting to classify any of these steps as good or bad, it can be said that there is no really serious danger to the system at present. Today's workers can realistically expect to receive their benefits as the system now stands, although there may have to be an increase in the tax rates after 2025.

It must be emphasized that all of these judgments are based on the validity of the trustees' assumptions. If the fertility rate is lower than expected, the problem will be exacerbated. Another important factor is productivity, as measured by the difference between the 4% price increases and the 5.75% wage increases. Materially lower productivity increases, if prolonged, would require substantial modification of the system.

The 4% inflation rate and the 5.75% increase in wages, as assumed by the trustees, would be considered quite reasonable by the general public today. It is instructive to note, therefore, that under these "reasonable" assumptions, by the year 2052 the average benefit being paid by the system at age 65 would be $289,520 per year and the average taxable wage would be $733,201 per year!

Solomon Islands

The Solomon Islands is a fully independent (as of July 7, 1978) parliamentary state and member of the Commonwealth of Nations. Until 1975 the area was called the British Solomon Islands Protectorate; on June 22 of that year the name was changed to the Solomon Islands, although its status continued unchanged until it became a self-governing protectorate on Jan. 2, 1976. The nation comprises a 1,450-km (900-mi) chain of islands and atolls in the western Pacific Ocean. Area (est.): 28,529 sq km (11,015 sq mi). Pop. (1978 est.): 214,000 (Melanesian, 93.8%; Polynesian, 4%; Gilbertese 1.4%; others 1.3%). Cap. and largest city: Honiara (pop., 1977 est., 15,700). Language: English (official), Pidgin (lingua franca), and some 90 local languages and dialects. Religion: Anglican 34.2%, Roman Catholic 18.7%, Seventh-day Adventist 9.7%, other Protestant 30.7%. Queen, Elizabeth II; governor-general in 1978, Baddeley Devesi; prime minister, Peter Kenilorea.

On July 7, 1978, the Solomon Islands, a British protectorate since 1893, became an independent state within the Commonwealth of Nations. The prime minister at independence was Peter Kenilorea (see BIOGRAPHIES), a 36-year-old former teacher and civil servant and an occasional lay preacher. A three-tier governmental structure comprising central, provincial, and local levels was established.

Independence had been delayed by controversy over citizenship rights for Gilbertese (resettled from their own overcrowded islands in the 1960s), Chinese, and European minorities and—a product of the Solomons' cultural diversity—over secessionist demands from the Western district, which wanted a clarification of the powers to be granted to provincial governments. The economy remained heavily oriented toward subsistence at a village level. Main exports were copra, fish (a Solomons-Japanese partnership), and timber; there was a growing palm oil industry and the prospect of bauxite mining.

The Solomon Islands was a member of the South Pacific Forum, and Honiara was chosen as headquarters for a fisheries agency to coordinate developments concerning the 200-mi economic zones of Forum members.   (BARRIE MACDONALD)

Somalia

Solomon Islands

Somalia

A republic of northeast Africa, the Somali Democratic Republic, or Somalia, is bounded by the Gulf of Aden, the Indian Ocean, Kenya, Ethiopia, and Djibouti. Area: 638,000 sq km (246,300 sq mi). Pop. (1978 est.): 3,446,000, mainly Hamitic, with Arabic and other admixtures. Cap. and largest city: Mogadishu (pop., 1976 UN est., 286,000). Language: Somali. Religion: predominantly Muslim. President of the Supreme Revolutionary Council in 1978, Maj. Gen. Muhammad Siyad Barrah.

For Pres. Muhammad Siyad Barrah's revolutionary regime, 1978 was the most difficult yet of the nine years since it came into existence. By the end of 1977, Somali government troops, supporting local guerrillas, had captured from Ethiopia nearly the whole of the Ogaden, a region populated by Somali nomads. It seemed as though the republic's long-standing aim of incorporating this "lost province" was being realized. Then, in February–March 1978, an Ethiopian counteroffensive, backed by Cuban troops and Soviet arms, recaptured Jijiga and later other towns. Deprived of outside support since it severed its own connections with the Soviet Union and Cuba the previous autumn, Somalia was forced to withdraw its troops from the region. Somalia continued to support guerrilla warfare, however, carried on by the two local organizations, the Western Somalia Liberation Front and the Somali Abo Liberation Front, which included Oromo tribesmen of the Harer region. In June the guerrillas recaptured the air base of Gode, and at the end of the year reports claimed they controlled all the area outside the towns. Observers believed that the scale of fighting in the Ogaden was on approximately the same level as before the invasion by regular Somali forces in the summer of 1977.

Soil Conservation:
see Environment

The defeat in the Ogaden was followed by an influx of refugees into Somalia; six camps were set up to shelter some of them. A UN mission report put the number at 150,000. Another consequence of the war was a steep rise in the cost of living, with 40% price increases for food and fuel.

On April 9 a group of army officers launched a coup, which was crushed within a few hours, though not without about 20 deaths. Seventeen of those responsible were tried, and they were executed in October. Others escaped to Kenya where they joined opponents of the Siyad Barrah regime. Another six officers had been executed, immediately after the Ogaden defeat, for antigovernment activity.

On a visit to China, April 13–18, Barrah signed an economic and technical cooperation agreement. In what appeared to be partly an attempt to revive national morale and counter disaffection, President Siyad Barrah in October announced that the coming year would see the promulgation of a new constitution and the long-promised restoration (in a new form) of the Somali Parliament, suspended in 1969. This, the president said, would be a place where the various Somali groups could express their views about policy and administration. There was also an amnesty for prisoners; 2,831 were freed, though it was not clear whether they included political prisoners.

International concern was aroused by the swarming of locusts in Somalia, as well as in other parts of the Horn of Africa. If the locusts were not brought under control, they would spread to other African countries and Arabia, possibly bringing famines in their wake. Although at least 21 swarms were destroyed in Somalia by international teams, efforts at control were hampered by the continuing war in the Ogaden, and many other swarms escaped. (VIRGINIA R. LULING)

See also Ethiopia.

South Africa

South Africa

The Republic. Occupying the southern tip of Africa, South Africa is bounded by Namibia (South West Africa), Botswana, Rhodesia (Zimbabwe), Mozambique, and Swaziland and by the Atlantic and Indian oceans on the west and east. South Africa entirely surrounds Lesotho and partially surrounds the two former Bantu homelands of Transkei (independent Oct. 26, 1976) and Bophuthatswana (independent Dec. 6, 1977), although the independence of the latter two is not recognized by the international community. Walvis Bay, part of Cape Province since 1910 but administered as part of South West Africa since 1922, was returned to the direct control of Cape Province on Sept. 1, 1977. Area (including Walvis Bay but excluding the two former homelands): 1,-140,943 sq km (440,521 sq mi). Pop. (1978 est.): 24,190,000, including (1977 est., excluding the two homelands) black (Bantu) 69%, white 18%, Coloured 10%, Asian 3%. Executive capital: Pretoria (pop., 1976 est., 634,400); judicial capital: Bloemfontein (pop., 1976 est., 234,900); legislative capital: Cape Town (pop., 1976 est., 842,600).

Largest city: Johannesburg (pop., 1976 est., 1,371,-000). Language: Afrikaans and English (official); Bantu languages predominate. Religion: mainly Christian. State presidents in 1978, Nicolaas J. Diederichs until August 21 and, from September 29, B. J. Vorster; prime ministers, B. J. Vorster until September 20 and, from September 29, P. W. Botha.

DOMESTIC AFFAIRS. After the death of State President Nicolaas J. Diederichs (*see* OBITUARIES) on Aug. 21, 1978, Prime Minister B. J. Vorster (*see* BIOGRAPHIES) was elected president on September 29. He was succeeded as prime minister by P. W. Botha (*see* BIOGRAPHIES), minister of defense, who retained that portfolio with a deputy minister, H. J. Coetzee, to assist him.

On assuming office Botha pledged his government to the ideal of national unity, the continued defense of South Africa against external aggression and the forces of subversion, and the creation of a cooperative economic community of southern African nations. A relatively minor reshuffle of Cabinet posts took place. The Ministry of Information, which had been the subject of controversy and investigation, was disbanded at the end of June and replaced by a Bureau for National and International Communications under the minister of foreign affairs.

Subsequent inquiries by government-appointed judicial commissions produced evidence of grave irregularities in the handling of the information department's secret funds and various projects. In view of the allegations the former minister of information, C. P. Mulder, resigned from the Cabinet, where he had been minister of plural relations and development. Opposition demands for the resignation of the government were rejected when a special session of Parliament debated the issue on December 7–8.

A five-year program for the streamlining of race relations and policies within the framework of separate development was foreshadowed by Mulder, who in January had taken over the Ministry of Bantu Administration and Development—renamed the Ministry of Plural Relations and Development—from M. C. Botha. ("Bantu" was dropped from official terminology in deference to the black population, and "black" was substituted.)

The department (headed by Piet Koornhof after Mulder's resignation) concentrated on the betterment of conditions in the black residential townships in or near the industrial areas. Forms of local autonomy were introduced under the system of elected community councils. In the larger places, particularly in the Johannesburg complex of Soweto, the councils were given semimunicipal status and the right of control over communal services and finances. Many blacks were opposed to the community councils and boycotted the elections, claiming that the representation they provided was "symbolic" and would only perpetuate the system of racial segregation. Plans for granting home ownership and property rights to residents on a long-term leasehold basis, including the right of inheritance, were finalized and building societies were encouraged to extend loan and mortgage facilities on property in those areas. Restrictions on traders in the black urban areas were lifted or modified, and permission was given for the opening of supermarkets under black control. Wage gaps between white and nonwhite workers were narrowed. Facilities were provided for the training of black workers. "Bantu education" was placed under a separate Department of Education and Training, and radical changes in the system were foreshadowed.

The government repeatedly reaffirmed the principle that the urban blacks were linked with the respective homelands and could claim no political rights or citizenship outside of those; thus Transkeians and Tswanas with independent homelands who were permanent residents in the "white" areas faced practical problems in connection with foreign travel documents, among other things. In the nonindependent homelands the tendency was toward the extension of administrative powers to the homeland authorities. Homelands with an economic potential were encouraged to seek investment from abroad, and several were successful in doing so. The Venda homeland in the northern Transvaal was seeking independence in 1979. In KwaZulu the chief minister, Gatsha Buthelezi, in January extended his Inkatha organization, originally a Zulu cultural movement, into an alliance with members of other black homelands as well as Coloured people and Indians.

Discussions on the constitutional proposals of 1977, including the election of a state president with executive powers and the establishment of three separate parliaments for the white, Coloured, and Indian populations and a Council of Cabinets as an umbrella body, continued. Opinion in the Coloured and Indian communities on various aspects of the proposals remained divided. The Coloured Labour Party opposed them on several grounds. Its main objections, shared by a section of the Indian Council, were that the proposals entrenched the principle of racial segregation and inequality and that the black urban population was excluded from political participation. The government indicated that it was prepared to consider modifications of the proposals. In the meantime, the South African Indian Council membership was enlarged, with more elected members and greater powers in its own sphere. The Natal Provincial Council decided to grant Indians and Coloureds direct representation in municipal councils in the province.

There was relatively little unrest of a racial nature in South Africa in 1978. The most serious incidents arose from the decision to destroy squatter camps mainly occupied "illegally" by blacks in the Cape peninsula. The strongest opposition both from the squatters, numbering more than 20,000, and from public opinion was encountered at the Crossroads site, where clashes with the police resulted in a number of injuries and at least one death. A scheme to remove the squatters, mostly Transkeians, to a settlement near the Transkei border in the Ciskei was shelved.

Isolated incidents of actual or suspected sabotage and murder in outlying areas raised fears of a possible spread of urban and other terrorism inspired by events beyond the border. Internal security was

Blacks and whites in Cape Town, South Africa, sat together on buses for the first time in ten years after easing of apartheid restrictions in February.

tightened under the Bureau of National Security (formerly the Bureau of State Security, or BOSS). Caches of arms were found in townships and in parts of the country near the eastern and northern borders, and infiltrators from adjoining territories were arrested. Trials on charges under the Terrorist Act and other security laws were held in various centres. Early in the year more than 700 persons of all races were known to be in some kind of detention. Some were released later, including Percy Qoboza, editor of the banned black newspaper *The World* (on March 10). There was strong public reaction to the death of a detainee who jumped from an upper floor at security headquarters in Port Elizabeth during questioning. A public inquiry absolved the police of any responsibility for his action. "Watchdog" arrangements for checking on the treatment of detainees in custody, which were instituted after the Steven Biko case in 1977, were tightened up after the later incident.

FOREIGN RELATIONS. Negotiations on the future independence of Namibia (South West Africa) were at the centre of South Africa's international relations throughout the year. Discussions on behalf of the territory were held at various levels with representatives of the five UN countries—the United States, Great Britain, France, West Germany, and Canada—charged by the UN Security Council with formulating an internationally acceptable basis for independence. The plan drafted by the five, in negotiation with South Africa, called for a cease-fire in the border fighting with the South West Africa People's Organization (SWAPO) insurgents, a free election under UN supervision, the presence of a UN peacekeeping and police force (UNTAG) in the transition to independence, and independence by Dec. 31, 1978. The proposals were endorsed by the Security Council, along with a further resolution declaring Walvis Bay (claimed by South Africa) an integral part of Namibia.

South Africa, while rejecting the latter demand,

accepted the main proposals on April 25, and SWAPO did so on July 12. A UN team under UN Secretary-General Kurt Waldheim's personal representative, Martii Ahtisaari of Finland, came to Namibia to report, in consultation with the South African administrator general, Justice Marthinus Steyn, on the implementation of the plan. Waldheim submitted proposals to the Security Council that included the dispatch of a UN force of up to 7,500 men and a police contingent to help in supervising elections and maintaining order, the reduction of South African troops in Namibia, and the holding of elections about April 1979.

The Security Council on September 29 adopted the Waldheim proposals and instructed him to go ahead. South Africa objected to several details, especially those relating to Walvis Bay and to the size and functions of UNTAG. It announced that it would proceed with plans for an election in December 1978 without UN supervision, but it kept the door open for further negotiations. SWAPO's position was equivocal, and border incidents continued. On October 16 negotiations were resumed at a conference in Pretoria attended by the foreign ministers of the five UN countries and agreement was reached. The ministers decided to recommend that a UN-supervised election be held on a fixed date in 1979 and that a UN mission under Ahtisaari should return to Windhoek to work out with the administrator general details relating to UNTAG and the election. The South African-sponsored election to a 50-member Constituent Assembly, held on December 5, was boycotted by SWAPO. On December 22 the Assembly, dominated by the conservative multiracial Democratic Turnhalle Alliance, accepted the Pretoria agreement in principle and SWAPO also indicated conditional acceptance.

In its relations with other countries and the West, the U.S. in particular, South Africa showed a growing resentment of criticisms of its race policies as a violation of human rights. It pointed at evidence of recent change and accused critics of "double standards." Emphasis was laid on its strategic position and its wealth of mineral and other resources to demonstrate that it was a desirable partner for the West as well as a potential target of world aggressors. Interdependence was the keynote of the relationship with the rest of southern Africa, as exemplified in the continued economic links with post-revolutionary Mozambique and the use by Zambia of South African railways and harbours.

THE ECONOMY. The 1978 national budget, presented on March 29 by the minister of finance, Owen Horwood, was framed in the context of a steadily rising gold price, a favourable balance of trade, a fluctuating but generally favourable balance of payments, higher foreign reserves, and signs of an upswing in the economy. The aim of the budget was to stimulate South Africa's real rate of growth and to curb and, if possible, lower the rate of inflation. State expenditure was cut in various directions, including defense; and new restrictions on bank credit, interest rates, and building society loans were relaxed during the year. A fiscal innovation was the introduction of a 4% general sales tax on goods and services.

Despite increased gold production costs some new long-term mining projects were launched on the strength of record gold earnings and world demand for uranium and other minerals such as chrome and its alloys. Gold reserves were revalued in terms of the greater price of gold.

Unemployment was still rife, especially among the black population, and was aggravated by the tendency toward industrial mechanization. Overseas capital, which in the past had been a factor in South Africa's industrial development, was slow in returning in any considerable volume. Codes of conduct for the treatment of black workers and the relations between employers and employees of other races were drawn up by organized commerce and industry as well as by the Trade Union Council of South Africa.

Bophuthatswana. The republic of Bophuthatswana consists of six discontinuous, landlocked geographic units, one of which borders Botswana on the northwest; it is otherwise entirely surrounded by South Africa. Area: 40,430 sq km (15,610 sq mi). Pop. (1978 est.): 1,245,000, including 99.6% Bantu, of whom Tswana 69.8%, Northern Sotho 7.5%. Capital: Mmabatho. Largest city: Ga-Rankuwa (pop., 1973 est., 64,200). Languages (official): Central Tswana, English, Afrikaans. Religion: predominantly Christian (Methodist, Lutheran, Anglican, and Bantu Christian churches). President in 1978, Lucas Mangope.

SOUTH AFRICA

Education. (1978) Primary, pupils 4,112,079; secondary, pupils 979,193; vocational, pupils 20,773; primary, secondary, and vocational, teachers 145,132; higher, students 136,293, teaching staff 10,597.

Finance. Monetary unit: rand, with (Sept. 18, 1978) a par value of R 0.87 to U.S $1 (free rate of R 1.70 = £1 sterling). Gold, SDR's, and foreign exchange (June 1978) U.S. $845 million. Budget (1977–78 est.): revenue R 7,585,000,000; expenditure R 8,785,000,000. Gross national product (1977) R 32,339,000,000. Money supply (June 1978) R 4,775,000,000. Cost of living (1975 = 100; June 1978) 134.3.

Foreign Trade. (Excluding crude oil and products; 1977) Imports R 5,452,000,000; exports R 8,685,000,000. Import sources: U.S. 19%; West Germany 18%; U.K. 16%; Japan 12%; France 5%. Export destinations (excluding gold): U.K. 23%; U.S. 14%; Japan 11%; West Germany 9%. Main exports: gold specie c. 32%; diamonds 11%; food 8%; iron and steel 7%; gold coin 5%; metal ores 5%.

Transport and Communications. Roads (excluding tracks; 1976) c. 230,000 km. Motor vehicles in use (1976): passenger 2,169,000; commercial 821,300. Railways: (excluding Namibia; 1976) 20,092 km; freight traffic (including Namibia; 1977) 78,495,000,000 net ton-km. Air traffic (1977): 6,488,000,000 passenger-km; freight 189,848,000 net ton-km. Shipping (1977): merchant vessels 100 gross tons and over 297; gross tonnage 476,324. Telephones (March 1977) 2,191,400. Radio receivers (Dec. 1975) 2,337,000. Television receivers (Jan. 1978) c. 950,000.

Agriculture. Production (in 000; metric tons; 1977): corn 9,714; wheat 1,815; sorghum 386; potatoes c. 800; tomatoes c. 270; sugar, raw value c. 2,140; peanuts c. 241; sunflower seed c. 476; oranges c. 630; grapefruit c. 90; pineapples c. 200; apples c. 260; grapes c. 1,180; tobacco c. 39; cotton, lint c. 30; wool c. 52; meat 908; milk 2,529; fish catch (1976) 638. Livestock (in 000; June 1977): cattle c. 12,800; sheep c. 31,200; pigs c. 1,400; goats c. 5,250; horses (1976) c. 230; chickens c. 27,000.

Industry. Index of manufacturing production (1975 = 100; 1977) 93.6. Fuel and power (in 000; 1977): coal (metric tons) 85,570; manufactured gas (cu m; 1976) c. 1,980,000; electricity (kw-hr) 80,199,000. Production (in 000; metric tons; 1977): cement 6,572; iron ore (60–65% metal content) 26,235; pig iron 6,904; crude steel 7,148; antimony concentrates (metal content; 1976) 11; copper ore (metal content; 1976) 197; chrome ore (oxide content; 1976) 1,087; manganese ore (metal content; 1976) 2,409; uranium (1976) 3.4; gold (troy oz) 22,500; diamonds (metric carats; 1976) 7,023; asbestos (1976) 370; petroleum products (1976) c. 12,370; fish meal (including Namibia; 1976) 212.

Bophuthatswana

Transkei

Since it attained independence on Dec. 6, 1977, the major unresolved issue of the new republic remained the rectification of its borders by the consolidation of the different parts into which it was divided. Pres. Lucas Mangope referred to it publicly and in discussions with the South African government. Minor border adjustments not involving land occupied by white farmers were made in the Transvaal and northern Cape Province by South African legislation early in 1978. Practical difficulties arising from the border situation were overcome by ad hoc agreements between the two governments with a minimum of inconvenience to travel and the conduct of trade. Meanwhile, Mangope concentrated on economic development. In the absence of international recognition, he was nevertheless able to interest private investors in his country.

Relations with South Africa, normally good, were temporarily strained by reported friction between Bophuthatswana border police and white miners from South Africa working at the Impala platinum mine near the border town of Rustenburg. An investigation ordered by Mangope showed that the affair was exaggerated. After an incident in which several armed men were intercepted by Tswana security police in an attempt to cross into South Africa through Bophuthatswana —two of them being shot—Mangope gave the assurance that he would not allow his country to be used as a base for anti-South Africa terrorism.

Transkei. Bordering the Indian Ocean and surrounded on land by South Africa, Transkei comprises three discontinuous geographic units, two of which are landlocked. Area: 41,002 sq km (15,-831 sq mi). Pop. (1978 est.): 2,178,000, including (1970) Bantu 99%, of whom 95% were Xhosa. Capital and largest city: Umtata (pop., 1978 est., 30,000). Language: Xhosa (official); English and Sesotho may be used for official purposes as well. Religion: Christian 65.8%, of which Methodist 25.2%; non-Christian 13.8%; 10.4% unspecified. President in 1978, Paramount Chief Botha Sigcau until December 1; prime minister, Kaiser Daliwonga Matanzima.

On the second anniversary of Transkei independence Prime Minister Kaiser Matanzima declared that although his country had not yet won international recognition—a situation for which he primarily blamed South Africa's race policies— Transkei was continuing to make great economic progress.

While economic and financial ties with South Africa were maintained, in spite of Matanzima's public criticisms of South Africa's policies, an open rift developed on the land question. Early in the year the South African government announced its intention to transfer the administration of East Griqualand, a flourishing pastoral area, from the Cape Province to Natal. Transkei claimed the territory on historical grounds as well as in terms of an understanding arrived at, Matanzima declared, during the independence negotiations. However, the South African decision was implemented in legislation passed by the Parliament in Cape Town, and Transkei severed diplomatic relations with South Africa. The further training of Transkeian military personnel by South Africa under a standing agreement was suspended, and Transkei announced that it would undertake its own training arrangements and appealed for foreign assistance.

Transkei's first president, Chief Botha Sigcau, died on December 1. Matanzima announced that he would resign as prime minister in order to stand for president. (LOUIS HOTZ)

See also Dependent States.

Southeast Asian Affairs

Intense competition by Communist powers to win the goodwill of non-Communist Southeast Asia set the tone in the region during 1978. This was a complete reversal of earlier Communist policies, which routinely condemned Southeast Asian governments as lackeys of Western powers and the Association of Southeast Asian Nations (ASEAN) as an instrument of neoimperialism. It was also the final repudiation of the domino theory which, in the aftermath of the Communist triumph in Indochina, predicted that the non-Communist states would fall victim to predatory Communism one by one.

ASEAN and Communist Feelers. The transformation was brought about by the fighting that erupted among the Communists themselves. The war between Vietnam and Cambodia was seen as directly encouraged by the hostility between the Soviet Union and China. So bitter was the enmity between the erstwhile comrades that each began actively canvassing international support. China started the drive in Southeast Asia, and the Soviet Union quickly followed suit.

Abandoning its position that ASEAN was a U.S. conspiracy, Moscow sought regular contacts with the regional grouping. Officials in the region interpreted this as a move to bolster Vietnam's standing among its neighbours. There was no doubt that Vietnam had begun to woo ASEAN members. Its June statement that the time was ripe to establish a "zone of peace, independence, and neutrality" in the region sounded almost like a public endorsement of ASEAN's concept of a "zone of peace, freedom, and neutrality."

Vietnamese soldiers captured many Cambodian prisoners in August after a skirmish in An Giang Province.

While welcoming the peace overtures, the non-Communist governments said they had to examine motives lest they be caught up in the Sino-Soviet rivalry. Singapore's Foreign Minister S. Rajaratnam brushed aside the Vietnamese proposal of a peace zone as a propaganda move intended to deflect attention from an ASEAN foreign ministers' conference then taking place in Thailand. Similarly, Indonesia's Mochtar Kusumaatmadja pointed out that ASEAN had its own concept of a peace zone and did not wish to be "identified with other concepts which may contain elements alien to ASEAN's concept."

Such statements reflected an unprecedented degree of coordination among Southeast Asian governments. Singapore's Lee Kuan Yew (see BIOGRAPHIES) said in August that the peoples and governments of ASEAN had learned valuable lessons from the conflicts between Vietnam and China and between Vietnam and Cambodia. Considerable solidarity had developed among them because "we have a common determination to prevent these catastrophes from spreading to us."

The spirit of coordination showed off to best advantage when Chinese Vice-Premier Teng Hsiao-p'ing visited Thailand, Malaysia, and Singapore in November. According to a carefully drawn action plan, his words were noted at his first port of call, Bangkok. Thai leaders showed nothing but courtesy to him, but swiftly informed fellow members that Teng had declined to disown Communist insurgents in Thailand. That brought out noticeable resistance to Teng at his second stop, Kuala Lumpur. The Malaysians told him bluntly that no outsiders would be allowed to meddle in their affairs. Since Teng had not softened in Kuala Lumpur either, Singapore spoke yet more bluntly, reminding their visitor not to mistake Singaporeans for overseas Chinese. The day Teng flew back home, Indonesia completed the action plan by declaring that it had been "seriously working" toward normalization of relations with China but would now have to reconsider its position.

If Teng's tough stand put Southeast Asian governments on guard, they did not seem unduly disturbed. The Communist Party of Thailand had not yet managed to carve out a "liberated zone." The Malayan Communist Party, after a spate of assassinations and bombings in 1975, appeared to have suffered a setback following a Malaysian-Thai agreement to launch combined military operations against them. Singapore had broken the back of front organizations, and the Communist Party of Indonesia remained decimated. The Philippine Communists were in limbo.

Political strategists in the region pointed out, however, that the insurgency leaders had no other choice but to remain on the defensive because the Communist countries were bickering among themselves while ASEAN nations were registering notable economic progress and political stability. Government leaders kept emphasizing that if vigilance was relaxed or the pace of economic advancement lost, the underground forces could regain some of their earlier momentum.

Regional Security. Doubts also persisted about big-power machinations in the region. Some leaders suggested that in the short run Southeast Asia could become the scene of a proxy war between China and the Soviet Union. That feeling was sparked by reports that the Soviets were building a big air base in central Laos while the Chinese were constructing another in Cambodia.

In the meantime, traditional U.S.-Soviet rivalry in the region seemed to go on. Japanese sources reported in May that the Soviet Union was increasing the size and fighting ability of its massive Pacific Fleet. More than 20 warships had been deployed in the Indian Ocean, 70% of them based in Siberian ports. In May the Soviet fleet conducted war games off the Bashi Channel between Taiwan and the Philippines. Reports that Soviet vessels had obtained the rights to base facilities in Cam Ranh Bay on Vietnam's east coast drew special attention to the exercises.

The U.S. continued to keep a low profile, although its Subic (naval) and Clark (air) bases in the Philippines gave it a position of advantage. In May official sources confirmed that U.S. military aircraft were using Singapore on their way to and from the Indian Ocean, but spokesmen emphasized that no base facilities were being sought.

Strategically, U.S. policy was seen by Southeast Asia as directed toward getting Japan to play a more active role in regional security. The idea appeared to have the backing of China, while some Southeast Asian leaders said such a development would be a natural extension of the economic role Japan was already playing. The apparent consensus prompted Vietnamese Prime Minister Pham Van Dong to warn, during his Southeast Asian tour in October, that the U.S., Japan, and China were forming a triumvirate that could threaten the region.

Economic Development. Even as ASEAN displayed unprecedented solidarity on political issues, its economic potential began attracting closer attention from industrialized countries. Officially organized "dialogues" were conducted between it and the U.S., the European Economic Community, Japan, and Australia. Economists predicted that the rapidly developing nations of the "Pacific basin" comprising Southeast Asia, Japan,

Korea, and Australia, would have an increasing impact on the world economy in the next decade. As if to emphasize this, businessmen from 16 countries in the area, meeting in Manila in May, signed a "Pacific Basin Charter on International Investments."

In March the 34th session of the UN Economic and Social Commission for Asia and the Pacific (ESCAP) met in Bangkok. A keynote resolution called for development strategies in the 1980s that would ensure social justice and establish a new international economic order that was more equitable for less developed countries. ESCAP also tried to reactivate the Lower Mekong development plan, welcoming the formation by Thailand, Vietnam, and Laos of an interim committee to coordinate investigations.

Islamic Activism. One topic that generated some discussion in the region during the year was the political impact of Islam. In Malaysia and Indonesia, the two Islamic countries of Southeast Asia, there were political moves by extremist Islamic elements. In the Philippines, Muslim separatists continued their guerrilla war despite prolonged attempts at reconciliation. A similar move by Muslims in the southern provinces of Thailand gave Islamic activism a regional flavour.

Commentators attributed the phenomenon to the general swing toward orthodoxy evident in the Islamic world as a whole and to material assistance extended by Libya to various groups in the region. One man arrested in southern Thailand in October for bomb throwing was found to be a Libyan citizen. The rebel Muslim leader of the Philippines had his headquarters in Libya, and Libyan financial assistance to various Islamic organizations in Malaysia and Indonesia was known to be considerable. For the present, however, the moderate Islamic leaders in those two countries were holding their own and helping to defuse the problems their neighbours faced.   (T. J. S. GEORGE)

See also articles on the various countries.
[976.B]

Space Exploration

The year began with a space spectacular that was neither planned nor applauded. On January 24 Cosmos 954, a Soviet ocean-surveillance satellite with a nuclear power supply, plunged into the atmosphere over the Queen Charlotte Islands off the coast of British Columbia. Several large radioactive pieces fell east of Great Slave Lake in Canada's Northwest Territories. Late in December 1977 the U.S. space tracking network had noted that the satellite was in trouble and reported the fact to both Canada and the U.S.S.R. Almost a month earlier, according to *Aviation Week & Space Technology* magazine, a group of British schoolboys had noted that the orbit of Cosmos 954 indicated that it would reenter the atmosphere. The usual practice of the Soviet Union is to send such satellites into much higher orbits when their missions are completed. At such altitudes their radioactivity poses no threat to the Earth's environment.

After the crash large U.S. and Canadian search teams explored the region in an effort to locate radioactive debris. They eventually found several chunks of the satellite, one of which was emitting considerable radiation. As a consequence of the crash the Soviet Union agreed to participate in a UN study on the safety measures used on Earth-orbital satellites with radioactive power supplies. The study could lead to sanctions against such satellites.

The U.S.S.R. on June 24 lost one of its most talented and distinguished space scientists with the death of Mstislav V. Keldysh (see OBITUARIES).

Manned Flight. The exploits of Soviet cosmonauts aboard the Salyut 6 space station dominated manned space activities in 1978. However, the highly successful program got off to an inauspicious start. Cosmonauts Vladimir V. Kovalenok and Valery V. Ryumin were launched aboard Soyuz 25 on Oct. 9, 1977, to rendezvous and dock with the space station. But mechanical difficulties in the automated docking procedure on the following day caused the mission to be aborted, and the crew returned to the Earth.

Success followed with Soyuz 26 launched on Dec. 10, 1977. Yuri V. Romanenko and Georgy M. Grechko successfully docked and worked in Salyut 6 for 96 days and 10 hours, returning to the Earth on March 16, 1978. In doing so, they broke the previous record for man in space set by U.S. astronauts on the Skylab 4 mission in 1973.

On Jan. 11, 1978, Salyut 6 was visited by Soyuz

No one had spent more time in space than Soviet cosmonauts Vladimir Kovalenok (left) and Aleksandr Ivanchenkov, who orbited the Earth for more than 139 days aboard the Soviet Salyut 6 space station. The two blasted off from Earth in June and did not return until November.

A. PUSHKARYOV—TASS/SOVFOTO

Major Satellites and Space Probes Launched Oct. 1, 1977–Sept. 30, 1978

Name/country/ launch vehicle/ scientific designation	Launch date, lifetime*	Physical characteristics Weight in kg†	Shape	Diam- eter in m†	Length or height in m†	Experiments	Orbital elements Perigee in km†	Apogee in km†	Period (min)	Inclination to Equator (degrees)
Soyuz 25/U.S.S.R./A II/ 1977-099A	10/9/77 10/11/77	6,570 (14,484)	sphere and cone	2.3 (7.55)	7.5 (24.61)	Aborted attempt to dock with Salyut 6 space station	280 (174)	318 (198)	90.2	51.6
ISSE 1/U.S./Delta/ 1977-102A	10/22/77	89 (196)	16-sided polyhedron	1.7 (5.58)	1.6 (5.25)	Effort to determine how sun controls Earth's near-space environment	862 (536)	137,377 (85,362)	3,440.8	31.1
ISSE 2/ESA/Delta/ 1977-102B	10/22/77	158 (348)	cylinder	1.3 (4.27)	1.1 (3.61)	Effort to determine how sun controls Earth's near-space environment	923 (574)	137,452 (85,409)	3,442	31.3
Meteosat/ESA/Delta/ 1977-108A	11/23/77	697 (1,537)	cylinder	2.1 (6.89)	3.2 (10.5)	First European weather satellite	34,913 (21,694)	35,692 (22,178)	1,411.5	0.7
Soyuz 26/U.S.S.R./A II/ 1977-113A	12/10/77 1/16/78	6,570 (14,484)	sphere and cone	2.3 (7.55)	7.5 (24.61)	Docked with Salyut 6; returned with Soyuz 27 crew	267 (166)	329 (204)	90.2	51.6
Meteor 2/U.S.S.R./A I/ 1977-117A	12/14/77	2,750 (6,063)	cylinder with two panels	1.5 (4.92)	5 (16.4)	Weather satellite	872 (542)	906 (563)	102.5	81.2
Sakura/Japan/Delta/ 1977-118A	12/15/77	676 (1,490)	cylinder	2.18 (7.15)	3.51 (11.52)	Experimental communications in geosynchronous orbit	35,567 (22,100)	36,157 (22,467)	1,439.9	0
Intelsat 4A (F-3)/U.S./Atlas Centaur/1978-002A	1/7/78	1,511 (3,331)	cylinder	2.4 (7.87)	2.8 (9.19)	Communications satellite	35,768 (22,225)	35,806 (22,249)	1,436.1	0.3
Soyuz 27/U.S.S.R./A II/ 1978-003A	1/10/78 3/16/78	6,570 (14,484)	sphere and cone	2.3 (7.55)	7.5 (24.61)	Ferried second crew to Salyut 6; returned with Soyuz 26 crew	330 (205)	350 (217)	91.3	51.6
Progress 1/U.S.S.R./A II/ 1978-008A	1/20/78 2/8/78	7,020 (15,476)	sphere and cone	2.2 (7.22)	8 (26.25)	Unmanned resupply vehicle for Salyut 6	329 (204)	348 (216)	91.2	51.6
China 8/China/‡/ 1978-011A	1/25/78 2/7/78	3,600 (7,937)	cylinder (probably)	‡	‡	Probably military test satellite; ejected recoverable package Jan. 30	161 (100)	479 (298)	90.9	57
International UV Explorer/ U.S.-ESA/Delta/1978-012A	1/26/78	671 (1,479)	cone with two solar panels	1.3 (4.27)	4.3 (14.11)	Study of celestial objects emitting ultraviolet radiation	25,678 (15,956)	45,873 (28,504)	1,435.6	28.6
EXOS 1/Japan/Mu-3H/ 1978-014A	2/4/78	103 (227)	cylinder	‡	‡	Study of auroras with ultraviolet television camera	636 (395)	3,979 (2,472)	134.2	65.3
Fleetsatcom 1/U.S./Atlas Centaur/1978-016A	2/9/78	1,884 (4,154)	hexagonal cylinder	2.4 (7.87)	1.27 (4.17)	Communications satellite	35,522 (22,072)	35,666 (22,162)	1,426.1	2.8
ISS B/Japan/N/ 1978-018A	2/16/78	140 (309)	cylinder	0.94 (3.08)	0.82 (2.69)	Ionospheric research	978 (608)	1,222 (759)	107.2	69.3
NavStar 1/U.S./Atlas Agena/ 1978-020A	2/22/78	736 (1,623)	cubical polyhedron with two solar panels	1.23 (4.04)	1.83 (6)	Navigational satellite	19,755 (12,275)	19,953 (12,398)	704.7	63.3
Soyuz 28/U.S.S.R./A II/ 1978-023A	3/2/78 3/10/78	6,570 (14,484)	sphere and cone	2.3 (7.55)	7.5 (24.61)	Ferried third crew to and from Salyut 6	334 (208)	353 (219)	91.3	51.6
Landsat 3/U.S./Delta/ 1978-026A	3/5/78	960 (2,116)	truncated cone with two panels	1.45 (4.76)	3 (9.84)	Earth resources experiments	900 (559)	918 (570)	103.2	99.4
Oscar 8/U.S./Delta/ 1978-026B	3/5/78	27 (60)	rectangular box	0.4 (1.31)	0.4 (1.31)	Amateur radio communications satellite	903 (561)	917 (570)	103.2	98.9
Intelsat 4A (F-6)/U.S./Atlas Centaur/1978-035A	3/31/78	1,480 (3,263)	cylinder	2.4 (7.87)	2.82 (9.25)	Communications satellite stationed over Indian Ocean	35,768 (22,225)	35,806 (22,249)	1,436	0.3
Yuri/Japan/Delta/ 1978-039A	4/7/78	678 (1,494)	boxlike with panels	‡	‡	First Japanese communications satellite in geosynchronous orbit	35,114 (21,819)	35,661 (22,159)	1,415.8	0
OTS 2/ESA/Delta/ 1978-044A	5/11/78	‡	cylinder	‡	‡	Communications satellite	35,782 (22,234)	35,794 (22,241)	1,436.1	0
NavStar 2/U.S./Atlas Agena F/ 1978-047A	5/13/78	433 (955)	cube with two curved sides	1.23 (4.04)	1.83 (6)	Navigational satellite	20,083 (12,479)	20,080 (12,601)	717.9	63.2
Pioneer Venus 1/U.S./Atlas Centaur/1978-051A	5/20/78	582 (1,283)	cylinder	2.5 (8.2)	4.5 (14.76)	Orbit Venus and photograph surface	Trajectory to Venus			
Soyuz 29/U.S.S.R./A II/ 1978-061A	6/15/78 9/3/78	6,570 (14,484)	sphere and cone	2.3 (7.55)	7.5 (24.61)	Ferried crew to Salyut 6; returned with Soyuz 31 crew	270 (168)	314 (195)	90	51.6
GOES 3/U.S./Delta/ 1978-062A	6/16/78	624 (1,375)	cylinder	1.91 (6.25)	2.69 (8.83)	Environmental satellite in geosynchronous orbit	35,769 (22,226)	35,805 (22,248)	1,436.1	0.9
Seasat 1/U.S./Atlas Agena F/ 1978-064A	6/26/78	2,291 (5,050)	cylinder with two solar panels	1.52 (5)	12.2 (40)	Study of various scientific areas of oceanography	770 (478)	798 (496)	100.5	108
Soyuz 30/U.S.S.R./A II/ 1978-065A	6/27/78 7/5/78	6,570 (14,484)	sphere and cone	2.3 (7.55)	7.5 (24.61)	Ferried crew to and from Salyut 6	264 (164)	310 (193)	90	51.6
Comstar D3/U.S./Atlas Centaur/1978-068A	6/29/78	1,518 (3,347)	cylinder	2.44 (8)	6.1 (20)	Domestic telephone service satellite	35,784 (22,235)	35,787 (22,237)	1,436.1	0.1
Progress 2/U.S.S.R./A II/ 1978-070A	7/7/78 8/4/78	7,000 (15,432)	sphere and cone	2.2 (7.22)	8 (26.25)	Unmanned resupply vehicle for Salyut 6	267 (166)	329 (204)	90.2	51.6
Geos 2/ESA/Delta/ 1978-071A	7/14/78	180 (397)	cylinder	1.6 (5.25)	1.1 (3.61)	Study of magnetosphere at geosynchronous altitude	35,593 (22,116)	36,573 (22,725)	1,436.3	0.7
Raduga 4/U.S.S.R./D le/ 1978-073A	7/18/78	5,000 (11,023)	cylinder	‡	‡	Communications satellite	36,473 (22,663)	36,731 (22,824)	1,478	0.4
Progress 3/U.S.S.R./A II/ 1978-077A	8/7/78 8/24/78	7,000 (15,432)	sphere and cone	2.2 (7.22)	8 (26.25)	Unmanned resupply vehicle for Salyut 6	267 (166)	329 (204)	90.2	51.6
Pioneer Venus 2/U.S./Atlas Centaur/1978-078A	8/8/78	904 (1,993)	cylinder	2.5 (8.2)	2.9 (9.51)	Carried 4 probes for atmosphere of Venus	Trajectory to Venus			
ISEE 3/U.S./Delta/ 1978-079A	8/12/78	469 (1,034)	‡	‡	‡	Interplanetary measurements of solar wind	181 (112)	108,920 (67,680)	67,352.9	1
Soyuz 31/U.S.S.R./A II/ 1978-081A	8/26/78 11/2/78	6,570 (14,484)	sphere and cone	2.3 (7.55)	7.5 (24.61)	Ferried crew to Salyut 6; returned with Soyuz 29 crew	337 (209)	353 (219)	91.4	51.6
Venera 11/U.S.S.R./D le/ 1978-084A	9/9/78	‡	‡	‡	‡	Flyby observations of Venus	Interplanetary trajectory			
Venera 12/U.S.S.R./D le/ 1978-086A	9/14/78	‡	‡	‡	‡	Flyby observations of Venus	Interplanetary trajectory			
EXOS 2/Japan/Mu-3H/ 1978-087A	9/16/78	154 (340)	cylinder	‡	‡	Aurora observations	221 (137)	30,102 (18,705)	524.3	0.7

*All dates are in universal time (UT).
†English units in parentheses: weight in pounds, dimensions in feet, apogee and perigee in statute miles.
‡Not available.

(MITCHELL R. SHARPE)

27 bearing Vladimir A. Dzhanibekov and Oleg G. Makarov. They worked with Romanenko and Grechko in Salyut 6 until returning to the Earth in the Soyuz 26 descent module on January 16. On January 20 the space station was resupplied by the unmanned Progress 1 vehicle that automatically rendezvoused and docked with it. This cargo craft delivered propellants and oxygen and food, water, and repair parts. The empty Progress was loaded with garbage and wastes from Salyut 6 and sent back into the atmosphere where it burned up on February 8.

On March 3 Romanenko and Grechko were joined by Aleksey A. Gubarev and Vladimir Remek in Soyuz 28. Remek, a Czechoslovak, was the first person other than one from the U.S. or the Soviet Union to enter space. This international crew worked aboard Salyut 6 until returning to the Earth on March 10. Romanenko and Grechko entered the Soyuz 27 spacecraft on March 16 and returned to the Earth.

Kovalenok and Aleksandr S. Ivanchenkov took Soyuz 29 into orbit on June 15. They too successfully docked with Salyut 6. Twelve days later they were joined by Soyuz 30 cosmonauts Pyotr Klimuk and Miroslaw Hermaszewski, a Pole, who assisted their two colleagues in scientific and engineering experiments until July 5. Klimuk and Hermaszewski then returned to the Earth in their own Soyuz.

Progress 2 arrived at Salyut 6 on July 7. Among its supplies were propellants, water, and a new electric furnace for manufacturing experiments. The empty vehicle was jettisoned on August 4. Four days later Progress 3 arrived with oxygen, regenerating equipment, and additional food and water. Indications were that Salyut 6 was being provisioned for long-term habitation.

Soyuz 31 docked with the space station on August 27. In it were Valery Bykovsky of the U.S.S.R. and Sigmund Jaehn of East Germany. They remained aboard until September 3, returning to the Earth in Soyuz 29. On September 20 Kovalenok and Ivanchenkov broke the manned space flight record set by Romanenko and Grechko.

On November 2, after a record 139 days and 14 hours in space, the two cosmonauts returned to the Earth in Soyuz 31. Soviet authorities said that preliminary medical checkups indicated the two had withstood the long flight well.

Skylab, the derelict U.S. space station still orbiting the Earth, responded to commands for a systems status check on March 4. The purpose of the contact by National Aeronautics and Space Administration (NASA) engineers was to determine if the craft could be maneuvered into a position that would lengthen its life until a visit by the space shuttle in late 1979 or early 1980. The huge space station had been dropping closer to the Earth than had been expected. Unsure of where it might reenter the atmosphere and how much of it might survive reentry, NASA wanted to keep it in orbit until a propulsion package carried aloft by shuttle could be attached to it. When ignited, the propulsion unit would send the Skylab into a much higher and more stable orbit or, alternatively, into a precisely controlled reentry into the atmosphere

where it would not endanger life. Maneuvers were made throughout the summer and fall, but by the year's end NASA had abandoned its plans to save the station. It was expected to burn up in the atmosphere when it fell to the Earth between mid-1979 and mid-1980.

In April the world learned that China would be the next nation to have a manned space program. The vice-premier for science and technology, Fang Yi, announced that China would have an operational manned space flight program within eight years.

Launch Vehicles. Ariane, the space launch vehicle being developed by the European Space Agency (ESA), took a step nearer operational status on Dec. 13, 1977. The first stage of the three-stage rocket was fired for the first time. Its four Viking 2 engines burned faultlessly for 111 seconds. On Jan. 10, 1978, its third stage was successfully test-fired, and a similar performance was turned in by its second stage on January 31. ESA in April gave approval for the production of five Arianes to be used in launching European satellites between 1981 and 1984.

Thirty-five candidate astronauts for the U.S. space shuttle reported to the Johnson Space Center in Houston, Texas, on July 10 to begin training. Twenty were mission specialists, and 15 were pilots. Among the candidates were six women. The 35 were selected from 8,079 applicants from around the world.

NASA, financially strapped for years and with little hope for larger budgets, proposed to ESA that it provide NASA with a second Spacelab in return for four free space shuttle missions. The offer of such a trade appeared to find favour with the European agency. In July Pres. Anwar as-Sadat of Egypt authorized the payment of $2,000 to NASA as earnest money for reserving space aboard the shuttle for Egyptian experiments. West Germany also made such a down payment toward two exclusively West German missions involving Spacelab.

Unmanned Satellites. On Oct. 22, 1977, a Delta rocket launched International Sun Earth Explorers 1 and 2 together. The former had been developed by NASA, while the latter was a product of ESA. Both satellites were designed to study the effects of the solar wind on the Earth's environment. On Nov. 23, 1977, NASA launched Meteosat, Europe's first weather satellite. Another Delta vehicle put Sakura, a Japanese communications satellite, into orbit on Dec. 15, 1977.

Landsat 1, launched in 1972, was retired on Jan. 16, 1978. Problems in keeping it pointed toward the Earth prompted the decision to shut down the satellite after it had produced more than 300,000 Earth-resources pictures. China greeted 1978 with the placing in orbit of China 8. On January 25 the satellite was launched from the nation's Shuang-cheng-tzu site and was the third such satellite to eject a recoverable payload while still in orbit.

Japan launched its Exos 1 on February 4 to study auroras and followed on February 16 with its HSS B to study the ionosphere. NavStar 1, the second satellite in a series that would ultimately total 24, was launched on February 22. NavStar 2 was orbited on May 13. When all 12 had been placed in orbit, they would provide an extremely accurate means of locating land, sea, and air craft.

That there was "gold in them thar stars" was indicated by data received from the International Ultraviolet Explorer, launched jointly by NASA and ESA in January. In April NASA scientists reported that the star Kappa Cancrii appears to contain as much as 100 billion tons of the metal.

ESA's OTS 2 communications satellite was launched on May 11 from the Kennedy Space Center in Florida. It was the first such European satellite to be placed in a geosynchronous orbit, allowing it to remain at a constant point above the Earth. It was to be used for three years in a series of tests to prepare members of the European Conference of Postal and Telecommunications Administrations for the use of such satellites after 1981.

Space Probes. The year 1978 opened with the U.S. Voyagers 1 and 2 experiencing difficulties on their journeys to Jupiter and Saturn. On February 22 mission controllers at the Jet Propulsion Laboratory in California were attempting to exercise the platform on which the cameras of Voyager 1 were mounted. The platform slowed down and finally stopped, refusing to obey commands. However, the condition cleared up in March. In April Voyager 2 developed problems in a radio receiver. Nevertheless, the two probes successfully navigated the 223 million-mi-wide asteroid belt between Mars and Jupiter in the early fall.

In late 1977 the malfunctioning solar wind detector of Pioneer 11 responded to a corrective measure taken by controllers at NASA's Ames Research Center. For the first time in nearly three years the instrument began sending data. In July the controllers sent final course adjustment commands to the probe, ensuring that it would approach within 18,000 mi of the edge of Saturn's outer ring and would swing under the rings to 15,000 mi from the planet's surface on Sept. 1, 1979.

Pioneer Venus 1 was launched on May 20 by a Centaur from the Kennedy Space Center for a rendezvous with Venus on December 4. The probe was designed to orbit the planet for at least eight months, collecting information on its upper atmosphere. On December 4 the craft went into an elliptical orbit around Venus, ranging in altitude above the surface from 113 to 41,000 mi. Among the first results of its measurements was the finding that the cloud tops over the planet's polar regions are about 40° F warmer than those over its equator.

Pioneer Venus 2 was launched on August 8. It carried four probes for making quantitative and qualitative chemical analyses of the Venusian atmosphere. The probes landed on the planet's surface on December 9. Among their first findings were surface temperatures of about 900° F and a larger quantity of argon in the atmosphere than had been expected. Also in December two Soviet probes, Venera 11 and 12, successfully landed on Venus.　　　　(MITCHELL R. SHARPE)

See also Astronomy; Defense; Earth Sciences; Industrial Review: *Aerospace; Telecommunications;* Television and Radio.

[738.C]

Spain

Spain

A constitutional monarchy of southwest Europe, Spain is bounded by Portugal, with which it shares the Iberian Peninsula, and by France. Area: 504,750 sq km (194, 885 sq mi), including the Balearic and Canary islands. Pop. (1978 est.): 37,109,-000, including the Balearics and Canaries. Cap. and largest city: Madrid (pop., 1978 est., 3,-994,200). Language: Spanish. Religion: Roman Catholic. King, Juan Carlos I; premier in 1978, Adolfo Suárez González.

The lower house of the Cortes approved the new constitution on July 21, 1978, by 258 votes to 2 with 14 abstentions, and on October 31 it was passed by both houses. The 169-article, democratic constitution for a constitutional monarchy was then approved in a national referendum (by 87% of the 68% of the electorate that voted) on December 6. The constitution stressed the unity of Spain but provided for autonomy for the regions, although the state remained responsible for law and justice throughout the country. Political movements for complete independence were outlawed. Immediate provisional local self-government was granted to 13 regions, but actual powers had been devolved only to Catalonia and the Basque provinces.

By October 1978 the Moncloa Pact between government, opposition parties, and trade unions for acceptance of economic austerity measures had been in operation for a year. The pact, which set out to reduce demand and inflation and to rejuvenate the economy, also included elements of social reform. That the main opposition parties had participated in its drafting was hailed as a considerable political achievement. Its key effects were: a reduction of the inflation rate from 26.4% in 1977 to 16–17% in 1978; higher growth rates, partly due to the good performance of the farming sector; equilibrium in the balance of payments as exports increased by over one-third, faster than the rate of growth of imports; high foreign reserves (U.S. $10 billion at the end of 1978); and a strengthening of the peseta as earnings from tourism, emigrant remittances, and investments rose. Unemployment increased in 1978, however, reaching 7.1%. An energy plan and financial legislation were still awaited.

Political tension leading to violence was concentrated in the Basque region and Madrid. By November the militant Basque separatist organization Euzkadi ta Azkatasuna (ETA; "Basque homeland and liberty") had claimed responsibility for more than 40 killings. Three police mutinies in the Basque country testified to the strain placed on the police force by ETA's campaign. Early in November the government approved a new tough security policy for the Basque provinces. The ETA campaign intensified, however, despite widespread counterdemonstrations by most parties throughout Spain. Meanwhile, a plot by disgruntled right-wing paramilitary and army officers to kidnap the Cabinet was foiled.

Labour unions and employers' federations be-

Education. (1975–76) Primary, pupils 6,393,804, teachers 193,370; secondary, pupils 818,403, teachers 48,694; vocational, pupils 305,254, teachers 28,283; teacher training, students 70,829, teachers 2,873; higher, students 461,076, teaching staff 26,565.

Finance. Monetary unit: peseta, with (Sept. 18, 1978) a free rate of 74.13 pesetas to U.S. $1 (145.25 pesetas = £1 sterling). Gold, SDR's, and convertible currencies (May 1978) U.S. $7,597,000,000. Budget (1977 actual): revenue 1,144,000,000,000 pesetas; expenditure 1,130,000,000,000 pesetas. Gross domestic product (1977) 8,797,000,000,000 pesetas. Money supply (June 1978) 2,931,000,000,000 pesetas. Cost of living (1975 = 100; June 1978) 168.6.

Foreign Trade. (1977) Imports 1,350,600,000,000 pesetas; exports 775.3 billion pesetas. Import sources: EEC 34% (West Germany 10%, France 8%, U.K. 5%, Italy 5%); U.S. 12%; Saudi Arabia 9%; Iran 7%. Export destinations: EEC 46% (France 16%, West Germany 11%, U.K. 6%, Italy 5%); U.S. 10%. Main exports: machinery 13%; fruit and vegetables 11%; iron and steel 7%; motor vehicles 9%; chemicals 6%; textiles and clothing 6%; footwear 5%. Tourism (1976): visitors 30,014,000; receipts U.S. $3,083,000,000.

Transport and Communications. Roads (1976) 145,328 km (including 1,426 km expressways). Motor vehicles in use (1976): passenger 5,351,362; commercial 1,051,605. Railways: (1976) 15,832 km (including 4,883 km electrified); traffic (1977) 17,163,000,000 passenger-km, freight 11,586,000,000 net ton-km. Air traffic (1977): 12,512,000,000 passenger-km; freight 350,944,000 net ton-km. Shipping (1977): merchant vessels 100 gross tons and over 2,726; gross tonnage 7,186,081. Telephones (Jan. 1977) 8,597,800. Radio receivers (Dec. 1975) 8,075,000. Television receivers (Dec. 1975) 6,525,000.

Agriculture. Production (in 000; metric tons; 1977): wheat 4,045; barley 6,707; oats 428; rye 218; corn 1,885; rice 379; potatoes 5,674; sugar, raw value 1,201; tomatoes 2,179; onions 992; cabbages (1976) c. 518; melons (1976) 815; watermelons (1976) 478; apples 718; pears (1976) 489; peaches (1976) 447; oranges 1,662; mandarin oranges and tangerines 702; lemons 325; sunflower seed 381; bananas 371; olives 1,772; olive oil 381; almonds (1976) 318; wine 2,219; tobacco c. 28; cotton, lint 40; cow's milk 5,533; hen's eggs 617; meat 2,174; fish catch (1976) 1,483. Livestock (in 000; 1977): cattle 4,500; pigs 9,008; sheep 15,590; goats 2,231; horses (1976) 268; mules (1976) 324; asses (1976) 274; chickens c. 52,000.

Industry. Index of industrial production (1975 = 100; 1977) 119. Fuel and power (in 000; metric tons; 1977): coal 11,727; lignite 5,789; crude oil 1,223; manufactured gas (cu m) c. 2,510,000; electricity (kw-hr) 93,702,000. Production (in 000; metric tons; 1977): cement 27,997; iron ore (50% metal content) 7,841; pig iron 6,919; crude steel 10,935; aluminum 211; copper 149; lead 89; zinc 157; petroleum products (1976) c. 48,230; sulfuric acid 3,274; fertilizers (nutrient content; 1976–77) nitrogenous 883, phosphate 592, potash 566; cotton yarn 82; cotton fabrics 66; wool yarn 35; man-made fibres 222; passenger cars (units) 1,028; commercial vehicles (units) 135. Merchant vessels launched (100 gross tons and over; 1977) 1,568,000 gross tons.

gan negotiations in midyear for agreements to replace the Moncloa Pact. At issue were the official guidelines to hold price and wage increases to around 12% and thus gain increased commitments for private and public investment. The authorities suggested that a doubling of the rate of growth of the economy in 1979 to about 4% would slow the increase in unemployment rates, while the employers hinted that hiring and firing practices would have to become more flexible. New legislation to encourage foreign investment in Spain, by raising the limits before government authorization was required, was under preparation. In August the government published plans to modernize the languishing public-sector steel and shipbuilding companies.

In mid-October the ruling Unión Centro Democrático (UCD), led by Premier Adolfo Suárez, held its first party congress in Madrid. Suárez had sought to homogenize the political makeup of the UCD, which was divided between Social Democrats grouped around Francisco Fernández Ordóñez and Liberals behind Joaquín Garrigues Walker. The consensus politics generated by the Moncloa Pact and the government's need to satisfy centre and centre-left opinion led to considerable internal strain, however, especially within the coalition's right wing.

Following the referendum on December 6, Suárez had a month to decide to dissolve the Cortes and call new general elections or to seek a vote of confidence based on the UCD vote and other parties' support in the Cortes. Doubts were expressed about future cooperation between the Socialist Party (PSOE) and the UCD. The PSOE wished to have the municipal elections, in which it expected to make gains, within 90 days of the referendum. The Communist Party reportedly wanted more time to consolidate its electoral power through the Comisiones Obreras (CCOO), its affiliated trade union, and was therefore likely to support Suárez in a vote of confidence.

On April 20 the European Economic Community (EEC) Commission responded favourably to Spain's 1977 application to join the Community, stating that full membership should be accomplished within ten years. During the first half of the transition period, Spain would adapt its laws to EEC requirements on competition, movement of goods and labour, external relations, and the EEC common agricultural policy (CAP) and would contribute to the EEC budget. At the end of the first period, the Commission would decide how much time to grant, up to five more years, for transition arrangements. On October 27 the EEC approved the opening of an office in Madrid in early 1979 and would assist Spanish rationalization of steel, fishing, textile, and shipbuilding capacity.

Up to the initial transitional phase, which could begin between 1981 and 1983, trade would be conducted under the 1970 preferential agreement. Currently about half of Spain's exports went to the EEC, which provided half of Spain's imports, excluding oil. On December 7 Spain and the seven European Free Trade Association (EFTA) countries signed an agreement lowering Spanish customs duties on industrial goods produced by EFTA countries by between 25 and 60%, while the EFTA countries agreed to introduce a general cut of 60% in their tariffs on Spanish imports. For agricultural products, EFTA countries would give concessions to Spain, which in return would lower its customs duties on farm imports from EFTA.

(MICHAEL WOOLLER)

See also Dependent States.

Speleology

In 1978 the second longest cave in the world, the Hölloch in Switzerland, was explored for an additional 4 km (2.5 mi); it thus became 133.2 km (82.7 mi) long. Another 22.2 km (13.8 mi) of passage found in the Optimisticheskaya cave in the Ukraine, U.S.S.R., brought its total length to 131.5 km (81.7 mi), and it remained third in the world list. At one point, however, it was only 800 m (2,625 ft) away from the fourth longest cave, the 102.6-km (63.7-mi) Ozyornaya, and the two caves might soon be joined.

Many very deep caves were extended even further. The "depth" of the Lamprechtsofen in

Austria being nearly all above the entrance, new discoveries were upward. In January the Salzburg Landesverein für Höhlenkunde reached a height of 867 m (2,844 ft) above the entrance. Three days later two Polish groups found two more upward branches. One of these brought them to a point 952 m (3,123 ft) above the entrance, thus giving the cave a total vertical extent of 962 m (3,156 ft) and making it the sixth deepest in the world. Explorations, also upward, in the Italian Antro di Corchia increased its overall vertical depth to 950 m (3,117 ft), so that it became the eighth deepest.

Progress was made, too, in the deep caves of America. A depth of 778 m (2,552 ft) was reached in the Mexican Sótano de Agua Lecarrizo. This made it the second deepest in the Western Hemisphere, but the cave was seen to continue even lower. With further exploration it was expected to connect with La Grieta, itself extended to a depth of 760 m (2,492 ft). In California, Bigfoot Cave became the deepest in the U.S., at 367 m (1,205 ft), when a connection was found between it and the higher-level Meatgrinder Cave.

There were many long explorations by divers in water-filled cave passages. The longest yet made was one of more than 2,000 m (6,562 ft) by Ian Lewis in a cave in the Nullarbor Plain (South Australia). In England the long underwater passage between Keld Head Spring and the Kingsdale Master Cave was finally penetrated. Oliver Statham and Geoffrey Yeadon, with the West German diver Jochen Hasenmayer, extended the previous Keld Head dives to 1,006 m (3,300 ft) in February. Later in the year Yeadon and Statham broke through to the underwater passages already known in the Kingsdale Master Cave. The length of this submerged link became 1,829 m (6,000 ft), the longest in Europe and the second longest in the world.

In the Royal Geographical Society's Mt. Mulu expedition in Sarawak, Borneo, a totally new type of limestone feature was found in one cave. Spikes of rock shaped by erosion or solution near the entrance all pointed directly toward the daylight. The cause of this was not yet fully understood but was probably associated with the effect of light on the growth of algae or bacteria that produce organic acids and thereby accelerate corrosion of the limestone.   (T. R. SHAW)

[232.A.5.a]

Sri Lanka

An Asian republic and member of the Commonwealth of Nations, Sri Lanka (Ceylon) occupies an island in the Indian Ocean off the southeast coast of peninsular India. Area: 65,610 sq km (25,332 sq mi). Pop. (1977 est.): 13,940,000, including Sinhalese about 72%; Tamil 21%; Moors 7%. Cap. and largest city: Colombo (pop., 1977 est., 616,000). Language: Sinhalese (official), Tamil, English. Religion (1971): Buddhist 67%; Hindu 18%; Christian 8%; Muslim 7%. Presidents in 1978, William Gopallawa and, from February 4, J. R. Jayawardene; prime ministers, J. R. Jayawardene and, from February 6, Ranasingle Premadasa.

Sri Lanka

Squash Rackets:
see Racket Games

Stamp Collecting:
see Philately and Numismatics

SRI LANKA
Education. (1976–77) Primary, pupils (state only) 1,385,001; secondary, pupils (state only) 1,076,502; primary and secondary (1973–74), teachers 98,925; vocational, pupils 4,778, teachers 1,239; teacher training, students 6,809, teachers (1974–75) 606; higher (1974–75), students 14,568, teaching staff 1,860.
Finance. Monetary unit: Sri Lanka rupee, with (Sept. 18, 1978) a free rate of SLRs 15.64 to U.S. $1 (SLRs 30.65 = £1 sterling). Gold, SDR's, and foreign exchange (June 1978) U.S. $309 million. Budget (1977 actual): revenue SLRs 6,686,000,000; expenditure SLRs 8,761,000,000. Gross domestic product (1977) SLRs 31,204,000,000. Money supply (May 1978) SLRs 5,841,000,000. Cost of living (Colombo; 1975 = 100; April 1978) 112.2.
Foreign Trade. (1977) Imports SLRs 6,061,000,000; exports SLRs 6,570,000,000. Import sources: Saudi Arabia 12%; Iran 9%; U.S. 8%; Japan 6%; India 6%; U.K. 5%; Australia 5%; Thailand 5%. Export destinations: Pakistan 8%; U.K. 8%; U.S. 7%; China c. 6%; Iraq 5%; Japan 5%. Main exports: tea 53%; rubber 14%; coconut products 5%.
Transport and Communications. Roads (1976) 31,150 km. Motor vehicles in use (1976): passenger 93,770; commercial 34,690. Railways: (1976) 1,498 km; traffic (1975–76) 2,990,000,000 passenger-km, freight 282 million net ton-km. Air traffic (1976): 305 million passenger-km; freight 2,660,000 net ton-km. Telephones (Jan. 1976) 72,000. Radio receivers (Dec. 1975) 530,000.
Agriculture. Production (in 000; metric tons; 1977): rice 1,706; cassava (1976) c. 791; sweet potatoes (1976) c. 220; onions c. 59; mangoes c. 69; lemons c. 52; pineapples c. 66; copra c. 160; tea c. 213; coffee c. 9; rubber 148. Livestock (in 000; June 1976): cattle 1,744; buffalo 854; sheep 30; goats 562; pigs 36; chickens 5,700.
Industry. Production (in 000; metric tons; 1976): salt 140; cement 422; graphite (exports; 1975) 10.4; petroleum products 1,358; cotton yarn 6.4; electricity (kw-hr) 1,202,000.

On Feb. 4, 1978, J. R. Jayawardene took office as the first elected president of Sri Lanka (renamed the Democratic Socialist Republic of Sri Lanka), and two days later Ranasingle Premadasa, deputy leader of the ruling United National Party, became prime minister. President Jayawardene's installation was boycotted by both the Tamil United Liberation Front and the Sri Lanka Freedom Party of former prime minister Mrs. Sirimavo Bandaranaike. The new French-style presidential constitution was formally promulgated on September 7. Its main provisions included election of the president and the National State Assembly for six-year terms and the holding of referenda on major issues.

In early April four police officers were murdered in the Tamil stronghold of Jaffna, supposedly by Tamil separatist terrorists. Isolated attacks on policemen and government officials followed, but security forces deployed in the area were able to keep violence in check. Antiterrorist legislation passed in May proscribed the Tamil Tiger Liberation Movement and similar groups.

Record production of food grains brought a modest improvement in the economy. The output of tea, the main export earner, rose by 6% in 1977, per capita income increased 2.6%, and the overall growth rate was 4.4% for the year. President Jayawardene's policy of free enterprise and tax exemption for foreign investors brought an increased flow of aid and capital investment, notably from the U.K. and the U.S. The International Monetary Fund granted a loan of $125 million.

Some 500 people were believed to have died when parts of the island were devastated by a cyclone on November 24.   (GOVINDAN UNNY)

Stock Exchanges

Despite international monetary troubles, political upheavals, and recession-prone economies, most of the world's major stock markets scored broadbased advances in 1978. Throughout Western Europe and the Asia-Pacific area, the diminishing rate of inflation among industrial countries, declining interest rates, and the trend toward political conservatism were the principal influences on stock price movements. But as often happens in equity price movements, unexplained psychological factors among the investing public held a strong control over the rises and falls in various markets. Of the 16 major stock price indexes, 11 were higher at the end of 1978 than at the end of 1977 (TABLE I).

Rising stock prices often occurred in spite of sluggish economic activity, high levels of unemployment, and social unrest. This reflected not only the tendency for stock price movements to anticipate future changes in economic and political conditions but also the uncertain state of investor confidence. Relatively high interest rates made bonds and other fixed-income securities strong competitors for equity-investment money. Similarly, soaring values for tangible assets, such as real estate and art, reduced the attraction of holding equities on a long-term basis.

On the other hand, given the depressed levels to which many common stocks had fallen in relation to the replacement value of their underlying assets, equities appeared to offer the potential for significant gains. Moreover, the trend in the rate of inflation continued to decelerate in most European countries and Japan in 1978. Because a drop in the inflation rate is generally accompanied by a cyclical decline in interest rates, the positive impact on stock price movements can be dramatic. A change in interest rates usually leads to a change in the rate at which investors discount the expected flow of corporate dividends and earnings. As a result a given flow of dividends is worth more when interest rates are low and less when rates are high. Similarly, the yields on bonds are lowered when interest rates decline, while the call factor on many bonds limits capital appreciation. The net effect is that falling inflation rates, coupled with cyclical declines in interest rates, increase the relative attractiveness of equities versus bonds and other fixed-income securities. (ROBERT H. TRIGG)

United States. The U.S. stock market reflected significant uncertainties in 1978 as a result of the nation's abnormal economic conditions. The Dow Jones industrial average ranged between a low of 742.12 on February 28 and a high of 907.74 on September 8, the smallest high and low figures in three years. The principal economic factors affecting the market were an annual inflation rate of 9%, abnormally high interest rates, and continued weakness in the value of the U.S. dollar. The drop in the exchange value of the dollar, coupled with credit tightening by the Federal Reserve Board, resulted in a decline of 55 points in the Dow Jones industrial average in the first seven trading ses-

sions of 1978 to a 2½-year low. By the end of February a three-year low of 742.12 was achieved before a moderate turnaround occurred in March and April on increasing volume. The "blue chips" moved narrowly throughout the year by comparison with the secondary stocks.

The volume of trading on the New York Stock Exchange rose 35% in 1978 with a turnover of 8,-304,315,509 shares, up from the level of 6,-153,169,391 the previous year. Turnover on the American Stock Exchange (Amex) rose 48% to a level of 1,037,873,935 shares, up from 700,984,895 in 1977, which, in turn, was a 40% increase over 1976. Similar growth was observed in the over-the-counter market, where the National Association of Securities Dealers reported a 43% gain to a level of 2,762,498,900. Bond turnover on the New York Stock Exchange dipped 2% to $4,554,013,000 in 1978, continuing a trend established during the previous year. A larger percentage decline occurred on the Amex, where a 7% drop was reflected by turnover of $265,550,000.

At the close of 1978 the price-earnings ratio on the Dow Jones industrial average was 7.9, as com-

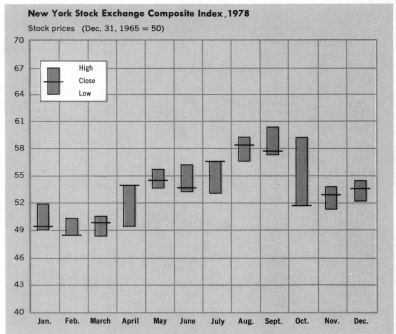

New York Stock Exchange Composite Index, 1978

Stock prices (Dec. 31, 1965 = 50)

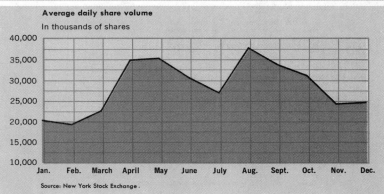

Average daily share volume

In thousands of shares

Source: New York Stock Exchange.

pared with 9.2 the previous year. Margin accounts on the New York Stock Exchange continued their long-term rise from a level of $9.6 billion in January to a peak of $12.3 billion in October. Bond yields continued to display a substantial negative spread as compared with stock dividends. Throughout 1978 bond yields drifted upward from a level of 8.2% to 9.12% by the year's end. Common-stock dividend yields fluctuated around the 5% level throughout 1978, closing at 5.04%.

Table I. Selected Major World Stock Price Indexes*

Country	1978 range High	1978 range Low	Year-end close 1977	Year-end close 1978	Percent change
Australia	567	411	477	542	+14%
Austria	2,318	2,238	2,306	2,277†	− 1
Belgium	101	90	91	98	+ 8
Denmark	99	88	96	89	− 7
France	83	48	53	77	+45
Germany, West	864	759	788	817	+ 4
Hong Kong	708	383	404	496	+23
Italy	82	55	56	69	+23
Japan	6,097	4,868	4,866	6,002	+23
Netherlands, The	93	76	80	81	+ 1
Singapore	415	252	264	349	+32
South Africa	282	194	211	269	+27
Spain	111	88	100	89	−11
Sweden	408	326	323	362	+12
Switzerland	324	262	301	289	− 4
United Kingdom	536	433	485	471	− 3

*Index numbers are rounded, and limited to countries for which at least 12 months' data were available on a weekly basis.
†As of Dec. 22, 1978.
Sources: *Barrons, The Economist, Financial Times,* and *The New York Times.*

Table II. U.S. Stock Market Prices

Month	Railroads (10 stocks) 1978	1977	Industrials (400 stocks) 1978	1977	Public utilities (40 stocks) 1978	1977	Composite (500 stocks) 1978	1977
January	46.13	50.24	99.34	115.17	52.40	54.01	90.25	103.81
February	44.69	49.27	97.95	112.14	51.60	52.88	88.98	100.96
March	43.61	50.21	97.65	111.88	51.72	52.14	88.82	100.57
April	44.77	52.83	102.07	109.89	52.16	52.57	92.71	99.05
May	46.05	54.14	107.70	109.10	51.71	53.68	97.41	98.76
June	44.92	53.06	107.96	109.46	52.25	55.29	97.66	99.29
July	43.97	53.12	107.39	110.12	52.32	55.24	97.19	100.18
August	47.26	49.19	114.99	107.50	53.35	55.42	103.92	97.75
September	48.19	48.11	115.11	105.94	52.54	54.61	103.86	96.23
October	47.63	46.23	111.56	103.18	51.28	54.26	100.58	93.74
November	...	46.44	...	103.71	...	54.46	...	94.28
December	...	46.46	...	103.13	...	54.54	...	93.82

Sources: U.S. Department of Commerce, *Survey of Current Business;* Board of Governors of the Federal Reserve System, *Federal Reserve Bulletin.* Prices are Standard and Poor's monthly averages of daily closing prices, with 1941–43=10.

Table III. U.S. Government Long-Term Bond Prices and Yields
Average price in dollars per $100 bond

Month	Average 1978	1977	Yield (%) 1978	1977	Month	Average 1978	1977	Yield (%) 1978	1977
January	53.74	59.73	7.50	6.68	July	49.97	57.48	8.09	6.97
February	53.09	56.23	7.60	7.15	August	51.32	57.30	7.87	7.00
March	52.90	55.83	7.63	7.20	September	51.67	57.77	7.82	6.94
April	52.15	56.31	7.74	7.14	October	50.11	56.68	8.07	7.08
May	51.34	56.06	7.87	7.17	November	...	56.24	...	7.14
June	50.91	57.38	7.94	6.99	December	...	55.62	...	7.23

Source: U.S. Department of Commerce, *Survey of Current Business.* Average prices are derived from average yields on the basis of an assumed 3% 20-year taxable U.S. Treasury bond. Yields are for U.S. Treasury bonds that are taxable and due or callable in ten years or more.

Table IV. U.S. Corporate Bond Prices and Yields
Average price in dollars per $100 bond

Month	Average 1978	1977	Yield (%) 1978	1977	Month	Average 1978	1977	Yield (%) 1978	1977
January	57.2	60.3	8.41	7.96	July	54.5	60.0	8.88	7.94
February	56.9	59.4	8.47	8.04	August	56.1	60.1	8.69	7.98
March	57.0	59.1	8.47	8.10	September	56.1	60.4	8.69	7.92
April	56.3	59.4	8.56	8.04	October	54.7	59.5	8.89	8.04
May	55.5	59.2	8.69	8.05	November	...	59.2	...	8.08
June	55.2	60.1	8.76	7.95	December	...	58.4	...	8.19

Source: U.S. Department of Commerce, *Survey of Current Business.* Average prices are based on Standard and Poor's composite index of A1+ issues. Yields are based on Moody's Aaa domestic corporate bond index.

Institutional investors were not active in the market in 1978, seeking alternative outlets for their funds. In the first quarter of 1978 private pension funds were net sellers of stock, and in the second and third quarters their net purchases were modest. Private pension fund commitments to the stock market were less than at any time since the 1940s. Mutual fund net subscriptions other than money market funds continued to show an adverse balance, with net sales exceeding $200 million per month in June and August.

The price of a seat on the New York Stock Exchange rose from a level of $45,000 in January to a high of $100,000 in October. On the American Stock Exchange a seat sold for $48,000 in January and, after dropping to the $30,000 range in February, rose to $52,000 in November. Customer debt to New York Stock Exchange member firms declined slightly to a year-end total of $10,830,000,-000, represented by 955,000 margin accounts. Stockbrokers increased the rates charged as commissions to investors with relatively small transactions.

The Standard and Poor composite index of 500 New York Stock Exchange stocks (TABLE II) began the year at 90.25 and declined in February and March to 88.82 before resuming a climb to a level of 103.86 in September. The 400 industrials in the index paralleled the composite, beginning at 99.34 in January, dipping to 97.65 in March, and then rising to a peak of 115.11 in September. Public utility stocks ranged very narrowly between a high of 53.35 in August and a low of 51.28 in October. Railroad stocks were generally lower than the previous year, reaching a bottom in March of 43.61, 13% below the corresponding month of 1977. The best industry average performance of 1978 among stock prices was achieved by aerospace shares, which gained 60.9%. Real estate issues followed with a 46.7% gain, airlines 43.2%, and recreational movies 41.2%. The poorest performance was turned in by retail department stores, down 15.9%; electric utilities were off 7.7%, gas utilities 4.6%, rubber and plastics 2.6%, and metals, iron, and steel 1.3%.

U.S. government long-term bond prices declined steadily between January and July 1978 and then rose irregularly (TABLE III). Bond prices were generally lower than in the previous year. An unusual aspect of 1978 was that it was one of the few years in which maturities over short terms were offering higher returns than those over long periods. Two-year Treasury notes, which normally yield at least 0.4% less than 30-year bonds, were yielding 1% more. The U.S. Treasury sold $3.2 billion of 52-week bills at an average return of 9.605%, the highest ever for such bills. The previous high was 9.56% in August 1974. About $135 billion of new bonds were sold publicly in 1978, including about $35 billion by the Treasury, $34 billion by other federal agencies, $20 billion by corporations, and $46 billion by local governments. Compared with 1977 these sales represented small increases. Average yields rose from 7.50% in January to 8.09% in July before slipping slightly below that record level. In July the year-to-year increase in average yield on new bond issues was 16%.

Corporate bond prices (TABLE IV) moved irregularly within a narrow range well below the levels of the previous year. The average was 57.2 in January and had declined to 54.5 by July. Bond yields were generally higher, rising from a level of 8.1% in January to a peak of 8.88% in July. The gain over July 1977 was 12%.

The options markets achieved all-time records for volume in 1978, with the 11 futures exchanges recording more than 57.5 million contracts with a value of about $1.6 trillion; this was a gain of 35% above the previous all-time high. Both the American Stock Exchange and the New York Stock Exchange took decisive steps toward increasing their participation in the options market.

The Chicago Board of Trade continued to be the nation's largest futures market, although its share of total volume slipped from 54 to 47% in 1978. A membership on the Chicago Mercantile Exchange sold for a record price of $275,000, the highest ever paid for a seat on any commodity futures exchange. A seat on the International Monetary Market Division, where contracts in foreign currencies, gold, and U.S. Treasury bills are traded, was quoted at $156,000 bid and $174,000 asked.

Canada. The Canadian stock market paralleled that of the U.S. in response to comparable economic developments. Real gross national product rose by 4%, while the consumer price index was up 9% for the year and unemployment rose to an average of 8.5%. The Canadian dollar dropped to a low of 84 cents at the year's end from 92.5 cents at the end of 1977. The prime lending rate was 12% versus 8.25% a year earlier.

The Toronto Stock Exchange (TSE) reflected sharp gains, due primarily to oil stocks reflecting export gains because of the low value of the Canadian dollar. The 300-share TSE composite index, which reached a low of 996.88 early in 1978, achieved a high of 1346.15 by the end of the year for an annual gain of 31%.

The average price-earnings ratio for stocks on the TSE was 9.07 and the average yield 4.32%. Among the industry leaders for 1978 were paper and forest products, the average price of which increased by 70.66%, and oils, which gained 40%.

Bond prices declined in 1978 due to the weakness of the Canadian dollar. Long-term Canadian bond averages reflected yields hovering about 9% throughout most of 1978, but they rose in the last quarter to close the year at 10%. The yields on 91-day Treasury bills rose during 1978 from 7.1% in January to 8% in mid-April, 9% in September, 10% in October, and 10.7% at the end of the year. (IRVING PFEFFER)

Western Europe. Stock markets in the four largest European economies followed divergent patterns in 1978. Great Britain and France experienced contrasting markets, with the former posting lower stock prices while the latter had the largest increase in equity prices among major world stock price indexes. Italy also enjoyed sharply higher prices, but the bull market in West Germany was relatively mild. Among the remaining European stock markets, higher prices prevailed in Sweden, Belgium, and The Netherlands, while

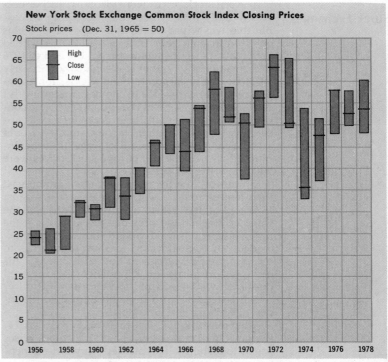

New York Stock Exchange Common Stock Index Closing Prices

Stock prices (Dec. 31, 1965 = 50)

High
Close
Low

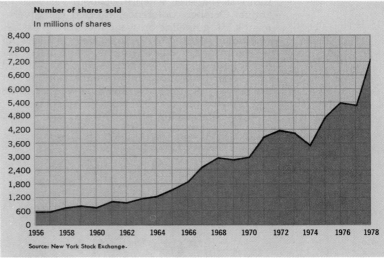

Number of shares sold
In millions of shares

Source: New York Stock Exchange.

lower prices were experienced in Spain, Denmark, Switzerland, and Austria.

In Great Britain the seesaw movement of prices on the London Stock Exchange in 1978 resulted in a small net loss in the leading averages. The *Financial Times* index of 30 industrial shares, which reached record highs in 1977, entered a downtrend in mid-January during which equity values were reduced by more than 9% before the first week of March. This poor performance occurred despite substantial improvement in Britain's annual inflation rate, which had dropped below 10% for the first time in four years. However, 6% of Britain's work force was unemployed. Moreover, the nation's international trade account was in deficit and worsening, thereby threatening to reverse the current account surplus achieved in 1977.

In April stock prices were virtually unchanged. A brief rally in May added 3% to equity values, but that was wiped out by the end of June. Yields on fixed-income securities, which had declined about four percentage points from the end of 1976 to the end of 1977, began to creep upward in early 1978. Domestic corporate bond yields, for example, reached nearly 13% at the beginning of July, compared with 11.9% at the end of 1977. Also contributing to bearish sentiment for equities was uncertainty over whether labour unions would accept a fourth year of statutory wage limits beginning in July. At the end of June stock prices were 5% below the 1977 close.

In mid-July the British government announced its intention to limit wage increases from August 1978 to August 1979 to 5%, which was half the wage ceiling for the previous year. At the same time, restrictions on dividend increases were extended but slightly eased to allow companies to increase their dividends in line with profits. This news restored investor confidence and reversed the downward trend of stock prices. The rally, which lasted well into September, pushed the index 15% above the June close.

After reaching its 1978 high on September 14, the stock market dropped about 11% before prices began to stabilize. The market's upward momentum was shattered when the Labour Party, at its annual October conference, rejected the government's 5% guideline on wage increases. That development subsequently triggered a series of strikes by major labour unions, particularly automobile and bakery workers. A mild rally carried prices nearly 5% above the November bottom, but the market backtracked in the final weeks of 1978 and finished the year 3% below the 1977 close.

After experiencing a bearish trend since 1976,

the stock market in France turned to the plus side in 1978. For the year as a whole the average rise in stock prices was 45%, the best performance among the major world stock price indexes. The bearish tone throughout most of 1977 had been based on investor fears that a leftist government would assume political power after the March 1978 general elections. Thus, the recovery in equity values began in mid-February as public opinion polls showed that popularity of the French leftist political parties was dropping. Yet the upward momentum in stock prices did not take hold until after the first round of voting March 12 revealed the Socialist-Communist political alliance would probably lose in the second round on March 19. When the surprisingly large margin of victory by the conservative coalition became known, the demand for stocks created an explosion in prices. Values on the Paris Bourse rose nearly 11% in the three days after the first round of voting, and by the end of March share prices were up 21% from the day before voting began.

The upward trend of the market was halted after the government announced that it planned to assume control of the financially ailing steel industry. Worker sit-ins at financially troubled firms to protest the loss of jobs also highlighted the unpleasant fact that French unemployment was abnormally high and likely to rise. Equity values fell 8% from early October to early December. A subsequent rebound was weak. As 1978 came to a close, stocks were 7% below the October high.

Despite social and political turmoil the Italian stock market reflected the country's improved economic and financial strength. The price index of shares traded on the Milan Stock Exchange climbed steadily throughout most of the year, but weakened in late October before finishing 1978 some 23% higher than during the previous year. However, this still left the index 31% below the 1972 highs.

The recovery in stock prices began in early January in the face of widespread terrorism and political violence. After the resignation of Premier Giulio Andreotti's government on January 16 a new ruling coalition was not formed until 56 days later, the longest period of political uncertainty since World War II. That coalition was headed by Andreotti, whose Christian Democrat Party subsequently scored impressive gains over the Communist Party in the May balloting for local and provincial offices. This period also witnessed the kidnapping and death of former premier Aldo Moro. On the economic front Italy's policy of economic restraint succeeded in reducing the rate of increase in consumer prices for the 12 months ended in February 1978 to 12.6%, compared with 20.5% in February 1977. By May the rate had slowed to 11.9%. At the same time, Italy's international payments account was likely to post a surplus for the second year in a row. The net gain in stock prices from the beginning of January to the end of May was over 13%.

In June the market fell almost 2% before resuming its advance. Economic predictions that Italy's output of goods and services would show a 4% increase in 1978 cheered investors. Stock prices

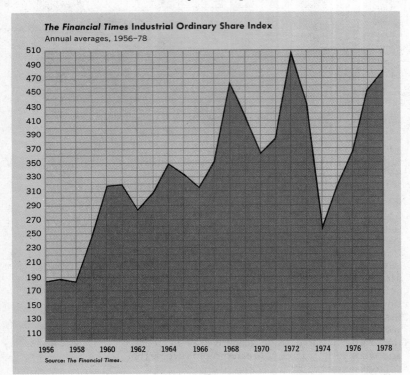

The Financial Times Industrial Ordinary Share Index
Annual averages, 1956–78

Source: The Financial Times.

jumped 17% in September, on top of a 7% rise in August. However, the market's upward momentum was soon broken. From the end of September to the end of November stock prices fell 11%. Among the market's chief worries were growing concern over sharp gains in the nation's money supply, which could ultimately reverse the declining rate of inflation, and uncertainty over whether the country would accept the economic and financial discipline necessary to produce long-term price stability.

The stock market in West Germany climbed to its highest level in eight years during 1978. In the January–June period prices on the Frankfurt Stock Exchange rose less than 1%. West Germany's success in keeping a lid on inflationary pressures outweighed investor concern over the economy's flagging pace. The rise in consumer prices for the 12 months ended May 1978 was 2.7%, down from 3.5% a year earlier. A major factor in controlling inflation was the rising value of the West German mark against the U.S. dollar in international currency markets. For 1978 as a whole the value of the mark in relation to the dollar increased 13%, after rising 11% in 1977. However, the mark's strength also squeezed export profits and encouraged West German companies to invest abroad rather than at home. The instability caused by widely fluctuating exchange rates was the major impetus behind Chancellor Helmut Schmidt's attempts to form a new European Monetary System linking nine European currencies.

During July, following the seven-nation economic summit meeting in Bonn, stock prices began a strong advance. To spur world economic recovery Schmidt pledged a $6 billion stimulus package, which, it was estimated, would add about one percentage point to West Germany's gross national product in 1979. From mid-July to mid-October equity values gained 9%. In November Pres. Jimmy Carter's program to bolster the value of the U.S. dollar in currency markets caused it to increase to 6% against the mark by the end of 1978. However, hopes for lessening dependence on the U.S. dollar by creating an alternative reserve currency were dealt a severe blow when first Great Britain declined to become a member of the European Monetary System, and then France refused to join until the issue of Common Market farm subsidies was resolved. After stumbling in November stock prices recovered some of their losses and finished the year with a net gain of 4%.

The trend of the stock market in Sweden was also higher. Prices on the Stockholm Exchange jumped 12% in 1978 after dropping 18% the year before. The recovery in stock prices. which began in late November 1977, did not encounter profit-taking until late February. But by that time equity values had increased 11%. The market's retreat was modest, with the entire decline being retraced by the end of March. The subsequent upswing lasted throughout the summer and reached its peak on August 4, 26% above the 1977 close.

Belgium experienced higher stock prices in 1978 after two years of declining equity values. Prices revealed a gain of nearly 3% through mid-February. A brief period of profit-taking was followed by a much sharper advance in which prices jumped 9% from March 10 to May 5. The uptrend came to a quick end, however, when bitter political disputes over government plans to reduce the $3 billion deficit and the timing of reforms giving autonomy to French- and Flemish-speaking districts forced the resignation of Prime Minister Léo Tindemans. From May 5 to June 30 equity values dropped 6%. Most of this loss was recovered by mid-September, however. The bullish bias of equity investors allowed the stock market to close the year with a net gain of 8%.

In The Netherlands the increase in the price index of issues listed on the Amsterdam Stock Exchange from year-end 1977 to year-end 1978 was 1%. Average share prices, which dropped 4% in 1977, slipped another 6% between mid-February and early April after a moderate rise to start the year. However, the stock market had its strongest rally over the next nine weeks when 13% was added to equity values. While the real rate of growth in gross national product in 1978 was expected to be relatively unchanged from that of the year before, the slowdown in the rate of inflation continued. Stock prices remained in a relatively narrow trading range during the summer. During the next buying wave prices reached their highest level on September 11 before profit-taking ended the rally. After sinking nearly 15% from the September high to the November close, prices recovered somewhat, but they were headed lower as 1978 came to an end.

Stocks in Spain generally performed poorly and were quite volatile. After dropping 33% in 1977 prices fell another 11% in 1978. Much of the decline could be attributed to the failure of the government to control inflation and reduce labour militancy. The crisis facing the country was reflected in domestic corporate bond yields, which reached record highs.

Currency unrest was the major influence on the Swiss stock market in 1978. The value of the Swiss franc had increased nearly 18% against the U.S. dollar in 1977, and it gained another 2% during January 1978. In February, however, as a means of discouraging the demand for Swiss currency the Swiss National Bank placed restrictions on the ability of nonresident foreign investors to buy Swiss securities. From February 14 to March 10 prices on the Zürich Stock Exchange plunged nearly 14%, the biggest selling wave since the October 1973 oil price increase.

The market fluctuated in a relatively narrow range between the February highs and the March lows until mid-September, when equity values were hit by another sinking spell as the U.S. dollar reached a record low of 1.4488 Swiss francs in foreign currency dealings. Moreover, the stock market continued weak even after the Swiss franc rose in value following massive intervention by the Swiss National Bank. The decline in equity values from September 8 to October 27 amounted to almost 8%. A revival of investor interest in equities was triggered by the West German-led initiative to promote greater financial stability in Europe by reducing European dependence on the U.S. dollar. The subsequent rally more than retraced the September decline, but stock prices finished 1978 4% lower than the year before and 39% below the record high recorded in 1972.

Other Countries. In Japan the increase in the index of leading industrial shares on the Tokyo Stock Exchange was 23% from the end of 1977 to the end of 1978. The rising value of the Japanese yen against the U.S. dollar was the dominant influence on economic trends. In fact, the yen's advance in relation to the dollar in 1978 as a whole (+ 19%) exceeded 1977's relatively large increase (+ 18%). While the yen's appreciation hurt Japanese exporters, domestic manufacturers greatly benefited from lower raw material costs. Japan's current-account surplus also remained relatively large, despite government efforts to curb exports and ease restrictions on imports. Moreover, high liquidity, surging corporate profits, and the continued easing of inflation rates added to the attractiveness of equity investments. For example, in September 1978 consumer prices were, on the average, 3.7% higher than a year earlier.

Stock prices recorded a new historical high on December 11 as the Tokyo Dow industrials index cleared the 6000 mark for the first time. The rally, which began in August, was accompanied by extraordinarily high trading volume. The buying stampede, mainly from financial institutions, reflected the increased profitability of major companies as well as the declining attractiveness of the bond market. The yield on Japanese government bonds, for example, averaged 5.47% in October, compared with 5.56% in May and 6.12% in December 1977. As 1978 came to a close, the stock market shrugged off the implications of the surprise selection of Masayoshi Ohira to replace Takeo Fukuda as prime minister and warnings from Tokyo Stock Exchange officials about the danger of speculating excessively in stocks.

The stock markets in Hong Kong and Singapore were also star performers in 1978. The index of 33 stocks traded on the Hong Kong Exchange rose 23%. Stock prices recorded gains of 18 and 16% in June and August, respectively, while prices fell 26% during November. The year's high was set on September 4 and the low on April 13.

The pattern of stock price movements in Singapore was quite similar to that in Hong Kong. However, the overall gain in equity values for the year as a whole was much larger (+ 32%). The December announcement that the U.S. and China would normalize diplomatic relations was bullish news in both Hong Kong and Singapore.

In Australia the trend of stock prices was also higher. Prices on the Sydney Stock Exchange gained 14% after rising 11% in 1977. The increase in consumer prices for the year ended June 1978 (7.9%) was substantially below the corresponding increase a year earlier (13.4%). Reflecting the trend toward lower interest rates, the Australian Savings Bond rate was reduced to 8¾% from 9% in November. At the year's close stock prices were 4% below the 1972 high and 14% under the all-time peak reached in 1970.

After overcoming a bearish trend during the first three months of the year, the stock market in South Africa was generally strong. For the year as a whole the average gain in industrial shares traded on the Johannesburg Stock Exchange was 27%. The resignation of Prime Minister B. J. Vorster in September proved to be only a temporary restraining influence on the uptrend in equity prices.

Commodity Prices. Sharply higher quotations generally prevailed in world commodity markets during 1978. *The Economist's* commodity price indicator, which measures spot prices in terms of the U.S. dollar for 29 internationally traded commodities, climbed nearly 14% from year-end 1977 to mid-December 1978. The index reached an all-time high on October 31, some 77% above its June 1975 trough and 2% higher than the previous peak recorded in April 1977. The decline in the dollar-based index following the October peak mainly reflected the strengthening of the U.S. dollar in world currency markets after the U.S. unveiled its dollar-rescue program on November 1.

The Economist's index of commodity prices has two major components: food and industrial raw materials. Although both components were higher near the end of 1978 that at the end of 1977, the rise in prices of industrial materials (+ 20%) was twice as large as for food prices (+ 9%). Much of the demand for raw materials was in anticipation of increasing economic activity in Europe. In addition, concern about strikes and stockpiling that might result from fear of still more price increases contributed to buildups of raw materials. Currency unrest also played a role as investors bought commodity futures as a hedge against the eroding purchasing power of the U.S. dollar.

Reuters United Kingdom commodity index, which measures spot or futures prices for 17 primary commodities weighted by their relative importance in international trade, climbed 5% from the end of 1977 to the end of 1978. This index reached its 1978 high on November 6, 8% above the 1977 close but almost 13% below the all-time high recorded in the spring of 1977.

The price of gold also reached a new peak in 1978. In late July the London gold quote surged past $200 per ounce for the first time, thereby exceeding the previous high set on Dec. 30, 1974. Thereafter, the price continued to climb more or less in a straight line until it hit $243.65 per ounce on October 31. After declining to $193.40 on November 30, it moved higher again and closed 1978 at $226 for a net gain of 37% for the year. Contributing to the strength of gold prices were high inflation rates, the sharp decline in the value of the U.S. dollar, and continued uncertainty over the course of the world economy.

Finally, among commodities with price structures unsuitable for trading in free markets, the price of crude oil continued to hold the spotlight in 1978. Because of an unfavourable supply-demand balance, the Organization of Petroleum Exporting Countries (OPEC) had to forgo raising oil prices. However, the depreciation of the U.S. dollar cut the real income of OPEC, while political turmoil in Iran reduced the flow of oil to world markets. In response, OPEC decided in mid-December to lift oil prices 14½% by Oct. 1, 1979.

(ROBERT H. TRIGG)

See also Economy, World.

Sudan

A republic of northeast Africa, the Sudan is bounded by Egypt, the Red Sea, Ethiopia, Kenya, Uganda, Zaire, the Central African Empire, Chad, and Libya. Area: 2,503,890 sq km (966,757 sq mi). Pop. (1978 est.): 17,141,000, including Arabs in the north and Negroes in the south. Cap. and largest city: Khartoum (pop., 1977 est., 1,089,-300). Language: Arabic, various tribal languages in the south. Religion: Muslim in the north; predominantly animist in the south. President in 1978, Maj. Gen. Gaafar Nimeiry; prime minister, Rashid Bakr.

In 1978 Pres. Gaafar Nimeiry continued his policy of strengthening his government by reconciling former dissidents. In March he appointed to the Central Committee of the Sudan Socialist Union — the only legal political organization — several dissident leaders who had responded to his earlier initiatives by returning from exile. Among them was former prime minister Sadik al-Mahdi, who had been the leader of the Umma Party and had been sentenced to death in 1976 for his role in the coup attempt of the previous year. On April 12 in London other exiled leaders signed a declaration of reconciliation whereby they disbanded the former National Front (which was behind the 1975 coup), provided for the return home of all its former members, and indicated their support for the present constitution.

In foreign relations progress was made toward reconciliation with Ethiopia (with provisions for an exchange of refugees between the two countries) and with Libya. However, Nimeiry's efforts as conciliator between Egypt, whose policy toward Israel he had backed, and other Arab states met with no success. Sudan's purchase of 12 F-5 fighter aircraft from the United States was confirmed in April.

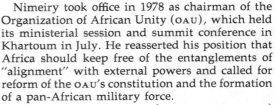

Sudan

SUDAN
Education. (1975–76) Primary, pupils 1,169,279, teachers 31,695; secondary, pupils 268,120, teachers 12,097; vocational, pupils 8,996, teachers 649; teacher training, students 4,723, teachers 420; higher, students 21,342, teaching staff 1,420.

Finance. Monetary unit: Sudanese pound, with (Sept. 18, 1978) a par value of Sud£0.40 to U.S. $1 (free rate of Sud£0.78 = £1 sterling). Gold, SDR's, and foreign exchange (June 1978) U.S. $21.9 million. Budget (1976–77 est.): revenue Sud£448 million; expenditure Sud£378 million. Money supply (June 1978) Sud£482,070,000. Cost of living (1975 = 100; Dec. 1977) 121.

Foreign Trade. (1977) Imports Sud£368,980,000; exports Sud£230,180,000. Import sources (1976): U.K. 20%; U.S. 9%; West Germany 8%; Italy 8%; Iraq 8%; Japan 7%; India 6%. Export destinations (1976): Italy 20%; Japan 7%; France 7%; West Germany 7%; Yugoslavia 5%; The Netherlands 5%. Main exports: cotton 60%; peanuts 11%; sesame seed 7%; gum arabic 5%.

Transport and Communications. Roads (1976) c. 50,-000 km (mainly tracks; including c. 550 km asphalted). Motor vehicles in use (1976): passenger c. 52,000; commercial (including buses) c. 27,000. Railways: (1976) 4,556 km; freight traffic (1973) 2,288,000,000 net ton-km. Air traffic (1976): 345 million passenger-km; freight 7.5 million net ton-km. Inland navigable waterways (1975) 4,068 km. Telephones (Jan. 1977) 43,300. Radio licenses (Dec. 1973) 1.3 million. Television receivers (Dec. 1975) 100,000.

Agriculture. Production (in 000; metric tons; 1977): wheat 336; millet c. 410; sorghum c. 1,600; sesame seed c. 265; cottonseed c. 350; peanuts c. 990; sugar, raw value (1976) c. 185; dates c. 106; cotton, lint 208; cow's milk c. 885; beef and veal c. 163; mutton and goat meat c. 120; timber (cu m) 22,371. Livestock (in 000; 1977): cattle 15,-892; sheep 15,248; goats 11,592; camels (1976) c. 2,827; asses (1976) c. 672; chickens c. 24,000.

Industry. Production (in 000; metric tons; 1976): petroleum products c. 1,120; electricity (kw-hr) c. 720,000; salt (1975) 75; cement (1975) 182.

Nimeiry took office in 1978 as chairman of the Organization of African Unity (OAU), which held its ministerial session and summit conference in Khartoum in July. He reasserted his position that Africa should keep free of the entanglements of "alignment" with external powers and called for reform of the OAU's constitution and the formation of a pan-African military force.

(VIRGINIA R. LULING)

Strikes:
see Industrial Relations
Sumo:
see Combat Sports
Surfing:
see Water Sports

Heavy rains brought vast flooding to the Gezira province of Sudan in July. Crops were wrecked, and half a million people were left homeless.

PASCALE VILLIERS LE MOY—CAMERA PRESS/PHOTO TRENDS

Suriname

Swaziland

Suriname

An independent republic of northern South America, Suriname is bounded by Guyana, Brazil, French Guiana, and the Atlantic Ocean. Area: 181,455 sq km (70,060 sq mi). Pop. (1977 est.): 448,000, including (1971) Hindustanis 37%, Creoles 30.8%, Indonesians 15.3%, Bush Negroes 10.3%, Amerindians 2.6%. Cap. and largest city: Paramaribo (pop., 1971, 102,300). Language: Dutch (official); English and Sranan (a creole) are lingua francas; Hindi, Javanese, Chinese, and various Amerindian languages are used within individual ethnic communities. Religion: predominantly Hindu, Christian, and Muslim. President in 1978, Johan Ferrier; prime minister, Henck Arron.

The new Cabinet, sworn in on Dec. 28, 1977, and led by Prime Minister Henck Arron, was confronted with serious economic and social difficulties, the most important being the rise of unemployment to about 30%. Some 10% of the population was employed by the civil service. Suriname maintained a positive balance of trade, however, thanks to the bauxite industry, which accounted for 90% of export income.

In the Commission for Development Cooperation between The Netherlands and Suriname, the Dutch delegation accused Suriname of neglecting poor farmers and lavishing money on prestige projects, while Suriname called the Dutch government unrealistic. A visit by the Dutch minister of development, Jan de Koning, in March 1978 was needed before negotiations could be resumed. In February Queen Juliana and Prince Bernhard of The Netherlands paid Suriname an official visit, the first by a head of state since independence in 1975. (DICK BOONSTRA)

Swaziland

A landlocked monarchy of southern Africa, Swaziland is bounded by South Africa and Mozambique. Area: 17,364 sq km (6,704 sq mi). Pop. (1976 prelim. census): 499,046. Cap. and largest city: Mbabane (pop., 1975 est., 24,000). Language: English and siSwati (official). Religion: Christian 60%; animist 40%. King, Sobhuza II; prime minister in 1978, Col. Maphevu Dlamini.

In July 1978 King Sobhuza II, the world's current longest-reigning sovereign, celebrated his 79th birthday. A new constitution (the previous one had been superseded in 1973 by government by royal decree) was completed by a royal commission; a team of counselors explained its provisions to the Tinkhundlas (local councils), which would nominate parliamentary candidates.

Ambrose Zwane, former leader of the banned Ngwane National Liberatory Congress, was arrested on February 9 but later escaped to Mozambique. Some 50 members of the Pan-Africanist Congress, a banned South African organization, were arrested in April, and it was announced that many would be deported. They were said to have broken new regulations, particularly those concerning the carrying of arms. Swaziland denied that the arrests had been made at the behest of South Africa.

The finance and foreign ministers of Swaziland and South Africa held economic discussions in April. Landlocked Swaziland initiated a charter mercantile marine, eventually to be based at Richard's Bay, South Africa.

Prince Makhosini Dlamini, prime minister from 1967 to 1976, died on April 28, 1978.

(MOLLY MORTIMER)

A Chinese technician inspects rice grown by Swazis. The teaching of rice cultivation is part of China's ten-year-old agricultural cooperation program in Swaziland.

SURINAME

Education. (1976–77) Primary, pupils 85,783, teachers 3,016; secondary, pupils 24,932, teachers 1,242; vocational, pupils 3,645, teachers 244; teacher training, students 1,998, teachers 182; higher (university only), students 938, teaching staff 113.

Finance. Monetary unit: Suriname guilder, with (Sept. 18, 1978) a par value of 1.785 Suriname guilder to U.S. $1 (3.51 Suriname guilders = £1 sterling). Gold, SDR's, and foreign exchange (June 1978) U.S. $141 million. Budget (1977 est.): revenue 541 million Suriname guilders; expenditure 581 million Suriname guilders.

Foreign Trade. (1975) Imports 467 million Suriname guilders; exports 495 million Suriname guilders. Import sources: U.S. c. 33%; Trinidad and Tobago c. 15%; The Netherlands c. 14%; Japan c. 6%; U.K. c. 5%. Export destinations: U.S. c. 39%; The Netherlands c. 13%; West Germany c. 10%; Norway c. 10%. Main exports: alumina 43%; bauxite 18%; aluminum 8%; rice 7%.

Transport and Communications. Roads (1977) c. 2,500 km. Motor vehicles in use (1976): passenger 28,800; commercial (including buses) 10,200. Railways (1977) 152 km. Telephones (Jan. 1977) 18,600. Radio receivers (Dec. 1975) 110,000. Television receivers (Dec. 1975) 34,000.

Agriculture. Production (in 000; metric tons; 1977): rice c. 182; oranges c. 5; grapefruit c. 3; bananas c. 46; sugar, raw value (1976) c. 11. Livestock (in 000; Jan. 1976): cattle c. 28; pigs c. 7; goats c. 6; chickens c. 908.

Industry. Production (in 000; metric tons; 1976): bauxite 4,669; alumina 1,130; aluminum 45; electricity (kw-hr) 1,335,000 (88% hydroelectric).

SWAZILAND

Education. (1976) Primary, pupils 92,721, teachers (1975) 2,363; secondary, pupils 17,396, teachers 885; vocational, pupils 613, teachers 72; teacher training, students 341, teachers 52; higher, students 1,150, teaching staff 136.

Finance and Trade. Monetary unit: lilangeni (emalangeni for more than 1), at par with the South African rand, with (Sept. 18, 1978) a par value of 0.87 lilangeni to U.S. $1 (free rate of 1.70 emalangeni = £1 sterling). Budget (1976–77 est.): revenue 70 million emalangeni; expenditure 75 million emalangeni. Foreign trade (1975): imports 134,566,000 emalangeni; exports 132,145,000 emalangeni. Export destinations (1970): U.K. 25%; Japan 24%; South Africa 21%. Main exports: sugar 54%; wood pulp 9%; iron ore 9%; asbestos 7%.

Agriculture. Production (in 000; metric tons; 1976): corn 110; rice *c.* 4; potatoes *c.* 7; sugar, raw value (1977) *c.* 239; pineapples *c.* 21; cotton, lint *c.* 6. Livestock (in 000; 1976): cattle *c.* 620; sheep *c.* 35; pigs *c.* 38; goats *c.* 260.

Industry. Production (in 000; metric tons; 1976): coal 126; iron ore (metal content) 1,217; asbestos 39; electricity (kw-hr) *c.* 244,000.

Sweden

A constitutional monarchy of northern Europe lying on the eastern side of the Scandinavian Peninsula, Sweden has common borders with Finland and Norway. Area: 449,964 sq km (173,732 sq mi). Pop. (1978 est.): 8,271,000. Cap. and largest city: Stockholm (pop., 1978 est., 658,400). Language: Swedish, with some Finnish and Lapp in the north. Religion: predominantly Lutheran. King, Carl XVI Gustaf; prime ministers in 1978, Thorbjörn Fälldin until October 5 and, from October 13, Ola Ullsten.

A vow to strengthen Sweden's trading position was made by Prime Minister Ola Ullsten (*see* BIOGRAPHIES) when his Liberal minority government came to power after his nomination on Oct. 13, 1978. Ullsten told the Riksdag (parliament) that Sweden was rapidly moving toward recovery, but unemployment had to be reduced and investment stepped up. Sweden's gross national product (GNP) rose by 2% in 1978 after a disastrous 2.5% decline in 1977. Ullsten's government anticipated that GNP would grow by 4% in 1979.

Ullsten's government took office after the collapse of Thorbjörn Fälldin's Centre-Conservative coalition, which held sway for only 24 months before splintering on the question of nuclear policy. Ullsten's Liberal Party held only 39 seats in the 349-seat unicameral Parliament, but he obtained passive support from the Centre and Social Democratic parties — the country's largest. Many observers saw his regime as merely custodial until the general elections due in September 1979. At that time, pollsters believed, the Social Democrats would have a good chance of returning to power under the leadership of Olof Palme. In his pledge to fight unemployment Ullsten noted that 2.6% of the work force was jobless and that 40% of the unemployed consisted of young people.

Ullsten, unlike his predecessor, was eager to push ahead energetically with Sweden's nuclear program. Six reactors were in operation, and more were ready for activation in an energy-hungry nation dependent upon imported oil. But he promised not to proceed further until a geological study

SWEDEN

Education. (1976–77) Primary, pupils 708,986, teachers 41,150; secondary, pupils 545,253, teachers 46,994; teacher training, students (1975–76) 12,622, teachers 1,100; higher (including 13 universities), students 125,800.

Finance. Monetary unit: krona, with (Sept. 18, 1978) a free rate of 4.42 kronor to U.S. $1 (8.67 kronor = £1 sterling). Gold, SDR's, and foreign exchange (June 1978) U.S. $4,178,000,000. Budget (1977–78 est.): revenue 111,558,-000,000 kronor; expenditure 120,002,000,000 kronor. Gross domestic product (1977) 351,320,000,000 kronor. Money supply (May 1978) 36,320,000,000 kronor. Cost of living (1975 = 100; June 1978) 134.9.

Foreign Trade. (1977) Imports 90,240,000,000 kronor; exports 84,305,000,000 kronor. Import sources: West Germany 19%; U.K. 11%; U.S. 7%; Denmark 7%; Finland 6%; Norway 6%; The Netherlands 5%. Export destinations: Norway 13%; U.K. 11%; West Germany 10%; Denmark 9%; Finland 6%; France 5%; U.S. 5%. Main exports: machinery 26%; motor vehicles 10%; paper 9%; iron and steel 7%; ships and boats 6%; wood pulp 6%; chemicals 5%; timber 5%.

Transport and Communications. Roads (1976) 124,837 km (including 735 km expressways). Motor vehicles in use (1976): passenger 2,881,300; commercial 165,-200. Railways: (1976) 12,066 km (including 7,479 km electrified); traffic (1977) 5,520,000,000 passenger-km, freight 14,220,000,000 net ton-km. Air traffic (including Swedish apportionment of international operations of Scandinavian Airlines System; 1977): 3,731,000,000 passenger-km; freight 183,870,000 net ton-km. Shipping (1977): merchant vessels 100 gross tons and over 728; gross tonnage 7,429,394. Telephones (June 1977) 5,673,-400. Radio licenses (Dec. 1976) 3,203,000. Television licenses (Dec. 1976) 2,988,000.

Agriculture. Production (in 000; metric tons; 1977): wheat *c.* 1,562; barley *c.* 1,992; oats *c.* 1,399; rye *c.* 364; potatoes 1,346; sugar, raw value *c.* 342; rapeseed 277; apples *c.* 144; cow's milk *c.* 3,247; beef and veal 147; pork 301; timber (cu m; 1976) 55,660; fish catch (1976) 209. Livestock (in 000; June 1977): cattle *c.* 1,876; sheep (1976) *c.* 382; pigs *c.* 2,585; chickens (1976) *c.* 11,692.

Industry. Index of industrial production (1975 = 100; 1977) 96. Production (in 000; metric tons; 1977): cement 2,529; electricity (kw-hr) 87,600,000 (63% hydroelectric in 1976); iron ore (60–65% metal content) 25,414; pig iron 2,310; crude steel 3,955; silver (1976) 0.14; petroleum products (1976) 14,427; sulfuric acid (1975) 793; manmade fibres (1976) 31; wood pulp (1976) mechanical *c.* 1,626, chemical *c.* 6,718; newsprint 1,111; other paper (1976) 3,810; passenger cars (units; 1976) 307. Merchant vessels launched (100 gross tons and over; 1977) 2,127,000 gross tons. New dwelling units (1977) 54,900.

Sweden

Parliamentary speaker Henry Allard (standing) presented the members of Sweden's new Liberal minority government to King Carl XVI Gustaf (head of table) in October.

determined where in Sweden radioactive wastes from reactors could be "safely stored"—the issue that had caused the collapse of the previous government. Ullsten was concerned about women's rights and, significantly, one-third of his ministers were women. However, the key Cabinet posts were filled by men.

Sweden's economic upswing was being shepherded by Erik Huss, the new industry minister, whose tasks were formidable. Real incomes had not yet returned to the 1976 levels. Private consumption dropped by 1% in 1977 and by an estimated 2% in 1978. Nonetheless, key industries were recovering after the 1977 debacle in which important industrial sectors suddenly stagnated or even collapsed. For example, the bottom fell out of shipbuilding, partly as a result of high production and wage costs. The industry was afterward partly nationalized. Forest industries were leading the way out of crisis, although pulp prices remained low. Paper performed better, and timber and steel started to move once again. The inflow of orders to the heavy-machinery sector, accounting for 40% of Swedish exports, proved encouraging, while Saab and Volvo, Sweden's two automotive groups, enjoyed brisk sales. In a deal first announced in May, the Norwegian government and private investors arranged to buy a 40% share in Volvo in order to revitalize the concern with fresh capital for technical development.

Massive foreign loans increased Sweden's foreign exchange reserves by nearly 10 billion kronor in 1978. Kronor devaluations totaling 18% since 1976 and a decision in August 1977 to leave the European currency "snake" were cited as prime factors behind the business upswing. A question facing policymakers was whether neutral Sweden should seek more intimate ties with the expanding European Economic Community (EEC). Full membership in the EEC was deemed not possible because of Sweden's nonalignment policy—in part dictated by the nation's geopolitical position in the Baltic area. Another question was whether to develop a new generation of domestically produced jet fighters. Sweden's powerful Air Force, spearheaded by the Viggen jet, was a mainstay in defense strategy, but the new B3LA project was fiercely debated because of the enormous projected costs. (ROGER NYE CHOATE)

Swimming

The world swimming championships, held in West Berlin, August 20–28, provided a showcase for the resurgence of U.S. women's swimming. Since 1973 East Germany had dominated women's swimming, having decisively defeated the U.S. team in the two preceding world championships (1973 and 1975) and also at the 1976 Olympic Games. In the 1978 tournament, however, the U.S. triumphed and the East Germans finished third.

The U.S. men continued their dominance of the sport, though not quite as impressively as in the 1976 Olympics. A significant development was the growing power of the Soviet Union's men's team. The ten-day tournament produced 13 world and 188 national records, including 15 set by U.S. swimmers. The swimming pool, designed for the 1936 Olympics, was completely renovated at a cost estimated by the 1978 organization committee at DM 14.1 million (approximately U.S. $7.5 million). A record 49 nations participated in the championships. The U.S. won 20 gold, 12 silver, and 4 bronze medals to lead all countries. Eleven of the gold medals were won by the men's team. The Soviet Union, the runner-up with four gold, four silver, and five bronze medals, was led by teenage breaststrokers Julia Bogdanova, 14, and Lina Kachushite, 15, and by Vladimir Salnikov, 18, winner of the 400- and 1,500-m freestyle events.

The dethroning of the East Germans was so complete that they were not able to win a gold medal until the final day, when world record holder Barbara Krause, 19, streaked home first in the 100-m freestyle. Their final medal count was one gold, seven silver, and four bronze. By contrast, they won 11 gold medals in the 1976 Olympics, all by women.

The big story of the tournament was Tracy Caulkins, 15, of Nashville, Tenn., who won five gold medals and one silver. She set world records in the 200-m individual medley (2 min 14.07 sec) and 400-m individual medley (4 min 40.83 sec); tied another world standard in the 200-m butterfly (2 min 9.87 sec); and helped her U.S. team win two relay gold medals, the 400-m freestyle team setting a world mark at 3 min 43.43 sec. She was also the runner-up in the 100-m breaststroke.

Named the outstanding swimmer at the world championships, Caulkins made her most sensational swim in the 400-m individual medley, dethroning the world record holder, East Germany's Ulrike Tauber. Her time of 4 min 40.83 sec was almost two seconds faster than the world standard of 4 min 42.77 sec set in the 1976 Olympics.

World Records Set in 1978

Event	Name	Country	Time
MEN			
200-m individual medley	Aleksandr Sidorenko	U.S.S.R.	2 min 05.24 sec
	Steve Lundquist	U.S.	2 min 04.39 sec
	Graham Smith	Canada	2 min 03.65 sec
400-m individual medley	Jesse Vassallo	U.S.	4 min 23.39 sec
			4 min 20.05 sec
400-m freestyle relay	U.S. national team (Jack Babashoff, Ambrose Gaines, James Montgomery, David McCagg)		3 min 19.74 sec
800-m freestyle relay	U.S. national team (Bruce Furniss, Billy Forrester, Bobby Hackett, Ambrose Gaines)		7 min 20.82 sec
WOMEN			
100-m freestyle	Barbara Krause	E. Ger.	55.41 sec
200-m freestyle	Barbara Krause	E. Ger.	1 min 59.04 sec
	Cynthia Woodhead	U.S.	1 min 58.53 sec
400-m freestyle	Kim Linehan	U.S.	4 min 07.66 sec
	Tracey Wickham	Australia	4 min 06.28 sec
800-m freestyle	Michelle Ford	Australia	8 min 34.86 sec
			8 min 31.30 sec
	Tracey Wickham	Australia	8 min 30.53 sec
			8 min 24.62 sec
1,500-m freestyle	Tracey Wickham	Australia	16 min 14.93 sec
200-m backstroke	Linda Jezek	U.S.	2 min 11.93 sec
100-m breaststroke	Julia Bogdanova	U.S.S.R.	1 min 10.31 sec
200-m breaststroke	Julia Bogdanova	U.S.S.R.	2 min 33.32 sec
	Lina Kachushite	U.S.S.R.	2 min 31.42 sec
100-m butterfly	Andrea Pollack	E. Ger.	59.46 sec
200-m butterfly	Andrea Pollack	E. Ger.	2 min 11.20 sec
			2 min 09.87 sec
	Tracy Caulkins	U.S.	2 min 09.87 sec
200-m individual medley	Tracy Caulkins	U.S.	2 min 15.09 sec
			2 min 14.07 sec
400-m individual medley	Tracy Caulkins	U.S.	4 min 40.83 sec
400-m freestyle relay	U.S. national team (Tracy Caulkins, Stephanie Elkins, Jill Sterkel, Cynthia Woodhead)		3 min 43.43 sec

Australia's Tracey Wickham, 15, showed that she must be considered the next star to emerge from that once-powerful swimming nation. In winning the 400-m freestyle in 4 min 6.28 sec she lowered the world record by more than one second.

Another outstanding competitor for the U.S. was 14-year-old Cynthia Woodhead, who was a threat in every freestyle event from the 100 m to the 800 m. She set a world mark of 1 min 58.53 sec in winning the 200-m freestyle, was runner-up in the 400-m and 800-m freestyles, and helped her relay teams to two gold medals with a time for her leg on the 400-m freestyle relay second only to East Germany's Barbara Krause.

Linda Jezek, 18, of Santa Clara, Calif., regained for the U.S. the backstroke titles that had been held by East Germany since 1973. Her clocking of 2 min 11.93 sec in the 200-m event erased the old world mark of 2 min 12.47 sec.

Lina Kachushite continued the Soviet stranglehold in women's breaststroke, as her 2 min 31.42 sec for the 200-m event erased the previous time of 2 min 33.32 sec set by her teammate Julia Bogdanova. The latter finished second and won the 100-m event.

In men's competition the U.S. unveiled a new teenage champion, Jesse Vassallo, who had just turned 17. Vassallo, after setting a world record in the 400-m individual medley at the U.S. national tournament in early August, further lowered his world best of 4 min 23.39 sec to 4 min 20.05 sec. A Puerto Rican by birth, Vassallo won his second gold medal in the 200-m backstroke and captured a silver in the 200-m individual medley. In that event Canada's Graham Smith (*see* BIOGRAPHIES) lowered the world mark from 2 min 4.39 sec to 2 min 3.65 sec.

WIDE WORLD

Greg Louganis was photographed at mid-spin during the ten-metre tower competition in the world swimming championships in West Berlin in August. The 18-year-old Californian won the gold medal in the platform diving event.

WIDE WORLD

Diving. Irina Kalinina of the Soviet Union, winner of the 1975 world event in springboard and runner-up in platform, won both events at the world meet in Berlin. On the springboard, Cynthia Potter and Jennifer Chandler of the U.S. finished second and third. In platform diving Martina Jaeschke of East Germany and Melissa Briley of the U.S. were second and third.

In men's diving Phil Boggs of the U.S. won his third successive world title on the springboard, trailed by Falk Hoffmann of East Germany and Giorgio Cagnotto of Italy. In the platform event 1976 Olympic silver medalist Greg Louganis of the U.S. moved up to win the gold medal, with Hoffmann again second and Vladimir Alenik of the U.S.S.R. third. (ALBERT SCHOENFIELD)

Stella Taylor, a 46-year-old marathon swimmer, embarked on a swim of over 100 miles from Orange Cay in The Bahamas to Florida in October. Rough seas and jellyfish stings forced her to abandon her efforts about 20 miles from Miami, Florida.

Switzerland

A federal republic in west central Europe consisting of a confederation of 26 cantons, Switzerland is bounded by West Germany, Austria, Liechtenstein, Italy, and France. Area: 41,293 sq km (15,943 sq mi). Pop. (1978 est.): 6,292,000. Cap.: Bern (pop., 1977 est., 146,500). Largest city: Zürich (pop., 1977 est., 382,900). Language (1970): German 65%; French 18%; Italian 12%; Romansh 1%. Religion (1970): Roman Catholic 49.4%; Protestant 47.7%. President in 1978, Willi Ritschard.

A historic event was the approval, in the federal plebiscite on Sept. 24, 1978, of a revision of the federal constitution creating the 26th canton of the Swiss Confederation, by 1,309,722 votes to 281,917 (82% of the voters at the customarily low participation rate of 41.5%). It ended years of controversy and was hailed by all as a victory of political common sense.

The new canton, Jura, was composed of three districts, all formerly part of the canton of Bern: Porrentruy, Franches-Montagnes, and Delémont. The (French-speaking) population numbered 67,000 (54,000 Catholics and 10,000 Protestants), or a little more than 1% of Switzerland's total. Territorially, Jura ranked 14th among the cantons, with 837 sq km (323 sq mi). Of its population, 58% was engaged in industry and 12% worked in

Switzerland

648

Syria

Syria

SWITZERLAND

Education. (1977–78) Primary, pupils 537,600, teachers (excluding craft teachers; 1961–62) 23,761; secondary, pupils 418,800, teachers (full time; 1961–62) 6,583; vocational, pupils 198,100; teacher training, students 12,100; higher (including 9 universities), students 67,900, teaching staff (universities and equivalent institutions only) 5,414.

Finance. Monetary unit: Swiss franc, with (Sept. 18, 1978) a free rate of SFr 1.58 to U.S. $1 (SFr 3.09 = £1 sterling). Gold and foreign exchange (June 1978) U.S. $13,-613,000,000. Budget (1977 actual): revenue SFr 12,-959,000,000; expenditure SFr 14,211,000,000. Gross national product (1977) SFr 152.3 billion. Money supply (May 1978) SFr 68,490,000,000. Cost of living (1975 = 100; June 1978) 104.4.

Foreign Trade. (1977) Imports SFr 42,932,000,000; exports SFr 42,011,000,000. Import sources: EEC 67% (West Germany 28%, France 12%, Italy 10%, U.K. 7%); U.S. 7%. Export destinations: EEC 46% (West Germany 17%, France 9%, Italy 8%, U.K. 6%); U.S. 7%; Austria 5%. Main exports: machinery 32%; chemicals 21%; watches and clocks 8%; precious metals and stones 6%; textile yarns and fabrics 5%. Tourism (1976): visitors 5,879,000; gross receipts U.S. $2,191,000,000.

Transport and Communications. Roads (1976) 62,093 km (including 680 km expressways). Motor vehicles in use (1976): passenger 1,863,600; commercial 168,580. Railways: (1975) 4,970 km (including 4,941 km electrified); traffic (1977) 8,028,000,000 passenger-km, freight 5,923,-000,000 net ton-km. Air traffic (1977): 9,269,000,000 passenger-km; freight 377,854,000 net ton-km. Shipping (1977): merchant vessels 100 gross tons and over 28; gross tonnage 252,746. Telephones (Jan. 1977) 4,016,300. Radio licenses (Dec. 1976) 2,107,900. Television licenses (Dec. 1976) 1,809,000.

Agriculture. Production (in 000; metric tons; 1977): wheat 388; barley 175; oats 45; corn (1976) c. 139; potatoes c. 870; rapeseed c. 21; apples c. 230; pears (1976) c. 90; sugar, raw value (1976) 83; wine c. 112; milk 3,460; butter 35; cheese c. 115; beef and veal 148; pork 261. Livestock (in 000; April 1977): cattle 2,001; sheep 368; pigs 2,065; chickens 6,053.

Industry. Index of industrial production (1975 = 100; 1977) 106. Production (in 000; metric tons; 1976): aluminum 78; cement 3,546; petroleum products 4,681; man-made fibres (1976) 82; cigarettes (units) 27,788,000; watches (exports; units) 42,143; manufactured gas (cu m) 94,000; electricity (kw-hr; 1977) 44,626,000.

agriculture (double the national average). Jura's constitution had progressive features, such as a provision for a department of women's affairs and enfranchisement at 18. The Christian Democrats represented about 30% of the electorate.

Elections to the Federal Parliament were not due until 1979 and the political scene was calm at the federal level. Discussion and government action revolved mostly around the issues submitted to popular plebiscites: an initiative to submit the construction of each new piece of highway to a plebiscite in the area concerned (rejected); a constitutional article conferring better defined powers of economic control on the federal government (accepted); the introduction of daylight saving time (rejected); an increase in the official price of milk (to help the dairy industry; accepted); a formula to facilitate abortion (rejected); an increase in federal aid to the universities (rejected); the banning of automobile traffic on 12 Sundays during the year (rejected); and the creation of a federal security police to supplement the existing cantonal police and to combat the increased threat of terrorism (rejected). A federal law for the protection of animals was accepted, but it was considered insufficient by lovers of wildlife. There was widespread dispute over whether the people should be called upon to decide on the construction of each

new nuclear power plant and whether a general moratorium should be imposed on the construction of new plants.

On December 3 the Federal Parliament elected Hans Hürlimann, Christian Democrat member of the Federal Council and minister of the interior, to the presidency of the Confederation for 1979. The draft "total revision" of the federal constitution aroused critical comment on various points, and its necessity was being questioned in some quarters. It called for reinforcement and modernization of fundamental rights, social institutions, private and public property rights, and the economy generally; the introduction of civil service as a substitute for military service; redistribution of responsibilities and powers between the cantons and the federal government; and the enfranchisement of all citizens at the age of 18.

Switzerland continued to boast one of the world's lowest rates of inflation. Unemployment remained within tolerable limits, although some export industries (watchmaking in particular) suffered from the continued overevaluation of the Swiss franc in world markets. Meanwhile, the growth rate stagnated at around 2 to 3.5%. The federal budget deficit caused concern; although it was less than had been expected, it had to be added to the SFr 5.2 billion in deficits accumulated since 1973.

In international relations, eventual adherence to the UN remained a topic of unenthusiastic public discussion, as did adhesion to the European Social Charter; the government continued to support the idea of UN membership. In March, at the Belgrade, Yugos., conference charged with following up the Helsinki agreements of 1975, the Swiss government continued to champion a set of formulas for the pacific solution of international conflicts.

(MELANIE STAERK)

Syria

A republic in southwestern Asia on the Mediterranean Sea, Syria is bordered by Turkey, Iraq, Jordan, Israel, and Lebanon. Area: 185,180 sq km (71,498 sq mi). Pop. (1977 est.): 7,845,000. Cap. and largest city: Damascus (pop., 1977 est., 1,097,-000). Language: Arabic (official); also Kurdish, Armenian, Turkish, and Circassian. Religion: predominantly Muslim. President in 1978, Gen. Hafez al-Assad; premiers, Abdul Rahman Khleifawi and, from March 27, Muhammad Ali al-Halabi.

In 1978 Syria tried to maintain a policy balanced between outright opposition to Egyptian Pres. Anwar as-Sadat's peace initiative with Israel and support for the Palestine Liberation Organization (PLO) on the one hand and the avoidance of war with Israel on the other. Its difficulties were increased by the involvement of its forces in Lebanon in fighting with Lebanese rightists and, until the latter part of the year, by its dispute with the rival Baathist regime in Iraq.

From the beginning of the year Syria accused Egypt of aiming at a separate peace agreement with Israel. Pres. Hafez al-Assad attended the anti-Sadat Front of Steadfastness summit meeting in

SYRIA

Education. (1976–77) Primary, pupils 1,287,287, teachers 39,415; secondary, pupils 374,365, teachers 28,158; vocational, pupils 22,487, teachers 2,446; teacher training, students 7,303, teachers 568; higher (1974–75), students 64,094, teaching staff 989.

Finance. Monetary unit: Syrian pound, with (Sept. 18, 1978) a par value of S£3.925 to U.S. $1 (free rate of S£7.69 = £1 sterling). Gold, SDR's, and foreign exchange (Sept. 1977) U.S. $717 million. Budget (total; 1978 est.) balanced at S£18,200 million. Gross domestic product (1976) S£22,957 million. Money supply (Sept. 1977) S£10,166 million. Cost of living (Damascus; 1975 = 100; March 1978) 130.

Foreign Trade. (1977) Imports S£10,605,000,000; exports S£4,199.2 million. Import sources: West Germany 14%; Saudi Arabia 10%; Romania 9%; France 8%; Italy 7%; Japan 6%. Export destinations: Italy 13%; U.S.S.R. c. 10%; West Germany 8%; France 7%; The Netherlands 7%; Belgium-Luxembourg 6%; Saudi Arabia 5%; U.K. 5%. Main exports: crude oil 58%; cotton 21%.

Transport and Communications. Roads (1975) c. 13,-300 km. Motor vehicles in use (1976): passenger 62,800; commercial (including buses) 55,900. Railways (1976): 1,-761 km; traffic 165.7 million passenger-km, freight 305.2 million net ton-km. Air traffic (1976): 712 million passenger-km; freight 7.6 million net ton-km. Telephones (Jan. 1977) 176,900. Radio receivers (June 1976) 1,232,000. Television receivers (Dec. 1975) 224,000.

Agriculture. Production (in 000; metric tons; 1977): wheat 1,217; barley 337; potatoes (1976) c. 135; pumpkins (1976) c. 120; cucumbers (1976) c. 180; tomatoes c. 550; onions c. 100; watermelons (1976) c. 500; melons (1976) c. 200; grapes c. 319; olives c. 238; cottonseed c. 245; cotton, lint c. 160. Livestock (in 000; 1977): sheep c. 6,817; goats c. 985; cattle (1976) c. 555; horses (1976) c. 55; asses (1976) c. 240; chickens c. 24,600.

Industry. Production (in 000; metric tons; 1976): cement 1,110; crude oil (1977) 10,680; natural gas (cu m) 454,000; petroleum products c. 2,830; cotton yarn 32; electricity (kw-hr) 1,862,000.

Algiers on February 2–4, but Algerian Pres. Houari Boumédienne's efforts to secure an Iraqi-Syrian reconciliation to strengthen the front failed because of Iraq's refusal to attend the talks.

Syria maintained close relations with the U.S.S.R. President Assad visited Moscow in February and again in October, after a visit to East Germany. Beginning in January there were increased Soviet military supplies to Syria including missiles, tanks, and planes. Syria also received some French and West German arms, partly financed by Libya. The defense allocation in Syria's 1978 budget was $1.1 billion, about one-quarter of the total and a 10% increase over 1977. Relations with the U.S. were generally cool, although Syria maintained contacts with Western countries. Assad visited West Germany in September and publicly disagreed with the Bonn government over President Sadat's peace initiative. Assad met U.S. Secretary of State Cyrus Vance in Damascus following the Camp David summit between Sadat and Israeli Prime Minister Menahem Begin in September, but refused to modify his opposition to the agreements. In August the U.S. Congress voted to cut U.S. aid to Syria although the cuts were later partially restored.

Syria's immediate preoccupation remained Lebanon, where 30,000 of its troops continued to form the bulk of the Arab Deterrent Force, costing Syria an estimated $70 million a month. Serious clashes between Syrians and Lebanese right-wing militia occurred in February. When Israel invaded southern Lebanon on March 14–15, Syria avoided war with Israel by keeping its forces north of the Litani River. In May Syria warned the Palestinians against their continuing clashes with the UN forces in south Lebanon. On the other hand, Syria roundly condemned the Lebanese parliamentary declaration of April 27 calling for an end to all Palestinian and non-Palestinian armed action on Lebanese territory.

Following the killing on June 13 of Tony Franjieh, Syria's principal ally among the Lebanese Christian leadership, Syria's relations with the Lebanese rightists deteriorated sharply. There were severe clashes in July and again in September and October. Syrian forces surrounded and bombarded Christian East Beirut, while Israeli planes regularly flew over the city to demonstrate their support for the Lebanese Christians. A hastily convened meeting of Arab foreign ministers in Lebanon arranged for Syrian forces to be withdrawn from the perimeter of East Beirut and replaced by non-Syrian troops; an uneasy calm was thus restored.

Syria's relations with Jordan cooled in the early part of the year because of King Hussein's refusal to condemn outright President Sadat's peace initiative, but they improved again after Hussein's visit to Damascus on July 20 when he gave assurances that Jordan would not join the negotiations. A major shift in Syria's Arab relations was achieved when President Assad visited Baghdad and on October 26 agreed with the Iraqi government to bury all their outstanding differences.

In a plebiscite held on February 8, President Assad was elected to a second seven-year term as president, beginning March 1978, by a huge majority. In accordance with the constitution a new Cabinet was then formed on March 30 under Premier Muhammad Ali al-Halabi.

(PETER MANSFIELD)

Table Tennis

Toward the end of 1977 the International Olympic Committee (IOC) extended formal recognition to the International Table Tennis Federation. This act did not of itself guarantee that table tennis would automatically be included in future Olympic Games, but it was a significant decision. The final decision would be left up to the host country, which would be guided by standards imposed by the IOC program commission.

Major tournaments during the year included the 11th European Championships, which were played in mid-March in Duisburg, West Germa-

1978 World Rankings

MEN	WOMEN
1. Mitsuru Kono (Japan)	1. Pak Yung Sun (North Korea)
2. Kua Yao-hua (China)	2. Chang Li (China)
3. Huang Liang (China)	3. Chang Te-ying (China)
4. Liang Ko-liang (China)	4. Ko Hsin-ai (China)
5. Gabor Gergely (Hung.)	5. Yang Ying (China)
6. Istvan Jonger (Hung.)	6. Chung Hyan Sook (South Korea)
7. Desmond Douglas (England)	7. Judit Magos (Hung.)
8. Milan Orlowski (Czech.)	8. Jill Hammersley (England)
9. Jacques Secretin (France)	9. Ann-Christin Hellman (Sweden)
10. Tibor Klampar (Hung.)	10. Kayoko Kawahigashi (Japan)

Wilfried Lieck and Wiebke Hendriksen of West Germany teamed up to win the European mixed doubles championship during the March tournament held in Duisburg, West Germany.

ny. Hungary overwhelmed the 29 other participating associations by capturing not only both team titles but the men's singles (Gabor Gergely) and the women's singles (Judit Magos) as well. The men's doubles was won by Gergely and Milan Orlowski (Czech.), the women's doubles by Maria Alexandru and Liana Mihut (Rom.), and the mixed doubles by Wilfried Lieck and Weibke Hendriksen (West Germany). In the European League, 27 national teams competed during the 1977–78 season. France won the Super Division, West Germany Division 1, Italy Division 2, and Turkey Division 3. In Europe Club competition, Sparta Prague won the men's cup and Statisztika Budapest the women's cup.

The Europe Top Twelve Players tournament was held in Prague, Czech., in late January. The top three finishers in the men's division were Gergely, Orlowski, and Stellan Bengtsson (Sweden). In the women's competition, Jill Hammersley (England) was followed by Bettine Vriesekoop (Neth.) and Valentina Popova (U.S.S.R.). The first African Clubs tournament, which was held in Egypt during March, was won by the Arab Contractors Club of Egypt. The first Latin-American championships, also held in March, took place in Mexico City. Mexico won the men's team title and Peru the women's team title. Venezuela dominated the individual events by winning both the men's and women's singles titles and the mixed doubles. Mexico's desire to promote and improve the quality of Latin-American table tennis was evident in October 1977 when the Mexican Federation, under the auspices of the Mexican Olympic Committee, welcomed representatives from 13 countries to a month-long seminar for coaches, organizers, and umpires.   (ARTHUR KINGSLEY VINT)

Taiwan

Taiwan, which consists of the islands of Formosa and Quemoy and other surrounding islands, is the seat of the Republic of China (Nationalist China).

Taiwan

It is north of the Philippines, southwest of Japan, and east of Hong Kong. The island of Formosa has an area of 35,779 sq km (13,814 sq mi); including its 77 outlying islands (14 in the Taiwan group and 63 in the Pescadores group), the area of Taiwan totals 35,982 sq km (13,893 sq mi). Pop. (1978 est.): 16,978,200. Cap. and largest city: Taipei (pop., 1978 est., 2,144,400). Presidents in 1978, Yen Chiakan and, from May 20, Chiang Ching-kuo; presidents of the Executive Yuan (premiers), Chiang Ching-kuo and, from May 29, Sun Yun-suan.

While the remarkable economic growth and steady political progress of Taiwan continued in 1978, its diplomatic position as the legal government of all China deteriorated further. On December 15 the U.S. announced that, as of Jan. 1, 1979, it would extend full diplomatic recognition to the People's Republic, at the same time breaking relations with the Nationalists and giving a year's notice of termination of the U.S.-Taiwan mutual security treaty. This left only 21 nations–none of them a great power–still maintaining diplomatic relations with Taiwan.

Although the Nationalists had been expecting the U.S. move since Pres. Richard M. Nixon's 1972 visit to Peking, Pres. Chiang Ching-kuo, on December 16, made a strong protest to Leonard Unger, the U.S. ambassador to Taipei. He also issued a statement denouncing the decision and stating that "the United States government cannot be expected to have the confidence of any free nation in the future." According to U.S. officials, all U.S. agreements with Taiwan except the mutual security treaty were to remain in force, unofficial cultural and economic contacts would be maintained, and the sale of certain defensive arms to the Nationalists would be continued. On December 27 a U.S. delegation headed by Deputy Secretary of State Warren Christopher, arriving in Taipei to discuss future relations between the two countries, was attacked by an angry mob, and Christopher was slightly injured when the windows of his car were broken. The talks, held after Chiang promised to ensure the delegation's safety, produced no tangible results.

Earlier in the year, Taiwan had interpreted as a deliberate snub U.S. Vice-Pres. Walter Mondale's failure to include Taiwan in his tour of Asia-Pacific nations. Similarly, the president's national security adviser, Zbigniew Brzezinsky, omitted Taiwan from his itinerary following his special mission to Peking, although he did make stops in Japan and South Korea. Either by design or by oversight, Brzezinsky arrived in Peking on May 20, the same day that former premier Chiang Ching-kuo was inaugurated as the Nationalists' third president, and no congratulatory message was sent to Chiang by the White House.

Political stability and unity were demonstrated in the smooth transfer of power in accordance with the 1948 constitution. The 1,248-member National Assembly held its sixth congress from February 19 to March 25 for the purpose of electing the president and vice-president. Chiang was elected president by 1,184 out of 1,204 votes, and former governor Shieh Tung-min, a Taiwanese, was elected vice-president by 941 out of 1,189. In his inauguration address on May 20, Chiang reiterated the Nationalist government's firm anti-Communist stand and its basic policy against establishing contact with any Communist regime, and pledged to maintain the Republic of China's place in the democratic camp.

On May 26 President Chiang appointed Sun Yun-suan as president of the Executive Yuan (premier). On May 29 Premier Sun was sworn in with the Executive Yuan (Cabinet), which was composed of over a dozen ministers, six of whom were born in Taiwan. Former Taipei mayor Lin Yang-kang and former Cabinet minister Lee Teng-hui, both Taiwanese, were named governor of Taiwan and mayor of Taipei, respectively. The prominence of native Taiwanese in the government marked a significant change in the dominant political position of the mainlanders.

The appointment of Sun, a former economics minister, as premier reflected Taiwan's increasing emphasis on economic growth as the best insurance for its future. Ten current development projects costing U.S. $4.5 billion, including nuclear power plants and petrochemical industries, were scheduled for completion in 1979, and 12 major projects with an estimated cost of $5.5 billion were initiated in 1978. The gross national product increased from $17 billion in 1976 to $20.8 billion in 1977; per capita income rose from $967 to $1,088.

Taiwan's economy continued to depend largely on foreign trade, with industrial products leading the export list. Trade totaled $17,836,700,000 in 1977 and had already reached more than $15.2 bil-

lion in the first eight months of 1978. The U.S. remained the country's number one trading partner, followed by Japan. To reduce its chronic trade surplus with the U.S., Taiwan sent special trade missions to the U.S. in January and June to purchase about $1 billion in additional American goods.   (HUNG-TI CHU)

Thousands of people packed the square outside the Sun Yat-sen Memorial Hall in Taipei after the inauguration of Chiang Ching-kuo as president of Nationalist China (Taiwan) in May.

TAIWAN

Education. (1976–77) Primary, pupils 2,341,413, teachers 64,974; secondary, pupils 1,240,803, teachers 51,945; vocational, pupils 296,493, teachers 10,447; higher, students 299,414, teaching staff 14,548.

Finance. Monetary unit: new Taiwan dollar, with (Sept. 18, 1978) a par value of NT$36 to U.S. $1 (free rate of NT$70.54 = £1 sterling). Gold and foreign exchange (June 1978) U.S. $1,462,000,000. Budget (1976–77 est.): revenue NT$170,181,000,000; expenditure NT$170,116,-000,000. Gross national product (1977) NT$740,640,000,-000. Money supply (May 1978) NT$176,240,000,000. Cost of living (1975 = 100; June 1978) 115.1.

Foreign Trade. (1977) Imports NT$323,840,000,000; exports NT$355,240,000,000. Import sources: Japan 31%; U.S. 23%; Kuwait 8%; Saudi Arabia 6%. Export destinations: U.S. 39%; Japan 12%; Hong Kong 7%. Main exports: clothing 14%; food 12%; textile yarns and fabrics 10%; telecommunications apparatus 9%; footwear 7%; veneers and plywood 5%.

Transport and Communications. Roads (1976) 17,172 km. Motor vehicles in use (1976): passenger 171,000; commercial 129,900. Railways (1976): 4,200 km; traffic 8,479,-000,000 passenger-km, freight 2,891,000,000 net ton-km. Air traffic (1976): 2,908,000,000 passenger-km; freight 171.6 million net ton-km. Shipping (1977): merchant vessels 100 gross tons and over 443; gross tonnage 1,559,000. Telephones (Dec. 1976) 1,396,000. Radio licenses (Dec. 1976) 1,493,100. Television licenses (Dec. 1976) 913,900.

Agriculture. Production (in 000; metric tons; 1976): rice 2,713; sweet potatoes 1,851; barley 644; corn 114; cassava 294; sugar, raw value 779; citrus fruit 384; bananas 213; pineapples 279; tea 25; pork c. 503; fish catch 811. Livestock (in 000; Dec. 1976): cattle 253; pigs 3,676; goats 211; chickens 28,354.

Industry. Production (in 000; metric tons; 1976): coal 3,236; crude oil 247; natural gas (cu m) 1,836,000; electricity (kw-hr) 26,877,000; cement 8,749; crude steel 597; sulfuric acid 449; petroleum products 10,470; cotton yarn 147; man-made fibres 341; paper c. 500; radio receivers (units) 6,849; television receivers (units) 3,850.

Tanzania

Tanzania

This republic, an East African member of the Commonwealth of Nations, consists of two parts: Tanganyika, on the Indian Ocean, bordered by Kenya, Uganda, Rwanda, Burundi, Zaire, Zambia, Malawi, and Mozambique; and Zanzibar, just off the coast, including Zanzibar Island, Pemba Island, and small islets. Total area of the united republic: 945,087 sq km (364,900 sq mi). Total pop. (1977 est.): 16,073,000, including (1966 est.) 98.9% African and 0.7% Indo-Pakistani. Cap. and largest city: Dar es Salaam (pop., 1977 est., 460,000) in Tanganyika. Language: English and Swahili. Religion (1967): traditional beliefs 34.6%; Christian 30.6%; Muslim 30.5%. President in 1978, Julius Nyerere.

The two main problems facing the government in 1978 were the need to strengthen the country's economy and uneasy relations with several of Tanzania's immediate neighbours. Some of the agricultural programs were not working well. The once efficient sisal industry was badly run down and, although West Germany made a grant of $7.5 million to replace worn-out and antiquated machinery, the real problem lay in the inefficiency of the nationalized sector. In other respects as well, West Germany was one of Tanzania's chief benefactors; it was agreed that West German aid, amounting in 1978 to $80 million ($55 million in cash and the rest in technical assistance), would take the form of a nonrepayable grant. The economy of Zanzibar, by contrast, was buoyant.

Relations with Zambia were strained because of disagreements over which section of the Rhode-

Target Sports

TANZANIA

Education. (1975–76) Primary, pupils 1,591,834, teachers 29,783; secondary and vocational, pupils 53,257, teachers 2,606; teacher training, pupils 9,930, teachers 612; higher, students 3,064, teaching staff (universities only) 434.

Finance. Monetary unit: Tanzanian shilling, with (Sept. 18, 1978) a free rate of TShs 7.58 to U.S. $1 (TShs 14.85 = £1 sterling). Gold, SDR's, and foreign exchange (June 1978) U.S. $180.2 million. Budget (1975–76 actual): revenue TShs 4,063,000,000; expenditure TShs 6,325,000,000. Gross national product (1976) TShs 22,322,000,000. Money supply (March 1978) TShs 6,122,000,000. Cost of living (1975 = 100; 1st quarter 1978) 126.1.

Foreign Trade. (1977) Imports TShs 5,975,000,000; exports TShs 4,161,000,000. Import sources (1976): U.K. 12%; Kenya 11%; Iran 9%; West Germany 8%; Japan 7%; China 6%; U.S. 6%. Export destinations: West Germany 14%; U.K. 13%; U.S. 9%; Singapore 7%; Italy 6%; Kenya 6%; Hong Kong 5%; India 5%. Main exports (1976): cotton 16%; coffee 13%; cloves 8%; sisal 6%; tobacco 5%; cashew nuts 5%; petroleum products 5%.

Transport and Communications. Roads (1975) c. 35,-000 km (including 19,200 km main roads). Motor vehicles in use (1976): passenger 42,000; commercial (including buses) 41,800. Railways (1977): c. 3,550 km. Air traffic (1976): 195 million passenger-km; freight 3.7 million net ton-km. Telephones (Jan. 1977) 68,000. Radio receivers (Dec. 1975) 232,000. Television receivers (Dec. 1974) c. 5,000.

Agriculture. Production (in 000; metric tons; 1977): corn 968; millet c. 150; sorghum c. 240; rice 194; sweet potatoes (1976) c. 441; cassava (1976) c. 5,100; sugar, raw value (1976) c. 103; dry beans c. 153; mangoes c. 174; bananas c. 790; cashew nuts (1976) 83; coffee 59; tobacco c. 21; cotton, lint c. 79; sisal c. 105; timber (cu m; 1976) 37,526; fish catch (1976) c. 181. Livestock (in 000; 1977): sheep c. 3,000; goats c. 4,700; cattle (1976) 14,362; asses c. 165; chickens c. 20,700.

Industry. Production (in 000; metric tons; 1976): cement 240; salt 22; diamonds (metric carats) c. 450; petroleum products 744; electricity (kw-hr) c. 685,000.

sian guerrilla movement should be supported and because, in February, Tanzania greatly increased the cost of storing Zambia's goods in Dar es Salaam in order to encourage a faster turnover. A small-scale border war with Uganda took place in October-November after mutual accusations of boundary infringements, while in spite of guarded optimism in Kenya, the Kenya-Tanzania border remained closed. (KENNETH INGHAM)

Target Sports

Archery. Archery continued to increase in popularity throughout the world in 1978 with new records being set by women in each of the four distances. These marks were established at regional tournaments because the world championships were not scheduled until 1979.

The records included, for men, 338 points at 70 m by Sante Spigarelli of Italy. In women's competition three Soviet archers set new individual records; they were Natalia Butuzova with 319 points at 70 m, Valentina Kovpan with 334 at 60 m, and Keto Lossaberidze with 329 at 50 m. In addition, the Soviet women's team set a new record of 3,772 points. Jadwiga Wilejto of Poland set a new women's record for 30 m of 349 points.

The archery championship of the Americas was held in Rio De Janeiro, Brazil, on November 25 and 26. This was the first time that a regional archery championship had taken place in South America. Seven nations participated with the United States dominating by winning first, second, and third for men and women and also taking first place in the team events.

Field archery continued to increase in popularity with 28 nations participating (38 women and 80 men) in the fifth world field archery championship in Geneva on September 16–17. Winners in the freestyle were Darrell Pace of the U.S. for men and Annemarie Lehmann of West Germany for women. Bare bow competition was won by Anders Rosenberg of Sweden for men and Suizuko Kobuchi of Japan for women.

Pursuing game animals and birds with bow and arrow continued to gain adherents in the U.S. with every one of the 50 states providing opportunities for the sport. The number of such hunters was listed at 1.5 million.

Shooting. The 42nd world shooting championships were held September 24-October 5 at Seoul, South Korea. Sponsored by the International Shooting Union, they attracted competitors from 63 non-Communist nations. U.S. shooters took 18 gold, 9 silver, and 6 bronze medals. Italy gained six golds, five silvers, and two bronzes. Finland won six golds, four silvers, and nine bronzes. Seven new world records were set.

TRAP AND SKEET. Eladio Vallduvi of Spain broke 198 of 200 targets to win the individual gold medal at trap. Silvano Basagni of Italy took the silver with one less. J. Ellis of Australia broke 195 to win the bronze. First place in the 600-bird team event went to the U.S. with a total of 580. A score of 576 placed the Japanese team second, while Spain was third. In women's trap competition Susan Nattrass of Canada shot a 195 to better her own world record of 192 set in 1977. W. Gentiletti of Italy was second with a score of 185, while M. Garcia of Spain was third with 179. The Italian women's trap team won first place with 387. Spain was second with 385, three points higher than the third-place U.S. team.

At skeet the Italian team took first place with a score of 578. L. Brunelli of Italy won the individual competition with a 197. The end of the three-day program—75 birds on each of the first two days and 50 on the last—found five competitors tied at 193 for second place. Three were eliminated by the ensuing shoot-off, but after remaining deadlocked at the end of three rounds, F. Roberti of Argentina and R. Garagnani of Italy each received silver medals. In women's skeet G. Hansburg of Italy won the individual title with a 189, but the West Germans took the team event with a 395.

RIFLES. U.S. shooters won 10 of the 13 team events and set a new world record score of 2,281 points for the standard big-bore rifle. Switzerland won the 300-m free rifle event with a team score of 1,537. Great Britain's 1,542 took the team kneeling small-bore free rifle match. The West Germans won the open air rifle competition with a score of 1,531. Individual gold medals were won by U.S. shooters S. Sandusky with a 50-m standard rifle score of 596, L. Bassham with a 50-m small-bore three-position score of 1,165, and L. Wigger with a 300-m free rifle three-position new world record score of 1,160. The standard big-bore rifle event was won for the U.S. by David Kimes's new world record score of 577. Wanda Jewell of the U.S., who won the standard small-bore rifle three-position event with a 580, also won the women's air rifle competition with a 385.

Great Britain took three individual first place titles. A. Allan's 599 points won the English Match, and J. Churchill's 390 were best in the small-bore free rifle kneeling event. After having trouble with his own rifle, M. Cooper fired a 379 to take the standing 300-m free rifle title, using one borrowed from Kimes. This score equaled the world record held by L. Wigger (U.S.). Swiss shooter W. Inderbitzen took first place in the 300-m free rifle prone match with a 399, while his countryman K. Bertschy won the kneeling event with a 391. E. Svensson of Sweden won the small-bore free rifle match with a 379. O. Schlipf of West Germany took the open air-rifle title with a 390.

On the running game targets at normal runs, the individual title went to J. Rinnikko of Finland with 572 points, while West Germany won the team title with 1,493. At mixed runs G. Mezzani of Italy won the individual championship with a new world record of 387. The Italian team's winning score was 1,517.

HANDGUNS. M. Minder of Switzerland shot a score of 577 to set a new free pistol world record four points higher than the old one. R. Skanaker of Sweden set a new world record for standard pistol with a 583. First place in rapid-fire pistol went to his countryman Ore Gunnarsson with 595. S. Makien of Finland took the centre-fire pistol event with a 592. Kim Dyer of the U.S. won the women's small-bore pistol match with a 590. The air pistol was won by P. Palokangas of Finland, who fired a 391. K. Hansson of Sweden shot a 382 to win the women's individual air pistol title. In team matches the free pistol event was won by Switzerland with 2,203. A score of 2,297 won the standard pistol event for the Finns. The rapid-fire match went to West Germany with 2,366 points. The centre-fire competition was won by Finland with 2,347. A score of 1,531 gave the Finns first place in the air pistol match.   (ROBERT N. SEARS)

Television and Radio

Radio and television service was available in some form in all major nations in 1978. Approximately 810 million radio sets were in use, of which 444 million, or 55%, were in the United States. Television sets numbered approximately 360 million, of which about 130 million, or 36%, were in the U.S.

The Soviet Union, with 64 million television sets, ranked next to the U.S., according to estimates published in the 1978 *Broadcasting Yearbook*, and Japan was third with 26.4 million. Other *Broadcasting* estimates included West Germany, 20.5 million; France, 14.5 million; Italy, 12.6 million; Brazil, 10.5 million; Canada, 9.9 million; Poland, 6.9 million; Spain, 6.8 million; Mexico, 5.4 million; East Germany, 5.2 million; The Netherlands, 5.1 million; and Argentina and Australia, 4 million each.

More than 6,700 television stations were on the air or under construction throughout the world. Approximately 2,200 were in the Far East, 2,110 in Western Europe, 1,050 in the U.S., 920 in Eastern Europe, 180 in South America, 105 in Mexico, 96 in Canada, and 45 in Africa. There were about 15,290 radio stations, mostly amplitude modulation (AM) but with a growing proportion of the frequency modulation (FM) type. The U.S. had 8,836, of which 4,259, or 48%, were FM.

Organization of Services. Broadcasting organizations throughout the world continued to exchange major news coverage by satellite. The funeral services for Pope Paul VI, the coronation of Pope John Paul I and subsequently his funeral, and the installation of Pope John Paul II were among the most widely distributed broadcasts. Segments of the news conference at which U.S. Pres. Jimmy Carter, Egyptian Pres. Anwar as-Sadat, and Israeli Prime Minister Menahem Begin announced the Camp David peace accords also were seen in many countries.

Relationships between broadcasters and cable

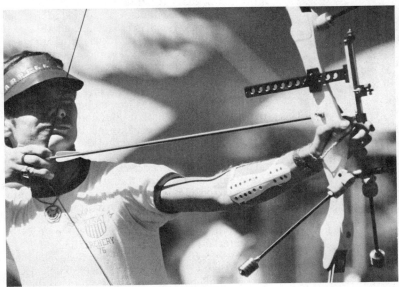

Archer Darrell Pace, 1976 Olympic gold medal winner, captured the men's archery event in the first U.S. National Sports Festival held at Colorado Springs in July.

RICH CLARKSON—SPORTS ILLUSTRATED © 1978 TIME, INC.

operators remained strained. The U.S. Supreme Court's refusal in late 1977 to review a decision stripping broadcasters of protection that had been granted by Federal Communications Commission (FCC) rules freed cable operators to compete more directly and aggressively with TV stations in sports and film programming. The FCC followed up by initiating an investigation into the economic relationship between cable and broadcast television in what it called an effort to replace "intuition" with factual information about cable's likely effect on local television stations. There were, at the time, approximately 4,000 cable systems operating in the U.S., serving 13 million homes, according to estimates compiled by *Broadcasting* magazine.

Broadcasters were stunned, as was the FCC, by a blow from another direction: the U.S. Court of Appeals for the District of Columbia struck down a major FCC policy that had given broadcasters a degree of protection that they felt they were entitled to. In cases in which new applicants seek the licenses of existing stations, the FCC had said it would renew the licenses of existing stations whenever those stations could show that they had provided "substantial" service to the public. The court ruled in September, however, that the existing stations must demonstrate "superior" service and even then might lose to challengers on other grounds, such as diversification of ownership or integration of ownership and management. Broadcasters feared that, no matter how high the quality of their service, they would be subject to challenge by—and lose their licenses to—newcomers who needed only to "promise" to provide better service or who, even without that promise, had no ownership ties to other media. Both the FCC and the broadcaster that lost the court decision, station

Carol Burnett says farewell on the final TV show of her hit series on March 29.

WIDE WORLD

WESH-TV in Daytona Beach, Fla., planned to appeal. Meanwhile, in December, the FCC gave preliminary approval to a plan that would create as many as 125 new AM radio stations by eliminating the "clear channel" stations that broadcast a powerful nighttime signal without local interference.

Congress approved new legislation authorizing increased federal funding of public broadcasting through 1983 and reducing, to $2 from the current $2.50, the amount that public broadcasters must raise for each matching federal dollar in the 1981–83 period. The legislation authorized $180 million in matching federal funds in 1981, $200 million in 1982, and $220 million in 1983.

The British government's White Paper *Broadcasting*, published in July 1978, accepted about half the recommendations of the Annan Committee on the Future of Broadcasting (whose report had appeared in April 1977), including that for a new Open Broadcasting Authority (OBA) to run a fourth television channel. The OBA would commission and buy programs with money gained by sponsorship, government funding, advertising, or other means, the aim always being to encourage novel and independently minded programming. Both British Broadcasting Corporation (BBC) and Independent Broadcasting Authority (IBA) local radio services would be expanded (in fact, each network was given nine more stations in October). Most controversial of the White Paper's proposals was that the BBC should be made more accountable through the setting up of management boards consisting of half government appointees and half BBC staff.

In Italy a new bill was introduced to regulate the thousands of private local stations that had sprung up since the Constitutional Court announced in 1974 and again in 1976 that the monopoly of Radiotelevisione Italiana (RAI) did not extend to local broadcasting. By mid-1978 there were 2,275 radio stations and 506 TV stations—all technically illegal—taking advantage of the court's decision. Under the proposed new legislation private stations could apply for licenses (costing 338,000 lire for a TV station and 100,000 lire for a radio station). Stations would be generally restricted to a radius of 15 km (9 mi). Every town of 10,000 inhabitants or more would have at least one radio station.

The tensions in French broadcasting between the Société Française de Production (SFP), the state production company, and the three state TV program companies resulted in October in a series of strikes that stopped both production and transmission. The strikes were triggered by SFP's deficit (about $50 million by the end of the year) and the high prices it charged the program companies.

The Australian Broadcasting Commission faced severe problems during the year due to government controls of spending and personnel. Its programs, however, continued to attract audiences. Against strong competition, the ABC secured in October the first rights, for the next ten years, to BBC material for showing in Australia.

The new regime in China gave the development of television a new, urgent priority. The existing two national channels would be supplemented by

WIDE WORLD

A winner for ABC in the fall TV network ratings war was "Battlestar Galactica."

three more, plus a local channel for Peking. The range of new programs broadcast during the summer included language lessons in English, French, and Japanese. The New China News Agency reported that there were more than one million TV sets in the country.

A new agreement for low- and medium-frequency radio broadcasting came into force on November 23. Made under the auspices of the International Telecommunication Union (ITU), it affected the ITU's regions 1 (Europe and Africa) and 3 (Asia and Australasia). The new frequency plan took account of the increase in the number and power of stations since the last agreement in 1948. Then there were 1,450 transmitters producing 82 Mw. In 1978 some 2,700 transmitters produced more than 214 Mw. Many of the industrial countries, which had gained numerous frequencies in 1948, had to give some of them up.

Programming. The U.S. continued to dominate the world TV market but in ever decreasing proportions. In 1978 the U.K. exported to the U.S. twice as much (£20 million) as it imported (£9 million). Australian TV also established itself as a major exporter. One Australian miniseries, "Against the Wind," tracing a young Irish girl's deportation to New South Wales at the end of the 18th century, rated as high as the U.S. miniseries "Holocaust."

Satellites were used increasingly for regular exchanges of programming. The Arab states started a regional exchange of programs by satellite, and the Asian-Pacific Broadcasting Union, ranging from Iran to Japan to Australia, substantially extended its network of satellite stations. Demand for satellites increasingly overran supply, sometimes

with dramatic results. During the transmission, via satellite, of the "Eurovision Song Contest," the hapless Israelis did not see their own entry in its winning moments because the satellite had to obey a prior booking to relay an Italian soccer match to South America.

U.S.-made mysteries, comedies, Westerns, made-for-television movies, and "miniseries"—dramatic programs in a limited number of episodes—were popular in 1978 in many countries. *Broadcasting* estimated that sales of U.S. programs and feature films to foreign broadcasters totaled $240 million in 1977, a 33% increase from the preceding year's record $180 million, and that they would reach at least $250 million in 1978. The gains came partly from price increases to offset rising production costs and partly from growing overseas demand for expensive made-for-TV movies and miniseries. In the latter group, some of the most widely sold were "Roots," "Washington: Behind Closed Doors," "Holocaust," "79 Park Avenue," "Rich Man, Poor Man," "Centennial," and the original miniseries trend-setter, "QB VII." Among regular television series, the most popular U.S. exports included "Kojak," "Starsky and Hutch," "Mod Squad," "Police Woman," "Hawaii Five-O," "The Six Million Dollar Man," "Gunsmoke," "Charlie's Angels," "Happy Days," and "The Mary Tyler Moore Show."

In preparing for the 1978–79 season in the U.S. the networks had canceled 12 shows, representing 17 hours of programming. ABC canceled 3½ hours, including "The Six Million Dollar Man," "Baretta," and "Fish." CBS cancellations, totaling 6½ hours, included "Kojak," "On Our Own," and "The Tony Randall Show." (CBS also lost three longtime audience favourites—"The Carol Burnett Show," "The Bob Newhart Show," and "Maude" —by decisions of their stars or producers not to continue.) NBC dropped "Police Woman," "The Bionic Woman," and "Black Sheep Squadron," among others, for a total of 7 hours.

To take their places, the networks relied heavily

Richard Chamberlain (left) and Robert Conrad starred in the NBC miniseries "Centennial," which began on October 1. The series was based on the novel by James A. Michener.

NBC PHOTO

on comedies and comedy-dramas. Inspired in large part by the success of the movie *Star Wars*, space fiction made its appearance in two series; these were "Battlestar Galactica," billed as "one of the most expensive programs ever made for television," and "Mork & Mindy," a comedy-drama featuring a character from the planet Ork, both on ABC. In all, 21 new series were introduced. *Broadcasting* estimated the cost of regular series and regularly scheduled movie nights at a record $730 million, 20% more than in 1977–78. Many of the new shows failed quickly, suggesting again the validity of the rule that not more than six out of ten new shows survive to a second year.

The three most popular shows, in terms of average audience ratings from mid-September through October, were ABC's "Three's Company," "Laverne & Shirley," and "Happy Days," in that order. The highest rated new series were ABC's "Mork & Mindy," which ranked fourth, and "Taxi!," another ABC comedy, which ranked tenth. Between them, in descending order, were five favourites that had been held over: "Little House on the Prairie" (NBC), "Charlie's Angels" (ABC), M*A*S*H" (CBS), and "Barney Miller" and "What's Happening!" (ABC). After "Taxi!," the most popular new shows were "Battlestar Galactica" and an NBC miniseries, "Centennial," in 11th and 12th places, respectively.

The largest audience of the year was won by "Holocaust," a four-part miniseries dealing with the annihilation of Jews by the Nazis, which was presented by NBC in April. For the four nights of the series, "Holocaust" averaged 31 in audience ratings, representing about 23.1 million homes a night and a 40% share of audience.

Britain, West Germany, Japan, Canada, and Australia were among the countries that bought "Holocaust." Audience ratings were generally high, reaching 41 in Australia compared with NBC's 31. In Israel reactions generally appeared to be lukewarm. In West Germany the series was bought by Westdeutscher Rundfunk, Cologne,

NBC's "Lifeline" won critical acclaim. The series, however, was canceled by NBC's new president, Fred Silverman, in mid-season.

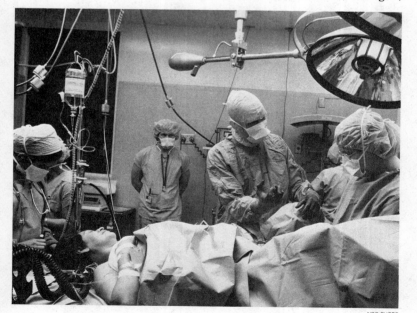

NBC PHOTO

but its showing was postponed until January 1979 and it would be preceded by two special documentaries to prepare the audience.

The movement in the U.S. toward "fourth networks," in which independently organized lineups of stations presented the same programs at substantially the same times, was represented in 1978 primarily by a coalition of stations under the name of "Operation Prime Time." In May more than 90 stations presented Operation Prime Time's four-hour production of John Jakes's "The Bastard" —which some stations retitled "The Kent Family Chronicles"—with better than average audience ratings in most markets. Three months later OPT presented Irwin Shaw's "Evening in Byzantium" on some 90 stations, again with generally good ratings, and in November they scheduled a two-part adaptation of Howard Fast's "The Immigrants."

Networks and stations in the U.S. continued to show concern about both the quality and the quantity of their children's programming. Networks increasingly deleted or attempted to improve conventional cartoon shows in their Saturday-morning lineups—traditionally children's time on television—and scheduled more children's specials.

Serials and game shows remained dominant in daytime television, with hour-long serials beginning to take over from the half-hour dramas that once reigned supreme. Expansion of one serial to an hour and a half—ABC's "Another World"—was being considered. In the period from January to August, according to estimates in *Broadcasting*, the daytime shows with the highest audience ratings were, in order, "Family Feud," a game show; "All My Children," "Another World," and "As the World Turns," all dramatic serials; and reruns of the prime-time "All in the Family."

In the 30th annual Emmy awards, the Academy of Television Arts and Sciences voted "Holocaust" the outstanding limited series of the year. "All in the Family" was voted the outstanding comedy series and "The Rockford Files" the outstanding drama series. Other winners included: American Ballet Theatre's "Giselle," for a classical program in the performing arts; "The Body Human," for an information series, and "The Great Whales," for an information special; "Halloween Is Grinch Night," for a children's special; "The Gathering," for a drama or comedy special; "Bette Midler—Ole Red Hair Is Back," for a comedy-variety or music special; "The Muppet Show," for a comedy-variety or music series; and "The Tonight Show Starring Johnny Carson," for outstanding program achievement. Edward Asner of "Lou Grant" and Sada Thompson of "Family" were named outstanding lead actor and actress in a drama series; and Carrol O'Connor and Jean Stapleton of "All in the Family" were named outstanding lead actor and actress in a comedy series.

Sports remained among the most popular television fare and became increasingly expensive. *Broadcasting* estimated that television and radio networks and stations paid $200,149,352 for rights to cover professional and college football games in 1978, a 142% increase from 1977, and $52,510,000 to cover major league baseball, less than 1% more than the year before and the smallest increase in a decade. Audiences remained large, although the average for regular-season football games was running slightly below 1977 levels. The Super Bowl football game in January 1978, however, attracted an estimated 86 million viewers in 34,410,000 homes to become the highest rated sports event ever broadcast in the U.S., second only to the final episode of "Roots" among all television programs. The World Series baseball championships in October also drew consistently large audiences, with the final game reaching a peak of 26,750,000 homes per average minute.

News and public affairs remained basic television fare, accounting for approximately one-fourth of air time. One of the most consistent users of television was President Carter, who made a dozen network appearances during the first nine months of 1978. His press conferences drew audiences generally estimated at 12 million to 15 million homes but ranging from 6.7 million for one held in the morning to 43.6 million for the one with President Sadat and Prime Minister Begin in the middle of prime evening viewing time.

Music, news, and public affairs remained the staples of radio programming. One long-sought right was attained in February when radio was allowed, for the first time, to present live coverage of a U.S. Senate debate—this one over the Panama Canal treaties. The proceedings were carried briefly by the CBS and NBC radio networks and for three days by National Public Radio. In June House floor proceedings were opened to radio coverage, but television was still excluded.

For its new fall season the Public Broadcasting Service scheduled six new television series, including three weekly public affairs offerings, a new series of feature films, and a new children's program. Among the new shows were "Cinema Showcase," featuring critically acclaimed art and documentary films; "The Long Search," a look at the world's 12 major religions; "Congressional Outlook," a documentary-style look at national political issues; "Sneak Previews," consisting of glimpses of current theatrical films; "Marie Curie," a miniseries based on the life of the scientist; and "Freestyle," an exploration of career choices in a series designed for youngsters aged 9 to 12.

Many European program-makers had a rough ride in 1978 as they faced financial cutbacks, government interventions, and labour union problems which were not directly related to programs but which nonetheless affected their capacity to make the programs they wished to make in the way they wished to make them. In the U.K. the BBC's director general, Ian Trethowan, publicly acknowledged that the BBC's inability to pay good wages (due to the government's reluctance to raise the license fee to a level deemed adequate by the corporation) could be clearly seen, by the viewer, in the worsening quality of the programs. The BBC's index of public satisfaction in its programs dropped to its lowest-ever level.

The rival ITV network, financed by advertising and enjoying a 30% increase in profits, was not slow to take advantage of the BBC's penury.

NBC PHOTO

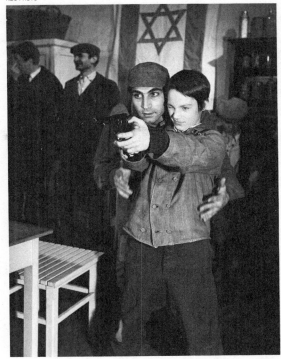

The four-part series "Holocaust" captured high ratings for NBC when it was viewed by 120 million in April.

Thames TV, the largest ITV company, persuaded not only the controller of BBC-1 to move to Thames but also many other senior management directors and technicians, including the former editors of "Panorama" and "Tonight"; the director of the prize-winning hospital series "Casualty"; and the BBC's (and the country's) top TV comedy duo, Eric Morecambe and Ernie Wise. Meanwhile, London Weekend Television (LWT) poached Bruce Forsyth, the presenter of the BBC's top-rated show, "The Generation Game." The rivalry between BBC and ITV burst into bitter hostility in November, with the former issuing a writ, when ITV completed a secret deal with the Football League that gave the network exclusive rights to all league games for the next three seasons for £5 million. Previously, the BBC and ITV had always negotiated jointly with the league and had paid around £1.5 million each. (As a measure of football's potential drawing power, an estimated 25 million British viewers—half the population—watched the year's World Cup transmissions from Argentina.)

The year's most controversial British programs were those dealing with current affairs in Northern Ireland. The biggest clash between the public authorities and broadcasters centred on a Thames TV "This Week" program on police brutality in Northern Ireland, which was banned by the IBA. A BBC staff director of 16 years' standing resigned when BBC management intervened in two films on the province (most notably to cut from a gravestone's epitaph the words "Murdered by British Paratroopers").

Most programs stirred no such controversy. Praise from all sides was heaped on the BBC's major documentary production, "The Body in Question," in which Jonathan Miller (actor, medical doctor, and theatre director) explored and explained with charm and lucidity the workings of the human body. In "The Voyage of Charles Darwin" (BBC), the team of documentary-makers that had dramatized "The Search for the Nile" followed the naturalist's journeys in HMS "Beagle." The BBC's "Living in the Past" recounted the experiences of a group of volunteers who, over 13 months, built and lived in an Iron Age village. The lure of nostalgia was brilliantly caught in Dennis Potter's serial "Pennies from Heaven."

Live sound broadcasting from the House of Commons started on April 3, some 55 years after the matter had first been debated and following a successful month-long experiment in 1975. The presence of microphones in the House had a marked effect. Chancellor Denis Healey acknowledged that his spring budget speech was shorter than usual and much simpler, and members doubled the number of questions in order to get heard by their constituents.

Programs in France were severely weakened by frequent strikes both at the state production company and in the program companies. A highly successful children's program was "Île aux Enfants," whose star puppet, Casimir, became a national figure, endorsing more than 200 French products. "Nouveau Vendredi" became the country's most respected current affairs series. It was produced and presented by a woman who had worked for both NBC and CBS and who used many U.S. techniques in her shows.

In Switzerland, where the Société Suisse de Radiodiffusion et Télévision (SSR) faced the problem of serving three main language groups living in fiercely independent cantons, it was decided to turn "Téléjournal," the nation's main news show, into a regional program. By early 1979 the German, Italian, and French language units of SSR would be broadcasting their own "Téléjournal" news programs.

The success throughout Europe of "Roots" and "Holocaust" and of other miniseries, when added to the regular flow of U.S. programming and the ever increasing amount of material that the European stations were buying from each other, resulted in many of the stations' schedules looking remarkably alike. In The Netherlands, for instance, the most popular programs were mostly of U.S. and U.K. origin (in about equal proportions), ranging from "All Creatures Great and Small" to "Mary Hartman, Mary Hartman." In Australia, too, the top shows were mostly British and U.S.

For the first time the three TV awards of the Prix Italia, the premier world festival, were won by one country. The BBC won the drama award with "The Spongers" and the documentary award with the first episode of "Casualty," a close-up look at scenes inside a hospital; LWT won the music prize with Kenneth MacMillan's "Mayerling," about the performance of a ballet.

Japan was one of the few industrial countries where the TV audience did not decline. In October the Ministry of Posts and Telecommunications began to issue licenses for multiplex sound broadcasting, which enabled broadcasters to transmit two sound signals alongside each picture. It could be used for stereo sound or to transmit a Japanese-language soundtrack of a foreign film.

Programming in third world countries changed little from previous years: a majority of imports leavened by domestic news, religious, educational, and often some drama material. The major trends were the increase in program exchange between less developed countries and an increase in the level of professional expertise.

(RUFUS W. CRATER; JOHN HOWKINS; SOL J. TAISHOFF)

Amateur Radio. The number of amateur radio operators continued to grow in 1978. The American Radio Relay League (ARRL), the leading organization of amateur (or "ham") radio operators, reported 368,601 amateur radio licenses outstanding in the U.S. as of October 31, a 7.5% gain in 12 months. The Citizens Radio Service (citizens band, or CB) boom of recent years, though it was waning, was credited with much of the increase. ARRL officials estimated that at least half of their new members were CBers who had become interested in the more sophisticated field of amateur radio. The number of ham operators throughout the world was put at about one million in November 1978.

When a disastrous tornado struck Bossier City, La., late in 1978, a network of ham operators served as communications links to the rest of the world. Earlier, during the flight of the "Double Eagle II" balloon across the Atlantic Ocean, amateur radio equipment on board enabled the balloonists to keep in touch with their engineers in Massachusetts after other on-board communications equipment broke down.

(RUFUS W. CRATER; SOL J. TAISHOFF)

See also Industrial Review: *Advertising; Telecommunications;* Motion Pictures; Music.
[613.D.4.b; 735; I.4–5]

"The Duchess of Duke Street," with Gemma Jones (left) in the title role, was a featured series from England on PBS.

Tennis

The growth of tennis as both a participant and a spectator sport continued in 1978, especially in the U.S. A survey there indicated that the number of players had grown from 10 million in 1968 to 29 million by 1978. In 1968 the U.S. Tennis Association (USTA) conducted 18 national championships for senior (over 35) men and women; in 1978, 62 such championship events were arranged.

The USTA spent $10 million in constructing a National Tennis Center on a 16-ac site in Flushing Meadow Park, Queens, N.Y. Comprising 27 outdoor and 9 indoor courts, the centre was the site of the U.S. Open championships and, with its Stadium Court arena holding 19,500 spectators, attracted a record Open attendance of 275,300 through 13 days of competition. At the Wimbledon championships unfavourable weather did not prevent the first week's attendance from being the highest ever recorded (198,197). The tournament had its third-highest total attendance with 335,258 and, on the first Wednesday, June 28, achieved a record daily total of 38,290. The Italian and French Open championships were similarly prosperous.

The USTA issued a list of prize money earnings for the year 1977. A total of 29 men and 8 women earned more than $100,000 each; the year before only 17 men and 5 women had accomplished this feat. Jimmy Connors (U.S.) was the top earner with $922,657. The top woman earner was Chris Evert (U.S.) with $503,134. There was a marked disparity between the amount of prize money awarded to men and the amount awarded to women; the 44th man on the list was credited with $63,632, the 44th woman with $4,350.

A lucrative circuit of women's tournaments in the U.S., promoted since 1970 by Virginia Slims cigarettes in conjunction with the Women's Tennis Association (WTA), came to an end in 1978 after disagreement about the format for 1979. It had comprised 32 players in 11 tournaments, each with prize money of $100,000; at the end of the season the top 8 had played for a final championship of $150,000.

In men's competition the series of tournaments promoted by World Championship Tennis (WCT), which in 1978 comprised eight qualifying tournaments, was incorporated into the year-long Colgate-Palmolive Grand Prix competition. There was no rapprochement with World Team Tennis (WTT), the U.S. league competition, and, although the men's game was not greatly affected, most of the leading women players were contracted to WTT teams and therefore were not available to compete in other events during much of the year. Soviet competitors did not play in any of the leading events in order to avoid playing South Africans.

The administrative organizations of the International Tennis Federation (ITF) and the Davis Cup Nations were joined. For the Davis Cup side of its activities the ITF retained the system of one nation, one vote, not adopting its own weighted voting system. The application of South Africa to compete in the Davis Cup in 1979 was refused.

Men's Competition. The Grand Prix for 1977 was won for the third time by Guillermo Vilas. At the end of the year he was 501 points ahead of his nearest rival, Brian Gottfried of the U.S., and his bonus prize was $300,000. He competed in 27 of the qualifying tournaments and won 14. In the subsequent Masters' Tournament, staged in Madison Square Garden, New York City, in early January 1978, Björn Borg of Sweden beat Vilas 6–3, 6–3

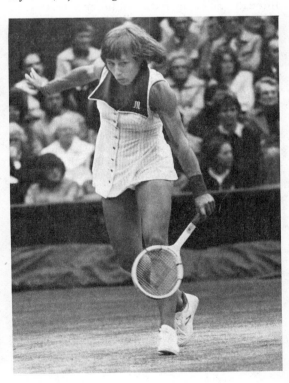

Björn Borg (left) defeated Victor Amaya to capture the men's singles crown at Wimbledon. Martina Navratilova (right) triumphed over Chris Evert in the women's singles.

PHOTOS, KEYSTONE

in a semifinal match. Jimmy Connors then beat Borg 6–4, 1–6, 6–4 in the final. The rules of the event occasioned criticism after both Vilas and Borg withdrew in the round-robin section without marring their qualification for the semifinal stage.

Vitas Gerulaitis of the U.S. won the Australian title, defeating John Lloyd of the U.K. 6–3, 7–6, 5–7, 3–6, 6–2 in the final. The 1978 championships were actually staged in the closing days of 1977 in Melbourne, Australia.

The final tournament of the WCT series was again staged in Dallas, Texas, in May. Gerulaitis beat Eddie Dibbs (U.S.) 6–3, 6–2, 6–1 to win the event. Disappointingly, an injury caused Borg to forfeit to Gerulaitis in the semifinal.

Borg came into his own in the Italian championships held in Rome in May. He beat Dibbs in the semifinal and Adriano Panatta of Italy in the final by 1–6, 6–3, 6–1, 4–6, 6–3. Panatta's triumph in his semifinal match against José Higueras of Spain was bizarre. With the match tied at one set apiece, the crowd became so noisily partisan in favour of Panatta that Higueras, who had won the opening set 6–0, withdrew in protest.

Borg maintained his invincibility in the French championships, contested in Paris in June, and in the final beat Vilas 6–1, 6–1, 6–3. The young Swede, who became 22 during the meet, did not lose a set in his seven tournament matches and conceded only 32 games in all.

In the Wimbledon championships at London in July, Borg won the men's singles for the third successive year, the first to do so since Fred Perry in 1934–36. His success came after a perilous opening match against Victor Amaya (U.S.), which he won 8–9, 6–1, 1–6, 6–3, 6–3. He played strongly for the rest of the tournament and was never better than in the final. He beat Connors 6–2, 6–2, 6–3 through one of the most skillful and devastating exhibitions seen in years.

In the U.S. the Open championships at Flushing Meadow Park in September, held on a fairly fast cement surface, were played the best two out of three sets until the fourth round. In one of the year's major upsets Butch Walts, a tall Californian, beat the defending champion, Vilas, 6–4, 7–6, 4–6, 6–7, 6–2 in the fourth round. Borg, seeded first, beat Gerulaitis in the semifinal, and at the same stage Connors, seeded second, beat John McEnroe of the U.S. In a disappointing final Connors overwhelmed Borg, who had an injured thumb, 6–4, 6–2, 6–2 to win for the third time out of five successive appearances in the finals.

In doubles competition the partnership of Australian-born Bob Hewitt and Frew McMillan (South Africa) was outstanding, even though Hewitt became 38 and McMillan became 36 during the year. They won tournaments in Philadelphia, Richmond, Va., St. Louis, Mo., Denver, Colo., Johannesburg, South Africa, and Queen's Club, London, before taking the Wimbledon title. It was their third success at Wimbledon following triumphs in 1967 and 1972. Hewitt had won with Fred Stolle (Australia) in 1962 and 1964.

In the U.S. Open Hewitt and McMillan lost in the quarterfinal to Martin Riessen and Sherwood Stewart of the U.S. In the final Riessen and Stewart were beaten by their compatriots Bob Lutz and Stan Smith, the champions of 1968.

Because of incidents in the 1977 Davis Cup competition with Great Britain, Ilie Nastase of Romania was banned from playing in the Davis Cup in 1978. Consequently, Romania, seeded to the semifinal of Section "A" of the European Zone, was easily beaten 5–0 by Czechoslovakia. Australia, the 1977 winners, won the Eastern Zone easily, beating Japan and New Zealand. In the interzone semifinals the U.S. beat Sweden by 3 matches to 2 and Great Britain beat Australia 3–2. In the Davis Cup finals, at Palm Springs, Calif., in December, the U.S. (Gottfried, Lutz, McEnroe, and Smith) beat Great Britain 4–1, the U.S. victories all being in straight sets.

Women's Competition. Chris Evert (U.S.) ended the 1977 season by winning not only the Colgate-Palmolive International Series, the equivalent of the men's Grand Prix, but also the subsequent Series championship at Palm Springs in November. In 1978 Evert competed less often than in 1977. The dominant player of the year was Martina Navratilova (*see* BIOGRAPHIES), in exile from Czechoslovakia and residing in the U.S.

Navratilova played in 11 of the 12 Virginia Slims tournaments staged in the U.S. between January and April and was beaten only by Evonne Goolagong Cawley (Australia) and by Tracy Austin (U.S.). She earned $214,350 in prize money. Cawley won the Australian championship. As in other years the Italian and French championships attracted comparatively few of the top-ranked women because many leading players were committed to WTT competition. The Italian title was won by Regina Marsikova (Czech.), and Virginia Ruzici (Rom.) won the French title. Navratilova won the Wimbledon singles. The event proceeded along copybook lines. For the first time, 16 players were seeded. Only the number 16 seed lost before the round of last 16 places. Evert, seeded one, Navratilova, two, Cawley, three, and Virginia Wade (U.K.), four, reached the semifinals. Wade, the defending champion, yielded to Evert. Navratilova beat Cawley in the semifinal and then won the final from Evert by 2–6, 6–4, 7–5.

Evert won the U.S. Open championship for the fourth consecutive year, a feat not achieved since Helen Jacobs (U.S.) won in 1932–35. Surprisingly, she did not play Navratilova in the final. Pam Shriver, from Lutherville, Md., beat Navratilova in a semifinal match by 7–6, 7–6 to become at 16 years 2 months (b. July 4, 1962) the youngest player ever to play for the title. In a well-contested final Evert beat Shriver 7–5, 6–4.

The annual contest between the women of the U.S. (Billie Jean King, Evert, Rosemary Casals, and JoAnne Russell) and Great Britain (Wade, Sue Barker, Michele Tyler, Sue Mappin, and Lesley Charles) broke new ground in November 1977, with a record total attendance over three days of 23,452, at the Coliseum Arena in Oakland, Calif. The U.S. won 7–0, the first such devastating score in 23 years.

In the finals of the Federation Cup in Melbourne in December, the U.S. (Austin, Evert, King) beat Australia 2–1. (LANCE TINGAY)

Thailand

A constitutional monarchy of Southeast Asia, Thailand is bordered by Burma, Laos, Cambodia, Malaysia, the Andaman Sea, and the Gulf of Thailand. Area: 542,373 sq km (209,411 sq mi). Pop. (1977 census): 44,035,100. Cap. and largest city: Bangkok (pop., 1977 census, 4,702,300). Language: Thai. Religion (1970): Buddhist 95.3%; Muslim 3.8%. King, Bhumibol Adulyadej; prime minister in 1978, Gen. Kriangsak Chamanand; chairman of the National Policy Council, Adm. Sa-ngad Chaloryu.

For Thailand 1978 was an unusually eventful year, with a concerted governmental drive to strengthen foreign relations taking precedence over the management of domestic politics. Prime Minister Kriangsak Chamanand set the pace personally with a series of foreign visits. Early in the year he traveled to other member countries of the Association of Southeast Asian Nations (ASEAN). He said his purposes were to promote ASEAN's cohesiveness, inform fellow members of his government's policies, and hold consultations on issues of common interest. Diplomatic reports noted, however, that a primary purpose was to coordinate ASEAN's views about China. When he

Thailand

journeyed to Peking in March–April, he seemed more a representative of the regional grouping than of Thailand alone. In May he became the first Thai prime minister in seven years to visit Burma.

Returning from Burma, Kriangsak said: "I don't have anything to worry about now that I've made friends with all neighbouring countries." That struck some of his countrymen as too optimistic. Cambodia, for one, remained a source of some concern despite an exchange of visits by the foreign ministers of the two countries. But few had any doubt about the success of Thailand's foreign policy efforts as the year drew to a close. Vietnamese Premier Pham Van Dong stopped in Bangkok at the start of an extended tour of ASEAN. Two months later, in November, Chinese Vice-Premier Teng Hsiao-p'ing also picked Bangkok as his first stop in a three-nation swing. In between, Soviet Deputy Foreign Minister Nikolay Firyubin came calling.

Thailand particularly wished to ease its security problems. Vietnam promised help in this respect; Pham Van Dong said categorically that his country would have no dealings with Communist insurgents in Thailand. Teng Hsiao-p'ing, however, pointedly refused to give any such assurance.

Kriangsak's relatively liberal approach to other countries did appear to improve the internal security situation. Some of the student radicals who had been forced underground by the previous government's oppressive policy were given amnesty, while others on trial were released. But the border with Cambodia remained troubled, with sporadic raids and a constant flow of Cambodian refugees straining Thai resources. The Communist insurgency in southern Thailand was said to have slowed down, but Muslim separatists periodically planted bombs at public places.

Domestic affairs were dominated by preparations for—and constant arguments over—general elections. Prime Minister Kriangsak's refusal to state whether he would take part in an election did not interfere with the government's avowed program of bringing about a democratic system.

By midyear a committee completed drafting a 191-clause constitution, Thailand's 13th in 46 years. It quickly generated controversy, largely due to a provision that made it unnecessary for the prime minister to be an elected member of Parliament. Nevertheless, it was passed by the appointed National Assembly at the end of November. Elections were to be held in March or April 1979.

The Board of Investment estimated at midyear that total private investment in the industrial sector during 1978 would exceed 10 billion baht (U.S. $500 million), as against 3.6 billion baht ($180 million) in 1977. Industrial activity was also said to have picked up. But the general economic picture was still unsatisfactory. The trade deficit in 1978 was expected to be about $1 billion because, while imports increased steeply, agricultural exports suffered a major setback. The worst drought in years was followed in September and October by exceptionally severe floods. Although the official death toll was below 100, some 300,000 people were forced to abandon their homes.

(T. J. S. GEORGE)

Textiles: *see* Industrial Review

THAILAND

Education. (1976–77) Primary, pupils 6,736,751, teachers 270,567; secondary, pupils 1,091,997, teachers 35,170; vocational, pupils 198,282, teachers 9,411; teacher training, students 44,156, teachers 5,639; higher, students 81,696, teaching staff (universities only) 7,757.

Finance. Monetary unit: baht, with (Sept. 18, 1978) a free rate of 20.04 baht to U.S. $1 (39.26 baht = £1 sterling). Gold, SDR's, and foreign exchange (June 1978) U.S. $2,119,000,000. Budget (1977 actual): revenue 53,818,000,000 baht; expenditure 66,012,000,000 baht. Gross national product (1977) 368,930,000,000 baht. Money supply (April 1978) 48,630,000,000 baht. Cost of living (1975 = 100; June 1978) 125.4.

Foreign Trade. (1977) Imports 94,177,000,000 baht; exports 71,198,000,000 baht. Import sources (1976): Japan 32%; U.S. 13%; Saudi Arabia 8%; Qatar 6%; West Germany 5%. Export destinations (1976): Japan 26%; The Netherlands 13%; U.S. 10%; Singapore 7%; Indonesia 5%; Hong Kong 5%. Main exports: rice 19%; tapioca 11%; sugar 10%; rubber 9%; tin 6%; corn 5%. Tourism (1976): visitors 1,098,000; gross receipts U.S. $197 million.

Transport and Communications. Roads (1976) 39,721 km. Motor vehicles in use (1976): passenger c. 363,100; commercial c. 267,000. Railways: (1975) 3,765 km; traffic (1976) 5,530,000,000 passenger-km, freight 2,630,000,000 net ton-km. Air traffic (1977): 3,418,000,000 passenger-km; freight 109.1 million net ton-km. Shipping (1977): merchant vessels 100 gross tons and over 100; gross tonnage 260,664. Telephones (Sept. 1976) 333,800. Radio receivers (Dec. 1975) 5.5 million. Television receivers (Dec. 1975) 761,000.

Agriculture. Production (in 000; metric tons; 1977): rice 13,590; corn 1,677; sweet potatoes (1976) c. 347; sorghum 112; cassava (1976) 7,850; dry beans c. 125; soybeans 98; peanuts c. 176; sugar, raw value c. 2,294; pineapples c. 500; bananas c. 1,546; tobacco c. 73; rubber 436; cotton, lint c. 22; jute and kenaf 237; timber (cu m; 1976) 21,119; fish catch (1976) 1,640. Livestock (in 000; 1977): cattle 4,547; buffalo 5,685; pigs 3,020; chickens c. 49,889.

Industry. Production (in 000; metric tons; 1976): cement 4,422; petroleum products c. 7,580; tin concentrates (metal content; 1977) 33; tungsten concentrates (oxide content) 2.2; lead concentrates (metal content) 0.9; manganese ore (metal content) 14; electricity (kw-hr) 10,295,000.

Theatre

The theatre in Western Europe faced new hardships. The cutbacks in public funding, noted in the annual report of the Arts Council of Great Britain, threatened such enterprises as the world-famous Joint Stock Company and the new British Theatre Institute. The Arts Council reduced the theatre portion of its 1978–79 arts budget by 10%.

Local authority grants also declined in real terms. A notable exception, the Hammersmith Borough Council, paid £3.2 million to rebuild the Lyric Theatre and saved the new Arts Centre at Peter Gill's Riverside Studios (with a grant of £65,000 to supplement its original £130,000). The new Conservative-led Greater London Council came under attack for severing the grants of the Royal Court and Open Space theatres and revoking the Half Moon Theatre's move into the reclaimed Wilton's Music Hall. However, the council's grant to the hard-hit National Theatre rose by 12½% to a much-needed £400,000. The British Centre of the International Theatre Institute (ITI), defunct since the withdrawal of Arts Council and British Council grants in 1975, was given new life as a Provisional Centre. Playwriting grants went to Ron Hutchinson (George Devine award), Richard O'Keefe (Arts Council Writing bursary), and David Halliwell and Snoo Wilson (sharers of the John Whiting playwrights award).

British Actors Equity Association set up a committee to offer help to victims of persecution. Chilean, Argentine, and Hungarian exile troupes were performing in West Germany, Italy, and France, and a handful of dissident Czechoslovaks were allowed out of the country to work abroad.

The annual report of the Royal Shakespeare Company (RSC) spoke of record-breaking atten-

dance at 35 productions in its four main stages and on tour. The engagement at the 190-seat Warehouse in London and the season at Newcastle upon Tyne were especially successful. In his tenth year in office Trevor Nunn was joined by Terry Hands as joint artistic director. Earned income of some £2,250,000 plus an Arts Council grant of £1.3 million and other grants left a deficit of £54,000.

Press criticism of Sir Peter Hall's management tended to obscure the National Theatre's achievements: 1,005 productions on its three stages and 708,960 in paid attendance for the year to April 1978. Earned income of more than £3,250,000 plus grants-in-aid (including £2,250,000 from the Arts Council) left a deficit of £406,436. Sir Peter defended his policy and received a clean bill of health from the Arts Council. Michael Rudman, retiring head of the Hampstead Theatre, and William Gaskill were to join the directing staff, alongside Hall, Christopher Morahan, and Bill Bryden.

Government and city authorities in France were criticized for their cutbacks in financial support. The labour unions condemned the arbitrary sacrifice of the arts to economy measures and denounced the crippling decision of Jean-Philippe Lecat, cultural minister, to annul his predecessor's grant to the Palais de Chaillot. Political conflict between artists and the authorities in both West and East Germany grew. One example was the removal of Claus Peymann from the State Theatre in Stuttgart, West Germany, despite its unrivaled record as the country's leading presenter of new works, original productions, and superb players. The brain drain from East Germany included directors Benno Besson and Matthias Langoff, playwright Thomas Brasch, and actress Katharina Thalbach. The refusal to let the Budapest Gaiety Theatre (Vígszinház) take its hit production of *Crime and Punishment*, staged by guest director Yury Liubimov from Moscow, to East Berlin was also political, as was the ban on a new play workshop at the state-run Deutsches Theatre.

Great Britain and Ireland. Hall's policy at the National Theatre of having writers stage their plays paid off in the case of David Hare's subversive *Plenty*, featuring Kate Nelligan at the Lyttelton; Arnold Wesker's romantic *Love Letters on Blue Paper*, in which Elizabeth Spriggs won a Society of West End Theatre (SWET) supporting role award, at the Cottesloe; and Edward Bond's spectacular pacifist-feminist *The Woman*, at the Olivier. Also at the Olivier, Ralph Koltai won a SWET award for his splendid set for Christopher Morahan's 150th Ibsen anniversary production of *Brand*, with Michael Bryant in the title role. Hall himself staged Chekhov's *The Cherry Orchard* and Shakespeare's *Macbeth* (with Albert Finney) at the Olivier, alongside Peter Wood's production of William Congreve's *The Double Dealer*, in which Dorothy Tutin won a SWET best actress award, and Morahan's production of John Galsworthy's *Strife*.

Peter Wood's production, at the Lyttelton, of Ferenc Molnar's *The Guardsman*, with Diana Rigg and Richard Johnson, and Morahan's revival of G. B. Shaw's *The Philanderer* compared favourably with Hall's neatly turned *Betrayal*, Harold Pinter's analytical drama of adultery. Among the new pro-

Elaine Paige starred in the surprise hit musical "Evita," which opened in London in June.

ductions at the Cottesloe were *Lark Rise*, Keith Dewhurst's dramatization of Flora Thompson's pastoral trilogy, and his own Cromwellian epic *The World Turned Upside Down*. At the RSC Hands won the SWET best director award for *Henry VI*; Alan Howard a best actor award in a revival for his scornful *Coriolanus*. Hands also staged the Jacobean thriller *The Changeling* and David Mercer's *Cousin Vladimir*. The Warehouse staged modern-dress versions of Alfred de Musset's *Lorenzaccio* and John Ford's *'Tis Pity She's a Whore* and Strindberg's *The Dance of Death*.

Peter Brook at Stratford staged an impressive *Antony and Cleopatra*, with Glenda Jackson and Alan Howard. Other productions in Britain outside London included a Russian season at the Leicester Haymarket, a festival of new works at the Sheffield Crucible, new plays by David Storey and Ronald Harwood at the Manchester Royal Exchange, and a challenging repertory at the Glasgow Citizens'. At the Mermaid, London, Tom Stoppard's *Every Good Boy Deserves Favour* and Brian Clark's ironic, much-awarded *Who's Life Is It Anyway?*, with Tom Conti as a paralyzed patient, topped the bill. Prospect, newly installed at the Old Vic, had an excellent record on tour, at the Edinburgh Festival, and in London, where its season included *Saint Joan* and *The Lady's Not for Burning*, each with Eileen Atkins, *King Lear*, with Anthony Quayle, and *Twelfth Night*, in which Robert Eddison's Feste won him a SWET supporting actor award. Landmarks of Michael Rudman's last season at the Hampstead were James Saunders's psychodrama *Bodies* and Michael Hastings's immigrant comedy *Gloo Joo*. The Open Space presented a Samuel Beckett double bill from Berlin, *Boo Hoo*, an American farce by Philip Magdalany, and Bertolt Brecht's *Respectable Wedding*, staged at the Half Moon with Goethe Institute sponsorship. The season at the Riverside included an enchanting *The Cherry Orchard* (director, Peter Gill), the same director's *The Changeling*, with Brian Cox, and three visitors: the Pip Simmons troupe, the Joint Stock with a Gaskill production, and the Catalan La Claca, in their antifascist mime-drama *Mori la Merma*, with decor by Joan Miró.

Other new productions included, at the Greenwich, under Alan Strachan, David Pownall's *An Audience Called Edouard*, inspired by Édouard Manet's "Le Déjeuner sur l'herbe;" at the Theatre Royal, Stratford, two plays with school backgrounds, by Tom McGrath and David Holman; at the New End, Simone Benmussa's *The Singular Life of Albert Nobbs*, based on George Moore's short story, and *Sticks and Bones* by David Rabe; at the Young Vic, under Michael Bogdanov, several modern-dress classics; at the Round House, Rabe's *Streamers* and Peter Barnes's modern-dress production of his own adaptation of Ben Jonson's *Bartholomew Fair*; and at the Royal Court and its subsidiary Theatre Upstairs, Nigel Williams's play of school life *Class Enemy*, Snoo Wilson's science fiction comedy *The Glad Hand*, and Leigh Jackson's *Eclipse*. U.S. plays included the musicals *Kismet* and *Annie*, Philip Hayes Dean's *Paul Robeson*, Tennessee Williams's *Vieux Carré*, and Ira Levin's *Deathtrap*.

The season's top musical hit was Tim Rice and

MARTHA SWOPE

(Left to right) Lester Rawlins, Brian Murray, and Barnard Hughes played in Hugh Leonard's "Da," which opened in New York City in May.

Andrew Lloyd Webber's SWET-awarded *Evita*, with SWET-awarded Elaine Paige as Eva Perón. Eduardo de Filippo's *Filumena* and Joan Plowright won the SWET awards for best comedy and best actress in a new play. Other commercial hits included *Waters of the Moon*, with Ingrid Bergman and Wendy Hiller, and Sir Noel Coward's *Look After Lulu*, both from Chichester; Australian Steve Spears's tragicomedy *The Elocution of Benjamin Franklin*, and *Bedroom Farce* and *Ten Times Table*, both by Alan Ayckbourn; two sexual farces, Royce Ryton's *The Unvarnished Truth* and C. Scott Forbes's *Mate!*, starring Britt Ekland; and Tom Stoppard's seriocomedy *Night and Day*, starring Diana Rigg (*Plays and Players* best actress award).

Hugh Leonard, new program director, unveiled the 20th Dublin Festival with the Abbey Theatre's production, by Soviet guest director Vladimir Monakhov, of Chekhov's *Uncle Vanya*, with Cyril Cusack, who also starred in *You Never Can Tell*, the Abbey's offering at the Malvern Shaw Festival. Thirty-year-old Joe Dowling succeeded Tomás Mac Anna as the youngest-ever director of the Abbey, now granted a £500,000 subsidy. The new Radio Telefís Eireann (RTE) Repertory players made their bow with a French guest to stage a Georges Feydeau farce. Other Dublin festival fare included the European premiere of Neil Simon's *Chapter Two*, Ulick O'Conor's triple bill of Noh-type plays, and Peter Luke's dramatization of Benedict Kiely's antiterrorist *Proxopera*.

France and Belgium. Hands's *Murder in the Cathedral* for the Comédie Française was followed by Feydeau's *A Flea in Your Ear*, a 19th-century *Britannicus*, Luigi Pirandello's *Six Characters in Search of an Author* (director, Antoine Bourseiller), and Carlo Goldoni's *Country Trilogy* (director, Giorgio Strehler). Théâtre de la Ville playbills included Maksim Gorky's *The Last Ones* (director, Lucian Pintilie); at the Théâtre de l'Est Parisien there was Brecht's *Puntila* and J.-P. Sartre's *Nekrassov*; at the Orsay, J.-L. Barrault's crazy-gang adaptation of Voltaire's *Zadig* and Jerome Savary's *1001 Nights* extravaganza with his Magic Circus; at the Chaillot, André-Louis Perinetti's gimmicky *Cyrano*; at the Espace Cardin, Marlowe's *Dr. Faustus* with Maria Casarès; at the Marais Festival, *Phèdre* with Ludmila Mikael; at the Paris Festival, Peter Brook's multinational *Measure for Measure*; and at the Avignon Festival, Benno Besson's staging of Brecht's *The Caucasian Chalk Circle*, with Nicole Serreau. There were also new plays in Paris by F. Arrabal, Jean Anouilh, Françoise Dorin, Marcel Mithois, and Robert Hossein.

Belgium saw René Kalisky's *The Passion According to Pier Paolo Pasolini*, staged by Albert-André Lheureux in the Botanical Gardens, Otomar Krejca's production of *Romeo and Juliet* for the Belgian National Theatre, Bernard de Coster's staging of Franz Kafka's *The Trial* at the Rideau, and Henri Ronse's of Frank Wedekind's *Lulu* at the Parc.

Switzerland, Germany, Austria, Italy. Gerhard Klingenberg in Zürich's rebuilt Schauspielhaus produced *William Tell*, followed by Roberto Guicciardini's *Candide*, Eugene O'Neill's *More Stately Mansions*, Max Frisch's *Biedermann* staged by Erwin Axer from Warsaw, and the world premiere of Herbert Meier's *Bräker*.

In Basel French director Bernard Sobel put on *Don Juan* and *Tartuffe*. At Geneva's Théâtre de Carouge, Matthias Langhoff and Manfred Karge produced East German Heiner Müller's *Prometheus*. *The Prince of Homburg* and Brecht's *Fazer*-fragment, also produced by Langhoff and Karge as guests of the Hamburg Schauspielhaus, were seen at the West Berlin Arts Festival, alongside Peter Stein's nightmarish production of Botho Strauss's *Reunion Trilogy* at the Schaubühne.

Highlights in West Berlin were Samuel Beckett's daunting production of *Play, Lovely Rita*, a study of Nazism by the former East German writer Thomas Brasch, and a sensational production of Brasch's *Rotter*, a "horrid fairy-tale" about Germans from Nazi times to present-day East Germany. As impressive were Peter Zadek's versions, for Hamburg's Thalia Theatre, of Trevor Griffiths' *Comedians* and, for Hamburg's Schauspielhaus, of Shakespeare's *A Winter's Tale*. East German playwright Stefan Schütz's *Kohlhaas*, based on a novella by Heinrich Kleist, was premiered in Kassel. In Munich's Residenz, Franco Enríquez produced *Agamemnon*, while at the Kammerspiele Ernst Wendt's production of Heiner Müller's *Germania, or Death in Berlin* nicely offset Dieter Dorn's *A Midsummer Night's Dream*.

Achim Benning began his new regime at Vienna's Burgtheater with East Berlin guest director Manfred Wekwerth's production of *The Prince of Homburg*, Hands's of *Troilus and Cressida*, Peter Wood's of Pinter's *Betrayal*, and the world premiere of Willi Pevny's *Dream of Happiness*, based on a play by Johann Nestroy. Other Austrian highlights were a doll's house *Marriage of Figaro* at the Salzburg Festival, Karl Paryla's return, after a 20-year absence, to stage Gorky's *Vassa Zheleznova* at the Volkstheater, and, at the Theater an der Wien, the premiere of Vaclav Havel's version of John Gay's *The Beggar's Opera*. Günther Rennert (*see* OBITUARIES) died midway during rehearsals of Goethe's *Stella* at the Josefstadt.

Franco Enríquez's Trieste production of Ödön von Horváth's *Stories of the Vienna Woods*, with Valeria Moriconi and Corrado Pani, was staged at the Burgtheater. The versatile Moriconi also starred in Enríquez's adaptation of *Héloise and Abelard* in San Miniato and in Pirandello's *The Life That I Gave Thee* in Brescia. Luca Ronconi's season included the world premiere of Pasolini's *Calderon* and Hugo von Hofmannsthal's *The Tower*, all in Prato, and two Arthur Schnitzler plays in Genoa. The world premiere of Hofmannsthal's *Electra* was given in Bolzano, while Luigi Squarzina staged Brecht's *Fear and Misery in the Third Reich* in Rome and Guicciardini produced Euripides' *Helen* at Syracuse. In Milan, Giorgio Strehler's cinematic version of *The Tempest*, with a female Ariel and a schoolgirl Miranda, was given in the Lirico.

Scandinavia and Eastern Europe. At Stockholm's Royal Dramatic five directors put on a vast happening, *Storm, A Play About Nuclear Energy*, with the entire staff of 350 performing. Sven Delblanc's play about Richard Strauss and Arne Törnqvist's about the socialist leader Karl Branting were others in Dramaten's repertory. Highlights at the City Theatre were *Othello*, staged by Johan Bergenstråhle, and Melchior Schedler's *Lazarillo*. Ralph Långbacka's production of Brecht's *Caucasian Chalk Circle* in Göteborg represented Sweden at the Warsaw Festival, and Theatre 9's multinational *Crossroads* in Wroclaw.

In Århus the Danish Odin Theatre of Eugenio Barba performed a new street play about Marco Polo, called *Millions*. Norway celebrated Ibsen's 150th birthday with a six-play season at the Oslo National and Charles Marowitz's collage of *Hedda* at the Bergen Festival. (*See* Special Report.) Notable Helsinki productions were Jouko Turkka's *The Ghost Sonata* and Arto af Hallström's *Othello* at the City Theatre, *An Enemy of the People* at the Swedish, and Henrik Tikannen's *Butterfly Wings* at the Little.

Veranda in the Forest by Ignaty Dvoretsky and a stylized *Othello* were Anatoly Efros's new productions at the Moscow Malaya Bronnaya. Adaptations of Vassily Bykov stories and Gogol's *Government Inspector* set in modern times were staged at the Taganka. *Cruel Games* by Aleksey Arbuzov and *Pickwick Papers* were Georgy Tovstonogov's new productions in Leningrad. *The Dead Class* won Poland the first prize at the Theatre of the Nations Festival at Caracas, Venezuela. At Warsaw's new Woli Theatre, Ludwik René staged *Galileo* with Tadeusz Lomnicki.

In Sofia, Bulg., the offerings included Yordan Radichkov's Bulgarian family saga *Lazaritsa* at the Satiric, Dragomir Assenov's *Beyond the Mirages* about Bulgarian emigrés at the Youth, and Stanislawa Przybyszweska's *The Danton Case* staged by Andrzej Wajda at the Army Theatre. The Budapest (Hung.) National's director Endre Marton was replaced by former critic Peter Nagy, who was joined by Gabor Szekely from Szolnok and Tamas Aser and Gabor Zsambeki from Kaposvar. Productions included, at the National, *Danton's Death* staged by Szekely, and Sandor Veores's *St. George and the Dragon*; at the Víg, Peter Vallo's production of Witold Gombrowicz's *Operette*; and, in the Carmelite Cloister of the reopened Royal Castle, Jozsef Ruszt's of Marlowe's *Dr. Faustus*. Andrej Hieng's Slovenian family tragedy with songs, *The Night of the Young Marrieds*, was a highlight of Yugoslavia's Novi Sad Festival.

(OSSIA TRILLING)

U.S. and Canada. Theatre in the U.S. and Canada is much more than the productions on Broadway, but to theatregoers everywhere and to stage professionals as well, theatre in New York symbolizes that in North America. A year's retrospective must begin there.

Broadway's 1978 season was distressing, not for the lack of good drama but because there indeed were fine new plays, two of them, and both were rejected by audiences. David Mamet's *The Water Engine* and Richard Wesley's *The Mighty Gents* were literary and theatrical dramas of compassion, power, and substance. But Broadway's audiences seemed to have drifted so far from drama that they apparently looked to the theatre only for entertainment. The Mamet and Wesley plays lasted several weeks between them. For Broadway audiences to support plays at all in 1978, they had to be showy or lightweight. One such 1978 success was *The Crucifer of Blood*, a new Sherlock Holmes mystery, played with tongue in cheek and elaborate production effects. The year's Tony award- and N.Y. Drama Critics award-winning play was Hugh Leonard's *Da*, a sentimental "Irish" play that made few demands on its audiences. The *Gin Game*, by Donald L. Coburn, won the Pulitzer Prize for 1978.

Even comedy, once a Broadway staple, fell on lean times. Neil Simon, the most (financially) successful playwright in theatre history, produced his annual new comedy, *Chapter Two*, an autobiographical play about the death of his wife and his remarriage. His best play to date, it went far to establish Simon as a comic playwright capable of depth. The year's only other comedy of note was Bernard Slade's *Tribute*, notable mainly for starring movie-actor Jack Lemmon and for proving Slade no flash in the pan (his first play, *Same Time Next Year*, closed late in 1978 after almost four years on Broadway).

Of course, the New York stage is best known for its musicals, the United States' best loved and only home-grown art form. But with inflation pushing the cost of these elaborate shows above the $1.5 million mark, fewer than ever were being produced. The year's best example was *On the Twentieth Century*, written by Betty Comden and Adolph Green, with music by Cy Coleman. *Timbuktu* was less successful, suggesting an end of the trend toward all-black versions of past hits (it was based on the 1953 musical *Kismet*).

Broadway's biggest musical hit in 1978 was *Ain't Misbehavin'*, a relatively inexpensive intimate revue celebrating the songs of Thomas "Fats" Waller. Capitalizing on the continuing nostalgia boom —in this case the World War II years—and being faithful to that era in musical staging, dance steps, costumes, and song presentation, *Ain't Misbehavin'* proved that a musical did not have to be elaborate to succeed.

Of the two dramas noted at the outset, *The Water Engine*, after a Chicago premiere, originated in New York at the New York Shakespeare Festival and *The Mighty Gents* was first produced at the Manhattan Theater Club. These institutions

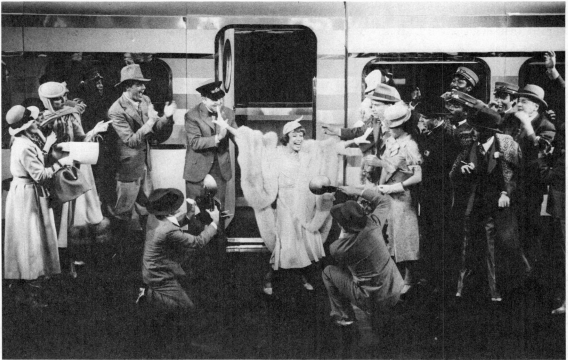

Imogene Coca (centre) was part of a large cast in the award-winning musical "On the Twentieth Century," with book and lyrics by Betty Comden and Adolph Green.

MARTHA SWOPE

emerged as two of New York's leading stages. Such nonprofit theatre, subsidized by government, foundation, and private contributions, offered an alternative stage for plays that commercial managements might not risk.These plays, whether classics or new, are essential to a theatre's life, and such institutions are New York's equivalent of the regional repertory theatres in other parts of the U.S. New York, once healthy with them, has seen their number dwindle. Lincoln Center's Vivian Beaumont Theatre remained closed in 1978, the cultural centre's second year without a theatre component. The Chelsea Theater Center and the BAM Repertory Company, both housed in the Brooklyn Academy of Music, struggled through the year with uneven productions. BAM's presentation of Samuel Beckett's *Waiting for Godot* was especially disappointing. Neither the Chelsea Theater Center nor the BAM Repertory Company produced anything between June and December, and their futures seemed indefinite.

New York's only source of theatre classics produced on the professional level was the Circle in the Square Theater. In 1978 it presented Molière's *Tartuffe* (with John Wood and Tammy Grimes), Shaw's *Saint Joan* (played by Lynn Redgrave), Feydeau's *Thirteen Rue De L'Amour* (starring Louis Jourdan), and a marvelous production of *Once in a Lifetime*, the 1930 satire of Hollywood by Moss Hart and George S. Kaufman.This was well-balanced programming, for the most part beautifully produced.

Many of the regional theatres in the U.S. continued to operate at standards as professional as Broadway's, sometimes even higher. The most prominent in 1978 were the Arena Stage, in Washington, D.C., Houston's Alley Theater, Chicago's Goodman Theater, the Mark Taper Forum in Los Angeles, San Francisco's American Conservatory Theater, The Guthrie Theater in Minneapolis, the Hartford (Conn.) Stage Company, Trinity Square Theatre in Providence, R.I., and two theatres in

New Haven, Conn., the Yale Repertory and the Long Wharf.

In 1978 these theatres presented such masterworks as *Macbeth, The Wild Duck, Hamlet, Rosmersholm, A Month in the Country,* and *The Winter's Tale.* The Guthrie Theater produced the U.S. premiere of Ibsen's *The Pretenders*; both Yale and the Arena Stage revived Ödön von Horváth's obscure *Tales from the Vienna Woods.* In other rewarding choices, such modern U.S. plays as Philip Barry's *The Philadelphia Story* and Tennessee Williams's *A Streetcar Named Desire* proved themselves destined to become classics. In a noteworthy trend, past U.S. masters such as Robert Sherwood, Maxwell Anderson, Clifford Odets, Lillian Hellman, William Inge, and Arthur Miller disappeared from the production schedules. All but Miller seemed doomed to obsolescence. Also, Bertolt Brecht, once the pet playwright of the regional theatres, went all but unproduced in 1978.

Canada's serious theatre in 1978 was almost all of the institutional kind, its commercial theatres devoting themselves mainly to Broadway shows. Over the 20-odd years of its existence Canada's Stratford Festival at Stratford, Ont., had established itself as the only institutional theatre on the North American continent in the international class. This large, wealthy theatre operated in true rotating repertory, changing its program daily, and though still devoted to Shakespeare it produced other classic and contemporary works as well. Stratford's 1978 season, with a huge company headed by Maggie Smith and Brian Bedford, could not have been duplicated by any other theatre in the U.S. or Canada. It included seven new full-size productions: *Macbeth, The Winter's Tale, Julius Caesar,* and *The Merry Wives of Windsor*; Chekhov's *Uncle Vanya*; John Whiting's *The Devils*; and Leonard Bernstein's *Candide. As You Like It* and Noel Coward's *Private Lives* were repeated from 1977 productions, and there were smaller-scale presentations of *Medea,* one-act plays by Beckett, and several new works.

Stratford overshadowed Canada's two-year-old National Arts Centre in Ottawa. However, the newer theatre was trying to be more representatively Canadian by producing work in both French and English. In 1978 it presented English-language versions of Shakespeare's *Troilus and Cressida,* Strindberg's *The Father,* and Tennessee Williams's *Camino Real* and French versions of Chekhov's *The Seagull* and Goldoni's *The Servant of Two Masters.* Oddly enough, none of the plays was Canadian nor were any of the French-language productions originally written in French.

In Vancouver the Manitoba Theatre Centre presented a sturdy, if unimaginative, schedule: Shakespeare's *Measure for Measure* and *A Midsummer Night's Dream*; Ibsen's *A Doll's House*; and three contemporary plays — Williams's *Night of the Iguana,* Peter Shaffer's *Royal Hunt of the Sun,* and David Storey's *The Contractor.* The Shaw Festival at Niagara-on-the-Lake, Ont., presented *Major Barbara* and *Heartbreak House,* as well as Ibsen's *John Gabriel Borkman.* (MARTIN GOTTFRIED)

See also Dance; Music.

[622]

Winner of the 1978 New York Drama Critics Award for best musical, "Ain't Misbehavin'" was a spirited collection of 30 songs made famous by composer-pianist Fats Waller.

MARTHA SWOPE

IBSEN'S INFLUENCE ON MODERN DRAMA

by Michael Meyer

Henrik Ibsen in 1863–64.

ROYAL NORWEGIAN EMBASSY, LONDON

March 20, 1978, marked the 150th anniversary of the birth of Henrik Ibsen, an event celebrated during the year by many special performances of his works in his native Norway and elsewhere. At such a time, it is appropriate to ask how great Ibsen's influence has been on the drama of today.

In the development of civilization some innovations, such as the wheel, have come to be so universally accepted that it is difficult to imagine there was ever a time when they did not exist. Ibsen's contributions to the drama were as basic as these. He achieved in his field what his three great contemporaries, Darwin, Marx, and Freud, achieved in theirs. He changed its face so utterly that nothing has been quite the same since.

Innovations. Ibsen was the first man to write a great tragedy in ordinary, everyday prose. When he began to write plays, in 1849, tragedy for the stage was written in verse, and that was an accepted fact like the Earth going round the Sun. Prose was all right for comedy—the Falstaff scenes of Shakespeare and *The School for Scandal*—but tragedy had to be in verse. Of course, this dogma had been questioned, and there had been attempts to write prose tragedies, especially in Germany. However, none of these had really worked, which seemed to confirm the general belief. One man had indeed written two great prose tragedies: Georg Büchner, before he died in 1837 at the age of 23, had created *Woyzeck* and *Danton's Death*. But nobody knew about these; the manuscript of *Woyzeck* was not discovered until more than 40 years later, and *Danton's Death* existed only in a botched version; also, more relevant to the argument, both were written in a splendidly flamboyant prose very akin to poetry. But in 1881, Ibsen wrote, in simple prose, *Ghosts*, a play that was as clearly a major tragedy as *Agamemnon* or *Othello*.

Michael Meyer is the author of Henrik Ibsen: The Making of a Dramatist *(1967),* Henrik Ibsen: The Farewell to Poetry *(1971), and* Henrik Ibsen: The Top of a Cold Mountain *(1971). He has also translated all the major plays of Ibsen and Strindberg.*

Moreover, a fact often forgotten today, *Ghosts* was a play not about dead or legendary heroes but about modern middle-class people. This was the second of Ibsen's fundamental innovations. He was the first man (again, excepting Büchner) to write a major tragedy about people called Mr. and Mrs. Previous stage tragedies had dealt with kings and queens, princes and princesses, or, at the lowest, Montagues and Capulets. Soon after Ibsen's plays began (belatedly) to be acted in England, in the 1890s, an English critic complained that they were "as if Apollo . . . were now told to take up his habitation in a back parlour in South Hampstead," continuing: "Tragedy is more likely to concern itself with Glamis Castle, Melrose Abbey, Carisbrooke or even Carlton House Terrace." Ibsen showed that tragedy could and did take place at least as frequently in back parlours as in castles and palaces.

The importance of these innovations can scarcely be exaggerated. Before Ibsen began to write, audiences did not regard stage characters in tragedies as ordinary human beings with whom they could identify. They looked on them as gods and goddesses, or at least as Homeric or Wagnerian heroes and heroines. Even Shakespeare's characters were acted thus, though one of Shakespeare's greatest qualities was that he made his kings life-size and fallible. From being the respected medium that it had been in Shakespeare's time, the drama had by the mid-1800s become a despised literary form, shunned by serious men (and women) of letters—so much so that many writers, when they did write plays, did so with the intent that they should never be performed but merely read. Ibsen showed that a dramatist could, like Shakespeare and the Greeks, study human character and relationships as sensitively and profoundly as the great novelists.

Third, Ibsen made the theatre, for the first time

667

since Euripides, a place of debate. In plays such as *The Pillars of Society, A Doll's House, Ghosts,* and *An Enemy of the People,* he discussed the kind of contemporary problems about which men and women read in the newspapers or argued on street corners. He thus turned the theatre from a home of entertainment and occasional catharsis into a place from which people emerged compelled to rethink basic principles that they had never before seriously questioned. No one had ever walked out of a Shakespeare play, in Shakespeare's time or since, in this state of mind. But that was the effect of Ibsen's plays on his contemporaries, like that of reading Darwin or Marx or Freud.

Technically, too, Ibsen's influence was immense. He threw out the old artificialities of plot of which even Shakespeare had been guilty and which playwrights since had taken for granted—mistaken identities, intercepted letters, overheard conversations, and the like. These devices are present in Ibsen's early plays, as late as *A Doll's House* (1879); thereafter, he eliminated them. Even more important, he was a master of subtext, the meaning behind the meaning, the art of making his characters say one thing but mean another. This, along with the subtlety of his characterization and relationships, embarrassed and repelled flamboyant players such as Sarah Bernhardt and Henry Irving but was eagerly embraced by the new generation of actors such as Stanislavsky and Eleonora Duse. To actresses, especially, his plays were a godsend. Other dramatists had created great women's roles, but in *A Doll's House, Ghosts, Rosmersholm, The Lady from the Sea,* and *Hedda Gabler* Ibsen wrote plays in which the *chief* part was a woman's—something that had not been done in any major stage tragedy since the Greeks (who wrote their female roles for male actors), apart from *Antony and Cleopatra* and the plays of Webster and Racine.

The great dramatists who succeeded Ibsen have almost without exception acknowledged their debt to him. August Strindberg read *Brand* as a youth and was stirred to try his hand at drama both by the message of revolt against social convention and by the poetry and imagination of Ibsen's style. He hailed Ibsen as "a Savonarola," though he later turned against him because of his championship of women. George Bernard Shaw discovered Ibsen through a chance acquaintanceship with William Archer struck up in the British Museum reading room; Archer, who knew Norwegian, read Ibsen's plays to him, translating off the cuff, and it was this that stimulated Shaw to abandon novels for the drama. Chekhov, knowing Ibsen only through bad translation, at first found him "dry, cold, a man of reason," but later declared him to be his "favourite

playwright." Pirandello declared: "After Shakespeare, I unhesitatingly place Ibsen first." Eugene O'Neill found him "much closer to me than Shakespeare." Even Bertolt Brecht, though he later moved away from Ibsen and decried him, was much influenced at the start of his career by Ibsen's challenge of social convention and defiance of the establishment.

Critical Reaction. A reaction inevitably set in, even before Ibsen's death. Max Beerbohm, reviewing *The Lady from the Sea* in 1902, noted with dismay that Ibsen already seemed old-fashioned. "But," he added, "time is a cyclist. The things of the day before yesterday are nearer to us than the things of yesterday, and nearer still are the things of the day before the day before. Ellida and the rest, creatures of yesterday, will grow gradually younger, and will doubtless be much admired at the end of the century." He was to be proved right. For a time, Ibsen's reputation declined, because what was most controversial about his plays, his challenge of social convention, lost its appeal as those conventions changed. Gradually, however, critics, actors, and playgoers came to realize that Ibsen the social reformer was less important than Ibsen the portrayer of human character and relationships. We are no longer shocked by a wife deciding to leave her husband, or by implied references to syphilis; yet *A Doll's House* and *Ghosts* survive triumphantly as human dramas. And Ibsen's later plays, which caused less controversy in his time because they dealt with less burning issues, plays such as *The Wild Duck, The Lady from the Sea, Hedda Gabler, The Master Builder,* and *Little Eyolf,* survive, as *Madame Bovary* and *War and Peace* survive, because of the profundity of the author's insight into the human predicament and because of his genius as a weaver of tales. Who, ignorant of the outcome at the beginning of the final act of any Ibsen play, could guess what that outcome would be or how it would be achieved? Yet how inevitable that outcome always seems.

The younger playwrights today in Great Britain and the United States tend to look on Strindberg rather than Ibsen as their immediate ancestor, because of Strindberg's talent for portraying people at their emotional boiling point, his terser, more fragmentary style, and his deliberate blurring of the frontier between reality and fantasy. But, almost without exception, they acknowledge Ibsen as responsible for the great breakthrough that transformed the drama from a kind of grand-opera-without-music into a medium fit for a modern thinker or a modern poet. As a Swedish critic, Martin Lamm, has written, Ibsen is the Rome of modern drama. All roads lead from him and to him.

Togo

A West African republic on the Bight of Benin, Togo is bordered by Ghana, Upper Volta, and Benin. Area: 56,785 sq km (21,925 sq mi). Pop. (1977 est.): 2,348,000. Cap. and largest city: Lomé (pop., 1976 est., 229,400). Language: French (official). Religion: animist; Muslim and Christian minorities. President in 1978, Gen. Gnassingbe Eyadema.

During 1978 Pres. Gnassingbe Eyadema was active as a mediator in the conflicts in Western Sahara and between Benin and Gabon and Tanzania and Uganda. After playing a major role in the freeing in December 1977 of eight Frenchmen held hostage by the Polisario guerrillas in Western Sahara, he helped to set up a meeting in Monrovia, Liberia, on March 17, 1978, attended by the presidents of Liberia, Guinea, Ivory Coast, Senegal, and The Gambia and himself. Another diplomatic success for Togo was the election in July of former Togolese foreign minister Edem Kodjo to the post of secretary-general of the Organization of African Unity.

President Eyadema, who approved French proposals for the creation of a joint African intervention force put forward at the fifth Franco-African conference in Paris, sent a contingent of soldiers to Zaire's Shaba Province in June to join the Moroccan-led force that replaced French and Belgian paratroops there.   (PHILIPPE DECRAENE)

TOGO
   Education. (1975–76) Primary, pupils 362,895, teachers 6,080; secondary, pupils 59,162, teachers 1,358; vocational, pupils 5,118, teachers 251; teacher training, students 310, teachers 25; higher, students 2,353, teaching staff 236.
   Finance. Monetary unit: CFA franc, with (Sept. 18, 1978) a par value of CFA Fr 50 to the French franc (free rate of CFA Fr 218.81 to U.S. $1; CFA Fr 428.75 = £1 sterling). Budget (1977 est.) balanced at CFA Fr 55,201,000,000.
   Foreign Trade. (1976) Imports CFA Fr 48,505,000,000; exports CFA Fr 24,914,000,000. Import sources: France 30%; U.K. 12%; West Germany 8%; The Netherlands 7%; Japan 5%; U.S. 5%. Export destinations: The Netherlands 33%; France 28%; West Germany 7%. Main exports: phosphates 52%; cocoa 17%; coffee 16%.

Tonga

An independent monarchy and member of the Commonwealth of Nations, Tonga is an island group in the Pacific Ocean east of Fiji. Area: 750 sq km (290 sq mi). Pop. (1976): 90,100. Cap.: Nukualofa (pop., 1976, 18,300). Language: English and Tongan. Religion: Christian. King, Taufa'ahau Tupou IV; prime minister in 1978, Prince Tu'ipelehake.

During 1978 Tonga continued to suffer from a balance of payments deficit and an inability to provide either wage employment or land for more than a fraction of its population. Only 10% of those who left school could find jobs, and the effects of New Zealand's restriction on short-term labour migration were still evident. Telecommunications facilities were improved by the opening of a satel-

TONGA
   Education. (1977–78) Primary, pupils 19,461, teachers 739; secondary, pupils 12,157, teachers 491; vocational, pupils 278, teachers 12; teacher training, students (1975) 117, teachers 11.
   Finance and Trade. Monetary unit: pa'anga, with (Sept. 18, 1978) a free rate of 0.70 pa'anga to U.S. $1 (1.38 pa'anga = £1 sterling). Budget (1975–76 est.): revenue 5,257,-000 pa'anga; expenditure 5,897,000 pa'anga. Foreign trade (1976): imports 11,655,000 pa'anga; exports 3,348,000 pa'anga. Import sources: New Zealand 40%; Australia 22%; U.K. 11%; Japan 6%; Fiji 5%. Export destinations: The Netherlands 30%; New Zealand 29%; West Germany 21%; U.K. 6%; Fiji 5%. Main exports: copra 54%; desiccated coconut 11%; bananas 8%; kava 6%; watermelons 5%.

lite-Earth station. The most noteworthy result of the 1978 elections was the election of a female commoner as a people's representative for the first time.

A 99-year monopoly of merchant banking and control of an industrial estate was given to the Bank of the South Pacific, which also agreed to finance a tourist hotel and to upgrade Fua'amotu airport. Developments came to a halt, however, when the U.S. sought the extradition from Australia of John Meier, the bank's principal financier, to answer charges related to unpaid taxes and penalties amounting to $6.5 million. The U.S. case failed because Tonga had given the defendant diplomatic status. Subsequently, the government withdrew the legislation relating to the bank on a technicality.

Celebrations, including a new coin issue, marked the 60th birthday of King Taufa'ahau Tupou IV. Tonga joined other members of the South Pacific Forum in establishing a joint agency for the management of 200-mi economic zones in the Southwest Pacific.   (BARRIE MACDONALD)

Track and Field Sports

Midway between the 1976 and 1980 Olympic Games, the 1978 track and field season featured a flood of world records and the celebration of two quadrennial regional championships.

Men's International Competition. Spirited competition marked both the XI Commonwealth Games and the 12th running of the European Championships. But it was in other competition that no less than 14 new world records were achieved, 8 of them in Olympic events. (All standard events in Table I except the 3,000 m are contested in the Olympic Games.)

It was likely that the year would be remembered primarily for the amazing exploits of Henry Rono. He accounted for four world marks in as many events and became the first man ever to break records for 3,000 m, 3,000-m steeplechase, 5,000 m, and 10,000 m. He was unbeaten until the end of a very long season when fatigue and minor but nagging injuries caught up with him.

Rono, the latest of Kenya's famed distance-running stars, set two of his records in the United States while competing for Washington State University. The other two were made in Europe. Rono's record splurge began in Berkeley, Calif.,

Togo

Tonga

Theology:
see Religion

Timber:
see Industrial Review

Tobacco:
see Industrial Review

Tobogganing:
see Winter Sports

Tourism:
see Industrial Review

Toys:
see Games and Toys

Dick Buerkle breaks the tape to set a new indoor track mile record at College Park, Maryland, in January. Buerkle covered the distance in 3 minutes 54.9 seconds.

where on April 8, before a small and unsuspecting audience, he ran 5,000 m in 13 min 8.4 sec. The time was a full 4.5 sec faster than the one-year-old existing mark.

An even smaller group of only 200 fans got their surprise gift when Rono ran the 3,000-m steeplechase in 8 min 5.4 sec at Seattle, Wash., on May 13. He knocked 2.6 sec off the old figure. After setting two meet — but not world — records in the U.S. national collegiate championships early in the month, Rono turned up in Vienna on June 11. There he proceeded to take the 10,000-m record away from fellow Kenyan Samson Kimobwa. The time was 27 min 22.5 sec, an improvement of 8 sec. The finale to Rono's spectacular record-breaking season came on June 27 at Oslo, Norway, where he sped the 3,000-m distance in 7 min 32.1 sec to chop 3.1 sec off the old mark.

Records escaped Rono for the rest of the summer, but victories did not. His most notable wins, two of them, came in the Commonwealth Games, which were celebrated in Edmonton, Alta., on August 6–12. Not pressed by any close competition, as in his record-breaking runs, Rono captured the steeplechase and 5,000 m as he pleased.

Only Rono was able to set records in standard Olympic events on the track. The remaining world marks were established in the field events and in two relays and two walks that are infrequently staged. A world best time of 8 min 13.5 sec was set in the two-mile run by Britain's Steve Ovett, but marks in nonmetric distances except for the one-mile were no longer officially recognized. Five of the eight field event records were bettered, all but one by a European. The lone new standard achieved by a U.S. athlete in an individual event came in the pole vault. Mike Tully, a student at the University of California at Los Angeles, cleared 5.71 m (18 ft 8¾ in) at Corvallis, Ore., on May 20. It was a clean, legal clearance, but the bar fell off while the height was being measured and acceptance of the record was in doubt.

Vladimir Yashchenko, a 19-year-old Soviet athlete who stunned the track world in 1977 with his first international high jump record, did it again in 1978. This time it was a clearance of 2.34 m (7 ft 8 in) at Tbilisi, U.S.S.R., on June 16. East Germans took over the shot put and discus records. Olympic champion Udo Beyer earned the shot put honours July 6 at Göteborg, Sweden, with a put of 22.15 m (72 ft 8 in). The discus mark went to Wolfgang Schmidt, who threw 71.14 m (233 ft 5 in) at East Berlin on August 9. There were two record setters in the hammer throw. First was Boris Zaichuk of the Soviet Union, who reached 80.14 m (262 ft 11 in) at Moscow on July 9 only to lose his record to Karl-Hans Riehm of West Germany. Riehm hurled the 16-lb hammer 80.32 m (263 ft 6 in) at Heidenheim, West Germany, on August 6.

In the nonstandard events, the University of Southern California ran the 4 × 200 m relay in 1 min 20.3 sec at Tempe, Ariz., May 27. It was only the second world record by U.S. trackmen in a notably unproductive season. Joel Andrews, James Sanford, Billy Mullins, and Clancy Edwards carried the baton. The other relay world best was the 7 min 8.1 sec time for 4 × 800 m, established by the Soviet Union at Podolsk on August 12. Vladimir Podolyakov, Nikolay Kirov, Vladimir Malozemlin, and Anatoliy Reshetnyak made up the team.

Raul Gonzales of Mexico accounted for the two remaining records, and he earned them both in one race. Walking at Førde, Norway, on May 19, Gonzales covered 50,000 m in 3 hr 52 min 24 sec and traveled 16 mi 1,637 yd in 2 hours.

The European Championships in Prague from August 31 to September 4 were hampered by bad weather. Some marks were not as good as expected, but the quality of the competition was excellent. The indoor version, held March 11 and 12 at Milan, Italy, was marked by the jumping of Yashchenko. His 2.35 m (7 ft 8½ in) leap was a new indoor best and remained 1 cm (½ in) better than his new outdoor standard established later in the year.

Milan was also the scene of what was to be the other big indoor competition of the season. It was the first tournament ever held between the U.S. and Europe, but neither team was at full strength, and the affair was not worthy of the name. Europe overwhelmed the U.S. in combined scoring for men and women, 141 to 80, with the U.S. women unable to win an event.

Women's International Competition. Marita Koch, a fast-rising East German sprinter, was to women's competition what Henry Rono was to men's. Unlike Rono she confined her record breaking to two events, but she put her name on the world record list a total of five times.

On May 28 at Erfurt, East Germany, Koch lowered the 200-m mark to 22.06 sec. One week later, on June 4 at Karl-Marx-Stadt, East Germany, she equaled her new mark. Still later in the season she ran the distance in 22.18 sec, giving her the three fastest times for the 200 m in history.

Deciding to concentrate on one event in the European Championships, Koch turned her attention to the 400 m. She ran a world record 49.19 sec at Leipzig, East Germany, on July 2 and cut another large chunk off that with a 49.02 sec at Potsdam, East Germany, on August 19. Her remarkable season reached its peak at Prague on August 31 when she captured the European title with her third 400-m record of the year. The time was 48.94 sec. Three days later Koch earned another gold medal when she anchored East Germany to a victory in the 4 × 400 m relay. Her lap of 48.3 sec was the fastest ever run by a woman and helped the quartet to a 3 min 21.2 sec clocking, the second fastest ever run by women.

Three other women put their names into the international record lists twice during the season. And all three, like Koch, capped the year with all-time bests in the European Championships. They were Sara Simeoni of Italy, a long-time challenger for high-jump honours, and two relative unknowns from the Soviet Union, long jumper Vilma Bardauskiene and 400-m hurdler Tatyana Selenzova.

Simeoni became the first woman to jump higher than 2 m when she added 1 cm to Rosemarie Ack-

ermann's highly regarded record by clearing 2.01 m (6 ft 7 in) at Brescia, Italy, on August 4. She repeated the height in the continental title meet, bettering Ackermann by 2 cm on August 31.

Bardauskiene surprised the track world when she jumped 7.07 m (23 ft 2¼ in) not once but twice at Kishinyov on August 18. She thus became the first female to better 7 m, and it did not take her long to do it again. Her championship victory was earned with a jump of 7.09 m (23 ft 3¼ in) on August 29.

Selenzova's heroics also came late in the season and followed a record run in the 400-m hurdles by Krystyna Kacperczyk of Poland, who was timed in 55.44 sec at West Berlin on August 18. Her mark lasted just one day before Selenzova ran the event in 55.31 sec at Podolsk, U.S.S.R. At Prague, on September 2, Selenzova dipped under 55 sec for the first time, lowering her new record to 54.89 sec.

Three more marks fell in standard events. Grazyna Rabsztyn of Poland sped over the 100-m hurdles in 12.48 sec at Fürth, West Germany, on June 10. The remaining two bests were achieved by East Germans, who continued to dominate the sport although challenged by a surprisingly strong Soviet Union contingent. Evelin Jahl, the Olympic discus titlist, claimed the world record in that event with a throw of 70.72 m (232 ft) at Dresden, East Germany, on August 12. And four of her countrywomen, Johanna Klier, Monika Hamann, Carla Bodendorf, and Marlies Gohr, clocked 42.27 sec to win the 4 × 100 m relay at Potsdam on August 19.

Overall, the world's women had a better year than the men, claiming new records in 7 of the 14 Olympic events. (The 400-m hurdles is not run in the Olympics.) Noteworthy performances in nonstandard events included an all-time best of 2 min 30.6 sec for 1,000 m by Tatyana Providokhina of the Soviet Union. And Loa Olafsson of Denmark turned in unofficial world records in the 5,000 m (15 min 8.8 sec) and 10,000 m (31 min 45.4 sec).

Indoors, the top performances were by Marlies Oelsner (later Gohr) with 7.12 sec for the 60 m in the European Championships; 1.95 m (6 ft 4¾ in) in the high jump by Simeoni; and 4 min 5 sec in the 1,500 m by Natalia Maracescu of Romania.

U.S. Competition. As was the case in 1977, only one individual U.S. trackman and one relay team made the world record lists in 1978 (*see* above). But three more men earned U.S. records, one of them doing it twice. The latter was James Butts, second-place finisher in the Olympic triple jump, who claimed the national record by leaping 17.21 m (56 ft 5½ in) and 17.24 m (56 ft 6¾ in). Doug Brown, a former record holder, regained the 3,000-m steeplechase honours when he ran the distance in 8 min 19.3 sec. And Greg Foster came within 0.01 sec of the world high-hurdle mark when he lowered the U.S. standard to 13.22 sec.

As in worldwide competition, the women in the U.S. were more productive than were the males. Official world records escaped them, but Kathy Mills of Penn State University ran a world's best of 15 min 35.5 sec in the 5,000 m, only to see that mark slashed by Olafsson five days later. National record breakers included: Brenda Morehead, 22.60

Table I. World 1978 Outdoor Records—Men

Event	Competitor, country, date	Performance
3,000 m	Henry Rono, Kenya, June 27	7 min 32.1 sec
3,000-m steeplechase	Henry Rono, Kenya, May 13	8 min 5.4 sec
5,000 m	Henry Rono, Kenya, April 8	13 min 8.4 sec
10,000 m	Henry Rono, Kenya, June 11	27 min 22.5 sec
High jump	Vladimir Yashchenko, U.S.S.R., June 16	2.34 m (7 ft 8 in)
Pole vault	Mike Tully, U.S., May 20	5.71 m (18 ft 8¾ in)
Shot put	Udo Beyer, East Germany, July 6	22.15 m (72 ft 8 in)
Discus	Wolfgang Schmidt, East Germany, Aug. 9	71.14 m (233 ft 5 in)
Hammer throw	Boris Zaichuk, U.S.S.R., July 9	80.14 m (262 ft 11 in)
	Karl-Hans Riehm, West Germany, Aug. 6	80.32 m (263 ft 6 in)
Nonstandard events		
Two mile*	Steve Ovett, U.K., Sept. 15	8 min 13.5 sec
4 × 200 m relay	University of Southern California, May 27	1 min 20.3 sec
4 × 800 m relay	U.S.S.R., Aug. 12	7 min 8.1 sec
2-hr walk	Raul Gonzales, Mexico, May 19	16 mi 1,637 yd
50,000-m walk	Raul Gonzales, Mexico, May 19	3 hr 52 min 24 sec

*World best; no official record.

Table II. World 1978 Outdoor Records—Women

Event	Competitor, country, date	Performance
200 m	Marita Koch, East Germany, May 28	22.06 sec
	Marita Koch, East Germany, June 4	22.06 sec
400 m	Marita Koch, East Germany, July 2	49.19 sec
	Marita Koch, East Germany, Aug. 19	49.02 sec
	Marita Koch, East Germany, Aug. 31	48.94 sec
100-m hurdles	Grazyna Rabsztyn, Poland, June 10	12.48 sec
400-m hurdles	Krystyna Kacperczyk, Poland, Aug. 18	55.44 sec
	Tatyana Selenzova, U.S.S.R., Aug. 19	55.31 sec
	Tatyana Selenzova, U.S.S.R., Sept. 2	54.89 sec
4 × 100 m relay	East Germany, Aug. 19	42.27 sec
High jump	Sara Simeoni, Italy, Aug. 4	2.01 m (6 ft 7 in)
	Sara Simeoni, Italy, Aug. 31	2.01 m (6 ft 7 in)
Long jump	Vilma Bardauskiene, U.S.S.R., Aug. 18	7.07 m (23 ft 2¼ in)
	Vilma Bardauskiene, U.S.S.R., Aug. 29	7.09 m (23 ft 3¼ in)
Discus throw	Evelin Jahl, East Germany, Aug. 12	70.72 m (232 ft)
Nonstandard events. World best; no official record		
1,000 m	Tatyana Providokhina, U.S.S.R., Aug. 20	2 min 30.6 sec
5,000 m	Kathy Mills, U.S., May 26	15 min 35.5 sec
	Loa Olafsson, Denmark, May 31	15 min 8.8 sec
10,000 m	Natalia Maracescu, Romania, Jan. 22	32 min 43.2 sec
	Loa Olafsson, Denmark, April 6	31 min 45.4 sec

sec for 200 m; Jan Merrill, 8 min 42.6 sec for 3,000 m; Patty Van Wolvelaere and Deby LaPlante, 13.14 sec and 13.13 sec for the 100-m hurdles; Louise Ritter, 1.90 m (6 ft 3 in) in the high jump; Jodi Anderson, 6.90 m (22 ft 7½ in) in the long jump; Maren Seidler, 18.45 m (60 ft 6½ in) in the shot put; and Jane Frederick, 4,651 and 4,704 points in the pentathlon. The latter was a changed event in 1978 because the 800-m run was substituted for the 200-m dash as one of the five events.

International team competition in the U.S. was limited to a dual meet between the U.S. and Soviet Union at Berkeley, Calif., on July 7–8. The U.S. men won 119–102, while the Soviet women won a close contest 75–71, giving the U.S. an overall victory of 190–177.

In collegiate team competition the University of Southern California, a perennial powerhouse, won the National Collegiate Athletic Association outdoor championships at Eugene, Ore. The indoor title, contested at Detroit, was won by the University of Texas at El Paso, its fourth triumph in five years. Los Angeles State University won the NCAA Division II title, while Occidental College, also in Los Angeles, captured the Division III crown, giving southern California schools all three NCAA titles. The National Association of Intercollegiate Athletics' crown went to Texas Southern University. California State University at Northridge won the national meet of the Association of Intercollegiate Athletics for Women.

In indoor competition, where no world records are accepted because conditions vary considerably, U.S. athletes accounted for a number of all-time bests, including four in standard events. Houston McTear ran 60 yd in 6.04 sec; Renaldo Nehemiah hurdled 60 yd in 7.07 sec; Mike Tully vaulted 5.59 m (18 ft 4 in) and 5.62 m (18 ft 5¼ in); Franklin Jacobs high jumped 2.32 m (7 ft 7¼ in) after Greg Joy of Canada did 2.31 m (7 ft 7 in) and before Yashchenko cleared 2.35 m (7 ft 8½ in); and Dick Buerkle ran one mile in 3 min 54.9 sec.

All-time indoor bests for women were turned

in by Merrill, 8 min 57.6 sec for 3,000 m; LaPlante, 7.53 sec for the 60-yd hurdles; and Deandra Carney, 6.72 sec for 60 yd.

Marathon Running and Cross Country. Bill Rodgers, a Boston businessman, dominated competition in the 26 mi 385 yd marathon, both in the U.S. and internationally. He had finished the 1977 season with a victory in the most important annual competition held outside the U.S. and won the two most prestigious races of 1978.

Rodgers won at Fukuoka, Japan, on Dec. 5, 1977, in the fast time of 2 hr 10 min 55 sec, defeating an international field. In 1978 he captured both the Boston and New York races, which, except for the Olympic Games contest, are the best-known marathons. His Boston victory came on April 17 when he ran the distance in 2 hr 10 min 13 sec, and he won at New York on October 22 in 2 hr 12 min 12 sec. It was his third consecutive New York triumph. The fastest time of the year, however, was the 2 hr 9 min 6 sec clocking for Shigeru Sou of Japan in winning the Beppu Mainchi race on February 5.

Two major championships were contested during the year. Gidemas Shahanga, a virtual unknown from Tanzania, won the Commonwealth Games on August 11 in 2 hr 15 min 40 sec. And the Soviet Union's Leonid Moiseyev became the European champion when he ran 2 hr 11 min 58 sec at Prague on September 3.

Grete Waitz of Norway, running her first marathon, won at New York in 2 hr 32 min 30 sec, the fastest time ever by a woman. And Julie Brown turned in a U.S. best when she took the Nike run at Eugene, Ore., on September 10 in 2 hr 36 min 24 sec. The leading woman in the Boston race was Gayle Barron at 2 hr 44 min 52 sec.

Interest in marathoning continued to burgeon in the U.S., highlighted by more than 11,000 runners at New York. More than 8,000 additional entries for that race were rejected because the course could not handle them.

The international cross country championships, held at Glasgow, Scotland, on March 25, were won by John Treacy of Ireland. He covered the muddy 12,300-m course in 39 min 25 sec. France edged the U.S. for the team title, Romania captured the women's title, and Waitz won the 4,728-m run in 16 min 19 sec.   (BERT NELSON)

[452.B.3.b]

Vladimir Yashchenko, a 19-year-old Soviet student, established a new men's indoor high jump record with a leap of 7 feet 8½ inches during the European indoor track and field championships held in Italy in March.

Transportation

Associated with the continued, though selective, growth in the world's economy during 1978 was the expansion of some elements of transport demand. It was not a year of major technological innovation; indeed, problems with the new giant Hovercraft services across the English Channel, the Soviet supersonic air transport, and high-speed trains underlined the difficulties of taking major steps in transport technology. Technological developments continued to occur in the operation of established systems. In this connection the use of microprocessors in the control of mechanical processes, vehicles, and whole systems increased.

In an increasingly busy and congested world, the avoidance of major disasters became more and more important, and the "Amoco Cadiz" oil tanker shipwreck, the road crash near San Carlos, Spain, and the California air disaster made the price of failure unfortunately clear.

The transportation problems of the less developed countries were attracting increased attention from the developed nations and the major international organizations. The World Bank was particularly active in fostering an improved approach to transport planning in the third world and providing aid for projects aimed at supporting the economic and social development of poorer countries.

Oil and energy conservation was an established feature of the transport policies of the major developed countries, but as yet few really effective measures to reduce oil consumption were in evidence. Probably the most notable energy-saving initiatives in the transport sector were the reduction of weight in new models of U.S. cars and increased railway electrification in some countries.

(DAVID BAYLISS)

AVIATION

For the air transport industry 1978 was a year of trauma, especially in the U.S., where Pres. Jimmy Carter's policies of liberalizing airline economic regulation began to take effect. The effect of "deregulation" was apparent in new discount fares, resulting in sharply increased traffic, and concern within the industry about its future stability. Internationally, the Carter administration's policies affected the field of bilateral air-service agreements, where U.S. pressure for liberalization began to be felt, and the International Air Transport Association (IATA), whose traffic conference machinery, used to fix fares, was threatened by the increasingly strict application of U.S. antitrust legislation.

After several years of intense public debate, the Airline Deregulation Act was signed into law by President Carter on October 24. Among its provisions was one allowing airlines to apply for "dormant" route authority—authority to operate routes held by other airlines but not used by them. The immediate result was an unprecedented scene outside the Civil Aeronautics Board (CAB) office in Washington, D.C., as airline representatives waited in line for nearly a week—with jostling, arguments, and alleged threats of violence—to lay claim to dormant routes or to protect the holder's title to such routes.

By the time the deregulation bill was signed, the CAB was already some way down the road to deregulation, and sharply discounted fares had led to an upsurge in airline traffic in the U.S. During January–September U.S. scheduled traffic rose 18.1% over the same period of 1977 and totaled 167,300,000,000 revenue passenger-miles, according to figures released by the Air Transport Association. By contrast, capacity increased only 5.4% to 266,200,000,000 available seat-miles, with the result that the passenger load factor increased sharply from 54.1% in the earlier period to 60.9%.

The potential decline in revenue caused by the new discounted fares was more than offset by the

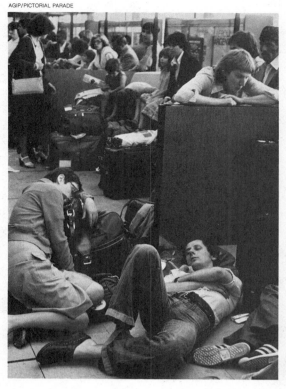

People had to sleep wherever they could when passengers were stranded in Orly Airport near Paris after air traffic controllers staged a work slowdown in July.

increased load factor, with the result that financial performance improved sharply. The 11 U.S. trunk airlines reported a net profit of just over $1 billion in the first nine months of 1978, compared with $511 million during the same period of 1977. Operating revenue at $15.8 billion was up 14.9%, while operating expenses rose 12.1% to $14.3 billion.

Internationally, the thrust of the U.S. negotiating policy was toward increased competition, determination of fares and rates by market forces rather than by government regulation, removal of restraints on airline capacity, liberalization of rules governing charters, and the multiple designation of airlines for particular routes. Bilateral agreements were reached between the U.S. and several countries during 1978—those with The Netherlands and Israel were notable for their liberal provisions—and many others were due to be negotiated in 1979.

The main effect of generally lowered fares was felt internationally on the North Atlantic, where there was a marked shift of traffic from charters to scheduled services. New services across the Atlantic included Laker Airways' low-fare Skytrain service between London and Los Angeles, which began on September 26 after the airline had been designated the second British carrier on the route.

Skytrain had already been operating between London and New York since 1977, and during the 1978 summer peak the other scheduled carriers reacted to the low-fare competition by introducing standby fares. The resulting lines of would-be travelers caused severe congestion problems in airport terminals. Laker passengers awaiting seats camped out in London streets. Traffic growth on the North Atlantic was demonstrated by a 19.6% increase in the number of scheduled passengers in

Trade, International: see Economy, World

Trade Unions: see Industrial Relations

Transkei: see South Africa

World Transportation

Country	Railways Traffic — Route length in 000 km	Passenger in 000,000 pass.-km	Freight in 000,000 net ton-km	Motor transport — Road length in 000 km	Vehicles in use Passenger in 000	Commercial in 000	Merchant shipping Ships of 100 tons and over — Number of vessels	Gross reg. tons in 000	Air traffic — Total km flown in 000,000	Passenger in 000,000 pass.-km	Freight in 000,000 net ton-km
EUROPE											
Austria	6.5	6,712	10,929	102.9	1,828.1	151.0	11	53	16.8	911	11.2
Belgium	4.0	7,660	6,468	114.8	2,700.5	237.3	271	1,595	47.8	4,051	348.2
Bulgaria	4.3	7,343	17,080	36.1	c.198.0[1]	c.43.0[1]	186	964	10.3	500	7.6
Cyprus	—	—	—	9.8	68.8	15.3	800	2,788	4.9	393	16.7
Czechoslovakia	13.2	17,920	71,550	145.5[1]	1,558.7	275.4	14	149	30.7	1,414	17.2
Denmark	2.5	3,415	1,805	66.5	1,339.8	248.6	1,407	5,331	37.8	2,567[2]	124.1[2]
Finland	6.0	2,974	6,399	73.8	1,032.9	132.7	337	2,262	30.0	1,395	38.5
France	34.3	51,670	66,225	795.8	16,230.0	2,145.0	1,327	11,614	265.6	27,284	1,669.3
Germany, East	14.3	22,704	52,142	118.9	2,052.2	248.6	447	1,487	26.3	1,448	50.5
Germany, West	31.8	38,408	55,747	469.6	19,180.5	1,260.0	1,975	9,592	180.3	15,904	1,268.7
Greece	2.5	1,583	844	36.6	495.7	218.8	3,344	29,517	43.5	4,354	58.3
Hungary	8.2	13,024	23,610	99.6	654.8	125.1	19	63	10.7	510	5.2
Ireland	2.0	794	534	89.0[1]	551.1	53.5	98	212	19.4	1,528	77.7
Italy	19.9	38,780	16,080	291.1[1]	16,221.3	1,060.0	1,690	11,111	134.6	10,780	468.2
Netherlands, The	2.8	8,018	2,805	86.4	3,760.0	316.0	1,254	5,290	95.1	11,497	753.0
Norway	4.2	2,010	2,632	78.1	1,022.9	138.7	2,738	27,801	52.3	3,470[2]	132.0[2]
Poland	23.9	44,311	135,407	300.8	1,290.1	467.1	773	3,448	26.0	1,666	15.7
Portugal	3.6	5,242	884	46.2[1]	1,034.0	288.0	350	1,281	34.9	3,010	91.5
Romania	11.0[1]	22,380[1]	67,560	c.95.0[1]	c.200.0	c.100.0	207	1,218	17.2	919	13.7
Spain	15.8	17,163	11,586	145.3	5,351.4	1,051.6	2,726	7,186	135.8	12,512	350.9
Sweden	12.1	5,520	14,220	124.8	2,881.3	165.2	728	7,429	63.5	3,731[2]	183.9[2]
Switzerland	5.0[1]	8,028	5,923	62.1	1,863.6	168.6	28	253	86.0	9,269	377.9
U.S.S.R.	268.8[1]	315,061	3,332,000	1,405.6	c.5,660.0	c.5,703.0	8,167	21,438	...	130,529	2,697.8
United Kingdom	18.4	28,600[3]	20,171[3]	368.4	14,355.0	1,795.0	3,432	31,646	300.5	31,871	1,019.1
Yugoslavia	10.0	10,356	22,230	c.113.5	1,732.1	152.4	459	2,285	30.6	2,150	20.6
ASIA											
Bangladesh	2.9	3,331[1]	639[1]	6.3	20.0	9.4	133	244	7.4	426	9.7
Burma	4.3	2,781	394	22.0	37.8	40.5	56	68	5.0	168	1.2
Cambodia	c.0.6	54[1]	10[1]	c.11.0	27.2[1]	11.0[1]	3	4	0.8	42	0.4
China	c.48.0	45,670[1]	301,000[1]	c.808.0	c.50.0	c.1,500.0	622	4,245	22.6	c.1,410	c.176.0
India	60.3[1]	159,940	154,310	1,232.3[1]	799.5	415.2	566	5,482	83.0	7,196	279.3
Indonesia	7.6	3,258	717	95.5	420.9	263.1	1,032	1,163	65.5	3,112	47.6
Iran	4.5[3]	2,126[1]	4,917[1]	c.52.0[1]	1,892.0	105.0	193	1,002	37.1	3,059	74.8
Iraq	2.0[1]	704	2,252	11.9[1]	98.6[1]	61.8[1]	110	1,135	11.5	1,221	32.5
Israel	0.9	280	449	10.7[1]	297.3	98.1	58	405	32.5	4,697	179.0
Japan	28.0[1]	311,860	41,585	1,078.4	18,475.6	11,387.2	9,642	40,036	276.4	22,813	1,126.6
Korea, South	5.7	c.16,900	10,276	45.5	96.1	87.5	1,042	2,495	38.6	4,519	355.1
Malaysia	1.8	1,273[4]	1,212[4]	21.3	430.4[1]	140.3[1]	179	564	29.9	2,100	48.4
Pakistan	8.8	12,957	8,677	49.9	196.1[1]	91.7[1]	84	476	35.3	3,410	148.3
Philippines	1.1[1]	780	40	112.9	386.2	281.0	504	1,147	41.5	3,050	111.9
Saudi Arabia	0.6	72[1]	66[1]	26.3	226.2	178.3	119	1,019	38.9	3,122	85.2
Syria	1.8	166	305	c.13.3[1]	62.8	55.9	32	21	9.8	712	7.6
Taiwan	4.2	8,479	2,891	17.2	171.0	129.9	443	1,559	20.0	2,908	171.6
Thailand	3.8[1]	5,530	2,630	39.7	c.363.1	c.267.0	100	261	36.5	3,418	109.1
Turkey	8.1	4,615	7,278	196.0	512.4	190.3	448	1,288	21.9	2,019	17.3
Vietnam	c.4.2	...	...	c.60.0	c.100.0	c.200.0	69	129	...	...	...
AFRICA											
Algeria	4.1	1,058[1]	1,901[1]	78.4[1]	204.1[1]	103.1[1]	112	1,056	28.7	1,881	8.8
Congo	0.8	246	508	c.11.0	19.0[1]	10.5[1]	14	4	2.8[5]	137[5]	14.2[5]
Egypt	4.9	8,831[1]	2,260[1]	26.0	245.6	57.4	176	408	20.9	1,739	21.9
Ethiopia	1.0	132[6]	260[6]	23.0	52.5	13.1	18	24	12.9	523	20.1
Gabon	—	—	—	6.9	c.10.1[1]	c.7.3[1]	15	99	4.7[5]	190[5]	14.4[5]
Ghana	1.0	431[1]	305[1]	35.0	64.0	46.0	79	183	3.5	194	4.4
Ivory Coast	0.8[1]	918[1]	529[1]	45.2	75.9[1]	13.7[1]	59	116	2.7[5]	151[5]	14.0[5]
Kenya	2.7[1]	...	3,650	50.1	83.7[1]	79.2[1]	19	15	13.1[7]	879[7]	19.7[7]
Liberia	0.5[1]	...	4,396[1]	7.3[1]	12.1[1]	10.0[1]	2,617	79,983	0.6	3	—
Libya	—	—	—	c.20.0	263.1[1]	131.3[1]	53	674	9.4	700	6.9
Malawi	0.6[1]	62	204	11.0[1]	10.2	10.6	—	—	3.2	122	4.7
Morocco	1.8	830	3,476	26.4[1]	347.4	145.7	91	270	19.5	1,264	18.2
Nigeria	3.5[1]	785[1]	972[1]	97.0[1]	c.150.0[1]	c.82.0[1]	94	336	10.2	470	8.4
Rhodesia	3.4[1]	...	4,660	78.9[1]	c.180.0[1]	c.70.0[1]	—	—	4.9	240	1.9
Senegal	1.0[1]	180	164	13.3[1]	48.0[1]	25.0[1]	75	28	2.5[5]	137[5]	13.9[5]
Somalia	—	—	—	c.17.1[1]	8.0[1]	8.0[1]	31	158	1.2	23	0.2
South Africa	20.1	...	78,495[8]	c.230.0	2,169.0	821.3	297	476	58.3	6,488	189.8
Sudan	4.6	...	2,288[1]	c.50.0	c.52.0	c.27.0	13	43	7.7	345	7.5
Tanzania	c.3.5	...	...	c.35.0[1]	42.0	41.8	22	36	5.1[7]	195[7]	3.7[7]
Tunisia	1.9	710	1,330	21.6	105.4	68.2	39	100	11.5	1,058	9.1
Uganda	1.3[1]	...	...	27.5	27.0[1]	14.1[1]	1	6	3.6[7]	197[7]	8.2[7]
Zaire	5.2[1]	447[1]	3,017[1]	c.145.0	84.8[1]	67.8[1]	34	110	14.9	690	54.8
Zambia	c.1.9	320[1]	897[1]	35.0	c.104.0	c.61.0	1	6	14.9	356	19.8
NORTH AND CENTRAL AMERICA											
Canada	70.5	2.942	197,089[1]	860.7[1]	8,870.0	2,112.0	1,283	2,823	297.6	24,910	620.0
Costa Rica	c.1.4	81[1]	14[1]	24.7	55.1[1]	37.2[1]	14	7	6.5	326	13.5
Cuba	14.7	695[1]	1,825[1]	27.0[1]	c.70.0[1]	c.33.0[1]	315	668	10.1	663	14.2
El Salvador	0.6	...	...	11.0[1]	41.0[1]	19.1[1]	2	2	6.8	195	14.0
Guatemala	0.9	...	117	13.4[1]	82.7	50.1	8	12	4.2	143	6.8
Honduras	1.8	174[1]	3[1]	9.2	20.5	30.2	63	105	5.1	257	3.6
Mexico	24.7[1]	4,058	34,821	193.4	2,641.0	976.7	311	674	98.3	7,833	83.4
Nicaragua	0.4	28[1]	14[1]	17.6	c.34.0	c.20.0	30	35	2.3	86	2.1
Panama	c.0.5	...	...	7.7	66.2[1]	19.6[1]	3,267	19,458	9.2	437	5.0
United States	331.3[1]	15,688[9]	1,146,492[9]	6,175.6	109,003.0	26,152.0	4,740	15,300	3,731.7	307,559	9,587.6
SOUTH AMERICA											
Argentina	40.1	14,481	11,039	207.3	2,588.0	1,101.0	401	1,677	68.4	4,801	126.7
Bolivia	3.8	310[1]	465[1]	37.1[1]	22.5[1]	30.1[1]	—	—	7.0	558	27.7
Brazil	33.0[1]	10,649[1]	55,220[1]	1,489.1	6,348.6	737.4	538	3,330	173.3	10,366	488.0
Chile	c.10.1	2,460	1,999	75.2	262.5	155.7[1]	143	406	20.8	1,228	75.7
Colombia	c.3.4	511	1,247	56.7	355.7	63.0	52	247	49.9	3,340	176.1
Ecuador	1.2[1]	65[1]	46[1]	21.5[1]	43.6[1]	68.4[1]	55	197	10.8	318	7.3
Paraguay	0.5	26[1]	30[1]	16.0[1]	c.25.9	c.14.8	26	22	2.6	83	1.0
Peru	c.3.4[1]	455[1]	707[1]	56.9	299.5	156.1	681	555	24.1	1,367	25.9
Uruguay	3.0	372	281[1]	49.6[1]	c.151.6[1]	c.85.7[1]	45	193	3.6	83	0.2
Venezuela	0.4	42[1]	15[1]	58.6	955.2[1]	369.4[1]	179	639	40.4	2,538	76.8
OCEANIA											
Australia	40.8[10]	...	30,820	837.9[1]	5,284.0	1,260.0	424	1,374	207.4	19,240	413.2
New Zealand	4.8	497	3,600	95.0[1]	1,210.2	230.8	102	199	48.7	3,608	121.9

Note: Data are for 1976 or 1977 unless otherwise indicated. (—) Indicates nil or negligible; (...) indicates not known; (c.) indicates provisional or estimated.
[1] Data given are the most recent available. [2] Including apportionment of traffic of Scandinavian Airlines System. [3] Excluding Northern Ireland. [4] Including Singapore.
[5] Including apportionment of traffic of Air Afrique (Gabon withdrew in 1976). [6] Including Djibouti traffic. [7] Including apportionment of former East African Airways Corporation (disbanded from 1977). [8] Including Namibia. [9] Principal railways. [10] State system only.

Sources: UN, *Statistical Yearbook 1977, Monthly Bulletin of Statistics, Annual Bulletin of Transport Statistics for Europe 1976*; Lloyd's Register of Shipping, *Statistical Tables 1977*; International Road Federation, *World Road Statistics 1977*.

(M. C. MacDONALD)

the first seven months of 1978. Charter passengers carried by IATA members alone showed a 23% decrease, reflecting the attractions of the new scheduled fares.

The total number of passengers carried by the world's airlines in 1977 (U.S.S.R. excluded), according to the International Civil Aviation Organization (ICAO), was 517 million, an increase of 8.8% over 1976; about 106 million passengers were carried by the national airline of the U.S.S.R. There were 25 accidents involving passenger fatalities on scheduled services in 1977 (U.S.S.R. excluded), ICAO reported, and 480 passengers died. The accident rate per 100,000 landings was 0.22, compared with 0.20 in 1976, when the rate was the lowest in the past 18 years. (DAVID WOOLLEY)

SHIPPING AND PORTS

Despite some seasonal upsurges in the world freight markets, both tanker and dry cargo, the overall world shipping picture remained gloomy in 1978. A demand for grain helped the market in the autumn, but it was short-term and tanker market rates barely covered operating costs.

By midyear the world merchant fleet totaled nearly 400 million gross registered tons (grt), or 654 million tons deadweight (dw), with 169 million tons dw under the Liberian flag. Japan's merchant fleet remained in second place with 65 million tons dw, and the U.K. fleet was third with 50 million tons dw. The international situation was reflected in the figures at the end of the year which showed 38 million tons dw of tankers and 12.5 million tons dw of dry cargo ships out of service. In nearly all sectors there was a buildup of tonnage in excess of requirements, particularly in the Europe–South Africa container service, where backup facilities at the South African ports failed to match the number of containers offered.

The great Persian Gulf import boom of the mid-1970s was responsible for a massive buildup of new port facilities in the Middle East, where the number of deepwater berths increased from 115 in 1975 to almost 500 by the end of 1978. Congestion virtually disappeared from the Gulf ports, and cutbacks in imports meant the end of a profitable operation for some shipowners. Work continued on deepening the Suez Canal to 53 ft. Ship traffic through the Suez in 1977 increased 5% over 1976. (W. D. EWART)

FREIGHT AND PIPELINES

One of the most important features of modern freight transport was the growth of specially designed multimodal systems. Perhaps the most obvious example was the container that could be moved by road, rail, ship, or barge. In the late 1970s these systems were growing faster than freight in general, the use of containers increasing at least twice as fast as freight traffic overall. In the U.K. the controversy over the 40-ton truck continued. These vehicles would improve the economy of freight transport and make the carrying of the large (40-ft) container economical, but concern about their safety and environmental effect led to strong resistance to their introduction.

During the year British Railways and the Société Nationale de Chemins de Fer introduced a plan for a single-bore tunnel beneath the English Channel. This would be essentially a railway tunnel, giving a major boost to freight and passenger movements between Great Britain and the European continent. The European Economic Community indicated a positive interest in the scheme. However, the Channel Tunnel project had been around for so long that doubts remained as to the likelihood of this latest plan coming to fruition.

In the U.S. the traditional use of gasoline engines for medium-weight trucks was giving way to the European practice of using the more efficient diesel engine for this purpose. Also Conrail (the East Coast rail freight organization) needed more government aid than had been planned. In this regard emphasis was placed on the automation of marshaling yards and more efficient terminal facilities.

Despite the awareness that oil and natural gas

Striking railway clerks picketed in front of idle engines in a rail yard near Chicago in September when strikes halted railway services on many lines.

supplies have a limited lifetime as large-scale energy sources, pipeline construction activity associated with transporting these materials continued at a high level. Major projects were under way in North America, the Soviet Union, and the Middle East, with lesser but substantial schemes in areas such as the North Sea and Central America. The range of materials transported by pipeline continued to expand and by 1978 included water, effluents, oil, gas, ammonia, ethylene, coal and other minerals, mail, and electronic components.

ROADS AND TRAFFIC

The need to foster and sustain economic activity provided the major stimulus for highway construction. From the need to halt the economic decline of the inner areas of long-established cities to helping farmers get their produce to local markets in less developed nations, economic significance was a dominant consideration.

Among the major projects in 1978 was the UN Development Program scheme for 3,200 km (2,000 mi) of rural feeder roads in West Africa. The Trans East Africa highway (8,000 km), the Pacific Coastal highway, and the expressway link between The Netherlands and Barcelona, Spain, provided examples of international trunk route projects.

The crossing of major topographical barriers has always been an exciting challenge for the highway engineer; the start of the second bridge over the Bosporus, the progress on the Humber Bridge in Britain, which would be the longest of its type in the world, and the opening of the Kwang Fu Bridge (Taiwan) and the Al Mikalla–Amein highway in Yemen (Aden) were testimony to this. The last project, which included a major new tunnel, cut down travel time between those two places from seven days to eight hours.

In cities traffic control became more widespread, and new methods continued to be developed. In the U.K. powers to regulate the use of off-street public parking garages were introduced, and area licensing of car use was being given serious consideration in Bangkok, Kuala Lumpur, and Stockholm.

INTERCITY RAIL

High-speed intercity rail services continued to increase, the nations offering them including Japan, Britain, France, West Germany, and the U.S. The Soviet Union and Italy expected to have lines in operation soon. British Rail's high-speed services on the east coast allowed the 640-km (400-mi) run from London to Edinburgh to be done in under five hours. The French railways produced the first model of their new 260-kph Train de Grande Vitesse.

Electrification was proceeding fastest in France and West Germany, with China planning to electrify its core network. For China this was part of a program of modernization that also included double tracking of all main routes, construction of six new main routes, dieselization of busy noncore services, and increased automation.

Many railways continued to have financial problems. The West German railways lost more than £1,100 million in their latest accounting year, and a state-owned group had to take over passenger services on Canadian National and Canadian Pacific railways. Exceptional in this respect was British Rail, which exceeded its financial targets.

The speeding up of intercity services made heavy demands on railway technology, particularly in ensuring ride comfort and keeping down energy consumption. Among the innovative applications becoming common were the use of thyristors to control traction current, tilting vehicles to increase comfort and stability when cornering at high speeds, and vehicle design borrowed from aerospace technology.

URBAN MASS TRANSIT

One of the most significant features of government support for urban mass transit was the renewal of design effort on urban buses. The special significance arose from the overwhelming importance of buses for passenger transport within urban areas. Current awareness of variations in operating conditions within individual countries meant that overall standardization gave way to requirements for a basic set of passenger and safety features. An example of this was the new U.S. requirement for new buses to provide facilities for boarding passengers in wheelchairs. In continental Europe, with low bridges and greater passenger tolerance of standing, the use of articulated buses was growing on heavily traveled routes.

At the other end of the public transport spectrum, the search for the best way to provide for low-intensity and dispersed demand prompted further innovation. In the U.K. there were a number of experiments in providing public transport in rural areas, and the law was changed to allow certain forms of car pools and extensions of community minibus services. The use of taxis grew, but institutionalized attempts to provide light bus transit had only limited success.

Despite the very high cost of building urban railway systems, this was an active field during the year. Extensions to established systems were made in Stockholm, Tokyo, Prague, Milan, Toronto, Montreal, and Moscow. New lines were opened in Lyon, France; Tashkent, U.S.S.R.; Amsterdam; and Atlanta, Ga.; and work was started on lines in Helsinki; Miami, Fla.; Gorky, U.S.S.R.; Caracas; and Calcutta. Technological innovation focused on improved train communication and control and automatic fare collection systems. Work was also being done on reducing energy consumption by the use of lightweight vehicles and energy recapture using regenerative braking and flywheels. New tramway systems were being planned and built in Calgary and Edmonton, Alta.; Buffalo, N.Y.; Tunis; and Hong Kong; and it seemed likely that this form of transportation would be accepted as a reasonable alternative to full rail systems. In the U.S. automatic small tramways, or "downtown people movers," were being planned in four cities. The largest project, in Los Angeles, involved 4.3 km (2.5 mi) of guideway.

(DAVID BAYLISS)

See also Energy; Engineering Projects; Environment; Industrial Review: *Aerospace*; *Automobiles*.

Trapshooting:
see Target Sports

MENACE ON THE RAILS

by David J. Umansky

The potential for disaster in a society that routinely transports billions of tons of explosives, flammable materials, poisons, corrosives, and other hazardous materials by truck, train, pipeline, airplane, ship, and barge was graphically illustrated in February 1978, when two railroad train derailments resulted in the deaths of 23 persons.

On Wednesday, February 22, a Louisville and Nashville Railroad freight train left the tracks while passing through Waverly, Tenn., in the north central part of the state. Among the cars that were derailed and lying on their sides were two "jumbo" tank cars, each containing more than 27,000 gal of liquid propane gas. No leaks were detected, and it was decided to right the cars. Following the successful completion of this operation, preparations were made to transfer the LPG to tank trucks.

David J. Umansky is director, Office of Public Affairs, in the U.S. Federal Railroad Administration.

On Friday afternoon, two days after the derailment had occurred and just before the transfer from the railroad cars to the tank trucks was to begin, one of the cars ruptured without warning. There was an explosion followed by a devastating fire. Fifteen people were killed and dozens more injured. The explosion and fire also destroyed two blocks of Waverly's business district.

Early the following Sunday morning, February 26, a southbound freight of the small Atlanta and St. Andrews Bay Railroad was derailed near Youngstown, Fla. Among the 52 locomotives and cars that jumped the tracks was a tank car carrying 90 tons of chlorine. The tank car was punctured, releasing chlorine gas that covered the surrounding land and portions of a highway with a poisonous greenish mist. Unable to see the gas because the sun had not yet risen and the night was foggy, motorists on the highway drove into the cloud, where they choked helplessly as their cars stalled. Eight persons died and at least 114 others were reported injured.

In Cades, Tenn., on the same day, an Illinois Central Gulf Railroad freight was derailed and a tank car containing caustic lye was punctured. There were no deaths or injuries in this incident, although residents of the area had to be evacuated.

Each of the accidents was investigated by the National Transportation Safety Board, a governmental body charged with making an inquiry into such accidents, issuing a finding as to the cause, and recommending procedures to prevent similar incidents in the future, and by the Federal Railroad Administra-

Eight people died of deadly chlorine gas fumes coming from a train that derailed near Youngstown, Florida, in February.

UPI COMPIX

tion, the agency of the United States Department of Transportation (DOT) responsible for enforcing railroad safety regulations. It was ruled that the Waverly derailment had been caused by a defective wheel and that the brake on that wheel had been locked. The Youngstown accident was blamed on sabotage, and the FBI was brought into the investigation; someone had tampered with the track. The Cades derailment was found to have been caused by dragging equipment.

The Nature of the Problem. These were by no means the first catastrophic accidents involving freight trains carrying hazardous materials, but the close proximity in time and the unusually high loss of life generated a national debate over the safety of the new large tank cars and the overall ability of the railroads to transport hazardous materials safely. Wide media coverage of the accidents and interviews with government officials and industry spokesmen made the general public aware, for the first time, of the nature of the problem.

In 1976 (the last year for which figures were available) U.S. railroads carried 80 million tons of hazardous materials in tank cars and 100 million tons in other types of cars; this compares with approximately 4 billion tons carried by trucks in 1977. By 1980 the total amount of dangerous substances transported by the railroad industry was expected to reach 200 million tons.

The regulations governing the interstate transportation of dangerous materials have evolved over the past 70 years, but—chlorine is an exception—most of the substances that are causing so much concern have been developed since World War II. About 20,000 substances are classified as "hazardous" by DOT, compared with about 1,000 before the war. Although no hard figures are available, it is estimated that the chemical industry produces some 1,000 new products a year, approximately half of which are added to the hazardous list. Among the substances listed as hazardous that are regularly shipped by train are chlorine, propane, anhydrous ammonia, cyanide, asphalt, hydrochloric acid, sulfuric acid, hydrogen peroxide, gasoline, and fuel oil.

According to the Federal Railroad Administration, 10,220 accidents were reported by the railroads in 1977. (An accident must be reported to the FRA if there are serious injuries to one or more railroad employees or other persons or if there is equipment damage totaling $2,300 or more.) Of these incidents, 808 involved one or more cars carrying hazardous materials; 1,072 such cars were damaged in these accidents, and 173 cars were damaged enough to cause them to release at least part of their cargoes. A total of 14,805 people were reportedly evacuated as a result.

Tracks and Tank Cars. Although none of the three accidents in February had been caused by track failure, the general condition of the nation's approximately 300,000 mi of track (including freight yards) was the major focus of attention in the discussion that followed. Beginning in the 1950s, many of the nation's financially hard-pressed railroads had put off repairs, and by the end of 1977 industry estimates placed the amount of deferred roadbed maintenance at $6.6 billion. There were suggestions, including some from government officials, that the track network should be nationalized so that federal funds could be used to rehabilitate and maintain the system. Studies of this idea were under way at year's end, but no concrete steps in that direction had been taken.

While the condition of the track received the most public notice, the pressure tank cars were generally perceived as presenting the greatest danger to people near an accident site. And although the railroads are the focus of concern in most derailments, virtually all of the cars are owned not by the railroads but by chemical, oil, and tank car leasing companies and other firms, which are responsible for meeting construction regulations.

Approximately 20,000 of these tankers are now in service. They can be identified by the Transportation Department code DOT 112 or DOT 114 on each car. Anhydrous ammonia is carried in some 3,500 cars, and about 16,500 tankers carry liquefied flammable gas. Over the years, tank cars have become larger and lighter in construction. The average product capacity has grown from 10,000 gal in the early 1950s to approximately 32,000 gal. There are federal regulations for marking these cars so their contents can be easily identified. In addition, there are rules governing where they can be placed in the

---

Hauling Hot Atoms

Regulations governing nuclear shipments are much stricter than those for other materials. A fleet of 50 specially armoured railroad cars is used to transport nuclear materials. The cars are built to withstand an impact of 30 mph, a 40-in drop onto a pin 6 in in diameter, and a half hour in a fire of 1,475° F.

To counter possible terrorist attacks, the cars are accompanied by plainclothes guards armed with a variety of powerful weapons and with walkie-talkies. Through 1978, no nuclear hijackings had been attempted, and no accidents involving nuclear-loaded cars had been reported.

Still, railroad men worry. They fear that the safety standards are not strict enough, and they petitioned the Interstate Commerce Commission for permission to enforce tougher regulations and to pass the added cost on to the shippers. The ICC denied the request, saying that present safeguards are adequate.

train in relation to the locomotives and cabooses and how far they must be separated from other cars carrying dangerous materials.

It was brought out during public discussion of the situation that there is an emergency service in existence to advise local officials on how to handle substances or containers involved in an accident. The service, called Chemtrec, was established by the Manufacturing Chemists Association. Basic assistance is provided through a toll-free telephone number which is manned 24 hours a day. The person on duty can give immediate expert advice to fire, police, civil defense, or other officials at the scene on the best way to deal with potentially destructive materials.

Moving Up the Timetable. The ability of the new "jumbo" tank cars to withstand the battering that takes place during a derailment has been seriously questioned. Late in 1976 DOT issued regulations for "retrofitting" or rebuilding these cars with new safety devices. It called for special coupling devices to help prevent the cars from separating during a derailment and to keep couplers from acting as spears that could puncture cars in front and rear. A second feature was a metal shield for each end of the car, designed to resist the head-on puncturing which is the most common type of damage to tank cars. Finally, cars that would carry flammable materials were to receive a thermal coating that would help keep their cargoes from exploding in the event of a fire outside the car. The department gave owners the option of substituting insulation and a steel jacket for the entire car for the head shields and spray-on coating. All of this work was to be done in stages, with the deadline for completion set at Dec. 31, 1981. Despite a great deal of research and testimony, the industry remained divided on which method would provide the best protection, although there was general agreement that additional protection was needed.

Following the accidents in February, the National Transportation Safety Board held hearings in Washington to determine the general safety of the pressure tank cars. After the hearings, the board recommended that the deadline for retrofitting of the cars be moved forward. The new schedule suggested by the board would have required that all tank cars be equipped with the new couplers and head shields by Dec. 25, 1978. The time limit for the thermal spray-on coating or insulation and steel jacket was not addressed.

At the same time the Federal Railroad Administration announced that it was considering a reduction in the timetable, and following the Safety Board meetings it held hearings to determine what action it should take. During the FRA hearings, industry representatives testified that a major problem in meeting shortened deadlines was the fact that many tank cars, especially those carrying anhydrous ammonia and propane, are used as storage containers by the buyers of those products. In many cases they are out of the hands of the owners or the railroads for long periods of time.

New regulations were issued on May 9, 1978. The deadline for replacing the couplers was moved forward from June 30, 1979, to Dec. 31, 1978; for head shields on tank cars carrying anhydrous ammonia or liquefied gas, there was a two-year reduction, from Dec. 31, 1981, to Dec. 31, 1979; and for the spray-on coating or the steel jacket and insulation on all remaining liquefied flammable gas cars, the timetable was cut back one year, from Dec. 31, 1981, to the same date in 1980. In addition, the Association of American Railroads, the railroad industry's trade association, recommended to its members that trains carrying compressed gases such as ammonia lower their speeds by ten miles per hour to minimize the effects of derailment.

The finding that wheel failure had caused the Waverly accident generated another unusual safety action by the Railroad Administration. An investigation revealed that this type of wheel had been involved in an unusually large number of accidents. The blame was placed on the high carbon content of the wheel, which caused it to crack when it became overheated. Approximately 100,000 of these wheels were in use throughout the industry in March, when an order was issued to remove all of them from service.

After March 31 no car could be used to carry hazardous materials if it had one or more of these wheels. By June 30 no car with this type of wheel could be used in the same train with cars carrying hazardous materials. Finally, all of the wheels had to be removed by the end of 1978. The Railroad Administration also ordered that every car be marked with a yellow circle if it had been inspected and found not to have any of the high-carbon wheels or if those wheels had been removed. A white circle was required if the car was still equipped with one or more of the wheels. In mid-June the Railroad Administration reported that 658,896 cars had been inspected and that 26,570 wheels had been replaced; more than 29,000 high-carbon wheels had been located but not yet removed.

By the end of the summer the controversy had died down and the media had turned their attention to other matters. The problem remained unsolved, however. Clearly, in an industrial society heavily dependent on the long-distance movement of potentially dangerous materials, safety would be an ongoing concern.

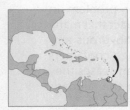

Trinidad and Tobago

Tunisia

Trinidad and Tobago

A republic and a member of the Commonwealth of Nations, Trinidad and Tobago consists of two islands off the coast of Venezuela, north of the Orinoco River delta. Area: 5,128 sq km (1,980 sq mi). Pop. (1977 est.): 1,115,000, including (1970) Negro 43%; East Indian 40%; mixed 14%. Cap. and largest city: Port-of-Spain (pop., 1973 est., 60,400). Language: English (official); Hindi, French, Spanish. Religion (1970): Christian 64%; Hindu 25%; Muslim 6%. President in 1978, Sir Ellis Clarke; prime minister, Eric Williams.

Recorded reserves for this wealthiest Commonwealth Caribbean nation, based on income from oil and gas, reached TT$4.1 billion in July 1978, or enough for 18 months' imports. The republic floated six substantial foreign currency loans in 1978. Continued rapid industrialization included construction of a liquefied natural gas plant, a steel plant, and an ammonia plant. The island's sugar industry, however, continued to incur heavy losses. Inflation remained at 11%, and toward the year's end attempts were made to lower the figure by reducing the money supply. Unemployment stood at about 15%.

Late in 1977 Trinidad proposed a multilateral aid program to overcome the Caribbean nations' balance of payments deficits. Without acknowledgment to Trinidad, the U.S. and other developed nations initiated the Caribbean Development Facility, but its failure as of late 1978 enabled Trinidad to open its own bilateral aid program to Barbados and the eastern Caribbean.

The United Labour Front (ULF) opposition split into two factions: one under Basdeo Panday and the other under Raffique Shah. The division strengthened the governing People's National Movement (PNM). Prime Minister Eric Williams stated that the PNM should consider the issue of his successor. (DAVID A. JESSOP)

Tunisia

A republic of North Africa lying on the Mediterranean Sea, Tunisia is bounded by Algeria and Libya. Area: 164,150 sq km (63,379 sq mi). Pop. (1977 est.): 6,065,000. Cap. and largest city: Tunis (pop., 1975 census, city proper 550,404; governorate 944,100). Language: Arabic (official). Religion: Muslim; Jewish and Christian minorities. President in 1978, Habib Bourguiba; prime minister, Hedi Nouira.

In 1978 a major confrontation arose between Tunisia's ruling Parti Socialist Destourien (PSD) and the labour unions. On January 10 Habib Achour, secretary-general of the General Union of Tunisian Workers (UGTT), resigned from the party political bureau to show his disapproval of the policies pursued by Prime Minister Hedi Nouira's government. On January 26 a general strike led to numerous clashes between police and demonstrators, resulting in many deaths; official sources put the number at about 40, though subsequent reports gave a figure of 51. Following this Habib Achour and several other union leaders were arrested, and Nouira spoke of a "premeditated plan"

TRINIDAD AND TOBAGO

Education. (1975–76) Primary, pupils 200,095, teachers 6,471; secondary, pupils 64,042, teachers 1,631; vocational, pupils 1,395, teachers 114; teacher training, students 1,188, teachers 116; higher, students 1,471, teaching staff 221.

Finance and Trade. Monetary unit: Trinidad and Tobago dollar, with (Sept. 18, 1978) a par value of TT$2.40 to U.S. $1 (free rate of TT$4.70 = £1 sterling). Gold, SDR's, and foreign exchange (June 1978) U.S. $1,529,000,000. Budget (1978 est.) balanced at TT$3,167,000,000. Foreign trade (1976): imports TT$4,512,700,000; exports TT$5,230,300,000. Import sources: Saudi Arabia 24%; U.S. 21%; U.K. 11%; Indonesia 10%; Iran 9%; Japan 5%. Export destinations: U.S. 70%; ship and air stores and bunkers 5%. Main exports: petroleum products 54%; crude oil 39%.

Transport and Communications. Roads (1976) c. 6,500 km. Motor vehicles in use (1976): passenger 105,000; commercial 21,000. There are no railways in operation. Air traffic (1976): 1,040,000,000 passenger-km; freight 24.2 million net ton-km. Shipping traffic (1976): goods loaded 20,315,000 metric tons, unloaded 12,998,000 metric tons. Telephones (Jan. 1977) 70,400. Radio licenses (Dec. 1974) 250,000. Television receivers (Dec. 1976) c. 125,000.

Agriculture. Production (in 000; metric tons; 1977): sugar, raw value c. 178; rice (1976) 21; tomatoes (1976) c. 10; oranges (1976) c. 12; grapefruit (1976) c. 11; copra c. 9; coffee c. 3; cocoa c. 4. Livestock (in 000; 1976): cattle c. 73; pigs c. 55; goats c. 42; poultry c. 6,480.

Industry. Production (in 000; metric tons; 1977): crude oil 11,831; natural gas (cu m) c. 1,690,000; petroleum products (1976) 14,897; cement 218; nitrogenous fertilizers (nutrient content; 1976–77) 46; electricity (kw-hr) 1,576,000.

TUNISIA

Education. (1977–78) Primary, pupils 957,107, teachers (1976–77) c. 23,983; secondary, pupils 194,709; vocational (1975–76), pupils 34,352; teacher training (1975–76), students 1,059; secondary, vocational, and teacher training, teachers (1975–76) 8,769; higher, students 23,137, teaching staff 3,089.

Finance. Monetary unit: Tunisian dinar, with (Sept. 18, 1978) a free rate of 0.39 dinar to U.S. $1 (0.77 dinar = £1 sterling). Gold, SDR's, and foreign exchange (June 1978) U.S. $261 million. Budget (total; 1976 est.) balanced at 641 million dinars. Gross domestic product (1977) 2,126,500,-000 dinars. Money supply (June 1978) 600,790,000 dinars. Cost of living (Tunis; 1975 = 100; June 1978) 118.3.

Foreign Trade. (1977) Imports 757.9 million dinars; exports 390.1 million dinars. Import sources: France 31%; West Germany 13%; Italy 10%; U.S. 6%. Export destinations: France 18%; West Germany 16%; Italy 14%; Greece 14%; U.S. 11%. Main exports (1976): crude oil 41%; phosphates 11%; olive oil 11%; chemicals 10%; clothing 9%. Tourism (1976): visitors 1,066,000; gross receipts U.S. $305 million.

Transport and Communications. Roads (1976) 21,595 km. Motor vehicles in use (1976): passenger 105,400; commercial 68,200. Railways: (1976) 1,928 km; traffic (1977) 710 million passenger-km, freight 1,330,000,000 net ton-km. Air traffic (1977): 1,058,000,000 passenger-km; freight 9,062,000 net ton-km. Telephones (Dec. 1975) 129,000. Radio receivers (Dec. 1975) 280,000. Television receivers (Dec. 1975) 176,000.

Agriculture. Production (in 000; metric tons; 1977): wheat 570; barley c. 95; potatoes (1976) c. 105; tomatoes c. 270; watermelons (1976) c. 160; wine c. 92; dates c. 50; olives c. 615; oranges 72. Livestock (in 000; 1976): sheep c. 3,526; cattle c. 880; goats c. 900; camels c. 195; poultry c. 14,839.

Industry. Production (in 000; metric tons; 1977): crude oil 4,262; natural gas (cu m) 230,000; cement 609; iron ore (53% metal content) 343; phosphate rock (1976) 3,301; lead 19; petroleum products (1976) 1,116; sulfuric acid 1,201; phosphate fertilizers (1976–77) c. 177; electricity (excluding most industrial production; kw-hr) 1,519,000.

Trucking Industry:
see Transportation

Trust Territories:
see Dependent States

to undermine the regime. A state of emergency was declared and a curfew imposed from January 26 to March 20.

In its attempt to regain control of the unions, the government demanded the calling of an extraordinary congress of the UGTT on February 25 and dismissed the 11 imprisoned members of its executive committee, confirming the appointment of a new secretary-general, Tijani Abid. This action caused widespread protests in France, and a delegation from the International Confederation of Free Trade Unions called for the liberation of the imprisoned unionists. The government ignored its appeal, and on March 22 Habib Achour was charged with subversion. A further sign of the regime's clampdown was the decision in April to charge Ahmad Mestiri, leader of the Social-Democratic opposition, with "defamation of the government," and later newspaper editor Hassib ben Amar was accused of defaming the armed forces.

The trial of the unionists opened in July, but in the following month the criminal court in Sousse ruled that the case fell under the jurisdiction of the State Security Court. On September 2, however, 35 unionists were provisionally released from custody and, after a tumultuous opening session in Tunis on September 14, the Security Court postponed its hearing until September 28. The prosecutor had called for the death penalty against 30 of the accused, and the defense lawyers walked out of the court in protest over the conduct of the trial. At the end of the trial, however, the verdicts were relatively mild. Habib Achour was sentenced to ten years at hard labour, and six of the defendants were acquitted.

In foreign affairs relations with France remained close. The failing health of Pres. Habib Bourguiba continued to weigh heavily on the country's political development and, following his hospitalization in Bonn, West Germany, in October, there were rumours about a possible successor to the presidency. (PHILIPPE DECRAENE)

Turkey

A republic of southeastern Europe and Asia Minor, Turkey is bounded by the Aegean Sea, the Black Sea, the U.S.S.R., Iran, Iraq, Syria, the Mediterranean Sea, Greece, and Bulgaria. Area: 779,452 sq km (300,948 sq mi), including 23,698 sq km in Europe. Pop. (1978 est.): 43,144,000. Cap.: Ankara (pop., 1975, 1,701,000). Largest city: Istanbul (pop., 1975, 2,547,000). Language: Turkish, Kurdish, Arabic. Religion: predominantly Muslim. President in 1978, Fahri Koruturk; prime minister, Bulent Ecevit.

Following the defeat on Dec. 31, 1977, of Suleyman Demirel's right-wing coalition government, a new government was formed on Jan. 5, 1978, under Bulent Ecevit, leader of the left-of-centre Republican People's Party (RPP). All the main portfolios went to the RPP. The Assembly endorsed the new government by 229 votes to 218 and, on February 28, approved its first budget. In September the Republican Reliance Party withdrew from the government.

Urgent problems facing Ecevit were political violence and a crisis in the economy. Some 262 people had been killed and more than 2,700 injured in over 1,200 incidents in 1977, and more than 600 political murders were committed in 1978. Late in the year religious and political violence in the eastern provinces led to the imposition of martial law. As for the economy, 1978 opened with a balance of payments deficit of $2.8 billion and overdue debt repayments of some $2.6 billion. On March 1 the Turkish lira was devalued by about 30%, and further small downward adjustments were made throughout the year. In April the International Monetary Fund granted Turkey a standby loan of $450 million, but disbursement was gradual and involved hard bargaining on the management of the economy. The price of oil was increased by 70% in September. Nevertheless, the fourth five-year plan, unveiled on August 31, set the annual growth target at 8% (as against 3% in 1977). During January–July prices increased at an annual rate of 57%.

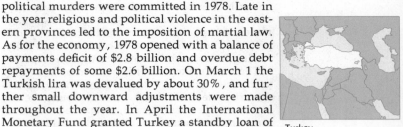

Turkey

TURKEY
Education. (1975–76) Primary, pupils 5,512,000, teachers 172,488; secondary, pupils 1,363,188, teachers 37,899; vocational, pupils 312,522, teachers 12,240; teacher training (1974–75), students 58,738, teachers 3,245; higher, students 322,965, teaching staff 15,274.

Finance. Monetary unit: Turkish lira, with (Sept. 18, 1978) a free rate of 24.17 liras to U.S. $1 (47.37 liras = £1 sterling). Gold, SDR's, and foreign exchange (April 1978) U.S. $1,077,000,000. Budget (1977–78 est.): revenue 203,-449,000,000 liras; expenditure 222,949,000,000 liras. Gross national product (1977) 817.4 billion liras. Money supply (April 1978) 221.1 billion liras. Cost of living (1975 = 100; June 1978) 234.3.

Foreign Trade. (1977) Imports 104,882,000,000 liras; exports 31,339,000,000 liras. Import sources: West Germany 16%; Iraq 12%; U.S. 9%; Italy 8%; U.K. 7%; Switzerland 6%; France 6%; Japan 5%; Libya 5%. Export destinations: West Germany 22%; Italy 9%; U.S. 7%; Switzerland 6%; France 5%; U.K. 5%; U.S.S.R. 5%. Main exports (1976): cotton 22%; fruit and vegetables 22%; tobacco 13%; textile yarns and fabrics 11%; clothing 5%. Tourism (1976): visitors 1,676,000; gross receipts U.S. $180 million.

Transport and Communications. Roads (1976) 195,982 km (including 189 km expressways). Motor vehicles in use (1976): passenger 512,400; commercial 190,300. Railways (1976): 8,138 km; traffic 4,615,000,000 passenger-km, freight 7,278,000,000 net ton-km. Air traffic (1976): 2,019,000,000 passenger-km; freight 17,320,000 net ton-km. Shipping (1977): merchant vessels 100 gross tons and over 448; gross tonnage 1,288,282. Telephones (Jan. 1977) 1,131,000. Radio licenses (Dec. 1976) 4,228,-000. Television receivers (Dec. 1976) 1,769,000.

Agriculture. Production (in 000; metric tons; 1977): wheat c. 16,715; barley c. 4,750; corn c. 1,200; rye 715; oats 380; potatoes c. 2,900; tomatoes c. 2,800; onions c. 780; sugar, raw value c. 1,140; sunflower seed c. 457; cottonseed c. 980; chick-peas c. 168; dry beans c. 160; cabbages (1976) c. 642; pumpkins (1976) c. 302; watermelons (1976) c. 4,087; cucumbers (1976) c. 397; oranges c. 513; lemons c. 275; apples c. 1,060; grapes c. 3,450; raisins c. 338; hazelnuts (1976) c. 260; olives c. 500; tea c. 58; tobacco c. 223; cotton, lint c. 570. Livestock (in 000; Dec. 1976): cattle 14,102; sheep 41,504; buffalo 1,056; goats 18,508; horses 853; asses 1,465; chickens 45,711.

Industry. Fuel and power (in 000; metric tons; 1977): crude oil 2,716; coal c. 4,400; lignite (1976) 7,440; electricity (kw-hr) 20,515,000. Production (in 000; metric tons; 1977): cement 13,843; iron ore (55–60% metal content) 3,187; pig iron 1,361; crude steel 1,396; petroleum products (1976) 12,792; sulfuric acid 199; fertilizers (nutrient content; 1976–77) nitrogenous 212, phosphate 357; chrome ore (oxide content; 1976) 346; manganese ore (metal content; 1976) 6.8; cotton yarn c. 115; man-made fibres (1976) 49.

see Engineering Projects

Turkey's external debts were considered at an Organization for Economic Cooperation and Development group meeting in Paris in May, and some $2 billion in debts were rescheduled by the end of November. As of that time, however, only some $600 million had been secured in new foreign trade credits (exclusive of credits tied to specific projects). Imports had to be cut back drastically, forcing industry to operate at only 50% capacity.

The most serious disorders occurred late in the year when fighting between Sunni Muslims and minority Alevis (Shi'ites), centred around the city of Maras, left over 97 dead, a reported one thousand or more wounded, and parts of the city in ruins. On December 26 Parliament approved the declaration of martial law in Istanbul, Ankara, and 11 eastern provinces.

The need for aid dominated Turkey's relations with its Western allies, which were further complicated by the continuing Aegean dispute with Greece and the Cyprus problem. Following U.S. Secretary of State Cyrus Vance's visit to Ankara in January and an exchange of letters with Greek Prime Minister Konstantinos Karamanlis in February, Ecevit and Karamanlis met in Montreux, Switz., in March. Subsequent talks did little to alleviate the Aegean dispute, however. Talks held in August on the Aegean air space dispute were also inconclusive. (*See* CYPRUS.)

Relations with the U.S. improved after the lifting of the arms embargo by Congress in August. On October 9, pending renegotiation of the U.S.-Turkish defense cooperation agreement, Turkey reopened, for one year, four of the U.S. defense installations previously closed down in retaliation for the embargo. In May Turkey announced that it would not participate in the program to increase NATO defense capabilities. The NATO Southeastern Europe Allied Ground Forces command in Izmir was handed to a Turkish general on June 30. Turkey's subsequent objection to a Greek proposal that the Aegean air command be given to a Greek officer remained unresolved. (*See* GREECE.)

Relations with the U.S.S.R. improved. Ecevit went to Moscow on June 21 and signed the long-delayed political document on friendly relations and cooperation, as well as agreements on the delimitation of the continental shelf in the Black Sea and on commercial and cultural relations.

(ANDREW MANGO)

Tuvalu

Tuvalu

A constitutional monarchy comprising nine main islands and their associated islets and reefs, Tuvalu is located in the western Pacific Ocean just south of the Equator and west of the International Date Line. Area: 26 sq km (9.5 sq mi). Pop. (1978 est.): 8,000, mostly Polynesians. Cap.: Funafuti (pop., 1976 est., 1,300). Queen, Elizabeth II; prime minister, Toalipi Lauti.

Tuvalu, formerly the Ellice Islands, achieved independence from Britain on Oct. 1, 1978—the third anniversary of its secession from the Gilbert and Ellice Islands Colony. Princess Margaret, Queen Elizabeth's representative at the celebra-

Uganda

TUVALU

Education. (1976) Primary, pupils 1,570, teachers 39; secondary, pupils 250, teachers 12.

Finance and Trade. Monetary unit: Australian dollar, with (Sept. 18, 1978) a free rate of A$0.87 to U.S.$1 (A$1.70 = £1 sterling). Budget (1977 est.) balanced at A$1,565,000 (including U.K. aid of A$676,000). Main export (1975): copra (valued at A$23,184).

---

tions, was prevented by illness from attending the final ceremony.

The new state's constitution provided for a prime minister to be chosen by and from the 12 members of the legislature, elected by universal adult suffrage. There were no political parties in Tuvalu. The first prime minister was Toalipi Lauti (*see* BIOGRAPHIES).

Tuvalu would receive from Britain a financial settlement that included budgetary assistance to 1980 of A$1.7 million, a general development grant of A$4.9 million, and a special development grant, without time limit, of A$4.7 million. Development expenditure was being concentrated on government buildings and services and on projects—especially agriculture and fisheries—likely to reduce the budget deficit. Customs and postage stamps were the main sources of government revenue. About 1,000 Tuvaluans lived overseas, and remittances were an important source of cash income for many villagers.

In September 1978 the South Pacific Forum, meeting at Niue, admitted Tuvalu as a full member.

(BARRIE MACDONALD)

Uganda

A republic and a member of the Commonwealth of Nations, Uganda is bounded by Sudan, Zaire, Rwanda, Tanzania, and Kenya. Area: 241,139 sq

---

UGANDA

Education. (1976) Primary, pupils 1,125,817, teachers 32,490; secondary, pupils 75,044, teachers 3,456; vocational, pupils 3,701, teachers 264; teacher training, students 6,328, teachers 364; higher, students 5,173, teaching staff 617.

Finance and Trade. Monetary unit: Uganda shilling, with (Sept. 18, 1978) a free rate of UShs 7.43 to U.S. $1 (UShs 14.55 = £1 sterling). Budget (1977–78 est.): revenue UShs 6,638,000,000; expenditure UShs 4,024,000,000. Foreign trade (1976): imports UShs 1,424,000,000; exports UShs 3,006,000,000. Import sources: Kenya 50%; U.K. 15%; West Germany 9%. Export destinations: U.S. 33%; U.K. 20%; France 6%; Italy 6%; Japan 6%. Main exports: coffee 83%; cotton 6%.

Transport and Communications. Roads (1976) 27,536 km. Motor vehicles in use (1974): passenger 27,000; commercial 14,100. Railways (1975) 1,301 km. Air traffic (1976): 197 million passenger-km; freight 8.2 million net ton-km. Telephones (Jan. 1977) 46,300. Radio receivers (Dec. 1975) 250,000. Television licenses (Dec. 1975) 70,000.

Agriculture. Production (in 000; metric tons; 1977): millet 471; sorghum 516; corn (1976) 623; sweet potatoes (1976) c. 664; cassava (1976) c. 1,000; peanuts c. 230; dry beans c. 264; bananas c. 350; coffee 202; tea 22; cotton, lint c. 41; timber (cu m; 1976) 14,611; fish catch (1976) 152. Livestock (in 000; Dec. 1975): cattle 4,900; sheep c. 1,100; goats c. 2,150; pigs c. 190; chickens c. 12,000.

Industry. Production (in 000; metric tons; 1976): cement 88; copper ore (metal content) 5.6; tungsten concentrates (oxide content) 0.07; phosphate rock 15; electricity (kw-hr) c. 729,000.

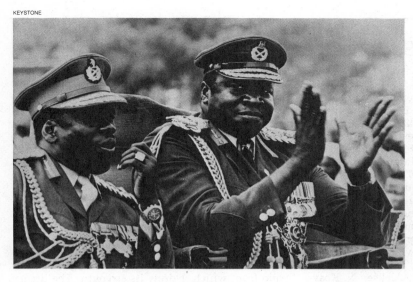

Ugandan Pres. Idi Amin (right) with Vice-Pres. Mustapha Adrisi before an armed rebellion broke out in southern Uganda led by people thought to be supporting Adrisi. Presumed dead in November, Adrisi had flown to Cairo after an automobile accident and reportedly asked for political asylum in Egypt.

km (93,104 sq mi), including 44,081 sq km of inland water. Pop. (1978 est.): 12,436,000, virtually all of whom are African. Cap. and largest city: Kampala (pop., 1975 UN est., 542,000). Language: English (official), Bantu, Nilotic, Nilo-Hamitic, and Sudanic. Religion: Christian, Muslim, traditional beliefs. President in 1978, Gen. Idi Amin.

In January 1978 Pres. Idi Amin declared the year as one of peace, love, unity, and reconciliation with neighbour countries. For internal politics, however, the prospects were not good, and late in the year a border war broke out with Tanzania. Domestically, President Amin felt his position threatened from a number of quarters. In January he warned Christian leaders against involvement in politics, and in February he accused some of the senior members of his own government of being implicated in the large-scale smuggling of coffee across the border into Kenya. Two months later the president again censured some of his military supporters, especially the finance minister, Brig. Moses Ali, whom he accused of giving preference to his friends in obtaining new cars.

Army discontent as a result of these charges centred on the vice-president and defense minister, Gen. Mustapha Adrisi. In mid-April Adrisi was injured in what was said to have been a car accident and was flown to Cairo for treatment. Then, on May 1, Amin announced that he had dismissed Lieut. Col. Nasur Ezega, commander of a mechanized regiment stationed in Masaka, for failure to report clashes between soldiers and Roman Catholic civilians in his district. This was followed by reports that the Army chief of staff, Maj. Gen. Isaac Lumago, and Brig. Moses Ali were under house arrest. Ali was dismissed from office at the end of July for misusing his position as chairman of a Cabinet committee on economic resources. Ali Towili, director of police training and former head of Amin's public safety unit, was also dismissed in May, along with the commissioner for prisons and the minister for tourism. Amin himself assumed responsibility for the Ministries of Tourism and of Information and Broadcasting, as well as taking over control of the Foreign Ministry in order, he said, to implement more effectively his policy of

love and reconciliation. The government was embarrassed on May 24 when a light aircraft containing four persons, one of them Bruce McKenzie, former minister of agriculture in Kenya, was destroyed by a bomb after leaving Entebbe Airport. All the occupants were killed.

Discontent with Amin's government resulted in attempts to assassinate the president. At the end of July a mutiny planned by three regiments of the Ugandan Army was only averted by the intervention of Palestinian troops flown in from Libya.

In October Amin charged that Tanzanian troops had invaded southwestern Uganda. This was denied by the Tanzanian government, which claimed that the report was an attempt by Amin to distract attention from Uganda's internal problems. At the end of October three battalions of Ugandan troops invaded Tanzania with tanks and heavy artillery and by November 2 claimed some 1,820 sq km of Tanzanian territory, mostly uninhabited swampland. Tanzania vowed to drive out the Ugandan troops and to try to oust "the idiot" Amin as president of Uganda. Meanwhile, Amin said that the best way to settle the border war would be to stage a boxing match between him and Tanzanian Pres. Julius Nyerere (see BIOGRAPHIES) with Muhammad Ali as referee. Further clashes were reported by Uganda late in November.

The high price of coffee on the world market left Uganda with a budget surplus in 1977, the first in several years. In the U.S., which had bought one-third of Uganda's exported coffee, the Senate voted 73 to 1 in July 1978 to ban trade with Uganda because of reports of atrocities there.

On Dec. 28, 1977, the Ugandan government had denied foreign currency to individuals or private firms wishing to import foreign goods, charging that businessmen were overcharging and banking their money abroad as the Asian trading community (expelled in 1972) had supposedly done. Partly as a result of this decision and partly due to their lack of business experience, many Africans found it necessary in 1978 to sublet their businesses to Arabs from Libya and the Middle East, who had access to foreign currency.

(KENNETH INGHAM)

Unemployment:
see Economy, World;
Social and Welfare
Services

Union of Soviet Socialist Republics

The Union of Soviet Socialist Republics is a federal state covering parts of eastern Europe and northern and central Asia. Area: 22,402,200 sq km (8,649,500 sq mi). Pop. (1977 est.): 258.9 million, including (1970) Russians 53%; Ukrainians 17%; Belorussians 4%; Uzbeks 4%; Tatars 2%. Cap. and largest city: Moscow (pop., 1977 est., 7,819,000). Language: officially Russian, but many others are spoken. Religion: about 40 religions are represented in the U.S.S.R., the major ones being Christian denominations. General secretary of the Communist Party of the Soviet Union and chairman of the Presidium of the Supreme Soviet (president) in 1978, Leonid Ilich Brezhnev; chairman of the Council of Ministers (premier), Aleksey N. Kosygin.

Domestic Affairs. After the obviously staged political "activity" connected with the adoption of the new Soviet constitution during 1977, the year 1978 seemed dull and uneventful. The constituent republics of the Soviet Union all adopted new fundamental laws in line with the new constitution, and the necessary adjustments were, of course, made to other relevant legislation. The personal ascendancy of Leonid Brezhnev continued unchallenged despite obvious signs that the general secretary of the Soviet Communist Party was having to contend with ill health. The changes in the composition of the Soviet leadership which occurred during 1978 confirmed Brezhnev's position; the promotions which took place generally advanced known supporters of his policies. In November Kyril Mazurov, a first deputy premier of the U.S.S.R. and a member of the Politburo who had exercised general oversight over industrial development, was relieved of all his posts for "reasons of health" and "at his own request." He was re-

placed in the Politburo by Konstantin Chernenko, one of the secretaries of the party's Central Committee, generally regarded as an able administrator and completely devoted to Brezhnev. Mazurov was from Belorussia, and after his departure the premier of the Belorussian Soviet Socialist Republic, Tikhon Kiselev, joined the central government as deputy premier. At the same time two new alternate members were appointed to the party's Politburo. They were Eduard Sheverdnadze, the first secretary of the Communist Party in Georgia, who had done much to clear up some of the corruption in that republic, and Nikolay Tikhonov, who replaced Mazurov as first deputy premier. Mikhail Gorbachev, the Communist Party boss of the Stavropol region, who had considerable experience in the management of agriculture, became national party secretary.

The current Soviet regime was essentially a conservative one, dedicated to preserving the status quo from which it drew its strength. The dreary record of repression of dissent and opposition to reform continued unabated, although the penalties handed out to some of the leading dissidents who were brought to trial were less harsh than had been expected. The Conference on Security and Cooperation in Europe, held in Belgrade, Yugos., to review the implementation of the Final Act of its Helsinki session in 1975, ended in March. This act included an agreement to facilitate the free movement of peoples and ideas across the East-West divide. However, the deliberations on human rights at Belgrade did not deter the Soviet authorities from persecuting their critics. In February Pjotr Wins, a member of the Ukrainian group set up to monitor the implementation of the Helsinki agreements, was arrested, to be later sent to prison as a "parasite."

In March there were reports that some Soviet psychiatrists were refusing to cooperate in the policy of confining dissidents to institutions for the mentally ill. A young medical orderly, Aleksandr Podrabinek, had become particularly prominent

Relatives and friends of Soviet dissident Anatoly Shcharansky wait outside the courthouse during his treason trial in July. Among them are (left to right) Ida Milgrom, Shcharansky's mother; and Soviet dissidents Aleksandr Lerner, Naum Meiman, and physicist Andrey Sakharov.

in drawing attention to this abuse. His brother Kyril was sentenced to 2½ years for illegal possession of arms in March and, in August, Aleksandr himself received the relatively mild sentence of five years of enforced residence ("internal exile") for slandering the U.S.S.R. His sentence coincided with the publication of a report to the Royal College of Psychiatrists in London which condemned the "widespread misuse of psychiatry for political purposes" in the Soviet Union.

The founder of the Helsinki monitoring group in Moscow, Yuri Orlov, who had been arrested in February 1977, was sentenced in May to seven years in a labour camp, to be followed by five years of internal exile. At the same time the Helsinki monitoring group in Georgia was destroyed by the arrest of three of its leaders, V. Rtskhiladze, Zviad Gamsakhurdia, and Merab Kostava; the last two pleaded guilty to slandering the Soviet Union, and Gamsakhurdia appeared on television to make an abject confession of his crimes. Two U.S. correspondents in Moscow, Craig Whitney of the *New York Times* and Harold Piper of the *Baltimore Sun*, were subsequently summoned for libel by the Soviet television authorities for casting doubts on the veracity of Gamsakhurdia's television performance. The U.S. journalists refused to cooperate in the court proceedings. They were ordered to print retractions in their respective papers and, when the papers refused, were fined; they paid the fines under protest. Surprisingly, their accreditation was not withdrawn.

In June two Jewish dissidents, Ida Nudel and Vladimir Slepak, were sentenced to four and five years, respectively, of internal exile for "hooliganism." But the most widely publicized trials took place in July. Aleksandr Ginzburg, held under arrest since February 1977, was sentenced to eight years in a severe labour camp for anti-Soviet propaganda; he had, in fact, administered the distribution of financial support to the families of political prisoners from funds made available by the exiled writer Aleksandr Solzhenitsyn. Anatoly Shcharansky (*see* BIOGRAPHIES), a young Jewish computer specialist and supporter of the Helsinki

monitoring group, whose arrest in March 1977 on charges of betraying the U.S.S.R. had caused some concern in the U.S., was sent to prison for three years, to be followed by ten years in a labour camp. Viktor Piatkus, a Lithuanian writer, and Lev Lukyanenko, a Ukrainian human rights activist, were each sentenced to ten years at hard labour and five years of internal exile. At the same time the Soviet press announced that the death sentence had been passed on Anatoly Filatov, who had been accused of high treason.

A group set up in Soviet Armenia to press for human rights was also destroyed by the Soviet police. In January Shagin Arutunyan was sentenced to three years in a labour camp, but the trial of Robert Nasaryan in December presented some difficulties because most of the prosecution witnesses gave evidence in favour of the accused. Nevertheless, Nasaryan was sent to prison for five years.

A new kind of dissent made its appearance in 1978. A small group of workers, led and inspired by Vladimir Klebanov, an unemployed miner, formed itself into a "free" union of workers and called for recognition of the rights of free association and proper collective bargaining. It appealed to the international labour movement for support but received little more than sympathy. The established leaders of dissent in the U.S.S.R., consisting mainly of intellectuals, remained aloof. There was no way in which Klebanov's ideas could be reconciled with the basic nature of the Soviet system, and he soon found himself in an institution for the insane. One of his main supporters, Vladimir Svirsky, was arrested in October. A month later the setting up in Moscow of a new free "interprofessional associated" group of workers was reported. Its founder, Mark Morozov, was arrested soon afterward.

The spate of trials caused a storm of protest in the West. Demands to move the 1980 Olympic Games from Moscow received no official support and soon petered out. Some Western scientists refused to attend international conferences held in the Soviet Union; there was some interruption of

---

U.S.S.R.

Education. (1976–77) Primary, pupils 35.6 million; secondary, pupils 10.9 million; primary and secondary, teachers 2,671,000; vocational, pupils 3,552,000; teacher training (1975–76), students 310,-348; vocational and teacher training, teachers 218,-428; higher, students 4,950,200, teaching staff 317,152.

Finance. Monetary unit: ruble, with (Sept. 18, 1978) a free rate of 0.67 ruble to U.S. $1 (1.31 ruble = £1 sterling). Budget (1978 est.): revenue 246.4 billion rubles; expenditure 246.2 billion rubles.

Foreign Trade. (1977) Imports 30,097,000,000 rubles; exports 33,256,000,000 rubles. Import sources: Eastern Europe 46% (East Germany 10%, Poland 10%, Bulgaria 8%, Czechoslovakia 8%, Hungary 7%); Cuba 6%; West Germany 6%; Japan 5%. Export destinations: Eastern Europe 46% (East Germany 11%, Poland 10%, Czechoslovakia 8%, Bulgaria 8%, Hungary 6%); Cuba 5%. Main exports: crude oil and products 28%; machinery and transport equipment 19%; gold c. 10%; iron and steel 6%; timber 5%.

Transport and Communications. Roads (1976) 1,405,600 km. Motor vehicles in use (1976): passenger c. 5,660,000; commercial (including buses) c. 5,-703,000. Railways: (1975) 268,800 km (including 130,500 km industrial); traffic (1976) 315,061,-000,000 passenger-km, freight (1977) 3,332,-000,000,000 net ton-km. Air traffic (1976): 130,529,000,000 passenger-km; freight 2,697,-800,000 net ton-km. Navigable inland waterways (1976) 146,400 km; freight traffic 222,700,000,000 ton-km. Shipping (1977): merchant vessels 100 gross tons and over 8,167; gross tonnage 21,438,291. Telephones (Jan. 1977) 18 million. Radio receivers (Dec. 1974) 116.1 million. Television receivers (Dec. 1976) 57.2 million.

Agriculture. Production (in 000; metric tons; 1977): wheat 92,042; barley 52,653; oats 18,379; rye 8,471; corn 10,993; rice 2,200; millet 2,000; potatoes c. 95,000; sugar, raw value c. 9,065; tomatoes c. 4,-733; watermelons (1976) c. 3,164; sunflower seed 5,870; cottonseed c. 5,694; linseed c. 340; soybeans c. 545; dry peas c. 5,560; wine c. 3,170; tea 99; tobacco c. 318; cotton, lint 2,716; flax fibres (1976) c. 503; wool 275; hen's eggs 3,360; milk 94,300; butter c. 1,400; cheese 1,415; meat c. 14,800; timber (cu m; 1976) 384,534; fish catch (1976) 10,134. Livestock (in 000; Jan. 1977): cattle 110,346; pigs 63,055; sheep 139,834; goats 5,539; horses (1976) 6,400; chickens 747,744.

Industry. Index of production (1975 = 100; 1977) 110. Fuel and power (in 000; metric tons; 1977): coal and lignite 722,000; crude oil 545,800; natural gas (cu m) 347,000,000; manufactured gas (cu m; 1976) 36,-400,000; electricity (kw-hr) 1,150,000,000. Production (in 000; metric tons; 1977): cement 127,000; iron ore (60% metal content) 240,000; pig iron 107,-000; steel 147,000; aluminum (1976) c. 1,600; copper (1976) c. 1,460; lead (1976) c. 500; zinc (1976) c. 720; magnesite (1976) c. 1,800; manganese ore (metal content; 1976) 2,992; tungsten concentrates (oxide content; 1976) c. 8; gold (troy oz) c. 8,000; silver (troy oz) c. 48,000; sulfuric acid 21,100; caustic soda 2,-660; plastics and resins 3,300; fertilizers (nutrient content; 1976) nitrogenous 8,531, phosphate 4,395, potash 8,310; newsprint (1976) 1,390; other paper (1976) 7,526; cotton fabrics (sq m) 6,820,000; woolen fabrics (sq m) 773,000; rayon and acetate fabrics (sq m) 1,648,000; passenger cars (units) 1,279; commercial vehicles (units) 781. New dwelling units completed (1976) 2,112,000.

cultural exchanges and labour union contacts; and several scheduled meetings between U.S. and Soviet officials, including the August session of the Soviet-American Joint Commission on Scientific and Technical Cooperation, were canceled. More significantly, U.S. Pres. Jimmy Carter placed restrictions on exports of oil-drilling equipment to the Soviet Union. He also stopped the proposed sale of U.S.-made computers which the Soviet news agency Tass had ordered for use during the 1980 Olympics.

Western European Communist parties, notably the French and the Spanish, joined in the chorus of protest against the trials, particularly the manner in which the rights of the defendants were being violated. None of this had any noticeable effect on the Soviet leadership, though on the credit side it should be noted that in January Andrew Klymchuk, a British student of Ukrainian origin, was released after he had admitted on television to having distributed "bourgeois-nationalist" propaganda material. Two fairly prominent physicists, V. Levich and Sergey Polikanov, were allowed to leave the country as was the dissident philosopher Aleksandr Zinoviev.

The continued activities of the dissidents obviously caused some concern to the Soviet leaders. In a major speech in Baku on September 22, Brezhnev himself claimed that they "include agents paid by the secret services of some Western countries," and he attacked Western criticism of the Soviet Union's repressive policies as "direct interference in our internal affairs, a flagrant violation of the spirit and letter of the Helsinki Final Act."

The difficulty of reconciling the policy of détente with the strict maintenance of ideological orthodoxy presented another problem. Brezhnev dealt with questions of ideological work and public morale at the 18th congress of the Communist Youth Movement (Komsomol) in May: "It is high time for workers on the ideological front to end the mechanical and thoughtless repetition of axiomatic

verities and fustian rhetoric." The Soviet media took a resolute stand in defending the U.S.S.R.'s position on human rights; several articles published in *Pravda* in May attacked racism and social inequality in the U.S. and criticized the U.S. for failing to ratify the UN conventions opposing racism and outlawing genocide.

In the first major revision of its travel rules in more than ten years, the Soviet Union in January added more than 20 towns and cities to those open to foreigners. They included the industrial city of Magnitogorsk and several towns in the Baltic states and in the area near Moscow. At the same time, however, Soviet authorities closed the border between the Kazakh Soviet Socialist Republic and China and barred all visitors from the Jewish Autonomous Oblast, which also lies on the Chinese border.

The Economy. With the exception of agriculture, the Soviet economy did little more than mark time during 1978. Industrial output rose 4.8% in the first nine months of the year, slightly less than the increase recorded for the same period in 1977. Oil production for 1978 was reported as 572.5 million metric tons, 2.5 million metric tons below target, and coal production as 729 million metric tons, a shortfall of 17 million metric tons. Despite these shortfalls, the overall statistics of energy production were impressive, though the authorities again appealed to the public to achieve economies in the consumption of energy, and ambitious plans for further developments in nuclear energy, based on the use of plutonium breeder reactors, were announced for the 1980s.

The Soviet Union's foreign debt continued to mount, thus reversing the more favourable trends reported in the second half of 1977. In the first six months of 1978 the deficit in the U.S.S.R.'s trade with the West stood at U.S. $2.9 billion, caused mainly by a slight decline of Soviet exports to the West and by the effects of price inflation affecting Soviet imports. The U.S.S.R. did maintain its tradi-

To exploit the vast region of Siberia, the Soviet government is building the Baykal-Amur Mainline Railway across 1,965 miles of wilderness from the town of Ust-Kut to Komsomolsk. The enormous project is expected to cost about $15 billion.

SIPA PRESS/BLACK STAR

tional surpluses in trading with the third world and with the other socialist countries. In a speech to the Supreme Soviet, Premier Aleksey Kosygin expressed his regret that Soviet trade with the U.S. accounted for only 2% of total Soviet foreign trade in 1977; Soviet purchases in the U.S. had declined by 30% in comparison with 1976.

Agriculture provided the main focus of attention. The Communist Party's Central Committee met in July to discuss this vital sector. Steps were taken to offer additional incentives to farmers, particularly with regard to livestock production. Great emphasis was placed on the need to produce more meat to satisfy growing consumer demand. As of Jan. 1, 1979, farmers would be paid increased bulk purchasing prices for milk, wool, mutton, and vegetables, but there would be no corresponding rise in retail prices. The minimum pension for collective farmers would be increased by 40% as of Jan. 1, 1980, and would ultimately be brought into line with the pensions paid to workers in industry. It was announced that investment in agriculture accounted for 25% of all budgetary investment, and officials were once again urged to encourage farmers to use their tiny private plots, the produce of which could be sold on a relatively free market. Improvements in rural housing conditions were promised, and the state bank agreed to write off debts caused by the disastrous failure of the 1975 harvest. More and better tractors were also to be made available.

The discovery of major new phosphate deposits in eastern Siberia held out prospects of a further increase in the production of chemical fertilizer, which had risen from 27 million metric tons in 1965 to 77 million metric tons in 1977. A problem in this area seemed to be the relatively low quality of the finished product and the lack of experience in its use.

The Soviet grain harvest was a record 230 million metric tons, thus reducing the nation's expected demand for grain imports. There were some difficulties in transporting and storing the grain, and there were some doubts as to its quality. But the achievement was impressive, even though the production of wine and meat fell below target.

Foreign Affairs. In most of the crises which disturbed the international system during 1978, the U.S.S.R. played a relatively passive role. President Carter's efforts to stabilize the Middle Eastern situation by persuading Israel and Egypt to conclude a peace treaty found no echo in Moscow; in his Baku speech in September, Brezhnev merely restated the Soviet position that Israel must give up the territories seized in the 1967 war, a Palestinian state should be set up, and the Palestine Liberation Organization must be included in any durable settlement.

The crisis in Iran late in 1978 seemed to have caught the Soviet Union by surprise. In April the U.S.S.R. had signed an agreement for the building of a pipeline across Iran, and in June a Soviet-Iranian commission met in Baku to make plans for educational and cultural cooperation in 1979–80. It seemed unlikely that the Soviet Union would like to see the shah of Iran replaced by a right-wing, religiously oriented regime, although the possibil-

There were short lines at the gas pumps after the Soviet Union doubled the price of gasoline in March to $1.10 a gallon for high octane.

ity of the ultimate ascendancy of the left-wing Tudeh Party undoubtedly provided a more attractive prospect.

The U.S.S.R. also made strenuous efforts to improve relations with another Muslim neighbour, Turkey. The latter's deteriorating relations with its NATO partners, especially with the U.S., brought about by Turkish policies in Cyprus, appeared to provide a useful opening for Soviet initiatives. The Soviet chief of staff visited Turkey in April, and Turkey's prime minister, Bulent Ecevit, traveled to Moscow in June.

During the year the Soviet Union had to cope with another kind of problem on its western periphery, in Eastern Europe. Although the Romanian president, Nicolae Ceausescu, joined the procession of Eastern European leaders who visited Brezhnev during the summer, at the end of November the U.S.S.R. was again faced by a Romanian challenge. Ceausescu not only refused to go along with Soviet proposals for a 3% increase in the military budgets of the Warsaw Pact countries but he subsequently announced his country's intention to reduce defense expenditures. He also firmly refused to endorse the Soviet Union's efforts to align the Warsaw Pact against China. The Romanians, having welcomed Premier Hua Kuofeng of China in the summer, naturally approved of the normalization of diplomatic relations between the U.S. and China as "an outstanding event in the service of peace and détente." The U.S.S.R. could not really condemn the establishment of full diplomatic relations between the two countries but nevertheless must have regarded it as the culmination of China's diplomatic campaign to isolate the Soviet Union.

The Soviet Union and the U.S. clashed early in the year over the issue of Soviet intervention in the war between Ethiopia and Somalia. The U.S.S.R. had sent arms and military advisers to Ethiopia, which was also benefiting from the presence of Cuban troops. President Carter accused the

United Arab Emirates

U.S.S.R. of "unwarranted interference" in the conflict. The Soviet Union responded by maintaining that the U.S. was distorting its aims and that it was only providing assistance to Ethiopia so that it could repel aggression from Somalia. Later in the year the U.S.S.R. said that neither it nor Cuba had played any role in the invasion of southern Zaire by Angola-based rebels.

Relations with the U.S. also became strained when Francis J. Crawford, a U.S. citizen and representative of International Harvester Co. in Moscow, was arrested and formally accused on June 17 of having "systematically sold large amounts of foreign currency at speculative prices to Soviet citizens." It was generally believed that the U.S.S.R. arrested Crawford in retaliation for the publicized arrest of two Soviet spies in New Jersey on May 20, such spies usually being arrested and deported without fanfare. Crawford was given a suspended five-year sentence and left the U.S.S.R. early in September.

Early in December, after two days of talks in Moscow, Brezhnev and Afghanistan Prime Minister Nur Mohammad Taraki committed their countries to a 20-year treaty of friendship and cooperation. They pledged, among other things, "to develop cooperation in the military field," though Taraki said that Afghanistan would remain officially nonaligned.

The signing of the Sino-Japanese Treaty of Peace and Friendship in August was described by the Soviet news agency Tass as being "fraught with danger to the stability of Asia," and it was followed by the withdrawal of the Soviet ambassador from Tokyo. Yet diplomatic contacts between the U.S.S.R. and China were not completely abandoned; a commercial and payments agreement was concluded in April, and talks of settling frontier disputes between the two countries were resumed at the same time. In May the Soviet Union apologized for a border incident on the Ussuri River. Nevertheless, the fundamental hostility between the two nations continued and was frequently expressed by both sides.

Thus the developments in U.S.-China relations, which dominated the international scene at the end of the year, must have caused considerable concern in Moscow. However, the Soviet Union was not deterred from continuing to negotiate with the U.S. about the most pressing issue in contemporary international relations, the second stage of an agreement on limiting strategic nuclear weapons. At the end of the year, agreement on SALT II appeared to be close, although some details remained to be settled. The most notable of these was the new Soviet practice, first used in a Pacific Ocean weapons test in July, of using complex telemetric codes to conceal data beamed from its nuclear warheads in order to prevent the U.S. from monitoring the tests. The continued use of this practice would, of course, make verification of any agreement problematic. Yet after difficult negotiations between U.S. Secretary of State Cyrus Vance and Soviet Foreign Minister Andrey Gromyko, held in Geneva at the end of December, it seemed possible that a treaty would be signed early in 1979.

(OTTO PICK)

Unions:
see Industrial Review

Unitarian Churches:
see Religion

United Church of
Canada:
see Religion

United Church of
Christ:
see Religion

United Arab Emirates

Consisting of Abu Dhabi, Ajman, Dubai, Fujairah, Ras al-Khaimah, Sharjah, and Umm al-Qaiwain, the United Arab Emirates is located on the eastern Arabian Peninsula. Area: 83,600 sq km (32,300 sq mi). Pop. (1978 est.): 860,000, of whom (1968) 68% were Arab, 15% Iranian, and 15% Indian and Pakistani. Cap.: Abu Dhabi town (pop., 1975, 95,000). Language: Arabic. Religion: Muslim. President in 1978, Sheikh Zaid ibn Sultan an-Nahayan; prime minister, Sheikh Maktum ibn Rashid al-Maktum.

In 1978 the United Arab Emirates (U.A.E.) underwent severe internal strains. On January 31 Pres. Sheikh Zaid ibn Sultan an-Nahayan announced the appointment of his son Sheikh Sultan ibn Zaid as commander in chief of the United Arab Emirates armed forces, into which troops of United Arab Emirates member states were to be finally amalgamated. Sheikh Rashid ibn Said al-Maktum of Dubai and his son, United Arab Emirates Defense Minister Sheikh Muhammad ibn Rashid al-Maktum, had not been consulted about the appointment of Sheikh Sultan, and Dubai troops were placed on alert.

In June Sheikh Rashid challenged Sheikh Zaid's actions as unconstitutional but denied that he intended to take Dubai out of the federation in retaliation for Sheikh Zaid's action. The ruler of Ras al-Khaimah also strongly criticized the federation for allegedly starving him of development funds. During the year the United Arab Emirates was in dispute with Oman over territory administered by Ras al-Khaimah but claimed by Oman; in May a decision to build an oil refinery in northern Ras al-Khaimah with Kuwaiti aid was strongly challenged by Oman.

In January the U.A.E. dirham was revalued by 0.5% against the U.S. dollar, and in March links with the dollar were formally cut and replaced by a link with the Special Drawing Rights of the International Monetary Fund. Federal spending allocations for 1978 were cut to $2.7 billion from the 1977 level of $3,350,000,000. The nation's economy suffered as a result of the saturation of the real estate market that followed the rapid rise in oil prices after 1973.

(PETER MANSFIELD)

UNITED ARAB EMIRATES

Education. (1976–77) Primary, pupils 60,742, teachers c. 3,876; secondary, pupils 14,511, teachers c. 1,579; vocational, pupils 625, teachers 270; teacher training, students 89, teachers (1975–76) 8.

Finance. Monetary unit: dirham, with (Sept. 18, 1978) a free rate of 3.85 dirhams to U.S. $1 (7.54 dirhams = £1 sterling). Gold and foreign exchange (June 1978) U.S. $667.6 million. Budget (federal; 1977–78 est.) balanced at 9,189,000,000 dirhams.

Foreign Trade. (1977) Imports 17,574,000,000 dirhams; exports 37,082,000,000 dirhams. Import sources (1976): Japan 17%; U.K. 17%; U.S. 13%; West Germany 7%; India 5%. Export destinations (1976): Japan 28%; France 13%; U.S. 12%; The Netherlands 10%; U.K. 8%; Spain 5%. Main export: crude oil 96%.

Industry. Production (in 000; metric tons): crude oil (1977) 98,305; petroleum products (1976) 302.

United Kingdom

A constitutional monarchy in northwestern Europe and member of the Commonwealth of Nations, the United Kingdom comprises the island of Great Britain (England, Scotland, and Wales) and Northern Ireland, together with many small islands. Area: 244,035 sq km (94,222 sq mi), including 3,084 sq km of inland water but excluding the crown dependencies of the Channel Islands and Isle of Man. Pop. (1978 est.): 55,870,000. Cap. and largest city: London (Greater London pop., 1977 est., 6,970,000). Language: English; some Welsh and Gaelic also are used. Religion: mainly Protestant with Catholic, Muslim, and Jewish minorities, in that order. Queen, Elizabeth II; prime minister in 1978, James Callaghan.

The Economy. For Great Britain 1978 was a boom year, better than any since 1973. Total output rose by between 5 and 6% during the 12 months, representing a rise of some 13% from the trough of 1975. Export volume increased by more than 5% when compared with 1977, which had itself been a remarkable year for growth in overseas sales. The fall in spending power experienced in 1977, which had been of the order of 8% over the year, was reversed. During the 1977–78 winter and for some time thereafter earnings rose twice as fast as prices, with the result that retail sales soared. Tax reductions in the autumn of 1977 and the summer of 1978 had a similar effect.

Some, but not all, of this improvement was attributable to the increasing income from North Sea oil. The positive effect of this on the balance of payments was some £1,000 million in 1977 and nearly twice as much in 1978. The British government chose to spend this windfall by increasing the purchasing power of consumers, which it did through real tax cuts; the policy was carried further by the increased strength of the pound sterling on the foreign exchange markets. The consequence was a decline in the cost of imported raw materials.

There was an evident underlying trend toward

United Kingdom

recovery even discounting the effect of North Sea oil. The recovery in production of manufactured goods that started in 1977 continued, though at a more sluggish pace, during the first nine months of 1978, and at the end of the year it seemed likely that Great Britain had held its recently improved share of world trade in manufactures. During the second quarter investment in plant and machinery by manufacturing industry reached its highest quarterly value in seven years. The rate of inflation was brought under control in 1978 for the first time since 1973. The increase in the retail price index in the 12 months to December 1977 was 12.1%. This fell to the long-sought "single figure" in January 1978, when it was 9.9%. By June it was 7.4%, less than a third of the crisis level of three years earlier. The rate stabilized at about 8% during the rest of 1978.

The government's continuing determination to maintain control over inflation was shown by its credit squeeze in early June. As a corrective to the judgment of three months earlier, "corset" controls were reimposed on the banks and interest rates were increased. This was only part of the strategy; the government insisted, against the declared opposition of the Trades Union Congress (TUC), that the preceding three years of wage controls would be followed by a fourth, with the target for pay increases set this time at 5%.

Economists differed on which factor was responsible for the decline in British inflation—the wage controls, the attempt to moderate the money supply, the strengthening pound, or the persistence of a historically high level of unemployment. The government proclaimed that its primary strategy in dealing with the problem was its "incomes policy." During the third phase of this policy, which ended in mid-1978, average earnings rose by 14.2%; this was substantially higher than the target of 10%. The hope was that the 5% fourth-phase target would not be exceeded by more than a few percentage points, but in early November the wage settlement with the workers at Ford Motor Co., worth some 17%, indicated that it was unlikely that the unions would take much notice of the target.

UNITED KINGDOM

Education. (1975–76) Primary, pupils 5,965,597, teachers 249,923; secondary and vocational, pupils 4,724,543, teachers 276,226; higher, students 677,700, teaching staff (universities only) 39,106.

Finance. Monetary unit: pound sterling, with (Sept. 18, 1978) a free rate of £0.51 to U.S. $1 (U.S. $1.96 = £1 sterling). Gold, SDR's, and foreign exchange (June 1978) U.S. $17,257,000,000. Budget (1978–79 est.): revenue £42,746 million; expenditure £51,378 million. Gross national product (1977) £140,070 million. Money supply (June 1978) £23,546 million. Cost of living (1975 = 100; June 1978) 146.3.

Foreign Trade. (1977) Imports £36,996 million; exports £33,308 million. Import sources: EEC 38% (West Germany 10%, France 7%, The Netherlands 7%, Belgium-Luxembourg 5%); U.S. 10%. Export destinations: EEC 36% (West Germany 8%, France 7%, The Netherlands 6%, Belgium-Luxembourg 5%, Ireland 5%); U.S. 9%. Main exports: nonelectrical machinery 18%; chemicals 12%; motor vehicles 8%; electrical machinery and equipment 8%; diamonds 6%; petroleum and products 6%. Tourism (1976): visitors 10,089,000; gross receipts U.S. $2,839,000,000.

Transport and Communications. Roads (1976) 368,370 km (including 2,332 km expressways). Motor vehicles in use (1976): passenger 14,355,000; commercial 1,795,000. Railways (1976): 18,354 km; traffic (excluding Northern Ireland) 28,600,000,000 passenger-km, freight (1977) 20,171,000,000 net ton-km. Air traffic (1977): 31,871,000,000 passenger-km; freight 1,019,080,000 net ton-km. Shipping (1977): merchant vessels 100 gross tons and over 3,432; gross tonnage 31,646,351. Shipping traffic (1976): goods loaded 55,626,000 metric tons, unloaded 181,489,000 metric tons. Telephones (March 1977) 22,012,000. Radio receivers (Dec. 1974) 42 million. Television licenses (Dec. 1977) 18,088,000.

Agriculture. Production (in 000; metric tons; 1977): wheat 5,229; barley 10,784; oats 771; potatoes 6,571; sugar, raw value c. 950; cabbages (1976) c. 674; cauliflower c. 274; green peas (1976) c. 715; carrots (1976) 555; apples c. 345; dry peas 109; tomatoes c. 176; onions c. 180; rapeseed 142; hen's eggs 807; cow's milk 15,041; butter 120; cheese 213; beef and veal c. 987; mutton and lamb c. 240; pork c. 906; wool 31; fish catch 824. Livestock (in 000; June 1977): cattle 13,926; sheep 28,054; pigs 7,673; poultry 117,768.

Industry. Index of production (1975 = 100; 1977) 102.1. Fuel and power (in 000; metric tons; 1977): coal 122,148; crude oil 37,538; natural gas (cu m) c. 39,960,000; electricity (kw-hr) 283,480,000. Production (in 000; metric tons; 1977): cement 15,458; iron ore (26% metal content) 3,745; pig iron 12,214; crude steel 20,410; petroleum products 86,340; sulfuric acid 3,405; fertilizers (nutrient content; 1976–77) nitrogenous 1,071, phosphate 428, potash 49; man-made fibres 552; cotton fabrics (m) 360,000; woolen fabrics (sq m) 150,000; rayon and acetate fabrics (m) 498,000; television receivers (units) 1,837; passenger cars (units) 1,316; commercial vehicles (units) 398. Merchant vessels launched (100 gross tons and over; 1977) 1,124,000 gross tons. New dwelling units completed (1977) 314,000.

As they are wont to do, Britons queued up—this time for bread when members of the bakers' union declared a national strike in November.

The government responded to the Ford settlement with an announcement that the company would be penalized by the withdrawal of public-sector business, but within a few weeks Parliament voted against this policy of "sanctions." It remained open to the government to put pressure on companies paying wages above the norm by denying them the right to increase prices. The mechanism for this policy, the Price Commission, was still in operation at the end of the year. In spite of continuing pressure from a number of unions for increases in wages far in excess of 5%, the opinion polls indicated that public support for incomes policy remained strong.

The underlying performance of the economy remained a cause for concern. The number of unemployed stayed at about 1.4 million during most of the year. Government expenditure, brought under some kind of restraint following the International Monetary Fund rescue visit during the closing months of 1976, was starting to rise again. Imports grew rapidly, with foreign cars capturing half the British market. Productivity remained low.

Partly for these reasons confidence in the ability of the British economy to compete on equal terms with the French and West German economies was not widespread. The proposed entry of Britain into the new European Monetary System encountered political opposition from those who had been against British membership in the European Economic Community and also from the left wing of the Labour Party; its possible effect on Britain's competitive position troubled others. Thus, in spite of much pressure from West Germany, British Prime Minister James Callaghan (see BIOGRAPHIES) decided, ostensibly on technical grounds, that Britain would not join the new system when it started in 1979, although it would attempt to manage its exchange rate as if it were a member. Industrial relations did not improve in 1978.

Work stoppages continued to plague British Leyland, hindering the motor company's planned recovery following the injection of government assistance. The similarly troubled Chrysler-UK was taken over by Peugeot-Citroën of France as part of the French firm's acquisition of Chrysler's European operations.

Disaffection among public employees was manifested in the strike of social workers and hospital personnel in London and elsewhere. The troubles of London's newspapers continued; the management of *The Times* and *Sunday Times* warned in April that if agreements on new technology and uninterrupted production could not be reached by November 30 publication of both newspapers and their associated journals would be suspended and staff members dismissed. When the deadline arrived, there was still no agreement and publication ceased. Shortly after Christmas the first 600 dismissals took effect, and at the year's end there was no sign that the principal trade union involved, the National Graphical Association, was ready to negotiate.

Politics. Prime Minister Callaghan's demonstration of an ability to govern in spite of a hung Parliament, a divided Labour Party, and TUC opposition to his principal policies was perhaps the outstanding political development of the year. At the start of 1978 Callaghan enjoyed the guaranteed support in Parliament of the Liberal Party, under the terms of the previous year's understanding with its leader, David Steel. Because this arrangement was due to come to an end in the autumn, Callaghan was widely expected to call a general election at about that time. Anticipation was at its height in the first week of September, when it seemed that the campaign had virtually begun; the Conservative Party opposition had already arranged an expensive election advertising campaign. But the prime minister took everyone by surprise and announced that there would be no election after all.

Callaghan's ability to remain in office depended in large part on the dwindling support for the smaller parties in Parliament, which in turn led those parties to vote for the government, or at least to abstain, on motions of confidence. The reduced support for the Scottish Nationalists and the concomitant increase in the prospects of the Labour Party in Scotland were demonstrated at by-elections, and this evidence was supported by opinion polls. Similar indications showed that the Liberal Party also was losing ground. Opinion polls taken in September suggested that only about 5% of the voters would support it at that time.

One reason given for the decline was the charge of conspiracy to murder against the former leader of the party, Jeremy Thorpe (*see* BIOGRAPHIES), but the polls indicated a withering away of the Liberal vote even before those charges were brought. Whatever the reasons, the Liberals, like the other small parties, stood to lose more from a general election during 1978 than they would gain. Thus Callaghan could rely on a combination of small-party votes and abstentions, as he did in the no-confidence vote in December that followed the defeat of his government's incomes policy.

Against this background the Conservatives appeared to fare no better than the general return of support to the larger parties would account for. In most tests of opinion the Conservative leader, Margaret Thatcher, was shown to be less popular than Prime Minister Callaghan, although the Conservative Party was ahead in polls of voting intentions at various times throughout the year. It also proved successful in increasing its support at by-elections.

One difficulty facing the Conservatives was the continued division on matters of policy between the official leadership under Thatcher and the segment of the party led by former prime minister Edward Heath. Toward the end of the year Heath made clear his support for Callaghan's incomes policy and his opposition to Thatcher's approach.

Devolution. One difficult policy question was at least partly cleared up during 1978, when the bills devolving some powers to elected assemblies for Scotland and Wales passed in Parliament after many months of debate. The bills were not to take effect until after referenda were held in both regions, probably in March 1979. The original expectation that the Conservatives would campaign heavily against a "yes" vote was modified by the Labour Party's demonstration that its support for the new assemblies in Scotland had done much to reduce the effectiveness of Scottish Nationalists. The new assemblies were to have limited powers, with ultimate control retained by the central government.

Although this fell far short of the separation demanded by the nationalists, the constitutional implications of devolution were much debated during 1978. One short-term consequence was that the case for increased representation of Northern Ireland in Parliament was much strengthened. A less predictable consequence was derived from the provision that any bill that passed its second reading in the Commons with the help of Scottish MP's would be subject to a second vote after 14 days allocated for further thinking. The provision was designed to meet the objection of English MP's, who protested that their say over Scottish affairs would be diminished by devolution while the influence of Scottish MP's over English affairs would remain the same. The constitutional question that arose, however, was whether this provision would ultimately lead to greater separation between the parts of the United Kingdom.

Foreign Relations. Early in January Prime Minister Callaghan visited India on an Asian tour that also included stops in Pakistan and Bangladesh. It was the first visit by a British prime minister to India in seven years. Callaghan and Indian Prime Minister Morarji Desai held talks that reportedly dealt with trade between the two nations.

Callaghan continued his travels in March when he journeyed to both West Germany and the U.S.

A fireman inspects the rubble of what had been a crowded restaurant near Belfast, Northern Ireland, until a bomb destroyed it. The blast, which killed 12 people, was believed by police to be the work of the Irish Republican Army.

The wreckage of a pier littered the beach at Margate, England, after savage storms crashed into the eastern coast in January.

for talks on world trade. Later, in an address to the UN General Assembly in June, he warned African nations to reject foreign interference in their affairs, a statement reflecting Britain's concern over the increasing involvement of the Soviet Union and Cuba in Africa.

In July the U.K. ordered five members of the Iraqi diplomatic staff in London to leave the country within a week. Two employees of Iraq's national airline and one employee of the Iraq Bank were also told to go. The British said that they were taking this action because of "increasing concern at the threat posed by terrorist activities in London, particularly against Arab targets." Iraq retaliated by expelling eight British diplomats and two senior employees of British Airways.

In an effort to break the deadlock reached in negotiations for a settlement in Rhodesia, Callaghan sent a personal emissary, Cledwyn Hughes, there in November. Hughes, chairman of the parliamentary Labour Party, was to try to secure the various factions' participation in a conference to be held in Britain in the new year.

The Bingham Report, published in September, charged that two British oil companies had over the years broken British sanctions against Rhodesia by taking part in arrangements designed to provide that nation with oil. This revelation caused strained relations between the U.K. and Zambia, and in an effort to improve the situation Callaghan met with Zambian Pres. Kenneth Kaunda in Nigeria. Additional British aid to Zambia was promised and in October was delivered in the form of a modern British antiaircraft system.

Northern Ireland. Violence continued in Northern Ireland during 1978, though on a reduced scale in comparison with some recent years. In February a bomb exploded in a restaurant in a Protestant area of Belfast, killing 12 and injuring more than 20. The Provisional Wing of the Irish Republican Army (IRA) was blamed, and 20 of its members were arrested. In November the IRA claimed responsibility for firebombings that damaged stores throughout Northern Ireland.

Roman Catholics marching in Londonderry in October to celebrate the tenth anniversary of a Catholic civil rights protest were attacked by Protestants. Many were hurt in the ensuing battle, including more than 60 policemen.

In a report published during the year Amnesty International accused the Royal Ulster Constabulary of maltreating suspected terrorists between 1975 and 1977. According to the report many of the allegations of beatings and the use of psychologically and physically exhausting methods of interrogation were corroborated by medical evidence. The constabulary claimed that the allegations were part of a propaganda campaign aimed at discrediting it. (*See* LAW.)

The Monarchy. In May Queen Elizabeth's sister, Princess Margaret, was granted a divorce, ending her 18-year-old marriage to Lord Snowdon. This marked a departure from the previous convention, whereby divorce was regarded as impossible for members of the royal family.

Queen Elizabeth II gave permission for her cousin, Prince Michael of Kent, and Baroness Marie-Christine von Reibnitz, a Roman Catholic divorcee, to marry. The pope, however, would not permit the couple to marry in a Catholic church. (Under the 1701 Act of Settlement a member of the royal family may not marry a Catholic; it was presumed that Prince Michael, the 16th in line of succession, was considered to be far enough removed from the throne.)

In May the queen and Prince Philip visited West Germany, and in July her majesty was invited to Canada, where she opened the Commonwealth Games in Edmonton, Alta. The queen later agreed to proposals limiting the role of the monarch as Canada's head of state and to various changes in Canada's constitution. However, the envisaged changes were not expected to "alter the essential relationship of the Crown to Canada."

(JOE ROGALY)

See also Commonwealth of Nations; Dependent States; Ireland.

United Nations

In reporting to the 33rd annual General Assembly (opened Sept. 19, 1978, recessed December 20; Indalecio Liévano of Colombia, president) on the United Nations' work for the year ended August 31, Secretary-General Kurt Waldheim emphasized the dangers of regional conflicts, particularly in southern Africa and the Middle East; deepening poverty and economic dislocation; a deteriorating environment; and the overshadowing threat posed by weapons of mass destruction.

Disarmament. From May 23 to July 1, the Assembly devoted its tenth special session to weaponry. This was the largest and most representative meeting on arms control in history and the first global meeting on the subject since the unsuccessful League of Nations World Disarmament Conference in 1932. On July 1 the Assembly adopted by consensus a "Final Document," designed "to lay the foundations" of an international strategy for general and complete disarmament.

In the document, delegates revamped their negotiating machinery. They created a Committee on Disarmament, "open to the nuclear-weapon States and to 32 to 35 other States." Membership was to be reviewed regularly, and the chairmanship would rotate monthly among all members. This committee would replace the Conference of the Committee on Disarmament, instituted in 1952 with 18 (later 31) members. The U.S. and the Soviet Union were permanent co-chairmen of the earlier body.

The Assembly also established a Disarmament Commission, composed of all UN members, to re-place the original commission, with the same name, established in 1952 but inactive since 1965. The new commission, which met for the first time on October 9, was to recommend approaches to disarmament problems, follow up the work of the special session, consider the elements of a comprehensive disarmament program, and report annually to the Assembly, which would now serve as the United Nations' main deliberative body on disarmament matters. The document looked forward, as an "ultimate goal," to "the complete elimination of nuclear weapons." Other priority objectives were agreements to limit and gradually reduce armed forces and stocks of conventional weapons, including chemical weapons, "excessively injurious" weapons, and weapons capable of "indiscriminate effects." The Assembly urged states to use resources freed through disarmament to promote the well-being of all peoples and to assist the less developed countries.

Peacekeeping. The principal manifestations of the UN security system during 1978 were its peacekeeping efforts in Cyprus, Lebanon, and other parts of the Middle East.

Despite the secretary-general's efforts, starting in January with talks in Ankara, Athens, and Nicosia, no agreed basis emerged for talks between the Greek and Turkish communities in Cyprus. On November 9 the General Assembly demanded, 110–4 (Iran, Pakistan, Turkey, Saudi Arabia) with 22 abstentions, that Turkey remove from Cyprus the "peace force" it sent there in 1974. It also insisted, 80–7 with 48 abstentions, that the Security Council use "all appropriate and practical measures" to enforce its own resolutions on Cyprus. Turkey, having ignored past UN resolutions on Cyprus, said that this one would merely "prolong the agony of the Cypriots." A 2,500-man UN force remained on the island to forestall conflict between the two communities.

Lebanon complained on March 15 to the secretary-general and to the Security Council that Israel, by invading southern Lebanon allegedly to destroy bases of the Palestine Liberation Organization (PLO), had committed "naked aggression." The attack followed a commando operation on

UN peacekeeping forces moved into the villages in the south of Lebanon after battles between Israeli and Palestinian forces.

Delegates stood for opening ceremonies in May of the United Nations General Assembly special disarmament session in New York City.

March 11 on the Haifa–Tel Aviv road by what Israel called a PLO "murder squad," in which 37 persons were killed and 82 wounded. Lebanon denied any connection with the PLO ambush and protested that it had "exerted tremendous efforts with the Palestinians and the Arab States in order to keep matters under control."

Responding on March 19 to Lebanon's complaints, the Security Council established, 12–0 (Czechoslovakia and the U.S.S.R. abstaining, China not participating), the UN Interim Force in Lebanon (UNIFIL). The Council charged UNIFIL with confirming that Israeli forces withdrew from Lebanon (Waldheim later reported that they had withdrawn on June 13), with restoring international peace and security, and with assisting Lebanon to regain effective control of its territory. The General Assembly, in special session, approved financial arrangements for UNIFIL on April 20–21, and the force numbered 6,000 men by year's end. It was unable to restore full authority to the Lebanese government, however.

To support UNIFIL, the Security Council on October 1 unanimously called upon "all those involved in hostilities in Lebanon to put an end to acts of violence and observe scrupulously an immediate and effective cease-fire . . . so that internal peace and national reconciliation could be restored . . . ." Waldheim continued his own mediatory efforts by dispatching Prince Sadruddin Aga Khan as his special envoy to Damascus and Beirut to try to effect a durable cease-fire.

Two other UN forces continued their work in the Middle East: the UN Emergency Force, separating Israeli and Egyptian troops in the Sinai while representatives of the two states conferred on a peace treaty, and the UN Disengagement Observer Force, on the Golan Heights between Israel and Syria.

Southern Africa. Namibia (South West Africa) and Rhodesia (Zimbabwe) dominated UN concerns in southern Africa in 1978. At a special session on Namibia (April 24–May 3), the General

Assembly adopted, 119–0 with 21 (mostly Western) abstentions, a Declaration and Program of Action on Namibia. It expressed "full support for the armed liberation struggle of the Namibian people" led by the South West Africa People's Organization (SWAPO) as "its sole and authoritative representative." South Africa on April 25 accepted Western (British, Canadian, French, U.S., and West German) proposals that called for free elections in Namibia with a substantial UN civil and military "presence" supervising them. The future of Walvis Bay, which the Assembly called "an integral part of Namibia" but which South Africa claimed as its own, was to be settled in negotiations between South Africa and the new Namibian government. SWAPO accepted this plan on July 12.

Acting on the South African and SWAPO agreement, the Security Council on July 27 approved, 13–0 (Czechoslovakia and the U.S.S.R. abstaining), a Namibian independence plan, asked the secretary-general to supervise elections there, and declared that Namibia's unity and territorial integrity, including Walvis Bay, must be assured. It adjured South Africa not to use Walvis Bay in any manner prejudicial to Namibian independence or to the viability of the Namibian economy. South Africa rejected the Security Council resolution as it related to Walvis Bay on July 31.

In response to that resolution, however, the secretary-general sent a survey team to Namibia. It stayed 17 days (August 6–22) and recommended a lapse of seven months from the time that the Security Council approved a UN operation in Namibia until elections took place. That meant delaying independence until 1979, but South African authorities set December as the month for elections, even though political parties in Namibia thought they needed more time to ensure free and fair balloting. The Security Council accepted the survey team's view, endorsed by Waldheim, and on September 29 it approved, 12–0 (Czechoslovakia and the U.S.S.R. abstaining; China not participating), the secretary-general's plan to send a 7,500-man military and civilian force to Namibia to arrange to register voters and conduct the elections. The Council also declared null and void "all unilateral measures taken by the illegal administration in Namibia in relation to the electoral process, including unilateral registration of voters, or transfer of power."

On November 13 the Council called, 10–0, for South Africa to cancel its election plans. It warned South Africa that if it refused to wait for UN-supervised elections, the Council would be compelled to initiate "appropriate actions under the Charter," including economic sanctions. Although Western powers abstained on the vote, the Canadian delegate, William Barton, said that the abstentions "should not be interpreted as a lack of sympathy for the resolution, or the direction in which it points."

The South African-sponsored elections resulted in a victory for the white-dominated Democratic Turnhalle Alliance, and the newly elected Constituent Assembly then moved to negotiate revised conditions (a smaller UN force; an end of aid to SWAPO) for a second, UN-sponsored election in

1979. South Africa itself, however, informed Waldheim on December 22 that it would accept his proposals to station a UN peacekeeping force in Namibia to supervise the new elections.

As regards Rhodesia, the Security Council on March 14 requested UN members not to recognize the "internal settlement" between the Ian Smith regime and all Rhodesian parties except the Patriotic Front, jointly headed by Joshua Nkomo and Robert Mugabe. Waldheim said in September that mounting unrest and violence in Rhodesia underlined the need for all principal parties to agree on arrangements for majority rule. No evidence of such agreement emerged by the end of the year, and the Smith regime, which had pledged itself to elections to establish majority rule in December, postponed them until April 20, 1979.

Other Matters. In August the International Bank for Reconstruction and Development issued the first of a series of annual reports on the progress and prospects of the world's less developed countries. It said that while these nations had made "very impressive" progress over the past 25 years, with improved living standards, increased life expectancy, more children going to school, and better economic management, the remaining problems were immense. Out of two billion people in "third-world" countries, about 800 million still lived in absolute poverty, a condition "so characterized by malnutrition, illiteracy, disease, squalid surroundings, high infant mortality, and low life expectancy as to be beyond any reasonable definition of human decency."

UN membership rose to 151 in 1978 with the admission of the Solomon Islands in September and of Dominica in December. Both were former British possessions.   (RICHARD N. SWIFT)

[522.B.2]

United States

The United States of America is a federal republic composed of 50 states, 49 of which are in North America and one of which consists of the Hawaiian Islands. Area: 9,363,123 sq km (3,615,122 sq mi), including 202,711 sq km of inland water but excluding the 156,192 sq km of the Great Lakes that lie within U.S. boundaries. Pop. (1978 est.): 218,863,000, including 87% white and 11.6% Negro. Language: English. Religion (1974 est.): Protestant 72.5 million; Roman Catholic 48.7 million; Jewish 6 million; Orthodox 3.7 million. Cap.: Washington, D.C. (pop., 1977 est., 690,000). Largest city: New York (pop., 1977 est., 7,312,200). President in 1978, Jimmy Carter.

The U.S. voters nudged Congress a step to the right in the off year elections on November 7, adding three Republicans in the Senate and 12 in the House of Representatives and thus allowing the GOP at least to entertain the notion that it was on the way back in national politics. The numbers themselves were not exactly the stuff of which a political renaissance ordinarily is made. Free to campaign in opposition to the White House as well as Congress for the first time in ten years, Republicans ought to have gained a few House seats. But

for a party that suffered badly in congressional voting in 1974 and failed to gain any of its strength back in 1976, 12 new House seats marked a beginning.

The three new Senate seats might represent something more than a beginning. As important as the numerical change was the fact that Republicans managed to gain Senate strength in a year when they were defending half the seats at stake, a far higher proportion than they held in the chamber as a whole. Taking incumbents and newcomers together, the GOP elected 20 senators in 1978—more than in any year since 1952.

Thus the congressional returns, combined with a net gain of 6 Republican governors for a new total of 18, allowed GOP leaders to claim overall success in the 1978 election. They did so even as the White House was pointing out—correctly—that the combined Democratic losses were relatively small compared with what has often befallen the party in power in midterm elections.

The administration of Pres. Jimmy Carter (*see* BIOGRAPHIES), whose relations with the 95th Congress generally were uneasy, was expected to be able to live with the probable new lineup of 59 Democrats and 41 Republicans in the Senate and 276 Democrats and 159 Republicans in the House. But it might have some reason to be disturbed by Republican gains at the statehouse level. The Republican Party appeared, for the time being at least, to have checked the severe erosion of its gubernatorial strength that began in 1970 when it controlled 32 governorships and sank to an embarrassing 12 in 1976.

Moderate Republicans were the clear winners in the November 7 gubernatorial elections. Of the new "big five" GOP governors, Richard Thornburgh of Pennsylvania and the reelected James Thompson of Illinois and William Milliken of Michigan were clearly identified with the party's left. James Rhodes, the veteran Republican narrowly returned to office in Ohio, was generally

United States

As a strike deadline approached, U.S. postal workers demonstrated outside New York City's main post office in July. Scattered strikes across the nation were ended or averted by a last minute settlement.

UPI COMPIX

local-minded but had always sided with the moderates in national politics. Only William Clements in Texas added to conservative influence at the big-state level.

The Republican left also reelected Robert Ray of Iowa, the dean of U.S. governors, to his fifth term. The right lost Meldrim Thomson, Jr., of New Hampshire, who had become nationally known for his outspoken extreme conservatism, and it also failed to elect Ted Strickland as governor of Colorado.

The congressional picture was different. Moderate and liberal Republicans probably held their own in Senate elections, gaining William Cohen in Maine, David Durenberger and Rudy Boschwitz in Minnesota, and Larry Pressler in South Dakota, all of whom replaced Democrats. But they lost national figures in Clifford Case in the New Jersey primary, Edward Brooke in the Massachusetts general election, and James Pearson of Kansas, who retired. Pearson's replacement, Nancy Landon Kassebaum (daughter of 1936 Republican presidential candidate Alf Landon), might also join the moderates. But Case and Brooke were replaced by Democrats.

Conservative Republicans, on the other hand, lost virtually nothing. They won unexpected victories by ousting liberal Democrats Dick Clark in Iowa and Thomas McIntyre in New Hampshire, and gained a potential national leader in William Armstrong of Colorado. Thad Cochran of Mississippi, that state's first Republican senator ever chosen by popular vote, was considered certain to join the right on fiscal and defense issues, although he was likely to be a moderate on many social and some race-related questions.

The Year in Congress. The byword of the 95th Congress, at its inception in January 1977, was reform. There was a Democratic president for the heavily Democratic Congress to work with for the first time in eight years. There was no more U.S. involvement in Indochina to preoccupy the legislators. Congress, it was thought, could turn its

attention to tax reform, welfare reform, election-law reform, labour-law reform, and a host of other measures, and thereby cure the ills that had been wrought upon U.S. society by many years of neglect.

These hopes were not realized. The 95th Congress compiled, perhaps, a respectable legislative record, but the sweeping social legislation that had been the core of the Democratic Party's platform—national health insurance, a new urban strategy, and the above-mentioned reforms—never got off the ground. Some blamed the failures on the ineptitude of President Carter and his staff. Some blamed the special-interest lobbyists. Still others saw a conservative mood sweeping the country.

Nevertheless, the year ended with some legislative victories for Carter, an achievement that had seemed impossible at the beginning of 1978. Indeed, the main development of the second session of the 95th Congress was that once the president narrowed his priorities and personally entered the fray to coordinate the lobbying on Capitol Hill he was able to win some important battles. Among the examples:

(1) Congress, on the last day of the session, approved the compromise natural gas pricing bill, the legislation that Carter had termed the most critical of the year. (2) The Senate ratified the Panama Canal treaties. (3) The Senate turned down a resolution that would have blocked the president from selling jet planes to Saudi Arabia, and Congress gave Carter authority to lift the arms embargo against Turkey. (4) Carter's veto of a popular public works appropriations bill, containing water projects that he called unnecessary, was upheld, although the president was opposed by the congressional Democratic leadership. (5) Congress adopted a measure restructuring the civil service system, legislation that might have the longest-lasting effect of any enacted by the 95th Congress.

But there was a price to be paid for these victories. The president's success when he pulled out all

---

UNITED STATES

Education. (1977–78) Primary and pre-primary, pupils 33.3 million, teachers 1,330,000; secondary and vocational, pupils 15.7 million, teachers 1,110,-000; higher (including teacher training colleges), students 11.3 million, teaching staff 700,000.

Finance. Monetary unit: U.S. dollar, with (Sept. 18, 1978) a free rate of U.S. $1.96 to £1 sterling. Gold, SDR's, and foreign exchange (June 1978) $14,-920,000,000. Federal budget (1978–79 est.): revenue $439.6 billion; expenditure $500.2 billion. Gross national product (1977) $1,887,200,000,000. Money supply (June 1978) $337.6 billion. Cost of living: (1975 = 100; June 1978) 121.2.

Foreign Trade. (1977) Imports $156,695,000,000; exports (excluding military aid exports of $63 million) $120,101,000,000. Import sources: Canada 20%; Japan 13%; West Germany 5%. Export destinations: Canada 21%; Japan 9%; West Germany 5%. Main exports: nonelectrical machinery 19%; motor vehicles 10%; chemicals 9%; electrical machinery and equipment 9%; cereals 7%; aircraft 5%. Tourism (1976): visitors 17,523,000; gross receipts U.S. $5,806,000,000.

Transport and Communications. Roads (1975) 6,175,577 km (including 64,653 km expressways). Motor vehicles in use (1976): passenger 109,003,000; commercial (including buses) 26,152,000. Railways

(1975): 331,311 km; traffic (class I railways only; 1976) 15,688,000,000 passenger km, freight 1,-146,492,000,000 net ton-km. Air traffic (1977): 307,-559,000,000 passenger-km (including domestic services 254,450,000,000 passenger-km); freight 9,587,638,000 net ton-km (including domestic services 6,254,644,000 net ton-km). Inland waterways: freight traffic (1975) 499,600,000,000 ton-km (including 144,800,000,000 ton-km on Great Lakes system and 249,200,000,000 ton-km on Mississippi River system). Shipping (1977): merchant vessels 100 gross tons and over 4,740; gross tonnage 15,299,681. Shipping traffic (1977): goods loaded 250,213,000 metric tons, unloaded 568,136,000 metric tons. Telephones (Jan. 1977) 155,173,000. Radio receivers (Dec. 1975) 402 million. Television receivers (Dec. 1974) 121.1 million.

Agriculture. Production (in 000; metric tons; 1977): corn 161,485; wheat 55,134; barley 9,056; oats 10,856; rye 432; rice 4,501; sorghum 20,083; sugar, raw value 5,429; potatoes 15,941; soybeans 46,712; dry beans 739; cabbages (1976) 1,271; lettuce (1976) 2,417; onions c. 1,549; tomatoes c. 8,160; apples 3,053; oranges 9,612; grapefruit 2,748; peaches (1976) 1,389; grapes 3,855; peanuts 1,627; sunflower seed 1,248; linseed 409; cottonseed 5,009; cotton, lint 3,156; tobacco 877; butter c. 496; cheese

1,845; hen's eggs 3,820; beef and veal 11,845; pork 6,012; timber (cu m; 1976) 341,397; fish catch (1976) 3,004. Livestock (in 000; Jan. 1977): cattle 122,810; sheep 12,766; pigs 54,934; horses (1976) c. 9,450; chickens c. 388,544.

Industry. Index of production (1975 = 100; 1977) 118; mining 106; manufacturing 119; electricity, gas, and water 104; construction 113. Unemployment (1977) 7%. Fuel and power (in 000; metric tons; 1977): coal 585,100; lignite 26,200; crude oil 403,-443; natural gas (cu m) 547,000,000; manufactured gas (cu m) 24,800,000; electricity (kw-hr) 2,185,404,-000. Production (in 000; metric tons; 1976): iron ore (61% metal content) 55,824; pig iron 73,821; crude steel 113,153; cement (shipments) 66,570; newsprint 3,190; other paper (1976) 50,886; petroleum products (1976) 641,841; sulfuric acid 31,191; caustic soda 9,509; plastics and resins (1976) 13,260; synthetic rubber 2,420; fertilizers (including Puerto Rico; nutrient content; 1976–77) nitrogenous 9,790, phosphate 7,131, potash 2,344; passenger cars (units) 9,-199; commercial vehicles (units) 3,440. Merchant vessels launched (100 gross tons and over; 1977) 1,038,000 gross tons. New dwelling units started (1977) 1,990,000.

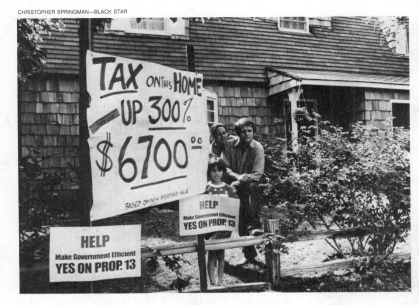

Proposition 13, which drastically reduced property taxes, was passed by the voters of California by a 2 to 1 margin in June. Property taxes in California were reduced by about 57% as a result of the measure.

the stops led to criticism from those who thought he had not worked hard enough to achieve passage of other legislation. Labour leaders, for example, believed that Carter had been lax in his support of a bill that would have changed the nation's labour law to give unions a stronger hand in collective bargaining. And many blacks criticized the president for not fighting hard enough to obtain passage of a strong full-employment measure. Moreover, the legislative victories were, in large part, the result of Republican support. Controversial proposals that did not have much Republican backing—the bill designed to control hospital costs, for example—were defeated.

Not surprisingly, the postmortem assessments of the 95th Congress depended on the political views of the assessors. Sen. Robert Byrd (Dem., W.Va.), the majority leader, said that he could not remember a Congress that had dealt with more difficult issues, and he gave Congress a grade of "A." The minority leader, Sen. Howard Baker, Jr. (Rep., Tenn.), declared that "we've got a Democratic president singing a Republican song."

Carter claimed success for the energy bill passed just before adjournment after two full years of debate, but it was easy to lose sight of the fact that the long-term national energy policy he had advocated at the outset of his presidency had been largely abandoned. Similarly, the tax-cut bill met Carter's fiscal limits, but it contained few of the so-called reform features of the president's original proposal. Furthermore, because Congress raised Social Security taxes and because inflation was increasing at an annual rate exceeding 8%, thereby pushing taxpayers into higher brackets, most Americans would have to pay more, not less, in taxes in 1979.

There were other winners and losers in the 95th Congress. Among the winners were the women's lobby, which got an extension of the time for ratification of the Equal Rights Amendment and no strong new federal rules against abortions; the health lobby, which blocked hospital-cost containment; New York City, which got a new infusion

of federal aid; and airline passengers, who could look forward to paying much lower fares as a result of legislation promoting competition in the airline industry.

For environmentalists Congress provided a mixed bag. Stiff rules on strip mining were adopted, the Endangered Species Act was extended, and construction of some environmentally unsound water projects was stopped. But Congress voted a delay in the application of automobile emission standards, and a measure restraining development in Alaska died in the rush toward adjournment. (*See* ARCTIC REGIONS.)

The big loser was organized labour. Its main projects—changes in the labour law and repeal of the law against common-situs picketing—fell victim to filibusters. A measure that would create a new Department of Education, a favourite of the National Education Association, was rejected.

In future years, the 95th Congress might be most remembered not for the laws it passed but for those its members violated. Rep. Charles C. Diggs, Jr. (Dem., Mich.) and former Rep. Richard T. Hanna (Dem., Calif.) were convicted of felonies. Other members and former members were indicted and more than a dozen senators and representatives were accused of unethical behaviour.

Foreign Affairs. The high point of President Carter's second year in office was the U.S.-sponsored Middle East summit at Camp David, Md., in September. Given little chance of success at the outset, the meeting concluded on September 17 with Israeli Prime Minister Menahem Begin and Egyptian Pres. Anwar as-Sadat (*see* NOBEL PRIZES) agreeing to a "framework" for a peace treaty between their two countries and for settlement of the broader Arab-Israeli issue of the West Bank and the Gaza Strip. Two documents governing those accords were signed at a subsequent White House ceremony by Begin and Sadat. Carter, who had been conducting the summit meeting since September 6, signed as a witness.

The terms of the Egyptian-Israeli accord required both nations to sign a peace treaty within

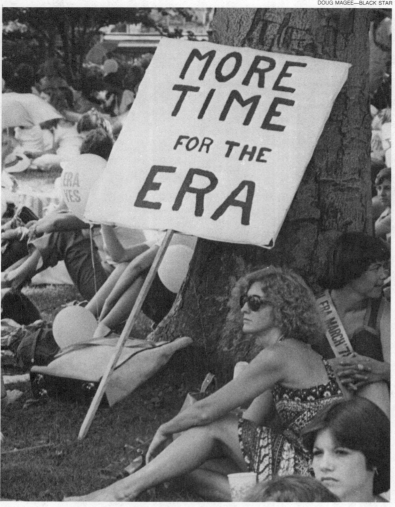

Weary marchers rested their tired feet after a crowd of almost 100,000 demonstrators marched on the Capitol in July to demand an extension of the deadline for ratification of the Equal Rights Amendment. Congress later voted to extend the deadline to June 30, 1982.

three months. Israel would withdraw from the Sinai and return it to Egypt. The area would be demilitarized. The Israeli withdrawal would occur in stages, with the first one taking place within three to nine months after the signing of the peace treaty. Normal diplomatic relations between Egypt and Israel would then be established.

The agreement dealing with the West Bank and Gaza Strip comprised several major points. Israel, Egypt, Jordan, and elected Palestinian representatives would negotiate the question of sovereignty of the Israeli-occupied territory after a five-year transition period. Israel and Jordan would sign a peace treaty at the end of that time. Israel was to keep troops in specified areas of the West Bank during the five-year period. Also, Israel would dissolve its military government and permit the Palestinians to elect representatives and to decide on a form of local government.

Egyptian and Israeli representatives opened negotiations for drafting a bilateral peace treaty in Washington, D.C., on October 12, and quick agreement was expected. However, the talks bogged down. The main obstacle was the linkage between the peace treaty and the future of the West Bank and Gaza Strip. The United States and Egypt contended that the two accords were linked

politically and morally, if not formally. Israel deemphasized any linkage, leading to charges that it was interested only in a separate peace with Egypt and would be quite happy to see the collapse of the West Bank-Gaza Strip negotiations.

In another dramatic development President Carter announced on December 15 that as of Jan. 1, 1979, the U.S. and China would reestablish full diplomatic relations with one another. These had been broken off in 1949 when the Chinese Communist forces under the leadership of Mao Tsetung defeated the Nationalist government army of Chiang Kai-shek. Chiang and his followers fled to Taiwan, where they established the Republic of China and gained the diplomatic recognition of the U.S. Under the terms of the new agreement the U.S. would break off formal diplomatic relations with Taiwan and terminate the 1954 mutual defense treaty that committed it to guarantee Taiwan's military security. A battle in the U.S. Senate over termination of the treaty was expected.

The Taiwanese reacted bitterly to the announcement, accusing the U.S. of a breach of faith. The Soviet Union appeared to take the move calmly, while Japan and many U.S. allies in Western Europe applauded the action.

Progress reportedly was made in 1978 in the U.S.-Soviet strategic arms limitation talks (SALT), but no agreement had been reached by the end of the year. The chief remaining points of contention were the questions of limitations on U.S. cruise missiles and the Soviet supersonic bomber called Backfire. Although Backfire was being deployed for a naval-strike role, it could, under certain circumstances, be used in a long-range mission against the U.S. The cruise missiles, actually small, pilotless jet airplanes, were potentially capable of great range and accuracy.

U.S. hopes for concluding the multilateral trade negotiations at Geneva received a jolt when Congress adjourned without extending the Carter administration's power to waive countervailing duties. Countervailing duties are those that are levied on subsidized imports so as to offset any price advantage they would otherwise enjoy in the U.S. market. The nine member countries of the European Economic Community were infuriated because Congress took no action. Denmark, in particular, was deeply concerned about the effect of the duties on its exports of canned hams, cheese, and butter cookies to the U.S. In a letter to EEC officials President Carter pledged to urge the new 96th Congress to waive the special duties. "The situation is extremely critical," chief U.S. trade negotiator Robert Strauss (see BIOGRAPHIES) told Business Week magazine in November. "If we don't complete the negotiations this year—and right now the Europeans are absolutely negative—we're in for a trade war."

Reduction of arms sales abroad continued to be a leading aim of the Carter administration in 1978. The president announced on February 1 that he had imposed an $8.6 billion ceiling on sales of arms to nonallied countries for the fiscal year ending September 30, an 8% cut from fiscal 1977. Sales to countries in the North Atlantic Treaty Organization, and to Japan, Australia, and New Zealand were not covered by the ceiling. Also, military construction projects were not counted as arms sales.

Most of the sales to nonallied nations were to countries in the Middle East. In his announcement, Carter stressed that a lower ceiling would "violate commitments already made, including our historic interest in the Middle East, and would ignore the continuing realities of world politics." However, a higher limit, Carter said, would "neglect our responsibility to set an example of restraint that others might follow."

Returning to the arms-sale issue at a news conference in Cranston, R. I., on February 17, the president said that he had pledged himself to cut down the volume of weapons sold worldwide "each succeeding year as long as I'm in office, barring some unpredictable worldwide military outbreak." To this end U.S. and Soviet negotiators met in Mexico City in December in an effort to reach agreement on ways of controlling exports of conventional weapons.

The U.S. registered a deficit in its 1977 balance of trade of $26.7 billion, the largest in the nation's history and four times that of 1976 and the deficit for 1978 was expected to be even higher. The chief cause of the deficit was the nation's increasing dependence on imported oil. In 1977 the U.S. imported $44.3 billion of oil, compared with $34 billion in 1976 and $25 billion in 1975. According to Courtenay Slater, chief economist for the Department of Commerce, "This heavy dependence on imported oil will continue to dominate the U.S. foreign trade picture, and a large deficit must again be expected in 1978." Other categories of imports that rose substantially in 1977 were machinery, iron and steel, automobiles, coffee, and sugar. Overall, imports rose 22% over 1976 while exports increased only 4.6%.

The strikes and violent disorders that disrupted Iran for much of 1978 created a dilemma for the Carter administration. In large part the protests were based on opposition to the politically repressive policies of Shah Mohammad Reza Pahlavi. Since concern for human rights abroad is one of the guiding principles of Carter's foreign policy, an expression of sympathy from the White House for the protesters' cause might have seemed in order. Instead, the White House issued a statement of strong support for the military government installed by the shah on November 6 to restore peace to the country. The statement reaffirmed the longstanding U.S. view of Iran as a bulwark of anti-Communism in the Middle East and as a dependable source of imported oil. Nevertheless, the protests mounted in intensity as the year drew to an end, forcing hundreds of families of U.S. nationals working in Iran to leave the country.

Domestic Affairs. On the domestic front the Carter administration's chief goal in 1978 was to combat inflation and halt the decline of the dollar's value in relation to that of other major currencies. In a speech to the American Society of Newspaper Editors on April 11, the president announced new steps his administration would take to fight inflation, chiefly by limiting wage increases for federal employees to 5.5% and freezing the pay of White House staff members and high-level officials in the executive branch. He ruled out the use of mandatory wage and price controls for the private sector but said he expected "American workers to follow the example of federal workers and accept a lower rate of wage increase."

The Carter program had little or no effect on either inflation or the condition of the dollar in foreign exchange markets. Accordingly, on October 24 the president unveiled a new anti-inflation plan designed to reduce the nation's inflation rate to 6–6.5% in 1979 from its 1978 level of more than 8%. In a nationally televised speech, he said, "If there is one thing I am asking of every American tonight, it is to give this plan a chance to work."

Carter hoped to slow inflation by persuading the public to accept voluntary wage-price guidelines, saying that mandatory controls were "extreme possibilities [that] wouldn't work." His guidelines included ceilings of 7% on pay increases and 5.75% on price increases, but there were many exceptions to these standards. The only unexpected feature of the plan was Carter's call for congressional enactment of "real wage insurance" to protect those who complied with the 7% pay limit.

One week later, on November 1, Carter announced a number of emergency measures to assist the dollar, including a pledge of "massive intervention" in currency markets to support the dollar, a quintupling of gold sales, and a sharp increase in the discount rate. The measures had an immediate and striking effect both in the United States and in other countries. On foreign exchange markets, the dollar rose by 7.5% against the Swiss franc, 7% against the West German mark, 5% against the Japanese yen, and 4.5% against the British pound. Reaction also was favourable on the New York Stock Exchange. The Dow Jones average rose by more than 35 points, a record single-day advance.

Voter resentment against inflation and the high cost of living found expression in movements to reduce taxes and limit government spending at the state and local level. California voters led the way June 6 when they overwhelmingly approved Proposition 13, a ballot initiative to cut property taxes by 57%. The emotional tax issue completely dominated the California primary and riveted national attention as well.

Proposition 13 limited the tax on real property to 1% of the full cash value of the property, according to the assessed value in 1975–76. It limited increases in assessed values to 2% a year, unless the property changed hands, in which case the property would be assessed at current market value. Moreover, it required a two-thirds vote of all state legislators for any increase in state taxes. A two-thirds vote of all registered voters was also required for local governments to levy any new taxes.

Ballot initiatives modeled after the California measure won approval in 13 states in the November 7 general election. Propositions that were almost duplicates of Proposition 13 were approved in Nevada and Idaho. They limited property taxes to 1% of market value. The proposal in Nevada would have to be approved again in 1980 to become law. Restrictions or recommendations to restrict taxing and spending also were approved in Alabama, Arizona, Hawaii, Illinois, Massachusetts, Missouri, North Dakota, South Dakota, Texas, Michigan, and in one large county in Maryland.

In November former president Richard Nixon visited France and the U.K. on his first European tour since his resignation in 1974. On a Paris television talk show and in an address at Oxford University he declared that his "political life is over" but said that he would speak out on important public issues. Although he was generally warmly received inside the debating hall at Oxford, outside Nixon was jeered by hundreds of demonstrators including many U.S. students.

Fraud and mismanagement at the General Services Administration were disclosed during the year in what one investigator described as perhaps "the biggest money scandal in the history of the federal government," one involving hundreds of millions of dollars. The probe of the GSA, which employed 35,000 and spent approximately $5 billion annually as the renter, builder, and purchasing agent for the federal government, spread throughout the country. Kickbacks for contracts awarded, illegal bidding procedures, and payment for work either never or only partially done were among the charges leveled against GSA employees. In July Joel Solomon, the head of the agency, fired his second in command, Robert Griffin, and vowed to conduct a thorough investigation of the staff and its operations. By the year's end more than 20 persons, both within and outside of the GSA, had pleaded guilty to charges of conspiracy to defraud the federal government.

In a decision handed down June 28, the U.S. Supreme Court voted 5 to 4 to affirm a lower court order requiring the University of California at Davis to admit Allan Bakke (see BIOGRAPHIES) to its medical school. Bakke, a 38-year-old white engineer, claimed that the school's minority-admissions program had made him a victim of "reverse discrimination." However, while the first vote of the justices ruled that the school's special admissions plan was unconstitutional, another 5–4 vote held that universities could consider race as one factor in choosing among applicants for admission.

The long-awaited Bakke decision was considered the most important civil-rights case to come before the Supreme Court in several years. The University of California claimed, and the court rejected, the argument that the court in the past had handed down broad rulings in support of the preferential treatment of minorities. Justice Lewis F. Powell, Jr., who cast the deciding vote in each aspect of the case, warned that in such areas as school desegregation, employment discrimination, and sex discrimination the court had "never approved a classification that aids persons perceived as members of relatively victimized groups at the expense of other innocent individuals in the absence of judicial, legislative or administrative findings of constitutional or statutory violations." Powell cited a 1977 case involving a Supreme Court award of retroactive seniority to black truck drivers as an example of this doctrine. He said that

the scope of judicial remedies to discrimination had not exceeded "the extent of the violations." (See LAW.)

The nation was stunned in November by a bizarre series of murders and suicides that claimed the lives of, among others, three public officials and many former residents of the San Francisco Bay area. U.S. congressman Leo Ryan, a resident of South San Francisco, and four other Americans were shot to death in Guyana on November 18 by members of the People's Temple, a California-based religious cult headed by the Rev. Jim Jones (see OBITUARIES). Ryan and his companions were gunned down as they and the remainder of their party were preparing to leave Guyana after a visit to Jonestown, a farm settlement established by People's Temple members. Ryan had organized the trip to investigate reports that Jonestown residents were mistreated and that many of them were being held there against their will.

An even more grisly story came to light the following day. Guyanese soldiers arriving at Jonestown were horrified to discover the bodies of hundreds of cult members who had been shot or had committed suicide by drinking a cyanide-laced soft drink. Among the dead were Jones and his wife. Guyanese authorities reported on November 21 that 409 persons were found dead at the jungle colony, but the actual toll, it was later determined, was 913. The bodies, including those of more than 200 children, were placed in metal caskets and flown to the United States for identification and burial or cremation.

The shock of the Guyana tragedy was still reverberating when San Francisco Mayor George Moscone and City Supervisor Harvey Milk were shot to death in their city hall offices on November 27. Dan White, a former member of the Board of Supervisors, San Francisco's city council, surrendered to police shortly afterward and was booked on two charges of murder. There was no known connection between the Guyana murder-suicides and the slayings of Moscone and Milk. Dianne Feinstein, president of the Board of Supervisors, was elected by other members of the board to fill out the remainder of Moscone's term as mayor.

The city of Cleveland, Ohio, on December 15 failed to pay off $15.5 million in short-term notes, becoming the first major U.S. municipality to default on a loan since the 1930s. Mayor Dennis Kucinich (see BIOGRAPHIES), who had narrowly escaped defeat in a recall vote earlier in the year, announced that he would lay off 20% of the city's work force on Jan. 2, 1979, to conserve cash. On December 22 the Cleveland city council approved Kucinich's proposal for two revenue-raising referenda on Feb. 27, 1979; these were whether the city income tax should be raised from 1 cent to 1½ cents on the dollar and whether the Municipal Electric Light plant owned by the city should be sold. On December 28 Kucinich announced that he had canceled the layoffs of the city workers because he had received assurances from the city's largest bank that it would wait until after February 27 to try to collect the loan that Cleveland had failed to pay.   (RICHARD L. WORSNOP)

See also Dependent States.

REBELLION DOWN ON THE FARM

by James C. Thomson

During the 1970s complaints by farmers that they have not been paid enough for their livestock and crops have been confusing to consumers angered by rapidly rising food prices. A look at supermarket shelves reveals that food prices rose at an annual rate of 16.8% during the first half of 1978. If farmers are so bad off, consumers ask, why is the retail cost of food continuing to rise at a record rate? Frustrated farmers ask the same question.

A strong tendency among both consumers and farmers is to blame food processors and distributors for the high prices. The middlemen's charges have, indeed, risen 328% in the last 25 years. During the same period the farm value of food has gone up 239%, while total consumer expenditures for food have increased 294%. A quarter century ago food marketing costs were 1.5 times the farm value of food. In 1978 they were double the farm value.

Over the same period, labour and packaging costs have risen faster than retail food prices, according to Howard Hjort, director of economics of the U.S. Department of Agriculture (USDA). Labour is the biggest marketing cost of food. It has increased at an annual rate of 10% since 1974. The labour component of food marketing amounted to $60 billion in 1977, or 48% of the total cost. Packaging accounts for 13% of the retail food bill, up 171% since 1963. Transportation costs have risen 10% annually since 1974 and account for 8% of the food bill.

Consumers will be interested to learn, however, that food prices in the U.S. have risen at a slower rate than in 10 of 15 other developed countries. Since 1970 U.S. food prices have gone up 76.8%; this compares with Canada, 99%; France, 109%; Italy, 180%; and the U.K., 203%.

Strike. For farmers, consumer complaints, escalating farm costs, and falling farm prices created an outrageous mix. When farm prices dropped below the cost of production, resentment exploded. The call for a nationwide strike to force higher farm

---

James C. Thomson, retired editor of Prairie Farmer *magazine, is the author of* American Farm Organizations *and* The Changing Agricultural Extension Service.

prices followed. Dec. 14, 1977, was widely publicized by the media as the strike date. It triggered demonstrations in various cities, marches on Washington, D.C., and more threats to withhold food from the nation's tables.

In Washington, farmers turned goats loose, buttonholed congressmen, and bowled over USDA guards who blocked their path in efforts to meet with Secretary of Agriculture Bob Bergland. To call public attention to their problems, farmers paraded through major cities across the nation. They disrupted traffic in busy business districts with slow-moving tractors and other vehicles.

About 100 demonstrators tied up Chicago traffic with 54 vehicles, including 14 tractors, in front of the Chicago Board of Trade. This is the world's largest commodity market, where more than $50 billion in grain contracts are traded annually. Some of this buying and selling is done by speculators. Though speculators are considered to perform a useful function in the market, the demonstrators denounced them and called the Board of Trade "another Las Vegas." They also called on government to guarantee farmers 100% of parity. Observers were disturbed by the demonstrators' lack of understanding of the meaning of 100% of parity and the purposes of the Board of Trade in facilitating the flow of goods. For a discussion of parity, *see* below.

One purpose of the demonstrations was well served. The media, especially television, gave the event wide coverage that frightened some consumers into thinking that farmers really intended to cut off food supplies. Unfortunately for the demonstrators, they received little more than vocal support from either leaders or members of most farm organizations.

Disparities. With the world's most efficient and most productive agriculture, why were both farmers and consumers unhappy at the same time? The complexity and vastness of the American food chain makes this a difficult question to answer. Agribusiness is America's largest industry by far. More than 30% of the nation's work force is employed in farm supply procurement and the production, transporting, exporting, and distribution of the nation's food supply. Farmers alone have invested more than $700 billion and will need another $200 billion in new capital by the end of the century.

To understand the farm problem one must understand the great disparities that exist among farmers with regard to such factors as the size and location of landholdings, income, capitalization, managerial ability, and education. For example, 215,000 farms, or 7.9% of the nation's 2.7 million farms, accounted for 70% of farm production in 1977. On the other hand, 1,670,000 farms, or 62%, produced 8%.

Farming in the U.S. is moving into fewer and stronger hands. Running a modern farm is a highly skilled operation requiring education, management ability, perfect timing, and a plethora of facts and experience that most people can never hope to match. Of the young men going into farming today, the USDA estimates that nearly 25% have college training. However, the USDA also estimates that 70% of all farms gross less than $20,000; net is roughly a fourth to a third of gross. This would seem to indicate that most farmers just barely eke out a living. Yet of this 70% virtually all, the USDA says, gain more than half of their incomes from off-farm sources.

At the other end of the scale, the top 200,000 farms netted an average $94,000 per unit in 1973, though this fell to $55,716 in 1976. These large farms have an average net worth of more than $2 million. Including the poorest, the average farm in the United States has $243,800 in assets and a debt load of $37,300.

Great variations also exist in soil types, climate, weather, and the types of crops and livestock produced. All of these exert some influence on a farmer's economic well-being.

Farm Organizations. The loosely organized group that named itself the American Agriculture Movement and called a strike in the winter of 1977–78 focused public attention on the economic plight of the farmer. However, the AAM did not gain widespread support; no more than 2% of the nation's farmers were involved.

Much of the farmer's political power is dispersed among four general farm organizations. Largest is the American Farm Bureau Federation with about 2.6 million members. Many of these members are nonfarmers. The AFBF is regarded as conservative but politically nonpartisan; most federal regulations are anathema to it. Consequently, the AFBF strongly approved of antigovernment Earl Butz, secretary of agriculture from 1971 to 1976.

Second largest and second oldest of the organizations is the National Farmers Union. The NFU is liberal, generally siding with labour unions and the Democratic Party. To the NFU the name Butz was poison. The National Grange is the oldest of the Big Four and perhaps the weakest politically. It is about as large as the NFU in membership, but it has few bona fide operating farmers as members.

The youngest farm group and the smallest in membership is the militant National Farmers Organization. The NFO was a spontaneous outgrowth of the farm unrest of the mid-1950s. It appealed to many farmers with its aggressive rallies and high-flown promises to drive farm prices up by means of withholding crops and demanding collective bargaining agreements from processors.

Violence followed in the wake of the NFO withholding actions as some farmers resisted. In recent years the NFO has lowered its voice and disclaimed violence, but its record has been less than spectacular. Withholding actions, violence, and efforts to consummate bargaining contracts with buyers have had little effect on farm prices and costs.

NFO membership reached a high-water mark of about 200,000 dues-paying members by the mid-1960s. As farmers lost faith in its results, membership dwindled and by 1978 was about 80,000.

The farm organizations reacted to the strike in various ways. All expressed degrees of support, ranging from strong among some Granges in the Northwest to icy cool by the Farm Bureau. The AFBF called the strike impractical and mildly chastised those who thought the low-income situation could be changed by a strike. As the crisis deepened, the AFBF leaders met in Chicago on Sept. 19, 1977, and authorized their president, Allan Grant, to seek a meeting with U.S. Pres. Jimmy Carter to discuss the farm income problem. Mainly because of overproduction and the loss of some overseas markets, farm income had plunged from $33.3 billion in 1973 to slightly more than $20 billion in 1977. During the same period farm costs were rising nearly 40%.

Strangely, President Carter refused to see Grant.

Parity

For more than 60 years the farmer has called on the federal government to guarantee him parity. Yet a recent poll by *Prairie Farmer* magazine indicated that most farmers cannot clearly define what the term means.

Parity is a yardstick that measures the relationship between the production items a farmer buys and the price of the product he sells. The base period is 1910–14, a time when those relationships were considered to be fair to the farmer. For this period the farm cost index was set at 100 and the farm price index at 100, a balance described as parity. By mid-1978 the farm price index had risen to 538 and the farm cost index to 744. By dividing the price index by the cost index one finds that farmers in mid-1978 were receiving 72% of parity, or 72% of what they consider ideal.

Presidents have promised farmers 100% of parity in their campaigns, but they have soon found out how impractical such a promise is. Secretary of Agriculture Bergland estimated that 100% of parity would cost the taxpayers $54 billion plus substantially higher food bills.

The fact is that farming techniques have changed tremendously since 1910–14, making the parity formula an anachronism. In the 1920s, before hybrid strains of corn had been developed, a farmer could produce about 4,000 bu of corn with horses and hand picking. In the late 1970s it was possible for his grandson to produce 80,000 bu.

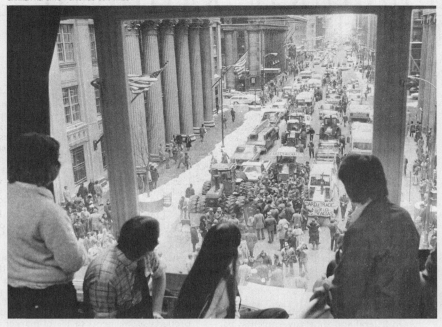

Farmers on foot and aboard large tractors jammed a busy Chicago street in a march on the Board of Trade in February. The farmers were demanding higher prices for their crops.

Instead, he chose to meet with AAM leaders at the White House. This organization had little standing among farmers and no dues-paying membership, while the AFBF represented 80% of the nation's commercial farmers.

Carter's action might be explained by the fact that the farm unrest of 1977 was most pronounced in two areas of the U.S. One was the Southeast, principally Georgia. The other was the Northwest, principally Washington. Both areas suffered from drought and poor crops. Coincidentally, the most influential man on the U.S. Senate Agriculture Committee was Sen. Herman Talmadge of Georgia and the most influential figure in the U.S. House Agriculture Committee was Thomas Foley of Washington. Because many of the members of the AAM were from their districts, both legislators listened carefully to the organization's protest. The end result was an unprecedented outflow of federal subsidies and the largest agriculture budget in U.S. history, nearly $20 billion.

Too Much Productivity? Since 1967 farm productivity per man has leaped 62%, while nonfarm business productivity was rising only 15%. Since 1960 the U.S. population has risen 20%, but farm production has increased 32%. Increasing productivity creates surpluses and drives down farm prices, thus penalizing the farmer for being productive.

In a laissez-faire economy this situation would right itself. The least efficient would be driven out of business. But farming also has a social dimension. Politicians try to protect farmers from potentially brutal market forces with price supports and subsidies. Efforts are made to sell more overseas and to give more away in welfare programs.

Efforts also are being made to liberalize trade in farm products through multilateral trade negotiations in Geneva. But farm leaders are becoming increasingly pessimistic about the outcome of these talks. The largest customers of U.S. farmers—the European Economic Community and Japan—along with most other nations are resisting U.S. efforts to export more to them. Even so, U.S. agricultural exports leaped from $6.2 billion in 1970 to an expected $24 billion in 1978. More than half of the nation's production of rice, hides, almonds, and soybeans is exported. The U.S. also sells 40% of its tallow, cotton, and wheat overseas as well as 30% of its corn, tobacco, and milo.

Future Prospects. Changing methods make the farm problem a chronic one. More food is being produced with less manpower. Farmers resist losing out to change. Politicians seeking votes spend tax money to shield farmers from the inevitable, and so the problem is exacerbated.

It is clear that rapid and turbulent change in U.S. agriculture will continue in spite of politicians. Farming now demands more education and greater management skills than it did in the past. Farms will continue to grow bigger and become fewer. The new farmer is younger, more aggressive, better educated, and more amenable to change than were his predecessors. A young farm leader elite is developing that could assume more control of the major organizations. The economic power of the farmers with large landholdings will increase as the number of farms dwindles. If big farmers use this monopoly power like some labour leaders, food consumers may have something to be worried about.

A broad-based revolt against rising taxes, symbolized by the catchword Proposition 13, swept across state governments during 1978, affecting virtually every statehouse by the end of the year. The movement took its name from a tax-cutting initiative that appeared on California's ballot in June, and it gave rise to major efforts to reduce property taxes nationwide.

Sensing a national mood favouring decreased government participation in the economy, legislators slowed the pace of lawmaking. Environmentalists did push through antinuclear and antilitter laws in several states. Casino gambling appeared outside Nevada for the first time, but otherwise the trend toward state-supervised games of chance slowed markedly.

Forty-two states held regular legislative sessions and 14 had special sessions during the year.

Party Strengths. Republicans marked up solid gains in both state legislative and gubernatorial elections in November. The number of states in which the GOP controlled both houses of the legislature rose from 4 to 12. Democrats continued to exercise dominance over 31 legislatures (down from 35), all except Colorado, Idaho, South Dakota, Wyoming, Arizona, Indiana, Kansas, North Dakota, Utah, New Hampshire, Vermont, and Iowa (where Republicans formed the majority in both houses); Maine, New York, Pennsylvania, and Montana (where each party controlled one house); Alaska and Minnesota (where Democrats controlled one chamber and the other was tied); and Nebraska (which has a nonpartisan, unicameral legislature).

Democrats took over three governorships from incumbent Republicans—in Kansas, New Hampshire, and South Carolina—and the Maine gubernatorial slot from an independent. But Republicans gained nine governorships previously held by Democrats (Minnesota, Nebraska, Nevada, Oregon, Tennessee, South Dakota, Wisconsin, Texas, and Pennsylvania). The gubernatorial lineup for 1979 was 32 Democrats and 18 Republicans.

Government Structures and Powers. For the first time in 50 years, states were considering two proposed U.S. constitutional amendments simultaneously. After extending the time limit for consideration of the Equal Rights Amendment to ban sex discrimination (*see* below), the U.S. Congress on August 22 approved a possible Twenty-eighth Amendment that would give full voting rights in Congress (two senators and one or two representatives) to the District of Columbia. By year's end, only three states—New Jersey, Ohio, and Michigan—had ratified it, and two more (Pennsylvania and California) had rejected it. Approval of 38 states within seven years would be required.

Five more states (Arizona, Kansas, Maryland, Montana, and Vermont) approved laws providing for periodic termination of state agencies unless specific reauthorization is given; 29 states had passed "sunset" laws since Colorado pioneered the concept in 1976.

Among states attempting to update their constitutions, Tennessee voters approved 12 of 13 proposed revisions of articles; Hawaii electors endorsed all 34 amendments put forward by a constitutional convention; and Florida voters rejected 8 amendments drafted by a constitutional revision committee.

New Mexico switched to a cabinet style of government; Pennsylvania established its budget office as a statutory agency; Arizona's governor ordered a change to modified zero-based budgeting; and Hawaii became the first state to adopt an official plan designed to limit and control growth. Legislators in two Midwestern states raised their own pay—by $8,000 annually to $28,000 in Illinois and by $5,000 to $22,500 in Ohio—despite complaints by Carter administration spokesmen that the increases violated voluntary federal wage-price guidelines.

Governmental Relations. Tensions between federal and state governments, particularly over federal preemption of lawmaking authority previously held by the states, eased noticeably during 1978. A report by the Advisory Commission on Intergovernmental Relations indicated that federal aid of all types to states surpassed $80 billion during the year, an increase of $11.9 billion over fiscal 1977. A frequently heard charge—that the federal government favoured Sunbelt (Southern and Southwestern) states in the expenditure of tax dollars—was contradicted by a General Services Administration study.

Disputes between states, of varying degrees of seriousness, were highly publicized. Missouri and Kansas settled a border quarrel that resulted from a shift in the Missouri River near St. Joseph in 1952. California claimed validity for an 1872 survey of the 120th meridian that would give it another 1,000 sq mi of Nevada-claimed real estate, including four casinos located near Lake Tahoe.

Tax Revolt. Resentment against state and local property taxes had festered throughout the nation for years, leading many states to grant piecemeal relief to the elderly, farmers, and others especially hard hit by escalating property values and taxes. In 1978, however, the movement turned into a full-scale tax revolt.

The rebellion had its roots in inflation and the accompanying dramatic increases in real estate values. The situation was especially critical in California, where a computerized property valuation system allowed assessors to keep assessments fully up to date with rising land values. A state treasury surplus of more than $6 billion had built up in recent years, but tax reform measures had failed to gain the two-thirds vote in the legislature needed for major changes in the state's financing structure. In 1977–78 two Californians, Howard Jarvis (*see* BIOGRAPHIES) and Paul Gann, led a petition drive that easily garnered more than 1.2 million signatures, well over the number required to place their tax-limitation initiative on the June 6 ballot. It was approved by more than 60% of California voters.

The measure rolled assessment rates back to 1975–76 levels and limited property tax rates to 1% of real market value. Increases in assessments were restricted to 2% annually, and new real estate levies were prohibited. The measure also required approval by two-thirds of local voters or state legislators for any further local or state tax increases. Substantial cutbacks in some local government services occurred, but the loss in local governmental revenue was cushioned by the huge state surplus; the state appropriated some $5 billion to offset the $7 billion in local taxes lost as a result of the initiative and promised to take over many spending functions previously held by local government.

Although Proposition 13-style measures eventually reached the ballot in more than a dozen jurisdictions, the net effect by year's end was far less than originally predicted. Voters in two other states, Idaho and Nevada, approved measures limiting property assessments to 1% of market value, but Nevada's action had to be ratified again in 1980 before it became effective. Electors in Michigan and Oregon defeated similar initiatives in November. However, voters in Alabama, Arizona, Hawaii, Illinois, Massachusetts, Michigan, Missouri, North Dakota, South Dakota, and Texas favoured some tax or spending restrictions. Ballot measures calling for further fiscal restraint were rejected in Arkansas, Colorado, Nebraska, and Oregon.

Finances and Taxes. The message was not lost on state legislators, who adopted a historic round of tax reductions during 1978. A survey by the Tax Foundation revealed that eight states increased taxes by a total of $200 million during the year, mainly by imposing higher motor fuel levies. But this was more than offset by tax reductions in 21 other states totaling some $2.5 billion, resulting in an overall reduction of about $2.3 billion annually. These reductions do not include the $7 billion cut in California's local property tax levies after the Proposition 13 initiative, nor do they reflect widespread legislative and voter action on local property taxes in other states throughout the year.

Eighteen state legislatures reduced personal income taxes, with California providing a historic one-time tax cut of $1 billion. Maine, Minnesota, New Mexico, New York, and Vermont lowered tax rates for most taxpayer categories, while 13 other states (Alaska, Arizona, California, Colorado, Idaho, Indiana, Kansas, Kentucky, Maryland, Mississippi, Ohio, Oregon, and Wisconsin) reduced their taxable income base by liberalizing credits, deductions, or exemptions. North Dakota voters mandated income tax reductions, and Arizona, California, and Colorado became the first states to adjust income tax frameworks to allow for inflation. Rhode Island was the only state to raise its income tax rate.

Only one state, Maine, reduced its corporate income tax rate, although others, including Colorado, Connecticut, Kansas, Louisiana, New York, and Virginia, took significant steps to relieve tax burdens on specific businesses. Tennessee, West Virginia, Kentucky, South Dakota, and Louisiana approved some new business taxes during the year.

Three states provided for alterations in sales tax rates: South Dakota raised its rate from 4 to 5%; Tennessee extended its 4.5% rate for another year, voiding a planned decrease; and New Mexico dropped its state sales tax level from 4 to 3.75% while allowing localities to increase their own rates.

Changes in levies on sales of cigarettes, motor fuel, and alcoholic beverages, ordinarily popular with lawmakers because of their low visibility, were scattered during the year. Idaho, Iowa, Michigan, Utah, and West Virginia increased motor fuel excises. Missouri and Oregon voters turned down proposed motor fuel tax hikes, and Delaware proceeded with a reduction in its gasoline tax rate. West Virginia raised cigarette taxes by five cents a pack, but Colorado let a similar increase lapse after a one-year trial. Some alcoholic drink taxes were increased in Michigan and South Dakota.

Figures accumulated in 1978 showed that state revenue from all sources totaled $204.5 billion during the 1977 fiscal year, an increase of 11.2% over the preceding 12 months. General revenue (excluding state liquor and state insurance trust revenue) amounted to $169.9 billion, up 11.7%. Total state expenditures rose 5.1% to $191.2 billion, creating a surplus of $13.3 billion for the year. General expenditures, not including outlays of state liquor stores and insurance trust systems, amounted to $166 billion, 8% above fiscal 1976. Of general revenue, some 59.5% came from state taxes and licenses; 11.8% from charges and miscellaneous revenue, including tuition; and 28.7% from intergovernmental revenue (mostly from the federal government).

The largest state outlay was $64 billion for education; of this, $21.2 billion went to state colleges and universities and $37 billion to local public schools. Other major outlays were $32.8 billion for public welfare, $17.5 billion for highways, and $12.6 billion for health and hospitals.

Ethics. Hawaii, Pennsylvania, and Kentucky adopted new ethics-financial disclosure regulations for public officials. Missouri, Montana, and Wisconsin approved new campaign finance reporting strictures. A state court in New York voided Gov. Hugh Carey's attempt to mandate financial disclosure by top state officials, but the New Jersey Supreme Court ruled a similar demand by Gov. Brendan Byrne to be legal. Kentucky became the first state to adopt a model procurement code, designed to set ethical standards and eliminate conflicts of interest in state purchasing.

Iowa approved a law requiring accountants to report negligent or careless performance by their colleagues. Fourteen states had similar laws for physicians, and eight more required state or local medical societies to report unprofessional conduct to authorities.

After several years of post-Watergate scandals involving top state officials, 1978 was a relatively light year for the discovery of official corruption. Former Alabama treasurer Melba Till Allen was sentenced to three years in prison on June 8 after being convicted of extortion. Wyoming Attorney General V. Frank Mendicino was indicted on five counts of misconduct by a state grand jury in May. Former Texas Supreme Court justice Donald B. Yarbrough was sentenced to five years' imprisonment on January 27 following his conviction for aggravated perjury. Samuel A. Harwell, a onetime financial analyst for the University of Houston in Texas, was indicted on securities fraud charges October 5; officials said he had devised a pyramid investment scheme involving government securities that collapsed in 1977, costing the state university some $17 million.

Education. The debate over equalizing per-pupil spending among school districts, which came to public attention after a California court decision in 1971, continued in 1978. Two more state courts, in Ohio and New York, declared that local property tax funding of school districts led to an unconstitutional denial of equal protection of the laws for children in poorer districts. Moves to equalize funding were made in Washington and Colorado during the year, and a survey by the Lawyers' Committee for Civil Rights Under Law revealed that school financing litigation was under way in another 14 states.

A drive to require minimum competency in mathematics and English skills as a precondition for high school graduation spread during the year. Kentucky, Kansas, Massachusetts, and Rhode Island set new standards, Oregon began administering a previously approved test, and Virginia scheduled a ninth-grade minimum reading and math test for 1981 graduates. Twelve states now demanded proof of competency for a diploma.

The U.S. Department of Health, Education, and Welfare began difficult negotiations with Southern states over integration in higher educational institutions. After approving desegregation plans in Arkansas, Florida, and Oklahoma, HEW threatened to cut off aid to Georgia and Virginia and actually moved to terminate funding for North Carolina before an agreement was reached.

Abortion. "Right to life" forces continued to press their advantage following a 1977 U.S. Supreme Court decision allowing states to halt public funding for nontherapeutic, or elective, abortions. Oregon voters defeated a proposal to cut off state reimbursements, but legislatures in Illinois, Massachusetts, and Pennsylvania overrode gubernatorial vetoes of severe restrictions on abortion funding. North Carolina cut its abortion reimbursement in half. Before a court ruling declared Virginia's restrictions illegal, only 11 states were still providing payments for low-income women desiring nontherapeutic abortions: Alaska, Colorado, Hawaii, Idaho, Maryland, Michigan, New York, North Carolina, Oregon, Washington, and West Virginia.

Lobbyists developed new tactics aimed at limiting or overturning the Supreme Court's 1973 decision prohibiting states from preventing elective abortions in the first three months of pregnancy. Lawmakers in Louisiana, Oklahoma, Illinois, and Kentucky approved laws making such abortions more difficult to obtain; however, laws in Missouri and Illinois declaring the fetus a ward of the state were declared unconstitutional. During the year four states —Delaware, Kentucky, Nebraska, and Pennsylvania—joined nine that had acted previously in calling for a U.S. constitutional convention on the abortion question. Such a convention is mandatory when two-thirds of the states (34) demand it. There was debate among legal experts as to whether the convention delegates could be legally limited to any single topic.

Drugs. Two more states, North Carolina and Nebraska, decriminalized possession of small amounts of marijuana during 1978, bringing to 11 the number of jurisdictions that had substituted light civil penalties (usually a fine) for criminal strictures on a first conviction. Florida, Louisiana, New Mexico, and Illinois approved legislation allowing cancer and/or glaucoma patients to use marijuana under a doctor's care. Michigan and Maine increased penalties for major drug pushers, and California and New York increased the severity of sentences for the sale of phencyclidine, a fad drug also known as PCP or angel dust.

Reversing a recent trend, the legal drinking age was raised during the year from 18 to 19 in Iowa and Montana and to 21 in Michigan. On the other hand, California removed liability from saloon keepers and bartenders for subsequent actions of their customers, and North Carolina permitted localities to allow liquor to be served by the drink. That left Oklahoma as the only state where liquor could not be served by the drink in public.

Idaho, Kansas, and New Jersey legalized laetrile; 16 states now permitted use of the drug in the treatment of cancer, even though the federal Food and Drug Administration had stated that there was no scientific evidence to support claims for its efficacy.

Law and Justice. Concern over imposition of the death penalty continued to dominate public debate on the criminal justice system. The U.S. Supreme Court voided a capital punishment law in Ohio on the grounds that it failed to allow juries to consider mitigating circumstances before imposing a death sentence. The decision jeopardized similar laws in a dozen states. Maryland legislators approved a new capital punishment law, and Oregon voters reinstated the death penalty by a solid margin. Governors in New York, New Jersey, and Pennsylvania vetoed capital punishment laws, but Pennsylvania legislators overrode the veto. California voters increased the number of crimes for which death could be imposed. Idaho joined Oklahoma and Texas in approving injection of lethal chemicals as an alternative to more traditional methods of execution.

Reacting to perceived dangers from specific crimes, Hawaii provided for extended jail terms for persons found guilty of victimizing the elderly, Michigan and Wisconsin toughened their laws against arson, and Florida approved a state computer crime law. Connecticut, Kansas, and Nebraska joined the states that provide compensation to innocent victims of crime, though the Kansas version, funded by a $1 fee levied on all parties in criminal and civil cases, was declared unconstitutional by the state attorney general. Ohio moved to join seven other states that permit cameras, tape recorders, and broadcast equipment in courtrooms under certain circumstances.

Nine more states—Arizona, Kentucky, Georgia, Indiana, Kansas, Maine, Iowa, New Mexico, and Wisconsin—adopted laws specifically forbidding use of children as prostitutes or in the making of pornography. Also continuing a recent trend, legislators in Idaho, Michigan, Nebraska, and Oklahoma acted to extend jail terms for certain crimes, either by providing mandatory minimum sentences or by denying parole in certain circumstances. Several states began cooperating to slow down "buttlegging," the smuggling of cigarettes from low- to high-tax states, said to involve some $400 million annually.

Delaware, Iowa, and New Jersey joined Oregon in allowing a spouse living with her husband to bring rape charges against him under aggravated circumstances (18 other states permitted such allegations if the couple were separated). The first test of such a law, a well publicized trial in Oregon in December, ended in the husband's acquittal.

Prisons. Partly as a result of new laws mandating minimum prison sentences for some crimes, populations of state penal facilities continued to rise during 1978. A survey by *Corrections* magazine in June reported that some 265,439 inmates were housed in state prisons on a typical day, about 12,000 more than in the previous year.

Although a number of states embarked on ambitious prison-construction projects, the pace of building failed to keep up with the prisoner population. Federal judges in Oklahoma and Maryland and a state judge in Tennessee found that conditions in those states' penal systems violated the Constitution; one result was the early release of 205 inmates in Maryland.

Health and Welfare. Advocates of a ban on public smoking won campaigns in Iowa and New Jersey, where statewide prohibitions on indoor smoking (except in designated areas) were mandated for public buildings and restaurants. In a major test of wills, tobacco companies poured $5 million into a campaign that helped defeat a California initiative to bar public smoking in that state.

Illinois and Arizona approved new laws governing the care of mental patients that expanded and detailed patient rights. New Jersey inaugurated a plan to require a second opinion before surgery paid for under the Blue Shield insurance plan; in 335 cases over eight months, the second opinion failed to confirm the need for surgery in 123 instances.

A Massachusetts court recognized the right of medical personnel—but not friends or relatives—to decide when the use of heroic lifesaving devices should be terminated in a hopeless case. Idaho, Montana, and Wisconsin joined 26 other states in abandoning a mandatory helmet requirement for motorcycle riders.

Gambling. Vermont opened the 14th state lottery during the year, and it was a financial success. So was the first casino operation in the U.S. outside Nevada, opened in May by Resorts International under state supervision in Atlantic City, N.J. Attempts to extend legal gambling in other states encountered bad luck, however. In a highly publicized election, Florida voters rejected casino gambling for Dade County (Miami Beach). Proposals for pari-mutuel horse race betting, legal in 33 other states, were turned down by voters in Minnesota, Texas, and Virginia. In other setbacks for gambling operations, courts in Colorado and Delaware declared that previously enacted laws authorizing sweepstakes and jai alai betting, respectively, were unconstitutional; the Illinois Supreme Court ruled that race track messenger services were illegal; and New Jersey voters, perhaps reacting to stories of irregularities at the initial casino operation, turned down a proposal to legalize jai alai wagering. The state later collected a $39,000 fine from Resorts International for lax accounting practices and credit rule violations.

Equal Rights. Supporters of a U.S. constitutional amendment to ban discrimination on account of sex won an important procedural victory in the U.S. Congress during the year but failed to make any substantive progress in the state legislatures. Although 35 states (of the 38 needed) had ratified the proposed Equal Rights Amendment, only one legislature has done so since 1975. At least eight states turned down attempts to ratify the amendment in 1978.

After heated debate, Congress extended the deadline for ratification by 39 months, from March 22, 1979, to June 30, 1982. Women's groups stepped up their economic boycott campaign against states that had not approved the proposed Twenty-seventh Amendment, and convention business in target jurisdictions was damaged measurably. Missouri and Nevada filed an antitrust suit against several pro-ERA groups over the boycott. Florida voters turned down a state ERA, but Iowa electors gave preliminary approval to a state anti-sex-bias amendment.

In extending the ERA deadline, Congress voted down an amendment that would have specifically allowed states to rescind a previous ratification. This had already been done by Idaho, Nebraska, and Tennessee, but the legality of such a step remained in doubt.

Recognizing the hardships that often accompany divorce, 17 states established programs to aid newly independent women. Hawaii rewrote its state constitution using sexually neutral language. Missouri voters turned down a right-to-work initiative bitterly opposed by labour union interests. A measure that would have allowed school districts to discriminate against homosexual teachers in employment was defeated by California voters, and an Ohio law prohibiting homosexual (but not heterosexual) sexual solicitation was declared unconstitutional by a state court. Voters enacted school busing bans in Massachusetts and Washington. On April 19 the U.S. Supreme Court voided a Tennessee law banning clergy from holding public office.

Environment. Three more states—Delaware, Connecticut, and Iowa—voted to join Maine, Michigan, Oregon, South Dakota, and Vermont in requiring a substantial deposit on all disposable beverage containers sold in the state. Michigan's mandatory deposit (effective December 3) was ten cents per can or bottle. Voters in Alaska and Nebraska rejected similar measures, however. The federal government penalized South Dakota $4.5 million in highway aid for failure to comply with billboard standards, and Maine enacted a tough law requiring removal of all billboards from nonbusiness property within four to six years.

Florida's governor closed the Green Swamp area of central Florida and the Florida Keys to development, although the state supreme court later cast doubt on the ability of the state administration to take such an action on its own. In Minnesota a long-running legal battle over the dumping of taconite iron tailings into Lake Superior was finally resolved when the Reserve Mining Co. agreed to construct a $370 million disposal site for the waste.

Several states, including Michigan, New York, Rhode Island, Wisconsin, and Montana, approved laws regulating the disposal of hazardous wastes. Illinois sued the U.S. Environmental Protection Agency for failing to meet an April 1978 deadline for implementing a hazardous waste control act passed by Congress in 1976.

Two state environmental efforts were rejected by the U.S. Supreme Court. On June 23 the high court voided New Jersey's attempt to ban importation and dumping of garbage from Pennsylvania; in the process, the garbage was classified as interstate commerce. On March 6 a Washington law declaring Puget Sound off limits to oil supertankers was overturned.

Energy. Voters in two states endorsed restrictive antinuclear measures: before any new construction, power companies would have to obtain voter approval in Montana and legislative permission in Hawaii. California, Minnesota, Ohio, and Wisconsin joined in a suit challenging the $560 million total liability limit on nuclear plant accidents set by federal legislation.

New Jersey, Iowa, and Vermont joined the states offering tax breaks to persons who install solar heating or cooling equipment. Gas pilot lights were banned on new appliances sold in Hawaii and Wisconsin.

Several important energy questions went to court. The U.S. Supreme Court upheld a Maryland law banning gas station ownership by major oil companies. Oklahoma, Texas, and Louisiana sued the U.S. Department of Energy over its natural gas pricing policy, which restricted income from gas shipped interstate. In turn, Louisiana was sued by the Federal Energy Regulatory Commission for its attempts to impose a first-use tax on gas piped from offshore wells under federal jurisdiction.

Consumer Protection. Several states moved to increase competition and reduce the cost of health care during 1978. Florida permitted dentists to advertise, and Missouri approved advertising for both dentists and doctors. Arizona, Kansas, Missouri, New York, and Vermont passed laws allowing druggists to advertise the availability of cheaper generic drugs that could be substituted for brand name products. New Jersey and New York moved to regulate hospital charges, but Pennsylvania temporarily ended its effort at hospital regulation after criticism from HEW.

So-called junk telephone calls, usually unsolicited attempts to sell merchandise or services, were severely restricted by Alaska, California, and Florida. The California regulation, promulgated by the state public service commission, required callers to state the nature and length of their message, identify the organization making the call, and obtain permission from the recipient before proceeding.

After the Vermont Supreme Court upheld a $1.5 million judgment against the Stratton ski area for injuries suffered by a downhill skier, the Vermont and New York legislatures approved laws governing liability in recreation areas featuring "inherent danger." The new laws, similar to measures in effect in Maine, New Hampshire, and Washington, generally made the operator responsible for accidents occurring on the uphill trip and the skier responsible for his own welfare on the way down.

Delaware and Minnesota provided a consumer advocate to intervene in utility matters. Florida and Georgia added a lay member to occupational regulatory boards. The California Supreme Court voided the state's fair trade law for liquor. Michigan enacted an "auto lemon" bill to protect car buyers, and several states established limits on the liability of manufacturers for product defects.   (DAVID C. BECKWITH)

AREA AND POPULATION

Area and Population of the States

State	AREA in sq mi Total	AREA in sq mi Inland water[1]	POPULATION (000) July 1, 1970	POPULATION (000) July 1, 1977[2]	Percent change 1970–77
Alabama	51,609	901	3,451	3,690	6.9
Alaska	586,412	19,980	305	407	33.4
Arizona	113,909	492	1,792	2,296	28.1
Arkansas	53,104	1,159	1,926	2,144	11.3
California	158,693	2,332	19,994	21,896	9.5
Colorado	104,247	481	2,225	2,619	17.7
Connecticut	5,009	147	3,039	3,108	2.3
Delaware	2,057	75	550	582	5.8
Dist. of Columbia	67	6	753	690	−8.4
Florida	58,560	4,470	6,845	8,452	23.5
Georgia	58,876	803	4,602	5,048	9.7
Hawaii	6,450	25	774	895	15.6
Idaho	83,557	880	717	857	19.5
Illinois	56,400	652	11,137	11,245	1.0
Indiana	36,291	194	5,208	5,330	2.3
Iowa	56,290	349	2,830	2,879	1.7
Kansas	82,264	477	2,248	2,326	3.5
Kentucky	40,395	745	3,224	3,458	7.3
Louisiana	48,523	3,593	3,644	3,921	7.6
Maine	33,215	2,295	995	1,085	9.0
Maryland	10,577	686	3,937	4,139	5.1
Massachusetts	8,257	431	5,699	5,782	1.5
Michigan	58,216	1,399	8,901	9,129	2.6
Minnesota	84,068	4,779	3,822	3,975	4.0
Mississippi	47,716	420	2,216	2,389	7.8
Missouri	69,686	691	4,693	4,801	2.3
Montana	147,138	1,551	697	761	9.2
Nebraska	77,227	744	1,490	1,561	4.8
Nevada	110,540	651	493	633	28.4
New Hampshire	9,304	277	742	849	14.4
New Jersey	7,836	315	7,195	7,329	1.9
New Mexico	121,666	254	1,018	1,190	16.9
New York	49,576	1,745	18,260	17,924	−1.8
North Carolina	52,586	3,788	5,091	5,525	8.5
North Dakota	70,665	1,392	618	653	5.7
Ohio	41,222	247	10,688	10,701	0.1
Oklahoma	69,919	1,137	2,572	2,811	9.3
Oregon	96,981	797	2,102	2,376	13.0
Pennsylvania	45,333	367	11,817	11,785	−0.3
Rhode Island	1,214	165	951	935	−1.7
South Carolina	31,055	830	2,596	2,876	10.8
South Dakota	77,047	1,092	666	689	3.4
Tennessee	42,244	916	3,932	4,299	9.3
Texas	267,338	5,204	11,254	12,830	14.0
Utah	84,916	2,820	1,069	1,268	18.6
Vermont	9,609	342	447	483	8.0
Virginia	40,817	1,037	4,653	5,135	10.4
Washington	68,192	1,622	3,414	3,658	7.1
West Virginia	24,181	111	1,746	1,859	6.5
Wisconsin	56,154	1,690	4,433	4,651	4.9
Wyoming	97,914	711	334	406	21.6
TOTAL U.S.	3,615,122	78,267	203,805	216,332[3]	6.1

[1] Excludes the Great Lakes and coastal waters.
[2] Preliminary.
[3] State figures do not add to total given because of rounding.
Source: U.S. Department of Commerce, Bureau of the Census, *Current Population Reports.*

Largest Metropolitan Areas[1]

Name	Population 1970 census	Population 1977 estimate	Percent change 1970–77	Land area in sq mi	Density per sq mi 1977
New York-Newark-Jersey City SCSA	17,033,367	16,590,400	−2.6	5,072	3,271
New York City	9,973,716	9,529,300	−4.5	1,384	6,885
Nassau-Suffolk	2,555,868	2,619,000	2.5	1,218	2,150
Newark	2,057,468	1,986,300	−3.5	1,008	1,970
Bridgeport[2]	792,814	799,100	0.8	627	1,274
Jersey City	607,839	572,300	−5.8	47	12,177
New Brunswick-Perth Amboy	583,813	592,100	1.4	312	1,898
Long Branch-Asbury Park	461,849	492,300	6.6	476	1,034
Los Angeles-Long Beach-Anaheim SCSA	9,980,859[3]	10,650,900	6.7	34,007	313
Los Angeles-Long Beach	7,041,980	7,126,800	1.2	4,069	1,751
Anaheim-Santa Ana-Garden Grove	1,421,233	1,786,300	25.7	782	2,284
Riverside-San Bernardino-Ontario	1,139,149[3]	1,277,400	12.1	27,293	47
Oxnard-Simi Valley-Ventura	378,497	460,400	21.6	1,863	247
Chicago-Gary SCSA	7,610,634[3]	7,564,000	−0.6	4,657	1,624
Chicago	6,977,267[3]	6,916,000	−0.9	3,719	1,860
Gary-Hammond-East Chicago	633,367	648,000	2.3	938	691
Philadelphia-Wilmington-Trenton SCSA	5,627,719	5,745,200	2.1	4,946	1,162
Philadelphia	4,824,110	4,908,000	1.7	3,553	1,381
Wilmington	499,493	518,800	3.9	1,165	445
Trenton	304,116	318,400	4.7	228	1,396
San Francisco-Oakland-San Jose SCSA	4,425,691[3]	4,723,300	6.7	5,390	876
San Francisco-Oakland	3,109,249[3]	3,214,000	3.4	2,480	1,296
San Jose	1,065,313	1,219,900	14.5	1,300	938
Vallejo-Fairfield-Napa	251,129	289,400	15.2	1,610	180
Detroit-Ann Arbor SCSA	4,669,154	4,620,400	−1.0	4,627	999
Detroit	4,435,051	4,370,200	−1.5	3,916	1,116
Ann Arbor	234,103	250,200	6.9	711	352
Boston-Lowell-Lawrence SCSA[2]	3,848,593	3,339,200	−13.2	3,114	1,072
Washington, D.C.	2,909,355	3,043,300	4.6	2,812	1,082
Cleveland-Akron-Lorain SCSA	2,999,811	2,958,300	−1.4	2,917	1,014
Cleveland	2,063,729	2,078,200	0.7	1,519	1,368
Akron	679,239	632,600	−6.9	903	700
Lorain-Elyria	256,843	247,500	−3.6	495	500
Houston-Galveston SCSA	2,169,128	2,886,200	33.1	7,193	401
Houston	1,999,316	2,704,200	35.3	6,794	398
Galveston-Texas City	169,812	182,000	7.2	399	456
Dallas-Fort Worth	2,378,353	2,653,000	11.5	8,360	317
St. Louis	2,410,492	2,367,700	−1.8	4,935	480
Pittsburgh	2,401,362	2,357,600	−1.8	3,049	773
Miami-Fort Lauderdale SCSA	1,887,892	2,298,700	21.8	3,261	705
Miami	1,267,792	1,423,600	12.3	2,042	697
Fort Lauderdale-Hollywood	620,100	875,100	41.1	1,219	718
Baltimore	2,071,016	2,148,500	3.7	2,259	951
Minneapolis-St. Paul	1,965,391	2,089,200	6.3	4,647	450
Atlanta	1,595,517	1,876,700	17.6	4,326	434
Seattle-Tacoma SCSA	1,836,949	1,851,900	0.8	5,902	314
Seattle-Everett	1,424,605	1,430,900	0.4	4,226	339
Tacoma	412,344	421,000	2.1	1,676	251
Cincinnati-Hamilton SCSA	1,613,414	1,703,000	5.6	2,620	650
Cincinnati	1,387,207	1,461,100	5.3	2,149	680
Hamilton-Middletown	226,207	241,900	6.9	471	514
San Diego	1,357,854	1,651,800	21.6	4,261	388
Milwaukee-Racine SCSA	1,574,722	1,591,800	1.1	1,793	888
Milwaukee	1,403,884	1,412,700	0.6	1,456	970
Racine	170,838	179,100	4.8	337	531
Denver-Boulder	1,239,545[3]	1,480,800	19.5	4,651	318
Tampa-St. Petersburg	1,088,549	1,388,500	27.6	2,045	679
Kansas City	1,273,926	1,318,800	3.5	3,341	395
Buffalo	1,349,211	1,292,100	−4.2	1,590	813
Phoenix	971,228	1,253,600	29.1	9,155	137

[1] Standard Metropolitan Statistical Area, SMSA, unless otherwise indicated; SCSA is a Standard Consolidated Statistical Area, which may be comprised of SMSA's.
[2] New England County Metropolitan Area.   [3] Revised.
Sources: U.S. Dept. of Commerce, Bureau of the Census, *Current Population Reports*; U.S. Dept. of Justice, FBI, *Uniform Crime Reports for the United States, 1977.*

Population Change

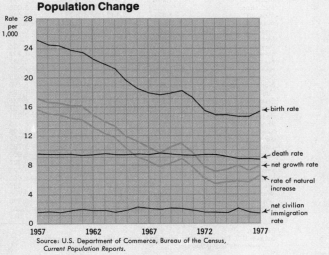

Source: U.S. Department of Commerce, Bureau of the Census, *Current Population Reports.*

Marriage and Divorce Rates

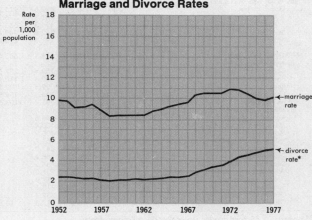

*Includes annulments.

Source: U.S. Department of Health, Education, and Welfare, Public Health Service, *Monthly Vital Statistics Report.*

707

Church Membership

Religious body	Total clergy	Inclusive membership
Adventists, Seventh-day	3,939	522,317
Baptist bodies		
American Baptist Association	5,870	1,350,000
American Baptist Churches in the U.S.A.	7,243	1,304,088
Baptist General Conference	991	120,222
Baptist Missionary Association of America	2,300	218,361
Conservative Baptist Association of America	...	300,000
Free Will Baptists	4,302	216,831
General Baptists (General Association of)	1,125	70,000
National Baptist Convention of America	28,574	2,668,799
National Baptist Convention, U.S.A., Inc.	27,500	5,500,000
Nat. Bap. Evang. Life and Soul Saving Assembly	137	57,674
National Primitive Baptist Convention, Inc.	636	250,000
Primitive Baptists	...	72,000
Progressive National Baptist Convention, Inc.	863	521,692
Regular Baptist Churches, General Assn. of	...	235,918
Southern Baptist Convention	55,500	13,078,239
United Free Will Baptist Church	915	100,000
Brethren (German Baptists): Church of the Brethren	1,929	177,534
Buddhist Churches of America	108	60,000
Christian and Missionary Alliance	1,454	152,841
Christian Church (Disciples of Christ)	6,596	1,256,849
Christian Churches and Churches of Christ	7,279	1,044,842
Christian Congregation	1,137	80,411
Church of God (Anderson, Ind.)	3,022	171,947
Church of the Nazarene	7,485	455,648
Churches of Christ	12,800	2,500,000
Community Churches, National Council of	210	125,000
Congregational Christian Churches, Natl. Assn. of	554	95,000
Eastern Churches		
American Carpatho-Russian Orth. Greek Catholic Ch.	68	100,000
Antiochian Orthodox Christian Archdiocese of N. Am.	132	152,000
Armenian Apostolic Church of America	34	125,000
Armenian Church of America, Diocese of the (Including Diocese of California)	60	326,500
Bulgarian Eastern Orthodox Church	11	86,000
Greek Orthodox Archdiocese of N. and S. America	655	1,950,000
Orthodox Church in America	498	1,000,000
Russian Orth. Ch. in the U.S.A., Patriarchal Parishes of	60	51,500
Russian Orthodox Church Outside Russia	168	55,000
Serbian Eastern Orth. Ch. for the U.S.A. and Canada	64	65,000
Syrian Orthodox Church of Antioch	14	50,000
Ukrainian Orthodox Church in the U.S.A.	131	87,745
Episcopal Church	12,302	2,818,830
Evangelical Covenant Church of America	716	74,060
Evangelical Free Church of America	960	100,000
Friends United Meeting	617	65,348
Independent Fundamental Churches of America	1,252	87,582

Religious body	Total clergy	Inclusive membership
Jehovah's Witnesses	none	554,018
Jewish congregations	6,400	5,775,935
Latter Day Saints		
Church of Jesus Christ of Latter-day Saints	20,490	2,486,261
Reorganized Church of Jesus Christ of L.D.S.	15,907	186,414
Lutherans		
American Lutheran Church	6,692	2,390,076
Evangelical Lutheran Churches, Association of	545	106,684
Lutheran Church in America	7,777	2,967,168
Lutheran Church—Missouri Synod	7,163	2,673,321
Wisconsin Evangelical Lutheran Synod	1,203	401,489
Mennonite Church	2,578	96,609
Methodists		
African Methodist Episcopal Church	3,870	1,950,000
African Methodist Episcopal Zion Church	6,820	1,083,391
Christian Methodist Episcopal Church	2,259	466,718
Free Methodist Church of North America	1,593	69,134
United Methodist Church	35,779	9,785,534
Moravian Church in America	215	53,468
North American Old Roman Catholic Church	116	60,214
Pentecostals		
Apostolic Overcoming Holy Church of God	350	75,000
Assemblies of God	13,928	1,283,892
Church of God	2,737	75,890
Church of God (Cleveland, Tenn.)	8,645	377,765
Church of God in Christ	6,000	425,000
Church of God in Christ, International	1,502	501,000
Church of God of Prophecy	5,679	65,801
International Church of the Foursquare Gospel	2,690	89,215
Pentecostal Church of God of America, Inc.	2,168	110,670
Pentecostal Holiness Church, Inc.	2,899	86,103
United Pentecostal Church, International	5,887	420,000
Polish National Catholic Church of America	141	282,411
Presbyterians		
Cumberland Presbyterian Church	704	93,200
Presbyterian Church in America	531	73,899
Presbyterian Church in the U.S.	5,187	869,693
United Presbyterian Church in the U.S.A.	13,835	2,561,234
Reformed bodies		
Christian Reformed Church in North America	858	210,088
Reformed Church in America	1,487	351,438
Roman Catholic Church	58,903	49,836,176
Salvation Army	5,025	396,238
Triumph the Church and Kingdom of God in Christ	1,375	54,307
Unitarian Universalist Association	904	184,240
United Church of Christ	9,739	1,785,652
Wesleyan Church	2,434	97,859

Table includes churches reporting a membership of 50,000 or more and represents the latest information available.
Source: National Council of Churches, *Yearbook of American and Canadian Churches,* 1979.

(CONSTANT H. JACQUET)

THE ECONOMY

Gross National Product and National Income

in billions of dollars

Item	1965[1]	1970[1]	1977	1978[2]
GROSS NATIONAL PRODUCT	688.1	982.4	1,887.2	2,083.2
By type of expenditure				
Personal consumption expenditures	430.2	618.8	1,206.5	1,324.9
Durable goods	62.8	84.9	178.4	198.0
Nondurable goods	188.6	264.7	479.0	519.8
Services	178.7	269.1	549.2	607.1
Gross private domestic investment	112.0	140.8	297.8	344.0
Fixed investment	102.5	137.0	282.3	325.1
Changes in business inventories	9.5	3.8	15.6	18.9
Net exports of goods and services	7.6	3.9	−11.1	−10.2
Exports	39.5	62.5	175.5	200.9
Imports	32.0	58.5	186.6	211.1
Government purchases of goods and services	138.4	218.9	394.0	424.5
Federal	67.3	95.6	145.1	147.2
State and local	71.1	123.2	248.9	277.3
By major type of product				
Goods output	336.6	456.2	832.6	911.2
Durable goods	133.6	170.8	341.3	375.1
Nondurable goods	203.1	285.4	491.3	536.1
Services	272.7	424.6	862.8	949.4
Structures	78.8	101.6	191.8	222.5
NATIONAL INCOME	566.0	798.4	1,515.3	1,683.6
By type of income				
Compensation of employees	396.5	609.2	1,153.4	1,287.5
Proprietors' income	56.7	65.1	99.8	110.1
Rental income of persons	17.1	18.6	22.5	22.2
Corporate profits	77.1	67.9	144.2	159.5
Net interest	18.5	37.5	95.4	104.5
By industry division[3]				
Agriculture, forestry, and fisheries	20.4	24.5	44.6	...
Mining and construction	35.9	51.6	100.4	...
Manufacturing	170.4	215.4	408.9	...
Nondurable goods	65.4	88.1	161.7	...
Durable goods	105.0	127.3	247.2	...
Transportation	23.1	30.3	58.4	...
Communications and public utilities	22.9	32.5	64.5	...
Wholesale and retail trade	84.7	122.2	237.0	...
Finance, insurance, and real estate	64.0	92.6	177.9	...
Services	64.1	103.3	213.1	...
Government and government enterprises	75.4	127.4	232.7	...
Other	4.7	4.6	17.3	18.6

[1] Revised. [2] Second quarter, seasonally adjusted at annual rates.
[3] Without capital consumption adjustment.
Source: U.S. Department of Commerce, Bureau of Economic Analysis, *Survey of Current Business.*

Personal Income Per Capita

State	1950	1960[1]	1970[1]	1977
Alabama	$ 880	$1,519	$2,948	$ 5,622
Alaska	2,384	2,809	4,644	10,568
Arizona	1,330	2,012	3,665	6,509
Arkansas	825	1,390	2,878	5,540
California	1,852	2,706	4,493	7,911
Colorado	1,487	2,252	3,855	7,160
Connecticut	1,875	2,838	4,917	8,061
Delaware	2,132	2,785	4,524	7,697
District of Columbia	2,221	2,983	5,079	8,999
Florida	1,281	1,947	3,738	6,684
Georgia	1,034	1,651	3,354	6,014
Hawaii	1,386	2,368	4,623	7,677
Idaho	1,295	1,850	3,290	5,980
Illinois	1,825	2,646	4,507	7,768
Indiana	1,512	2,178	3,772	6,921
Iowa	1,485	1,983	3,751	6,878
Kansas	1,443	2,160	3,853	7,134
Kentucky	981	1,586	3,112	5,945
Louisiana	1,120	1,668	3,090	5,913
Maine	1,186	1,862	3,302	5,734
Maryland	1,602	2,341	4,309	7,572
Massachusetts	1,633	2,461	4,340	7,258
Michigan	1,701	2,357	4,180	7,619
Minnesota	1,410	2,075	3,859	7,129
Mississippi	755	1,222	2,626	5,030
Missouri	1,431	2,112	3,781	6,654
Montana	1,622	2,035	3,500	6,125
Nebraska	1,490	2,110	3,789	6,720
Nevada	2,018	2,799	4,563	7,988
New Hampshire	1,323	2,135	3,737	6,536
New Jersey	1,834	2,727	4,701	7,994
New Mexico	1,177	1,843	3,077	5,857
New York	1,873	2,740	4,712	7,537
North Carolina	1,037	1,590	3,252	5,935
North Dakota	1,263	1,704	3,086	6,190
Ohio	1,620	2,345	4,020	7,084
Oklahoma	1,143	1,876	3,387	6,346
Oregon	1,620	2,220	3,719	7,007
Pennsylvania	1,541	2,269	3,971	7,011
Rhode Island	1,605	2,217	3,959	6,775
South Carolina	893	1,397	2,990	5,628
South Dakota	1,242	1,784	3,123	5,957
Tennessee	994	1,576	3,119	5,785
Texas	1,349	1,936	3,606	6,803
Utah	1,309	1,979	3,227	5,923
Vermont	1,121	1,847	3,468	5,823
Virginia	1,228	1,864	3,712	6,865
Washington	1,674	2,360	4,053	7,528
West Virginia	1,065	1,621	3,061	5,986
Wisconsin	1,477	2,188	3,812	6,890
Wyoming	1,668	2,247	3,815	7,562
United States	1,496	2,222	3,966	7,019

[1] Revised.
Source: U.S. Department of Commerce, Bureau of Economic Analysis, *Survey of Current Business.*

Average Employee Earnings

September figures

Industry	HOURLY 1977	HOURLY 1978[1]	WEEKLY 1977	WEEKLY 1978[1]
MANUFACTURING				
Durable goods				
Lumber and wood products	$5.24	$5.74	$212.22	$230.17
Furniture and fixtures	4.43	4.76	175.87	187.54
Stone, clay, and glass products	5.91	6.46	244.08	271.97
Primary metal industries	7.64	8.44	317.82	356.17
Fabricated metal products	6.01	6.45	247.61	265.74
Nonelectrical machinery	6.38	6.88	267.32	290.34
Electrical equipment and supplies	5.51	5.94	225.36	241.16
Transportation equipment	7.37	8.05	316.91	342.93
Instruments and related products	5.37	5.77	219.10	238.30
Nondurable goods				
Food and kindred products	5.45	5.87	220.18	236.56
Tobacco manufactures	5.53	6.10	215.12	234.24
Textile mill products	4.10	4.42	166.05	179.45
Apparel and related products	3.68	4.00	131.01	143.60
Paper and allied products	6.11	6.68	263.95	287.91
Printing and publishing	6.22	6.58	237.60	250.70
Chemicals and allied products	6.56	7.13	274.21	299.46
Petroleum and coal products	7.88	8.66	340.42	384.50
Rubber and plastics products	5.21	5.58	213.61	231.01
Leather and leather products	3.64	3.92	134.32	145.43
NONMANUFACTURING				
Metal mining	7.52	8.52	302.30	354.43
Coal mining	8.44	9.87	367.14	391.84
Oil and gas extraction	6.47	7.16	290.50	322.20
Contract construction	8.26	8.87	303.14	332.63
Local and suburban transportation	6.37	6.91	260.53	276.40
Electric, gas, and sanitary services	7.23	7.76	297.88	324.37
Wholesale trade	5.47	6.01	212.24	233.79
Retail trade	3.90	4.24	122.85	131.02
Hotels, tourist courts, and motels[2]	3.33	3.66	103.56	114.19
Banking	3.96	4.25	144.54	155.98

[1] Preliminary.   [2] Excludes tips.   Source: U.S. Dept. of Labor, Bureau of Labor Statistics, *Employment and Earnings.*

Unemployment Trends

quarterly averages, seasonally adjusted

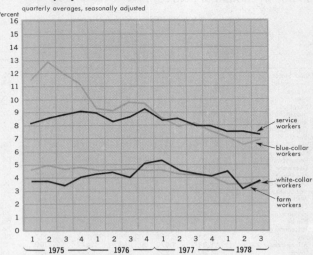

Source: U.S. Department of Labor, Bureau of Labor Statistics, *Monthly Labor Review.*

Value of Agricultural Products, with Fisheries, 1977

in thousands of dollars

State	Corn (grain)	Hay	Soybeans	Wheat	Tobacco	Cotton (lint)	Potatoes	Cattle, calves	Hogs, pigs	Sheep, lambs	Milk[1]	Eggs[2]	Chickens[2]	FISHERIES
Alabama	22,294	53,928	188,160	5,292	1,223	60,749	18,512	223,171	86,308	36	75,719	160,742	7,540	37,244[3]
Alaska	...	...	...	26,514	...	...	...	485	162	4	2,957	620	31	326,245
Arizona	6,600	94,965	...	26,514	...	320,573	8,986	204,235	16,608	7,700	95,147	5,635	154	...
Arkansas	4,672	61,074	592,020	52,767	...	263,592	...	240,098	46,203	82	74,888	181,070	14,743	1,999[3]
California	65,900	479,198	...	116,960	...	754,921	124,943	608,994	16,271	28,565	1,190,020	353,272	6,240	194,957
Colorado	153,178	159,201	...	123,065	...	...	32,941	638,260	36,621	34,609	91,222	22,437	586	...
Connecticut	...	10,626	...	...	22,827	...	2,516	5,929	1,167	133	68,016	51,996	1,617	2,379
Delaware	20,202	3,431	27,428	2,266	...	...	4,697	2,591	7,835	41	14,330	7,285	417	778
Florida	16,744	28,476	43,164	829	30,904	1,152	42,454	192,611	29,513	44	241,449	114,674	4,634	95,485
Georgia	49,200	46,248	124,260	7,425	155,106	18,547	13	139,345	177,806	13	135,870	290,588	10,997	9,096
Hawaii	...	...	...	...	...	...	...	17,245	7,722	...	23,550	12,408	225	9,412
Idaho	5,418	209,573	...	124,989	...	...	251,370	232,485	6,574	20,178	145,120	8,000	384	38
Illinois	2,421,090	198,378	1,768,230	146,996	...	...	1,380	381,722	931,590	4,250	234,608	65,399	1,655	931
Indiana	1,266,840	127,544	745,362	114,390	22,705	...	6,830	251,654	566,659	3,370	226,546	137,182	4,381	118
Iowa	2,182,400	339,575	1,327,428	6,605	...	...	1,821	1,073,674	2,024,620	13,258	384,144	70,474	2,700	891
Kansas	322,560	227,642	142,758	741,428	...	160	...	975,315	303,042	5,570	140,402	19,478	1,433	8
Kentucky	253,800	142,278	222,666	20,276	571,847	...	...	290,257	140,272	862	235,503	23,445	1,287	820[3]
Louisiana	6,760	33,605	352,688	1,928	209	159,034	917	142,372	15,826	175	117,502	32,741	1,937	137,936
Maine	...	18,020	...	...	...	...	127,440	6,684	1,115	259	69,351	101,695	4,658	61,997
Maryland	84,240	38,690	44,928	9,387	32,890[3]	...	1,032	29,755	19,789	417	164,952	17,479	1,126	30,787
Massachusetts	...	15,378	...	...	8,800	...	4,795	5,363	5,858	208	67,740	20,620	1,099	114,017
Michigan	353,813	159,880	112,752	66,000	...	...	45,516	168,197	94,676	3,488	461,341	63,240	2,073	3,275
Minnesota	1,170,000	394,596	726,758	330,142	...	...	41,202	434,334	544,568	8,622	835,452	78,440	1,137	1,283
Mississippi	11,520	53,912	433,985	7,140	...	415,800	679	205,336	42,727	63	88,031	98,216	6,353	26,341
Missouri	420,660	279,300	770,400	123,923	6,670	59,333	...	655,021	524,079	3,465	276,869	48,764	5,239	149
Montana	1,720	212,932	...	304,998	...	...	9,072	299,480	25,403	8,834	28,792	8,313	259	...
Nebraska	1,257,300	250,044	212,636	227,150	...	...	6,053	1,018,645	434,272	5,479	122,438	25,557	503	21
Nevada	...	49,664	...	4,056	...	...	14,700	58,353	1,300	3,259	19,404	134	8	...
New Hampshire	...	11,285	...	...	...	...	433	4,238	972	178	36,849	12,163	760	1,473
New Jersey	13,965	22,185	22,391	2,734	...	...	8,867	8,942	6,278	139	57,585	22,524	841	38,480
New Mexico	21,033	63,506	...	19,644	...	41,213	1,929	225,695	8,499	7,739	48,266	14,160	307	...
New York	107,520	269,062	1,495	12,968	...	...	52,065	84,313	15,660	1,422	1,004,390	81,213	2,674	30,790
North Carolina	185,309	39,075	166,980	12,600	866,237	11,606	16,969	73,538	243,180	140	182,212	163,982	14,663	28,855
North Dakota	30,620	137,233	21,660	565,700	...	...	58,240	286,194	36,704	5,779	79,703	3,052	109	79
Ohio	741,195	199,248	623,864	151,998	28,025	...	13,334	226,128	245,659	10,591	447,523	78,649	3,361	1,978
Oklahoma	16,749	186,560	31,460	412,425	...	95,674	...	670,296	41,719	2,009	113,232	25,162	976	503[3]
Oregon	2,907	146,220	...	122,364	...	...	70,043	158,749	13,354	10,752	106,883	23,843	527	48,532
Pennsylvania	240,120	272,230	11,561	20,048	14,118[3]	...	31,238	139,623	78,917	1,963	821,950	131,700	11,630	246
Rhode Island	...	990	...	...	...	...	3,678	500	952	36	6,321	2,962	85	22,920
South Carolina	42,408	24,354	148,200	5,923	170,899	28,248	...	47,981	58,130	14	61,490	58,968	1,898	9,497
South Dakota	228,330	226,512	46,208	186,781	...	...	3,239	609,556	230,752	27,152	145,958	19,011	524	288
Tennessee	97,273	80,080	270,710	22,680	173,853	58,262	3,139	237,487	136,302	252	198,058	47,829	2,506	1,249[3]
Texas	319,251	229,124	103,740	264,375	...	1,331,677	26,855	1,887,864	114,746	49,849	363,757	123,562	6,190	134,237
Utah	2,835	107,757	...	12,026	...	...	4,056	82,362	7,044	17,168	89,575	13,456	145	...
Vermont	...	43,981	...	...	...	...	1,363	19,174	1,197	202	217,860	7,572	184	...
Virginia	66,220	83,391	46,139	13,981	163,965	62	17,557	122,647	57,392	4,643	198,336	44,567	2,705	55,351
Washington	11,957	133,760	...	268,458	...	...	138,752	138,045	8,879	1,414	256,267	44,275	1,312	80,785
West Virginia	8,192	42,330	...	682	3,443	...	878	35,217	9,980	3,195	33,933	10,001	492	7
Wisconsin	557,700	660,110	32,966	6,398	20,127	...	70,348	277,129	205,559	2,946	1,937,876	43,941	2,776	3,623
Wyoming	5,483	74,575	...	12,167	...	...	1,363	188,359	3,418	19,428	12,078	1,067	23	...
TOTAL U.S.	12,796,002	6,741,726	9,362,997	4,678,478	2,293,848	3,621,068	1,275,261	14,025,653	7,633,879	319,991	12,051,465	2,993,563	138,104	1,515,100

[1] Farm value.   [2] Gross income, Dec. 1, 1976–Nov. 30, 1977.   [3] Estimate.   [4] Decrease in inventory and death loss of sheep resulted in deficit in number of pounds produced.

Sources: U.S. Department of Agriculture, Statistical Reporting Service, Crop Reporting Board, *Crop Values, Meat Animals, Milk, Poultry*; U.S. Department of Commerce, National Oceanic and Atmospheric Administration, National Marine Fisheries Service, *Fisheries of the United States, 1977.*

Income by Industrial Source, 1977

State and region	SOURCES OF PERSONAL INCOME: Total personal income	Farm income	Govt. income disbursements: Federal	Govt. income disbursements: State, local	Private nonfarm income	SOURCES OF LABOUR AND PROPRIETORS' INCOME % OF TOTAL: Total	Farms	Mining	Construction	Mfg.	Wholesale, retail trade	Finance, insurance, real estate	Transportation, communications, public util.	Service	Govt.	Other
United States	$1,518,390	$26,730	$67,215	$132,255	$937,052	$1,163,252	%2.3	%1.6	%6.0	%26.2	%16.7	%5.6	%7.5	%16.6	%17.1	%0.4
New England	87,932	365	2,528	7,011	54,515	64,419	0.6	0.1	4.9	31.2	16.1	6.4	6.1	19.5	14.8	0.4
Maine	6,220	111	348	494	3,598	4,550	2.4	0.1	6.9	27.4	16.6	4.3	6.5	16.2	18.5	1.0
New Hampshire	5,547	22	181	406	3,274	3,884	0.6	0.2	7.0	32.3	16.9	5.2	5.5	17.0	15.1	0.3
Vermont	2,814	71	78	262	1,688	2,099	3.4	0.4	6.4	27.7	15.1	4.6	6.5	19.2	16.2	0.4
Massachusetts	41,964	61	1,184	3,590	26,321	31,156	0.2	[2]	4.4	28.6	16.5	6.4	6.7	21.5	15.3	0.4
Rhode Island	6,332	9	225	560	3,765	4,559	0.2	[2]	4.6	33.4	15.6	5.5	4.7	18.3	17.2	0.4
Connecticut	25,055	92	512	1,699	15,868	18,171	0.5	0.2	4.7	36.4	15.2	7.5	5.4	17.6	12.2	0.3
Mideast	318,332	1,226	14,806	28,849	197,251	242,131	0.5	0.5	4.5	25.8	15.9	6.9	8.1	19.5	18.0	0.3
New York	135,089	351	3,177	14,049	85,205	102,781	0.3	0.2	3.4	23.0	16.2	9.5	8.7	21.6	16.8	0.3
New Jersey	58,589	109	1,621	4,691	34,245	40,666	0.3	0.1	4.5	30.5	17.6	5.1	8.6	17.6	15.5	0.3
Pennsylvania	82,630	559	2,316	6,046	54,022	62,944	0.9	1.7	5.7	33.5	15.4	4.9	7.7	16.7	13.3	0.2
Delaware	4,477	61	153	360	2,948	3,522	1.7	0.2	6.1	39.0	13.7	4.4	5.9	14.1	14.6	0.2
Maryland	31,337	145	2,882	2,892	15,855	21,775	0.7	0.1	6.8	17.2	17.5	5.3	6.5	19.1	26.5	0.3
District of Columbia	6,210	[1]	4,656	811	4,976	10,443	[2]	[2]	2.4	2.7	6.8	4.3	6.0	24.6	52.4	0.7
Great Lakes	301,646	5,242	6,445	24,417	201,053	237,157	2.2	0.8	5.3	37.5	15.6	4.6	6.6	14.1	13.0	0.2
Michigan	69,554	590	1,110	6,366	47,562	55,629	1.1	0.5	4.6	43.8	13.9	3.7	5.3	13.5	13.4	0.2
Ohio	75,809	816	1,866	5,507	52,243	60,432	1.3	1.0	5.2	39.2	15.7	4.2	6.9	14.0	12.2	0.2
Indiana	36,890	832	791	2,638	25,157	29,417	2.8	0.7	5.8	41.4	14.9	4.2	6.6	11.7	11.6	0.2
Illinois	87,346	1,593	2,192	7,116	55,991	66,892	2.4	1.0	5.6	30.0	17.3	5.9	7.8	15.9	13.9	0.2
Wisconsin	32,047	1,411	486	2,790	20,100	24,787	5.7	0.2	6.1	34.6	15.5	4.6	6.0	13.8	13.2	0.3
Plains	115,316	6,084	3,976	9,734	68,517	88,312	6.9	1.0	6.6	22.9	18.3	5.3	8.4	14.7	15.5	0.3
Minnesota	28,337	1,870	562	2,612	17,300	22,343	8.4	1.2	6.2	23.8	18.1	5.3	7.6	14.8	14.2	0.3
Iowa	19,802	1,265	343	1,714	11,456	14,777	8.6	0.2	7.0	26.5	18.0	5.3	6.8	13.5	13.9	0.3
Missouri	31,943	774	1,392	2,397	20,896	25,460	3.0	0.6	5.8	26.3	18.2	5.3	9.7	15.8	14.9	0.2
North Dakota	4,044	404	290	352	1,992	3,039	13.3	2.2	9.5	6.4	20.4	4.4	8.4	13.8	21.1	0.4
South Dakota	4,104	519	240	353	1,878	2,990	17.4	1.5	7.2	9.6	18.7	4.5	7.2	13.8	19.8	0.4
Nebraska	10,491	666	429	980	5,880	7,955	8.4	0.5	7.6	15.7	19.1	6.4	9.6	14.6	17.7	0.3
Kansas	16,594	587	721	1,326	9,116	11,749	5.0	2.7	7.0	21.3	17.9	5.2	8.7	14.4	17.4	0.3
Southeast	295,466	5,956	17,539	24,704	174,757	222,957	2.7	2.4	6.7	24.2	17.0	5.0	7.7	15.0	18.9	0.4
Virginia	35,246	243	4,357	2,981	18,364	25,946	0.9	1.4	6.7	19.8	15.1	4.6	7.2	15.6	28.3	0.2
West Virginia	11,129	31	257	886	7,337	8,511	0.4	17.2	7.5	23.9	14.0	3.1	8.4	11.9	13.4	0.1
Kentucky	20,561	526	1,088	1,434	12,601	15,649	3.4	6.7	6.4	26.8	15.3	4.0	7.5	13.5	16.1	0.2
Tennessee	24,869	404	1,154	2,019	16,429	20,006	2.0	0.6	5.9	31.0	17.7	4.9	6.7	15.0	15.9	0.2
North Carolina	32,791	1,051	1,699	2,917	20,385	26,052	4.0	0.2	5.4	32.6	15.9	4.2	6.5	13.0	17.7	0.3
South Carolina	16,186	195	1,250	1,364	9,815	12,624	1.5	0.2	6.6	34.2	14.5	4.1	5.7	12.0	20.7	0.4
Georgia	30,358	416	2,016	2,689	19,187	24,308	1.7	0.4	5.4	24.2	19.4	5.6	9.2	14.3	19.4	0.3
Florida	56,496	929	2,369	4,803	29,399	37,500	2.5	0.4	6.9	13.4	20.2	7.3	8.9	20.6	19.1	0.8
Alabama	20,745	351	1,434	1,774	12,510	16,068	2.2	1.7	7.1	28.2	15.9	4.5	7.0	13.1	20.0	0.3
Mississippi	12,019	614	653	1,021	6,890	9,179	6.7	1.7	6.4	27.5	15.5	4.2	6.5	12.9	18.2	0.4
Louisiana	23,187	411	825	1,952	15,137	18,326	2.2	7.8	9.8	17.5	17.7	4.6	9.6	15.2	15.2	0.4
Arkansas	11,878	784	436	864	6,703	8,788	8.9	1.2	6.8	26.9	16.4	4.4	7.4	12.8	14.8	0.4
Southwest	127,032	2,079	7,069	10,567	77,739	97,454	2.1	6.0	8.0	18.5	18.5	5.4	7.9	15.1	18.1	0.4
Oklahoma	17,839	455	1,143	1,382	10,056	13,036	3.5	9.0	6.3	17.5	23.5	4.9	8.2	13.8	19.4	0.3
Texas	87,280	1,183	4,374	6,729	55,858	68,144	1.7	5.5	8.3	20.0	19.2	5.5	8.0	15.1	16.3	0.4
New Mexico	6,970	146	669	853	3,654	5,321	2.7	9.0	8.1	7.1	16.0	4.1	8.0	16.1	28.6	0.3
Arizona	14,943	295	882	1,602	8,172	10,952	2.7	4.2	8.1	15.8	22.4	5.8	6.9	16.1	22.7	0.5
Rocky Mountain	39,123	789	2,669	3,706	23,306	30,470	2.6	5.3	8.6	15.4	17.7	5.2	8.6	15.4	20.9	0.3
Montana	4,661	146	277	522	2,512	3,457	4.2	3.9	8.7	11.1	18.7	4.3	10.6	15.0	23.1	0.3
Idaho	5,128	202	260	466	3,036	3,964	5.1	1.3	9.5	19.1	18.3	4.7	7.6	15.3	18.3	0.7
Wyoming	3,073	64	161	284	1,934	2,443	2.6	23.2	12.0	5.5	14.3	3.3	9.9	10.6	18.2	0.3
Colorado	18,752	281	1,349	1,756	11,236	14,622	1.9	3.7	7.5	16.4	18.0	6.0	8.1	16.8	21.2	0.3
Utah	7,510	96	621	679	4,588	5,984	1.6	5.2	9.1	16.9	17.6	4.8	8.7	14.3	21.7	0.2
Far West	222,459	4,804	10,501	22,050	133,396	170,750	2.8	0.6	6.1	21.3	17.4	5.7	7.2	19.1	19.1	0.7
Washington	27,534	557	1,620	2,568	16,144	20,888	2.7	0.2	7.7	22.0	18.1	5.2	7.3	15.9	20.0	0.8
Oregon	16,651	304	512	1,678	10,401	12,894	2.4	0.2	6.9	25.7	19.1	5.1	7.8	15.2	17.0	0.6
Nevada	5,059	34	267	463	3,392	4,155	0.8	1.6	9.5	5.2	15.0	4.3	8.2	37.5	17.6	0.3
California	173,214	3,909	8,103	17,342	103,460	132,814	2.9	0.6	5.7	21.3	17.2	5.9	7.1	19.4	19.2	0.7
Alaska	4,311	4	642	576	3,151	4,375	0.1	4.2	22.1	5.1	10.7	3.6	10.5	15.1	27.9	0.9
Hawaii	6,773	180	1,040	642	3,366	5,228	3.4	[2]	7.2	5.7	16.3	6.6	9.2	18.9	32.2	0.5

Dollar figures in millions. Percentages may not add to 100.0 because of rounding.
[1] Less than $500,000. [2] Less than 0.05%.
Source: U.S. Department of Commerce, Bureau of Economic Analysis, *Survey of Current Business*.

Farms and Farm Income

State	Number of farms 1978[1]	Land in farms 1978 in 000 acres[1]	CASH RECEIPTS, 1977, IN $000[1] Farm marketings: Total	Crops	Livestock and products
Alabama	76,000	14,400	1,496,430	569,018	927,412
Alaska	310	1,690[2]	11,472	7,099	4,373
Arizona	6,600	40,700	1,198,399	689,670	508,729
Arkansas	68,000	17,300	2,468,809	1,294,356	1,174,453
California	75,000	34,000	9,369,883	6,455,902	2,913,981
Colorado	29,000	39,000	2,059,881	561,179	1,498,702
Connecticut	4,000	470	233,737	104,096	129,641
Delaware	3,500	655	260,682	80,738	179,944
Florida	38,500	14,000	2,625,728	1,880,025	745,703
Georgia	69,000	17,000	2,194,120	960,290	1,233,830
Hawaii	4,100	2,300	324,688	259,748	64,940
Idaho	26,900	15,600	1,169,840	694,013	475,827
Illinois	117,000	28,900	5,792,386	3,919,833	1,872,553
Indiana	95,000	17,100	3,239,472	1,973,597	1,265,875
Iowa	128,000	34,100	7,064,884	2,764,855	4,300,029
Kansas	76,000	48,500	3,848,883	1,624,850	2,224,033
Kentucky	117,000	15,500	1,805,801	1,064,616	741,185
Louisiana	43,000	11,100	1,257,018	851,024	405,994
Maine	7,600	1,690	417,828	154,754	263,074
Maryland	17,400	2,900	657,467	229,185	428,282
Massachusetts	5,300	670	213,943	108,759	105,184
Michigan	72,000	11,400	1,823,656	983,013	840,643
Minnesota	114,000	30,600	4,322,534	2,083,735	2,238,799
Mississippi	78,000	16,200	1,713,736	918,342	795,394
Missouri	133,000	32,600	2,870,237	1,193,166	1,677,071
Montana	22,900	62,100	957,152	443,364	513,788
Nebraska	68,000	48,000	3,979,670	1,723,374	2,256,296
Nevada	2,100	9,000	147,124	45,171	101,353
New Hampshire	3,000	580	78,503	23,386	55,117
New Jersey	8,300	1,010	351,066	252,054	99,012
New Mexico	12,800	47,300	790,789	221,455	569,334
New York	57,000	11,100	1,725,123	524,815	1,200,308
North Carolina	115,000	13,100	2,622,248	1,554,421	1,067,827
North Dakota	41,500	41,700	1,539,310	1,055,999	483,311
Ohio	108,000	16,800	2,793,615	1,636,905	1,156,710
Oklahoma	85,000	36,700	1,925,815	766,100	1,159,715
Oregon	34,000	19,200	1,034,205	677,877	356,328
Pennsylvania	72,000	10,000	1,903,223	600,268	1,302,955
Rhode Island	740	68	26,324	15,083	11,241
South Carolina	45,000	7,700	783,869	506,631	277,238
South Dakota	43,000	45,500	1,610,207	493,140	1,117,067
Tennessee	110,000	14,600	1,370,363	694,347	676,016
Texas	197,000	139,800	6,909,746	3,385,038	3,524,708
Utah	13,400	12,900	363,462	96,232	267,230
Vermont	6,700	1,800	266,742	21,576	245,166
Virginia	61,000	9,900	1,004,356	444,516	559,840
Washington	36,500	16,200	1,707,688	1,199,977	507,711
West Virginia	26,000	4,600	147,915	42,441	105,474
Wisconsin	99,000	19,000	3,151,842	595,940	2,555,902
Wyoming	8,000	35,300	452,163	72,368	379,795
TOTAL U.S.	2,680,150	1,072,333	96,084,034	48,518,341	47,565,093

[1] Preliminary. [2] Exclusive of grazing land leased from the U.S. Government, Alaska farmland totals about 70,000 acres.
Source: U.S. Department of Agriculture, Statistical Reporting Service and Economic Research Service.

Principal Minerals Produced

State	Principal minerals, in order of value, 1975	Value in $000		% of U.S. total	
		1974	1975	1974	1975
Alabama	Coal, petroleum, cement, stone	$764,746	$968,973	1.39	1.56
Alaska	Petroleum, natural gas, stone, sand and gravel	448,437	480,745	0.81	0.77
Arizona	Copper, molybdenum, cement, sand and gravel	1,562,234	1,288,423	2.83	2.07
Arkansas	Petroleum, bromine, natural gas, stone	406,821	436,441	0.74	0.70
California	Petroleum, cement, natural gas, sand and gravel	2,797,080	3,152,937	5.07	5.06
Colorado	Petroleum, molybdenum, coal, cement	750,299	960,800	1.36	1.54
Connecticut	Stone, sand and gravel, feldspar, lime	35,362	33,010	0.06	0.05
Delaware	Sand and gravel, magnesium compounds, clays	3,793	1,906	0.01	0.01
Florida	Phosphate rock, petroleum, stone, cement	1,043,895	1,775,500	1.89	2.85
Georgia	Clays, stone, cement, sand and gravel	363,100	333,387	0.66	0.54
Hawaii	Stone, cement, sand and gravel, pumice	42,042	49,710	0.08	0.08
Idaho	Phosphate rock, silver, zinc, lead	208,558	233,788	0.38	0.38
Illinois	Coal, petroleum, stone, sand and gravel	1,149,210	1,490,598	2.08	2.39
Indiana	Coal, cement, stone, petroleum	440,690	541,600	0.80	0.87
Iowa	Cement, stone, sand and gravel, coal	176,720	195,740	0.32	0.31
Kansas	Petroleum, natural gas, natural gas liquids, cement	889,398	970,611	1.61	1.56
Kentucky	Coal, petroleum, stone, natural gas	2,563,210	2,738,859	4.65	4.40
Louisiana	Petroleum, natural gas, natural gas liquids, sulfur	8,146,578	8,513,275	14.77	13.67
Maine	Cement, sand and gravel, zinc, stone	36,348	36,741	0.07	0.06
Maryland	Coal, stone, cement, sand and gravel	172,880	164,919	0.31	0.26
Massachusetts	Stone, sand and gravel, lime, clays	62,109	58,846	0.11	0.09
Michigan	Iron ore, petroleum, cement, copper	1,040,067	1,291,653	1.89	2.07
Minnesota	Iron ore, sand and gravel, stone, cement	1,026,366	1,097,088	1.86	1.76
Mississippi	Petroleum, natural gas, sand and gravel, cement	391,155	410,009	0.71	0.66
Missouri	Lead, cement, stone, iron ore	691,049	722,728	1.25	1.16
Montana	Petroleum, copper, coal, cement	574,801	573,150	1.04	0.92
Nebraska	Petroleum, cement, sand and gravel, stone	98,634	111,905	0.18	0.18
Nevada	Copper, gold, sand and gravel, cement	257,876	258,390	0.47	0.41
New Hampshire	Sand and gravel, stone, clays, gem stones	13,691	17,107	0.02	0.03
New Jersey	Stone, sand and gravel, zinc, titanium concentrate	140,748	123,702	0.26	0.20
New Mexico	Petroleum, natural gas, copper, potassium salts	1,941,544	2,091,541	3.52	3.36
New York	Cement, stone, zinc, salt	440,573	397,728	0.80	0.64
North Carolina	Stone, phosphate rock, lithium minerals	155,869	152,880	0.28	0.25
North Dakota	Petroleum, coal, sand and gravel, natural gas	159,427	201,504	0.29	0.32
Ohio	Coal, petroleum, stone, lime	1,107,670	1,356,454	2.01	2.18
Oklahoma	Petroleum, natural gas, natural gas liquids, coal	2,123,690	2,267,095	3.85	3.64
Oregon	Stone, sand and gravel, cement, nickel	103,920	106,004	0.19	0.17
Pennsylvania	Coal, cement, stone, lime	2,374,512	2,907,838	4.30	4.67
Rhode Island	Sand and gravel, stone, gem stones	5,982	6,198	0.01	0.01
South Carolina	Cement, stone, sand and gravel, clays	105,171	115,467	0.19	0.19
South Dakota	Gold, cement, stone, sand and gravel	102,627	101,821	0.19	0.16
Tennessee	Coal, stone, zinc, cement	395,608	424,768	0.71	0.68
Texas	Petroleum, natural gas, natural gas liquids, cement	13,711,144	15,529,931	24.85	24.94
Utah	Petroleum, copper, coal, gold	952,045	966,407	1.72	1.55
Vermont	Stone, asbestos, sand and gravel, talc	35,453	28,779	0.06	0.05
Virginia	Coal, stone, cement, sand and gravel	1,058,207	1,261,974	1.92	2.03
Washington	Cement, coal, sand and gravel, stone	143,916	158,505	0.26	0.25
West Virginia	Coal, natural gas, petroleum, natural gas liquids	2,403,177	3,390,021	4.36	5.44
Wisconsin	Sand and gravel, stone, iron ore, cement	114,763	132,260	0.21	0.21
Wyoming	Petroleum, sodium compounds, coal, natural gas	1,437,200	1,644,438	2.60	2.64
TOTAL U.S.		$55,172,000	$62,275,000	100.00	100.00

Source: U.S. Department of the Interior, Bureau of Mines, *Minerals Yearbook*.

Services

Kind of service	NUMBER OF SERVICES		NUMBER OF EMPLOYEES [1]	
	1975	1976	1975	1976
Hotels and other lodging places	45,060	46,122	839,699	890,512
Hotels, tourist courts, and motels	34,365	35,147	780,647	829,157
Rooming and boarding houses	4,312	4,010	34,809	33,282
Camps and trailering parks	3,644	3,957	13,338	15,434
Sporting and recreational camps	1,800	1,844	7,919	8,990
Personal services	161,058	159,719	875,056	880,718
Laundry, cleaning, garment services	46,250	44,869	363,623	356,130
Photographic studios, portrait	5,001	5,441	26,678	28,563
Beauty shops	70,468	70,174	268,925	274,485
Barber shops	12,154	11,521	27,681	27,586
Shoe repair and hat cleaning shops	3,216	3,100	7,497	7,537
Funeral service and crematories	14,590	14,472	70,814	71,121
Miscellaneous personal services	9,101	9,692	108,511	113,062
Business services	123,024	133,804	1,956,452	2,126,688
Advertising	9,180	9,589	112,927	114,325
Credit reporting and collection	5,658	5,627	58,531	60,210
Mailing, reproduction, stenographic	11,024	11,755	88,409	93,081
Building services	20,854	22,740	356,955	383,502
Employment agencies	6,138	6,314	58,920	72,768
Temporary help supply services	3,133	3,331	186,600	233,322
Computer and data processing services	6,517	7,476	157,989	174,595
Research and development laboratories	1,810	2,004	71,423	73,189
Management and public relations	17,896	20,192	188,170	218,386
Detective and protective services	5,533	5,841	253,125	248,050
Equipment rental and leasing	9,539	10,327	76,446	80,911
Photofinishing laboratories	2,191	2,341	55,822	56,292
Auto repair, services, and garages	84,814	91,653	409,979	444,165
Automobile rentals, without drivers	7,294	7,256	75,527	73,638
Automobile parking	6,076	7,001	33,716	32,910
Automotive repair shops	64,309	69,468	250,570	282,297
Automotive services, except repair	6,988	7,520	49,476	53,073
Car washes	5,144	5,286	39,457	40,792
Miscellaneous repair services	44,435	47,874	227,399	242,767
Radio and television repair	8,733	9,112	37,333	37,674
Motion pictures	14,515	14,748	181,241	184,607
Motion picture production	3,097	3,220	53,057	52,963
Motion picture distribution	1,088	1,126	14,539	15,358
Motion picture theatres	10,301	10,289	113,340	115,752

Kind of service	NUMBER OF SERVICES		NUMBER OF EMPLOYEES [1]	
	1975	1976	1975	1976
Amusement and recreation services	42,732	44,903	522,563	563,380
Producers, orchestras, entertainers	5,966	6,112	59,269	63,110
Bowling and billiard establishments	7,895	7,859	98,578	102,433
Racing, including track operation	1,685	1,782	38,817	...
Public golf courses	2,081	2,127	12,588	13,879
Amusement parks	508	552	27,171	30,299
Membership sports, recreation clubs	8,648	9,009	130,630	136,465
Health services	255,141	263,576	3,922,194	4,089,115
Physicians' offices	121,171	124,122	544,763	566,495
Dentists' offices	74,045	76,359	235,456	252,295
Osteopathic physicians' offices	4,359	4,336	14,787	15,354
Chiropractors' offices	5,982	6,502	10,902	12,593
Optometrists' offices	9,669	10,132	23,372	25,016
Nursing and personal care facilities	11,879	11,790	684,284	736,309
Hospitals	5,380	5,333	2,143,106	2,194,141
Medical and dental laboratories	8,963	9,459	79,035	84,785
Outpatient care facilities	4,679	5,419	90,091	104,513
Legal services	82,512	85,758	338,138	363,088
Educational services	25,345	25,521	957,131	983,431
Elementary and secondary schools	14,115	14,007	312,947	312,374
Colleges and universities	2,296	2,317	522,766	548,118
Libraries and information centres	1,416	1,469	16,463	16,371
Correspondence and vocational schools	2,869	2,891	45,601	46,919
Social services	39,893	43,036	647,918	723,119
Residential care	5,073	5,575	136,113	149,659
Museums, botanical, zoological gardens	790	871	21,779	23,398
Membership organizations	131,255	135,628	1,025,253	1,071,128
Business associations	11,651	12,077	66,972	70,343
Professional organizations	3,471	3,746	33,092	36,712
Labour organizations	21,140	22,265	154,538	164,129
Civic and social organizations	32,532	33,854	262,049	270,039
Political organizations	972	1,371	3,548	6,286
Religious organizations	54,526	54,986	434,567	447,938
Miscellaneous services	62,883	67,554	617,914	639,767
Engineering, architectural services	28,017	29,468	336,890	345,003
Noncommercial research organizations	2,199	2,349	57,606	60,357
Accounting, auditing and bookkeeping	29,917	32,657*	208,470	218,534
TOTAL [2]	1,117,606	1,164,782	12,657,563	13,340,684

[1] Mid-March pay period.　　[2] Includes administrative and auxiliary businesses not shown separately.
Source: U.S. Department of Commerce, Bureau of the Census, *County Business Patterns 1975* and *1976*.

Principal Manufactures, 1976

monetary figures in millions of dollars

Industry	Employees (000)	Cost of labour¹	Cost of materials	Value of shipments	Value added by mfg.
Food and kindred products	1,536	$17,289	$128,618	$180,930	$52,760
Meat products	311	3,474	38,252	45,827	7,530
Dairy products	164	1,908	19,657	24,830	5,261
Preserved fruits and vegetables	222	2,032	10,935	17,722	6,799
Grain mill products	114	1,453	15,133	21,189	6,083
Beverages	204	2,629	12,241	21,069	8,833
Tobacco products	65	704	4,659	8,786	4,128
Textile mill products	876	7,368	22,194	36,389	14,495
Apparel and other textile products	1,271	8,563	18,150	34,758	16,860
Lumber and wood products	629	6,143	18,121	31,239	13,454
Furniture and fixtures	426	3,772	6,946	14,232	7,370
Paper and allied products	615	8,046	27,877	48,218	20,604
Printing and publishing	1,086	12,680	15,288	42,838	27,647
Chemicals and allied products	851	12,365	53,725	104,139	51,408
Industrial chemicals	251	4,032	20,237	37,296	17,513
Plastics materials and synthetics	153	2,187	10,688	17,156	6,648
Drugs	151	2,223	3,813	13,016	9,333
Soap, cleaners, and toilet goods	110	1,415	6,383	14,741	8,469
Paints, allied products	60	810	3,438	5,931	2,562
Agricultural chemicals	52	722	5,448	9,195	3,763
Petroleum and coal products	144	2,437	69,392	82,347	13,169
Rubber, misc. plastics products	627	6,742	15,885	31,765	15,950
Leather and leather products	247	1,805	3,691	7,176	3,559
Stone, clay, and glass products	599	7,086	14,056	30,635	16,773
Primary metal industries	1,106	16,975	59,932	93,002	34,182
Blast furnace, basic steel products	532	9,166	30,231	46,687	17,274
Iron, steel foundries	216	2,966	4,361	9,787	5,496
Primary nonferrous metals	59	963	6,909	9,970	2,980
Nonferrous drawing and rolling	171	2,339	13,653	18,753	5,360
Nonferrous foundries	85	951	1,653	3,389	1,738
Fabricated metal products	1,471	18,382	38,720	77,507	39,145
Ordnance and accessories	75	976	1,115	2,804	1,664
Machinery, except electrical	1,960	$26,480	$48,648	$105,525	$57,357
Engines and turbines	125	1,939	4,935	9,009	4,200
Farm and garden machinery	146	1,949	5,776	10,534	4,783
Construction and related mach.	312	4,378	10,234	19,741	9,646
Metalworking machinery	290	3,954	3,867	11,278	7,458
Special industry machinery	196	2,556	4,159	9,454	5,175
General industrial machinery	281	3,746	6,184	14,196	8,043
Service industry machines	173	2,152	5,587	10,660	5,214
Office, computing machines	229	3,277	5,664	13,723	8,102
Electric and electronic equipment	1,578	19,253	32,831	73,867	41,746
Electric distributing equip.	104	1,193	2,018	4,688	2,702
Electrical industrial apparatus	195	2,284	3,691	8,453	4,916
Household appliances	157	1,699	4,847	9,161	4,454
Electric lighting, wiring equip.	159	1,700	3,228	7,342	4,204
Radio, TV receiving equipment	90	956	3,302	5,823	2,544
Communication equipment	422	6,050	7,513	19,138	11,656
Electronic components, access.	323	3,763	5,008	12,433	7,568
Transportation equipment	1,668	26,442	85,892	141,026	55,657
Motor vehicles and equipment	797	13,019	65,343	95,381	30,948
Aircraft and parts	408	6,665	10,087	23,463	12,735
Ship, boat building, repairing	207	2,605	3,481	7,516	4,032
Railroad equipment	50	740	2,077	3,616	1,455
Guided missiles, space vehicles	142	2,723	2,347	7,142	5,027
Instruments and related products	518	6,598	8,989	25,030	16,386
Measuring, controlling devices	169	2,100	2,143	6,180	4,102
Medical instruments and supplies	111	1,248	1,892	4,766	2,956
Photographic equipment and supplies	107	1,732	2,915	8,845	6,077
Miscellaneous manufacturing industries	410	3,868	7,580	16,286	8,822
All establishments, including administrative and auxiliary	18,753	233,389	681,194	1,185,695	511,471

¹ Payroll only.   Source: U.S. Department of Commerce, *Annual Survey of Manufactures 1976.*

Business Activity

Category of activity	WHOLESALING				RETAILING				SERVICES			
	1960	1965	1970	1975	1960	1965	1970	1975	1960	1965	1970	1975
Number of businesses (in 000)												
Sole proprietorships	306	265	274	336	1,548	1,554	1,689	1,765	1,966	2,208	2,507	3,034
Active partnerships	41	32	30	31	238	202	170	162	159	169	176	199
Active corporations	117	147	166	221	217	288	351	394	121	188	281	437
Business receipts (in $000,000)												
Sole proprietorships	17,061	17,934	21,556	33,339	65,439	77,760	89,315	112,453	23,256	29,789	40,869	55,997
Active partnerships	12,712	10,879	11,325	16,009	24,787	23,244	23,546	29,133	9,281	12,442	18,791	30,167
Active corporations	130,637	171,414	234,885	512,958	125,787	183,925	274,808	457,422	22,106	36,547	66,460	131,013
Net profit (less loss; in $000,000)												
Sole proprietorships	1,305	1,483	1,806	2,861	3,869	5,019	5,767	6,724	8,060	11,008	15,063	18,385
Active partnerships	587	548	557	820	1,612	1,654	1,603	1,836	3,056	4,402	6,189	7,224
Active corporations	2,130	3,288	4,441	14,920	2,225	4,052	5,217	8,443	849	1,505	1,199	3,498

Data refer to accounting periods ending between July 1 of year shown and June 30 of following year.
Source: U.S. Department of the Treasury, Internal Revenue Service, *Statistics of Income: Business Income Tax Returns* and *Corporation Income Tax Returns.*

Retail Sales

in millions of dollars

Kind of business	1960	1965	1970	1977
Durable goods stores¹	70,560	94,186	114,288	238,815
Automotive group	39,579	56,884	64,966	143,682
Passenger car, other automotive dealers	37,038	53,484	59,388	131,418
Tire, battery, accessory dealers	2,541	3,400	5,578	12,264
Furniture and appliance group	10,591	13,352	17,778	34,499
Furniture, home furnishings stores	...	...	10,483	20,843
Household appliance, TV, radio stores	...	...	6,073	10,654
Building materials, hardware, farm equipment group	11,222	12,388	20,494	37,958
Lumberyards, building materials dealers	8,567	9,731	11,995	26,706
Hardware stores	2,655	2,657	3,351	6,431
Nondurable goods stores¹	148,969	189,942	261,239	469,529
Apparel group	13,631	15,765	19,810	33,527
Men's, boys' wear stores	2,644	...	4,630	6,694
Women's apparel, accessory stores	5,295	...	7,582	12,814
Family clothing stores	...	...	3,360	6,928
Shoe stores	2,437	...	3,501	5,766
Drug and proprietary stores	7,538	9,186	13,352	22,380
Eating and drinking places	16,146	20,201	29,689	63,825
Food group	54,023	64,016	86,114	156,313
Grocery stores	48,610	...	79,756	145,900
Meat and fish markets	...	...	2,244	...
Bakeries	...	...	1,303	2,136
Gasoline service stations	17,588	20,611	27,994	56,538
General merchandise group	...	42,299	61,320	89,231
Department stores and dry goods general merchandise stores	...	...	45,000	81,273
Variety stores	...	...	6,959	7,958
Mail-order houses (department store merchandise)	...	...	3,853	6,751
Liquor stores	4,893	5,674	7,980	13,084
TOTAL	219,529	284,128	375,527	708,344

¹Includes some kinds of business not shown separately.
Source: U.S. Department of Commerce, Bureau of the Census, *Monthly Retail Trade,* Bureau of Economic Analysis, *1975 Business Statistics.*

Sales of Merchant Wholesalers

in millions of dollars

Kind of business	1960	1965	1970	1977
Durable goods¹	56,803	82,861	111,970	285,605
Motor vehicles, automotive equipment	7,883	12,140	19,482	54,046
Electrical goods	8,660	12,681	16,667	31,745
Furniture, home furnishings	2,910	3,777	5,199	11,026
Hardware, plumbing, heating equipment	6,422	8,413	10,858	22,404
Lumber, construction supplies	6,680	9,765	10,863	26,181
Machinery, equipment, supplies	14,287	20,561	27,638	82,003
Metals, metalwork (except scrap)	5,708	9,162	13,647	29,000
Scrap, waste materials	3,296	4,789	6,040	9,632
Nondurable goods¹	80,477	104,470	135,029	356,498
Groceries and related products	27,661	38,068	53,411	110,766
Beer, wine, distilled alcoholic beverages	7,424	9,464	13,332	23,371
Drugs, chemicals, allied products	5,370	7,180	9,135	10,868
Tobacco, tobacco products	4,164	5,014	6,232	8,868
Dry goods, apparel	6,675	8,804	10,577	19,595
Paper, paper products	4,153	5,612	7,679	15,482
Farm products	11,683	13,711	13,987	70,051
Other nondurable goods	13,346	16,966	22,632	48,762
TOTAL	137,281	187,331	246,999	642,104

¹Includes some kinds of business not shown separately.
Source: U.S. Dept. of Commerce, Bureau of the Census, *Monthly Wholesale Trade.*

Commercial Banks[1]

December 31, 1977

State	Number of banks	Total assets or liabilities $000,000	SELECTED ASSETS ($000,000) Loans[2]	Invest-ments	Reserves, cash, and bank balances	SELECTED LIABILITIES ($000,000) Deposits Total	Demand	Time	Capital accounts
Ala.	310	13,579	10,999	3,539	1,573	11,701	4,490	4,915	1,063
Alaska	12	1,769	1,363	363	212	1,519	726	435	143
Ariz.	17	8,730	6,625	1,479	1,231	7,601	2,981	2,504	543
Ark.	259	8,552	6,882	2,155	950	7,447	2,926	2,822	676
Calif.	220	124,788	89,069	20,575	17,012	101,015	37,518	35,993	7,823
Colo.	288	11,231	8,605	2,166	1,606	9,635	4,344	2,649	818
Conn.	71	10,383	7,497	1,990	1,717	8,987	4,193	2,154	702
Del.	17	3,075	2,475	1,210	339	2,428	985	833	220
D.C.	16	5,379	4,061	1,292	795	4,392	2,334	924	433
Fla.	676	33,986	26,090	11,081	4,335	29,702	12,347	8,059	2,610
Ga.	440	17,970	12,685	3,067	2,719	14,583	7,105	5,313	1,469
Hawaii	8	3,492	2,841	857	373	3,116	1,163	910	250
Idaho	24	3,777	3,118	844	456	3,288	1,181	1,209	256
Ill.	1,235	87,225	70,129	22,787	9,872	68,837	24,503	28,460	6,361
Ind.	407	25,556	20,472	7,307	2,606	21,804	7,493	9,399	1,854
Iowa	649	16,094	13,376	4,222	1,618	14,225	4,484	6,032	1,251
Kan.	615	12,476	9,838	3,400	1,361	10,804	4,118	4,394	1,032
Ky.	343	14,104	10,987	3,448	1,592	12,182	5,235	4,675	1,089
La.	254	17,214	13,284	4,674	2,128	14,725	6,024	5,759	1,309
Maine	43	2,731	2,329	643	264	2,391	788	626	205
Md.	108	12,478	9,942	2,499	1,468	10,618	4,198	2,545	911
Mass.	145	20,704	14,390	4,233	3,093	16,334	8,044	3,668	1,569
Mich.	361	41,776	33,136	10,252	4,997	36,094	11,109	12,194	3,035
Minn.	752	21,742	17,629	5,489	2,519	18,028	6,223	7,323	1,638
Miss.	184	8,341	6,577	2,275	1,030	7,351	2,779	3,566	626
Mo.	712	26,049	19,196	6,635	3,666	21,286	9,273	7,434	1,927
Mont.	157	4,006	3,374	1,031	408	3,600	1,225	1,512	297
Neb.	451	8,568	6,642	1,810	1,128	7,395	2,951	3,176	685
Nev.	8	2,719	2,150	689	349	2,431	1,061	702	207
N.H.	78	2,434	2,043	479	262	2,164	658	509	188
N.J.	188	29,504	24,002	9,016	3,219	25,710	9,430	7,204	2,097
N.M.	83	4,303	3,356	1,047	520	3,831	1,490	1,602	308
N.Y.	231	194,203	121,369	26,525	43,752	140,230	77,688	44,787	15,998
N.C.	89	17,324	13,006	3,712	2,403	14,419	6,160	4,425	1,361
N.D.	170	3,476	2,916	961	295	3,144	1,049	1,419	282
Ohio	486	43,278	33,927	12,018	4,993	36,264	13,125	11,217	3,647
Okla.	476	15,102	11,605	3,899	2,072	13,144	5,356	5,536	1,182
Ore.	53	9,715	7,206	1,873	995	7,766	3,050	2,484	670
Pa.	381	64,866	51,736	15,901	6,901	51,830	17,570	19,892	4,953
R.I.	14	4,733	3,902	912	406	3,772	991	1,547	341
S.C.	88	5,779	4,439	1,441	739	4,967	2,680	1,249	478
S.D.	157	3,822	3,278	1,010	361	3,443	1,008	1,704	304
Tenn.	346	18,127	14,167	4,197	2,246	15,840	5,626	6,921	1,339
Texas	1,377	71,760	53,278	17,746	10,612	60,275	27,452	23,774	5,358
Utah	71	5,006	3,996	969	623	4,374	1,645	1,592	373
Vt.	30	1,844	1,627	416	132	1,678	415	485	133
Va.	279	18,882	15,340	4,443	2,145	16,418	5,849	6,045	1,412
Wash.	86	15,054	11,002	2,140	2,049	12,203	4,926	4,066	966
W.Va.	227	8,129	6,651	2,662	699	6,980	2,209	2,426	674
Wis.	623	21,449	17,331	5,220	2,129	18,539	6,063	6,897	1,534
Wyo.	82	2,425	1,963	660	292	2,156	792	871	192
TOTAL	14,397	1,129,712	843,905	249,257	159,264	922,665	377,034	326,837	84,795

[1] Detail may not add to total given due to rounding; excludes noninsured banks.
[2] Includes investment securities, trading account securities, federal funds sold, and securities purchased under agreements to resell.
Source: Federal Deposit Insurance Corporation, *Assets and Liabilities—Commercial and Mutual Savings Banks—December 31, 1977, 1977 Report of Income.*

Life Insurance, 1977

Number of policies in 000s; value in $000,000

State	Total Number of policies	Total Value	Ordinary Number of policies	Ordinary Value	Group Number of certificates	Group Value	Industrial Number of policies	Industrial Value	Credit[1] Number of policies	Credit[1] Value
Ala.	11,981	$41,538	1,859	$20,064	1,571	$15,550	6,819	$2,674	1,732	$3,250
Alaska	622	5,443	122	2,128	358	2,966	10	3	132	346
Ariz.	4,709	28,024	1,670	15,978	1,400	9,692	150	88	1,489	2,266
Ark.	2,675	17,163	908	9,181	623	6,284	505	283	639	1,415
Calif.	30,051	250,191	10,410	124,641	12,022	113,610	2,011	1,388	5,608	10,552
Colo.	4,400	34,547	1,686	18,821	1,427	13,499	235	172	1,052	2,055
Conn.	5,634	44,903	2,348	21,682	1,824	21,339	302	212	1,160	1,670
Del.	1,430	10,224	500	4,106	384	5,417	236	153	310	548
D.C.	2,436	15,099	435	3,916	936	10,319	506	285	559	579
Fla.	15,387	88,277	4,945	49,096	3,423	31,363	3,735	2,540	3,284	5,278
Ga.	12,458	62,685	3,059	31,107	2,515	24,774	4,505	2,926	2,379	3,878
Hawaii	1,636	14,449	568	7,764	696	5,948	5	2	367	735
Idaho	1,321	9,046	510	4,923	475	3,418	26	12	310	693
Ill.	22,308	154,143	9,141	79,073	6,039	66,387	3,224	1,966	3,904	6,717
Ind.	10,179	65,033	3,977	33,037	2,626	27,238	1,664	996	1,912	3,762
Iowa	4,846	36,078	2,496	20,710	1,310	13,124	243	126	797	2,118
Kan.	4,053	27,992	1,881	17,092	1,049	9,118	331	177	792	1,605
Ky.	6,426	33,256	2,058	16,017	1,317	13,795	1,700	959	1,351	2,485
La.	9,315	43,270	1,987	21,549	1,682	16,372	3,822	2,279	1,824	3,070
Maine	1,938	10,589	708	5,571	695	4,248	78	50	457	720
Md.	8,073	50,902	2,793	25,956	1,782	21,359	1,817	1,037	1,681	2,550
Mass.	9,060	65,271	3,923	32,620	2,377	29,827	823	505	1,937	2,319
Mich.	16,089	121,976	5,482	46,995	5,520	67,763	1,957	1,187	3,130	6,031
Minn.	6,164	49,950	2,462	23,732	2,258	23,883	249	135	1,195	2,200
Miss.	3,831	19,926	874	9,917	823	7,507	760	507	1,374	1,995
Mo.	8,631	56,285	3,567	28,595	2,288	24,133	1,274	735	1,502	2,822
Mont.	1,090	7,417	421	4,452	335	2,334	25	10	309	621
Neb.	2,665	20,016	1,355	12,196	698	6,753	126	67	486	1,000
Nev.	1,301	9,163	255	3,348	503	4,444	9	5	534	1,366
N.H.	1,405	9,700	647	5,514	339	3,567	95	61	324	558
N.J.	11,811	102,073	5,432	50,308	3,164	47,571	1,396	1,060	1,819	3,134
N.M.	1,823	11,698	566	5,790	665	4,974	76	43	516	891
N.Y.	27,063	216,592	11,332	102,024	7,613	103,974	1,980	1,359	6,138	9,615
N.C.	11,943	58,775	3,526	29,990	2,233	22,641	3,695	2,132	2,489	4,012
N.D.	942	7,158	428	4,235	283	2,308	4	2	227	613
Ohio	20,423	136,906	8,054	68,500	5,132	58,474	3,371	2,105	3,866	7,827
Okla.	4,259	30,375	1,652	16,282	1,097	11,715	406	239	1,104	2,139
Ore.	3,146	25,204	1,177	12,463	1,147	11,246	85	41	737	1,454
Pa.	24,521	142,783	9,807	71,916	5,486	59,906	4,589	2,703	4,639	8,258
R.I.	1,876	11,792	785	6,370	593	4,862	181	109	317	451
S.C.	7,507	30,025	2,269	15,187	1,345	11,194	2,588	1,557	1,305	2,087
S.D.	943	7,179	507	4,576	225	2,074	5	2	206	527
Tenn.	9,330	49,206	2,445	23,159	2,209	20,791	2,639	1,599	2,037	3,657
Texas	23,135	153,478	7,819	79,871	6,392	62,168	3,634	2,301	5,290	9,138
Utah	2,073	13,371	670	7,058	858	5,262	89	36	456	1,015
Vt.	764	5,046	339	2,823	194	1,892	36	23	195	308
Va.	10,440	63,541	3,220	29,970	2,375	28,746	2,542	1,465	2,303	3,360
Wash.	5,038	40,090	1,876	20,344	1,990	17,872	170	78	1,002	1,796
W.Va.	3,229	17,267	969	7,588	757	7,890	601	369	902	1,420
Wis.	7,299	52,843	3,364	28,599	2,414	21,766	480	279	1,041	2,199
Wyo.	570	4,477	244	2,497	182	1,690	4	3	140	297
TOTAL U.S.	390,249	$2,582,815	139,528	$1,289,321	105,649	$1,115,047	65,813	$39,045	79,259	$139,402

[1] Life insurance on loans of ten years' or less duration.
Source: Institute of Life Insurance, *Life Insurance Fact Book '78.*

Savings and Loan Associations

Dec. 31, 1977 [1]

State	Number of assns.	Total assets ($000,000)	Per capita assets
Alabama	60	$3,791	$1,034
Alaska	4	277	726
Arizona	16	4,457	1,964
Arkansas	71	3,280	1,555
California	165	83,312	3,871
Colorado	46	6,688	2,589
Connecticut	37	3,439	1,103
Delaware	20	250	429
District of Columbia	16	4,448	6,337
Florida	122	34,583	4,107
Georgia	96	8,432	1,697
Guam	2	51	544
Hawaii	10	2,535	2,858
Idaho	11	833	1,002
Illinois	396	34,208	3,046
Indiana	166	8,424	1,589
Iowa	78	5,679	1,979
Kansas	85	5,590	2,420
Kentucky	107	4,633	1,352
Louisiana	118	6,140	1,599
Maine	21	553	517
Maryland	190	7,289	1,759
Massachusetts	166	7,323	1,261
Michigan	66	13,265	1,457
Minnesota	65	8,178	2,063
Mississippi	61	2,184	928
Missouri	114	11,917	2,494
Montana	14	835	1,109
Nebraska	44	3,933	2,532
Nevada	7	1,518	2,488
New Hampshire	17	894	1,087
New Jersey	222	17,698	2,412
New Mexico	43	2,476	2,120
New York	132	23,044	1,274
North Carolina	178	8,956	1,638
North Dakota	11	1,669	2,596
Ohio	404	30,908	2,891
Oklahoma	59	4,224	1,527
Oregon	28	5,335	2,291
Pennsylvania	416	19,431	1,638
Puerto Rico	12	1,399	437
Rhode Island	6	659	711
South Carolina	73	4,844	1,701
South Dakota	18	826	1,204
Tennessee	96	5,529	1,312
Texas	330	24,316	1,947
Utah	13	2,820	2,297
Vermont	7	212	446
Virginia	81	6,731	1,338
Washington	49	7,281	2,016
West Virginia	36	1,175	645
Wisconsin	118	9,867	2,141
Wyoming	13	616	1,580
TOTAL U.S.	4,770	$459,282	$2,114

[1] Preliminary. Components do not add to totals because of differences in reporting dates and accounting systems.
Source: U.S. League of Savings Associations, *Savings and Loan Fact Book '78.*

GOVERNMENT AND POLITICS

The National Executive

December 15, 1978

Department, bureau, or office	Executive official and official title
PRESIDENT OF THE UNITED STATES	Jimmy Carter
Vice-President	Walter F. Mondale
EXECUTIVE OFFICE OF THE PRESIDENT	
Assistant to the President	Zbigniew Brzezinski
	Hamilton Jordan
	Timothy E. Kraft
Press Secretary to the President	Joseph L. Powell
Counsel to the President	Robert J. Lipshutz
Special Assistant to the President	Joseph W. Aragon
Office of Management and Budget	James T. McIntyre, Jr., director
Council of Economic Advisers	Charles L. Schultze, chairman
National Security Council	[1]
Central Intelligence Agency	Adm. Stansfield Turner, director
Domestic Policy Staff	Stuart E. Eizenstat, executive director
Office of the Special Representative	
for Trade Negotiations	Robert S. Strauss, special representative
Council on Environmental Quality	Charles H. Warren, chairman
Council on Wage and Price Stability	Barry P. Bosworth, director
Office of Science and Technology	
Policy	Frank Press, director
Office of Administration	Richard Harden, director
DEPARTMENT OF STATE	Cyrus R. Vance, secretary
	Warren M. Christopher, deputy secretary
Political Affairs	David D. Newsom, undersecretary
Economic Affairs	Richard N. Cooper, undersecretary
Security Assistance, Science and	
Technology	Lucy Wilson Benson, undersecretary
Management	Ben H. Read, deputy undersecretary
Ambassador at Large	Ellsworth Bunker
	Elliot L. Richardson
	Arthur J. Goldberg
	Gerard C. Smith
Counselor of the Department	Matthew Nimetz
Agency for International Development	John J. Gilligan, administrator
Permanent Mission to the Organization	
of American States	Gale W. McGee, permanent representative
Sinai Support Mission	C. William Kontos, director
Mission to the United Nations	Andrew J. Young, representative
African Affairs	Richard M. Moose, asst. secretary
European Affairs	George S. Vest, asst. secretary
East Asian and Pacific Affairs	Richard C. Holbrooke, asst. secretary
Inter-American Affairs	Viron P. Vaky, asst. secretary
Near Eastern and South Asian Affairs	Harold H. Saunders, asst. secretary
International Organization Affairs	C. William Maynes, asst. secretary
DEPARTMENT OF THE TREASURY	W. Michael Blumenthal, secretary
	Robert Carswell, deputy secretary
Monetary Affairs	Anthony M. Solomon, undersecretary
Comptroller of the Currency	John G. Heimann, comptroller
Bur. of Government Financial Operations	Dario A. Pagliai, commissioner
U.S. Customs Service	Robert E. Chasen, commissioner
Bureau of Engraving and Printing	Seymour Berry, director
Bureau of the Mint	Stella B. Hackel, director
Bureau of the Public Debt	H. J. Hintgen, commissioner
Internal Revenue Service	Jerome Kurtz, commissioner
Office of the Treasurer	Azie Taylor Morton, treasurer
Savings Bond Division	Azie Taylor Morton, national director
U.S. Secret Service	H. Stuart Knight, director
Bureau of Alcohol, Tobacco and Firearms	John G. Krogman, director (acting)
Federal Law Enforcement Training	
Center	Arthur F. Brandstatter, director
DEPARTMENT OF DEFENSE	Harold Brown, secretary
	Charles W. Duncan, Jr., deputy secretary
Joint Chiefs of Staff	Gen. David C. Jones, USAF, chairman
Chief of Staff, Army	Gen. Bernard W. Rogers, USA
Chief of Naval Operations	Adm. Thomas B. Hayward, USN
Chief of Staff, Air Force	Gen. Lew Allen, Jr., USAF
Commandant of the Marine Corps	Gen. Louis H. Wilson, USMC
Department of the Army	Clifford L. Alexander, Jr., secretary
Department of the Navy	W. Graham Claytor, Jr., secretary
Department of the Air Force	John Stetson, secretary
DEPARTMENT OF JUSTICE	
Attorney General	Griffin B. Bell
Solicitor General	Wade H. McCree, Jr.
Community Relations Service	Gilbert G. Pompa, director
Law Enforcement Assistance Admin.	Henry S. Dogin, administrator (acting)
Antitrust Division	John H. Shenefield, asst. attorney general
Civil Division	Barbara A. Babcock, asst. attorney general
Civil Rights Division	Drew S. Days III, asst. attorney general
Criminal Division	Philip B. Heymann, asst. attorney general
Land and Natural Resources Division	James W. Moorman, asst. attorney general
Tax Division	M. Carr Ferguson, asst. attorney general
Office of Management and Finance	Kevin D. Rooney, asst. attorney general
Federal Bureau of Investigation	William H. Webster, director
Bureau of Prisons	Norman A. Carlson, director
Immigration and Naturalization Service	Leonel J. Castillo, commissioner
Drug Enforcement Administration	Peter B. Bensinger, administrator
U.S. Marshals Service	William E. Hall, Jr., director
DEPARTMENT OF THE INTERIOR	Cecil D. Andrus, secretary
	James A. Joseph, undersecretary
Fish and Wildlife and Parks	Robert L. Herbst, asst. secretary
National Park Service	William J. Whalen, director
Fish and Wildlife Service	Lynn A. Greenwalt, director
Heritage Conservation and	
Recreation Service	Chris T. Delaporte, director

Department, bureau, or office	Executive official and official title
Energy and Minerals	Joan M. Davenport, asst. secretary
Office of Minerals Policy and	
Research Analysis	Hermann Enzer, director
Geological Survey	William Menard, director
Bureau of Mines	Roger Markle, director
Office of Surface Mining Reclamation	
and Enforcement	Walter N. Heine, director
Land and Water Resources	Guy R. Martin, asst. secretary
Bureau of Land Management	W. Frank Gregg, director
Bureau of Reclamation	R. Keith Higginson, commissioner
Indian Affairs	Forrest J. Gerard, assistant secretary
DEPARTMENT OF AGRICULTURE	Bob Bergland, secretary
	Vacancy (deputy secretary)
Rural Development	Alex P. Mercure, asst. secretary
Rural Electrification Administration	Robert W. Feragen, administrator
Farmers Home Administration	Gordon Cavanaugh, administrator
Marketing Services	P. R. (Bobby) Smith, asst. secretary
Agricultural Marketing Service	Barbara L. Schlei, administrator
International Affairs and Commodity	
Programs	Dale E. Hathaway, asst. secretary
Commodity Credit Corporation	Dale E. Hathaway, president
Conservation, Research, and Education	M. Rupert Cutler, asst. secretary
Forest Service	John R. McGuire, chief
Soil Conservation Service	Ronello M. Davis, administrator
Economics, Policy Analysis, and Budget	Howard W. Hjort, director
Economics, Statistics, and	
Cooperatives Service	Kenneth R. Farrell, administrator (acting)
Food and Consumer Services	Carol Tucker Foreman, asst. secretary
DEPARTMENT OF COMMERCE	Juanita M. Kreps, secretary
	Sidney L. Harman, undersecretary
Industry and Trade	Frank Weil, asst. secretary
Chief Economist	Courtenay M. Slater
Bureau of the Census	Manuel D. Plotkin, director
Bureau of Economic Analysis	George Jaszi, director
Science and Technology	Jordan Baruch, asst. secretary
Office of Environmental Affairs	Sidney R. Galler, deputy asst. secretary
National Bureau of Standards	Ernest Ambler, director
Patent and Trademark Office	Donald W. Banner, commissioner
Maritime Affairs	Robert J. Blackwell, asst. secretary
Tourism	Fabian Chavez, Jr., asst. secretary
National Oceanic and Atmospheric	
Administration	Richard A. Frank, administrator
DEPARTMENT OF LABOR	Ray Marshall, secretary
	Robert J. Brown, undersecretary
Administration and Management	Alfred M. Zuck, asst. secretary
Employment and Training	Ernest G. Green, asst. secretary
Labor-Management Relations	Francis X. Burkhardt, asst. secretary
Occupational Safety and Health	Eula Bingham, asst. secretary
Labor Statistics	Janet L. Norwood, commissioner (acting)
Mine Safety and Health	Robert B. Lagather, asst. secretary
DEPARTMENT OF HEALTH, EDUCATION,	
AND WELFARE	Joseph A. Califano, Jr., secretary
	Hale Champion, undersecretary
Office of Human Development Services	Arabella Martinez, asst. secretary
Education Division	Mary F. Berry, asst. secretary
Office of Education	Ernest L. Boyer, commissioner
National Institute of Education	Patricia Albjerg Graham, director
Public Health Service	Julius B. Richmond, M.D., asst. secretary
Food and Drug Administration	Donald Kennedy, commissioner
National Institutes of Health	Donald S. Fredrickson, director
Health Resources Administration	Henry A. Foley, administrator
Health Services Administration	George I. Lythcott, M.D., administrator
Center for Disease Control	William H. Foege, M.D., director
Alcohol, Drug Abuse, and Mental	
Health Administration	Gerald L. Klerman, administrator
Health Care Financing Administration	Leonard D. Schaeffer, administrator
Social Security Administration	Stanford G. Ross, commissioner
Office of Child Support Enforcement	Stanford G. Ross, director
DEPARTMENT OF HOUSING	
AND URBAN DEVELOPMENT	Patricia Roberts Harris, secretary
	Jay Janis, undersecretary
Community Planning and Development	Robert C. Embry, asst. secretary
Federal Housing Commissioner	Lawrence B. Simons
Fair Housing and Equal Opportunity	Vacancy (asst. secretary)
Policy Development and Research	Donna E. Shalala, asst. secretary
DEPARTMENT OF TRANSPORTATION	Brock Adams, secretary
	Alan A. Butchman, deputy secretary
United States Coast Guard	Adm. John B. Hayes, USCG, commandant
Federal Aviation Administration	Langhorne M. Bond, administrator
Federal Highway Administration	Karl S. Bowers, administrator
National Highway Traffic Safety	
Administration	Joan B. Claybrook, administrator
Federal Railroad Administration	John M. Sullivan, administrator
Urban Mass Transportation Admin.	Richard S. Page, administrator
St. Lawrence Seaway Development Corp.	David W. Oberlin, administrator
Research and Special Programs	
Administration	James D. Palmer, administrator
DEPARTMENT OF ENERGY	James R. Schlesinger, secretary
	John F. O'Leary, deputy secretary
	Dale D. Myers, undersecretary
Federal Energy Regulatory Commission	Charles B. Curtis, chairman
General Counsel	Lynn R. Coleman, general counsel
Office of the Executive Secretariat	Raymond L. Walters, director

[1] Council comprised of the President of the United States and certain other members.

Senate January 1979

State, name, and party	Term expires
Ala.—Heflin, Howell (D)	1985
Stewart, Donald (D)	1981
Alaska—Stevens, Ted (R)	1985
Gravel, Mike (D)	1981
Ariz.—DeConcini, Dennis (D)	1983
Goldwater, Barry M. (R)	1981
Ark.—Bumpers, Dale (D)	1981
Pryor, David (D)	1985
Calif.—Cranston, Alan (D)	1981
Hayakawa, S. I. (R)	1983
Colo.—Hart, Gary W. (D)	1981
Armstrong, William L. (R)	1985
Conn.—Ribicoff, Abraham (D)	1981
Weicker, Lowell P., Jr. (R)	1983
Del.—Biden, Joseph R., Jr. (D)	1985
Roth, William V., Jr. (R)	1983
Fla.—Stone, Richard (D)	1981
Chiles, Lawton M. (D)	1983
Ga.—Nunn, Sam (D)	1985
Talmadge, Herman E. (D)	1981
Hawaii—Inouye, Daniel K. (D)	1981
Matsunaga, Spark M. (D)	1983
Idaho—Church, Frank (D)	1981
McClure, James A. (R)	1985
Ill.—Percy, Charles H. (R)	1985
Stevenson, Adlai E., III (D)	1981
Ind.—Bayh, Birch (D)	1981
Lugar, Richard G. (R)	1983
Iowa—Jepsen, Roger (R)	1985
Culver, John C. (D)	1981
Kan.—Dole, Robert J. (R)	1981
Kassebaum, Nancy L. (R)	1985
Ky.—Ford, Wendell H. (D)	1981
Huddleston, Walter (D)	1985
La.—Long, Russell B. (D)	1981
Johnston, J. Bennett, Jr. (D)	1985
Maine—Muskie, Edmund S. (D)	1983
Cohen, William S. (R)	1985
Md.—Sarbanes, Paul S. (D)	1983
Mathias, Charles McC., Jr. (R)	1981
Mass.—Tsongas, Paul E. (D)	1985
Kennedy, Edward M. (D)	1983
Mich.—Levin, Carl (D)	1985
Riegle, Donald W., Jr. (D)	1983
Minn.—Durenberger, David (R)	1983
Boschwitz, Rudy (R)	1985
Miss.—Stennis, John C. (D)	1983
Cochran, Thad (R)	1985
Mo.—Danforth, John C. (R)	1983
Eagleton, Thomas F. (D)	1981
Mont.—Baucus, Max (D)	1985
Melcher, John (D)	1983
Neb.—Exon, J. J. (D)	1985
Zorinsky, Edward (D)	1983
Nev.—Laxalt, Paul (R)	1981
Cannon, Howard W. (D)	1983
N.H.—Durkin, John A. (D)	1981
Humphrey, Gordon (R)	1985
N.J.—Bradley, Bill (D)	1985
Williams, Harrison A., Jr. (D)	1983
N.M.—Domenici, Pete V. (R)	1985
Schmitt, Harrison H. (R)	1983
N.Y.—Javits, Jacob K. (R)	1981
Moynihan, Daniel P. (D)	1983
N.C.—Helms, Jesse (R)	1985
Morgan, Robert B. (D)	1981
N.D.—Young, Milton R. (R)	1981
Burdick, Quentin N. (D)	1983
Ohio—Glenn, John H., Jr. (D)	1981
Metzenbaum, Howard M. (D)	1983
Okla.—Bellmon, Henry L. (R)	1981
Boren, David L. (D)	1985
Ore.—Hatfield, Mark O. (R)	1985
Packwood, Robert W. (R)	1981
Pa.—Heinz, H. John, III (R)	1983
Schweiker, Richard S. (R)	1981
R.I.—Pell, Claiborne (D)	1985
Chafee, John H. (R)	1983
S.C.—Thurmond, Strom (R)	1985
Hollings, Ernest F. (D)	1981
S.D.—McGovern, George (D)	1981
Pressler, Larry (R)	1985
Tenn.—Sasser, James R. (D)	1983
Baker, Howard H., Jr. (R)	1985
Texas—Tower, John G. (R)	1985
Bentsen, Lloyd M. (D)	1983
Utah—Garn, Jake (R)	1981
Hatch, Orrin G. (R)	1983
Vt.—Leahy, Patrick J. (D)	1981
Stafford, Robert T. (R)	1983
Va.—Warner, John W. (R)	1985
Byrd, Harry F., Jr. (I)	1983
Wash.—Jackson, Henry M. (D)	1983
Magnuson, Warren G. (D)	1981
W.Va.—Byrd, Robert C. (D)	1983
Randolph, Jennings (D)	1985
Wis.—Nelson, Gaylord (D)	1981
Proxmire, William (D)	1983
Wyo.—Wallop, Malcolm (R)	1983
Simpson, Alan K. (R)	1985

House of Representatives

membership at the opening of the first session of the 96th Congress in January 1979

State, district, name, party

Ala.—1. Edwards, Jack (R)
2. Dickinson, W. L. (R)
3. Nichols, William (D)
4. Bevill, Tom (D)
5. Flippo, Ronnie G. (D)
6. Buchanan, John H., Jr. (R)
7. Shelby, Richard C. (D)
Alaska—Young, Don (R)
Ariz.—1. Rhodes, John J. (R)
2. Udall, Morris K. (D)
3. Stump, Bob (D)
4. Rudd, Eldon D. (R)
Ark.—1. Alexander, Bill (D)
2. Bethune, Ed (R)
3. Hammerschmidt, J. P. (R)
4. Anthony, Beryl F. (D)
Calif.—1. Johnson, Harold T. (D)
2. Clausen, Don H. (R)
3. Matsui, Robert T. (D)
4. Fazio, Vic (D)
5. Burton, John L. (D)
6. Burton, Phillip (D)
7. Miller, George, III (D)
8. Dellums, Ronald V. (D)
9. Stark, Fortney H. (D)
10. Edwards, Don (D)
11. (vacancy)[1]
12. McCloskey, Paul N., Jr. (R)
13. Mineta, Norman Y. (D)
14. Shumway, Norman D. (R)
15. Coelho, Tony (D)
16. Panetta, Leon E. (D)
17. Pashayan, Charles, Jr. (R)
18. Thomas, William (R)
19. Lagomarsino, Robert J. (R)
20. Goldwater, Barry M., Jr. (R)
21. Corman, James C. (D)
22. Moorhead, Carlos J. (R)
23. Beilenson, Anthony C. (D)
24. Waxman, Henry A. (D)
25. Roybal, Edward R. (D)
26. Rousselot, John H. (R)
27. Dornan, Robert K. (R)
28. Dixon, Julian C. (D)
29. Hawkins, Augustus F. (D)
30. Danielson, George E. (D)
31. Wilson, Charles H. (D)
32. Anderson, Glenn M. (D)
33. Grisham, Wayne (R)
34. Lungren, Daniel E. (R)
35. Lloyd, Jim (D)
36. Brown, George E., Jr. (D)
37. Lewis, Jerry (R)
38. Patterson, Jerry M. (D)
39. Dannemeyer, W. E. (R)
40. Badham, Robert E. (R)
41. Wilson, Bob (R)
42. Van Deerlin, Lionel (D)
43. Burgener, Clair W. (R)
Colo.—1. Schroeder, Patricia (D)
2. Wirth, Timothy E. (D)
3. Kogovsek, Ray (D)
4. Johnson, J. P. (R)
5. Kramer, Ken (R)
Conn.—1. Cotter, William R. (D)
2. Dodd, Christopher J. (D)
3. Giaimo, Robert N. (D)
4. McKinney, Stewart B. (R)
5. Ratchford, William R. (D)
6. Moffett, Toby (D)
Del.—Evans, Thomas, Jr. (R)
Fla.—1. Hutto, Earl D. (D)
2. Fuqua, Don (D)
3. Bennett, Charles E. (D)
4. Chappell, William, Jr. (D)
5. Kelly, Richard (R)
6. Young, C. William (R)
7. Gibbons, Sam (D)
8. Ireland, Andrew P. (D)
9. Nelson, Bill (D)
10. Bafalis, L. A. (R)
11. Mica, Dan (D)
12. Stack, Edward J. (D)
13. Lehman, William (D)
14. Pepper, Claude (D)
15. Fascell, Dante B. (D)
Ga.—1. Ginn, R. B. (D)
2. Mathis, Dawson (D)
3. Brinkley, Jack (D)
4. Levitas, Elliott H. (D)
5. Fowler, Wyche, Jr. (D)
6. Gingrich, Newt (R)
7. McDonald, Lawrence P. (D)
8. Evans, Billy Lee (D)
9. Jenkins, Edgar L. (D)
10. Barnard, Doug (D)
Hawaii—1. Heftel, Cecil (D)
2. Akaka, Daniel (D)
Idaho—1. Symms, S. D. (R)
2. Hansen, George V. (R)

Srate, district, name, party

Ill.—1. Stewart, Bennett (D)
2. Murphy, Morgan (D)
3. Russo, Martin A. (D)
4. Derwinski, Edward J. (R)
5. Fary, John G. (D)
6. Hyde, Henry J. (R)
7. Collins, Cardiss (D)
8. Rostenkowski, Dan (D)
9. Yates, Sidney R. (D)
10. Mikva, Abner J. (D)
11. Annunzio, Frank (D)
12. Crane, Philip M. (R)
13. McClory, Robert (R)
14. Erlenborn, J. N. (R)
15. Corcoran, Tom (R)
16. Anderson, John B. (R)
17. O'Brien, G. M. (R)
18. Michel, Robert H. (R)
19. Railsback, Thomas F. (R)
20. Findley, Paul (R)
21. Madigan, E. R. (R)
22. Crane, Daniel B. (R)
23. Price, Melvin (D)
24. Simon, Paul (D)
Ind.—1. Benjamin, Adam (D)
2. Fithian, Floyd J. (D)
3. Brademas, John (D)
4. Quayle, J. Danforth (R)
5. Hillis, Elwood H. (R)
6. Evans, David W. (D)
7. Myers, John (R)
8. Deckard, H. Joel (R)
9. Hamilton, L. H. (D)
10. Sharp, Philip R. (D)
11. Jacobs, Andrew, Jr. (D)
Iowa—1. Leach, James (R)
2. Tauke, Tom (R)
3. Grassley, Charles E. (R)
4. Smith, Neal (D)
5. Harkin, Tom (D)
6. Bedell, Berkley (D)
Kan.—1. Sebelius, Keith G. (R)
2. Jeffries, Jim (R)
3. Winn, Larry, Jr. (R)
4. Glickman, Dan (D)
5. Whittaker, Robert (R)
Ky.—1. Hubbard, Carroll, Jr. (D)
2. Natcher, William H. (D)
3. Mazzoli, Romano L. (D)
4. Snyder, Gene (R)
5. Carter, Tim L. (R)
6. Hopkins, Larry J. (R)
7. Perkins, Carl D. (D)
La.—1. Livingston, Bob (R)
2. Boggs, Lindy (D)
3. Treen, David C. (R)
4. Leach, Claude (D)
5. Huckaby, Jerry (D)
6. Moore, W. Henson, III (R)
7. Breaux, John B. (D)
8. Long, Gillis W. (D)
Maine—1. Emery, David F. (R)
2. Snowe, Olympia J. (R)
Md.—1. Bauman, Robert E. (R)
2. Long, Clarence D. (D)
3. Mikulski, Barbara A. (D)
4. Holt, Marjorie S. (R)
5. Spellman, Gladys N. (D)
6. Byron, Beverly (D)
7. Mitchell, Parren J. (D)
8. Barnes, Michael D. (D)
Mass.—1. Conte, Silvio O. (R)
2. Boland, Edward P. (D)
3. Early, Joseph D. (D)
4. Drinan, Robert F. (D)
5. Shannon, James M. (D)
6. Mavroules, Nicholas (D)
7. Markey, Edward J. (D)
8. O'Neill, Thomas P., Jr. (D)
9. Moakley, John J. (D)
10. Heckler, Margaret (R)
11. Donnelly, Brian J. (D)
12. Studds, Gerry E. (D)
Mich.—1. Conyers, John, Jr. (D)
2. Pursell, Carl D. (R)
3. Wolpe, Howard (D)
4. Stockman, David A. (R)
5. Sawyer, Harold S. (R)
6. Carr, Bob (D)
7. Kildee, Dale E. (D)
8. Traxler, Bob (D)
9. Vander Jagt, Guy (R)
10. Albosta, Donald J. (D)
11. Davis, Robert W. (R)
12. Bonior, David E. (D)
13. Diggs, Charles C., Jr. (D)
14. Nedzi, Lucien N. (D)
15. Ford, W. D. (D)
16. Dingell, John D. (D)
17. Brodhead, William M. (D)
18. Blanchard, James J. (D)
19. Broomfield, William S. (R)
Minn.—1. Erdahl, Arlen (R)
2. Hagedorn, Tom (R)
3. Frenzel, William (R)
4. Vento, Bruce F. (D)
5. Sabo, Martin Olav (D)
6. Nolan, Richard (D)
7. Stangeland, Arlan (R)
8. Oberstar, James L. (D)
Miss.—1. Whitten, Jamie L. (D)
2. Bowen, D. R. (D)

State, district, name, party

3. Montgomery, G. V. (D)
4. Hinson, Jon C. (R)
5. Lott, Trent (R)
Mo.—1. Clay, William (D)
2. Young, Robert A. (D)
3. Gephardt, Richard A. (D)
4. Skelton, Ike (D)
5. Bolling, Richard (D)
6. Coleman, E. Thomas (R)
7. Taylor, Gene (R)
8. Ichord, Richard H. (D)
9. Volkmer, Harold L. (D)
10. Burlison, Bill D. (D)
Mont.—1. Williams, Pat (D)
2. Marlenee, Ron (R)
Neb.—1. Bereuter, D. K. (R)
2. Cavanaugh, John J. (D)
3. Smith, Virginia (R)
Nev.—Santini, James (D)
N.H.—1. D'Amours, Norman (D)
2. Cleveland, James C. (R)
N.J.—1. Florio, James J. (D)
2. Hughes, William J. (D)
3. Howard, J. J. (D)
4. Thompson, Frank, Jr. (D)
5. Fenwick, Millicent (R)
6. Forsythe, Edwin B. (R)
7. Maguire, Andrew (D)
8. Roe, Robert A. (D)
9. Hollenbeck, Harold C. (R)
10. Rodino, Peter W., Jr. (D)
11. Minish, Joseph G. (D)
12. Rinaldo, M. J. (R)
13. Courter, James A. (R)
14. Guarini, Frank J. (D)
15. Patten, Edward J. (D)
N.M.—1. Lujan, Manuel, Jr. (R)
2. Runnels, Harold L. (D)
N.Y.—1. Carney, William (R)
2. Downey, Thomas J. (D)
3. Ambro, Jerome A., Jr. (D)
4. Lent, Norman F. (R)
5. Wydler, John W. (R)
6. Wolff, L. L. (D)
7. Addabbo, Joseph P. (D)
8. Rosenthal, Benjamin S. (D)
9. Ferraro, Geraldine (D)
10. Biaggi, Mario (D)
11. Scheuer, James H. (D)
12. Chisholm, Shirley (D)
13. Solarz, Stephen J. (D)
14. Richmond, Frederick W. (D)
15. Zeferetti, Leo C. (D)
16. Holtzman, Elizabeth (D)
17. Murphy, John M. (D)
18. Green, S. William (R)
19. Rangel, Charles B. (D)
20. Weiss, Theodore S. (D)
21. Garcia, Robert (D)
22. Bingham, J. B. (D)
23. Peyser, Peter A. (D)
24. Ottinger, Richard L. (D)
25. Fish, Hamilton, Jr. (R)
26. Gilman, B. A. (R)
27. McHugh, Matthew F. (D)
28. Stratton, Samuel S. (D)
29. Solomon, Gerald (R)
30. McEwen, Robert (R)
31. Mitchell, D. J. (R)
32. Hanley, James M. (D)
33. Lee, Gary A. (R)
34. Horton, Frank J. (R)
35. Conable, B., Jr. (R)
36. LaFalce, John J. (D)
37. Nowak, Henry J. (D)
38. Kemp, Jack F. (R)
39. Lundine, Stanley N. (D)
N.C.—1. Jones, Walter B. (D)
2. Fountain, L. H. (D)
3. Whitley, Charles (D)
4. Andrews, Ike F. (D)
5. Neal, Stephen L. (D)
6. Preyer, L. R. (D)
7. Rose, C. G., III (D)
8. Hefner, Bill (D)
9. Martin, J. G. (R)
10. Broyhill, James T. (R)
11. Gudger, Lamar (D)
N.D.—Andrews, Mark (R)
Ohio—1. Gradison, Willis D. (R)
2. Luken, Thomas A. (D)
3. Hall, Tony P. (D)
4. Guyer, Tennyson (R)
5. Latta, Delbert L. (R)
6. Harsha, William H. (R)
7. Brown, Clarence J. (R)
8. Kindness, Thomas N. (R)
9. Ashley, Thomas L. (D)
10. Miller, Clarence E. (R)
11. Stanton, J. William (R)
12. Devine, Samuel L. (R)
13. Pease, Donald J. (D)
14. Seiberling, John F., Jr. (D)
15. Wylie, Chalmers P. (R)
16. Regula, R. S. (R)
17. Ashbrook, John M. (R)
18. Applegate, Douglas (D)
19. Williams, Lyle (R)
20. Oakar, Mary Rose (D)
21. Stokes, Louis (D)
22. Vanik, Charles A. (D)
23. Mottl, Ronald M. (D)

State, district, name, party

Okla.—1. Jones, James R. (D)
2. Synar, Mike (D)
3. Watkins, Wes (D)
4. Steed, Tom (D)
5. Edwards, Mickey (R)
6. English, Glenn (D)
Ore.—1. AuCoin, Les (D)
2. Ullman, Al (D)
3. Duncan, Robert (D)
4. Weaver, James (D)
Pa.—1. Myers, Michael (D)
2. Gray, William H., III (D)
3. Lederer, Raymond F. (D)
4. Dougherty, C. F. (R)
5. Schulze, Richard T. (R)
6. Yatron, Gus (D)
7. Edgar, Robert W. (D)
8. Kostmayer, Peter H. (D)
9. Shuster, E. G. (R)
10. McDade, Joseph M. (R)
11. Flood, Daniel J. (D)
12. Murtha, John P. (D)
13. Coughlin, R. L. (R)
14. Moorhead, William S. (D)
15. Ritter, Donald L. (R)
16. Walker, Robert S. (R)
17. Ertel, Allen E. (D)
18. Walgren, Doug (D)
19. Goodling, William F. (R)
20. Gaydos, Joseph (D)
21. Bailey, Don (D)
22. Murphy, Austin J. (D)
23. Clinger, William F., Jr. (R)
24. Marks, Marc L. (R)
25. Atkinson, Eugene V. (D)
R.I.—1. St. Germain, Fernand (D)
2. Beard, Edward P. (D)
S.C.—1. Davis, Mendel (D)
2. Spence, Floyd D. (R)
3. Derrick, Butler C., Jr. (D)
4. Campbell, Carroll A., Jr. (R)
5. Holland, Kenneth L. (D)
6. Jenrette, John W., Jr. (D)
S.D.—1. Daschle, Thomas A. (D)
2. Abdnor, James (R)
Tenn.—1. Quillen, James H. (R)
2. Duncan, John J. (R)
3. Lloyd Bouquards, Marilyn (D)
4. Gore, Albert, Jr. (D)
5. Boner, Bill (D)
6. Beard, Robin L., Jr. (R)
7. Jones, Edward (D)
8. Ford, Harold E. (D)
Texas—1. Hall, Sam B. (D)
2. Wilson, Charles (D)
3. Collins, James M. (R)
4. Roberts, Ray (D)
5. Mattox, Jim (D)
6. Gramm, Phil (D)
7. Archer, William R. (R)
8. Eckhardt, Robert C. (D)
9. Brooks, Jack (D)
10. Pickle, J. J. (D)
11. Leath, J. Marvin (D)
12. Wright, James C., Jr. (D)
13. Hightower, Jack (D)
14. Wyatt, Joe (D)
15. de la Garza, E. (D)
16. White, Richard C. (D)
17. Stenholm, Charles W. (D)
18. Leland, Mickey (D)
19. Hance, Kent (D)
20. Gonzalez, Henry B. (D)
21. Loeffler, Tom (R)
22. Paul, Ron (R)
23. Kazen, Abraham, Jr. (D)
24. Frost, Martin (D)
Utah—1. McKay, K. Gunn (D)
2. Marriott, Dan (R)
Vt.—Jeffords, James M. (R)
Va.—1. Trible, Paul S. (R)
2. Whitehurst, G. W. (R)
3. Satterfield, D. E., III (D)
4. Daniel, R. W. (R)
5. Daniel, W. C. (D)
6. Butler, M. C. (R)
7. Robinson, J. Kenneth (R)
8. Harris, Herbert E. (D)
9. Wampler, William C. (R)
10. Fisher, Joseph L. (D)
Wash.—1. Pritchard, Joel (R)
2. Swift, Al (D)
3. Bonker, Don (D)
4. McCormack, Mike (D)
5. Foley, Thomas S. (D)
6. Dicks, Norman D. (D)
7. Lowry, Mike (D)
W.Va.—1. Mollohan, R. H. (D)
2. Staggers, Harley O. (D)
3. Slack, John M., Jr. (D)
4. Rahall, Nick Joe (D)
Wis.—1. Aspin, Leslie (D)
2. Kastenmeier, Robert W. (D)
3. Baldus, Alvin J. (D)
4. Zablocki, Clement J. (D)
5. Reuss, Henry S. (D)
6. (vacancy)[2]
7. Obey, David R. (D)
8. Roth, Tobias A. (R)
9. Sensenbrenner, F. J. (R)
Wyo.—Cheney, Richard (R)

Supreme Court

Chief Justice Warren Earl Burger (appointed 1969)

Associate Justices (year appointed)

William J. Brennan, Jr.	(1956)	Harry A. Blackmun	(1970)
Potter Stewart	(1958)	Lewis F. Powell, Jr.	(1972)
Byron R. White	(1962)	William H. Rehnquist	(1972)
Thurgood Marshall	(1967)	John Paul Stevens	(1975)

[1] Rep. Leo J. Ryan died Nov. 18, 1978. [2] Rep. William A. Steiger died Dec. 4, 1978.

The Federal Administrative Budget

in millions of dollars; fiscal years ending Sept. 30

Source and function	1977	1978 estimate	1979 estimate
BUDGET RECEIPTS	$356,900	$400,400	$439,600
Individual income taxes	156,700	178,800	190,100
Corporation income taxes	54,900	58,900	62,500
Excise taxes	17,500	20,200	25,500
Social insurance taxes and contributions	108,700	124,100	141,900
Estate and gift taxes	7,300	5,600	6,100
Customs duties	5,200	5,800	6,400
Miscellaneous receipts	6,500	6,900	7,200
BUDGET EXPENDITURES	401,900	462,200	500,200
National defense	97,500	107,600	117,800
Department of Defense military functions	95,600	105,300	115,200
Atomic energy defense activities	1,900	2,300	2,500
Defense-related activities	−100	[1]	[1]
International affairs	4,800	6,700	7,700
Conduct of foreign affairs	1,000	1,100	1,200
Foreign economic and financial assistance	4,200	5,300	5,400
Foreign information and exchange activities	400	400	500
International financial programs	−800	−[1]	700
Military assistance	500	500	500
General science, space, and technology	4,700	4,800	5,100
Agriculture	5,500	9,100	5,400
Farm income stabilization	4,500	7,900	4,200
Agricultural research and services	1,100	1,200	1,300
Natural resources and environment	10,000	12,100	12,200
Water resources	3,200	3,700	3,400
Conservation and land management	1,300	2,100	1,600
Recreational resources	1,000	1,300	1,500
Pollution control and abatement	4,300	4,900	5,600
Other natural resources	1,000	1,200	1,300
Energy	4,200	7,800	9,600
Energy supply	3,300	4,200	4,100
Energy conservation	100	600	1,400
Commerce and housing credit	[1]	3,500	3,000
Mortgage credit and thrift insurance	−3,300	500	−300
Payment to the Postal Service	2,300	1,800	1,800
Other advancement and regulation	1,100	1,300	1,400
Transportation	14,600	16,300	17,400
Air transportation	2,800	3,300	3,400
Water transportation	1,700	1,900	2,000
Ground transportation	10,000	11,100	12,000
Other transportation	100	100	100
Community and regional development	6,300	9,700	8,700
Community development	3,500	4,000	4,000
Area and regional development	$2,100	$4,000	$4,000
Disaster relief and insurance	600	1,700	1,000
Education, training, employment, and social services	21,000	27,500	30,400
Elementary, secondary, and vocational education	5,100	5,700	6,500
Higher education	3,100	3,800	4,300
Research and general education aids	900	1,200	1,200
Training and employment	6,900	10,900	12,800
Social Services	4,600	5,500	5,100
Health	38,800	44,300	49,700
Health care services	34,500	39,900	45,100
Health research and education	3,500	3,500	3,700
Consumer and occupational health and safety	700	800	900
Income security	137,000	147,600	160,000
General retirement and disability insurance	88,600	98,200	108,400
Federal employee retirement and disability	9,500	10,800	12,000
Unemployment compensation	15,300	12,400	11,800
Public assistance and other income supplements	23,600	26,300	27,800
Veterans benefits and services	18,000	18,900	19,300
Income security for veterans	9,200	9,700	10,300
Veterans education, training, and rehabilitation	3,700	3,100	2,600
Hospital and medical care for veterans	4,700	5,400	5,800
Other veterans benefits and services	500	600	700
Administration of justice	3,600	4,000	4,200
Federal law enforcement activities	1,700	1,900	2,000
Federal litigative and judicial activities	800	1,000	1,100
Federal correctional activities	200	300	400
Criminal justice assistance	800	800	700
General government	3,400	4,100	4,300
Legislative functions	800	900	900
Central fiscal operations	1,900	2,200	2,400
General property and records management	100	400	400
Other general government	500	600	600
General purpose fiscal assistance	9,500	9,900	9,600
Interest	38,100	43,800	49,000
Allowances for contingencies, civilian agency pay raises	—	—	2,800
Undistributed offsetting receipts	−15,100	−15,600	−16,000
Employer share, employee retirement	−4,500	−5,000	−5,200
Interest received by trust funds	−8,100	−8,600	−9,100
Rents and royalties on the Outer Continental Shelf	−2,400	−2,000	−1,800

[1] Less than $50,000,000. Source: Executive Office of the President, Office of Management and Budget, *The United States Budget in Brief: Fiscal Year 1979.*

State Government Revenue, Expenditure, and Debt

1977 in thousands of dollars

State	GENERAL REVENUE: Total	State taxes: Total	State taxes: General sales	State taxes: Individual income	Intergov-ernmental	Charges & misc.	GENERAL EXPENDITURE: Total	Education	Highways	Public welfare	Hospi-tals	DEBT: Total	Issued 1977[1]	Retired 1977[1]
Ala.	2,649,994	1,403,674	454,754	261,895	897,438	348,882	2,966,281	1,231,256	373,199	367,027	170,287	997,145	73,193	55,050
Alaska	1,220,263	773,474	—	210,338	274,065	172,724	1,147,589	344,075	161,561	56,382	13,662	916,584	146,141	26,617
Ariz.	1,734,733	1,160,068	502,911	190,591	370,650	204,015	1,865,661	851,805	240,763	112,138	70,206	103,206	13,700	2,346
Ark.	1,395,087	802,913	274,295	163,781	465,629	126,545	1,521,155	565,521	248,329	236,524	67,609	140,494	7,373	5,906
Calif.	20,737,318	12,589,124	4,314,027	3,620,933	6,394,124	1,754,070	22,439,586	6,975,305	1,077,130	5,450,070	574,667	6,742,567	556,250	316,620
Colo.	2,001,520	1,077,285	359,570	338,920	612,671	311,564	2,151,503	971,570	247,584	292,718	104,149	197,266	53,364	9,909
Conn.	2,327,037	1,457,139	583,478	59,333	544,265	325,633	2,656,060	649,931	171,460	419,592	152,985	3,173,424	375,460	204,102
Del.	638,263	390,882	—	168,000	138,040	109,341	696,692	268,246	57,470	73,959	26,573	742,708	84,654	65,259
Fla.	4,851,120	3,274,802	1,398,590	—	1,153,534	422,784	5,391,507	2,205,579	584,523	442,093	223,368	2,003,353	320,965	57,446
Ga.	3,180,603	1,906,506	687,415	495,639	987,802	286,295	3,440,030	1,360,676	353,033	516,951	179,329	1,268,456	47,885	69,200
Hawaii	1,228,873	685,703	341,017	203,018	351,205	191,965	1,502,093	477,559	93,769	193,002	74,786	1,486,277	176,410	56,789
Idaho	659,704	367,823	103,860	112,470	226,611	65,270	772,627	268,872	134,969	75,275	13,664	52,256	12,705	1,276
Ill.	8,166,462	5,319,547	1,842,319	1,413,368	2,132,120	714,795	9,939,241	3,104,160	1,132,536	2,112,789	466,009	4,053,846	892,600	150,266
Ind.	3,437,094	2,162,900	1,045,571	479,259	770,161	504,033	3,456,564	1,406,796	442,652	390,706	164,598	587,394	28,840	22,734
Iowa	2,154,486	1,292,507	346,785	447,409	595,833	266,146	2,552,312	1,003,837	406,840	330,185	137,934	123,951	2,930	4,849
Kan.	1,604,009	969,005	326,708	209,171	435,569	199,435	1,718,799	676,251	236,322	292,006	114,765	402,809	93,600	22,804
Ky.	2,650,503	1,560,385	463,841	338,160	773,344	316,774	2,848,694	1,019,853	416,641	462,417	74,820	2,040,599	164,530	120,489
La.	3,216,145	1,718,665	481,677	133,614	980,516	516,964	3,646,738	1,199,560	530,779	438,553	249,888	1,769,239	381,245	68,392
Maine	862,847	468,462	169,665	75,157	282,023	112,362	981,474	292,498	111,554	171,482	25,238	564,071	60,935	33,383
Md.	3,491,869	2,127,712	465,840	806,740	829,424	534,733	3,918,843	1,261,732	401,761	570,286	218,266	3,051,080	543,165	148,064
Mass.	4,968,600	2,934,261	441,878	1,191,531	1,491,274	543,065	5,520,145	1,349,860	350,066	1,456,925	238,082	5,167,658	621,798	275,929
Mich.	7,891,575	4,843,716	1,406,985	1,465,467	2,128,063	919,796	9,070,835	2,885,497	739,828	1,989,567	348,558	1,950,959	216,741	98,977
Minn.	3,867,665	2,485,565	466,658	956,933	951,633	430,467	4,157,681	1,747,894	382,703	621,991	169,186	1,236,667	355,350	115,911
Miss.	1,759,384	969,251	475,465	131,598	590,715	199,418	1,922,027	747,739	285,188	229,327	76,251	812,088	76,704	33,343
Mo.	2,632,790	1,598,094	596,434	389,594	792,632	242,064	2,790,077	1,026,457	397,613	438,851	164,972	440,415	156,739	62,745
Mont.	669,969	312,399	—	111,862	271,008	86,562	783,421	248,310	161,395	69,768	27,484	101,392	21,470	5,020
Neb.	1,044,090	612,918	198,736	170,595	295,568	135,604	1,042,162	331,119	195,279	132,630	65,146	59,297	885	5,639
Nev.	527,434	329,069	115,744	—	148,843	49,522	632,780	205,149	86,839	47,227	10,816	54,603	5,000	3,560
N.H.	461,530	200,231	—	7,066	168,813	92,486	677,139	152,514	110,284	81,033	43,839	363,177	97,360	19,305
N.J.	5,370,256	3,103,725	913,100	709,653	1,505,267	761,264	6,827,632	1,854,559	301,204	1,142,687	295,341	4,051,767	344,516	111,104
N.M.	1,215,326	597,604	257,239	26,639	337,725	279,997	1,137,043	525,000	125,531	106,846	51,927	212,068	39,220	14,070
N.Y.	18,805,597	10,743,249	2,218,162	4,526,975	5,877,917	2,184,431	21,252,546	5,525,006	689,445	4,430,883	1,104,205	20,012,019	2,732,524	833,591
N.C.	4,026,279	2,384,780	511,501	782,092	1,231,466	410,033	4,357,782	1,908,358	453,332	447,717	280,904	807,475	150,849	43,767
N.D.	677,857	296,330	110,224	55,037	226,177	155,350	678,657	233,411	111,088	64,588	22,800	67,326	—	2,760
Ohio	6,061,522	3,570,771	1,135,466	614,879	1,702,109	788,642	8,168,648	2,548,122	788,533	1,093,536	344,745	3,205,246	283,848	137,216
Okla.	2,110,124	1,139,000	205,092	216,833	606,314	364,810	2,138,132	857,453	265,640	360,597	110,107	937,252	8,690	24,885
Ore.	1,965,340	973,145	—	561,895	625,042	367,153	2,272,393	686,897	236,975	342,602	97,101	2,431,243	483,065	53,402
Pa.	8,588,406	5,590,840	1,524,515	1,178,071	2,311,999	685,567	11,207,936	3,085,146	946,529	2,297,639	590,875	6,383,946	649,935	194,192
R.I.	850,549	438,841	141,770	103,784	262,524	149,184	972,252	251,894	37,597	215,870	63,402	640,327	186,075	56,340
S.C.	2,135,404	1,187,589	415,277	290,393	633,949	313,866	2,334,336	890,839	181,763	236,880	130,311	1,311,389	305,685	61,760
S.D.	492,966	200,115	101,023	—	190,802	102,049	528,910	154,994	94,947	67,692	39,790	231,533	90,730	2,485
Tenn.	2,625,899	1,529,531	733,641	22,385	833,681	262,687	2,854,020	1,055,959	444,901	413,964	131,415	1,203,163	264,205	48,428
Texas	8,090,170	4,750,065	1,695,848	—	2,082,534	1,257,571	7,829,437	3,820,465	700,921	1,173,648	585,831	2,124,976	127,962	84,438
Utah	1,040,213	531,276	226,949	158,268	352,032	156,905	1,177,333	547,872	129,616	117,010	44,451	145,536	—	6,756
Vt.	485,906	229,803	32,497	70,334	183,611	72,492	535,769	149,266	59,998	84,159	15,019	454,547	64,577	26,305
Va.	3,576,392	2,053,823	426,848	714,086	964,624	557,945	3,926,729	1,385,452	651,649	495,607	255,010	872,519	148,590	43,808
Wash.	3,449,022	2,100,035	1,172,572	—	956,337	392,650	4,092,803	1,562,472	375,671	529,850	100,778	1,411,775	241,894	57,450
W.Va.	1,552,183	903,413	447,435	164,671	503,813	144,957	1,832,035	589,724	341,657	187,034	59,044	1,334,820	241,455	74,541
Wis.	4,227,293	2,733,294	667,939	1,144,073	1,048,769	445,230	4,455,535	1,437,968	323,523	873,401	140,302	1,684,708	424,725	74,865
Wyo.	488,464	233,336	94,580	—	185,301	69,827	448,313	136,535	103,797	25,706	12,085	73,279	—	2,056
TOTAL	169,866,135	101,084,645	30,895,901	25,492,510	48,675,566	20,105,924	191,237,957	64,037,013	17,496,387	32,779,390	8,742,580	90,199,895	12,376,537	4,016,149

Fiscal year ending June 30, 1977, except Alabama, September 30; New York, March 31; and Texas, August 31. [1] Long term only.
Source: U.S. Department of Commerce, Bureau of the Census, *State Government Finances in 1977.*

EDUCATION

Public Elementary and Secondary Schools

Fall 1977 estimates

State	ENROLLMENT		INSTRUCTIONAL STAFF				TEACHERS' AVERAGE ANNUAL SALARIES		STUDENT-TEACHER RATIO		Expenditure per pupil
	Elementary	Secondary	Total [1]	Principals and supervisors	Teachers, elementary	Teachers, secondary	Elementary	Secondary	Elementary	Secondary	
Alabama	379,321	382,559	39,002	2,000	17,976	19,026	$11,761	$11,995	21.3	20.1	$1,259
Alaska	51,325	39,019	5,690	379	2,564	2,351	22,475	22,614	20.0	16.6	3,123
Arizona	393,985	158,657	27,285	1,054	16,932	7,257	13,406	14,896	23.3	21.9	1,374
Arkansas	240,447	218,331	25,023	1,286	10,909	11,554	9,814	10,221	22.0	18.9	1,201
California	2,451,854	1,703,831	201,090	9,840	109,100	72,550	16,240	18,800	22.5	23.5	1,649
Colorado	306,000	262,000	34,580	1,550	15,475	14,475	13,825	14,201	19.8	18.1	1,613
Connecticut	416,769	200,156	40,541	2,113	21,450	14,850	14,340	14,726	19.4	13.5	1,907
Delaware	57,967	60,033	6,884	372	2,489	3,537	13,497	14,016	23.3	17.0	1,970
District of Columbia	66,323	54,349	7,015	473	3,587	2,435	...	...	18.5	22.3	2,173
Florida	776,714	758,856	87,322	3,945	38,066	36,417	11,064	11,430	20.4	20.8	1,450
Georgia	672,681	427,056	55,808	2,340	33,105	20,363	12,000	12,461	20.3	21.0	1,213
Hawaii	90,977	81,372	9,346	619	4,370	3,511	18,188	17,143	20.8	23.2	1,447
Idaho	105,591	95,842	10,692	575	4,908	4,653	11,517	11,947	21.5	20.6	...
Illinois	1,451,745	718,795	121,238	6,766	54,919	52,394	14,659	16,151	26.4	13.7	1,910
Indiana	585,665	558,375	59,772	3,599	26,243	27,125	13,227	13,941	22.3	20.6	1,331
Iowa	306,345	282,415	39,044	1,380	15,859	17,473	12,899	13,837	19.3	16.2	1,899
Kansas	266,232	179,893	29,381	1,526	13,839	11,935	11,382	13,061	19.2	15.1	1,613
Kentucky	438,047	256,132	36,550	1,950	20,475	12,025	11,435	12,305	21.4	21.3	1,207
Louisiana	443,000	396,000	45,621	2,190	23,322	18,086	13,712	14,203	19.0	21.9	1,556
Maine	169,865	75,975	13,608	1,192	7,380	4,936	11,247	12,313	23.0	15.4	1,366
Maryland	421,044	415,788	49,337	3,397	20,720	22,508	15,511	16,080	20.3	18.5	1,649
Massachusetts	583,070	581,700	74,900	4,700	30,700	34,500	15,000	15,300	19.0	16.9	1,974
Michigan	1,029,052	998,597	100,591	6,902	45,532	41,202	18,710	17,128	22.6	24.2	...
Minnesota	410,672	435,380	50,020	2,128	20,125	24,462	14,258	15,384	20.4	17.8	1,859
Mississippi	280,142	225,893	27,842	1,590	13,835	11,012	10,285	10,770	20.2	20.5	1,159
Missouri	614,938	316,294	55,634	3,257	24,428	23,893	11,911	12,365	25.2	13.2	...
Montana	108,447	58,395	10,695	635	5,516	3,984	12,082	13,211	19.7	14.6	1,804
Nebraska	159,126	145,205	20,319	999	9,407	8,437	11,230	12,328	16.9	17.2	1,450
Nevada	73,069	69,589	6,965	405	3,045	3,005	14,064	14,233	24.0	23.2	1,445
New Hampshire	104,632	69,986	10,339	580	4,780	4,374	10,966	11,700	21.9	16.0	1,355
New Jersey	864,717	514,821	90,300	5,600	47,500	29,000	15,197	15,758	18.2	17.8	2,115
New Mexico	142,689	139,027	16,355	1,810	6,875	6,900	12,585	13,025	20.8	20.1	1,403
New York	1,597,667	1,630,881	187,100	13,010	77,180	87,090	17,800	18,200	26.7	18.7	2,282
North Carolina	823,061	368,714	61,650	3,731	37,302	17,862	12,574	13,652	22.1	20.6	1,251
North Dakota	58,105	66,980	8,191	335	4,416	3,068	11,121	11,620	13.2	21.8	1,483
Ohio	1,290,125	885,465	122,000	7,000	54,000	51,300	12,990	13,885	23.9	17.3	1,469
Oklahoma	319,200	278,700	34,100	1,820	15,600	15,300	11,180	11,660	20.5	18.2	1,361
Oregon	275,930	202,100	28,110	2,290	13,125	10,665	13,650	14,245	21.0	18.9	1,809
Pennsylvania	1,053,300	1,076,800	126,500	5,400	54,800	57,600	14,150	14,550	19.2	18.7	1,928
Rhode Island	83,833	84,135	10,476	546	4,994	4,127	14,026	15,223	16.8	20.4	1,741
South Carolina	382,449	243,534	33,608	2,270	17,509	11,819	11,003	11,750	21.8	20.6	1,267
South Dakota	93,888	49,643	9,412	500	5,343	2,954	10,800	11,016	17.6	16.8	1,322
Tennessee	538,648	339,776	46,105	2,310	24,605	15,751	11,680	12,353	21.9	21.6	1,263
Texas	1,518,000	1,342,000	168,900	8,500	79,370	72,130	12,600	13,050	26.1	22.6	1,257
Utah	173,386	143,789	14,615	849	6,643	6,351	12,822	13,275	26.1	22.6	1,279
Vermont	61,557	41,377	7,510	890	3,276	2,894	10,867	11,649	18.8	14.3	1,488
Virginia	662,072	420,112	63,130	4,370	33,767	24,993	12,350	13,450	19.6	16.8	1,492
Washington	395,237	381,226	39,556	2,840	17,902	15,789	15,750	16,679	22.1	24.1	1,734
West Virginia	234,174	166,861	23,520	1,619	11,214	9,558	11,807	12,325	20.9	17.5	...
Wisconsin	501,498	416,365	57,500	2,100	30,000	25,400	13,500	14,100	16.7	16.4	1,909
Wyoming	48,470	40,530	6,055	400	2,700	2,725	12,955	13,605	18.0	14.9	1,770
TOTAL U.S.	24,573,051	19,059,309	2,456,827	137,932	1,169,177	1,007,606	$13,902	$14,680	21.0	18.9	$1,634

Kindergartens included in elementary schools; junior high schools, in secondary schools.
[1] Includes librarians, guidance and psychological personnel, and related educational workers.
Source: National Education Association, Research Division, *Estimates of School Statistics, 1977–78* (Copyright 1978. All rights reserved. Used by permission).

Universities and Colleges

state statistics

State	NUMBER OF INSTITUTIONS 1977–1978		Enrollment [1,2] fall, 1977	EARNED DEGREES CONFERRED 1975–1976			State	NUMBER OF INSTITUTIONS 1977–1978		Enrollment [1,2] fall, 1977	EARNED DEGREES CONFERRED 1975–1976		
	Total	Public		Bachelor's and first professional	Master's except first professional	Doctor's		Total	Public		Bachelor's and first professional	Master's except first professional	Doctor's
Alabama	57	36	160,377	15,519	6,116	226	Montana	12	9	30,730	3,907	680	70
Alaska	16	13	29,312	475	211	8	Nebraska	30	16	81,329	8,492	1,552	178
Arizona	23	17	181,440	9,519	4,278	387	Nevada	6	5	31,412	1,490	469	24
Arkansas	32	19	71,071	7,270	1,670	120	New Hampshire	24	10	39,319	5,377	797	67
California	257	135	1,790,808	91,161	30,798	3,799	New Jersey	65	31	300,890	27,029	8,108	691
Colorado	41	27	153,896	14,876	5,186	726	New Mexico	19	16	54,310	5,211	1,594	167
Connecticut	46	22	149,268	14,270	6,403	579	New York	291	83	944,832	90,891	40,001	3,626
Delaware	10	6	30,894	2,808	459	68	North Carolina	120	73	255,956	24,672	4,957	734
District of Columbia	19	3	83,871	9,246	5,046	524	North Dakota	15	11	32,241	3,684	453	66
Florida	74	37	364,204	28,920	8,227	1,411	Ohio	132	62	452,811	46,136	12,281	1,665
Georgia	67	34	173,819	18,052	8,168	568	Oklahoma	44	29	149,994	14,033	4,082	416
Hawaii	11	8	47,038	3,653	1,131	116	Oregon	43	21	141,554	11,350	3,068	409
Idaho	9	6	40,250	2,946	615	70	Pennsylvania	179	61	475,366	58,034	14,327	1,809
Illinois	154	63	658,655	48,872	17,735	2,025	Rhode Island	13	3	63,721	6,555	1,737	194
Indiana	64	24	221,970	25,387	9,697	1,208	South Carolina	56	31	123,779	11,670	3,737	207
Iowa	61	22	126,094	14,973	2,411	568	South Dakota	17	7	30,982	3,781	720	45
Kansas	52	29	127,671	12,273	3,272	385	Tennessee	70	24	188,661	19,168	5,280	585
Kentucky	39	9	131,667	12,990	4,877	259	Texas	148	95	647,840	54,937	15,549	1,502
Louisiana	31	20	153,988	17,182	4,339	332	Utah	14	9	88,584	9,087	2,260	407
Maine	25	10	40,125	4,804	695	41	Vermont	24	6	29,413	4,281	1,246	39
Maryland	54	32	218,012	17,024	5,404	612	Virginia	71	39	255,969	21,223	5,284	534
Massachusetts	119	33	376,821	40,784	14,079	2,018	Washington	49	33	259,480	17,854	3,824	512
Michigan	95	45	481,436	39,380	16,005	1,498	West Virginia	28	17	80,968	8,071	2,219	121
Minnesota	65	30	188,871	19,563	2,941	497	Wisconsin	59	30	241,164	22,022	5,712	899
Mississippi	46	27	98,397	9,452	3,299	280	Wyoming	8	8	19,706	1,343	388	57
Missouri	82	28	221,152	23,557	7,534	686							
							TOTAL U.S.	3,086	1,464	11,342,118	985,254	310,921	34,035

Excludes service academies. [1] Excludes non–degree-credit students. [2] Preliminary.
Source: U.S. Department of Health, Education, and Welfare, National Center for Education Statistics, *Digest of Education Statistics, Education Directory,* and *Earned Degrees Conferred.*

Universities and Colleges, 1977–78[1]

Selected four-year schools

Institution	Location	Year Founded	Total Students[2]	Total Faculty[3]	Bound Library volumes
ALABAMA					
Alabama A. & M. U.	Normal	1875	4,425	315	255,600
Alabama State U.	Montgomery	1874	4,200	179	145,000
Auburn U.	Auburn	1856	17,977	1,052	927,000
Birmingham-Southern	Birmingham	1856	1,256	85	100,000
Jacksonville State U.	Jacksonville	1883	7,011	275	227,000
Troy State U.	Troy	1887	4,343	216	260,000
Tuskegee Institute	Tuskegee Institute	1881	3,616	343	225,000
U. of Alabama	University	1831	17,048	861	1,185,000
U. of South Alabama	Mobile	1963	6,971	387	200,000
ALASKA					
U. of Alaska	Fairbanks	1917	22,000	350	303,500
ARIZONA					
Arizona State U.	Tempe	1885	35,278	1,715	1,350,500
Northern Arizona U.	Flagstaff	1899	11,536	550	811,100
U. of Arizona	Tucson	1885	30,722	1,820	1,990,000
ARKANSAS					
Arkansas State U.	State University	1909	7,303	360	500,000
U. of Arkansas	Fayetteville	1871	14,752	492	832,400
U. of A. at Little Rock	Little Rock	1927	9,330	385	285,768
U. of Central Arkansas	Conway	1907	5,355	261	212,500
CALIFORNIA					
California Inst. of Tech.	Pasadena	1891	1,500	278	323,000
Cal. Polytech. State U.	San Luis Obispo	1901	15,502	1,073	525,000
Cal. State Polytech. U.	Pomona	1938	14,090	868	326,400
Cal. State U., Chico	Chico	1887	12,791	791	498,620
Cal. State U., Dominguez Hills	Dominguez Hills	1960	6,993	268	202,200
Cal. State U., Fresno	Fresno	1911	15,240	980	553,900
Cal. State U., Fullerton	Fullerton	1957	16,529	1,250	495,300
Cal. State U., Hayward	Hayward	1957	12,000	679	490,000
Cal. State U., Long Beach	Long Beach	1949	31,336	2,316	655,200
Cal. State U., Los Angeles	Los Angeles	1947	26,270	1,400	800,000
Cal. State U., Northridge	Northridge	1958	28,077	1,510	600,000
Cal. State U., Sacramento	Sacramento	1947	20,094	875[4]	629,100
Golden Gate U.	San Francisco	1901	9,100	800	250,000
Humboldt State U.	Arcata	1913	7,824	459	235,000
Loyola Marymount U.	Los Angeles	1911	6,024	380	358,300
Occidental	Los Angeles	1887	1,886	132	320,000
San Francisco State U.	San Francisco	1899	24,035	1,630	500,000
San Jose State U.	San Jose	1857	28,308	1,697	700,000
Sonoma State U.	Rohnert Park	1960	5,860	392	268,700
Stanford U.	Stanford	1885	12,354	1,072	4,363,600
U. of C., Berkeley	Berkeley	1868	28,384	1,884	4,900,000
U. of C., Davis	Davis	1905	17,367	1,208	1,400,000
U. of C., Irvine	Irvine	1960	9,408	621	780,000
U. of C., Los Angeles	Los Angeles	1919	31,752	2,509	3,900,000
U. of C., Riverside	Riverside	1868	4,909	369	1,220,000
U. of C., San Diego	La Jolla	1912	10,378	770	540,000
U. of C., Santa Barbara	Santa Barbara	1944	14,695	746	880,000
U. of C., Santa Cruz	Santa Cruz	1965	6,104	365	450,000
U. of the Pacific	Stockton	1851	6,050	402	230,000
U. of San Francisco	San Francisco	1855	6,326	355	320,000
U. of Santa Clara	Santa Clara	1851	6,295	316	397,000
U. of Southern California	Los Angeles	1880	28,402	1,686	1,650,000
COLORADO					
Colorado	Colorado Springs	1874	1,928	195	280,000
Colorado School of Mines	Golden	1874	2,400	170	158,000
Colorado State U.	Fort Collins	1870	17,812	1,150	1,000,000
Metropolitan State	Denver	1963	13,637	479[4]	425,300
U. S. Air Force Academy	USAF Academy	1954	4,400	500	470,000
U. of Colorado	Boulder	1876	21,766	541[4]	1,525,800
U. of Denver	Denver	1864	7,835	593	1,250,000
U. of Northern Colorado	Greeley	1889	11,048	820	503,000
U. of Southern Colorado	Pueblo	1933	5,200	465	125,000
CONNECTICUT					
Central Connecticut State	New Britain	1849	11,751	535	275,000
Southern Connecticut State	New Haven	1893	11,179	727	327,800
Trinity	Hartford	1823	2,078	169	597,000
U. S. Coast Guard Acad.	New London	1876	1,100	130	90,000
U. of Bridgeport	Bridgeport	1927	8,050	358	295,400
U. of Connecticut	Storrs	1881	20,854	1,349	1,476,700
U. of Hartford	West Hartford	1877	9,217	624	260,000
Wesleyan U.	Middletown	1831	2,350	252	772,000
Western Connecticut State	Danbury	1903	5,496	288	133,600
Yale U.	New Haven	1701	9,000	1,500	6,692,600
DELAWARE					
Delaware State	Dover	1891	2,366	118	128,400
U. of Delaware	Newark	1833	15,400	1,050	1,000,000
DISTRICT OF COLUMBIA					
American U.	Washington	1893	12,583	579	514,200
Catholic U. of America	Washington	1887	7,400	533	900,000
George Washington U.	Washington	1821	22,120	2,573	710,900
Georgetown U.	Washington	1789	11,384	2,491	839,300
Howard U.	Washington	1867	10,150	1,856	1,012,500
FLORIDA					
Florida A. & M. U.	Tallahassee	1887	5,472	398	273,800
Florida State U.	Tallahassee	1857	21,465	960	1,266,300
Florida Tech. U.	Orlando	1963	10,605	397	371,800
Rollins	Winter Park	1885	4,227	112	174,700
U. of Florida	Gainesville	1853	29,952	2,748	1,900,000
U. of Miami	Coral Gables	1925	18,034	1,307	1,132,100
U. of South Florida	Tampa	1960	19,407	964	494,200
GEORGIA					
Atlanta U.	Atlanta	1865	1,117	167	300,000
Augusta	Augusta	1925	3,685	170	219,200
Emory U.	Atlanta	1836	7,183	833	2,005,800
Georgia	Milledgeville	1889	3,599	191	130,000
Georgia Inst. of Tech.	Atlanta	1885	10,113	518	850,000
Georgia Southern	Statesboro	1906	6,000	360	170,000
Georgia State U.	Atlanta	1913	21,000	1,005	550,000
Mercer U.	Macon	1833	1,910	130	180,000
Morehouse[5]	Atlanta	1867	1,405	110	297,300
Oglethorpe U.	Atlanta	1835	830	44	60,000
Spelman[6]	Atlanta	1881	1,262	102	44,000
U. of Georgia	Athens	1785	22,974	1,204	1,719,200
HAWAII					
Brigham Young U.-Hawaii	Laie	1955	1,770	121	105,000
U. of Hawaii	Honolulu	1907	21,160	1,403	1,435,000
IDAHO					
Boise State U.	Boise	1932	9,099	425	232,300
Idaho State U.	Pocatello	1901	10,737	374	305,000
U. of Idaho	Moscow	1889	8,334	540	500,000
ILLINOIS					
Augustana	Rock Island	1860	2,363	143	213,600
Bradley U.	Peoria	1897	5,050	361	300,000
Chicago State U.	Chicago	1869	7,025	349	210,800
Concordia Teachers	River Forest	1864	1,118	103	120,300
De Paul U.	Chicago	1898	11,052	336	390,000
Eastern Illinois U.	Charleston	1895	9,585	542	423,600
Illinois Inst. of Tech.	Chicago	1892	7,155	737	1,343,200
Illinois State U.	Normal	1857	19,039	1,049	744,800
Knox	Galesburg	1837	1,026	90	186,000
Lake Forest	Lake Forest	1857	2,000	94	200,000
Loyola U. of Chicago	Chicago	1870	15,202	1,800	703,300
Northeastern Ill. State U.	Chicago	1869	10,093	460	337,300
Northern Illinois U.	De Kalb	1895	21,690	1,184	823,000
Northwestern U.	Evanston	1851	15,323	1,673	2,500,000
Southern Illinois U.	Carbondale	1869	22,549	1,605	1,514,700
SIU at Edwardsville	Edwardsville	1957	12,060	839	697,400
U. of Chicago	Chicago	1891	9,480	1,120	3,334,200
U. of Illinois	Urbana	1867	33,946	2,574	5,494,800
U. of I. at Chicago Circle	Chicago	1965	20,693	2,013	951,300
Western Illinois U.	Macomb	1899	12,739	772	500,000
Wheaton	Wheaton	1860	2,353	185	170,000
INDIANA					
Ball State U.	Muncie	1918	17,139	881	931,700
Butler U.	Indianapolis	1855	5,267	249	182,000
De Pauw U.	Greencastle	1837	2,416	183	338,500
Indiana State U.	Terre Haute	1865	11,474	709	500,000
Indiana U.	Bloomington	1820	31,884	1,468	3,379,710
Purdue U.	West Lafayette	1869	30,445	1,249	1,357,800
U. of Evansville	Evansville	1854	4,653	281	250,000
U. of Notre Dame du Lac	Notre Dame	1842	8,731	686	1,346,600
Valparaiso U.	Valparaiso	1859	4,484	300	250,000
IOWA					
Coe	Cedar Rapids	1851	1,243	136	170,000
Drake U.	Des Moines	1881	6,458	382	415,000
Grinnell	Grinnell	1846	1,256	120	250,000
Iowa State U.	Ames	1858	23,138	1,611	1,200,000
U. of Iowa	Iowa City	1847	22,990	1,455	2,136,900
U. of Northern Iowa	Cedar Falls	1876	10,455	637	482,500
KANSAS					
Emporia State U.	Emporia	1863	6,000	299	550,000
Kansas State U.	Manhattan	1863	19,045	1,004	820,000
U. of Kansas	Lawrence	1866	24,300	1,363	2,000,000
Witchita State U.	Wichita	1895	15,937	813	525,000
KENTUCKY					
Berea	Berea	1855	1,442	136	170,000
Eastern Kentucky U.	Richmond	1906	13,679[4]	567[4]	582,200
Kentucky State U.	Frankfort	1886	2,389	154	155,000
Murray State U.	Murray	1922	7,740	417	312,000
U. of Kentucky	Lexington	1865	39,516	1,875	1,555,000
U. of Louisville	Louisville	1798	18,365	1,363	930,100
Western Kentucky U.	Bowling Green	1907	13,586	670	643,000
LOUISIANA					
Grambling State U.	Grambling	1901	4,003	200[4]	165,000
Louisiana State U.	Baton Rouge	1860	25,828	1,095	1,660,000
Louisiana Tech U.	Ruston	1894	9,105	392	733,200
Northeast Louisiana U.	Monroe	1931	7,630	395	288,900
Northwestern State U.	Natchitoches	1884	6,500	300	200,000
Southern U.	Baton Rouge	1880	8,097	453	338,600
Tulane U.	New Orleans	1834	9,462	893	1,200,000
U. of Southwestern La.	Lafayette	1898	13,010	591	430,000
MAINE					
Bates	Lewiston	1864	1,385	121	250,000
Bowdoin	Brunswick	1794	1,381	112	550,000
Colby	Waterville	1813	1,667	127	398,000
U. of Maine, Farmington	Farmington	1864	1,936	91[4]	76,100
U. of Maine at Orono	Orono	1865	10,970	464	522,000
U. of Southern Maine	Portland	1878	8,000	366	280,000
MARYLAND					
Goucher[6]	Towson	1885	1,022	125	183,500
Johns Hopkins U.	Baltimore	1876	9,208	1,667	2,064,900
Morgan State U.	Baltimore	1867	5,601	450	181,700
Towson State U.	Baltimore	1866	13,499	810	337,000
U.S. Naval Academy	Annapolis	1845	4,169	546	370,000
U. of Maryland	College Park	1807	37,866	2,882	1,800,000
MASSACHUSETTS					
Amherst	Amherst	1821	1,539	164	511,400
Boston	Chestnut Hill	1863	13,968	855	1,000,000
Boston U.	Boston	1869	24,000	1,326	1,234,000
Brandeis U.	Waltham	1948	3,555	404	700,000
Clark U.	Worcester	1887	2,375	196	365,000
Harvard U.	Cambridge	1636	21,095	3,019	9,574,600
Holy Cross	Worcester	1843	2,460	190	340,000
Mass. Inst. of Tech.	Cambridge	1861	8,712	1,587	1,700,000
Mt. Holyoke[6]	South Hadley	1837	1,934	216	422,200
Northeastern U.	Boston	1898	36,132	1,800	743,200
Radcliffe[6]	Cambridge	1879	1,988	. . .	. . .
Salem State	Salem	1854	7,850	275	170,000
Simmons[6]	Boston	1899	2,634	231	200,000

Institution	Location	Year founded	Total students[2]	Total faculty[3]	Bound library volumes
Smith	Northampton	1871	2,719	260	853,800
Tufts U.	Medford	1852	6,371	990	492,000
U. of Lowell	Lowell	1895	9,731	412	275,000
U. of Massachusetts	Amherst	1863	23,900	1,475	1,500,000
Wellesley[6]	Wellesley	1870	2,144	270	600,000
Wheaton[6]	Norton	1834	1,174	121	190,000
Williams	Williamstown	1793	1,995	182	485,000
MICHIGAN					
Albion	Albion	1835	1,794	121	210,000
Central Michigan U.	Mt. Pleasant	1892	16,287	741	600,000
Eastern Michigan U.	Ypsilanti	1849	19,104	757	387,600
Ferris State	Big Rapids	1884	10,208	594	235,000
Hope	Holland	1866	2,400	170	181,000
Michigan State U.	East Lansing	1855	43,749	2,695	2,500,000
Michigan Tech U.	Houghton	1885	7,130	472	427,300
Northern Michigan U.	Marquette	1899	8,208	354	266,500
U. of Detroit	Detroit	1877	8,158	245	479,000
U. of Michigan	Ann Arbor	1817	35,000	6,000	5,000,000
Wayne State U.	Detroit	1868	34,389	2,200	1,755,500
Western Michigan U.	Kalamazoo	1903	20,617	1,090	685,800
MINNESOTA					
Carleton	Northfield	1866	1,681	141	360,000
Concordia	Moorhead	1891	2,647	196	230,300
Gustavus Adolphus	St. Peter	1862	2,265	160	166,300
Hamline U.	St. Paul	1854	1,816	148	150,000
Macalester	St. Paul	1874	1,744	151	280,000
Mankato State U.	Mankato	1867	10,075	530	495,000
Moorhead State U.	Moorhead	1885	6,204	255	233,600
St. Catherine[6]	St. Paul	1905	2,000	130	200,000
St. Cloud State U.	St. Cloud	1869	11,606	521	551,000
St. John's U.[5]	Collegeville	1857	1,940	109	270,000
St. Olaf	Northfield	1874	2,960	240	296,400
St. Thomas	St. Paul	1885	4,500	148	190,900
U. of Minnesota	Minneapolis	1851	55,114	4,266	3,300,000
Winona State U.	Winona	1858	4,210	203	165,000
MISSISSIPPI					
Alcorn State U.	Lorman	1871	2,653	126	124,000
Jackson State U.	Jackson	1877	7,718	350	220,000
Mississippi	Clinton	1826	3,500	150	152,000
Mississippi U. for Women	Columbus	1884	2,862	162	293,700
Mississippi State U.	Mississippi State	1878	10,478	526	652,700
U. of Mississippi	University	1848	9,655	438	488,300
U. of Southern Mississippi	Hattiesburg	1912	9,806	670	506,000
MISSOURI					
Central Missouri State U.	Warrensburg	1871	10,250	465	300,000
Northeast Missouri State U.	Kirksville	1867	5,500	299	235,000
St. Louis U.	St. Louis	1818	10,167	1,714	970,000
Southeast Missouri State U.	Cape Girardeau	1873	8,584	427	290,000
Southwest Missouri State U.	Springfield	1906	12,600	599	315,000
U. of Missouri-Columbia	Columbia	1839	23,474	3,954	1,882,400
U. of Missouri-Kansas City	Kansas City	1933	10,554	1,063	591,100
U. of Missouri-Rolla	Rolla	1870	5,100	336	272,000
U. of Missouri-St. Louis	St. Louis	1963	11,474	339	306,700
Washington U.	St. Louis	1853	11,359	2,000	1,500,000
MONTANA					
Montana State U.	Bozeman	1893	9,400	411[4]	374,400
U. of Montana	Missoula	1893	8,267	450[4]	500,000
NEBRASKA					
Creighton U.	Omaha	1878	5,027	867	467,100
U. of Nebraska	Lincoln	1869	22,256	1,198	1,400,000
U. of Nebraska at Omaha	Omaha	1908	15,058	707	400,000
NEVADA					
U. of Nevada-Las Vegas	Las Vegas	1951	6,851	299[4]	330,000
U. of Nevada-Reno	Reno	1864	9,181	364[4]	568,000
NEW HAMPSHIRE					
Dartmouth	Hanover	1769	3,700	430	1,000,000
U. of New Hampshire	Durham	1866	12,175	626	710,000
NEW JERSEY					
Glassboro State	Glassboro	1923	11,000	435	338,000
Jersey City State	Jersey City	1927	11,285	345	150,000
Kean Col. of N. J.	Union	1855	13,748	449	195,000
Montclair State	Upper Montclair	1908	14,700	780	297,900
Princeton U.	Princeton	1746	6,000	589[4]	3,000,000
Rider	Lawrenceville	1865	5,871	338	292,000
Rutgers State U.	New Brunswick	1766	46,306	2,200	2,000,000
Seton Hall U.	South Orange	1856	9,902	568	300,000
Stevens Inst. of Tech.	Hoboken	1870	2,472	156	90,000
Trenton State	Trenton	1855	5,696	516	330,000
Upsala	East Orange	1893	1,500	115	135,000
William Patterson	Wayne	1855	10,494	590	273,700
NEW MEXICO					
New Mexico State U.	Las Cruces	1888	11,605	696	555,000
U. of New Mexico	Albuquerque	1889	21,547	1,271	900,000
NEW YORK					
Adelphi U.	Garden City	1896	10,500	545	300,000
Alfred U.	Alfred	1836	2,100	170	200,000
Canisius	Buffalo	1870	4,274	257	208,500
City U. of New York					
Bernard M. Baruch	New York	1919	14,173	718	228,000
Brooklyn	Brooklyn	1930	19,402	1,467	739,000
City	New York	1847	14,000	750	900,000
Herbert H. Lehman	Bronx	1931	11,417	753	286,000
Hunter	New York	1870	17,816	1,270	446,100
Queens	Flushing	1937	19,068	1,310	473,000
Richmond	Staten Island	1965	3,976	262	165,000
York	Jamaica	1966	4,927	256	110,000
Colgate U.	Hamilton	1819	3,000	324	319,000
Columbia U.	New York	1754	15,157	3,766	4,500,000
Barnard[6]	New York	1889	2,214	185	145,000
Teachers	New York	1887	6,107	222	450,000
Cornell U.	Ithaca	1865	16,340	1,812	4,000,000

Institution	Location	Year founded	Total students[2]	Total faculty[3]	Bound library volumes
Elmira	Elmira	1855	2,950	158	140,000
Fordham U.	Bronx	1841	13,863	810	927,200
Hamilton	Clinton	1812	960	85	325,900
Hofstra U.	Hempstead	1935	10,800	560	720,000
Ithaca	Ithaca	1892	4,415	320	247,000
Juilliard School	New York	1905	1,175	200	50,000
Long Island U.	Greenvale	1926	24,400	1,000	488,000
Manhattan[5]	Bronx	1853	4,591	276	180,400
Marymount[5]	Tarrytown	1907	1,940	140	52,000
New School for Soc. Res.	New York	1919	27,000	1,500	175,000
New York U.	New York	1831	42,052	5,723	2,533,900
Niagara U.	Niagara University	1856	4,352	292	209,300
Polytechnic Inst. of N.Y.	Brooklyn	1854	4,583	342	251,500
Pratt Inst.	Brooklyn	1887	4,050	493	215,000
Rensselaer Polytech. Inst.	Troy	1824	6,853	406	276,600
Rochester Inst. of Tech.	Rochester	1829	12,577	1,049	142,000
St. Bonaventure U.	St. Bonaventure	1856	2,715	161	200,000
St. John's U.	Jamaica	1870	13,858	723	888,400
St. Lawrence U.	Canton	1856	2,276	152	270,800
State U. of N.Y. at Albany	Albany	1844	14,600	840	900,000
SUNY at Buffalo	Buffalo	1846	24,579	1,895	1,810,700
SUNY at Stony Brook	Stony Brook	1957	16,361	1,013	1,072,100
State U. Colleges					
Brockport	Brockport	1867	10,033	490	311,200
Buffalo	Buffalo	1867	11,101	528[4]	350,000
Cortland	Cortland	1868	5,615	322	234,800
Fredonia	Fredonia	1867	5,090	260	310,800
Geneseo	Geneseo	1867	5,845	597	289,600
New Paltz	New Paltz	1828	7,543	423	276,900
Oneonta	Oneonta	1889	6,400	366	300,000
Oswego	Oswego	1861	9,143	468	305,400
Plattsburgh	Plattsburgh	1889	5,970	309	266,500
Potsdam	Potsdam	1816	5,045	301	232,900
Syracuse U.	Syracuse	1870	15,127	1,213	1,752,500
U.S. Merchant Marine Acad.	Kings Point	1938	1,110	80	100,000
U.S. Military Academy	West Point	1802	4,417	625	400,000
U. of Rochester	Rochester	1850	8,031	503	1,700,000
Vassar	Poughkeepsie	1861	2,200	221	500,000
Wagner	Staten Island	1883	2,500	226	175,000
Yeshiva U.	New York	1886	3,985	2,493	789,000
NORTH CAROLINA					
Appalachian State U.	Boone	1899	9,668	536	371,600
Catawba	Salisbury	1851	978	58	130,200
Davidson	Davidson	1837	1,362	100	235,000
Duke U.	Durham	1838	9,018	1,551	2,869,600
East Carolina U.	Greenville	1907	11,968	649	532,600
Lenoir Rhyne	Hickory	1891	1,273	105	100,000
N. Carolina A. & T. St. U.	Greensboro	1891	5,611	297	273,600
N. Carolina State U.	Raleigh	1887	17,471	902	800,000
U. of N.C. at Chapel Hill	Chapel Hill	1789	20,126	1,972	2,373,600
U. of N.C. at Greensboro	Greensboro	1891	9,855	587	1,075,000
Wake Forest U.	Winston-Salem	1834	4,516	781	660,000
Western Carolina U.	Cullowhee	1889	6,380	307	231,000
NORTH DAKOTA					
North Dakota State U.	Fargo	1890	7,576	345[4]	325,000
U. of North Dakota	Grand Forks	1883	8,632	460	320,000
OHIO					
Antioch	Yellow Springs	1852	1,486	75	230,000
Bowling Green State U.	Bowling Green	1910	16,416	721	550,000
Case Western Reserve U.	Cleveland	1826	8,300	1,700	1,576,000
Cleveland State U.	Cleveland	1964	17,915	767	375,300
Denison U.	Granville	1831	2,125	181	360,000
John Carroll U.	Cleveland	1886	4,000	176	100,000
Kent State U.	Kent	1910	27,700	1,056	1,100,000
Kenyon	Gambier	1824	1,470	102[4]	250,000
Marietta	Marietta	1835	1,496	116	236,700
Miami U.	Oxford	1809	16,004	765	988,000
Oberlin	Oberlin	1833	2,700	226	700,000
Ohio State U.	Columbus	1870	51,002	3,533[4]	3,407,700
Ohio U.	Athens	1804	13,310	823	985,700
U. of Akron	Akron	1870	22,608	1,012	768,400
U. of Cincinnati	Cincinnati	1819	33,742	2,220	730,000
U. of Dayton	Dayton	1850	8,275	450	445,000
U. of Toledo	Toledo	1872	17,257	804	1,038,800
Wooster	Wooster	1866	1,800	156	200,000
Xavier U.	Cincinnati	1831	6,493	276	189,000
Youngstown State U.	Youngstown	1908	15,696	729	350,000
OKLAHOMA					
Central State U.	Edmond	1890	11,876	429	496,700
Oklahoma State U.	Stillwater	1890	21,000	1,163	1,200,000
U. of Oklahoma	Norman	1890	19,719	1,534	1,463,200
U. of Tulsa	Tulsa	1894	6,100	290	838,000
OREGON					
Lewis and Clark	Portland	1867	2,299	269	168,000
Oregon State U.	Corvallis	1868	16,502	1,122	760,000
Portland State U.	Portland	1946	14,241	556	522,500
Reed	Portland	1909	1,142	105	267,400
U. of Oregon	Eugene	1872	16,701	1,326	1,377,200
PENNSYLVANIA					
Allegheny	Meadville	1815	1,912	120	254,300
Bryn Mawr[6]	Bryn Mawr	1885	1,601	175	435,000
Bucknell U.	Lewisburg	1846	3,200	257	400,000
Carnegie-Mellon U.	Pittsburgh	1900	5,049	411	554,300
Dickinson	Carlisle	1773	1,710	127[4]	250,000
Drexel U.	Philadelphia	1891	9,687	277	350,000
Duquesne U.	Pittsburgh	1878	7,130	510	380,000
Edinboro State	Edinboro	1857	6,382	433	318,100
Franklin and Marshall	Lancaster	1787	1,986	132	248,000
Gettysburg	Gettysburg	1832	1,951	163	237,700
Indiana U. of Pa.	Indiana	1875	11,727	582	400,000
Juniata	Huntingdon	1876	1,141	92	188,000
Lafayette	Easton	1826	2,323	163	315,000
La Salle	Philadelphia	1863	6,337	345	260,000
Lehigh U.	Bethlehem	1865	6,200	374	565,000
Moravian	Bethlehem	1742	1,240	79	141,000
Muhlenberg	Allentown	1848	1,705	121	170,000

Selected four-year schools

Institution	Location	Year founded	Total students [2]	Total faculty [3]	Bound library volumes
Pennsylvania State U.	University Park	1855	35,647	1,584	1,467,600
St. Joseph's	Philadelphia	1851	5,696	292	165,400
Slippery Rock State	Slippery Rock	1889	5,845	338	836,000
Susquehanna U.	Selinsgrove	1858	1,635	121	101,000
Swarthmore	Swarthmore	1864	1,293	169	510,000
Temple U.	Philadelphia	1884	36,339	2,426	1,446,000
U. of Pennsylvania	Philadelphia	1740	20,538	4,722	2,750,000
U. of Pittsburgh	Pittsburgh	1787	29,743	4,461	1,769,700
Ursinus	Collegeville	1869	1,034	90	134,000
Villanova U.	Villanova	1842	6,768	380	420,000
West Chester State	West Chester	1812	9,168	491	330,000
PUERTO RICO					
Inter American U.	San Juan	1912	23,296	1,042	260,000
U. of Puerto Rico	Río Piedras	1903	26,042	1,476	879,000
RHODE ISLAND					
Brown U.	Providence	1764	7,044	467	1,595,300
Rhode Island	Providence	1854	5,200	364	205,000
U. of Rhode Island	Kingston	1892	10,435	750	616,700
SOUTH CAROLINA					
The Citadel [5]	Charleston	1842	3,357	156	339,000
Clemson U.	Clemson	1889	11,478	676 [4]	650,700
Furman U.	Greenville	1826	2,929	139	238,000
U. of South Carolina	Columbia	1801	24,783	1,120 [4]	1,700,000
SOUTH DAKOTA					
South Dakota State U.	Brookings	1881	6,537	468	398,000
U. of South Dakota	Vermillion	1882	5,734	550	420,000
TENNESSEE					
Fisk U.	Nashville	1867	1,281	96	182,800
Memphis State U.	Memphis	1909	22,149	775	698,900
Middle Tennessee State U.	Murfreesboro	1911	10,223	450	570,000
Tennessee State U.	Nashville	1909	5,698	287	214,400
Tennessee Tech. U.	Cookeville	1915	7,256	312	327,100
U. of Tennessee	Knoxville	1794	25,965	1,390	1,312,100
Vanderbilt U.	Nashville	1873	7,269	1,687	1,405,300
TEXAS					
Austin	Sherman	1849	1,198	88	166,200
Baylor U.	Waco	1845	9,386	467	837,500
East Texas State U.	Commerce	1889	9,282	470	550,000
Hardin-Simmons U.	Abilene	1891	1,649	123	155,000
Lamar U.	Beaumont	1923	12,800	496	430,000
North Texas State U.	Denton	1890	15,733	1,114	1,119,800
Prairie View A. & M.	Prairie View	1876	5,400	410 [4]	195,700
Rice U.	Houston	1891	3,700	445	991,800
Sam Houston State U.	Huntsville	1879	10,918	356 [4]	559,700
Southern Methodist U.	Dallas	1911	9,105	630	1,479,200
Southwest Texas State U.	San Marcos	1899	14,600	641	474,700
Stephen F. Austin State U.	Nacogdoches	1923	10,731	798	673,500
Texas A. & I. U.	Kingsville	1925	6,283	255	416,000
Texas A. & M. U.	College Station	1876	30,255	1,360 [4]	1,100,000
Texas Christian U.	Fort Worth	1873	6,159	416	794,500
Texas Southern U.	Houston	1947	8,500	427	270,000
Texas Tech. U.	Lubbock	1923	22,176	1,386	2,500,000
U. of Houston	Houston	1927	30,000	1,750	1,100,000
U. of Texas at Arlington	Arlington	1895	16,201	1,050	635,000
U. of Texas at Austin	Austin	1881	41,660	1,756 [4]	4,000,000
U. of Texas at El Paso	El Paso	1913	15,836	487	433,200
West Texas State U.	Canyon	1909	6,701	277	686,600
UTAH					
Brigham Young U.	Provo	1875	35,882	1,315	1,500,000
U. of Utah	Salt Lake City	1850	21,444	1,316	1,500,000
Utah State U.	Logan	1888	9,526	850	420,100
Weber State	Ogden	1889	9,695	440	272,300
VERMONT					
Bennington	Bennington	1925	657	57	10,000
Middlebury	Middlebury	1800	1,870	166	371,500
U. of Vermont	Burlington	1791	10,702	699	800,000
VIRGINIA					
James Madison U.	Harrisonburg	1908	7,926	446	247,800
Old Dominion U.	Norfolk	1930	13,968	735	416,900
U. of Richmond	Richmond	1830	4,220	311	248,800
U. of Virginia	Charlottesville	1819	15,903	1,451	2,231,600
Virginia Commonwealth U.	Richmond	1838	18,437	1,727	478,200
Virginia Military Inst. [5]	Lexington	1839	1,328	103	253,100
Va. Polytech. Inst. & State U.	Blacksburg	1872	20,000	1,530	1,300,000
Washington & Lee U. [5]	Lexington	1749	1,710	162	293,400
William & Mary	Williamsburg	1693	6,129	413	1,500,000
WASHINGTON					
Central Washington U.	Ellensburg	1891	7,900	379	289,000
Eastern Washington U.	Cheney	1890	7,137	429	228,400
Gonzaga U.	Spokane	1887	3,100	203	365,000
U. of Washington	Seattle	1861	34,500	2,382	2,276,500
Washington State U.	Pullman	1890	16,665	993	1,108,300
Western Washington U.	Bellingham	1893	9,800	484	500,000
Whitman	Walla Walla	1859	1,090	79	247,834
WEST VIRGINIA					
Bethany	Bethany	1840	941	77	140,000
Marshall U.	Huntington	1837	11,221	500	365,800
West Virginia U.	Morgantown	1867	18,565	1,850	870,800
WISCONSIN					
Beloit	Beloit	1846	1,013	105	224,000
Lawrence U.	Appleton	1847	1,184	133	220,000
Marquette U.	Milwaukee	1881	12,001	740	600,000
St. Norbert	De Pere	1898	1,526	102	85,000
U. of W.-Eau Claire	Eau Claire	1916	10,494	530	362,500
U. of W.-Green Bay	Green Bay	1965	3,642	167	300,000
U. of W.-La Crosse	La Crosse	1909	8,431	464 [4]	503,700
U. of W.-Madison	Madison	1848	39,022	2,155	3,238,200
U. of W.-Milwaukee	Milwaukee	1956	24,281	1,667	1,063,000
U. of W.-Oshkosh	Oshkosh	1871	10,068	482 [4]	328,700
U. of W.-Platteville	Platteville	1866	4,641	325	188,300
U. of W.-River Falls	River Falls	1874	5,000	241	179,600
U. of W.-Stevens Point	Stevens Point	1894	8,993	520	470,000
U. of W.-Stout	Menomonie	1893	6,471	334 [4]	170,000
U. of W.-Superior	Superior	1896	2,282	213	203,000
U. of W.-Whitewater	Whitewater	1868	9,601	393	262,200
WYOMING					
U. of Wyoming	Laramie	1886	9,200	850	1,000,000

[1] Latest data available; coeducational unless otherwise indicated. [2] Total includes part-time students. [3] Total includes part-time or full-time equivalent faculty. [4] Total includes full-time equivalent only. [5] Men's school. [6] Women's school.

LIVING CONDITIONS

Health Personnel and Facilities

State	Physicians 1977 [1]	Dentists 1977	Registered Nurses [2]	Hospital facilities 1977 Hospitals	Beds	Nursing homes 1976 Facilities	Beds
Alabama	3,951	1,232	10,235	149	25,198	217	19,489
Alaska	366	210	2,030	26	1,697	11	782
Arizona	4,221	1,104	12,383	80	11,140	71	5,914
Arkansas	2,253	688	5,033	97	13,589	217	19,803
California	47,172	13,369	103,385	625	115,378	3,500	138,219
Colorado	4,871	1,568	15,515	103	15,075	243	22,731
Connecticut	7,113	2,078	23,612	64	19,079	356	24,573
Delaware	908	258	4,389	16	4,688	29	2,228
District of Columbia	3,383	633	5,545	20	9,850	70	2,873
Florida	16,001	3,946	38,398	247	54,854	335	33,097
Georgia	6,383	2,053	17,423	188	31,173	325	29,455
Hawaii	1,567	549	4,117	28	3,868	144	3,188
Idaho	874	418	3,755	51	3,697	67	4,823
Illinois	18,995	5,653	60,806	286	76,135	936	88,311
Indiana	6,401	2,156	21,481	136	34,458	506	37,611
Iowa	3,325	1,318	17,812	141	21,549	552	33,874
Kansas	3,221	1,049	12,655	162	18,116	393	23,195
Kentucky	4,320	1,393	11,734	122	18,749	321	20,950
Louisiana	5,266	1,499	11,524	160	25,016	205	19,135
Maine	1,488	468	7,440	54	7,326	307	9,020
Maryland	9,351	2,452	22,462	83	24,865	191	19,154
Massachusetts	14,185	3,933	56,567	193	47,635	869	50,940
Michigan	13,519	4,589	46,681	252	52,423	704	66,750
Minnesota	7,015	2,333	23,638	189	31,141	517	43,036
Mississippi	2,248	716	6,288	114	16,930	147	9,023
Missouri	7,379	2,213	18,823	169	35,667	474	33,746
Montana	915	412	4,429	65	5,119	107	5,335
Nebraska	2,135	901	9,798	108	11,473	284	23,349
Nevada	778	313	2,564	25	3,243	37	1,638
New Hampshire	1,374	438	7,044	33	4,997	115	6,378
New Jersey	13,107	4,464	51,061	140	45,199	467	33,976
New Mexico	1,586	478	4,077	54	6,552	72	3,366
New York	46,614	11,982	125,794	383	140,779	1,027	104,523
North Carolina	7,403	2,041	21,366	160	34,220	722	24,614
North Dakota	725	281	3,653	61	5,999	103	6,878
Ohio	16,201	4,906	57,052	248	67,769	953	64,903
Oklahoma	3,223	1,109	8,698	142	17,286	362	26,650
Oregon	4,134	1,600	11,382	88	12,031	283	17,189
Pennsylvania	20,619	5,932	96,414	318	89,368	676	61,891
Rhode Island	1,822	484	6,638	21	6,841	120	7,330
South Carolina	3,304	1,045	10,187	89	17,337	119	8,701
South Dakota	631	295	3,852	70	5,978	154	8,386
Tennessee	6,108	1,874	12,051	164	31,235	290	20,092
Texas	17,309	5,442	40,372	568	77,951	1,105	102,139
Utah	1,971	776	4,531	40	5,036	104	4,613
Vermont	1,031	265	4,521	19	3,075	263	5,130
Virginia	7,541	2,429	23,935	135	32,212	341	25,435
Washington	6,163	2,511	21,953	128	16,250	370	30,344
West Virginia	2,389	650	7,314	83	15,510	127	5,585
Wisconsin	6,512	2,485	23,318	172	29,757	530	52,577
Wyoming	423	187	1,922	30	2,584	30	1,923
TOTAL U.S.	369,791	111,178	1,127,657	7,099	1,407,097	20,468	1,414,865

[1] Non-federal only. [2] Latest data available. Sources: American Medical Association, *Physician Distribution and Licensure in the U.S., 1976;* American Dental Association, *Distribution of Dentists in the United States by State, Region, District, and County, 1976;* American Nurses' Association; American Hospital Association, *Hospital Statistics, 1978 Edition;* U.S. Department of Health, Education, and Welfare, Public Health Service.

Crime Rates per 100,000 Population

State or metropolitan area	VIOLENT CRIME										PROPERTY CRIME							
	Total		Murder		Rape		Robbery		Assault		Total		Burglary		Larceny		Auto theft	
	1972	1977	1972	1977	1972	1977	1972	1977	1972	1977	1972	1977	1972	1977	1972	1977	1972	1977
Alabama	313.2	414.4	14.1	14.2	18.8	25.2	68.6	96.8	211.7	278.3	1,529.0	3,298.2	776.1	1,135.5	557.8	1,881.9	195.0	280.7
Alaska	370.5	443.2	9.5	10.8	**41.8**	**51.6**	66.5	96.8	252.6	284.0	2,756.0	5,454.8	970.8	1,331.7	1,287.1	3,369.8	498.2	753.3
Arizona	448.9	494.2	7.3	9.5	33.4	34.2	120.8	138.2	287.4	312.3	3,297.0	**7,253.0**	1,615.9	2,346.1	1,251.3	**4,467.4**	429.8	439.5
Arkansas	244.7	322.9	10.4	8.8	17.3	27.6	54.8	83.2	162.2	203.4	1,362.1	3,018.1	663.1	972.6	594.8	1,862.1	104.2	183.4
California	540.7	706.0	8.8	11.5	39.7	49.4	238.6	287.0	253.7	358.0	**4,065.5**	6,302.7	**1,949.2**	2,139.4	1,435.1	3,499.8	681.3	663.5
Colorado	405.4	511.9	8.3	6.3	38.4	42.0	141.4	170.7	217.3	292.9	3,649.1	6,315.6	1,580.1	1,935.2	1,479.7	3,903.2	589.3	477.1
Connecticut	199.2	282.3	3.2	4.2	8.9	16.8	79.1	129.5	107.9	131.8	2,271.3	4,559.8	956.8	1,346.0	845.4	2,620.7	469.1	593.2
Delaware	386.0	382.1	6.9	6.0	14.2	24.9	130.1	157.0	234.9	194.2	2,776.5	5,828.0	1,249.4	1,682.6	1,035.9	3,678.4	491.2	467.0
Florida	554.5	686.8	12.7	10.2	26.4	39.6	189.4	187.9	**326.0**	449.1	3,365.7	6,051.8	1,605.1	1,859.9	1,394.4	3,840.5	366.1	351.4
Georgia	377.6	439.8	**18.5**	11.7	20.8	31.1	134.3	140.5	204.0	256.5	2,091.3	3,819.2	1,081.7	1,351.1	702.9	2,170.2	306.7	297.9
Hawaii	155.5	224.8	6.8	7.2	21.3	25.5	55.4	128.0	72.1	64.1	2,856.4	6,321.3	1,335.6	1,911.5	1,122.4	3,920.4	398.4	489.4
Idaho	143.5	236.9	3.8	5.5	15.6	19.4	20.6	39.6	103.4	172.5	1,990.9	3,888.0	754.6	1,050.8	1,052.4	2,599.6	183.9	237.6
Illinois	508.1	452.0	8.8	9.9	23.3	21.8	260.1	211.3	215.9	209.0	1,975.8	4,442.1	846.1	1,085.0	686.7	2,828.5	443.0	528.6
Indiana	233.9	310.6	6.0	7.4	20.3	26.5	106.6	123.2	100.9	153.5	2,039.9	3,962.3	880.9	1,086.2	810.8	2,498.7	348.1	377.4
Iowa	87.4	144.0	1.7	2.3	8.6	10.6	26.7	41.2	50.3	89.8	1,374.0	3,717.5	521.6	812.5	683.3	2,685.1	169.1	219.9
Kansas	209.8	309.8	4.0	6.6	17.8	22.0	68.9	100.7	119.1	180.5	1,929.6	4,254.0	906.6	1,270.4	791.0	2,739.3	232.0	244.3
Kentucky	225.7	233.6	9.8	10.1	15.7	19.1	83.2	81.1	117.1	123.3	1,541.0	2,779.8	650.2	872.2	609.0	1,662.1	281.8	245.4
Louisiana	422.4	524.8	13.2	15.5	23.0	30.9	133.4	142.9	252.8	335.5	2,048.1	3,973.1	903.1	1,165.5	788.5	2,469.9	356.4	337.7
Maine	103.8	224.7	5.3	2.4	7.8	13.5	21.1	38.7	69.6	170.0	1,414.3	3,850.7	698.0	1,253.1	560.8	2,350.7	155.5	246.9
Maryland	651.2	693.8	12.5	8.0	26.0	34.8	324.1	292.1	288.6	358.9	2,728.1	5,006.2	1,111.7	1,400.0	1,082.2	3,177.7	534.2	428.5
Massachusetts	295.2	425.3	3.7	3.1	13.5	20.8	152.8	169.9	125.2	231.6	3,096.2	4,983.7	1,242.3	1,532.2	881.4	2,311.3	**972.4**	**1,140.1**
Michigan	555.2	584.7	11.0	9.3	29.3	38.9	289.3	261.9	225.6	274.6	3,264.3	5,227.3	1,582.3	1,522.7	1,208.0	3,159.0	473.9	545.5
Minnesota	174.5	193.8	2.4	2.7	14.7	19.5	84.4	85.9	72.9	85.8	2,081.5	4,037.0	927.2	1,134.7	817.0	2,559.3	337.3	343.1
Mississippi	312.7	288.7	15.4	14.3	17.5	19.6	39.9	65.7	240.0	189.1	1,007.4	2,299.9	540.0	915.6	346.8	1,239.9	120.5	144.4
Missouri	383.4	460.4	8.3	9.6	25.5	28.3	175.6	189.0	174.0	233.5	2,270.8	4,120.8	1,100.6	1,318.3	699.7	2,424.2	470.5	378.4
Montana	150.1	218.0	2.5	5.4	10.8	16.7	33.2	39.2	103.5	156.8	1,776.6	3,887.3	708.2	804.9	821.4	2,773.2	247.0	309.2
Nebraska	173.0	199.4	2.9	3.9	13.9	18.1	52.7	64.7	103.5	112.7	1,547.2	3,325.2	556.7	760.0	729.0	2,316.1	261.6	249.1
Nevada	429.6	743.0	13.5	**15.8**	34.0	49.1	190.1	323.1	192.0	355.0	3,807.0	7,225.0	1,757.5	**2,453.1**	**1,486.1**	4,212.6	563.4	559.2
New Hampshire	63.7	113.1	1.7	3.2	7.0	10.7	13.4	23.2	41.6	76.0	1,314.0	3,679.0	596.6	1,041.7	592.6	2,343.9	124.8	293.4
New Jersey	374.3	392.0	6.5	5.6	16.9	21.0	210.1	180.4	140.8	185.1	2,658.7	4,721.8	1,194.3	1,435.8	878.3	2,774.5	586.2	511.5
New Mexico	415.8	500.9	11.1	8.8	32.7	39.1	119.0	109.6	253.1	343.4	3,001.5	4,686.7	1,402.1	1,418.7	1,230.0	3,008.6	369.5	259.5
New York	**744.1**	**831.8**	11.0	10.7	22.4	29.4	**467.4**	**472.6**	243.2	319.1	2,744.4	5,255.8	1,256.3	1,728.0	923.2	2,782.0	565.0	745.8
North Carolina	414.5	407.1	12.8	10.6	14.2	17.0	62.3	61.3	325.2	318.3	1,518.5	3,384.0	752.0	1,154.1	618.3	2,037.8	148.2	192.1
North Dakota	45.9	67.1	1.3	0.9	4.9	9.0	8.9	13.3	30.9	43.8	978.0	2,433.8	357.1	446.1	530.2	1,843.0	90.7	144.7
Ohio	299.4	406.7	7.5	7.8	19.9	27.3	160.6	190.5	111.4	181.1	2,061.7	4,313.2	901.3	1,216.0	717.8	2,696.8	442.6	400.4
Oklahoma	232.6	316.6	7.0	8.6	19.0	29.2	63.6	73.8	143.1	205.0	1,868.8	3,843.0	942.9	1,288.2	661.3	2,228.1	264.6	326.8
Oregon	297.6	455.8	5.5	4.9	26.3	39.9	109.5	124.1	156.3	286.9	3,145.6	5,531.4	1,468.8	1,636.4	1,290.2	3,506.1	386.6	388.9
Pennsylvania	267.4	282.8	6.0	5.6	15.2	19.0	145.6	130.3	100.6	128.0	1,512.8	2,834.7	742.3	877.5	437.1	1,624.1	333.5	333.2
Rhode Island	250.4	301.6	1.3	3.6	8.3	10.5	81.7	86.5	159.1	201.0	3,017.0	5,125.0	1,124.0	1,489.5	996.9	2,844.1	896.2	791.4
South Carolina	385.8	636.2	16.8	11.9	21.4	33.0	66.0	105.9	281.6	**485.3**	1,901.5	4,201.1	992.3	1,613.6	695.9	2,342.4	213.2	245.1
South Dakota	111.3	189.1	1.2	2.0	11.3	13.5	15.6	17.9	83.2	155.7	1,167.5	2,422.4	472.8	570.5	587.3	1,704.4	107.4	147.5
Tennessee	319.0	389.5	11.3	10.1	19.9	29.7	10.1	145.8	186.7	203.9	1,782.6	3,350.2	894.3	1,259.7	587.4	1,776.5	300.9	314.0
Texas	350.9	407.7	12.3	13.3	23.8	33.8	118.2	152.4	196.6	208.2	2,304.7	4,989.4	1,206.7	1,603.1	768.6	2,988.7	329.3	397.6
Utah	183.2	240.0	2.9	3.5	18.3	20.3	62.3	68.8	99.7	147.3	2,358.3	4,510.6	913.2	1,171.6	1,167.3	3,004.6	277.7	334.5
Vermont	96.3	149.5	1.7	1.4	10.8	15.9	10.6	30.8	73.2	101.2	1,350.0	3,814.5	738.3	1,348.2	497.6	2,201.0	114.1	265.2
Virginia	297.6	290.0	9.6	9.0	19.5	23.3	109.4	92.1	159.1	165.7	1,734.6	3,734.0	790.0	986.2	678.0	2,521.2	266.6	226.7
Washington	250.6	374.9	4.2	4.3	21.8	39.6	87.6	106.2	137.0	224.8	2,910.3	5,352.8	1,381.4	1,605.6	1,197.6	3,386.9	331.3	360.3
West Virginia	129.1	152.3	6.1	6.0	8.2	13.2	31.6	42.2	83.2	90.9	927.7	2,102.4	413.0	597.4	405.1	1,341.7	109.7	163.3
Wisconsin	96.4	131.5	2.8	2.8	8.3	12.9	36.7	52.2	48.6	63.7	1,686.7	3,681.9	638.5	846.9	815.4	2,614.2	232.7	220.7
Wyoming	148.1	240.9	4.1	5.4	13.9	21.9	33.9	39.7	96.2	173.9	1,758.0	3,865.8	596.2	811.6	958.0	2,772.2	203.8	282.0
Baltimore	956.6	971.9	17.6	10.2	31.4	41.0	507.7	417.6	399.9	**503.1**	3,095.1	5,461.2	1,356.2	1,518.7	1,115.9	3,415.2	622.9	527.4
Boston	350.4	515.6	4.6	3.6	15.1	22.6	201.3	238.5	129.4	251.0	3,053.6	5,192.4	1,112.6	1,489.3	836.1	2,271.2	**1,104.8**	**1,431.9**
Chicago	671.7	560.5	11.5	13.7	28.5	24.6	373.8	289.4	257.9	232.7	2,241.8	5,124.3	919.8	1,190.8	712.9	3,196.5	609.1	737.1
Cleveland	483.0	600.8	16.1	14.2	27.0	32.6	302.7	364.9	137.2	189.0	2,459.9	4,346.6	849.3	1,237.3	509.4	2,194.1	1,101.2	915.2
Detroit	821.1	825.6	17.3	14.1	33.1	47.5	507.1	454.3	263.6	309.7	3,997.1	5,848.1	1,855.9	1,661.3	1,357.3	3,296.7	783.9	890.1
Houston	459.9	468.9	17.3	**18.0**	30.1	45.9	255.9	268.4	156.6	136.6	3,109.7	5,557.9	1,711.4	1,736.8	818.4	3,133.1	580.0	687.9
Los Angeles	853.0	1,004.1	12.8	16.0	**56.0**	**64.9**	377.7	429.0	406.6	494.2	**4,578.7**	6,009.0	**2,237.3**	2,199.9	1,365.6	2,899.8	975.8	909.4
Minneapolis	325.3	309.2	3.8	3.6	26.2	28.3	165.8	148.8	129.5	128.5	3,172.3	5,082.5	1,408.8	1,477.1	1,166.6	3,129.3	597.0	476.1
Newark	638.9	571.8	10.7	7.7	28.5	31.0	382.1	279.5	217.6	253.7	3,064.2	4,797.2	1,426.5	1,450.8	873.0	2,750.0	764.7	596.4
New York	**1,357.1**	**1,339.3**	**19.1**	17.1	37.0	42.8	**877.4**	**810.2**	**423.6**	469.2	3,737.1	6,103.4	1,747.4	2,112.7	1,100.2	2,897.7	889.5	1,092.9
Philadelphia	441.1	430.3	10.7	8.9	19.9	27.2	254.7	212.2	155.8	182.0	2,146.9	3,606.0	1,021.3	1,118.0	545.2	2,003.7	580.4	484.3
Pittsburgh	284.8	319.0	3.9	4.8	19.1	20.9	151.4	155.2	110.4	138.2	1,603.7	2,649.6	717.6	825.6	484.6	1,396.2	401.5	427.8
St. Louis	559.5	663.9	12.7	13.0	34.5	38.9	277.6	311.5	234.8	300.5	3,027.6	5,142.5	1,500.1	1,610.8	776.3	2,941.2	751.3	590.6
San Francisco	643.0	768.8	8.6	11.9	45.2	51.9	341.9	378.6	247.3	326.5	4,362.8	**7,170.2**	2,045.4	**2,255.1**	**1,488.8**	**4,170.0**	828.7	745.1
Washington, D.C.	669.3	604.5	12.4	10.3	42.0	36.1	375.0	352.9	239.9	205.2	2,811.0	5,223.3	1,123.7	1,387.1	1,079.1	3,439.5	608.1	396.7

Boldface: highest rate among states or listed metropolitan areas. Source: U.S. Department of Justice, Federal Bureau of Investigation, *Uniform Crime Reports*.

TRANSPORTATION AND TRADE

Transportation

State	Road and street mi[1] 1977	Motor vehicles in 000s, 1977[2]			Railroad mileage 1976[3]	Airports 1978	Pipeline mileage 1977[4]
		Total	Auto-mobiles	Trucks and buses			
Ala.	86,676	2,668	2,021	647	4,534	142	1,660
Alaska	9,930	276	171	105	20	763	193
Ariz.	55,746	1,536	1,112	424	2,036	209	1,355
Ark.	77,451	1,393	930	463	3,522	167	3,071
Calif.	172,841	14,748	11,740	3,008	7,291	813	10,352
Colo.	86,106	2,112	1,575	537	3,384	261	2,396
Conn.	19,044	2,136	1,965	171	634	103	94
Del.	5,244	378	309	69	291	32	3
D.C.	1,101	273	252	21	30	17	[5]
Fla.	98,094	6,140	5,039	1,101	4,104	438	288
Ga.	102,826	3,512	2,728	784	5,417	275	2,024
Hawaii	3,794	526	448	78	—	53	—
Idaho	57,788	723	448	275	2,631	190	633
Ill.	133,559[3]	6,905	5,674	1,231	10,555	876	10,914
Ind.	91,662	3,592	2,744	848	6,357	306	4,552
Iowa	112,460	2,261	1,636	625	7,539	253	4,581
Kan.	134,621	1,917	1,316	601	7,524	351	17,152
Ky.	69,706	2,444	1,768	676	3,517	97	2,444
La.	54,814	2,394	1,722	672	3,710	282	9,460
Maine	21,670	730	581	149	1,660	162	353
Md.	26,113	2,578	2,196	382	1,062	142	219
Mass.	32,867	3,284	2,944	340	1,404	139	242
Mich.	118,998	5,959	4,891	1,068	5,914	413	4,861
Minn.	128,456	2,845	2,118	727	7,294	336	2,841
Miss.	67,708	1,503	1,057	446	3,432	154	3,246
Mo.	117,223	3,013	2,284	729	6,010	365	7,142
Mont.	77,902	667	407	260	4,862	169	3,232
Neb.	96,894	1,331	942	389	5,360	305	3,317
Nev.	50,068	535	393	142	1,573	118	275
N.H.	15,333	547	462	85	751	54	190
N.J.	33,126	4,444	4,012	432	1,679	254	494
N.M.	70,858	925	621	304	2,057	139	6,960
N.Y.	109,419	7,717	6,760	957	5,266	490	1,586
N.C.	91,187	4,048	3,117	931	4,116	258	896
N.D.	106,430	582	344	238	5,060	211	1,773
Ohio	110,620[6]	7,553	6,506	1,047	7,677	569	6,524
Okla.	109,606	2,332	1,576	756	4,897	285	20,710
Ore.	108,278	1,844	1,474	370	3,043	301	414
Pa.	116,880	8,629	7,328	1,301	7,888	651	8,097
R.I.	5,537	605	528	77	139	24	17
S.C.	61,294	1,853	1,471	382	3,033	126	668
S.D.	82,426	554	352	202	3,352	134	642
Tenn.	81,567	2,885	2,214	671	3,181	144	739
Texas	257,649	9,358	6,864	2,494	13,273	1,250	65,966
Utah	48,501	914	624	290	1,726	93	1,118
Vt.	13,909[3]	317	252	65	767	60	177
Va.	63,430	3,368	2,825	543	3,849	249	824
Wash.	84,326	2,832	2,092	740	4,723	350	783
W.Va.	37,244	1,025	785	240	3,460	71	3,511
Wis.	105,520	2,739	2,269	470	5,733	332	926
Wyo.	32,854	385	226	159	1,778	93	7,151
TOTAL	3,857,356	143,835	114,113	29,722	199,115	14,069	227,066

[1] Includes federally controlled roads. [2] Estimated registration, excluding military. Detail may not add to totals because of rounding. [3] Preliminary. [4] Petroleum and products only. [5] Included with Maryland. [6] 1976. Sources: ICC; Dept. of Transportation, FAA, FHWA; Dept. of Energy; Motor Vehicles Manufacturers Assn.

Communications Facilities

State	Post Offices Sept. 30, 1978	TELEPHONES Jan. 1, 1978 Total	Residential	Radio AM	FM	TV	Public TV stations 1977	Daily Number	Circulation	Weekly* Number	Circulation	Sunday Number	Circulation
Alabama	620	2,309,442	1,763,468	137	70	17	9	25	732,098	109	462,548	17	671,390
Alaska	190	223,000	124,880	20	7	7	4	7	88,708	11	22,005	1	49,311
Arizona	212	1,629,694	1,183,229	60	28	11	2	17	563,532	51	449,819	5	480,097
Arkansas	640	1,331,712	1,007,219	87	51	8	4	33	360,186	117	348,231	16	455,310
California	1,122	18,103,632	12,965,153	229	185	57	14	125	6,081,840	435	5,600,835	44	5,139,437
Colorado	407	2,037,835	1,441,313	69	44	11	2	27	835,954	117	519,310	9	837,976
Connecticut	247	2,520,885	1,879,009	38	26	5	4	26	889,778	52	494,759	7	650,998
Delaware	55	487,227	358,752	10	8	—	—	3	161,224	14	95,633	2	148,833
District of Columbia	1	1,041,487	507,008	6	9	5	—	2	890,549	. . .	. . .	2	1,099,505
Florida	460	6,820,674	5,048,481	201	113	30	10	51	2,411,832	132	752,639	34	2,398,479
Georgia	644	3,727,524	2,783,986	178	83	18	10	37	1,042,698	204	1,048,955	14	1,020,709
Hawaii	76	630,021	409,514	26	8	10	2	5	311,343	3	102,803	2	210,841
Idaho	262	614,772	453,625	43	17	8	3	15	201,070	59	127,841	6	165,645
Illinois	1,265	9,442,720	7,037,941	125	128	22	6	88	3,243,038	583	3,227,328	23	2,741,523
Indiana	753	3,879,655	2,998,622	86	98	18	7	79	1,664,526	185	638,252	18	1,172,860
Iowa	952	2,142,508	1,623,936	74	64	14	8	40	901,044	341	770,225	9	766,514
Kansas	693	1,790,992	1,346,901	59	39	12	2	51	647,091	231	433,732	14	446,879
Kentucky	1,227	2,123,529	1,615,217	117	83	11	14	27	780,876	143	576,308	13	616,031
Louisiana	532	2,591,942	1,972,465	94	55	16	3	26	860,005	97	510,889	14	775,749
Maine	495	741,924	574,031	36	27	7	5	9	278,679	38	161,348	1	112,902
Maryland	427	3,241,071	2,433,847	52	33	6	4	13	699,828	75	780,087	4	673,927
Massachusetts	428	4,298,362	3,136,615	66	43	11	3	46	2,016,116	145	1,137,158	8	1,457,034
Michigan	857	6,769,342	5,157,834	128	107	24	7	52	2,457,209	256	1,517,694	14	2,237,415
Minnesota	857	2,967,265	2,195,605	91	68	13	5	30	1,109,546	332	988,635	12	1,069,555
Mississippi	465	1,403,614	1,086,842	107	66	10	8	25	395,425	99	285,195	10	289,837
Missouri	965	3,533,552	2,644,819	109	71	22	3	54	1,682,814	272	1,573,006	16	1,140,459
Montana	369	544,655	400,146	45	19	12	—	11	195,045	67	139,582	7	190,553
Nebraska	548	1,200,836	898,301	48	30	14	9	19	492,523	197	458,538	4	369,720
Nevada	92	627,027	421,930	22	12	8	1	9	189,618	16	40,390	4	170,265
New Hampshire	241	642,993	490,445	26	16	2	5	9	177,954	25	179,441	2	70,079
New Jersey	520	6,127,506	4,580,224	38	34	5	4	27	1,722,018	189	1,656,645	13	1,349,920
New Mexico	328	755,964	531,159	57	28	9	3	21	256,119	21	150,570	12	227,583
New York	1,630	13,187,030	9,473,921	162	118	30	12	76	6,809,813	398	2,504,768	32	6,295,360
North Carolina	776	3,711,050	2,802,560	209	86	18	9	51	1,322,720	118	524,118	22	1,069,762
North Dakota	443	477,873	353,169	26	13	11	2	10	144,860	89	178,065	2	49,984
Ohio	1,082	7,548,359	5,730,280	124	132	24	12	96	3,405,601	240	1,526,703	23	2,414,030
Oklahoma	632	2,119,319	1,558,758	67	49	10	4	54	863,046	194	367,411	46	898,756
Oregon	349	1,759,050	1,277,392	78	29	12	4	22	664,844	92	615,680	5	568,919
Pennsylvania	1,790	9,260,846	7,054,558	177	122	25	9	106	3,886,526	222	1,540,966	14	3,057,795
Rhode Island	55	681,794	514,498	15	7	2	1	7	362,644	14	85,017	2	221,425
South Carolina	393	1,874,630	1,408,508	107	53	12	7	20	586,883	71	269,533	8	469,255
South Dakota	404	473,256	355,047	33	16	10	2	13	177,283	144	195,099	3	101,798
Tennessee	569	2,921,239	2,209,312	155	69	18	5	34	1,177,702	125	554,472	14	980,210
Texas	1,509	9,572,605	6,922,203	288	170	54	7	112	3,416,383	500	1,307,823	87	3,589,840
Utah	212	936,932	688,531	35	16	3	2	5	270,887	52	172,248	4	264,438
Vermont	287	329,812	240,264	19	11	2	4	8	125,179	18	59,237	4	73,487
Virginia	900	3,499,260	2,597,740	136	72	15	7	33	1,067,363	99	608,234	14	820,282
Washington	467	2,786,380	2,036,544	95	44	14	6	23	1,083,440	138	1,052,847	13	1,050,731
West Virginia	1,021	1,037,003	793,075	62	31	9	3	28	469,090	73	266,399	9	382,587
Wisconsin	775	3,272,967	2,437,777	98	92	17	7	36	1,227,779	235	742,346	6	851,493
Wyoming	168	319,379	225,943	29	9	3	—	10	92,811	28	71,516	3	61,746
TOTAL U.S.	30,412	162,072,146	119,752,597	4,399	2,809	712	268	1,753	61,495,140	7,466	37,892,883	668	52,429,234

*Excluding District of Columbia.   Sources: U.S. Postal Service; Federal Communications Commission; American Telephone and Telegraph Co., The Editor & Publisher Co., Inc., *International Year Book, 1978* (Copyright 1978. All rights reserved. Used by permission.); National Newspaper Association; Corporation for Public Broadcasting.

Major Trading Partners, by Value

in millions of dollars

Country	EXPORTS 1972	1977	IMPORTS 1972	1977
North America	16,025	34,412	18,495	40,961
Canada	12,415[1]	25,749	14,927	29,356
Mexico	1,982	4,806	1,632	4,685
South America	3,661	9,276	3,434	9,344
Argentina	396	731	201	383
Brazil	1,243	2,482	942	2,246
Chile	186	520	83	261
Colombia	317	782	284	822
Peru	293	500	334	499
Venezuela	924	3,171	1,297	4,072
Europe	16,180	36,296	15,744	28,331
Belgium and Luxembourg	1,138	3,117	968	1,441
France	1,609	3,503	1,369	3,031
Germany, West	2,807	5,982	4,250	7,215
Italy	1,434	2,788	1,757	3,038
Netherlands, The	1,871	4,796	639	1,477
Spain	930	1,875	600	970
Sweden	472	1,099	601	990
Switzerland	672	1,359	619	1,085
United Kingdom	2,658	5,380	2,987	5,068
U.S.S.R.	542	1,628	95	234
Asia	11,353	32,411	15,134	49,592
Hong Kong	489	1,292	1,249	2,916
India	350	779	427	781
Indonesia	308	763	278	3,491
Iran	558	2,731	199	2,789
Israel	537	1,447	222	570
Japan	4,963	10,522	9,064	18,623
Korea, South	735	2,371	708	2,895
Malaysia	128	561	301	1,322
Philippines	365	876	491	1,103
Saudi Arabia	314	3,575	194	6,359
Singapore	385	1,172	265	875
Taiwan	628	1,798	1,293	3,681
Oceania	1,034	2,877	1,145	1,720
Australia	842	2,356	807	1,185
Africa	1,500	4,563	1,578	16,854
Algeria	98	527	104	3,065
Nigeria	114	958	271	6,096
South Africa[2]	602	1,071	325	1,275
Total	49,759[1]	120,163[1]	55,583[1]	146,817[1]

[1] Includes shipments to or from unidentified countries.   [2] Includes South West Africa.
Source: U.S. Department of Commerce, Domestic and International Business Administration, *Overseas Business Reports*.

Major Commodities Traded, 1977

in millions of dollars

Item	Total[1]	Canada	American Republics	Western Europe	Far East[2]
TOTAL EXPORTS	120,163	25,749[3]	16,346	33,752	21,220
Agricultural commodities					
Grains and preparations	8,755	110	880	1,758	2,426
Soybeans	4,393	97	127	2,508	1,225
Cotton, including linters, wastes	1,548	72	6	225	1,148
Nonagricultural commodities					
Ores and scrap metals	784	145	37	403	185
Coal, coke, and briquettes	2,730	792	212	709	938
Chemicals	10,827	1,539	2,350	3,737	1,932
Machinery	33,343	6,927	5,589	9,213	4,540
Agricultural machines, tractors, parts	2,780	1,012	562	527	133
Electrical apparatus	10,285	1,615	1,731	2,779	2,117
Transport equipment[4]	16,171	7,499	1,930	2,102	1,340
Civilian aircraft and parts	4,679	201	392	1,407	980
Paper manufactures	1,517	372	366	378	137
Metal manufactures	2,339	712	375	400	181
Iron and steel mill products[5]	1,608	605	354	201	121
Yarn, fabrics, and clothing	1,859	368	425	648	115
Other exports	34,289	6,511	3,695	11,470	6,932
TOTAL IMPORTS	146,817	29,356	16,335	27,417	36,405
Agricultural commodities					
Meat and preparations	1,273	74	276	261	5
Fish	2,056	418	506	416	426
Coffee	3,861	—	2,646	6	269
Sugar	1,079	29	533	11	292
Nonagricultural commodities					
Ores and scrap metal	2,234	995	444	77	55
Petroleum, crude	33,714	1,612	2,705	751	2,885
Petroleum products	7,812	343	2,343	904	428
Chemicals	5,432	1,451	212	2,465	554
Machinery	17,937	3,014	1,218	5,519	8,015
Transport equipment	17,557	7,697	207	3,928	5,668
Automobiles, new	10,626	3,795	[6]	2,940	5,441
Iron and steel mill products	5,281	584	99	1,959	2,468
Nonferrous metals	3,369	1,227	416	712	576
Textiles other than clothing	1,772	49	162	541	922
Other imports	43,440	11,863	4,568	9,867	13,842

[1] Includes areas not shown separately.   [2] Includes Japan, East and South Asia.
[3] Excludes grains and oilseeds transshipped through Canada to unidentified overseas countries.   [4] Excludes parts for tractors.   [5] Excludes pig iron.
[6] Less than $500,000.   Source: U.S. Dept. of Commerce, Domestic and International Business Administration, *Overseas Business Reports*.

Upper Volta

A republic of West Africa, Upper Volta is bordered by Mali, Niger, Benin, Togo, Ghana, and Ivory Coast. Area: 274,200 sq km (105,869 sq mi). Pop. (1978 est.): 6,464,000. Cap. and largest city: Ouagadougou (pop., 1975 est., 168,600). Language: French (official). Religion: animist; Muslim and Christian minorities. President in 1978, Gen. Sangoulé Lamizana; premiers, General Lamizana and, from July 7, Joseph Conombo.

Legislative elections on April 30, 1978, marked a return to parliamentary democracy, under the constitution approved in November 1977. With all parties allowed to participate, eight parties fielded 367 candidates for the 57 seats. However, the poll attracted only about 40% of the electorate.

Four candidates contested the presidential election, including the incumbent president, Gen. Sangoulé Lamizana. After an indecisive first round, Lamizana was reelected on May 28 with 56.2% of the vote. His chief rival, Macaire Ouedraogo, was considered to be a spokesman for former president Maurice Yaméogo, who was deposed in 1966 and forbidden by law to take part in the election.

On July 7, Joseph Conombo, a former minister in the French government, became premier of the first government of the Third Republic of Upper Volta. He was elected by 29 votes, with one against and 27 abstentions, suggesting that the country's parliamentarians had not put aside their quarrels.

(PHILIPPE DECRAENE)

UPPER VOLTA

Education. (1977–78) Primary, pupils 160,528, teachers 3,204; secondary, pupils 16,992, teachers 710; vocational, pupils 3,213, teachers 174; teacher training, students 623, teachers 33; higher, students 1,673, teaching staff 124.
Finance. Monetary unit: CFA franc, with (Sept. 18, 1978) a par value of CFA Fr 50 to the French franc (free rate of CFA Fr 218.81 = U.S. $1; CFA Fr 428.75 = £1 sterling). Budget (1977 est.) balanced at CFA Fr 23.1 billion.
Foreign Trade. (1976) Imports CFA Fr 34,420,000,000; exports CFA Fr 12,690,000,000. Import sources (1975): France 43%; Ivory Coast 20%; U.S. 7%. Export destinations (1975): Ivory Coast 48%; France 19%; Italy 7%; U.K. 6%; Togo 5%. Main exports (1975): livestock 36%; hides and skins 22%; cotton 16%; peanuts 15%; karité nuts 7%; sesame seed 6%.

Uruguay

A republic of South America, Uruguay is on the Atlantic Ocean and is bounded by Brazil and Argentina. Area: 176,215 sq km (68,037 sq mi). Pop. (1977 est.): 2,814,000, including (1961) white 89%; mestizo 10%. Cap. and largest city: Montevideo (pop., 1975, 1,229,700). Language: Spanish. Religion: mainly Roman Catholic. President in 1978, Aparicio Méndez.

In December 1977 the government had ratified plans for a new constitution by 1980. Presidential elections, planned for 1981, would be restricted to one candidate chosen jointly by the two traditional parties, Partido Blanco and Partido Colorado.

URUGUAY

Education. (1976) Primary, pupils 382,759, teachers 15,-679; secondary, pupils 141,731, teachers 13,980; vocational, pupils (1975) 38,343, teachers (1973) 3,953; teacher training, students (1975) 3,997, teachers (1973) 341; higher, students 39,927, teaching staff 2,149.
Finance. Monetary unit: new peso, with (Sept. 18, 1978) a free commercial rate of 6.47 new pesos to U.S. $1 (12.68 new pesos = £1 sterling). Gold, SDR's, and foreign exchange (June 1978) U.S. $469 million. Budget (1977 actual): revenue 2,937,500,000,000 new pesos; expenditure 3,177,100,000 new pesos. Gross domestic product (1976) 12,537,100,000 new pesos. Cost of living: (Montevideo; 1975 = 100; June 1978) 335.2.
Foreign Trade. (1977) Imports U.S. $729.9 million; exports U.S. $607.5 million. Import sources: Brazil 13%; Argentina 12%; U.S. 10%; Iraq 9%; West Germany 7%; Nigeria 7%; U.K. 5%. Export destinations: Brazil 16%; U.S. 14%; West Germany 12%; The Netherlands 7%; Argentina 6%; U.K. 5%. Main exports: wool 20%; meat 18%; hides 5%.
Transport and Communications. Roads (1973) 49,634 km. Motor vehicles in use (1974): passenger c. 151,600; commercial (including buses) c. 85,700. Railways (1976): 2,987 km; traffic 372 million passenger-km, freight (1975) 281 million net ton-km. Air traffic (1976): 83 million passenger-km; freight 200,000 net ton-km. Shipping (1977): merchant vessels 100 gross tons and over 45; gross tonnage 192,792. Telephones (Jan. 1977) 258,000. Radio receivers (Dec. 1975) 1.5 million. Television receivers (Dec. 1975) 351,000.
Agriculture. Production (in 000; metric tons; 1977): wheat c. 160; corn c. 121; rice 228; sorghum c. 120; potatoes (1976) 166; sweet potatoes (1976) c. 85; sugar, raw value (1976) 148; linseed 46; sunflower seed 34; apples (1976) c. 34; peaches (1976) c. 40; oranges c. 43; wine c. 95; wool 38; beef and veal c. 314. Livestock (in 000; May 1977): cattle 10,241; sheep (1976) 15,974; pigs c. 310; horses (1976) c. 418; chickens (1976) c. 7,400.
Industry. Production (in 000; metric tons; 1976): crude steel 15; cement 672; petroleum products 1,795; electricity (kw-hr) c. 2,800,000.

In February Gen. Gregorio Alvarez assumed power as commander in chief of the armed forces (and hence virtual ruler of the country), but conflicts among army leaders continued. On June 27 the head of military intelligence, Gen. Amaury Prantl, was arrested (he had accused Alvarez and other officers of abuses). The Organization of American States refused Uruguay's offer to act as host to its 1978 General Assembly because of human-rights concerns.

The government's market-oriented economic strategy continued to be based on export development. The low level of wages and the country's location between Argentina and Brazil were offered as attractive advantages for foreign investors. New trade agreements were reached with Brazil and the European Economic Community, and exports to the U.S. increased. Economic growth for 1978 was expected to be about 3%.

(MARTA BEKERMANN DE FAINBOIM)

Vatican City State

This independent sovereignty is surrounded by but is not part of Rome. As a state with territorial limits, it is properly distinguished from the Holy See, which constitutes the worldwide administrative and legislative body for the Roman Catholic Church. The area of Vatican City is 44 ha (108.8 ac). Pop. (1978 est.): 729. As sovereign pontiff, John Paul II is the chief of state. Vatican City is

Upper Volta

Uruguay

Vatican City

Universities:
see Education

Urban Mass Transit:
see Transportation

U.S.S.R.:
see Union of Soviet Socialist Republics

ALAIN DEJEAN—SYGMA

A throng of more than 50,000 mourners jammed St. Peter's Square on October 4 for the funeral of Pope John Paul I. The pope was entombed in St. Peter's Basilica.

administered by a pontifical commission of five cardinals, of which the secretary of state, Jean Cardinal Villot, is president.

Three popes in a year, a pontificate that lasted only 34 days, and, for the first time, a Pole elected to the Roman pontificate made 1978 an extraordinary year. Pope Paul VI (*see* OBITUARIES) showed signs of failing health in the spring when he did not take certain services during Holy Week. He addressed an anguished appeal to the members of the Red Brigades who had abducted the president of the Italian Christian Democrat Party, Aldo Moro, in March. He received Pres. Anwar as-Sadat of Egypt and King Hussein of Jordan and in July left for his summer residence of Castel Gandolfo, where he died suddenly on August 6.

An unusually brief conclave led unexpectedly to the election on August 26 of the patriarch of Venice, Albino Cardinal Luciani, as Pope John Paul I. His smiling simplicity soon won him widespread popularity, but on September 28 he died in bed of a heart attack (*see* OBITUARIES). A new conclave was summoned, and on October 16, confounding all the forecasts, it elected Karol Cardinal Wojtyla, archbishop of Krakow, Poland, who chose the papal name John Paul II (*see* BIOGRAPHIES).

(MAX BERGERRE)

See also Religion: *Roman Catholic Church.*

Venezuela

A republic of northern South America, Venezuela is bounded by Colombia, Brazil, Guyana, and the Caribbean Sea. Area: 899,180 sq km (347,175 sq mi). Pop. (1978 est.): 13,122,000, including mestizo 69%; white 20%; Negro 9%; Indian 2%. Cap.

Venezuela

and largest city: Caracas (metro. area pop., 1978 est., 2,755,000). Language: Spanish. Religion: predominantly Roman Catholic. President in 1978, Carlos Andrés Pérez.

Political affairs in Venezuela in 1978 were dominated by the presidential election, held on December 3. The campaign opened on April 1 with eight candidates. Television personality Renny Ottolina, who had announced his candidacy as an independent, had died in March in an air crash; in his place the former minister of information, Diego Arria Salicetti, stood as an antiparty candidate.

The principal issues of the campaign focused on housing, health, education, and the quality of public services. Under the constitution Pres. Carlos Andrés Pérez was prohibited from running for reelection until two intervening five-year presidential terms had passed. In the election Luis Herrera Campins, leader of the Social Christian Party (COPEI, equivalent of Christian Democratic), emerged a clear winner and was nominated as president-elect on December 4. His victory was a blow to the ruling Acción Democrática, whose candidate, Luis Piñerúa Ordaz, was supported by President Pérez.

Production of petroleum declined in 1978 and by October 9 had reached an average of only 2,130,000 bbl a day, compared with 2,280,000 bbl in the corresponding period of 1977. The fall in output caused concern about public finances, since the 1978 budget had been based on a production level of 2.2 million bbl a day. The budget was cut by about 6% overall to compensate for the loss of income, and when output recovered later in the year it was decided to base the 1979 budget on a conservative daily average of 2,170,000 bbl.

The state oil company, Petróleos de Venezuela

(Petrovén), placed emphasis on conserving stocks and exploration to compensate for declining reserves and to satisfy the increased demand for light and medium grades of crude oil. Offshore drilling was started in the Orinoco River delta with the sinking in October of the first of six deep wells. Other offshore projects were planned for the Golfo de la Vela and the Golfo Triste. Secondary recovery in existing oil fields was increased, and priority was given to the expansion of the country's four major refineries in order to meet demand for lighter crudes.

No further steps were taken to develop the Orinoco heavy-oil belt, where reserves were estimated at 700,000,000,000 bbl, as compared with 60,000,000,000 bbl in the rest of the country, although an agreement was signed in October with West Germany for the study of extraction and processing techniques. Negotiations also began for the acquisition of a minority shareholding in the refineries owned by Exxon and Shell in Aruba and Curaçao, respectively. In October the former minister of mines, Juan Pablo Pérez Alfonzo, publicly criticized the management of the nationalized oil industry by charging that Petrovén sold oil below the prices of the Organization of Petroleum Exporting Countries and acted in response to foreign interests rather than those of its stockholders.

Other projects started in 1978 included construction work on the Caracas underground railway and the formation of a coal-mining company in

Zulia state. The latter was expected to supply the planned Zulia steelworks with four million tons of coal annually as of 1980.

Increased imports of capital goods for development projects and of consumer goods, coupled with reduced oil exports, caused serious concern over the balance of payments, which was expected to show a large deficit. Imports were forecast to exceed exports by about $2 billion, as compared with a small trade surplus in 1977. A ban was imposed on the importation of about 500 items, including nonessential domestic goods, but this was not expected to be sufficient. Lower rates of growth were expected and considered necessary to contain inflation, which grew at a rate of 6.8% in the first half of the year.

During the September disturbances in Nicaragua, Venezuela sent aircraft and guns to Costa Rica for defense purposes and pressed for the overthrow of Gen. Anastasio Somoza, president of Nicaragua.   (SARAH CAMERON)

Veterinary Science

Worldwide, the number of veterinarians and veterinary schools continued to grow in 1978. There were indications that some Western countries, among them Belgium and Italy, were training more veterinarians than they could absorb. Australia also had a surplus, but it stemmed from the depression in cattle and sheep farming following long droughts. A continuing shortage of veterinary scientists in the third world was exacerbated because many graduates there preferred to work in the cities rather than in the rural areas where their services were most needed.

An innovation with important implications for animal breeding was the availability for veterinary use of hormonal products with a potent effect on the female reproductive organs. Thus, in artificial insemination programs, prostaglandins or the synthetic prostaglandin analogue, cloprostenol, enabled estrus ("heat") to be synchronized in a number of animals, allowing inseminations to be

The two French stallions believed to have brought contagious equine metritis, a venereal disease of horses, into the U.S. are Lyphard (left) and Caro. The disease was discovered in Kentucky in March and caused losses of millions of dollars to Thoroughbred horse breeders.

VENEZUELA

Education. (1974–75) Primary, pupils 1,990,123, teachers 63,198; secondary, pupils 583,163; vocational, pupils 34,240; teacher training, students 13,807; secondary, vocational, and teacher training, teachers 35,671; higher (1975–76), students 213,542, teaching staff 15,792.

Finance. Monetary unit: bolivar, with (Sept. 18, 1978) a par value of 4.29 bolivares to U.S. $1 (free rate of 8.40 bolivares = £1 sterling). Gold, SDR's, and foreign exchange (June 1978) U.S. $6,240,000,000. Budget (1977 actual): revenue 40,506,000,000 bolivares; expenditure 49,984,000,000 bolivares. Gross national product (1976) 133,520,000,000 bolivares. Money supply (May 1978) 40,-514,000,000 bolivares. Cost of living (Caracas; 1975 = 100; June 1978) 122.7.

Foreign Trade. (1977) Imports (fob) c. 36,615,000,000 bolivares; exports 40,960,000,000 bolivares. Import sources (1976): U.S. 41%; West Germany 9%; Japan 8%; Italy 5%. Export destinations (1976): U.S. 33%; Netherlands Antilles 20%; Canada 13%. Main exports: crude oil 63%; petroleum products 33%.

Transport and Communications. Roads (1976) 58,560 km. Motor vehicles in use (1975): passenger 955,200; commercial 369,400. Railways: (1976) 419 km; traffic (1971) 42 million passenger-km, freight 15 million net ton-km. Air traffic (1976): 2,538,000,000 passenger-km; freight 76,830,000 net ton-km. Shipping (1977): merchant vessels 100 gross tons and over 179; gross tonnage 639,396. Telephones (Jan. 1977) 742,000. Radio receivers (Dec. 1975) 2,050,000. Television receivers (Dec. 1975) 1,284,000.

Agriculture. Production (in 000; metric tons; 1977): corn c. 800; rice 508; sorghum c. 325; potatoes 190; cassava (1976) c. 353; sugar, raw value c. 460; tomatoes c. 102; sesame seed c. 80; bananas c. 1,050; oranges c. 258; coffee c. 40; cocoa c. 17; tobacco c. 15; cotton, lint c. 19; beef and veal c. 273. Livestock (in 000; 1977): cattle c. 9,654; pigs c. 1,997; sheep c. 104; goats c. 1,285; horses (1976) c. 457; asses (1976) c. 557; poultry c. 30,000.

Industry. Production (in 000; metric tons; 1977): crude oil 116,821; natural gas (cu m) c. 11,300,000; petroleum products (1976) 40,019; iron ore (64% metal content) 13,-684; cement (1976) 3,538; gold (troy oz; 1976) 16; diamonds (metric carats; 1976) 850; electricity (kw-hr; 1976) 23,276,000.

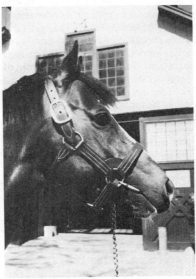

© THE GUARDIAN

Two litters of test-tube piglets were born in England in November. Embryos that had been fertilized in the U.S. were flown to Staffordshire, then transplanted into sows there.

made at a planned time. Prostaglandins also made the technique of breeding by embryo transfer more feasible. Embryo transfer involves transferring a minute fertilized ovum from a mated cow to another in which it grows to term. Thus a pedigree calf can be born to a nonpedigree mother. By using prostaglandins, veterinarians could ensure that a recipient cow is physiologically ready to accept an embryo from a donor animal.

Swine fever (hog cholera) had been eradicated from many countries, but a related disease, African swine fever, was appearing in a number of places outside the African continent. The virus responsible was carried in infected pork—harmless to humans—used in meals for aircraft passengers. The infection was passed on when uneaten meals and food scraps prepared in one country were fed to pigs in the country of destination. This was the cause of a serious outbreak of African swine fever in Brazil. Similarly, food waste from ships caused outbreaks in Malta and Sardinia. Incineration of such imported food waste would be necessary to eliminate the risk. The epidemiological patterns of other viral diseases, notably foot-and-mouth disease, were also influenced by the effects of long-distance transport, in this case by the growth of international trade in live cattle.

Contagious equine metritis, a venereal disease of horses first found in Europe and Australia, traveled to the U.S., possibly from France. The U.S. Department of Agriculture placed restrictions on the movement of Thoroughbred horses from Kentucky for breeding purposes. Affected countries introduced rigorous control measures in an effort to stamp out the disease, which may cause sterility and spontaneous abortions. In the U.K. all breeding horses had to be tested for the infection and the

Vietnam

results kept in a central register at Newmarket, the main centre for Thoroughbred studs. The microorganism responsible for the disease was isolated, but it could not be identified with any known species. British scientists therefore proposed it as a new species of the genus *Hemophilus, H. equigenitalis.* Difficulties in positively eradicating the infection led to renewed calls to allow artificial insemination in Thoroughbred horses, which would effectively prevent the spread of the disease.

(EDWARD BODEN)

[353.C]

Vietnam

The Socialist Republic of Vietnam is a southeast Asian state bordered in the north by China, in the west by Laos and Cambodia, and in the south and east by the South China Sea. Area: 338,392 sq km (130,654 sq mi). Pop. (1977 est.): 51,152,000. Capital: Hanoi (pop., 1976 est., 1,443,500). Largest city: Ho Chi Minh City (formerly Saigon; pop., 1976 est., 3,460,500; government authorities report an estimated 700,000 people have been resettled outside the city since 1976). Language: Vietnamese, French, English. Religion: Buddhist, animist, Confucian, Christian (Roman Catholic), Hoa Hao and Cao Dai religious sects. Secretary of the Communist Party in 1978, Le Duan; president, Ton Duc Thang; premier, Pham Van Dong.

Border conflicts with Cambodia on the one side and China on the other kept Vietnam on tenterhooks for much of 1978. In late 1977 some 60,000 men had been thrown into a punitive strike against Cambodia, although Vietnam's main-line forces had not been involved and the Cambodians

---

VIETNAM

Education. (1975–76) Primary, pupils 7,403,715, teachers 204,988; secondary and vocational, pupils 2,915,753, teachers 108,454; higher, students 80,323, teaching staff 9,642.

Finance. Monetary unit: dong, with (Sept. 18, 1978) a free rate of 2.18 dong to U.S. $1 (4.27 dong = £1 sterling). Budget (1977 est.) balanced at 8,950,000,000 dong.

Foreign Trade. (1976) Imports c. U.S. $900 million; exports U.S. $300 million. Import sources: U.S.S.R. c. 33%; China c. 11%; Japan c. 19%; East Germany c. 5%. Export destinations: U.S.S.R. c. 28%; China c. 17%; Japan c. 15%; Hong Kong c. 7%; East Germany c. 7%; Singapore c. 6%. Main exports (1974): clothing c. 10%; fish c. 10%; rubber c. 10%; coal c. 5%; beverages c. 5%.

Transport and Communications. Roads (1977) c. 60,-000 km. Motor vehicles in use (1976): passenger c. 100,-000; commercial (including buses) c. 200,000. Railways: (1977) c. 4,230 km; traffic (South only; 1973) 170 million passenger-km, freight 1.3 million net ton-km. Air traffic (South only; 1975): 120 million passenger-km; freight 1 million net ton-km. Navigable waterways (1976) c. 6,000 km. Telephones (South only; Dec. 1973) 47,000. Radio receivers (Dec. 1976) c. 5 million. Television receivers (Dec. 1976) c. 2 million.

Agriculture. Production (in 000; metric tons; 1977): rice 11,250; sweet potatoes (1976) c. 1,200; cassava (1976) c. 1,150; bananas c. 510; tea (1976) c. 9; coffee (1976) c. 8; tobacco c. 21; jute c. 31; rubber (1976) c. 20; pork c. 425; timber (cu m; 1976) 18,832; fish catch (1976) c. 1,010. Livestock (in 000; 1976): cattle c. 1,850; buffalo c. 2,260; pigs c. 11,500; chickens c. 56,000; ducks c. 36,000.

Industry. Production (in 000; metric tons; 1976): coal c. 4,250; cement c. 700; salt c. 350; phosphate rock c. 1,400; phosphate fertilizers (1976–77) c. 110; electricity (kw-hr) c. 2,500,000.

beat back the attack. Subsequently, thousands of former cadres demobilized after the Vietnam war were brought back into service, and by midyear some nine divisions were said to be battle-ready along the border. There were no immediate military moves, however; instead, emphasis was placed on propaganda. By April direct exhortations were going out to Cambodian soldiers to turn their guns on "the present power-holders in Phnom Penh." Military activity was resumed in late November, leading to speculation that Vietnam was beginning a dry-season offensive. In early December Radio Hanoi announced the formation of a Kampuchean United Front for National Salvation dedicated to the overthrow of the Pol Pot government. By year's end Vietnamese forces had reportedly penetrated deep into Cambodian territory.

Sino-Vietnamese relations were strained by China's support for the otherwise friendless Phnom Penh regime, as well as by a dispute over Vietnam's treatment of its ethnic Chinese minority. The ideological base for what developed into a campaign against ethnic Chinese was a decision by the Ho Chi Minh City People's Committee in March to implement the policy of "socialist transformation of private industry and commerce in the southern provinces." This was to be achieved by "abolishing capitalist trade and shifting capitalist traders to production." By month's end some 30,-000 private businessmen in the city—a vast majority of them Chinese—had ceased their activities. In the north rumours spread that war between Vietnam and China was imminent.

The result was an exodus of Chinese from Vietnam, on foot through high passes along the northern border and by fishing boat across the Gulf of Thailand. Checkpoints in the north became scenes of high tension as Vietnamese and Chinese faced each other, sometimes trading abuses, sometimes rocks, and sometimes shots. The escapees who preferred the sea routes became part of a mostly tragic saga. Scores of overcrowded boats miraculously turned up in ports as far away as Australia; some of the refugees were picked up at sea, and an unknown number were lost without a trace.

China protested vehemently and warned of grave consequences. In June two Chinese ships left Canton to take stranded refugees to the "motherland" but were not allowed to enter Vietnamese waters. In July China officially announced it had canceled its entire aid program to Vietnam. Chinese media charged that the Soviet Union was the instigator of trouble, while Hanoi roundly accused China of masterminding both the atrocities inside Cambodia and the border fighting between Cambodia and Vietnam.

The bitter feuding with its Communist neighbours evidently forced Hanoi to reactivate its vast military machine. In midyear Radio Hanoi reported that regional armed units of battalion and regimental size had been set up in areas northeast of Hanoi. By August there were reports of a "general mobilization." The party newspaper *Nhan Dan* said that five million young people aged from 18 to 30 had been registered for a new paramilitary organization called the National Task Force.

The worst floods to hit Vietnam in 35 years damaged over half a million homes and killed more than 100 people. Workers struggle to rescue a rice crop in the village of Hoang Long.

Another consequence was a reassessment by Hanoi of its relations with the Association of Southeast Asian Nations (ASEAN). Gone were the days when Vietnam saw the regional grouping as a U.S. conspiracy. In an all-out effort to cement relations with the ASEAN countries, Premier Pham Van Dong made personal visits to them in September–October. He repeatedly pledged that Vietnam would not support insurgents in other countries—a promise that was greeted with particular enthusiasm in Thailand. On the whole, however, ASEAN countries were cautious.

Hanoi's search for support was by no means confined to Southeast Asia. In the first half of the year some 30 delegations visited foreign capitals from Bonn to Baghdad. Vietnam appealed to the U.S. for normalization of relations "without conditions." It asked all countries for help in coping with a cereals deficit of some two million tons and, in September, for assistance in fighting floods. It took loans from the International Monetary Fund and the Japanese Fund for External Economic Cooperation and joined the Soviet bloc Council for Mutual Economic Assistance (Comecon) in midyear. The U.S. continued to refuse any assistance, but several other Western countries and the World Bank showed a willingness to help.

In May the government announced the unification of northern and southern currencies. The new dong's value against foreign currencies was unchanged at about 2.18 dong to a U.S. dollar. Simultaneously, a campaign was launched to limit the supply of money; all citizens were told how much cash they could keep and that anything above the limit would be confiscated unless a satisfactory explanation could be given. (T. J. S. GEORGE)

See also China.

Water Sports

Motorboating. Defending world offshore powerboat racing champion Betty Cook became in 1978 the first woman to win the United States driving title. The Newport Beach, Calif., resident trailed Joey Ippolito of Hollandale, Fla., by 220 points going into the season's final race, the Guy Lombardo Gold Cup, at Freeport, N.Y. But Ippolito was forced from the race by engine trouble, and Cook drove her 38-ft Scarab, "Kaama," to victory, taking the U.S. title, 1,700 points to 1,520 for Ippolito. The North and South American continental championships went to Billy Martin of Clark, N.J., who swept eight of his first ten races during the year, in Argentina, Uruguay, Panama, and the U.S.

Cook, Martin, and Ippolito were selected to be the U.S. entries in the world offshore championships, scheduled to be held in Argentina. Both Cook and Ippolito drove 38-ft Scarabs, Cook's powered by twin Mercruiser 482s and Ippolito's by Kickhaefer Aeromarine 454s. Martin's "Bounty Hunter" was a superlight Cigarette, also Mercruiser-powered and formerly owned by designer Don Aronow.

In unlimited hydroplane racing, veteran driver Bill Muncey in 1978 maintained his domination of the sport. He won six of the seven races on the circuit, his seventh Gold Cup at Owensboro, Ky., and the 50th unlimited victory of his career. He lost only the Tri-Cities, Wash., Regatta, when his Rolls-Royce-powered "Atlas Van Lines" developed engine trouble and Ron Snyder drove his "Miss Budweiser" to victory. Muncey's 50th win and his 50th birthday both occurred during the annual regatta in San Diego, Calif., in September.

Three new racing teams joined the unlimited circuit during the year. They were Squire Shops of Seattle, Wash., Circus Circus of Las Vegas, Nev., and Chuck King and Roger Janke of Orange,

Calif., who campaigned on behalf of three regional sponsors. The Unlimited Hydroplane Commission gave its highest award, the J. Lee Schoenith Trophy, to Ole Bardahl. The only other winner was the late Guy Lombardo.

Ken Magoon postponed his attempt to set a new transatlantic powerboat speed record. He cited technical problems and said he would make the attempt in the early summer of 1979.

(ALBERT W. LIMBURG)

River Sports. The fastest-growing of the river sports during 1978 was rafting, with greatly improved equipment becoming generally available. Also during the year U.S. canoeists and kayakers were venturing onto the nation's more challenging white-water rivers in increasing numbers. The era of the familiar heavy, bulbous canoe might be passing. Several sleek, straight-sided models designed by naval architects and built of new synthetic materials were introduced in 1978.

A long debate over the Boundary Waters Canoe Area in northern Minnesota culminated in the passage of new federal legislation conferring official "Wilderness" status on a large portion of the region. A landmark park-management proposal, designed to limit access to the Grand Canyon in Arizona, received widespread public response; a rewrite of the plan was subsequently scheduled.

The 14th world flat-water championships were held in Belgrade, Yugos. East Germany and Czechoslovakia dominated the various canoeing and kayaking races. The U.S. team made a surprisingly strong showing, with Brent Turner and Steve Kelly from the men's team and Leslie Klein and Ann Turner from the women's placing in the top ten in their events. In the U.S. national white-water competition, held in North Carolina in May, Eric Evans won the men's kayaking class for the ninth time.

Marathon racing, the "citizens' racing" of canoeing and kayaking, grew quickly in 1978, and might be the sport's biggest form of racing in terms

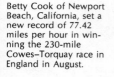

Betty Cook of Newport Beach, California, set a new record of 77.42 miles per hour in winning the 230-mile Cowes–Torquay race in England in August.

of number of participants. Marathon races were usually held on relatively moderate rivers, and there were enough different classes to accommodate boats of almost every description.

(ERIC LEAPER)

Water Skiing. Great Britain's Mike Hazelwood continued in 1978 to assert his mastery over the world's best water skiers by adding the Australian Moomba Masters and the U.S. Masters overall titles to the world championship he captured in 1977. Cindy Todd of Pierson, Fla., the world women's champion, also won the overall in the two Masters tournaments, but she lost in her bid for the U.S. national open overall crown to her teammate Deena Brush of West Sacramento, Calif.

In the U.S. national championships at Tivoli Gardens, Mich., in August, Brush won both the slalom and jumping events. Cyndi Benzel of Prior Lake, Minn., won the national open women's tricks title. Ricky McCormick of Winter Haven, Fla., successfully defended his U.S. national open overall title in the men's competition, but the individual events were won by Bob LaPoint of Castro Valley, Calif., in slalom, Cory Pickos of Eagle Lake, Fla., in tricks, and Robert Kempton of Tampa, Fla., in jumping.

Todd moved back into the winner's circle at the Group I (Western Hemisphere) Championships in September and set a new world women's slalom record of 58 buoys. Brush won the jumping title, while Maria Victoria Carrasco, the world women's tricks champion from Caracas, Venezuela, won in her specialty. Carlos Suarez of Caracas, who held the men's world tricks title, scored a record 7,950 points in tricks that gave him the edge in the Group I men's overall competition. McCormick won jumping, and LaPoint took the slalom. U.S. skiers won the team title, just as they had at the 1977 world meet, with Venezuela second and Canada third.

(THOMAS C. HARDMAN)

Surfing. The International Professional Surfing Association 1977 season ended with South Africa's Shaun Tomson capturing first place in the Hawaiian Tropic World Cup. This achievement carried him to the top spot in the IPS ratings, with a total of 5,948 points. Wayne Bartholomew of Australia finished a strong second with 5,385 points. Among the total of 51 professional surfers, South Africans, Hawaiians, and Australians gained the first 18 places.

The seventh world amateur surfing championships were held under the auspices of the International Professional Surfing Association at Nahoon Reef, East London, South Africa, July 3–14, 1978. Participating were teams from the U.S. (except Hawaii), South Africa, the U.K., France, and Hawaii. Political problems prevented Australia from competing and dampened the ardour of the contestants. Anthony Brodowicz, surfing brilliantly in six-foot classic waves, won the championship for South Africa.

(JACK FLANAGAN)

Water Polo. As they had done at the 1976 Olympic Games, Hungary and Italy battled it out for the top spot at the third world water polo championships, held in West Berlin in August. The game between the two perennial powers ended deadlocked 4–4, but a tie was all Italy needed to win the gold medal as Hungary had been tied earlier by the U.S.S.R. Yugoslavia defeated the U.S.S.R. 6–4 as those two teams finished third and fourth. The U.S. team continued its comeback effort by finishing fifth, followed by Romania, West Germany, and Bulgaria. Notably absent from the top finishers was The Netherlands, which fell from 3rd in Montreal to 13th.

For the first time ever a major international tournament was held in North America, as Canada, Mexico, and the United States acted as joint hosts for the first annual Can-Am-Mex series. Seven countries competed, with Hungary capturing first with a record of 16 wins, 1 loss, and 1 tie. Yugoslavia took second place, followed by West Germany and the United States.

The men's Amateur Athletic Union outdoor national championship was once again won by Concord, as Walter Bricker led his team to a 5–4 victory over runner-up West Valley. The 1977 National Collegiate Athletic Association championships were held in the East for the first time, with Brown University in Providence, R.I., acting as host. University of California (Berkeley) won the tournament with good team play, while California (Irvine) paced by Gary Figueroa, took second. Stanford took third-place honours, with Pepperdine finishing fourth to complete a California sweep.

(WILLIAM ENSIGN FRADY)

Western Samoa

A constitutional monarchy and member of the Commonwealth of Nations, Western Samoa is an island group in the South Pacific Ocean, about 2,600 km E of New Zealand and 3,500 km S of Hawaii. Area: 2,849 sq km (1,100 sq mi), with two major islands, Savai'i (1,813 sq km) and Upolu (1,036 sq km), and seven smaller islands. Pop. (1977 est.): 153,000. Cap. and largest city: Apia (pop., 1976 census, 32,100). Language: Samoan and English. Religion (1976): Congregational 50%, Roman Catholic 22%, Methodist 16%, others 12%. Head of state (*O le Ao o le Malo*) in 1978, Malietoa Tanumafili II; prime minister, Tupuola Taisi Tufuga Efi.

During 1978 Western Samoa enjoyed a continued recovery from the economic low point of 1975. Rising copra and cocoa prices and increased production helped to offset the loss in remittance income caused by a decline in the number of mi-

Western Samoa

WESTERN SAMOA

Education. (1977) Primary, pupils 41,280, teachers 1,346; secondary, pupils 9,087, teachers 468; vocational, pupils 231, teachers 48; teacher training, students 427, teachers 20.

Finance and Trade. Monetary unit: tala, with (Sept. 18, 1978) a free rate of 0.59 tala to U.S. $1 (1.17 tala = £1 sterling). Budget (1976 est.): revenue 16,255,000 tala; expenditure 16,321,000 tala. Foreign trade (1977): imports 32,254,000 tala; exports 11,577,000 tala. Import sources: New Zealand 29%; Australia 17%; Japan 15%; U.S. 9%; West Germany 8%; Fiji c. 5%; Singapore 5%. Export destinations: West Germany 46%; New Zealand 16%; The Netherlands 10%; U.S. 10%; Japan 7%. Main exports: cocoa 51%; copra 40%.

Weather:
see Earth Sciences

Weight Lifting:
see Gymnastics and Weight Lifting

Welfare:
see Social and Welfare Services

grants working in New Zealand. There was continued emphasis on increasing the productivity of village agriculture and on discouraging dependence on imports. Government revenue was expected to rise by 18% to reach $22 million, sufficient to allow a slight surplus on the budget and some $6 million for development projects. Foreign aid grants, mostly from New Zealand and Australia, totaled $8.6 million. A new shipping venture (related to the development of the South Pacific Forum shipping line) was to be financed by West Germany.

Prime Minister Tupuola Efi traveled to Australia to attend the Commonwealth heads of government regional meeting in Sydney in February. While there he called for the involvement of all interested countries (including the U.S.) in the proposed South Pacific Forum joint agency for the management of 200-mi economic zones in the Southwest Pacific; it was a viewpoint that was not universally popular with his Forum colleagues.

(BARRIE MACDONALD)

Winter Sports

The major sports on snow and ice continued their worldwide expansion during 1978. More indoor rinks brought a general increase in the number of skaters and curlers. Improved tracks in Europe and the U.S. added to the facilities for bobsledders and tobogganists. Winter resorts throughout the world lured even more skiers.

Skiing. The respective organizers of the Alpine and Nordic competitions cooperated more than in previous years. There was a marked increase in participation in long-distance cross-country events outside their traditional northern European stronghold, particularly in North America.

ALPINE RACING. The 12th World Cup series, generally considered more prestigious than the biennial world championships—the former measuring consistency throughout a season as opposed

Hanni Wenzel was the first skier from Liechtenstein ever to win the women's World Cup, awarded on the basis of a series of skiing events spread over a period of four months.

SVEN SIMON/KATHERINE YOUNG

to form at one meeting—consisted of 23 men's and 23 women's events spread over four months of meetings in Austria, France, Italy, Switzerland, the U.S., West Germany, and Yugoslavia.

Supreme in both slalom and giant slalom, Ingemar Stenmark (*see* BIOGRAPHIES) of Sweden took the men's trophy for a third successive time, again without even attempting a downhill race. Phil Mahre of the U.S. and Andreas Wenzel of Liechtenstein finished second and third. Franz Klammer of Austria was once more the outstanding downhiller, the results underlining a growing tendency to specialize. Stenmark won his 28th World Cup race—the men's record—since joining the circuit in 1974, having finished among the top three in 54 of 72 races entered.

Hanni Wenzel, sister of Andreas, became the first winner from Liechtenstein of the women's World Cup. Hers was, however, a somewhat hollow victory over Austria's Annemarie Proell-Moser, who would have won her sixth trophy by five points had she not been disqualified from one event when her ski suit did not conform with new regulations. Lise-Marie Morerod of Switzerland, the defending champion, finished third after again proving best in giant slalom. Wenzel topped the slalom list and Moser the downhill. Moser extended her seemingly untouchable career record number of World Cup race wins to 51, including 28 in the downhill.

The concurrently decided Nations' Cup was won for the sixth consecutive year by Austria, again topping both men's and women's standings. Switzerland was runner-up for a fourth straight year, and the U.S. finished third.

Thirty-five nations sent 304 competitors (192 men, 112 women) to the 25th world championships in Alpine events at Garmisch-Partenkirchen, West Germany, on January 29–February 5. Approximately 170,000 spectators attended, and the men's downhill alone drew nearly 50,000, a record for an Alpine competition.

Stenmark gained two gold medals, decisively winning the giant slalom with more than two seconds to spare from runner-up Wenzel and his third-placed Liechtenstein compatriot, Willi Frommelt. Stenmark's other victory was in the slalom, which he won by more than half a second from Piero Gros of Italy; Paul Frommelt, brother of Willi, finished third. Josef Walcher of Austria won the downhill, only 0.07 sec ahead of Michael Veith of West Germany, with another Austrian, Werner Grissmann, third. Wenzel won the Alpine combination, with Josef Ferstl (West Germany) and Pete Patterson (U.S.) second and third; Stenmark did not qualify because he did not compete in the downhill.

In the women's events Moser took gold medals in the downhill and combination and also gained a bronze in the giant slalom, which was won narrowly by Maria Epple (West Germany) from Morerod. Second and third in the downhill were Irene Epple, sister of Maria, and Doris De Agostini (Switz.). Lea Sölkner of Austria won the slalom from Pamela Behr of West Germany. Another Austrian, Monika Kaserer, was third despite making the fastest second run. Wenzel and Fabienne Serrat

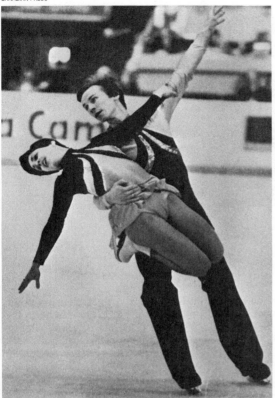

Soviet skaters Irina Rodnina and Aleksandr Zaitsev won their sixth consecutive victory in the pairs title in the world figure skating championships in Ottawa in March.

of France finished second and third in the combined. But for Moser, members of the Wenzel family would have taken corresponding men's and women's titles.

André Arnold of Austria attained the world professional title on the North American 13-event circuit, defeating the Swiss favourite, Josef Odermatt, runner-up for the third time. Jim Hunter of Canada was third. The first women's professional title, decided over three events, went to Lyndall Heyer (U.S.), ahead of Judy Nagel (U.S.) and Toril Forland (Norway).

NORDIC EVENTS. The 32nd world championships in Nordic events at Lahti, Fin., on February 17–26, were contested by 370 competitors (285 men, 85 women) from 28 nations; 173,500 spectators attended. A highlight of the tournament was the winning of medals for the first time by cross-country racers from Poland and France. Josef Luszczek was Polish victor in the 15 km, more than two seconds ahead of Evgeny Belyaev (U.S.S.R.) and Juha Mieto (Fin.). Sergey Saveliev and Nikolai Zimyatov of the U.S.S.R. took the first two places in the 30 km, Luszczek finishing third. Sven-Åke Lundbäck (Sweden) won the grueling 50 km from Belyaev, with Frenchman Jean-Paul Pierrat placing third. Sweden, Finland, and Norway finished in that order in the 4 × 10-km relay. Konrad Winkler and Ulrich Wehling of East Germany finished first and third in the Nordic combination, with Rauno Miettinen of Finland placing second.

Tapio Räisänen of Finland won the spectacu-

lar 90-m jumping, followed by Alois Lipburger (Austria) and Falko Weisspflog (East Germany). The 70-m jump was an unexpected success for another East German, Mathias Buse, relegating his more experienced compatriot, Henry Glass, to second place ahead of Aleksey Borovitin (U.S.S.R.).

Zinaida Amosova gained two gold medals and one bronze in the women's cross-country events, winning both the 10 km and 20 km and helping the Soviet team to finish third in the 4 × 5-km relay, behind the Finnish victors and East Germany. Helena Takalo won the 5 km from her fellow Finn Hilkka Riihivuori, with Raisa Smetanina (U.S.S.R.) third. Smetanina and Riihivuori reversed the order in the 10 km behind Galina Kulakova, the veteran Soviet winner of four Olympic gold medals.

East German ski-shooters dominated the world biathlon championships, held from February 27 to March 5 at Hochfilzen, Austria. Frank Ulrich, key racer in the team relay victory, also won the 10 km and placed second in the 20 km behind Odd Lirhus of Norway.

OTHER EVENTS. Professional freestyle, the highly specialized, increasingly popular form of spectacular acrobatic and balletic skiing, made more headway in North America than in Europe. The men's World Trophy was retained by John Eaves of Canada, and the women's was captured by Genia Fuller of the U.S. Steven McKinney of the U.S. broke the world speed skiing record on July 14, hurtling down a glacier above Cervinia, Italy, at 123.044 mph.

Ice Skating. Although increased cost tended to reduce the number of new rinks run by private enterprise, a trend to municipal ownership resulted in new facilities close to many people who had previously been without them.

FIGURE SKATING. All four titles were defended, but only one retained—indeed a rarity—at the world figure and dance championships in Ottawa on March 7–11, involving 106 skaters from 19 nations. Higher and more difficult jumps were a main feature of a men's event, which ended so near to a three-way tie that the new champion, Charles Tickner of the U.S., was placed first by only two of the nine judges. Four placed Jan Hoffmann of East Germany in front and three chose Britain's Robin Cousins, but the complex scoring system marginally favoured Tickner. Despite this enthralling cliff-hanger and the humbling of Vladimir Kovalev, the fourth-placed defending champion from the U.S.S.R., the little-known Vern Taylor of Canada, who finished only 12th, almost overshadowed all others by achieving the first triple axel jump in international competition —a mighty leap from a forward takeoff involving three and a half midair rotations. Tickner reached his peak with a combination of two great triple toe loop jumps joined by a three turn. Hoffmann might have succeeded to the title had he not fallen from a triple lutz. Cousins landed three triples and was adjudged the best of all in free skating, losing only because he was narrowly outscored in figures.

Anett Pötzsch became the third East German to capture the women's title. Linda Fratianne, the

Winter Sports

A new course record in the two-man bobsled event was set at Lake Placid, New York, in February by the Swiss team of Erich Scharer and Josef Benz. They drove the course in 1:05.12.

deposed U.S. champion, clearly outpointed Pötzsch in the free skating but could not close the gap established by the new titleholder in the figures. Mindful of her initial advantage, Pötzsch proceeded with caution but clinched the issue with two characteristic triple salchow jumps. Although the technical highlights of the third-place finisher, Susanna Driano of Italy, were almost flawless, her linking footwork and choreographic presentation were not so impressive.

Several records were shattered when Aleksandr Zaitsev and Irina Rodnina retained, with apparent ease, the pairs title they first gained in 1973. The slick Soviet pair provided five action-packed minutes with admirable cohesion, excelling with a triple twist lift, throw axel, death spiral, and superbly timed double jumps. It was the sixth consecu-

tive victory for this pair, two more than any other, but for Rodnina it was a tenth straight win — including four with her previous partner, Aleksey Ulanov. This equaled the largest number of world victories in any figure skating event, a distinction shared with two great pre-World War II soloists, Sonja Henie (Norway) and Ulrich Salchow (Sweden). A keen tussle for second place was won by the East Germans, Uwe Bewersdorff and Manuela Mager, edging out the more spectacular U.S. pair, Randy Gardner and Tai Babilonia.

The most surprising title upset occurred in the ice dance when Gennadi Karponosov and Natalia Linichuk dethroned their Soviet compatriots Andrey Minekov and Irina Moiseyeva, who placed second. Warren Maxwell and Janet Thompson of the U.K., second-place finishers in 1977, slipped to fourth behind their long-standing Hungarian rivals, Andras Sallay and Krisztina Regöczy.

The international ice stage made way for the understudies when 81 skaters from 21 countries took part in the first official world junior championships, on March 21–25 at Mégève, France. With entrants limited by age to 16 for singles and 18 for doubles, Canadians were most successful, with Dennis Coi winning the boys' event and Paul Marini and Barbara Underhill the pairs. Jill Sawyer of the U.S. took the girls' title, and the ice dance went to Sergey Panomarenko and Tatiana Durasova of the U.S.S.R.

SPEED SKATING. Eric Heiden of the U.S. retained the men's world speed championship in Göteborg, Sweden, on February 25–26. Jan Egil Storholt of Norway was again runner-up, with Sergey Marchuk (U.S.S.R.) third. Heiden won three of the four events, the 10,000 m going to the Norwegian veteran Sten Stensen.

The women's world speed championship, in Helsinki on March 4–5, was dominated by Eastern Europeans. Tatyana Averina, who took two Olympic gold medals in 1976, won from her Soviet compatriot Galina Stepanskaya, with Marion Dittmann third for East Germany. Averina won the two middle distance events and Dittmann the

The U.S. curling rink, shown here in action, won the 20th world curling championship in Winnipeg, Manitoba, in April.

CANADIAN PRESS

3,000 m, but the 500 m went to another Soviet skater, Valentina Golovenkina.

The separate world sprint titles for men and women, contested on February 11–12 over the new Olympic circuit at Lake Placid, N.Y., were won, respectively, by Heiden and Liubov Sadchikova of the U.S.S.R.

Three new world records were established. In March, Heiden lowered the 3,000 m to 4 min 7.01 sec at Inzell, West Germany, and reduced the 1,-000 m to 1 min 14.99 sec at Savalen, Norway. In April, Khalida Vorobyeva of the U.S.S.R. clocked the women's 1,500 m in 2 min 7.18 sec at Medeo, Alma-Ata, U.S.S.R.

Bobsledding. Highlight of the season was a successful testing of the renovated Mt. Van Hoevenberg track at Lake Placid, suitably improved for the 1980 Olympic events with two years to spare and in time to stage the 45th world championships on February 4–12. This event attracted competitors from 13 nations. The titles were retained by the defending champions, East Germany and Switzerland.

Horst Schonau steered the winning East German four-man sled with an aggregate time for the four runs 0.17 sec faster than the Swiss runners-up, driven by Erich Scharer. Meinhard Nehmer, the defending champion, finished third.

Scharer proved to be the outstanding rider of the meeting, not only capturing the two-man title with brakeman Josef Benz, but setting new track records in both events and thereby earning the Stan Benham Memorial Trophy, awarded annually in memory of the U.S. world champion (1949 and 1950). Like Schonau, Scharer also defeated a compatriot who was the title defender, Hans Hiltebrand, this time humbled in fourth spot behind runner-up Nehmer and the third-placed West German sled driven by Jakob Resch.

Tobogganing. Paul Hildgartner of Italy won the men's title in the 24th world luge championships on a fast, tightly curved track in Imst, Austria, on January 21–22. Close runner-up was Anton Winkler of West Germany, ahead of the third-placed Austrian veteran Manfred Schmid. Vera Sosulya achieved a women's victory for the U.S.S.R., followed by Andrea Fendt of West Germany and Angelika Schäfferer from Austria.

Swiss riders achieved grand slams in both the major classic events for skeleton tobogganists on the Cresta Run at St.-Moritz, Switz. Christian Nater won the 69th Grand National over the full course, with Bruno Bischofberger runner-up. Third was Gianni Bibbia, son of Nino, winner of the event a record eight times and, remarkably at 55, the sixth-place finisher. The 55th Curzon Cup from Junction was regained by Poldi Berchtold, the 1975 victor and holder of the track record, with runner-up Urs Nater followed by his brother, Christian.

Curling. The 20th world curling championship for the Air Canada Silver Broom, in Winnipeg, Man., from March 27 to April 2, was won by a U.S. rink from Superior, Wis., comprising Bob Nichols, Bill Strum, Tom Locken, and Bob Christman. They beat Kristian Soerum's rink from Norway 6–4 in the final. It was the second title in

three years for the U.S., which had defeated Tom Schaeffer's Swedish defending champions 6–5 in the semifinals. Norway made its first appearance in the final round after pulling the surprise of the tournament with a 6–2 triumph over Mike Chernoff's Canadian rink in the other semifinal. Spectators at the final numbered 9,172 and a record 102,193 attended the seven-day tournament.

Canada, represented by a Calgary rink skipped by Paul Gowsell, retained the fourth world junior championship (under 21), sponsored by Uniroyal at Grindelwald, Switz., on March 11–17. Scotland was runner-up with Sweden and Norway third and fourth, respectively.   (HOWARD BASS)

See also Ice Hockey.
[452.B.4.g–h]

Yemen, People's Democratic Republic of

A people's republic in the southern coastal region of the Arabian Peninsula, Yemen (Aden) is bordered by Yemen (San'a'), Saudi Arabia, and Oman. Area: 287,680 sq km (111,074 sq mi). Pop. (1977 est.): 1,797,000. Cap. and largest city: Aden (pop., 1973, 132,500). Language: Arabic. Religion: Muslim. Chairmen of the Presidential Council in 1978, Salem Ali Rubayyi until June 26, Ali Nasir Muhammad Husani from July 1, and Abd-al Fattah Ismail from December 27; prime minister from July 1, Ali Nasir Muhammad Husani.

People's Democratic Republic of Yemen

In 1978 the People's Democratic Republic of Yemen (Aden; South Yemen) increased its pro-Soviet orientation following elimination of the relatively moderate Pres. Salem Ali Rubayyi. In January and February South Yemen forces were involved in serious border clashes with Saudi Arabia. The Saudis were alarmed over events in the Horn of Africa, where Cuban-trained South Yemen troops were supporting the Ethiopians while Aden was being used as a staging area for Soviet arms and

---

YEMEN, PEOPLE'S DEMOCRATIC REPUBLIC OF

Education. (1974–75) Primary, pupils 196,466, teachers 6,467; secondary, pupils 38,389, teachers 1,656; vocational, pupils 676, teachers (1973–74) 142; teacher training, students 631, teachers 47; higher, students 934, teaching staff 92.

Finance and Trade. Monetary unit: Yemen dinar, with (Sept. 18, 1978) a par value of 0.345 dinar to U.S. $1 (free rate of 0.68 dinar = £1 sterling). Budget (1976–77 actual): revenue 24,760,000 dinars; expenditure 39,150,000 dinars. Foreign trade (1976): imports 115.7 million dinars; exports 61.2 million dinars. Import sources: Kuwait *c.* 13%; Japan *c.* 10%; U.K. 6%. Export destinations: Canada *c.* 71%; Japan *c.* 9%. Main export: petroleum products 83%.

Transport. Roads (1976) 10,494 km (including 1,356 km with improved surface). Motor vehicles in use (1976): passenger 11,900; commercial (including buses) 10,500. There are no railways. Shipping traffic (1974): goods loaded 2,-308,000 metric tons, unloaded 3,780,000 metric tons.

Agriculture. Production (in 000; metric tons; 1976): millet and sorghum *c.* 65; wheat *c.* 12; watermelons *c.* 38; dates 41; cotton, lint *c.* 3; fish catch *c.* 127. Livestock (in 000; 1976): cattle *c.* 102; sheep *c.* 930; goats *c.* 1,230; camels *c.* 40; chickens *c.* 1,400.

Industry. Production (in 000; metric tons; 1976): petroleum products *c.* 1,760; salt *c.* 75; electricity (kw-hr) 180,000.

Wood Products:
see Industrial Review

World Bank:
see Economy, World

Wrestling:
see Combat Sports

Yachting:
see Sailing

Cuban troops en route to Ethiopia. However, during the first part of the year there were still tentative moves toward rapprochement with Saudi Arabia and other conservative Arabian states, sponsored by the president but opposed by the powerful secretary-general of the United Political Organization, Abd-al Fattah Ismail.

The split was worsened by Ismail's declared intention to merge all political forces into a single Marxist Vanguard Party. The power struggle came to a head following the murder on June 24 of the Yemen Arab Republic's president, Ahmad al-Ghashmi, by a bomb carried by an envoy of President Ali Rubayyi. On June 26, after fighting in Aden, Ismail emerged victorious and Ali Rubayyi and two of his ministers were executed. Ali Nasir Muhammad Husani, chairman of the Presidential Council from July 1, remained prime minister after Ismail's election as chairman on December 27.

(PETER MANSFIELD)

Yemen Arab Republic

Yugoslavia

Yemen Arab Republic

A republic situated in the southwestern coastal region of the Arabian Peninsula, Yemen (San'a') is bounded by Yemen (Aden), Saudi Arabia, and the Red Sea. Area: 200,000 sq km (77,200 sq mi). Pop. (1975): 5,237,900. Cap. and largest city: San'a' (pop., 1975, 134,600). Language: Arabic. Religion: Muslim. Presidents in 1978, Col. Ahmad al-Ghashmi to June 24 and, from July 17, Col. Ali Abdullah Saleh; premier, Abdel-Aziz Abdel-Ghani.

In February 1978 Pres. Ahmad al-Ghashmi announced a "return to democracy" for the Yemen Arab Republic (San'a'; North Yemen) with the formation of a 99-member Constituent People's Assembly, to sit for three years. In April the new five-year presidency, to which Ghashmi was elected by the Assembly, replaced the Command Council. When Ghashmi was assassinated on June 24 by a bomb carried by an envoy from the People's Democratic Republic of Yemen (Aden; South Yemen), the new political system allowed a smooth transition. A four-man Command Council was formed and one of its members, Col. Ali Ab-

---

YEMEN ARAB REPUBLIC

Education. (1976–77) Primary, pupils 221,482, teachers (1975–76) 6,604; secondary, pupils 24,873, teachers (1975–76) c. 1,172; vocational, pupils 503, teachers (1975–76) 60; teacher training, students 1,650, teachers (1975–76) 113; higher, students (1975–76) 2,408, teaching staff (1973–74) 58.

Finance and Trade. Monetary unit: rial, with (Sept. 18, 1978) a par value of 4.56 rials to U.S. $1 (free rate of 8.89 rials = £1 sterling). Budget (1977–78 est.): revenue 1,550,000,000 rials; expenditure 2,053,000,000 rials. Foreign trade: imports (1976) 1,882,200,000 rials; exports (1977) 50,610,000 rials. Import sources: Saudi Arabia 12%; Japan 10%; India 7%; Australia 7%; U.K. 6%; China 6%; The Netherlands 6%. Export destinations (1976): Japan 42%; China 33%; Yemen (Aden) 27%; Italy 18%; Saudi Arabia 16%. Main exports: cotton 49%; coffee 17%; hides and skins 12%.

Agriculture. Production (in 000; metric tons; 1977): barley c. 80; corn (1976) 104; wheat (1976) 90; sorghum c. 800; potatoes (1976) 86; grapes c. 43; dates c. 70; coffee c. 5; tobacco (1976) 6; cotton, lint c. 10. Livestock (in 000; 1976): cattle c. 1,000; sheep c. 3,200; goats c. 7,400; camels c. 120; asses c. 640.

---

dullah Saleh, was elected president by the Assembly on July 17.

President Saleh, a member of the powerful Hashed tribal confederation, endeavoured to ease the chronic tension between northern tribesmen and urban political groups by bringing tribal leaders into the Assembly. An attempted coup by dissident army officers on October 15 failed, and on November 5, 12 of the 13 convicted participants were executed.

Difficult relations with South Yemen were exacerbated by the assassination. North Yemen exonerated the South Yemen president, Salem Ali Rubayyi, who was himself executed in a coup on June 26, and blamed the militant Marxists who now dominated the Aden regime. Relations with Saudi Arabia remained close, and Saudi aid was substantial.

(PETER MANSFIELD)

Yugoslavia

A federal socialist republic, Yugoslavia is bordered by Italy, Austria, Hungary, Romania, Bulgaria, Greece, Albania, and the Adriatic Sea. Area: 255,804 sq km (98,766 sq mi). Pop. (1978 est.): 21,912,000. Cap. and largest city: Belgrade (pop., 1975 UN est., 870,000). Language: Serbo-Croatian, Slovenian, and Macedonian. Religion (1953): Orthodox 41%; Roman Catholic 32%; Muslim 12%. President of the republic for life and president of the League of Communists in 1977, Marshal Tito (Josip Broz); president of the Federal Executive Council (premier), Veselin Djuranovic.

Throughout 1978 Yugoslavia pursued an active policy in Europe and among the nonaligned nations. In March Foreign Minister Milos Minic traveled to Sudan, Ethiopia, and Somalia attempting to mediate the conflict in the Horn of Africa. In April and May Minic visited countries in South and Southeast Asia.

At the 11th congress of the Yugoslav League of Communists, held in Belgrade June 20–23, a newly streamlined 24-member Presidium was elected, with Stane Dolanc as its secretary. The concept of "self-managing pluralism" was put forward in a report by Edvard Kardelj, the party's chief ideologist and senior man after Tito. (Kardelj became seriously ill in the second half of the year, and on October 19 Branko Mikulic, a Croat leader from Bosnia, was elected Tito's deputy in the Presidium for 12 months.)

At the congress Josip Vrhovec, Yugoslavia's foreign minister since May 16, criticized Cuba (without mentioning it by name) for its "hegemonistic" and "divisive" policy in the nonaligned grouping, as also did Minic. These criticisms of Cuba and its backer in Africa, the Soviet Union, were echoed by President Tito at the conference of foreign ministers of nonaligned countries in Belgrade (July 25–30). The visit to Yugoslavia in August by the Chinese Communist Party leader Hua Kuo-feng was criticized in the Soviet press and led to a cooling of relations. In September Tito canceled his planned meeting with Pres. Leonid I. Brezhnev of the Soviet Union. Relations with Bulgaria also deteriorated, again over Macedonia.

Chinese Communist Party Chairman Hua Kuo-feng addressed his Yugoslavian hosts at a banquet in Belgrade in August. At Hua's left is President Tito.

In contrast, Yugoslavia's relations with the West developed well. Tito visited the U.S. in March, when Pres. Jimmy Carter endorsed Yugoslavia's nonaligned stance and expressed support for its territorial integrity. Purchases of $1.4 million of U.S. military equipment were authorized in 1978, and Yugoslav Minister of Defense Gen. Nikola Ljubicic visited the U.S. in September to discuss further arms acquisitions. Also in September, Stane Potocar, chief of Yugoslavia's general staff, visited China, North Korea, and India. The Italian Communist Party's chief foreign relations expert, Giancarlo Pajetta, visited Yugoslavia in August at the time of Hua Kuo-feng's visit. Press reports suggested that Yugoslavia was helping to bring about a resumption of contacts between the Chinese and Italian parties. Italian Communist Party leader Enrico Berlinguer visited Yugoslavia in October. The prince of Wales was welcomed in November.

The Helsinki Accords Review Conference

At the close of the 35-nation summit meeting of the Conference on Security and Cooperation in Europe in Helsinki, Fin., July 30–Aug. 1, 1975, the participants decided to review at a meeting two years later the progress achieved in implementing the provisions of the Helsinki Final Act. Preparations for this follow-up meeting were completed in the summer of 1977, and it was held in Belgrade, Yugos., from Oct. 4, 1977, to March 9, 1978.

From the outset it was clear that deep differences of opinion existed among the participants. The NATO and European Economic Community (EEC) nations saw the Belgrade gathering as an opportunity for a full and frank review of the achievements and failures of the Helsinki process, especially the so-called Basket III of the Final Act which dealt with cooperation in humanitarian and informational fields. The neutral and nonaligned states broadly supported the NATO and EEC positions, especially on human rights, but also showed a great preoccupation with security issues.

On the Soviet bloc side, Romania took an independent line close to that of the neutral and nonaligned states. However, the rest of the Soviet bloc wanted only a perfunctory treatment of the Final Act implementation, with each government simply reporting what it had done. This was a clear reflection of the fear of the Soviet and Eastern European governments that the conference could give a further boost to their own domestic human rights campaigners, who had already made the Helsinki act the basis for their activities.

To divert attention from the human rights issues, the Soviet Union and its allies proposed conferences on energy, transport, the environment, and other topics from Helsinki's Basket II. They also tried to use the Belgrade meeting as a forum for attacking NATO's security policy by, for example, pressing for a pledge by both NATO and the Warsaw Pact not to take in new members—a move designed to make more difficult Spain's future entry into NATO. As far as public opinion outside the Soviet bloc was concerned, these tactics failed. The calls for human rights measures at Belgrade were incomparably better received than Soviet slogans for a "military détente."

Nevertheless, at the Belgrade conference the Soviet Union managed to prevent the adoption of any further commitments in the human rights field. Deep disagreements over the content of the Concluding Document prolonged the conference by more than two months beyond its provisional closing date of Dec. 22, 1977. In the end, the non-Communist nations decided to accept a document without "teeth" rather than see the whole Helsinki process stopped completely. Another follow-up meeting was scheduled to begin in Madrid on Nov. 11, 1980.

YUGOSLAVIA
YUGOSLAVIA

Education. (1976–77) Primary, pupils 1,456,809, teachers 58,801; secondary, pupils 1,786,330, teachers 83,377; vocational, pupils 483,969, teachers 40,-415; teacher training, students 9,535, teachers 791; higher, students 256,420, teaching staff 16,202.

Finance. Monetary unit: dinar, with (Sept. 18, 1978) a free rate of 18.79 dinars to U.S. $1 (36.81 dinars = £1 sterling). Gold, SDR's, and foreign exchange (June 1978) U.S. $2,069,000,000. Budget (1976 actual): revenue 134,220,000,000 dinars; expenditure 145,240,000,000 dinars. Gross material product (1976) 593 billion dinars. Money supply (June 1977) 225.1 billion dinars. Cost of living (1975 = 100; June 1978) 146.4.

Foreign Trade. (1977) Imports 176,290,000,000 dinars; exports 96,150,000,000 dinars. Import sources: West Germany 16%; U.S.S.R. 14%; Italy 11%; U.S. 6%; France 5%; Iraq 5%. Export destinations: U.S.S.R. 22%; Italy 13%; West Germany 7%; U.S. 6%. Main exports: machinery 19%; food 10%; textiles 8%; ships and boats 8%; chemicals 6%; tim-ber 6%; nonferrous metals 6%. Tourism (1976): visitors 5,572,000; gross receipts U.S. $802 million.

Transport and Communications. Roads (1976) *c.* 113,510 km. Motor vehicles in use (1976): passenger 1,732,100; commercial 152,360. Railways: (1976) 9,967 km; traffic (1977) 10,356,000,000 passenger-km, freight 22,230,000,000 net ton-km. Air traffic (1976): 2,150,000,000 passenger-km; freight 20.6 million net ton-km. Shipping (1977): merchant vessels 100 gross tons and over 459; gross tonnage 2,-284,526. Telephones (Jan. 1977) 1,430,600. Radio licenses (Dec. 1976) 4,526,000. Television licenses (Dec. 1976) 3,463,000.

Agriculture. Production (in 000; metric tons; 1977): wheat 5,622; barley 650; oats 309; corn 9,856; potatoes *c.* 2,854; sunflower seed 437; sugar, raw value *c.* 765; onions *c.* 280; tomatoes *c.* 440; cabbages (1976) *c.* 710; chillies and peppers (1976) *c.* 315; watermelons (1976) *c.* 556; plums (1976) *c.* 569; apples 367; wine 638; tobacco 62; beef and veal *c.* 325; pork *c.* 660; timber (cu m; 1976) 14,036. Live-stock (in 000; Jan. 1977): cattle 5,641; sheep 7,481; pigs 7,326; horses 812; chickens 53,779.

Industry. Fuel and power (in 000; metric tons; 1977): coal 509; lignite 38,595; crude oil 3,950; natural gas (cu m) *c.* 1,900,000; manufactured gas (cu m; 1976) *c.* 230,000; electricity (kw-hr) 48,630,000. Production (in 000; metric tons; 1977): cement 8,005; iron ore (35% metal content) 4,451; pig iron 2,108; crude steel 2,584; antimony ore (metal content; 1976) 2; chrome ore (oxide content; 1976) 0.7; magnesite (1976) 391; manganese ore (metal content; 1976) 6.6; aluminum 200; copper 121; lead 130; zinc 99; gold (troy oz; 1976) 157; silver (troy oz; 1976) 6,400; petroleum products (1976) *c.* 10,980; sulfuric acid 937; cotton yarn 121; wool yarn 46; man-made fibres 90; wood pulp (1976) 538; newsprint 96; other paper (1976) 533; television receivers (units) 402; passenger cars (units) 180; commercial vehicles (units) 48. Merchant vessels launched (100 gross tons and over; 1977) 285,000 gross tons.

The crackdown on the so-called Cominformists (hard-line Communists friendly to Moscow) reached a climax on April 13 with the sentencing to 20 years' imprisonment of Mileta Perovic, who had led anti-Tito Communists in the Soviet Union but disappeared from Western Europe in 1977. The authorities also continued their pursuit of Croat nationalists. Vjenceslav Cizek, who had disappeared from West Germany in 1977, was given a 15-year sentence on August 8. On November 1 five young Croats were sentenced in Zagreb for allegedly working for Croat separatism and for supplying information to exiled Croat journalist Bruno Busic. Busic had been murdered in Paris on October 16. In September West Germany refused to extradite eight Yugoslav citizens, six of them Croats, accused by Yugoslavia of terrorist activity; in retaliation, Yugoslavia, in November, released four suspected West German terrorists arrested on Yugoslav soil in May.

Industrial production increased by 8.2% in the first half of 1978 as compared with the first half of 1977. In the first nine months of 1978 exports amounted to $4.3 billion and imports to $7.7 billion, but the trade deficit was reduced by 14% as compared with the first nine months of 1977. Over 30 strikes for higher pay occurred in the first half of 1978, most of them in Croatia.　　(K. F. CVIIC)

Yiddish Literature:
see Literature
Yiddish Literature:
see Literature

Zaire

A republic of equatorial Africa, Zaire is bounded by the Central African Empire, Sudan, Uganda, Rwanda, Burundi, Tanzania, Zambia, Angola, Congo, and the Atlantic Ocean. Area: 2,344,885 sq km (905,365 sq mi). Pop. (1978 est.): 26,478,000. Cap. and largest city: Kinshasa (pop., 1974, 1,733,-800). Language: French; Bantu dialects. Religion: animist approximately 50%; Christian 43%. President in 1978, Mobutu Sese Seko; prime minister, Mpinga Kasenga.

With an inflation rate of the order of 70%, an external debt of more than U.S. $2 billion, and with the price of copper showing little sign of rising, Zaire faced a difficult year in 1978. The loss of $15 million by the Tokyo-based Compagnie de Dé-veloppement Minière du Zaire in 1977–78 was a measure of the country's problems. The revitalization of agriculture was one of Zaire's most pressing needs. In spite of the fertility of much of the soil, exports of coffee, rubber, and palm oil had fallen badly, and a country that in 1960 had exported a considerable amount of surplus corn now found it necessary to import the greater part of its food. Fears of famine were aggravated by grave

Zaire

ZAIRE
ZAIRE

Education. (1973–74) Primary, pupils 3,538,257, teachers (1972–73) 80,481; secondary, pupils 225,606; vocational, pupils 47,579; teacher training, students 62,018; secondary, vocational, and teacher training, teachers 14,-483; higher, students (1974–75) 21,021, teaching staff 2,-550.

Finance. Monetary unit: zaire, with (Sept. 18, 1978) a free rate of 0.79 zaire to U.S. $1 (1.54 zaires = £1 sterling). Gold, SDR's, and foreign exchange (June 1978) U.S. $313,-670,000. Budget (1975 actual): revenue 431.9 million zaires; expenditure 710.5 million zaires. Gross national product (1976) 2,829,000,000 zaires. Money supply (May 1978) 1,184,510,000 zaires. Cost of living (Kinshasa; 1975 = 100; June 1978) 434.7.

Foreign Trade. (1977) Imports 522.7 million zaires; exports 846.9 million zaires. Import sources (1976): Belgium-Luxembourg 16%; France *c.* 15%; U.S. 12%; West Germany *c.* 10%; The Netherlands *c.* 5%; Spain *c.* 5%. Export destinations (1976): Belgium-Luxembourg *c.* 44%; U.S. *c.* 14%; Italy *c.* 9%; France *c.* 8%; Japan *c.* 6%; West Germany *c.* 6%; U.K. *c.* 5%. Main exports: copper 41%; coffee 20%; cobalt 11%; diamonds 7%.

Transport and Communications. Roads (1976) *c.* 145,-000 km. Motor vehicles in use (1974): passenger 84,800; commercial 67,800. Railways: (1975) 5,245 km; traffic (1973) 447 million passenger-km, freight 3,017,000,000 net ton-km. Air traffic (1976): 690 million passenger-km; freight 54.8 million net ton-km. Shipping (1977): merchant vessels 100 gross tons and over 34; gross tonnage 109,785. Inland waterways (including Zaire River; 1976) *c.* 16,400 km. Telephones (Dec. 1975) 48,000. Radio receivers (Dec. 1974) 2,448,000. Television receivers (Dec. 1975) 7,000.

Agriculture. Production (in 000; metric tons; 1977): rice *c.* 220; corn *c.* 515; sweet potatoes (1976) *c.* 300; cassava (1976) 9,832; peanuts 312; palm kernels *c.* 72; palm oil *c.* 175; sugar, raw value (1976) *c.* 74; mangoes *c.* 86; bananas *c.* 83; oranges *c.* 105; coffee *c.* 90; rubber *c.* 27; cotton, lint *c.* 14; timber (cu m; 1976) *c.* 13,690; fish catch (1976) *c.* 118. Livestock (in 000; Dec. 1975): cattle 1,144; sheep *c.* 711; goats *c.* 2,256; pigs 627; poultry *c.* 10,992.

Industry. Production (in 000; metric tons; 1976): copper 274; tin 0.6; zinc 61; manganese ore (metal content) 95; gold (troy oz) 86; silver (troy oz) 2,500; diamonds (metric carats) 11,820; crude oil (1977) 1,126; coal (1977) *c.* 110; petroleum products 335; electricity (kw-hr) *c.* 3,502,000.

French Legionnaires checked identification papers searching for rebels in Kolwezi in Shaba Province. France sent in troops when Zaire requested help in repulsing Katangese rebels who invaded the province from Angola in May.

inadequacies in the system of transport and communications.

The U.S. Agency for International Development promised $20 million during 1978, half of it to finance food imports, but foreign sources generally were wary of providing assistance in view of the obvious shortcomings in the country's administration. Nor were they uncritical of Pres. Mobutu Sese Seko himself and of the vast private fortune he was believed to have amassed. Within the country there was wide-ranging opposition to the president, but it was weakened by its many divisions.

Early in March it was announced that 91 people had been arrested on charges of organizing an armed revolt against the government and of attempting to blow up the Inga Dam hydroelectric installations. Fifteen others, officers in the armed services, had been executed for mutiny after an immediate court-martial. Of the 91, 13 army officers and civilians were executed after trial and 63 were given prison sentences. These measures were followed by clashes involving relatives of the executed men, and a further 66 people were arrested.

In the middle of May, Katangese rebels of the Congo National Liberation Front (FNLC) crossed the border into Shaba Province from bases in Angola and attacked the towns of Kolwezi and Mutshatsha. Zairian troops put up little effective resistance, and the president at once called for help from Belgium, France, Morocco, the U.S., and China. France sent paratroops, who quickly seized Kolwezi and reported atrocities against white civilians. Belgium, after a brief hesitation, also sent troops, while the U.S. supplied military equipment. It was French troops, however, who were responsible for driving the rebels back over the border, after which they and the Belgians withdrew. Their intervention did not go uncriticized. Some of the Communist powers and the Organization of African Unity deplored external involvement in an African territory. China, however, gave its full approval, and in June Foreign Minister Huang Hua visited Zaire.

The raid, although summarily dealt with, had serious effects both on the economy and on the country's political stability. There was an immediate threat to the world's cobalt supplies, 47% of which were supplied by Zaire in 1977; 85% of that total, and that of the highest grade, had come from the mines around Kolwezi. The temporary closure of the mines and the subsequent flooding after electricity supplies were cut off seriously affected production. The problem was aggravated because a number of European technicians, vital to the industry, had fled the country.

In these circumstances Zaire's approach to outside sources for financial assistance met with a cool response. A meeting of representatives of some of the Western powers and the International Monetary Fund (IMF) in Brussels in mid-June resulted in offers of monetary help from West Germany, Canada, and the European Economic Community, together with 40,000 tons of cereal and 1,900 tons of dried milk. This fell far short of the $1 billion tentatively mentioned by Zaire, and even these offers were made only on condition that Zaire surrender control of the national central bank and the Ministry of Finance to IMF representatives. Events in Shaba, however, had alerted the Western powers to the danger that Zaire's important mineral resources might fall into hostile hands.

Another summit meeting of francophone African states in Paris produced help of a different kind in the shape of an African security force (mostly Moroccan and francophone African), the first elements of which were flown to Lumbumbashi by the U.S. Air Force on June 5. The need for their presence was reinforced by rumours that the rebels were preparing another attack and because it was feared that a large proportion of the poverty-stricken inhabitants might support the rebels.

In one area there was a gleam of hope. In July talks began in Brazzaville, Congo, between Zaire and Angola aimed at reducing tension, and on October 17 Pres. Agostinho Neto of Angola and President Mobutu signed a cooperation agreement in Luanda. It was agreed that Angolans should inspect the controversial rocket testing range set up by the West German missile concern OTRAG in Zaire and dispel rumours of its military significance. As a further result of the rapprochement, the Benguela Railway, which had been closed as a result of guerrilla activity in Angola and upon which Zaire depended heavily for the export of its minerals, was officially reopened in November.

(KENNETH INGHAM)

Zambia

Zambia

A republic and a member of the Commonwealth of Nations, Zambia is bounded by Tanzania, Malawi, Mozambique, Rhodesia, Namibia (South West Africa), Angola, and Zaire. Area: 752,614 sq km (290,586 sq mi). Pop. (1978 est.): 5,514,000, about 99% of whom are Africans. Cap. and largest city: Lusaka (pop., 1976 est., 483,000). Language: English and Bantu. Religion: predominantly animist, with Roman Catholic (21%), Protestant, Hindu, and Muslim minorities. President in 1978, Kenneth Kaunda; prime ministers, Mainza Chona and, from June 15, Daniel Lisulo.

Zambia's economy in 1978 was in a desperate

Rhodesian troops attacked terrorist strongholds in October. Bodies of suspected guerrillas lie on the ground outside an ammunition storage building at a ZAPU guerrilla training camp.

WIDE WORLD

Zanzibar:
see Tanzania

Zoology:
see Life Sciences

ZAMBIA

Education. (1976) Primary, pupils 907,867, teachers 19,-300; secondary, pupils 78,805, teachers 3,538; vocational, pupils 5,392, teachers 481; teacher training, students 2,780, teachers 229; higher, students 3,447, teaching staff 412.

Finance. Monetary unit: kwacha, with (Sept. 18, 1978) a free rate of 0.80 kwacha to U.S. $1 (1.56 kwachas = £1 sterling). Gold, SDR's, and foreign exchange (June 1978) U.S. $99 million. Budget (1977 actual): revenue 500.2 million kwachas; expenditure 709.8 million kwachas. Gross national product (1977) 1,842,000,000 kwachas. Cost of living (1975 = 100; Feb. 1978) 159.1.

Foreign Trade. (1977) Imports 645,220,000 kwachas; exports 708,570,000 kwachas. Import sources (1976): U.K. 24%; Saudi Arabia 13%; U.S. 11%; South Africa 8%; West Germany 7%; Italy 6%; Japan 5%. Export destinations (1976): Japan 17%; U.S. 15%; West Germany 14%; U.K. 14%; Italy 9%; France 6%; India 5%. Main export: copper 91%.

Transport and Communications. Roads (1972) 34,963 km. Motor vehicles in use (1976): passenger *c.* 104,000; commercial (including buses) *c.* 61,000. Railways (1976) *c.* 1,934 km (including *c.* 890 km of the 1,870-km Tanzam railway). Air traffic (1976): 356 million passenger-km; freight 19.8 million net ton-km. Telephones (Jan. 1977) *c.* 55,400. Radio receivers (Dec. 1975) *c.* 100,000. Television receivers (Dec. 1974) 22,000.

Agriculture. Production (in 000; metric tons; 1977): corn *c.* 980; cassava (1976) *c.* 163; millet *c.* 86; sorghum *c.* 51; peanuts *c.* 32; sugar, raw value (1976) *c.* 85; tobacco *c.* 7; cotton, lint *c.* 4. Livestock (in 000; 1976): cattle *c.* 2,300; sheep *c.* 50; goats *c.* 283; pigs *c.* 106; chickens *c.* 8,628.

Industry. Production (in 000; metric tons; 1976): copper 695; coal (1977) 780; lead 14; zinc 37; petroleum products *c.* 800; electricity (kw-hr) 7,034,000.

---

state due to the continuing low price of copper and the high cost of imported food. In his New Year's message of January 1, Pres. Kenneth Kaunda (*see* BIOGRAPHIES) said that government subsidies on food would be scrapped, and shortly afterward the finance minister introduced an austerity budget. In March the International Monetary Fund promised a U.S. $390 million loan on various conditions. Kaunda appealed to China for help in increasing the efficiency of the railway link with Dar es Salaam in Tanzania, but although China agreed, the president had to reopen the railway link with South Africa through Rhodesia in October.

The challenge to Kaunda's political position from former vice-president Simon Kapwepwe and Harry Nkumbula, the former leader of the African National Congress, was checked in September when the ruling United National Independence Party amended the party's constitution to prevent anyone other than Kaunda from being nominated for the presidency in the December 12 election. Although his position became still more difficult in October after devastating Rhodesian air raids on guerrilla camps near Lusaka, he was massively reelected and sworn in for a fourth term on December 15.

(KENNETH INGHAM)

Zoos and Botanical Gardens

Zoos. As part of the extensive international cooperation among zoos to implement breeding programs on a worldwide basis, there was a determined effort in 1978 to multiply the number of primates in captivity. Recent evidence showed

Zoos and Botanical Gardens

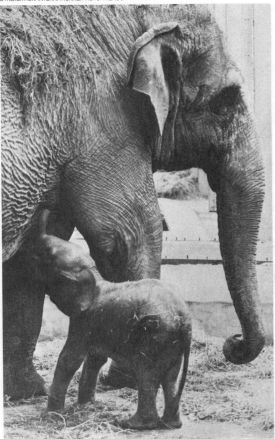

A rare crossbred elephant, having an Indian mother and an African father, was born at Chester Zoo in England. Unhappily, the infant died after 10 days.

after G. S. Mottershead, the zoo's founder and director, who died in May (*see* OBITUARIES). Unhappily, the baby succumbed to an intestinal infection at the age of ten days. Jubilee, Chester's baby Indian elephant born in May 1977, continued to make good progress.

Several zoos underwent modernization and expansion during the year. A new Penguin House, designed for several species, was opened at the West Berlin Zoo. Renovation work was carried out at the London Zoo and at Edinburgh and Calderpark (Glasgow) in Scotland. The Artis Zoo in Amsterdam opened a completely new building for small mammals in which certain climatic zones could be simulated. In Paris the Jardin des Plantes was to be expanded and modernized.

Heidelberg, West Germany, and Oklahoma City zoos opened areas representative of Africa and South America, respectively. The areas housed mammals, birds, reptiles, and plant life of a given faunal region. Oklahoma City Zoo incorporated an educational centre in its South American scheme, a mode of exhibiting animals that was being used increasingly.

A new zoological garden was opened to the public on June 1, 1978, at Santa Cruz, Bolivia. When fully established the animal collection was to be largely representative of South American species. The establishment of this completely new zoo coincided with the rediscovery of a bird which had been thought to be extinct. The white-winged guan (*Penelope albipennis*), the last recorded specimen of which had been seen in 1877, was found in northwestern Peru by John O'Neill of Louisiana State University and was soon protected by law. Some of these birds might make their way to the Santa Cruz collection. (J. O. L. KING)

Hsing-Hsing and Ling-Ling, giant pandas given to the United States by China in 1972, have yet to mate. Officials from the Washington, D.C., National Zoo went to China in June to seek advice from zoo keepers there.

that the number of gorillas in the wild state was at a low level, and those in Rwanda and Zaire faced an increased threat of poaching. A mountain gorilla fund was established, and captive breeding remained a priority. San Diego, Calif., Seattle, Wash., and many other U.S. and European zoos had breeding projects under way.

Although chimpanzee and orangutan births were no longer great news items, they were still important. It was anticipated that gorilla births would also become less of a sensation one day, which would redound to the credit of zoos. The Zürich (Switz.) Zoo hoped to acquire a group of gorillas for its new ape house. The Jersey (Channel Islands) Wildlife Preservation Trust launched an appeal to construct a new gorilla complex. London Zoo lost its famous gorilla Guy, who died at age 32 after undergoing dental surgery.

Many zoos endured financial difficulties because of inflation, and so in Britain a successful venture to aid them was launched with the slogan "Save Our Species" (sos). Proceeds were to be divided among zoos to help cover their costs.

A survey of elephants in the British Isles was conducted by Mary-Elizabeth Raw. After details of the survey had been published, Chester (England) Zoo recorded the birth of the world's first crossbred elephant. The male calf had an African father and an Indian mother and was named Motty

Zoos and Botanical Gardens

New York's famed Botanical Garden Conservatory reopened in March after two years of reconstruction at a cost of $5 million. Crowds packed the conservatory after the reopening.

Botanical Gardens. The educational and conservational functions of botanical gardens received much attention at a number of conferences during 1978. The second Kew Conservation Conference in England, the 12th Conference on Problems of Botanical Gardens at Leipzig, East Germany, the International Conference of the Technical Heads of Botanical Gardens at Göttingen, West Germany, and the meeting of the American Association of Botanical Gardens and Arboreta at Hamilton, Ont., all gave evidence of increasing efforts by garden administrations to improve and widen facilities for information, teaching, research, and the implementation of protective measures for endangered plants within their regions. Other matters discussed were the role of botanical gardens in the training of future professional gardeners; measures to maintain efficiency while continuing to lose personnel because of enforced economies; and the use of electronic data storing as an essential aid in the management of collections.

The growing emphasis on plant conservation was stressed by the provision of specially arranged grounds at a number of gardens; these included the Conservatoire botanique du Stangalarc'h at Brest in Brittany, France, and the Conservatoire des espèces méditerranéennes de Porquerolles on the French Riviera. Successful work in this field was also reported from the botanical gardens at Tübingen, West Germany; Cambridge, England; Poznan, Poland; Bratislava, Czech.; Viera y Clavijo, Canary Islands, Spain; La Plata, Arg.; Jalapa, Mexico; and from a number of gardens in South Africa, the U.S.S.R., and Hawaii. The establishment of more gene banks as "Noah's Arks" for the survival of plants was also reported and would undoubtedly play a major role in the conservation of threatened species.

A new 106-ha botanical garden was being established during the year at Maracaibo, Venezuela. There were also plans for gardens at the new universities at Bayreuth, Osnabrück, Regensburg, and Ulm in West Germany and for new gardens in Berlin, Dresden, Greifswald, Karl-Marx-Stadt, and Leipzig in East Germany.

At the Royal Botanic Gardens, Kew, Queen Charlotte's Cottage was reopened to the public on May 20 after extensive restoration. The cottage, built about 1772 in woods in the southern part of the gardens, was used as a rural retreat by George III and his family. Also at Kew, construction continued on the new pyramid-shaped temperate house with its surrounding water-filled moat designed to produce a flow of cool, humid air. The development of new research departments and nurseries for tropical plants was also in progress.

After two years of renovation financed with a $5 million gift by philanthropist Enid Haupt, the New York Botanical Garden Conservatory reopened in March. A glass structure with a dome 90 ft high and with ten interconnecting pavilions, the conservatory covers nearly an acre in New York City. During the restoration hundreds of glass panes were replaced along with the heating and ventilating systems. A new underground passageway was designed for displays of aquatic plants, mushrooms, and mosses.   (JOHANNES APEL)
[355.C.6]

CONTRIBUTORS

Names of contributors to the Britannica Book of the Year *with the articles written by them.*
The arrangement is alphabetical by last name.

AARSDAL, STENER. Economic and Political Journalist, *Borsen*, Copenhagen.
Biographies (*in part*); **Denmark**

ADAMS, ANDREW M. Free-lance Foreign Correspondent; Editor and Publisher, *Sumo World* magazine. Author of *Ninja: The Invisible Assassins; Born to Die; The Cherry Blossom Squadrons.*
Combat Sports: *Judo; Karate; Kendo; Sumo*

AGRELLA, JOSEPH C. Correspondent, *Blood-Horse* magazine; former Turf Editor, *Chicago Sun-Times.* Co-author of *Ten Commandments for Professional Handicapping; American Race Horses.*
Equestrian Sports: *Thoroughbred Racing and Steeplechasing* (*in part*)

AIELLO, LESLIE C. Lecturer, Department of Anthropology, University College, London.
Anthropology

ALLABY, MICHAEL. Free-lance Writer and Lecturer. Author of *The Eco-Activists; Who Will Eat?; A Blueprint for Survival; Home Farm;* Co-author of *Robots Behind the Plow.* Editor of *The Survival Handbook; Dictionary of the Environment.*
Environment (*in part*)

ALLAN, J. A. Lecturer in Geography, School of Oriental and African Studies, University of London.
Libya

ALSTON, REX. Broadcaster and Journalist; retired BBC Commentator. Author of *Taking the Air; Over to Rex Alston; Test Commentary; Watching Cricket.*
Cricket

ANDERSON, PETER J. Assistant Director, Institute of Polar Studies, Ohio State University, Columbus.
Antarctic

APEL, JOHANNES. Curator, Botanic Garden, University of Hamburg. Author of *Gärtnerisch-Botanische Briefe.*
Zoos and Botanical Gardens: *Botanical Gardens*

ARCHIBALD, JOHN J. Feature Writer and TV Columnist, *St. Louis Post-Dispatch.* Author of *Bowling for Boys and Girls.*
Bowling: *Tenpin Bowling* (*in part*); *Duckpins*

ARNOLD, BRUCE. Free-lance Journalist and Writer, Dublin. Parliamentary Correspondent, *Irish Independent.*
Ireland

ARRINGTON, LEONARD J. Church Historian, Church of Jesus Christ of Latter-day Saints. Author of *Great Basin Kingdom; An Economic History of the Latter-day Saints; Charles C. Rich; Mormon General and Western Frontiersman; Building the City of God: Community and Cooperation Among the Mormons.*
Religion: *Church of Jesus Christ of Latter-day Saints*

AYTON, CYRIL J. Editor, *Motorcycle Sport*, London.
Motor Sports: *Motorcycles*

BARFORD, MICHAEL F. Editor and Director, *World Tobacco*, London.
Industrial Review: *Tobacco*

BARGAD, WARREN. Milton D. Ratner Professor of Hebrew Literature, Spertus College of Judaica, Chicago. Author of *Hayim Hazaz: Novelist of Ideas; Anthology of Israeli Poetry.*
Literature: *Hebrew*

BARGHOORN, FREDERICK C. Professor of Political Science, Yale University. Author of *Politics in the U.S.S.R.*
Special Preprint: *Soviet Union*

BASS, HOWARD. Journalist and Broadcaster. Editor, *Winter Sports*, 1948–69. Winter Sports Correspondent, *Daily Telegraph* and *Sunday Telegraph*, London; *The Olympian*, New York City; *Canadian Skater*, Ottawa; *Skate*, London; *Skating*, Boston; *Ski Racing*, Denver; *Sport & Recreation*, London. Author of *The Sense in Sport; This Skating Age; The Magic of Skiing; International Encyclopaedia of Winter Sports; Let's Go Skating.*
Biographies (*in part*); **Ice Hockey:** *European and International*; **Winter Sports**

BAYLISS, DAVID. Chief Planner (Transportation), Greater London Council. Co-author of *Developing Patterns of Urbanization; Uses of Economics.* Advisory Editor of *Models in Urban and Regional Planning.*
Transportation (*in part*)

BEALL, JOHN V. Business Development Engineer, Fluor Mining & Metals, Inc. Author of sections 1 and 34, *Mining Engineering Handbook.* Frequent Contributor to *Mining Engineering.*
Mining and Quarrying (*in part*)

BEATTIE, ROGER A. Member of Secretariat, International Social Security Association, Geneva.
Social and Welfare Services (*in part*)

BEATTY, JAMES R. Research Fellow, B. F. Goodrich Research and Development Center, Brecksville, Ohio. Co-author of *Concepts in Compounding; Physical Testing of Elastomers and Polymers in Applied Polymer Science.*
Industrial Review: *Rubber*

BECKWITH, DAVID C. Managing Editor, *Legal Times of Washington*, Washington, D.C.
United States Statistical Supplement: *Developments in the States in 1978*

BENTLEY, STUART. Principal Lecturer in Sociology, Sheffield City Polytechnic, England. Co-author of *Work, Race, Immigration.*
Migration, International; Race Relations

BERGERRE, MAX. Correspondent ANSA for Vatican Affairs, Rome.
Vatican City State

BICKELHAUPT, DAVID L. Professor of Insurance and Finance, College of Administrative Science, Ohio State University, Columbus. Author of *Transition to Multiple-Line Insurance Companies; General Insurance* (9th ed.).
Industrial Review: *Insurance*

BILEFIELD, LIONEL. Technical Journalist.
Industrial Review: *Paints and Varnishes*

BINSTED, ARTHUR T. E. Former Chairman, British Bottlers' Institute, London.
Industrial Review: *Alcoholic Beverages* (*in part*)

BODDY, WILLIAM C. Editor, *Motor Sport.* Full Member, Guild of Motoring Writers. Author of *The History of Brooklands Motor Course; The World's Land Speed Record; Continental Sports Cars; The Bugatti Story; History of Montlhéry.*
Motor Sports: *Grand Prix Racing*

BODEN, EDWARD. Editor, *The Veterinary Record*; Executive Editor, *Research in Veterinary Science.*
Veterinary Science

BOERMA, ADDEKE HENDRIK. Director General, Food and Agriculture Organization of the United Nations, Rome, 1968–76.
Special Preprint: *Food Supply of the World*

BOLT, PETER H. Secretary, British Committee, World Methodist Council. Author of *A Way of Loving.*
Religion: *Methodist Churches*

BOONSTRA, DICK. Assistant Professor, Department of Political Science, Free University, Amsterdam.
Biographies (*in part*); **Netherlands, The; Suriname**

BOOTH, JOHN NICHOLLS. Lecturer and Writer; Co-founder, Japan Free Religious Association; Senior Pastor of a number of U.S. churches. Author of *The Quest for Preaching Power; Introducing Unitarian Universalism.*
Religion: *Unitarian (Universalist) Churches*

BOSWALL, JEFFERY. Producer of Sound and Television Programs, British Broadcasting Corporation Natural History Unit, Bristol, England.
Life Sciences: *Ornithology*

BOYLE, C. L. Lieutenant Colonel, R.A. (retired). Chairman, Survival Service Commission, International Union for Conservation of Nature and Natural Resources, 1958–63; Secretary, Fauna Preservation Society, London, 1950–63.
Environment (*in part*)

BRACKMAN, ARNOLD C. Asian Affairs Specialist. Author of *Indonesian Commu-*

nism: A History; Southeast Asia's Second Front: The Power Struggle in the Malay Archipelago; The Communist Collapse in Indonesia; The Last Emperor.
Indonesia

BRADSHER, HENRY S. Diplomatic Correspondent, *Washington (D.C.) Star.*
Philippines

BRAIDWOOD, ROBERT J. Professor Emeritus of Old World Prehistory, University of Chicago; Field Director, Prehistoric Project of the Oriental Institute, Chicago. Author of *Prehistoric Men* (8th ed.); *Courses Toward Urban Life.*
Archaeology: *Eastern Hemisphere*

BRAZEE, RUTLAGE J. Program Manager for Seismological Research, U.S. Nuclear Regulatory Commission, Washington, D.C.
Earth Sciences: *Geophysics*

BRECHER, KENNETH. Associate Professor of Physics, Massachusetts Institute of Technology.
Astronomy

BRUNO, HAL. Director of Political Coverage, ABC News, Washington, D.C.
Biographies (in part)

BURDIN, JOEL L. Associate Director, American Association of Colleges for Teacher Education; Editor, *Journal of Teacher Education;* Executive Secretary, Associated Organizations for Teacher Education. Co-author of *A Reader's Guide to the Comprehensive Models for Preparing Elementary Teachers; Elementary School Curriculum and Instruction.*
Education (in part)

BURKE, DONALD P. Executive Editor, *Chemical Week,* New York City.
Industrial Review: *Chemicals*

BURKS, ARDATH W. Professor of Asian Studies, Rutgers University, New Brunswick, N.J. Author of *The Government of Japan; East Asia: China, Korea, Japan.*
Japan

BUSS, ROBIN. Lecturer in French, Woolwich College of Further Education, London.
Literature: *French* (in part)

BUTLER, FRANK. Sports Editor, *News of the World,* London. Author of *A History of Boxing in Britain.*
Combat Sports: *Boxing*

CALHOUN, DAVID R. Editor, Encyclopædia Britannica, Yearbooks.
Biographies (in part); **Gambling** (in part)

CAMERON, SARAH. Economist, Lloyds Bank International Ltd., London.
Colombia; Dominican Republic; Venezuela

CASEMENT, RICHARD. Science Correspondent, *The Economist,* London. Author of *Urban Traffic: Policies in Congestion.*
Industrial Review: *Special Report*

CASSIDY, RICHARD J. Public Relations Officer, British Gas Corporation. Author of *Britain's Gas* (in preparation).
Energy: *Natural Gas*

CASSIDY, VICTOR M. Writer and Editor, currently at work on a biography of Wyndham Lewis.
Biographies (in part)

CEGIELSKI, CHARLES M. Associate Editor, Encyclopædia Britannica, Yearbooks.
Biographies (in part); **Life Sciences:** *Introduction*

CHALMEY, LUCIEN. Honorary Secretary-General, Union Internationale des Producteurs et Distributeurs d'Énergie Électrique, Paris.
Energy: *Electricity*

CHAPMAN, KENNETH F. Editor, *Philatelic Magazine;* Philatelic Correspondent, *The Times,* London. Author of *Good Stamp Collecting; Commonwealth Stamp Collecting.*
Philately and Numismatics: *Stamps*

CHAPMAN, ROBIN. Senior Economist, Lloyds Bank International Ltd., London.
Haiti

CHAPPELL, DUNCAN. Professor, Department of Legal Studies, Latrobe University, Melbourne, Australia. Co-author of *The Police and the Public in Australia and New Zealand.* Co-editor of *The Australian Criminal Justice System* (1st and 2nd ed.); *Violence and Criminal Justice; Forcible Rape: the Crime, the Victim and the Offender.*
Crime and Law Enforcement

CHOATE, ROGER NYE. Stockholm Correspondent, *The Times,* London.
Biographies (in part); **Sweden**

CHU, HUNG-TI. Expert in Far Eastern Affairs; Former International Civil Servant and University Professor.
China; Taiwan

CLARKE, R. O. Principal Administrator, Social Affairs and Industrial Relations Division, Organization for Economic Cooperation and Development, Paris. Co-author of *Workers' Participation in Management in Britain.*
Industrial Relations

CLEVELAND, WILLIAM A. Geography Editor, *Encyclopædia Britannica* and Britannica Yearbooks.
Mining and Quarrying (in part)

CLIFTON, DONALD F. Professor of Metallurgy, University of Idaho.
Materials Sciences: *Metallurgy*

CLOUD, STANLEY W. White House Washington Correspondent and Editor, Time-Life News Service.
Biographies (in part)

COGLE, T. C. J. Editor, *Electrical Review,* London.
Industrial Review: *Electrical*

COLLINS, L. J. D. Lecturer in Bulgarian History, University of London.
Cyprus

COPPOCK, CHARLES DENNIS. President, English Lacrosse Union. Author of "Men's Lacrosse" in *The Oxford Companion to Sports and Games.*
Field Hockey and Lacrosse: *Lacrosse* (in part)

COSTIN, STANLEY H. British Correspondent, *Herrenjournal International* and *Men's Wear, Australasia.* Council of Management Member, British Men's Fashion Association Ltd. Former President, Men's Fashion Writers International.
Fashion and Dress (in part)

CRATER, RUFUS W. Chief Correspondent, *Broadcasting,* Washington, D.C.
Television and Radio (in part)

CROSS, COLIN J. Editor, *The Polo Magazine,* U.K.
Equestrian Sports: *Polo*

CROSSLAND, NORMAN. Bonn Correspondent, *The Economist,* London.
German Democratic Republic; Germany, Federal Republic of

CVIIC, K. F. Leader Writer and East European Specialist, *The Economist,* London.
Yugoslavia

DAIFUKU, HIROSHI. Chief, Section for Operations and Training, Cultural Heritage Division, UNESCO, Paris.
Historic Preservation

DAUME, DAPHNE. Editor, Encyclopædia Britannica, Yearbooks.
Biographies (in part); **Guyana** (in part)

DAVID, TUDOR. Managing Editor, *Education,* London.
Education (in part)

DAVIES, JOHN. Education Secretary, The Publishers Association, London.
Publishing: *Books* (in part)

DAVIS, DONALD A. Editor, *Drug & Cosmetic Industry,* New York City. Contributor to *The Science and Technology of Aerosol Packaging; Advances in Cosmetic Technology* (forthcoming).
Industrial Review: *Pharmaceuticals*

d'EÇA, RAUL. Retired from foreign service with U.S. Information Service. Co-author of *Latin American History.*
Brazil

DECRAENE, PHILIPPE. Member of editorial staff, *Le Monde,* Paris. Editor in Chief, *Revue française d'Études politiques africaines.* Author of *Le Panafricanisme; Tableau des Partis Politiques Africains; Lettres de l'Afrique Atlantique.*
Benin; Biographies (in part); **Cameroon; Central African Empire; Chad; Comoros; Congo; Djibouti; Gabon; Guinea; Ivory Coast; Madagascar; Mali; Mauritania; Niger; Senegal; Togo; Tunisia; Upper Volta**

de FAINBOIM, MARTA BEKERMANN. Economist, Lloyds Bank International Ltd., London.
Peru; Uruguay

de la BARRE, KENNETH. Staff Scientist, Arctic Institute of North America, Calgary, Montreal.
Arctic Regions

DE PUY, NORMAN R. Pastor and Executive Minister, First Baptist Church of Dearborn, Mich. Author of *The Bible Alive.*
Religion: *Baptist Churches*

DESAUTELS, PAUL E. Curator, Department of Mineral Sciences, National Museum of Natural History, Smithsonian Institution, Washington, D.C. Author of *The Mineral Kingdom; The Gem Kingdom.*
Industrial Review: *Gemstones*

DIRNBACHER, ELFRIEDE. Austrian Civil Servant.
Austria

DOWBOR, PAUL. Economist, Lloyds Bank International Ltd., London.
Latin-American Affairs

DUNICAN, PETER. Chairman, Ove Arup Partnership, London.
Engineering Projects: *Buildings*

EIU. The Economist Intelligence Unit, London.
Economy, World (*in part*)

ENGELS, JAN R. Editor, *Vooruitgang* (Quarterly of the Belgian Party for Freedom and Progress), Brussels.
Belgium

EVANS, JOSEPH H. Secretary, United Church of Christ, New York City.
Religion: *United Church of Christ*

EWART, W. D. Editor and Director, *Fairplay International Shipping Weekly*, London. Author of *Marine Engines; Atomic Submarines; Hydrofoils and Hovercraft; Building a Ship.* Editor of *World Atlas of Shipping.*
Industrial Review: *Shipbuilding;* **Transportation** (*in part*)

FAIRBANK, JENTY. Director of Information Services, International Headquarters, The Salvation Army. Author of *William and Catherine Booth: God's Soldiers.*
Religion: *Salvation Army*

FARR, D. M. L. Professor of History, Carleton University, Ottawa. Co-author of *The Canadian Experience.*
Canada

FENDELL, ROBERT J. Auto Editor, *Science & Mechanics;* Auto Contributor, *Gentlemen's Quarterly.* Author of *The New Era Car Book and Auto Survival Guide.* Co-author of *Encyclopedia of Motor Racing Greats.*
Motor Sports: *U.S. Racing*

FERRIER, R. W. Group Historian and Archivist, British Petroleum Company Ltd., London.
Energy: *Petroleum*

FIDDICK, PETER. Specialist Writer, *The Guardian*, London.
Publishing: *Introduction; Newspapers (in part); Magazines (in part)*

FIELDS, DONALD. Helsinki Correspondent, BBC, *The Guardian*, and *The Sunday Times*, London.
Finland

FIRTH, DAVID. Editor, *The Friend*, London; formerly Editor, *Quaker Monthly*, London.
Religion: *Religious Society of Friends*

FISHER, DAVID. Civil Engineer, Freeman Fox & Partners, London; formerly

Executive Editor, *Engineering*, London.
Engineering Projects: *Bridges*

FLANAGAN, JACK. Special Group Travel Newspaper Columnist.
Water Sports: *Surfing*

FOWELL, R. J. Lecturer, Department of Mining Engineering, University of Newcastle upon Tyne, England.
Energy: *Coal*

FRADY, WILLIAM ENSIGN, III. Editor, *Water Polo Scoreboard*, Newport Beach, Calif.
Water Sports: *Water Polo*

FRANKLIN, HAROLD. Editor, *English Bridge Quarterly.* Bridge Correspondent, *Yorkshire Post; Yorkshire Evening Post.* Broadcaster. Author of *Best of Bridge on the Air.*
Contract Bridge

FRANZ, FREDERICK W. President, Watch Tower Bible and Tract Society of Pennsylvania.
Religion: *Jehovah's Witnesses*

FRAWLEY, MARGARET-LOUISE. Press Officer, All-England Women's Lacrosse Association.
Field Hockey and Lacrosse: *Lacrosse (in part)*

FRIDOVICH, IRWIN. James B. Duke Professor of Biochemistry, Duke University Medical Center, Durham, N.C. Contributor to *Oxidase and Redox Systems; Molecular Mechanisms of Oxygen Activation.*
Life Sciences: *Molecular Biology (in part)*

FRIEDLY, ROBERT LOUIS. Executive Director, Office of Communication, Christian Church (Disciples of Christ), Indianapolis, Ind.
Religion: *Disciples of Christ*

FRISKIN, SYDNEY E. Hockey Correspondent, *The Times*, London.
Field Hockey and Lacrosse: *Field Hockey*

FROST, DAVID. Rugby Union Correspondent, *The Guardian*, London.
Football: *Rugby*

GADDUM, PETER W. Chairman, H. T. Gaddum and Company Ltd., Silk Merchants, Macclesfield, Cheshire, England. Honorary President, International Silk Association, Lyons. Author of *Silk—How and Where It Is Produced.*
Industrial Review: *Textiles (in part)*

GANADO, ALBERT. Lawyer, Malta.
Malta

GBGB. Gaming Board of Great Britain.
Gambling (*in part*)

GEORGE, T. J. S. Editor, *Asiaweek*, Hong Kong. Author of *Krishna Menon: A Biography; Lew Kuan Yew's Singapore.*
Biographies (*in part*); **Cambodia; Korea; Laos; Southeast Asian Affairs; Thailand; Vietnam**

GILL, JOSEPH B. City Editor, *Republic*, Columbus, Ind.
Architecture: *Special Report*

GILLESPIE, HUGH M. Director of Communications, International Road Federa-

tion, Washington, D.C.; Consultant, U.S. National Academy of Sciences. Editor, *Transportation Research News.*
Engineering Projects: *Roads*

GJESTER, FAY. Oslo Correspondent, *Financial Times*, London.
Norway

GOLDSMITH, ARTHUR. Editorial Director, *Popular Photography*, New York City. Author of *The Photography Game; The Nude in Photography.* Co-author of *The Eye of Eisenstaedt.*
Photography

GOLOMBEK, HARRY. British Chess Champion, 1947, 1949, and 1955. Chess Correspondent, *The Times* and *Observer*, London. Author of *Penguin Handbook of the Game of Chess; A History of Chess.*
Biographies (*in part*); **Chess**

GOODWIN, R. M. Free-lance Writer, London.
Equestrian Sports: *Thoroughbred Racing and Steeplechasing (in part)*

GOODWIN, ROBERT E. Executive Director, Billiard Congress of America, Chicago, Publisher-Editor of various trade magazines.
Billiard Games

GOTTFRIED, MARTIN. Drama Critic, *Saturday Review*, New York City. Author of *A Theater Divided; Opening Nights.*
Theatre (*in part*)

GOULD, DONALD W. Medical Correspondent, *New Statesman*, London.
Health and Disease: *Overview (in part); Mental Health*

GREEN, BENNY. Jazz Critic, *Observer*, London; Record Reviewer, British Broadcasting Corporation. Author of *The Reluctant Art; Blame It on My Youth; 58 Minutes to London; Jazz Decade; Drums in My Ears.* Contributor to *Encyclopedia of Jazz.*
Music: *Jazz*

GRIFFITHS, A. R. G. Senior Lecturer in History, Flinders University of South Australia. Author of *Contemporary Australia.*
Australia; Australia: *Special Report;* **Nauru; Papua New Guinea**

GROSSBERG, ROBERT H. Executive Director, U.S. Amateur Jai Alai Players Association, Miami, Fla.
Court Games: *Jai Alai*

GROSSMAN, JOEL W. Director, Archaeological Survey Office, Rutgers University, New Brunswick, N.J.
Archaeology: *Western Hemisphere*

HARDMAN, THOMAS C. Editor and Publisher, *The Water Skier*, American Water Ski Association. Co-author of *Let's Go Water Skiing.*
Water Sports: *Water Skiing*

HARRIES, DAVID A. Director, Kinnear Moodie (1973) Ltd., Peterborough, England.
Engineering Projects: *Tunnels*

HARRIS, RICHARD. Deputy Foreign Editor and Asian Specialist, *The Times*,

London. Author of *Independence and After*; *America and East Asia*.
China: *Special Report*

HASEGAWA, RYUSAKU. Editor, TBS-Britannica Co., Ltd., Tokyo.
Baseball (*in part*)

HAWKLAND, WILLIAM D. Professor of Law, University of Illinois, Urbana-Champaign. Author of *Sale and Bulk Sale Under the Uniform Commercial Code*; *Cases on Bills and Notes*; *Transactional Guide of the Uniform Commercial Code*; *Cases on Sales and Security*.
Law: *Court Decisions*

HAWLEY, H. B. Specialist, Human Nutrition and Food Science, Switzerland.
Food Processing

HEBBLETHWAITE, PETER. Lecturer, Wadham College, Oxford, England. Author of *Bernanos*; *The Council Fathers and Atheism*; *Understanding the Synod*; *The Runaway Church*; *Christian-Marxist Dialogue and Beyond*.
Biographies (*in part*); **Religion:** *Roman Catholic Church*

HENDERSHOTT, MYRL C. Professor of Oceanography, Scripps Institution of Oceanography, La Jolla, Calif.
Earth Sciences: *Oceanography*

HERMAN, ROBIN CATHY. Sports Reporter, *New York Times*.
Ice Hockey: *North American*

HESS, MARVIN G. Executive Vice-President, National Wrestling Coaches Association, Salt Lake City, Utah.
Combat Sports: *Wrestling*

HINDIN, HARVEY J. Communications Editor, *Electronics* magazine, New York City. Author of numerous articles on electronics and mathematics.
Industrial Review: *Telecommunications*

HOBDAY, JULIA. Editor, *Toys International*, London.
Games and Toys

HOPE, THOMAS W. President, Hope Reports, Inc. Rochester, N.Y. Author of *Hope Reports AV-USA*; *Hope Reports Education and Media*; *Hope Reports Perspective*.
Motion Pictures (*in part*)

HORRY, JOHN H. Former Secretary, International Squash Rackets Federation. Contributor to *The Oxford Companion to Sports and Games*.
Racket Games: *Squash Rackets*

HOTZ, LOUIS. Former Editorial Writer, *Johannesburg (S.Af.) Star*. Co-author and contributor to *The Jews in South Africa: A History*.
South Africa

HOWKINS, JOHN. Editor, *InterMedia*, International Institute of Communications, London. Author of *Understanding Television*.
Television and Radio (*in part*)

HUNNINGS, NEVILLE MARCH. General Editor, European Law Centre Ltd., London. Editor of *Common Market Law Reports*, *Commercial Laws of Europe*, *European*

Commercial Cases, and *Eurolaw Commercial Intelligence*. Author of *Film Censors and the Law*. Co-editor of *Legal Problems of an Enlarged European Community*.
Law: *International Law*

INGHAM, KENNETH. Professor of History, University of Bristol, England. Author of *Reformers in India*; *A History of East Africa*.
Angola; Cape Verde; Guinea-Bissau; Kenya; Malawi; Mozambique; Rhodesia; São Tomé and Príncipe; Tanzania; Uganda; Zaire; Zambia

JACQUET, CONSTANT H. Staff Associate for Information Services, Office of Research, Evaluation and Planning, National Council of Churches. Editor of *Yearbook of American and Canadian Churches*.
United States Statistical Supplement: *Church Membership Table*

JARDINE, ADRIAN. Company Director and Public Relations Consultant. Member, Guild of Yachting Writers.
Sailing

JASPERT, W. PINCUS. Technical Editorial Consultant. European Editor, North American Publishing Company, Philadelphia. Member, Inter-Comprint Planning Committee; Member, Society of Photographic Engineers and Scientists. Editor of *Encyclopaedia of Type Faces*.
Industrial Review: *Printing*

JESSOP, DAVID A. Editor, *West Indies Chronicle* and *Insight*. Consultant on Caribbean affairs.
Bahamas, The; Barbados; Biographies (*in part*); **Dependent States** (*in part*); **Dominica; Grenada; Guyana** (*in part*); **Jamaica; Trinidad and Tobago**

JOFFÉ, GEORGE. Journalist and Writer on North African Affairs.
Algeria; Morocco

JONES, C. M. Consultant, *World Bowls*; Editor, *Tennis*. Member, British Society of Sports Psychology; Associate Member, British Association of National Coaches. Author of *Winning Bowls*; *How to Become a Champion*; numerous books on tennis. Co-author of *Tackle Bowls My Way*; *Bryant on Bowls*.
Bowling: *Lawn Bowls*

JONES, W. GLYN. Professor of Scandinavian Studies, University of Newcastle upon Tyne, England. Author of *Johannes Jørgensens modne år*; *Johannes Jörgensen*; *Denmark*; *William Heinesen*; *Færo og kosmos*.
Literature: *Danish*

JOSEPH, LOU. Manager of Media Relations, Bureau of Public Information, American Dental Association. Author of *A Doctor Discusses Allergy: Facts and Fiction*; *Natural Childbirth*; *Diabetes*.
Health and Disease: *Dentistry*

JUSTIN, KAREN. Assistant Editor, Encyclopædia Britannica, Yearbooks.
Biographies (*in part*)

KATZ, WILLIAM A. Professor, School of Library Science, State University of New York, Albany. Author of *Magazines for*

Libraries (2nd ed. and supplement); *Magazine Selection*.
Publishing: *Magazines* (*in part*)

KELLEHER, JOHN A. Editor, *The Dominion*, Wellington, N.Z.
New Zealand

KELLMAN, JEROLD L. Editor-in-Chief, Publications International, Ltd. Author of *Presidents of the United States*; Contributor to *The People's Almanac*.
Biographies (*in part*); **Computers**

KENNEDY, RICHARD M. Agricultural Economist, Foreign Demand and Competition Division, Economic Research Service, U.S. Department of Agriculture.
Agriculture and Food Supplies

KERRIGAN, ANTHONY. Visiting Professor, University of Illinois. Editor and Translator of *Selected Works* of Miguel de Unamuno (7 vol.) and of works of Jorge Luis Borges. Author of *At the Front Door of the Atlantic*.
Literature: *Spanish* (*in part*)

KILIAN, MICHAEL D. Columnist, *Chicago Tribune*; News Commentator, WBBM Radio, Chicago.
Aerial Sports

KILLHEFFER, JOHN V. Associate Editor, *Encyclopædia Britannica*.
Nobel Prizes (*in part*)

KIMCHE, JON. Editor, *Afro-Asian Affairs*, London. Author of *There Could Have Been Peace: The Untold Story of Why We Failed With Palestine and Again with Israel*; *Seven Fallen Pillars*; *Second Arab Awakening*.
Biographies (*in part*); **Israel**

KIND, JOSHUA B. Associate Professor of Art History, Northern Illinois University, De Kalb. Author of *Rouault*; *Naive Art in Illinois 1830–1976*.
Museums (*in part*)

KING, J. O. L. Professor of Animal Husbandry, University of Liverpool, England. Author of *Veterinary Dietetics*; *An Introduction to Animal Husbandry*.
Zoos and Botanical Gardens: *Zoos*

KITAGAWA, JOSEPH MITSUO. Professor of History of Religions and Dean of the Divinity School, University of Chicago. Author of *Religions of the East*; *Religion in Japanese History*.
Religion: *Buddhism*

KLARE, HUGH J. Chairman, Gloucestershire Probation Training Committee, England. Secretary, Howard League for Penal Reform 1950–71. Author of *People in Prison*. Regular Contributor to *Justice of the Peace*.
Prisons and Penology

KNECHT, JEAN. Formerly Assistant Foreign Editor, *Le Monde*, Paris; formerly Permanent Correspondent in Washington and Vice-President of the Association de la Presse Diplomatique Française.
France

KOPPER, PHILIP. Free-lance Writer, Washington, D.C.
Biographies (*in part*); **Nobel Prizes** (*in part*)

KOVAN, RICHARD W. Deputy Editor, *Nuclear Engineering International*, London.
Industrial Review: *Nuclear Industry*

KWAN-TERRY, JOHN. Senior Lecturer, Department of English Language and Literature, University of Singapore. Editor of *The Teaching of Languages in Institutions of Higher Learning in Southeast Asia.*
Literature: *Chinese*

LAMB, KEVIN M. Sports Writer, *Chicago Sun-Times.*
Biographies (*in part*); **Football:** *U.S. Football; Canadian Football*

LARSON, ROY. Religion Editor, *Chicago Sun-Times.*
Religion: *Introduction*

LATHAM, ARTHUR. Associate Editor, Encyclopædia Britannica, Yearbooks.
Biographies (*in part*)

LEAPER, ERIC. Executive Director, National Organization for River Sports, Colorado Springs, Colo.
Water Sports: *River Sports*

LEGUM, COLIN. Associate Editor, *The Observer*; Editor, *Middle East Contemporary Survey* and *Africa Contemporary Record*, London. Author of *Must We Lose Africa?; Congo Disaster; Pan-Africanism: A Political Guide; South Africa: Crisis for the West.*
African Affairs; Biographies (*in part*)

LEIFER, MICHAEL. Reader in International Relations, London School of Economics and Political Science. Author of *Dilemmas of Statehood in Southeast Asia.*
Malaysia; Singapore

LENNOX-KERR, PETER. European Editor, *Textile World.* Author of *Index to Man-Made Fibres Book.* Editor of *Nonwovens '71*; Publisher of *OE-Report*, New Mills, England.
Industrial Review: *Textiles* (*in part*)

LEVE, CHARLES S. Editor, *National Racquetball* magazine; National Director, U.S. Racquetball Association and National Racquetball Club, Inc. Author of *Inside Racquetball*; Co-author of *Winning Racquetball.*
Racket Games: *Racquetball*

LIMBURG, ALBERT W. Public Relations Director, Boating Industry Associations, Chicago.
Water Sports: *Motorboating*

LITTEL, FRANKLIN H. Professor of Religion, Temple University, Philadelphia, Pa. Co-editor of *Weltkirchenlexikon*; Author of *Macmillan Atlas History of Christianity.*
Religion: *World Church Membership*

LOEFFLER, EDWARD J. Technical Director, National Machine Tool Builders' Association, McLean, Va.
Industrial Review: *Machinery and Machine Tools*

LOGAN, ROBERT G. Sportswriter, *Chicago Tribune.* Author of *The Bulls and Chicago — A Stormy Affair.*
Basketball (*in part*)

LUCHTING, WOLFGANG A. Professor of German and Hispanoamerican Languages and Literatures, Washington State University, Pullman. Author of *Pasos a desnivel; J. R. Ribeyro y sus dobles.*
Biographies (*in part*); **Literature:** *Spanish* (*in part*)

LULING, VIRGINIA R. Social Anthropologist.
Somalia; Sudan

LUNDE, ANDERS S. Consultant; Adjunct Professor, Department of Biostatistics, University of North Carolina. Author of *Systems of Demographic Measurement: The Single Round Retrospective Interview Survey.*
Demography

MACDONALD, BARRIE. Senior Lecturer in History, Massey University, Palmerston North, N.Z. Author of several articles on the history and politics of Pacific islands.
Biographies (*in part*); **Dependent States** (*in part*); **Fiji; Solomon Islands; Tonga; Tuvalu; Western Samoa**

MacDONALD, M. C. Director, World Economics Ltd., London.
Agriculture and Food Supplies: *grain table;* **Transportation:** *table;* statistical sections of articles on the various countries

MACDONALD, TREVOR J. Manager, International Affairs, British Steel Corporation.
Industrial Review: *Iron and Steel*

MACGREGOR-MORRIS, PAMELA. Equestrian Correspondent, *The Times* and *Horse and Hound*, London. Author of books on equestrian topics.
Equestrian Sports: *Show Jumping*

McLACHLAN, KEITH S. Lecturer, School of Oriental and African Studies, University of London.
Iran

McRAE, HAMISH. Financial Editor, *The Guardian*, London. Co-author of *Capital City: London as a Financial Centre; The Second Great Crash.*
Feature Article: *Another Day, a Different Dollar*

MALLETT, H. M. F. Editor, *Wool Record Weekly Market Report*, Bradford, England.
Industrial Review: *Textiles* (*in part*)

MANGO, ANDREW. Orientalist and Broadcaster.
Turkey

MANSFIELD, PETER. Free-lance Writer on Middle Eastern affairs.
Bahrain; Biographies (*in part*); **Egypt; Iraq; Jordan; Kuwait; Lebanon; Middle Eastern Affairs; Oman; Qatar; Saudi Arabia; Syria; United Arab Emirates; Yemen, People's Democratic Republic of; Yemen Arab Republic**

MARSHALL, J. G. SCOTT. Horticultural Consultant.
Gardening (*in part*)

MARTY, MARTIN E. Fairfax M. Cone Distinguished Service Professor, University of Chicago; Associate Editor, *The Christian Century.*
Religion: *Special Report*

MARYLES, DAISY G. Associate Editor, Bookselling and Marketing, *Publishers Weekly*, New York City.
Publishing: *Books* (*in part*)

MATEJA, JAMES L. Auto Editor and Financial Reporter, *Chicago Tribune.*
Industrial Review: *Automobiles*

MATTHÍASSON, BJÖRN. Economist, European Free Trade Association, Geneva.
Iceland

MAURON, PAUL. Director, International Vine and Wine Office, Paris.
Industrial Review: *Alcoholic Beverages* (*in part*)

MAZIE, DAVID M. Associate of Carl T. Rowan, syndicated columnist. Free-lance Writer.
Social and Welfare Services (*in part*)

MAZRUI, ALI A. Professor of Political Science, University of Michigan, Ann Arbor; Visiting Professor (1977–78) in Modern Commonwealth History, University of Leeds, England. Author of *Political Values and the Educated Class in Africa; Africa's International Relations; Towards a Pax Africana.*
Feature Article: *Question Mark over Africa*

MAZZE, EDWARD MARK. Dean and Professor of Marketing, W. Paul Stillman School of Business, Seton Hall University, South Orange, N.J. Author of *Personal Selling: Choice Against Chance; Introduction to Marketing: Readings in the Discipline.*
Consumerism (*in part*); **Industrial Review:** *Advertising*

MELLBLOM, NEIL B. Director, News Bureau, Lutheran Council in the USA, New York City.
Religion: *Lutheran Churches*

MELLOR, CHRISTINE. Economist, Lloyds Bank International Ltd., London.
Costa Rica; Guatemala

MERRIAM, MONIQUE. Economist, Lloyds Bank International Ltd., London.
Chile; Ecuador; Paraguay

MEYENDORFF, JOHN. Professor of Church History and Patristics, St. Vladimir's Orthodox Theological Seminary; Professor of History, Fordham University, New York City. Author of *Christ in Eastern Christian Thought; Byzantine Theology.*
Religion: *The Orthodox Church; Eastern Non-Chalcedonian Churches*

MEYER, MICHAEL. Writer. Author of *Henrik Ibsen: The Making of a Dramatist; Henrik Ibsen: The Farewell to Poetry; Henrik Ibsen: The Top of a Cold Mountain.* Translator of works of Ibsen and Strindberg.
Theatre: *Special Report*

MILES, PETER W. Chairman, Department of Entomology, University of Adelaide, Australia.
Life Sciences: *Entomology*

MILLIKIN, SANDRA. Architectural Historian.
Architecture; Art Exhibitions; Museums (*in part*)

MITCHELL, K. K. Lecturer, Department of Physical Education, University of Leeds, England. Honorary General Secretary, English Basket Ball Association.
Basketball (*in part*)

MODIANO, MARIO. Athens Correspondent, *The Times*, London.
Greece

MODRICH, PAUL LAWRENCE. Assistant Professor of Biochemistry, Duke University Medical Center, Durham, N.C.
Life Sciences: *Molecular Biology* (*in part*)

MOFFAT, A. I. B. Senior Lecturer, Department of Civil Engineering, University of Newcastle upon Tyne, England. Editor of *Inspection, Operation and Maintenance of Existing Dams*.
Engineering Projects: *Dams*

MONACO, ALBERT M., JR. Executive Director, United States Volleyball Association, San Francisco, Calif.
Court Games: *Volleyball*

MOORE, JOHN E. Staff Hydrologist, Water Resources Division, U.S. Geological Survey.
Earth Sciences: *Hydrology*

MORGAN, HAZEL. Free-lance Writer and Singer, London.
Music: *Popular*

MORRIS, DESMOND. Research Fellow, Wolfson College, University of Oxford. Author of *The Naked Ape; The Human Zoo; Manwatching: A Field Guide to Human Behaviour*.
Football: *Special Report*

MORRISON, DONALD. Associate Editor, *Time* magazine.
Publishing: *Newspapers* (*in part*)

MORTIMER, MOLLY. Commonwealth Correspondent, *The Spectator*, London. Author of *Trusteeship in Practice; Kenya*.
Botswana; Burundi; Commonwealth of Nations; Dependent States (*in part*); **Equatorial Guinea; Gambia, The; Ghana; Lesotho; Liberia; Maldives; Mauritius; Nigeria; Rwanda; Seychelles; Sierra Leone; Swaziland**

MOSHANSKY, MOZELLE A. Free-lance Musician; Music Journalist, *The Daily Telegraph, Classical Music Weekly*, and BBC Radio. Editor and Author on musical topics.
Biographies (*in part*); **Music:** *Introduction; Opera; Symphonic*

MUCK, TERRY CHARLES. Editor, *Handball* magazine, Skokie, Ill.
Court Games: *Handball*

MULLINS, STEPHANIE. Historian, London.
Biographies (*in part*)

NAYLOR, ERNEST. Professor of Marine Biology, University of Liverpool; Director, Marine Biological Laboratory, Port Erin, Isle of Man. Author of *British Marine Isopods*.
Life Sciences: *Marine Biology*

NEILL, JOHN. Technical Manager, Submerged Combustion Ltd. Author of

Climbers' Club Guides; *Cwm Silyn and Tremadoc, Snowdon South;* Alpine Club Guide: *Selected Climbs in the Pennine Alps*.
Mountaineering

NELSON, BERT. Editor, *Track and Field News*. Author of *Little Red Book; The Decathlon Book; Olympic Track and Field; Of People and Things*.
Track and Field Sports

NETSCHERT, BRUCE C. Vice-President, National Economic Research Associates, Inc., Washington, D.C. Author of *The Future Supply of Oil and Gas*. Co-author of *Energy in the American Economy: 1850–1975*.
Energy: *World Summary*

NEUSNER, JACOB. University Professor, Brown University, Providence, R.I. Author of *Invitation to the Talmud; A History of the Mishnaic Law of Purities*.
Religion: *Judaism*

NOEL, H. S. Free-lance Journalist; Former Managing Editor, *World Fishing*, London.
Fisheries

NORMAN, GERALDINE. Saleroom Correspondent, *The Times*, London. Author of *The Sale of Works of Art; Nineteenth Century Painters and Painting: A Dictionary;* Co-author of *The Fake's Progress*.
Art Sales

NOVALES, RONALD R. Professor of Biological Sciences, Northwestern University, Evanston, Ill. Contributor to *Handbook of Physiology; Comparative Animal Physiology; Frontiers of Hormone Research*.
Life Sciences: *Zoology Overview*

OSBORNE, KEITH. Editor, *Rowing*, 1961–63; Honorary Editor, *British Rowing Almanack*, 1961– . Author of *Boat Racing in Britain, 1715–1975*.
Rowing

OSTERBIND, CARTER C. Director, Bureau of Economic and Business Research, University of Florida. Editor of *Income in Retirement; Migration, Mobility, and Aging; Social Goals, Social Programs and the Aging*.
Industrial Review: *Building and Construction*

OVSYANNIKOV, ALEKSEY. Editor in Chief, *Knizhnoye Obozreniye*, Moscow.
Literature: *Russian* (*in part*)

PAGE, SHEILA A. B. Research Officer, National Institute of Economic and Social Research, London.
Economy, World (*in part*)

PALMER, JOHN. European Editor, *The Guardian*, London.
European Unity

PALMER, S. B. Senior Lecturer, Department of Applied Physics, University of Hull, England.
Physics

PARKER, SANDY. Publisher, *Sandy Parker Reports*, a weekly newsletter of the fur industry; Business Editor, *Fur Chic Magazine*.
Industrial Review: *Furs*

PARNELL, COLIN. Consultant Editor, *Wine and Spirit*, London. Publisher, *De-*

canter Magazine, London.
Industrial Review: *Alcoholic Beverages* (*in part*)

PASKOV, DAVID. Journalist, Agence France-Presse, Paris.
Biographies (*in part*)

PAUL, CHARLES ROBERT, JR. Director of Communications, U.S. Olympic Committee, Colorado Springs, Colo. Author of *The Olympic Games, 1968*.
Gymnastics and Weight Lifting

PENFOLD, ROBIN C. Free-lance Writer specializing in industrial topics. Editor, *Shell Polymers*. Author of *A Journalist's Guide to Plastics*.
Industrial Review: *Plastics*

PERTILE, LINO. Lecturer in Italian, University of Sussex, England.
Literature: *Italian*

PETHERICK, KARIN. Crown Princess Louise Lecturer in Swedish, University College, London.
Literature: *Swedish*

PFEFFER, IRVING. Attorney. President, Dover Insurance Co., Ltd. Author of *The Financing of Small Business; Perspectives on Insurance*.
Stock Exchanges (*in part*)

PHINNEY, ALLISON W. Manager, Committees on Publication, The First Church of Christ, Scientist, Boston.
Religion: *Church of Christ, Scientist*

PICK, OTTO. Professor of International Relations, University of Surrey, Guildford, England. Co-author of *Collective Security*.
Union of Soviet Socialist Republics

PLOTKIN, FREDERICK S. Professor of English Literature and Chairman, Division of Humanities, Stern College, Yeshiva University, New York City. Author of *Milton's Inward Jerusalem; Faith and Reason; Judaism and Tragic Theology*.
Literature: *United States*

PRASAD, H. Y. SHARADA. Director, Indian Institute of Mass Communication, New Delhi, India.
India

RANGER, ROBIN. Associate Professor, Department of Political Science, St. Francis Xavier University, Antigonish, Nova Scotia; Department of National Defence Fellow in Strategic Studies (1978–79). Author of *Arms and Politics*.
Defense; Defense: *Special Report*

RAPPAPORT, PAUL. Director, Solar Energy Research Institute, Golden, Colo.
Feature Article: *Toward a Sun-Powered World*

RAY, G. F. Senior Research Fellow, National Institute of Economic and Social Research, London; Visiting Professor, University of Surrey, Guildford, England.
Industrial Review: *Introduction*

REBELO, L. S. Lecturer, Department of Portuguese Studies, King's College, University of London.
Literature: *Portuguese* (*in part*)

REIBSTEIN, JOAN NATALIE. Associate Editor, Wesleyan University Press, Middletown, Conn.
Biographies (*in part*)

REICHELDERFER, F. W. Consultant on Atmospheric Sciences; Former Director, Weather Bureau, U.S. Department of Commerce, Washington, D.C.
Earth Sciences: *Meteorology*

REID, J. H. Senior Lecturer in German, University of Nottingham, England. Co-editor of *Renaissance and Modern Studies*. Author of *Heinrich Böll: Withdrawal and Re-emergence*; Co-author of *Critical Strategies: German Fiction in the Twentieth Century*.
Literature: *German*

ROBINSON, DAVID. Film Critic, *The Times*, London. Author of *Buster Keaton*; *The Great Funnies—A History of Screen Comedy*; *A History of World Cinema*.
Biographies (*in part*); **Motion Pictures** (*in part*)

RODERICK, JOHN. Longtime Foreign Correspondent. Author of *What You Should Know About China*.
Biographies (*in part*)

ROGALY, JOE. Assistant Editor, *Financial Times*, London.
United Kingdom

SAEKI, SHOICHI. Professor of Comparative Literature, University of Tokyo. Author of *In Search of Japanese Ego*.
Literature: *Japanese*

SAINT-AMOUR, ROBERT. Professor, Department of Literary Studies, University of Quebec at Montreal.
Literature: *French* (*in part*)

SAMUELSON, PAUL A. Institute Professor, Department of Economics, Massachusetts Institute of Technology. Author of *Economics*; *Foundations of Economic Analysis*.
Feature Article: *The Roots of Inflation*

SARAHETE, YRJÖ. General Secretary, Fédération Internationale des Quilleurs, Helsinki.
Bowling: *Tenpin Bowling* (*in part*)

SCHOENFIELD, ALBERT. Co-publisher, *Swimming World*; Vice-Chairman, U.S. Olympic Swimming Committee. Contributor to *The Technique of Water Polo*; *The History of Swimming*; *Competitive Swimming as I See It*.
Swimming

SCHÖPFLIN, GEORGE. Lecturer in East European Political Institutions, London School of Economics and School of Slavonic and East European Studies, University of London.
Czechoslovakia

SCHULMAN, ELIAS. Associate Professor, Queens College, City University of New York. Author of *Israel Tsinberg, His Life and Works*; *A History of Yiddish Literature in America*; *Soviet-Yiddish Literature*.
Literature: *Yiddish*

SEARS, ROBERT N. Senior Associate Technical Editor, *The American Rifleman*.
Target Sports (*in part*)

SHACKLEFORD, CAMILLE. Director, International Tourism Consultants.
Industrial Review: *Tourism*

SHARPE, MITCHELL R. Science Writer; Historian, Alabama Space and Rocket Center, Huntsville. Author of *Living in Space: The Environment of the Astronaut*; *Yuri Gagarin, First Man in Space*; *"It Is I, Seagull": Valentina Tereshkova, First Woman in Space*; *Satellites and Probes, the Development of Unmanned Spaceflight*.
Space Exploration

SHAW, T. R. Commander, Royal Navy. Member, British Cave Research Assn.
Speleology

SHENK, CLAYTON B. Executive Secretary, U.S. National Archery Association.
Target Sports (*in part*)

SIMPSON, NOEL. Managing Director, Sydney Bloodstock Proprietary Ltd., Sydney, Australia.
Equestrian Sports: *Harness Racing*

SMEDLEY, GLENN B. Public Relations Director, American Numismatic Association.
Philately and Numismatics: *Coins*

SMITH, R. W. Dean, Graduate School, University of the Pacific, Stockton, Calif. Editor of *Venture of Islam* by M. G. S. Hodgson.
Religion: *Islam*

SMOGORZEWSKI, K. M. Writer on contemporary history. Founder and Editor, *Free Europe*, London. Author of *The United States and Great Britain*; *Poland's Access to the Sea*.
Albania; Andorra; Biographies (*in part*); **Bulgaria; Hungary; Liechtenstein; Luxembourg; Monaco; Mongolia; Poland; Political Parties; Romania; San Marino**

SNIDER, ARTHUR J. Science Writer, *Chicago Sun-Times*. Author of *Learning How to Live with Heart Trouble*; *Learning How to Live with Nervous Tension*; *Learning How to Live with High Blood Pressure*.
Health and Disease: *Overview* (*in part*)

SPELMAN, ROBERT A. President, Home Furnishings Services, Washington, D.C.
Industrial Review: *Furniture*

STAERK, MELANIE. Member, Swiss Press Association. Former Member, Swiss National Commission for UNESCO.
Switzerland

STEEN, LYNN ARTHUR. Professor of Mathematics, St. Olaf College, Northfield, Minn. Author of *Counterexamples in Topology*; *Annotated Bibliography of Expository Writing in the Mathematical Sciences*.
Mathematics

STERN, IRWIN. Assistant Professor of Portuguese, Columbia University, New York City. Author of *Júlio Dinis e o romance português (1860–1870)*; Co-editor of *Modern Iberian Literature: A Library of Literary Criticism*.
Literature: *Portuguese* (*in part*)

STEVENSON, TOM. Garden Columnist, *Baltimore News American*; *Washington Post*;

Washington Post-Los Angeles Times News Service. Book Editor, *American Horticulturist*. Author of *Pruning Guide for Trees, Shrubs, and Vines*; *Lawn Guide*.
Gardening (*in part*)

STØVERUD, TORBJØRN. W. P. Ker Senior Lecturer in Norwegian, University College, London.
Literature: *Norwegian*

STRAUSS, MICHAEL. Feature and Sports Writer, *New York Times*. Author of *The New York Times Ski Guide to the United States*.
Combat Sports: *Fencing*

SULLIVAN, H. PATRICK. Professor of Religion, Vassar College, Poughkeepsie, N.Y.
Religion: *Hinduism*

SURO, ROBERTO. Correspondent, Midwest Bureau, *Time* magazine.
Migration, International: *Special Report*

SWEETINBURGH, THELMA. Paris Fashion Correspondent for the British Wool Textile Industry.
Fashion and Dress (*in part*)

SWIFT, RICHARD N. Professor of Politics, New York University, New York City. Author of *International Law: Current and Classic*; *World Affairs and the College Curriculum*.
United Nations

SYNAN, VINSON. Assistant General Superintendent, Pentecostal Holiness Church. Author of *The Holiness-Pentecostal Movement*; *The Old Time Power*.
Religion: *Pentecostal Churches*

TAISHOFF, SOL J. Editor, *Broadcasting*, Washington, D.C.
Television and Radio (*in part*)

TALLAN, NORMAN M. Chief, Processing and High Temperature Materials Branch, Air Force Base, Dayton, Ohio. Editor of *Electrical Conductivity in Ceramics and Glass*.
Materials Sciences: *Ceramics*

TARADASH, DANIEL. President, Writers Guild of America, West, 1977–79; former President, Academy of Motion Picture Arts and Sciences. Screenwriter for *From Here to Eternity* and *Picnic*.
Motion Pictures: *Special Report*

TATTERSALL, ARTHUR. Textile Trade Statistician, Manchester, England.
Industrial Review: *Textiles* (*in part*)

TEITELBAUM, MICHAEL S. University Lecturer in Demography, University of Oxford; Fellow of Nuffield College. Editor of *Sex Differences: Social and Biological Perspectives*; *The British Fertility Decline* (in preparation).
Feature Article: *As Societies Age*

TERRY, WALTER, JR. Dance Critic, *Saturday Review* magazine, New York City. Author of *The Dance in America*; *The Ballet Companion*.
Dance (*in part*)

THOMAS, HARFORD. Retired City and Financial Editor, *The Guardian*, London.
Biographies (*in part*)

THOMPSON, ANTHONY. European Linguist Research Fellow, CLW, Aberystwyth, Wales. General Secretary, International Federation of Library Associations, 1962–70. Author of *Library Buildings of Britain and Europe.*
Libraries

THOMSON, JAMES C. Retired Editor, *Prairie Farmer* magazine. Author of *American Farm Organizations; The Changing Agricultural Extension Service.*
United States: *Special Report*

TINGAY, LANCE. Lawn Tennis Correspondent, the *Daily Telegraph*, London. Author of *100 Years of Wimbledon; Tennis, A Pictorial History.*
Tennis

TINKER, JON. Director, Earthscan, a service of the International Institute for Environment and Development.
Environment: *Special Report*

TRIGG, ROBERT H. Director, Economic Research, Committee Policy Studies Section, New York Stock Exchange.
Stock Exchanges (*in part*)

TRILLING, OSSIA. Vice-President, International Association of Theatre Critics (1956–77). Co-editor and Contributor, *International Theatre.* Contributor, BBC, the *Financial Times*, London.
Theatre (*in part*)

TRINDADE, INGRID T. Secretary, Department of Cooperation and Witness, World Alliance of Reformed Churches.
Religion: *Presbyterian, Reformed, and Congregational Churches*

TRUSSELL, TAIT. Administrative Vice-President, American Forest Institute.
Industrial Review: *Wood Products*

UMANSKY, DAVID J. Director, Office of Public Affairs, Federal Railroad Administration, Washington, D.C.
Transportation: *Special Report*

UNHCR. The Office of the United Nations High Commissioner for Refugees.
Refugees

UNNY, GOVINDAN. Agence France-Presse Special Correspondent for India, Nepal, and Sri Lanka.
Afghanistan; Bangladesh; Bhutan; Biographies (*in part*)**; Burma; Nepal; Pakistan; Sri Lanka**

VALE, NORMAN K. Retired Director of News Services, The United Church of Canada.
Religion: *United Church of Canada*

van den HOVEN, ISOLA. Writer on Consumer Affairs, The Hague, Neth.
Consumerism (*in part*)

VAN GORKOM, JEROME W. Chairman of the Board and Chief Executive Officer, Trans Union Corp., Lincolnshire, Ill. Member, Advisory Council on Social Security, U.S. Department of Health, Education, and Welfare.
Social and Welfare Services: *Special Report*

van PRAAG, JACK H. National Public Relations Director, U.S. Badminton Assn.
Racket Games: *Badminton*

VERDI, ROBERT WILLIAM. Sportswriter, *Chicago Tribune.*
Baseball (*in part*)

VIANSSON-PONTÉ, PIERRE. Editorial Adviser and Leader Writer, *Le Monde*, Paris. Author of *Les Gaullistes; The King and His Court: Les Politiques.*
Biographies (*in part*)

VINT, ARTHUR KINGSLEY. Counselor, International Table Tennis Federation, Sussex, England.
Table Tennis

WADLEY, J. B. Writer and Broadcaster on cycling. Editor of *Guinness Guide to Bicycling.* Author of *Tour de France 1970, 1971, and 1973; Old Roads and New.*
Cycling

WARD, PETER. Head, Ward News Service, Parliamentary Press Gallery, Ottawa; Contributing Editor, *Canadian Business* magazine.
Canada: *Special Report*

WARD-THOMAS, P. A. Golf Correspondent, *Country Life*, London.
Golf

WAY, DIANE L. Research Assistant, Ontario Historical Studies Series.
Biographies (*in part*)

WEBB, HENRY, JR. Retired from U.S. Foreign Service.
El Salvador; Honduras; Nicaragua

WEBB, W. L. Literary Editor, *The Guardian*, London and Manchester.
Literature: *Introduction; United Kingdom; Russian* (*in part*)*; Eastern European*

WEBSTER, PETER L. Associate Professor, Department of Botany, University of Massachusetts. Co-author of *The Cell.*
Life Sciences: *Botany*

WEEDEN, CYRIL. Assistant Director, Glass Manufacturers' Federation, London.
Industrial Review: *Glass*

WIJNGAARD, BARBARA. Economist, Lloyds Bank International Ltd., London.
Argentina; Mexico

WILKINSON, GORDON. Head, Communications Section, Research and Development Division, Rentokil Ltd., Crawley, England. Chemistry Consultant, *New Scientist*, London. Author of *Industrial Timber Preservation.*
Chemistry.

WILKINSON, PAUL. Reader in Politics, University of Wales. Author of *Political Terrorism; Terrorism and the Liberal State.*
Feature Article: *Terrorism—Weapon of the Weak*

WILLEY, DAVID DOUGLAS. Rome Correspondent, BBC.
Biographies (*in part*)**; Italy**

WILLIAMS, PETER. Editor, *Dance and Dancers*, London. Chairman, Arts Council, Great Britain's Dance Theatre Committee; Chairman, British Council's Drama Advisory Committee.
Dance (*in part*)

WILLIAMSON, TREVOR. Chief Sports Subeditor, *Daily Telegraph*, London.
Biographies (*in part*)**; Football:** *Association Football*

WILSON, MICHAEL. Employed with Carl Byoir & Associates Ltd., London.
Industrial Review: *Aerospace*

WINSBURY, REX. Editorial Director, Fintel Ltd., London. Author of *New Technology and the Press; New Technology and the Journalist.*
Publishing: *Special Report*

WITTE, RANDALL E. Associate Editor, *The Western Horseman* magazine.
Rodeo

WOOD, CHRISTINA. Free-lance Sportswriter.
Racket Games: *Rackets; Real Tennis*

WOOD, KENNETH H. Editor, *Adventist Review.* Author of *Meditations for Moderns; Relevant Religion.*
Religion: *Seventh-day Adventist Church*

WOODS, ELIZABETH. Writer. Author of *The Yellow Volkswagen; Gone.*
Literature: *English* (*in part*)

WOOLLER, MICHAEL. Economist, Lloyds Bank International Ltd., London.
Biographies (*in part*)**; Bolivia; Cuba; Portugal; Spain**

WOOLLEY, DAVID. Editor, *Airports International*, London.
Transportation (*in part*)

WORSNOP, RICHARD L. Associate Editor, Editorial Research Reports, Washington, D.C.
United States

WRIGHT, ALMON R. Retired Senior Historian, U.S. Department of State.
Panama

WYLLIE, PETER JOHN. Homer J. Livingston Professor, University of Chicago. Author of *The Dynamic Earth.*
Earth Sciences: *Geology and Geochemistry*

YANG, WINSTON L. Y. Professor of Chinese Studies, Department of Asian Studies, Seton Hall University, South Orange, N.J. Author of *Modern Chinese Fiction; Teng Hsiao-p'ing: A Political Biography* (forthcoming).
Biographies (*in part*)

YOUNG, M. NORVEL. Chancellor, Pepperdine University, Malibu, Calif.; Chairman of the Board, 20th Century Christian Publishing Co. Author of *Preachers of Today; History of Colleges Connected with Churches of Christ; The Church Is Building.*
Religion: *Churches of Christ*

YOUNG, SUSAN. News Editor, *Church Times*, London.
Religion: *Anglican Communion*

ZANDER, MICHAEL. Professor of Law, London School of Economics and Political Science. Author of *Social Workers, Their Clients and the Law; Legal Services for the Community;* Editor of *Family Guide to the Law.*
Law: *Special Report*

Index

The black type entries are article headings in the *Book of the Year.*
These black type article entries do not show page notations because
they are to be found in their alphabetical position in the body of the
book. They show the dates of the issues of the *Book of the Year* in which
the articles appear. For example "Archaeology 79, 78, 77" indicates
that the article "Archaeology" is to be found in the 1979, 1978, and
1977 *Book of the Year.*

The light type headings that are indented under black type article headings refer to material elsewhere in the text related to the subject under
which they are listed. The light type headings that are not indented refer
to information in the text not given a special article. Biographies and obituaries are listed as cross references to the sections "Biographies" and
"Obituaries" within the article *People of the Year.* References to illustrations
are preceded by the abbreviation "il."

All headings, whether consisting of a single word or more, are treated for
the purpose of alphabetization as single complete headings. Names beginning with "Mc" and "Mac" are alphabetized as "Mac"; "St." is treated as
"Saint."

G

N